DATE DUE

DEMCO 38-296

GALE CITY & METRO RANKINGS REPORTER

GALE

CITY & METRO

RANKINGS

REPORTER

SECOND EDITION

3,000 Rankings of U.S. Cities and Metro Areas on a Variety of

Topics, Including Arts and Leisure, Demographics, Education,

Government Expenditures, Taxes, etc., from Government,

Business, and General Interest Sources.

HELEN S. FISHER, EDITOR

GALE

DETROIT • NEW YORK • TORONTO • LONDON

Helen S. Fisher, *Editor*

Editorial Code and Data, Inc. Staff

Robert S. Lazich and Susan M. Turner, *Contributing Editors*
Gary Alampi, *Programmer Analyst*
Sherae Carroll, *Data Entry Associate*

Gale Research Staff

Camille A. Killens, *Associate Editor*
Lawrence W. Baker, *Managing Editor*
Mary Beth Trimper, *Production Director*
Evi Seoud, *Assistant Production Manager*
Shanna Heilveil, *Production Assistant*

Cover design by Mark Howell

ISSN: 1077-9132
ISBN: 0-7876-0061-X

Printed in the United States of America
by Gale Research

10 9 8 7 6 5 4 3 2 1

Table of Contents

CHAPTER 1 - ENVIRONMENT AND NATURAL RESOURCES continued:

PART II - SOCIAL PROFILE

CHAPTER 13 - OCCUPATIONS continued:

CHAPTER 13 - OCCUPATIONS continued:

Table 1277 Top 25 MSAs For Employment As Mining Engineers, 1990: Whites 514
Table 1278 Top 25 MSAs For Employment As Motion Picture Projectionists, 1990: Blacks 514
Table 1279 Top 25 MSAs For Employment As Motion Picture Projectionists, 1990: Whites 514
Table 1280 Top 25 MSAs For Employment As Musicians and Composers, 1990: Blacks 515
Table 1281 Top 25 MSAs For Employment As Musicians and Composers, 1990: Whites 515
Table 1282 Top 25 MSAs For Employment As Nuclear Engineers, 1990: Blacks 516
Table 1283 Top 25 MSAs For Employment As Nuclear Engineers, 1990: Whites 516
Table 1284 Top 25 MSAs For Employment As Nursery Workers, 1990: Blacks 517
Table 1285 Top 25 MSAs For Employment As Nursery Workers, 1990: Whites 517
Table 1286 Top 25 MSAs For Employment As Occupational Therapists, 1990: Blacks 518
Table 1287 Top 25 MSAs For Employment As Occupational Therapists, 1990: Whites 518
Table 1288 Top 25 MSAs For Employment As Optometrists, 1990: Blacks 518
Table 1289 Top 25 MSAs For Employment As Optometrists, 1990: Whites 519
Table 1290 Top 25 MSAs For Employment As Painters, Sculptors, Craft-artists, and Artist Printmakers, 1990: Blacks 519
Table 1291 Top 25 MSAs For Employment As Painters, Sculptors, Craft-artists, and Artist Printmakers, 1990: Whites 520
Table 1292 Top 25 MSAs For Employment As Personnel and Labor Relations Managers, 1990: Blacks 520
Table 1293 Top 25 MSAs For Employment As Personnel and Labor Relations Managers, 1990: Whites 521
Table 1294 Top 25 MSAs For Employment As Petroleum Engineers, 1990: Blacks 521
Table 1295 Top 25 MSAs For Employment As Petroleum Engineers, 1990: Whites 521
Table 1296 Top 25 MSAs For Employment As Pharmacists, 1990: Blacks 522
Table 1297 Top 25 MSAs For Employment As Pharmacists, 1990: Whites 522
Table 1298 Top 25 MSAs For Employment As Photographers, 1990: Blacks 523
Table 1299 Top 25 MSAs For Employment As Photographers, 1990: Whites 523
Table 1300 Top 25 MSAs For Employment As Physical Education Teachers, 1990: Blacks 524
Table 1301 Top 25 MSAs For Employment As Physical Education Teachers, 1990: Whites 524
Table 1302 Top 25 MSAs For Employment As Physical Therapists, 1990: Blacks 524
Table 1303 Top 25 MSAs For Employment As Physical Therapists, 1990: Whites 525
Table 1304 Top 25 MSAs For Employment As Physicians' Assistants, 1990: Blacks 525
Table 1305 Top 25 MSAs For Employment As Physicians' Assistants, 1990: Whites 526
Table 1306 Top 25 MSAs For Employment As Physicians, 1990: Blacks 526
Table 1307 Top 25 MSAs For Employment As Physicians, 1990: Whites 527
Table 1308 Top 25 MSAs For Employment As Physicists and Astronomers, 1990: Blacks 527
Table 1309 Top 25 MSAs For Employment As Physicists and Astronomers, 1990: Whites 528
Table 1310 Top 25 MSAs For Employment As Physics Teachers, 1990: Blacks 528
Table 1311 Top 25 MSAs For Employment As Physics Teachers, 1990: Whites 528
Table 1312 Top 25 MSAs For Employment As Podiatrists, 1990: Blacks 529
Table 1313 Top 25 MSAs For Employment As Podiatrists, 1990: Whites 529
Table 1314 Top 25 MSAs For Employment As Police and Detectives, Public Service, 1990: Blacks 530
Table 1315 Top 25 MSAs For Employment As Police and Detectives, Public Service, 1990: Whites 530
Table 1316 Top 25 MSAs For Employment As Political Science Teachers, 1990: Blacks 531
Table 1317 Top 25 MSAs For Employment As Political Science Teachers, 1990: Whites 531
Table 1318 Top 25 MSAs For Employment As Power Plant Operators, 1990: Blacks 531
Table 1319 Top 25 MSAs For Employment As Power Plant Operators, 1990: Whites 532
Table 1320 Top 25 MSAs For Employment As Precious Stones and Metals Workers, 1990: Blacks 532
Table 1321 Top 25 MSAs For Employment As Precious Stones and Metals Workers, 1990: Whites 533
Table 1322 Top 25 MSAs For Employment As Printing Press Operators, 1990: Blacks 533
Table 1323 Top 25 MSAs For Employment As Printing Press Operators, 1990: Whites 534
Table 1324 Top 25 MSAs For Employment As Private Household Cleaners and Servants, 1990: Blacks 534
Table 1325 Top 25 MSAs For Employment As Private Household Cleaners and Servants, 1990: Whites 535
Table 1326 Top 25 MSAs For Employment As Proofreaders, 1990: Blacks 535
Table 1327 Top 25 MSAs For Employment As Proofreaders, 1990: Whites 536
Table 1328 Top 25 MSAs For Employment As Psychologists, 1990: Blacks 536
Table 1329 Top 25 MSAs For Employment As Psychologists, 1990: Whites 536
Table 1330 Top 25 MSAs For Employment As Psychology Teachers, 1990: Blacks 537
Table 1331 Top 25 MSAs For Employment As Psychology Teachers, 1990: Whites 537
Table 1332 Top 25 MSAs For Employment As Railroad Brake, Signal, and Switch Operators, 1990: Blacks 538
Table 1333 Top 25 MSAs For Employment As Railroad Brake, Signal, and Switch Operators, 1990: Whites 538
Table 1334 Top 25 MSAs For Employment As Railroad Conductors and Yardmasters, 1990: Blacks 539
Table 1335 Top 25 MSAs For Employment As Railroad Conductors and Yardmasters, 1990: Whites 539
Table 1336 Top 25 MSAs For Employment As Registered Nurses, 1990: Blacks 539
Table 1337 Top 25 MSAs For Employment As Registered Nurses, 1990: Whites 540
Table 1338 Top 25 MSAs For Employment As Respiratory Therapists, 1990: Blacks 540
Table 1339 Top 25 MSAs For Employment As Respiratory Therapists, 1990: Whites 541
Table 1340 Top 25 MSAs For Employment As Roofers, 1990: Blacks 541
Table 1341 Top 25 MSAs For Employment As Roofers, 1990: Whites 542
Table 1342 Top 25 MSAs For Employment As Sailors and Deckhands, 1990: Blacks 542
Table 1343 Top 25 MSAs For Employment As Sailors and Deckhands, 1990: Whites 543

CHAPTER 13 - OCCUPATIONS continued:

CHAPTER 13 - OCCUPATIONS continued:

PART V - ECONOMIC PROFILE

CHAPTER 16 - GENERAL ECONOMIC PROFILE continued:

PART VI - GOVERNMENT

INTRODUCTION

Gale City & Metro Rankings Reporter (GCMRR), now in its second edition, is a compilation of statistical rankings of more than 300 cities and Metropolitan Statistical Areas (MSAs) of the United States. It contains more than 3,000 tables covering statistics on topics such as cost of living, crime, education, employment, environment, government, health, housing, income, industry, leisure activities, occupations, population, poverty, and recreation.

Data for *GCMRR-2* were gathered from a variety of sources: federal, state, and local governments; associations and societies; and newspapers and periodicals.

GCMRR-2 presents comprehensive information on cities and MSAs for serious reference and analytical work by library professionals, business persons, researchers, students, and the general public.

SCOPE

An attempt was made to provide data on physical, cultural, social, economic, and demographic categories as well as on subjects of more general interest such as entertainment, sports, recreation, and tourism.

One of its chief objectives is to cover as many topics as possible. Depending on the topic, this required limiting the rankings to 50, 25, or 10 cities or MSAs. In rare instances, data on a topic relating to all MSAs, cities, and counties provided by a particular source have been ranked. In those cases in which the number of locations has been limited, a notation to that effect is given in a note in the table. The listings provide rankings for "good" as well as "bad" categories—e.g., acreage of national parks to crime statistics, respectively.

The Location Index can be consulted to find information for a specific city or MSA. For information on cities and MSAs that have not been included in a table, users can check the source block that appears at the end of each table. The corresponding "Listing of Sources" will direct the user to the original source material.

If the source materials provided data on fewer than 25 or 10 cities, all of the cities have been included in the tables.

For some of the more general topics, such as total population, total Asian population, total female population, school enrollment, and the like, all 284 MSAs appearing in the *1990 Census of Population and Housing* are listed. These tables are typically found at the beginning of a chapter or topic heading.

The majority of tables contain data from the late 1980s or the early 1990s. More recent data were preferred. Only in rare instances, where recent data were not available, was earlier information included. Approximately 400 tables from the first edition of GCMRR have been repeated in this second edition. These tables (primarily taken from the 1990 Census of Population and Housing) provide data on first ancestry, immigration, income, marital status, population, poverty, and women-owned businesses. The degree of detail, the variety, and the fact that much of the material will not be updated until after the Census of Population in the year 2000 led to the decision to include them in the second edition of GCMRR.

RANKINGS

A ranking based solely on numbers may be misleading in that the more populous cities and MSAs will almost always rank at or near the top.

GCMRR-2 highlights the more significant aspects of the data presented by emphasizing *per capita-* or *percentage*-based rankings. These rankings are more likely to provide an accurate view of a city's culture, society, environment, trends, etc. For instance—

– the Rochester, New York area ranks first in the number of black family child care providers per 100,000 population. The St. Louis, Missouri area ranks first in the number of whites employed in the same occupation...

– the Greenville, South Carolina area ranks first in the number of black physicians per 100,000 population. The Mobile, Alabama area ranks first in the number of white physicians per 100,000 population...

– the Pittsburgh, Pennsylvania area ranks first in the number of black tailors per 100,000 population. The Salt Lake City, Utah area ranks first in the number white tailors per 100,000 population.,.

– the Atlanta, Georgia area ranks first in the number of male nuclear engineers per 100,000 population; the Detroit-Ann Arbor, Michigan, area ranks first in the number of women nuclear engineers per 100,000 population.

– Indianapolis, Indiana, ranks first in the number of persons employed as authors per 100,000 population—this holds true for both men and women.

– the Kansas City area holds first place in the number of women funeral directors per 100,000 population; the area of Portland-Vancouver, Oregon-Washington, ranks first in the number of men funeral directors per 100,000 population.

– Persons in Johnstown, Pennsylvania, were most likely to live in the same house in 1990 that they had occupied in 1985.

– Persons in Killeen-Temple, Texas, were most likely to have lived abroad in 1985.

– Cities in New York rank first in the number of persons in the 30-44 age group who moved there in the period between March 1993 and March 1994 (61,000); cities in California rank first in the number of persons in the same age group who moved out during that same period (135,000).

– the New York area ranks first in the number of females who moved in during the period of March 1993-94 (107,000); the Los Angeles area ranks first in the number of females who moved out (250,000).

– the Dallas-Fort Worth, Texas area ranks first in the number of males who moved in during the period between March 1993-94; the Los Angeles area ranks first in the number of males who moved out (279,000).

– Central American persons rank first in percentage of population in cities in California— except for the Hondurans, who rank first in New Orleans, Louisiana; and the Panamanians, who rank first in Fayetteville, North Carolina.

– Albany, Georgia, ranks first in black population. It also ranks first in percentage of black women householders with children who are living *below* poverty level, as well as first in percentage of black male householders with children who are living *above* poverty.

– Enid, Oklahoma, takes last place in percentage of total population and first place in percentage of population living outside of urban areas.

FORMAT OF TABLES

Table Layout

Rankings are presented in tabular format. Tables are grouped by chapter and subtopic.

SAMPLE ENTRY

Key

1 **Entry number:** Shown between two stars. May be used for locating an entry from the index.

2 **Sub-topic:** Gives a broad description for a group of tables.

3 **Table title:** Always shown in bold type.

4 **Explanatory headnotes:** Gives infomation about an entry to help make data more understandable. Further information may also be supplied in the notes field (see number 10).

5 **Footnote number:** A reference to the notes field. The number will not be present if a note is more general.

6 **List of cities or MSAs:** Almost always in rank order.

7 **Data column:** If figures show per capita or percentage calculations, they were most likely computed by the editors; otherwise, the figures are from the original source.

8 **Ranking:** For first column of data.

9 **Source note:** All entries cite the source of the table, the date of publication, and the page number, if given in the original. In cases where the publisher obtained the information from another source, that publication will be listed as the "primary source."

10 **Footnote field:** Gives further explanatory information about the content of a table, if needed. Often deals with a particular part of a table, if numbered.

3 **2** **1** **7** **8**

905
First Ancestry

Persons, by First Ancestry, 1990: French Canadian

4 Data provided for all respondents who reported "French Canadian" as their sole ancestry, and those who reported "French Canadian" as their first ancestry.
[Table shows the top 50 areas]

MSA[1]	% of total population	Rank
Huoma—Thibodaux, LA	37.915	1
Lafayette, LA	32.605	2
Lewiston—Auburn, ME	24.263	3
Lake Charles, LA	21.768	4
Manchester, NH	17.505	5
Fitchburg—Leominster, MA	11.864	6
Burlington, VT	8.573	7
Baton Rouge, LA	8.409	8
Beaumont—Port Arthur, TX	8.249	9
Portsmouth—Dover—Rochester, NH—ME	8.201	10
Providence—Pawtucket—Fall River, RI—MA	7.200	11
Springfield, MA	7.077	12
Bangor, ME	6.605	13
New Bedford, MA	6.441	14
Alexandria, LA	5.790	15
Worcester, MA	5.681	16
Portland, ME	5.130	17
New Orleans, LA	4.125	18
Pittsfield, MA	4.068	19
New London—Norwich, CT—RI	4.017	20
Glen Falls, NY	3.981	21
Hartford—New Britain—Middletown, CT	3.674	22
Boston—Lawrence—Salem, MA—NH	3.550	23
Waterbury, CT	3.171	24
Kankakee, IL	3.125	25
Albany—Schenectady—Troy, NY	2.194	26
Saginaw—Bay City—Midland, MI	2.094	27
Biloxi—Gulfport, MS	2.091	28
Flint, MI	2.048	29
Monroe, LA	1.991	30
Syracuse, NY	1.956	31
Green Bay, WI	1.743	32
New Haven —Meriden, CT	1.635	33
Shreveport, LA	1.584	34
Muskegon, MI	1.527	35
Pascagoula, MS	1.420	36
Detroit—Ann Arbor, MI	1.343	37
Utica—Rome, NY	1.302	38
Lansing—East Lansing, MI	1.227	39
Fort Walton Beach, FL	1.226	40
Jacksonville, NC	1.205	41
Eau Clair, WI	1.168	42
Houston—Galveston—Brazoria, TX	1.119	43
Daytona Beach, FL	1.108	44
Fort Pierce, FL	1.106	45
Anchorage, AK	1.099	46
Melbourne—Titusville—Palm Bay, FL	1.094	47
Ocala, FL	1.065	48
Sarasota, FL	1.032	49
Poughkeepsie, NY	1.027	50

5 **6**

9 *Source*: U.S. Bureau of the Census, Data User Services Division, 1990 Census of Population and Housing, Summary Tape Fiole 3C, United States Summary, CD-ROM, February 1992.

10 *Note*: This is just a sample note to show what one would look like.

Headnotes and footnotes have been provided to aid in the interpretation of data.

Table Contents

Table contents are sorted by rank (in ascending order), or alphabetically. When two or more areas have the same value, they are given the same ranking. The location names are then alphabetically sorted.

Rankings Values and Ranks

The first column of each table shows the number or ratio of the item being measured, e.g., number of miles, dollars, or persons; percentage of total population; percentage of housing units; percentage of population age 25+, etc. The second column shows the city's rank based on that measurement.

Data used for comparisons are taken from the same years as the data in the first column. In most cases, data used to calculate per capita and percentage columns were obtained from the source material itself or from the U.S. Bureau of the Census. Nearly all 1990 population and housing data are based on the *1990 Census of Population and Housing*. Population data for other years were obtained from *Statistical Abstract of the United States: 1992 (112th edition)*.

ARRANGEMENT

The *Table of Contents* shows the true order of all sections, chapters, topics, and tables as they appear in *GCMRR-2*. Table and page numbers are provided. *Parts* appear in large bold print. *Chapters*, numbered sequentially and also in bold print, are followed by *topics*, in italics; table titles are then listed under the topics. The table numbers are found on the left and the page numbers on which those tables appear are on the right.

The major parts included in *GCMRR-2* are:

- **Part I - Physical Profile:** This section includes data on the environment, toxic chemical releases, weather and climate, and national parks.

- **Part II - Social Profile:** Provides rankings for population by race, ethnicity, and age; immigration; marital status; geographic mobility; cost of living; housing; taxes; transportation; health and health care; and living arrangements.

- **Part III - Education and Culture:** Lists rankings for ancestry and language; school enrollment; education expenditures; educational attainment by age, race, and ethnicity; and number of teachers.

- **Part IV - Jobs and Income:** Rankings are provided for government employment; employment by age, race, industry, and sex; unemployment; income; occupations; and poverty.

- **Part V - Economic Profile:** This section covers consumer expenditures, imports and exports, construction industry, manufacturing, services industry, wholesale trade, retail trade, transportation sector, and the utilities sector.

- **Part VI - Government:** Ranks revenues and expenditures for federal, county, and city governments; and law and criminal justice statistics.

- **Part VII - Leisure Time:** Provides rankings for TV viewing; parks and recreation; travel and tourism; and sports activities.

SOURCES

More than 175 sources were used to compile *GCMRR-2*. They include federal government documents, newspapers and periodicals, and associations and societies. For a complete list, see the "Listing of Sources".

INDEXES

Two indexes are included in *GCMRR-2* Both provide page and table numbers.

- **Location Index:** Every city or MSA name included in *GCMRR-2* is presented in alphabetical order.

- **Keyword Index:** This index is based on keywords and topics found in each table. It also includes non-geographical terms relating to the subject matter of the ranking.

LISTING OF SOURCES

Sources are listed in alphabetical order in this section. Each source entry is followed by the numbers of the tables in which that source was used.

ACKNOWLEDGMENTS

For contributing entries, advice, suggestions, technical assistance, and other invaluable support during the production of *GCMRR-2*, the editors thank Gary Alampi of ECDI, the National Association of Regulatory Utilities Commissioners (NARUC) and the American Public Transit Association (APTA).

COMMENTS AND SUGGESTIONS

Although every effort has been made to maintain accuracy, errors may occasionally occur. The editors would be grateful if these were brought to their attention for correction in future editions of *GCMRR*. Comments about *GCMRR* or suggestions for its improvement are always welcome.

Please contact:
Editors
Gale City and Metro Rankings Reporter
Gale Research Inc.
835 Penobscot Building
Detroit, Michigan 48226-4094
Phone: (313) 961-2242 or
(800) 347-GALE
Fax: (313) 961-6815

Abbreviations and Acronyms

0	Zero or rounds to less than half the unit of measurement shown
AFB	Air Force Base
AGT	Automated Guideway Transportation system
AIDS	Acquired Immunodeficiency Syndrome
APT	Airport
B	Base figure is too small from which to derive a figure that meets statistical standards for reliability
BIF	Bank Insurance Fund
BJA	Bureau of Justice Assistance
BJS	Bureau of Justice Statistics
CALM	Centralized Accounting for Local Management
CBD	Central Business District
CBO	Congressional Budget Office
CEWG	Community Epidemiology Work Group (National Institute on Drug Abuse)
CMSA	Consolidated Metropolitan Statistical Area
CO	Carbon Monoxide
CPI	Consumer Price Index
CPU	Passenger Car Equivalent Unit
CSI	Customer Satisfaction Index (U.S. Postal Service)
CTA	Central Transit Authority
DOT	Department of Transportation
DPM	Downtown People Mover (Automated Guideway/Commuter Rail System)
DUF	Drug Use Forecasting (program) (National Institute of Justice)
DVMT	Daily Vehicle-Miles of Travel
DoD	Department of Defense
EMS	Emergency Medical Services
EPA	Environmental Protection Agency
FAA	Federal Aviation Administration
FAS	Free Alongside Ship
FHA	Federal Housing Administration
FHLB	Federal Home Loan Bank
FIRE	Finance, Insurance, and Real Estate
FTEE	Full-Time Equivalency Employment
FY	Fiscal Year
GAO	General Accounting Office
HCFA	Health Care Financing Administration
HIV	Human Immunodeficiency Virus
HPMS	Highway Performance Monitoring System
HUD	Department of Housing and Urban Development
IDU	Injecting Drug User
IHS	Indian Health Service
IPC	Individuals, Partnerships, and Corporations
IPO	Initial Public Offering
ISD	Independent School District
KWH	Kilowatt Hour
LSD	Lysergic Acid Diethylamide
M & R	Maintenance and Repair
MBTA	Massachusetts Bay Transit Authority
MSA	Metropolitan Statistical Area
Muni	Municipal
NAAQS	National Ambient Air Quality Standards (EPA)
NAS	Naval Air Station
NEA	National Endowment for the Arts
NECMA	New England County Metropolitan Area
NFIB	National Federation of Independent Business Foundation
NJT	New Jersey Transit
NO2	Nitrogen Dioxide
NOW	Negotiable Order of Withdrawal (Banking term)
PB	Plumbum (Lead)
PBX	Private Branch Exchange (Telephone)
PCP	Phencyclidine
PM	Particulate Matter
PMSA	Primary Metropolitan Statistical Area

RTD	Rapid Transit District	**TD**	Transit District
SAIF	Savings Association Insurance Fund	**TRI**	Toxic Release Inventory
SBIR	Small Business Innovation Research program	**TS**	Transit System
		UCR	Uniform Crime Reporting (program) (FBI)
SCRTD	Southern California Rapid Transit District	**WMATA**	Washington Metropolitan Area Transit Authority
SEPTA	Southeast Pennsylvania Transit Authority	**WTD**	Wet Tons per Day
SO2	Sulfur Dioxide	**X**	Not applicable because column heading, stubline, or other contingencies make an entry impossibly absurd, or meaningless
SORTA	Southern Ohio Rapid Transit Authority		
T	Trace (Precipitation)	**Y**	Relevant attribute is present
TA	Transit Authority		
TASC	Treatment and Alternatives to Street Crimes		

PART I

PHYSICAL PROFILE

Contents

Chapter 1

ENVIRONMENT AND NATURAL RESOURCES

Topics Covered

Air Quality
Chemicals
Chemical Weapons
Farms
Land Area
Livestock
National Parks
Sewerage Systems
Toxic Chemical Releases
Toxic Waste
Water and Water Use
Weather and Climate

★4322★
Air Quality
Emergency Room Visits, 1993-94: Estimated Number of Visits Related to Exposure to Ozone

[Number of visits is estimated]

City	Total visits	Rank
Los Angeles, CA	132,015	1
New York, NY	108,663	2
San Diego, CA	59,820	3
Detroit, MI	45,324	4
Houston, TX	38,841	5
Philadelphia, PA	35,802	6
Baltimore, MD	25,584	7
Washington, DC	24,090	8
Saint Louis, MO	22,368	9
Dallas, TX	16,632	10
Milwaukee, WI	12,870	11
Hartford, CT	10,263	12
New Haven, CT	5,331	13

Source: Love, Jacqueline, "Ozone Levels Still Called Health Threat for Region," *Detroit Free Press*, 20 June 1996, p. 6B.

★4323★
Air Quality
Emergency Room Visits, 1993-94: Percentage Related to Exposure to Ozone

City	Percentage	Rank
Los Angeles, CA	8.5	1
Baltimore, MD	7.9	2
Washington, DC	7.6	3
Dallas, TX	7.5	4
Hartford, CT	7.5	4
New Haven, CT	7.4	5
Philadelphia, PA	7.3	6
San Diego, CA	7.3	6
Saint Louis, MO	7.3	6
Houston, TX	7.2	7
New York, NY	6.9	8
Detroit, MI	6.3	9
Milwaukee, WI	6.3	9

Source: Love, Jacqueline, "Ozone Levels Still Called Health Threat for Region," *Detroit Free Press*, 20 June 1996, p. 6B.

★500★
Air Quality
Failure to Meet NAAQS for Ozone, 1991-93: Average Number of Days Exceeding Standards

Metropolitan area	1991-93 average	Rank
Los Angeles South Coast Air, CA[1]	104.3	1
Southeast Desert Modified AQMD, CA[2]	59.3	2
San Joaquin Valley, CA	18.9	3
Ventura County, CA	15.9	4
Portland, ME	11.8	5
San Diego, CA	11.8	5
Philadelphia, PA-NJ-DE-MD CMSA	10.3	6
Sacramento, CA	9.7	7
Greater Connecticut, CT[3]	7.5	8
Houston-Galveston-Brazoria, TX CMSA	6.3	9
New York, NY-NJ-CT CMSA[4]	6.1	10
Baltimore, MD	4.8	11
Chicago-Gary-Lake County, IL-IN-WI CMSA	4.7	12
Springfield, MA	4.6	13
Atlanta, GA	4.2	14
Phoenix, AZ	4.0	15
Providence, RI[5]	4.0	15
Milwaukee-Racine, WI CMSA	3.9	16
El Paso, TX	3.7	17
Grand Rapids, MI	3.4	18
Boston-Lawrence-Salem, MA-NH CMSA[6]	3.1	19
Kent County and Queen Anne's County, MD[7]	2.8	20
Beaumont-Port Arthur, TX	2.7	21
Sheboygan, WI	2.6	22
Knox and Lincoln Counties, ME[7]	2.3	23

Source: U.S. Bureau of the Census, *Statistical Abstract of the United States, 1995*, (115th edition), Washington, D.C.: U.S. Government Printing Office, 1995, p. 234. Primary source: U.S. Environmental Protection Agency, published in 1993 Air Quality Update, October 1994. *Notes:* "NAAQS" stands for "National Ambient Air Quality Standards." Data are shown only for the top 25 areas. 1. Primarily represents Los Angeles and Orange Counties. 2. Represents primarily San Joaquin, Turlock, Merced, Madera, Fresno, Kings, Tulare, and Kern Counties. 3. Primarily represents Hartford-New Haven area. 4. Excludes the Connecticut portion. 5. Covers entire State of Rhode Island. 6. Includes also both the Worcester, MA, and New Bedford, MA, MSAs. 7. Not a metropolitan area.

★501★
Air Quality
Failure to Meet NAAQS for Ozone, 1993: Number of Days Exceeding Standards

Metropolitan area	1993[1]	Rank
Los Angeles South Coast Air, CA[2]	97.6	1
Southeast Desert Modified AQMD, CA[3]	72.6	2
San Joaquin Valley, CA	27.5	3
Houston-Galveston-Brazoria, TX CMSA	10.4	4

[Continued]

★501★
Failure to Meet NAAQS for Ozone, 1993: Number of Days Exceeding Standards
[Continued]

Metropolitan area	1993[1]	Rank
Ventura County, CA	9.0	5
Baltimore, MD	6.2	6
Springfield, MA	6.2	6
Greater Connecticut, CT[4]	6.0	7
New York, NY-NJ-CT CMSA[5]	6.0	7
Philadelphia, PA-NJ-DE-MD CMSA	5.2	8
Atlanta, GA	4.3	9
El Paso, TX	4.1	10
Boston-Lawrence-Salem, MA-NH CMSA[6]	4.0	11
San Diego, CA	4.0	11
Portland, ME	3.8	12
Sacramento, CA	3.6	13
Richmond-Petersburg, VA	3.1	14
Washington, DC-MD-VA	3.1	14
Baton Rouge, LA	3.0	15
Norfolk-Virginia Beach-Newport News, VA	3.0	15
Chicago-Gary-Lake County, IL-IN-WI CMSA	2.4	16
Milwaukee-Racine, WI CMSA	2.4	16
Dallas-Fort Worth, TX CMSA	2.3	17
Charlotte-Gastonia-Rock Hill, NC-SC[7]	2.1	18
Nashville, TN	2.1	18

Source: U.S. Bureau of the Census, *Statistical Abstract of the United States, 1995*, (115th edition), Washington, D.C.: U.S. Government Printing Office, 1995, p. 234. Primary source: U.S. Environmental Protection Agency, published in 1993 Air Quality Update, October 1994. *Notes:* "NAAQS" stands for "National Ambient Air Quality Standards." Data are shown only for the top 25 areas. 1. May represent a different monitoring location than that used to calculate average. 2. Primarily represents Los Angeles and Orange Counties. 3. Represents primarily San Joaquin, Turlock, Merced, Madera, Fresno, Kings, Tulare, and Kern Counties. 4. Primarily represents Hartford-New Haven area. 5. Excludes the Connecticut portion. 6. Includes also both the Worcester, MA, and New Bedford, MA MSAs. 7. Excludes York County, SC.

★4324★
Air Quality
Hospital Admissions, 1993-94: Estimated Number Related to Exposure to Ozone
[Number of admissions is estimated]

City	Total admissions	Rank
Los Angeles, CA	44,005	1
New York, NY	36,221	2
San Diego, CA	19,940	3
Detroit, MI	15,108	4
Houston, TX	12,947	5
Philadelphia, PA	11,934	6
Baltimore, MD	8,528	7
Washington, DC	8,030	8
Saint Louis, MO	7,456	9
Dallas, TX	5,544	10
Milwaukee, WI	4,290	11

[Continued]

★4324★
Hospital Admissions, 1993-94: Estimated Number Related to Exposure to Ozone
[Continued]

City	Total admissions	Rank
Hartford, CT	3,421	12
New Haven, CT	1,777	13

Source: Love, Jacqueline, "Ozone Levels Still Called Health Threat for Region," *Detroit Free Press*, 20 June 1996, p. 6B.

★4325★
Air Quality
Hospital Admissions, 1993-94: Percentage Related to Exposure to Ozone

City	Percentage	Rank
Los Angeles, CA	8.5	1
Baltimore, MD	7.9	2
Washington, DC	7.6	3
Dallas, TX	7.5	4
Hartford, CT	7.5	4
New Haven, CT	7.4	5
Philadelphia, PA	7.3	6
San Diego, CA	7.3	6
Saint Louis, MO	7.3	6
Houston, TX	7.2	7
New York, NY	6.9	8
Detroit, MI	6.3	9
Milwaukee, WI	6.3	9

Source: Love, Jacqueline, "Ozone Levels Still Called Health Threat for Region," *Detroit Free Press*, 20 June 1996, p. 6B.

★4487★
Chemicals
Chemicals Shipping, 1994
[In thousands of tons]

City/Port	Tons	Rank
Beaumont, TX	3,723	4
Chocolate Bayou, TX	1,043	6
Corpus Christi, TX	4,212	3
Freeport, TX	3,428	5
Houston, TX	11,793	1
New Orleans, LA	744	8
Port Arthur, TX	777	7
South Louisiana, LA	307	9
Texas City, TX	6,219	2

Source: "Chemical Traffic," *Chemical Week*, 12 June 1996, p. 40. Primary source: U.S. Army Corps of Engineers.

★8★
Chemical Weapons
Chemical Weapons Stored, 1995

Data refer to weapons stored since the Cold War era. These weapons are scheduled for destruction by the year 2006.

[In tons]

City	Tons	Rank
Umatilla, OR	3,717.38	2
Tooele, UT	13,616	7
Newport, IN	1,269.33	6
Edgewood, MD	1,624.87	5
Richmond, KY	523.41	8
Anniston, AL	2,253.63	4
Pine Bluff, AR	3,849.71	1
Pueblo, CO	2,611.05	3

Source: Komarow, Steve, "Army Unveils Chemical Cache," *USA TODAY*, 23 January 1996, p. 3A. Primary source: U.S. Department of Defense.

★9★
Farms
Farm Subsidies, 1985-1994: Amounts

[In millions of dollars]

City	1985-94 subsidies[1]	Rank
Bakersfield, CA	192	4
Lamesa, TX	251	2
Lubbock, TX	247	3
Plainview, TX	172	5
Stuttgart, AR	280	1

Source: Ingersoll, Bruce, "Rice Farmers in Arkansas are Raising Cain as They Would Lose Most if U.S. Ends Subsidies," *Wall Street Journal*, 12 September 1995, p. A24. Primary source: Environmental Working Group; U.S. Department of Agriculture. *Note:* 1. Subsidy payments by zip code.

★10★
Farms
Government Subsidies to Farms, 1994-95: Number of Farmers in Communities Receiving the Largest Amounts

City	Farmers	Rank
Bakersfield, CA	1,607	3
Lamesa, TX	1,506	4
Lubbock, TX	5,077	1
Plainview, TX	1,668	2
Stuttgart, AR	886	5

Source: Ingersoll, Bruce, "Rice Farmers in Arkansas are Raising Cain as They Would Lose Most if U.S. Ends Subsidies," *Wall Street Journal*, 12 September 1995, p. A24. Primary source: Environmental Working Group; U.S. Department of Agriculture.

★11★
Land Area
Land Area, 1990: 25 Cities With the Least Square Mileage

Data refer to cities with populations of 200,000 or more.

[In square miles]

City/MSA	Miles	Rank
Akron, OH	62.2	21
Anaheim, CA	44.3	7
Baton Rouge, LA	73.9	23
Boston, MA	48.4	9
Buffalo, NY	40.6	6
Cincinnati, OH	77.2	25
Cleveland, OH	77.0	24
Jersey City, NJ	14.9	1
Long Beach, CA	50.0	10
Louisville, KY	62.1	22
Miami, FL	35.6	4
Minneapolis, MN	54.9	14
Newark, NJ	23.8	2
Norfolk, VA	53.8	13
Oakland, CA	56.1	16
Pittsburgh, PA	55.6	15
Richmond, VA	60.1	18
Rochester, NY	35.8	5
Saint Louis, MO	61.9	20
Saint Paul, MN	52.8	12
Saint Petersburg, FL	59.2	17
San Francisco, CA	46.7	8
Santa Ana, CA	27.1	3
Stockton, CA	52.6	11
Washington, DC	61.4	19

Source: U.S. Department of Commerce, Economics and Statistics Administration, Bureau of the Census, *County and City Data Book 1994: A Statistical Abstract Supplement*, Washington, D.C.: U.S. Government Printing Office, August 1994, p. xxvii.

★12★
Land Area
Land Area, 1990: 25 Cities With the Most Square Mileage

Data refer to cities with populations of 200,000 or more.

[In square miles]

City/MSA	Miles	Rank
Anchorage, AK	1,697.6	1
Jacksonville, FL	758.7	2
Oklahoma City, OK	608.2	3
Houston, TX	539.9	4
Nashville-Davidson, TN	473.3	5
Los Angeles, CA	469.3	6
Phoenix, AZ	419.9	7
Indianapolis, IN	361.7	8
Dallas, TX	342.4	9
San Antonio, TX	333.0	10
San Diego, CA	324.0	11
Kansas City, MO	311.5	12
New York, NY	308.9	13
Lexington-Fayette, KY	284.5	14

[Continued]

★12★

Land Area, 1990: 25 Cities With the Most Square Mileage

[Continued]

City/MSA	Miles	Rank
Fort Worth, TX	281.1	15
Memphis, TN	256.0	16
Virginia Beach, VA	248.3	17
El Paso, TX	245.4	18
Chicago, IL	227.2	19
Austin, TX	217.8	20
Columbus, OH	190.9	21
Tulsa, OK	183.5	22
Colorado Springs, CO	183.2	23
New Orleans, LA	180.6	24
Charlotte, NC	174.3	25

Source: U.S. Department of Commerce, Economics and Statistics Administration, Bureau of the Census, *County and City Data Book 1994: A Statistical Abstract Supplement,* Washington, D.C.: U.S. Government Printing Office, August 1994, p. xxvii.

★13★

Livestock

Dairy Goats, 1995: Leading Counties

County	Number	Rank
Anderson County, SC	548	20
Charles County, MD	966	9
Clackamas County, OR	858	10
Columbia County, NY	1,080	6
Columbia County, WI	1,447	4
Crawford County, WI	526	22
Dane County, WI	786	12
Douglas County, OR	585	19
Frederick County, MD	639	16
Fresno County, CA	1,104	5
Kings County, CA	3,416	1
Maricopa County, AZ	657	14
Merced County, CA	1,736	2
Monterey County, CA	1,030	8
Polk County, MO	640	15
Portage County, WI	545	21
San Bernardino County, CA	1,063	7
San Diego County, CA	624	18
Sonoma County, CA	770	13
Stanislaus County, CA	1,583	3
Tioga County, NY	629	17
Waller County, TX	846	11

Source: Dairy Goat Journal, (March 1996), p. 28.

★14★

National Parks

Affiliated Areas of the National Park Service, 1995

The law by which the National Park Service administers areas of land or water for park, monument, historic, parkway, recreational, or other purposes, specifically excludes properties that are neither federally owned nor directly administered by the National Park Service but which use some National Park Service Assistance.

City/Location	Acreage	Rank
Brookneal, VA	117	5
Dunseith, ND	2,330.30	4
Fredericksburg, VA	14,004	2
Gering, NE	83.36	7
Lansing, MI	52	8
Lubec, ME	2,721.50	3
Madison, WI	32,500	1
Newport, RI	0.23	13
Oregon City, OR	0.63	11
Philadelphia, PA	3.71	10
Richmond, VA	20.63	9
River Forest, IL	91.20	6
Washington, DC	0.35	12

Source: U.S. Department of the Interior, National Park Service, *The National Parks: Index 1995,* Washington, D.C.: U.S. Department of the Interior, 1995, p. 104.

★15★

Sewerage Systems

Sewerage Systems Cleanups, 1996: Costs in Selected Cities

[In millions of dollars]

City	Spending amount ($millions)	Rank
Seattle, WA	585	1
Boston, MA	370	2
Saint Paul, MN	300	3
Portland, ME	52	4

Source: Aeppel, Timothy, "Giant Sewage Storage Tank Shakes City," *Wall Street Journal,* 22 January 1996, p. B1.

★16★

Toxic Chemical Releases

Deaths Caused By Toxic Pollutants, 1995: Leading Cities

City	Number of deaths	Rank
Los Angeles, CA	5,873	1
New York, NY	4,024	2
Chicago, IL	3,479	3
Philadelphia, PA	2,599	4
Detroit, MI	2,123	5
Riverside-San Bernardino, CA	1,905	6
San Francisco-Oakland, CA	1,270	7
Pittsburgh, PA	1,216	8

[Continued]

★16★

Deaths Caused By Toxic Pollutants, 1995: Leading Cities

[Continued]

City	Number of deaths	Rank
Saint Louis, MO	1,195	9
Cleveland, OH	1,161	10

Source: "Fine Pollutants in Air Cause Many Deaths, Study Suggests," *New York Times,* 9 May 1996, p. A8. Primary source: Environmental Protection Agency; Natural Resources Defense Council.

★17★

Toxic Chemical Releases

High Particle Pollution, 1990-1994: Leading MSAs

Data refer to the concentration of particles of 10 microns or smaller, in micrograms per cubic meter of air.

[In micrograms per cubic meter of air]

MSA	Concentration of particles	Rank
Visalia-Tulare-Porterville, CA	60.4	1
Bakersfield, CA	54.8	2
Fresno, CA	51.7	3
Riverside-San Bernardino, CA	48.1	4
Stockton, CA	44.8	5
Los Angeles-Long Beach, CA	43.8	6
Phoenix, AZ	39.5	7
Spokane, WA	38.7	8
Reno, NV	38.5	9
Las Vegas, NV	38.3	10
Anaheim-Santa Ana, CA	38.1	11
Medford, OR	37.9	12
Saint Joseph, MO	37.6	13
Yuba City, CA	37.4	14
Steubenville-Weirton, OH-WV	36.6	15
Provo-Orem, UT	36.5	16
Cleveland, OH	35.6	17
Omaha, NE-IA	35.5	18
Atlanta, GA	35.1	19
Chattanooga, TN-GA	34.9	20
Paterson-Clifton-Passaic, NJ	34.8	21
San Diego, CA	34.8	21
Boise, ID	34.0	22
Chicago, IL	33.7	23
Roanoke, VA	33.7	23
Philadelphia, PA-NJ	33.5	24
Detroit, MI	33.2	25
Salt Lake City-Ogden, UT	33.2	25
Yakima, WA	33.1	26
Chico, CA	33.1	26

Source: "Fine Pollutants in Air Cause Many Deaths, Study Suggests," *New York Times,* 9 May 1996, p. A8. Primary source: Environmental Protection Agency; Natural Resources Defense Council. *Note:* "MSA" stands for "Metropolitan Statistical Area."

★18★

Toxic Chemical Releases

Toxic Chemical Releases, 1992: 1,1,1-trichloroethane

County	Releases	Rank
Los Angeles County, CA	12,596,880	1
Orange County, CA	4,846,869	2
Cook County, IL	4,280,892	3
New Haven County, CT	2,431,782	4
Cuyahoga County, OH	2,371,458	5
Fairfield County, CT	2,133,773	6
Hartford County, CT	2,017,608	7
Salt Lake County, UT	1,849,689	8
San Diego County, CA	1,728,603	9
Jackson County, IN	1,641,999	10
Maricopa County, AZ	1,611,785	11
Union County, OH	1,602,806	12
Milwaukee County, WI	1,559,277	13
Montgomery County, PA	1,487,206	14
Elkhart County, IN	1,461,728	15
Hamilton County, OH	1,447,705	16
Greenville County, SC	1,385,996	17
Dallas County, TX	1,377,206	18
Davidson County, TN	1,363,945	19
Franklin County, MO	1,286,915	20

Source: U.S. Environmental Protection Agency, "Toxic Release Inventory, 1992." In *National Economic, Social, and Environmental Data Bank* [CD-ROM]. Prepared by U.S. Department of Commerce, Economics, and Statistics Administration, Washington, D.C.: U.S. Department of Commerce, National Economic, Social, and Environmental Data Bank, Economics and Statistics Administration, Office of Business Analysis, February 1995.

★19★

Toxic Chemical Releases

Toxic Chemical Releases, 1992: 1,1,2,2-tetrachloroethane

County	Releases	Rank
Calcasieu Parish, LA	79,955	1
Brazoria County, TX	41,710	2
Harris County, TX	23,985	3
Union County, NJ	22,166	4
San Patricio County, TX	12,587	5
Denver County, CO	10,000	6
Allegheny County, PA	4,600	7
Marshall County, KY	1,307	8
Iberville Parish, LA	1,260	9
York County, SC	765	10
Ascension Parish, LA	706	11
Clay County, FL	211	12
Sullivan County, TN	70	13
Sedgwick County, KS	27	14
Ralls County, MO	2	15

Source: U.S. Environmental Protection Agency, "Toxic Release Inventory, 1992." In *National Economic, Social, and Environmental Data Bank* [CD-ROM]. Prepared by U.S. Department of Commerce, Economics, and Statistics Administration, Washington, D.C.: U.S. Department of Commerce, National Economic, Social, and Environmental Data Bank, Economics and Statistics Administration, Office of Business Analysis, February 1995.

★20★
Toxic Chemical Releases

Toxic Chemical Releases, 1992: 1,1,2-trichloroethane

County	Releases	Rank
Saint Louis City/County, MO	1,242,850	1
Harris County, TX	425,470	2
Custer County, OK	272,911	3
Calcasieu Parish, LA	206,173	4
Marshall County, KY	165,807	5
Floyd County, IA	99,255	6
San Patricio County, TX	45,317	7
Habersham County, GA	43,420	8
Washington County, MN	30,004	9
Brazoria County, TX	28,130	10
Middlesex County, MA	16,610	11
Brown County, TX	13,466	12
Iberville Parish, LA	11,078	13
Cook County, IL	10,554	14
St James Parish, LA	6,065	15
Monroe County, NY	6,061	16
Ascension Parish, LA	2,170	17
Jefferson County, WI	2,070	18
Jefferson County, TX	333	19
Clay County, FL	316	20

Source: U.S. Environmental Protection Agency, "Toxic Release Inventory, 1992." In *National Economic, Social, and Environmental Data Bank* [CD-ROM]. Prepared by U.S. Department of Commerce, Economics, and Statistics Administration, Washington, D.C.: U.S. Department of Commerce, National Economic, Social, and Environmental Data Bank, Economics and Statistics Administration, Office of Business Analysis, February 1995.

★21★
Toxic Chemical Releases

Toxic Chemical Releases, 1992: 1,1-dimethyl Hydrazine

County	Releases	Rank
Sacramento County, CA	8,711	1
Calcasieu Parish, LA	361	2
Ascension Parish, LA	104	3
Washington County, AL	88	4

Source: U.S. Environmental Protection Agency, "Toxic Release Inventory, 1992." In *National Economic, Social, and Environmental Data Bank* [CD-ROM]. Prepared by U.S. Department of Commerce, Economics, and Statistics Administration, Washington, D.C.: U.S. Department of Commerce, National Economic, Social, and Environmental Data Bank, Economics and Statistics Administration, Office of Business Analysis, February 1995.

★22★
Toxic Chemical Releases

Toxic Chemical Releases, 1992: 1,2,4-trichlorobenzene

County	Releases	Rank
Henderson County, KY	157,050	1
Jefferson County, TX	135,405	2
Hamilton County, OH	123,645	3
St Clair County, IL	94,630	4
Harris County, TX	80,000	5

[Continued]

★22★

Toxic Chemical Releases, 1992: 1,2,4-trichlorobenzene
[Continued]

County	Releases	Rank
Mecklenburg County, VA	68,831	6
Rockingham County, NC	61,605	7
Chesterfield County, SC	54,005	8
Schuylkill County, PA	45,050	9
Mecklenburg County, NC	36,624	10
Carter County, OK	29,300	11
Grayson County, TX	28,285	12
Somerset County, NJ	27,786	13
Rutherford County, NC	27,683	14
Brevard County, FL	27,608	15
Anson County, NC	23,550	16
Dale County, AL	22,750	17
Gaston County, NC	21,824	18
Grays Harbor County, WA	21,650	19
Hoke County, NC	20,948	20

Source: U.S. Environmental Protection Agency, "Toxic Release Inventory, 1992." In *National Economic, Social, and Environmental Data Bank* [CD-ROM]. Prepared by U.S. Department of Commerce, Economics, and Statistics Administration, Washington, D.C.: U.S. Department of Commerce, National Economic, Social, and Environmental Data Bank, Economics and Statistics Administration, Office of Business Analysis, February 1995.

★23★
Toxic Chemical Releases

Toxic Chemical Releases, 1992: 1,2,4-trimethylbenzene

County	Releases	Rank
Colbert County, AL	518,574	1
Lancaster County, SC	238,404	2
Lake County, IN	152,418	3
Morton County, ND	133,297	4
Sullivan County, TN	132,352	5
Wayne County, MI	130,199	6
Montgomery County, KS	127,000	7
Jackson County, MS	116,176	8
Eau Claire County, WI	111,735	9
Jefferson County, TX	107,797	10
Polk County, GA	105,457	11
Los Angeles County, CA	98,997	12
Brown County, WI	90,040	13
York County, VA	88,000	14
Kewaunee County, WI	86,527	15
Galveston County, TX	83,615	16
Westchester County, NY	83,175	17
Niagara County, NY	72,284	18
Muskogee County, OK	67,350	19
St Louis County, MO	66,613	20

Source: U.S. Environmental Protection Agency, "Toxic Release Inventory, 1992." In *National Economic, Social, and Environmental Data Bank* [CD-ROM]. Prepared by U.S. Department of Commerce, Economics, and Statistics Administration, Washington, D.C.: U.S. Department of Commerce, National Economic, Social, and Environmental Data Bank, Economics and Statistics Administration, Office of Business Analysis, February 1995.

★24★
Toxic Chemical Releases
Toxic Chemical Releases, 1992: 1,2-butylene Oxide

County	Releases	Rank
Midland County, MI	43,776	1
Rutherford County, TN	11,138	2
Orange County, CA	10,355	3
Calcasieu Parish, LA	7,232	4
Brazoria County, TX	7,100	5
Ouachita Parish, LA	6,100	6
Shelby County, TN	1,250	7
Ascension Parish, LA	1,156	8
Vermillion County, IN	1,010	9
Spartanburg County, SC	785	10
Harris County, TX	769	11
Erie County, NY	700	12
Georgetown County, SC	425	13
Nassau County, NY	260	14
Travis County, TX	250	15
Montgomery County, TX	158	16

Source: U.S. Environmental Protection Agency, "Toxic Release Inventory, 1992." In *National Economic, Social, and Environmental Data Bank* [CD-ROM]. Prepared by U.S. Department of Commerce, Economics, and Statistics Administration, Washington, D.C.: U.S. Department of Commerce, National Economic, Social, and Environmental Data Bank, Economics and Statistics Administration, Office of Business Analysis, February 1995.

★25★
Toxic Chemical Releases
Toxic Chemical Releases, 1992: 1,2-dibromoethane

County	Releases	Rank
Orleans County, NY	69,895	1
Salem County, NJ	20,313	2
Columbia County, AR	16,750	3
Union County, AR	11,689	4
Washington County, OH	10,702	5
Los Angeles County, CA	1,390	6
Honolulu County, HI	500	7
Harris County, TX	500	7
Jefferson County, TX	500	7
Moore County, TX	385	8
Kern County, CA	300	9
Salt Lake County, UT	250	10
St Bernard Parish, LA	110	11
Contra Costa County, CA	92	12
West Baton Rouge Parish, LA	68	13
East Baton Rouge Parish, LA	59	14
Live Oak County, TX	6	15
Dakota County, MN	4	16

Source: U.S. Environmental Protection Agency, "Toxic Release Inventory, 1992." In *National Economic, Social, and Environmental Data Bank* [CD-ROM]. Prepared by U.S. Department of Commerce, Economics, and Statistics Administration, Washington, D.C.: U.S. Department of Commerce, National Economic, Social, and Environmental Data Bank, Economics and Statistics Administration, Office of Business Analysis, February 1995.

★26★
Toxic Chemical Releases
Toxic Chemical Releases, 1992: 1,2-dichlorobenzene

County	Releases	Rank
Harris County, TX	828,374	1
Dutchess County, NY	480,600	2
Posey County, IN	273,357	3
Cocke County, TN	270,098	4
Chambers County, TX	264,373	5
Independence County, AR	191,120	6
Worcester County, MA	167,976	7
Marinette County, WI	121,800	8
Centre County, PA	120,500	9
St Clair County, IL	108,500	10
New Castle County, DE	85,507	11
Marshall County, WV	66,382	12
Placer County, CA	47,950	13
Berkshire County, MA	40,844	14
Salem County, NJ	37,121	15
Ascension Parish, LA	32,459	16
Tallapoosa County, AL	25,988	17
Union County, NJ	24,458	18
Luzerne County, PA	24,145	19
Brevard County, FL	22,947	20

Source: U.S. Environmental Protection Agency, "Toxic Release Inventory, 1992." In *National Economic, Social, and Environmental Data Bank* [CD-ROM]. Prepared by U.S. Department of Commerce, Economics, and Statistics Administration, Washington, D.C.: U.S. Department of Commerce, National Economic, Social, and Environmental Data Bank, Economics and Statistics Administration, Office of Business Analysis, February 1995.

★27★
Toxic Chemical Releases
Toxic Chemical Releases, 1992: 1,2-dichloroethane

County	Releases	Rank
Lake County, IN	1,842,250	1
Jefferson County, WV	1,140,273	2
Calcasieu Parish, LA	1,095,247	3
Charleston County, SC	981,872	4
Ascension Parish, LA	924,333	5
Weld County, CO	882,622	6
Marshall County, KY	698,999	7
Rowan County, NC	412,820	8
Harris County, TX	292,752	9
Iberville Parish, LA	195,905	10
Brazoria County, TX	152,860	11
Calhoun County, TX	124,145	12
Muskegon County, MI	119,796	13
East Baton Rouge Parish, LA	117,908	14
Jackson County, MO	102,837	15
Orleans County, NY	86,630	16
Rensselaer County, NY	86,400	17
Northumberland County, PA	77,210	18
Salem County, NJ	67,735	19
Wexford County, MI	62,509	20

Source: U.S. Environmental Protection Agency, "Toxic Release Inventory, 1992." In *National Economic, Social, and Environmental Data Bank* [CD-ROM]. Prepared by U.S. Department of Commerce, Economics, and Statistics Administration, Washington, D.C.: U.S. Department of Commerce, National Economic, Social, and Environmental Data Bank, Economics and Statistics Administration, Office of Business Analysis, February 1995.

★28★
Toxic Chemical Releases

Toxic Chemical Releases, 1992: 1,2-dichloroethylene

County	Releases	Rank
Durham County, NC	68,800	1
Calcasieu Parish, LA	43,715	2
Sedgwick County, KS	7,972	3
Marshall County, KY	4,390	4
Brazoria County, TX	2,021	5
Harris County, TX	1,155	6
Ascension Parish, LA	721	7
Honolulu County, HI	255	8
Galveston County, TX	3	9

Source: U.S. Environmental Protection Agency, "Toxic Release Inventory, 1992." In *National Economic, Social, and Environmental Data Bank* [CD-ROM]. Prepared by U.S. Department of Commerce, Economics, and Statistics Administration, Washington, D.C.: U.S. Department of Commerce, National Economic, Social, and Environmental Data Bank, Economics and Statistics Administration, Office of Business Analysis, February 1995.

★29★
Toxic Chemical Releases

Toxic Chemical Releases, 1992: 1,2-dichloropropane

County	Releases	Rank
Monroe County, NY	390,495	1
Milwaukee County, WI	288,669	2
Brazoria County, TX	151,400	3
Franklin City/County, VA	133,073	4
Iberville Parish, LA	59,180	5
Burlington County, NJ	10,025	6
St Charles Parish, LA	4,603	7
New Castle County, DE	1,100	8
Sedgwick County, KS	852	9
Jefferson County, TX	230	10
Los Angeles County, CA	192	11
Contra Costa County, CA	52	12

Source: U.S. Environmental Protection Agency, "Toxic Release Inventory, 1992." In *National Economic, Social, and Environmental Data Bank* [CD-ROM]. Prepared by U.S. Department of Commerce, Economics, and Statistics Administration, Washington, D.C.: U.S. Department of Commerce, National Economic, Social, and Environmental Data Bank, Economics and Statistics Administration, Office of Business Analysis, February 1995.

★30★
Toxic Chemical Releases

Toxic Chemical Releases, 1992: 1,3-butadiene

County	Releases	Rank
Jefferson County, TX	968,122	1
Harris County, TX	950,517	2
Orange County, TX	432,019	3
Brazoria County, TX	389,505	4
Hamilton County, TN	228,162	5
Wood County, WV	199,000	6
Daviess County, KY	163,302	7
Jefferson County, KY	144,840	8
Summit County, OH	139,336	9

[Continued]

★30★
Toxic Chemical Releases

Toxic Chemical Releases, 1992: 1,3-butadiene
[Continued]

County	Releases	Rank
Muscatine County, IA	133,000	10
St Charles Parish, LA	116,022	11
Lake County, OH	105,335	12
Calcasieu Parish, LA	103,724	13
Ector County, TX	101,666	14
East Baton Rouge Parish, LA	97,228	15
New London County, CT	78,300	16
Galveston County, TX	76,641	17
Erie County, NY	71,817	18
Nueces County, TX	69,155	19
Beaver County, PA	69,032	20

Source: U.S. Environmental Protection Agency, "Toxic Release Inventory, 1992." In *National Economic, Social, and Environmental Data Bank* [CD-ROM]. Prepared by U.S. Department of Commerce, Economics, and Statistics Administration, Washington, D.C.: U.S. Department of Commerce, National Economic, Social, and Environmental Data Bank, Economics and Statistics Administration, Office of Business Analysis, February 1995.

★31★
Toxic Chemical Releases

Toxic Chemical Releases, 1992: 1,3-dichlorobenzene

County	Releases	Rank
New Castle County, DE	5,347	1
Marshall County, WV	4,150	2
St Clair County, IL	1,463	3
Calcasieu Parish, LA	1	4

Source: U.S. Environmental Protection Agency, "Toxic Release Inventory, 1992." In *National Economic, Social, and Environmental Data Bank* [CD-ROM]. Prepared by U.S. Department of Commerce, Economics, and Statistics Administration, Washington, D.C.: U.S. Department of Commerce, National Economic, Social, and Environmental Data Bank, Economics and Statistics Administration, Office of Business Analysis, February 1995.

★32★
Toxic Chemical Releases

Toxic Chemical Releases, 1992: 1,3-dichloropropylene

County	Releases	Rank
Brazoria County, TX	45,810	1
St Charles Parish, LA	9,500	2
New Castle County, DE	3,885	3
Contra Costa County, CA	874	4
San Benito County, CA	500	5
Mc Henry County, IL	255	6
Midland County, MI	227	7

Source: U.S. Environmental Protection Agency, "Toxic Release Inventory, 1992." In *National Economic, Social, and Environmental Data Bank* [CD-ROM]. Prepared by U.S. Department of Commerce, Economics, and Statistics Administration, Washington, D.C.: U.S. Department of Commerce, National Economic, Social, and Environmental Data Bank, Economics and Statistics Administration, Office of Business Analysis, February 1995.

★33★
Toxic Chemical Releases

Toxic Chemical Releases, 1992: 1,4-dichlorobenzene

County	Releases	Rank
Marshall County, WV	359,200	1
Worcester County, MA	283,156	2
St Clair County, IL	180,400	3
New Castle County, DE	69,296	4
Seneca County, OH	40,200	5
Wabash County, IN	36,090	6
Hutchinson County, TX	16,300	7
Lucas County, OH	14,511	8
Hampshire County, MA	8,255	9
Cook County, IL	6,600	10
Fulton County, GA	1,369	11
Washington County, OK	302	12
Passaic County, NJ	250	13
Pinellas County, FL	35	14
Pike County, MO	35	14
San Diego County, CA	10	15
Saint Louis City/County, MO	5	16
Calcasieu Parish, LA	1	17

Source: U.S. Environmental Protection Agency, "Toxic Release Inventory, 1992." In *National Economic, Social, and Environmental Data Bank* [CD-ROM]. Prepared by U.S. Department of Commerce, Economics, and Statistics Administration, Washington, D.C.: U.S. Department of Commerce, National Economic, Social, and Environmental Data Bank, Economics and Statistics Administration, Office of Business Analysis, February 1995.

★34★
Toxic Chemical Releases

Toxic Chemical Releases, 1992: 1,4-dioxane

County	Releases	Rank
San Diego County, CA	141,974	1
Spartanburg County, SC	102,755	2
Rowan County, NC	89,005	3
St Charles Parish, LA	65,092	4
Hennepin County, MN	46,013	5
Monroe County, NY	40,602	6
Mobile County, AL	39,350	7
Greenville County, SC	39,250	8
Richland County, SC	38,000	9
Lenoir County, NC	37,180	10
Union County, OH	36,261	11
East Baton Rouge Parish, LA	35,900	12
Salt Lake County, UT	34,856	13
Brunswick County, NC	25,774	14
Darlington County, SC	23,851	15
Montgomery County, PA	23,832	16
Mc Leod County, MN	23,663	17
Orange County, CA	23,007	18
Davidson County, TN	22,021	19
Brazoria County, TX	21,600	20

Source: U.S. Environmental Protection Agency, "Toxic Release Inventory, 1992." In *National Economic, Social, and Environmental Data Bank* [CD-ROM]. Prepared by U.S. Department of Commerce, Economics, and Statistics Administration, Washington, D.C.: U.S. Department of Commerce, National Economic, Social, and Environmental Data Bank, Economics and Statistics Administration, Office of Business Analysis, February 1995.

★35★
Toxic Chemical Releases

Toxic Chemical Releases, 1992: 2,3-dichloropropene

County	Releases	Rank
Harris County, TX	201,640	1
Brazoria County, TX	90,350	2
Tippecanoe County, IN	720	3

Source: U.S. Environmental Protection Agency, "Toxic Release Inventory, 1992." In *National Economic, Social, and Environmental Data Bank* [CD-ROM]. Prepared by U.S. Department of Commerce, Economics, and Statistics Administration, Washington, D.C.: U.S. Department of Commerce, National Economic, Social, and Environmental Data Bank, Economics and Statistics Administration, Office of Business Analysis, February 1995.

★36★
Toxic Chemical Releases

Toxic Chemical Releases, 1992: 2,4,6-trichlorophenol

County	Releases	Rank
Midland County, MI	157	1

Source: U.S. Environmental Protection Agency, "Toxic Release Inventory, 1992." In *National Economic, Social, and Environmental Data Bank* [CD-ROM]. Prepared by U.S. Department of Commerce, Economics, and Statistics Administration, Washington, D.C.: U.S. Department of Commerce, National Economic, Social, and Environmental Data Bank, Economics and Statistics Administration, Office of Business Analysis, February 1995.

★37★
Toxic Chemical Releases

Toxic Chemical Releases, 1992: 2,4-d

County	Releases	Rank
Buchanan County, MO	49,358	1
Yellowstone County, MT	12,955	2
Hendry County, FL	10,412	3
Jefferson County, TX	2,605	4
Freeborn County, MN	1,804	5
Lucas County, OH	1,565	6
Cook County, IL	1,060	7
Wyandotte County, KS	1,005	8
Henry County, OH	1,000	9
Page County, IA	750	10
Union County, OH	543	11
Multnomah County, OR	510	12
Talladega County, AL	500	13
Cherokee County, KS	260	14
Coahoma County, MS	260	14
Hamilton County, IA	250	15
Stanly County, NC	250	15
Los Angeles County, CA	250	15
Midland County, MI	136	16
Bartow County, GA	75	17

Source: U.S. Environmental Protection Agency, "Toxic Release Inventory, 1992." In *National Economic, Social, and Environmental Data Bank* [CD-ROM]. Prepared by U.S. Department of Commerce, Economics, and Statistics Administration, Washington, D.C.: U.S. Department of Commerce, National Economic, Social, and Environmental Data Bank, Economics and Statistics Administration, Office of Business Analysis, February 1995.

★38★

Toxic Chemical Releases

Toxic Chemical Releases, 1992: 2,4-diaminoanisole

County	Releases	Rank
Jackson County, MS	26	1

Source: U.S. Environmental Protection Agency, "Toxic Release Inventory, 1992." In *National Economic, Social, and Environmental Data Bank* [CD-ROM]. Prepared by U.S. Department of Commerce, Economics, and Statistics Administration, Washington, D.C.: U.S. Department of Commerce, National Economic, Social, and Environmental Data Bank, Economics and Statistics Administration, Office of Business Analysis, February 1995.

★39★

Toxic Chemical Releases

Toxic Chemical Releases, 1992: 2,4-diaminoanisole Sulfate

County	Releases	Rank
Kings County, NY	250	1

Source: U.S. Environmental Protection Agency, "Toxic Release Inventory, 1992." In *National Economic, Social, and Environmental Data Bank* [CD-ROM]. Prepared by U.S. Department of Commerce, Economics, and Statistics Administration, Washington, D.C.: U.S. Department of Commerce, National Economic, Social, and Environmental Data Bank, Economics and Statistics Administration, Office of Business Analysis, February 1995.

★40★

Toxic Chemical Releases

Toxic Chemical Releases, 1992: 2,4-diaminotoluene

County	Releases	Rank
Orangeburg County, SC	4,170	1
Rensselaer County, NY	1,006	2
Essex/Passaic County, NJ	503	3

Source: U.S. Environmental Protection Agency, "Toxic Release Inventory, 1992." In *National Economic, Social, and Environmental Data Bank* [CD-ROM]. Prepared by U.S. Department of Commerce, Economics, and Statistics Administration, Washington, D.C.: U.S. Department of Commerce, National Economic, Social, and Environmental Data Bank, Economics and Statistics Administration, Office of Business Analysis, February 1995.

★41★

Toxic Chemical Releases

Toxic Chemical Releases, 1992: 2,4-dichlorophenol

County	Releases	Rank
Jefferson County, TX	81,460	1
Midland County, MI	400	2
Phillips County, AR	250	3
Monroe County, NY	9	4

Source: U.S. Environmental Protection Agency, "Toxic Release Inventory, 1992." In *National Economic, Social, and Environmental Data Bank* [CD-ROM]. Prepared by U.S. Department of Commerce, Economics, and Statistics Administration, Washington, D.C.: U.S. Department of Commerce, National Economic, Social, and Environmental Data Bank, Economics and Statistics Administration, Office of Business Analysis, February 1995.

★42★

Toxic Chemical Releases

Toxic Chemical Releases, 1992: 2,4-dimethylphenol

County	Releases	Rank
Harris County, TX	43,000	1
Porter County, IN	26,600	2
Catawba County, NC	5,250	3
Tuscaloosa County, AL	2,037	4
Shelby County, TN	1,738	5
Skagit County, WA	1,250	6
Audrain County, MO	1,005	7
Saint Louis City/County, MO	636	8
Middlesex County, NJ	500	9
Schenectady County, NY	364	10
Union County, NJ	288	11
Carbon County, WY	251	12
Allegheny County, PA	202	13
Dakota County, MN	58	14
Orange County, TX	27	15
Iberville Parish, LA	5	16
Butler County, KS	2	17

Source: U.S. Environmental Protection Agency, "Toxic Release Inventory, 1992." In *National Economic, Social, and Environmental Data Bank* [CD-ROM]. Prepared by U.S. Department of Commerce, Economics, and Statistics Administration, Washington, D.C.: U.S. Department of Commerce, National Economic, Social, and Environmental Data Bank, Economics and Statistics Administration, Office of Business Analysis, February 1995.

★43★

Toxic Chemical Releases

Toxic Chemical Releases, 1992: 2,4-dinitrophenol

County	Releases	Rank
Jefferson County, TX	112,760	1
Sullivan County, TN	87,121	2
Allegheny County, PA	12,148	3
Westmoreland County, PA	12,078	4
Ector County, TX	6,288	5
Mecklenburg County, NC	1,607	6
Erie County, NY	297	7
Galveston County, TX	255	8
Harris County, TX	198	9
Jackson County, MS	10	10

Source: U.S. Environmental Protection Agency, "Toxic Release Inventory, 1992." In *National Economic, Social, and Environmental Data Bank* [CD-ROM]. Prepared by U.S. Department of Commerce, Economics, and Statistics Administration, Washington, D.C.: U.S. Department of Commerce, National Economic, Social, and Environmental Data Bank, Economics and Statistics Administration, Office of Business Analysis, February 1995.

★44★

Toxic Chemical Releases

Toxic Chemical Releases, 1992: 2,4-dinitrotoluene

County	Releases	Rank
Ascension Parish, LA	234,572	1
Chambers County, TX	16,279	2
Salem County, NJ	4,428	3
Marshall County, WV	1,875	4
Pulaski County, VA	1,079	5
Wakulla County, FL	50	6
Jackson County, MS	19	7
Clark County, IN	1	8

Source: U.S. Environmental Protection Agency, "Toxic Release Inventory, 1992." In *National Economic, Social, and Environmental Data Bank* [CD-ROM]. Prepared by U.S. Department of Commerce, Economics, and Statistics Administration, Washington, D.C.: U.S. Department of Commerce, National Economic, Social, and Environmental Data Bank, Economics and Statistics Administration, Office of Business Analysis, February 1995.

★45★

Toxic Chemical Releases

Toxic Chemical Releases, 1992: 2,6-dinitrotoluene

County	Releases	Rank
Ascension Parish, LA	62,448	1
Chambers County, TX	4,380	2
Marshall County, WV	555	3

Source: U.S. Environmental Protection Agency, "Toxic Release Inventory, 1992." In *National Economic, Social, and Environmental Data Bank* [CD-ROM]. Prepared by U.S. Department of Commerce, Economics, and Statistics Administration, Washington, D.C.: U.S. Department of Commerce, National Economic, Social, and Environmental Data Bank, Economics and Statistics Administration, Office of Business Analysis, February 1995.

★46★

Toxic Chemical Releases

Toxic Chemical Releases, 1992: 2,6-xylidine

County	Releases	Rank
Salem County, NJ	1,923	1

Source: U.S. Environmental Protection Agency, "Toxic Release Inventory, 1992." In *National Economic, Social, and Environmental Data Bank* [CD-ROM]. Prepared by U.S. Department of Commerce, Economics, and Statistics Administration, Washington, D.C.: U.S. Department of Commerce, National Economic, Social, and Environmental Data Bank, Economics and Statistics Administration, Office of Business Analysis, February 1995.

★47★

Toxic Chemical Releases

Toxic Chemical Releases, 1992: 2-ethoxyethanol

County	Releases	Rank
Sullivan County, TN	112,200	1
Ramsey County, MN	102,005	2
Douglas County, MN	98,250	3
Sedgwick County, KS	96,010	4
Jefferson County, KY	95,481	5

[Continued]

★47★

Toxic Chemical Releases, 1992: 2-ethoxyethanol
[Continued]

County	Releases	Rank
Santa Clara County, CA	86,200	6
Wayne County, MI	76,986	7
Oakland County, MI	36,250	8
Alameda County, CA	30,594	9
Clark County, IN	30,465	10
Jackson County, MS	27,296	11
Franklin County, OH	26,939	12
Albemarle County, VA	26,727	13
King County, WA	26,000	14
Macomb County, MI	24,600	15
De Kalb County, GA	23,117	16
Madison County, TN	23,013	17
Goodhue County, MN	20,914	18
Bedford County, TN	20,425	19
Pickaway County, OH	20,000	20

Source: U.S. Environmental Protection Agency, "Toxic Release Inventory, 1992." In *National Economic, Social, and Environmental Data Bank* [CD-ROM]. Prepared by U.S. Department of Commerce, Economics, and Statistics Administration, Washington, D.C.: U.S. Department of Commerce, National Economic, Social, and Environmental Data Bank, Economics and Statistics Administration, Office of Business Analysis, February 1995.

★48★

Toxic Chemical Releases

Toxic Chemical Releases, 1992: 2-methoxyethanol

County	Releases	Rank
Delaware County, PA	1,022,800	1
Rockland County, NY	861,900	2
Barceloneta County, PR	461,511	3
Hampton County, SC	343,590	4
La Crosse County, WI	149,800	5
Middlesex County, MA	141,770	6
Merrimack County, NH	117,428	7
Monroe County, NY	101,602	8
Worcester County, MA	97,784	9
Sullivan County, TN	56,001	10
Westchester County, NY	51,866	11
Riverside County, CA	50,000	12
Los Angeles County, CA	49,272	13
Dutchess County, NY	49,007	14
Hampshire County, MA	43,833	15
Hampden County, MA	38,732	16
Rensselaer County, NY	37,999	17
Brunswick County, NC	35,223	18
Somerset County, NJ	29,420	19
St. Louis County, MO	28,104	20

Source: U.S. Environmental Protection Agency, "Toxic Release Inventory, 1992." In *National Economic, Social, and Environmental Data Bank* [CD-ROM]. Prepared by U.S. Department of Commerce, Economics, and Statistics Administration, Washington, D.C.: U.S. Department of Commerce, National Economic, Social, and Environmental Data Bank, Economics and Statistics Administration, Office of Business Analysis, February 1995.

★49★

Toxic Chemical Releases

Toxic Chemical Releases, 1992: 2-nitrophenol

County	Releases	Rank
St Clair County, IL	39,500	1
Iberville Parish, LA	1,027	2

Source: U.S. Environmental Protection Agency, "Toxic Release Inventory, 1992." In *National Economic, Social, and Environmental Data Bank* [CD-ROM]. Prepared by U.S. Department of Commerce, Economics, and Statistics Administration, Washington, D.C.: U.S. Department of Commerce, National Economic, Social, and Environmental Data Bank, Economics and Statistics Administration, Office of Business Analysis, February 1995.

★50★

Toxic Chemical Releases

Toxic Chemical Releases, 1992: 2-nitropropane

County	Releases	Rank
Harris County, TX	92,380	1
Ouachita Parish, LA	69,100	2
Cook County, IL	6,800	3
Phillips County, AR	5,605	4
Bergen County, NJ	3,693	5
Sioux County, IA	750	6
Ralls County, MO	120	7
Ottawa County, MI	5	8

Source: U.S. Environmental Protection Agency, "Toxic Release Inventory, 1992." In *National Economic, Social, and Environmental Data Bank* [CD-ROM]. Prepared by U.S. Department of Commerce, Economics, and Statistics Administration, Washington, D.C.: U.S. Department of Commerce, National Economic, Social, and Environmental Data Bank, Economics and Statistics Administration, Office of Business Analysis, February 1995.

★51★

Toxic Chemical Releases

Toxic Chemical Releases, 1992: 2-phenylphenol

County	Releases	Rank
Sullivan County, TN	8,693	1
Somerset County, NJ	2,577	2
Wyandotte County, KS	800	3
San Bernardino County, CA	785	4
Orange County, FL	750	5
Will County, IL	677	6
Saint Louis City/County, MO	500	7
Los Angeles County, CA	500	7
Midland County, MI	480	8
Huntington County, IN	260	9
Riverside County, CA	260	9
Hamilton County, OH	250	10
Milwaukee County, WI	250	10
Lucas County, OH	245	11
Sandusky County, OH	5	12

Source: U.S. Environmental Protection Agency, "Toxic Release Inventory, 1992." In *National Economic, Social, and Environmental Data Bank* [CD-ROM]. Prepared by U.S. Department of Commerce, Economics, and Statistics Administration, Washington, D.C.: U.S. Department of Commerce, National Economic, Social, and Environmental Data Bank, Economics and Statistics Administration, Office of Business Analysis, February 1995.

★52★

Toxic Chemical Releases

Toxic Chemical Releases, 1992: 3,3'-dichlorobenzidine

County	Releases	Rank
Muskegon County, MI	16,960	1
Will County, IL	260	2
Ottawa County, MI	52	3
Passaic County, NJ	10	4

Source: U.S. Environmental Protection Agency, "Toxic Release Inventory, 1992." In *National Economic, Social, and Environmental Data Bank* [CD-ROM]. Prepared by U.S. Department of Commerce, Economics, and Statistics Administration, Washington, D.C.: U.S. Department of Commerce, National Economic, Social, and Environmental Data Bank, Economics and Statistics Administration, Office of Business Analysis, February 1995.

★53★

Toxic Chemical Releases

Toxic Chemical Releases, 1992: 3,3'-dimethoxybenzidine

County	Releases	Rank
Essex/Passaic County, NJ	36	1
Passaic County, NJ	5	2
Berks County, PA	4	3

Source: U.S. Environmental Protection Agency, "Toxic Release Inventory, 1992." In *National Economic, Social, and Environmental Data Bank* [CD-ROM]. Prepared by U.S. Department of Commerce, Economics, and Statistics Administration, Washington, D.C.: U.S. Department of Commerce, National Economic, Social, and Environmental Data Bank, Economics and Statistics Administration, Office of Business Analysis, February 1995.

★54★

Toxic Chemical Releases

Toxic Chemical Releases, 1992: 3,3'-dimethylbenzidine

County	Releases	Rank
Passaic County, NJ	5	1

Source: U.S. Environmental Protection Agency, "Toxic Release Inventory, 1992." In *National Economic, Social, and Environmental Data Bank* [CD-ROM]. Prepared by U.S. Department of Commerce, Economics, and Statistics Administration, Washington, D.C.: U.S. Department of Commerce, National Economic, Social, and Environmental Data Bank, Economics and Statistics Administration, Office of Business Analysis, February 1995.

★55★

Toxic Chemical Releases

Toxic Chemical Releases, 1992: 4,4'-diaminodiphenyl Ether

County	Releases	Rank
Pickaway County, OH	6,612	1
Greenville County, SC	500	2
Salem County, NJ	313	3

Source: U.S. Environmental Protection Agency, "Toxic Release Inventory, 1992." In *National Economic, Social, and Environmental Data Bank* [CD-ROM]. Prepared by U.S. Department of Commerce, Economics, and Statistics Administration, Washington, D.C.: U.S. Department of Commerce, National Economic, Social, and Environmental Data Bank, Economics and Statistics Administration, Office of Business Analysis, February 1995.

★56★
Toxic Chemical Releases

Toxic Chemical Releases, 1992: 4,4'-isopropylidenediphenol

County	Releases	Rank
Harris County, TX	672,390	1
Scioto County, OH	219,650	2
Posey County, IN	134,311	3
Cook County, IL	38,771	4
Brazoria County, TX	22,899	5
Ocean County, NJ	21,902	6
Hampshire County, MA	20,000	7
Spartanburg County, SC	18,019	8
Baltimore City/County, MD	15,650	9
Outagamie County, WI	14,328	10
Beaver County, PA	11,010	11
Pickaway County, OH	8,100	12
Cuyahoga County, OH	6,568	13
Macomb County, MI	6,128	14
New Castle County, DE	5,729	15
Milwaukee County, WI	5,571	16
Allegheny County, PA	5,016	17
Wood County, WI	4,800	18
Chambers County, TX	4,618	19
Jefferson County, KY	4,216	20

Source: U.S. Environmental Protection Agency, "Toxic Release Inventory, 1992." In *National Economic, Social, and Environmental Data Bank* [CD-ROM]. Prepared by U.S. Department of Commerce, Economics, and Statistics Administration, Washington, D.C.: U.S. Department of Commerce, National Economic, Social, and Environmental Data Bank, Economics and Statistics Administration, Office of Business Analysis, February 1995.

★57★
Toxic Chemical Releases

Toxic Chemical Releases, 1992: 4,4'-methylenebis(2-Chloro Aniline)

County	Releases	Rank
Cattaraugus County, NY	1,250	1
Cumberland County, ME	1,200	2
Summit County, OH	1,000	3
Marion County, FL	750	4
Bureau County, IL	250	5
Preble County, OH	250	5
Baltimore City/County, MD	160	6
Shelby County, TN	5	7
Los Angeles County, CA	5	7

Source: U.S. Environmental Protection Agency, "Toxic Release Inventory, 1992." In *National Economic, Social, and Environmental Data Bank* [CD-ROM]. Prepared by U.S. Department of Commerce, Economics, and Statistics Administration, Washington, D.C.: U.S. Department of Commerce, National Economic, Social, and Environmental Data Bank, Economics and Statistics Administration, Office of Business Analysis, February 1995.

★58★
Toxic Chemical Releases

Toxic Chemical Releases, 1992: 4,4'-methylenedianiline

County	Releases	Rank
Ascension Parish, LA	88,736	1
Chambers County, TX	30,146	2
Crawford County, WI	21,000	3
Harris County, TX	9,750	4
Marshall County, WV	9,681	5
Brown County, MN	7,106	6
Los Angeles County, CA	4,780	7
Ocean County, NJ	3,837	8
New Haven County, CT	3,049	9
Pulaski County, AR	2,401	10
Cabell County, WV	1,001	11
Sedgwick County, KS	750	12
Wichita County, TX	750	12
Tulsa County, OK	729	13
Gaston County, NC	500	14
Spartanburg County, SC	500	14
Clay County, MO	255	15
Columbia County, AR	250	16
Schenectady County, NY	250	16
Camden County, NJ	212	17

Source: U.S. Environmental Protection Agency, "Toxic Release Inventory, 1992." In *National Economic, Social, and Environmental Data Bank* [CD-ROM]. Prepared by U.S. Department of Commerce, Economics, and Statistics Administration, Washington, D.C.: U.S. Department of Commerce, National Economic, Social, and Environmental Data Bank, Economics and Statistics Administration, Office of Business Analysis, February 1995.

★59★
Toxic Chemical Releases

Toxic Chemical Releases, 1992: 4,6-dinitro-o-cresol

County	Releases	Rank
Galveston County, TX	204,740	1
Harris County, TX	44,210	2
East Baton Rouge Parish, LA	411	3
St James Parish Parish, LA	140	4
Jackson County, MS	5	5
Fresno County, CA	1	6

Source: U.S. Environmental Protection Agency, "Toxic Release Inventory, 1992." In *National Economic, Social, and Environmental Data Bank* [CD-ROM]. Prepared by U.S. Department of Commerce, Economics, and Statistics Administration, Washington, D.C.: U.S. Department of Commerce, National Economic, Social, and Environmental Data Bank, Economics and Statistics Administration, Office of Business Analysis, February 1995.

★60★
Toxic Chemical Releases

Toxic Chemical Releases, 1992: 4-nitrophenol

County	Releases	Rank
St Clair County, IL	333,300	1
Saint Louis City/County, MO	135,400	2
St Charles Parish, LA	2,759	3
Bergen County, NJ	750	4

[Continued]

★60★

Toxic Chemical Releases, 1992: 4-nitrophenol
[Continued]

County	Releases	Rank
Sullivan County, TN	34	5
Clinton County, PA	32	6

Source: U.S. Environmental Protection Agency, "Toxic Release Inventory, 1992." In *National Economic, Social, and Environmental Data Bank* [CD-ROM]. Prepared by U.S. Department of Commerce, Economics, and Statistics Administration, Washington, D.C.: U.S. Department of Commerce, National Economic, Social, and Environmental Data Bank, Economics and Statistics Administration, Office of Business Analysis, February 1995.

★61★

Toxic Chemical Releases

Toxic Chemical Releases, 1992: 5-nitro-o-anisidine

County	Releases	Rank
Passaic County, NJ	15	1

Source: U.S. Environmental Protection Agency, "Toxic Release Inventory, 1992." In *National Economic, Social, and Environmental Data Bank* [CD-ROM]. Prepared by U.S. Department of Commerce, Economics, and Statistics Administration, Washington, D.C.: U.S. Department of Commerce, National Economic, Social, and Environmental Data Bank, Economics and Statistics Administration, Office of Business Analysis, February 1995.

★62★

Toxic Chemical Releases

Toxic Chemical Releases, 1992: Acetaldehyde

County	Releases	Rank
Matagorda County, TX	1,298,113	1
Harris County, TX	798,598	2
Gray County, TX	752,000	3
Sullivan County, TN	696,003	4
Spartanburg County, SC	523,005	5
Richland County, SC	491,400	6
Brunswick County, NC	454,832	7
Rowan County, NC	385,800	8
Harrison County, TX	290,000	9
Morgan County, AL	268,500	10
Transylvania County, NC	242,005	11
Lenoir County, NC	231,570	12
Scioto County, OH	190,250	13
Ascension Parish, LA	177,300	14
Darlington County, SC	167,901	15
Galveston County, TX	156,009	16
Davidson County, TN	136,000	17
Baltimore City/County, MD	135,603	18
Mason County, WV	119,100	19
Greenville County, SC	116,785	20

Source: U.S. Environmental Protection Agency, "Toxic Release Inventory, 1992." In *National Economic, Social, and Environmental Data Bank* [CD-ROM]. Prepared by U.S. Department of Commerce, Economics, and Statistics Administration, Washington, D.C.: U.S. Department of Commerce, National Economic, Social, and Environmental Data Bank, Economics and Statistics Administration, Office of Business Analysis, February 1995.

★63★

Toxic Chemical Releases

Toxic Chemical Releases, 1992: Acetamide

County	Releases	Rank
Calhoun County, TX	35	1
Pickaway County, OH	5	2

Source: U.S. Environmental Protection Agency, "Toxic Release Inventory, 1992." In *National Economic, Social, and Environmental Data Bank* [CD-ROM]. Prepared by U.S. Department of Commerce, Economics, and Statistics Administration, Washington, D.C.: U.S. Department of Commerce, National Economic, Social, and Environmental Data Bank, Economics and Statistics Administration, Office of Business Analysis, February 1995.

★64★

Toxic Chemical Releases

Toxic Chemical Releases, 1992: Acetone

County	Releases	Rank
Sullivan County, TN	31,448,147	1
Giles County, VA	10,548,509	2
Galveston County, TX	5,703,110	3
Marion County, IN	4,625,381	4
Kanawha County, WV	4,106,888	5
Onondaga County, NY	3,197,135	6
York County, SC	3,193,015	7
Hopewell City/County, VA	2,902,743	8
Barceloneta County, PR	2,704,544	9
Johnson County, IN	2,588,322	10
Kalamazoo County, MI	2,462,568	11
Tippecanoe County, IN	2,406,195	12
Monroe County, NY	2,350,744	13
Harris County, TX	2,292,484	14
Philadelphia County, PA	2,247,364	15
Posey County, IN	2,177,370	16
Hawkins County, TN	1,975,666	17
Scioto County, OH	1,967,955	18
Blackford County, IN	1,934,548	19
Pinal County, AZ	1,846,553	20

Source: U.S. Environmental Protection Agency, "Toxic Release Inventory, 1992." In *National Economic, Social, and Environmental Data Bank* [CD-ROM]. Prepared by U.S. Department of Commerce, Economics, and Statistics Administration, Washington, D.C.: U.S. Department of Commerce, National Economic, Social, and Environmental Data Bank, Economics and Statistics Administration, Office of Business Analysis, February 1995.

★65★

Toxic Chemical Releases

Toxic Chemical Releases, 1992: Acetonitrile

County	Releases	Rank
Jefferson Parish, LA	12,000,624	1
Allen County, OH	3,398,450	2
Brazoria County, TX	1,564,178	3
Marion County, IN	1,282,439	4
Calhoun County, TX	1,211,523	5
Jefferson County, TX	832,872	6
Harris County, TX	608,979	7
Union County, NJ	394,900	8
Tippecanoe County, IN	394,650	9
Ottawa County, MI	250,862	10
Galveston County, TX	235,305	11

[Continued]

★65★

Toxic Chemical Releases, 1992: Acetonitrile
[Continued]

County	Releases	Rank
Kalamazoo County, MI	208,067	12
Chester County, PA	196,400	13
Vermillion County, IN	185,010	14
St Charles Parish, LA	134,004	15
Rockland County, NY	85,220	16
Giles County, VA	61,204	17
Victoria County, TX	53,674	18
Orange County, TX	53,330	19
Bergen County, NJ	44,880	20

Source: U.S. Environmental Protection Agency, "Toxic Release Inventory, 1992." In *National Economic, Social, and Environmental Data Bank* [CD-ROM]. Prepared by U.S. Department of Commerce, Economics, and Statistics Administration, Washington, D.C.: U.S. Department of Commerce, National Economic, Social, and Environmental Data Bank, Economics and Statistics Administration, Office of Business Analysis, February 1995.

★66★
Toxic Chemical Releases

Toxic Chemical Releases, 1992: Acrolein

County	Releases	Rank
Matagorda County, TX	38,370	1
Brazoria County, TX	33,541	2
Galveston County, TX	28,512	3
St Charles Parish, LA	14,179	4
Calhoun County, TX	7,627	5
Harris County, TX	2,730	6
Jefferson Parish, LA	250	7
Liberty County, TX	2	8

Source: U.S. Environmental Protection Agency, "Toxic Release Inventory, 1992." In *National Economic, Social, and Environmental Data Bank* [CD-ROM]. Prepared by U.S. Department of Commerce, Economics, and Statistics Administration, Washington, D.C.: U.S. Department of Commerce, National Economic, Social, and Environmental Data Bank, Economics and Statistics Administration, Office of Business Analysis, February 1995.

★67★
Toxic Chemical Releases

Toxic Chemical Releases, 1992: Acrylamide

County	Releases	Rank
Calhoun County, TX	2,400,742	1
Jefferson Parish, LA	1,400,624	2
Galveston County, TX	417,400	3
Suffolk City/County, VA	37,660	4
Kanawha County, WV	30,528	5
Alameda County, CA	22,626	6
St John The Baptist Parish, LA	10,127	7
Montgomery County, MD	9,100	8
Beaver County, PA	6,421	9
Midland County, MI	6,364	10
Marshall County, KY	5,225	11
Wharton County, TX	3,129	12
New Haven County, CT	2,417	13
Muscogee County, GA	2,190	14
Kalamazoo County, MI	2,000	15

[Continued]

★67★

Toxic Chemical Releases, 1992: Acrylamide
[Continued]

County	Releases	Rank
Mecklenburg County, NC	1,500	16
St Louis County, MO	1,251	17
Bucks County, PA	1,250	18
Cook County, IL	1,103	19
Worcester County, MA	1,084	20

Source: U.S. Environmental Protection Agency, "Toxic Release Inventory, 1992." In *National Economic, Social, and Environmental Data Bank* [CD-ROM]. Prepared by U.S. Department of Commerce, Economics, and Statistics Administration, Washington, D.C.: U.S. Department of Commerce, National Economic, Social, and Environmental Data Bank, Economics and Statistics Administration, Office of Business Analysis, February 1995.

★68★
Toxic Chemical Releases

Toxic Chemical Releases, 1992: Acrylic Acid

County	Releases	Rank
Jefferson Parish, LA	9,100,250	1
Calhoun County, TX	8,301,709	2
Allen County, OH	4,100,740	3
Brazoria County, TX	183,000	4
Hamilton County, TN	122,822	5
Harris County, TX	99,944	6
Morgan County, IL	94,496	7
Suffolk City/County, VA	55,415	8
Marion County, IA	51,005	9
Will County, IL	50,598	10
Portsmouth City/County, VA	33,327	11
Warren County, KY	28,750	12
Kankakee County, IL	23,305	13
St Charles Parish, LA	22,063	14
Mecklenburg County, NC	21,354	15
Kanawha County, WV	16,828	16
Fairfield County, CT	15,272	17
Suffolk County, NY	11,160	18
Guilford County, NC	10,050	19
Gray County, TX	10,000	20

Source: U.S. Environmental Protection Agency, "Toxic Release Inventory, 1992." In *National Economic, Social, and Environmental Data Bank* [CD-ROM]. Prepared by U.S. Department of Commerce, Economics, and Statistics Administration, Washington, D.C.: U.S. Department of Commerce, National Economic, Social, and Environmental Data Bank, Economics and Statistics Administration, Office of Business Analysis, February 1995.

★69★
Toxic Chemical Releases

Toxic Chemical Releases, 1992: Acrylonitrile

County	Releases	Rank
Brazoria County, TX	1,597,949	1
Allen County, OH	1,415,250	2
Calhoun County, TX	1,329,637	3
Wood County, WV	921,180	4
Jefferson Parish, LA	506,724	5
Muscatine County, IA	501,222	6
Harris County, TX	465,894	7

[Continued]

★69★

Toxic Chemical Releases, 1992: Acrylonitrile
[Continued]

County	Releases	Rank
Hancock County, MS	295,729	8
La Salle County, IL	288,042	9
Kershaw County, SC	266,128	10
Jefferson County, KY	213,105	11
Jefferson County, TX	210,599	12
Morgan County, AL	171,023	13
Galveston County, TX	165,110	14
Summit County, OH	145,760	15
Kanawha County, WV	126,130	16
Santa Rosa County, FL	110,798	17
Hamilton County, OH	87,640	18
Aususta County, VA	60,461	19
Williamsburg City/County, VA	49,549	20

Source: U.S. Environmental Protection Agency, "Toxic Release Inventory, 1992." In *National Economic, Social, and Environmental Data Bank* [CD-ROM]. Prepared by U.S. Department of Commerce, Economics, and Statistics Administration, Washington, D.C.: U.S. Department of Commerce, National Economic, Social, and Environmental Data Bank, Economics and Statistics Administration, Office of Business Analysis, February 1995.

★70★

Toxic Chemical Releases

Toxic Chemical Releases, 1992: Allyl Alcohol

County	Releases	Rank
St John The Baptist Parish, LA	191,871	1
Wayne County, MI	185,238	2
Summit County, OH	170,330	3
Harris County, TX	9,870	4
Marshall County, KY	5,481	5
Morris County, NJ	5,244	6
Kershaw County, SC	4,695	7
Kanawha County, WV	3,887	8
Rowan County, NC	3,498	9
Middlesex County, NJ	1,500	10
Crittenden County, AR	1,000	11
Providence County, RI	842	12
Tippecanoe County, IN	505	13
Kern County, CA	505	13
Brazoria County, TX	140	14
Pettis County, MO	49	15
Ellis County, TX	10	16

Source: U.S. Environmental Protection Agency, "Toxic Release Inventory, 1992." In *National Economic, Social, and Environmental Data Bank* [CD-ROM]. Prepared by U.S. Department of Commerce, Economics, and Statistics Administration, Washington, D.C.: U.S. Department of Commerce, National Economic, Social, and Environmental Data Bank, Economics and Statistics Administration, Office of Business Analysis, February 1995.

★71★

Toxic Chemical Releases

Toxic Chemical Releases, 1992: Allyl Chloride

County	Releases	Rank
Harris County, TX	171,991	1
St Charles Parish, LA	91,000	2
Glynn County, GA	63,148	3
St John The Baptist Parish, LA	46,641	4
Rowan County, NC	24,002	5
Brazoria County, TX	12,000	6
Passaic County, NJ	11,208	7
Marshall County, KY	10,399	8
Sedgwick County, KS	6,155	9
Niagara County, NY	2,755	10
Midland County, MI	2,587	11
Tyler County, WV	1,657	12
Macomb County, MI	1,335	13
Salem County, NJ	1,005	14
Worcester County, MA	500	15
Portsmouth City/County, VA	378	16
Crittenden County, AR	255	17
Phillips County, AR	255	17
Cocke County, TN	27	18
Fort Bend County, TX	20	19

Source: U.S. Environmental Protection Agency, "Toxic Release Inventory, 1992." In *National Economic, Social, and Environmental Data Bank* [CD-ROM]. Prepared by U.S. Department of Commerce, Economics, and Statistics Administration, Washington, D.C.: U.S. Department of Commerce, National Economic, Social, and Environmental Data Bank, Economics and Statistics Administration, Office of Business Analysis, February 1995.

★72★

Toxic Chemical Releases

Toxic Chemical Releases, 1992: Alpha-naphthylamine

County	Releases	Rank
Berks County, PA	534	1
Gaston County, NC	500	2

Source: U.S. Environmental Protection Agency, "Toxic Release Inventory, 1992." In *National Economic, Social, and Environmental Data Bank* [CD-ROM]. Prepared by U.S. Department of Commerce, Economics, and Statistics Administration, Washington, D.C.: U.S. Department of Commerce, National Economic, Social, and Environmental Data Bank, Economics and Statistics Administration, Office of Business Analysis, February 1995.

★73★

Toxic Chemical Releases

Toxic Chemical Releases, 1992: Aluminum (Fume Or Dust)

County	Releases	Rank
Mclean County, KY	7,503,050	1
Onondaga County, NY	1,736,839	2
Camden County, NJ	1,335,337	3
Boyd County, KY	831,205	4
Butler County, OH	641,550	5
Whitley County, IN	395,200	6
Will County, IL	382,830	7
Allen County, IN	329,408	8

[Continued]

★73★

Toxic Chemical Releases, 1992: Aluminum (Fume Or Dust)
[Continued]

County	Releases	Rank
Jefferson County, KY	255,582	9
Mayes County, OK	194,947	10
Shelby County, IN	183,429	11
Creek County, OK	183,000	12
Madison County, IL	180,400	13
Rock Island County, IL	161,894	14
Saint Louis City/County, MO	156,200	15
Johnson County, MO	148,739	16
Middlesex County, NJ	143,357	17
Butler County, KY	130,000	18
Roane County, TN	130,000	18
Wayne County, MI	120,760	19

Source: U.S. Environmental Protection Agency, "Toxic Release Inventory, 1992." In *National Economic, Social, and Environmental Data Bank* [CD-ROM]. Prepared by U.S. Department of Commerce, Economics, and Statistics Administration, Washington, D.C.: U.S. Department of Commerce, National Economic, Social, and Environmental Data Bank, Economics and Statistics Administration, Office of Business Analysis, February 1995.

★74★
Toxic Chemical Releases

Toxic Chemical Releases, 1992: Aluminum Oxide (Fibrous Forms)

County	Releases	Rank
Camden County, NJ	1,403,900	1
Pinal County, AZ	892,819	2
Mercer County, PA	684,000	3
Los Angeles County, CA	648,004	4
Sheboygan County, WI	550,400	5
De Kalb County, IN	481,490	6
Hamilton County, OH	346,620	7
San Bernardino County, CA	261,496	8
Geauga County, OH	248,450	9
Wright County, MO	180,940	10
Seneca County, OH	177,600	11
La Porte County, IN	153,000	12
Cattaraugus County, NY	122,571	13
St Louis County, MN	108,810	14
Coffee County, GA	96,755	15
La Salle County, IL	88,209	16
Mayes County, OK	87,800	17
Sandusky County, OH	78,782	18
Stark County, OH	77,097	19
Multnomah County, OR	77,000	20

Source: U.S. Environmental Protection Agency, "Toxic Release Inventory, 1992." In *National Economic, Social, and Environmental Data Bank* [CD-ROM]. Prepared by U.S. Department of Commerce, Economics, and Statistics Administration, Washington, D.C.: U.S. Department of Commerce, National Economic, Social, and Environmental Data Bank, Economics and Statistics Administration, Office of Business Analysis, February 1995.

★75★
Toxic Chemical Releases

Toxic Chemical Releases, 1992: Ammonia

County	Releases	Rank
Brazoria County, TX	60,343,069	1
Jefferson Parish, LA	51,467,070	2
Galveston County, TX	36,963,661	3
Ascension Parish, LA	29,091,706	4
St James Parish, LA	23,198,365	5
Jefferson County, TX	18,287,233	6
Calhoun County, TX	17,874,849	7
Calcasieu Parish, LA	17,464,224	8
St Louis County, MO	16,380,610	9
Los Angeles County, CA	15,222,034	10
Allen County, OH	14,195,700	11
Kenai Peninsula County, AK	13,744,064	12
Yazoo County, MS	12,284,469	13
Hamilton County, OH	8,325,226	14
Saint Louis City/County, MO	8,266,155	15
Maury County, TN	7,677,955	16
Manatee County, FL	7,645,750	17
Columbia County, AR	7,240,000	18
Harris County, TX	6,710,398	19
St Charles Parish, LA	6,409,766	20

Source: U.S. Environmental Protection Agency, "Toxic Release Inventory, 1992." In *National Economic, Social, and Environmental Data Bank* [CD-ROM]. Prepared by U.S. Department of Commerce, Economics, and Statistics Administration, Washington, D.C.: U.S. Department of Commerce, National Economic, Social, and Environmental Data Bank, Economics and Statistics Administration, Office of Business Analysis, February 1995.

★76★
Toxic Chemical Releases

Toxic Chemical Releases, 1992: Ammonium Nitrate (Solution)

County	Releases	Rank
Jefferson County, TX	15,000,120	1
Escambia County, FL	14,000,000	2
Laramie County, WY	6,469,090	3
San Bernardino County, CA	2,300,000	4
Rogers County, OK	2,263,250	5
Utah County, UT	1,623,191	6
Mayes County, OK	1,623,005	7
Orange County, CA	1,536,965	8
Wyandotte County, KS	1,525,003	9
Hopewell City/County, VA	1,142,054	10
Chatham County, GA	1,125,500	11
Pike County, MO	1,035,640	12
Caddo Parish, LA	1,001,100	13
Ascension Parish, LA	999,547	14
Douglas County, KS	950,250	15
Erie County, PA	816,000	16
Okeechobee County, FL	769,453	17
Brazos County, TX	721,250	18
Yazoo County, MS	631,421	19
Sequoyah County, OK	554,540	20

Source: U.S. Environmental Protection Agency, "Toxic Release Inventory, 1992." In *National Economic, Social, and Environmental Data Bank* [CD-ROM]. Prepared by U.S. Department of Commerce, Economics, and Statistics Administration, Washington, D.C.: U.S. Department of Commerce, National Economic, Social, and Environmental Data Bank, Economics and Statistics Administration, Office of Business Analysis, February 1995.

★77★
Toxic Chemical Releases

Toxic Chemical Releases, 1992: Ammonium Sulfate (Solution)

County	Releases	Rank
St Clair County, IL	10,790,339	1
Shelby County, TN	9,981,801	2
Middlesex County, NJ	5,924,180	3
Cook County, IL	5,900,005	4
Maury County, TN	4,875,546	5
Essex County, NJ	4,643,559	6
Manati County, PR	2,841,602	7
Ascension Parish, LA	2,227,227	8
Sullivan County, TN	2,100,000	9
Milwaukee County, WI	1,862,955	10
Harris County, TX	1,607,700	11
Franklin County, OH	1,558,531	12
Moore County, TX	1,471,700	13
Humphreys County, TN	1,401,800	14
Onondaga County, NY	1,300,000	15
Dakota County, NE	1,226,604	16
Dakota County, MN	1,179,700	17
Barceloneta County, PR	1,115,488	18
Whitfield County, GA	1,107,400	19
Bannock County, ID	1,087,000	20

Source: U.S. Environmental Protection Agency, "Toxic Release Inventory, 1992." In *National Economic, Social, and Environmental Data Bank* [CD-ROM]. Prepared by U.S. Department of Commerce, Economics, and Statistics Administration, Washington, D.C.: U.S. Department of Commerce, National Economic, Social, and Environmental Data Bank, Economics and Statistics Administration, Office of Business Analysis, February 1995.

★78★
Toxic Chemical Releases

Toxic Chemical Releases, 1992: Aniline

County	Releases	Rank
Ascension Parish, LA	2,413,620	1
Cook County, IL	972,539	2
Cabell County, WV	399,555	3
Erie County, NY	297,136	4
St Clair County, IL	224,875	5
Summit County, OH	168,800	6
Chambers County, TX	148,920	7
New Haven County, CT	109,308	8
Scioto County, OH	102,000	9
Jefferson County, TX	82,173	10
Pr County, PR	56,505	11
New Castle County, DE	52,080	12
Harris County, TX	51,550	13
Providence County, RI	46,565	14
Niagara County, NY	46,292	15
Wake County, NC	31,750	16
Orangeburg County, SC	22,830	17
Marshall County, WV	20,883	18
Putnam County, WV	15,200	19
Muskegon County, MI	14,660	20

Source: U.S. Environmental Protection Agency, "Toxic Release Inventory, 1992." In *National Economic, Social, and Environmental Data Bank* [CD-ROM]. Prepared by U.S. Department of Commerce, Economics, and Statistics Administration, Washington, D.C.: U.S. Department of Commerce, National Economic, Social, and Environmental Data Bank, Economics and Statistics Administration, Office of Business Analysis, February 1995.

★79★
Toxic Chemical Releases

Toxic Chemical Releases, 1992: Anthracene

County	Releases	Rank
Jefferson County, AL	483,762	1
Galveston County, TX	308,100	2
Allegheny County, PA	20,929	3
Wayne County, MI	18,506	4
Lake County, IN	17,550	5
Lawrence County, OH	16,140	6
Madison County, IL	8,006	7
Cowlitz County, WA	7,305	8
Cuyahoga County, OH	6,795	9
Calhoun County, TX	6,430	10
Washington County, OH	5,522	11
Northampton County, PA	4,810	12
Brooke County, WV	4,621	13
Jefferson County, OH	3,300	14
Usa County, VI	2,707	15
Seneca County, OH	2,676	16
Marshall County, KY	2,309	17
Cook County, IL	2,120	18
Boyd County, KY	2,094	19
Spartanburg County, SC	2,055	20

Source: U.S. Environmental Protection Agency, "Toxic Release Inventory, 1992." In *National Economic, Social, and Environmental Data Bank* [CD-ROM]. Prepared by U.S. Department of Commerce, Economics, and Statistics Administration, Washington, D.C.: U.S. Department of Commerce, National Economic, Social, and Environmental Data Bank, Economics and Statistics Administration, Office of Business Analysis, February 1995.

★80★
Toxic Chemical Releases

Toxic Chemical Releases, 1992: Antimony

County	Releases	Rank
Sheboygan County, WI	95,715	1
Los Angeles County, CA	67,470	2
Bexar County, TX	46,457	3
Jefferson County, AL	42,325	4
Collin County, TX	40,440	5
Shelby County, TN	24,681	6
Marion County, IN	24,190	7
Denver County, CO	20,788	8
Dakota County, MN	19,200	9
Franklin County, OH	19,036	10
Dallas County, TX	16,787	11
Webb County, TX	15,250	12
Pike County, AL	15,202	13
Lowndes County, MS	14,634	14
Ottawa County, MI	11,931	15
Nueces County, TX	10,633	16
Troup County, GA	8,994	17
Muscogee County, GA	7,929	18
Lake County, IN	6,160	19
Fulton County, GA	5,200	20

Source: U.S. Environmental Protection Agency, "Toxic Release Inventory, 1992." In *National Economic, Social, and Environmental Data Bank* [CD-ROM]. Prepared by U.S. Department of Commerce, Economics, and Statistics Administration, Washington, D.C.: U.S. Department of Commerce, National Economic, Social, and Environmental Data Bank, Economics and Statistics Administration, Office of Business Analysis, February 1995.

★81★

Toxic Chemical Releases

Toxic Chemical Releases, 1992: Antimony Compounds

County	Releases	Rank
Gila County, AZ	1,328,445	1
Marion County, IN	742,879	2
Douglas County, NE	580,650	3
Lewis and Clark County, MT	284,482	4
Saginaw County, MI	140,800	5
Northampton County, PA	96,295	6
Centre County, PA	86,109	7
Brazoria County, TX	79,255	8
Richland County, SC	77,059	9
East Baton Rouge Parish, LA	69,577	10
Dyer County, TN	58,250	11
Muskegon County, MI	46,032	12
Cleveland County, NC	38,765	13
Medina County, OH	37,567	14
Steuben County, NY	37,006	15
Orange County, NY	36,126	16
Morris County, NJ	34,223	17
Jefferson County, KY	30,405	18
Dekalb County, TN	29,035	19
Holt County, MO	27,969	20

Source: U.S. Environmental Protection Agency, "Toxic Release Inventory, 1992." In *National Economic, Social, and Environmental Data Bank* [CD-ROM]. Prepared by U.S. Department of Commerce, Economics, and Statistics Administration, Washington, D.C.: U.S. Department of Commerce, National Economic, Social, and Environmental Data Bank, Economics and Statistics Administration, Office of Business Analysis, February 1995.

★82★

Toxic Chemical Releases

Toxic Chemical Releases, 1992: Arsenic

County	Releases	Rank
Cabarrus County, NC	168,046	1
Garfield County, CO	56,800	2
Jefferson County, AL	42,335	3
Palm Beach County, FL	31,034	4
Los Angeles County, CA	16,492	5
George County, MS	15,385	6
Collin County, TX	12,301	7
Pike County, AL	11,329	8
Rockbridge County, VA	9,650	9
Shelby County, TN	7,617	10
Marion County, IN	7,267	11
Berks County, PA	6,127	12
Dakota County, MN	5,878	13
Chatham County, NC	4,292	14
Powell County, KY	3,300	15
Muscogee County, GA	2,754	16
San Joaquin County, CA	2,709	17
Florence County, SC	2,703	18
Cook County, IL	2,700	19
Dallas County, TX	2,214	20

Source: U.S. Environmental Protection Agency, "Toxic Release Inventory, 1992." In *National Economic, Social, and Environmental Data Bank* [CD-ROM]. Prepared by U.S. Department of Commerce, Economics, and Statistics Administration, Washington, D.C.: U.S. Department of Commerce, National Economic, Social, and Environmental Data Bank, Economics and Statistics Administration, Office of Business Analysis, February 1995.

★83★

Toxic Chemical Releases

Toxic Chemical Releases, 1992: Arsenic Compounds

County	Releases	Rank
Salt Lake County, UT	17,320,955	1
Gila County, AZ	994,033	2
Lewis and Clark County, MT	347,686	3
Floyd County, IA	106,440	4
Dekalb County, GA	77,641	5
Harris County, TX	71,540	6
York County, SC	66,095	7
El Paso County, TX	48,650	8
Douglas County, NE	48,140	9
Jefferson County, MO	46,003	10
Brazos County, TX	37,630	11
Berkeley County, WV	29,622	12
Douglas County, KS	27,259	13
East Baton Rouge Parish, LA	26,949	14
Halifax County, NC	24,253	15
Potter County, TX	22,510	16
Pierce County, GA	21,255	17
Shelby County, TN	16,960	18
Marion County, IN	13,788	19
Mecklenburg County, NC	11,203	20

Source: U.S. Environmental Protection Agency, "Toxic Release Inventory, 1992." In *National Economic, Social, and Environmental Data Bank* [CD-ROM]. Prepared by U.S. Department of Commerce, Economics, and Statistics Administration, Washington, D.C.: U.S. Department of Commerce, National Economic, Social, and Environmental Data Bank, Economics and Statistics Administration, Office of Business Analysis, February 1995.

★84★

Toxic Chemical Releases

Toxic Chemical Releases, 1992: Asbestos (Friable)

County	Releases	Rank
Orange County, CA	1,514,946	1
Middlesex County, NJ	1,460,145	2
Nueces County, TX	956,400	3
Dekalb County, TN	855,861	4
Washington County, AL	748,546	5
Harris County, TX	384,015	6
Wayne County, NY	355,209	7
Stokes County, NC	234,877	8
Northampton County, PA	193,020	9
Montgomery County, OH	187,930	10
Iberville Parish, LA	165,005	11
Union County, KY	137,520	12
Noble County, IN	113,900	13
Knox County, OH	112,731	14
Crawford County, AR	111,750	15
Bradley County, TN	99,403	16
Lancaster County, PA	92,650	17
Montgomery County, PA	67,000	18
Shelby County, TN	57,600	19
Utah County, UT	47,768	20

Source: U.S. Environmental Protection Agency, "Toxic Release Inventory, 1992." In *National Economic, Social, and Environmental Data Bank* [CD-ROM]. Prepared by U.S. Department of Commerce, Economics, and Statistics Administration, Washington, D.C.: U.S. Department of Commerce, National Economic, Social, and Environmental Data Bank, Economics and Statistics Administration, Office of Business Analysis, February 1995.

★85★
Toxic Chemical Releases
Toxic Chemical Releases, 1992: Barium

County	Releases	Rank
Putnam County, OH	168,760	1
Saginaw County, MI	108,750	2
Sequoyah County, OK	78,327	3
Jefferson County, AL	68,250	4
Utah County, UT	58,869	5
Mason County, WV	54,771	6
Ramsey County, MN	50,000	7
Madison County, IL	49,287	8
Tarrant County, TX	31,684	9
Dallas County, TX	26,395	10
Crawford County, OH	25,500	11
Nez Perce County, ID	25,100	12
Jefferson County, TX	24,499	13
Bernalillo County, NM	23,605	14
Stearns County, MN	17,162	15
Fulton County, OH	15,163	16
Franklin County, PA	15,005	17
Union County, IA	14,963	18
Miami County, OH	13,560	19
Cuyahoga County, OH	12,570	20

Source: U.S. Environmental Protection Agency, "Toxic Release Inventory, 1992." In *National Economic, Social, and Environmental Data Bank* [CD-ROM]. Prepared by U.S. Department of Commerce, Economics, and Statistics Administration, Washington, D.C.: U.S. Department of Commerce, National Economic, Social, and Environmental Data Bank, Economics and Statistics Administration, Office of Business Analysis, February 1995.

★86★
Toxic Chemical Releases
Toxic Chemical Releases, 1992: Barium Compounds

County	Releases	Rank
Bartow County, GA	5,730,067	1
St Clair County, IL	2,381,969	2
Rowan County, NC	1,911,300	3
Winchester County, VA	1,412,800	4
Pinal County, AZ	1,293,000	5
Niagara County, NY	1,233,817	6
Centre County, PA	1,132,743	7
Gila County, AZ	1,053,600	8
Grant County, NM	977,000	9
Salt Lake County, UT	960,075	10
Madison County, IL	668,705	11
Humphreys County, TN	585,695	12
Hidalgo County, NM	581,000	13
La Salle County, IL	370,810	14
Lamar County, TX	366,000	15
Dyer County, TN	335,688	16
Waukesha County, WI	289,023	17
Montgomery County, OH	251,145	18
Fayette County, KY	247,958	19
Dekalb County, TN	241,154	20

Source: U.S. Environmental Protection Agency, "Toxic Release Inventory, 1992." In *National Economic, Social, and Environmental Data Bank* [CD-ROM]. Prepared by U.S. Department of Commerce, Economics, and Statistics Administration, Washington, D.C.: U.S. Department of Commerce, National Economic, Social, and Environmental Data Bank, Economics and Statistics Administration, Office of Business Analysis, February 1995.

★87★
Toxic Chemical Releases
Toxic Chemical Releases, 1992: Benzal Chloride

County	Releases	Rank
Gloucester County, NJ	37,006	1
Hamilton County, TN	1,514	2
Niagara County, NY	240	3

Source: U.S. Environmental Protection Agency, "Toxic Release Inventory, 1992." In *National Economic, Social, and Environmental Data Bank* [CD-ROM]. Prepared by U.S. Department of Commerce, Economics, and Statistics Administration, Washington, D.C.: U.S. Department of Commerce, National Economic, Social, and Environmental Data Bank, Economics and Statistics Administration, Office of Business Analysis, February 1995.

★88★
Toxic Chemical Releases
Toxic Chemical Releases, 1992: Benzene

County	Releases	Rank
Lake County, IN	2,437,406	1
Allegheny County, PA	2,411,010	2
Butler County, OH	1,639,010	3
Brooke County, WV	1,568,791	4
Madison County, IL	1,229,162	5
Harris County, TX	1,134,127	6
Galveston County, TX	1,062,074	7
Brazoria County, TX	1,046,130	8
Jefferson County, TX	1,027,292	9
Richmond County, GA	766,722	10
York County, SC	602,719	11
Jefferson County, AL	581,472	12
Northampton County, PA	557,754	13
Calcasieu Parish, LA	531,327	14
Wayne County, MI	452,180	15
Nueces County, TX	380,572	16
Erie County, NY	363,607	17
Giles County, VA	344,001	18
Boyd County, KY	340,140	19
Los Angeles County, CA	308,530	20

Source: U.S. Environmental Protection Agency, "Toxic Release Inventory, 1992." In *National Economic, Social, and Environmental Data Bank* [CD-ROM]. Prepared by U.S. Department of Commerce, Economics, and Statistics Administration, Washington, D.C.: U.S. Department of Commerce, National Economic, Social, and Environmental Data Bank, Economics and Statistics Administration, Office of Business Analysis, February 1995.

★89★
Toxic Chemical Releases
Toxic Chemical Releases, 1992: Benzoic Trichloride

County	Releases	Rank
Hamilton County, TN	4,985	1
Niagara County, NY	1,698	2
Rensselaer County, NY	992	3
Washington County, OH	755	4

Source: U.S. Environmental Protection Agency, "Toxic Release Inventory, 1992." In *National Economic, Social, and Environmental Data Bank* [CD-ROM]. Prepared by U.S. Department of Commerce, Economics, and Statistics Administration, Washington, D.C.: U.S. Department of Commerce, National Economic, Social, and Environmental Data Bank, Economics and Statistics Administration, Office of Business Analysis, February 1995.

★90★
Toxic Chemical Releases

Toxic Chemical Releases, 1992: Benzoyl Chloride

County	Releases	Rank
Hamilton County, TN	652,452	1
Harrison County, TX	68,251	2
Harris County, TX	4,750	3
Niagara County, NY	4,143	4
Brazoria County, TX	1,420	5
Saline County, KS	505	6
Lorain County, OH	310	7
Erie County, NY	265	8
Washington County, OH	255	9
Allegheny County, PA	250	10
Livingston County, NY	240	11
New Haven County, CT	200	12
Glynn County, GA	113	13
Los Angeles County, CA	15	14
Tuscarawas County, OH	5	15
Bergen County, NJ	3	16
Sullivan County, TN	3	16
Kent County, RI	1	17

Source: U.S. Environmental Protection Agency, "Toxic Release Inventory, 1992." In *National Economic, Social, and Environmental Data Bank* [CD-ROM]. Prepared by U.S. Department of Commerce, Economics, and Statistics Administration, Washington, D.C.: U.S. Department of Commerce, National Economic, Social, and Environmental Data Bank, Economics and Statistics Administration, Office of Business Analysis, February 1995.

★91★
Toxic Chemical Releases

Toxic Chemical Releases, 1992: Benzoyl Peroxide

County	Releases	Rank
Los Angeles County, CA	43,220	1
Berkeley County, WV	16,800	2
Barry County, MI	12,245	3
Livingston County, NY	7,300	4
Niagara County, NY	2,773	5
Beaver County, PA	2,360	6
Saline County, KS	1,794	7
Bristol City/County, VA	1,610	8
Scott County, KY	1,330	9
Montgomery County, PA	1,245	10
Mercer County, WV	908	11
Mesa County, CO	818	12
Erie County, NY	634	13
Bexar County, TX	255	14
New Haven County, CT	250	15
Tuscarawas County, OH	250	15
Allegheny County, PA	250	15
Burlington County, NJ	212	16
Muscogee County, GA	190	17
San Francisco County, CA	189	18

Source: U.S. Environmental Protection Agency, "Toxic Release Inventory, 1992." In *National Economic, Social, and Environmental Data Bank* [CD-ROM]. Prepared by U.S. Department of Commerce, Economics, and Statistics Administration, Washington, D.C.: U.S. Department of Commerce, National Economic, Social, and Environmental Data Bank, Economics and Statistics Administration, Office of Business Analysis, February 1995.

★92★
Toxic Chemical Releases

Toxic Chemical Releases, 1992: Benzyl Chloride

County	Releases	Rank
Gloucester County, NJ	231,410	1
Berkeley County, SC	51,678	2
Providence County, RI	16,236	3
Florence County, SC	12,750	4
Middlesex County, NJ	11,300	5
Philadelphia County, PA	8,844	6
Sullivan County, TN	5,715	7
Ottawa County, MI	5,200	8
Harris County, TX	3,321	9
Ector County, TX	1,693	10
Hutchinson County, TX	1,610	11
Salem County, NJ	1,505	12
St Louis County, MO	1,000	13
Shelby County, TN	793	14
Carroll County, KY	784	15
Guilford County, NC	755	16
Richland County, SC	750	17
Bexar County, TX	500	18
Houston County, TX	500	18
Spartanburg County, SC	500	18

Source: U.S. Environmental Protection Agency, "Toxic Release Inventory, 1992." In *National Economic, Social, and Environmental Data Bank* [CD-ROM]. Prepared by U.S. Department of Commerce, Economics, and Statistics Administration, Washington, D.C.: U.S. Department of Commerce, National Economic, Social, and Environmental Data Bank, Economics and Statistics Administration, Office of Business Analysis, February 1995.

★93★
Toxic Chemical Releases

Toxic Chemical Releases, 1992: Beryllium

County	Releases	Rank
Ottawa County, OH	7,765	1
Jackson County, MI	1,500	2
Berks County, PA	16	3
Muscogee County, GA	5	4
Macomb County, MI	5	4
Wayne County, OH	5	4
Chester County, PA	4	5

Source: U.S. Environmental Protection Agency, "Toxic Release Inventory, 1992." In *National Economic, Social, and Environmental Data Bank* [CD-ROM]. Prepared by U.S. Department of Commerce, Economics, and Statistics Administration, Washington, D.C.: U.S. Department of Commerce, National Economic, Social, and Environmental Data Bank, Economics and Statistics Administration, Office of Business Analysis, February 1995.

★94★

Toxic Chemical Releases

Toxic Chemical Releases, 1992: Beryllium Compounds

County	Releases	Rank
Berks County, PA	40,885	1
Pima County, AZ	472	2
Dakota County, MN	65	3

Source: U.S. Environmental Protection Agency, "Toxic Release Inventory, 1992." In *National Economic, Social, and Environmental Data Bank* [CD-ROM]. Prepared by U.S. Department of Commerce, Economics, and Statistics Administration, Washington, D.C.: U.S. Department of Commerce, National Economic, Social, and Environmental Data Bank, Economics and Statistics Administration, Office of Business Analysis, February 1995.

★95★

Toxic Chemical Releases

Toxic Chemical Releases, 1992: Biphenyl

County	Releases	Rank
New Castle County, DE	203,495	1
Galveston County, TX	197,694	2
Whitfield County, GA	176,986	3
Gordon County, GA	159,440	4
Midland County, MI	113,358	5
Lee County, SC	104,000	6
Schuylkill County, PA	89,420	7
Harris County, TX	88,477	8
Richland County, SC	82,763	9
Gaston County, NC	81,942	10
Tallapoosa County, AL	80,961	11
Spartanburg County, SC	77,300	12
Lauderdale County, AL	75,440	13
Henry County, VA	67,671	14
Bristol County, MA	63,601	15
Brunswick County, NC	59,099	16
Providence County, RI	58,779	17
Darlington County, SC	53,763	18
Orange County, TX	53,209	19
Hamblen County, TN	52,000	20

Source: U.S. Environmental Protection Agency, "Toxic Release Inventory, 1992." In *National Economic, Social, and Environmental Data Bank* [CD-ROM]. Prepared by U.S. Department of Commerce, Economics, and Statistics Administration, Washington, D.C.: U.S. Department of Commerce, National Economic, Social, and Environmental Data Bank, Economics and Statistics Administration, Office of Business Analysis, February 1995.

★96★

Toxic Chemical Releases

Toxic Chemical Releases, 1992: Bis(2-chloro-1-methylethyl) Ether

County	Releases	Rank
Iberville Parish, LA	16,400	1
Brazoria County, TX	1,830	2

Source: U.S. Environmental Protection Agency, "Toxic Release Inventory, 1992." In *National Economic, Social, and Environmental Data Bank* [CD-ROM]. Prepared by U.S. Department of Commerce, Economics, and Statistics Administration, Washington, D.C.: U.S. Department of Commerce, National Economic, Social, and Environmental Data Bank, Economics and Statistics Administration, Office of Business Analysis, February 1995.

★97★

Toxic Chemical Releases

Toxic Chemical Releases, 1992: Bis(2-chloroethyl) Ether

County	Releases	Rank
Shelby County, TN	20,780	1
Washington County, MO	15,406	2
Harris County, TX	12,660	3
St James Parish, LA	3,243	4
San Patricio County, TX	2,521	5
New Castle County, DE	910	6
Middlesex County, NJ	505	7
Ector County, TX	250	8
Calcasieu Parish, LA	74	9

Source: U.S. Environmental Protection Agency, "Toxic Release Inventory, 1992." In *National Economic, Social, and Environmental Data Bank* [CD-ROM]. Prepared by U.S. Department of Commerce, Economics, and Statistics Administration, Washington, D.C.: U.S. Department of Commerce, National Economic, Social, and Environmental Data Bank, Economics and Statistics Administration, Office of Business Analysis, February 1995.

★98★

Toxic Chemical Releases

Toxic Chemical Releases, 1992: Bis(2-ethylhexyl) Adipate

County	Releases	Rank
Dyer County, TN	31,600	1
Whitley County, IN	26,500	2
Suffolk County, MA	25,780	3
Portage County, OH	20,100	4
Franklin County, OH	20,000	5
Allen County, IN	16,500	6
Hudson County, NJ	12,200	7
Sullivan County, TN	11,124	8
Sangamon County, IL	10,709	9
Kent County, MD	10,198	10
Stanislaus County, CA	9,600	11
Cook County, IL	9,117	12
Madison County, AL	9,100	13
Essex County, NJ	8,500	14
St Joseph County, IN	8,270	15
Merced County, CA	8,105	16
Middlesex County, NJ	7,942	17
Lenawee County, MI	7,500	18
Gordon County, GA	6,432	19
Hamilton County, OH	5,304	20

Source: U.S. Environmental Protection Agency, "Toxic Release Inventory, 1992." In *National Economic, Social, and Environmental Data Bank* [CD-ROM]. Prepared by U.S. Department of Commerce, Economics, and Statistics Administration, Washington, D.C.: U.S. Department of Commerce, National Economic, Social, and Environmental Data Bank, Economics and Statistics Administration, Office of Business Analysis, February 1995.

★99★
Toxic Chemical Releases

Toxic Chemical Releases, 1992: Bis(chloromethyl) Ether

County	Releases	Rank
Burlington County, NJ	3	1
Philadelphia County, PA	2	2

Source: U.S. Environmental Protection Agency, "Toxic Release Inventory, 1992." In *National Economic, Social, and Environmental Data Bank* [CD-ROM]. Prepared by U.S. Department of Commerce, Economics, and Statistics Administration, Washington, D.C.: U.S. Department of Commerce, National Economic, Social, and Environmental Data Bank, Economics and Statistics Administration, Office of Business Analysis, February 1995.

★100★
Toxic Chemical Releases

Toxic Chemical Releases, 1992: Bromoform

County	Releases	Rank
Columbia County, AR	72,000	1
Hancock County, MS	5	2

Source: U.S. Environmental Protection Agency, "Toxic Release Inventory, 1992." In *National Economic, Social, and Environmental Data Bank* [CD-ROM]. Prepared by U.S. Department of Commerce, Economics, and Statistics Administration, Washington, D.C.: U.S. Department of Commerce, National Economic, Social, and Environmental Data Bank, Economics and Statistics Administration, Office of Business Analysis, February 1995.

★101★
Toxic Chemical Releases

Toxic Chemical Releases, 1992: Bromomethane

County	Releases	Rank
Brunswick County, NC	790,880	1
Sebastian County, AR	552,160	2
Berkeley County, SC	341,000	3
Morgan County, AL	210,970	4
Union County, AR	126,155	5
Davidson County, TN	101,000	6
Sullivan County, TN	93,000	7
Yuma County, AZ	44,100	8
Dauphin County, PA	40,490	9
Columbia County, AR	39,300	10
Erie County, NY	39,000	11
Du Page County, IL	32,000	12
Cook County, IL	25,000	13
Fulton County, GA	24,000	14
Middlesex County, MA	18,200	15
Allegheny County, PA	17,000	16
Lebanon County, PA	15,718	17
Bergen County, NJ	15,500	18
Kankakee County, IL	14,400	19
Macomb County, MI	14,233	20

Source: U.S. Environmental Protection Agency, "Toxic Release Inventory, 1992." In *National Economic, Social, and Environmental Data Bank* [CD-ROM]. Prepared by U.S. Department of Commerce, Economics, and Statistics Administration, Washington, D.C.: U.S. Department of Commerce, National Economic, Social, and Environmental Data Bank, Economics and Statistics Administration, Office of Business Analysis, February 1995.

★102★
Toxic Chemical Releases

Toxic Chemical Releases, 1992: Butyl Acrylate

County	Releases	Rank
Hampden County, MA	102,470	1
Harris County, TX	72,856	2
Bucks County, PA	39,893	3
Berks County, PA	27,920	4
Los Angeles County, CA	26,892	5
St Charles Parish, LA	25,642	6
Cook County, IL	22,004	7
Orange County, TX	21,485	8
Mobile County, AL	17,873	9
Clinton County, PA	17,770	10
St Louis County, MO	16,080	11
Daviess County, KY	14,700	12
Allegheny County, PA	14,440	13
Brazoria County, TX	13,503	14
Kenton County, KY	13,262	15
Jefferson County, KY	12,298	16
Knox County, TN	8,650	17
Summit County, OH	6,722	18
Alameda County, CA	5,325	19
Lucas County, OH	5,320	20

Source: U.S. Environmental Protection Agency, "Toxic Release Inventory, 1992." In *National Economic, Social, and Environmental Data Bank* [CD-ROM]. Prepared by U.S. Department of Commerce, Economics, and Statistics Administration, Washington, D.C.: U.S. Department of Commerce, National Economic, Social, and Environmental Data Bank, Economics and Statistics Administration, Office of Business Analysis, February 1995.

★103★
Toxic Chemical Releases

Toxic Chemical Releases, 1992: Butyl Benzyl Phthalate

County	Releases	Rank
Kankakee County, IL	277,000	1
Delaware County, PA	117,320	2
Gloucester County, NJ	98,821	3
Grayson County, TX	95,250	4
Wayne County, MI	82,795	5
Coshocton County, OH	60,021	6
Dane County, WI	42,250	7
Lehigh County, PA	39,200	8
Davidson County, TN	37,250	9
Wichita County, TX	29,211	10
Fulton County, GA	25,060	11
Dearborn County, IN	23,593	12
Niagara County, NY	20,549	13
Vanderburgh County, IN	19,450	14
Franklin County, OH	16,770	15
Richmond City/County, VA	14,647	16
Cook County, IL	12,322	17
Mercer County, NJ	12,086	18
Alameda County, CA	11,750	19
Troup County, GA	11,300	20

Source: U.S. Environmental Protection Agency, "Toxic Release Inventory, 1992." In *National Economic, Social, and Environmental Data Bank* [CD-ROM]. Prepared by U.S. Department of Commerce, Economics, and Statistics Administration, Washington, D.C.: U.S. Department of Commerce, National Economic, Social, and Environmental Data Bank, Economics and Statistics Administration, Office of Business Analysis, February 1995.

★104★
Toxic Chemical Releases

Toxic Chemical Releases, 1992: Butyraldehyde

County	Releases	Rank
Hampden County, MA	409,330	1
Sullivan County, TN	131,000	2
Harrison County, TX	106,000	3
Galveston County, TX	73,315	4
Wayne County, MI	37,558	5
Harris County, TX	28,869	6
Brazoria County, TX	27,700	7
Nueces County, TX	24,000	8
Matagorda County, TX	19,508	9
Kanawha County, WV	11,430	10
Morgan County, AL	5,351	11
Putnam County, WV	4,190	12
Bladen County, NC	3,412	13
Lucas County, OH	1,750	14
Marshall County, KY	1,699	15
Monmouth County, NJ	750	16
Blair County, PA	250	17
Hopewell City/County, VA	248	18
Marion County, IN	12	19
Peoria County, IL	5	20

Source: U.S. Environmental Protection Agency, "Toxic Release Inventory, 1992." In *National Economic, Social, and Environmental Data Bank* [CD-ROM]. Prepared by U.S. Department of Commerce, Economics, and Statistics Administration, Washington, D.C.: U.S. Department of Commerce, National Economic, Social, and Environmental Data Bank, Economics and Statistics Administration, Office of Business Analysis, February 1995.

★105★
Toxic Chemical Releases

Toxic Chemical Releases, 1992: C.I. Basic Green 4

County	Releases	Rank
Essex/Passaic County, NJ	648	1
Morrison County, MN	505	2
Greenville County, SC	364	3
Culpeper County, VA	255	4

Source: U.S. Environmental Protection Agency, "Toxic Release Inventory, 1992." In *National Economic, Social, and Environmental Data Bank* [CD-ROM]. Prepared by U.S. Department of Commerce, Economics, and Statistics Administration, Washington, D.C.: U.S. Department of Commerce, National Economic, Social, and Environmental Data Bank, Economics and Statistics Administration, Office of Business Analysis, February 1995.

★106★
Toxic Chemical Releases

Toxic Chemical Releases, 1992: C.I. Disperse Yellow 3

County	Releases	Rank
Gaston County, NC	1,452	1
Murray County, GA	250	2

Source: U.S. Environmental Protection Agency, "Toxic Release Inventory, 1992." In *National Economic, Social, and Environmental Data Bank* [CD-ROM]. Prepared by U.S. Department of Commerce, Economics, and Statistics Administration, Washington, D.C.: U.S. Department of Commerce, National Economic, Social, and Environmental Data Bank, Economics and Statistics Administration, Office of Business Analysis, February 1995.

★107★
Toxic Chemical Releases

Toxic Chemical Releases, 1992: C.I. Food Red 15

County	Releases	Rank
Rensselaer County, NY	272	1

Source: U.S. Environmental Protection Agency, "Toxic Release Inventory, 1992." In *National Economic, Social, and Environmental Data Bank* [CD-ROM]. Prepared by U.S. Department of Commerce, Economics, and Statistics Administration, Washington, D.C.: U.S. Department of Commerce, National Economic, Social, and Environmental Data Bank, Economics and Statistics Administration, Office of Business Analysis, February 1995.

★108★
Toxic Chemical Releases

Toxic Chemical Releases, 1992: C.I. Solvent Yellow 3

County	Releases	Rank
Pima County, AZ	10	1

Source: U.S. Environmental Protection Agency, "Toxic Release Inventory, 1992." In *National Economic, Social, and Environmental Data Bank* [CD-ROM]. Prepared by U.S. Department of Commerce, Economics, and Statistics Administration, Washington, D.C.: U.S. Department of Commerce, National Economic, Social, and Environmental Data Bank, Economics and Statistics Administration, Office of Business Analysis, February 1995.

★109★
Toxic Chemical Releases

Toxic Chemical Releases, 1992: Cadmium

County	Releases	Rank
Montgomery County, TN	76,426	1
Cuyahoga County, OH	54,093	2
Polk County, FL	40,311	3
Wayne County, MI	30,036	4
Sauk County, WI	23,146	5
Bristol County, MA	17,498	6
Rock County, WI	14,896	7
Ottawa County, MI	13,665	8
Cook County, IL	11,533	9
Morgan County, AL	8,600	10
St Clair County, IL	8,090	11
Blackford County, IN	7,955	12
Northampton County, PA	7,296	13
Saginaw County, MI	6,605	14
Fond Du Lac County, WI	5,115	15
St Louis County, MO	4,632	16
Warren County, MO	4,080	17
Van Wert County, OH	3,632	18
Montgomery County, PA	3,260	19
Berks County, PA	2,331	20

Source: U.S. Environmental Protection Agency, "Toxic Release Inventory, 1992." In *National Economic, Social, and Environmental Data Bank* [CD-ROM]. Prepared by U.S. Department of Commerce, Economics, and Statistics Administration, Washington, D.C.: U.S. Department of Commerce, National Economic, Social, and Environmental Data Bank, Economics and Statistics Administration, Office of Business Analysis, February 1995.

★110★

Toxic Chemical Releases

Toxic Chemical Releases, 1992: Cadmium Compounds

County	Releases	Rank
Salt Lake County, UT	568,250	1
Lewis and Clark County, MT	136,009	2
Alachua County, FL	130,059	3
Gila County, AZ	107,124	4
Kings County, NY	73,200	5
Wayne County, MI	67,250	6
Jefferson County, KY	49,715	7
Morgan County, AL	25,990	8
Snohomish County, WA	24,729	9
Jefferson County, MO	23,697	10
Bannock County, ID	18,798	11
Allegheny County, PA	16,437	12
Cuyahoga County, OH	15,794	13
Geauga County, OH	15,750	14
Huron County, OH	15,505	15
Cook County, IL	13,114	16
Mc Lennan County, TX	11,037	17
Johnson County, TX	9,911	18
El Paso County, TX	9,750	19
Columbiana County, OH	9,630	20

Source: U.S. Environmental Protection Agency, "Toxic Release Inventory, 1992." In *National Economic, Social, and Environmental Data Bank* [CD-ROM]. Prepared by U.S. Department of Commerce, Economics, and Statistics Administration, Washington, D.C.: U.S. Department of Commerce, National Economic, Social, and Environmental Data Bank, Economics and Statistics Administration, Office of Business Analysis, February 1995.

★111★

Toxic Chemical Releases

Toxic Chemical Releases, 1992: Calcium Cyanamide

County	Releases	Rank
Johnson County, KS	52,620	1

Source: U.S. Environmental Protection Agency, "Toxic Release Inventory, 1992." In *National Economic, Social, and Environmental Data Bank* [CD-ROM]. Prepared by U.S. Department of Commerce, Economics, and Statistics Administration, Washington, D.C.: U.S. Department of Commerce, National Economic, Social, and Environmental Data Bank, Economics and Statistics Administration, Office of Business Analysis, February 1995.

★112★

Toxic Chemical Releases

Toxic Chemical Releases, 1992: Captan

County	Releases	Rank
Lake County, OH	21,755	1
Weld County, CO	10,389	2
St Louis County, MO	8,560	3
Fairfield County, CT	2,232	4
Lowndes County, GA	1,260	5
Crisp County, GA	1,250	6
Tunica County, MS	1,250	6
Dodge County, NE	1,000	7
Cook County, GA	760	8

[Continued]

★112★

Toxic Chemical Releases, 1992: Captan
[Continued]

County	Releases	Rank
Shelby County, TN	755	9
Cecil County, MD	505	10
Phillips County, AR	500	11
Tazewell County, IL	352	12
Owyhee County, ID	319	13
Oldham County, KY	255	14
Fresno County, CA	250	15
Erie County, NY	54	16
Peach County, GA	40	17
Yuma County, AZ	6	18
Hancock County, MS	5	19

Source: U.S. Environmental Protection Agency, "Toxic Release Inventory, 1992." In *National Economic, Social, and Environmental Data Bank* [CD-ROM]. Prepared by U.S. Department of Commerce, Economics, and Statistics Administration, Washington, D.C.: U.S. Department of Commerce, National Economic, Social, and Environmental Data Bank, Economics and Statistics Administration, Office of Business Analysis, February 1995.

★113★

Toxic Chemical Releases

Toxic Chemical Releases, 1992: Carbaryl

County	Releases	Rank
Kanawha County, WV	4,914	1
Cecil County, MD	4,535	2
St Louis County, MO	1,482	3
Crisp County, GA	1,250	4
Tunica County, MS	1,250	4
Liberty County, TX	1,250	4
Buchanan County, MO	1,210	5
Roanoke County, VA	1,005	6
Dodge County, NE	1,000	7
Bexar County, TX	750	8
Contra Costa County, CA	561	9
Weld County, CO	510	10
St. Louis City/County, MO	505	11
Oldham County, KY	500	12
Essex County, NJ	500	12
Fresno County, CA	435	13
Cook County, GA	260	14
Lorain County, OH	250	15
Peach County, GA	120	16
Coahoma County, MS	10	17

Source: U.S. Environmental Protection Agency, "Toxic Release Inventory, 1992." In *National Economic, Social, and Environmental Data Bank* [CD-ROM]. Prepared by U.S. Department of Commerce, Economics, and Statistics Administration, Washington, D.C.: U.S. Department of Commerce, National Economic, Social, and Environmental Data Bank, Economics and Statistics Administration, Office of Business Analysis, February 1995.

★114★
Toxic Chemical Releases
Toxic Chemical Releases, 1992: Carbon Disulfide

County	Releases	Rank
Mobile County, AL	46,208,861	1
Hamblen County, TN	22,500,000	2
Carter County, TN	4,623,000	3
St Mary Parish, LA	4,038,937	4
Vermilion County, IL	3,101,750	5
Fountain County, IN	1,810,178	6
Loudon County, TN	1,700,000	7
Shawnee County, KS	1,290,250	8
Mississippi County, AR	1,201,300	9
Erie County, NY	1,140,129	10
Cook County, IL	1,031,050	11
Maury County, TN	943,900	12
West Baton Rouge Parish, LA	929,056	13
Iberia Parish, LA	902,000	14
Barceloneta County, PR	856,100	15
Marshall County, WV	682,313	16
Washington County, OH	640,000	17
Kay County, OK	588,965	18
Union County, AR	475,695	19
Evangeline Parish, LA	470,480	20

Source: U.S. Environmental Protection Agency, "Toxic Release Inventory, 1992." In *National Economic, Social, and Environmental Data Bank* [CD-ROM]. Prepared by U.S. Department of Commerce, Economics, and Statistics Administration, Washington, D.C.: U.S. Department of Commerce, National Economic, Social, and Environmental Data Bank, Economics and Statistics Administration, Office of Business Analysis, February 1995.

★115★
Toxic Chemical Releases
Toxic Chemical Releases, 1992: Carbon Tetrachloride

County	Releases	Rank
Jefferson County, TX	402,530	1
Mobile County, AL	312,702	2
Brazoria County, TX	307,736	3
Colbert County, AL	213,600	4
Baltimore City/County, MD	205,726	5
Harris County, TX	153,532	6
Sedgwick County, KS	131,037	7
Ascension Parish, LA	129,834	8
New Castle County, DE	124,475	9
Marshall County, WV	118,571	10
Shelby County, TN	107,968	11
Contra Costa County, CA	61,590	12
Calcasieu Parish, LA	54,704	13
Posey County, IN	52,596	14
Midland County, MI	48,317	15
Iberville Parish, LA	41,876	16
Philadelphia County, PA	41,257	17
St Charles Parish, LA	41,247	18
Crawford County, OH	40,440	19
Lake County, OH	33,250	20

Source: U.S. Environmental Protection Agency, "Toxic Release Inventory, 1992." In *National Economic, Social, and Environmental Data Bank* [CD-ROM]. Prepared by U.S. Department of Commerce, Economics, and Statistics Administration, Washington, D.C.: U.S. Department of Commerce, National Economic, Social, and Environmental Data Bank, Economics and Statistics Administration, Office of Business Analysis, February 1995.

★116★
Toxic Chemical Releases
Toxic Chemical Releases, 1992: Carbonyl Sulfide

County	Releases	Rank
Humphreys County, TN	8,500,000	1
Harrison County, MS	5,400,000	2
St Mary Parish, LA	872,664	3
New Castle County, DE	582,000	4
Monroe County, MS	421,000	5
Iberia Parish, LA	340,000	6
West Baton Rouge Parish, LA	316,679	7
Contra Costa County, CA	305,000	8
Chatham County, GA	247,000	9
Washington County, OH	230,000	10
Marshall County, WV	219,270	11
Calcasieu Parish, LA	180,000	12
Grant County, KS	157,679	13
Howard County, TX	129,954	14
Evangeline Parish, LA	122,283	15
Kay County, OK	120,027	16
Union County, AR	109,780	17
Russell County, AL	78,483	18
Hutchinson County, TX	77,744	19
Aransas County, TX	58,000	20

Source: U.S. Environmental Protection Agency, "Toxic Release Inventory, 1992." In *National Economic, Social, and Environmental Data Bank* [CD-ROM]. Prepared by U.S. Department of Commerce, Economics, and Statistics Administration, Washington, D.C.: U.S. Department of Commerce, National Economic, Social, and Environmental Data Bank, Economics and Statistics Administration, Office of Business Analysis, February 1995.

★117★
Toxic Chemical Releases
Toxic Chemical Releases, 1992: Catechol

County	Releases	Rank
Clatsop County, OR	166,110	1
Harris County, TX	88,795	2
Middlesex County, NJ	46,000	3
Humboldt County, CA	38,220	4
Wood County, WI	37,000	5
Columbia County, OR	35,331	6
Erie County, PA	33,390	7
Allegany County, MD	33,000	8
Maricopa County, AZ	32,300	9
Gulf County, FL	23,000	10
Hopewell City/County, VA	21,000	11
Navajo County, AZ	19,352	12
Bibb County, GA	18,000	13
Missoula County, MT	17,800	14
Haywood County, NC	17,600	15
Charleston County, SC	17,255	16
Carlton County, MN	15,246	17
Bay County, FL	11,853	18
Clark County, WA	11,650	19
Chatham County, GA	11,140	20

Source: U.S. Environmental Protection Agency, "Toxic Release Inventory, 1992." In *National Economic, Social, and Environmental Data Bank* [CD-ROM]. Prepared by U.S. Department of Commerce, Economics, and Statistics Administration, Washington, D.C.: U.S. Department of Commerce, National Economic, Social, and Environmental Data Bank, Economics and Statistics Administration, Office of Business Analysis, February 1995.

★118★
Toxic Chemical Releases

Toxic Chemical Releases, 1992: Chloramben

County	Releases	Rank
Logan County, IL	15,601	1

Source: U.S. Environmental Protection Agency, "Toxic Release Inventory, 1992." In *National Economic, Social, and Environmental Data Bank* [CD-ROM]. Prepared by U.S. Department of Commerce, Economics, and Statistics Administration, Washington, D.C.: U.S. Department of Commerce, National Economic, Social, and Environmental Data Bank, Economics and Statistics Administration, Office of Business Analysis, February 1995.

★119★
Toxic Chemical Releases

Toxic Chemical Releases, 1992: Chlordane

County	Releases	Rank
Shelby County, TN	5,040	1
Hancock County, MS	5	2

Source: U.S. Environmental Protection Agency, "Toxic Release Inventory, 1992." In *National Economic, Social, and Environmental Data Bank* [CD-ROM]. Prepared by U.S. Department of Commerce, Economics, and Statistics Administration, Washington, D.C.: U.S. Department of Commerce, National Economic, Social, and Environmental Data Bank, Economics and Statistics Administration, Office of Business Analysis, February 1995.

★120★
Toxic Chemical Releases

Toxic Chemical Releases, 1992: Chlorine

County	Releases	Rank
Tooele County, UT	88,150,000	1
Douglas County, IL	3,885,422	2
Washington County, ME	858,202	3
Coos County, NH	690,250	4
Brazoria County, TX	609,826	5
Warren County, MS	521,636	6
Warrick County, IN	502,200	7
Scott County, IA	380,008	8
Koochiching County, MN	370,000	9
San Bernardino County, CA	359,739	10
Harris County, TX	347,473	11
Wasco County, OR	321,700	12
Clarke County, AL	300,350	13
Penobscot County, ME	285,679	14
Madison County, IL	237,570	15
Spokane County, WA	229,845	16
Camden County, GA	221,713	17
Bay County, FL	218,089	18
Cowlitz County, WA	212,870	19
Bradley County, TN	198,898	20

Source: U.S. Environmental Protection Agency, "Toxic Release Inventory, 1992." In *National Economic, Social, and Environmental Data Bank* [CD-ROM]. Prepared by U.S. Department of Commerce, Economics, and Statistics Administration, Washington, D.C.: U.S. Department of Commerce, National Economic, Social, and Environmental Data Bank, Economics and Statistics Administration, Office of Business Analysis, February 1995.

★121★
Toxic Chemical Releases

Toxic Chemical Releases, 1992: Chlorine Dioxide

County	Releases	Rank
Coos County, NH	640,250	1
Monroe County, AL	370,250	2
York County, SC	265,414	3
Dallas County, AL	260,005	4
Jasper County, TX	226,500	5
Bay County, FL	203,147	6
Humboldt County, CA	192,505	7
Penobscot County, ME	177,995	8
Washington County, ME	175,000	9
Columbus County, NC	170,000	10
Allegany County, MD	160,035	11
Craven County, NC	142,605	12
Columbia County, OR	129,173	13
Oxford County, ME	119,354	14
Nez Perce County, ID	114,250	15
Choctaw County, AL	110,000	16
Clatsop County, OR	100,005	17
Walla Walla County, WA	96,410	18
Camden County, GA	93,005	19
Isle Of Wight County, VA	92,110	20

Source: U.S. Environmental Protection Agency, "Toxic Release Inventory, 1992." In *National Economic, Social, and Environmental Data Bank* [CD-ROM]. Prepared by U.S. Department of Commerce, Economics, and Statistics Administration, Washington, D.C.: U.S. Department of Commerce, National Economic, Social, and Environmental Data Bank, Economics and Statistics Administration, Office of Business Analysis, February 1995.

★122★
Toxic Chemical Releases

Toxic Chemical Releases, 1992: Chloroacetic Acid

County	Releases	Rank
Hopewell City/County, VA	17,780	1
Somerset County, NJ	5,604	2
Saint Louis City/County, MO	2,700	3
Ashtabula County, OH	1,800	4
Midland County, MI	1,451	5
Gaston County, NC	1,296	6
Niagara County, NY	755	7
Passaic County, NJ	753	8
Hamilton County, TN	750	9
Mobile County, AL	587	10
East Baton Rouge Parish, LA	522	11
Los Angeles County, CA	505	12
Dade County, FL	500	13
New London County, CT	255	14
Middlesex County, NJ	255	14
St Charles Parish, LA	44	15
Clinton County, PA	43	16
Blair County, PA	15	17
Harris County, TX	15	17
Ector County, TX	10	18

Source: U.S. Environmental Protection Agency, "Toxic Release Inventory, 1992." In *National Economic, Social, and Environmental Data Bank* [CD-ROM]. Prepared by U.S. Department of Commerce, Economics, and Statistics Administration, Washington, D.C.: U.S. Department of Commerce, National Economic, Social, and Environmental Data Bank, Economics and Statistics Administration, Office of Business Analysis, February 1995.

★123★

Toxic Chemical Releases

Toxic Chemical Releases, 1992: Chlorobenzene

County	Releases	Rank
Washington County, OH	2,682,163	1
Mobile County, AL	1,152,010	2
Kanawha County, WV	1,060,472	3
Harris County, TX	917,869	4
Marshall County, WV	541,533	5
Ascension Parish, LA	357,142	6
St Clair County, IL	274,740	7
Philadelphia County, PA	127,346	8
Chambers County, TX	119,047	9
Midland County, MI	117,886	10
Calcasieu Parish, LA	117,833	11
Saint Louis City/County, MO	109,360	12
Charleston County, SC	89,614	13
Hamilton County, OH	83,026	14
New Castle County, DE	79,287	15
Essex County, NJ	36,348	16
Centre County, PA	32,610	17
Muscatine County, IA	22,807	18
Marion County, MO	14,510	19
Orange County, TX	11,309	20

Source: U.S. Environmental Protection Agency, "Toxic Release Inventory, 1992." In *National Economic, Social, and Environmental Data Bank* [CD-ROM]. Prepared by U.S. Department of Commerce, Economics, and Statistics Administration, Washington, D.C.: U.S. Department of Commerce, National Economic, Social, and Environmental Data Bank, Economics and Statistics Administration, Office of Business Analysis, February 1995.

★124★

Toxic Chemical Releases

Toxic Chemical Releases, 1992: Chloroethane

County	Releases	Rank
Jefferson County, MO	870,000	1
Harrison County, TX	472,400	2
Lawrence County, OH	465,000	3
Calcasieu Parish, LA	361,278	4
Whitfield County, GA	360,000	5
Frederick County, VA	310,900	6
Will County, IL	274,000	7
Beaufort County, SC	245,460	8
Los Angeles County, CA	185,000	9
New London County, CT	163,505	10
Ascension Parish, LA	162,411	11
Midland County, MI	145,998	12
Salem County, NJ	102,906	13
Matagorda County, TX	96,579	14
Cameron County, PA	91,830	15
Ellis County, TX	33,000	16
Hopewell City/County, VA	31,855	17
Galveston County, TX	13,969	18
Harris County, TX	10,249	19
Brazoria County, TX	10,028	20

Source: U.S. Environmental Protection Agency, "Toxic Release Inventory, 1992." In *National Economic, Social, and Environmental Data Bank* [CD-ROM]. Prepared by U.S. Department of Commerce, Economics, and Statistics Administration, Washington, D.C.: U.S. Department of Commerce, National Economic, Social, and Environmental Data Bank, Economics and Statistics Administration, Office of Business Analysis, February 1995.

★125★

Toxic Chemical Releases

Toxic Chemical Releases, 1992: Chloroform

County	Releases	Rank
Haywood County, NC	1,086,101	1
Nez Perce County, ID	921,000	2
Glynn County, GA	854,800	3
Columbus County, NC	840,610	4
Mobile County, AL	799,950	5
Cowlitz County, WA	674,030	6
Snohomish County, WA	667,200	7
Choctaw County, AL	625,000	8
Lawrence County, AL	565,210	9
Saint Louis City/County, MO	514,440	10
Taylor County, FL	485,311	11
Erie County, PA	427,200	12
Wayne County, GA	394,400	13
York County, SC	389,196	14
Washington County, ME	366,575	15
Harris County, TX	360,907	16
Richmond County, GA	360,400	17
Morehouse Parish, LA	347,439	18
Clatsop County, OR	344,700	19
Sedgwick County, KS	342,671	20

Source: U.S. Environmental Protection Agency, "Toxic Release Inventory, 1992." In *National Economic, Social, and Environmental Data Bank* [CD-ROM]. Prepared by U.S. Department of Commerce, Economics, and Statistics Administration, Washington, D.C.: U.S. Department of Commerce, National Economic, Social, and Environmental Data Bank, Economics and Statistics Administration, Office of Business Analysis, February 1995.

★126★

Toxic Chemical Releases

Toxic Chemical Releases, 1992: Chloromethane

County	Releases	Rank
Harris County, TX	1,487,301	1
East Baton Rouge Parish, LA	680,921	2
Midland County, MI	657,150	3
Tyler County, WV	541,366	4
Carroll County, KY	445,406	5
Cook County, IL	439,262	6
Harrison County, TX	380,380	7
Washington County, OH	367,110	8
Greene County, MO	324,408	9
Peoria County, IL	292,516	10
Grundy County, IL	259,005	11
New London County, CT	244,950	12
Rockingham County, VA	236,400	13
Charleston County, SC	203,054	14
Galveston County, TX	154,413	15
Sedgwick County, KS	126,400	16
Shelby County, TN	119,831	17
Calcasieu Parish, LA	116,867	18
Marshall County, WV	102,900	19
Kanawha County, WV	101,104	20

Source: U.S. Environmental Protection Agency, "Toxic Release Inventory, 1992." In *National Economic, Social, and Environmental Data Bank* [CD-ROM]. Prepared by U.S. Department of Commerce, Economics, and Statistics Administration, Washington, D.C.: U.S. Department of Commerce, National Economic, Social, and Environmental Data Bank, Economics and Statistics Administration, Office of Business Analysis, February 1995.

★127★

Toxic Chemical Releases

Toxic Chemical Releases, 1992: Chloromethyl Methyl Ether

County	Releases	Rank
Burlington County, NJ	91	1
Philadelphia County, PA	33	2

Source: U.S. Environmental Protection Agency, "Toxic Release Inventory, 1992." In *National Economic, Social, and Environmental Data Bank* [CD-ROM]. Prepared by U.S. Department of Commerce, Economics, and Statistics Administration, Washington, D.C.: U.S. Department of Commerce, National Economic, Social, and Environmental Data Bank, Economics and Statistics Administration, Office of Business Analysis, February 1995.

★128★

Toxic Chemical Releases

Toxic Chemical Releases, 1992: Chlorophenols

County	Releases	Rank
Jefferson County, TX	929,505	1
Sedgwick County, KS	52,600	2
Philadelphia County, PA	1,322	3
Somerset County, NJ	1,250	4
Cleveland County, NC	750	5
Cook County, IL	510	6
Multnomah County, OR	500	7
Midland County, MI	347	8
Lucas County, OH	179	9
Jackson County, MO	155	10

Source: U.S. Environmental Protection Agency, "Toxic Release Inventory, 1992." In *National Economic, Social, and Environmental Data Bank* [CD-ROM]. Prepared by U.S. Department of Commerce, Economics, and Statistics Administration, Washington, D.C.: U.S. Department of Commerce, National Economic, Social, and Environmental Data Bank, Economics and Statistics Administration, Office of Business Analysis, February 1995.

★129★

Toxic Chemical Releases

Toxic Chemical Releases, 1992: Chloroprene

County	Releases	Rank
Jefferson County, KY	524,159	1
Harris County, TX	322,190	2
Calhoun County, TX	25,000	3
Marshall County, KY	2,672	4
Bergen County, NJ	2,278	5
Summit County, OH	1,738	6
Pinellas County, FL	500	7
Brazoria County, TX	2	8

Source: U.S. Environmental Protection Agency, "Toxic Release Inventory, 1992." In *National Economic, Social, and Environmental Data Bank* [CD-ROM]. Prepared by U.S. Department of Commerce, Economics, and Statistics Administration, Washington, D.C.: U.S. Department of Commerce, National Economic, Social, and Environmental Data Bank, Economics and Statistics Administration, Office of Business Analysis, February 1995.

★130★

Toxic Chemical Releases

Toxic Chemical Releases, 1992: Chlorothalonil

County	Releases	Rank
Harris County, TX	208,534	1
Franklin County, OH	1,790	2
Cook County, IL	1,421	3
Lowndes County, GA	1,260	4
St Louis County, MO	848	5
Dallas County, TX	758	6
Guilford County, NC	688	7
Baltimore City/County, MD	468	8
Jefferson County, KY	374	9
Buchanan County, MO	344	10
Clayton County, GA	318	11
Orange County, FL	154	12
Mississippi County, AR	142	13
Fulton County, GA	85	14
Berks County, PA	82	15
Crisp County, GA	49	16
Dade County, FL	10	17
Lebanon County, PA	1	18

Source: U.S. Environmental Protection Agency, "Toxic Release Inventory, 1992." In *National Economic, Social, and Environmental Data Bank* [CD-ROM]. Prepared by U.S. Department of Commerce, Economics, and Statistics Administration, Washington, D.C.: U.S. Department of Commerce, National Economic, Social, and Environmental Data Bank, Economics and Statistics Administration, Office of Business Analysis, February 1995.

★131★

Toxic Chemical Releases

Toxic Chemical Releases, 1992: Chromium

County	Releases	Rank
Cambria County, PA	1,141,856	1
Milwaukee County, WI	952,180	2
La Porte County, IN	701,847	3
Madison County, IN	573,743	4
Union County, MS	551,500	5
Rock County, WI	467,195	6
Winnebago County, IL	409,301	7
Mahoning County, OH	339,422	8
Marquette County, MI	339,085	9
Cuyahoga County, OH	320,209	10
Stark County, OH	302,764	11
Utah County, UT	237,205	12
Harris County, TX	205,139	13
Madison County, IL	199,881	14
Calhoun County, AL	199,267	15
Galveston County, TX	190,180	16
Lawrence County, IN	176,640	17
Wayne County, MI	173,863	18
Berks County, PA	165,593	19
Beaver County, PA	145,988	20

Source: U.S. Environmental Protection Agency, "Toxic Release Inventory, 1992." In *National Economic, Social, and Environmental Data Bank* [CD-ROM]. Prepared by U.S. Department of Commerce, Economics, and Statistics Administration, Washington, D.C.: U.S. Department of Commerce, National Economic, Social, and Environmental Data Bank, Economics and Statistics Administration, Office of Business Analysis, February 1995.

★ 132 ★
Toxic Chemical Releases

Toxic Chemical Releases, 1992: Chromium Compounds

County	Releases	Rank
New Hanover County, NC	7,444,278	1
Lake County, IN	2,656,288	2
Gila County, AZ	2,222,200	3
Montgomery County, OH	1,755,463	4
Garland County, AR	1,690,250	5
Nueces County, TX	1,143,201	6
Cabell County, WV	882,015	7
Milwaukee County, WI	701,029	8
Washington County, OH	670,000	9
Washington County, PA	550,204	10
Cook County, IL	520,508	11
Lorain County, OH	492,545	12
Creek County, OK	458,941	13
Angelina County, TX	331,475	14
Jefferson County, AL	321,316	15
La Porte County, IN	317,990	16
Westmoreland County, PA	282,252	17
Sacramento County, CA	282,013	18
Black Hawk County, IA	271,479	19
Chatham County, GA	253,730	20

Source: U.S. Environmental Protection Agency, "Toxic Release Inventory, 1992." In *National Economic, Social, and Environmental Data Bank* [CD-ROM]. Prepared by U.S. Department of Commerce, Economics, and Statistics Administration, Washington, D.C.: U.S. Department of Commerce, National Economic, Social, and Environmental Data Bank, Economics and Statistics Administration, Office of Business Analysis, February 1995.

★ 133 ★
Toxic Chemical Releases

Toxic Chemical Releases, 1992: Cobalt

County	Releases	Rank
Hampton City/County, VA	103,015	1
Wayne County, MI	35,053	2
Galveston County, TX	32,259	3
Essex County, NJ	18,603	4
Worcester County, MA	12,543	5
New Hanover County, NC	10,600	6
Benton County, AR	10,338	7
Greenville County, SC	9,347	8
Callaway County, MO	8,010	9
Boyd County, KY	7,552	10
Bergen County, NJ	5,250	11
Rock Island County, IL	4,840	12
Muskegon County, MI	4,410	13
Berks County, PA	4,390	14
Mercer County, PA	4,026	15
Washtenaw County, MI	3,500	16
Lake County, OH	3,383	17
Stark County, OH	3,042	18
Macomb County, MI	2,839	19
Spartanburg County, SC	2,802	20

Source: U.S. Environmental Protection Agency, "Toxic Release Inventory, 1992." In *National Economic, Social, and Environmental Data Bank* [CD-ROM]. Prepared by U.S. Department of Commerce, Economics, and Statistics Administration, Washington, D.C.: U.S. Department of Commerce, National Economic, Social, and Environmental Data Bank, Economics and Statistics Administration, Office of Business Analysis, February 1995.

★ 134 ★
Toxic Chemical Releases

Toxic Chemical Releases, 1992: Cobalt Compounds

County	Releases	Rank
Morgan County, AL	153,250	1
Gila County, AZ	153,200	2
Brunswick County, NC	101,155	3
Berkeley County, SC	30,300	4
Mc Leod County, MN	25,705	5
Jefferson Parish, LA	18,274	6
Lake County, OH	17,001	7
Lorain County, OH	16,188	8
Sandusky County, OH	15,193	9
Will County, IL	13,880	10
Smith County, TX	13,077	11
Douglas County, NE	12,805	12
Washington County, PA	12,284	13
Hamilton County, TN	11,711	14
Victoria County, TX	10,950	15
La Porte County, IN	10,141	16
Multnomah County, OR	9,526	17
St Clair County, IL	8,545	18
Ascension Parish, LA	7,540	19
Sullivan County, TN	7,515	20

Source: U.S. Environmental Protection Agency, "Toxic Release Inventory, 1992." In *National Economic, Social, and Environmental Data Bank* [CD-ROM]. Prepared by U.S. Department of Commerce, Economics, and Statistics Administration, Washington, D.C.: U.S. Department of Commerce, National Economic, Social, and Environmental Data Bank, Economics and Statistics Administration, Office of Business Analysis, February 1995.

★ 135 ★
Toxic Chemical Releases

Toxic Chemical Releases, 1992: Copper

County	Releases	Rank
Pinal County, AZ	10,146,957	1
Lancaster County, PA	2,352,941	2
Passaic County, NJ	632,372	3
Franklin County, PA	579,369	4
Madison County, IL	570,801	5
Galveston County, TX	561,630	6
Orange County, FL	491,084	7
Elkhart County, IN	490,766	8
Bristol County, MA	481,113	9
Whitley County, IN	366,287	10
Los Angeles County, CA	364,457	11
Howard County, IN	319,950	12
Cook County, IL	298,409	13
Collin County, TX	296,750	14
Onondaga County, NY	296,692	15
Marion County, IN	270,480	16
Montgomery County, TN	227,072	17
Orange County, CA	208,100	18
Monongalia County, WV	189,250	19
Erie County, OH	173,855	20

Source: U.S. Environmental Protection Agency, "Toxic Release Inventory, 1992." In *National Economic, Social, and Environmental Data Bank* [CD-ROM]. Prepared by U.S. Department of Commerce, Economics, and Statistics Administration, Washington, D.C.: U.S. Department of Commerce, National Economic, Social, and Environmental Data Bank, Economics and Statistics Administration, Office of Business Analysis, February 1995.

★136★
Toxic Chemical Releases

Toxic Chemical Releases, 1992: Copper Compounds

County	Releases	Rank
Salt Lake County, UT	39,423,971	1
Ontonagon County, MI	18,420,600	2
Hidalgo County, NM	14,257,755	3
Gila County, AZ	11,985,142	4
Grant County, NM	6,724,000	5
Lewis and Clark County, MT	1,321,586	6
Saratoga County, NY	1,305,805	7
St Clair County, IL	1,213,234	8
Lexington County, SC	1,156,762	9
Cook County, IL	672,598	10
Sacramento County, CA	443,220	11
King County, WA	358,234	12
La Salle County, IL	316,064	13
Berks County, PA	314,289	14
De Witt County, IL	280,750	15
El Paso County, TX	206,950	16
Iron County, MO	203,198	17
Wyandotte County, KS	201,057	18
Calcasieu Parish, LA	176,707	19
Elmore County, AL	167,456	20

Source: U.S. Environmental Protection Agency, "Toxic Release Inventory, 1992." In *National Economic, Social, and Environmental Data Bank* [CD-ROM]. Prepared by U.S. Department of Commerce, Economics, and Statistics Administration, Washington, D.C.: U.S. Department of Commerce, National Economic, Social, and Environmental Data Bank, Economics and Statistics Administration, Office of Business Analysis, February 1995.

★137★
Toxic Chemical Releases

Toxic Chemical Releases, 1992: Creosote

County	Releases	Rank
Todd County, KY	1,138,931	1
Jackson County, IL	810,076	2
Florence County, SC	437,983	3
Travis County, TX	372,620	4
Hampshire County, WV	363,652	5
Tuscaloosa County, AL	330,800	6
Rapides Parish, LA	286,950	7
Brunswick County, NC	267,926	8
Adams County, CO	229,509	9
Pearl River County, MS	191,900	10
Lawrence County, OH	182,405	11
Brooke County, WV	180,233	12
Pike County, IN	137,769	13
King County, WA	131,055	14
Roanoke County, VA	112,489	15
Chatham County, GA	90,000	16
Jefferson County, AL	83,050	17
Beauregard Parish, LA	76,473	18
Multnomah County, OR	71,923	19
Blount County, AL	68,700	20

Source: U.S. Environmental Protection Agency, "Toxic Release Inventory, 1992." In *National Economic, Social, and Environmental Data Bank* [CD-ROM]. Prepared by U.S. Department of Commerce, Economics, and Statistics Administration, Washington, D.C.: U.S. Department of Commerce, National Economic, Social, and Environmental Data Bank, Economics and Statistics Administration, Office of Business Analysis, February 1995.

★138★
Toxic Chemical Releases

Toxic Chemical Releases, 1992: Cresol (Mixed Isomers)

County	Releases	Rank
Harris County, TX	916,876	1
Orange County, TX	633,579	2
Allen County, IN	233,746	3
Victoria County, TX	215,349	4
Tippecanoe County, IN	130,253	5
Lawrence County, IN	116,445	6
Christian County, KY	85,565	7
Venango County, PA	84,508	8
Schenectady County, NY	78,489	9
Scotland County, NC	77,350	10
Lake County, IL	49,532	11
Los Angeles County, CA	45,243	12
Oldham County, KY	35,193	13
Calcasieu Parish, LA	33,142	14
Williamson County, TN	31,513	15
Winnebago County, IL	23,000	16
Putnam County, WV	17,986	17
Cuyahoga County, OH	14,708	18
Westmoreland County, PA	14,123	19
Catawba County, NC	13,500	20

Source: U.S. Environmental Protection Agency, "Toxic Release Inventory, 1992." In *National Economic, Social, and Environmental Data Bank* [CD-ROM]. Prepared by U.S. Department of Commerce, Economics, and Statistics Administration, Washington, D.C.: U.S. Department of Commerce, National Economic, Social, and Environmental Data Bank, Economics and Statistics Administration, Office of Business Analysis, February 1995.

★139★
Toxic Chemical Releases

Toxic Chemical Releases, 1992: Cumene

County	Releases	Rank
Philadelphia County, PA	1,368,814	1
Butler County, KS	380,540	2
Harris County, TX	375,334	3
Glynn County, GA	365,782	4
Iberville Parish, LA	363,721	5
Scioto County, OH	353,960	6
Posey County, IN	225,869	7
Jefferson County, TX	190,701	8
Cook County, IL	132,617	9
New Haven County, CT	114,514	10
Gloucester County, NJ	97,165	11
Galveston County, TX	65,870	12
Boyd County, KY	65,259	13
Wood County, WV	63,180	14
Lancaster County, SC	57,196	15
Nueces County, TX	53,732	16
Alachua County, FL	52,087	17
Jackson County, MS	50,250	18
Colbert County, AL	38,893	19
Calhoun County, AL	33,118	20

Source: U.S. Environmental Protection Agency, "Toxic Release Inventory, 1992." In *National Economic, Social, and Environmental Data Bank* [CD-ROM]. Prepared by U.S. Department of Commerce, Economics, and Statistics Administration, Washington, D.C.: U.S. Department of Commerce, National Economic, Social, and Environmental Data Bank, Economics and Statistics Administration, Office of Business Analysis, February 1995.

★140★
Toxic Chemical Releases

Toxic Chemical Releases, 1992: Cumene Hydroperoxide

County	Releases	Rank
Scioto County, OH	214,010	1
Harrison County, TX	32,473	2
Butler County, KS	32,000	3
Harris County, TX	31,581	4
Calhoun County, MI	14,100	5
Lee County, MS	7,415	6
Wayne County, MI	5,255	7
Philadelphia County, PA	4,300	8
Lenawee County, MI	4,096	9
Posey County, IN	2,530	10
Peoria County, IL	1,600	11
Brazoria County, TX	1,413	12
Livingston County, NY	786	13
Sabana Grande County, PR	755	14
Vermilion County, IL	588	15
Los Angeles County, CA	512	16
Gloucester County, NJ	500	17
Waupaca County, WI	500	17
Iberville Parish, LA	496	18
Jackson County, MO	490	19

Source: U.S. Environmental Protection Agency, "Toxic Release Inventory, 1992." In *National Economic, Social, and Environmental Data Bank* [CD-ROM]. Prepared by U.S. Department of Commerce, Economics, and Statistics Administration, Washington, D.C.: U.S. Department of Commerce, National Economic, Social, and Environmental Data Bank, Economics and Statistics Administration, Office of Business Analysis, February 1995.

★141★
Toxic Chemical Releases

Toxic Chemical Releases, 1992: Cupferron

County	Releases	Rank
Saint Louis City/County, MO	1,010	1
Harris County, TX	34	2
Hancock County, MS	5	3

Source: U.S. Environmental Protection Agency, "Toxic Release Inventory, 1992." In *National Economic, Social, and Environmental Data Bank* [CD-ROM]. Prepared by U.S. Department of Commerce, Economics, and Statistics Administration, Washington, D.C.: U.S. Department of Commerce, National Economic, Social, and Environmental Data Bank, Economics and Statistics Administration, Office of Business Analysis, February 1995.

★142★
Toxic Chemical Releases

Toxic Chemical Releases, 1992: Cyanide Compounds

County	Releases	Rank
Jefferson County, TX	1,001,535	1
Calhoun County, TX	900,017	2
Allen County, OH	680,000	3
Victoria County, TX	574,588	4
Orange County, TX	532,710	5
Cook County, IL	318,230	6
Baltimore County, MD	231,780	7

[Continued]

★142★

Toxic Chemical Releases, 1992: Cyanide Compounds
[Continued]

County	Releases	Rank
Montgomery County, AL	216,870	8
Iberia Parish, LA	201,000	9
Harris County, TX	162,161	10
Galveston County, TX	155,275	11
Multnomah County, OR	142,116	12
Allegheny County, PA	141,321	13
Hartford County, CT	126,426	14
Wayne County, MI	125,504	15
Lake County, IN	117,834	16
Brooke County, WV	67,050	17
Washington County, OH	51,600	18
Fond Du Lac County, WI	45,706	19
Aransas County, TX	38,000	20

Source: U.S. Environmental Protection Agency, "Toxic Release Inventory, 1992." In *National Economic, Social, and Environmental Data Bank* [CD-ROM]. Prepared by U.S. Department of Commerce, Economics, and Statistics Administration, Washington, D.C.: U.S. Department of Commerce, National Economic, Social, and Environmental Data Bank, Economics and Statistics Administration, Office of Business Analysis, February 1995.

★143★
Toxic Chemical Releases

Toxic Chemical Releases, 1992: Cyclohexane

County	Releases	Rank
Orange County, TX	3,989,474	1
Washington County, OH	1,930,510	2
Escambia County, FL	1,335,000	3
Cook County, IL	846,475	4
Brazoria County, TX	793,235	5
Harris County, TX	686,774	6
Marion County, IA	654,005	7
Brookings County, SD	460,576	8
Jefferson County, TX	410,073	9
Hutchinson County, TX	387,964	10
Mc Leod County, MN	326,457	11
Ramsey County, MN	317,910	12
Calcasieu Parish, LA	305,880	13
Bucks County, PA	300,750	14
Worcester County, MA	291,347	15
Richmond County, GA	289,822	16
Victoria County, TX	271,645	17
Monroe County, NY	265,316	18
Marion County, AL	201,400	19
Guayama County, PR	183,111	20

Source: U.S. Environmental Protection Agency, "Toxic Release Inventory, 1992." In *National Economic, Social, and Environmental Data Bank* [CD-ROM]. Prepared by U.S. Department of Commerce, Economics, and Statistics Administration, Washington, D.C.: U.S. Department of Commerce, National Economic, Social, and Environmental Data Bank, Economics and Statistics Administration, Office of Business Analysis, February 1995.

★144★
Toxic Chemical Releases

Toxic Chemical Releases, 1992: Decabromodiphenyl Oxide

County	Releases	Rank
Dyer County, TN	206,750	1
Union County, AR	205,663	2
Northampton County, PA	71,547	3
Albany County, NY	32,851	4
Medina County, OH	28,100	5
Greenville County, SC	27,767	6
Nevada County, AR	23,709	7
Whitfield County, GA	23,000	8
York County, PA	22,209	9
Columbia County, AR	22,000	10
Washington County, NY	21,000	11
Guilford County, NC	18,800	12
Limestone County, TX	17,000	13
Morris County, NJ	14,250	14
Livingston County, MI	14,184	15
Gaston County, NC	12,025	16
Summit County, OH	10,635	17
Nueces County, TX	10,000	18
Mercer County, NJ	9,976	19
Catawba County, NC	8,344	20

Source: U.S. Environmental Protection Agency, "Toxic Release Inventory, 1992." In *National Economic, Social, and Environmental Data Bank* [CD-ROM]. Prepared by U.S. Department of Commerce, Economics, and Statistics Administration, Washington, D.C.: U.S. Department of Commerce, National Economic, Social, and Environmental Data Bank, Economics and Statistics Administration, Office of Business Analysis, February 1995.

★145★
Toxic Chemical Releases

Toxic Chemical Releases, 1992: Di(2-ethylhexyl) Phthalate

County	Releases	Rank
Wayne County, MI	340,384	1
Cumberland County, NC	164,767	2
Bristol County, MA	148,891	3
Lancaster County, PA	134,948	4
Cook County, IL	123,135	5
Middlesex County, NJ	111,566	6
Harrison County, IN	109,386	7
Los Angeles County, CA	100,496	8
Racine County, WI	91,250	9
Dyer County, TN	86,093	10
Hamblen County, TN	77,700	11
Ashland County, OH	69,408	12
Hudson County, NJ	68,250	13
Washington County, NY	66,609	14
Henry County, VA	61,956	15
Tarrant County, TX	58,625	16
Greene County, AR	56,300	17
Fairfield County, CT	52,473	18
St Charles County, MO	48,260	19
Iosco County, MI	47,885	20

Source: U.S. Environmental Protection Agency, "Toxic Release Inventory, 1992." In *National Economic, Social, and Environmental Data Bank* [CD-ROM]. Prepared by U.S. Department of Commerce, Economics, and Statistics Administration, Washington, D.C.: U.S. Department of Commerce, National Economic, Social, and Environmental Data Bank, Economics and Statistics Administration, Office of Business Analysis, February 1995.

★146★
Toxic Chemical Releases

Toxic Chemical Releases, 1992: Diaminotoluene (Mixed Isomers)

County	Releases	Rank
Ascension Parish, LA	663,375	1
Chambers County, TX	377,081	2
Harris County, TX	279,800	3
Calcasieu Parish, LA	30,026	4
Berkeley County, SC	6,689	5
Marshall County, WV	3,582	6
Hamilton County, OH	1,576	7
Wayne County, MI	725	8
Brazoria County, TX	673	9
Palo Pinto County, TX	500	10
East Baton Rouge Parish, LA	95	11
Los Angeles County, CA	87	12

Source: U.S. Environmental Protection Agency, "Toxic Release Inventory, 1992." In *National Economic, Social, and Environmental Data Bank* [CD-ROM]. Prepared by U.S. Department of Commerce, Economics, and Statistics Administration, Washington, D.C.: U.S. Department of Commerce, National Economic, Social, and Environmental Data Bank, Economics and Statistics Administration, Office of Business Analysis, February 1995.

★147★
Toxic Chemical Releases

Toxic Chemical Releases, 1992: Dibenzofuran

County	Releases	Rank
Jefferson County, AL	51,474	1
Wayne County, MI	46,387	2
Allegheny County, PA	18,001	3
Lawrence County, OH	16,800	4
Northampton County, PA	4,510	5
Washington County, OH	4,203	6
Brooke County, WV	1,915	7
Jefferson County, OH	1,900	8
Cook County, IL	1,500	9
Vigo County, IN	1,000	10
Madison County, IL	960	11
St Clair County, AL	750	12
Sussex County, DE	750	12
Hillsborough County, FL	750	12
Porter County, IN	750	12
Scioto County, OH	750	12
Forsyth County, NC	750	12
Hudson County, NJ	750	12
Graves County, KY	606	13
Brazoria County, TX	510	14

Source: U.S. Environmental Protection Agency, "Toxic Release Inventory, 1992." In *National Economic, Social, and Environmental Data Bank* [CD-ROM]. Prepared by U.S. Department of Commerce, Economics, and Statistics Administration, Washington, D.C.: U.S. Department of Commerce, National Economic, Social, and Environmental Data Bank, Economics and Statistics Administration, Office of Business Analysis, February 1995.

★148★

Toxic Chemical Releases

Toxic Chemical Releases, 1992: Dibutyl Phthalate

County	Releases	Rank
Escambia County, FL	141,100	1
Forsyth County, NC	26,680	2
Bedford County, TN	25,640	3
Wayne County, MI	18,660	4
Waukesha County, WI	13,375	5
Montgomery County, TN	13,361	6
Harris County, TX	9,520	7
Middlesex County, MA	8,004	8
Genesee County, MI	7,000	9
Cook County, IL	6,334	10
Colonial Height County, VA	5,406	11
Transylvania County, NC	5,113	12
Madison County, KY	5,000	13
Oswego County, NY	4,900	14
Middlesex County, NJ	4,884	15
Gregg County, TX	4,495	16
Monroe County, NY	4,399	17
New Hanover County, NC	4,329	18
Sangamon County, IL	4,320	19
Hawkins County, TN	3,823	20

Source: U.S. Environmental Protection Agency, "Toxic Release Inventory, 1992." In *National Economic, Social, and Environmental Data Bank* [CD-ROM]. Prepared by U.S. Department of Commerce, Economics, and Statistics Administration, Washington, D.C.: U.S. Department of Commerce, National Economic, Social, and Environmental Data Bank, Economics and Statistics Administration, Office of Business Analysis, February 1995.

★149★

Toxic Chemical Releases

Toxic Chemical Releases, 1992: Dichlorobenzene (Mixed Isomers)

County	Releases	Rank
Bergen County, NJ	181,600	1
Penobscot County, ME	59,283	2
Washington County, OH	42,552	3
Orange County, CA	16,005	4
Calcasieu Parish, LA	11,608	5
Mecklenburg County, NC	11,112	6
Dallas County, TX	3,000	7
Bexar County, TX	1,275	8
Spartanburg County, SC	750	9
Marshall County, WV	750	9
Lake County, OH	492	10
St Mary Parish, LA	250	11
Maury County, TN	250	11
Union County, NJ	100	12

Source: U.S. Environmental Protection Agency, "Toxic Release Inventory, 1992." In *National Economic, Social, and Environmental Data Bank* [CD-ROM]. Prepared by U.S. Department of Commerce, Economics, and Statistics Administration, Washington, D.C.: U.S. Department of Commerce, National Economic, Social, and Environmental Data Bank, Economics and Statistics Administration, Office of Business Analysis, February 1995.

★150★

Toxic Chemical Releases

Toxic Chemical Releases, 1992: Dichlorobromomethane

County	Releases	Rank
Calcasieu Parish, LA	632	1

Source: U.S. Environmental Protection Agency, "Toxic Release Inventory, 1992." In *National Economic, Social, and Environmental Data Bank* [CD-ROM]. Prepared by U.S. Department of Commerce, Economics, and Statistics Administration, Washington, D.C.: U.S. Department of Commerce, National Economic, Social, and Environmental Data Bank, Economics and Statistics Administration, Office of Business Analysis, February 1995.

★151★

Toxic Chemical Releases

Toxic Chemical Releases, 1992: Dichloromethane

County	Releases	Rank
Monroe County, NY	5,860,880	1
Posey County, IN	4,763,540	2
Kalamazoo County, MI	4,225,102	3
Lee County, MS	3,844,655	4
Barceloneta County, PR	3,311,027	5
Los Angeles County, CA	3,205,341	6
Catawba County, NC	2,431,851	7
Vermillion County, IN	2,419,205	8
Broome County, NY	2,062,600	9
Elkhart County, IN	1,902,837	10
Bradford County, PA	1,557,850	11
Cook County, IL	1,554,537	12
Dougherty County, GA	1,548,000	13
Randolph County, NC	1,463,203	14
Salt Lake County, UT	1,447,103	15
Washtenaw County, MI	1,439,623	16
Cuyahoga County, OH	1,371,170	17
Lancaster County, NE	1,176,546	18
Tippecanoe County, IN	1,117,905	19
Canadian County, OK	1,115,962	20

Source: U.S. Environmental Protection Agency, "Toxic Release Inventory, 1992." In *National Economic, Social, and Environmental Data Bank* [CD-ROM]. Prepared by U.S. Department of Commerce, Economics, and Statistics Administration, Washington, D.C.: U.S. Department of Commerce, National Economic, Social, and Environmental Data Bank, Economics and Statistics Administration, Office of Business Analysis, February 1995.

★152★

Toxic Chemical Releases

Toxic Chemical Releases, 1992: Dichlorvos

County	Releases	Rank
Doniphan County, KS	3,175	1
St Louis County, MO	806	2
Washington County, IA	260	3
Hancock County, MS	250	4
Cayey County, PR	250	4
Dallas County, TX	250	4
Harris County, TX	250	4
Marion County, IA	30	5

[Continued]

★152★

Toxic Chemical Releases, 1992: Dichlorvos
[Continued]

County	Releases	Rank
Los Angeles County, CA	30	5
Washington County, GA	5	6

Source: U.S. Environmental Protection Agency, "Toxic Release Inventory, 1992." In *National Economic, Social, and Environmental Data Bank* [CD-ROM]. Prepared by U.S. Department of Commerce, Economics, and Statistics Administration, Washington, D.C.: U.S. Department of Commerce, National Economic, Social, and Environmental Data Bank, Economics and Statistics Administration, Office of Business Analysis, February 1995.

★153★
Toxic Chemical Releases

Toxic Chemical Releases, 1992: Dicofol

County	Releases	Rank
Cook County, GA	260	1
Washington County, MS	255	2
Fresno County, CA	36	3
Crisp County, GA	8	4

Source: U.S. Environmental Protection Agency, "Toxic Release Inventory, 1992." In *National Economic, Social, and Environmental Data Bank* [CD-ROM]. Prepared by U.S. Department of Commerce, Economics, and Statistics Administration, Washington, D.C.: U.S. Department of Commerce, National Economic, Social, and Environmental Data Bank, Economics and Statistics Administration, Office of Business Analysis, February 1995.

★154★
Toxic Chemical Releases

Toxic Chemical Releases, 1992: Diethanolamine

County	Releases	Rank
Los Angeles County, CA	1,917,953	1
Howard County, IN	270,300	2
Peoria County, IL	255,915	3
New Castle County, DE	171,709	4
Harris County, TX	156,522	5
Wayne County, MI	134,174	6
Penuelas County, PR	130,286	7
Gratiot County, MI	114,000	8
St Charles Parish, LA	100,005	9
Cook County, IL	97,734	10
Passaic County, NJ	96,783	11
Berks County, PA	95,528	12
Marion County, IN	87,469	13
Porter County, IN	86,900	14
Lake County, IN	71,250	15
Lucas County, OH	62,862	16
Essex/Passaic County, NJ	59,176	17
Bergen County, NJ	56,265	18
Genesee County, MI	55,251	19
Pecos County, TX	48,638	20

Source: U.S. Environmental Protection Agency, "Toxic Release Inventory, 1992." In *National Economic, Social, and Environmental Data Bank* [CD-ROM]. Prepared by U.S. Department of Commerce, Economics, and Statistics Administration, Washington, D.C.: U.S. Department of Commerce, National Economic, Social, and Environmental Data Bank, Economics and Statistics Administration, Office of Business Analysis, February 1995.

★155★
Toxic Chemical Releases

Toxic Chemical Releases, 1992: Diethyl Phthalate

County	Releases	Rank
Mc Leod County, MN	428,530	1
Hudson County, NJ	77,950	2
Greenville County, SC	19,780	3
Fulton County, GA	15,850	4
Wood County, WI	14,100	5
Chesterfield County, SC	13,365	6
Sullivan County, TN	11,385	7
Hartford County, CT	8,237	8
Blackford County, IN	4,808	9
Philadelphia County, PA	3,858	10
Tarrant County, TX	3,705	11
Harrison County, TX	2,923	12
Monmouth County, NJ	2,849	13
Sacramento County, CA	1,720	14
Guilford County, NC	1,640	15
Passaic County, NJ	1,265	16
Delaware County, PA	1,005	17
Essex County, NJ	1,000	18
Montgomery County, PA	957	19
Du Page County, IL	750	20

Source: U.S. Environmental Protection Agency, "Toxic Release Inventory, 1992." In *National Economic, Social, and Environmental Data Bank* [CD-ROM]. Prepared by U.S. Department of Commerce, Economics, and Statistics Administration, Washington, D.C.: U.S. Department of Commerce, National Economic, Social, and Environmental Data Bank, Economics and Statistics Administration, Office of Business Analysis, February 1995.

★156★
Toxic Chemical Releases

Toxic Chemical Releases, 1992: Diethyl Sulfate

County	Releases	Rank
New Castle County, DE	2,726	1
Galveston County, TX	1,947	2
Delaware County, PA	984	3
Harris County, TX	855	4
Essex County, NJ	527	5
Lehigh County, PA	500	6
Rock County, WI	500	6
Guilford County, NC	290	7
Bradley County, TN	265	8
Northumberland County, PA	260	9
Rowan County, NC	250	10
Passaic County, NJ	250	10
Morgan County, AL	230	11
Blair County, PA	115	12
Hamilton County, OH	15	13
Allendale County, SC	15	13
Bergen County, NJ	11	14
Whitfield County, GA	10	15
Payne County, OK	10	15
Mecklenburg County, NC	9	16

Source: U.S. Environmental Protection Agency, "Toxic Release Inventory, 1992." In *National Economic, Social, and Environmental Data Bank* [CD-ROM]. Prepared by U.S. Department of Commerce, Economics, and Statistics Administration, Washington, D.C.: U.S. Department of Commerce, National Economic, Social, and Environmental Data Bank, Economics and Statistics Administration, Office of Business Analysis, February 1995.

★157★

Toxic Chemical Releases

Toxic Chemical Releases, 1992: Dimethyl Phthalate

County	Releases	Rank
Frederick County, VA	244,000	1
Guilford County, NC	58,978	2
Orange County, FL	31,616	3
Niagara County, NY	30,244	4
Bucks County, PA	17,360	5
St Louis County, MO	13,700	6
Los Angeles County, CA	7,887	7
Lancaster County, SC	7,806	8
Brazoria County, TX	7,500	9
Trumbull County, OH	6,428	10
Cumberland County, TN	6,380	11
Chesterfield County, SC	4,565	12
Washington County, AR	4,315	13
Middlesex County, MA	3,959	14
Huntingdon County, PA	3,532	15
New Hanover County, NC	3,261	16
Blount County, TN	2,846	17
Adams County, NE	2,840	18
Fayette County, OH	2,722	19
Allegheny County, PA	2,275	20

Source: U.S. Environmental Protection Agency, "Toxic Release Inventory, 1992." In *National Economic, Social, and Environmental Data Bank* [CD-ROM]. Prepared by U.S. Department of Commerce, Economics, and Statistics Administration, Washington, D.C.: U.S. Department of Commerce, National Economic, Social, and Environmental Data Bank, Economics and Statistics Administration, Office of Business Analysis, February 1995.

★158★

Toxic Chemical Releases

Toxic Chemical Releases, 1992: Dimethyl Sulfate

County	Releases	Rank
Contra Costa County, CA	2,522	1
Rockingham County, VA	2,067	2
Kanawha County, WV	1,206	3
Clinton County, PA	1,166	4
Cook County, IL	550	5
Rensselaer County, NY	503	6
Middlesex County, NJ	500	7
Union County, NJ	455	8
Clinton County, NY	293	9
Rock County, WI	275	10
York County, SC	250	11
Hamilton County, OH	129	12
Gaston County, NC	78	13
Jackson County, MO	61	14
Los Angeles County, CA	42	15
Sullivan County, TN	14	16
Pettis County, MO	13	17
Richmond County, GA	10	18
Washington County, OH	10	18
Payne County, OK	10	18

Source: U.S. Environmental Protection Agency, "Toxic Release Inventory, 1992." In *National Economic, Social, and Environmental Data Bank* [CD-ROM]. Prepared by U.S. Department of Commerce, Economics, and Statistics Administration, Washington, D.C.: U.S. Department of Commerce, National Economic, Social, and Environmental Data Bank, Economics and Statistics Administration, Office of Business Analysis, February 1995.

★159★

Toxic Chemical Releases

Toxic Chemical Releases, 1992: Dinitrotoluene (Mixed Isomers)

County	Releases	Rank
Harris County, TX	697,300	1
Calcasieu Parish, LA	12,785	2
Salem County, NJ	7,633	3

Source: U.S. Environmental Protection Agency, "Toxic Release Inventory, 1992." In *National Economic, Social, and Environmental Data Bank* [CD-ROM]. Prepared by U.S. Department of Commerce, Economics, and Statistics Administration, Washington, D.C.: U.S. Department of Commerce, National Economic, Social, and Environmental Data Bank, Economics and Statistics Administration, Office of Business Analysis, February 1995.

★160★

Toxic Chemical Releases

Toxic Chemical Releases, 1992: Epichlorohydrin

County	Releases	Rank
Harris County, TX	746,591	1
Brazoria County, TX	108,000	2
Sedgwick County, KS	66,000	3
Ocean County, NJ	54,470	4
New Castle County, DE	53,100	5
St Charles Parish, LA	41,560	6
Washington County, AL	31,200	7
Vermilion County, IL	20,187	8
Forrest County, MS	17,742	9
Hampden County, MA	17,560	10
Washington County, RI	11,913	11
Iberville Parish, LA	8,390	12
Allegheny County, PA	7,421	13
Essex County, NJ	6,520	14
Jefferson County, KY	5,488	15
Middlesex County, NJ	5,109	16
Humacao County, PR	4,210	17
Mecklenburg County, NC	3,710	18
Glynn County, GA	3,057	19
Kalamazoo County, MI	2,750	20

Source: U.S. Environmental Protection Agency, "Toxic Release Inventory, 1992." In *National Economic, Social, and Environmental Data Bank* [CD-ROM]. Prepared by U.S. Department of Commerce, Economics, and Statistics Administration, Washington, D.C.: U.S. Department of Commerce, National Economic, Social, and Environmental Data Bank, Economics and Statistics Administration, Office of Business Analysis, February 1995.

★161★

Toxic Chemical Releases

Toxic Chemical Releases, 1992: Ethyl Acrylate

County	Releases	Rank
Harris County, TX	78,665	1
Bucks County, PA	61,047	2
St Charles Parish, LA	21,722	3
Jefferson County, KY	21,308	4
De Soto County, MS	19,900	5
Lorain County, OH	10,200	6
Knox County, TN	8,620	7
Cook County, IL	8,560	8

[Continued]

★161★

Toxic Chemical Releases, 1992: Ethyl Acrylate

[Continued]

County	Releases	Rank
Daviess County, KY	7,317	9
Allegheny County, PA	5,720	10
Galveston County, TX	5,164	11
Greenville County, SC	3,510	12
Hampden County, MA	3,460	13
Somerset County, NJ	3,039	14
Knox County, KY	3,021	15
Shelby County, TN	3,001	16
Burlington County, NJ	2,831	17
Pickaway County, OH	2,280	18
Suffolk City/County, VA	2,211	19
Aiken County, SC	2,005	20

Source: U.S. Environmental Protection Agency, "Toxic Release Inventory, 1992." In *National Economic, Social, and Environmental Data Bank* [CD-ROM]. Prepared by U.S. Department of Commerce, Economics, and Statistics Administration, Washington, D.C.: U.S. Department of Commerce, National Economic, Social, and Environmental Data Bank, Economics and Statistics Administration, Office of Business Analysis, February 1995.

★162★

Toxic Chemical Releases

Toxic Chemical Releases, 1992: Ethyl Chloroformate

County	Releases	Rank
Harris County, TX	1,770	1
Kanawha County, WV	52	2

Source: U.S. Environmental Protection Agency, "Toxic Release Inventory, 1992." In *National Economic, Social, and Environmental Data Bank* [CD-ROM]. Prepared by U.S. Department of Commerce, Economics, and Statistics Administration, Washington, D.C.: U.S. Department of Commerce, National Economic, Social, and Environmental Data Bank, Economics and Statistics Administration, Office of Business Analysis, February 1995.

★163★

Toxic Chemical Releases

Toxic Chemical Releases, 1992: Ethylbenzene

County	Releases	Rank
Brown County, TX	603,757	1
Harris County, TX	562,605	2
Galveston County, TX	360,199	3
Montgomery County, OH	296,008	4
Wayne County, MI	266,597	5
Union County, OH	264,414	6
Jefferson County, TX	251,908	7
Westchester County, NY	251,250	8
Rutherford County, TN	250,882	9
Vernon County, MO	234,696	10
Genesee County, MI	213,319	11
St Louis County, MO	203,797	12
St Charles County, MO	195,005	13
Lowndes County, MS	170,945	14
Brazoria County, TX	170,756	15
Washington County, MN	152,742	16
Ramsey County, MN	148,603	17

[Continued]

★163★

Toxic Chemical Releases, 1992: Ethylbenzene

[Continued]

County	Releases	Rank
Worcester County, MA	143,397	18
Iberville Parish, LA	134,040	19
Lowndes County, GA	132,820	20

Source: U.S. Environmental Protection Agency, "Toxic Release Inventory, 1992." In *National Economic, Social, and Environmental Data Bank* [CD-ROM]. Prepared by U.S. Department of Commerce, Economics, and Statistics Administration, Washington, D.C.: U.S. Department of Commerce, National Economic, Social, and Environmental Data Bank, Economics and Statistics Administration, Office of Business Analysis, February 1995.

★164★

Toxic Chemical Releases

Toxic Chemical Releases, 1992: Ethylene

County	Releases	Rank
Harris County, TX	5,214,880	1
Brazoria County, TX	4,265,085	2
Harrison County, TX	3,100,000	3
Jefferson County, TX	2,914,486	4
Marshall County, KY	1,956,519	5
Grundy County, IL	1,780,621	6
Calhoun County, TX	1,632,732	7
Calcasieu Parish, LA	1,606,362	8
East Baton Rouge Parish, LA	1,574,870	9
Orange County, TX	1,521,172	10
Ector County, TX	1,424,140	11
Ascension Parish, LA	1,351,935	12
Galveston County, TX	1,150,312	13
Douglas County, IL	989,514	14
Clinton County, IA	950,000	15
Montgomery County, KS	920,000	16
Iberville Parish, LA	824,245	17
St Charles Parish, LA	578,269	18
Nueces County, TX	483,644	19
Brooke County, WV	410,000	20

Source: U.S. Environmental Protection Agency, "Toxic Release Inventory, 1992." In *National Economic, Social, and Environmental Data Bank* [CD-ROM]. Prepared by U.S. Department of Commerce, Economics, and Statistics Administration, Washington, D.C.: U.S. Department of Commerce, National Economic, Social, and Environmental Data Bank, Economics and Statistics Administration, Office of Business Analysis, February 1995.

★165★

Toxic Chemical Releases

Toxic Chemical Releases, 1992: Ethylene Glycol

County	Releases	Rank
Linn County, IA	4,084,040	1
Kanawha County, WV	3,973,173	2
Middlesex County, NJ	2,845,068	3
Hopewell City/County, VA	2,683,656	4
Jefferson County, TX	1,979,871	5
Mason County, WV	1,479,001	6
Ascension Parish, LA	1,049,800	7
Henry County, VA	852,729	8
Lake County, IN	704,765	9

[Continued]

★ 165 ★

Toxic Chemical Releases, 1992: Ethylene Glycol
[Continued]

County	Releases	Rank
Denver County, CO	639,898	10
Harris County, TX	514,595	11
Darlington County, SC	502,833	12
Fulton County, GA	463,610	13
Santa Clara County, CA	459,763	14
Greenville County, SC	389,381	15
Porter County, IN	389,169	16
Chatham County, NC	351,520	17
Macon County, IL	339,760	18
Rowan County, NC	327,671	19
Pickaway County, OH	277,407	20

Source: U.S. Environmental Protection Agency, "Toxic Release Inventory, 1992." In *National Economic, Social, and Environmental Data Bank* [CD-ROM]. Prepared by U.S. Department of Commerce, Economics, and Statistics Administration, Washington, D.C.: U.S. Department of Commerce, National Economic, Social, and Environmental Data Bank, Economics and Statistics Administration, Office of Business Analysis, February 1995.

★ 166 ★

Toxic Chemical Releases

Toxic Chemical Releases, 1992: Ethylene Oxide

County	Releases	Rank
Harris County, TX	216,419	1
Ascension Parish, LA	159,400	2
Aibonito County, PR	136,600	3
Delaware County, PA	130,600	4
Kanawha County, WV	127,167	5
Hopewell City/County, VA	118,105	6
Baxter County, AR	110,000	7
Newton County, GA	107,996	8
Richmond County, GA	104,000	9
Bolivar County, MS	99,000	10
Jayuya County, PR	83,200	11
Grundy County, IL	67,805	12
Lake County, IN	66,297	13
Shelby County, TN	62,560	14
Jefferson County, KY	41,247	15
Providence County, RI	40,787	16
Wayne County, MI	39,681	17
Lake County, IL	39,076	18
Rock County, WI	37,803	19
Erie County, NY	36,903	20

Source: U.S. Environmental Protection Agency, "Toxic Release Inventory, 1992." In *National Economic, Social, and Environmental Data Bank* [CD-ROM]. Prepared by U.S. Department of Commerce, Economics, and Statistics Administration, Washington, D.C.: U.S. Department of Commerce, National Economic, Social, and Environmental Data Bank, Economics and Statistics Administration, Office of Business Analysis, February 1995.

★ 167 ★

Toxic Chemical Releases

Toxic Chemical Releases, 1992: Ethylene Thiourea

County	Releases	Rank
Mercer County, NJ	8,236	1
Peoria County, IL	5,575	2
Summit County, OH	1,500	3
Geauga County, OH	1,005	4
Fairfield County, CT	510	5
Cook County, IL	68	6
Hamilton County, TN	5	7

Source: U.S. Environmental Protection Agency, "Toxic Release Inventory, 1992." In *National Economic, Social, and Environmental Data Bank* [CD-ROM]. Prepared by U.S. Department of Commerce, Economics, and Statistics Administration, Washington, D.C.: U.S. Department of Commerce, National Economic, Social, and Environmental Data Bank, Economics and Statistics Administration, Office of Business Analysis, February 1995.

★ 168 ★

Toxic Chemical Releases

Toxic Chemical Releases, 1992: Fluometuron

County	Releases	Rank
Gaston County, NC	81,000	1
Buchanan County, MO	1,853	2
Lowndes County, GA	1,260	3
Tift County, GA	260	4
Mississippi County, AR	134	5

Source: U.S. Environmental Protection Agency, "Toxic Release Inventory, 1992." In *National Economic, Social, and Environmental Data Bank* [CD-ROM]. Prepared by U.S. Department of Commerce, Economics, and Statistics Administration, Washington, D.C.: U.S. Department of Commerce, National Economic, Social, and Environmental Data Bank, Economics and Statistics Administration, Office of Business Analysis, February 1995.

★ 169 ★

Toxic Chemical Releases

Toxic Chemical Releases, 1992: Formaldehyde

County	Releases	Rank
Nueces County, TX	2,520,830	1
Ouachita Parish, LA	2,505,147	2
Philadelphia County, PA	2,492,134	3
St Charles Parish, LA	2,120,536	4
Brazoria County, TX	1,623,130	5
Kalamazoo County, MI	1,226,475	6
Cuyahoga County, OH	857,973	7
Hampden County, MA	836,475	8
Saint Louis City/County, MO	483,062	9
New Haven County, CT	433,577	10
Defiance County, OH	385,462	11
Licking County, OH	336,070	12
Pike County, MO	335,000	13
Mc Minn County, TN	326,806	14
Beltrami County, MN	323,759	15
Sawyer County, WI	314,185	16
Chatham County, NC	281,652	17
Sheboygan County, WI	244,616	18

[Continued]

★169★

Toxic Chemical Releases, 1992: Formaldehyde
[Continued]

County	Releases	Rank
Lucas County, OH	226,812	19
Cowlitz County, WA	217,201	20

Source: U.S. Environmental Protection Agency, "Toxic Release Inventory, 1992." In *National Economic, Social, and Environmental Data Bank* [CD-ROM]. Prepared by U.S. Department of Commerce, Economics, and Statistics Administration, Washington, D.C.: U.S. Department of Commerce, National Economic, Social, and Environmental Data Bank, Economics and Statistics Administration, Office of Business Analysis, February 1995.

★170★
Toxic Chemical Releases

Toxic Chemical Releases, 1992: Freon 113

County	Releases	Rank
Los Angeles County, CA	1,479,281	1
Santa Clara County, CA	1,242,793	2
Cook County, IL	1,161,381	3
Orange County, CA	994,833	4
Tarrant County, TX	755,907	5
Middlesex County, MA	716,422	6
Salt Lake County, UT	680,465	7
Hartford County, CT	661,396	8
Pinellas County, FL	636,237	9
San Diego County, CA	578,162	10
Snohomish County, WA	556,467	11
Hillsborough County, NH	542,775	12
Monroe County, NY	523,523	13
New Haven County, CT	515,383	14
Essex County, MA	510,527	15
King County, WA	492,758	16
Milwaukee County, WI	455,910	17
Montgomery County, PA	446,076	18
Genesee County, MI	428,240	19
Jackson County, MO	423,833	20

Source: U.S. Environmental Protection Agency, "Toxic Release Inventory, 1992." In *National Economic, Social, and Environmental Data Bank* [CD-ROM]. Prepared by U.S. Department of Commerce, Economics, and Statistics Administration, Washington, D.C.: U.S. Department of Commerce, National Economic, Social, and Environmental Data Bank, Economics and Statistics Administration, Office of Business Analysis, February 1995.

★171★
Toxic Chemical Releases

Toxic Chemical Releases, 1992: Glycol Ethers

County	Releases	Rank
Cook County, IL	2,827,518	1
Wayne County, MI	1,851,975	2
Oakland County, MI	1,496,100	3
Los Angeles County, CA	1,483,221	4
York County, ME	1,110,817	5
Bergen County, NJ	989,358	6
Rutherford County, TN	985,971	7
Jefferson County, KY	926,130	8
Allegheny County, PA	866,182	9
Hamilton County, OH	831,131	10

[Continued]

★171★

Toxic Chemical Releases, 1992: Glycol Ethers
[Continued]

County	Releases	Rank
Scott County, KY	820,000	11
Milwaukee County, WI	800,959	12
Essex County, NJ	772,134	13
Marion County, AL	763,600	14
Orange County, NY	670,781	15
Middlesex County, NJ	663,589	16
Fulton County, GA	657,321	17
Brooke County, WV	650,808	18
Chesterfield County, SC	633,500	19
Montgomery County, OH	621,699	20

Source: U.S. Environmental Protection Agency, "Toxic Release Inventory, 1992." In *National Economic, Social, and Environmental Data Bank* [CD-ROM]. Prepared by U.S. Department of Commerce, Economics, and Statistics Administration, Washington, D.C.: U.S. Department of Commerce, National Economic, Social, and Environmental Data Bank, Economics and Statistics Administration, Office of Business Analysis, February 1995.

★172★
Toxic Chemical Releases

Toxic Chemical Releases, 1992: Heptachlor

County	Releases	Rank
Shelby County, TN	89,162	1

Source: U.S. Environmental Protection Agency, "Toxic Release Inventory, 1992." In *National Economic, Social, and Environmental Data Bank* [CD-ROM]. Prepared by U.S. Department of Commerce, Economics, and Statistics Administration, Washington, D.C.: U.S. Department of Commerce, National Economic, Social, and Environmental Data Bank, Economics and Statistics Administration, Office of Business Analysis, February 1995.

★173★
Toxic Chemical Releases

Toxic Chemical Releases, 1992: Hexachloro-1,3-butadiene

County	Releases	Rank
Calcasieu Parish, LA	77,072	1
Saint Louis City/County, MO	8,490	2
Brazoria County, TX	4,044	3
Ascension Parish, LA	1,147	4
Sedgwick County, KS	387	5
Niagara County, NY	63	6
Iberville Parish, LA	51	7

Source: U.S. Environmental Protection Agency, "Toxic Release Inventory, 1992." In *National Economic, Social, and Environmental Data Bank* [CD-ROM]. Prepared by U.S. Department of Commerce, Economics, and Statistics Administration, Washington, D.C.: U.S. Department of Commerce, National Economic, Social, and Environmental Data Bank, Economics and Statistics Administration, Office of Business Analysis, February 1995.

★174★
Toxic Chemical Releases

Toxic Chemical Releases, 1992: Hexachlorobenzene

County	Releases	Rank
Harris County, TX	34,089	1
Contra Costa County, CA	13,332	2
Shelby County, TN	3,548	3
Brazoria County, TX	2,320	4
Ascension Parish, LA	1,027	5
Sedgwick County, KS	271	6
Calcasieu Parish, LA	158	7
Iberville Parish, LA	100	8

Source: U.S. Environmental Protection Agency, "Toxic Release Inventory, 1992." In *National Economic, Social, and Environmental Data Bank* [CD-ROM]. Prepared by U.S. Department of Commerce, Economics, and Statistics Administration, Washington, D.C.: U.S. Department of Commerce, National Economic, Social, and Environmental Data Bank, Economics and Statistics Administration, Office of Business Analysis, February 1995.

★175★
Toxic Chemical Releases

Toxic Chemical Releases, 1992: Hexachlorocyclopentadiene

County	Releases	Rank
Shelby County, TN	105,986	1
Niagara County, NY	21,157	2
Jefferson County, TX	1,720	3
Preble County, OH	750	4

Source: U.S. Environmental Protection Agency, "Toxic Release Inventory, 1992." In *National Economic, Social, and Environmental Data Bank* [CD-ROM]. Prepared by U.S. Department of Commerce, Economics, and Statistics Administration, Washington, D.C.: U.S. Department of Commerce, National Economic, Social, and Environmental Data Bank, Economics and Statistics Administration, Office of Business Analysis, February 1995.

★176★
Toxic Chemical Releases

Toxic Chemical Releases, 1992: Hexachloroethane

County	Releases	Rank
Cuyahoga County, OH	38,548	1
Calcasieu Parish, LA	33,962	2
Lenawee County, MI	32,695	3
Iberville Parish, LA	22,391	4
Morgan County, AL	5,350	5
Brazoria County, TX	2,139	6
Sedgwick County, KS	1,650	7
Ascension Parish, LA	775	8
Pemiscot County, MO	500	9
Contra Costa County, CA	87	10
Newton County, MS	10	11
Middlesex County, NJ	10	11

Source: U.S. Environmental Protection Agency, "Toxic Release Inventory, 1992." In *National Economic, Social, and Environmental Data Bank* [CD-ROM]. Prepared by U.S. Department of Commerce, Economics, and Statistics Administration, Washington, D.C.: U.S. Department of Commerce, National Economic, Social, and Environmental Data Bank, Economics and Statistics Administration, Office of Business Analysis, February 1995.

★177★
Toxic Chemical Releases

Toxic Chemical Releases, 1992: Hydrazine

County	Releases	Rank
Chambers County, TX	20,732	1
Sacramento County, CA	8,655	2
York County, SC	7,905	3
Shelby County, TN	4,213	4
Morgan County, AL	3,400	5
Harris County, TX	3,296	6
Madison County, IL	2,790	7
Chenango County, NY	2,277	8
Calcasieu Parish, LA	1,943	9
Rockingham County, VA	1,260	10
Essex County, NJ	1,250	11
Middlesex County, NJ	1,250	11
Colbert County, AL	1,125	12
Marshall County, WV	864	13
Ocean County, NJ	780	14
Butler County, PA	755	15
Cocke County, TN	677	16
Brazoria County, TX	665	17
Jackson County, MO	539	18
Winnebago County, IL	500	19

Source: U.S. Environmental Protection Agency, "Toxic Release Inventory, 1992." In *National Economic, Social, and Environmental Data Bank* [CD-ROM]. Prepared by U.S. Department of Commerce, Economics, and Statistics Administration, Washington, D.C.: U.S. Department of Commerce, National Economic, Social, and Environmental Data Bank, Economics and Statistics Administration, Office of Business Analysis, February 1995.

★178★
Toxic Chemical Releases

Toxic Chemical Releases, 1992: Hydrazine Sulfate

County	Releases	Rank
Ascension Parish, LA	138,941	1
Essex County, NJ	505	2
Hancock County, MS	250	3
Somerset County, NJ	2	4

Source: U.S. Environmental Protection Agency, "Toxic Release Inventory, 1992." In *National Economic, Social, and Environmental Data Bank* [CD-ROM]. Prepared by U.S. Department of Commerce, Economics, and Statistics Administration, Washington, D.C.: U.S. Department of Commerce, National Economic, Social, and Environmental Data Bank, Economics and Statistics Administration, Office of Business Analysis, February 1995.

★179★
Toxic Chemical Releases

Toxic Chemical Releases, 1992: Hydrochloric Acid

County	Releases	Rank
Sedgwick County, KS	45,516,046	1
Humphreys County, TN	41,390,000	2
Harrison County, MS	33,472,005	3
St Clair County, IL	16,685,750	4
Jefferson County, KY	9,877,435	5
Union County, AR	9,619,459	6

[Continued]

★179★

Toxic Chemical Releases, 1992: Hydrochloric Acid
[Continued]

County	Releases	Rank
Harris County, TX	9,130,954	7
Ashtabula County, OH	8,565,417	8
Douglas County, IL	7,485,464	9
Tooele County, UT	7,052,360	10
Wayne County, MI	6,202,634	11
Lake County, IN	5,312,776	12
Niagara County, NY	5,016,139	13
Polk County, FL	4,189,391	14
Porter County, IN	3,565,568	15
Cook County, IL	3,412,601	16
Butler County, OH	3,119,335	17
Ketchikan Gatew County, AK	2,689,000	18
Cuyahoga County, OH	2,643,568	19
Brazoria County, TX	2,293,808	20

Source: U.S. Environmental Protection Agency, "Toxic Release Inventory, 1992." In *National Economic, Social, and Environmental Data Bank* [CD-ROM]. Prepared by U.S. Department of Commerce, Economics, and Statistics Administration, Washington, D.C.: U.S. Department of Commerce, National Economic, Social, and Environmental Data Bank, Economics and Statistics Administration, Office of Business Analysis, February 1995.

★180★

Toxic Chemical Releases

Toxic Chemical Releases, 1992: Hydrogen Cyanide

County	Releases	Rank
Brazoria County, TX	975,506	1
Orange County, TX	520,871	2
Victoria County, TX	180,328	3
Harris County, TX	134,404	4
Douglas County, WI	87,960	5
York County, SC	82,750	6
Sacramento County, CA	72,450	7
Salt Lake County, UT	68,464	8
Calhoun County, TX	46,000	9
Galveston County, TX	36,600	10
Allen County, OH	14,800	11
Orangeburg County, SC	12,000	12
Iberville Parish, LA	7,543	13
Washington County, AL	6,950	14
Kanawha County, WV	6,606	15
Jefferson County, TX	6,100	16
Roane County, TN	4,290	17
Jefferson Parish, LA	3,600	18
Hillsborough County, NH	3,252	19
Mobile County, AL	2,863	20

Source: U.S. Environmental Protection Agency, "Toxic Release Inventory, 1992." In *National Economic, Social, and Environmental Data Bank* [CD-ROM]. Prepared by U.S. Department of Commerce, Economics, and Statistics Administration, Washington, D.C.: U.S. Department of Commerce, National Economic, Social, and Environmental Data Bank, Economics and Statistics Administration, Office of Business Analysis, February 1995.

★181★

Toxic Chemical Releases

Toxic Chemical Releases, 1992: Hydrogen Fluoride

County	Releases	Rank
Milam County, TX	1,305,634	1
Warrick County, IN	918,540	2
Muskingum County, OH	854,435	3
Blount County, TN	577,848	4
Hancock County, KY	549,247	5
Clark County, WA	490,582	6
Allegheny County, PA	379,455	7
Flathead County, MT	372,100	8
Spokane County, WA	372,000	9
Monroe County, OH	295,159	10
New Madrid County, MO	277,044	11
Cowlitz County, WA	260,255	12
Chelan County, WA	223,300	13
Travis County, TX	216,670	14
Multnomah County, OR	194,957	15
Westmoreland County, PA	193,337	16
Stanly County, NC	185,644	17
Worcester County, MA	185,117	18
Washington County, PA	155,540	19
Montgomery County, PA	153,643	20

Source: U.S. Environmental Protection Agency, "Toxic Release Inventory, 1992." In *National Economic, Social, and Environmental Data Bank* [CD-ROM]. Prepared by U.S. Department of Commerce, Economics, and Statistics Administration, Washington, D.C.: U.S. Department of Commerce, National Economic, Social, and Environmental Data Bank, Economics and Statistics Administration, Office of Business Analysis, February 1995.

★182★

Toxic Chemical Releases

Toxic Chemical Releases, 1992: Hydroquinone

County	Releases	Rank
Harris County, TX	218,603	1
Marinette County, WI	120,813	2
Niagara County, NY	112,305	3
Brazoria County, TX	100,000	4
Jefferson Parish, LA	82,000	5
New Haven County, CT	34,734	6
Calhoun County, TX	9,932	7
Bergen County, NJ	6,301	8
Broome County, NY	5,100	9
Allen County, OH	3,855	10
Gray County, TX	3,005	11
Monroe County, NY	2,719	12
Summit County, OH	2,390	13
Nassau County, NY	2,331	14
Cook County, IL	2,134	15
Gwinnett County, GA	1,327	16
Camden County, NJ	1,247	17
Jefferson County, WV	1,116	18
Riverside County, CA	1,000	19
Los Angeles County, CA	923	20

Source: U.S. Environmental Protection Agency, "Toxic Release Inventory, 1992." In *National Economic, Social, and Environmental Data Bank* [CD-ROM]. Prepared by U.S. Department of Commerce, Economics, and Statistics Administration, Washington, D.C.: U.S. Department of Commerce, National Economic, Social, and Environmental Data Bank, Economics and Statistics Administration, Office of Business Analysis, February 1995.

Toxic Chemical Releases

★183★

Toxic Chemical Releases, 1992: Isobutyraldehyde

County	Releases	Rank
Mobile County, AL	285,860	1
Harrison County, TX	116,001	2
Essex County, NJ	49,886	3
Harris County, TX	43,741	4
Brazoria County, TX	18,905	5
Galveston County, TX	13,774	6
Hopewell City/County, VA	12,210	7
Nueces County, TX	10,100	8
Sullivan County, TN	9,624	9
Duval County, FL	4,900	10
Matagorda County, TX	3,530	11
Independence County, AR	325	12
Philadelphia County, PA	82	13

Source: U.S. Environmental Protection Agency, "Toxic Release Inventory, 1992." In *National Economic, Social, and Environmental Data Bank* [CD-ROM]. Prepared by U.S. Department of Commerce, Economics, and Statistics Administration, Washington, D.C.: U.S. Department of Commerce, National Economic, Social, and Environmental Data Bank, Economics and Statistics Administration, Office of Business Analysis, February 1995.

★184★

Toxic Chemical Releases

Toxic Chemical Releases, 1992: Isopropyl Alcohol (Manufacturing)

County	Releases	Rank
Will County, IL	379,241	1
Ouachita Parish, LA	296,142	2
Los Angeles County, CA	168,957	3
Jackson County, OH	144,600	4
Cook County, IL	143,005	5
Hall County, GA	141,274	6
Middlesex County, MA	140,950	7
Racine County, WI	134,030	8
Greene County, MO	131,448	9
Hamblen County, TN	113,184	10
Dorchester County, SC	103,915	11
Caldwell County, NC	102,297	12
Catawba County, NC	85,248	13
Lunenburg County, VA	82,811	14
Ontario County, NY	82,807	15
Union County, KY	75,890	16
Oswego County, NY	75,300	17
Montgomery County, IN	65,500	18
Haywood County, NC	60,101	19
Mecklenburg County, NC	57,433	20

Source: U.S. Environmental Protection Agency, "Toxic Release Inventory, 1992." In *National Economic, Social, and Environmental Data Bank* [CD-ROM]. Prepared by U.S. Department of Commerce, Economics, and Statistics Administration, Washington, D.C.: U.S. Department of Commerce, National Economic, Social, and Environmental Data Bank, Economics and Statistics Administration, Office of Business Analysis, February 1995.

★185★

Toxic Chemical Releases

Toxic Chemical Releases, 1992: Isosafrole

County	Releases	Rank
Milwaukee County, WI	255	1

Source: U.S. Environmental Protection Agency, "Toxic Release Inventory, 1992." In *National Economic, Social, and Environmental Data Bank* [CD-ROM]. Prepared by U.S. Department of Commerce, Economics, and Statistics Administration, Washington, D.C.: U.S. Department of Commerce, National Economic, Social, and Environmental Data Bank, Economics and Statistics Administration, Office of Business Analysis, February 1995.

★186★

Toxic Chemical Releases

Toxic Chemical Releases, 1992: Lead

County	Releases	Rank
Bexar County, TX	1,599,935	1
Los Angeles County, CA	1,149,203	2
Berks County, PA	952,085	3
Pike County, AL	755,178	4
Collin County, TX	720,340	5
Putnam County, OH	712,405	6
Marion County, IN	587,337	7
Galveston County, TX	562,674	8
Shelby County, TN	531,454	9
Marion County, OH	516,254	10
Jefferson County, AL	445,839	11
Wayne County, MI	408,460	12
Madison County, IL	401,239	13
Pinal County, AZ	376,340	14
Franklin County, OH	367,405	15
Sheboygan County, WI	320,845	16
Lancaster County, PA	317,931	17
Richland County, OH	311,585	18
Hillsborough County, FL	272,873	19
Mercer County, PA	227,326	20

Source: U.S. Environmental Protection Agency, "Toxic Release Inventory, 1992." In *National Economic, Social, and Environmental Data Bank* [CD-ROM]. Prepared by U.S. Department of Commerce, Economics, and Statistics Administration, Washington, D.C.: U.S. Department of Commerce, National Economic, Social, and Environmental Data Bank, Economics and Statistics Administration, Office of Business Analysis, February 1995.

★187★

Toxic Chemical Releases

Toxic Chemical Releases, 1992: Lead Compounds

County	Releases	Rank
Salt Lake County, UT	30,241,165	1
Jefferson County, MO	3,606,546	2
Lewis and Clark County, MT	3,109,622	3
Gila County, AZ	2,856,567	4
Iron County, MO	1,880,644	5
Cook County, IL	1,046,141	6
Chemung County, NY	920,270	7
Centre County, PA	835,547	8
Steuben County, NY	832,888	9
Passaic County, NJ	770,919	10

[Continued]

★187★

Toxic Chemical Releases, 1992: Lead Compounds
[Continued]

County	Releases	Rank
San Bernardino County, CA	757,060	11
Lake County, IN	680,947	12
Marion County, IN	617,089	13
Douglas County, NE	608,700	14
Trumbull County, OH	464,042	15
Allegheny County, PA	460,672	16
Cuyahoga County, OH	450,022	17
Whiteside County, IL	395,609	18
Peoria County, IL	371,400	19
Orange County, TX	371,190	20

Source: U.S. Environmental Protection Agency, "Toxic Release Inventory, 1992." In *National Economic, Social, and Environmental Data Bank* [CD-ROM]. Prepared by U.S. Department of Commerce, Economics, and Statistics Administration, Washington, D.C.: U.S. Department of Commerce, National Economic, Social, and Environmental Data Bank, Economics and Statistics Administration, Office of Business Analysis, February 1995.

★188★

Toxic Chemical Releases

Toxic Chemical Releases, 1992: Lindane

County	Releases	Rank
Weld County, CO	2,546	1
Tunica County, MS	760	2
Oldham County, KY	750	3
Dodge County, NE	500	4
Camden County, GA	198	5
Owyhee County, ID	55	6
Tazewell County, IL	28	7
Cook County, GA	10	8
Bergen County, NJ	5	9
Harris County, TX	5	9
Grand Forks County, ND	4	10

Source: U.S. Environmental Protection Agency, "Toxic Release Inventory, 1992." In *National Economic, Social, and Environmental Data Bank* [CD-ROM]. Prepared by U.S. Department of Commerce, Economics, and Statistics Administration, Washington, D.C.: U.S. Department of Commerce, National Economic, Social, and Environmental Data Bank, Economics and Statistics Administration, Office of Business Analysis, February 1995.

★189★

Toxic Chemical Releases

Toxic Chemical Releases, 1992: M-cresol

County	Releases	Rank
Allegheny County, PA	13,256	1
Cook County, IL	8,563	2
Venango County, PA	3,550	3
Providence County, RI	1,505	4
Payne County, OK	1,287	5
Monroe County, NY	566	6
Allen County, IN	500	7
Jackson County, MS	500	7
Muskegon County, MI	408	8
Kershaw County, SC	83	9

[Continued]

★189★

Toxic Chemical Releases, 1992: M-cresol
[Continued]

County	Releases	Rank
Santa Clara County, CA	61	10
Jefferson County, KY	10	11
Sullivan County, TN	4	12

Source: U.S. Environmental Protection Agency, "Toxic Release Inventory, 1992." In *National Economic, Social, and Environmental Data Bank* [CD-ROM]. Prepared by U.S. Department of Commerce, Economics, and Statistics Administration, Washington, D.C.: U.S. Department of Commerce, National Economic, Social, and Environmental Data Bank, Economics and Statistics Administration, Office of Business Analysis, February 1995.

★190★

Toxic Chemical Releases

Toxic Chemical Releases, 1992: M-dinitrobenzene

County	Releases	Rank
Salem County, NJ	8,218	1
Jackson County, MS	6	2

Source: U.S. Environmental Protection Agency, "Toxic Release Inventory, 1992." In *National Economic, Social, and Environmental Data Bank* [CD-ROM]. Prepared by U.S. Department of Commerce, Economics, and Statistics Administration, Washington, D.C.: U.S. Department of Commerce, National Economic, Social, and Environmental Data Bank, Economics and Statistics Administration, Office of Business Analysis, February 1995.

★191★

Toxic Chemical Releases

Toxic Chemical Releases, 1992: M-xylene

County	Releases	Rank
Jackson County, MS	191,500	1
St Bernard Parish, LA	150,600	2
Hancock County, KY	146,600	3
Will County, IL	128,800	4
Guayama County, PR	119,772	5
Morgan County, AL	97,805	6
Allegheny County, PA	70,632	7
Galveston County, TX	63,300	8
Contra Costa County, CA	57,492	9
Marion County, KS	55,018	10
Honolulu County, HI	51,305	11
Elkhart County, IN	29,871	12
Los Angeles County, CA	29,429	13
Jefferson County, TX	27,770	14
Harris County, TX	27,436	15
Burke County, NC	24,705	16
Monroe County, NY	17,300	17
Moore County, TX	13,900	18
Jefferson County, AL	12,000	19
Worcester County, MA	11,780	20

Source: U.S. Environmental Protection Agency, "Toxic Release Inventory, 1992." In *National Economic, Social, and Environmental Data Bank* [CD-ROM]. Prepared by U.S. Department of Commerce, Economics, and Statistics Administration, Washington, D.C.: U.S. Department of Commerce, National Economic, Social, and Environmental Data Bank, Economics and Statistics Administration, Office of Business Analysis, February 1995.

★192★
Toxic Chemical Releases
Toxic Chemical Releases, 1992: Maleic Anhydride

County	Releases	Rank
St Clair County, IL	646,609	1
Escambia County, FL	602,151	2
Will County, IL	234,361	3
Wayne County, WV	121,790	4
East Baton Rouge Parish, LA	62,740	5
Harris County, TX	37,520	6
Allegheny County, PA	35,272	7
Clinton County, IA	35,010	8
Galveston County, TX	33,024	9
Saint Louis City/County, MO	30,703	10
Beaver County, PA	15,371	11
Lowndes County, GA	11,097	12
St Louis County, MO	10,063	13
Shelby County, TN	9,582	14
Harrison County, TX	7,200	15
Lake County, OH	6,797	16
Middlesex County, NJ	5,703	17
Duval County, FL	5,132	18
Chautauqua County, NY	4,665	19
Ventura County, CA	4,425	20

Source: U.S. Environmental Protection Agency, "Toxic Release Inventory, 1992." In *National Economic, Social, and Environmental Data Bank* [CD-ROM]. Prepared by U.S. Department of Commerce, Economics, and Statistics Administration, Washington, D.C.: U.S. Department of Commerce, National Economic, Social, and Environmental Data Bank, Economics and Statistics Administration, Office of Business Analysis, February 1995.

★193★
Toxic Chemical Releases
Toxic Chemical Releases, 1992: Maneb

County	Releases	Rank
Brazos County, TX	3,615	1
Lowndes County, GA	1,260	2
Cecil County, MD	1,005	3
Dodge County, NE	500	4
Oldham County, KY	255	5
Grand Forks County, ND	11	6

Source: U.S. Environmental Protection Agency, "Toxic Release Inventory, 1992." In *National Economic, Social, and Environmental Data Bank* [CD-ROM]. Prepared by U.S. Department of Commerce, Economics, and Statistics Administration, Washington, D.C.: U.S. Department of Commerce, National Economic, Social, and Environmental Data Bank, Economics and Statistics Administration, Office of Business Analysis, February 1995.

★194★
Toxic Chemical Releases
Toxic Chemical Releases, 1992: Manganese

County	Releases	Rank
Madison County, IN	3,732,971	1
Saginaw County, MI	2,431,763	2
Utah County, UT	2,429,515	3
Wayne County, MI	1,691,292	4
Racine County, WI	938,865	5

[Continued]

★194★
Toxic Chemical Releases, 1992: Manganese
[Continued]

County	Releases	Rank
Madison County, IL	905,691	6
Cuyahoga County, OH	833,847	7
Milwaukee County, WI	825,757	8
Mercer County, PA	743,691	9
Cumberland County, PA	623,782	10
Cambria County, PA	575,756	11
Sheboygan County, WI	556,350	12
Lucas County, OH	539,980	13
Sandusky County, OH	464,505	14
Richland County, OH	431,606	15
Etowah County, AL	426,603	16
Cook County, IL	348,814	17
Middlesex County, NJ	276,102	18
Lawrence County, IN	264,835	19
Tioga County, PA	211,483	20

Source: U.S. Environmental Protection Agency, "Toxic Release Inventory, 1992." In *National Economic, Social, and Environmental Data Bank* [CD-ROM]. Prepared by U.S. Department of Commerce, Economics, and Statistics Administration, Washington, D.C.: U.S. Department of Commerce, National Economic, Social, and Environmental Data Bank, Economics and Statistics Administration, Office of Business Analysis, February 1995.

★195★
Toxic Chemical Releases
Toxic Chemical Releases, 1992: Manganese Compounds

County	Releases	Rank
Lake County, IN	40,682,520	1
Washington County, OH	10,533,300	2
Bucks County, PA	7,992,230	3
Passaic County, NJ	6,066,618	4
Monroe County, MS	4,530,400	5
Whiteside County, IL	3,628,055	6
Cuyahoga County, OH	3,296,533	7
Lewis and Clark County, MT	3,013,043	8
Tipton County, TN	2,449,841	9
Trumbull County, OH	2,236,788	10
Clark County, NV	2,164,300	11
Humphreys County, TN	1,634,456	12
Northumberland County, PA	1,601,187	13
Cook County, IL	1,598,544	14
Waupaca County, WI	1,595,447	15
Shelby County, AL	1,563,215	16
Jefferson County, AL	1,550,123	17
Defiance County, OH	1,405,010	18
La Salle County, IL	1,321,406	19
Wayne County, MI	1,249,510	20

Source: U.S. Environmental Protection Agency, "Toxic Release Inventory, 1992." In *National Economic, Social, and Environmental Data Bank* [CD-ROM]. Prepared by U.S. Department of Commerce, Economics, and Statistics Administration, Washington, D.C.: U.S. Department of Commerce, National Economic, Social, and Environmental Data Bank, Economics and Statistics Administration, Office of Business Analysis, February 1995.

★ 196 ★

Toxic Chemical Releases

Toxic Chemical Releases, 1992: Mercury

County	Releases	Rank
Elkhart County, IN	44,131	1
Iberville Parish, LA	26,442	2
Calcasieu Parish, LA	26,024	3
Colbert County, AL	16,576	4
Mobile County, AL	14,903	5
Marshall County, KY	13,217	6
Niagara County, NY	10,888	7
New Castle County, DE	8,485	8
Richmond County, GA	6,061	9
Whatcom County, WA	5,550	10
Bradley County, TN	5,241	11
Crawford County, OH	4,522	12
Marshall County, WV	4,070	13
Ashtabula County, OH	1,804	14
Penobscot County, ME	1,565	15
Glynn County, GA	1,559	16
Columbus County, NC	1,206	17
Davidson County, NC	567	18
Albany County, NY	512	19
Hancock County, MS	500	20

Source: U.S. Environmental Protection Agency, "Toxic Release Inventory, 1992." In *National Economic, Social, and Environmental Data Bank* [CD-ROM]. Prepared by U.S. Department of Commerce, Economics, and Statistics Administration, Washington, D.C.: U.S. Department of Commerce, National Economic, Social, and Environmental Data Bank, Economics and Statistics Administration, Office of Business Analysis, February 1995.

★ 197 ★

Toxic Chemical Releases

Toxic Chemical Releases, 1992: Mercury Compounds

County	Releases	Rank
Somerset County, NJ	14,854	1
Wood County, WV	8,549	2
Geauga County, OH	7,521	3
Lancaster County, SC	2,153	4
Erie County, PA	1,675	5
Huron County, OH	1,005	6
Hancock County, MS	505	7
Essex County, NJ	265	8
Dade County, FL	255	9
San Mateo County, CA	255	9
Ventura County, CA	250	10
Dane County, WI	250	10
Dakota County, MN	88	11
Hamilton County, OH	49	12
Ascension Parish, LA	37	13
Montgomery County, PA	15	14
Bennington County, VT	15	14
Albany County, NY	14	15
Orange County, CA	13	16
Cerro Gordo County, IA	5	17

Source: U.S. Environmental Protection Agency, "Toxic Release Inventory, 1992." In *National Economic, Social, and Environmental Data Bank* [CD-ROM]. Prepared by U.S. Department of Commerce, Economics, and Statistics Administration, Washington, D.C.: U.S. Department of Commerce, National Economic, Social, and Environmental Data Bank, Economics and Statistics Administration, Office of Business Analysis, February 1995.

★ 198 ★

Toxic Chemical Releases

Toxic Chemical Releases, 1992: Methanol

County	Releases	Rank
Harris County, TX	18,744,079	1
Humboldt County, CA	12,422,250	2
Essex County, NJ	9,923,743	3
Bay County, FL	9,819,300	4
Chatham County, GA	9,593,277	5
Sacramento County, CA	8,692,280	6
Hopewell City/County, VA	7,889,490	7
Hamilton County, OH	7,771,921	8
Wood County, WI	7,270,100	9
Philadelphia County, PA	6,576,112	10
Columbia County, OR	6,561,806	11
Alleghany County, VA	6,478,750	12
Gulf County, FL	6,090,005	13
Union County, NJ	5,713,052	14
Hampton County, SC	5,123,212	15
Bergen County, NJ	5,112,119	16
Charleston County, SC	5,079,946	17
Ascension Parish, LA	4,847,428	18
Kalamazoo County, MI	4,640,733	19
Passaic County, NJ	4,592,501	20

Source: U.S. Environmental Protection Agency, "Toxic Release Inventory, 1992." In *National Economic, Social, and Environmental Data Bank* [CD-ROM]. Prepared by U.S. Department of Commerce, Economics, and Statistics Administration, Washington, D.C.: U.S. Department of Commerce, National Economic, Social, and Environmental Data Bank, Economics and Statistics Administration, Office of Business Analysis, February 1995.

★ 199 ★

Toxic Chemical Releases

Toxic Chemical Releases, 1992: Methoxychlor

County	Releases	Rank
Weld County, CO	1,505	1
Crisp County, GA	1,250	2
Tunica County, MS	760	3
St Louis County, MO	319	4
Putnam County, WV	15	5

Source: U.S. Environmental Protection Agency, "Toxic Release Inventory, 1992." In *National Economic, Social, and Environmental Data Bank* [CD-ROM]. Prepared by U.S. Department of Commerce, Economics, and Statistics Administration, Washington, D.C.: U.S. Department of Commerce, National Economic, Social, and Environmental Data Bank, Economics and Statistics Administration, Office of Business Analysis, February 1995.

★ 200 ★

Toxic Chemical Releases

Toxic Chemical Releases, 1992: Methyl Acrylate

County	Releases	Rank
Orange County, TX	769,427	1
Gray County, TX	63,000	2
Washington County, AL	35,000	3
Allen County, OH	26,950	4
Hampden County, MA	21,350	5
Aususta County, VA	11,519	6
Daviess County, KY	11,200	7
Cuyahoga County, OH	5,112	8

[Continued]

★200★

Toxic Chemical Releases, 1992: Methyl Acrylate

[Continued]

County	Releases	Rank
Middlesex County, NJ	5,010	9
Kershaw County, SC	5,003	10
Knox County, TN	4,670	11
York County, ME	3,830	12
Jefferson County, KY	3,193	13
Washington County, MN	2,500	14
Mc Henry County, IL	2,450	15
East Baton Rouge Parish, LA	2,363	16
Jefferson County, TX	2,251	17
Passaic County, NJ	2,000	18
Bucks County, PA	2,000	18
Greenville County, SC	1,951	19

Source: U.S. Environmental Protection Agency, "Toxic Release Inventory, 1992." In *National Economic, Social, and Environmental Data Bank* [CD-ROM]. Prepared by U.S. Department of Commerce, Economics, and Statistics Administration, Washington, D.C.: U.S. Department of Commerce, National Economic, Social, and Environmental Data Bank, Economics and Statistics Administration, Office of Business Analysis, February 1995.

★201★

Toxic Chemical Releases

Toxic Chemical Releases, 1992: Methyl Ethyl Ketone

County	Releases	Rank
Mc Leod County, MN	11,827,498	1
Cook County, IL	3,689,200	2
Colbert County, AL	3,588,025	3
Frederick County, VA	3,122,297	4
Lowndes County, MS	2,473,819	5
Harris County, TX	2,287,577	6
Sedgwick County, KS	1,982,035	7
Forsyth County, NC	1,774,268	8
King County, WA	1,630,077	9
Anderson County, SC	1,534,502	10
Franklin County, OH	1,480,847	11
Alcorn County, MS	1,399,855	12
Brown County, TX	1,333,875	13
Macomb County, MI	1,258,916	14
Middlesex County, MA	1,222,258	15
Blackford County, IN	1,155,536	16
Snohomish County, WA	1,103,222	17
Mississippi County, AR	1,102,220	18
Houston County, AL	1,090,970	19
Marion County, IA	1,045,350	20

Source: U.S. Environmental Protection Agency, "Toxic Release Inventory, 1992." In *National Economic, Social, and Environmental Data Bank* [CD-ROM]. Prepared by U.S. Department of Commerce, Economics, and Statistics Administration, Washington, D.C.: U.S. Department of Commerce, National Economic, Social, and Environmental Data Bank, Economics and Statistics Administration, Office of Business Analysis, February 1995.

★202★

Toxic Chemical Releases

Toxic Chemical Releases, 1992: Methyl Hydrazine

County	Releases	Rank
Los Angeles County, CA	1	1

Source: U.S. Environmental Protection Agency, "Toxic Release Inventory, 1992." In *National Economic, Social, and Environmental Data Bank* [CD-ROM]. Prepared by U.S. Department of Commerce, Economics, and Statistics Administration, Washington, D.C.: U.S. Department of Commerce, National Economic, Social, and Environmental Data Bank, Economics and Statistics Administration, Office of Business Analysis, February 1995.

★203★

Toxic Chemical Releases

Toxic Chemical Releases, 1992: Methyl Iodide

County	Releases	Rank
Galveston County, TX	24,900	1
Harris County, TX	9,694	2
Westchester County, NY	500	3
Sullivan County, TN	36	4

Source: U.S. Environmental Protection Agency, "Toxic Release Inventory, 1992." In *National Economic, Social, and Environmental Data Bank* [CD-ROM]. Prepared by U.S. Department of Commerce, Economics, and Statistics Administration, Washington, D.C.: U.S. Department of Commerce, National Economic, Social, and Environmental Data Bank, Economics and Statistics Administration, Office of Business Analysis, February 1995.

★204★

Toxic Chemical Releases

Toxic Chemical Releases, 1992: Methyl Isobutyl Ketone

County	Releases	Rank
Onondaga County, NY	1,562,645	1
Glynn County, GA	1,448,734	2
Oakland County, MI	1,268,942	3
Berks County, PA	1,149,354	4
Los Angeles County, CA	846,595	5
Cook County, IL	832,945	6
Frederick County, VA	690,691	7
Kent County, MI	579,035	8
Rutherford County, TN	571,884	9
Lowndes County, MS	571,552	10
St Louis County, MO	489,189	11
Colbert County, AL	391,419	12
Middlesex County, NJ	380,186	13
Sullivan County, TN	375,018	14
Jefferson County, KY	371,153	15
Franklin County, OH	351,116	16
Tippecanoe County, IN	339,316	17
Henry County, VA	325,541	18
Genesee County, MI	320,771	19
Saint Louis City/County, MO	303,572	20

Source: U.S. Environmental Protection Agency, "Toxic Release Inventory, 1992." In *National Economic, Social, and Environmental Data Bank* [CD-ROM]. Prepared by U.S. Department of Commerce, Economics, and Statistics Administration, Washington, D.C.: U.S. Department of Commerce, National Economic, Social, and Environmental Data Bank, Economics and Statistics Administration, Office of Business Analysis, February 1995.

★205★

Toxic Chemical Releases

Toxic Chemical Releases, 1992: Methyl Isocyanate

County	Releases	Rank
Kanawha County, WV	13,868	1
Flathead County, MT	1,000	2
Jefferson County, TX	5	3

Source: U.S. Environmental Protection Agency, "Toxic Release Inventory, 1992." In *National Economic, Social, and Environmental Data Bank* [CD-ROM]. Prepared by U.S. Department of Commerce, Economics, and Statistics Administration, Washington, D.C.: U.S. Department of Commerce, National Economic, Social, and Environmental Data Bank, Economics and Statistics Administration, Office of Business Analysis, February 1995.

★206★

Toxic Chemical Releases

Toxic Chemical Releases, 1992: Methyl Methacrylate

County	Releases	Rank
Harris County, TX	851,989	1
Bucks County, PA	357,426	2
Jefferson Parish, LA	338,300	3
York County, ME	253,587	4
Jefferson County, KY	244,488	5
Clearfield County, PA	105,000	6
Wood County, WV	100,960	7
De Soto County, MS	98,400	8
Sabana Grande County, PR	77,500	9
Erie County, NY	68,578	10
New Haven County, CT	59,922	11
Tarrant County, TX	58,727	12
Fairfield County, CT	51,349	13
Worcester County, MA	48,670	14
Mobile County, AL	47,101	15
Shelby County, TN	46,650	16
Kanawha County, WV	42,736	17
Clay County, MO	40,505	18
Boone County, KY	37,000	19
Will County, IL	36,865	20

Source: U.S. Environmental Protection Agency, "Toxic Release Inventory, 1992." In *National Economic, Social, and Environmental Data Bank* [CD-ROM]. Prepared by U.S. Department of Commerce, Economics, and Statistics Administration, Washington, D.C.: U.S. Department of Commerce, National Economic, Social, and Environmental Data Bank, Economics and Statistics Administration, Office of Business Analysis, February 1995.

★207★

Toxic Chemical Releases

Toxic Chemical Releases, 1992: Methyl Tert-butyl Ether

County	Releases	Rank
Harris County, TX	1,228,471	1
Jackson County, MS	231,250	2
Nueces County, TX	197,395	3
Guayama County, PR	150,141	4
Jefferson County, TX	134,336	5
Moore County, TX	114,561	6

[Continued]

★207★

Toxic Chemical Releases, 1992: Methyl Tert-butyl Ether

[Continued]

County	Releases	Rank
Los Angeles County, CA	97,444	7
Howard County, TX	96,840	8
Middlesex County, NJ	95,951	9
Delaware County, PA	85,400	10
St James Parish, LA	68,045	11
Union County, NJ	57,794	12
Boyd County, KY	55,100	13
St Charles Parish, LA	52,120	14
East Baton Rouge Parish, LA	39,600	15
Jones County, TX	35,470	16
Kay County, OK	35,235	17
Tuscaloosa County, AL	30,165	18
Sheboygan County, WI	30,061	19
Laramie County, WY	28,250	20

Source: U.S. Environmental Protection Agency, "Toxic Release Inventory, 1992." In *National Economic, Social, and Environmental Data Bank* [CD-ROM]. Prepared by U.S. Department of Commerce, Economics, and Statistics Administration, Washington, D.C.: U.S. Department of Commerce, National Economic, Social, and Environmental Data Bank, Economics and Statistics Administration, Office of Business Analysis, February 1995.

★208★

Toxic Chemical Releases

Toxic Chemical Releases, 1992: Methylene Bromide

County	Releases	Rank
Kershaw County, SC	56,072	1
Tarrant County, TX	15,900	2
Hamilton County, TN	12,000	3
Shelby County, TN	6,083	4
Baltimore City/County, MD	4,753	5
Columbia County, AR	750	6

Source: U.S. Environmental Protection Agency, "Toxic Release Inventory, 1992." In *National Economic, Social, and Environmental Data Bank* [CD-ROM]. Prepared by U.S. Department of Commerce, Economics, and Statistics Administration, Washington, D.C.: U.S. Department of Commerce, National Economic, Social, and Environmental Data Bank, Economics and Statistics Administration, Office of Business Analysis, February 1995.

★209★

Toxic Chemical Releases

Toxic Chemical Releases, 1992: Methylenebis (Phenylisocyanate)

County	Releases	Rank
Calhoun County, AL	324,999	1
Ascension Parish, LA	286,704	2
Madison County, IN	208,750	3
Harris County, TX	181,370	4
Lee County, AL	110,070	5
Whitley County, IN	107,500	6
Ottawa County, MI	106,569	7
Allen County, IN	81,900	8

[Continued]

★209★

Toxic Chemical Releases, 1992: Methylenebis (Phenylisocyanate)
[Continued]

County	Releases	Rank
Dillon County, SC	65,000	9
Mercer County, NJ	55,120	10
Wexford County, MI	54,633	11
Vermilion County, IL	54,000	12
Los Angeles County, CA	53,748	13
Mayes County, OK	49,963	14
Barry County, MO	43,910	15
Lawrence County, OH	34,070	16
Gregg County, TX	32,205	17
Douglas County, NE	31,000	18
Northampton County, PA	30,970	19
Woodbury County, IA	30,310	20

Source: U.S. Environmental Protection Agency, "Toxic Release Inventory, 1992." In *National Economic, Social, and Environmental Data Bank* [CD-ROM]. Prepared by U.S. Department of Commerce, Economics, and Statistics Administration, Washington, D.C.: U.S. Department of Commerce, National Economic, Social, and Environmental Data Bank, Economics and Statistics Administration, Office of Business Analysis, February 1995.

★210★
Toxic Chemical Releases

Toxic Chemical Releases, 1992: Michler's Ketone

County	Releases	Rank
Essex County, NJ	27,591	1

Source: U.S. Environmental Protection Agency, "Toxic Release Inventory, 1992." In *National Economic, Social, and Environmental Data Bank* [CD-ROM]. Prepared by U.S. Department of Commerce, Economics, and Statistics Administration, Washington, D.C.: U.S. Department of Commerce, National Economic, Social, and Environmental Data Bank, Economics and Statistics Administration, Office of Business Analysis, February 1995.

★211★
Toxic Chemical Releases

Toxic Chemical Releases, 1992: Molybdenum Trioxide

County	Releases	Rank
La Porte County, IN	229,632	1
Jefferson Parish, LA	173,805	2
Galveston County, TX	96,000	3
Bradford County, PA	66,422	4
Los Angeles County, CA	47,577	5
Nueces County, TX	38,880	6
Lee County, IA	25,800	7
Baltimore County, MD	24,553	8
Calhoun County, TX	23,483	9
Washington County, PA	21,041	10
Jefferson County, KY	19,918	11
Cook County, IL	17,083	12
Northampton County, PA	16,034	13
Brazoria County, TX	15,910	14
Cabell County, WV	15,203	15

[Continued]

★211★

Toxic Chemical Releases, 1992: Molybdenum Trioxide
[Continued]

County	Releases	Rank
Harris County, TX	14,507	16
Contra Costa County, CA	12,776	17
Androscoggin County, ME	11,319	18
Jefferson County, TX	9,520	19
Salt Lake County, UT	9,406	20

Source: U.S. Environmental Protection Agency, "Toxic Release Inventory, 1992." In *National Economic, Social, and Environmental Data Bank* [CD-ROM]. Prepared by U.S. Department of Commerce, Economics, and Statistics Administration, Washington, D.C.: U.S. Department of Commerce, National Economic, Social, and Environmental Data Bank, Economics and Statistics Administration, Office of Business Analysis, February 1995.

★212★
Toxic Chemical Releases

Toxic Chemical Releases, 1992: N,N-dimethylaniline

County	Releases	Rank
New Haven County, CT	168,001	1
Erie County, NY	57,412	2
Polk County, TN	43,087	3
Hamilton County, OH	30,088	4
Onondaga County, NY	25,028	5
Sullivan County, TN	15,412	6
Essex County, NJ	15,301	7
Kanawha County, WV	9,031	8
Mobile County, AL	5,870	9
Bergen County, NJ	2,149	10
Porter County, IN	1,336	11
Monroe County, NY	587	12
Rensselaer County, NY	508	13
Spartanburg County, SC	500	14
Peach County, GA	250	15
Salem County, NJ	153	16
Duval County, FL	17	17
Allegheny County, PA	7	18

Source: U.S. Environmental Protection Agency, "Toxic Release Inventory, 1992." In *National Economic, Social, and Environmental Data Bank* [CD-ROM]. Prepared by U.S. Department of Commerce, Economics, and Statistics Administration, Washington, D.C.: U.S. Department of Commerce, National Economic, Social, and Environmental Data Bank, Economics and Statistics Administration, Office of Business Analysis, February 1995.

★213★
Toxic Chemical Releases

Toxic Chemical Releases, 1992: N-butyl Alcohol

County	Releases	Rank
Escambia County, FL	2,401,539	1
Lake County, IN	1,792,821	2
Union County, NJ	1,491,541	3
Harris County, TX	1,264,879	4
Galveston County, TX	1,145,149	5
Monroe County, PA	1,142,537	6
Brown County, TX	1,048,246	7

[Continued]

★213★

Toxic Chemical Releases, 1992: N-butyl Alcohol
[Continued]

County	Releases	Rank
Hampden County, MA	980,105	8
Los Angeles County, CA	923,947	9
Barceloneta County, PR	814,919	10
Middlesex County, NJ	678,273	11
St Louis County, MO	649,090	12
Lucas County, OH	633,293	13
Cook County, IL	609,008	14
Wayne County, MI	593,555	15
Caldwell County, NC	560,932	16
Fulton County, GA	526,672	17
Chesterfield County, SC	485,500	18
Jefferson County, CO	476,033	19
Clay County, MO	473,287	20

Source: U.S. Environmental Protection Agency, "Toxic Release Inventory, 1992." In *National Economic, Social, and Environmental Data Bank* [CD-ROM]. Prepared by U.S. Department of Commerce, Economics, and Statistics Administration, Washington, D.C.: U.S. Department of Commerce, National Economic, Social, and Environmental Data Bank, Economics and Statistics Administration, Office of Business Analysis, February 1995.

★214★
Toxic Chemical Releases

Toxic Chemical Releases, 1992: N-dioctyl Phthalate

County	Releases	Rank
Harford County, MD	54,130	1
Lake County, IL	28,000	2
Dane County, WI	27,240	3
Bristol County, MA	19,755	4
Pulaski County, VA	15,155	5
Guilford County, NC	11,260	6
Preble County, OH	8,250	7
Butler County, KS	8,100	8
Monroe County, MS	8,038	9
Summit County, OH	6,556	10
Middlesex County, MA	6,040	11
Waukesha County, WI	5,006	12
Knox County, IL	4,100	13
Rockdale County, GA	3,962	14
Gloucester County, NJ	2,030	15
Allegheny County, PA	1,972	16
Cuyahoga County, OH	1,772	17
Lancaster County, PA	1,593	18
Jackson County, MO	1,333	19
Harris County, TX	1,295	20

Source: U.S. Environmental Protection Agency, "Toxic Release Inventory, 1992." In *National Economic, Social, and Environmental Data Bank* [CD-ROM]. Prepared by U.S. Department of Commerce, Economics, and Statistics Administration, Washington, D.C.: U.S. Department of Commerce, National Economic, Social, and Environmental Data Bank, Economics and Statistics Administration, Office of Business Analysis, February 1995.

★215★
Toxic Chemical Releases

Toxic Chemical Releases, 1992: N-nitrosodiphenylamine

County	Releases	Rank
Ascension Parish, LA	1,853,445	1

Source: U.S. Environmental Protection Agency, "Toxic Release Inventory, 1992." In *National Economic, Social, and Environmental Data Bank* [CD-ROM]. Prepared by U.S. Department of Commerce, Economics, and Statistics Administration, Washington, D.C.: U.S. Department of Commerce, National Economic, Social, and Environmental Data Bank, Economics and Statistics Administration, Office of Business Analysis, February 1995.

★216★
Toxic Chemical Releases

Toxic Chemical Releases, 1992: Naphthalene

County	Releases	Rank
Galveston County, TX	686,629	1
Allegheny County, PA	544,075	2
Calhoun County, TX	401,370	3
Harris County, TX	306,119	4
Brooke County, WV	300,007	5
Du Page County, IL	296,381	6
Wayne County, MI	281,227	7
Lake County, IN	222,515	8
Jefferson County, AL	179,246	9
Lawrence County, OH	126,540	10
Douglas County, NE	111,505	11
Northampton County, PA	99,300	12
Cerro Gordo County, IA	98,244	13
Clay County, MS	88,400	14
Tallapoosa County, AL	79,026	15
Madison County, IL	74,455	16
Cook County, IL	74,451	17
Marion County, IN	68,330	18
Cuyahoga County, OH	66,074	19
Sedgwick County, KS	64,150	20

Source: U.S. Environmental Protection Agency, "Toxic Release Inventory, 1992." In *National Economic, Social, and Environmental Data Bank* [CD-ROM]. Prepared by U.S. Department of Commerce, Economics, and Statistics Administration, Washington, D.C.: U.S. Department of Commerce, National Economic, Social, and Environmental Data Bank, Economics and Statistics Administration, Office of Business Analysis, February 1995.

★217★
Toxic Chemical Releases

Toxic Chemical Releases, 1992: Nickel

County	Releases	Rank
Douglas County, OR	2,467,709	1
Wayne County, MI	501,640	2
Stark County, OH	362,052	3
Lawrence County, TN	336,563	4
Cambria County, PA	318,489	5
Rock County, WI	231,715	6
Winnebago County, IL	215,302	7
Hampton City/County, VA	178,015	8
Elkhart County, IN	172,549	9
Cuyahoga County, OH	160,998	10

[Continued]

★217★

Toxic Chemical Releases, 1992: Nickel
[Continued]

County	Releases	Rank
Beaver County, PA	151,519	11
Cook County, IL	145,426	12
Madison County, IL	122,503	13
Norfolk County, MA	108,655	14
Allen County, OH	106,831	15
Milwaukee County, WI	106,451	16
Lawrence County, IN	88,445	17
Berks County, PA	80,222	18
Galveston County, TX	76,708	19
New Madrid County, MO	76,250	20

Source: U.S. Environmental Protection Agency, "Toxic Release Inventory, 1992." In *National Economic, Social, and Environmental Data Bank* [CD-ROM]. Prepared by U.S. Department of Commerce, Economics, and Statistics Administration, Washington, D.C.: U.S. Department of Commerce, National Economic, Social, and Environmental Data Bank, Economics and Statistics Administration, Office of Business Analysis, February 1995.

★218★
Toxic Chemical Releases

Toxic Chemical Releases, 1992: Nickel Compounds

County	Releases	Rank
Wayne County, MI	1,938,819	1
Gila County, AZ	1,112,408	2
Garland County, AR	1,054,250	3
Orange County, TX	668,392	4
Victoria County, TX	396,473	5
Allegheny County, PA	181,533	6
Ascension Parish, LA	178,516	7
Westmoreland County, PA	176,843	8
Jefferson County, KY	171,711	9
Alachua County, FL	160,262	10
Franklin County, OH	152,248	11
Los Angeles County, CA	142,032	12
Northampton County, PA	128,220	13
Hamilton County, OH	123,418	14
Jefferson County, TX	123,382	15
New Haven County, CT	111,302	16
Lake County, IN	104,240	17
Washington County, PA	94,937	18
Mecklenburg County, NC	85,431	19
Cook County, IL	85,027	20

Source: U.S. Environmental Protection Agency, "Toxic Release Inventory, 1992." In *National Economic, Social, and Environmental Data Bank* [CD-ROM]. Prepared by U.S. Department of Commerce, Economics, and Statistics Administration, Washington, D.C.: U.S. Department of Commerce, National Economic, Social, and Environmental Data Bank, Economics and Statistics Administration, Office of Business Analysis, February 1995.

★219★
Toxic Chemical Releases

Toxic Chemical Releases, 1992: Nitric Acid

County	Releases	Rank
Victoria County, TX	27,928,930	1
Harris County, TX	8,396,172	2
Ouachita Parish, LA	3,303,600	3
Allegheny County, PA	2,412,155	4
Muskingum County, OH	2,100,450	5
Cuyahoga County, OH	1,383,246	6
Westmoreland County, PA	1,183,420	7
Meeker County, MN	1,101,092	8
Shelby County, OH	1,026,888	9
Cook County, IL	943,657	10
Chester County, PA	938,310	11
Wayne County, MI	733,467	12
New London County, CT	722,500	13
Tulsa County, OK	678,550	14
Gloucester County, NJ	667,924	15
Orange County, TX	665,619	16
Berks County, PA	628,160	17
New Haven County, CT	623,005	18
Galveston County, TX	621,500	19
St Louis County, MO	511,550	20

Source: U.S. Environmental Protection Agency, "Toxic Release Inventory, 1992." In *National Economic, Social, and Environmental Data Bank* [CD-ROM]. Prepared by U.S. Department of Commerce, Economics, and Statistics Administration, Washington, D.C.: U.S. Department of Commerce, National Economic, Social, and Environmental Data Bank, Economics and Statistics Administration, Office of Business Analysis, February 1995.

★220★
Toxic Chemical Releases

Toxic Chemical Releases, 1992: Nitrilotriacetic Acid

County	Releases	Rank
Washington County, AL	7,705	1
Wayne County, MI	1,555	2
De Kalb County, GA	1,005	3
Monroe County, PA	1,005	3
Los Angeles County, CA	505	4
Whitfield County, GA	250	5

Source: U.S. Environmental Protection Agency, "Toxic Release Inventory, 1992." In *National Economic, Social, and Environmental Data Bank* [CD-ROM]. Prepared by U.S. Department of Commerce, Economics, and Statistics Administration, Washington, D.C.: U.S. Department of Commerce, National Economic, Social, and Environmental Data Bank, Economics and Statistics Administration, Office of Business Analysis, February 1995.

★221★
Toxic Chemical Releases

Toxic Chemical Releases, 1992: Nitrobenzene

County	Releases	Rank
Ascension Parish, LA	568,160	1
Jefferson County, TX	128,833	2
Wake County, NC	44,655	3
Montgomery County, AL	12,350	4
Jackson County, MS	11,424	5

[Continued]

★221★

Toxic Chemical Releases, 1992: Nitrobenzene
[Continued]

County	Releases	Rank
Fairfield County, CT	6,010	6
Marshall County, WV	4,397	7
Clay County, FL	2,947	8
Washington County, AL	2,500	9
Niagara County, NY	1,483	10
Harris County, TX	1,048	11
Essex County, NJ	1,000	12
Saint Louis City/County, MO	845	13
Greenville County, SC	500	14
Jefferson Parish, LA	5	15
Ralls County, MO	1	16

Source: U.S. Environmental Protection Agency, "Toxic Release Inventory, 1992." In *National Economic, Social, and Environmental Data Bank* [CD-ROM]. Prepared by U.S. Department of Commerce, Economics, and Statistics Administration, Washington, D.C.: U.S. Department of Commerce, National Economic, Social, and Environmental Data Bank, Economics and Statistics Administration, Office of Business Analysis, February 1995.

★222★
Toxic Chemical Releases

Toxic Chemical Releases, 1992: Nitroglycerin

County	Releases	Rank
Morris County, NJ	24,271	1
Dade County, FL	22,345	2
Mineral County, WV	16,900	3
Pulaski County, VA	15,169	4
Jasper County, MO	11,061	5
Wakulla County, FL	1,019	6
Schuylkill County, PA	750	7
Williamson County, IL	439	8
Jackson County, MO	255	9
Salt Lake County, UT	137	10
Santa Clara County, CA	5	11
Clark County, IN	2	12

Source: U.S. Environmental Protection Agency, "Toxic Release Inventory, 1992." In *National Economic, Social, and Environmental Data Bank* [CD-ROM]. Prepared by U.S. Department of Commerce, Economics, and Statistics Administration, Washington, D.C.: U.S. Department of Commerce, National Economic, Social, and Environmental Data Bank, Economics and Statistics Administration, Office of Business Analysis, February 1995.

★223★
Toxic Chemical Releases

Toxic Chemical Releases, 1992: O-anisidine

County	Releases	Rank
Berks County, PA	5,610	1
Gaston County, NC	1,105	2
Allendale County, SC	750	3
Harris County, TX	255	4
Kent County, RI	221	5

Source: U.S. Environmental Protection Agency, "Toxic Release Inventory, 1992." In *National Economic, Social, and Environmental Data Bank* [CD-ROM]. Prepared by U.S. Department of Commerce, Economics, and Statistics Administration, Washington, D.C.: U.S. Department of Commerce, National Economic, Social, and Environmental Data Bank, Economics and Statistics Administration, Office of Business Analysis, February 1995.

★224★
Toxic Chemical Releases

Toxic Chemical Releases, 1992: O-cresol

County	Releases	Rank
Cook County, IL	55,718	1
Los Angeles County, CA	24,375	2
Albany County, NY	17,278	3
Allegheny County, PA	14,624	4
Ocean County, NJ	11,614	5
Niagara County, NY	11,530	6
Harris County, TX	9,305	7
Galveston County, TX	5,600	8
Providence County, RI	2,045	9
Schenectady County, NY	1,510	10
Washington County, AL	750	11
Summit County, OH	750	11
Darke County, OH	550	12
Madison County, KY	520	13
Newaygo County, MI	500	14
Sacramento County, CA	500	14
Posey County, IN	462	15
Brazoria County, TX	434	16
Sheboygan County, WI	287	17
New Castle County, DE	260	18

Source: U.S. Environmental Protection Agency, "Toxic Release Inventory, 1992." In *National Economic, Social, and Environmental Data Bank* [CD-ROM]. Prepared by U.S. Department of Commerce, Economics, and Statistics Administration, Washington, D.C.: U.S. Department of Commerce, National Economic, Social, and Environmental Data Bank, Economics and Statistics Administration, Office of Business Analysis, February 1995.

★225★
Toxic Chemical Releases

Toxic Chemical Releases, 1992: O-dinitrobenzene

County	Releases	Rank
Salem County, NJ	1,138	1
Jackson County, MS	2	2

Source: U.S. Environmental Protection Agency, "Toxic Release Inventory, 1992." In *National Economic, Social, and Environmental Data Bank* [CD-ROM]. Prepared by U.S. Department of Commerce, Economics, and Statistics Administration, Washington, D.C.: U.S. Department of Commerce, National Economic, Social, and Environmental Data Bank, Economics and Statistics Administration, Office of Business Analysis, February 1995.

★226★
Toxic Chemical Releases

Toxic Chemical Releases, 1992: O-toluidine

County	Releases	Rank
Niagara County, NY	12,395	1
Harris County, TX	12,004	2
Berks County, PA	8,486	3
Passaic County, NJ	8,410	4
Ascension Parish, LA	7,302	5
Chambers County, TX	4,618	6
Jackson County, MS	1,257	7
Montgomery County, PA	750	8
Sedgwick County, KS	505	9

[Continued]

★226★

Toxic Chemical Releases, 1992: O-toluidine

[Continued]

County	Releases	Rank
Scioto County, OH	500	10
Calcasieu Parish, LA	464	11
Salem County, NJ	420	12
Bergen County, NJ	11	13
Mecklenburg County, NC	6	14
Jefferson Parish, LA	5	15

Source: U.S. Environmental Protection Agency, "Toxic Release Inventory, 1992." In *National Economic, Social, and Environmental Data Bank* [CD-ROM]. Prepared by U.S. Department of Commerce, Economics, and Statistics Administration, Washington, D.C.: U.S. Department of Commerce, National Economic, Social, and Environmental Data Bank, Economics and Statistics Administration, Office of Business Analysis, February 1995.

★227★
Toxic Chemical Releases

Toxic Chemical Releases, 1992: O-xylene

County	Releases	Rank
Brunswick County, NC	718,449	1
Davidson County, TN	257,000	2
Wayne County, WV	184,894	3
Guayama County, PR	124,261	4
New Haven County, CT	121,473	5
St Bernard Parish, LA	103,500	6
Jackson County, MS	101,500	7
Harris County, TX	78,094	8
Hudson County, NJ	73,185	9
Galveston County, TX	64,950	10
Will County, IL	62,758	11
Nueces County, TX	55,235	12
Sullivan County, TN	51,300	13
Morgan County, AL	49,605	14
Marion County, MO	37,610	15
Contra Costa County, CA	37,384	16
Allegheny County, PA	34,141	17
Dane County, WI	24,800	18
Honolulu County, HI	24,505	19
Crawford County, KS	23,928	20

Source: U.S. Environmental Protection Agency, "Toxic Release Inventory, 1992." In *National Economic, Social, and Environmental Data Bank* [CD-ROM]. Prepared by U.S. Department of Commerce, Economics, and Statistics Administration, Washington, D.C.: U.S. Department of Commerce, National Economic, Social, and Environmental Data Bank, Economics and Statistics Administration, Office of Business Analysis, February 1995.

★228★
Toxic Chemical Releases

Toxic Chemical Releases, 1992: P-anisidine

County	Releases	Rank
Hamilton County, OH	15	1
Rensselaer County, NY	5	2
Berkeley County, SC	5	2

Source: U.S. Environmental Protection Agency, "Toxic Release Inventory, 1992." In *National Economic, Social, and Environmental Data Bank* [CD-ROM]. Prepared by U.S. Department of Commerce, Economics, and Statistics Administration, Washington, D.C.: U.S. Department of Commerce, National Economic, Social, and Environmental Data Bank, Economics and Statistics Administration, Office of Business Analysis, February 1995.

★229★
Toxic Chemical Releases

Toxic Chemical Releases, 1992: P-cresidine

County	Releases	Rank
Hamilton County, OH	18,985	1
Cook County, IL	2,450	2
Allendale County, SC	255	3

Source: U.S. Environmental Protection Agency, "Toxic Release Inventory, 1992." In *National Economic, Social, and Environmental Data Bank* [CD-ROM]. Prepared by U.S. Department of Commerce, Economics, and Statistics Administration, Washington, D.C.: U.S. Department of Commerce, National Economic, Social, and Environmental Data Bank, Economics and Statistics Administration, Office of Business Analysis, February 1995.

★230★
Toxic Chemical Releases

Toxic Chemical Releases, 1992: P-cresol

County	Releases	Rank
Cook County, IL	1,089,238	1
Crawford County, KS	25,013	2
Schenectady County, NY	24,109	3
Allegheny County, PA	16,789	4
Los Angeles County, CA	15,950	5
Gaston County, NC	12,095	6
Washington County, AL	8,570	7
New Haven County, CT	3,475	8
Providence County, RI	2,505	9
Venango County, PA	2,090	10
Middlesex County, NJ	2,043	11
Ascension Parish, LA	2,027	12
Jefferson County, TX	1,936	13
Jefferson County, KY	500	14
Hamilton County, OH	185	15
Sullivan County, TN	4	16

Source: U.S. Environmental Protection Agency, "Toxic Release Inventory, 1992." In *National Economic, Social, and Environmental Data Bank* [CD-ROM]. Prepared by U.S. Department of Commerce, Economics, and Statistics Administration, Washington, D.C.: U.S. Department of Commerce, National Economic, Social, and Environmental Data Bank, Economics and Statistics Administration, Office of Business Analysis, February 1995.

★231★
Toxic Chemical Releases

Toxic Chemical Releases, 1992: P-dinitrobenzene

County	Releases	Rank
Salem County, NJ	823	1

Source: U.S. Environmental Protection Agency, "Toxic Release Inventory, 1992." In *National Economic, Social, and Environmental Data Bank* [CD-ROM]. Prepared by U.S. Department of Commerce, Economics, and Statistics Administration, Washington, D.C.: U.S. Department of Commerce, National Economic, Social, and Environmental Data Bank, Economics and Statistics Administration, Office of Business Analysis, February 1995.

★232★
Toxic Chemical Releases

Toxic Chemical Releases, 1992: P-nitrosodiphenylamine

County	Releases	Rank
Morgan County, AL	1,324	1

Source: U.S. Environmental Protection Agency, "Toxic Release Inventory, 1992." In *National Economic, Social, and Environmental Data Bank* [CD-ROM]. Prepared by U.S. Department of Commerce, Economics, and Statistics Administration, Washington, D.C.: U.S. Department of Commerce, National Economic, Social, and Environmental Data Bank, Economics and Statistics Administration, Office of Business Analysis, February 1995.

★233★
Toxic Chemical Releases

Toxic Chemical Releases, 1992: P-phenylenediamine

County	Releases	Rank
Chesterfield County, VA	40,800	1
Fairfield County, CT	23,449	2
Jefferson County, TX	540	3
Bristol County, MA	440	4
Posey County, IN	266	5
Kings County, NY	250	6
Summit County, OH	60	7
Salem County, NJ	58	8

Source: U.S. Environmental Protection Agency, "Toxic Release Inventory, 1992." In *National Economic, Social, and Environmental Data Bank* [CD-ROM]. Prepared by U.S. Department of Commerce, Economics, and Statistics Administration, Washington, D.C.: U.S. Department of Commerce, National Economic, Social, and Environmental Data Bank, Economics and Statistics Administration, Office of Business Analysis, February 1995.

★234★
Toxic Chemical Releases

Toxic Chemical Releases, 1992: P-xylene

County	Releases	Rank
New Hanover County, NC	2,468,004	1
Morgan County, AL	866,015	2
Brunswick County, NC	629,884	3
Berkeley County, SC	532,000	4
Usa County, VI	253,500	5
Guayama County, PR	225,658	6
Davidson County, TN	187,000	7
Jackson County, MS	183,500	8
St Bernard Parish, LA	120,400	9
Galveston County, TX	118,501	10
Nueces County, TX	112,793	11
Richland County, SC	93,700	12
Sullivan County, TN	60,020	13
Allegheny County, PA	36,090	14
Contra Costa County, CA	27,430	15
Honolulu County, HI	16,805	16
Jefferson County, TX	15,630	17
Los Angeles County, CA	12,827	18

[Continued]

★234★

Toxic Chemical Releases, 1992: P-xylene
[Continued]

County	Releases	Rank
Harris County, TX	12,140	19
Moore County, TX	5,380	20

Source: U.S. Environmental Protection Agency, "Toxic Release Inventory, 1992." In *National Economic, Social, and Environmental Data Bank* [CD-ROM]. Prepared by U.S. Department of Commerce, Economics, and Statistics Administration, Washington, D.C.: U.S. Department of Commerce, National Economic, Social, and Environmental Data Bank, Economics and Statistics Administration, Office of Business Analysis, February 1995.

★235★
Toxic Chemical Releases

Toxic Chemical Releases, 1992: Parathion

County	Releases	Rank
Weld County, CO	19,366	1
Cook County, GA	7,684	2
Fresno County, CA	53	3
Peach County, GA	30	4
Tunica County, MS	25	5
Yuma County, AZ	21	6
Coahoma County, MS	10	7
Finney County, KS	5	8

Source: U.S. Environmental Protection Agency, "Toxic Release Inventory, 1992." In *National Economic, Social, and Environmental Data Bank* [CD-ROM]. Prepared by U.S. Department of Commerce, Economics, and Statistics Administration, Washington, D.C.: U.S. Department of Commerce, National Economic, Social, and Environmental Data Bank, Economics and Statistics Administration, Office of Business Analysis, February 1995.

★236★
Toxic Chemical Releases

Toxic Chemical Releases, 1992: Pentachlorophenol

County	Releases	Rank
Brunswick County, NC	31,830	1
Monroe County, AL	14,678	2
Jefferson County, KY	10,210	3
Escambia County, AL	6,555	4
Bibb County, AL	5,870	5
Sevier County, AR	4,746	6
Stone County, MS	3,788	7
Fulton County, GA	3,632	8
San Joaquin County, CA	3,421	9
Florence County, SC	2,605	10
Multnomah County, OR	2,208	11
Rapides Parish, LA	2,185	12
Ramsey County, MN	1,792	13
King County, WA	1,315	14
Jasper County, MO	1,115	15
Shelby County, TN	1,005	16
Bristol County, MA	795	17
Clark County, WA	760	18

[Continued]

★236★

Toxic Chemical Releases, 1992: Pentachlorophenol
[Continued]

County	Releases	Rank
Mineral County, NV	750	19
Washington County, OR	750	19

Source: U.S. Environmental Protection Agency, "Toxic Release Inventory, 1992." In *National Economic, Social, and Environmental Data Bank* [CD-ROM]. Prepared by U.S. Department of Commerce, Economics, and Statistics Administration, Washington, D.C.: U.S. Department of Commerce, National Economic, Social, and Environmental Data Bank, Economics and Statistics Administration, Office of Business Analysis, February 1995.

★237★
Toxic Chemical Releases

Toxic Chemical Releases, 1992: Peracetic Acid

County	Releases	Rank
Clinton County, MI	3,642	1
Erie County, NY	2,533	2
Kalamazoo County, MI	1,305	3
Clark County, OH	1,000	4
St Charles Parish, LA	524	5
Vermillion County, IN	510	6
Des Moines County, IA	505	7
Ramsey County, MN	500	8
Will County, IL	250	9
Sandusky County, OH	250	9
Steele County, MN	66	10
Gloucester County, NJ	2	11

Source: U.S. Environmental Protection Agency, "Toxic Release Inventory, 1992." In *National Economic, Social, and Environmental Data Bank* [CD-ROM]. Prepared by U.S. Department of Commerce, Economics, and Statistics Administration, Washington, D.C.: U.S. Department of Commerce, National Economic, Social, and Environmental Data Bank, Economics and Statistics Administration, Office of Business Analysis, February 1995.

★238★
Toxic Chemical Releases

Toxic Chemical Releases, 1992: Phenol

County	Releases	Rank
Harris County, TX	3,833,954	1
Cook County, IL	1,338,312	2
Ogle County, IL	943,771	3
Los Angeles County, CA	934,019	4
Bergen County, NJ	817,391	5
Jefferson County, TX	708,224	6
Monongalia County, WV	545,034	7
Niagara County, NY	524,011	8
Galveston County, TX	521,226	9
Calcasieu Parish, LA	501,002	10
Brazoria County, TX	462,384	11
Cuyahoga County, OH	434,756	12
Butler County, OH	415,250	13
Philadelphia County, PA	368,885	14
Defiance County, OH	341,637	15
Scioto County, OH	332,190	16
Butler County, KS	322,747	17

[Continued]

★238★

Toxic Chemical Releases, 1992: Phenol
[Continued]

County	Releases	Rank
Hardin County, OH	299,805	18
Tippecanoe County, IN	287,369	19
Allen County, IN	256,060	20

Source: U.S. Environmental Protection Agency, "Toxic Release Inventory, 1992." In *National Economic, Social, and Environmental Data Bank* [CD-ROM]. Prepared by U.S. Department of Commerce, Economics, and Statistics Administration, Washington, D.C.: U.S. Department of Commerce, National Economic, Social, and Environmental Data Bank, Economics and Statistics Administration, Office of Business Analysis, February 1995.

★239★
Toxic Chemical Releases

Toxic Chemical Releases, 1992: Phosgene

County	Releases	Rank
Brazoria County, TX	1,197	1
Calcasieu Parish, LA	766	2
Kanawha County, WV	765	3
Salem County, NJ	701	4
Niagara County, NY	695	5
Cocke County, TN	590	6
Harris County, TX	510	7
Chambers County, TX	500	8
Ottawa County, MI	270	9
Livingston County, NY	206	10
Marshall County, WV	101	11
Ascension Parish, LA	79	12
Sedgwick County, KS	68	13
Midland County, MI	58	14
Mobile County, AL	51	15
Somerset County, NJ	24	16
Summit County, OH	16	17
Allendale County, SC	10	18
Middlesex County, NJ	2	19

Source: U.S. Environmental Protection Agency, "Toxic Release Inventory, 1992." In *National Economic, Social, and Environmental Data Bank* [CD-ROM]. Prepared by U.S. Department of Commerce, Economics, and Statistics Administration, Washington, D.C.: U.S. Department of Commerce, National Economic, Social, and Environmental Data Bank, Economics and Statistics Administration, Office of Business Analysis, February 1995.

★240★
Toxic Chemical Releases

Toxic Chemical Releases, 1992: Phosphoric Acid

County	Releases	Rank
St James Parish, LA	66,988,405	1
Beaufort County, NC	24,324,000	2
Polk County, FL	22,076,061	3
Hamilton County, FL	9,000,000	4
Ascension Parish, LA	7,477,000	5
St Charles Parish, LA	2,136,020	6
Macon County, IL	1,484,104	7
Cook County, IL	570,167	8
Lucas County, OH	530,134	9
Buchanan County, MO	377,517	10

[Continued]

★240★

Toxic Chemical Releases, 1992: Phosphoric Acid
[Continued]

County	Releases	Rank
Kent County, MI	358,785	11
Milwaukee County, WI	323,666	12
Hillsborough County, FL	302,623	13
Tioga County, PA	300,000	14
Davidson County, TN	265,853	15
Scotland County, NC	254,730	16
Jefferson County, KY	253,894	17
Covington City/County, VA	233,600	18
Los Angeles County, CA	226,355	19
Travis County, TX	215,875	20

Source: U.S. Environmental Protection Agency, "Toxic Release Inventory, 1992." In *National Economic, Social, and Environmental Data Bank* [CD-ROM]. Prepared by U.S. Department of Commerce, Economics, and Statistics Administration, Washington, D.C.: U.S. Department of Commerce, National Economic, Social, and Environmental Data Bank, Economics and Statistics Administration, Office of Business Analysis, February 1995.

★241★
Toxic Chemical Releases

Toxic Chemical Releases, 1992: Phosphorus (Yellow Or White)

County	Releases	Rank
Bannock County, ID	2,185,513	1
Itawamba County, MS	11,400	2
St Clair County, IL	6,711	3
Caribou County, ID	3,831	4
St Louis County, MO	3,474	5
Silver Bow County, MT	3,050	6
Mason County, KY	2,980	7
Madison County, IL	2,073	8
Sedgwick County, KS	1,800	9
Mobile County, AL	1,405	10
Sussex County, DE	1,037	11
Maury County, TN	847	12
Allen County, IN	840	13
Fond Du Lac County, WI	781	14
Arapahoe County, CO	750	15
Cook County, IL	750	15
Hillsdale County, MI	535	16
Calhoun County, AL	510	17
Mercer County, PA	500	18
Oakland County, MI	300	19

Source: U.S. Environmental Protection Agency, "Toxic Release Inventory, 1992." In *National Economic, Social, and Environmental Data Bank* [CD-ROM]. Prepared by U.S. Department of Commerce, Economics, and Statistics Administration, Washington, D.C.: U.S. Department of Commerce, National Economic, Social, and Environmental Data Bank, Economics and Statistics Administration, Office of Business Analysis, February 1995.

★242★
Toxic Chemical Releases

Toxic Chemical Releases, 1992: Phthalic Anhydride

County	Releases	Rank
Cook County, IL	931,033	1
Harris County, TX	738,784	2
Hudson County, NJ	340,050	3
East Baton Rouge Parish, LA	332,231	4
Galveston County, TX	133,100	5
Allegheny County, PA	92,584	6
Will County, IL	76,224	7
Jefferson County, KY	42,408	8
Clay County, MO	38,688	9
Baltimore City/County, MD	38,144	10
Essex County, NJ	28,026	11
Baxter County, AR	21,100	12
Escambia County, FL	18,349	13
Erie County, NY	15,900	14
Gloucester County, NJ	13,020	15
Hamilton County, OH	11,548	16
Winnebago County, IL	9,450	17
Kent County, MI	9,000	18
Adams County, PA	8,810	19
Multnomah County, OR	8,610	20

Source: U.S. Environmental Protection Agency, "Toxic Release Inventory, 1992." In *National Economic, Social, and Environmental Data Bank* [CD-ROM]. Prepared by U.S. Department of Commerce, Economics, and Statistics Administration, Washington, D.C.: U.S. Department of Commerce, National Economic, Social, and Environmental Data Bank, Economics and Statistics Administration, Office of Business Analysis, February 1995.

★243★
Toxic Chemical Releases

Toxic Chemical Releases, 1992: Picric Acid

County	Releases	Rank
Jefferson County, TX	1,200,000	1
Victoria County, TX	34,930	2
Escambia County, FL	15,000	3
Jackson County, MS	1,047	4
Mecklenburg County, NC	4	5

Source: U.S. Environmental Protection Agency, "Toxic Release Inventory, 1992." In *National Economic, Social, and Environmental Data Bank* [CD-ROM]. Prepared by U.S. Department of Commerce, Economics, and Statistics Administration, Washington, D.C.: U.S. Department of Commerce, National Economic, Social, and Environmental Data Bank, Economics and Statistics Administration, Office of Business Analysis, February 1995.

★244★
Toxic Chemical Releases

Toxic Chemical Releases, 1992: Polychlorinated Biphenyls (PCBs)

County	Releases	Rank
Oakland County, MI	1,381,074	1
Henderson County, KY	323,250	2
Angelina County, TX	294,430	3
St Louis County, MO	121,000	4
Santa Barbara County, CA	116,356	5

[Continued]

★244★

Toxic Chemical Releases, 1992: Polychlorinated Biphenyls (PCBs)
[Continued]

County	Releases	Rank
Essex County, MA	91,123	6
Jefferson County, KY	77,347	7
Mobile County, AL	38,204	8
Greenville County, SC	34,000	9
Middlesex County, NJ	26,366	10
Klamath County, OR	22,600	11
Pierce County, WA	22,417	12
Summit County, OH	21,927	13
Rutherford County, TN	14,444	14
St Lawrence County, NY	13,673	15
Vanderburgh County, IN	12,044	16
Mc Curtain County, OK	11,600	17
Gloucester County, NJ	9,005	18
Gila County, AZ	7,763	19
Brown County, WI	6,000	20

Source: U.S. Environmental Protection Agency, "Toxic Release Inventory, 1992." In *National Economic, Social, and Environmental Data Bank* [CD-ROM]. Prepared by U.S. Department of Commerce, Economics, and Statistics Administration, Washington, D.C.: U.S. Department of Commerce, National Economic, Social, and Environmental Data Bank, Economics and Statistics Administration, Office of Business Analysis, February 1995.

★245★
Toxic Chemical Releases

Toxic Chemical Releases, 1992: Propionaldehyde

County	Releases	Rank
Sullivan County, TN	658,004	1
Brazoria County, TX	190,509	2
Harrison County, TX	64,000	3
Galveston County, TX	35,314	4
Escambia County, FL	32,000	5
Lehigh County, PA	11,309	6
Matagorda County, TX	10,664	7
Grundy County, IL	5,600	8
Harris County, TX	4,420	9
Marion County, IN	4,217	10
Jefferson County, TX	3,256	11
Iberville Parish, LA	2,890	12
Passaic County, NJ	2,435	13
Chester County, SC	519	14
Monmouth County, NJ	255	15
Essex County, NJ	5	16

Source: U.S. Environmental Protection Agency, "Toxic Release Inventory, 1992." In *National Economic, Social, and Environmental Data Bank* [CD-ROM]. Prepared by U.S. Department of Commerce, Economics, and Statistics Administration, Washington, D.C.: U.S. Department of Commerce, National Economic, Social, and Environmental Data Bank, Economics and Statistics Administration, Office of Business Analysis, February 1995.

★246★
Toxic Chemical Releases

Toxic Chemical Releases, 1992: Propoxur

County	Releases	Rank
De Kalb County, GA	510	1
Henrico County, VA	255	2
Hancock County, MS	250	3
Harris County, TX	250	3
Racine County, WI	35	4
Jackson County, MO	31	5

Source: U.S. Environmental Protection Agency, "Toxic Release Inventory, 1992." In *National Economic, Social, and Environmental Data Bank* [CD-ROM]. Prepared by U.S. Department of Commerce, Economics, and Statistics Administration, Washington, D.C.: U.S. Department of Commerce, National Economic, Social, and Environmental Data Bank, Economics and Statistics Administration, Office of Business Analysis, February 1995.

★247★
Toxic Chemical Releases

Toxic Chemical Releases, 1992: Propylene

County	Releases	Rank
Harris County, TX	4,053,973	1
St Clair County, MI	3,967,600	2
Jefferson County, TX	2,659,065	3
Brazoria County, TX	2,091,337	4
Montgomery County, KS	1,607,500	5
Galveston County, TX	1,376,591	6
Ector County, TX	955,872	7
Harrison County, TX	920,000	8
St Charles Parish, LA	814,548	9
East Baton Rouge Parish, LA	788,200	10
Calcasieu Parish, LA	785,290	11
Wayne County, WV	519,000	12
Howard County, TX	337,131	13
York County, VA	308,000	14
Los Angeles County, CA	273,686	15
Grundy County, IL	247,000	16
Ascension Parish, LA	214,912	17
Skagit County, WA	197,850	18
Nueces County, TX	192,790	19
Contra Costa County, CA	179,240	20

Source: U.S. Environmental Protection Agency, "Toxic Release Inventory, 1992." In *National Economic, Social, and Environmental Data Bank* [CD-ROM]. Prepared by U.S. Department of Commerce, Economics, and Statistics Administration, Washington, D.C.: U.S. Department of Commerce, National Economic, Social, and Environmental Data Bank, Economics and Statistics Administration, Office of Business Analysis, February 1995.

★248★
Toxic Chemical Releases

Toxic Chemical Releases, 1992: Propylene Oxide

County	Releases	Rank
Harris County, TX	345,713	1
New Haven County, CT	248,774	2
Kanawha County, WV	164,492	3
Brazoria County, TX	141,944	4
Wayne County, MI	125,097	5
Mason County, WV	100,110	6
Camden County, NJ	88,800	7

[Continued]

★248★

Toxic Chemical Releases, 1992: Propylene Oxide
[Continued]

County	Releases	Rank
Iberville Parish, LA	58,001	8
Wilbarger County, TX	46,148	9
Tippecanoe County, IN	39,480	10
Glenn County, CA	36,000	11
San Diego County, CA	30,786	12
Gloucester County, NJ	30,005	13
Guilford County, NC	24,689	14
Stanislaus County, CA	22,015	15
Monroe County, NY	21,513	16
Marion County, IN	20,858	17
Broome County, NY	20,766	18
Jefferson County, TX	20,651	19
Lake County, IN	20,425	20

Source: U.S. Environmental Protection Agency, "Toxic Release Inventory, 1992." In *National Economic, Social, and Environmental Data Bank* [CD-ROM]. Prepared by U.S. Department of Commerce, Economics, and Statistics Administration, Washington, D.C.: U.S. Department of Commerce, National Economic, Social, and Environmental Data Bank, Economics and Statistics Administration, Office of Business Analysis, February 1995.

★249★
Toxic Chemical Releases

Toxic Chemical Releases, 1992: Propyleneimine

County	Releases	Rank
Bergen County, NJ	750	1
Middlesex County, MA	81	2
Burlington County, NJ	63	3
De Kalb County, GA	4	4
Dallas County, TX	2	5
Warren County, VA	2	5

Source: U.S. Environmental Protection Agency, "Toxic Release Inventory, 1992." In *National Economic, Social, and Environmental Data Bank* [CD-ROM]. Prepared by U.S. Department of Commerce, Economics, and Statistics Administration, Washington, D.C.: U.S. Department of Commerce, National Economic, Social, and Environmental Data Bank, Economics and Statistics Administration, Office of Business Analysis, February 1995.

★250★
Toxic Chemical Releases

Toxic Chemical Releases, 1992: Pyridine

County	Releases	Rank
Harris County, TX	240,834	1
Allen County, OH	210,250	2
Barceloneta County, PR	151,875	3
Pickaway County, OH	90,097	4
Calhoun County, TX	90,071	5
Marion County, IN	73,392	6
Manati County, PR	53,053	7
Baltimore City/County, MD	49,874	8
Sheboygan County, WI	34,415	9
Monroe County, NY	23,045	10
Orange County, NY	11,300	11
Ottawa County, MI	10,315	12
Pitt County, NC	10,110	13

[Continued]

★250★

Toxic Chemical Releases, 1992: Pyridine
[Continued]

County	Releases	Rank
Sullivan County, TN	7,869	14
Northumberland County, PA	7,563	15
Kanawha County, WV	4,733	16
Kalamazoo County, MI	3,750	17
Tippecanoe County, IN	3,300	18
Pittsylvania County, VA	2,910	19
Vermillion County, IN	2,660	20

Source: U.S. Environmental Protection Agency, "Toxic Release Inventory, 1992." In *National Economic, Social, and Environmental Data Bank* [CD-ROM]. Prepared by U.S. Department of Commerce, Economics, and Statistics Administration, Washington, D.C.: U.S. Department of Commerce, National Economic, Social, and Environmental Data Bank, Economics and Statistics Administration, Office of Business Analysis, February 1995.

★251★
Toxic Chemical Releases

Toxic Chemical Releases, 1992: Quinoline

County	Releases	Rank
Etowah County, AL	14,950	1
Allegheny County, PA	11,554	2
Lawrence County, OH	7,320	3
Wayne County, MI	5,402	4
Cook County, IL	2,916	5
Tippecanoe County, IN	2,700	6
Jefferson County, AL	1,364	7
Vigo County, IN	1,000	8
Brooke County, WV	505	9
Harris County, TX	500	10
Porter County, IN	250	11
Baltimore County, MD	165	12
Graves County, KY	144	13
Lake County, IN	110	14
Northampton County, PA	89	15
Erie County, NY	83	16
Trumbull County, OH	72	17
Utah County, UT	72	17
Cuyahoga County, OH	62	18
Pearl River County, MS	53	19

Source: U.S. Environmental Protection Agency, "Toxic Release Inventory, 1992." In *National Economic, Social, and Environmental Data Bank* [CD-ROM]. Prepared by U.S. Department of Commerce, Economics, and Statistics Administration, Washington, D.C.: U.S. Department of Commerce, National Economic, Social, and Environmental Data Bank, Economics and Statistics Administration, Office of Business Analysis, February 1995.

★252★
Toxic Chemical Releases

Toxic Chemical Releases, 1992: Quinone

County	Releases	Rank
Sullivan County, TN	1,602	1
Matagorda County, TX	5	2

Source: U.S. Environmental Protection Agency, "Toxic Release Inventory, 1992." In *National Economic, Social, and Environmental Data Bank* [CD-ROM]. Prepared by U.S. Department of Commerce, Economics, and Statistics Administration, Washington, D.C.: U.S. Department of Commerce, National Economic, Social, and Environmental Data Bank, Economics and Statistics Administration, Office of Business Analysis, February 1995.

★253★
Toxic Chemical Releases
Toxic Chemical Releases, 1992: Quintozene

County	Releases	Rank
Union County, OH	832	1
Phillips County, AR	255	2
Tazewell County, IL	26	3

Source: U.S. Environmental Protection Agency, "Toxic Release Inventory, 1992." In *National Economic, Social, and Environmental Data Bank* [CD-ROM]. Prepared by U.S. Department of Commerce, Economics, and Statistics Administration, Washington, D.C.: U.S. Department of Commerce, National Economic, Social, and Environmental Data Bank, Economics and Statistics Administration, Office of Business Analysis, February 1995.

★254★
Toxic Chemical Releases
Toxic Chemical Releases, 1992: Saccharin (Manufacturing)

County	Releases	Rank
Rutherford County, TN	3,200	1
Hamilton County, OH	1,175	2
Mercer County, NJ	675	3

Source: U.S. Environmental Protection Agency, "Toxic Release Inventory, 1992." In *National Economic, Social, and Environmental Data Bank* [CD-ROM]. Prepared by U.S. Department of Commerce, Economics, and Statistics Administration, Washington, D.C.: U.S. Department of Commerce, National Economic, Social, and Environmental Data Bank, Economics and Statistics Administration, Office of Business Analysis, February 1995.

★255★
Toxic Chemical Releases
Toxic Chemical Releases, 1992: Safrole

County	Releases	Rank
Milwaukee County, WI	17	1

Source: U.S. Environmental Protection Agency, "Toxic Release Inventory, 1992." In *National Economic, Social, and Environmental Data Bank* [CD-ROM]. Prepared by U.S. Department of Commerce, Economics, and Statistics Administration, Washington, D.C.: U.S. Department of Commerce, National Economic, Social, and Environmental Data Bank, Economics and Statistics Administration, Office of Business Analysis, February 1995.

★256★
Toxic Chemical Releases
Toxic Chemical Releases, 1992: Sec-butyl Alcohol

County	Releases	Rank
Escambia County, FL	173,152	1
St Charles Parish, LA	111,000	2
Niagara County, NY	65,738	3
Hamilton County, TN	53,050	4
Harris County, TX	49,617	5
East Baton Rouge Parish, LA	44,153	6
Kane County, IL	40,600	7
Montgomery County, OH	40,246	8
Jefferson County, KY	37,624	9
Cook County, IL	32,966	10

[Continued]

★256★
Toxic Chemical Releases, 1992: Sec-butyl Alcohol
[Continued]

County	Releases	Rank
Franklin County, OH	24,941	11
Erie County, PA	20,750	12
Lenawee County, MI	16,750	13
Genesee County, MI	16,179	14
Fairfield County, CT	15,350	15
Oakland County, MI	15,058	16
Hamilton County, OH	14,500	17
Wayne County, MI	14,300	18
Van Zandt County, TX	13,500	19
Bartholomew County, IN	12,750	20

Source: U.S. Environmental Protection Agency, "Toxic Release Inventory, 1992." In *National Economic, Social, and Environmental Data Bank* [CD-ROM]. Prepared by U.S. Department of Commerce, Economics, and Statistics Administration, Washington, D.C.: U.S. Department of Commerce, National Economic, Social, and Environmental Data Bank, Economics and Statistics Administration, Office of Business Analysis, February 1995.

★257★
Toxic Chemical Releases
Toxic Chemical Releases, 1992: Selenium

County	Releases	Rank
Pinal County, AZ	171,283	1
Monroe County, NY	15,076	2
Berks County, PA	4,114	3
Calhoun County, AL	1,750	4
Grant County, KY	1,500	5
Hillsborough County, NH	750	6
Calhoun County, IA	510	7
Hampden County, MA	500	8
King County, WA	500	8
Jefferson County, KY	255	9
Washington County, IA	250	10
Lincoln Parish, LA	250	10
Tulsa County, OK	250	10
Nueces County, TX	186	11
Jackson County, MI	15	12
Middlesex County, NJ	15	12
Harrison County, MS	6	13

Source: U.S. Environmental Protection Agency, "Toxic Release Inventory, 1992." In *National Economic, Social, and Environmental Data Bank* [CD-ROM]. Prepared by U.S. Department of Commerce, Economics, and Statistics Administration, Washington, D.C.: U.S. Department of Commerce, National Economic, Social, and Environmental Data Bank, Economics and Statistics Administration, Office of Business Analysis, February 1995.

★258★
Toxic Chemical Releases
Toxic Chemical Releases, 1992: Selenium Compounds

County	Releases	Rank
Salt Lake County, UT	132,805	1
Iberia Parish, LA	41,201	2
Gila County, AZ	28,800	3
Potter County, TX	11,260	4
Wichita County, TX	10,100	5
Jackson County, MS	3,550	6
Lake County, IL	3,265	7
Huron County, OH	2,455	8
Jefferson County, KY	1,119	9
Middlesex County, NJ	1,007	10
Worcester County, MA	755	11
La Salle County, IL	750	12
Polk County, IA	750	12
Cuyahoga County, OH	713	13
Dakota County, MN	691	14
Essex County, NJ	510	15
Somerset County, NJ	510	15
Cook County, IL	505	16
Cobb County, GA	505	16
St Charles County, MO	505	16

Source: U.S. Environmental Protection Agency, "Toxic Release Inventory, 1992." In *National Economic, Social, and Environmental Data Bank* [CD-ROM]. Prepared by U.S. Department of Commerce, Economics, and Statistics Administration, Washington, D.C.: U.S. Department of Commerce, National Economic, Social, and Environmental Data Bank, Economics and Statistics Administration, Office of Business Analysis, February 1995.

★259★
Toxic Chemical Releases
Toxic Chemical Releases, 1992: Silver

County	Releases	Rank
Middlesex County, NJ	3,945	1
Kanawha County, WV	3,220	2
Contra Costa County, CA	1,336	3
Bristol County, MA	1,288	4
Providence County, RI	1,011	5
Linn County, IA	1,000	6
Toa Baja County, PR	1,000	6
Ascension Parish, LA	764	7
Warren County, NY	755	8
Niagara County, NY	709	9
Fond Du Lac County, WI	691	10
Ottawa County, MI	576	11
Essex County, NJ	515	12
Cambria County, PA	510	13
Luquillo County, PR	505	14
Pinal County, AZ	500	15
Hamilton County, OH	500	15
Bergen County, NJ	500	15
Morgan County, TN	500	15
King County, WA	500	15

Source: U.S. Environmental Protection Agency, "Toxic Release Inventory, 1992." In *National Economic, Social, and Environmental Data Bank* [CD-ROM]. Prepared by U.S. Department of Commerce, Economics, and Statistics Administration, Washington, D.C.: U.S. Department of Commerce, National Economic, Social, and Environmental Data Bank, Economics and Statistics Administration, Office of Business Analysis, February 1995.

★260★
Toxic Chemical Releases
Toxic Chemical Releases, 1992: Silver Compounds

County	Releases	Rank
Salt Lake County, UT	58,100	1
Los Angeles County, CA	18,000	2
Monroe County, NY	10,963	3
Lewis and Clark County, MT	10,912	4
Union County, NJ	5,180	5
Gila County, AZ	4,923	6
Kanawha County, WV	4,665	7
St Clair County, IL	3,770	8
Bristol County, MA	2,112	9
Harris County, TX	1,420	10
Douglas County, NE	1,255	11
Cook County, IL	775	12
Potter County, TX	760	13
Orange County, NY	729	14
Jefferson County, TX	620	15
Jasper County, MO	510	16
Lexington County, SC	415	17
Transylvania County, NC	349	18
New London County, CT	265	19
Guilford County, NC	265	19

Source: U.S. Environmental Protection Agency, "Toxic Release Inventory, 1992." In *National Economic, Social, and Environmental Data Bank* [CD-ROM]. Prepared by U.S. Department of Commerce, Economics, and Statistics Administration, Washington, D.C.: U.S. Department of Commerce, National Economic, Social, and Environmental Data Bank, Economics and Statistics Administration, Office of Business Analysis, February 1995.

★261★
Toxic Chemical Releases
Toxic Chemical Releases, 1992: Sodium Hydroxide (Solution)

County	Releases	Rank
Newton County, MO	17,650	1
Kay County, OK	785	2
Cabell County, WV	750	3
Tarrant County, TX	10	4
Milwaukee County, WI	5	5

Source: U.S. Environmental Protection Agency, "Toxic Release Inventory, 1992." In *National Economic, Social, and Environmental Data Bank* [CD-ROM]. Prepared by U.S. Department of Commerce, Economics, and Statistics Administration, Washington, D.C.: U.S. Department of Commerce, National Economic, Social, and Environmental Data Bank, Economics and Statistics Administration, Office of Business Analysis, February 1995.

★262★
Toxic Chemical Releases
Toxic Chemical Releases, 1992: Sodium Sulfate (Solution)

County	Releases	Rank
Walker County, GA	800,000	1

Source: U.S. Environmental Protection Agency, "Toxic Release Inventory, 1992." In *National Economic, Social, and Environmental Data Bank* [CD-ROM]. Prepared by U.S. Department of Commerce, Economics, and Statistics Administration, Washington, D.C.: U.S. Department of Commerce, National Economic, Social, and Environmental Data Bank, Economics and Statistics Administration, Office of Business Analysis, February 1995.

★263★
Toxic Chemical Releases

Toxic Chemical Releases, 1992: Styrene

County	Releases	Rank
East Baton Rouge Parish, LA	2,296,126	1
Ouachita Parish, LA	1,582,594	2
Chesapeake City/County, VA	1,401,646	3
Harris County, TX	1,095,189	4
Los Angeles County, CA	1,087,179	5
Elkhart County, IN	1,034,215	6
Jefferson County, TX	1,002,575	7
Wood County, WV	848,500	8
Orange County, CA	797,144	9
La Salle County, IL	721,066	10
Mississippi County, AR	720,106	11
Whitfield County, GA	599,400	12
Muscatine County, IA	546,666	13
Marshall County, IN	541,232	14
Worcester County, MA	508,980	15
Galveston County, TX	506,381	16
Waukesha County, WI	503,003	17
Will County, IL	446,935	18
Hamilton County, OH	444,527	19
St Joseph County, MI	435,584	20

Source: U.S. Environmental Protection Agency, "Toxic Release Inventory, 1992." In *National Economic, Social, and Environmental Data Bank* [CD-ROM]. Prepared by U.S. Department of Commerce, Economics, and Statistics Administration, Washington, D.C.: U.S. Department of Commerce, National Economic, Social, and Environmental Data Bank, Economics and Statistics Administration, Office of Business Analysis, February 1995.

★264★
Toxic Chemical Releases

Toxic Chemical Releases, 1992: Styrene Oxide

County	Releases	Rank
St Charles Parish, LA	2,153	1
Monmouth County, NJ	255	2
Essex County, NJ	5	3
Passaic County, NJ	5	3
Galveston County, TX	5	3

Source: U.S. Environmental Protection Agency, "Toxic Release Inventory, 1992." In *National Economic, Social, and Environmental Data Bank* [CD-ROM]. Prepared by U.S. Department of Commerce, Economics, and Statistics Administration, Washington, D.C.: U.S. Department of Commerce, National Economic, Social, and Environmental Data Bank, Economics and Statistics Administration, Office of Business Analysis, February 1995.

★265★
Toxic Chemical Releases

Toxic Chemical Releases, 1992: Sulfuric Acid

County	Releases	Rank
Jefferson Parish, LA	80,011,510	1
Harris County, TX	15,334,271	2
Sedgwick County, KS	13,237,868	3
Berks County, PA	13,082,194	4
St James Parish, LA	11,213,764	5
Grays Harbor County, WA	8,141,620	6
Hinds County, MS	7,402,655	7
Potter County, TX	5,920,005	8

[Continued]

★265★
Toxic Chemical Releases

Toxic Chemical Releases, 1992: Sulfuric Acid
[Continued]

County	Releases	Rank
Ascension Parish, LA	5,901,726	9
Cook County, IL	5,499,515	10
St Clair County, IL	4,638,654	11
Tulsa County, OK	4,465,076	12
El Paso County, TX	3,819,924	13
Brown County, WI	3,631,547	14
Allegheny County, PA	3,284,056	15
Angelina County, TX	3,155,101	16
Union County, AR	3,063,502	17
Orange County, TX	2,693,697	18
Muskingum County, OH	2,611,090	19
Chesterfield County, VA	1,824,350	20

Source: U.S. Environmental Protection Agency, "Toxic Release Inventory, 1992." In *National Economic, Social, and Environmental Data Bank* [CD-ROM]. Prepared by U.S. Department of Commerce, Economics, and Statistics Administration, Washington, D.C.: U.S. Department of Commerce, National Economic, Social, and Environmental Data Bank, Economics and Statistics Administration, Office of Business Analysis, February 1995.

★266★
Toxic Chemical Releases

Toxic Chemical Releases, 1992: Tert-butyl Alcohol

County	Releases	Rank
Harris County, TX	3,836,446	1
Livingston County, NY	303,570	2
Hopewell City/County, VA	239,120	3
St Clair County, IL	134,230	4
Kalamazoo County, MI	101,026	5
Essex County, NJ	80,409	6
Harrison County, TX	76,462	7
Nueces County, TX	70,500	8
Dougherty County, GA	34,700	9
Mc Leod County, MN	30,404	10
Franklin County, MO	27,799	11
Nassau County, NY	25,192	12
Rock Island County, IL	23,900	13
Middlesex County, NJ	21,915	14
Cook County, IL	19,570	15
Cortland County, NY	16,220	16
Orange County, TX	10,810	17
Rutherford County, TN	10,241	18
Union County, AR	9,900	19
Monroe County, NY	9,720	20

Source: U.S. Environmental Protection Agency, "Toxic Release Inventory, 1992." In *National Economic, Social, and Environmental Data Bank* [CD-ROM]. Prepared by U.S. Department of Commerce, Economics, and Statistics Administration, Washington, D.C.: U.S. Department of Commerce, National Economic, Social, and Environmental Data Bank, Economics and Statistics Administration, Office of Business Analysis, February 1995.

★ 267 ★
Toxic Chemical Releases

Toxic Chemical Releases, 1992: Tetrachloroethylene

County	Releases	Rank
Los Angeles County, CA	2,083,950	1
Marion County, IN	1,544,477	2
Orange County, CA	965,815	3
Calcasieu Parish, LA	944,161	4
Scott County, IA	921,529	5
Cook County, IL	723,398	6
Sedgwick County, KS	674,351	7
Cuyahoga County, OH	662,981	8
Nassau County, NY	603,685	9
Dutchess County, NY	471,100	10
Hartford County, CT	441,368	11
Saint Louis City/County, MO	431,000	12
Payne County, OK	424,705	13
Broome County, NY	380,145	14
Niagara County, NY	379,186	15
Fairfield County, CT	375,205	16
Lorain County, OH	347,450	17
Brazoria County, TX	327,386	18
Philadelphia County, PA	321,804	19
Muskegon County, MI	281,590	20

Source: U.S. Environmental Protection Agency, "Toxic Release Inventory, 1992." In *National Economic, Social, and Environmental Data Bank* [CD-ROM]. Prepared by U.S. Department of Commerce, Economics, and Statistics Administration, Washington, D.C.: U.S. Department of Commerce, National Economic, Social, and Environmental Data Bank, Economics and Statistics Administration, Office of Business Analysis, February 1995.

★ 268 ★
Toxic Chemical Releases

Toxic Chemical Releases, 1992: Tetrachlorvinphos

County	Releases	Rank
Mobile County, AL	86,000	1
Doniphan County, KS	6,228	2
Essex County, NJ	4,300	3
Dodge County, NE	1,000	4
St Louis County, MO	882	5
East Baton Rouge Parish, LA	500	6

Source: U.S. Environmental Protection Agency, "Toxic Release Inventory, 1992." In *National Economic, Social, and Environmental Data Bank* [CD-ROM]. Prepared by U.S. Department of Commerce, Economics, and Statistics Administration, Washington, D.C.: U.S. Department of Commerce, National Economic, Social, and Environmental Data Bank, Economics and Statistics Administration, Office of Business Analysis, February 1995.

★ 269 ★
Toxic Chemical Releases

Toxic Chemical Releases, 1992: Thallium

County	Releases	Rank
Nueces County, TX	1,171	1
King County, WA	500	2

Source: U.S. Environmental Protection Agency, "Toxic Release Inventory, 1992." In *National Economic, Social, and Environmental Data Bank* [CD-ROM]. Prepared by U.S. Department of Commerce, Economics, and Statistics Administration, Washington, D.C.: U.S. Department of Commerce, National Economic, Social, and Environmental Data Bank, Economics and Statistics Administration, Office of Business Analysis, February 1995.

★ 270 ★
Toxic Chemical Releases

Toxic Chemical Releases, 1992: Thallium Compounds

County	Releases	Rank
El Paso County, TX	515	1

Source: U.S. Environmental Protection Agency, "Toxic Release Inventory, 1992." In *National Economic, Social, and Environmental Data Bank* [CD-ROM]. Prepared by U.S. Department of Commerce, Economics, and Statistics Administration, Washington, D.C.: U.S. Department of Commerce, National Economic, Social, and Environmental Data Bank, Economics and Statistics Administration, Office of Business Analysis, February 1995.

★ 271 ★
Toxic Chemical Releases

Toxic Chemical Releases, 1992: Thiourea

County	Releases	Rank
Potter County, TX	5,060	1
Santa Clara County, CA	2,450	2
Broome County, NY	1,800	3
Cook County, IL	1,010	4
Tarrant County, TX	910	5
Los Angeles County, CA	860	6
Hancock County, WV	816	7
De Kalb County, GA	760	8
Franklin County, OH	760	8
Middlesex County, NJ	760	8
King County, CA	760	8
King County, WA	760	8
Oakland County, MI	755	9
Maricopa County, AZ	750	10
Glenn County, CA	750	10
Solano County, CA	750	10
Morris County, NJ	700	11
Washington County, AL	510	12
Muskegon County, MI	510	12
Coles County, IL	505	13

Source: U.S. Environmental Protection Agency, "Toxic Release Inventory, 1992." In *National Economic, Social, and Environmental Data Bank* [CD-ROM]. Prepared by U.S. Department of Commerce, Economics, and Statistics Administration, Washington, D.C.: U.S. Department of Commerce, National Economic, Social, and Environmental Data Bank, Economics and Statistics Administration, Office of Business Analysis, February 1995.

★272★
Toxic Chemical Releases
Toxic Chemical Releases, 1992: Thorium Dioxide

County	Releases	Rank
Hamilton County, TN	411,270	1
Clackamas County, OR	250	2
Cuyahoga County, OH	128	3

Source: U.S. Environmental Protection Agency, "Toxic Release Inventory, 1992." In *National Economic, Social, and Environmental Data Bank* [CD-ROM]. Prepared by U.S. Department of Commerce, Economics, and Statistics Administration, Washington, D.C.: U.S. Department of Commerce, National Economic, Social, and Environmental Data Bank, Economics and Statistics Administration, Office of Business Analysis, February 1995.

★273★
Toxic Chemical Releases
Toxic Chemical Releases, 1992: Titanium Tetrachloride

County	Releases	Rank
Mobile County, AL	1,508,100	1
Harris County, TX	289,002	2
Matagorda County, TX	171,594	3
Humphreys County, TN	18,000	4
Middlesex County, NJ	14,361	5
Harrison County, MS	12,000	6
Chatham County, GA	7,700	7
Jefferson County, TX	2,500	8
Monroe County, MS	1,800	9
Contra Costa County, CA	1,350	10
Ashtabula County, OH	1,303	11
New Castle County, DE	540	12
Linn County, OR	500	13
Salem County, NJ	475	14
Baltimore City/County, MD	250	15
Charleston County, SC	250	15
Calcasieu Parish, LA	100	16
Calhoun County, AR	75	17
Niagara County, NY	28	18
Lenawee County, MI	24	19

Source: U.S. Environmental Protection Agency, "Toxic Release Inventory, 1992." In *National Economic, Social, and Environmental Data Bank* [CD-ROM]. Prepared by U.S. Department of Commerce, Economics, and Statistics Administration, Washington, D.C.: U.S. Department of Commerce, National Economic, Social, and Environmental Data Bank, Economics and Statistics Administration, Office of Business Analysis, February 1995.

★274★
Toxic Chemical Releases
Toxic Chemical Releases, 1992: Toluene

County	Releases	Rank
Mc Leod County, MN	7,451,465	1
Jefferson County, KY	7,276,617	2
Cook County, IL	5,185,899	3
Harris County, TX	5,169,964	4
St Clair County, MI	3,443,325	5
Richland County, SC	3,428,805	6
Hawkins County, TN	3,410,716	7
Kosciusko County, IN	3,303,015	8

[Continued]

★274★
Toxic Chemical Releases, 1992: Toluene
[Continued]

County	Releases	Rank
Lancaster County, NE	3,277,033	9
Catawba County, NC	3,211,886	10
Bucks County, PA	3,048,106	11
Lake County, OH	3,006,839	12
Lancaster County, PA	2,977,850	13
Marion County, IA	2,586,850	14
Ascension Parish, LA	2,485,776	15
Middlesex County, NJ	2,370,637	16
Anne Arundel County, MD	2,157,141	17
Alcorn County, MS	2,122,302	18
Kent County, MI	2,086,804	19
Chester County, PA	2,074,546	20

Source: U.S. Environmental Protection Agency, "Toxic Release Inventory, 1992." In *National Economic, Social, and Environmental Data Bank* [CD-ROM]. Prepared by U.S. Department of Commerce, Economics, and Statistics Administration, Washington, D.C.: U.S. Department of Commerce, National Economic, Social, and Environmental Data Bank, Economics and Statistics Administration, Office of Business Analysis, February 1995.

★275★
Toxic Chemical Releases
Toxic Chemical Releases, 1992: Toluene-2,4-diisocyanate

County	Releases	Rank
Williams County, OH	19,800	1
Morgan County, AL	15,949	2
Cook County, IL	14,607	3
Mc Henry County, IL	12,005	4
Jefferson County, KY	10,628	5
Chambers County, TX	9,625	6
Knox County, KY	8,313	7
Ascension Parish, LA	7,461	8
Lancaster County, NE	5,900	9
Marshall County, WV	5,418	10
Copiah County, MS	4,850	11
Los Angeles County, CA	3,888	12
Orange County, CA	3,855	13
Philadelphia County, PA	2,960	14
Hudson County, NJ	2,100	15
Monroe County, IN	1,236	16
Essex County, MA	1,134	17
Martin County, MN	970	18
Meade County, KY	836	19
Du Page County, IL	760	20

Source: U.S. Environmental Protection Agency, "Toxic Release Inventory, 1992." In *National Economic, Social, and Environmental Data Bank* [CD-ROM]. Prepared by U.S. Department of Commerce, Economics, and Statistics Administration, Washington, D.C.: U.S. Department of Commerce, National Economic, Social, and Environmental Data Bank, Economics and Statistics Administration, Office of Business Analysis, February 1995.

★276★

Toxic Chemical Releases

Toxic Chemical Releases, 1992: Toluene-2,6-diisocyanate

County	Releases	Rank
Wayne County, MI	15,007	1
Morgan County, AL	4,169	2
Cook County, IL	3,783	3
Mc Henry County, IL	2,905	4
Jefferson County, KY	2,848	5
Knox County, KY	2,267	6
Ascension Parish, LA	1,887	7
Marshall County, WV	1,357	8
Orange County, CA	1,005	9
Washington County, TX	750	10
Du Page County, IL	515	11
Greene County, MO	505	12
Seminole County, FL	500	13
De Kalb County, GA	500	13
Elkhart County, IN	500	13
Macomb County, MI	500	13
Cuyahoga County, OH	500	13
Chickasaw County, MS	500	13
Dallas County, TX	500	13
Yolo County, CA	500	13

Source: U.S. Environmental Protection Agency, "Toxic Release Inventory, 1992." In *National Economic, Social, and Environmental Data Bank* [CD-ROM]. Prepared by U.S. Department of Commerce, Economics, and Statistics Administration, Washington, D.C.: U.S. Department of Commerce, National Economic, Social, and Environmental Data Bank, Economics and Statistics Administration, Office of Business Analysis, February 1995.

★277★

Toxic Chemical Releases

Toxic Chemical Releases, 1992: Toluenediisocyanate (Mixed Isomers)

County	Releases	Rank
Calcasieu Parish, LA	97,988	1
Mc Lennan County, TX	19,210	2
Richmond City/County, VA	17,502	3
Wayne County, MI	7,858	4
Volusia County, FL	4,647	5
Fulton County, GA	3,931	6
Monroe County, NY	3,740	7
Plymouth County, MA	2,536	8
Boulder County, CO	1,575	9
Kent County, RI	1,500	10
Washington County, TN	1,500	10
Los Angeles County, CA	1,467	11
Kern County, CA	1,400	12
Lee County, MS	1,381	13
St Charles County, MO	1,250	14
Catawba County, NC	1,204	15
Orange County, CA	1,005	16
Hamilton County, TN	1,000	17
Tarrant County, TX	996	18
Brazoria County, TX	980	19

Source: U.S. Environmental Protection Agency, "Toxic Release Inventory, 1992." In *National Economic, Social, and Environmental Data Bank* [CD-ROM]. Prepared by U.S. Department of Commerce, Economics, and Statistics Administration, Washington, D.C.: U.S. Department of Commerce, National Economic, Social, and Environmental Data Bank, Economics and Statistics Administration, Office of Business Analysis, February 1995.

★278★

Toxic Chemical Releases

Toxic Chemical Releases, 1992: Total All Chemicals

County	Releases	Rank
Salt Lake County, UT 0arris County, TX TXCAA, MO 0efferson Parish, LA, VAVAO	87,215,731,109,	000,0001
St James Parish, LA	39,719,101,803,	0004
Tooele County, UT	95,212,486	5
Brazoria County, TX	83,781,729	6
Sedgwick County, KS	69,570,471	7
Lake County, IN	67,703,042	8
Ascension Parish, LA	66,963,144	9
Cook County, IL	66,551,185	10
Mobile County, AL	62,855,438	11
Galveston County, TX	61,478,311	12
Jefferson County, TX	57,172,625	13
Los Angeles County, CA	55,931,737	14
Humphreys County, TN	54,188,792	15
Wayne County, MI	53,291,192	16
St Clair County, IL	46,339,925	17
Gila County, AZ	44,520,294	18
Sullivan County, TN	41,080,956	19
Lewis and Clark County, MT	40,319,456	20

Source: U.S. Environmental Protection Agency, "Toxic Release Inventory, 1992." In *National Economic, Social, and Environmental Data Bank* [CD-ROM]. Prepared by U.S. Department of Commerce, Economics, and Statistics Administration, Washington, D.C.: U.S. Department of Commerce, National Economic, Social, and Environmental Data Bank, Economics and Statistics Administration, Office of Business Analysis, February 1995.

★279★

Toxic Chemical Releases

Toxic Chemical Releases, 1992: Toxaphene

County	Releases	Rank
Washington County, MS	2,200	1

Source: U.S. Environmental Protection Agency, "Toxic Release Inventory, 1992." In *National Economic, Social, and Environmental Data Bank* [CD-ROM]. Prepared by U.S. Department of Commerce, Economics, and Statistics Administration, Washington, D.C.: U.S. Department of Commerce, National Economic, Social, and Environmental Data Bank, Economics and Statistics Administration, Office of Business Analysis, February 1995.

★280★

Toxic Chemical Releases

Toxic Chemical Releases, 1992: Trichlorfon

County	Releases	Rank
Johnson County, KS	1,115	1
Leavenworth County, KS	505	2
Jackson County, MO	19	3
Lebanon County, PA	3	4

Source: U.S. Environmental Protection Agency, "Toxic Release Inventory, 1992." In *National Economic, Social, and Environmental Data Bank* [CD-ROM]. Prepared by U.S. Department of Commerce, Economics, and Statistics Administration, Washington, D.C.: U.S. Department of Commerce, National Economic, Social, and Environmental Data Bank, Economics and Statistics Administration, Office of Business Analysis, February 1995.

Toxic Chemical Releases

★281★
Toxic Chemical Releases

Toxic Chemical Releases, 1992: Trichloroethylene

County	Releases	Rank
Sedgwick County, KS	2,439,857	1
Cook County, IL	1,951,433	2
Grenada County, MS	1,279,640	3
Bristol County, MA	940,964	4
Laurens County, GA	901,203	5
King County, WA	879,286	6
Cobb County, GA	853,166	7
Kent County, MI	816,150	8
Tarrant County, TX	797,107	9
Chautauqua County, NY	761,329	10
Wayne County, MI	565,928	11
Montgomery County, PA	522,750	12
Fayette County, IN	520,920	13
Harrison County, IN	479,639	14
St Louis County, MO	461,626	15
Essex County, NJ	421,500	16
Winnebago County, IL	421,172	17
Kent County, DE	413,600	18
Montgomery County, AL	402,046	19
Calcasieu Parish, LA	388,434	20

Source: U.S. Environmental Protection Agency, "Toxic Release Inventory, 1992." In *National Economic, Social, and Environmental Data Bank* [CD-ROM]. Prepared by U.S. Department of Commerce, Economics, and Statistics Administration, Washington, D.C.: U.S. Department of Commerce, National Economic, Social, and Environmental Data Bank, Economics and Statistics Administration, Office of Business Analysis, February 1995.

★282★
Toxic Chemical Releases

Toxic Chemical Releases, 1992: Trifluralin

County	Releases	Rank
Tippecanoe County, IN	43,655	1
Muscatine County, IA	20,785	2
Washington County, MS	18,255	3
Buchanan County, MO	5,484	4
La Salle County, IL	4,126	5
Lowndes County, GA	1,260	6
Lucas County, OH	755	7
Mercer County, NJ	755	7
Lorain County, OH	750	8
Dodge County, NE	500	9
Ellis County, TX	500	9
Hamilton County, IA	250	10
Red Willow County, NE	250	10
Niagara County, NY	194	11
Mississippi County, AR	156	12
Jackson County, MO	106	13
Yuma County, AZ	37	14
Vermilion County, IL	19	15
Stark County, IL	10	16
Polk County, IA	8	17

Source: U.S. Environmental Protection Agency, "Toxic Release Inventory, 1992." In *National Economic, Social, and Environmental Data Bank* [CD-ROM]. Prepared by U.S. Department of Commerce, Economics, and Statistics Administration, Washington, D.C.: U.S. Department of Commerce, National Economic, Social, and Environmental Data Bank, Economics and Statistics Administration, Office of Business Analysis, February 1995.

★283★
Toxic Chemical Releases

Toxic Chemical Releases, 1992: Urethane

County	Releases	Rank
Allen County, IN	2,800	1
Bergen County, NJ	2,278	2
Dallas County, TX	1,275	3
Butte County, CA	1,000	4
Passaic County, NJ	750	5
Sedgwick County, KS	20	6

Source: U.S. Environmental Protection Agency, "Toxic Release Inventory, 1992." In *National Economic, Social, and Environmental Data Bank* [CD-ROM]. Prepared by U.S. Department of Commerce, Economics, and Statistics Administration, Washington, D.C.: U.S. Department of Commerce, National Economic, Social, and Environmental Data Bank, Economics and Statistics Administration, Office of Business Analysis, February 1995.

★284★
Toxic Chemical Releases

Toxic Chemical Releases, 1992: Vanadium (Fume or Dust)

County	Releases	Rank
Madison County, IL	37,467	1
Guernsey County, OH	35,340	2
Nueces County, TX	28,826	3
Los Angeles County, CA	8,332	4
St Louis County, MO	3,474	5
Carbon County, WY	1,719	6
Westmoreland County, PA	1,660	7
Butler County, OH	1,000	8
Calhoun County, AL	770	9
Baltimore City/County, MD	515	10
Arapahoe County, CO	500	11
Gloucester County, NJ	500	11
Halifax County, VA	260	12
Onondaga County, NY	255	13
Beaver County, PA	255	13
Peoria County, IL	250	14
Bartholomew County, IN	10	15
Wyandot County, OH	10	15
Hamilton County, OH	5	16
Kay County, OK	5	16

Source: U.S. Environmental Protection Agency, "Toxic Release Inventory, 1992." In *National Economic, Social, and Environmental Data Bank* [CD-ROM]. Prepared by U.S. Department of Commerce, Economics, and Statistics Administration, Washington, D.C.: U.S. Department of Commerce, National Economic, Social, and Environmental Data Bank, Economics and Statistics Administration, Office of Business Analysis, February 1995.

★285★
Toxic Chemical Releases

Toxic Chemical Releases, 1992: Vinyl Acetate

County	Releases	Rank
Orange County, TX	3,030,658	1
Harris County, TX	1,658,738	2
Victoria County, TX	839,698	3
Marshall County, KY	635,394	4
Matagorda County, TX	435,499	5

[Continued]

★285★

Toxic Chemical Releases, 1992: Vinyl Acetate

[Continued]

County	Releases	Rank
East Baton Rouge Parish, LA	420,326	6
Grundy County, IL	350,389	7
Galveston County, TX	337,562	8
Hampden County, MA	147,000	9
Burlington County, NJ	99,894	10
Kanawha County, WV	95,302	11
Montgomery County, PA	91,855	12
Morgan County, IL	88,378	13
Lake County, OH	87,227	14
Passaic County, NJ	71,627	15
Hamilton County, OH	59,420	16
Calhoun County, TX	56,529	17
Clinton County, IA	54,000	18
Wayne County, MI	48,484	19
Sangamon County, IL	47,791	20

Source: U.S. Environmental Protection Agency, "Toxic Release Inventory, 1992." In *National Economic, Social, and Environmental Data Bank* [CD-ROM]. Prepared by U.S. Department of Commerce, Economics, and Statistics Administration, Washington, D.C.: U.S. Department of Commerce, National Economic, Social, and Environmental Data Bank, Economics and Statistics Administration, Office of Business Analysis, February 1995.

★286★

Toxic Chemical Releases

Toxic Chemical Releases, 1992: Vinyl Bromide

County	Releases	Rank
Morgan County, AL	1,470	1
Columbia County, AR	5	2

Source: U.S. Environmental Protection Agency, "Toxic Release Inventory, 1992." In *National Economic, Social, and Environmental Data Bank* [CD-ROM]. Prepared by U.S. Department of Commerce, Economics, and Statistics Administration, Washington, D.C.: U.S. Department of Commerce, National Economic, Social, and Environmental Data Bank, Economics and Statistics Administration, Office of Business Analysis, February 1995.

★287★

Toxic Chemical Releases

Toxic Chemical Releases, 1992: Vinyl Chloride

County	Releases	Rank
Harris County, TX	166,517	1
New Castle County, DE	163,474	2
Montgomery County, PA	139,849	3
Salem County, NJ	88,035	4
Marshall County, KY	83,130	5
Sangamon County, IL	76,036	6
Niagara County, NY	72,946	7
Oklahoma County, OK	65,712	8
Monroe County, MS	64,005	9
Calcasieu Parish, LA	55,198	10
Burlington County, NJ	54,968	11
Ascension Parish, LA	54,277	12
Iberville Parish, LA	48,405	13
Ashtabula County, OH	39,100	14
Calhoun County, TX	20,650	15

[Continued]

★287★

Toxic Chemical Releases, 1992: Vinyl Chloride

[Continued]

County	Releases	Rank
West Baton Rouge Parish, LA	20,008	16
Santa Rosa County, FL	13,250	17
Madison County, IN	12,138	18
Brazoria County, TX	9,770	19
Jefferson County, KY	9,100	20

Source: U.S. Environmental Protection Agency, "Toxic Release Inventory, 1992." In *National Economic, Social, and Environmental Data Bank* [CD-ROM]. Prepared by U.S. Department of Commerce, Economics, and Statistics Administration, Washington, D.C.: U.S. Department of Commerce, National Economic, Social, and Environmental Data Bank, Economics and Statistics Administration, Office of Business Analysis, February 1995.

★288★

Toxic Chemical Releases

Toxic Chemical Releases, 1992: Vinylidene Chloride

County	Releases	Rank
Calcasieu Parish, LA	199,441	1
Whitfield County, GA	134,730	2
Daviess County, KY	36,011	3
Midland County, MI	22,573	4
Brazoria County, TX	18,429	5
Mc Henry County, IL	13,205	6
Morgan County, AL	3,030	7
Tippecanoe County, IN	2,200	8
Kanawha County, WV	2,055	9
Alleghany County, VA	1,712	10
Portage County, OH	1,059	11
Gaston County, NC	1,006	12
Erie County, NY	932	13
Weld County, CO	690	14
Lake County, IL	530	15
Jefferson County, KY	270	16
Ascension Parish, LA	171	17
Sedgwick County, KS	169	18
Monroe County, NY	96	19
Harris County, TX	50	20

Source: U.S. Environmental Protection Agency, "Toxic Release Inventory, 1992." In *National Economic, Social, and Environmental Data Bank* [CD-ROM]. Prepared by U.S. Department of Commerce, Economics, and Statistics Administration, Washington, D.C.: U.S. Department of Commerce, National Economic, Social, and Environmental Data Bank, Economics and Statistics Administration, Office of Business Analysis, February 1995.

★289★

Toxic Chemical Releases

Toxic Chemical Releases, 1992: Xylene (Mixed Isomers)

County	Releases	Rank
Salt Lake County, UT	6,743,062	1
Wayne County, MI	3,890,748	2
Cook County, IL	3,287,290	3
Brown County, TX	2,588,989	4
Kent County, MI	2,341,212	5

[Continued]

Toxic Chemical Releases, 1992: Xylene (Mixed Isomers)
[Continued]

County	Releases	Rank
Woodford County, KY	2,064,003	6
Harris County, TX	1,958,394	7
St Louis County, MO	1,917,857	8
Adams County, MS	1,829,610	9
Montgomery County, OH	1,828,753	10
Union County, OH	1,780,851	11
Tippecanoe County, IN	1,666,112	12
Jefferson County, KY	1,641,286	13
Frederick County, VA	1,470,728	14
Oakland County, MI	1,406,015	15
Los Angeles County, CA	1,405,106	16
Huron County, OH	1,398,246	17
Genesee County, MI	1,328,895	18
Clay County, MO	1,268,628	19
Trumbull County, OH	1,247,891	20

Source: U.S. Environmental Protection Agency, "Toxic Release Inventory, 1992." In *National Economic, Social, and Environmental Data Bank* [CD-ROM]. Prepared by U.S. Department of Commerce, Economics, and Statistics Administration, Washington, D.C.: U.S. Department of Commerce, National Economic, Social, and Environmental Data Bank, Economics and Statistics Administration, Office of Business Analysis, February 1995.

★290★
Toxic Chemical Releases

Toxic Chemical Releases, 1992: Zinc (Fume or Dust)

County	Releases	Rank
Saginaw County, MI	5,981,350	1
Madison County, IL	3,172,490	2
Middlesex County, NJ	2,841,543	3
Montgomery County, TN	2,379,935	4
Richland County, OH	2,207,484	5
Marshall County, OK	1,246,888	6
Boyd County, KY	394,745	7
Winnebago County, IL	349,676	8
Cook County, IL	201,439	9
Bedford County, VA	174,750	10
Daviess County, KY	174,605	11
Jefferson County, AL	160,403	12
Box Elder County, UT	156,371	13
Ottawa County, MI	153,750	14
St John The Baptist Parish, LA	150,411	15
Sheboygan County, WI	126,209	16
Hamilton County, TN	125,128	17
Fairfield County, CT	124,637	18
Waukesha County, WI	122,760	19
Mercer County, PA	118,630	20

Source: U.S. Environmental Protection Agency, "Toxic Release Inventory, 1992." In *National Economic, Social, and Environmental Data Bank* [CD-ROM]. Prepared by U.S. Department of Commerce, Economics, and Statistics Administration, Washington, D.C.: U.S. Department of Commerce, National Economic, Social, and Environmental Data Bank, Economics and Statistics Administration, Office of Business Analysis, February 1995.

★291★
Toxic Chemical Releases

Toxic Chemical Releases, 1992: Zinc Compounds

County	Releases	Rank
Lewis and Clark County, MT	32,058,971	1
Gila County, AZ	22,614,844	2
Wayne County, MI	21,394,434	3
Jefferson County, MO	10,409,599	4
Hidalgo County, NM	7,931,520	5
Salt Lake County, UT	7,410,055	6
Jefferson County, OH	6,527,100	7
Brooke County, WV	6,500,592	8
Iron County, MO	6,220,234	9
San Bernardino County, CA	5,539,595	10
Whiteside County, IL	4,994,238	11
Cook County, IL	4,168,199	12
Lake County, IN	3,711,130	13
Peoria County, IL	3,421,537	14
Orange County, TX	2,678,929	15
Hamblen County, TN	2,314,665	16
Butler County, OH	2,279,740	17
Lincoln County, WI	2,233,590	18
Douglas County, NE	1,907,050	19
Mississippi County, AR	1,780,005	20

Source: U.S. Environmental Protection Agency, "Toxic Release Inventory, 1992." In *National Economic, Social, and Environmental Data Bank* [CD-ROM]. Prepared by U.S. Department of Commerce, Economics, and Statistics Administration, Washington, D.C.: U.S. Department of Commerce, National Economic, Social, and Environmental Data Bank, Economics and Statistics Administration, Office of Business Analysis, February 1995.

★292★
Toxic Chemical Releases

Toxic Chemical Releases, 1992: Zineb

County	Releases	Rank
Cecil County, MD	1,005	1

Source: U.S. Environmental Protection Agency, "Toxic Release Inventory, 1992." In *National Economic, Social, and Environmental Data Bank* [CD-ROM]. Prepared by U.S. Department of Commerce, Economics, and Statistics Administration, Washington, D.C.: U.S. Department of Commerce, National Economic, Social, and Environmental Data Bank, Economics and Statistics Administration, Office of Business Analysis, February 1995.

★293★
Toxic Waste

Counties With Highest Chemical Hazards Risks, 1995: Number of Storage Facilities

Data refer to the leading ten counties.

County	Facilities	Rank
Harris County, TX	153	3
Los Angeles County, CA	260	1
Cook County, IL	251	2
Cuyahoga County, OH	98	4
Wayne County, MI	88	5
Mobile County, AL	22	7
Ascension County, LA	16	8
Niagara County, NY	24	6

[Continued]

★293★

Counties With Highest Chemical Hazards Risks, 1995: Number of Storage Facilities
[Continued]

County	Facilities	Rank
Jefferson County, TX	24	6
Brazoria County, TX	16	8

Source: Fairly, Peter, "'Nowhere to Hide' from Chemical Hazard, Says Report," *Chemical Week,* 23 August 1995, p. 9. Primary source: U.S. Public Interest Research Group (US PIRG; Washington, DC); National Environmental Law Center (NELC; Boston).

★294★
Toxic Waste

Counties With Highest Chemical Hazards Risks, 1995: Toxic Chemical Storage

Data refer to the leading ten counties.

[In pounds]

County	Pounds	Rank
Ascension County, LA	311,684,300	3
Brazoria County, TX	122,099,203	4
Cook County, IL	37,030,205	6
Cuyahoga County, OH	12,265,001	10
Harris County, TX	439,645,914	1
Jefferson County, TX	53,502,606	5
Los Angeles County, CA	359,110,309	2
Mobile County, AL	32,416,301	7
Niagara County, NY	20,354,102	8
Wayne County, MI	15,655,304	9

Source: Fairly, Peter, "'Nowhere to Hide' from Chemical Hazard, Says Report," *Chemical Week,* 23 August 1995, p. 9. Primary source: U.S. Public Interest Research Group (US PIRG; Washington, DC); National Environmental Law Center (NELC; Boston).

★295★
Water and Water Use

Rivers Administered By the National Park Service, 1995

Data refer to cities/areas which primarily are responsible for administering the rivers. The user should note, however, that the length of the river may encompass more than one locale.

[In miles of river administered]

City/Location	Length of river system	Rank
Anchorage, AK	86.0	10
Big Bend National Park, TX	191.2	6
Bushkill, PA	40.0	17
Eagle, AR	208	3
Fairbanks, AK	721.0	1
Fresno, CA	81.0	11
Glen Jean, WV	11.0	18
Kalispell, MT	77.6	12
King Salmon, AK	132.0	8
Kotzebue, AK	70.0	14
Narrowsburg, NY	73.4	13

[Continued]

★295★

Rivers Administered By the National Park Service, 1995
[Continued]

City/Location	Length of river system	Rank
National Park, CA	54.0	15
O'Neill, NE	202.0	5
Philadelphia, PA	164.4	7
Porterville, CA	206.5	4
Saint Croix Falls, WI	252.0	2
Three Rivers, CA	103.0	9
Warburg, TN	45.0	16
Yosemite National Park, CA	81.0	11

Source: U.S. Department of the Interior, National Park Service, *The National Parks: Index 1995,* Washington, D.C.: U.S. Department of the Interior, 1995, p. 104.

★296★
Weather and Climate

Snowfall Averages in the Snowiest Cities
[In annual inches]

City	Inches	Rank
Blue Canyon, CA	240.8	1
Caribou, ME	110.4	5
Flagstaff, AZ	99.9	8
Lander, WY	102.5	7
Marquette, MI	128.6	2
Mount Shasta, CA	104.9	6
Muskegon, MI	97.0	10
Sault Sainte Marie, MI	116.7	3
Sexton Summit, OR	97.8	9
Syracuse, NY	111.6	4

Source: "Snowiest Cities in USA," *USA TODAY,* 2 February 1996, p. 8A. Primary source: *The USA TODAY Weather Almanac. Note:* Data for Alaska are not included in the table.

PART II

SOCIAL PROFILE

Contents

Chapter 2

POPULATION

Topics Covered

General Population
Older American Population
Asian Population
Hispanic Population
Native American Population
Pacific Islander Population
Population Changes
Population Density
County Population
Metropolitan Population
Population Projections
CMSA Population
Population By Age Group
Population By Race

★297★
General Population
Families, 1990

MSA	Number	Rank
New York – Northern New Jersey – Long Island, NY – NJ – CT	4,598,623	1
Los Angeles – Anaheim – Riverside, CA	3,447,770	2
Chicago – Gary – Lake County, IL – IN – WI	2,042,356	3
San Francisco – Oakland – San Jose, CA	1,528,920	4
Philadelphia – Wilmington – Trenton, PA – NJ – DE – MD	1,521,413	5
Detroit – Ann Arbor, MI	1,225,500	6
Boston – Lawrence – Salem, MA – NH	1,042,977	7
Dallas – Fort Worth, TX	1,010,612	8
Washington, DC – MD – VA	980,971	9
Houston – Galveston – Brazoria, TX	947,604	10
Miami – Fort Lauderdale, FL	822,497	11
Atlanta, GA	748,828	12
Cleveland – Akron – Lorain, OH	739,669	13
Seattle – Tacoma, WA	659,731	14
Saint Louis, MO – IL	650,177	15
Minneapolis – Saint Paul, MN – WI	634,667	16
Baltimore, MD	625,590	17
Pittsburgh – Beaver Valley, PA	618,136	18
San Diego, CA	605,144	19
Tampa – Saint Petersburg – Clearwater, FL	579,152	20
Phoenix, AZ	552,909	21
Denver – Boulder, CO	478,989	22
Cincinnati – Hamilton, OH – KY – IN	460,608	23
Kansas City, MO – KS	420,874	24
Milwaukee – Racine, WI	419,702	25
Portland – Vancouver, OR – WA	387,162	26
Sacramento, CA	381,692	27
Norfolk – Virginia Beach – Newport News, VA	361,467	28
Columbus, OH	357,649	29
Indianapolis, IN	335,627	30
San Antonio, TX	332,315	31
Charlotte – Gastonia – Rock Hill, NC – SC	319,242	32
New Orleans, LA	318,544	33
Buffalo – Niagara Falls, NY	315,700	34
Providence – Pawtucket – Fall River, RI – MA	299,617	35
Hartford – New Britain – Middletown, CT	288,785	36
Orlando, FL	280,105	37
Nashville, TN	266,208	38
Greensboro – Winston-Salem – High Point, NC	264,293	39
Salt Lake City – Ogden, UT	262,143	40
Louisville, KY – IN	261,379	41
Rochester, NY	260,038	42
Dayton – Springfield, OH	259,821	43
Oklahoma City, OK	257,571	44
Memphis, TN – AR – MS	256,849	45

[Continued]

★297★
Families, 1990
[Continued]

MSA	Number	Rank
Birmingham, AL	251,213	46
West Palm Beach – Boca Raton – Delray Beach, FL	244,633	47
Jacksonville, FL	243,636	48
Richmond – Petersburg, VA	230,490	49
Albany – Schenectady – Troy, NY	225,804	50
Honolulu, HI	199,597	51
Scranton – Wilkes-Barre, PA	198,121	52
Tulsa, OK	195,735	53
Las Vegas, NV	191,468	54
Austin, TX	188,253	55
Raleigh – Durham, NC	188,248	56
Allentown – Bethlehem – Easton, PA – NJ	188,241	57
Grand Rapids, MI	180,571	58
Greenville – Spartanburg, SC	175,921	59
Tucson, AZ	170,709	60
Knoxville, TN	170,513	61
Syracuse, NY	167,693	62
Fresno, CA	163,716	63
Omaha, NE – IA	162,579	64
Harrisburg – Lebanon – Carlisle, PA	158,943	65
Toledo, OH	158,791	66
El Paso, TX	144,088	67
Little Rock – North Little Rock, AR	139,377	68
Bakersfield, CA	137,814	69
New Haven – Meriden, CT	137,583	70
Baton Rouge, LA	136,939	71
Springfield, MA	136,800	72
Youngstown – Warren, OH	136,488	73
Wichita, KS	131,435	74
Charleston, SC	130,968	75
Mobile, AL	130,249	76
Johnson City – Kingsport – Bristol, TN – VA	127,078	77
Albuquerque, NM	125,628	78
Chattanooga, TN – GA	121,833	79
Stockton, CA	118,345	80
Flint, MI	116,872	81
York, PA	116,758	82
Columbia, SC	116,038	83
Lakeland – Winter Haven, FL	115,537	84
Melbourne – Titusville – Palm Bay, FL	114,375	85
Worcester, MA	113,716	86
Lancaster, PA	112,965	87
Canton, OH	109,517	88
Saginaw – Bay City – Midland, MI	109,208	89
Lansing – East Lansing, MI	106,447	90
Augusta, GA – SC	105,858	91
Colorado Springs, CO	104,914	92
Des Moines, IA	104,788	93
Daytona Beach, FL	103,410	94
Jackson, MS	102,077	95
Fort Myers – Cape Coral, FL	100,231	96
Beaumont – Port Arthur, TX	99,478	97

[Continued]

★297★

Families, 1990
[Continued]

MSA	Number	Rank
Fort Wayne, IN	97,291	98
Modesto, CA	95,264	99
Davenport – Rock Island – Moline, IA – IL	94,999	100
Spokane, WA	94,956	101
Pensacola, FL	94,100	102
Peoria, IL	92,250	103
Reading, PA	92,046	104
Lexington-Fayette, KY	91,786	105
Corpus Christi, TX	89,695	106
Shreveport, LA	89,057	107
Huntington – Ashland, WV – KY – OH	88,842	108
McAllen – Edinburg – Mission, TX	88,615	109
Santa Barbara – Santa Maria – Lompoc, CA	87,510	110
Madison, WI	87,346	111
Sarasota, FL	84,614	112
Salinas – Seaside – Monterey, CA	84,038	113
Appleton – Oshkosh – Neenah, WI	83,410	114
Atlantic City, NJ	83,111	115
Utica – Rome, NY	81,683	116
Rockford, IL	77,755	117
Visalia – Tulare – Porterville, CA	77,542	118
Evansville, IN – KY	77,234	119
Montgomery, AL	76,609	120
Macon – Warner Robins, GA	75,366	121
Eugene – Springfield, OR	74,065	122
Fort Pierce, FL	73,773	123
Salem, OR	71,941	124
Charleston, WV	71,638	125
Erie, PA	71,459	126
Fayetteville, NC	70,801	127
New London – Norwich, CT – RI	70,595	128
Binghamton, NY	69,553	129
Johnstown, PA	66,742	130
Huntsville, AL	66,269	131
Poughkeepsie, NY	65,338	132
Reno, NV	64,947	133
Killeen – Temple, TX	64,881	134
Springfield, MO	64,429	135
Savannah, GA	64,359	136
Hickory – Morganton, NC	64,049	137
South Bend – Mishawaka, IN	63,998	138
Duluth, MN – WI	63,892	139
Columbus, GA – AL	63,240	140
Roanoke, VA	62,450	141
Bradenton, FL	62,354	142
Brownsville – Harlingen, TX	60,903	143
Waterbury, CT	59,524	144
Portsmouth – Dover – Rochester, NH – ME	58,409	145
Ocala, FL	57,770	146
Anchorage, AK	57,519	147
Provo – Orem, UT	56,750	148
Portland, ME	56,446	149
Kalamazoo, MI	56,066	150

[Continued]

★297★

Families, 1990
[Continued]

MSA	Number	Rank
Tallahassee, FL	55,849	151
Lubbock, TX	55,696	152
Boise, ID	54,635	153
Lafayette, LA	54,029	154
Lincoln, NE	53,360	155
Biloxi – Gulfport, MS	52,108	156
Amarillo, TX	51,029	157
Springfield, IL	50,975	158
Bremerton, WA	50,802	159
Green Bay, WI	50,732	160
Fort Smith, AR – OK	49,767	161
Asheville, NC	49,499	162
Houma – Thibodaux, LA	48,758	163
Yakima, WA	48,609	164
Waco, TX	48,399	165
Fort Collins – Loveland, CO	47,521	166
New Bedford, MA	47,274	167
Gainesville, FL	46,974	168
Chico, CA	46,712	169
Saint Cloud, MN	46,471	170
Lake Charles, LA	45,308	171
Cedar Rapids, IA	45,165	172
Wheeling, WV – OH	44,503	173
Benton Harbor, MI	44,392	174
Longview – Marshall, TX	44,308	175
Naples, FL	44,136	176
Clarksville – Hopkinsville, TN – KY	44,098	177
Merced, CA	43,830	178
Olympia, WA	43,428	179
Topeka, KS	43,025	180
Parkersburg – Marietta, WV – OH	42,736	181
Muskegon, MI	42,602	182
Elkhart – Goshen, IN	41,939	183
Anderson, SC	41,770	184
Tyler, TX	41,538	185
Lima, OH	41,510	186
Redding, CA	40,707	187
Steubenville – Weirton, OH – WV	40,649	188
Medford, OR	40,559	189
Richland – Kennewick – Pasco, WA	40,304	190
Fort Walton Beach, FL	39,885	191
Jackson, MI	39,211	192
Champaign – Urbana – Rantoul, IL	38,957	193
Waterloo – Cedar Falls, IA	38,731	194
Manchester, NH	38,351	195
Florence, AL	38,250	196
Joplin, MO	37,921	197
Decatur, AL	37,874	198
Janesville – Beloit, WI	37,767	199
Tuscaloosa, AL	37,716	200
Lynchburg, VA	37,676	201
Athens, GA	37,563	202
Fargo – Moorhead, ND – MN	37,506	203
Jamestown – Dunkirk, NY	37,449	204
Battle Creek, MI	36,840	205
Monroe, LA	36,705	206
Dothan, AL	36,198	207

[Continued]

★297★
Families, 1990
[Continued]

MSA	Number	Rank
Anderson, IN	36,087	208
Altoona, PA	36,051	209
Panama City, FL	35,726	210
Mansfield, OH	35,096	211
Eau Claire, WI	35,024	212
Alexandria, LA	34,275	213
Greeley, CO	34,057	214
Terre Haute, IN	33,870	215
Sharon, PA	33,619	216
Pueblo, CO	33,574	217
Las Cruces, NM	33,471	218
Texarkana, TX – Texarkana, AR	33,076	219
Jacksonville, NC	32,974	220
Decatur, IL	32,601	221
Hagerstown, MD	32,581	222
Bellingham, WA	32,528	223
Wichita Falls, TX	32,511	224
Wilmington, NC	32,492	225
Williamsport, PA	32,443	226
Sioux Falls, SD	32,327	227
Yuba City, CA	32,286	228
Charlottesville, VA	31,953	229
Odessa, TX	31,862	230
Pascagoula, MS	31,855	231
Anniston, AL	31,759	232
Burlington, VT	31,484	233
Abilene, TX	31,107	234
Wausau, WI	31,092	235
Burlington, NC	31,073	236
Billings, MT	31,007	237
Glens Falls, NY	30,976	238
Danville, VA	30,871	239
Bloomington – Normal, IL	30,653	240
Sioux City, IA – NE	30,609	241
Santa Fe, NM	30,531	242
Fayetteville – Springdale, AR	30,421	243
Muncie, IN	30,286	244
Florence, SC	30,155	245
Laredo, TX	29,735	246
Albany, GA	29,631	247
Lawton, OK	29,175	248
Lafayette – West Lafayette, IN	28,975	249
Midland, TX	28,833	250
Gadsden, AL	28,585	251
Sheboygan, WI	28,195	252
Cumberland, MD – WV	28,180	253
Yuma, AZ	28,110	254
Rochester, MN	28,097	255
Kokomo, IN	27,327	256
Fitchburg – Leominster, MA	27,258	257
Sherman – Denison, TX	26,800	258
State College, PA	26,456	259
Columbia, MO	25,939	260
San Angelo, TX	25,657	261
Bryan – College Station, TX	25,435	262
Kankakee, IL	25,003	263
Elmira, NY	24,895	264

[Continued]

★297★
Families, 1990
[Continued]

MSA	Number	Rank
Owensboro, KY	24,120	265
La Crosse, WI	24,117	266
Lewiston – Auburn, ME	23,549	267
Bloomington, IN	23,121	268
Bismarck, ND	22,435	269
Saint Joseph, MO	22,410	270
Bangor, ME	22,112	271
Dubuque, IA	22,096	272
Pine Bluff, AR	22,091	273
Rapid City, SD	22,050	274
Pittsfield, MA	21,573	275
Jackson, TN	21,418	276
Great Falls, MT	21,289	277
Iowa City, IA	20,478	278
Cheyenne, WY	20,127	279
Victoria, TX	20,033	280
Lawrence, KS	17,297	281
Grand Forks, ND	17,232	282
Casper, WY	16,799	283
Enid, OK	15,917	284

Source: U.S. Bureau of the Census, Data User Services Division, *1990 Census of Population and Housing*, Summary Tape File 3C, United States Summary, CD- ROM, February 1992.

★298★
General Population

Households, 1990

MSA	Number	Rank
New York – Northern New Jersey – Long Island, NY – NJ-CT	6,617,074	1
Los Angeles – Anaheim – Riverside, CA	4,909,218	2
Chicago – Gary – Lake County, IL – IN – WI	2,903,236	3
San Francisco – Oakland – San Jose, CA	2,334,992	4
Philadelphia – Wilmington – Trenton, PA – NJ – DE – MD	2,151,624	5
Detroit – Ann Arbor, MI	1,724,767	6
Boston – Lawrence – Salem, MA – NH	1,545,347	7
Washington, DC – MD – VA	1,460,785	8
Dallas – Fort Worth, TX	1,452,215	9
Houston – Galveston – Brazoria, TX	1,333,707	10
Miami – Fort Lauderdale, FL	1,220,097	11
Cleveland – Akron – Lorain, OH	1,058,648	12
Atlanta, GA	1,056,929	13
Seattle – Tacoma, WA	1,003,337	14
Minneapolis – Saint Paul, MN – WI	935,760	15
Saint Louis, MO – IL	923,639	16
Pittsburgh – Beaver Valley, PA	891,071	17
San Diego, CA	887,719	18
Baltimore, MD	879,968	19
Tampa – Saint Petersburg – Clearwater, FL	870,999	20

[Continued]

★298★

Households, 1990
[Continued]

MSA	Number	Rank
Phoenix, AZ	808,162	21
Denver – Boulder, CO	739,001	22
Cincinnati – Hamilton, OH – KY – IN	652,333	23
Kansas City, MO – KS	602,514	24
Milwaukee – Racine, WI	601,967	25
Portland – Vancouver, OR – WA	576,083	26
Sacramento, CA	557,811	27
Columbus, OH	525,558	28
Norfolk – Virginia Beach – Newport News, VA	494,145	29
Indianapolis, IN	480,406	30
Buffalo – Niagara Falls, NY	460,707	31
New Orleans, LA	454,417	32
San Antonio, TX	451,731	33
Charlotte – Gastonia – Rock Hill, NC – SC	440,458	34
Providence – Pawtucket – Fall River, RI – MA	428,869	35
Hartford – New Britain – Middletown, CT	411,507	36
Orlando, FL	402,519	37
Nashville, TN	375,849	38
Rochester, NY	374,856	39
Greensboro – Winston-Salem – High Point, NC	372,191	40
Oklahoma City, OK	368,502	41
Louisville, KY – IN	367,421	42
West Palm Beach – Boca Raton – Delray Beach, FL	366,131	43
Dayton – Springfield, OH	364,346	44
Memphis, TN – AR – MS	357,166	45
Salt Lake City – Ogden, UT	347,121	46
Birmingham, AL	344,912	47
Jacksonville, FL	343,043	48
Albany – Schenectady – Troy, NY	335,818	49
Richmond – Petersburg, VA	331,771	50
Austin, TX	303,921	51
Raleigh – Durham, NC	287,835	52
Las Vegas, NV	287,684	53
Scranton – Wilkes-Barre, PA	280,648	54
Tulsa, OK	277,423	55
Honolulu, HI	265,625	56
Tucson, AZ	262,129	57
Allentown – Bethlehem – Easton, PA – NJ	259,034	58
Grand Rapids, MI	245,230	59
Syracuse, NY	243,972	60
Greenville – Spartanburg, SC	240,878	61
Knoxville, TN	237,614	62
Omaha, NE – IA	232,395	63
Toledo, OH	230,721	64
Harrisburg – Lebanon – Carlisle, PA	226,267	65
Fresno, CA	221,133	66
New Haven – Meriden, CT	199,198	67
Springfield, MA	196,725	68
Little Rock – North Little Rock, AR	195,058	69

[Continued]

★298★

Households, 1990
[Continued]

MSA	Number	Rank
Baton Rouge, LA	188,297	70
Wichita, KS	187,099	71
Youngstown – Warren, OH	186,902	72
Albuquerque, NM	185,445	73
Bakersfield, CA	182,116	74
El Paso, TX	178,514	75
Charleston, SC	177,484	76
Mobile, AL	174,530	77
Johnson City – Kingsport – Bristol, TN – VA	170,626	78
Chattanooga, TN – GA	165,970	79
Columbia, SC	163,407	80
Melbourne – Titusville – Palm Bay, FL	161,928	81
Flint, MI	161,501	82
Worcester, MA	161,381	83
Stockton, CA	158,659	84
Lansing – East Lansing, MI	156,994	85
York, PA	156,830	86
Lakeland – Winter Haven, FL	155,870	87
Daytona Beach, FL	153,315	88
Des Moines, IA	153,282	89
Lancaster, PA	151,352	90
Canton, OH	148,995	91
Saginaw – Bay City – Midland, MI	148,098	92
Colorado Springs, CO	147,227	93
Augusta, GA – SC	142,723	94
Madison, WI	142,231	95
Spokane, WA	141,859	96
Fort Myers – Cape Coral, FL	140,046	97
Jackson, MS	139,571	98
Davenport – Rock Island – Moline, IA – IL	135,962	99
Fort Wayne, IN	135,876	100
Beaumont – Port Arthur, TX	134,164	101
Lexington-Fayette, KY	134,039	102
Santa Barbara – Santa Maria – Lompoc, CA	130,378	103
Peoria, IL	129,511	104
Pensacola, FL	128,776	105
Reading, PA	127,849	106
Sarasota, FL	125,764	107
Modesto, CA	125,731	108
Shreveport, LA	123,806	109
Atlantic City, NJ	123,442	110
Huntington – Ashland, WV – KY – OH	119,654	111
Corpus Christi, TX	118,333	112
Utica – Rome, NY	117,237	113
Appleton – Oshkosh – Neenah, WI	115,895	114
Salinas – Seaside – Monterey, CA	113,340	115
Eugene – Springfield, OR	110,940	116
Evansville, IN – KY	108,685	117
Rockford, IL	107,759	118
Montgomery, AL	105,425	119
McAllen – Edinburg – Mission, TX	103,514	120
Macon – Warner Robins, GA	102,886	121

[Continued]

★298★
Households, 1990
[Continued]

MSA	Number	Rank
Reno, NV	102,430	122
Salem, OR	101,743	123
Erie, PA	101,652	124
Fort Pierce, FL	101,183	125
Binghamton, NY	100,504	126
Charleston, WV	100,134	127
New London – Norwich, CT – RI	98,397	128
Visalia – Tulare – Porterville, CA	97,726	129
Duluth, MN – WI	95,604	130
Springfield, MO	93,389	131
South Bend – Mishawaka, IN	92,171	132
Fayetteville, NC	91,823	133
Johnstown, PA	91,696	134
Huntsville, AL	91,361	135
Bradenton, FL	91,263	136
Savannah, GA	89,701	137
Poughkeepsie, NY	89,627	138
Roanoke, VA	89,617	139
Tallahassee, FL	88,332	140
Columbus, GA – AL	86,350	141
Hickory – Morganton, NC	85,393	142
Portland, ME	84,809	143
Portsmouth – Dover – Rochester, NH – ME	84,266	144
Waterbury, CT	84,186	145
Killeen – Temple, TX	84,175	146
Kalamazoo, MI	84,021	147
Anchorage, AK	83,043	148
Lincoln, NE	82,836	149
Lubbock, TX	81,362	150
Ocala, FL	78,564	151
Gainesville, FL	78,493	152
Boise, ID	77,502	153
Springfield, IL	76,163	154
Lafayette, LA	75,000	155
Brownsville – Harlingen, TX	73,550	156
Green Bay, WI	72,384	157
Amarillo, TX	72,252	158
Chico, CA	71,778	159
Biloxi – Gulfport, MS	71,307	160
Asheville, NC	70,755	161
Fort Collins – Loveland, CO	70,574	162
Waco, TX	70,153	163
Provo – Orem, UT	70,011	164
Bremerton, WA	69,488	165
Fort Smith, AR – OK	66,964	166
Yakima, WA	66,174	167
New Bedford, MA	65,482	168
Cedar Rapids, IA	65,242	169
Saint Cloud, MN	64,335	170
Champaign – Urbana – Rantoul, IL	63,993	171
Topeka, KS	63,587	172
Wheeling, WV – OH	62,858	173
Olympia, WA	62,047	174
Naples, FL	61,646	175
Benton Harbor, MI	61,390	176
Houma – Thibodaux, LA	61,065	177

[Continued]

★298★
Households, 1990
[Continued]

MSA	Number	Rank
Longview – Marshall, TX	60,916	178
Lake Charles, LA	60,276	179
Parkersburg – Marietta, WV – OH	57,958	180
Fargo – Moorhead, ND – MN	57,892	181
Muskegon, MI	57,827	182
Athens, GA	57,655	183
Medford, OR	57,400	184
Tyler, TX	56,807	185
Manchester, NH	56,645	186
Elkhart – Goshen, IN	56,555	187
Clarksville – Hopkinsville, TN – KY	56,030	188
Redding, CA	55,940	189
Anderson, SC	55,704	190
Waterloo – Cedar Falls, IA	55,575	191
Merced, CA	55,548	192
Lima, OH	55,363	193
Steubenville – Weirton, OH – WV	55,143	194
Tuscaloosa, AL	55,045	195
Richland – Kennewick – Pasco, WA	54,632	196
Jackson, MI	53,891	197
Jamestown – Dunkirk, NY	53,667	198
Fort Walton Beach, FL	53,372	199
Joplin, MO	53,130	200
Lynchburg, VA	52,609	201
Janesville – Beloit, WI	52,251	202
Battle Creek, MI	51,856	203
Florence, AL	50,768	204
Monroe, LA	50,531	205
Eau Claire, WI	50,502	206
Altoona, PA	50,325	207
Anderson, IN	49,857	208
Decatur, AL	49,163	209
Terre Haute, IN	49,045	210
Panama City, FL	48,791	211
Charlottesville, VA	48,718	212
Bellingham, WA	48,645	213
Dothan, AL	48,377	214
Burlington, VT	48,293	215
Wilmington, NC	47,983	216
Mansfield, OH	47,859	217
Sioux Falls, SD	47,850	218
Greeley, CO	47,566	219
Pueblo, CO	47,241	220
Bloomington – Normal, IL	46,896	221
Decatur, IL	46,068	222
Alexandria, LA	45,782	223
Sharon, PA	45,676	224
Lafayette – West Lafayette, IN	45,509	225
Wichita Falls, TX	45,384	226
Muncie, IN	45,106	227
Las Cruces, NM	45,043	228
Santa Fe, NM	44,998	229
Williamsport, PA	44,994	230
Billings, MT	44,877	231
Texarkana, TX – Texarkana, AR	44,739	232
Hagerstown, MD	44,671	233
Bryan – College Station, TX	43,904	234

[Continued]

★298★

Households, 1990
[Continued]

MSA	Number	Rank
Fayetteville – Springdale, AR	43,655	235
Abilene, TX	43,217	236
Sioux City, IA – NE	43,027	237
Yuba City, CA	42,909	238
Glens Falls, NY	42,823	239
Anniston, AL	42,806	240
Burlington, NC	42,798	241
State College, PA	42,784	242
Odessa, TX	42,396	243
Danville, VA	42,313	244
Columbia, MO	42,089	245
Wausau, WI	41,534	246
Jacksonville, NC	40,545	247
Pascagoula, MS	40,433	248
Rochester, MN	40,161	249
Florence, SC	39,998	250
Cumberland, MD – WV	39,768	251
Bloomington, IN	39,374	252
Albany, GA	39,258	253
Midland, TX	38,967	254
Sheboygan, WI	38,658	255
Gadsden, AL	38,453	256
Fitchburg – Leominster, MA	38,239	257
Lawton, OK	37,676	258
Kokomo, IN	37,395	259
La Crosse, WI	36,847	260
Sherman – Denison, TX	36,799	261
Iowa City, IA	36,118	262
Yuma, AZ	35,827	263
San Angelo, TX	35,638	264
Elmira, NY	35,184	265
Kankakee, IL	34,588	266
Laredo, TX	34,510	267
Lewiston – Auburn, ME	34,026	268
Owensboro, KY	33,110	269
Bangor, ME	32,901	270
Saint Joseph, MO	32,368	271
Pittsfield, MA	31,569	272
Bismarck, ND	31,485	273
Dubuque, IA	30,689	274
Rapid City, SD	30,634	275
Great Falls, MT	30,206	276
Lawrence, KS	30,105	277
Pine Bluff, AR	29,955	278
Jackson, TN	29,541	279
Cheyenne, WY	28,302	280
Victoria, TX	26,269	281
Grand Forks, ND	25,455	282
Casper, WY	23,758	283
Enid, OK	22,627	284

Source: U.S. Bureau of the Census, Data User Services Division, *1990 Census of Population and Housing*, Summary Tape File 3C, United States Summary, CD-ROM, February 1992.

★299★

General Population

Female Population, 1990

MSA	% female	Rank
Sarasota, FL	53.1	1
Monroe, LA	53.0	2
Altoona, PA	52.9	3
Gadsden, AL	52.9	3
Springfield, IL	52.9	3
Springfield, MA	52.9	3
Bradenton, FL	52.8	4
Burlington, NC	52.8	4
Jackson, MS	52.8	4
Jackson, TN	52.8	4
Pittsburgh – Beaver Valley, PA	52.8	4
Roanoke, VA	52.8	4
Shreveport, LA	52.8	4
Wheeling, WV – OH	52.8	4
Birmingham, AL	52.7	5
Cumberland, MD – WV	52.7	5
Danville, VA	52.7	5
Florence, SC	52.7	5
Lynchburg, VA	52.7	5
Saint Joseph, MO	52.7	5
Asheville, NC	52.6	6
Muncie, IN	52.6	6
Wilmington, NC	52.6	6
Charleston, WV	52.5	7
Decatur, IL	52.5	7
Macon – Warner Robins, GA	52.5	7
New Bedford, MA	52.5	7
New Orleans, LA	52.5	7
Scranton – Wilkes-Barre, PA	52.5	7
Youngstown – Warren, OH	52.5	7
Albany, GA	52.4	8
Anderson, SC	52.4	8
Buffalo – Niagara Falls, NY	52.4	8
Chattanooga, TN – GA	52.4	8
Richmond – Petersburg, VA	52.4	8
Bloomington – Normal, IL	52.3	9
Cleveland – Akron – Lorain, OH	52.3	9
Huntington – Ashland, WV – KY – OH	52.3	9
Louisville, KY – IN	52.3	9
Memphis, TN – AR – MS	52.3	9
Mobile, AL	52.3	9
New York – Northern New Jersey – Long Island, NY – NJ – CT	52.3	9
Owensboro, KY	52.3	9
Steubenville – Weirton, OH – WV	52.3	9
Tampa – Saint Petersburg – Clearwater, FL	52.3	9
Des Moines, IA	52.2	10
Enid, OK	52.2	10
Evansville, IN – KY	52.2	10
Flint, MI	52.2	10
Florence, AL	52.2	10
Greensboro – Winston-Salem – High Point, NC	52.2	10
Kokomo, IN	52.2	10
Miami – Fort Lauderdale, FL	52.2	10
Montgomery, AL	52.2	10

[Continued]

★ 299 ★

Female Population, 1990
[Continued]

MSA	% female	Rank
Parkersburg – Marietta, WV – OH	52.2	10
Portland, ME	52.2	10
Providence – Pawtucket – Fall River, RI – MA	52.2	10
Saint Louis, MO – IL	52.2	10
Sherman – Denison, TX	52.2	10
Tallahassee, FL	52.2	10
Waterbury, CT	52.2	10
Waterloo – Cedar Falls, IA	52.2	10
Alexandria, LA	52.1	11
Brownsville – Harlingen, TX	52.1	11
Little Rock – North Little Rock, AR	52.1	11
New Haven – Meriden, CT	52.1	11
Toledo, OH	52.1	11
Atlantic City, NJ	52.0	12
Benton Harbor, MI	52.0	12
Canton, OH	52.0	12
Cincinnati – Hamilton, OH – KY – IN	52.0	12
Indianapolis, IN	52.0	12
Johnstown, PA	52.0	12
Kalamazoo, MI	52.0	12
Knoxville, TN	52.0	12
La Crosse, WI	52.0	12
Laredo, TX	52.0	12
Lexington-Fayette, KY	52.0	12
Peoria, IL	52.0	12
Philadelphia – Wilmington – Trenton, PA – NJ – DE – MD	52.0	12
Pittsfield, MA	52.0	12
Pueblo, CO	52.0	12
Savannah, GA	52.0	12
Springfield, MO	52.0	12
Tyler, TX	52.0	12
Amarillo, TX	51.9	13
Boston – Lawrence – Salem, MA – NH	51.9	13
Dayton – Springfield, OH	51.9	13
Joplin, MO	51.9	13
Lewiston – Auburn, ME	51.9	13
Longview – Marshall, TX	51.9	13
Ocala, FL	51.9	13
Sioux Falls, SD	51.9	13
Texarkana, TX – Texarkana, AR	51.9	13
Topeka, KS	51.9	13
West Palm Beach – Boca Raton – Delray Beach, FL	51.9	13
Athens, GA	51.8	14
Bloomington, IN	51.8	14
Charlotte – Gastonia – Rock Hill, NC – SC	51.8	14
Detroit – Ann Arbor, MI	51.8	14
Erie, PA	51.8	14
Greenville – Spartanburg, SC	51.8	14
Johnson City – Kingsport – Bristol, TN – VA	51.8	14
McAllen – Edinburg – Mission, TX	51.8	14
Milwaukee – Racine, WI	51.8	14

[Continued]

★ 299 ★

Female Population, 1990
[Continued]

MSA	% female	Rank
Nashville, TN	51.8	14
Raleigh – Durham, NC	51.8	14
Saginaw – Bay City – Midland, MI	51.8	14
South Bend – Mishawaka, IN	51.8	14
Syracuse, NY	51.8	14
Albany – Schenectady – Troy, NY	51.7	15
Allentown – Bethlehem – Easton, PA – NJ	51.7	15
Baltimore, MD	51.7	15
Bangor, ME	51.7	15
Davenport – Rock Island – Moline, IA – IL	51.7	15
Dubuque, IA	51.7	15
Jamestown – Dunkirk, NY	51.7	15
Kansas City, MO – KS	51.7	15
Lansing – East Lansing, MI	51.7	15
Reading, PA	51.7	15
Rochester, NY	51.7	15
Anniston, AL	51.6	16
Baton Rouge, LA	51.6	16
Beaumont – Port Arthur, TX	51.6	16
Binghamton, NY	51.6	16
Burlington, VT	51.6	16
Charlottesville, VA	51.6	16
Daytona Beach, FL	51.6	16
Eau Claire, WI	51.6	16
Fort Myers – Cape Coral, FL	51.6	16
Harrisburg – Lebanon – Carlisle, PA	51.6	16
Hartford – New Britain – Middletown, CT	51.6	16
Kankakee, IL	51.6	16
Lakeland – Winter Haven, FL	51.6	16
Manchester, NH	51.6	16
Pine Bluff, AR	51.6	16
Sioux City, IA – NE	51.6	16
Tulsa, OK	51.6	16
Tuscaloosa, AL	51.6	16
Williamsport, PA	51.6	16
Worcester, MA	51.6	16
Abilene, TX	51.5	17
Battle Creek, MI	51.5	17
Billings, MT	51.5	17
Cedar Rapids, IA	51.5	17
Chicago – Gary – Lake County, IL – IN – WI	51.5	17
El Paso, TX	51.5	17
Fort Smith, AR – OK	51.5	17
Lake Charles, LA	51.5	17
Midland, TX	51.5	17
Omaha, NE – IA	51.5	17
Rochester, MN	51.5	17
Rockford, IL	51.5	17
Sharon, PA	51.5	17
Atlanta, GA	51.4	18
Augusta, GA – SC	51.4	18
Columbia, MO	51.4	18

[Continued]

★299★

Female Population, 1990
[Continued]

MSA	% female	Rank
Columbia, SC	51.4	18
Dothan, AL	51.4	18
Elmira, NY	51.4	18
Fitchburg – Leominster, MA	51.4	18
Fort Wayne, IN	51.4	18
Lafayette, LA	51.4	18
Lancaster, PA	51.4	18
Odessa, TX	51.4	18
San Antonio, TX	51.4	18
Chico, CA	51.3	19
Columbus, OH	51.3	19
Duluth, MN – WI	51.3	19
Eugene – Springfield, OR	51.3	19
Grand Rapids, MI	51.3	19
Janesville – Beloit, WI	51.3	19
Oklahoma City, OK	51.3	19
Olympia, WA	51.3	19
Pensacola, FL	51.3	19
San Angelo, TX	51.3	19
Spokane, WA	51.3	19
Waco, TX	51.3	19
Washington, DC – MD – VA	51.3	19
Albuquerque, NM	51.2	20
Bismarck, ND	51.2	20
Decatur, AL	51.2	20
Green Bay, WI	51.2	20
Houma – Thibodaux, LA	51.2	20
Jacksonville, FL	51.2	20
Medford, OR	51.2	20
Portsmouth – Dover – Rochester, NH – ME	51.2	20
Terre Haute, IN	51.2	20
Tucson, AZ	51.2	20
Victoria, TX	51.2	20
Elkhart – Goshen, IN	51.1	21
Fort Pierce, FL	51.1	21
Hickory – Morganton, NC	51.1	21
Mansfield, OH	51.1	21
Minneapolis – Saint Paul, MN – WI	51.1	21
Muskegon, MI	51.1	21
Wichita Falls, TX	51.1	21
York, PA	51.1	21
Anderson, IN	51.0	22
Casper, WY	51.0	22
Corpus Christi, TX	51.0	22
Lincoln, NE	51.0	22
Modesto, CA	51.0	22
Portland – Vancouver, OR – WA	51.0	22
Sacramento, CA	51.0	22
Wichita, KS	51.0	22
Redding, CA	50.9	23
Appleton – Oshkosh – Neenah, WI	50.8	24
Fargo – Moorhead, ND – MN	50.8	24
Lima, OH	50.8	24
Lubbock, TX	50.8	24
Panama City, FL	50.8	24
Pascagoula, MS	50.8	24

[Continued]

★299★

Female Population, 1990
[Continued]

MSA	% female	Rank
Phoenix, AZ	50.8	24
Boise, ID	50.7	25
Dallas – Fort Worth, TX	50.7	25
Denver – Boulder, CO	50.7	25
Fort Collins – Loveland, CO	50.7	25
Great Falls, MT	50.7	25
Huntsville, AL	50.7	25
Madison, WI	50.7	25
Naples, FL	50.7	25
Orlando, FL	50.7	25
Salem, OR	50.7	25
Utica – Rome, NY	50.7	25
Wausau, WI	50.7	25
Fresno, CA	50.6	26
Greeley, CO	50.6	26
Melbourne – Titusville – Palm Bay, FL	50.6	26
Provo – Orem, UT	50.6	26
Santa Fe, NM	50.6	26
Bellingham, WA	50.5	27
Fayetteville – Springdale, AR	50.5	27
Iowa City, IA	50.5	27
Lawrence, KS	50.5	27
Seattle – Tacoma, WA	50.5	27
Sheboygan, WI	50.5	27
Gainesville, FL	50.4	28
Las Cruces, NM	50.4	28
Rapid City, SD	50.4	28
Salt Lake City – Ogden, UT	50.4	28
Visalia – Tulare – Porterville, CA	50.4	28
Yakima, WA	50.4	28
Cheyenne, WY	50.3	29
Columbus, GA – AL	50.3	29
San Francisco – Oakland – San Jose, CA	50.3	29
Yuba City, CA	50.3	29
Charleston, SC	50.2	30
Glens Falls, NY	50.2	30
Houston – Galveston – Brazoria, TX	50.2	30
Biloxi – Gulfport, MS	50.1	31
Austin, TX	50.0	32
Los Angeles – Anaheim – Riverside, CA	50.0	32
Poughkeepsie, NY	50.0	32
Richland – Kennewick – Pasco, WA	50.0	32
Colorado Springs, CO	49.9	33
Norfolk – Virginia Beach – Newport News, VA	49.9	33
Saint Cloud, MN	49.8	34
Santa Barbara – Santa Maria – Lompoc, CA	49.8	34
Bakersfield, CA	49.7	35
Champaign – Urbana – Rantoul, IL	49.6	36
Hagerstown, MD	49.6	36
Merced, CA	49.5	37
New London – Norwich, CT – RI	49.5	37

[Continued]

★ 299 ★

Female Population, 1990

[Continued]

MSA	% female	Rank
Fort Walton Beach, FL	49.4	38
Reno, NV	49.4	38
Stockton, CA	49.4	38
Lafayette – West Lafayette, IN	49.3	39
Las Vegas, NV	49.3	39
Jackson, MI	49.2	40
San Diego, CA	49.1	41
Bremerton, WA	49.0	42
Honolulu, HI	49.0	42
Yuma, AZ	49.0	42
Grand Forks, ND	48.8	43
Anchorage, AK	48.6	44
Bryan – College Station, TX	48.3	45
Fayetteville, NC	48.3	45
Salinas – Seaside – Monterey, CA	48.3	45
State College, PA	48.3	45
Lawton, OK	48.0	46
Killeen – Temple, TX	47.9	47
Clarksville – Hopkinsville, TN – KY	47.7	48
Jacksonville, NC	40.4	49

Source: U.S. Bureau of the Census, Data User Services Division, *1990 Census of Population and Housing,* Summary Tape File 3C, United States Summary, CD-ROM, February 1992.

★ 300 ★

General Population

Male Population, 1990

MSA	% male	Rank
Jacksonville, NC	59.6	1
Clarksville – Hopkinsville, TN – KY	52.3	2
Killeen – Temple, TX	52.1	3
Lawton, OK	52.0	4
Bryan – College Station, TX	51.7	5
Fayetteville, NC	51.7	5
Salinas – Seaside – Monterey, CA	51.7	5
State College, PA	51.7	5
Anchorage, AK	51.4	6
Grand Forks, ND	51.2	7
Bremerton, WA	51.0	8
Honolulu, HI	51.0	8
Yuma, AZ	51.0	8
San Diego, CA	50.9	9
Jackson, MI	50.8	10
Lafayette – West Lafayette, IN	50.7	11
Las Vegas, NV	50.7	11
Fort Walton Beach, FL	50.6	12
Reno, NV	50.6	12
Stockton, CA	50.6	12
Merced, CA	50.5	13
New London – Norwich, CT – RI	50.5	13
Champaign – Urbana – Rantoul, IL	50.4	14
Hagerstown, MD	50.4	14
Bakersfield, CA	50.3	15
Saint Cloud, MN	50.2	16
Santa Barbara – Santa Maria – Lompoc, CA	50.2	16

[Continued]

★ 300 ★

Male Population, 1990

[Continued]

MSA	% male	Rank
Colorado Springs, CO	50.1	17
Norfolk – Virginia Beach – Newport News, VA	50.1	17
Austin, TX	50.0	18
Los Angeles – Anaheim – Riverside, CA	50.0	18
Poughkeepsie, NY	50.0	18
Richland – Kennewick – Pasco, WA	50.0	18
Biloxi – Gulfport, MS	49.9	19
Charleston, SC	49.8	20
Glens Falls, NY	49.8	20
Houston – Galveston – Brazoria, TX	49.8	20
Cheyenne, WY	49.7	21
Columbus, GA – AL	49.7	21
San Francisco – Oakland – San Jose, CA	49.7	21
Yuba City, CA	49.7	21
Gainesville, FL	49.6	22
Las Cruces, NM	49.6	22
Rapid City, SD	49.6	22
Salt Lake City – Ogden, UT	49.6	22
Visalia – Tulare – Porterville, CA	49.6	22
Yakima, WA	49.6	22
Bellingham, WA	49.5	23
Fayetteville – Springdale, AR	49.5	23
Iowa City, IA	49.5	23
Lawrence, KS	49.5	23
Seattle – Tacoma, WA	49.5	23
Sheboygan, WI	49.5	23
Fresno, CA	49.4	24
Greeley, CO	49.4	24
Melbourne – Titusville – Palm Bay, FL	49.4	24
Provo – Orem, UT	49.4	24
Santa Fe, NM	49.4	24
Boise, ID	49.3	25
Dallas – Fort Worth, TX	49.3	25
Denver – Boulder, CO	49.3	25
Fort Collins – Loveland, CO	49.3	25
Great Falls, MT	49.3	25
Huntsville, AL	49.3	25
Madison, WI	49.3	25
Naples, FL	49.3	25
Orlando, FL	49.3	25
Salem, OR	49.3	25
Utica – Rome, NY	49.3	25
Wausau, WI	49.3	25
Appleton – Oshkosh – Neenah, WI	49.2	26
Fargo – Moorhead, ND – MN	49.2	26
Lima, OH	49.2	26
Lubbock, TX	49.2	26
Panama City, FL	49.2	26
Pascagoula, MS	49.2	26
Phoenix, AZ	49.2	26
Redding, CA	49.1	27
Anderson, IN	49.0	28

[Continued]

★300★

Male Population, 1990
[Continued]

MSA	% male	Rank
Casper, WY	49.0	28
Corpus Christi, TX	49.0	28
Lincoln, NE	49.0	28
Modesto, CA	49.0	28
Portland–Vancouver, OR–WA	49.0	28
Sacramento, CA	49.0	28
Wichita, KS	49.0	28
Elkhart–Goshen, IN	48.9	29
Fort Pierce, FL	48.9	29
Hickory–Morganton, NC	48.9	29
Mansfield, OH	48.9	29
Minneapolis–Saint Paul, MN–WI	48.9	29
Muskegon, MI	48.9	29
Wichita Falls, TX	48.9	29
York, PA	48.9	29
Albuquerque, NM	48.8	30
Bismarck, ND	48.8	30
Decatur, AL	48.8	30
Green Bay, WI	48.8	30
Houma–Thibodaux, LA	48.8	30
Jacksonville, FL	48.8	30
Medford, OR	48.8	30
Portsmouth–Dover–Rochester, NH–ME	48.8	30
Terre Haute, IN	48.8	30
Tucson, AZ	48.8	30
Victoria, TX	48.8	30
Chico, CA	48.7	31
Columbus, OH	48.7	31
Duluth, MN–WI	48.7	31
Eugene–Springfield, OR	48.7	31
Grand Rapids, MI	48.7	31
Janesville–Beloit, WI	48.7	31
Oklahoma City, OK	48.7	31
Olympia, WA	48.7	31
Pensacola, FL	48.7	31
San Angelo, TX	48.7	31
Spokane, WA	48.7	31
Waco, TX	48.7	31
Washington, DC–MD–VA	48.7	31
Atlanta, GA	48.6	32
Augusta, GA–SC	48.6	32
Columbia, MO	48.6	32
Columbia, SC	48.6	32
Dothan, AL	48.6	32
Elmira, NY	48.6	32
Fitchburg–Leominster, MA	48.6	32
Fort Wayne, IN	48.6	32
Lafayette, LA	48.6	32
Lancaster, PA	48.6	32
Odessa, TX	48.6	32
San Antonio, TX	48.6	32
Abilene, TX	48.5	33
Battle Creek, MI	48.5	33
Billings, MT	48.5	33
Cedar Rapids, IA	48.5	33
Chicago–Gary–Lake County, IL–IN–WI	48.5	33

[Continued]

★300★

Male Population, 1990
[Continued]

MSA	% male	Rank
El Paso, TX	48.5	33
Fort Smith, AR–OK	48.5	33
Lake Charles, LA	48.5	33
Midland, TX	48.5	33
Omaha, NE–IA	48.5	33
Rochester, MN	48.5	33
Rockford, IL	48.5	33
Sharon, PA	48.5	33
Anniston, AL	48.4	34
Baton Rouge, LA	48.4	34
Beaumont–Port Arthur, TX	48.4	34
Binghamton, NY	48.4	34
Burlington, VT	48.4	34
Charlottesville, VA	48.4	34
Daytona Beach, FL	48.4	34
Eau Claire, WI	48.4	34
Fort Myers–Cape Coral, FL	48.4	34
Harrisburg–Lebanon–Carlisle, PA	48.4	34
Hartford–New Britain–Middletown, CT	48.4	34
Kankakee, IL	48.4	34
Lakeland–Winter Haven, FL	48.4	34
Manchester, NH	48.4	34
Pine Bluff, AR	48.4	34
Sioux City, IA–NE	48.4	34
Tulsa, OK	48.4	34
Tuscaloosa, AL	48.4	34
Williamsport, PA	48.4	34
Worcester, MA	48.4	34
Albany–Schenectady–Troy, NY	48.3	35
Allentown–Bethlehem–Easton, PA–NJ	48.3	35
Baltimore, MD	48.3	35
Bangor, ME	48.3	35
Davenport–Rock Island–Moline, IA–IL	48.3	35
Dubuque, IA	48.3	35
Jamestown–Dunkirk, NY	48.3	35
Kansas City, MO–KS	48.3	35
Lansing–East Lansing, MI	48.3	35
Reading, PA	48.3	35
Rochester, NY	48.3	35
Athens, GA	48.2	36
Bloomington, IN	48.2	36
Charlotte–Gastonia–Rock Hill, NC–SC	48.2	36
Detroit–Ann Arbor, MI	48.2	36
Erie, PA	48.2	36
Greenville–Spartanburg, SC	48.2	36
Johnson City–Kingsport–Bristol, TN–VA	48.2	36
McAllen–Edinburg–Mission, TX	48.2	36
Milwaukee–Racine, WI	48.2	36
Nashville, TN	48.2	36
Raleigh–Durham, NC	48.2	36
Saginaw–Bay City–Midland, MI	48.2	36

[Continued]

★300★

Male Population, 1990
[Continued]

MSA	% male	Rank
South Bend – Mishawaka, IN	48.2	36
Syracuse, NY	48.2	36
Amarillo, TX	48.1	37
Boston – Lawrence – Salem, MA – NH	48.1	37
Dayton – Springfield, OH	48.1	37
Joplin, MO	48.1	37
Lewiston – Auburn, ME	48.1	37
Longview – Marshall, TX	48.1	37
Ocala, FL	48.1	37
Sioux Falls, SD	48.1	37
Texarkana, TX – Texarkana, AR	48.1	37
Topeka, KS	48.1	37
West Palm Beach – Boca Raton – Delray Beach, FL	48.1	37
Atlantic City, NJ	48.0	38
Benton Harbor, MI	48.0	38
Canton, OH	48.0	38
Cincinnati – Hamilton, OH – KY – IN	48.0	38
Indianapolis, IN	48.0	38
Johnstown, PA	48.0	38
Kalamazoo, MI	48.0	38
Knoxville, TN	48.0	38
La Crosse, WI	48.0	38
Laredo, TX	48.0	38
Lexington-Fayette, KY	48.0	38
Peoria, IL	48.0	38
Philadelphia – Wilmington – Trenton, PA – NJ – DE – MD	48.0	38
Pittsfield, MA	48.0	38
Pueblo, CO	48.0	38
Savannah, GA	48.0	38
Springfield, MO	48.0	38
Tyler, TX	48.0	38
Alexandria, LA	47.9	39
Brownsville – Harlingen, TX	47.9	39
Little Rock – North Little Rock, AR	47.9	39
New Haven – Meriden, CT	47.9	39
Toledo, OH	47.9	39
Des Moines, IA	47.8	40
Enid, OK	47.8	40
Evansville, IN – KY	47.8	40
Flint, MI	47.8	40
Florence, AL	47.8	40
Greensboro – Winston-Salem – High Point, NC	47.8	40
Kokomo, IN	47.8	40
Miami – Fort Lauderdale, FL	47.8	40
Montgomery, AL	47.8	40
Parkersburg – Marietta, WV – OH	47.8	40
Portland, ME	47.8	40
Providence – Pawtucket – Fall River, RI – MA	47.8	40
Saint Louis, MO – IL	47.8	40
Sherman – Denison, TX	47.8	40
Tallahassee, FL	47.8	40
Waterbury, CT	47.8	40

[Continued]

★300★

Male Population, 1990
[Continued]

MSA	% male	Rank
Waterloo – Cedar Falls, IA	47.8	40
Bloomington – Normal, IL	47.7	41
Cleveland – Akron – Lorain, OH	47.7	41
Huntington – Ashland, WV – KY – OH	47.7	41
Louisville, KY – IN	47.7	41
Memphis, TN – AR – MS	47.7	41
Mobile, AL	47.7	41
New York – Northern New Jersey – Long Island, NY – NJ – CT	47.7	41
Owensboro, KY	47.7	41
Steubenville – Weirton, OH – WV	47.7	41
Tampa – Saint Petersburg – Clearwater, FL	47.7	41
Albany, GA	47.6	42
Anderson, SC	47.6	42
Buffalo – Niagara Falls, NY	47.6	42
Chattanooga, TN – GA	47.6	42
Richmond – Petersburg, VA	47.6	42
Charleston, WV	47.5	43
Decatur, IL	47.5	43
Macon – Warner Robins, GA	47.5	43
New Bedford, MA	47.5	43
New Orleans, LA	47.5	43
Scranton – Wilkes-Barre, PA	47.5	43
Youngstown – Warren, OH	47.5	43
Asheville, NC	47.4	44
Muncie, IN	47.4	44
Wilmington, NC	47.4	44
Birmingham, AL	47.3	45
Cumberland, MD – WV	47.3	45
Danville, VA	47.3	45
Florence, SC	47.3	45
Lynchburg, VA	47.3	45
Saint Joseph, MO	47.3	45
Bradenton, FL	47.2	46
Burlington, NC	47.2	46
Jackson, MS	47.2	46
Jackson, TN	47.2	46
Pittsburgh – Beaver Valley, PA	47.2	46
Roanoke, VA	47.2	46
Shreveport, LA	47.2	46
Wheeling, WV – OH	47.2	46
Altoona, PA	47.1	47
Gadsden, AL	47.1	47
Springfield, IL	47.1	47
Springfield, MA	47.1	47
Monroe, LA	47.0	48
Sarasota, FL	46.9	49

Source: U.S. Bureau of the Census, Data User Services Division, *1990 Census of Population and Housing,* Summary Tape File 3C, United States Summary, CD-ROM, February 1992.

★301★

General Population

Most Populous Cities in the U.S., 1990

[In millions]

City	Population	Rank
New York, NY	7.3	1
Los Angeles, CA	3.5	2
Chicago, IL	2.8	3
Houston, TX	1.6	4
Philadelphia, PA	1.6	4

Source: State Government News, p. 29, October 1991. *Notes:* Cities with the same population were ranked equally by the editors of *City and Metropolitan Area Rankings*.

★302★

General Population

Total Population, 1990

MSA	Number	Rank
New York – Northern New Jersey – Long Island, NY – NJ – CT	18,087,251	1
Los Angeles – Anaheim – Riverside, CA	14,531,529	2
Chicago – Gary – Lake County, IL – IN – WI	8,065,633	3
San Francisco – Oakland – San Jose, CA	6,253,311	4
Philadelphia – Wilmington – Trenton, PA – NJ – DE – MD	5,899,345	5
Detroit – Ann Arbor, MI	4,665,236	6
Boston – Lawrence – Salem, MA – NH	4,171,747	7
Washington, DC – MD – VA	3,923,574	8
Dallas – Fort Worth, TX	3,885,415	9
Houston – Galveston – Brazoria, TX	3,711,043	10
Miami – Fort Lauderdale, FL	3,192,582	11
Atlanta, GA	2,833,511	12
Cleveland – Akron – Lorain, OH	2,759,823	13
Seattle – Tacoma, WA	2,559,164	14
San Diego, CA	2,498,016	15
Minneapolis – Saint Paul, MN – WI	2,464,124	16
Saint Louis, MO – IL	2,444,099	17
Baltimore, MD	2,382,172	18
Pittsburgh – Beaver Valley, PA	2,242,798	19
Phoenix, AZ	2,122,101	20
Tampa – Saint Petersburg – Clearwater, FL	2,067,959	21
Denver – Boulder, CO	1,848,319	22
Cincinnati – Hamilton, OH – KY – IN	1,744,124	23
Milwaukee – Racine, WI	1,607,183	24
Kansas City, MO – KS	1,566,280	25
Sacramento, CA	1,481,102	26
Portland – Vancouver, OR – WA	1,477,895	27
Norfolk – Virginia Beach – Newport News, VA	1,396,107	28
Columbus, OH	1,377,419	29
San Antonio, TX	1,302,099	30
Indianapolis, IN	1,249,822	31
New Orleans, LA	1,238,816	32
Buffalo – Niagara Falls, NY	1,189,288	33

[Continued]

★302★

Total Population, 1990

[Continued]

MSA	Number	Rank
Charlotte – Gastonia – Rock Hill, NC – SC	1,162,093	34
Providence – Pawtucket – Fall River, RI – MA	1,141,525	35
Hartford – New Britain – Middletown, CT	1,085,895	36
Orlando, FL	1,072,748	37
Salt Lake City – Ogden, UT	1,072,227	38
Rochester, NY	1,002,410	39
Nashville, TN	985,026	40
Memphis, TN – AR – MS	981,747	41
Oklahoma City, OK	958,839	42
Louisville, KY – IN	952,662	43
Dayton – Springfield, OH	951,270	44
Greensboro – Winston-Salem – High Point, NC	942,091	45
Birmingham, AL	907,810	46
Jacksonville, FL	906,727	47
Albany – Schenectady – Troy, NY	874,304	48
Richmond – Petersburg, VA	865,640	49
West Palm Beach – Boca Raton – Delray Beach, FL	863,518	50
Honolulu, HI	836,231	51
Austin, TX	781,572	52
Las Vegas, NV	741,459	53
Raleigh – Durham, NC	735,480	54
Scranton – Wilkes-Barre, PA	734,175	55
Tulsa, OK	708,954	56
Grand Rapids, MI	688,399	57
Allentown – Bethlehem – Easton, PA – NJ	686,688	58
Fresno, CA	667,490	59
Tucson, AZ	666,880	60
Syracuse, NY	659,864	61
Greenville – Spartanburg, SC	640,861	62
Omaha, NE – IA	618,262	63
Toledo, OH	614,128	64
Knoxville, TN	604,816	65
El Paso, TX	591,610	66
Harrisburg – Lebanon – Carlisle, PA	587,986	67
Bakersfield, CA	543,477	68
New Haven – Meriden, CT	530,240	69
Springfield, MA	529,484	70
Baton Rouge, LA	528,264	71
Little Rock – North Little Rock, AR	513,117	72
Charleston, SC	506,875	73
Youngstown – Warren, OH	492,619	74
Wichita, KS	485,270	75
Stockton, CA	480,628	76
Albuquerque, NM	480,577	77
Mobile, AL	476,923	78
Columbia, SC	453,331	79
Worcester, MA	436,941	80
Johnson City – Kingsport – Bristol, TN – VA	436,047	81
Chattanooga, TN – GA	433,210	82

[Continued]

★302★

Total Population, 1990
[Continued]

MSA	Number	Rank
Lansing – East Lansing, MI	432,674	83
Flint, MI	430,459	84
Lancaster, PA	422,822	85
York, PA	417,848	86
Lakeland – Winter Haven, FL	405,382	87
Saginaw – Bay City – Midland, MI	399,320	88
Melbourne – Titusville – Palm Bay, FL	398,978	89
Colorado Springs, CO	397,014	90
Augusta, GA – SC	396,809	91
Jackson, MS	395,396	92
Canton, OH	394,106	93
Des Moines, IA	392,928	94
McAllen – Edinburg – Mission, TX	383,545	95
Daytona Beach, FL	370,712	96
Modesto, CA	370,522	97
Santa Barbara – Santa Maria – Lompoc, CA	369,608	98
Madison, WI	367,085	99
Fort Wayne, IN	363,811	100
Spokane, WA	361,364	101
Beaumont – Port Arthur, TX	361,226	102
Salinas – Seaside – Monterey, CA	355,660	103
Davenport – Rock Island – Moline, IA – IL	350,861	104
Corpus Christi, TX	349,894	105
Lexington-Fayette, KY	348,428	106
Pensacola, FL	344,406	107
Peoria, IL	339,172	108
Reading, PA	336,523	109
Fort Myers – Cape Coral, FL	335,113	110
Shreveport, LA	334,341	111
Atlantic City, NJ	319,416	112
Utica – Rome, NY	316,633	113
Appleton – Oshkosh – Neenah, WI	315,121	114
Huntington – Ashland, WV – KY – OH	312,529	115
Visalia – Tulare – Porterville, CA	311,921	116
Montgomery, AL	292,517	117
Rockford, IL	283,719	118
Eugene – Springfield, OR	282,912	119
Macon – Warner Robins, GA	281,103	120
Evansville, IN – KY	278,990	121
Salem, OR	278,024	122
Sarasota, FL	277,776	123
Erie, PA	275,572	124
Fayetteville, NC	274,566	125
New London – Norwich, CT – RI	266,819	126
Binghamton, NY	264,497	127
Provo – Orem, UT	263,590	128
Brownsville – Harlingen, TX	260,120	129
Poughkeepsie, NY	259,462	130
Killeen – Temple, TX	255,301	131
Reno, NV	254,667	132
Fort Pierce, FL	251,071	133
Charleston, WV	250,454	134
South Bend – Mishawaka, IN	247,052	135

[Continued]

★302★

Total Population, 1990
[Continued]

MSA	Number	Rank
Columbus, GA – AL	243,072	136
Savannah, GA	242,622	137
Johnstown, PA	241,247	138
Springfield, MO	240,593	139
Duluth, MN – WI	239,971	140
Huntsville, AL	238,912	141
Tallahassee, FL	233,598	142
Anchorage, AK	226,338	143
Roanoke, VA	224,477	144
Portsmouth – Dover – Rochester, NH – ME	223,692	145
Kalamazoo, MI	223,411	146
Lubbock, TX	222,636	147
Hickory – Morganton, NC	221,700	148
Waterbury, CT	221,629	149
Portland, ME	215,481	150
Lincoln, NE	213,641	151
Bradenton, FL	211,707	152
Lafayette, LA	208,740	153
Boise, ID	205,775	154
Gainesville, FL	204,111	155
Biloxi – Gulfport, MS	197,125	156
Ocala, FL	194,833	157
Green Bay, WI	194,594	158
Saint Cloud, MN	190,921	159
Bremerton, WA	189,731	160
Springfield, IL	189,550	161
Waco, TX	189,123	162
Yakima, WA	188,823	163
Amarillo, TX	187,547	164
Fort Collins – Loveland, CO	186,136	165
Houma – Thibodaux, LA	182,842	166
Chico, CA	182,120	167
Merced, CA	178,403	168
Fort Smith, AR – OK	175,911	169
New Bedford, MA	175,705	170
Asheville, NC	174,821	171
Champaign – Urbana – Rantoul, IL	173,025	172
Clarksville – Hopkinsville, TN – KY	169,439	173
Cedar Rapids, IA	168,767	174
Lake Charles, LA	168,134	175
Longview – Marshall, TX	162,431	176
Benton Harbor, MI	161,378	177
Olympia, WA	161,238	178
Topeka, KS	160,976	179
Wheeling, WV – OH	159,301	180
Muskegon, MI	158,983	181
Athens, GA	156,267	182
Elkhart – Goshen, IN	156,198	183
Lima, OH	154,340	184
Fargo – Moorhead, ND – MN	153,296	185
Naples, FL	152,099	186
Tyler, TX	151,309	187
Tuscaloosa, AL	150,522	188
Richland – Kennewick – Pasco, WA	150,033	189
Jacksonville, NC	149,838	190
Jackson, MI	149,756	191

[Continued]

★302★
Total Population, 1990
[Continued]

MSA	Number	Rank
Parkersburg – Marietta, WV – OH	149,169	192
Manchester, NH	147,867	193
Redding, CA	147,036	194
Waterloo – Cedar Falls, IA	146,611	195
Medford, OR	146,389	196
Anderson, SC	145,196	197
Fort Walton Beach, FL	143,776	198
Steubenville – Weirton, OH – WV	142,523	199
Lynchburg, VA	142,199	200
Monroe, LA	142,191	201
Jamestown – Dunkirk, NY	141,895	202
Janesville – Beloit, WI	139,510	203
Eau Claire, WI	137,543	204
Battle Creek, MI	135,982	205
Las Cruces, NM	135,510	206
Joplin, MO	134,910	207
Laredo, TX	133,239	208
Greeley, CO	131,821	209
Alexandria, LA	131,556	210
Decatur, AL	131,556	210
Burlington, VT	131,441	211
Florence, AL	131,327	212
Charlottesville, VA	131,107	213
Dothan, AL	130,964	214
Terre Haute, IN	130,812	215
Anderson, IN	130,669	216
Lafayette – West Lafayette, IN	130,598	217
Altoona, PA	130,542	218
Bloomington – Normal, IL	129,180	219
Bellingham, WA	127,780	220
Panama City, FL	126,994	221
Mansfield, OH	126,137	222
Sioux Falls, SD	123,809	223
State College, PA	123,786	224
Pueblo, CO	123,051	225
Yuba City, CA	122,643	226
Wichita Falls, TX	122,378	227
Bryan – College Station, TX	121,862	228
Hagerstown, MD	121,393	229
Sharon, PA	121,003	230
Wilmington, NC	120,284	231
Texarkana, TX – Texarkana, AR	120,132	232
Muncie, IN	119,659	233
Abilene, TX	119,655	234
Odessa, TX	118,934	235
Williamsport, PA	118,710	236
Glens Falls, NY	118,539	237
Decatur, IL	117,206	238
Santa Fe, NM	117,043	239
Anniston, AL	116,034	240
Wausau, WI	115,400	241
Pascagoula, MS	115,243	242
Sioux City, IA – NE	115,018	243
Florence, SC	114,344	244
Billings, MT	113,419	245
Fayetteville – Springdale, AR	113,409	246
Albany, GA	112,561	247

[Continued]

★302★
Total Population, 1990
[Continued]

MSA	Number	Rank
Columbia, MO	112,379	248
Lawton, OK	111,486	249
Bloomington, IN	108,978	250
Danville, VA	108,711	251
Burlington, NC	108,213	252
Yuma, AZ	106,895	253
Midland, TX	106,611	254
Rochester, MN	106,470	255
Sheboygan, WI	103,877	256
Fitchburg – Leominster, MA	102,797	257
Cumberland, MD – WV	101,643	258
Gadsden, AL	99,840	259
San Angelo, TX	98,458	260
La Crosse, WI	97,904	261
Kokomo, IN	96,946	262
Kankakee, IL	96,255	263
Iowa City, IA	96,119	264
Elmira, NY	95,195	265
Sherman – Denison, TX	95,021	266
Bangor, ME	88,704	267
Lewiston – Auburn, ME	88,074	268
Owensboro, KY	87,189	269
Dubuque, IA	86,403	270
Pine Bluff, AR	85,487	271
Bismarck, ND	83,831	272
Saint Joseph, MO	83,083	273
Lawrence, KS	81,798	274
Rapid City, SD	81,343	275
Pittsfield, MA	79,271	276
Jackson, TN	77,982	277
Great Falls, MT	77,691	278
Victoria, TX	74,361	279
Cheyenne, WY	73,142	280
Grand Forks, ND	70,683	281
Casper, WY	61,226	282
Enid, OK	56,735	283

Source: U.S. Bureau of the Census, Data User Services Division, *1990 Census of Population and Housing*, Summary Tape File 3C, United States Summary, CD- ROM, February 1992.

★303★
General Population
Total Population, 1990: Residing on Farms
[Table shows the top 50 areas]

MSA	% residing on farms	Rank
Saint Cloud, MN	7.1836	1
Wausau, WI	6.9731	2
Dubuque, IA	5.9732	3
Greeley, CO	5.6653	4
Eau Claire, WI	5.5008	5
Merced, CA	4.9848	6
Yakima, WA	4.8919	7
Lima, OH	4.4059	8
Lancaster, PA	4.3002	9

[Continued]

★303★
Total Population, 1990: Residing on Farms
[Continued]

MSA	% residing on farms	Rank
Iowa City, IA	4.2125	10
Fayetteville – Springdale, AR	3.9336	11
Joplin, MO	3.9256	12
Bismarck, ND	3.8399	13
Waterloo – Cedar Falls, IA	3.8346	14
Visalia – Tulare – Porterville, CA	3.7506	15
Elkhart – Goshen, IN	3.7491	16
Owensboro, KY	3.7195	17
Kokomo, IN	3.6845	18
Salem, OR	3.5137	19
Yuba City, CA	3.4123	20
Modesto, CA	3.3434	21
Kankakee, IL	3.3390	22
Rochester, MN	3.3174	23
Danville, VA	3.3171	24
Fargo – Moorhead, ND – MN	3.2343	25
Sioux City, IA – NE	3.1899	26
Enid, OK	3.1726	27
Bloomington – Normal, IL	3.0980	28
Jamestown – Dunkirk, NY	3.0142	29
Johnson City – Kingsport – Bristol, TN – VA	2.9951	30
Appleton – Oshkosh – Neenah, WI	2.9633	31
Lexington-Fayette, KY	2.9211	32
Sheboygan, WI	2.8909	33
Bellingham, WA	2.8142	34
Janesville – Beloit, WI	2.7690	35
Fresno, CA	2.7626	36
Florence, SC	2.6858	37
Fort Wayne, IN	2.6813	38
Sioux Falls, SD	2.6185	39
Terre Haute, IN	2.4822	40
Davenport – Rock Island – Moline, IA – IL	2.4409	41
Richland – Kennewick – Pasco, WA	2.4348	42
Lansing – East Lansing, MI	2.4286	43
Mansfield, OH	2.3617	44
Great Falls, MT	2.3413	45
Decatur, AL	2.2135	46
Clarksville – Hopkinsville, TN – KY	2.1955	47
Stockton, CA	2.1507	48
La Crosse, WI	2.1480	49
Peoria, IL	2.1364	50

Source: U.S. Bureau of the Census, Data User Services Division, *1990 Census of Population and Housing*, Summary Tape File 3C, United States Summary, CD-ROM, February 1992.

★304★
General Population
Total Population, 1990: Residing in Nonfarm Areas

[Table shows the top 50 areas]

MSA	% not residing on farms	Rank
Ocala, FL	59.3	1
Johnstown, PA	57.4	2
Hickory – Morganton, NC	54.8	3
York, PA	51.3	4
Glens Falls, NY	50.8	5
Anderson, SC	50.2	6
Decatur, AL	47.1	7
Athens, GA	46.9	8
Sharon, PA	46.9	8
Danville, VA	46.8	9
Jackson, MI	46.1	10
Florence, AL	45.5	11
Florence, SC	45.0	12
Charlottesville, VA	44.7	13
Jamestown – Dunkirk, NY	44.6	14
Benton Harbor, MI	44.3	15
Williamsport, PA	44.2	16
Parkersburg – Marietta, WV – OH	43.7	17
Tyler, TX	43.2	18
Poughkeepsie, NY	43.1	19
Hagerstown, MD	42.5	20
Steubenville – Weirton, OH – WV	42.5	20
Huntington – Ashland, WV – KY – OH	42.4	21
Saint Cloud, MN	42.3	22
Johnson City – Kingsport – Bristol, TN – VA	41.6	23
State College, PA	41.0	24
Cumberland, MD – WV	40.0	25
Wheeling, WV – OH	40.0	25
Greensboro – Winston-Salem – High Point, NC	39.7	26
Olympia, WA	39.6	27
Harrisburg – Lebanon – Carlisle, PA	38.3	28
Knoxville, TN	38.2	29
Lancaster, PA	38.1	30
Bellingham, WA	37.9	31
Redding, CA	37.9	31
Texarkana, TX – Texarkana, AR	37.9	31
Utica – Rome, NY	37.9	31
Asheville, NC	37.0	32
Greenville – Spartanburg, SC	37.0	32
Joplin, MO	36.9	33
Portland, ME	36.8	34
Reading, PA	36.7	35
Wausau, WI	36.7	35
Fort Smith, AR – OK	36.5	36
Scranton – Wilkes-Barre, PA	36.2	37
Sherman – Denison, TX	36.1	38
Binghamton, NY	35.6	39
Portsmouth – Dover – Rochester, NH – ME	35.6	39

[Continued]

★304★

Total Population, 1990: Residing in Nonfarm Areas

[Continued]

MSA	% not residing on farms	Rank
Houma–Thibodaux, LA	34.8	40
Bremerton, WA	34.2	41

Source: U.S. Bureau of the Census, Data User Services Division, *1990 Census of Population and Housing*, Summary Tape File 3C, United States Summary, CD- ROM, February 1992.

★305★

General Population

Total Population, 1990: Residing Inside Urbanized Areas

[Table shows the top 50 areas]

MSA	% residing in urban areas	Rank
Miami–Fort Lauderdale, FL	98.8	1
Anchorage, AK	98.0	2
Salt Lake City–Ogden, UT	97.8	3
Albuquerque, NM	95.6	4
El Paso, TX	95.1	5
Los Angeles–Anaheim– Riverside, CA	95.0	6
Norfolk–Virginia Beach– Newport News, VA	94.8	7
Odessa, TX	94.7	8
Las Vegas, NV	94.0	9
San Diego, CA	94.0	9
Chicago–Gary–Lake County, IL–IN–WI	93.7	10
New York–Northern New Jersey–Long Island, NY– NJ–CT	93.7	10
Phoenix, AZ	93.7	10
San Francisco–Oakland–San Jose, CA	93.6	11
Laredo, TX	92.8	12
West Palm Beach–Boca Raton– Delray Beach, FL	91.7	13
Denver–Boulder, CO	90.3	14
Lincoln, NE	90.1	15
Columbus, GA–AL	89.9	16
Melbourne–Titusville–Palm Bay, FL	89.7	17
Abilene, TX	89.5	18
Honolulu, HI	89.3	19
Colorado Springs, CO	88.9	20
Bradenton, FL	88.7	21
Santa Barbara–Santa Maria– Lompoc, CA	88.7	21
Bryan–College Station, TX	88.3	22
Omaha, NE–IA	88.0	23
Orlando, FL	88.0	23
Sarasota, FL	87.8	24
New Orleans, LA	87.7	25
Seattle–Tacoma, WA	87.6	26

[Continued]

★305★

Total Population, 1990: Residing Inside Urbanized Areas

[Continued]

MSA	% residing in urban areas	Rank
Springfield, MA	87.6	26
Saint Joseph, MO	87.3	27
Cleveland–Akron–Lorain, OH	87.2	28
Midland, TX	87.2	28
Washington, DC–MD–VA	87.0	29
San Angelo, TX	86.8	30
Tucson, AZ	86.8	30
San Antonio, TX	86.7	31
South Bend–Mishawaka, IN	86.7	31
Fayetteville, NC	86.6	32
Philadelphia–Wilmington– Trenton, PA–NJ–DE–MD	86.6	32
Pueblo, CO	86.4	33
Dallas–Fort Worth, TX	86.1	34
Detroit–Ann Arbor, MI	85.8	35
Casper, WY	85.4	36
New Haven–Meriden, CT	85.2	37
Tampa–Saint Petersburg– Clearwater, FL	85.2	37
Providence–Pawtucket–Fall River, RI–MA	85.1	38
Lubbock, TX	84.5	39

Source: U.S. Bureau of the Census, Data User Services Division, *1990 Census of Population and Housing*, Summary Tape File 3C, United States Summary, CD- ROM, February 1992.

★306★

General Population

Total Population, 1990: Residing Outside Urbanized Areas

[Table shows the top 50 areas]

MSA	% not residing in urban areas	Rank
Enid, OK	79.38	1
Jamestown–Dunkirk, NY	52.40	2
Chico, CA	45.36	3
Visalia–Tulare–Porterville, CA	41.94	4
Merced, CA	39.08	5
Houma–Thibodaux, LA	28.62	6
Bakersfield, CA	28.06	7
Modesto, CA	23.54	8
Fort Collins–Loveland, CO	23.38	9
Santa Fe, NM	22.01	10
Longview–Marshall, TX	21.96	11
Fort Myers–Cape Coral, FL	20.36	12
Stockton, CA	19.93	13
Dothan, AL	19.80	14
Lima, OH	19.42	15
Medford, OR	19.41	16
Duluth, MN–WI	18.54	17
Atlantic City, NJ	18.31	18
Clarksville–Hopkinsville, TN–KY	17.59	19
Lexington-Fayette, KY	17.52	20

[Continued]

★306★

Total Population, 1990: Residing Outside Urbanized Areas

[Continued]

MSA	% not residing in urban areas	Rank
Yakima, WA	17.15	21
Salem, OR	16.89	22
Yuma, AZ	16.59	23
Nashville, TN	16.27	24
Wichita Falls, TX	15.80	25
Parkersburg – Marietta, WV – OH	15.73	26
Little Rock – North Little Rock, AR	15.61	27
Naples, FL	15.52	28
Fresno, CA	15.15	29
Champaign – Urbana – Rantoul, IL	14.80	30
Joplin, MO	14.61	31
Beaumont – Port Arthur, TX	14.28	32
Anniston, AL	13.42	33
Wichita, KS	13.40	34
Madison, WI	13.34	35
Grand Forks, ND	13.22	36
Portsmouth – Dover – Rochester, NH – ME	12.79	37
Bellingham, WA	12.76	38
Austin, TX	12.68	39
Hickory – Morganton, NC	12.61	40
Anderson, SC	12.48	41
Lancaster, PA	12.48	41
Battle Creek, MI	12.47	42
Lakeland – Winter Haven, FL	12.44	43
Sharon, PA	12.41	44
Des Moines, IA	12.28	45
Corpus Christi, TX	12.13	46
Tulsa, OK	11.90	47
Dayton – Springfield, OH	11.89	48
Saint Cloud, MN	11.85	49

Source: U.S. Bureau of the Census, Data User Services Division, *1990 Census of Population and Housing,* Summary Tape File 3C, United States Summary, CD- ROM, February 1992.

★307★

General Population

Population, 1992: The 25 Least Populous Places

Data refer to cities with populations of 200,000 or more.

City/MSA	Number	Rank
Mobile, AL	201,896	1
Richmond, VA	202,263	2
Stockton, CA	219,621	3
Raleigh, NC	220,524	4
Akron, OH	223,621	5
Baton Rouge, LA	224,704	6
Jersey City, NJ	228,575	7
Lexington-Fayette, KY	232,562	8
Rochester, NY	234,163	9
Saint Petersburg, FL	235,306	10
Riverside, CA	238,601	11
Aurora, CO	239,626	12
Anchorage, AK	245,866	13

[Continued]

★307★

Population, 1992: The 25 Least Populous Places

[Continued]

City/MSA	Number	Rank
Norfolk, VA	253,768	14
Birmingham, AL	264,984	15
Corpus Christi, TX	266,412	16
Newark, NJ	267,849	17
Saint Paul, MN	268,266	18
Louisville, KY	271,038	19
Anaheim, CA	274,162	20
Arlington, TX	275,907	21
Tampa, FL	284,737	22
Santa Ana, CA	288,024	23
Las Vegas, NV	295,516	24
Colorado Springs, CO	295,815	25

Source: U.S. Department of Commerce, Economics and Statistics Administration, Bureau of the Census, *County and City Data Book 1994: A Statistical Abstract Supplement,* Washington, D.C.: U.S. Government Printing Office, August 1994, p. xxvii.

★308★

General Population

Population, 1992: The 25 Most Populous Places

Data refer to cities with populations of 200,000 or more.

City/MSA	Number	Rank
New York, NY	7,311,966	1
Los Angeles, CA	3,489,779	2
Chicago, IL	2,768,483	3
Houston, TX	1,690,180	4
Philadelphia, PA	1,552,572	5
San Diego, CA	1,148,851	6
Dallas, TX	1,022,497	7
Phoenix, AZ	1,012,230	8
Detroit, MI	1,012,110	9
San Antonio, TX	966,437	10
San Jose, CA	801,331	11
Indianapolis, IN	746,538	12
San Francisco, CA	728,921	13
Baltimore, MD	726,096	14
Jacksonville, FL	661,177	15
Columbus, OH	642,987	16
Milwaukee, WI	617,043	17
Memphis, TN	610,275	18
Washington, DC	585,221	19
Boston, MA	551,675	20
El Paso, TX	543,813	21
Seattle, WA	519,598	22
Cleveland, OH	502,539	23
Nashville-Davidson, TN	495,012	24
Austin, TX	492,329	25

Source: U.S. Department of Commerce, Economics and Statistics Administration, Bureau of the Census, *County and City Data Book 1994: A Statistical Abstract Supplement,* Washington, D.C.: U.S. Government Printing Office, August 1994, p. xxvii.

★309★

Older American Population

Elderly Population (County Estimates), 1991, By Age for Counties With A Minimum of 20% Elderly: Number of Persons Age 65 and Older

County	Number	Rank
Pinellas County, FL	225,437	1
Palm Beach County, FL	214,992	2
Pasco County, FL	92,474	3
Sarasota County, FL	91,802	4
Lee County, FL	85,696	5
Manatee County, FL	60,795	6
Lake County, FL	43,392	7
Charlotte County, FL	39,357	8
Hernando County, FL	32,611	9
Citrus County, FL	30,405	10
Martin County, FL	28,358	11
Indian River County, FL	25,088	12
Highlands County, FL	23,346	13
Baxter County, AR	9,360	14
Kerr County, TX	9,163	15
Flagler County, FL	7,896	16
Roscommon County, MI	5,140	17
Gogebic County, MI	4,391	18
Gillespie County, TX	4,297	19
Llano County, TX	4,015	20
Sharp County, AR	3,968	21
Bosque County, TX	3,764	22
Polk County, NC	3,636	23
Iron County, MI	3,575	24
Sierra County, NM	3,218	25

Source: U.S. Bureau of the Census, Current Population Reports, Special Studies, P23-190, *65+ In the United States,* Washington, D.C.: U.S. Government Printing Office, 1996, pp. 8-17. Primary source: U.S. Bureau of the Census, Population Division, *Estimates of the Population of Counties, by Age, Sex, and Race: 1991,* PE-9, November 1993. *Note:* Data are shown only for the top 25 areas.

★310★

Older American Population

Elderly Population (County Estimates), 1991, By Age for Counties With A Minimum of 20% Elderly: Number of Persons Age 85 and Older

County	Number	Rank
Pinellas County, FL	27,857	1
Palm Beach County, FL	19,181	2
Sarasota County, FL	9,076	3
Pasco County, FL	6,918	4
Manatee County, FL	6,156	5
Lee County, FL	6,117	6
Lake County, FL	3,515	7
Charlotte County, FL	2,829	8
Martin County, FL	2,040	9
Citrus County, FL	1,969	10
Indian River County, FL	1,757	11
Hernando County, FL	1,678	12
Highlands County, FL	1,667	13
Kerr County, TX	916	14
Baxter County, AR	754	15
Gillespie County, TX	559	16

[Continued]

★310★

Elderly Population (County Estimates), 1991, By Age for Counties With A Minimum of 20% Elderly: Number of Persons Age 85 and Older

[Continued]

County	Number	Rank
Cloud County, KS	481	17
Gogebic County, MI	466	18
Bosque County, TX	436	19
Polk County, NC	408	20
Flagler County, FL	345	21
Llano County, TX	341	22
Sharp County, AR	335	23
Cedar County, MO	323	24
Coleman County, TX	323	24

Source: U.S. Bureau of the Census, Current Population Reports, Special Studies, P23-190, *65+ In the United States,* Washington, D.C.: U.S. Government Printing Office, 1996, pp. 8-17. Primary source: U.S. Bureau of the Census, Population Division, *Estimates of the Population of Counties, by Age, Sex, and Race: 1991,* PE-9, November 1993. *Note:* Data are shown only for the top 25 areas.

★311★

Older American Population

Elderly Population (County Estimates), 1991, By Age for Counties With A Minimum of 20% Elderly: Percentage of Persons Age 65 and Older

County	Percentage	Rank
Kalawao County, HI	34.6	1
Llano County, TX	34.2	2
Charlotte County, FL	33.8	3
Highlands County, FL	33.3	4
Pasco County, FL	32.4	5
Sarasota County, FL	31.9	6
Hernando County, FL	30.7	7
Sierra County, NM	30.7	7
Citrus County, FL	30.2	8
Keweenaw County, MI	30.2	8
McIntosh County, ND	30.0	9
Elk County, KS	29.9	10
Baxter County, AR	29.4	11
Pawnee County, NE	28.7	12
Smith County, KS	28.3	13
Hickory County, MO	28.2	14
Manatee County, FL	28.1	15
Republic County, KS	28.1	15
McPherson County, SD	27.9	16
Hamilton County, TX	27.7	17
Lake County, FL	27.5	18
Osborne County, KS	27.5	18
Martin County, FL	27.4	19
Furnas County, NE	27.3	20
Hooker County, NE	27.3	20

Source: U.S. Bureau of the Census, Current Population Reports, Special Studies, P23-190, *65+ In the United States,* Washington, D.C.: U.S. Government Printing Office, 1996, pp. 8-17. Primary source: U.S. Bureau of the Census, Population Division, *Estimates of the Population of Counties, by Age, Sex, and Race: 1991,* PE-9, November 1993. *Note:* Data are shown only for the top 25 areas.

★312★

Older American Population

Elderly Population (County Estimates), 1991, By Age for Counties With A Minimum of 20% Elderly: Percentage of Persons Age 85 and Older

County	Percentage	Rank
Kalawao County, HI	5.4	1
Smith County, KS	5.4	1
Farnas County, NE	5.2	2
Lincoln County, KS	5.0	3
Hooker County, NE	4.7	4
Nelson County, ND	4.7	4
Decatur County, KS	4.6	5
Osborne County, KS	4.6	5
Elk County, KS	4.5	6
Gentry County, MO	4.5	6
Thayer County, NE	4.5	6
Cloud County, KS	4.4	7
Republic County, KS	4.4	7
Webster County, NE	4.4	7
Worth County, MO	4.4	7
Franklin County, NE	4.3	8
Comanche County, KS	4.2	9
McIntosh County, ND	4.2	9
Washington County, KS	4.2	9
Wayne County, IA	4.2	9
Bedford (City), VA	4.1	10
Boyd County, NE	4.1	10
Clifton Forge (City), VA	4.0	11
Hamilton County, TX	4.0	11
Pawnee County, NE	4.0	11

Source: U.S. Bureau of the Census, Current Population Reports, Special Studies, P23-190, *65+ In the United States,* Washington, D.C.: U.S. Government Printing Office, 1996, pp. 8-17. Primary source: U.S. Bureau of the Census, Population Division, *Estimates of the Population of Counties, by Age, Sex, and Race: 1991,* PE-9, November 1993. *Note:* Data are shown only for the top 25 areas.

★313★

Older American Population

Elderly Population (County Estimates), 1991, By Age: Number of Persons Age 65 and Older

Data refer to the population in counties with 10,000 or more elderly citizens.

County	Number	Rank
Los Angeles County, CA	865,309	1
Hudson County, NJ	704,300	2
Cook County, IL	632,961	3
Queens County, NY	283,449	4
San Diego County, CA	278,661	5
Kings County, NY	278,058	6
Dade County, FL	276,841	7
Maricopa County, AZ	275,009	8
Broward County, FL	266,547	9
Wayne County, MI	265,302	10
Philadelphia County, PA	238,498	11
Allegheny County, PA	234,118	12
Pinellas County, FL	225,437	13
Orange County, CA	223,136	14
Cuyahoga County, OH	223,059	15

[Continued]

★313★

Elderly Population (County Estimates), 1991, By Age: Number of Persons Age 65 and Older

[Continued]

County	Number	Rank
Palm Beach County, FL	214,992	16
Harris County, TX	204,589	17
New York County, NY	195,734	18
Nassau County, NY	183,085	19
Middlesex County, MA	176,444	20
King County, WA	168,632	21
Riverside County, CA	162,026	22
Dallas County, TX	155,976	23
Erie County, NY	148,167	24
Suffolk County, NY	142,209	25

Source: U.S. Bureau of the Census, Current Population Reports, Special Studies, P23-190, *65+ In the United States,* Washington, D.C.: U.S. Government Printing Office, 1996, pp. 8-17. Primary source: U.S. Bureau of the Census, Population Division, *Estimates of the Population of Counties, by Age, Sex, and Race: 1991,* PE-9, November 1993. *Note:* Data are shown only for the top 25 areas.

★314★

Older American Population

Elderly Population (County Estimates), 1991, By Age: Number of Persons Age 85 and Older

Data refer to the population in counties with 10,000 or more elderly citizens.

County	Number	Rank
Los Angeles County, CA	85,507	1
Cook County, IL	58,941	2
Dade County, FL	31,187	3
Queens County, NY	28,851	4
Pinellas County, FL	27,857	5
Kings County, NY	26,911	6
Broward County, FL	26,049	7
San Diego County, CA	25,626	8
Wayne County, MI	24,718	9
Maricopa County, AZ	23,584	10
Orange County, CA	23,407	11
New York County, NY	22,819	12
Philadelphia County, PA	22,486	13
Allegheny County, PA	20,964	14
Cuyahoga County, OH	20,714	15
Middlesex County, MA	20,422	16
Palm Beach County, FL	19,181	17
Harris County, TX	17,547	18
King County, WA	17,242	19
Bronx County, NY	16,954	20
Nassau County, NY	16,438	21
Dallas County, TX	15,506	22
Hennepin County, MN	15,184	23
Milwaukee County, WI	14,766	24
Suffolk County, NY	14,255	25

Source: U.S. Bureau of the Census, Current Population Reports, Special Studies, P23-190, *65+ In the United States,* Washington, D.C.: U.S. Government Printing Office, 1996, pp. 8-17. Primary source: U.S. Bureau of the Census, Population Division, *Estimates of the Population of Counties, by Age, Sex, and Race: 1991,* PE-9, November 1993. *Note:* Data are shown only for the top 25 areas.

★315★

Older American Population

Elderly Population (County Estimates), 1991, By Age: Percentage of Persons Age 65 and Older

Data refer to the population in counties with 10,000 or more elderly citizens.

County	Percent	Rank
Pasco County, FL	32.4	1
Sarasota County, FL	32.3	2
Pinellas County, FL	26.1	3
Lee County, FL	24.7	4
Palm Beach County, FL	24.3	5
Ocean County, MD	23.5	6
Volusia County, FL	22.8	7
Broward County, FL	20.7	8
Luzerne County, PA	19.9	9
Polk County, FL	18.5	10
Allegheny County, PA	17.5	11
Westmoreland County, PA	17.3	12
Brevard County, FL	16.6	13
Saint Louis (City), MO	16.6	13
Cuyahoga County, OH	15.8	14
Providence County, RI	15.8	14
Delaware County, PA	15.6	15
Bergen County, NJ	15.4	16
Erie County, NY	15.2	17
Montgomery County, PA	15.2	17
Philadelphia County, PA	15.2	17
Union County, NJ	15.1	18
Hampden County, MA	14.9	19
New Haven County, CT	14.8	20
Bristol County, MA	14.7	21

Source: U.S. Bureau of the Census, Current Population Reports, Special Studies, P23-190, *65+ In the United States,* Washington, D.C.: U.S. Government Printing Office, 1996, pp. 8-17. Primary source: U.S. Bureau of the Census, Population Division, *Estimates of the Population of Counties, by Age, Sex, and Race: 1991,* PE-9, November 1993. *Note:* Data are shown only for the top 25 areas.

★316★

Older American Population

Elderly Population (County Estimates), 1991, By Age: Percentage of Persons Age 85 and Older

Data refer to the population in counties with 10,000 or more elderly citizens.

County	Percentage	Rank
Pinellas County, FL	3.2	1
Sarasota County, FL	3.2	1
Pasco County, FL	2.4	2
Palm Beach County, FL	2.2	3
Volusia County, FL	2.2	3
Ocean County, NJ	2.1	4
Saint Louis City, MO	2.1	4
Broward County, FL	2.0	5
Lee County, FL	1.8	6
Luzerne County, PA	1.8	6
Hampden County, MA	1.7	7
Providence County, RI	1.7	7
Allegheny County, PA	1.6	8
Dade County, FL	1.6	8
Denver County, CO	1.6	8

[Continued]

★316★

Elderly Population (County Estimates), 1991, By Age: Percentage of Persons Age 85 and Older

[Continued]

County	Percentage	Rank
Essex County, MA	1.6	8
Montgomery County, PA	1.6	8
Multnomah County, OR	1.6	8
New Haven County, CT	1.6	8
Norfolk County, MA	1.6	8
San Francisco County, CA	1.6	8
Westchester County, NY	1.6	8
Worcester County, MA	1.6	8
Bristol County, MA	1.5	9
Cuyahoga County, OH	1.5	9

Source: U.S. Bureau of the Census, Current Population Reports, Special Studies, P23-190, *65+ In the United States,* Washington, D.C.: U.S. Government Printing Office, 1996, pp. 8-17. Primary source: U.S. Bureau of the Census, Population Division, *Estimates of the Population of Counties, by Age, Sex, and Race: 1991,* PE-9, November 1993. *Note:* Data are shown only for the top 25 areas.

★317★

Asian Population

Asian Population, 1990: Asian Indian

[Table shows the top 50 areas]

MSA	% of total population	Rank
Yuba City, CA	3.7817	1
Merced, CA	1.3430	2
New York – Northern New Jersey – Long Island, NY – NJ – CT	1.0617	3
Washington, DC – MD – VA	0.9115	4
Bryan – College Station, TX	0.8460	5
San Francisco – Oakland – San Jose, CA	0.8082	6
Lafayette – West Lafayette, IN	0.7856	7
Fresno, CA	0.7464	8
Modesto, CA	0.7368	9
Poughkeepsie, NY	0.7327	10
Chicago – Gary – Lake County, IL – IN – WI	0.7194	11
Houston – Galveston – Brazoria, TX	0.6871	12
State College, PA	0.6544	13
Champaign – Urbana – Rantoul, IL	0.6421	14
Stockton, CA	0.5990	15
Huntsville, AL	0.5215	16
Iowa City, IA	0.4921	17
Lawrence, KS	0.4792	18
Los Angeles – Anaheim – Riverside, CA	0.4722	19
Gainesville, FL	0.4551	20
Raleigh – Durham, NC	0.4442	21
Philadelphia – Wilmington – Trenton, PA – NJ – DE – MD	0.4403	22
Dallas – Fort Worth, TX	0.4361	23
Sacramento, CA	0.4243	24
Austin, TX	0.4212	25
Orlando, FL	0.4201	26
Boston – Lawrence – Salem, MA – NH	0.4020	27

[Continued]

★317★

Asian Population, 1990: Asian Indian
[Continued]

MSA	% of total population	Rank
Charlottesville, VA	0.3890	28
Sheboygan, WI	0.3860	29
Hartford – New Britain – Middletown, CT	0.3848	30
Detroit – Ann Arbor, MI	0.3674	31
Baltimore, MD	0.3476	32
Worcester, MA	0.3332	33
Miami – Fort Lauderdale, FL	0.3290	34
Columbia, MO	0.3212	35
Lansing – East Lansing, MI	0.3173	36
Atlanta, GA	0.3159	37
Rochester, MN	0.3128	38
Augusta, GA – SC	0.3120	39
Bloomington – Normal, IL	0.3120	39
Kalamazoo, MI	0.3048	40
Atlantic City, NJ	0.3040	41
Albany – Schenectady – Troy, NY	0.3007	42
New Haven – Meriden, CT	0.2963	43
Madison, WI	0.2939	44
West Palm Beach – Boca Raton – Delray Beach, FL	0.2930	45
Visalia – Tulare – Porterville, CA	0.2889	46
Bloomington, IN	0.2881	47
Tallahassee, FL	0.2877	48
Salinas – Seaside – Monterey, CA	0.2840	49

Source: U.S. Bureau of the Census, Data User Services Division, *1990 Census of Population and Housing,* Summary Tape File 3C, United States Summary, CD-ROM, February 1992.

★318★

Asian Population

Asian Population, 1990: Cambodian

[Table shows the top 50 areas]

MSA	% of total population	Rank
Stockton, CA	2.26745	1
Modesto, CA	1.07659	2
Rochester, MN	0.73542	3
Fresno, CA	0.48690	4
Columbia, MO	0.40844	5
Providence – Pawtucket – Fall River, RI – MA	0.40498	6
Seattle – Tacoma, WA	0.35387	7
Boston – Lawrence – Salem, MA – NH	0.28683	8
Los Angeles – Anaheim – Riverside, CA	0.24673	9
Olympia, WA	0.20343	10
San Francisco – Oakland – San Jose, CA	0.18542	11
Sioux City, IA – NE	0.17997	12
San Diego, CA	0.17630	13
Portland, ME	0.16475	14
Bellingham, WA	0.16121	15

[Continued]

★318★

Asian Population, 1990: Cambodian
[Continued]

MSA	% of total population	Rank
Portland – Vancouver, OR – WA	0.14798	16
Richmond – Petersburg, VA	0.11702	17
Washington, DC – MD – VA	0.10541	18
Pittsfield, MA	0.09840	19
Columbus, OH	0.09815	20
Des Moines, IA	0.09544	21
Minneapolis – Saint Paul, MN – WI	0.09042	22
Salem, OR	0.08524	23
Springfield, MA	0.08423	24
Lawton, OK	0.08342	25
Philadelphia – Wilmington – Trenton, PA – NJ – DE – MD	0.08211	26
Houston – Galveston – Brazoria, TX	0.07801	27
Dallas – Fort Worth, TX	0.07791	28
Greensboro – Winston-Salem – High Point, NC	0.07727	29
Redding, CA	0.07481	30
Wichita, KS	0.07357	31
Lancaster, PA	0.07190	32
Madison, WI	0.06974	33
Mobile, AL	0.06731	34
Salt Lake City – Ogden, UT	0.06678	35
Chattanooga, TN – GA	0.06671	36
Jacksonville, FL	0.06474	37
Charlotte – Gastonia – Rock Hill, NC – SC	0.06041	38
Janesville – Beloit, WI	0.06021	39
Atlanta, GA	0.06003	40
Jamestown – Dunkirk, NY	0.05497	41
Tyler, TX	0.05353	42
Denver – Boulder, CO	0.05021	43
Bakersfield, CA	0.04968	44
South Bend – Mishawaka, IN	0.04898	45
Phoenix, AZ	0.04675	46
Manchester, NH	0.04666	47
Memphis, TN – AR – MS	0.04665	48
Portsmouth – Dover – Rochester, NH – ME	0.04515	49
Norfolk – Virginia Beach – Newport News, VA	0.04326	50

Source: U.S. Bureau of the Census, Data User Services Division, *1990 Census of Population and Housing,* Summary Tape File 3C, United States Summary, CD-ROM, February 1992.

★319★
Asian Population
Asian Population, 1990: Chinese

[Table shows the top 50 areas]

MSA	% of total poupulation	Rank
Honolulu, HI	7.5761	1
San Francisco – Oakland – San Jose, CA	5.3097	2
Los Angeles – Anaheim – Riverside, CA	2.1180	3
Sacramento, CA	2.0173	4
New York – Northern New Jersey – Long Island, NY – NJ – CT	1.7722	5
Champaign – Urbana – Rantoul, IL	1.5408	6
Iowa City, IA	1.4950	7
Lafayette – West Lafayette, IN	1.4411	8
Lawrence, KS	1.3387	9
State College, PA	1.3087	10
Stockton, CA	1.1941	11
Boston – Lawrence – Salem, MA – NH	1.1634	12
Seattle – Tacoma, WA	1.1307	13
Bryan – College Station, TX	1.0947	14
Washington, DC – MD – VA	1.0227	15
Columbia, MO	0.9957	16
Reno, NV	0.9691	17
Houston – Galveston – Brazoria, TX	0.8333	18
Poughkeepsie, NY	0.7650	19
San Diego, CA	0.7591	20
Bloomington, IN	0.7524	21
Madison, WI	0.7143	22
Austin, TX	0.6921	23
Santa Barbara – Santa Maria – Lompoc, CA	0.6612	24
Portland – Vancouver, OR – WA	0.6477	25
Gainesville, FL	0.6438	26
Salinas – Seaside – Monterey, CA	0.6284	27
Fresno, CA	0.6217	28
Raleigh – Durham, NC	0.6041	29
Las Vegas, NV	0.5441	30
Chicago – Gary – Lake County, IL – IN – WI	0.5331	31
Athens, GA	0.5318	32
Charlottesville, VA	0.5278	33
Chico, CA	0.5150	34
New Haven – Meriden, CT	0.5134	35
Tucson, AZ	0.4867	36
Eugene – Springfield, OR	0.4811	37
Philadelphia – Wilmington – Trenton, PA – NJ – DE – MD	0.4609	38
Dallas – Fort Worth, TX	0.4379	39
Binghamton, NY	0.4250	40
Atlantic City, NJ	0.4239	41
Modesto, CA	0.4156	42
Phoenix, AZ	0.4134	43
Miami – Fort Lauderdale, FL	0.4118	44
Lansing – East Lansing, MI	0.4042	45
Huntsville, AL	0.3926	46
Fort Collins – Loveland, CO	0.3857	47
Tallahassee, FL	0.3857	47

[Continued]

★319★
Asian Population, 1990: Chinese
[Continued]

MSA	% of total poupulation	Rank
Rochester, MN	0.3813	48
Atlanta, GA	0.3682	49

Source: U.S. Bureau of the Census, Data User Services Division, *1990 Census of Population and Housing*, Summary Tape File 3C, United States Summary, CD-ROM, February 1992.

★320★
Asian Population
Asian Population, 1990: Filipino

[Table shows the top 50 areas]

MSA	% of total population	Rank
Honolulu, HI	14.2369	1
San Francisco – Oakland – San Jose, CA	4.1641	2
San Diego, CA	3.8601	3
Stockton, CA	3.3281	4
Salinas – Seaside – Monterey, CA	3.2326	5
Bremerton, WA	2.4292	6
Los Angeles – Anaheim – Riverside, CA	2.0309	7
Anchorage, AK	1.5375	8
Bakersfield, CA	1.5268	9
Santa Barbara – Santa Maria – Lompoc, CA	1.5238	10
Norfolk – Virginia Beach – Newport News, VA	1.4309	11
Sacramento, CA	1.3746	12
Seattle – Tacoma, WA	1.3543	13
Reno, NV	1.3186	14
Visalia – Tulare – Porterville, CA	1.3122	15
Las Vegas, NV	1.0690	16
Jacksonville, FL	0.9039	17
Fort Walton Beach, FL	0.8666	18
Jacksonville, NC	0.8095	19
Chicago – Gary – Lake County, IL – IN – WI	0.7919	20
Yuba City, CA	0.7730	21
Modesto, CA	0.7265	22
Pensacola, FL	0.6887	23
Charleston, SC	0.6885	24
Washington, DC – MD – VA	0.6630	25
Merced, CA	0.6513	26
New York – Northern New Jersey – Long Island, NY – NJ – CT	0.5860	27
Fresno, CA	0.5733	28
New London – Norwich, CT – RI	0.5611	29
Olympia, WA	0.4962	30
Yuma, AZ	0.4949	31
Cheyenne, WY	0.4498	32
Killeen – Temple, TX	0.4418	33
Lawton, OK	0.4395	34
Rapid City, SD	0.4315	35
Houston – Galveston – Brazoria, TX	0.4216	36

[Continued]

★ 320 ★
Asian Population, 1990: Filipino
[Continued]

MSA	% of total population	Rank
Yakima, WA	0.4041	37
Colorado Springs, CO	0.3899	38
Biloxi – Gulfport, MS	0.3840	39
Orlando, FL	0.3718	40
Portland – Vancouver, OR – WA	0.3540	41
Great Falls, MT	0.3514	42
Champaign – Urbana – Rantoul, IL	0.3398	43
Charlottesville, VA	0.3379	44
Abilene, TX	0.3368	45
Richland – Kennewick – Pasco, WA	0.3166	46
Grand Forks, ND	0.3141	47
Panama City, FL	0.3040	48
Corpus Christi, TX	0.3021	49
Enid, OK	0.2996	50

Source: U.S. Bureau of the Census, Data User Services Division, *1990 Census of Population and Housing*, Summary Tape File 3C, United States Summary, CD-ROM, February 1992.

★ 321 ★
Asian Population
Asian Population, 1990: Hmong
[Table shows the top 50 areas]

MSA	% of total population	Rank
Merced, CA	3.643436	1
Fresno, CA	2.913002	2
Yuba City, CA	2.128943	3
La Crosse, WI	2.065288	4
Wausau, WI	1.720971	5
Eau Claire, WI	1.207622	6
Stockton, CA	1.103348	7
Sheboygan, WI	1.092638	8
Green Bay, WI	0.862308	9
Minneapolis – Saint Paul, MN – WI	0.702765	10
Chico, CA	0.676477	11
Appleton – Oshkosh – Neenah, WI	0.639120	12
Visalia – Tulare – Porterville, CA	0.596946	13
Sacramento, CA	0.374789	14
Modesto, CA	0.307674	15
Milwaukee – Racine, WI	0.231025	16
Madison, WI	0.223382	17
Santa Barbara – Santa Maria – Lompoc, CA	0.190743	18
Hickory – Morganton, NC	0.142986	19
Rochester, MN	0.132432	20
Duluth, MN – WI	0.122932	21
Spokane, WA	0.122591	22
Redding, CA	0.108137	23
Providence – Pawtucket – Fall River, RI – MA	0.103809	24
Lansing – East Lansing, MI	0.091293	25
Fitchburg – Leominster, MA	0.085606	26
San Diego, CA	0.081465	27
Des Moines, IA	0.080676	28

[Continued]

★ 321 ★
Asian Population, 1990: Hmong
[Continued]

MSA	% of total population	Rank
Lancaster, PA	0.071898	29
Denver – Boulder, CO	0.065303	30
Saginaw – Bay City – Midland, MI	0.049835	31
Detroit – Ann Arbor, MI	0.036247	32
Kansas City, MO – KS	0.034221	33
Portland – Vancouver, OR – WA	0.034103	34
Salem, OR	0.032731	35
Richland – Kennewick – Pasco, WA	0.032659	36
Rockford, IL	0.026435	37
Kankakee, IL	0.023895	38
Tulsa, OK	0.023415	39
Omaha, NE – IA	0.021835	40
Sioux City, IA – NE	0.020866	41
Syracuse, NY	0.020610	42
Fort Wayne, IN	0.017317	43
Salt Lake City – Ogden, UT	0.017161	44
Seattle – Tacoma, WA	0.013911	45
Janesville – Beloit, WI	0.013619	46
Atlanta, GA	0.013305	47
Los Angeles – Anaheim – Riverside, CA	0.010749	48
Springfield, MA	0.008688	49
Grand Forks, ND	0.007074	50

Source: U.S. Bureau of the Census, Data User Services Division, *1990 Census of Population and Housing*, Summary Tape File 3C, United States Summary, CD-ROM, February 1992.

★ 322 ★
Asian Population
Asian Population, 1990: Japanese
[Table shows the top 50 areas]

MSA	% of total population	Rank
Honolulu, HI	23.7652	1
San Francisco – Oakland – San Jose, CA	1.3034	2
Los Angeles – Anaheim – Riverside, CA	1.2172	3
Salinas – Seaside – Monterey, CA	1.1806	4
Sacramento, CA	1.1452	5
Seattle – Tacoma, WA	1.0707	6
Fresno, CA	1.0692	7
Santa Barbara – Santa Maria – Lompoc, CA	0.8509	8
Stockton, CA	0.8137	9
Yuba City, CA	0.7917	10
San Diego, CA	0.7308	11
Anchorage, AK	0.6044	12
Portland – Vancouver, OR – WA	0.5283	13
Spokane, WA	0.5020	14
Greeley, CO	0.4893	15
Lafayette – West Lafayette, IN	0.4747	16
Merced, CA	0.4742	17
Champaign – Urbana – Rantoul, IL	0.4641	18

[Continued]

★322★

Asian Population, 1990: Japanese
[Continued]

MSA	% of total population	Rank
Olympia, WA	0.4577	19
Salt Lake City – Ogden, UT	0.4496	20
Denver – Boulder, CO	0.4441	21
Eugene – Springfield, OR	0.4351	22
Jacksonville, NC	0.4271	23
Colorado Springs, CO	0.4267	24
Las Vegas, NV	0.3969	25
Bremerton, WA	0.3958	26
Bellingham, WA	0.3475	27
Visalia – Tulare – Porterville, CA	0.3347	28
Fort Collins – Loveland, CO	0.3326	29
Reno, NV	0.3326	29
Lawton, OK	0.3229	30
Battle Creek, MI	0.3206	31
Salem, OR	0.3194	32
Bloomington – Normal, IL	0.3135	33
Bloomington, IN	0.3037	34
Richland – Kennewick – Pasco, WA	0.2986	35
Provo – Orem, UT	0.2781	36
New York – Northern New Jersey – Long Island, NY – NJ – CT	0.2736	37
Iowa City, IA	0.2715	38
Medford, OR	0.2623	39
Yuma, AZ	0.2591	40
Rochester, MN	0.2536	41
Washington, DC – MD – VA	0.2519	42
Tucson, AZ	0.2485	43
Lawrence, KS	0.2482	44
Chico, CA	0.2471	45
Chicago – Gary – Lake County, IL – IN – WI	0.2407	46
Boise, ID	0.2352	47
Cheyenne, WY	0.2338	48
Killeen – Temple, TX	0.2315	49

Source: U.S. Bureau of the Census, Data User Services Division, *1990 Census of Population and Housing,* Summary Tape File 3C, United States Summary, CD-ROM, February 1992.

★323★

Asian Population

Asian Population, 1990: Korean
[Table shows the top 50 areas]

MSA	% of total population	Rank
Honolulu, HI	2.7103	1
Los Angeles – Anaheim – Riverside, CA	1.3364	2
Anchorage, AK	1.2645	3
Salinas – Seaside – Monterey, CA	1.1927	4
Killeen – Temple, TX	1.1018	5
Washington, DC – MD – VA	1.0082	6
Lawton, OK	0.9983	7
Seattle – Tacoma, WA	0.9412	8
Iowa City, IA	0.9072	9

[Continued]

★323★

Asian Population, 1990: Korean
[Continued]

MSA	% of total population	Rank
Olympia, WA	0.8621	10
Colorado Springs, CO	0.8317	11
Champaign – Urbana – Rantoul, IL	0.8213	12
Clarksville – Hopkinsville, TN – KY	0.7430	13
Fayetteville, NC	0.6767	14
San Francisco – Oakland – San Jose, CA	0.6687	15
New York – Northern New Jersey – Long Island, NY – NJ – CT	0.6573	16
Bryan – College Station, TX	0.6417	17
State College, PA	0.5106	18
Bloomington, IN	0.4973	19
Baltimore, MD	0.4881	20
Portland – Vancouver, OR – WA	0.4675	21
Columbus, GA – AL	0.4645	22
Chicago – Gary – Lake County, IL – IN – WI	0.4576	23
Lawrence, KS	0.4316	24
Las Vegas, NV	0.4278	25
Lafayette – West Lafayette, IN	0.4257	26
Madison, WI	0.4078	27
Philadelphia – Wilmington – Trenton, PA – NJ – DE – MD	0.4064	28
Minneapolis – Saint Paul, MN – WI	0.3816	29
Denver – Boulder, CO	0.3744	30
Sacramento, CA	0.3710	31
Athens, GA	0.3673	32
Santa Barbara – Santa Maria – Lompoc, CA	0.3634	33
Fort Walton Beach, FL	0.3596	34
Reno, NV	0.3444	35
Atlanta, GA	0.3377	36
Lansing – East Lansing, MI	0.3374	37
Columbia, MO	0.3373	38
Eugene – Springfield, OR	0.3358	39
Anniston, AL	0.3344	40
Kalamazoo, MI	0.3312	41
Fitchburg – Leominster, MA	0.3249	42
Augusta, GA – SC	0.3211	43
Bremerton, WA	0.3162	44
Gainesville, FL	0.3155	45
Huntsville, AL	0.3143	46
Austin, TX	0.3057	47
Charlottesville, VA	0.3020	48
Yuba City, CA	0.2919	49
Dallas – Fort Worth, TX	0.2859	50

Source: U.S. Bureau of the Census, Data User Services Division, *1990 Census of Population and Housing,* Summary Tape File 3C, United States Summary, CD-ROM, February 1992.

★324★
Asian Population
Asian Population, 1990: Laotian
[Table shows the top 50 areas]

MSA	% of total population	Rank
Fresno, CA	1.36182	1
Merced, CA	1.17543	2
Visalia – Tulare – Porterville, CA	1.10509	3
Redding, CA	0.94127	4
Fort Smith, AR – OK	0.91410	5
Stockton, CA	0.90839	6
Modesto, CA	0.64746	7
Sacramento, CA	0.59874	8
Amarillo, TX	0.57586	9
Sioux City, IA – NE	0.45384	10
Chico, CA	0.40633	11
Des Moines, IA	0.39880	12
Fitchburg – Leominster, MA	0.37355	13
Richland – Kennewick – Pasco, WA	0.33259	14
San Diego, CA	0.28659	15
Rockford, IL	0.25377	16
Yuba City, CA	0.25195	17
Nashville, TN	0.23228	18
Rochester, MN	0.21602	19
Binghamton, NY	0.21248	20
Minneapolis – Saint Paul, MN – WI	0.21160	21
Honolulu, HI	0.20114	22
Portland – Vancouver, OR – WA	0.20103	23
Providence – Pawtucket – Fall River, RI – MA	0.19702	24
Portsmouth – Dover – Rochester, NH – ME	0.18508	25
Seattle – Tacoma, WA	0.17353	26
Hickory – Morganton, NC	0.17185	27
San Francisco – Oakland – San Jose, CA	0.16794	28
Wichita, KS	0.15867	29
Dallas – Fort Worth, TX	0.14441	30
Milwaukee – Racine, WI	0.14379	31
Elkhart – Goshen, IN	0.14277	32
Salt Lake City – Ogden, UT	0.13318	33
Olympia, WA	0.12466	34
Montgomery, AL	0.12410	35
Iowa City, IA	0.10716	36
Las Vegas, NV	0.10709	37
Sheboygan, WI	0.10686	38
Santa Barbara – Santa Maria – Lompoc, CA	0.10660	39
Rochester, NY	0.10575	40
Atlanta, GA	0.10295	41
Salem, OR	0.10071	42
Hartford – New Britain – Middletown, CT	0.09421	43
Boise, ID	0.09331	44
Fayetteville – Springdale, AR	0.09259	45
Columbus, OH	0.08756	46
Sioux Falls, SD	0.08642	47
Denver – Boulder, CO	0.08456	48
Anchorage, AK	0.08395	49
Lansing – East Lansing, MI	0.08367	50

Source: U.S. Bureau of the Census, Data User Services Division, *1990 Census of Population and Housing,* Summary Tape File 3C, United States Summary, CD-ROM, February 1992.

★325★
Asian Population
Asian Population, 1990: Thai
[Table shows the top 50 areas]

MSA	% of total population	Rank
Fort Walton Beach, FL	0.42358	1
Las Vegas, NV	0.20608	2
Los Angeles – Anaheim – Riverside, CA	0.16038	3
Honolulu, HI	0.13310	4
Columbia, MO	0.12814	5
Reno, NV	0.12173	6
Merced, CA	0.11715	7
Abilene, TX	0.11366	8
Fayetteville, NC	0.11291	9
Washington, DC – MD – VA	0.11072	10
Killeen – Temple, TX	0.10380	11
Cheyenne, WY	0.09844	12
Anchorage, AK	0.09543	13
Amarillo, TX	0.09064	14
Lawton, OK	0.08701	15
Champaign – Urbana – Rantoul, IL	0.08322	16
Enid, OK	0.08284	17
Des Moines, IA	0.07966	18
Shreveport, LA	0.07866	19
Colorado Springs, CO	0.07859	20
Bryan – College Station, TX	0.07714	21
Jacksonville, NC	0.07608	22
Seattle – Tacoma, WA	0.07264	23
Panama City, FL	0.07087	24
Sacramento, CA	0.06650	25
Rapid City, SD	0.06639	26
Melbourne – Titusville – Palm Bay, FL	0.06517	27
Richland – Kennewick – Pasco, WA	0.06465	28
Dallas – Fort Worth, TX	0.06434	29
San Francisco – Oakland – San Jose, CA	0.06043	30
Austin, TX	0.06014	31
Spokane, WA	0.05894	32
Chicago – Gary – Lake County, IL – IN – WI	0.05702	33
Tucson, AZ	0.05698	34
Lafayette – West Lafayette, IN	0.05590	35
Huntsville, AL	0.05483	36
Iowa City, IA	0.05306	37
Albany, GA	0.05153	38
Oklahoma City, OK	0.05100	39
Yuba City, CA	0.05055	40
Kalamazoo, MI	0.04879	41
Tampa – Saint Petersburg – Clearwater, FL	0.04686	42
San Antonio, TX	0.04577	43
Salt Lake City – Ogden, UT	0.04551	44
Olympia, WA	0.04527	45
Denver – Boulder, CO	0.04507	46
Lafayette, LA	0.04503	47
Portland – Vancouver, OR – WA	0.04432	48
Salinas – Seaside – Monterey, CA	0.04386	49
San Diego, CA	0.04359	50

Source: U.S. Bureau of the Census, Data User Services Division, *1990 Census of Population and Housing,* Summary Tape File 3C, United States Summary, CD-ROM, February 1992.

★ 326 ★
Asian Population
Asian Population, 1990: Vietnamese
[Table shows the top 50 areas]

MSA	% of total population	Rank
Stockton, CA	1.4219	1
San Francisco – Oakland – San Jose, CA	1.3590	2
Biloxi – Gulfport, MS	1.3332	3
Beaumont – Port Arthur, TX	1.0769	4
Los Angeles – Anaheim – Riverside, CA	1.0010	5
Houston – Galveston – Brazoria, TX	0.8883	6
New Orleans, LA	0.8752	7
San Diego, CA	0.8231	8
Sacramento, CA	0.7270	9
Wichita, KS	0.6943	10
Fort Smith, AR – OK	0.6435	11
Honolulu, HI	0.6318	12
Washington, DC – MD – VA	0.5985	13
Amarillo, TX	0.5839	14
Wichita Falls, TX	0.5736	15
Seattle – Tacoma, WA	0.5553	16
Olympia, WA	0.5501	17
Oklahoma City, OK	0.5186	18
Panama City, FL	0.5142	19
Portland – Vancouver, OR – WA	0.5142	19
Dallas – Fort Worth, TX	0.4915	20
Rochester, MN	0.4884	21
Worcester, MA	0.4804	22
Salinas – Seaside – Monterey, CA	0.4665	23
Houma – Thibodaux, LA	0.4397	24
Modesto, CA	0.4011	25
Lancaster, PA	0.3888	26
Pascagoula, MS	0.3887	27
Austin, TX	0.3678	28
Pensacola, FL	0.3478	29
Denver – Boulder, CO	0.3373	30
Bellingham, WA	0.3342	31
Minneapolis – Saint Paul, MN – WI	0.3290	32
Harrisburg – Lebanon – Carlisle, PA	0.3267	33
Lincoln, NE	0.3057	34
Orlando, FL	0.2952	35
Baton Rouge, LA	0.2910	36
Grand Rapids, MI	0.2885	37
Lafayette, LA	0.2884	38
Fresno, CA	0.2845	39
Santa Barbara – Santa Maria – Lompoc, CA	0.2776	40
Boston – Lawrence – Salem, MA – NH	0.2665	41
Bryan – College Station, TX	0.2651	42
Savannah, GA	0.2597	43
Champaign – Urbana – Rantoul, IL	0.2560	44
Richland – Kennewick – Pasco, WA	0.2473	45
Albuquerque, NM	0.2460	46
Salt Lake City – Ogden, UT	0.2287	47

[Continued]

★ 326 ★
Asian Population, 1990: Vietnamese
[Continued]

MSA	% of total population	Rank
Mobile, AL	0.2281	48
Salem, OR	0.2216	49

Source: U.S. Bureau of the Census, Data User Services Division, *1990 Census of Population and Housing,* Summary Tape File 3C, United States Summary, CD-ROM, February 1992.

★ 327 ★
Hispanic Population
Central American Population, 1990: Guatemalan
[Table shows the top 50 areas]

MSA	% of total population	Rank
Los Angeles – Anaheim – Riverside, CA	0.96101	1
Providence – Pawtucket – Fall River, RI – MA	0.38904	2
Miami – Fort Lauderdale, FL	0.28854	3
Washington, DC – MD – VA	0.23948	4
San Francisco – Oakland – San Jose, CA	0.21034	5
Santa Barbara – Santa Maria – Lompoc, CA	0.20508	6
Reno, NV	0.19908	7
Chicago – Gary – Lake County, IL – IN – WI	0.19562	8
Brownsville – Harlingen, TX	0.18953	9
Naples, FL	0.18606	10
New Orleans, LA	0.16637	11
Houston – Galveston – Brazoria, TX	0.16615	12
New York – Northern New Jersey – Long Island, NY – NJ – CT	0.15707	13
West Palm Beach – Boca Raton – Delray Beach, FL	0.15298	14
Boston – Lawrence – Salem, MA – NH	0.15250	15
Santa Fe, NM	0.14866	16
Fort Pierce, FL	0.13940	17
Fort Myers – Cape Coral, FL	0.11608	18
San Diego, CA	0.10408	19
Bakersfield, CA	0.09936	20
Albuquerque, NM	0.08802	21
Visalia – Tulare – Porterville, CA	0.07951	22
Greeley, CO	0.07889	23
Modesto, CA	0.07449	24
Dallas – Fort Worth, TX	0.06681	25
Fresno, CA	0.06592	26
Orlando, FL	0.06451	27
Las Vegas, NV	0.06271	28
San Antonio, TX	0.06236	29
Medford, OR	0.06216	30
Waco, TX	0.06186	31
Bradenton, FL	0.05574	32
Phoenix, AZ	0.05240	33

[Continued]

★327★

Central American Population, 1990: Guatemalan
[Continued]

MSA	% of total population	Rank
Portland – Vancouver, OR – WA	0.05102	34
El Paso, TX	0.04547	35
Merced, CA	0.04540	36
Corpus Christi, TX	0.04458	37
Salt Lake City – Ogden, UT	0.04430	38
Bloomington, IN	0.04405	39
Iowa City, IA	0.04057	40
Provo – Orem, UT	0.04021	41
Salinas – Seaside – Monterey, CA	0.03993	42
Anchorage, AK	0.03976	43
Stockton, CA	0.03912	44
Austin, TX	0.03851	45
Sacramento, CA	0.03801	46
Columbus, GA – AL	0.03703	47
Tucson, AZ	0.03464	48
Elkhart – Goshen, IN	0.03201	49
Allentown – Bethlehem – Easton, PA – NJ	0.03160	50

Source: U.S. Bureau of the Census, Data User Services Division, *1990 Census of Population and Housing*, Summary Tape File 3C, United States Summary, CD-ROM, February 1992.

★328★

Hispanic Population

Central American Population, 1990: Honduran
[Table shows the top 50 areas]

MSA	% of total population	Rank
New Orleans, LA	0.78301	1
Miami – Fort Lauderdale, FL	0.61687	2
New York – Northern New Jersey – Long Island, NY – NJ – CT	0.18626	3
Los Angeles – Anaheim – Riverside, CA	0.17494	4
Houston – Galveston – Brazoria, TX	0.16157	5
Brownsville – Harlingen, TX	0.15262	6
Naples, FL	0.09402	7
Washington, DC – MD – VA	0.08984	8
Boston – Lawrence – Salem, MA – NH	0.07989	9
Salinas – Seaside – Monterey, CA	0.07620	10
Tyler, TX	0.07204	11
Tampa – Saint Petersburg – Clearwater, FL	0.07152	12
Bradenton, FL	0.06518	13
West Palm Beach – Boca Raton – Delray Beach, FL	0.06253	14
Beaumont – Port Arthur, TX	0.06063	15
Orlando, FL	0.05975	16
Iowa City, IA	0.05826	17
McAllen – Edinburg – Mission, TX	0.05553	18
Dallas – Fort Worth, TX	0.05021	19
Manchester, NH	0.04869	20

[Continued]

★328★

Central American Population, 1990: Honduran
[Continued]

MSA	% of total population	Rank
Melbourne – Titusville – Palm Bay, FL	0.04762	21
Bryan – College Station, TX	0.04759	22
Columbus, GA – AL	0.04525	23
Killeen – Temple, TX	0.04426	24
Jacksonville, NC	0.04138	25
Baton Rouge, LA	0.04070	26
Chicago – Gary – Lake County, IL – IN – WI	0.04032	27
Austin, TX	0.03992	28
San Diego, CA	0.03799	29
San Francisco – Oakland – San Jose, CA	0.03748	30
San Antonio, TX	0.03656	31
Ocala, FL	0.03644	32
Reno, NV	0.03495	33
Poughkeepsie, NY	0.03469	34
Sarasota, FL	0.03456	35
El Paso, TX	0.03262	36
Tuscaloosa, AL	0.03255	37
Clarksville – Hopkinsville, TN – KY	0.03246	38
Tallahassee, FL	0.03211	39
Fresno, CA	0.03116	40
Gainesville, FL	0.03038	41
Fort Walton Beach, FL	0.02991	42
Sioux City, IA – NE	0.02956	43
Las Vegas, NV	0.02954	44
Waterbury, CT	0.02888	45
Benton Harbor, MI	0.02850	46
Fargo – Moorhead, ND – MN	0.02740	47
Visalia – Tulare – Porterville, CA	0.02725	48
Shreveport, LA	0.02722	49
Charleston, SC	0.02703	50

Source: U.S. Bureau of the Census, Data User Services Division, *1990 Census of Population and Housing*, Summary Tape File 3C, United States Summary, CD-ROM, February 1992.

★329★

Hispanic Population

Central American Population, 1990: Nicaraguan
[Table shows the top 50 areas]

MSA	% of total population	Rank
Miami – Fort Lauderdale, FL	2.36238	1
San Francisco – Oakland – San Jose, CA	0.48712	2
New Orleans, LA	0.33968	3
Los Angeles – Anaheim – Riverside, CA	0.27508	4
Abilene, TX	0.24738	5
Washington, DC – MD – VA	0.20390	6
Merced, CA	0.14518	7
West Palm Beach – Boca Raton – Delray Beach, FL	0.14383	8

[Continued]

★329★

Central American Population, 1990: Nicaraguan
[Continued]

MSA	% of total population	Rank
Brownsville – Harlingen, TX	0.10764	9
Las Vegas, NV	0.10412	10
Beaumont – Port Arthur, TX	0.10409	11
Modesto, CA	0.10256	12
Gainesville, FL	0.10142	13
Houston – Galveston – Brazoria, TX	0.09668	14
Santa Fe, NM	0.08800	15
Baton Rouge, LA	0.08178	16
Austin, TX	0.07933	17
New York – Northern New Jersey – Long Island, NY – NJ – CT	0.07778	18
Bryan – College Station, TX	0.06483	19
Sacramento, CA	0.06347	20
Stockton, CA	0.06013	21
Salinas – Seaside – Monterey, CA	0.05286	22
Orlando, FL	0.04819	23
Richland – Kennewick – Pasco, WA	0.04732	24
San Antonio, TX	0.04715	25
Cumberland, MD – WV	0.04526	26
Monroe, LA	0.04431	27
Laredo, TX	0.03828	28
Albuquerque, NM	0.03766	29
Dallas – Fort Worth, TX	0.03462	30
Bakersfield, CA	0.03422	31
San Diego, CA	0.03379	32
Fayetteville, NC	0.03314	33
Columbia, MO	0.03292	34
Billings, MT	0.03262	35
Atlantic City, NJ	0.03225	36
Jacksonville, NC	0.03203	37
Reno, NV	0.03181	38
New Haven – Meriden, CT	0.03150	39
Tampa – Saint Petersburg – Clearwater, FL	0.03134	40
Lawton, OK	0.03050	41
Santa Barbara – Santa Maria – Lompoc, CA	0.03003	42
Jamestown – Dunkirk, NY	0.02960	43
McAllen – Edinburg – Mission, TX	0.02920	44
Corpus Christi, TX	0.02801	45
Anchorage, AK	0.02783	46
Yuma, AZ	0.02619	47
Rochester, NY	0.02474	48
Tucson, AZ	0.02459	49
Naples, FL	0.02433	50

Source: U.S. Bureau of the Census, Data User Services Division, *1990 Census of Population and Housing,* Summary Tape File 3C, United States Summary, CD-ROM, February 1992.

★330★

Hispanic Population

Central American Population, 1990: Panamanian
[Table shows the top 50 areas]

MSA	% of total population	Rank
Fayetteville, NC	0.36421	1
Killeen – Temple, TX	0.29690	2
Columbus, GA – AL	0.25383	3
Miami – Fort Lauderdale, FL	0.24660	4
Clarksville – Hopkinsville, TN – KY	0.23312	5
Lawton, OK	0.21976	6
Colorado Springs, CO	0.19596	7
Jacksonville, NC	0.17886	8
Salinas – Seaside – Monterey, CA	0.15998	9
New York – Northern New Jersey – Long Island, NY – NJ – CT	0.14984	10
Fort Walton Beach, FL	0.14954	11
Rapid City, SD	0.12171	12
El Paso, TX	0.10581	13
Washington, DC – MD – VA	0.09632	14
Orlando, FL	0.09536	15
Norfolk – Virginia Beach – Newport News, VA	0.08703	16
Dothan, AL	0.08094	17
Yuma, AZ	0.07578	18
Augusta, GA – SC	0.07434	19
Olympia, WA	0.07256	20
Tampa – Saint Petersburg – Clearwater, FL	0.06722	21
San Diego, CA	0.06617	22
Austin, TX	0.06269	23
San Antonio, TX	0.06267	24
Melbourne – Titusville – Palm Bay, FL	0.06216	25
Columbia, SC	0.05559	26
San Francisco – Oakland – San Jose, CA	0.05351	27
Bremerton, WA	0.05323	28
Huntsville, AL	0.05274	29
Fort Collins – Loveland, CO	0.05265	30
Los Angeles – Anaheim – Riverside, CA	0.05218	31
Pensacola, FL	0.04936	32
Tallahassee, FL	0.04837	33
Albuquerque, NM	0.04578	34
New Orleans, LA	0.04553	35
Las Vegas, NV	0.04532	36
Poughkeepsie, NY	0.04509	37
Sarasota, FL	0.04320	38
Honolulu, HI	0.04090	39
Bloomington, IN	0.03946	40
Rochester, MN	0.03945	41
Abilene, TX	0.03844	42
Champaign – Urbana – Rantoul, IL	0.03814	43
Richmond – Petersburg, VA	0.03754	44
Savannah, GA	0.03751	45
Jacksonville, FL	0.03739	46
Glens Falls, NY	0.03712	47
Biloxi – Gulfport, MS	0.03653	48

[Continued]

★330★

Central American Population, 1990: Panamanian
[Continued]

MSA	% of total population	Rank
Fort Myers – Cape Coral, FL	0.03611	49
Gainesville, FL	0.03478	50

Source: U.S. Bureau of the Census, Data User Services Division, *1990 Census of Population and Housing*, Summary Tape File 3C, United States Summary, CD-ROM, February 1992.

★331★

Hispanic Population

Central American Population, 1990: Salvadoran
[Table shows the top 50 areas]

MSA	% of total population	Rank
Los Angeles – Anaheim – Riverside, CA	1.89098	1
Washington, DC – MD – VA	1.32260	2
Houston – Galveston – Brazoria, TX	1.09066	3
San Francisco – Oakland – San Jose, CA	0.83856	4
Reno, NV	0.42722	5
New York – Northern New Jersey – Long Island, NY – NJ – CT	0.35205	6
Brownsville – Harlingen, TX	0.34292	7
Salinas – Seaside – Monterey, CA	0.32053	8
Dallas – Fort Worth, TX	0.29657	9
Miami – Fort Lauderdale, FL	0.28560	10
Las Vegas, NV	0.27945	11
Bakersfield, CA	0.25889	12
Fresno, CA	0.23731	13
Boston – Lawrence – Salem, MA – NH	0.20953	14
Merced, CA	0.15751	15
Sherman – Denison, TX	0.15260	16
Santa Barbara – Santa Maria – Lompoc, CA	0.14421	17
Austin, TX	0.14061	18
Richland – Kennewick – Pasco, WA	0.13664	19
Modesto, CA	0.13360	20
Visalia – Tulare – Porterville, CA	0.13273	21
Worcester, MA	0.10734	22
Sacramento, CA	0.10391	23
West Palm Beach – Boca Raton – Delray Beach, FL	0.10237	24
Stockton, CA	0.09820	25
Bryan – College Station, TX	0.09683	26
Tucson, AZ	0.09387	27
New Orleans, LA	0.09009	28
Chico, CA	0.08731	29
Laredo, TX	0.08631	30
San Diego, CA	0.08435	31
Providence – Pawtucket – Fall River, RI – MA	0.07937	32
Chicago – Gary – Lake County, IL – IN – WI	0.07645	33

[Continued]

★331★

Central American Population, 1990: Salvadoran
[Continued]

MSA	% of total population	Rank
San Antonio, TX	0.07403	34
Jacksonville, NC	0.07141	35
McAllen – Edinburg – Mission, TX	0.06753	36
Phoenix, AZ	0.06479	37
Victoria, TX	0.06455	38
Provo – Orem, UT	0.06411	39
Tallahassee, FL	0.06164	40
Yuma, AZ	0.06081	41
Atlantic City, NJ	0.06011	42
Pittsfield, MA	0.05803	43
Odessa, TX	0.05802	44
Las Cruces, NM	0.05608	45
Albuquerque, NM	0.05369	46
Yakima, WA	0.05349	47
Salt Lake City – Ogden, UT	0.05195	48
Santa Fe, NM	0.05041	49
Atlanta, GA	0.04856	50

Source: U.S. Bureau of the Census, Data User Services Division, *1990 Census of Population and Housing*, Summary Tape File 3C, United States Summary, CD-ROM, February 1992.

★332★

Hispanic Population

Cuban Population, 1990
[Table shows the top 50 areas]

MSA	% of total population	Rank
Miami – Fort Lauderdale, FL	18.3701	1
West Palm Beach – Boca Raton – Delray Beach, FL	2.0052	2
Naples, FL	1.8363	3
Tampa – Saint Petersburg – Clearwater, FL	1.6409	4
Orlando, FL	0.9406	5
New York – Northern New Jersey – Long Island, NY – NJ – CT	0.8804	6
Las Vegas, NV	0.8257	7
Gainesville, FL	0.7898	8
Tallahassee, FL	0.6032	9
New Orleans, LA	0.4670	10
Los Angeles – Anaheim – Riverside, CA	0.4150	11
Fort Pierce, FL	0.3808	12
Sarasota, FL	0.3445	13
Daytona Beach, FL	0.3391	14
Ocala, FL	0.3326	15
Lakeland – Winter Haven, FL	0.3313	16
Fort Myers – Cape Coral, FL	0.3271	17
Melbourne – Titusville – Palm Bay, FL	0.3128	18
Fort Walton Beach, FL	0.2671	19
Jacksonville, FL	0.2639	20
Jacksonville, NC	0.2496	21
Houston – Galveston – Brazoria, TX	0.2394	22

[Continued]

★332★

Cuban Population, 1990
[Continued]

MSA	% of total population	Rank
Washington, DC – MD – VA	0.2346	23
Panama City, FL	0.2173	24
Bradenton, FL	0.2121	25
Atlanta, GA	0.2113	26
Chicago – Gary – Lake County, IL – IN – WI	0.2106	27
Hartford – New Britain – Middletown, CT	0.1859	28
Atlantic City, NJ	0.1759	29
Poughkeepsie, NY	0.1673	30
Boston – Lawrence – Salem, MA – NH	0.1565	31
New Haven – Meriden, CT	0.1562	32
Laredo, TX	0.1471	33
Fayetteville, NC	0.1424	34
Anchorage, AK	0.1401	35
Dallas – Fort Worth, TX	0.1341	36
Grand Rapids, MI	0.1341	36
Rochester, NY	0.1319	37
Philadelphia – Wilmington – Trenton, PA – NJ – DE – MD	0.1307	38
Worcester, MA	0.1305	39
Bryan – College Station, TX	0.1297	40
San Francisco – Oakland – San Jose, CA	0.1283	41
La Crosse, WI	0.1277	42
Austin, TX	0.1244	43
Pensacola, FL	0.1243	44
San Diego, CA	0.1225	45
Savannah, GA	0.1216	46
Tuscaloosa, AL	0.1216	46
Santa Barbara – Santa Maria – Lompoc, CA	0.1193	47
Glens Falls, NY	0.1173	48

Source: U.S. Bureau of the Census, Data User Services Division, *1990 Census of Population and Housing,* Summary Tape File 3C, United States Summary, CD-ROM, February 1992.

★333★

Hispanic Population

Dominican (Dominican Republic) Population, 1990

[Table shows the top 50 areas]

MSA	% of total population	Rank
New York – Northern New Jersey – Long Island, NY – NJ – CT	2.24446	1
Miami – Fort Lauderdale, FL	0.84458	2
Providence – Pawtucket – Fall River, RI – MA	0.81829	3
Boston – Lawrence – Salem, MA – NH	0.69602	4
Orlando, FL	0.24983	5
Waterbury, CT	0.19853	6

[Continued]

★333★

Dominican (Dominican Republic) Population, 1990
[Continued]

MSA	% of total population	Rank
Atlantic City, NJ	0.17782	7
Poughkeepsie, NY	0.16611	8
Anchorage, AK	0.14006	9
West Palm Beach – Boca Raton – Delray Beach, FL	0.13376	10
Worcester, MA	0.13366	11
New Bedford, MA	0.12692	12
Fitchburg – Leominster, MA	0.12452	13
Killeen – Temple, TX	0.11947	14
Washington, DC – MD – VA	0.11941	15
Glens Falls, NY	0.11895	16
Allentown – Bethlehem – Easton, PA – NJ	0.10849	17
Elmira, NY	0.10820	18
Jacksonville, NC	0.10745	19
Springfield, MA	0.09538	20
Hartford – New Britain – Middletown, CT	0.09218	21
Reading, PA	0.09212	22
Sarasota, FL	0.08100	23
Albany – Schenectady – Troy, NY	0.08052	24
Tampa – Saint Petersburg – Clearwater, FL	0.07640	25
Binghamton, NY	0.07599	26
Jamestown – Dunkirk, NY	0.07541	27
Lawton, OK	0.07445	28
Rochester, NY	0.07392	29
Manchester, NH	0.07304	30
Philadelphia – Wilmington – Trenton, PA – NJ – DE – MD	0.06077	31
Utica – Rome, NY	0.05937	32
Fayetteville, NC	0.05900	33
Lancaster, PA	0.05842	34
Pittsfield, MA	0.05803	35
Ocala, FL	0.05595	36
Fort Pierce, FL	0.05218	37
New London – Norwich, CT – RI	0.05097	38
Las Vegas, NV	0.05071	39
Colorado Springs, CO	0.04886	40
Lewiston – Auburn, ME	0.04655	41
Melbourne – Titusville – Palm Bay, FL	0.04537	42
New Haven – Meriden, CT	0.04451	43
Jacksonville, FL	0.04312	44
Salinas – Seaside – Monterey, CA	0.04274	45
Norfolk – Virginia Beach – Newport News, VA	0.04169	46
Tallahassee, FL	0.04152	47
Clarksville – Hopkinsville, TN – KY	0.03836	48
Charleston, SC	0.03827	49
Buffalo – Niagara Falls, NY	0.03801	50

Source: U.S. Bureau of the Census, Data User Services Division, *1990 Census of Population and Housing,* Summary Tape File 3C, United States Summary, CD-ROM, February 1992.

★334★
Hispanic Population
Hispanic Population, 1990: American Indian, Eskimo, or Aleut

[Table shows the top 50 areas]

MSA	% of total population	Rank
Rapid City, SD	0.54215	1
Tucson, AZ	0.39752	2
Santa Barbara – Santa Maria – Lompoc, CA	0.39555	3
Albuquerque, NM	0.36623	4
Santa Fe, NM	0.36226	5
Yakima, WA	0.34371	6
Pueblo, CO	0.28931	7
Lawton, OK	0.27986	8
Stockton, CA	0.27256	9
Fresno, CA	0.26922	10
Merced, CA	0.26905	11
Phoenix, AZ	0.25465	12
Bakersfield, CA	0.21675	13
Salinas – Seaside – Monterey, CA	0.21537	14
Sioux City, IA – NE	0.21475	15
Great Falls, MT	0.21109	16
Visalia – Tulare – Porterville, CA	0.20133	17
Anchorage, AK	0.19042	18
Sacramento, CA	0.18216	19
Lawrence, KS	0.17849	20
San Diego, CA	0.17430	21
Modesto, CA	0.17273	22
Oklahoma City, OK	0.17000	23
Los Angeles – Anaheim – Riverside, CA	0.16876	24
Reno, NV	0.16688	25
Denver – Boulder, CO	0.16096	26
Enid, OK	0.15334	27
Greeley, CO	0.15248	28
Brownsville – Harlingen, TX	0.15032	29
Yuma, AZ	0.14968	30
Redding, CA	0.14894	31
Colorado Springs, CO	0.14811	32
Fort Collins – Loveland, CO	0.14452	33
Yuba City, CA	0.14351	34
Las Vegas, NV	0.13622	35
Medford, OR	0.13457	36
San Antonio, TX	0.13401	37
Tulsa, OK	0.13245	38
Chico, CA	0.13068	39
San Francisco – Oakland – San Jose, CA	0.13035	40
El Paso, TX	0.12897	41
McAllen – Edinburg – Mission, TX	0.12645	42
Casper, WY	0.12250	43
Bremerton, WA	0.10857	44
Olympia, WA	0.10543	45
Green Bay, WI	0.09918	46
Salem, OR	0.09711	47
Corpus Christi, TX	0.09660	48
Las Cruces, NM	0.09593	49
Boise, ID	0.09428	50

Source: U.S. Bureau of the Census, Data User Services Division, *1990 Census of Population and Housing,* Summary Tape File 3C, United States Summary, CD-ROM, February 1992.

★335★
Hispanic Population
Hispanic Population, 1990: Asian or Pacific Islander

[Table shows the top 50 areas]

MSA	% of total population	Rank
Honolulu, HI	3.05035	1
Stockton, CA	0.56967	2
Salinas – Seaside – Monterey, CA	0.54856	3
San Francisco – Oakland – San Jose, CA	0.44007	4
San Diego, CA	0.42386	5
Merced, CA	0.37163	6
Visalia – Tulare – Porterville, CA	0.36804	7
Santa Barbara – Santa Maria – Lompoc, CA	0.35768	8
Bakersfield, CA	0.33562	9
Bremerton, WA	0.33468	10
Los Angeles – Anaheim – Riverside, CA	0.30176	11
Fresno, CA	0.25798	12
Sacramento, CA	0.25744	13
Yuba City, CA	0.23890	14
Modesto, CA	0.22050	15
Anchorage, AK	0.20235	16
Yuma, AZ	0.16839	17
Albuquerque, NM	0.16626	18
Jacksonville, NC	0.16418	19
Seattle – Tacoma, WA	0.15853	20
Norfolk – Virginia Beach – Newport News, VA	0.15737	21
Lawton, OK	0.14800	22
Yakima, WA	0.14723	23
Killeen – Temple, TX	0.13631	24
Cheyenne, WY	0.13262	25
Las Vegas, NV	0.12597	26
Reading, PA	0.12540	27
Colorado Springs, CO	0.12493	28
New York – Northern New Jersey – Long Island, NY – NJ – CT	0.12193	29
El Paso, TX	0.12052	30
Tucson, AZ	0.11876	31
Fort Walton Beach, FL	0.11754	32
Jacksonville, FL	0.11558	33
Fayetteville, NC	0.11218	34
Reno, NV	0.11073	35
San Antonio, TX	0.10168	36
Clarksville – Hopkinsville, TN – KY	0.09974	37
Corpus Christi, TX	0.09374	38
Houston – Galveston – Brazoria, TX	0.08917	39
Denver – Boulder, CO	0.08808	40
Chicago – Gary – Lake County, IL – IN – WI	0.08740	41
Columbus, GA – AL	0.08351	42
Fitchburg – Leominster, MA	0.08171	43
Washington, DC – MD – VA	0.07891	44
Pensacola, FL	0.07636	45
Santa Fe, NM	0.07604	46
Champaign – Urbana – Rantoul, IL	0.07571	47
Pueblo, CO	0.07558	48

[Continued]

★335★
Hispanic Population, 1990: Asian or Pacific Islander
[Continued]

MSA	% of total population	Rank
Atlantic City, NJ	0.07451	49
Alexandria, LA	0.07449	50

Source: U.S. Bureau of the Census, Data User Services Division, *1990 Census of Population and Housing,* Summary Tape File 3C, United States Summary, CD-ROM, February 1992.

★336★
Hispanic Population
Mexican Population, 1990
[Table shows the top 50 areas]

MSA	% of total population	Rank
Laredo, TX	90.810	1
McAllen – Edinburg – Mission, TX	82.266	2
Brownsville – Harlingen, TX	77.695	3
El Paso, TX	66.654	4
Las Cruces, NM	51.486	5
Corpus Christi, TX	48.289	6
San Antonio, TX	43.926	7
Yuma, AZ	40.016	8
Visalia – Tulare – Porterville, CA	36.341	9
Fresno, CA	32.786	10
Victoria, TX	31.703	11
Odessa, TX	29.652	12
Merced, CA	29.571	13
Salinas – Seaside – Monterey, CA	29.255	14
Los Angeles – Anaheim – Riverside, CA	25.713	15
Bakersfield, CA	25.165	16
San Angelo, TX	23.970	17
Pueblo, CO	23.719	18
Santa Barbara – Santa Maria – Lompoc, CA	23.477	19
Tucson, AZ	22.079	20
Yakima, WA	21.914	21
Lubbock, TX	20.997	22
Stockton, CA	20.226	23
Midland, TX	19.656	24
Albuquerque, NM	19.526	25
Modesto, CA	19.107	26
Austin, TX	18.131	27
Greeley, CO	17.569	28
San Diego, CA	17.362	29
Houston – Galveston – Brazoria, TX	16.790	30
Phoenix, AZ	14.418	31
Santa Fe, NM	14.282	32
Abilene, TX	12.646	33
Richland – Kennewick – Pasco, WA	11.979	34
Yuba City, CA	11.600	35
Bryan – College Station, TX	11.580	36
Amarillo, TX	11.519	37
Dallas – Fort Worth, TX	11.311	38

[Continued]

★336★
Mexican Population, 1990
[Continued]

MSA	% of total population	Rank
Waco, TX	11.171	39
San Francisco – Oakland – San Jose, CA	10.354	40
Sacramento, CA	8.938	41
Killeen – Temple, TX	8.317	42
Denver – Boulder, CO	8.142	43
Naples, FL	8.125	44
Wichita Falls, TX	7.630	45
Chicago – Gary – Lake County, IL – IN – WI	7.523	46
Las Vegas, NV	7.226	47
Cheyenne, WY	7.115	48
Salem, OR	6.378	49
Reno, NV	6.040	50

Source: U.S. Bureau of the Census, Data User Services Division, *1990 Census of Population and Housing,* Summary Tape File 3C, United States Summary, CD-ROM, February 1992.

★337★
Hispanic Population
Puerto Rican Population, 1990
[Table shows the top 50 areas]

MSA	% of total population	Rank
Springfield, MA	7.613	1
New York – Northern New Jersey – Long Island, NY – NJ – CT	6.834	2
Waterbury, CT	5.614	3
Hartford – New Britain – Middletown, CT	5.215	4
Fitchburg – Leominster, MA	5.129	5
Orlando, FL	4.820	6
New Haven – Meriden, CT	4.215	7
Atlantic City, NJ	3.842	8
Reading, PA	3.815	9
Worcester, MA	3.203	10
Miami – Fort Lauderdale, FL	2.965	11
Allentown – Bethlehem – Easton, PA – NJ	2.934	12
Lancaster, PA	2.904	13
New Bedford, MA	2.649	14
Philadelphia – Wilmington – Trenton, PA – NJ – DE – MD	2.538	15
Jamestown – Dunkirk, NY	2.307	16
Rochester, NY	2.034	17
Killeen – Temple, TX	2.004	18
Honolulu, HI	1.936	19
Poughkeepsie, NY	1.910	20
Chicago – Gary – Lake County, IL – IN – WI	1.900	21
New London – Norwich, CT – RI	1.860	22
Boston – Lawrence – Salem, MA – NH	1.804	23
Fort Myers – Cape Coral, FL	1.746	24

[Continued]

★ 337 ★

Puerto Rican Population, 1990
[Continued]

MSA	% of total population	Rank
Fayetteville, NC	1.660	25
Jacksonville, NC	1.654	26
Tampa – Saint Petersburg – Clearwater, FL	1.632	27
Lawton, OK	1.579	28
Daytona Beach, FL	1.573	29
West Palm Beach – Boca Raton – Delray Beach, FL	1.430	30
Buffalo – Niagara Falls, NY	1.322	31
Ocala, FL	1.301	32
Utica – Rome, NY	1.259	33
Naples, FL	1.210	34
Melbourne – Titusville – Palm Bay, FL	1.199	35
Cleveland – Akron – Lorain, OH	1.198	36
Providence – Pawtucket – Fall River, RI – MA	1.152	37
Columbus, GA – AL	1.140	38
Clarksville – Hopkinsville, TN – KY	1.115	39
Harrisburg – Lebanon – Carlisle, PA	1.065	40
Milwaukee – Racine, WI	0.955	41
Albany – Schenectady – Troy, NY	0.933	42
Fort Pierce, FL	0.899	43
York, PA	0.886	44
Fort Walton Beach, FL	0.836	45
Youngstown – Warren, OH	0.823	46
Elmira, NY	0.818	47
Gainesville, FL	0.802	48
Erie, PA	0.785	49
Jacksonville, FL	0.768	50

Source: U.S. Bureau of the Census, Data User Services Division, *1990 Census of Population and Housing*, Summary Tape File 3C, United States Summary, CD-ROM, February 1992.

★ 338 ★

Hispanic Population

South American Population, 1990: Colombian
[Table shows the top 50 areas]

MSA	% of total population	Rank
Miami – Fort Lauderdale, FL	2.0649	1
New York – Northern New Jersey – Long Island, NY – NJ – CT	0.8765	2
Providence – Pawtucket – Fall River, RI – MA	0.4525	3
Orlando, FL	0.4388	4
West Palm Beach – Boca Raton – Delray Beach, FL	0.3882	5
Houston – Galveston – Brazoria, TX	0.2875	6
Los Angeles – Anaheim – Riverside, CA	0.2092	7
Washington, DC – MD – VA	0.2036	8

[Continued]

★ 338 ★

South American Population, 1990: Colombian
[Continued]

MSA	% of total population	Rank
Tampa – Saint Petersburg – Clearwater, FL	0.2026	9
Atlantic City, NJ	0.1985	10
Gainesville, FL	0.1950	11
Tallahassee, FL	0.1901	12
Boston – Lawrence – Salem, MA – NH	0.1843	13
Naples, FL	0.1736	14
Anchorage, AK	0.1728	15
Poughkeepsie, NY	0.1692	16
Ocala, FL	0.1601	17
Hartford – New Britain – Middletown, CT	0.1580	18
Fort Myers – Cape Coral, FL	0.1435	19
Las Vegas, NV	0.1351	20
Fort Pierce, FL	0.1338	21
Melbourne – Titusville – Palm Bay, FL	0.1271	22
Chicago – Gary – Lake County, IL – IN – WI	0.1198	23
Worcester, MA	0.1188	24
Atlanta, GA	0.1160	25
Manchester, NH	0.1150	26
Lawton, OK	0.1112	27
Daytona Beach, FL	0.1033	28
Allentown – Bethlehem – Easton, PA – NJ	0.1005	29
Fitchburg – Leominster, MA	0.1002	30
New Haven – Meriden, CT	0.1000	31
San Francisco – Oakland – San Jose, CA	0.0989	32
Greenville – Spartanburg, SC	0.0972	33
San Diego, CA	0.0965	34
Salinas – Seaside – Monterey, CA	0.0964	35
Reno, NV	0.0915	36
Lancaster, PA	0.0906	37
Waterbury, CT	0.0902	38
Lexington-Fayette, KY	0.0898	39
Jacksonville, FL	0.0886	40
Springfield, MA	0.0867	41
Rochester, MN	0.0855	42
Philadelphia – Wilmington – Trenton, PA – NJ – DE – MD	0.0826	43
New Orleans, LA	0.0814	44
Lafayette, LA	0.0776	45
Terre Haute, IN	0.0734	46
Scranton – Wilkes-Barre, PA	0.0711	47
Burlington, VT	0.0708	48
Dallas – Fort Worth, TX	0.0691	49
Austin, TX	0.0681	50

Source: U.S. Bureau of the Census, Data User Services Division, *1990 Census of Population and Housing*, Summary Tape File 3C, United States Summary, CD-ROM, February 1992.

★339★
Hispanic Population
South American Population, 1990: Ecuadorian
[Table shows the top 50 areas]

MSA	% of total population	Rank
New York – Northern New Jersey – Long Island, NY – NJ – CT	0.65061	1
Miami – Fort Lauderdale, FL	0.33399	2
Los Angeles – Anaheim – Riverside, CA	0.15928	3
Fitchburg – Leominster, MA	0.13911	4
Washington, DC – MD – VA	0.12025	5
Chicago – Gary – Lake County, IL – IN – WI	0.10541	6
West Palm Beach – Boca Raton – Delray Beach, FL	0.08813	7
Orlando, FL	0.08492	8
New Haven – Meriden, CT	0.06903	9
Poughkeepsie, NY	0.06591	10
Santa Barbara – Santa Maria – Lompoc, CA	0.05438	11
Allentown – Bethlehem – Easton, PA – NJ	0.05403	12
Daytona Beach, FL	0.05341	13
Waterbury, CT	0.05053	14
Sarasota, FL	0.04824	15
Houston – Galveston – Brazoria, TX	0.04718	16
Tampa – Saint Petersburg – Clearwater, FL	0.04700	17
Fayetteville, NC	0.04516	18
Boston – Lawrence – Salem, MA – NH	0.04351	19
New Orleans, LA	0.04262	20
Providence – Pawtucket – Fall River, RI – MA	0.04240	21
Fort Myers – Cape Coral, FL	0.04237	22
Columbus, GA – AL	0.04196	23
Bryan – College Station, TX	0.04103	24
Ocala, FL	0.03901	25
Fort Pierce, FL	0.03704	26
Worcester, MA	0.03662	27
Charlotte – Gastonia – Rock Hill, NC – SC	0.03614	28
Pensacola, FL	0.03513	29
Bakersfield, CA	0.03422	30
San Francisco – Oakland – San Jose, CA	0.03421	31
Melbourne – Titusville – Palm Bay, FL	0.03409	32
Atlantic City, NJ	0.03381	33
Provo – Orem, UT	0.03339	34
Gainesville, FL	0.03283	35
Jacksonville, NC	0.03137	36
Texarkana, TX – Texarkana, AR	0.02997	37
San Diego, CA	0.02962	38
New London – Norwich, CT – RI	0.02886	39
Las Vegas, NV	0.02819	40
El Paso, TX	0.02603	41
Syracuse, NY	0.02576	42
Hartford – New Britain – Middletown, CT	0.02542	43

[Continued]

★339★
Hispanic Population
South American Population, 1990: Ecuadorian
[Continued]

MSA	% of total population	Rank
Iowa City, IA	0.02497	44
Wichita, KS	0.02493	45
Yuma, AZ	0.02339	46
Columbia, SC	0.02338	47
Brownsville – Harlingen, TX	0.02307	48
South Bend – Mishawaka, IN	0.02307	48
Abilene, TX	0.02173	49

Source: U.S. Bureau of the Census, Data User Services Division, *1990 Census of Population and Housing,* Summary Tape File 3C, United States Summary, CD-ROM, February 1992.

★340★
Hispanic Population
South American Population, 1990: Peruvian
[Table shows the top 50 areas]

MSA	% of total population	Rank
Miami – Fort Lauderdale, FL	0.64130	1
New York – Northern New Jersey – Long Island, NY – NJ – CT	0.31195	2
Washington, DC – MD – VA	0.29613	3
Hartford – New Britain – Middletown, CT	0.20380	4
Los Angeles – Anaheim – Riverside, CA	0.20162	5
San Francisco – Oakland – San Jose, CA	0.19829	6
Athens, GA	0.13950	7
West Palm Beach – Boca Raton – Delray Beach, FL	0.09264	8
Provo – Orem, UT	0.08953	9
Salinas – Seaside – Monterey, CA	0.08885	10
Sarasota, FL	0.08352	11
Anchorage, AK	0.08350	12
Orlando, FL	0.08035	13
Houston – Galveston – Brazoria, TX	0.07418	14
Champaign – Urbana – Rantoul, IL	0.06935	15
San Diego, CA	0.06425	16
Gainesville, FL	0.06026	17
Salt Lake City – Ogden, UT	0.06025	18
Boston – Lawrence – Salem, MA – NH	0.05763	19
Santa Barbara – Santa Maria – Lompoc, CA	0.05736	20
Naples, FL	0.05391	21
Tucson, AZ	0.05383	22
Chicago – Gary – Lake County, IL – IN – WI	0.05373	23
Poughkeepsie, NY	0.05357	24
Melbourne – Titusville – Palm Bay, FL	0.05339	25
Denver – Boulder, CO	0.05335	26
Bakersfield, CA	0.05281	27

[Continued]

★340★

South American Population, 1990: Peruvian

[Continued]

MSA	% of total population	Rank
Las Cruces, NM	0.05166	28
Sacramento, CA	0.05118	29
Tampa – Saint Petersburg – Clearwater, FL	0.04826	30
Dallas – Fort Worth, TX	0.04630	31
Atlanta, GA	0.04623	32
Providence – Pawtucket – Fall River, RI – MA	0.04582	33
Bryan – College Station, TX	0.04513	34
Manchester, NH	0.04463	35
Modesto, CA	0.04426	36
Fort Pierce, FL	0.04421	37
Lawrence, KS	0.04401	38
Reno, NV	0.04359	39
Fort Collins – Loveland, CO	0.04298	40
Yuba City, CA	0.04240	41
Las Vegas, NV	0.04140	42
Stockton, CA	0.03995	43
Seattle – Tacoma, WA	0.03943	44
New Haven – Meriden, CT	0.03942	45
Springfield, MA	0.03909	46
Fort Myers – Cape Coral, FL	0.03879	47
Austin, TX	0.03800	48
El Paso, TX	0.03769	49
Jacksonville, NC	0.03537	50

Source: U.S. Bureau of the Census, Data User Services Division, *1990 Census of Population and Housing*, Summary Tape File 3C, United States Summary, CD-ROM, February 1992.

★341★

Native American Population

American Indian, Eskimo, or Aleut Population, 1990: Aleut

[Table shows the top 50 areas]

MSA	% of total population	Rank
Anchorage, AK	1.15314	1
Sherman – Denison, TX	0.05893	2
Seattle – Tacoma, WA	0.05857	3
Bremerton, WA	0.05429	4
Olympia, WA	0.04962	5
Bradenton, FL	0.04109	6
Bellingham, WA	0.03913	7
Santa Fe, NM	0.02819	8
Charlottesville, VA	0.02593	9
Portland – Vancouver, OR – WA	0.02429	10
Salem, OR	0.02194	11
Redding, CA	0.02176	12
Honolulu, HI	0.02057	13
Fresno, CA	0.01918	14
Waterbury, CT	0.01715	15
Stockton, CA	0.01706	16
Colorado Springs, CO	0.01688	17
Fort Collins – Loveland, CO	0.01612	18

[Continued]

American Indian, Eskimo, or Aleut Population, 1990: Aleut

[Continued]

MSA	% of total population	Rank
Sacramento, CA	0.01580	19
Panama City, FL	0.01496	20
Wichita Falls, TX	0.01471	21
Appleton – Oshkosh – Neenah, WI	0.01460	22
San Diego, CA	0.01397	23
Bakersfield, CA	0.01380	24
Florence, SC	0.01312	25
Greeley, CO	0.01290	26
Charleston, WV	0.01278	27
Madison, WI	0.01226	28
Pine Bluff, AR	0.01170	29
Biloxi – Gulfport, MS	0.01167	30
San Francisco – Oakland – San Jose, CA	0.01151	31
Austin, TX	0.01100	32
Reno, NV	0.01099	33
Odessa, TX	0.01009	34
Yakima, WA	0.01006	35
Rapid City, SD	0.00983	36
Fort Smith, AR – OK	0.00966	37
Salinas – Seaside – Monterey, CA	0.00956	38
Yuma, AZ	0.00935	39
Spokane, WA	0.00913	40
Laredo, TX	0.00901	41
Eugene – Springfield, OR	0.00884	42
Los Angeles – Anaheim – Riverside, CA	0.00848	43
Atlantic City, NJ	0.00814	44
Santa Barbara – Santa Maria – Lompoc, CA	0.00812	45
Canton, OH	0.00787	46
Dallas – Fort Worth, TX	0.00762	47
Pueblo, CO	0.00731	48
Merced, CA	0.00729	49
Tulsa, OK	0.00719	50

Source: U.S. Bureau of the Census, Data User Services Division, *1990 Census of Population and Housing*, Summary Tape File 3C, United States Summary, CD-ROM, February 1992.

★342★

Native American Population

American Indian, Eskimo, or Aleut Population, 1990: American Indian

[Table shows the top 50 areas]

MSA	% of total population	Rank
Rapid City, SD	7.209	1
Tulsa, OK	6.811	2
Fort Smith, AR – OK	5.352	3
Oklahoma City, OK	4.793	4
Lawton, OK	4.555	5
Yakima, WA	4.445	6
Great Falls, MT	4.042	7

[Continued]

★342★
American Indian, Eskimo, or Aleut Population, 1990: American Indian
[Continued]

MSA	% of total population	Rank
Houma – Thibodaux, LA	3.727	8
Albuquerque, NM	3.326	9
Bellingham, WA	3.000	10
Tucson, AZ	2.997	11
Anchorage, AK	2.966	12
Billings, MT	2.919	13
Lawrence, KS	2.613	14
Redding, CA	2.594	15
Santa Fe, NM	2.330	16
Enid, OK	2.149	17
Yuba City, CA	2.144	18
Bismarck, ND	2.026	19
Reno, NV	1.926	20
Chico, CA	1.916	21
Decatur, AL	1.906	22
Joplin, MO	1.895	23
Duluth, MN – WI	1.884	24
Green Bay, WI	1.839	25
Phoenix, AZ	1.795	26
Sioux City, IA – NE	1.721	27
Medford, OR	1.694	28
Fayetteville, NC	1.663	29
Bremerton, WA	1.647	30
Grand Forks, ND	1.596	31
Olympia, WA	1.521	32
Salem, OR	1.509	33
Yuma, AZ	1.491	34
Spokane, WA	1.415	35
Fayetteville – Springdale, AR	1.384	36
Visalia – Tulare – Porterville, CA	1.323	37
Bakersfield, CA	1.310	38
Sherman – Denison, TX	1.303	39
Sacramento, CA	1.196	40
Sioux Falls, SD	1.191	41
Seattle – Tacoma, WA	1.187	42
Stockton, CA	1.186	43
Modesto, CA	1.175	44
Topeka, KS	1.128	45
Wichita, KS	1.125	46
Fresno, CA	1.108	47
Eugene – Springfield, OR	1.102	48
Bangor, ME	1.059	49
Cheyenne, WY	1.051	50

Source: U.S. Bureau of the Census, Data User Services Division, *1990 Census of Population and Housing,* Summary Tape File 3C, United States Summary, CD-ROM, February 1992.

★343★
Native American Population
American Indian, Eskimo, or Aleut Population, 1990: Eskimo
[Table shows the top 50 areas]

MSA	% of total population	Rank
Anchorage, AK	2.46843	1
Seattle – Tacoma, WA	0.04306	2
Bremerton, WA	0.03742	3
Spokane, WA	0.03348	4
Redding, CA	0.03333	5
Columbus, GA – AL	0.02880	6
Bellingham, WA	0.02270	7
Longview – Marshall, TX	0.02216	8
Rapid City, SD	0.02213	9
Billings, MT	0.02116	10
Lawrence, KS	0.01956	11
Tyler, TX	0.01784	12
Fort Walton Beach, FL	0.01739	13
Clarksville – Hopkinsville, TN – KY	0.01712	14
Manchester, NH	0.01691	15
Salem, OR	0.01619	16
Portland – Vancouver, OR – WA	0.01577	17
Sacramento, CA	0.01452	18
Odessa, TX	0.01429	19
Decatur, AL	0.01368	20
Lafayette – West Lafayette, IN	0.01302	21
Eugene – Springfield, OR	0.01272	22
Oklahoma City, OK	0.01272	22
Bangor, ME	0.01240	23
Florence, SC	0.01224	24
Boise, ID	0.01215	25
Olympia, WA	0.01178	26
Rockford, IL	0.01163	27
Burlington, VT	0.01141	28
Greeley, CO	0.01138	29
Salt Lake City – Ogden, UT	0.01138	29
Pensacola, FL	0.01103	30
Gainesville, FL	0.01078	31
Augusta, GA – SC	0.01058	32
Medford, OR	0.01025	33
Reno, NV	0.01021	34
Portsmouth – Dover – Rochester, NH – ME	0.00983	35
Colorado Springs, CO	0.00982	36
Sarasota, FL	0.00972	37
Honolulu, HI	0.00957	38
San Francisco – Oakland – San Jose, CA	0.00953	39
Albany, GA	0.00888	40
Poughkeepsie, NY	0.00886	41
Denver – Boulder, CO	0.00871	42
Kansas City, MO – KS	0.00862	43
Montgomery, AL	0.00855	44
Stockton, CA	0.00853	45
Youngstown – Warren, OH	0.00853	45
Anderson, IN	0.00842	46
Duluth, MN – WI	0.00833	47

Source: U.S. Bureau of the Census, Data User Services Division, *1990 Census of Population and Housing,* Summary Tape File 3C, United States Summary, CD-ROM, February 1992.

★344★
Pacific Islander Population
Micronesian Population, 1990: Guamanian
[Table shows the top 50 areas]

MSA	% of total population	Rank
Bremerton, WA	0.44221	1
Honolulu, HI	0.24431	2
Killeen – Temple, TX	0.23345	3
Salinas – Seaside – Monterey, CA	0.22971	4
San Diego, CA	0.21409	5
Olympia, WA	0.17986	6
Lawton, OK	0.13634	7
Columbus, GA – AL	0.12630	8
Fayetteville, NC	0.10926	9
San Francisco – Oakland – San Jose, CA	0.10396	10
Clarksville – Hopkinsville, TN – KY	0.09856	11
Seattle – Tacoma, WA	0.08143	12
Fort Walton Beach, FL	0.08138	13
Jacksonville, NC	0.07942	14
Merced, CA	0.07847	15
Bellingham, WA	0.07122	16
Stockton, CA	0.06533	17
Anchorage, AK	0.06230	18
Colorado Springs, CO	0.06070	19
Los Angeles – Anaheim – Riverside, CA	0.06031	20
Yuma, AZ	0.05894	21
El Paso, TX	0.05713	22
Santa Barbara – Santa Maria – Lompoc, CA	0.05682	23
Las Cruces, NM	0.05608	24
Las Vegas, NV	0.05112	25
Sacramento, CA	0.04996	26
Eugene – Springfield, OR	0.04984	27
Pine Bluff, AR	0.04913	28
Salem, OR	0.04460	29
Great Falls, MT	0.04119	30
San Angelo, TX	0.03961	31
Portland – Vancouver, OR – WA	0.03904	32
Albuquerque, NM	0.03745	33
Fresno, CA	0.03700	34
Redding, CA	0.03196	35
Norfolk – Virginia Beach – Newport News, VA	0.03094	36
Spokane, WA	0.03044	37
Yuba City, CA	0.02691	38
San Antonio, TX	0.02673	39
Dothan, AL	0.02672	40
Modesto, CA	0.02672	40
Lawrence, KS	0.02567	41
Champaign – Urbana – Rantoul, IL	0.02543	42
Wichita Falls, TX	0.02533	43
Visalia – Tulare – Porterville, CA	0.02501	44
Jacksonville, FL	0.02393	45
Pensacola, FL	0.02207	46
Austin, TX	0.02162	47
Oklahoma City, OK	0.02065	48
Washington, DC – MD – VA	0.01965	49

Source: U.S. Bureau of the Census, Data User Services Division, *1990 Census of Population and Housing*, Summary Tape File 3C, United States Summary, CD-ROM, February 1992.

★345★
Pacific Islander Population
Micronesian Population, 1990: Melanesian
[Table shows the top 50 areas]

MSA	% of total population	Rank
Modesto, CA	0.14088	1
Sacramento, CA	0.07987	2
San Francisco – Oakland – San Jose, CA	0.04332	3
Honolulu, HI	0.04257	4
Salinas – Seaside – Monterey, CA	0.03824	5
Stockton, CA	0.02726	6
Eugene – Springfield, OR	0.01873	7
Portland – Vancouver, OR – WA	0.01360	8
Seattle – Tacoma, WA	0.01114	9
Bloomington, IN	0.01101	10
Lawton, OK	0.00807	11
Reno, NV	0.00668	12
Muncie, IN	0.00585	13
Los Angeles – Anaheim – Riverside, CA	0.00531	14
Salt Lake City – Ogden, UT	0.00457	15
Olympia, WA	0.00372	16
Milwaukee – Racine, WI	0.00249	17
Provo – Orem, UT	0.00190	18
San Diego, CA	0.00180	19
Dallas – Fort Worth, TX	0.00160	20
Fresno, CA	0.00150	21
Tucson, AZ	0.00150	21
Waterloo – Cedar Falls, IA	0.00136	22
Atlanta, GA	0.00134	23
Denver – Boulder, CO	0.00130	24
Houston – Galveston – Brazoria, TX	0.00129	25
Lancaster, PA	0.00118	26
Baltimore, MD	0.00113	27
Springfield, MA	0.00113	27
Rochester, NY	0.00100	28
Providence – Pawtucket – Fall River, RI – MA	0.00096	29
Tampa – Saint Petersburg – Clearwater, FL	0.00087	30
Boston – Lawrence – Salem, MA – NH	0.00079	31
Saint Louis, MO – IL	0.00078	32
New Orleans, LA	0.00073	33
Grand Rapids, MI	0.00058	34
New York – Northern New Jersey – Long Island, NY – NJ – CT	0.00052	35
Washington, DC – MD – VA	0.00043	36
Philadelphia – Wilmington – Trenton, PA – NJ – DE – MD	0.00017	37
Detroit – Ann Arbor, MI	0.00011	38
Abilene, TX	0.00000	39
Albany, GA	0.00000	39
Albany – Schenectady – Troy, NY	0.00000	39
Albuquerque, NM	0.00000	39
Alexandria, LA	0.00000	39
Allentown – Bethlehem – Easton, PA – NJ	0.00000	39
Anchorage, AK	0.00000	39

[Continued]

★345★

Micronesian Population, 1990: Melanesian
[Continued]

MSA	% of total population	Rank
Anniston, AL	0.00000	39
Atlantic City, NJ	0.00000	39
Augusta, GA–SC	0.00000	39

Source: U.S. Bureau of the Census, Data User Services Division, 1990 Census of Population and Housing, Summary Tape File 3C, United States Summary, CD-ROM, February 1992.

★346★

Pacific Islander Population

Polynesian Population, 1990: Hawaiian
[Table shows the top 50 areas]

MSA	% of total population	Rank
Honolulu, HI	10.78338	1
Bremerton, WA	0.20186	2
Olympia, WA	0.19908	3
Anchorage, AK	0.19484	4
Salinas–Seaside–Monterey, CA	0.18501	5
Las Vegas, NV	0.17506	6
San Francisco–Oakland–San Jose, CA	0.16212	7
San Diego, CA	0.16029	8
Provo–Orem, UT	0.15858	9
Yuba City, CA	0.15655	10
Merced, CA	0.15134	11
Sacramento, CA	0.12774	12
Killeen–Temple, TX	0.12691	13
Seattle–Tacoma, WA	0.12117	14
Colorado Springs, CO	0.11738	15
Clarksville–Hopkinsville, TN–KY	0.10328	16
Greeley, CO	0.10089	17
Portland–Vancouver, OR–WA	0.09947	18
Jacksonville, NC	0.09811	19
Stockton, CA	0.09779	20
Bakersfield, CA	0.09421	21
Reno, NV	0.09228	22
Los Angeles–Anaheim–Riverside, CA	0.09179	23
Cheyenne, WY	0.09024	24
Fayetteville, NC	0.08996	25
Eugene–Springfield, OR	0.08978	26
Modesto, CA	0.08663	27
Pueblo, CO	0.07720	28
Salt Lake City–Ogden, UT	0.07219	29
Fort Walton Beach, FL	0.06747	30
Yuma, AZ	0.06736	31
Abilene, TX	0.06686	32
Lawton, OK	0.06548	33
Spokane, WA	0.06088	34
Medford, OR	0.05943	35
Lincoln, NE	0.05898	36
Santa Barbara–Santa Maria–Lompoc, CA	0.05844	37
Grand Forks, ND	0.05801	38

[Continued]

★346★

Polynesian Population, 1990: Hawaiian
[Continued]

MSA	% of total population	Rank
Visalia–Tulare–Porterville, CA	0.04937	39
Redding, CA	0.04829	40
Fresno, CA	0.04794	41
Phoenix, AZ	0.04769	42
Orlando, FL	0.04689	43
Sioux Falls, SD	0.04685	44
Dothan, AL	0.04581	45
Salem, OR	0.04532	46
Boise, ID	0.04519	47
Savannah, GA	0.04451	48
Pensacola, FL	0.04413	49
New London–Norwich, CT–RI	0.04123	50

Source: U.S. Bureau of the Census, Data User Services Division, 1990 Census of Population and Housing, Summary Tape File 3C, United States Summary, CD-ROM, February 1992.

★347★

Pacific Islander Population

Polynesian Population, 1990: Tongan
[Table shows the top 50 areas]

MSA	% of total population	Rank
Honolulu, HI	1.72560	1
Anchorage, AK	0.20942	2
San Diego, CA	0.17854	3
Lawton, OK	0.12916	4
Salt Lake City–Ogden, UT	0.12777	5
Bremerton, WA	0.12439	6
San Francisco–Oakland–San Jose, CA	0.12163	7
Seattle–Tacoma, WA	0.11199	8
Los Angeles–Anaheim–Riverside, CA	0.10078	9
Clarksville–Hopkinsville, TN–KY	0.09915	10
Salinas–Seaside–Monterey, CA	0.09841	11
Provo–Orem, UT	0.09446	12
Fayetteville, NC	0.07102	13
Jacksonville, NC	0.04004	14
Las Cruces, NM	0.03985	15
Kansas City, MO–KS	0.03320	16
Las Vegas, NV	0.02967	17
Fresno, CA	0.02936	18
Sacramento, CA	0.02842	19
Colorado Springs, CO	0.02796	20
Santa Barbara–Santa Maria–Lompoc, CA	0.02733	21
Bakersfield, CA	0.02521	22
Modesto, CA	0.02348	23
San Angelo, TX	0.02336	24
Richland–Kennewick–Pasco, WA	0.02266	25
Columbus, GA–AL	0.02263	26
Atlantic City, NJ	0.02254	27
Great Falls, MT	0.02188	28
Pensacola, FL	0.02091	29

[Continued]

★347★
Polynesian Population, 1990: Tongan
[Continued]

MSA	% of total population	Rank
Sharon, PA	0.01983	30
Chico, CA	0.01977	31
Olympia, WA	0.01799	32
Eugene–Springfield, OR	0.01767	33
Portland–Vancouver, OR–WA	0.01719	34
Spokane, WA	0.01716	35
Stockton, CA	0.01623	36
Reno, NV	0.01610	37
Savannah, GA	0.01525	38
Medford, OR	0.01435	39
Yuma, AZ	0.01403	40
El Paso, TX	0.01369	41
Decatur, IL	0.01365	42
Billings, MT	0.01323	43
Norfolk–Virginia Beach–Newport News, VA	0.01289	44
Melbourne–Titusville–Palm Bay, FL	0.01203	45
Tucson, AZ	0.01170	46
Davenport–Rock Island–Moline, IA–IL	0.01140	47
Raleigh–Durham, NC	0.01047	48
Kokomo, IN	0.01032	49
Killeen–Temple, TX	0.01018	50

Source: U.S. Bureau of the Census, Data User Services Division, *1990 Census of Population and Housing,* Summary Tape File 3C, United States Summary, CD-ROM, February 1992.

★348★
Population Changes
Population Changes, 1980-1992: 25 Cities With the Greatest Growth Rate

Data refer to cities with populations of 200,000 or more.

City/MSA	Rate	Rank
Mesa, AZ	94.6	1
Las Vegas, NV	79.5	2
Fresno, CA	72.9	3
Arlington, TX	72.3	4
Virginia Beach, VA	59.1	5
Aurora, CO	51.1	6
Stockton, CA	48.1	7
Raleigh, NC	46.8	8
Austin, TX	42.3	9
Santa Ana, CA	41.2	10
Anchorage, AK	41.0	11
Riverside, CA	39.9	12
Sacramento, CA	38.8	13
Colorado Springs, CO	37.5	14
Charlotte, NC	32.0	15
San Diego, CA	31.2	16
Phoenix, AZ	28.2	17
El Paso, TX	27.9	18
San Jose, CA	27.3	19
Tucson, AZ	25.6	20

[Continued]

★348★
Population Changes, 1980-1992: 25 Cities With the Greatest Growth Rate
[Continued]

City/MSA	Rate	Rank
Anaheim, CA	24.9	21
San Antonio, TX	23.0	22
Jacksonville, FL	22.2	23
Long Beach, CA	21.4	24
Portland, OR	21.0	25

Source: U.S. Department of Commerce, Economics and Statistics Administration, Bureau of the Census, *County and City Data Book 1994: A Statistical Abstract Supplement,* Washington, D.C.: U.S. Government Printing Office, August 1994, p. xxvii.

★349★
Population Changes
Population Changes, 1980-1992: 25 Cities With the Slowest Growth Rate

Data refer to cities with populations of 200,000 or more.

City/MSA	Rate	Rank
Akron, OH	-5.7	17
Atlanta, GA	-7.1	15
Baltimore, MD	-7.7	13
Birmingham, AL	-6.8	16
Buffalo, NY	-9.7	8
Chicago, IL	-7.9	12
Cincinnati, OH	-5.5	19
Cleveland, OH	-12.4	6
Corpus Christi, TX	-14.8	4
Detroit, MI	-15.9	2
Kansas City, MO	-3.7	21
Louisville, KY	-9.3	9
Memphis, TN	-5.6	18
Milwaukee, WI	-3.0	23
Minneapolis, MN	-2.2	24
New Orleans, LA	-12.2	7
Newark, NJ	-18.6	1
Norfolk, VA	-4.9	20
Philadelphia, PA	-8.0	11
Pittsburgh, PA	-13.5	5
Richmond, VA	-7.7	14
Rochester, NY	-3.1	22
Saint Louis, MO	-15.3	3
Toledo, OH	-7.1	15
Washington, DC	-8.3	10

Source: U.S. Department of Commerce, Economics and Statistics Administration, Bureau of the Census, *County and City Data Book 1994: A Statistical Abstract Supplement,* Washington, D.C.: U.S. Government Printing Office, August 1994, p. xxvii.

★350★

Population Changes

Population of Metropolitan Areas, 1994: Percent Change Since 1990

City	Per-cent	Rank
Akron, OH PMSA	2.9	79
Albany-Schenectady-Troy, NY MSA	1.6	90
Albuquerque, NM MSA	9.6	28
Allentown-Bethlehem-Easton, PA MSA	2.8	80
Anchorage, AK MSA	12.1	13
Ann Arbor, MI PMSA	5.1	58
Appleton-Oshkosh-Neenah, WI MSA	5.4	55
Atlanta, GA MSA	12.6	9
Atlantic City-Cape May, NJ PMSA	3.3	75
Augusta-Aiken, GA-SC MSA	8.0	35
Austin-San Marcos, TX MSA	13.9	8
Bakersfield, CA MSA	11.8	14
Baltimore, MD PMSA	3.2	76
Baton Rouge, LA MSA	5.7	52
Beaumont-Port Arthur, TX MSA	3.2	76
Bergen-Passaic, NJ PMSA	2.0	86
Biloxi-Gulfport-Pascagoula, MS MSA	8.6	31
Binghamton, NY MSA	-1.0	103
Birmingham, AL MSA	3.8	70
Boise City, ID MSA	17.5	3
Boulder-Longmont, CO PMSA	10.8	17
Brazoria, TX PMSA	10.3	22
Bremerton, WA PMSA	16.2	4
Brownsville-Harlingen-San Benito, TX MSA	15.2	6
Canton-Massillon, OH MSA	2.1	85
Charleston, WV MSA	1.7	89
Charleston-North Charleston, SC MSA	3.0	78
Charlotte-Gastonia-Rock Hill, NC-SC MSA	8.5	32
Chattanooga, TN-GA MSA	3.5	73
Chicago, IL PMSA	3.5	73
Chicago-Gary-Kenosha, IL-IN-WI CMSA	3.5	73
Cincinnati, OH-KY-IN PMSA	3.6	72
Cincinnati-Hamilton, OH-KY-IN CMSA	4.2	67
Cleveland-Akron, OH CMSA	1.4	91
Cleveland-Lorain-Elyria, OH PMSA	0.9	95
Colorado Springs, CO MSA	14.0	7
Columbia, SC MSA	7.1	44
Columbus, GA-AL MSA	5.1	58
Columbus, OH MSA	5.8	51
Corpus Christi, TX MSA	7.4	41
Dallas, TX PMSA	8.3	33
Dallas-Fort Worth, TX CMSA	8.1	34
Davenport-Moline-Rock Island, IA-IL MSA	2.0	86
Dayton-Springfield, OH MSA	0.5	98

[Continued]

★350★

Population of Metropolitan Areas, 1994: Percent Change Since 1990

[Continued]

City	Per-cent	Rank
Daytona Beach, FL MSA	10.3	22
Denver, CO PMSA	10.7	18
Denver-Boulder-Greeley, CO CMSA	10.6	19
Des Moines, IA MSA	6.0	49
Detroit, MI PMSA	0.9	95
Detroit-Ann Arbor-Flint, MI CMSA	1.3	92
Dutchess County, NY PMSA	0.8	96
El Paso, TX MSA	12.4	11
Erie, PA MSA	1.7	89
Eugene-Springfield, OR MSA	5.7	52
Evansville-Henderson, IN-KY MSA	2.7	81
Fayetteville, NC MSA	4.6	63
Flint, MI PMSA	0.7	97
Fort Lauderdale, FL PMSA	10.2	23
Fort Myers-Cape Coral, FL MSA	9.6	28
Fort Pierce-Port St. Lucie, FL MSA	10.8	17
Fort Wayne, IN MSA	2.8	80
Fort Worth-Arlington, TX PMSA	7.6	39
Fresno, CA MSA	10.5	20
Galveston-Texas City, TX PMSA	8.0	35
Gary, IN PMSA	2.5	83
Grand Rapids-Muskegon-Holland, MI MSA	5.0	59
Greeley, CO PMSA	9.3	29
Greensboro-Winston-Salem-High Point, NC MSA	5.4	55
Greenville-Spartanburg-Anderson, SC MSA	5.2	57
Hagerstown, MD PMSA	4.3	66
Hamilton-Middletown, OH PMSA	7.3	42
Harrisburg-Lebanon-Carlisle, PA MSA	3.7	71
Hickory-Morganton, NC MSA	4.6	63
Honolulu, HI MSA	4.6	63
Houston, TX PMSA	10.0	24
Houston-Galveston-Brazoria, TX CMSA	9.9	25
Huntington-Ashland, WV-KY-OH MSA	1.2	93
Huntsville, AL MSA	7.9	36
Indianapolis, IN MSA	5.9	50
Jackson, MS MSA	4.2	67
Jacksonville, FL MSA	7.2	43
Jersey City, NJ PMSA	-0.1	101
Johnson City-Kingsport-Bristol, TN-VA MSA	3.3	75
Kalamazoo-Battle Creek, MI MSA	3.1	77
Kankakee, IL PMSA	5.2	57
Kansas City, MO-KS MSA	4.1	68
Kenosha, WI PMSA	7.5	40
Killeen-Temple, TX MSA	12.5	10
Knoxville, TN MSA	7.7	38

[Continued]

★350★

Population of Metropolitan Areas, 1994: Percent Change Since 1990
[Continued]

City	Per-cent	Rank
Lafayette, LA MSA	4.7	62
Lakeland-Winter Haven, FL MSA	6.0	49
Lancaster, PA MSA	4.7	62
Lansing-East Lansing, MI MSA	0.8	96
Las Vegas, NV-AZ MSA	26.2	1
Lexington, KY MSA	6.1	48
Little Rock-North Little Rock, AR MSA	4.8	61
Los Angeles-Long Beach, CA PMSA	3.2	76
Los Angeles-Riverside-Orange County, CA CMSA	5.3	56
Louisville, KY-IN MSA	3.4	74
Macon, GA MSA	5.6	53
Madison, WI MSA	6.3	47
McAllen-Edinburg-Mission, TX MSA	20.2	2
Melbourne-Titusville-Palm Bay, FL MSA	11.2	15
Memphis, TN-AR-MS MSA	4.8	61
Miami, FL PMSA	4.5	64
Miami-Fort Lauderdale, FL CMSA	6.7	46
Middlesex-Somerset-Hunterdon, NJ PMSA	4.8	61
Milwaukee-Racine, WI CMSA	1.9	87
Milwaukee-Waukesha, WI PMSA	1.6	90
Minneapolis-Saint Paul, MN-WI MSA	5.9	50
Mobile, AL MSA	7.4	41
Modesto, CA MSA	9.8	26
Monmouth-Ocean, NJ PMSA	4.9	60
Montgomery, AL MSA	6.7	46
Nashville, TN MSA	8.6	31
Nassau-Suffolk, NY PMSA	1.6	90
New Orleans, LA MSA	1.8	88
New York, NY PMSA	0.4	99
Newark, NJ PMSA	0.9	95
Newburgh, NY-PA PMSA	6.1	48
Norfolk-Virginia Beach-Newport News, VA-NC MSA	5.9	50
Oakland, CA PMSA	4.9	60
Oklahoma City, OK MSA	5.1	58
Olympia, WA PMSA	16.1	5
Omaha, NE-IA MSA	3.6	72
Orange County, CA PMSA	5.5	54
Orlando, FL MSA	11.2	15
Pensacola, FL MSA	7.7	38
Peoria-Pekin, IL MSA	1.3	92
Philadelphia, PA-NJ PMSA	0.5	98
Philadelphia-Wilmington-Atlantic City, PA-NJ-DE-MD CMSA	1.1	94
Phoenix-Mesa, AZ MSA	10.5	20
Pittsburgh, PA MSA	0.3	100

[Continued]

★350★

Population of Metropolitan Areas, 1994: Percent Change Since 1990
[Continued]

City	Per-cent	Rank
Portland-Salem, OR-WA CMSA	10.5	20
Portland-Vancouver, OR-WA PMSA	10.6	19
Provo-Orem, UT MSA	10.4	21
Racine, WI PMSA	3.8	70
Raleigh-Durham-Chapel Hill, NC MSA	12.4	11
Reading, PA MSA	3.3	75
Reno, NV MSA	11.1	16
Richmond-Petersburg, VA MSA	5.9	50
Riverside-San Bernardino, CA PMSA	12.3	12
Rochester, NY MSA	2.6	82
Rockford, IL MSA	5.2	57
Sacramento, CA PMSA	7.6	39
Sacramento-Yolo, CA CMSA	7.2	43
Saginaw-Bay City-Midland, MI MSA	0.7	97
Saint Louis, MO-IL MSA	1.8	88
Salem, OR PMSA	10.0	24
Salinas, CA MSA	-1.1	104
Salt Lake City-Ogden, UT MSA	9.9	25
San Antonio, TX MSA	8.5	32
San Diego, CA MSA	5.4	55
San Francisco, CA PMSA	2.6	82
San Francisco-Oakland-San Jose, CA CMSA	4.2	67
San Jose, CA PMSA	4.0	69
Santa Barbara-Santa Maria-Lompoc, CA MSA	2.9	79
Santa Cruz-Watsonville, CA PMSA	2.3	84
Santa Rosa, CA PMSA	5.7	52
Sarasota-Bradenton, FL MSA	5.8	51
Savannah, GA MSA	6.9	45
Scranton-Wilkes-Barre-Hazleton, PA MSA	-0.2	102
Seattle-Bellevue-Everett, WA PMSA	7.2	43
Seattle-Tacoma-Bremerton, WA CMSA	8.6	31
Shreveport-Bossier City, LA MSA	0.5	98
South Bend, IN MSA	3.4	74
Spokane, WA MSA	9.6	28
Springfield, MO MSA	9.3	29
Stockton-Lodi, CA MSA	7.8	37
Syracuse, NY MSA	1.6	90
Tacoma, WA PMSA	8.9	30
Tallahassee, FL MSA	8.5	32
Tampa-Saint Petersburg-Clearwater, FL MSA	4.3	66
Trenton, NJ PMSA	1.1	94
Tucson, AZ MSA	9.7	27
Tulsa, OK MSA	4.8	61
Utica-Rome, NY MSA	-0.1	101

[Continued]

★350★

Population of Metropolitan Areas, 1994: Percent Change Since 1990
[Continued]

City	Per-cent	Rank
Vallejo-Fairfield-Napa, CA PMSA	7.2	43
Ventura, CA PMSA	5.0	59
Vineland-Millville-Bridgeton, NJ PMSA	0.5	98
Visalia-Tulare-Porterville, CA MSA	10.0	24
Washington, DC-MD-VA-WV PMSA	5.9	50
Washington-Baltimore, DC-MD-VA-WV CMSA	4.9	60
West Palm Beach-Boca Raton, FL MSA	10.5	20
Wichita, KS MSA	4.4	65
Wilmington-Newark, DE-MD PMSA	5.0	59
Yolo, CA PMSA	3.7	71
York, PA MSA	5.4	55
Youngstown-Warren, OH MSA	0.5	98

Source: U.S. Bureau of the Census, *Statistical Abstract of the United States: 1995,* (115th edition), Washington, D.C.: U.S. Government Printing Office, 1995, p. 40. Primary source: U.S. Bureau of the Census, unpublished data.

★351★

Population Density

Population Density, 1992: 25 Cities With the Fewest Number of Persons Per Square Mile

Data refer to cities with populations of 200,000 or more.

City/MSA	Number	Rank
Anchorage, AK	145	1
Oklahoma City, OK	746	2
Lexington-Fayette, KY	817	3
Jacksonville, FL	871	4
Nashville-Davidson, TN	1,046	5
Kansas City, MO	1,385	6
Colorado Springs, CO	1,615	7
Fort Worth, TX	1,617	8
Virginia Beach, VA	1,680	9
Mobile, AL	1,711	10
Birmingham, AL	1,784	11
Aurora, CO	1,808	12
Tulsa, OK	2,045	13
Indianapolis, IN	2,064	14
El Paso, TX	2,216	15
Austin, TX	2,260	16
Memphis, TN	2,384	17
Charlotte, NC	2,388	18
Phoenix, AZ	2,411	19
Raleigh, NC	2,503	20
Tampa, FL	2,619	21
Tucson, AZ	2,656	22
Wichita, KS	2,708	23

[Continued]

★351★

Population Density, 1992: 25 Cities With the Fewest Number of Persons Per Square Mile
[Continued]

City/MSA	Number	Rank
New Orleans, LA	2,711	24
Mesa, AZ	2,732	25

Source: U.S. Department of Commerce, Economics and Statistics Administration, Bureau of the Census, *County and City Data Book 1994: A Statistical Abstract Supplement,* Washington, D.C.: U.S. Government Printing Office, August 1994, p. xxvii.

★352★

Population Density

Population Density, 1992: 25 Cities With the Greatest Number of Persons Per Square Mile

Data refer to cities with populations of 200,000 or more.

City/MSA	Number	Rank
New York, NY	23,671	1
San Francisco, CA	15,609	2
Jersey City, NJ	15,341	3
Chicago, IL	12,185	4
Philadelphia, PA	11,492	5
Boston, MA	11,398	6
Newark, NJ	11,254	7
Santa Ana, CA	10,628	8
Miami, FL	10,309	9
Washington, DC	9,531	10
Baltimore, MD	8,986	11
Long Beach, CA	8,775	12
Buffalo, NY	7,963	13
Los Angeles, CA	7,436	14
Detroit, MI	7,297	15
Oakland, CA	6,653	16
Minneapolis, MN	6,606	17
Pittsburgh, PA	6,598	18
Rochester, NY	6,541	19
Cleveland, OH	6,526	20
Milwaukee, WI	6,421	21
Saint Louis, MO	6,199	22
Seattle, WA	6,193	23
Anaheim, CA	6,189	24
Saint Paul, MN	5,081	25

Source: U.S. Department of Commerce, Economics and Statistics Administration, Bureau of the Census, *County and City Data Book 1994: A Statistical Abstract Supplement,* Washington, D.C.: U.S. Government Printing Office, August 1994, p. xxvii.

★353★
County Population
Population of Counties of 500,000 Persons and More, 1992

County	Population	Rank
Allegheny, PA	1,334,396	15
Baltimore, MD	705,138	48
Bergen, NJ	834,983	37
Bexar, TX	1,233,096	19
Broward, FL	1,301,274	17
Bucks, PA	556,279	67
Camden, NJ	397,631	73
Clark, NV	845,633	34
Contra Costa, CA	840,585	36
Cook, IL	5,139,341	2
Cuyogoga, OH	1,411,209	12
Dade, FL	2,007,972	7
Dallas, TX	1,913,395	8
DeKalb, GA	563,517	66
Delaware, PA	549,506	69
DuPage, IL	816,116	38
El Paso, TX	628,472	57
Erie, NY	972,289	26
Essex, MA	669,984	53
Essex, NJ	773,420	40
Fairfax, VA	857,020	32
Franklin, OH	992,095	25
Fresno, CA	705,613	47
Fulton, GA	665,765	54
Hamilton, OH	872,026	30
Harris, TX	2,971,755	3
Hennepin, MN	1,041,332	23
Hillsborough, FL	858,552	31
Hudson, NJ	554,950	68
Jackson, MO	634,057	56
Jefferson, KY	670,837	52
Kern, CA	587,680	63
King, WA	1,557,537	9
Los Angeles, CA	9,053,645	1
Macomb, MI	728,220	43
Middlesex, MA	1,394,408	13
Middlesex, NJ	684,456	51
Milwaukee, WI	951,884	27
Monmouth, NJ	565,928	65
Monroe, NY	724,418	44
Montgomery, MD	781,022	39
Montgomery, OH	578,642	64
Montgomery, PA	689,996	49
Multnomah, OR	600,811	62
Nassau, NY	1,302,067	16
Norfolk, MA	620,957	58
Oakland, MI	1,118,611	21
Oklahoma, OK	612,713	61
Orange, CA	2,484,789	5
Orange, FL	714,579	45
Palm Beach, FL	900,655	28
Pierce, WA	619,648	59
Pinellas, FL	854,976	33
Prince Georges, MD	750,614	42
Riverside, CA	1,288,435	18
Sacramento, CA	1,093,237	22
Saint Louis, MO	1,000,690	24

[Continued]

★353★
Population of Counties of 500,000 Persons and More, 1992
[Continued]

County	Population	Rank
Salt Lake, UT	763,526	41
San Bernardino, CA	1,534,343	10
San Diego, CA	2,601,055	4
San Mateo, CA	663,531	55
Santa Clara, CA	1,528,527	11
Shelby, TN	844,847	35
Suffolk, NY	1,338,204	14
Summit, OH	523,191	70
Tarrant, TX	1,220,119	20
Travis, TX	613,159	60
Tulsa, OK	519,847	71
Union, NJ	493,340	72
Ventura, CA	686,560	50
Wayne, MI	2,096,179	6
Westchester, NY	881,822	29
Worcester, MA	708,164	46

Source: U.S. Department of Commerce, Economics and Statistics Administration, U.S. Bureau of the Census, *County and City Data Book 1994: A Statistical Abstract Supplement,* Washington, D.C.: U.S. Government Printing Office, August 1994, n.p.

★354★
Metropolitan Population
Population of Selected Metropolitan Areas, 1994

Data are estimated.

City/MSA	Number	Rank
Benton Harbor, MI MSA	161,737	15
Boston – Worcester – Lawrence, MA-NH-ME-CT CMSA	5,497,284	7
Chicago – Gary – Kenosha, IL-IN-WI CMSA	8,526,804	3
Dallas – Fort Worth, TX CMSA	4,362,483	9
Detroit – Ann Arbor – Flint, MI	5,255,700	8
Grand Rapids – Muskegon – Holland, MI MSA	984,990	11
Houston – Galveston – Brazoria, TX CMSA	4,098,776	10
Jackson, MI MSA	153,290	16
Kalamazoo – Battle Creek, MI MSA	442,637	12
Lansing – East Lansing, MI MSA	436,129	13
Los Angeles – Riverside – Orange County, CA CMSA	15,302,275	2
New York – Northern New Jersey – Long Island, NY-NJ-CT-PA CMSA	19,796,430	1
Philadelphia – Wilmington – Atlantic City, PA-NJ-DE-MD CMSA	5,959,301	6
Saginaw – Bay City – Midland, MI MSA	402,306	14

[Continued]

★354★

Population of Selected Metropolitan Areas, 1994
[Continued]

City/MSA	Number	Rank
San Francisco – Oakland – San Jose, CA CMSA	6,513,322	5
Washington – Baltimore, DC-MD-VA-WV CMSA	7,051,495	4

Source: "Population Rankings," *Crain's Small Business,* (January 1996), p. 18. Primary source: U.S. Bureau of the Census.

★355★
Metropolitan Population

Population of Metropolitan Areas, 1994
[In thousands]

City	1994 July	Rank
Akron, OH PMSA	677	86
Albany-Schenectady-Troy, NY MSA	875	77
Albuquerque, NM MSA	646	89
Allentown-Bethlehem-Easton, PA MSA	612	95
Anchorage, AK MSA	254	165
Ann Arbor, MI PMSA	515	105
Appleton-Oshkosh-Neenah, WI MSA	332	144
Atlanta, GA MSA	3,331	17
Atlantic City-Cape May, NJ PMSA	330	145
Augusta-Aiken, GA-SC MSA	448	114
Austin-San Marcos, TX MSA	964	73
Bakersfield, CA MSA	609	97
Baltimore, MD PMSA	2,458	28
Baton Rouge, LA MSA	558	99
Beaumont-Port Arthur, TX MSA	373	132
Bergen-Passaic, NJ PMSA	1,304	57
Biloxi-Gulfport-Pascagoula, MS MSA	339	143
Binghamton, NY MSA	262	162
Birmingham, AL MSA	872	80
Boise City, ID MSA	348	139
Boulder-Longmont, CO PMSA	250	167
Brazoria, TX PMSA	212	170
Bremerton, WA PMSA	220	169
Brownsville-Harlingen-San Benito, TX MSA	300	152
Buffalo-Niagara Falls, NY MSA	1,189	59
Canton-Massillon, OH MSA	402	126
Charleston, WV MSA	255	164
Charleston-North Charleston, SC MSA	522	103
Charlotte-Gastonia-Rock Hill, NC-SC MSA	1,260	58
Chattanooga, TN-GA MSA	439	117
Chicago, IL PMSA	7,668	5
Chicago-Gary-Kenosha, IL-IN-WI CMSA	8,527	4
Cincinnati, OH-KY-IN PMSA	1,581	45

[Continued]

★355★

Population of Metropolitan Areas, 1994
[Continued]

City	1994 July	Rank
Cincinnati-Hamilton, OH-KY-IN CMSA	1,894	38
Cleveland-Akron, OH CMSA	2,899	20
Cleveland-Lorain-Elyria, OH PMSA	2,222	30
Colorado Springs, CO MSA	452	112
Columbia, SC MSA	486	108
Columbus, GA-AL MSA	274	161
Columbus, OH MSA	1,423	53
Corpus Christi, TX MSA	376	131
Dallas, TX PMSA	2,898	21
Dallas-Fort Worth, TX, CMSA	4,362	12
Davenport-Moline-Rock Island, IA-IL MSA	358	136
Dayton-Springfield, OH MSA	956	74
Daytona Beach, FL MSA	440	116
Denver, CO PMSA	1,796	39
Denver-Boulder-Greeley, CO CMSA	2,190	31
Des Moines, IA MSA	416	122
Detroit, MI PMSA	4,307	13
Detroit-Ann Arbor-Flint, MI CMSA	5,255	9
Dutchess County, NY PMSA	261	163
El Paso, TX MSA	665	87
Erie, PA MSA	280	158
Eugene-Springfield, OR MSA	299	153
Evansville-Henderson, IN-KY MSA	287	156
Fayetteville, NC MSA	287	156
Flint, MI PMSA	433	119
Fort Lauderdale, FL PMSA	1,383	54
Fort Myers-Cape Coral, FL MSA	367	134
Fort Pierce-Port St. Lucie, FL MSA	278	159
Fort Wayne, IN MSA	469	110
Fort Worth-Arlington, TX PMSA	1,464	48
Fresno, CA MSA	835	81
Galveston-Texas City, TX PMSA	235	168
Gary, IN PMSA	620	93
Grand Rapids-Muskegon-Holland, MI MSA	985	69
Greeley, CO PMSA	144	174
Greensboro-Winston-Salem-High Point, NC MSA	1,107	61
Greenville-Spartanburg-Anderson, SC MSA	873	79
Hagerstown, MD PMSA	127	177
Hamilton-Middletown, OH PMSA	313	148
Harrisburg-Lebanon-Carlisle, PA MSA	610	96
Hickory-Morganton, NC MSA	306	151
Honolulu, HI MSA	874	78
Houston, TX PMSA	3,653	15
Houston-Galveston-Brazoria, TX CMSA	4,099	14
Huntington-Ashland, WV-KY-OH MSA	316	147

[Continued]

★355★
Population of Metropolitan Areas, 1994
[Continued]

City	1994 July	Rank
Huntsville, AL MSA	316	147
Indianapolis, IN MSA	1,462	49
Jackson, MS MSA	412	123
Jacksonville, FL MSA	972	71
Jersey City, NJ PMSA	552	100
Johnson City-Kingsport-Bristol, TN-VA MSA	451	113
Kalamazoo-Battle Creek, MI MSA	443	115
Kankakee, IL PMSA	101	178
Kansas City, MO-KS MSA	1,647	41
Kenosha, WI PMSA	138	176
Killeen-Temple, TX MSA	287	156
Knoxville, TN MSA	631	92
Lafayette, LA MSA	361	135
Lakeland-Winter Haven, FL MSA	430	121
Lancaster, PA MSA	443	115
Lansing-East Lansing, MI MSA	436	118
Las Vegas, NV-AZ MSA	1,076	63
Lexington, KY MSA	431	120
Little Rock-North Little Rock, AR MSA	538	102
Los Angeles-Long Beach, CA PMSA	9,150	2
Los Angeles-Riverside-Orange County, CA CMSA	15,302	1
Louisville, KY-IN MSA	981	70
Macon, GA MSA	307	150
Madison, WI MSA	390	128
McAllen-Edinburg-Mission, TX MSA	461	111
Melbourne-Titusville-Palm Bay, FL MSA	443	115
Memphis, TN-AR-MS MSA	1,056	66
Miami, FL PMSA	2,025	35
Miami-Fort Lauderdale, FL CMSA	3,408	16
Middlesex-Somerset-Hunterdon, NJ PMSA	1,069	65
Milwaukee-Racine, WI CMSA	1,637	43
Milwaukee-Waukesha, WI PMSA	1,456	50
Minneapolis-Saint Paul, MN-WI MSA	2,688	22
Mobile, AL MSA	512	106
Modesto, CA MSA	407	125
Monmouth-Ocean, NJ PMSA	1,035	67
Montgomery, AL MSA	312	149
Nashville, TN MSA	1,070	64
Nassau-Suffolk, NY PMSA	2,651	23
New Orleans, LA MSA	1,309	56
New York, NY PMSA	8,584	3
Newark, NJ PMSA	1,934	37
Newburgh, NY-PA PMSA	356	137
Norfolk-Virginia Beach-Newport News, VA-NC MSA	1,529	47
Oakland, CA PMSA	2,182	32
Oklahoma City, OK MSA	1,007	68

[Continued]

★355★
Population of Metropolitan Areas, 1994
[Continued]

City	1994 July	Rank
Olympia, WA PMSA	187	171
Omaha, NE-IA MSA	663	88
Orange County, CA PMSA	2,543	25
Orlando, FL MSA	1,361	55
Pensacola, FL MSA	371	133
Peoria-Pekin, IL MSA	344	141
Philadelphia, PA-NJ PMSA	4,949	10
Philadelphia-Wilmington-Atlantic City, PA-NJ-DE-MD CMSA	5,957	8
Phoenix-Mesa, AZ MSA	2,473	27
Pittsburgh, PA MSA	2,402	29
Portland-Salem, OR-WA CMSA	1,982	36
Portland-Vancouver, OR-WA PMSA	1,676	40
Provo-Orem, UT MSA	291	154
Racine, WI PMSA	182	172
Raleigh-Durham-Chapel Hill, NC MSA	965	72
Reading, PA MSA	348	139
Reno, NV MSA	283	157
Richmond-Petersburg, VA MSA	917	76
Riverside-San Bernardino, CA PMSA	2,907	19
Rochester, NY MSA	1,090	62
Rockford, IL MSA	347	140
Sacramento, CA PMSA	1,441	51
Sacramento-Yolo, CA CMSA	1,588	44
Saginaw-Bay City-Midland, MI MSA	402	126
Saint Louis, MO-IL MSA	2,536	26
Salem, OR PMSA	306	151
Salinas, CA MSA	352	138
Salt Lake City-Ogden, UT MSA	1,178	60
San Antonio, TX MSA	1,437	52
San Diego, CA MSA	2,632	24
San Francisco, CA PMSA	1,646	42
San Francisco-Oakland-San Jose, CA CMSA	6,513	7
San Jose, CA PMSA	1,557	46
Santa Barbara-Santa Maria-Lompoc, CA MSA	380	129
Santa Cruz-Watsonville, CA PMSA	235	168
Santa Rosa, CA PMSA	410	124
Sarasota-Bradenton, FL MSA	518	104
Savannah, GA MSA	276	160
Scranton-Wilkes-Barre-Hazleton, PA MSA	637	91
Seattle-Bellevue-Everett, WA PMSA	2,180	33
Seattle-Tacoma-Bremerton, WA CMSA	3,225	18
Shreveport-Bossier City, LA MSA	378	130
South Bend, IN MSA	255	164
Spokane, WA MSA	396	127

[Continued]

★355★

Population of Metropolitan Areas, 1994
[Continued]

City	1994 July	Rank
Springfield, MO MSA	289	155
Stockton-Lodi, CA MSA	518	104
Syracuse, NY MSA	754	82
Tacoma, WA PMSA	638	90
Tallahassee, FL MSA	253	166
Tampa-Saint Petersburg-Clearwater, FL MSA	2,157	34
Toledo, OH MSA	614	94
Trenton, NJ PMSA	329	146
Tucson, AZ MSA	732	84
Tulsa, OK MSA	743	83
Utica-Rome, NY MSA	316	147
Vallejo-Fairfield-Napa, CA PMSA	483	109
Ventura, CA PMSA	703	85
Vineland-Millville-Bridgeton, NJ PMSA	139	175
Visalia-Tulare-Porterville, CA MSA	343	142
Washington, DC-MD-VA-WV PMSA	4,474	11
Washington-Baltimore, DC-MD-VA-WV CMSA	7,059	6
West Palm Beach-Boca Raton, FL MSA	955	75
Wichita, KS MSA	507	107
Wilmington-Newark, DE-MD PMSA	539	101
Yolo, CA PMSA	146	173
York, PA MSA	358	136
Youngstown-Warren, OH MSA	604	98

Source: U.S. Bureau of the Census, *Statistical Abstract of the United States: 1995,* (115th edition), Washington, D.C.: U.S. Government Printing Office, 1995, p. 40. Primary source: U.S. Bureau of the Census, unpublished data.

★356★

Metropolitan Population

Population, 1993: Cities With 100,00 to 249,999 Persons

City	Pop.	Rank
Aurora, CO	246,610	1
Riverside, CA	241,041	2
St. Petersburg, FL	238,727	3
Rochester, NY	235,301	4
Lexington, KY	235,094	5
Jersey City, NJ	230,298	6
Baton Rouge, LA	225,544	7
Akron, OH	225,040	8
Raleigh, NC	224,057	9
Stockton, CA	211,867	10
Richmond, VA	205,331	11
Mobile, AL	204,286	12
Bakersfield, CA	198,908	13
Lincoln, NE	198,228	14
Jackson, MS	198,227	15

[Continued]

★356★

Population, 1993: Cities With 100,00 to 249,999 Persons
[Continued]

City	Pop.	Rank
Shreveport, LA	197,379	16
Madison, WI	196,919	17
Des Moines, IA	195,485	18
Garland, TX	194,930	19
Montgomery, AL	194,399	20
Greensboro, NC	192,951	21
Grand Rapids, MI	192,121	22
Lubbock, TX	191,639	23
Spokane, WA	191,511	24
Columbus, GA	190,331	25

Source: Maguire, Kathleen, and Ann L. Pastore, eds., *Sourcebook of Criminal Justice Statistics 1994,* U.S. Department of Justice, Bureau of Justice Statistics, Washington, D.C.: U.S. Government Printing Office, 1995, p. 320. Primary source: National Rifle Association of America, Institute for Legislative Action; data were made available through the Federal Bureau of Investigation's Uniform Crime Reporting Program.

★357★

Metropolitan Population

Population, 1993: Cities With 250,000 or More Persons

City	Pop.	Rank
New York, NY	7,347,257	1
Los Angeles, CA	3,525,317	2
Chicago, IL	2,788,996	3
Houston, TX	1,724,327	4
Philadelphia, PA	1,559,534	5
San Diego, CA	1,160,603	6
Dallas, TX	1,042,619	7
Phoenix, AZ	1,039,369	8
Detroit, MI[1]	1,020,062	9
San Antonio, TX	985,456	10
Honolulu, HI	875,455	11
San Jose, CA	809,528	12
San Francisco, CA	736,377	13
Baltimore, MD	732,968	14
Las Vegas, NV	717,441	15
Jacksonville, FL	672,310	16
Columbus, OH	646,933	17
Milwaukee, WI	623,114	18
Memphis, TN	618,981	19
Washington, DC	578,000	20
El Paso, TX	554,515	21
Boston, MA	553,870	22
Seattle, WA	531,274	23
Nashville, TN	513,648	24
Cleveland, OH	505,730	25

Source: Maguire, Kathleen, and Ann L. Pastore, eds., *Sourcebook of Criminal Justice Statistics 1994,* U.S. Department of Justice, Bureau of Justice Statistics, Washington, D.C.: U.S. Government Printing Office, 1995, p. 320. Primary source: National Rifle Association of America, Institute for Legislative Action; data were made available through the Federal Bureau of Investigation's Uniform Crime Reporting Program.

★358★
Metropolitan Population
Population, 1995: Selected Cities

City	Population	Rank
Baltimore, MD	787,000	4
Chicago, IL	3,005,000	1
Detroit, MI	1,011,274	3
Houston, TX	1,595,000	2
Orlando, FL	128,000	7
San Francisco, CA	679,000	5
Seattle, WA	494,000	6

Source: Gray, Madison J., "Becoming 'World Class' City Requires New Amenities for Dining, Fun," *Detroit News*, 21 December 1995, p. 1K. Primary source: U.S. Department of Commerce 1992 Census of Retail Trade (Geographic Area Series), Bureau of the Census; U.S. Department of Commerce 1992 Census of Service Industries (Geographic Area Series), Bureau of the Census.

★359★
Population Projections
Population Projections, 2000, CMSAs

[In thousands]

City/MSA	Thousands	Rank
Chicago-Gary-Kenosha, IL-IN-WI CMSA	8,906	3
Cincinnati-Hamilton, OH-KY-IN CMSA	1,982	15
Cleveland-Akron, OH CMSA	2,920	12
Dallas-Fort Worth, TX CMSA	4,760	8
Denver-Boulder-Greeley, CO CMSA	2,404	13
Detroit-Ann Arbor-Flint, MI CMSA	5,315	7
Houston-Galveston-Brazoria, TX CMSA	4,496	9
Los Angeles-Riverside-Orange County, CA CMSA	16,733	2
Miami-Fort Lauderdale, FL CMSA	3,698	10
Milwaukee-Racine, WI CMSA	1,685	17
New York-Northern New Jersey-Long Island, NY-NJ-CT-PA CMSA	20,175	1
Philadelphia-Wilmington-Atlantic City, PA-NJ-DE-MD CMSA	6,218	6
Portland-Salem, OR-WA CMSA	2,160	14
Sacramento-Yolo, CA CMSA	1,826	16
San Francisco-Oakland-San Jose, CA CMSA	6,986	5
Seattle-Tacoma-Bremerton, WA CMSA	3,580	11
Washington-Baltimore, DC-MD-VA-WV CMSA	7,594	4

Source: U.S. Department of Commerce, Economics and Statistics Administration, Bureau of Economic Analysis, *Survey of Current Business*, vol. 76, no. 6, Washington, D.C.: U.S. Government Printing Office, (June 1996), p. 67. *Note:* "CMSA" stands for "Consolidated Metropolitan Statistical Area."

★360★
Population Projections
Population Projections, 2005, CMSAs

[In thousands]

City/MSA	Thousands	Rank
Chicago-Gary-Kenosha, IL-IN-WI CMSA	9,219	3
Cincinnati-Hamilton, OH-KY-IN CMSA	2,048	15
Cleveland-Akron, OH CMSA	2,945	12
Dallas-Fort Worth, TX CMSA	5,056	8
Denver-Boulder-Greeley, CO CMSA	2,571	13
Detroit-Ann Arbor-Flint, MI CMSA	5,366	7
Houston-Galveston-Brazoria, TX CMSA	4,757	9
Los Angeles-Riverside-Orange County, CA CMSA	17,746	2
Miami-Fort Lauderdale, FL CMSA	3,917	10
Milwaukee-Racine, WI CMSA	1,729	17
New York-Northern New Jersey-Long Island, NY-NJ-CT-PA CMSA	20,515	1
Philadelphia-Wilmington-Atlantic City, PA-NJ-DE-MD CMSA	6,388	6
Portland-Salem, OR-WA CMSA	2,300	14
Sacramento-Yolo, CA CMSA	1,997	16
San Francisco-Oakland-San Jose, CA CMSA	7,347	5
Seattle-Tacoma-Bremerton, WA CMSA	3,861	11
Washington-Baltimore, DC-MD-VA-WV CMSA	7,996	4

Source: U.S. Department of Commerce, Economics and Statistics Administration, Bureau of Economic Analysis, *Survey of Current Business*, vol. 76, no. 6, Washington, D.C.: U.S. Government Printing Office, (June 1996), p. 67. *Note:* "CMSA" stands for "Consolidated Metropolitan Statistical Area."

★361★
CMSA Population
Population, 1993, CMSAs

[In thousands]

City/MSA	Thousands	Rank
Chicago-Gary-Kenosha, IL-IN-WI CMSA	8,466	3
Cincinnati-Hamilton, OH-KY-IN CMSA	1,881	15
Cleveland-Akron, OH CMSA	2,894	12
Dallas-Fort Worth, TX CMSA	4,279	8
Denver-Boulder-Greeley, CO CMSA	2,146	13
Detroit-Ann Arbor-Flint, MI CMSA	5,246	7
Houston-Galveston-Brazoria, TX CMSA	4,028	9
Los Angeles-Riverside-Orange County, CA CMSA	15,210	2
Miami-Fort Lauderdale, FL CMSA	3,354	10
Milwaukee-Racine, WI CMSA	1,634	16

[Continued]

★361★

Population, 1993, CMSAs
[Continued]

City/MSA	Thousands	Rank
New York-Northern New Jersey-Long Island, NY-NJ-CT-PA CMSA	19,646	1
Philadelphia-Wilmington-Atlantic City, PA-NJ-DE-MD CMSA	5,941	6
Portland-Salem, OR-WA CMSA	1,944	14
Sacramento-Yolo, CA CMSA	1,576	17
San Francisco-Oakland-San Jose, CA CMSA	6,469	5
Seattle-Tacoma-Bremerton, WA CMSA	3,189	11
Washington-Baltimore, DC-MD-VA-WV CMSA	6,986	4

Source: U.S. Department of Commerce, Economics and Statistics Administration, Bureau of Economic Analysis, *Survey of Current Business*, vol. 76, no. 6, Washington, D.C.: U.S. Government Printing Office, (June 1996), p. 67. *Note:* "CMSA" stands for "Consolidated Metropolitan Statistical Area."

★362★

Population By Age Group

Persons Under One Year Old, 1990
[Table shows the top 50 areas]

MSA	% of total population	Rank
Provo – Orem, UT	2.32	1
Jacksonville, NC	1.88	2
Laredo, TX	1.86	3
Merced, CA	1.73	4
Bakersfield, CA	1.72	5
Killeen – Temple, TX	1.72	5
Odessa, TX	1.70	6
Rapid City, SD	1.68	7
Anchorage, AK	1.66	8
Fresno, CA	1.64	9
Salt Lake City – Ogden, UT	1.63	10
McAllen – Edinburg – Mission, TX	1.62	11
Clarksville – Hopkinsville, TN – KY	1.61	12
El Paso, TX	1.60	13
Brownsville – Harlingen, TX	1.59	14
Grand Rapids, MI	1.59	14
Las Cruces, NM	1.59	14
Visalia – Tulare – Porterville, CA	1.59	14
Fayetteville, NC	1.58	15
Houma – Thibodaux, LA	1.58	15
Midland, TX	1.58	15
Modesto, CA	1.58	15
Great Falls, MT	1.57	16
Grand Forks, ND	1.56	17
Richland – Kennewick – Pasco, WA	1.56	17
Bremerton, WA	1.55	18
Columbus, GA – AL	1.54	19
Norfolk – Virginia Beach – Newport News, VA	1.54	19
Lawton, OK	1.53	20
Charleston, SC	1.50	21

[Continued]

★362★

Persons Under One Year Old, 1990
[Continued]

MSA	% of total population	Rank
Los Angeles – Anaheim – Riverside, CA	1.50	21
Salinas – Seaside – Monterey, CA	1.50	21
Colorado Springs, CO	1.49	22
Omaha, NE – IA	1.48	23
Reno, NV	1.48	23
Yuma, AZ	1.48	23
Dallas – Fort Worth, TX	1.47	24
Houston – Galveston – Brazoria, TX	1.47	24
Minneapolis – Saint Paul, MN – WI	1.47	24
Sioux Falls, SD	1.47	24
Amarillo, TX	1.46	25
Elkhart – Goshen, IN	1.46	25
Muskegon, MI	1.46	25
Yuba City, CA	1.46	25
Jackson, MI	1.45	26
San Diego, CA	1.45	26
Wichita, KS	1.45	26
Rochester, NY	1.44	27
Wichita Falls, TX	1.44	27
Yakima, WA	1.44	27

Source: U.S. Bureau of the Census, Data User Services Division, *1990 Census of Population and Housing*, Summary Tape File 3C, United States Summary, CD-ROM, February 1992.

★363★

Population By Age Group

Persons Age 5, 1990
[Table shows the top 50 areas]

MSA	% of total population	Rank
Casper, WY	2.22	1
Merced, CA	2.17	2
Odessa, TX	2.02	3
Provo – Orem, UT	2.02	3
Salt Lake City – Ogden, UT	2.00	4
Bakersfield, CA	1.98	5
Midland, TX	1.98	5
Richland – Kennewick – Pasco, WA	1.98	5
Laredo, TX	1.97	6
McAllen – Edinburg – Mission, TX	1.97	6
Yuba City, CA	1.96	7
Fresno, CA	1.92	8
Visalia – Tulare – Porterville, CA	1.92	8
Brownsville – Harlingen, TX	1.89	9
Modesto, CA	1.88	10
Rapid City, SD	1.87	11
Victoria, TX	1.87	11
Anchorage, AK	1.86	12
Lafayette, LA	1.85	13
El Paso, TX	1.84	14
Bremerton, WA	1.81	15
Yakima, WA	1.81	15

[Continued]

★363★
Persons Age 5, 1990
[Continued]

MSA	% of total population	Rank
Corpus Christi, TX	1.79	16
Grand Rapids, MI	1.79	16
Muskegon, MI	1.79	16
Stockton, CA	1.79	16
Baton Rouge, LA	1.78	17
San Antonio, TX	1.78	17
Alexandria, LA	1.74	18
Greeley, CO	1.74	18
Rochester, MN	1.74	18
Green Bay, WI	1.73	19
Owensboro, KY	1.73	19
Fort Wayne, IN	1.72	20
Houma – Thibodaux, LA	1.72	20
Lawton, OK	1.72	20
Saint Cloud, MN	1.72	20
Sioux City, IA – NE	1.72	20
Appleton – Oshkosh – Neenah, WI	1.71	21
Charleston, SC	1.71	21
Pensacola, FL	1.71	21
Houston – Galveston – Brazoria, TX	1.70	22
Monroe, LA	1.70	22
Boise, ID	1.69	23
Kankakee, IL	1.69	23
New Orleans, LA	1.69	23
San Angelo, TX	1.69	23
Jackson, MS	1.68	24
Las Cruces, NM	1.68	24
Salinas – Seaside – Monterey, CA	1.68	24

Source: U.S. Bureau of the Census, Data User Services Division, *1990 Census of Population and Housing*, Summary Tape File 3C, United States Summary, CD-ROM, February 1992.

★364★
Population By Age Group
Persons Age 18, 1990
[Table shows the top 50 areas]

MSA	% of total population	Rank
Bryan – College Station, TX	3.40	1
Bloomington, IN	3.35	2
Lafayette – West Lafayette, IN	2.99	3
Champaign – Urbana – Rantoul, IL	2.90	4
Provo – Orem, UT	2.68	5
Bloomington – Normal, IL	2.63	6
Columbia, MO	2.51	7
Gainesville, FL	2.46	8
Lawrence, KS	2.46	8
Muncie, IN	2.42	9
State College, PA	2.41	10
Bangor, ME	2.27	11
Tallahassee, FL	2.15	12
Athens, GA	2.13	13
Tuscaloosa, AL	2.13	13

[Continued]

★364★
Persons Age 18, 1990
[Continued]

MSA	% of total population	Rank
Iowa City, IA	2.09	14
Charlottesville, VA	2.08	15
Jacksonville, NC	2.08	15
McAllen – Edinburg – Mission, TX	2.02	16
Pine Bluff, AR	2.00	17
Lansing – East Lansing, MI	1.99	18
Burlington, VT	1.96	19
Cumberland, MD – WV	1.94	20
La Crosse, WI	1.93	21
Kalamazoo, MI	1.92	22
Wichita Falls, TX	1.92	22
Eau Claire, WI	1.91	23
Las Cruces, NM	1.91	23
Anniston, AL	1.90	24
Brownsville – Harlingen, TX	1.90	24
El Paso, TX	1.89	25
Waco, TX	1.88	26
Grand Forks, ND	1.87	27
Laredo, TX	1.87	27
Lubbock, TX	1.87	27
Fayetteville – Springdale, AR	1.86	28
Springfield, MO	1.82	29
Erie, PA	1.81	30
Monroe, LA	1.81	30
Baton Rouge, LA	1.78	31
Columbia, SC	1.78	31
San Angelo, TX	1.78	31
Greenville – Spartanburg, SC	1.77	32
Santa Barbara – Santa Maria – Lompoc, CA	1.77	32
Syracuse, NY	1.77	32
Lawton, OK	1.76	33
Biloxi – Gulfport, MS	1.75	34
Fargo – Moorhead, ND – MN	1.75	34
Fayetteville, NC	1.75	34
Jamestown – Dunkirk, NY	1.75	34

Source: U.S. Bureau of the Census, Data User Services Division, *1990 Census of Population and Housing*, Summary Tape File 3C, United States Summary, CD-ROM, February 1992.

★365★
Population By Age Group
Persons Age 19, 1990
[Table shows the top 50 areas]

MSA	% of total population	Rank
Bloomington, IN	6.09	1
Bryan – College Station, TX	5.68	2
Lawrence, KS	5.58	3
Lafayette – West Lafayette, IN	5.41	4
Iowa City, IA	4.34	5
State College, PA	4.30	6
Champaign – Urbana – Rantoul, IL	4.16	7
Columbia, MO	4.14	8

[Continued]

★365★
Persons Age 19, 1990
[Continued]

MSA	% of total population	Rank
Muncie, IN	3.98	9
Jacksonville, NC	3.94	10
Bloomington–Normal, IL	3.84	11
Gainesville, FL	3.53	12
Athens, GA	3.43	13
Tuscaloosa, AL	3.18	14
Bangor, ME	3.13	15
Charlottesville, VA	3.10	16
Tallahassee, FL	3.09	17
Grand Forks, ND	3.04	18
Provo–Orem, UT	3.02	19
Fargo–Moorhead, ND–MN	2.95	20
Burlington, VT	2.91	21
La Crosse, WI	2.75	22
Lincoln, NE	2.74	23
Lansing–East Lansing, MI	2.73	24
Lubbock, TX	2.71	25
Fayetteville, NC	2.65	26
Kalamazoo, MI	2.64	27
Terre Haute, IN	2.64	27
Fayetteville–Springdale, AR	2.60	28
Waco, TX	2.59	29
Madison, WI	2.53	30
Waterloo–Cedar Falls, IA	2.52	31
Lawton, OK	2.50	32
Eau Claire, WI	2.46	33
Killeen–Temple, TX	2.45	34
Clarksville–Hopkinsville, TN–KY	2.44	35
Abilene, TX	2.43	36
Austin, TX	2.43	36
Springfield, MO	2.43	36
Fort Collins–Loveland, CO	2.40	37
Saint Cloud, MN	2.36	38
Greeley, CO	2.35	39
Raleigh–Durham, NC	2.32	40
Santa Barbara–Santa Maria–Lompoc, CA	2.30	41
Anniston, AL	2.29	42
San Angelo, TX	2.29	42
Wilmington, NC	2.26	43
Columbus, GA–AL	2.25	44
Wichita Falls, TX	2.23	45
Las Cruces, NM	2.22	46

Source: U.S. Bureau of the Census, Data User Services Division, *1990 Census of Population and Housing*, Summary Tape File 3C, United States Summary, CD-ROM, February 1992.

★366★
Population By Age Group
Persons Age 20, 1990
[Table shows the top 50 areas]

MSA	% of total population	Rank
State College, PA	6.09	1
Bryan–College Station, TX	5.91	2
Bloomington, IN	5.90	3
Lawrence, KS	5.39	4
Lafayette–West Lafayette, IN	4.88	5
Jacksonville, NC	4.78	6
Iowa City, IA	4.22	7
Champaign–Urbana–Rantoul, IL	4.15	8
Columbia, MO	4.03	9
Bloomington–Normal, IL	3.94	10
Athens, GA	3.80	11
Gainesville, FL	3.57	12
Muncie, IN	3.57	12
Tallahassee, FL	3.30	13
Fargo–Moorhead, ND–MN	3.15	14
Bangor, ME	3.14	15
Grand Forks, ND	3.07	16
Tuscaloosa, AL	3.04	17
Fayetteville, NC	2.97	18
Charlottesville, VA	2.91	19
Clarksville–Hopkinsville, TN–KY	2.86	20
Burlington, VT	2.77	21
Kalamazoo, MI	2.73	22
Lawton, OK	2.71	23
Lansing–East Lansing, MI	2.69	24
La Crosse, WI	2.65	25
Killeen–Temple, TX	2.63	26
Saint Cloud, MN	2.62	27
Las Cruces, NM	2.60	28
Madison, WI	2.60	28
Fayetteville–Springdale, AR	2.59	29
Lincoln, NE	2.59	29
Springfield, MO	2.52	30
Provo–Orem, UT	2.51	31
Santa Barbara–Santa Maria–Lompoc, CA	2.50	32
Eau Claire, WI	2.48	33
Lubbock, TX	2.47	34
Austin, TX	2.45	35
Greeley, CO	2.42	36
Waco, TX	2.41	37
Fort Collins–Loveland, CO	2.40	38
Bellingham, WA	2.36	39
Terre Haute, IN	2.29	40
Waterloo–Cedar Falls, IA	2.26	41
Raleigh–Durham, NC	2.24	42
Chico, CA	2.21	43
Wilmington, NC	2.20	44
Abilene, TX	2.18	45
Norfolk–Virginia Beach–Newport News, VA	2.16	46
Anniston, AL	2.14	47

Source: U.S. Bureau of the Census, Data User Services Division, *1990 Census of Population and Housing*, Summary Tape File 3C, United States Summary, CD-ROM, February 1992.

★367★

Population By Age Group

Persons Age 21, 1990

[Table shows the top 50 areas]

MSA	% of total population	Rank
State College, PA	6.84	1
Bryan – College Station, TX	6.08	2
Lawrence, KS	5.34	3
Jacksonville, NC	5.29	4
Bloomington, IN	5.05	5
Lafayette – West Lafayette, IN	4.94	6
Iowa City, IA	4.53	7
Champaign – Urbana – Rantoul, IL	4.19	8
Columbia, MO	3.85	9
Athens, GA	3.82	10
Bloomington – Normal, IL	3.78	11
Gainesville, FL	3.47	12
Grand Forks, ND	3.28	13
Muncie, IN	3.12	14
Tallahassee, FL	3.09	15
Burlington, VT	3.00	16
Charlottesville, VA	2.96	17
Tuscaloosa, AL	2.83	18
Fayetteville, NC	2.81	19
Fargo – Moorhead, ND – MN	2.74	20
Lansing – East Lansing, MI	2.71	21
Madison, WI	2.67	22
Killeen – Temple, TX	2.65	23
Clarksville – Hopkinsville, TN – KY	2.63	24
Provo – Orem, UT	2.61	25
Lynchburg, VA	2.51	26
Saint Cloud, MN	2.51	26
Lincoln, NE	2.50	27
Kalamazoo, MI	2.47	28
Lawton, OK	2.46	29
Lubbock, TX	2.44	30
Bangor, ME	2.41	31
Fayetteville – Springdale, AR	2.41	31
La Crosse, WI	2.41	31
Waco, TX	2.37	32
Santa Barbara – Santa Maria – Lompoc, CA	2.34	33
Austin, TX	2.33	34
Eau Claire, WI	2.33	34
Waterloo – Cedar Falls, IA	2.33	34
Fort Collins – Loveland, CO	2.32	35
Bellingham, WA	2.26	36
Raleigh – Durham, NC	2.19	37
Springfield, MO	2.19	37
Chico, CA	2.13	38
Las Cruces, NM	2.12	39
Norfolk – Virginia Beach – Newport News, VA	2.10	40
San Diego, CA	2.07	41
Charleston, SC	1.96	42
South Bend – Mishawaka, IN	1.96	42
Portsmouth – Dover – Rochester, NH – ME	1.95	43

Source: U.S. Bureau of the Census, Data User Services Division, *1990 Census of Population and Housing,* Summary Tape File 3C, United States Summary, CD-ROM, February 1992.

★368★

Population By Age Group

Persons Age 22 to 24, 1990

[Table shows the top 50 areas]

MSA	% of total population	Rank
Jacksonville, NC	11.1	1
Bryan – College Station, TX	11.0	2
Iowa City, IA	9.7	3
Lawrence, KS	9.1	4
Bloomington, IN	8.7	5
State College, PA	8.5	6
Provo – Orem, UT	7.9	7
Lafayette – West Lafayette, IN	7.8	8
Champaign – Urbana – Rantoul, IL	7.4	9
Grand Forks, ND	7.4	9
Columbia, MO	7.3	10
Gainesville, FL	7.3	10
Athens, GA	7.1	11
Clarksville – Hopkinsville, TN – KY	7.1	11
Killeen – Temple, TX	7.1	11
Fayetteville, NC	6.8	12
Tallahassee, FL	6.8	12
Lubbock, TX	6.6	13
Madison, WI	6.4	14
Bloomington – Normal, IL	6.2	15
Lincoln, NE	6.2	15
Austin, TX	6.1	16
Fargo – Moorhead, ND – MN	6.1	16
Charlottesville, VA	5.9	17
La Crosse, WI	5.9	17
Lawton, OK	5.9	17
Muncie, IN	5.9	17
Lansing – East Lansing, MI	5.8	18
Norfolk – Virginia Beach – Newport News, VA	5.8	18
Saint Cloud, MN	5.8	18
San Diego, CA	5.8	18
Tuscaloosa, AL	5.8	18
Fayetteville – Springdale, AR	5.7	19
Raleigh – Durham, NC	5.7	19
Bangor, ME	5.6	20
Burlington, VT	5.6	20
Charleston, SC	5.6	20
Chico, CA	5.6	20
Kalamazoo, MI	5.6	20
Salinas – Seaside – Monterey, CA	5.5	21
Lexington-Fayette, KY	5.4	22
Santa Barbara – Santa Maria – Lompoc, CA	5.4	22
Boston – Lawrence – Salem, MA – NH	5.3	23
Columbus, GA – AL	5.3	23
Honolulu, HI	5.3	23
Abilene, TX	5.2	24
Columbus, OH	5.2	24
Fort Collins – Loveland, CO	5.2	24
Rapid City, SD	5.2	24
Los Angeles – Anaheim – Riverside, CA	5.1	25

Source: U.S. Bureau of the Census, Data User Services Division, *1990 Census of Population and Housing,* Summary Tape File 3C, United States Summary, CD-ROM, February 1992.

★369★

Population By Age Group

Persons Age 25 to 29, 1990

[Table shows the top 50 areas]

MSA	% of total population	Rank
Jacksonville, NC	13.1	1
Fayetteville, NC	11.4	2
Iowa City, IA	11.4	2
Killeen – Temple, TX	11.3	3
Austin, TX	11.0	4
Clarksville – Hopkinsville, TN – KY	11.0	4
Grand Forks, ND	10.8	5
Dallas – Fort Worth, TX	10.7	6
Raleigh – Durham, NC	10.5	7
Norfolk – Virginia Beach – Newport News, VA	10.4	8
Washington, DC – MD – VA	10.4	8
Charleston, SC	10.3	9
Fort Walton Beach, FL	10.3	9
San Diego, CA	10.3	9
Anchorage, AK	10.1	10
Atlanta, GA	10.1	10
Madison, WI	10.1	10
Huntsville, AL	10.0	11
Los Angeles – Anaheim – Riverside, CA	10.0	11
Minneapolis – Saint Paul, MN – WI	10.0	11
New London – Norwich, CT – RI	10.0	11
Champaign – Urbana – Rantoul, IL	9.9	12
Colorado Springs, CO	9.9	12
Lawton, OK	9.9	12
Orlando, FL	9.9	12
Salinas – Seaside – Monterey, CA	9.9	12
Boston – Lawrence – Salem, MA – NH	9.8	13
Charlottesville, VA	9.8	13
Columbia, MO	9.8	13
Fitchburg – Leominster, MA	9.8	13
Manchester, NH	9.8	13
Honolulu, HI	9.7	14
Las Vegas, NV	9.7	14
Rapid City, SD	9.7	14
Sioux Falls, SD	9.7	14
Columbus, OH	9.6	15
Gainesville, FL	9.6	15
Lexington-Fayette, KY	9.6	15
Rochester, MN	9.6	15
San Francisco – Oakland – San Jose, CA	9.6	15
Columbia, SC	9.5	16
Houston – Galveston – Brazoria, TX	9.5	16
Lubbock, TX	9.5	16
Portsmouth – Dover – Rochester, NH – ME	9.5	16
Columbus, GA – AL	9.4	17
Indianapolis, IN	9.4	17
Jacksonville, FL	9.4	17
Lawrence, KS	9.4	17

[Continued]

★369★

Population By Age Group

Persons Age 25 to 29, 1990

[Continued]

MSA	% of total population	Rank
Phoenix, AZ	9.4	17
Seattle – Tacoma, WA	9.4	17

Source: U.S. Bureau of the Census, Data User Services Division, *1990 Census of Population and Housing*, Summary Tape File 3C, United States Summary, CD-ROM, February 1992.

★370★

Population By Age Group

Persons Age 30 to 34, 1990

[Table shows the top 50 areas]

MSA	% of total population	Rank
Anchorage, AK	11.4	1
Austin, TX	10.6	2
Denver – Boulder, CO	10.6	2
Midland, TX	10.6	2
Rochester, MN	10.6	2
Dallas – Fort Worth, TX	10.5	3
Houston – Galveston – Brazoria, TX	10.4	4
Minneapolis – Saint Paul, MN – WI	10.3	5
Raleigh – Durham, NC	10.3	5
Atlanta, GA	10.2	6
San Francisco – Oakland – San Jose, CA	10.1	7
Seattle – Tacoma, WA	10.1	7
Washington, DC – MD – VA	10.1	7
Reno, NV	10.0	8
Burlington, VT	9.9	9
Huntsville, AL	9.9	9
Lafayette, LA	9.9	9
San Diego, CA	9.9	9
Colorado Springs, CO	9.8	10
Fort Collins – Loveland, CO	9.8	10
Los Angeles – Anaheim – Riverside, CA	9.8	10
Madison, WI	9.8	10
Manchester, NH	9.8	10
Norfolk – Virginia Beach – Newport News, VA	9.8	10
Orlando, FL	9.8	10
Salinas – Seaside – Monterey, CA	9.8	10
Albuquerque, NM	9.6	11
Boston – Lawrence – Salem, MA – NH	9.6	11
Charleston, SC	9.6	11
Fort Walton Beach, FL	9.6	11
Grand Forks, ND	9.6	11
Nashville, TN	9.6	11
Odessa, TX	9.6	11
Wichita, KS	9.6	11
Baltimore, MD	9.5	12
Casper, WY	9.5	12
Columbia, SC	9.5	12

[Continued]

★370★
Persons Age 30 to 34, 1990
[Continued]

MSA	% of total population	Rank
Columbus, OH	9.5	12
Indianapolis, IN	9.5	12
Portland, ME	9.5	12
Richmond – Petersburg, VA	9.5	12
Sacramento, CA	9.5	12
Sioux Falls, SD	9.5	12
Billings, MT	9.4	13
Green Bay, WI	9.4	13
Hartford – New Britain – Middletown, CT	9.4	13
Jacksonville, NC	9.4	13
Kansas City, MO – KS	9.4	13
Lexington-Fayette, KY	9.4	13
Portsmouth – Dover – Rochester, NH – ME	9.4	13

Source: U.S. Bureau of the Census, Data User Services Division, *1990 Census of Population and Housing*, Summary Tape File 3C, United States Summary, CD-ROM, February 1992.

★371★
Population By Age Group
Persons Age 35 to 39, 1990
[Table shows the top 50 areas]

MSA	% of total population	Rank
Anchorage, AK	10.5	1
Santa Fe, NM	9.9	2
Denver – Boulder, CO	9.6	3
Olympia, WA	9.4	4
Portland – Vancouver, OR – WA	9.4	4
Austin, TX	9.3	5
Fort Collins – Loveland, CO	9.2	6
Seattle – Tacoma, WA	9.2	6
Atlanta, GA	9.1	7
Boise, ID	9.1	7
Casper, WY	9.1	7
Houston – Galveston – Brazoria, TX	9.1	7
San Francisco – Oakland – San Jose, CA	9.1	7
Washington, DC – MD – VA	9.1	7
Madison, WI	9.0	8
Reno, NV	9.0	8
Bismarck, ND	8.9	9
Bremerton, WA	8.9	9
Burlington, VT	8.9	9
Minneapolis – Saint Paul, MN – WI	8.9	9
Portland, ME	8.9	9
Raleigh – Durham, NC	8.9	9
Richmond – Petersburg, VA	8.9	9
Eugene – Springfield, OR	8.8	10
Sacramento, CA	8.8	10
Albuquerque, NM	8.7	11
Bellingham, WA	8.7	11

[Continued]

★371★
Persons Age 35 to 39, 1990
[Continued]

MSA	% of total population	Rank
Billings, MT	8.7	11
Dallas – Fort Worth, TX	8.7	11
Nashville, TN	8.7	11
Springfield, IL	8.7	11
Colorado Springs, CO	8.6	12
Medford, OR	8.6	12
Wilmington, NC	8.6	12
Charleston, WV	8.5	13
Columbia, SC	8.5	13
Greeley, CO	8.5	13
Rapid City, SD	8.5	13
Rochester, MN	8.5	13
Sioux Falls, SD	8.5	13
Des Moines, IA	8.4	14
Fort Wayne, IN	8.4	14
Green Bay, WI	8.4	14
Kansas City, MO – KS	8.4	14
Lexington-Fayette, KY	8.4	14
Midland, TX	8.4	14
Omaha, NE – IA	8.4	14
Poughkeepsie, NY	8.4	14
Richland – Kennewick – Pasco, WA	8.4	14
Topeka, KS	8.4	14

Source: U.S. Bureau of the Census, Data User Services Division, *1990 Census of Population and Housing*, Summary Tape File 3C, United States Summary, CD-ROM, February 1992.

★372★
Population By Age Group
Persons Age 40 to 44, 1990
[Table shows the top 50 areas]

MSA	% of total population	Rank
Santa Fe, NM	9.3	1
Anchorage, AK	8.6	2
Denver – Boulder, CO	8.6	2
Washington, DC – MD – VA	8.5	3
Olympia, WA	8.4	4
Portland – Vancouver, OR – WA	8.4	4
Atlanta, GA	8.3	5
San Francisco – Oakland – San Jose, CA	8.3	5
Reno, NV	8.2	6
Boise, ID	8.1	7
Eugene – Springfield, OR	8.1	7
Seattle – Tacoma, WA	8.1	7
Cheyenne, WY	7.9	8
Richmond – Petersburg, VA	7.9	8
Bremerton, WA	7.8	9
Fort Collins – Loveland, CO	7.8	9
Hickory – Morganton, NC	7.8	9
Portland, ME	7.8	9
Raleigh – Durham, NC	7.8	9
Columbia, SC	7.7	10

[Continued]

★372★

Persons Age 40 to 44, 1990
[Continued]

MSA	% of total population	Rank
Poughkeepsie, NY	7.7	10
Roanoke, VA	7.7	10
Sacramento, CA	7.7	10
Albuquerque, NM	7.6	11
Asheville, NC	7.6	11
Baltimore, MD	7.6	11
Charlotte – Gastonia – Rock Hill, NC – SC	7.6	11
Houston – Galveston – Brazoria, TX	7.6	11
Lexington-Fayette, KY	7.6	11
Medford, OR	7.6	11
York, PA	7.6	11
Anderson, IN	7.5	12
Bangor, ME	7.5	12
Bellingham, WA	7.5	12
Burlington, NC	7.5	12
Chattanooga, TN – GA	7.5	12
Greensboro – Winston-Salem – High Point, NC	7.5	12
Harrisburg – Lebanon – Carlisle, PA	7.5	12
Jackson, MI	7.5	12
Knoxville, TN	7.5	12
Kokomo, IN	7.5	12
Louisville, KY – IN	7.5	12
Madison, WI	7.5	12
Minneapolis – Saint Paul, MN – WI	7.5	12
Nashville, TN	7.5	12
Parkersburg – Marietta, WV – OH	7.5	12
Rochester, NY	7.5	12
Springfield, IL	7.5	12
Tulsa, OK	7.5	12
Battle Creek, MI	7.4	13

Source: U.S. Bureau of the Census, Data User Services Division, *1990 Census of Population and Housing*, Summary Tape File 3C, United States Summary, CD-ROM, February 1992.

★373★

Population By Age Group

Persons Age 45 to 49, 1990
[Table shows the top 50 areas]

MSA	% of total population	Rank
Santa Fe, NM	7.0	1
Johnson City – Kingsport – Bristol, TN – VA	6.7	2
Anderson, SC	6.6	3
Washington, DC – MD – VA	6.6	3
Kokomo, IN	6.5	4
Anchorage, AK	6.4	5
Atlanta, GA	6.3	6
Decatur, AL	6.3	6
Hickory – Morganton, NC	6.3	6

[Continued]

★373★

Persons Age 45 to 49, 1990
[Continued]

MSA	% of total population	Rank
Las Vegas, NV	6.3	6
Medford, OR	6.3	6
Olympia, WA	6.3	6
Chattanooga, TN – GA	6.2	7
Greensboro – Winston-Salem – High Point, NC	6.2	7
Pascagoula, MS	6.2	7
Poughkeepsie, NY	6.2	7
Reno, NV	6.2	7
Roanoke, VA	6.2	7
San Francisco – Oakland – San Jose, CA	6.2	7
Wilmington, NC	6.2	7
Anderson, IN	6.1	8
Baltimore, MD	6.1	8
Burlington, NC	6.1	8
Greenville – Spartanburg, SC	6.1	8
Hartford – New Britain – Middletown, CT	6.1	8
Huntington – Ashland, WV – KY – OH	6.1	8
New York – Northern New Jersey – Long Island, NY – NJ – CT	6.1	8
Panama City, FL	6.1	8
Parkersburg – Marietta, WV – OH	6.1	8
Portland – Vancouver, OR – WA	6.1	8
Seattle – Tacoma, WA	6.1	8
Tulsa, OK	6.1	8
Asheville, NC	6.0	9
Billings, MT	6.0	9
Charlotte – Gastonia – Rock Hill, NC – SC	6.0	9
Danville, VA	6.0	9
Denver – Boulder, CO	6.0	9
Florence, AL	6.0	9
Florence, SC	6.0	9
Knoxville, TN	6.0	9
Mansfield, OH	6.0	9
Redding, CA	6.0	9
Richmond – Petersburg, VA	6.0	9
Rochester, MN	6.0	9
Rockford, IL	6.0	9
Saginaw – Bay City – Midland, MI	6.0	9
Flint, MI	5.9	10
Gadsden, AL	5.9	10
Peoria, IL	5.9	10
York, PA	5.9	10

Source: U.S. Bureau of the Census, Data User Services Division, *1990 Census of Population and Housing*, Summary Tape File 3C, United States Summary, CD-ROM, February 1992.

★374★
Population By Age Group
Persons Age 50 to 54, 1990
[Table shows the top 50 areas]

MSA	% of total population	Rank
Johnson City – Kingsport – Bristol, TN – VA	5.9	1
Mansfield, OH	5.7	2
Florence, AL	5.6	3
Hickory – Morganton, NC	5.6	3
Santa Fe, NM	5.6	3
Steubenville – Weirton, OH – WV	5.6	3
Huntsville, AL	5.5	4
Kokomo, IN	5.5	4
Charleston, WV	5.4	5
Danville, VA	5.4	5
Decatur, AL	5.4	5
Huntington – Ashland, WV – KY – OH	5.4	5
Anderson, IN	5.3	6
Burlington, NC	5.3	6
Las Vegas, NV	5.3	6
Parkersburg – Marietta, WV – OH	5.3	6
Chattanooga, TN – GA	5.2	7
Cumberland, MD – WV	5.2	7
Fort Smith, AR – OK	5.2	7
Fort Walton Beach, FL	5.2	7
Knoxville, TN	5.2	7
Pascagoula, MS	5.2	7
Reno, NV	5.2	7
Asheville, NC	5.1	8
Gadsden, AL	5.1	8
Janesville – Beloit, WI	5.1	8
New York – Northern New Jersey – Long Island, NY – NJ – CT	5.1	8
Pensacola, FL	5.1	8
Wheeling, WV – OH	5.1	8
Anderson, SC	5.0	9
Beaumont – Port Arthur, TX	5.0	9
Cedar Rapids, IA	5.0	9
Dayton – Springfield, OH	5.0	9
Flint, MI	5.0	9
Great Falls, MT	5.0	9
Greensboro – Winston-Salem – High Point, NC	5.0	9
Greenville – Spartanburg, SC	5.0	9
Melbourne – Titusville – Palm Bay, FL	5.0	9
Owensboro, KY	5.0	9
Panama City, FL	5.0	9
Poughkeepsie, NY	5.0	9
Saginaw – Bay City – Midland, MI	5.0	9
Benton Harbor, MI	4.9	10
Hagerstown, MD	4.9	10
Miami – Fort Lauderdale, FL	4.9	10
Pittsburgh – Beaver Valley, PA	4.9	10
Roanoke, VA	4.9	10
Sharon, PA	4.9	10
Washington, DC – MD – VA	4.9	10
Youngstown – Warren, OH	4.9	10

Source: U.S. Bureau of the Census, Data User Services Division, *1990 Census of Population and Housing*, Summary Tape File 3C, United States Summary, CD-ROM, February 1992.

★375★
Population By Age Group
Persons Age 55 to 59, 1990
[Table shows the top 50 areas]

MSA	% of total population	Rank
Steubenville – Weirton, OH – WV	5.5	1
Melbourne – Titusville – Palm Bay, FL	5.4	2
Fort Myers – Cape Coral, FL	5.3	3
Florence, AL	5.2	4
Johnson City – Kingsport – Bristol, TN – VA	5.1	5
Naples, FL	5.1	5
Sarasota, FL	5.1	5
Burlington, NC	5.0	6
Charleston, WV	5.0	6
Enid, OK	5.0	6
Fort Walton Beach, FL	5.0	6
Gadsden, AL	5.0	6
Hickory – Morganton, NC	5.0	6
Mansfield, OH	5.0	6
Ocala, FL	5.0	6
Pittsfield, MA	5.0	6
Wheeling, WV – OH	5.0	6
Altoona, PA	4.9	7
Chattanooga, TN – GA	4.9	7
Danville, VA	4.9	7
Decatur, IL	4.9	7
Huntington – Ashland, WV – KY – OH	4.9	7
Huntsville, AL	4.9	7
Johnstown, PA	4.9	7
Kokomo, IN	4.9	7
Pittsburgh – Beaver Valley, PA	4.9	7
Pueblo, CO	4.9	7
Reading, PA	4.9	7
Sharon, PA	4.9	7
Sherman – Denison, TX	4.9	7
Anderson, SC	4.8	8
Anniston, AL	4.8	8
Buffalo – Niagara Falls, NY	4.8	8
Decatur, AL	4.8	8
Fort Pierce, FL	4.8	8
Pascagoula, MS	4.8	8
Roanoke, VA	4.8	8
Scranton – Wilkes-Barre, PA	4.8	8
Williamsport, PA	4.8	8
Youngstown – Warren, OH	4.8	8
Anderson, IN	4.7	9
Cumberland, MD – WV	4.7	9
Daytona Beach, FL	4.7	9
Flint, MI	4.7	9
Greensboro – Winston-Salem – High Point, NC	4.7	9
Hagerstown, MD	4.7	9
Lakeland – Winter Haven, FL	4.7	9
Owensboro, KY	4.7	9
Topeka, KS	4.7	9
Wichita Falls, TX	4.7	9

Source: U.S. Bureau of the Census, Data User Services Division, *1990 Census of Population and Housing*, Summary Tape File 3C, United States Summary, CD-ROM, February 1992.

★376★
Population By Age Group
Persons Age 60 and 61, 1990

[Table shows the top 50 areas]

MSA	% of total population	Rank
Sarasota, FL	2.73	1
Naples, FL	2.52	2
Fort Myers – Cape Coral, FL	2.48	3
Ocala, FL	2.48	3
Fort Pierce, FL	2.41	4
Sharon, PA	2.33	5
Steubenville – Weirton, OH – WV	2.29	6
Cumberland, MD – WV	2.27	7
Johnstown, PA	2.27	7
Pittsburgh – Beaver Valley, PA	2.26	8
Bradenton, FL	2.24	9
Gadsden, AL	2.21	10
Melbourne – Titusville – Palm Bay, FL	2.19	11
Daytona Beach, FL	2.17	12
Danville, VA	2.10	13
Charleston, WV	2.09	14
Wheeling, WV – OH	2.09	14
Decatur, IL	2.08	15
Burlington, NC	2.07	16
Youngstown – Warren, OH	2.07	16
Panama City, FL	2.06	17
Scranton – Wilkes-Barre, PA	2.05	18
Lakeland – Winter Haven, FL	2.04	19
Huntington – Ashland, WV – KY – OH	2.03	20
Tampa – Saint Petersburg – Clearwater, FL	2.03	20
Enid, OK	2.02	21
Florence, AL	2.02	21
West Palm Beach – Boca Raton – Delray Beach, FL	2.02	21
Anderson, IN	2.01	22
Asheville, NC	2.01	22
Benton Harbor, MI	2.01	22
Roanoke, VA	2.01	22
Reading, PA	2.00	23
Allentown – Bethlehem – Easton, PA – NJ	1.99	24
Buffalo – Niagara Falls, NY	1.99	24
Parkersburg – Marietta, WV – OH	1.99	24
Lake Charles, LA	1.98	25
Canton, OH	1.97	26
Peoria, IL	1.97	26
Sherman – Denison, TX	1.96	27
Casper, WY	1.95	28
New Bedford, MA	1.94	29
Muncie, IN	1.93	30
Owensboro, KY	1.93	30
Beaumont – Port Arthur, TX	1.92	31
Duluth, MN – WI	1.92	31
Jamestown – Dunkirk, NY	1.92	31
Johnson City – Kingsport – Bristol, TN – VA	1.92	31

[Continued]

★376★

Persons Age 60 and 61, 1990
[Continued]

MSA	% of total population	Rank
Binghamton, NY	1.91	32
Tyler, TX	1.91	32

Source: U.S. Bureau of the Census, Data User Services Division, *1990 Census of Population and Housing*, Summary Tape File 3C, United States Summary, CD-ROM, February 1992.

★377★
Population By Age Group
Persons Age 62 to 64, 1990

[Table shows the top 50 areas]

MSA	% of total population	Rank
Naples, FL	4.5	1
Sarasota, FL	4.5	1
Fort Myers – Cape Coral, FL	4.4	2
Fort Pierce, FL	4.4	2
Ocala, FL	4.4	2
Bradenton, FL	4.3	3
Daytona Beach, FL	4.0	4
Cumberland, MD – WV	3.7	5
Lakeland – Winter Haven, FL	3.7	5
Pittsburgh – Beaver Valley, PA	3.6	6
Steubenville – Weirton, OH – WV	3.6	6
Wheeling, WV – OH	3.6	6
Danville, VA	3.5	7
Scranton – Wilkes-Barre, PA	3.5	7
Sharon, PA	3.5	7
Tampa – Saint Petersburg – Clearwater, FL	3.5	7
West Palm Beach – Boca Raton – Delray Beach, FL	3.5	7
Youngstown – Warren, OH	3.5	7
Altoona, PA	3.4	8
Johnstown, PA	3.4	8
Melbourne – Titusville – Palm Bay, FL	3.4	8
Charleston, WV	3.3	9
Pueblo, CO	3.3	9
Huntington – Ashland, WV – KY – OH	3.2	10
Johnson City – Kingsport – Bristol, TN – VA	3.2	10
Allentown – Bethlehem – Easton, PA – NJ	3.1	11
Anderson, SC	3.1	11
Asheville, NC	3.1	11
Atlantic City, NJ	3.1	11
Buffalo – Niagara Falls, NY	3.1	11
Burlington, NC	3.1	11
Elmira, NY	3.1	11
Medford, OR	3.1	11
Parkersburg – Marietta, WV – OH	3.1	11
Pittsfield, MA	3.1	11
Reading, PA	3.1	11

[Continued]

★377★

Persons Age 62 to 64, 1990

[Continued]

MSA	% of total population	Rank
Roanoke, VA	3.1	11
Battle Creek, MI	3.0	12
Beaumont – Port Arthur, TX	3.0	12
Canton, OH	3.0	12
Florence, AL	3.0	12
Gadsden, AL	3.0	12
Glens Falls, NY	3.0	12
Hagerstown, MD	3.0	12
Jamestown – Dunkirk, NY	3.0	12
Panama City, FL	3.0	12
Sioux City, IA – NE	3.0	12
South Bend – Mishawaka, IN	3.0	12
Utica – Rome, NY	3.0	12
Williamsport, PA	3.0	12

Source: U.S. Bureau of the Census, Data User Services Division, *1990 Census of Population and Housing,* Summary Tape File 3C, United States Summary, CD-ROM, February 1992.

★378★

Population By Age Group

Persons Age 65 to 69, 1990

[Table shows the top 50 areas]

MSA	% of total population	Rank
Sarasota, FL	9.6	1
Fort Myers – Cape Coral, FL	8.4	2
Bradenton, FL	8.2	3
Fort Pierce, FL	8.2	3
Ocala, FL	8.1	4
Naples, FL	7.7	5
Daytona Beach, FL	7.2	6
West Palm Beach – Boca Raton – Delray Beach, FL	6.7	7
Tampa – Saint Petersburg – Clearwater, FL	6.5	8
Lakeland – Winter Haven, FL	6.2	9
Melbourne – Titusville – Palm Bay, FL	6.1	10
Johnstown, PA	5.9	11
Steubenville – Weirton, OH – WV	5.8	12
Pittsburgh – Beaver Valley, PA	5.7	13
Scranton – Wilkes-Barre, PA	5.7	13
Cumberland, MD – WV	5.6	14
Sharon, PA	5.6	14
Wheeling, WV – OH	5.6	14
Danville, VA	5.5	15
Youngstown – Warren, OH	5.5	15
Chico, CA	5.4	16
Altoona, PA	5.3	17
Asheville, NC	5.3	17
Gadsden, AL	5.3	17
Atlantic City, NJ	5.1	18
Burlington, NC	5.1	18
New Bedford, MA	5.1	18

[Continued]

★378★

Persons Age 65 to 69, 1990

[Continued]

MSA	% of total population	Rank
Pittsfield, MA	5.1	18
Buffalo – Niagara Falls, NY	5.0	19
Johnson City – Kingsport – Bristol, TN – VA	5.0	19
Medford, OR	5.0	19
Roanoke, VA	5.0	19
Saint Joseph, MO	5.0	19
Utica – Rome, NY	5.0	19
Anderson, SC	4.9	20
Canton, OH	4.9	20
Charleston, WV	4.9	20
Reading, PA	4.9	20
Williamsport, PA	4.9	20
Allentown – Bethlehem – Easton, PA – NJ	4.8	21
Duluth, MN – WI	4.8	21
Florence, AL	4.8	21
Providence – Pawtucket – Fall River, RI – MA	4.8	21
Pueblo, CO	4.8	21
Redding, CA	4.8	21
Terre Haute, IN	4.8	21
Cleveland – Akron – Lorain, OH	4.7	22
Erie, PA	4.7	22
Huntington – Ashland, WV – KY – OH	4.7	22
Sherman – Denison, TX	4.7	22

Source: U.S. Bureau of the Census, Data User Services Division, *1990 Census of Population and Housing,* Summary Tape File 3C, United States Summary, CD-ROM, February 1992.

★379★

Population By Age Group

Persons Age 70 to 74, 1990

[Table shows the top 50 areas]

MSA	% of total population	Rank
Sarasota, FL	8.4	1
Bradenton, FL	7.5	2
Fort Myers – Cape Coral, FL	7.0	3
Fort Pierce, FL	6.9	4
West Palm Beach – Boca Raton – Delray Beach, FL	6.8	5
Naples, FL	6.7	6
Ocala, FL	6.4	7
Daytona Beach, FL	6.1	8
Tampa – Saint Petersburg – Clearwater, FL	5.7	9
Johnstown, PA	5.1	10
Lakeland – Winter Haven, FL	5.1	10
Chico, CA	4.8	11
Scranton – Wilkes-Barre, PA	4.8	11
Melbourne – Titusville – Palm Bay, FL	4.7	12

[Continued]

★379★

Persons Age 70 to 74, 1990
[Continued]

MSA	% of total population	Rank
Pittsburgh – Beaver Valley, PA	4.7	12
Wheeling, WV – OH	4.7	12
Cumberland, MD – WV	4.5	13
Medford, OR	4.5	13
Sharon, PA	4.5	13
Steubenville – Weirton, OH – WV	4.5	13
Altoona, PA	4.4	14
Duluth, MN – WI	4.4	14
Youngstown – Warren, OH	4.4	14
Elmira, NY	4.3	15
New Bedford, MA	4.3	15
Allentown – Bethlehem – Easton, PA – NJ	4.2	16
Atlantic City, NJ	4.2	16
Gadsden, AL	4.2	16
Miami – Fort Lauderdale, FL	4.2	16
Pittsfield, MA	4.2	16
Sherman – Denison, TX	4.2	16
Buffalo – Niagara Falls, NY	4.1	17
Danville, VA	4.1	17
Utica – Rome, NY	4.1	17
Yuma, AZ	4.1	17
Asheville, NC	4.0	18
Charleston, WV	4.0	18
Jamestown – Dunkirk, NY	4.0	18
Pueblo, CO	4.0	18
Reading, PA	4.0	18
Waterbury, CT	4.0	18
Kankakee, IL	3.9	19
Providence – Pawtucket – Fall River, RI – MA	3.9	19
Redding, CA	3.9	19
Springfield, MA	3.9	19
Terre Haute, IN	3.9	19
Williamsport, PA	3.9	19
Erie, PA	3.8	20
Hagerstown, MD	3.8	20
Joplin, MO	3.8	20

Source: U.S. Bureau of the Census, Data User Services Division, *1990 Census of Population and Housing,* Summary Tape File 3C, United States Summary, CD-ROM, February 1992.

★380★

Population By Age Group

Persons Age 75 to 79, 1990
[Table shows the top 50 areas]

MSA	% of total population	Rank
Sarasota, FL	6.85	1
Bradenton, FL	5.77	2
West Palm Beach – Boca Raton – Delray Beach, FL	5.44	3
Fort Myers – Cape Coral, FL	5.01	4
Fort Pierce, FL	4.74	5

[Continued]

★380★

Persons Age 75 to 79, 1990
[Continued]

MSA	% of total population	Rank
Tampa – Saint Petersburg – Clearwater, FL	4.44	6
Naples, FL	4.41	7
Daytona Beach, FL	4.38	8
Ocala, FL	4.36	9
Scranton – Wilkes-Barre, PA	3.86	10
Wheeling, WV – OH	3.83	11
Miami – Fort Lauderdale, FL	3.68	12
Lakeland – Winter Haven, FL	3.65	13
Johnstown, PA	3.57	14
Duluth, MN – WI	3.56	15
Sharon, PA	3.50	16
Chico, CA	3.49	17
Pittsburgh – Beaver Valley, PA	3.48	18
Sherman – Denison, TX	3.43	19
Cumberland, MD – WV	3.40	20
Steubenville – Weirton, OH – WV	3.39	21
Gadsden, AL	3.37	22
Enid, OK	3.35	23
Medford, OR	3.35	23
Saint Joseph, MO	3.34	24
Altoona, PA	3.32	25
Pittsfield, MA	3.32	25
Waterbury, CT	3.26	26
Atlantic City, NJ	3.24	27
New Bedford, MA	3.21	28
Jamestown – Dunkirk, NY	3.18	29
Reading, PA	3.15	30
Joplin, MO	3.14	31
Utica – Rome, NY	3.14	31
Melbourne – Titusville – Palm Bay, FL	3.12	32
Terre Haute, IN	3.04	33
Asheville, NC	3.01	34
Buffalo – Niagara Falls, NY	2.97	35
Providence – Pawtucket – Fall River, RI – MA	2.97	35
Youngstown – Warren, OH	2.97	35
Pueblo, CO	2.96	36
Sheboygan, WI	2.96	36
Salem, OR	2.95	37
Springfield, IL	2.95	37
Allentown – Bethlehem – Easton, PA – NJ	2.94	38
Danville, VA	2.92	39
Texarkana, TX – Texarkana, AR	2.92	39
Parkersburg – Marietta, WV – OH	2.91	40
Charleston, WV	2.90	41
Binghamton, NY	2.87	42

Source: U.S. Bureau of the Census, Data User Services Division, *1990 Census of Population and Housing,* Summary Tape File 3C, United States Summary, CD-ROM, February 1992.

★381★

Population By Age Group

Persons Age 80 to 84 Years, 1990

[Table shows the top 50 areas]

MSA	% of total population	Rank
Sarasota, FL	4.35	1
Bradenton, FL	3.94	2
West Palm Beach – Boca Raton – Delray Beach, FL	3.37	3
Daytona Beach, FL	2.95	4
Tampa – Saint Petersburg – Clearwater, FL	2.88	5
Fort Myers – Cape Coral, FL	2.68	6
Naples, FL	2.52	7
Miami – Fort Lauderdale, FL	2.46	8
Fort Pierce, FL	2.41	9
Enid, OK	2.39	10
Duluth, MN – WI	2.35	11
Saint Joseph, MO	2.33	12
Cumberland, MD – WV	2.30	13
Scranton – Wilkes-Barre, PA	2.30	13
Sherman – Denison, TX	2.24	14
Joplin, MO	2.23	15
Altoona, PA	2.22	16
Jamestown – Dunkirk, NY	2.21	17
Lakeland – Winter Haven, FL	2.16	18
Jackson, TN	2.14	19
Johnstown, PA	2.13	20
Waterbury, CT	2.11	21
Asheville, NC	2.09	22
Chico, CA	2.08	23
Reading, PA	2.08	23
Wheeling, WV – OH	2.06	24
Atlantic City, NJ	2.04	25
Dubuque, IA	2.04	25
New Bedford, MA	2.03	26
Sheboygan, WI	2.03	26
Pittsburgh – Beaver Valley, PA	2.02	27
Pittsfield, MA	2.02	27
Sharon, PA	2.02	27
Terre Haute, IN	2.01	28
Williamsport, PA	1.97	29
Salem, OR	1.96	30
Medford, OR	1.95	31
Ocala, FL	1.94	32
Roanoke, VA	1.94	32
Sioux City, IA – NE	1.93	33
Providence – Pawtucket – Fall River, RI – MA	1.90	34
Decatur, IL	1.89	35
Tyler, TX	1.88	36
Utica – Rome, NY	1.88	36
Springfield, IL	1.87	37
Texarkana, TX – Texarkana, AR	1.87	37
Peoria, IL	1.86	38
Yakima, WA	1.86	38
Allentown – Bethlehem – Easton, PA – NJ	1.85	39
Danville, VA	1.85	39

Source: U.S. Bureau of the Census, Data User Services Division, *1990 Census of Population and Housing,* Summary Tape File 3C, United States Summary, CD-ROM, February 1992.

★382★

Population By Age Group

Persons Age 85 and Over, 1990

[Table shows the top 50 areas]

MSA	% of total population	Rank
Sarasota, FL	3.01	1
Bradenton, FL	2.64	2
Daytona Beach, FL	2.13	3
Tampa – Saint Petersburg – Clearwater, FL	2.05	4
Pittsfield, MA	2.01	5
West Palm Beach – Boca Raton – Delray Beach, FL	2.01	5
Saint Joseph, MO	1.97	6
Asheville, NC	1.82	7
Sherman – Denison, TX	1.82	7
New Bedford, MA	1.80	8
Fort Myers – Cape Coral, FL	1.77	9
Jamestown – Dunkirk, NY	1.77	9
Lewiston – Auburn, ME	1.77	9
Duluth, MN – WI	1.75	10
Enid, OK	1.75	10
Roanoke, VA	1.73	11
Sioux City, IA – NE	1.73	11
Elmira, NY	1.72	12
Miami – Fort Lauderdale, FL	1.70	13
Cumberland, MD – WV	1.69	14
Terre Haute, IN	1.69	14
Altoona, PA	1.66	15
Waterloo – Cedar Falls, IA	1.66	15
Decatur, IL	1.64	16
Eau Claire, WI	1.64	16
Salem, OR	1.64	16
Wheeling, WV – OH	1.64	16
Atlantic City, NJ	1.63	17
Dubuque, IA	1.61	18
Glens Falls, NY	1.61	18
Sharon, PA	1.61	18
Sheboygan, WI	1.60	19
Topeka, KS	1.60	19
Utica – Rome, NY	1.60	19
Springfield, MA	1.59	20
La Crosse, WI	1.58	21
Parkersburg – Marietta, WV – OH	1.57	22
Scranton – Wilkes-Barre, PA	1.57	22
Danville, VA	1.56	23
Providence – Pawtucket – Fall River, RI – MA	1.55	24
Worcester, MA	1.55	24
Johnstown, PA	1.54	25
Sioux Falls, SD	1.54	25
Wichita Falls, TX	1.54	25
Albany – Schenectady – Troy, NY	1.53	26
Waterbury, CT	1.53	26
Williamsport, PA	1.53	26
Davenport – Rock Island – Moline, IA – IL	1.52	27
Springfield, MO	1.52	27
Peoria, IL	1.51	28

Source: U.S. Bureau of the Census, Data User Services Division, *1990 Census of Population and Housing,* Summary Tape File 3C, United States Summary, CD-ROM, February 1992.

★383★
Population By Race
American Indian, Eskimo, or Aleut Population, 1990

MSA	% of total population	Rank
Rapid City, SD	7.241	1
Tulsa, OK	6.820	2
Anchorage, AK	6.587	3
Fort Smith, AR – OK	5.363	4
Oklahoma City, OK	4.809	5
Lawton, OK	4.555	6
Yakima, WA	4.459	7
Great Falls, MT	4.042	8
Houma – Thibodaux, LA	3.727	9
Albuquerque, NM	3.331	10
Bellingham, WA	3.062	11
Tucson, AZ	3.004	12
Billings, MT	2.940	13
Redding, CA	2.649	14
Lawrence, KS	2.632	15
Santa Fe, NM	2.362	16
Enid, OK	2.149	17
Yuba City, CA	2.149	17
Bismarck, ND	2.026	18
Reno, NV	1.947	19
Chico, CA	1.929	20
Decatur, AL	1.920	21
Joplin, MO	1.906	22
Duluth, MN – WI	1.897	23
Green Bay, WI	1.845	24
Phoenix, AZ	1.805	25
Bremerton, WA	1.739	26
Sioux City, IA – NE	1.725	27
Medford, OR	1.704	28
Fayetteville, NC	1.667	29
Grand Forks, ND	1.602	30
Olympia, WA	1.583	31
Salem, OR	1.547	32
Yuma, AZ	1.501	33
Spokane, WA	1.458	34
Fayetteville – Springdale, AR	1.392	35
Sherman – Denison, TX	1.369	36
Bakersfield, CA	1.332	37
Visalia – Tulare – Porterville, CA	1.323	38
Seattle – Tacoma, WA	1.289	39
Sacramento, CA	1.226	40
Stockton, CA	1.212	41
Sioux Falls, SD	1.199	42
Modesto, CA	1.178	43
Wichita, KS	1.135	44
Fresno, CA	1.130	45
Topeka, KS	1.128	46
Eugene – Springfield, OR	1.124	47
Bangor, ME	1.071	48
Cheyenne, WY	1.055	49
Santa Barbara – Santa Maria – Lompoc, CA	1.052	50
Pensacola, FL	0.997	51
Fargo – Moorhead, ND – MN	0.990	52
Portland – Vancouver, OR – WA	0.984	53
Minneapolis – Saint Paul, MN – WI	0.947	54

[Continued]

★383★
American Indian, Eskimo, or Aleut Population, 1990
[Continued]

MSA	% of total population	Rank
Merced, CA	0.942	55
Las Vegas, NV	0.936	56
Appleton – Oshkosh – Neenah, WI	0.922	57
Muskegon, MI	0.915	58
Colorado Springs, CO	0.905	59
Salinas – Seaside – Monterey, CA	0.882	60
San Diego, CA	0.861	61
Pueblo, CO	0.848	62
Amarillo, TX	0.817	63
Panama City, FL	0.802	64
Salt Lake City – Ogden, UT	0.794	65
Richland – Kennewick – Pasco, WA	0.781	66
Boise, ID	0.776	67
Springfield, MO	0.755	68
Denver – Boulder, CO	0.736	69
Casper, WY	0.732	70
Jacksonville, NC	0.726	71
Wichita Falls, TX	0.709	72
Las Cruces, NM	0.704	73
Flint, MI	0.673	74
Lansing – East Lansing, MI	0.669	75
Syracuse, NY	0.664	76
Provo – Orem, UT	0.660	77
Mobile, AL	0.653	78
San Francisco – Oakland – San Jose, CA	0.653	78
Killeen – Temple, TX	0.640	79
Buffalo – Niagara Falls, NY	0.638	80
Odessa, TX	0.626	81
Los Angeles – Anaheim – Riverside, CA	0.602	82
Longview – Marshall, TX	0.597	83
Fort Collins – Loveland, CO	0.591	84
Lincoln, NE	0.589	85
Fort Walton Beach, FL	0.587	86
Greeley, CO	0.584	87
Huntsville, AL	0.578	88
New London – Norwich, CT – RI	0.555	89
Alexandria, LA	0.543	90
Milwaukee – Racine, WI	0.543	90
Texarkana, TX – Texarkana, AR	0.535	91
Kansas City, MO – KS	0.522	92
Eau Claire, WI	0.521	93
Battle Creek, MI	0.520	94
Grand Rapids, MI	0.516	95
Omaha, NE – IA	0.514	96
Dallas – Fort Worth, TX	0.513	97
Benton Harbor, MI	0.511	98
Kokomo, IN	0.510	99
Saginaw – Bay City – Midland, MI	0.494	100
Honolulu, HI	0.473	101
Pine Bluff, AR	0.466	102
Clarksville – Hopkinsville, TN – KY	0.463	103
Saint Cloud, MN	0.458	104
La Crosse, WI	0.456	105

[Continued]

★383★

American Indian, Eskimo, or Aleut Population, 1990
[Continued]

MSA	% of total population	Rank
Ocala, FL	0.447	106
Florence, AL	0.434	107
San Angelo, TX	0.430	108
Wilmington, NC	0.421	109
El Paso, TX	0.415	110
Detroit – Ann Arbor, MI	0.414	111
Dothan, AL	0.413	112
Jackson, MI	0.409	113
Charlotte – Gastonia – Rock Hill, NC – SC	0.404	114
Little Rock – North Little Rock, AR	0.399	115
Midland, TX	0.391	116
Janesville – Beloit, WI	0.389	117
Melbourne – Titusville – Palm Bay, FL	0.381	118
Norfolk – Virginia Beach – Newport News, VA	0.381	118
Lakeland – Winter Haven, FL	0.374	119
Saint Joseph, MO	0.374	119
Kalamazoo, MI	0.373	120
Austin, TX	0.372	121
Naples, FL	0.366	122
Sheboygan, WI	0.365	123
Lubbock, TX	0.362	124
Madison, WI	0.361	125
Providence – Pawtucket – Fall River, RI – MA	0.361	125
Bradenton, FL	0.359	126
San Antonio, TX	0.359	126
Charleston, SC	0.358	127
Corpus Christi, TX	0.358	127
Tyler, TX	0.354	128
Jacksonville, FL	0.351	129
Gadsden, AL	0.347	130
Orlando, FL	0.345	131
Biloxi – Gulfport, MS	0.342	132
Davenport – Rock Island – Moline, IA – IL	0.341	133
Abilene, TX	0.340	134
Greensboro – Winston-Salem – High Point, NC	0.338	135
Elkhart – Goshen, IN	0.335	136
Daytona Beach, FL	0.329	137
Shreveport, LA	0.328	138
Tampa – Saint Petersburg – Clearwater, FL	0.327	139
Houston – Galveston – Brazoria, TX	0.319	140
Columbus, GA – AL	0.317	141
Elmira, NY	0.316	142
Wausau, WI	0.316	142
Burlington, NC	0.315	143
Fort Wayne, IN	0.311	144
New Orleans, LA	0.310	145
Washington, DC – MD – VA	0.309	146

[Continued]

★383★

American Indian, Eskimo, or Aleut Population, 1990
[Continued]

MSA	% of total population	Rank
Albany, GA	0.307	147
Jamestown – Dunkirk, NY	0.307	147
Bloomington, IN	0.306	148
Muncie, IN	0.306	148
Richmond – Petersburg, VA	0.302	149
Asheville, NC	0.301	150
Portland, ME	0.299	151
Fort Myers – Cape Coral, FL	0.296	152
South Bend – Mishawaka, IN	0.294	153
Beaumont – Port Arthur, TX	0.289	154
Savannah, GA	0.289	154
New Bedford, MA	0.287	155
Columbia, MO	0.285	156
Knoxville, TN	0.284	157
Lafayette, LA	0.283	158
Rockford, IL	0.281	159
Baltimore, MD	0.279	160
Lake Charles, LA	0.276	161
Raleigh – Durham, NC	0.274	162
Bryan – College Station, TX	0.273	163
Waco, TX	0.273	163
Des Moines, IA	0.271	164
Anderson, IN	0.270	165
Nashville, TN	0.270	165
Chattanooga, TN – GA	0.268	166
Steubenville – Weirton, OH – WV	0.265	167
Augusta, GA – SC	0.264	168
Manchester, NH	0.263	169
Champaign – Urbana – Rantoul, IL	0.262	170
Anniston, AL	0.261	171
Canton, OH	0.260	172
Rochester, NY	0.260	172
Burlington, VT	0.258	173
Montgomery, AL	0.251	174
Johnson City – Kingsport – Bristol, TN – VA	0.250	175
Portsmouth – Dover – Rochester, NH – ME	0.247	176
Tallahassee, FL	0.241	177
Brownsville – Harlingen, TX	0.236	178
Waterbury, CT	0.236	178
Saint Louis, MO – IL	0.234	179
Sarasota, FL	0.234	179
Fitchburg – Leominster, MA	0.232	180
Dayton – Springfield, OH	0.231	181
Pittsfield, MA	0.230	182
Columbia, SC	0.229	183
Utica – Rome, NY	0.228	184
Birmingham, AL	0.226	185
Pascagoula, MS	0.225	186
New York – Northern New Jersey – Long Island, NY – NJ – CT	0.223	187
Peoria, IL	0.223	187
Columbus, OH	0.221	188
Memphis, TN – AR – MS	0.221	188

[Continued]

★383★

American Indian, Eskimo, or Aleut Population, 1990
[Continued]

MSA	% of total population	Rank
Toledo, OH	0.221	188
Worcester, MA	0.221	188
Lewiston – Auburn, ME	0.220	189
Atlanta, GA	0.218	190
Indianapolis, IN	0.216	191
Parkersburg – Marietta, WV – OH	0.215	192
Hickory – Morganton, NC	0.213	193
Evansville, IN – KY	0.212	194
Terre Haute, IN	0.212	194
Albany – Schenectady – Troy, NY	0.211	195
Fort Pierce, FL	0.208	196
Philadelphia – Wilmington – Trenton, PA – NJ – DE – MD	0.208	196
Chicago – Gary – Lake County, IL – IN – WI	0.205	197
Macon – Warner Robins, GA	0.204	198
Gainesville, FL	0.203	199
Rochester, MN	0.203	199
Cleveland – Akron – Lorain, OH	0.202	200
Glens Falls, NY	0.202	200
Atlantic City, NJ	0.200	201
Lexington-Fayette, KY	0.198	202
Hagerstown, MD	0.194	203
Hartford – New Britain – Middletown, CT	0.194	203
Springfield, IL	0.192	204
Boston – Lawrence – Salem, MA – NH	0.190	205
Victoria, TX	0.190	205
Williamsport, PA	0.188	206
Athens, GA	0.187	207
Tuscaloosa, AL	0.187	207
Louisville, KY – IN	0.185	208
Monroe, LA	0.184	209
State College, PA	0.184	209
Lima, OH	0.183	210
Miami – Fort Lauderdale, FL	0.182	211
Baton Rouge, LA	0.181	212
Binghamton, NY	0.180	213
Poughkeepsie, NY	0.177	214
Cedar Rapids, IA	0.175	215
Youngstown – Warren, OH	0.175	215
Lynchburg, VA	0.173	216
West Palm Beach – Boca Raton – Delray Beach, FL	0.172	217
New Haven – Meriden, CT	0.170	218
Anderson, SC	0.169	219
Bloomington – Normal, IL	0.169	219
McAllen – Edinburg – Mission, TX	0.168	220
Lafayette – West Lafayette, IN	0.167	221
Owensboro, KY	0.167	221
Waterloo – Cedar Falls, IA	0.164	222
Greenville – Spartanburg, SC	0.160	223
Mansfield, OH	0.156	224
Cincinnati – Hamilton, OH – KY – IN	0.155	225

[Continued]

★383★

American Indian, Eskimo, or Aleut Population, 1990
[Continued]

MSA	% of total population	Rank
Springfield, MA	0.150	226
Harrisburg – Lebanon – Carlisle, PA	0.144	227
Charlottesville, VA	0.138	228
Erie, PA	0.138	228
Huntington – Ashland, WV – KY – OH	0.133	229
Kankakee, IL	0.132	230
Decatur, IL	0.131	231
Lancaster, PA	0.131	231
Iowa City, IA	0.130	232
Charleston, WV	0.125	233
Roanoke, VA	0.125	233
Wheeling, WV – OH	0.119	234
York, PA	0.118	235
Danville, VA	0.114	236
Pittsburgh – Beaver Valley, PA	0.108	237
Sharon, PA	0.107	238
Allentown – Bethlehem – Easton, PA – NJ	0.104	239
Reading, PA	0.100	240
Florence, SC	0.099	241
Altoona, PA	0.096	242
Dubuque, IA	0.090	243
Jackson, MS	0.089	244
Johnstown, PA	0.082	245
Scranton – Wilkes-Barre, PA	0.078	246
Jackson, TN	0.063	247
Laredo, TX	0.030	248
Cumberland, MD – WV	0.027	249

Source: U.S. Bureau of the Census, Data User Services Division, *1990 Census of Population and Housing,* Summary Tape File 3C, United States Summary, CD-ROM, February 1992.

★384★

Population By Race

Asian or Pacific Islander Population, 1990

MSA	% of total population	Rank
Honolulu, HI	63.07	1
San Francisco – Oakland – San Jose, CA	14.84	2
Stockton, CA	12.44	3
Los Angeles – Anaheim – Riverside, CA	9.22	4
Yuba City, CA	9.06	5
Fresno, CA	8.58	6
Merced, CA	8.31	7
San Diego, CA	7.95	8
Salinas – Seaside – Monterey, CA	7.78	9
Sacramento, CA	7.75	10
Seattle – Tacoma, WA	6.42	11
Washington, DC – MD – VA	5.14	12

[Continued]

★384★

Asian or Pacific Islander Population, 1990
[Continued]

MSA	% of total population	Rank
Modesto, CA	5.09	13
New York – Northern New Jersey – Long Island, NY – NJ – CT	4.79	14
Anchorage, AK	4.76	15
Champaign – Urbana – Rantoul, IL	4.59	16
Santa Barbara – Santa Maria – Lompoc, CA	4.48	17
Bremerton, WA	4.46	18
Visalia – Tulare – Porterville, CA	4.38	19
Iowa City, IA	3.88	20
Reno, NV	3.85	21
Lafayette – West Lafayette, IN	3.77	22
Olympia, WA	3.71	23
Bryan – College Station, TX	3.66	24
Las Vegas, NV	3.52	25
Houston – Galveston – Brazoria, TX	3.51	26
Portland – Vancouver, OR – WA	3.44	27
Lawrence, KS	3.24	28
Chicago – Gary – Lake County, IL – IN – WI	3.17	29
State College, PA	3.13	30
Bakersfield, CA	3.02	31
Rochester, MN	2.95	32
Boston – Lawrence – Salem, MA – NH	2.88	33
Columbia, MO	2.81	34
Killeen – Temple, TX	2.81	34
Chico, CA	2.78	35
La Crosse, WI	2.76	36
Lawton, OK	2.65	37
Minneapolis – Saint Paul, MN – WI	2.64	38
Fort Walton Beach, FL	2.54	39
Bloomington, IN	2.50	40
Norfolk – Virginia Beach – Newport News, VA	2.50	40
Dallas – Fort Worth, TX	2.47	41
Colorado Springs, CO	2.44	42
Austin, TX	2.35	43
Salt Lake City – Ogden, UT	2.35	43
Madison, WI	2.34	44
Denver – Boulder, CO	2.29	45
Gainesville, FL	2.23	46
Poughkeepsie, NY	2.23	46
Biloxi – Gulfport, MS	2.19	47
Wausau, WI	2.11	48
Richland – Kennewick – Pasco, WA	2.08	49
Philadelphia – Wilmington – Trenton, PA – NJ – DE – MD	2.06	50
Fort Smith, AR – OK	2.05	51
Jacksonville, NC	2.04	52
Fayetteville, NC	2.03	53
Eugene – Springfield, OR	1.96	54
Charlottesville, VA	1.94	55
Sheboygan, WI	1.94	55
Orlando, FL	1.90	56

[Continued]

★384★

Asian or Pacific Islander Population, 1990
[Continued]

MSA	% of total population	Rank
Raleigh – Durham, NC	1.90	56
Bellingham, WA	1.88	57
Lansing – East Lansing, MI	1.88	57
Wichita, KS	1.84	58
Spokane, WA	1.83	59
Tucson, AZ	1.82	60
Redding, CA	1.81	61
Eau Claire, WI	1.79	62
Panama City, FL	1.78	63
Atlanta, GA	1.76	64
Baltimore, MD	1.76	64
Oklahoma City, OK	1.76	64
Huntsville, AL	1.73	65
Fitchburg – Leominster, MA	1.72	66
Worcester, MA	1.70	67
Amarillo, TX	1.69	68
New Orleans, LA	1.69	68
Salem, OR	1.69	68
Pensacola, FL	1.68	69
Atlantic City, NJ	1.67	70
Beaumont – Port Arthur, TX	1.66	71
Phoenix, AZ	1.66	71
Providence – Pawtucket – Fall River, RI – MA	1.66	71
Jacksonville, FL	1.64	72
Clarksville – Hopkinsville, TN – KY	1.60	73
Albuquerque, NM	1.54	74
Kalamazoo, MI	1.54	74
Binghamton, NY	1.51	75
New Haven – Meriden, CT	1.51	75
Columbus, OH	1.50	76
Des Moines, IA	1.50	76
Wichita Falls, TX	1.48	77
Fort Collins – Loveland, CO	1.47	78
Athens, GA	1.46	79
Detroit – Ann Arbor, MI	1.46	79
Provo – Orem, UT	1.45	80
Augusta, GA – SC	1.41	81
Hartford – New Britain – Middletown, CT	1.41	81
Lincoln, NE	1.39	82
New London – Norwich, CT – RI	1.38	83
Sioux City, IA – NE	1.38	83
Bloomington – Normal, IL	1.37	84
Richmond – Petersburg, VA	1.36	85
Green Bay, WI	1.33	86
Rochester, NY	1.32	87
Miami – Fort Lauderdale, FL	1.29	88
Grand Forks, ND	1.28	89
Melbourne – Titusville – Palm Bay, FL	1.26	90
Yuma, AZ	1.26	90
Albany – Schenectady – Troy, NY	1.25	91
Columbus, GA – AL	1.24	92
San Antonio, TX	1.23	93
Milwaukee – Racine, WI	1.21	94

[Continued]

Asian or Pacific Islander Population, 1990
[Continued]

MSA	% of total population	Rank
Rockford, IL	1.18	95
Abilene, TX	1.17	96
Tallahassee, FL	1.17	96
Boise, ID	1.16	97
Charleston, SC	1.16	97
Cheyenne, WY	1.15	98
El Paso, TX	1.15	98
Appleton – Oshkosh – Neenah, WI	1.14	99
Rapid City, SD	1.14	99
Syracuse, NY	1.14	99
Lancaster, PA	1.12	100
Lubbock, TX	1.12	100
Omaha, NE – IA	1.11	101
Tampa – Saint Petersburg – Clearwater, FL	1.11	101
Grand Rapids, MI	1.09	102
Lexington-Fayette, KY	1.07	103
Allentown – Bethlehem – Easton, PA – NJ	1.06	104
West Palm Beach – Boca Raton – Delray Beach, FL	1.06	104
Burlington, VT	1.05	105
Great Falls, MT	1.05	105
Greeley, CO	1.04	106
Yakima, WA	1.04	106
Harrisburg – Lebanon – Carlisle, PA	1.03	107
Savannah, GA	1.03	107
Kansas City, MO – KS	1.02	108
Manchester, NH	1.02	108
Baton Rouge, LA	1.01	109
Cleveland – Akron – Lorain, OH	1.00	110
Columbia, SC	0.99	111
Las Cruces, NM	0.99	111
Toledo, OH	0.99	111
Medford, OR	0.97	112
Portsmouth – Dover – Rochester, NH – ME	0.97	112
Nashville, TN	0.95	113
Springfield, MA	0.95	113
South Bend – Mishawaka, IN	0.94	114
Charlotte – Gastonia – Rock Hill, NC – SC	0.93	115
Saint Louis, MO – IL	0.93	115
Tulsa, OK	0.93	115
Buffalo – Niagara Falls, NY	0.92	116
Dayton – Springfield, OH	0.91	117
Fayetteville – Springdale, AR	0.91	117
Portland, ME	0.91	117
San Angelo, TX	0.90	118
Benton Harbor, MI	0.88	119
Cedar Rapids, IA	0.88	119
Bangor, ME	0.87	120
Enid, OK	0.87	120
Midland, TX	0.86	121
Dothan, AL	0.85	122

[Continued]

Asian or Pacific Islander Population, 1990
[Continued]

MSA	% of total population	Rank
Lafayette, LA	0.85	122
Terre Haute, IN	0.84	123
Memphis, TN – AR – MS	0.82	124
Pascagoula, MS	0.81	125
Topeka, KS	0.81	125
Indianapolis, IN	0.80	126
Roanoke, VA	0.80	126
Cincinnati – Hamilton, OH – KY – IN	0.79	127
Fargo – Moorhead, ND – MN	0.79	127
Santa Fe, NM	0.79	127
Tuscaloosa, AL	0.79	127
Waco, TX	0.75	128
Waterloo – Cedar Falls, IA	0.75	128
Anniston, AL	0.74	129
Battle Creek, MI	0.74	129
Reading, PA	0.74	129
Fort Wayne, IN	0.73	130
Alexandria, LA	0.72	131
Corpus Christi, TX	0.72	131
Pittsfield, MA	0.72	131
Sherman – Denison, TX	0.72	131
Elmira, NY	0.71	132
Knoxville, TN	0.71	132
Mobile, AL	0.71	132
Peoria, IL	0.71	132
Springfield, IL	0.69	133
Utica – Rome, NY	0.69	133
Waterbury, CT	0.69	133
Elkhart – Goshen, IN	0.68	134
Greensboro – Winston-Salem – High Point, NC	0.68	134
Hickory – Morganton, NC	0.68	134
Pueblo, CO	0.68	134
Davenport – Rock Island – Moline, IA – IL	0.67	135
Flint, MI	0.67	135
Pittsburgh – Beaver Valley, PA	0.67	135
Sioux Falls, SD	0.66	136
Springfield, MO	0.66	136
Greenville – Spartanburg, SC	0.65	137
Janesville – Beloit, WI	0.65	137
Macon – Warner Robins, GA	0.64	138
Chattanooga, TN – GA	0.63	139
Joplin, MO	0.63	139
Louisville, KY – IN	0.63	139
Saginaw – Bay City – Midland, MI	0.63	139
Bradenton, FL	0.62	140
Little Rock – North Little Rock, AR	0.62	140
Daytona Beach, FL	0.61	141
Houma – Thibodaux, LA	0.60	142
Montgomery, AL	0.60	142
Muncie, IN	0.59	143
Jamestown – Dunkirk, NY	0.58	144
Lakeland – Winter Haven, FL	0.57	145
Charleston, WV	0.56	146
Duluth, MN – WI	0.56	146

[Continued]

★ 384 ★

Asian or Pacific Islander Population, 1990
[Continued]

MSA	% of total population	Rank
Kankakee, IL	0.56	146
Monroe, LA	0.56	146
Shreveport, LA	0.56	146
Asheville, NC	0.54	147
Hagerstown, MD	0.54	147
Lewiston – Auburn, ME	0.54	147
Mansfield, OH	0.54	147
York, PA	0.54	147
Victoria, TX	0.53	148
Fort Pierce, FL	0.52	149
Kokomo, IN	0.52	149
Erie, PA	0.51	150
Ocala, FL	0.51	150
Sarasota, FL	0.50	151
Birmingham, AL	0.49	152
Dubuque, IA	0.49	152
Fort Myers – Cape Coral, FL	0.49	152
Gadsden, AL	0.49	152
Wilmington, NC	0.49	152
Jackson, MS	0.47	153
Scranton – Wilkes-Barre, PA	0.47	153
Tyler, TX	0.47	153
Evansville, IN – KY	0.46	154
Bismarck, ND	0.44	155
Muskegon, MI	0.44	155
Canton, OH	0.43	156
Cumberland, MD – WV	0.43	156
Texarkana, TX – Texarkana, AR	0.43	156
Albany, GA	0.42	157
Saint Cloud, MN	0.42	157
Billings, MT	0.41	158
Decatur, IL	0.41	158
Glens Falls, NY	0.41	158
Lynchburg, VA	0.41	158
Parkersburg – Marietta, WV – OH	0.41	158
Williamsport, PA	0.41	158
New Bedford, MA	0.40	159
Youngstown – Warren, OH	0.39	160
Lima, OH	0.37	161
Wheeling, WV – OH	0.37	161
Huntington – Ashland, WV – KY – OH	0.36	162
Naples, FL	0.35	163
Jackson, TN	0.34	164
Casper, WY	0.33	165
Jackson, MI	0.32	166
Longview – Marshall, TX	0.32	166
Laredo, TX	0.31	167
Sharon, PA	0.31	167
Florence, SC	0.30	168
Anderson, SC	0.29	169
Johnson City – Kingsport – Bristol, TN – VA	0.29	169
McAllen – Edinburg – Mission, TX	0.29	169
Altoona, PA	0.28	170
Danville, VA	0.28	170

[Continued]

★ 384 ★

Asian or Pacific Islander Population, 1990
[Continued]

MSA	% of total population	Rank
Anderson, IN	0.27	171
Odessa, TX	0.27	171
Pine Bluff, AR	0.27	171
Steubenville – Weirton, OH – WV	0.27	171
Brownsville – Harlingen, TX	0.25	172
Lake Charles, LA	0.25	172
Burlington, NC	0.22	173
Saint Joseph, MO	0.22	173
Florence, AL	0.21	174
Owensboro, KY	0.21	174
Decatur, AL	0.19	175
Johnstown, PA	0.17	176

Source: U.S. Bureau of the Census, Data User Services Division, *1990 Census of Population and Housing*, Summary Tape File 3C, United States Summary, CD-ROM, February 1992.

★ 385 ★

Population By Race

Black Population, 1990

MSA	% of total population	Rank
Albany, GA	45.685	1
Pine Bluff, AR	43.057	2
Jackson, MS	42.464	3
Memphis, TN – AR – MS	40.675	4
Florence, SC	38.713	5
Columbus, GA – AL	37.576	6
Montgomery, AL	35.931	7
Savannah, GA	35.480	8
Shreveport, LA	34.948	9
New Orleans, LA	34.783	10
Macon – Warner Robins, GA	34.629	11
Fayetteville, NC	31.851	12
Danville, VA	31.683	13
Augusta, GA – SC	31.060	14
Jackson, TN	31.002	15
Monroe, LA	30.976	16
Columbia, SC	30.405	17
Charleston, SC	30.228	18
Tallahassee, FL	30.148	19
Baton Rouge, LA	29.608	20
Richmond – Petersburg, VA	29.155	21
Norfolk – Virginia Beach – Newport News, VA	28.509	22
Alexandria, LA	27.879	23
Mobile, AL	27.340	24
Birmingham, AL	27.017	25
Washington, DC – MD – VA	26.563	26
Atlanta, GA	25.956	27
Tuscaloosa, AL	25.940	28
Baltimore, MD	25.826	29
Raleigh – Durham, NC	24.912	30
Lafayette, LA	24.586	31
Beaumont – Port Arthur, TX	23.443	32

[Continued]

★385★

Black Population, 1990
[Continued]

MSA	% of total population	Rank
Lake Charles, LA	22.910	33
Longview – Marshall, TX	22.064	34
Texarkana, TX – Texarkana, AR	22.052	35
Lynchburg, VA	21.194	36
Dothan, AL	21.152	37
Detroit – Ann Arbor, MI	20.876	38
Tyler, TX	20.813	39
Clarksville – Hopkinsville, TN – KY	20.545	40
Pascagoula, MS	20.480	41
Huntsville, AL	20.134	42
Wilmington, NC	19.984	43
Jacksonville, FL	19.965	44
Charlotte – Gastonia – Rock Hill, NC – SC	19.917	45
Jacksonville, NC	19.881	46
Little Rock – North Little Rock, AR	19.855	47
Flint, MI	19.531	48
Killeen – Temple, TX	19.448	49
Greensboro – Winston-Salem – High Point, NC	19.305	50
Burlington, NC	19.248	51
Gainesville, FL	19.169	52
Chicago – Gary – Lake County, IL – IN – WI	19.150	53
Anniston, AL	18.658	54
Philadelphia – Wilmington – Trenton, PA – NJ – DE – MD	18.647	55
Miami – Fort Lauderdale, FL	18.536	56
Athens, GA	18.495	57
New York – Northern New Jersey – Long Island, NY – NJ – CT	18.200	58
Biloxi – Gulfport, MS	17.930	59
Houston – Galveston – Brazoria, TX	17.899	60
Lawton, OK	17.838	61
Greenville – Spartanburg, SC	17.403	62
Saint Louis, MO – IL	17.276	63
Anderson, SC	16.595	64
Pensacola, FL	16.245	65
Cleveland – Akron – Lorain, OH	15.983	66
Waco, TX	15.579	67
Nashville, TN	15.462	68
Benton Harbor, MI	15.389	69
Kankakee, IL	15.044	70
Charlottesville, VA	14.485	71
Houma – Thibodaux, LA	14.482	72
Dallas – Fort Worth, TX	14.266	73
Gadsden, AL	13.885	74
Atlantic City, NJ	13.858	75
Indianapolis, IN	13.726	76
Muskegon, MI	13.532	77
Lakeland – Winter Haven, FL	13.399	78
Chattanooga, TN – GA	13.388	79
Milwaukee – Racine, WI	13.323	80
Dayton – Springfield, OH	13.282	81
Louisville, KY – IN	13.091	82

[Continued]

★385★

Black Population, 1990
[Continued]

MSA	% of total population	Rank
Kansas City, MO – KS	12.797	83
Ocala, FL	12.773	84
West Palm Beach – Boca Raton – Delray Beach, FL	12.381	85
Orlando, FL	12.379	86
Florence, AL	12.362	87
Roanoke, VA	12.237	88
Fort Pierce, FL	12.185	89
New Haven – Meriden, CT	12.122	90
Decatur, IL	12.053	91
Columbus, OH	11.948	92
Cincinnati – Hamilton, OH – KY – IN	11.638	93
Toledo, OH	11.347	94
Decatur, AL	11.213	95
Bryan – College Station, TX	11.191	96
Youngstown – Warren, OH	11.104	97
Lexington-Fayette, KY	10.686	98
Panama City, FL	10.530	99
Oklahoma City, OK	10.490	100
Battle Creek, MI	10.373	101
Buffalo – Niagara Falls, NY	10.237	102
South Bend – Mishawaka, IN	9.704	103
Saginaw – Bay City – Midland, MI	9.702	104
Champaign – Urbana – Rantoul, IL	9.601	105
Las Vegas, NV	9.506	106
Rochester, NY	9.286	107
Austin, TX	9.207	108
Wichita Falls, TX	9.060	109
Daytona Beach, FL	9.021	110
Fort Walton Beach, FL	9.021	110
Kalamazoo, MI	8.916	111
Tampa – Saint Petersburg – Clearwater, FL	8.902	112
Hartford – New Britain – Middletown, CT	8.669	113
San Francisco – Oakland – San Jose, CA	8.563	114
Los Angeles – Anaheim – Riverside, CA	8.440	115
Fort Wayne, IN	8.285	116
Poughkeepsie, NY	8.283	117
Omaha, NE – IA	8.255	118
Rockford, IL	8.175	119
Tulsa, OK	8.136	120
Topeka, KS	8.103	121
Asheville, NC	8.070	122
Jackson, MI	8.017	123
Pittsburgh – Beaver Valley, PA	7.977	124
Lima, OH	7.962	125
Hickory – Morganton, NC	7.857	126
Melbourne – Titusville – Palm Bay, FL	7.840	127
Bradenton, FL	7.786	128
Midland, TX	7.782	129
Mansfield, OH	7.778	130
Springfield, IL	7.605	131

[Continued]

★385★

Black Population, 1990
[Continued]

MSA	% of total population	Rank
Lubbock, TX	7.562	132
Anderson, IN	7.543	133
Wichita, KS	7.534	134
Peoria, IL	7.445	135
Columbia, MO	7.404	136
Lansing – East Lansing, MI	7.217	137
Colorado Springs, CO	7.117	138
Waterbury, CT	6.854	139
Sacramento, CA	6.844	140
San Antonio, TX	6.813	141
Sherman – Denison, TX	6.812	142
Harrisburg – Lebanon – Carlisle, PA	6.660	143
Springfield, MA	6.636	144
Victoria, TX	6.610	145
Fort Myers – Cape Coral, FL	6.569	146
Salinas – Seaside – Monterey, CA	6.377	147
Anchorage, AK	6.367	148
San Diego, CA	6.305	149
Canton, OH	6.282	150
Abilene, TX	6.238	151
Hagerstown, MD	6.075	152
Grand Rapids, MI	5.935	153
Knoxville, TN	5.933	154
Waterloo – Cedar Falls, IA	5.864	155
Syracuse, NY	5.856	156
Evansville, IN – KY	5.764	157
Muncie, IN	5.756	158
Boston – Lawrence – Salem, MA – NH	5.660	159
Stockton, CA	5.594	160
Charleston, WV	5.520	161
Bakersfield, CA	5.461	162
Davenport – Rock Island – Moline, IA – IL	5.388	163
Elmira, NY	5.387	164
Denver – Boulder, CO	5.223	165
Erie, PA	5.222	166
Amarillo, TX	5.053	167
Fresno, CA	4.924	168
Merced, CA	4.920	169
Sharon, PA	4.802	170
Odessa, TX	4.767	171
Seattle – Tacoma, WA	4.756	172
Albany – Schenectady – Troy, NY	4.727	173
Janesville – Beloit, WI	4.686	174
Terre Haute, IN	4.643	175
New London – Norwich, CT – RI	4.590	176
Naples, FL	4.573	177
Elkhart – Goshen, IN	4.549	178
Kokomo, IN	4.465	179
Utica – Rome, NY	4.352	180
Sarasota, FL	4.285	181
Bloomington – Normal, IL	4.226	182
Lawrence, KS	4.053	183
San Angelo, TX	4.034	184

[Continued]

★385★

Black Population, 1990
[Continued]

MSA	% of total population	Rank
Owensboro, KY	3.966	185
Steubenville – Weirton, OH – WV	3.913	186
Corpus Christi, TX	3.829	187
Fort Smith, AR – OK	3.812	188
El Paso, TX	3.716	189
Des Moines, IA	3.715	190
Minneapolis – Saint Paul, MN – WI	3.626	191
Enid, OK	3.529	192
Phoenix, AZ	3.501	193
Saint Joseph, MO	3.223	194
Providence – Pawtucket – Fall River, RI – MA	3.176	195
Tucson, AZ	3.127	196
Honolulu, HI	3.075	197
Cheyenne, WY	2.979	198
Reading, PA	2.925	199
York, PA	2.860	200
Madison, WI	2.837	201
Portland – Vancouver, OR – WA	2.771	202
Yuma, AZ	2.761	203
Santa Barbara – Santa Maria – Lompoc, CA	2.749	204
Yuba City, CA	2.748	205
Albuquerque, NM	2.732	206
Bremerton, WA	2.585	207
Bloomington, IN	2.538	208
New Bedford, MA	2.434	209
Cumberland, MD – WV	2.280	210
Williamsport, PA	2.273	211
Lancaster, PA	2.264	212
Lincoln, NE	2.258	213
Worcester, MA	2.166	214
State College, PA	2.146	215
Reno, NV	2.145	216
Fitchburg – Leominster, MA	2.143	217
Iowa City, IA	2.091	218
Huntington – Ashland, WV – KY – OH	2.082	219
Glens Falls, NY	2.020	220
Grand Forks, ND	1.993	221
Pittsfield, MA	1.970	222
Allentown – Bethlehem – Easton, PA – NJ	1.960	223
Johnson City – Kingsport – Bristol, TN – VA	1.951	224
Cedar Rapids, IA	1.924	225
Lafayette – West Lafayette, IN	1.908	226
Sioux City, IA – NE	1.857	227
Wheeling, WV – OH	1.782	228
Pueblo, CO	1.716	229
Olympia, WA	1.680	230
Modesto, CA	1.630	231
Jamestown – Dunkirk, NY	1.620	232
Binghamton, NY	1.588	233
Johnstown, PA	1.578	234
Las Cruces, NM	1.564	235

[Continued]

★385★

Black Population, 1990

[Continued]

MSA	% of total population	Rank
Springfield, MO	1.507	236
Rapid City, SD	1.501	237
Visalia – Tulare – Porterville, CA	1.458	238
Richland – Kennewick – Pasco, WA	1.445	239
Spokane, WA	1.402	240
Fayetteville – Springdale, AR	1.366	241
Great Falls, MT	1.295	242
Chico, CA	1.152	243
Yakima, WA	1.105	244
Portsmouth – Dover – Rochester, NH – ME	1.089	245
Scranton – Wilkes-Barre, PA	1.020	246
Parkersburg – Marietta, WV – OH	0.997	247
Salt Lake City – Ogden, UT	0.938	248
Joplin, MO	0.925	249
Altoona, PA	0.823	250
Salem, OR	0.795	251
Burlington, VT	0.794	252
Redding, CA	0.762	253
Rochester, MN	0.741	254
Eugene – Springfield, OR	0.731	255
Manchester, NH	0.726	256
Sioux Falls, SD	0.631	257
Portland, ME	0.624	258
Bangor, ME	0.609	259
Casper, WY	0.583	260
Fort Collins – Loveland, CO	0.568	261
Boise, ID	0.564	262
Duluth, MN – WI	0.550	263
Santa Fe, NM	0.540	264
Green Bay, WI	0.528	265
Lewiston – Auburn, ME	0.509	266
La Crosse, WI	0.498	267
Bellingham, WA	0.484	268
Sheboygan, WI	0.445	269
Greeley, CO	0.398	270
Saint Cloud, MN	0.393	271
Dubuque, IA	0.353	272
Brownsville – Harlingen, TX	0.347	273
Billings, MT	0.335	274
Eau Claire, WI	0.295	275
Fargo – Moorhead, ND – MN	0.286	276
Appleton – Oshkosh – Neenah, WI	0.274	277
McAllen – Edinburg – Mission, TX	0.266	278
Medford, OR	0.169	279
Bismarck, ND	0.104	280
Provo – Orem, UT	0.095	281
Laredo, TX	0.074	282
Wausau, WI	0.067	283

Source: U.S. Bureau of the Census, Data User Services Division, *1990 Census of Population and Housing,* Summary Tape File 3C, United States Summary, CD-ROM, February 1992.

★386★

Population By Race

White Population, 1990

MSA	% of total population	Rank
Dubuque, IA	98.9	1
Altoona, PA	98.7	2
Saint Cloud, MN	98.6	3
Lewiston – Auburn, ME	98.5	4
Parkersburg – Marietta, WV – OH	98.3	5
Scranton – Wilkes-Barre, PA	98.2	6
Johnstown, PA	98.1	7
Portland, ME	98.1	7
Burlington, VT	97.7	8
Wheeling, WV – OH	97.6	9
Appleton – Oshkosh – Neenah, WI	97.4	10
Fargo – Moorhead, ND – MN	97.4	10
Huntington – Ashland, WV – KY – OH	97.4	10
Johnson City – Kingsport – Bristol, TN – VA	97.4	10
Portsmouth – Dover – Rochester, NH – ME	97.4	10
Wausau, WI	97.4	10
Casper, WY	97.3	11
Eau Claire, WI	97.3	11
Manchester, NH	97.3	11
Sioux Falls, SD	97.3	11
Bangor, ME	97.2	12
Bismarck, ND	97.2	12
Cumberland, MD – WV	97.2	12
Glens Falls, NY	97.0	13
Duluth, MN – WI	96.9	14
Springfield, MO	96.9	14
Williamsport, PA	96.9	14
Boise, ID	96.8	15
Cedar Rapids, IA	96.8	15
Pittsfield, MA	96.6	16
Sheboygan, WI	96.5	17
Binghamton, NY	96.4	18
Joplin, MO	96.4	18
Provo – Orem, UT	96.4	18
La Crosse, WI	96.1	19
Green Bay, WI	96.0	20
Jamestown – Dunkirk, NY	96.0	20
Fayetteville – Springdale, AR	95.9	21
Rochester, MN	95.9	21
York, PA	95.7	22
Medford, OR	95.6	23
Owensboro, KY	95.6	23
Steubenville – Weirton, OH – WV	95.5	24
Billings, MT	95.3	25
Eugene – Springfield, OR	95.3	25
Saint Joseph, MO	95.3	25
Lincoln, NE	95.0	26
Spokane, WA	94.8	27
Fort Collins – Loveland, CO	94.7	28
Sarasota, FL	94.7	28
Sharon, PA	94.7	28
Allentown – Bethlehem – Easton, PA – NJ	94.6	29
Grand Forks, ND	94.5	30

[Continued]

★386★

White Population, 1990
[Continued]

MSA	% of total population	Rank
Bloomington, IN	94.3	31
Kokomo, IN	94.3	31
Lancaster, PA	94.2	32
State College, PA	94.2	32
Redding, CA	94.1	33
Terre Haute, IN	94.1	33
Utica – Rome, NY	94.0	34
Des Moines, IA	93.9	35
Madison, WI	93.9	35
Bloomington – Normal, IL	93.8	36
Janesville – Beloit, WI	93.8	36
Charleston, WV	93.7	37
Elkhart – Goshen, IN	93.7	37
Reading, PA	93.7	37
Erie, PA	93.6	38
Lafayette – West Lafayette, IN	93.6	38
Bellingham, WA	93.5	39
Evansville, IN – KY	93.5	39
Iowa City, IA	93.5	39
Sioux City, IA – NE	93.5	39
Worcester, MA	93.5	39
Salt Lake City – Ogden, UT	93.4	40
Albany – Schenectady – Troy, NY	93.2	41
Fitchburg – Leominster, MA	93.0	42
Great Falls, MT	93.0	42
Muncie, IN	93.0	42
Waterloo – Cedar Falls, IA	93.0	42
Canton, OH	92.9	43
Hagerstown, MD	92.9	43
Knoxville, TN	92.9	43
Elmira, NY	92.8	44
Enid, OK	92.8	44
Providence – Pawtucket – Fall River, RI – MA	92.6	45
Minneapolis – Saint Paul, MN – WI	92.2	46
Davenport – Rock Island – Moline, IA – IL	92.1	47
New London – Norwich, CT – RI	92.1	47
Olympia, WA	92.1	47
New Bedford, MA	91.9	48
Syracuse, NY	91.9	48
Salem, OR	91.8	49
Anderson, IN	91.6	50
Naples, FL	91.5	51
Portland – Vancouver, OR – WA	91.5	51
Harrisburg – Lebanon – Carlisle, PA	91.4	52
Springfield, IL	91.4	52
Fort Myers – Cape Coral, FL	91.3	53
Las Cruces, NM	91.3	53
Mansfield, OH	91.3	53
Peoria, IL	91.2	54
Hickory – Morganton, NC	91.1	55
Lima, OH	91.1	55
Pittsburgh – Beaver Valley, PA	91.1	55
Asheville, NC	91.0	56

[Continued]

★386★

White Population, 1990
[Continued]

MSA	% of total population	Rank
Chico, CA	90.8	57
Grand Rapids, MI	90.8	57
Jackson, MI	90.6	58
Cheyenne, WY	90.5	59
Bremerton, WA	90.1	60
Bradenton, FL	89.9	61
Melbourne – Titusville – Palm Bay, FL	89.9	61
Sherman – Denison, TX	89.9	61
Fort Wayne, IN	89.8	62
Rapid City, SD	89.4	63
Columbia, MO	89.1	64
Lawrence, KS	89.1	64
Omaha, NE – IA	89.1	64
Boston – Lawrence – Salem, MA – NH	89.0	65
Greeley, CO	89.0	65
Waterbury, CT	88.9	66
Daytona Beach, FL	88.7	67
Rockford, IL	88.7	67
Poughkeepsie, NY	88.5	68
Fort Smith, AR – OK	88.4	69
Kalamazoo, MI	88.4	69
Reno, NV	88.4	69
Tampa – Saint Petersburg – Clearwater, FL	88.4	69
Lansing – East Lansing, MI	88.2	70
South Bend – Mishawaka, IN	88.0	71
Topeka, KS	87.9	72
Lexington-Fayette, KY	87.8	73
Youngstown – Warren, OH	87.7	74
Rochester, NY	87.6	75
Wichita, KS	87.5	76
Battle Creek, MI	87.4	77
Cincinnati – Hamilton, OH – KY – IN	87.3	78
Buffalo – Niagara Falls, NY	87.2	79
Decatur, IL	87.2	79
Fort Walton Beach, FL	87.1	80
Florence, AL	86.9	81
Saginaw – Bay City – Midland, MI	86.9	81
Denver – Boulder, CO	86.7	82
Roanoke, VA	86.7	82
Decatur, AL	86.6	83
Richland – Kennewick – Pasco, WA	86.6	83
Springfield, MA	86.6	83
Panama City, FL	86.5	84
Seattle – Tacoma, WA	86.5	84
Colorado Springs, CO	86.2	85
Hartford – New Britain – Middletown, CT	86.1	86
Columbus, OH	86.0	87
Louisville, KY – IN	85.9	88
Toledo, OH	85.9	88
Chattanooga, TN – GA	85.6	89
Fort Pierce, FL	85.6	89
Ocala, FL	85.6	89

[Continued]

★386★

White Population, 1990
[Continued]

MSA	% of total population	Rank
Dayton – Springfield, OH	85.3	90
Gadsden, AL	85.1	91
Indianapolis, IN	85.0	92
Phoenix, AZ	84.9	93
West Palm Beach – Boca Raton – Delray Beach, FL	84.9	93
Pueblo, CO	84.8	94
Amarillo, TX	84.7	95
Champaign – Urbana – Rantoul, IL	84.6	96
Kansas City, MO – KS	84.4	97
Lakeland – Winter Haven, FL	84.4	97
Muskegon, MI	84.3	98
Abilene, TX	84.0	99
Wichita Falls, TX	84.0	99
Kankakee, IL	83.5	100
New Haven – Meriden, CT	83.4	101
Tulsa, OK	83.4	101
Milwaukee – Racine, WI	83.2	102
Charlottesville, VA	83.1	103
Nashville, TN	83.1	103
Anderson, SC	82.8	104
Orlando, FL	82.8	104
Benton Harbor, MI	82.7	105
Santa Fe, NM	82.7	105
Brownsville – Harlingen, TX	82.4	106
Cleveland – Akron – Lorain, OH	82.0	107
Midland, TX	81.7	108
Greenville – Spartanburg, SC	81.6	109
Atlantic City, NJ	81.5	110
Las Vegas, NV	81.3	111
Oklahoma City, OK	81.3	111
Saint Louis, MO – IL	81.3	111
San Angelo, TX	81.1	112
Houma – Thibodaux, LA	81.0	113
Anchorage, AK	80.8	114
Pensacola, FL	80.6	115
Modesto, CA	80.4	116
Anniston, AL	80.1	117
Burlington, NC	80.0	118
Athens, GA	79.6	119
Victoria, TX	79.6	119
Greensboro – Winston-Salem – High Point, NC	79.5	120
Biloxi – Gulfport, MS	79.3	121
Lubbock, TX	79.3	121
Sacramento, CA	79.1	122
Wilmington, NC	79.0	123
Little Rock – North Little Rock, AR	78.9	124
Tucson, AZ	78.9	124
Charlotte – Gastonia – Rock Hill, NC – SC	78.5	125
Pascagoula, MS	78.3	126
Flint, MI	78.2	127
Lynchburg, VA	78.1	128
Bryan – College Station, TX	77.8	129
Yuba City, CA	77.8	129

[Continued]

★386★

White Population, 1990
[Continued]

MSA	% of total population	Rank
Gainesville, FL	77.7	130
Jacksonville, FL	77.4	131
Waco, TX	77.4	131
Huntsville, AL	77.3	132
Dothan, AL	77.2	133
Santa Barbara – Santa Maria – Lompoc, CA	77.2	133
Albuquerque, NM	77.1	134
Odessa, TX	77.0	135
Philadelphia – Wilmington – Trenton, PA – NJ – DE – MD	77.0	135
Austin, TX	76.9	136
El Paso, TX	76.6	137
Texarkana, TX – Texarkana, AR	76.6	137
Detroit – Ann Arbor, MI	76.5	138
Miami – Fort Lauderdale, FL	76.5	138
Lake Charles, LA	76.3	139
Clarksville – Hopkinsville, TN – KY	75.9	140
Corpus Christi, TX	75.9	140
Yuma, AZ	75.7	141
Dallas – Fort Worth, TX	75.3	142
Longview – Marshall, TX	75.3	142
San Antonio, TX	75.2	143
San Diego, CA	75.1	144
Tyler, TX	75.1	144
McAllen – Edinburg – Mission, TX	74.8	145
Jacksonville, NC	74.6	146
Yakima, WA	73.9	147
Lafayette, LA	73.8	148
Stockton, CA	73.5	149
Beaumont – Port Arthur, TX	73.1	150
Tuscaloosa, AL	72.9	151
Raleigh – Durham, NC	72.5	152
Birmingham, AL	72.2	153
Baltimore, MD	71.8	154
Chicago – Gary – Lake County, IL – IN – WI	71.6	155
Lawton, OK	71.6	155
Atlanta, GA	71.3	156
Mobile, AL	71.1	157
Killeen – Temple, TX	71.0	158
Alexandria, LA	70.7	159
Laredo, TX	70.5	160
New York – Northern New Jersey – Long Island, NY – NJ – CT	70.3	161
Bakersfield, CA	69.8	162
San Francisco – Oakland – San Jose, CA	69.4	163
Baton Rouge, LA	68.9	164
Richmond – Petersburg, VA	68.8	165
Jackson, TN	68.5	166
Monroe, LA	68.0	167
Charleston, SC	67.9	168
Columbia, SC	67.9	168
Danville, VA	67.9	168
Norfolk – Virginia Beach – Newport News, VA	67.9	168

[Continued]

★386★

White Population, 1990
[Continued]

MSA	% of total population	Rank
Tallahassee, FL	67.8	169
Houston – Galveston – Brazoria, TX	67.6	170
Merced, CA	67.5	171
Augusta, GA – SC	66.7	172
Visalia – Tulare – Porterville, CA	65.9	173
Washington, DC – MD – VA	65.8	174
Los Angeles – Anaheim – Riverside, CA	64.7	175
Macon – Warner Robins, GA	64.3	176
Salinas – Seaside – Monterey, CA	63.9	177
Shreveport, LA	63.9	177
Fresno, CA	63.5	178
Montgomery, AL	63.0	179
Savannah, GA	62.9	180
New Orleans, LA	62.2	181
Fayetteville, NC	62.0	182
Florence, SC	60.8	183
Columbus, GA – AL	59.4	184
Memphis, TN – AR – MS	58.1	185
Jackson, MS	56.9	186
Pine Bluff, AR	56.1	187
Albany, GA	53.3	188
Honolulu, HI	31.7	189

Source: U.S. Bureau of the Census, Data User Services Division, *1990 Census of Population and Housing*, Summary Tape File 3C, United States Summary, CD-ROM, February 1992.

Chapter 3

IMMIGRANT POPULATION

Topics Covered

Aliens
Illegal Immigrants
Immigrant Population
Immigrants Admitted, By Country of Birth
Immigrants Admitted, By Time Period
Naturalized Citizens
Nonimmigrants Admitted, By Region of Citizenship
Nonimmigrants Admitted, By Country of Citizenship
Refugees and Asylees

★387★

Aliens

Aliens Deported and Required to Depart From the Central Region of the United States, 1994: Totals

The total number from all three regions (i.e., Eastern, Central, and Western) is 1,068,170. The total number of persons deported and required to depart from the Central Region of the United States is 363,750.

City/MSA	Number	Rank
Chicago, IL	603	7
Dallas, TX	7,067	4
Denver, CO	2,564	5
El Paso, TX	89,360	3
Harlingen, TX	133,963	1
Helena, MT	214	10
Houston, TX	1,446	6
Kansas City, MO	462	8
Omaha, NE	71	11
Saint Paul, MN	240	9
San Antonio, TX	127,760	2

Source: U.S. Department of Justice, Immigration and Naturalization Service, *Statistical Yearbook of the Immigration and Naturalization Service, 1994*, Washington, D.C.: U.S. Government Printing Office, 1996, p. 171.

★388★

Aliens

Aliens Deported and Required to Depart From the Eastern Region of the United States, 1994: Totals

The total number from all three regions (i.e., Eastern, Central, and Western) is 1,068,170. The total number of persons deported and required to depart from the Eastern Region of the United States is 13,751.

City/MSA	Number	Rank
Atlanta, GA	602	7
Baltimore, MD	247	11
Boston, MA	624	6
Buffalo, NY	1,932	2
Cleveland, OH	141	13
Detroit, MI	545	8
Miami, FL	1,526	3
New Orleans, LA	2,820	1
New York, NY	827	4
Newark, NJ	266	10
Philadelphia, PA	267	9
Portland, ME	675	5
Washington, DC	233	12

Source: U.S. Department of Justice, Immigration and Naturalization Service, *Statistical Yearbook of the Immigration and Naturalization Service, 1994*, Washington, D.C.: U.S. Government Printing Office, 1996, p. 171.

★389★

Aliens

Aliens Deported and Required to Depart From the Western Region of the United States, 1994: Totals

The total number from all three regions (i.e., Eastern, Central, and Western) is 1,068,170. The total number of persons deported and required to depart from the Western Region of the United States is 690,669.

City/MSA	Number	Rank
Anchorage, AK	81	8
Honolulu, HI	435	6
Los Angeles, CA	12,202	4
Phoenix, AZ	161,564	2
Portland, OR	208	7
San Diego, CA	490,822	1
San Francisco, CA	20,911	3
Seattle, WA	4,446	5

Source: U.S. Department of Justice, Immigration and Naturalization Service, *Statistical Yearbook of the Immigration and Naturalization Service, 1994*, Washington, D.C.: U.S. Government Printing Office, 1996, p. 171.

★390★

Aliens

Aliens Deported From the Central Region of the United States, 1994: Totals

The total number from all three regions (i.e., Eastern, Central, and Western) is 39,620. The total number of persons deported from the Central Region of the United States is 10,852.

City/MSA	Number	Rank
Chicago, IL	252	7
Dallas, TX	514	6
Denver, CO	1,703	4
El Paso, TX	2,515	1
Harlingen, TX	1,928	3
Helena, MT	104	9
Houston, TX	1,327	5
Kansas City, MO	157	8
Omaha, NE	42	11
Saint Paul, MN	81	10
San Antonio, TX	2,229	2

Source: U.S. Department of Justice, Immigration and Naturalization Service, *Statistical Yearbook of the Immigration and Naturalization Service, 1994*, Washington, D.C.: U.S. Government Printing Office, 1996, p. 171.

★391★

Aliens

Aliens Deported From the Eastern Region of the United States, 1994: Totals

The total number from all three regions (i.e., Eastern, Central, and Western) is 39,620. The total number of persons deported from the Eastern Region of the United States is 6,190.

City/MSA	Number	Rank
Atlanta, GA	247	6
Baltimore, MD	172	9
Boston, MA	543	4
Buffalo, NY	265	5

[Continued]

★391★

Aliens Deported From the Eastern Region of the United States, 1994: Totals
[Continued]

City/MSA	Number	Rank
Cleveland, OH	37	12
Detroit, MI	60	11
Miami, FL	797	2
New Orleans, LA	2,707	1
New York, NY	594	3
Newark, NJ	175	8
Philadelphia, PA	185	7
Portland, ME	34	13
Washington, DC	129	10

Source: U.S. Department of Justice, Immigration and Naturalization Service, *Statistical Yearbook of the Immigration and Naturalization Service, 1994*, Washington, D.C.: U.S. Government Printing Office, 1996, p. 171.

★392★
Aliens

Aliens Deported From the Western Region of the United States, 1994: Totals

The total number from all three regions (i.e., Eastern, Central, and Western) is 39,620. The total number of persons deported from the Western Region of the United States is 22,578.

City/MSA	Number	Rank
Anchorage, AK	32	8
Honolulu, HI	115	7
Los Angeles, CA	5,683	2
Phoenix, AZ	4,138	3
Portland, OR	145	6
San Diego, CA	9,215	1
San Francisco, CA	840	5
Seattle, WA	2,410	4

Source: U.S. Department of Justice, Immigration and Naturalization Service, *Statistical Yearbook of the Immigration and Naturalization Service, 1994*, Washington, D.C.: U.S. Government Printing Office, 1996, p. 171.

★393★
Aliens

Aliens Required to Depart From the Central Region of the United States, 1994: Totals

The total number from all three regions (i.e., Eastern, Central, and Western) is 1,028,550. The total number of persons required to depart from the Central Region of the United States is 352,898.

City/MSA	Number	Rank
Chicago, IL	351	6
Dallas, TX	6,553	4
Denver, CO	861	5
El Paso, TX	86,845	3
Harlingen, TX	132,035	1
Helena, MT	110	10
Houston, TX	119	9
Kansas City, MO	305	7
Omaha, NE	29	11

[Continued]

★393★

Aliens Required to Depart From the Central Region of the United States, 1994: Totals
[Continued]

City/MSA	Number	Rank
Saint Paul, MN	159	8
San Antonio, TX	125,531	2

Source: U.S. Department of Justice, Immigration and Naturalization Service, *Statistical Yearbook of the Immigration and Naturalization Service, 1994*, Washington, D.C.: U.S. Government Printing Office, 1996, p. 171.

★394★
Aliens

Aliens Required to Depart From the Eastern Region of the United States, 1994: Totals

The total number from all three regions (i.e., Eastern, Central, and Western) is 1,028,550. The total number of persons required to depart from the Eastern Region of the United States is 7,561.

City/MSA	Number	Rank
Atlanta, GA	355	5
Baltimore, MD	75	12
Boston, MA	81	11
Buffalo, NY	1,667	1
Cleveland, OH	104	8
Detroit, MI	485	4
Miami, FL	729	2
New Orleans, LA	113	7
New York, NY	233	6
Newark, NJ	91	9
Philadelphia, PA	82	10
Portland, ME	641	3
Washington, DC	104	8

Source: U.S. Department of Justice, Immigration and Naturalization Service, *Statistical Yearbook of the Immigration and Naturalization Service, 1994*, Washington, D.C.: U.S. Government Printing Office, 1996, p. 171.

★395★
Aliens

Aliens Required to Depart From the Western Region of the United States, 1994: Totals

The total number from all three regions (i.e., Eastern, Central, and Western) is 1,028,550. The total number of persons required to depart from the Western Region of the United States is 668,091.

City/MSA	Number	Rank
Anchorage, AK	49	8
Honolulu, HI	320	6
Los Angeles, CA	6,519	4
Phoenix, AZ	157,426	2
Portland, OR	63	7
San Diego, CA	481,607	1
San Francisco, CA	20,071	3
Seattle, WA	2,036	5

Source: U.S. Department of Justice, Immigration and Naturalization Service, *Statistical Yearbook of the Immigration and Naturalization Service, 1994*, Washington, D.C.: U.S. Government Printing Office, 1996, p. 171.

★396★

Illegal Immigrants

Apprehensions of Illegal Immigrants, 1996

City	Number	Rank
Del Rio, TX	11,021	6
El Centro, CA	7,572	7
El Paso, TX	14,411	4
Laredo, TX	11,858	5
Marfa, TX	1,119	9
McAllen, TX	20,157	3
San Diego, CA	58,582	1
Tucson, AZ	41,967	2
Yuma, AZ	2,770	8

Source: "Border Apprehensions On the Rise," *USA TODAY*, 9 February 1996, p. 12A. Primary source: Immigration and Naturalization Service.

★397★

Immigrant Population

Foreign-Born Population, 1990

[Top 10 areas]

Cities	Total	Rank
New York, NY	2,082,931	1
Los Angeles, CA	1,336,665	2
Chicago, IL	469,187	3
Houston, TX	290,374	4
San Francisco, CA	246,034	5
San Diego, CA	232,138	6
Miami, FL	214,128	7
San Jose, CA	207,041	8
Santa Ana, CA	149,445	9
Hialeah, FL	132,372	10

Source: Nation's Cities Weekly, Vol 16, No. 8, p. 2, February 22, 1993, Washington, DC: National League of Cities. Primary source: Bureau of the Census: *"The Foreign Born Population in the United States 1990."*

★398★

Immigrant Population

Foreign-Born Population, 1990: Percentage of Total U.S. Population

[Top 10 areas]

Cities	Total	Rank
New York, NY	70.4	1
Los Angeles, CA	59.7	2
Chicago, IL	59.4	3
Houston, TX	55.1	4
San Francisco, CA	51.8	5
San Diego, CA	51.3	6
Miami, FL	50.9	7
San Jose, CA	40.3	8
Santa Ana, CA	49.0	9
Hialeah, FL	48.4	10

Source: Nation's Cities Weekly, Vol. 16, No. 8, p. 2, February 22, 1993, Washington, DC: National League of Cities. Primary source: Bureau of the Census: *"The Foreign Born Population in the United States 1990."*

★399★

Immigrant Population

Popular Destinations for Immigrants, 1990-95: Leading Metro Areas

Data refer to the total change in immigration between 1990 and 1995. According to the source, "People in increasing numbers are leaving most of the ten large metro areas that are the destinations for more than 2/3 of all immigrants arriving from abroad. They are headed for other metro areas and smaller communities that are receiving relatively few immigrants. They are in search, largely, of people like themselves."

City/MSA	Numbers	Rank
Los Angeles, CA	792,712	1
New York, NY	705,939	2
San Francisco, CA	262,519	3
Chicago, IL	216,309	4
Miami, FL	157,059	5
Washington, DC	125,479	6
Houston, TX	110,323	7
San Diego, CA	85,025	8
Boston, MA	74,316	9
Dallas, TX	72,246	10

Source: Tilove, Jonathan, "Demographic Balkanization?," *Detroit News,* 19 May 1996, p. 5B.

★400★

Immigrants Admitted, By Country of Birth

Immigrants Admitted, 1994, By Selected Country of Birth: All Countries (Least Popular MSAs)

The total number of immigrants admitted to the United States from all countries in fiscal year 1994 is 804,416. The number of immigrants living in metropolitan areas that are not MSAs is 44,806; in "other" MSAs, 126,031; in "unknown areas," 201.

City/MSA	Immigrants admitted to the U.S.	Rank
Bakersfield, CA	3,032	7
Baltimore, MD	4,914	19
Bridgeport-Stamford-Norwalk-Danbury, CT	3,785	11
Cleveland-Lorain-Elyria, OH	3,333	8
Denver, CO	4,387	17
El Paso, TX	4,537	18
Fort Worth-Arlington, TX	3,455	9
Hartford, CT	3,458	10
Las Vegas, NV	2,687	3
McAllen-Edinburg-Mission, TX	3,805	12
Orlando, FL	3,914	13
Phoenix-Mesa, AZ	5,264	20
Providence-Warwick-Pawtucket, RI	2,776	5
Saint Louis, MO-IL	2,669	2
Salinas, CA	2,706	4
San Antonio, TX	2,960	6
Stockton-Lodi, CA	2,482	1
Tampa-Saint Petersburg-Clearwater, FL	4,300	16
Ventura, CA	4,109	15
West Palm Beach-Boca Raton, FL	3,961	14

Source: U.S. Department of Justice, Immigration and Naturalization Service, *Statistical Yearbook of the Immigration and Naturalization Service, 1994,* Washington, D.C.: U.S. Government Printing Office, 1996, p. 64.

★401★
Immigrants Admitted, By Country of Birth

Immigrants Admitted, 1994, By Selected Country of Birth and Selected MSA of Intended Residence: All Countries (Most Popular MSAs)

The total number of immigrants admitted to the United States from all countries in fiscal year 1994 is 804,416. The number of immigrants living in metropolitan areas that are not MSAs is 44,806; in "other" MSAs, 126,031; in "unknown areas," 201.

City/MSA	Immigrants admitted to the U.S.	Rank
Bergen-Passaic, NJ	11,606	14
Boston-Lawrence-Lowell-Brockton, MA	18,709	6
Chicago, IL	40,081	3
Dallas, TX	9,453	18
Detroit, MI	8,736	20
Houston, TX	17,600	8
Los Angeles-Long Beach, CA	77,112	2
Miami, FL	29,108	4
Nassau-Suffolk, NY	10,649	16
New York, NY	124,423	1
Newark, NJ	12,040	13
Oakland, CA	13,701	12
Orange County, CA	15,502	10
Philadelphia, PA-NJ	11,535	15
Riverside-San Bernardino, CA	9,163	19
San Diego, CA	14,212	11
San Francisco, CA	18,641	7
San Jose, CA	16,207	9
Seattle-Bellevue-Everett, WA	10,504	17
Washington, DC-MD-VA	25,021	5

Source: U.S. Department of Justice, Immigration and Naturalization Service, *Statistical Yearbook of the Immigration and Naturalization Service, 1994,* Washington, D.C.: U.S. Government Printing Office, 1996, p. 64.

★402★
Immigrants Admitted, By Country of Birth

Immigrants Admitted, 1994, By Selected Country of Birth: Canada (Least Popular MSAs)

The total number of immigrants admitted to the United States from Canada in fiscal year 1994 is 16,068. The number of immigrants living in metropolitan areas that are not MSAs is 1,995; in "other" MSAs, 5,385; in "unknown areas," 9.

City/MSA	Immigrants admitted to the U.S.	Rank
Bakersfield, CA	22	16
Baltimore, MD	74	6
Bergen-Passaic, NJ	87	4
Bridgeport-Stamford-Norwalk-Danbury, CT	114	1
El Paso, TX	13	18
Fort Worth-Arlington, TX	58	9
Fresno, CA	31	14
Hartford, CT	57	10
Jersey City, NJ	27	15
Las Vegas, NV	87	4

[Continued]

★402★
Immigrants Admitted, 1994, By Selected Country of Birth: Canada (Least Popular MSAs)
[Continued]

City/MSA	Immigrants admitted to the U.S.	Rank
McAllen-Edinburg-Mission, TX	36	12
Middlesex-Somerset-Hunterdon, NJ	67	7
Nassau-Suffolk, NY	85	5
Providence-Warwick-Pawtucket, RI	33	13
Sacramento, CA	65	8
Saint Louis, MO-IL	92	3
Salinas, CA	14	17
San Antonio, TX	105	2
Stockton-Lodi, CA	6	19
Ventura, CA	41	11

Source: U.S. Department of Justice, Immigration and Naturalization Service, *Statistical Yearbook of the Immigration and Naturalization Service, 1994,* Washington, D.C.: U.S. Government Printing Office, 1996, p. 64.

★403★
Immigrants Admitted, By Country of Birth

Immigrants Admitted, 1994, By Selected Country of Birth: Canada (Most Popular MSAs)

The total number of immigrants admitted to the United States from Canada in fiscal year 1994 is 16,068. The number of immigrants living in metropolitan areas that are not MSAs is 1,995; in "other" MSAs, 5,385; in "unknown areas," 9.

City/MSA	Immigrants admitted to the U.S.	Rank
Detroit, MI	637	1
Los Angeles-Long Beach, CA	535	2
New York, NY	518	3
Fort Lauderdale, FL	472	4
Chicago, IL	436	5
Tampa-Saint Petersburg-Clearwater, FL	373	6
Seattle-Bellevue-Everett, WA	368	7
Boston-Lawrence-Lowell-Brockton, MA	335	8
Phoenix-Mesa, AZ	274	9
Atlanta, GA	266	10
Houston, TX	255	11
West Palm Beach-Boca Raton, FL	227	12
Washington, DC-MD-VA	223	13
Orange County, CA	200	14
San Diego, CA	196	15
Miami, FL	192	16
Minneapolis-Saint Paul, MN-WI	191	17
Orlando, FL	189	18
Dallas, TX	185	19
Oakland, CA	184	20

Source: U.S. Department of Justice, Immigration and Naturalization Service, *Statistical Yearbook of the Immigration and Naturalization Service, 1994,* Washington, D.C.: U.S. Government Printing Office, 1996, p. 64.

★404★
Immigrants Admitted, By Country of Birth

Immigrants Admitted, 1994, By Selected Country of Birth: China, Mainland (Least Popular MSAs)

The total number of immigrants admitted to the United States from Mainland China in fiscal year 1994 is 53,985. The number of immigrants living in metropolitan areas that are not MSAs is 2,112; in "other" MSAs, 9,509; in "unknown areas," 0.

City/MSA	Immigrants admitted to the U.S.	Rank
McAllen-Edinburgh-Mission, TX	5	1
El Paso, TX	21	2
Bakersfield, CA	25	3
Salinas, CA	30	4
San Antonio, TX	60	5
Stockton-Lodi, CA	69	6
Fort Worth-Arlington, TX	70	7
Fresno, CA	73	8
West Palm Beach-Boca Raton, FL	80	9
Ventura, CA	102	10
Tampa-Saint Petersburg-Clearwater, FL	103	11
Orlando, FL	104	12
Fort Lauderdale, FL	109	13
Bridgeport-Stamford-Norwalk-Danbury, CT	130	14
Las Vegas, NV	150	15
Hartford, CT	169	16
Providence-Warwick-Pawtucket, RI	171	17
Cleveland-Lorain-Elyria, OH	183	18
Denver, CO	201	19
Miami, FL	203	20

Source: U.S. Department of Justice, Immigration and Naturalization Service, *Statistical Yearbook of the Immigration and Naturalization Service, 1994,* Washington, D.C.: U.S. Government Printing Office, 1996, p. 64.

★405★
Immigrants Admitted, By Country of Birth

Immigrants Admitted, 1994, By Selected Country of Birth: China, Mainland (Most Popular MSAs)

The total number of immigrants admitted to the United States from Mainland China in fiscal year 1994 is 53,985. The number of immigrants living in metropolitan areas that are not MSAs is 2,112; in "other" MSAs, 9,509; in "unknown areas," 0.

City/MSA	Immigrants admitted to the U.S.	Rank
New York, NY	10,163	1
Los Angeles-Long Beach, CA	6,183	2
San Francisco, CA	3,934	3
Oakland, CA	2,327	4
San Jose, CA	1,945	5
Washington, DC-MD-VA	1,849	6
Boston-Lawrence-Lowell-Brockton, MA	1,727	7
Chicago, IL	1,420	8
Philadelphia, PA-NJ	1,107	9

[Continued]

★405★

Immigrants Admitted, 1994, By Selected Country of Birth: China, Mainland (Most Popular MSAs)
[Continued]

City/MSA	Immigrants admitted to the U.S.	Rank
Houston, TX	846	10
Orange County, CA	827	11
Honolulu, HI	714	12
Seattle-Bellevue-Everett, WA	667	13
San Diego, CA	631	14
Middlesex-Somerset-Hunterdon, NJ	621	15
Nassau-Suffolk, NY	589	16
Baltimore, MD	488	17
Newark, NJ	465	18
Dallas, TX	433	19
Minneapolis-Saint Paul, MN-WI	400	20

Source: U.S. Department of Justice, Immigration and Naturalization Service, *Statistical Yearbook of the Immigration and Naturalization Service, 1994,* Washington, D.C.: U.S. Government Printing Office, 1996, p. 64.

★406★
Immigrants Admitted, By Country of Birth

Immigrants Admitted, 1994, By Selected Country of Birth: Colombia (Least Popular MSAs)

The total number of immigrants admitted to the United States from Colombia in fiscal year 1994 is 10,847. The number of immigrants living in metropolitan areas that are not MSAs is 281; in "other" MSAs, 996; in "unknown areas," 0.

City/MSA	Immigrants admitted to the U.S.	Rank
Fresno, CA	1	1
McAllen-Edinburg-Mission, TX	2	2
Stockton-Lodi, CA	3	3
Honolulu, HI	4	4
El Paso, TX	5	5
Sacramento, CA	5	5
Bakersfield, CA	6	6
Salinas, CA	6	6
Portland-Vancouver, OR-WA	9	7
Saint Louis, MO-IL	13	8
Cleveland-Lorain-Elyria, OH	14	9
San Antonio, TX	17	10
Detroit, MI	18	11
San Jose, CA	21	12
Las Vegas, NV	23	13
Phoenix-Mesa, AZ	23	13

Source: U.S. Department of Justice, Immigration and Naturalization Service, *Statistical Yearbook of the Immigration and Naturalization Service, 1994,* Washington, D.C.: U.S. Government Printing Office, 1996, p. 64.

★407★
Immigrants Admitted, By Country of Birth

Immigrants Admitted, 1994, By Selected Country of Birth: Colombia (Most Popular MSAs)

The total number of immigrants admitted to the United States from Colombia in fiscal year 1994 is 10,847. The number of immigrants living in metropolitan areas that are not MSAs is 281; in "other" MSAs, 996; in "unknown areas," 0.

City/MSA	Immigrants admitted to the U.S.	Rank
New York, NY	2,364	1
Miami, FL	1,735	2
Bergen-Passaic, NJ	574	3
Newark, NJ	571	4
Fort Lauderdale, FL	439	5
Nassau-Suffolk, NY	399	6
Jersey City, NJ	359	7
Los Angeles-Long Beach, CA	316	8
Washington, DC-MD-VA	289	9
Chicago, IL	217	10
Houston, TX	215	11
Boston-Lawrence-Lowell-Brockton, MA	197	12
Bridgeport-Stamford-Norwalk-Danbury, CT	165	13
Orlando, FL	158	14
Atlanta, GA	142	15
Providence-Warwick-Pawtucket, RI	138	16
West Palm Beach-Boca Raton, FL	138	16
Middlesex-Somerset-Hunterdon, NJ	128	17
Tampa-Saint Petersburg-Clearwater, FL	122	18
Philadelphia, PA-NJ	110	19
Orange County, CA	93	20

Source: U.S. Department of Justice, Immigration and Naturalization Service, *Statistical Yearbook of the Immigration and Naturalization Service, 1994,* Washington, D.C.: U.S. Government Printing Office, 1996, p. 64.

★408★
Immigrants Admitted, By Country of Birth

Immigrants Admitted, 1994, By Selected Country of Birth: Cuba (Least Popular MSAs)

The total number of immigrants admitted to the United States from Cuba in fiscal year 1994 is 14,727. The number of immigrants living in metropolitan areas that are not MSAs is 189; in "other" MSAs, 440; in "unknown areas," 0.

City/MSA	Immigrants admitted to the U.S.	Rank
Salinas, CA	0	1
Bakersfield, CA	1	2
Honolulu, HI	1	2
McAllen-Edinburg-Mission, TX	1	2
Providence-Warwick-Pawtucket, RI	1	2
Stockton-Lodi, CA	1	2

[Continued]

★408★
Immigrants Admitted, 1994, By Selected Country of Birth: Cuba (Least Popular MSAs)
[Continued]

City/MSA	Immigrants admitted to the U.S.	Rank
Cleveland-Lorain-Elyria, OH	2	3
Denver, CO	2	3
Portland-Vancouver, OR-WA	2	3
Ventura, CA	2	3
Baltimore, MD	3	4
El Paso, TX	3	4
Sacramento, CA	3	4
Saint Louis, MO-IL	3	4

Source: U.S. Department of Justice, Immigration and Naturalization Service, *Statistical Yearbook of the Immigration and Naturalization Service, 1994,* Washington, D.C.: U.S. Government Printing Office, 1996, p. 64.

★409★
Immigrants Admitted, By Country of Birth

Immigrants Admitted, 1994, By Selected Country of Birth: Cuba (Most Popular MSAs)

The total number of immigrants admitted to the United States from Cuba in fiscal year 1994 is 14,727. The number of immigrants living in metropolitan areas that are not MSAs is 189; in "other" MSAs, 440; in "unknown areas," 0.

City/MSA	Immigrants admitted to the U.S.	Rank
Miami, FL	11,453	1
Jersey City, NJ	421	2
New York, NY	192	3
Los Angeles-Long Beach, CA	281	4
Fort Lauderdale, FL	268	5
New York, NY	192	6
Las Vegas, NV	165	7
West Palm Beach-Boca Raton, FL	156	8
Newark, NJ	118	9
Orlando, FL	96	10
Chicago, IL	80	11
Bergen-Passaic, NJ	51	12
San Francisco, CA	49	13
Washington, DC-MD-VA	34	14
Boston-Lawrence-Lowell-Brockton, MA	29	15
Houston, TX	29	15
Seattle-Bellevue-Everett, WA	24	16
Atlanta, GA	23	17
Philadelphia, PA-NJ	23	17
Dallas, TX	22	18
Middlesex-Somerset-Hunterdon, NJ	20	19
Nassau-Suffolk, NY	19	20
Orange County, CA	19	20

Source: U.S. Department of Justice, Immigration and Naturalization Service, *Statistical Yearbook of the Immigration and Naturalization Service, 1994,* Washington, D.C.: U.S. Government Printing Office, 1996, p. 64.

★410★
Immigrants Admitted, By Country of Birth
Immigrants Admitted, 1994, By Selected Country of Birth: Dominican Republic (Least Popular MSAs)

The total number of immigrants admitted to the United States from the Dominican Republic in fiscal year 1994 is 51,189. The number of immigrants living in metropolitan areas that are not MSAs is 3,883; in "other" MSAs, 1,446; in "unknown areas," 0.

City/MSA	Immigrants admitted to the U.S.	Rank
Fresno, CA	0	1
Honolulu, HI	0	1
McAllen-Edinburg-Mission, TX	0	1
Portland-Vancouver, OR-WA	0	1
El Paso, TX	1	2
Bakersfield, CA	1	2
Salinas, CA	1	2
Denver, CO	2	3
Saint Louis, MO-IL	2	3
Seattle-Bellevue-Everett, WA	4	4
Riverside-San Bernardino, CA	4	4
Sacramento, CA	4	4
Ventura, CA	4	4
San Jose, CA	5	5
Stockton-Lodi, CA	6	6
Dallas, TX	7	7
Orange County, CA	8	8
San Antonio, TX	9	9
Fort Worth-Arlington, TX	12	10
Cleveland-Lorain-Elyria, OH	12	10

Source: U.S. Department of Justice, Immigration and Naturalization Service, *Statistical Yearbook of the Immigration and Naturalization Service, 1994*, Washington, D.C.: U.S. Government Printing Office, 1996, p. 64.

★411★
Immigrants Admitted, By Country of Birth
Immigrants Admitted, 1994, By Selected Country of Birth: Dominican Republic (Most Popular MSAs)

The total number of immigrants admitted to the United States from the Dominican Republic in fiscal year 1994 is 51,189. The number of immigrants living in metropolitan areas that are not MSAs is 3,883; in "other" MSAs, 1,446; in "unknown areas," 0.

City/MSA	Immigrants admitted to the U.S.	Rank
Bergen-Passaic, NJ	2,144	3
Boston-Lawrence-Lowell-Brockton, MA	2,420	2
Bridgeport-Stamford-Norwalk-Danbury, CT	114	15
Chicago, IL	104	16
Fort Lauderdale, FL	187	12
Hartford, CT	63	19
Houston, TX	65	18
Jersey City, NJ	1,422	5
Los Angeles-Long Beach, CA	41	20

[Continued]

★411★
Immigrants Admitted, 1994, By Selected Country of Birth: Dominican Republic (Most Popular MSAs)
[Continued]

City/MSA	Immigrants admitted to the U.S.	Rank
Miami, FL	1,779	4
Middlesex-Somerset-Hunterdon, NJ	732	8
Nassau-Suffolk, NY	1,033	6
New York, NY	26,992	1
Newark, NJ	760	7
Orlando, FL	144	13
Philadelphia, PA-NJ	289	11
Providence-Warwick-Pawtucket, RI	634	9
Tampa-Saint Petersburg-Clearwater, FL	94	17
Washington, DC-MD-VA	387	10
West Palm Beach-Boca Raton, FL	120	14

Source: U.S. Department of Justice, Immigration and Naturalization Service, *Statistical Yearbook of the Immigration and Naturalization Service, 1994*, Washington, D.C.: U.S. Government Printing Office, 1996, p. 64.

★412★
Immigrants Admitted, By Country of Birth
Immigrants Admitted, 1994, By Selected Country of Birth: El Salvador (Least Popular MSAs)

The total number of immigrants admitted to the United States from El Salvador in fiscal year 1994 is 17,644. The number of immigrants living in metropolitan areas that are not MSAs is 314; in "other" MSAs, 713; in "unknown areas," 0.

City/MSA	Immigrants admitted to the U.S.	Rank
Honolulu, HI	1	1
Saint Louis, MO-IL	3	2
Detroit, MI	5	3
Hartford, CT	6	4
Cleveland-Lorain-Elyria, OH	9	5
Denver, CO	9	5
El Paso, TX	9	5
Orlando, FL	12	6
Stockton-Lodi, CA	12	6
Providence-Warwick-Pawtucket, RI	14	7
McAllen-Edinburg-Mission, TX	17	8
Bridgeport-Stamford-Norwalk-Danbury, CT	22	9
Middlesex-Somerset-Hunterdon, NJ	23	10
Philadelphia, PA-NJ	23	10
Seattle-Bellevue-Everett, WA	23	10
West Palm Beach-Boca Raton, FL	23	10
Minneapolis-Saint Paul, MN-WI	24	11

[Continued]

★412★

Immigrants Admitted, 1994, By Selected Country of Birth: El Salvador (Least Popular MSAs)

[Continued]

City/MSA	Immigrants admitted to the U.S.	Rank
Portland-Vancouver, OR-WA	29	12
Fort Worth-Arlington, TX	30	13
Baltimore, MD	31	14

Source: U.S. Department of Justice, Immigration and Naturalization Service, *Statistical Yearbook of the Immigration and Naturalization Service, 1994*, Washington, D.C.: U.S. Government Printing Office, 1996, p. 64.

★413★

Immigrants Admitted, By Country of Birth

Immigrants Admitted, 1994, By Selected Country of Birth: El Salvador (Most Popular MSAs)

The total number of immigrants admitted to the United States from El Salvador in fiscal year 1994 is 17,644. The number of immigrants living in metropolitan areas that are not MSAs is 314; in "other" MSAs, 713; in "unknown areas," 0.

City/MSA	Immigrants admitted to the U.S.	Rank
Atlanta, GA	62	20
Bakersfield, CA	82	18
Bergen-Passaic, NJ	104	16
Boston-Lawrence-Lowell-Brockton, MA	221	11
Chicago, IL	158	14
Dallas, TX	368	7
Fresno, CA	90	17
Houston, TX	1,853	3
Jersey City, NJ	252	10
Las Vegas, NV	70	19
Los Angeles-Long Beach, CA	5,963	1
Miami, FL	219	12
Nassau-Suffolk, NY	974	4
New York, NY	948	5
Newark, NJ	159	13
Oakland, CA	219	12
Orange County, CA	311	8
Riverside-San Bernardino, CA	259	9
San Francisco, CA	640	6
San Jose, CA	117	15
Ventura, CA	62	20
Washington, DC-MD-VA	2,853	2

Source: U.S. Department of Justice, Immigration and Naturalization Service, *Statistical Yearbook of the Immigration and Naturalization Service, 1994*, Washington, D.C.: U.S. Government Printing Office, 1996, p. 64.

★414★

Immigrants Admitted, By Country of Birth

Immigrants Admitted, 1994, By Selected Country of Birth: Germany (Least Popular MSAs)

The total number of immigrants admitted to the United States from Germany in fiscal year 1994 is 6,992. The number of immigrants living in metropolitan areas that are not MSAs is 1,202; in "other" MSAs, 2,469; in "unknown areas," 1.

City/MSA	Immigrants admitted to the U.S.	Rank
McAllen-Edinburg-Mission, TX	8	1
Stockton-Lodi, CA	8	1
Jersey City, NJ	9	2
Salinas, CA	11	3
Fresno, CA	12	4
Bakersfield, CA	14	5
Ventura, CA	19	6
Fort Worth-Arlington, TX	25	7
Providence-Warwick-Pawtucket, RI	25	7
Sacramento, CA	25	7
Hartford, CT	28	8
Las Vegas, NV	29	9
Middlesex-Somerset-Hunterdon, NJ	29	9
Honolulu, HI	34	10
Cleveland-Lorain-Elyria, OH	39	11
Bridgeport-Stamford-Norwalk-Danbury, CT	40	12
San Antonio, TX	40	12
Saint Louis, MO-IL	41	13
West Palm Beach-Boca Raton, FL	42	14
Bergen-Passaic, NJ	46	15

Source: U.S. Department of Justice, Immigration and Naturalization Service, *Statistical Yearbook of the Immigration and Naturalization Service, 1994*, Washington, D.C.: U.S. Government Printing Office, 1996, p. 64.

★415★

Immigrants Admitted, By Country of Birth

Immigrants Admitted, 1994, By Selected Country of Birth: Germany (Most Popular MSAs)

The total number of immigrants admitted to the United States from Germany in fiscal year 1994 is 6,992. The number of immigrants living in metropolitan areas that are not MSAs is 1,202; in "other" MSAs, 2,469; in "unknown areas," 1.

City/MSA	Immigrants admitted to the U.S.	Rank
Los Angeles-Long Beach, CA	331	1
New York, NY	253	2
Washington, DC-MD-VA	170	3
Chicago, IL	156	4
Boston-Lawrence-Lowell-Brockton, MA	119	5
San Francisco, CA	112	6
Atlanta, GA	105	7
San Diego, CA	99	8
Philadelphia, PA-NJ	97	9

[Continued]

★415★

Immigrants Admitted, 1994, By Selected Country of Birth: Germany (Most Popular MSAs)
[Continued]

City/MSA	Immigrants admitted to the U.S.	Rank
Tampa-Saint Petersburg-Clearwater, FL	96	10
Detroit, MI	90	11
San Jose, CA	85	12
Houston, TX	82	13
Phoenix-Mesa, AZ	81	14
Orange County, CA	71	15
Minneapolis-Saint Paul, MN-WI	70	16
Fort Lauderdale, FL	67	17
Seattle-Bellevue-Everett, WA	65	18
Baltimore, MD	62	19
Oakland, CA	61	20

Source: U.S. Department of Justice, Immigration and Naturalization Service, *Statistical Yearbook of the Immigration and Naturalization Service, 1994,* Washington, D.C.: U.S. Government Printing Office, 1996, p. 64.

★416★
Immigrants Admitted, By Country of Birth

Immigrants Admitted, 1994, By Selected Country of Birth: Guatemala

The total number of immigrants admitted to the United States from Guatemala in fiscal year 1994 is 7,389. The number of immigrants living in metropolitan areas that are not MSAs is 296; in "other" MSAs, 633; in "unknown areas," 0.

City/MSA	Immigrants admitted the U.S.	Rank
Atlanta, GA	9	34
Bakersfield, CA	19	28
Baltimore, MD	17	29
Bergen-Passaic, NJ	55	16
Boston-Lawrence-Lowell-Brockton, MA	160	9
Bridgeport-Stamford-Norwalk-Danbury, CT	36	21
Chicago, IL	457	2
Cleveland-Lorain-Elyria, OH	5	37
Dallas, TX	95	13
Denver, CO	16	30
Detroit, MI	14	32
El Paso, TX	1	39
Fort Lauderdale, FL	28	23
Fort Worth-Arlington, TX	2	38
Fresno, CA	21	27
Hartford, CT	8	35
Honolulu, HI	2	38
Houston, TX	194	7
Jersey City, NJ	44	19
Las Vegas, NV	22	26
Los Angeles-Long Beach, CA	2,752	1
McAllen-Edinburg-Mission, TX	9	34
Miami, FL	205	5

[Continued]

★416★

Immigrants Admitted, 1994, By Selected Country of Birth: Guatemala
[Continued]

City/MSA	Immigrants admitted the U.S.	Rank
Middlesex-Somerset-Hunterdon, NJ	28	23
Minneapolis-Saint Paul, MN-WI	23	25
Nassau-Suffolk, NY	172	8
New York, NY	406	3
Newark, NJ	126	12
Oakland, CA	74	14
Orange County, CA	200	6
Orlando, FL	25	24
Philadelphia, PA-NJ	39	20
Phoenix-Mesa, AZ	56	15
Portland-Vancouver, OR-WA	28	23
Providence-Warwick-Pawtucket, RI	156	10
Riverside-San Bernardino, CA	172	8
Sacramento, CA	9	34
Saint Louis, MO-IL	10	33
Salinas, CA	6	36
San Antonio, TX	56	15
San Diego, CA	25	24
San Francisco, CA	149	11
San Jose, CA	46	18
Seattle-Bellevue-Everett, WA	15	31
Stockton-Lodi, CA	10	33
Tampa-Saint Petersburg-Clearwater, FL	35	22
Ventura, CA	50	17
Washington, DC-MD-VA	344	4
West Palm Beach-Boca Raton, FL	25	24

Source: U.S. Department of Justice, Immigration and Naturalization Service, *Statistical Yearbook of the Immigration and Naturalization Service, 1994,* Washington, D.C.: U.S. Government Printing Office, 1996, p. 64.

★417★
Immigrants Admitted, By Country of Birth

Immigrants Admitted, 1994, By Selected Country of Birth: Guyana

The total number of immigrants admitted to the United States from Guyana in fiscal year 1994 is 7,662. The number of immigrants living in metropolitan areas that are not MSAs is 104; in "other" MSAs, 317; in "unknown areas," 0.

City/MSA	Immigrants admitted to the U.S.	Rank
Atlanta, GA	53	13
Bakersfield, CA	0	32
Baltimore, MD	30	19
Bergen-Passaic, NJ	56	12
Boston-Lawrence-Lowell-Brockton, MA	43	15

[Continued]

★417★
Immigrants Admitted, 1994, By Selected Country of Birth: Guyana
[Continued]

City/MSA	Immigrants admitted to the U.S.	Rank
Bridgeport-Stamford-Norwalk-Danbury, CT	26	20
Chicago, IL	32	18
Cleveland-Lorain-Elyria, OH	35	17
Dallas, TX	16	23
Denver, CO	1	31
Detroit, MI	7	26
El Paso, TX	0	32
Fort Lauderdale, FL	169	6
Fort Worth-Arlington, TX	7	26
Fresno, CA	0	32
Hartford, CT	46	14
Honolulu, HI	1	31
Houston, TX	26	20
Jersey City, NJ	136	7
Las Vegas, NV	6	27
Los Angeles-Long Beach, CA	60	10
McAllen-Edinburg-Mission, TX	0	32
Miami, FL	207	4
Middlesex-Somerset-Hunterdon, NJ	57	11
Minneapolis-Saint Paul, MN-WI	135	8
Nassau-Suffolk, NY	197	5
New York, NY	5,021	1
Newark, NJ	377	2
Oakland, CA	13	24
Orange County, CA	20	21
Orlando, FL	80	9
Philadelphia, PA-NJ	42	16
Phoenix-Mesa, AZ	1	31
Portland-Vancouver, OR-WA	0	32
Providence-Warwick-Pawtucket, RI	1	31
Riverside-San Bernardino, CA	11	25
Sacramento, CA	4	28
Saint Louis, MO-IL	2	30
Salinas, CA	0	32
San Antonio, TX	2	30
San Diego, CA	6	27
San Francisco, CA	6	27
San Jose, CA	17	22
Seattle-Bellevue-Everett, WA	3	29
Stockton-Lodi, CA	0	32
Tampa-Saint Petersburg-Clearwater, FL	13	24
Ventura, CA	1	31
Washington, DC-MD-VA	249	3
West Palm Beach-Boca Raton, FL	26	20

Source: U.S. Department of Justice, Immigration and Naturalization Service, *Statistical Yearbook of the Immigration and Naturalization Service, 1994,* Washington, D.C.: U.S. Government Printing Office, 1996, p. 64.

★418★
Immigrants Admitted, By Country of Birth
Immigrants Admitted, 1994, By Selected Country of Birth: Haiti

The total number of immigrants admitted to the United States from Haiti in fiscal year 1994 is 13,333. The number of immigrants living in metropolitan areas that are not MSAs is 241; in "other" MSAs, 837; in "unknown areas," 0.

City/MSA	Immigrants admitted to the U.S.	Rank
Atlanta, GA	33	17
Bakersfield, CA	0	33
Baltimore, MD	15	22
Bergen-Passaic, NJ	39	16
Boston-Lawrence-Lowell-Brockton, MA	930	5
Bridgeport-Stamford-Norwalk-Danbury, CT	288	8
Chicago, IL	92	12
Cleveland-Lorain-Elyria, OH	2	31
Dallas, TX	2	31
Denver, CO	4	29
Detroit, MI	4	29
El Paso, TX	0	33
Fort Lauderdale, FL	1,144	4
Fort Worth-Arlington, TX	2	31
Fresno, CA	0	33
Hartford, CT	19	19
Honolulu, HI	1	32
Houston, TX	16	21
Jersey City, NJ	88	13
Las Vegas, NV	2	31
Los Angeles-Long Beach, CA	27	18
McAllen-Edinburg-Mission, TX	0	33
Miami, FL	2,294	2
Middlesex-Somerset-Hunterdon, NJ	17	20
Minneapolis-Saint Paul, MN-WI	11	25
Nassau-Suffolk, NY	387	7
New York, NY	4,085	1
Newark, NJ	1,150	3
Oakland, CA	7	27
Orange County, CA	4	29
Orlando, FL	233	9
Philadelphia, PA-NJ	125	11
Phoenix-Mesa, AZ	3	30
Portland-Vancouver, OR-WA	10	26
Providence-Warwick-Pawtucket, RI	55	15
Riverside-San Bernardino, CA	3	30
Sacramento, CA	0	33
Saint Louis, MO-IL	5	28
Salinas, CA	0	33
San Antonio, TX	1	32
San Diego, CA	13	24
San Francisco, CA	14	23
San Jose, CA	1	32
Seattle-Bellevue-Everett, WA	11	25
Stockton-Lodi, CA	0	33
Tampa-Saint Petersburg-Clearwater, FL	56	14

[Continued]

★418★

Immigrants Admitted, 1994, By Selected Country of Birth: Haiti

[Continued]

City/MSA	Immigrants admitted to the U.S.	Rank
Ventura, CA	0	33
Washington, DC-MD-VA	154	10
West Palm Beach-Boca Raton, FL	903	6

Source: U.S. Department of Justice, Immigration and Naturalization Service, *Statistical Yearbook of the Immigration and Naturalization Service, 1994*, Washington, D.C.: U.S. Government Printing Office, 1996, p. 64.

★419★

Immigrants Admitted, By Country of Birth

Immigrants Admitted, 1994, By Selected Country of Birth: Hong Kong

The total number of immigrants admitted to the United States from Hong Kong in fiscal year 1994 is 7,731. The number of immigrants living in metropolitan areas that are not MSAs is 236; in "other" MSAs, 771; in "unknown areas," 1.

City/MSA	Immigrants admitted to the U.S.	Rank
Atlanta, GA	57	19
Bakersfield, CA	11	36
Baltimore, MD	45	23
Bergen-Passaic, NJ	56	20
Boston-Lawrence-Lowell-Brockton, MA	221	8
Bridgeport-Stamford-Norwalk-Danbury, CT	30	29
Chicago, IL	201	9
Cleveland-Lorain-Elyria, OH	25	31
Dallas, TX	65	18
Denver, CO	20	33
Detroit, MI	27	30
El Paso, TX	3	40
Fort Lauderdale, FL	50	21
Fort Worth-Arlington, TX	17	35
Fresno, CA	17	35
Hartford, CT	7	38
Honolulu, HI	239	7
Houston, TX	176	10
Jersey City, NJ	35	28
Las Vegas, NV	39	26
Los Angeles-Long Beach, CA	1,067	2
McAllen-Edinburg-Mission, TX	0	41
Miami, FL	48	22
Middlesex-Somerset-Hunterdon, NJ	73	16
Minneapolis-Saint Paul, MN-WI	56	20
Nassau-Suffolk, NY	82	15
New York, NY	1,159	1
Newark, NJ	70	17
Oakland, CA	525	4

[Continued]

★419★

Immigrants Admitted, 1994, By Selected Country of Birth: Hong Kong

[Continued]

City/MSA	Immigrants admitted to the U.S.	Rank
Orange County, CA	136	12
Orlando, FL	9	37
Philadelphia, PA-NJ	102	14
Phoenix-Mesa, AZ	27	30
Portland-Vancouver, OR-WA	40	25
Providence-Warwick-Pawtucket, RI	18	34
Riverside-San Bernardino, CA	57	19
Sacramento, CA	118	13
Saint Louis, MO-IL	42	24
Salinas, CA	9	37
San Antonio, TX	9	37
San Diego, CA	73	16
San Francisco, CA	909	3
San Jose, CA	272	5
Seattle-Bellevue-Everett, WA	245	6
Stockton-Lodi, CA	38	27
Tampa-Saint Petersburg-Clearwater, FL	11	36
Ventura, CA	4	39
Washington, DC-MD-VA	161	11
West Palm Beach-Boca Raton, FL	21	32

Source: U.S. Department of Justice, Immigration and Naturalization Service, *Statistical Yearbook of the Immigration and Naturalization Service, 1994*, Washington, D.C.: U.S. Government Printing Office, 1996, p. 64.

★420★

Immigrants Admitted, By Country of Birth

Immigrants Admitted, 1994, By Selected Country of Birth: India

The total number of immigrants admitted to the United States from India in fiscal year 1994 is 34,921. The number of immigrants living in metropolitan areas that are not MSAs is 1,629; in "other" MSAs, 7,120; in "unknown areas," 2.

City/MSA	Immigrants admitted to the U.S.	Rank
Atlanta, GA	460	18
Bakersfield, CA	135	33
Baltimore, MD	305	22
Bergen-Passaic, NJ	607	15
Boston-Lawrence-Lowell-Brockton, MA	642	13
Bridgeport-Stamford-Norwalk-Danbury, CT	194	27
Chicago, IL	2,994	2
Cleveland-Lorain-Elyria, OH	279	25
Dallas, TX	573	17
Denver, CO	77	38
Detroit, MI	802	10

[Continued]

★420★
Immigrants Admitted, 1994, By Selected Country of Birth: India
[Continued]

City/MSA	Immigrants admitted to the U.S.	Rank
El Paso, TX	10	45
Fort Lauderdale, FL	130	35
Fort Worth-Arlington, TX	157	31
Fresno, CA	312	21
Hartford, CT	157	31
Honolulu, HI	36	42
Houston, TX	1,061	7
Jersey City, NJ	623	14
Las Vegas, NV	28	44
Los Angeles-Long Beach, CA	1,339	5
McAllen-Edinburg-Mission, TX	5	46
Miami, FL	99	36
Middlesex-Somerset-Hunterdon, NJ	1,253	6
Minneapolis-Saint Paul, MN-WI	157	31
Nassau-Suffolk, NY	705	11
New York, NY	4,008	1
Newark, NJ	694	12
Oakland, CA	1,049	8
Orange County, CA	583	16
Orlando, FL	167	29
Philadelphia, PA-NJ	1,011	9
Phoenix-Mesa, AZ	160	30
Portland-Vancouver, OR-WA	134	34
Providence-Warwick-Pawtucket, RI	39	41
Riverside-San Bernardino, CA	292	24
Sacramento, CA	294	23
Saint Louis, MO-IL	209	26
Salinas, CA	34	43
San Antonio, TX	52	40
San Diego, CA	155	32
San Francisco, CA	350	19
San Jose, CA	1,473	3
Seattle-Bellevue-Everett, WA	342	20
Stockton-Lodi, CA	167	29
Tampa-Saint Petersburg-Clearwater, FL	193	28
Ventura, CA	83	37
Washington, DC-MD-VA	1,464	4
West Palm Beach-Boca Raton, FL	76	39

Source: U.S. Department of Justice, Immigration and Naturalization Service, *Statistical Yearbook of the Immigration and Naturalization Service, 1994*, Washington, D.C.: U.S. Government Printing Office, 1996, p. 64.

★421★
Immigrants Admitted, By Country of Birth
Immigrants Admitted, 1994, By Selected Country of Birth: Iran

The total number of immigrants admitted to the United States from Iran in fiscal year 1994 is 11,422. The number of immigrants living in metropolitan areas that are not MSAs is 265; in "other" MSAs, 1,565; in "unknown areas," 0.

City/MSA	Immigrants admitted to the U.S.	Rank
Atlanta, GA	181	12
Bakersfield, CA	11	38
Baltimore, MD	111	16
Bergen-Passaic, NJ	66	24
Boston-Lawrence-Lowell-Brockton, MA	158	15
Bridgeport-Stamford-Norwalk-Danbury, CT	17	36
Chicago, IL	183	11
Cleveland-Lorain-Elyria, OH	36	31
Dallas, TX	200	10
Denver, CO	97	19
Detroit, MI	59	26
El Paso, TX	8	40
Fort Lauderdale, FL	42	29
Fort Worth-Arlington, TX	55	27
Fresno, CA	47	28
Hartford, CT	20	35
Honolulu, HI	10	39
Houston, TX	232	9
Jersey City, NJ	16	37
Las Vegas, NV	29	33
Los Angeles-Long Beach, CA	3,723	1
McAllen-Edinburg-Mission, TX	0	42
Miami, FL	59	26
Middlesex-Somerset-Hunterdon, NJ	28	34
Minneapolis-Saint Paul, MN-WI	68	22
Nassau-Suffolk, NY	177	13
New York, NY	333	5
Newark, NJ	36	31
Oakland, CA	300	6
Orange County, CA	697	3
Orlando, FL	59	26
Philadelphia, PA-NJ	87	20
Phoenix-Mesa, AZ	61	25
Portland-Vancouver, OR-WA	67	23
Providence-Warwick-Pawtucket, RI	17	36
Riverside-San Bernardino, CA	102	17
Sacramento, CA	98	18
Saint Louis, MO-IL	32	32
Salinas, CA	11	38
San Antonio, TX	41	30
San Diego, CA	246	7
San Francisco, CA	233	8
San Jose, CA	474	4
Seattle-Bellevue-Everett, WA	161	14
Stockton-Lodi, CA	3	41
Tampa-Saint Petersburg-Clearwater, FL	36	31

★421★
Immigrants Admitted, 1994, By Selected Country of Birth: Iran
[Continued]

City/MSA	Immigrants admitted to the U.S.	Rank
Ventura, CA	83	21
Washington, DC-MD-VA	754	2
West Palm Beach-Boca Raton, FL	28	34

Source: U.S. Department of Justice, Immigration and Naturalization Service, *Statistical Yearbook of the Immigration and Naturalization Service, 1994*, Washington, D.C.: U.S. Government Printing Office, 1996, p. 64.

★422★
Immigrants Admitted, By Country of Birth
Immigrants Admitted, 1994, By Selected Country of Birth: Iraq

The total number of immigrants admitted to the United States from Iraq in fiscal year 1994 is 6,025. The number of immigrants living in metropolitan areas that are not MSAs is 85; in "other" MSAs, 1,478; in "unknown areas," 0.

City/MSA	Immigrants admitted to the U.S.	Rank
Atlanta, GA	18	23
Bakersfield, CA	2	32
Baltimore, MD	10	26
Bergen-Passaic, NJ	20	21
Boston-Lawrence-Lowell-Brockton, MA	64	11
Bridgeport-Stamford-Norwalk-Danbury, CT	2	32
Chicago, IL	549	3
Cleveland-Lorain-Elyria, OH	55	13
Dallas, TX	354	4
Denver, CO	28	20
Detroit, MI	1,379	1
El Paso, TX	4	30
Fort Lauderdale, FL	6	29
Fort Worth-Arlington, TX	79	10
Fresno, CA	8	27
Hartford, CT	30	19
Honolulu, HI	0	34
Houston, TX	33	17
Jersey City, NJ	1	33
Las Vegas, NV	7	28
Los Angeles-Long Beach, CA	206	5
McAllen-Edinburg-Mission, TX	0	34
Miami, FL	19	22
Middlesex-Somerset-Hunterdon, NJ	10	26
Minneapolis-Saint Paul, MN-WI	18	23
Nassau-Suffolk, NY	6	29
New York, NY	62	12
Newark, NJ	2	32
Oakland, CA	18	23

[Continued]

★422★
Immigrants Admitted, 1994, By Selected Country of Birth: Iraq
[Continued]

City/MSA	Immigrants admitted to the U.S.	Rank
Orange County, CA	34	16
Orlando, FL	11	25
Philadelphia, PA-NJ	37	15
Phoenix-Mesa, AZ	89	8
Portland-Vancouver, OR-WA	34	16
Providence-Warwick-Pawtucket, RI	1	33
Riverside-San Bernardino, CA	32	18
Sacramento, CA	14	24
Saint Louis, MO-IL	84	9
Salinas, CA	3	31
San Antonio, TX	3	31
San Diego, CA	794	2
San Francisco, CA	79	10
San Jose, CA	53	14
Seattle-Bellevue-Everett, WA	97	7
Stockton-Lodi, CA	0	34
Tampa-Saint Petersburg-Clearwater, FL	4	30
Ventura, CA	4	30
Washington, DC-MD-VA	98	6
West Palm Beach-Boca Raton, FL	0	34

Source: U.S. Department of Justice, Immigration and Naturalization Service, *Statistical Yearbook of the Immigration and Naturalization Service, 1994*, Washington, D.C.: U.S. Government Printing Office, 1996, p. 64.

★423★
Immigrants Admitted, By Country of Birth
Immigrants Admitted, 1994, By Selected Country of Birth: Ireland

The total number of immigrants admitted to the United States from Ireland in fiscal year 1994 is 17,256. The number of immigrants living in metropolitan areas that are not MSAs is 695; in "other" MSAs, 2,445; in "unknown areas," 0.

City/MSA	Immigrants admitted to the U.S.	Rank
Atlanta, GA	140	16
Bakersfield, CA	2	45
Baltimore, MD	90	24
Bergen-Passaic, NJ	314	8
Boston-Lawrence-Lowell-Brockton, MA	2,482	2
Bridgeport-Stamford-Norwalk-Danbury, CT	221	11
Chicago, IL	1,059	3
Cleveland-Lorain-Elyria, OH	74	29
Dallas, TX	83	27
Denver, CO	50	31
Detroit, MI	46	34

[Continued]

★423★

Immigrants Admitted, 1994, By Selected Country of Birth: Ireland

[Continued]

City/MSA	Immigrants admitted to the U.S.	Rank
El Paso, TX	5	43
Fort Lauderdale, FL	149	15
Fort Worth-Arlington, TX	13	39
Fresno, CA	4	44
Hartford, CT	96	23
Honolulu, HI	8	42
Houston, TX	105	22
Jersey City, NJ	128	18
Las Vegas, NV	34	36
Los Angeles-Long Beach, CA	463	7
McAllen-Edinburg-Mission, TX	1	46
Miami, FL	84	26
Middlesex-Somerset-Hunterdon, NJ	115	20
Minneapolis-Saint Paul, MN-WI	68	30
Nassau-Suffolk, NY	726	5
New York, NY	4,122	1
Newark, NJ	255	10
Oakland, CA	118	19
Orange County, CA	174	12
Orlando, FL	84	26
Philadelphia, PA-NJ	472	6
Phoenix-Mesa, AZ	82	28
Portland-Vancouver, OR-WA	47	33
Providence-Warwick-Pawtucket, RI	68	30
Riverside-San Bernardino, CA	42	35
Sacramento, CA	50	31
Saint Louis, MO-IL	49	32
Salinas, CA	11	40
San Antonio, TX	20	38
San Diego, CA	173	13
San Francisco, CA	960	4
San Jose, CA	167	14
Seattle-Bellevue-Everett, WA	137	17
Stockton-Lodi, CA	9	41
Tampa-Saint Petersburg-Clearwater, FL	113	21
Ventura, CA	26	37
Washington, DC-MD-VA	291	9
West Palm Beach-Boca Raton, FL	86	25

Source: U.S. Department of Justice, Immigration and Naturalization Service, *Statistical Yearbook of the Immigration and Naturalization Service, 1994*, Washington, D.C.: U.S. Government Printing Office, 1996, p. 64.

★424★

Immigrants Admitted, By Country of Birth

Immigrants Admitted, 1994, By Selected Country of Birth: Jamaica

The total number of immigrants admitted to the United States from Jamaica in fiscal year 1994 is 14,349. The number of residents living in metropolitan areas that are not MSAs is 238; in "other" MSAs, 1,285; in "unknown areas," 0.

City/MSA	Immigrants admitted to the U.S.	Rank
Atlanta, GA	162	15
Bakersfield, CA	2	38
Baltimore, MD	155	17
Bergen-Passaic, NJ	254	11
Boston-Lawrence-Lowell-Brockton, MA	258	10
Bridgeport-Stamford-Norwalk-Danbury, CT	231	13
Chicago, IL	217	14
Cleveland-Lorain-Elyria, OH	32	22
Dallas, TX	27	23
Denver, CO	4	36
Detroit, MI	46	21
El Paso, TX	1	39
Fort Lauderdale, FL	1,264	2
Fort Worth-Arlington, TX	8	32
Fresno, CA	3	37
Hartford, CT	395	8
Honolulu, HI	3	37
Houston, TX	102	19
Jersey City, NJ	22	24
Las Vegas, NV	9	31
Los Angeles-Long Beach, CA	139	18
McAllen-Edinburg-Mission, TX	3	37
Miami, FL	1,155	3
Middlesex-Somerset-Hunterdon, NJ	54	20
Minneapolis-Saint Paul, MN-WI	18	28
Nassau-Suffolk, NY	464	4
New York, NY	5,595	1
Newark, NJ	445	6
Oakland, CA	18	28
Orange County, CA	20	26
Orlando, FL	244	12
Philadelphia, PA-NJ	340	9
Phoenix-Mesa, AZ	1	39
Portland-Vancouver, OR-WA	7	33
Providence-Warwick-Pawtucket, RI	22	24
Riverside-San Bernardino, CA	21	25
Sacramento, CA	11	29
Saint Louis, MO-IL	8	32
Salinas, CA	1	39
San Antonio, TX	5	35
San Diego, CA	19	27
San Francisco, CA	11	29
San Jose, CA	6	34
Seattle-Bellevue-Everett, WA	10	30
Stockton-Lodi, CA	0	40
Tampa-Saint Petersburg-Clearwater, FL	158	16

[Continued]

★424★

Immigrants Admitted, 1994, By Selected Country of Birth: Jamaica
[Continued]

City/MSA	Immigrants admitted to the U.S.	Rank
Ventura, CA	3	37
Washington, DC-MD-VA	455	5
West Palm Beach-Boca Raton, FL	397	7

Source: U.S. Department of Justice, Immigration and Naturalization Service, *Statistical Yearbook of the Immigration and Naturalization Service, 1994*, Washington, D.C.: U.S. Government Printing Office, 1996, p. 64.

★425★
Immigrants Admitted, By Country of Birth

Immigrants Admitted, 1994, By Selected Country of Birth: Japan

The total number of immigrants admitted to the United States from Japan in fiscal year 1994 is 6,093. The number of immigrants living in metropolitan areas that are not MSAs is 535; in "other" MSAs, 1,074; in "unknown areas," 22.

City/MSA	Immigrants admitted to the U.S.	Rank
Atlanta, GA	76	16
Bakersfield, CA	4	41
Baltimore, MD	21	31
Bergen-Passaic, NJ	157	8
Boston-Lawrence-Lowell-Brockton, MA	89	13
Bridgeport-Stamford-Norwalk-Danbury, CT	44	20
Chicago, IL	140	10
Cleveland-Lorain-Elyria, OH	12	35
Dallas, TX	32	24
Denver, CO	34	23
Detroit, MI	81	14
El Paso, TX	6	39
Fort Lauderdale, FL	11	36
Fort Worth-Arlington, TX	13	34
Fresno, CA	15	33
Hartford, CT	10	37
Honolulu, HI	455	3
Houston, TX	52	18
Jersey City, NJ	30	25
Las Vegas, NV	21	31
Los Angeles-Long Beach, CA	782	1
McAllen-Edinburg-Mission, TX	1	43
Miami, FL	29	26
Middlesex-Somerset-Hunterdon, NJ	17	32
Minneapolis-Saint Paul, MN-WI	41	21
Nassau-Suffolk, NY	77	15
New York, NY	561	2
Newark, NJ	32	24
Oakland, CA	124	11

[Continued]

★425★

Immigrants Admitted, 1994, By Selected Country of Birth: Japan
[Continued]

City/MSA	Immigrants admitted to the U.S.	Rank
Orange County, CA	199	6
Orlando, FL	27	28
Philadelphia, PA-NJ	49	19
Phoenix-Mesa, AZ	40	22
Portland-Vancouver, OR-WA	76	16
Providence-Warwick-Pawtucket, RI	5	40
Riverside-San Bernardino, CA	53	17
Sacramento, CA	21	31
Saint Louis, MO-IL	23	30
Salinas, CA	21	31
San Antonio, TX	28	27
San Diego, CA	180	7
San Francisco, CA	214	5
San Jose, CA	155	9
Seattle-Bellevue-Everett, WA	224	4
Stockton-Lodi, CA	3	42
Tampa-Saint Petersburg-Clearwater, FL	25	29
Ventura, CA	30	25
Washington, DC-MD-VA	113	12
West Palm Beach-Boca Raton, FL	7	38

Source: U.S. Department of Justice, Immigration and Naturalization Service, *Statistical Yearbook of the Immigration and Naturalization Service, 1994*, Washington, D.C.: U.S. Government Printing Office, 1996, p. 64.

★426★
Immigrants Admitted, By Country of Birth

Immigrants Admitted, 1994, By Selected Country of Birth: Korea

The total number of immigrants admitted to the United States from Korea in fiscal year 1994 is 16,011. The number of immigrants living in metropolitan areas that are not MSAs is 978; in "other" MSAs, 2,662; in "unknown areas," 7.

City/MSA	Immigrants admitted to the U.S.	Rank
Atlanta, GA	74	27
Bakersfield, CA	13	44
Baltimore, MD	307	10
Bergen-Passaic, NJ	547	6
Boston-Lawrence-Lowell-Brockton, MA	145	19
Bridgeport-Stamford-Norwalk-Danbury, CT	46	34
Chicago, IL	690	4
Cleveland-Lorain-Elyria, OH	37	36
Dallas, TX	163	18
Denver, CO	123	24
Detroit, MI	44	35

[Continued]

★426★

Immigrants Admitted, 1994, By Selected Country of Birth: Korea
[Continued]

City/MSA	Immigrants admitted to the U.S.	Rank
El Paso, TX	36	37
Fort Lauderdale, FL	272	12
Fort Worth-Arlington, TX	68	28
Fresno, CA	11	45
Hartford, CT	23	40
Honolulu, HI	324	9
Houston, TX	140	20
Jersey City, NJ	55	30
Las Vegas, NV	89	25
Los Angeles-Long Beach, CA	3,070	1
McAllen-Edinburg-Mission, TX	2	46
Miami, FL	17	42
Middlesex-Somerset-Hunterdon, NJ	133	22
Minneapolis-Saint Paul, MN-WI	210	13
Nassau-Suffolk, NY	186	15
New York, NY	1,463	2
Newark, NJ	129	23
Oakland, CA	202	14
Orange County, CA	633	5
Orlando, FL	31	39
Philadelphia, PA-NJ	424	7
Phoenix-Mesa, AZ	84	26
Portland-Vancouver, OR-WA	168	16
Providence-Warwick-Pawtucket, RI	11	45
Riverside-San Bernardino, CA	136	21
Sacramento, CA	0	47
Saint Louis, MO-IL	52	32
Salinas, CA	56	29
San Antonio, TX	33	38
San Diego, CA	129	23
San Francisco, CA	166	17
San Jose, CA	278	11
Seattle-Bellevue-Everett, WA	369	8
Stockton-Lodi, CA	15	43
Tampa-Saint Petersburg-Clearwater, FL	51	33
Ventura, CA	53	31
Washington, DC-MD-VA	809	3
West Palm Beach-Boca Raton, FL	19	41

Source: U.S. Department of Justice, Immigration and Naturalization Service, *Statistical Yearbook of the Immigration and Naturalization Service, 1994*, Washington, D.C.: U.S. Government Printing Office, 1996, p. 64.

★427★
Immigrants Admitted, By Country of Birth

Immigrants Admitted, 1994, By Selected Country of Birth: Mexico

The total number of immigrants admitted to the United States from Mexico in fiscal year 1994 is 111,398. The number of immigrants living in metropolitan areas that are not MSAs is 12,634; in "other" MSAs, 22,595; in "unknown areas," 5.

City/MSA	Immigrants admitted to the U.S.	Rank
Atlanta, GA	332	27
Bakersfield, CA	2,182	12
Baltimore, MD	35	44
Bergen-Passaic, NJ	188	33
Boston-Lawrence-Lowell-Brockton, MA	65	39
Bridgeport-Stamford-Norwalk-Danbury, CT	43	40
Chicago, IL	7,469	2
Cleveland-Lorain-Elyria, OH	35	44
Dallas, TX	2,658	10
Denver, CO	1,155	18
Detroit, MI	193	32
El Paso, TX	4,149	5
Fort Lauderdale, FL	112	35
Fort Worth-Arlington, TX	1,073	20
Fresno, CA	3,188	9
Hartford, CT	15	48
Honolulu, HI	20	47
Houston, TX	4,806	3
Jersey City, NJ	41	41
Las Vegas, NV	554	23
Los Angeles-Long Beach, CA	15,605	1
McAllen-Edinburg-Mission, TX	3,612	8
Miami, FL	265	29
Middlesex-Somerset-Hunterdon, NJ	40	42
Minneapolis-Saint Paul, MN-WI	110	36
Nassau-Suffolk, NY	79	38
New York, NY	1,086	19
Newark, NJ	38	43
Oakland, CA	1,382	16
Orange County, CA	3,789	7
Orlando, FL	115	34
Philadelphia, PA-NJ	337	26
Phoenix-Mesa, AZ	2,063	13
Portland-Vancouver, OR-WA	541	24
Providence-Warwick-Pawtucket, RI	23	46
Riverside-San Bernardino, CA	4,257	4
Sacramento, CA	519	25
Saint Louis, MO-IL	29	45
Salinas, CA	1,840	14
San Antonio, TX	1,732	15
San Diego, CA	3,991	6
San Francisco, CA	977	21
San Jose, CA	1,357	17
Seattle-Bellevue-Everett, WA	205	31
Stockton-Lodi, CA	762	22
Tampa-Saint Petersburg-Clearwater, FL	224	30

[Continued]

★427★

Immigrants Admitted, 1994, By Selected Country of Birth: Mexico

[Continued]

City/MSA	Immigrants admitted to the U.S.	Rank
Ventura, CA	2,473	11
Washington, DC-MD-VA	281	28
West Palm Beach-Boca Raton, FL	98	37

Source: U.S. Department of Justice, Immigration and Naturalization Service, *Statistical Yearbook of the Immigration and Naturalization Service, 1994,* Washington, D.C.: U.S. Government Printing Office, 1996, p. 64.

★428★

Immigrants Admitted, By Country of Birth

Immigrants Admitted, 1994, By Selected Country of Birth: Pakistan

The total number of immigrants admitted to the United States from Pakistan in fiscal year 1994 is 8,698. The number of immigrants living in metropolitan areas that are not MSAs is 325; in "other" MSAs, 1,414; in "unknown areas," 0.

City/MSA	Immigrants admitted to the U.S.	Rank
Atlanta, GA	149	11
Bakersfield, CA	19	32
Baltimore, MD	86	18
Bergen-Passaic, NJ	82	19
Boston-Lawrence-Lowell-Brockton, MA	86	18
Bridgeport-Stamford-Norwalk-Danbury, CT	42	24
Chicago, IL	644	3
Cleveland-Lorain-Elyria, OH	27	28
Dallas, TX	157	10
Denver, CO	22	31
Detroit, MI	202	7
El Paso, TX	1	37
Fort Lauderdale, FL	75	20
Fort Worth-Arlington, TX	55	22
Fresno, CA	27	28
Hartford, CT	38	26
Honolulu, HI	11	34
Houston, TX	406	4
Jersey City, NJ	111	16
Las Vegas, NV	24	30
Los Angeles-Long Beach, CA	347	5
McAllen-Edinburg-Mission, TX	4	35
Miami, FL	110	17
Middlesex-Somerset-Hunterdon, NJ	124	14
Minneapolis-Saint Paul, MN-WI	25	29
Nassau-Suffolk, NY	262	6
New York, NY	1,732	1
Newark, NJ	110	17
Oakland, CA	176	9

[Continued]

★428★

Immigrants Admitted, 1994, By Selected Country of Birth: Pakistan

[Continued]

City/MSA	Immigrants admitted to the U.S.	Rank
Orange County, CA	130	13
Orlando, FL	44	23
Philadelphia, PA-NJ	132	12
Phoenix-Mesa, AZ	31	27
Portland-Vancouver, OR-WA	22	31
Providence-Warwick-Pawtucket, RI	4	35
Riverside-San Bernardino, CA	114	15
Sacramento, CA	65	21
Saint Louis, MO-IL	38	26
Salinas, CA	3	36
San Antonio, TX	11	34
San Diego, CA	40	25
San Francisco, CA	75	20
San Jose, CA	178	8
Seattle-Bellevue-Everett, WA	44	23
Stockton-Lodi, CA	82	19
Tampa-Saint Petersburg-Clearwater, FL	40	25
Ventura, CA	19	32
Washington, DC-MD-VA	716	2
West Palm Beach-Boca Raton, FL	17	33

Source: U.S. Department of Justice, Immigration and Naturalization Service, *Statistical Yearbook of the Immigration and Naturalization Service, 1994,* Washington, D.C.: U.S. Government Printing Office, 1996, p. 64.

★429★

Immigrants Admitted, By Country of Birth

Immigrants Admitted, 1994, By Selected Country of Birth: Peru

The total number of immigrants admitted to the United States from Peru in fiscal year 1994 is 9,177. The number of immigrants living in metropolitan areas that are not MSAs is 226; in "other" MSAs, 785; in "unknown areas," 0.

City/MSA	Immigrants admitted to the U.S.	Rank
Atlanta, GA	68	22
Bakersfield, CA	12	38
Baltimore, MD	38	28
Bergen-Passaic, NJ	762	3
Boston-Lawrence-Lowell-Brockton, MA	70	20
Bridgeport-Stamford-Norwalk-Danbury, CT	88	19
Chicago, IL	169	11
Cleveland-Lorain-Elyria, OH	19	35
Dallas, TX	55	24
Denver, CO	52	25
Detroit, MI	16	36

[Continued]

★429★
Immigrants Admitted, 1994, By Selected Country of Birth: Peru
[Continued]

City/MSA	Immigrants admitted to the U.S.	Rank
El Paso, TX	2	42
Fort Lauderdale, FL	255	9
Fort Worth-Arlington, TX	12	38
Fresno, CA	5	40
Hartford, CT	127	15
Honolulu, HI	9	39
Houston, TX	113	16
Jersey City, NJ	343	7
Las Vegas, NV	33	29
Los Angeles-Long Beach, CA	661	5
McAllen-Edinburg-Mission, TX	3	41
Miami, FL	941	2
Middlesex-Somerset-Hunterdon, NJ	131	14
Minneapolis-Saint Paul, MN-WI	30	31
Nassau-Suffolk, NY	312	8
New York, NY	1,393	1
Newark, NJ	426	6
Oakland, CA	148	13
Orange County, CA	167	12
Orlando, FL	67	23
Philadelphia, PA-NJ	55	24
Phoenix-Mesa, AZ	29	32
Portland-Vancouver, OR-WA	25	33
Providence-Warwick-Pawtucket, RI	22	34
Riverside-San Bernardino, CA	105	17
Sacramento, CA	14	37
Saint Louis, MO-IL	16	36
Salinas, CA	5	40
San Antonio, TX	31	30
San Diego, CA	51	26
San Francisco, CA	231	10
San Jose, CA	98	18
Seattle-Bellevue-Everett, WA	33	29
Stockton-Lodi, CA	3	41
Tampa-Saint Petersburg-Clearwater, FL	70	20
Ventura, CA	40	27
Washington, DC-MD-VA	725	4
West Palm Beach-Boca Raton, FL	69	21

Source: U.S. Department of Justice, Immigration and Naturalization Service, *Statistical Yearbook of the Immigration and Naturalization Service, 1994*, Washington, D.C.: U.S. Government Printing Office, 1996, p. 64.

★430★
Immigrants Admitted, By Country of Birth
Immigrants Admitted, 1994, By Selected Country of Birth: Philippines

The total number of immigrants admitted to the United States from Philippines in fiscal year 1994 is 53,535. The number of immigrants living in metropolitan areas that are not MSAs is 5,104; in "other" MSAs, 7,108; in "unknown areas," 121.

City/MSA	Immigrants admitted to the U.S.	Rank
Atlanta, GA	168	35
Bakersfield, CA	280	26
Baltimore, MD	206	32
Bergen-Passaic, NJ	591	16
Boston-Lawrence-Lowell-Brockton, MA	210	31
Bridgeport-Stamford-Norwalk-Danbury, CT	71	44
Chicago, IL	2,391	6
Cleveland-Lorain-Elyria, OH	81	42
Dallas, TX	241	28
Denver, CO	127	38
Detroit, MI	317	23
El Paso, TX	47	47
Fort Lauderdale, FL	123	39
Fort Worth-Arlington, TX	61	46
Fresno, CA	191	34
Hartford, CT	67	45
Honolulu, HI	3,258	3
Houston, TX	760	13
Jersey City, NJ	697	14
Las Vegas, NV	505	18
Los Angeles-Long Beach, CA	7,476	1
McAllen-Edinburg-Mission, TX	37	49
Miami, FL	223	30
Middlesex-Somerset-Hunterdon, NJ	360	22
Minneapolis-Saint Paul, MN-WI	105	41
Nassau-Suffolk, NY	283	25
New York, NY	3,423	2
Newark, NJ	673	15
Oakland, CA	2,340	7
Orange County, CA	1,152	10
Orlando, FL	149	37
Philadelphia, PA-NJ	475	19
Phoenix-Mesa, AZ	227	29
Portland-Vancouver, OR-WA	250	27
Providence-Warwick-Pawtucket, RI	42	48
Riverside-San Bernardino, CA	955	12
Sacramento, CA	538	17
Saint Louis, MO-IL	153	36
Salinas, CA	297	24
San Antonio, TX	116	40
San Diego, CA	3,199	4
San Francisco, CA	2,882	5
San Jose, CA	1,984	8
Seattle-Bellevue-Everett, WA	1,196	9
Stockton-Lodi, CA	448	20
Tampa-Saint Petersburg-Clearwater, FL	200	33

[Continued]

★430★
Immigrants Admitted, 1994, By Selected Country of Birth: Philippines
[Continued]

City/MSA	Immigrants admitted to the U.S.	Rank
Ventura, CA	440	21
Washington, DC-MD-VA	1,111	11
West Palm Beach-Boca Raton, FL	75	43

Source: U.S. Department of Justice, Immigration and Naturalization Service, *Statistical Yearbook of the Immigration and Naturalization Service, 1994,* Washington, D.C.: U.S. Government Printing Office, 1996, p. 64.

★431★
Immigrants Admitted, By Country of Birth
Immigrants Admitted, 1994, By Selected Country of Birth: Poland

The total number of immigrants admitted to the United States from Poland in fiscal year 1994 is 28,048. The number of immigrants living in metropolitan areas that are not MSAs is 427; in "other" MSAs, 2,321; in "unknown areas," 1.

City/MSA	Immigrants admitted to the U.S.	Rank
Atlanta, GA	135	15
Bakersfield, CA	4	39
Baltimore, MD	68	22
Bergen-Passaic, NJ	1,481	3
Boston-Lawrence-Lowell-Brockton, MA	250	12
Bridgeport-Stamford-Norwalk-Danbury, CT	299	11
Chicago, IL	11,098	1
Cleveland-Lorain-Elyria, OH	173	14
Dallas, TX	36	29
Denver, CO	76	20
Detroit, MI	570	7
El Paso, TX	4	39
Fort Lauderdale, FL	133	16
Fort Worth-Arlington, TX	18	37
Fresno, CA	4	39
Hartford, CT	968	5
Honolulu, HI	0	41
Houston, TX	35	30
Jersey City, NJ	368	10
Las Vegas, NV	19	36
Los Angeles-Long Beach, CA	191	13
McAllen-Edinburg-Mission, TX	0	41
Miami, FL	55	25
Middlesex-Somerset-Hunterdon, NJ	418	9
Minneapolis-Saint Paul, MN-WI	41	28
Nassau-Suffolk, NY	692	6
New York, NY	5,665	2
Newark, NJ	1,026	4
Oakland, CA	77	19

[Continued]

★431★
Immigrants Admitted, 1994, By Selected Country of Birth: Poland
[Continued]

City/MSA	Immigrants admitted to the U.S.	Rank
Orange County, CA	71	21
Orlando, FL	22	35
Philadelphia, PA-NJ	465	8
Phoenix-Mesa, AZ	55	25
Portland-Vancouver, OR-WA	30	32
Providence-Warwick-Pawtucket, RI	111	17
Riverside-San Bernardino, CA	26	33
Sacramento, CA	19	36
Saint Louis, MO-IL	25	34
Salinas, CA	2	40
San Antonio, TX	31	31
San Diego, CA	58	24
San Francisco, CA	47	27
San Jose, CA	59	23
Seattle-Bellevue-Everett, WA	103	18
Stockton-Lodi, CA	0	41
Tampa-Saint Petersburg-Clearwater, FL	111	17
Ventura, CA	5	38
Washington, DC-MD-VA	103	18
West Palm Beach-Boca Raton, FL	52	26

Source: U.S. Department of Justice, Immigration and Naturalization Service, *Statistical Yearbook of the Immigration and Naturalization Service, 1994,* Washington, D.C.: U.S. Government Printing Office, 1996, p. 64.

★432★
Immigrants Admitted, By Country of Birth
Immigrants Admitted, 1994, By Selected Country of Birth: Taiwan

The total number of immigrants admitted to the United States from Taiwan in fiscal year 1994 is 10,032. The number of immigrants living in metropolitan areas that are not MSAs is 361; in "other" MSAs, 1,440; in "unknown areas," 1.

City/MSA	Immigrants admitted to the U.S.	Rank
Atlanta, GA	92	19
Bakersfield, CA	3	42
Baltimore, MD	50	25
Bergen-Passaic, NJ	109	17
Boston-Lawrence-Lowell-Brockton, MA	118	15
Bridgeport-Stamford-Norwalk-Danbury, CT	22	33
Chicago, IL	224	9
Cleveland-Lorain-Elyria, OH	47	27
Dallas, TX	169	12
Denver, CO	36	28
Detroit, MI	52	24

[Continued]

★432★

Immigrants Admitted, 1994, By Selected Country of Birth: Taiwan

[Continued]

City/MSA	Immigrants admitted to the U.S.	Rank
El Paso, TX	6	41
Fort Lauderdale, FL	21	34
Fort Worth-Arlington, TX	57	21
Fresno, CA	18	36
Hartford, CT	12	40
Honolulu, HI	73	20
Houston, TX	330	7
Jersey City, NJ	34	30
Las Vegas, NV	29	31
Los Angeles-Long Beach, CA	2,342	1
McAllen-Edinburg-Mission, TX	1	43
Miami, FL	34	30
Middlesex-Somerset-Hunterdon, NJ	187	10
Minneapolis-Saint Paul, MN-WI	49	26
Nassau-Suffolk, NY	110	16
New York, NY	653	3
Newark, NJ	133	14
Oakland, CA	347	5
Orange County, CA	555	4
Orlando, FL	35	29
Philadelphia, PA-NJ	104	18
Phoenix-Mesa, AZ	54	22
Portland-Vancouver, OR-WA	36	28
Providence-Warwick-Pawtucket, RI	12	40
Riverside-San Bernardino, CA	142	13
Sacramento, CA	53	23
Saint Louis, MO-IL	28	32
Salinas, CA	13	39
San Antonio, TX	16	37
San Diego, CA	142	13
San Francisco, CA	317	8
San Jose, CA	788	2
Seattle-Bellevue-Everett, WA	183	11
Stockton-Lodi, CA	6	41
Tampa-Saint Petersburg-Clearwater, FL	22	33
Ventura, CA	19	35
Washington, DC-MD-VA	333	6
West Palm Beach-Boca Raton, FL	14	38

Source: U.S. Department of Justice, Immigration and Naturalization Service, *Statistical Yearbook of the Immigration and Naturalization Service, 1994,* Washington, D.C.: U.S. Government Printing Office, 1996, p. 64.

★433★

Immigrants Admitted, By Country of Birth

Immigrants Admitted, 1994, By Selected Country of Birth: Soviet Union

The total number of immigrants admitted to the United States from the Soviet Union in fiscal year 1994 is 63,420. The number of immigrants living in metropolitan areas that are not MSAs is 1,113; in "other" MSAs, 9,039; in "unknown areas," 1.

City/MSA	Immigrants admitted to the U.S.	Rank
Atlanta, GA	572	18
Bakersfield, CA	5	45
Baltimore, MD	1,394	10
Bergen-Passaic, NJ	534	19
Boston-Lawrence-Lowell-Brockton, MA	1,967	6
Bridgeport-Stamford-Norwalk-Danbury, CT	195	30
Chicago, IL	2,885	3
Cleveland-Lorain-Elyria, OH	981	12
Dallas, TX	421	22
Denver, CO	603	17
Detroit, MI	734	13
El Paso, TX	7	44
Fort Lauderdale, FL	163	31
Fort Worth-Arlington, TX	44	38
Fresno, CA	163	31
Hartford, CT	282	26
Honolulu, HI	22	42
Houston, TX	267	27
Jersey City, NJ	73	37
Las Vegas, NV	40	39
Los Angeles-Long Beach, CA	7,710	2
McAllen-Edinburg-Mission, TX	2	46
Miami, FL	315	25
Middlesex-Somerset-Hunterdon, NJ	320	24
Minneapolis-Saint Paul, MN-WI	718	16
Nassau-Suffolk, NY	200	29
New York, NY	18,157	1
Newark, NJ	720	15
Oakland, CA	408	23
Orange County, CA	134	32
Orlando, FL	44	38
Philadelphia, PA-NJ	1,868	7
Phoenix-Mesa, AZ	123	33
Portland-Vancouver, OR-WA	1,679	9
Providence-Warwick-Pawtucket, RI	245	28
Riverside-San Bernardino, CA	119	34
Sacramento, CA	1,984	5
Saint Louis, MO-IL	439	20
Salinas, CA	24	41
San Antonio, TX	38	40
San Diego, CA	426	21
San Francisco, CA	2,395	4
San Jose, CA	728	14
Seattle-Bellevue-Everett, WA	1,861	8
Stockton-Lodi, CA	1	47
Tampa-Saint Petersburg-Clearwater, FL	85	35

[Continued]

★433★

Immigrants Admitted, 1994, By Selected Country of Birth: Soviet Union

[Continued]

City/MSA	Immigrants admitted to the U.S.	Rank
Ventura, CA	16	43
Washington, DC-MD-VA	1,079	11
West Palm Beach-Boca Raton, FL	77	36

Source: U.S. Department of Justice, Immigration and Naturalization Service, *Statistical Yearbook of the Immigration and Naturalization Service, 1994,* Washington, D.C.: U.S. Government Printing Office, 1996, p. 64.

★434★

Immigrants Admitted, By Country of Birth

Immigrants Admitted, 1994, By Selected Country of Birth: United Kingdom

The total number of immigrants admitted to the United States from the United Kingdom in fiscal year 1994 is 16,326. The number of immigrants living in metropolitan areas that are not MSAs is 1,246; in "other" MSAs, 4,113; in "unknown areas," 0.

City/MSA	Immigrants admitted to the U.S.	Rank
Atlanta, GA	334	9
Bakersfield, CA	23	46
Baltimore, MD	94	32
Bergen-Passaic, NJ	131	29
Boston-Lawrence-Lowell-Brockton, MA	581	3
Bridgeport-Stamford-Norwalk-Danbury, CT	192	21
Chicago, IL	448	6
Cleveland-Lorain-Elyria, OH	75	36
Dallas, TX	188	22
Denver, CO	160	25
Detroit, MI	222	16
El Paso, TX	13	48
Fort Lauderdale, FL	255	14
Fort Worth-Arlington, TX	64	38
Fresno, CA	45	42
Hartford, CT	68	37
Honolulu, HI	46	41
Houston, TX	378	8
Jersey City, NJ	57	40
Las Vegas, NV	80	34
Los Angeles-Long Beach, CA	1,077	2
McAllen-Edinburg-Mission, TX	3	49
Miami, FL	156	26
Middlesex-Somerset-Hunterdon, NJ	151	27
Minneapolis-Saint Paul, MN-WI	146	28
Nassau-Suffolk, NY	208	19
New York, NY	1,424	1
Newark, NJ	196	20
Oakland, CA	234	15

[Continued]

★434★

Immigrants Admitted, 1994, By Selected Country of Birth: United Kingdom

[Continued]

City/MSA	Immigrants admitted to the U.S.	Rank
Orange County, CA	284	13
Orlando, FL	317	10
Philadelphia, PA-NJ	457	5
Phoenix-Mesa, AZ	178	23
Portland-Vancouver, OR-WA	130	30
Providence-Warwick-Pawtucket, RI	39	44
Riverside-San Bernardino, CA	124	31
Sacramento, CA	44	43
Saint Louis, MO-IL	77	35
Salinas, CA	26	45
San Antonio, TX	59	39
San Diego, CA	219	18
San Francisco, CA	478	4
San Jose, CA	294	12
Seattle-Bellevue-Everett, WA	220	17
Stockton-Lodi, CA	17	47
Tampa-Saint Petersburg-Clearwater, FL	308	11
Ventura, CA	83	33
Washington, DC-MD-VA	389	7
West Palm Beach-Boca Raton, FL	170	24

Source: U.S. Department of Justice, Immigration and Naturalization Service, *Statistical Yearbook of the Immigration and Naturalization Service, 1994,* Washington, D.C.: U.S. Government Printing Office, 1996, p. 64.

★435★

Immigrants Admitted, By Country of Birth

Immigrants Admitted, 1994, By Selected Country of Birth: Trinidad

The total number of immigrants admitted to the United States from Trinidad in fiscal year 1994 is 6,292. The number of immigrants living in metropolitan areas that are not MSAs is 138; in "other" MSAs, 447; in "unknown areas," 0.

City/MSA	Immigrants admitted to the U.S.	Rank
Atlanta, GA	40	18
Bakersfield, CA	1	34
Baltimore, MD	113	9
Bergen-Passaic, NJ	63	14
Boston-Lawrence-Lowell-Brockton, MA	131	8
Bridgeport-Stamford-Norwalk-Danbury, CT	25	19
Chicago, IL	25	19
Cleveland-Lorain-Elyria, OH	15	23
Dallas, TX	24	20
Denver, CO	4	31
Detroit, MI	4	31

[Continued]

★435★

Immigrants Admitted, 1994, By Selected Country of Birth: Trinidad

[Continued]

City/MSA	Immigrants admitted to the U.S.	Rank
El Paso, TX	1	34
Fort Lauderdale, FL	276	3
Fort Worth-Arlington, TX	18	22
Fresno, CA	0	35
Hartford, CT	19	21
Honolulu, HI	1	34
Houston, TX	83	11
Jersey City, NJ	61	15
Las Vegas, NV	3	32
Los Angeles-Long Beach, CA	79	12
McAllen-Edinburg-Mission, TX	2	33
Miami, FL	230	4
Middlesex-Somerset-Hunterdon, NJ	48	16
Minneapolis-Saint Paul, MN-WI	11	26
Nassau-Suffolk, NY	193	5
New York, NY	3,256	1
Newark, NJ	179	7
Oakland, CA	6	29
Orange County, CA	9	28
Orlando, FL	91	10
Philadelphia, PA-NJ	180	6
Phoenix-Mesa, AZ	12	25
Portland-Vancouver, OR-WA	2	33
Providence-Warwick-Pawtucket, RI	9	28
Riverside-San Bernardino, CA	13	24
Sacramento, CA	4	31
Saint Louis, MO-IL	5	30
Salinas, CA	0	35
San Antonio, TX	4	31
San Diego, CA	11	26
San Francisco, CA	9	28
San Jose, CA	3	32
Seattle-Bellevue-Everett, WA	10	27
Stockton-Lodi, CA	0	35
Tampa-Saint Petersburg-Clearwater, FL	46	17
Ventura, CA	0	35
Washington, DC-MD-VA	307	2
West Palm Beach-Boca Raton, FL	75	13

Source: U.S. Department of Justice, Immigration and Naturalization Service, *Statistical Yearbook of the Immigration and Naturalization Service, 1994,* Washington, D.C.: U.S. Government Printing Office, 1996, p. 64.

★436★

Immigrants Admitted, By Country of Birth

Immigrants Admitted, 1994, By Selected Country of Birth: Vietnam

The total number of immigrants admitted to the United States from Vietnam in fiscal year 1994 is 41,345. The number of immigrants living in metropolitan areas that are not MSAs is 1,139; in "other" MSAs, 10,029; in "unknown areas," 1.

City/MSA	Immigrants admitted to the U.S.	Rank
Atlanta, GA	1,400	7
Bakersfield, CA	11	44
Baltimore, MD	107	29
Bergen-Passaic, NJ	11	44
Boston-Lawrence-Lowell-Brockton, MA	1,068	9
Bridgeport-Stamford-Norwalk-Danbury, CT	88	33
Chicago, IL	621	16
Cleveland-Lorain-Elyria, OH	89	32
Dallas, TX	913	11
Denver, CO	429	18
Detroit, MI	64	38
El Paso, TX	8	45
Fort Lauderdale, FL	81	34
Fort Worth-Arlington, TX	795	12
Fresno, CA	79	35
Hartford, CT	149	27
Honolulu, HI	342	21
Houston, TX	2,051	4
Jersey City, NJ	93	31
Las Vegas, NV	81	34
Los Angeles-Long Beach, CA	3,118	2
McAllen-Edinburg-Mission, TX	0	46
Miami, FL	31	42
Middlesex-Somerset-Hunterdon, NJ	95	30
Minneapolis-Saint Paul, MN-WI	621	16
Nassau-Suffolk, NY	56	40
New York, NY	375	19
Newark, NJ	116	28
Oakland, CA	923	10
Orange County, CA	2,936	3
Orlando, FL	323	22
Philadelphia, PA-NJ	711	15
Phoenix-Mesa, AZ	294	25
Portland-Vancouver, OR-WA	725	14
Providence-Warwick-Pawtucket, RI	17	43
Riverside-San Bernardino, CA	310	24
Sacramento, CA	759	13
Saint Louis, MO-IL	320	23
Salinas, CA	65	37
San Antonio, TX	62	39
San Diego, CA	1,141	8
San Francisco, CA	552	17
San Jose, CA	3,706	1
Seattle-Bellevue-Everett, WA	1,771	6
Stockton-Lodi, CA	259	26
Tampa-Saint Petersburg-Clearwater, FL	343	20

[Continued]

★436★

Immigrants Admitted, 1994, By Selected Country of Birth: Vietnam

[Continued]

City/MSA	Immigrants admitted to the U.S.	Rank
Ventura, CA	70	36
Washington, DC-MD-VA	1,952	5
West Palm Beach-Boca Raton, FL	45	41

Source: U.S. Department of Justice, Immigration and Naturalization Service, *Statistical Yearbook of the Immigration and Naturalization Service, 1994,* Washington, D.C.: U.S. Government Printing Office, 1996, p. 64.

★437★

Immigrants Admitted, By Time Period

Immigrants Admitted: 1987 to 1990

[Table shows the top 50 areas]

MSA	% of total population	Rank
Los Angeles – Anaheim – Riverside, CA	5.177	1
Miami – Fort Lauderdale, FL	4.578	2
Merced, CA	3.523	3
Laredo, TX	3.522	4
Fresno, CA	3.474	5
McAllen – Edinburg – Mission, TX	3.339	6
San Francisco – Oakland – San Jose, CA	3.319	7
El Paso, TX	3.217	8
Visalia – Tulare – Porterville, CA	3.214	9
Santa Barbara – Santa Maria – Lompoc, CA	3.198	10
Salinas – Seaside – Monterey, CA	3.170	11
San Diego, CA	3.061	12
New York – Northern New Jersey – Long Island, NY – NJ – CT	2.938	13
Washington, DC – MD – VA	2.687	14
Yuma, AZ	2.524	15
Brownsville – Harlingen, TX	2.484	16
Lawrence, KS	2.353	17
Bryan – College Station, TX	2.326	18
Honolulu, HI	2.276	19
Lafayette – West Lafayette, IN	2.263	20
Iowa City, IA	2.194	21
Yuba City, CA	2.169	22
Stockton, CA	2.154	23
Yakima, WA	2.101	24
Las Cruces, NM	2.003	25
Modesto, CA	1.985	26
Bakersfield, CA	1.935	27
Houston – Galveston – Brazoria, TX	1.888	28
Naples, FL	1.855	29
Champaign – Urbana – Rantoul, IL	1.845	30
Boston – Lawrence – Salem, MA – NH	1.843	31

[Continued]

★437★

Immigrants Admitted: 1987 to 1990

[Continued]

MSA	% of total population	Rank
Reno, NV	1.780	32
Bloomington, IN	1.759	33
Richland – Kennewick – Pasco, WA	1.743	34
Chicago – Gary – Lake County, IL – IN – WI	1.582	35
Sacramento, CA	1.581	36
Columbia, MO	1.560	37
Las Vegas, NV	1.549	38
State College, PA	1.524	39
West Palm Beach – Boca Raton – Delray Beach, FL	1.457	40
Tucson, AZ	1.456	41
Gainesville, FL	1.323	42
Austin, TX	1.285	43
Dallas – Fort Worth, TX	1.267	44
Providence – Pawtucket – Fall River, RI – MA	1.256	45
Phoenix, AZ	1.250	46
Madison, WI	1.217	47
Seattle – Tacoma, WA	1.209	48
Rochester, MN	1.152	49
Salem, OR	1.141	50

Source: U.S. Bureau of the Census, Data User Services Division, *1990 Census of Population and Housing,* Summary Tape File 3C, United States Summary, CD-ROM, February 1992.

★438★

Immigrants Admitted, By Time Period

Immigrants Admitted: 1960 to 1964

[Table shows the top 50 areas]

MSA	% of total population	Rank
Miami – Fort Lauderdale, FL	4.074	1
El Paso, TX	1.902	2
Laredo, TX	1.679	3
Yuma, AZ	1.679	3
Las Cruces, NM	1.360	4
Salinas – Seaside – Monterey, CA	1.306	5
Los Angeles – Anaheim – Riverside, CA	1.231	6
McAllen – Edinburg – Mission, TX	1.195	7
New York – Northern New Jersey – Long Island, NY – NJ – CT	1.195	7
San Francisco – Oakland – San Jose, CA	1.174	8
Brownsville – Harlingen, TX	1.171	9
San Diego, CA	1.118	10
Santa Barbara – Santa Maria – Lompoc, CA	1.065	11
New Bedford, MA	1.063	12
Fitchburg – Leominster, MA	1.039	13
Stockton, CA	0.912	14
West Palm Beach – Boca Raton – Delray Beach, FL	0.898	15

[Continued]

★438★

Immigrants Admitted: 1960 to 1964
[Continued]

MSA	% of total population	Rank
Tucson, AZ	0.781	16
Las Vegas, NV	0.778	17
Honolulu, HI	0.760	18
Hartford – New Britain – Middletown, CT	0.741	19
Modesto, CA	0.729	20
Yuba City, CA	0.683	21
Poughkeepsie, NY	0.668	22
Manchester, NH	0.666	23
Merced, CA	0.666	23
Visalia – Tulare – Porterville, CA	0.665	24
Fresno, CA	0.661	25
Boston – Lawrence – Salem, MA – NH	0.634	26
Tampa – Saint Petersburg – Clearwater, FL	0.620	27
Bakersfield, CA	0.607	28
Chicago – Gary – Lake County, IL – IN – WI	0.603	29
Sacramento, CA	0.602	30
Bellingham, WA	0.588	31
Lawton, OK	0.581	32
Washington, DC – MD – VA	0.575	33
Naples, FL	0.571	34
Orlando, FL	0.571	34
San Antonio, TX	0.571	34
Colorado Springs, CO	0.547	35
Reno, NV	0.540	36
Waterbury, CT	0.539	37
Melbourne – Titusville – Palm Bay, FL	0.529	38
Seattle – Tacoma, WA	0.526	39
Providence – Pawtucket – Fall River, RI – MA	0.519	40
Fort Walton Beach, FL	0.509	41
Springfield, MA	0.504	42
New Haven – Meriden, CT	0.502	43
Anchorage, AK	0.486	44
San Angelo, TX	0.448	45

Source: U.S. Bureau of the Census, Data User Services Division, 1990 Census of Population and Housing, Summary Tape File 3C, United States Summary, CD-ROM, February 1992.

★439★

Immigrants Admitted, By Time Period

Immigrants Admitted: 1965 to 1969

[Table shows the top 50 areas]

MSA	% of total population	Rank
Miami – Fort Lauderdale, FL	4.630	1
New Bedford, MA	3.164	2
Yuma, AZ	2.162	3
Laredo, TX	1.942	4
New York – Northern New Jersey – Long Island, NY – NJ – CT	1.910	5

[Continued]

★439★

Immigrants Admitted: 1965 to 1969
[Continued]

MSA	% of total population	Rank
El Paso, TX	1.827	6
Brownsville – Harlingen, TX	1.784	7
McAllen – Edinburg – Mission, TX	1.744	8
Los Angeles – Anaheim – Riverside, CA	1.694	9
Salinas – Seaside – Monterey, CA	1.635	10
San Francisco – Oakland – San Jose, CA	1.477	11
Providence – Pawtucket – Fall River, RI – MA	1.402	12
Merced, CA	1.379	13
Honolulu, HI	1.373	14
San Diego, CA	1.251	15
Visalia – Tulare – Porterville, CA	1.167	16
Las Cruces, NM	1.126	17
Modesto, CA	1.107	18
Stockton, CA	1.084	19
Santa Barbara – Santa Maria – Lompoc, CA	1.071	20
Hartford – New Britain – Middletown, CT	1.032	21
Waterbury, CT	1.031	22
Boston – Lawrence – Salem, MA – NH	0.950	23
West Palm Beach – Boca Raton – Delray Beach, FL	0.945	24
Chicago – Gary – Lake County, IL – IN – WI	0.936	25
Washington, DC – MD – VA	0.818	26
Las Vegas, NV	0.791	27
San Antonio, TX	0.786	28
Yuba City, CA	0.780	29
Tucson, AZ	0.754	30
Fresno, CA	0.743	31
Bakersfield, CA	0.729	32
Orlando, FL	0.729	32
Houston – Galveston – Brazoria, TX	0.713	33
Manchester, NH	0.678	34
New Haven – Meriden, CT	0.661	35
Sacramento, CA	0.651	36
Bellingham, WA	0.643	37
Naples, FL	0.642	38
Tampa – Saint Petersburg – Clearwater, FL	0.634	39
Poughkeepsie, NY	0.628	40
Springfield, MA	0.627	41
Odessa, TX	0.605	42
Seattle – Tacoma, WA	0.597	43
Lawton, OK	0.578	44
Rochester, NY	0.542	45
Melbourne – Titusville – Palm Bay, FL	0.524	46
Killeen – Temple, TX	0.511	47

[Continued]

★439★

Immigrants Admitted: 1965 to 1969

[Continued]

MSA	% of total population	Rank
Detroit – Ann Arbor, MI	0.500	48
Worcester, MA	0.471	49

Source: U.S. Bureau of the Census, Data User Services Division, *1990 Census of Population and Housing,* Summary Tape File 3C, United States Summary, CD-ROM, February 1992.

★440★

Immigrants Admitted, By Time Period

Immigrants Admitted: 1970 to 1974

[Table shows the top 50 areas]

MSA	% of total population	Rank
Miami – Fort Lauderdale, FL	3.677	1
McAllen – Edinburg – Mission, TX	3.455	2
El Paso, TX	3.402	3
Yuma, AZ	3.125	4
Brownsville – Harlingen, TX	3.116	5
Los Angeles – Anaheim – Riverside, CA	3.036	6
Laredo, TX	2.810	7
Salinas – Seaside – Monterey, CA	2.737	8
Merced, CA	2.533	9
New Bedford, MA	2.429	10
New York – Northern New Jersey – Long Island, NY – NJ – CT	2.352	11
Honolulu, HI	2.286	12
Las Cruces, NM	2.149	13
Visalia – Tulare – Porterville, CA	2.067	14
San Francisco – Oakland – San Jose, CA	1.902	15
Modesto, CA	1.836	16
San Diego, CA	1.788	17
Santa Barbara – Santa Maria – Lompoc, CA	1.676	18
Fresno, CA	1.658	19
Stockton, CA	1.486	20
Chicago – Gary – Lake County, IL – IN – WI	1.458	21
Providence – Pawtucket – Fall River, RI – MA	1.400	22
Bakersfield, CA	1.335	23
Houston – Galveston – Brazoria, TX	1.291	24
Washington, DC – MD – VA	1.261	25
Yuba City, CA	1.204	26
Odessa, TX	1.148	27
San Antonio, TX	1.116	28
Yakima, WA	1.084	29
West Palm Beach – Boca Raton – Delray Beach, FL	1.024	30
Las Vegas, NV	1.017	31
Boston – Lawrence – Salem, MA – NH	0.939	32
Waterbury, CT	0.931	33

[Continued]

★440★

Immigrants Admitted: 1970 to 1974

[Continued]

MSA	% of total population	Rank
Tucson, AZ	0.888	34
Sacramento, CA	0.868	35
Hartford – New Britain – Middletown, CT	0.851	36
Dallas – Fort Worth, TX	0.809	37
Orlando, FL	0.795	38
Richland – Kennewick – Pasco, WA	0.784	39
Killeen – Temple, TX	0.780	40
Naples, FL	0.766	41
Midland, TX	0.739	42
Anchorage, AK	0.729	43
Austin, TX	0.710	44
Champaign – Urbana – Rantoul, IL	0.699	45
San Angelo, TX	0.696	46
Phoenix, AZ	0.691	47
Poughkeepsie, NY	0.680	48
Reno, NV	0.675	49
Tampa – Saint Petersburg – Clearwater, FL	0.629	50

Source: U.S. Bureau of the Census, Data User Services Division, *1990 Census of Population and Housing,* Summary Tape File 3C, United States Summary, CD-ROM, February 1992.

★441★

Immigrants Admitted, By Time Period

Immigrants Admitted: 1975 to 1979

[Table shows the top 50 areas]

MSA	% of total population	Rank
Los Angeles – Anaheim – Riverside, CA	4.743	1
McAllen – Edinburg – Mission, TX	4.231	2
Merced, CA	3.899	3
Brownsville – Harlingen, TX	3.723	4
Yuma, AZ	3.641	5
Laredo, TX	3.634	6
Salinas – Seaside – Monterey, CA	3.596	7
El Paso, TX	3.456	8
San Francisco – Oakland – San Jose, CA	3.204	9
Miami – Fort Lauderdale, FL	3.053	10
Fresno, CA	3.025	11
Visalia – Tulare – Porterville, CA	2.955	12
San Diego, CA	2.699	13
Houston – Galveston – Brazoria, TX	2.599	14
Honolulu, HI	2.574	15
Modesto, CA	2.415	16
New Bedford, MA	2.347	17
Stockton, CA	2.280	18
Las Cruces, NM	2.272	19
New York – Northern New Jersey – Long Island, NY – NJ – CT	2.265	20
Santa Barbara – Santa Maria – Lompoc, CA	2.212	21

[Continued]

★441★

Immigrants Admitted: 1975 to 1979
[Continued]

MSA	% of total population	Rank
Bakersfield, CA	2.208	22
Odessa, TX	2.157	23
Yakima, WA	1.993	24
Yuba City, CA	1.919	25
Washington, DC – MD – VA	1.728	26
Chicago – Gary – Lake County, IL – IN – WI	1.720	27
Dallas – Fort Worth, TX	1.533	28
Midland, TX	1.456	29
Providence – Pawtucket – Fall River, RI – MA	1.438	30
Sacramento, CA	1.316	31
Richland – Kennewick – Pasco, WA	1.299	32
Reno, NV	1.273	33
Las Vegas, NV	1.245	34
Bryan – College Station, TX	1.206	35
West Palm Beach – Boca Raton – Delray Beach, FL	1.142	36
Seattle – Tacoma, WA	1.116	37
Austin, TX	1.112	38
San Antonio, TX	1.092	39
San Angelo, TX	1.081	40
Boston – Lawrence – Salem, MA – NH	1.076	41
Orlando, FL	0.996	42
Albuquerque, NM	0.978	43
Tucson, AZ	0.975	44
Naples, FL	0.968	45
Phoenix, AZ	0.964	46
Bellingham, WA	0.865	47
Tyler, TX	0.849	48
Beaumont – Port Arthur, TX	0.835	49
Greeley, CO	0.835	49

Source: U.S. Bureau of the Census, Data User Services Division, *1990 Census of Population and Housing*, Summary Tape File 3C, United States Summary, CD-ROM, February 1992.

★442★

Immigrants Admitted, By Time Period

Immigrants Admitted: 1980 to 1981
[Table shows the top 50 areas]

MSA	% of total population	Rank
Miami – Fort Lauderdale, FL	4.6792	1
Los Angeles – Anaheim – Riverside, CA	3.3013	2
McAllen – Edinburg – Mission, TX	2.9775	3
Brownsville – Harlingen, TX	2.8441	4
Laredo, TX	2.5998	5
Merced, CA	2.4456	6
Stockton, CA	2.2693	7
Fresno, CA	2.2048	8
Houston – Galveston – Brazoria, TX	2.1811	9

[Continued]

★442★

Immigrants Admitted: 1980 to 1981
[Continued]

MSA	% of total population	Rank
El Paso, TX	2.1164	10
San Francisco – Oakland – San Jose, CA	2.0992	11
Salinas – Seaside – Monterey, CA	2.0534	12
Visalia – Tulare – Porterville, CA	1.9611	13
New York – Northern New Jersey – Long Island, NY – NJ – CT	1.7262	14
San Diego, CA	1.6615	15
Santa Barbara – Santa Maria – Lompoc, CA	1.6085	16
Modesto, CA	1.5551	17
Las Cruces, NM	1.3940	18
Yuba City, CA	1.3079	19
Bakersfield, CA	1.2994	20
Dallas – Fort Worth, TX	1.2767	21
Naples, FL	1.2696	22
Honolulu, HI	1.2311	23
West Palm Beach – Boca Raton – Delray Beach, FL	1.2249	24
Washington, DC – MD – VA	1.1841	25
Sacramento, CA	1.1838	26
Yuma, AZ	1.1030	27
Odessa, TX	1.0678	28
Las Vegas, NV	1.0367	29
Reno, NV	1.0198	30
Yakima, WA	1.0062	31
Chicago – Gary – Lake County, IL – IN – WI	0.9906	32
Midland, TX	0.9755	33
Austin, TX	0.8841	34
San Antonio, TX	0.8171	35
New Bedford, MA	0.7928	36
Boston – Lawrence – Salem, MA – NH	0.7873	37
Tucson, AZ	0.7561	38
Providence – Pawtucket – Fall River, RI – MA	0.7464	39
Orlando, FL	0.7463	40
Richland – Kennewick – Pasco, WA	0.7012	41
Phoenix, AZ	0.6818	42
Seattle – Tacoma, WA	0.6588	43
Bryan – College Station, TX	0.6516	44
Amarillo, TX	0.6068	45
Albuquerque, NM	0.6053	46
Hartford – New Britain – Middletown, CT	0.6044	47
Chico, CA	0.5914	48
Fort Pierce, FL	0.5616	49
Tampa – Saint Petersburg – Clearwater, FL	0.5423	50

Source: U.S. Bureau of the Census, Data User Services Division, *1990 Census of Population and Housing*, Summary Tape File 3C, United States Summary, CD-ROM, February 1992.

★443★

Immigrants Admitted, By Time Period

Immigrants Admitted: 1982 to 1984

[Table shows the top 50 areas]

MSA	% of total population	Rank
Los Angeles – Anaheim – Riverside, CA	2.8297	1
Miami – Fort Lauderdale, FL	2.6126	2
San Francisco – Oakland – San Jose, CA	2.2554	3
Laredo, TX	2.2201	4
Salinas – Seaside – Monterey, CA	2.0503	5
Stockton, CA	1.9864	6
New York – Northern New Jersey – Long Island, NY – NJ – CT	1.9291	7
Fresno, CA	1.8400	8
Merced, CA	1.7545	9
McAllen – Edinburg – Mission, TX	1.7372	10
Visalia – Tulare – Porterville, CA	1.6956	11
San Diego, CA	1.6737	12
El Paso, TX	1.6614	13
Honolulu, HI	1.6335	14
Brownsville – Harlingen, TX	1.5943	15
Santa Barbara – Santa Maria – Lompoc, CA	1.5635	16
Modesto, CA	1.5494	17
Washington, DC – MD – VA	1.5099	18
Houston – Galveston – Brazoria, TX	1.3893	19
Las Cruces, NM	1.3733	20
Bakersfield, CA	1.3320	21
Yakima, WA	1.1948	22
Yuma, AZ	1.1600	23
Dallas – Fort Worth, TX	1.1106	24
Reno, NV	1.0174	25
Boston – Lawrence – Salem, MA – NH	0.9563	26
West Palm Beach – Boca Raton – Delray Beach, FL	0.9350	27
Sacramento, CA	0.8870	28
Chicago – Gary – Lake County, IL – IN – WI	0.8794	29
Naples, FL	0.8113	30
Austin, TX	0.8053	31
Yuba City, CA	0.7868	32
Bryan – College Station, TX	0.7738	33
Las Vegas, NV	0.7716	34
Champaign – Urbana – Rantoul, IL	0.7484	35
Richland – Kennewick – Pasco, WA	0.7392	36
New Bedford, MA	0.7382	37
Seattle – Tacoma, WA	0.7218	38
Providence – Pawtucket – Fall River, RI – MA	0.7131	39
Phoenix, AZ	0.6753	40
Anchorage, AK	0.6649	41
San Antonio, TX	0.6635	42
Gainesville, FL	0.6340	43
Tucson, AZ	0.5986	44
Orlando, FL	0.5938	45
Hartford – New Britain – Middletown, CT	0.5926	46

[Continued]

★443★

Immigrants Admitted: 1982 to 1984

[Continued]

MSA	% of total population	Rank
Portland – Vancouver, OR – WA	0.5315	47
Killeen – Temple, TX	0.5296	48
Midland, TX	0.5159	49
Iowa City, IA	0.5119	50

Source: U.S. Bureau of the Census, Data User Services Division, *1990 Census of Population and Housing*, Summary Tape File 3C, United States Summary, CD-ROM, February 1992.

★444★

Immigrants Admitted, By Time Period

Immigrants Admitted: 1985 to 1986

[Table shows the top 50 areas]

MSA	% of total population	Rank
Los Angeles – Anaheim – Riverside, CA	2.8784	1
Miami – Fort Lauderdale, FL	2.6430	2
Fresno, CA	2.1170	3
Salinas – Seaside – Monterey, CA	2.1088	4
Stockton, CA	2.0658	5
Visalia – Tulare – Porterville, CA	1.9829	6
Merced, CA	1.9803	7
San Francisco – Oakland – San Jose, CA	1.8884	8
Laredo, TX	1.8831	9
New York – Northern New Jersey – Long Island, NY – NJ – CT	1.7774	10
Santa Barbara – Santa Maria – Lompoc, CA	1.7681	11
McAllen – Edinburg – Mission, TX	1.7651	12
San Diego, CA	1.7086	13
Yuma, AZ	1.5838	14
El Paso, TX	1.5334	15
Modesto, CA	1.5224	16
Yuba City, CA	1.4783	17
Yakima, WA	1.4495	18
Naples, FL	1.4458	19
Washington, DC – MD – VA	1.4340	20
Brownsville – Harlingen, TX	1.4086	21
Bakersfield, CA	1.3526	22
Honolulu, HI	1.3491	23
Houston – Galveston – Brazoria, TX	1.1182	24
West Palm Beach – Boca Raton – Delray Beach, FL	1.0783	25
Reno, NV	0.9911	26
Richland – Kennewick – Pasco, WA	0.9805	27
Las Cruces, NM	0.9756	28
Bryan – College Station, TX	0.9018	29
Boston – Lawrence – Salem, MA – NH	0.9009	30
Chicago – Gary – Lake County, IL – IN – WI	0.8861	31
Dallas – Fort Worth, TX	0.8814	32

[Continued]

★444★

Immigrants Admitted: 1985 or 1986

[Continued]

MSA	% of total population	Rank
Iowa City, IA	0.8281	33
Las Vegas, NV	0.8026	34
Tucson, AZ	0.7896	35
Phoenix, AZ	0.7895	36
Austin, TX	0.7600	37
Providence – Pawtucket – Fall River, RI – MA	0.7578	38
Sacramento, CA	0.7260	39
New Bedford, MA	0.6630	40
Champaign – Urbana – Rantoul, IL	0.6548	41
Salem, OR	0.6435	42
State College, PA	0.6406	43
Columbia, MO	0.6256	44
Tyler, TX	0.6107	45
Lawrence, KS	0.6076	46
Anchorage, AK	0.5872	47
Seattle – Tacoma, WA	0.5694	48
Lafayette – West Lafayette, IN	0.5674	49
Chico, CA	0.5590	50

Source: U.S. Bureau of the Census, Data User Services Division, *1990 Census of Population and Housing,* Summary Tape File 3C, United States Summary, CD-ROM, February 1992.

★445★

Immigrants Admitted, By Time Period

Immigrants Admitted: Before 1950

[Table shows the top 50 areas]

MSA	% of total population	Rank
West Palm Beach – Boca Raton – Delray Beach, FL	2.563	1
Laredo, TX	2.231	2
Sarasota, FL	2.197	3
McAllen – Edinburg – Mission, TX	2.145	4
New York – Northern New Jersey – Long Island, NY – NJ – CT	2.035	5
Lewiston – Auburn, ME	2.034	6
Brownsville – Harlingen, TX	1.964	7
Miami – Fort Lauderdale, FL	1.952	8
New Bedford, MA	1.896	9
Waterbury, CT	1.873	10
El Paso, TX	1.737	11
Daytona Beach, FL	1.618	12
Fitchburg – Leominster, MA	1.616	13
Fort Pierce, FL	1.572	14
Tampa – Saint Petersburg – Clearwater, FL	1.571	15
Bradenton, FL	1.560	16
Hartford – New Britain – Middletown, CT	1.508	17
Manchester, NH	1.495	18
Boston – Lawrence – Salem, MA – NH	1.493	19
Providence – Pawtucket – Fall River, RI – MA	1.462	20

[Continued]

★445★

Immigrants Admitted: Before 1950

[Continued]

MSA	% of total population	Rank
Bellingham, WA	1.444	21
Santa Barbara – Santa Maria – Lompoc, CA	1.431	22
Pittsfield, MA	1.425	23
Fort Myers – Cape Coral, Fl	1.407	24
Springfield, MA	1.360	25
Detroit – Ann Arbor, MI	1.309	26
Honolulu, HI	1.304	27
San Francisco – Oakland – San Jose, CA	1.291	28
Buffalo – Niagara Falls, NY	1.290	29
Naples, FL	1.286	30
Poughkeepsie, NY	1.259	31
Worcester, MA	1.257	32
New Haven – Meriden, CT	1.238	33
Salinas – Seaside – Monterey, CA	1.234	34
Stockton, CA	1.172	35
Fresno, CA	1.148	36
Albany – Schenectady – Troy, NY	1.130	37
Rochester, NY	1.114	38
New London – Norwich, CT – RI	1.094	39
Atlantic City, NJ	1.057	40
Utica – Rome, NY	1.036	41
Chicago – Gary – Lake County, IL – IN – WI	1.031	42
Los Angeles – Anaheim – Riverside, CA	1.019	43
Tucson, AZ	1.017	44
Cleveland – Akron – Lorain, OH	1.008	45
San Diego, CA	0.964	46
Visalia – Tulare – Porterville, CA	0.964	46
Ocala, FL	0.949	47
Portland, ME	0.944	48
Youngstown – Warren, OH	0.944	48

Source: U.S. Bureau of the Census, Data User Services Division, *1990 Census of Population and Housing,* Summary Tape File 3C, United States Summary, CD-ROM, February 1992.

★446★

Naturalized Citizens

Naturalized Citizens, 1994, By Selected Country of Former Allegiance: All Countries

The total number of citizens naturalized in the United States in fiscal year 1994 is 407,398. The number of naturalized citizens living in metropolitan areas that are not MSAs is 17,722; in "other" MSAs, 53,181; in "unknown areas," 22,196.

City/MSA	Number	Rank
Atlanta, GA	4,286	22
Baltimore, MD	2,400	30
Bergen-Passaic, NJ	5,994	13
Boston-Lawrence-Lowell-Brockton, MA	10,822	9
Bridgeport-Stamford-Norwalk-Danbury, CT	2,100	34

[Continued]

★446★

Naturalized Citizens, 1994, By Selected Country of Former Allegiance: All Countries
[Continued]

City/MSA	Number	Rank
Chicago, IL	16,430	4
Cleveland-Lorain-Elyria, OH	1,790	40
Dallas, TX	4,423	21
Denver, CO	1,965	36
Detroit, MI	5,866	15
Fort Lauderdale, FL	5,101	17
Fort Worth-Arlington, TX	1,738	41
Fresno, CA	2,062	35
Hartford, CT	2,146	33
Honolulu, HI	3,991	24
Houston, TX	10,865	8
Jersey City, NJ	4,603	19
Las Vegas, NV	1,164	46
Lincoln, NE	3,762	25
Los Angeles-Long Beach, CA	24,221	2
Miami, FL	20,540	3
Middlesex-Somerset-Hunterdon, NJ	3,703	26
Minneapolis-Saint Paul, MN-WI	2,576	28
Modesto, CA	1,160	47
Monmouth-Ocean, NJ	1,027	50
Nassau-Suffolk, NY	5,989	14
New Bedford-Fall River-Attleboro, MA	1,810	39
New Orleans, LA	1,108	48
New York, NY	56,971	1
Newark, NJ	7,275	11
Oakland, CA	9,945	10
Orange County, CA	5,782	16
Orlando, FL	2,355	31
Philadelphia, PA-NJ	7,268	12
Phoenix-Mesa, AZ	1,900	38
Portland-Vancouver, OR-WA	1,948	37
Providence-Warwick-Pawtucket, RI	2,217	32
Riverside-San Bernardino, CA	3,095	27
Sacramento, CA	4,106	23
San Antonio, TX	1,477	44
San Diego, CA	4,443	20
San Francisco, CA	12,809	6
San Jose, CA	11,460	7
Seattle-Bellevue-Everett, WA	5,028	18
Stockton-Lodi, CA	1,659	42
Tampa-Saint Petersburg-Clearwater, FL	1,539	43
Vallejo-Fairfield-Napa, CA	1,422	45
Washington, DC-MD-VA	14,368	5
West Palm Beach-Boca Raton, FL	2,499	29
Worcester-Fitchburg-Leominster, MA	1,091	49

Source: U.S. Department of Justice, Immigration and Naturalization Service, *Statistical Yearbook of the Immigration and Naturalization Service, 1994,* Washington, D.C.: U.S. Government Printing Office, 1996, p. 146.

★447★

Naturalized Citizens

Naturalized Citizens, 1994, By Selected Country of Former Allegiance: Canada

The total number of citizens from Canada naturalized in the United States in fiscal year 1994 is 8,782. The number of naturalized citizens living in metropolitan areas that are not MSAs is 1,011; in "other" MSAs, 2,412; in "unknown areas," 375.

City/MSA	Number	Rank
Atlanta, GA	132	11
Baltimore, MD	57	33
Bergen-Passaic, NJ	61	32
Boston-Lawrence-Lowell-Brockton, MA	321	2
Bridgeport-Stamford-Norwalk-Danbury, CT	96	20
Chicago, IL	175	8
Cleveland-Lorain-Elyria, OH	66	31
Dallas, TX	94	21
Denver, CO	101	19
Detroit, MI	448	1
Fort Lauderdale, FL	234	4
Fort Worth-Arlington, TX	40	37
Fresno, CA	6	45
Hartford, CT	123	15
Honolulu, HI	41	36
Houston, TX	92	22
Jersey City, NJ	8	43
Las Vegas, NV	38	38
Lincoln, NE	2	47
Los Angeles-Long Beach, CA	220	6
Miami, FL	76	26
Middlesex-Somerset-Hunterdon, NJ	50	35
Minneapolis-Saint Paul, MN-WI	128	13
Modesto, CA	7	44
Monmouth-Ocean, NJ	29	40
Nassau-Suffolk, NY	88	23
New Bedford-Fall River-Attleboro, MA	36	39
New Orleans, LA	6	45
New York, NY	279	3
Newark, NJ	56	34
Oakland, CA	163	9
Orange County, CA	114	16
Orlando, FL	69	30
Philadelphia, PA-NJ	131	12
Phoenix-Mesa, AZ	127	14
Portland-Vancouver, OR-WA	105	18
Providence-Warwick-Pawtucket, RI	36	39
Riverside-San Bernardino, CA	73	28
Sacramento, CA	38	38
San Antonio, TX	12	42
San Diego, CA	82	24
San Francisco, CA	198	7
San Jose, CA	74	27
Seattle-Bellevue-Everett, WA	227	5
Stockton-Lodi, CA	4	46
Tampa-Saint Petersburg-Clearwater, FL	71	29
Vallejo-Fairfield-Napa, CA	25	41

[Continued]

★447★

Naturalized Citizens, 1994, By Selected Country of Former Allegiance: Canada
[Continued]

City/MSA	Number	Rank
Washington, DC-MD-VA	134	10
West Palm Beach-Boca Raton, FL	113	17
Worcester-Fitchburg-Leominster, MA	78	25

Source: U.S. Department of Justice, Immigration and Naturalization Service, *Statistical Yearbook of the Immigration and Naturalization Service, 1994*, Washington, D.C.: U.S. Government Printing Office, 1996, p. 146.

★448★
Naturalized Citizens

Naturalized Citizens, 1994, By Selected Country of Former Allegiance: China (Mainland)

The total number of citizens from Mainland China naturalized in the United States in fiscal year 1994 is 20,828. The number of naturalized citizens living in metropolitan areas that are not MSAs is 398; in "other" MSAs, 1,593; in "unknown areas," 846.

City/MSA	Number	Rank
Atlanta, GA	114	19
Baltimore, MD	107	20
Bergen-Passaic, NJ	79	24
Boston-Lawrence-Lowell-Brockton, MA	1,037	5
Bridgeport-Stamford-Norwalk-Danbury, CT	28	42
Chicago, IL	695	7
Cleveland-Lorain-Elyria, OH	71	26
Dallas, TX	76	25
Denver, CO	62	30
Detroit, MI	126	18
Fort Lauderdale, FL	70	27
Fort Worth-Arlington, TX	22	45
Fresno, CA	56	32
Hartford, CT	26	43
Honolulu, HI	350	11
Houston, TX	346	12
Jersey City, NJ	57	31
Las Vegas, NV	40	37
Lincoln, NE	3	48
Los Angeles-Long Beach, CA	1,386	3
Miami, FL	98	21
Middlesex-Somerset-Hunterdon, NJ	114	19
Minneapolis-Saint Paul, MN-WI	67	28
Modesto, CA	25	44
Monmouth-Ocean, NJ	54	33
Nassau-Suffolk, NY	155	14
New Bedford-Fall River-Attleboro, MA	8	47
New Orleans, LA	30	40
New York, NY	4,689	1
Newark, NJ	134	17
Oakland, CA	1,223	4

[Continued]

★448★

Naturalized Citizens, 1994, By Selected Country of Former Allegiance: China (Mainland)
[Continued]

City/MSA	Number	Rank
Orange County, CA	152	15
Orlando, FL	49	35
Philadelphia, PA-NJ	356	10
Phoenix-Mesa, AZ	90	22
Portland-Vancouver, OR-WA	141	16
Providence-Warwick-Pawtucket, RI	66	29
Riverside-San Bernardino, CA	51	34
Sacramento, CA	315	13
San Antonio, TX	19	46
San Diego, CA	87	23
San Francisco, CA	3,409	2
San Jose, CA	776	6
Seattle-Bellevue-Everett, WA	423	9
Stockton-Lodi, CA	57	31
Tampa-Saint Petersburg-Clearwater, FL	47	36
Vallejo-Fairfield-Napa, CA	29	41
Washington, DC-MD-VA	508	8
West Palm Beach-Boca Raton, FL	37	38
Worcester-Fitchburg-Leominster, MA	31	39

Source: U.S. Department of Justice, Immigration and Naturalization Service, *Statistical Yearbook of the Immigration and Naturalization Service, 1994*, Washington, D.C.: U.S. Government Printing Office, 1996, p. 146.

★449★
Naturalized Citizens

Naturalized Citizens, 1994, By Selected Country of Former Allegiance: Colombia

The total number of citizens from Colombia naturalized in the United States in fiscal year 1994 is 12,067. The number of naturalized citizens living in metropolitan areas that are not MSAs is 243; in "other" MSAs, 830; in "unknown areas," 373.

City/MSA	Number	Rank
Atlanta, GA	144	16
Baltimore, MD	36	26
Bergen-Passaic, NJ	592	3
Boston-Lawrence-Lowell-Brockton, MA	188	14
Bridgeport-Stamford-Norwalk-Danbury, CT	129	17
Chicago, IL	318	9
Cleveland-Lorain-Elyria, OH	24	33
Dallas, TX	51	24
Denver, CO	21	35
Detroit, MI	17	37
Fort Lauderdale, FL	515	5
Fort Worth-Arlington, TX	26	32
Fresno, CA	7	43
Hartford, CT	63	21
Honolulu, HI	5	44

[Continued]

Naturalized Citizens, 1994, By Selected Country of Former Allegiance: Colombia
[Continued]

City/MSA	Number	Rank
Houston, TX	361	7
Jersey City, NJ	346	8
Las Vegas, NV	22	34
Lincoln, NE	1	45
Los Angeles-Long Beach, CA	306	10
Miami, FL	1,949	2
Middlesex-Somerset-Hunterdon, NJ	127	18
Minneapolis-Saint Paul, MN-WI	21	35
Modesto, CA	11	40
Monmouth-Ocean, NJ	28	30
Nassau-Suffolk, NY	370	6
New Bedford-Fall River-Attleboro, MA	9	42
New Orleans, LA	35	27
New York, NY	2,791	1
Newark, NJ	569	4
Oakland, CA	52	23
Orange County, CA	74	20
Orlando, FL	198	13
Philadelphia, PA-NJ	127	18
Phoenix-Mesa, AZ	29	29
Portland-Vancouver, OR-WA	16	38
Providence-Warwick-Pawtucket, RI	167	15
Riverside-San Bernardino, CA	43	25
Sacramento, CA	12	39
San Antonio, TX	27	31
San Diego, CA	24	33
San Francisco, CA	62	22
San Jose, CA	32	28
Seattle-Bellevue-Everett, WA	22	34
Stockton-Lodi, CA	5	44
Tampa-Saint Petersburg-Clearwater, FL	103	19
Vallejo-Fairfield-Napa, CA	10	41
Washington, DC-MD-VA	298	11
West Palm Beach-Boca Raton, FL	218	12
Worcester-Fitchburg-Leominster, MA	20	36

Source: U.S. Department of Justice, Immigration and Naturalization Service, *Statistical Yearbook of the Immigration and Naturalization Service, 1994,* Washington, D.C.: U.S. Government Printing Office, 1996, p. 146.

Naturalized Citizens, 1994, By Selected Country of Former Allegiance: Cuba

The total number of citizens from Cuba naturalized in the United States in fiscal year 1994 is 15,896. The number of naturalized citizens living in metropolitan areas that are not MSAs is 193; in "other" MSAs, 466; in "unknown areas," 432.

City/MSA	Number	Rank
Atlanta, GA	62	15
Baltimore, MD	3	37
Bergen-Passaic, NJ	138	10
Boston-Lawrence-Lowell-Brockton, MA	45	20
Bridgeport-Stamford-Norwalk-Danbury, CT	24	26
Chicago, IL	137	11
Cleveland-Lorain-Elyria, OH	2	38
Dallas, TX	33	23
Denver, CO	2	38
Detroit, MI	15	27
Fort Lauderdale, FL	330	7
Fort Worth-Arlington, TX	13	28
Fresno, CA	2	38
Hartford, CT	7	33
Honolulu, HI	0	40
Houston, TX	109	12
Jersey City, NJ	713	2
Las Vegas, NV	60	16
Lincoln, NE	0	40
Los Angeles-Long Beach, CA	564	4
Miami, FL	10,131	1
Middlesex-Somerset-Hunterdon, NJ	51	18
Minneapolis-Saint Paul, MN-WI	6	34
Modesto, CA	1	39
Monmouth-Ocean, NJ	10	30
Nassau-Suffolk, NY	51	18
New Bedford-Fall River-Attleboro, MA	0	40
New Orleans, LA	48	19
New York, NY	656	3
Newark, NJ	376	5
Oakland, CA	36	22
Orange County, CA	63	14
Orlando, FL	147	9
Philadelphia, PA-NJ	32	24
Phoenix-Mesa, AZ	10	30
Portland-Vancouver, OR-WA	12	29
Providence-Warwick-Pawtucket, RI	8	32
Riverside-San Bernardino, CA	53	17
Sacramento, CA	5	35
San Antonio, TX	3	37
San Diego, CA	4	36
San Francisco, CA	37	21
San Jose, CA	31	25
Seattle-Bellevue-Everett, WA	12	29
Stockton-Lodi, CA	2	38
Tampa-Saint Petersburg-Clearwater, FL	325	8
Vallejo-Fairfield-Napa, CA	3	37

[Continued]

★450★

Naturalized Citizens, 1994, By Selected Country of Former Allegiance: Cuba
[Continued]

City/MSA	Number	Rank
Washington, DC-MD-VA	67	13
West Palm Beach-Boca Raton, FL	357	6
Worcester-Fitchburg-Leominster, MA	9	31

Source: U.S. Department of Justice, Immigration and Naturalization Service, *Statistical Yearbook of the Immigration and Naturalization Service, 1994,* Washington, D.C.: U.S. Government Printing Office, 1996, p. 146.

★451★

Naturalized Citizens

Naturalized Citizens, 1994, By Selected Country of Former Allegiance: Dominican Republic

The total number of citizens from the Dominican Republic naturalized in the United States in fiscal year 1994 is 11,399. The number of naturalized citizens living in metropolitan areas that are not MSAs is 404; in "other" MSAs, 842; in "unknown areas," 268.

City/MSA	Number	Rank
Atlanta, GA	28	18
Baltimore, MD	13	21
Bergen-Passaic, NJ	389	5
Boston-Lawrence-Lowell-Brockton, MA	530	3
Bridgeport-Stamford-Norwalk-Danbury, CT	47	15
Chicago, IL	41	16
Cleveland-Lorain-Elyria, OH	12	22
Dallas, TX	13	21
Denver, CO	3	29
Detroit, MI	5	27
Fort Lauderdale, FL	110	10
Fort Worth-Arlington, TX	5	27
Fresno, CA	0	32
Hartford, CT	10	23
Honolulu, HI	5	27
Houston, TX	39	17
Jersey City, NJ	433	4
Las Vegas, NV	0	32
Lincoln, NE	0	32
Los Angeles-Long Beach, CA	22	20
Miami, FL	643	2
Middlesex-Somerset-Hunterdon, NJ	109	11
Minneapolis-Saint Paul, MN-WI	6	26
Modesto, CA	0	32
Monmouth-Ocean, NJ	12	22
Nassau-Suffolk, NY	197	7
New Bedford-Fall River-Attleboro, MA	8	24
New Orleans, LA	1	31
New York, NY	6,388	1
Newark, NJ	206	6
Oakland, CA	6	26

[Continued]

★451★

Naturalized Citizens, 1994, By Selected Country of Former Allegiance: Dominican Republic
[Continued]

City/MSA	Number	Rank
Orange County, CA	7	25
Orlando, FL	86	12
Philadelphia, PA-NJ	50	14
Phoenix-Mesa, AZ	4	28
Portland-Vancouver, OR-WA	1	31
Providence-Warwick-Pawtucket, RI	183	8
Riverside-San Bernardino, CA	6	26
Sacramento, CA	0	32
San Antonio, TX	6	26
San Diego, CA	7	25
San Francisco, CA	6	26
San Jose, CA	3	29
Seattle-Bellevue-Everett, WA	1	31
Stockton-Lodi, CA	2	30
Tampa-Saint Petersburg-Clearwater, FL	25	19
Vallejo-Fairfield-Napa, CA	0	32
Washington, DC-MD-VA	130	9
West Palm Beach-Boca Raton, FL	59	13
Worcester-Fitchburg-Leominster, MA	28	18

Source: U.S. Department of Justice, Immigration and Naturalization Service, *Statistical Yearbook of the Immigration and Naturalization Service, 1994,* Washington, D.C.: U.S. Government Printing Office, 1996, p. 146.

★452★

Naturalized Citizens

Naturalized Citizens, 1994, By Selected Country of Former Allegiance: Guyana

The total number of citizens from Guyana naturalized in the United States in fiscal year 1994 is 6,066. The number of naturalized citizens living in metropolitan areas that are not MSAs is 52; in "other" MSAs, 237; in "unknown areas," 69.

City/MSA	Number	Rank
Atlanta, GA	58	10
Baltimore, MD	19	20
Bergen-Passaic, NJ	31	16
Boston-Lawrence-Lowell-Brockton, MA	46	14
Bridgeport-Stamford-Norwalk-Danbury, CT	8	29
Chicago, IL	16	23
Cleveland-Lorain-Elyria, OH	23	17
Dallas, TX	10	27
Denver, CO	5	32
Detroit, MI	17	22
Fort Lauderdale, FL	89	7
Fort Worth-Arlington, TX	6	31
Fresno, CA	1	36
Hartford, CT	54	12
Honolulu, HI	2	35

[Continued]

★452★
Naturalized Citizens, 1994, By Selected Country of Former Allegiance: Guyana
[Continued]

City/MSA	Number	Rank
Houston, TX	32	15
Jersey City, NJ	146	4
Las Vegas, NV	0	37
Lincoln, NE	0	37
Los Angeles-Long Beach, CA	21	18
Miami, FL	84	8
Middlesex-Somerset-Hunterdon, NJ	55	11
Minneapolis-Saint Paul, MN-WI	65	9
Modesto, CA	0	37
Monmouth-Ocean, NJ	11	26
Nassau-Suffolk, NY	138	5
New Bedford-Fall River-Attleboro, MA	0	37
New Orleans, LA	4	33
New York, NY	3,892	1
Newark, NJ	315	2
Oakland, CA	20	19
Orange County, CA	3	34
Orlando, FL	98	6
Philadelphia, PA-NJ	48	13
Phoenix-Mesa, AZ	2	35
Portland-Vancouver, OR-WA	0	37
Providence-Warwick-Pawtucket, RI	1	36
Riverside-San Bernardino, CA	4	33
Sacramento, CA	0	37
San Antonio, TX	1	36
San Diego, CA	6	31
San Francisco, CA	9	28
San Jose, CA	2	35
Seattle-Bellevue-Everett, WA	3	34
Stockton-Lodi, CA	0	37
Tampa-Saint Petersburg-Clearwater, FL	13	25
Vallejo-Fairfield-Napa, CA	7	30
Washington, DC-MD-VA	311	3
West Palm Beach-Boca Raton, FL	14	24
Worcester-Fitchburg-Leominster, MA	18	21

Source: U.S. Department of Justice, Immigration and Naturalization Service, *Statistical Yearbook of the Immigration and Naturalization Service, 1994*, Washington, D.C.: U.S. Government Printing Office, 1996, p. 146.

★453★
Naturalized Citizens
Naturalized Citizens, 1994, By Selected Country of Former Allegiance: Haiti

The total number of citizens from Haiti naturalized in the United States in fiscal year 1994 is 7,982. The number of naturalized citizens living in metropolitan areas that are not MSAs is 68; in "other" MSAs, 263; in "unknown areas," 84.

City/MSA	Number	Rank
Atlanta, GA	25	16
Baltimore, MD	10	21
Bergen-Passaic, NJ	24	17
Boston-Lawrence-Lowell-Brockton, MA	715	3
Bridgeport-Stamford-Norwalk-Danbury, CT	184	8
Chicago, IL	76	12
Cleveland-Lorain-Elyria, OH	2	28
Dallas, TX	4	26
Denver, CO	3	27
Detroit, MI	9	22
Fort Lauderdale, FL	403	5
Fort Worth-Arlington, TX	1	29
Fresno, CA	1	29
Hartford, CT	16	18
Honolulu, HI	0	30
Houston, TX	7	23
Jersey City, NJ	44	14
Las Vegas, NV	1	29
Lincoln, NE	0	30
Los Angeles-Long Beach, CA	12	20
Miami, FL	1,199	2
Middlesex-Somerset-Hunterdon, NJ	25	16
Minneapolis-Saint Paul, MN-WI	5	25
Modesto, CA	0	30
Monmouth-Ocean, NJ	54	13
Nassau-Suffolk, NY	319	6
New Bedford-Fall River-Attleboro, MA	4	26
New Orleans, LA	3	27
New York, NY	3,119	1
Newark, NJ	668	4
Oakland, CA	6	24
Orange County, CA	3	27
Orlando, FL	104	10
Philadelphia, PA-NJ	101	11
Phoenix-Mesa, AZ	1	29
Portland-Vancouver, OR-WA	1	29
Providence-Warwick-Pawtucket, RI	27	15
Riverside-San Bernardino, CA	3	27
Sacramento, CA	1	29
San Antonio, TX	1	29
San Diego, CA	0	30
San Francisco, CA	0	30
San Jose, CA	4	26
Seattle-Bellevue-Everett, WA	2	28
Stockton-Lodi, CA	0	30
Tampa-Saint Petersburg-Clearwater, FL	14	19
Vallejo-Fairfield-Napa, CA	0	30

[Continued]

★453★

Naturalized Citizens, 1994, By Selected Country of Former Allegiance: Haiti

[Continued]

City/MSA	Number	Rank
Washington, DC-MD-VA	152	9
West Palm Beach-Boca Raton, FL	204	7
Worcester-Fitchburg-Leominster, MA	10	21

Source: U.S. Department of Justice, Immigration and Naturalization Service, *Statistical Yearbook of the Immigration and Naturalization Service, 1994,* Washington, D.C.: U.S. Government Printing Office, 1996, p. 146.

★454★

Naturalized Citizens

Naturalized Citizens, 1994, By Selected Country of Former Allegiance: India

The total number of citizens from India naturalized in the United States in fiscal year 1994 is 20,454. The number of naturalized citizens living in metropolitan areas that are not MSAs is 816; in "other" MSAs, 3,892; in "unknown areas," 691.

City/MSA	Number	Rank
Atlanta, GA	376	15
Baltimore, MD	242	18
Bergen-Passaic, NJ	499	11
Boston-Lawrence-Lowell-Brockton, MA	540	9
Bridgeport-Stamford-Norwalk-Danbury, CT	158	23
Chicago, IL	1,699	1
Cleveland-Lorain-Elyria, OH	160	22
Dallas, TX	351	17
Denver, CO	63	38
Detroit, MI	502	10
Fort Lauderdale, FL	89	32
Fort Worth-Arlington, TX	79	35
Fresno, CA	155	24
Hartford, CT	125	26
Honolulu, HI	15	48
Houston, TX	660	6
Jersey City, NJ	375	16
Las Vegas, NV	21	46
Lincoln, NE	5	49
Los Angeles-Long Beach, CA	469	13
Miami, FL	93	30
Middlesex-Somerset-Hunterdon, NJ	900	4
Minneapolis-Saint Paul, MN-WI	104	27
Modesto, CA	84	34
Monmouth-Ocean, NJ	101	28
Nassau-Suffolk, NY	433	14
New Bedford-Fall River-Attleboro, MA	18	47
New Orleans, LA	46	41
New York, NY	1,672	2
Newark, NJ	494	12
Oakland, CA	586	8

[Continued]

★454★

Naturalized Citizens, 1994, By Selected Country of Former Allegiance: India

[Continued]

City/MSA	Number	Rank
Orange County, CA	196	19
Orlando, FL	92	31
Philadelphia, PA-NJ	798	5
Phoenix-Mesa, AZ	87	33
Portland-Vancouver, OR-WA	38	45
Providence-Warwick-Pawtucket, RI	45	42
Riverside-San Bernardino, CA	92	31
Sacramento, CA	194	20
San Antonio, TX	41	43
San Diego, CA	39	44
San Francisco, CA	168	21
San Jose, CA	643	7
Seattle-Bellevue-Everett, WA	146	25
Stockton-Lodi, CA	97	29
Tampa-Saint Petersburg-Clearwater, FL	56	39
Vallejo-Fairfield-Napa, CA	48	40
Washington, DC-MD-VA	1,021	3
West Palm Beach-Boca Raton, FL	74	36
Worcester-Fitchburg-Leominster, MA	66	37

Source: U.S. Department of Justice, Immigration and Naturalization Service, *Statistical Yearbook of the Immigration and Naturalization Service, 1994,* Washington, D.C.: U.S. Government Printing Office, 1996, p. 146.

★455★

Naturalized Citizens

Naturalized Citizens, 1994, By Selected Country of Former Allegiance: Iran

The total number of citizens from Iran naturalized in the United States in fiscal year 1994 is 8,746. The number of naturalized citizens living in metropolitan areas that are not MSAs is 169; in "other" MSAs, 1,293; in "unknown areas," 771.

City/MSA	Number	Rank
Atlanta, GA	154	12
Baltimore, MD	102	17
Bergen-Passaic, NJ	71	21
Boston-Lawrence-Lowell-Brockton, MA	177	11
Bridgeport-Stamford-Norwalk-Danbury, CT	27	33
Chicago, IL	178	10
Cleveland-Lorain-Elyria, OH	19	38
Dallas, TX	194	9
Denver, CO	67	23
Detroit, MI	45	27
Fort Lauderdale, FL	39	29
Fort Worth-Arlington, TX	51	26
Fresno, CA	30	31
Hartford, CT	28	32
Honolulu, HI	8	42

[Continued]

★455★

Naturalized Citizens, 1994, By Selected Country of Former Allegiance: Iran

[Continued]

City/MSA	Number	Rank
Houston, TX	259	6
Jersey City, NJ	5	43
Las Vegas, NV	27	33
Lincoln, NE	4	44
Los Angeles-Long Beach, CA	1,312	1
Miami, FL	75	18
Middlesex-Somerset-Hunterdon, NJ	26	34
Minneapolis-Saint Paul, MN-WI	70	22
Modesto, CA	62	24
Monmouth-Ocean, NJ	15	39
Nassau-Suffolk, NY	255	7
New Bedford-Fall River-Attleboro, MA	5	43
New Orleans, LA	9	41
New York, NY	310	3
Newark, NJ	31	30
Oakland, CA	264	4
Orange County, CA	262	5
Orlando, FL	55	25
Philadelphia, PA-NJ	103	16
Phoenix-Mesa, AZ	67	23
Portland-Vancouver, OR-WA	73	20
Providence-Warwick-Pawtucket, RI	13	40
Riverside-San Bernardino, CA	43	28
Sacramento, CA	137	14
San Antonio, TX	23	36
San Diego, CA	144	13
San Francisco, CA	239	8
San Jose, CA	460	2
Seattle-Bellevue-Everett, WA	128	15
Stockton-Lodi, CA	8	42
Tampa-Saint Petersburg-Clearwater, FL	25	35
Vallejo-Fairfield-Napa, CA	21	37
Washington, DC-MD-VA	74	19
West Palm Beach-Boca Raton, FL	25	35
Worcester-Fitchburg-Leominster, MA	19	38

Source: U.S. Department of Justice, Immigration and Naturalization Service, *Statistical Yearbook of the Immigration and Naturalization Service, 1994*, Washington, D.C.: U.S. Government Printing Office, 1996, p. 146.

★456★

Naturalized Citizens

Naturalized Citizens, 1994, By Selected Country of Former Allegiance: Jamaica

The total number of citizens from Jamaica naturalized in the United States in fiscal year 1994 is 12,173. The number of naturalized citizens living in metropolitan areas that are not MSAs is 183; in "other" MSAs, 766; in "unknown areas," 137.

City/MSA	Number	Rank
Atlanta, GA	177	14
Baltimore, MD	106	16
Bergen-Passaic, NJ	244	10
Boston-Lawrence-Lowell-Brockton, MA	212	11
Bridgeport-Stamford-Norwalk-Danbury, CT	178	13
Chicago, IL	121	15
Cleveland-Lorain-Elyria, OH	32	22
Dallas, TX	25	23
Denver, CO	3	35
Detroit, MI	51	20
Fort Lauderdale, FL	1,256	2
Fort Worth-Arlington, TX	6	32
Fresno, CA	4	34
Hartford, CT	416	5
Honolulu, HI	5	33
Houston, TX	85	18
Jersey City, NJ	21	24
Las Vegas, NV	4	34
Lincoln, NE	1	36
Los Angeles-Long Beach, CA	77	19
Miami, FL	1,226	3
Middlesex-Somerset-Hunterdon, NJ	96	17
Minneapolis-Saint Paul, MN-WI	8	30
Modesto, CA	0	37
Monmouth-Ocean, NJ	25	23
Nassau-Suffolk, NY	396	6
New Bedford-Fall River-Attleboro, MA	0	37
New Orleans, LA	3	35
New York, NY	4,568	1
Newark, NJ	381	7
Oakland, CA	19	25
Orange County, CA	6	32
Orlando, FL	196	12
Philadelphia, PA-NJ	279	8
Phoenix-Mesa, AZ	3	35
Portland-Vancouver, OR-WA	1	36
Providence-Warwick-Pawtucket, RI	10	29
Riverside-San Bernardino, CA	19	25
Sacramento, CA	14	26
San Antonio, TX	10	29
San Diego, CA	10	29
San Francisco, CA	12	27
San Jose, CA	7	31
Seattle-Bellevue-Everett, WA	12	27
Stockton-Lodi, CA	1	36
Tampa-Saint Petersburg-Clearwater, FL	46	21
Vallejo-Fairfield-Napa, CA	5	33

[Continued]

★456★

Naturalized Citizens, 1994, By Selected Country of Former Allegiance: Jamaica

[Continued]

City/MSA	Number	Rank
Washington, DC-MD-VA	443	4
West Palm Beach-Boca Raton, FL	256	9
Worcester-Fitchburg-Leominster, MA	11	28

Source: U.S. Department of Justice, Immigration and Naturalization Service, *Statistical Yearbook of the Immigration and Naturalization Service, 1994*, Washington, D.C.: U.S. Government Printing Office, 1996, p. 146.

★457★

Naturalized Citizens

Naturalized Citizens, 1994, By Selected Country of Former Allegiance: Korea

The total number of citizens from Korea naturalized in the United States in fiscal year 1994 is 11,389. The number of naturalized citizens living in metropolitan areas that are not MSAs is 547; in "other" MSAs, 1,842; in "unknown areas," 794.

City/MSA	Number	Rank
Atlanta, GA	259	10
Baltimore, MD	257	11
Bergen-Passaic, NJ	269	9
Boston-Lawrence-Lowell-Brockton, MA	101	20
Bridgeport-Stamford-Norwalk-Danbury, CT	13	39
Chicago, IL	544	4
Cleveland-Lorain-Elyria, OH	53	27
Dallas, TX	141	15
Denver, CO	105	18
Detroit, MI	96	21
Fort Lauderdale, FL	14	38
Fort Worth-Arlington, TX	29	33
Fresno, CA	26	34
Hartford, CT	11	40
Honolulu, HI	390	6
Houston, TX	142	14
Jersey City, NJ	38	31
Las Vegas, NV	40	29
Lincoln, NE	6	43
Los Angeles-Long Beach, CA	1,162	1
Miami, FL	11	40
Middlesex-Somerset-Hunterdon, NJ	73	23
Minneapolis-Saint Paul, MN-WI	63	25
Modesto, CA	4	45
Monmouth-Ocean, NJ	29	33
Nassau-Suffolk, NY	129	16
New Bedford-Fall River-Attleboro, MA	5	44
New Orleans, LA	9	41
New York, NY	948	2
Newark, NJ	84	22
Oakland, CA	189	12

[Continued]

★457★

Naturalized Citizens, 1994, By Selected Country of Former Allegiance: Korea

[Continued]

City/MSA	Number	Rank
Orange County, CA	277	7
Orlando, FL	39	30
Philadelphia, PA-NJ	405	5
Phoenix-Mesa, AZ	54	26
Portland-Vancouver, OR-WA	127	17
Providence-Warwick-Pawtucket, RI	4	45
Riverside-San Bernardino, CA	72	24
Sacramento, CA	103	19
San Antonio, TX	43	28
San Diego, CA	32	32
San Francisco, CA	152	13
San Jose, CA	405	5
Seattle-Bellevue-Everett, WA	274	8
Stockton-Lodi, CA	9	41
Tampa-Saint Petersburg-Clearwater, FL	18	36
Vallejo-Fairfield-Napa, CA	22	35
Washington, DC-MD-VA	906	3
West Palm Beach-Boca Raton, FL	7	42
Worcester-Fitchburg-Leominster, MA	17	37

Source: U.S. Department of Justice, Immigration and Naturalization Service, *Statistical Yearbook of the Immigration and Naturalization Service, 1994*, Washington, D.C.: U.S. Government Printing Office, 1996, p. 146.

★458★

Naturalized Citizens

Naturalized Citizens, 1994, By Selected Country of Former Allegiance: Mexico

The total number of citizens from Mexico naturalized in the United States in fiscal year 1994 is 39,310. The number of naturalized citizens living in metropolitan areas that are not MSAs is 3,627; in "other" MSAs, 7,649; in "unknown areas," 6,264.

City/MSA	Number	Rank
Atlanta, GA	79	25
Baltimore, MD	8	42
Bergen-Passaic, NJ	27	31
Boston-Lawrence-Lowell-Brockton, MA	22	34
Bridgeport-Stamford-Norwalk-Danbury, CT	7	43
Chicago, IL	3,498	2
Cleveland-Lorain-Elyria, OH	14	39
Dallas, TX	887	6
Denver, CO	309	16
Detroit, MI	106	22
Fort Lauderdale, FL	25	33
Fort Worth-Arlington, TX	302	18
Fresno, CA	638	9
Hartford, CT	11	41
Honolulu, HI	26	32

[Continued]

★458★

Naturalized Citizens, 1994, By Selected Country of Former Allegiance: Mexico
[Continued]

City/MSA	Number	Rank
Houston, TX	2,614	3
Jersey City, NJ	12	40
Las Vegas, NV	205	19
Lincoln, NE	11	41
Los Angeles-Long Beach, CA	5,613	1
Miami, FL	90	24
Middlesex-Somerset-Hunterdon, NJ	15	38
Minneapolis-Saint Paul, MN-WI	55	27
Modesto, CA	305	17
Monmouth-Ocean, NJ	6	44
Nassau-Suffolk, NY	20	35
New Bedford-Fall River-Attleboro, MA	0	47
New Orleans, LA	17	37
New York, NY	182	20
Newark, NJ	15	38
Oakland, CA	595	10
Orange County, CA	732	8
Orlando, FL	35	29
Philadelphia, PA-NJ	31	30
Phoenix-Mesa, AZ	420	12
Portland-Vancouver, OR-WA	47	28
Providence-Warwick-Pawtucket, RI	3	46
Riverside-San Bernardino, CA	1,066	4
Sacramento, CA	321	15
San Antonio, TX	807	7
San Diego, CA	988	5
San Francisco, CA	366	13
San Jose, CA	567	11
Seattle-Bellevue-Everett, WA	75	26
Stockton-Lodi, CA	326	14
Tampa-Saint Petersburg-Clearwater, FL	19	36
Vallejo-Fairfield-Napa, CA	123	21
Washington, DC-MD-VA	91	23
West Palm Beach-Boca Raton, FL	35	29
Worcester-Fitchburg-Leominster, MA	4	45

Source: U.S. Department of Justice, Immigration and Naturalization Service, *Statistical Yearbook of the Immigration and Naturalization Service, 1994,* Washington, D.C.: U.S. Government Printing Office, 1996, p. 146.

★459★
Naturalized Citizens

Naturalized Citizens, 1994, By Selected Country of Former Allegiance: Philippines

The total number of citizens from the Philippines naturalized in the United States in fiscal year 1994 is 37,304. The number of naturalized citizens living in metropolitan areas that are not MSAs is 3,054; in "other" MSAs, 4,150; in "unknown areas," 1,957.

City/MSA	Number	Rank
Atlanta, GA	103	34
Baltimore, MD	171	26
Bergen-Passaic, NJ	377	19
Boston-Lawrence-Lowell-Brockton, MA	152	29
Bridgeport-Stamford-Norwalk-Danbury, CT	35	46
Chicago, IL	1,482	7
Cleveland-Lorain-Elyria, OH	77	39
Dallas, TX	172	25
Denver, CO	89	37
Detroit, MI	238	22
Fort Lauderdale, FL	106	32
Fort Worth-Arlington, TX	53	42
Fresno, CA	104	33
Hartford, CT	45	44
Honolulu, HI	2,036	4
Houston, TX	448	14
Jersey City, NJ	472	13
Las Vegas, NV	227	24
Lincoln, NE	3,656	1
Los Angeles-Long Beach, CA	2,771	2
Miami, FL	164	28
Middlesex-Somerset-Hunterdon, NJ	235	23
Minneapolis-Saint Paul, MN-WI	88	38
Modesto, CA	35	46
Monmouth-Ocean, NJ	98	35
Nassau-Suffolk, NY	227	24
New Bedford-Fall River-Attleboro, MA	9	48
New Orleans, LA	52	43
New York, NY	1,466	8
Newark, NJ	400	18
Oakland, CA	1,950	5
Orange County, CA	437	16
Orlando, FL	97	36
Philadelphia, PA-NJ	416	17
Phoenix-Mesa, AZ	119	30
Portland-Vancouver, OR-WA	169	27
Providence-Warwick-Pawtucket, RI	37	45
Riverside-San Bernardino, CA	349	20
Sacramento, CA	438	15
San Antonio, TX	114	31
San Diego, CA	1,349	9
San Francisco, CA	2,353	3
San Jose, CA	1,785	6
Seattle-Bellevue-Everett, WA	941	10
Stockton-Lodi, CA	311	21
Tampa-Saint Petersburg-Clearwater, FL	66	41
Vallejo-Fairfield-Napa, CA	738	12

[Continued]

★459★

Naturalized Citizens, 1994, By Selected Country of Former Allegiance: Philippines

[Continued]

City/MSA	Number	Rank
Washington, DC-MD-VA	800	11
West Palm Beach-Boca Raton, FL	71	40
Worcester-Fitchburg-Leominster, MA	15	47

Source: U.S. Department of Justice, Immigration and Naturalization Service, *Statistical Yearbook of the Immigration and Naturalization Service, 1994*, Washington, D.C.: U.S. Government Printing Office, 1996, p. 146.

★460★

Naturalized Citizens

Naturalized Citizens, 1994, By Selected Country of Former Allegiance: Poland

The total number of citizens from Poland naturalized in the United States in fiscal year 1994 is 6,857. The number of naturalized citizens that are living in metropolitan areas that are not MSAs is 158; in "other" MSAs, 973; in "unknown areas," 147.

City/MSA	Number	Rank
Atlanta, GA	31	27
Baltimore, MD	43	22
Bergen-Passaic, NJ	242	5
Boston-Lawrence-Lowell-Brockton, MA	170	8
Bridgeport-Stamford-Norwalk-Danbury, CT	62	15
Chicago, IL	1,806	1
Cleveland-Lorain-Elyria, OH	81	12
Dallas, TX	26	28
Denver, CO	55	17
Detroit, MI	261	4
Fort Lauderdale, FL	41	24
Fort Worth-Arlington, TX	7	35
Fresno, CA	2	38
Hartford, CT	314	3
Honolulu, HI	6	36
Houston, TX	52	18
Jersey City, NJ	78	14
Las Vegas, NV	9	34
Lincoln, NE	3	37
Los Angeles-Long Beach, CA	80	13
Miami, FL	32	26
Middlesex-Somerset-Hunterdon, NJ	143	9
Minneapolis-Saint Paul, MN-WI	31	27
Modesto, CA	1	39
Monmouth-Ocean, NJ	32	26
Nassau-Suffolk, NY	103	10
New Bedford-Fall River-Attleboro, MA	12	33
New Orleans, LA	2	38
New York, NY	786	2
Newark, NJ	199	7
Oakland, CA	43	22

[Continued]

★460★

Naturalized Citizens, 1994, By Selected Country of Former Allegiance: Poland

[Continued]

City/MSA	Number	Rank
Orange County, CA	25	29
Orlando, FL	15	32
Philadelphia, PA-NJ	227	6
Phoenix-Mesa, AZ	26	28
Portland-Vancouver, OR-WA	19	30
Providence-Warwick-Pawtucket, RI	31	27
Riverside-San Bernardino, CA	9	34
Sacramento, CA	12	33
San Antonio, TX	16	31
San Diego, CA	44	21
San Francisco, CA	56	16
San Jose, CA	50	19
Seattle-Bellevue-Everett, WA	95	11
Stockton-Lodi, CA	0	40
Tampa-Saint Petersburg-Clearwater, FL	42	23
Vallejo-Fairfield-Napa, CA	3	37
Washington, DC-MD-VA	78	14
West Palm Beach-Boca Raton, FL	33	25
Worcester-Fitchburg-Leominster, MA	45	20

Source: U.S. Department of Justice, Immigration and Naturalization Service, *Statistical Yearbook of the Immigration and Naturalization Service, 1994*, Washington, D.C.: U.S. Government Printing Office, 1996, p. 146.

★461★

Naturalized Citizens

Naturalized Citizens, 1994, By Selected Country of Former Allegiance: Portugal

The total number of citizens from Portugal naturalized in the United States in fiscal year 1994 is 5,997. The number of naturalized citizens living in metropolitan areas that are not MSAs is 133; in "other" MSAs, 557; in "unknown areas," 180.

City/MSA	Number	Rank
Atlanta, GA	6	30
Baltimore, MD	3	33
Bergen-Passaic, NJ	53	16
Boston-Lawrence-Lowell-Brockton, MA	572	4
Bridgeport-Stamford-Norwalk-Danbury, CT	93	10
Chicago, IL	8	28
Cleveland-Lorain-Elyria, OH	3	33
Dallas, TX	5	31
Denver, CO	1	35
Detroit, MI	3	33
Fort Lauderdale, FL	7	29
Fort Worth-Arlington, TX	0	36
Fresno, CA	34	23
Hartford, CT	64	13
Honolulu, HI	3	33

[Continued]

★461★

Naturalized Citizens, 1994, By Selected Country of Former Allegiance: Portugal

[Continued]

City/MSA	Number	Rank
Houston, TX	7	29
Jersey City, NJ	155	8
Las Vegas, NV	2	34
Lincoln, NE	0	36
Los Angeles-Long Beach, CA	59	14
Miami, FL	18	25
Middlesex-Somerset-Hunterdon, NJ	85	11
Minneapolis-Saint Paul, MN-WI	3	33
Modesto, CA	221	5
Monmouth-Ocean, NJ	38	21
Nassau-Suffolk, NY	56	15
New Bedford-Fall River-Attleboro, MA	1,441	1
New Orleans, LA	1	35
New York, NY	167	7
Newark, NJ	628	3
Oakland, CA	174	6
Orange County, CA	5	31
Orlando, FL	12	27
Philadelphia, PA-NJ	44	19
Phoenix-Mesa, AZ	5	31
Portland-Vancouver, OR-WA	4	32
Providence-Warwick-Pawtucket, RI	672	2
Riverside-San Bernardino, CA	35	22
Sacramento, CA	32	24
San Antonio, TX	0	36
San Diego, CA	12	27
San Francisco, CA	78	12
San Jose, CA	136	9
Seattle-Bellevue-Everett, WA	12	27
Stockton-Lodi, CA	52	17
Tampa-Saint Petersburg-Clearwater, FL	4	32
Vallejo-Fairfield-Napa, CA	12	27
Washington, DC-MD-VA	45	18
West Palm Beach-Boca Raton, FL	14	26
Worcester-Fitchburg-Leominster, MA	43	20

Source: U.S. Department of Justice, Immigration and Naturalization Service, *Statistical Yearbook of the Immigration and Naturalization Service, 1994*, Washington, D.C.: U.S. Government Printing Office, 1996, p. 146.

★462★

Naturalized Citizens

Naturalized Citizens, 1994, By Selected Country of Former Allegiance: Taiwan

The total number of citizens from Taiwan naturalized in the United States in fiscal year 1994 is 9,450. The total provided by the source for non-MSAs is 230; for "other" MSAs, 1,065; for "unknown," 688.

City/MSA	Number	Rank
Atlanta, GA	125	16
Baltimore, MD	71	21
Bergen-Passaic, NJ	106	18
Boston-Lawrence-Lowell-Brockton, MA	154	13
Bridgeport-Stamford-Norwalk-Danbury, CT	18	35
Chicago, IL	188	11
Cleveland-Lorain-Elyria, OH	12	39
Dallas, TX	200	10
Denver, CO	38	29
Detroit, MI	74	20
Fort Lauderdale, FL	15	36
Fort Worth-Arlington, TX	59	23
Fresno, CA	18	35
Hartford, CT	22	33
Honolulu, HI	67	22
Houston, TX	273	8
Jersey City, NJ	19	34
Las Vegas, NV	25	32
Lincoln, NE	0	45
Los Angeles-Long Beach, CA	1,299	1
Miami, FL	18	35
Middlesex-Somerset-Hunterdon, NJ	214	9
Minneapolis-Saint Paul, MN-WI	28	31
Modesto, CA	1	44
Monmouth-Ocean, NJ	52	27
Nassau-Suffolk, NY	127	15
New Bedford-Fall River-Attleboro, MA	2	43
New Orleans, LA	8	41
New York, NY	844	3
Newark, NJ	122	17
Oakland, CA	531	4
Orange County, CA	338	7
Orlando, FL	31	30
Philadelphia, PA-NJ	136	14
Phoenix-Mesa, AZ	55	25
Portland-Vancouver, OR-WA	43	28
Providence-Warwick-Pawtucket, RI	2	43
Riverside-San Bernardino, CA	89	19
Sacramento, CA	53	26
San Antonio, TX	18	35
San Diego, CA	56	24
San Francisco, CA	407	5
San Jose, CA	907	2
Seattle-Bellevue-Everett, WA	176	12
Stockton-Lodi, CA	10	40
Tampa-Saint Petersburg-Clearwater, FL	5	42
Vallejo-Fairfield-Napa, CA	14	37
Washington, DC-MD-VA	370	6

[Continued]

★462★

Naturalized Citizens, 1994, By Selected Country of Former Allegiance: Taiwan

[Continued]

City/MSA	Number	Rank
West Palm Beach-Boca Raton, FL	13	38
Worcester-Fitchburg-Leominster, MA	14	37

Source: U.S. Department of Justice, Immigration and Naturalization Service, *Statistical Yearbook of the Immigration and Naturalization Service, 1994,* Washington, D.C.: U.S. Government Printing Office, 1996, p. 146.

★463★

Naturalized Citizens

Naturalized Citizens, 1994, By Selected Country of Former Allegiance: United Kingdom

The total number of citizens from the United Kingdom who were naturalized in the United States in fiscal year 1994 is 15,003. The total provided by the source for non-MSAs is 932; for "other" MSAs, 2,589; for "unknown," 552.

City/MSA	Number	Rank
Atlanta, GA	194	14
Baltimore, MD	107	28
Bergen-Passaic, NJ	140	20
Boston-Lawrence-Lowell-Brockton, MA	575	5
Bridgeport-Stamford-Norwalk-Danbury, CT	123	23
Chicago, IL	291	11
Cleveland-Lorain-Elyria, OH	87	30
Dallas, TX	119	24
Denver, CO	72	33
Detroit, MI	214	13
Fort Lauderdale, FL	140	20
Fort Worth-Arlington, TX	53	37
Fresno, CA	47	39
Hartford, CT	78	32
Honolulu, HI	176	16
Houston, TX	373	8
Jersey City, NJ	49	38
Las Vegas, NV	42	41
Lincoln, NE	6	48
Los Angeles-Long Beach, CA	667	4
Miami, FL	150	17
Middlesex-Somerset-Hunterdon, NJ	149	18
Minneapolis-Saint Paul, MN-WI	80	31
Modesto, CA	19	46
Monmouth-Ocean, NJ	65	35
Nassau-Suffolk, NY	221	12
New Bedford-Fall River-Attleboro, MA	18	47
New Orleans, LA	24	45
New York, NY	1,905	1
Newark, NJ	185	15
Oakland, CA	733	3
Orange County, CA	131	21

[Continued]

★463★

Naturalized Citizens, 1994, By Selected Country of Former Allegiance: United Kingdom

[Continued]

City/MSA	Number	Rank
Orlando, FL	113	26
Philadelphia, PA-NJ	316	9
Phoenix-Mesa, AZ	96	29
Portland-Vancouver, OR-WA	112	27
Providence-Warwick-Pawtucket, RI	61	36
Riverside-San Bernardino, CA	96	29
Sacramento, CA	146	19
San Antonio, TX	33	42
San Diego, CA	128	22
San Francisco, CA	1,180	2
San Jose, CA	408	7
Seattle-Bellevue-Everett, WA	303	10
Stockton-Lodi, CA	29	44
Tampa-Saint Petersburg-Clearwater, FL	69	34
Vallejo-Fairfield-Napa, CA	32	43
Washington, DC-MD-VA	415	6
West Palm Beach-Boca Raton, FL	115	25
Worcester-Fitchburg-Leominster, MA	45	40

Source: U.S. Department of Justice, Immigration and Naturalization Service, *Statistical Yearbook of the Immigration and Naturalization Service, 1994,* Washington, D.C.: U.S. Government Printing Office, 1996, p. 146.

★464★

Naturalized Citizens

Naturalized Citizens, 1994, By Selected Country of Former Allegiance: Vietnam

The total number of citizens from Vietnam who were naturalized in the United States in fiscal year 1994 is 26,833. The total provided by the source for non-MSAs is 616; for "other" MSAs, 3,902; for "unknown," 1,620.

City/MSA	Number	Rank
Atlanta, GA	328	17
Baltimore, MD	55	33
Bergen-Passaic, NJ	10	44
Boston-Lawrence-Lowell-Brockton, MA	948	6
Bridgeport-Stamford-Norwalk-Danbury, CT	45	35
Chicago, IL	253	20
Cleveland-Lorain-Elyria, OH	43	36
Dallas, TX	423	14
Denver, CO	250	21
Detroit, MI	65	30
Fort Lauderdale, FL	45	35
Fort Worth-Arlington, TX	337	16
Fresno, CA	82	28
Hartford, CT	73	29
Honolulu, HI	239	23
Houston, TX	1,586	4

[Continued]

★ 464 ★

Naturalized Citizens, 1994, By Selected Country of Former Allegiance: Vietnam

[Continued]

City/MSA	Number	Rank
Jersey City, NJ	57	32
Las Vegas, NV	36	38
Lincoln, NE	19	42
Los Angeles-Long Beach, CA	1,739	2
Miami, FL	24	41
Middlesex-Somerset-Hunterdon, NJ	47	34
Minneapolis-Saint Paul, MN-WI	375	15
Modesto, CA	45	35
Monmouth-Ocean, NJ	2	45
Nassau-Suffolk, NY	55	33
New Bedford-Fall River-Attleboro, MA	13	43
New Orleans, LA	279	18
New York, NY	508	13
Newark, NJ	55	33
Oakland, CA	902	9
Orange County, CA	1,718	3
Orlando, FL	177	25
Philadelphia, PA-NJ	842	10
Phoenix-Mesa, AZ	106	27
Portland-Vancouver, OR-WA	337	16
Providence-Warwick-Pawtucket, RI	29	40
Riverside-San Bernardino, CA	216	24
Sacramento, CA	1,014	5
San Antonio, TX	42	37
San Diego, CA	522	12
San Francisco, CA	914	8
San Jose, CA	3,457	1
Seattle-Bellevue-Everett, WA	701	11
Stockton-Lodi, CA	241	22
Tampa-Saint Petersburg-Clearwater, FL	154	26
Vallejo-Fairfield-Napa, CA	34	39
Washington, DC-MD-VA	940	7
West Palm Beach-Boca Raton, FL	58	31
Worcester-Fitchburg-Leominster, MA	255	19

Source: U.S. Department of Justice, Immigration and Naturalization Service, *Statistical Yearbook of the Immigration and Naturalization Service, 1994,* Washington, D.C.: U.S. Government Printing Office, 1996, p. 146.

★ 465 ★

Nonimmigrants Admitted, By Region of Citizenship

Nonimmigrants Admitted, 1994, By Selected Region of Citizenship: All Regions

City/MSA	Nonimmigrants admitted to the U.S.	Rank
Los Angeles, CA	2,681,447	3
Miami, FL	3,650,970	1
New York, NY	3,432,306	2
Newark, NJ	631,406	6
Orlando, FL	875,214	5
San Francisco, CA	1,119,554	4
Washington, DC	603,697	7

Source: U.S. Department of Justice, Immigration and Naturalization Service, *Statistical Yearbook of the Immigration and Naturalization Service, 1994,* Washington, D.C.: U.S. Government Printing Office, 1996, p. 118.

★ 466 ★

Nonimmigrants Admitted, By Region of Citizenship

Nonimmigrants Admitted, 1994, By Selected Region of Citizenship: Africa

City/MSA	Nonimmigrants admitted to the U.S.	Rank
Los Angeles, CA	13,429	4
Miami, FL	23,989	2
New York, NY	107,839	1
Newark, NJ	7,641	5
Orlando, FL	3,469	7
San Francisco, CA	3,790	6
Washington, DC	20,554	3

Source: U.S. Department of Justice, Immigration and Naturalization Service, *Statistical Yearbook of the Immigration and Naturalization Service, 1994,* Washington, D.C.: U.S. Government Printing Office, 1996, p. 118.

★ 467 ★

Nonimmigrants Admitted, By Region of Citizenship

Nonimmigrants Admitted, 1994, By Selected Region of Citizenship: Asia

City/MSA	Nonimmigrants admitted to the U.S.	Rank
Los Angeles, CA	1,097,167	1
Miami, FL	111,639	4
New York, NY	703,350	2
Newark, NJ	85,756	6
Orlando, FL	18,243	7
San Francisco, CA	631,558	3
Washington, DC	89,960	5

Source: U.S. Department of Justice, Immigration and Naturalization Service, *Statistical Yearbook of the Immigration and Naturalization Service, 1994,* Washington, D.C.: U.S. Government Printing Office, 1996, p. 118.

★468★
Nonimmigrants Admitted, By Region of Citizenship

Nonimmigrants Admitted, 1994, By Selected Region of Citizenship: Caribbean

City/MSA	Nonimmigrants admitted to the U.S.	Rank
Los Angeles, CA	1,844	5
Miami, FL	514,389	1
New York, NY	166,381	2
Newark, NJ	11,515	3
Orlando, FL	11,100	4
San Francisco, CA	524	7
Washington, DC	780	6

Source: U.S. Department of Justice, Immigration and Naturalization Service, *Statistical Yearbook of the Immigration and Naturalization Service, 1994*, Washington, D.C.: U.S. Government Printing Office, 1996, p. 118.

★469★
Nonimmigrants Admitted, By Region of Citizenship

Nonimmigrants Admitted, 1994, By Selected Region of Citizenship: Central America

City/MSA	Nonimmigrants admitted to the U.S.	Rank
Los Angeles, CA	59,024	2
Miami, FL	338,480	1
New York, NY	17,587	3
Newark, NJ	635	7
Orlando, FL	7,754	4
San Francisco, CA	6,199	6
Washington, DC	7,144	5

Source: U.S. Department of Justice, Immigration and Naturalization Service, *Statistical Yearbook of the Immigration and Naturalization Service, 1994*, Washington, D.C.: U.S. Government Printing Office, 1996, p. 118.

★470★
Nonimmigrants Admitted, By Region of Citizenship

Nonimmigrants Admitted, 1994, By Selected Region of Citizenship: Europe

City/MSA	Nonimmigrants admitted to the U.S.	Rank
Los Angeles, CA	789,447	3
Miami, FL	981,983	2
New York, NY	1,993,317	1
Newark, NJ	483,400	5
Orlando, FL	686,781	4
San Francisco, CA	381,004	7
Washington, DC	423,114	6

Source: U.S. Department of Justice, Immigration and Naturalization Service, *Statistical Yearbook of the Immigration and Naturalization Service, 1994*, Washington, D.C.: U.S. Government Printing Office, 1996, p. 118.

★471★
Nonimmigrants Admitted, By Region of Citizenship

Nonimmigrants Admitted, 1994, By Selected Region of Citizenship: North America

City/MSA	Nonimmigrants admitted to the U.S.	Rank
Los Angeles, CA	348,828	2
Miami, FL	1,021,795	1
New York, NY	268,167	3
Newark, NJ	38,825	6
Orlando, FL	89,999	4
San Francisco, CA	64,886	5
Washington, DC	28,179	7

Source: U.S. Department of Justice, Immigration and Naturalization Service, *Statistical Yearbook of the Immigration and Naturalization Service, 1994*, Washington, D.C.: U.S. Government Printing Office, 1996, p. 118.

★472★
Nonimmigrants Admitted, By Region of Citizenship

Nonimmigrants Admitted, 1994, By Selected Region of Citizenship: Oceania

City/MSA	Nonimmigrants admitted to the U.S.	Rank
Los Angeles, CA	317,186	1
Miami, FL	13,247	4
New York, NY	27,299	2
Newark, NJ	6,524	6
Orlando, FL	1,887	7
San Francisco, CA	20,829	3
Washington, DC	11,894	5

Source: U.S. Department of Justice, Immigration and Naturalization Service, *Statistical Yearbook of the Immigration and Naturalization Service, 1994*, Washington, D.C.: U.S. Government Printing Office, 1996, p. 118.

★473★
Nonimmigrants Admitted, By Region of Citizenship

Nonimmigrants Admitted, 1994, By Selected Region of Citizenship: South America

City/MSA	Nonimmigrants admitted to the U.S.	Rank
Los Angeles, CA	99,204	3
Miami, FL	1,474,508	1
New York, NY	312,135	2
Newark, NJ	6,537	7
Orlando, FL	71,960	4
San Francisco, CA	9,237	6
Washington, DC	23,635	5

Source: U.S. Department of Justice, Immigration and Naturalization Service, *Statistical Yearbook of the Immigration and Naturalization Service, 1994*, Washington, D.C.: U.S. Government Printing Office, 1996, p. 118.

★474★
Nonimmigrants Admitted, By Country of Citizenship

Nonimmigrants Admitted, 1994, By Selected Country of Citizenship: Argentina

City/MSA	Nonimmigrants admitted to the U.S.	Rank
Los Angeles, CA	16,976	3
Miami, FL	280,117	1
New York, NY	68,335	2
Newark, NJ	1,300	6
Orlando, FL	1,612	5
San Francisco, CA	1,201	7
Washington, DC	5,907	4

Source: U.S. Department of Justice, Immigration and Naturalization Service, *Statistical Yearbook of the Immigration and Naturalization Service, 1994*, Washington, D.C.: U.S. Government Printing Office, 1996, p. 118.

★475★
Nonimmigrants Admitted, By Country of Citizenship

Nonimmigrants Admitted, 1994, By Selected Country of Citizenship: Austria

City/MSA	Nonimmigrants admitted to the U.S.	Rank
Los Angeles, CA	18,800	3
Miami, FL	23,798	2
New York, NY	50,818	1
Newark, NJ	4,489	6
Orlando, FL	4,331	7
San Francisco, CA	9,448	4
Washington, DC	4,921	5

Source: U.S. Department of Justice, Immigration and Naturalization Service, *Statistical Yearbook of the Immigration and Naturalization Service, 1994*, Washington, D.C.: U.S. Government Printing Office, 1996, p. 118.

★476★
Nonimmigrants Admitted, By Country of Citizenship

Nonimmigrants Admitted, 1994, By Selected Country of Citizenship: Bangladesh

City/MSA	Nonimmigrants admitted to the U.S.	Rank
Los Angeles, CA	1,802	2
Miami, FL	356	5
New York, NY	8,531	1
Newark, NJ	497	4
Orlando, FL	32	7
San Francisco, CA	303	6
Washington, DC	681	3

Source: U.S. Department of Justice, Immigration and Naturalization Service, *Statistical Yearbook of the Immigration and Naturalization Service, 1994*, Washington, D.C.: U.S. Government Printing Office, 1996, p. 118.

★477★
Nonimmigrants Admitted, By Country of Citizenship

Nonimmigrants Admitted, 1994, By Selected Country of Citizenship: Belize

City/MSA	Nonimmigrants admitted to the U.S.	Rank
Los Angeles, CA	1,621	2
Miami, FL	10,002	1
New York, NY	163	4
Newark, NJ	30	6
Orlando, FL	13	7
San Francisco, CA	209	3
Washington, DC	94	5

Source: U.S. Department of Justice, Immigration and Naturalization Service, *Statistical Yearbook of the Immigration and Naturalization Service, 1994*, Washington, D.C.: U.S. Government Printing Office, 1996, p. 118.

★478★
Nonimmigrants Admitted, By Country of Citizenship

Nonimmigrants Admitted, 1994, By Selected Country of Citizenship: Canada

City/MSA	Nonimmigrants admitted to the U.S.	Rank
Los Angeles, CA	3,022	3
Miami, FL	3,240	2
New York, NY	4,703	1
Newark, NJ	1,180	5
Orlando, FL	471	7
San Francisco, CA	2,219	4
Washington, DC	1,104	6

Source: U.S. Department of Justice, Immigration and Naturalization Service, *Statistical Yearbook of the Immigration and Naturalization Service, 1994*, Washington, D.C.: U.S. Government Printing Office, 1996, p. 118.

★479★
Nonimmigrants Admitted, By Country of Citizenship

Nonimmigrants Admitted, 1994, By Selected Country of Citizenship: Egypt

City/MSA	Nonimmigrants admitted to the U.S.	Rank
Los Angeles, CA	2,954	2
Miami, FL	995	4
New York, NY	20,731	1
Newark, NJ	695	5
Orlando, FL	349	7
San Francisco, CA	368	6
Washington, DC	1,748	3

Source: U.S. Department of Justice, Immigration and Naturalization Service, *Statistical Yearbook of the Immigration and Naturalization Service, 1994*, Washington, D.C.: U.S. Government Printing Office, 1996, p. 118.

★480★
Nonimmigrants Admitted, By Country of Citizenship
Nonimmigrants Admitted, 1994, By Selected Country of Citizenship: Kenya

City/MSA	Nonimmigrants admitted to the U.S.	Rank
Los Angeles, CA	516	3
Miami, FL	331	5
New York, NY	2,306	1
Newark, NJ	338	4
Orlando, FL	191	7
San Francisco, CA	219	6
Washington, DC	906	2

Source: U.S. Department of Justice, Immigration and Naturalization Service, *Statistical Yearbook of the Immigration and Naturalization Service, 1994*, Washington, D.C.: U.S. Government Printing Office, 1996, p. 118.

★481★
Nonimmigrants Admitted, By Country of Citizenship
Nonimmigrants Admitted, 1994, By Selected Country of Citizenship: Netherlands Antilles

City/MSA	Nonimmigrants admitted to the U.S.	Rank
Los Angeles, CA	22	5
Miami, FL	6,824	1
New York, NY	309	2
Newark, NJ	130	4
Orlando, FL	239	3
San Francisco, CA	11	6
Washington, DC	6	7

Source: U.S. Department of Justice, Immigration and Naturalization Service, *Statistical Yearbook of the Immigration and Naturalization Service, 1994*, Washington, D.C.: U.S. Government Printing Office, 1996, p. 118.

★482★
Nonimmigrants Admitted, By Country of Citizenship
Nonimmigrants Admitted, 1994, By Selected Country of Citizenship: New Zealand

City/MSA	Nonimmigrants admitted to the U.S.	Rank
Los Angeles, CA	80,207	1
Miami, FL	2,891	4
New York, NY	5,291	2
Newark, NJ	1,563	6
Orlando, FL	380	7
San Francisco, CA	2,444	5
Washington, DC	3,862	3

Source: U.S. Department of Justice, Immigration and Naturalization Service, *Statistical Yearbook of the Immigration and Naturalization Service, 1994*, Washington, D.C.: U.S. Government Printing Office, 1996, p. 118.

★483★
Nonimmigrants Admitted, By Country of Citizenship
Nonimmigrants Admitted, 1994, By Selected Country of Citizenship: Peru

City/MSA	Nonimmigrants admitted to the U.S.	Rank
Los Angeles, CA	12,189	2
Miami, FL	125,650	1
New York, NY	3,253	3
Newark, NJ	366	6
Orlando, FL	220	7
San Francisco, CA	646	4
Washington, DC	488	5

Source: U.S. Department of Justice, Immigration and Naturalization Service, *Statistical Yearbook of the Immigration and Naturalization Service, 1994*, Washington, D.C.: U.S. Government Printing Office, 1996, p. 118.

★484★
Nonimmigrants Admitted, By Country of Citizenship
Nonimmigrants Admitted, 1994, By Selected Country of Citizenship: South Africa

City/MSA	Nonimmigrants admitted to the U.S.	Rank
Los Angeles, CA	5,153	3
Miami, FL	17,608	2
New York, NY	29,011	1
Newark, NJ	1,470	6
Orlando, FL	1,695	5
San Francisco, CA	1,291	7
Washington, DC	4,253	4

Source: U.S. Department of Justice, Immigration and Naturalization Service, *Statistical Yearbook of the Immigration and Naturalization Service, 1994*, Washington, D.C.: U.S. Government Printing Office, 1996, p. 118.

★485★
Refugees and Asylees
Refugees/Asylees Granted Lawful Permanent Resident Status, 1994, By Selected Country of Birth: All Countries

The total number of refugees and asylees granted lawful permanent resident status in the United States in fiscal year 1994, from all countries, is 121,434. The number of refugees and asylees living in metropolitan areas that are not MSAs is 2,383; in "other" MSAs, 16,364; in "unknown areas," 0.

City/MSA	Number	Rank
Atlanta, GA	2,109	15
Baltimore, MD	1,469	22
Bergen-Passaic, NJ	526	35
Boston-Lawrence-Lowell-Brockton, MA	3,109	9
Charlotte-Gastonia-Rock Hill, NC-SC	480	38
Chicago, IL	3,981	5
Cleveland-Lorain-Elyria, OH	1,091	23

[Continued]

★485★
Refugees/Asylees Granted Lawful Permanent Resident Status, 1994, By Selected Country of Birth: All Countries
[Continued]

City/MSA	Number	Rank
Columbus, OH	380	46
Dallas, TX	1,596	21
Denver, CO	1,022	24
Detroit, MI	1,885	16
Fort Lauderdale, FL	594	34
Fort Worth-Arlington, TX	717	28
Fresno, CA	1,780	18
Hartford, CT	415	43
Houston, TX	1,734	19
Jacksonville, FL	615	31
Jersey City, NJ	414	44
Kansas City, MO-KS	602	33
Los Angeles-Long Beach, CA	7,895	3
Merced, CA	513	36
Miami, FL	10,995	2
Milwaukee-Waukesha, WI	876	26
Minneapolis-Saint Paul, MN-WI	2,660	11
Nashville, TN	647	30
New Orleans, LA	345	50
New York, NY	18,807	1
Newark, NJ	952	25
Oakland, CA	1,839	17
Orange County, CA	1,663	20
Orlando, FL	446	41
Philadelphia, PA-NJ	2,416	14
Phoenix-Mesa, AZ	455	40
Portland-Vancouver, OR-WA	2,444	13
Rochester, NY	377	47
Sacramento, CA	3,406	7
Saint Louis, MO-IL	871	27
Salt Lake City-Ogden, UT	468	39
San Diego, CA	2,551	12
San Francisco, CA	2,885	10
San Jose, CA	3,900	6
Seattle-Bellevue-Everett, WA	4,115	4
Spokane, WA	439	42
Springfield, MA	392	45
Stockton-Lodi, CA	612	32
Tacoma, WA	499	37
Tampa-Saint Petersburg-Clearwater, FL	660	29
Washington, DC-MD-VA	3,345	8
West Palm Beach-Boca Raton, FL	346	49
Yolo, CA	348	48

Source: U.S. Department of Justice, Immigration and Naturalization Service, *Statistical Yearbook of the Immigration and Naturalization Service, 1994,* Washington, D.C.: U.S. Government Printing Office, 1996, p. 92.

★486★
Refugees and Asylees
Refugees/Asylees Granted Lawful Permanent Resident Status, 1994, By Selected Country of Birth: Albania

The total number of refugees and asylees from Albania who were granted lawful permanent resident status in the United States in fiscal year 1994 is 733. The number of refugees and asylees living in metropolitan areas that are not MSAs is 19; in "other" MSAs, 103; in "unknown areas," 0.

City/MSA	Number	Rank
Atlanta, GA	0	20
Baltimore, MD	16	11
Bergen-Passaic, NJ	17	10
Boston-Lawrence-Lowell-Brockton, MA	67	2
Charlotte-Gastonia-Rock Hill, NC-SC	0	20
Chicago, IL	39	4
Cleveland-Lorain-Elyria, OH	5	16
Columbus, OH	0	20
Dallas, TX	4	17
Denver, CO	4	17
Detroit, MI	61	3
Fort Lauderdale, FL	0	20
Fort Worth-Arlington, TX	0	20
Fresno, CA	0	20
Hartford, CT	26	6
Houston, TX	0	20
Jacksonville, FL	37	5
Jersey City, NJ	1	19
Kansas City, MO-KS	0	20
Los Angeles-Long Beach, CA	7	14
Merced, CA	0	20
Miami, FL	2	18
Milwaukee-Waukesha, WI	10	12
Minneapolis-Saint Paul, MN-WI	1	19
Nashville, TN	0	20
New Orleans, LA	0	20
New York, NY	173	1
Newark, NJ	18	9
Oakland, CA	0	20
Orange County, CA	0	20
Orlando, FL	6	15
Philadelphia, PA-NJ	18	9
Phoenix-Mesa, AZ	17	10
Portland-Vancouver, OR-WA	0	20
Rochester, NY	0	20
Sacramento, CA	0	20
Saint Louis, MO-IL	9	13
Salt Lake City-Ogden, UT	0	20
San Diego, CA	5	16
San Francisco, CA	10	12
San Jose, CA	0	20
Seattle-Bellevue-Everett, WA	20	8
Spokane, WA	0	20
Springfield, MA	0	20
Stockton-Lodi, CA	0	20
Tacoma, WA	0	20
Tampa-Saint Petersburg-Clearwater, FL	16	11
Washington, DC-MD-VA	21	7

[Continued]

★486★

Refugees/Asylees Granted Lawful Permanent Resident Status, 1994, By Selected Country of Birth: Albania
[Continued]

City/MSA	Number	Rank
West Palm Beach-Boca Raton, FL	1	19
Yolo, CA	0	20

Source: U.S. Department of Justice, Immigration and Naturalization Service, *Statistical Yearbook of the Immigration and Naturalization Service, 1994*, Washington, D.C.: U.S. Government Printing Office, 1996, p. 92.

★487★
Refugees and Asylees

Refugees/Asylees Granted Lawful Permanent Resident Status, 1994, By Selected Country of Birth: Afghanistan

The total number of refugees and asylees from Afghanistan who were granted lawful permanent resident status in the United States in fiscal year 1994 is 1,665. The number of refugees and asylees living in metropolitan that are not MSAs is 11; in "other" MSAs, 227; in "unknown areas," 0.

City/MSA	Number	Rank
Atlanta, GA	42	9
Baltimore, MD	0	22
Bergen-Passaic, NJ	9	17
Boston-Lawrence-Lowell-Brockton, MA	0	22
Charlotte-Gastonia-Rock Hill, NC-SC	7	19
Chicago, IL	10	16
Cleveland-Lorain-Elyria, OH	0	22
Columbus, OH	1	21
Dallas, TX	1	21
Denver, CO	13	15
Detroit, MI	0	22
Fort Lauderdale, FL	0	22
Fort Worth-Arlington, TX	7	19
Fresno, CA	0	22
Hartford, CT	0	22
Houston, TX	2	20
Jacksonville, FL	0	22
Jersey City, NJ	1	21
Kansas City, MO-KS	26	11
Los Angeles-Long Beach, CA	137	4
Merced, CA	0	22
Miami, FL	0	22
Milwaukee-Waukesha, WI	1	21
Minneapolis-Saint Paul, MN-WI	1	21
Nashville, TN	9	17
New Orleans, LA	0	22
New York, NY	184	2
Newark, NJ	43	8
Oakland, CA	356	1
Orange County, CA	37	10
Orlando, FL	0	22

[Continued]

★487★

Refugees/Asylees Granted Lawful Permanent Resident Status, 1994, By Selected Country of Birth: Afghanistan
[Continued]

City/MSA	Number	Rank
Philadelphia, PA-NJ	10	16
Phoenix-Mesa, AZ	20	13
Portland-Vancouver, OR-WA	1	21
Rochester, NY	8	18
Sacramento, CA	14	14
Saint Louis, MO-IL	0	22
Salt Lake City-Ogden, UT	14	14
San Diego, CA	111	5
San Francisco, CA	14	14
San Jose, CA	57	7
Seattle-Bellevue-Everett, WA	84	6
Spokane, WA	0	22
Springfield, MA	0	22
Stockton-Lodi, CA	13	15
Tacoma, WA	0	22
Tampa-Saint Petersburg-Clearwater, FL	0	22
Washington, DC-MD-VA	171	3
West Palm Beach-Boca Raton, FL	0	22
Yolo, CA	23	12

Source: U.S. Department of Justice, Immigration and Naturalization Service, *Statistical Yearbook of the Immigration and Naturalization Service, 1994*, Washington, D.C.: U.S. Government Printing Office, 1996, p. 92.

★488★
Refugees and Asylees

Refugees/Asylees Granted Lawful Permanent Resident Status, 1994, By Selected Country of Birth: China (Mainland)

The total number of refugees and asylees from Mainland China who were granted lawful permanent resident status in the United States in fiscal year 1994 is 774. The number of refugees and asylees living in metropolitan areas that are not MSAs is 21; in "other" MSAs, 74; in "unknown areas," 0.

City/MSA	Number	Rank
Atlanta, GA	2	15
Baltimore, MD	4	13
Bergen-Passaic, NJ	1	16
Boston-Lawrence-Lowell-Brockton, MA	9	9
Charlotte-Gastonia-Rock Hill, NC-SC	3	14
Chicago, IL	13	7
Cleveland-Lorain-Elyria, OH	1	16
Columbus, OH	0	17
Dallas, TX	5	12
Denver, CO	4	13
Detroit, MI	1	16
Fort Lauderdale, FL	3	14
Fort Worth-Arlington, TX	0	17

[Continued]

★488★

Refugees/Asylees Granted Lawful Permanent Resident Status, 1994, By Selected Country of Birth: China (Mainland)

[Continued]

City/MSA	Number	Rank
Fresno, CA	0	17
Hartford, CT	0	17
Houston, TX	8	10
Jacksonville, FL	0	17
Jersey City, NJ	0	17
Kansas City, MO-KS	1	16
Los Angeles-Long Beach, CA	59	2
Merced, CA	0	17
Miami, FL	8	10
Milwaukee-Waukesha, WI	2	15
Minneapolis-Saint Paul, MN-WI	5	12
Nashville, TN	0	17
New Orleans, LA	2	15
New York, NY	422	1
Newark, NJ	0	17
Oakland, CA	15	6
Orange County, CA	5	12
Orlando, FL	0	17
Philadelphia, PA-NJ	6	11
Phoenix-Mesa, AZ	0	17
Portland-Vancouver, OR-WA	2	15
Rochester, NY	2	15
Sacramento, CA	3	14
Saint Louis, MO-IL	1	16
Salt Lake City-Ogden, UT	2	15
San Diego, CA	1	16
San Francisco, CA	39	3
San Jose, CA	19	4
Seattle-Bellevue-Everett, WA	10	8
Spokane, WA	0	17
Springfield, MA	0	17
Stockton-Lodi, CA	0	17
Tacoma, WA	0	17
Tampa-Saint Petersburg-Clearwater, FL	3	14
Washington, DC-MD-VA	17	5
West Palm Beach-Boca Raton, FL	0	17
Yolo, CA	0	17

Source: U.S. Department of Justice, Immigration and Naturalization Service, *Statistical Yearbook of the Immigration and Naturalization Service, 1994,* Washington, D.C.: U.S. Government Printing Office, 1996, p. 92.

★489★

Refugees and Asylees

Refugees/Asylees Granted Lawful Permanent Resident Status, 1994, By Selected Country of Birth: Cuba

The total number of refugees and asylees from Cuba who were granted lawful permanent resident status in the United States in fiscal year 1994 is 11,998. The number of refugees and asylees living in metropolitan areas that are not MSAs is 137; in "other" MSAs, 552; for "unknown areas," 0.

City/MSA	Number	Rank
Atlanta, GA	12	20
Baltimore, MD	1	27
Bergen-Passaic, NJ	38	12
Boston-Lawrence-Lowell-Brockton, MA	19	17
Charlotte-Gastonia-Rock Hill, NC-SC	2	26
Chicago, IL	51	10
Cleveland-Lorain-Elyria, OH	2	26
Columbus, OH	0	28
Dallas, TX	19	17
Denver, CO	2	26
Detroit, MI	4	24
Fort Lauderdale, FL	219	4
Fort Worth-Arlington, TX	2	26
Fresno, CA	4	24
Hartford, CT	4	24
Houston, TX	25	14
Jacksonville, FL	6	23
Jersey City, NJ	279	2
Kansas City, MO-KS	30	13
Los Angeles-Long Beach, CA	191	5
Merced, CA	0	28
Miami, FL	9,555	1
Milwaukee-Waukesha, WI	1	27
Minneapolis-Saint Paul, MN-WI	6	23
Nashville, TN	3	25
New Orleans, LA	20	16
New York, NY	123	7
Newark, NJ	72	9
Oakland, CA	12	20
Orange County, CA	10	21
Orlando, FL	86	8
Philadelphia, PA-NJ	14	19
Phoenix-Mesa, AZ	8	22
Portland-Vancouver, OR-WA	0	28
Rochester, NY	16	18
Sacramento, CA	2	26
Saint Louis, MO-IL	2	26
Salt Lake City-Ogden, UT	2	26
San Diego, CA	3	25
San Francisco, CA	42	11
San Jose, CA	4	24
Seattle-Bellevue-Everett, WA	20	16
Spokane, WA	0	28
Springfield, MA	0	28
Stockton-Lodi, CA	1	27
Tacoma, WA	0	28
Tampa-Saint Petersburg-Clearwater, FL	248	3
Washington, DC-MD-VA	22	15

[Continued]

★489★

Refugees/Asylees Granted Lawful Permanent Resident Status, 1994, By Selected Country of Birth: Cuba
[Continued]

City/MSA	Number	Rank
West Palm Beach-Boca Raton, FL	127	6
Yolo, CA	0	28

Source: U.S. Department of Justice, Immigration and Naturalization Service, *Statistical Yearbook of the Immigration and Naturalization Service, 1994,* Washington, D.C.: U.S. Government Printing Office, 1996, p. 92.

★490★
Refugees and Asylees

Refugees/Asylees Granted Lawful Permanent Resident Status, 1994, By Selected Country of Birth: Ethiopia

The total number of refugees and asylees from Ethiopia who were granted lawful permanent resident status in the United States in fiscal year 1994 is 2,730. The number of refugees and asylees living in metropolitan areas that are not MSAs is 43; in "other" MSAs, 394; in "unknown areas," 0.

City/MSA	Number	Rank
Atlanta, GA	152	3
Baltimore, MD	9	28
Bergen-Passaic, NJ	6	30
Boston-Lawrence-Lowell-Brockton, MA	84	9
Charlotte-Gastonia-Rock Hill, NC-SC	11	26
Chicago, IL	81	10
Cleveland-Lorain-Elyria, OH	3	32
Columbus, OH	69	12
Dallas, TX	112	7
Denver, CO	51	13
Detroit, MI	2	33
Fort Lauderdale, FL	0	35
Fort Worth-Arlington, TX	10	27
Fresno, CA	33	17
Hartford, CT	2	33
Houston, TX	48	14
Jacksonville, FL	20	22
Jersey City, NJ	1	34
Kansas City, MO-KS	20	22
Los Angeles-Long Beach, CA	120	5
Merced, CA	0	35
Miami, FL	4	31
Milwaukee-Waukesha, WI	1	34
Minneapolis-Saint Paul, MN-WI	114	6
Nashville, TN	25	19
New Orleans, LA	7	29
New York, NY	21	21
Newark, NJ	2	33
Oakland, CA	70	11
Orange County, CA	13	24
Orlando, FL	4	31

[Continued]

★490★

Refugees/Asylees Granted Lawful Permanent Resident Status, 1994, By Selected Country of Birth: Ethiopia
[Continued]

City/MSA	Number	Rank
Philadelphia, PA-NJ	21	21
Phoenix-Mesa, AZ	24	20
Portland-Vancouver, OR-WA	29	18
Rochester, NY	19	23
Sacramento, CA	2	33
Saint Louis, MO-IL	42	15
Salt Lake City-Ogden, UT	1	34
San Diego, CA	124	4
San Francisco, CA	37	16
San Jose, CA	88	8
Seattle-Bellevue-Everett, WA	336	2
Spokane, WA	6	30
Springfield, MA	1	34
Stockton-Lodi, CA	1	34
Tacoma, WA	0	35
Tampa-Saint Petersburg-Clearwater, FL	12	25
Washington, DC-MD-VA	456	1
West Palm Beach-Boca Raton, FL	0	35
Yolo, CA	0	35

Source: U.S. Department of Justice, Immigration and Naturalization Service, *Statistical Yearbook of the Immigration and Naturalization Service, 1994,* Washington, D.C.: U.S. Government Printing Office, 1996, p. 92.

★491★
Refugees and Asylees

Refugees/Asylees Granted Lawful Permanent Resident Status, 1994, By Selected Country of Birth: Haiti

The total number of refugees and asylees from Haiti who were granted lawful permanent resident status in the United States in fiscal year 1994 is 664. The number of refugees and asylees living in metropolitan areas that are not MSAs is 16; in "other" MSAs, 75; in "unknown areas," 0.

City/MSA	Number	Rank
Atlanta, GA	6	12
Baltimore, MD	0	18
Bergen-Passaic, NJ	1	17
Boston-Lawrence-Lowell-Brockton, MA	48	5
Charlotte-Gastonia-Rock Hill, NC-SC	0	18
Chicago, IL	0	18
Cleveland-Lorain-Elyria, OH	0	18
Columbus, OH	0	18
Dallas, TX	0	18
Denver, CO	2	16
Detroit, MI	0	18
Fort Lauderdale, FL	65	3
Fort Worth-Arlington, TX	0	18
Fresno, CA	0	18

[Continued]

★491★

Refugees/Asylees Granted Lawful Permanent Resident Status, 1994, By Selected Country of Birth: Haiti

[Continued]

City/MSA	Number	Rank
Hartford, CT	0	18
Houston, TX	2	16
Jacksonville, FL	17	9
Jersey City, NJ	7	11
Kansas City, MO-KS	23	7
Los Angeles-Long Beach, CA	0	18
Merced, CA	0	18
Miami, FL	144	1
Milwaukee-Waukesha, WI	0	18
Minneapolis-Saint Paul, MN-WI	0	18
Nashville, TN	0	18
New Orleans, LA	9	10
New York, NY	49	4
Newark, NJ	30	6
Oakland, CA	0	18
Orange County, CA	0	18
Orlando, FL	49	4
Philadelphia, PA-NJ	5	13
Phoenix-Mesa, AZ	0	18
Portland-Vancouver, OR-WA	9	10
Rochester, NY	5	13
Sacramento, CA	0	18
Saint Louis, MO-IL	4	14
Salt Lake City-Ogden, UT	0	18
San Diego, CA	0	18
San Francisco, CA	3	15
San Jose, CA	0	18
Seattle-Bellevue-Everett, WA	0	18
Spokane, WA	0	18
Springfield, MA	0	18
Stockton-Lodi, CA	0	18
Tacoma, WA	0	18
Tampa-Saint Petersburg-Clearwater, FL	19	8
Washington, DC-MD-VA	1	17
West Palm Beach-Boca Raton, FL	75	2
Yolo, CA	0	18

Source: U.S. Department of Justice, Immigration and Naturalization Service, Statistical Yearbook of the Immigration and Naturalization Service, 1994, Washington, D.C.: U.S. Government Printing Office, 1996, p. 92.

★492★

Refugees and Asylees

Refugees/Asylees Granted Lawful Permanent Resident Status, 1994, By Selected Country of Birth: Iran

The total number of refugees and asylees from Iran who were granted lawful permanent resident status in the United States in fiscal year 1994 is 2,186. The number of refugees and asylees living in metropolitan areas that are not MSAs is 48; in "other" MSAs, 251; for "unknown areas," 0.

City/MSA	Number	Rank
Atlanta, GA	15	11
Baltimore, MD	15	11
Bergen-Passaic, NJ	4	20
Boston-Lawrence-Lowell-Brockton, MA	12	13
Charlotte-Gastonia-Rock Hill, NC-SC	3	21
Chicago, IL	38	5
Cleveland-Lorain-Elyria, OH	1	23
Columbus, OH	2	22
Dallas, TX	11	14
Denver, CO	16	10
Detroit, MI	2	22
Fort Lauderdale, FL	0	24
Fort Worth-Arlington, TX	2	22
Fresno, CA	8	17
Hartford, CT	0	24
Houston, TX	7	18
Jacksonville, FL	10	15
Jersey City, NJ	0	24
Kansas City, MO-KS	9	16
Los Angeles-Long Beach, CA	1,309	1
Merced, CA	0	24
Miami, FL	2	22
Milwaukee-Waukesha, WI	2	22
Minneapolis-Saint Paul, MN-WI	3	21
Nashville, TN	9	16
New Orleans, LA	0	24
New York, NY	113	2
Newark, NJ	6	19
Oakland, CA	28	6
Orange County, CA	23	7
Orlando, FL	3	21
Philadelphia, PA-NJ	1	23
Phoenix-Mesa, AZ	2	22
Portland-Vancouver, OR-WA	0	24
Rochester, NY	1	23
Sacramento, CA	13	12
Saint Louis, MO-IL	1	23
Salt Lake City-Ogden, UT	4	20
San Diego, CA	17	9
San Francisco, CA	20	8
San Jose, CA	100	3
Seattle-Bellevue-Everett, WA	23	7
Spokane, WA	0	24
Springfield, MA	0	24
Stockton-Lodi, CA	0	24
Tacoma, WA	0	24
Tampa-Saint Petersburg-Clearwater, FL	1	23
Washington, DC-MD-VA	51	4

[Continued]

★492★

Refugees/Asylees Granted Lawful Permanent Resident Status, 1994, By Selected Country of Birth: Iran

[Continued]

City/MSA	Number	Rank
West Palm Beach-Boca Raton, FL	0	24
Yolo, CA	0	24

Source: U.S. Department of Justice, Immigration and Naturalization Service, *Statistical Yearbook of the Immigration and Naturalization Service, 1994,* Washington, D.C.: U.S. Government Printing Office, 1996, p. 92.

★493★

Refugees and Asylees

Refugees/Asylees Granted Lawful Permanent Resident Status, 1994, By Selected Country of Birth: Iraq

The total number of refugees and asylees from Iraq who were granted lawful permanent resident status in the United States in fiscal year 1994 is 4,400. The number of refugees and asylees living in metropolitan areas that are not MSAs is 41; in "other" MSAs, 787; in "unknown areas," 0.

City/MSA	Number	Rank
Atlanta, GA	17	22
Baltimore, MD	3	31
Bergen-Passaic, NJ	7	29
Boston-Lawrence-Lowell-Brockton, MA	46	16
Charlotte-Gastonia-Rock Hill, NC-SC	0	34
Chicago, IL	349	3
Cleveland-Lorain-Elyria, OH	52	14
Columbus, OH	27	19
Dallas, TX	345	4
Denver, CO	16	23
Detroit, MI	859	1
Fort Lauderdale, FL	0	34
Fort Worth-Arlington, TX	70	11
Fresno, CA	0	34
Hartford, CT	27	19
Houston, TX	10	27
Jacksonville, FL	87	7
Jersey City, NJ	0	34
Kansas City, MO-KS	13	25
Los Angeles-Long Beach, CA	82	9
Merced, CA	1	33
Miami, FL	10	27
Milwaukee-Waukesha, WI	0	34
Minneapolis-Saint Paul, MN-WI	15	24
Nashville, TN	308	5
New Orleans, LA	7	29
New York, NY	29	18
Newark, NJ	1	33
Oakland, CA	4	30
Orange County, CA	16	23
Orlando, FL	10	27

[Continued]

★493★

Refugees/Asylees Granted Lawful Permanent Resident Status, 1994, By Selected Country of Birth: Iraq

[Continued]

City/MSA	Number	Rank
Philadelphia, PA-NJ	24	21
Phoenix-Mesa, AZ	73	10
Portland-Vancouver, OR-WA	26	20
Rochester, NY	3	31
Sacramento, CA	9	28
Saint Louis, MO-IL	84	8
Salt Lake City-Ogden, UT	48	15
San Diego, CA	629	2
San Francisco, CA	69	12
San Jose, CA	32	17
Seattle-Bellevue-Everett, WA	96	6
Spokane, WA	0	34
Springfield, MA	0	34
Stockton-Lodi, CA	0	34
Tacoma, WA	11	26
Tampa-Saint Petersburg-Clearwater, FL	2	32
Washington, DC-MD-VA	55	13
West Palm Beach-Boca Raton, FL	0	34
Yolo, CA	0	34

Source: U.S. Department of Justice, Immigration and Naturalization Service, *Statistical Yearbook of the Immigration and Naturalization Service, 1994,* Washington, D.C.: U.S. Government Printing Office, 1996, p. 92.

★494★

Refugees and Asylees

Refugees/Asylees Granted Lawful Permanent Resident Status, 1994, By Selected Country of Birth: Laos

The total number of refugees and asylees from Laos who were granted lawful permanent resident status in the United States in fiscal year 1994 is 4,482. The number of refugees and asylees living in metropolitan areas that are not MSAs is 315; in "other" MSAs, 937; in "unknown areas," 0.

City/MSA	Number	Rank
Atlanta, GA	18	17
Baltimore, MD	1	26
Bergen-Passaic, NJ	4	23
Boston-Lawrence-Lowell-Brockton, MA	7	21
Charlotte-Gastonia-Rock Hill, NC-SC	6	22
Chicago, IL	6	22
Cleveland-Lorain-Elyria, OH	1	26
Columbus, OH	8	20
Dallas, TX	20	15
Denver, CO	32	12
Detroit, MI	57	9
Fort Lauderdale, FL	0	27
Fort Worth-Arlington, TX	10	19

[Continued]

★494★

Refugees/Asylees Granted Lawful Permanent Resident Status, 1994, By Selected Country of Birth: Laos
[Continued]

City/MSA	Number	Rank
Fresno, CA	890	1
Hartford, CT	0	27
Houston, TX	2	25
Jacksonville, FL	0	27
Jersey City, NJ	0	27
Kansas City, MO-KS	27	13
Los Angeles-Long Beach, CA	22	14
Merced, CA	286	4
Miami, FL	0	27
Milwaukee-Waukesha, WI	152	6
Minneapolis-Saint Paul, MN-WI	710	2
Nashville, TN	12	18
New Orleans, LA	0	27
New York, NY	4	23
Newark, NJ	0	27
Oakland, CA	76	7
Orange County, CA	6	22
Orlando, FL	0	27
Philadelphia, PA-NJ	8	20
Phoenix-Mesa, AZ	4	23
Portland-Vancouver, OR-WA	47	10
Rochester, NY	8	20
Sacramento, CA	464	3
Saint Louis, MO-IL	1	26
Salt Lake City-Ogden, UT	4	23
San Diego, CA	43	11
San Francisco, CA	3	24
San Jose, CA	7	21
Seattle-Bellevue-Everett, WA	62	8
Spokane, WA	10	19
Springfield, MA	0	27
Stockton-Lodi, CA	181	5
Tacoma, WA	2	25
Tampa-Saint Petersburg-Clearwater, FL	2	25
Washington, DC-MD-VA	8	20
West Palm Beach-Boca Raton, FL	0	27
Yolo, CA	19	16

Source: U.S. Department of Justice, Immigration and Naturalization Service, *Statistical Yearbook of the Immigration and Naturalization Service, 1994,* Washington, D.C.: U.S. Government Printing Office, 1996, p. 92.

★495★

Refugees and Asylees

Refugees/Asylees Granted Lawful Permanent Resident Status, 1994, By Selected Country of Birth: Liberia

The total number of refugees and asylees from Liberia who were granted lawful permanent resident status in the United States in fiscal year 1994 is 851. The number of refugees and asylees living in metropolitan areas that are not MSAs is 5; in "other" MSAs, 201; in "unknown areas," 0.

City/MSA	Number	Rank
Atlanta, GA	7	15
Baltimore, MD	26	7
Bergen-Passaic, NJ	0	20
Boston-Lawrence-Lowell-Brockton, MA	11	12
Charlotte-Gastonia-Rock Hill, NC-SC	19	9
Chicago, IL	19	9
Cleveland-Lorain-Elyria, OH	12	11
Columbus, OH	3	17
Dallas, TX	29	6
Denver, CO	0	20
Detroit, MI	2	18
Fort Lauderdale, FL	0	20
Fort Worth-Arlington, TX	0	20
Fresno, CA	0	20
Hartford, CT	0	20
Houston, TX	16	10
Jacksonville, FL	1	19
Jersey City, NJ	1	19
Kansas City, MO-KS	35	5
Los Angeles-Long Beach, CA	8	14
Merced, CA	0	20
Miami, FL	3	17
Milwaukee-Waukesha, WI	3	17
Minneapolis-Saint Paul, MN-WI	60	4
Nashville, TN	0	20
New Orleans, LA	1	19
New York, NY	114	1
Newark, NJ	60	4
Oakland, CA	19	9
Orange County, CA	0	20
Orlando, FL	1	19
Philadelphia, PA-NJ	74	3
Phoenix-Mesa, AZ	20	8
Portland-Vancouver, OR-WA	5	16
Rochester, NY	0	20
Sacramento, CA	1	19
Saint Louis, MO-IL	1	19
Salt Lake City-Ogden, UT	0	20
San Diego, CA	0	20
San Francisco, CA	8	14
San Jose, CA	0	20
Seattle-Bellevue-Everett, WA	9	13
Spokane, WA	0	20
Springfield, MA	0	20
Stockton-Lodi, CA	0	20
Tacoma, WA	0	20
Tampa-Saint Petersburg-Clearwater, FL	1	19
Washington, DC-MD-VA	75	2

[Continued]

★495★

Refugees/Asylees Granted Lawful Permanent Resident Status, 1994, By Selected Country of Birth: Liberia
[Continued]

City/MSA	Number	Rank
West Palm Beach-Boca Raton, FL	1	19
Yolo, CA	0	20

Source: U.S. Department of Justice, Immigration and Naturalization Service, *Statistical Yearbook of the Immigration and Naturalization Service, 1994,* Washington, D.C.: U.S. Government Printing Office, 1996, p. 92.

★496★
Refugees and Asylees

Refugees/Asylees Granted Lawful Permanent Resident Status, 1994, By Selected Country of Birth: Nicaragua

The total number of refugees and asylees from Nicaragua who were granted lawful permanent resident status in the United States in fiscal year 1994 is 966. The number of refugees and asylees living in metropolitan areas that are not MSAs is 12; in "other" MSAs, 95; in "unknown areas," 0.

City/MSA	Number	Rank
Atlanta, GA	3	16
Baltimore, MD	0	19
Bergen-Passaic, NJ	0	19
Boston-Lawrence-Lowell-Brockton, MA	0	19
Charlotte-Gastonia-Rock Hill, NC-SC	5	14
Chicago, IL	2	17
Cleveland-Lorain-Elyria, OH	1	18
Columbus, OH	0	19
Dallas, TX	8	11
Denver, CO	0	19
Detroit, MI	0	19
Fort Lauderdale, FL	14	9
Fort Worth-Arlington, TX	1	18
Fresno, CA	0	19
Hartford, CT	0	19
Houston, TX	19	7
Jacksonville, FL	0	19
Jersey City, NJ	3	16
Kansas City, MO-KS	0	19
Los Angeles-Long Beach, CA	90	2
Merced, CA	3	16
Miami, FL	526	1
Milwaukee-Waukesha, WI	2	17
Minneapolis-Saint Paul, MN-WI	0	19
Nashville, TN	0	19
New Orleans, LA	20	6
New York, NY	4	15
Newark, NJ	0	19
Oakland, CA	23	5
Orange County, CA	6	13
Orlando, FL	0	19

[Continued]

★496★

Refugees/Asylees Granted Lawful Permanent Resident Status, 1994, By Selected Country of Birth: Nicaragua
[Continued]

City/MSA	Number	Rank
Philadelphia, PA-NJ	0	19
Phoenix-Mesa, AZ	3	16
Portland-Vancouver, OR-WA	0	19
Rochester, NY	0	19
Sacramento, CA	0	19
Saint Louis, MO-IL	0	19
Salt Lake City-Ogden, UT	0	19
San Diego, CA	3	16
San Francisco, CA	43	4
San Jose, CA	13	10
Seattle-Bellevue-Everett, WA	0	19
Spokane, WA	0	19
Springfield, MA	0	19
Stockton-Lodi, CA	0	19
Tacoma, WA	0	19
Tampa-Saint Petersburg-Clearwater, FL	7	12
Washington, DC-MD-VA	45	3
West Palm Beach-Boca Raton, FL	15	8
Yolo, CA	0	19

Source: U.S. Department of Justice, Immigration and Naturalization Service, *Statistical Yearbook of the Immigration and Naturalization Service, 1994,* Washington, D.C.: U.S. Government Printing Office, 1996, p. 92.

★497★
Refugees and Asylees

Refugees/Asylees Granted Lawful Permanent Resident Status, 1994, By Selected Country of Birth: Romania

The total number of refugees and asylees from Romania who were granted lawful permanent resident status in the United States in fiscal year 1994 is 1,199. The number of refugees and asylees living in metropolitan areas that are not MSAs is 33; in "other" MSAs, 179; in "unknown areas," 0.

City/MSA	Number	Rank
Atlanta, GA	20	10
Baltimore, MD	7	18
Bergen-Passaic, NJ	4	21
Boston-Lawrence-Lowell-Brockton, MA	10	16
Charlotte-Gastonia-Rock Hill, NC-SC	9	17
Chicago, IL	190	1
Cleveland-Lorain-Elyria, OH	13	13
Columbus, OH	1	24
Dallas, TX	12	14
Denver, CO	15	12
Detroit, MI	77	3
Fort Lauderdale, FL	45	6
Fort Worth-Arlington, TX	0	25

[Continued]

★497★

Refugees/Asylees Granted Lawful Permanent Resident Status, 1994, By Selected Country of Birth: Romania
[Continued]

City/MSA	Number	Rank
Fresno, CA	0	25
Hartford, CT	11	15
Houston, TX	17	11
Jacksonville, FL	9	17
Jersey City, NJ	1	24
Kansas City, MO-KS	1	24
Los Angeles-Long Beach, CA	42	7
Merced, CA	0	25
Miami, FL	5	20
Milwaukee-Waukesha, WI	0	25
Minneapolis-Saint Paul, MN-WI	13	13
Nashville, TN	3	22
New Orleans, LA	1	24
New York, NY	115	2
Newark, NJ	6	19
Oakland, CA	25	9
Orange County, CA	42	7
Orlando, FL	0	25
Philadelphia, PA-NJ	15	12
Phoenix-Mesa, AZ	30	8
Portland-Vancouver, OR-WA	73	4
Rochester, NY	0	25
Sacramento, CA	46	5
Saint Louis, MO-IL	6	19
Salt Lake City-Ogden, UT	4	21
San Diego, CA	1	24
San Francisco, CA	3	22
San Jose, CA	11	15
Seattle-Bellevue-Everett, WA	73	4
Spokane, WA	2	23
Springfield, MA	0	25
Stockton-Lodi, CA	0	25
Tacoma, WA	0	25
Tampa-Saint Petersburg-Clearwater, FL	3	22
Washington, DC-MD-VA	25	9
West Palm Beach-Boca Raton, FL	1	24
Yolo, CA	0	25

Source: U.S. Department of Justice, Immigration and Naturalization Service, *Statistical Yearbook of the Immigration and Naturalization Service, 1994,* Washington, D.C.: U.S. Government Printing Office, 1996, p. 92.

★498★

Refugees and Asylees

Refugees/Asylees Granted Lawful Permanent Resident Status, 1994, By Selected Country of Birth: Somalia

The total number of refugees and asylees from Somalia who were granted lawful permanent resident status in the United States in fiscal year 1994 is 1,572. The number of refugees and asylees living in metropolitan areas that are not MSAs is 56; in "other" MSAs, 155; in "unknown areas," 0.

City/MSA	Number	Rank
Atlanta, GA	99	5
Baltimore, MD	1	23
Bergen-Passaic, NJ	0	24
Boston-Lawrence-Lowell-Brockton, MA	130	3
Charlotte-Gastonia-Rock Hill, NC-SC	5	20
Chicago, IL	40	9
Cleveland-Lorain-Elyria, OH	1	23
Columbus, OH	8	17
Dallas, TX	40	9
Denver, CO	6	19
Detroit, MI	6	19
Fort Lauderdale, FL	0	24
Fort Worth-Arlington, TX	8	17
Fresno, CA	8	17
Hartford, CT	7	18
Houston, TX	13	14
Jacksonville, FL	6	19
Jersey City, NJ	2	22
Kansas City, MO-KS	18	13
Los Angeles-Long Beach, CA	35	11
Merced, CA	0	24
Miami, FL	0	24
Milwaukee-Waukesha, WI	12	15
Minneapolis-Saint Paul, MN-WI	119	4
Nashville, TN	68	7
New Orleans, LA	0	24
New York, NY	11	16
Newark, NJ	0	24
Oakland, CA	6	19
Orange County, CA	2	22
Orlando, FL	0	24
Philadelphia, PA-NJ	37	10
Phoenix-Mesa, AZ	4	21
Portland-Vancouver, OR-WA	23	12
Rochester, NY	0	24
Sacramento, CA	0	24
Saint Louis, MO-IL	23	12
Salt Lake City-Ogden, UT	1	23
San Diego, CA	329	1
San Francisco, CA	0	24
San Jose, CA	41	8
Seattle-Bellevue-Everett, WA	93	6
Spokane, WA	0	24
Springfield, MA	0	24
Stockton-Lodi, CA	0	24
Tacoma, WA	0	24
Tampa-Saint Petersburg-Clearwater, FL	0	24
Washington, DC-MD-VA	159	2

[Continued]

★498★

Refugees/Asylees Granted Lawful Permanent Resident Status, 1994, By Selected Country of Birth: Somalia
[Continued]

City/MSA	Number	Rank
West Palm Beach-Boca Raton, FL	0	24
Yolo, CA	0	24

Source: U.S. Department of Justice, Immigration and Naturalization Service, Statistical Yearbook of the Immigration and Naturalization Service, 1994, Washington, D.C.: U.S. Government Printing Office, 1996, p. 92.

★499★
Refugees and Asylees

Refugees/Asylees Granted Lawful Permanent Resident Status, 1994, By Selected Country of Birth: Soviet Union

The total number of refugees and asylees from the Soviet Union who were granted lawful permanent resident status in the United States in fiscal year 1994 is 50,756. The number of refugees and asylees living in metropolitan areas that are not MSAs is 605; in "other" MSAs, 5,020; in "unknown areas," 0.

City/MSA	Number	Rank
Atlanta, GA	481	19
Baltimore, MD	1,263	10
Bergen-Passaic, NJ	394	20
Boston-Lawrence-Lowell-Brockton, MA	1,616	7
Charlotte-Gastonia-Rock Hill, NC-SC	74	38
Chicago, IL	2,507	3
Cleveland-Lorain-Elyria, OH	890	11
Columbus, OH	185	33
Dallas, TX	311	24
Denver, CO	509	18
Detroit, MI	604	14
Fort Lauderdale, FL	137	36
Fort Worth-Arlington, TX	20	46
Fresno, CA	88	37
Hartford, CT	235	30
Houston, TX	172	35
Jacksonville, FL	268	28
Jersey City, NJ	37	44
Kansas City, MO-KS	223	31
Los Angeles-Long Beach, CA	3,479	2
Merced, CA	2	48
Miami, FL	256	29
Milwaukee-Waukesha, WI	517	17
Minneapolis-Saint Paul, MN-WI	631	12
Nashville, TN	44	43
New Orleans, LA	5	47
New York, NY	16,721	1
Newark, NJ	624	13
Oakland, CA	294	25
Orange County, CA	53	42
Orlando, FL	25	45

[Continued]

★499★

Refugees/Asylees Granted Lawful Permanent Resident Status, 1994, By Selected Country of Birth: Soviet Union
[Continued]

City/MSA	Number	Rank
Philadelphia, PA-NJ	1,611	8
Phoenix-Mesa, AZ	67	40
Portland-Vancouver, OR-WA	1,582	9
Rochester, NY	223	31
Sacramento, CA	1,939	5
Saint Louis, MO-IL	370	21
Salt Lake City-Ogden, UT	180	34
San Diego, CA	312	23
San Francisco, CA	2,144	4
San Jose, CA	549	16
Seattle-Bellevue-Everett, WA	1,714	6
Spokane, WA	287	26
Springfield, MA	314	22
Stockton-Lodi, CA	0	49
Tacoma, WA	190	32
Tampa-Saint Petersburg-Clearwater, FL	54	41
Washington, DC-MD-VA	585	15
West Palm Beach-Boca Raton, FL	68	39
Yolo, CA	277	27

Source: U.S. Department of Justice, Immigration and Naturalization Service, Statistical Yearbook of the Immigration and Naturalization Service, 1994, Washington, D.C.: U.S. Government Printing Office, 1996, p. 92.

★500★
Refugees and Asylees

Refugees/Asylees Granted Lawful Permanent Resident Status, 1994, By Selected Country of Birth: Thailand

The total number of refugees and asylees from Thailand who were granted lawful permanent resident status in the United States in fiscal year 1994 is 3,076. The number of refugees and asylees living in metropolitan areas that are not MSAs is 158; in "other" MSAs, 671; in "unknown areas," 0.

City/MSA	Number	Rank
Atlanta, GA	4	19
Baltimore, MD	0	23
Bergen-Passaic, NJ	0	23
Boston-Lawrence-Lowell-Brockton, MA	19	11
Charlotte-Gastonia-Rock Hill, NC-SC	3	20
Chicago, IL	5	18
Cleveland-Lorain-Elyria, OH	0	23
Columbus, OH	4	19
Dallas, TX	2	21
Denver, CO	13	13
Detroit, MI	46	8
Fort Lauderdale, FL	0	23
Fort Worth-Arlington, TX	2	21

[Continued]

★500★

Refugees/Asylees Granted Lawful Permanent Resident Status, 1994, By Selected Country of Birth: Thailand
[Continued]

City/MSA	Number	Rank
Fresno, CA	640	1
Hartford, CT	1	22
Houston, TX	2	21
Jacksonville, FL	0	23
Jersey City, NJ	0	23
Kansas City, MO-KS	3	20
Los Angeles-Long Beach, CA	15	12
Merced, CA	214	4
Miami, FL	0	23
Milwaukee-Waukesha, WI	104	6
Minneapolis-Saint Paul, MN-WI	472	2
Nashville, TN	0	23
New Orleans, LA	0	23
New York, NY	5	18
Newark, NJ	0	23
Oakland, CA	70	7
Orange County, CA	9	16
Orlando, FL	4	19
Philadelphia, PA-NJ	5	18
Phoenix-Mesa, AZ	1	22
Portland-Vancouver, OR-WA	11	14
Rochester, NY	0	23
Sacramento, CA	319	3
Saint Louis, MO-IL	0	23
Salt Lake City-Ogden, UT	1	22
San Diego, CA	20	10
San Francisco, CA	4	19
San Jose, CA	10	15
Seattle-Bellevue-Everett, WA	35	9
Spokane, WA	6	17
Springfield, MA	0	23
Stockton-Lodi, CA	181	5
Tacoma, WA	4	19
Tampa-Saint Petersburg-Clearwater, FL	3	20
Washington, DC-MD-VA	1	22
West Palm Beach-Boca Raton, FL	0	23
Yolo, CA	9	16

Source: U.S. Department of Justice, Immigration and Naturalization Service, *Statistical Yearbook of the Immigration and Naturalization Service, 1994*, Washington, D.C.: U.S. Government Printing Office, 1996, p. 92.

★501★
Refugees and Asylees

Refugees/Asylees Granted Lawful Permanent Resident Status, 1994, By Selected Country of Birth: Vietnam

The total number of refugees and asylees from Vietnam who were granted lawful permanent resident status in the United States in fiscal year 1994 is 27,318. The number of refugees and asylees living in metropolitan areas that are not MSAs is 732; in "other" MSAs, 5,640; in "unknown areas," 1.

City/MSA	Number	Rank
Atlanta, GA	1,169	7
Baltimore, MD	68	36
Bergen-Passaic, NJ	3	48
Boston-Lawrence-Lowell-Brockton, MA	874	8
Charlotte-Gastonia-Rock Hill, NC-SC	278	19
Chicago, IL	379	17
Cleveland-Lorain-Elyria, OH	65	38
Columbus, OH	24	45
Dallas, TX	569	11
Denver, CO	283	18
Detroit, MI	46	42
Fort Lauderdale, FL	51	40
Fort Worth-Arlington, TX	556	12
Fresno, CA	59	39
Hartford, CT	67	37
Houston, TX	1,247	6
Jacksonville, FL	84	33
Jersey City, NJ	67	37
Kansas City, MO-KS	146	30
Los Angeles-Long Beach, CA	1,861	2
Merced, CA	7	47
Miami, FL	18	46
Milwaukee-Waukesha, WI	48	41
Minneapolis-Saint Paul, MN-WI	422	16
Nashville, TN	86	32
New Orleans, LA	252	22
New York, NY	231	25
Newark, NJ	40	43
Oakland, CA	652	10
Orange County, CA	1,392	3
Orlando, FL	235	24
Philadelphia, PA-NJ	490	15
Phoenix-Mesa, AZ	156	29
Portland-Vancouver, OR-WA	526	13
Rochester, NY	80	34
Sacramento, CA	515	14
Saint Louis, MO-IL	213	26
Salt Lake City-Ogden, UT	170	28
San Diego, CA	779	9
San Francisco, CA	259	21
San Jose, CA	2,835	1
Seattle-Bellevue-Everett, WA	1,353	5
Spokane, WA	127	31
Springfield, MA	74	35
Stockton-Lodi, CA	182	27
Tacoma, WA	272	20
Tampa-Saint Petersburg-Clearwater, FL	245	23
Washington, DC-MD-VA	1,362	4

[Continued]

★501★

Refugees/Asylees Granted Lawful Permanent Resident Status, 1994, By Selected Country of Birth: Vietnam

[Continued]

City/MSA	Number	Rank
West Palm Beach-Boca Raton, FL	28	44
Yolo, CA	0	49

Source: U.S. Department of Justice, Immigration and Naturalization Service, *Statistical Yearbook of the Immigration and Naturalization Service, 1994*, Washington, D.C.: U.S. Government Printing Office, 1996, p. 92.

Chapter 4

OUTMIGRANT POPULATION

Topic Covered

Geographical Mobility

★502★

Geographical Mobility

Outmigrant Population in Large MSAs, March 1993 to March 1994: Black

[In thousands]

MSAs	Number	Rank
Boston-Lawrence-Salem, MA-NH CMSA	1	8
Chicago-Gary-Lake County, IL-IN-WI CMSA	70	1
Dallas-Fort Worth, TX CMSA	30	4
Detroit-Ann Arbor, MI CMSA	44	3
Houston-Galveston-Brazoria, TX CMSA	19	7
Los Angeles-Anaheim-Riverside, CA CMSA	24	6
New York-Northern New Jersey		9
Philadelphia-Wilmington-Trenton, PA-NJ-DE-MD CMSA	24	6
San Francisco-Oakland-San Jose, CA CMSA	29	5
Washington, DC-MD-VA MSA	54	2
Long Island, NY-NJ-CT CMSA	30	4

Source: Hansen, Kristin A., *Geographical Mobility: March 1993 to March 1994*, U.S. Bureau of the Census, *Current Population Reports* series, P20-485, Washington, D.C.: U.S. Government Printing Office, 1995, p. 164. *Notes:* "MSA" stands for "Metropolitan Statistical Area." "CMSA" stands for "Consolidated Metropolitan Statistical Area."

★503★

Geographical Mobility

Outmigrant Population in Large MSAs, March 1993 to March 1994: Hispanic

[In thousands]

MSAs	Number[1]	Rank
Boston-Lawrence-Salem, MA-NH CMSA	1	8
Chicago-Gary-Lake County, IL-IN-WI CMSA	8	5
Dallas-Fort Worth, TX CMSA	11	4
Detroit-Ann Arbor, MI CMSA	1	8
Houston-Galveston-Brazoria, TX CMSA	25	3
Los Angeles-Anaheim-Riverside, CA CMSA	115	1
New York-Northern New Jersey		9
Philadelphia-Wilmington-Trenton, PA-NJ-DE-MD CMSA	2	7
San Francisco-Oakland-San Jose, CA CMSA	6	6
Washington, DC-MD-VA MSA	2	7
Long Island, NY-NJ-CT CMSA	38	2

Source: Hansen, Kristin A., *Geographical Mobility: March 1993 to March 1994*, U.S. Bureau of the Census, *Current Population Reports* series, P20-485, Washington, D.C.: U.S. Government Printing Office, 1995, p. 164. *Notes:* "MSA" stands for "Metropolitan Statistical Area." "CMSA" stands for "Consolidated Metropolitan Statistical Area." 1. Persons of Hispanic origin may be of any race.

★504★

Geographical Mobility

Outmigrant Population in Large MSAs, March 1993 to March 1994: White

[In thousands]

MSAs	Number	Rank
Boston-Lawrence-Salem, MA-NH CMSA	131	4
Chicago-Gary-Lake County, IL-IN-WI CMSA	100	6
Dallas-Fort Worth, TX CMSA	194	3
Detroit-Ann Arbor, MI CMSA	69	8
Houston-Galveston-Brazoria, TX CMSA	88	7
Los Angeles-Anaheim-Riverside, CA CMSA	461	1
New York-Northern New Jersey		10
Philadelphia-Wilmington-Trenton, PA-NJ-DE-MD CMSA	116	5
San Francisco-Oakland-San Jose, CA CMSA	88	7
Washington, DC-MD-VA MSA	52	9
Long Island, NY-NJ-CT CMSA	259	2

Source: Hansen, Kristin A., *Geographical Mobility: March 1993 to March 1994*, U.S. Bureau of the Census, *Current Population Reports* series, P20-485, Washington, D.C.: U.S. Government Printing Office, 1995, p. 164. *Notes:* "MSA" stands for "Metropolitan Statistical Area." "CMSA" stands for "Consolidated Metropolitan Statistical Area."

★505★

Geographical Mobility

Outmigrant Population in Large MSAs, March 1993 to March 1994: Females

[In thousands]

MSAs	Number	Rank
Boston-Lawrence-Salem, MA-NH CMSA	72	7
Chicago-Gary-Lake County, IL-IN-WI CMSA	122	3
Dallas-Fort Worth, TX CMSA	113	4
Detroit-Ann Arbor, MI CMSA	60	8
Houston-Galveston-Brazoria, TX CMSA	59	9
Los Angeles-Anaheim-Riverside, CA CMSA	250	1
New York-Northern New Jersey		11
Philadelphia-Wilmington-Trenton, PA-NJ-DE-MD CMSA	73	6
San Francisco-Oakland-San Jose, CA CMSA	75	5
Washington, DC-MD-VA MSA	52	10
Long Island, NY-NJ-CT CMSA	176	2

Source: Hansen, Kristin A., *Geographical Mobility: March 1993 to March 1994*, U.S. Bureau of the Census, *Current Population Reports* series, P20-485, Washington, D.C.: U.S. Government Printing Office, 1995, p. 164. *Notes:* "MSA" stands for "Metropolitan Statistical Area." "CMSA" stands for "Consolidated Metropolitan Statistical Area."

★506★

Geographical Mobility

Outmigrant Population in Large MSAs, March 1993 to March 1994: Males

[In thousands]

MSAs	Number	Rank
Boston-Lawrence-Salem, MA-NH CMSA	60	7
Chicago-Gary-Lake County, IL-IN-WI CMSA	100	4
Dallas-Fort Worth, TX CMSA	119	3
Detroit-Ann Arbor, MI CMSA	55	8
Houston-Galveston-Brazoria, TX CMSA	52	10
Los Angeles-Anaheim-Riverside, CA CMSA	279	1
New York-Northern New Jersey		11
Philadelphia-Wilmington-Trenton, PA-NJ-DE-MD CMSA	66	6
San Francisco-Oakland-San Jose, CA CMSA	73	5
Washington, DC-MD-VA MSA	54	9
Long Island, NY-NJ-CT CMSA	166	2

Source: Hansen, Kristin A., *Geographical Mobility: March 1993 to March 1994*, U.S. Bureau of the Census, *Current Population Reports* series, P20-485, Washington, D.C.: U.S. Government Printing Office, 1995, p. 164. *Notes:* "MSA" stands for "Metropolitan Statistical Area." "CMSA" stands for "Consolidated Metropolitan Statistical Area."

★507★

Geographical Mobility

Outmigrant Population in Large MSAs, March 1993 to March 1994: Persons Age One Year Old and Older

[In thousands]

MSAs	Number	Rank
Boston-Lawrence-Salem, MA-NH CMSA	132	7
Chicago-Gary-Lake County, IL-IN-WI CMSA	222	4
Dallas-Fort Worth, TX CMSA	231	3
Detroit-Ann Arbor, MI CMSA	115	8
Houston-Galveston-Brazoria, TX CMSA	110	9
Los Angeles-Anaheim-Riverside, CA CMSA	529	1
New York-Northern New Jersey		11
Philadelphia-Wilmington-Trenton, PA-NJ-DE-MD CMSA	140	6
San Francisco-Oakland-San Jose, CA CMSA	148	5
Washington, DC-MD-VA MSA	106	10
Long Island, NY-NJ-CT CMSA	342	2

Source: Hansen, Kristin A., *Geographical Mobility: March 1993 to March 1994*, U.S. Bureau of the Census, *Current Population Reports* series, P20-485, Washington, D.C.: U.S. Government Printing Office, 1995, p. 164. *Notes:* "MSA" stands for "Metropolitan Statistical Area." "CMSA" stands for "Consolidated Metropolitan Statistical Area."

★508★

Geographical Mobility

Outmigrant Population in Large MSAs, March 1993 to March 1994: Persons Age One to Four Years

[In thousands]

MSAs	Number	Rank
Boston-Lawrence-Salem, MA-NH CMSA	9	7
Chicago-Gary-Lake County, IL-IN-WI CMSA	15	3
Dallas-Fort Worth, TX CMSA	10	6
Detroit-Ann Arbor, MI CMSA	16	2
Houston-Galveston-Brazoria, TX CMSA	15	3
Los Angeles-Anaheim-Riverside, CA CMSA	30	1
New York-Northern New Jersey		9
Philadelphia-Wilmington-Trenton, PA-NJ-DE-MD CMSA	12	5
San Francisco-Oakland-San Jose, CA CMSA	8	8
Washington, DC-MD-VA MSA	-	9
Long Island, NY-NJ-CT CMSA	13	4

Source: Hansen, Kristin A., *Geographical Mobility: March 1993 to March 1994*, U.S. Bureau of the Census, *Current Population Reports* series, P20-485, Washington, D.C.: U.S. Government Printing Office, 1995, p. 164. *Notes:* "MSA" stands for "Metropolitan Statistical Area." "CMSA" stands for "Consolidated Metropolitan Statistical Area."

★509★

Geographical Mobility

Outmigrant Population in Large MSAs, March 1993 to March 1994: Persons Age Five to Nine Years

[In thousands]

MSAs	Number	Rank
Boston-Lawrence-Salem, MA-NH CMSA	13	6
Chicago-Gary-Lake County, IL-IN-WI CMSA	21	3
Dallas-Fort Worth, TX CMSA	24	2
Detroit-Ann Arbor, MI CMSA	21	3
Houston-Galveston-Brazoria, TX CMSA	16	5
Los Angeles-Anaheim-Riverside, CA CMSA	42	1
New York-Northern New Jersey		10
Philadelphia-Wilmington-Trenton, PA-NJ-DE-MD CMSA	8	7
San Francisco-Oakland-San Jose, CA CMSA	6	8
Washington, DC-MD-VA MSA	4	9
Long Island, NY-NJ-CT CMSA	18	4

Source: Hansen, Kristin A., *Geographical Mobility: March 1993 to March 1994*, U.S. Bureau of the Census, *Current Population Reports* series, P20-485, Washington, D.C.: U.S. Government Printing Office, 1995, p. 164. *Notes:* "MSA" stands for "Metropolitan Statistical Area." "CMSA" stands for "Consolidated Metropolitan Statistical Area."

★510★
Geographical Mobility

Outmigrant Population in Large MSAs, March 1993 to March 1994: Persons Age Ten to Fourteen Years

[In thousands]

MSAs	Number	Rank
Boston-Lawrence-Salem, MA-NH CMSA	16	3
Chicago-Gary-Lake County, IL-IN-WI CMSA	16	3
Dallas-Fort Worth, TX CMSA	26	2
Detroit-Ann Arbor, MI CMSA	6	8
Houston-Galveston-Brazoria, TX CMSA	7	7
Los Angeles-Anaheim-Riverside, CA CMSA	33	1
New York-Northern New Jersey		9
Philadelphia-Wilmington-Trenton, PA-NJ-DE-MD CMSA	9	6
San Francisco-Oakland-San Jose, CA CMSA	13	4
Washington, DC-MD-VA MSA	12	5
Long Island, NY-NJ-CT CMSA	12	5

Source: Hansen, Kristin A., *Geographical Mobility: March 1993 to March 1994,* U.S. Bureau of the Census, *Current Population Reports* series, P20-485, Washington, D.C.: U.S. Government Printing Office, 1995, p. 164. *Notes:* "MSA" stands for "Metropolitan Statistical Area." "CMSA" stands for "Consolidated Metropolitan Statistical Area."

★511★
Geographical Mobility

Outmigrant Population in Large MSAs, March 1993 to March 1994: Persons Age 15 to 19 Years

[In thousands]

MSAs	Number	Rank
Boston-Lawrence-Salem, MA-NH CMSA	6	8
Chicago-Gary-Lake County, IL-IN-WI CMSA	18	3
Dallas-Fort Worth, TX CMSA	9	7
Detroit-Ann Arbor, MI CMSA	6	8
Houston-Galveston-Brazoria, TX CMSA	9	7
Los Angeles-Anaheim-Riverside, CA CMSA	43	1
New York-Northern New Jersey		9
Philadelphia-Wilmington-Trenton, PA-NJ-DE-MD CMSA	11	6
San Francisco-Oakland-San Jose, CA CMSA	12	5
Washington, DC-MD-VA MSA	16	4
Long Island, NY-NJ-CT CMSA	26	2

Source: Hansen, Kristin A., *Geographical Mobility: March 1993 to March 1994,* U.S. Bureau of the Census, *Current Population Reports* series, P20-485, Washington, D.C.: U.S. Government Printing Office, 1995, p. 164. *Notes:* "MSA" stands for "Metropolitan Statistical Area." "CMSA" stands for "Consolidated Metropolitan Statistical Area."

★512★
Geographical Mobility

Outmigrant Population in Large MSAs, March 1993 to March 1994: Persons Age 20 to 24 Years

[In thousands]

MSAs	Number	Rank
Boston-Lawrence-Salem, MA-NH CMSA	7	9
Chicago-Gary-Lake County, IL-IN-WI CMSA	31	3
Dallas-Fort Worth, TX CMSA	14	5
Detroit-Ann Arbor, MI CMSA	9	8
Houston-Galveston-Brazoria, TX CMSA	11	7
Los Angeles-Anaheim-Riverside, CA CMSA	56	1
New York-Northern New Jersey		11
Philadelphia-Wilmington-Trenton, PA-NJ-DE-MD CMSA	12	6
San Francisco-Oakland-San Jose, CA CMSA	23	4
Washington, DC-MD-VA MSA	3	10
Long Island, NY-NJ-CT CMSA	37	2

Source: Hansen, Kristin A., *Geographical Mobility: March 1993 to March 1994,* U.S. Bureau of the Census, *Current Population Reports* series, P20-485, Washington, D.C.: U.S. Government Printing Office, 1995, p. 164. *Notes:* "MSA" stands for "Metropolitan Statistical Area." "CMSA" stands for "Consolidated Metropolitan Statistical Area."

★513★
Geographical Mobility

Outmigrant Population in Large MSAs, March 1993 to March 1994: Persons Age 25 to 29 Years

[In thousands]

MSAs	Number	Rank
Boston-Lawrence-Salem, MA-NH CMSA	10	8
Chicago-Gary-Lake County, IL-IN-WI CMSA	23	3
Dallas-Fort Worth, TX CMSA	23	3
Detroit-Ann Arbor, MI CMSA	14	7
Houston-Galveston-Brazoria, TX CMSA	16	6
Los Angeles-Anaheim-Riverside, CA CMSA	55	1
New York-Northern New Jersey		10
Philadelphia-Wilmington-Trenton, PA-NJ-DE-MD CMSA	21	4
San Francisco-Oakland-San Jose, CA CMSA	19	5
Washington, DC-MD-VA MSA	7	9
Long Island, NY-NJ-CT CMSA	41	2

Source: Hansen, Kristin A., *Geographical Mobility: March 1993 to March 1994,* U.S. Bureau of the Census, *Current Population Reports* series, P20-485, Washington, D.C.: U.S. Government Printing Office, 1995, p. 164. *Notes:* "MSA" stands for "Metropolitan Statistical Area." "CMSA" stands for "Consolidated Metropolitan Statistical Area."

★514★
Geographical Mobility

Outmigrant Population in Large MSAs, March 1993 to March 1994: Persons Age 30 to 44 Years

[In thousands]

MSAs	Number	Rank
Boston-Lawrence-Salem, MA-NH CMSA	45	6
Chicago-Gary-Lake County, IL-IN-WI CMSA	57	4
Dallas-Fort Worth, TX CMSA	97	2
Detroit-Ann Arbor, MI CMSA	27	9
Houston-Galveston-Brazoria, TX CMSA	21	10
Los Angeles-Anaheim-Riverside, CA CMSA	135	1
New York-Northern New Jersey		11
Philadelphia-Wilmington-Trenton, PA-NJ-DE-MD CMSA	39	7
San Francisco-Oakland-San Jose, CA CMSA	46	5
Washington, DC-MD-VA MSA	36	8
Long Island, NY-NJ-CT CMSA	92	3

Source: Hansen, Kristin A., *Geographical Mobility: March 1993 to March 1994*, U.S. Bureau of the Census, *Current Population Reports* series, P20-485, Washington, D.C.: U.S. Government Printing Office, 1995, p. 164. *Notes:* "MSA" stands for "Metropolitan Statistical Area." "CMSA" stands for "Consolidated Metropolitan Statistical Area."

★515★
Geographical Mobility

Outmigrant Population in Large MSAs, March 1993 to March 1994: Persons Age 45 to 64 Years

[In thousands]

MSAs	Number	Rank
Boston-Lawrence-Salem, MA-NH CMSA	18	5
Chicago-Gary-Lake County, IL-IN-WI CMSA	33	3
Dallas-Fort Worth, TX CMSA	17	6
Detroit-Ann Arbor, MI CMSA	8	9
Houston-Galveston-Brazoria, TX CMSA	10	8
Los Angeles-Anaheim-Riverside, CA CMSA	87	1
New York-Northern New Jersey		10
Philadelphia-Wilmington-Trenton, PA-NJ-DE-MD CMSA	11	7
San Francisco-Oakland-San Jose, CA CMSA	11	7
Washington, DC-MD-VA MSA	27	4
Long Island, NY-NJ-CT CMSA	72	2

Source: Hansen, Kristin A., *Geographical Mobility: March 1993 to March 1994*, U.S. Bureau of the Census, *Current Population Reports* series, P20-485, Washington, D.C.: U.S. Government Printing Office, 1995, p. 164. *Notes:* "MSA" stands for "Metropolitan Statistical Area." "CMSA" stands for "Consolidated Metropolitan Statistical Area."

★516★
Geographical Mobility

Outmigrant Population in Large MSAs, March 1993 to March 1994: Persons Age 65 Years and Older

[In thousands]

MSAs	Number	Rank
Boston-Lawrence-Salem, MA-NH CMSA	7	6
Chicago-Gary-Lake County, IL-IN-WI CMSA	7	6
Dallas-Fort Worth, TX CMSA	12	4
Detroit-Ann Arbor, MI CMSA	6	7
Houston-Galveston-Brazoria, TX CMSA	6	7
Los Angeles-Anaheim-Riverside, CA CMSA	47	1
New York-Northern New Jersey		9
Philadelphia-Wilmington-Trenton, PA-NJ-DE-MD CMSA	17	3
San Francisco-Oakland-San Jose, CA CMSA	11	5
Washington, DC-MD-VA MSA	1	8
Long Island, NY-NJ-CT CMSA	30	2

Source: Hansen, Kristin A., *Geographical Mobility: March 1993 to March 1994*, U.S. Bureau of the Census, *Current Population Reports* series, P20-485, Washington, D.C.: U.S. Government Printing Office, 1995, p. 164. *Notes:* "MSA" stands for "Metropolitan Statistical Area." "CMSA" stands for "Consolidated Metropolitan Statistical Area."

★517★
Geographical Mobility

Outmigrants From the State of Michigan, 1995

Data refer to those areas in which former residents of the state of Michigan decided to settle.

City	Number	Rank
Atlanta, GA	1,518	26
Atlanta, GA	2,007	19
Atlanta, GA	944	45
Atlanta, GA	975	43
Boston, MA	888	47
Bradenton, FL	2,944	10
Brooksville, FL	2,114	17
Charlotte, NC	1,415	28
Cocoa, FL	1,520	25
Columbia, TN	1,303	35
Columbus, OH	1,270	36
Dallas, TX	1,365	32
Daytona Beach, FL	2,156	16
Fort Lauderdale, FL	3,001	9
Fort Myers, FL	2,559	13
Fort Myers, FL	4,442	4
Fort Pierce, FL	928	46
Inverness, FL	1,511	27
Jacksonville, FL	1,375	31
Lakeland-Winter Haven, FL	3,067	8
Las Vegas, NV	2,915	11
Los Angeles, CA	2,308	14
Memphis, TN	1,003	42
Naples, FL	1,694	22

[Continued]

★517★

Outmigrants From the State of Michigan, 1995
[Continued]

City	Number	Rank
Nashville, TN	1,113	39
Nashville, TN	1,389	30
New Port Richey, FL	4,016	5
New York, NY	1,243	37
Ocala, FL	1,590	24
Orlando, FL	1,175	38
Orlando, FL	2,057	18
Orlando, FL	3,093	7
Phoenix, AZ	6,314	1
Raleigh, NC	1,052	41
Riverside, CA	1,408	29
Sacramento, CA	833	48
Saint Petersburg, FL	5,097	2
San Bernardino, CA	1,061	40
San Diego, CA	4,595	3
San Jose, CA	1,900	21
Santa Ana-Anaheim, CA	1,683	23
Sarasota, FL	2,822	12
Seattle, WA	803	50
Sebring, FL	965	44
Tampa, FL	1,964	20
Tucson, AZ	2,198	15
Washington, DC	1,311	34
Washington, DC	822	49
West Palm Beach, FL	1,326	33
West Palm Beach, FL	3,610	6

Source: "Settling In the Sun," *Detroit Free Press,* 9 October 1995, p. 6A.

Chapter 5

MARITAL STATUS

Topics Covered

Marital Status of Men
Marital Status of Women
Marital Status of Parents

★518★

Marital Status of Men

Men, 1990: Divorced

[Table shows the top 50 areas]

MSA	% of all men	Rank
Las Vegas, NV	11.0	1
Reno, NV	10.9	2
Santa Fe, NM	9.0	3
Anderson, IN	8.6	4
Anchorage, AK	8.0	5
Jackson, MI	8.0	5
Albuquerque, NM	7.7	6
Cheyenne, WY	7.6	7
Tampa – Saint Petersburg – Clearwater, FL	7.5	8
Denver – Boulder, CO	7.4	9
Eugene – Springfield, OR	7.4	9
Portland – Vancouver, OR – WA	7.4	9
Redding, CA	7.4	9
Battle Creek, MI	7.3	10
Daytona Beach, FL	7.3	10
Jacksonville, FL	7.3	10
Salem, OR	7.3	10
Seattle – Tacoma, WA	7.3	10
Topeka, KS	7.3	10
Biloxi – Gulfport, MS	7.2	11
Boise, ID	7.2	11
Medford, OR	7.2	11
Oklahoma City, OK	7.2	11
Panama City, FL	7.2	11
Tucson, AZ	7.2	11
Bradenton, FL	7.1	12
Miami – Fort Lauderdale, FL	7.1	12
Muskegon, MI	7.1	12
Orlando, FL	7.1	12
Casper, WY	7.0	13
Evansville, IN – KY	7.0	13
Fort Myers – Cape Coral, Fl	7.0	13
Fort Walton Beach, FL	7.0	13
Indianapolis, IN	7.0	13
Kokomo, IN	7.0	13
Phoenix, AZ	7.0	13
Pueblo, CO	7.0	13
Sarasota, FL	7.0	13
Spokane, WA	7.0	13
Chattanooga, TN – GA	6.9	14
Olympia, WA	6.9	14
Pensacola, FL	6.9	14
Sacramento, CA	6.9	14
Tulsa, OK	6.9	14
Great Falls, MT	6.8	15
Jackson, TN	6.8	15
Lakeland – Winter Haven, FL	6.8	15
Louisville, KY – IN	6.8	15
Melbourne – Titusville – Palm Bay, FL	6.8	15
Ocala, FL	6.8	15

Source: U.S. Bureau of the Census, Data User Services Division, *1990 Census of Population and Housing,* Summary Tape File 3C, United States Summary, CD- ROM, February 1992.

★519★

Marital Status of Men

Men, 1990: Married

[Table shows the top 50 areas]

MSA	% of all men	Rank
Sarasota, FL	56.7	1
Fort Myers – Cape Coral, Fl	53.4	2
Bradenton, FL	53.1	3
Fort Pierce, FL	51.9	4
Naples, FL	51.7	5
Florence, AL	51.5	6
Ocala, FL	51.5	6
Johnson City – Kingsport – Bristol, TN – VA	51.1	7
Parkersburg – Marietta, WV – OH	50.4	8
Anderson, SC	49.8	9
Gadsden, AL	49.8	9
Decatur, AL	49.7	10
Joplin, MO	49.7	10
West Palm Beach – Boca Raton – Delray Beach, FL	49.6	11
Enid, OK	49.5	12
Huntington – Ashland, WV – KY – OH	49.5	12
Sherman – Denison, TX	49.5	12
Steubenville – Weirton, OH – WV	49.5	12
Charleston, WV	49.3	13
Fort Smith, AR – OK	49.3	13
Melbourne – Titusville – Palm Bay, FL	49.3	13
Burlington, NC	49.2	14
York, PA	49.2	14
Kokomo, IN	49.1	15
Hickory – Morganton, NC	49.0	16
Asheville, NC	48.9	17
Cumberland, MD – WV	48.8	18
Knoxville, TN	48.8	18
Lakeland – Winter Haven, FL	48.8	18
Wheeling, WV – OH	48.7	19
Tampa – Saint Petersburg – Clearwater, FL	48.5	20
Johnstown, PA	48.4	21
Sheboygan, WI	48.4	21
Medford, OR	48.2	22
Canton, OH	48.1	23
Daytona Beach, FL	48.1	23
Altoona, PA	48.0	24
Allentown – Bethlehem – Easton, PA – NJ	47.9	25
Evansville, IN – KY	47.9	25
Tyler, TX	47.9	25
Chattanooga, TN – GA	47.8	26
Owensboro, KY	47.8	26
Sharon, PA	47.8	26
Reading, PA	47.7	27
Rochester, MN	47.7	27
Wausau, WI	47.6	28
Lancaster, PA	47.4	29
Mansfield, OH	47.4	29

[Continued]

★519★

Men, 1990: Married

[Continued]

MSA	% of all men	Rank
Decatur, IL	47.3	30
Tulsa, OK	47.3	30

Source: U.S. Bureau of the Census, Data User Services Division, *1990 Census of Population and Housing*, Summary Tape File 3C, United States Summary, CD- ROM, February 1992.

★520★

Marital Status of Men

Men, 1990: Never Married

[Table shows the top 50 areas]

MSA	% of all men	Rank
Bryan – College Station, TX	42.1	1
State College, PA	41.7	2
Bloomington, IN	38.8	3
Iowa City, IA	38.4	4
Lawrence, KS	38.0	5
Lafayette – West Lafayette, IN	36.2	6
Champaign – Urbana – Rantoul, IL	35.2	7
Gainesville, FL	34.4	8
Columbia, MO	32.5	9
Tallahassee, FL	30.7	10
Charlottesville, VA	30.6	11
Madison, WI	30.5	12
Athens, GA	30.4	13
Burlington, VT	29.7	14
Boston – Lawrence – Salem, MA – NH	29.4	15
Jacksonville, NC	29.4	15
Bloomington – Normal, IL	29.2	16
Austin, TX	28.6	17
Bangor, ME	28.4	18
Fargo – Moorhead, ND – MN	28.4	18
Santa Barbara – Santa Maria – Lompoc, CA	28.1	19
San Diego, CA	28.0	20
San Francisco – Oakland – San Jose, CA	27.8	21
Tuscaloosa, AL	27.8	21
Washington, DC – MD – VA	27.8	21
New York – Northern New Jersey – Long Island, NY – NJ – CT	27.7	22
Los Angeles – Anaheim – Riverside, CA	27.6	23
Grand Forks, ND	27.5	24
Raleigh – Durham, NC	27.5	24
Honolulu, HI	27.4	25
Lincoln, NE	27.4	25
Lansing – East Lansing, MI	27.2	26
Kalamazoo, MI	26.9	27
Muncie, IN	26.7	28
New Haven – Meriden, CT	26.6	29
Saint Cloud, MN	26.6	29
La Crosse, WI	26.4	30

[Continued]

★520★

Men, 1990: Never Married

[Continued]

MSA	% of all men	Rank
Poughkeepsie, NY	26.4	30
Worcester, MA	26.1	31
Hartford – New Britain – Middletown, CT	26.0	32
Chicago – Gary – Lake County, IL – IN – WI	25.9	33
Fayetteville, NC	25.9	33
Philadelphia – Wilmington – Trenton, PA – NJ – DE – MD	25.9	33
Springfield, MA	25.8	34
Albany – Schenectady – Troy, NY	25.7	35
Columbia, SC	25.7	35
Atlantic City, NJ	25.5	36
Syracuse, NY	25.4	37
Baltimore, MD	25.2	38
Detroit – Ann Arbor, MI	25.0	39

Source: U.S. Bureau of the Census, Data User Services Division, *1990 Census of Population and Housing*, Summary Tape File 3C, United States Summary, CD- ROM, February 1992.

★521★

Marital Status of Men

Men, 1990: Separated From Spouse

[Table shows the top 50 areas]

MSA	% of all men	Rank
Danville, VA	2.86	1
Florence, SC	2.84	2
Baltimore, MD	2.77	3
Shreveport, LA	2.66	4
Richmond – Petersburg, VA	2.57	5
Norfolk – Virginia Beach – Newport News, VA	2.51	6
New Orleans, LA	2.44	7
Charleston, SC	2.42	8
Washington, DC – MD – VA	2.40	9
Hagerstown, MD	2.38	10
Memphis, TN – AR – MS	2.35	11
Charlotte – Gastonia – Rock Hill, NC – SC	2.32	12
Fayetteville, NC	2.29	13
Hickory – Morganton, NC	2.25	14
Columbia, SC	2.24	15
Asheville, NC	2.19	16
Greensboro – Winston-Salem – High Point, NC	2.17	17
Alexandria, LA	2.16	18
Glens Falls, NY	2.13	19
Burlington, NC	2.12	20
Philadelphia – Wilmington – Trenton, PA – NJ – DE – MD	2.11	21
Wilmington, NC	2.10	22
Atlantic City, NJ	2.09	23
Albany – Schenectady – Troy, NY	2.08	24

[Continued]

★521★

Men, 1990: Separated From Spouse
[Continued]

MSA	% of all men	Rank
Greenville – Spartanburg, SC	2.08	24
Houston – Galveston – Brazoria, TX	2.05	25
Lynchburg, VA	2.04	26
New York – Northern New Jersey – Long Island, NY – NJ – CT	2.01	27
Lake Charles, LA	2.00	28
Miami – Fort Lauderdale, FL	1.98	29
Utica – Rome, NY	1.97	30
Raleigh – Durham, NC	1.96	31
Jackson, MI	1.93	32
Columbus, GA – AL	1.92	33
Las Vegas, NV	1.92	33
Elmira, NY	1.89	34
Jacksonville, NC	1.89	34
Pueblo, CO	1.88	35
Rochester, NY	1.88	35
Macon – Warner Robins, GA	1.87	36
Albany, GA	1.86	37
Killeen – Temple, TX	1.85	38
Odessa, TX	1.85	38
Erie, PA	1.84	39
Syracuse, NY	1.83	40
Augusta, GA – SC	1.82	41
Jackson, MS	1.82	41
Monroe, LA	1.82	41
Roanoke, VA	1.80	42
Corpus Christi, TX	1.79	43

Source: U.S. Bureau of the Census, Data User Services Division, *1990 Census of Population and Housing*, Summary Tape File 3C, United States Summary, CD- ROM, February 1992.

★522★

Marital Status of Men

Men, 1990: Widowed
[Table shows the top 50 areas]

MSA	% of all men	Rank
Sarasota, FL	3.46	1
Bradenton, FL	3.40	2
Wheeling, WV – OH	3.09	3
Fort Myers – Cape Coral, Fl	2.95	4
Atlantic City, NJ	2.94	5
Daytona Beach, FL	2.94	5
Altoona, PA	2.93	6
Scranton – Wilkes-Barre, PA	2.90	7
Fort Pierce, FL	2.89	8
Pittsburgh – Beaver Valley, PA	2.89	8
Johnstown, PA	2.88	9
West Palm Beach – Boca Raton – Delray Beach, FL	2.85	10
Tampa – Saint Petersburg – Clearwater, FL	2.84	11
Steubenville – Weirton, OH – WV	2.72	12

[Continued]

★522★

Men, 1990: Widowed
[Continued]

MSA	% of all men	Rank
Utica – Rome, NY	2.63	13
Pittsfield, MA	2.60	14
Buffalo – Niagara Falls, NY	2.58	15
Sharon, PA	2.53	16
Cumberland, MD – WV	2.50	17
Ocala, FL	2.50	17
Youngstown – Warren, OH	2.48	18
Duluth, MN – WI	2.45	19
Miami – Fort Lauderdale, FL	2.45	19
Naples, FL	2.45	19
Waterbury, CT	2.45	19
Pine Bluff, AR	2.41	20
Pueblo, CO	2.39	21
Lakeland – Winter Haven, FL	2.38	22
Allentown – Bethlehem – Easton, PA – NJ	2.37	23
Lewiston – Auburn, ME	2.36	24
Reading, PA	2.36	24
Danville, VA	2.32	25
Gadsden, AL	2.32	25
Providence – Pawtucket – Fall River, RI – MA	2.32	25
Burlington, NC	2.31	26
Glens Falls, NY	2.31	26
Decatur, IL	2.30	27
Jackson, TN	2.30	27
Saint Joseph, MO	2.30	27
Springfield, MA	2.30	27
Cleveland – Akron – Lorain, OH	2.29	28
Philadelphia – Wilmington – Trenton, PA – NJ – DE – MD	2.29	28
New York – Northern New Jersey – Long Island, NY – NJ – CT	2.28	29
Roanoke, VA	2.28	29
Anderson, SC	2.27	30
New Bedford, MA	2.27	30
Asheville, NC	2.26	31
Jamestown – Dunkirk, NY	2.26	31
New Haven – Meriden, CT	2.25	32
Binghamton, NY	2.24	33

Source: U.S. Bureau of the Census, Data User Services Division, *1990 Census of Population and Housing*, Summary Tape File 3C, United States Summary, CD- ROM, February 1992.

★523★

Marital Status of Women

Women, 1990: Divorced
[Table shows the top 50 areas]

MSA	% of all women	Rank
Reno, NV	12.7	1
Las Vegas, NV	12.2	2
Santa Fe, NM	11.1	3
Albuquerque, NM	10.6	4

[Continued]

★523★

Women, 1990: Divorced
[Continued]

MSA	% of all women	Rank
Anchorage, AK	10.3	5
Denver – Boulder, CO	10.3	5
Spokane, WA	10.1	6
Portland – Vancouver, OR – WA	9.9	7
Battle Creek, MI	9.8	8
Oklahoma City, OK	9.8	8
Redding, CA	9.8	8
Sacramento, CA	9.8	8
Seattle – Tacoma, WA	9.8	8
Topeka, KS	9.8	8
Anderson, IN	9.7	9
Jacksonville, FL	9.7	9
Olympia, WA	9.7	9
Tulsa, OK	9.7	9
Eugene – Springfield, OR	9.6	10
Miami – Fort Lauderdale, FL	9.6	10
Tucson, AZ	9.6	10
Medford, OR	9.5	11
Phoenix, AZ	9.5	11
Boise, ID	9.4	12
Flint, MI	9.4	12
Indianapolis, IN	9.4	12
Pensacola, FL	9.4	12
Tampa – Saint Petersburg – Clearwater, FL	9.4	12
Cheyenne, WY	9.3	13
Salem, OR	9.3	13
San Diego, CA	9.3	13
San Francisco – Oakland – San Jose, CA	9.3	13
Tallahassee, FL	9.3	13
Austin, TX	9.2	14
Orlando, FL	9.2	14
Saint Joseph, MO	9.2	14
Kansas City, MO – KS	9.1	15
Louisville, KY – IN	9.1	15
Pueblo, CO	9.1	15
Springfield, IL	9.1	15
Amarillo, TX	9.0	16
Billings, MT	9.0	16
Casper, WY	9.0	16
Chattanooga, TN – GA	9.0	16
Columbus, OH	9.0	16
Dallas – Fort Worth, TX	9.0	16
Dayton – Springfield, OH	9.0	16
Columbus, GA – AL	8.9	17
Lexington-Fayette, KY	8.9	17
Little Rock – North Little Rock, AR	8.9	17

Source: U.S. Bureau of the Census, Data User Services Division, *1990 Census of Population and Housing,* Summary Tape File 3C, United States Summary, CD- ROM, February 1992.

★524★

Marital Status of Women

Women, 1990: Married

[Table shows the top 50 areas]

MSA	% of all women	Rank
Naples, FL	50.0	1
Fort Myers – Cape Coral, Fl	49.7	2
Sarasota, FL	49.7	2
Fort Pierce, FL	48.9	3
Melbourne – Titusville – Palm Bay, FL	47.6	4
Decatur, AL	47.4	5
Florence, AL	47.2	6
Bradenton, FL	47.0	7
Johnson City – Kingsport – Bristol, TN – VA	47.0	7
Ocala, FL	47.0	7
Jacksonville, NC	46.9	8
Sheboygan, WI	46.9	8
York, PA	46.9	8
Wausau, WI	46.7	9
Fort Walton Beach, FL	46.5	10
Hickory – Morganton, NC	46.4	11
Bremerton, WA	46.2	12
Fort Smith, AR – OK	46.2	12
Parkersburg – Marietta, WV – OH	46.1	13
Joplin, MO	45.8	14
Panama City, FL	45.7	15
West Palm Beach – Boca Raton – Delray Beach, FL	45.5	16
Enid, OK	45.4	17
Great Falls, MT	45.4	17
Lakeland – Winter Haven, FL	45.4	17
Medford, OR	45.4	17
Hagerstown, MD	45.2	18
Kokomo, IN	45.2	18
Daytona Beach, FL	45.1	19
Cheyenne, WY	45.0	20
Anderson, SC	44.9	21
Huntington – Ashland, WV – KY – OH	44.9	21
Huntsville, AL	44.8	22
Killeen – Temple, TX	44.8	22
Lancaster, PA	44.8	22
Elkhart – Goshen, IN	44.7	23
Steubenville – Weirton, OH – WV	44.7	23
Yuma, AZ	44.7	23
Casper, WY	44.6	24
Clarksville – Hopkinsville, TN – KY	44.6	24
Knoxville, TN	44.6	24
Rochester, MN	44.6	24
Allentown – Bethlehem – Easton, PA – NJ	44.5	25
Charleston, WV	44.5	25
Colorado Springs, CO	44.5	25
Fayetteville – Springdale, AR	44.5	25
Mansfield, OH	44.5	25
Sherman – Denison, TX	44.5	25
Appleton – Oshkosh – Neenah, WI	44.4	26
Sharon, PA	44.4	26

Source: U.S. Bureau of the Census, Data User Services Division, *1990 Census of Population and Housing,* Summary Tape File 3C, United States Summary, CD- ROM, February 1992.

★525★

Marital Status of Women

Women, 1990: Never Married

[Table shows the top 50 areas]

MSA	% of all women	Rank
Bloomington, IN	36.2	1
Bryan–College Station, TX	34.0	2
Lawrence, KS	33.8	3
Iowa City, IA	33.4	4
State College, PA	32.8	5
Columbia, MO	29.4	6
Lafayette–West Lafayette, IN	28.4	7
Champaign–Urbana–Rantoul, IL	28.0	8
Gainesville, FL	27.9	9
Tallahassee, FL	27.8	10
Bloomington–Normal, IL	27.6	11
Burlington, VT	27.3	12
Athens, GA	27.0	13
Charlottesville, VA	26.0	14
Madison, WI	26.0	14
Boston–Lawrence–Salem, MA–NH	25.4	15
Washington, DC–MD–VA	24.3	16
La Crosse, WI	24.2	17
Raleigh–Durham, NC	24.2	17
Tuscaloosa, AL	23.9	18
Kalamazoo, MI	23.8	19
Lansing–East Lansing, MI	23.8	19
Fargo–Moorhead, ND–MN	23.5	20
Muncie, IN	23.5	20
New York–Northern New Jersey–Long Island, NY–NJ–CT	23.5	20
Bangor, ME	23.1	21
Springfield, MA	23.1	21
Lincoln, NE	22.7	22
New Haven–Meriden, CT	22.6	23
Austin, TX	22.5	24
Philadelphia–Wilmington–Trenton, PA–NJ–DE–MD	21.9	25
Columbia, SC	21.8	26
Provo–Orem, UT	21.8	26
Syracuse, NY	21.7	27
Santa Barbara–Santa Maria–Lompoc, CA	21.6	28
Grand Forks, ND	21.4	29
Worcester, MA	21.4	29
Buffalo–Niagara Falls, NY	21.3	30
Chicago–Gary–Lake County, IL–IN–WI	21.3	30
Hartford–New Britain–Middletown, CT	21.3	30
Jackson, MS	21.3	30
Albany–Schenectady–Troy, NY	21.2	31
Saint Cloud, MN	21.2	31
Providence–Pawtucket–Fall River, RI–MA	21.1	32
Rochester, NY	21.1	32
Detroit–Ann Arbor, MI	21.0	33
New Orleans, LA	20.9	34
Dubuque, IA	20.8	35

[Continued]

★525★

Women, 1990: Never Married

[Continued]

MSA	% of all women	Rank
Lynchburg, VA	20.8	35
Baltimore, MD	20.7	36

Source: U.S. Bureau of the Census, Data User Services Division, *1990 Census of Population and Housing,* Summary Tape File 3C, United States Summary, CD-ROM, February 1992.

★526★

Marital Status of Women

Women, 1990: Separated From Spouse

[Table shows the top 50 areas]

MSA	% of all women	Rank
Florence, SC	3.77	1
Fayetteville, NC	3.72	2
Baltimore, MD	3.58	3
Danville, VA	3.56	4
Memphis, TN–AR–MS	3.55	5
Norfolk–Virginia Beach–Newport News, VA	3.55	5
Shreveport, LA	3.44	6
New Orleans, LA	3.42	7
Columbus, GA–AL	3.41	8
Albany, GA	3.38	9
Wilmington, NC	3.21	10
New York–Northern New Jersey–Long Island, NY–NJ–CT	3.17	11
Monroe, LA	3.12	12
Charleston, SC	3.09	13
Washington, DC–MD–VA	2.98	14
Richmond–Petersburg, VA	2.97	15
Columbia, SC	2.95	16
Charlotte–Gastonia–Rock Hill, NC–SC	2.92	17
Jacksonville, NC	2.89	18
Augusta, GA–SC	2.87	19
Greensboro–Winston-Salem–High Point, NC	2.87	19
Brownsville–Harlingen, TX	2.86	20
Alexandria, LA	2.85	21
Lake Charles, LA	2.80	22
Savannah, GA	2.80	22
Atlantic City, NJ	2.77	23
Burlington, NC	2.74	24
Philadelphia–Wilmington–Trenton, PA–NJ–DE–MD	2.74	24
Houston–Galveston–Brazoria, TX	2.71	25
Hickory–Morganton, NC	2.69	26
Jackson, MS	2.68	27
Fresno, CA	2.67	28
Merced, CA	2.67	28
Greenville–Spartanburg, SC	2.63	29
McAllen–Edinburg–Mission, TX	2.63	29
Laredo, TX	2.61	30

[Continued]

★526★

Women, 1990: Separated From Spouse
[Continued]

MSA	% of all women	Rank
Macon – Warner Robins, GA	2.61	30
Bakersfield, CA	2.59	31
Corpus Christi, TX	2.59	31
Baton Rouge, LA	2.57	32
Miami – Fort Lauderdale, FL	2.57	32
Raleigh – Durham, NC	2.56	33
Los Angeles – Anaheim – Riverside, CA	2.55	34
Rochester, NY	2.55	34
El Paso, TX	2.53	35
San Antonio, TX	2.53	35
Elmira, NY	2.52	36
Chico, CA	2.51	37
Sacramento, CA	2.48	38
Pine Bluff, AR	2.45	39

Source: U.S. Bureau of the Census, Data User Services Division, *1990 Census of Population and Housing,* Summary Tape File 3C, United States Summary, CD-ROM, February 1992.

★527★

Marital Status of Women

Women, 1990: Widowed

[Table shows the top 50 areas]

MSA	% of all women	Rank
Sarasota, FL	15.8	1
Bradenton, FL	14.9	2
Scranton – Wilkes-Barre, PA	13.9	3
Johnstown, PA	13.6	4
Wheeling, WV – OH	13.6	4
Daytona Beach, FL	13.5	5
Cumberland, MD – WV	13.4	6
Gadsden, AL	13.4	6
West Palm Beach – Boca Raton – Delray Beach, FL	13.4	6
Pittsburgh – Beaver Valley, PA	13.2	7
Steubenville – Weirton, OH – WV	13.2	7
Tampa – Saint Petersburg – Clearwater, FL	13.1	8
Altoona, PA	13.0	9
Danville, VA	13.0	9
Asheville, NC	12.5	10
Atlantic City, NJ	12.4	11
Sharon, PA	12.3	12
Sherman – Denison, TX	12.3	12
Terre Haute, IN	12.3	12
Charleston, WV	12.2	13
Pine Bluff, AR	12.2	13
Roanoke, VA	12.2	13
Duluth, MN – WI	12.1	14
Saint Joseph, MO	12.1	14
Johnson City – Kingsport – Bristol, TN – VA	12.0	15
Pittsfield, MA	12.0	15

[Continued]

★527★

Women, 1990: Widowed
[Continued]

MSA	% of all women	Rank
Burlington, NC	11.9	16
Joplin, MO	11.9	16
Ocala, FL	11.9	16
Utica – Rome, NY	11.9	16
Fort Myers – Cape Coral, Fl	11.8	17
Fort Pierce, FL	11.8	17
Huntington – Ashland, WV – KY – OH	11.8	17
Anniston, AL	11.7	18
Buffalo – Niagara Falls, NY	11.7	18
Jackson, TN	11.7	18
Parkersburg – Marietta, WV – OH	11.7	18
Texarkana, TX – Texarkana, AR	11.7	18
Anderson, SC	11.6	19
Birmingham, AL	11.6	19
Longview – Marshall, TX	11.6	19
Miami – Fort Lauderdale, FL	11.6	19
Elmira, NY	11.5	20
Florence, AL	11.5	20
New Bedford, MA	11.5	20
Enid, OK	11.3	21
Florence, SC	11.2	22
Waterbury, CT	11.2	22
Youngstown – Warren, OH	11.2	22
Providence – Pawtucket – Fall River, RI – MA	11.1	23

Source: U.S. Bureau of the Census, Data User Services Division, *1990 Census of Population and Housing,* Summary Tape File 3C, United States Summary, CD-ROM, February 1992.

★528★

Marital Status of Parents

Single Parents, 1990: Highest Numbers

Data show percentage of single-parent households among all households with children under 18.

[In percentages]

City	Percentage	Rank
Albany, GA	37.3	1
New York, NY	35.9	2
Flint, MI	35.3	3
Jersey City, NJ	34.3	4
New Orleans, LA	33.6	5
Memphis, TN	33.2	6
Shreveport, LA	32.2	7
Vineland-Millville-Bridgeton, NJ	31.8	8
Monroe, LA	31.8	8
Columbia, GA	31.7	9

Source: "Single Parents," *St. Louis Post-Dispatch,* 10 January 1995, p. 6A. Primary source: U.S. Census Bureau.

★529★

Marital Status of Parents

Single Parents, 1990: Lowest Numbers

Data show percentage of single-parent households among all households with children under 18.

[In percentages]

City	Percentage	Rank
Danbury, CT	13.4	7
Lake County, IL	15.4	3
Middlesex-Somerset-Hunterdon, NJ	14.8	5
Nashua, NH	15.1	4
Nassau-Suffolk, NY	13.9	6
Provo-Orem, UT	12.0	8
Saint Cloud, MN	15.6	1
Sheboygan, WI	15.5	2
State College, PA	15.1	4
Wausau, WI	13.9	6

Source: "Single Parents," *St. Louis Post-Dispatch*, 10 January 1995, p. 6A. Primary source: U.S. Census Bureau.

Chapter 6

COST OF LIVING

Topics Covered

Cable Television
Consumer Expenditures
Daycare
Funeral Prices

★530★

Cable Television

Cable Television Rates, 1996 (Selected Cities): Amounts

Data refer to Time Warner rates under its contract with the Federal Communications Commission.

[In dollars per month]

City	Rate	Rank
Austin, TX	24.33	3
Franklin, WI	23.24	4
New York, NY	27.16	1
Portland, OR	25.02	2

Source: Robichaux, Mark, "FCC's 'Social Contract' for Cable Companies Draws Ire," *Wall Street Journal,* 29 January 1996, p. B4.

★531★

Cable Television

Cable Television Rates, 1996 (Selected Cities): Percent Change From Previous Rates

Data refer to Time Warner rates under its contract with the Federal Communications Commission.

City	Percent change	Rank
Austin, TX	+11	3
Franklin, WI	+12	2
New York, NY	+12	2
Portland, OR	+13	1

Source: Robichaux, Mark, "FCC's 'Social Contract' for Cable Companies Draws Ire," *Wall Street Journal,* 29 January 1996, p. B4.

★532★

Consumer Expenditures

Average Annual Consumer Expenditures, 1993, By Type: Total Expenditures

Data refer to expenditures for food; housing (including shelter); apparel and services; transportation (including vehicle purchases and purchases of gasoline and motor oil); and health care. Metropolitan areas are those defined as of June 30, 1983.

[In dollars]

MSA	Dollars	Rank
Anchorage, AK MSA	39,804	3
Atlanta, GA MSA	36,893	7
Baltimore, MD MSA	30,820	21
Boston-Lawrence-Salem, MA-NH CMSA	33,631	15
Buffalo-Niagara Falls, NY CMSA	24,297	26
Chicago-Gary-Lake County, IL-IN-WI CMSA	35,370	10
Cincinnati-Hamilton, OH-KY-IN CMSA	32,751	17
Cleveland-Akron-Lorain, OH CMSA	27,677	24
Dallas-Fort Worth, TX CMSA	37,258	6
Detroit-Ann Arbor, MI CMSA	32,542	19
Honolulu, HI MSA	38,997	4

[Continued]

★532★

Average Annual Consumer Expenditures, 1993, By Type: Total Expenditures

[Continued]

MSA	Dollars	Rank
Houston-Galveston-Brazoria, TX CMSA	34,062	14
Kansas City, MO-KS CMSA	33,089	16
Los Angeles-Long Beach, CA PMSA	35,319	12
Miami-Fort Lauderdale, FL CMSA	30,744	22
Milwaukee, WI PMSA	32,690	18
Minneapolis-Saint Paul, MN-WI MSA	38,775	5
New York-Northern New Jersey-Long Island, NY-NJ-CT CMSA	35,760	9
Philadelphia-Wilmington-Trenton, PA-NJ-DE-MD CMSA	34,591	13
Pittsburgh-Beaver Valley, PA CMSA	28,976	23
Portland-Vancouver, OR-WA CMSA	32,027	20
Saint Louis-East Saint Louis-Alton, MO-IL CMSA	27,656	25
San Diego, CA MSA	35,320	11
San Francisco-Oakland-San Jose, CA CMSA	40,969	1
Seattle-Tacoma, WA CMSA	36,211	8
Washington, DC-MD-VA MSA	40,507	2

Source: U.S. Bureau of the Census, *Statistical Abstract of the United States: 1995,* (115th edition), Washington, D.C.: U.S. Government Printing Office, 1995, p. 468. Primary source: U.S. Bureau of Labor Statistics, *Consumer Expenditures in 1993;* and unpublished data.

★533★

Consumer Expenditures

Average Annual Consumer Expenditures, 1993, By Type: Apparel and Services

Metropolitan areas are those defined as of June 30, 1983.

[In dollars]

MSA	Dollars	Rank
Anchorage, AK MSA	1,905	16
Atlanta, GA MSA	2,103	5
Baltimore, MD MSA	1,753	20
Boston-Lawrence-Salem, MA-NH CMSA	1,990	11
Buffalo-Niagara Falls, NY CMSA	1,313	25
Chicago-Gary-Lake County, IL-IN-WI CMSA	2,285	3
Cincinnati-Hamilton, OH-KY-IN CMSA	2,003	10
Cleveland-Akron-Lorain, OH CMSA	1,503	24
Dallas-Fort Worth, TX CMSA	1,837	18
Detroit-Ann Arbor, MI CMSA	1,936	13
Honolulu, HI MSA	2,086	6

[Continued]

★533★
Average Annual Consumer Expenditures, 1993, By Type: Apparel and Services
[Continued]

MSA	Dollars	Rank
Houston-Galveston-Brazoria, TX CMSA	1,819	19
Kansas City, MO-KS CMSA	2,016	8
Los Angeles-Long Beach, CA PMSA	1,980	12
Miami-Fort Lauderdale, FL CMSA	1,625	23
Milwaukee, WI PMSA	1,934	14
Minneapolis-Saint Paul, MN-WI MSA	2,014	9
New York-Northern New Jersey-Long Island, NY-NJ-CT CMSA	2,435	1
Philadelphia-Wilmington-Trenton, PA-NJ-DE-MD CMSA	2,422	2
Pittsburgh-Beaver Valley, PA CMSA	2,185	4
Portland-Vancouver, OR-WA CMSA	1,654	22
Saint Louis-East Saint Louis-Alton, MO-IL MSA	1,211	26
San Diego, CA MSA	1,752	21
San Francisco-Oakland-San Jose, CA CMSA	1,849	17
Seattle-Tacoma, WA CMSA	1,923	15
Washington, DC-MD-VA MSA	2,027	7

Source: U.S. Bureau of the Census, *Statistical Abstract of the United States: 1995*, (115th edition), Washington, D.C.: U.S. Government Printing Office, 1995, p. 468. Primary source: U.S. Bureau of Labor Statistics, *Consumer Expenditures in 1993*; and unpublished data.

★534★
Consumer Expenditures
Average Annual Consumer Expenditures, 1993, By Type: Food

Metropolitan areas are those defined as of June 30, 1983.

[In dollars]

MSA	Dollars	Rank
Anchorage, AK MSA	5,192	4
Atlanta, GA MSA	4,210	24
Baltimore, MD MSA	4,574	16
Boston-Lawrence-Salem, MA-NH CMSA	4,329	22
Buffalo-Niagara Falls, NY CMSA	4,663	15
Chicago-Gary-Lake County, IL-IN-WI CMSA	5,060	5
Cincinnati-Hamilton, OH-KY-IN CMSA	4,801	9
Cleveland-Akron-Lorain, OH CMSA	4,368	21
Dallas-Fort Worth, TX CMSA	4,898	8
Detroit-Ann Arbor, MI CMSA	4,307	23
Honolulu, HI MSA	7,104	1

[Continued]

★534★
Average Annual Consumer Expenditures, 1993, By Type: Food
[Continued]

MSA	Dollars	Rank
Houston-Galveston-Brazoria, TX CMSA	4,705	13
Kansas City, MO-KS CMSA	4,492	17
Los Angeles-Long Beach, CA PMSA	4,725	11
Miami-Fort Lauderdale, FL CMSA	4,934	7
Milwaukee, WI PMSA	4,444	19
Minneapolis-Saint Paul, MN-WI CMSA	4,898	8
New York-Northern New Jersey-Long Island, NY-NJ-CT CMSA	5,241	3
Philadelphia-Wilmington-Trenton, PA-NJ-DE-MD CMSA	4,700	14
Pittsburgh-Beaver Valley, PA CMSA	4,476	18
Portland-Vancouver, OR-WA CMSA	4,434	20
Saint Louis-East Saint Louis-Alton, MO-IL CMSA	4,188	25
San Diego, CA MSA	4,739	10
San Francisco-Oakland-San Jose, CA CMSA	5,337	2
Seattle-Tacoma, WA CMSA	4,722	12
Washington, DC-MD-VA MSA	5,031	6

Source: U.S. Bureau of the Census, *Statistical Abstract of the United States: 1995*, (115th edition), Washington, D.C.: U.S. Government Printing Office, 1995, p. 468. Primary source: U.S. Bureau of Labor Statistics, *Consumer Expenditures in 1993*; and unpublished data.

★535★
Consumer Expenditures
Average Annual Consumer Expenditures, 1993, By Type: Gasoline and Motor Oil

Metropolitan areas are those defined as of June 30, 1983.

[In dollars]

MSA	Dollars	Rank
Anchorage, AK MSA	957	15
Atlanta, GA MSA	1,066	6
Baltimore, MD MSA	916	18
Boston-Lawrence-Salem, MA-NH CMSA	968	14
Buffalo-Niagara Falls, NY CMSA	713	25
Chicago-Gary-Lake County, IL-IN-WI CMSA	1,001	12
Cincinnati-Hamilton, OH-KY-IN CMSA	1,077	5
Cleveland-Akron-Lorain, OH CMSA	854	20
Dallas-Fort Worth, TX CMSA	1,201	1
Detroit-Ann Arbor, MI CMSA	1,019	10
Honolulu, HI MSA	819	23

[Continued]

★535★

Average Annual Consumer Expenditures, 1993, By Type: Gasoline and Motor Oil
[Continued]

MSA	Dollars	Rank
Houston-Galveston-Brazoria, TX CMSA	1,106	2
Kansas City, MO-KS CMSA	1,043	9
Los Angeles-Long Beach, CA PMSA	1,045	8
Miami-Fort Lauderdale, FL CMSA	931	17
Milwaukee, WI PMSA	1,012	11
Minneapolis-Saint Paul, MN-WI MSA	1,082	4
New York-Northern New Jersey-Long Island, NY-NJ-CT CMSA	826	22
Philadelphia-Wilmington-Trenton, PA-NJ-DE-MD CMSA	828	21
Pittsburgh-Beaver Valley, PA CMSA	800	24
Portland-Vancouver, OR-WA CMSA	942	16
Saint Louis-East Saint Louis-Alton, MO-IL CMSA	908	19
San Diego, CA MSA	1,054	7
San Francisco-Oakland-San Jose, CA CMSA	1,087	3
Seattle-Tacoma, WA CMSA	1,082	4
Washington, DC-MD-VA MSA	976	13

Source: U.S. Bureau of the Census, Statistical Abstract of the United States: 1995, (115th edition), Washington, D.C.: U.S. Government Printing Office, 1995, p. 468. Primary source: U.S. Bureau of Labor Statistics, Consumer Expenditures in 1993; and unpublished data.

★536★
Consumer Expenditures

Average Annual Consumer Expenditures, 1993, By Type: Health Care

Metropolitan areas are those defined as of June 30, 1983.

[In dollars]

MSA	Dollars	Rank
Anchorage, AK MSA	1,904	4
Atlanta, GA MSA	1,971	1
Baltimore, MD MSA	1,608	17
Boston-Lawrence-Salem, MA-NH CMSA	1,640	15
Buffalo-Niagara Falls, NY CMSA	1,399	25
Chicago-Gary-Lake County, IL-IN-WI CMSA	1,825	6
Cincinnati-Hamilton, OH-KY-IN CMSA	1,656	14
Cleveland-Akron-Lorain, OH CMSA	1,681	12
Dallas-Fort Worth, TX CMSA	1,916	2
Detroit-Ann Arbor, MI CMSA	1,255	26
Honolulu, HI MSA	1,661	13

[Continued]

★536★

Average Annual Consumer Expenditures, 1993, By Type: Health Care
[Continued]

MSA	Dollars	Rank
Houston-Galveston-Brazoria, TX CMSA	1,813	7
Kansas City, MO-KS CMSA	1,915	3
Los Angeles-Long Beach, CA PMSA	1,519	23
Miami-Fort Lauderdale, FL CMSA	1,583	20
Milwaukee, WI PMSA	1,602	18
Minneapolis-Saint Paul, MN-WI MSA	1,687	11
New York-Northern New Jersey-Long Island, NY-NJ-CT CMSA	1,689	10
Philadelphia-Wilmington-Trenton, PA-NJ-DE-MD CMSA	1,803	8
Pittsburgh-Beaver Valley, PA CMSA	1,903	5
Portland-Vancouver, OR-WA CMSA	1,573	21
Saint Louis-East Saint Louis-Alton, MO-IL CMSA	1,609	16
San Diego, CA MSA	1,561	22
San Francisco-Oakland-San Jose, CA CMSA	1,444	24
Seattle-Tacoma, WA CMSA	1,594	19
Washington, DC-MD-VA MSA	1,723	9

Source: U.S. Bureau of the Census, Statistical Abstract of the United States: 1995, (115th edition), Washington, D.C.: U.S. Government Printing Office, 1995, p. 468. Primary source: U.S. Bureau of Labor Statistics, Consumer Expenditures in 1993; and unpublished data.

★537★
Consumer Expenditures

Average Annual Consumer Expenditures, 1993, By Type: Housing

Metropolitan areas are those defined as of June 30, 1983.

[In dollars]

MSA	Dollars[1]	Rank
Anchorage, AK MSA	13,104	3
Atlanta, GA MSA	12,690	6
Baltimore, MD MSA	10,690	16
Boston-Lawrence-Salem, MA-NH CMSA	12,338	9
Buffalo-Niagara Falls, NY CMSA	7,865	26
Chicago-Gary-Lake County, IL-IN-WI CMSA	11,708	13
Cincinnati-Hamilton, OH-KY-IN CMSA	9,940	21
Cleveland-Akron-Lorain, OH CMSA	8,191	25
Dallas-Fort Worth, TX CMSA	11,401	14
Detroit-Ann Arbor, MI CMSA	10,718	15
Honolulu, HI MSA	12,261	10

[Continued]

★ 537 ★

Average Annual Consumer Expenditures, 1993, By Type: Housing
[Continued]

MSA	Dollars[1]	Rank
Houston-Galveston-Brazoria, TX CMSA	10,060	19
Kansas City, MO-KS CMSA	9,887	22
Los Angeles-Long Beach, CA PMSA	12,750	5
Miami-Fort Lauderdale, FL CMSA	10,018	20
Milwaukee, WI PMSA	10,162	18
Minneapolis-Saint Paul, MN-WI MSA	12,398	8
New York-Northern New Jersey-Long Island, NY-NJ-CT CMSA	13,080	4
Philadelphia-Wilmington-Trenton, PA-NJ-DE-MD CMSA	12,180	11
Pittsburgh-Beaver Valley, PA CMSA	8,607	23
Portland-Vancouver, OR-WA CMSA	10,487	17
Saint Louis-East Saint Louis-Alton, MO-IL CMSA	8,297	24
San Diego, CA MSA	12,413	7
San Francisco-Oakland-San Jose, CA CMSA	14,155	2
Seattle-Tacoma, WA CMSA	11,813	12
Washington, DC-MD-VA MSA	14,233	1

Source: U.S. Bureau of the Census, *Statistical Abstract of the United States: 1995*, (115th edition), Washington, D.C.: U.S. Government Printing Office, 1995, p. 468. Primary source: U.S. Bureau of Labor Statistics, *Consumer Expenditures in 1993;* and unpublished data. *Note:* 1. Includes expenditures not shown separately.

★ 538 ★

Consumer Expenditures

Average Annual Consumer Expenditures, 1993, By Type: Shelter

Metropolitan areas are those defined as of June 30, 1983.

[In dollars]

MSA	Dollars	Rank
Anchorage, AK MSA	8,239	7
Atlanta, GA MSA	7,241	10
Baltimore, MD MSA	6,425	15
Boston-Lawrence-Salem, MA-NH CMSA	7,784	8
Buffalo-Niagara Falls, NY CMSA	4,641	23
Chicago-Gary-Lake County, IL-IN-WI CMSA	6,814	12
Cincinnati-Hamilton, OH-KY-IN CMSA	5,493	20
Cleveland-Akron-Lorain, OH CMSA	4,443	24
Dallas-Fort Worth, TX CMSA	6,180	17
Detroit-Ann Arbor, MI CMSA	6,201	16
Honolulu, HI MSA	8,352	6

[Continued]

★ 538 ★

Average Annual Consumer Expenditures, 1993, By Type: Shelter
[Continued]

MSA	Dollars	Rank
Houston-Galveston-Brazoria, TX CMSA	5,247	21
Kansas City, MO-KS CMSA	4,989	22
Los Angeles-Long Beach, CA PMSA	8,533	3
Miami-Fort Lauderdale, FL CMSA	6,152	18
Milwaukee, WI PMSA	6,082	19
Minneapolis-Saint Paul, MN-WI MSA	6,985	11
New York-Northern New Jersey-Long Island, NY-NJ-CT CMSA	8,487	4
Philadelphia-Wilmington-Trenton, PA-NJ-DE-MD CMSA	6,737	13
Pittsburgh-Beaver Valley, PA CMSA	4,295	26
Portland-Vancouver, OR-WA CMSA	6,519	14
Saint Louis-East Saint Louis-Alton, MO-IL CMSA	4,358	25
San Diego, CA MSA	8,433	5
San Francisco-Oakland-San Jose, CA CMSA	9,658	1
Seattle-Tacoma, WA CMSA	7,361	9
Washington, DC-MD-VA MSA	8,901	2

Source: U.S. Bureau of the Census, *Statistical Abstract of the United States: 1995*, (115th edition), Washington, D.C.: U.S. Government Printing Office, 1995, p. 468. Primary source: U.S. Bureau of Labor Statistics, *Consumer Expenditures in 1993;* and unpublished data.

★ 539 ★

Consumer Expenditures

Average Annual Consumer Expenditures, 1993, By Type: Transportation

Data include expenditures for vehicle purchases and purchases of gasoline and motor oil. Metropolitan areas are those defined as of June 30, 1983.

[In dollars]

MSA	Dollars[1]	Rank
Anchorage, AK MSA	6,536	5
Atlanta, GA MSA	6,368	9
Baltimore, MD MSA	4,067	25
Boston-Lawrence-Salem, MA-NH CMSA	5,525	18
Buffalo-Niagara Falls, NY CMSA	3,960	26
Chicago-Gary-Lake County, IL-IN-WI CMSA	6,396	7
Cincinnati-Hamilton, OH-KY-IN CMSA	6,021	11
Cleveland-Akron-Lorain, OH CMSA	5,266	20
Dallas-Fort Worth, TX CMSA	7,444	1

[Continued]

★539★

Average Annual Consumer Expenditures, 1993, By Type: Transportation

[Continued]

MSA	Dollars[1]	Rank
Detroit-Ann Arbor, MI CMSA	6,832	3
Honolulu, HI MSA	5,490	19
Houston-Galveston-Brazoria, TX CMSA	6,388	8
Kansas City, MO-KS CMSA	6,526	6
Los Angeles-Long Beach, CA PMSA	5,911	14
Miami-Fort Lauderdale, FL CMSA	5,596	17
Milwaukee, WI PMSA	6,154	10
Minneapolis-Saint Paul, MN-WI MSA	5,917	13
New York-Northern New Jersey-Long Island, NY-NJ-CT CMSA	4,882	22
Philadelphia-Wilmington-Trenton, PA-NJ-DE-MD CMSA	4,858	23
Pittsburgh-Beaver Valley, PA CMSA	4,981	21
Portland-Vancouver, OR-WA CMSA	5,827	15
Saint Louis-East Saint Louis-Alton, MO-IL CMSA	4,832	24
San Diego, CA MSA	5,985	12
San Francisco-Oakland-San Jose, CA CMSA	7,017	2
Seattle-Tacoma, WA CMSA	6,712	4
Washington, DC-MD-VA MSA	5,753	16

Source: U.S. Bureau of the Census, *Statistical Abstract of the United States: 1995*, (115th edition), Washington, D.C.: U.S. Government Printing Office, 1995, p. 468. Primary source: U.S. Bureau of Labor Statistics, *Consumer Expenditures in 1993;* and unpublished data. *Note:* 1. Includes expenditures not shown separately.

★540★
Consumer Expenditures

Average Annual Consumer Expenditures, 1993, By Type: Vehicle Purchases

Metropolitan areas are those defined as of June 30, 1983.

[In dollars]

MSA	Dollars	Rank
Anchorage, AK MSA	2,394	13
Atlanta, GA MSA	2,702	10
Baltimore, MD MSA	1,184	26
Boston-Lawrence-Salem, MA-NH CMSA	2,343	15
Buffalo-Niagara Falls, NY CMSA	1,394	24
Chicago-Gary-Lake County, IL-IN-WI CMSA	2,926	5
Cincinnati-Hamilton, OH-KY-IN CMSA	2,515	11
Cleveland-Akron-Lorain, OH CMSA	2,447	12
Dallas-Fort Worth, TX CMSA	3,620	1

[Continued]

★540★

Average Annual Consumer Expenditures, 1993, By Type: Vehicle Purchases

[Continued]

MSA	Dollars	Rank
Detroit-Ann Arbor, MI CMSA	3,213	2
Honolulu, HI MSA	1,809	22
Houston-Galveston-Brazoria, TX CMSA	2,770	8
Kansas City, MO-KS CMSA	2,822	6
Los Angeles-Long Beach, CA PMSA	2,197	19
Miami-Fort Lauderdale, FL CMSA	2,216	17
Milwaukee, WI PMSA	3,153	3
Minneapolis-Saint Paul, MN-WI MSA	2,369	14
New York-Northern New Jersey-Long Island, NY-NJ-CT CMSA	1,337	25
Philadelphia-Wilmington-Trenton, PA-NJ-DE-MD CMSA	1,423	23
Pittsburgh-Beaver Valley, PA CMSA	2,108	20
Portland-Vancouver, OR-WA CMSA	2,715	9
Saint Louis-East Saint Louis-Alton, MO-IL CMSA	2,208	18
San Diego, CA MSA	2,263	16
San Francisco-Oakland-San Jose, CA CMSA	2,929	4
Seattle-Tacoma, WA CMSA	2,783	7
Washington, DC-MD-VA MSA	1,918	21

Source: U.S. Bureau of the Census, *Statistical Abstract of the United States: 1995*, (115th edition), Washington, D.C.: U.S. Government Printing Office, 1995, p. 468. Primary source: U.S. Bureau of Labor Statistics, *Consumer Expenditures in 1993;* and unpublished data.

★541★
Daycare

Daycare Costs, 1993: Highest

[In dollars per week]

City	Cost per week	Rank
Anchorage, AK	96	7
Boston, MA	122	1
Buffalo, NY	91	9
Chicago, IL	91	9
Hartford, CT	92	8
Manchester, NH	103	5
Minneapolis, MN	120	2
New York, NY	118	3
Philadelphia, PA	105	4
Washington, DC	101	6

Source: Gunsch, Dawn, "For Your Information: A New Administration Means New Regulation," *Personnel Journal,* (March 1993), p. 15.

★542★
Daycare

Daycare Costs, 1993: Lowest

[In dollars per week]

City	Cost per week	Rank
Boise, ID	58	7
Casper, WY	47	2
Columbia, SC	59	8
Jackson, MS	46	1
Little Rock, AR	58	7
Mobile, AL	49	3
New Orleans, LA	55	5
Salt Lake City, UT	46	1
Tampa, FL	57	6
Tucson, AZ	50	4

Source: Gunsch, Dawn, "For Your Information: A New Administration Means New Regulation," *Personnel Journal,* (March 1993), p. 15.

★543★
Daycare

Daycare Costs, 1996: Highest

Data refer to the median monthly fees for a 3-year-old in a for-profit center 5 days per week, 8 hours per day.

[In dollars per month]

City	Cost	Rank
New York, NY	589	1
Boston, MA	579	2
Minneapolis, MN	537	3
Philadelphia, PA	503	4
Washington, DC	486	5

Source: "Where Daycare Is No Bargain," USA SNAPSHOTS, *USA TODAY,* 18 March 1996, p. 1D. Primary source: Runzheimer International analysis.

★544★
Daycare

Daycare Costs, 1996: Lowest

Data refer to the median monthly fees for a 3-year-old in a for-profit center 5 days per week, 8 hours per day.

[In dollars per month]

City	Cost	Rank
Casper, WY	217	1
Mobile, AL	217	1
Jackson, MS	231	2
Tampa, FL	246	3
New Orleans, LA	256	4

Source: "Where Daycare Is No Bargain," USA SNAPSHOTS, *USA TODAY,* 19 March 1996, p. 1D. Primary source: Runzheimer International analysis.

★545★
Daycare

Daycare Costs, By Age of Child(ren), 1996: One Year Old

Data refer to costs for full day care.

[In dollars]

City	Cost	Rank
Boston, MA	228.00	1
Boulder, CO	165.00	2
Dallas, TX	89.00	6
Durham, NC	99.00	5
Minneapolis, MN	161.00	3
Oakland, CA	145.00	4
Orlando, FL	83.00	7

Source: "Child Care Fees Across the Nation," *Child Care Information Exchange,* (July 1996), p. 89.

★546★
Daycare

Daycare Costs, By Age of Child(ren), 1996: Three Years Old

Data refer to costs for full day care.

[In dollars]

City	Cost	Rank
Boston, MA	170.00	1
Boulder, CO	120.00	3
Dallas, TX	71.00	7
Durham, NC	89.00	5
Minneapolis, MN	116.00	4
Oakland, CA	125.00	2
Orlando, FL	73.00	6

Source: "Child Care Fees Across the Nation," *Child Care Information Exchange,* (July 1996), p. 89.

★547★
Daycare

Daycare Costs, By Age of Child(ren), 1996: Six Years Old

Data refer to costs for afternoon only day care.

[In dollars]

City	Cost	Rank
Boston, MA	128.00	1
Boulder, CO	66.00	4
Dallas, TX	51.00	6
Durham, NC	54.00	5
Minneapolis, MN	72.00	2
Oakland, CA	70.00	3
Orlando, FL	38.00	7

Source: "Child Care Fees Across the Nation," *Child Care Information Exchange,* (July 1996), p. 89.

★548★

Funeral Prices

Burial Costs, 1995: Selected Cities

Data refer to costs for direct burial, i.e., no visitation or other options.

City	Costs	Rank
Baltimore, MD	1,035	2
Boston, MA	952	3
Chicago, IL	640	8
Dallas-Houston, TX	875	4
Denver, CO	1,122	1
Los Angeles, CA	610	9
New York-Long Island, NY	545	11
Phoenix, AZ	800	5
Pittsburgh, PA	650	7
Saint Louis, MO	400	12
Seattle, WA	629	6
Tampa, FL	581	10

Source: "Funeral/Cremation Price Survey," *Consumers Digest,* (September/October 1995), p. 55.

★549★

Funeral Prices

Cremation Costs, 1995: Selected Cities

City	Cremation	Rank
Baltimore, MD	695	1
Boston, MA	695	1
Chicago, IL	390	8
Dallas-Houston, TX	575	3
Denver, CO	586	2
Los Angeles, CA	415	7
New York-Long Island, NY	390	8
Phoenix, AZ	375	9
Pittsburgh, PA	390	8
Saint Louis, MO	445	5
Seattle, WA	497	4
Tampa, FL	431	6

Source: "Funeral/Cremation Price Survey," *Consumers Digest,* (September/October 1995), p. 55.

Chapter 7

HEALTH AND HEALTH CONDITIONS

Topics Covered

Drug Use and Abuse
Alcohol Use
Cocaine Use
Cocaine and Heroin Use
Crack or Freebase Use
Illegal Steroid Use
Injected-Drug Use
Marijuana Use
Methamphetamine Use
Tobacco Use
Eating Habits
Exercise Habits
Self-Image
Youth Risk Behavior
Diseases: AIDS
Diseases: Back Problems
Diseases: Breast Cancer
Diseases: Coronary Disease
Emergency Medical Services
Vital Statistics
Costs for Illegal Drugs
Medical Insurance

★550★

Drug Use and Abuse

High School Students Who Reported Being Offered, Sold, or Given Illegal Drugs on School Property, 1993: Females

Data refer to the 12-month period preceding the survey.

[In percentages]

City/MSA	Female	Rank
Boston, MA	18.1	5
Chicago, IL	13.8	9
Dallas, TX	16.2	6
Fort Lauderdale, FL	18.5	4
Jersey City, NJ	10.7	11
Miami, FL	23.7	2
New Orleans, LA	9.7	12
New York City, NY	14.5	8
Philadelphia, PA	15.4	7
San Diego, CA	31.4	1
Seattle, WA	22.5	3
Washington, DC	13.3	10

Source: U.S. Department of Health and Human Services, Public Health Service, Centers for Disease Control and Prevention (CDC), CDC Surveillance Summaries, MMWR: Morbidity and Mortality Weekly Report, 24 March, 1995, vol. 44, no. SS-1, *Youth Risk Behavior Surveillance—United States, 1993,* Atlanta, GA: Centers for Disease Control and Prevention, 1995, p. 46. *Notes:* Data for New Orleans, Louisiana; New York City, New York; Philadelphia, Pennsylvania; and San Francisco, California, are unweighted. Survey covers selected sites.

★551★

Drug Use and Abuse

High School Students Who Reported Being Offered, Sold, or Given Illegal Drugs on School Property, 1993: Males

Data refer to the 12-month period preceding the survey.

[In percentages]

City/MSA	Male	Rank
Boston, MA	25.3	7
Chicago, IL	19.3	10
Dallas, TX	26.9	6
Fort Lauderdale, FL	30.4	4
Jersey City, NJ	19.7	9
Miami, FL	36.6	2
New Orleans, LA	17.3	12
New York City, NY	28.9	5
Philadelphia, PA	22.9	8
San Diego, CA	42.0	1
Seattle, WA	33.5	3
Washington, DC	18.6	11

Source: U.S. Department of Health and Human Services, Public Health Service, Centers for Disease Control and Prevention (CDC), CDC Surveillance Summaries, MMWR: Morbidity and Mortality Weekly Report, 24 March, 1995, vol. 44, no. SS-1, *Youth Risk Behavior Surveillance—United States, 1993,* Atlanta, GA: Centers for Disease Control and Prevention, 1995, p. 46. *Notes:* Data for New Orleans, Louisiana; New York City, New York; Philadelphia, Pennsylvania; and San Francisco, California, are unweighted. Survey covers selected sites.

★552★

Drug Use and Abuse

High School Students Who Reported Being Offered, Sold, or Given Illegal Drugs on School Property, 1993: Total

Data refer to the 12-month period preceding the survey.

[In percentages]

City/MSA	Total	Rank
Boston, MA	21.7	5
Chicago, IL	16.5	9
Dallas, TX	21.2	7
Fort Lauderdale, FL	24.5	4
Jersey City, NJ	15.2	11
Miami, FL	30.3	2
New Orleans, LA	12.8	12
New York City, NY	21.3	6
Philadelphia, PA	18.9	8
San Diego, CA	36.7	1
Seattle, WA	28.0	3
Washington, DC	15.7	10

Source: U.S. Department of Health and Human Services, Public Health Service, Centers for Disease Control and Prevention (CDC), CDC Surveillance Summaries, MMWR: Morbidity and Mortality Weekly Report, 24 March, 1995, vol. 44, no. SS-1, *Youth Risk Behavior Surveillance—United States, 1993,* Atlanta, GA: Centers for Disease Control and Prevention, 1995, p. 46. *Notes:* Data for New Orleans, Louisiana; New York City, New York; Philadelphia, Pennsylvania; and San Francisco, California, are unweighted. Survey covers selected sites.

★553★

Alcohol Use

High School Students Currently Using Alcohol, 1993: Females

Data refer to high school students who drank alcohol on more than one of the 30 days preceding the survey.

[In percentages]

City/MSA	Female	Rank
Boston, MA	35.6	10
Chicago, IL	38.6	8
Dallas, TX	42.4	5
Fort Lauderdale, FL	42.8	4
Jersey City, NJ	34.8	11
Miami, FL	36.0	9
New Orleans, LA	43.1	3
New York City, NY	31.4	13
Philadelphia, PA	40.8	6
San Diego, CA	43.7	1
San Francisco, CA	31.8	12
Seattle, WA	43.6	2
Washington, DC	40.1	7

Source: U.S. Department of Health and Human Services, Public Health Service, Centers for Disease Control and Prevention (CDC), CDC Surveillance Summaries, MMWR: Morbidity and Mortality Weekly Report, 24 March, 1995, vol. 44, no. SS-1, *Youth Risk Behavior Surveillance—United States, 1993,* Atlanta, GA: Centers for Disease Control and Prevention, 1995, p. 41. *Notes:* Data for New Orleans, Louisiana; New York City, New York; Philadelphia, Pennsylvania; and San Francisco, California, are unweighted. Survey covers selected sites.

★554★
Alcohol Use

High School Students Currently Using Alcohol, 1993: Males

Data refer to high school students who drank alcohol on more than one of the 30 days preceding the survey.

[In percentages]

City/MSA	Male	Rank
Boston, MA	44.9	7
Chicago, IL	39.7	11
Dallas, TX	51.1	1
Fort Lauderdale, FL	45.0	6
Jersey City, NJ	50.3	2
Miami, FL	37.7	12
New Orleans, LA	48.9	3
New York City, NY	45.3	5
Philadelphia, PA	41.9	10
San Diego, CA	43.5	8
San Francisco, CA	34.3	13
Seattle, WA	48.7	4
Washington, DC	42.7	9

Source: U.S. Department of Health and Human Services, Public Health Service, Centers for Disease Control and Prevention (CDC), CDC Surveillance Summaries, MMWR: Morbidity and Mortality Weekly Report, 24 March, 1995, vol. 44, no. SS-1, *Youth Risk Behavior Surveillance—United States, 1993,* Atlanta, GA: Centers for Disease Control and Prevention, 1995, p. 41. *Notes:* Data for New Orleans, Louisiana; New York City, New York; Philadelphia, Pennsylvania; and San Francisco, California, are unweighted. Survey covers selected sites.

★555★
Alcohol Use

High School Students Currently Using Alcohol, 1993: Total

Data refer to high school students who drank alcohol on more than one of the 30 days preceding the survey.

[In percentages]

City/MSA	Total	Rank
Boston, MA	40.1	9
Chicago, IL	39.2	10
Dallas, TX	46.4	1
Fort Lauderdale, FL	43.9	4
Jersey City, NJ	42.4	6
Miami, FL	36.8	12
New Orleans, LA	45.4	3
New York City, NY	37.9	11
Philadelphia, PA	41.4	7
San Diego, CA	43.7	5
San Francisco, CA	32.9	13
Seattle, WA	46.1	2
Washington, DC	41.3	8

Source: U.S. Department of Health and Human Services, Public Health Service, Centers for Disease Control and Prevention (CDC), CDC Surveillance Summaries, MMWR: Morbidity and Mortality Weekly Report, 24 March, 1995, vol. 44, no. SS-1, *Youth Risk Behavior Surveillance—United States, 1993,* Atlanta, GA: Centers for Disease Control and Prevention, 1995, p. 41. *Notes:* Data for New Orleans, Louisiana; New York City, New York; Philadelphia, Pennsylvania; and San Francisco, California, are unweighted. Survey covers selected sites.

★556★
Alcohol Use

High School Students Who Indulged in Episodes of Heavy Drinking, 1993: Females

Data refer to high school students who drank five or more drinks of alcohol on at least one occasion during more than one of the 30 days preceding the survey.

[In percentages]

City/MSA	Female	Rank
Boston, MA	15.1	7
Chicago, IL	15.3	6
Dallas, TX	19.3	3
Fort Lauderdale, FL	15.9	5
Jersey City, NJ	19.5	2
Miami, FL	11.0	11
New Orleans, LA	13.3	10
New York City, NY	9.2	12
Philadelphia, PA	19.5	2
San Diego, CA	19.6	1
San Francisco, CA	14.0	8
Seattle, WA	16.4	4
Washington, DC	13.8	9

Source: U.S. Department of Health and Human Services, Public Health Service, Centers for Disease Control and Prevention (CDC), CDC Surveillance Summaries, MMWR: Morbidity and Mortality Weekly Report, 24 March, 1995, vol. 44, no. SS-1, *Youth Risk Behavior Surveillance—United States, 1993,* Atlanta, GA: Centers for Disease Control and Prevention, 1995, p. 41. *Notes:* Data for New Orleans, Louisiana; New York City, New York; Philadelphia, Pennsylvania; and San Francisco, California, are unweighted. Survey covers selected sites.

★557★
Alcohol Use

High School Students Who Indulged in Episodes of Heavy Drinking, 1993: Males

Data refer to high school students who drank five or more drinks of alcohol on at least one occasion during more than one of the 30 days preceding the survey.

[In percentages]

City/MSA	Male	Rank
Boston, MA	25.6	3
Chicago, IL	21.0	9
Dallas, TX	30.7	1
Fort Lauderdale, FL	24.7	5
Jersey City, NJ	26.1	2
Miami, FL	17.6	11
New Orleans, LA	23.3	7
New York City, NY	19.6	10
Philadelphia, PA	24.0	6
San Diego, CA	25.0	4
San Francisco, CA	17.3	12
Seattle, WA	22.4	8
Washington, DC	19.6	10

Source: U.S. Department of Health and Human Services, Public Health Service, Centers for Disease Control and Prevention (CDC), CDC Surveillance Summaries, MMWR: Morbidity and Mortality Weekly Report, 24 March, 1995, vol. 44, no. SS-1, *Youth Risk Behavior Surveillance—United States, 1993,* Atlanta, GA: Centers for Disease Control and Prevention, 1995, p. 41. *Notes:* Data for New Orleans, Louisiana; New York City, New York; Philadelphia, Pennsylvania; and San Francisco, California, are unweighted. Survey covers selected sites.

★558★

Alcohol Use

High School Students Who Indulged in Episodes of Heavy Drinking, 1993: Total

Data refer to high school students who drank five or more drinks of alcohol on at least one occasion during more than one of the 30 days preceding the survey.

[In percentages]

City/MSA	Total	Rank
Boston, MA	20.3	5
Chicago, IL	18.1	7
Dallas, TX	24.7	1
Fort Lauderdale, FL	20.3	5
Jersey City, NJ	22.7	2
Miami, FL	14.3	11
New Orleans, LA	17.4	8
New York City, NY	14.1	12
Philadelphia, PA	21.7	4
San Diego, CA	22.4	3
San Francisco, CA	15.6	10
Seattle, WA	19.4	6
Washington, DC	16.4	9

Source: U.S. Department of Health and Human Services, Public Health Service, Centers for Disease Control and Prevention (CDC), CDC Surveillance Summaries, MMWR: Morbidity and Mortality Weekly Report, 24 March, 1995, vol. 44, no. SS-1, *Youth Risk Behavior Surveillance—United States, 1993*, Atlanta, GA: Centers for Disease Control and Prevention, 1995, p. 41. *Notes:* Data for New Orleans, Louisiana; New York City, New York; Philadelphia, Pennsylvania; and San Francisco, California, are unweighted. Survey covers selected sites.

★559★

Alcohol Use

High School Students With Lifetime Alcohol Use, 1993: Females

Data refer to high school students who have ever had one drink of alcohol.

[In percentages]

City/MSA	Female	Rank
Boston, MA	63.9	9
Chicago, IL	70.5	7
Dallas, TX	76.6	2
Fort Lauderdale, FL	77.5	1
Jersey City, NJ	62.4	10
Miami, FL	75.4	3
New Orleans, LA	76.6	2
New York City, NY	69.5	8
Philadelphia, PA	75.1	4
San Diego, CA	73.0	6
San Francisco, CA	60.1	11
Washington, DC	74.3	5

Source: U.S. Department of Health and Human Services, Public Health Service, Centers for Disease Control and Prevention (CDC), CDC Surveillance Summaries, MMWR: Morbidity and Mortality Weekly Report, 24 March, 1995, vol. 44, no. SS-1, *Youth Risk Behavior Surveillance—United States, 1993*, Atlanta, GA: Centers for Disease Control and Prevention, 1995, p. 41. *Notes:* Data for New Orleans, Louisiana; New York City, New York; Philadelphia, Pennsylvania; and San Francisco, California, are unweighted. Survey covers selected sites.

★560★

Alcohol Use

High School Students With Lifetime Alcohol Use, 1993: Males

Data refer to high school students who have ever had one drink of alcohol.

[In percentages]

City/MSA	Male	Rank
Boston, MA	71.1	10
Chicago, IL	69.4	11
Dallas, TX	81.8	1
Fort Lauderdale, FL	76.5	4
Jersey City, NJ	78.0	3
Miami, FL	75.6	6
New Orleans, LA	79.3	2
New York City, NY	76.0	5
Philadelphia, PA	73.9	8
San Diego, CA	71.5	9
San Francisco, CA	61.1	12
Washington, DC	74.0	7

Source: U.S. Department of Health and Human Services, Public Health Service, Centers for Disease Control and Prevention (CDC), CDC Surveillance Summaries, MMWR: Morbidity and Mortality Weekly Report, 24 March, 1995, vol. 44, no. SS-1, *Youth Risk Behavior Surveillance—United States, 1993*, Atlanta, GA: Centers for Disease Control and Prevention, 1995, p. 41. *Notes:* Data for New Orleans, Louisiana; New York City, New York; Philadelphia, Pennsylvania; and San Francisco, California, are unweighted. Survey covers selected sites.

★561★

Alcohol Use

High School Students With Lifetime Alcohol Use, 1993: Total

Data refer to high school students who have ever had one drink of alcohol.

[In percentages]

City/MSA	Total	Rank
Boston, MA	67.4	11
Chicago, IL	70.0	9
Dallas, TX	79.0	1
Fort Lauderdale, FL	77.0	3
Jersey City, NJ	69.9	10
Miami, FL	75.5	4
New Orleans, LA	77.6	2
New York City, NY	72.6	7
Philadelphia, PA	74.6	5
San Diego, CA	72.3	8
San Francisco, CA	60.5	12
Washington, DC	74.2	6

Source: U.S. Department of Health and Human Services, Public Health Service, Centers for Disease Control and Prevention (CDC), CDC Surveillance Summaries, MMWR: Morbidity and Mortality Weekly Report, 24 March, 1995, vol. 44, no. SS-1, *Youth Risk Behavior Surveillance—United States, 1993*, Atlanta, GA: Centers for Disease Control and Prevention, 1995, p. 41. *Notes:* Data for New Orleans, Louisiana; New York City, New York; Philadelphia, Pennsylvania; and San Francisco, California, are unweighted. Survey covers selected sites.

★562★
Alcohol Use

High School Students Who Reported Using Alcohol on School Property, 1993: Females

Data refer to high school students who drank alcohol on school property on more than one of the 30 days preceding the survey.

[In percentages]

City/MSA	Female	Rank
Boston, MA	4.1	6
Chicago, IL	6.0	4
Dallas, TX	7.5	2
Fort Lauderdale, FL	2.7	9
Jersey City, NJ	8.4	1
Miami, FL	3.5	8
New Orleans, LA	3.9	7
New York City, NY	2.7	9
Philadelphia, PA	3.9	7
San Diego, CA	6.1	3
Seattle, WA	6.0	4
Washington, DC	5.3	5

Source: U.S. Department of Health and Human Services, Public Health Service, Centers for Disease Control and Prevention (CDC), CDC Surveillance Summaries, MMWR: Morbidity and Mortality Weekly Report, 24 March, 1995, vol. 44, no. SS-1, *Youth Risk Behavior Surveillance—United States, 1993*, Atlanta, GA: Centers for Disease Control and Prevention, 1995, p. 46. *Notes:* Data for New Orleans, Louisiana; New York City, New York; Philadelphia, Pennsylvania; and San Francisco, California, are unweighted. Survey covers selected sites.

★563★
Alcohol Use

High School Students Who Reported Using Alcohol on School Property, 1993: Males

Data refer to high school students who drank alcohol on school property on more than one of the 30 days preceding the survey.

[In percentages]

City/MSA	Male	Rank
Boston, MA	7.6	8
Chicago, IL	6.9	11
Dallas, TX	8.9	4
Fort Lauderdale, FL	7.1	10
Jersey City, NJ	16.1	1
Miami, FL	4.6	12
New Orleans, LA	7.7	7
New York City, NY	7.8	6
Philadelphia, PA	7.2	9
San Diego, CA	9.2	3
Seattle, WA	8.5	5
Washington, DC	9.4	2

Source: U.S. Department of Health and Human Services, Public Health Service, Centers for Disease Control and Prevention (CDC), CDC Surveillance Summaries, MMWR: Morbidity and Mortality Weekly Report, 24 March, 1995, vol. 44, no. SS-1, *Youth Risk Behavior Surveillance—United States, 1993*, Atlanta, GA: Centers for Disease Control and Prevention, 1995, p. 46. *Notes:* Data for New Orleans, Louisiana; New York City, New York; Philadelphia, Pennsylvania; and San Francisco, California, are unweighted. Survey covers selected sites.

★564★
Alcohol Use

High School Students Who Reported Using Alcohol on School Property, 1993: Total

Data refer to high school students who drank alcohol on school property on more than one of the 30 days preceding the survey.

[In percentages]

City/MSA	Total	Rank
Boston, MA	5.9	7
Chicago, IL	6.5	6
Dallas, TX	8.2	2
Fort Lauderdale, FL	4.9	11
Jersey City, NJ	12.2	1
Miami, FL	4.1	12
New Orleans, LA	5.4	9
New York City, NY	5.1	10
Philadelphia, PA	5.5	8
San Diego, CA	7.7	3
Seattle, WA	7.3	4
Washington, DC	7.2	5

Source: U.S. Department of Health and Human Services, Public Health Service, Centers for Disease Control and Prevention (CDC), CDC Surveillance Summaries, MMWR: Morbidity and Mortality Weekly Report, 24 March, 1995, vol. 44, no. SS-1, *Youth Risk Behavior Surveillance—United States, 1993*, Atlanta, GA: Centers for Disease Control and Prevention, 1995, p. 46. *Notes:* Data for New Orleans, Louisiana; New York City, New York; Philadelphia, Pennsylvania; and San Francisco, California, are unweighted. Survey covers selected sites.

★565★
Cocaine Use

High School Students Currently Using Cocaine, 1993: Females

Data refer to high school students who used cocaine one or more times during the 30 days preceding the survey.

[In percentages]

City/MSA	Females	Rank
Boston, MA	0.9	7
Chicago, IL	0.9	7
Dallas, TX	0.9	7
Fort Lauderdale, FL	1.1	6
Jersey City, NJ	1.2	5
Miami, FL	1.7	2
New Orleans, LA	0.7	8
New York City, NY	0.0	9
Philadelphia, PA	1.1	6
San Diego, CA	3.6	1
San Francisco, CA	1.6	3
Seattle, WA	1.3	4
Washington, DC	0.7	8

Source: U.S. Department of Health and Human Services, Public Health Service, Centers for Disease Control and Prevention (CDC), CDC Surveillance Summaries, MMWR: Morbidity and Mortality Weekly Report, 24 March, 1995, vol. 44, no. SS-1, *Youth Risk Behavior Surveillance—United States, 1993*, Atlanta, GA: Centers for Disease Control and Prevention, 1995, p. 43. *Notes:* Data for New Orleans, Louisiana; New York City, New York; Philadelphia, Pennsylvania; and San Francisco, California, are unweighted. Survey covers selected sites.

★566★
Cocaine Use
High School Students Currently Using Cocaine, 1993: Males

Data refer to high school students who used cocaine one or more times during the 30 days preceding the survey.

[In percentages]

City/MSA	Males	Rank
Boston, MA	3.0	4
Chicago, IL	2.9	5
Dallas, TX	2.5	7
Fort Lauderdale, FL	2.7	6
Jersey City, NJ	0.9	11
Miami, FL	3.0	4
New Orleans, LA	1.3	10
New York City, NY	0.9	11
Philadelphia, PA	2.3	8
San Diego, CA	5.0	1
San Francisco, CA	3.6	3
Seattle, WA	4.4	2
Washington, DC	1.8	9

Source: U.S. Department of Health and Human Services, Public Health Service, Centers for Disease Control and Prevention (CDC), CDC Surveillance Summaries, MMWR: Morbidity and Mortality Weekly Report, 24 March, 1995, vol. 44, no. SS-1, *Youth Risk Behavior Surveillance—United States, 1993,* Atlanta, GA: Centers for Disease Control and Prevention, 1995, p. 43. *Notes:* Data for New Orleans, Louisiana; New York City, New York; Philadelphia, Pennsylvania; and San Francisco, California, are unweighted. Survey covers selected sites.

★567★
Cocaine Use
High School Students Currently Using Cocaine, 1993: Total

Data refer to high school students who used cocaine one or more times during the 30 days preceding the survey.

[In percentages]

City/MSA	Total	Rank
Boston, MA	1.9	6
Chicago, IL	2.0	5
Dallas, TX	1.7	7
Fort Lauderdale, FL	1.9	6
Jersey City, NJ	1.2	8
Miami, FL	2.3	4
New Orleans, LA	0.9	9
New York City, NY	0.4	10
Philadelphia, PA	1.7	7
San Diego, CA	4.3	1
San Francisco, CA	2.6	3
Seattle, WA	2.8	2
Washington, DC	1.2	8

Source: U.S. Department of Health and Human Services, Public Health Service, Centers for Disease Control and Prevention (CDC), CDC Surveillance Summaries, MMWR: Morbidity and Mortality Weekly Report, 24 March, 1995, vol. 44, no. SS-1, *Youth Risk Behavior Surveillance—United States, 1993,* Atlanta, GA: Centers for Disease Control and Prevention, 1995, p. 43. *Notes:* Data for New Orleans, Louisiana; New York City, New York; Philadelphia, Pennsylvania; and San Francisco, California, are unweighted. Survey covers selected sites.

★568★
Cocaine Use
High School Students With Lifetime Cocaine Use, 1993: Females

Data refer to high school students who have ever tried any form of cocaine, including powder, crack, or freebase.

[In percentages]

City/MSA	Female	Rank
Boston, MA	2.1	8
Chicago, IL	2.4	7
Dallas, TX	3.7	4
Fort Lauderdale, FL	2.7	6
Jersey City, NJ	3.0	5
Miami, FL	4.0	3
New Orleans, LA	1.1	9
New York City, NY	1.1	9
Philadelphia, PA	3.0	5
San Diego, CA	8.3	1
San Francisco, CA	5.0	2
Washington, DC	1.1	9

Source: U.S. Department of Health and Human Services, Public Health Service, Centers for Disease Control and Prevention (CDC), CDC Surveillance Summaries, MMWR: Morbidity and Mortality Weekly Report, 24 March, 1995, vol. 44, no. SS-1, *Youth Risk Behavior Surveillance—United States, 1993,* Atlanta, GA: Centers for Disease Control and Prevention, 1995, p. 43. *Notes:* Data for New Orleans, Louisiana; New York City, New York; Philadelphia, Pennsylvania; and San Francisco, California, are unweighted. Survey covers selected sites.

★569★
Cocaine Use
High School Students With Lifetime Cocaine Use, 1993: Males

Data refer to high school students who have ever tried any form of cocaine, including powder, crack, or freebase.

[In percentages]

City/MSA	Male	Rank
Boston, MA	5.6	5
Chicago, IL	5.4	6
Dallas, TX	6.6	3
Fort Lauderdale, FL	4.3	8
Jersey City, NJ	2.1	11
Miami, FL	6.0	4
New Orleans, LA	2.6	9
New York City, NY	1.8	12
Philadelphia, PA	4.8	7
San Diego, CA	9.3	1
San Francisco, CA	6.9	2
Washington, DC	2.5	10

Source: U.S. Department of Health and Human Services, Public Health Service, Centers for Disease Control and Prevention (CDC), CDC Surveillance Summaries, MMWR: Morbidity and Mortality Weekly Report, 24 March, 1995, vol. 44, no. SS-1, *Youth Risk Behavior Surveillance—United States, 1993,* Atlanta, GA: Centers for Disease Control and Prevention, 1995, p. 43. *Notes:* Data for New Orleans, Louisiana; New York City, New York; Philadelphia, Pennsylvania; and San Francisco, California, are unweighted. Survey covers selected sites.

★570★

Cocaine Use

High School Students With Lifetime Cocaine Use, 1993: Total

Data refer to high school students who have ever tried any form of cocaine, including powder, crack, or freebase.

[In percentages]

City/MSA	Total	Rank
Boston, MA	3.8	6
Chicago, IL	4.0	4
Dallas, TX	5.1	3
Fort Lauderdale, FL	3.5	7
Jersey City, NJ	2.5	8
Miami, FL	5.1	3
New Orleans, LA	1.7	10
New York City, NY	1.4	11
Philadelphia, PA	3.9	5
San Diego, CA	8.8	1
San Francisco, CA	5.9	2
Washington, DC	1.8	9

Source: U.S. Department of Health and Human Services, Public Health Service, Centers for Disease Control and Prevention (CDC), CDC Surveillance Summaries, MMWR: Morbidity and Mortality Weekly Report, 24 March, 1995, vol. 44, no. SS-1, *Youth Risk Behavior Surveillance—United States, 1993,* Atlanta, GA: Centers for Disease Control and Prevention, 1995, p. 43. *Notes:* Data for New Orleans, Louisiana; New York City, New York; Philadelphia, Pennsylvania; and San Francisco, California, are unweighted. Survey covers selected sites.

★571★

Cocaine and Heroin Use

Cocaine-to-Heroin Use Ratios, 1994: Selected Cities

Data refer to emergency room mentions per 100,000 population.

City	Ratio	Rank
Atlanta, GA	17:1	1
Miami, FL	11:1	2
New Orleans, LA	8:1	3

Source: National Institutes of Health, Division of Epidemiology and Prevention Research, National Institute on Drug Abuse, *Epidemiologic Trends in Drug Abuse,* Community Epidemiology Work Group (CEWG), Rockville, Maryland: National Institutes of Health, December 1994, n.p.

★572★

Crack or Freebase Use

High School Students With Lifetime Crack Use or Lifetime Freebase Use, 1993: Females

Data refer to high school students who ever used crack or freebase.

[In percentages]

City/MSA	Female	Rank
Boston, MA	1.1	7
Chicago, IL	1.3	6
Dallas, TX	1.7	4
Fort Lauderdale, FL	1.3	6
Jersey City, NJ	1.9	3
Miami, FL	1.9	3
New Orleans, LA	0.9	8

[Continued]

★572★

High School Students With Lifetime Crack Use or Lifetime Freebase Use, 1993: Females

[Continued]

City/MSA	Female	Rank
New York City, NY	0.2	10
Philadelphia, PA	1.5	5
San Diego, CA	4.5	1
San Francisco, CA	2.2	2
Washington, DC	0.8	9

Source: U.S. Department of Health and Human Services, Public Health Service, Centers for Disease Control and Prevention (CDC), CDC Surveillance Summaries, MMWR: Morbidity and Mortality Weekly Report, 24 March, 1995, vol. 44, no. SS-1, *Youth Risk Behavior Surveillance—United States, 1993,* Atlanta, GA: Centers for Disease Control and Prevention, 1995, p. 43. *Notes:* Data for New Orleans, Louisiana; New York City, New York; Philadelphia, Pennsylvania; and San Francisco, California, are unweighted. Survey covers selected sites.

★573★

Crack or Freebase Use

High School Students With Lifetime Crack Use or Lifetime Freebase Use, 1993: Males

Data refer to high school students who ever used crack or freebase.

[In percentages]

City/MSA	Male	Rank
Boston, MA	2.5	6
Chicago, IL	3.1	3
Dallas, TX	2.9	4
Fort Lauderdale, FL	2.4	7
Jersey City, NJ	1.0	10
Miami, FL	2.6	5
New Orleans, LA	0.8	11
New York City, NY	1.4	9
Philadelphia, PA	3.1	3
San Diego, CA	5.4	1
San Francisco, CA	5.0	2
Washington, DC	1.7	8

Source: U.S. Department of Health and Human Services, Public Health Service, Centers for Disease Control and Prevention (CDC), CDC Surveillance Summaries, MMWR: Morbidity and Mortality Weekly Report, 24 March, 1995, vol. 44, no. SS-1, *Youth Risk Behavior Surveillance—United States, 1993,* Atlanta, GA: Centers for Disease Control and Prevention, 1995, p. 43. *Notes:* Data for New Orleans, Louisiana; New York City, New York; Philadelphia, Pennsylvania; and San Francisco, California, are unweighted. Survey covers selected sites.

★574★

Crack or Freebase Use

High School Students With Lifetime Crack Use or Lifetime Freebase Use, 1993: Total

Data refer to high school students who ever used crack or freebase.

[In percentages]

City/MSA	Total	Rank
Boston, MA	1.8	5
Chicago, IL	2.3	3
Dallas, TX	2.3	3
Fort Lauderdale, FL	1.8	5

[Continued]

★574★

High School Students With Lifetime Crack Use or Lifetime Freebase Use, 1993: Total

[Continued]

City/MSA	Total	Rank
Jersey City, NJ	1.5	6
Miami, FL	2.3	3
New Orleans, LA	0.8	8
New York City, NY	0.7	9
Philadelphia, PA	2.2	4
San Diego, CA	5.0	1
San Francisco, CA	3.6	2
Washington, DC	1.3	7

Source: U.S. Department of Health and Human Services, Public Health Service, Centers for Disease Control and Prevention (CDC), CDC Surveillance Summaries, MMWR: Morbidity and Mortality Weekly Report, 24 March, 1995, vol. 44, no. SS-1, *Youth Risk Behavior Surveillance—United States, 1993,* Atlanta, GA: Centers for Disease Control and Prevention, 1995, p. 43. *Notes:* Data for New Orleans, Louisiana; New York City, New York; Philadelphia, Pennsylvania; and San Francisco, California, are unweighted. Survey covers selected sites.

★575★

Illegal Steroid Use

High School Students With Lifetime Illegal Steroid Use, 1993: Females

Data refer to high school students who have ever used illegal steroids.

[In percentages]

City/MSA	Female	Rank
Boston, MA	2.4	2
Chicago, IL	1.8	4
Dallas, TX	1.3	5
Fort Lauderdale, FL	0.9	8
Jersey City, NJ	1.3	5
Miami, FL	1.9	3
New Orleans, LA	0.9	8
New York City, NY	1.3	5
Philadelphia, PA	2.4	2
San Diego, CA	2.6	1
San Francisco, CA	1.1	6
Washington, DC	1.0	7

Source: U.S. Department of Health and Human Services, Public Health Service, Centers for Disease Control and Prevention (CDC), CDC Surveillance Summaries, MMWR: Morbidity and Mortality Weekly Report, 24 March, 1995, vol. 44, no. SS-1, *Youth Risk Behavior Surveillance—United States, 1993,* Atlanta, GA: Centers for Disease Control and Prevention, 1995, p. 43. *Notes:* Data for New Orleans, Louisiana; New York City, New York; Philadelphia, Pennsylvania; and San Francisco, California, are unweighted. Survey covers selected sites.

★576★

Illegal Steroid Use

High School Students With Lifetime Illegal Steroid Use, 1993: Males

Data refer to high school students who have ever used illegal steroids.

[In percentages]

City/MSA	Male	Rank
Boston, MA	5.4	1
Chicago, IL	4.5	2
Dallas, TX	2.8	8
Fort Lauderdale, FL	4.5	2
Jersey City, NJ	4.1	4
Miami, FL	4.1	4
New Orleans, LA	2.5	9
New York City, NY	4.5	2
Philadelphia, PA	4.0	5
San Diego, CA	4.3	3
San Francisco, CA	3.6	7
Washington, DC	3.9	6

Source: U.S. Department of Health and Human Services, Public Health Service, Centers for Disease Control and Prevention (CDC), CDC Surveillance Summaries, MMWR: Morbidity and Mortality Weekly Report, 24 March, 1995, vol. 44, no. SS-1, *Youth Risk Behavior Surveillance—United States, 1993,* Atlanta, GA: Centers for Disease Control and Prevention, 1995, p. 43. *Notes:* Data for New Orleans, Louisiana; New York City, New York; Philadelphia, Pennsylvania; and San Francisco, California, are unweighted. Survey covers selected sites.

★577★

Illegal Steroid Use

High School Students With Lifetime Illegal Steroid Use, 1993: Total

Data refer to high school students who have ever used illegal steroids.

[In percentages]

City/MSA	Total	Rank
Boston, MA	3.8	1
Chicago, IL	3.2	3
Dallas, TX	2.0	8
Fort Lauderdale, FL	2.7	6
Jersey City, NJ	2.8	5
Miami, FL	3.1	4
New Orleans, LA	1.6	9
New York City, NY	2.8	5
Philadelphia, PA	3.2	3
San Diego, CA	3.4	2
San Francisco, CA	2.4	7
Washington, DC	2.4	7

Source: U.S. Department of Health and Human Services, Public Health Service, Centers for Disease Control and Prevention (CDC), CDC Surveillance Summaries, MMWR: Morbidity and Mortality Weekly Report, 24 March, 1995, vol. 44, no. SS-1, *Youth Risk Behavior Surveillance—United States, 1993,* Atlanta, GA: Centers for Disease Control and Prevention, 1995, p. 43. *Notes:* Data for New Orleans, Louisiana; New York City, New York; Philadelphia, Pennsylvania; and San Francisco, California, are unweighted. Survey covers selected sites.

★578★

Injected-Drug Use

High School Students With Lifetime Injected-Drug Use, 1993: Females

Data refer to high school students who have ever injected illegal drugs not prescribed by a physician.

[In percentages]

City/MSA	Female	Rank
Boston, MA	0.8	4
Chicago, IL	0.5	7
Dallas, TX	0.5	7
Fort Lauderdale, FL	1.0	3
Jersey City, NJ	0.7	5
Miami, FL	1.3	1
New Orleans, LA	0.5	7
New York City, NY	0.6	6
Philadelphia, PA	0.7	5
San Diego, CA	1.2	2
San Francisco, CA	1.3	1
Washington, DC	1.0	3

Source: U.S. Department of Health and Human Services, Public Health Service, Centers for Disease Control and Prevention (CDC), CDC Surveillance Summaries, MMWR: Morbidity and Mortality Weekly Report, 24 March, 1995, vol. 44, no. SS-1, *Youth Risk Behavior Surveillance—United States, 1993,* Atlanta, GA: Centers for Disease Control and Prevention, 1995, p. 43. *Notes:* Data for New Orleans, Louisiana; New York City, New York; Philadelphia, Pennsylvania; and San Francisco, California, are unweighted. Survey covers selected sites.

★579★

Injected-Drug Use

High School Students With Lifetime Injected-Drug Use, 1993: Males

Data refer to high school students who have ever injected illegal drugs not prescribed by a physician.

[In percentages]

City/MSA	Male	Rank
Boston, MA	3.0	2
Chicago, IL	2.3	3
Dallas, TX	1.7	5
Fort Lauderdale, FL	2.3	3
Jersey City, NJ	1.4	6
Miami, FL	3.0	2
New Orleans, LA	0.5	8
New York City, NY	1.1	7
Philadelphia, PA	2.3	3
San Diego, CA	3.8	1
San Francisco, CA	2.3	3
Washington, DC	2.0	4

Source: U.S. Department of Health and Human Services, Public Health Service, Centers for Disease Control and Prevention (CDC), CDC Surveillance Summaries, MMWR: Morbidity and Mortality Weekly Report, 24 March, 1995, vol. 44, no. SS-1, *Youth Risk Behavior Surveillance—United States, 1993,* Atlanta, GA: Centers for Disease Control and Prevention, 1995, p. 43. *Notes:* Data for New Orleans, Louisiana; New York City, New York; Philadelphia, Pennsylvania; and San Francisco, California, are unweighted. Survey covers selected sites.

★580★

Injected-Drug Use

High School Students With Lifetime Injected-Drug Use, 1993: Total

Data refer to high school students who have ever injected illegal drugs not prescribed by a physician.

[In percentages]

City/MSA	Total	Rank
Boston, MA	1.9	3
Chicago, IL	1.5	6
Dallas, TX	1.1	9
Fort Lauderdale, FL	1.7	5
Jersey City, NJ	1.2	8
Miami, FL	2.2	2
New Orleans, LA	0.5	11
New York City, NY	0.8	10
Philadelphia, PA	1.4	7
San Diego, CA	2.6	1
San Francisco, CA	1.8	4
Washington, DC	1.5	6

Source: U.S. Department of Health and Human Services, Public Health Service, Centers for Disease Control and Prevention (CDC), CDC Surveillance Summaries, MMWR: Morbidity and Mortality Weekly Report, 24 March, 1995, vol. 44, no. SS-1, *Youth Risk Behavior Surveillance—United States, 1993,* Atlanta, GA: Centers for Disease Control and Prevention, 1995, p. 43. *Notes:* Data for New Orleans, Louisiana; New York City, New York; Philadelphia, Pennsylvania; and San Francisco, California, are unweighted. Survey covers selected sites.

★581★

Marijuana Use

High School Students Who Reported Using Marijuana on School Property, 1993: Females

Data refer to high school students who used marijuana one or more times during the 30 days preceding the survey.

[In percentages]

City/MSA	Female	Rank
Boston, MA	3.9	5
Chicago, IL	3.4	7
Dallas, TX	2.4	10
Fort Lauderdale, FL	3.2	8
Jersey City, NJ	3.5	6
Miami, FL	3.4	7
New Orleans, LA	2.5	9
New York City, NY	2.2	11
Philadelphia, PA	6.0	2
San Diego, CA	6.3	1
Seattle, WA	5.8	3
Washington, DC	4.1	4

Source: U.S. Department of Health and Human Services, Public Health Service, Centers for Disease Control and Prevention (CDC), CDC Surveillance Summaries, MMWR: Morbidity and Mortality Weekly Report, 24 March, 1995, vol. 44, no. SS-1, *Youth Risk Behavior Surveillance—United States, 1993,* Atlanta, GA: Centers for Disease Control and Prevention, 1995, p. 46. *Notes:* Data for New Orleans, Louisiana; New York City, New York; Philadelphia, Pennsylvania; and San Francisco, California, are unweighted. Survey covers selected sites.

★ 582 ★

Marijuana Use

High School Students Who Reported Using Marijuana on School Property, 1993: Males

Data refer to high school students who used marijuana one or more times during the 30 days preceding the survey.

[In percentages]

City/MSA	Male	Rank
Boston, MA	9.2	5
Chicago, IL	7.8	8
Dallas, TX	7.1	11
Fort Lauderdale, FL	8.9	6
Jersey City, NJ	6.9	12
Miami, FL	7.2	10
New Orleans, LA	7.9	7
New York City, NY	7.7	9
Philadelphia, PA	11.0	4
San Diego, CA	12.1	3
Seattle, WA	12.3	2
Washington, DC	13.7	1

Source: U.S. Department of Health and Human Services, Public Health Service, Centers for Disease Control and Prevention (CDC), CDC Surveillance Summaries, MMWR: Morbidity and Mortality Weekly Report, 24 March, 1995, vol. 44, no. SS-1, *Youth Risk Behavior Surveillance—United States, 1993,* Atlanta, GA: Centers for Disease Control and Prevention, 1995, p. 46. *Notes:* Data for New Orleans, Louisiana; New York City, New York; Philadelphia, Pennsylvania; and San Francisco, California, are unweighted. Survey covers selected sites.

★ 583 ★

Marijuana Use

High School Students Who Reported Using Marijuana on School Property, 1993: Total

Data refer to high school students who used marijuana one or more times during the 30 days preceding the survey.

[In percentages]

City/MSA	Total	Rank
Boston, MA	6.5	5
Chicago, IL	5.6	7
Dallas, TX	4.6	11
Fort Lauderdale, FL	6.0	6
Jersey City, NJ	5.3	8
Miami, FL	5.3	8
New Orleans, LA	4.7	10
New York City, NY	4.8	9
Philadelphia, PA	8.3	4
San Diego, CA	9.3	1
Seattle, WA	9.0	2
Washington, DC	8.4	3

Source: U.S. Department of Health and Human Services, Public Health Service, Centers for Disease Control and Prevention (CDC), CDC Surveillance Summaries, MMWR: Morbidity and Mortality Weekly Report, 24 March, 1995, vol. 44, no. SS-1, *Youth Risk Behavior Surveillance—United States, 1993,* Atlanta, GA: Centers for Disease Control and Prevention, 1995, p. 46. *Notes:* Data for New Orleans, Louisiana; New York City, New York; Philadelphia, Pennsylvania; and San Francisco, California, are unweighted. Survey covers selected sites.

★ 584 ★

Marijuana Use

High School Students Currently Using Marijuana, 1993: Females

Data refer to high school students who have ever used marijuana one or more times during the 30 days preceding the survey.

[In percentages]

City/MSA	Female	Rank
Boston, MA	14.1	4
Chicago, IL	11.3	7
Dallas, TX	9.1	11
Fort Lauderdale, FL	13.4	5
Jersey City, NJ	10.6	9
Miami, FL	9.7	10
New Orleans, LA	10.7	8
New York City, NY	8.1	12
Philadelphia, PA	19.9	1
San Diego, CA	18.6	2
San Francisco, CA	17.8	3
Seattle, WA	18.6	2
Washington, DC	12.7	6

Source: U.S. Department of Health and Human Services, Public Health Service, Centers for Disease Control and Prevention (CDC), CDC Surveillance Summaries, MMWR: Morbidity and Mortality Weekly Report, 24 March, 1995, vol. 44, no. SS-1, *Youth Risk Behavior Surveillance—United States, 1993,* Atlanta, GA: Centers for Disease Control and Prevention, 1995, p. 41. *Notes:* Data for New Orleans, Louisiana; New York City, New York; Philadelphia, Pennsylvania; and San Francisco, California, are unweighted. Survey covers selected sites.

★ 585 ★

Marijuana Use

High School Students Currently Using Marijuana, 1993: Males

Data refer to high school students who have ever used marijuana one or more times during the 30 days preceding the survey.

[In percentages]

City/MSA	Male	Rank
Boston, MA	21.7	6
Chicago, IL	17.3	11
Dallas, TX	19.0	9
Fort Lauderdale, FL	22.5	5
Jersey City, NJ	18.2	10
Miami, FL	18.2	10
New Orleans, LA	19.6	8
New York City, NY	15.6	12
Philadelphia, PA	25.9	2
San Diego, CA	26.5	1
San Francisco, CA	20.6	7
Seattle, WA	25.4	3
Washington, DC	24.6	4

Source: U.S. Department of Health and Human Services, Public Health Service, Centers for Disease Control and Prevention (CDC), CDC Surveillance Summaries, MMWR: Morbidity and Mortality Weekly Report, 24 March, 1995, vol. 44, no. SS-1, *Youth Risk Behavior Surveillance—United States, 1993,* Atlanta, GA: Centers for Disease Control and Prevention, 1995, p. 41. *Notes:* Data for New Orleans, Louisiana; New York City, New York; Philadelphia, Pennsylvania; and San Francisco, California, are unweighted. Survey covers selected sites.

★586★
Marijuana Use

High School Students Currently Using Marijuana, 1993: Total

Data refer to high school students who have ever used marijuana one or more times during the 30 days preceding the survey.

[In percentages]

City/MSA	Total	Rank
Boston, MA	17.8	7
Chicago, IL	14.3	9
Dallas, TX	13.7	11
Fort Lauderdale, FL	17.9	6
Jersey City, NJ	14.4	8
Miami, FL	14.0	10
New Orleans, LA	14.3	9
New York City, NY	11.8	12
Philadelphia, PA	22.7	1
San Diego, CA	22.6	2
San Francisco, CA	19.2	4
Seattle, WA	22.0	3
Washington, DC	18.1	5

Source: U.S. Department of Health and Human Services, Public Health Service, Centers for Disease Control and Prevention (CDC), CDC Surveillance Summaries, MMWR: Morbidity and Mortality Weekly Report, 24 March, 1995, vol. 44, no. SS-1, *Youth Risk Behavior Surveillance—United States, 1993*, Atlanta, GA: Centers for Disease Control and Prevention, 1995, p. 41. *Notes:* Data for New Orleans, Louisiana; New York City, New York; Philadelphia, Pennsylvania; and San Francisco, California, are unweighted. Survey covers selected sites.

★587★
Marijuana Use

High School Students With Lifetime Marijuana Use, 1993: Females

Data refer to high school students who have ever used marijuana.

[In percentages]

City/MSA	Female	Rank
Boston, MA	26.7	4
Chicago, IL	24.6	7
Dallas, TX	23.2	8
Fort Lauderdale, FL	26.4	5
Jersey City, NJ	22.1	9
Miami, FL	19.3	11
New Orleans, LA	25.1	6
New York City, NY	19.3	11
Philadelphia, PA	37.7	1
San Diego, CA	32.7	2
San Francisco, CA	31.1	3
Washington, DC	21.4	10

Source: U.S. Department of Health and Human Services, Public Health Service, Centers for Disease Control and Prevention (CDC), CDC Surveillance Summaries, MMWR: Morbidity and Mortality Weekly Report, 24 March, 1995, vol. 44, no. SS-1, *Youth Risk Behavior Surveillance—United States, 1993*, Atlanta, GA: Centers for Disease Control and Prevention, 1995, p. 41. *Notes:* Data for New Orleans, Louisiana; New York City, New York; Philadelphia, Pennsylvania; and San Francisco, California, are unweighted. Survey covers selected sites.

★588★
Marijuana Use

High School Students With Lifetime Marijuana Use, 1993: Males

Data refer to high school students who have ever used marijuana.

[In percentages]

City/MSA	Male	Rank
Boston, MA	35.0	7
Chicago, IL	28.6	12
Dallas, TX	35.7	6
Fort Lauderdale, FL	35.8	5
Jersey City, NJ	30.6	10
Miami, FL	31.3	9
New Orleans, LA	37.2	4
New York City, NY	28.7	11
Philadelphia, PA	43.9	1
San Diego, CA	40.3	2
San Francisco, CA	32.6	8
Washington, DC	37.5	3

Source: U.S. Department of Health and Human Services, Public Health Service, Centers for Disease Control and Prevention (CDC), CDC Surveillance Summaries, MMWR: Morbidity and Mortality Weekly Report, 24 March, 1995, vol. 44, no. SS-1, *Youth Risk Behavior Surveillance—United States, 1993*, Atlanta, GA: Centers for Disease Control and Prevention, 1995, p. 41. *Notes:* Data for New Orleans, Louisiana; New York City, New York; Philadelphia, Pennsylvania; and San Francisco, California, are unweighted. Survey covers selected sites.

★589★
Marijuana Use

High School Students With Lifetime Marijuana Use, 1993: Total

Data refer to high school students who have ever used marijuana.

[In percentages]

City/MSA	Total	Rank
Boston, MA	30.7	5
Chicago, IL	26.6	9
Dallas, TX	29.0	7
Fort Lauderdale, FL	31.1	4
Jersey City, NJ	26.3	10
Miami, FL	25.3	11
New Orleans, LA	30.0	6
New York City, NY	23.8	12
Philadelphia, PA	40.5	1
San Diego, CA	36.5	2
San Francisco, CA	31.8	3
Washington, DC	28.8	8

Source: U.S. Department of Health and Human Services, Public Health Service, Centers for Disease Control and Prevention (CDC), CDC Surveillance Summaries, MMWR: Morbidity and Mortality Weekly Report, 24 March, 1995, vol. 44, no. SS-1, *Youth Risk Behavior Surveillance—United States, 1993*, Atlanta, GA: Centers for Disease Control and Prevention, 1995, p. 41. *Notes:* Data for New Orleans, Louisiana; New York City, New York; Philadelphia, Pennsylvania; and San Francisco, California, are unweighted. Survey covers selected sites.

★590★

Methamphetamine Use

Methamphetamine Abuse, 1994: Number of Emergency Room Episodes

City	Number	Rank
Dallas, TX	155	6
Denver, Co	143	7
Los Angeles-Long Beach, CA	1,418	1
Phoenix, AZ	770	4
San Diego, CA	966	3
San Francisco, CA	1,150	2
Seattle, WA	259	5

Source: "Speed Freaks," *U.S. News & World Report,* 13 November 1995, p. 51. Primary source: Substance Abuse and Mental Health Services Administration, Drug Abuse Warning Network.

★591★

Tobacco Use

High School Students Who Reported Using Cigarettes on School Property, 1993: Females

Data refer to high school students who used cigarettes on more than one of the 30 days preceding the survey.

[In percentages]

City/MSA	Female	Rank
Boston, MA	12.1	4
Chicago, IL	7.5	8
Dallas, TX	4.9	10
Fort Lauderdale, FL	8.8	6
Jersey City, NJ	17.1	1
Miami, FL	10.4	5
New Orleans, LA	3.4	11
New York City, NY	8.5	7
Philadelphia, PA	16.3	2
San Diego, CA	7.0	9
Seattle, WA	13.4	3
Washington, DC	3.1	12

Source: U.S. Department of Health and Human Services, Public Health Service, Centers for Disease Control and Prevention (CDC), CDC Surveillance Summaries, MMWR: Morbidity and Mortality Weekly Report, 24 March, 1995, vol. 44, no. SS-1, *Youth Risk Behavior Surveillance—United States, 1993,* Atlanta, GA: Centers for Disease Control and Prevention, 1995, p. 46. *Notes:* Data for New Orleans, Louisiana; New York City, New York; Philadelphia, Pennsylvania; and San Francisco, California, are unweighted. Survey covers selected sites.

★592★

Tobacco Use

High School Students Who Reported Using Cigarettes on School Property, 1993: Males

Data refer to high school students who used cigarettes on more than one of the 30 days preceding the survey.

[In percentages]

City/MSA	Male	Rank
Boston, MA	10.4	6
Chicago, IL	9.2	8
Dallas, TX	8.0	9
Fort Lauderdale, FL	11.1	4

[Continued]

★592★

High School Students Who Reported Using Cigarettes on School Property, 1993: Males

[Continued]

City/MSA	Male	Rank
Jersey City, NJ	16.9	1
Miami, FL	9.3	7
New Orleans, LA	4.8	11
New York City, NY	10.6	5
Philadelphia, PA	11.7	3
San Diego, CA	10.4	6
Seattle, WA	13.6	2
Washington, DC	7.4	10

Source: U.S. Department of Health and Human Services, Public Health Service, Centers for Disease Control and Prevention (CDC), CDC Surveillance Summaries, MMWR: Morbidity and Mortality Weekly Report, 24 March, 1995, vol. 44, no. SS-1, *Youth Risk Behavior Surveillance—United States, 1993,* Atlanta, GA: Centers for Disease Control and Prevention, 1995, p. 46. *Notes:* Data for New Orleans, Louisiana; New York City, New York; Philadelphia, Pennsylvania; and San Francisco, California, are unweighted. Survey covers selected sites.

★593★

Tobacco Use

High School Students Who Reported Using Cigarettes on School Property, 1993: Total

Data refer to high school students who used cigarettes on more than one of the 30 days preceding the survey.

[In percentages]

City/MSA	Total	Rank
Boston, MA	11.2	4
Chicago, IL	8.4	8
Dallas, TX	6.5	9
Fort Lauderdale, FL	9.9	5
Jersey City, NJ	17.0	1
Miami, FL	9.9	5
New Orleans, LA	4.0	11
New York City, NY	9.5	6
Philadelphia, PA	14.1	2
San Diego, CA	8.7	7
Seattle, WA	13.6	3
Washington, DC	5.1	10

Source: U.S. Department of Health and Human Services, Public Health Service, Centers for Disease Control and Prevention (CDC), CDC Surveillance Summaries, MMWR: Morbidity and Mortality Weekly Report, 24 March, 1995, vol. 44, no. SS-1, *Youth Risk Behavior Surveillance—United States, 1993,* Atlanta, GA: Centers for Disease Control and Prevention, 1995, p. 46. *Notes:* Data for New Orleans, Louisiana; New York City, New York; Philadelphia, Pennsylvania; and San Francisco, California, are unweighted. Survey covers selected sites.

★594★

Tobacco Use

High School Students Who Reported Using Smokeless Tobacco on School Property, 1993: Females

Data refer to high school students who reported using chewing tobacco or snuff during the days preceding the survey.

[In percentages]

City/MSA	Female	Rank
Boston, MA	0.4	4
Chicago, IL	0.0	7
Dallas, TX	0.3	5
Fort Lauderdale, FL	0.5	3
Jersey City, NJ	1.0	1
Miami, FL	0.5	3
New Orleans, LA	0.7	2
New York City, NY	0.0	7
Philadelphia, PA	0.4	4
San Diego, CA	0.4	4
Washington, DC	0.1	6

Source: U.S. Department of Health and Human Services, Public Health Service, Centers for Disease Control and Prevention (CDC), CDC Surveillance Summaries, MMWR: Morbidity and Mortality Weekly Report, 24 March, 1995, vol. 44, no. SS-1, *Youth Risk Behavior Surveillance—United States, 1993*, Atlanta, GA: Centers for Disease Control and Prevention, 1995, p. 46. *Notes:* Data for New Orleans, Louisiana; New York City, New York; Philadelphia, Pennsylvania; and San Francisco, California, are unweighted. Survey covers selected sites.

★595★

Tobacco Use

High School Students Who Reported Using Smokeless Tobacco on School Property, 1993: Males

Data refer to high school students who reported using chewing tobacco or snuff during the days preceding the survey.

[In percentages]

City/MSA	Male	Rank
Boston, MA	2.3	5
Chicago, IL	2.0	7
Dallas, TX	3.7	3
Fort Lauderdale, FL	4.8	1
Jersey City, NJ	1.0	10
Miami, FL	3.0	4
New Orleans, LA	1.7	8
New York City, NY	1.6	9
Philadelphia, PA	1.0	10
San Diego, CA	4.3	2
Washington, DC	2.1	6

Source: U.S. Department of Health and Human Services, Public Health Service, Centers for Disease Control and Prevention (CDC), CDC Surveillance Summaries, MMWR: Morbidity and Mortality Weekly Report, 24 March, 1995, vol. 44, no. SS-1, *Youth Risk Behavior Surveillance—United States, 1993*, Atlanta, GA: Centers for Disease Control and Prevention, 1995, p. 46. *Notes:* Data for New Orleans, Louisiana; New York City, New York; Philadelphia, Pennsylvania; and San Francisco, California, are unweighted. Survey covers selected sites.

★596★

Tobacco Use

High School Students Who Reported Using Smokeless Tobacco on School Property, 1993: Total

Data refer to high school students who reported using chewing tobacco or snuff during the days preceding the survey.

[In percentages]

City/MSA	Total	Rank
Boston, MA	1.3	5
Chicago, IL	1.1	6
Dallas, TX	1.9	3
Fort Lauderdale, FL	2.6	1
Jersey City, NJ	1.0	7
Miami, FL	1.7	4
New Orleans, LA	1.1	6
New York City, NY	0.7	8
Philadelphia, PA	0.7	8
San Diego, CA	2.3	2
Washington, DC	1.0	7

Source: U.S. Department of Health and Human Services, Public Health Service, Centers for Disease Control and Prevention (CDC), CDC Surveillance Summaries, MMWR: Morbidity and Mortality Weekly Report, 24 March, 1995, vol. 44, no. SS-1, *Youth Risk Behavior Surveillance—United States, 1993*, Atlanta, GA: Centers for Disease Control and Prevention, 1995, p. 46. *Notes:* Data for New Orleans, Louisiana; New York City, New York; Philadelphia, Pennsylvania; and San Francisco, California, are unweighted. Survey covers selected sites.

★597★

Eating Habits

High School Students Who Ate No More Than Two Servings of Foods Typically High in Fat Content, 1993: Females

Data refer to high school students who ate no more than two servings of the following foods: hamburgers, hot dogs, or sausage; french fries or potato chips; and doughnuts, pie, or cake.

[In percentages]

City/MSA	Female	Rank
Boston, MA	76.9	5
Chicago, IL	60.3	11
Dallas, TX	72.5	8
Fort Lauderdale, FL	82.7	1
Jersey City, NJ	75.9	6
Miami, FL	72.9	7
New Orleans, LA	65.4	10
New York City, NY	80.2	2
Philadelphia, PA	70.9	9
San Diego, CA	79.5	4
San Francisco, CA	79.8	3
Washington, DC	72.9	7

Source: U.S. Department of Health and Human Services, Public Health Service, Centers for Disease Control and Prevention (CDC), CDC Surveillance Summaries, MMWR: Morbidity and Mortality Weekly Report, 24 March, 1995, vol. 44, no. SS-1, *Youth Risk Behavior Surveillance—United States, 1993*, Atlanta, GA: Centers for Disease Control and Prevention, 1995, p. 53. *Notes:* Data for New Orleans, Louisiana; New York City, New York; Philadelphia, Pennsylvania; and San Francisco, California, are unweighted. Survey covers selected sites.

★598★

Eating Habits

High School Students Who Ate No More Than Two Servings of Foods Typically High in Fat Content, 1993: Males

Data refer to high school students who ate no more than two servings of the following foods: hamburgers, hot dogs, or sausage; french fries or potato chips; and doughnuts, pie, or cake.

[In percentages]

City/MSA	Male	Rank
Boston, MA	68.1	3
Chicago, IL	52.9	10
Dallas, TX	60.5	6
Fort Lauderdale, FL	64.7	4
Jersey City, NJ	64.5	5
Miami, FL	64.7	4
New Orleans, LA	55.5	9
New York City, NY	70.5	2
Philadelphia, PA	58.5	8
San Diego, CA	64.5	5
San Francisco, CA	73.8	1
Washington, DC	58.7	7

Source: U.S. Department of Health and Human Services, Public Health Service, Centers for Disease Control and Prevention (CDC), CDC Surveillance Summaries, MMWR: Morbidity and Mortality Weekly Report, 24 March, 1995, vol. 44, no. SS-1, *Youth Risk Behavior Surveillance—United States, 1993,* Atlanta, GA: Centers for Disease Control and Prevention, 1995, p. 53. *Notes:* Data for New Orleans, Louisiana; New York City, New York; Philadelphia, Pennsylvania; and San Francisco, California, are unweighted. Survey covers selected sites.

★599★

Eating Habits

High School Students Who Ate No More Than Two Servings of Foods Typically High in Fat Content, 1993: Total

Data refer to high school students who ate no more than two servings of the following foods: hamburgers, hot dogs, or sausage; french fries or potato chips; and doughnuts, pie, or cake.

[In percentages]

City/MSA	Total	Rank
Boston, MA	72.6	4
Chicago, IL	56.9	12
Dallas, TX	66.8	8
Fort Lauderdale, FL	73.7	3
Jersey City, NJ	70.3	6
Miami, FL	68.8	7
New Orleans, LA	61.4	11
New York City, NY	75.6	2
Philadelphia, PA	65.1	10
San Diego, CA	71.9	5
San Francisco, CA	77.0	1
Washington, DC	66.4	9

Source: U.S. Department of Health and Human Services, Public Health Service, Centers for Disease Control and Prevention (CDC), CDC Surveillance Summaries, MMWR: Morbidity and Mortality Weekly Report, 24 March, 1995, vol. 44, no. SS-1, *Youth Risk Behavior Surveillance—United States, 1993,* Atlanta, GA: Centers for Disease Control and Prevention, 1995, p. 53. *Notes:* Data for New Orleans, Louisiana; New York City, New York; Philadelphia, Pennsylvania; and San Francisco, California, are unweighted. Survey covers selected sites.

★600★

Eating Habits

High School Students Who Reported Eating Fruits and Vegetables, 1993: Females

Data refer to high school students who consumed fruit, fruit juice, green salad, and cooked vegetables.

[In percentages]

City/MSA	Female	Rank
Boston, MA	12.8	4
Chicago, IL	10.8	7
Dallas, TX	9.1	11
Fort Lauderdale, FL	12.4	5
Jersey City, NJ	9.6	9
Miami, FL	9.7	8
New Orleans, LA	8.2	12
New York City, NY	13.7	3
Philadelphia, PA	9.3	10
San Diego, CA	16.4	2
San Francisco, CA	18.1	1
Washington, DC	12.2	6

Source: U.S. Department of Health and Human Services, Public Health Service, Centers for Disease Control and Prevention (CDC), CDC Surveillance Summaries, MMWR: Morbidity and Mortality Weekly Report, 24 March, 1995, vol. 44, no. SS-1, *Youth Risk Behavior Surveillance—United States, 1993,* Atlanta, GA: Centers for Disease Control and Prevention, 1995, p. 53. *Notes:* Data for New Orleans, Louisiana; New York City, New York; Philadelphia, Pennsylvania; and San Francisco, California, are unweighted. Survey covers selected sites.

★601★

Eating Habits

High School Students Who Reported Eating Fruits and Vegetables, 1993: Males

Data refer to high school students who consumed fruit, fruit juice, green salad, and cooked vegetables.

[In percentages]

City/MSA	Male	Rank
Boston, MA	14.6	7
Chicago, IL	14.1	8
Dallas, TX	11.0	12
Fort Lauderdale, FL	17.1	4
Jersey City, NJ	13.6	9
Miami, FL	15.0	6
New Orleans, LA	15.3	5
New York City, NY	17.4	3
Philadelphia, PA	12.4	11
San Diego, CA	20.6	2
San Francisco, CA	24.7	1
Washington, DC	13.2	10

Source: U.S. Department of Health and Human Services, Public Health Service, Centers for Disease Control and Prevention (CDC), CDC Surveillance Summaries, MMWR: Morbidity and Mortality Weekly Report, 24 March, 1995, vol. 44, no. SS-1, *Youth Risk Behavior Surveillance—United States, 1993,* Atlanta, GA: Centers for Disease Control and Prevention, 1995, p. 53. *Notes:* Data for New Orleans, Louisiana; New York City, New York; Philadelphia, Pennsylvania; and San Francisco, California, are unweighted. Survey covers selected sites.

★602★

Eating Habits

High School Students Who Reported Eating Fruits and Vegetables, 1993: Total

Data refer to high school students who consumed fruit, fruit juice, green salad, and cooked vegetables.

[In percentages]

City/MSA	Total	Rank
Boston, MA	13.7	5
Chicago, IL	12.3	8
Dallas, TX	10.0	12
Fort Lauderdale, FL	14.7	4
Jersey City, NJ	11.7	9
Miami, FL	12.4	7
New Orleans, LA	11.1	10
New York City, NY	15.4	3
Philadelphia, PA	10.8	11
San Diego, CA	18.5	2
San Francisco, CA	21.2	1
Washington, DC	12.7	6

Source: U.S. Department of Health and Human Services, Public Health Service, Centers for Disease Control and Prevention (CDC), CDC Surveillance Summaries, MMWR: Morbidity and Mortality Weekly Report, 24 March, 1995, vol. 44, no. SS-1, *Youth Risk Behavior Surveillance—United States, 1993*, Atlanta, GA: Centers for Disease Control and Prevention, 1995, p. 53. *Notes:* Data for New Orleans, Louisiana; New York City, New York; Philadelphia, Pennsylvania; and San Francisco, California, are unweighted. Survey covers selected sites.

★603★

Exercise Habits

High School Students Who Attended Physical Education Classes Daily, 1993: Females

[In percentages]

City/MSA	Female	Rank
Boston, MA	9.7	12
Chicago, IL	85.2	1
Dallas, TX	28.6	9
Fort Lauderdale, FL	22.0	10
Jersey City, NJ	69.2	2
Miami, FL	31.1	7
New Orleans, LA	51.2	4
New York City, NY	52.1	3
Philadelphia, PA	28.9	8
San Diego, CA	50.5	5
San Francisco, CA	43.0	6
Washington, DC	21.9	11

Source: U.S. Department of Health and Human Services, Public Health Service, Centers for Disease Control and Prevention (CDC), CDC Surveillance Summaries, MMWR: Morbidity and Mortality Weekly Report, 24 March, 1995, vol. 44, no. SS-1, *Youth Risk Behavior Surveillance—United States, 1993*, Atlanta, GA: Centers for Disease Control and Prevention, 1995, p. 55. *Notes:* Data for New Orleans, Louisiana; New York City, New York; Philadelphia, Pennsylvania; and San Francisco, California, are unweighted. Survey covers selected sites.

★604★

Exercise Habits

High School Students Who Attended Physical Education Classes Daily, 1993: Males

[In percentages]

City/MSA	Male	Rank
Boston, MA	9.8	11
Chicago, IL	75.9	1
Dallas, TX	35.4	9
Fort Lauderdale, FL	35.4	9
Jersey City, NJ	70.8	2
Miami, FL	35.8	8
New Orleans, LA	51.7	5
New York City, NY	56.3	3
Philadelphia, PA	37.5	7
San Diego, CA	54.9	4
San Francisco, CA	49.7	6
Washington, DC	20.5	10

Source: U.S. Department of Health and Human Services, Public Health Service, Centers for Disease Control and Prevention (CDC), CDC Surveillance Summaries, MMWR: Morbidity and Mortality Weekly Report, 24 March, 1995, vol. 44, no. SS-1, *Youth Risk Behavior Surveillance—United States, 1993*, Atlanta, GA: Centers for Disease Control and Prevention, 1995, p. 55. *Notes:* Data for New Orleans, Louisiana; New York City, New York; Philadelphia, Pennsylvania; and San Francisco, California, are unweighted. Survey covers selected sites.

★605★

Exercise Habits

High School Students Who Attended Physical Education Classes Daily, 1993: Total

[In percentages]

City/MSA	Total	Rank
Boston, MA	9.8	12
Chicago, IL	80.5	1
Dallas, TX	31.9	9
Fort Lauderdale, FL	28.7	10
Jersey City, NJ	69.8	2
Miami, FL	33.5	7
New Orleans, LA	51.3	5
New York City, NY	54.1	3
Philadelphia, PA	32.9	8
San Diego, CA	52.6	4
San Francisco, CA	46.1	6
Washington, DC	21.3	11

Source: U.S. Department of Health and Human Services, Public Health Service, Centers for Disease Control and Prevention (CDC), CDC Surveillance Summaries, MMWR: Morbidity and Mortality Weekly Report, 24 March, 1995, vol. 44, no. SS-1, *Youth Risk Behavior Surveillance—United States, 1993*, Atlanta, GA: Centers for Disease Control and Prevention, 1995, p. 55. *Notes:* Data for New Orleans, Louisiana; New York City, New York; Philadelphia, Pennsylvania; and San Francisco, California, are unweighted. Survey covers selected sites.

★606★

Exercise Habits

High School Students Who Participated in Strengthening Exercises, 1993: Females

Data refer to high school students who engaged in push-ups, sit-ups, or lifting weights, during more than 4 of the 7 days preceding the survey.

[In percentages]

City/MSA	Female	Rank
Boston, MA	20.4	10
Chicago, IL	27.8	2
Dallas, TX	23.3	5
Fort Lauderdale, FL	22.5	6
Jersey City, NJ	18.5	11
Miami, FL	24.1	4
New Orleans, LA	21.5	8
New York City, NY	25.4	3
Philadelphia, PA	20.7	9
San Diego, CA	30.5	1
San Francisco, CA	21.7	7
Washington, DC	18.3	12

Source: U.S. Department of Health and Human Services, Public Health Service, Centers for Disease Control and Prevention (CDC), CDC Surveillance Summaries, MMWR: Morbidity and Mortality Weekly Report, 24 March, 1995, vol. 44, no. SS-1, *Youth Risk Behavior Surveillance—United States, 1993,* Atlanta, GA: Centers for Disease Control and Prevention, 1995, p. 55. *Notes:* Data for New Orleans, Louisiana; New York City, New York; Philadelphia, Pennsylvania; and San Francisco, California, are unweighted. Survey covers selected sites.

★607★

Exercise Habits

High School Students Who Participated in Strengthening Exercises, 1993: Males

Data refer to high school students who engaged in push-ups, sit-ups, or lifting weights, during more than 4 of the 7 days preceding the survey.

[In percentages]

City/MSA	Male	Rank
Boston, MA	33.0	12
Chicago, IL	43.8	4
Dallas, TX	39.7	6
Fort Lauderdale, FL	41.4	5
Jersey City, NJ	44.4	3
Miami, FL	39.4	7
New Orleans, LA	37.7	9
New York City, NY	47.3	1
Philadelphia, PA	38.7	8
San Diego, CA	46.3	2
San Francisco, CA	35.9	10
Washington, DC	33.2	11

Source: U.S. Department of Health and Human Services, Public Health Service, Centers for Disease Control and Prevention (CDC), CDC Surveillance Summaries, MMWR: Morbidity and Mortality Weekly Report, 24 March, 1995, vol. 44, no. SS-1, *Youth Risk Behavior Surveillance—United States, 1993,* Atlanta, GA: Centers for Disease Control and Prevention, 1995, p. 55. *Notes:* Data for New Orleans, Louisiana; New York City, New York; Philadelphia, Pennsylvania; and San Francisco, California, are unweighted. Survey covers selected sites.

★608★

Exercise Habits

High School Students Who Participated in Strengthening Exercises, 1993: Total

Data refer to high school students who engaged in push-ups, sit-ups, or lifting weights, during more than 4 of the 7 days preceding the survey.

[In percentages]

City/MSA	Total	Rank
Boston, MA	26.3	11
Chicago, IL	35.3	3
Dallas, TX	31.1	7
Fort Lauderdale, FL	32.0	4
Jersey City, NJ	31.3	6
Miami, FL	31.8	5
New Orleans, LA	28.1	10
New York City, NY	35.6	2
Philadelphia, PA	29.3	8
San Diego, CA	38.4	1
San Francisco, CA	28.5	9
Washington, DC	25.0	12

Source: U.S. Department of Health and Human Services, Public Health Service, Centers for Disease Control and Prevention (CDC), CDC Surveillance Summaries, MMWR: Morbidity and Mortality Weekly Report, 24 March, 1995, vol. 44, no. SS-1, *Youth Risk Behavior Surveillance—United States, 1993,* Atlanta, GA: Centers for Disease Control and Prevention, 1995, p. 55. *Notes:* Data for New Orleans, Louisiana; New York City, New York; Philadelphia, Pennsylvania; and San Francisco, California, are unweighted. Survey covers selected sites.

★609★

Exercise Habits

High School Students Who Participated in Stretching Exercises, 1993: Female

Data refer to high school students who engaged in exercises of the following types: touching toes, bending knees, or stretching legs, during more than 4 of the 7 days preceding the survey.

[In percentages]

City/MSA	Female	Rank
Boston, MA	22.8	12
Chicago, IL	37.8	2
Dallas, TX	29.2	9
Fort Lauderdale, FL	30.8	8
Jersey City, NJ	31.5	7
Miami, FL	34.5	4
New Orleans, LA	27.6	10
New York City, NY	36.4	3
Philadelphia, PA	31.6	6
San Diego, CA	50.0	1
San Francisco, CA	33.6	5
Washington, DC	24.4	11

Source: U.S. Department of Health and Human Services, Public Health Service, Centers for Disease Control and Prevention (CDC), CDC Surveillance Summaries, MMWR: Morbidity and Mortality Weekly Report, 24 March, 1995, vol. 44, no. SS-1, *Youth Risk Behavior Surveillance—United States, 1993,* Atlanta, GA: Centers for Disease Control and Prevention, 1995, p. 55. *Notes:* Data for New Orleans, Louisiana; New York City, New York; Philadelphia, Pennsylvania; and San Francisco, California, are unweighted. Survey covers selected sites.

★610★
Exercise Habits
High School Students Who Participated in Stretching Exercises, 1993: Male

Data refer to high school students who engaged in exercises of the following types: touching toes, bending knees, or stretching legs, during more than 4 of the 7 days preceding the survey.

[In percentages]

City/MSA	Male	Rank
Boston, MA	26.8	12
Chicago, IL	34.1	9
Dallas, TX	35.9	7
Fort Lauderdale, FL	36.0	6
Jersey City, NJ	37.2	5
Miami, FL	39.5	3
New Orleans, LA	33.2	10
New York City, NY	45.0	2
Philadelphia, PA	35.0	8
San Diego, CA	53.2	1
San Francisco, CA	38.3	4
Washington, DC	27.1	11

Source: U.S. Department of Health and Human Services, Public Health Service, Centers for Disease Control and Prevention (CDC), CDC Surveillance Summaries, MMWR: Morbidity and Mortality Weekly Report, 24 March, 1995, vol. 44, no. SS-1, *Youth Risk Behavior Surveillance—United States, 1993*, Atlanta, GA: Centers for Disease Control and Prevention, 1995, p. 55. *Notes:* Data for New Orleans, Louisiana; New York City, New York; Philadelphia, Pennsylvania; and San Francisco, California, are unweighted. Survey covers selected sites.

★611★
Exercise Habits
High School Students Who Participated in Stretching Exercises, 1993: Total

Data refer to high school students who engaged in exercises of the following types: touching toes, bending knees, or stretching legs, during more than 4 of the 7 days preceding the survey.

[In percentages]

City/MSA	Total	Rank
Boston, MA	24.8	12
Chicago, IL	35.8	4
Dallas, TX	32.4	9
Fort Lauderdale, FL	33.4	7
Jersey City, NJ	34.3	6
Miami, FL	37.0	3
New Orleans, LA	29.8	10
New York City, NY	40.3	2
Philadelphia, PA	33.2	8
San Diego, CA	51.6	1
San Francisco, CA	35.7	5
Washington, DC	25.7	11

Source: U.S. Department of Health and Human Services, Public Health Service, Centers for Disease Control and Prevention (CDC), CDC Surveillance Summaries, MMWR: Morbidity and Mortality Weekly Report, 24 March, 1995, vol. 44, no. SS-1, *Youth Risk Behavior Surveillance—United States, 1993*, Atlanta, GA: Centers for Disease Control and Prevention, 1995, p. 55. *Notes:* Data for New Orleans, Louisiana; New York City, New York; Philadelphia, Pennsylvania; and San Francisco, California, are unweighted. Survey covers selected sites.

★612★
Exercise Habits
High School Students Who Participated in Vigorous Physical Activity, 1993: Females

Data refer to high school students who engaged in activities that caused sweating and hard breathing for more than 20 minutes on more than 3 of the 7 days preceding the survey.

[In percentages]

City/MSA	Female	Rank
Boston, MA	42.6	9
Chicago, IL	56.3	4
Dallas, TX	47.3	7
Fort Lauderdale, FL	46.5	8
Jersey City, NJ	41.3	11
Miami, FL	48.3	6
New Orleans, LA	41.2	12
New York City, NY	57.6	3
Philadelphia, PA	41.9	10
San Diego, CA	59.8	1
San Francisco, CA	50.7	5
Seattle, WA	58.0	2
Washington, DC	37.5	13

Source: U.S. Department of Health and Human Services, Public Health Service, Centers for Disease Control and Prevention (CDC), CDC Surveillance Summaries, MMWR: Morbidity and Mortality Weekly Report, 24 March, 1995, vol. 44, no. SS-1, *Youth Risk Behavior Surveillance—United States, 1993*, Atlanta, GA: Centers for Disease Control and Prevention, 1995, p. 55. *Notes:* Data for New Orleans, Louisiana; New York City, New York; Philadelphia, Pennsylvania; and San Francisco, California, are unweighted. Survey covers selected sites.

★613★
Exercise Habits
High School Students Who Participated in Vigorous Physical Activity, 1993: Males

Data refer to high school students who engaged in activities that caused sweating and hard breathing for more than 20 minutes on more than 3 of the 7 days preceding the survey.

[In percentages]

City/MSA	Male	Rank
Boston, MA	58.3	11
Chicago, IL	67.2	6
Dallas, TX	63.2	9
Fort Lauderdale, FL	74.2	3
Jersey City, NJ	58.1	12
Miami, FL	65.5	7
New Orleans, LA	63.5	8
New York City, NY	80.8	1
Philadelphia, PA	63.0	10
San Diego, CA	77.4	2
San Francisco, CA	69.5	5
Seattle, WA	70.6	4
Washington, DC	53.4	13

Source: U.S. Department of Health and Human Services, Public Health Service, Centers for Disease Control and Prevention (CDC), CDC Surveillance Summaries, MMWR: Morbidity and Mortality Weekly Report, 24 March, 1995, vol. 44, no. SS-1, *Youth Risk Behavior Surveillance—United States, 1993*, Atlanta, GA: Centers for Disease Control and Prevention, 1995, p. 55. *Notes:* Data for New Orleans, Louisiana; New York City, New York; Philadelphia, Pennsylvania; and San Francisco, California, are unweighted. Survey covers selected sites.

★614★

Exercise Habits

High School Students Who Participated in Vigorous Physical Activity, 1993: Total

Data refer to high school students who engaged in activities that caused sweating and hard breathing for more than 20 minutes on more than 3 of the 7 days preceding the survey.

[In percentages]

City/MSA	Total	Rank
Boston, MA	50.2	11
Chicago, IL	61.4	4
Dallas, TX	54.9	8
Fort Lauderdale, FL	60.3	5
Jersey City, NJ	49.6	12
Miami, FL	57.0	7
New Orleans, LA	50.3	10
New York City, NY	68.5	2
Philadelphia, PA	51.9	9
San Diego, CA	68.6	1
San Francisco, CA	59.5	6
Seattle, WA	64.4	3
Washington, DC	44.8	13

Source: U.S. Department of Health and Human Services, Public Health Service, Centers for Disease Control and Prevention (CDC), CDC Surveillance Summaries, MMWR: Morbidity and Mortality Weekly Report, 24 March, 1995, vol. 44, no. SS-1, *Youth Risk Behavior Surveillance—United States, 1993,* Atlanta, GA: Centers for Disease Control and Prevention, 1995, p. 55. *Notes:* Data for New Orleans, Louisiana; New York City, New York; Philadelphia, Pennsylvania; and San Francisco, California, are unweighted. Survey covers selected sites.

★615★

Exercise Habits

High School Students Who Were Enrolled in Physical Education Classes, 1993: Females

[In percentages]

City/MSA	Female	Rank
Boston, MA	62.5	4
Chicago, IL	94.3	1
Dallas, TX	33.2	11
Fort Lauderdale, FL	28.3	12
Jersey City, NJ	84.2	2
Miami, FL	39.4	10
New Orleans, LA	56.3	7
New York City, NY	82.2	3
Philadelphia, PA	56.8	6
San Diego, CA	60.5	5
San Francisco, CA	54.2	8
Washington, DC	41.6	9

Source: U.S. Department of Health and Human Services, Public Health Service, Centers for Disease Control and Prevention (CDC), CDC Surveillance Summaries, MMWR: Morbidity and Mortality Weekly Report, 24 March, 1995, vol. 44, no. SS-1, *Youth Risk Behavior Surveillance—United States, 1993,* Atlanta, GA: Centers for Disease Control and Prevention, 1995, p. 55. *Notes:* Data for New Orleans, Louisiana; New York City, New York; Philadelphia, Pennsylvania; and San Francisco, California, are unweighted. Survey covers selected sites.

★616★

Exercise Habits

High School Students Who Were Enrolled in Physical Education Classes, 1993: Males

[In percentages]

City/MSA	Male	Rank
Boston, MA	62.7	5
Chicago, IL	91.4	1
Dallas, TX	45.4	11
Fort Lauderdale, FL	46.5	9
Jersey City, NJ	84.8	2
Miami, FL	46.0	10
New Orleans, LA	59.7	8
New York City, NY	83.1	3
Philadelphia, PA	62.2	6
San Diego, CA	69.9	4
San Francisco, CA	61.7	7
Washington, DC	45.1	12

Source: U.S. Department of Health and Human Services, Public Health Service, Centers for Disease Control and Prevention (CDC), CDC Surveillance Summaries, MMWR: Morbidity and Mortality Weekly Report, 24 March, 1995, vol. 44, no. SS-1, *Youth Risk Behavior Surveillance—United States, 1993,* Atlanta, GA: Centers for Disease Control and Prevention, 1995, p. 55. *Notes:* Data for New Orleans, Louisiana; New York City, New York; Philadelphia, Pennsylvania; and San Francisco, California, are unweighted. Survey covers selected sites.

★617★

Exercise Habits

High School Students Who Were Enrolled in Physical Education Classes, 1993: Total

[In percentages]

City/MSA	Total	Rank
Boston, MA	62.7	5
Chicago, IL	92.6	1
Dallas, TX	39.0	11
Fort Lauderdale, FL	37.4	12
Jersey City, NJ	84.4	2
Miami, FL	42.8	10
New Orleans, LA	57.6	8
New York City, NY	82.5	3
Philadelphia, PA	59.2	6
San Diego, CA	65.2	4
San Francisco, CA	57.7	7
Washington, DC	43.2	9

Source: U.S. Department of Health and Human Services, Public Health Service, Centers for Disease Control and Prevention (CDC), CDC Surveillance Summaries, MMWR: Morbidity and Mortality Weekly Report, 24 March, 1995, vol. 44, no. SS-1, *Youth Risk Behavior Surveillance—United States, 1993,* Atlanta, GA: Centers for Disease Control and Prevention, 1995, p. 55. *Notes:* Data for New Orleans, Louisiana; New York City, New York; Philadelphia, Pennsylvania; and San Francisco, California, are unweighted. Survey covers selected sites.

★618★
Self-Image

High School Students Who Thought They Were Overweight, 1993: Females

[In percentages]

City/MSA	Female	Rank
Boston, MA	36.2	5
Chicago, IL	35.1	6
Dallas, TX	39.1	4
Fort Lauderdale, FL	41.6	1
Jersey City, NJ	29.5	12
Miami, FL	33.6	8
New Orleans, LA	30.3	11
New York City, NY	34.9	7
Philadelphia, PA	31.3	10
San Diego, CA	39.9	3
San Francisco, CA	40.9	2
Washington, DC	31.8	9

Source: U.S. Department of Health and Human Services, Public Health Service, Centers for Disease Control and Prevention (CDC), CDC Surveillance Summaries, MMWR: Morbidity and Mortality Weekly Report, 24 March, 1995, vol. 44, no. SS-1, *Youth Risk Behavior Surveillance—United States, 1993,* Atlanta, GA: Centers for Disease Control and Prevention, 1995, p. 53. *Notes:* Data for New Orleans, Louisiana; New York City, New York; Philadelphia, Pennsylvania; and San Francisco, California, are unweighted. Survey covers selected sites.

★619★
Self-Image

High School Students Who Thought They Were Overweight, 1993: Males

[In percentages]

City/MSA	Male	Rank
Boston, MA	18.6	9
Chicago, IL	21.4	5
Dallas, TX	22.2	3
Fort Lauderdale, FL	23.6	1
Jersey City, NJ	14.6	12
Miami, FL	22.0	4
New Orleans, LA	17.7	10
New York City, NY	22.3	2
Philadelphia, PA	16.6	11
San Diego, CA	20.4	7
San Francisco, CA	21.3	6
Washington, DC	20.2	8

Source: U.S. Department of Health and Human Services, Public Health Service, Centers for Disease Control and Prevention (CDC), CDC Surveillance Summaries, MMWR: Morbidity and Mortality Weekly Report, 24 March, 1995, vol. 44, no. SS-1, *Youth Risk Behavior Surveillance—United States, 1993,* Atlanta, GA: Centers for Disease Control and Prevention, 1995, p. 53. *Notes:* Data for New Orleans, Louisiana; New York City, New York; Philadelphia, Pennsylvania; and San Francisco, California, are unweighted. Survey covers selected sites.

★620★
Self-Image

High School Students Who Thought They Were Overweight, 1993: Total

[In percentages]

City/MSA	Total	Rank
Boston, MA	27.5	8
Chicago, IL	28.5	6
Dallas, TX	31.0	3
Fort Lauderdale, FL	32.5	1
Jersey City, NJ	22.0	12
Miami, FL	27.7	7
New Orleans, LA	25.1	10
New York City, NY	28.9	5
Philadelphia, PA	24.3	11
San Diego, CA	30.1	4
San Francisco, CA	31.7	2
Washington, DC	26.6	9

Source: U.S. Department of Health and Human Services, Public Health Service, Centers for Disease Control and Prevention (CDC), CDC Surveillance Summaries, MMWR: Morbidity and Mortality Weekly Report, 24 March, 1995, vol. 44, no. SS-1, *Youth Risk Behavior Surveillance—United States, 1993,* Atlanta, GA: Centers for Disease Control and Prevention, 1995, p. 53. *Notes:* Data for New Orleans, Louisiana; New York City, New York; Philadelphia, Pennsylvania; and San Francisco, California, are unweighted. Survey covers selected sites.

★621★
Self-Image

High School Students Who Were Attempting Weight Loss, 1993: Females

[In percentages]

City/MSA	Female	Rank
Boston, MA	47.8	7
Chicago, IL	46.2	9
Dallas, TX	52.0	3
Fort Lauderdale, FL	58.0	1
Jersey City, NJ	41.3	12
Miami, FL	48.1	6
New Orleans, LA	41.2	13
New York City, NY	47.7	8
Philadelphia, PA	43.7	11
San Diego, CA	53.9	2
San Francisco, CA	51.2	4
Seattle, WA	50.7	5
Washington, DC	44.1	10

Source: U.S. Department of Health and Human Services, Public Health Service, Centers for Disease Control and Prevention (CDC), CDC Surveillance Summaries, MMWR: Morbidity and Mortality Weekly Report, 24 March, 1995, vol. 44, no. SS-1, *Youth Risk Behavior Surveillance—United States, 1993,* Atlanta, GA: Centers for Disease Control and Prevention, 1995, p. 53. *Notes:* Data for New Orleans, Louisiana; New York City, New York; Philadelphia, Pennsylvania; and San Francisco, California, are unweighted. Survey covers selected sites.

★622★

Self-Image

High School Students Who Were Attempting Weight Loss, 1993: Males

[In percentages]

City/MSA	Male	Rank
Boston, MA	24.6	3
Chicago, IL	27.6	1
Dallas. TX	25.0	2
Fort Lauderdale, FL	23.0	6
Jersey City, NJ	15.5	13
Miami, FL	23.1	5
New Orleans, LA	16.2	12
New York City, NY	23.9	4
Philadelphia, PA	17.1	11
San Diego, CA	21.6	7
San Francisco, CA	21.2	8
Seattle, WA	18.3	10
Washington, DC	19.2	9

Source: U.S. Department of Health and Human Services, Public Health Service, Centers for Disease Control and Prevention (CDC), CDC Surveillance Summaries, MMWR: Morbidity and Mortality Weekly Report, 24 March, 1995, vol. 44, no. SS-1, *Youth Risk Behavior Surveillance—United States, 1993*, Atlanta, GA: Centers for Disease Control and Prevention, 1995, p. 53. *Notes:* Data for New Orleans, Louisiana; New York City, New York; Philadelphia, Pennsylvania; and San Francisco, California, are unweighted. Survey covers selected sites.

★623★

Self-Image

High School Students Who Were Attempting Weight Loss, 1993: Total

[In percentages]

City/MSA	Total	Rank
Boston, MA	36.4	6
Chicago, IL	37.2	4
Dallas, TX	39.1	2
Fort Lauderdale, FL	40.5	1
Jersey City, NJ	28.5	12
Miami, FL	35.3	7
New Orleans, LA	30.9	11
New York City, NY	36.4	6
Philadelphia, PA	31.1	10
San Diego, CA	37.7	3
San Francisco, CA	37.0	5
Seattle, WA	34.4	8
Washington, DC	32.8	9

Source: U.S. Department of Health and Human Services, Public Health Service, Centers for Disease Control and Prevention (CDC), CDC Surveillance Summaries, MMWR: Morbidity and Mortality Weekly Report, 24 March, 1995, vol. 44, no. SS-1, *Youth Risk Behavior Surveillance—United States, 1993*, Atlanta,. GA: Centers for Disease Control and Prevention, 1995, p. 53. *Notes:* Data for New Orleans, Louisiana; New York City, New York; Philadelphia, Pennsylvania; and San Francisco, California, are unweighted. Survey covers selected sites.

★624★

Youth Risk Behavior

High School Students Who Carried A Gun, 1993: Females

Data refer to incidences occurring over a period of 30 days.

[In percentages]

City/MSA	Female	Rank
Boston, MA	4.1	6
Chicago, IL	3.6	7
Dallas, TX	6.1	1
Washington, DC	6.0	2
Fort Lauderdale, FL	3.0	8
Jersey City, NJ	3.0	8
Miami, FL	5.0	3
San Diego, CA	2.1	9
Seattle, WA	3.6	7
New Orleans, LA	4.4	5
New York City, NY	2.0	10
Philadelphia, PA	4.8	4
San Francisco, CA	3.0	8

Source: U.S. Department of Health and Human Services, Public Health Service, Centers for Disease Control and Prevention (CDC), CDC Surveillance Summaries, MMWR: Morbidity and Mortality Weekly Report, 24 March, 1995, vol. 44, no. SS-1, *Youth Risk Behavior Surveillance—United States, 1993*, Atlanta, GA: Centers for Disease Control and Prevention, 1995, p. 25. *Notes:* Data for New Orleans, Louisiana; New York City, New York; Philadelphia, Pennsylvania; and San Francisco, California, are unweighted. Survey covers selected sites.

★625★

Youth Risk Behavior

High School Students Who Carried A Gun, 1993: Males

Data refer to incidences occurring over a period of 30 days.

[In percentages]

City/MSA	Male	Rank
Boston, MA	15.7	7
Chicago, IL	15.0	9
Dallas, TX	22.7	2
Washington, DC	23.1	1
Fort Lauderdale, FL	12.5	11
Jersey City, NJ	20.6	3
Miami, FL	16.3	6
San Diego, CA	13.5	8
Seattle, WA	15.4	5
New Orleans, LA	18.3	10
New York City, NY	13.6	4
Philadelphia, PA	19.2	12
San Francisco, CA	10.7	13

Source: U.S. Department of Health and Human Services, Public Health Service, Centers for Disease Control and Prevention (CDC), CDC Surveillance Summaries, MMWR: Morbidity and Mortality Weekly Report, 24 March, 1995, vol. 44, no. SS-1, *Youth Risk Behavior Surveillance—United States, 1993*, Atlanta, GA: Centers for Disease Control and Prevention, 1995, p. 25. *Notes:* Data for New Orleans, Louisiana; New York City, New York; Philadelphia, Pennsylvania; and San Francisco, California, are unweighted. Survey covers selected sites.

★626★
Youth Risk Behavior

High School Students Who Carried A Gun, 1993: Total

Data refer to incidences occurring over a period of 30 days.

[In percentages]

City/MSA	Total	Rank
Boston, MA	10.0	6
Chicago, IL	9.2	8
Dallas, TX	14.0	1
Fort Lauderdale, FL	7.8	9
Jersey City, NJ	11.6	3
Miami, FL	10.9	4
New Orleans, LA	10.1	5
New York City, NY	7.5	11
Philadelphia, PA	11.6	3
San Diego, CA	7.7	10
San Francisco, CA	6.6	12
Seattle, WA	9.6	7
Washington, DC	13.7	2

Source: U.S. Department of Health and Human Services, Public Health Service, Centers for Disease Control and Prevention (CDC), CDC Surveillance Summaries, MMWR: Morbidity and Mortality Weekly Report, 24 March, 1995, vol. 44, no. SS-1, *Youth Risk Behavior Surveillance—United States, 1993,* Atlanta, GA: Centers for Disease Control and Prevention, 1995, p. 25. *Notes:* Data for New Orleans, Louisiana; New York City, New York; Philadelphia, Pennsylvania; and San Francisco, California, are unweighted. Survey covers selected sites.

★627★
Youth Risk Behavior

High School Students Who Carried A Weapon, 1993: Females

Data refer to incidences occurring over a period of 30 days. "Weapon" as used in this table includes guns, knives, and clubs.

[In percentages]

City/MSA	Female	Rank
Boston, MA	17.8	5
Chicago, IL	17.9	4
Dallas, TX	13.9	9
Washington, DC	27.4	1
Fort Lauderdale, FL	9.9	12
Jersey City, NJ	24.6	2
Miami, FL	14.5	8
San Diego, CA	9.5	13
Seattle, WA	12.6	10
New Orleans, LA	15.6	7
New York City, NY	16.4	6
Philadelphia, PA	23.1	3
San Francisco, CA	11.9	11

Source: U.S. Department of Health and Human Services, Public Health Service, Centers for Disease Control and Prevention (CDC), CDC Surveillance Summaries, MMWR: Morbidity and Mortality Weekly Report, 24 March, 1995, vol. 44, no. SS-1, *Youth Risk Behavior Surveillance—United States, 1993,* Atlanta, GA: Centers for Disease Control and Prevention, 1995, p. 25. *Notes:* Data for New Orleans, Louisiana; New York City, New York; Philadelphia, Pennsylvania; and San Francisco, California, are unweighted. Survey covers selected sites.

★628★
Youth Risk Behavior

High School Students Who Carried A Weapon, 1993: Males

Data refer to incidences occurring over a period of 30 days. "Weapon" as used in this table includes guns, knives, and clubs.

[In percentages]

City/MSA	Male	Rank
Boston, MA	36.9	5
Chicago, IL	27.6	11
Dallas, TX	37.3	4
Washington, DC	40.9	2
Fort Lauderdale, FL	31.9	8
Jersey City, NJ	46.1	1
Miami, FL	32.6	7
San Diego, CA	32.6	7
Seattle, WA	31.5	9
New Orleans, LA	27.7	10
New York City, NY	34.7	6
Philadelphia, PA	39.0	3
San Francisco, CA	26.9	12

Source: U.S. Department of Health and Human Services, Public Health Service, Centers for Disease Control and Prevention (CDC), CDC Surveillance Summaries, MMWR: Morbidity and Mortality Weekly Report, 24 March, 1995, vol. 44, no. SS-1, *Youth Risk Behavior Surveillance—United States, 1993,* Atlanta, GA: Centers for Disease Control and Prevention, 1995, p. 25. *Notes:* Data for New Orleans, Louisiana; New York City, New York; Philadelphia, Pennsylvania; and San Francisco, California, are unweighted. Survey covers selected sites.

★629★
Youth Risk Behavior

High School Students Who Carried A Weapon, 1993: Total

Data refer to incidences occurring over a period of 30 days. "Weapon" as used in this table includes guns, knives, and clubs.

[In percentages]

City/MSA	Total	Rank
Boston, MA	27.5	4
Chicago, IL	22.7	8
Dallas, TX	25.0	6
Fort Lauderdale, FL	20.9	11
Jersey City, NJ	35.3	1
Miami, FL	23.7	7
New Orleans, LA	20.6	12
New York City, NY	25.1	5
Philadelphia, PA	30.6	3
San Diego, CA	21.0	10
San Francisco, CA	19.1	13
Seattle, WA	22.1	9
Washington, DC	33.5	2

Source: U.S. Department of Health and Human Services, Public Health Service, Centers for Disease Control and Prevention (CDC), CDC Surveillance Summaries, MMWR: Morbidity and Mortality Weekly Report, 24 March, 1995, vol. 44, no. SS-1, *Youth Risk Behavior Surveillance—United States, 1993,* Atlanta, GA: Centers for Disease Control and Prevention, 1995, p. 25. *Notes:* Data for New Orleans, Louisiana; New York City, New York; Philadelphia, Pennsylvania; and San Francisco, California, are unweighted. Survey covers selected sites.

★630★

Youth Risk Behavior

Weapons-Carrying By High School Students, 1993: Rate for Females

Data refer to incidences occurring over a period of 30 days.

City/MSA	Female	Rank
Boston, MA	71.9	4
Chicago, IL	66.2	5
Dallas, TX	49.9	9
Fort Lauderdale, FL	38.6	12
Jersey City, NJ	83.5	3
Miami, FL	54.6	7
New Orleans, LA	54.1	8
New York City, NY	60.3	6
Philadelphia, PA	91.4	2
San Diego, CA	29.6	13
San Francisco, CA	42.5	11
Seattle, WA	46.9	10
Washington, DC	109.7	1

Source: U.S. Department of Health and Human Services, Public Health Service, Centers for Disease Control and Prevention (CDC), CDC Surveillance Summaries, MMWR: Morbidity and Mortality Weekly Report, 24 March, 1995, vol. 44, no. SS-1, *Youth Risk Behavior Surveillance—United States, 1993*, Atlanta, GA: Centers for Disease Control and Prevention, 1995, p. 25. *Notes:* Data for New Orleans, Louisiana; New York City, New York; Philadelphia, Pennsylvania; and San Francisco, California, are unweighted. Survey covers selected sites.

★631★

Youth Risk Behavior

Weapons-Carrying By High School Students, 1993: Rate for Males

Data refer to incidences occurring over a period of 30 days.

City/MSA	Male	Rank
Boston, MA	153.3	5
Chicago, IL	95.0	13
Dallas, TX	156.1	4
Fort Lauderdale, FL	128.8	10
Jersey City, NJ	184.9	1
Miami, FL	131.1	8
New Orleans, LA	99.1	12
New York City, NY	143.1	6
Philadelphia, PA	169.3	3
San Diego, CA	129.2	9
San Francisco, CA	110.7	11
Seattle, WA	133.2	7
Washington, DC	171.5	2

Source: U.S. Department of Health and Human Services, Public Health Service, Centers for Disease Control and Prevention (CDC), CDC Surveillance Summaries, MMWR: Morbidity and Mortality Weekly Report, 24 March, 1995, vol. 44, no. SS-1, *Youth Risk Behavior Surveillance—United States, 1993*, Atlanta, GA: Centers for Disease Control and Prevention, 1995, p. 25. *Notes:* Data for New Orleans, Louisiana; New York City, New York; Philadelphia, Pennsylvania; and San Francisco, California, are unweighted. Survey covers selected sites.

★632★

Youth Risk Behavior

Weapons-Carrying By High School Students, 1993: Total Rate

Data refer to incidences occurring over a period of 30 days.

City/MSA	Total	Rank
Boston, MA	113.1	4
Chicago, IL	80.6	10
Dallas, TX	100.1	5
Fort Lauderdale, FL	83.9	9
Jersey City, NJ	133.4	2
Miami, FL	93.5	7
New Orleans, LA	72.7	13
New York City, NY	99.7	6
Philadelphia, PA	128.3	3
San Diego, CA	78.9	11
San Francisco, CA	75.2	12
Seattle, WA	90.3	8
Washington, DC	137.6	1

Source: U.S. Department of Health and Human Services, Public Health Service, Centers for Disease Control and Prevention (CDC), CDC Surveillance Summaries, MMWR: Morbidity and Mortality Weekly Report, 24 March, 1995, vol. 44, no. SS-1, *Youth Risk Behavior Surveillance—United States, 1993*, Atlanta, GA: Centers for Disease Control and Prevention, 1995, p. 25. *Notes:* Data for New Orleans, Louisiana; New York City, New York; Philadelphia, Pennsylvania; and San Francisco, California, are unweighted. Survey covers selected sites.

★633★

Diseases: AIDS

AIDS Cases Reported in Adults and Adolescents to 1995: Highest Cumulative Totals

Data refer to cases per 100,000 population, in metropolitan areas with 500,000 or more persons.

City/MSA	Number	Rank
New York, NY	79,984	1
Los Angeles, CA	30,885	2
San Francisco, CA	22,800	3
Miami, FL	15,975	4
Washington, DC	14,435	5
Chicago, IL	14,165	6
Houston, TX	12,459	7
Newark, NJ	11,521	8
Philadelphia, PA	11,489	9
Atlanta, GA	10,355	10
Boston, MA	9,337	11
Dallas, TX	8,691	12
Baltimore, MD	8,448	13
Fort Lauderdale, FL	8,019	14
San Diego, CA	7,299	15
Oakland, CA	5,918	16
Tampa-Saint Petersburg, FL	5,474	17
Detroit, MI	5,083	18
Seattle, WA	4,942	19
Jersey City, NJ	4,680	20
Riverside-San Bernardino, CA	4,617	21
West Palm Beach, FL	4,566	22
Nassau-Suffolk, NY	4,439	23

[Continued]

★633★

AIDS Cases Reported in Adults and Adolescents to 1995: Highest Cumulative Totals
[Continued]

City/MSA	Number	Rank
New Orleans, LA	4,404	24
Denver, CO	4,225	25

Source: U.S. Department of Health and Human Services, Public Health Service, Centers for Disease Control and Prevention, National Center for HIV, STD, and TB Prevention, *HIV/AIDS Surveillance Report,* Year-end edition, vol.7, no. 2, Atlanta, Georgia: Centers for Disease Control and Prevention, p. 8. *Notes:* "AIDS" stands for "Acquired Immune Deficiency Syndrome,"; "STD" stands for "Sexually Transmitted Diseases,"; "TB" stands for "Tuberculosis."

★634★

Diseases: AIDS

AIDS Cases Reported in Adults and Adolescents to 1995: Lowest Cumulative Totals

Data refer to cases per 100,000 population, in metropolitan areas with 500,000 or more persons.

City/MSA	Number	Rank
Youngstown, OH	232	1
Ann Arbor, MI	272	2
Scranton, PA	284	3
Akron, OH	319	4
Toledo, OH	373	5
Gary, IN	429	6
Knoxville, TN	434	7
Wichita, KS	454	8
Omaha, NE	480	9
Allentown, PA	489	10
Stockton, CA	508	11
Grand Rapids, MI	527	12
Ventura, CA	532	13
Tacoma, WA	540	14
El Paso, TX	549	15
Harrisburg, PA	549	15
Bakersfield, CA	615	16
Dayton, OH	646	17
Albuquerque, NM	680	18
Little Rock, AR	686	19
Syracuse, NY	732	20
Mobile, AL	736	21
Tulsa, OK	744	22
Fresno, CA	792	23
Louisville, KY	807	24
Baton Rouge, LA	851	25

Source: U.S. Department of Health and Human Services, Public Health Service, Centers for Disease Control and Prevention, National Center for HIV, STD, and TB Prevention, *HIV/AIDS Surveillance Report,* Year-end edition, vol.7, no. 2, Atlanta, Georgia: Centers for Disease Control and Prevention, p. 8. *Notes:* "AIDS" stands for "Acquired Immune Deficiency Syndrome,"; "STD" stands for "Sexually Transmitted Diseases,"; "TB" stands for "Tuberculosis."

★635★

Diseases: AIDS

AIDS Cases Reported in Children Under Age 13, to 1995: Highest Cumulative Totals

Data refer to cases per 100,000 population, in metropolitan areas with 500,000 or more persons.

City/MSA	Number	Rank
New York, NY	1,620	1
Miami, FL	397	2
Newark, NJ	570	3
Washington, DC	205	4
Los Angeles, CA	200	5
Fort Lauderdale, FL	182	6
Baltimore, MD	173	7
Chicago, IL	170	8
Philadelphia, PA	163	9
West Palm Beach, FL	159	10
Boston, MA	149	11
Houston, TX	114	12
New Haven, CT	106	13
Jersey City, NJ	101	14
Atlanta, GA	84	15
Nassau-Suffolk, NY	76	16
Tampa-Saint Petersburg, FL	74	17
Bergen-Passaic, NJ	64	18
Jacksonville, FL	62	19
Orlando, FL	62	19
Middlesex, NJ	61	20
Detroit, MI	60	21
New Orleans, LA	51	22
Norfolk, VA	51	22
Monmouth-Ocean City, NJ	50	23

Source: U.S. Department of Health and Human Services, Public Health Service, Centers for Disease Control and Prevention, National Center for HIV, STD, and TB Prevention, *HIV/AIDS Surveillance Report,* Year-end edition, vol.7, no. 2, Atlanta, Georgia: Centers for Disease Control and Prevention, p. 8. *Notes:* "AIDS" stands for "Acquired Immune Deficiency Syndrome,"; "STD" stands for "Sexually Transmitted Diseases,"; "TB" stands for "Tuberculosis."

★636★

Diseases: AIDS

AIDS Cases Reported in Children Under Age 13, to 1995: Lowest Cumulative Totals

Data refer to cases per 100,000 population, in metropolitan areas with 500,000 or more persons.

City/MSA	Number	Rank
Albuquerque, NM	2	1
Allentown, PA	6	4
Ann Arbor, MI	5	3
Bakersfield, CA	3	2
Dayton, OH	8	6
El Paso, TX	2	1
Fresno, CA	8	6
Gary, IN	3	2
Grand Rapids, MI	3	2
Greenville, SC	2	1
Harrisburg, PA	5	3
Knoxville, TN	5	3
Louisville, KY	8	6
Mobile, AL	9	7

[Continued]

★636★

AIDS Cases Reported in Children Under Age 13, to 1995: Lowest Cumulative Totals
[Continued]

City/MSA	Number	Rank
Oklahoma City, OK	2	1
Omaha, NE	2	1
Rochester, NY	8	6
Scranton, PA	3	2
Syracuse, NY	7	5
Tacoma, WA	7	5
Toledo, OH	8	6
Tucson, AZ	6	4
Tulsa, OK	6	4
Ventura, CA	2	1
Wichita, KS	2	1

Source: U.S. Department of Health and Human Services, Public Health Service, Centers for Disease Control and Prevention, National Center for HIV, STD, and TB Prevention, *HIV/AIDS Surveillance Report,* Year-end edition, vol.7, no. 2, Atlanta, Georgia: Centers for Disease Control and Prevention, p. 8. *Notes:* "AIDS" stands for "Acquired Immune Deficiency Syndrome,"; "STD" stands for "Sexually Transmitted Diseases,"; "TB" stands for "Tuberculosis."

★637★

Diseases: AIDS

AIDS Cases Reported, 1995: Lowest Number Reported

Data refer to rates per 100,000 population, in metropolitan areas with 500,000 or more persons.

City/MSA	Number	Rank
Akron, OH	37	1
Toledo, OH	37	1
Youngstown, OH	40	2
Scranton, PA	47	3
Dayton, OH	48	4
Ann Arbor, MI	54	5
Knoxville, TN	69	6
Ventura, CA	70	7
Tacoma, WA	73	8
Stockton, CA	74	9
Gary, IN	77	10
Omaha, NE	78	11
Buffalo, NY	84	12
Little Rock, AR	86	13
Allentown, PA	88	14
Tulsa, OK	91	15
Albuquerque, NM	92	16
Grand Rapids, MI	98	17
Wichita, KS	99	18
Syracuse, NY	106	19
Mobile, AL	118	20
Oklahoma City, OK	118	20
Tucson, AZ	120	21
Baton Rouge, LA	121	22
Greenville, SC	126	23

Source: U.S. Department of Health and Human Services, Public Health Service, Centers for Disease Control and Prevention, National Center for HIV, STD, and TB Prevention, *HIV/AIDS Surveillance Report,* Year-end edition, vol.7, no. 2, Atlanta, Georgia: Centers for Disease Control and Prevention, p. 8. *Notes:* "AIDS" stands for "Acquired Immune Deficiency Syndrome,"; "STD" stands for "Sexually Transmitted Diseases,"; "TB" stands for "Tuberculosis."

★638★

Diseases: AIDS

AIDS Cases Reported, 1995: Highest Number Reported

Data refer to cases per 100,000 population, in metropolitan areas with 500,000 or more persons.

City/MSA	Number	Rank
New York, NY	10,496	1
Los Angeles, CA	3,997	2
Miami, FL	2,381	3
San Francisco, CA	2,135	4
Washington, DC	2,130	5
Chicago, IL	1,912	6
Philadelphia, PA	1,810	7
Baltimore, MD	1,715	8
Newark, NJ	1,681	9
Atlanta, GA	1,556	10
Dallas, TX	1,289	11
Fort Lauderdale, FL	1,271	12
Boston, MA	1,266	13
Houston, TX	1,158	14
San Diego, CA	1,068	15
New Haven, CT	948	16
West Palm Beach, FL	810	17
Detroit, MI	794	18
Riverside-San Bernardino, CA	768	19
Jersey City, NJ	760	20
Orlando, FL	709	21
Tampa-Saint Petersburg, FL	709	21
Oakland, CA	655	22
Seattle, WA	645	23
Norfolk, VA	603	24
New Orleans, LA	594	25

Source: U.S. Department of Health and Human Services, Public Health Service, Centers for Disease Control and Prevention, National Center for HIV, STD, and TB Prevention, *HIV/AIDS Surveillance Report,* Year-end edition, vol.7, no. 2, Atlanta, Georgia: Centers for Disease Control and Prevention, p. 8. *Notes:* "AIDS" stands for "Acquired Immune Deficiency Syndrome,"; "HIV" stands for "Human Immunodeficiency Virus,"; "STD" stands for "Sexually Transmitted Diseases,"; "TB" stands for "Tuberculosis."

★639★

Diseases: AIDS

AIDS Cases Reported, 1995: Highest Rates

Data refer to rates per 100,000 population, in metropolitan areas with 500,000 or more persons.

City/MSA	Rate	Rank
Jersey City, NJ	138.1	1
San Francisco, CA	129.7	2
New York, NY	122.5	3
Miami, FL	117.2	4
Fort Lauderdale, FL	90.0	5
Newark, NJ	86.8	6
West Palm Beach, FL	83.3	7
Baltimore, MD	69.4	8
New Haven, CT	58.3	9
Orlando, FL	51.0	10
Hartford, CT	50.3	11
Wilmington, DE	48.5	12
Washington, DC	47.2	13

[Continued]

★639★

AIDS Cases Reported, 1995: Highest Rates
[Continued]

City/MSA	Rate	Rank
Jacksonville, FL	46.4	14
Atlanta, GA	45.3	15
New Orleans, LA	45.2	16
Los Angeles, CA	43.7	17
Dallas, TX	43.6	18
Bergen-Passaic, NJ	42.7	19
San Diego, CA	40.4	20
Norfolk, VA	39.1	21
Philadelphia, PA	36.6	22
Las Vegas, NV	33.8	23
Tampa-Saint Petersburg, FL	32.5	24
Middlesex, NJ	32.4	25
Monmouth-Ocean City, NJ	32.4	25

Source: U.S. Department of Health and Human Services, Public Health Service, Centers for Disease Control and Prevention, National Center for HIV, STD, and TB Prevention, *HIV/AIDS Surveillance Report,* Year-end edition, vol.7, no. 2, Atlanta, Georgia: Centers for Disease Control and Prevention, p. 8. *Notes:* "AIDS" stands for "Acquired Immune Deficiency Syndrome,"; "STD" stands for "Sexually Transmitted Diseases,"; "TB" stands for "Tuberculosis."

★640★

Diseases: AIDS

AIDS Cases Reported, 1995: Lowest Rates

Data refer to cases per 100,000 population, in metropolitan areas with 500,000 or more persons.

City/MSA	Rate	Rank
Dayton, OH	5.0	1
Akron, OH	5.5	2
Toledo, OH	6.0	3
Youngstown, OH	6.6	4
Buffalo, NY	7.1	5
Scranton, PA	7.4	6
Grand Rapids, MI	9.8	7
Pittsburgh, PA	9.8	7
Ventura, CA	9.9	8
Ann Arbor, MI	10.3	9
Knoxville, TN	10.8	10
Tacoma, WA	11.2	11
Salt Lake City, UT	11.3	12
Oklahoma City, OK	11.6	13
Omaha, NE	11.6	13
Minneapolis-Saint Paul, MN	11.7	14
Cincinnati, OH	12.2	15
Tulsa, OK	12.2	15
Gary, IN	12.4	16
Columbus, OH	13.4	17
Milwaukee, WI	13.4	17
Albuquerque, NM	13.9	18
Stockton, CA	14.1	19
Syracuse, NY	14.1	19
Greenville, SC	14.2	20

Source: U.S. Department of Health and Human Services, Public Health Service, Centers for Disease Control and Prevention, National Center for HIV, STD, and TB Prevention, *HIV/AIDS Surveillance Report,* Year-end edition, vol.7, no. 2, Atlanta, Georgia: Centers for Disease Control and Prevention, p. 8. *Notes:* "AIDS" stands for "Acquired Immune Deficiency Syndrome,"; "HIV" stands for "Human Immunodeficiency Virus,"; "STD" stands for "Sexually Transmitted Diseases,"; "TB" stands for "Tuberculosis."

★641★

Diseases: AIDS

AIDS Cases Reported, to 1995: Highest Cumulative Totals

Data refer to cases in adults, adolescents, and children under age 13 per 100,000 population, in metropolitan areas with 500,000 or more persons.

City/MSA	Number	Rank
Atlanta, GA	10,439	10
Baltimore, MD	8,621	13
Boston, MA	9,486	11
Chicago, IL	14,335	6
Dallas, TX	8,725	12
Detroit, MI	5,143	18
Fort Lauderdale, FL	8,201	14
Houston, TX	12,573	7
Jersey City, NJ	4,781	20
Los Angeles, CA	31,085	2
Miami, FL	16,372	4
Nassau-Suffolk, NY	4,515	23
New Haven, CT	4,305	25
New Orleans, LA	4,455	24
New York, NY	81,604	1
Newark, NJ	11,791	8
Oakland, CA	5,951	16
Philadelphia, PA	11,652	9
Riverside-San Bernardino, CA	4,659	22
San Diego, CA	7,344	15
San Francisco, CA	22,835	3
Seattle, WA	4,956	19
Tampa-Saint Petersburg, FL	5,548	17
Washington, DC	14,640	5
West Palm Beach, FL	4,725	21

Source: U.S. Department of Health and Human Services, Public Health Service, Centers for Disease Control and Prevention, National Center for HIV, STD, and TB Prevention, *HIV/AIDS Surveillance Report,* Year-end edition, vol.7, no. 2, Atlanta, Georgia: Centers for Disease Control and Prevention, p. 8. *Notes:* "AIDS" stands for "Acquired Immune Deficiency Syndrome,"; "STD" stands for "Sexually Transmitted Diseases,"; "TB" stands for "Tuberculosis."

★642★

Diseases: AIDS

AIDS Cases Reported, to 1995: Lowest Cumulative Totals

Data refer to cases in adults, adolescents, and children under age 13 per 100,000 population, in metropolitan areas with 500,000 or more persons.

City/MSA	Number	Rank
Youngstown, OH	232	1
Ann Arbor, MI	277	2
Scranton, PA	287	3
Akron, OH	319	4
Toledo, OH	381	5
Gary, IN	432	6
Knoxville, TN	439	7
Omaha, NE	452	8
Wichita, KS	456	9
Allentown, PA	495	10
Stockton, Ca	520	11
Grand Rapids, MI	530	12
Ventura, CA	534	13
Tacoma, WA	547	14

[Continued]

★642★

AIDS Cases Reported, to 1995: Lowest Cumulative Totals

[Continued]

City/MSA	Number	Rank
El Paso, TX	551	15
Harrisburg, PA	554	16
Bakersfield, CA	618	17
Dayton, OH	654	18
Albuquerque, NM	682	19
Little Rock, AR	696	20
Syracuse, NY	739	21
Mobile, AL	745	22
Tulsa, OK	750	23
Fresno, CA	800	24
Louisville, KY	815	25

Source: U.S. Department of Health and Human Services, Public Health Service, Centers for Disease Control and Prevention, National Center for HIV, STD, and TB Prevention, *HIV/AIDS Surveillance Report,* Year-end edition, vol.7, no. 2, Atlanta, Georgia: Centers for Disease Control and Prevention, p. 8. *Notes:* "AIDS" stands for "Acquired Immune Deficiency Syndrome,"; "STD" stands for "Sexually Transmitted Diseases,"; "TB" stands for "Tuberculosis."

★643★

Diseases: Back Problems

Back Surgery Rates, 1994

[Rate per 1,000 persons]

City	Rate	Rank
Atlanta, GA	2.4	9
Boston, MA	1.9	10
Chicago, IL	1.7	11
Denver, CO	3.2	3
Houston, TX	2.8	6
Los Angeles, CA	3.0	4
Manhattan, NY	1.2	13
Miami, FL	1.4	12
Saint Louis, MO	2.8	7
Salt Lake City, UT	4.0	1
San Francisco, CA	2.5	8
Seattle, WA	3.5	2
Tucson, AZ	4.0	1
Washington, DC	2.9	5

Source: Chang, Trina, "Back Surgery," *American Health,* (May 19960, p. 25.

★644★

Diseases: Breast Cancer

Breast-Sparing Surgery for Women Over Age 65, 1994 (Highest Percentages)

Breast-sparing surgery includes lumpectomies and partial mastectomies.

[In percentages]

City	Percentages	Rank
Boston, MA	32.0	3
Elyria, OH	48.0	1
Los Angeles, CA	22.0	6
Manhattan, NY	29.0	5

[Continued]

★644★

Breast-Sparing Surgery for Women Over Age 65, 1994 (Highest Percentages)

[Continued]

City	Percentages	Rank
Paterson, NJ	38.0	2
Philadelphia, PA	31.0	4

Source: Chang, Trina, "Breast Cancer Surgery," *American Health,* (May 1996), p. 25.

★645★

Diseases: Breast Cancer

Breast-Sparing Surgery for Women Over Age 65, 1994 (Lowest Percentages)

Breast-sparing surgery includes lumpectomies and partial mastectomies.

[In percentages]

City	Percentages	Rank
Fort Collins, CO	5.0	2
Fort Smith, AR	4.0	3
Houston, TX	13.0	1
Ogden, UT	2.0	4
Rapid City, SD	1.0	5
Yakima, WA	4.0	3

Source: Chang, Trina, "Breast Cancer Surgery," *American Health,* (May 1996), p. 25.

★646★

Diseases: Coronary Disease

Coronary Bypass Surgery, 1995: Average Costs for Medicare Patients

City	Amount	Rank
Los Angeles, CA	65,309	1
Philadelphia, PA	64,016	2
San Diego, CA	63,923	3
San Francisco, CA	58,342	4
New Orleans, LA	55,738	5
Chicago, IL	53,211	6
Phoenix, AZ	51,171	7
Birmingham, AL	51,023	8
Houston, TX	50,193	9
Kansas City, MO	49,431	10
Dallas, TX	47,542	11
Boston, MA	44,864	12
Minneapolis-Saint Paul, MN	42,015	13
New York City, NY	38,902	14
Cleveland, OH	37,349	15
Atlanta, GA	36,426	16
Seattle, WA	34,291	17
Baltimore, MD	23,390	18

Source: Chang, Trina, "The Bill for Bypass Surgery," *American Health,* (April 1995), p. 37.

★647★
Emergency Medical Services

Emergency Medical Services (EMS), 1996: Runs Per Vehicle Per Year

City	Number	Rank
Boston, MA	5,700	3
Chicago, IL	3,830	5
Cleveland, OH	5,000	4
Detroit, MI	8,250	1
Pittsburgh, PA	7,800	2

Source: "Bogus Calls Keep EMS On Run," *Detroit Free Press,* 21 June 1996, p. 8A. Primary source: City of Detroit, Michigan. *Note:* "EMS" stands for "Emergency Medical Services."

★648★
Emergency Medical Services

Emergency Medical Services (EMS), 1996: Runs Per Year

City	Number	Rank
Boston, MA	104,000	3
Chicago, IL	226,000	1
Cleveland, OH	90,000	4
Detroit, MI	132,000	2
Pittsburgh, PA	63,000	5

Source: "Bogus Calls Keep EMS On Run," *Detroit Free Press,* 21 June 1996, p. 8A. Primary source: City of Detroit, Michigan. *Note:* "EMS" stands for "Emergency Medical Services."

★649★
Emergency Medical Services

Emergency Medical Services (EMS), 1996: Staff

City	Number	Rank
Boston, MA	290	2
Chicago, IL	634	1
Cleveland, OH	235	4
Detroit, MI	240	3
Pittsburgh, PA	160	5

Source: "Bogus Calls Keep EMS On Run," *Detroit Free Press,* 21 June 1996, p. 8A. Primary source: City of Detroit, Michigan. *Note:* "EMS" stands for "Emergency Medical Services."

★650★
Emergency Medical Services

Emergency Medical Services (EMS), 1996: Vehicles

City	Number	Rank
Boston, MA	18	2
Chicago, IL	59	1
Cleveland, OH	18	2
Detroit, MI	16	3
Pittsburgh, PA	11	4

Source: "Bogus Calls Keep EMS On Run," *Detroit Free Press,* 21 June 1996, p. 8A. Primary source: City of Detroit, Michigan. *Note:* "EMS" stands for "Emergency Medical Services."

★651★
Vital Statistics

Births, 1988: Birth Rates in the 20 Largest Metropolitan Areas

[Rate is per 1,000 population]

City/MSA	Rate	Rank
New York-Northern New Jersey-Long Island, NY-NJ-CT-PA CMSA/NECMA[1]	15.8	10
Los Angeles-Riverside-Orange County, CA CMSA	19.9	1
Chicago-Gary-Kenosha, IL-IN-WI CMSA	17.3	5
Washington-Baltimore, DC-MD-VA-WV CMSA	16.4	7
San Francisco-Oakland-San Jose, CA CMSA	16.3	8
Philadelphia-Wilmington-Atlantic City, PA-NJ-DE-MD CMSA	16.1	9
Boston-Brockton-Nashua, MA-NH NECMA	15.2	11
Detroit-Ann Arbor-Flint, MI CMSA	15.2	11
Dallas-Fort Worth, TX CMSA	18.9	2
Houston-Galveston-Brazoria, TX CMSA	18.7	3
Miami-Fort Lauderdale, FL CMSA	15.8	10
Seattle-Tacoma-Bremerton, WA CMSA	15.8	10
Atlanta, GA MSA	17.3	12
Cleveland-Akron, OH CMSA	14.7	14
Minneapolis-Saint Paul, MN-WI MSA	16.8	6
San Diego, CA MSA	18.7	3
Saint Louis, MO-IL MSA	16.1	9
Pittsburgh, PA MSA	12.5	14
Phoenix-Mesa, AZ MSA	18.6	4
Tampa-Saint Petersburg-Clearwater, FL MSA	13.6	13

Source: U.S. Bureau of the Census, *Statistical Abstract of the United States: 1995,* (115th edition), Washington, D.C.: U.S. Government Printing Office, 1995, p. 78. Primary source: U.S. National Center for Health Statistics, *Vital Statistics of the United States,* annual; and unpublished data. *Notes:* "CMSA" stands for "Consolidated Metropolitan Statistical Area." "MSA" stands for "Metropolitan Statistical Area," and "NECMA" stands for "New England County Metropolitan Area." 1. Includes parts of New Haven County, CT, not in the CMSA; excludes parts of Litchfield and Middlesex Counties, CT, in the CMSA.

★652★
Vital Statistics

Births, 1988: Number in the 20 Largest Metropolitan Areas

[In thousands]

City/MSA	Number	Rank
Atlanta, GA MSA	49,123	11
Boston-Brockton-Nashua, MA-NH NECMA	85,666	7
Chicago-Gary-Kenosha, IL-IN-WI CMSA	141,570	3
Cleveland-Akron, OH CMSA	42,012	15

[Continued]

★652★

Births, 1988: Number in the 20 Largest Metropolitan Areas

[Continued]

City/MSA	Number	Rank
Dallas-Fort Worth, TX CMSA	74,017	9
Detroit-Ann Arbor-Flint, MI CMSA	78,425	8
Houston-Galveston-Brazoria, TX CMSA	67,130	10
Los Angeles-Riverside-Orange County, CA CMSA	276,991	2
Miami-Fort Lauderdale, FL CMSA	48,638	12
Minneapolis-Saint Paul, MN-WI MSA	41,436	16
New York-Northern New Jersey-Long Island, NY-NJ-CT-PA CMSA/NECMA[1]	307,126	1
Philadelphia-Wilmington-Atlantic City, PA-NJ-DE-MD CMSA	94,245	6
Phoenix-Mesa, AZ MSA	40,216	17
Pittsburgh, PA MSA	30,134	19
Saint Louis, MO-IL MSA	40,097	18
San Diego, CA MSA	44,096	14
San Francisco-Oakland-San Jose, CA CMSA	99,474	5
Seattle-Tacoma-Bremerton, WA CMSA	44,475	13
Tampa-Saint Petersburg-Clearwater, FL MSA	27,201	20
Washington-Baltimore, DC-MD-VA-WV CMSA	107,954	4

Source: U.S. Bureau of the Census, *Statistical Abstract of the United States: 1995*, (115th edition), Washington, D.C.: U.S. Government Printing Office, 1995, p. 78. Primary source: U.S. National Center for Health Statistics, *Vital Statistics of the United States*, annual; and unpublished data. *Notes:* "CMSA" stands for "Consolidated Metropolitan Statistical Area." "MSA" stands for "Metropolitan Statistical Area," and "NECMA" stands for "New England County Metropolitan Area." 1. Includes parts of New Haven County, CT, not in the CMSA; excludes parts of Litchfield and Middlesex Counties, CT, in the CMSA.

★653★

Vital Statistics

Deaths, 1988: Death Rates in the 20 Largest Metropolitan Areas

[Rate is per 1,000 population]

City/MSA	Rate	Rank
New York-Northern New Jersey-Long Island, NY-NJ-CT-PA CMSA/NECMA[1]	9.7	5
Los Angeles-Riverside-Orange County, CA CMSA	7.3	14
Chicago-Gary-Kenosha, IL-IN-WI CMSA	8.7	10
Washington-Baltimore, DC-MD-VA-WV CMSA	7.7	12
San Francisco-Oakland-San Jose, CA CMSA	7.8	11
Philadelphia-Wilmington-Atlantic City, PA-NJ-DE-MD CMSA	10.0	4

[Continued]

★653★

Deaths, 1988: Death Rates in the 20 Largest Metropolitan Areas

[Continued]

City/MSA	Rate	Rank
Boston-Brockton-Nashua, MA-NH NECMA	9.0	8
Detroit-Ann Arbor-Flint, MI CMSA	8.8	9
Dallas-Fort Worth, TX CMSA	6.5	17
Houston-Galveston-Brazoria, TX CMSA	6.3	18
Miami-Fort Lauderdale, FL CMSA	10.7	3
Seattle-Tacoma-Bremerton, WA CMSA	7.3	14
Atlanta, GA MSA	6.8	16
Cleveland-Akron, OH CMSA	9.6	6
Minneapolis-Saint Paul, MN-WI MSA	6.8	16
San Diego, CA MSA	7.0	15
Saint Louis, MO-IL MSA	9.4	7
Pittsburgh, PA MSA	11.3	2
Phoenix-Mesa, AZ MSA	7.5	13
Tampa-Saint Petersburg-Clearwater, FL MSA	12.4	1

Source: U.S. Bureau of the Census, *Statistical Abstract of the United States: 1995*, (115th edition), Washington, D.C.: U.S. Government Printing Office, 1995, p. 78. Primary source: U.S. National Center for Health Statistics, *Vital Statistics of the United States*, annual; and unpublished data. *Notes:* "CMSA" stands for "Consolidated Metropolitan Statistical Area." "MSA" stands for "Metropolitan Statistical Area." "NECMA" stands for New England County Metropolitan Area." 1. Includes parts of New Haven County, CT, not in the CMSA; excludes parts of Litchfield and Middlesex Counties, CT, in the CMSA.

★654★

Vital Statistics

Deaths, 1988: Number in the 20 Largest Metropolitan Areas

[In thousands]

City/MSA	Number	Rank
Atlanta, GA MSA	19,235	17
Boston-Brockton-Nashua, MA-NH NECMA	50,656	6
Chicago-Gary-Kenosha, IL-IN-WI CMSA	71,500	3
Cleveland-Akron, OH CMSA	27,524	10
Dallas-Fort Worth, TX CMSA	25,596	12
Detroit-Ann Arbor-Flint, MI CMSA	45,227	8
Houston-Galveston-Brazoria, TX CMSA	22,579	15
Los Angeles-Riverside-Orange County, CA CMSA	101,850	2
Miami-Fort Lauderdale, FL CMSA	32,785	9
Minneapolis-Saint Paul, MN-WI MSA	16,896	18
New York-Northern New Jersey-Long Island, NY-NJ-CT-PA CMSA/NECMA[1]	189,362	1
Philadelphia-Wilmington-Atlantic City, PA-NJ-DE-MD CMSA	58,748	4

[Continued]

★654★

Deaths, 1988: Number in the 20 Largest Metropolitan Areas

[Continued]

City/MSA	Number	Rank	
Phoenix-Mesa, AZ MSA	16,315	20	
Pittsburgh, PA MSA	27,206	11	
Saint Louis, MO-IL MSA	23,302	14	
San Diego, CA MSA	16,658	19	
San Francisco-Oakland-San Jose, CA CMSA	47,356	7	
Seattle-Tacoma-Bremerton, WA CMSA	20,447	16	
Tampa-Saint Petersburg-Clearwater, FL MSA	24,903	13	
Washington-Baltimore, DC-MD-VA-WV CMSA	50,890	5	k

Source: U.S. Bureau of the Census, *Statistical Abstract of the United States: 1995,* (115th edition), Washington, D.C.: U.S. Government Printing Office, 1995, p. 78. Primary source: U.S. National Center for Health Statistics, *Vital Statistics of the United States,* annual; and unpublished data. *Notes:* "CMSA" stands for "Consolidated Metropolitan Statistical Area." "MSA" stands for "Metropolitan Statistical Area." "NECMA" stands for New England County Metropolitan Area." 1. Includes parts of New Haven County, CT, not in the CMSA; excludes parts of Litchfield and Middlesex Counties, CT, in the CMSA.

★655★

Vital Statistics

Infants' Deaths, 1988: Death Rates in the 20 Largest Metropolitan Areas

[Rates are per 1,000 registered live births]

City/MSA	Rate[1]	Rank
New York-Northern New Jersey-Long Island, NY-NJ-CT-PA CMSA/NECMA[2]	10.9	8
Los Angeles-Riverside-Orange County, CA CMSA	8.9	13
Chicago-Gary-Kenosha, IL-IN-WI CMSA	11.9	2
Washington-Baltimore, DC-MD-VA-WV CMSA	11.5	4
San Francisco-Oakland-San Jose, CA CMSA	7.8	16
Philadelphia-Wilmington-Atlantic City, PA-NJ-DE-MD CMSA	11.7	3
Boston-Brockton-Nashua, MA-NH NECMA	7.7	17
Detroit-Ann Arbor-Flint, MI CMSA	12.3	1
Dallas-Fort Worth, TX CMSA	8.8	14
Houston-Galveston-Brazoria, TX CMSA	9.6	12
Miami-Fort Lauderdale, FL CMSA	11.1	6
Seattle-Tacoma-Bremerton, WA CMSA	8.9	13
Atlanta, GA MSA	11.3	5
Cleveland-Akron, OH CMSA	11.0	7
Minneapolis-Saint Paul, MN-WI MSA	7.8	16

[Continued]

★655★

Infants' Deaths, 1988: Death Rates in the 20 Largest Metropolitan Areas

[Continued]

City/MSA	Rate[1]	Rank
San Diego, CA MSA	7.1	18
Saint Louis, MO-IL MSA	9.7	11
Pittsburgh, PA MSA	8.6	15
Phoenix-Mesa, AZ MSA	9.9	10
Tampa-Saint Petersburg-Clearwater, FL MSA	10.7	9

Source: U.S. Bureau of the Census, *Statistical Abstract of the United States: 1995,* (115th edition), Washington, D.C.: U.S. Government Printing Office, 1995, p. 78. Primary source: U.S. National Center for Health Statistics, *Vital Statistics of the United States,* annual; and unpublished data. *Notes:* "CMSA" stands for "Consolidated Metropolitan Statistical Area." "MSA" stands for "Metropolitan Statistical Area." "NECMA" stands for "New England County Metropolitan Area." 1. Infants under 1 year, excluding fetal deaths. 2. Includes parts of New Haven County, CT, not in the CMSA; excludes parts of Litchfield and Middlesex Counties, CT, in the CMSA.

★656★

Vital Statistics

Infants' Deaths, 1988: Number in the 20 Largest Metropolitan Areas

[In thousands]

City	Number[1]	Rank
Atlanta, GA MSA	554	11
Boston-Brockton-Nashua, MA-NH NECMA	659	8
Chicago-Gary-Kenosha, IL-IN-WI CMSA	1,678	3
Cleveland-Akron, OH CMSA	463	13
Dallas-Fort Worth, TX CMSA	654	9
Detroit-Ann Arbor-Flint, MI CMSA	967	6
Houston-Galveston-Brazoria, TX CMSA	644	10
Los Angeles-Riverside-Orange County, CA CMSA	2,458	2
Miami-Fort Lauderdale, FL CMSA	542	12
Minneapolis-Saint Paul, MN-WI MSA	322	17
New York-Northern New Jersey-Long Island, NY-NJ-CT-PA CMSA/NECMA[2]	3,354	1
Philadelphia-Wilmington-Atlantic City, PA-NJ-DE-MD CMSA	1,100	5
Phoenix-Mesa, AZ MSA	398	14
Pittsburgh, PA MSA	260	20
Saint Louis, MO-IL MSA	390	16
San Diego, CA MSA	315	18
San Francisco-Oakland-San Jose, CA CMSA	774	7
Seattle-Tacoma-Bremerton, WA CMSA	395	15

[Continued]

★656★

Infants' Deaths, 1988: Number in the 20 Largest Metropolitan Areas

[Continued]

City	Number[1]	Rank
Tampa-Saint Petersburg-Clearwater, FL MSA	290	19
Washington-Baltimore, DC-MD-VA-WV CMSA	1,243	4

Source: U.S. Bureau of the Census, *Statistical Abstract of the United States: 1995,* (115th edition), Washington, D.C.: U.S. Government Printing Office, 1995, p. 78. Primary source: U.S. National Center for Health Statistics, *Vital Statistics of the United States,* annual; and unpublished data. *Notes:* "CMSA" stands for "Consolidated Metropolitan Statistical Area." "MSA" stands for "Metropolitan Statistical Area." "NECMA" stands for "New England County Metropolitan Area." 1. Infants under 1 year, excluding fetal deaths. 2. Includes parts of New Haven County, CT, not in the CMSA; excludes parts of Litchfield and Middlesex Counties, CT, in the CMSA.

★657★

Vital Statistics

Deaths Caused By Heroin Use, 1994, Selected Cities: Percent Change Since 1991

City	Percent change	Rank
New York, NY	-9	1
Los Angeles, CA	+49	3
Philadelphia, PA	+68	4
Baltimore, MD	+93	6
Chicago, IL	+71	5
New Orleans, LA	+733	9
Newark, NJ	+193	8
San Francisco, CA	+104	7
Detroit, MI	+33	2

Source: "Heroin Use on the Increase," *Detroit Free Press,* 18 June 1996, p. 3A. Primary source: Partnership for a Drug Free America.

★658★

Vital Statistics

Deaths Caused By Heroin Use, 1994, Selected Cities: Total Deaths

City	Number	Rank
New York, NY	531	1
Los Angeles, CA	472	2
Philadelphia, PA	402	3
Baltimore, MD	339	4
Chicago, IL	294	5
New Orleans, LA	257	6
Newark, NJ	199	7
San Francisco, CA	167	8
Detroit, MI	109	9

Source: "Heroin Use on the Increase," *Detroit Free Press,* 18 June 1996, p. 3A. Primary source: Partnership for a Drug Free America.

★659★

Vital Statistics

Deaths Caused By Methamphetamine Use, 1994: Increased Percent Change From 1991

According to the source, "Results from a new government survey... show that the nation's medical examiners reported a 144% increase in methamphetamine-related deaths from 1992 to 1994."

City	Percent	Rank
Phoenix, AZ	1,009	1
San Diego, CA	187	2
Los Angeles, CA	121	3
San Francisco, CA	68	4

Source: Davis, Robert, "'Meth' Use in the '90s" A Growing 'Epidemic,'" *USA TODAY,* 7 September 1995, p. 7A. Primary source: Drug Abuse Warning Network.

★660★

Vital Statistics

Deaths Caused By Methamphetamine Use, 1994: Selected Cities

According to the source, "Results from a new government survey... show that the nation's medical examiners reported a 144% increase in methamphetamine-related deaths from 1992 to 1994."

City	Number	Rank
Los Angeles, CA	219	1
San Diego, CA	172	2
Phoenix, AZ	122	3
San Francisco, CA	69	4

Source: Davis, Robert, "'Meth' Use in the '90s" A Growing 'Epidemic,'" *USA TODAY,* 7 September 1995, p. 7A. Primary source: Drug Abuse Warning Network.

★661★

Vital Statistics

Immunizations of Children, 1995-96: Highest Rates

Data refer to immunizations of children 19-35 months of age against the following diseases: diphtheria, pertussis, tetanus, polio, measles, mumps, and rubella.

[In percentages]

City/MSA	Percentage	Rank
Boston, MA	87	1
Santa Clara, CA	85	2
Cuyahoga County, OH (Cleveland)	84	3
El Paso, TX	82	4
Marion County, IN	81	5

Source: Stevens, Carol, "Vaccination Rate Embarrasses State: Michigan Ranks Worst in Nation for Getting Kids Immunized," *The Detroit News and Free Press,* 19 May 1996, p. 1A. Primary source: Centers for Disease Control and Prevention, February 1996; Michigan Department of Community Health.

★662★
Vital Statistics
Immunizations of Children, 1995-96: Lowest Rates

Data refer to immunizations of children 19-35 months of age against the following diseases: diphtheria, pertussis, tetanus, polio, measles, mumps, and rubella.

[In percentages]

City/MSA	Percentage	Rank
Detroit, MI	52	1
Chicago, IL	61	2
Houston, TX	62	3
Newark, NJ	62	3
Bexar County, TX (San Antonio, TX)	67	4

Source: Stevens, Carol, "Vaccination Rate Embarrasses State: Michigan Ranks Worst in Nation for Getting Kids Immunized," *The Detroit News and Free Press,* 19 May 1996, p. 1A. Primary source: Centers for Disease Control and Prevention, February 1996; Michigan Department of Community Health.

★663★
Costs for Illegal Drugs
Cocaine Prices, 1994: Highest Prices (Selected Cities)

[In dollars per gram]

City	Price	Rank
Honolulu, HI	125	1
New Orleans, LA	125	1
Washington, DC	120	2

Source: National Institutes of Health, Division of Epidemiology and Prevention Research, National Institute on Drug Abuse, *Epidemiologic Trends in Drug Abuse,* Community Epidemiology Work Group (CEWG), Rockville, Maryland: National Institutes of Health, December 1994, n.p.

★664★
Costs for Illegal Drugs
Cocaine Prices, 1994: Lowest Prices (Selected Cities)

[In dollars per gram]

City	Price	Rank
Seattle, WA	30	1
Chicago, IL	35	2
Saint Louis, MO	36	3

Source: National Institutes of Health, Division of Epidemiology and Prevention Research, National Institute on Drug Abuse, *Epidemiologic Trends in Drug Abuse,* Community Epidemiology Work Group (CEWG), Rockville, Maryland: National Institutes of Health, December 1994, n.p.

★665★
Medical Insurance
Persons Covered By Health Maintenance Organizations, 1994: Largest Markets

[In percentage of population]

City	Percent	Rank
Boston, MA	35	4
Los Angeles, CA	35	4
Minneapolis-Saint Paul, MN	39	3
Portland, OR	64	1
Rochester, NY	63	2
Sacramento, CA	35	4
San Diego, CA	35	4
San Francisco-Oakland, CA	39	3

Source: "Health Care Fact: Largest Managed Care Markets," *AHA News,* 16 October 1995, p. 2. Primary source: InterStudy Competitive Edge, 1995.

Chapter 8

HOUSING AND MOBILITY

Topics Covered

Demolitions
Federal Assistance
Geographic Mobility
Home Ownership
Housing
Housing Costs
Housing Construction
Occupancy
Vacancies

★666★

Demolitions

Housing Projects Slated for Demolition, 1996: Costs

Data refer to units slated for demolition under a HUD (Department of Housing and Urban Development) program, HOPE VI, through which 32 housing authorities have received $1.5 billion.

City/MSA	Cost	Rank
Baltimore, MD	7,200,000	1
Charlotte, NC	895,593	4
Denver, CO	315,000	8
El Paso, TX	316,000	7
Milwaukee, WI	874,055	5
New Orleans, LA	2,772,000	2
San Antonio, TX	1,000,000	3
Washington, DC	580,000	6

Source: "High-Rises Fall to HUD's New Plans," *ENR,* (The McGraw-Hill Construction Weekly), 11 September 1995, p. 8. Primary source: U.S. Department of Housing and Urban Development (HUD).

★667★

Demolitions

Housing Projects Slated for Demolition, 1996: Costs of Replacement Housing

Data refer to units slated for demolition under a HUD (Department of Housing and Urban Development) program, HOPE VI, through which 32 housing authorities have received $1.5 billion.

City/MSA	Cost	Rank
Baltimore, MD	25,350,000	3
Charlotte, NC	23,851,272	4
El Paso, TX	9,672,000	7
Milwaukee, WI	10,528,668	6
New Orleans, LA	36,300,000	1
San Antonio, TX	32,841,498	2
Washington, DC	17,277,000	5

Source: "High-Rises Fall to HUD's New Plans," *ENR,* (The McGraw-Hill Construction Weekly), 11 September 1995, p. 8. Primary source: U.S. Department of Housing and Urban Development (HUD).

★668★

Demolitions

Housing Projects Slated for Demolition, 1996: Number of Units

Data refer to units slated for demolition under a HUD (Department of Housing and Urban Development) program, HOPE VI, through which 32 housing authorities have received $1.5 billion.

City/MSA	Number	Rank
Baltimore, MD	771	1
Charlotte, NC	300	4
Denver, CO	100	8
El Paso, TX	124	6
Milwaukee, WI	119	7
New Orleans, LA	660	2
San Antonio, TX	421	3
Washington, DC	134	5

Source: "High-Rises Fall to HUD's New Plans," *ENR,* (The McGraw-Hill Construction Weekly), 11 September 1995, p. 8. Primary source: U.S. Department of Housing and Urban Development (HUD).

★669★

Federal Assistance

HUD Block Grant Funding Per Capita, 1995: Cities With the Highest Amounts

[In annual dollars per person]

City/MSA	Amount per capita	Rank
Saint Louis, MO	78.03	1
Buffalo, NY	71.07	2
Cleveland, OH	66.87	3
Detroit, MI	55.91	4
Rochester, NY	53.17	5

Source: Loeb, Penny, "Fast Pucks: Waste, Fraud and Abuse," *U.S. News & World Report,* 27 March 1995, p. 26. Primary source: *U.S. News & World Report* basic data; U.S. Census Bureau; U.S. Department of Housing and Urban Development. *Note:* "HUD" stands for "U.S. Department of Housing and Urban Development."

★670★

Federal Assistance

HUD Block Grant Funding Per Capita, 1995: Cities With the Lowest Amounts

[In annual dollars per person]

City/MSA	Amount per capita	Rank
Baton Rouge, LA	17.06	1
Jackson, MS	19.97	4
Macon, GA	19.93	3
Memphis, TN	19.76	2
Shreveport, LA	21.12	5

Source: Loeb, Penny, "Fast Pucks: Waste, Fraud and Abuse," *U.S. News & World Report,* 27 March 1995, p. 26. Primary source: *U.S. News & World Report* basic data; U.S. Census Bureau; U.S. Department of Housing and Urban Development. *Note:* "HUD" stands for "U.S. Department of Housing and Urban Development."

★671★

Geographic Mobility

Inmigration, 1993-94, By Age: 1 to 4 Years

[In thousands]

MSA	1 to 4 years	Rank
Boston-Lawrence-Salem, MA-NH CMSA	4	5
Chicago-Gary-Lake County, IL-IN-WI CMSA	5	4
Dallas-Fort Worth, TX CMSA	15	2
Detroit-Ann Arbor, MI CMSA	2	6
Houston-Galveston-Brazoria, TX CMSA	2	6
Los Angeles-Anaheim-Riverside, CA CMSA	5	4
New York-Northern New Jersey-Long Island, NY-NJ-CT CMSA	19	1
Philadelphia-Wilmington-Trenton, PA-NJ-DE-MD CMSA	5	4

[Continued]

★671★

Inmigration, 1993-94, By Age: 1 to 4 Years
[Continued]

MSA	1 to 4 years	Rank
San Francisco-Oakland-San Jose, CA CMSA	10	3
Washington, DC-MD-VA MSA	10	3

Source: Hansen, Kristin A., *Geographical Mobility: March 1993 to March 1994*, U.S. Bureau of the Census, Current Population Reports, P20-485, Washington, D.C.: U.S. Government Printing Office, 1995, p. 164. *Notes:* "CMSA" stands for "Consolidated Metropolitan Statistical Area." "MSA" stands for "Metropolitan Statistical Area."

★672★
Geographic Mobility

Inmigration, 1993-94, By Age: 5 to 9 Years
[In thousands]

MSA	5 to 9 years	Rank
Boston-Lawrence-Salem, MA-NH CMSA	3	7
Chicago-Gary-Lake County, IL-IN-WI CMSA	12	3
Dallas-Fort Worth, TX CMSA	20	1
Detroit-Ann Arbor, MI CMSA	3	7
Houston-Galveston-Brazoria, TX CMSA	11	4
Los Angeles-Anaheim-Riverside, CA CMSA	13	2
New York-Northern New Jersey-Long Island, NY-NJ-CT CMSA	7	5
Philadelphia-Wilmington-Trenton, PA-NJ-DE-MD CMSA	5	6
Washington, DC-MD-VA MSA	12	3

Source: Hansen, Kristin A., *Geographical Mobility: March 1993 to March 1994*, U.S. Bureau of the Census, Current Population Reports, P20-485, Washington, D.C.: U.S. Government Printing Office, 1995, p. 164. *Notes:* "CMSA" stands for "Consolidated Metropolitan Statistical Area." "MSA" stands for "Metropolitan Statistical Area."

★673★
Geographic Mobility

Inmigration, 1993-94, By Age: 10 to 14 Years
[In thousands]

MSA	10 to 14 years	Rank
Boston-Lawrence-Salem, MA-NH CMSA	3	8
Chicago-Gary-Lake County, IL-IN-WI CMSA	8	3
Dallas-Fort Worth, TX CMSA	20	1
Detroit-Ann Arbor, MI CMSA	3	8
Houston-Galveston-Brazoria, TX CMSA	3	8
Los Angeles-Anaheim-Riverside, CA CMSA	7	4

[Continued]

★673★

Inmigration, 1993-94, By Age: 10 to 14 Years
[Continued]

MSA	10 to 14 years	Rank
New York-Northern New Jersey-Long Island, NY-NJ-CT CMSA	6	5
Philadelphia-Wilmington-Trenton, PA-NJ-DE-MD CMSA	5	6
San Francisco-Oakland-San Jose, CA CMSA	4	7
Washington, DC-MD-VA CMSA	10	2

Source: Hansen, Kristin A., *Geographical Mobility: March 1993 to March 1994*, U.S. Bureau of the Census, Current Population Reports, P20-485, Washington, D.C.: U.S. Government Printing Office, 1995, p. 164. *Notes:* "CMSA" stands for "Consolidated Metropolitan Statistical Area." "MSA" stands for "Metropolitan Statistical Area."

★674★
Geographic Mobility

Inmigration, 1993-94, By Age: 15 to 19 Years
[In thousands]

MSA	15 to 19 years	Rank
Boston-Lawrence-Salem, MA-NH CMSA	8	5
Chicago-Gary-Lake County, IL-IN-WI CMSA	14	2
Dallas-Fort Worth, TX CMSA	6	7
Detroit-Ann Arbor, MI CMSA	7	6
Houston-Galveston-Brazoria, TX CMSA	12	3
Los Angeles-Anaheim-Riverside, CA CMSA	19	1
New York-Northern New Jersey-Long Island, NY-NJ-CT CMSA	19	1
Philadelphia-Wilmington-Trenton, PA-NJ-DE-MD CMSA	9	4
San Francisco-Oakland-San Jose, CA CMSA	4	8
Washington, DC-MD-VA MSA	3	9

Source: Hansen, Kristin A., *Geographical Mobility: March 1993 to March 1994*, U.S. Bureau of the Census, Current Population Reports, P20-485, Washington, D.C.: U.S. Government Printing Office, 1995, p. 164. *Notes:* "CMSA" stands for "Consolidated Metropolitan Statistical Area." "MSA" stands for "Metropolitan Statistical Area."

★675★

Geographic Mobility

Inmigration, 1993-94, By Age: 20 to 24 Years

[In thousands]

MSA	20 to 24 years	Rank
Boston-Lawrence-Salem, MA-NH CMSA	17	7
Chicago-Gary-Lake County, IL-IN-WI CMSA	33	3
Dallas-Fort Worth, TX CMSA	27	4
Detroit-Ann Arbor, MI CMSA	10	8
Houston-Galveston-Brazoria, TX CMSA	23	6
Los Angeles-Anaheim-Riverside, CA CMSA	43	2
New York-Northern New Jersey-Long Island, NY-NJ-CT CMSA	24	5
Philadelphia-Wilmington-Trenton, PA-NJ-DE-MD CMSA	23	6
San Francisco-Oakland-San Jose, CA CMSA	27	4
Washington, DC-MD-VA MSA	44	1

Source: Hansen, Kristin A., *Geographical Mobility: March 1993 to March 1994*, U.S. Bureau of the Census, Current Population Reports, P20-485, Washington, D.C.: U.S. Government Printing Office, 1995, p. 164. *Notes:* "CMSA" stands for "Consolidated Metropolitan Statistical Area." "MSA stands for "Metropolitan Statistical Area."

★676★

Geographic Mobility

Inmigration, 1993-94, By Age: 25 to 29 Years

[In thousands]

MSA	25 to 29 years	Rank
Boston-Lawrence-Salem, MA-NH CMSA	11	7
Chicago-Gary-Lake County, IL-IN-WI CMSA	28	3
Dallas-Fort Worth, TX CMSA	18	6
Detroit-Ann Arbor, MI CMSA	9	8
Houston-Galveston-Brazoria, TX CMSA	28	3
Los Angeles-Anaheim-Riverside, CA CMSA	20	5
New York-Northern New Jersey-Long Island, NY-NJ-CT CMSA	41	1
Philadelphia-Wilmington-Trenton, PA-NJ-DE-MD CMSA	5	9
San Francisco-Oakland-San Jose, CA CMSA	38	2
Washington, DC-MD-VA MSA	27	4

Source: Hansen, Kristin A., *Geographical Mobility: March 1993 to March 1994*, U.S. Bureau of the Census, Current Population Reports, P20-485, Washington, D.C.: U.S. Government Printing Office, 1995, p. 164. *Notes:* "CMSA" stands for "Consolidated Metropolitan Statistical Area." "MSA" stands for "Metropolitan Statistical Area."

★677★

Geographic Mobility

Inmigration, 1993-94, By Age: 30 to 44 Years

[In thousands]

MSA	30 to 44 years	Rank
Boston-Lawrence-Salem, MA-NH CMSA	21	9
Chicago-Gary-Lake County, IL-IN-WI CMSA	36	5
Dallas-Fort Worth, TX CMSA	54	2
Detroit-Ann Arbor, MI CMSA	23	8
Houston-Galveston-Brazoria, TX CMSA	24	7
Los Angeles-Anaheim-Riverside, CA CMSA	44	3
New York-Northern New Jersey-Long Island, NY-NJ-CT CMSA	61	1
Philadelphia-Wilmington-Trenton, PA-NJ-DE-MD CMSA	15	10
San Francisco-Oakland-San Jose, CA CMSA	42	4
Washington, DC-MD-VA CMSA	34	6

Source: Hansen, Kristin A., *Geographical Mobility: March 1993 to March 1994*, U.S. Bureau of the Census, Current Population Reports, P20-485, Washington, D.C.: U.S. Government Printing Office, 1995, p. 164. *Notes:* "CMSA" stands for "Consolidated Metropolitan Statistical Area." "MSA" stands for "Metropolitan Statistical Area."

★678★

Geographic Mobility

Inmigration, 1993-94, By Age: 45 to 64 Years

[In thousands]

MSA	45 to 64 years	Rank
Boston-Lawrence-Salem, MA-NH CMSA	9	6
Chicago-Gary-Lake County, IL-IN-WI CMSA	18	2
Dallas-Fort Worth, TX CMSA	17	3
Detroit-Ann Arbor, MI CMSA	3	8
Houston-Galveston-Brazoria, TX CMSA	34	1
Los Angeles-Anaheim-Riverside, CA CMSA	18	2
New York-Northern New Jersey-Long Island, NY-NJ-CT CMSA	11	4
Philadelphia-Wilmington-Trenton, PA-NJ-DE-MD CMSA	11	4
San Francisco-Oakland-San Jose, CA CMSA	10	5
Washington, DC-MD-VA MSA	6	7

Source: Hansen, Kristin A., *Geographical Mobility: March 1993 to March 1994*, U.S. Bureau of the Census, Current Population Reports, P20-485, Washington, D.C.: U.S. Government Printing Office, 1995, p. 164. *Notes:* "CMSA" stands for "Consolidated Metropolitan Statistical Area." "MSA" stands for "Metropolitan Statistical Area."

★679★
Geographic Mobility

Inmigration, 1993-94, By Age: 65 Years and Older

[In thousands]

MSA	65 years and over	Rank
Boston-Lawrence-Salem, MA-NH CMSA	5	4
Dallas-Fort Worth, TX CMSA	5	4
Detroit-Ann Arbor, MI CMSA	6	3
Houston-Galveston-Brazoria, TX CMSA	3	5
Los Angeles-Anaheim-Riverside, CA CMSA	9	2
New York-Northern New Jersey-Long Island, NY-NJ-CT CMSA	9	2
Philadelphia-Wilmington-Trenton, PA-NJ-DE-MD CMSA	1	6
San Francisco-Oakland-San Jose, CA CMSA	11	1

Source: Hansen, Kristin A., *Geographical Mobility: March 1993 to March 1994*, U.S. Bureau of the Census, Current Population Reports, P20-485, Washington, D.C.: U.S. Government Printing Office, 1995, p. 164. *Notes:* "CMSA" stands for "Consolidated Metropolitan Statistical Area." "MSA" stands for "Metropolitan Statistical Area."

★680★
Geographic Mobility

Inmigration, 1993-94, By Ethnicity: Hispanic

[In thousands]

MSA	Hispanic	Rank
Boston-Lawrence-Salem, MA-NH CMSA	10	6
Chicago-Gary-Lake County, IL-IN-WI CMSA	12	5
Dallas-Fort Worth, TX CMSA	25	3
Detroit-Ann Arbor, MI CMSA	2	9
Houston-Galveston-Brazoria, TX CMSA	7	8
Los Angeles-Anaheim-Riverside, CA CMSA	29	2
New York-Northern New Jersey-Long Island, NY-NJ-CT CMSA	41	1
Philadelphia-Wilmington-Trenton, PA-NJ-DE-MD CMSA	8	7
San Francisco-Oakland-San Jose, CA CMSA	22	4

Source: Hansen, Kristin A., *Geographical Mobility: March 1993 to March 1994*, U.S. Bureau of the Census, Current Population Reports, P20-485, Washington, D.C.: U.S. Government Printing Office, 1995, p. 164. *Notes:* Persons of Hispanic origin may be of any race. "CMSA" stands for "Consolidated Metropolitan Statistical Area." "MSA" stands for "Metropolitan Statistical Area."

★681★
Geographic Mobility

Inmigration, 1993-94, By Race: Black

[In thousands]

MSA	Black	Rank
Boston-Lawrence-Salem, MA-NH CMSA	13	7
Chicago-Gary-Lake County, IL-IN-WI CMSA	59	1
Dallas-Fort Worth, TX CMSA	15	6
Detroit-Ann Arbor, MI CMSA	2	9
Houston-Galveston-Brazoria, TX CMSA	34	3
Los Angeles-Anaheim-Riverside, CA CMSA	35	2
New York-Northern New Jersey-Long Island, NY-NJ-CT CMSA	20	4
Philadelphia-Wilmington-Trenton, PA-NJ-DE-MD CMSA	19	5
San Francisco-Oakland-San Jose, CA CMSA	3	8

Source: Hansen, Kristin A., *Geographical Mobility: March 1993 to March 1994*, U.S. Bureau of the Census, Current Population Reports, P20-485, Washington, D.C.: U.S. Government Printing Office, 1995, p. 164. *Notes:* "CMSA" stands for "Consolidated Metropolitan Statistical Area." "MSA" stands for "Metropolitan Statistical Area."

★682★
Geographic Mobility

Inmigration, 1993-94, By Race: White

[In thousands]

MSA	White	Rank
Boston-Lawrence-Salem, MA-NH CMSA	69	8
Chicago-Gary-Lake County, IL-IN-WI CMSA	82	7
Dallas-Fort Worth, TX CMSA	152	2
Detroit-Ann Arbor, MI CMSA	61	9
Houston-Galveston-Brazoria, TX CMSA	103	6
Los Angeles-Anaheim-Riverside, CA CMSA	115	5
New York-Northern New Jersey-Long Island, NY-NJ-CT CMSA	166	1
Philadelphia-Wilmington-Trenton, PA-NJ-DE-MD CMSA	59	10
San Francisco-Oakland-San Jose, CA CMSA	136	4
Washington, DC-MD-VA MSA	139	3

Source: Hansen, Kristin A., *Geographical Mobility: March 1993 to March 1994*, U.S. Bureau of the Census, Current Population Reports, P20-485, Washington, D.C.: U.S. Government Printing Office, 1995, p. 164. *Notes:* "CMSA" stands for "Consolidated Metropolitan Statistical Area." "MSA" stands for "Metropolitan Statistical Area."

★683★
Geographic Mobility
Inmigration, 1993-94, By Sex: Females
[In thousands]

MSA	Female	Rank
Boston-Lawrence-Salem, MA-NH CMSA	28	9
Chicago-Gary-Lake County, IL-IN-WI CMSA	73	4
Dallas-Fort Worth, TX CMSA	60	7
Detroit-Ann Arbor, MI CMSA	25	10
Houston-Galveston-Brazoria, TX CMSA	67	6
Los Angeles-Anaheim-Riverside, CA CMSA	80	3
New York-Northern New Jersey-Long Island, NY-NJ-CT CMSA	107	1
Philadelphia-Wilmington-Trenton, PA-NJ-DE-MD CMSA	48	8
San Francisco-Oakland-San Jose, CA CMSA	82	2
Washington, DC-MD-VA MSA	71	5

Source: Hansen, Kristin A., Geographical Mobility: March 1993 to March 1994, U.S. Bureau of the Census, Current Population Reports, P20-485, Washington, D.C.: U.S. Government Printing Office, 1995, p. 164. Notes: "CMSA" stands for "Consolidated Metropolitan Statistical Area." "MSA" stands for "Metropolitan Statistical Area."

★684★
Geographic Mobility
Inmigration, 1993-94, By Sex: Males
[In thousands]

MSA	Male	Rank
Boston-Lawrence-Salem, MA-NH CMSA	54	8
Chicago-Gary-Lake County, IL-IN-WI CMSA	82	4
Dallas-Fort Worth, TX CMSA	123	1
Detroit-Ann Arbor, MI CMSA	40	9
Houston-Galveston-Brazoria, TX CMSA	72	6
Los Angeles-Anaheim-Riverside, CA CMSA	98	2
New York-Northern New Jersey-Long Island, NY-NJ-CT CMSA	89	3
Philadelphia-Wilmington-Trenton, PA-NJ-DE-MD CMSA	31	10
San Francisco-Oakland-San Jose, CA CMSA	64	7
Washington, DC-MD-VA MSA	76	5

Source: Hansen, Kristin A., Geographical Mobility: March 1993 to March 1994, U.S. Bureau of the Census, Current Population Reports, P20-485, Washington, D.C.: U.S. Government Printing Office, 1995, p. 164. Notes: "CMSA" stands for "Consolidated Metropolitan Statistical Area." "MSA" stands for "Metropolitan Statistical Area."

★685★
Geographic Mobility
Outmigration, 1993-94, By Age: 1 to 4 Years
[In thousands]

MSA	1 to 4 years	Rank
Boston-Lawrence-Salem, MA-NH CMSA	9	7
Chicago-Gary-Lake County, IL-IN-WI CMSA	15	3
Dallas-Fort Worth, TX CMSA	10	6
Detroit-Ann Arbor, MI CMSA	16	2
Houston-Galveston-Brazoria, TX CMSA	15	3
Los Angeles-Anaheim-Riverside, CA CMSA	30	1
New York-Northern New Jersey-Long Island, NY-NJ-CT CMSA	13	4
Philadelphia-Wilmington-Trenton, PA-NJ-DE-MD CMSA	12	5
San Francisco-Oakland-San Jose, CA CMSA	8	8

Source: Hansen, Kristin A., Geographical Mobility: March 1993 to March 1994, U.S. Bureau of the Census, Current Population Reports, P20-485, Washington, D.C.: U.S. Government Printing Office, 1995, p. 164. Notes: "CMSA" stands for "Consolidated Metropolitan Statistical Area." "MSA" stands for "Metropolitan Statistical Area."

★686★
Geographic Mobility
Outmigration, 1993-94, By Age: 5 to 9 Years
[In thousands]

MSA	5 to 9 years	Rank
Boston-Lawrence-Salem, MA-NH CMSA	13	6
Chicago-Gary-Lake County, IL-IN-WI CMSA	21	3
Dallas-Fort Worth, TX CMSA	24	2
Detroit-Ann Arbor, MI CMSA	21	3
Houston-Galveston-Brazoria, TX CMSA	16	5
Los Angeles-Anaheim-Riverside, CA CMSA	42	1
New York-Northern New Jersey-Long Island, NY-NJ-CT CMSA	18	4
Philadelphia-Wilmington-Trenton, PA-NJ-DE-MD CMSA	8	7
San Francisco-Oakland-San Jose, CA CMSA	6	8
Washington, DC-MD-VA MSA	4	9

Source: Hansen, Kristin A., Geographical Mobility: March 1993 to March 1994, U.S. Bureau of the Census, Current Population Reports, P20-485, Washington, D.C.: U.S. Government Printing Office, 1995, p. 164. Notes: "CMSA" stands for "Consolidated Metropolitan Statistical Area." "MSA" stands for "Metropolitan Statistical Area."

★687★
Geographic Mobility
Outmigration, 1993-94, By Age: 10 to 14 Years
[In thousands]

MSA	10 to 14 years	Rank
Boston-Lawrence-Salem, MA-NH CMSA	16	3
Chicago-Gary-Lake County, IL-IN-WI CMSA	16	3
Dallas-Fort Worth, TX CMSA	26	2
Detroit-Ann Arbor, MI CMSA	6	8
Houston-Galveston-Brazoria, TX CMSA	7	7
Los Angeles-Anaheim-Riverside, CA CMSA	33	1
New York-Northern New Jersey-Long Island, NY-NJ-CT CMSA	12	5
Philadelphia-Wilmington-Trenton, PA-NJ-DE-MD CMSA	9	6
San Francisco-Oakland-San Jose, CA CMSA	13	4
Washington, DC-MD-VA MSA	12	5

Source: Hansen, Kristin A., *Geographical Mobility: March 1993 to March 1994*, U.S. Bureau of the Census, Current Population Reports, P20-485, Washington, D.C.: U.S. Government Printing Office, 1995, p. 164. *Notes:* "CMSA" stands for "Consolidated Metropolitan Statistical Area." "MSA" stands for "Metropolitan Statistical Area."

★688★
Geographic Mobility
Outmigration, 1993-94, By Age: 15 to 19 Years
[In thousands]

MSA	15 to 19 years	Rank
Boston-Lawrence-Salem, MA-NH CMSA	6	8
Chicago-Gary-Lake County, IL-IN-WI CMSA	18	3
Dallas-Fort Worth, TX CMSA	9	7
Detroit-Ann Arbor, MI CMSA	6	8
Houston-Galveston-Brazoria, TX CMSA	9	7
Los Angeles-Anaheim-Riverside, CA CMSA	43	1
New York-Northern New Jersey-Long Island, NY-NJ-CT CMSA	26	2
Philadelphia-Wilmington-Trenton, PA-NJ-DE-MD CMSA	11	6
San Francisco-Oakland-San Jose, CA CMSA	12	5
Washington, DC-MD-VA MSA	16	4

Source: Hansen, Kristin A., *Geographical Mobility: March 1993 to March 1994*, U.S. Bureau of the Census, Current Population Reports, P20-485, Washington, D.C.: U.S. Government Printing Office, 1995, p. 164. *Notes:* "CMSA" stands for "Consolidated Metropolitan Statistical Area." "MSA" stands for "Metropolitan Statistical Area."

★689★
Geographic Mobility
Outmigration, 1993-94, By Age: 20 to 24 Years
[In thousands]

MSA	20 to 24 years	Rank
Boston-Lawrence-Salem, MA-NH CMSA	7	9
Chicago-Gary-Lake County, IL-IN-WI CMSA	31	3
Dallas-Fort Worth, TX CMSA	14	5
Detroit-Ann Arbor, MI CMSA	9	8
Houston-Galveston-Brazoria, TX CMSA	11	7
Los Angeles-Anaheim-Riverside, CA CMSA	56	1
New York-Northern New Jersey-Long Island, NY-NJ-CT CMSA	37	2
Philadelphia-Wilmington-Trenton, PA-NJ-DE-MD CMSA	12	6
San Francisco-Oakland-San Jose, CA CMSA	23	4
Washington, DC-MD-VA MSA	3	10

Source: Hansen, Kristin A., *Geographical Mobility: March 1993 to March 1994*, U.S. Bureau of the Census, Current Population Reports, P20-485, Washington, D.C.: U.S. Government Printing Office, 1995, p. 164. *Notes:* "CMSA" stands for "Consolidated Metropolitan Statistical Area." "MSA" stands for "Metropolitan Statistical Area."

★690★
Geographic Mobility
Outmigration, 1993-94, By Age: 25 to 29 Years
[In thousands]

MSA	25 to 29 years	Rank
Boston-Lawrence-Salem, MA-NH CMSA	10	8
Chicago-Gary-Lake County, IL-IN-WI CMSA	23	3
Dallas-Fort Worth, TX CMSA	23	3
Detroit-Ann Arbor, MI CMSA	14	7
Houston-Galveston-Brazoria, TX CMSA	16	6
Los Angeles-Anaheim-Riverside, CA CMSA	55	1
New York-Northern New Jersey-Long Island, NY-NJ-CT CMSA	41	2
Philadelphia-Wilmington-Trenton, PA-NJ-DE-MD CMSA	21	4
San Francisco-Oakland-San Jose, CA CMSA	19	5
Washington, DC-MD-VA MSA	7	9

Source: Hansen, Kristin A., *Geographical Mobility: March 1993 to March 1994*, U.S. Bureau of the Census, Current Population Reports, P20-485, Washington, D.C.: U.S. Government Printing Office, 1995, p. 164. *Notes:* "CMSA" stands for "Consolidated Metropolitan Statistical Area." "MSA" stands for "Metropolitan Statistical Area."

★691★
Geographic Mobility

Outmigration, 1993-94, By Age: 30 to 44 Years

[In thousands]

MSA	30 to 44 years	Rank
Boston-Lawrence-Salem, MA-NH CMSA	45	6
Chicago-Gary-Lake County, IL-IN-WI CMSA	57	4
Dallas-Fort Worth, TX CMSA	97	2
Detroit-Ann Arbor, MI CMSA	27	9
Houston-Galveston-Brazoria, TX CMSA	21	10
Los Angeles-Anaheim-Riverside, CA CMSA	135	1
New York-Northern New Jersey-Long Island, NY-NJ-CT CMSA	92	3
Philadelphia-Wilmington-Trenton, PA-NJ-DE-MD CMSA	39	7
San Francisco-Oakland-San Jose, CA CMSA	46	5
Washington, DC-MD-VA CMSA	36	8

Source: Hansen, Kristin A., *Geographical Mobility: March 1993 to March 1994*, U.S. Bureau of the Census, Current Population Reports, P20-485, Washington, D.C.: U.S. Government Printing Office, 1995, p. 164. *Notes:* "CMSA" stands for "Consolidated Metropolitan Statistical Area." "MSA" stands for "Metropolitan Statistical Area."

★692★
Geographic Mobility

Outmigration, 1993-94, By Age: 45 to 64 Years

[In thousands]

MSA	45 to 64 years	Rank
Boston-Lawrence-Salem, MA-NH CMSA	18	5
Chicago-Gary-Lake County, IL-IN-WI CMSA	33	3
Dallas-Fort Worth, TX CMSA	17	6
Detroit-Ann Arbor, MI CMSA	8	9
Houston-Galveston-Brazoria, TX CMSA	10	8
Los Angeles-Anaheim-Riverside, CA CMSA	87	1
New York-Northern New Jersey-Long Island, NY-NJ-CT CMSA	72	2
Philadelphia-Wilmington-Trenton, PA-NJ-DE-MD CMSA	11	7
San Francisco-Oakland-San Jose, CA CMSA	11	7
Washington, DC-MD-VA MSA	27	4

Source: Hansen, Kristin A., *Geographical Mobility: March 1993 to March 1994*, U.S. Bureau of the Census, Current Population Reports, P20-485, Washington, D.C.: U.S. Government Printing Office, 1995, p. 164. *Notes:* "CMSA" stands for "Consolidated Metropolitan Statistical Area." "MSA" stands for "Metropolitan Statistical Area."

★693★
Geographic Mobility

Outmigration, 1993-94, By Age: 65 Years and Older

[In thousands]

MSA	65 years and over	Rank
Boston-Lawrence-Salem, MA-NH CMSA	7	6
Chicago-Gary-Lake County, IL-IN-WI CMSA	7	6
Dallas-Fort Worth, TX CMSA	12	4
Detroit-Ann Arbor, MI CMSA	5	8
Houston-Galveston-Brazoria, TX CMSA	6	7
Los Angeles-Anaheim-Riverside, CA CMSA	47	1
New York-Northern New Jersey-Long Island, NY-NJ-CT CMSA	30	2
Philadelphia-Wilmington-Trenton, PA-NJ-DE-MD CMSA	17	3
San Francisco-Oakland-San Jose, CA CMSA	11	5
Washington, DC-MD-VA MSA	1	9

Source: Hansen, Kristin A., *Geographical Mobility: March 1993 to March 1994*, U.S. Bureau of the Census, Current Population Reports, P20-485, Washington, D.C.: U.S. Government Printing Office, 1995, p. 164. *Notes:* "CMSA" stands for "Consolidated Metropolitan Statistical Area." "MSA" stands for "Metropolitan Statistical Area."

★694★
Geographic Mobility

Outmigration, 1993-94, By Ethnicity: Hispanic

[In thousands]

MSA	Hispanic	Rank
Boston-Lawrence-Salem, MA-NH CMSA	1	8
Chicago-Gary-Lake County, IL-IN-WI CMSA	8	5
Dallas-Fort Worth, TX CMSA	11	4
Detroit-Ann Arbor, MI CMSA	1	8
Houston-Galveston-Brazoria, TX CMSA	25	3
Los Angeles-Anaheim-Riverside, CA CMSA	115	1
New York-Northern New Jersey-Long Island, NY-NJ-CT CMSA	38	2
Philadelphia-Wilmington-Trenton, PA-NJ-DE-MD CMSA	2	7
San Francisco-Oakland-San Jose, CA CMSA	6	6
Washington, DC-MD-VA MSA	2	7

Source: Hansen, Kristin A., *Geographical Mobility: March 1993 to March 1994*, U.S. Bureau of the Census, Current Population Reports, P20-485, Washington, D.C.: U.S. Government Printing Office, 1995, p. 164. *Notes:* Persons of Hispanic origin may be of any race. "CMSA" stands for "Consolidated Metropolitan Statistical Area." "MSA" stands for "Metropolitan Statistical Area."

★695★
Geographic Mobility
Outmigration, 1993-94, By Race: Black
[In thousands]

MSA	Black	Rank
Boston-Lawrence-Salem, MA-NH CMSA	1	8
Chicago-Gary-Lake County, IL-IN-WI CMSA	70	1
Dallas-Fort Worth, TX CMSA	30	4
Detroit-Ann Arbor, MI CMSA	44	3
Houston-Galveston-Brazoria, TX CMSA	19	7
Los Angeles-Anaheim-Riverside, CA CMSA	24	6
New York-Northern New Jersey-Long Island, NY-NJ-CT CMSA	30	4
Philadelphia-Wilmington-Trenton, PA-NJ-DE-MD CMSA	24	6
San Francisco-Oakland-San Jose, CA CMSA	29	5
Washington, DC-MD-VA MSA	54	2

Source: Hansen, Kristin A., Geographical Mobility: March 1993 to March 1994, U.S. Bureau of the Census, Current Population Reports, P20-485, Washington, D.C.: U.S. Government Printing Office, 1995, p. 164.

★696★
Geographic Mobility
Outmigration, 1993-94, By Race: White
[In thousands]

MSA	White	Rank
Boston-Lawrence-Salem, MA-NH CMSA	131	4
Chicago-Gary-Lake County, IL-IN-WI CMSA	100	6
Dallas-Fort Worth, TX CMSA	194	3
Detroit-Ann Arbor, MI CMSA	69	9
Houston-Galveston-Brazoria, TX CMSA	83	8
Los Angeles-Anaheim-Riverside, CA CMSA	461	1
New York-Northern New Jersey-Long Island, NY-NJ-CT CMSA	259	2
Philadelphia-Wilmington-Trenton, PA-NJ-DE-MD CMSA	116	5
San Francisco-Oakland-San Jose, CA CMSA	88	7
Washington, DC-MD-VA MSA	52	10

Source: Hansen, Kristin A., Geographical Mobility: March 1993 to March 1994, U.S. Bureau of the Census, Current Population Reports, P20-485, Washington, D.C.: U.S. Government Printing Office, 1995, p. 164. Notes: "CMSA" stands for "Consolidated Metropolitan Statistical Area." "MSA" stands for "Metropolitan Statistical Area."

★697★
Geographic Mobility
Outmigration, 1993-94, By Sex: Females
[In thousands]

MSA	Female	Rank
Boston-Lawrence-Salem, MA-NH CMSA	72	7
Chicago-Gary-Lake County, IL-IN-WI CMSA	122	3
Dallas-Fort Worth, TX CMSA	113	4
Detroit-Ann Arbor, MI CMSA	60	8
Houston-Galveston-Brazoria, TX CMSA	59	9
Los Angeles-Anaheim-Riverside, CA CMSA	250	1
New York-Northern New Jersey-Long Island, NY-NJ-CT CMSA	176	2
Philadelphia-Wilmington-Trenton, PA-NJ-DE-MD CMSA	73	6
San Francisco-Oakland-San Jose, CA CMSA	75	5
Washington, DC-MD-VA MSA	52	10

Source: Hansen, Kristin A., Geographical Mobility: March 1993 to March 1994, U.S. Bureau of the Census, Current Population Reports, P20-485, Washington, D.C.: U.S. Government Printing Office, 1995, p. 164. Notes: "CMSA" stands for "Consolidated Metropolitan Statistical Area." "MSA stands for Metropolitan Statistical Area."

★698★
Geographic Mobility
Outmigration, 1993-94, By Sex: Males
[In thousands]

MSA	Male	Rank
Boston-Lawrence-Salem, MA-NH CMSA	60	7
Chicago-Gary-Lake County, IL-IN-WI CMSA	100	4
Dallas-Fort Worth, TX CMSA	119	3
Detroit-Ann Arbor, MI CMSA	55	8
Houston-Galveston-Brazoria, TX CMSA	52	10
Los Angeles-Anaheim-Riverside, CA CMSA	279	1
New York-Northern New Jersey-Long Island, NY-NJ-CT CMSA	166	2
Philadelphia-Wilmington-Trenton, PA-NJ-DE-MD CMSA	66	6
San Francisco-Oakland-San Jose, CA CMSA	73	5
Washington, DC-MD-VA MSA	54	9

Source: Hansen, Kristin A., Geographical Mobility: March 1993 to March 1994, U.S. Bureau of the Census, Current Population Reports, P20-485, Washington, D.C.: U.S. Government Printing Office, 1995, p. 164. Notes: "CMSA" stands for "Consolidated Metropolitan Statistical Area." "MSA" stands for "Metropolitan Statistical Area."

★699★

Home Ownership

Home Ownership Rates, 1993: Highest

Data refer to 10 of the 61 largest metropolitan areas.

[In percentages]

City	1993	Rank
Birmingham, AL	70.4	9
Detroit, MI	72.0	5
Greensboro-Winston Salem-High Point, NC	72.1	4
Middlesex-Somerset-Hunterdon, NJ	73.8	3
Monmouth-Ocean, NJ	75.3	2
Nassau-Suffolk, NY	80.2	1
Philadelphia, PA-NJ	71.5	6
Phoenix, AZ	70.3	10
Pittsburgh, PA	70.8	7
Rochester, NY	70.7	8

Source: Callis, Robert R. Housing Vacancies and Homeownership, Annual Statistics: 1993, U.S. Bureau of the Census, Current Housing Reports, Series H111/93-A, Washington, D.C.: U.S. Government Printing Office, 1994, p. 38.

★700★

Home Ownership

Home Ownership Rates, 1993: Lowest

Data refer to 10 of the 61 largest metropolitan areas.

[In percentages]

City	1993	Rank
Dallas, TX	52.9	7
Honolulu, HI	52.4	6
Houston, TX	55.4	10
Los Angeles-Long Beach, CA	49.5	2
Miami-Hialeah, FL	52.3	5
Nashville, TN	54.2	8
New Orleans, LA	52.1	4
New York, NY	34.0	1
San Antonio, TX	54.5	9
San Francisco, CA	50.3	3

Source: Callis, Robert R. Housing Vacancies and Homeownership, Annual Statistics: 1993, U.S. Bureau of the Census, Current Housing Reports, Series H111/93-A, Washington, D.C.: U.S. Government Printing Office, 1994, p. 38.

★701★

Housing

Home Loans Made to Persons in the Low-to-Moderate Income Ranges, 1994: Percentage Increase Since 1990

According to the source, "Lending... is on the rise around Chicago, in part because of increased federal pressure to comply with the Community Reinvestment Act."

City/MSA	Percentage	Rank
McHenry County, IL	127	1
DuPage County, IL	103	2
Lake County, IL	101	3
Will County, IL	100	4

[Continued]

★701★

Home Loans Made to Persons in the Low-to-Moderate Income Ranges, 1994: Percentage Increase Since 1990

[Continued]

City/MSA	Percentage	Rank
Cook County, IL	93	5
Kane County, IL	92	6
Chicago, IL	58	7

Source: Schmeltzer, John, "Mortgage Tide Shifts to Low Incomes: Banks Own Up to Reinvestment Mandate," Chicago Tribune, 8 May 1996, p. C1. Primary source: Woodstock Institute. Notes: According to the source, "low-to-moderate" income for 1990 is defined as $34,000 or less; for 1994 , $38,000 or less."

★702★

Housing

Home Loans Made to Persons in the Low-to-Moderate Income Ranges, 1994: Total

According to the source, "Lending... is on the rise around Chicago, in part because of increased federal pressure to comply with the Community Reinvestment Act."

City/MSA	Number	Rank
Cook County, IL	11,935	1
Chicago, IL	8,855	2
DuPage County, IL	3,463	3
Lake County, IL	2,431	4
Will County, IL	2,227	5
Kane County, IL	1,946	6
McHenry County, IL	1,228	7

Source: Schmeltzer, John, "Mortgage Tide Shifts to Low Incomes: Banks Own Up to Reinvestment Mandate," Chicago Tribune, 8 May 1996, p. C1. Primary source: Woodstock Institute. Notes: According to the source, "low-to-moderate" income for 1990 is defined as $34,000 or less; for 1994 , $38,000 or less."

★703★

Housing

Vacation Home Sales, 1996: Average Prices

City	Average sale	Rank
Atlantic Beach, NC	99,267	22
Bar Harbor, ME	115,872	21
Branson, MO	92,537	23
Cape Cod, MA	115,883	20
Carmel, CA	450,845	4
Fort Myers, FL	138,264	18
Hamptons, NY	427,929	5
Highlands, NC	214,311	12
Hilton Head, SC	169,972	15
Jersey Shore, NJ	240,093	10
Key Biscayne, FL	515,000	2
Lake Geneva, WI	196,999	13
North Lake Tahoe, CA	418,485	6
Ocean City, MD	138,713	17
Orcas Island, WA	316,955	8
Palm Springs, CA	258,264	9
Santa Fe, NM	217,012	11
South Padre Island, TX	135,888	19

[Continued]

★703★

Vacation Home Sales, 1996: Average Prices
[Continued]

City	Average sale	Rank
Sun Valley, ID	344,261	7
Telluride, CO	491,127	3
Traverse City, MI	138,788	16
Wailea, HI	619,933	1
White Fish, MT	173,975	14

Source: "Dow Jones Real Estate Index: Vacation Home Prices," *Wall Street Journal,* 29 March 1996, p. B8. Primary source: Coldwell Bankers, Corp.

★704★

Housing Costs

Apartment Rental Prices, 1995: Leading Cities/ Counties

Data refer to rents charged during the fourth quarter of 1995. The national average is $697 per month.

[In dollars per month]

City	Rents	Rank
San Francisco, CA	1,105	1
Orange County, CA	959	2
Los Angeles, CA	864	3
Chicago, IL	842	4

Source: "Having Fun," *Wall Street Journal,* 5 April 1996, p. B8. Primary source: M/PF Research, Inc. (Dallas, Texas).

★705★

Housing Costs

Cost of Houses, 1994

Data refer to prices for a 4-bedroom house with 2,200 square feet of living space.

[Dollars in thousands]

City	Cost	Rank
Atlanta, GA	153,778	7
Denver, CO	161,725	6
Pittsburgh, PA	179,633	5
Portland, OR	194,313	4
Sacramento, CA	208,375	3
San Diego, CA	243,880	2
San Francisco, CA	566,000	1

Source: McCarthy, Mike, "Buyers Still In Control of Residential Real Estate," *Business Journal,* 5 June 1995, p. 26. Primary source: Coldwell Banker.

★706★

Housing Costs

Home Prices, 1994: Median

City	Median price	Rank
Brazoria, TX	88,000	1
Davenport-Moline-Rock Island, IA-IL	63,000	9
Duluth-Superior, MN-WI	68,500	7
Grand Rapids-Muskegon-Holland, MI	80,000	2
Jackson, MI	65,000	8
Kokomo, IN	70,000	6
Lansing, MI	78,500	3
Lima, OH	62,000	10
Lincoln, NE	73,000	5
Vineland-Millville-Bridgeton, NJ	74,000	4

Source: "Go Midwest, Young Home Buyer," *Builder,* (January 1995), p. 80. Primary source: NAHB.

★707★

Housing Costs

Housing Affordability, 1996: Cities With the Smallest Percentage of Affordable Homes

Data refer to cities with populations of over 1 million in which there is the smallest percentage of homes that householders could afford when they are earning the median income for these areas.

City/MSA	Percentage	Rank
San Francisco, CA	21.0	1
New York, NY	35.0	2
Portland, OR	37.0	3
San Jose, CA	41.0	4
San Diego, CA	46.0	5

Source: "Penthouse Prices," *USA SNAPSHOTS, USA TODAY,* 22 May 1996, p. 1B. Primary source: National Association of Home Builders survey.

★708★

Housing Costs

Housing Markets For Single-Family Homes, 1995: Least Affordable

[In percentages]

City	Single-family home costs[1]	Rank
Boston, MA	39.7	6
Honolulu, HI	60.6	2
Los Angeles, CA	51.8	3
New York, NY	49.3	4
Oakland-East Bay, CA	40.8	5
San Diego, CA	36.0	7
San Francisco, CA	63.0	1
San Jose, CA	34.1	8
Sarasota-Bradenton, FL	33.3	9
Tucson, AZ	28.7	10

Source: "Dallas-Ft. Worth Area Tops Affordable Housing List," *American City & County,* (November 1995), p. 64. Primary source: E&Y Kenneth Levanthal Real Estate Group. *Note:* 1. Reflects a percentage of disposable median household income.

★709★
Housing Costs

Housing Markets for Single-Family Homes, 1995: Most Affordable

[In percentages]

City	Single-family home costs[1]	Rank
Central New Jersey, NJ	23.0	1
Dallas-Fort Worth	16.5	10
Houston, TX	18.6	7
Indianapolis, IN	19.0	6
Jacksonville, FL	18.3	9
Kansas City, MO	18.4	8
Louisville, KY	19.8	2
Oklahoma City, OK	19.2	5
Richmond, VA	19.7	3
Saint Louis, MO	19.4	4

Source: "Dallas-Ft. Worth Area Tops Affordable Housing List," *American City & County,* (November 1995), p. 64. Primary source: E&Y Kenneth Levanthal Real Estate Group. *Note:* 1. Reflects a percentage of disposable median household income.

★710★
Housing Costs

Housing Markets, 1995: Least Affordable

[In percentages]

City	Composite housing costs[1]	Rank
Boston, MA	33.2	6
Honolulu, HI	48.8	2
Los Angeles, CA	40.7	4
New York, NY	41.3	3
Oakland-East Bay, CA	34.7	5
San Diego, CA	34.7	5
San Francisco, CA	49.2	1
San Jose, CA	30.7	8
Sarasota-Bradenton, FL	31.0	7
Tucson, AZ	31.0	7

Source: "Dallas-Ft. Worth Area Tops Affordable Housing List," *American City & County,* (November 1995), p. 64. Primary source: E&Y Kenneth Levanthal Real Estate Group. *Notes:* 1. Reflects a percentage of disposable median household income. The composite figure is a simple average of the single family home and rental components.

★711★
Housing Costs

Housing Markets, 1995: Most Affordable

[In percentages]

City	Composite housing costs[1]	Rank
Central New Jersey, NJ	20.4	2
Dallas-Fort Worth, TX	17.8	8
Houston, TX	18.4	7
Indianapolis, IN	19.6	6
Jacksonville, FL	20.3	3

[Continued]

★711★
Housing Markets, 1995: Most Affordable
[Continued]

City	Composite housing costs[1]	Rank
Kansas City, MO	19.6	6
Louisville, KY	19.9	4
Oklahoma City, OK	19.6	6
Richmond, VA	19.8	5
Saint Louis, MO	21.0	1

Source: "Dallas-Ft. Worth Area Tops Affordable Housing List," *American City & County,* (November 1995), p. 64. Primary source: E&Y Kenneth Levanthal Real Estate Group. *Notes:* 1. Reflects a percentage of disposable median household income. The composite figure is a simple average of the single family home and rental components.

★712★
Housing Costs

Kitchen Remodeling, 1995: Average Cost

City	Cost	Rank
Atlanta, GA	20,427	10
Boston, MA	27,255	2
Des Moines, IA	22,115	7
Kansas City, MO	23,256	6
Louisville, KY	21,887	8
Portland, OR	24,255	4
Raleigh-Durham, NC	19,852	11
Reno, NV	23,624	5
Ridgewood, NJ	25,885	3
San Francisco, CA	28,999	1
Tulsa, OK	20,836	9

Source: Auerbach, Jonathan, "A Guide to What's Cooking In Kitchens," *Wall Street Journal,* 17 November 1995, p. B12. Primary source: *Remodeling Magazine.*

★713★
Housing Costs

Kitchen Remodeling, 1995: Resale Value

City	Value	Rank
Atlanta, GA	25,163	3
Boston, MA	24,625	4
Des Moines, IA	12,600	11
Kansas City, MO	24,588	5
Louisville, KY	19,267	8
Portland, OR	20,150	7
Raleigh-Durham, NC	22,500	6
Reno, NV	16,667	9
Ridgewood, NJ	26,875	2
San Francisco, CA	35,333	1
Tulsa, OK	16,292	10

Source: Auerbach, Jonathan, "A Guide to What's Cooking In Kitchens," *Wall Street Journal,* 17 November 1995, p. B12. Primary source: *Remodeling Magazine.*

★714★

Housing Costs

Most Affordable Places to Purchase A Home, 1994, Based on Median Income

City	Median income	Rank
Brazoria, TX	45,700	1
Davenport-Moline-Rock Island, IA-IL	39,800	6
Duluth-Superior, MN-WI	36,300	10
Grand Rapids-Muskegon-Holland, MI	44,000	3
Jackson, MI	39,700	7
Kokomo, IN	41,900	5
Lansing, MI	45,400	2
Lima, OH	38,600	8
Lincoln, NE	43,600	4
Vineland-Millville-Bridgeton, NJ	38,400	9

Source: "Go Midwest, Young Home Buyer," *Builder,* (January 1995), p. 80. Primary source: NAHB.

★715★

Housing Costs

Rental Costs, 1995: Least Affordable

[In percentages]

City	Rental costs[1]	Rank
Boston, MA	26.8	10
Honolulu, HI	37.1	1
Los Angeles, CA	29.6	6
New York, NY	33.3	4
Oakland-East Bay, CA	28.7	8
San Diego, CA	30.8	5
San Francisco, CA	35.5	2
San Jose, CA	27.3	9
Sarasota-Bradenton, FL	28.8	7
Tucson, AZ	33.4	3

Source: "Dallas-Ft. Worth Area Tops Affordable Housing List," *American City & County,* (November 1995), p. 64. Primary source: E&Y Kenneth Levanthal Real Estate Group. *Note:* 1. Reflects a percentage of disposable median household income.

★716★

Housing Costs

Rental Costs, 1995: Most Affordable

[In percentages]

City	Rental costs[1]	Rank
Central New Jersey, NJ	17.8	9
Dallas-Fort Worth, TX	19.1	7
Houston, TX	18.2	8
Indianapolis, IN	20.1	5
Jacksonville, FL	22.3	2
Kansas City, MO	20.9	3
Louisville, KY	20.0	6
Oklahoma City, OK	20.0	6

[Continued]

★716★

Rental Costs, 1995: Most Affordable

[Continued]

City	Rental costs[1]	Rank
Richmond, VA	20.2	4
Saint Louis, MO	22.6	1

Source: "Dallas-Ft. Worth Area Tops Affordable Housing List," *American City & County,* (November 1995), p. 64. Primary source: E&Y Kenneth Levanthal Real Estate Group. *Note:* 1. Reflects a percentage of disposable median household income.

★717★

Housing Costs

Rental Rates, 1995: Highest

Data refer to the rates for a two-bedroom apartment.

[In dollars per month (average)]

City/MSA	Rent	Rank
Manhattan, NY	2,810	1
San Francisco, CA	1,178	2
Honolulu, HI	1,170	3
Westchester County, NY	1,074	4
Marin County, CA	1,057	5
Hilton Head, SC	1,055	6

Source: "Where Rent Is A Killer," USA SNAPSHOTS, *USA TODAY,* 16 May 1996, p.1B. Primary source: American Chamber of Commerce Research Association (ACCRA) *Cost of Living Index.*

★718★

Housing Construction

Annual Construction of Housing Units, 1993, Selected Areas: Total Units Authorized (Highest Numbers)

Data refer to authorized construction in permit-issuing places. Totals include one-family houses.

[In thousands]

MSA	Units	Rank
Atlanta, GA MSA	35.0	1
Chicago-Gary-Lake County, IL-IN-WI CMSA	34.0	2
Dallas, TX PMSA	19.9	9
Dallas-Fort Worth, TX CMSA	26.2	6
Las Vegas, NV MSA	19.0	10
Los Angeles-Anaheim-Riverside, CA CMSA	28.2	4
Miami-Fort Lauderdale, FL CMSA	21.3	8
New York-Northern New Jersey-Long Island, NY-NJ-CT CMSA	31.6	3
Phoenix, AZ MSA	24.9	7
Washington, DC-MD-VA MSA	27.9	5

Source: U.S. Department of Commerce, Economics and Statistics Administration, Bureau of the Census, *New Residential Construction in Selected Metropolitan Areas, Fourth Quarter 1993,* Current Construction Reports, C21/93-Q4, Washington, D.C.: U.S. Government Printing Office, March 1994, p. 4. *Notes:* "CMSA" stands for "Consolidated Metropolitan Statistical Area." "MSA stands for "Metropolitan Statistical Area." "PMSA" stands for "Primary Metropolitan Statistical Area."

★719★

Housing Construction

Annual Construction of Housing Units, 1993, Selected Areas: Total Units Authorized (Lowest Numbers)

Data refer to authorized construction in permit-issuing places. Totals include one-family houses.

[In thousands]

MSA	Units	Rank
Anaheim-Santa Ana, CA PMSA	6.3	5
Colorado Springs, CO MSA	3.7	2
Jacksonville, FL MSA	7.5	7
Los Angeles-Long Beach, CA PMSA	7.6	8
New Orleans, LA MSA	3.6	1
New York, NY PMSA	7.3	6
Sacramento, CA MSA	8.6	9
Salt Lake City-Ogden, UT MSA	8.7	10
San Antonio, TX MSA	5.8	3
San Diego, CA MSA	5.8	3
Tucson, AZ MSA	6.2	4

Source: U.S. Department of Commerce, Economics and Statistics Administration, Bureau of the Census, *New Residential Construction in Selected Metropolitan Areas, Fourth Quarter 1993*, Current Construction Reports, C21/93-Q4, Washington, D.C.: U.S. Government Printing Office, March 1994, p. 4. *Notes:* "CMSA" stands for "Consolidated Metropolitan Statistical Area." "MSA stands for "Metropolitan Statistical Area." "PMSA" stands for "Primary Metropolitan Statistical Area."

★720★

Housing Construction

Annual Construction of Housing Units, 1993, Selected Areas: Units Authorized But Not Started At End of Period (Highest Numbers)

Data refer to authorized construction in permit-issuing places. Totals include one-family houses.

[In thousands]

MSA	Units	Rank
Atlanta, GA MSA	3.0	8
Baltimore, MD MSA	3.4	7
Dallas, TX PMSA	1.6	10
Dallas-Fort Worth, TX CMSA	1.9	9
Fort Lauderdale-Hollywood-Pompano Beach, FL PMSA	3.4	7
Los Angeles-Anaheim-Riverside, CA CMSA	4.4	4
Los Angeles-Long Beach, CA PMSA	1.9	9
Miami-Fort Lauderdale, FL CMSA	7.5	2
Miami-Hialeah, FL PMSA	4.0	5
New York, NY PMSA	3.4	7
New York-Northern New Jersey-Long Island, NY-NJ-CT CMSA	11.1	1
Orlando, FL MSA	3.4	7
Seattle, WA PMSA	3.0	8

[Continued]

★720★

Annual Construction of Housing Units, 1993, Selected Areas: Units Authorized But Not Started At End of Period (Highest Numbers)

[Continued]

MSA	Units	Rank
Seattle-Tacoma, WA CMSA	3.9	6
Washington, DC-MD-VA MSA	7.4	3

Source: U.S. Department of Commerce, Economics and Statistics Administration, Bureau of the Census, *New Residential Construction in Selected Metropolitan Areas, Fourth Quarter 1993*, Current Construction Reports, C21/93-Q4, Washington, D.C.: U.S. Government Printing Office, March 1994, p. 4. *Notes:* "CMSA" stands for "Consolidated Metropolitan Statistical Area." "MSA" stands for "Metropolitan Statistical Area." "PMSA" stands for "Primary Metropolitan Statistical Area."

★721★

Housing Construction

Annual Construction of Housing Units, 1993, Selected Areas: Units Authorized But Not Started At End of Period (Lowest Numbers)

Data refer to authorized construction in permit-issuing places. Totals include one-family houses.

[In thousands]

MSA	Units	Rank
Denver, CO PMSA	0.4	1
Denver-Boulder, CO CMSA	0.5	2
Jacksonville, FL MSA	0.8	5
Las Vegas, NV MSA	0.6	3
Norfolk-Virginia Beach-Newport News, VA MSA	0.4	1
Sacramento, CA MSA	0.6	3
Saint Louis, MO-IL MSA	0.7	4
Tucson, AZ MSA	0.5	2
West Palm Beach-Boca Raton-Delray Beach, FL MSA	0.5	2

Source: U.S. Department of Commerce, Economics and Statistics Administration, Bureau of the Census, *New Residential Construction in Selected Metropolitan Areas, Fourth Quarter 1993*, Current Construction Reports, C21/93-Q4, Washington, D.C.: U.S. Government Printing Office, March 1994, p. 4. *Notes:* "CMSA" stands for "Consolidated Metropolitan Statistical Area." "MSA" stands for "Metropolitan Statistical Area." "PMSA" stands for "Primary Metropolitan Statistical Area."

★722★

Housing Construction

Annual Construction of Housing Units, 1993, Selected Areas: Units Completed (Highest Numbers)

Data refer to authorized construction in permit-issuing places. Totals include one-family houses.

[In thousands]

MSA	Units	Rank
Atlanta, GA MSA	28.7	3
Chicago-Gary-Lake County, IL-IN-WI CMSA	32.3	2
Dallas-Fort Worth, TX CMSA	22.0	6
Las Vegas, NV MSA	17.6	9
Los Angeles-Anaheim-Riverside, CA CMSA	34.6	1
Miami-Fort Lauderdale, FL CMSA	17.9	8
Minneapolis-Saint Paul, MN-WI MSA	16.7	10
New York-Northern New Jersey-Long Island, NY-NJ-CT CMSA	25.4	4
Phoenix, AZ MSA	20.5	7
Washington, DC-MD-VA MSA	25.0	5

Source: U.S. Department of Commerce, Economics and Statistics Administration, Bureau of the Census, *New Residential Construction in Selected Metropolitan Areas, Fourth Quarter 1993,* Current Construction Reports, C21/93-Q4, Washington, D.C.: U.S. Government Printing Office, March 1994, p. 4. *Notes:* "CMSA" stands for "Consolidated Metropolitan Statistical Area." "MSA" stands for "Metropolitan Statistical Area." "PMSA" stands for "Primary Metropolitan Statistical Area."

★723★

Housing Construction

Annual Construction of Housing Units, 1993, Selected Areas: Units Completed (Lowest Numbers)

Data refer to authorized construction in permit-issuing places. Totals include one-family houses.

[In thousands]

MSA	Units	Rank
Anaheim-Santa Ana, CA PMSA	6.3	7
Colorado Springs, CO MSA	3.1	1
Jacksonville, FL MSA	7.6	9
New Orleans, LA MSA	3.2	2
New York, NY PMSA	5.8	5
Norfolk-Virginia Beach-Newport News, VA MSA	7.8	10
Sacramento, CA MSA	7.8	10
Salt Lake City-Ogden, UT MSA	6.2	6
San Antonio, TX MSA	4.2	3
San Diego, CA MSA	7.1	8
Tucson, AZ MSA	4.4	4

Source: U.S. Department of Commerce, Economics and Statistics Administration, Bureau of the Census, *New Residential Construction in Selected Metropolitan Areas, Fourth Quarter 1993,* Current Construction Reports, C21/93-Q4, Washington, D.C.: U.S. Government Printing Office, March 1994, p. 4. *Notes:* "CMSA" stands for "Consolidated Metropolitan Statistical Area." "MSA" stands for "Metropolitan Statistical Area." "PMSA" stands for "Primary Metropolitan Statistical Area."

★724★

Housing Construction

Annual Construction of Housing Units, 1993, Selected Areas: Units Started (Highest Numbers)

Data refer to authorized construction in permit-issuing places. Totals include one-family houses.

[In thousands]

MSA	Units	Rank
Atlanta, GA MSA	32.7	2
Chicago-Gary-Lake County, IL-IN-WI CMSA	33.1	1
Dallas, TX PMSA	18.9	9
Dallas-Fort Worth, TX CMSA	25.2	6
Las Vegas, NV MSA	19.1	8
Los Angeles-Anaheim-Riverside, CA CMSA	28.6	3
Miami-Fort Lauderdale, FL CMSA	18.2	10
Minneapolis-Saint Paul, MN-WI MSA	18.2	10
New York-Northern New Jersey-Long Island, NY-NJ-CT CMSA	28.2	4
Phoenix, AZ MSA	24.0	7
Washington, DC-MD-VA MSA	25.9	5

Source: U.S. Department of Commerce, Economics and Statistics Administration, Bureau of the Census, *New Residential Construction in Selected Metropolitan Areas, Fourth Quarter 1993,* Current Construction Reports, C21/93-Q4, Washington, D.C.: U.S. Government Printing Office, March 1994, p. 4. *Notes:* "CMSA" stands for "Consolidated Metropolitan Statistical Area." "MSA" stands for "Metropolitan Statistical Area." "PMSA" stands for "Primary Metropolitan Statistical Area."

★725★

Housing Construction

Annual Construction of Housing Units, 1993, Selected Areas: Units Started (Lowest Numbers)

Data refer to authorized construction in permit-issuing places. Totals include one-family houses.

[In thousands]

MSA	Units	Rank
Anaheim-Santa Ana, CA PMSA	6.1	6
Colorado Springs, CO MSA	3.6	2
Jacksonville, FL MSA	7.3	7
Los Angeles-Long Beach, CA PMSA	8.0	10
Miami-Hialeah, FL PMSA	7.7	8
New Orleans, LA MSA	3.5	1
New York, NY PMSA	5.6	5
San Antonio, TX MSA	5.4	3
San Diego, CA MSA	5.5	4
Tucson, AZ MSA	5.6	5

Source: U.S. Department of Commerce, Economics and Statistics Administration, Bureau of the Census, *New Residential Construction in Selected Metropolitan Areas, Fourth Quarter 1993,* Current Construction Reports, C21/93-Q4, Washington, D.C.: U.S. Government Printing Office, March 1994, p. 4. *Notes:* "CMSA" stands for "Consolidated Metropolitan Statistical Area." "MSA" stands for "Metropolitan Statistical Area." "PMSA" stands for "Primary Metropolitan Statistical Area."

★726★
Housing Construction

Annual Construction of Housing Units, 1993, Selected Areas: Units Under Construction At End of Period (Highest Numbers)

Data refer to authorized construction in permit-issuing places. Totals include one-family houses.

[In thousands]

MSA	Units	Rank
Atlanta, GA MSA	12.8	5
Chicago-Gary-Lake County, IL-IN-WI CMSA	17.3	3
Dallas-Fort Worth, TX CMSA	9.9	9
Las Vegas, NV MSA	8.7	10
Los Angeles-Anaheim-Riverside, CA CMSA	19.6	2
Miami-Fort Lauderdale, FL CMSA	13.5	4
New York-Northern New Jersey-Long Island, NY-NJ-CT CMSA	28.9	1
Phoenix, AZ MSA	10.4	8
Seattle-Tacoma, WA CMSA	10.5	7
Washington, DC-MD-VA MSA	11.0	6

Source: U.S. Department of Commerce, Economics and Statistics Administration, Bureau of the Census, *New Residential Construction in Selected Metropolitan Areas, Fourth Quarter 1993,* Current Construction Reports, C21/93-Q4, Washington, D.C.: U.S. Government Printing Office, March 1994, p. 4. *Notes:* "CMSA" stands for "Consolidated Metropolitan Statistical Area." "MSA" stands for "Metropolitan Statistical Area." "PMSA" stands for "Primary Metropolitan Statistical Area."

★727★
Housing Construction

Annual Construction of Housing Units, 1993, Selected Areas: Units Under Construction At End of Period (Lowest Numbers)

Data refer to authorized construction in permit-issuing places. Totals include one-family houses.

[In thousands]

MSA	Units	Rank
Anaheim-Santa Ana, CA PMSA	4.1	10
Colorado Springs, CO MSA	1.4	1
Jacksonville, FL MSA	1.8	3
New Orleans, LA MSA	1.5	2
Norfolk-Virginia Beach-Newport News, VA MSA	3.9	9
Orlando, FL MSA	3.6	7
Sacramento, CA MSA	3.7	8
San Antonio, TX MSA	2.5	4
San Diego, CA MSA	3.4	6
Tucson, AZ MSA	3.1	5

Source: U.S. Department of Commerce, Economics and Statistics Administration, Bureau of the Census, *New Residential Construction in Selected Metropolitan Areas, Fourth Quarter 1993,* Current Construction Reports, C21/93-Q4, Washington, D.C.: U.S. Government Printing Office, March 1994, p. 4. *Notes:* "CMSA" stands for "Consolidated Metropolitan Statistical Area." "MSA" stands for "Metropolitan Statistical Area." "PMSA" stands for "Primary Metropolitan Statistical Area."

★728★
Housing Construction

Annual Construction of One-Family Houses Units, 1993, Selected Areas: Total Houses Authorized (Highest Numbers)

Data refer to authorized construction in permit-issuing places.

[In thousands]

MSA	Units	Rank
Atlanta, GA MSA	31.4	1
Chicago-Gary-Lake County, IL-IN-WI CMSA	27.8	2
Dallas-Fort Worth, TX CMSA	21.5	7
Las Vegas, NV MSA	15.7	9
Los Angeles-Anaheim-Riverside, CA CMSA	22.5	6
Miami-Fort Lauderdale, FL CMSA	15.6	10
Minneapolis-Saint Paul, MN-WI MSA	16.0	8
New York-Northern New Jersey-Long Island, NY-NJ-CT CMSA	23.3	4
Phoenix, AZ MSA	22.6	5
Washington, DC-MD-VA MSA	24.2	3

Source: U.S. Department of Commerce, Economics and Statistics Administration, Bureau of the Census, *New Residential Construction in Selected Metropolitan Areas, Fourth Quarter 1993,* Current Construction Reports, C21/93-Q4, Washington, D.C.: U.S. Government Printing Office, March 1994, p. 4. *Notes:* "CMSA" stands for "Consolidated Metropolitan Statistical Area." "MSA" stands for "Metropolitan Statistical Area." "PMSA" stands for "Primary Metropolitan Statistical Area."

★729★
Housing Construction

Annual Construction of One-Family Houses Units, 1993, Selected Areas: Total Houses Authorized (Lowest Numbers)

Data refer to authorized construction in permit-issuing places.

[In thousands]

MSA	Units	Rank
Anaheim-Santa Ana, CA PMSA	4.4	5
Colorado Springs, CO MSA	3.6	3
Los Angeles-Long Beach, CA PMSA	4.7	7
Miami-Hialeah, FL PMSA	5.8	9
New Orleans, LA MSA	3.4	2
New York, NY PMSA	2.8	1
Salt Lake City-Ogden, UT MSA	7.0	10
San Antonio, TX MSA	4.5	6
San Diego, CA MSA	4.2	4
Tucson, AZ MSA	5.4	8
West Palm Beach-Boca Raton-Delray Beach, FL MSA	7.0	10

Source: U.S. Department of Commerce, Economics and Statistics Administration, Bureau of the Census, *New Residential Construction in Selected Metropolitan Areas, Fourth Quarter 1993,* Current Construction Reports, C21/93-Q4, Washington, D.C.: U.S. Government Printing Office, March 1994, p. 4. *Notes:* "CMSA" stands for "Consolidated Metropolitan Statistical Area." "MSA" stands for "Metropolitan Statistical Area." "PMSA" stands for "Primary Metropolitan Statistical Area."

★730★

Housing Construction

Annual Construction of One-Family Houses, 1993, Selected Areas: Houses Authorized But Not Started At End of Period

Data refer to authorized construction in permit-issuing places.

[In thousands]

MSA	Houses	Rank
Atlanta, GA MSA	1.8	5
Baltimore, MD MSA	2.6	3
Chicago-Gary-Lake County, IL-IN-WI CMSA	1.4	8
Fort Lauderdale-Hollywood-Pompano Beach, FL PMSA	1.6	6
Los Angeles-Anaheim-Riverside, CA CMSA	1.9	4
Miami-Hialeah, FL PMSA	1.0	10
New York-Northern New Jersey-Long Island, NY-NJ-CT CMSA	7.6	1
Phoenix, AZ MSA	1.3	9
Seattle-Tacoma, WA CMSA	1.5	7
Washington, DC-MD-VA MSA	5.4	2

Source: U.S. Department of Commerce, Economics and Statistics Administration, Bureau of the Census, *New Residential Construction in Selected Metropolitan Areas, Fourth Quarter 1993*, Current Construction Reports, C21/93-Q4, Washington, D.C.: U.S. Government Printing Office, March 1994, p. 4. *Notes:* "CMSA" stands for "Consolidated Metropolitan Statistical Area." "MSA" stands for "Metropolitan Statistical Area." "PMSA" stands for "Primary Metropolitan Statistical Area."

★731★

Housing Construction

Annual Construction of One-Family Houses, 1993, Selected Areas: Houses Authorized But Not Started At End of Period

Data refer to authorized construction in permit-issuing places.

[In thousands]

MSA	Houses	Rank
Anaheim-Santa Ana, CA PMSA	0.3	10
Charlotte-Gastonia-Rock Hill, NC-SC MSA	0.6	7
Chicago-Gary-Lake County, IL-IN-WI CMSA	1.4	1
Dallas-Fort Worth, TX CMSA	0.9	4
Denver, CO PMSA	0.4	9
Los Angeles-Long Beach, CA PMSA	0.5	8
Miami-Hialeah, FL PMSA	1.0	3
Phoenix, AZ MSA	1.3	2
Saint Louis, MO-IL MSA	0.7	6
San Diego, CA MSA	0.8	5

Source: U.S. Department of Commerce, Economics and Statistics Administration, Bureau of the Census, *New Residential Construction in Selected Metropolitan Areas, Fourth Quarter 1993*, Current Construction Reports, C21/93-Q4, Washington, D.C.: U.S. Government Printing Office, March 1994, p. 4. *Notes:* "CMSA" stands for "Consolidated Metropolitan Statistical Area." "MSA" stands for "Metropolitan Statistical Area." "PMSA" stands for "Primary Metropolitan Statistical Area."

★732★

Housing Construction

Annual Construction of One-Family Houses, 1993, Selected Areas: Houses Completed (Lowest Numbers)

Data refer to authorized construction in permit-issuing places.

[In thousands]

MSA	Houses	Rank
Anaheim-Santa Ana, CA PMSA	3.7	7
Colorado Springs, CO MSA	3.1	8
Los Angeles-Long Beach, CA PMSA	5.9	2
Miami-Hialeah, FL PMSA	5.4	3
New Orleans, LA MSA	3.0	9
New York, NY PMSA	2.6	10
Salt Lake City-Ogden, UT MSA	6.0	1
San Antonio, TX MSA	4.1	6
San Diego, CA MSA	4.4	4
Tucson, AZ MSA	4.3	5

Source: U.S. Department of Commerce, Economics and Statistics Administration, Bureau of the Census, *New Residential Construction in Selected Metropolitan Areas, Fourth Quarter 1993*, Current Construction Reports, C21/93-Q4, Washington, D.C.: U.S. Government Printing Office, March 1994, p. 4. *Notes:* "CMSA" stands for "Consolidated Metropolitan Statistical Area." "MSA" stands for "Metropolitan Statistical Area." "PMSA" stands for "Primary Metropolitan Statistical Area."

★733★

Housing Construction

Annual Construction of One-Family Houses, 1993, Selected Areas: Houses Completed (Highest Numbers)

Data refer to authorized construction in permit-issuing places.

[In thousands]

MSA	Houses	Rank
Atlanta, GA MSA	27.4	1
Chicago-Gary-Lake County, IL-IN-WI CMSA	26.7	2
Dallas, TX PMSA	14.0	10
Dallas-Fort Worth, TX CMSA	19.2	6
Las Vegas, NV MSA	14.4	9
Los Angeles-Anaheim-Riverside, CA CMSA	23.8	3
Minneapolis-Saint Paul, MN-WI MSA	14.9	8
New York-Northern New Jersey-Long Island, NY-NJ-CT CMSA	19.3	5
Phoenix, AZ MSA	18.6	7
Washington, DC-MD-VA MSA	21.7	4

Source: U.S. Department of Commerce, Economics and Statistics Administration, Bureau of the Census, *New Residential Construction in Selected Metropolitan Areas, Fourth Quarter 1993*, Current Construction Reports, C21/93-Q4, Washington, D.C.: U.S. Government Printing Office, March 1994, p. 4. *Notes:* "CMSA" stands for "Consolidated Metropolitan Statistical Area." "MSA" stands for "Metropolitan Statistical Area." "PMSA" stands for "Primary Metropolitan Statistical Area."

★ 734 ★

Housing Construction

Annual Construction of One-Family Houses, 1993, Selected Areas: Houses Started (Lowest Numbers)

Data refer to authorized construction in permit-issuing places.

[In thousands]

MSA	Houses	Rank
Anaheim-Santa Ana, CA PMSA	4.3	6
Colorado Springs, CO MSA	3.6	8
Jacksonville, FL MSA	6.9	2
Los Angeles-Long Beach, CA PMSA	4.7	5
Miami-Hialeah, FL PMSA	5.7	3
New Orleans, LA MSA	3.3	9
New York, NY PMSA	2.7	10
San Diego, CA MSA	4.1	7
Tucson, AZ MSA	5.3	4
West Palm Beach-Boca Raton-Delray Beach, FL MSA	7.0	1

Source: U.S. Department of Commerce, Economics and Statistics Administration, Bureau of the Census, *New Residential Construction in Selected Metropolitan Areas, Fourth Quarter 1993,* Current Construction Reports, C21/93-Q4, Washington, D.C.: U.S. Government Printing Office, March 1994, p. 4. *Notes:* "CMSA" stands for "Consolidated Metropolitan Statistical Area." "MSA" stands for "Metropolitan Statistical Area." "PMSA" stands for "Primary Metropolitan Statistical Area."

★ 736 ★

Housing Construction

Annual Construction of One-Family Houses, 1993, Selected Areas: Houses Under Construction At End of Period (Lowest Numbers)

Data refer to authorized construction in permit-issuing places.

[In thousands]

MSA	Houses	Rank
Anaheim-Santa Ana, CA PMSA	2.3	6
Colorado Springs, CO MSA	1.4	9
Jacksonville, FL MSA	1.5	8
New Orleans, LA MSA	1.3	10
New York, NY PMSA	2.5	5
Norfolk-Virginia Beach-Newport News, VA MSA	2.7	3
Orlando, FL MSA	2.6	4
San Antonio, TX MSA	2.0	7
Tucson, AZ MSA	2.9	2
West Palm Beach-Boca Raton-Delray Beach, FL MSA	3.3	1

Source: U.S. Department of Commerce, Economics and Statistics Administration, Bureau of the Census, *New Residential Construction in Selected Metropolitan Areas, Fourth Quarter 1993,* Current Construction Reports, C21/93-Q4, Washington, D.C.: U.S. Government Printing Office, March 1994, p. 4. *Notes:* "CMSA" stands for "Consolidated Metropolitan Statistical Area." "MSA" stand for "Metropolitan Statistical Area." "PMSA" stands for "Primary Metropolitan Statistical Area."

★ 735 ★

Housing Construction

Annual Construction of One-Family Houses, 1993, Selected Areas: Houses Started (Highest Numbers)

Data refer to authorized construction in permit-issuing places.

[In thousands]

MSA	Houses	Rank
Atlanta, GA MSA	30.2	1
Chicago-Gary-Lake County, IL-IN-WI CMSA	27.7	2
Dallas, TX PMSA	15.5	10
Dallas-Fort Worth, TX CMSA	21.4	7
Las Vegas, NV MSA	15.7	9
Los Angeles-Anaheim-Riverside, CA CMSA	22.5	4
Minneapolis-Saint Paul, MN-WI MSA	16.1	8
New York-Northern New Jersey-Long Island, NY-NJ-CT CMSA	22.0	5
Phoenix, AZ MSA	21.6	6
Washington, DC-MD-VA MSA	23.0	3

Source: U.S. Department of Commerce, Economics and Statistics Administration, Bureau of the Census, *New Residential Construction in Selected Metropolitan Areas, Fourth Quarter 1993,* Current Construction Reports, C21/93-Q4, Washington, D.C.: U.S. Government Printing Office, March 1994, p. 4. *Notes:* "CMSA" stands for "Consolidated Metropolitan Statistical Area." "MSA" stands for "Metropolitan Statistical Area." "PMSA" stands for "Primary Metropolitan Statistical Area."

★ 737 ★

Housing Construction

Annual Construction of One-Family Houses, 1993, Selected Areas: Houses Under Construction At End of Period (Highest Numbers)

Data refer to authorized construction in permit-issuing places.

[In thousands]

MSA	Houses	Rank
Atlanta, GA MSA	11.1	4
Chicago-Gary-Lake County, IL-IN-WI CMSA	12.5	2
Dallas-Fort Worth, TX CMSA	6.8	8
Denver-Boulder, CO CMSA	6.4	10
Los Angeles-Anaheim-Riverside, CA CMSA	12.4	3
Miami-Fort Lauderdale, FL CMSA	8.7	6
New York-Northern New Jersey-Long Island, NY-NJ-CT CMSA	19.2	1
Phoenix, AZ MSA	8.6	7
Riverside-San Bernardino, CA PMSA	6.7	9
Washington, DC-MD-VA MSA	9.1	5

Source: U.S. Department of Commerce, Economics and Statistics Administration, Bureau of the Census, *New Residential Construction in Selected Metropolitan Areas, Fourth Quarter 1993,* Current Construction Reports, C21/93-Q4, Washington, D.C.: U.S. Government Printing Office, March 1994, p. 4. *Notes:* "CMSA" stands for "Consolidated Metropolitan Statistical Area." "MSA" stand for "Metropolitan Statistical Area." "PMSA" stands for "Primary Metropolitan Statistical Area."

★738★

Housing Construction

Housing Startups, 1994

City	1994 starts	Rank
Atlanta, GA	39,551	1
Boston, MA	17,378	8
Chicago, IL	31,516	3
Dallas, TX	22,740	6
Houston, TX	19,336	7
Las Vegas, NV	26,187	5
Minneapolis-Saint Paul, MN	17,357	9
Orlando, FL	16,380	10
Phoenix, AZ	34,096	2
Washington, DC	30,810	4

Source: "Top 10 Housing Markets: 1995," *Builder,* (January 1995), p. 53. Primary source: NAHB.

★739★

Housing Construction

Housing Startups, 1995: Projected

City	Projected	Rank
Atlanta, GA	37,850	1
Boston, MA	17,298	8
Chicago, IL	31,169	2
Dallas, TX	23,023	6
Houston, TX	19,588	7
Las Vegas, NV	26,550	5
Minneapolis-Saint Paul, MN	17,194	9
Orlando, FL	16,942	10
Phoenix, AZ	30,203	3
Washington, DC	30,077	4

Source: "Top 10 Housing Markets: 1995," *Builder,* (January 1995), p. 53. Primary source: NAHB.

★740★

Housing Construction

Percent Change In Housing Startups Since 1994, 1995

Data are based on projected 1995 starts.

City	Percent change	Rank
Atlanta, GA	-4.3	8
Boston, MA	-0.5	4
Chicago, IL	-1.1	6
Dallas, TX	+1.3	3
Houston, TX	+1.3	3
Las Vegas, NV	+1.4	2
Minneapolis-Saint Paul, MN	-0.9	5
Orlando, FL	+3.4	1
Phoenix, AZ	-11.4	9
Washington, DC	-2.4	7

Source: "Top 10 Housing Markets: 1995," *Builder,* (January 1995), p. 53. Primary source: NAHB.

★741★

Housing Construction

Quarterly Construction of Housing Units, 1993, Selected Areas: Total Units Authorized (Highest Numbers)

Data refer to authorized construction in permit-issuing places for the fourth quarter of 1993. One-family houses are included in the totals.

[In thousands]

MSA	Units	Rank
Atlanta, GA MSA	9.0	3
Chicago, IL PMSA	4.8	10
Chicago-Gary-Lake County, IL-IN-WI CMSA	9.4	2
Dallas-Fort Worth, TX CMSA	6.4	6
Las Vegas, NV MSA	5.3	7
Miami-Fort Lauderdale, FL CMSA	5.0	8
New York-Northern New Jersey-Long Island, NY-NJ-CT CMSA	10.0	1
Phoenix, AZ MSA	6.9	5
Seattle-Tacoma, WA CMSA	4.9	9
Washington, DC-MD-VA MSA	7.0	4

Source: U.S. Department of Commerce, Economics and Statistics Administration, Bureau of the Census, *New Residential Construction in Selected Metropolitan Areas, Fourth Quarter 1993,* Current Construction Reports, C21/93-Q4, Washington, D.C.: U.S. Government Printing Office, March 1994, p. 4. *Notes:* "CMSA" "Consolidated Metropolitan Statistical Area." "MSA" stands for "Metropolitan Statistical Area." "PMSA" stands for "Primary Metropolitan Statistical Area."

★742★

Housing Construction

Quarterly Construction of Housing Units, 1993, Selected Areas: Total Units Authorized (Lowest Numbers)

Data refer to authorized construction in permit-issuing places for the fourth quarter of 1993. One-family houses are included in the totals.

[In thousands]

MSA	Units	Rank
Anaheim-Santa Ana, CA PMSA	1.3	8
Colorado Springs, CO	1.0	9
Jacksonville, FL MSA	1.7	6
Miami-Hialeah, FL PMSA	1.6	7
New Orleans, LA MSA	0.8	10
Norfolk-Virginia Beach-Newport News, VA MSA	2.1	3
Sacramento, CA MSA	2.3	1
Salt Lake City-Ogden, UT MSA	2.2	2
San Antonio, TX MSA	2.0	4
Tucson, AZ MSA	1.8	5

Source: U.S. Department of Commerce, Economics and Statistics Administration, Bureau of the Census, *New Residential Construction in Selected Metropolitan Areas, Fourth Quarter 1993,* Current Construction Reports, C21/93-Q4, Washington, D.C.: U.S. Government Printing Office, March 1994, p. 4. *Notes:* "CMSA" "Consolidated Metropolitan Statistical Area." "MSA" stands for "Metropolitan Statistical Area." "PMSA" stands for "Primary Metropolitan Statistical Area."

★743★

Housing Construction

Quarterly Construction of Housing Units, 1993, Selected Areas: Units Authorized But Not Started At End of Period

Data refer to authorized construction in permit-issuing places during the fourth quarter of 1993. One-family houses are included in the totals.

[In thousands]

MSA	Units	Rank
Atlanta, GA MSA	3.0	8
Baltimore, MD MSA	3.4	7
Dallas, TX PMSA	1.6	10
Dallas-Fort Worth, TX CMSA	1.9	9
Los Angeles-Anaheim-Riverside, CA CMSA	4.4	4
Miami-Fort Lauderdale, FL CMSA	7.5	2
Miami-Hialeah, FL PMSA	4.0	5
New York-Northern New Jersey-Long Island, NY-NJ-CT CMSA	11.1	1
Seattle-Tacoma, WA CMSA	3.9	6
Washington, DC-MD-VA MSA	7.4	3

Source: U.S. Department of Commerce, Economics and Statistics Administration, Bureau of the Census, *New Residential Construction in Selected Metropolitan Areas, Fourth Quarter 1993*, Current Construction Reports, C21/93-Q4, Washington, D.C.: U.S. Government Printing Office, March 1994, p. 4. *Notes:* "CMSA" stands for "Consolidated Metropolitan Statistical Area." "MSA" stands for "Metropolitan Statistical Area." "PMSA" stands for "Primary Metropolitan Statistical Area."

★744★

Housing Construction

Quarterly Construction of Housing Units, 1993, Selected Areas: Units Authorized But Not Started At End of Period

Data refer to authorized construction in permit-issuing places during the fourth quarter of 1993. One-family houses are included in the totals.

[In thousands]

MSA	Units	Rank
Anaheim-Santa Ana, CA PMSA	0.9	5
Charlotte-Gastonia-Rock Hill, NC-SC MSA	0.7	7
Denver, CO PMSA	0.4	10
Denver-Boulder, CO CMSA	0.5	9
Houston, TX PMSA	1.3	2
Houston-Galveston-Brazoria, TX CMSA	1.4	1
Jacksonville, FL MSA	0.8	6
Las Vegas, NV MSA	0.6	8
San Antonio, TX MSA	1.2	3
San Diego, CA MSA	1.0	4

Source: U.S. Department of Commerce, Economics and Statistics Administration, Bureau of the Census, *New Residential Construction in Selected Metropolitan Areas, Fourth Quarter 1993*, Current Construction Reports, C21/93-Q4, Washington, D.C.: U.S. Government Printing Office, March 1994, p. 4. *Notes:* "CMSA" stands for "Consolidated Metropolitan Statistical Area." "MSA" stands for "Metropolitan Statistical Area." "PMSA" stands for "Primary Metropolitan Statistical Area."

★745★

Housing Construction

Quarterly Construction of Housing Units, 1993, Selected Areas: Units Completed

Data refer to authorized construction in permit-issuing places for the fourth quarter of 1993. One-family houses are included in the totals.

[In thousands]

MSA	Units	Rank
Atlanta, GA MSA	7.8	3
Chicago, IL PMSA	5.4	8
Chicago-Gary-Lake County, IL-IN-WI CMSA	11.0	1
Dallas-Fort Worth, TX CMSA	5.3	9
Las Vegas, NV MSA	5.8	6
Los Angeles-Anaheim-Riverside, CA CMSA	9.8	2
Miami-Fort Lauderdale, FL CMSA	5.5	7
Minneapolis-Saint Paul, MN-WI MSA	5.1	10
New York-Northern New Jersey-Long Island, NY-NJ-CT CMSA	7.4	4
Washington, DC-MD-VA MSA	6.9	5

Source: U.S. Department of Commerce, Economics and Statistics Administration, Bureau of the Census, *New Residential Construction in Selected Metropolitan Areas, Fourth Quarter 1993*, Current Construction Reports, C21/93-Q4, Washington, D.C.: U.S. Government Printing Office, March 1994, p. 4. *Notes:* "CMSA" stands for "Consolidated Metropolitan Statistical Area." "MSA" stands for "Metropolitan Statistical Area." "PMSA" stands for "Primary Metropolitan Statistical Area."

★746★

Housing Construction

Quarterly Construction of Housing Units, 1993, Selected Areas: Units Completed

Data refer to authorized construction in permit-issuing places for the fourth quarter of 1993. One-family houses are included in the totals.

[In thousands]

MSA	Units	Rank
Anaheim-Santa Ana, CA PMSA	2.0	4
Colorado Springs, CO MSA	0.7	10
Jacksonville, FL MSA	2.1	3
New Orleans, LA MSA	1.0	9
New York, NY PMSA	1.6	6
Norfolk-Virginia Beach-Newport News, VA MSA	2.3	1
Sacramento, CA MSA	2.2	2
San Antonio, TX MSA	1.3	7
San Diego, CA MSA	1.7	5
Tucson, AZ MSA	1.2	8

Source: U.S. Department of Commerce, Economics and Statistics Administration, Bureau of the Census, *New Residential Construction in Selected Metropolitan Areas, Fourth Quarter 1993*, Current Construction Reports, C21/93-Q4, Washington, D.C.: U.S. Government Printing Office, March 1994, p. 4. *Notes:* "CMSA" stands for "Consolidated Metropolitan Statistical Area." "MSA" stands for "Metropolitan Statistical Area." "PMSA" stands for "Primary Metropolitan Statistical Area."

★747★

Housing Construction

Quarterly Construction of Housing Units, 1993, Selected Areas: Units Started

Data refer to authorized construction in permit-issuing places for the fourth quarter of 1993. One-family houses are included in the totals.

[In thousands]

MSA	Units	Rank
Anaheim-Santa Ana, CA PMSA	1.2	8
Colorado Springs, CO MSA	0.8	10
Fort Lauderdale-Hollywood-Pompano Beach, FL PMSA	2.5	2
Jacksonville, FL MSA	1.7	5
Los Angeles-Long Beach, CA PMSA	1.5	6
New Orleans, LA MSA	1.0	9
New York, NY PMSA	1.3	7
Norfolk-Virginia Beach-Newport News, VA MSA	2.0	4
Sacramento, CA MSA	2.2	3
Saint Louis, MO-IL MSA	2.6	1

Source: U.S. Department of Commerce, Economics and Statistics Administration, Bureau of the Census, *New Residential Construction in Selected Metropolitan Areas, Fourth Quarter 1993*, Current Construction Reports, C21/93-Q4, Washington, D.C.: U.S. Government Printing Office, March 1994, p. 4. *Notes:* "CMSA" stands for "Consolidated Metropolitan Statistical Area." "MSA" stands for "Metropolitan Statistical Area." "PMSA" "Primary Metropolitan Statistical Area."

★748★

Housing Construction

Quarterly Construction of Housing Units, 1993, Selected Areas: Units Started

Data refer to authorized construction in permit-issuing places for the fourth quarter of 1993. One-family houses are included in the totals.

[In thousands]

MSA	Units	Rank
Atlanta, GA MSA	8.5	2
Chicago, IL PMSA	4.2	10
Chicago-Gary-Lake County, IL-IN-WI CMSA	9.0	1
Dallas, TX PMSA	4.5	9
Dallas-Fort Worth, TX CMSA	6.0	5
Las Vegas, NV MSA	5.1	7
Minneapolis-Saint Paul, MN-WI MSA	4.9	8
New York-Northern New Jersey-Long Island, NY-NJ-CT CMSA	6.6	4
Phoenix, AZ MSA	6.7	3
Washington, DC-MD-VA MSA	5.9	6

Source: U.S. Department of Commerce, Economics and Statistics Administration, Bureau of the Census, *New Residential Construction in Selected Metropolitan Areas, Fourth Quarter 1993*, Current Construction Reports, C21/93-Q4, Washington, D.C.: U.S. Government Printing Office, March 1994, p. 4. *Notes:* "CMSA" stands for "Consolidated Metropolitan Statistical Area." "MSA" stands for "Metropolitan Statistical Area." "PMSA" "Primary Metropolitan Statistical Area."

★749★

Housing Construction

Quarterly Construction of Housing Units, 1993, Selected Areas: Units Under Construction At End of Period

Data refer to authorized construction in permit-issuing places for the fourth quarter of 1993. One-family houses are included in the totals.

[In thousands]

MSA	Units	Rank
Anaheim-Santa Ana, CA PMSA	4.1	1
Colorado Springs, CO MSA	1.4	10
Jacksonville, FL MSA	1.8	8
New Orleans, LA MSA	1.5	9
Norfolk-Virginia Beach-Newport News, VA MSA	3.9	2
Orlando, FL MSA	3.6	4
Sacramento, CA MSA	3.7	3
San Antonio, TX MSA	2.5	7
San Diego, CA MSA	3.4	5
Tucson, AZ MSA	3.1	6

Source: U.S. Department of Commerce, Economics and Statistics Administration, Bureau of the Census, *New Residential Construction in Selected Metropolitan Areas, Fourth Quarter 1993*, Current Construction Reports, C21/93-Q4, Washington, D.C.: U.S. Government Printing Office, March 1994, p. 4. *Notes:* "CMSA" stands for "Consolidated Metropolitan Statistical Area." "MSA" stands for "Metropolitan Statistical Area." "PMSA" stands for "Primary Metropolitan Statistical Area."

★750★

Housing Construction

Quarterly Construction of Housing Units, 1993, Selected Areas: Units Under Construction At End of Period

Data refer to authorized construction in permit-issuing places for the fourth quarter of 1993. One-family houses are included in the totals.

[In thousands]

MSA	Units	Rank
Atlanta, GA MSA	12.8	5
Chicago-Gary-Lake County, IL-IN-WI CMSA	17.3	3
Dallas-Fort Worth, TX CMSA	9.9	9
Las Vegas, NV MSA	8.7	10
Los Angeles-Anaheim-Riverside, CA CMSA	19.6	2
Miami-Fort Lauderdale, FL CMSA	13.5	4
New York-Northern New Jersey-Long Island, NY-NJ-CT CMSA	28.9	1
Phoenix, AZ MSA	10.4	8
Seattle-Tacoma, WA CMSA	10.5	7
Washington, DC-MD-VA MSA	11.0	6

Source: U.S. Department of Commerce, Economics and Statistics Administration, Bureau of the Census, *New Residential Construction in Selected Metropolitan Areas, Fourth Quarter 1993*, Current Construction Reports, C21/93-Q4, Washington, D.C.: U.S. Government Printing Office, March 1994, p. 4. *Notes:* "CMSA" stands for "Consolidated Metropolitan Statistical Area." "MSA" stands for "Metropolitan Statistical Area." "PMSA" stands for "Primary Metropolitan Statistical Area."

★751★

Housing Construction

Quarterly Construction of One-Family Houses, 1993, Selected Areas: Houses Completed

Data refer to authorized construction in permit-issuing places for the fourth quarter of 1993.

[In thousands]

MSA	Houses	Rank
Atlanta, GA MSA	7.3	3
Chicago, IL PMSA	4.2	10
Chicago-Gary-Lake County, IL-IN-WI CMSA	9.1	1
Dallas-Fort Worth, TX CMSA	4.8	8
Las Vegas, NV MSA	4.9	7
Los Angeles-Anaheim-Riverside, CA CMSA	7.4	2
Minneapolis-Saint Paul, MN-WI MSA	4.6	9
New York-Northern New Jersey-Long Island, NY-NJ-CT CMSA	5.6	5
Phoenix, AZ MSA	5.2	6
Washington, DC-MD-VA MSA	6.0	4

Source: U.S. Department of Commerce, Economics and Statistics Administration, Bureau of the Census, *New Residential Construction in Selected Metropolitan Areas, Fourth Quarter 1993,* Current Construction Reports, C21/93-Q4, Washington, D.C.: U.S. Government Printing Office, March 1994, p. 4. *Notes:* "CMSA" stands for "Consolidated Metropolitan Statistical Area." "PMSA" stands for "Primary Metropolitan Statistical Area." "MSA" stands for "Metropolitan Statistical Area."

★752★

Housing Construction

Quarterly Construction of One-Family Houses, 1993, Selected Areas: Houses Completed

Data refer to authorized construction in permit-issuing places for the fourth quarter of 1993.

[In thousands]

MSA	Houses	Rank
Anaheim-Santa Ana, CA PMSA	1.3	7
Colorado Springs, CO MSA	0.7	10
Fort Lauderdale-Hollywood-Pompano Beach, FL PMSA	2.2	1
Jacksonville, FL MSA	2.0	3
Los Angeles-Long Beach, CA PMSA	1.5	6
Miami-Hialeah, FL PMSA	1.6	5
New Orleans, LA MSA	1.0	9
Orlando, FL MSA	2.1	2
San Antonio, TX MSA	1.2	8
Seattle, WA PMSA	1.9	4

Source: U.S. Department of Commerce, Economics and Statistics Administration, Bureau of the Census, *New Residential Construction in Selected Metropolitan Areas, Fourth Quarter 1993,* Current Construction Reports, C21/93-Q4, Washington, D.C.: U.S. Government Printing Office, March 1994, p. 4. *Notes:* "CMSA" stands for "Consolidated Metropolitan Statistical Area." "PMSA" stands for "Primary Metropolitan Statistical Area." "MSA" stands for "Metropolitan Statistical Area."

★753★

Housing Construction

Quarterly Construction of One-Family Houses, 1993, Selected Areas: Houses Started

Data refer to authorized construction in permit-issuing places during the fourth quarter of 1993.

[In thousands]

MSA	Houses	Rank
Atlanta, GA MSA	7.4	2
Chicago, IL PMSA	3.5	10
Chicago-Gary-Lake County, IL-IN-WI CMSA	7.9	1
Dallas-Fort Worth, TX CMSA	4.9	7
Las Vegas, NV MSA	4.0	9
Los Angeles-Anaheim-Riverside, CA CMSA	5.2	5
Minneapolis-Saint Paul, MN-WI MSA	4.1	8
New York-Northern New Jersey-Long Island, NY-NJ-CT CMSA	5.3	4
Phoenix, AZ MSA	5.6	3
Washington, DC-MD-VA MSA	5.0	6

Source: U.S. Department of Commerce, Economics and Statistics Administration, Bureau of the Census, *New Residential Construction in Selected Metropolitan Areas, Fourth Quarter 1993,* Current Construction Reports, C21/93-Q4, Washington, D.C.: U.S. Government Printing Office, March 1994, p. 4. *Notes:* "CMSA" stands for "Consolidated Metropolitan Statistical Area." "PMSA" stands for "Primary Metropolitan Statistical Area." "MSA" stands for "Metropolitan Statistical Area."

★754★

Housing Construction

Quarterly Construction of One-Family Houses, 1993, Selected Areas: Houses Started

Data refer to authorized construction in permit-issuing places during the fourth quarter of 1993.

[In thousands]

MSA	Houses	Rank
Anaheim-Santa Ana, CA PMSA	1.0	9
Charlotte-Gastonia-Rock Hill, NC-SC MSA	2.2	1
Colorado Springs, CO MSA	0.8	10
Jacksonville, FL MSA	1.7	5
Norfolk-Virginia Beach-Newport News, VA MSA	1.6	6
Orlando, FL MSA	2.0	3
Sacramento, CA MSA	2.1	2
Salt Lake City-Ogden, UT MSA	1.5	7
San Antonio, TX MSA	1.4	8
Seattle, WA PMSA	1.9	4

Source: U.S. Department of Commerce, Economics and Statistics Administration, Bureau of the Census, *New Residential Construction in Selected Metropolitan Areas, Fourth Quarter 1993,* Current Construction Reports, C21/93-Q4, Washington, D.C.: U.S. Government Printing Office, March 1994, p. 4. *Notes:* "CMSA" stands for "Consolidated Metropolitan Statistical Area." "PMSA" stands for "Primary Metropolitan Statistical Area." "MSA" stands for "Metropolitan Statistical Area."

★755★

Housing Construction

Quarterly Construction of One-Family Houses, 1993, Selected Areas: Houses Under Construction At End of Period

Data refer to authorized construction in permit-issuing places during the fourth quarter of 1993.

[In thousands]

MSA	Houses	Rank
Anaheim-Santa Ana, CA PMSA	2.3	6
Colorado Springs, CO MSA	1.4	9
Jacksonville, FL MSA	1.5	8
Los Angeles-Long Beach, CA PMSA	2.7	3
New Orleans, LA MSA	1.3	10
New York, NY PMSA	2.5	5
Orlando, FL MSA	2.6	4
Sacramento, CA MSA	3.3	1
San Antonio, TX MSA	2.0	7
Tucson, AZ MSA	2.9	2

Source: U.S. Department of Commerce, Economics and Statistics Administration, Bureau of the Census, *New Residential Construction in Selected Metropolitan Areas, Fourth Quarter 1993*, Current Construction Reports, C21/93-Q4, Washington, D.C.: U.S. Government Printing Office, March 1994, p. 4. *Notes:* "CMSA" stands for "Consolidated Metropolitan Statistical Area." "PMSA" stands for "Primary Metropolitan Statistical Area." "MSA" stands for "Metropolitan Statistical Area."

★756★

Housing Construction

Quarterly Construction of One-Family Houses, 1993, Selected Areas: Houses Under Construction At End of Period

Data refer to authorized construction in permit-issuing places during the fourth quarter of 1993.

[In thousands]

MSA	Houses	Rank
Atlanta, GA MSA	11.1	4
Chicago-Gary-Lake County, IL-IN-WI CMSA	12.5	2
Dallas-Fort Worth, TX CMSA	6.8	8
Denver-Boulder, CO CMSA	6.4	10
Los Angeles-Anaheim-Riverside, CA CMSA	12.4	3
Miami-Fort Lauderdale, FL CMSA	8.7	6
New York-Northern New Jersey-Long Island, NY-NJ-CT CMSA	19.2	1
Phoenix, AZ MSA	8.6	7
Riverside-San Bernardino, CA PMSA	6.7	9
Washington, DC-MD-VA MSA	9.1	5

Source: U.S. Department of Commerce, Economics and Statistics Administration, Bureau of the Census, *New Residential Construction in Selected Metropolitan Areas, Fourth Quarter 1993*, Current Construction Reports, C21/93-Q4, Washington, D.C.: U.S. Government Printing Office, March 1994, p. 4. *Notes:* "CMSA" stands for "Consolidated Metropolitan Statistical Area." "PMSA" stands for "Primary Metropolitan Statistical Area." "MSA" stands for "Metropolitan Statistical Area."

★757★

Housing Construction

Quarterly Construction of One-Family Houses, 1993, Selected Areas: Total Houses Authorized

Data refer to authorized construction in permit-issuing places during the fourth quarter of 1993.

[In thousands]

MSA	Houses	Rank
Anaheim-Santa Ana, CA PMSA	1.1	7
Colorado Springs, CO MSA	0.9	9
Jacksonville, FL MSA	1.6	4
Los Angeles-Long Beach, CA PMSA	1.0	8
New Orleans, LA MSA	0.8	10
Norfolk-Virginia Beach-Newport News, VA MSA	1.8	3
Sacramento, CA MSA	1.9	2
San Diego, CA MSA	1.4	6
Seattle, WA PMSA	2.0	1
West Palm Beach-Boca Raton-Delray Beach, FL MSA	1.5	5

Source: U.S. Department of Commerce, Economics and Statistics Administration, Bureau of the Census, *New Residential Construction in Selected Metropolitan Areas, Fourth Quarter 1993*, Current Construction Reports, C21/93-Q4, Washington, D.C.: U.S. Government Printing Office, March 1994, p. 4. *Notes:* "CMSA" stands for "Consolidated Metropolitan Statistical Area." "MSA" stands for "Metropolitan Statistical Area." "PMSA" stands for "Primary Metropolitan Statistical Area."

★758★

Housing Construction

Quarterly Construction of One-Family Houses, 1993, Selected Areas: Total Houses Authorized

Data refer to authorized construction in permit-issuing places during the fourth quarter of 1993.

[In thousands]

MSA	Houses	Rank
Atlanta, GA MSA	8.0	1
Chicago-Gary-Lake County, IL-IN-WI CMSA	7.4	2
Dallas-Fort Worth, TX CMSA	5.0	7
Las Vegas, NV MSA	4.0	8
Los Angeles-Anaheim-Riverside, CA CMSA	5.3	6
Miami-Fort Lauderdale, FL CMSA	3.6	10
Minneapolis-Saint Paul, MN-WI MSA	3.9	9
New York-Northern New Jersey-Long Island, NY-NJ-CT CMSA	6.4	3
Phoenix, AZ MSA	6.2	4
Washington, DC-MD-VA MSA	5.7	5

Source: U.S. Department of Commerce, Economics and Statistics Administration, Bureau of the Census, *New Residential Construction in Selected Metropolitan Areas, Fourth Quarter 1993*, Current Construction Reports, C21/93-Q4, Washington, D.C.: U.S. Government Printing Office, March 1994, p. 4. *Notes:* "CMSA" stands for "Consolidated Metropolitan Statistical Area." "MSA" stands for "Metropolitan Statistical Area." "PMSA" stands for "Primary Metropolitan Statistical Area."

★759★
Housing Construction

Quarterly Construction of One-Family Housing Units, 1993, Selected Areas: Units Authorized But Not Started At End of Period

Data refer to authorized construction in permit-issuing places during the fourth quarter of 1993.

[In thousands]

MSA	Houses	Rank
Anaheim-Santa Ana, CA PMSA	0.3	10
Charlotte-Gastonia-Rock Hill, NC-SC MSA	0.6	7
Chicago-Gary-Lake County, IL-IN-WI CMSA	1.4	1
Dallas-Fort Worth, TX CMSA	0.9	4
Denver, CO PMSA	0.4	9
Los Angeles-Long Beach, CA PMSA	0.5	8
Miami-Hialeah, FL PMSA	1.0	3
Phoenix, AZ MSA	1.3	2
Saint Louis, MO-IL MSA	0.7	6
San Diego, CA MSA	0.8	5

Source: U.S. Department of Commerce, Economics and Statistics Administration, Bureau of the Census, *New Residential Construction in Selected Metropolitan Areas, Fourth Quarter 1993*, Current Construction Reports, C21/93-Q4, Washington, D.C.: U.S. Government Printing Office, March 1994, p. 4. *Notes:* "CMSA" stands for "Consolidated Metropolitan Statistical Area." "PMSA" stands for "Primary Metropolitan Statistical Area." "MSA" stands for "Metropolitan Statistical Area."

★760★
Housing Construction

Quarterly Construction of One-Family Housing Units, 1993, Selected Areas: Units Authorized But Not Started At End of Period

Data refer to authorized construction in permit-issuing places during the fourth quarter of 1993.

[In thousands]

MSA	Houses	Rank
Atlanta, GA MSA	1.8	5
Baltimore, MD MSA	2.6	3
Chicago-Gary-Lake County, IL-IN-WI CMSA	1.4	8
Fort Lauderdale-Hollywood-Pompano Beach, FL PMSA	1.6	6
Los Angeles-Anaheim-Riverside, CA CMSA	1.9	4
Miami-Hialeah, FL PMSA	1.0	10
New York-Northern New Jersey-Long Island, NY-NJ-CT CMSA	7.6	1
Phoenix, AZ MSA	1.3	9
Seattle-Tacoma, WA CMSA	1.5	7
Washington, DC-MD-VA MSA	5.4	2

Source: U.S. Department of Commerce, Economics and Statistics Administration, Bureau of the Census, *New Residential Construction in Selected Metropolitan Areas, Fourth Quarter 1993*, Current Construction Reports, C21/93-Q4, Washington, D.C.: U.S. Government Printing Office, March 1994, p. 4. *Notes:* "CMSA" stands for "Consolidated Metropolitan Statistical Area." "PMSA" stands for "Primary Metropolitan Statistical Area." "MSA" stands for "Metropolitan Statistical Area."

★761★
Occupancy

Apartment Occupancy, 1996: Areas With the Highest Rates

City	Rate	Rank
San Jose, CA	99.6	1
Newark, NJ	99.4	2
San Francisco, CA	98.9	3
Middlesex, NJ	98.3	4
Salt Lake City, UT	96.7	5
Oakland, CA	96.5	6
Richmond, VA	96.4	7
Jacksonville, FL	96.0	8
Portland, OR	95.9	9
Seattle, WA	95.9	10

Source: "No Vacancies," *Wall Street Journal*, 21 June 1996, p. B12. Primary source: M/PF Research, Inc., Dallas, Texas.

★762★
Vacancies

Vacancy Rates In Selected Markets, 1996, By Type: Downtown Areas

[In percentages]

City	Downtown	Rank
Albuquerque, NM	20.7	4
Atlanta, GA	7.9	17
Charleston, SC	15.9	10
Charlotte, NC	13.1	12
Chattanooga, TN	30.0	1
Chicago, IL	5.0	21
Cincinnati, OH	18.6	8
Cleveland, OH	10.0	15
Dallas, TX	18.0	9
Denver, CO	21.0	3
Detroit, MI	20.4	5
Fort Worth, TX	15.0	11
Honolulu, HI	4.9	22
Houston, TX	13.0	13
Las Vegas, NV	4.0	23
Long Island, NY	20.0	6
Los Angeles County, CA	25.0	2
Manchester, NH	10.0	15
Miami, FL	2.5	24
Minneapolis, MN	19.1	7
New Orleans, LA	11.0	14
Omaha, NE	8.0	16
Orange County, CA	10.0	15
Phoenix, AZ	8.0	16
Saint Louis, MO	7.0	18
Salt Lake City, UT	5.4	20
San Francisco, CA	6.56	19
Seattle, WA	10.0	15
Springfield, MA	30.0	1

Source: "Will Virtual Vacancy Belie the Numbers?" *Chain Store Age*, (May 1996), p. 72. Primary source: New America Network 1996 Real Estate Planning Guide.

★763★

Vacancies

Vacancy Rates In Selected Markets, 1996, By Type: Neighborhood Centers

[In percentages].

City	Neighborhood centers	Rank
Albuquerque, NM	9.5	10
Atlanta, GA	9.8	9
Buffalo, NY	12.0	5
Charleston, SC	12.0	5
Charlotte, NC	8.8	12
Chattanooga, TN	9.0	11
Chicago, IL	14.0	4
Cincinnati, OH	8.0	14
Cleveland, OH	11.3	6
Dallas, TX	14.1	3
Denver, CO	6.0	18
Detroit, MI	5.2	19
Fort Worth, TX	15.0	2
Honolulu, HI	7.8	15
Houston, TX	14.0	4
Las Vegas, NV	9.0	11
Long Island, NY	10.0	8
Los Angeles, CA	10.0	8
Manchester, NH	8.0	14
Miami, FL	7.7	16
Minneapolis, MN	10.1	7
New Orleans, LA	8.0	14
Omaha, NE	8.4	13
Orange County, CA	7.5	17
Phoenix, AZ	6.0	18
Salt Lake City, UT	3.9	22
Seattle, WA	4.3	21
Springfield, MA	25.0	1
St. Louis, MO	5.0	20

Source: "Will Virtual Vacancy Belie the Numbers?" *Chain Store Age,* (May 1996), p. 72. Primary source: New America Network 1996 Real Estate Planning Guide.

★764★

Vacancies

Vacancy Rates In Selected Markets, 1996, By Type: Power Centers

[In percentages]

City	Power centers	Rank
Albuquerque, NM	1.08	19
Atlanta, GA	21.4	1
Buffalo, NY	10.0	5
Charleston, SC	10.0	5
Charlotte, NC	4.3	13
Chicago, IL	8.0	8
Cincinnati, OH	5.0	12
Cleveland, OH	5.9	10
Dallas, TX	12.4	4
Denver, CO	10.0	5
Detroit, MI	8.5	7
Fort Worth, TX	10.0	5
Honolulu, HI	15.4	3

[Continued]

★764★

Vacancy Rates In Selected Markets, 1996, By Type: Power Centers

[Continued]

City	Power centers	Rank
Houston, TX	15.9	2
Las Vegas, NV	6.0	9
Long Island, NY	3.0	16
Los Angeles, CA	5.0	12
Manchester, NH	6.0	9
Miami, FL	5.1	11
Minneapolis, MN	8.9	6
New Orleans, LA	5.0	12
Omaha, NE	4.2	14
Orange County, CA	6.0	9
Phoenix, AZ	2.0	18
Salt Lake City, UT	3.3	15
Seattle, WA	2.5	17
Springfield, MA	10.0	5
St. Louis, MO	3.0	16

Source: "Will Virtual Vacancy Belie the Numbers?" *Chain Store Age,* (May 1996), p. 72. Primary source: New America Network 1996 Real Estate Planning Guide.

★765★

Vacancies

Vacancy Rates In Selected Markets, 1996, By Type: Regional Malls

[In percentages].

City	Regional malls	Rank
Albuquerque, NM	0.8	18
Atlanta, GA	2.7	15
Charleston, SC	10.0	4
Charlotte, NC	1.8	17
Chattanooga, TN	5.0	10
Chicago, IL	15.0	1
Cincinnati, OH	5.0	10
Cleveland, OH	10.0	4
Dallas, TX	6.4	8
Denver, CO	3.4	13
Detroit, MI	7.0	7
Honolulu, HI	0.4	19
Houston, TX	12.5	3
Las Vegas, NV	4.0	11
Los Angeles, CA	10.0	4
Manchester, NH	5.0	10
Minneapolis, MN	5.7	9
New Orleans, LA	8.0	6
Omaha, NE	13.5	2
Orange County, CA	8.5	5
Phoenix, AZ	2.0	16
Salt Lake City, UT	3.8	12
Seattle, WA	3.0	14
Springfield, MA	8.0	6
St. Louis, MO	4.0	11

Source: "Will Virtual Vacancy Belie the Numbers?" *Chain Store Age,* (May 1996), p. 72. Primary source: New America Network 1996 Real Estate Planning Guide.

★766★
Vacancies
Homeowner Vacancy Rates, 1993: Highest

Data refer to 18 of the 61 largest metropolitan areas.

[In percentages]

City	1993	Rank
Atlanta, GA	1.9	10
Baltimore, MD	2.2	8
Dayton-Springfield, OH	2.2	8
Fort Lauderdale-Hollywood-Pompano Beach, FL	3.1	2
Fort Worth-Arlington, TX	2.5	5
Houston, TX	2.0	9
Indianapolis, IN	2.2	8
Jacksonville, FL	2.8	3
Middlesex-Somerset-Hunterdon, NJ	2.2	8
New York, NY	2.7	4
Oklahoma City, OK	2.2	8
Orlando, FL	2.8	3
Saint Louis, MO-IL	2.4	6
San Bernardino-Riverside, CA	2.5	5
San Diego, CA	2.3	7
San Francisco, CA	1.8	11
Tampa-Saint Petersburg-Clearwater, FL	3.4	1
Washington, DC-MD-VA	2.5	5

Source: Callis, Robert R., *Housing Vacancies and Homeownership, Annual Statistics: 1993*, U.S. Bureau of the Census, Current Housing Reports, Series H111/93-A, Washington, D.C.: U.S. Government Printing Office, 1994, p. 20.

★767★
Vacancies
Homeowner Vacancy Rates, 1993: Lowest

Data refer to 17 of the 61 largest metropolitan areas.

[In percentages]

City	1993	Rank
Boston, MA	0.8	6
Cincinnati, OH-KY-IN	0.9	7
Cleveland, OH	0.7	5
Detroit, MI	0.9	7
Hartford, CT	0.7	5
Kansas City, MO-KS	0.6	4
Memphis, TN-AR-MS	0.8	6
Nashville, TN	0.7	5
Nassau-Suffolk, NY	0.7	5
New York, NY	2.7	4
Portland, OR	0.1	1
Rochester, NY	0.9	7
Sacramento, CA	0.8	6
Salt Lake City-Ogden, UT	0.4	2
San Antonio, TX	0.5	3
San Jose, CA	0.7	5
Seattle, WA	0.9	7

Source: Callis, Robert R., *Housing Vacancies and Homeownership, Annual Statistics: 1993*, U.S. Bureau of the Census, Current Housing Reports, Series H111/93-A, Washington, D.C.: U.S. Government Printing Office, 1994, p. 20.

★768★
Vacancies
Rental Vacancy Rates, 1993: Highest

Data refer to 10 of the 61 largest metropolitan areas.

[In percentages]

City	1993	Rank
Dallas, TX	10.7	6
Houston, TX	12.0	5
Indianapolis, IN	9.8	10
Kansas City, MO-KS	13.2	3
Louisville, KY-IN	15.3	2
Norfolk-Virginia Beach-Newport News, VA	10.4	7
Oklahoma City, OK	21.2	1
Orlando, FL	10.7	6
Philadelphia, PA-NJ	12.3	4
Richmond-Petersburg, VA	10.1	9
Sacramento, CA	10.3	8
San Bernardino-Riverside, CA	10.3	8

Source: Callis, Robert R., *Housing Vacancies and Homeownership, Annual Statistics: 1993*, U.S. Bureau of the Census, Current Housing Reports, Series H111/93-A, Washington, D.C.: U.S. Government Printing Office, 1994, p. 19.

★769★
Vacancies
Rental Vacancy Rates, 1993: Lowest

Data refer to 10 of the 61 largest metropolitan areas.

[In percentages]

City	1993	Rank
Buffalo, NY	5.4	10
Denver, CO	4.9	6
Honolulu, HI	3.9	4
Miami-Hialeah, FL	3.6	3
Minneapolis-Saint Paul, MN-WI	5.2	9
New York, NY	5.0	7
Oakland, CA	4.5	5
Pittsburgh, PA	5.1	8
Salt Lake City-Ogden, UT	2.9	1
San Antonio, TX	3.5	2

Source: Callis, Robert R., *Housing Vacancies and Homeownership, Annual Statistics: 1993*, U.S. Bureau of the Census, Current Housing Reports, Series H111/93-A, Washington, D.C.: U.S. Government Printing Office, 1994, p. 19.

PART III

EDUCATION AND CULTURE

Contents

Chapter 9

EDUCATION

Topics Covered

Degrees Conferred
Enrollment
Finances and Expenditures
Teachers

★770★
Degrees Conferred

Associate's Degrees Conferred at College and University Campuses Enrolling More Than 14,600 Students: 1991-92

Table includes data for publicly and privately controlled 2- and 4-year institutions.

Institution	Earned degrees conferred 1991-92 associate	Rank
Community College of the Air Force	10,000	1
Miami-Dade Community College	5,019	2
Nassau Community College	3,139	3
Macomb Community College	2,704	4
Saint Petersburg Junior College	2,578	5
Northern Virginia Community College	2,191	6
Saint Louis Community College, Forest Park	2,023	7
Oakland Community College	1,970	8
Community College of Allegheny County	1,948	9
Florida Community College, Jacksonville	1,897	10
Valencia Community College	1,879	11
Broward Community College	1,814	12
Hillsborough Community College	1,755	13
College of Du Page	1,719	14
Palm Beach Community College	1,624	15
Lansing Community College	1,525	16
Cuyahoga Community College District	1,490	17
University of Florida	1,411	18
Community College of Rhode Island	1,393	19
Tarrant County Junior College District	1,346	20
Milwaukee Area Technical College	1,313	21
William Rainey Harper College	1,290	22
City College of San Francisco	1,289	23
CUNY, Borough of Manhattan Community College	1,264	24
Sinclair Community College	1,228	25

Source: U.S. Department of Education, Office of Educational Research and Improvement, National Center for Education Statistics, *Digest of Education Statistics 1994*, NCES 94-115, Lanham, Maryland: Bernan 1995, p. 218. *Notes:* - Data not available or not applicable. Data are shown only for the top 25 areas.

★771★
Degrees Conferred

Associate's Degrees Conferred at Historically Black Colleges and Universities: Fall 1992

Table includes data for publicly and privately controlled 2- and 4-year institutions.

Institution	Enrollment, 1992 associate	Rank
Alabama A&M University, AL[1]	1	35
Alabama State University, AL	4	34
Albany State College, GA	-	36
Alcorn State University, MS	28	24
Allen University, SC	-	36
Arkansas Baptist College, AR	-	36
Barber-Scotia College, NC	-	36
Benedict College, SC	-	36
Bennett College, NC	-	36
Bethune-Cookman College, FL	-	36
Bishop State Community College, AL	197	5
Bluefield State College, WV	222	2
Bowie State University, MD	-	36
C.A. Fredd State Technical College, AL	-	36
Carver State Technical College, AL	37	19
Central State University, OH	4	34
Cheyney University of Pennsylvania, PA	-	36
Clafin College, SC	-	36
Clark Atlanta University, GA	-	36
Clinton Junior College, SC[2]	-	36
Coahoma Community College, MS	142	6
Concordia College, AL	45	18
Coppin State College, MD	-	36
Delaware State College, DE	-	36
Denmark Technical College, SC	75	12
Dillard University, LA	-	36
Edward Waters College, FL	-	36
Elizabeth City State University, NC	-	36
Fayetteville State University, NC	17	27
Fisk University, TN	-	36
Florida A&M University, FL[1]	11	31
Florida Memorial College, FL	-	36
Fort Valley State College, GA[1]	1	35
Grambling State University, LA	57	16
Hampton University, VA	-	36
Harris-Stowe State College, MO	-	36
Hinds Community College, Utica Campus, MS	92	11
Howard University, DC	-	36
Huston-Tilotson College, TX	-	36
Interdenominational Theological Center, GA	-	36
J.F. Drake Technical College, AL	32	22
Jackson State University, MS	-	36
Jarvis Christian College, TX	-	36
Johnson C. Smith University, NC	-	36
Kentucky State University, KY[1]	72	13

[Continued]

★771★

Associate's Degrees Conferred at Historically Black Colleges and Universities: Fall 1992

[Continued]

Institution	Enrollment, 1992 associate	Rank
Knoxville College, TN	35	21
Lane College, TN	-	36
Langston University, OK[1]	-	36
Lawson State Community College, AL	102	9
Le Moyne-Owen College, TN	-	36
Lewis College of Business, MI	29	23
Lincoln University, MO[1]	99	10
Lincoln University, PA	-	36
Livingstone College, NC	-	36
Mary Holmes College, MS	105	8
Meharry Medical College, TN	-	36
Miles College, AL	-	36
Mississippi Valley State University, MS	-	36
Morehouse College, GA	-	36
Morehouse School of Medicine, GA	-	36
Morgan State University, MD	-	36
Morris Brown College, GA	-	36
Morris College, SC	-	36
Norfolk State University, VA	58	15
North Carolina Agricultural and Technical	-	36
North Carolina Central University, NC	-	36
Oakwood College, AL	16	28
Paine College, GA	-	36
Paul Quinn College, TX	-	36
Philander Smith College, AR	-	36
Prairie View A&M University, TX[1]	-	36
Rust College, MS	-	36
Savannah State College, GA	1	35
Selma University, AL	6	32
Shaw University, NC	15	29
Shorter College, AR	13	30
South Carolina State College, SC[1]	-	36
Southern University and A&M College, Baton Rouge, LA[1]	27	25
Southern University, New Orleans, LA	36	20
Southern University, Shreveport-Bossier City Campus, LA	63	14
Southwestern Christian College, TX	36	20
Spelman College, GA	-	36
St. Augustine's College, NC	-	36
St. Paul's College, VA	-	36
St. Phillip's College, TX	220	3
Stillman College, AL	-	36
Talladega College, AL	-	36

[Continued]

★771★

Associate's Degrees Conferred at Historically Black Colleges and Universities: Fall 1992

[Continued]

Institution	Enrollment, 1992 associate	Rank
Tennessee State University, TN[1]	219	4
Texas College, TX	-	36
Texas Southern University, TX	-	36
Tougaloo College, MS	5	33
Trenholm College, AL	24	26
Tuskegee University, AL[1]	-	36
University of Arkansas, Pine Bluff, AR[1]	-	36
University of Maryland, Eastern Shore, MD[1]	-	36
University of the District of Columbia, DC[1]	225	1
University of the Virgin Islands, St. Thomas Campus, VI[1]	47	17
Virginia State University, VA[1]	-	36
Virginia Union University, VA	-	36
Voorhees College, SC	1	35
West Virginia State College, WV	141	7
Wilberforce University, OH	-	36
Wiley College, TX	-	36
Winston-Salem State University, NC	-	36
Xavier University of Louisiana, LA	-	36
State University, NC[1]	-	36

Source: U.S. Department of Education, Office of Educational Research and Improvement, National Center for Education Statistics, *Digest of Education Statistics 1994,* NCES 94-115, Lanham, Maryland: Bernan 1995, p. 225. Primary source: U.S. Department of Education, National Center for Education Statistics, Integrated Postsecondary Education Data System (IPEDS), "Fall Enrollment, 1992," "Completions, 1991-92," and "Finance, 1991-92," surveys. Table prepared June 1994. *Notes:* - Data not reported or not applicable. 1. Land-grant institution. 2. Lost accreditation.

★772★

Degrees Conferred

Bachelor's Degrees Conferred at College and University Campuses Enrolling More Than 14,600 Students: 1991-92

Table includes data for publicly and privately controlled 2- and 4-year institutions.

Institution	Earned degrees conferred 1991-92 bachelor's	Rank
Pennsylvania State U., Main Campus	8,361	1
Michigan State University	7,706	2
University of Texas, Austin	7,666	3
Ohio State University, Main Campus	7,214	4

[Continued]

★772★

Bachelor's Degrees Conferred at College and University Campuses Enrolling More Than 14,600 Students: 1991-92

[Continued]

Institution	Earned degrees conferred 1991-92 bachelor's	Rank
Texas A&M University	6,929	5
University of Wisconsin, Madison	6,345	6
University of Illinois, Urbana Campus	6,175	7
Arizona State University	6,012	8
University of California, Berkeley	5,999	9
Purdue University, Main Campus	5,726	10
University of California, Los Angeles	5,726	10
Florida State University	5,587	11
U. of Maryland, College Park Campus	5,563	12
San Diego Mesa College	5,532	13
University of Florida	5,459	14
University of Minnesota, Twin Cities	5,441	15
Indiana University, Bloomington	5,404	16
University of Washington	5,372	17
Unviersity of Michigan, Ann Arbor	5,341	18
Bringham Young University	5,326	19
Rutgers University, New Brunswick	5,232	20
University of South Florida	4,816	21
Southern Illinois University, Carbondale	4,759	22
California State University, Long Beach	4,674	23
University of Arizona	4,587	24

Source: U.S. Department of Education, Office of Educational Research and Improvement, National Center for Education Statistics, *Digest of Education Statistics 1994*, NCES 94-115, Lanham, Maryland: Bernan 1995, p. 218. *Notes:* - Data not available or not applicable. Data are shown only for the top 25 areas.

★773★

Degrees Conferred

Bachelor's Degrees Conferred at Historically Black Colleges and Universities: Fall 1992

Table includes data for publicly and privately controlled 2- and 4-year institutions.

Institution	Enrollment, 1992 bachelor's	Rank
Alabama A&M University, AL[1]	380	22
Alabama State University, AL	242	40
Albany State College, GA	247	39
Alcorn State University, MS	289	31
Allen University, SC	-	78
Arkansas Baptist College, AR	31	75

[Continued]

★773★

Bachelor's Degrees Conferred at Historically Black Colleges and Universities: Fall 1992

[Continued]

Institution	Enrollment, 1992 bachelor's	Rank
Barber-Scotia College, NC	56	71
Benedict College, SC	180	49
Bennett College, NC	79	64
Bethune-Cookman College, FL	253	38
Bishop State Community College, AL	-	78
Bluefield State College, WV	282	33
Bowie State University, MD	307	29
C.A. Fredd State Technical College, AL	-	78
Carver State Technical College, AL	-	78
Central State University, OH	289	31
Cheyney University of Pennsylvania, PA	148	51
Clafin College, SC	113	58
Clark Atlanta University, GA	360	23
Clinton Junior College, SC[2]	-	78
Coahoma Community College, MS	-	78
Concordia College, AL	-	78
Coppin State College, MD	235	41
Delaware State College, DE	260	36
Denmark Technical College, SC	-	78
Dillard University, LA	199	47
Edward Waters College, FL	98	60
Elizabeth City State University, NC	327	27
Fayetteville State University, NC	350	25
Fisk University, TN	160	50
Florida A&M University, FL[1]	847	4
Florida Memorial College, FL	266	34
Fort Valley State College, GA[1]	231	42
Grambling State University, LA	565	10
Hampton University, VA	912	2
Harris-Stowe State College, MO	68	67
Hinds Community College, Utica Campus, MS	-	78
Howard University, DC	1,328	1
Huston-Tilotson College, TX	68	67
Interdenominational Theological Center, GA	-	78
J.F. Drake Technical College, AL	-	78
Jackson State University, MS	639	7
Jarvis Christian College, TX	61	68
Johnson C. Smith University, NC	262	35
Kentucky State University, KY[1]	146	52
Knoxville College, TN	60	69
Lane College, TN	60	69
Langston University, OK[1]	415	17
Lawson State Community College, AL	-	78
Le Moyne-Owen College, TN	100	59

[Continued]

★773★

Bachelor's Degrees Conferred at Historically Black Colleges and Universities: Fall 1992
[Continued]

Institution	Enrollment, 1992 bachelor's	Rank
Lewis College of Business, MI	-	78
Lincoln University, MO[1]	259	37
Lincoln University, PA	207	45
Livingstone College, NC	59	70
Mary Holmes College, MS	-	78
Meharry Medical College, TN	-	78
Miles College, AL	76	65
Mississippi Valley State University, MS	206	46
Morehouse College, GA	448	15
Morehouse School of Medicine, GA	-	78
Morgan State University, MD	515	12
Morris Brown College, GA	89	62
Morris College, SC	135	54
Norfolk State University, VA	659	6
North Carolina Agricultural and Technical		78
North Carolina Central University, NC	509	13
Oakwood College, AL	148	51
Paine College, GA	59	70
Paul Quinn College, TX	68	67
Philander Smith College, AR	52	73
Prairie View A&M University, TX[1]	576	9
Rust College, MS	142	53
Savannah State College, GA	218	43
Selma University, AL	9	76
Shaw University, NC	288	32
Shorter College, AR	-	78
South Carolina State College, SC[1]	555	11
Southern University and A&M College, Baton Rouge, LA[1]	848	3
Southern University, New Orleans, LA	306	30
Southern University, Shreveport-Bossier City Campus, LA	-	78
Southwestern Christian College, TX	6	77
Spelman College, GA	358	24
St. Augustine's College, NC	186	48
St. Paul's College, VA	55	72
St. Phillip's College, TX	-	78
Stillman College, AL	114	57
Talladega College, AL	76	65
Tennessee State University, TN[1]	634	8
Texas College, TX	32	74
Texas Southern University, TX	407	19
Tougaloo College, MS	87	63
Trenholm College, AL	-	78

[Continued]

★773★

Bachelor's Degrees Conferred at Historically Black Colleges and Universities: Fall 1992
[Continued]

Institution	Enrollment, 1992 bachelor's	Rank
Tuskegee University, AL[1]	413	18
University of Arkansas, Pine Bluff, AR[1]	321	28
University of Maryland, Eastern Shore, MD[1]	217	44
University of the District of Columbia, DC[1]	500	14
University of the Virgin Islands, St. Thomas Campus, VI[1]	117	56
Virginia State University, VA[1]	423	16
Virginia Union University, VA	125	55
Voorhees College, SC	71	66
West Virginia State College, WV	396	20
Wilberforce University, OH	95	61
Wiley College, TX	31	75
Winston-Salem State University, NC	390	21
Xavier University of Louisiana, LA	343	26
State University, NC[1]	838	5

Source: U.S. Department of Education, Office of Educational Research and Improvement, National Center for Education Statistics, *Digest of Education Statistics 1994,* NCES 94-115, Lanham, Maryland: Bernan 1995, p. 225. Primary source: U.S. Department of Education, National Center for Education Statistics, Integrated Postsecondary Education Data System (IPEDS), "Fall Enrollment, 1992," "Completions, 1991-92," and "Finance, 1991-92," surveys. Table prepared June 1994. *Notes:* - Data not reported or not applicable. 1. Land-grant institution. 2. Lost accreditation.

★774★

Degrees Conferred

Doctoral Degrees Conferred at College and University Campuses Enrolling More Than 14,600 Students: 1991-92

Table includes data for publicly and privately controlled 2- and 4-year institutions.

Institution	Earned degrees conferred 1991-92 doctor's	Rank
University of California, Berkeley	798	1
University of Illinois, Urbana Campus	775	2
University of Wisconsin, Madison	680	3
Unviersity of Michigan, Ann Arbor	676	4
Ohio State University, Main Campus	671	5
University of Texas, Austin	671	5
University of Minnesota, Twin Cities	651	6
Columbia University, New York	630	7

[Continued]

★774★

Doctoral Degrees Conferred at College and University Campuses Enrolling More Than 14,600 Students: 1991-92

[Continued]

Institution	Earned degrees conferred 1991-92 doctor's	Rank
University of California, Los Angeles	613	8
Stanford University	569	9
Pennsylvania State U., Main Campus	541	10
U. of Maryland, College Park Campus	506	11
Harvard University	501	12
Purdue University, Main Campus	478	13
University of Pennsylvania	477	14
Michigan State University	476	15
Texas A&M University	472	16
University of Massachusetts at Amherst	409	17
New York University	404	18
Rutgers University, New Brunswick	402	19
Indiana University, Bloomington	398	20
University of Washington	396	21
University of Iowa	380	22
Virginia Polytechnic Inst. and State University	366	23
University of Florida	364	24

Source: U.S. Department of Education, Office of Educational Research and Improvement, National Center for Education Statistics, *Digest of Education Statistics 1994*, NCES 94-115, Lanham, Maryland: Bernan 1995, p. 218. *Notes:* - Data not available or not applicable. Data are shown only for the top 25 areas.

★775★
Degrees Conferred

Doctorates Conferred at Historically Black Colleges and Universities: Fall 1992

Table includes data for publicly and privately controlled 2- and 4-year institutions.

Institution	Enrollment, 1992 doctor's	Rank
Alabama A&M University, AL[1]	1	9
Alabama State University, AL	-	10
Albany State College, GA	-	10
Alcorn State University, MS	-	10
Allen University, SC	-	10
Arkansas Baptist College, AR	-	10
Barber-Scotia College, NC	-	10
Benedict College, SC	-	10
Bennett College, NC	-	10
Bethune-Cookman College, FL	-	10
Bishop State Community College, AL	-	10

[Continued]

Institution	Enrollment, 1992 doctor's	Rank
Bluefield State College, WV	-	10
Bowie State University, MD	-	10
C.A. Fredd State Technical College, AL	-	10
Carver State Technical College, AL	-	10
Central State University, OH	-	10
Cheyney University of Pennsylvania, PA	-	10
Clafin College, SC	-	10
Clark Atlanta University, GA	40	2
Clinton Junior College, SC[2]	-	10
Coahoma Community College, MS	-	10
Concordia College, AL	-	10
Coppin State College, MD	-	10
Delaware State College, DE	-	10
Denmark Technical College, SC	-	10
Dillard University, LA	-	10
Edward Waters College, FL	-	10
Elizabeth City State University, NC	-	10
Fayetteville State University, NC	-	10
Fisk University, TN	-	10
Florida A&M University, FL[1]	2	8
Florida Memorial College, FL	-	10
Fort Valley State College, GA[1]	-	10
Grambling State University, LA	1	9
Hampton University, VA	-	10
Harris-Stowe State College, MO	-	10
Hinds Community College, Utica Campus, MS	-	10
Howard University, DC	72	1
Huston-Tilotson College, TX	-	10
Interdenominational Theological Center, GA	3	7
J.F. Drake Technical College, AL	-	10
Jackson State University, MS	8	5
Jarvis Christian College, TX	-	10
Johnson C. Smith University, NC	-	10
Kentucky State University, KY[1]	-	10
Knoxville College, TN	-	10
Lane College, TN	-	10
Langston University, OK[1]	-	10
Lawson State Community College, AL	-	10
Le Moyne-Owen College, TN	-	10
Lewis College of Business, MI	-	10
Lincoln University, MO[1]	-	10
Lincoln University, PA	-	10
Livingstone College, NC	-	10
Mary Holmes College, MS	-	10
Meharry Medical College, TN	8	5

[Continued]

★775★

Doctorates Conferred at Historically Black Colleges and Universities: Fall 1992

[Continued]

Institution	Enrollment, 1992 doctor's	Rank
Miles College, AL	-	10
Mississippi Valley State University, MS	-	10
Morehouse College, GA	-	10
Morehouse School of Medicine, GA	-	10
Morgan State University, MD	7	6
Morris Brown College, GA	-	10
Morris College, SC	-	10
Norfolk State University, VA	-	10
North Carolina Agricultural and Technical		10
North Carolina Central University, NC	-	10
Oakwood College, AL	-	10
Paine College, GA	-	10
Paul Quinn College, TX	-	10
Philander Smith College, AR	-	10
Prairie View A&M University, TX[1]	-	10
Rust College, MS	-	10
Savannah State College, GA	-	10
Selma University, AL	-	10
Shaw University, NC	-	10
Shorter College, AR	-	10
South Carolina State College, SC[1]	8	5
Southern University and A&M College, Baton Rouge, LA[1]	1	9
Southern University, New Orleans, LA	-	10
Southern University, Shreveport-Bossier City Campus, LA	-	10
Southwestern Christian College, TX	-	10
Spelman College, GA	-	10
St. Augustine's College, NC	-	10
St. Paul's College, VA	-	10
St. Phillip's College, TX	-	10
Stillman College, AL	-	10
Talladega College, AL	-	10
Tennessee State University, TN[1]	34	3
Texas College, TX	19	4
Texas Southern University, TX	-	10
Tougaloo College, MS	-	10
Trenholm College, AL	-	10
Tuskegee University, AL[1]	-	10
University of Arkansas, Pine Bluff, AR[1]	-	10
University of Maryland, Eastern Shore, MD[1]	1	9
University of the District of Columbia, DC[1]	-	10

[Continued]

★775★

Doctorates Conferred at Historically Black Colleges and Universities: Fall 1992

[Continued]

Institution	Enrollment, 1992 doctor's	Rank
University of the Virgin Islands, St. Thomas Campus, VI[1]	-	10
Virginia State University, VA[1]	-	10
Virginia Union University, VA	-	10
Voorhees College, SC	-	10
West Virginia State College, WV	-	10
Wilberforce University, OH	-	10
Wiley College, TX	-	10
Winston-Salem State University, NC	-	10
Xavier University of Louisiana, LA	-	10
State University, NC[1]	-	10

Source: U.S. Department of Education, Office of Educational Research and Improvement, National Center for Education Statistics, *Digest of Education Statistics 1994*, NCES 94-115, Lanham, Maryland: Bernan 1995, p. 225. Primary source: U.S. Department of Education, National Center for Education Statistics, Integrated Postsecondary Education Data System (IPEDS), "Fall Enrollment, 1992," "Completions, 1991-92," and "Finance, 1991-92," surveys. Table prepared June 1994. *Notes:* - Data not reported or not applicable. 1. Land-grant institution. 2. Lost accreditation.

★776★

Degrees Conferred

First Professional Degrees Conferred at College and University Campuses Enrolling More Than 14,600 Students: 1991-92

Table includes data for publicly and privately controlled 2- and 4-year institutions.

Institution	Earned degrees conferred 1991-92 first professional	Rank
Arizona State University	146	64
Auburn University, Main Campus	81	76
Boston University	654	7
Bringham Young University	150	63
Cleveland State University	308	32
Colorado State University	127	67
Columbia University, New York	543	12
De Paul University	289	35
East Carolina University	70	79
Florida State University	164	59
George Mason University	186	52
George Washington University	590	11
Georgia State University	167	57
Harvard University	765	2
Indiana U. - Purdue U. at Indianapolis	543	12
Indiana University, Bloomington	261	41
Iowa State University	65	80

[Continued]

★776★

★776★

First Professional Degrees Conferred at College and University Campuses Enrolling More Than 14,600 Students: 1991-92
[Continued]

Institution	Earned degrees conferred 1991-92 first professional	Rank
Kansas State U. of Agr. and App. Sci.	91	72
La. St. U. & A&M Hebert Laws Center	296	33
Loyola University of Chicago	426	25
Memphis State University	128	66
Michigan State University	308	32
Mississippi State University	42	83
New York University	764	3
North Carolina State University, Raleigh	62	81
Northeastern University	178	54
Northern Illinois University	100	71
Northwestern University	434	24
Ohio State University, Main Campus	664	6
Ohio University, Main Campus	77	77
Oklahoma State University, Main Campus	51	82
Purdue University, Main Campus	82	75
Rutgers University, New Brunswick	10	85
SUNY at Buffalo	462	21
SUNY at Stony Brook	123	68
Saint John's University of New York	419	26
Southern Illinois University, Carbondale	155	61
Stanford University	258	42
Syracuse University, Main Campus	235	45
Temple University	624	9
Texas A&M University	156	60
Texas Tech. University	191	51
University of Akron, Main Campus	166	58
University of Alabama	178	54
University of Alabama at Birmingham	229	47
University of Arizona	277	39
University of California, Berkeley	341	30
University of California, Davis	374	27
University of California, Irvine	82	75
University of California, Los Angeles	533	13
University of California, San Diego	120	69
University of Cincinnati, Main Campus	279	38
University of Colorado at Boulder	151	62

[Continued]

First Professional Degrees Conferred at College and University Campuses Enrolling More Than 14,600 Students: 1991-92
[Continued]

Institution	Earned degrees conferred 1991-92 first professional	Rank
University of Connecticut	205	50
University of Florida	693	5
University of Georgia	288	36
University of Hawaii Manoa	116	70
University of Houston-University Park	486	17
University of Illinois at Chicago	464	20
University of Illinois, Urbana Campus	271	40
University of Iowa	502	16
University of Kansas, Main Campus	185	53
University of Kentucky	285	37
University of Louisville	295	34
University of Minnesota, Twin Cities	629	8
University of Missouri, Columbia	315	31
University of Missouri, Saint Louis	39	84
University of Nebraska, Lincoln	139	65
University of New Mexico, Main Campus	176	55
University of North Carolina, Chapel Hill	467	19
University of Oklahoma, Norman Campus	234	46
University of Oregon	155	61
University of Pennsylvania	608	10
University of Pittsburgh, Main Campus	439	23
University of Rhode Island	4	86
University of South Carolina, Columbia	343	29
University of South Florida	89	73
University of Southern California	1,064	1
University of Tennessee, Knoxville	215	48
University of Texas, Austin	511	15
University of Toledo	169	56
University of Utah	214	49
University of Virginia, Main Campus	516	14
University of Washington	356	28
University of Wisconsin, Madison	470	18
Unversity of Michigan, Ann Arbor	724	4
Virginia Commonwealth University	239	44
Virginia Polytechnic Inst. and State University	76	78

[Continued]

★776★

First Professional Degrees Conferred at College and University Campuses Enrolling More Than 14,600 Students: 1991-92

[Continued]

Institution	Earned degrees conferred 1991-92 first professional	Rank
Washington State University	88	74
Wayne State University	461	22
West Virginia University	242	43
Wright State University, Main Campus	82	75

Source: U.S. Department of Education, Office of Educational Research and Improvement, National Center for Education Statistics, *Digest of Education Statistics 1994*, NCES 94-115, Lanham, Maryland: Bernan 1995, p. 218.

★777★

Degrees Conferred

First Professional Degrees Conferred at Historically Black Colleges and Universities: Fall 1992

Table includes data for publicly and privately controlled 2- and 4-year institutions.

Institution	Enrollment, 1992 first professional	Rank
Alabama A&M University, AL[1]	-	12
Alabama State University, AL	-	12
Albany State College, GA	-	12
Alcorn State University, MS	-	12
Allen University, SC	-	12
Arkansas Baptist College, AR	-	12
Barber-Scotia College, NC	-	12
Benedict College, SC	-	12
Bennett College, NC	-	12
Bethune-Cookman College, FL	-	12
Bishop State Community College, AL	-	12
Bluefield State College, WV	-	12
Bowie State University, MD	-	12
C.A. Fredd State Technical College, AL	-	12
Carver State Technical College, AL	-	12
Central State University, OH	-	12
Cheyney University of Pennsylvania, PA	-	12
Clafin College, SC	-	12
Clark Atlanta University, GA	-	12
Clinton Junior College, SC[2]	-	12
Coahoma Community College, MS	-	12
Concordia College, AL	-	12

[Continued]

★777★

First Professional Degrees Conferred at Historically Black Colleges and Universities: Fall 1992

[Continued]

Institution	Enrollment, 1992 first professional	Rank
Coppin State College, MD	-	12
Delaware State College, DE	-	12
Denmark Technical College, SC	-	12
Dillard University, LA	-	12
Edward Waters College, FL	-	12
Elizabeth City State University, NC	-	12
Fayetteville State University, NC	-	12
Fisk University, TN	-	12
Florida A&M University, FL[1]	10	9
Florida Memorial College, FL	-	12
Fort Valley State College, GA[1]	-	12
Grambling State University, LA	-	12
Hampton University, VA	-	12
Harris-Stowe State College, MO	-	12
Hinds Community College, Utica Campus, MS	-	12
Howard University, DC	179	1
Huston-Tilotson College, TX	-	12
Interdenominational Theological Center, GA	52	6
J.F. Drake Technical College, AL	-	12
Jackson State University, MS	-	12
Jarvis Christian College, TX	-	12
Johnson C. Smith University, NC	-	12
Kentucky State University, KY[1]	-	12
Knoxville College, TN	-	12
Lane College, TN	-	12
Langston University, OK[1]	-	12
Lawson State Community College, AL	-	12
Le Moyne-Owen College, TN	-	12
Lewis College of Business, MI	-	12
Lincoln University, MO[1]	-	12
Lincoln University, PA	-	12
Livingstone College, NC	5	11
Mary Holmes College, MS	-	12
Meharry Medical College, TN	62	5
Miles College, AL	-	12
Mississippi Valley State University, MS	-	12
Morehouse College, GA	-	12
Morehouse School of Medicine, GA	19	8
Morgan State University, MD	-	12
Morris Brown College, GA	-	12
Morris College, SC	-	12
Norfolk State University, VA	-	12
North Carolina Agricultural and Technical		12
North Carolina Central University, NC	97	4

[Continued]

★777★

First Professional Degrees Conferred at Historically Black Colleges and Universities: Fall 1992

[Continued]

Institution	Enrollment, 1992 first professional	Rank
Oakwood College, AL	-	12
Paine College, GA	-	12
Paul Quinn College, TX	-	12
Philander Smith College, AR	-	12
Prairie View A&M University, TX[1]	-	12
Rust College, MS	-	12
Savannah State College, GA	-	12
Selma University, AL	-	12
Shaw University, NC	-	12
Shorter College, AR	-	12
South Carolina State College, SC[1]	-	12
Southern University and A&M College, Baton Rouge, LA[1]	110	3
Southern University, New Orleans, LA	-	12
Southern University, Shreveport-Bossier City Campus, LA	-	12
Southwestern Christian College, TX	-	12
Spelman College, GA	-	12
St. Augustine's College, NC	-	12
St. Paul's College, VA	-	12
St. Phillip's College, TX	-	12
Stillman College, AL	-	12
Talladega College, AL	-	12
Tennessee State University, TN[1]	-	12
Texas College, TX	-	12
Texas Southern University, TX	166	2
Tougaloo College, MS	-	12
Trenholm College, AL	-	12
Tuskegee University, AL[1]	50	7
University of Arkansas, Pine Bluff, AR[1]	-	12
University of Maryland, Eastern Shore, MD[1]	-	12
University of the District of Columbia, DC[1]	-	12
University of the Virgin Islands, St. Thomas Campus, VI[1]	-	12
Virginia State University, VA[1]	-	12
Virginia Union University, VA	-	12
Voorhees College, SC	-	12
West Virginia State College, WV	-	12
Wilberforce University, OH	-	12
Wiley College, TX	-	12
Winston-Salem State University, NC	-	12

[Continued]

★777★

First Professional Degrees Conferred at Historically Black Colleges and Universities: Fall 1992

[Continued]

Institution	Enrollment, 1992 first professional	Rank
Xavier University of Louisiana, LA	6	10
State University, NC[1]	-	12

Source: U.S. Department of Education, Office of Educational Research and Improvement, National Center for Education Statistics, *Digest of Education Statistics 1994*, NCES 94-115, Lanham, Maryland: Bernan 1995, p. 225. Primary source: U.S. Department of Education, National Center for Education Statistics, Integrated Postsecondary Education Data System (IPEDS), "Fall Enrollment, 1992," "Completions, 1991-92," and "Finance, 1991-92," surveys. Table prepared June 1994. *Notes:* - Data not reported or not applicable. 1. Land-grant institution. 2. Lost accreditation.

★778★

Degrees Conferred

Master's Degrees Conferred at College and University Campuses Enrolling More Than 14,600 Students: 1991-92

Table includes data for publicly and privately controlled 2- and 4-year institutions.

Institution	Earned degrees conferred 1991-92 master's	Rank
New York University	4,324	1
Columbia University, New York	4,259	2
Harvard University	2,949	3
Unviersity of Michigan, Ann Arbor	2,759	4
Boston University	2,511	5
University of Illinois, Urbana Campus	2,305	6
University of California, Santa Barbara	2,266	7
University of California, Irvine	2,216	8
University of Texas, Austin	2,197	9
Ohio State University, Main Campus	2,193	10
University of Minnesota, Twin Cities	2,142	11
Central Michigan University	2,052	12
University of Pennsylvania	2,016	13
University of Delaware	2,014	14
University of Wisconsin, Madison	1,993	15
Northwestern University	1,986	16
Wayne State University	1,974	17
University of Washington	1,932	18
University of Pittsburgh, Main Campus	1,913	19
Stanford University	1,845	20
University of South Carolina, Columbia	1,832	21

[Continued]

★778★

Master's Degrees Conferred at College and University Campuses Enrolling More Than 14,600 Students: 1991-92

[Continued]

Institution	Earned degrees conferred 1991-92 master's	Rank
Michigan State University	1,743	22
Southwestern College	1,727	23
Indiana University, Bloomington	1,694	24
Syracuse University, Main Campus	1,592	25

Source: U.S. Department of Education, Office of Educational Research and Improvement, National Center for Education Statistics, *Digest of Education Statistics 1994*, NCES 94-115, Lanham, Maryland: Bernan 1995, p. 218. *Notes:* - Data not available or not applicable. Data are shown only for the top 25 areas.

★779★

Degrees Conferred

Master's Degrees Conferred at Historically Black Colleges and Universities: Fall 1992

Table includes data for publicly and privately controlled 2- and 4-year institutions.

Institution	Enrollment, 1992 master's	Rank
Alabama A&M University, AL[1]	304	1
Alabama State University, AL	104	16
Albany State College, GA	52	28
Alcorn State University, MS	60	25
Allen University, SC	-	37
Arkansas Baptist College, AR	-	37
Barber-Scotia College, NC	-	37
Benedict College, SC	-	37
Bennett College, NC	-	37
Bethune-Cookman College, FL	-	37
Bishop State Community College, AL	-	37
Bluefield State College, WV	-	37
Bowie State University, MD	258	4
C.A. Fredd State Technical College, AL	-	37
Carver State Technical College, AL	-	37
Central State University, OH	-	37
Cheyney University of Pennsylvania, PA	94	19
Clafin College, SC	-	37
Clark Atlanta University, GA	278	2
Clinton Junior College, SC[2]	-	37
Coahoma Community College, MS	-	37
Concordia College, AL	-	37
Coppin State College, MD	62	24
Delaware State College, DE	59	26
Denmark Technical College, SC	-	37

[Continued]

★779★

Master's Degrees Conferred at Historically Black Colleges and Universities: Fall 1992

[Continued]

Institution	Enrollment, 1992 master's	Rank
Dillard University, LA	-	37
Edward Waters College, FL	-	37
Elizabeth City State University, NC	-	37
Fayetteville State University, NC	105	15
Fisk University, TN	10	34
Florida A&M University, FL[1]	97	18
Florida Memorial College, FL	-	37
Fort Valley State College, GA[1]	54	27
Grambling State University, LA	132	12
Hampton University, VA	78	21
Harris-Stowe State College, MO	-	37
Hinds Community College, Utica Campus, MS	-	37
Howard University, DC	269	3
Huston-Tilotson College, TX	-	37
Interdenominational Theological Center, GA	-	37
J.F. Drake Technical College, AL	-	37
Jackson State University, MS	182	8
Jarvis Christian College, TX	-	37
Johnson C. Smith University, NC	-	37
Kentucky State University, KY[1]	25	31
Knoxville College, TN	-	37
Lane College, TN	-	37
Langston University, OK[1]	7	35
Lawson State Community College, AL	-	37
Le Moyne-Owen College, TN	-	37
Lewis College of Business, MI	-	37
Lincoln University, MO[1]	60	25
Lincoln University, PA	85	20
Livingstone College, NC	-	37
Mary Holmes College, MS	-	37
Meharry Medical College, TN	13	33
Miles College, AL	-	37
Mississippi Valley State University, MS	3	36
Morehouse College, GA	-	37
Morehouse School of Medicine, GA	-	37
Morgan State University, MD	106	14
Morris Brown College, GA	-	37
Morris College, SC	-	37
Norfolk State University, VA	129	13
North Carolina Agricultural and Technical		37
North Carolina Central University, NC	165	9
Oakwood College, AL	-	37
Paine College, GA	-	37
Paul Quinn College, TX	-	37
Philander Smith College, AR	-	37

[Continued]

★779★

Master's Degrees Conferred at Historically Black Colleges and Universities: Fall 1992

[Continued]

Institution	Enrollment, 1992 master's	Rank
Prairie View A&M University, TX[1]	184	7
Rust College, MS	-	37
Savannah State College, GA	10	34
Selma University, AL	-	37
Shaw University, NC	-	37
Shorter College, AR	-	37
South Carolina State College, SC[1]	66	23
Southern University and A&M College, Baton Rouge, LA[1]	151	10
Southern University, New Orleans, LA	41	29
Southern University, Shreveport-Bossier City Campus, LA	-	37
Southwestern Christian College, TX	-	37
Spelman College, GA	-	37
St. Augustine's College, NC	-	37
St. Paul's College, VA	-	37
St. Phillip's College, TX	-	37
Stillman College, AL	-	37
Talladega College, AL	-	37
Tennessee State University, TN[1]	151	10
Texas College, TX	-	37
Texas Southern University, TX	197	6
Tougaloo College, MS	-	37
Trenholm College, AL	-	37
Tuskegee University, AL[1]	52	28
University of Arkansas, Pine Bluff, AR[1]	-	37
University of Maryland, Eastern Shore, MD[1]	24	32
University of the District of Columbia, DC[1]	133	11
University of the Virgin Islands, St. Thomas Campus, VI[1]	38	30
Virginia State University, VA[1]	76	22
Virginia Union University, VA	-	37
Voorhees College, SC	-	37
West Virginia State College, WV	-	37
Wilberforce University, OH	-	37
Wiley College, TX	-	37
Winston-Salem State University, NC	-	37
Xavier University of Louisiana, LA	101	17
State University, NC[1]	207	5

Source: U.S. Department of Education, Office of Educational Research and Improvement, National Center for Education Statistics, *Digest of Education Statistics 1994,* NCES 94-115, Lanham, Maryland: Bernan 1995, p. 225. Primary source: U.S. Department of Education, National Center for Education Statistics, Integrated Postsecondary Education Data System (IPEDS), "Fall Enrollment, 1992," "Completions, 1991-92," and "Finance, 1991-92," surveys. Table prepared June 1994. *Notes:* - Data not reported or not applicable. 1. Land-grant institution. 2. Lost accreditation.

★780★

Degrees Conferred

Where Most Adults Aged 25 Years and Older Have a Minimum of A Bachelor's Degree, 1995

Data refer to adults residing in locations with a minimum of 2500 persons.

[In percentages]

City	Most educated places	Rank
Stanford, CA	90.9	1
Chevy Chase, MD	80.2	2
Winnetka, IL	79.2	3
Scarsdale, NY	74.7	4
Portola Valley, CA	74.1	5

Source: "USA's Most Educational Places," USA SNAPSHOTS, *USA TODAY,* 26 December, 1995, p. 1A. Primary source: *101 Smartest Spots,* G. Scott Thomas analysis for *American Demographics.*

★781★

Enrollment

Black Enrollment in Historically Black Colleges and Universities: Fall 1992

Table includes data for publicly and privately controlled 2- and 4-year institutions.

Institution	Enrollment, 1992 black	Rank
Alabama A&M University, AL[1]	4,006	19
Alabama State University, AL	5,380	10
Albany State College, GA	2,632	29
Alcorn State University, MS	2,751	27
Allen University, SC	221	100
Arkansas Baptist College, AR	307	97
Barber-Scotia College, NC	690	76
Benedict College, SC	2,310	33
Bennett College, NC	611	82
Bethune-Cookman College, FL	2,226	35
Bishop State Community College, AL	1,566	45
Bluefield State College, WV	189	101
Bowie State University, MD	3,230	22
C.A. Fredd State Technical College, AL	305	98
Carver State Technical College, AL	369	93
Central State University, OH	2,854	26
Cheyney University of Pennsylvania, PA	1,456	51
Clafin College, SC	1,031	62
Clark Atlanta University, GA	4,221	18
Clinton Junior College, SC[2]	-	105
Coahoma Community College, MS	841	70
Concordia College, AL	345	95
Coppin State College, MD	2,693	28
Delaware State College, DE	1,823	41
Denmark Technical College, SC	572	85

[Continued]

★781★

Black Enrollment in Historically Black Colleges and Universities: Fall 1992
[Continued]

Institution	Enrollment, 1992 black	Rank
Dillard University, LA	1,504	46
Edward Waters College, FL	591	83
Elizabeth City State University, NC	1,489	48
Fayetteville State University, NC	2,444	31
Fisk University, TN	857	69
Florida A&M University, FL[1]	8,394	5
Florida Memorial College, FL	1,269	55
Fort Valley State College, GA[1]	2,354	32
Grambling State University, LA	7,120	7
Hampton University, VA	4,912	12
Harris-Stowe State College, MO	1,490	47
Hinds Community College, Utica Campus, MS	933	64
Howard University, DC	9,188	3
Huston-Tilotson College, TX	438	91
Interdenominational Theological Center, GA	357	94
J.F. Drake Technical College, AL	393	92
Jackson State University, MS	5,832	9
Jarvis Christian College, TX	587	84
Johnson C. Smith University, NC	1,272	54
Kentucky State University, KY[1]	1,263	56
Knoxville College, TN	904	66
Lane College, TN	532	88
Langston University, OK[1]	1,699	43
Lawson State Community College, AL	1,975	38
Le Moyne-Owen College, TN	1,201	57
Lewis College of Business, MI	319	96
Lincoln University, MO[1]	1,041	61
Lincoln University, PA	1,361	52
Livingstone College, NC	670	77
Mary Holmes College, MS	715	75
Meharry Medical College, TN	553	87
Miles College, AL	749	73
Mississippi Valley State University, MS	2,199	36
Morehouse College, GA	2,932	25
Morehouse School of Medicine, GA	136	104
Morgan State University, MD	5,015	11
Morris Brown College, GA	1,955	40
Morris College, SC	790	72
Norfolk State University, VA	7,234	6
North Carolina Agricultural and Technical		105
North Carolina Central University, NC	4,751	15
Oakwood College, AL	1,153	58
Paine College, GA	663	78
Paul Quinn College, TX	914	65
Philander Smith College, AR	818	71

[Continued]

★781★

Black Enrollment in Historically Black Colleges and Universities: Fall 1992
[Continued]

Institution	Enrollment, 1992 black	Rank
Prairie View A&M University, TX[1]	4,894	13
Rust College, MS	1,066	60
Savannah State College, GA	2,575	30
Selma University, AL	284	99
Shaw University, NC	2,307	34
Shorter College, AR	139	103
South Carolina State College, SC[1]	4,744	16
Southern University and A&M College, Baton Rouge, LA[1]	9,773	1
Southern University, New Orleans, LA	4,307	17
Southern University, Shreveport-Bossier City Campus, LA	962	63
Southwestern Christian College, TX	183	102
Spelman College, GA	1,973	39
St. Augustine's College, NC	1,737	42
St. Paul's College, VA	640	80
St. Phillip's College, TX	1,352	53
Stillman College, AL	872	67
Talladega College, AL	869	68
Tennessee State University, TN[1]	4,779	14
Texas College, TX	519	89
Texas Southern University, TX	8,950	4
Tougaloo College, MS	1,131	59
Trenholm College, AL	563	86
Tuskegee University, AL[1]	3,335	21
University of Arkansas, Pine Bluff, AR[1]	3,004	23
University of Maryland, Eastern Shore, MD[1]	1,675	44
University of the District of Columbia, DC[1]	9,614	2
University of the Virgin Islands, St. Thomas Campus, VI[1]	1,466	50
Virginia State University, VA[1]	4,001	20
Virginia Union University, VA	1,479	49
Voorhees College, SC	662	79
West Virginia State College, WV	624	81
Wilberforce University, OH	734	74
Wiley College, TX	510	90
Winston-Salem State University, NC	2,124	37
Xavier University of Louisiana, LA	2,997	24
State University, NC[1]	6,534	8

Source: U.S. Department of Education, Office of Educational Research and Improvement, National Center for Education Statistics, *Digest of Education Statistics 1994*, NCES 94-115, Lanham, Maryland: Bernan 1995, p. 225. Primary source: U.S. Department of Education, National Center for Education Statistics, Integrated Postsecondary Education Data System (IPEDS), "Fall Enrollment, 1992," "Completions, 1991-92," and "Finance, 1991-92," surveys. Table prepared June 1994. *Notes:* - Data not reported or not applicable. 1. Land-grant institution. 2. Lost accreditation.

★782★

Enrollment

Enrollment at College and University Campuses Enrolling More Than 14,000 Students: Fall 1991 and 1992

Table includes data for publicly and privately controlled 2- and 4-year institutions.

Institution	Total enrollment, fall 1992	Rank
University of Minnesota, Twin Cities	54,671	1
Ohio State University, Main Campus	52,179	2
Miami-Dade Community College	51,768	3
University of Texas, Austin	49,253	4
Arizona State University	43,628	5
University of Wisconsin, Madison	41,824	6
Texas A&M University	41,710	7
Michigan State University	39,138	8
Pennsylvania State U., Main Campus	38,446	9
University of Illinois, Urbana Campus	38,396	10
Northern Virginia Community College	38,343	11
Purdue University, Main Campus	37,746	12
Houston Community College System	37,410	13
University of Florida	36,447	14
Indiana University, Bloomington	36,071	15
University of Michigan, Ann Arbor	35,476	16
University of California, Los Angeles	35,403	17
University of Arizona	35,118	18
Wayne State University	34,945	19
University of Washington	34,597	20
Community College of the Air Force	34,294	21
University of South Florida	34,145	22
New York University	33,695	23
Rutgers University, New Brunswick	33,577	24
University of Houston-University Park	33,022	25

Source: U.S. Department of Education, Office of Educational Research and Improvement, National Center for Education Statistics, *Digest of Education Statistics 1994*, NCES 94-115, Lanham, Maryland: Bernan 1995, p. 218. *Note:* Data are shown only for the top 25 areas.

★783★

Enrollment

Enrollment at the Largest College and University Campuses: Fall 1992

Table includes data for publicly and privately controlled 2- and 4-year institutions.

Institution	Total enrollment fall 1992	Rank
University of Minnesota, Twin Cities	54,671	1
Ohio State University, Main Campus	52,179	2
Miami-Dade Community College	51,768	3
University of Texas, Austin	49,253	4
Arizona State University	43,628	5
University of Wisconsin, Madison	41,824	6
Texas A&M University	41,710	7
Michigan State University	39,138	8
Pennsylvania State U, Main Campus	38,446	9
University of Illinois, Urbana Campus	38,396	10
Northern Virginia Community College	38,343	11
Purdue University, Main Campus	37,746	12
Houston Community College System	37,410	13
University of Florida	36,447	14
Indiana University, Bloomington	36,071	15
University of Michigan, Ann Arbor	35,476	16
University of California, Los Angeles	35,403	17
University of Arizona	35,118	18
Wayne State University	34,945	19
University of Washington	34,597	20
Community College of the Air Force	34,294	21
University of South Florida	34,145	22
New York University	33,695	23
Rutgers University, New Brunswick	33,577	24
University of Houston-University Park	33,022	25

Source: U.S. Department of Education, Office of Educational Research and Improvement, National Center for Education Statistics, *Digest of Education Statistics 1994*, NCES 94-115, Lanham, Maryland: Bernan 1995, p. 217. Primary source: U.S. Department of Education. National Center for Education Statistics, Integrated Postsecondary Education Data System (IPEDS), "Fall Enrollment, 1992" survey. Table prepared May 1994. *Note:* Data are shown only for the top 25 areas.

★784★
Enrollment
Enrollment in Historically Black Colleges and Universities, Fall 1992: Total Enrollment

Table includes data for publicly and privately controlled 2- and 4-year institutions.

Institution	Enrollment, 1992 total	Rank
Alabama A&M University, AL[1]	5,068	18
Alabama State University, AL	5,488	15
Albany State College, GA	3,106	31
Alcorn State University, MS	2,919	36
Allen University, SC	228	96
Arkansas Baptist College, AR	311	94
Barber-Scotia College, NC	705	78
Benedict College, SC	2,414	44
Bennett College, NC	635	83
Bethune-Cookman College, FL	2,301	45
Bishop State Community College, AL	2,757	38
Bluefield State College, WV	2,931	35
Bowie State University, MD	4,809	19
C.A. Fredd State Technical College, AL	330	92
Carver State Technical College, AL	400	89
Central State University, OH	3,236	30
Cheyney University of Pennsylvania, PA	1,548	54
Clafin College, SC	1,040	64
Clark Atlanta University, GA	4,480	22
Clinton Junior College, SC[2]	-	100
Coahoma Community College, MS	851	73
Concordia College, AL	356	91
Coppin State College, MD	2,944	33
Delaware State College, DE	2,936	34
Denmark Technical College, SC	597	85
Dillard University, LA	1,511	55
Edward Waters College, FL	627	84
Elizabeth City State University, NC	2,019	50
Fayetteville State University, NC	3,902	25
Fisk University, TN	872	71
Florida A&M University, FL[1]	9,487	5
Florida Memorial College, FL	1,489	56
Fort Valley State College, GA[1]	2,537	41
Grambling State University, LA	7,533	9
Hampton University, VA	5,582	14
Harris-Stowe State College, MO	1,978	51
Hinds Community College, Utica Campus, MS	983	65
Howard University, DC	10,667	3
Huston-Tilotson College, TX	536	87
Interdenominational Theological Center, GA	382	90
J.F. Drake Technical College, AL	870	72
Jackson State University, MS	6,203	10
Jarvis Christian College, TX	597	85
Johnson C. Smith University, NC	1,278	59
Kentucky State University, KY[1]	2,541	40

[Continued]

★784★
Enrollment in Historically Black Colleges and Universities, Fall 1992: Total Enrollment
[Continued]

Institution	Enrollment, 1992 total	Rank
Knoxville College, TN	914	69
Lane College, TN	534	88
Langston University, OK[1]	3,315	28
Lawson State Community College, AL	2,041	48
Le Moyne-Owen College, TN	1,205	60
Lewis College of Business, MI	322	93
Lincoln University, MO[1]	4,030	24
Lincoln University, PA	1,476	57
Livingstone College, NC	677	81
Mary Holmes College, MS	790	75
Meharry Medical College, TN	681	79
Miles College, AL	751	76
Mississippi Valley State University, MS	2,213	46
Morehouse College, GA	2,990	32
Morehouse School of Medicine, GA	162	98
Morgan State University, MD	5,402	16
Morris Brown College, GA	2,094	47
Morris College, SC	792	74
Norfolk State University, VA	8,624	6
North Carolina Agricultural and Technical		100
North Carolina Central University, NC	5,681	12
Oakwood College, AL	1,334	58
Paine College, GA	680	80
Paul Quinn College, TX	934	67
Philander Smith College, AR	938	66
Prairie View A&M University, TX[1]	5,660	13
Rust College, MS	1,132	61
Savannah State College, GA	2,872	37
Selma University, AL	285	95
Shaw University, NC	2,483	42
Shorter College, AR	161	99
South Carolina State College, SC[1]	5,071	17
Southern University and A&M College, Baton Rouge, LA[1]	10,403	4
Southern University, New Orleans, LA	4,591	21
Southern University, Shreveport-Bossier City Campus, LA	1,067	63
Southwestern Christian College, TX	217	97
Spelman College, GA	2,026	49
St. Augustine's College, NC	1,918	52
St. Phillip's College, TX	6,166	11
Stillman College, AL	888	70
Tennessee State University, TN[1]	7,591	8

[Continued]

★784★

Enrollment in Historically Black Colleges and Universities, Fall 1992: Total Enrollment
[Continued]

Institution	Enrollment, 1992 total	Rank
Texas College, TX	543	86
Texas Southern University, TX	10,777	2
Tougaloo College, MS	1,131	62
Trenholm College, AL	918	68
Tuskegee University, AL[1]	3,598	27
University of Arkansas, Pine Bluff, AR[1]	3,709	26
University of Maryland, Eastern Shore, MD[1]	2,430	43
University of the District of Columbia, DC[1]	11,578	1
University of the Virgin Islands, St. Thomas Campus, VI[1]	1,856	53
Virginia State University, VA[1]	4,435	23
Virginia Union University, VA	1,511	55
Voorhees College, SC	665	82
West Virginia State College, WV	4,793	20
Wilberforce University, OH	750	77
Wiley College, TX	534	88
Winston-Salem State University, NC	2,728	39
Xavier University of Louisiana, LA	3,303	29
State University, NC[1]	7,723	7

Source: U.S. Department of Education, Office of Educational Research and Improvement, National Center for Education Statistics, *Digest of Education Statistics 1994*, NCES 94-115, Lanham, Maryland: Bernan 1995, p. 225. Primary source: U.S. Department of Education, National Center for Education Statistics, Integrated Postsecondary Education Data System (IPEDS), "Fall Enrollment, 1992," "Completions, 1991-92," and "Finance, 1991-92," surveys. Table prepared June 1994. *Notes:* - Data not reported or not applicable. 1. Land-grant institution. 2. Lost accreditation.

★785★
Enrollment

Enrollment in the Largest Public School Districts: Fall 1992

School District	Enrollment, fall 1992	Rank
New York, NY	983,971	1
Los Angeles, CA	639,781	2
Chicago, IL	411,582	3
Dade County, FL	303,346	4
Philadelphia, PA	201,496	5
Houston, TX	198,013	6
Broward County, FL	178,060	7
Detroit, MI	172,330	9
Dallas, TX	139,711	10
Clark County, NV	136,188	11
Fairfax County, VA	133,425	12
Hillsborough County, FL	132,224	13
San Diego, CA	125,116	14

[Continued]

★785★

Enrollment in the Largest Public School Districts: Fall 1992
[Continued]

School District	Enrollment, fall 1992	Rank
Duval County, FL	117,663	15
Palm Beach County, FL	116,466	16
Prince George's County, MD	113,132	17
Baltimore City, MD	110,662	18
Orange County, FL	110,136	19
Montgomery County, MD	110,037	20
Memphis City, TN	106,490	21
Pinellas County, FL	98,048	22
Milwaukee City, WI	94,300	23
Jefferson County, KY	93,440	24
Baltimore County, MD	93,270	25

Source: U.S. Department of Education, Office of Educational Research and Improvement, National Center for Education Statistics, *Digest of Education Statistics 1994*, NCES-94-115, Lanham, Maryland: Bernan 1995, p. 103. Primary source: U.S. Department of Education, National Center for Education Statistics, Common Care of Data survey. Table prepared May 1994. *Notes:* "ISD" stands for "Independent School District." Data are shown only for the top 25 areas.

★786★
Enrollment

Full-Time Enrollment at Colleges and University Campuses Enrolling More Than 14,600 Students: Fall 1992

Table includes data for publicly and privately controlled 2- and 4-year institutions.

Institution	Enrollment, by attendance status, fall 1992 full-time	Rank
University of Texas, Austin	42,524	1
Ohio State University, Main Campus	41,087	2
Texas A&M University	37,171	3
University of Wisconsin, Madison	34,916	4
Pennsylvania State U., Main Campus	33,851	5
University of California, Los Angeles	32,761	6
University of Illinois, Urbana Campus	32,524	7
University of Michigan, Ann Arbor	31,997	8
Purdue University, Main Campus	31,436	9
Michigan State University	31,425	10
University of Florida	30,560	11
Indiana University, Bloomington	30,091	12
Brigham Young University	29,042	13
Arizona State University	28,818	14
University of Washington	28,058	15
University of California, Berkeley	27,760	16
University of Arizona	26,766	17

[Continued]

★786★

Full-Time Enrollment at Colleges and University Campuses Enrolling More Than 14,600 Students: Fall 1992

[Continued]

Institution	Enrollment, by attendance status, fall 1992 full-time	Rank
Rutgers University, New Brunswick	24,271	18
University of Georgia	24,218	19
U. of Maryland, College Park Campus	24,051	20
Florida State University	22,494	21
University of Minnesota, Twin Cities	22,351	22
Virginia Polytechnic Inst. and State University	22,236	23
Boston University	21,752	24
University of Colorado at Boulder	21,736	25

Source: U.S. Department of Education, Office of Educational Research and Improvement, National Center for Education Statistics, *Digest of Education Statistics 1994*, NCES 94-115, Lanham, Maryland: Bernan 1995, p. 218. *Notes:* - Data not available or not applicable. Data are shown only for the top 25 areas.

★787★

Enrollment

Full-Time Equivalent Enrollment at College and University Campuses Enrolling More Than 14,600 Students: Fall 1992

Table includes data for publicly and privately controlled 2- and 4-year institutions.

[Dollars in thousands]

Institution	Full-time-equivalent enrollment, fall 1992	Rank
Ohio State University, Main Campus	45,361	1
University of Texas, Austin	45,177	2
Texas A&M University	38,920	3
University of Wisconsin, Madison	37,622	4
Pennsylvania State U., Main Campus	35,606	5
University of Minnesota, Twin Cities	35,105	6
University of Illinois, Urbana Campus	34,756	7
Arizona State University	34,520	8
Michigan State University	34,394	9
Purdue University, Main Campus	33,901	10
University of California, Los Angeles	33,778	11
University of Michigan, Ann Arbor	33,306	12

[Continued]

★787★

Full-Time Equivalent Enrollment at College and University Campuses Enrolling More Than 14,600 Students: Fall 1992

[Continued]

Institution	Full-time-equivalent enrollment, fall 1992	Rank
University of Florida	32,837	13
Indiana University, Bloomington	32,387	14
University of Washington	30,636	15
Bringham Young University	30,313	16
University of Arizona	29,994	17
Miami-Dade Community College	29,938	18
University of California, Berkeley	28,863	19
Rutgers University, New Brunswick	27,796	20
U. of Maryland, College Park Campus	27,424	21
New York University	25,941	22
University of Georgia	25,880	23
Florida State University	24,776	24
University of Houston-University Park	24,514	25

Source: U.S. Department of Education, Office of Educational Research and Improvement, National Center for Education Statistics, *Digest of Education Statistics 1994*, NCES 94-115, Lanham, Maryland: Bernan 1995, p. 218. *Note:* Data are shown only for the top 25 areas.

★788★

Enrollment

Men Enrolled at College and University Campuses Enrolling More Than 14,600 Students: Fall 1992

Table includes data for publicly and privately controlled 2- and 4-year institutions.

Institution	Enrollment, by sex, fall 1992 men	Rank
Ohio State University, Main Campus	27,467	1
University of Minnesota, Twin Cities	26,818	2
University of Texas, Austin	26,576	3
Texas A&M University	24,250	4
Purdue University, Main Campus	21,962	5
Arizona State University	21,930	6
Pennsylvania State U., Main Campus	21,727	7
University of Illinois, Urbana Campus	21,469	8
Miami-Dade Community College	21,442	9
University of Wisconsin, Madison	21,321	10
University of Florida	19,892	11
University of Michigan, Ann Arbor	19,517	12

[Continued]

★788★

Men Enrolled at College and University Campuses Enrolling More Than 14,600 Students: Fall 1992

[Continued]

Institution	Enrollment, by sex, fall 1992 men	Rank
Michigan State University	19,055	13
University of California, Los Angeles	18,391	14
University of Arizona	18,077	15
Northern Virginia Community College	17,809	16
University of Washington	17,382	17
U. of Maryland, College Park Campus	17,230	18
Indiana University, Bloomington	17,017	19
North Carolina State University, Raleigh	16,957	20
University of California, Berkeley	16,823	21
University of Houston-University Park	16,807	22
Houston Community College System	16,684	23
University of Southern California	16,561	24
Brigham Young University	16,324	25

Source: U.S. Department of Education, Office of Educational Research and Improvement, National Center for Education Statistics, *Digest of Education Statistics 1994*, NCES 94-115, Lanham, Maryland: Bernan 1995, p. 218. *Note:* Data are shown only for the top 25 areas.

★789★
Enrollment

Part-Time Enrollment at College and University Campuses Enrolling More Than 14,600 Students: Fall 1992

Table includes data for publicly and privately controlled 2- and 4-year institutions.

Institution	Enrollment, by attendance status, fall 1992 part-time	Rank
Miami-Dade Community College	32,870	1
University of Minnesota, Twin Cities	32,320	2
Northern Virginia Community College	29,162	3
Houston Community College System	28,899	4
Saint Louis Community College, Forest Park	23,199	5
College of Du Page	23,062	6
Pima Community College	22,482	7
Central Piedmont Community College	21,987	8

[Continued]

★789★

Part-Time Enrollment at College and University Campuses Enrolling More Than 14,600 Students: Fall 1992

[Continued]

Institution	Enrollment, by attendance status, fall 1992 part-time	Rank
City College of San Francisco	21,863	9
Community College of the Air Force	21,600	10
Rancho Santiago College	20,729	11
Oakland Community College	20,575	12
Tarrant County Junior College District	20,278	13
Macomb Community College	19,936	14
Wayne State University	19,183	15
Austin Community College	18,850	16
International Correspondence Schools	18,728	17
El Camino College	18,613	18
Pasadena City College	18,178	19
De Anza College	17,606	20
Broward Community College	17,400	21
Milwaukee Area Technical College	17,388	22
Santa Rosa Junior College	17,314	23
Santa Monica College	17,083	24
Cuyahoga Community College District	17,052	25

Source: U.S. Department of Education, Office of Educational Research and Improvement, National Center for Education Statistics, *Digest of Education Statistics 1994*, NCES 94-115, Lanham, Maryland: Bernan 1995, p. 218. *Note:* Data are shown only for the top 25 areas.

★790★
Enrollment

Postbaccalaureate Enrollment at College and University Campuses Enrolling More Than 14,600 Students: Fall 1992

Table includes data for publicly and privately controlled 2- and 4-year institutions.

Institution	Enrollment, by level, fall 1992 post-baccalaureate	Rank
New York University	18,459	1
Harvard University	14,158	2
Wayne State University	14,080	3
University of Texas, Austin	13,342	4
Unviersity of Michigan, Ann Arbor	13,240	5
Ohio State University, Main Campus	13,224	6
Columbia University, New York	13,156	7

[Continued]

★790★

Postbaccalaureate Enrollment at College and University Campuses Enrolling More Than 14,600 Students: Fall 1992

[Continued]

Institution	Enrollment, by level, fall 1992 post-baccalaureate	Rank
University of Southern California	13,123	8
University of Minnesota, Twin Cities	13,067	9
University of Wisconsin, Madison	12,233	10
University of California, Los Angeles	11,756	11
Arizona State University	11,724	12
George Washington University	11,469	13
University of Pennsylvania	11,085	14
University of Illinois, Urbana Campus	11,048	15
Boston University	10,458	16
University of South Carolina, Columbia	10,329	17
Temple University	10,290	18
University of Pittsburgh, Main Campus	9,940	19
University of Iowa	9,341	20
U. of Maryland, College Park Campus	9,241	21
University of Florida	9,149	22
University of Washington	9,116	23
University of Virginia, Main Campus	8,921	24
University of California, Berkeley	8,909	25

Source: U.S. Department of Education, Office of Educational Research and Improvement, National Center for Education Statistics, *Digest of Education Statistics 1994*, NCES 94-115, Lanham, Maryland: Bernan 1995, p. 218. *Notes:* - Data not available or not applicable. Data are shown only for the top 25 areas.

★791★

Enrollment

Undergraduate Enrollment at College and University Campuses Enrolling More Than 14,600 Students: Fall 1992

Table includes data for publicly and privately controlled 2- and 4-year institutions.

Institution	Enrollment, by level, fall 1992 undergraduate	Rank
Miami-Dade Community College	51,768	1
University of Minnesota, Twin Cities	41,604	2
Ohio State University, Main Campus	38,955	3
Northern Virginia Community College	38,343	4

[Continued]

★791★

Undergraduate Enrollment at College and University Campuses Enrolling More Than 14,600 Students: Fall 1992

[Continued]

Institution	Enrollment, by level, fall 1992 undergraduate	Rank
Houston Community College System	37,410	5
University of Texas, Austin	35,911	6
Community College of the Air Force	34,294	7
Texas A&M University	33,479	8
Saint Louis Community College, Forest Park	32,005	9
Arizona State University	31,904	10
Pennsylvania State U., Main Campus	31,805	11
College of Du Page	31,621	12
Purdue University, Main Campus	31,199	13
Michigan State University	30,726	14
Pima Community College	30,175	15
City College of San Francisco	29,708	16
University of Wisconsin, Madison	29,591	17
Brigham Young University	29,452	18
Tarrant County Junior College District	28,516	19
Indiana University, Bloomington	28,149	20
University of Illinois, Urbana Campus	27,348	21
University of Florida	27,298	22
Macomb Community College	26,498	23
Central Piedmont Community College	26,428	24
University of Arizona	26,347	25

Source: U.S. Department of Education, Office of Educational Research and Improvement, National Center for Education Statistics, *Digest of Education Statistics 1994*, NCES 94-115, Lanham, Maryland: Bernan 1995, p. 218. *Note:* Data are shown only for the top 25 areas.

★792★

Enrollment

Women Enrolled at College and University Campuses Enrolling More Than 14,600 Students: Fall 1992

Table includes data for publicly and privately controlled 2- and 4-year institutions.

Institution	Enrollment, by sex, fall 1992 women	Rank
Miami-Dade Community College	30,326	1
University of Minnesota, Twin Cities	27,853	2
Ohio State University, Main Campus	24,712	3
University of Texas, Austin	22,677	4
Arizona State University	21,698	5
Houston Community College System	20,726	6
Northern Virginia Community College	20,534	7
University of Wisconsin, Madison	20,503	8
Michigan State University	20,083	9
Community College of the Air Force	20,045	10
Saint Louis Community College, Forest Park	19,398	11
University of South Florida	19,362	12
Indiana University, Bloomington	19,054	13
Wayne State University	18,940	14
New York University	18,556	15
College of Du Page	18,100	16
Rutgers University, New Brunswick	17,944	17
Texas A&M University	17,460	18
University of Washington	17,215	19
University of Arizona	17,041	20
University of California, Los Angeles	17,012	21
University of Illinois, Urbana Campus	16,927	22
Pennsylvania State U., Main Campus	16,719	23
California State University, Northridge	16,714	24
University of Florida	16,555	25

Source: U.S. Department of Education. Office of Educational Research and Improvement. National Center for Education Statistics. *Digest of Education Statistics 1994*, NCES 94-115. Lanham, Maryland: Bernan 1995, p. 218. *Note:* Data are shown only for the top 25 areas.

★793★

Finances and Expenditures

Current-Fund Expenditures at Historically Black Colleges and Universities: Fall 1992

Table includes data for publicly and privately controlled 2- and 4-year institutions.

Institution	Expenditures, 1991-92 (in thousands) current-fund expenditures	Rank
Alabama A&M University, AL[1]	48,979	17
Alabama State University, AL	36,788	22
Albany State College, GA	20,801	47
Alcorn State University, MS	28,153	34
Allen University, SC	3,180	96
Arkansas Baptist College, AR	1,696	101
Barber-Scotia College, NC	7,452	80
Benedict College, SC	17,015	56
Bennett College, NC	9,557	69
Bethune-Cookman College, FL	27,474	37
Bishop State Community College, AL	7,950	77
Bluefield State College, WV	10,916	64
Bowie State University, MD	29,390	31
C.A. Fredd State Technical College, AL	2,003	100
Carver State Technical College, AL	3,019	97
Central State University, OH	37,516	21
Cheyney University of Pennsylvania, PA	22,285	45
Clafin College, SC	9,098	70
Clark Atlanta University, GA	73,482	6
Clinton Junior College, SC[2]	-	104
Coahoma Community College, MS	7,540	79
Concordia College, AL	2,658	99
Coppin State College, MD	20,197	49
Delaware State College, DE	34,591	24
Denmark Technical College, SC	5,569	88
Dillard University, LA	17,481	53
Edward Waters College, FL	6,603	84
Elizabeth City State University, NC	23,344	42
Fayetteville State University, NC	31,200	28
Fisk University, TN	11,543	61
Florida A&M University, FL[1]	92,658	3
Florida Memorial College, FL	14,416	58
Fort Valley State College, GA[1]	24,136	40
Grambling State University, LA	53,661	16
Hampton University, VA	64,804	9
Harris-Stowe State College, MO	7,561	78
Hinds Community College, Utica Campus, MS	0	104
Howard University, DC	453,386	1
Huston-Tilotson College, TX	7,294	81
Interdenominational Theological Center, GA	4,833	93
J.F. Drake Technical College, AL	3,766	94
Jackson State University, MS	57,569	13
Jarvis Christian College, TX	9,660	68

[Continued]

★793★

Current-Fund Expenditures at Historically Black Colleges and Universities: Fall 1992

[Continued]

Institution	Expenditures, 1991-92 (in thousands) current-fund expenditures	Rank
Johnson C. Smith University, NC	17,151	54
Kentucky State University, KY[1]	33,309	27
Knoxville College, TN	13,748	59
Lane College, TN	6,870	82
Langston University, OK[1]	23,020	44
Lawson State Community College, AL	8,347	74
Le Moyne-Owen College, TN	8,605	71
Lewis College of Business, MI	1,471	102
Lincoln University, MO[1]	27,611	36
Lincoln University, PA	23,705	41
Livingstone College, NC	8,394	72
Mary Holmes College, MS	6,464	86
Meharry Medical College, TN	73,070	7
Miles College, AL	6,039	87
Mississippi Valley State University, MS	19,257	50
Morehouse College, GA	35,253	23
Morehouse School of Medicine, GA	33,937	26
Morgan State University, MD	54,463	15
Morris Brown College, GA	28,439	33
Morris College, SC	8,189	75
Norfolk State University, VA	59,111	12
North Carolina Agricultural and Technical		104
North Carolina Central University, NC	48,586	18
Oakwood College, AL	17,146	55
Paine College, GA	7,965	76
Paul Quinn College, TX	10,367	66
Philander Smith College, AR	5,498	89
Prairie View A&M University, TX[1]	60,864	11
Rust College, MS	11,226	62
Savannah State College, GA	21,215	46
Selma University, AL	3,604	95
Shaw University, NC	18,374	52
Shorter College, AR	858	103
South Carolina State College, SC[1]	45,106	20
Southern University and A&M College, Baton Rouge, LA[1]	75,357	5
Southern University, New Orleans, LA	19,222	51
Southern University, Shreveport-Bossier City Campus, LA	6,752	83
Southwestern Christian College, TX	2,806	98
Spelman College, GA	30,012	30

[Continued]

★793★

Current-Fund Expenditures at Historically Black Colleges and Universities: Fall 1992

[Continued]

Institution	Expenditures, 1991-92 (in thousands) current-fund expenditures	Rank
St. Augustine's College, NC	23,205	43
St. Paul's College, VA	8,378	73
St. Phillip's College, TX	25,698	39
Stillman College, AL	10,718	65
Talladega College, AL	9,802	67
Tennessee State University, TN[1]	56,780	14
Texas College, TX	4,916	92
Texas Southern University, TX	67,401	8
Tougaloo College, MS	11,109	63
Trenholm College, AL	5,322	90
Tuskegee University, AL[1]	62,792	10
University of Arkansas, Pine Bluff, AR[1]	26,530	38
University of Maryland, Eastern Shore, MD[1]	30,839	29
University of the District of Columbia, DC[1]	99,535	2
University of the Virgin Islands, St. Thomas Campus, VI[1]	29,258	32
Virginia State University, VA[1]	45,137	19
Virginia Union University, VA	14,915	57
Voorhees College, SC	6,513	85
West Virginia State College, WV	20,600	48
Wilberforce University, OH	11,618	60
Wiley College, TX	5,171	91
Winston-Salem State University, NC	27,820	35
Xavier University of Louisiana, LA	34,085	25
State University, NC[1]	78,808	4

Source: U.S. Department of Education, Office of Educational Research and Improvement, National Center for Education Statistics, *Digest of Education Statistics 1994*, NCES 94-115, Lanham, Maryland: Bernan 1995, p. 225. Primary source: U.S. Department of Education, National Center for Education Statistics, Integrated Postsecondary Education Data System (IPEDS), "Fall Enrollment, 1992," "Completions, 1991-92," and "Finance, 1991-92," surveys. Table prepared June 1994. *Notes:* - Data not reported or not applicable. 1. Land-grant institution. 2. Lost accreditation.

★794★

Finances and Expenditures

Current-Fund Expenditures of College and University Campuses Enrolling More Than 14,600 Students: 1991-92

Table includes data for publicly and privately controlled 2- and 4-year institutions.

[Dollars in thousands]

Ins	Financial statistics, 1991-92, in thousands current-fund	Rank
Unviersity of Michigan, Ann Arbor	1,737,727	1
University of California, Los Angeles	1,632,399	2
Stanford University	1,467,368	3
University of Minnesota, Twin Cities	1,387,189	4
University of Pennsylvania	1,342,529	5
Harvard University	1,261,519	6
Ohio State University, Main Campus	1,261,009	7
University of Wisconsin, Madison	1,248,135	8
New York University	1,229,140	9
University of Washington	1,103,080	10
University of California, Davis	970,834	11
Columbia University, New York	961,738	12
University of California, San Diego	922,972	13
University of Southern California	905,836	14
University of Iowa	894,979	15
University of California, Berkeley	822,011	16
Michigan State University	783,603	17
University of Florida	778,139	18
University of Alabama at Birmingham	763,533	19
University of Illinois, Urbana Campus	756,113	20
University of Virginia, Main Campus	747,966	21
University of Texas, Austin	736,810	22
Indiana U. - Purdue U. at Indianapolis	719,023	23
Texas A&M University	709,608	24
University of North Carolina, Chapel Hill	709,139	25

Source: U.S. Department of Education, Office of Educational Research and Improvement, National Center for Education Statistics, *Digest of Education Statistics 1994,* NCES 94-115, Lanham, Maryland: Bernan 1995, p. 218. *Note:* Data are shown only for the top 25 areas.

★795★

Finances and Expenditures

Current-Fund Revenues of College and University Campuses Enrolling More Than 14,600 Students: 1991-92

Table includes data for publicly and privately controlled 2- and 4-year institutions.

[Dollars in thousands]

Institution	Financial statistics, 1991-92, in thousands current-fund revenues	Rank
Harvard University	1,125,894	1
University of California, Los Angeles	1,070,734	2
University of Minnesota, Twin Cities	1,002,226	3
Stanford University	978,189	4
Unviersity of Michigan, Ann Arbor	951,450	5
University of Wisconsin, Madison	942,242	6
Columbia University, New York	923,030	7
Ohio State University, Main Campus	845,589	8
University of Washington	833,699	9
New York University	796,350	10
University of California, Berkeley	765,911	11
University of Pennsylvania	729,864	12
University of Florida	702,766	13
University of Southern California	664,398	14
University of Illinois, Urbana Campus	664,255	15
Texas A&M University	645,252	16
University of Texas, Austin	637,231	17
Michigan State University	635,234	18
University of North Carolina, Chapel Hill	629,628	19
Pennsylvania State U., Main Campus	604,882	20
University of California, Davis	601,885	21
University of California, San Diego	600,470	22
Boston University	570,046	23
Northwestern University	555,449	24
University of Arizona	550,016	25

Source: U.S. Department of Education, Office of Educational Research and Improvement, National Center for Education Statistics, *Digest of Education Statistics 1994,* NCES 94-115, Lanham, Maryland: Bernan 1995, p. 218. *Note:* Data are shown only for the top 25 areas.

★796★

Educational and General Expenditures at Historically Black Colleges and Universities: Fall 1992

Table includes data for publicly and privately controlled 2- and 4-year institutions.

Institution	Expenditures, 1991-92 (in thousands) educational and general	Rank
Alabama A&M University, AL[1]	44,753	16
Alabama State University, AL	30,746	25
Albany State College, GA	17,985	48
Alcorn State University, MS	24,165	37
Allen University, SC	3,180	95
Arkansas Baptist College, AR	1,563	101
Barber-Scotia College, NC	6,270	82
Benedict College, SC	15,110	54
Bennett College, NC	8,553	69
Bethune-Cookman College, FL	23,226	38
Bishop State Community College, AL	7,303	76
Bluefield State College, WV	9,941	61
Bowie State University, MD	25,869	31
C.A. Fredd State Technical College, AL	1,990	100
Carver State Technical College, AL	2,975	96
Central State University, OH	31,291	23
Cheyney University of Pennsylvania, PA	19,662	43
Clafin College, SC	7,706	72
Clark Atlanta University, GA	69,189	4
Clinton Junior College, SC[2]	-	104
Coahoma Community College, MS	6,840	79
Concordia College, AL	2,389	99
Coppin State College, MD	18,931	45
Delaware State College, DE	30,635	26
Denmark Technical College, SC	4,675	92
Dillard University, LA	15,514	53
Edward Waters College, FL	6,132	83
Elizabeth City State University, NC	19,805	42
Fayetteville State University, NC	26,386	30
Fisk University, TN	9,893	62
Florida A&M University, FL[1]	83,245	3
Florida Memorial College, FL	13,310	56
Fort Valley State College, GA[1]	21,346	40
Grambling State University, LA	42,956	17
Hampton University, VA	56,196	9
Harris-Stowe State College, MO	7,561	74
Hinds Community College, Utica Campus, MS	0	104
Howard University, DC	287,402	1
Huston-Tilotson College, TX	6,548	81
Interdenominational Theological Center, GA	4,730	91
J.F. Drake Technical College, AL	3,600	94

[Continued]

★796★

Educational and General Expenditures at Historically Black Colleges and Universities: Fall 1992

[Continued]

Institution	Expenditures, 1991-92 (in thousands) educational and general	Rank
Jackson State University, MS	46,709	13
Jarvis Christian College, TX	8,691	68
Johnson C. Smith University, NC	14,666	55
Kentucky State University, KY[1]	30,219	27
Knoxville College, TN	12,193	59
Lane College, TN	5,650	85
Langston University, OK[1]	18,269	47
Lawson State Community College, AL	7,999	71
Le Moyne-Owen College, TN	8,197	70
Lewis College of Business, MI	1,450	102
Lincoln University, MO[1]	25,256	33
Lincoln University, PA	20,625	41
Livingstone College, NC	7,503	75
Mary Holmes College, MS	5,798	84
Meharry Medical College, TN	45,382	15
Miles College, AL	5,420	87
Mississippi Valley State University, MS	16,369	52
Morehouse College, GA	30,747	24
Morehouse School of Medicine, GA	33,937	20
Morgan State University, MD	46,414	14
Morris Brown College, GA	24,423	35
Morris College, SC	7,070	77
Norfolk State University, VA	47,879	12
North Carolina Agricultural and Technical		104
North Carolina Central University, NC	41,102	18
Oakwood College, AL	13,272	57
Paine College, GA	6,985	78
Paul Quinn College, TX	9,730	63
Philander Smith College, AR	4,878	89
Prairie View A&M University, TX[1]	48,876	11
Rust College, MS	9,363	65
Savannah State College, GA	17,837	49
Selma University, AL	2,849	97
Shaw University, NC	17,073	50
Shorter College, AR	786	103
South Carolina State College, SC[1]	36,033	19
Southern University and A&M College, Baton Rouge, LA[1]	64,846	6
Southern University, New Orleans, LA	18,377	46
Southern University, Shreveport-Bossier City Campus, LA	6,590	80

[Continued]

★796★

Educational and General Expenditures at Historically Black Colleges and Universities: Fall 1992

[Continued]

Institution	Expenditures, 1991-92 (in thousands) educational and general	Rank
Southwestern Christian College, TX	2,452	98
Spelman College, GA	24,553	34
St. Augustine's College, NC	19,157	44
St. Paul's College, VA	7,638	73
St. Phillip's College, TX	25,487	32
Stillman College, AL	9,183	66
Talladega College, AL	8,728	67
Tennessee State University, TN[1]	52,372	10
Texas College, TX	4,481	93
Texas Southern University, TX	60,951	7
Tougaloo College, MS	10,225	60
Trenholm College, AL	5,112	88
Tuskegee University, AL[1]	56,197	8
University of Arkansas, Pine Bluff, AR[1]	24,264	36
University of Maryland, Eastern Shore, MD[1]	27,500	28
University of the District of Columbia, DC[1]	98,973	2
University of the Virgin Islands, St. Thomas Campus, VI[1]	26,808	29
Virginia State University, VA[1]	33,539	21
Virginia Union University, VA	12,601	58
Voorhees College, SC	5,604	86
West Virginia State College, WV	16,884	51
Wilberforce University, OH	9,723	64
Wiley College, TX	4,750	90
Winston-Salem State University, NC	23,157	39
Xavier University of Louisiana, LA	31,555	22
State University, NC[1]	67,859	5

Source: U.S. Department of Education, Office of Educational Research and Improvement, National Center for Education Statistics, *Digest of Education Statistics 1994*, NCES 94-115, Lanham, Maryland: Bernan 1995, p. 225. Primary source: U.S. Department of Education, National Center for Education Statistics, Integrated Postsecondary Education Data System (IPEDS), "Fall Enrollment, 1992," "Completions, 1991-92," and "Finance, 1991-92," surveys. Table prepared June 1994. *Notes:* 1. Land-grant Rank. 2. Lost accreditation.

★797★

Finances and Expenditures

Educational and General Expenditures of College and University Campuses Enrolling More Than 14,600 Students: 1991-92

Table includes data for publicly and privately controlled 2- and 4-year institutions.

[Dollars in thousands]

	Financial statistics, 1991-92, in thousands educational	Rank
Unviersity of Michigan, Ann Arbor	1,967,522	1
University of California, Los Angeles	1,665,644	2
Stanford University	1,583,489	3
University of Pennsylvania	1,499,200	4
Harvard University	1,449,086	5
University of Minnesota, Twin Cities	1,420,170	6
New York University	1,305,650	7
Ohio State University, Main Campus	1,278,831	8
University of Wisconsin, Madison	1,277,431	9
University of Washington	1,164,839	10
Columbia University, New York	1,041,138	11
University of California, Davis	1,030,819	12
University of California, San Diego	959,392	13
University of Southern California	949,427	14
University of Iowa	924,714	15
University of Texas, Austin	874,493	16
University of California, Berkeley	839,912	17
University of Alabama at Birmingham	822,523	18
University of Virginia, Main Campus	816,790	19
Michigan State University	812,022	20
University of Florida	788,305	21
University of Illinois, Urbana Campus	775,956	22
University of Cincinnati, Main Campus	769,556	23
Pennsylvania State U., Main Campus	754,180	24
Texas A&M University	750,949	25

Source: U.S. Department of Education, Office of Educational Research and Improvement, National Center for Education Statistics, *Digest of Education Statistics 1994*, NCES 94-115, Lanham, Maryland: Bernan 1995, p. 218. *Notes:* - Data not available or not applicable. Data are shown only for the top 25 areas.

★798★
Finances and Expenditures

Federal Budget Allocations for Urban Schools, 1995-96: Lunch Program

City	School lunch program	Rank
Atlanta, GA	$11,453,583	7
Birmingham, AL	7,537,821	9
Boston, MA	0	19
Broward County, FL	20,911,372	4
Buffalo, NY	0	19
Chicago, IL	79,886,860	1
Columbus, OH	8,939,328	8
Dade County, FL	48,380,000	2
Dallas, TX	0	19
Denver, CO	7,056,966	12
Detroit, MI	0	19
El Paso, TX	0	19
Houston, TX	0	19
Indianapolis, IN	7,257,000	10
Long Beach, CA	12,209,256	6
Memphis, TN	0	19
Minneapolis, MN	6,902,557	13
New York, NY	0	19
Newark, NJ	0	19
Norfolk, VA	5,535,000	15
Oakland, CA	0	19
Omaha, NE	4,714,447	18
Philadelphia, PA	28,370,360	3
Pittsburgh, PA	0	19
Portland, OR	5,445,347	16
Providence, RI	0	19
Saint Louis, MO	0	19
Saint Paul, MN	5,982,699	14
San Diego, CA	16,334,634	5
San Francisco, CA	7,166,800	11
Seattle, WA	4,730,698	17

Source: Thompson, Garland, L., "School Dropouts: Despite Progress, Minority Rates Still Exceed Whites," *Black Issues in Higher Education*, 15 June 1995, p. 24. Primary source: Council of Great City Schools, "Effect of House Committee Proposed Fiscal Year 95 Rescissions."

★799★
Finances and Expenditures

Federal Budget Allocations for Urban Schools, 1995-96: Total

City	Total federal allocations	Rank
Atlanta, GA	$33,385,510	10
Birmingham, AL	18,970,713	22
Boston, MA	23,263,677	16
Broward County, FL	43,967,352	7
Buffalo, NY	23,728,854	15
Chicago, IL	244,861,159	2
Columbus, OH	31,613,210	11
Dade County, FL	119,587,575	3
Dallas, TX	41,046,353	8

[Continued]

★799★

Federal Budget Allocations for Urban Schools, 1995-96: Total
[Continued]

City	Total federal allocations	Rank
Denver, CO	23,235,161	17
Detroit, MI	97,761,067	5
El Paso, TX	18,613,272	23
Houston, TX	51,655,523	6
Indianapolis, IN	22,479,194	18
Long Beach, CA	23,947,881	14
Memphis, TN	28,184,559	13
Minneapolis, MN	19,642,569	21
New York, NY	430,974,774	1
Newark, NJ	28,199,440	12
Norfolk, VA	14,019,014	29
Oakland, CA	15,896,926	27
Omaha, NE	12,950,627	30
Philadelphia, PA	113,681,750	4
Pittsburgh, PA	16,199,805	26
Portland, OR	16,967,885	25
Providence, RI	11,410,570	31
Saint Louis, MO	21,655,608	19
Saint Paul, MN	18,081,768	24
San Diego, CA	40,168,907	9
San Francisco, CA	21,407,054	20
Seattle, WA	14,199,918	28

Source: Thompson, Garland L., "School Dropouts: Despite Progress, Minority Rates Still Exceed Whites," *Black Issues in Higher Education*, 15 June 1995, p. 24. Primary source: Council of Great City Schools, "Effect of House Committee Proposed Fiscal Year 95 Rescissions."

★800★
Teachers

Demand For Teachers, 1996-97: Projected Number

City (School District)	Numbers	Rank
Los Angeles, CA	1,600	2
Chicago, IL	1,000	3
Dade County, FL	2,500	1
Broward County, FL	800	4
Houston, TX	1,000	3
Dallas, TX	800	4
Long Beach, CA	700	5
Memphis, TN	500	6
San Diego, CA	500	6
Jefferson County, KY	450	7
New Orleans, LA	300	8

Source: Henry, Tamara, "Urban Area Teacher Shortages," *USA TODAY*, 22 May 1996, p. 7D. Primary source: "The Urban Teacher Challenge: A Report on Teacher Recruitment and Demand in Selected Great City Schools."

★801★
Teachers

Teachers in the Largest School Districts, 1995: Total Number

City (School District)	Numbers	Rank
Los Angeles, CA	28,000	1
Chicago, IL	28,000	1
Dade County, FL	19,000	2
Broward County, FL	12,000	3
Houston, TX	12,000	4
Dallas, TX	8,984	5
Long Beach, CA	7,000	6
Memphis, TN	6,000	7
San Diego, CA	6,000	7
Jefferson County, KY	5,600	8
New Orleans, LA	5,000	9

Source: Henry, Tamara, "Urban Area Teacher Shortages," *USA TODAY*, 22 May 1996, p. 7D. Primary source: "The Urban Teacher Challenge: A Report on Teacher Recruitment and Demand in Selected Great City Schools."

Chapter 10

ANCESTRY AND LANGUAGE

Topic Covered

First Ancestry

★802★

First Ancestry

Persons, By First Ancestry, 1990: Arab

Data provided for all respondents who reported "Arab" as their sole ancestry, and those who reported "Arab" as their first ancestry.

[Table shows the top 50 areas]

MSA	% of total population	Rank
Detroit – Ann Arbor, MI	1.1715	1
Utica – Rome, NY	0.9734	2
Worcester, MA	0.8592	3
Toledo, OH	0.8018	4
Allentown – Bethlehem – Easton, PA – NJ	0.6505	5
Wheeling, WV – OH	0.6459	6
Lansing – East Lansing, MI	0.6437	7
Washington, DC – MD – VA	0.6247	8
Boston – Lawrence – Salem, MA – NH	0.6229	9
Flint, MI	0.5870	10
Jacksonville, FL	0.5644	11
New Bedford, MA	0.5595	12
Cleveland – Akron – Lorain, OH	0.5580	13
New York – Northern New Jersey – Long Island, NY – NJ – CT	0.5428	14
Providence – Pawtucket – Fall River, RI – MA	0.5324	15
Pittsfield, MA	0.5210	16
Iowa City, IA	0.5160	17
Los Angeles – Anaheim – Riverside, CA	0.5077	18
Youngstown – Warren, OH	0.4957	19
Scranton – Wilkes-Barre, PA	0.4741	20
Syracuse, NY	0.4637	21
Binghamton, NY	0.4597	22
Miami – Fort Lauderdale, FL	0.4542	23
Cedar Rapids, IA	0.4539	24
Pittsburgh – Beaver Valley, PA	0.4447	25
San Diego, CA	0.4390	26
Charleston, WV	0.4364	27
Bryan – College Station, TX	0.4292	28
Peoria, IL	0.4237	29
Manchester, NH	0.4213	30
San Francisco – Oakland – San Jose, CA	0.4129	31
Bloomington, IN	0.4083	32
Canton, OH	0.4083	32
Columbia, MO	0.4040	33
Roanoke, VA	0.3978	34
Tucson, AZ	0.3920	35
Lawrence, KS	0.3912	36
Orlando, FL	0.3880	37
West Palm Beach – Boca Raton – Delray Beach, FL	0.3820	38
Buffalo – Niagara Falls, NY	0.3809	39
Lafayette, LA	0.3804	40
New London – Norwich, CT – RI	0.3797	41
El Paso, TX	0.3764	42
Burlington, VT	0.3736	43
Waterbury, CT	0.3718	44
Houston – Galveston – Brazoria, TX	0.3693	45

[Continued]

★802★

First Ancestry

Persons, By First Ancestry, 1990: Arab

[Continued]

MSA	% of total population	Rank
Austin, TX	0.3658	46
Champaign – Urbana – Rantoul, IL	0.3653	47
Wichita, KS	0.3643	48
Raleigh – Durham, NC	0.3640	49

Source: U.S. Bureau of the Census, Data User Services Division, *1990 Census of Population and Housing*, Summary Tape File 3C, United States Summary, CD-ROM, February 1992.

★803★

First Ancestry

Persons, By First Ancestry, 1990: Austrian

Data provided for all respondents who listed "Austrian" as their sole ancestry, and those who listed "Austrian" as their first ancestry.

[Table shows the top 50 areas]

MSA	% of total population	Rank
Allentown – Bethlehem – Easton, PA – NJ	1.1037	1
West Palm Beach – Boca Raton – Delray Beach, FL	0.9538	2
New York – Northern New Jersey – Long Island, NY – NJ – CT	0.6659	3
Miami – Fort Lauderdale, FL	0.5773	4
Scranton – Wilkes-Barre, PA	0.5274	5
Eau Claire, WI	0.4828	6
Pittsfield, MA	0.4554	7
Sarasota, FL	0.4302	8
Milwaukee – Racine, WI	0.3940	9
Pittsburgh – Beaver Valley, PA	0.3870	10
Syracuse, NY	0.3763	11
Pueblo, CO	0.3755	12
Poughkeepsie, NY	0.3712	13
Great Falls, MT	0.3617	14
Casper, WY	0.3528	15
Albany – Schenectady – Troy, NY	0.3428	16
South Bend – Mishawaka, IN	0.3388	17
Santa Fe, NM	0.3366	18
Chicago – Gary – Lake County, IL – IN – WI	0.3313	19
Waterbury, CT	0.3280	20
Colorado Springs, CO	0.3274	21
Hartford – New Britain – Middletown, CT	0.3252	22
State College, PA	0.3207	23
Burlington, VT	0.3180	24
Billings, MT	0.3174	25
Johnstown, PA	0.3117	26
Philadelphia – Wilmington – Trenton, PA – NJ – DE – MD	0.3112	27
Cleveland – Akron – Lorain, OH	0.3106	28
New Haven – Meriden, CT	0.3070	29
Denver – Boulder, CO	0.3049	30
Fort Pierce, FL	0.3011	31

[Continued]

★ 803 ★

Persons, By First Ancestry, 1990: Austrian

[Continued]

MSA	% of total population	Rank
Washington, DC – MD – VA	0.2972	32
Binghamton, NY	0.2953	33
Reno, NV	0.2886	34
Seattle – Tacoma, WA	0.2759	35
San Francisco – Oakland – San Jose, CA	0.2726	36
Olympia, WA	0.2698	37
Minneapolis – Saint Paul, MN – WI	0.2688	38
Harrisburg – Lebanon – Carlisle, PA	0.2665	39
Fort Collins – Loveland, CO	0.2638	40
Anchorage, AK	0.2598	41
Sheboygan, WI	0.2590	42
Springfield, IL	0.2575	43
Mansfield, OH	0.2529	44
Gainesville, FL	0.2528	45
Tucson, AZ	0.2528	45
Buffalo – Niagara Falls, NY	0.2520	46
Santa Barbara – Santa Maria – Lompoc, CA	0.2462	47
Tampa – Saint Petersburg – Clearwater, FL	0.2455	48
Fort Myers – Cape Coral, Fl	0.2450	49

Source: U.S. Bureau of the Census, Data User Services Division, *1990 Census of Population and Housing,* Summary Tape File 3C, United States Summary, CD-ROM, February 1992.

★ 804 ★

First Ancestry

Persons, By First Ancestry, 1990: Belgian

Data provided for all respondents who reported "Belgian" as their sole ancestry, and those who reported "Belgian" as their first ancestry.

[Table shows the top 50 areas]

MSA	% of total population	Rank
Green Bay, WI	8.5799	1
Davenport – Rock Island – Moline, IA – IL	3.7670	2
South Bend – Mishawaka, IN	2.1542	3
Alexandria, LA	1.2025	4
Appleton – Oshkosh – Neenah, WI	0.6845	5
Detroit – Ann Arbor, MI	0.5475	6
Duluth, MN – WI	0.3984	7
Cedar Rapids, IA	0.2957	8
Saginaw – Bay City – Midland, MI	0.2782	9
Lansing – East Lansing, MI	0.2681	10
Jackson, MI	0.2678	11
Muskegon, MI	0.2661	12
Manchester, NH	0.2644	13
Elkhart – Goshen, IN	0.2420	14
Billings, MT	0.2372	15
Great Falls, MT	0.2214	16
Iowa City, IA	0.2206	17

[Continued]

★ 804 ★

Persons, By First Ancestry, 1990: Belgian

[Continued]

MSA	% of total population	Rank
Kansas City, MO – KS	0.2103	18
Madison, WI	0.2073	19
Peoria, IL	0.1934	20
Milwaukee – Racine, WI	0.1827	21
Sioux Falls, SD	0.1817	22
Rochester, NY	0.1776	23
Battle Creek, MI	0.1765	24
Sheboygan, WI	0.1742	25
Rockford, IL	0.1664	26
Bloomington – Normal, IL	0.1641	27
Steubenville – Weirton, OH – WV	0.1635	28
Omaha, NE – IA	0.1598	29
Benton Harbor, MI	0.1593	30
Rochester, MN	0.1503	31
Saint Cloud, MN	0.1440	32
Minneapolis – Saint Paul, MN – WI	0.1419	33
Champaign – Urbana – Rantoul, IL	0.1410	34
La Crosse, WI	0.1410	34
Eugene – Springfield, OR	0.1357	35
Toledo, OH	0.1347	36
Wausau, WI	0.1343	37
Flint, MI	0.1338	38
Kalamazoo, MI	0.1338	38
Fort Myers – Cape Coral, Fl	0.1295	39
Lawrence, KS	0.1271	40
Pittsburgh – Beaver Valley, PA	0.1264	41
Fort Collins – Loveland, CO	0.1241	42
Bellingham, WA	0.1229	43
Des Moines, IA	0.1211	44
Melbourne – Titusville – Palm Bay, FL	0.1198	45
Grand Rapids, MI	0.1187	46
Kankakee, IL	0.1174	47
Colorado Springs, CO	0.1164	48

Source: U.S. Bureau of the Census, Data User Services Division, *1990 Census of Population and Housing,* Summary Tape File 3C, United States Summary, CD-ROM, February 1992.

★ 805 ★

First Ancestry

Persons, By First Ancestry, 1990: Canadian

Data provided for all respondents who reported "Canadian" as their sole ancestry, and for those who reported "Canadian" as their first ancestry.

[Table shows the top 50 areas]

MSA	% of total population	Rank
Lewiston – Auburn, ME	1.4828	1
Manchester, NH	1.3850	2
Bangor, ME	0.9729	3
Boston – Lawrence – Salem, MA – NH	0.8643	4
Portland, ME	0.8275	5

[Continued]

★ 805 ★

Persons, By First Ancestry, 1990: Canadian
[Continued]

MSA	% of total population	Rank
Bellingham, WA	0.8178	6
Fitchburg – Leominster, MA	0.8064	7
Portsmouth – Dover – Rochester, NH – ME	0.7667	8
Burlington, VT	0.5805	9
Worcester, MA	0.5296	10
Springfield, MA	0.5230	11
Providence – Pawtucket – Fall River, RI – MA	0.4056	12
Flint, MI	0.3891	13
Bradenton, FL	0.3883	14
Detroit – Ann Arbor, MI	0.3751	15
New Bedford, MA	0.3699	16
Naples, FL	0.3695	17
Daytona Beach, FL	0.3620	18
Fort Pierce, FL	0.3509	19
Ocala, FL	0.3290	20
Buffalo – Niagara Falls, NY	0.3268	21
Santa Barbara – Santa Maria – Lompoc, CA	0.3268	21
Seattle – Tacoma, WA	0.3175	22
Waterbury, CT	0.3064	23
Olympia, WA	0.3027	24
Hartford – New Britain – Middletown, CT	0.3012	25
Glens Falls, NY	0.3003	26
Jackson, MI	0.2998	27
Rochester, NY	0.2993	28
West Palm Beach – Boca Raton – Delray Beach, FL	0.2972	29
Sarasota, FL	0.2941	30
Tampa – Saint Petersburg – Clearwater, FL	0.2930	31
Provo – Orem, UT	0.2815	32
Melbourne – Titusville – Palm Bay, FL	0.2797	33
Portland – Vancouver, OR – WA	0.2742	34
Lansing – East Lansing, MI	0.2612	35
Fort Myers – Cape Coral, Fl	0.2611	36
Spokane, WA	0.2604	37
Pittsfield, MA	0.2573	38
Miami – Fort Lauderdale, FL	0.2500	39
New London – Norwich, CT – RI	0.2451	40
Syracuse, NY	0.2363	41
San Diego, CA	0.2326	42
Bremerton, WA	0.2266	43
Medford, OR	0.2261	44
Orlando, FL	0.2135	45
New Haven – Meriden, CT	0.2114	46
Los Angeles – Anaheim – Riverside, CA	0.2107	47
Albany – Schenectady – Troy, NY	0.2106	48
Salem, OR	0.2047	49

Source: U.S. Bureau of the Census, Data User Services Division, *1990 Census of Population and Housing*, Summary Tape File 3C, United States Summary, CD-ROM, February 1992.

★ 806 ★

First Ancestry

Persons, By First Ancestry, 1990: Czech

Data provided for all respondents who reported "Czech" as their sole ancestry, and those who reported "Czech" as their first ancestry.

[Table shows the top 50 areas]

MSA	% of total population	Rank
Cedar Rapids, IA	6.754	1
Victoria, TX	4.354	2
Lincoln, NE	4.176	3
Iowa City, IA	3.659	4
Omaha, NE – IA	3.045	5
Waco, TX	2.715	6
Bryan – College Station, TX	2.486	7
Grand Forks, ND	1.964	8
Green Bay, WI	1.693	9
Enid, OK	1.627	10
Killeen – Temple, TX	1.455	11
Eau Claire, WI	1.381	12
Rapid City, SD	1.335	13
La Crosse, WI	1.307	14
Austin, TX	1.301	15
Cleveland – Akron – Lorain, OH	1.290	16
Bismarck, ND	1.262	17
Minneapolis – Saint Paul, MN – WI	1.118	18
Chicago – Gary – Lake County, IL – IN – WI	1.082	19
Great Falls, MT	1.034	20
Corpus Christi, TX	1.017	21
Waterloo – Cedar Falls, IA	1.012	22
Madison, WI	1.006	23
Sioux City, IA – NE	0.989	24
Wausau, WI	0.975	25
Rochester, MN	0.970	26
Houston – Galveston – Brazoria, TX	0.965	27
Sioux Falls, SD	0.886	28
San Angelo, TX	0.884	29
Fort Collins – Loveland, CO	0.861	30
Milwaukee – Racine, WI	0.855	31
Fargo – Moorhead, ND – MN	0.851	32
Saint Cloud, MN	0.824	33
Casper, WY	0.817	34
Billings, MT	0.745	35
Janesville – Beloit, WI	0.685	36
Benton Harbor, MI	0.652	37
Duluth, MN – WI	0.648	38
Des Moines, IA	0.638	39
Denver – Boulder, CO	0.609	40
Appleton – Oshkosh – Neenah, WI	0.602	41
Oklahoma City, OK	0.589	42
Dallas – Fort Worth, TX	0.573	43
Steubenville – Weirton, OH – WV	0.554	44
Eugene – Springfield, OR	0.552	45
Greeley, CO	0.545	46
Wheeling, WV – OH	0.533	47
Kankakee, IL	0.529	48
Cheyenne, WY	0.526	49
Flint, MI	0.526	49

Source: U.S. Bureau of the Census, Data User Services Division, *1990 Census of Population and Housing*, Summary Tape File 3C, United States Summary, CD-ROM, February 1992.

★807★

First Ancestry

Persons, By First Ancestry, 1990: Danish

Data provided for all respondents who reported "Danish" as their sole ancestry, and for those who reported "Danish" as their first ancestry.

[Table shows the top 50 areas]

MSA	% of total population	Rank
Provo – Orem, UT	6.165	1
Salt Lake City – Ogden, UT	4.883	2
Omaha, NE – IA	2.847	3
Sioux City, IA – NE	2.807	4
Sioux Falls, SD	2.435	5
Waterloo – Cedar Falls, IA	2.290	6
Boise, ID	1.989	7
Lincoln, NE	1.832	8
Rochester, MN	1.596	9
Des Moines, IA	1.533	10
Eugene – Springfield, OR	1.420	11
Billings, MT	1.337	12
Iowa City, IA	1.260	13
Casper, WY	1.227	14
Bremerton, WA	1.169	15
Santa Barbara – Santa Maria – Lompoc, CA	1.152	16
Cedar Rapids, IA	1.150	17
Rapid City, SD	1.126	18
Minneapolis – Saint Paul, MN – WI	1.104	19
Portland – Vancouver, OR – WA	1.104	19
Bellingham, WA	1.075	20
Cheyenne, WY	1.071	21
Reno, NV	1.056	22
Seattle – Tacoma, WA	1.047	23
Spokane, WA	1.042	24
Great Falls, MT	1.017	25
Fort Collins – Loveland, CO	1.015	26
Chico, CA	0.980	27
Janesville – Beloit, WI	0.939	28
Green Bay, WI	0.932	29
Fargo – Moorhead, ND – MN	0.931	30
Milwaukee – Racine, WI	0.921	31
Medford, OR	0.901	32
Portland, ME	0.898	33
Salem, OR	0.897	34
Richland – Kennewick – Pasco, WA	0.878	35
Anchorage, AK	0.859	36
Olympia, WA	0.854	37
Redding, CA	0.854	37
Grand Forks, ND	0.835	38
Las Vegas, NV	0.828	39
Greeley, CO	0.818	40
Sacramento, CA	0.802	41
Denver – Boulder, CO	0.785	42
Fresno, CA	0.778	43
Bismarck, ND	0.756	44
Muskegon, MI	0.754	45
Madison, WI	0.740	46
Kankakee, IL	0.733	47
Eau Claire, WI	0.728	48

Source: U.S. Bureau of the Census, Data User Services Division, 1990 Census of Population and Housing, Summary Tape File 3C, United States Summary, CD-ROM, February 1992.

★808★

First Ancestry

Persons, By First Ancestry, 1990: Dutch

Data provided for all respondents who reported "Dutch" as their sole ancestry, and those who reported "Dutch" as their first ancestry.

[Table shows the top 50 areas]

MSA	% of total population	Rank
Grand Rapids, MI	25.524	1
Kalamazoo, MI	11.975	2
Muskegon, MI	9.365	3
Bellingham, WA	9.091	4
Sheboygan, WI	7.585	5
Appleton – Oshkosh – Neenah, WI	5.904	6
Sioux Falls, SD	5.171	7
Green Bay, WI	4.778	8
Lafayette – West Lafayette, IN	3.478	9
Battle Creek, MI	3.406	10
Des Moines, IA	3.328	11
Rochester, NY	3.180	12
Elkhart – Goshen, IN	3.072	13
Sioux City, IA – NE	2.924	14
Enid, OK	2.905	15
Lansing – East Lansing, MI	2.831	16
Allentown – Bethlehem – Easton, PA – NJ	2.807	17
Hickory – Morganton, NC	2.803	18
Joplin, MO	2.740	19
Williamsport, PA	2.733	20
Albany – Schenectady – Troy, NY	2.731	21
Elmira, NY	2.697	22
Benton Harbor, MI	2.617	23
Jackson, MI	2.600	24
Knoxville, TN	2.541	25
Bradenton, FL	2.433	26
Decatur, IL	2.433	26
Parkersburg – Marietta, WV – OH	2.419	27
Medford, OR	2.352	28
Jamestown – Dunkirk, NY	2.333	29
Fayetteville – Springdale, AR	2.315	30
Salt Lake City – Ogden, UT	2.308	31
Tulsa, OK	2.276	32
Yakima, WA	2.269	33
Poughkeepsie, NY	2.235	34
Salem, OR	2.234	35
Asheville, NC	2.226	36
Richland – Kennewick – Pasco, WA	2.224	37
Saint Joseph, MO	2.223	38
Binghamton, NY	2.222	39
Reading, PA	2.206	40
Johnson City – Kingsport – Bristol, TN – VA	2.205	41
Iowa City, IA	2.188	42
Oklahoma City, OK	2.177	43
Wichita, KS	2.171	44
Fort Collins – Loveland, CO	2.151	45
State College, PA	2.147	46
Eugene – Springfield, OR	2.127	47
Glens Falls, NY	2.124	48
Terre Haute, IN	2.118	49

Source: U.S. Bureau of the Census, Data User Services Division, 1990 Census of Population and Housing, Summary Tape File 3C, United States Summary, CD-ROM, February 1992.

★809★

First Ancestry

Persons, By First Ancestry, 1990: English

Data provided for all respondents who reported "English" as their sole ancestry, and for those who responded "English" as their first ancestry.

[Table shows the top 50 areas]

MSA	% of total population	Rank
Provo–Orem, UT	39.21	1
Salt Lake City–Ogden, UT	31.75	2
Portland, ME	21.79	3
Bangor, ME	20.34	4
Portsmouth–Dover–Rochester, NH–ME	19.22	5
Boise, ID	18.11	6
Charlottesville, VA	15.84	7
Medford, OR	15.69	8
Redding, CA	15.18	9
Lynchburg, VA	15.11	10
Sarasota, FL	14.86	11
Asheville, NC	14.76	12
Lewiston–Auburn, ME	14.57	13
Burlington, VT	14.45	14
Raleigh–Durham, NC	14.43	15
Owensboro, KY	14.38	16
Richmond–Petersburg, VA	14.34	17
Lexington-Fayette, KY	14.25	18
Elmira, NY	14.17	19
Charleston, WV	14.01	20
Springfield, MO	13.93	21
Bradenton, FL	13.90	22
Binghamton, NY	13.83	23
Chico, CA	13.82	24
Roanoke, VA	13.82	24
Wilmington, NC	13.76	25
Eugene–Springfield, OR	13.73	26
Athens, GA	13.58	27
Casper, WY	13.38	28
Battle Creek, MI	13.23	29
Huntington–Ashland, WV–KY–OH	13.19	30
Jackson, MI	13.11	31
Daytona Beach, FL	13.08	32
Midland, TX	12.94	33
Knoxville, TN	12.88	34
Melbourne–Titusville–Palm Bay, FL	12.85	35
Glens Falls, NY	12.71	36
Joplin, MO	12.68	37
Greenville–Spartanburg, SC	12.64	38
Panama City, FL	12.64	38
Fort Myers–Cape Coral, Fl	12.63	39
Naples, FL	12.63	39
Johnson City–Kingsport–Bristol, TN–VA	12.58	40
Olympia, WA	12.57	41
Nashville, TN	12.55	42
Fayetteville–Springdale, AR	12.53	43
Ocala, FL	12.51	44
Danville, VA	12.50	45

[Continued]

★809★

Persons, By First Ancestry, 1990: English

[Continued]

MSA	% of total population	Rank
Lansing–East Lansing, MI	12.41	46
Lakeland–Winter Haven, FL	12.40	47

Source: U.S. Bureau of the Census, Data User Services Division, 1990 Census of Population and Housing, Summary Tape File 3C, United States Summary, CD-ROM, February 1992.

★810★

First Ancestry

Persons, By First Ancestry, 1990: Finnish

Data provided for all respondents who reported "Finnish" as their sole ancestry, and those who reported "Finnish" as their first ancestry.

[Table shows the top 50 areas]

MSA	% of total population	Rank
Duluth, MN–WI	11.0205	1
Fitchburg–Leominster, MA	3.7219	2
Minneapolis–Saint Paul, MN–WI	1.1853	3
Great Falls, MT	0.8765	4
Portland–Vancouver, OR–WA	0.8440	5
Saint Cloud, MN	0.7448	6
Worcester, MA	0.6491	7
Bremerton, WA	0.6446	8
Olympia, WA	0.6183	9
Fargo–Moorhead, ND–MN	0.5721	10
Green Bay, WI	0.5545	11
West Palm Beach–Boca Raton–Delray Beach, FL	0.5539	12
Detroit–Ann Arbor, MI	0.5529	13
Seattle–Tacoma, WA	0.5256	14
Lansing–East Lansing, MI	0.5189	15
Billings, MT	0.4955	16
Grand Forks, ND	0.4683	17
Elmira, NY	0.4591	18
Anchorage, AK	0.4590	19
Muskegon, MI	0.4541	20
Wausau, WI	0.4393	21
Eugene–Springfield, OR	0.4284	22
Bellingham, WA	0.3897	23
Rapid City, SD	0.3799	24
Spokane, WA	0.3689	25
Lewiston–Auburn, ME	0.3679	26
Sheboygan, WI	0.3668	27
Rochester, MN	0.3578	28
Milwaukee–Racine, WI	0.3529	29
Jackson, MI	0.3365	30
Salem, OR	0.3223	31
Portland, ME	0.3221	32
New London–Norwich, CT–RI	0.3208	33
Richland–Kennewick–Pasco, WA	0.3139	34
Bismarck, ND	0.3030	35
Grand Rapids, MI	0.3027	36
Madison, WI	0.2956	37
Appleton–Oshkosh–Neenah, WI	0.2897	38

[Continued]

★810★

Persons, By First Ancestry, 1990: Finnish

[Continued]

MSA	% of total population	Rank
Redding, CA	0.2863	39
Flint, MI	0.2839	40
Youngstown – Warren, OH	0.2726	41
Chico, CA	0.2680	42
Boise, ID	0.2658	43
Kalamazoo, MI	0.2645	44
Reno, NV	0.2643	45
Boston – Lawrence – Salem, MA – NH	0.2638	46
Medford, OR	0.2562	47
Saginaw – Bay City – Midland, MI	0.2527	48
Fort Collins – Loveland, CO	0.2514	49
Portsmouth – Dover – Rochester, NH – ME	0.2486	50

Source: U.S. Bureau of the Census, Data User Services Division, *1990 Census of Population and Housing*, Summary Tape File 3C, United States Summary, CD-ROM, February 1992.

★811★

First Ancestry

Persons, By First Ancestry, 1990: French (exc. Basque)

Data provided for all respondents who reported "French" as their sole ancestry, and those who reported "French" as their first ancestry.

[Table shows the top 50 areas]

MSA	% of total population	Rank
Lewiston – Auburn, ME	21.02	1
Burlington, VT	20.35	2
Fitchburg – Leominster, MA	16.39	3
Houma – Thibodaux, LA	16.13	4
Manchester, NH	15.90	5
Glens Falls, NY	13.59	6
Worcester, MA	13.31	7
New Orleans, LA	12.22	8
Springfield, MA	12.14	9
Bangor, ME	11.76	10
Lafayette, LA	11.74	11
Portsmouth – Dover – Rochester, NH – ME	11.34	12
Portland, ME	10.90	13
Kankakee, IL	10.62	14
Lake Charles, LA	10.56	15
Pittsfield, MA	10.55	16
Baton Rouge, LA	10.54	17
Providence – Pawtucket – Fall River, RI – MA	10.31	18
Biloxi – Gulfport, MS	9.84	19
New Bedford, MA	9.37	20
Alexandria, LA	8.25	21
New London – Norwich, CT – RI	7.56	22
Hartford – New Britain – Middletown, CT	6.90	23

[Continued]

★811★

Persons, By First Ancestry, 1990: French (exc. Basque)

[Continued]

MSA	% of total population	Rank
Saginaw – Bay City – Midland, MI	6.75	24
Albany – Schenectady – Troy, NY	6.17	25
Pascagoula, MS	6.16	26
Beaumont – Port Arthur, TX	6.10	27
Waterbury, CT	5.72	28
Syracuse, NY	5.10	29
Boston – Lawrence – Salem, MA – NH	4.96	30
Green Bay, WI	4.92	31
Utica – Rome, NY	4.53	32
Muskegon, MI	4.45	33
Flint, MI	4.44	34
Shreveport, LA	4.20	35
Monroe, LA	4.18	36
Duluth, MN – WI	3.76	37
Grand Forks, ND	3.73	38
Sioux City, IA – NE	3.59	39
Detroit – Ann Arbor, MI	3.56	40
Ocala, FL	3.52	41
Toledo, OH	3.48	42
Redding, CA	3.46	43
Bremerton, WA	3.43	44
Fort Wayne, IN	3.41	45
Medford, OR	3.41	45
Spokane, WA	3.41	45
Yakima, WA	3.40	46
Sarasota, FL	3.39	47
Daytona Beach, FL	3.37	48

Source: U.S. Bureau of the Census, Data User Services Division, *1990 Census of Population and Housing*, Summary Tape File 3C, United States Summary, CD-ROM, February 1992.

★812★

First Ancestry

Persons, By First Ancestry, 1990: French Canadian

Data provided for all respondents who reported "French Canadian" and their sole ancestry, and those who reported "French Canadian" as their first ancestry.

[Table shows the top 50 areas]

MSA	% of total population	Rank
Houma – Thibodaux, LA	37.915	1
Lafayette, LA	32.605	2
Lewiston – Auburn, ME	24.263	3
Lake Charles, LA	21.768	4
Manchester, NH	17.505	5
Fitchburg – Leominster, MA	11.864	6
Burlington, VT	8.573	7
Baton Rouge, LA	8.409	8
Beaumont – Port Arthur, TX	8.249	9
Portsmouth – Dover – Rochester, NH – ME	8.201	10

[Continued]

★812★

Persons, By First Ancestry, 1990: French Canadian
[Continued]

MSA	% of total population	Rank
Providence – Pawtucket – Fall River, RI – MA	7.200	11
Springfield, MA	7.077	12
Bangor, ME	6.605	13
New Bedford, MA	6.441	14
Alexandria, LA	5.790	15
Worcester, MA	5.681	16
Portland, ME	5.130	17
New Orleans, LA	4.125	18
Pittsfield, MA	4.068	19
New London – Norwich, CT – RI	4.017	20
Glens Falls, NY	3.981	21
Hartford – New Britain – Middletown, CT	3.674	22
Boston – Lawrence – Salem, MA – NH	3.550	23
Waterbury, CT	3.171	24
Kankakee, IL	3.125	25
Albany – Schenectady – Troy, NY	2.194	26
Saginaw – Bay City – Midland, MI	2.094	27
Biloxi – Gulfport, MS	2.091	28
Flint, MI	2.048	29
Monroe, LA	1.991	30
Syracuse, NY	1.956	31
Green Bay, WI	1.743	32
New Haven – Meriden, CT	1.635	33
Shreveport, LA	1.584	34
Muskegon, MI	1.527	35
Pascagoula, MS	1.420	36
Detroit – Ann Arbor, MI	1.343	37
Utica – Rome, NY	1.302	38
Lansing – East Lansing, MI	1.227	39
Fort Walton Beach, FL	1.226	40
Jacksonville, NC	1.205	41
Eau Claire, WI	1.168	42
Houston – Galveston – Brazoria, TX	1.119	43
Daytona Beach, FL	1.108	44
Fort Pierce, FL	1.106	45
Anchorage, AK	1.099	46
Melbourne – Titusville – Palm Bay, FL	1.094	47
Ocala, FL	1.065	48
Sarasota, FL	1.032	49
Poughkeepsie, NY	1.027	50

Source: U.S. Bureau of the Census, Data User Services Division, *1990 Census of Population and Housing*, Summary Tape File 3C, United States Summary, CD-ROM, February 1992.

★813★
First Ancestry

Persons, By First Ancestry, 1990: German

Data provided for all respondents who reported "German" as their sole ancestry, and those who reported "German" as their first ancestry.

[Table shows the top 50 areas]

MSA	% of total population	Rank
Bismarck, ND	63.6	1
Sheboygan, WI	62.4	2
Dubuque, IA	62.2	3
Appleton – Oshkosh – Neenah, WI	59.1	4
Wausau, WI	58.1	5
Saint Cloud, MN	57.7	6
York, PA	54.5	7
Lancaster, PA	52.1	8
Waterloo – Cedar Falls, IA	48.8	9
Williamsport, PA	47.6	10
Lima, OH	47.0	11
Reading, PA	47.0	11
Altoona, PA	46.9	12
La Crosse, WI	46.8	13
Eau Claire, WI	46.1	14
Harrisburg – Lebanon – Carlisle, PA	45.7	15
Lincoln, NE	45.2	16
Sioux Falls, SD	44.4	17
Fort Wayne, IN	43.2	18
Rochester, MN	42.4	19
Elkhart – Goshen, IN	40.7	20
Cedar Rapids, IA	40.2	21
Milwaukee – Racine, WI	40.0	22
Green Bay, WI	39.9	23
Madison, WI	39.8	24
Hagerstown, MD	39.0	25
Sioux City, IA – NE	39.0	25
Evansville, IN – KY	38.9	26
Johnstown, PA	38.6	27
Janesville – Beloit, WI	38.5	28
Fargo – Moorhead, ND – MN	37.9	29
Iowa City, IA	37.6	30
Bloomington – Normal, IL	37.4	31
Peoria, IL	37.4	31
Cincinnati – Hamilton, OH – KY – IN	37.2	32
Rapid City, SD	37.1	33
Cumberland, MD – WV	36.6	34
State College, PA	36.1	35
Canton, OH	35.3	36
Mansfield, OH	35.3	36
Toledo, OH	35.0	37
Billings, MT	34.4	38
Saint Louis, MO – IL	34.4	38
Minneapolis – Saint Paul, MN – WI	34.3	39
Davenport – Rock Island – Moline, IA – IL	34.0	40
Allentown – Bethlehem – Easton, PA – NJ	33.6	41
Omaha, NE – IA	33.2	42
Lafayette – West Lafayette, IN	32.9	43

[Continued]

★813★

Persons, By First Ancestry, 1990: German

[Continued]

MSA	% of total population	Rank
Topeka, KS	32.9	43
Greeley, CO	32.7	44

Source: U.S. Bureau of the Census, Data User Services Division, *1990 Census of Population and Housing*, Summary Tape File 3C, United States Summary, CD-ROM, February 1992.

★814★

First Ancestry

Persons, By First Ancestry, 1990: Greek

Data provided for all respondents who reported "Greek" as their sole ancestry, and those who reported "Greek" as their first ancestry.

[Table shows the top 50 areas]

MSA	% of total population	Rank
Manchester, NH	2.629	1
Boston – Lawrence – Salem, MA – NH	1.385	2
Portsmouth – Dover – Rochester, NH – ME	1.134	3
Fitchburg – Leominster, MA	1.047	4
Youngstown – Warren, OH	1.013	5
Chicago – Gary – Lake County, IL – IN – WI	0.971	6
Worcester, MA	0.968	7
Canton, OH	0.940	8
New York – Northern New Jersey – Long Island, NY – NJ – CT	0.933	9
New London – Norwich, CT – RI	0.923	10
Springfield, MA	0.884	11
Steubenville – Weirton, OH – WV	0.841	12
Tampa – Saint Petersburg – Clearwater, FL	0.805	13
Portland, ME	0.687	14
Wheeling, WV – OH	0.685	15
Salt Lake City – Ogden, UT	0.652	16
Reading, PA	0.640	17
Poughkeepsie, NY	0.632	18
Baltimore, MD	0.619	19
Pittsfield, MA	0.606	20
New Haven – Meriden, CT	0.604	21
Washington, DC – MD – VA	0.583	22
New Bedford, MA	0.569	23
Hartford – New Britain – Middletown, CT	0.549	24
Detroit – Ann Arbor, MI	0.537	25
Pittsburgh – Beaver Valley, PA	0.529	26
Daytona Beach, FL	0.520	27
Atlantic City, NJ	0.518	28
Allentown – Bethlehem – Easton, PA – NJ	0.493	29
Albany – Schenectady – Troy, NY	0.492	30
San Francisco – Oakland – San Jose, CA	0.492	30

[Continued]

★814★

Persons, By First Ancestry, 1990: Greek

[Continued]

MSA	% of total population	Rank
West Palm Beach – Boca Raton – Delray Beach, FL	0.492	30
Cleveland – Akron – Lorain, OH	0.477	31
Casper, WY	0.469	32
Las Vegas, NV	0.468	33
Champaign – Urbana – Rantoul, IL	0.459	34
Wilmington, NC	0.440	35
Fort Pierce, FL	0.435	36
Pensacola, FL	0.431	37
Providence – Pawtucket – Fall River, RI – MA	0.424	38
Philadelphia – Wilmington – Trenton, PA – NJ – DE – MD	0.421	39
Miami – Fort Lauderdale, FL	0.415	40
Sacramento, CA	0.414	41
Reno, NV	0.410	42
Lansing – East Lansing, MI	0.407	43
South Bend – Mishawaka, IN	0.407	43
Bradenton, FL	0.406	44
Rochester, NY	0.401	45
Cheyenne, WY	0.399	46
Olympia, WA	0.398	47

Source: U.S. Bureau of the Census, Data User Services Division, *1990 Census of Population and Housing*, Summary Tape File 3C, United States Summary, CD-ROM, February 1992.

★815★

First Ancestry

Persons, By First Ancestry, 1990: Hungarian

Data provided for all respondents who reported "Hungarian" as their sole ancestry, and those who reported "Hungarian" as their first ancestry.

[Table shows the top 50 areas]

MSA	% of total population	Rank
South Bend – Mishawaka, IN	3.255	1
Cleveland – Akron – Lorain, OH	2.985	2
Allentown – Bethlehem – Easton, PA – NJ	2.394	3
Youngstown – Warren, OH	2.008	4
Toledo, OH	1.754	5
Johnstown, PA	1.749	6
Sharon, PA	1.572	7
Pittsburgh – Beaver Valley, PA	1.388	8
Steubenville – Weirton, OH – WV	1.374	9
Wheeling, WV – OH	1.303	10
Flint, MI	1.168	11
Canton, OH	1.124	12
Detroit – Ann Arbor, MI	0.981	13
West Palm Beach – Boca Raton – Delray Beach, FL	0.978	14
New York – Northern New Jersey – Long Island, NY – NJ – CT	0.967	15
Poughkeepsie, NY	0.840	16

[Continued]

★815★

Persons, By First Ancestry, 1990: Hungarian

[Continued]

MSA	% of total population	Rank
Sarasota, FL	0.835	17
New Haven – Meriden, CT	0.824	18
Erie, PA	0.723	19
Buffalo – Niagara Falls, NY	0.704	20
Naples, FL	0.700	21
Kalamazoo, MI	0.670	22
State College, PA	0.668	23
Miami – Fort Lauderdale, FL	0.659	24
Saginaw – Bay City – Midland, MI	0.655	25
Columbus, OH	0.653	26
Waterbury, CT	0.638	27
Muskegon, MI	0.599	28
Fort Myers – Cape Coral, Fl	0.596	29
Dayton – Springfield, OH	0.593	30
Philadelphia – Wilmington – Trenton, PA – NJ – DE – MD	0.593	30
Benton Harbor, MI	0.581	31
Tampa – Saint Petersburg – Clearwater, FL	0.569	32
Mansfield, OH	0.567	33
Harrisburg – Lebanon – Carlisle, PA	0.533	34
Scranton – Wilkes-Barre, PA	0.522	35
Milwaukee – Racine, WI	0.515	36
Elkhart – Goshen, IN	0.513	37
Chicago – Gary – Lake County, IL – IN – WI	0.499	38
Melbourne – Titusville – Palm Bay, FL	0.496	39
Bradenton, FL	0.492	40
Daytona Beach, FL	0.477	41
Fort Pierce, FL	0.469	42
Phoenix, AZ	0.464	43
Atlantic City, NJ	0.462	44
Las Vegas, NV	0.450	45
Burlington, VT	0.439	46
Springfield, IL	0.439	46
Binghamton, NY	0.426	47
Lansing – East Lansing, MI	0.424	48

Source: U.S. Bureau of the Census, Data User Services Division, *1990 Census of Population and Housing*, Summary Tape File 3C, United States Summary, CD-ROM, February 1992.

★816★

First Ancestry

Persons, By First Ancestry, 1990: Irish

Data provided for all respondents who reported "Irish" as their sole ancestry, and those who reported "Irish" as their first ancestry.

[Table shows the top 50 areas]

MSA	% of total population	Rank
Boston – Lawrence – Salem, MA – NH	21.06	1
Pittsfield, MA	18.47	2
Worcester, MA	16.91	3
Albany – Schenectady – Troy, NY	16.40	4
Poughkeepsie, NY	15.97	5
Portland, ME	15.03	6
Glens Falls, NY	14.82	7
Atlantic City, NJ	14.52	8
Philadelphia – Wilmington – Trenton, PA – NJ – DE – MD	14.17	9
Syracuse, NY	14.14	10
Decatur, AL	14.10	11
Florence, AL	14.06	12
Binghamton, NY	14.03	13
Elmira, NY	13.98	14
Anderson, SC	13.85	15
Portsmouth – Dover – Rochester, NH – ME	13.74	16
Scranton – Wilkes-Barre, PA	13.67	17
Owensboro, KY	13.65	18
Springfield, MA	13.62	19
Manchester, NH	13.61	20
Dubuque, IA	13.45	21
Providence – Pawtucket – Fall River, RI – MA	13.33	22
Fort Smith, AR – OK	13.29	23
Waterbury, CT	13.27	24
Gadsden, AL	13.16	25
Fayetteville – Springdale, AR	13.15	26
Bangor, ME	13.12	27
Texarkana, TX – Texarkana, AR	13.02	28
Huntington – Ashland, WV – KY – OH	12.55	29
Chattanooga, TN – GA	12.50	30
Sherman – Denison, TX	12.44	31
Fitchburg – Leominster, MA	12.31	32
New London – Norwich, CT – RI	12.27	33
Wichita Falls, TX	12.23	34
Knoxville, TN	12.22	35
Utica – Rome, NY	12.16	36
Burlington, VT	12.11	37
New Haven – Meriden, CT	12.08	38
Springfield, MO	12.02	39
Nashville, TN	11.84	40
Longview – Marshall, TX	11.78	41
Louisville, KY – IN	11.71	42
Steubenville – Weirton, OH – WV	11.66	43
Monroe, LA	11.65	44
Springfield, IL	11.64	45
Johnson City – Kingsport – Bristol, TN – VA	11.60	46
Tulsa, OK	11.58	47

[Continued]

★816★

Persons, By First Ancestry, 1990: Irish

[Continued]

MSA	% of total population	Rank
Jackson, TN	11.57	48
Greenville – Spartanburg, SC	11.53	49
Hartford – New Britain – Middletown, CT	11.49	50

Source: U.S. Bureau of the Census, Data User Services Division, *1990 Census of Population and Housing*, Summary Tape File 3C, United States Summary, CD-ROM, February 1992.

★817★

First Ancestry

Persons, By First Ancestry, 1990: Italian

Data provided for all respondents who reported "Italian" as their sole ancestry, and those who reported "Italian" as their first ancestry.

[Table shows the top 50 areas]

MSA	% of total population	Rank
Waterbury, CT	22.05	1
New Haven – Meriden, CT	21.99	2
Utica – Rome, NY	16.75	3
Poughkeepsie, NY	15.77	4
Atlantic City, NJ	15.26	5
Pittsfield, MA	14.93	6
New York – Northern New Jersey – Long Island, NY – NJ – CT	14.76	7
Providence – Pawtucket – Fall River, RI – MA	14.31	8
Rochester, NY	13.97	9
Youngstown – Warren, OH	13.60	10
Albany – Schenectady – Troy, NY	13.55	11
Hartford – New Britain – Middletown, CT	13.15	12
Scranton – Wilkes-Barre, PA	13.04	13
Boston – Lawrence – Salem, MA – NH	12.38	14
Buffalo – Niagara Falls, NY	12.33	15
Syracuse, NY	12.28	16
Steubenville – Weirton, OH – WV	12.10	17
New London – Norwich, CT – RI	11.98	18
Pittsburgh – Beaver Valley, PA	11.89	19
Jamestown – Dunkirk, NY	11.37	20
Philadelphia – Wilmington – Trenton, PA – NJ – DE – MD	11.28	21
Fitchburg – Leominster, MA	11.15	22
Worcester, MA	9.41	23
Binghamton, NY	9.28	24
Erie, PA	9.07	25
Sharon, PA	8.58	26
Allentown – Bethlehem – Easton, PA – NJ	8.48	27
Springfield, MA	8.16	28
Elmira, NY	7.69	29
West Palm Beach – Boca Raton – Delray Beach, FL	7.49	30

[Continued]

★817★

Persons, By First Ancestry, 1990: Italian

[Continued]

MSA	% of total population	Rank
Fort Pierce, FL	7.14	31
Cleveland – Akron – Lorain, OH	7.01	32
Altoona, PA	6.82	33
Glens Falls, NY	6.47	34
Johnstown, PA	6.38	35
Wheeling, WV – OH	6.38	35
Canton, OH	6.37	36
Pueblo, CO	6.35	37
Tampa – Saint Petersburg – Clearwater, FL	6.11	38
New Orleans, LA	6.03	39
Portland, ME	6.03	39
Las Vegas, NV	6.02	40
Daytona Beach, FL	5.88	41
Chicago – Gary – Lake County, IL – IN – WI	5.86	42
Reading, PA	5.77	43
Fort Myers – Cape Coral, Fl	5.73	44
Melbourne – Titusville – Palm Bay, FL	5.62	45
Naples, FL	5.60	46
Reno, NV	5.51	47
Sarasota, FL	5.34	48

Source: U.S. Bureau of the Census, Data User Services Division, *1990 Census of Population and Housing*, Summary Tape File 3C, United States Summary, CD-ROM, February 1992.

★818★

First Ancestry

Persons, By First Ancestry, 1990: Lithuanian

Data provided for all respondents who reported "Lithuanian" as their sole ancestry, and those who reported "Lithuanian" as their first ancestry.

[Table shows the top 50 areas]

MSA	% of total population	Rank
Waterbury, CT	2.2132	1
Scranton – Wilkes-Barre, PA	2.0373	2
Worcester, MA	1.8833	3
Hartford – New Britain – Middletown, CT	0.9669	4
Springfield, IL	0.9095	5
Chicago – Gary – Lake County, IL – IN – WI	0.8092	6
Boston – Lawrence – Salem, MA – NH	0.7062	7
Sheboygan, WI	0.6402	8
New Haven – Meriden, CT	0.6203	9
Binghamton, NY	0.6019	10
Grand Rapids, MI	0.5481	11
Rockford, IL	0.5421	12
Kankakee, IL	0.5215	13
Pittsburgh – Beaver Valley, PA	0.5202	14
Fitchburg – Leominster, MA	0.4767	15

[Continued]

★818★

Persons, By First Ancestry, 1990: Lithuanian
[Continued]

MSA	% of total population	Rank
Manchester, NH	0.4720	16
Springfield, MA	0.4601	17
Philadelphia – Wilmington – Trenton, PA – NJ – DE – MD	0.4465	18
Albany – Schenectady – Troy, NY	0.4255	19
Lewiston – Auburn, ME	0.4246	20
Baltimore, MD	0.4227	21
Cleveland – Akron – Lorain, OH	0.4131	22
Allentown – Bethlehem – Easton, PA – NJ	0.4008	23
West Palm Beach – Boca Raton – Delray Beach, FL	0.3898	24
New London – Norwich, CT – RI	0.3849	25
State College, PA	0.3789	26
Atlantic City, NJ	0.3747	27
Benton Harbor, MI	0.3600	28
Pittsfield, MA	0.3557	29
Naples, FL	0.3445	30
Harrisburg – Lebanon – Carlisle, PA	0.3424	31
Reading, PA	0.3399	32
Champaign – Urbana – Rantoul, IL	0.3387	33
Omaha, NE – IA	0.3214	34
Detroit – Ann Arbor, MI	0.3111	35
Muskegon, MI	0.3107	36
Daytona Beach, FL	0.3037	37
Sioux City, IA – NE	0.3034	38
New York – Northern New Jersey – Long Island, NY – NJ – CT	0.3028	39
Rochester, NY	0.2958	40
Tampa – Saint Petersburg – Clearwater, FL	0.2886	41
Sarasota, FL	0.2876	42
Utica – Rome, NY	0.2751	43
Johnstown, PA	0.2744	44
Portsmouth – Dover – Rochester, NH – ME	0.2740	45
Washington, DC – MD – VA	0.2578	46
Janesville – Beloit, WI	0.2552	47
Providence – Pawtucket – Fall River, RI – MA	0.2539	48
Miami – Fort Lauderdale, FL	0.2469	49
Iowa City, IA	0.2455	50

Source: U.S. Bureau of the Census, Data User Services Division, *1990 Census of Population and Housing,* Summary Tape File 3C, United States Summary, CD-ROM, February 1992.

★819★
First Ancestry

Persons, By First Ancestry, 1990: Norwegian

Data provided for all respondents who reported "Norwegian" as their sole ancestry, and those who reported "Norwegian" as their first ancestry.

[Table shows the top 50 areas]

MSA	% of total population	Rank
Fargo – Moorhead, ND – MN	26.179	1
Grand Forks, ND	25.203	2
La Crosse, WI	16.427	3
Eau Claire, WI	14.511	4
Sioux Falls, SD	14.173	5
Rochester, MN	12.037	6
Janesville – Beloit, WI	9.872	7
Bismarck, ND	9.807	8
Duluth, MN – WI	9.775	9
Madison, WI	9.657	10
Minneapolis – Saint Paul, MN – WI	9.092	11
Billings, MT	7.769	12
Rapid City, SD	6.972	13
Great Falls, MT	6.927	14
Saint Cloud, MN	5.825	15
Bremerton, WA	5.548	16
Seattle – Tacoma, WA	5.400	17
Bellingham, WA	5.351	18
Spokane, WA	4.308	19
Olympia, WA	4.247	20
Sioux City, IA – NE	3.839	21
Waterloo – Cedar Falls, IA	3.677	22
Eugene – Springfield, OR	3.312	23
Portland – Vancouver, OR – WA	3.287	24
Richland – Kennewick – Pasco, WA	3.204	25
Salem, OR	2.984	26
Des Moines, IA	2.972	27
Cedar Rapids, IA	2.952	28
Casper, WY	2.901	29
Wausau, WI	2.769	30
Rockford, IL	2.747	31
Anchorage, AK	2.719	32
Iowa City, IA	2.594	33
Medford, OR	2.554	34
Appleton – Oshkosh – Neenah, WI	2.380	35
Boise, ID	2.214	36
Green Bay, WI	2.142	37
Milwaukee – Racine, WI	2.052	38
Fort Collins – Loveland, CO	1.986	39
Yakima, WA	1.851	40
Chico, CA	1.790	41
Colorado Springs, CO	1.721	42
Cheyenne, WY	1.716	43
Reno, NV	1.621	44
Redding, CA	1.540	45
Denver – Boulder, CO	1.532	46
Phoenix, AZ	1.417	47
Omaha, NE – IA	1.402	48
Salt Lake City – Ogden, UT	1.294	49
Provo – Orem, UT	1.258	50

Source: U.S. Bureau of the Census, Data User Services Division, *1990 Census of Population and Housing,* Summary Tape File 3C, United States Summary, CD-ROM, February 1992.

★820★
First Ancestry

Persons, By First Ancestry, 1990: Polish

Data provided for all respondents who reported "Polish" as their sole ancestry, and those who reported "Polish" as their first ancestry.

[Table shows the top 50 areas]

MSA	% of total population	Rank
Buffalo – Niagara Falls, NY	15.35	1
Scranton – Wilkes-Barre, PA	14.84	2
Wausau, WI	12.44	3
Springfield, MA	11.29	4
Erie, PA	10.92	5
South Bend – Mishawaka, IN	10.71	6
Milwaukee – Racine, WI	9.48	7
Hartford – New Britain – Middletown, CT	9.17	8
Saginaw – Bay City – Midland, MI	9.15	9
Detroit – Ann Arbor, MI	9.06	10
Utica – Rome, NY	9.03	11
Chicago – Gary – Lake County, IL – IN – WI	8.77	12
Jamestown – Dunkirk, NY	8.41	13
Green Bay, WI	8.02	14
Toledo, OH	7.68	15
Pittsburgh – Beaver Valley, PA	7.05	16
Pittsfield, MA	6.92	17
Wheeling, WV – OH	6.86	18
Johnstown, PA	6.75	19
New London – Norwich, CT – RI	6.49	20
Worcester, MA	6.40	21
Albany – Schenectady – Troy, NY	6.12	22
Cleveland – Akron – Lorain, OH	5.92	23
Steubenville – Weirton, OH – WV	5.92	23
Jackson, MI	5.77	24
New Haven – Meriden, CT	5.68	25
Grand Rapids, MI	5.64	26
Saint Cloud, MN	5.37	27
Binghamton, NY	5.30	28
Syracuse, NY	5.28	29
Duluth, MN – WI	5.03	30
Reading, PA	4.93	31
Muskegon, MI	4.81	32
Philadelphia – Wilmington – Trenton, PA – NJ – DE – MD	4.60	33
Waterbury, CT	4.55	34
Elmira, NY	4.46	35
New York – Northern New Jersey – Long Island, NY – NJ – CT	4.43	36
Manchester, NH	4.03	37
Allentown – Bethlehem – Easton, PA – NJ	3.99	38
Poughkeepsie, NY	3.96	39
Flint, MI	3.89	40
Baltimore, MD	3.88	41
West Palm Beach – Boca Raton – Delray Beach, FL	3.71	42
Appleton – Oshkosh – Neenah, WI	3.69	43
Eau Claire, WI	3.69	43
Rochester, NY	3.68	44
Grand Forks, ND	3.66	45

[Continued]

★820★

Persons, By First Ancestry, 1990: Polish
[Continued]

MSA	% of total population	Rank
Omaha, NE – IA	3.50	46
Minneapolis – Saint Paul, MN – WI	3.49	47
New Bedford, MA	3.45	48

Source: U.S. Bureau of the Census, Data User Services Division, *1990 Census of Population and Housing*, Summary Tape File 3C, United States Summary, CD-ROM, February 1992.

★821★
First Ancestry

Persons, By First Ancestry, 1990: Portuguese

Data provided for all respondents who reported "Portuguese" as their sole ancestry, and those who reported "Portuguese" as their first ancestry.

[Table shows the top 50 areas]

MSA	% of total ancestry	Rank
New Bedford, MA	35.3524	1
Providence – Pawtucket – Fall River, RI – MA	11.7248	2
Merced, CA	6.9965	3
Modesto, CA	4.5428	4
Visalia – Tulare – Porterville, CA	2.9947	5
Stockton, CA	2.6101	6
Honolulu, HI	2.6066	7
Waterbury, CT	2.2687	8
Boston – Lawrence – Salem, MA – NH	1.8192	9
San Francisco – Oakland – San Jose, CA	1.7409	10
Springfield, MA	1.7177	11
New London – Norwich, CT – RI	1.5175	12
Chico, CA	1.5133	13
Sacramento, CA	1.3906	14
Salinas – Seaside – Monterey, CA	1.2265	15
Redding, CA	1.2174	16
Fresno, CA	1.1657	17
Yuba City, CA	1.1228	18
Hartford – New Britain – Middletown, CT	0.9855	19
Reno, NV	0.8666	20
Santa Barbara – Santa Maria – Lompoc, CA	0.8625	21
Medford, OR	0.7029	22
Fitchburg – Leominster, MA	0.6206	23
New York – Northern New Jersey – Long Island, NY – NJ – CT	0.5295	24
Manchester, NH	0.5099	25
San Diego, CA	0.5088	26
New Haven – Meriden, CT	0.4868	27
Worcester, MA	0.4834	28
Pittsfield, MA	0.4453	29
Bakersfield, CA	0.4208	30
Portsmouth – Dover – Rochester, NH – ME	0.4073	31

[Continued]

★821★

Persons, By First Ancestry, 1990: Portuguese

[Continued]

MSA	% of total ancestry	Rank
Bangor, ME	0.3100	32
Eugene – Springfield, OR	0.2877	33
Las Vegas, NV	0.2796	34
Springfield, IL	0.2764	35
Allentown – Bethlehem – Easton, PA – NJ	0.2730	36
Bremerton, WA	0.2714	37
Burlington, VT	0.2708	38
Poughkeepsie, NY	0.2559	39
West Palm Beach – Boca Raton – Delray Beach, FL	0.2461	40
Casper, WY	0.2401	41
Fort Pierce, FL	0.2394	42
Daytona Beach, FL	0.2279	43
Portland – Vancouver, OR – WA	0.2278	44
Los Angeles – Anaheim – Riverside, CA	0.2245	45
Naples, FL	0.2163	46
Fort Myers – Cape Coral, Fl	0.2146	47
Tampa – Saint Petersburg – Clearwater, FL	0.2144	48
Portland, ME	0.2107	49
Melbourne – Titusville – Palm Bay, FL	0.2065	50

Source: U.S. Bureau of the Census, Data User Services Division, *1990 Census of Population and Housing*, Summary Tape File 3C, United States Summary, CD-ROM, February 1992.

★822★

First Ancestry

Persons, By First Ancestry, 1990: Russian

Data provided for all respondents who reported "Russian" as their sole ancestry, and those who reported "Russian" as their first ancestry.

[Table shows the top 50 areas]

MSA	% of total population	Rank
West Palm Beach – Boca Raton – Delray Beach, FL	4.555	1
Miami – Fort Lauderdale, FL	3.099	2
New York – Northern New Jersey – Long Island, NY – NJ – CT	3.074	3
Philadelphia – Wilmington – Trenton, PA – NJ – DE – MD	2.101	4
Boston – Lawrence – Salem, MA – NH	2.034	5
New Haven – Meriden, CT	1.940	6
Scranton – Wilkes-Barre, PA	1.860	7
Binghamton, NY	1.852	8
Atlantic City, NJ	1.822	9
Washington, DC – MD – VA	1.570	10
Hartford – New Britain – Middletown, CT	1.546	11
Poughkeepsie, NY	1.504	12

[Continued]

★822★

Persons, By First Ancestry, 1990: Russian

[Continued]

MSA	% of total population	Rank
Baltimore, MD	1.395	13
Los Angeles – Anaheim – Riverside, CA	1.352	14
Chicago – Gary – Lake County, IL – IN – WI	1.262	15
San Francisco – Oakland – San Jose, CA	1.248	16
Sarasota, FL	1.241	17
Salem, OR	1.186	18
Albany – Schenectady – Troy, NY	1.149	19
Pittsburgh – Beaver Valley, PA	1.097	20
Waterbury, CT	1.070	21
Cleveland – Akron – Lorain, OH	1.069	22
New London – Norwich, CT – RI	1.023	23
Springfield, MA	1.022	24
Pittsfield, MA	0.986	25
Santa Fe, NM	0.983	26
Las Vegas, NV	0.950	27
San Diego, CA	0.925	28
Denver – Boulder, CO	0.912	29
Tucson, AZ	0.910	30
Santa Barbara – Santa Maria – Lompoc, CA	0.892	31
Burlington, VT	0.882	32
Portland, ME	0.881	33
Detroit – Ann Arbor, MI	0.853	34
State College, PA	0.853	34
Worcester, MA	0.838	35
Madison, WI	0.835	36
Syracuse, NY	0.807	37
Bloomington, IN	0.805	38
Johnstown, PA	0.799	39
Gainesville, FL	0.792	40
Allentown – Bethlehem – Easton, PA – NJ	0.784	41
Erie, PA	0.784	41
Portland – Vancouver, OR – WA	0.782	42
Phoenix, AZ	0.780	43
Providence – Pawtucket – Fall River, RI – MA	0.778	44
Lawrence, KS	0.770	45
Manchester, NH	0.764	46
Rochester, NY	0.746	47
Charlottesville, VA	0.733	48

Source: U.S. Bureau of the Census, Data User Services Division, *1990 Census of Population and Housing*, Summary Tape File 3C, United States Summary, CD-ROM, February 1992.

★823★

First Ancestry

Persons, By First Ancestry, 1990: Scotch-Irish

Data provided for all respondents who reported "Scotch-Irish" as their sole ancestry, and those who reported "Scotch-Irish" as their first ancestry.

[Table shows the top 50 areas]

MSA	% of total population	Rank
Wilmington, NC	7.04	1
Charlotte – Gastonia – Rock Hill, NC – SC	6.23	2
Asheville, NC	6.04	3
Anderson, SC	4.91	4
Greenville – Spartanburg, SC	4.79	5
Florence, SC	4.66	6
Knoxville, TN	4.65	7
Sharon, PA	4.48	8
Raleigh – Durham, NC	4.46	9
Columbia, SC	4.30	10
Burlington, NC	4.18	11
Nashville, TN	4.13	12
Fayetteville, NC	4.11	13
Roanoke, VA	3.96	14
Jackson, MS	3.94	15
Greensboro – Winston-Salem – High Point, NC	3.84	16
Johnson City – Kingsport – Bristol, TN – VA	3.84	16
Casper, WY	3.62	17
Steubenville – Weirton, OH – WV	3.56	18
Pensacola, FL	3.51	19
Hickory – Morganton, NC	3.46	20
Wheeling, WV – OH	3.45	21
Bangor, ME	3.42	22
Fort Walton Beach, FL	3.37	23
Mobile, AL	3.35	24
Abilene, TX	3.33	25
Amarillo, TX	3.33	25
Tallahassee, FL	3.32	26
Lynchburg, VA	3.29	27
Jackson, TN	3.25	28
Montgomery, AL	3.25	28
Midland, TX	3.23	29
Panama City, FL	3.22	30
Charlottesville, VA	3.21	31
San Angelo, TX	3.19	32
Tyler, TX	3.18	33
Waco, TX	3.16	34
Shreveport, LA	3.14	35
Austin, TX	3.11	36
Birmingham, AL	3.11	36
Florence, AL	3.10	37
Huntsville, AL	3.10	37
Memphis, TN – AR – MS	3.09	38
Athens, GA	3.05	39
Pascagoula, MS	3.03	40
Springfield, MO	3.03	40
Lexington-Fayette, KY	3.00	41
Enid, OK	2.94	42

[Continued]

★823★

Persons, By First Ancestry, 1990: Scotch-Irish

[Continued]

MSA	% of total population	Rank
Atlanta, GA	2.92	43
Lubbock, TX	2.91	44

Source: U.S. Bureau of the Census, Data User Services Division, *1990 Census of Population and Housing*, Summary Tape File 3C, United States Summary, CD-ROM, February 1992.

★824★

First Ancestry

Persons, By First Ancestry, 1990: Scottish

Data provided for all respondents who reported "Scottish" as their sole ancestry, and those who reported "Scottish" as their first ancestry.

[Table shows the top 50 areas]

MSA	% of total population	Rank
Portland, ME	4.234	1
Bangor, ME	3.797	2
Portsmouth – Dover – Rochester, NH – ME	3.336	3
Provo – Orem, UT	3.106	4
Cumberland, MD – WV	3.063	5
Burlington, VT	2.816	6
Asheville, NC	2.737	7
Salt Lake City – Ogden, UT	2.707	8
Bellingham, WA	2.685	9
Boise, ID	2.619	10
Medford, OR	2.607	11
Wilmington, NC	2.475	12
Casper, WY	2.458	13
Raleigh – Durham, NC	2.423	14
Glens Falls, NY	2.404	15
Bremerton, WA	2.394	16
Seattle – Tacoma, WA	2.391	17
Portland – Vancouver, OR – WA	2.381	18
Sarasota, FL	2.365	19
Eugene – Springfield, OR	2.283	20
Olympia, WA	2.218	21
Manchester, NH	2.216	22
Spokane, WA	2.193	23
Boston – Lawrence – Salem, MA – NH	2.172	24
Tallahassee, FL	2.168	25
Great Falls, MT	2.166	26
Lewiston – Auburn, ME	2.162	27
Melbourne – Titusville – Palm Bay, FL	2.161	28
Fort Collins – Loveland, CO	2.147	29
Bradenton, FL	2.142	30
Bloomington, IN	2.102	31
Redding, CA	2.095	32
Anchorage, AK	2.072	33
Naples, FL	2.068	34
Charlottesville, VA	2.065	35
Chico, CA	2.063	36

[Continued]

★824★

Persons, By First Ancestry, 1990: Scottish

[Continued]

MSA	% of total population	Rank
Athens, GA	2.039	37
Fort Myers – Cape Coral, Fl	2.027	38
Salem, OR	2.026	39
New London – Norwich, CT – RI	2.023	40
Fort Walton Beach, FL	2.018	41
Fort Pierce, FL	2.016	42
Daytona Beach, FL	1.997	43
Billings, MT	1.982	44
Santa Barbara – Santa Maria – Lompoc, CA	1.982	44
Greenville – Spartanburg, SC	1.953	45
Reno, NV	1.936	46
Knoxville, TN	1.923	47
Lexington-Fayette, KY	1.919	48
Tampa – Saint Petersburg – Clearwater, FL	1.884	49

Source: U.S. Bureau of the Census, Data User Services Division, *1990 Census of Population and Housing*, Summary Tape File 3C, United States Summary, CD-ROM, February 1992.

★825★

First Ancestry

Persons, By First Ancestry, 1990: Slovak

Data provided for all respondents who reported "Slovak" as their sole ancestry, and those who reported "Slovak" as their first ancestry.

[Table shows the top 50 areas]

MSA	% of total population	Rank
Johnstown, PA	7.129	1
Youngstown – Warren, OH	6.453	2
Pittsburgh – Beaver Valley, PA	5.447	3
Sharon, PA	4.853	4
Scranton – Wilkes-Barre, PA	4.794	5
Binghamton, NY	4.435	6
Allentown – Bethlehem – Easton, PA – NJ	3.860	7
Cleveland – Akron – Lorain, OH	3.691	8
Steubenville – Weirton, OH – WV	3.455	9
State College, PA	2.858	10
Erie, PA	2.496	11
Wheeling, WV – OH	2.035	12
Canton, OH	1.586	13
Pueblo, CO	1.391	14
Reading, PA	1.235	15
Duluth, MN – WI	1.208	16
Harrisburg – Lebanon – Carlisle, PA	1.151	17
Altoona, PA	1.053	18
Chicago – Gary – Lake County, IL – IN – WI	0.934	19
Flint, MI	0.811	20
Poughkeepsie, NY	0.774	21
Milwaukee – Racine, WI	0.768	22

[Continued]

★825★

Persons, By First Ancestry, 1990: Slovak

[Continued]

MSA	% of total population	Rank
Great Falls, MT	0.757	23
Fort Myers – Cape Coral, Fl	0.724	24
Springfield, IL	0.700	25
Sheboygan, WI	0.690	26
Iowa City, IA	0.688	27
Saginaw – Bay City – Midland, MI	0.687	28
Toledo, OH	0.660	29
Philadelphia – Wilmington – Trenton, PA – NJ – DE – MD	0.658	30
Muskegon, MI	0.657	31
Detroit – Ann Arbor, MI	0.650	32
New York – Northern New Jersey – Long Island, NY – NJ – CT	0.642	33
Sarasota, FL	0.642	33
Waterbury, CT	0.621	34
Lansing – East Lansing, MI	0.604	35
Naples, FL	0.592	36
Lancaster, PA	0.573	37
Daytona Beach, FL	0.555	38
Glens Falls, NY	0.552	39
Omaha, NE – IA	0.547	40
Elmira, NY	0.538	41
Tampa – Saint Petersburg – Clearwater, FL	0.537	42
Cedar Rapids, IA	0.530	43
Victoria, TX	0.527	44
Albany – Schenectady – Troy, NY	0.526	45
Columbus, OH	0.524	46
Hartford – New Britain – Middletown, CT	0.516	47
Mansfield, OH	0.515	48
West Palm Beach – Boca Raton – Delray Beach, FL	0.502	49

Source: U.S. Bureau of the Census, Data User Services Division, *1990 Census of Population and Housing*, Summary Tape File 3C, United States Summary, CD-ROM, February 1992.

★826★

First Ancestry

Persons, By First Ancestry, 1990: SubSaharan African

Data provided for all respondents who reported "SubSaharan African" as their sole ancestry, and those who reported "SubSaharan African" as their first ancestry.

[Table shows the top 50 areas]

MSA	% of total population	Rank
New Bedford, MA	4.7904	1
Providence – Pawtucket – Fall River, RI – MA	1.0673	2
Washington, DC – MD – VA	1.0212	3
Boston – Lawrence – Salem, MA – NH	0.5283	4

[Continued]

★826★

Persons, By First Ancestry, 1990: SubSaharan African

[Continued]

MSA	% of total population	Rank
Columbia, MO	0.5170	5
Atlanta, GA	0.4780	6
Gainesville, FL	0.4287	7
New York – Northern New Jersey – Long Island, NY – NJ – CT	0.4255	8
Raleigh – Durham, NC	0.4239	9
Tallahassee, FL	0.3861	10
Houston – Galveston – Brazoria, TX	0.3413	11
Columbus, GA – AL	0.3345	12
Champaign – Urbana – Rantoul, IL	0.3231	13
Dallas – Fort Worth, TX	0.3180	14
Iowa City, IA	0.3069	15
New Haven – Meriden, CT	0.2925	16
Austin, TX	0.2906	17
San Francisco – Oakland – San Jose, CA	0.2897	18
Benton Harbor, MI	0.2826	19
Columbia, SC	0.2799	20
Huntsville, AL	0.2783	21
Lincoln, NE	0.2687	22
Worcester, MA	0.2609	23
Baton Rouge, LA	0.2573	24
Baltimore, MD	0.2439	25
Abilene, TX	0.2432	26
Waterbury, CT	0.2432	26
Jackson, MS	0.2398	27
Ocala, FL	0.2351	28
Albany, GA	0.2345	29
New Orleans, LA	0.2322	30
Savannah, GA	0.2246	31
Bryan – College Station, TX	0.2232	32
Montgomery, AL	0.2150	33
Dayton – Springfield, OH	0.2142	34
Philadelphia – Wilmington – Trenton, PA – NJ – DE – MD	0.2134	35
Miami – Fort Lauderdale, FL	0.2064	36
Athens, GA	0.2048	37
Columbus, OH	0.2023	38
Los Angeles – Anaheim – Riverside, CA	0.2022	39
Chicago – Gary – Lake County, IL – IN – WI	0.1990	40
Wilmington, NC	0.1970	41
Minneapolis – Saint Paul, MN – WI	0.1920	42
Charlotte – Gastonia – Rock Hill, NC – SC	0.1918	43
Nashville, TN	0.1914	44
San Diego, CA	0.1894	45
Lansing – East Lansing, MI	0.1891	46
Lawton, OK	0.1866	47
Hartford – New Britain – Middletown, CT	0.1865	48
Little Rock – North Little Rock, AR	0.1857	49

Source: U.S. Bureau of the Census, Data User Services Division, *1990 Census of Population and Housing*, Summary Tape File 3C, United States Summary, CD-ROM, February 1992.

★827★

First Ancestry

Persons, By First Ancestry, 1990: Swedish

Data provided for all respondents who reported "Swedish" as their sole ancestry, and those who reported "Swedish" as their first ancestry.

[Table shows the top 50 areas]

MSA	% of total ancestry	Rank
Jamestown – Dunkirk, NY	12.395	1
Duluth, MN – WI	11.749	2
Rockford, IL	9.424	3
Minneapolis – Saint Paul, MN – WI	8.394	4
Davenport – Rock Island – Moline, IA – IL	5.967	5
Saint Cloud, MN	4.715	6
Fargo – Moorhead, ND – MN	4.037	7
Muskegon, MI	3.942	8
Worcester, MA	3.902	9
Sioux City, IA – NE	3.821	10
Lincoln, NE	3.768	11
Bellingham, WA	3.727	12
Seattle – Tacoma, WA	3.598	13
Salt Lake City – Ogden, UT	3.572	14
Provo – Orem, UT	3.477	15
Spokane, WA	3.449	16
Olympia, WA	3.304	17
Bremerton, WA	3.283	18
Sioux Falls, SD	3.199	19
Des Moines, IA	3.173	20
Omaha, NE – IA	3.158	21
Portland – Vancouver, OR – WA	3.095	22
Greeley, CO	3.089	23
Fort Collins – Loveland, CO	3.056	24
Boise, ID	3.053	25
Rochester, MN	3.044	26
Grand Forks, ND	2.999	27
Cheyenne, WY	2.864	28
Richland – Kennewick – Pasco, WA	2.672	29
Eugene – Springfield, OR	2.659	30
Great Falls, MT	2.653	31
Topeka, KS	2.636	32
Casper, WY	2.574	33
Rapid City, SD	2.537	34
Medford, OR	2.502	35
Denver – Boulder, CO	2.436	36
Billings, MT	2.406	37
Bismarck, ND	2.263	38
Lawrence, KS	2.258	39
Iowa City, IA	2.215	40
Salem, OR	2.194	41
Bloomington – Normal, IL	2.192	42
Eau Claire, WI	2.111	43
Anchorage, AK	2.091	44
Redding, CA	2.066	45
Chico, CA	2.014	46
Modesto, CA	1.949	47
Yakima, WA	1.882	48
Janesville – Beloit, WI	1.879	49
Erie, PA	1.874	50

Source: U.S. Bureau of the Census, Data User Services Division, *1990 Census of Population and Housing*, Summary Tape File 3C, United States Summary, CD-ROM, February 1992.

★828★

First Ancestry

Persons, By First Ancestry, 1990: Ukrainian

Data provided for all respondents who reported "Ukrainian" as their sole ancestry, and those who reported "Ukrainian" as their first ancestry.

[Table shows the top 50 areas]

MSA	% of total population	Rank
Scranton – Wilkes-Barre, PA	1.3678	1
Allentown – Bethlehem – Easton, PA – NJ	1.3409	2
Elmira, NY	1.3047	3
Youngstown – Warren, OH	0.9573	4
Pittsburgh – Beaver Valley, PA	0.8872	5
Binghamton, NY	0.8862	6
Utica – Rome, NY	0.8764	7
Johnstown, PA	0.8655	8
Rochester, NY	0.8263	9
Syracuse, NY	0.8041	10
Albany – Schenectady – Troy, NY	0.7389	11
Philadelphia – Wilmington – Trenton, PA – NJ – DE – MD	0.6997	12
Cleveland – Akron – Lorain, OH	0.6172	13
Reading, PA	0.5682	14
Buffalo – Niagara Falls, NY	0.5443	15
Hartford – New Britain – Middletown, CT	0.5410	16
Detroit – Ann Arbor, MI	0.4850	17
New York – Northern New Jersey – Long Island, NY – NJ – CT	0.4843	18
Pittsfield, MA	0.4718	19
Poughkeepsie, NY	0.4521	20
Sarasota, FL	0.4097	21
New London – Norwich, CT – RI	0.4063	22
State College, PA	0.4063	22
Erie, PA	0.4057	23
Bismarck, ND	0.3972	24
New Haven – Meriden, CT	0.3960	25
Wheeling, WV – OH	0.3854	26
Sharon, PA	0.3611	27
Atlantic City, NJ	0.3575	28
Waterbury, CT	0.3407	29
Chicago – Gary – Lake County, IL – IN – WI	0.3307	30
West Palm Beach – Boca Raton – Delray Beach, FL	0.3223	31
Manchester, NH	0.3097	32
Harrisburg – Lebanon – Carlisle, PA	0.2992	33
Saint Joseph, MO	0.2877	34
Springfield, MA	0.2750	35
Baltimore, MD	0.2514	36
Providence – Pawtucket – Fall River, RI – MA	0.2500	37
Grand Forks, ND	0.2349	38
Washington, DC – MD – VA	0.2327	39
Minneapolis – Saint Paul, MN – WI	0.2319	40
Tampa – Saint Petersburg – Clearwater, FL	0.2316	41
Bellingham, WA	0.2230	42
Fort Pierce, FL	0.2199	43

[Continued]

★828★

Persons, By First Ancestry, 1990: Ukrainian

[Continued]

MSA	% of total population	Rank
Muskegon, MI	0.2195	44
Eugene – Springfield, OR	0.2131	45
Daytona Beach, FL	0.2126	46
Fort Myers – Cape Coral, FI	0.2101	47
Miami – Fort Lauderdale, FL	0.2063	48
Seattle – Tacoma, WA	0.2010	49

Source: U.S. Bureau of the Census, Data User Services Division, *1990 Census of Population and Housing*, Summary Tape File 3C, United States Summary, CD-ROM, February 1992.

★829★

First Ancestry

Persons, By First Ancestry, 1990: United States or American

The Bureau of the Census accepted "American" as a unique ethnicity if it was given as the only response, was given as part of an ambiguous response, or was given with State names as a response. Other distinct groups who reported "American Indian," "Mexican American," and "African American," were identified separately.

[Table shows the top 50 areas]

MSA	% of total population	Rank
Florence, AL	25.85	1
Decatur, AL	21.16	2
Gadsden, AL	21.00	3
Dothan, AL	19.49	4
Tuscaloosa, AL	17.40	5
Anniston, AL	16.16	6
Danville, VA	15.43	7
Johnson City – Kingsport – Bristol, TN – VA	15.31	8
Charleston, WV	15.24	9
Anderson, SC	15.20	10
Birmingham, AL	14.97	11
Huntington – Ashland, WV – KY – OH	14.82	12
Hickory – Morganton, NC	14.69	13
Burlington, NC	14.06	14
Chattanooga, TN – GA	14.03	15
Montgomery, AL	13.61	16
Jackson, TN	13.57	17
Huntsville, AL	13.15	18
Panama City, FL	13.05	19
Lynchburg, VA	12.91	20
Pascagoula, MS	12.88	21
Fort Smith, AR – OK	12.80	22
Florence, SC	12.61	23
Albany, GA	12.57	24
Mobile, AL	12.53	25
Greensboro – Winston-Salem – High Point, NC	12.49	26
Sherman – Denison, TX	12.40	27
Knoxville, TN	12.33	28
Owensboro, KY	12.25	29
Augusta, GA – SC	12.21	30
Macon – Warner Robins, GA	11.99	31

[Continued]

★ 829 ★

Persons, By First Ancestry, 1990: United States or American
[Continued]

MSA	% of total population	Rank
Greenville – Spartanburg, SC	11.90	32
Nashville, TN	11.88	33
Athens, GA	11.76	34
Monroe, LA	11.73	35
Fayetteville – Springdale, AR	11.70	36
Columbus, GA – AL	11.69	37
Roanoke, VA	11.56	38
Anderson, IN	11.39	39
Saint Joseph, MO	11.10	40
Texarkana, TX – Texarkana, AR	11.02	41
Lexington-Fayette, KY	10.94	42
Alexandria, LA	10.80	43
Clarksville – Hopkinsville, TN – KY	10.62	44
Pine Bluff, AR	10.53	45
Asheville, NC	10.50	46
Charlottesville, VA	10.50	46
Louisville, KY – IN	10.39	47
Savannah, GA	10.35	48
Longview – Marshall, TX	10.26	49

Source: U.S. Bureau of the Census, Data User Services Division, *1990 Census of Population and Housing,* Summary Tape File 3C, United States Summary, CD-ROM, February 1992.

★ 830 ★
First Ancestry

Persons, By First Ancestry, 1990: Welsh

Data provided for all respondents who reported "Welsh" as their sole ancestry, and those who reported "Welsh" as their first ancestry.

[Table shows the top 50 areas]

MSA	% of total population	Rank
Scranton – Wilkes-Barre, PA	3.180	1
Utica – Rome, NY	2.314	2
Provo – Orem, UT	1.696	3
Binghamton, NY	1.483	4
Cumberland, MD – WV	1.388	5
Youngstown – Warren, OH	1.363	6
Sharon, PA	1.350	7
Columbus, OH	1.338	8
Glens Falls, NY	1.286	9
Allentown – Bethlehem – Easton, PA – NJ	1.276	10
Canton, OH	1.205	11
Salt Lake City – Ogden, UT	1.161	12
Johnstown, PA	1.153	13
Boise, ID	1.143	14
Lima, OH	1.035	15
Williamsport, PA	0.993	16
State College, PA	0.978	17
Steubenville – Weirton, OH – WV	0.941	18
Harrisburg – Lebanon – Carlisle, PA	0.922	19

[Continued]

★ 830 ★

Persons, By First Ancestry, 1990: Welsh
[Continued]

MSA	% of total population	Rank
Elmira, NY	0.885	20
Lawrence, KS	0.868	21
Fort Collins – Loveland, CO	0.867	22
Terre Haute, IN	0.854	23
Des Moines, IA	0.852	24
Sarasota, FL	0.841	25
Altoona, PA	0.830	26
Reading, PA	0.800	27
Iowa City, IA	0.795	28
Lancaster, PA	0.795	28
Casper, WY	0.794	29
Eugene – Springfield, OR	0.779	30
Olympia, WA	0.775	31
Colorado Springs, CO	0.737	32
Bellingham, WA	0.736	33
Portland – Vancouver, OR – WA	0.734	34
Syracuse, NY	0.732	35
Seattle – Tacoma, WA	0.722	36
Bremerton, WA	0.718	37
Topeka, KS	0.718	37
Reno, NV	0.706	38
Huntington – Ashland, WV – KY – OH	0.700	39
Parkersburg – Marietta, WV – OH	0.700	39
Pittsburgh – Beaver Valley, PA	0.682	40
Daytona Beach, FL	0.680	41
Chico, CA	0.678	42
Bradenton, FL	0.671	43
Cedar Rapids, IA	0.657	44
Anderson, IN	0.656	45
Charlottesville, VA	0.653	46
Spokane, WA	0.652	47

Source: U.S. Bureau of the Census, Data User Services Division, *1990 Census of Population and Housing,* Summary Tape File 3C, United States Summary, CD-ROM, February 1992.

★ 831 ★
First Ancestry

Persons, By First Ancestry, 1990: West Indian (exc. Hispanic origin)

Data provided for all respondents who reported "West Indian (except of Hispanic origin)" as their sole ancestry, and those who reported "West Indian (except of Hispanic origin)" as their first ancestry.

[Table shows the top 50 areas]

MSA	% of total population	Rank
Miami – Fort Lauderdale, FL	5.0327	1
New York – Northern New Jersey – Long Island, NY – NJ – CT	2.7757	2
West Palm Beach – Boca Raton – Delray Beach, FL	2.3672	3
Naples, FL	1.4622	4
Orlando, FL	1.3542	5
Hartford – New Britain – Middletown, CT	1.2855	6

[Continued]

★831★

Persons, By First Ancestry, 1990: West Indian (exc. Hispanic origin)

[Continued]

MSA	% of total population	Rank
Boston – Lawrence – Salem, MA – NH	1.0682	7
Fort Pierce, FL	0.9818	8
Washington, DC – MD – VA	0.8215	9
Poughkeepsie, NY	0.7897	10
Gainesville, FL	0.6545	11
Jacksonville, NC	0.6374	12
Lakeland – Winter Haven, FL	0.5898	13
Ocala, FL	0.5882	14
Melbourne – Titusville – Palm Bay, FL	0.5860	15
New Haven – Meriden, CT	0.5318	16
Springfield, MA	0.4470	17
Tulsa, OK	0.4450	18
Waterbury, CT	0.4133	19
Tallahassee, FL	0.3985	20
Fort Myers – Cape Coral, Fl	0.3769	21
Rochester, NY	0.3714	22
Tampa – Saint Petersburg – Clearwater, FL	0.3655	23
Philadelphia – Wilmington – Trenton, PA – NJ – DE – MD	0.3605	24
Killeen – Temple, TX	0.3600	25
Oklahoma City, OK	0.3489	26
Fayetteville, NC	0.3212	27
Baltimore, MD	0.3150	28
Huntsville, AL	0.3114	29
Atlanta, GA	0.2926	30
Fort Smith, AR – OK	0.2911	31
Benton Harbor, MI	0.2888	32
Lawton, OK	0.2816	33
Atlantic City, NJ	0.2793	34
Elmira, NY	0.2784	35
Sherman – Denison, TX	0.2726	36
Clarksville – Hopkinsville, TN – KY	0.2674	37
Houston – Galveston – Brazoria, TX	0.2666	38
Norfolk – Virginia Beach – Newport News, VA	0.2650	39
Worcester, MA	0.2650	39
Jacksonville, FL	0.2480	40
Daytona Beach, FL	0.2444	41
Albany – Schenectady – Troy, NY	0.2431	42
New London – Norwich, CT – RI	0.2391	43
Utica – Rome, NY	0.2255	44
Los Angeles – Anaheim – Riverside, CA	0.2161	45
Bradenton, FL	0.2140	46
Fort Walton Beach, FL	0.2045	47
Fayetteville – Springdale, AR	0.1975	48
Chicago – Gary – Lake County, IL – IN – WI	0.1919	49

Source: U.S. Bureau of the Census, Data User Services Division, *1990 Census of Population and Housing*, Summary Tape File 3C, United States Summary, CD-ROM, February 1992.

★832★

First Ancestry

Persons, By First Ancestry, 1990: Yugoslavian

Data provided for all respondents who reported "Yugoslavian" as their sole or first ancestry.

[Table shows the top 50 areas]

MSA	% of total population	Rank
Duluth, MN – WI	2.3936	1
Cleveland – Akron – Lorain, OH	1.5501	2
Pueblo, CO	1.4986	3
Steubenville – Weirton, OH – WV	1.2103	4
Johnstown, PA	0.8933	5
Pittsburgh – Beaver Valley, PA	0.8707	6
Sheboygan, WI	0.7066	7
Sharon, PA	0.6934	8
Youngstown – Warren, OH	0.5383	9
Milwaukee – Racine, WI	0.5166	10
Bellingham, WA	0.4852	11
Chicago – Gary – Lake County, IL – IN – WI	0.4834	12
Canton, OH	0.4621	13
Wheeling, WV – OH	0.4187	14
Billings, MT	0.4144	15
Great Falls, MT	0.3424	16
Anchorage, AK	0.3318	17
Detroit – Ann Arbor, MI	0.3163	18
Harrisburg – Lebanon – Carlisle, PA	0.2888	19
Mansfield, OH	0.2569	20
Seattle – Tacoma, WA	0.2524	21
Reno, NV	0.2521	22
South Bend – Mishawaka, IN	0.2384	23
Sacramento, CA	0.2145	24
San Francisco – Oakland – San Jose, CA	0.2071	25
Las Vegas, NV	0.2001	26
Naples, FL	0.1999	27
Saint Cloud, MN	0.1943	28
Redding, CA	0.1938	29
New York – Northern New Jersey – Long Island, NY – NJ – CT	0.1933	30
Phoenix, AZ	0.1886	31
Portland – Vancouver, OR – WA	0.1863	32
Richland – Kennewick – Pasco, WA	0.1846	33
Bloomington, IN	0.1835	34
Salinas – Seaside – Monterey, CA	0.1791	35
San Diego, CA	0.1785	36
Minneapolis – Saint Paul, MN – WI	0.1771	37
Salt Lake City – Ogden, UT	0.1755	38
Columbus, OH	0.1745	39
Biloxi – Gulfport, MS	0.1699	40
Pascagoula, MS	0.1666	41
Kankakee, IL	0.1662	42
Champaign – Urbana – Rantoul, IL	0.1595	43
Fresno, CA	0.1576	44
Los Angeles – Anaheim – Riverside, CA	0.1574	45
Medford, OR	0.1564	46
Lafayette – West Lafayette, IN	0.1524	47
Spokane, WA	0.1514	48

[Continued]

★832★

Persons, By First Ancestry, 1990: Yugoslavian
[Continued]

MSA	% of total population	Rank
Denver – Boulder, CO	0.1496	49
State College, PA	0.1470	50

Source: U.S. Bureau of the Census, Data User Services Division, *1990 Census of Population and Housing*, Summary Tape File 3C, United States Summary, CD-ROM, February 1992.

PART IV

JOBS AND INCOME

Contents

Chapter 11

EMPLOYMENT

Topics Covered

New Employment Opportunities
Employment in Government
Employment Projections
Employment Projections: By Industry
Employment (Nonfarm Payrolls)
Employment, By Occupation
Employment, By Race
Employment (Civilian Labor Force Characteristics)
Job Growth
Distribution of Employed Persons, By Occupation
Distribution of Employed Hispanics, By Occupation
Distribution of Employed Persons, By Race and Occupation
Distribution of Employed Persons, By Sex and Occupation
Unemployment
Hours and Earnings
United States Postal Service

★833★
New Employment Opportunities
Cities In Which Jobs Are Being Generated, 1995: Number of Companies

City	Number of companies	Rank
New York, NY	196	1
San Francisco, CA	145	2
Los Angeles, CA	109	3
Boston, MA	99	4
Dallas-Fort Worth, TX	95	5
Chicago, IL	87	6
Houston, TX	82	7
Minneapolis-Saint Paul, MN	65	8
Philadelphia, PA	61	9
Atlanta, GA	48	10

Source: "Lose Some, Win Some," *Business Week,* 11 September 1995, p. 6. Primary source: Hoover's Masterlist Database, the Reference Press, Inc.

★834★
New Employment Opportunities
Job Growth, 1995-96: Leading Metropolitan Areas

City/MSA	Jobs gained 1995-1996	Rank
Atlanta, GA	88,800	1
Los Angeles, CA	84,000	2
Chicago, IL	77,400	3
Detroit, MI	60,000	4
Dallas, TX	59,100	5
Phoenix, AZ	53,900	6
Las Vegas, NV	49,200	7
Houston, TX	44,100	8
Portland, OR	41,900	9
San Jose, CA	41,800	10

Source: "Employment Leaders," *Wall Street Journal,* 31 May 1996, p. B8.

★835★
Employment in Government
Employment in City Government, 1992: Full-Time Equivalent Employment

[In thousands]

City	Thousands	Rank
Albuquerque, NM	6	20
Anaheim, CA	3	23
Arlington, TX	2	24
Atlanta, GA	8	18
Austin, TX	11	15
Baltimore, MD	27	6
Birmingham, AL	4	22
Boston, MA	21	9
Buffalo, NY	13	13
Charlotte, NC	5	21
Chicago, IL	41	4
Cincinnati, OH	7	19
Cleveland, OH	8	18

[Continued]

★835★
Employment in City Government, 1992: Full-Time Equivalent Employment
[Continued]

City	Thousands	Rank
Colorado Springs, CO	5	21
Columbus, OH	8	18
Dallas, TX	14	12
Denver, CO	12	14
Detroit, MI	19	10
El Paso, TX	5	21
Fort Worth, TX	5	21
Fresno, CA	3	23
Honolulu, HI	9	17
Houston, TX	21	9
Indianapolis, IN	13	13
Jacksonville, FL	10	16
Kansas City, MO	6	20
Long Beach, CA	5	21
Los Angeles, CA	50	2
Louisville, KY	4	22
Memphis, TN	22	8
Mesa, AZ	2	24
Miami, FL	4	22
Milwaukee, WI	8	18
Minneapolis, MN	6	20
Nashville-Davidson, TN	17	11
New Orleans, LA	10	16
New York, NY	415	1
Newark, NJ	4	22
Norfolk, VA	10	16
Oakland, CA	5	21
Oklahoma City, OK	5	21
Omaha, NE	3	23
Philadelphia, PA	30	5
Phoenix, AZ	11	15
Pittsburgh, PA	5	21
Portland, OR	5	21
Sacramento, CA	4	22
Saint Louis, MO	7	19
Saint Paul, MN	3	23
San Antonio, TX	13	13
San Diego, CA	9	17
San Francisco, CA	26	7
San Jose, CA	6	20
Santa Ana, CA	2	24
Seattle, WA	10	16
Tampa, FL	4	22
Toledo, OH	3	23
Tucson, AZ	5	21
Tulsa, OK	4	22
Virginia Beach, VA	14	12
Washington, DC	46	3
Wichita, KS	3	23

Source: U.S. Bureau of the Census, *Statistical Abstract of the United States: 1995,* (115th edition), Washington, D.C.: U.S. Government Printing Office, 1995, p. 328. Primary source: U.S. Bureau of the Census, *City Employment,* series GE, no. 2, annual; and unpublished data.

★836★

Employment in Government

Employment in City Government, 1992: Full-Time Equivalent Employment Per 10,000 Population

City	Per 10,000	Rank
Albuquerque, NM	147	26
Anaheim, CA	98	48
Arlington, TX	73	55
Atlanta, GA	197	13
Austin, TX	246	12
Baltimore, MD	372	5
Birmingham, AL	145	28
Boston, MA	361	7
Buffalo, NY	390	4
Charlotte, NC	115	40
Chicago, IL	148	25
Cincinnati, OH	191	14
Cleveland, OH	167	20
Colorado Springs, CO	181	17
Columbus, OH	125	35
Dallas, TX	137	31
Denver, CO	266	11
Detroit, MI	180	18
El Paso, TX	99	47
Fort Worth, TX	114	41
Fresno, CA	73	55
Honolulu, HI	111	42
Houston, TX	129	34
Indianapolis, IN	172	19
Jacksonville, FL	156	23
Kansas City, MO	146	27
Long Beach, CA	123	36
Los Angeles, CA	140	29
Louisville, KY	160	22
Memphis, TN	366	6
Mesa, AZ	82	52
Miami, FL	101	46
Milwaukee, WI	133	32
Minneapolis, MN	161	21
Nashville-Davidson, TN	340	10
New Orleans, LA	149	24
New York, NY	557	2
Newark, NJ	139	30
Norfolk, VA	394	3
Oakland, CA	130	33
Oklahoma City, OK	104	45
Omaha, NE	81	53
Philadelphia, PA	189	15
Phoenix, AZ	110	43
Pittsburgh, PA	145	28
Portland, OR	104	45
Sacramento, CA	107	44
Saint Louis, MO	188	16
Saint Paul, MN	119	38
San Antonio, TX	140	29
San Diego, CA	93	50
San Francisco, CA	354	9
San Jose, CA	76	54
Santa Ana, CA	64	56

[Continued]

★836★

Employment in City Government, 1992: Full-Time Equivalent Employment Per 10,000 Population

[Continued]

City	Per 10,000	Rank
Seattle, WA	197	13
Tampa, FL	140	29
Toledo, OH	86	51
Tucson, AZ	118	39
Tulsa, OK	120	37
Virginia Beach, VA	356	8
Washington, DC	763	1
Wichita, KS	97	49

Source: U.S. Bureau of the Census, *Statistical Abstract of the United States: 1995*, (115th edition), Washington, D.C.: U.S. Government Printing Office, 1995, p. 328. Primary source: U.S. Bureau of the Census, *City Employment*, series GE, no. 2, annual; and unpublished data.

★837★

Employment in Government

Employment in City Government, 1992: Payroll

[In millions of dollars; as of October 1992]

City	Millions	Rank
Albuquerque, NM	12	29
Anaheim, CA	10	31
Arlington, TX	5	35
Atlanta, GA	18	23
Austin, TX	27	18
Baltimore, MD	70	7
Birmingham, AL	9	32
Boston, MA	61	8
Buffalo, NY	36	13
Charlotte, NC	11	30
Chicago, IL	135	4
Cincinnati, OH	20	22
Cleveland, OH	20	22
Colorado Springs, CO	13	28
Columbus, OH	20	22
Dallas, TX	36	13
Denver, CO	35	14
Detroit, MI	49	11
El Paso, TX	11	30
Fort Worth, TX	11	30
Fresno, CA	8	33
Honolulu, HI	29	17
Houston, TX	51	10
Indianapolis, IN	26	19
Jacksonville, FL	27	18
Kansas City, MO	16	25
Long Beach, CA	18	23
Los Angeles, CA	188	2
Louisville, KY	8	33
Memphis, TN	53	9
Mesa, AZ	7	34
Miami, FL	14	27
Milwaukee, WI	23	21
Minneapolis, MN	18	23

[Continued]

★837★

Employment in City Government, 1992: Payroll
[Continued]

City	Millions	Rank
Nashville-Davidson, TN	40	12
New Orleans, LA	12	29
New York, NY	1,307	1
Newark, NJ	12	29
Norfolk, VA	24	20
Oakland, CA	17	24
Oklahoma City, OK	12	29
Omaha, NE	8	33
Philadelphia, PA	92	6
Phoenix, AZ	32	15
Pittsburgh, PA	14	27
Portland, OR	15	26
Sacramento, CA	13	28
Saint Louis, MO	18	23
Saint Paul, MN	11	30
San Antonio, TX	32	15
San Diego, CA	29	17
San Francisco, CA	99	5
San Jose, CA	24	20
Santa Ana, CA	9	32
Seattle, WA	35	14
Tampa, FL	11	30
Toledo, OH	9	32
Tucson, AZ	12	29
Tulsa, OK	11	30
Virginia Beach, VA	30	16
Washington, DC	138	3
Wichita, KS	7	34

Source: U.S. Bureau of the Census, *Statistical Abstract of the United States: 1995*, (115th edition), Washington, D.C.: U.S. Government Printing Office, 1995, p. 328. Primary source: U.S. Bureau of the Census, *City Employment*, series GE, no. 2, annual; and unpublished data.

★838★

Employment in Government

Employment in City Government, 1992: Total Employment

[In thousands]

City	Thousands	Rank
Albuquerque, NM	7	20
Anaheim, CA	1	26
Arlington, TX	2	25
Atlanta, GA	8	19
Austin, TX	12	15
Baltimore, MD	28	6
Birmingham, AL	4	23
Boston, MA	21	9
Buffalo, NY	14	13
Charlotte, NC	5	22
Chicago, IL	41	4
Cincinnati, OH	8	19
Cleveland, OH	9	18
Colorado Springs, CO	5	22
Columbus, OH	8	19
Dallas, TX	14	13

[Continued]

★838★

Employment in City Government, 1992: Total Employment
[Continued]

City	Thousands	Rank
Denver, CO	14	13
Detroit, MI	19	10
El Paso, TX	5	22
Fort Worth, TX	5	22
Fresno, CA	3	24
Honolulu, HI	11	16
Houston, TX	21	9
Indianapolis, IN	13	14
Jacksonville, FL	11	16
Kansas City, MO	6	21
Long Beach, CA	6	21
Los Angeles, CA	50	2
Louisville, KY	4	23
Memphis, TN	24	8
Mesa, AZ	2	25
Miami, FL	4	23
Milwaukee, WI	9	18
Minneapolis, MN	7	20
Nashville-Davidson, TN	18	11
New Orleans, LA	10	17
New York, NY	442	1
Newark, NJ	3	24
Norfolk, VA	11	16
Oakland, CA	6	21
Oklahoma City, OK	5	22
Omaha, NE	3	24
Philadelphia, PA	31	5
Phoenix, AZ	11	16
Pittsburgh, PA	7	20
Portland, OR	5	22
Sacramento, CA	4	23
Saint Louis, MO	8	19
Saint Paul, MN	3	24
San Antonio, TX	14	13
San Diego, CA	11	16
San Francisco, CA	26	7
San Jose, CA	7	20
Santa Ana, CA	2	25
Seattle, WA	11	16
Tampa, FL	4	23
Toledo, OH	3	24
Tucson, AZ	5	22
Tulsa, OK	4	23
Virginia Beach, VA	15	12
Washington, DC	48	3
Wichita, KS	3	24

Source: U.S. Bureau of the Census, *Statistical Abstract of the United States: 1995*, (115th edition), Washington, D.C.: U.S. Government Printing Office, 1995, p. 328. Primary source: U.S. Bureau of the Census, *City Employment*, series GE, no. 2, annual; and unpublished data.

★839★

Employment Projections

Employment Projections, 2000, CMSAs: Number of Jobs

[In thousands of jobs]

City/MSA	Number	Rank
Chicago-Gary-Kenosha, IL-IN-WI CMSA	5,298	3
Cincinnati-Hamilton, OH-KY-IN CMSA	1,168	15
Cleveland-Akron, OH CMSA	1,700	12
Dallas-Fort Worth, TX CMSA	3,077	7
Denver-Boulder-Greeley, CO CMSA	1,646	13
Detroit-Ann Arbor-Flint, MI CMSA	2,894	8
Houston-Galveston-Brazoria, TX CMSA	2,627	9
Los Angeles-Riverside-Orange County, CA CMSA	8,707	2
Miami-Fort Lauderdale, FL CMSA	2,006	11
Milwaukee-Racine, WI CMSA	1,071	16
New York-Northern New Jersey-Long Island, NY-NJ-CT-PA CMSA	11,168	1
Philadelphia-Wilmington-Atlantic City, PA-NJ-DE-MD CMSA	3,469	6
Portland-Salem, OR-WA CMSA	1,294	14
Sacramento-Yolo, CA CMSA	1,032	17
San Francisco-Oakland-San Jose, CA CMSA	4,382	5
Seattle-Tacoma-Bremerton, WA CMSA	2,243	10
Washington-Baltimore, DC-MD-VA-WV CMSA	4,931	4

Source: U.S. Department of Commerce, Economics and Statistics Administration, Bureau of Economic Analysis, *Survey of Current Business*, vol. 76, no. 6, Washington, D.C.: U.S. Government Printing Office, (June 1996), p. 67. *Note:* "CMSA" stands for "Consolidated Metropolitan Statistical Area."

★840★

Employment Projections

Employment Projections, 2005, CMSAs: Number of Jobs

[In thousands of jobs]

City/MSA	Number	Rank
Chicago-Gary-Kenosha, IL-IN-WI CMSA	5,601	3
Cincinnati-Hamilton, OH-KY-IN CMSA	1,236	15
Cleveland-Akron, OH CMSA	1,755	13
Dallas-Fort Worth, TX CMSA	3,334	7
Denver-Boulder-Greeley, CO CMSA	1,788	12
Detroit-Ann Arbor-Flint, MI CMSA	2,987	8
Houston-Galveston-Brazoria, TX CMSA	2,825	9
Los Angeles-Riverside-Orange County, CA CMSA	9,411	2

[Continued]

★840★

Employment Projections, 2005, CMSAs: Number of Jobs

[Continued]

City/MSA	Number	Rank
Miami-Fort Lauderdale, FL CMSA	2,156	11
Milwaukee-Racine, WI CMSA	1,121	17
New York-Northern New Jersey-Long Island, NY-NJ-CT-PA CMSA	11,625	1
Philadelphia-Wilmington-Atlantic City, PA-NJ-DE-MD CMSA	3,628	6
Portland-Salem, OR-WA CMSA	1,398	14
Sacramento-Yolo, CA CMSA	1,159	16
San Francisco-Oakland-San Jose, CA CMSA	4,723	5
Seattle-Tacoma-Bremerton, WA CMSA	2,456	10
Washington-Baltimore, DC-MD-VA-WV CMSA	5,264	4

Source: U.S. Department of Commerce, Economics and Statistics Administration, Bureau of Economic Analysis, *Survey of Current Business*, vol. 76, no. 6, Washington, D.C.: U.S. Government Printing Office, (June 1996), p. 67. *Note:* "CMSA" stands for "Consolidated Metropolitan Statistical Area."

★841★

Employment Projections: By Industry

Numerical Change in Employment in the Fastest Growing Metropolitan Areas, 1993-2005, By Industry: All Industries

Data refer to employment changes in selected metropolitan areas. The U.S. average is 27,205,500.

City/MSA	Numerical change	Rank
Austin-San Marcos, TX	209,007	7
Fort Collins-Loveland, CO	42,648	15
Fort Myers-Cape Coral, FL	69,223	11
Fort Pierce-Port Saint Lucie, FL	42,585	16
Las Vegas, NV-AZ	253,862	6
Naples, FL	44,154	13
Olympia, WA	35,514	17
Orange County, CA	524,571	1
Orlando, FL	335,573	4
Phoenix-Mesa, AZ	469,264	2
Provo-Orem, UT	58,935	12
Punta Gorda, FL	20,173	20
Redding, CA	28,264	19
Riverside-San Bernardino, CA	415,737	3
Sacramento, CA	286,908	5
San Luis Obispo-Atascadero-Paso Robles, CA	42,928	14
Santa Fe, NM	31,417	18
Santa Rosa, CA	81,618	10
Sarasota-Bradenton, FL	105,269	9
West Palm Beach-Boca Raton, FL	172,248	8

Source: U.S. Department of Commerce, Economics and Statistics Administration, Bureau of Economic Analysis, *Survey of Current Business*, vol. 76, no. 6, Washington, D.C.: U.S. Government Printing Office, (June 1996), p. 61.

★842★

Employment Projections: By Industry

Numerical Change in Employment in the Fastest Growing Metropolitan Areas, 1993-2005, By Industry: Agricultural Services, Forestry, and Fishing

Data refer to employment changes in selected metropolitan areas and include United States residents employed by international organizations, foreign embassies, and consulates in the United States. The U.S. total is 602,180.

City/MSA	Numerical change	Rank
Austin-San Marcos, TX	3,124	7
Fort Collins-Loveland, CO	1,182	14
Fort Myers-Cape Coral, FL	948	15
Fort Pierce-Port Saint Lucie, FL	4,378	5
Las Vegas, NV-AZ	2,778	8
Naples, FL	1,633	12
Olympia, WA	624	18
Orange County, CA	8,530	2
Orlando, FL	2,696	9
Phoenix-Mesa, AZ	6,232	4
Provo-Orem, UT	831	16
Punta Gorda, FL	325	19
Redding, CA	696	17
Riverside-San Bernardino, CA	9,861	1
Sacramento, CA	3,853	6
San Luis Obispo-Atascadero-Paso Robles, CA	1,356	13
Santa Fe, NM	302	20
Santa Rosa, CA	2,341	10
Sarasota-Bradenton, FL	2,076	11
West Palm Beach-Boca Raton, FL	8,119	3

Source: U.S. Department of Commerce, Economics and Statistics Administration, Bureau of Economic Analysis, *Survey of Current Business*, vol. 76, no. 6, Washington, D.C.: U.S. Government Printing Office, (June 1996), p. 61.

★843★

Employment Projections: By Industry

Numerical Change in Employment in the Fastest Growing Metropolitan Areas, 1993-2005, By Industry: Construction

Data refer to employment changes in selected metropolitan areas. The U.S. total is 1,410,938.

City/MSA	Numerical change	Rank
Austin-San Marcos, TX	8,975	7
Fort Collins-Loveland, CO	2,102	17
Fort Myers-Cape Coral, FL	5,971	10
Fort Pierce-Port Saint Lucie, FL	2,630	14
Las Vegas, NV-AZ	22,055	4
Naples, FL	3,947	11
Olympia, WA	1,957	19
Orange County, CA	26,448	3
Orlando, FL	15,266	6
Phoenix-Mesa, AZ	28,687	1
Provo-Orem, UT	3,772	12
Punta Gorda, FL	1,580	20

[Continued]

★843★

Numerical Change in Employment in the Fastest Growing Metropolitan Areas, 1993-2005, By Industry: Construction

[Continued]

City/MSA	Numerical change	Rank
Redding, CA	2,308	16
Riverside-San Bernardino, CA	26,462	2
Sacramento, CA	18,249	5
San Luis Obispo-Atascadero-Paso Robles, CA	2,399	15
Santa Fe, NM	1,967	18
Santa Rosa, CA	6,609	9
Sarasota-Bradenton, FL	3,337	13
West Palm Beach-Boca Raton, FL	7,183	8

Source: U.S. Department of Commerce, Economics and Statistics Administration, Bureau of Economic Analysis, *Survey of Current Business*, vol. 76, no. 6, Washington, D.C.: U.S. Government Printing Office, (June 1996), p. 61.

★844★

Employment Projections: By Industry

Numerical Change in Employment in the Fastest Growing Metropolitan Areas, 1993-2005, By Industry: Farming

Data refer to employment changes in selected metropolitan areas. The U.S. total is - 101,750.

City/MSA	Numerical change	Rank
Austin-San Marcos, TX	82	9
Fort Collins-Loveland, CO	57	10
Fort Myers-Cape Coral, FL	462	3
Fort Pierce-Port Saint Lucie, FL	-60	15
Las Vegas, NV-AZ	30	13
Naples, FL	2,789	1
Olympia, WA	-63	16
Orange County, CA	55	11
Orlando, FL	-911	20
Phoenix-Mesa, AZ	-113	18
Provo-Orem, UT	-97	17
Punta Gorda, FL	84	8
Redding, CA	47	12
Riverside-San Bernardino, CA	439	4
Sacramento, CA	362	6
San Luis Obispo-Atascadero-Paso Robles, CA	176	7
Santa Fe, NM	16	14
Santa Rosa, CA	657	2
Sarasota-Bradenton, FL	437	5
West Palm Beach-Boca Raton, FL	-603	19

Source: U.S. Department of Commerce, Economics and Statistics Administration, Bureau of Economic Analysis, *Survey of Current Business*, vol. 76, no. 6, Washington, D.C.: U.S. Government Printing Office, (June 1996), p. 61.

★845★
Employment Projections: By Industry

Numerical Change in Employment in the Fastest Growing Metropolitan Areas, 1993-2005, By Industry: Federal Civilian Government

Data refer to employment changes in selected metropolitan areas. The U.S. total is - 113,175.

City/MSA	Numerical change	Rank
Austin-San Marcos, TX	280	7
Fort Collins-Loveland, CO	216	10
Fort Myers-Cape Coral, FL	248	9
Fort Pierce-Port Saint Lucie, FL	113	12
Las Vegas, NV-AZ	1,280	4
Naples, FL	76	14
Olympia, WA	58	15
Orange County, CA	1,602	2
Orlando, FL	1,431	3
Phoenix-Mesa, AZ	2,566	1
Provo-Orem, UT	47	16
Punta Gorda, FL	35	18
Redding, CA	93	13
Riverside-San Bernardino, CA	1,149	5
Sacramento, CA	-2,229	20
San Luis Obispo-Atascadero-Paso Robles, CA	46	17
Santa Fe, NM	-33	19
Santa Rosa, CA	199	11
Sarasota-Bradenton, FL	252	8
West Palm Beach-Boca Raton, FL	642	6

Source: U.S. Department of Commerce, Economics and Statistics Administration, Bureau of Economic Analysis, *Survey of Current Business,* vol. 76, no. 6, Washington, D.C.: U.S. Government Printing Office, (June 1996), p. 60.

★846★
Employment Projections: By Industry

Numerical Change in Employment in the Fastest Growing Metropolitan Areas, 1993-2005, By Industry: Federal Military Government

Data refer to employment changes in selected metropolitan areas. The U.S. total is - 107,522.

City/MSA	Numerical change	Rank
Austin-San Marcos, TX	-898	16
Fort Collins-Loveland, CO	-12	4
Fort Myers-Cape Coral, FL	-45	9
Fort Pierce-Port Saint Lucie, FL	-32	8
Las Vegas, NV-AZ	509	1
Naples, FL	-16	5
Olympia, WA	-26	7
Orange County, CA	48	2
Orlando, FL	-2,742	19
Phoenix-Mesa, AZ	-139	14
Provo-Orem, UT	-108	12
Punta Gorda, FL	-9	3
Redding, CA	-19	6
Riverside-San Bernardino, CA	-2,124	18
Sacramento, CA	-1,172	17

[Continued]

★846★

Numerical Change in Employment in the Fastest Growing Metropolitan Areas, 1993-2005, By Industry: Federal Military Government
[Continued]

City/MSA	Numerical change	Rank
San Luis Obispo-Atascadero-Paso Robles, CA	-32	8
Santa Fe, NM	-48	10
Santa Rosa, CA	-163	15
Sarasota-Bradenton, FL	-62	11
West Palm Beach-Boca Raton, FL	-110	13

Source: U.S. Department of Commerce, Economics and Statistics Administration, Bureau of Economic Analysis, *Survey of Current Business,* vol. 76, no. 6, Washington, D.C.: U.S. Government Printing Office, (June 1996), p. 61.

★847★
Employment Projections: By Industry

Numerical Change in Employment in the Fastest Growing Metropolitan Areas, 1993-2005, By Industry: Finance, Insurance, and Real Estate

Data refer to employment changes in selected metropolitan areas. The U.S. total is 1,822,156.

City/MSA	Numerical change	Rank
Austin-San Marcos, TX	15,203	7
Fort Collins-Loveland, CO	1,443	18
Fort Myers-Cape Coral, FL	4,328	10
Fort Pierce-Port Saint Lucie, FL	1,760	14
Las Vegas, NV-AZ	16,961	6
Naples, FL	2,477	13
Olympia, WA	1,549	16
Orange County, CA	51,468	1
Orlando, FL	19,034	5
Phoenix-Mesa, AZ	40,321	2
Provo-Orem, UT	1,448	17
Punta Gorda, FL	571	20
Redding, CA	1,400	19
Riverside-San Bernardino, CA	21,374	4
Sacramento, CA	25,586	3
San Luis Obispo-Atascadero-Paso Robles, CA	3,892	11
Santa Fe, NM	1,685	15
Santa Rosa, CA	5,166	9
Sarasota-Bradenton, FL	2,900	12
West Palm Beach-Boca Raton, FL	12,537	8

Source: U.S. Department of Commerce, Economics and Statistics Administration, Bureau of Economic Analysis, *Survey of Current Business,* vol. 76, no. 6, Washington, D.C.: U.S. Government Printing Office, (June 1996), p. 61.

★848★
Employment Projections: By Industry

Numerical Change in Employment in the Fastest Growing Metropolitan Areas, 1993-2005, By Industry: Manufacturing (Durable Goods)

Data refer to employment changes in selected metropolitan areas. The U.S. total is - 188,816.

City/MSA	Numerical change	Rank
Austin-San Marcos, TX	14,723	1
Fort Collins-Loveland, CO	1,088	8
Fort Myers-Cape Coral, FL	195	15
Fort Pierce-Port Saint Lucie, FL	272	13
Las Vegas, NV-AZ	2,165	5
Naples, FL	267	14
Olympia, WA	6	17
Orange County, CA	-227	19
Orlando, FL	1,688	7
Phoenix-Mesa, AZ	8,127	2
Provo-Orem, UT	313	12
Punta Gorda, FL	111	16
Redding, CA	-42	18
Riverside-San Bernardino, CA	7,709	3
Sacramento, CA	2,513	4
San Luis Obispo-Atascadero-Paso Robles, CA	613	10
Santa Fe, NM	511	11
Santa Rosa, CA	1,830	6
Sarasota-Bradenton, FL	1,086	9
West Palm Beach-Boca Raton, FL	-229	20

Source: U.S. Department of Commerce, Economics and Statistics Administration, Bureau of Economic Analysis, *Survey of Current Business*, vol. 76, no. 6, Washington, D.C.: U.S. Government Printing Office, (June 1996), p. 61.

★849★
Employment Projections: By Industry

Numerical Change in Employment in the Fastest Growing Metropolitan Areas, 1993-2005, By Industry: Manufacturing (Nondurable Goods)

Data refer to employment changes in selected metropolitan areas. The U.S. total is 337,083.

City/MSA	Numerical change	Rank
Austin-San Marcos, TX	1,647	10
Fort Collins-Loveland, CO	843	12
Fort Myers-Cape Coral, FL	644	15
Fort Pierce-Port Saint Lucie, FL	262	18
Las Vegas, NV-AZ	3,058	6
Naples, FL	251	19
Olympia, WA	485	16
Orange County, CA	14,169	1
Orlando, FL	3,277	4
Phoenix-Mesa, AZ	9,569	2
Provo-Orem, UT	1,995	9
Punta Gorda, FL	120	20
Redding, CA	705	14
Riverside-San Bernardino, CA	8,626	3
Sacramento, CA	3,269	5

[Continued]

★849★

Numerical Change in Employment in the Fastest Growing Metropolitan Areas, 1993-2005, By Industry: Manufacturing (Nondurable Goods)

[Continued]

City/MSA	Numerical change	Rank
San Luis Obispo-Atascadero-Paso Robles, CA	792	13
Santa Fe, NM	436	17
Santa Rosa, CA	2,370	7
Sarasota-Bradenton, FL	1,526	11
West Palm Beach-Boca Raton, FL	2,209	8

Source: U.S. Department of Commerce, Economics and Statistics Administration, Bureau of Economic Analysis, *Survey of Current Business*, vol. 76, no. 6, Washington, D.C.: U.S. Government Printing Office, (June 1996), p. 61.

★850★
Employment Projections: By Industry

Numerical Change in Employment in the Fastest Growing Metropolitan Areas, 1993-2005, By Industry: Mining

Data refer to employment changes in selected metropolitan areas. The U.S. total is - 95,711.

City/MSA	Numerical change	Rank
Austin-San Marcos, TX	158	2
Fort Collins-Loveland, CO	-32	17
Fort Myers-Cape Coral, FL	7	12
Fort Pierce-Port Saint Lucie, FL	9	11
Las Vegas, NV-AZ	4	13
Naples, FL	106	3
Olympia, WA	21	8
Orange County, CA	-346	19
Orlando, FL	73	5
Phoenix-Mesa, AZ	1,015	1
Provo-Orem, UT	-21	15
Redding, CA	39	6
Riverside-San Bernardino, CA	-202	18
Sacramento, CA	37	7
San Luis Obispo-Atascadero-Paso Robles, CA	19	9
Santa Fe, NM	12	10
Santa Rosa, CA	-5	14
Sarasota-Bradenton, FL	-29	16
West Palm Beach-Boca Raton, FL	92	4

Source: U.S. Department of Commerce, Economics and Statistics Administration, Bureau of Economic Analysis, *Survey of Current Business*, vol. 76, no. 6, Washington, D.C.: U.S. Government Printing Office, (June 1996), p. 61.

★851★

Employment Projections: By Industry

Numerical Change in Employment in the Fastest Growing Metropolitan Areas, 1993-2005, By Industry: Retail Trade

Data refer to employment changes in selected metropolitan areas. The U.S. total is 4,469,102.

City/MSA	Numerical change	Rank
Austin-San Marcos, TX	31,097	7
Fort Collins-Loveland, CO	9,305	13
Fort Myers-Cape Coral, FL	13,186	11
Fort Pierce-Port Saint Lucie, FL	8,466	15
Las Vegas, NV-AZ	39,640	6
Naples, FL	8,572	14
Olympia, WA	5,797	19
Orange County, CA	83,025	2
Orlando, FL	56,172	4
Phoenix-Mesa, AZ	73,554	3
Provo-Orem, UT	10,530	12
Punta Gorda, FL	5,149	20
Redding, CA	5,861	18
Riverside-San Bernardino, CA	83,683	1
Sacramento, CA	46,716	5
San Luis Obispo-Atascadero-Paso Robles, CA	8,396	16
Santa Fe, NM	6,176	17
Santa Rosa, CA	15,211	9
Sarasota-Bradenton, FL	13,959	10
West Palm Beach-Boca Raton, FL	29,408	8

Source: U.S. Department of Commerce, Economics and Statistics Administration, Bureau of Economic Analysis, *Survey of Current Business,* vol. 76, no. 6, Washington, D.C.: U.S. Government Printing Office, (June 1996), p. 61.

★852★

Employment Projections: By Industry

Numerical Change in Employment in the Fastest Growing Metropolitan Areas, 1993-2005, By Industry: Services

Data refer to employment changes in selected metropolitan areas. The U.S. total is 14,139,037.

City/MSA	Numerical change	Rank
Austin-San Marcos, TX	93,813	7
Fort Collins-Loveland, CO	17,774	14
Fort Myers-Cape Coral, FL	30,339	11
Fort Pierce-Port Saint Lucie, FL	17,373	15
Las Vegas, NV-AZ	125,731	5
Naples, FL	19,887	13
Olympia, WA	13,596	18
Orange County, CA	247,528	1
Orlando, FL	186,408	3
Phoenix-Mesa, AZ	206,693	2
Provo-Orem, UT	29,871	12
Punta Gorda, FL	9,462	20
Redding, CA	11,782	19
Riverside-San Bernardino, CA	172,817	4
Sacramento, CA	119,416	6

[Continued]

★852★

Numerical Change in Employment in the Fastest Growing Metropolitan Areas, 1993-2005, By Industry: Services
[Continued]

City/MSA	Numerical change	Rank
San Luis Obispo-Atascadero-Paso Robles, CA	16,832	16
Santa Fe, NM	13,936	17
Santa Rosa, CA	36,406	10
Sarasota-Bradenton, FL	70,461	9
West Palm Beach-Boca Raton, FL	86,387	8

Source: U.S. Department of Commerce, Economics and Statistics Administration, Bureau of Economic Analysis, *Survey of Current Business,* vol. 76, no. 6, Washington, D.C.: U.S. Government Printing Office, (June 1996), p. 61.

★853★

Employment Projections: By Industry

Numerical Change in Employment in the Fastest Growing Metropolitan Areas, 1993-2005, By Industry: State and Local Government

Data refer to employment changes in selected metropolitan areas. The U.S. total is 2,721,129.

City/MSA	Numerical change	Rank
Austin-San Marcos, TX	28,460	5
Fort Collins-Loveland, CO	6,082	13
Fort Myers-Cape Coral, FL	8,164	10
Fort Pierce-Port Saint Lucie, FL	4,206	17
Las Vegas, NV-AZ	21,137	7
Naples, FL	2,351	19
Olympia, WA	9,782	9
Orange County, CA	31,560	4
Orlando, FL	22,988	6
Phoenix-Mesa, AZ	47,985	3
Provo-Orem, UT	6,306	11
Punta Gorda, FL	1,767	20
Redding, CA	3,021	18
Riverside-San Bernardino, CA	51,448	2
Sacramento, CA	53,454	1
San Luis Obispo-Atascadero-Paso Robles, CA	4,998	16
Santa Fe, NM	5,365	14
Santa Rosa, CA	6,132	12
Sarasota-Bradenton, FL	5,004	15
West Palm Beach-Boca Raton, FL	12,783	8

Source: U.S. Department of Commerce, Economics and Statistics Administration, Bureau of Economic Analysis, *Survey of Current Business,* vol. 76, no. 6, Washington, D.C.: U.S. Government Printing Office, (June 1996), p. 61.

★854★

Employment Projections: By Industry

Numerical Change in Employment in the Fastest Growing Metropolitan Areas, 1993-2005, By Industry: Transportation and Public Utilities

Data refer to employment changes in selected metropolitan areas. The U.S. total is 1,140,979.

City/MSA	Numerical change	Rank
Austin-San Marcos, TX	6,681	7
Fort Collins-Loveland, CO	1,196	15
Fort Myers-Cape Coral, FL	2,799	9
Fort Pierce-Port Saint Lucie, FL	2,040	12
Las Vegas, NV-AZ	9,753	5
Naples, FL	937	16
Olympia, WA	590	17
Orange County, CA	14,910	4
Orlando, FL	17,974	2
Phoenix-Mesa, AZ	22,251	1
Provo-Orem, UT	508	19
Punta Gorda, FL	571	18
Redding, CA	1,369	14
Riverside-San Bernardino, CA	17,398	3
Sacramento, CA	8,045	6
San Luis Obispo-Atascadero-Paso Robles, CA	2,492	10
Santa Fe, NM	261	20
Santa Rosa, CA	2,458	11
Sarasota-Bradenton, FL	1,413	13
West Palm Beach-Boca Raton, FL	6,094	8

Source: U.S. Department of Commerce, Economics and Statistics Administration, Bureau of Economic Analysis, *Survey of Current Business*, vol. 76, no. 6, Washington, D.C.: U.S. Government Printing Office, (June 1996), p. 61.

★855★

Employment Projections: By Industry

Numerical Change in Employment in the Fastest Growing Metropolitan Areas, 1993-2005, By Industry: Wholesale Trade

Data refer to employment changes in selected metropolitan areas. The U.S. total is 1,169,869.

City/MSA	Numerical change	Rank
Austin-San Marcos, TX	5,662	8
Fort Collins-Loveland, CO	1,403	13
Fort Myers-Cape Coral, FL	1,977	12
Fort Pierce-Port Saint Lucie, FL	1,167	14
Las Vegas, NV-AZ	8,760	6
Naples, FL	877	18
Olympia, WA	1,138	15
Orange County, CA	45,800	1
Orlando, FL	12,320	4
Phoenix-Mesa, AZ	22,515	2
Provo-Orem, UT	3,538	9
Punta Gorda, FL	406	20
Redding, CA	1,003	16
Riverside-San Bernardino, CA	17,098	3
Sacramento, CA	8,806	5

[Continued]

★855★

Numerical Change in Employment in the Fastest Growing Metropolitan Areas, 1993-2005, By Industry: Wholesale Trade
[Continued]

City/MSA	Numerical change	Rank
San Luis Obispo-Atascadero-Paso Robles, CA	948	17
Santa Fe, NM	832	19
Santa Rosa, CA	2,368	11
Sarasota-Bradenton, FL	2,909	10
West Palm Beach-Boca Raton, FL	7,738	7

Source: U.S. Department of Commerce, Economics and Statistics Administration, Bureau of Economic Analysis, *Survey of Current Business*, vol. 76, no. 6, Washington, D.C.: U.S. Government Printing Office, (June 1996), p. 61.

★856★

Employment Projections: By Industry

Numerical Change in Employment in the Slowest Growing Metropolitan Areas, 1993-2005, By Industry: Agricultural Services, Forestry, and Fishing

Data refer to employment changes in selected metropolitan areas and include United States residents employed by international organizations, foreign embassies, and consulates in the United States. The U.S. total is 602,180.

City/MSA	Numerical change	Rank
Benton Harbor, MI	205	8
Cleveland-Lorain-Elyria, OH	3,793	2
Cumberland, MD-WV	65	16
Danville, VA	83	14
Detroit, MI	4,625	1
Duluth-Superior, MN-WI	324	4
Flint, MI	523	3
Great Falls, MT	160	10
Jackson, MI	230	7
Jamestown, NY	240	6
Jersey City, NJ	79	15
Pine Bluff, AR	172	9
Pueblo, CO	96	12
Steubenville-Weirton, OH-WV	157	11
Wheeling, WV-OH	94	13
Wichita Falls, TX	271	5

Source: U.S. Department of Commerce, Economics and Statistics Administration, Bureau of Economic Analysis, *Survey of Current Business*, vol. 76, no. 6, Washington, D.C.: U.S. Government Printing Office, (June 1996), p. 61.

★857★

Employment Projections: By Industry

Numerical Change in Employment in the Slowest Growing Metropolitan Areas, 1993-2005, By Industry: All Industries

Data refer to employment changes in selected metropolitan areas. The U.S. total is 27,205,500.

City/MSA	Numerical change	Rank
Benton Harbor, MI	8,021	8
Cleveland-Lorain-Elyria, OH	106,057	3
Cumberland, MD-WV	3,760	15
Danville, VA	2,388	20
Detroit, MI	183,608	2
Duluth-Superior, MN-WI	12,173	7
Flint, MI	15,088	5
Great Falls, MT	3,576	16
Jackson, MI	6,610	12
Jamestown, NY	7,182	11
Jersey City, NJ	22,527	4
Mansfield, OH	7,974	9
New York, NY	289,053	1
Pine Bluff, AR	2,392	19
Pueblo, CO	5,561	14
Steubenville-Weirton, OH-WV	2,544	18
Utica-Rome, NY	13,989	6
Waterloo-Cedar Falls, IA	7,557	10
Wheeling, WV-OH	3,278	17
Wichita Falls, TX	5,800	13

Source: U.S. Department of Commerce, Economics and Statistics Administration, Bureau of Economic Analysis, *Survey of Current Business*, vol. 76, no. 6, Washington, D.C.: U.S. Government Printing Office, (June 1996), p. 61.

★858★

Employment Projections: By Industry

Numerical Change in Employment in the Slowest Growing Metropolitan Areas, 1993-2005, By Industry: Construction

Data refer to employment changes in selected metropolitan areas. The U.S. total is 1,410,938.

City/MSA	Numerical change	Rank
Benton Harbor, MI	643	8
Cleveland-Lorain-Elyria, OH	7,674	1
Cumberland, MD-WV	-158	20
Danville, VA	352	11
Detroit, MI	4,698	2
Duluth-Superior, MN-WI	812	5
Flint, MI	1,194	4
Great Falls, MT	-38	19
Jackson, MI	288	13
Jamestown, NY	365	10
Jersey City, NJ	699	7
Mansfield, OH	242	16
New York, NY	3,673	3
Pine Bluff, AR	501	9
Pueblo, CO	202	17
Steubenville-Weirton, OH-WV	287	14
Utica-Rome, NY	756	6

[Continued]

★858★

Numerical Change in Employment in the Slowest Growing Metropolitan Areas, 1993-2005, By Industry: Construction

[Continued]

City/MSA	Numerical change	Rank
Waterloo-Cedar Falls, IA	284	15
Wheeling, WV-OH	79	18
Wichita Falls, TX	349	12

Source: U.S. Department of Commerce, Economics and Statistics Administration, Bureau of Economic Analysis, *Survey of Current Business*, vol. 76, no. 6, Washington, D.C.: U.S. Government Printing Office, (June 1996), p. 61.

★859★

Employment Projections: By Industry

Numerical Change in Employment in the Slowest Growing Metropolitan Areas, 1993-2005, By Industry: Farming

Data refer to employment changes in selected metropolitan areas. The U.S. total is - 101,750.

City/MSA	Numerical change	Rank
Benton Harbor, MI	-193	15
Cleveland-Lorain-Elyria, OH	-412	17
Cumberland, MD-WV	-26	6
Danville, VA	-371	16
Detroit, MI	-630	18
Duluth-Superior, MN-WI	-64	9
Flint, MI	-98	11
Great Falls, MT	29	1
Jackson, MI	-45	8
Jamestown, NY	0	3
Jersey City, NJ	0	3
Mansfield, OH	-164	14
New York, NY	-30	7
Pine Bluff, AR	-102	12
Pueblo, CO	-18	5
Steubenville-Weirton, OH-WV	-30	7
Utica-Rome, NY	-17	4
Waterloo-Cedar Falls, IA	-113	13
Wheeling, WV-OH	-81	10
Wichita Falls, TX	1	2

Source: U.S. Department of Commerce, Economics and Statistics Administration, Bureau of Economic Analysis, *Survey of Current Business*, vol. 76, no. 6, Washington, D.C.: U.S. Government Printing Office, (June 1996), p. 60.

★860★

Employment Projections: By Industry

Numerical Change in Employment in the Slowest Growing Metropolitan Areas, 1993-2005, By Industry: Federal Civilian Government

Data refer to employment changes in selected metropolitan areas. The U.S. total is - 113,175.

City/MSA	Numerical change	Rank
Benton Harbor, MI	-35	2
Cleveland-Lorain-Elyria, OH	-2,068	18
Cumberland, MD-WV	-39	4
Danville, VA	-33	1
Detroit, MI	-4,252	19
Duluth-Superior, MN-WI	-225	13
Flint, MI	-63	8
Great Falls, MT	-194	11
Jackson, MI	-53	6
Jamestown, NY	-36	3
Jersey City, NJ	-779	17
Mansfield, OH	-70	9
New York, NY	-10,985	20
Pine Bluff, AR	-216	12
Pueblo, CO	-361	14
Steubenville-Weirton, OH-WV	-55	7
Utica-Rome, NY	-602	16
Waterloo-Cedar Falls, IA	-44	5
Wheeling, WV-OH	-96	10
Wichita Falls, TX	-478	15

Source: U.S. Department of Commerce, Economics and Statistics Administration, Bureau of Economic Analysis, *Survey of Current Business,* vol. 76, no. 6, Washington, D.C.: U.S. Government Printing Office, (June 1996), p. 61.

★861★

Employment Projections: By Industry

Numerical Change in Employment in the Slowest Growing Metropolitan Areas, 1993-2005, By Industry: Federal Military Government

Data refer to employment changes in selected metropolitan areas. The U.S. total is - 107,522.

City/MSA	Numerical change	Rank
Benton Harbor, MI	-60	11
Cleveland-Lorain-Elyria, OH	-551	16
Cumberland, MD-WV	-22	6
Danville, VA	-35	7
Detroit, MI	-1,854	18
Duluth-Superior, MN-WI	-71	13
Flint, MI	-150	15
Great Falls, MT	-37	9
Jackson, MI	-50	10
Jamestown, NY	-36	8
Jersey City, NJ	-69	12
Mansfield, OH	-35	7
New York, NY	-3,500	19
Pine Bluff, AR	-12	4
Pueblo, CO	-13	5
Steubenville-Weirton, OH-WV	22	3
Utica-Rome, NY	-731	17

[Continued]

★861★

Numerical Change in Employment in the Slowest Growing Metropolitan Areas, 1993-2005, By Industry: Federal Military Government

[Continued]

City/MSA	Numerical change	Rank
Waterloo-Cedar Falls, IA	-79	14
Wheeling, WV-OH	38	2
Wichita Falls, TX	877	1

Source: U.S. Department of Commerce, Economics and Statistics Administration, Bureau of Economic Analysis, *Survey of Current Business,* vol. 76, no. 6, Washington, D.C.: U.S. Government Printing Office, (June 1996), p. 61.

★862★

Employment Projections: By Industry

Numerical Change in Employment in the Slowest Growing Metropolitan Areas, 1993-2005, By Industry: Finance, Insurance, and Real Estate

Data refer to employment changes in selected metropolitan areas. The U.S. total is 1,822,156.

City/MSA	Numerical change	Rank
Benton Harbor, MI	380	8
Cleveland-Lorain-Elyria, OH	12,009	3
Cumberland, MD-WV	110	16
Danville, VA	-38	18
Detroit, MI	18,932	2
Duluth-Superior, MN-WI	135	13
Flint, MI	298	9
Great Falls, MT	-142	19
Jackson, MI	428	7
Jamestown, NY	-379	20
Jersey City, NJ	6,656	4
Mansfield, OH	122	14
New York, NY	43,616	1
Pine Bluff, AR	176	12
Pueblo, CO	-31	17
Steubenville-Weirton, OH-WV	257	10
Utica-Rome, NY	1,104	5
Waterloo-Cedar Falls, IA	508	6
Wheeling, WV-OH	111	15
Wichita Falls, TX	236	11

Source: U.S. Department of Commerce, Economics and Statistics Administration, Bureau of Economic Analysis, *Survey of Current Business,* vol. 76, no. 6, Washington, D.C.: U.S. Government Printing Office, (June 1996), p. 61.

★863★
Employment Projections: By Industry

Numerical Change in Employment in the Slowest Growing Metropolitan Areas, 1993-2005, By Industry: Manufacturing (Durable Goods)

Data refer to employment changes in selected metropolitan areas. The U.S. total is - 188,816.

City/MSA	Numerical change	Rank
Benton Harbor, MI	-617	9
Cleveland-Lorain-Elyria, OH	-15,537	17
Cumberland, MD-WV	-111	4
Danville, VA	125	1
Detroit, MI	-27,721	18
Duluth-Superior, MN-WI	-63	3
Flint, MI	-4,941	16
Great Falls, MT	-131	5
Jackson, MI	-770	10
Jamestown, NY	-1,592	13
Jersey City, NJ	-2,132	14
Mansfield, OH	-440	6
New York, NY	-29,947	19
Pine Bluff, AR	40	2
Pueblo, CO	-563	7
Steubenville-Weirton, OH-WV	-886	11
Utica-Rome, NY	-3,105	15
Waterloo-Cedar Falls, IA	-1,436	12
Wheeling, WV-OH	-613	8

Source: U.S. Department of Commerce, Economics and Statistics Administration, Bureau of Economic Analysis, *Survey of Current Business,* vol. 76, no. 6, Washington, D.C.: U.S. Government Printing Office, (June 1996), p. 61.

★864★
Employment Projections: By Industry

Numerical Change in Employment in the Slowest Growing Metropolitan Areas, 1993-2005, By Industry: Manufacturing (Nondurable Goods)

Data refer to employment changes in selected metropolitan areas. The U.S. total is 337,083.

City/MSA	Numerical change	Rank
Benton Harbor, MI	54	6
Cleveland-Lorain-Elyria, OH	179	4
Cumberland, MD-WV	-680	15
Danville, VA	-740	16
Detroit, MI	-4,990	17
Duluth-Superior, MN-WI	-403	13
Flint, MI	324	3
Great Falls, MT	33	8
Jackson, MI	-72	9
Jamestown, NY	-111	11
Jersey City, NJ	-7,735	18
Mansfield, OH	76	5
New York, NY	-44,584	19
Pine Bluff, AR	463	1
Pueblo, CO	44	7
Steubenville-Weirton, OH-WV	-186	12
Utica-Rome, NY	-472	14

[Continued]

★864★

Numerical Change in Employment in the Slowest Growing Metropolitan Areas, 1993-2005, By Industry: Manufacturing (Nondurable Goods)
[Continued]

City/MSA	Numerical change	Rank
Waterloo-Cedar Falls, IA	351	2
Wheeling, WV-OH	-105	10

Source: U.S. Department of Commerce, Economics and Statistics Administration, Bureau of Economic Analysis, *Survey of Current Business,* vol. 76, no. 6, Washington, D.C.: U.S. Government Printing Office, (June 1996), p. 61.

★865★
Employment Projections: By Industry

Numerical Change in Employment in the Slowest Growing Metropolitan Areas, 1993-2005, By Industry: Mining

Data refer to employment changes in selected metropolitan areas. The U.S. total is - 95,711.

City/MSA	Numerical change	Rank
Benton Harbor, MI	-16	4
Cleveland-Lorain-Elyria, OH	-230	11
Cumberland, MD-WV	-66	7
Detroit, MI	-161	8
Duluth-Superior, MN-WI	-198	10
Flint, MI	-28	5
Great Falls, MT	0	2
Jackson, MI	-43	6
Jamestown, NY	14	1
Pueblo, CO	-5	3
Steubenville-Weirton, OH-WV	-180	9
Wheeling, WV-OH	-493	12
Wichita Falls, TX	-1,079	13

Source: U.S. Department of Commerce, Economics and Statistics Administration, Bureau of Economic Analysis, *Survey of Current Business,* vol. 76, no. 6, Washington, D.C.: U.S. Government Printing Office, (June 1996), p. 61.

★866★
Employment Projections: By Industry

Numerical Change in Employment in the Slowest Growing Metropolitan Areas, 1993-2005, By Industry: Retail Trade

Data refer to employment changes in selected metropolitan areas. The U.S. total is 4,469,102.

City/MSA	Numerical change	Rank
Benton Harbor, MI	1,597	9
Cleveland-Lorain-Elyria, OH	7,918	2
Cumberland, MD-WV	1,118	13
Danville, VA	557	16
Detroit, MI	23,442	1
Duluth-Superior, MN-WI	2,617	6
Flint, MI	5,253	3

[Continued]

★866★

Numerical Change in Employment in the Slowest Growing Metropolitan Areas, 1993-2005, By Industry: Retail Trade

[Continued]

City/MSA	Numerical change	Rank
Great Falls, MT	808	15
Jackson, MI	1,364	11
Jamestown, NY	1,800	7
Jersey City, NJ	4,866	4
Mansfield, OH	1,419	10
New York, NY	-22,063	20
Pine Bluff, AR	179	19
Pueblo, CO	1,248	12
Steubenville-Weirton, OH-WV	289	18
Utica-Rome, NY	3,940	5
Waterloo-Cedar Falls, IA	1,738	8
Wheeling, WV-OH	486	17
Wichita Falls, TX	1,107	14

Source: U.S. Department of Commerce, Economics and Statistics Administration, Bureau of Economic Analysis, *Survey of Current Business*, vol. 76, no. 6, Washington, D.C.: U.S. Government Printing Office, (June 1996), p. 61.

★867★

Employment Projections: By Industry

Numerical Change in Employment in the Slowest Growing Metropolitan Areas, 1993-2005, By Industry: Services

Data refer to employment changes in selected metropolitan areas. The U.S. total is 14,139,037.

City/MSA	Numerical change	Rank
Benton Harbor, MI	4,211	12
Cleveland-Lorain-Elyria, OH	85,596	3
Cumberland, MD-WV	3,418	15
Danville, VA	1,811	19
Detroit, MI	155,701	2
Duluth-Superior, MN-WI	7,968	7
Flint, MI	12,732	5
Great Falls, MT	2,812	17
Jackson, MI	3,821	13
Jamestown, NY	5,342	8
Jersey City, NJ	13,496	4
Mansfield, OH	4,653	9
New York, NY	310,349	1
Pine Bluff, AR	671	20
Pueblo, CO	4,409	11
Steubenville-Weirton, OH-WV	2,383	18
Utica-Rome, NY	11,187	6
Waterloo-Cedar Falls, IA	4,410	10
Wheeling, WV-OH	3,307	16
Wichita Falls, TX	3,619	14

Source: U.S. Department of Commerce, Economics and Statistics Administration, Bureau of Economic Analysis, *Survey of Current Business*, vol. 76, no. 6, Washington, D.C.: U.S. Government Printing Office, (June 1996), p. 61.

★868★

Employment Projections: By Industry

Numerical Change in Employment in the Slowest Growing Metropolitan Areas, 1993-2005, By Industry: Transportation and Public Utilities

Data refer to employment changes in selected metropolitan areas. The U.S. total is 1,140,979.

City/MSA	Numerical change	Rank
Benton Harbor, MI	551	3
Cleveland-Lorain-Elyria, OH	-952	17
Danville, VA	141	12
Detroit, MI	2,903	1
Duluth-Superior, MN-WI	328	7
Flint, MI	192	10
Great Falls, MT	-99	14
Jackson, MI	-13	13
Jamestown, NY	417	6
Jersey City, NJ	-1,459	19
Mansfield, OH	533	4
New York, NY	-1,056	18
Pine Bluff, AR	-814	16
Pueblo, CO	-153	15
Steubenville-Weirton, OH-WV	226	9
Utica-Rome, NY	642	2
Waterloo-Cedar Falls, IA	156	11
Wheeling, WV-OH	319	8
Wichita Falls, TX	443	5

Source: U.S. Department of Commerce, Economics and Statistics Administration, Bureau of Economic Analysis, *Survey of Current Business*, vol. 76, no. 6, Washington, D.C.: U.S. Government Printing Office, (June 1996), p. 61.

★869★

Employment Projections: By Industry

Numerical Change in Employment in the Slowest Growing Metropolitan Areas, 1993-2005, By Industry: Wholesale Trade

Data refer to employment changes in selected metropolitan areas. The U.S. total is 1,169,869.

City/MSA	Numerical change	Rank
Benton Harbor, MI	208	7
Cleveland-Lorain-Elyria, OH	1,676	3
Danville, VA	19	16
Detroit, MI	11,581	1
Duluth-Superior, MN-WI	57	15
Flint, MI	-956	18
Great Falls, MT	-7	17
Jackson, MI	185	9
Jamestown, NY	196	8
Jersey City, NJ	5,403	2
Mansfield, OH	342	6
New York, NY	-2,266	19
Pine Bluff, AR	116	13
Pueblo, CO	175	10
Steubenville-Weirton, OH-WV	99	14
Utica-Rome, NY	705	5
Waterloo-Cedar Falls, IA	718	4

[Continued]

★869★

Numerical Change in Employment in the Slowest Growing Metropolitan Areas, 1993-2005, By Industry: Wholesale Trade

[Continued]

City/MSA	Numerical change	Rank
Wheeling, WV-OH	154	11
Wichita Falls, TX	151	12

Source: U.S. Department of Commerce, Economics and Statistics Administration, Bureau of Economic Analysis, *Survey of Current Business*, vol. 76, no. 6, Washington, D.C.: U.S. Government Printing Office, (June 1996), p. 61.

★870★

Employment Projections: By Industry

Percent Change in Employment in the Fastest Growing Metropolitan Areas, 1993-2005, By Industry: All Industries

Data refer to employment changes in selected metropolitan areas. The U.S. average is 19%.

City/MSA	Percent change	Rank
Austin-San Marcos, TX	36	10
Fort Collins-Loveland, CO	36	10
Fort Myers-Cape Coral, FL	40	6
Fort Pierce-Port Saint Lucie, FL	37	9
Las Vegas, NV-AZ	45	2
Naples, FL	44	3
Olympia, WA	38	8
Orange County, CA	35	11
Orlando, FL	42	5
Phoenix-Mesa, AZ	35	11
Provo-Orem, UT	43	4
Punta Gorda, FL	49	1
Redding, CA	38	8
Riverside-San Bernardino, CA	40	6
Sacramento, CA	38	8
San Luis Obispo-Atascadero-Paso Robles, CA	40	6
Santa Fe, NM	36	10
Santa Rosa, CA	38	8
Sarasota-Bradenton, FL	39	7
West Palm Beach-Boca Raton, FL	35	11

Source: U.S. Department of Commerce, Economics and Statistics Administration, Bureau of Economic Analysis, *Survey of Current Business*, vol. 76, no. 6, Washington, D.C.: U.S. Government Printing Office, (June 1996), p. 60.

★871★

Employment Projections: By Industry

Percent Change in Employment in the Fastest Growing Metropolitan Areas, 1993-2005, By Industry: Agricultural Services, Forestry, and Fishing

Data refer to employment changes in selected metropolitan areas and include United States residents employed by international organizations, foreign embassies, and consulates in the United States. The U.S. average is 40%.

City/MSA	Percent change	Rank
Austin-San Marcos, TX	61	5
Fort Collins-Loveland, CO	67	3
Fort Myers-Cape Coral, FL	29	16
Fort Pierce-Port Saint Lucie, FL	50	7
Las Vegas, NV-AZ	64	4
Naples, FL	31	15
Olympia, WA	42	12
Orange County, CA	49	8
Orlando, FL	23	17
Phoenix-Mesa, AZ	38	14
Provo-Orem, UT	69	2
Punta Gorda, FL	40	13
Redding, CA	72	1
Riverside-San Bernardino, CA	48	9
Sacramento, CA	48	9
San Luis Obispo-Atascadero-Paso Robles, CA	49	8
Santa Fe, NM	54	6
Santa Rosa, CA	61	5
Sarasota-Bradenton, FL	44	11
West Palm Beach-Boca Raton, FL	47	10

Source: U.S. Department of Commerce, Economics and Statistics Administration, Bureau of Economic Analysis, *Survey of Current Business*, vol. 76, no. 6, Washington, D.C.: U.S. Government Printing Office, (June 1996), p. 60.

★872★

Employment Projections: By Industry

Percent Change in Employment in the Fastest Growing Metropolitan Areas, 1993-2005, By Industry: Construction

Data refer to employment changes in selected metropolitan areas. The U.S. average is 20%.

City/MSA	Percent change	Rank
Austin-San Marcos, TX	31	12
Fort Collins-Loveland, CO	29	14
Fort Myers-Cape Coral, FL	38	8
Fort Pierce-Port Saint Lucie, FL	30	13
Las Vegas, NV-AZ	48	1
Naples, FL	44	5
Olympia, WA	39	7
Orange County, CA	39	7
Orlando, FL	33	11
Phoenix-Mesa, AZ	37	9
Provo-Orem, UT	45	4
Punta Gorda, FL	41	6

[Continued]

★872★

Percent Change in Employment in the Fastest Growing Metropolitan Areas, 1993-2005, By Industry: Construction

[Continued]

City/MSA	Percent change	Rank
Redding, CA	46	3
Riverside-San Bernardino, CA	39	7
Sacramento, CA	41	6
San Luis Obispo-Atascadero-Paso Robles, CA	36	10
Santa Fe, NM	38	8
Santa Rosa, CA	47	2
Sarasota-Bradenton, FL	21	16
West Palm Beach-Boca Raton, FL	25	15

Source: U.S. Department of Commerce, Economics and Statistics Administration, Bureau of Economic Analysis, *Survey of Current Business,* vol. 76, no. 6, Washington, D.C.: U.S. Government Printing Office, (June 1996), p. 60.

★873★

Employment Projections: By Industry

Percent Change in Employment in the Fastest Growing Metropolitan Areas, 1993-2005, By Industry: Farming

Data refer to employment changes in selected metropolitan areas. The U.S. average is - 3%.

City/MSA	Percent change	Rank
Austin-San Marcos, TX	1	9
Fort Collins-Loveland, CO	4	6
Fort Myers-Cape Coral, FL	15	3
Fort Pierce-Port Saint Lucie, FL	-2	11
Las Vegas, NV-AZ	3	7
Naples, FL	28	1
Olympia, WA	-5	13
Orange County, CA	1	9
Orlando, FL	-9	14
Phoenix-Mesa, AZ	-1	10
Provo-Orem, UT	-4	12
Punta Gorda, FL	17	2
Redding, CA	3	7
Riverside-San Bernardino, CA	2	8
Sacramento, CA	6	5
San Luis Obispo-Atascadero-Paso Robles, CA	4	6
Santa Fe, NM	4	6
Santa Rosa, CA	9	4
Sarasota-Bradenton, FL	9	4
West Palm Beach-Boca Raton, FL	-5	13

Source: U.S. Department of Commerce, Economics and Statistics Administration, Bureau of Economic Analysis, *Survey of Current Business,* vol. 76, no. 6, Washington, D.C.: U.S. Government Printing Office, (June 1996), p. 60.

★874★

Employment Projections: By Industry

Percent Change in Employment in the Fastest Growing Metropolitan Areas, 1993-2005, By Industry: Federal Civilian Government

Data refer to employment changes in selected metropolitan areas. The U.S. average is - 4%.

City/MSA	Percent change	Rank
Austin-San Marcos, TX	2	10
Fort Collins-Loveland, CO	10	5
Fort Myers-Cape Coral, FL	16	1
Fort Pierce-Port Saint Lucie, FL	15	2
Las Vegas, NV-AZ	15	2
Naples, FL	14	3
Olympia, WA	6	8
Orange County, CA	9	6
Orlando, FL	13	4
Phoenix-Mesa, AZ	13	4
Provo-Orem, UT	5	9
Punta Gorda, FL	15	2
Redding, CA	7	7
Riverside-San Bernardino, CA	6	8
Sacramento, CA	-11	12
San Luis Obispo-Atascadero-Paso Robles, CA	6	8
Santa Fe, NM	-2	11
Santa Rosa, CA	10	5
Sarasota-Bradenton, FL	14	3
West Palm Beach-Boca Raton, FL	16	1

Source: U.S. Department of Commerce, Economics and Statistics Administration, Bureau of Economic Analysis, *Survey of Current Business,* vol. 76, no. 6, Washington, D.C.: U.S. Government Printing Office, (June 1996), p. 60.

★875★

Employment Projections: By Industry

Percent Change in Employment in the Fastest Growing Metropolitan Areas, 1993-2005, By Industry: Federal Military Government

Data refer to employment changes in selected metropolitan areas. The U.S. average is - 4%.

City/MSA	Percent change	Rank
Austin-San Marcos, TX	-22	13
Fort Collins-Loveland, CO	-2	4
Fort Myers-Cape Coral, FL	-5	7
Fort Pierce-Port Saint Lucie, FL	-4	6
Las Vegas, NV-AZ	5	1
Naples, FL	-4	6
Olympia, WA	-3	5
Orange County, CA	0	2
Orlando, FL	-17	12
Phoenix-Mesa, AZ	-1	3
Provo-Orem, UT	-5	7
Punta Gorda, FL	-3	5
Redding, CA	-5	7
Riverside-San Bernardino, CA	-8	9
Sacramento, CA	-14	11

[Continued]

★875★
Percent Change in Employment in the Fastest Growing Metropolitan Areas, 1993-2005, By Industry: Federal Military Government
[Continued]

City/MSA	Percent change	Rank
San Luis Obispo-Atascadero-Paso Robles, CA	-6	8
Santa Fe, NM	-8	9
Santa Rosa, CA	-10	10
Sarasota-Bradenton, FL	-5	7
West Palm Beach-Boca Raton, FL	-4	6

Source: U.S. Department of Commerce, Economics and Statistics Administration, Bureau of Economic Analysis, *Survey of Current Business*, vol. 76, no. 6, Washington, D.C.: U.S. Government Printing Office, (June 1996), p. 60.

★876★
Employment Projections: By Industry
Percent Change in Employment in the Fastest Growing Metropolitan Areas, 1993-2005, By Industry: Finance, Insurance, and Real Estate

Data refer to employment changes in selected metropolitan areas. The U.S. average is 18%.

City/MSA	Percent change	Rank
Austin-San Marcos, TX	32	5
Fort Collins-Loveland, CO	20	11
Fort Myers-Cape Coral, FL	25	10
Fort Pierce-Port Saint Lucie, FL	20	11
Las Vegas, NV-AZ	44	1
Naples, FL	25	10
Olympia, WA	29	8
Orange County, CA	32	5
Orlando, FL	30	7
Phoenix-Mesa, AZ	31	6
Provo-Orem, UT	25	10
Punta Gorda, FL	16	12
Redding, CA	30	7
Riverside-San Bernardino, CA	32	5
Sacramento, CA	36	3
San Luis Obispo-Atascadero-Paso Robles, CA	41	2
Santa Fe, NM	33	4
Santa Rosa, CA	27	9
Sarasota-Bradenton, FL	14	13
West Palm Beach-Boca Raton, FL	27	9

Source: U.S. Department of Commerce, Economics and Statistics Administration, Bureau of Economic Analysis, *Survey of Current Business*, vol. 76, no. 6, Washington, D.C.: U.S. Government Printing Office, (June 1996), p. 60.

★877★
Employment Projections: By Industry
Percent Change in Employment in the Fastest Growing Metropolitan Areas, 1993-2005, By Industry: Manufacturing (Durable Goods)

Data refer to employment changes in selected metropolitan areas. The U.S. average is - 2%.

City/MSA	Percent change	Rank
Austin-San Marcos, TX	29	1
Fort Collins-Loveland, CO	8	11
Fort Myers-Cape Coral, FL	6	12
Fort Pierce-Port Saint Lucie, FL	9	10
Las Vegas, NV-AZ	23	3
Naples, FL	20	4
Olympia, WA	0	15
Orange County, CA	0	15
Orlando, FL	5	13
Phoenix-Mesa, AZ	8	11
Provo-Orem, UT	3	14
Punta Gorda, FL	19	5
Redding, CA	-1	16
Riverside-San Bernardino, CA	12	8
Sacramento, CA	11	9
San Luis Obispo-Atascadero-Paso Robles, CA	16	6
Santa Fe, NM	25	2
Santa Rosa, CA	13	7
Sarasota-Bradenton, FL	9	10
West Palm Beach-Boca Raton, FL	-1	16

Source: U.S. Department of Commerce, Economics and Statistics Administration, Bureau of Economic Analysis, *Survey of Current Business*, vol. 76, no. 6, Washington, D.C.: U.S. Government Printing Office, (June 1996), p. 60.

★878★
Employment Projections: By Industry
Percent Change in Employment in the Fastest Growing Metropolitan Areas, 1993-2005, By Industry: Manufacturing (Nondurable Goods)

Data refer to employment changes in selected metropolitan areas. The U.S. average is 4%.

City/MSA	Percent change	Rank
Austin-San Marcos, TX	14	12
Fort Collins-Loveland, CO	26	5
Fort Myers-Cape Coral, FL	22	8
Fort Pierce-Port Saint Lucie, FL	10	13
Las Vegas, NV-AZ	40	1
Naples, FL	25	6
Olympia, WA	20	9
Orange County, CA	19	10
Orlando, FL	17	11
Phoenix-Mesa, AZ	25	6
Provo-Orem, UT	33	2
Punta Gorda, FL	26	5
Redding, CA	33	2
Riverside-San Bernardino, CA	27	4
Sacramento, CA	20	9

[Continued]

★878★

Percent Change in Employment in the Fastest Growing Metropolitan Areas, 1993-2005, By Industry: Manufacturing (Nondurable Goods)

[Continued]

City/MSA	Percent change	Rank
San Luis Obispo-Atascadero-Paso Robles, CA	26	5
Santa Fe, NM	32	3
Santa Rosa, CA	26	5
Sarasota-Bradenton, FL	22	8
West Palm Beach-Boca Raton, FL	24	7

Source: U.S. Department of Commerce, Economics and Statistics Administration, Bureau of Economic Analysis, *Survey of Current Business*, vol. 76, no. 6, Washington, D.C.: U.S. Government Printing Office, (June 1996), p. 60.

★879★

Employment Projections: By Industry

Percent Change in Employment in the Fastest Growing Metropolitan Areas, 1993-2005, By Industry: Mining

Data refer to employment changes in selected metropolitan areas. The U.S. average is - 11%.

City/MSA	Percent change	Rank
Austin-San Marcos, TX	3	9
Fort Collins-Loveland, CO	-7	12
Fort Myers-Cape Coral, FL	4	8
Fort Pierce-Port Saint Lucie, FL	8	6
Las Vegas, NV-AZ	0	10
Naples, FL	17	2
Olympia, WA	18	1
Orange County, CA	-14	15
Orlando, FL	9	5
Phoenix-Mesa, AZ	16	3
Provo-Orem, UT	-23	16
Redding, CA	13	4
Riverside-San Bernardino, CA	-10	13
Sacramento, CA	4	8
San Luis Obispo-Atascadero-Paso Robles, CA	6	7
Santa Fe, NM	3	9
Santa Rosa, CA	-1	11
Sarasota-Bradenton, FL	-12	14
West Palm Beach-Boca Raton, FL	8	6

Source: U.S. Department of Commerce, Economics and Statistics Administration, Bureau of Economic Analysis, *Survey of Current Business*, vol. 76, no. 6, Washington, D.C.: U.S. Government Printing Office, (June 1996), p. 60.

★880★

Employment Projections: By Industry

Percent Change in Employment in the Fastest Growing Metropolitan Areas, 1993-2005, By Industry: Retail Trade

Data refer to employment changes in selected metropolitan areas. The U.S. average is 19%.

City/MSA	Percent change	Rank
Austin-San Marcos, TX	33	12
Fort Collins-Loveland, CO	38	8
Fort Myers-Cape Coral, FL	36	10
Fort Pierce-Port Saint Lucie, FL	36	10
Las Vegas, NV-AZ	43	4
Naples, FL	44	3
Olympia, WA	37	9
Orange County, CA	34	11
Orlando, FL	39	7
Phoenix-Mesa, AZ	31	13
Provo-Orem, UT	45	2
Punta Gorda, FL	51	1
Redding, CA	40	6
Riverside-San Bernardino, CA	41	5
Sacramento, CA	36	10
San Luis Obispo-Atascadero-Paso Robles, CA	38	8
Santa Fe, NM	40	6
Santa Rosa, CA	39	7
Sarasota-Bradenton, FL	27	14
West Palm Beach-Boca Raton, FL	31	13

Source: U.S. Department of Commerce, Economics and Statistics Administration, Bureau of Economic Analysis, *Survey of Current Business*, vol. 76, no. 6, Washington, D.C.: U.S. Government Printing Office, (June 1996), p. 60.

★881★

Employment Projections: By Industry

Percent Change in Employment in the Fastest Growing Metropolitan Areas, 1993-2005, By Industry: Services

Data refer to employment changes in selected metropolitan areas. The U.S. average is 35%.

City/MSA	Percent change	Rank
Austin-San Marcos, TX	54	9
Fort Collins-Loveland, CO	57	6
Fort Myers-Cape Coral, FL	55	8
Fort Pierce-Port Saint Lucie, FL	51	10
Las Vegas, NV-AZ	50	11
Naples, FL	62	3
Olympia, WA	59	4
Orange County, CA	51	10
Orlando, FL	63	2
Phoenix-Mesa, AZ	50	11
Provo-Orem, UT	55	8
Punta Gorda, FL	66	1
Redding, CA	54	9
Riverside-San Bernardino, CA	58	5
Sacramento, CA	55	8

[Continued]

★881★
Percent Change in Employment in the Fastest Growing Metropolitan Areas, 1993-2005, By Industry: Services
[Continued]

City/MSA	Percent change	Rank
San Luis Obispo-Atascadero-Paso Robles, CA	56	7
Santa Fe, NM	48	12
Santa Rosa, CA	66	1
Sarasota-Bradenton, FL	62	3
West Palm Beach-Boca Raton, FL	50	11

Source: U.S. Department of Commerce, Economics and Statistics Administration, Bureau of Economic Analysis, *Survey of Current Business,* vol. 76, no. 6, Washington, D.C.: U.S. Government Printing Office, (June 1996), p. 60.

★882★
Employment Projections: By Industry
Percent Change in Employment in the Fastest Growing Metropolitan Areas, 1993-2005, By Industry: State and Local Government

Data refer to employment changes in selected metropolitan areas. The U.S. average is 17%.

City/MSA	Percent change	Rank
Austin-San Marcos, TX	25	12
Fort Collins-Loveland, CO	33	7
Fort Myers-Cape Coral, FL	40	3
Fort Pierce-Port Saint Lucie, FL	35	5
Las Vegas, NV-AZ	46	1
Naples, FL	35	5
Olympia, WA	34	6
Orange County, CA	29	10
Orlando, FL	34	6
Phoenix-Mesa, AZ	33	7
Provo-Orem, UT	40	3
Punta Gorda, FL	41	2
Redding, CA	32	8
Riverside-San Bernardino, CA	38	4
Sacramento, CA	35	5
San Luis Obispo-Atascadero-Paso Robles, CA	33	7
Santa Fe, NM	23	13
Santa Rosa, CA	26	11
Sarasota-Bradenton, FL	23	13
West Palm Beach-Boca Raton, FL	30	9

Source: U.S. Department of Commerce, Economics and Statistics Administration, Bureau of Economic Analysis, *Survey of Current Business,* vol. 76, no. 6, Washington, D.C.: U.S. Government Printing Office, (June 1996), p. 60.

★883★
Employment Projections: By Industry
Percent Change in Employment in the Fastest Growing Metropolitan Areas, 1993-2005, By Industry: Transportation and Public Utilities

Data refer to employment changes in selected metropolitan areas. The U.S. average is 17%.

City/MSA	Percent change	Rank
Austin-San Marcos, TX	38	5
Fort Collins-Loveland, CO	40	3
Fort Myers-Cape Coral, FL	39	4
Fort Pierce-Port Saint Lucie, FL	39	4
Las Vegas, NV-AZ	39	4
Naples, FL	37	6
Olympia, WA	26	12
Orange County, CA	35	8
Orlando, FL	43	2
Phoenix-Mesa, AZ	36	7
Provo-Orem, UT	20	14
Punta Gorda, FL	46	1
Redding, CA	32	10
Riverside-San Bernardino, CA	38	5
Sacramento, CA	29	11
San Luis Obispo-Atascadero-Paso Robles, CA	43	2
Santa Fe, NM	19	15
Santa Rosa, CA	34	9
Sarasota-Bradenton, FL	22	13
West Palm Beach-Boca Raton, FL	37	6

Source: U.S. Department of Commerce, Economics and Statistics Administration, Bureau of Economic Analysis, *Survey of Current Business,* vol. 76, no. 6, Washington, D.C.: U.S. Government Printing Office, (June 1996), p. 60.

★884★
Employment Projections: By Industry
Percent Change in Employment in the Fastest Growing Metropolitan Areas, 1993-2005, By Industry: Wholesale Trade

Data refer to employment changes in selected metropolitan areas. The U.S. average is 18%.

City/MSA	Percent change	Rank
Austin-San Marcos, TX	32	17
Fort Collins-Loveland, CO	50	3
Fort Myers-Cape Coral, FL	36	13
Fort Pierce-Port Saint Lucie, FL	37	12
Las Vegas, NV-AZ	53	2
Naples, FL	40	10
Olympia, WA	46	7
Orange County, CA	48	5
Orlando, FL	32	17
Phoenix-Mesa, AZ	33	16
Provo-Orem, UT	74	1
Punta Gorda, FL	49	4
Redding, CA	35	14
Riverside-San Bernardino, CA	43	8
Sacramento, CA	34	15

[Continued]

★ 884 ★

Percent Change in Employment in the Fastest Growing Metropolitan Areas, 1993-2005, By Industry: Wholesale Trade

[Continued]

City/MSA	Percent change	Rank
San Luis Obispo-Atascadero-Paso Robles, CA	35	14
Santa Fe, NM	47	6
Santa Rosa, CA	31	18
Sarasota-Bradenton, FL	38	11
West Palm Beach-Boca Raton, FL	41	9

Source: U.S. Department of Commerce, Economics and Statistics Administration, Bureau of Economic Analysis, *Survey of Current Business*, vol. 76, no. 6, Washington, D.C.: U.S. Government Printing Office, (June 1996), p. 60.

★ 885 ★

Employment Projections: By Industry

Percent Change in Employment in the Slowest Growing Metropolitan Areas, 1993-2005, By Industry: All Industries

Data refer to employment changes in selected metropolitan areas. The U.S. average is 19%.

City/MSA	Percent change	Rank
Benton Harbor, MI	10	1
Cleveland-Lorain-Elyria, OH	9	2
Cumberland, MD-WV	9	2
Danville, VA	4	7
Detroit, MI	8	3
Duluth-Superior, MN-WI	10	1
Flint, MI	8	3
Great Falls, MT	8	3
Jackson, MI	10	1
Jamestown, NY	10	1
Jersey City, NJ	8	3
Mansfield, OH	9	2
New York, NY	6	5
Pine Bluff, AR	6	5
Pueblo, CO	10	1
Steubenville-Weirton, OH-WV	4	7
Utica-Rome, NY	9	2
Waterloo-Cedar Falls, IA	10	1
Wheeling, WV-OH	5	6
Wichita Falls, TX	7	4

Source: U.S. Department of Commerce, Economics and Statistics Administration, Bureau of Economic Analysis, *Survey of Current Business*, vol. 76, no. 6, Washington, D.C.: U.S. Government Printing Office, (June 1996), p. 60.

★ 886 ★

Employment Projections: By Industry

Percent Change in Employment in the Slowest Growing Metropolitan Areas, 1993-2005, By Industry: Agricultural Services, Forestry, and Fishing

Data refer to employment changes in selected metropolitan areas and include United States residents employed by international organizations, foreign embassies, and consulates in the United States. The U.S. average is 40%.

City/MSA	Percent change	Rank
Benton Harbor, MI	31	11
Cleveland-Lorain-Elyria, OH	43	5
Cumberland, MD-WV	30	12
Danville, VA	33	10
Detroit, MI	35	9
Duluth-Superior, MN-WI	40	7
Flint, MI	46	3
Great Falls, MT	42	6
Jackson, MI	45	4
Jamestown, NY	33	10
Jersey City, NJ	31	11
Pine Bluff, AR	55	1
Pueblo, CO	25	14
Steubenville-Weirton, OH-WV	49	2
Wheeling, WV-OH	26	13
Wichita Falls, TX	38	8

Source: U.S. Department of Commerce, Economics and Statistics Administration, Bureau of Economic Analysis, *Survey of Current Business*, vol. 76, no. 6, Washington, D.C.: U.S. Government Printing Office, (June 1996), p. 60.

★ 887 ★

Employment Projections: By Industry

Percent Change in Employment in the Slowest Growing Metropolitan Areas, 1993-2005, By Industry: Construction

Data refer to employment changes in selected metropolitan areas. The U.S. average is 20%.

City/MSA	Percent change	Rank
Benton Harbor, MI	20	2
Cleveland-Lorain-Elyria, OH	14	4
Cumberland, MD-WV	-7	15
Danville, VA	12	6
Detroit, MI	6	11
Duluth-Superior, MN-WI	15	3
Flint, MI	14	4
Great Falls, MT	-2	14
Jackson, MI	10	8
Jamestown, NY	12	6
Jersey City, NJ	12	6
Mansfield, OH	7	10
New York, NY	3	12
Pine Bluff, AR	29	1
Pueblo, CO	7	10
Steubenville-Weirton, OH-WV	10	8
Utica-Rome, NY	13	5
Waterloo-Cedar Falls, IA	9	9

[Continued]

★887★

Percent Change in Employment in the Slowest Growing Metropolitan Areas, 1993-2005, By Industry: Construction

[Continued]

City/MSA	Percent change	Rank
Wheeling, WV-OH	2	13
Wichita Falls, TX	11	7

Source: U.S. Department of Commerce, Economics and Statistics Administration, Bureau of Economic Analysis, *Survey of Current Business*, vol. 76, no. 6, Washington, D.C.: U.S. Government Printing Office, (June 1996), p. 60.

★888★

Employment Projections: By Industry

Percent Change in Employment in the Slowest Growing Metropolitan Areas, 1993-2005, By Industry: Farming

Data refer to employment changes in selected metropolitan areas. The U.S. average is - 3%.

City/MSA	Percent change	Rank
Benton Harbor, MI	-7	8
Cleveland-Lorain-Elyria, OH	-6	7
Cumberland, MD-WV	-4	6
Danville, VA	-18	11
Detroit, MI	-8	9
Duluth-Superior, MN-WI	-4	6
Flint, MI	-8	9
Great Falls, MT	3	1
Jackson, MI	-3	5
Jamestown, NY	0	2
Jersey City, NJ	0	2
Mansfield, OH	-7	8
New York, NY	-7	8
Pine Bluff, AR	-10	10
Pueblo, CO	-2	4
Steubenville-Weirton, OH-WV	-4	6
Utica-Rome, NY	-1	3
Waterloo-Cedar Falls, IA	-7	8
Wheeling, WV-OH	-6	7
Wichita Falls, TX	0	2

Source: U.S. Department of Commerce, Economics and Statistics Administration, Bureau of Economic Analysis, *Survey of Current Business*, vol. 76, no. 6, Washington, D.C.: U.S. Government Printing Office, (June 1996), p. 60.

★889★

Employment Projections: By Industry

Percent Change in Employment in the Slowest Growing Metropolitan Areas, 1993-2005, By Industry: Federal Civilian Government

Data refer to employment changes in selected metropolitan areas. The U.S. average is - 4%.

City/MSA	Percent change	Rank
Benton Harbor, MI	-8	2
Cleveland-Lorain-Elyria, OH	-10	4
Cumberland, MD-WV	-12	6
Danville, VA	-12	6
Detroit, MI	-14	8
Duluth-Superior, MN-WI	-12	6
Flint, MI	-5	1
Great Falls, MT	-12	6
Jackson, MI	-13	7
Jamestown, NY	-9	3
Jersey City, NJ	-8	2
Mansfield, OH	-9	3
New York, NY	-14	8
Pine Bluff, AR	-11	5
Pueblo, CO	-42	11
Steubenville-Weirton, OH-WV	-14	8
Utica-Rome, NY	-15	9
Waterloo-Cedar Falls, IA	-8	2
Wheeling, WV-OH	-14	8
Wichita Falls, TX	-19	10

Source: U.S. Department of Commerce, Economics and Statistics Administration, Bureau of Economic Analysis, *Survey of Current Business*, vol. 76, no. 6, Washington, D.C.: U.S. Government Printing Office, (June 1996), p. 60.

★890★

Employment Projections: By Industry

Percent Change in Employment in the Slowest Growing Metropolitan Areas, 1993-2005, By Industry: Federal Military Government

Data refer to employment changes in selected metropolitan areas. The U.S. average is - 4%.

City/MSA	Percent change	Rank
Benton Harbor, MI	-12	12
Cleveland-Lorain-Elyria, OH	-7	9
Cumberland, MD-WV	-4	7
Danville, VA	-7	9
Detroit, MI	-13	13
Duluth-Superior, MN-WI	-6	8
Flint, MI	-12	12
Great Falls, MT	-1	4
Jackson, MI	-11	11
Jamestown, NY	-9	10
Jersey City, NJ	-4	7
Mansfield, OH	-6	8
New York, NY	-12	12
Pine Bluff, AR	-2	5
Pueblo, CO	-3	6
Steubenville-Weirton, OH-WV	4	3
Utica-Rome, NY	-15	14

[Continued]

★890★

Percent Change in Employment in the Slowest Growing Metropolitan Areas, 1993-2005, By Industry: Federal Military Government

[Continued]

City/MSA	Percent change	Rank
Waterloo-Cedar Falls, IA	-11	11
Wheeling, WV-OH	6	2
Wichita Falls, TX	13	1

Source: U.S. Department of Commerce, Economics and Statistics Administration, Bureau of Economic Analysis, *Survey of Current Business,* vol. 76, no. 6, Washington, D.C.: U.S. Government Printing Office, (June 1996), p. 60.

★891★

Employment Projections: By Industry

Percent Change in Employment in the Slowest Growing Metropolitan Areas, 1993-2005, By Industry: Finance, Insurance, and Real Estate

Data refer to employment changes in selected metropolitan areas. The U.S. average is 18%.

City/MSA	Percent change	Rank
Benton Harbor, MI	9	7
Cleveland-Lorain-Elyria, OH	13	3
Cumberland, MD-WV	5	10
Danville, VA	-2	13
Detroit, MI	11	5
Duluth-Superior, MN-WI	3	11
Flint, MI	3	11
Great Falls, MT	-5	14
Jackson, MI	14	2
Jamestown, NY	-15	15
Jersey City, NJ	25	1
Mansfield, OH	3	11
New York, NY	7	8
Pine Bluff, AR	9	7
Pueblo, CO	-1	12
Steubenville-Weirton, OH-WV	10	6
Utica-Rome, NY	10	6
Waterloo-Cedar Falls, IA	12	4
Wheeling, WV-OH	3	11
Wichita Falls, TX	6	9

Source: U.S. Department of Commerce, Economics and Statistics Administration, Bureau of Economic Analysis, *Survey of Current Business,* vol. 76, no. 6, Washington, D.C.: U.S. Government Printing Office, (June 1996), p. 60.

★892★

Employment Projections: By Industry

Percent Change in Employment in the Slowest Growing Metropolitan Areas, 1993-2005, By Industry: Manufacturing (Durable Goods)

Data refer to employment changes in selected metropolitan areas. The U.S. average is - 2%.

City/MSA	Percent change	Rank
Benton Harbor, MI	-4	5
Cleveland-Lorain-Elyria, OH	-10	9
Cumberland, MD-WV	-5	6
Danville, VA	4	1
Detroit, MI	-8	8
Duluth-Superior, MN-WI	-1	3
Flint, MI	-12	10
Great Falls, MT	-59	17
Jackson, MI	-8	8
Jamestown, NY	-15	12
Jersey City, NJ	-37	16
Mansfield, OH	-2	4
New York, NY	-30	15
Pine Bluff, AR	1	2
Pueblo, CO	-14	11
Steubenville-Weirton, OH-WV	-7	7
Utica-Rome, NY	-20	13
Waterloo-Cedar Falls, IA	-14	11
Wheeling, WV-OH	-23	14

Source: U.S. Department of Commerce, Economics and Statistics Administration, Bureau of Economic Analysis, *Survey of Current Business,* vol. 76, no. 6, Washington, D.C.: U.S. Government Printing Office, (June 1996), p. 60.

★893★

Employment Projections: By Industry

Percent Change in Employment in the Slowest Growing Metropolitan Areas, 1993-2005, By Industry: Manufacturing (Nondurable Goods)

Data refer to employment changes in selected metropolitan areas. The U.S. average is 4%.

City/MSA	Percent change	Rank
Benton Harbor, MI	1	7
Cleveland-Lorain-Elyria, OH	0	8
Cumberland, MD-WV	-16	14
Danville, VA	-6	10
Detroit, MI	-6	10
Duluth-Superior, MN-WI	-10	12
Flint, MI	9	2
Great Falls, MT	3	5
Jackson, MI	-3	9
Jamestown, NY	-3	9
Jersey City, NJ	-27	16
Mansfield, OH	2	6
New York, NY	-17	15
Pine Bluff, AR	10	1
Pueblo, CO	4	4
Steubenville-Weirton, OH-WV	-13	13
Utica-Rome, NY	-8	11

[Continued]

★893★

Percent Change in Employment in the Slowest Growing Metropolitan Areas, 1993-2005, By Industry: Manufacturing (Nondurable Goods)

[Continued]

City/MSA	Percent change	Rank
Waterloo-Cedar Falls, IA	8	3
Wheeling, WV-OH	-3	9

Source: U.S. Department of Commerce, Economics and Statistics Administration, Bureau of Economic Analysis, *Survey of Current Business*, vol. 76, no. 6, Washington, D.C.: U.S. Government Printing Office, (June 1996), p. 60.

★894★

Employment Projections: By Industry

Percent Change in Employment in the Slowest Growing Metropolitan Areas, 1993-2005, By Industry: Mining

Data refer to employment changes in selected metropolitan areas. The U.S. average is - 11%.

City/MSA	Percent change	Rank
Benton Harbor, MI	-10	6
Cleveland-Lorain-Elyria, OH	-12	7
Cumberland, MD-WV	-30	11
Detroit, MI	-7	5
Duluth-Superior, MN-WI	-4	3
Flint, MI	-10	6
Great Falls, MT	0	2
Jackson, MI	-17	8
Jamestown, NY	4	1
Pueblo, CO	-6	4
Steubenville-Weirton, OH-WV	-27	10
Wheeling, WV-OH	-33	12
Wichita Falls, TX	-25	9

Source: U.S. Department of Commerce, Economics and Statistics Administration, Bureau of Economic Analysis, *Survey of Current Business*, vol. 76, no. 6, Washington, D.C.: U.S. Government Printing Office, (June 1996), p. 60.

★895★

Employment Projections: By Industry

Percent Change in Employment in the Slowest Growing Metropolitan Areas, 1993-2005, By Industry: Retail Trade

Data refer to employment changes in selected metropolitan areas. The U.S. average is 19%.

City/MSA	Percent change	Rank
Benton Harbor, MI	11	5
Cleveland-Lorain-Elyria, OH	4	10
Cumberland, MD-WV	12	4
Danville, VA	6	9
Detroit, MI	6	9
Duluth-Superior, MN-WI	10	6
Flint, MI	13	3

[Continued]

★895★

Employment Projections: By Industry

Percent Change in Employment in the Slowest Growing Metropolitan Areas, 1993-2005, By Industry: Retail Trade

[Continued]

City/MSA	Percent change	Rank
Great Falls, MT	9	7
Jackson, MI	10	6
Jamestown, NY	13	3
Jersey City, NJ	14	2
Mansfield, OH	8	8
New York, NY	-5	12
Pine Bluff, AR	3	11
Pueblo, CO	10	6
Steubenville-Weirton, OH-WV	3	11
Utica-Rome, NY	15	1
Waterloo-Cedar Falls, IA	12	4
Wheeling, WV-OH	3	11
Wichita Falls, TX	9	7

Source: U.S. Department of Commerce, Economics and Statistics Administration, Bureau of Economic Analysis, *Survey of Current Business*, vol. 76, no. 6, Washington, D.C.: U.S. Government Printing Office, (June 1996), p. 60.

★896★

Employment Projections: By Industry

Percent Change in Employment in the Slowest Growing Metropolitan Areas, 1993-2005, By Industry: Services

Data refer to employment changes in selected metropolitan areas. The U.S. average is 35%.

City/MSA	Percent change	Rank
Benton Harbor, MI	20	9
Cleveland-Lorain-Elyria, OH	23	6
Cumberland, MD-WV	29	1
Danville, VA	16	11
Detroit, MI	23	6
Duluth-Superior, MN-WI	22	7
Flint, MI	24	5
Great Falls, MT	21	8
Jackson, MI	23	6
Jamestown, NY	28	2
Jersey City, NJ	21	8
Mansfield, OH	20	9
New York, NY	18	10
Pine Bluff, AR	7	13
Pueblo, CO	26	4
Steubenville-Weirton, OH-WV	15	12
Utica-Rome, NY	27	3
Waterloo-Cedar Falls, IA	21	8
Wheeling, WV-OH	15	12
Wichita Falls, TX	18	10

Source: U.S. Department of Commerce, Economics and Statistics Administration, Bureau of Economic Analysis, *Survey of Current Business*, vol. 76, no. 6, Washington, D.C.: U.S. Government Printing Office, (June 1996), p. 60.

★897★

Employment Projections: By Industry

Numerical Change in Employment in the Slowest Growing Metropolitan Areas, 1993-2005, By Industry: State and Local Government

Data refer to employment changes in selected metropolitan areas. The U.S. total is 2,721,129.

City/MSA	Numerical change	Rank
Benton Harbor, MI	1,095	7
Cleveland-Lorain-Elyria, OH	6,963	2
Cumberland, MD-WV	531	13
Danville, VA	521	15
Detroit, MI	1,333	5
Duluth-Superior, MN-WI	957	10
Flint, MI	810	11
Great Falls, MT	381	16
Jackson, MI	1,341	4
Jamestown, NY	963	9
Jersey City, NJ	3,502	3
Mansfield, OH	1,093	8
New York, NY	41,809	1
Pine Bluff, AR	1,216	6
Pueblo, CO	530	14
Steubenville-Weirton, OH-WV	162	19
Utica-Rome, NY	330	17
Waterloo-Cedar Falls, IA	744	12
Wheeling, WV-OH	77	20
Wichita Falls, TX	193	18

Source: U.S. Department of Commerce, Economics and Statistics Administration, Bureau of Economic Analysis, *Survey of Current Business,* vol. 76, no. 6, Washington, D.C.: U.S. Government Printing Office, (June 1996), p. 61.

★898★

Employment Projections: By Industry

Percent Change in Employment in the Slowest Growing Metropolitan Areas, 1993-2005, By Industry: State and Local Government

Data refer to employment changes in selected metropolitan areas. The U.S. average is 17%.

City/MSA	Percent change	Rank
Benton Harbor, MI	13	3
Cleveland-Lorain-Elyria, OH	6	9
Cumberland, MD-WV	9	7
Danville, VA	10	6
Detroit, MI	1	14
Duluth-Superior, MN-WI	5	10
Flint, MI	4	11
Great Falls, MT	10	6
Jackson, MI	15	2
Jamestown, NY	10	6
Jersey City, NJ	11	5
Mansfield, OH	12	4
New York, NY	7	8
Pine Bluff, AR	20	1
Pueblo, CO	6	9
Steubenville-Weirton, OH-WV	3	12
Utica-Rome, NY	1	14

[Continued]

★898★

Percent Change in Employment in the Slowest Growing Metropolitan Areas, 1993-2005, By Industry: State and Local Government

[Continued]

City/MSA	Percent change	Rank
Waterloo-Cedar Falls, IA	7	8
Wheeling, WV-OH	1	14
Wichita Falls, TX	2	13

Source: U.S. Department of Commerce, Economics and Statistics Administration, Bureau of Economic Analysis, *Survey of Current Business,* vol. 76, no. 6, Washington, D.C.: U.S. Government Printing Office, (June 1996), p. 60.

★899★

Employment Projections: By Industry

Percent Change in Employment in the Slowest Growing Metropolitan Areas, 1993-2005, By Industry: Transportation and Public Utilities

Data refer to employment changes in selected metropolitan areas. The U.S. average is 17%.

City/MSA	Percent change	Rank
Benton Harbor, MI	17	1
Cleveland-Lorain-Elyria, OH	-2	12
Danville, VA	10	5
Detroit, MI	3	10
Duluth-Superior, MN-WI	4	9
Flint, MI	4	9
Great Falls, MT	-6	14
Jackson, MI	0	11
Jamestown, NY	15	2
Jersey City, NJ	-5	13
Mansfield, OH	11	4
New York, NY	0	11
Pine Bluff, AR	-34	16
Pueblo, CO	-7	15
Steubenville-Weirton, OH-WV	6	8
Utica-Rome, NY	13	3
Waterloo-Cedar Falls, IA	7	7
Wheeling, WV-OH	8	6
Wichita Falls, TX	13	3

Source: U.S. Department of Commerce, Economics and Statistics Administration, Bureau of Economic Analysis, *Survey of Current Business,* vol. 76, no. 6, Washington, D.C.: U.S. Government Printing Office, (June 1996), p. 60.

★900★

Employment Projections: By Industry

Percent Change in Employment in the Slowest Growing Metropolitan Areas, 1993-2005, By Industry: Wholesale Trade

Data refer to employment changes in selected metropolitan areas. The U.S. average is 18%.

City/MSA	Percent change	Rank
Benton Harbor, MI	8	5
Cleveland-Lorain-Elyria, OH	2	9
Danville, VA	1	10
Detroit, MI	10	4
Duluth-Superior, MN-WI	1	10
Flint, MI	-12	13
Great Falls, MT	0	11
Jackson, MI	8	5
Jamestown, NY	8	5
Jersey City, NJ	21	1
Mansfield, OH	10	4
New York, NY	-1	12
Pine Bluff, AR	8	5
Pueblo, CO	12	3
Steubenville-Weirton, OH-WV	7	6
Utica-Rome, NY	14	2
Waterloo-Cedar Falls, IA	21	1
Wheeling, WV-OH	5	8
Wichita Falls, TX	6	7

Source: U.S. Department of Commerce, Economics and Statistics Administration, Bureau of Economic Analysis, *Survey of Current Business*, vol. 76, no. 6, Washington, D.C.: U.S. Government Printing Office, (June 1996), p. 60.

★901★

Employment (Nonfarm Payrolls)

Employees on Nonfarm Payrolls, July 1995, By Industry: All Industries (Highest Numbers)

[In thousands; not seasonally adjusted]

City	Total	Rank
Atlanta, GA	1,836.7	8
Baltimore, MD PMSA	1,122.6	17
Boston, MA	1,787.6	9
Chicago, IL	3,878.3	1
Cleveland-Lorain-Elyria, OH	1,101.6	18
Dallas, TX	1,587.9	11
Detroit, MI	2,005.7	7
Houston, TX	1,752.4	10
Los Angeles-Long Beach, CA	3,715.2	3
Minneapolis-Saint Paul, MN	1,538.3	12
Nassau-Suffolk, NY	1,077.4	19
New York City, NY	3,310.1	4
New York, NY PMSA	3,807.0	2
Orange County, CA	1,130.0	16
Philadelphia, PA PMSA	2,157.3	6
Phoenix-Mesa, AZ	1,173.2	15
Pittsburgh, PA	1,036.1	20
Saint Louis, MO	1,238.5	13
Seattle-Bellevue-Everett, WA	1,177.0	14
Washington, DC PMSA	2,407.6	5

Source: U.S. Department of Labor, Bureau of Labor Statistics, *Employment and Earnings*, Washington, D.C.: U.S. Government Printing Office, September 1995, p. 84.

★902★

Employment (Nonfarm Payrolls)

Employees on Nonfarm Payrolls, July 1995, By Industry: All Industries (Lowest Numbers)

[In thousands; not seasonally adjusted]

City	Total	Rank
Barre-Montpelier, VT	29.3	3
Bismarck, ND	46.5	18
Bristol, VA	35.7	5
Casper, WY	28.9	2
Danville, VA	41.8	13
Elmira, NY	41.3	12
Enid, OK	24.4	1
Grand Forks, ND	47.1	20
Kankakee, IL	41.3	12
Kenosha, WI	45.2	16
Las Cruces, NM	46.1	17
Lawrence, KS	40.0	8
Lawton, OK	38.7	6
Lewiston-Auburn, ME	40.4	10
Owensboro, KY	43.1	14
Pittsfield, MA	41.1	11
Rapid City, SD	47.0	19
San Angelo, TX	40.2	9
Sharon, PA	44.6	15
Sherman-Denison, TX	39.2	7
Victoria, TX	32.8	4

Source: U.S. Department of Labor, Bureau of Labor Statistics, *Employment and Earnings*, Washington, D.C.: U.S. Government Printing Office, September 1995, p. 84.

★903★

Employment (Nonfarm Payrolls)

Employees on Nonfarm Payrolls, July 1995, By Industry: Government (Highest Numbers)

[In thousands; not seasonally adjusted]

City	Government	Rank
Atlanta, GA	241.1	7
Baltimore, MD PMSA	203.5	11
Boston, MA	207.2	10
Chicago, IL	459.2	5
Dallas, TX	183.2	13
Detroit, MI	213.1	9
Houston, TX	229.8	8
Los Angeles-Long Beach, CA	522.5	4
Minneapolis-Saint Paul, MN	200.5	12
Nassau-Suffolk, NY	166.5	16
New York City, NY	551.0	3
New York, NY PMSA	632.1	2
Northern Virginia, VA	171.5	15
Oakland, CA	162.9	17
Philadelphia, PA PMSA	287.8	6
Sacramento, CA	158.9	20
San Diego, CA	173.3	14
Seattle-Bellevue-Everett, WA	162.1	18
Suburban Maryland-Washington, DC	160.2	19
Washington, DC PMSA	805.7	1

Source: U.S. Department of Labor, Bureau of Labor Statistics, *Employment and Earnings*, Washington, D.C.: U.S. Government Printing Office, September 1995, p. 84.

★904★

Employment (Nonfarm Payrolls)

Employees on Nonfarm Payrolls, July 1995, By Industry: Government (Lowest Numbers)

[In thousands; not seasonally adjusted]

City	Government	Rank
Dubuque, IA	3.4	1
Lewiston-Auburn, ME	3.9	2
Enid, OK	4.0	3
Pittsfield, MA	4.7	4
Casper, WY	4.7	4
Sherman-Denison, TX	4.8	5
Danville, VA	5.0	6
Bristol, VA	5.1	7
Sharon, PA	5.3	8
Decatur, IL	5.5	9
Owensboro, KY	5.5	9
Victoria, TX	5.5	9
Elkhart-Goshen, IN	5.6	10
Barre-Montpelier, VT	5.8	11
Sheboygan, WI	5.8	11
Kokomo, IN	6.0	12
Steubenville-Weirton, OH	6.0	12
Kenosha, WI	6.1	13
Wausau, WI	6.2	14
Sioux City, IA	6.3	15

Source: U.S. Department of Labor, Bureau of Labor Statistics, *Employment and Earnings,* Washington, D.C.: U.S. Government Printing Office, September 1995, p. 84.

★905★

Employment (Nonfarm Payrolls)

Employees on Nonfarm Payrolls, July 1995, By Industry: Finance, Insurance, and Real Estate (Highest Numbers)

[In thousands; not seasonally adjusted]

City	Finance insurance and real estate	Rank
New York, NY PMSA	513.5	1
New York City, NY	480.6	2
Chicago, IL	313.8	3
Los Angeles-Long Beach, CA	238.5	4
Philadelphia, PA PMSA	156.9	5
Boston, MA	153.2	6
Washington, DC PMSA	136.3	7
Dallas, TX	132.0	8
Atlanta, GA	118.9	9
Detroit, MI	111.5	10
Minneapolis-Saint Paul, MN	111.4	11
San Francisco, CA	99.9	12
Houston, TX	99.4	13
Phoenix-Mesa, AZ	91.3	14
Orange County, CA	90.2	15
Nassau-Suffolk, NY	82.9	16
Saint Louis, MO	79.4	17
Denver, CO	74.4	18

[Continued]

★905★

Employees on Nonfarm Payrolls, July 1995, By Industry: Finance, Insurance, and Real Estate (Highest Numbers)

[Continued]

City	Finance insurance and real estate	Rank
Seattle-Bellevue-Everett, WA	73.8	19
Baltimore, MD PMSA	73.4	20

Source: U.S. Department of Labor, Bureau of Labor Statistics, *Employment and Earnings,* Washington, D.C.: U.S. Government Printing Office, September 1995, p. 84. *Note:* "FIRE" stands for "finance, insurance, and real estate."

★906★

Employment (Nonfarm Payrolls)

Employees on Nonfarm Payrolls, July 1995, By Industry: Finance, Insurance, and Real Estate (Lowest Numbers)

[In thousands; not seasonally adjusted]

City	Finance insurance and real estate	Rank
Casper, WY	1.1	1
Enid, OK	1.1	1
Bristol, VA	1.2	2
Danville, VA	1.4	3
Dover, DE	1.4	3
Elmira, NY	1.4	3
Pine Bluff, AR	1.4	3
Sharon, PA	1.5	4
Fitchburg-Leominster, MA	1.6	5
Kenosha, WI	1.6	5
Kokomo, IN	1.6	5
San Angelo, TX	1.6	5
Dubuque, IA	1.7	6
Grand Forks, ND	1.7	6
Kankakee, IL	1.7	6
Lawton, OK	1.7	6
Rapid City, SD	1.7	6
Steubenville-Weirton, OH	1.7	6
Victoria, TX	1.7	6
Iowa City, IA	1.8	7

Source: U.S. Department of Labor, Bureau of Labor Statistics, *Employment and Earnings,* Washington, D.C.: U.S. Government Printing Office, September 1995, p. 84. *Note:* "FIRE" stands for "finance, insurance, and real estate."

★907★
Employment (Nonfarm Payrolls)

Employees on Nonfarm Payrolls, July 1995, By Industry: Manufacturing (Highest Numbers)

[In thousands; not seasonally adjusted]

City	Manufacturing	Rank
Atlanta, GA	211.5	12
Boston, MA	220.4	11
Charlotte-Gastonia-Rock Hill, NC	150.8	20
Chicago, IL	654.0	1
Cincinnati, OH	140.7	22
Cleveland-Lorain-Elyria, OH	226.7	10
Dallas, TX	230.1	8
Detroit, MI	432.7	3
Grand Rapids-Muskegon-Holland, MI	150.0	21
Greensboro-Winston-Salem-High Point, NC	170.5	18
Houston, TX	187.6	15
Los Angeles-Long Beach, CA	626.8	2
Milwaukee-Waukesha, WI	178.3	17
Minneapolis-Saint Paul, MN	277.5	7
New York City, NY	280.4	6
New York, NY PMSA	336.2	4
Newark, NJ	138.6	23
Orange County, CA	205.0	13
Philadelphia, PA PMSA	308.4	5
Phoenix-Mesa, AZ	155.8	19
Pittsburgh, PA	134.2	25
Portland-Vancouver, OR	137.4	24
Saint Louis, MO	198.4	14
San Jose, CA	227.3	9
Seattle-Bellevue-Everett, WA	185.0	16

Source: U.S. Department of Labor, Bureau of Labor Statistics, *Employment and Earnings,* Washington, D.C.: U.S. Government Printing Office, September 1995, p. 80.

★908★
Employment (Nonfarm Payrolls)

Employees on Nonfarm Payrolls, July 1995, By Industry: Manufacturing (Lowest Numbers)

[In thousands; not seasonally adjusted]

City	Manufacturing	Rank
Abilene, TX	3.3	8
Alexandria, LA	3.3	8
Anchorage, AK	2.6	6
Barnstable-Yarmouth, MA	2.2	4
Barre-Montpelier, VT	3.7	9
Bismarck, ND	2.6	6
Bryan-College Station, TX	3.9	10
Casper, WY	1.7	2
Dover, DE	6.1	20
Enid, OK	1.9	3
Gainesville, FL	6.0	19
Grand Forks, ND	3.1	7
Houma, LA	6.2	21
Iowa City, IA	4.5	14
Laredo, TX	1.4	1
Las Cruces, NM	2.4	5
Lawrence, KS	5.2	16

[Continued]

Employees on Nonfarm Payrolls, July 1995, By Industry: Manufacturing (Lowest Numbers)
[Continued]

City	Manufacturing	Rank
Lawton, OK	4.1	11
Rapid City, SD	4.2	12
San Angelo, TX	5.4	17
Santa Fe, NM	2.2	4
Springfield, IL	4.3	13
Tallahassee, FL	5.0	15
Texarkana, TX	5.5	18
Victoria, TX	3.1	7

Source: U.S. Department of Labor, Bureau of Labor Statistics, *Employment and Earnings,* Washington, D.C.: U.S. Government Printing Office, September 1995, p. 80.

★909★
Employment (Nonfarm Payrolls)

Employees on Nonfarm Payrolls, July 1995, By Industry: Mining (Highest Numbers)

[In thousands; not seasonally adjusted]

City	Mining	Rank
Houston, TX	65.9	1
Dallas, TX	13.5	2
New Orleans, LA	12.9	3
Odessa-Midland, TX	12.6	4
Lafayette, LA	11.7	5
Bakersfield, CA	11.1	6
Tulsa, OK	8.2	7
Denver, CO	7.8	8
Oklahoma City, OK	7.2	9
Houma, LA	6.5	10
Los Angeles-Long Beach, CA	6.0	11
Duluth-Superior, MN	5.2	12
Phoenix-Mesa, AZ	5.1	13
Fort Worth-Arlington, TX	4.4	14
Lakeland-Winter Haven, FL	3.8	15

Source: U.S. Department of Labor, Bureau of Labor Statistics, *Employment and Earnings,* Washington, D.C.: U.S. Government Printing Office, September 1995, p. 84.

★910★
Employment (Nonfarm Payrolls)

Employees on Nonfarm Payrolls, July 1995, By Industry: Mining (Lowest Numbers)

[In thousands; not seasonally adjusted]

City	Mining	Rank
Alexandria, LA	.1	1
Lawton, OK	.1	1
Medford-Ashland, OR	.1	1
Pittsfield, MA	.1	1
San Jose, CA	.1	1
Stockton-Lodi, CA	.1	1
Texarkana, TX	.1	1
Baltimore, MD PMSA	.2	2
Eugene-Springfield, OR	.2	2

[Continued]

★910★

Employees on Nonfarm Payrolls, July 1995, By Industry: Mining (Lowest Numbers)

[Continued]

City	Mining	Rank
Fort Lauderdale, FL	.2	2
Lexington, KY	.2	2
Lubbock, TX	.2	2
Providence-Fall River-Warwick, RI	.2	2
Salem, OR	.2	2
Salinas, CA	.2	2

Source: U.S. Department of Labor, Bureau of Labor Statistics, *Employment and Earnings,* Washington, D.C.: U.S. Government Printing Office, September 1995, p. 84.

★911★

Employment (Nonfarm Payrolls)

Employees on Nonfarm Payrolls, July 1995, By Industry: Services (Highest Numbers)

[In thousands; not seasonally adjusted]

City	Services	Rank
Atlanta, GA	537.1	9
Baltimore, MD PMSA	359.3	15
Boston, MA	883.6	5
Chicago, IL	1,162.0	4
Dallas, TX	453.5	11
Detroit, MI	601.3	8
Houston, TX	510.8	10
Los Angeles-Long Beach, CA	1,190.9	2
Minneapolis-Saint Paul, MN	441.6	12
Nassau-Suffolk, NY	339.3	20
New York City, NY	1,162.7	3
New York, NY PMSA	1,329.8	1
Northern Virginia, VA	344.8	18
Orange County, CA	339.6	19
Philadelphia, PA PMSA	738.0	7
Phoenix-Mesa, AZ	349.6	17
Pittsburgh, PA	352.9	16
Saint Louis, MO	380.1	13
Tampa-Saint Petersburg-Clearwater, FL	373.2	14
Washington, DC PMSA	873.7	6

Source: U.S. Department of Labor, Bureau of Labor Statistics, *Employment and Earnings,* Washington, D.C.: U.S. Government Printing Office, September 1995, p. 84.

★912★

Employment (Nonfarm Payrolls)

Employees on Nonfarm Payrolls, July 1995, By Industry: Services (Lowest Numbers)

[In thousands; not seasonally adjusted]

City	Services	Rank
Barre-Montpelier, VT	8.0	4
Bristol, VA	6.6	2
Casper, WY	7.8	3
Danville, VA	8.5	7

[Continued]

★912★

Employees on Nonfarm Payrolls, July 1995, By Industry: Services (Lowest Numbers)

[Continued]

City	Services	Rank
Dover, DE	10.9	16
Elmira, NY	10.0	12
Enid, OK	6.3	1
Kankakee, IL	11.1	17
Kenosha, WI	10.7	15
Kokomo, IN	8.7	8
Laredo, TX	9.8	11
Las Cruces, NM	10.0	12
Lawrence, KS	9.1	9
Lawton, OK	8.3	6
Pine Bluff, AR	8.2	5
San Angelo, TX	10.5	13
Sheboygan, WI	10.6	14
Sherman-Denison, TX	9.6	10
Victoria, TX	8.5	7
Wausau, WI	11.4	18

Source: U.S. Department of Labor, Bureau of Labor Statistics, *Employment and Earnings,* Washington, D.C.: U.S. Government Printing Office, September 1995, p. 84.

★913★

Employment (Nonfarm Payrolls)

Employees on Nonfarm Payrolls, July 1995, By Industry: Transportation and Public Utilities (Highest Numbers)

[In thousands; not seasonally adjusted]

City	Transportation and public utilities	Rank
Atlanta, GA	142.3	5
Boston, MA	76.9	15
Chicago, IL	230.5	1
Dallas, TX	102.8	8
Denver, CO	77.7	14
Detroit, MI	89.3	10
Houston, TX	120.5	6
Kansas City, MO	66.9	19
Los Angeles-Long Beach, CA	200.8	3
Miami, FL	76.2	16
Minneapolis-Saint Paul, MN	78.9	11
New York City, NY	198.9	4
New York, NY PMSA	225.6	2
Newark, NJ	81.1	12
Philadelphia, PA PMSA	102.7	9
Pittsburgh, PA	63.8	20
Saint Louis, MO	78.9	13
San Francisco, CA	74.0	17
Seattle-Bellevue-Everett, WA	72.8	18
Washington, DC PMSA	110.2	7

Source: U.S. Department of Labor, Bureau of Labor Statistics, *Employment and Earnings,* Washington, D.C.: U.S. Government Printing Office, September 1995, p. 80.

★914★

Employment (Nonfarm Payrolls)

Employees on Nonfarm Payrolls, July 1995, By Industry: Transportation and Public Utilities (Lowest Numbers)

[In thousands; not seasonally adjusted]

City	Transportation and public utilities	Rank
Athens, GA	1.5	6
Barre-Montpelier, VT	1.0	1
Bloomington, IN	1.8	9
Bristol, VA	1.3	4
Casper, WY	1.6	7
Danville, VA	1.4	5
Dover, DE	1.5	6
Dubuque, IA	1.9	10
Elmira, NY	1.5	6
Fitchburg-Leominster, MA	1.8	9
Gainesville, FL	1.9	10
Glens Falls, NY	1.7	8
Kokomo, IN	1.2	3
Las Cruces, NM	1.5	6
Lawrence, KS	1.1	2
Lewiston-Auburn, ME	1.7	8
Pittsfield, MA	1.1	2
Santa Fe, NM	1.2	3
Sherman-Denison, TX	1.8	9
Victoria, TX	1.5	6

Source: U.S. Department of Labor, Bureau of Labor Statistics, *Employment and Earnings*, Washington, D.C.: U.S. Government Printing Office, September 1995, p. 80.

★915★

Employment (Nonfarm Payrolls)

Employees on Nonfarm Payrolls, July 1995, By Industry: Wholesale and Retail Trade (Highest Numbers)

[In thousands; not seasonally adjusted]

City	Wholesale and retail trade	Rank
Atlanta, GA	495.4	5
Baltimore, MD PMSA	262.9	18
Boston, MA	391.6	11
Chicago, IL	901.5	1
Cleveland-Lorain-Elyria, OH	257.3	19
Dallas, TX	406.6	10
Detroit, MI	481.0	6
Houston, TX	416.4	9
Los Angeles-Long Beach, CA	817.4	2
Minneapolis-Saint Paul, MN	362.0	12
Nassau-Suffolk, NY	282.8	17
New York City, NY	544.7	4
New York, NY PMSA	655.9	3
Orange County, CA	285.2	16
Philadelphia, PA PMSA	479.0	7
Phoenix-Mesa, AZ	285.9	15

[Continued]

★915★

Employees on Nonfarm Payrolls, July 1995, By Industry: Wholesale and Retail Trade (Highest Numbers)

[Continued]

City	Wholesale and retail trade	Rank
Pittsburgh, PA	254.3	20
Saint Louis, MO	298.4	13
Seattle-Bellevue-Everett, WA	290.0	14
Washington, DC PMSA	464.6	8

Source: U.S. Department of Labor, Bureau of Labor Statistics, *Employment and Earnings*, Washington, D.C.: U.S. Government Printing Office, September 1995, p. 80.

★916★

Employment (Nonfarm Payrolls)

Employees on Nonfarm Payrolls, July 1995, By Industry: Wholesale and Retail Trade (Lowest Numbers)

[In thousands; not seasonally adjusted]

City	Wholesale and retail trade	Rank
Barre-Montpelier, VT	6.6	1
Enid, OK	6.8	2
Pine Bluff, AR	7.3	3
Casper, WY	8.3	4
Danville, VA	8.7	5
Lawton, OK	9.0	6
Victoria, TX	9.2	7
Bristol, VA	9.3	8
Sherman-Denison, TX	9.5	9
San Angelo, TX	9.8	10
Sheboygan, WI	9.8	10
Pittsfield, MA	10.2	11
Lewiston-Auburn, ME	10.3	12
Lawrence, KS	10.5	13
Las Cruces, NM	10.7	14
Vineland-Millville-Bridgeton, NJ	10.7	14
Kankakee, IL	10.8	15
Elmira, NY	10.9	16
Steubenville-Weirton, OH	10.9	16
Fitchburg-Leominster, MA	11.1	17

Source: U.S. Department of Labor, Bureau of Labor Statistics, *Employment and Earnings*, Washington, D.C.: U.S. Government Printing Office, September 1995, p. 80.

★917★
Employment (Nonfarm Payrolls)

Employees on Nonfarm Payrolls, July 1995: By Industry: Construction (Highest Numbers)

[In thousands; not seasonally adjusted]

City	Construction	Rank
Chicago, IL	155.3	1
Houston, TX	122.0	2
Washington, DC PMSA	121.3	3
New York, NY PMSA	113.9	4
Los Angeles-Long Beach, CA	112.3	5
New York City, NY	90.5	6
Atlanta, GA	88.9	7
Philadelphia, PA PMSA	84.5	8
Phoenix-Mesa, AZ	80.3	9
Detroit, MI	76.1	10
Dallas, TX	66.2	11
Saint Louis, MO	64.9	12
Seattle-Bellevue-Everett, WA	64.7	13
Baltimore, MD PMSA	63.8	14
Minneapolis-Saint Paul, MN	60.3	15
Suburban Maryland-Washington, DC	55.5	16
Boston, MA	54.2	17
Northern Virginia, VA	54.0	18
Denver, CO	53.6	19
Orange County, CA	49.1	20

Source: U.S. Department of Labor, Bureau of Labor Statistics, *Employment and Earnings*, Washington, D.C.: U.S. Government Printing Office, September 1995, p. 84.

★918★
Employment (Nonfarm Payrolls)

Employees on Nonfarm Payrolls, July 1995: By Industry: Construction (Lowest Numbers)

[In thousands; not seasonally adjusted]

City	Construction	Rank
Pine Bluff, AR	.7	1
Enid, OK	.9	2
Bristol, VA	1.3	3
Elmira, NY	1.5	4
Pittsfield, MA	1.5	4
Sharon, PA	1.6	5
Kokomo, IN	1.7	6
Casper, WY	1.8	7
Fitchburg-Leominster, MA	1.8	7
Lawton, OK	1.8	7
Lewiston-Auburn, ME	1.8	7
San Angelo, TX	1.8	7
Victoria, TX	1.9	8
Vineland-Millville-Bridgeton, NJ	1.9	8
Jackson, MI	2.0	9
Kenosha, WI	2.0	9
Laredo, TX	2.0	9
Kankakee, IL	2.5	11
Abilene, TX	2.1	10
Danville, VA	2.1	10

Source: U.S. Department of Labor, Bureau of Labor Statistics, *Employment and Earnings*, Washington, D.C.: U.S. Government Printing Office, September 1995, p. 84.

★919★
Employment, By Occupation

Taxicab Drivers, 1996

City/MSA	Drivers	Rank
New York, NY	11,787	1
Chicago, IL	5,500	2
Houston, TX	2,049	3
Los Angeles, CA	1,850	4
Philadelphia, PA	1,500	5

Source: Minzesheimer, Bob, "To Be NYC Cabbie, Fare's Not Cheap: Medallions Auctioned for $175,000," *USA TODAY*, 20 May 1996, p. 2A. Primary source: International Taxicab and Livery Association; U.S. Bureau of the Census.

★920★
Employment, By Occupation

Foodservice Workers, 1995

Data provided include noncitizens, naturalized citizens, and native-born citizens.

City	Number	Rank
Baltimore, MD	26,000	9
Chicago, IL	82,000	3
Dallas, TX	37,000	6
Detroit, MI	32,000	7
Houston, TX	54,000	4
Indianapolis, IN	28,000	8
Los Angeles, CA	96,000	2
New York, NY	169,000	1
Philadelphia, PA	48,000	5
Phoenix, AZ	25,000	10

Source: Rousseau, Rita, "Immigration: the Reluctant Enforcers," *Restaurants & Institutions*, 1 October, 1995, p. 40. Primary source: Population Use Microsample Data (5% sample) from 1990 U.S. Census, analyzed for *R&I* by the Center for Governmental Studies, Northern Illinois University, DeKalb; foodservice employment includes restaurant workers and other food retail workers; population includes metropolitan area. *Notes:* Figures are based on self-reported data; therefore, undocumented workers are included, but are severely underrepresented.

★921★
Employment, By Occupation

Telecommunications Jobs, 1996

Data refer to job openings in firms with less than 1,000 employees.

City	Number	Rank
Dallas, TX	4,439	2
New York, NY	3,278	5
Richardson, TX	2,667	6
San Diego, CA	3,831	3
San Jose, CA	5,156	1
Santa Clara, CA	2,276	7
Sunnyvale, CA	3,336	4

Source: Hostetler, Michele, "Area Rings Up Plethora of Telecom Work," *Business Journal*, 25-31 March, 1995, p. 1. Primary source: CorpTech, Inc.

★922★

Employment, By Race

Minority Lawyers, 1994: Percentage Employed As Associates (Selected Cities)

Minorities constitute approximately 8.36% of all lawyers employed as associates in the United States.

City	Percentage	Rank
Miami, FL	26.65	1
San Francisco, CA	16.17	2
Los Angeles, CA	13.5	3
Seattle, WA	10.16	4
New York, NY	9.78	5
Washington, DC	8.52	6
Atlanta, GA	7.35	7
Dallas, TX	6.63	8
Houston, TX	6.41	9
Chicago, IL	6.04	10
Boston, MA	5.09	11

Source: "Lawyers in the Minority," *Wall Street Journal,* 7 April 1995, p. B5. Primary source: 1994 survey by the National Association for Law Placement. *Notes:* "Minorities" refers to African-Americans, Hispanics, Asians, and Native Americans.

★923★

Employment, By Race

Minority Lawyers, 1994: Percentage Employed As Partners (Selected Cities)

Minorities constitute approximately 2.68% of all lawyers employed as partners in the United States.

City	Percentage	Rank
Atlanta, GA	2.22	8
Boston, MA	1.75	10
Chicago, IL	1.63	11
Dallas, TX	1.79	9
Houston, TX	3.36	4
Los Angeles, CA	5.76	2
Miami, FL	8.45	1
New York, NY	2.74	6
San Francisco, CA	5.33	3
Seattle, WA	2.85	5
Washington, DC	2.28	7

Source: "Lawyers in the Minority," *Wall Street Journal,* 7 April 1995, p. B5. Primary source: 1994 survey by the National Association for Law Placement. *Notes:* "Minorities" refers to African-Americans, Hispanics, Asians, and Native Americans.

★924★

Employment (Civilian Labor Force Characteristics)

Civilian Labor Force Participation Rate in Central Cities, 1993: Total

Data refer to selected central cities.

Central Cities	Total	Rank
Baltimore, MD	66.9	5
Chicago, IL	63.4	10
Cleveland, OH	56.8	12
Dallas, TX	73.1	1
Detroit, MI	53.4	16
Washington, DC	66.8	6

[Continued]

★924★

Civilian Labor Force Participation Rate in Central Cities, 1993: Total
[Continued]

Central Cities	Total	Rank
Houston, TX	69.0	4
Indianapolis, IN	71.7	2
Los Angeles, CA	64.8	7
Milwaukee, WI	66.9	5
New York, NY	55.9	13
Philadelphia, PA	55.1	14
Phoenix, AZ	71.0	3
Saint Louis, IL-MO	54.2	15
San Antonio, TX	61.2	11
San Diego, CA	63.9	9
San Francisco, CA	64.0	8

Source: U.S. Department of Labor, Bureau of Labor Statistics, *Geographic Profile of Employment and Unemployment, 1993,* Washington, D.C.: U.S. Government Printing Office, September 1994, p. 95.

★925★

Employment (Civilian Labor Force Characteristics)

Civilian Labor Force Participation Rate in MSAs, 1993: (Highest)

Data refer to selected metropolitan statistical areas.

MSA	Total	Rank
Minneapolis-Saint Paul, MN MSA	77.0	1
Dallas-Fort Worth, TX CMSA	75.6	2
Kansas City, MO MSA	74.2	3
Denver-Boulder, CO CMSA	74.0	4
Washington, DC MSA	73.6	5
Salt Lake City-Ogden, UT MSA	73.3	6
Seattle, WA PMSA	73.0	7
Atlanta, GA MSA	72.5	8
Anaheim-Santa Ana, CA PMSA	72.1	9
Indianapolis, IN MSA	72.0	10

Source: U.S. Department of Labor, Bureau of Labor Statistics, *Geographic Profile of Employment and Unemployment, 1993,* Washington, D.C.: U.S. Government Printing Office, September 1994, p. 95.

★926★

Employment (Civilian Labor Force Characteristics)

Civilian Labor Force Participation Rate in MSAs, 1993: (Lowest)

Data refer to selected metropolitan statistical areas.

MSA	Total	Rank
New York, NY PMSA	58.0	1
Pittsburgh-Beaver Valley, PA CMSA	59.0	2
Fort Lauderdale-Hollywood-Pompano Beach, FL	60.4	3
New Orleans, LA MSA	61.8	4
Miami-Hialeah, FL PMSA	61.9	5
Buffalo-Niagara Falls, NY CMSA	62.6	6
Tampa-Saint Petersburg-Clearwater, FL MSA	62.9	7

[Continued]

★926★

Civilian Labor Force Participation Rate in MSAs, 1993: (Lowest)
[Continued]

MSA	Total	Rank
San Antonio, TX MSA	63.1	8
Oakland, CA PMSA	63.6	9
Los Angeles-Long Beach, CA PMSA	63.8	10

Source: U.S. Department of Labor, Bureau of Labor Statistics, *Geographic Profile of Employment and Unemployment, 1993,* Washington, D.C.: U.S. Government Printing Office, September 1994, p. 95.

★927★

Employment (Civilian Labor Force Characteristics)

Civilian Labor Force Participation Rate of Men in Central Cities, 1993

Data refer to selected central cities.

Central cities	Rate	Rank
Baltimore, MD	74.4	7
Chicago, IL	72.3	10
Cleveland, OH	66.5	14
Dallas, TX	82.9	1
Detroit, MI	62.5	16
Washington, DC	73.1	8
Houston, TX	78.3	3
Indianapolis, IN	76.9	4
Los Angeles, CA	75.4	5
Milwaukee, WI	72.8	9
New York, NY	66.7	13
Philadelphia, PA	64.6	15
Phoenix, AZ	79.6	2
San Antonio, TX	69.9	12
San Diego, CA	75.0	6
San Francisco, CA	71.5	11

Source: U.S. Department of Labor, Bureau of Labor Statistics, *Geographic Profile of Employment and Unemployment, 1993,* Washington, D.C.: U.S. Government Printing Office, September 1994, p. 95.

★928★

Employment (Civilian Labor Force Characteristics)

Civilian Labor Force Participation Rate of Men, 1993: (Highest)

Data refer to selected metropolitan statistical areas.

MSA	Rate	Rank
Dallas-Fort Worth, TX CMSA	85.8	1
Minneapolis-Saint Paul, MN MSA	83.9	2
Anaheim-Santa Ana, CA PMSA	82.6	3
Houston, TX PMSA	81.6	4
Kansas City, MO MSA	81.5	5
Seattle, WA PMSA	81.2	6
Salt Lake City-Ogden, UT MSA	81.1	7
Denver-Boulder, CO CMSA	80.9	8
Atlanta, GA MSA	80.2	9
Indianapolis, IN MSA	80.1	10

Source: U.S. Department of Labor, Bureau of Labor Statistics, *Geographic Profile of Employment and Unemployment, 1993,* Washington, D.C.: U.S. Government Printing Office, September 1994, p. 95.

★929★

Employment (Civilian Labor Force Characteristics)

Civilian Labor Force Participation Rate of Men, 1993: (Lowest)

Data refer to selected metropolitan statistical areas.

MSA	Rate	Rank
Pittsburgh-Beaver Valley, PA CMSA	68.1	1
Fort Lauderdale-Hollywood-Pompano Beach, FL PMSA	68.8	2
New Orleans, LA MSA	68.8	2
Buffalo-Niagara Falls, NY CMSA	70.1	3
Tampa-Saint Petersburg-Clearwater, FL MSA	70.6	4
Sacramento, CA MSA	72.4	5
San Antonio, TX MSA	72.4	5
Memphis, TN MSA	72.6	6
New York, NY MSA	73.9	7
Philadelphia, PA PMSA	73.9	7

Source: U.S. Department of Labor, Bureau of Labor Statistics, *Geographic Profile of Employment and Unemployment, 1993,* Washington, D.C.: U.S. Government Printing Office, September 1994, p. 95.

★930★

Employment (Civilian Labor Force Characteristics)

Civilian Labor Force Participation Rate of Women in Central Cities, 1993

Data refer to selected central cities.

Central cities	Rate	Rank
Baltimore, MD	60.8	6
Chicago, IL	55.8	9
Cleveland, OH	48.4	14
Dallas, TX	63.8	2
Detroit, MI	46.1	17
Washington, DC	61.5	5
Houston, TX	60.0	7
Indianapolis, IN	67.5	1
Los Angeles, CA	54.2	10
Milwaukee, WI	61.8	4
New York, NY	46.8	16
Philadelphia, PA	47.4	15
Phoenix, AZ	62.8	3
Saint Louis, IL-MO	50.7	13
San Antonio, TX	53.3	12
San Diego, CA	54.1	11
San Francisco, CA	56.1	8

Source: U.S. Department of Labor, Bureau of Labor Statistics, *Geographic Profile of Employment and Unemployment, 1993,* Washington, D.C.: U.S. Government Printing Office, September 1994, p. 95.

★931★

Employment (Civilian Labor Force Characteristics)

Civilian Labor Force Participation Rate of Women, 1993: (Highest)

Data refer to selected metropolitan statistical areas.

MSA	Rate	Rank
Minneapolis-Saint Paul, MN MSA	70.7	1
Washington, DC MSA	68.3	2
Kansas City, MO MSA	68.0	3
Denver-Boulder, CO CMSA	67.5	4
Milwaukee, WI PMSA	65.8	5
Salt Lake City-Ogden, UT MSA	65.8	5
Atlanta, GA MSA	65.7	6
Dallas-Fort Worth, TX CMSA	65.3	7
Indianapolis, IN MSA	65.3	7
Charlotte-Gastonia-Rock Hill, NC-SC MSA	64.4	8

Source: U.S. Department of Labor, Bureau of Labor Statistics, *Geographic Profile of Employment and Unemployment, 1993,* Washington, D.C.: U.S. Government Printing Office, September 1994, p. 95.

★932★

Employment (Civilian Labor Force Characteristics)

Civilian Labor Force Participation Rate of Women, 1993: (Lowest)

Data refer to selected metropolitan statistical areas.

MSA	Rate	Rank
New York, NY PMSA	49.1	1
Miami-Hialeah, FL PMSA	51.1	2
Fort Lauderdale-Hollywood-Pompano Beach, FL PMSA	52.8	3
Los Angeles-Long Beach, CA PMSA	53.2	4
Oakland, CA PMSA	54.0	5
Pittsburgh-Beaver Valley, PA CMSA	54.0	5
Riverside-San Bernardino, CA PMSA	54.0	5
San Antonio, TX MSA	54.6	6
Philadelphia, PA PMSA	55.1	7
Cleveland, OH PMSA	55.3	8

Source: U.S. Department of Labor, Bureau of Labor Statistics, *Geographic Profile of Employment and Unemployment, 1993,* Washington, D.C.: U.S. Government Printing Office, September 1994, p. 95.

★933★

Employment (Civilian Labor Force Characteristics)

Civilian Labor Force, 1994: Total

[In thousands]

City	Thousands	Rank
Los Angeles-Long Beach, CA[1]	4,396.0	1
Chicago, IL	3,964.6	2
New York, NY	3,830.2	3
Washington, DC-MD-VA-WV	2,585.3	4
Philadelphia, PA-NJ	2,434.8	5
Detroit, MI	2,131.0	6
Houston, TX	1,958.8	7

[Continued]

★933★

Civilian Labor Force, 1994: Total

[Continued]

City	Thousands	Rank
Atlanta, GA	1,846.6	8
Boston, MA-NH	1,753.9	9
Dallas, TX	1,672.6	10
Minneapolis-Saint Paul, MN-WI	1,580.4	11
Nassau-Suffolk, NY	1,359.1	12
Orange County, CA	1,342.1	13
Saint Louis, MO-IL[2]	1,279.3	14
Riverside-San Bernardino, CA	1,273.7	15
Phoenix-Mesa, AZ	1,267.0	16
San Diego, CA	1,234.5	17
Baltimore, MD	1,218.2	18
Seattle-Bellevue-Everett, WA	1,193.8	19
Pittsburgh, PA	1,137.0	20
Oakland, CA	1,135.7	21
Cleveland-Lorain-Elyria, OH	1,085.6	22
Tampa-Saint Petersburg-Clearwater, FL	1,083.4	23
Miami, FL	1,039.2	24
Denver, CO	1,014.7	25

Source: U.S. Bureau of the Census, *Statistical Abstract of the United States: 1995,* (115th edition), Washington, D.C.: U.S. Government Printing Office, 1995, p. 402. Primary source: U.S. Bureau of Labor Statistics, *Employment and Earnings,* May 1995. *Notes:* Data are shown only for the top 25 areas. 1. Derived from the Current Population Survey. 2. Excludes the part of Sullivan City in Crawford County, Missouri.

★934★

Job Growth

Job Growth, 1982-1992

[In percent]

City	Percentage	Rank
Atlanta, GA	46.0	1
Chicago, IL	17.0	7
Dallas-Fort Worth, TX	35.0	2
Denver, CO	22.0	6
Detroit-Ann Arbor, MI	22.0	6
Los Angeles-Long Beach, CA	26.0	4
Miami-Fort Lauderdale, FL	23.0	5
San Francisco-San Jose, CA	23.0	5
Seattle-Tacoma, WA	46.0	1
Washington-Baltimore, DC-MD	30.0	3

Source: Johnson, Kirk, and Thomas J. Lueck, "Economy in the New York Region Is Recovering, But Pace is Slow," *New York Times,* 19 February, 1996, p. A12. Primary source: Bureau of Labor Statistics; Fleet Financial Group, Hartford, Connecticut; Dun and Bradstreet, Economic Analysis Department.

★935★
Distribution of Employed Persons, By Occupation

Percent Distribution of All Employed Persons in Selected Cities, 1994, By Occupation: Administrative Support, Including Clerical

City	Percent	Rank
Baltimore, MD	24.0	1
Chicago, IL	17.6	8
Cleveland, OH	17.7	7
Dallas, TX	13.9	14
Detroit, MI	17.0	9
Houston, TX	16.1	11
Indianapolis, IN	19.0	3
Los Angeles, CA	15.9	12
Milwaukee, WI	18.8	4
New York, NY	18.8	4
Philadelphia, PA	21.4	2
Phoenix, AZ	17.6	8
Saint Louis, MO	18.5	5
San Antonio, TX	14.3	13
San Diego, CA	13.6	15
San Francisco, CA	18.4	6
Washington, DC	16.3	10

Source: U.S. Department of Labor, Bureau of Labor Statistics, *Geographic Profile of Employment and Unemployment, 1994,* Bulletin 2469, Washington, D.C.: U.S. Government Printing Office, December 1995, p. 103.

★936★
Distribution of Employed Persons, By Occupation

Percent Distribution of All Employed Persons in Selected Cities, 1994, By Occupation: Executive, Administrative, and Managerial

City	Percent	Rank
Baltimore, MD	10.8	13
Chicago, IL	11.6	11
Cleveland, OH	6.3	17
Dallas, TX	13.5	3
Detroit, MI	10.9	12
Houston, TX	12.1	10
Indianapolis, IN	12.3	9
Los Angeles, CA	12.8	7
Milwaukee, WI	13.2	5
New York, NY	13.1	6
Philadelphia, PA	9.9	14
Phoenix, AZ	13.3	4
Saint Louis, MO	8.5	15
San Antonio, TX	8.3	16
San Diego, CA	19.1	1
San Francisco, CA	12.5	8
Washington, DC	17.7	2

Source: U.S. Department of Labor, Bureau of Labor Statistics, *Geographic Profile of Employment and Unemployment, 1994,* Bulletin 2469, Washington, D.C.: U.S. Government Printing Office, December 1995, p. 103.

★937★
Distribution of Employed Persons, By Occupation

Percent Distribution of All Employed Persons in Selected Cities, 1994, By Occupation: Handlers, Equipment Cleaners, Helpers, and Laborers

City	Percent	Rank
Baltimore, MD	4.6	7
Chicago, IL	5.8	3
Cleveland, OH	5.4	5
Dallas, TX	5.3	6
Detroit, MI	3.2	13
Houston, TX	7.5	1
Indianapolis, IN	5.5	4
Los Angeles, CA	4.5	8
Milwaukee, WI	4.4	9
New York, NY	3.3	12
Philadelphia, PA	4.4	9
Phoenix, AZ	3.8	11
Saint Louis, MO	5.3	6
San Antonio, TX	5.9	2
San Diego, CA	4.4	9
San Francisco, CA	4.2	10
Washington, DC	2.1	14

Source: U.S. Department of Labor, Bureau of Labor Statistics, *Geographic Profile of Employment and Unemployment, 1994,* Bulletin 2469, Washington, D.C.: U.S. Government Printing Office, December 1995, p. 103.

★938★
Distribution of Employed Persons, By Occupation

Percent Distribution of All Employed Persons in Selected Cities, 1994, By Occupation: Machine Operators, Assemblers, and Inspectors

City	Percent	Rank
Baltimore, MD	3.3	13
Chicago, IL	8.8	2
Cleveland, OH	8.4	4
Dallas, TX	7.0	6
Detroit, MI	12.8	1
Houston, TX	2.9	15
Indianapolis, IN	4.8	11
Los Angeles, CA	8.7	3
Milwaukee, WI	7.7	5
New York, NY	5.1	9
Philadelphia, PA	5.0	10
Phoenix, AZ	3.8	12
Saint Louis, MO	5.6	7
San Antonio, TX	5.2	8
San Diego, CA	3.1	14
San Francisco, CA	3.3	13
Washington, DC	1.3	16

Source: U.S. Department of Labor, Bureau of Labor Statistics, *Geographic Profile of Employment and Unemployment, 1994,* Bulletin 2469, Washington, D.C.: U.S. Government Printing Office, December 1995, p. 103.

★939★

Distribution of Employed Persons, By Occupation

Percent Distribution of All Employed Persons in Selected Cities, 1994, By Occupation: Precision Production, Craft, and Repair

City	Percent	Rank
Baltimore, MD	8.4	12
Chicago, IL	9.3	11
Cleveland, OH	14.9	1
Dallas, TX	11.7	4
Detroit, MI	9.7	10
Houston, TX	9.9	9
Indianapolis, IN	10.9	6
Los Angeles, CA	10.4	7
Milwaukee, WI	7.5	13
New York, NY	7.5	13
Philadelphia, PA	10.0	8
Phoenix, AZ	14.8	2
Saint Louis, MO	11.1	5
San Antonio, TX	12.8	3
San Diego, CA	6.8	14
San Francisco, CA	5.2	15
Washington, DC	5.0	16

Source: U.S. Department of Labor, Bureau of Labor Statistics, *Geographic Profile of Employment and Unemployment, 1994,* Bulletin 2469, Washington, D.C.: U.S. Government Printing Office, December 1995, p. 103.

★940★

Distribution of Employed Persons, By Occupation

Percent Distribution of All Employed Persons in Selected Cities, 1994, By Occupation: Professional Specialty

City	Percent	Rank
Baltimore, MD	11.3	14
Chicago, IL	15.9	5
Cleveland, OH	6.1	17
Dallas, TX	12.4	11
Detroit, MI	10.0	16
Houston, TX	11.5	13
Indianapolis, IN	12.6	10
Los Angeles, CA	14.1	7
Milwaukee, WI	14.7	6
New York, NY	16.4	4
Philadelphia, PA	13.8	9
Phoenix, AZ	11.7	12
Saint Louis, MO	13.9	8
San Antonio, TX	10.4	15
San Diego, CA	17.2	3
San Francisco, CA	20.3	2
Washington, DC	25.0	1

Source: U.S. Department of Labor, Bureau of Labor Statistics, *Geographic Profile of Employment and Unemployment, 1994,* Bulletin 2469, Washington, D.C.: U.S. Government Printing Office, December 1995, p. 103.

★941★

Distribution of Employed Persons, By Occupation

Percent Distribution of All Employed Persons in Selected Cities, 1994, By Occupation: Sales

City	Percent	Rank
Baltimore, MD	8.0	16
Chicago, IL	9.6	13
Cleveland, OH	8.4	14
Dallas, TX	11.2	8
Detroit, MI	8.2	15
Houston, TX	13.8	3
Indianapolis, IN	14.6	2
Los Angeles, CA	10.6	9
Milwaukee, WI	9.8	12
New York, NY	10.2	10
Philadelphia, PA	10.0	11
Phoenix, AZ	13.2	4
Saint Louis, MO	12.9	5
San Antonio, TX	14.7	1
San Diego, CA	12.8	6
San Francisco, CA	12.6	7
Washington, DC	6.6	17

Source: U.S. Department of Labor, Bureau of Labor Statistics, *Geographic Profile of Employment and Unemployment, 1994,* Bulletin 2469, Washington, D.C.: U.S. Government Printing Office, December 1995, p. 103.

★942★

Distribution of Employed Persons, By Occupation

Percent Distribution of All Employed Persons in Selected Cities, 1994, By Occupation: Service Occupations

City	Percent	Rank
Baltimore, MD	20.1	3
Chicago, IL	15.0	14
Cleveland, OH	23.0	1
Dallas, TX	15.5	13
Detroit, MI	20.8	2
Houston, TX	16.4	10
Indianapolis, IN	11.8	16
Los Angeles, CA	16.1	11
Milwaukee, WI	17.5	7
New York, NY	19.1	5
Philadelphia, PA	16.8	8
Phoenix, AZ	13.3	15
Saint Louis, MO	16.6	9
San Antonio, TX	20.0	4
San Diego, CA	15.5	13
San Francisco, CA	15.7	12
Washington, DC	18.3	6

Source: U.S. Department of Labor, Bureau of Labor Statistics, *Geographic Profile of Employment and Unemployment, 1994,* Bulletin 2469, Washington, D.C.: U.S. Government Printing Office, December 1995, p. 103.

★943★

Distribution of Employed Persons, By Occupation

Percent Distribution of All Employed Persons in Selected Cities, 1994, By Occupation: Technicians and Related Support

City	Percent	Rank
Baltimore, MD	2.8	6
Chicago, IL	2.5	7
Cleveland, OH	1.7	11
Dallas, TX	2.1	10
Detroit, MI	2.8	6
Houston, TX	3.0	5
Indianapolis, IN	4.5	1
Los Angeles, CA	2.4	8
Milwaukee, WI	1.7	11
New York, NY	2.5	7
Philadelphia, PA	3.3	4
Phoenix, AZ	3.5	3
Saint Louis, MO	2.5	7
San Antonio, TX	2.3	9
San Diego, CA	2.8	6
San Francisco, CA	2.3	9
Washington, DC	4.1	2

Source: U.S. Department of Labor, Bureau of Labor Statistics, *Geographic Profile of Employment and Unemployment, 1994*, Bulletin 2469, Washington, D.C.: U.S. Government Printing Office, December 1995, p. 103.

★944★

Distribution of Employed Persons, By Occupation

Percent Distribution of All Employed Persons in Selected Cities, 1994, By Occupation: Transportation and Material Moving

City	Percent	Rank
Baltimore, MD	5.7	2
Chicago, IL	3.3	11
Cleveland, OH	6.6	1
Dallas, TX	4.6	6
Detroit, MI	4.2	9
Houston, TX	4.7	5
Indianapolis, IN	2.6	14
Los Angeles, CA	2.5	15
Milwaukee, WI	4.4	7
New York, NY	3.8	10
Philadelphia, PA	5.0	4
Phoenix, AZ	3.2	12
Saint Louis, MO	5.1	3
San Antonio, TX	4.2	9
San Diego, CA	2.6	14
San Francisco, CA	4.3	8
Washington, DC	2.9	13

Source: U.S. Department of Labor, Bureau of Labor Statistics, *Geographic Profile of Employment and Unemployment, 1994*, Bulletin 2469, Washington, D.C.: U.S. Government Printing Office, December 1995, p. 103.

★945★

Distribution of Employed Persons, By Occupation

Percent Distribution of All Employed Persons in Selected MSAs, 1994, By Occupation: Administrative Support, Including Clerical

MSA	Percent	Rank
Anaheim-Santa Ana, CA PMSA	15.4	24
Atlanta, GA	16.1	18
Baltimore, MD	17.2	9
Bergen-Passaic, NJ PMSA	16.7	13
Boston, MA PMSA	16.3	16
Buffalo-Niagara Falls, NY CMSA	14.1	30
Charlotte-Gastonia-Rock Hill, NC-SC	13.2	34
Chicago, IL PMSA	17.4	7
Cincinnati, OH PMSA	15.7	21
Cleveland, OH PMSA	15.4	24
Columbus, OH	17.3	8
Dallas-Fort Worth, TX CMSA	14.7	27
Dayton-Springfield, OH	13.7	32
Denver-Boulder, CO CMSA	16.3	16
Detroit, MI PMSA	15.0	25
Fort Lauderdale-Hollywood-Pompano Beach, FL PMSA	17.0	11
Hartford-New Britain-Middletown, CT CMSA	15.9	19
Houston, TX PMSA	16.5	14
Indianapolis, IN	16.8	12
Kansas City, KS-MO	19.6	1
Los Angeles-Long Beach, CA PMSA	16.8	12
Louisville, KY	16.4	15
Memphis, TN	17.1	10
Miami-Hialeah, FL PMSA	17.2	9
Milwaukee, WI PMSA	14.4	29
Minneapolis-Saint Paul, MN	18.2	4
Nassau-Suffolk, NY PMSA	19.2	2
New Orleans, LA	16.7	13
New York, NY PMSA	17.9	6
Newark, NJ PMSA	17.1	10
Norfolk-Virginia Beach-Newport News, VA	18.1	5
Oakland, CA PMSA	15.6	22
Oklahoma City, OK	13.9	31
Philadelphia, PA PMSA	18.7	3
Phoenix, AZ	16.8	12
Pittsburgh-Beaver Valley, PA	14.8	26
Portland, OR PMSA	15.5	23
Providence-Pawtucket-Fall River, MA-RI CMSA	14.8	26
Riverside-San Bernardino, CA PMSA	15.8	20
Rochester, NY	13.4	33
Sacramento, CA	16.2	17
Saint Louis, MO-IL	16.5	14
Salt Lake City-Ogden, UT	17.2	9
San Antonio, TX	15.9	19
San Diego, CA	15.0	25
San Francisco, CA PMSA	15.5	23
San Jose, CA PMSA	14.5	28
Seattle, WA PMSA	13.0	35

[Continued]

★945★

Percent Distribution of All Employed Persons in Selected MSAs, 1994, By Occupation: Administrative Support, Including Clerical

[Continued]

MSA	Percent	Rank
Tampa-Saint Petersburg-Clearwater, FL	16.5	14
Washington, DC	16.1	18

Source: U.S. Department of Labor, Bureau of Labor Statistics, *Geographic Profile of Employment and Unemployment, 1994*, Bulletin 2469, Washington, D.C.: U.S. Government Printing Office, December 1995, p. 103. *Notes:* "CMSA" stands for "Consolidated Metropolitan Statistical Area." "MSA" stands for "Metropolitan Statistical Area." "PMSA" stands for "Primary Metropolitan Statistical Area."

★946★

Distribution of Employed Persons, By Occupation

Percent Distribution of All Employed Persons in Selected MSAs, 1994, By Occupation: Executive, Administrative, and Managerial

MSA	Percent	Rank
Anaheim-Santa Ana, CA PMSA	18.9	3
Atlanta, GA	17.9	6
Baltimore, MD	16.3	11
Bergen-Passaic, NJ PMSA	18.0	5
Boston, MA PMSA	17.1	9
Buffalo-Niagara Falls, NY CMSA	11.3	36
Charlotte-Gastonia-Rock Hill, NC-SC	14.2	23
Chicago, IL PMSA	14.7	20
Cincinnati, OH PMSA	13.0	30
Cleveland, OH PMSA	14.5	21
Columbus, OH	16.7	10
Dallas-Fort Worth, TX CMSA	15.9	13
Dayton-Springfield, OH	11.6	35
Denver-Boulder, CO CMSA	15.7	14
Detroit, MI PMSA	13.9	24
Fort Lauderdale-Hollywood-Pompano Beach, FL PMSA	14.2	23
Hartford-New Britain-Middletown, CT CMSA	15.0	18
Houston, TX PMSA	14.2	23
Indianapolis, IN	16.3	11
Kansas City, KS-MO	15.7	14
Los Angeles-Long Beach, CA PMSA	13.4	27
Louisville, KY	13.5	26
Memphis, TN	11.7	34
Miami-Hialeah, FL PMSA	12.1	33
Milwaukee, WI PMSA	15.4	15
Minneapolis-Saint Paul, MN	15.3	16
Nassau-Suffolk, NY PMSA	15.4	15
New Orleans, LA	15.3	16
New York, NY PMSA	14.2	23
Newark, NJ PMSA	16.7	10
Norfolk-Virginia Beach-Newport News, VA	10.8	37
Oakland, CA PMSA	17.8	7
Oklahoma City, OK	14.7	20

[Continued]

★946★

Percent Distribution of All Employed Persons in Selected MSAs, 1994, By Occupation: Executive, Administrative, and Managerial

[Continued]

MSA	Percent	Rank
Philadelphia, PA PMSA	14.4	22
Phoenix, AZ	15.1	17
Pittsburgh-Beaver Valley, PA	12.4	32
Portland, OR PMSA	18.8	4
Providence-Pawtucket-Fall River, MA-RI CMSA	13.1	29
Riverside-San Bernardino, CA PMSA	13.3	28
Rochester, NY	12.7	31
Sacramento, CA	14.9	19
Saint Louis, MO-IL	13.6	25
Salt Lake City-Ogden, UT	15.7	14
San Antonio, TX	8.6	38
San Diego, CA	16.1	12
San Francisco, CA PMSA	19.1	2
San Jose, CA PMSA	17.9	6
Seattle, WA PMSA	17.5	8
Tampa-Saint Petersburg-Clearwater, FL	14.4	22
Washington, DC	21.3	1

Source: U.S. Department of Labor, Bureau of Labor Statistics, *Geographic Profile of Employment and Unemployment, 1994*, Bulletin 2469, Washington, D.C.: U.S. Government Printing Office, December 1995, p. 103. *Notes:* "CMSA" stands for "Consolidated Metropolitan Statistical Area." "MSA" stands for "Metropolitan Statistical Area." "PMSA" stands for "Primary Metropolitan Statistical Area."

★947★

Distribution of Employed Persons, By Occupation

Percent Distribution of All Employed Persons in Selected MSAs, 1994, By Occupation: Handlers, Equipment Cleaners, Helpers, and Laborers

MSA	Percent	Rank
Anaheim-Santa Ana, CA PMSA	3.9	14
Atlanta, GA	4.2	12
Baltimore, MD	2.9	23
Bergen-Passaic, NJ PMSA	3.2	20
Boston, MA PMSA	2.6	26
Buffalo-Niagara Falls, NY CMSA	3.1	21
Charlotte-Gastonia-Rock Hill, NC-SC	5.9	2
Chicago, IL PMSA	4.5	9
Cincinnati, OH PMSA	4.3	11
Cleveland, OH PMSA	3.5	17
Columbus, OH	4.7	8
Dallas-Fort Worth, TX CMSA	4.8	7
Dayton-Springfield, OH	5.3	4
Denver-Boulder, CO CMSA	3.4	18
Detroit, MI PMSA	3.5	17
Fort Lauderdale-Hollywood-Pompano Beach, FL PMSA	4.4	10
Hartford-New Britain-Middletown, CT CMSA	3.1	21
Houston, TX PMSA	4.9	6

[Continued]

★947★

Percent Distribution of All Employed Persons in Selected MSAs, 1994, By Occupation: Handlers, Equipment Cleaners, Helpers, and Laborers

[Continued]

MSA	Percent	Rank
Indianapolis, IN	4.5	9
Kansas City, KS-MO	3.5	17
Los Angeles-Long Beach, CA PMSA	4.3	11
Louisville, KY	5.6	3
Memphis, TN	6.7	1
Miami-Hialeah, FL PMSA	4.7	8
Milwaukee, WI PMSA	3.4	18
Minneapolis-Saint Paul, MN	3.2	20
Nassau-Suffolk, NY PMSA	3.6	16
New Orleans, LA	2.7	25
New York, NY PMSA	3.0	22
Newark, NJ PMSA	4.1	13
Norfolk-Virginia Beach-Newport News, VA	4.4	10
Oakland, CA PMSA	4.3	11
Oklahoma City, OK	3.3	19
Philadelphia, PA PMSA	3.4	18
Phoenix, AZ	3.7	15
Pittsburgh-Beaver Valley, PA	4.5	9
Portland, OR PMSA	2.7	25
Providence-Pawtucket-Fall River, MA-RI CMSA	3.5	17
Riverside-San Bernardino, CA PMSA	3.5	17
Rochester, NY	2.7	25
Sacramento, CA	3.3	19
Saint Louis, MO-IL	4.4	10
Salt Lake City-Ogden, UT	4.3	11
San Antonio, TX	5.0	5
San Diego, CA	3.5	17
San Francisco, CA PMSA	3.2	20
San Jose, CA PMSA	2.8	24
Seattle, WA PMSA	4.3	11
Tampa-Saint Petersburg-Clearwater, FL	2.7	25
Washington, DC	1.8	27

Source: U.S. Department of Labor, Bureau of Labor Statistics, *Geographic Profile of Employment and Unemployment, 1994,* Bulletin 2469, Washington, D.C.: U.S. Government Printing Office, December 1995, p. 103. *Notes:* "CMSA" stands for "Consolidated Metropolitan Statistical Area." "MSA" stands for "Metropolitan Statistical Area." "PMSA" stands for "Primary Metropolitan Statistical Area."

★948★

Distribution of Employed Persons, By Occupation

Percent Distribution of All Employed Persons in Selected MSAs, 1994, By Occupation: Machine Operators, Assemblers, and Inspectors

MSA	Percent	Rank
Anaheim-Santa Ana, CA PMSA	6.3	9
Atlanta, GA	4.6	20
Baltimore, MD	2.5	32
Bergen-Passaic, NJ PMSA	5.9	11

[Continued]

★948★

Percent Distribution of All Employed Persons in Selected MSAs, 1994, By Occupation: Machine Operators, Assemblers, and Inspectors

[Continued]

MSA	Percent	Rank
Boston, MA PMSA	3.0	30
Buffalo-Niagara Falls, NY CMSA	6.2	10
Charlotte-Gastonia-Rock Hill, NC-SC	11.1	1
Chicago, IL PMSA	5.8	12
Cincinnati, OH PMSA	5.8	12
Cleveland, OH PMSA	7.1	8
Columbus, OH	4.8	18
Dallas-Fort Worth, TX CMSA	5.2	14
Dayton-Springfield, OH	9.1	3
Denver-Boulder, CO CMSA	3.2	29
Detroit, MI PMSA	8.1	6
Fort Lauderdale-Hollywood-Pompano Beach, FL PMSA	1.9	34
Hartford-New Britain-Middletown, CT CMSA	4.1	22
Houston, TX PMSA	3.4	27
Indianapolis, IN	4.7	19
Kansas City, KS-MO	3.7	25
Los Angeles-Long Beach, CA PMSA	7.2	7
Louisville, KY	8.7	4
Memphis, TN	6.2	10
Miami-Hialeah, FL PMSA	3.3	28
Milwaukee, WI PMSA	8.3	5
Minneapolis-Saint Paul, MN	5.0	16
Nassau-Suffolk, NY PMSA	2.4	33
New Orleans, LA	4.0	23
New York, NY PMSA	4.4	21
Newark, NJ PMSA	5.0	16
Norfolk-Virginia Beach-Newport News, VA	3.5	26
Oakland, CA PMSA	5.0	16
Oklahoma City, OK	5.2	14
Philadelphia, PA PMSA	4.1	22
Phoenix, AZ	3.5	26
Pittsburgh-Beaver Valley, PA	4.9	17
Portland, OR PMSA	4.1	22
Providence-Pawtucket-Fall River, MA-RI CMSA	9.9	2
Riverside-San Bernardino, CA PMSA	4.6	20
Rochester, NY	6.3	9
Sacramento, CA	2.7	31
Saint Louis, MO-IL	5.2	14
Salt Lake City-Ogden, UT	5.1	15
San Antonio, TX	5.3	13
San Diego, CA	3.8	24
San Francisco, CA PMSA	2.5	32
San Jose, CA PMSA	4.6	20
Seattle, WA PMSA	3.3	28

[Continued]

★948★

Percent Distribution of All Employed Persons in Selected MSAs, 1994, By Occupation: Machine Operators, Assemblers, and Inspectors
[Continued]

MSA	Percent	Rank
Tampa-Saint Petersburg-Clearwater, FL	3.8	24
Washington, DC	1.6	35

Source: U.S. Department of Labor, Bureau of Labor Statistics, *Geographic Profile of Employment and Unemployment, 1994,* Bulletin 2469, Washington, D.C.: U.S. Government Printing Office, December 1995, p. 103. *Notes:* "CMSA" stands for "Consolidated Metropolitan Statistical Area." "MSA" stands for "Metropolitan Statistical Area." "PMSA" stands for "Primary Metropolitan Statistical Area."

★949★

Distribution of Employed Persons, By Occupation

Percent Distribution of All Employed Persons in Selected MSAs, 1994, By Occupation: Precision Production, Craft, and Repair

MSA	Percent	Rank
Anaheim-Santa Ana, CA PMSA	8.2	32
Atlanta, GA	9.9	18
Baltimore, MD	9.3	24
Bergen-Passaic, NJ PMSA	9.1	26
Boston, MA PMSA	7.6	35
Buffalo-Niagara Falls, NY CMSA	10.4	15
Charlotte-Gastonia-Rock Hill, NC-SC	10.8	12
Chicago, IL PMSA	10.4	15
Cincinnati, OH PMSA	11.1	10
Cleveland, OH PMSA	11.1	10
Columbus, OH	9.2	25
Dallas-Fort Worth, TX CMSA	10.6	13
Dayton-Springfield, OH	12.2	3
Denver-Boulder, CO CMSA	8.6	29
Detroit, MI PMSA	11.3	8
Fort Lauderdale-Hollywood-Pompano Beach, FL PMSA	14.2	1
Hartford-New Britain-Middletown, CT CMSA	9.6	21
Houston, TX PMSA	10.5	14
Indianapolis, IN	11.5	7
Kansas City, KS-MO	10.3	16
Los Angeles-Long Beach, CA PMSA	11.0	11
Louisville, KY	10.0	17
Memphis, TN	8.6	29
Miami-Hialeah, FL PMSA	10.5	14
Milwaukee, WI PMSA	9.6	21
Minneapolis-Saint Paul, MN	8.5	30
Nassau-Suffolk, NY PMSA	9.6	21
New Orleans, LA	9.6	21
New York, NY PMSA	7.7	34
Newark, NJ PMSA	9.5	22
Norfolk-Virginia Beach-Newport News, VA	11.7	6
Oakland, CA PMSA	9.4	23
Oklahoma City, OK	8.9	28

[Continued]

★949★

Percent Distribution of All Employed Persons in Selected MSAs, 1994, By Occupation: Precision Production, Craft, and Repair
[Continued]

MSA	Percent	Rank
Philadelphia, PA PMSA	10.0	17
Phoenix, AZ	12.0	5
Pittsburgh-Beaver Valley, PA	9.7	20
Portland, OR PMSA	9.0	27
Providence-Pawtucket-Fall River, MA-RI CMSA	10.8	12
Riverside-San Bernardino, CA PMSA	13.2	2
Rochester, NY	8.6	29
Sacramento, CA	8.3	31
Saint Louis, MO-IL	9.5	22
Salt Lake City-Ogden, UT	11.2	9
San Antonio, TX	12.1	4
San Diego, CA	9.4	23
San Francisco, CA PMSA	7.6	35
San Jose, CA PMSA	9.4	23
Seattle, WA PMSA	9.8	19
Tampa-Saint Petersburg-Clearwater, FL	11.5	7
Washington, DC	7.9	33

Source: U.S. Department of Labor, Bureau of Labor Statistics, *Geographic Profile of Employment and Unemployment, 1994,* Bulletin 2469, Washington, D.C.: U.S. Government Printing Office, December 1995, p. 103. *Notes:* "CMSA" stands for "Consolidated Metropolitan Statistical Area." "MSA" stands for "Metropolitan Statistical Area." "PMSA" stands for "Primary Metropolitan Statistical Area."

★950★

Distribution of Employed Persons, By Occupation

Percent Distribution of All Employed Persons in Selected MSAs, 1994, By Occupation: Professional Specialties

MSA	Percent	Rank
Anaheim-Santa Ana, CA PMSA	13.4	33
Atlanta, GA	15.2	24
Baltimore, MD	18.0	7
Bergen-Passaic, NJ PMSA	15.1	25
Boston, MA PMSA	23.4	1
Buffalo-Niagara Falls, NY CMSA	16.7	15
Charlotte-Gastonia-Rock Hill, NC-SC	12.8	35
Chicago, IL PMSA	16.4	17
Cincinnati, OH PMSA	17.5	10
Cleveland, OH PMSA	14.3	29
Columbus, OH	15.8	21
Dallas-Fort Worth, TX CMSA	14.3	29
Dayton-Springfield, OH	15.0	26
Denver-Boulder, CO CMSA	18.6	6
Detroit, MI PMSA	14.6	28
Fort Lauderdale-Hollywood-Pompano Beach, FL PMSA	11.9	37
Hartford-New Britain-Middletown, CT CMSA	17.9	8
Houston, TX PMSA	14.3	29

[Continued]

★950★

Percent Distribution of All Employed Persons in Selected MSAs, 1994, By Occupation: Professional Specialties

[Continued]

MSA	Percent	Rank
Indianapolis, IN	11.7	38
Kansas City, KS-MO	13.6	32
Los Angeles-Long Beach, CA PMSA	14.1	30
Louisville, KY	13.6	32
Memphis, TN	12.8	35
Miami-Hialeah, FL PMSA	12.5	36
Milwaukee, WI PMSA	17.2	12
Minneapolis-Saint Paul, MN	15.7	22
Nassau-Suffolk, NY PMSA	16.4	17
New Orleans, LA	15.5	23
New York, NY PMSA	17.4	11
Newark, NJ PMSA	16.3	18
Norfolk-Virginia Beach-Newport News, VA	14.6	28
Oakland, CA PMSA	15.9	20
Oklahoma City, OK	17.0	13
Philadelphia, PA PMSA	16.6	16
Phoenix, AZ	13.2	34
Pittsburgh-Beaver Valley, PA	17.6	9
Portland, OR PMSA	17.0	13
Providence-Pawtucket-Fall River, MA-RI CMSA	14.9	27
Riverside-San Bernardino, CA PMSA	12.8	35
Rochester, NY	20.4	3
Sacramento, CA	16.9	14
Saint Louis, MO-IL	16.4	17
Salt Lake City-Ogden, UT	14.1	30
San Antonio, TX	10.8	39
San Diego, CA	16.0	19
San Francisco, CA PMSA	19.0	4
San Jose, CA PMSA	16.7	15
Seattle, WA PMSA	18.7	5
Tampa-Saint Petersburg-Clearwater, FL	14.0	31
Washington, DC	20.8	2

Source: U.S. Department of Labor, Bureau of Labor Statistics, *Geographic Profile of Employment and Unemployment, 1994*, Bulletin 2469, Washington, D.C.: U.S. Government Printing Office, December 1995, p. 103. *Notes:* "CMSA" stands for "Consolidated Metropolitan Statistical Area." "MSA" stands for "Metropolitan Statistical Area." "PMSA" stands for "Primary Metropolitan Statistical Area."

★951★

Distribution of Employed Persons, By Occupation

Percent Distribution of All Employed Persons in Selected MSAs, 1994, By Occupation: Sales

MSA	Percent	Rank
Anaheim-Santa Ana, CA PMSA	14.2	7
Atlanta, GA	12.9	17
Baltimore, MD	11.4	26
Bergen-Passaic, NJ PMSA	14.1	8
Boston, MA PMSA	11.0	29

[Continued]

★951★

Percent Distribution of All Employed Persons in Selected MSAs, 1994, By Occupation: Sales

[Continued]

MSA	Percent	Rank
Buffalo-Niagara Falls, NY CMSA	11.7	24
Charlotte-Gastonia-Rock Hill, NC-SC	12.7	19
Chicago, IL PMSA	11.6	25
Cincinnati, OH PMSA	12.7	19
Cleveland, OH PMSA	11.6	25
Columbus, OH	11.6	25
Dallas-Fort Worth, TX CMSA	12.8	18
Dayton-Springfield, OH	12.0	21
Denver-Boulder, CO CMSA	14.3	6
Detroit, MI PMSA	12.5	20
Fort Lauderdale-Hollywood-Pompano Beach, FL PMSA	14.9	3
Hartford-New Britain-Middletown, CT CMSA	11.4	26
Houston, TX PMSA	14.2	7
Indianapolis, IN	15.9	1
Kansas City, KS-MO	13.3	13
Los Angeles-Long Beach, CA PMSA	11.9	22
Louisville, KY	11.3	27
Memphis, TN	14.6	5
Miami-Hialeah, FL PMSA	14.6	5
Milwaukee, WI PMSA	11.1	28
Minneapolis-Saint Paul, MN	11.8	23
Nassau-Suffolk, NY PMSA	13.9	10
New Orleans, LA	12.8	18
New York, NY PMSA	10.5	32
Newark, NJ PMSA	11.3	27
Norfolk-Virginia Beach-Newport News, VA	14.0	9
Oakland, CA PMSA	10.6	31
Oklahoma City, OK	15.4	2
Philadelphia, PA PMSA	12.5	20
Phoenix, AZ	13.4	12
Pittsburgh-Beaver Valley, PA	13.1	15
Portland, OR PMSA	14.1	8
Providence-Pawtucket-Fall River, MA-RI CMSA	10.5	32
Riverside-San Bernardino, CA PMSA	13.0	16
Rochester, NY	10.9	30
Sacramento, CA	10.6	31
Saint Louis, MO-IL	13.2	14
Salt Lake City-Ogden, UT	12.0	21
San Antonio, TX	14.7	4
San Diego, CA	13.7	11
San Francisco, CA PMSA	13.1	15
San Jose, CA PMSA	10.5	32
Seattle, WA PMSA	13.3	13
Tampa-Saint Petersburg-Clearwater, FL	13.7	11
Washington, DC	10.0	33

Source: U.S. Department of Labor, Bureau of Labor Statistics, *Geographic Profile of Employment and Unemployment, 1994*, Bulletin 2469, Washington, D.C.: U.S. Government Printing Office, December 1995, p. 103. *Notes:* "CMSA" stands for "Consolidated Metropolitan Statistical Area." "MSA" stands for "Metropolitan Statistical Area." "PMSA" stands for "Primary Metropolitan Statistical Area."

★952★

Distribution of Employed Persons, By Occupation

Percent Distribution of All Employed Persons in Selected MSAs, 1994, By Occupation: Service Occupations

MSA	Percent	Rank
Anaheim-Santa Ana, CA PMSA	13.2	16
Atlanta, GA	12.0	25
Baltimore, MD	12.9	18
Bergen-Passaic, NJ PMSA	9.5	31
Boston, MA PMSA	12.4	21
Buffalo-Niagara Falls, NY CMSA	17.3	3
Charlotte-Gastonia-Rock Hill, NC-SC	11.1	29
Chicago, IL PMSA	12.2	23
Cincinnati, OH PMSA	11.8	27
Cleveland, OH PMSA	14.2	10
Columbus, OH	11.9	26
Dallas-Fort Worth, TX CMSA	12.6	19
Dayton-Springfield, OH	12.3	22
Denver-Boulder, CO CMSA	11.6	28
Detroit, MI PMSA	13.1	17
Fort Lauderdale-Hollywood-Pompano Beach, FL PMSA	15.0	7
Hartford-New Britain-Middletown, CT CMSA	13.5	14
Houston, TX PMSA	12.2	23
Indianapolis, IN	10.3	30
Kansas City, KS-MO	12.3	22
Los Angeles-Long Beach, CA PMSA	14.0	11
Louisville, KY	12.6	19
Memphis, TN	12.2	23
Miami-Hialeah, FL PMSA	16.5	4
Milwaukee, WI PMSA	13.9	12
Minneapolis-Saint Paul, MN	13.3	15
Nassau-Suffolk, NY PMSA	12.1	24
New Orleans, LA	15.0	7
New York, NY PMSA	18.3	1
Newark, NJ PMSA	12.0	25
Norfolk-Virginia Beach-Newport News, VA	15.6	5
Oakland, CA PMSA	13.1	17
Oklahoma City, OK	12.4	21
Philadelphia, PA PMSA	12.3	22
Phoenix, AZ	13.3	15
Pittsburgh-Beaver Valley, PA	13.3	15
Portland, OR PMSA	11.1	29
Providence-Pawtucket-Fall River, MA-RI CMSA	15.1	6
Riverside-San Bernardino, CA PMSA	11.8	27
Rochester, NY	14.7	9
Sacramento, CA	15.0	7
Saint Louis, MO-IL	11.9	26
Salt Lake City-Ogden, UT	11.8	27
San Antonio, TX	17.8	2
San Diego, CA	14.8	8
San Francisco, CA PMSA	12.6	19
San Jose, CA PMSA	13.5	14
Seattle, WA PMSA	12.2	23

[Continued]

★952★

Percent Distribution of All Employed Persons in Selected MSAs, 1994, By Occupation: Service Occupations

[Continued]

MSA	Percent	Rank
Tampa-Saint Petersburg-Clearwater, FL	13.8	13
Washington, DC	12.5	20

Source: U.S. Department of Labor, Bureau of Labor Statistics, *Geographic Profile of Employment and Unemployment, 1994,* Bulletin 2469, Washington, D.C.: U.S. Government Printing Office, December 1995, p. 103. *Notes:* "CMSA" stands for "Consolidated Metropolitan Statistical Area." "MSA" stands for "Metropolitan Statistical Area." "PMSA" stands for "Primary Metropolitan Statistical Area."

★953★

Distribution of Employed Persons, By Occupation

Percent Distribution of All Employed Persons in Selected MSAs, 1994, By Occupation: Technicians and Related Support

MSA	Percent	Rank
Anaheim-Santa Ana, CA PMSA	2.8	17
Atlanta, GA	3.0	15
Baltimore, MD	3.2	14
Bergen-Passaic, NJ PMSA	4.3	4
Boston, MA PMSA	3.4	12
Buffalo-Niagara Falls, NY CMSA	3.0	15
Charlotte-Gastonia-Rock Hill, NC-SC	3.2	14
Chicago, IL PMSA	2.9	16
Cincinnati, OH PMSA	3.5	11
Cleveland, OH PMSA	2.8	17
Columbus, OH	3.4	12
Dallas-Fort Worth, TX CMSA	3.3	13
Dayton-Springfield, OH	3.2	14
Denver-Boulder, CO CMSA	3.9	8
Detroit, MI PMSA	3.3	13
Fort Lauderdale-Hollywood-Pompano Beach, FL PMSA	2.6	19
Hartford-New Britain-Middletown, CT CMSA	4.4	3
Houston, TX PMSA	3.3	13
Indianapolis, IN	3.6	10
Kansas City, KS-MO	3.4	12
Los Angeles-Long Beach, CA PMSA	2.6	19
Louisville, KY	4.1	6
Memphis, TN	3.6	10
Miami-Hialeah, FL PMSA	2.0	21
Milwaukee, WI PMSA	3.2	14
Minneapolis-Saint Paul, MN	4.8	2
Nassau-Suffolk, NY PMSA	2.7	18
New Orleans, LA	2.7	18
New York, NY PMSA	2.7	18
Newark, NJ PMSA	3.2	14
Norfolk-Virginia Beach-Newport News, VA	2.9	16
Oakland, CA PMSA	2.7	18
Oklahoma City, OK	3.6	10

[Continued]

★953★

Percent Distribution of All Employed Persons in Selected MSAs, 1994, By Occupation: Technicians and Related Support

[Continued]

MSA	Percent	Rank
Philadelphia, PA PMSA	3.3	13
Phoenix, AZ	4.2	5
Pittsburgh-Beaver Valley, PA	4.0	7
Portland, OR PMSA	2.9	16
Providence-Pawtucket-Fall River, MA-RI CMSA	2.8	17
Riverside-San Bernardino, CA PMSA	3.6	10
Rochester, NY	6.0	1
Sacramento, CA	3.9	8
Saint Louis, MO-IL	4.3	4
Salt Lake City-Ogden, UT	3.7	9
San Antonio, TX	2.7	18
San Diego, CA	2.7	18
San Francisco, CA PMSA	2.5	20
San Jose, CA PMSA	4.4	3
Seattle, WA PMSA	4.0	7
Tampa-Saint Petersburg-Clearwater, FL	2.7	18
Washington, DC	4.0	7

Source: U.S. Department of Labor, Bureau of Labor Statistics, *Geographic Profile of Employment and Unemployment, 1994,* Bulletin 2469, Washington, D.C.: U.S. Government Printing Office, December 1995, p. 103. *Notes:* "CMSA" stands for "Consolidated Metropolitan Statistical Area." "MSA" stands for "Metropolitan Statistical Area." "PMSA" stands for "Primary Metropolitan Statistical Area."

★954★

Distribution of Employed Persons, By Occupation

Percent Distribution of All Employed Persons in Selected MSAs, 1994, By Occupation: Transportation and Material Moving

MSA	Percent	Rank
Anaheim-Santa Ana, CA PMSA	2.4	26
Atlanta, GA	3.3	17
Baltimore, MD	5.2	3
Bergen-Passaic, NJ PMSA	3.6	14
Boston, MA PMSA	2.5	25
Buffalo-Niagara Falls, NY CMSA	4.8	4
Charlotte-Gastonia-Rock Hill, NC-SC	4.0	11
Chicago, IL PMSA	3.3	17
Cincinnati, OH PMSA	3.3	17
Cleveland, OH PMSA	4.2	9
Columbus, OH	3.3	17
Dallas-Fort Worth, TX CMSA	4.0	11
Dayton-Springfield, OH	4.0	11
Denver-Boulder, CO CMSA	3.4	16
Detroit, MI PMSA	3.6	14
Fort Lauderdale-Hollywood-Pompano Beach, FL PMSA	2.6	24
Hartford-New Britain-Middletown, CT CMSA	3.4	16
Houston, TX PMSA	4.6	6

[Continued]

★954★

Percent Distribution of All Employed Persons in Selected MSAs, 1994, By Occupation: Transportation and Material Moving

[Continued]

MSA	Percent	Rank
Indianapolis, IN	3.2	18
Kansas City, KS-MO	3.4	16
Los Angeles-Long Beach, CA PMSA	3.1	19
Louisville, KY	3.7	13
Memphis, TN	5.6	2
Miami-Hialeah, FL PMSA	4.7	5
Milwaukee, WI PMSA	2.9	21
Minneapolis-Saint Paul, MN	3.5	15
Nassau-Suffolk, NY PMSA	3.2	18
New Orleans, LA	4.7	5
New York, NY PMSA	3.4	16
Newark, NJ PMSA	4.1	10
Norfolk-Virginia Beach-Newport News, VA	2.9	21
Oakland, CA PMSA	4.0	11
Oklahoma City, OK	3.9	12
Philadelphia, PA PMSA	3.5	15
Phoenix, AZ	2.8	22
Pittsburgh-Beaver Valley, PA	4.2	9
Portland, OR PMSA	2.3	27
Providence-Pawtucket-Fall River, MA-RI CMSA	3.5	15
Riverside-San Bernardino, CA PMSA	6.0	1
Rochester, NY	3.0	20
Sacramento, CA	4.3	8
Saint Louis, MO-IL	3.7	13
Salt Lake City-Ogden, UT	4.0	11
San Antonio, TX	4.5	7
San Diego, CA	2.9	21
San Francisco, CA PMSA	3.7	13
San Jose, CA PMSA	2.7	23
Seattle, WA PMSA	2.9	21
Tampa-Saint Petersburg-Clearwater, FL	3.7	13
Washington, DC	2.8	22

Source: U.S. Department of Labor, Bureau of Labor Statistics, *Geographic Profile of Employment and Unemployment, 1994,* Bulletin 2469, Washington, D.C.: U.S. Government Printing Office, December 1995, p. 103. *Notes:* "CMSA" stands for "Consolidated Metropolitan Statistical Area." "MSA" stands for "Metropolitan Statistical Area." "PMSA" stands for "Primary Metropolitan Statistical Area."

★955★

Distribution of Employed Hispanics, By Occupation

Percent Distribution of Employed Hispanic Persons in Selected Cities, 1994, By Occupation: Administrative Support, Including Clerical

City	Percent	Rank
Chicago, IL	15.7	3
Dallas, TX	7.6	8
Houston, TX	8.9	7
Los Angeles, CA	12.8	5

[Continued]

★955★

Percent Distribution of Employed Hispanic Persons in Selected Cities, 1994, By Occupation: Administrative Support, Including Clerical

[Continued]

City	Percent	Rank
New York, NY	18.0	2
Phoenix, AZ	15.3	4
San Antonio, TX	11.9	6
San Diego, CA	7.5	9
San Francisco, CA	18.9	1
Washington, DC	4.3	10

Source: U.S. Department of Labor, Bureau of Labor Statistics, *Geographic Profile of Employment and Unemployment, 1994*, Bulletin 2469, Washington, D.C.: U.S. Government Printing Office, December 1995, p. 103.

★956★

Distribution of Employed Hispanics, By Occupation

Percent Distribution of Employed Hispanic Persons in Selected Cities, 1994, By Occupation: Executive, Administrative, and Managerial

City	Percent	Rank
Chicago, IL	6.1	7
Dallas, TX	4.8	8
Houston, TX	4.2	10
Los Angeles, CA	4.3	9
New York, NY	7.7	5
Phoenix, AZ	10.4	2
San Antonio, TX	6.6	6
San Diego, CA	8.5	4
San Francisco, CA	8.6	3
Washington, DC	12.4	1

Source: U.S. Department of Labor, Bureau of Labor Statistics, *Geographic Profile of Employment and Unemployment, 1994*, Bulletin 2469, Washington, D.C.: U.S. Government Printing Office, December 1995, p. 103.

★957★

Distribution of Employed Hispanics, By Occupation

Percent Distribution of Employed Hispanic Persons in Selected Cities, 1994, By Occupation: Handlers, Equipment Cleaners, Helpers, and Laborers

City	Percent	Rank
Chicago, IL	9.8	6
Dallas, TX	11.9	3
Houston, TX	15.4	1
Los Angeles, CA	7.4	8
New York, NY	4.3	10
Phoenix, AZ	11.2	4
San Antonio, TX	8.8	7
San Diego, CA	10.3	5
San Francisco, CA	12.6	2
Washington, DC	4.8	9

Source: U.S. Department of Labor, Bureau of Labor Statistics, *Geographic Profile of Employment and Unemployment, 1994*, Bulletin 2469, Washington, D.C.: U.S. Government Printing Office, December 1995, p. 103.

★958★

Distribution of Employed Hispanics, By Occupation

Percent Distribution of Employed Hispanic Persons in Selected Cities, 1994, By Occupation: Machine Operators, Assemblers, and Inspectors

City	Percent	Rank
Chicago, IL	23.5	1
Dallas, TX	14.5	3
Houston, TX	4.6	8
Los Angeles, CA	17.5	2
New York, NY	10.4	4
Phoenix, AZ	7.5	5
San Antonio, TX	7.4	6
San Diego, CA	6.7	7
San Francisco, CA	3.3	10
Washington, DC	4.0	9

Source: U.S. Department of Labor, Bureau of Labor Statistics, *Geographic Profile of Employment and Unemployment, 1994*, Bulletin 2469, Washington, D.C.: U.S. Government Printing Office, December 1995, p. 103.

★959★

Distribution of Employed Hispanics, By Occupation

Percent Distribution of Employed Hispanic Persons in Selected Cities, 1994, By Occupation: Precision Production, Craft, and Repair

City	Percent	Rank
Chicago, IL	12.2	6
Dallas, TX	21.7	1
Houston, TX	18.7	2
Los Angeles, CA	15.9	4
New York, NY	9.1	7
Phoenix, AZ	18.4	3
San Antonio, TX	15.7	5
San Diego, CA	9.0	8
San Francisco, CA	5.5	10
Washington, DC	8.1	9

Source: U.S. Department of Labor, Bureau of Labor Statistics, *Geographic Profile of Employment and Unemployment, 1994*, Bulletin 2469, Washington, D.C.: U.S. Government Printing Office, December 1995, p. 103.

★960★

Distribution of Employed Hispanics, By Occupation

Percent Distribution of Employed Hispanic Persons in Selected Cities, 1994, By Occupation: Professional Specialty

City	Percent	Rank
Chicago, IL	5.6	4
Dallas, TX	6.5	2
Houston, TX	2.6	8
Los Angeles, CA	3.9	7
New York, NY	6.8	1
Phoenix, AZ	5.1	5
San Antonio, TX	5.1	5
San Diego, CA	4.7	6

[Continued]

★960★

Percent Distribution of Employed Hispanic Persons in Selected Cities, 1994, By Occupation: Professional Specialty

[Continued]

City	Percent	Rank
San Francisco, CA	6.2	3
Washington, DC	6.5	2

Source: U.S. Department of Labor, Bureau of Labor Statistics, Geographic Profile of Employment and Unemployment, 1994, Bulletin 2469, Washington, D.C.: U.S. Government Printing Office, December 1995, p. 103.

★961★

Distribution of Employed Hispanics, By Occupation

Percent Distribution of Employed Hispanic Persons in Selected Cities, 1994, By Occupation: Sales

City	Percent	Rank
Chicago, IL	6.3	8
Dallas, TX	4.8	10
Houston, TX	7.9	4
Los Angeles, CA	6.0	9
New York, NY	8.9	3
Phoenix, AZ	6.4	7
San Antonio, TX	11.4	2
San Diego, CA	14.5	1
San Francisco, CA	6.7	6
Washington, DC	7.5	5

Source: U.S. Department of Labor, Bureau of Labor Statistics, Geographic Profile of Employment and Unemployment, 1994, Bulletin 2469, Washington, D.C.: U.S. Government Printing Office, December 1995, p. 103.

★962★

Distribution of Employed Hispanics, By Occupation

Percent Distribution of Employed Hispanic Persons in Selected Cities, 1994, By Occupation: Service Occupations

City	Percent	Rank
Chicago, IL	14.4	10
Dallas, TX	16.1	9
Houston, TX	27.3	4
Los Angeles, CA	24.5	5
New York, NY	27.9	2
Phoenix, AZ	18.5	8
San Antonio, TX	22.9	7
San Diego, CA	27.8	3
San Francisco, CA	24.3	6
Washington, DC	45.3	1

Source: U.S. Department of Labor, Bureau of Labor Statistics, Geographic Profile of Employment and Unemployment, 1994, Bulletin 2469, Washington, D.C.: U.S. Government Printing Office, December 1995, p. 103.

★963★

Distribution of Employed Hispanics, By Occupation

Percent Distribution of Employed Hispanic Persons in Selected Cities, 1994, By Occupation: Technicians and Related Support

City	Percent	Rank
Chicago, IL	1.3	4
Dallas, TX	(3)	7
Houston, TX	.2	6
Los Angeles, CA	1.2	5
New York, NY	2.2	2
Phoenix, AZ	1.2	5
San Antonio, TX	1.9	3
San Diego, CA	(3)	7
San Francisco, CA	(3)	7
Washington, DC	3.3	1

Source: U.S. Department of Labor, Bureau of Labor Statistics, Geographic Profile of Employment and Unemployment, 1994, Bulletin 2469, Washington, D.C.: U.S. Government Printing Office, December 1995, p. 103.

★964★

Distribution of Employed Hispanics, By Occupation

Percent Distribution of Employed Hispanic Persons in Selected Cities, 1994, By Occupation: Transportation and Material Moving

City	Percent	Rank
Chicago, IL	3.4	7
Dallas, TX	6.1	2
Houston, TX	5.0	5
Los Angeles, CA	2.7	9
New York, NY	4.7	6
Phoenix, AZ	2.3	10
San Antonio, TX	6.0	3
San Diego, CA	5.6	4
San Francisco, CA	12.5	1
Washington, DC	2.9	8

Source: U.S. Department of Labor, Bureau of Labor Statistics, Geographic Profile of Employment and Unemployment, 1994, Bulletin 2469, Washington, D.C.: U.S. Government Printing Office, December 1995, p. 103.

★965★

Distribution of Employed Hispanics, By Occupation

Percent Distribution of Employed Hispanic Persons in Selected MSAs, 1994, By Occupation: Administrative Support, Including Clerical

MSA	Percent	Rank
Anaheim-Santa Ana, CA PMSA	13.9	10
Bergen-Passaic, NJ PMSA	17.6	5
Boston, MA PMSA	11.1	19
Chicago, IL PMSA	13.3	12
Dallas-Fort Worth, TX CMSA	9.4	22
Denver-Boulder, CO CMSA	19.3	2
Detroit, MI PMSA	23.2	1
Fort Lauderdale-Hollywood- Pompano Beach, FL PMSA	12.5	14
Houston, TX PMSA	10.0	20

[Continued]

★965★

Percent Distribution of Employed Hispanic Persons in Selected MSAs, 1994, By Occupation: Administrative Support, Including Clerical
[Continued]

MSA	Percent	Rank
Los Angeles-Long Beach, CA PMSA	14.7	8
Miami-Hialeah, FL PMSA	17.4	6
Nassau-Suffolk, NY PMSA	18.8	3
New York, NY PMSA	17.4	6
Newark, NJ PMSA	13.8	11
Oakland, CA PMSA	11.6	17
Philadelphia, PA PMSA	14.6	9
Phoenix, AZ	12.3	15
Portland, OR PMSA	5.0	26
Providence-Pawtucket-Fall River, MA-RI CMSA	5.9	25
Riverside-San Bernardino, CA PMSA	13.8	11
Sacramento, CA	11.5	18
Salt Lake City-Ogden, UT	17.8	4
San Antonio, TX	12.8	13
San Diego, CA	8.6	24
San Francisco, CA PMSA	16.1	7
San Jose, CA PMSA	11.7	16
Tampa-Saint Petersburg-Clearwater, FL	8.7	23
Washington, DC	9.7	21

Source: U.S. Department of Labor, Bureau of Labor Statistics, *Geographic Profile of Employment and Unemployment, 1994,* Bulletin 2469, Washington, D.C.: U.S. Government Printing Office, December 1995, p. 103. *Notes:* "CMSA" stands for "Consolidated Metropolitan Statistical Area." "MSA" stands for "Metropolitan Statistical Area." "PMSA" stands for "Primary Metropolitan Statistical Area."

★966★

Distribution of Employed Hispanics, By Occupation

Percent Distribution of Employed Hispanic Persons in Selected MSAs, 1994, By Occupation: Executive, Administrative, and Managerial

MSA	Percent	Rank
Anaheim-Santa Ana, CA PMSA	7.3	13
Bergen-Passaic, NJ PMSA	6.9	15
Boston, MA PMSA	7.6	11
Chicago, IL PMSA	6.1	20
Dallas-Fort Worth, TX CMSA	6.4	18
Denver-Boulder, CO CMSA	7.5	12
Detroit, MI PMSA	6.2	19
Fort Lauderdale-Hollywood-Pompano Beach, FL PMSA	15.0	1
Houston, TX PMSA	5.5	23
Los Angeles-Long Beach, CA PMSA	5.6	22
Miami-Hialeah, FL PMSA	11.1	3
Nassau-Suffolk, NY PMSA	5.9	21
New York, NY PMSA	7.7	10
Newark, NJ PMSA	2.8	25

[Continued]

★966★

Percent Distribution of Employed Hispanic Persons in Selected MSAs, 1994, By Occupation: Executive, Administrative, and Managerial
[Continued]

MSA	Percent	Rank
Oakland, CA PMSA	10.7	5
Philadelphia, PA PMSA	6.8	16
Phoenix, AZ	10.1	6
Portland, OR PMSA	12.4	2
Providence-Pawtucket-Fall River, MA-RI CMSA	3.4	24
Riverside-San Bernardino, CA PMSA	8.8	9
Sacramento, CA	11.0	4
Salt Lake City-Ogden, UT	5.5	23
San Antonio, TX	6.6	17
San Diego, CA	6.9	15
San Francisco, CA PMSA	7.2	14
San Jose, CA PMSA	7.6	11
Tampa-Saint Petersburg-Clearwater, FL	9.6	8
Washington, DC	9.7	7

Source: U.S. Department of Labor, Bureau of Labor Statistics, *Geographic Profile of Employment and Unemployment, 1994,* Bulletin 2469, Washington, D.C.: U.S. Government Printing Office, December 1995, p. 103. *Notes:* "CMSA" stands for "Consolidated Metropolitan Statistical Area." "MSA" stands for "Metropolitan Statistical Area." "PMSA" stands for "Primary Metropolitan Statistical Area."

★967★

Distribution of Employed Hispanics, By Occupation

Percent Distribution of Employed Hispanic Persons in Selected MSAs, 1994, By Occupation: Handlers, Equipment Cleaners, Helpers, and Laborers

MSA	Percent	Rank
Anaheim-Santa Ana, CA PMSA	7.3	10
Bergen-Passaic, NJ PMSA	6.7	12
Boston, MA PMSA	8.0	8
Chicago, IL PMSA	9.4	4
Dallas-Fort Worth, TX CMSA	11.8	1
Denver-Boulder, CO CMSA	5.4	15
Detroit, MI PMSA	8.6	6
Fort Lauderdale-Hollywood-Pompano Beach, FL PMSA	5.3	16
Houston, TX PMSA	11.8	1
Los Angeles-Long Beach, CA PMSA	7.9	9
Miami-Hialeah, FL PMSA	5.2	17
Nassau-Suffolk, NY PMSA	9.7	3
New York, NY PMSA	4.1	20
Newark, NJ PMSA	8.0	8
Oakland, CA PMSA	10.6	2
Philadelphia, PA PMSA	6.8	11
Phoenix, AZ	10.6	2
Portland, OR PMSA	1.0	23
Providence-Pawtucket-Fall River, MA-RI CMSA	2.6	22

[Continued]

★967★

Percent Distribution of Employed Hispanic Persons in Selected MSAs, 1994, By Occupation: Handlers, Equipment Cleaners, Helpers, and Laborers

[Continued]

MSA	Percent	Rank
Riverside-San Bernardino, CA PMSA	6.0	13
Sacramento, CA	5.1	18
Salt Lake City-Ogden, UT	8.3	7
San Antonio, TX	7.3	10
San Diego, CA	9.3	5
San Francisco, CA PMSA	8.3	7
San Jose, CA PMSA	5.7	14
Tampa-Saint Petersburg-Clearwater, FL	4.9	19
Washington, DC	3.9	21

Source: U.S. Department of Labor, Bureau of Labor Statistics, *Geographic Profile of Employment and Unemployment, 1994*, Bulletin 2469, Washington, D.C.: U.S. Government Printing Office, December 1995, p. 103. *Notes:* "CMSA" stands for "Consolidated Metropolitan Statistical Area." "MSA" stands for "Metropolitan Statistical Area." "PMSA" stands for "Primary Metropolitan Statistical Area."

★968★

Distribution of Employed Hispanics, By Occupation

Percent Distribution of Employed Hispanic Persons in Selected MSAs, 1994, By Occupation: Machine Operators, Assemblers, and Inspectors

MSA	Percent	Rank
Anaheim-Santa Ana, CA PMSA	15.1	6
Bergen-Passaic, NJ PMSA	18.9	4
Boston, MA PMSA	9.7	14
Chicago, IL PMSA	22.1	2
Dallas-Fort Worth, TX CMSA	13.2	8
Denver-Boulder, CO CMSA	5.4	22
Detroit, MI PMSA	5.2	23
Fort Lauderdale-Hollywood-Pompano Beach, FL PMSA	5.6	21
Houston, TX PMSA	6.2	20
Los Angeles-Long Beach, CA PMSA	14.7	7
Miami-Hialeah, FL PMSA	4.8	24
Nassau-Suffolk, NY PMSA	9.7	14
New York, NY PMSA	9.9	13
Newark, NJ PMSA	20.6	3
Oakland, CA PMSA	8.4	16
Philadelphia, PA PMSA	15.3	5
Phoenix, AZ	7.0	18
Portland, OR PMSA	6.6	19
Providence-Pawtucket-Fall River, MA-RI CMSA	40.7	1
Riverside-San Bernardino, CA PMSA	12.0	10
Sacramento, CA	11.2	11
Salt Lake City-Ogden, UT	12.8	9
San Antonio, TX	8.1	17
San Diego, CA	9.0	15

[Continued]

★968★

Percent Distribution of Employed Hispanic Persons in Selected MSAs, 1994, By Occupation: Machine Operators, Assemblers, and Inspectors

[Continued]

MSA	Percent	Rank
San Francisco, CA PMSA	4.0	25
San Jose, CA PMSA	10.5	12
Tampa-Saint Petersburg-Clearwater, FL	5.4	22
Washington, DC	2.6	26

Source: U.S. Department of Labor, Bureau of Labor Statistics, *Geographic Profile of Employment and Unemployment, 1994*, Bulletin 2469, Washington, D.C.: U.S. Government Printing Office, December 1995, p. 103. *Notes:* "CMSA" stands for "Consolidated Metropolitan Statistical Area." "MSA" stands for "Metropolitan Statistical Area." "PMSA" stands for "Primary Metropolitan Statistical Area."

★969★

Distribution of Employed Hispanics, By Occupation

Percent Distribution of Employed Hispanic Persons in Selected MSAs, 1994, By Occupation: Precision Production, Craft, and Repair

MSA	Percent	Rank
Anaheim-Santa Ana, CA PMSA	7.8	21
Bergen-Passaic, NJ PMSA	10.8	18
Boston, MA PMSA	7.5	22
Chicago, IL PMSA	12.9	12
Dallas-Fort Worth, TX CMSA	20.6	2
Denver-Boulder, CO CMSA	10.8	18
Detroit, MI PMSA	12.7	13
Fort Lauderdale-Hollywood-Pompano Beach, FL PMSA	21.9	1
Houston, TX PMSA	18.4	4
Los Angeles-Long Beach, CA PMSA	14.5	9
Miami-Hialeah, FL PMSA	12.4	14
Nassau-Suffolk, NY PMSA	14.3	10
New York, NY PMSA	9.1	20
Newark, NJ PMSA	15.1	7
Oakland, CA PMSA	6.3	23
Philadelphia, PA PMSA	9.1	20
Phoenix, AZ	18.0	5
Portland, OR PMSA	11.9	15
Providence-Pawtucket-Fall River, MA-RI CMSA	13.7	11
Riverside-San Bernardino, CA PMSA	14.6	8
Sacramento, CA	3.8	24
Salt Lake City-Ogden, UT	19.7	3
San Antonio, TX	14.6	8
San Diego, CA	11.3	16
San Francisco, CA PMSA	11.3	16
San Jose, CA PMSA	16.6	6

[Continued]

★969★
Percent Distribution of Employed Hispanic Persons in Selected MSAs, 1994, By Occupation: Precision Production, Craft, and Repair
[Continued]

MSA	Percent	Rank
Tampa-Saint Petersburg- Clearwater, FL	11.2	17
Washington, DC	10.3	19

Source: U.S. Department of Labor, Bureau of Labor Statistics, Geographic Profile of Employment and Unemployment, 1994, Bulletin 2469, Washington, D.C.: U.S. Government Printing Office, December 1995, p. 103. Notes: "CMSA" stands for "Consolidated Metropolitan Statistical Area." "MSA" stands for "Metropolitan Statistical Area." "PMSA" stands for "Primary Metropolitan Statistical Area."

★970★
Distribution of Employed Hispanics, By Occupation
Percent Distribution of Employed Hispanic Persons in Selected MSAs, 1994, By Occupation: Professional Specialties

MSA	Percent	Rank
Anaheim-Santa Ana, CA PMSA	5.8	14
Bergen-Passaic, NJ PMSA	4.1	23
Boston, MA PMSA	11.8	3
Chicago, IL PMSA	5.7	15
Dallas-Fort Worth, TX CMSA	4.8	20
Denver-Boulder, CO CMSA	6.5	10
Detroit, MI PMSA	13.3	1
Fort Lauderdale-Hollywood- Pompano Beach, FL PMSA	6.4	11
Houston, TX PMSA	4.1	23
Los Angeles-Long Beach, CA PMSA	4.8	20
Miami-Hialeah, FL PMSA	7.6	7
Nassau-Suffolk, NY PMSA	6.6	9
New York, NY PMSA	6.6	9
Newark, NJ PMSA	4.7	21
Oakland, CA PMSA	8.5	5
Philadelphia, PA PMSA	13.0	2
Phoenix, AZ	6.0	13
Portland, OR PMSA	.6	24
Providence-Pawtucket-Fall River, MA-RI CMSA	7.2	8
Riverside-San Bernardino, CA PMSA	4.5	22
Sacramento, CA	6.1	12
Salt Lake City-Ogden, UT	4.5	22
San Antonio, TX	5.3	18
San Diego, CA	5.6	16
San Francisco, CA PMSA	5.4	17
San Jose, CA PMSA	5.1	19
Tampa-Saint Petersburg- Clearwater, FL	8.4	6
Washington, DC	11.7	4

Source: U.S. Department of Labor, Bureau of Labor Statistics, Geographic Profile of Employment and Unemployment, 1994, Bulletin 2469, Washington, D.C.: U.S. Government Printing Office, December 1995, p. 103. Notes: "CMSA" stands for "Consolidated Metropolitan Statistical Area." "MSA" stands for "Metropolitan Statistical Area." "PMSA" stands for "Primary Metropolitan Statistical Area."

★971★
Distribution of Employed Hispanics, By Occupation
Percent Distribution of Employed Hispanic Persons in Selected MSAs, 1994, By Occupation: Sales

MSA	Percent	Rank
Anaheim-Santa Ana, CA PMSA	12.6	4
Bergen-Passaic, NJ PMSA	7.0	20
Boston, MA PMSA	6.6	22
Chicago, IL PMSA	6.6	22
Dallas-Fort Worth, TX CMSA	6.6	22
Denver-Boulder, CO CMSA	14.9	2
Detroit, MI PMSA	7.9	16
Fort Lauderdale-Hollywood- Pompano Beach, FL PMSA	7.8	17
Houston, TX PMSA	10.7	7
Los Angeles-Long Beach, CA PMSA	8.3	14
Miami-Hialeah, FL PMSA	16.1	1
Nassau-Suffolk, NY PMSA	8.8	12
New York, NY PMSA	8.6	13
Newark, NJ PMSA	8.0	15
Oakland, CA PMSA	5.7	23
Philadelphia, PA PMSA	10.6	8
Phoenix, AZ	5.7	23
Portland, OR PMSA	7.6	19
Providence-Pawtucket-Fall River, MA-RI CMSA	7.7	18
Riverside-San Bernardino, CA PMSA	10.4	9
Sacramento, CA	4.9	24
Salt Lake City-Ogden, UT	9.1	11
San Antonio, TX	11.8	5
San Diego, CA	13.5	3
San Francisco, CA PMSA	10.1	10
San Jose, CA PMSA	6.7	21
Tampa-Saint Petersburg- Clearwater, FL	10.4	9
Washington, DC	11.3	6

Source: U.S. Department of Labor, Bureau of Labor Statistics, Geographic Profile of Employment and Unemployment, 1994, Bulletin 2469, Washington, D.C.: U.S. Government Printing Office, December 1995, p. 103. Notes: "CMSA" stands for "Consolidated Metropolitan Statistical Area." "MSA" stands for "Metropolitan Statistical Area." "PMSA" stands for "Primary Metropolitan Statistical Area."

★972★
Distribution of Employed Hispanics, By Occupation
Percent Distribution of Employed Hispanic Persons in Selected MSAs, 1994, By Occupation: Service Occupations

MSA	Percent	Rank
Anaheim-Santa Ana, CA PMSA	24.1	7
Bergen-Passaic, NJ PMSA	14.6	23
Boston, MA PMSA	30.4	2
Chicago, IL PMSA	16.8	18
Dallas-Fort Worth, TX CMSA	18.2	16
Denver-Boulder, CO CMSA	19.5	14
Detroit, MI PMSA	14.5	24
Fort Lauderdale-Hollywood- Pompano Beach, FL PMSA	17.3	17

[Continued]

★972★

Percent Distribution of Employed Hispanic Persons in Selected MSAs, 1994, By Occupation: Service Occupations
[Continued]

MSA	Percent	Rank
Houston, TX PMSA	22.3	11
Los Angeles-Long Beach, CA PMSA	20.5	13
Miami-Hialeah, FL PMSA	16.2	19
Nassau-Suffolk, NY PMSA	11.0	26
New York, NY PMSA	28.7	3
Newark, NJ PMSA	14.9	22
Oakland, CA PMSA	23.9	8
Philadelphia, PA PMSA	11.5	25
Phoenix, AZ	19.4	15
Portland, OR PMSA	24.9	5
Providence-Pawtucket-Fall River, MA-RI CMSA	15.7	21
Riverside-San Bernardino, CA PMSA	15.8	20
Sacramento, CA	26.2	4
Salt Lake City-Ogden, UT	16.8	18
San Antonio, TX	22.0	12
San Diego, CA	23.4	9
San Francisco, CA PMSA	24.7	6
San Jose, CA PMSA	22.8	10
Tampa-Saint Petersburg-Clearwater, FL	15.8	20
Washington, DC	33.2	1

Source: U.S. Department of Labor, Bureau of Labor Statistics, *Geographic Profile of Employment and Unemployment, 1994,* Bulletin 2469, Washington, D.C.: U.S. Government Printing Office, December 1995, p. 103. *Notes:* "CMSA" stands for "Consolidated Metropolitan Statistical Area." "MSA" stands for "Metropolitan Statistical Area." "PMSA" stands for "Primary Metropolitan Statistical Area."

★973★
Distribution of Employed Hispanics, By Occupation

Percent Distribution of Employed Hispanic Persons in Selected MSAs, 1994, By Occupation: Technicians and Related Support

MSA	Percent	Rank
Anaheim-Santa Ana, CA PMSA	.6	14
Bergen-Passaic, NJ PMSA	4.1	3
Boston, MA PMSA	2.4	6
Chicago, IL PMSA	1.5	10
Dallas-Fort Worth, TX CMSA	.7	13
Denver-Boulder, CO CMSA	5.7	1
Detroit, MI PMSA	(3)	16
Fort Lauderdale-Hollywood-Pompano Beach, FL PMSA	2.4	6
Houston, TX PMSA	1.5	10
Los Angeles-Long Beach, CA PMSA	1.6	9
Miami-Hialeah, FL PMSA	1.9	8
Nassau-Suffolk, NY PMSA	4.5	2
New York, NY PMSA	2.3	7

[Continued]

★973★

Percent Distribution of Employed Hispanic Persons in Selected MSAs, 1994, By Occupation: Technicians and Related Support
[Continued]

MSA	Percent	Rank
Newark, NJ PMSA	1.6	9
Oakland, CA PMSA	.7	13
Philadelphia, PA PMSA	3.9	4
Phoenix, AZ	1.4	11
Portland, OR PMSA	1.3	12
Providence-Pawtucket-Fall River, MA-RI CMSA	(3)	16
Riverside-San Bernardino, CA PMSA	2.6	5
Sacramento, CA	1.4	11
Salt Lake City-Ogden, UT	1.4	11
San Antonio, TX	2.3	7
San Diego, CA	.7	13
San Francisco, CA PMSA	(3)	16
San Jose, CA PMSA	1.5	10
Tampa-Saint Petersburg-Clearwater, FL	.3	15
Washington, DC	2.6	5

Source: U.S. Department of Labor, Bureau of Labor Statistics, *Geographic Profile of Employment and Unemployment, 1994,* Bulletin 2469, Washington, D.C.: U.S. Government Printing Office, December 1995, p. 103. *Notes:* "CMSA" stands for "Consolidated Metropolitan Statistical Area." "MSA" stands for "Metropolitan Statistical Area." "PMSA" stands for "Primary Metropolitan Statistical Area."

★974★
Distribution of Employed Hispanics, By Occupation

Percent Distribution of Employed Hispanic Persons in Selected MSAs, 1994, By Occupation: Transportation and Material Moving

MSA	Percent	Rank
Anaheim-Santa Ana, CA PMSA	2.7	22
Bergen-Passaic, NJ PMSA	9.1	3
Boston, MA PMSA	2.8	21
Chicago, IL PMSA	3.9	17
Dallas-Fort Worth, TX CMSA	4.4	15
Denver-Boulder, CO CMSA	4.6	13
Detroit, MI PMSA	8.4	5
Fort Lauderdale-Hollywood-Pompano Beach, FL PMSA	4.1	16
Houston, TX PMSA	5.5	10
Los Angeles-Long Beach, CA PMSA	4.5	14
Miami-Hialeah, FL PMSA	5.3	11
Nassau-Suffolk, NY PMSA	6.0	9
New York, NY PMSA	4.4	15
Newark, NJ PMSA	8.7	4
Oakland, CA PMSA	9.4	1
Philadelphia, PA PMSA	5.5	10
Phoenix, AZ	2.8	21
Portland, OR PMSA	2.0	24
Providence-Pawtucket-Fall River, MA-RI CMSA	2.3	23

[Continued]

★974★

Percent Distribution of Employed Hispanic Persons in Selected MSAs, 1994, By Occupation: Transportation and Material Moving
[Continued]

MSA	Percent	Rank
Riverside-San Bernardino, CA PMSA	6.6	6
Sacramento, CA	3.0	20
Salt Lake City-Ogden, UT	3.7	18
San Antonio, TX	6.3	8
San Diego, CA	4.7	12
San Francisco, CA PMSA	9.2	2
San Jose, CA PMSA	3.2	19
Tampa-Saint Petersburg-Clearwater, FL	6.5	7
Washington, DC	2.8	21

Source: U.S. Department of Labor, Bureau of Labor Statistics, *Geographic Profile of Employment and Unemployment, 1994,* Bulletin 2469, Washington, D.C.: U.S. Government Printing Office, December 1995, p. 103. *Notes:* "CMSA" stands for "Consolidated Metropolitan Statistical Area." "MSA" stands for "Metropolitan Statistical Area." "PMSA" stands for "Primary Metropolitan Statistical Area."

★975★

Distribution of Employed Persons, By Race and Occupation

Percent Distribution of Employed Black Persons in Selected Cities, 1994, By Occupation: Administrative Support, Including Clerical

City	Percent	Rank
Baltimore, MD	25.1	2
Chicago, IL	21.7	7
Cleveland, OH	24.6	3
Dallas, TX	18.9	8
Detroit, MI	18.2	10
Houston, TX	23.7	4
Indianapolis, IN	27.8	1
Los Angeles, CA	22.2	5
Milwaukee, WI	18.1	11
New York, NY	22.1	6
Philadelphia, PA	18.6	9
Washington, DC	23.7	4

Source: U.S. Department of Labor, Bureau of Labor Statistics, *Geographic Profile of Employment and Unemployment, 1994,* Bulletin 2469, Washington, D.C.: U.S. Government Printing Office, December 1995, p. 103.

★976★

Distribution of Employed Persons, By Race and Occupation

Percent Distribution of Employed Black Persons in Selected Cities, 1994, By Occupation: Executive, Administrative, and Managerial

City	Percent	Rank
Baltimore, MD	9.7	5
Chicago, IL	8.1	9
Cleveland, OH	4.1	12
Dallas, TX	11.2	3
Detroit, MI	9.9	4
Houston, TX	9.5	6
Indianapolis, IN	5.8	11
Los Angeles, CA	14.4	1
Milwaukee, WI	6.9	10
New York, NY	8.7	7
Philadelphia, PA	8.3	8
Washington, DC	12.2	2

Source: U.S. Department of Labor, Bureau of Labor Statistics, *Geographic Profile of Employment and Unemployment, 1994,* Bulletin 2469, Washington, D.C.: U.S. Government Printing Office, December 1995, p. 103.

★977★

Distribution of Employed Persons, By Race and Occupation

Percent Distribution of Employed Black Persons in Selected Cities, 1994, By Occupation: Handlers, Equipment Cleaners, Helpers, and Laborers

City	Percent	Rank
Baltimore, MD	5.5	5
Chicago, IL	6.1	4
Cleveland, OH	6.2	3
Dallas, TX	4.5	8
Detroit, MI	3.6	10
Houston, TX	6.7	2
Indianapolis, IN	9.9	1
Los Angeles, CA	4.6	7
Milwaukee, WI	4.5	8
New York, NY	3.7	9
Philadelphia, PA	4.9	6
Washington, DC	3.2	11

Source: U.S. Department of Labor, Bureau of Labor Statistics, *Geographic Profile of Employment and Unemployment, 1994,* Bulletin 2469, Washington, D.C.: U.S. Government Printing Office, December 1995, p. 103.

★978★

Distribution of Employed Persons, By Race and Occupation

Percent Distribution of Employed Black Persons in Selected Cities, 1994, By Occupation: Machine Operators, Assemblers, and Inspectors

City	Percent	Rank
Baltimore, MD	3.3	9
Chicago, IL	4.9	6
Cleveland, OH	6.2	4
Dallas, TX	4.1	8

[Continued]

★978★

Percent Distribution of Employed Black Persons in Selected Cities, 1994, By Occupation: Machine Operators, Assemblers, and Inspectors

[Continued]

City	Percent	Rank
Detroit, MI	13.3	1
Houston, TX	3.0	10
Indianapolis, IN	12.4	2
Los Angeles, CA	1.8	12
Milwaukee, WI	8.7	3
New York, NY	4.2	7
Philadelphia, PA	5.6	5
Washington, DC	2.0	11

Source: U.S. Department of Labor, Bureau of Labor Statistics, *Geographic Profile of Employment and Unemployment, 1994,* Bulletin 2469, Washington, D.C.: U.S. Government Printing Office, December 1995, p. 103.

★979★

Distribution of Employed Persons, By Race and Occupation

Percent Distribution of Employed Black Persons in Selected Cities, 1994, By Occupation: Precision Production, Craft, and Repair

City	Percent	Rank
Baltimore, MD	7.1	5
Chicago, IL	6.8	7
Cleveland, OH	2.8	10
Dallas, TX	8.7	1
Detroit, MI	7.8	2
Houston, TX	5.4	9
Indianapolis, IN	5.9	8
Los Angeles, CA	7.3	4
Milwaukee, WI	7.1	5
New York, NY	7.7	3
Philadelphia, PA	7.7	3
Washington, DC	7.0	6

Source: U.S. Department of Labor, Bureau of Labor Statistics, *Geographic Profile of Employment and Unemployment, 1994,* Bulletin 2469, Washington, D.C.: U.S. Government Printing Office, December 1995, p. 103.

★980★

Distribution of Employed Persons, By Race and Occupation

Percent Distribution of Employed Black Persons in Selected Cities, 1994, By Occupation: Professional Specialty

City	Percent	Rank
Baltimore, MD	6.8	9
Chicago, IL	15.8	1
Cleveland, OH	6.2	10
Dallas, TX	5.9	11
Detroit, MI	10.2	6
Houston, TX	7.4	8
Indianapolis, IN	1.6	12
Los Angeles, CA	12.0	5
Milwaukee, WI	9.8	7

[Continued]

★980★

Percent Distribution of Employed Black Persons in Selected Cities, 1994, By Occupation: Professional Specialty

[Continued]

City	Percent	Rank
New York, NY	12.2	4
Philadelphia, PA	13.0	3
Washington, DC	13.8	2

Source: U.S. Department of Labor, Bureau of Labor Statistics, *Geographic Profile of Employment and Unemployment, 1994,* Bulletin 2469, Washington, D.C.: U.S. Government Printing Office, December 1995, p. 103.

★981★

Distribution of Employed Persons, By Race and Occupation

Percent Distribution of Employed Black Persons in Selected Cities, 1994, By Occupation: Sales

City	Percent	Rank
Baltimore, MD	8.0	6
Chicago, IL	7.9	7
Cleveland, OH	9.7	4
Dallas, TX	9.8	3
Detroit, MI	7.8	8
Houston, TX	11.2	2
Indianapolis, IN	6.1	11
Los Angeles, CA	9.3	5
Milwaukee, WI	14.3	1
New York, NY	6.5	9
Philadelphia, PA	6.3	10
Washington, DC	6.3	10

Source: U.S. Department of Labor, Bureau of Labor Statistics, *Geographic Profile of Employment and Unemployment, 1994,* Bulletin 2469, Washington, D.C.: U.S. Government Printing Office, December 1995, p. 103.

★982★

Distribution of Employed Persons, By Race and Occupation

Percent Distribution of Employed Black Persons in Selected Cities, 1994, By Occupation: Service Occupations

City	Percent	Rank
Baltimore, MD	25.1	5
Chicago, IL	19.8	9
Cleveland, OH	29.6	1
Dallas, TX	27.1	3
Detroit, MI	21.4	8
Houston, TX	18.3	12
Indianapolis, IN	24.4	6
Los Angeles, CA	19.2	10
Milwaukee, WI	18.7	11
New York, NY	27.6	2
Philadelphia, PA	26.4	4
Washington, DC	21.7	7

Source: U.S. Department of Labor, Bureau of Labor Statistics, *Geographic Profile of Employment and Unemployment, 1994,* Bulletin 2469, Washington, D.C.: U.S. Government Printing Office, December 1995, p. 103.

★983★

Distribution of Employed Persons, By Race and Occupation

Percent Distribution of Employed Black Persons in Selected Cities, 1994, By Occupation: Technicians and Related Support

City	Percent	Rank
Baltimore, MD	1.9	8
Chicago, IL	3.6	4
Cleveland, OH	.3	11
Dallas, TX	1.4	10
Detroit, MI	2.8	6
Houston, TX	4.4	1
Indianapolis, IN	3.2	5
Los Angeles, CA	4.2	2
Milwaukee, WI	1.7	9
New York, NY	2.6	7
Philadelphia, PA	2.8	6
Washington, DC	4.1	3

Source: U.S. Department of Labor, Bureau of Labor Statistics, *Geographic Profile of Employment and Unemployment, 1994*, Bulletin 2469, Washington, D.C.: U.S. Government Printing Office, December 1995, p. 103.

★984★

Distribution of Employed Persons, By Race and Occupation

Percent Distribution of Employed Black Persons in Selected Cities, 1994, By Occupation: Transportation and Material Moving

City	Percent	Rank
Baltimore, MD	7.3	4
Chicago, IL	4.7	8
Cleveland, OH	8.9	2
Dallas, TX	6.5	5
Detroit, MI	4.4	10
Houston, TX	8.6	3
Indianapolis, IN	(3)	12
Los Angeles, CA	3.8	11
Milwaukee, WI	10.2	1
New York, NY	4.5	9
Philadelphia, PA	6.3	6
Washington, DC	5.0	7

Source: U.S. Department of Labor, Bureau of Labor Statistics, *Geographic Profile of Employment and Unemployment, 1994*, Bulletin 2469, Washington, D.C.: U.S. Government Printing Office, December 1995, p. 103.

★985★

Distribution of Employed Persons, By Race and Occupation

Percent Distribution of Employed Black Persons in Selected MSAs, 1994, By Occupation: Administrative Support, Including Clerical

MSA	Percent	Rank
Atlanta, GA	17.9	24
Baltimore, MD	22.8	10
Bergen-Passaic, NJ PMSA	22.7	11
Boston, MA PMSA	20.9	15
Charlotte-Gastonia-Rock Hill, NC-SC	13.7	30

[Continued]

★985★

Percent Distribution of Employed Black Persons in Selected MSAs, 1994, By Occupation: Administrative Support, Including Clerical
[Continued]

MSA	Percent	Rank
Chicago, IL PMSA	22.2	12
Cincinnati, OH PMSA	18.7	21
Cleveland, OH PMSA	24.4	6
Columbus, OH	24.8	5
Dallas-Fort Worth, TX CMSA	18.5	22
Denver-Boulder, CO CMSA	29.8	1
Detroit, MI PMSA	17.5	27
Fort Lauderdale-Hollywood-Pompano Beach, FL PMSA	18.4	23
Houston, TX PMSA	20.9	15
Kansas City, KS-MO	23.6	9
Los Angeles-Long Beach, CA PMSA	23.8	8
Memphis, TN	14.7	29
Miami-Hialeah, FL PMSA	16.3	28
Milwaukee, WI PMSA	17.7	25
Minneapolis-Saint Paul, MN	20.9	15
Nassau-Suffolk, NY PMSA	26.9	2
New Orleans, LA	20.3	17
New York, NY PMSA	21.5	14
Newark, NJ PMSA	20.3	17
Norfolk-Virginia Beach-Newport News, VA	17.6	26
Oakland, CA PMSA	25.3	4
Oklahoma City, OK	21.6	13
Philadelphia, PA PMSA	19.7	20
Pittsburgh-Beaver Valley, PA	20.2	18
Portland, OR PMSA	9.4	33
Providence-Pawtucket-Fall River, MA-RI CMSA	12.4	31
Riverside-San Bernardino, CA PMSA	10.4	32
Rochester, NY	8.0	34
Saint Louis, MO-IL	20.0	19
San Diego, CA	25.4	3
Tampa-Saint Petersburg-Clearwater, FL	20.7	16
Washington, DC	24.3	7

Source: U.S. Department of Labor, Bureau of Labor Statistics, *Geographic Profile of Employment and Unemployment, 1994*, Bulletin 2469, Washington, D.C.: U.S. Government Printing Office, December 1995, p. 103. *Notes:* "CMSA" stands for "Consolidated Metropolitan Statistical Area." "MSA" stands for "Metropolitan Statistical Area." "PMSA" stands for "Primary Metropolitan Statistical Area."

★986★

Distribution of Employed Persons, By Race and Occupation

Percent Distribution of Employed Black Persons in Selected MSAs, 1994, By Occupation: Executive, Administrative, and Managerial

MSA	Percent	Rank
Atlanta, GA	12.3	9
Baltimore, MD	11.2	13
Bergen-Passaic, NJ PMSA	15.1	3
Boston, MA PMSA	10.4	17
Charlotte-Gastonia-Rock Hill, NC-SC	5.3	30
Chicago, IL PMSA	9.7	18
Cincinnati, OH PMSA	7.3	24
Cleveland, OH PMSA	7.8	22
Columbus, OH	12.9	6
Dallas-Fort Worth, TX CMSA	10.8	15
Denver-Boulder, CO CMSA	4.3	33
Detroit, MI PMSA	11.1	14
Fort Lauderdale-Hollywood-Pompano Beach, FL PMSA	5.1	31
Houston, TX PMSA	8.6	20
Kansas City, KS-MO	12.8	7
Los Angeles-Long Beach, CA PMSA	12.7	8
Memphis, TN	7.5	23
Miami-Hialeah, FL PMSA	10.5	16
Milwaukee, WI PMSA	7.2	25
Minneapolis-Saint Paul, MN	13.2	5
Nassau-Suffolk, NY PMSA	11.7	11
New Orleans, LA	6.5	28
New York, NY PMSA	8.9	19
Newark, NJ PMSA	11.6	12
Norfolk-Virginia Beach-Newport News, VA	6.8	27
Oakland, CA PMSA	12.2	10
Oklahoma City, OK	6.9	26
Philadelphia, PA PMSA	7.3	24
Pittsburgh-Beaver Valley, PA	5.7	29
Portland, OR PMSA	12.3	9
Providence-Pawtucket-Fall River, MA-RI CMSA	1.4	34
Riverside-San Bernardino, CA PMSA	20.4	1
Rochester, NY	8.1	21
Saint Louis, MO-IL	4.5	32
San Diego, CA	13.7	4
Tampa-Saint Petersburg-Clearwater, FL	7.8	22
Washington, DC	15.6	2

Source: U.S. Department of Labor, Bureau of Labor Statistics, *Geographic Profile of Employment and Unemployment, 1994*, Bulletin 2469, Washington, D.C.: U.S. Government Printing Office, December 1995, p. 103. *Notes:* "CMSA" stands for "Consolidated Metropolitan Statistical Area." "MSA" stands for "Metropolitan Statistical Area." "PMSA" stands for "Primary Metropolitan Statistical Area."

★987★

Distribution of Employed Persons, By Race and Occupation

Percent Distribution of Employed Black Persons in Selected MSAs, 1994, By Occupation: Handlers, Equipment Cleaners, Helpers, and Laborers

MSA	Percent	Rank
Atlanta, GA	5.7	12
Baltimore, MD	5.9	11
Bergen-Passaic, NJ PMSA	4.5	16
Boston, MA PMSA	3.5	24
Charlotte-Gastonia-Rock Hill, NC-SC	11.3	2
Chicago, IL PMSA	6.5	8
Cincinnati, OH PMSA	11.8	1
Cleveland, OH PMSA	4.4	17
Columbus, OH	4.3	18
Dallas-Fort Worth, TX CMSA	6.1	10
Denver-Boulder, CO CMSA	7.3	7
Detroit, MI PMSA	3.6	23
Fort Lauderdale-Hollywood-Pompano Beach, FL PMSA	9.8	4
Houston, TX PMSA	5.6	13
Kansas City, KS-MO	4.3	18
Los Angeles-Long Beach, CA PMSA	3.8	21
Memphis, TN	10.8	3
Miami-Hialeah, FL PMSA	7.3	7
Milwaukee, WI PMSA	4.5	16
Minneapolis-Saint Paul, MN	.4	29
Nassau-Suffolk, NY PMSA	3.4	25
New Orleans, LA	2.5	26
New York, NY PMSA	3.6	23
Newark, NJ PMSA	6.2	9
Norfolk-Virginia Beach-Newport News, VA	9.0	5
Oakland, CA PMSA	10.8	3
Oklahoma City, OK	2.2	28
Philadelphia, PA PMSA	4.1	19
Pittsburgh-Beaver Valley, PA	7.9	6
Portland, OR PMSA	3.9	20
Providence-Pawtucket-Fall River, MA-RI CMSA	5.6	13
Riverside-San Bernardino, CA PMSA	3.8	21
Rochester, NY	3.7	22
Saint Louis, MO-IL	4.6	15
San Diego, CA	4.6	15
Tampa-Saint Petersburg-Clearwater, FL	5.3	14
Washington, DC	2.3	27

Source: U.S. Department of Labor, Bureau of Labor Statistics, *Geographic Profile of Employment and Unemployment, 1994*, Bulletin 2469, Washington, D.C.: U.S. Government Printing Office, December 1995, p. 103. *Notes:* "CMSA" stands for "Consolidated Metropolitan Statistical Area." "MSA" stands for "Metropolitan Statistical Area." "PMSA" stands for "Primary Metropolitan Statistical Area."

★988★

Distribution of Employed Persons, By Race and Occupation

Percent Distribution of Employed Black Persons in Selected MSAs, 1994, By Occupation: Machine Operators, Assemblers, and Inspectors

MSA	Percent	Rank
Atlanta, GA	7.9	12
Baltimore, MD	2.8	26
Bergen-Passaic, NJ PMSA	5.9	16
Boston, MA PMSA	6.7	14
Charlotte-Gastonia-Rock Hill, NC-SC	17.9	1
Chicago, IL PMSA	3.9	23
Cincinnati, OH PMSA	4.2	21
Cleveland, OH PMSA	5.8	17
Columbus, OH	8.3	10
Dallas-Fort Worth, TX CMSA	6.0	15
Denver-Boulder, CO CMSA	9.6	7
Detroit, MI PMSA	12.2	4
Fort Lauderdale-Hollywood-Pompano Beach, FL PMSA	3.0	25
Houston, TX PMSA	4.0	22
Kansas City, KS-MO	4.2	21
Los Angeles-Long Beach, CA PMSA	2.4	28
Memphis, TN	10.0	5
Miami-Hialeah, FL PMSA	2.4	28
Milwaukee, WI PMSA	8.5	9
Minneapolis-Saint Paul, MN	9.2	8
Nassau-Suffolk, NY PMSA	2.7	27
New Orleans, LA	4.0	22
New York, NY PMSA	4.2	21
Newark, NJ PMSA	5.5	19
Norfolk-Virginia Beach-Newport News, VA	5.5	19
Oakland, CA PMSA	7.0	13
Oklahoma City, OK	5.5	19
Philadelphia, PA PMSA	5.6	18
Pittsburgh-Beaver Valley, PA	5.2	20
Portland, OR PMSA	9.9	6
Providence-Pawtucket-Fall River, MA-RI CMSA	13.5	3
Riverside-San Bernardino, CA PMSA	3.6	24
Rochester, NY	16.9	2
Saint Louis, MO-IL	8.0	11
San Diego, CA	3.0	25
Tampa-Saint Petersburg-Clearwater, FL	5.6	18
Washington, DC	1.0	29

Source: U.S. Department of Labor, Bureau of Labor Statistics, *Geographic Profile of Employment and Unemployment, 1994*, Bulletin 2469, Washington, D.C.: U.S. Government Printing Office, December 1995, p. 103. *Notes:* "CMSA" stands for "Consolidated Metropolitan Statistical Area." "MSA" stands for "Metropolitan Statistical Area." "PMSA" stands for "Primary Metropolitan Statistical Area."

★989★

Distribution of Employed Persons, By Race and Occupation

Percent Distribution of Employed Black Persons in Selected MSAs, 1994, By Occupation: Precision Production, Craft, and Repair

MSA	Percent	Rank
Atlanta, GA	7.0	19
Baltimore, MD	5.6	23
Bergen-Passaic, NJ PMSA	6.9	20
Boston, MA PMSA	4.2	25
Charlotte-Gastonia-Rock Hill, NC-SC	6.9	20
Chicago, IL PMSA	7.6	17
Cincinnati, OH PMSA	8.2	14
Cleveland, OH PMSA	3.7	28
Columbus, OH	8.2	14
Dallas-Fort Worth, TX CMSA	10.5	4
Denver-Boulder, CO CMSA	3.9	27
Detroit, MI PMSA	8.4	12
Fort Lauderdale-Hollywood-Pompano Beach, FL PMSA	12.0	2
Houston, TX PMSA	5.6	23
Kansas City, KS-MO	8.3	13
Los Angeles-Long Beach, CA PMSA	9.4	9
Memphis, TN	7.0	19
Miami-Hialeah, FL PMSA	7.6	17
Milwaukee, WI PMSA	6.9	20
Minneapolis-Saint Paul, MN	9.9	7
Nassau-Suffolk, NY PMSA	10.0	6
New Orleans, LA	9.4	9
New York, NY PMSA	7.9	16
Newark, NJ PMSA	8.7	11
Norfolk-Virginia Beach-Newport News, VA	14.3	1
Oakland, CA PMSA	9.5	8
Oklahoma City, OK	11.2	3
Philadelphia, PA PMSA	7.4	18
Pittsburgh-Beaver Valley, PA	2.5	29
Portland, OR PMSA	4.0	26
Providence-Pawtucket-Fall River, MA-RI CMSA	9.0	10
Riverside-San Bernardino, CA PMSA	6.1	21
Rochester, NY	5.7	22
Saint Louis, MO-IL	4.5	24
San Diego, CA	6.9	20
Tampa-Saint Petersburg-Clearwater, FL	10.2	5
Washington, DC	8.1	15

Source: U.S. Department of Labor, Bureau of Labor Statistics, *Geographic Profile of Employment and Unemployment, 1994*, Bulletin 2469, Washington, D.C.: U.S. Government Printing Office, December 1995, p. 103. *Notes:* "CMSA" stands for "Consolidated Metropolitan Statistical Area." "MSA" stands for "Metropolitan Statistical Area." "PMSA" stands for "Primary Metropolitan Statistical Area."

★990★
Distribution of Employed Persons, By Race and Occupation

Percent Distribution of Employed Black Persons in Selected MSAs, 1994, By Occupation: Professional Specialties

MSA	Percent	Rank
Atlanta, GA	10.5	17
Baltimore, MD	11.4	15
Bergen-Passaic, NJ PMSA	9.0	22
Boston, MA PMSA	14.9	4
Charlotte-Gastonia-Rock Hill, NC-SC	6.9	28
Chicago, IL PMSA	14.0	6
Cincinnati, OH PMSA	12.6	10
Cleveland, OH PMSA	9.2	21
Columbus, OH	10.1	18
Dallas-Fort Worth, TX CMSA	7.7	26
Denver-Boulder, CO CMSA	4.4	33
Detroit, MI PMSA	11.7	13
Fort Lauderdale-Hollywood-Pompano Beach, FL PMSA	8.6	23
Houston, TX PMSA	9.9	19
Kansas City, KS-MO	8.2	24
Los Angeles-Long Beach, CA PMSA	13.1	7
Memphis, TN	7.8	25
Miami-Hialeah, FL PMSA	10.7	16
Milwaukee, WI PMSA	9.9	19
Minneapolis-Saint Paul, MN	4.9	32
Nassau-Suffolk, NY PMSA	9.3	20
New Orleans, LA	11.5	14
New York, NY PMSA	12.5	11
Newark, NJ PMSA	12.7	9
Norfolk-Virginia Beach-Newport News, VA	12.3	12
Oakland, CA PMSA	7.2	27
Oklahoma City, OK	5.8	30
Philadelphia, PA PMSA	14.3	5
Pittsburgh-Beaver Valley, PA	12.7	9
Portland, OR PMSA	5.6	31
Providence-Pawtucket-Fall River, MA-RI CMSA	15.6	3
Riverside-San Bernardino, CA PMSA	21.3	1
Rochester, NY	11.5	14
Saint Louis, MO-IL	17.8	2
San Diego, CA	6.6	29
Tampa-Saint Petersburg-Clearwater, FL	13.0	8
Washington, DC	13.0	8

Source: U.S. Department of Labor, Bureau of Labor Statistics, *Geographic Profile of Employment and Unemployment, 1994,* Bulletin 2469, Washington, D.C.: U.S. Government Printing Office, December 1995, p. 103. *Notes:* "CMSA" stands for "Consolidated Metropolitan Statistical Area." "MSA" stands for "Metropolitan Statistical Area." "PMSA" stands for "Primary Metropolitan Statistical Area."

★991★
Distribution of Employed Persons, By Race and Occupation

Percent Distribution of Employed Black Persons in Selected MSAs, 1994, By Occupation: Sales

MSA	Percent	Rank
Atlanta, GA	10.8	6
Baltimore, MD	7.5	16
Bergen-Passaic, NJ PMSA	7.0	19
Boston, MA PMSA	10.0	9
Charlotte-Gastonia-Rock Hill, NC-SC	7.0	19
Chicago, IL PMSA	9.0	12
Cincinnati, OH PMSA	6.2	24
Cleveland, OH PMSA	9.9	10
Columbus, OH	4.5	27
Dallas-Fort Worth, TX CMSA	9.1	11
Denver-Boulder, CO CMSA	10.7	7
Detroit, MI PMSA	8.5	13
Fort Lauderdale-Hollywood-Pompano Beach, FL PMSA	12.3	3
Houston, TX PMSA	8.5	13
Kansas City, KS-MO	4.0	29
Los Angeles-Long Beach, CA PMSA	9.9	10
Memphis, TN	12.2	4
Miami-Hialeah, FL PMSA	7.3	17
Milwaukee, WI PMSA	14.0	2
Minneapolis-Saint Paul, MN	6.7	21
Nassau-Suffolk, NY PMSA	6.4	23
New Orleans, LA	11.5	5
New York, NY PMSA	6.5	22
Newark, NJ PMSA	4.6	26
Norfolk-Virginia Beach-Newport News, VA	7.7	15
Oakland, CA PMSA	4.8	25
Oklahoma City, OK	7.1	18
Philadelphia, PA PMSA	8.0	14
Pittsburgh-Beaver Valley, PA	10.2	8
Portland, OR PMSA	17.8	1
Providence-Pawtucket-Fall River, MA-RI CMSA	4.2	28
Riverside-San Bernardino, CA PMSA	6.4	23
Rochester, NY	6.9	20
Saint Louis, MO-IL	9.0	12
San Diego, CA	8.5	13
Tampa-Saint Petersburg-Clearwater, FL	8.5	13
Washington, DC	8.0	14

Source: U.S. Department of Labor, Bureau of Labor Statistics, *Geographic Profile of Employment and Unemployment, 1994,* Bulletin 2469, Washington, D.C.: U.S. Government Printing Office, December 1995, p. 103. *Notes:* "CMSA" stands for "Consolidated Metropolitan Statistical Area." "MSA" stands for "Metropolitan Statistical Area." "PMSA" stands for "Primary Metropolitan Statistical Area."

★992★

Distribution of Employed Persons, By Race and Occupation

Percent Distribution of Employed Black Persons in Selected MSAs, 1994, By Occupation: Service Occupations

MSA	Percent	Rank
Atlanta, GA	19.3	27
Baltimore, MD	22.7	16
Bergen-Passaic, NJ PMSA	20.6	21
Boston, MA PMSA	22.8	15
Charlotte-Gastonia-Rock Hill, NC-SC	21.7	18
Chicago, IL PMSA	18.6	30
Cincinnati, OH PMSA	23.1	14
Cleveland, OH PMSA	23.9	12
Columbus, OH	19.4	26
Dallas-Fort Worth, TX CMSA	21.1	19
Denver-Boulder, CO CMSA	25.9	7
Detroit, MI PMSA	19.8	24
Fort Lauderdale-Hollywood-Pompano Beach, FL PMSA	23.5	13
Houston, TX PMSA	18.8	28
Kansas City, KS-MO	29.0	4
Los Angeles-Long Beach, CA PMSA	16.5	32
Memphis, TN	20.0	23
Miami-Hialeah, FL PMSA	25.9	7
Milwaukee, WI PMSA	19.6	25
Minneapolis-Saint Paul, MN	25.8	8
Nassau-Suffolk, NY PMSA	22.6	17
New Orleans, LA	24.2	11
New York, NY PMSA	27.9	5
Newark, NJ PMSA	20.1	22
Norfolk-Virginia Beach-Newport News, VA	21.0	20
Oakland, CA PMSA	14.6	35
Oklahoma City, OK	34.3	2
Philadelphia, PA PMSA	24.8	9
Pittsburgh-Beaver Valley, PA	26.2	6
Portland, OR PMSA	24.7	10
Providence-Pawtucket-Fall River, MA-RI CMSA	34.4	1
Riverside-San Bernardino, CA PMSA	15.6	33
Rochester, NY	31.5	3
Saint Louis, MO-IL	18.7	29
San Diego, CA	18.4	31
Tampa-Saint Petersburg-Clearwater, FL	18.8	28
Washington, DC	15.4	34

Source: U.S. Department of Labor, Bureau of Labor Statistics, *Geographic Profile of Employment and Unemployment, 1994,* Bulletin 2469, Washington, D.C.: U.S. Government Printing Office, December 1995, p. 103. *Notes:* "CMSA" stands for "Consolidated Metropolitan Statistical Area." "MSA" stands for "Metropolitan Statistical Area." "PMSA" stands for "Primary Metropolitan Statistical Area."

★993★

Distribution of Employed Persons, By Race and Occupation

Percent Distribution of Employed Black Persons in Selected MSAs, 1994, By Occupation: Technicians and Related Support

MSA	Percent	Rank
Atlanta, GA	2.1	20
Baltimore, MD	2.0	21
Bergen-Passaic, NJ PMSA	4.3	6
Boston, MA PMSA	2.8	15
Charlotte-Gastonia-Rock Hill, NC-SC	1.7	23
Chicago, IL PMSA	3.4	12
Cincinnati, OH PMSA	3.6	10
Cleveland, OH PMSA	2.3	19
Columbus, OH	2.9	14
Dallas-Fort Worth, TX CMSA	1.9	22
Denver-Boulder, CO CMSA	.5	27
Detroit, MI PMSA	2.6	16
Fort Lauderdale-Hollywood-Pompano Beach, FL PMSA	1.9	22
Houston, TX PMSA	5.6	3
Kansas City, KS-MO	2.8	15
Los Angeles-Long Beach, CA PMSA	3.8	9
Memphis, TN	2.5	17
Miami-Hialeah, FL PMSA	1.2	26
Milwaukee, WI PMSA	1.6	24
Minneapolis-Saint Paul, MN	3.1	13
Nassau-Suffolk, NY PMSA	2.1	20
New Orleans, LA	2.4	18
New York, NY PMSA	2.6	16
Newark, NJ PMSA	3.5	11
Norfolk-Virginia Beach-Newport News, VA	1.5	25
Oakland, CA PMSA	3.5	11
Oklahoma City, OK	1.7	23
Philadelphia, PA PMSA	2.9	14
Pittsburgh-Beaver Valley, PA	4.1	8
Portland, OR PMSA	10.2	1
Providence-Pawtucket-Fall River, MA-RI CMSA	2.6	16
Riverside-San Bernardino, CA PMSA	5.3	4
Rochester, NY	4.2	7
Saint Louis, MO-IL	5.3	4
San Diego, CA	9.3	2
Tampa-Saint Petersburg-Clearwater, FL	2.0	21
Washington, DC	5.2	5

Source: U.S. Department of Labor, Bureau of Labor Statistics, *Geographic Profile of Employment and Unemployment, 1994,* Bulletin 2469, Washington, D.C.: U.S. Government Printing Office, December 1995, p. 103. *Notes:* "CMSA" stands for "Consolidated Metropolitan Statistical Area." "MSA" stands for "Metropolitan Statistical Area." "PMSA" stands for "Primary Metropolitan Statistical Area."

★994★

Distribution of Employed Persons, By Race and Occupation

Percent Distribution of Employed Black Persons in Selected MSAs, 1994, By Occupation: Transportation and Material Moving

MSA	Percent	Rank
Atlanta, GA	5.8	12
Baltimore, MD	7.2	6
Bergen-Passaic, NJ PMSA	3.9	20
Boston, MA PMSA	3.9	20
Charlotte-Gastonia-Rock Hill, NC-SC	5.9	11
Chicago, IL PMSA	4.8	15
Cincinnati, OH PMSA	4.3	17
Cleveland, OH PMSA	7.7	4
Columbus, OH	4.2	18
Dallas-Fort Worth, TX CMSA	6.6	7
Denver-Boulder, CO CMSA	1.9	26
Detroit, MI PMSA	4.0	19
Fort Lauderdale-Hollywood-Pompano Beach, FL PMSA	2.2	25
Houston, TX PMSA	10.4	1
Kansas City, KS-MO	1.7	27
Los Angeles-Long Beach, CA PMSA	3.9	20
Memphis, TN	6.2	10
Miami-Hialeah, FL PMSA	8.6	3
Milwaukee, WI PMSA	10.0	2
Minneapolis-Saint Paul, MN	5.8	12
Nassau-Suffolk, NY PMSA	4.9	14
New Orleans, LA	6.5	8
New York, NY PMSA	4.2	18
Newark, NJ PMSA	6.4	9
Norfolk-Virginia Beach-Newport News, VA	3.2	22
Oakland, CA PMSA	3.3	21
Oklahoma City, OK	3.1	23
Philadelphia, PA PMSA	5.7	13
Pittsburgh-Beaver Valley, PA	4.6	16
Portland, OR PMSA	(3)	28
Providence-Pawtucket-Fall River, MA-RI CMSA	(3)	28
Riverside-San Bernardino, CA PMSA	3.9	20
Rochester, NY	3.3	21
Saint Louis, MO-IL	7.6	5
San Diego, CA	3.0	24
Tampa-Saint Petersburg-Clearwater, FL	6.2	10
Washington, DC	6.6	7

Source: U.S. Department of Labor, Bureau of Labor Statistics, *Geographic Profile of Employment and Unemployment, 1994*, Bulletin 2469, Washington, D.C.: U.S. Government Printing Office, December 1995, p. 103. *Notes:* "CMSA" stands for "Consolidated Metropolitan Statistical Area." "MSA" stands for "Metropolitan Statistical Area." "PMSA" stands for "Primary Metropolitan Statistical Area."

★995★

Distribution of Employed Persons, By Race and Occupation

Percent Distribution of Employed White Persons in Selected Cities, 1994, By Occupation: Administrative Support, Including Clerical

City	Percent	Rank
Baltimore, MD	22.3	2
Chicago, IL	15.4	8
Cleveland, OH	13.4	14
Dallas, TX	12.6	15
Detroit, MI	11.7	16
Houston, TX	13.8	13
Indianapolis, IN	17.0	6
Los Angeles, CA	15.0	9
Milwaukee, WI	18.8	3
New York, NY	17.8	4
Philadelphia, PA	22.9	1
Phoenix, AZ	17.1	5
Saint Louis, MO	15.9	7
San Antonio, TX	14.3	10
San Diego, CA	14.0	12
San Francisco, CA	14.1	11
Washington, DC	8.4	17

Source: U.S. Department of Labor, Bureau of Labor Statistics, *Geographic Profile of Employment and Unemployment, 1994*, Bulletin 2469, Washington, D.C.: U.S. Government Printing Office, December 1995, p. 103.

★996★

Distribution of Employed Persons, By Race and Occupation

Percent Distribution of Employed White Persons in Selected Cities, 1994, By Occupation: Executive, Administrative, and Managerial

City	Percent	Rank
Baltimore, MD	12.9	10
Chicago, IL	14.0	8
Cleveland, OH	8.1	16
Dallas, TX	14.2	6
Detroit, MI	16.1	3
Houston, TX	12.6	11
Indianapolis, IN	14.1	7
Los Angeles, CA	12.3	12
Milwaukee, WI	15.8	4
New York, NY	15.7	5
Philadelphia, PA	11.4	13
Phoenix, AZ	13.8	9
Saint Louis, MO	10.1	14
San Antonio, TX	8.5	15
San Diego, CA	20.9	2
San Francisco, CA	12.3	12
Washington, DC	24.1	1

Source: U.S. Department of Labor, Bureau of Labor Statistics, *Geographic Profile of Employment and Unemployment, 1994*, Bulletin 2469, Washington, D.C.: U.S. Government Printing Office, December 1995, p. 103.

★997★

Distribution of Employed Persons, By Race and Occupation

Percent Distribution of Employed White Persons in Selected Cities, 1994, By Occupation: Handlers, Equipment Cleaners, Helpers, and Laborers

City	Percent	Rank
Baltimore, MD	3.0	12
Chicago, IL	5.6	4
Cleveland, OH	5.1	5
Dallas, TX	5.7	3
Detroit, MI	1.0	13
Houston, TX	7.9	1
Indianapolis, IN	4.4	8
Los Angeles, CA	4.6	7
Milwaukee, WI	4.1	9
New York, NY	3.3	11
Philadelphia, PA	4.1	9
Phoenix, AZ	3.9	10
Saint Louis, MO	7.9	1
San Antonio, TX	6.4	2
San Diego, CA	3.9	10
San Francisco, CA	4.9	6
Washington, DC	.7	14

Source: U.S. Department of Labor, Bureau of Labor Statistics, Geographic Profile of Employment and Unemployment, 1994, Bulletin 2469, Washington, D.C.: U.S. Government Printing Office, December 1995, p. 103.

★998★

Distribution of Employed Persons, By Race and Occupation

Percent Distribution of Employed White Persons in Selected Cities, 1994, By Occupation: Machine Operators, Assemblers, and Inspectors

City	Percent	Rank
Baltimore, MD	3.2	12
Chicago, IL	9.1	4
Cleveland, OH	9.3	3
Dallas, TX	7.8	5
Detroit, MI	11.3	1
Houston, TX	3.0	13
Indianapolis, IN	2.9	14
Los Angeles, CA	9.9	2
Milwaukee, WI	7.4	6
New York, NY	4.4	9
Philadelphia, PA	3.5	11
Phoenix, AZ	3.9	10
Saint Louis, MO	6.2	7
San Antonio, TX	5.0	8
San Diego, CA	1.5	15
San Francisco, CA	1.5	15
Washington, DC	.5	16

Source: U.S. Department of Labor, Bureau of Labor Statistics, Geographic Profile of Employment and Unemployment, 1994, Bulletin 2469, Washington, D.C.: U.S. Government Printing Office, December 1995, p. 103.

★999★

Distribution of Employed Persons, By Race and Occupation

Percent Distribution of Employed White Persons in Selected Cities, 1994, By Occupation: Precision Production, Craft, and Repair

City	Percent	Rank
Baltimore, MD	10.9	10
Chicago, IL	10.3	11
Cleveland, OH	23.3	1
Dallas, TX	12.4	6
Detroit, MI	18.2	2
Houston, TX	11.5	8
Indianapolis, IN	12.1	7
Los Angeles, CA	11.1	9
Milwaukee, WI	7.7	12
New York, NY	7.5	13
Philadelphia, PA	11.5	8
Phoenix, AZ	14.8	4
Saint Louis, MO	15.2	3
San Antonio, TX	12.8	5
San Diego, CA	5.2	15
San Francisco, CA	5.4	14
Washington, DC	2.9	16

Source: U.S. Department of Labor, Bureau of Labor Statistics, Geographic Profile of Employment and Unemployment, 1994, Bulletin 2469, Washington, D.C.: U.S. Government Printing Office, December 1995, p. 103.

★1000★

Distribution of Employed Persons, By Race and Occupation

Percent Distribution of Employed White Persons in Selected Cities, 1994, By Occupation: Professional Specialty

City	Percent	Rank
Baltimore, MD	18.5	5
Chicago, IL	16.5	7
Cleveland, OH	5.9	16
Dallas, TX	15.3	8
Detroit, MI	7.9	15
Houston, TX	12.9	11
Indianapolis, IN	15.2	9
Los Angeles, CA	14.4	10
Milwaukee, WI	16.8	6
New York, NY	18.9	4
Philadelphia, PA	14.4	10
Phoenix, AZ	12.0	12
Saint Louis, MO	9.9	14
San Antonio, TX	10.1	13
San Diego, CA	20.0	3
San Francisco, CA	26.3	2
Washington, DC	38.6	1

Source: U.S. Department of Labor, Bureau of Labor Statistics, Geographic Profile of Employment and Unemployment, 1994, Bulletin 2469, Washington, D.C.: U.S. Government Printing Office, December 1995, p. 103.

★1001★

Distribution of Employed Persons, By Race and Occupation

Percent Distribution of Employed White Persons in Selected Cities, 1994, By Occupation: Sales

City	Percent	Rank
Baltimore, MD	8.1	13
Chicago, IL	10.9	10
Cleveland, OH	7.8	14
Dallas, TX	11.6	9
Detroit, MI	10.4	11
Houston, TX	13.9	5
Indianapolis, IN	16.8	1
Los Angeles, CA	9.9	12
Milwaukee, WI	8.1	13
New York, NY	10.9	10
Philadelphia, PA	12.7	8
Phoenix, AZ	13.0	7
Saint Louis, MO	13.7	6
San Antonio, TX	15.0	2
San Diego, CA	14.4	3
San Francisco, CA	14.1	4
Washington, DC	7.1	15

Source: U.S. Department of Labor, Bureau of Labor Statistics, *Geographic Profile of Employment and Unemployment, 1994*, Bulletin 2469, Washington, D.C.: U.S. Government Printing Office, December 1995, p. 103.

★1002★

Distribution of Employed Persons, By Race and Occupation

Percent Distribution of Employed White Persons in Selected Cities, 1994, By Occupation: Service Occupations

City	Percent	Rank
Baltimore, MD	11.1	14
Chicago, IL	12.8	12
Cleveland, OH	17.6	3
Dallas, TX	11.4	13
Detroit, MI	18.0	2
Houston, TX	16.2	5
Indianapolis, IN	8.8	15
Los Angeles, CA	16.0	6
Milwaukee, WI	16.9	4
New York, NY	15.5	8
Philadelphia, PA	11.4	13
Phoenix, AZ	13.1	10
Saint Louis, MO	15.9	7
San Antonio, TX	18.8	1
San Diego, CA	12.9	11
San Francisco, CA	15.1	9
Washington, DC	12.9	11

Source: U.S. Department of Labor, Bureau of Labor Statistics, *Geographic Profile of Employment and Unemployment, 1994*, Bulletin 2469, Washington, D.C.: U.S. Government Printing Office, December 1995, p. 103.

★1003★

Distribution of Employed Persons, By Race and Occupation

Percent Distribution of Employed White Persons in Selected Cities, 1994, By Occupation: Technicians and Related Support

City	Percent	Rank
Baltimore, MD	4.4	2
Chicago, IL	2.0	9
Cleveland, OH	2.5	6
Dallas, TX	2.2	7
Detroit, MI	1.7	10
Houston, TX	2.5	6
Indianapolis, IN	4.8	1
Los Angeles, CA	2.0	9
Milwaukee, WI	1.7	10
New York, NY	2.5	6
Philadelphia, PA	3.7	4
Phoenix, AZ	3.3	5
Saint Louis, MO	3.3	5
San Antonio, TX	2.2	7
San Diego, CA	2.1	8
San Francisco, CA	2.2	7
Washington, DC	3.9	3

Source: U.S. Department of Labor, Bureau of Labor Statistics, *Geographic Profile of Employment and Unemployment, 1994*, Bulletin 2469, Washington, D.C.: U.S. Government Printing Office, December 1995, p. 103.

★1004★

Distribution of Employed Persons, By Race and Occupation

Percent Distribution of Employed White Persons in Selected Cities, 1994, By Occupation: Transportation and Material Moving

City	Percent	Rank
Baltimore, MD	3.0	9
Chicago, IL	2.7	11
Cleveland, OH	5.3	1
Dallas, TX	4.3	3
Detroit, MI	3.7	5
Houston, TX	3.4	6
Indianapolis, IN	2.9	10
Los Angeles, CA	2.4	12
Milwaukee, WI	2.3	13
New York, NY	3.4	6
Philadelphia, PA	4.1	4
Phoenix, AZ	3.1	8
Saint Louis, MO	2.0	14
San Antonio, TX	4.6	2
San Diego, CA	3.2	7
San Francisco, CA	4.6	2
Washington, DC	.6	15

Source: U.S. Department of Labor, Bureau of Labor Statistics, *Geographic Profile of Employment and Unemployment, 1994*, Bulletin 2469, Washington, D.C.: U.S. Government Printing Office, December 1995, p. 103.

★1005★

Distribution of Employed Persons, By Race and Occupation

Percent Distribution of Employed White Persons in Selected MSAs, 1994, By Occupation: Administrative Support, Including Clerical

MSA	Percent	Rank
Anaheim-Santa Ana, CA PMSA	15.3	23
Atlanta, GA	15.5	21
Baltimore, MD	15.6	20
Bergen-Passaic, NJ PMSA	16.3	14
Boston, MA PMSA	16.2	15
Buffalo-Niagara Falls, NY CMSA	13.3	34
Charlotte-Gastonia-Rock Hill, NC-SC	13.4	33
Chicago, IL PMSA	16.5	12
Cincinnati, OH PMSA	15.4	22
Cleveland, OH PMSA	13.7	31
Columbus, OH	16.8	10
Dallas-Fort Worth, TX CMSA	14.4	28
Dayton-Springfield, OH	13.4	33
Denver-Boulder, CO CMSA	15.7	19
Detroit, MI PMSA	14.8	26
Fort Lauderdale-Hollywood-Pompano Beach, FL PMSA	16.8	10
Hartford-New Britain-Middletown, CT CMSA	15.7	19
Houston, TX PMSA	16.1	16
Indianapolis, IN	15.6	20
Kansas City, KS-MO	19.1	1
Los Angeles-Long Beach, CA PMSA	15.9	18
Louisville, KY	17.0	9
Memphis, TN	18.9	2
Miami-Hialeah, FL PMSA	17.5	7
Milwaukee, WI PMSA	14.1	29
Minneapolis-Saint Paul, MN	17.9	6
Nassau-Suffolk, NY PMSA	18.8	3
New Orleans, LA	14.9	25
New York, NY PMSA	16.8	10
Newark, NJ PMSA	16.4	13
Norfolk-Virginia Beach-Newport News, VA	18.6	4
Oakland, CA PMSA	13.4	33
Oklahoma City, OK	13.2	35
Philadelphia, PA PMSA	18.5	5
Phoenix, AZ	16.6	11
Pittsburgh-Beaver Valley, PA	14.5	27
Portland, OR PMSA	16.0	17
Providence-Pawtucket-Fall River, MA-RI CMSA	15.0	24
Riverside-San Bernardino, CA PMSA	16.2	15
Rochester, NY	14.1	29
Sacramento, CA	16.4	13
Saint Louis, MO-IL	16.1	16
Salt Lake City-Ogden, UT	17.3	8
San Antonio, TX	16.0	17
San Diego, CA	15.5	21
San Francisco, CA PMSA	13.8	30
San Jose, CA PMSA	14.4	28
Seattle, WA PMSA	13.0	36

[Continued]

★1005★

Percent Distribution of Employed White Persons in Selected MSAs, 1994, By Occupation: Administrative Support, Including Clerical

[Continued]

MSA	Percent	Rank
Tampa-Saint Petersburg-Clearwater, FL	16.1	16
Washington, DC	13.6	32

Source: U.S. Department of Labor, Bureau of Labor Statistics, *Geographic Profile of Employment and Unemployment, 1994,* Bulletin 2469, Washington, D.C.: U.S. Government Printing Office, December 1995, p. 103. *Notes:* "CMSA" stands for "Consolidated Metropolitan Statistical Area." "MSA" stands for "Metropolitan Statistical Area." "PMSA" stands for "Primary Metropolitan Statistical Area."

★1006★

Distribution of Employed Persons, By Race and Occupation

Percent Distribution of Employed White Persons in Selected MSAs, 1994, By Occupation: Executive, Administrative, and Managerial

MSA	Percent	Rank
Anaheim-Santa Ana, CA PMSA	18.8	7
Atlanta, GA	20.7	2
Baltimore, MD	17.9	12
Bergen-Passaic, NJ PMSA	18.5	8
Boston, MA PMSA	17.8	13
Buffalo-Niagara Falls, NY CMSA	11.6	38
Charlotte-Gastonia-Rock Hill, NC-SC	16.6	18
Chicago, IL PMSA	16.3	20
Cincinnati, OH PMSA	13.7	32
Cleveland, OH PMSA	15.8	24
Columbus, OH	17.2	15
Dallas-Fort Worth, TX CMSA	17.1	16
Dayton-Springfield, OH	11.3	39
Denver-Boulder, CO CMSA	16.6	18
Detroit, MI PMSA	14.4	31
Fort Lauderdale-Hollywood-Pompano Beach, FL PMSA	16.5	19
Hartford-New Britain-Middletown, CT CMSA	15.0	29
Houston, TX PMSA	15.4	27
Indianapolis, IN	18.0	11
Kansas City, KS-MO	16.2	21
Los Angeles-Long Beach, CA PMSA	13.1	34
Louisville, KY	13.7	32
Memphis, TN	16.0	22
Miami-Hialeah, FL PMSA	12.3	37
Milwaukee, WI PMSA	16.2	21
Minneapolis-Saint Paul, MN	15.7	25
Nassau-Suffolk, NY PMSA	15.9	23
New Orleans, LA	19.8	4
New York, NY PMSA	16.8	17
Newark, NJ PMSA	18.3	10
Norfolk-Virginia Beach-Newport News, VA	12.6	36
Oakland, CA PMSA	18.4	9
Oklahoma City, OK	15.6	26

[Continued]

★1006★

Percent Distribution of Employed White Persons in Selected MSAs, 1994, By Occupation: Executive, Administrative, and Managerial

[Continued]

MSA	Percent	Rank
Philadelphia, PA PMSA	15.9	23
Phoenix, AZ	15.7	25
Pittsburgh-Beaver Valley, PA	12.8	35
Portland, OR PMSA	19.1	6
Providence-Pawtucket-Fall River, MA-RI CMSA	13.6	33
Riverside-San Bernardino, CA PMSA	13.1	34
Rochester, NY	13.1	34
Sacramento, CA	14.9	30
Saint Louis, MO-IL	15.3	28
Salt Lake City-Ogden, UT	15.8	24
San Antonio, TX	8.8	40
San Diego, CA	16.8	17
San Francisco, CA PMSA	19.9	3
San Jose, CA PMSA	19.2	5
Seattle, WA PMSA	17.3	14
Tampa-Saint Petersburg-Clearwater, FL	15.4	27
Washington, DC	23.7	1

Source: U.S. Department of Labor, Bureau of Labor Statistics, *Geographic Profile of Employment and Unemployment, 1994,* Bulletin 2469, Washington, D.C.: U.S. Government Printing Office, December 1995, p. 103. *Notes:* "CMSA" stands for "Consolidated Metropolitan Statistical Area." "MSA" stands for "Metropolitan Statistical Area." "PMSA" stands for "Primary Metropolitan Statistical Area."

★1007★

Distribution of Employed Persons, By Race and Occupation

Percent Distribution of Employed White Persons in Selected MSAs, 1994, By Occupation: Handlers, Equipment Cleaners, Helpers, and Laborers

MSA	Percent	Rank
Anaheim-Santa Ana, CA PMSA	4.0	11
Atlanta, GA	3.3	16
Baltimore, MD	1.9	24
Bergen-Passaic, NJ PMSA	3.0	19
Boston, MA PMSA	2.6	21
Buffalo-Niagara Falls, NY CMSA	3.1	18
Charlotte-Gastonia-Rock Hill, NC-SC	4.5	6
Chicago, IL PMSA	4.1	10
Cincinnati, OH PMSA	3.4	15
Cleveland, OH PMSA	3.3	16
Columbus, OH	4.6	5
Dallas-Fort Worth, TX CMSA	4.6	5
Dayton-Springfield, OH	5.4	1
Denver-Boulder, CO CMSA	3.0	19
Detroit, MI PMSA	3.4	15
Fort Lauderdale-Hollywood-Pompano Beach, FL PMSA	3.0	19
Hartford-New Britain-Middletown, CT CMSA	3.0	19

[Continued]

★1007★

Percent Distribution of Employed White Persons in Selected MSAs, 1994, By Occupation: Handlers, Equipment Cleaners, Helpers, and Laborers

[Continued]

MSA	Percent	Rank
Houston, TX PMSA	4.8	3
Indianapolis, IN	3.8	12
Kansas City, KS-MO	3.3	16
Los Angeles-Long Beach, CA PMSA	4.7	4
Louisville, KY	5.3	2
Memphis, TN	3.2	17
Miami-Hialeah, FL PMSA	4.2	9
Milwaukee, WI PMSA	3.2	17
Minneapolis-Saint Paul, MN	3.4	15
Nassau-Suffolk, NY PMSA	3.7	13
New Orleans, LA	2.8	20
New York, NY PMSA	2.8	20
Newark, NJ PMSA	3.7	13
Norfolk-Virginia Beach-Newport News, VA	2.3	23
Oakland, CA PMSA	3.8	12
Oklahoma City, OK	3.5	14
Philadelphia, PA PMSA	3.3	16
Phoenix, AZ	3.7	13
Pittsburgh-Beaver Valley, PA	4.3	8
Portland, OR PMSA	2.6	21
Providence-Pawtucket-Fall River, MA-RI CMSA	3.4	15
Riverside-San Bernardino, CA PMSA	3.7	13
Rochester, NY	2.6	21
Sacramento, CA	3.5	14
Saint Louis, MO-IL	4.4	7
Salt Lake City-Ogden, UT	4.3	8
San Antonio, TX	5.4	1
San Diego, CA	3.0	19
San Francisco, CA PMSA	3.5	14
San Jose, CA PMSA	2.6	21
Seattle, WA PMSA	4.4	7
Tampa-Saint Petersburg-Clearwater, FL	2.4	22
Washington, DC	1.6	25

Source: U.S. Department of Labor, Bureau of Labor Statistics, *Geographic Profile of Employment and Unemployment, 1994,* Bulletin 2469, Washington, D.C.: U.S. Government Printing Office, December 1995, p. 103. *Notes:* "CMSA" stands for "Consolidated Metropolitan Statistical Area." "MSA" stands for "Metropolitan Statistical Area." "PMSA" stands for "Primary Metropolitan Statistical Area."

★1008★

Distribution of Employed Persons, By Race and Occupation

Percent Distribution of Employed White Persons in Selected MSAs, 1994, By Occupation: Machine Operators, Assemblers, and Inspectors

MSA	Percent	Rank
Anaheim-Santa Ana, CA PMSA	6.3	9
Atlanta, GA	2.6	29
Baltimore, MD	2.4	30
Bergen-Passaic, NJ PMSA	5.8	12
Boston, MA PMSA	2.6	29
Buffalo-Niagara Falls, NY CMSA	6.0	10
Charlotte-Gastonia-Rock Hill, NC-SC	9.0	3
Chicago, IL PMSA	5.5	13
Cincinnati, OH PMSA	5.9	11
Cleveland, OH PMSA	7.2	8
Columbus, OH	4.1	19
Dallas-Fort Worth, TX CMSA	4.4	17
Dayton-Springfield, OH	9.2	2
Denver-Boulder, CO CMSA	2.4	30
Detroit, MI PMSA	7.3	7
Fort Lauderdale-Hollywood-Pompano Beach, FL PMSA	1.7	32
Hartford-New Britain-Middletown, CT CMSA	4.0	20
Houston, TX PMSA	3.2	25
Indianapolis, IN	3.7	21
Kansas City, KS-MO	3.7	21
Los Angeles-Long Beach, CA PMSA	7.8	6
Louisville, KY	8.3	4
Memphis, TN	3.0	27
Miami-Hialeah, FL PMSA	3.5	23
Milwaukee, WI PMSA	8.1	5
Minneapolis-Saint Paul, MN	4.4	17
Nassau-Suffolk, NY PMSA	2.2	31
New Orleans, LA	3.7	21
New York, NY PMSA	3.6	22
Newark, NJ PMSA	4.8	15
Norfolk-Virginia Beach-Newport News, VA	2.7	28
Oakland, CA PMSA	4.3	18
Oklahoma City, OK	4.7	16
Philadelphia, PA PMSA	3.6	22
Phoenix, AZ	3.4	24
Pittsburgh-Beaver Valley, PA	4.8	15
Portland, OR PMSA	3.5	23
Providence-Pawtucket-Fall River, MA-RI CMSA	9.3	1
Riverside-San Bernardino, CA PMSA	4.7	16
Rochester, NY	5.2	14
Sacramento, CA	2.6	29
Saint Louis, MO-IL	4.7	16
Salt Lake City-Ogden, UT	4.8	15
San Antonio, TX	5.2	14
San Diego, CA	2.7	28
San Francisco, CA PMSA	1.7	32
San Jose, CA PMSA	3.6	22
Seattle, WA PMSA	3.1	26

[Continued]

★1008★

Percent Distribution of Employed White Persons in Selected MSAs, 1994, By Occupation: Machine Operators, Assemblers, and Inspectors
[Continued]

MSA	Percent	Rank
Tampa-Saint Petersburg-Clearwater, FL	3.2	25
Washington, DC	1.7	32

Source: U.S. Department of Labor, Bureau of Labor Statistics, *Geographic Profile of Employment and Unemployment, 1994,* Bulletin 2469, Washington, D.C.: U.S. Government Printing Office, December 1995, p. 103. *Notes:* "CMSA" stands for "Consolidated Metropolitan Statistical Area." "MSA" stands for "Metropolitan Statistical Area." "PMSA" stands for "Primary Metropolitan Statistical Area."

★1009★

Distribution of Employed Persons, By Race and Occupation

Percent Distribution of Employed White Persons in Selected MSAs, 1994, By Occupation: Precision Production, Craft, and Repair

MSA	Percent	Rank
Anaheim-Santa Ana, CA PMSA	8.2	35
Atlanta, GA	11.4	12
Baltimore, MD	10.7	17
Bergen-Passaic, NJ PMSA	9.6	27
Boston, MA PMSA	8.0	36
Buffalo-Niagara Falls, NY CMSA	10.7	17
Charlotte-Gastonia-Rock Hill, NC-SC	11.7	10
Chicago, IL PMSA	11.0	15
Cincinnati, OH PMSA	11.5	11
Cleveland, OH PMSA	12.6	3
Columbus, OH	9.3	29
Dallas-Fort Worth, TX CMSA	10.5	19
Dayton-Springfield, OH	12.5	4
Denver-Boulder, CO CMSA	8.8	32
Detroit, MI PMSA	12.0	7
Fort Lauderdale-Hollywood-Pompano Beach, FL PMSA	14.7	1
Hartford-New Britain-Middletown, CT CMSA	10.4	20
Houston, TX PMSA	11.8	9
Indianapolis, IN	12.2	6
Kansas City, KS-MO	10.6	18
Los Angeles-Long Beach, CA PMSA	11.3	13
Louisville, KY	9.9	24
Memphis, TN	10.0	23
Miami-Hialeah, FL PMSA	11.0	15
Milwaukee, WI PMSA	9.8	25
Minneapolis-Saint Paul, MN	8.5	33
Nassau-Suffolk, NY PMSA	9.7	26
New Orleans, LA	9.8	25
New York, NY PMSA	7.7	37
Newark, NJ PMSA	9.7	26
Norfolk-Virginia Beach-Newport News, VA	10.5	19
Oakland, CA PMSA	10.1	22
Oklahoma City, OK	8.9	31

[Continued]

★1009★

Percent Distribution of Employed White Persons in Selected MSAs, 1994, By Occupation: Precision Production, Craft, and Repair

[Continued]

MSA	Percent	Rank
Philadelphia, PA PMSA	10.5	19
Phoenix, AZ	11.9	8
Pittsburgh-Beaver Valley, PA	10.3	21
Portland, OR PMSA	9.2	30
Providence-Pawtucket-Fall River, MA-RI CMSA	10.9	16
Riverside-San Bernardino, CA PMSA	13.2	2
Rochester, NY	8.9	31
Sacramento, CA	8.9	31
Saint Louis, MO-IL	10.5	19
Salt Lake City-Ogden, UT	11.2	14
San Antonio, TX	12.3	5
San Diego, CA	9.2	30
San Francisco, CA PMSA	8.3	34
San Jose, CA PMSA	9.5	28
Seattle, WA PMSA	10.0	23
Tampa-Saint Petersburg-Clearwater, FL	11.7	10
Washington, DC	7.4	38

Source: U.S. Department of Labor, Bureau of Labor Statistics, *Geographic Profile of Employment and Unemployment, 1994,* Bulletin 2469, Washington, D.C.: U.S. Government Printing Office, December 1995, p. 103. *Notes:* "CMSA" stands for "Consolidated Metropolitan Statistical Area." "MSA" stands for "Metropolitan Statistical Area." "PMSA" stands for "Primary Metropolitan Statistical Area."

★1010★

Distribution of Employed Persons, By Race and Occupation

Percent Distribution of Employed White Persons in Selected MSAs, 1994, By Occupation: Professional Specialties

MSA	Percent	Rank
Anaheim-Santa Ana, CA PMSA	13.5	34
Atlanta, GA	17.7	12
Baltimore, MD	20.0	5
Bergen-Passaic, NJ PMSA	15.4	24
Boston, MA PMSA	23.7	2
Buffalo-Niagara Falls, NY CMSA	16.8	15
Charlotte-Gastonia-Rock Hill, NC-SC	14.3	31
Chicago, IL PMSA	16.9	14
Cincinnati, OH PMSA	18.1	10
Cleveland, OH PMSA	15.1	27
Columbus, OH	16.1	21
Dallas-Fort Worth, TX CMSA	15.3	25
Dayton-Springfield, OH	15.6	23
Denver-Boulder, CO CMSA	19.9	6
Detroit, MI PMSA	14.8	28
Fort Lauderdale-Hollywood-Pompano Beach, FL PMSA	12.3	38
Hartford-New Britain-Middletown, CT CMSA	18.5	9
Houston, TX PMSA	14.8	28

[Continued]

★1010★

Percent Distribution of Employed White Persons in Selected MSAs, 1994, By Occupation: Professional Specialties

[Continued]

MSA	Percent	Rank
Indianapolis, IN	12.8	37
Kansas City, KS-MO	14.4	30
Los Angeles-Long Beach, CA PMSA	14.2	32
Louisville, KY	13.9	33
Memphis, TN	16.3	19
Miami-Hialeah, FL PMSA	12.9	36
Milwaukee, WI PMSA	18.1	10
Minneapolis-Saint Paul, MN	16.2	20
Nassau-Suffolk, NY PMSA	16.7	16
New Orleans, LA	17.2	13
New York, NY PMSA	19.8	7
Newark, NJ PMSA	16.7	16
Norfolk-Virginia Beach-Newport News, VA	15.2	26
Oakland, CA PMSA	16.5	17
Oklahoma City, OK	18.0	11
Philadelphia, PA PMSA	16.8	15
Phoenix, AZ	13.4	35
Pittsburgh-Beaver Valley, PA	17.7	12
Portland, OR PMSA	17.7	12
Providence-Pawtucket-Fall River, MA-RI CMSA	14.7	29
Riverside-San Bernardino, CA PMSA	12.0	39
Rochester, NY	21.2	4
Sacramento, CA	16.2	20
Saint Louis, MO-IL	15.8	22
Salt Lake City-Ogden, UT	14.2	32
San Antonio, TX	10.6	40
San Diego, CA	18.0	11
San Francisco, CA PMSA	21.6	3
San Jose, CA PMSA	16.4	18
Seattle, WA PMSA	19.2	8
Tampa-Saint Petersburg-Clearwater, FL	14.2	32
Washington, DC	23.9	1

Source: U.S. Department of Labor, Bureau of Labor Statistics, *Geographic Profile of Employment and Unemployment, 1994,* Bulletin 2469, Washington, D.C.: U.S. Government Printing Office, December 1995, p. 103. *Notes:* "CMSA" stands for "Consolidated Metropolitan Statistical Area." "MSA" stands for "Metropolitan Statistical Area." "PMSA" stands for "Primary Metropolitan Statistical Area."

★1011★

Distribution of Employed Persons, By Race and Occupation

Percent Distribution of Employed White Persons in Selected MSAs, 1994, By Occupation: Sales

MSA	Percent	Rank
Anaheim-Santa Ana, CA PMSA	14.6	10
Atlanta, GA	13.9	14
Baltimore, MD	12.8	19
Bergen-Passaic, NJ PMSA	14.8	9
Boston, MA PMSA	11.3	28

[Continued]

★1011★

Percent Distribution of Employed White Persons in Selected MSAs, 1994, By Occupation: Sales
[Continued]

MSA	Percent	Rank
Buffalo-Niagara Falls, NY CMSA	12.0	23
Charlotte-Gastonia-Rock Hill, NC-SC	14.3	11
Chicago, IL PMSA	12.5	21
Cincinnati, OH PMSA	13.7	15
Cleveland, OH PMSA	12.0	23
Columbus, OH	12.7	20
Dallas-Fort Worth, TX CMSA	13.4	17
Dayton-Springfield, OH	12.3	22
Denver-Boulder, CO CMSA	14.8	9
Detroit, MI PMSA	13.4	17
Fort Lauderdale-Hollywood-Pompano Beach, FL PMSA	15.7	6
Hartford-New Britain-Middletown, CT CMSA	11.5	27
Houston, TX PMSA	15.0	8
Indianapolis, IN	16.9	2
Kansas City, KS-MO	14.3	11
Los Angeles-Long Beach, CA PMSA	11.6	26
Louisville, KY	11.9	24
Memphis, TN	16.3	5
Miami-Hialeah, FL PMSA	16.5	3
Milwaukee, WI PMSA	10.9	29
Minneapolis-Saint Paul, MN	12.3	22
Nassau-Suffolk, NY PMSA	14.3	11
New Orleans, LA	13.7	15
New York, NY PMSA	11.3	28
Newark, NJ PMSA	13.0	18
Norfolk-Virginia Beach-Newport News, VA	17.1	1
Oakland, CA PMSA	12.3	22
Oklahoma City, OK	16.4	4
Philadelphia, PA PMSA	13.4	17
Phoenix, AZ	13.5	16
Pittsburgh-Beaver Valley, PA	13.4	17
Portland, OR PMSA	14.3	11
Providence-Pawtucket-Fall River, MA-RI CMSA	10.9	29
Riverside-San Bernardino, CA PMSA	13.7	15
Rochester, NY	11.5	27
Sacramento, CA	10.1	31
Saint Louis, MO-IL	14.1	12
Salt Lake City-Ogden, UT	11.8	25
San Antonio, TX	15.1	7
San Diego, CA	15.0	8
San Francisco, CA PMSA	14.0	13
San Jose, CA PMSA	11.5	27
Seattle, WA PMSA	14.1	12
Tampa-Saint Petersburg-Clearwater, FL	14.6	10
Washington, DC	10.7	30

Source: U.S. Department of Labor, Bureau of Labor Statistics, *Geographic Profile of Employment and Unemployment, 1994,* Bulletin 2469, Washington, D.C.: U.S. Government Printing Office, December 1995, p. 103. *Notes:* "CMSA" stands for "Consolidated Metropolitan Statistical Area." "MSA" stands for "Metropolitan Statistical Area." "PMSA" stands for "Primary Metropolitan Statistical Area."

★1012★
Distribution of Employed Persons, By Race and Occupation

Percent Distribution of Employed White Persons in Selected MSAs, 1994, By Occupation: Service Occupations

MSA	Percent	Rank
Anaheim-Santa Ana, CA PMSA	13.6	7
Atlanta, GA	8.2	32
Baltimore, MD	9.5	29
Bergen-Passaic, NJ PMSA	8.4	30
Boston, MA PMSA	11.5	15
Buffalo-Niagara Falls, NY CMSA	16.8	1
Charlotte-Gastonia-Rock Hill, NC-SC	8.3	31
Chicago, IL PMSA	10.8	21
Cincinnati, OH PMSA	10.3	25
Cleveland, OH PMSA	12.3	13
Columbus, OH	11.0	20
Dallas-Fort Worth, TX CMSA	11.2	18
Dayton-Springfield, OH	11.2	18
Denver-Boulder, CO CMSA	10.3	25
Detroit, MI PMSA	11.8	14
Fort Lauderdale-Hollywood-Pompano Beach, FL PMSA	13.0	10
Hartford-New Britain-Middletown, CT CMSA	11.8	14
Houston, TX PMSA	11.1	19
Indianapolis, IN	8.4	30
Kansas City, KS-MO	10.1	27
Los Angeles-Long Beach, CA PMSA	14.3	6
Louisville, KY	11.2	18
Memphis, TN	5.8	33
Miami-Hialeah, FL PMSA	14.3	6
Milwaukee, WI PMSA	14.3	6
Minneapolis-Saint Paul, MN	12.7	11
Nassau-Suffolk, NY PMSA	11.4	16
New Orleans, LA	10.4	24
New York, NY PMSA	15.0	4
Newark, NJ PMSA	9.8	28
Norfolk-Virginia Beach-Newport News, VA	13.0	10
Oakland, CA PMSA	13.3	8
Oklahoma City, OK	10.8	21
Philadelphia, PA PMSA	10.3	25
Phoenix, AZ	13.1	9
Pittsburgh-Beaver Valley, PA	12.4	12
Portland, OR PMSA	10.2	26
Providence-Pawtucket-Fall River, MA-RI CMSA	14.5	5
Riverside-San Bernardino, CA PMSA	11.3	17
Rochester, NY	13.0	10
Sacramento, CA	15.1	3
Saint Louis, MO-IL	10.6	23
Salt Lake City-Ogden, UT	11.8	14
San Antonio, TX	16.7	2
San Diego, CA	12.7	11
San Francisco, CA PMSA	10.1	27
San Jose, CA PMSA	13.1	9
Seattle, WA PMSA	11.1	19

[Continued]

★1012★

Percent Distribution of Employed White Persons in Selected MSAs, 1994, By Occupation: Service Occupations

[Continued]

MSA	Percent	Rank
Tampa-Saint Petersburg-Clearwater, FL	13.0	10
Washington, DC	10.7	22

Source: U.S. Department of Labor, Bureau of Labor Statistics, *Geographic Profile of Employment and Unemployment, 1994,* Bulletin 2469, Washington, D.C.: U.S. Government Printing Office, December 1995, p. 103. *Notes:* "CMSA" stands for "Consolidated Metropolitan Statistical Area." "MSA" stands for "Metropolitan Statistical Area." "PMSA" stands for "Primary Metropolitan Statistical Area."

★1013★

Distribution of Employed Persons, By Race and Occupation

Percent Distribution of Employed White Persons in Selected MSAs, 1994, By Occupation: Technicians and Related Support

MSA	Percent	Rank
Anaheim-Santa Ana, CA PMSA	2.3	22
Atlanta, GA	3.5	11
Baltimore, MD	3.6	10
Bergen-Passaic, NJ PMSA	4.2	5
Boston, MA PMSA	3.3	13
Buffalo-Niagara Falls, NY CMSA	3.0	15
Charlotte-Gastonia-Rock Hill, NC-SC	3.6	10
Chicago, IL PMSA	2.7	18
Cincinnati, OH PMSA	3.5	11
Cleveland, OH PMSA	2.9	16
Columbus, OH	3.5	11
Dallas-Fort Worth, TX CMSA	3.6	10
Dayton-Springfield, OH	3.3	13
Denver-Boulder, CO CMSA	4.3	4
Detroit, MI PMSA	3.3	13
Fort Lauderdale-Hollywood-Pompano Beach, FL PMSA	2.7	18
Hartford-New Britain-Middletown, CT CMSA	4.2	5
Houston, TX PMSA	2.7	18
Indianapolis, IN	3.7	9
Kansas City, KS-MO	3.5	11
Los Angeles-Long Beach, CA PMSA	2.4	21
Louisville, KY	4.2	5
Memphis, TN	4.6	3
Miami-Hialeah, FL PMSA	2.3	22
Milwaukee, WI PMSA	3.4	12
Minneapolis-Saint Paul, MN	4.9	2
Nassau-Suffolk, NY PMSA	2.8	17
New Orleans, LA	2.9	16
New York, NY PMSA	2.7	18
Newark, NJ PMSA	3.2	14
Norfolk-Virginia Beach-Newport News, VA	3.6	10
Oakland, CA PMSA	2.1	23
Oklahoma City, OK	3.5	11

[Continued]

★1013★

Percent Distribution of Employed White Persons in Selected MSAs, 1994, By Occupation: Technicians and Related Support

[Continued]

MSA	Percent	Rank
Philadelphia, PA PMSA	3.3	13
Phoenix, AZ	4.2	5
Pittsburgh-Beaver Valley, PA	4.0	7
Portland, OR PMSA	2.6	19
Providence-Pawtucket-Fall River, MA-RI CMSA	2.8	17
Riverside-San Bernardino, CA PMSA	3.3	13
Rochester, NY	5.9	1
Sacramento, CA	3.7	9
Saint Louis, MO-IL	4.1	6
Salt Lake City-Ogden, UT	3.7	9
San Antonio, TX	2.5	20
San Diego, CA	2.4	21
San Francisco, CA PMSA	2.3	22
San Jose, CA PMSA	3.5	11
Seattle, WA PMSA	3.8	8
Tampa-Saint Petersburg-Clearwater, FL	2.6	19
Washington, DC	3.6	10

Source: U.S. Department of Labor, Bureau of Labor Statistics, *Geographic Profile of Employment and Unemployment, 1994,* Bulletin 2469, Washington, D.C.: U.S. Government Printing Office, December 1995, p. 103. *Notes:* "CMSA" stands for "Consolidated Metropolitan Statistical Area." "MSA" stands for "Metropolitan Statistical Area." "PMSA" stands for "Primary Metropolitan Statistical Area."

★1014★

Distribution of Employed Persons, By Race and Occupation

Percent Distribution of Employed White Persons in Selected MSAs, 1994, By Occupation: Transportation and Material Moving

MSA	Percent	Rank
Anaheim-Santa Ana, CA PMSA	2.3	23
Atlanta, GA	2.1	25
Baltimore, MD	4.6	5
Bergen-Passaic, NJ PMSA	3.6	12
Boston, MA PMSA	2.5	21
Buffalo-Niagara Falls, NY CMSA	5.1	2
Charlotte-Gastonia-Rock Hill, NC-SC	3.5	13
Chicago, IL PMSA	3.1	16
Cincinnati, OH PMSA	3.3	14
Cleveland, OH PMSA	3.6	12
Columbus, OH	3.3	14
Dallas-Fort Worth, TX CMSA	3.7	11
Dayton-Springfield, OH	4.1	7
Denver-Boulder, CO CMSA	3.3	14
Detroit, MI PMSA	3.5	13
Fort Lauderdale-Hollywood-Pompano Beach, FL PMSA	2.7	20
Hartford-New Britain-Middletown, CT CMSA	3.8	10
Houston, TX PMSA	3.5	13

[Continued]

★1014★

Percent Distribution of Employed White Persons in Selected MSAs, 1994, By Occupation: Transportation and Material Moving
[Continued]

MSA	Percent	Rank
Indianapolis, IN	3.5	13
Kansas City, KS-MO	3.6	12
Los Angeles-Long Beach, CA PMSA	3.2	15
Louisville, KY	4.1	7
Memphis, TN	5.1	2
Miami-Hialeah, FL PMSA	4.0	8
Milwaukee, WI PMSA	2.2	24
Minneapolis-Saint Paul, MN	3.5	13
Nassau-Suffolk, NY PMSA	3.2	15
New Orleans, LA	3.9	9
New York, NY PMSA	2.9	18
Newark, NJ PMSA	3.7	11
Norfolk-Virginia Beach-Newport News, VA	2.8	19
Oakland, CA PMSA	4.2	6
Oklahoma City, OK	3.8	10
Philadelphia, PA PMSA	3.0	17
Phoenix, AZ	2.8	19
Pittsburgh-Beaver Valley, PA	4.2	6
Portland, OR PMSA	2.4	22
Providence-Pawtucket-Fall River, MA-RI CMSA	3.6	12
Riverside-San Bernardino, CA PMSA	6.5	1
Rochester, NY	2.9	18
Sacramento, CA	4.8	4
Saint Louis, MO-IL	2.9	18
Salt Lake City-Ogden, UT	4.0	8
San Antonio, TX	4.9	3
San Diego, CA	3.2	15
San Francisco, CA PMSA	3.2	15
San Jose, CA PMSA	2.9	18
Seattle, WA PMSA	2.9	18
Tampa-Saint Petersburg-Clearwater, FL	3.3	14
Washington, DC	1.4	26

Source: U.S. Department of Labor, Bureau of Labor Statistics, *Geographic Profile of Employment and Unemployment, 1994,* Bulletin 2469, Washington, D.C.: U.S. Government Printing Office, December 1995, p. 103. *Notes:* "CMSA" stands for "Consolidated Metropolitan Statistical Area." "MSA" stands for "Metropolitan Statistical Area." "PMSA" stands for "Primary Metropolitan Statistical Area."

★1015★

Distribution of Employed Persons, By Sex and Occupation

Percent Distribution of Employed Men in Selected Cities, 1994, By Occupation: Administrative Support, Including Clerical

City	Percent	Rank
Baltimore, MD	6.7	14
Chicago, IL	8.9	5
Cleveland, OH	7.4	10
Dallas, TX	6.7	14

[Continued]

★1015★

Percent Distribution of Employed Men in Selected Cities, 1994, By Occupation: Administrative Support, Including Clerical
[Continued]

City	Percent	Rank
Detroit, MI	8.0	9
Houston, TX	7.1	11
Indianapolis, IN	5.4	15
Los Angeles, CA	8.1	8
Milwaukee, WI	10.1	4
New York, NY	10.7	3
Philadelphia, PA	12.7	1
Phoenix, AZ	8.2	7
San Antonio, TX	6.8	13
San Diego, CA	7.0	12
San Francisco, CA	11.1	2
Washington, DC	8.4	6

Source: U.S. Department of Labor, Bureau of Labor Statistics, *Geographic Profile of Employment and Unemployment, 1994,* Bulletin 2469, Washington, D.C.: U.S. Government Printing Office, December 1995, p. 103.

★1016★

Distribution of Employed Persons, By Sex and Occupation

Percent Distribution of Employed Men in Selected Cities, 1994, By Occupation: Executive, Administrative, and Managerial

City	Percent	Rank
Baltimore, MD	11.9	9
Chicago, IL	10.8	11
Cleveland, OH	6.3	15
Dallas, TX	12.8	6
Detroit, MI	9.9	12
Houston, TX	11.8	10
Indianapolis, IN	14.4	3
Los Angeles, CA	12.1	8
Milwaukee, WI	14.2	4
New York, NY	13.2	5
Philadelphia, PA	9.7	13
Phoenix, AZ	12.7	7
San Antonio, TX	6.4	14
San Diego, CA	19.8	1
San Francisco, CA	11.9	9
Washington, DC	17.2	2

Source: U.S. Department of Labor, Bureau of Labor Statistics, *Geographic Profile of Employment and Unemployment, 1994,* Bulletin 2469, Washington, D.C.: U.S. Government Printing Office, December 1995, p. 103.

★1017★

Distribution of Employed Persons, By Sex and Occupation

Percent Distribution of Employed Men in Selected Cities, 1994, By Occupation: Handlers, Equipment Cleaners, Helpers, and Laborers

City	Percent	Rank
Baltimore, MD	8.4	6
Chicago, IL	8.7	4
Cleveland, OH	8.9	3
Dallas, TX	8.1	7
Detroit, MI	4.0	13
Houston, TX	11.1	1
Indianapolis, IN	9.2	2
Los Angeles, CA	7.0	8
Milwaukee, WI	7.0	8
New York, NY	5.5	12
Philadelphia, PA	6.8	9
Phoenix, AZ	6.1	11
San Antonio, TX	8.6	5
San Diego, CA	6.7	10
San Francisco, CA	6.1	11
Washington, DC	3.3	14

Source: U.S. Department of Labor, Bureau of Labor Statistics, *Geographic Profile of Employment and Unemployment, 1994,* Bulletin 2469, Washington, D.C.: U.S. Government Printing Office, December 1995, p. 103.

★1018★

Distribution of Employed Persons, By Sex and Occupation

Percent Distribution of Employed Men in Selected Cities, 1994, By Occupation: Machine Operators, Assemblers, and Inspectors

City	Percent	Rank
Baltimore, MD	4.8	10
Chicago, IL	10.3	2
Cleveland, OH	10.3	2
Dallas, TX	8.5	4
Detroit, MI	15.0	1
Houston, TX	3.8	11
Indianapolis, IN	7.1	6
Los Angeles, CA	9.7	3
Milwaukee, WI	7.9	5
New York, NY	4.8	10
Philadelphia, PA	4.9	9
Phoenix, AZ	5.4	8
San Antonio, TX	6.7	7
San Diego, CA	3.2	12
San Francisco, CA	2.6	13
Washington, DC	1.8	14

Source: U.S. Department of Labor, Bureau of Labor Statistics, *Geographic Profile of Employment and Unemployment, 1994,* Bulletin 2469, Washington, D.C.: U.S. Government Printing Office, December 1995, p. 103.

★1019★

Distribution of Employed Persons, By Sex and Occupation

Percent Distribution of Employed Men in Selected Cities, 1994, By Occupation: Precision Production, Craft, and Repair

City	Percent	Rank
Baltimore, MD	13.5	10
Chicago, IL	15.5	9
Cleveland, OH	23.4	1
Dallas, TX	18.4	5
Detroit, MI	17.8	6
Houston, TX	15.5	9
Indianapolis, IN	19.5	3
Los Angeles, CA	16.6	8
Milwaukee, WI	13.0	12
New York, NY	13.1	11
Philadelphia, PA	17.4	7
Phoenix, AZ	22.4	2
San Antonio, TX	19.4	4
San Diego, CA	10.7	13
San Francisco, CA	7.6	15
Washington, DC	9.1	14

Source: U.S. Department of Labor, Bureau of Labor Statistics, *Geographic Profile of Employment and Unemployment, 1994,* Bulletin 2469, Washington, D.C.: U.S. Government Printing Office, December 1995, p. 103.

★1020★

Distribution of Employed Persons, By Sex and Occupation

Percent Distribution of Employed Men in Selected Cities, 1994, By Occupation: Professional Specialty

City	Percent	Rank
Baltimore, MD	13.7	6
Chicago, IL	13.3	7
Cleveland, OH	5.5	15
Dallas, TX	9.7	12
Detroit, MI	7.1	14
Houston, TX	11.2	9
Indianapolis, IN	15.3	4
Los Angeles, CA	12.8	8
Milwaukee, WI	11.1	10
New York, NY	14.0	5
Philadelphia, PA	10.4	11
Phoenix, AZ	11.2	9
San Antonio, TX	7.8	13
San Diego, CA	16.6	3
San Francisco, CA	19.6	2
Washington, DC	25.1	1

Source: U.S. Department of Labor, Bureau of Labor Statistics, *Geographic Profile of Employment and Unemployment, 1994,* Bulletin 2469, Washington, D.C.: U.S. Government Printing Office, December 1995, p. 103.

★1021★

Distribution of Employed Persons, By Sex and Occupation

Percent Distribution of Employed Men in Selected Cities, 1994, By Occupation: Sales

City	Percent	Rank
Baltimore, MD	9.3	11
Chicago, IL	9.1	12
Cleveland, OH	5.6	16
Dallas, TX	9.7	10
Detroit, MI	8.6	13
Houston, TX	13.5	4
Indianapolis, IN	16.2	1
Los Angeles, CA	10.8	8
Milwaukee, WI	8.2	14
New York, NY	11.3	7
Philadelphia, PA	9.8	9
Phoenix, AZ	11.8	6
San Antonio, TX	14.5	3
San Diego, CA	12.7	5
San Francisco, CA	15.0	2
Washington, DC	6.2	15

Source: U.S. Department of Labor, Bureau of Labor Statistics, *Geographic Profile of Employment and Unemployment, 1994,* Bulletin 2469, Washington, D.C.: U.S. Government Printing Office, December 1995, p. 103.

★1022★

Distribution of Employed Persons, By Sex and Occupation

Percent Distribution of Employed Men in Selected Cities, 1994, By Occupation: Service Occupations

City	Percent	Rank
Baltimore, MD	18.2	2
Chicago, IL	14.4	10
Cleveland, OH	17.6	6
Dallas, TX	12.4	13
Detroit, MI	19.2	1
Houston, TX	12.9	12
Indianapolis, IN	3.9	16
Los Angeles, CA	13.0	11
Milwaukee, WI	17.2	7
New York, NY	17.8	5
Philadelphia, PA	15.6	9
Phoenix, AZ	10.2	15
San Antonio, TX	18.0	3
San Diego, CA	12.1	14
San Francisco, CA	15.9	8
Washington, DC	17.9	4

Source: U.S. Department of Labor, Bureau of Labor Statistics, *Geographic Profile of Employment and Unemployment, 1994,* Bulletin 2469, Washington, D.C.: U.S. Government Printing Office, December 1995, p. 103.

★1023★

Distribution of Employed Persons, By Sex and Occupation

Percent Distribution of Employed Men in Selected Cities, 1994, By Occupation: Technicians and Related Support

City	Percent	Rank
Baltimore, MD	3.1	4
Chicago, IL	2.5	6
Cleveland, OH	1.7	11
Dallas, TX	2.2	8
Detroit, MI	2.0	10
Houston, TX	2.4	7
Indianapolis, IN	2.6	5
Los Angeles, CA	2.5	6
Milwaukee, WI	2.1	9
New York, NY	2.4	7
Philadelphia, PA	2.6	5
Phoenix, AZ	3.6	2
San Antonio, TX	1.5	12
San Diego, CA	3.2	3
San Francisco, CA	2.5	6
Washington, DC	4.3	1

Source: U.S. Department of Labor, Bureau of Labor Statistics, *Geographic Profile of Employment and Unemployment, 1994,* Bulletin 2469, Washington, D.C.: U.S. Government Printing Office, December 1995, p. 103.

★1024★

Distribution of Employed Persons, By Sex and Occupation

Percent Distribution of Employed Men in Selected Cities, 1994, By Occupation: Transportation and Material Moving

City	Percent	Rank
Baltimore, MD	10.2	2
Chicago, IL	5.5	9
Cleveland, OH	11.1	1
Dallas, TX	7.3	6
Detroit, MI	7.6	5
Houston, TX	7.3	6
Indianapolis, IN	4.6	11
Los Angeles, CA	4.0	12
Milwaukee, WI	8.7	4
New York, NY	6.9	7
Philadelphia, PA	9.6	3
Phoenix, AZ	5.4	10
San Antonio, TX	7.3	6
San Diego, CA	4.6	11
San Francisco, CA	6.8	8
Washington, DC	5.5	9

Source: U.S. Department of Labor, Bureau of Labor Statistics, *Geographic Profile of Employment and Unemployment, 1994,* Bulletin 2469, Washington, D.C.: U.S. Government Printing Office, December 1995, p. 103.

★1025★

Distribution of Employed Persons, By Sex and Occupation

Percent Distribution of Employed Men in Selected MSAs, 1994, By Occupation: Administrative Support, Including Clerical

MSA	Percent	Rank
Anaheim-Santa Ana, CA PMSA	7.1	13
Atlanta, GA	6.0	20
Baltimore, MD	5.9	21
Bergen-Passaic, NJ PMSA	7.2	12
Boston, MA PMSA	7.5	9
Buffalo-Niagara Falls, NY CMSA	5.3	26
Charlotte-Gastonia-Rock Hill, NC-SC	4.7	30
Chicago, IL PMSA	7.5	9
Cincinnati, OH PMSA	7.4	10
Cleveland, OH PMSA	4.6	31
Columbus, OH	8.9	2
Dallas-Fort Worth, TX CMSA	6.2	19
Dayton-Springfield, OH	4.2	32
Denver-Boulder, CO CMSA	7.3	11
Detroit, MI PMSA	5.2	27
Fort Lauderdale-Hollywood-Pompano Beach, FL PMSA	6.3	18
Hartford-New Britain-Middletown, CT CMSA	5.5	24
Houston, TX PMSA	6.0	20
Indianapolis, IN	3.9	34
Kansas City, KS-MO	7.8	7
Los Angeles-Long Beach, CA PMSA	7.6	8
Louisville, KY	6.6	16
Memphis, TN	7.6	8
Miami-Hialeah, FL PMSA	7.3	11
Milwaukee, WI PMSA	6.5	17
Minneapolis-Saint Paul, MN	7.9	6
Nassau-Suffolk, NY PMSA	7.2	12
New Orleans, LA	8.7	3
New York, NY PMSA	9.9	1
Newark, NJ PMSA	7.1	13
Norfolk-Virginia Beach-Newport News, VA	6.8	15
Oakland, CA PMSA	7.3	11
Oklahoma City, OK	5.9	21
Philadelphia, PA PMSA	8.3	5
Phoenix, AZ	7.8	7
Pittsburgh-Beaver Valley, PA	5.8	22
Portland, OR PMSA	5.4	25
Providence-Pawtucket-Fall River, MA-RI CMSA	5.8	22
Riverside-San Bernardino, CA PMSA	4.8	29
Rochester, NY	4.1	33
Sacramento, CA	6.5	17
Saint Louis, MO-IL	5.6	23
Salt Lake City-Ogden, UT	7.9	6
San Antonio, TX	6.6	16
San Diego, CA	5.9	21
San Francisco, CA PMSA	7.8	7
San Jose, CA PMSA	4.7	30
Seattle, WA PMSA	5.1	28

[Continued]

★1025★

Percent Distribution of Employed Men in Selected MSAs, 1994, By Occupation: Administrative Support, Including Clerical

[Continued]

MSA	Percent	Rank
Tampa-Saint Petersburg-Clearwater, FL	6.9	14
Washington, DC	8.5	4

Source: U.S. Department of Labor, Bureau of Labor Statistics, *Geographic Profile of Employment and Unemployment, 1994*, Bulletin 2469, Washington, D.C.: U.S. Government Printing Office, December 1995, p. 103. *Notes:* "CMSA" stands for "Consolidated Metropolitan Statistical Area." "MSA" stands for "Metropolitan Statistical Area." "PMSA" stands for "Primary Metropolitan Statistical Area."

★1026★

Distribution of Employed Persons, By Sex and Occupation

Percent Distribution of Employed Men in Selected MSAs, 1994, By Occupation: Executive, Administrative, and Managerial

MSA	Percent	Rank
Anaheim-Santa Ana, CA PMSA	21.0	2
Atlanta, GA	18.9	7
Baltimore, MD	15.6	22
Bergen-Passaic, NJ PMSA	19.6	4
Boston, MA PMSA	19.1	6
Buffalo-Niagara Falls, NY CMSA	13.4	36
Charlotte-Gastonia-Rock Hill, NC-SC	16.2	18
Chicago, IL PMSA	15.5	23
Cincinnati, OH PMSA	14.4	32
Cleveland, OH PMSA	15.8	21
Columbus, OH	17.3	10
Dallas-Fort Worth, TX CMSA	16.6	15
Dayton-Springfield, OH	13.8	35
Denver-Boulder, CO CMSA	16.6	15
Detroit, MI PMSA	14.7	30
Fort Lauderdale-Hollywood-Pompano Beach, FL PMSA	13.8	35
Hartford-New Britain-Middletown, CT CMSA	16.9	13
Houston, TX PMSA	14.2	33
Indianapolis, IN	16.9	13
Kansas City, KS-MO	15.0	27
Los Angeles-Long Beach, CA PMSA	13.0	39
Louisville, KY	16.1	19
Memphis, TN	13.8	35
Miami-Hialeah, FL PMSA	14.0	34
Milwaukee, WI PMSA	16.0	20
Minneapolis-Saint Paul, MN	17.1	11
Nassau-Suffolk, NY PMSA	19.2	5
New Orleans, LA	17.0	12
New York, NY PMSA	14.8	29
Newark, NJ PMSA	19.1	6
Norfolk-Virginia Beach-Newport News, VA	13.3	37
Oakland, CA PMSA	18.2	8
Oklahoma City, OK	15.3	25

[Continued]

★1026★

Percent Distribution of Employed Men in Selected MSAs, 1994, By Occupation: Executive, Administrative, and Managerial

[Continued]

MSA	Percent	Rank
Philadelphia, PA PMSA	16.3	17
Phoenix, AZ	15.4	24
Pittsburgh-Beaver Valley, PA	13.4	36
Portland, OR PMSA	19.7	3
Providence-Pawtucket-Fall River, MA-RI CMSA	14.9	28
Riverside-San Bernardino, CA PMSA	12.3	40
Rochester, NY	13.1	38
Sacramento, CA	15.1	26
Saint Louis, MO-IL	14.5	31
Salt Lake City-Ogden, UT	16.5	16
San Antonio, TX	7.9	41
San Diego, CA	16.7	14
San Francisco, CA PMSA	17.6	9
San Jose, CA PMSA	19.2	5
Seattle, WA PMSA	17.6	9
Tampa-Saint Petersburg-Clearwater, FL	15.0	27
Washington, DC	21.6	1

Source: U.S. Department of Labor, Bureau of Labor Statistics, Geographic Profile of Employment and Unemployment, 1994, Bulletin 2469, Washington, D.C.: U.S. Government Printing Office, December 1995, p. 103. Notes: "CMSA" stands for "Consolidated Metropolitan Statistical Area." "MSA" stands for "Metropolitan Statistical Area." "PMSA" stands for "Primary Metropolitan Statistical Area."

★1027★

Distribution of Employed Persons, By Sex and Occupation

Percent Distribution of Employed Men in Selected MSAs, 1994, By Occupation: Handlers, Equipment Cleaners, Helpers, and Laborers

MSA	Percent	Rank
Anaheim-Santa Ana, CA PMSA	5.9	17
Atlanta, GA	5.9	17
Baltimore, MD	5.1	23
Bergen-Passaic, NJ PMSA	4.8	26
Boston, MA PMSA	4.1	30
Buffalo-Niagara Falls, NY CMSA	5.2	22
Charlotte-Gastonia-Rock Hill, NC-SC	8.5	3
Chicago, IL PMSA	6.8	11
Cincinnati, OH PMSA	6.2	15
Cleveland, OH PMSA	5.9	17
Columbus, OH	6.6	13
Dallas-Fort Worth, TX CMSA	7.0	9
Dayton-Springfield, OH	7.2	7
Denver-Boulder, CO CMSA	5.2	22
Detroit, MI PMSA	5.3	21
Fort Lauderdale-Hollywood-Pompano Beach, FL PMSA	7.3	6
Hartford-New Britain-Middletown, CT CMSA	4.4	28
Houston, TX PMSA	7.5	5

[Continued]

★1027★

Percent Distribution of Employed Men in Selected MSAs, 1994, By Occupation: Handlers, Equipment Cleaners, Helpers, and Laborers

[Continued]

MSA	Percent	Rank
Indianapolis, IN	7.1	8
Kansas City, KS-MO	5.5	19
Los Angeles-Long Beach, CA PMSA	6.7	12
Louisville, KY	9.0	2
Memphis, TN	9.1	1
Miami-Hialeah, FL PMSA	7.5	5
Milwaukee, WI PMSA	5.6	18
Minneapolis-Saint Paul, MN	5.4	20
Nassau-Suffolk, NY PMSA	6.3	14
New Orleans, LA	4.0	31
New York, NY PMSA	5.0	24
Newark, NJ PMSA	6.7	12
Norfolk-Virginia Beach-Newport News, VA	6.2	15
Oakland, CA PMSA	6.8	11
Oklahoma City, OK	4.3	29
Philadelphia, PA PMSA	5.3	21
Phoenix, AZ	6.1	16
Pittsburgh-Beaver Valley, PA	6.9	10
Portland, OR PMSA	4.8	26
Providence-Pawtucket-Fall River, MA-RI CMSA	4.9	25
Riverside-San Bernardino, CA PMSA	4.9	25
Rochester, NY	4.7	27
Sacramento, CA	5.5	19
Saint Louis, MO-IL	6.9	10
Salt Lake City-Ogden, UT	6.6	13
San Antonio, TX	7.7	4
San Diego, CA	5.2	22
San Francisco, CA PMSA	4.9	25
San Jose, CA PMSA	3.6	32
Seattle, WA PMSA	6.7	12
Tampa-Saint Petersburg-Clearwater, FL	4.7	27
Washington, DC	3.0	33

Source: U.S. Department of Labor, Bureau of Labor Statistics, Geographic Profile of Employment and Unemployment, 1994, Bulletin 2469, Washington, D.C.: U.S. Government Printing Office, December 1995, p. 103. Notes: "CMSA" stands for "Consolidated Metropolitan Statistical Area." "MSA" stands for "Metropolitan Statistical Area." "PMSA" stands for "Primary Metropolitan Statistical Area."

★1028★

Distribution of Employed Persons, By Sex and Occupation

Percent Distribution of Employed Men in Selected MSAs, 1994, By Occupation: Machine Operators, Assemblers, and Inspectors

MSA	Percent	Rank
Anaheim-Santa Ana, CA PMSA	6.8	15
Atlanta, GA	5.1	26
Baltimore, MD	3.3	36
Bergen-Passaic, NJ PMSA	6.4	18

[Continued]

★1028★

Percent Distribution of Employed Men in Selected MSAs, 1994, By Occupation: Machine Operators, Assemblers, and Inspectors

[Continued]

MSA	Percent	Rank
Boston, MA PMSA	3.6	34
Buffalo-Niagara Falls, NY CMSA	8.9	7
Charlotte-Gastonia-Rock Hill, NC-SC	9.4	6
Chicago, IL PMSA	6.5	17
Cincinnati, OH PMSA	6.9	14
Cleveland, OH PMSA	8.4	9
Columbus, OH	5.8	23
Dallas-Fort Worth, TX CMSA	6.2	20
Dayton-Springfield, OH	11.1	1
Denver-Boulder, CO CMSA	4.0	33
Detroit, MI PMSA	10.1	5
Fort Lauderdale-Hollywood-Pompano Beach, FL PMSA	2.1	40
Hartford-New Britain-Middletown, CT CMSA	6.3	19
Houston, TX PMSA	4.6	30
Indianapolis, IN	7.0	13
Kansas City, KS-MO	4.7	29
Los Angeles-Long Beach, CA PMSA	8.7	8
Louisville, KY	10.4	3
Memphis, TN	6.8	15
Miami-Hialeah, FL PMSA	2.3	38
Milwaukee, WI PMSA	10.3	4
Minneapolis-Saint Paul, MN	5.8	23
Nassau-Suffolk, NY PMSA	2.2	39
New Orleans, LA	6.1	21
New York, NY PMSA	4.3	31
Newark, NJ PMSA	5.1	26
Norfolk-Virginia Beach-Newport News, VA	5.4	25
Oakland, CA PMSA	6.0	22
Oklahoma City, OK	6.9	14
Philadelphia, PA PMSA	4.9	28
Phoenix, AZ	4.6	30
Pittsburgh-Beaver Valley, PA	6.2	20
Portland, OR PMSA	5.6	24
Providence-Pawtucket-Fall River, MA-RI CMSA	10.6	2
Riverside-San Bernardino, CA PMSA	6.7	16
Rochester, NY	7.4	10
Sacramento, CA	3.4	35
Saint Louis, MO-IL	7.2	12
Salt Lake City-Ogden, UT	5.8	23
San Antonio, TX	7.3	11
San Diego, CA	4.7	29
San Francisco, CA PMSA	2.9	37
San Jose, CA PMSA	4.3	31
Seattle, WA PMSA	5.0	27

[Continued]

★1028★

Percent Distribution of Employed Men in Selected MSAs, 1994, By Occupation: Machine Operators, Assemblers, and Inspectors

[Continued]

MSA	Percent	Rank
Tampa-Saint Petersburg-Clearwater, FL	4.2	32
Washington, DC	2.3	38

Source: U.S. Department of Labor, Bureau of Labor Statistics, *Geographic Profile of Employment and Unemployment, 1994,* Bulletin 2469, Washington, D.C.: U.S. Government Printing Office, December 1995, p. 103. *Notes:* "CMSA" stands for "Consolidated Metropolitan Statistical Area." "MSA" stands for "Metropolitan Statistical Area." "PMSA" stands for "Primary Metropolitan Statistical Area."

★1029★

Distribution of Employed Persons, By Sex and Occupation

Percent Distribution of Employed Men in Selected MSAs, 1994, By Occupation: Precision Production, Craft, and Repair

MSA	Percent	Rank
Anaheim-Santa Ana, CA PMSA	13.0	39
Atlanta, GA	16.6	23
Baltimore, MD	15.5	30
Bergen-Passaic, NJ PMSA	15.7	29
Boston, MA PMSA	13.3	38
Buffalo-Niagara Falls, NY CMSA	19.0	9
Charlotte-Gastonia-Rock Hill, NC-SC	18.7	11
Chicago, IL PMSA	17.4	17
Cincinnati, OH PMSA	18.6	12
Cleveland, OH PMSA	18.5	13
Columbus, OH	15.7	29
Dallas-Fort Worth, TX CMSA	16.7	22
Dayton-Springfield, OH	21.0	3
Denver-Boulder, CO CMSA	14.3	35
Detroit, MI PMSA	19.1	8
Fort Lauderdale-Hollywood-Pompano Beach, FL PMSA	24.3	1
Hartford-New Britain-Middletown, CT CMSA	16.1	26
Houston, TX PMSA	17.2	19
Indianapolis, IN	20.8	4
Kansas City, KS-MO	19.1	8
Los Angeles-Long Beach, CA PMSA	17.5	16
Louisville, KY	17.1	20
Memphis, TN	14.4	34
Miami-Hialeah, FL PMSA	18.2	14
Milwaukee, WI PMSA	14.7	32
Minneapolis-Saint Paul, MN	14.5	33
Nassau-Suffolk, NY PMSA	16.0	27
New Orleans, LA	16.9	21
New York, NY PMSA	13.5	37
Newark, NJ PMSA	16.3	25
Norfolk-Virginia Beach-Newport News, VA	20.5	5
Oakland, CA PMSA	14.3	35
Oklahoma City, OK	14.4	34

[Continued]

★1029★

Percent Distribution of Employed Men in Selected MSAs, 1994, By Occupation: Precision Production, Craft, and Repair

[Continued]

MSA	Percent	Rank
Philadelphia, PA PMSA	17.1	20
Phoenix, AZ	18.8	10
Pittsburgh-Beaver Valley, PA	16.4	24
Portland, OR PMSA	15.8	28
Providence-Pawtucket-Fall River, MA-RI CMSA	17.8	15
Riverside-San Bernardino, CA PMSA	21.3	2
Rochester, NY	13.3	38
Sacramento, CA	14.2	36
Saint Louis, MO-IL	17.3	18
Salt Lake City-Ogden, UT	18.7	11
San Antonio, TX	19.3	6
San Diego, CA	15.5	30
San Francisco, CA PMSA	12.3	40
San Jose, CA PMSA	15.0	31
Seattle, WA PMSA	16.3	25
Tampa-Saint Petersburg-Clearwater, FL	19.2	7
Washington, DC	13.5	37

Source: U.S. Department of Labor, Bureau of Labor Statistics, *Geographic Profile of Employment and Unemployment, 1994*, Bulletin 2469, Washington, D.C.: U.S. Government Printing Office, December 1995, p. 103. *Notes:* "CMSA" stands for "Consolidated Metropolitan Statistical Area." "MSA" stands for "Metropolitan Statistical Area." "PMSA" stands for "Primary Metropolitan Statistical Area."

★1030★

Distribution of Employed Persons, By Sex and Occupation

Percent Distribution of Employed Men in Selected MSAs, 1994, By Occupation: Professional Specialties

MSA	Percent	Rank
Anaheim-Santa Ana, CA PMSA	13.5	22
Atlanta, GA	14.2	18
Baltimore, MD	18.0	6
Bergen-Passaic, NJ PMSA	11.9	31
Boston, MA PMSA	22.1	1
Buffalo-Niagara Falls, NY CMSA	13.2	25
Charlotte-Gastonia-Rock Hill, NC-SC	10.5	36
Chicago, IL PMSA	14.9	15
Cincinnati, OH PMSA	15.1	13
Cleveland, OH PMSA	13.7	21
Columbus, OH	12.6	28
Dallas-Fort Worth, TX CMSA	12.3	29
Dayton-Springfield, OH	11.7	32
Denver-Boulder, CO CMSA	17.4	7
Detroit, MI PMSA	14.1	19
Fort Lauderdale-Hollywood-Pompano Beach, FL PMSA	10.4	37
Hartford-New Britain-Middletown, CT CMSA	13.7	21
Houston, TX PMSA	12.8	27

[Continued]

★1030★

Percent Distribution of Employed Men in Selected MSAs, 1994, By Occupation: Professional Specialties

[Continued]

MSA	Percent	Rank
Indianapolis, IN	14.5	16
Kansas City, KS-MO	11.4	34
Los Angeles-Long Beach, CA PMSA	13.1	26
Louisville, KY	11.4	34
Memphis, TN	11.6	33
Miami-Hialeah, FL PMSA	11.2	35
Milwaukee, WI PMSA	16.4	10
Minneapolis-Saint Paul, MN	14.4	17
Nassau-Suffolk, NY PMSA	14.2	18
New Orleans, LA	15.8	12
New York, NY PMSA	14.9	15
Newark, NJ PMSA	13.9	20
Norfolk-Virginia Beach-Newport News, VA	11.4	34
Oakland, CA PMSA	14.5	16
Oklahoma City, OK	16.6	9
Philadelphia, PA PMSA	14.5	16
Phoenix, AZ	12.2	30
Pittsburgh-Beaver Valley, PA	16.4	10
Portland, OR PMSA	15.0	14
Providence-Pawtucket-Fall River, MA-RI CMSA	13.4	23
Riverside-San Bernardino, CA PMSA	10.0	38
Rochester, NY	21.6	2
Sacramento, CA	17.0	8
Saint Louis, MO-IL	13.7	21
Salt Lake City-Ogden, UT	11.4	34
San Antonio, TX	7.4	39
San Diego, CA	16.2	11
San Francisco, CA PMSA	19.2	5
San Jose, CA PMSA	19.3	4
Seattle, WA PMSA	16.6	9
Tampa-Saint Petersburg-Clearwater, FL	13.3	24
Washington, DC	19.9	3

Source: U.S. Department of Labor, Bureau of Labor Statistics, *Geographic Profile of Employment and Unemployment, 1994*, Bulletin 2469, Washington, D.C.: U.S. Government Printing Office, December 1995, p. 103. *Notes:* "CMSA" stands for "Consolidated Metropolitan Statistical Area." "MSA" stands for "Metropolitan Statistical Area." "PMSA" stands for "Primary Metropolitan Statistical Area."

★1031★

Distribution of Employed Persons, By Sex and Occupation

Percent Distribution of Employed Men in Selected MSAs, 1994, By Occupation: Sales

MSA	Percent	Rank
Anaheim-Santa Ana, CA PMSA	12.4	15
Atlanta, GA	12.9	11
Baltimore, MD	13.1	9
Bergen-Passaic, NJ PMSA	14.8	5
Boston, MA PMSA	10.9	25

[Continued]

★1031★

Percent Distribution of Employed Men in Selected MSAs, 1994, By Occupation: Sales

[Continued]

MSA	Percent	Rank
Buffalo-Niagara Falls, NY CMSA	10.7	26
Charlotte-Gastonia-Rock Hill, NC-SC	11.3	22
Chicago, IL PMSA	11.1	24
Cincinnati, OH PMSA	11.5	20
Cleveland, OH PMSA	11.1	24
Columbus, OH	12.7	12
Dallas-Fort Worth, TX CMSA	12.6	13
Dayton-Springfield, OH	12.2	17
Denver-Boulder, CO CMSA	14.8	5
Detroit, MI PMSA	11.7	18
Fort Lauderdale-Hollywood-Pompano Beach, FL PMSA	12.9	11
Hartford-New Britain-Middletown, CT CMSA	11.2	23
Houston, TX PMSA	15.3	3
Indianapolis, IN	15.5	1
Kansas City, KS-MO	14.8	5
Los Angeles-Long Beach, CA PMSA	11.7	18
Louisville, KY	9.9	32
Memphis, TN	13.6	8
Miami-Hialeah, FL PMSA	14.5	6
Milwaukee, WI PMSA	10.1	30
Minneapolis-Saint Paul, MN	12.3	16
Nassau-Suffolk, NY PMSA	14.3	7
New Orleans, LA	8.1	34
New York, NY PMSA	11.4	21
Newark, NJ PMSA	10.6	27
Norfolk-Virginia Beach-Newport News, VA	10.5	28
Oakland, CA PMSA	9.9	32
Oklahoma City, OK	15.3	3
Philadelphia, PA PMSA	12.5	14
Phoenix, AZ	12.6	13
Pittsburgh-Beaver Valley, PA	11.6	19
Portland, OR PMSA	14.9	4
Providence-Pawtucket-Fall River, MA-RI CMSA	10.1	30
Riverside-San Bernardino, CA PMSA	11.2	23
Rochester, NY	12.9	11
Sacramento, CA	10.0	31
Saint Louis, MO-IL	12.7	12
Salt Lake City-Ogden, UT	11.3	22
San Antonio, TX	15.4	2
San Diego, CA	13.0	10
San Francisco, CA PMSA	13.6	8
San Jose, CA PMSA	8.8	33
Seattle, WA PMSA	13.1	9
Tampa-Saint Petersburg-Clearwater, FL	13.1	9
Washington, DC	10.4	29

Source: U.S. Department of Labor, Bureau of Labor Statistics, *Geographic Profile of Employment and Unemployment,* 1994, Bulletin 2469, Washington, D.C.: U.S. Government Printing Office, December 1995, p. 103. *Notes:* "CMSA" stands for "Consolidated Metropolitan Statistical Area." "MSA" stands for "Metropolitan Statistical Area." "PMSA" stands for "Primary Metropolitan Statistical Area."

★1032★

Distribution of Employed Persons, By Sex and Occupation

Percent Distribution of Employed Men in Selected MSAs, 1994, By Occupation: Service Occupations

MSA	Percent	Rank
Anaheim-Santa Ana, CA PMSA	12.2	7
Atlanta, GA	10.7	17
Baltimore, MD	10.3	21
Bergen-Passaic, NJ PMSA	8.1	35
Boston, MA PMSA	10.9	16
Buffalo-Niagara Falls, NY CMSA	11.8	8
Charlotte-Gastonia-Rock Hill, NC-SC	9.0	30
Chicago, IL PMSA	11.1	14
Cincinnati, OH PMSA	9.3	27
Cleveland, OH PMSA	10.7	17
Columbus, OH	9.1	29
Dallas-Fort Worth, TX CMSA	10.0	23
Dayton-Springfield, OH	7.8	36
Denver-Boulder, CO CMSA	8.9	31
Detroit, MI PMSA	9.2	28
Fort Lauderdale-Hollywood-Pompano Beach, FL PMSA	14.4	3
Hartford-New Britain-Middletown, CT CMSA	12.6	5
Houston, TX PMSA	9.4	26
Indianapolis, IN	4.5	37
Kansas City, KS-MO	9.9	24
Los Angeles-Long Beach, CA PMSA	11.7	9
Louisville, KY	8.7	32
Memphis, TN	7.8	36
Miami-Hialeah, FL PMSA	13.4	4
Milwaukee, WI PMSA	11.3	13
Minneapolis-Saint Paul, MN	11.0	15
Nassau-Suffolk, NY PMSA	9.9	24
New Orleans, LA	11.1	14
New York, NY PMSA	17.0	1
Newark, NJ PMSA	10.6	18
Norfolk-Virginia Beach-Newport News, VA	13.4	4
Oakland, CA PMSA	11.6	10
Oklahoma City, OK	8.6	33
Philadelphia, PA PMSA	10.4	20
Phoenix, AZ	10.5	19
Pittsburgh-Beaver Valley, PA	10.9	16
Portland, OR PMSA	8.3	34
Providence-Pawtucket-Fall River, MA-RI CMSA	12.6	5
Riverside-San Bernardino, CA PMSA	12.3	6
Rochester, NY	10.5	19
Sacramento, CA	11.1	14
Saint Louis, MO-IL	9.7	25
Salt Lake City-Ogden, UT	10.2	22
San Antonio, TX	15.3	2
San Diego, CA	11.4	12
San Francisco, CA PMSA	11.5	11
San Jose, CA PMSA	11.4	12
Seattle, WA PMSA	9.3	27

[Continued]

★1032★

Percent Distribution of Employed Men in Selected MSAs, 1994, By Occupation: Service Occupations

[Continued]

MSA	Percent	Rank
Tampa-Saint Petersburg-Clearwater, FL	10.7	17
Washington, DC	10.0	23

Source: U.S. Department of Labor, Bureau of Labor Statistics, *Geographic Profile of Employment and Unemployment, 1994,* Bulletin 2469, Washington, D.C.: U.S. Government Printing Office, December 1995, p. 103. *Notes:* "CMSA" stands for "Consolidated Metropolitan Statistical Area." "MSA" stands for "Metropolitan Statistical Area." "PMSA" stands for "Primary Metropolitan Statistical Area."

★1033★

Distribution of Employed Persons, By Sex and Occupation

Percent Distribution of Employed Men in Selected MSAs, 1994, By Occupation: Technicians and Related Support

MSA	Percent	Rank
Anaheim-Santa Ana, CA PMSA	2.8	18
Atlanta, GA	2.7	19
Baltimore, MD	3.0	17
Bergen-Passaic, NJ PMSA	4.3	4
Boston, MA PMSA	3.0	17
Buffalo-Niagara Falls, NY CMSA	2.2	24
Charlotte-Gastonia-Rock Hill, NC-SC	3.0	17
Chicago, IL PMSA	2.7	19
Cincinnati, OH PMSA	3.1	16
Cleveland, OH PMSA	2.2	24
Columbus, OH	3.7	10
Dallas-Fort Worth, TX CMSA	3.4	13
Dayton-Springfield, OH	2.7	19
Denver-Boulder, CO CMSA	3.9	8
Detroit, MI PMSA	3.3	14
Fort Lauderdale-Hollywood-Pompano Beach, FL PMSA	1.8	26
Hartford-New Britain-Middletown, CT CMSA	4.3	4
Houston, TX PMSA	2.6	20
Indianapolis, IN	2.5	21
Kansas City, KS-MO	3.2	15
Los Angeles-Long Beach, CA PMSA	2.7	19
Louisville, KY	3.2	15
Memphis, TN	3.1	16
Miami-Hialeah, FL PMSA	1.1	27
Milwaukee, WI PMSA	2.6	20
Minneapolis-Saint Paul, MN	4.8	2
Nassau-Suffolk, NY PMSA	3.3	14
New Orleans, LA	1.8	26
New York, NY PMSA	2.4	22
Newark, NJ PMSA	2.7	19
Norfolk-Virginia Beach-Newport News, VA	4.2	5
Oakland, CA PMSA	2.3	23
Oklahoma City, OK	3.8	9

[Continued]

★1033★

Percent Distribution of Employed Men in Selected MSAs, 1994, By Occupation: Technicians and Related Support

[Continued]

MSA	Percent	Rank
Philadelphia, PA PMSA	3.1	16
Phoenix, AZ	4.1	6
Pittsburgh-Beaver Valley, PA	3.5	12
Portland, OR PMSA	3.0	17
Providence-Pawtucket-Fall River, MA-RI CMSA	2.2	24
Riverside-San Bernardino, CA PMSA	3.2	15
Rochester, NY	5.7	1
Sacramento, CA	3.6	11
Saint Louis, MO-IL	4.4	3
Salt Lake City-Ogden, UT	3.7	10
San Antonio, TX	1.9	25
San Diego, CA	2.8	18
San Francisco, CA PMSA	2.7	19
San Jose, CA PMSA	4.8	2
Seattle, WA PMSA	3.9	8
Tampa-Saint Petersburg-Clearwater, FL	2.2	24
Washington, DC	4.0	7

Source: U.S. Department of Labor, Bureau of Labor Statistics, *Geographic Profile of Employment and Unemployment, 1994,* Bulletin 2469, Washington, D.C.: U.S. Government Printing Office, December 1995, p. 103. *Notes:* "CMSA" stands for "Consolidated Metropolitan Statistical Area." "MSA" stands for "Metropolitan Statistical Area." "PMSA" stands for "Primary Metropolitan Statistical Area."

★1034★

Distribution of Employed Persons, By Sex and Occupation

Percent Distribution of Employed Men in Selected MSAs, 1994, By Occupation: Transportation and Material Moving

MSA	Percent	Rank
Anaheim-Santa Ana, CA PMSA	3.9	32
Atlanta, GA	5.8	19
Baltimore, MD	8.7	3
Bergen-Passaic, NJ PMSA	6.3	14
Boston, MA PMSA	4.3	31
Buffalo-Niagara Falls, NY CMSA	8.0	4
Charlotte-Gastonia-Rock Hill, NC-SC	6.8	11
Chicago, IL PMSA	5.6	21
Cincinnati, OH PMSA	5.7	20
Cleveland, OH PMSA	6.9	10
Columbus, OH	5.6	21
Dallas-Fort Worth, TX CMSA	6.3	14
Dayton-Springfield, OH	6.2	15
Denver-Boulder, CO CMSA	6.2	15
Detroit, MI PMSA	5.7	20
Fort Lauderdale-Hollywood-Pompano Beach, FL PMSA	4.4	30
Hartford-New Britain-Middletown, CT CMSA	5.9	18
Houston, TX PMSA	7.5	7

[Continued]

★1034★

Percent Distribution of Employed Men in Selected MSAs, 1994, By Occupation: Transportation and Material Moving
[Continued]

MSA	Percent	Rank
Indianapolis, IN	5.6	21
Kansas City, KS-MO	6.5	12
Los Angeles-Long Beach, CA PMSA	4.9	26
Louisville, KY	6.4	13
Memphis, TN	10.3	1
Miami-Hialeah, FL PMSA	7.6	6
Milwaukee, WI PMSA	5.2	23
Minneapolis-Saint Paul, MN	6.1	16
Nassau-Suffolk, NY PMSA	5.0	25
New Orleans, LA	8.7	3
New York, NY PMSA	6.1	16
Newark, NJ PMSA	7.0	9
Norfolk-Virginia Beach-Newport News, VA	5.5	22
Oakland, CA PMSA	6.5	12
Oklahoma City, OK	6.1	16
Philadelphia, PA PMSA	6.0	17
Phoenix, AZ	4.5	29
Pittsburgh-Beaver Valley, PA	6.8	11
Portland, OR PMSA	3.4	33
Providence-Pawtucket-Fall River, MA-RI CMSA	5.9	18
Riverside-San Bernardino, CA PMSA	9.9	2
Rochester, NY	5.1	24
Sacramento, CA	7.2	8
Saint Louis, MO-IL	6.0	17
Salt Lake City-Ogden, UT	6.4	13
San Antonio, TX	7.8	5
San Diego, CA	4.9	26
San Francisco, CA PMSA	5.9	18
San Jose, CA PMSA	4.3	31
Seattle, WA PMSA	4.7	27
Tampa-Saint Petersburg-Clearwater, FL	6.4	13
Washington, DC	4.6	28

Source: U.S. Department of Labor, Bureau of Labor Statistics, *Geographic Profile of Employment and Unemployment, 1994,* Bulletin 2469, Washington, D.C.: U.S. Government Printing Office, December 1995, p. 103. *Notes:* "CMSA" stands for "Consolidated Metropolitan Statistical Area." "MSA" stands for "Metropolitan Statistical Area." "PMSA" stands for "Primary Metropolitan Statistical Area."

★1035★

Distribution of Employed Persons, By Sex and Occupation

Percent Distribution of Employed Women in Selected Cities, 1994, By Occupation: Administrative Support, Including Clerical

City	Percent	Rank
Baltimore, MD	40.0	1
Chicago, IL	27.6	9
Cleveland, OH	30.4	4
Dallas, TX	23.0	13

[Continued]

★1035★

Percent Distribution of Employed Women in Selected Cities, 1994, By Occupation: Administrative Support, Including Clerical
[Continued]

City	Percent	Rank
Detroit, MI	26.1	11
Houston, TX	28.7	6
Indianapolis, IN	31.1	2
Los Angeles, CA	26.7	10
Milwaukee, WI	28.0	7
New York, NY	27.9	8
Philadelphia, PA	31.0	3
Phoenix, AZ	29.8	5
San Antonio, TX	24.6	12
San Diego, CA	21.5	14
San Francisco, CA	28.7	6
Washington, DC	24.6	12

Source: U.S. Department of Labor, Bureau of Labor Statistics, *Geographic Profile of Employment and Unemployment, 1994,* Bulletin 2469, Washington, D.C.: U.S. Government Printing Office, December 1995, p. 103.

★1036★

Distribution of Employed Persons, By Sex and Occupation

Percent Distribution of Employed Women in Selected Cities, 1994, By Occupation: Executive, Administrative, and Managerial

City	Percent	Rank
Baltimore, MD	9.8	15
Chicago, IL	12.5	8
Cleveland, OH	6.2	16
Dallas, TX	14.3	3
Detroit, MI	12.0	11
Houston, TX	12.4	9
Indianapolis, IN	10.5	13
Los Angeles, CA	13.9	5
Milwaukee, WI	12.2	10
New York, NY	12.9	7
Philadelphia, PA	10.2	14
Phoenix, AZ	14.0	4
San Antonio, TX	11.0	12
San Diego, CA	18.3	1
San Francisco, CA	13.4	6
Washington, DC	18.2	2

Source: U.S. Department of Labor, Bureau of Labor Statistics, *Geographic Profile of Employment and Unemployment, 1994,* Bulletin 2469, Washington, D.C.: U.S. Government Printing Office, December 1995, p. 103.

★ 1037 ★

Distribution of Employed Persons, By Sex and Occupation

Percent Distribution of Employed Women in Selected Cities, 1994, By Occupation: Handlers, Equipment Cleaners, Helpers, and Laborers

City	Percent	Rank
Baltimore, MD	1.0	9
Chicago, IL	2.5	2
Cleveland, OH	1.0	9
Dallas, TX	1.8	5
Detroit, MI	2.3	3
Houston, TX	2.6	1
Indianapolis, IN	2.2	4
Los Angeles, CA	1.0	9
Milwaukee, WI	1.7	6
New York, NY	.9	10
Philadelphia, PA	1.8	5
Phoenix, AZ	.8	11
San Antonio, TX	2.2	4
San Diego, CA	1.5	7
San Francisco, CA	1.4	8
Washington, DC	.8	11

Source: U.S. Department of Labor, Bureau of Labor Statistics, *Geographic Profile of Employment and Unemployment, 1994*, Bulletin 2469, Washington, D.C.: U.S. Government Printing Office, December 1995, p. 103.

★ 1038 ★

Distribution of Employed Persons, By Sex and Occupation

Percent Distribution of Employed Women in Selected Cities, 1994, By Occupation: Machine Operators, Assemblers, and Inspectors

City	Percent	Rank
Baltimore, MD	1.9	13
Chicago, IL	7.0	4
Cleveland, OH	6.2	5
Dallas, TX	5.1	7
Detroit, MI	10.7	1
Houston, TX	1.7	15
Indianapolis, IN	2.8	12
Los Angeles, CA	7.2	3
Milwaukee, WI	7.5	2
New York, NY	5.4	6
Philadelphia, PA	5.0	8
Phoenix, AZ	1.8	14
San Antonio, TX	3.2	10
San Diego, CA	3.1	11
San Francisco, CA	4.3	9
Washington, DC	.8	16

Source: U.S. Department of Labor, Bureau of Labor Statistics, *Geographic Profile of Employment and Unemployment, 1994*, Bulletin 2469, Washington, D.C.: U.S. Government Printing Office, December 1995, p. 103.

★ 1039 ★

Distribution of Employed Persons, By Sex and Occupation

Percent Distribution of Employed Women in Selected Cities, 1994, By Occupation: Precision Production, Craft, and Repair

City	Percent	Rank
Baltimore, MD	3.7	3
Chicago, IL	2.2	6
Cleveland, OH	4.3	2
Dallas, TX	3.3	4
Detroit, MI	1.5	11
Houston, TX	2.2	6
Indianapolis, IN	3.3	4
Los Angeles, CA	1.9	8
Milwaukee, WI	1.6	10
New York, NY	1.2	12
Philadelphia, PA	1.8	9
Phoenix, AZ	4.9	1
San Antonio, TX	3.0	5
San Diego, CA	2.1	7
San Francisco, CA	1.9	8
Washington, DC	.8	13

Source: U.S. Department of Labor, Bureau of Labor Statistics, *Geographic Profile of Employment and Unemployment, 1994*, Bulletin 2469, Washington, D.C.: U.S. Government Printing Office, December 1995, p. 103.

★ 1040 ★

Distribution of Employed Persons, By Sex and Occupation

Percent Distribution of Employed Women in Selected Cities, 1994, By Occupation: Professional Specialty

City	Percent	Rank
Baltimore, MD	9.2	15
Chicago, IL	18.9	4
Cleveland, OH	6.8	16
Dallas, TX	15.8	9
Detroit, MI	12.8	11
Houston, TX	11.8	13
Indianapolis, IN	10.2	14
Los Angeles, CA	15.9	8
Milwaukee, WI	18.5	5
New York, NY	19.1	3
Philadelphia, PA	17.6	7
Phoenix, AZ	12.5	12
San Antonio, TX	14.1	10
San Diego, CA	18.0	6
San Francisco, CA	21.3	2
Washington, DC	24.8	1

Source: U.S. Department of Labor, Bureau of Labor Statistics, *Geographic Profile of Employment and Unemployment, 1994*, Bulletin 2469, Washington, D.C.: U.S. Government Printing Office, December 1995, p. 103.

★1041★

Distribution of Employed Persons, By Sex and Occupation

Percent Distribution of Employed Women in Selected Cities, 1994, By Occupation: Sales

City	Percent	Rank
Baltimore, MD	6.8	14
Chicago, IL	10.2	9
Cleveland, OH	11.8	6
Dallas, TX	13.1	5
Detroit, MI	7.9	12
Houston, TX	14.1	3
Indianapolis, IN	13.2	4
Los Angeles, CA	10.3	8
Milwaukee, WI	11.4	7
New York, NY	9.0	11
Philadelphia, PA	10.3	8
Phoenix, AZ	15.0	1
San Antonio, TX	14.9	2
San Diego, CA	13.1	5
San Francisco, CA	9.3	10
Washington, DC	6.9	13

Source: U.S. Department of Labor, Bureau of Labor Statistics, *Geographic Profile of Employment and Unemployment, 1994,* Bulletin 2469, Washington, D.C.: U.S. Government Printing Office, December 1995, p. 103.

★1042★

Distribution of Employed Persons, By Sex and Occupation

Percent Distribution of Employed Women in Selected Cities, 1994, By Occupation: Service Occupations

City	Percent	Rank
Baltimore, MD	21.9	4
Chicago, IL	15.6	14
Cleveland, OH	29.8	1
Dallas, TX	19.3	9
Detroit, MI	22.5	3
Houston, TX	21.3	5
Indianapolis, IN	18.8	10
Los Angeles, CA	20.3	7
Milwaukee, WI	17.7	12
New York, NY	20.5	6
Philadelphia, PA	18.2	11
Phoenix, AZ	17.4	13
San Antonio, TX	22.8	2
San Diego, CA	19.5	8
San Francisco, CA	15.5	15
Washington, DC	18.8	10

Source: U.S. Department of Labor, Bureau of Labor Statistics, *Geographic Profile of Employment and Unemployment, 1994,* Bulletin 2469, Washington, D.C.: U.S. Government Printing Office, December 1995, p. 103.

★1043★

Distribution of Employed Persons, By Sex and Occupation

Percent Distribution of Employed Women in Selected Cities, 1994, By Occupation: Technicians and Related Support

City	Percent	Rank
Baltimore, MD	2.5	9
Chicago, IL	2.6	8
Cleveland, OH	1.7	13
Dallas, TX	2.0	12
Detroit, MI	3.6	5
Houston, TX	3.9	3
Indianapolis, IN	6.1	1
Los Angeles, CA	2.2	11
Milwaukee, WI	1.3	14
New York, NY	2.7	7
Philadelphia, PA	4.1	2
Phoenix, AZ	3.4	6
San Antonio, TX	3.4	6
San Diego, CA	2.3	10
San Francisco, CA	2.0	12
Washington, DC	3.8	4

Source: U.S. Department of Labor, Bureau of Labor Statistics, *Geographic Profile of Employment and Unemployment, 1994,* Bulletin 2469, Washington, D.C.: U.S. Government Printing Office, December 1995, p. 103.

★1044★

Distribution of Employed Persons, By Sex and Occupation

Percent Distribution of Employed Women in Selected Cities, 1994, By Occupation: Transportation and Material Moving

City	Percent	Rank
Baltimore, MD	1.5	1
Chicago, IL	.6	6
Cleveland, OH	1.1	3
Dallas, TX	1.3	2
Detroit, MI	.7	5
Houston, TX	1.1	3
Indianapolis, IN	.8	4
Los Angeles, CA	.4	7
Milwaukee, WI	(3)	10
New York, NY	.3	8
Philadelphia, PA	(3)	10
Phoenix, AZ	.4	7
San Antonio, TX	(3)	10
San Diego, CA	.3	8
San Francisco, CA	.7	5
Washington, DC	.2	9

Source: U.S. Department of Labor, Bureau of Labor Statistics, *Geographic Profile of Employment and Unemployment, 1994,* Bulletin 2469, Washington, D.C.: U.S. Government Printing Office, December 1995, p. 103.

★1045★

Distribution of Employed Persons, By Sex and Occupation

Percent Distribution of Employed Women in Selected MSAs, 1994, By Occupation: Administrative Support, Including Clerical

MSA	Percent	Rank
Anaheim-Santa Ana, CA PMSA	26.1	26
Atlanta, GA	27.7	19
Baltimore, MD	29.5	6
Bergen-Passaic, NJ PMSA	28.1	16
Boston, MA PMSA	26.1	26
Buffalo-Niagara Falls, NY CMSA	23.5	36
Charlotte-Gastonia-Rock Hill, NC-SC	23.0	38
Chicago, IL PMSA	29.0	11
Cincinnati, OH PMSA	25.4	31
Cleveland, OH PMSA	27.8	18
Columbus, OH	27.6	20
Dallas-Fort Worth, TX CMSA	25.5	30
Dayton-Springfield, OH	25.2	32
Denver-Boulder, CO CMSA	27.0	23
Detroit, MI PMSA	26.9	24
Fort Lauderdale-Hollywood-Pompano Beach, FL PMSA	29.8	5
Hartford-New Britain-Middletown, CT CMSA	26.8	25
Houston, TX PMSA	30.3	4
Indianapolis, IN	29.3	8
Kansas City, KS-MO	31.9	2
Los Angeles-Long Beach, CA PMSA	29.0	11
Louisville, KY	27.5	21
Memphis, TN	26.8	25
Miami-Hialeah, FL PMSA	28.8	12
Milwaukee, WI PMSA	23.3	37
Minneapolis-Saint Paul, MN	29.2	9
Nassau-Suffolk, NY PMSA	34.1	1
New Orleans, LA	25.4	31
New York, NY PMSA	26.9	24
Newark, NJ PMSA	29.1	10
Norfolk-Virginia Beach-Newport News, VA	29.4	7
Oakland, CA PMSA	26.0	27
Oklahoma City, OK	23.3	37
Philadelphia, PA PMSA	30.5	3
Phoenix, AZ	28.2	15
Pittsburgh-Beaver Valley, PA	25.4	31
Portland, OR PMSA	27.3	22
Providence-Pawtucket-Fall River, MA-RI CMSA	24.9	33
Riverside-San Bernardino, CA PMSA	30.5	3
Rochester, NY	23.8	35
Sacramento, CA	28.6	13
Saint Louis, MO-IL	29.0	11
Salt Lake City-Ogden, UT	28.3	14
San Antonio, TX	28.3	14
San Diego, CA	25.6	29
San Francisco, CA PMSA	25.4	31
San Jose, CA PMSA	25.8	28
Seattle, WA PMSA	22.6	39

[Continued]

★1045★

Percent Distribution of Employed Women in Selected MSAs, 1994, By Occupation: Administrative Support, Including Clerical
[Continued]

MSA	Percent	Rank
Tampa-Saint Petersburg-Clearwater, FL	27.9	17
Washington, DC	24.3	34

Source: U.S. Department of Labor, Bureau of Labor Statistics, *Geographic Profile of Employment and Unemployment, 1994,* Bulletin 2469, Washington, D.C.: U.S. Government Printing Office, December 1995, p. 103. *Notes:* "CMSA" stands for "Consolidated Metropolitan Statistical Area." "MSA" stands for "Metropolitan Statistical Area." "PMSA" stands for "Primary Metropolitan Statistical Area."

★1046★

Distribution of Employed Persons, By Sex and Occupation

Percent Distribution of Employed Women in Selected MSAs, 1994, By Occupation: Executive, Administrative, and Managerial

MSA	Percent	Rank
Anaheim-Santa Ana, CA PMSA	16.3	8
Atlanta, GA	16.8	5
Baltimore, MD	16.9	4
Bergen-Passaic, NJ PMSA	16.1	9
Boston, MA PMSA	14.8	14
Buffalo-Niagara Falls, NY CMSA	9.0	36
Charlotte-Gastonia-Rock Hill, NC-SC	11.8	29
Chicago, IL PMSA	13.9	20
Cincinnati, OH PMSA	11.4	30
Cleveland, OH PMSA	12.9	25
Columbus, OH	16.0	10
Dallas-Fort Worth, TX CMSA	15.1	13
Dayton-Springfield, OH	9.0	36
Denver-Boulder, CO CMSA	14.6	16
Detroit, MI PMSA	12.8	26
Fort Lauderdale-Hollywood-Pompano Beach, FL PMSA	14.6	16
Hartford-New Britain-Middletown, CT CMSA	12.9	25
Houston, TX PMSA	14.3	17
Indianapolis, IN	15.8	11
Kansas City, KS-MO	16.4	7
Los Angeles-Long Beach, CA PMSA	14.1	18
Louisville, KY	10.4	33
Memphis, TN	9.7	35
Miami-Hialeah, FL PMSA	9.8	34
Milwaukee, WI PMSA	14.7	15
Minneapolis-Saint Paul, MN	13.5	23
Nassau-Suffolk, NY PMSA	10.7	32
New Orleans, LA	13.3	24
New York, NY PMSA	13.6	22
Newark, NJ PMSA	13.8	21
Norfolk-Virginia Beach-Newport News, VA	8.3	37
Oakland, CA PMSA	17.2	3
Oklahoma City, OK	14.0	19

[Continued]

★1046★

Percent Distribution of Employed Women in Selected MSAs, 1994, By Occupation: Executive, Administrative, and Managerial
[Continued]

MSA	Percent	Rank
Philadelphia, PA PMSA	12.3	28
Phoenix, AZ	14.8	14
Pittsburgh-Beaver Valley, PA	11.1	31
Portland, OR PMSA	17.6	2
Providence-Pawtucket-Fall River, MA-RI CMSA	11.1	31
Riverside-San Bernardino, CA PMSA	14.6	16
Rochester, NY	12.3	28
Sacramento, CA	14.6	16
Saint Louis, MO-IL	12.5	27
Salt Lake City-Ogden, UT	14.6	16
San Antonio, TX	9.7	35
San Diego, CA	15.3	12
San Francisco, CA PMSA	20.9	1
San Jose, CA PMSA	16.5	6
Seattle, WA PMSA	17.2	3
Tampa-Saint Petersburg-Clearwater, FL	13.6	22
Washington, DC	20.9	1

Source: U.S. Department of Labor, Bureau of Labor Statistics, *Geographic Profile of Employment and Unemployment, 1994,* Bulletin 2469, Washington, D.C.: U.S. Government Printing Office, December 1995, p. 103. *Notes:* "CMSA" stands for "Consolidated Metropolitan Statistical Area." "MSA" stands for "Metropolitan Statistical Area." "PMSA" stands for "Primary Metropolitan Statistical Area."

★1047★

Distribution of Employed Persons, By Sex and Occupation

Percent Distribution of Employed Women in Selected MSAs, 1994, By Occupation: Handlers, Equipment Cleaners, Helpers, and Laborers

MSA	Percent	Rank
Anaheim-Santa Ana, CA PMSA	1.3	16
Atlanta, GA	2.2	7
Baltimore, MD	.6	22
Bergen-Passaic, NJ PMSA	1.4	15
Boston, MA PMSA	.8	20
Buffalo-Niagara Falls, NY CMSA	.8	20
Charlotte-Gastonia-Rock Hill, NC-SC	2.8	3
Chicago, IL PMSA	1.9	10
Cincinnati, OH PMSA	2.3	6
Cleveland, OH PMSA	.8	20
Columbus, OH	2.4	5
Dallas-Fort Worth, TX CMSA	2.0	9
Dayton-Springfield, OH	3.0	2
Denver-Boulder, CO CMSA	1.3	16
Detroit, MI PMSA	1.4	15
Fort Lauderdale-Hollywood-Pompano Beach, FL PMSA	1.0	19
Hartford-New Britain-Middletown, CT CMSA	1.8	11
Houston, TX PMSA	1.5	14

[Continued]

★1047★

Percent Distribution of Employed Women in Selected MSAs, 1994, By Occupation: Handlers, Equipment Cleaners, Helpers, and Laborers
[Continued]

MSA	Percent	Rank
Indianapolis, IN	1.9	10
Kansas City, KS-MO	1.4	15
Los Angeles-Long Beach, CA PMSA	1.2	17
Louisville, KY	1.8	11
Memphis, TN	4.3	1
Miami-Hialeah, FL PMSA	1.4	15
Milwaukee, WI PMSA	.8	20
Minneapolis-Saint Paul, MN	.8	20
Nassau-Suffolk, NY PMSA	.4	24
New Orleans, LA	1.2	17
New York, NY PMSA	.8	20
Newark, NJ PMSA	1.0	19
Norfolk-Virginia Beach-Newport News, VA	2.5	4
Oakland, CA PMSA	1.1	18
Oklahoma City, OK	2.1	8
Philadelphia, PA PMSA	1.3	16
Phoenix, AZ	.7	21
Pittsburgh-Beaver Valley, PA	1.7	12
Portland, OR PMSA	.2	25
Providence-Pawtucket-Fall River, MA-RI CMSA	2.0	9
Riverside-San Bernardino, CA PMSA	1.7	12
Rochester, NY	.5	23
Sacramento, CA	.6	22
Saint Louis, MO-IL	1.7	12
Salt Lake City-Ogden, UT	1.6	13
San Antonio, TX	1.6	13
San Diego, CA	1.6	13
San Francisco, CA PMSA	1.1	18
San Jose, CA PMSA	1.9	10
Seattle, WA PMSA	1.3	16
Tampa-Saint Petersburg-Clearwater, FL	.4	24
Washington, DC	.5	23

Source: U.S. Department of Labor, Bureau of Labor Statistics, *Geographic Profile of Employment and Unemployment, 1994,* Bulletin 2469, Washington, D.C.: U.S. Government Printing Office, December 1995, p. 103. *Notes:* "CMSA" stands for "Consolidated Metropolitan Statistical Area." "MSA" stands for "Metropolitan Statistical Area." "PMSA" stands for "Primary Metropolitan Statistical Area."

★1048★

Distribution of Employed Persons, By Sex and Occupation

Percent Distribution of Employed Women in Selected MSAs, 1994, By Occupation: Machine Operators, Assemblers, and Inspectors

MSA	Percent	Rank
Anaheim-Santa Ana, CA PMSA	5.7	6
Atlanta, GA	4.2	17
Baltimore, MD	1.6	33
Bergen-Passaic, NJ PMSA	5.1	10

[Continued]

★1048★

Percent Distribution of Employed Women in Selected MSAs, 1994, By Occupation: Machine Operators, Assemblers, and Inspectors

[Continued]

MSA	Percent	Rank
Boston, MA PMSA	2.4	27
Buffalo-Niagara Falls, NY CMSA	3.3	22
Charlotte-Gastonia-Rock Hill, NC-SC	13.0	1
Chicago, IL PMSA	5.0	11
Cincinnati, OH PMSA	4.5	15
Cleveland, OH PMSA	5.5	8
Columbus, OH	3.5	20
Dallas-Fort Worth, TX CMSA	3.9	18
Dayton-Springfield, OH	6.6	4
Denver-Boulder, CO CMSA	2.3	28
Detroit, MI PMSA	5.7	6
Fort Lauderdale-Hollywood-Pompano Beach, FL PMSA	1.6	33
Hartford-New Britain-Middletown, CT CMSA	1.9	30
Houston, TX PMSA	1.8	31
Indianapolis, IN	2.5	26
Kansas City, KS-MO	2.8	23
Los Angeles-Long Beach, CA PMSA	5.3	9
Louisville, KY	6.7	3
Memphis, TN	5.6	7
Miami-Hialeah, FL PMSA	4.6	14
Milwaukee, WI PMSA	6.1	5
Minneapolis-Saint Paul, MN	4.2	17
Nassau-Suffolk, NY PMSA	2.6	25
New Orleans, LA	1.7	32
New York, NY PMSA	4.6	14
Newark, NJ PMSA	4.9	12
Norfolk-Virginia Beach-Newport News, VA	1.7	32
Oakland, CA PMSA	3.7	19
Oklahoma City, OK	3.3	22
Philadelphia, PA PMSA	3.3	22
Phoenix, AZ	2.1	29
Pittsburgh-Beaver Valley, PA	3.4	21
Portland, OR PMSA	2.3	28
Providence-Pawtucket-Fall River, MA-RI CMSA	9.2	2
Riverside-San Bernardino, CA PMSA	1.7	32
Rochester, NY	5.0	11
Sacramento, CA	1.9	30
Saint Louis, MO-IL	2.8	23
Salt Lake City-Ogden, UT	4.3	16
San Antonio, TX	2.7	24
San Diego, CA	2.8	23
San Francisco, CA PMSA	1.9	30
San Jose, CA PMSA	4.8	13
Seattle, WA PMSA	1.3	34

[Continued]

★1048★

Percent Distribution of Employed Women in Selected MSAs, 1994, By Occupation: Machine Operators, Assemblers, and Inspectors

[Continued]

MSA	Percent	Rank
Tampa-Saint Petersburg-Clearwater, FL	3.3	22
Washington, DC	.8	35

Source: U.S. Department of Labor, Bureau of Labor Statistics, *Geographic Profile of Employment and Unemployment, 1994,* Bulletin 2469, Washington, D.C.: U.S. Government Printing Office, December 1995, p. 103. *Notes:* "CMSA" stands for "Consolidated Metropolitan Statistical Area." "MSA" stands for "Metropolitan Statistical Area." "PMSA" stands for "Primary Metropolitan Statistical Area."

★1049★

Distribution of Employed Persons, By Sex and Occupation

Percent Distribution of Employed Women in Selected MSAs, 1994, By Occupation: Precision Production, Craft, and Repair

MSA	Percent	Rank
Anaheim-Santa Ana, CA PMSA	2.0	12
Atlanta, GA	2.2	11
Baltimore, MD	2.5	8
Bergen-Passaic, NJ PMSA	1.2	19
Boston, MA PMSA	1.3	18
Buffalo-Niagara Falls, NY CMSA	1.3	18
Charlotte-Gastonia-Rock Hill, NC-SC	1.7	15
Chicago, IL PMSA	2.3	10
Cincinnati, OH PMSA	2.5	8
Cleveland, OH PMSA	2.6	7
Columbus, OH	1.3	18
Dallas-Fort Worth, TX CMSA	2.8	6
Dayton-Springfield, OH	1.4	17
Denver-Boulder, CO CMSA	1.9	13
Detroit, MI PMSA	2.0	12
Fort Lauderdale-Hollywood-Pompano Beach, FL PMSA	2.0	12
Hartford-New Britain-Middletown, CT CMSA	2.9	5
Houston, TX PMSA	1.9	13
Indianapolis, IN	2.5	8
Kansas City, KS-MO	1.1	20
Los Angeles-Long Beach, CA PMSA	2.4	9
Louisville, KY	1.9	13
Memphis, TN	2.5	8
Miami-Hialeah, FL PMSA	1.4	17
Milwaukee, WI PMSA	3.8	1
Minneapolis-Saint Paul, MN	2.2	11
Nassau-Suffolk, NY PMSA	1.6	16
New Orleans, LA	1.6	16
New York, NY PMSA	1.1	20
Newark, NJ PMSA	1.4	17
Norfolk-Virginia Beach-Newport News, VA	2.9	5
Oakland, CA PMSA	3.4	3
Oklahoma City, OK	2.5	8

[Continued]

★1049★

Percent Distribution of Employed Women in Selected MSAs, 1994, By Occupation: Precision Production, Craft, and Repair
[Continued]

MSA	Percent	Rank
Philadelphia, PA PMSA	1.9	13
Phoenix, AZ	3.4	3
Pittsburgh-Beaver Valley, PA	1.8	14
Portland, OR PMSA	1.1	20
Providence-Pawtucket-Fall River, MA-RI CMSA	2.9	5
Riverside-San Bernardino, CA PMSA	2.4	9
Rochester, NY	3.5	2
Sacramento, CA	.8	21
Saint Louis, MO-IL	.5	22
Salt Lake City-Ogden, UT	2.2	11
San Antonio, TX	2.6	7
San Diego, CA	2.4	9
San Francisco, CA PMSA	1.6	16
San Jose, CA PMSA	3.0	4
Seattle, WA PMSA	1.7	15
Tampa-Saint Petersburg-Clearwater, FL	2.4	9
Washington, DC	1.9	13

Source: U.S. Department of Labor, Bureau of Labor Statistics, *Geographic Profile of Employment and Unemployment, 1994,* Bulletin 2469, Washington, D.C.: U.S. Government Printing Office, December 1995, p. 103. *Notes:* "CMSA" stands for "Consolidated Metropolitan Statistical Area." "MSA" stands for "Metropolitan Statistical Area." "PMSA" stands for "Primary Metropolitan Statistical Area."

★1050★
Distribution of Employed Persons, By Sex and Occupation

Percent Distribution of Employed Women in Selected MSAs, 1994, By Occupation: Professional Specialties

MSA	Percent	Rank
Anaheim-Santa Ana, CA PMSA	13.2	39
Atlanta, GA	16.3	26
Baltimore, MD	18.0	17
Bergen-Passaic, NJ PMSA	18.9	14
Boston, MA PMSA	24.8	1
Buffalo-Niagara Falls, NY CMSA	20.4	5
Charlotte-Gastonia-Rock Hill, NC-SC	15.4	30
Chicago, IL PMSA	18.2	16
Cincinnati, OH PMSA	20.2	6
Cleveland, OH PMSA	15.0	33
Columbus, OH	19.8	8
Dallas-Fort Worth, TX CMSA	16.9	22
Dayton-Springfield, OH	19.1	12
Denver-Boulder, CO CMSA	20.0	7
Detroit, MI PMSA	15.2	31
Fort Lauderdale-Hollywood-Pompano Beach, FL PMSA	13.7	38
Hartford-New Britain-Middletown, CT CMSA	22.2	2
Houston, TX PMSA	16.3	26

[Continued]

★1050★

Percent Distribution of Employed Women in Selected MSAs, 1994, By Occupation: Professional Specialties
[Continued]

MSA	Percent	Rank
Indianapolis, IN	8.9	40
Kansas City, KS-MO	16.0	27
Los Angeles-Long Beach, CA PMSA	15.5	29
Louisville, KY	16.0	27
Memphis, TN	14.0	37
Miami-Hialeah, FL PMSA	14.2	36
Milwaukee, WI PMSA	18.0	17
Minneapolis-Saint Paul, MN	17.0	21
Nassau-Suffolk, NY PMSA	19.1	12
New Orleans, LA	15.1	32
New York, NY PMSA	20.2	6
Newark, NJ PMSA	19.2	11
Norfolk-Virginia Beach-Newport News, VA	17.8	18
Oakland, CA PMSA	17.5	19
Oklahoma City, OK	17.4	20
Philadelphia, PA PMSA	19.0	13
Phoenix, AZ	14.5	35
Pittsburgh-Beaver Valley, PA	19.1	12
Portland, OR PMSA	19.4	10
Providence-Pawtucket-Fall River, MA-RI CMSA	16.4	25
Riverside-San Bernardino, CA PMSA	16.6	24
Rochester, NY	19.2	11
Sacramento, CA	16.8	23
Saint Louis, MO-IL	19.5	9
Salt Lake City-Ogden, UT	17.4	20
San Antonio, TX	15.4	30
San Diego, CA	15.7	28
San Francisco, CA PMSA	18.6	15
San Jose, CA PMSA	13.7	38
Seattle, WA PMSA	21.2	4
Tampa-Saint Petersburg-Clearwater, FL	14.9	34
Washington, DC	21.7	3

Source: U.S. Department of Labor, Bureau of Labor Statistics, *Geographic Profile of Employment and Unemployment, 1994,* Bulletin 2469, Washington, D.C.: U.S. Government Printing Office, December 1995, p. 103. *Notes:* "CMSA" stands for "Consolidated Metropolitan Statistical Area." "MSA" stands for "Metropolitan Statistical Area." "PMSA" stands for "Primary Metropolitan Statistical Area."

★1051★
Distribution of Employed Persons, By Sex and Occupation

Percent Distribution of Employed Women in Selected MSAs, 1994, By Occupation: Sales

MSA	Percent	Rank
Anaheim-Santa Ana, CA PMSA	16.5	4
Atlanta, GA	13.0	21
Baltimore, MD	9.7	36
Bergen-Passaic, NJ PMSA	13.2	19
Boston, MA PMSA	11.0	34

[Continued]

★ 1051 ★

Percent Distribution of Employed Women in Selected MSAs, 1994, By Occupation: Sales

[Continued]

MSA	Percent	Rank
Buffalo-Niagara Falls, NY CMSA	12.8	22
Charlotte-Gastonia-Rock Hill, NC-SC	14.4	12
Chicago, IL PMSA	12.1	28
Cincinnati, OH PMSA	14.1	14
Cleveland, OH PMSA	12.3	26
Columbus, OH	10.1	35
Dallas-Fort Worth, TX CMSA	13.0	21
Dayton-Springfield, OH	11.8	29
Denver-Boulder, CO CMSA	13.6	16
Detroit, MI PMSA	13.4	17
Fort Lauderdale-Hollywood-Pompano Beach, FL PMSA	17.3	3
Hartford-New Britain-Middletown, CT CMSA	11.5	31
Houston, TX PMSA	12.7	23
Indianapolis, IN	16.3	5
Kansas City, KS-MO	11.7	30
Los Angeles-Long Beach, CA PMSA	12.2	27
Louisville, KY	12.8	22
Memphis, TN	15.5	7
Miami-Hialeah, FL PMSA	14.7	10
Milwaukee, WI PMSA	12.2	27
Minneapolis-Saint Paul, MN	11.3	33
Nassau-Suffolk, NY PMSA	13.3	18
New Orleans, LA	17.9	1
New York, NY PMSA	9.5	38
Newark, NJ PMSA	12.2	27
Norfolk-Virginia Beach-Newport News, VA	17.5	2
Oakland, CA PMSA	11.5	31
Oklahoma City, OK	15.6	6
Philadelphia, PA PMSA	12.5	24
Phoenix, AZ	14.3	13
Pittsburgh-Beaver Valley, PA	14.9	9
Portland, OR PMSA	13.1	20
Providence-Pawtucket-Fall River, MA-RI CMSA	11.0	34
Riverside-San Bernardino, CA PMSA	15.4	8
Rochester, NY	8.6	39
Sacramento, CA	11.4	32
Saint Louis, MO-IL	13.8	15
Salt Lake City-Ogden, UT	12.7	23
San Antonio, TX	13.8	15
San Diego, CA	14.5	11
San Francisco, CA PMSA	12.4	25
San Jose, CA PMSA	12.5	24
Seattle, WA PMSA	13.4	17
Tampa-Saint Petersburg-Clearwater, FL	14.4	12
Washington, DC	9.6	37

Source: U.S. Department of Labor, Bureau of Labor Statistics, *Geographic Profile of Employment and Unemployment, 1994*, Bulletin 2469, Washington, D.C.: U.S. Government Printing Office, December 1995, p. 103. *Notes:* "CMSA" stands for "Consolidated Metropolitan Statistical Area." "MSA" stands for "Metropolitan Statistical Area." "PMSA" stands for "Primary Metropolitan Statistical Area."

★ 1052 ★

Distribution of Employed Persons, By Sex and Occupation

Percent Distribution of Employed Women in Selected MSAs, 1994, By Occupation: Service Occupations

MSA	Percent	Rank
Anaheim-Santa Ana, CA PMSA	14.6	28
Atlanta, GA	13.4	36
Baltimore, MD	15.8	21
Bergen-Passaic, NJ PMSA	11.1	37
Boston, MA PMSA	14.2	31
Buffalo-Niagara Falls, NY CMSA	23.0	1
Charlotte-Gastonia-Rock Hill, NC-SC	13.6	34
Chicago, IL PMSA	13.5	35
Cincinnati, OH PMSA	14.8	26
Cleveland, OH PMSA	18.2	9
Columbus, OH	15.4	22
Dallas-Fort Worth, TX CMSA	15.9	20
Dayton-Springfield, OH	17.9	10
Denver-Boulder, CO CMSA	14.9	25
Detroit, MI PMSA	17.8	11
Fort Lauderdale-Hollywood-Pompano Beach, FL PMSA	15.8	21
Hartford-New Britain-Middletown, CT CMSA	14.4	29
Houston, TX PMSA	15.9	20
Indianapolis, IN	15.8	21
Kansas City, KS-MO	14.7	27
Los Angeles-Long Beach, CA PMSA	16.9	15
Louisville, KY	17.1	14
Memphis, TN	16.7	17
Miami-Hialeah, FL PMSA	20.0	4
Milwaukee, WI PMSA	16.8	16
Minneapolis-Saint Paul, MN	15.8	21
Nassau-Suffolk, NY PMSA	14.9	25
New Orleans, LA	19.4	6
New York, NY PMSA	19.8	5
Newark, NJ PMSA	13.7	33
Norfolk-Virginia Beach-Newport News, VA	17.8	11
Oakland, CA PMSA	15.0	24
Oklahoma City, OK	16.9	15
Philadelphia, PA PMSA	14.6	28
Phoenix, AZ	16.8	16
Pittsburgh-Beaver Valley, PA	16.3	18
Portland, OR PMSA	14.4	29
Providence-Pawtucket-Fall River, MA-RI CMSA	17.7	12
Riverside-San Bernardino, CA PMSA	11.1	37
Rochester, NY	19.3	7
Sacramento, CA	20.1	3
Saint Louis, MO-IL	14.3	30
Salt Lake City-Ogden, UT	13.7	33
San Antonio, TX	21.0	2
San Diego, CA	18.7	8
San Francisco, CA PMSA	14.0	32
San Jose, CA PMSA	16.0	19
Seattle, WA PMSA	15.9	20

[Continued]

★1052★

Percent Distribution of Employed Women in Selected MSAs, 1994, By Occupation: Service Occupations

[Continued]

MSA	Percent	Rank
Tampa-Saint Petersburg-Clearwater, FL	17.4	13
Washington, DC	15.3	23

Source: U.S. Department of Labor, Bureau of Labor Statistics, *Geographic Profile of Employment and Unemployment, 1994,* Bulletin 2469, Washington, D.C.: U.S. Government Printing Office, December 1995, p. 103. *Notes:* "CMSA" stands for "Consolidated Metropolitan Statistical Area." "MSA" stands for "Metropolitan Statistical Area." "PMSA" stands for "Primary Metropolitan Statistical Area."

★1053★

Distribution of Employed Persons, By Sex and Occupation

Percent Distribution of Employed Women in Selected MSAs, 1994, By Occupation: Technicians and Related Support

MSA	Percent	Rank
Anaheim-Santa Ana, CA PMSA	2.7	20
Atlanta, GA	3.4	14
Baltimore, MD	3.4	14
Bergen-Passaic, NJ PMSA	4.3	6
Boston, MA PMSA	3.7	12
Buffalo-Niagara Falls, NY CMSA	3.8	11
Charlotte-Gastonia-Rock Hill, NC-SC	3.3	15
Chicago, IL PMSA	3.0	18
Cincinnati, OH PMSA	4.0	9
Cleveland, OH PMSA	3.4	14
Columbus, OH	3.2	16
Dallas-Fort Worth, TX CMSA	3.2	16
Dayton-Springfield, OH	3.8	11
Denver-Boulder, CO CMSA	3.9	10
Detroit, MI PMSA	3.3	15
Fort Lauderdale-Hollywood-Pompano Beach, FL PMSA	3.6	13
Hartford-New Britain-Middletown, CT CMSA	4.5	5
Houston, TX PMSA	4.2	7
Indianapolis, IN	4.6	4
Kansas City, KS-MO	3.6	13
Los Angeles-Long Beach, CA PMSA	2.5	22
Louisville, KY	5.1	2
Memphis, TN	4.1	8
Miami-Hialeah, FL PMSA	3.1	17
Milwaukee, WI PMSA	4.0	9
Minneapolis-Saint Paul, MN	4.8	3
Nassau-Suffolk, NY PMSA	2.0	24
New Orleans, LA	3.7	12
New York, NY PMSA	3.0	18
Newark, NJ PMSA	3.8	11
Norfolk-Virginia Beach-Newport News, VA	1.6	25
Oakland, CA PMSA	3.3	15
Oklahoma City, OK	3.3	15

[Continued]

★1053★

Percent Distribution of Employed Women in Selected MSAs, 1994, By Occupation: Technicians and Related Support

[Continued]

MSA	Percent	Rank
Philadelphia, PA PMSA	3.6	13
Phoenix, AZ	4.2	7
Pittsburgh-Beaver Valley, PA	2.9	19
Portland, OR PMSA	3.4	14
Providence-Pawtucket-Fall River, MA-RI CMSA	4.2	7
Riverside-San Bernardino, CA PMSA	4.2	7
Rochester, NY	6.3	1
Sacramento, CA	4.2	7
Saint Louis, MO-IL	4.0	9
Salt Lake City-Ogden, UT	3.6	13
San Antonio, TX	3.7	12
San Diego, CA	2.6	21
San Francisco, CA PMSA	2.1	23
San Jose, CA PMSA	3.9	10
Seattle, WA PMSA	4.0	9
Tampa-Saint Petersburg-Clearwater, FL	3.4	14
Washington, DC	4.0	9

Source: U.S. Department of Labor, Bureau of Labor Statistics, *Geographic Profile of Employment and Unemployment, 1994,* Bulletin 2469, Washington, D.C.: U.S. Government Printing Office, December 1995, p. 103. *Notes:* "CMSA" stands for "Consolidated Metropolitan Statistical Area." "MSA" stands for "Metropolitan Statistical Area." "PMSA" stands for "Primary Metropolitan Statistical Area."

★1054★

Distribution of Employed Persons, By Sex and Occupation

Percent Distribution of Employed Women in Selected MSAs, 1994, By Occupation: Transportation and Material Moving

MSA	Percent	Rank
Anaheim-Santa Ana, CA PMSA	0.4	11
Atlanta, GA	.4	11
Baltimore, MD	1.4	1
Bergen-Passaic, NJ PMSA	.4	11
Boston, MA PMSA	.5	10
Buffalo-Niagara Falls, NY CMSA	1.4	1
Charlotte-Gastonia-Rock Hill, NC-SC	.7	8
Chicago, IL PMSA	.6	9
Cincinnati, OH PMSA	.6	9
Cleveland, OH PMSA	1.1	4
Columbus, OH	.6	9
Dallas-Fort Worth, TX CMSA	1.0	5
Dayton-Springfield, OH	1.2	3
Denver-Boulder, CO CMSA	.3	12
Detroit, MI PMSA	1.1	4
Fort Lauderdale-Hollywood-Pompano Beach, FL PMSA	.5	10
Hartford-New Britain-Middletown, CT CMSA	.8	7
Houston, TX PMSA	.9	6

[Continued]

★ 1054 ★

Percent Distribution of Employed Women in Selected MSAs, 1994, By Occupation: Transportation and Material Moving

[Continued]

MSA	Percent	Rank
Indianapolis, IN	.8	7
Kansas City, KS-MO	.1	14
Los Angeles-Long Beach, CA PMSA	.7	8
Louisville, KY	.6	9
Memphis, TN	.7	8
Miami-Hialeah, FL PMSA	1.4	1
Milwaukee, WI PMSA	.3	12
Minneapolis-Saint Paul, MN	.8	7
Nassau-Suffolk, NY PMSA	1.0	5
New Orleans, LA	.3	12
New York, NY PMSA	.3	12
Newark, NJ PMSA	.7	8
Norfolk-Virginia Beach-Newport News, VA	.3	12
Oakland, CA PMSA	.8	7
Oklahoma City, OK	1.3	2
Philadelphia, PA PMSA	.6	9
Phoenix, AZ	.7	8
Pittsburgh-Beaver Valley, PA	1.1	4
Portland, OR PMSA	.9	6
Providence-Pawtucket-Fall River, MA-RI CMSA	.8	7
Riverside-San Bernardino, CA PMSA	.8	7
Rochester, NY	.6	9
Sacramento, CA	.6	9
Saint Louis, MO-IL	1.1	4
Salt Lake City-Ogden, UT	1.0	5
San Antonio, TX	.2	13
San Diego, CA	.5	10
San Francisco, CA PMSA	.8	7
San Jose, CA PMSA	.9	6
Seattle, WA PMSA	.6	9
Tampa-Saint Petersburg-Clearwater, FL	.4	11
Washington, DC	.8	7

Source: U.S. Department of Labor, Bureau of Labor Statistics, *Geographic Profile of Employment and Unemployment, 1994,* Bulletin 2469, Washington, D.C.: U.S. Government Printing Office, December 1995, p. 103. *Notes:* "CMSA" stands for "Consolidated Metropolitan Statistical Area." "MSA" stands for "Metropolitan Statistical Area." "PMSA" stands for "Primary Metropolitan Statistical Area."

★ 1055 ★
Unemployment

Unemployment Rate in Central Cities, 1993, By Sex: Men

Data refer to selected cities.

Central city	Men	Rank
Baltimore, MD	12.7	3
Chicago, IL	12.1	5
Cleveland, OH	12.4	4
Dallas, TX	8.8	10

[Continued]

★ 1055 ★

Unemployment Rate in Central Cities, 1993, By Sex: Men

[Continued]

Central city	Men	Rank
Detroit, MI	14.5	1
Washington, DC	8.6	11
Houston, TX	8.4	12
Indianapolis, IN	6.7	15
Los Angeles, CA	10.6	7
Milwaukee, WI	9.8	8
New York, NY	11.4	6
Philadelphia, PA	13.0	2
Phoenix, AZ	9.1	9
San Antonio, TX	7.0	14
San Diego, CA	8.4	12
San Francisco, CA	7.1	13

Source: U.S. Department of Labor, Bureau of Labor Statistics, *Geographic Profile of Employment and Unemployment, 1993,* Washington, D.C.: U.S. Government Printing Office, September 1994, p. 95.

★ 1056 ★
Unemployment

Unemployment Rate in Central Cities, 1993, By Sex: Women

Data refer to selected cities.

Central city	Women	Rank
Baltimore, MD	10.0	5
Chicago, IL	9.1	7
Cleveland, OH	9.0	8
Dallas, TX	10.6	3
Detroit, MI	12.9	2
Washington, DC	8.4	11
Houston, TX	10.2	4
Indianapolis, IN	5.1	15
Los Angeles, CA	9.0	8
Milwaukee, WI	7.0	13
New York, NY	8.7	10
Philadelphia, PA	9.8	6
Phoenix, AZ	6.2	14
Saint Louis, IL-MO	16.3	1
San Antonio, TX	7.5	12
San Diego, CA	8.7	10
San Francisco, CA	8.9	9

Source: U.S. Department of Labor, Bureau of Labor Statistics, *Geographic Profile of Employment and Unemployment, 1993,* Washington, D.C.: .U.S. Government Printing Office, September 1994, p. 95.

★1057★
Unemployment

Unemployment Rate in Central Cities, 1993: Total

Data refer to selected cities.

Central city	Total	Rank
Baltimore, MD	11.4	4
Chicago, IL	10.7	6
Cleveland, OH	10.9	5
Dallas, TX	9.6	9
Detroit, MI	13.7	2
Washington, DC	8.5	11
Houston, TX	9.2	10
Indianapolis, IN	5.8	15
Los Angeles, CA	9.9	8
Milwaukee, WI	8.4	12
New York, NY	10.2	7
Philadelphia, PA	11.5	3
Phoenix, AZ	7.8	13
Saint Louis, IL-MO	15.8	1
San Antonio, TX	7.2	14
San Diego, CA	8.5	11
San Francisco, CA	7.9	12

Source: U.S. Department of Labor, Bureau of Labor Statistics, *Geographic Profile of Employment and Unemployment, 1993*, Washington, D.C.: U.S. Government Printing Office, September 1994, p. 95.

★1058★
Unemployment

Unemployment Rate in MSAs, 1993, By Sex: Men (Highest Rates)

Data refer to selected metropolitan statistical areas.

MSA	Men	Rank
Chicago, IL PMSA	8.7	8
Hartford-New Britain-Middletown, CT CMSA	8.4	10
Los Angeles-Long Beach, CA PMSA	10.5	2
New York, NY PMSA	10.4	3
Newark, NJ PMSA	9.8	4
Norfolk-Virginia Beach-Newport News, VA MSA	9.5	6
Oakland, CA PMSA	8.6	9
Pittsburgh-Beaver Valley, PA CMSA	8.6	9
Providence-Pawtucket-Fall River, RI-MA CMSA	8.7	8
Riverside-San Bernardino, CA PMSA	11.6	1
Sacramento, CA MSA	9.3	7
San Diego, CA MSA	9.6	5

Source: U.S. Department of Labor, Bureau of Labor Statistics, *Geographic Profile of Employment and Unemployment, 1993*, Washington, D.C.: U.S. Government Printing Office, September 1994, p. 95.

★1059★
Unemployment

Unemployment Rate in MSAs, 1993, By Sex: Women (Highest Rates)

Data refer to selected metropolitan statistical areas.

MSA	Women	Rank
Anaheim-Santa Ana, CA PMSA	7.6	10
Los Angeles-Long Beach, CA PMSA	8.6	6
Memphis, TN MSA	9.8	9
Miami-Hialeah, FL PMSA	9.0	4
New Orleans, LA MSA	10.1	3
New York, NY PMSA	8.0	8
Oakland, CA PMSA	11.1	1
Riverside-San Bernardino, CA PMSA	10.8	2
Saint Louis, MO-IL MSA	8.1	7
San Diego, CA MSA	8.8	5

Source: U.S. Department of Labor, Bureau of Labor Statistics, *Geographic Profile of Employment and Unemployment, 1993*, Washington, D.C.: .U.S. Government Printing Office, September 1994, p. 95.

★1060★
Unemployment

Unemployment Rate in MSAs, 1993, By Sex: Men (Lowest Rates)

Data refer to selected metropolitan statistical areas.

MSA	Men	Rank
Atlanta, GA MSA	5.4	7
Charlotte-Gastonia-Rock Hill, NC-SC MSA	4.9	3
Columbus, OH MSA	5.5	8
Denver-Boulder, CO CMSA	5.0	4
Indianapolis, IN MSA	4.7	2
Kansas City, MO MSA	5.4	7
Louisville, KY MSA	4.7	2
Milwaukee, WI PMSA	5.2	6
Salt Lake City-Ogden, UT MSA	3.6	1
Washington, DC MSA	5.1	5

Source: U.S. Department of Labor, Bureau of Labor Statistics, *Geographic Profile of Employment and Unemployment, 1993*, Washington, D.C.: U.S. Government Printing Office, September 1994, p. 95.

★1061★
Unemployment

Unemployment Rate in MSAs, 1993, By Sex: Women (Lowest Rates)

Data refer to selected metropolitan statistical areas.

MSA	Women	Rank
Atlanta, GA MSA	4.8	6
Bergen-Passaic, NJ PMSA	5.1	7
Charlotte-Gastonia-Rock Hill, NC-SC MSA	5.3	8
Columbus, OH MSA	4.3	4
Denver-Boulder, CO CMSA	3.5	2
Indianapolis, IN MSA	4.3	4

[Continued]

★1061★

Unemployment Rate in MSAs, 1993, By Sex: Women (Lowest Rates)
[Continued]

MSA	Women	Rank
Louisville, KY MSA	2.9	1
Milwaukee, WI PMSA	4.1	3
Minneapolis-Saint Paul, MN MSA	4.1	3
Rochester, NY MSA	4.3	4
Salt Lake City-Ogden, UT MSA	4.4	5
Washington, DC MSA	5.3	8

Source: U.S. Department of Labor, Bureau of Labor Statistics, *Geographic Profile of Employment and Unemployment, 1993,* Washington, D.C.: .U.S. Government Printing Office, September 1994, p. 95.

★1062★
Unemployment

Unemployment Rate in MSAs, 1993: Highest

Data refer to selected metropolitan statistical areas.

MSA	Total	Rank
Anaheim-Santa Ana, CA PMSA	7.8	8
Chicago, IL PMSA	7.9	7
Houston, TX PMSA	7.4	10
Los Angeles-Long Beach, CA PMSA	9.7	2
Miami-Hialeah, FL PMSA	8.2	6
New Orleans, LA MSA	9.0	4
New York, NY PMSA	9.3	3
Newark, NJ PMSA	8.6	5
Norfolk-Virginia Beach-Newport News, VA MSA	8.2	6
Oakland, CA PMSA	9.7	2
Philadelphia, PA PMSA	7.5	9
Pittsburgh-Beaver Valley, PA CMSA	7.4	10
Providence-Pawtucket-Fall River, RI-MA CMSA	7.8	8
Riverside-San Bernardino, CA PMSA	11.3	1
Sacramento, CA MSA	7.9	7
San Diego, CA MSA	9.3	3
San Jose, CA PMSA	7.5	9

Source: U.S. Department of Labor, Bureau of Labor Statistics, *Geographic Profile of Employment and Unemployment, 1993,* Washington, D.C.: U.S. Government Printing Office, September 1994, p. 95.

★1063★
Unemployment

Unemployment Rate in MSAs, 1993: Lowest

Data refer to selected metropolitan statistical areas.

MSA	Total	Rank
Atlanta, GA MSA	5.1	7
Charlotte-Gastonia-Rock Hill, NC-SC MSA	5.1	7
Cincinnati, OH PMSA	6.0	11
Columbus, OH MSA	5.0	6

[Continued]

★1063★

Unemployment Rate in MSAs, 1993: Lowest
[Continued]

MSA	Total	Rank
Dayton-Springfield, OH MSA	6.1	12
Denver-Boulder, CO CMSA	4.3	3
Indianapolis, IN MSA	4.5	4
Kansas City, MO-KS MSA	5.8	10
Louisville, KY MSA	3.9	1
Milwaukee, WI PMSA	4.6	5
Minneapolis-Saint Paul, MN MSA	5.4	9
Rochester, NY MSA	5.0	6
Salt Lake City-Ogden, UT MSA	4.0	2
Seattle, WA PMSA	6.0	11
Tampa-Saint Petersburg-Clearwater, FL MSA	6.1	12
Washington, DC MSA	5.2	8

Source: U.S. Department of Labor, Bureau of Labor Statistics, *Geographic Profile of Employment and Unemployment, 1993,* Washington, D.C.: U.S. Government Printing Office, September 1994, p. 95.

★1064★
Unemployment

Unemployment Rate, 1994

[In thousands]

City	Rate	Rank
Los Angeles-Long Beach, CA[1]	9.4	1
Riverside-San Bernardino, CA	9.4	1
New York, NY	8.1	2
Miami, FL	8.0	3
Providence, Fall River-Warwick, RI-MA	7.5	4
New Orleans, LA	7.4	5
Sacramento, CA	7.3	6
San Diego, CA	7.2	7
Bergen-Passaic, NJ	7.1	8
Newark, NJ	7.0	9
Fort Lauderdale, FL	6.5	10
Houston, TX	6.4	11
Las Vegas, NV-AZ	6.3	12
Oakland, CA	6.3	12
San Jose, CA	6.3	12
Buffalo-Niagara Falls, NY	6.2	13
Pittsburgh, PA	6.2	13
Baltimore, MD	6.0	14
Hartford, CT	5.9	15
Philadelphia, PA-NJ	5.9	15
Cleveland-Lorain-Elyria, OH	5.8	16
Orange County, CA	5.8	16
Orlando, FL	5.8	16
Detroit, MI	5.7	17
Nassau-Suffolk, NY	5.7	17

Source: U.S. Bureau of the Census, *Statistical Abstract of the United States: 1995,* (115th edition), Washington, D.C.: U.S. Government Printing Office, 1995, p. 402. Primary source: U.S. Bureau of Labor Statistics, *Employment and Earnings,* May 1995. *Notes:* Data are shown only for the top 25 areas. 1. Derived from the Current Population Survey.

★ 1065 ★

Hours and Earnings

Average Annual Pay, 1993

[In dollars]

City	1993[1]	Rank
Albany-Schenectady-Troy, NY	26,604	47
Anchorage, AK	33,782	9
Ann Arbor, MI	27,930	35
Atlanta, GA	28,359	32
Baltimore, MD	27,236	41
Bergen-Passaic, NJ	34,126	8
Bloomington-Normal, IL	26,285	56
Boston-Worcester-Lawrence-		62
Boulder-Longmont, CO	26,215	57
Brazoria, TX	28,453	31
Chicago, IL	30,720	16
Cincinnati, OH-KY-IN	26,465	53
Cleveland-Lorain-Elyria, OH	26,989	44
Dallas, TX	29,489	25
Decatur, IL	26,040	61
Denver, CO	28,607	30
Detroit, MI	31,622	15
Dutchess County, NY	29,730	23
Flint, MI	30,512	18
Fort Worth-Arlington, TX	26,622	46
Hartford, CT	32,555	12
Honolulu, HI	27,253	40
Houston, TX	30,069	20
Huntsville, AL	29,243	27
Indianapolis, IN	26,587	48
Jersey City, NJ	32,815	11
Kokomo, IN	29,672	24
Lansing-East Lansing, MI	26,848	45
Los Angeles-Long Beach, CA	31,760	13
Melbourne-Titusville-Palm Bay, FL	26,095	59
Middlesex-Somerset-Hunterdon, NJ	35,573	3
Milwaukee-Waukesha, WI	26,202	58
Minneapolis-St. Paul, MN-WI	28,345	33
Monmouth-Ocean, NJ	28,045	34
Nassau-Suffolk, NY	30,226	19
New Haven-Bridgeport-Stamford-		62
New London-Norwich, CT	28,630	29
New York, NY	39,381	1
Newark, NJ	35,129	5
Oakland, CA	31,701	14
Orange County, CA	29,916	21
Philadelphia, PA-NJ	29,839	22
Pittsburgh, PA	26,478	52
Portland-Vancouver, OR-WA	26,360	54
Raleigh-Durham-Chapel Hill, NC	26,063	60
Rochester, MN	27,624	38
Rochester, NY	27,645	37
Sacramento, CA	27,476	39
Saginaw-Bay City-Midland, MI	27,686	36
San Diego, CA	26,531	51
San Francisco, CA	35,278	4
San Jose, CA	38,040	2
Seattle-Bellevue-Everett, WA	29,399	26
Springfield, IL	26,998	43

[Continued]

★ 1065 ★

Average Annual Pay, 1993

[Continued]

City	1993[1]	Rank
St. Louis, MO-IL	26,544	50
Trenton, NJ	34,365	7
Ventura, CA	26,567	49
Washington, DC-MD-VA-WV	33,170	10
West Palm Beach-Boca Raton, FL	26,348	55
Wilmington-Newark, DE-MD	29,232	28
Yolo, CA	27,187	42
Danbury-Waterbury, CT	35,058	6
Lowell-Brockton, MA-NH	30,642	17

Source: U.S. Bureau of the Census, *Statistical Abstract of the United States: 1995,* (115th edition), Washington, DC: U.S. Government Printing Office, 1995, p. 432. Primary source: U.S. Bureau of Labor Statistics, USDL News Release 94-516, *Average Annual Pay Levels in Metropolitan Areas, 1993. Note:* 1. Preliminary.

★ 1066 ★

Hours and Earnings

Average Annual Pay in Areas of New York, 1993

City/MSA	Amount	Rank
Albany-Schenectady-Troy, NY	26,604	5
Binghamton, NY	25,548	7
Buffalo-Niagara Falls, NY	25,016	8
Dutchess County, NY	29,730	3
Elmira, NY	22,254	11
Glens Falls, NY	22,971	9
Long Island (Nassau-Suffolk), NY	30,226	2
New York City, NY	39,381	1
Rochester, NY	27,645	4
Syracuse, NY	25,873	6
Utica-Rome, NY	22,549	10

Source: "The Other NY," *Site Selection,* (October 1995), p. 6. Primary source: Bureau of Labor Statistics, U.S. Department of Labor, 1993.

★ 1067 ★

Hours and Earnings

Average Hourly Earnings of Production Workers on Manufacturing Payrolls, July 1995 (Highest Earnings)

[In dollars per hour; not seasonally adjusted]

City	Average hourly earnings	Rank
Ann Arbor, MI	16.87	8
Baton Rouge, LA	16.17	12
Bloomington-Normal, IL	17.19	7
Buffalo-Niagara Falls, NY	15.72	14
Cedar Rapids, IA	15.43	20
Detroit, MI	17.61	5
Flint, MI	21.16	1
Gary, IN	18.12	3
Hamilton-Middletown, OH	16.43	11
Janesville-Beloit, WI	16.85	9

[Continued]

★1067★

Average Hourly Earnings of Production Workers on Manufacturing Payrolls, July 1995 (Highest Earnings)

[Continued]

City	Average hourly earnings	Rank
Kokomo, IN	19.76	2
Lansing-East Lansing, MI	17.71	4
Lima, OH	15.58	16
Muncie, IN	15.45	19
Oakland, CA	15.58	16
Parkersburg-Marietta, WV	15.56	17
Saginaw-Bay City-Midland, MI	17.32	6
Steubenville-Weirton, OH	16.78	10
Toledo, OH	15.63	15
Wilmington-Newark, DE	15.95	13
Youngstown-Warren, OH	15.54	18

Source: U.S. Department of Labor, Bureau of Labor Statistics, *Employment and Earnings*, Washington, D.C.: U.S. Government Printing Office, September 1995, p. 121.

★1068★

Hours and Earnings

Average Hourly Earnings of Production Workers on Manufacturing Payrolls, July 1995 (Lowest Earnings)

[In dollars per hour; not seasonally adjusted]

City	Average hourly earnings	Rank
Altoona, PA	10.56	16
Asheville, NC	10.04	9
Binghamton, NY	10.23	12
Bristol, VA	10.16	11
Charlottesville, VA	10.13	10
Chattanooga, TN	10.70	18
Fargo-Moorhead, ND	9.97	8
Fayetteville-Springdale-Rogers, AR	9.56	3
Fort Smith, AR	9.88	5
Jackson, MS	10.43	14
Johnstown, PA	9.85	4
Knoxville, TN	10.80	20
Lewiston-Auburn, ME	9.95	7
Newburgh, NY	10.69	17
Rapid City, SD	9.45	2
Salem, OR	10.79	19
San Antonio, TX	9.42	1
Sioux City, IA	10.55	15
Sioux Falls, SD	9.92	6
Springfield, MO	10.33	13
Williamsport, PA	10.80	20

Source: U.S. Department of Labor, Bureau of Labor Statistics, *Employment and Earnings*, Washington, D.C.: U.S. Government Printing Office, September 1995, p. 121.

★1069★

Hours and Earnings

Average Weekly Earnings of Production Workers on Manufacturing Payrolls, July 1995 (Highest Earnings)

[In dollars per week; not seasonally adjusted]

City	Average weekly earnings	Rank
Ann Arbor, MI	681.55	13
Baton Rouge, LA	714.71	11
Bloomington-Normal, IL	766.67	5
Detroit, MI	741.38	7
Flint, MI	998.75	1
Gary, IN	732.05	8
Hamilton-Middletown, OH	729.49	9
Janesville-Beloit, WI	754.88	6
Kokomo, IN	825.97	2
Lansing-East Lansing, MI	773.93	4
Lima, OH	674.61	15
Parkersburg-Marietta, WV	675.30	14
Saginaw-Bay City-Midland, MI	784.60	3
Steubenville-Weirton, OH	723.22	10
Youngstown-Warren, OH	689.77	12

Source: U.S. Department of Labor, Bureau of Labor Statistics, *Employment and Earnings*, Washington, D.C.: U.S. Government Printing Office, September 1995, p. 121.

★1070★

Hours and Earnings

Average Weekly Earnings of Production Workers on Manufacturing Payrolls, July 1995 (Lowest Earnings)

[In dollars per week; not seasonally adjusted]

City	Average weekly earnings	Rank
Bloomington, IN	401.12	5
Fayetteville-Springdale-Rogers, AR	400.58	3
Fort Smith, AR	404.09	7
Johnstown, PA	400.90	4
Lewiston-Auburn, ME	372.13	1
New York City, NY	408.44	9
Portland, ME	403.29	6
Rapid City, SD	378.95	2
Salem, OR	411.10	10
Sioux Falls, SD	407.71	8

Source: U.S. Department of Labor, Bureau of Labor Statistics, *Employment and Earnings*, Washington, D.C.: U.S. Government Printing Office, September 1995, p. 121.

★1071★

Hours and Earnings

Average Weekly Hours of Production Workers on Manufacturing Payrolls, July 1995 (Fewest Hours)

[In hours per week; not seasonally adjusted]

City	Average weekly hours	Rank
Bloomington, IN	36.3	1
Burlington, VT	38.1	8
Elkhart-Goshen, IN	38.0	7
Eugene-Springfield, OR	39.1	16
Fargo-Moorhead, ND	38.9	14
Greensboro-Winston-Salem-High Point, NC	39.0	15
Jackson, MI	38.8	13
Kenosha, WI	38.3	10
Knoxville, TN	38.1	8
La Crosse, WI	38.8	13
Lewiston-Auburn, ME	37.4	3
Madison, WI	38.3	10
Nashua, NH	37.7	5
Nassau-Suffolk, NY	38.8	13
New York City, NY	37.3	2
New York, NY PMSA	37.8	6
Newburgh, NY	38.5	11
Portland, ME	36.3	1
Portsmouth-Rochester, NH	37.5	4
Providence-Fall River-Warwick, RI	39.0	15
Racine, WI	38.2	9
Salem, OR	38.1	8
South Bend, IN	38.7	12
Wheeling, WV	38.9	14

Source: U.S. Department of Labor, Bureau of Labor Statistics, *Employment and Earnings,* Washington, D.C.: U.S. Government Printing Office, September 1995, p. 121.

★1072★

Hours and Earnings

Average Weekly Hours of Production Workers on Manufacturing Payrolls, July 1995 (Most Hours)

[In hours per week; not seasonally adjusted]

City	Average weekly hours	Rank
Baton Rouge, LA	44.2	8
Bloomington-Normal, IL	44.6	6
Charleston, WV	45.4	3
Cincinnati, OH	43.2	15
Eau Claire, WI	44.1	9
Flint, MI	47.2	1
Hamilton-Middletown, OH	44.4	7
Hartford, CT	43.2	15
Houston, TX	43.8	10
Janesville-Beloit, WI	44.8	5
Lafayette, IN	43.5	12
Lansing-East Lansing, MI	43.7	11
Lima, OH	43.3	14

[Continued]

★1072★

Average Weekly Hours of Production Workers on Manufacturing Payrolls, July 1995 (Most Hours)

[Continued]

City	Average weekly hours	Rank
Mobile, AL	43.5	12
New Orleans, LA	43.2	15
Parkersburg-Marietta, WV	43.4	13
Richmond-Petersburg, VA	43.4	13
Saginaw-Bay City-Midland, MI	45.3	4
Saint Louis, MO	44.2	8
Savannah, GA	46.4	2
Terre Haute, IN	44.8	5
Wausau, WI	43.3	14

Source: U.S. Department of Labor, Bureau of Labor Statistics, *Employment and Earnings,* Washington, D.C.: U.S. Government Printing Office, September 1995, p. 121.

★1073★

Hours and Earnings

Employment Earnings, 2000, CMSAs: Projections

[In millions of 1987 dollars]

City/MSA	Millions of 1987 dollars	Rank
Chicago-Gary-Kenosha, IL-IN-WI CMSA	139,469	3
Cincinnati-Hamilton, OH-KY-IN CMSA	25,803	15
Cleveland-Akron, OH CMSA	39,641	12
Dallas-Fort Worth, TX CMSA	75,490	8
Denver-Boulder-Greeley, CO CMSA	37,959	13
Detroit-Ann Arbor-Flint, MI CMSA	76,087	7
Houston-Galveston-Brazoria, TX CMSA	68,375	9
Los Angeles-Riverside-Orange County, CA CMSA	224,857	2
Miami-Fort Lauderdale, FL CMSA	44,295	11
Milwaukee-Racine, WI CMSA	24,026	17
New York-Northern New Jersey-Long Island, NY-NJ-CT-PA CMSA	346,215	1
Philadelphia-Wilmington-Atlantic City, PA-NJ-DE-MD CMSA	88,833	6
Portland-Salem, OR-WA CMSA	28,584	14
Sacramento-Yolo, CA CMSA	24,081	16
San Francisco-Oakland-San Jose, CA CMSA	123,732	5
Seattle-Tacoma-Bremerton, WA CMSA	54,400	10
Washington-Baltimore, DC-MD-VA-WV CMSA	128,423	4

Source: U.S. Department of Commerce, Economics and Statistics Administration, Bureau of Economic Analysis, *Survey of Current Business,* vol. 76, no. 6, Washington, D.C.: U.S. Government Printing Office, (June 1996), p. 67. *Note:* "CMSA" stands for "Consolidated Metropolitan Statistical Area."

★1074★
Hours and Earnings
Employment Earnings, 2005, CMSAs: Projections

[In millions of 1987 dollars]

City/MSA	Millions of 1987 dollars	Rank
Chicago-Gary-Kenosha, IL-IN-WI CMSA	151,733	3
Cincinnati-Hamilton, OH-KY-IN CMSA	28,166	15
Cleveland-Akron, OH CMSA	42,190	13
Dallas-Fort Worth, TX CMSA	84,287	7
Denver-Boulder-Greeley, CO CMSA	42,616	12
Detroit-Ann Arbor-Flint, MI CMSA	80,619	8
Houston-Galveston-Brazoria, TX CMSA	75,446	9
Los Angeles-Riverside-Orange County, CA CMSA	250,626	2
Miami-Fort Lauderdale, FL CMSA	49,342	11
Milwaukee-Racine, WI CMSA	25,932	17
New York-Northern New Jersey-Long Island, NY-NJ-CT-PA CMSA	371,448	1
Philadelphia-Wilmington-Atlantic City, PA-NJ-DE-MD CMSA	95,878	6
Portland-Salem, OR-WA CMSA	31,876	14
Sacramento-Yolo, CA CMSA	27,957	16
San Francisco-Oakland-San Jose, CA CMSA	137,303	5
Seattle-Tacoma-Bremerton, WA CMSA	61,298	10
Washington-Baltimore, DC-MD-VA-WV CMSA	140,878	4

Source: U.S. Department of Commerce, Economics and Statistics Administration, Bureau of Economic Analysis, *Survey of Current Business,* vol. 76, no. 6, Washington, D.C.: U.S. Government Printing Office, (June 1996), p. 67. *Note:* "CMSA" stands for "Consolidated Metropolitan Statistical Area."

★1075★
Hours and Earnings
Employment Earnings, CMSAs, 1993

[In millions of 1987 dollars]

City/MSA	Millions of 1987 dollars	Rank
Chicago-Gary-Kenosha, IL-IN-WI CMSA	121,709	3
Cincinnati-Hamilton, OH-KY-IN CMSA	22,052	15
Cleveland-Akron, OH CMSA	35,774	12
Dallas-Fort Worth, TX CMSA	62,266	8
Denver-Boulder-Greeley, CO CMSA	31,148	13
Detroit-Ann Arbor-Flint, MI CMSA	69,026	7
Houston-Galveston-Brazoria, TX CMSA	57,048	9
Los Angeles-Riverside-Orange County, CA CMSA	189,587	2

[Continued]

★1075★
Employment Earnings, CMSAs, 1993
[Continued]

City/MSA	Millions of 1987 dollars	Rank
Miami-Fort Lauderdale, FL CMSA	36,879	11
Milwaukee-Racine, WI CMSA	21,295	16
New York-Northern New Jersey-Long Island, NY-NJ-CT-PA CMSA	308,610	1
Philadelphia-Wilmington-Atlantic City, PA-NJ-DE-MD CMSA	78,182	6
Portland-Salem, OR-WA CMSA	23,594	14
Sacramento-Yolo, CA CMSA	18,738	17
San Francisco-Oakland-San Jose, CA CMSA	104,968	5
Seattle-Tacoma-Bremerton, WA CMSA	45,165	10
Washington-Baltimore, DC-MD-VA-WV CMSA	110,195	4

Source: U.S. Department of Commerce, Economics and Statistics Administration, Bureau of Economic Analysis, *Survey of Current Business,* vol. 76, no. 6, Washington, D.C.: U.S. Government Printing Office, (June 1996), p. 67. *Note:* "CMSA" stands for "Consolidated Metropolitan Statistical Area."

★1076★
Hours and Earnings
Employment in City Government, 1992: Average Earnings

[In dollars; for October 1992]

City	Dollars	Rank
Albuquerque, NM	2,100	57
Anaheim, CA	4,235	2
Arlington, TX	2,721	33
Atlanta, GA	2,373	49
Austin, TX	2,496	40
Baltimore, MD	2,613	37
Birmingham, AL	2,293	52
Boston, MA	2,949	25
Buffalo, NY	2,986	23
Charlotte, NC	2,436	44
Chicago, IL	3,269	13
Cincinnati, OH	3,092	20
Cleveland, OH	2,742	32
Colorado Springs, CO	2,594	38
Columbus, OH	2,782	31
Dallas, TX	2,642	36
Denver, CO	2,859	30
Detroit, MI	2,700	34
El Paso, TX	2,220	55
Fort Worth, TX	2,277	53
Fresno, CA	3,043	21
Honolulu, HI	3,139	16
Houston, TX	2,404	48
Indianapolis, IN	2,164	56
Jacksonville, FL	2,888	28
Kansas City, MO	2,485	41

[Continued]

★1076★

Employment in City Government, 1992: Average Earnings
[Continued]

City	Dollars	Rank
Long Beach, CA	3,627	8
Los Angeles, CA	3,815	7
Louisville, KY	1,965	58
Memphis, TN	2,361	50
Mesa, AZ	2,908	26
Miami, FL	3,994	4
Milwaukee, WI	2,782	31
Minneapolis, MN	3,097	19
Nashville-Davidson, TN	2,430	45
New Orleans, LA	1,623	59
New York, NY	3,154	15
Newark, NJ	3,220	14
Norfolk, VA	2,349	51
Oakland, CA	3,985	5
Oklahoma City, OK	2,567	39
Omaha, NE	3,138	17
Philadelphia, PA	3,092	20
Phoenix, AZ	3,104	18
Pittsburgh, PA	3,092	20
Portland, OR	3,363[1]	12
Sacramento, CA	3,384	11
Saint Louis, MO	2,405	47
Saint Paul, MN	3,429	10
San Antonio, TX	2,472	42
San Diego, CA	2,894	27
San Francisco, CA	3,881	6
San Jose, CA	4,206	3
Santa Ana, CA	5,162	1
Seattle, WA	3,494	9
Tampa, FL	2,861	29
Toledo, OH	2,955	24
Tucson, AZ	2,645	35
Tulsa, OK	2,463	43
Virginia Beach, VA	2,275	54
Washington, DC	3,022	22
Wichita, KS	2,429	46

Source: U.S. Bureau of the Census, *Statistical Abstract of the United States: 1995*, (115th edition), Washington, D.C.: U.S. Government Printing Office, 1995, p. 328. Primary source: U.S. Bureau of the Census, *City Employment*, series GE, no. 2, annual; and unpublished data. *Note:* 1. 1991 data.

★1077★

Hours and Earnings

Network Voice Analysts, 1995: Annual Salaries

According to the source, responsibilities for this position include evaluating, selecting, installing, and maintaining voice communications equipment and services. Nationally, the pay ranges from $35,000 per year to $55,000 per year.

City	Salary	Rank
Atlanta, GA	39,100	14
Boston, MA	42,300	10
Chicago, IL	47,100	4
Cleveland, OH	33,000	19
Dallas-Fort Worth, TX	43,100	9

[Continued]

★1077★

Network Voice Analysts, 1995: Annual Salaries
[Continued]

City	Salary	Rank
Denver, CO	44,400	6
Detroit, MI	33,700	18
Los Angeles, CA	50,100	1
Miami, FL	38,400	15
Minneapolis-Saint Paul, MN	43,800	8
New York, NY	49,300	2
Philadelphia, PA	40,500	12
Phoenix, AZ	37,100	16
Portland, OR	36,900	17
Raleigh-Durham, NC	40,700	11
Saint Louis, MO	39,500	13
San Diego, CA	44,100	7
San Francisco-San Jose, CA	47,400	3
Seattle, WA	39,100	14
Washington, DC	44,700	5

Source: "The Network Paycheck," *Network World*, 5 June 1995, p. 50. Primary source: EDP, Irving, Texas.

★1078★

Hours and Earnings

Wages for Logistics Industry Professionals, 1994: Leading Cities

[In dollars per year]

City/County	Amount	Rank
Atlanta, GA	51,002	11
Boston, MA	52,838	7
Chicago, IL	56,050	5
Cleveland-Akron, OH	48,436	12
Dallas-Fort Worth, TX	51,566	8
Detroit, MI	51,142	10
Houston, TX	51,357	9
Los Angeles-Orange County, CA	56,829	3
New York City, NY	57,662	2
Northern New Jersey, NJ	63,063	1
Philadelphia, PA	55,059	6
San Francisco-Oakland, CA	56,438	4

Source: "Money For Nothing? Not Hardly!" *Traffic Management*, (April 1995), p. 33. Primary source: *Traffic Management* survey of logistics industry professionals.

★1079★

United States Postal Service

Overnight First-Class Mail Delivery Service, 1996

According to the source, "For the first time since 1990, an average of 90% of first-class, overnight mail is being delivered on time to local destinations... " Performance was rated from March 2 through May 24 of 1996. Overnight deliveries of mail have been tracked by the accounting firm of Price Waterhouse since 1990.

[In percentages]

City	Rating	Rank
Wichita, KS	96	1
Honolulu, HI	95	2
San Diego, CA	95	2
Buffalo, NY	94	3
Charleston, WV	94	3
City of Industry, CA	94	3
Columbia, SC	94	3
Harrisburg, PA	94	3
Macon, GA	94	3
Sioux Falls, SD	94	3
Austin, TX	93	4
Des Moines, IA	93	4
Jacksonville, FL	93	4
Omaha, NE	93	4
Pittsburgh, PA	93	4
Portland, ME	93	4
Salt Lake City, UT	93	4
San Jose, CA	93	4
Santa Ana, CA	93	4
Seattle, WA	93	4
Van Nuys, CA	93	4
Akron, OH	92	5
Billings, MT	92	5
Cleveland, OH	92	5
Columbus, OH	92	5

Source: Castaneda, Carol J., "Postal Service: 90% On-Time Record Is Something to Write Home About," *USA TODAY*, 5 June 1996, p. 8A. Primary source: U.S. Postal Service. *Note:* Data are shown only for the top 25 areas.

Chapter 12

EMPLOYMENT-TO-POPULATION RATIOS

Topic Covered

Employment-to-Population Ratios

★1080★

Employment-to-Population Ratios

Employment-Population Ratio in Central Cities, 1993, By Sex: Men

Data refer to selected cities.

Central city	Men	Rank
Baltimore, MD	64.9	10
Chicago, IL	63.5	11
Cleveland, OH	58.2	13
Dallas, TX	75.6	1
Detroit, MI	53.5	15
Washington, DC	66.8	7
Houston, TX	71.6	4
Indianapolis, IN	71.7	3
Los Angeles, CA	67.4	6
Milwaukee, WI	65.7	9
New York, NY	59.1	12
Philadelphia, PA	56.2	14
Phoenix, AZ	72.4	2
San Antonio, TX	65.0	9
San Diego, CA	68.7	5
San Francisco, CA	66.4	8

Source: U.S. Department of Labor, Bureau of Labor Statistics, *Geographic Profile of Employment and Unemployment, 1993,* Washington, D.C.: U.S. Government Printing Office, September 1994, p. 95.

★1081★

Employment-to-Population Ratios

Employment-Population Ratio in Central Cities, 1993: Total

Data refer to selected central cities.

Central city	Total	Rank
Baltimore, MD	59.3	7
Chicago, IL	56.6	11
Cleveland, OH	50.6	13
Dallas, TX	66.1	2
Detroit, MI	46.1	15
Washington, DC	61.2	5
Houston, TX	62.6	4
Indianapolis, IN	67.5	1
Los Angeles, CA	58.4	9
Milwaukee, WI	61.3	6
New York, NY	50.2	12
Philadelphia, PA	48.8	14
Phoenix, AZ	65.5	3
San Antonio, TX	56.8	10
San Diego, CA	58.4	9
San Francisco, CA	58.9	8

Source: U.S. Department of Labor, Bureau of Labor Statistics, *Geographic Profile of Employment and Unemployment, 1993,* Washington, D.C.: U.S. Government Printing Office, September 1994, p. 95.

★1082★

Employment-to-Population Ratios

Employment-Population Ratio in MSAs, 1993, By Sex: Men (Highest Ratios)

Data refer to selected metropolitan areas and cities.

MSA	Men	Rank
Anaheim-Santa Ana, CA PMSA	76.0	7
Atlanta, GA MSA	75.9	8
Charlotte-Gastonia-Rock Hill, NC-SC MSA	75.3	10
Dallas-Fort Worth, TX CMSA	80.5	1
Denver-Boulder, CO CMSA	76.9	5
Houston, TX PMSA	75.7	9
Indianapolis, IN MSA	76.3	6
Kansas City, MO MSA	77.1	4
Minneapolis-Saint Paul, MN MSA	78.3	2
Salt Lake City-Ogden, UT MSA	78.2	3

Source: U.S. Department of Labor, Bureau of Labor Statistics, *Geographic Profile of Employment and Unemployment, 1993,* Washington, D.C.: U.S. Government Printing Office, September 1994, p. 95.

★1083★

Employment-to-Population Ratios

Employment-Population Ratio in MSAs, 1993: (Highest)

Data refer to selected metropolitan statistical areas and cities.

MSA	Total	Rank
Atlanta, GA MSA	68.8	7
Dallas-Fort Worth, TX CMSA	70.7	3
Denver-Boulder, CO CMSA	70.8	2
Indianapolis, IN MSA	68.7	8
Kansas City, MO MSA	69.9	5
Milwaukee, WI PMSA	68.2	10
Minneapolis-Saint Paul, MN MSA	72.8	1
Salt Lake City-Ogden, UT MSA	70.4	4
Seattle, WA PMSA	68.6	9
Washington, DC MSA	69.8	6

Source: U.S. Department of Labor, Bureau of Labor Statistics, *Geographic Profile of Employment and Unemployment, 1993,* Washington, D.C.: U.S. Government Printing Office, September 1994, p. 95.

★1084★

Employment-to-Population Ratios

Employment-Population Ratio in MSAs, 1993: (Lowest)

Data refer to selected metropolitan statistical areas.

MSA	Total	Rank
Buffalo-Niagara Falls, NY CMSA	58.5	10
Fort Lauderdale-Hollywood-Pompano Beach, FL PMSA	56.2	4
Los Angeles-Long Beach, CA PMSA	57.7	9
Miami-Hialeah, FL PMSA	56.8	6
New Orleans, LA MSA	56.3	5
New York, NY PMSA	52.6	2
Oakland, CA PMSA	57.4	8

[Continued]

★1084★

Employment-Population Ratio in MSAs, 1993: (Lowest)
[Continued]

MSA	Total	Rank
Pittsburgh-Beaver Valley, PA CMSA	54.7	3
Riverside-San Bernardino, CA PMSA	57.1	7
Sacramento, CA MSA	59.0	12
Saint Louis, MO-IL MSA	45.6	1
San Antonio, TX MSA	58.7	11

Source: U.S. Department of Labor, Bureau of Labor Statistics, *Geographic Profile of Employment and Unemployment, 1993,* Washington, D.C.: U.S. Government Printing Office, September 1994, p. 95.

★1085★

Employment-to-Population Ratios

Employment-Population Ratios in Central Cities, 1993, By Sex: Women

Data refer to selected cities.

MSA	Women	Rank
Baltimore, MD	54.7	6
Chicago, IL	50.8	9
Cleveland, OH	44.1	13
Dallas, TX	57.0	4
Detroit, MI	40.1	17
Washington, DC	56.3	5
Houston, TX	53.9	7
Indianapolis, IN	64.1	1
Los Angeles, CA	49.3	11
Milwaukee, WI	57.5	3
New York, NY	42.8	14
Philadelphia, PA	42.7	15
Phoenix, AZ	59.0	2
Saint Louis, IL-MO	42.5	16
San Antonio, TX	49.2	12
San Diego, CA	49.4	10
San Francisco, CA	51.1	8

Source: U.S. Department of Labor, Bureau of Labor Statistics, *Geographic Profile of Employment and Unemployment, 1993,* Washington, D.C.: U.S. Government Printing Office, September 1994, p. 95.

★1086★

Employment-to-Population Ratios

Employment-Population Ratios in MSAs, 1993, By Sex: Men (Lowest Ratios)

Data refer to selected metropolitan statistical areas.

MSA	Men	Rank
New York, NY PMSA	61.3	1
Pittsburgh-Beaver Valley, PA CMSA	62.2	2
New Orleans, LA MSA	63.2	3
Fort Lauderdale-Hollywood-Pompano Beach, FL PMSA	64.3	4
Buffalo-Niagara Falls, NY CMSA	64.8	5

[Continued]

★1086★

Employment-Population Ratios in MSAs, 1993, By Sex: Men (Lowest Ratios)
[Continued]

MSA	Men	Rank
Sacramento, CA MSA	65.7	6
Tampa-Saint Petersburg-Clearwater, FL MSA	66.0	7
Riverside-San Bernardino, CA PMSA	66.7	8
San Antonio, TX MSA	67.0	9
Los Angeles-Long Beach, CA PMSA	67.1	10

Source: U.S. Department of Labor, Bureau of Labor Statistics, *Geographic Profile of Employment and Unemployment, 1993,* Washington, D.C.: U.S. Government Printing Office, September 1994, p. 95.

★1087★

Employment-to-Population Ratios

Employment-Population Ratios in MSAs, 1993, By Sex: Women (Highest Ratios)

Data refer to selected metropolitan statistical areas.

MSA	Women	Rank
Atlanta, GA MSA	62.6	7
Charlotte-Gastonia-Rock Hill, NC-SC MSA	61.0	10
Denver-Boulder, CO CMSA	65.1	2
Hartford-New Britain-Middletown, CT CMSA	61.0	10
Indianapolis, IN MSA	62.4	8
Kansas City, MO MSA	63.7	4
Milwaukee, WI PMSA	63.2	5
Minneapolis-Saint Paul, MN MSA	67.8	1
Salt Lake City-Ogden, UT MSA	62.9	6
Washington, DC MSA	64.7	3

Source: U.S. Department of Labor, Bureau of Labor Statistics, *Geographic Profile of Employment and Unemployment, 1993,* Washington, D.C.: U.S. Government Printing Office, September 1994, p. 95.

★1088★

Employment-to-Population Ratios

Employment-Population Ratios in MSAs, 1993, By Sex: Women (Lowest Ratios)

Data refer to selected metropolitan statistical areas.

MSA	Women	Rank
Fort Lauderdale-Hollywood-Pompano Beach, FL PMSA	48.9	5
Los Angeles-Long Beach, CA PMSA	48.7	4
Miami-Hialeah, FL PMSA	46.5	2
New Orleans, LA MSA	50.4	7
New York, NY PMSA	45.2	1
Oakland, CA PMSA	48.0	6
Pittsburgh-Beaver Valley, PA CMSA	48.0	6
Riverside-San Bernardino, CA PMSA	48.2	3

[Continued]

★1088★

Employment-Population Ratios in MSAs, 1993, By Sex: Women (Lowest Ratios)

[Continued]

MSA	Women	Rank
San Antonio, TX MSA	51.0	9
San Diego, CA MSA	50.5	8

Source: U.S. Department of Labor, Bureau of Labor Statistics, *Geographic Profile of Employment and Unemployment, 1993*, Washington, D.C.: U.S. Government Printing Office, September 1994, p. 95.

Chapter 13

OCCUPATIONS

Topic Covered

Occupations, By Race/Sex

★ 1089 ★

Occupations, By Race/Sex

Top 25 MSAs For Employment As Accountants and Auditors, 1990: Blacks

MSA/CMSA	Employees per 100,000 pop.	Rank
Orlando, FL MSA	19,146	1
Washington, DC – MD – VA MSA	10,504	2
Los Angeles – Anaheim – Riverside, CA CMSA	6,465	3
Chicago – Gary – Lake County, IL – IN – WI CMSA	6,315	4
Atlanta, GA MSA	5,682	5
Philadelphia – Wilmington – Trenton, PA – NJ – DE – MD CMSA	4,935	6
Houston – Galveston – Brazoria, TX CMSA	3,630	7
San Francisco – Oakland – San Jose, CA CMSA	3,477	8
Detroit – Ann Arbor, MI CMSA	3,265	9
Dallas – Fort Worth, TX CMSA	2,982	10
Baltimore, MD MSA	2,074	11
Miami – Fort Lauderdale, FL CMSA	1,796	12
Cleveland – Akron – Lorain, OH CMSA	1,495	13
Boston – Lawrence – Salem, MA – NH CMSA	1,440	14
Memphis, TN – AR – MS MSA	1,428	15
New Orleans, LA MSA	1,295	16
St. Louis, MO – IL MSA	1,145	17
Richmond – Petersburg, VA MSA	1,104	18
Norfolk – Virginia Beach – Newport News, VA MSA	957	19
Raleigh – Durham, NC MSA	873	20
Kansas City, MO – KS MSA	819	21
Columbus, OH MSA	718	22
Cincinnati – Hamilton, OH – KY – IN CMSA	696	23
Indianapolis, IN MSA	695	24
Columbia, SC MSA	678	25

Source: U.S. Department of Commerce, Bureau of the Census, Data User Services Division, *1990 Census of Population and Housing, Equal Employment Opportunity File, CD-90-EE0-1, January 1993,* CD-ROM.

★ 1090 ★

Occupations, By Race/Sex

Top 25 MSAs For Employment As Accountants and Auditors, 1990: Whites

MSA/CMSA	Employees per 100,000 pop.	Rank
Portland – Vancouver, OR – WA CMSA	138,010	1
Los Angeles – Anaheim – Riverside, CA CMSA	73,543	2
Chicago – Gary – Lake County, IL – IN – WI CMSA	57,006	3
San Francisco – Oakland – San Jose, CA CMSA	41,835	4

[Continued]

★ 1090 ★

Top 25 MSAs For Employment As Accountants and Auditors, 1990: Whites

[Continued]

MSA/CMSA	Employees per 100,000 pop.	Rank
Boston – Lawrence – Salem, MA – NH CMSA	41,285	5
Philadelphia – Wilmington – Trenton, PA – NJ – DE – MD CMSA	40,839	6
Dallas – Fort Worth, TX CMSA	35,729	7
Washington, DC – MD – VA MSA	35,084	8
Houston – Galveston – Brazoria, TX CMSA	29,638	9
Detroit – Ann Arbor, MI CMSA	25,954	10
Minneapolis – St. Paul, MN – WI MSA	23,493	11
Atlanta, GA MSA	23,309	12
Miami – Fort Lauderdale, FL CMSA	19,833	13
Seattle – Tacoma, WA CMSA	18,185	14
Denver – Boulder, CO CMSA	17,771	15
Cleveland – Akron – Lorain, OH CMSA	16,994	16
St. Louis, MO – IL MSA	16,858	17
Baltimore, MD MSA	15,396	18
Phoenix, AZ MSA	13,856	19
San Diego, CA MSA	13,372	20
Pittsburgh – Beaver Valley, PA CMSA	13,165	21
Cincinnati – Hamilton, OH – KY – IN CMSA	12,555	22
Kansas City, MO – KS MSA	12,170	23
Tampa – St. Petersburg – Clearwater, FL MSA	12,014	24
Milwaukee – Racine, WI CMSA	10,678	25

Source: U.S. Department of Commerce, Bureau of the Census, Data User Services Division, *1990 Census of Population and Housing, Equal Employment Opportunity File, CD-90-EE0-1, January 1993,* CD-ROM.

★ 1091 ★

Occupations, By Race/Sex

Top 25 MSAs For Employment As Actors and Directors, 1990: Blacks

MSA/CMSA	Employees per 100,000 pop.	Rank
Nashville, TN MSA	2,101	1
Los Angeles – Anaheim – Riverside, CA CMSA	1,635	2
Washington, DC – MD – VA MSA	531	3
Chicago – Gary – Lake County, IL – IN – WI CMSA	389	4
Atlanta, GA MSA	198	5
San Francisco – Oakland – San Jose, CA CMSA	193	6
Detroit – Ann Arbor, MI CMSA	176	7
Baltimore, MD MSA	173	8
Philadelphia – Wilmington – Trenton, PA – NJ – DE – MD CMSA	158	9

[Continued]

★1091★

Top 25 MSAs For Employment As Actors and Directors, 1990: Blacks

[Continued]

MSA/CMSA	Employees per 100,000 pop.	Rank
Houston – Galveston – Brazoria, TX CMSA	125	10
Miami – Fort Lauderdale, FL CMSA	101	11
Boston – Lawrence – Salem, MA – NH CMSA	99	12
Norfolk – Virginia Beach – Newport News, VA MSA	84	13
Pittsburgh – Beaver Valley, PA CMSA	78	14
New Orleans, LA MSA	73	15
Minneapolis – St. Paul, MN – WI MSA	64	16
Dallas – Fort Worth, TX CMSA	62	17
Raleigh – Durham, NC MSA	61	18
Milwaukee – Racine, WI CMSA	52	19
Kansas City, MO – KS MSA	45	20
Charlotte – Gastonia – Rock Hill, NC – SC MSA	45	20
Orlando, FL MSA	44	21
Indianapolis, IN MSA	44	21
Tampa – St. Petersburg – Clearwater, FL MSA	44	21
Jackson, MS MSA	43	22

Source: U.S. Department of Commerce, Bureau of the Census, Data User Services Division, *1990 Census of Population and Housing, Equal Employment Opportunity File, CD-90-EE0-1, January 1993*, CD-ROM.

★1092★

Occupations, By Race/Sex

Top 25 MSAs For Employment As Actors and Directors, 1990: Whites

MSA/CMSA	Employees per 100,000 pop.	Rank
Baltimore, MD MSA	23,404	1
New York – Northern New Jersey – Long Island, NY – NJ – CT CMSA	18,936	2
Chicago – Gary – Lake County, IL – IN – WI CMSA	3,447	3
San Francisco – Oakland – San Jose, CA CMSA	2,829	4
Washington, DC – MD – VA MSA	2,487	5
Boston – Lawrence – Salem, MA – NH CMSA	2,315	6
Philadelphia – Wilmington – Trenton, PA – NJ – DE – MD CMSA	1,603	7
Miami – Fort Lauderdale, FL CMSA	1,508	8
Dallas – Fort Worth, TX CMSA	1,243	9
Seattle – Tacoma, WA CMSA	1,205	10
Detroit – Ann Arbor, MI CMSA	1,200	11

[Continued]

★1092★

Top 25 MSAs For Employment As Actors and Directors, 1990: Whites

[Continued]

MSA/CMSA	Employees per 100,000 pop.	Rank
Atlanta, GA MSA	1,191	12
Minneapolis – St. Paul, MN – WI MSA	1,168	13
Denver – Boulder, CO CMSA	934	14
San Diego, CA MSA	781	15
Portland – Vancouver, OR – WA CMSA	777	16
Houston – Galveston – Brazoria, TX CMSA	773	17
Orlando, FL MSA	768	18
Baltimore, MD MSA	734	19
Phoenix, AZ MSA	611	20
Nashville, TN MSA	605	21
Pittsburgh – Beaver Valley, PA CMSA	560	22
St. Louis, MO – IL MSA	552	23
Tampa – St. Petersburg – Clearwater, FL MSA	526	24
Cleveland – Akron – Lorain, OH CMSA	499	25

Source: U.S. Department of Commerce, Bureau of the Census, Data User Services Division, *1990 Census of Population and Housing, Equal Employment Opportunity File, CD-90-EE0-1, January 1993*, CD-ROM.

★1093★

Occupations, By Race/Sex

Top 25 MSAs For Employment As Administrators, Protective Services, 1990: Blacks

MSA/CMSA	Employees per 100,000 pop.	Rank
Denver – Boulder, CO CMSA	649	1
Los Angeles – Anaheim – Riverside, CA CMSA	308	2
Washington, DC – MD – VA MSA	293	3
Detroit – Ann Arbor, MI CMSA	231	4
Baltimore, MD MSA	200	5
Philadelphia – Wilmington – Trenton, PA – NJ – DE – MD CMSA	130	6
Miami – Fort Lauderdale, FL CMSA	127	7
San Francisco – Oakland – San Jose, CA CMSA	112	8
Atlanta, GA MSA	108	9
Chicago – Gary – Lake County, IL – IN – WI CMSA	108	9
Dallas – Fort Worth, TX CMSA	79	10
New Orleans, LA MSA	68	11
Memphis, TN – AR – MS MSA	61	12
Boston – Lawrence – Salem, MA – NH CMSA	59	13
Richmond – Petersburg, VA MSA	56	14
Columbia, SC MSA	53	15

[Continued]

★1093★

Top 25 MSAs For Employment As Administrators, Protective Services, 1990: Blacks

[Continued]

MSA/CMSA	Employees per 100,000 pop.	Rank
Dayton – Springfield, OH MSA	52	16
Nashville, TN MSA	47	17
Sacramento, CA MSA	45	18
Norfolk – Virginia Beach – Newport News, VA MSA	42	19
St. Louis, MO – IL MSA	42	19
Columbus, OH MSA	37	20
Tampa – St. Petersburg – Clearwater, FL MSA	35	21
Raleigh – Durham, NC MSA	35	21
Cleveland – Akron – Lorain, OH CMSA	34	22

Source: U.S. Department of Commerce, Bureau of the Census, Data User Services Division, *1990 Census of Population and Housing, Equal Employment Opportunity File, CD-90-EE0-1, January 1993*, CD-ROM.

★1094★

Occupations, By Race/Sex

Top 25 MSAs For Employment As Administrators, Protective Services, 1990: Whites

MSA/CMSA	Employees per 100,000 pop.	Rank
Phoenix, AZ MSA	2,023	1
Los Angeles – Anaheim – Riverside, CA CMSA	1,289	2
Chicago – Gary – Lake County, IL – IN – WI CMSA	1,017	3
Philadelphia – Wilmington – Trenton, PA – NJ – DE – MD CMSA	968	4
Boston – Lawrence – Salem, MA – NH CMSA	906	5
Washington, DC – MD – VA MSA	800	6
San Francisco – Oakland – San Jose, CA CMSA	795	7
Baltimore, MD MSA	533	8
Miami – Fort Lauderdale, FL CMSA	486	9
Detroit – Ann Arbor, MI CMSA	480	10
St. Louis, MO – IL MSA	471	11
Sacramento, CA MSA	452	12
Dallas – Fort Worth, TX CMSA	407	13
Seattle – Tacoma, WA CMSA	381	14
Cleveland – Akron – Lorain, OH CMSA	368	15
Columbus, OH MSA	361	16
Denver – Boulder, CO CMSA	360	17
Phoenix, AZ MSA	356	18
San Diego, CA MSA	345	19
Atlanta, GA MSA	343	20
Tampa – St. Petersburg – Clearwater, FL MSA	340	21

[Continued]

★1094★

Top 25 MSAs For Employment As Administrators, Protective Services, 1990: Whites

[Continued]

MSA/CMSA	Employees per 100,000 pop.	Rank
Minneapolis – St. Paul, MN – WI MSA	337	22
Houston – Galveston – Brazoria, TX CMSA	308	23
Cincinnati – Hamilton, OH – KY – IN CMSA	301	24
Pittsburgh – Beaver Valley, PA CMSA	294	25

Source: U.S. Department of Commerce, Bureau of the Census, Data User Services Division, *1990 Census of Population and Housing, Equal Employment Opportunity File, CD-90-EE0-1, January 1993*, CD-ROM.

★1095★

Occupations, By Race/Sex

Top 25 MSAs For Employment As Aerospace Engineers, 1990: Blacks

MSA/CMSA	Employees per 100,000 pop.	Rank
New Orleans, LA MSA	1,746	1
Dallas – Fort Worth, TX CMSA	287	2
St. Louis, MO – IL MSA	233	3
San Francisco – Oakland – San Jose, CA CMSA	214	4
Houston – Galveston – Brazoria, TX CMSA	193	5
New York – Northern New Jersey – Long Island, NY – NJ – CT CMSA	167	6
Seattle – Tacoma, WA CMSA	162	7
Washington, DC – MD – VA MSA	128	8
Cincinnati – Hamilton, OH – KY – IN CMSA	120	9
Philadelphia – Wilmington – Trenton, PA – NJ – DE – MD CMSA	113	10
San Diego, CA MSA	113	10
New Orleans, LA MSA	76	11
Orlando, FL MSA	75	12
Huntsville, AL MSA	59	13
Hartford – New Britain – Middletown, CT CMSA	46	14
Baltimore, MD MSA	43	15
Atlanta, GA MSA	42	16
Miami – Fort Lauderdale, FL CMSA	38	17
Denver – Boulder, CO CMSA	37	18
Sacramento, CA MSA	34	19
Melbourne – Titusville – Palm Bay, FL MSA	32	20
West Palm Beach – Boca Raton – Delray Beach, FL MSA	32	20

[Continued]

★1095★

Top 25 MSAs For Employment As Aerospace Engineers, 1990: Blacks

[Continued]

MSA/CMSA	Employees per 100,000 pop.	Rank
Wichita, KS MSA	32	20
Cleveland – Akron – Lorain, OH CMSA	31	21
Kansas City, MO – KS MSA	31	21

Source: U.S. Department of Commerce, Bureau of the Census, Data User Services Division, *1990 Census of Population and Housing, Equal Employment Opportunity File, CD-90-EE0-1, January 1993,* CD-ROM.

★1096★

Occupations, By Race/Sex

Top 25 MSAs For Employment As Aerospace Engineers, 1990: Men

MSA/CMSA	Employees per 100,000 pop.	Rank
Pittsburgh – Beaver Valley, PA CMSA	35,507	1
Seattle – Tacoma, WA CMSA	12,904	2
Dallas – Fort Worth, TX CMSA	7,214	3
San Francisco – Oakland – San Jose, CA CMSA	6,610	4
St. Louis, MO – IL MSA	5,367	5
New York – Northern New Jersey – Long Island, NY – NJ – CT CMSA	5,148	6
San Diego, CA MSA	3,666	7
Phoenix, AZ MSA	3,343	8
Denver – Boulder, CO CMSA	3,180	9
Houston – Galveston – Brazoria, TX CMSA	2,863	10
Hartford – New Britain – Middletown, CT CMSA	2,667	11
Philadelphia – Wilmington – Trenton, PA – NJ – DE – MD CMSA	2,220	12
Melbourne – Titusville – Palm Bay, FL MSA	2,198	13
Wichita, KS MSA	2,151	14
Cincinnati – Hamilton, OH – KY – IN CMSA	2,141	15
West Palm Beach – Boca Raton – Delray Beach, FL MSA	1,947	16
Huntsville, AL MSA	1,800	17
Washington, DC – MD – VA MSA	1,792	18
Boston – Lawrence – Salem, MA – NH CMSA	1,615	19
Orlando, FL MSA	1,528	20
Salt Lake City – Ogden, UT MSA	1,102	21
Atlanta, GA MSA	1,035	22
Albany – Schenectady – Troy, NY MSA	1,019	23

[Continued]

★1096★

Top 25 MSAs For Employment As Aerospace Engineers, 1990: Men

[Continued]

MSA/CMSA	Employees per 100,000 pop.	Rank
Cleveland – Akron – Lorain, OH CMSA	1,011	24
Baltimore, MD MSA	857	25

Source: U.S. Department of Commerce, Bureau of the Census, Data User Services Division, *1990 Census of Population and Housing, Equal Employment Opportunity File, CD-90-EE0-1, January 1993,* CD-ROM.

★1097★

Occupations, By Race/Sex

Top 25 MSAs For Employment As Aerospace Engineers, 1990: Women

MSA/CMSA	Employees per 100,000 pop.	Rank
Providence – Pawtucket – Fall River, RI – MA CMSA	3,557	1
Seattle – Tacoma, WA CMSA	894	2
Dallas – Fort Worth, TX CMSA	679	3
San Francisco – Oakland – San Jose, CA CMSA	602	4
Houston – Galveston – Brazoria, TX CMSA	519	5
St. Louis, MO – IL MSA	471	6
Denver – Boulder, CO CMSA	438	7
Melbourne – Titusville – Palm Bay, FL MSA	293	8
New York – Northern New Jersey – Long Island, NY – NJ – CT CMSA	266	9
San Diego, CA MSA	262	10
Huntsville, AL MSA	240	11
Washington, DC – MD – VA MSA	225	12
Philadelphia – Wilmington – Trenton, PA – NJ – DE – MD CMSA	217	13
Cincinnati – Hamilton, OH – KY – IN CMSA	213	14
Phoenix, AZ MSA	189	15
Hartford – New Britain – Middletown, CT CMSA	165	16
Boston – Lawrence – Salem, MA – NH CMSA	147	17
Orlando, FL MSA	142	18
Albany – Schenectady – Troy, NY MSA	131	19
Wichita, KS MSA	126	20
Baltimore, MD MSA	97	21
Sacramento, CA MSA	92	22
Atlanta, GA MSA	90	23
Tucson, AZ MSA	90	23
West Palm Beach – Boca Raton – Delray Beach, FL MSA	86	24

Source: U.S. Department of Commerce, Bureau of the Census, Data User Services Division, *1990 Census of Population and Housing, Equal Employment Opportunity File, CD-90-EE0-1, January 1993,* CD-ROM.

★ 1098 ★

Occupations, By Race/Sex

Top 25 MSAs For Employment As Agriculture and Forestry Teachers, 1990: Men

MSA/CMSA	Employees per 100,000 pop.	Rank
Duluth, MN – WI MSA	24	1
Honolulu, HI MSA	23	2
Raleigh – Durham, NC MSA	19	3
State College, PA MSA	17	4
Miami – Fort Lauderdale, FL CMSA	15	5
Rochester, NY MSA	14	6
Burlington, VT MSA	14	6
Modesto, CA MSA	13	7
Appleton – Oshkosh – Neenah, WI MSA	13	7
Baton Rouge, LA MSA	13	7
Columbia, MO MSA	13	7
Davenport – Rock Island – Moline, IA – IL MSA	11	8
Lansing – East Lansing, MI MSA	10	9
Bryan – College Station, TX MSA	10	9
New York – Northern New Jersey – Long Island, NY – NJ – CT CMSA	9	10
Wausau, WI MSA	9	10
Detroit – Ann Arbor, MI CMSA	9	10
Athens, GA MSA	9	10
Madison, WI MSA	8	11
Richmond – Petersburg, VA MSA	8	11
Sacramento, CA MSA	8	11
Syracuse, NY MSA	8	11
Visalia – Tulare – Porterville, CA MSA	8	11
Fort Smith, AR – OK MSA	8	11
Greenville – Spartanburg, SC MSA	8	11

Source: U.S. Department of Commerce, Bureau of the Census, Data User Services Division, *1990 Census of Population and Housing, Equal Employment Opportunity File, CD-90-EE0-1, January 1993,* CD-ROM.

★ 1099 ★

Occupations, By Race/Sex

Top 25 MSAs For Employment As Agriculture and Forestry Teachers, 1990: Women

MSA/CMSA	Employees per 100,000 pop.	Rank
Denver – Boulder, CO CMSA	18	1
San Francisco – Oakland – San Jose, CA CMSA	16	2
Boston – Lawrence – Salem, MA – NH CMSA	13	3
Chicago – Gary – Lake County, IL – IN – WI CMSA	12	4
Lafayette – West Lafayette, IN MSA	11	5
New York – Northern New Jersey – Long Island, NY – NJ – CT CMSA	11	5

[Continued]

★ 1099 ★

Top 25 MSAs For Employment As Agriculture and Forestry Teachers, 1990: Women

[Continued]

MSA/CMSA	Employees per 100,000 pop.	Rank
Boise City, ID MSA	10	6
State College, PA MSA	10	6
Asheville, NC MSA	9	7
Benton Harbor, MI MSA	9	7
Kansas City, MO – KS MSA	9	7
Albany – Schenectady – Troy, NY MSA	8	8
Little Rock – North Little Rock, AR MSA	8	8
Los Angeles – Anaheim – Riverside, CA CMSA	8	8
Portland – Vancouver, OR – WA CMSA	8	8
San Diego, CA MSA	8	8
Denver – Boulder, CO CMSA	7	9
Oklahoma City, OK MSA	7	9
Lubbock, TX MSA	6	10
Olympia, WA MSA	6	10
Scranton – Wilkes-Barre, PA MSA	6	10
Dayton – Springfield, OH MSA	5	11
Washington, DC – MD – VA MSA	5	11
Seattle – Tacoma, WA CMSA	4	12
Indianapolis, IN MSA	2	13

Source: U.S. Department of Commerce, Bureau of the Census, Data User Services Division, *1990 Census of Population and Housing, Equal Employment Opportunity File, CD-90-EE0-1, January 1993,* CD-ROM.

★ 1100 ★

Occupations, By Race/Sex

Top 25 MSAs For Employment As Air Traffic Controllers, 1990: Men

MSA/CMSA	Employees per 100,000 pop.	Rank
Norfolk – Virginia Beach – Newport News, VA MSA	1,937	1
Los Angeles – Anaheim – Riverside, CA CMSA	1,467	2
Dallas – Fort Worth, TX CMSA	1,267	3
Chicago – Gary – Lake County, IL – IN – WI CMSA	1,148	4
Washington, DC – MD – VA MSA	1,050	5
Miami – Fort Lauderdale, FL CMSA	984	6
San Francisco – Oakland – San Jose, CA CMSA	963	7
Atlanta, GA MSA	890	8
Houston – Galveston – Brazoria, TX CMSA	854	9
Seattle – Tacoma, WA CMSA	694	10
Minneapolis – St. Paul, MN – WI MSA	667	11
Denver – Boulder, CO CMSA	629	12
Cleveland – Akron – Lorain, OH CMSA	566	13

[Continued]

★1100★

Top 25 MSAs For Employment As Air Traffic Controllers, 1990: Men
[Continued]

MSA/CMSA	Employees per 100,000 pop.	Rank
Kansas City, MO–KS MSA	563	14
Memphis, TN–AR–MS MSA	541	15
Boston–Lawrence–Salem, MA–NH CMSA	539	16
Jacksonville, FL MSA	532	17
San Diego, CA MSA	503	18
Phoenix, AZ MSA	431	19
Salt Lake City–Ogden, UT MSA	414	20
Detroit–Ann Arbor, MI CMSA	400	21
Philadelphia–Wilmington–Trenton, PA–NJ–DE–MD CMSA	398	22
Anchorage, AK MSA	372	23
Indianapolis, IN MSA	358	24
Baltimore, MD MSA	357	25

Source: U.S. Department of Commerce, Bureau of the Census, Data User Services Division, *1990 Census of Population and Housing, Equal Employment Opportunity File, CD-90-EE0-1, January 1993,* CD-ROM.

★1101★

Occupations, By Race/Sex

Top 25 MSAs For Employment As Air Traffic Controllers, 1990: Women

MSA/CMSA	Employees per 100,000 pop.	Rank
Raleigh–Durham, NC MSA	678	1
Los Angeles–Anaheim–Riverside, CA CMSA	455	2
Miami–Fort Lauderdale, FL CMSA	336	3
Washington, DC–MD–VA MSA	314	4
Dallas–Fort Worth, TX CMSA	305	5
San Francisco–Oakland–San Jose, CA CMSA	294	6
Chicago–Gary–Lake County, IL–IN–WI CMSA	279	7
Atlanta, GA MSA	254	8
Houston–Galveston–Brazoria, TX CMSA	249	9
Seattle–Tacoma, WA CMSA	248	10
San Diego, CA MSA	175	11
St. Louis, MO–IL MSA	158	12
Honolulu, HI MSA	157	13
Phoenix, AZ MSA	153	14
Cleveland–Akron–Lorain, OH CMSA	144	15
Boston–Lawrence–Salem, MA–NH CMSA	143	16
Jacksonville, FL MSA	140	17
Minneapolis–St. Paul, MN–WI MSA	136	18
Denver–Boulder, CO CMSA	128	19
Detroit–Ann Arbor, MI CMSA	117	20

[Continued]

★1101★

Top 25 MSAs For Employment As Air Traffic Controllers, 1990: Women
[Continued]

MSA/CMSA	Employees per 100,000 pop.	Rank
Philadelphia–Wilmington–Trenton, PA–NJ–DE–MD CMSA	117	20
Pittsburgh–Beaver Valley, PA CMSA	113	21
Memphis, TN–AR–MS MSA	110	22
Baltimore, MD MSA	109	23
Kansas City, MO–KS MSA	105	24

Source: U.S. Department of Commerce, Bureau of the Census, Data User Services Division, *1990 Census of Population and Housing, Equal Employment Opportunity File, CD-90-EE0-1, January 1993,* CD-ROM.

★1102★

Occupations, By Race/Sex

Top 25 MSAs For Employment As Aircraft Engine Mechanics, 1990: Men

MSA/CMSA	Employees per 100,000 pop.	Rank
Boston–Lawrence–Salem, MA–NH CMSA	9,470	1
San Francisco–Oakland–San Jose, CA CMSA	7,405	2
New York–Northern New Jersey–Long Island, NY–NJ–CT CMSA	5,957	3
Atlanta, GA MSA	4,745	4
Miami–Fort Lauderdale, FL CMSA	4,615	5
Seattle–Tacoma, WA CMSA	4,394	6
Dallas–Fort Worth, TX CMSA	3,954	7
Tulsa, OK MSA	3,162	8
San Diego, CA MSA	2,808	9
Minneapolis–St. Paul, MN–WI MSA	2,652	10
Chicago–Gary–Lake County, IL–IN–WI CMSA	2,439	11
Phoenix, AZ MSA	2,275	12
San Antonio, TX MSA	2,209	13
Oklahoma City, OK MSA	1,923	14
Denver–Boulder, CO CMSA	1,762	15
Kansas City, MO–KS MSA	1,717	16
Philadelphia–Wilmington–Trenton, PA–NJ–DE–MD CMSA	1,708	17
Houston–Galveston–Brazoria, TX CMSA	1,640	18
St. Louis, MO–IL MSA	1,554	19
Salt Lake City–Ogden, UT MSA	1,534	20
Detroit–Ann Arbor, MI CMSA	1,493	21
Jacksonville, FL MSA	1,490	22
Norfolk–Virginia Beach–Newport News, VA MSA	1,472	23

[Continued]

★1102★

Top 25 MSAs For Employment As Aircraft Engine Mechanics, 1990: Men

[Continued]

MSA/CMSA	Employees per 100,000 pop.	Rank
Pittsburgh – Beaver Valley, PA CMSA	1,400	24
Wichita, KS MSA	1,282	25

Source: U.S. Department of Commerce, Bureau of the Census, Data User Services Division, *1990 Census of Population and Housing, Equal Employment Opportunity File,* CD-90-EE0-1, January 1993, CD-ROM.

★1103★

Occupations, By Race/Sex

Top 25 MSAs For Employment As Aircraft Engine Mechanics, 1990: Women

MSA/CMSA	Employees per 100,000 pop.	Rank
Abilene, TX MSA	627	1
Seattle – Tacoma, WA CMSA	273	2
San Diego, CA MSA	214	3
Oklahoma City, OK MSA	208	4
San Francisco – Oakland – San Jose, CA CMSA	187	5
New York – Northern New Jersey – Long Island, NY – NJ – CT CMSA	172	6
Dallas – Fort Worth, TX CMSA	152	7
Norfolk – Virginia Beach – Newport News, VA MSA	136	8
Atlanta, GA MSA	109	9
San Antonio, TX MSA	99	10
Boston – Lawrence – Salem, MA – NH CMSA	91	11
Miami – Fort Lauderdale, FL CMSA	91	11
St. Louis, MO – IL MSA	88	12
Kansas City, MO – KS MSA	78	13
Philadelphia – Wilmington – Trenton, PA – NJ – DE – MD CMSA	74	14
Cincinnati – Hamilton, OH – KY – IN CMSA	65	15
Pensacola, FL MSA	62	16
Salt Lake City – Ogden, UT MSA	59	17
Corpus Christi, TX MSA	58	18
Hartford – New Britain – Middletown, CT CMSA	58	18
Macon – Warner Robins, GA MSA	58	18
Sacramento, CA MSA	58	18
Tulsa, OK MSA	58	18
Jacksonville, FL MSA	57	19
Bakersfield, CA MSA	53	20

Source: U.S. Department of Commerce, Bureau of the Census, Data User Services Division, *1990 Census of Population and Housing, Equal Employment Opportunity File,* CD-90-EE0-1, January 1993, CD-ROM.

★1104★

Occupations, By Race/Sex

Top 25 MSAs For Employment As Airplane Pilots and Navigators, 1990: Blacks

MSA/CMSA	Employees per 100,000 pop.	Rank
Tampa – St. Petersburg – Clearwater, FL MSA	160	1
New York – Northern New Jersey – Long Island, NY – NJ – CT CMSA	137	2
Atlanta, GA MSA	125	3
Miami – Fort Lauderdale, FL CMSA	111	4
San Francisco – Oakland – San Jose, CA CMSA	100	5
Washington, DC – MD – VA MSA	96	6
Dallas – Fort Worth, TX CMSA	86	7
Philadelphia – Wilmington – Trenton, PA – NJ – DE – MD CMSA	80	8
Memphis, TN – AR – MS MSA	65	9
Charlotte – Gastonia – Rock Hill, NC – SC MSA	56	10
San Diego, CA MSA	53	11
Phoenix, AZ MSA	41	12
Pittsburgh – Beaver Valley, PA CMSA	40	13
Denver – Boulder, CO CMSA	39	14
Chicago – Gary – Lake County, IL – IN – WI CMSA	38	15
Detroit – Ann Arbor, MI CMSA	34	16
Norfolk – Virginia Beach – Newport News, VA MSA	31	17
Honolulu, HI MSA	30	18
Bakersfield, CA MSA	26	19
Seattle – Tacoma, WA CMSA	23	20
Nashville, TN MSA	22	21
Pensacola, FL MSA	20	22
Sacramento, CA MSA	17	23
Milwaukee – Racine, WI CMSA	17	23
Boston – Lawrence – Salem, MA – NH CMSA	17	23

Source: U.S. Department of Commerce, Bureau of the Census, Data User Services Division, *1990 Census of Population and Housing, Equal Employment Opportunity File,* CD-90-EE0-1, January 1993, CD-ROM.

★1105★

Occupations, By Race/Sex

Top 25 MSAs For Employment As Airplane Pilots and Navigators, 1990: Whites

MSA/CMSA	Employees per 100,000 pop.	Rank
Phoenix, AZ MSA	5,621	1
Los Angeles – Anaheim – Riverside, CA CMSA	4,511	2
Atlanta, GA MSA	4,349	3
New York – Northern New Jersey – Long Island, NY – NJ – CT CMSA	4,035	4

[Continued]

★1106★

Occupations, By Race/Sex

★1105★

Top 25 MSAs For Employment As Airplane Pilots and Navigators, 1990: Whites

[Continued]

MSA/CMSA	Employees per 100,000 pop.	Rank
Chicago – Gary – Lake County, IL – IN – WI CMSA	3,507	5
Miami – Fort Lauderdale, FL CMSA	2,969	6
San Francisco – Oakland – San Jose, CA CMSA	2,920	7
Seattle – Tacoma, WA CMSA	2,876	8
Denver – Boulder, CO CMSA	2,674	9
Minneapolis – St. Paul, MN – WI MSA	2,421	10
Houston – Galveston – Brazoria, TX CMSA	2,367	11
San Diego, CA MSA	2,087	12
Phoenix, AZ MSA	1,994	13
Memphis, TN – AR – MS MSA	1,539	14
Philadelphia – Wilmington – Trenton, PA – NJ – DE – MD CMSA	1,530	15
Washington, DC – MD – VA MSA	1,450	16
St. Louis, MO – IL MSA	1,283	17
Detroit – Ann Arbor, MI CMSA	1,250	18
Pittsburgh – Beaver Valley, PA CMSA	1,191	19
Charlotte – Gastonia – Rock Hill, NC – SC MSA	1,082	20
Boston – Lawrence – Salem, MA – NH CMSA	915	21
Kansas City, MO – KS MSA	886	22
Portland – Vancouver, OR – WA CMSA	880	23
Las Vegas, NV MSA	872	24
Baltimore, MD MSA	865	25

Source: U.S. Department of Commerce, Bureau of the Census, Data User Services Division, *1990 Census of Population and Housing, Equal Employment Opportunity File, CD-90-EE0-1, January 1993,* CD-ROM.

★1106★

Occupations, By Race/Sex

Top 25 MSAs For Employment As Announcers, 1990: Blacks

MSA/CMSA	Employees per 100,000 pop.	Rank
Richmond – Petersburg, VA MSA	398	1
Los Angeles – Anaheim – Riverside, CA CMSA	254	2
Atlanta, GA MSA	177	3
Chicago – Gary – Lake County, IL – IN – WI CMSA	176	4
Washington, DC – MD – VA MSA	174	5
Philadelphia – Wilmington – Trenton, PA – NJ – DE – MD CMSA	149	6
San Francisco – Oakland – San Jose, CA CMSA	141	7

[Continued]

★1106★

Top 25 MSAs For Employment As Announcers, 1990: Blacks

[Continued]

MSA/CMSA	Employees per 100,000 pop.	Rank
Houston – Galveston – Brazoria, TX CMSA	139	8
Detroit – Ann Arbor, MI CMSA	131	9
Dallas – Fort Worth, TX CMSA	120	10
Baltimore, MD MSA	113	11
Norfolk – Virginia Beach – Newport News, VA MSA	95	12
Indianapolis, IN MSA	88	13
Cleveland – Akron – Lorain, OH CMSA	81	14
Miami – Fort Lauderdale, FL CMSA	81	14
Baton Rouge, LA MSA	76	15
Richmond – Petersburg, VA MSA	73	16
Cincinnati – Hamilton, OH – KY – IN CMSA	72	17
Milwaukee – Racine, WI CMSA	71	18
Memphis, TN – AR – MS MSA	69	19
St. Louis, MO – IL MSA	68	20
New Orleans, LA MSA	66	21
Tampa – St. Petersburg – Clearwater, FL MSA	62	22
Boston – Lawrence – Salem, MA – NH CMSA	61	23
Pittsburgh – Beaver Valley, PA CMSA	59	24

Source: U.S. Department of Commerce, Bureau of the Census, Data User Services Division, *1990 Census of Population and Housing, Equal Employment Opportunity File, CD-90-EE0-1, January 1993,* CD-ROM.

★1107★

Occupations, By Race/Sex

Top 25 MSAs For Employment As Announcers, 1990: Whites

MSA/CMSA	Employees per 100,000 pop.	Rank
Austin, TX MSA	2,563	1
Los Angeles – Anaheim – Riverside, CA CMSA	2,057	2
Chicago – Gary – Lake County, IL – IN – WI CMSA	1,104	3
Washington, DC – MD – VA MSA	1,004	4
Philadelphia – Wilmington – Trenton, PA – NJ – DE – MD CMSA	864	5
Boston – Lawrence – Salem, MA – NH CMSA	782	6
Dallas – Fort Worth, TX CMSA	743	7
San Francisco – Oakland – San Jose, CA CMSA	678	8
Detroit – Ann Arbor, MI CMSA	668	9
Miami – Fort Lauderdale, FL CMSA	565	10

[Continued]

★1107★

Top 25 MSAs For Employment As Announcers, 1990: Whites
[Continued]

MSA/CMSA	Employees per 100,000 pop.	Rank
Atlanta, GA MSA	537	11
Houston – Galveston – Brazoria, TX CMSA	528	12
Minneapolis – St. Paul, MN – WI MSA	454	13
Seattle – Tacoma, WA CMSA	450	14
St. Louis, MO – IL MSA	448	15
Cleveland – Akron – Lorain, OH CMSA	424	16
Pittsburgh – Beaver Valley, PA CMSA	415	17
Phoenix, AZ MSA	415	17
Denver – Boulder, CO CMSA	404	18
San Diego, CA MSA	378	19
Tampa – St. Petersburg – Clearwater, FL MSA	373	20
Cincinnati – Hamilton, OH – KY – IN CMSA	371	21
San Antonio, TX MSA	325	22
Nashville, TN MSA	310	23
Buffalo – Niagara Falls, NY CMSA	307	24

Source: U.S. Department of Commerce, Bureau of the Census, Data User Services Division, *1990 Census of Population and Housing, Equal Employment Opportunity File, CD-90-EE0-1, January 1993*, CD-ROM.

★1108★

Occupations, By Race/Sex

Top 25 MSAs For Employment As Architects, 1990: Blacks

MSA/CMSA	Employees per 100,000 pop.	Rank
Pittsburgh – Beaver Valley, PA CMSA	734	1
Washington, DC – MD – VA MSA	547	2
Los Angeles – Anaheim – Riverside, CA CMSA	378	3
Chicago – Gary – Lake County, IL – IN – WI CMSA	250	4
Atlanta, GA MSA	207	5
Philadelphia – Wilmington – Trenton, PA – NJ – DE – MD CMSA	195	6
San Francisco – Oakland – San Jose, CA CMSA	169	7
Detroit – Ann Arbor, MI CMSA	164	8
Miami – Fort Lauderdale, FL CMSA	131	9
Houston – Galveston – Brazoria, TX CMSA	117	10
Baltimore, MD MSA	85	11
Norfolk – Virginia Beach – Newport News, VA MSA	79	12
Dallas – Fort Worth, TX CMSA	75	13

[Continued]

★1108★

Top 25 MSAs For Employment As Architects, 1990: Blacks
[Continued]

MSA/CMSA	Employees per 100,000 pop.	Rank
Kansas City, MO – KS MSA	65	14
St. Louis, MO – IL MSA	61	15
Cleveland – Akron – Lorain, OH CMSA	60	16
Birmingham, AL MSA	56	17
Boston – Lawrence – Salem, MA – NH CMSA	45	18
Minneapolis – St. Paul, MN – WI MSA	42	19
Indianapolis, IN MSA	39	20
San Antonio, TX MSA	36	21
San Diego, CA MSA	35	22
Phoenix, AZ MSA	35	22
Dayton – Springfield, OH MSA	34	23
Tampa – St. Petersburg – Clearwater, FL MSA	32	24

Source: U.S. Department of Commerce, Bureau of the Census, Data User Services Division, *1990 Census of Population and Housing, Equal Employment Opportunity File, CD-90-EE0-1, January 1993*, CD-ROM.

★1109★

Occupations, By Race/Sex

Top 25 MSAs For Employment As Architects, 1990: Whites

MSA/CMSA	Employees per 100,000 pop.	Rank
Tampa – St. Petersburg – Clearwater, FL MSA	15,407	1
Los Angeles – Anaheim – Riverside, CA CMSA	9,901	2
San Francisco – Oakland – San Jose, CA CMSA	7,133	3
Chicago – Gary – Lake County, IL – IN – WI CMSA	6,308	4
Boston – Lawrence – Salem, MA – NH CMSA	5,460	5
Washington, DC – MD – VA MSA	5,411	6
Philadelphia – Wilmington – Trenton, PA – NJ – DE – MD CMSA	4,418	7
Seattle – Tacoma, WA CMSA	3,221	8
Dallas – Fort Worth, TX CMSA	2,921	9
Atlanta, GA MSA	2,775	10
San Diego, CA MSA	2,622	11
Miami – Fort Lauderdale, FL CMSA	2,505	12
Houston – Galveston – Brazoria, TX CMSA	2,455	13
Minneapolis – St. Paul, MN – WI MSA	2,232	14
Detroit – Ann Arbor, MI CMSA	2,183	15
Denver – Boulder, CO CMSA	2,021	16
Baltimore, MD MSA	1,732	17

[Continued]

★1109★

Top 25 MSAs For Employment As Architects, 1990: Whites

[Continued]

MSA/CMSA	Employees per 100,000 pop.	Rank
St. Louis, MO – IL MSA	1,606	18
Phoenix, AZ MSA	1,593	19
Sacramento, CA MSA	1,490	20
Cleveland – Akron – Lorain, OH CMSA	1,393	21
Portland – Vancouver, OR – WA CMSA	1,342	22
Tampa – St. Petersburg – Clearwater, FL MSA	1,276	23
Columbus, OH MSA	1,148	24
Pittsburgh – Beaver Valley, PA CMSA	1,126	25

Source: U.S. Department of Commerce, Bureau of the Census, Data User Services Division, *1990 Census of Population and Housing, Equal Employment Opportunity File, CD-90-EE0-1, January 1993,* CD-ROM.

★1110★

Occupations, By Race/Sex

Top 25 MSAs For Employment As Archivists and Curators, 1990: Blacks

MSA/CMSA	Employees per 100,000 pop.	Rank
Jacksonville, FL MSA	283	1
Washington, DC – MD – VA MSA	282	2
Philadelphia – Wilmington – Trenton, PA – NJ – DE – MD CMSA	103	3
St. Louis, MO – IL MSA	96	4
Chicago – Gary – Lake County, IL – IN – WI CMSA	76	5
Los Angeles – Anaheim – Riverside, CA CMSA	57	6
Baltimore, MD MSA	47	7
San Francisco – Oakland – San Jose, CA CMSA	37	8
Houston – Galveston – Brazoria, TX CMSA	36	9
Richmond – Petersburg, VA MSA	32	10
Norfolk – Virginia Beach – Newport News, VA MSA	25	11
Boston – Lawrence – Salem, MA – NH CMSA	24	12
Cleveland – Akron – Lorain, OH CMSA	22	13
Columbia, SC MSA	20	14
Miami – Fort Lauderdale, FL CMSA	20	14
Dayton – Springfield, OH MSA	20	14
Buffalo – Niagara Falls, NY CMSA	18	15
Roanoke, VA MSA	16	16
Atlanta, GA MSA	16	16
Detroit – Ann Arbor, MI CMSA	16	16
New Orleans, LA MSA	15	17

[Continued]

★1110★

Top 25 MSAs For Employment As Archivists and Curators, 1990: Blacks

[Continued]

MSA/CMSA	Employees per 100,000 pop.	Rank
Orlando, FL MSA	14	18
Dallas – Fort Worth, TX CMSA	13	19
Las Vegas, NV MSA	13	19
Knoxville, TN MSA	13	19

Source: U.S. Department of Commerce, Bureau of the Census, Data User Services Division, *1990 Census of Population and Housing, Equal Employment Opportunity File, CD-90-EE0-1, January 1993,* CD-ROM.

★1111★

Occupations, By Race/Sex

Top 25 MSAs For Employment As Archivists and Curators, 1990: Whites

MSA/CMSA	Employees per 100,000 pop.	Rank
Phoenix, AZ MSA	2,913	1
Washington, DC – MD – VA MSA	1,689	2
Los Angeles – Anaheim – Riverside, CA CMSA	1,139	3
Boston – Lawrence – Salem, MA – NH CMSA	926	4
Chicago – Gary – Lake County, IL – IN – WI CMSA	868	5
San Francisco – Oakland – San Jose, CA CMSA	826	6
Philadelphia – Wilmington – Trenton, PA – NJ – DE – MD CMSA	756	7
Detroit – Ann Arbor, MI CMSA	400	8
Baltimore, MD MSA	346	9
Minneapolis – St. Paul, MN – WI MSA	333	10
St. Louis, MO – IL MSA	305	11
Kansas City, MO – KS MSA	247	12
Cleveland – Akron – Lorain, OH CMSA	243	13
Seattle – Tacoma, WA CMSA	230	14
New Haven – Meriden, CT MSA	224	15
Dallas – Fort Worth, TX CMSA	218	16
Houston – Galveston – Brazoria, TX CMSA	204	17
Miami – Fort Lauderdale, FL CMSA	200	18
Albany – Schenectady – Troy, NY MSA	194	19
San Diego, CA MSA	191	20
Atlanta, GA MSA	184	21
Indianapolis, IN MSA	183	22
Denver – Boulder, CO CMSA	183	22
Pittsburgh – Beaver Valley, PA CMSA	179	23
Hartford – New Britain – Middletown, CT CMSA	175	24

Source: U.S. Department of Commerce, Bureau of the Census, Data User Services Division, *1990 Census of Population and Housing, Equal Employment Opportunity File, CD-90-EE0-1, January 1993,* CD-ROM.

★1112★

Occupations, By Race/Sex

Top 25 MSAs For Employment As Art, Drama, and Music Teachers, 1990: Blacks

MSA/CMSA	Employees per 100,000 pop.	Rank
Pittsburgh – Beaver Valley, PA CMSA	83	1
Washington, DC – MD – VA MSA	72	2
New Orleans, LA MSA	45	3
New York – Northern New Jersey – Long Island, NY – NJ – CT CMSA	42	4
Houston – Galveston – Brazoria, TX CMSA	39	5
Detroit – Ann Arbor, MI CMSA	28	6
Cincinnati – Hamilton, OH – KY – IN CMSA	25	7
Sacramento, CA MSA	25	7
Pittsburgh – Beaver Valley, PA CMSA	25	7
Cleveland – Akron – Lorain, OH CMSA	23	8
Columbia, SC MSA	22	9
Baton Rouge, LA MSA	20	10
San Francisco – Oakland – San Jose, CA CMSA	19	11
Hartford – New Britain – Middletown, CT CMSA	18	12
Philadelphia – Wilmington – Trenton, PA – NJ – DE – MD CMSA	18	12
Austin, TX MSA	18	12
Santa Barbara – Santa Maria – Lompoc, CA MSA	18	12
Dayton – Springfield, OH MSA	17	13
Dallas – Fort Worth, TX CMSA	16	14
Boston – Lawrence – Salem, MA – NH CMSA	16	14
Chicago – Gary – Lake County, IL – IN – WI CMSA	16	14
Raleigh – Durham, NC MSA	15	15
Pine Bluff, AR MSA	14	16
Augusta, GA – SC MSA	13	17
Norfolk – Virginia Beach – Newport News, VA MSA	13	17

Source: U.S. Department of Commerce, Bureau of the Census, Data User Services Division, *1990 Census of Population and Housing, Equal Employment Opportunity File, CD-90-EE0-1, January 1993,* CD-ROM.

★1113★

Occupations, By Race/Sex

Top 25 MSAs For Employment As Art, Drama, and Music Teachers, 1990: Whites

MSA/CMSA	Employees per 100,000 pop.	Rank
Asheville, NC MSA	1,186	1
Los Angeles – Anaheim – Riverside, CA CMSA	867	2
Chicago – Gary – Lake County, IL – IN – WI CMSA	669	3
San Francisco – Oakland – San Jose, CA CMSA	539	4
Boston – Lawrence – Salem, MA – NH CMSA	496	5
Philadelphia – Wilmington – Trenton, PA – NJ – DE – MD CMSA	439	6
Washington, DC – MD – VA MSA	331	7
Detroit – Ann Arbor, MI CMSA	287	8
Minneapolis – St. Paul, MN – WI MSA	273	9
Dallas – Fort Worth, TX CMSA	263	10
Seattle – Tacoma, WA CMSA	244	11
Baltimore, MD MSA	233	12
Cleveland – Akron – Lorain, OH CMSA	229	13
Cincinnati – Hamilton, OH – KY – IN CMSA	207	14
San Diego, CA MSA	189	15
Houston – Galveston – Brazoria, TX CMSA	185	16
Phoenix, AZ MSA	174	17
Pittsburgh – Beaver Valley, PA CMSA	174	17
Bloomington, IN MSA	168	18
Greenville – Spartanburg, SC MSA	157	19
Portland – Vancouver, OR – WA CMSA	154	20
Austin, TX MSA	154	20
St. Louis, MO – IL MSA	152	21
Kansas City, MO – KS MSA	150	22
Raleigh – Durham, NC MSA	146	23

Source: U.S. Department of Commerce, Bureau of the Census, Data User Services Division, *1990 Census of Population and Housing, Equal Employment Opportunity File, CD-90-EE0-1, January 1993,* CD-ROM.

★1114★

Occupations, By Race/Sex

Top 25 MSAs For Employment As Athletes, 1990: Blacks

MSA/CMSA	Employees per 100,000 pop.	Rank
Denver – Boulder, CO CMSA	527	1
Los Angeles – Anaheim – Riverside, CA CMSA	420	2
San Francisco – Oakland – San Jose, CA CMSA	293	3
Washington, DC – MD – VA MSA	265	4
Detroit – Ann Arbor, MI CMSA	216	5
Philadelphia – Wilmington – Trenton, PA – NJ – DE – MD CMSA	201	6
Atlanta, GA MSA	199	7
Chicago – Gary – Lake County, IL – IN – WI CMSA	192	8
Houston – Galveston – Brazoria, TX CMSA	164	9
Miami – Fort Lauderdale, FL CMSA	157	10
Dallas – Fort Worth, TX CMSA	132	11
Cleveland – Akron – Lorain, OH CMSA	112	12
Richmond – Petersburg, VA MSA	89	13
Tampa – St. Petersburg – Clearwater, FL MSA	87	14
Kansas City, MO – KS MSA	83	15
Greensboro – Winston-Salem – High Point, NC MSA	72	16
Sacramento, CA MSA	67	17
Nashville, TN MSA	65	18
Boston – Lawrence – Salem, MA – NH CMSA	63	19
Phoenix, AZ MSA	63	19
Charlotte – Gastonia – Rock Hill, NC – SC MSA	63	19
St. Louis, MO – IL MSA	63	19
Pittsburgh – Beaver Valley, PA CMSA	62	20
Cincinnati – Hamilton, OH – KY – IN CMSA	60	21
Baltimore, MD MSA	57	22

Source: U.S. Department of Commerce, Bureau of the Census, Data User Services Division, *1990 Census of Population and Housing, Equal Employment Opportunity File, CD-90-EE0-1, January 1993,* CD-ROM.

★1115★

Occupations, By Race/Sex

Top 25 MSAs For Employment As Athletes, 1990: Whites

MSA/CMSA	Employees per 100,000 pop.	Rank
Baltimore, MD MSA	3,952	1
Los Angeles – Anaheim – Riverside, CA CMSA	3,580	2
San Francisco – Oakland – San Jose, CA CMSA	1,804	3
Chicago – Gary – Lake County, IL – IN – WI CMSA	1,662	4
Philadelphia – Wilmington – Trenton, PA – NJ – DE – MD CMSA	1,632	5
Boston – Lawrence – Salem, MA – NH CMSA	1,612	6
Miami – Fort Lauderdale, FL CMSA	1,343	7
Detroit – Ann Arbor, MI CMSA	1,131	8
San Diego, CA MSA	1,088	9
Dallas – Fort Worth, TX CMSA	1,045	10
Washington, DC – MD – VA MSA	936	11
Seattle – Tacoma, WA CMSA	924	12
Baltimore, MD MSA	892	13
St. Louis, MO – IL MSA	862	14
Tampa – St. Petersburg – Clearwater, FL MSA	854	15
Houston – Galveston – Brazoria, TX CMSA	832	16
Phoenix, AZ MSA	831	17
Minneapolis – St. Paul, MN – WI MSA	754	18
Cleveland – Akron – Lorain, OH CMSA	725	19
Atlanta, GA MSA	682	20
Cincinnati – Hamilton, OH – KY – IN CMSA	628	21
Denver – Boulder, CO CMSA	613	22
Pittsburgh – Beaver Valley, PA CMSA	590	23
Orlando, FL MSA	544	24
Oklahoma City, OK MSA	542	25

Source: U.S. Department of Commerce, Bureau of the Census, Data User Services Division, *1990 Census of Population and Housing, Equal Employment Opportunity File, CD-90-EE0-1, January 1993,* CD-ROM.

★1116★

Occupations, By Race/Sex

Top 25 MSAs For Employment As Auctioneers, 1990: Blacks

MSA/CMSA	Employees per 100,000 pop.	Rank
Raleigh – Durham, NC MSA	19	1
Los Angeles – Anaheim – Riverside, CA CMSA	19	1
Washington, DC – MD – VA MSA	15	2
York, PA MSA	10	3

[Continued]

★1116★

Top 25 MSAs For Employment As Auctioneers, 1990: Blacks

[Continued]

MSA/CMSA	Employees per 100,000 pop.	Rank
Philadelphia – Wilmington – Trenton, PA – NJ – DE – MD CMSA	10	3
Anderson, IN MSA	9	4
Chattanooga, TN – GA MSA	9	4
San Francisco – Oakland – San Jose, CA CMSA	8	5
New York – Northern New Jersey – Long Island, NY – NJ – CT CMSA	8	5
St. Louis, MO – IL MSA	8	5
Stockton, CA MSA	7	6
Jackson, MS MSA	6	7
Kansas City, MO – KS MSA	6	7
Parkersburg – Marietta, WV – OH MSA	0	8
Norfolk – Virginia Beach – Newport News, VA MSA	0	8
Panama City, FL MSA	0	8
Omaha, NE – IA MSA	0	8
Orlando, FL MSA	0	8
Phoenix, AZ MSA	0	8
Ocala, FL MSA	0	8
Oklahoma City, OK MSA	0	8
Muncie, IN MSA	0	8
New Orleans, LA MSA	0	8
Naples, FL MSA	0	8
New Haven – Meriden, CT MSA	0	8

Source: U.S. Department of Commerce, Bureau of the Census, Data User Services Division, *1990 Census of Population and Housing, Equal Employment Opportunity File, CD-90-EE0-1, January 1993,* CD-ROM.

★1117★

Occupations, By Race/Sex

Top 25 MSAs For Employment As Auctioneers, 1990: Whites

MSA/CMSA	Employees per 100,000 pop.	Rank
Columbus, OH MSA	242	1
Los Angeles – Anaheim – Riverside, CA CMSA	223	2
Philadelphia – Wilmington – Trenton, PA – NJ – DE – MD CMSA	154	3
Lancaster, PA MSA	122	4
San Francisco – Oakland – San Jose, CA CMSA	112	5
Dallas – Fort Worth, TX CMSA	109	6
Houston – Galveston – Brazoria, TX CMSA	98	7
Miami – Fort Lauderdale, FL CMSA	89	8
Chicago – Gary – Lake County, IL – IN – WI CMSA	85	9

[Continued]

★1117★

Top 25 MSAs For Employment As Auctioneers, 1990: Whites

[Continued]

MSA/CMSA	Employees per 100,000 pop.	Rank
Detroit – Ann Arbor, MI CMSA	81	10
Boston – Lawrence – Salem, MA – NH CMSA	80	11
Tampa – St. Petersburg – Clearwater, FL MSA	80	11
Phoenix, AZ MSA	75	12
Sharon, PA MSA	71	13
Baltimore, MD MSA	66	14
Pittsburgh – Beaver Valley, PA CMSA	66	14
Oklahoma City, OK MSA	61	15
Fort Wayne, IN MSA	59	16
Columbia, MO MSA	57	17
Indianapolis, IN MSA	57	17
Cincinnati – Hamilton, OH – KY – IN CMSA	53	18
Washington, DC – MD – VA MSA	53	18
Columbus, OH MSA	52	19
Kansas City, MO – KS MSA	50	20
Cleveland – Akron – Lorain, OH CMSA	49	21

Source: U.S. Department of Commerce, Bureau of the Census, Data User Services Division, *1990 Census of Population and Housing, Equal Employment Opportunity File, CD-90-EE0-1, January 1993,* CD-ROM.

★1118★

Occupations, By Race/Sex

Top 25 MSAs For Employment As Authors, 1990: Blacks

MSA/CMSA	Employees per 100,000 pop.	Rank
San Diego, CA MSA	475	1
Washington, DC – MD – VA MSA	407	2
Los Angeles – Anaheim – Riverside, CA CMSA	300	3
Chicago – Gary – Lake County, IL – IN – WI CMSA	287	4
San Francisco – Oakland – San Jose, CA CMSA	116	5
Detroit – Ann Arbor, MI CMSA	93	6
Atlanta, GA MSA	91	7
Philadelphia – Wilmington – Trenton, PA – NJ – DE – MD CMSA	88	8
Houston – Galveston – Brazoria, TX CMSA	56	9
Dayton – Springfield, OH MSA	55	10
St. Louis, MO – IL MSA	54	11
Denver – Boulder, CO CMSA	44	12
Boston – Lawrence – Salem, MA – NH CMSA	44	12
Cleveland – Akron – Lorain, OH CMSA	40	13

[Continued]

★1118★

Top 25 MSAs For Employment As Authors, 1990: Blacks
[Continued]

MSA/CMSA	Employees per 100,000 pop.	Rank
Indianapolis, IN MSA	37	14
Miami – Fort Lauderdale, FL CMSA	34	15
Memphis, TN – AR – MS MSA	33	16
Huntsville, AL MSA	32	17
Minneapolis – St. Paul, MN – WI MSA	31	18
Richmond – Petersburg, VA MSA	30	19
Baltimore, MD MSA	29	20
Seattle – Tacoma, WA CMSA	29	20
Charleston, SC MSA	27	21
Norfolk – Virginia Beach – Newport News, VA MSA	21	22
Portland – Vancouver, OR – WA CMSA	21	22

Source: U.S. Department of Commerce, Bureau of the Census, Data User Services Division, *1990 Census of Population and Housing, Equal Employment Opportunity File, CD-90-EE0-1,* January 1993, CD-ROM.

★1119★
Occupations, By Race/Sex

Top 25 MSAs For Employment As Authors, 1990: Whites

MSA/CMSA	Employees per 100,000 pop.	Rank
Houston – Galveston – Brazoria, TX CMSA	15,162	1
Los Angeles – Anaheim – Riverside, CA CMSA	12,656	2
San Francisco – Oakland – San Jose, CA CMSA	5,734	3
Washington, DC – MD – VA MSA	5,306	4
Chicago – Gary – Lake County, IL – IN – WI CMSA	3,220	5
Boston – Lawrence – Salem, MA – NH CMSA	2,991	6
Philadelphia – Wilmington – Trenton, PA – NJ – DE – MD CMSA	2,349	7
Seattle – Tacoma, WA CMSA	1,747	8
Minneapolis – St. Paul, MN – WI MSA	1,719	9
Dallas – Fort Worth, TX CMSA	1,618	10
San Diego, CA MSA	1,380	11
Denver – Boulder, CO CMSA	1,365	12
Atlanta, GA MSA	1,164	13
Detroit – Ann Arbor, MI CMSA	1,112	14
Houston – Galveston – Brazoria, TX CMSA	967	15
Phoenix, AZ MSA	918	16
Miami – Fort Lauderdale, FL CMSA	909	17
Portland – Vancouver, OR – WA CMSA	784	18

[Continued]

★1119★

Top 25 MSAs For Employment As Authors, 1990: Whites
[Continued]

MSA/CMSA	Employees per 100,000 pop.	Rank
St. Louis, MO – IL MSA	712	19
Austin, TX MSA	708	20
Baltimore, MD MSA	686	21
Sacramento, CA MSA	639	22
Raleigh – Durham, NC MSA	635	23
Pittsburgh – Beaver Valley, PA CMSA	622	24
Cleveland – Akron – Lorain, OH CMSA	614	25

Source: U.S. Department of Commerce, Bureau of the Census, Data User Services Division, *1990 Census of Population and Housing, Equal Employment Opportunity File, CD-90-EE0-1,* January 1993, CD-ROM.

★1120★
Occupations, By Race/Sex

Top 25 MSAs For Employment As Baggage Porters and Bellhops, 1990: Blacks

MSA/CMSA	Employees per 100,000 pop.	Rank
Baton Rouge, LA MSA	1,253	1
Miami – Fort Lauderdale, FL CMSA	681	2
Los Angeles – Anaheim – Riverside, CA CMSA	570	3
Atlanta, GA MSA	547	4
Washington, DC – MD – VA MSA	427	5
Chicago – Gary – Lake County, IL – IN – WI CMSA	410	6
Philadelphia – Wilmington – Trenton, PA – NJ – DE – MD CMSA	399	7
Dallas – Fort Worth, TX CMSA	388	8
Las Vegas, NV MSA	342	9
Orlando, FL MSA	259	10
Detroit – Ann Arbor, MI CMSA	259	10
St. Louis, MO – IL MSA	253	11
San Francisco – Oakland – San Jose, CA CMSA	244	12
Houston – Galveston – Brazoria, TX CMSA	243	13
New Orleans, LA MSA	207	14
Baltimore, MD MSA	183	15
Memphis, TN – AR – MS MSA	173	16
Denver – Boulder, CO CMSA	171	17
Cincinnati – Hamilton, OH – KY – IN CMSA	138	18
Cleveland – Akron – Lorain, OH CMSA	131	19
Boston – Lawrence – Salem, MA – NH CMSA	123	20
Tampa – St. Petersburg – Clearwater, FL MSA	123	20
West Palm Beach – Boca Raton – Delray Beach, FL MSA	95	21

[Continued]

★1120★

Top 25 MSAs For Employment As Baggage Porters and Bellhops, 1990: Blacks
[Continued]

MSA/CMSA	Employees per 100,000 pop.	Rank
Atlantic City, NJ MSA	84	22
Phoenix, AZ MSA	80	23

Source: U.S. Department of Commerce, Bureau of the Census, Data User Services Division, 1990 Census of Population and Housing, Equal Employment Opportunity File, CD-90-EE0-1, January 1993, CD-ROM.

★1121★

Occupations, By Race/Sex

Top 25 MSAs For Employment As Baggage Porters and Bellhops, 1990: Whites

MSA/CMSA	Employees per 100,000 pop.	Rank
Milwaukee – Racine, WI CMSA	1,682	1
Los Angeles – Anaheim – Riverside, CA CMSA	1,275	2
Miami – Fort Lauderdale, FL CMSA	1,078	3
Chicago – Gary – Lake County, IL – IN – WI CMSA	1,011	4
Las Vegas, NV MSA	1,007	5
Dallas – Fort Worth, TX CMSA	1,003	6
San Francisco – Oakland – San Jose, CA CMSA	752	7
Phoenix, AZ MSA	706	8
Orlando, FL MSA	690	9
Minneapolis – St. Paul, MN – WI MSA	502	10
Pittsburgh – Beaver Valley, PA CMSA	498	11
Detroit – Ann Arbor, MI CMSA	469	12
Washington, DC – MD – VA MSA	464	13
Denver – Boulder, CO CMSA	434	14
Atlanta, GA MSA	417	15
Seattle – Tacoma, WA CMSA	414	16
Salt Lake City – Ogden, UT MSA	392	17
Houston – Galveston – Brazoria, TX CMSA	378	18
Boston – Lawrence – Salem, MA – NH CMSA	362	19
San Diego, CA MSA	353	20
Tampa – St. Petersburg – Clearwater, FL MSA	344	21
Philadelphia – Wilmington – Trenton, PA – NJ – DE – MD CMSA	332	22
St. Louis, MO – IL MSA	241	23
Baltimore, MD MSA	238	24
Portland – Vancouver, OR – WA CMSA	193	25

Source: U.S. Department of Commerce, Bureau of the Census, Data User Services Division, 1990 Census of Population and Housing, Equal Employment Opportunity File, CD-90-EE0-1, January 1993, CD-ROM.

★1122★

Occupations, By Race/Sex

Top 25 MSAs For Employment As Bakers, 1990: Blacks

MSA/CMSA	Employees per 100,000 pop.	Rank
Richmond – Petersburg, VA MSA	1,962	1
Chicago – Gary – Lake County, IL – IN – WI CMSA	1,076	2
Philadelphia – Wilmington – Trenton, PA – NJ – DE – MD CMSA	967	3
Atlanta, GA MSA	766	4
Detroit – Ann Arbor, MI CMSA	738	5
Miami – Fort Lauderdale, FL CMSA	684	6
Los Angeles – Anaheim – Riverside, CA CMSA	601	7
Washington, DC – MD – VA MSA	524	8
St. Louis, MO – IL MSA	456	9
New Orleans, LA MSA	416	10
Houston – Galveston – Brazoria, TX CMSA	369	11
Dallas – Fort Worth, TX CMSA	360	12
Memphis, TN – AR – MS MSA	323	13
San Francisco – Oakland – San Jose, CA CMSA	312	14
Norfolk – Virginia Beach – Newport News, VA MSA	247	15
Charlotte – Gastonia – Rock Hill, NC – SC MSA	236	16
Baltimore, MD MSA	233	17
Richmond – Petersburg, VA MSA	208	18
Birmingham, AL MSA	199	19
Indianapolis, IN MSA	182	20
Cleveland – Akron – Lorain, OH CMSA	176	21
Greensboro – Winston-Salem – High Point, NC MSA	174	22
Boston – Lawrence – Salem, MA – NH CMSA	167	23
Greenville – Spartanburg, SC MSA	158	24
Jackson, MS MSA	147	25

Source: U.S. Department of Commerce, Bureau of the Census, Data User Services Division, 1990 Census of Population and Housing, Equal Employment Opportunity File, CD-90-EE0-1, January 1993, CD-ROM.

★1123★

Occupations, By Race/Sex

Top 25 MSAs For Employment As Bakers, 1990: Whites

MSA/CMSA	Employees per 100,000 pop.	Rank
Sioux City, IA – NE MSA	9,376	1
Los Angeles – Anaheim – Riverside, CA CMSA	5,946	2
Chicago – Gary – Lake County, IL – IN – WI CMSA	4,040	3
San Francisco – Oakland – San Jose, CA CMSA	3,142	4
Philadelphia – Wilmington – Trenton, PA – NJ – DE – MD CMSA	3,132	5
Boston – Lawrence – Salem, MA – NH CMSA	2,936	6
Detroit – Ann Arbor, MI CMSA	2,397	7
Pittsburgh – Beaver Valley, PA CMSA	1,822	8
Minneapolis – St. Paul, MN – WI MSA	1,536	9
Cleveland – Akron – Lorain, OH CMSA	1,535	10
Miami – Fort Lauderdale, FL CMSA	1,484	11
Seattle – Tacoma, WA CMSA	1,464	12
Houston – Galveston – Brazoria, TX CMSA	1,362	13
Dallas – Fort Worth, TX CMSA	1,321	14
St. Louis, MO – IL MSA	1,274	15
Baltimore, MD MSA	1,210	16
Washington, DC – MD – VA MSA	1,094	17
Providence – Pawtucket – Fall River, RI – MA CMSA	1,089	18
Buffalo – Niagara Falls, NY CMSA	1,085	19
San Diego, CA MSA	1,033	20
Portland – Vancouver, OR – WA CMSA	982	21
Phoenix, AZ MSA	973	22
Denver – Boulder, CO CMSA	924	23
Milwaukee – Racine, WI CMSA	916	24
Rochester, NY MSA	859	25

Source: U.S. Department of Commerce, Bureau of the Census, Data User Services Division, *1990 Census of Population and Housing, Equal Employment Opportunity File, CD-90-EE0-1, January 1993,* CD-ROM.

★1124★

Occupations, By Race/Sex

Top 25 MSAs For Employment As Barbers, 1990: Blacks

MSA/CMSA	Employees per 100,000 pop.	Rank
Charleston, WV MSA	1,190	1
Philadelphia – Wilmington – Trenton, PA – NJ – DE – MD CMSA	633	2
Washington, DC – MD – VA MSA	583	3
Chicago – Gary – Lake County, IL – IN – WI CMSA	468	4
Atlanta, GA MSA	359	5
Houston – Galveston – Brazoria, TX CMSA	333	6
Miami – Fort Lauderdale, FL CMSA	283	7
Los Angeles – Anaheim – Riverside, CA CMSA	278	8
Norfolk – Virginia Beach – Newport News, VA MSA	262	9
Detroit – Ann Arbor, MI CMSA	251	10
Baltimore, MD MSA	221	11
Dallas – Fort Worth, TX CMSA	217	12
San Francisco – Oakland – San Jose, CA CMSA	183	13
St. Louis, MO – IL MSA	165	14
Charlotte – Gastonia – Rock Hill, NC – SC MSA	163	15
Buffalo – Niagara Falls, NY CMSA	144	16
Cleveland – Akron – Lorain, OH CMSA	129	17
Kansas City, MO – KS MSA	115	18
Jacksonville, FL MSA	111	19
Cincinnati – Hamilton, OH – KY – IN CMSA	95	20
Augusta, GA – SC MSA	92	21
Memphis, TN – AR – MS MSA	91	22
Louisville, KY – IN MSA	90	23
Indianapolis, IN MSA	89	24
Seattle – Tacoma, WA CMSA	87	25

Source: U.S. Department of Commerce, Bureau of the Census, Data User Services Division, *1990 Census of Population and Housing, Equal Employment Opportunity File, CD-90-EE0-1, January 1993,* CD-ROM.

★1125★

Occupations, By Race/Sex

Top 25 MSAs For Employment As Barbers, 1990: Whites

MSA/CMSA	Employees per 100,000 pop.	Rank
Rochester, NY MSA	3,476	1
Los Angeles – Anaheim – Riverside, CA CMSA	2,319	2
Chicago – Gary – Lake County, IL – IN – WI CMSA	1,981	3
Philadelphia – Wilmington – Trenton, PA – NJ – DE – MD CMSA	1,568	4

[Continued]

★1125★

Top 25 MSAs For Employment As Barbers, 1990: Whites

[Continued]

MSA/CMSA	Employees per 100,000 pop.	Rank
San Francisco – Oakland – San Jose, CA CMSA	1,299	5
Boston – Lawrence – Salem, MA – NH CMSA	1,106	6
Detroit – Ann Arbor, MI CMSA	1,063	7
Dallas – Fort Worth, TX CMSA	993	8
Miami – Fort Lauderdale, FL CMSA	944	9
Minneapolis – St. Paul, MN – WI MSA	871	10
St. Louis, MO – IL MSA	815	11
Houston – Galveston – Brazoria, TX CMSA	764	12
Cleveland – Akron – Lorain, OH CMSA	746	13
Pittsburgh – Beaver Valley, PA CMSA	746	13
Cincinnati – Hamilton, OH – KY – IN CMSA	732	14
Phoenix, AZ MSA	703	15
Washington, DC – MD – VA MSA	664	16
Tampa – St. Petersburg – Clearwater, FL MSA	638	17
Seattle – Tacoma, WA CMSA	633	18
Baltimore, MD MSA	580	19
Atlanta, GA MSA	564	20
San Diego, CA MSA	556	21
Denver – Boulder, CO CMSA	505	22
Kansas City, MO – KS MSA	502	23
Columbus, OH MSA	494	24

Source: U.S. Department of Commerce, Bureau of the Census, Data User Services Division, *1990 Census of Population and Housing, Equal Employment Opportunity File, CD-90-EE0-1, January 1993*, CD-ROM.

★1126★

Occupations, By Race/Sex

Top 25 MSAs For Employment As Bartenders, 1990: Blacks

MSA/CMSA	Employees per 100,000 pop.	Rank
Columbus, OH MSA	1,071	1
Chicago – Gary – Lake County, IL – IN – WI CMSA	880	2
Philadelphia – Wilmington – Trenton, PA – NJ – DE – MD CMSA	764	3
Los Angeles – Anaheim – Riverside, CA CMSA	508	4
Atlanta, GA MSA	369	5
San Francisco – Oakland – San Jose, CA CMSA	335	6
Houston – Galveston – Brazoria, TX CMSA	333	7

[Continued]

★1126★

Top 25 MSAs For Employment As Bartenders, 1990: Blacks

[Continued]

MSA/CMSA	Employees per 100,000 pop.	Rank
New Orleans, LA MSA	322	8
Detroit – Ann Arbor, MI CMSA	320	9
Washington, DC – MD – VA MSA	312	10
St. Louis, MO – IL MSA	232	11
Dallas – Fort Worth, TX CMSA	214	12
Milwaukee – Racine, WI CMSA	187	13
Cleveland – Akron – Lorain, OH CMSA	177	14
Las Vegas, NV MSA	175	15
Seattle – Tacoma, WA CMSA	145	16
Baltimore, MD MSA	131	17
Indianapolis, IN MSA	128	18
Boston – Lawrence – Salem, MA – NH CMSA	128	18
Pittsburgh – Beaver Valley, PA CMSA	124	19
Norfolk – Virginia Beach – Newport News, VA MSA	123	20
Memphis, TN – AR – MS MSA	120	21
Miami – Fort Lauderdale, FL CMSA	118	22
Denver – Boulder, CO CMSA	109	23
Baton Rouge, LA MSA	100	24

Source: U.S. Department of Commerce, Bureau of the Census, Data User Services Division, *1990 Census of Population and Housing, Equal Employment Opportunity File, CD-90-EE0-1, January 1993*, CD-ROM.

★1127★

Occupations, By Race/Sex

Top 25 MSAs For Employment As Bartenders, 1990: Whites

MSA/CMSA	Employees per 100,000 pop.	Rank
Glens Falls, NY MSA	16,768	1
Los Angeles – Anaheim – Riverside, CA CMSA	12,292	2
Chicago – Gary – Lake County, IL – IN – WI CMSA	9,808	3
San Francisco – Oakland – San Jose, CA CMSA	6,794	4
Philadelphia – Wilmington – Trenton, PA – NJ – DE – MD CMSA	6,159	5
Boston – Lawrence – Salem, MA – NH CMSA	6,098	6
Detroit – Ann Arbor, MI CMSA	4,843	7
Miami – Fort Lauderdale, FL CMSA	4,787	8
Pittsburgh – Beaver Valley, PA CMSA	4,325	9
Seattle – Tacoma, WA CMSA	4,086	10
Dallas – Fort Worth, TX CMSA	4,005	11
Milwaukee – Racine, WI CMSA	3,986	12

[Continued]

★1127★

Top 25 MSAs For Employment As Bartenders, 1990: Whites
[Continued]

MSA/CMSA	Employees per 100,000 pop.	Rank
Minneapolis – St. Paul, MN – WI MSA	3,615	13
Las Vegas, NV MSA	3,483	14
Tampa – St. Petersburg – Clearwater, FL MSA	3,352	15
San Diego, CA MSA	3,339	16
Cleveland – Akron – Lorain, OH CMSA	3,149	17
Washington, DC – MD – VA MSA	3,133	18
Houston – Galveston – Brazoria, TX CMSA	3,101	19
Phoenix, AZ MSA	3,086	20
St. Louis, MO – IL MSA	3,014	21
Denver – Boulder, CO CMSA	2,730	22
Portland – Vancouver, OR – WA CMSA	2,569	23
Atlanta, GA MSA	2,480	24
Baltimore, MD MSA	2,418	25

Source: U.S. Department of Commerce, Bureau of the Census, Data User Services Division, *1990 Census of Population and Housing, Equal Employment Opportunity File, CD-90-EE0-1, January 1993,* CD-ROM.

★1128★

Occupations, By Race/Sex

Top 25 MSAs For Employment As Biological and Life Scientists, 1990: Blacks

MSA/CMSA	Employees per 100,000 pop.	Rank
Dayton – Springfield, OH MSA	432	1
Washington, DC – MD – VA MSA	303	2
Philadelphia – Wilmington – Trenton, PA – NJ – DE – MD CMSA	121	3
Raleigh – Durham, NC MSA	91	4
Baltimore, MD MSA	88	5
Atlanta, GA MSA	84	6
Chicago – Gary – Lake County, IL – IN – WI CMSA	81	7
Detroit – Ann Arbor, MI CMSA	61	8
Los Angeles – Anaheim – Riverside, CA CMSA	59	9
Richmond – Petersburg, VA MSA	56	10
Boston – Lawrence – Salem, MA – NH CMSA	49	11
Memphis, TN – AR – MS MSA	44	12
San Francisco – Oakland – San Jose, CA CMSA	43	13
Nashville, TN MSA	36	14
Dallas – Fort Worth, TX CMSA	33	15
Houston – Galveston – Brazoria, TX CMSA	31	16
Toledo, OH MSA	25	17
Madison, WI MSA	25	17

[Continued]

★1128★

Top 25 MSAs For Employment As Biological and Life Scientists, 1990: Blacks
[Continued]

MSA/CMSA	Employees per 100,000 pop.	Rank
St. Louis, MO – IL MSA	23	18
Tampa – St. Petersburg – Clearwater, FL MSA	22	19
New Orleans, LA MSA	22	19
Gainesville, FL MSA	21	20
Athens, GA MSA	21	20
Kalamazoo, MI MSA	20	21
Indianapolis, IN MSA	20	21

Source: U.S. Department of Commerce, Bureau of the Census, Data User Services Division, *1990 Census of Population and Housing, Equal Employment Opportunity File, CD-90-EE0-1, January 1993,* CD-ROM.

★1129★

Occupations, By Race/Sex

Top 25 MSAs For Employment As Biological and Life Scientists, 1990: Whites

MSA/CMSA	Employees per 100,000 pop.	Rank
Chicago – Gary – Lake County, IL – IN – WI CMSA	3,189	1
San Francisco – Oakland – San Jose, CA CMSA	2,933	2
Washington, DC – MD – VA MSA	2,436	3
Philadelphia – Wilmington – Trenton, PA – NJ – DE – MD CMSA	2,188	4
Los Angeles – Anaheim – Riverside, CA CMSA	2,040	5
Boston – Lawrence – Salem, MA – NH CMSA	1,900	6
Chicago – Gary – Lake County, IL – IN – WI CMSA	1,614	7
Seattle – Tacoma, WA CMSA	1,191	8
San Diego, CA MSA	1,096	9
Baltimore, MD MSA	855	10
Detroit – Ann Arbor, MI CMSA	772	11
Raleigh – Durham, NC MSA	759	12
St. Louis, MO – IL MSA	691	13
Denver – Boulder, CO CMSA	688	14
Sacramento, CA MSA	679	15
Minneapolis – St. Paul, MN – WI MSA	634	16
Madison, WI MSA	627	17
Portland – Vancouver, OR – WA CMSA	622	18
Atlanta, GA MSA	598	19
Houston – Galveston – Brazoria, TX CMSA	526	20
Dallas – Fort Worth, TX CMSA	503	21
Gainesville, FL MSA	482	22
Cincinnati – Hamilton, OH – KY – IN CMSA	436	23

[Continued]

★1129★

Top 25 MSAs For Employment As Biological and Life Scientists, 1990: Whites

[Continued]

MSA/CMSA	Employees per 100,000 pop.	Rank
Miami – Fort Lauderdale, FL CMSA	424	24
Indianapolis, IN MSA	377	25

Source: U.S. Department of Commerce, Bureau of the Census, Data User Services Division, *1990 Census of Population and Housing, Equal Employment Opportunity File, CD-90-EE0-1, January 1993,* CD-ROM.

★1130★

Occupations, By Race/Sex

Top 25 MSAs For Employment As Biological Science Teachers, 1990: Blacks

MSA/CMSA	Employees per 100,000 pop.	Rank
Pine Bluff, AR MSA	15	1
Tallahassee, FL MSA	11	2
Jacksonville, FL MSA	10	3
New York – Northern New Jersey – Long Island, NY – NJ – CT CMSA	10	3
Nashville, TN MSA	9	4
Columbus, OH MSA	7	5
Sacramento, CA MSA	7	5
Raleigh – Durham, NC MSA	7	5
Omaha, NE – IA MSA	0	6
Olympia, WA MSA	0	6
Phoenix, AZ MSA	0	6
Panama City, FL MSA	0	6
Oklahoma City, OK MSA	0	6
Ocala, FL MSA	0	6
Orlando, FL MSA	0	6
Norfolk – Virginia Beach – Newport News, VA MSA	0	6
Muncie, IN MSA	0	6
New Haven – Meriden, CT MSA	0	6
Muskegon, MI MSA	0	6
Poughkeepsie, NY MSA	0	6
New Orleans, LA MSA	0	6
Odessa, TX MSA	0	6
Owensboro, KY MSA	0	6
Reno, NV MSA	0	6
Pine Bluff, AR MSA	0	6

Source: U.S. Department of Commerce, Bureau of the Census, Data User Services Division, *1990 Census of Population and Housing, Equal Employment Opportunity File, CD-90-EE0-1, January 1993,* CD-ROM.

★1131★

Occupations, By Race/Sex

Top 25 MSAs For Employment As Biological Science Teachers, 1990: Whites

MSA/CMSA	Employees per 100,000 pop.	Rank
San Diego, CA MSA	358	1
Los Angeles – Anaheim – Riverside, CA CMSA	229	2
Boston – Lawrence – Salem, MA – NH CMSA	194	3
Philadelphia – Wilmington – Trenton, PA – NJ – DE – MD CMSA	125	4
Columbus, OH MSA	119	5
Washington, DC – MD – VA MSA	103	6
Raleigh – Durham, NC MSA	90	7
San Francisco – Oakland – San Jose, CA CMSA	88	8
Dallas – Fort Worth, TX CMSA	87	9
San Diego, CA MSA	83	10
Baltimore, MD MSA	82	11
Detroit – Ann Arbor, MI CMSA	73	12
Austin, TX MSA	65	13
Providence – Pawtucket – Fall River, RI – MA CMSA	61	14
Chicago – Gary – Lake County, IL – IN – WI CMSA	59	15
Madison, WI MSA	58	16
Oklahoma City, OK MSA	53	17
Sacramento, CA MSA	51	18
Seattle – Tacoma, WA CMSA	46	19
St. Louis, MO – IL MSA	43	20
Rochester, NY MSA	42	21
Jackson, MS MSA	42	21
Milwaukee – Racine, WI CMSA	41	22
Champaign – Urbana – Rantoul, IL MSA	40	23
Houston – Galveston – Brazoria, TX CMSA	40	23

Source: U.S. Department of Commerce, Bureau of the Census, Data User Services Division, *1990 Census of Population and Housing, Equal Employment Opportunity File, CD-90-EE0-1, January 1993,* CD-ROM.

★1132★

Occupations, By Race/Sex

Top 25 MSAs For Employment As Bridge, Lock, and Lighthouse Tenders, 1990: Blacks

MSA/CMSA	Employees per 100,000 pop.	Rank
Sacramento, CA MSA	118	1
Chicago – Gary – Lake County, IL – IN – WI CMSA	59	2
Cleveland – Akron – Lorain, OH CMSA	38	3
Norfolk – Virginia Beach – Newport News, VA MSA	24	4
Little Rock – North Little Rock, AR MSA	19	5

[Continued]

★1132★

Top 25 MSAs For Employment As Bridge, Lock, and Lighthouse Tenders, 1990: Blacks
[Continued]

MSA/CMSA	Employees per 100,000 pop.	Rank
Detroit – Ann Arbor, MI CMSA	18	6
Charleston, SC MSA	16	7
Washington, DC – MD – VA MSA	16	7
Nashville, TN MSA	16	7
Pittsburgh – Beaver Valley, PA CMSA	14	8
New Orleans, LA MSA	14	8
Jacksonville, FL MSA	14	8
Greensboro – Winston-Salem – High Point, NC MSA	14	8
Atlanta, GA MSA	12	9
Baltimore, MD MSA	12	9
Milwaukee – Racine, WI CMSA	10	10
Philadelphia – Wilmington – Trenton, PA – NJ – DE – MD CMSA	10	10
Mobile, AL MSA	9	11
Florence, AL MSA	9	11
Wilmington, NC MSA	8	12
Richmond – Petersburg, VA MSA	8	12
West Palm Beach – Boca Raton – Delray Beach, FL MSA	7	13
Florence, SC MSA	7	13
Tallahassee, FL MSA	7	13
Jamestown – Dunkirk, NY	7	13

Source: U.S. Department of Commerce, Bureau of the Census, Data User Services Division, *1990 Census of Population and Housing, Equal Employment Opportunity File, CD-90-EE0-1, January 1993, CD-ROM.*

★1133★

Occupations, By Race/Sex

Top 25 MSAs For Employment As Bridge, Lock, and Lighthouse Tenders, 1990: Whites

MSA/CMSA	Employees per 100,000 pop.	Rank
Lafayette, LA MSA	422	1
Miami – Fort Lauderdale, FL CMSA	156	2
Tampa – St. Petersburg – Clearwater, FL MSA	119	3
Chicago – Gary – Lake County, IL – IN – WI CMSA	111	4
Norfolk – Virginia Beach – Newport News, VA MSA	103	5
Houma – Thibodaux, LA MSA	101	6
New Orleans, LA MSA	96	7
Pittsburgh – Beaver Valley, PA CMSA	96	7
Jacksonville, FL MSA	79	8
Detroit – Ann Arbor, MI CMSA	77	9
San Francisco – Oakland – San Jose, CA CMSA	64	10
Huntington – Ashland, WV – KY – OH MSA	60	11

[Continued]

★1133★

Top 25 MSAs For Employment As Bridge, Lock, and Lighthouse Tenders, 1990: Whites
[Continued]

MSA/CMSA	Employees per 100,000 pop.	Rank
Minneapolis – St. Paul, MN – WI MSA	57	12
Portland – Vancouver, OR – WA CMSA	56	13
Atlantic City, NJ MSA	55	14
Milwaukee – Racine, WI CMSA	49	15
Boston – Lawrence – Salem, MA – NH CMSA	49	15
New London – Norwich, CT – RI MSA	44	16
Melbourne – Titusville – Palm Bay, FL MSA	43	17
West Palm Beach – Boca Raton – Delray Beach, FL MSA	43	17
Cincinnati – Hamilton, OH – KY – IN CMSA	41	18
Biloxi – Gulfport, MS MSA	41	18
Sarasota, FL MSA	40	19
Seattle – Tacoma, WA CMSA	40	19
Fort Myers – Cape CoraL, Fl MSA	40	19

Source: U.S. Department of Commerce, Bureau of the Census, Data User Services Division, *1990 Census of Population and Housing, Equal Employment Opportunity File, CD-90-EE0-1, January 1993, CD-ROM.*

★1134★

Occupations, By Race/Sex

Top 25 MSAs For Employment As Bus Drivers, 1990: Blacks

MSA/CMSA	Employees per 100,000 pop.	Rank
Tampa – St. Petersburg – Clearwater, FL MSA	14,388	1
Chicago – Gary – Lake County, IL – IN – WI CMSA	7,614	2
Los Angeles – Anaheim – Riverside, CA CMSA	6,094	3
Washington, DC – MD – VA MSA	5,272	4
Philadelphia – Wilmington – Trenton, PA – NJ – DE – MD CMSA	4,241	5
San Francisco – Oakland – San Jose, CA CMSA	2,856	6
Houston – Galveston – Brazoria, TX CMSA	2,568	7
Miami – Fort Lauderdale, FL CMSA	2,393	8
Atlanta, GA MSA	2,318	9
Dallas – Fort Worth, TX CMSA	2,220	10
Detroit – Ann Arbor, MI CMSA	2,218	11
Baltimore, MD MSA	2,044	12
St. Louis, MO – IL MSA	1,938	13
Cleveland – Akron – Lorain, OH CMSA	1,809	14

[Continued]

★1134★

Top 25 MSAs For Employment As Bus Drivers, 1990: Blacks
[Continued]

MSA/CMSA	Employees per 100,000 pop.	Rank
New Orleans, LA MSA	1,498	15
Norfolk – Virginia Beach – Newport News, VA MSA	1,299	16
Milwaukee – Racine, WI CMSA	1,276	17
Boston – Lawrence – Salem, MA – NH CMSA	1,209	18
Richmond – Petersburg, VA MSA	859	19
Memphis, TN – AR – MS MSA	832	20
Raleigh – Durham, NC MSA	820	21
Pittsburgh – Beaver Valley, PA CMSA	790	22
Charlotte – Gastonia – Rock Hill, NC – SC MSA	762	23
Kansas City, MO – KS MSA	762	23
Greensboro – Winston-Salem – High Point, NC MSA	686	24

Source: U.S. Department of Commerce, Bureau of the Census, Data User Services Division, *1990 Census of Population and Housing, Equal Employment Opportunity File, CD-90-EE0-1, January 1993,* CD-ROM.

★1135★
Occupations, By Race/Sex

Top 25 MSAs For Employment As Bus Drivers, 1990: Whites

MSA/CMSA	Employees per 100,000 pop.	Rank
Washington, DC – MD – VA MSA	26,444	1
Los Angeles – Anaheim – Riverside, CA CMSA	8,713	2
Philadelphia – Wilmington – Trenton, PA – NJ – DE – MD CMSA	8,432	3
Chicago – Gary – Lake County, IL – IN – WI CMSA	7,231	4
Boston – Lawrence – Salem, MA – NH CMSA	5,662	5
Minneapolis – St. Paul, MN – WI MSA	4,919	6
Seattle – Tacoma, WA CMSA	4,747	7
Detroit – Ann Arbor, MI CMSA	4,692	8
San Francisco – Oakland – San Jose, CA CMSA	4,287	9
Pittsburgh – Beaver Valley, PA CMSA	4,219	10
Washington, DC – MD – VA MSA	3,962	11
Cleveland – Akron – Lorain, OH CMSA	3,434	12
Houston – Galveston – Brazoria, TX CMSA	3,315	13
Atlanta, GA MSA	3,036	14
St. Louis, MO – IL MSA	2,971	15
Portland – Vancouver, OR – WA CMSA	2,874	16

[Continued]

★1135★

Top 25 MSAs For Employment As Bus Drivers, 1990: Whites
[Continued]

MSA/CMSA	Employees per 100,000 pop.	Rank
Buffalo – Niagara Falls, NY CMSA	2,620	17
Phoenix, AZ MSA	2,615	18
Cincinnati – Hamilton, OH – KY – IN CMSA	2,509	19
Baltimore, MD MSA	2,397	20
Dallas – Fort Worth, TX CMSA	2,340	21
Albany – Schenectady – Troy, NY MSA	2,316	22
Denver – Boulder, CO CMSA	2,315	23
Rochester, NY MSA	2,273	24
Tampa – St. Petersburg – Clearwater, FL MSA	2,251	25

Source: U.S. Department of Commerce, Bureau of the Census, Data User Services Division, *1990 Census of Population and Housing, Equal Employment Opportunity File, CD-90-EE0-1, January 1993,* CD-ROM.

★1136★
Occupations, By Race/Sex

Top 25 MSAs For Employment As Business and Promotion Agents, 1990: Blacks

MSA/CMSA	Employees per 100,000 pop.	Rank
Charlotte – Gastonia – Rock Hill, NC – SC MSA	400	1
Los Angeles – Anaheim – Riverside, CA CMSA	252	2
Washington, DC – MD – VA MSA	158	3
Chicago – Gary – Lake County, IL – IN – WI CMSA	87	4
Baltimore, MD MSA	84	5
Houston – Galveston – Brazoria, TX CMSA	83	6
Atlanta, GA MSA	78	7
Dallas – Fort Worth, TX CMSA	65	8
San Francisco – Oakland – San Jose, CA CMSA	59	9
Miami – Fort Lauderdale, FL CMSA	55	10
Norfolk – Virginia Beach – Newport News, VA MSA	50	11
Detroit – Ann Arbor, MI CMSA	42	12
Las Vegas, NV MSA	41	13
Cincinnati – Hamilton, OH – KY – IN CMSA	37	14
Cleveland – Akron – Lorain, OH CMSA	36	15
Philadelphia – Wilmington – Trenton, PA – NJ – DE – MD CMSA	33	16
Louisville, KY – IN MSA	27	17
Boston – Lawrence – Salem, MA – NH CMSA	24	18
Kansas City, MO – KS MSA	24	18

[Continued]

★1136★

Top 25 MSAs For Employment As Business and Promotion Agents, 1990: Blacks
[Continued]

MSA/CMSA	Employees per 100,000 pop.	Rank
Lexington-Fayette, KY MSA	23	19
Birmingham, AL MSA	21	20
Denver – Boulder, CO CMSA	21	20
Nashville, TN MSA	20	21
Fayetteville, NC MSA	19	22
St. Louis, MO – IL MSA	19	22

Source: U.S. Department of Commerce, Bureau of the Census, Data User Services Division, *1990 Census of Population and Housing, Equal Employment Opportunity File, CD-90-EE0-1, January 1993,* CD-ROM.

★1137★

Occupations, By Race/Sex

Top 25 MSAs For Employment As Business and Promotion Agents, 1990: Whites

MSA/CMSA	Employees per 100,000 pop.	Rank
Columbus, OH MSA	4,418	1
Los Angeles – Anaheim – Riverside, CA CMSA	3,810	2
Chicago – Gary – Lake County, IL – IN – WI CMSA	1,412	3
San Francisco – Oakland – San Jose, CA CMSA	1,084	4
Washington, DC – MD – VA MSA	834	5
Boston – Lawrence – Salem, MA – NH CMSA	703	6
Dallas – Fort Worth, TX CMSA	596	7
Miami – Fort Lauderdale, FL CMSA	586	8
Philadelphia – Wilmington – Trenton, PA – NJ – DE – MD CMSA	561	9
Atlanta, GA MSA	482	10
San Diego, CA MSA	461	11
Seattle – Tacoma, WA CMSA	420	12
Minneapolis – St. Paul, MN – WI MSA	415	13
Detroit – Ann Arbor, MI CMSA	414	14
Phoenix, AZ MSA	403	15
Houston – Galveston – Brazoria, TX CMSA	399	16
Denver – Boulder, CO CMSA	395	17
Nashville, TN MSA	372	18
Portland – Vancouver, OR – WA CMSA	308	19
Cleveland – Akron – Lorain, OH CMSA	273	20
Cincinnati – Hamilton, OH – KY – IN CMSA	249	21
Kansas City, MO – KS MSA	248	22
Indianapolis, IN MSA	239	23

[Continued]

★1137★

Top 25 MSAs For Employment As Business and Promotion Agents, 1990: Whites
[Continued]

MSA/CMSA	Employees per 100,000 pop.	Rank
Sacramento, CA MSA	239	23
Las Vegas, NV MSA	236	24

Source: U.S. Department of Commerce, Bureau of the Census, Data User Services Division, *1990 Census of Population and Housing, Equal Employment Opportunity File, CD-90-EE0-1, January 1993,* CD-ROM.

★1138★

Occupations, By Race/Sex

Top 25 MSAs For Employment As Business, Commerce, and Marketing Teachers, 1990: Blacks

MSA/CMSA	Employees per 100,000 pop.	Rank
Portland, ME MSA	69	1
Detroit – Ann Arbor, MI CMSA	19	2
New York – Northern New Jersey – Long Island, NY – NJ – CT CMSA	19	2
San Francisco – Oakland – San Jose, CA CMSA	18	3
Houston – Galveston – Brazoria, TX CMSA	15	4
Fayetteville, NC MSA	14	5
Hartford – New Britain – Middletown, CT CMSA	12	6
Chattanooga, TN – GA MSA	11	7
Milwaukee – Racine, WI CMSA	11	7
New Orleans, LA MSA	10	8
Little Rock – North Little Rock, AR MSA	9	9
Nashville, TN MSA	9	9
Rochester, NY MSA	9	9
Atlanta, GA MSA	8	10
Birmingham, AL MSA	8	10
Baton Rouge, LA MSA	8	10
Raleigh – Durham, NC MSA	8	10
Albany – Schenectady – Troy, NY MSA	7	11
Minneapolis – St. Paul, MN – WI MSA	7	11
Cincinnati – Hamilton, OH – KY – IN CMSA	7	11
West Palm Beach – Boca Raton – Delray Beach, FL MSA	6	12
Greensboro – Winston-Salem – High Point, NC MSA	5	13
Decatur, AL MSA	3	14
Cedar Rapids, IA MSA	0	15
Bryan – College Station, TX MSA	0	15

Source: U.S. Department of Commerce, Bureau of the Census, Data User Services Division, *1990 Census of Population and Housing, Equal Employment Opportunity File, CD-90-EE0-1, January 1993,* CD-ROM.

★1139★

Occupations, By Race/Sex

Top 25 MSAs For Employment As Business, Commerce, and Marketing Teachers, 1990: Whites

MSA/CMSA	Employees per 100,000 pop.	Rank
Pittsburgh – Beaver Valley, PA CMSA	210	1
Philadelphia – Wilmington – Trenton, PA – NJ – DE – MD CMSA	128	2
Los Angeles – Anaheim – Riverside, CA CMSA	106	3
Chicago – Gary – Lake County, IL – IN – WI CMSA	104	4
Boston – Lawrence – Salem, MA – NH CMSA	99	5
Washington, DC – MD – VA MSA	89	6
San Francisco – Oakland – San Jose, CA CMSA	88	7
Houston – Galveston – Brazoria, TX CMSA	84	8
Dallas – Fort Worth, TX CMSA	66	9
Columbus, OH MSA	65	10
Detroit – Ann Arbor, MI CMSA	61	11
Atlanta, GA MSA	55	12
Seattle – Tacoma, WA CMSA	52	13
San Antonio, TX MSA	51	14
Cleveland – Akron – Lorain, OH CMSA	49	15
Tampa – St. Petersburg – Clearwater, FL MSA	47	16
Phoenix, AZ MSA	46	17
Sacramento, CA MSA	42	18
Pittsburgh – Beaver Valley, PA CMSA	38	19
Birmingham, AL MSA	37	20
Baltimore, MD MSA	36	21
Omaha, NE – IA MSA	35	22
Toledo, OH MSA	33	23
Charlotte – Gastonia – Rock Hill, NC – SC MSA	33	23
Mobile, AL MSA	32	24

Source: U.S. Department of Commerce, Bureau of the Census, Data User Services Division, *1990 Census of Population and Housing, Equal Employment Opportunity File, CD-90-EEO-1, January 1993*, CD-ROM.

★1140★

Occupations, By Race/Sex

Top 25 MSAs For Employment As Butchers and Meat Cutters, 1990: Blacks

MSA/CMSA	Employees per 100,000 pop.	Rank
Tallahassee, FL MSA	1,506	1
Chicago – Gary – Lake County, IL – IN – WI CMSA	1,154	2
Detroit – Ann Arbor, MI CMSA	977	3
Philadelphia – Wilmington – Trenton, PA – NJ – DE – MD CMSA	929	4

[Continued]

★1140★

Top 25 MSAs For Employment As Butchers and Meat Cutters, 1990: Blacks
[Continued]

MSA/CMSA	Employees per 100,000 pop.	Rank
Washington, DC – MD – VA MSA	655	5
Jackson, MS MSA	609	6
Los Angeles – Anaheim – Riverside, CA CMSA	608	7
Atlanta, GA MSA	537	8
Baltimore, MD MSA	529	9
New Orleans, LA MSA	458	10
Houston – Galveston – Brazoria, TX CMSA	425	11
Birmingham, AL MSA	393	12
Miami – Fort Lauderdale, FL CMSA	363	13
St. Louis, MO – IL MSA	348	14
Memphis, TN – AR – MS MSA	326	15
Dallas – Fort Worth, TX CMSA	324	16
Montgomery, AL MSA	316	17
Norfolk – Virginia Beach – Newport News, VA MSA	307	18
Fayetteville, NC MSA	299	19
Milwaukee – Racine, WI CMSA	253	20
Athens, GA MSA	248	21
Charlotte – Gastonia – Rock Hill, NC – SC MSA	245	22
Cleveland – Akron – Lorain, OH CMSA	243	23
Omaha, NE – IA MSA	243	23
Macon – Warner Robins, GA MSA	242	24

Source: U.S. Department of Commerce, Bureau of the Census, Data User Services Division, *1990 Census of Population and Housing, Equal Employment Opportunity File, CD-90-EEO-1, January 1993*, CD-ROM.

★1141★

Occupations, By Race/Sex

Top 25 MSAs For Employment As Butchers and Meat Cutters, 1990: Whites

MSA/CMSA	Employees per 100,000 pop.	Rank
Atlanta, GA MSA	11,490	1
Los Angeles – Anaheim – Riverside, CA CMSA	6,388	2
Chicago – Gary – Lake County, IL – IN – WI CMSA	5,812	3
Philadelphia – Wilmington – Trenton, PA – NJ – DE – MD CMSA	4,474	4
San Francisco – Oakland – San Jose, CA CMSA	3,427	5
Detroit – Ann Arbor, MI CMSA	3,018	6
Boston – Lawrence – Salem, MA – NH CMSA	2,744	7
Miami – Fort Lauderdale, FL CMSA	2,684	8
Pittsburgh – Beaver Valley, PA CMSA	2,081	9

[Continued]

★1141★

Top 25 MSAs For Employment As Butchers and Meat Cutters, 1990: Whites

[Continued]

MSA/CMSA	Employees per 100,000 pop.	Rank
Cleveland – Akron – Lorain, OH CMSA	1,911	10
Minneapolis – St. Paul, MN – WI MSA	1,883	11
Houston – Galveston – Brazoria, TX CMSA	1,859	12
Dallas – Fort Worth, TX CMSA	1,834	13
St. Louis, MO – IL MSA	1,787	14
Tampa – St. Petersburg – Clearwater, FL MSA	1,627	15
Cincinnati – Hamilton, OH – KY – IN CMSA	1,614	16
Baltimore, MD MSA	1,593	17
Seattle – Tacoma, WA CMSA	1,569	18
Washington, DC – MD – VA MSA	1,433	19
Atlanta, GA MSA	1,381	20
Denver – Boulder, CO CMSA	1,325	21
Omaha, NE – IA MSA	1,259	22
Milwaukee – Racine, WI CMSA	1,187	23
Phoenix, AZ MSA	1,182	24
Portland – Vancouver, OR – WA CMSA	1,148	25

Source: U.S. Department of Commerce, Bureau of the Census, Data User Services Division, *1990 Census of Population and Housing, Equal Employment Opportunity File, CD-90-EE0-1, January 1993,* CD-ROM.

★1142★

Occupations, By Race/Sex

Top 25 MSAs For Employment As Cabinet Makers and Bench Carpenters, 1990: Blacks

MSA/CMSA	Employees per 100,000 pop.	Rank
Milwaukee – Racine, WI CMSA	458	1
Miami – Fort Lauderdale, FL CMSA	141	2
Atlanta, GA MSA	138	3
Los Angeles – Anaheim – Riverside, CA CMSA	126	4
Baltimore, MD MSA	108	5
Washington, DC – MD – VA MSA	107	6
Philadelphia – Wilmington – Trenton, PA – NJ – DE – MD CMSA	102	7
Memphis, TN – AR – MS MSA	77	8
Chicago – Gary – Lake County, IL – IN – WI CMSA	72	9
Greensboro – Winston-Salem – High Point, NC MSA	72	9
San Francisco – Oakland – San Jose, CA CMSA	70	10
Dallas – Fort Worth, TX CMSA	65	11
Richmond – Petersburg, VA MSA	38	12
Macon – Warner Robins, GA MSA	37	13

[Continued]

★1142★

Top 25 MSAs For Employment As Cabinet Makers and Bench Carpenters, 1990: Blacks

[Continued]

MSA/CMSA	Employees per 100,000 pop.	Rank
Indianapolis, IN MSA	36	14
Birmingham, AL MSA	32	15
Cleveland – Akron – Lorain, OH CMSA	31	16
Huntsville, AL MSA	31	16
Columbus, OH MSA	28	17
Pensacola, FL MSA	28	17
Nashville, TN MSA	26	18
Lakeland – Winter Haven, FL MSA	25	19
Norfolk – Virginia Beach – Newport News, VA MSA	25	19
Louisville, KY – IN MSA	23	20
Montgomery, AL MSA	23	20

Source: U.S. Department of Commerce, Bureau of the Census, Data User Services Division, *1990 Census of Population and Housing, Equal Employment Opportunity File, CD-90-EE0-1, January 1993,* CD-ROM.

★1143★

Occupations, By Race/Sex

Top 25 MSAs For Employment As Cabinet Makers and Bench Carpenters, 1990: Whites

MSA/CMSA	Employees per 100,000 pop.	Rank
San Antonio, TX MSA	3,606	1
Los Angeles – Anaheim – Riverside, CA CMSA	3,567	2
San Francisco – Oakland – San Jose, CA CMSA	1,749	3
Chicago – Gary – Lake County, IL – IN – WI CMSA	1,547	4
Minneapolis – St. Paul, MN – WI MSA	1,320	5
Seattle – Tacoma, WA CMSA	1,062	6
Philadelphia – Wilmington – Trenton, PA – NJ – DE – MD CMSA	1,030	7
Miami – Fort Lauderdale, FL CMSA	995	8
Atlanta, GA MSA	976	9
Sacramento, CA MSA	915	10
Detroit – Ann Arbor, MI CMSA	859	11
Dallas – Fort Worth, TX CMSA	849	12
Tampa – St. Petersburg – Clearwater, FL MSA	792	13
Boston – Lawrence – Salem, MA – NH CMSA	754	14
Portland – Vancouver, OR – WA CMSA	734	15
Phoenix, AZ MSA	694	16
Washington, DC – MD – VA MSA	659	17
San Diego, CA MSA	589	18
Cleveland – Akron – Lorain, OH CMSA	538	19

[Continued]

★1143★

Top 25 MSAs For Employment As Cabinet Makers and Bench Carpenters, 1990: Whites

[Continued]

MSA/CMSA	Employees per 100,000 pop.	Rank
Milwaukee – Racine, WI CMSA	536	20
Baltimore, MD MSA	521	21
Kansas City, MO – KS MSA	502	22
Salt Lake City – Ogden, UT MSA	428	23
Columbus, OH MSA	419	24
Houston – Galveston – Brazoria, TX CMSA	408	25

Source: U.S. Department of Commerce, Bureau of the Census, Data User Services Division, *1990 Census of Population and Housing, Equal Employment Opportunity File, CD-90-EE0-1, January 1993*, CD-ROM.

★1144★

Occupations, By Race/Sex

Top 25 MSAs For Employment As Captains and Other Officers, Fishing Vessels, 1990: Blacks

MSA/CMSA	Employees per 100,000 pop.	Rank
Alexandria, LA MSA	28	1
Tampa – St. Petersburg – Clearwater, FL MSA	14	2
Houston – Galveston – Brazoria, TX CMSA	10	3
Charleston, SC MSA	7	4
New York – Northern New Jersey – Long Island, NY – NJ – CT CMSA	6	5
Pascagoula, MS MSA	6	5
Pittsburgh – Beaver Valley, PA CMSA	4	6
Savannah, GA MSA	2	7
Madison, WI MSA	0	8
Memphis, TN – AR – MS MSA	0	8
Midland, TX MSA	0	8
Mobile, AL MSA	0	8
Merced, CA MSA	0	8
Modesto, CA MSA	0	8
Minneapolis – St. Paul, MN – WI MSA	0	8
Manchester, NH MSA	0	8
Milwaukee – Racine, WI CMSA	0	8
Medford, OR MSA	0	8
Melbourne – Titusville – Palm Bay, FL MSA	0	8
Louisville, KY – IN MSA	0	8
Parkersburg – Marietta, WV – OH MSA	0	8
Norfolk – Virginia Beach – Newport News, VA MSA	0	8
Odessa, TX MSA	0	8
Panama City, FL MSA	0	8
Muskegon, MI MSA	0	8

Source: U.S. Department of Commerce, Bureau of the Census, Data User Services Division, *1990 Census of Population and Housing, Equal Employment Opportunity File, CD-90-EE0-1, January 1993*, CD-ROM.

★1145★

Occupations, By Race/Sex

Top 25 MSAs For Employment As Captains and Other Officers, Fishing Vessels, 1990: Whites

MSA/CMSA	Employees per 100,000 pop.	Rank
Dayton – Springfield, OH MSA	379	1
New York – Northern New Jersey – Long Island, NY – NJ – CT CMSA	294	2
San Diego, CA MSA	201	3
Houma – Thibodaux, LA MSA	160	4
Providence – Pawtucket – Fall River, RI – MA CMSA	144	5
New Bedford, MA MSA	142	6
Miami – Fort Lauderdale, FL CMSA	136	7
Boston – Lawrence – Salem, MA – NH CMSA	124	8
Mobile, AL MSA	124	8
Tampa – St. Petersburg – Clearwater, FL MSA	119	9
Portland, ME MSA	112	10
West Palm Beach – Boca Raton – Delray Beach, FL MSA	111	11
Los Angeles – Anaheim – Riverside, CA CMSA	107	12
Brownsville – Harlingen, TX MSA	94	13
Fort Myers – Cape Coral, Fl MSA	92	14
Atlantic City, NJ MSA	90	15
San Francisco – Oakland – San Jose, CA CMSA	68	16
New Orleans, LA MSA	67	17
Jacksonville, FL MSA	61	18
Houston – Galveston – Brazoria, TX CMSA	52	19
Fort Walton Beach, FL MSA	52	19
Anchorage, AK MSA	48	20
Philadelphia – Wilmington – Trenton, PA – NJ – DE – MD CMSA	46	21
Corpus Christi, TX MSA	45	22
Panama City, FL MSA	42	23

Source: U.S. Department of Commerce, Bureau of the Census, Data User Services Division, *1990 Census of Population and Housing, Equal Employment Opportunity File, CD-90-EE0-1, January 1993*, CD-ROM.

★1146★

Occupations, By Race/Sex

Top 25 MSAs For Employment As Chemical Engineers, 1990: Blacks

MSA/CMSA	Employees per 100,000 pop.	Rank
Rapid City, SD MSA	236	1
New York – Northern New Jersey – Long Island, NY – NJ – CT CMSA	221	2
Philadelphia – Wilmington – Trenton, PA – NJ – DE – MD CMSA	159	3
Cincinnati – Hamilton, OH – KY – IN CMSA	153	4
Chicago – Gary – Lake County, IL – IN – WI CMSA	119	5
St. Louis, MO – IL MSA	64	6
Beaumont – Port Arthur, TX MSA	60	7
Washington, DC – MD – VA MSA	52	8
Cleveland – Akron – Lorain, OH CMSA	51	9
Los Angeles – Anaheim – Riverside, CA CMSA	47	10
Baton Rouge, LA MSA	43	11
Minneapolis – St. Paul, MN – WI MSA	40	12
Greenville – Spartanburg, SC MSA	39	13
San Francisco – Oakland – San Jose, CA CMSA	38	14
Saginaw – Bay City – Midland, MI MSA	38	14
Knoxville, TN MSA	36	15
New Orleans, LA MSA	35	16
Baltimore, MD MSA	34	17
Salt Lake City – Ogden, UT MSA	28	18
Lake Charles, LA MSA	27	19
Detroit – Ann Arbor, MI CMSA	27	19
Memphis, TN – AR – MS MSA	26	20
Augusta, GA – SC MSA	26	20
Miami – Fort Lauderdale, FL CMSA	25	21
Louisville, KY – IN MSA	23	22

Source: U.S. Department of Commerce, Bureau of the Census, Data User Services Division, *1990 Census of Population and Housing, Equal Employment Opportunity File, CD-90-EE0-1, January 1993,* CD-ROM.

★1147★

Occupations, By Race/Sex

Top 25 MSAs For Employment As Chemical Engineers, 1990: Whites

MSA/CMSA	Employees per 100,000 pop.	Rank
Chicago – Gary – Lake County, IL – IN – WI CMSA	5,016	1
New York – Northern New Jersey – Long Island, NY – NJ – CT CMSA	4,283	2
Philadelphia – Wilmington – Trenton, PA – NJ – DE – MD CMSA	3,700	3
Chicago – Gary – Lake County, IL – IN – WI CMSA	2,670	4
San Francisco – Oakland – San Jose, CA CMSA	1,482	5
Los Angeles – Anaheim – Riverside, CA CMSA	1,394	6
Minneapolis – St. Paul, MN – WI MSA	1,307	7
Cleveland – Akron – Lorain, OH CMSA	1,235	8
Cincinnati – Hamilton, OH – KY – IN CMSA	1,085	9
Saginaw – Bay City – Midland, MI MSA	1,049	10
Baton Rouge, LA MSA	1,047	11
Boston – Lawrence – Salem, MA – NH CMSA	910	12
Detroit – Ann Arbor, MI CMSA	819	13
St. Louis, MO – IL MSA	805	14
Beaumont – Port Arthur, TX MSA	683	15
Allentown – Bethlehem – Easton, PA – NJ MSA	662	16
New Orleans, LA MSA	624	17
Johnson City – Kingsport – Bristol, TN – VA MSA	624	17
Pittsburgh – Beaver Valley, PA CMSA	590	18
Charleston, WV MSA	558	19
Augusta, GA – SC MSA	557	20
Baltimore, MD MSA	545	21
Knoxville, TN MSA	543	22
Buffalo – Niagara Falls, NY CMSA	543	22
Richmond – Petersburg, VA MSA	448	23

Source: U.S. Department of Commerce, Bureau of the Census, Data User Services Division, *1990 Census of Population and Housing, Equal Employment Opportunity File, CD-90-EE0-1, January 1993,* CD-ROM.

★1148★

Occupations, By Race/Sex

Top 25 MSAs For Employment As Chemistry Teachers, 1990: Blacks

MSA/CMSA	Employees per 100,000 pop.	Rank
Pensacola, FL MSA	27	1
Washington, DC – MD – VA MSA	17	2
New Orleans, LA MSA	16	3
Houston – Galveston – Brazoria, TX CMSA	11	4
Tallahassee, FL MSA	11	4
Dallas – Fort Worth, TX CMSA	10	5
Baltimore, MD MSA	9	6
Richmond – Petersburg, VA MSA	9	6
Norfolk – Virginia Beach – Newport News, VA MSA	9	6
Cincinnati – Hamilton, OH – KY – IN CMSA	8	7
Athens, GA MSA	8	7
Chicago – Gary – Lake County, IL – IN – WI CMSA	6	8
San Francisco – Oakland – San Jose, CA CMSA	5	9
Minneapolis – St. Paul, MN – WI MSA	4	10
Lubbock, TX MSA	0	11
Mansfield, OH MSA	0	11
Lincoln, NE MSA	0	11
Los Angeles – Anaheim – Riverside, CA CMSA	0	11
Lewiston – Auburn, ME MSA	0	11
Milwaukee – Racine, WI CMSA	0	11
Longview – Marshall, TX MSA	0	11
Little Rock – North Little Rock, AR MSA	0	11
Monroe, LA MSA	0	11
Melbourne – Titusville – Palm Bay, FL MSA	0	11
Modesto, CA MSA	0	11

Source: U.S. Department of Commerce, Bureau of the Census, Data User Services Division, *1990 Census of Population and Housing, Equal Employment Opportunity File, CD-90-EE0-1,* January 1993, CD-ROM.

★1149★

Occupations, By Race/Sex

Top 25 MSAs For Employment As Chemistry Teachers, 1990: Whites

MSA/CMSA	Employees per 100,000 pop.	Rank
Cleveland – Akron – Lorain, OH CMSA	236	1
Chicago – Gary – Lake County, IL – IN – WI CMSA	189	2
Los Angeles – Anaheim – Riverside, CA CMSA	173	3
Philadelphia – Wilmington – Trenton, PA – NJ – DE – MD CMSA	128	4

[Continued]

★1149★

Top 25 MSAs For Employment As Chemistry Teachers, 1990: Whites

[Continued]

MSA/CMSA	Employees per 100,000 pop.	Rank
Boston – Lawrence – Salem, MA – NH CMSA	123	5
San Francisco – Oakland – San Jose, CA CMSA	114	6
Madison, WI MSA	99	7
Houston – Galveston – Brazoria, TX CMSA	83	8
Denver – Boulder, CO CMSA	76	9
Baltimore, MD MSA	70	10
Hartford – New Britain – Middletown, CT CMSA	67	11
Raleigh – Durham, NC MSA	67	11
Detroit – Ann Arbor, MI CMSA	59	12
Dallas – Fort Worth, TX CMSA	57	13
Cleveland – Akron – Lorain, OH CMSA	51	14
Indianapolis, IN MSA	48	15
Pittsburgh – Beaver Valley, PA CMSA	47	16
New Orleans, LA MSA	46	17
Syracuse, NY MSA	46	17
Fort Collins – Loveland, CO MSA	45	18
Austin, TX MSA	44	19
State College, PA MSA	43	20
San Diego, CA MSA	42	21
St. Louis, MO – IL MSA	41	22
Minneapolis – St. Paul, MN – WI MSA	41	22

Source: U.S. Department of Commerce, Bureau of the Census, Data User Services Division, *1990 Census of Population and Housing, Equal Employment Opportunity File, CD-90-EE0-1,* January 1993, CD-ROM.

★1150★

Occupations, By Race/Sex

Top 25 MSAs For Employment As Chemists, Except Biochemists, 1990: Blacks

MSA/CMSA	Employees per 100,000 pop.	Rank
Charlotte – Gastonia – Rock Hill, NC – SC MSA	1,000	1
Philadelphia – Wilmington – Trenton, PA – NJ – DE – MD CMSA	616	2
Chicago – Gary – Lake County, IL – IN – WI CMSA	478	3
Washington, DC – MD – VA MSA	408	4
Houston – Galveston – Brazoria, TX CMSA	381	5
Baltimore, MD MSA	358	6
Los Angeles – Anaheim – Riverside, CA CMSA	319	7
San Francisco – Oakland – San Jose, CA CMSA	248	8

[Continued]

★1150★

Top 25 MSAs For Employment As Chemists, Except Biochemists, 1990: Blacks
[Continued]

MSA/CMSA	Employees per 100,000 pop.	Rank
Atlanta, GA MSA	228	9
Cleveland – Akron – Lorain, OH CMSA	204	10
Dallas – Fort Worth, TX CMSA	178	11
Detroit – Ann Arbor, MI CMSA	153	12
St. Louis, MO – IL MSA	152	13
Raleigh – Durham, NC MSA	139	14
Memphis, TN – AR – MS MSA	135	15
Charlotte – Gastonia – Rock Hill, NC – SC MSA	126	16
Indianapolis, IN MSA	125	17
Columbia, SC MSA	121	18
Miami – Fort Lauderdale, FL CMSA	106	19
Cincinnati – Hamilton, OH – KY – IN CMSA	95	20
Richmond – Petersburg, VA MSA	92	21
Baton Rouge, LA MSA	92	21
Buffalo – Niagara Falls, NY CMSA	82	22
Dayton – Springfield, OH MSA	77	23
Boston – Lawrence – Salem, MA – NH CMSA	75	24

Source: U.S. Department of Commerce, Bureau of the Census, Data User Services Division, 1990 Census of Population and Housing, Equal Employment Opportunity File, CD-90-EE0-1, January 1993, CD-ROM.

★1151★

Occupations, By Race/Sex

Top 25 MSAs For Employment As Chemists, Except Biochemists, 1990: Whites

MSA/CMSA	Employees per 100,000 pop.	Rank
Phoenix, AZ MSA	10,109	1
Philadelphia – Wilmington – Trenton, PA – NJ – DE – MD CMSA	6,251	2
Chicago – Gary – Lake County, IL – IN – WI CMSA	5,382	3
San Francisco – Oakland – San Jose, CA CMSA	4,791	4
Los Angeles – Anaheim – Riverside, CA CMSA	3,700	5
Houston – Galveston – Brazoria, TX CMSA	3,511	6
Washington, DC – MD – VA MSA	2,892	7
Boston – Lawrence – Salem, MA – NH CMSA	2,850	8
Cleveland – Akron – Lorain, OH CMSA	2,187	9
St. Louis, MO – IL MSA	2,073	10
Detroit – Ann Arbor, MI CMSA	1,880	11
Minneapolis – St. Paul, MN – WI MSA	1,811	12

[Continued]

★1151★

Top 25 MSAs For Employment As Chemists, Except Biochemists, 1990: Whites
[Continued]

MSA/CMSA	Employees per 100,000 pop.	Rank
Pittsburgh – Beaver Valley, PA CMSA	1,776	13
Denver – Boulder, CO CMSA	1,622	14
Dallas – Fort Worth, TX CMSA	1,602	15
Cincinnati – Hamilton, OH – KY – IN CMSA	1,570	16
Raleigh – Durham, NC MSA	1,511	17
Baltimore, MD MSA	1,390	18
Rochester, NY MSA	1,243	19
Indianapolis, IN MSA	1,210	20
San Diego, CA MSA	1,165	21
Atlanta, GA MSA	1,041	22
Columbus, OH MSA	1,026	23
Saginaw – Bay City – Midland, MI MSA	998	24
Milwaukee – Racine, WI CMSA	884	25

Source: U.S. Department of Commerce, Bureau of the Census, Data User Services Division, 1990 Census of Population and Housing, Equal Employment Opportunity File, CD-90-EE0-1, January 1993, CD-ROM.

★1152★

Occupations, By Race/Sex

Top 25 MSAs For Employment As Chief Executives and General Administrators, Public Administration, 1990: Blacks

MSA/CMSA	Employees per 100,000 pop.	Rank
Memphis, TN – AR – MS MSA	316	1
Los Angeles – Anaheim – Riverside, CA CMSA	158	2
Detroit – Ann Arbor, MI CMSA	156	3
Chicago – Gary – Lake County, IL – IN – WI CMSA	154	4
Washington, DC – MD – VA MSA	139	5
Philadelphia – Wilmington – Trenton, PA – NJ – DE – MD CMSA	127	6
Houston – Galveston – Brazoria, TX CMSA	79	7
Norfolk – Virginia Beach – Newport News, VA MSA	56	8
San Francisco – Oakland – San Jose, CA CMSA	51	9
St. Louis, MO – IL MSA	48	10
Cleveland – Akron – Lorain, OH CMSA	45	11
Dallas – Fort Worth, TX CMSA	38	12
New Orleans, LA MSA	37	13
Miami – Fort Lauderdale, FL CMSA	33	14
Greensboro – Winston-Salem – High Point, NC MSA	32	15

[Continued]

★1152★

Top 25 MSAs For Employment As Chief Executives and General Administrators, Public Administration, 1990: Blacks
[Continued]

MSA/CMSA	Employees per 100,000 pop.	Rank
Cincinnati – Hamilton, OH – KY – IN CMSA	32	15
San Antonio, TX MSA	31	16
Tampa – St. Petersburg – Clearwater, FL MSA	30	17
Boston – Lawrence – Salem, MA – NH CMSA	28	18
Richmond – Petersburg, VA MSA	25	19
Baltimore, MD MSA	25	19
Columbia, SC MSA	24	20
Worcester, MA MSA	23	21
Jackson, MS MSA	22	22
Asheville, NC MSA	22	22

Source: U.S. Department of Commerce, Bureau of the Census, Data User Services Division, 1990 Census of Population and Housing, Equal Employment Opportunity File, CD-90-EE0-1, January 1993, CD-ROM.

★1153★

Occupations, By Race/Sex

Top 25 MSAs For Employment As Chief Executives and General Administrators, Public Administration, 1990: Whites

MSA/CMSA	Employees per 100,000 pop.	Rank
New Orleans, LA MSA	1,232	1
Los Angeles – Anaheim – Riverside, CA CMSA	613	2
Chicago – Gary – Lake County, IL – IN – WI CMSA	436	3
San Francisco – Oakland – San Jose, CA CMSA	391	4
Philadelphia – Wilmington – Trenton, PA – NJ – DE – MD CMSA	341	5
Washington, DC – MD – VA MSA	311	6
Detroit – Ann Arbor, MI CMSA	282	7
Boston – Lawrence – Salem, MA – NH CMSA	224	8
Baltimore, MD MSA	204	9
Houston – Galveston – Brazoria, TX CMSA	194	10
Dallas – Fort Worth, TX CMSA	190	11
Cleveland – Akron – Lorain, OH CMSA	178	12
Miami – Fort Lauderdale, FL CMSA	174	13
St. Louis, MO – IL MSA	151	14
Tampa – St. Petersburg – Clearwater, FL MSA	150	15
San Diego, CA MSA	146	16
Minneapolis – St. Paul, MN – WI MSA	143	17

[Continued]

★1153★

Top 25 MSAs For Employment As Chief Executives and General Administrators, Public Administration, 1990: Whites
[Continued]

MSA/CMSA	Employees per 100,000 pop.	Rank
Sacramento, CA MSA	138	18
Denver – Boulder, CO CMSA	134	19
Seattle – Tacoma, WA CMSA	125	20
Pittsburgh – Beaver Valley, PA CMSA	115	21
Columbus, OH MSA	109	22
Milwaukee – Racine, WI CMSA	107	23
Albany – Schenectady – Troy, NY MSA	104	24
Buffalo – Niagara Falls, NY CMSA	101	25

Source: U.S. Department of Commerce, Bureau of the Census, Data User Services Division, 1990 Census of Population and Housing, Equal Employment Opportunity File, CD-90-EE0-1, January 1993, CD-ROM.

★1154★

Occupations, By Race/Sex

Top 25 MSAs For Employment As Child Care Workers, Private Household, 1990: Blacks

MSA/CMSA	Employees per 100,000 pop.	Rank
San Antonio, TX MSA	3,218	1
Washington, DC – MD – VA MSA	1,045	2
Chicago – Gary – Lake County, IL – IN – WI CMSA	560	3
Houston – Galveston – Brazoria, TX CMSA	531	4
Philadelphia – Wilmington – Trenton, PA – NJ – DE – MD CMSA	473	5
Los Angeles – Anaheim – Riverside, CA CMSA	439	6
Atlanta, GA MSA	386	7
Miami – Fort Lauderdale, FL CMSA	350	8
Dallas – Fort Worth, TX CMSA	340	9
Detroit – Ann Arbor, MI CMSA	312	10
Baltimore, MD MSA	308	11
New Orleans, LA MSA	283	12
Memphis, TN – AR – MS MSA	235	13
Norfolk – Virginia Beach – Newport News, VA MSA	220	14
St. Louis, MO – IL MSA	211	15
Birmingham, AL MSA	211	15
Cleveland – Akron – Lorain, OH CMSA	204	16
San Francisco – Oakland – San Jose, CA CMSA	185	17
Boston – Lawrence – Salem, MA – NH CMSA	137	18
Shreveport, LA MSA	135	19
Baton Rouge, LA MSA	124	20

[Continued]

★1154★

Top 25 MSAs For Employment As Child Care Workers, Private Household, 1990: Blacks

[Continued]

MSA/CMSA	Employees per 100,000 pop.	Rank
Charleston, SC MSA	124	20
Charlotte – Gastonia – Rock Hill, NC – SC MSA	124	20
Richmond – Petersburg, VA MSA	123	21
Columbia, SC MSA	117	22

Source: U.S. Department of Commerce, Bureau of the Census, Data User Services Division, *1990 Census of Population and Housing, Equal Employment Opportunity File, CD-90-EE0-1,* January 1993, CD-ROM.

★1155★

Occupations, By Race/Sex

Top 25 MSAs For Employment As Child Care Workers, Private Household, 1990: Whites

MSA/CMSA	Employees per 100,000 pop.	Rank
Stockton, CA MSA	7,557	1
New York – Northern New Jersey – Long Island, NY – NJ – CT CMSA	7,147	2
San Francisco – Oakland – San Jose, CA CMSA	3,755	3
Chicago – Gary – Lake County, IL – IN – WI CMSA	3,685	4
Washington, DC – MD – VA MSA	2,755	5
Boston – Lawrence – Salem, MA – NH CMSA	2,591	6
Detroit – Ann Arbor, MI CMSA	2,143	7
Seattle – Tacoma, WA CMSA	2,128	8
Philadelphia – Wilmington – Trenton, PA – NJ – DE – MD CMSA	2,034	9
Houston – Galveston – Brazoria, TX CMSA	1,909	10
Dallas – Fort Worth, TX CMSA	1,743	11
San Diego, CA MSA	1,678	12
Minneapolis – St. Paul, MN – WI MSA	1,651	13
Denver – Boulder, CO CMSA	1,512	14
Phoenix, AZ MSA	1,406	15
Portland – Vancouver, OR – WA CMSA	1,335	16
Baltimore, MD MSA	1,248	17
Miami – Fort Lauderdale, FL CMSA	1,238	18
Atlanta, GA MSA	1,235	19
Cleveland – Akron – Lorain, OH CMSA	1,231	20
St. Louis, MO – IL MSA	1,096	21
Pittsburgh – Beaver Valley, PA CMSA	1,071	22
Kansas City, MO – KS MSA	952	23

[Continued]

★1155★

Top 25 MSAs For Employment As Child Care Workers, Private Household, 1990: Whites

[Continued]

MSA/CMSA	Employees per 100,000 pop.	Rank
Sacramento, CA MSA	923	24
Norfolk – Virginia Beach – Newport News, VA MSA	916	25

Source: U.S. Department of Commerce, Bureau of the Census, Data User Services Division, *1990 Census of Population and Housing, Equal Employment Opportunity File, CD-90-EE0-1,* January 1993, CD-ROM.

★1156★

Occupations, By Race/Sex

Top 25 MSAs For Employment As Clergy, 1990: Blacks

MSA/CMSA	Employees per 100,000 pop.	Rank
Kansas City, MO – KS MSA	2,283	1
Chicago – Gary – Lake County, IL – IN – WI CMSA	982	2
Los Angeles – Anaheim – Riverside, CA CMSA	927	3
Philadelphia – Wilmington – Trenton, PA – NJ – DE – MD CMSA	852	4
Washington, DC – MD – VA MSA	807	5
Dallas – Fort Worth, TX CMSA	590	6
Detroit – Ann Arbor, MI CMSA	542	7
Atlanta, GA MSA	517	8
Houston – Galveston – Brazoria, TX CMSA	487	9
Miami – Fort Lauderdale, FL CMSA	404	10
Memphis, TN – AR – MS MSA	400	11
San Francisco – Oakland – San Jose, CA CMSA	382	12
Baltimore, MD MSA	354	13
Cleveland – Akron – Lorain, OH CMSA	298	14
Boston – Lawrence – Salem, MA – NH CMSA	277	15
Charlotte – Gastonia – Rock Hill, NC – SC MSA	253	16
Norfolk – Virginia Beach – Newport News, VA MSA	232	17
St. Louis, MO – IL MSA	224	18
Columbus, OH MSA	223	19
Greensboro – Winston-Salem – High Point, NC MSA	214	20
Pittsburgh – Beaver Valley, PA CMSA	198	21
Cincinnati – Hamilton, OH – KY – IN CMSA	197	22
Birmingham, AL MSA	197	22
Nashville, TN MSA	183	23
Kansas City, MO – KS MSA	172	24

Source: U.S. Department of Commerce, Bureau of the Census, Data User Services Division, *1990 Census of Population and Housing, Equal Employment Opportunity File, CD-90-EE0-1,* January 1993, CD-ROM.

★1157★
Occupations, By Race/Sex

Top 25 MSAs For Employment As Clergy, 1990: Whites

MSA/CMSA	Employees per 100,000 pop.	Rank
Albany – Schenectady – Troy, NY MSA	11,917	1
Los Angeles – Anaheim – Riverside, CA CMSA	9,998	2
Chicago – Gary – Lake County, IL – IN – WI CMSA	6,891	3
Dallas – Fort Worth, TX CMSA	5,129	4
Philadelphia – Wilmington – Trenton, PA – NJ – DE – MD CMSA	5,098	5
San Francisco – Oakland – San Jose, CA CMSA	4,635	6
Boston – Lawrence – Salem, MA – NH CMSA	3,800	7
Detroit – Ann Arbor, MI CMSA	3,681	8
Atlanta, GA MSA	3,201	9
Minneapolis – St. Paul, MN – WI MSA	3,161	10
Washington, DC – MD – VA MSA	3,036	11
St. Louis, MO – IL MSA	2,915	12
Houston – Galveston – Brazoria, TX CMSA	2,891	13
Seattle – Tacoma, WA CMSA	2,878	14
Cleveland – Akron – Lorain, OH CMSA	2,764	15
Pittsburgh – Beaver Valley, PA CMSA	2,676	16
Tampa – St. Petersburg – Clearwater, FL MSA	2,260	17
Cincinnati – Hamilton, OH – KY – IN CMSA	2,116	18
Phoenix, AZ MSA	2,052	19
Kansas City, MO – KS MSA	2,024	20
San Diego, CA MSA	1,995	21
Charlotte – Gastonia – Rock Hill, NC – SC MSA	1,993	22
Denver – Boulder, CO CMSA	1,974	23
Baltimore, MD MSA	1,947	24
Indianapolis, IN MSA	1,877	25

Source: U.S. Department of Commerce, Bureau of the Census, Data User Services Division, *1990 Census of Population and Housing, Equal Employment Opportunity File,* CD-90-EE0-1, January 1993, CD-ROM.

★1158★
Occupations, By Race/Sex

Top 25 MSAs For Employment As Computer Operators, 1990: Blacks

MSA/CMSA	Employees per 100,000 pop.	Rank
Olympia, WA MSA	15,830	1
Chicago – Gary – Lake County, IL – IN – WI CMSA	5,930	2
Washington, DC – MD – VA MSA	5,718	3
Los Angeles – Anaheim – Riverside, CA CMSA	5,159	4
Philadelphia – Wilmington – Trenton, PA – NJ – DE – MD CMSA	3,972	5
Atlanta, GA MSA	3,228	6
Dallas – Fort Worth, TX CMSA	2,828	7
Detroit – Ann Arbor, MI CMSA	2,533	8
Houston – Galveston – Brazoria, TX CMSA	2,485	9
Baltimore, MD MSA	2,239	10
San Francisco – Oakland – San Jose, CA CMSA	2,166	11
St. Louis, MO – IL MSA	1,360	12
Miami – Fort Lauderdale, FL CMSA	1,320	13
Cleveland – Akron – Lorain, OH CMSA	1,284	14
Richmond – Petersburg, VA MSA	1,216	15
Norfolk – Virginia Beach – Newport News, VA MSA	1,211	16
Boston – Lawrence – Salem, MA – NH CMSA	1,122	17
Memphis, TN – AR – MS MSA	1,113	18
Kansas City, MO – KS MSA	1,053	19
New Orleans, LA MSA	886	20
Columbus, OH MSA	785	21
Charlotte – Gastonia – Rock Hill, NC – SC MSA	670	22
Raleigh – Durham, NC MSA	646	23
Jacksonville, FL MSA	630	24
Nashville, TN MSA	621	25

Source: U.S. Department of Commerce, Bureau of the Census, Data User Services Division, *1990 Census of Population and Housing, Equal Employment Opportunity File,* CD-90-EE0-1, January 1993, CD-ROM.

★1159★
Occupations, By Race/Sex

Top 25 MSAs For Employment As Computer Operators, 1990: Whites

MSA/CMSA	Employees per 100,000 pop.	Rank
Orlando, FL MSA	41,075	1
Los Angeles – Anaheim – Riverside, CA CMSA	22,571	2
Chicago – Gary – Lake County, IL – IN – WI CMSA	19,072	3
Philadelphia – Wilmington – Trenton, PA – NJ – DE – MD CMSA	15,409	4

[Continued]

★1159★

Top 25 MSAs For Employment As Computer Operators, 1990: Whites

[Continued]

MSA/CMSA	Employees per 100,000 pop.	Rank
Boston – Lawrence – Salem, MA – NH CMSA	11,769	5
Dallas – Fort Worth, TX CMSA	11,707	6
San Francisco – Oakland – San Jose, CA CMSA	10,388	7
Detroit – Ann Arbor, MI CMSA	10,195	8
Houston – Galveston – Brazoria, TX CMSA	7,870	9
Washington, DC – MD – VA MSA	7,554	10
Minneapolis – St. Paul, MN – WI MSA	7,487	11
Atlanta, GA MSA	7,408	12
St. Louis, MO – IL MSA	6,841	13
Cleveland – Akron – Lorain, OH CMSA	6,635	14
Miami – Fort Lauderdale, FL CMSA	6,307	15
Seattle – Tacoma, WA CMSA	6,241	16
Denver – Boulder, CO CMSA	5,857	17
Baltimore, MD MSA	5,699	18
Kansas City, MO – KS MSA	5,003	19
Phoenix, AZ MSA	4,928	20
Cincinnati – Hamilton, OH – KY – IN CMSA	4,807	21
Pittsburgh – Beaver Valley, PA CMSA	4,782	22
Tampa – St. Petersburg – Clearwater, FL MSA	4,781	23
Columbus, OH MSA	4,726	24
Hartford – New Britain – Middletown, CT CMSA	4,104	25

Source: U.S. Department of Commerce, Bureau of the Census, Data User Services Division, *1990 Census of Population and Housing, Equal Employment Opportunity File, CD-90-EE0-1, January 1993,* CD-ROM.

★1160★

Occupations, By Race/Sex

Top 25 MSAs For Employment As Computer Programmers, 1990: Blacks

MSA/CMSA	Employees per 100,000 pop.	Rank
Birmingham, AL MSA	5,993	1
Washington, DC – MD – VA MSA	4,883	2
Chicago – Gary – Lake County, IL – IN – WI CMSA	2,384	3
Los Angeles – Anaheim – Riverside, CA CMSA	2,052	4
Philadelphia – Wilmington – Trenton, PA – NJ – DE – MD CMSA	1,807	5
Atlanta, GA MSA	1,685	6
Detroit – Ann Arbor, MI CMSA	1,207	7
San Francisco – Oakland – San Jose, CA CMSA	1,160	8

[Continued]

★1160★

Top 25 MSAs For Employment As Computer Programmers, 1990: Blacks

[Continued]

MSA/CMSA	Employees per 100,000 pop.	Rank
Houston – Galveston – Brazoria, TX CMSA	1,105	9
Dallas – Fort Worth, TX CMSA	1,044	10
Baltimore, MD MSA	981	11
St. Louis, MO – IL MSA	736	12
Raleigh – Durham, NC MSA	650	13
Boston – Lawrence – Salem, MA – NH CMSA	615	14
Cleveland – Akron – Lorain, OH CMSA	432	15
Miami – Fort Lauderdale, FL CMSA	429	16
Richmond – Petersburg, VA MSA	359	17
Norfolk – Virginia Beach – Newport News, VA MSA	346	18
Hartford – New Britain – Middletown, CT CMSA	343	19
Columbus, OH MSA	322	20
Denver – Boulder, CO CMSA	296	21
Austin, TX MSA	289	22
Columbia, SC MSA	280	23
Charlotte – Gastonia – Rock Hill, NC – SC MSA	269	24
Kansas City, MO – KS MSA	264	25

Source: U.S. Department of Commerce, Bureau of the Census, Data User Services Division, *1990 Census of Population and Housing, Equal Employment Opportunity File, CD-90-EE0-1, January 1993,* CD-ROM.

★1161★

Occupations, By Race/Sex

Top 25 MSAs For Employment As Computer Programmers, 1990: Whites

MSA/CMSA	Employees per 100,000 pop.	Rank
Anchorage, AK MSA	52,379	1
Los Angeles – Anaheim – Riverside, CA CMSA	27,578	2
San Francisco – Oakland – San Jose, CA CMSA	25,303	3
Chicago – Gary – Lake County, IL – IN – WI CMSA	22,696	4
Washington, DC – MD – VA MSA	21,203	5
Boston – Lawrence – Salem, MA – NH CMSA	18,002	6
Philadelphia – Wilmington – Trenton, PA – NJ – DE – MD CMSA	17,886	7
Dallas – Fort Worth, TX CMSA	17,086	8
Minneapolis – St. Paul, MN – WI MSA	12,824	9
Detroit – Ann Arbor, MI CMSA	11,293	10
Atlanta, GA MSA	10,657	11
Denver – Boulder, CO CMSA	10,346	12

[Continued]

★1161★

Top 25 MSAs For Employment As Computer Programmers, 1990: Whites

[Continued]

MSA/CMSA	Employees per 100,000 pop.	Rank
Houston – Galveston – Brazoria, TX CMSA	9,953	13
Seattle – Tacoma, WA CMSA	8,629	14
Baltimore, MD MSA	8,129	15
St. Louis, MO – IL MSA	7,197	16
San Diego, CA MSA	6,629	17
Cleveland – Akron – Lorain, OH CMSA	6,319	18
Phoenix, AZ MSA	6,191	19
Raleigh – Durham, NC MSA	5,842	20
Miami – Fort Lauderdale, FL CMSA	5,805	21
Hartford – New Britain – Middletown, CT CMSA	5,729	22
Kansas City, MO – KS MSA	5,525	23
Columbus, OH MSA	5,168	24
Pittsburgh – Beaver Valley, PA CMSA	5,106	25

Source: U.S. Department of Commerce, Bureau of the Census, Data User Services Division, *1990 Census of Population and Housing, Equal Employment Opportunity File, CD-90-EE0-1,* January 1993, CD-ROM.

★1162★

Occupations, By Race/Sex

Top 25 MSAs For Employment As Computer Science Teachers, 1990: Blacks

MSA/CMSA	Employees per 100,000 pop.	Rank
Baltimore, MD MSA	40	1
Memphis, TN – AR – MS MSA	30	2
San Francisco – Oakland – San Jose, CA CMSA	15	3
New York – Northern New Jersey – Long Island, NY – NJ – CT CMSA	11	4
Columbia, MO MSA	10	5
Washington, DC – MD – VA MSA	9	6
Nashville, TN MSA	9	6
Tyler, TX MSA	7	7
Norfolk – Virginia Beach – Newport News, VA MSA	7	7
Phoenix, AZ MSA	7	7
Atlanta, GA MSA	6	8
New Haven – Meriden, CT MSA	6	8
Greensboro – Winston-Salem – High Point, NC MSA	6	8
Philadelphia – Wilmington – Trenton, PA – NJ – DE – MD CMSA	3	9
Miami – Fort Lauderdale, FL CMSA	2	10
Parkersburg – Marietta, WV – OH MSA	0	11

[Continued]

★1162★

Top 25 MSAs For Employment As Computer Science Teachers, 1990: Blacks

[Continued]

MSA/CMSA	Employees per 100,000 pop.	Rank
Orlando, FL MSA	0	11
Naples, FL MSA	0	11
Olympia, WA MSA	0	11
Owensboro, KY MSA	0	11
Muncie, IN MSA	0	11
Odessa, TX MSA	0	11
Panama City, FL MSA	0	11
Pascagoula, MS MSA	0	11
Reno, NV MSA	0	11

Source: U.S. Department of Commerce, Bureau of the Census, Data User Services Division, *1990 Census of Population and Housing, Equal Employment Opportunity File, CD-90-EE0-1,* January 1993, CD-ROM.

★1163★

Occupations, By Race/Sex

Top 25 MSAs For Employment As Computer Science Teachers, 1990: Whites

MSA/CMSA	Employees per 100,000 pop.	Rank
Champaign – Urbana – Rantoul, IL MSA	233	1
New York – Northern New Jersey – Long Island, NY – NJ – CT CMSA	125	2
San Francisco – Oakland – San Jose, CA CMSA	117	3
Boston – Lawrence – Salem, MA – NH CMSA	115	4
Miami – Fort Lauderdale, FL CMSA	107	5
Chicago – Gary – Lake County, IL – IN – WI CMSA	100	6
Philadelphia – Wilmington – Trenton, PA – NJ – DE – MD CMSA	90	7
Pittsburgh – Beaver Valley, PA CMSA	82	8
Portland – Vancouver, OR – WA CMSA	58	9
Dallas – Fort Worth, TX CMSA	53	10
Seattle – Tacoma, WA CMSA	47	11
Houston – Galveston – Brazoria, TX CMSA	45	12
Kansas City, MO – KS MSA	42	13
Denver – Boulder, CO CMSA	42	13
Spokane, WA MSA	41	14
Madison, WI MSA	39	15
Raleigh – Durham, NC MSA	36	16
Phoenix, AZ MSA	35	17
Milwaukee – Racine, WI CMSA	35	17
Washington, DC – MD – VA MSA	31	18
San Diego, CA MSA	29	19
Atlanta, GA MSA	29	19

[Continued]

★1163★

Top 25 MSAs For Employment As Computer Science Teachers, 1990: Whites
[Continued]

MSA/CMSA	Employees per 100,000 pop.	Rank
Lynchburg, VA MSA	28	20
Sacramento, CA MSA	27	21
Nashville, TN MSA	27	21

Source: U.S. Department of Commerce, Bureau of the Census, Data User Services Division, *1990 Census of Population and Housing, Equal Employment Opportunity File, CD-90-EE0-1, January 1993,* CD-ROM.

★1164★
Occupations, By Race/Sex

Top 25 MSAs For Employment As Computer Systems Analysts and Scientists, 1990: Blacks

MSA/CMSA	Employees per 100,000 pop.	Rank
Owensboro, KY MSA	4,355	1
New York – Northern New Jersey – Long Island, NY – NJ – CT CMSA	3,721	2
Los Angeles – Anaheim – Riverside, CA CMSA	1,617	3
Chicago – Gary – Lake County, IL – IN – WI CMSA	1,459	4
Philadelphia – Wilmington – Trenton, PA – NJ – DE – MD CMSA	1,055	5
Atlanta, GA MSA	983	6
San Francisco – Oakland – San Jose, CA CMSA	942	7
Baltimore, MD MSA	816	8
Dallas – Fort Worth, TX CMSA	800	9
Detroit – Ann Arbor, MI CMSA	607	10
Boston – Lawrence – Salem, MA – NH CMSA	592	11
Houston – Galveston – Brazoria, TX CMSA	507	12
St. Louis, MO – IL MSA	357	13
Cleveland – Akron – Lorain, OH CMSA	284	14
Raleigh – Durham, NC MSA	266	15
Columbus, OH MSA	266	15
Dayton – Springfield, OH MSA	256	16
Hartford – New Britain – Middletown, CT CMSA	229	17
Minneapolis – St. Paul, MN – WI MSA	217	18
Seattle – Tacoma, WA CMSA	217	18
Cincinnati – Hamilton, OH – KY – IN CMSA	204	19
Richmond – Petersburg, VA MSA	201	20
Greensboro – Winston-Salem – High Point, NC MSA	187	21

[Continued]

★1164★

Top 25 MSAs For Employment As Computer Systems Analysts and Scientists, 1990: Blacks
[Continued]

MSA/CMSA	Employees per 100,000 pop.	Rank
Denver – Boulder, CO CMSA	181	22
Tampa – St. Petersburg – Clearwater, FL MSA	165	23

Source: U.S. Department of Commerce, Bureau of the Census, Data User Services Division, *1990 Census of Population and Housing, Equal Employment Opportunity File, CD-90-EE0-1, January 1993,* CD-ROM.

★1165★
Occupations, By Race/Sex

Top 25 MSAs For Employment As Computer Systems Analysts and Scientists, 1990: Whites

MSA/CMSA	Employees per 100,000 pop.	Rank
Hartford – New Britain – Middletown, CT CMSA	34,430	1
San Francisco – Oakland – San Jose, CA CMSA	23,251	2
Washington, DC – MD – VA MSA	23,023	3
Los Angeles – Anaheim – Riverside, CA CMSA	20,802	4
Boston – Lawrence – Salem, MA – NH CMSA	20,622	5
Chicago – Gary – Lake County, IL – IN – WI CMSA	16,623	6
Philadelphia – Wilmington – Trenton, PA – NJ – DE – MD CMSA	13,259	7
Dallas – Fort Worth, TX CMSA	12,137	8
Seattle – Tacoma, WA CMSA	10,352	9
Minneapolis – St. Paul, MN – WI MSA	8,342	10
Baltimore, MD MSA	8,286	11
Detroit – Ann Arbor, MI CMSA	7,945	12
Atlanta, GA MSA	7,848	13
Houston – Galveston – Brazoria, TX CMSA	7,403	14
Denver – Boulder, CO CMSA	7,307	15
San Diego, CA MSA	6,263	16
Phoenix, AZ MSA	5,325	17
St. Louis, MO – IL MSA	4,971	18
Cleveland – Akron – Lorain, OH CMSA	4,413	19
Hartford – New Britain – Middletown, CT CMSA	4,027	20
Portland – Vancouver, OR – WA CMSA	3,731	21
Pittsburgh – Beaver Valley, PA CMSA	3,593	22
Columbus, OH MSA	3,428	23
Cincinnati – Hamilton, OH – KY – IN CMSA	3,335	24
Raleigh – Durham, NC MSA	3,298	25

Source: U.S. Department of Commerce, Bureau of the Census, Data User Services Division, *1990 Census of Population and Housing, Equal Employment Opportunity File, CD-90-EE0-1, January 1993,* CD-ROM.

★1166★
Occupations, By Race/Sex
Top 25 MSAs For Employment As Cooks, 1990: Blacks

MSA/CMSA	Employees per 100,000 pop.	Rank
Tampa – St. Petersburg – Clearwater, FL MSA	19,379	1
Chicago – Gary – Lake County, IL – IN – WI CMSA	15,208	2
Atlanta, GA MSA	11,174	3
Philadelphia – Wilmington – Trenton, PA – NJ – DE – MD CMSA	11,063	4
Detroit – Ann Arbor, MI CMSA	10,582	5
Houston – Galveston – Brazoria, TX CMSA	9,567	6
Dallas – Fort Worth, TX CMSA	9,346	7
Washington, DC – MD – VA MSA	9,031	8
Miami – Fort Lauderdale, FL CMSA	8,561	9
Baltimore, MD MSA	7,192	10
Los Angeles – Anaheim – Riverside, CA CMSA	6,739	11
St. Louis, MO – IL MSA	6,615	12
Memphis, TN – AR – MS MSA	6,441	13
New Orleans, LA MSA	6,396	14
Norfolk – Virginia Beach – Newport News, VA MSA	5,697	15
Cleveland – Akron – Lorain, OH CMSA	4,825	16
Birmingham, AL MSA	4,347	17
Charlotte – Gastonia – Rock Hill, NC – SC MSA	4,068	18
Richmond – Petersburg, VA MSA	3,991	19
San Francisco – Oakland – San Jose, CA CMSA	3,764	20
Raleigh – Durham, NC MSA	3,381	21
Kansas City, MO – KS MSA	3,177	22
Indianapolis, IN MSA	3,170	23
Jackson, MS MSA	3,130	24
Baton Rouge, LA MSA	2,970	25

Source: U.S. Department of Commerce, Bureau of the Census, Data User Services Division, *1990 Census of Population and Housing, Equal Employment Opportunity File, CD-90-EE0-1,* January 1993, CD-ROM.

★1167★
Occupations, By Race/Sex
Top 25 MSAs For Employment As Cooks, 1990: Whites

MSA/CMSA	Employees per 100,000 pop.	Rank
Orlando, FL MSA	58,498	1
Los Angeles – Anaheim – Riverside, CA CMSA	51,608	2
Chicago – Gary – Lake County, IL – IN – WI CMSA	31,333	3
Detroit – Ann Arbor, MI CMSA	25,682	4
San Francisco – Oakland – San Jose, CA CMSA	24,405	5

[Continued]

★1167★
Top 25 MSAs For Employment As Cooks, 1990: Whites
[Continued]

MSA/CMSA	Employees per 100,000 pop.	Rank
Philadelphia – Wilmington – Trenton, PA – NJ – DE – MD CMSA	23,303	6
Boston – Lawrence – Salem, MA – NH CMSA	22,751	7
Minneapolis – St. Paul, MN – WI MSA	18,090	8
Dallas – Fort Worth, TX CMSA	15,992	9
Cleveland – Akron – Lorain, OH CMSA	15,733	10
Pittsburgh – Beaver Valley, PA CMSA	15,545	11
St. Louis, MO – IL MSA	14,856	12
Seattle – Tacoma, WA CMSA	14,693	13
Houston – Galveston – Brazoria, TX CMSA	12,907	14
Miami – Fort Lauderdale, FL CMSA	12,753	15
Tampa – St. Petersburg – Clearwater, FL MSA	12,182	16
Phoenix, AZ MSA	11,678	17
Washington, DC – MD – VA MSA	11,599	18
Cincinnati – Hamilton, OH – KY – IN CMSA	11,356	19
Denver – Boulder, CO CMSA	11,155	20
San Diego, CA MSA	11,097	21
Atlanta, GA MSA	10,812	22
Portland – Vancouver, OR – WA CMSA	10,145	23
Milwaukee – Racine, WI CMSA	9,353	24
Columbus, OH MSA	9,172	25

Source: U.S. Department of Commerce, Bureau of the Census, Data User Services Division, *1990 Census of Population and Housing, Equal Employment Opportunity File, CD-90-EE0-1,* January 1993, CD-ROM.

★1168★
Occupations, By Race/Sex
Top 25 MSAs For Employment As Cooks, Private Household, 1990: Blacks

MSA/CMSA	Employees per 100,000 pop.	Rank
Orlando, FL MSA	226	1
Dallas – Fort Worth, TX CMSA	92	2
Los Angeles – Anaheim – Riverside, CA CMSA	89	3
New Orleans, LA MSA	85	4
San Francisco – Oakland – San Jose, CA CMSA	71	5
Birmingham, AL MSA	58	6
Miami – Fort Lauderdale, FL CMSA	56	7
Houston – Galveston – Brazoria, TX CMSA	55	8

[Continued]

★ 1168 ★

Top 25 MSAs For Employment As Cooks, Private Household, 1990: Blacks
[Continued]

MSA/CMSA	Employees per 100,000 pop.	Rank
Memphis, TN – AR – MS MSA	55	8
Baltimore, MD MSA	54	9
Chicago – Gary – Lake County, IL – IN – WI CMSA	53	10
Norfolk – Virginia Beach – Newport News, VA MSA	44	11
Indianapolis, IN MSA	43	12
Detroit – Ann Arbor, MI CMSA	43	12
Tallahassee, FL MSA	37	13
Cincinnati – Hamilton, OH – KY – IN CMSA	36	14
Tulsa, OK MSA	35	15
Washington, DC – MD – VA MSA	31	16
Charleston, SC MSA	30	17
Louisville, KY – IN MSA	30	17
Columbia, SC MSA	30	17
Richmond – Petersburg, VA MSA	29	18
San Antonio, TX MSA	28	19
Atlanta, GA MSA	26	20
Greensboro – Winston-Salem – High Point, NC MSA	25	21

Source: U.S. Department of Commerce, Bureau of the Census, Data User Services Division, *1990 Census of Population and Housing, Equal Employment Opportunity File, CD-90-EE0-1, January 1993*, CD-ROM.

★ 1169 ★

Occupations, By Race/Sex

Top 25 MSAs For Employment As Cooks, Private Household, 1990: Whites

MSA/CMSA	Employees per 100,000 pop.	Rank
Salt Lake City – Ogden, UT MSA	544	1
Los Angeles – Anaheim – Riverside, CA CMSA	399	2
San Francisco – Oakland – San Jose, CA CMSA	186	3
Philadelphia – Wilmington – Trenton, PA – NJ – DE – MD CMSA	150	4
Boston – Lawrence – Salem, MA – NH CMSA	141	5
Miami – Fort Lauderdale, FL CMSA	117	6
Chicago – Gary – Lake County, IL – IN – WI CMSA	105	7
West Palm Beach – Boca Raton – Delray Beach, FL MSA	104	8
Detroit – Ann Arbor, MI CMSA	79	9
Phoenix, AZ MSA	67	10
Santa Barbara – Santa Maria – Lompoc, CA MSA	66	11
Washington, DC – MD – VA MSA	65	12
Pittsburgh – Beaver Valley, PA CMSA	57	13

[Continued]

★ 1169 ★

Top 25 MSAs For Employment As Cooks, Private Household, 1990: Whites
[Continued]

MSA/CMSA	Employees per 100,000 pop.	Rank
San Diego, CA MSA	47	14
Denver – Boulder, CO CMSA	42	15
Fort Pierce, FL MSA	41	16
Cincinnati – Hamilton, OH – KY – IN CMSA	41	16
Dallas – Fort Worth, TX CMSA	40	17
St. Louis, MO – IL MSA	38	18
Providence – Pawtucket – Fall River, RI – MA CMSA	35	19
Buffalo – Niagara Falls, NY CMSA	34	20
Houston – Galveston – Brazoria, TX CMSA	34	20
Syracuse, NY MSA	34	20
Louisville, KY – IN MSA	33	21
Fresno, CA MSA	33	21

Source: U.S. Department of Commerce, Bureau of the Census, Data User Services Division, *1990 Census of Population and Housing, Equal Employment Opportunity File, CD-90-EE0-1, January 1993*, CD-ROM.

★ 1170 ★

Occupations, By Race/Sex

Top 25 MSAs For Employment As Correctional Institution Officers, 1990: Blacks

MSA/CMSA	Employees per 100,000 pop.	Rank
Nashville, TN MSA	6,001	1
Philadelphia – Wilmington – Trenton, PA – NJ – DE – MD CMSA	2,736	2
Baltimore, MD MSA	2,544	3
Washington, DC – MD – VA MSA	1,813	4
Chicago – Gary – Lake County, IL – IN – WI CMSA	1,417	5
Houston – Galveston – Brazoria, TX CMSA	1,200	6
Miami – Fort Lauderdale, FL CMSA	993	7
Los Angeles – Anaheim – Riverside, CA CMSA	861	8
Columbia, SC MSA	860	9
Memphis, TN – AR – MS MSA	729	10
Atlanta, GA MSA	667	11
Detroit – Ann Arbor, MI CMSA	647	12
Richmond – Petersburg, VA MSA	557	13
San Francisco – Oakland – San Jose, CA CMSA	511	14
Montgomery, AL MSA	488	15
Birmingham, AL MSA	410	16
Raleigh – Durham, NC MSA	357	17
Baton Rouge, LA MSA	342	18
Buffalo – Niagara Falls, NY CMSA	306	19
Orlando, FL MSA	283	20
San Diego, CA MSA	275	21

[Continued]

★1170★

Top 25 MSAs For Employment As Correctional Institution Officers, 1990: Blacks

[Continued]

MSA/CMSA	Employees per 100,000 pop.	Rank
Nashville, TN MSA	270	22
West Palm Beach – Boca Raton – Delray Beach, FL MSA	261	23
St. Louis, MO – IL MSA	260	24
Kansas City, MO – KS MSA	254	25

Source: U.S. Department of Commerce, Bureau of the Census, Data User Services Division, *1990 Census of Population and Housing, Equal Employment Opportunity File, CD-90-EE0-1, January 1993,* CD-ROM.

★1171★

Occupations, By Race/Sex

Top 25 MSAs For Employment As Correctional Institution Officers, 1990: Whites

MSA/CMSA	Employees per 100,000 pop.	Rank
Orlando, FL MSA	6,379	1
Philadelphia – Wilmington – Trenton, PA – NJ – DE – MD CMSA	2,902	2
Los Angeles – Anaheim – Riverside, CA CMSA	1,936	3
San Francisco – Oakland – San Jose, CA CMSA	1,728	4
Boston – Lawrence – Salem, MA – NH CMSA	1,604	5
Buffalo – Niagara Falls, NY CMSA	1,529	6
Houston – Galveston – Brazoria, TX CMSA	1,305	7
Sacramento, CA MSA	1,239	8
Chicago – Gary – Lake County, IL – IN – WI CMSA	1,183	9
Seattle – Tacoma, WA CMSA	1,134	10
Utica – Rome, NY MSA	1,048	11
Albany – Schenectady – Troy, NY MSA	1,018	12
Hagerstown, MD MSA	981	13
Miami – Fort Lauderdale, FL CMSA	974	14
Providence – Pawtucket – Fall River, RI – MA CMSA	935	15
Killeen – Temple, TX MSA	884	16
Phoenix, AZ MSA	879	17
Minneapolis – St. Paul, MN – WI MSA	830	18
Kansas City, MO – KS MSA	816	19
Elmira, NY MSA	780	20
Dallas – Fort Worth, TX CMSA	741	21
Pittsburgh – Beaver Valley, PA CMSA	719	22
Lansing – East Lansing, MI MSA	713	23

[Continued]

★1171★

Top 25 MSAs For Employment As Correctional Institution Officers, 1990: Whites

[Continued]

MSA/CMSA	Employees per 100,000 pop.	Rank
Bakersfield, CA MSA	709	24
Tampa – St. Petersburg – Clearwater, FL MSA	702	25

Source: U.S. Department of Commerce, Bureau of the Census, Data User Services Division, *1990 Census of Population and Housing, Equal Employment Opportunity File, CD-90-EE0-1, January 1993,* CD-ROM.

★1172★

Occupations, By Race/Sex

Top 25 MSAs For Employment As Counselors, Educational and Vocational, 1990: Blacks

MSA/CMSA	Employees per 100,000 pop.	Rank
Mobile, AL MSA	4,216	1
Los Angeles – Anaheim – Riverside, CA CMSA	1,714	2
Washington, DC – MD – VA MSA	1,573	3
Philadelphia – Wilmington – Trenton, PA – NJ – DE – MD CMSA	1,509	4
Chicago – Gary – Lake County, IL – IN – WI CMSA	1,466	5
Detroit – Ann Arbor, MI CMSA	983	6
San Francisco – Oakland – San Jose, CA CMSA	859	7
Baltimore, MD MSA	831	8
Houston – Galveston – Brazoria, TX CMSA	730	9
Miami – Fort Lauderdale, FL CMSA	641	10
Atlanta, GA MSA	566	11
Cleveland – Akron – Lorain, OH CMSA	534	12
St. Louis, MO – IL MSA	529	13
Dallas – Fort Worth, TX CMSA	512	14
Raleigh – Durham, NC MSA	444	15
Greensboro – Winston-Salem – High Point, NC MSA	403	16
Memphis, TN – AR – MS MSA	354	17
San Diego, CA MSA	345	18
New Orleans, LA MSA	337	19
Norfolk – Virginia Beach – Newport News, VA MSA	330	20
Sacramento, CA MSA	266	21
Charlotte – Gastonia – Rock Hill, NC – SC MSA	257	22
Pittsburgh – Beaver Valley, PA CMSA	252	23
Boston – Lawrence – Salem, MA – NH CMSA	242	24
Baton Rouge, LA MSA	240	25

Source: U.S. Department of Commerce, Bureau of the Census, Data User Services Division, *1990 Census of Population and Housing, Equal Employment Opportunity File, CD-90-EE0-1, January 1993,* CD-ROM.

★1173★

Occupations, By Race/Sex

Top 25 MSAs For Employment As Counselors, Educational and Vocational, 1990: Whites

MSA/CMSA	Employees per 100,000 pop.	Rank
Denver – Boulder, CO CMSA	14,470	1
Los Angeles – Anaheim – Riverside, CA CMSA	8,073	2
Boston – Lawrence – Salem, MA – NH CMSA	4,853	3
San Francisco – Oakland – San Jose, CA CMSA	4,579	4
Philadelphia – Wilmington – Trenton, PA – NJ – DE – MD CMSA	4,557	5
Chicago – Gary – Lake County, IL – IN – WI CMSA	4,356	6
Washington, DC – MD – VA MSA	3,203	7
Detroit – Ann Arbor, MI CMSA	2,706	8
Dallas – Fort Worth, TX CMSA	2,518	9
Seattle – Tacoma, WA CMSA	2,448	10
Minneapolis – St. Paul, MN – WI MSA	2,328	11
Pittsburgh – Beaver Valley, PA CMSA	2,065	12
Houston – Galveston – Brazoria, TX CMSA	1,968	13
Miami – Fort Lauderdale, FL CMSA	1,908	14
Cleveland – Akron – Lorain, OH CMSA	1,880	15
San Diego, CA MSA	1,859	16
Baltimore, MD MSA	1,766	17
St. Louis, MO – IL MSA	1,741	18
Denver – Boulder, CO CMSA	1,600	19
Portland – Vancouver, OR – WA CMSA	1,559	20
Cincinnati – Hamilton, OH – KY – IN CMSA	1,548	21
Atlanta, GA MSA	1,486	22
Providence – Pawtucket – Fall River, RI – MA CMSA	1,476	23
Tampa – St. Petersburg – Clearwater, FL MSA	1,436	24
Rochester, NY MSA	1,402	25

Source: U.S. Department of Commerce, Bureau of the Census, Data User Services Division, *1990 Census of Population and Housing, Equal Employment Opportunity File, CD-90-EE0-1, January 1993,* CD-ROM.

★1174★

Occupations, By Race/Sex

Top 25 MSAs For Employment As Dancers, 1990: Blacks

MSA/CMSA	Employees per 100,000 pop.	Rank
Raleigh – Durham, NC MSA	411	1
Los Angeles – Anaheim – Riverside, CA CMSA	133	2
Chicago – Gary – Lake County, IL – IN – WI CMSA	95	3
Washington, DC – MD – VA MSA	92	4
Philadelphia – Wilmington – Trenton, PA – NJ – DE – MD CMSA	90	5
Detroit – Ann Arbor, MI CMSA	65	6
Atlanta, GA MSA	42	7
Miami – Fort Lauderdale, FL CMSA	40	8
Las Vegas, NV MSA	40	8
Cleveland – Akron – Lorain, OH CMSA	36	9
San Francisco – Oakland – San Jose, CA CMSA	34	10
Houston – Galveston – Brazoria, TX CMSA	33	11
Dayton – Springfield, OH MSA	27	12
Omaha, NE – IA MSA	25	13
Atlantic City, NJ MSA	24	14
Dallas – Fort Worth, TX CMSA	24	14
Sacramento, CA MSA	20	15
New Orleans, LA MSA	19	16
Albany – Schenectady – Troy, NY MSA	18	17
Denver – Boulder, CO CMSA	17	18
Tulsa, OK MSA	17	18
Muskegon, MI MSA	15	19
Minneapolis – St. Paul, MN – WI MSA	14	20
Charlotte – Gastonia – Rock Hill, NC – SC MSA	14	20
Tampa – St. Petersburg – Clearwater, FL MSA	14	20

Source: U.S. Department of Commerce, Bureau of the Census, Data User Services Division, *1990 Census of Population and Housing, Equal Employment Opportunity File, CD-90-EE0-1, January 1993,* CD-ROM.

★1175★

Occupations, By Race/Sex

Top 25 MSAs For Employment As Dancers, 1990: Whites

MSA/CMSA	Employees per 100,000 pop.	Rank
Sacramento, CA MSA	2,291	1
Los Angeles – Anaheim – Riverside, CA CMSA	1,449	2
Las Vegas, NV MSA	710	3
Philadelphia – Wilmington – Trenton, PA – NJ – DE – MD CMSA	523	4

[Continued]

★1175★

Top 25 MSAs For Employment As Dancers, 1990: Whites
[Continued]

MSA/CMSA	Employees per 100,000 pop.	Rank
Houston – Galveston – Brazoria, TX CMSA	512	5
Dallas – Fort Worth, TX CMSA	462	6
San Francisco – Oakland – San Jose, CA CMSA	456	7
Miami – Fort Lauderdale, FL CMSA	456	7
Detroit – Ann Arbor, MI CMSA	411	8
Atlanta, GA MSA	366	9
Chicago – Gary – Lake County, IL – IN – WI CMSA	362	10
Orlando, FL MSA	360	11
Washington, DC – MD – VA MSA	352	12
Seattle – Tacoma, WA CMSA	317	13
Tampa – St. Petersburg – Clearwater, FL MSA	288	14
Boston – Lawrence – Salem, MA – NH CMSA	271	15
Phoenix, AZ MSA	261	16
Cleveland – Akron – Lorain, OH CMSA	230	17
San Diego, CA MSA	219	18
Minneapolis – St. Paul, MN – WI MSA	213	19
Norfolk – Virginia Beach – Newport News, VA MSA	209	20
Austin, TX MSA	204	21
Indianapolis, IN MSA	183	22
Baltimore, MD MSA	182	23
Portland – Vancouver, OR – WA CMSA	180	24

Source: U.S. Department of Commerce, Bureau of the Census, Data User Services Division, *1990 Census of Population and Housing, Equal Employment Opportunity File, CD-90-EE0-1, January 1993,* CD-ROM.

★1176★

Occupations, By Race/Sex

Top 25 MSAs For Employment As Data-entry Keyers, 1990: Blacks

MSA/CMSA	Employees per 100,000 pop.	Rank
Raleigh – Durham, NC MSA	18,680	1
Chicago – Gary – Lake County, IL – IN – WI CMSA	7,843	2
Los Angeles – Anaheim – Riverside, CA CMSA	6,583	3
Washington, DC – MD – VA MSA	6,281	4
Philadelphia – Wilmington – Trenton, PA – NJ – DE – MD CMSA	6,051	5
Atlanta, GA MSA	4,920	6
Dallas – Fort Worth, TX CMSA	3,539	7
Baltimore, MD MSA	3,474	8

[Continued]

★1176★

Top 25 MSAs For Employment As Data-entry Keyers, 1990: Blacks
[Continued]

MSA/CMSA	Employees per 100,000 pop.	Rank
Detroit – Ann Arbor, MI CMSA	2,984	9
Houston – Galveston – Brazoria, TX CMSA	2,832	10
San Francisco – Oakland – San Jose, CA CMSA	2,764	11
Miami – Fort Lauderdale, FL CMSA	2,051	12
Memphis, TN – AR – MS MSA	1,818	13
St. Louis, MO – IL MSA	1,774	14
Cleveland – Akron – Lorain, OH CMSA	1,747	15
Columbus, OH MSA	1,686	16
Kansas City, MO – KS MSA	1,484	17
Boston – Lawrence – Salem, MA – NH CMSA	1,473	18
Richmond – Petersburg, VA MSA	1,415	19
Raleigh – Durham, NC MSA	1,201	20
Norfolk – Virginia Beach – Newport News, VA MSA	1,149	21
Jacksonville, FL MSA	1,148	22
Cincinnati – Hamilton, OH – KY – IN CMSA	1,058	23
Indianapolis, IN MSA	1,026	24
Birmingham, AL MSA	963	25

Source: U.S. Department of Commerce, Bureau of the Census, Data User Services Division, *1990 Census of Population and Housing, Equal Employment Opportunity File, CD-90-EE0-1, January 1993,* CD-ROM.

★1177★

Occupations, By Race/Sex

Top 25 MSAs For Employment As Data-entry Keyers, 1990: Whites

MSA/CMSA	Employees per 100,000 pop.	Rank
Austin, TX MSA	33,811	1
Los Angeles – Anaheim – Riverside, CA CMSA	24,288	2
Chicago – Gary – Lake County, IL – IN – WI CMSA	18,374	3
Philadelphia – Wilmington – Trenton, PA – NJ – DE – MD CMSA	13,551	4
Boston – Lawrence – Salem, MA – NH CMSA	12,293	5
Minneapolis – St. Paul, MN – WI MSA	10,950	6
Dallas – Fort Worth, TX CMSA	10,774	7
San Francisco – Oakland – San Jose, CA CMSA	10,538	8
Detroit – Ann Arbor, MI CMSA	7,783	9
Seattle – Tacoma, WA CMSA	6,494	10
Miami – Fort Lauderdale, FL CMSA	6,386	11

[Continued]

★1177★

Top 25 MSAs For Employment As Data-entry Keyers, 1990: Whites
[Continued]

MSA/CMSA	Employees per 100,000 pop.	Rank
Washington, DC – MD – VA MSA	6,304	12
Atlanta, GA MSA	6,167	13
Houston – Galveston – Brazoria, TX CMSA	6,165	14
Phoenix, AZ MSA	5,954	15
Denver – Boulder, CO CMSA	5,748	16
Cleveland – Akron – Lorain, OH CMSA	5,739	17
Kansas City, MO – KS MSA	5,657	18
St. Louis, MO – IL MSA	5,549	19
Columbus, OH MSA	5,139	20
Cincinnati – Hamilton, OH – KY – IN CMSA	4,951	21
Tampa – St. Petersburg – Clearwater, FL MSA	4,793	22
Baltimore, MD MSA	4,751	23
Milwaukee – Racine, WI CMSA	4,696	24
Pittsburgh – Beaver Valley, PA CMSA	4,420	25

Source: U.S. Department of Commerce, Bureau of the Census, Data User Services Division, *1990 Census of Population and Housing, Equal Employment Opportunity File, CD-90-EE0-1, January 1993,* CD-ROM.

★1178★

Occupations, By Race/Sex

Top 25 MSAs For Employment As Dental Assistants, 1990: Blacks

MSA/CMSA	Employees per 100,000 pop.	Rank
Charleston, SC MSA	1,705	1
Los Angeles – Anaheim – Riverside, CA CMSA	706	2
Chicago – Gary – Lake County, IL – IN – WI CMSA	683	3
Detroit – Ann Arbor, MI CMSA	504	4
Washington, DC – MD – VA MSA	456	5
Houston – Galveston – Brazoria, TX CMSA	284	6
Atlanta, GA MSA	277	7
San Francisco – Oakland – San Jose, CA CMSA	268	8
Philadelphia – Wilmington – Trenton, PA – NJ – DE – MD CMSA	224	9
Baltimore, MD MSA	220	10
Miami – Fort Lauderdale, FL CMSA	196	11
Cleveland – Akron – Lorain, OH CMSA	165	12
Dallas – Fort Worth, TX CMSA	156	13
St. Louis, MO – IL MSA	154	14
Memphis, TN – AR – MS MSA	109	15
Norfolk – Virginia Beach – Newport News, VA MSA	104	16

[Continued]

★1178★

Top 25 MSAs For Employment As Dental Assistants, 1990: Blacks
[Continued]

MSA/CMSA	Employees per 100,000 pop.	Rank
Augusta, GA – SC MSA	100	17
Raleigh – Durham, NC MSA	99	18
Nashville, TN MSA	96	19
San Diego, CA MSA	96	19
Boston – Lawrence – Salem, MA – NH CMSA	94	20
Birmingham, AL MSA	89	21
New Orleans, LA MSA	83	22
Jacksonville, FL MSA	83	22
Jackson, MS MSA	82	23

Source: U.S. Department of Commerce, Bureau of the Census, Data User Services Division, *1990 Census of Population and Housing, Equal Employment Opportunity File, CD-90-EE0-1, January 1993,* CD-ROM.

★1179★

Occupations, By Race/Sex

Top 25 MSAs For Employment As Dental Assistants, 1990: Whites

MSA/CMSA	Employees per 100,000 pop.	Rank
Kansas City, MO – KS MSA	12,734	1
Los Angeles – Anaheim – Riverside, CA CMSA	7,482	2
Chicago – Gary – Lake County, IL – IN – WI CMSA	5,089	3
Philadelphia – Wilmington – Trenton, PA – NJ – DE – MD CMSA	4,110	4
San Francisco – Oakland – San Jose, CA CMSA	4,028	5
Detroit – Ann Arbor, MI CMSA	3,485	6
Boston – Lawrence – Salem, MA – NH CMSA	3,221	7
Seattle – Tacoma, WA CMSA	2,329	8
Dallas – Fort Worth, TX CMSA	2,320	9
Minneapolis – St. Paul, MN – WI MSA	2,081	10
Washington, DC – MD – VA MSA	1,981	11
Cleveland – Akron – Lorain, OH CMSA	1,944	12
Houston – Galveston – Brazoria, TX CMSA	1,798	13
San Diego, CA MSA	1,728	14
St. Louis, MO – IL MSA	1,700	15
Miami – Fort Lauderdale, FL CMSA	1,687	16
Denver – Boulder, CO CMSA	1,639	17
Pittsburgh – Beaver Valley, PA CMSA	1,443	18
Portland – Vancouver, OR – WA CMSA	1,431	19
Atlanta, GA MSA	1,427	20
Baltimore, MD MSA	1,371	21

[Continued]

★1179★

Top 25 MSAs For Employment As Dental Assistants, 1990: Whites

[Continued]

MSA/CMSA	Employees per 100,000 pop.	Rank
Milwaukee – Racine, WI CMSA	1,359	22
Phoenix, AZ MSA	1,307	23
Sacramento, CA MSA	1,278	24
Tampa – St. Petersburg – Clearwater, FL MSA	1,267	25

Source: U.S. Department of Commerce, Bureau of the Census, Data User Services Division, *1990 Census of Population and Housing, Equal Employment Opportunity File, CD-90-EE0-1, January 1993*, CD-ROM.

★1180★

Occupations, By Race/Sex

Top 25 MSAs For Employment As Dental Hygienists, 1990: Blacks

MSA/CMSA	Employees per 100,000 pop.	Rank
Orlando, FL MSA	281	1
Washington, DC – MD – VA MSA	134	2
Philadelphia – Wilmington – Trenton, PA – NJ – DE – MD CMSA	99	3
Los Angeles – Anaheim – Riverside, CA CMSA	88	4
Baltimore, MD MSA	76	5
Atlanta, GA MSA	69	6
Detroit – Ann Arbor, MI CMSA	57	7
Miami – Fort Lauderdale, FL CMSA	54	8
Chicago – Gary – Lake County, IL – IN – WI CMSA	34	9
Birmingham, AL MSA	33	10
Augusta, GA – SC MSA	32	11
San Francisco – Oakland – San Jose, CA CMSA	31	12
Nashville, TN MSA	30	13
Anniston, AL MSA	26	14
Cleveland – Akron – Lorain, OH CMSA	25	15
Houston – Galveston – Brazoria, TX CMSA	23	16
Greensboro – Winston-Salem – High Point, NC MSA	23	16
Flint, MI MSA	20	17
Atlantic City, NJ MSA	17	18
Phoenix, AZ MSA	17	18
Kansas City, MO – KS MSA	17	18
Norfolk – Virginia Beach – Newport News, VA MSA	16	19
Boston – Lawrence – Salem, MA – NH CMSA	16	19
Omaha, NE – IA MSA	14	20
Fresno, CA MSA	12	21

Source: U.S. Department of Commerce, Bureau of the Census, Data User Services Division, *1990 Census of Population and Housing, Equal Employment Opportunity File, CD-90-EE0-1, January 1993*, CD-ROM.

★1181★

Occupations, By Race/Sex

Top 25 MSAs For Employment As Dental Hygienists, 1990: Whites

MSA/CMSA	Employees per 100,000 pop.	Rank
Austin, TX MSA	4,863	1
Los Angeles – Anaheim – Riverside, CA CMSA	2,543	2
San Francisco – Oakland – San Jose, CA CMSA	2,349	3
Chicago – Gary – Lake County, IL – IN – WI CMSA	2,221	4
Detroit – Ann Arbor, MI CMSA	1,939	5
Boston – Lawrence – Salem, MA – NH CMSA	1,872	6
Philadelphia – Wilmington – Trenton, PA – NJ – DE – MD CMSA	1,563	7
Minneapolis – St. Paul, MN – WI MSA	1,414	8
Seattle – Tacoma, WA CMSA	1,196	9
Miami – Fort Lauderdale, FL CMSA	1,126	10
Washington, DC – MD – VA MSA	1,111	11
Atlanta, GA MSA	1,079	12
Dallas – Fort Worth, TX CMSA	1,039	13
Portland – Vancouver, OR – WA CMSA	818	14
Houston – Galveston – Brazoria, TX CMSA	757	15
Cleveland – Akron – Lorain, OH CMSA	752	16
Phoenix, AZ MSA	711	17
Denver – Boulder, CO CMSA	663	18
Buffalo – Niagara Falls, NY CMSA	650	19
Baltimore, MD MSA	611	20
Milwaukee – Racine, WI CMSA	607	21
San Diego, CA MSA	581	22
Cincinnati – Hamilton, OH – KY – IN CMSA	575	23
Rochester, NY MSA	541	24
Pittsburgh – Beaver Valley, PA CMSA	511	25

Source: U.S. Department of Commerce, Bureau of the Census, Data User Services Division, *1990 Census of Population and Housing, Equal Employment Opportunity File, CD-90-EE0-1, January 1993*, CD-ROM.

★1182★

Occupations, By Race/Sex

Top 25 MSAs For Employment As Dentists, 1990: Blacks

MSA/CMSA	Employees per 100,000 pop.	Rank
Columbus, OH MSA	796	1
Washington, DC – MD – VA MSA	469	2
Detroit – Ann Arbor, MI CMSA	259	3
Los Angeles – Anaheim – Riverside, CA CMSA	254	4

[Continued]

★1182★

Top 25 MSAs For Employment As Dentists, 1990: Blacks
[Continued]

MSA/CMSA	Employees per 100,000 pop.	Rank
Chicago – Gary – Lake County, IL – IN – WI CMSA	207	5
Philadelphia – Wilmington – Trenton, PA – NJ – DE – MD CMSA	174	6
San Francisco – Oakland – San Jose, CA CMSA	157	7
Baltimore, MD MSA	141	8
Cleveland – Akron – Lorain, OH CMSA	116	9
Memphis, TN – AR – MS MSA	108	10
Houston – Galveston – Brazoria, TX CMSA	104	11
Atlanta, GA MSA	103	12
Nashville, TN MSA	98	13
St. Louis, MO – IL MSA	83	14
Kansas City, MO – KS MSA	78	15
Miami – Fort Lauderdale, FL CMSA	71	16
Dallas – Fort Worth, TX CMSA	69	17
Jackson, MS MSA	65	18
Charleston, SC MSA	56	19
Boston – Lawrence – Salem, MA – NH CMSA	54	20
Pittsburgh – Beaver Valley, PA CMSA	49	21
Buffalo – Niagara Falls, NY CMSA	41	22
New Orleans, LA MSA	40	23
Norfolk – Virginia Beach – Newport News, VA MSA	36	24
Augusta, GA – SC MSA	33	25

Source: U.S. Department of Commerce, Bureau of the Census, Data User Services Division, *1990 Census of Population and Housing, Equal Employment Opportunity File, CD-90-EE0-1,* January 1993, CD-ROM.

★1183★

Occupations, By Race/Sex

Top 25 MSAs For Employment As Dentists, 1990: Whites

MSA/CMSA	Employees per 100,000 pop.	Rank
Cincinnati – Hamilton, OH – KY – IN CMSA	15,153	1
Los Angeles – Anaheim – Riverside, CA CMSA	6,959	2
Chicago – Gary – Lake County, IL – IN – WI CMSA	5,229	3
San Francisco – Oakland – San Jose, CA CMSA	4,548	4
Philadelphia – Wilmington – Trenton, PA – NJ – DE – MD CMSA	3,718	5
Boston – Lawrence – Salem, MA – NH CMSA	3,248	6

[Continued]

★1183★

Top 25 MSAs For Employment As Dentists, 1990: Whites
[Continued]

MSA/CMSA	Employees per 100,000 pop.	Rank
Detroit – Ann Arbor, MI CMSA	3,128	7
Washington, DC – MD – VA MSA	2,589	8
Dallas – Fort Worth, TX CMSA	2,298	9
Seattle – Tacoma, WA CMSA	2,006	10
Miami – Fort Lauderdale, FL CMSA	2,003	11
Minneapolis – St. Paul, MN – WI MSA	1,933	12
Houston – Galveston – Brazoria, TX CMSA	1,911	13
Pittsburgh – Beaver Valley, PA CMSA	1,844	14
Cleveland – Akron – Lorain, OH CMSA	1,695	15
Atlanta, GA MSA	1,669	16
Baltimore, MD MSA	1,463	17
San Diego, CA MSA	1,463	17
Denver – Boulder, CO CMSA	1,393	18
St. Louis, MO – IL MSA	1,341	19
Kansas City, MO – KS MSA	1,218	20
Phoenix, AZ MSA	1,155	21
Milwaukee – Racine, WI CMSA	1,115	22
Portland – Vancouver, OR – WA CMSA	1,060	23
Cincinnati – Hamilton, OH – KY – IN CMSA	1,040	24

Source: U.S. Department of Commerce, Bureau of the Census, Data User Services Division, *1990 Census of Population and Housing, Equal Employment Opportunity File, CD-90-EE0-1,* January 1993, CD-ROM.

★1184★

Occupations, By Race/Sex

Top 25 MSAs For Employment As Dietitians, 1990: Blacks

MSA/CMSA	Employees per 100,000 pop.	Rank
Memphis, TN – AR – MS MSA	2,568	1
Chicago – Gary – Lake County, IL – IN – WI CMSA	881	2
Philadelphia – Wilmington – Trenton, PA – NJ – DE – MD CMSA	768	3
Washington, DC – MD – VA MSA	704	4
Detroit – Ann Arbor, MI CMSA	583	5
Baltimore, MD MSA	508	6
Los Angeles – Anaheim – Riverside, CA CMSA	472	7
Houston – Galveston – Brazoria, TX CMSA	471	8
Atlanta, GA MSA	405	9
Miami – Fort Lauderdale, FL CMSA	386	10
Dallas – Fort Worth, TX CMSA	377	11

[Continued]

★1184★

Top 25 MSAs For Employment As Dietitians, 1990: Blacks
[Continued]

MSA/CMSA	Employees per 100,000 pop.	Rank
Cleveland – Akron – Lorain, OH CMSA	274	12
San Francisco – Oakland – San Jose, CA CMSA	264	13
Memphis, TN – AR – MS MSA	257	14
Boston – Lawrence – Salem, MA – NH CMSA	214	15
St. Louis, MO – IL MSA	213	16
New Orleans, LA MSA	195	17
Raleigh – Durham, NC MSA	173	18
Indianapolis, IN MSA	165	19
Norfolk – Virginia Beach – Newport News, VA MSA	163	20
Nashville, TN MSA	149	21
Richmond – Petersburg, VA MSA	149	21
Kansas City, MO – KS MSA	147	22
Pittsburgh – Beaver Valley, PA CMSA	137	23
Greensboro – Winston-Salem – High Point, NC MSA	132	24

Source: U.S. Department of Commerce, Bureau of the Census, Data User Services Division, *1990 Census of Population and Housing, Equal Employment Opportunity File, CD-90-EE0-1, January 1993,* CD-ROM.

★1185★

Occupations, By Race/Sex

Top 25 MSAs For Employment As Dietitians, 1990: Whites

MSA/CMSA	Employees per 100,000 pop.	Rank
San Diego, CA MSA	3,828	1
Los Angeles – Anaheim – Riverside, CA CMSA	2,733	2
Boston – Lawrence – Salem, MA – NH CMSA	1,773	3
Chicago – Gary – Lake County, IL – IN – WI CMSA	1,631	4
Philadelphia – Wilmington – Trenton, PA – NJ – DE – MD CMSA	1,558	5
San Francisco – Oakland – San Jose, CA CMSA	1,377	6
Detroit – Ann Arbor, MI CMSA	1,124	7
Dallas – Fort Worth, TX CMSA	965	8
St. Louis, MO – IL MSA	917	9
Seattle – Tacoma, WA CMSA	916	10
Cleveland – Akron – Lorain, OH CMSA	869	11
Minneapolis – St. Paul, MN – WI MSA	858	12
Washington, DC – MD – VA MSA	839	13
Pittsburgh – Beaver Valley, PA CMSA	738	14

[Continued]

★1185★

Top 25 MSAs For Employment As Dietitians, 1990: Whites
[Continued]

MSA/CMSA	Employees per 100,000 pop.	Rank
Cincinnati – Hamilton, OH – KY – IN CMSA	668	15
Buffalo – Niagara Falls, NY CMSA	659	16
Miami – Fort Lauderdale, FL CMSA	643	17
Houston – Galveston – Brazoria, TX CMSA	610	18
Atlanta, GA MSA	588	19
Columbus, OH MSA	588	19
Tampa – St. Petersburg – Clearwater, FL MSA	566	20
Milwaukee – Racine, WI CMSA	553	21
Dayton – Springfield, OH MSA	505	22
San Diego, CA MSA	503	23
Kansas City, MO – KS MSA	496	24

Source: U.S. Department of Commerce, Bureau of the Census, Data User Services Division, *1990 Census of Population and Housing, Equal Employment Opportunity File, CD-90-EE0-1, January 1993,* CD-ROM.

★1186★

Occupations, By Race/Sex

Top 25 MSAs For Employment As Dressmakers, 1990: Blacks

MSA/CMSA	Employees per 100,000 pop.	Rank
Raleigh – Durham, NC MSA	1,295	1
Philadelphia – Wilmington – Trenton, PA – NJ – DE – MD CMSA	443	2
Atlanta, GA MSA	318	3
Miami – Fort Lauderdale, FL CMSA	309	4
Chicago – Gary – Lake County, IL – IN – WI CMSA	300	5
Memphis, TN – AR – MS MSA	239	6
Washington, DC – MD – VA MSA	235	7
Detroit – Ann Arbor, MI CMSA	197	8
St. Louis, MO – IL MSA	186	9
Birmingham, AL MSA	181	10
Houston – Galveston – Brazoria, TX CMSA	173	11
Los Angeles – Anaheim – Riverside, CA CMSA	172	12
Cleveland – Akron – Lorain, OH CMSA	163	13
Richmond – Petersburg, VA MSA	152	14
New Orleans, LA MSA	146	15
Baltimore, MD MSA	132	16
Charlotte – Gastonia – Rock Hill, NC – SC MSA	132	16
Norfolk – Virginia Beach – Newport News, VA MSA	130	17
Dallas – Fort Worth, TX CMSA	96	18

[Continued]

★1186★

Top 25 MSAs For Employment As Dressmakers, 1990: Blacks

[Continued]

MSA/CMSA	Employees per 100,000 pop.	Rank
San Francisco – Oakland – San Jose, CA CMSA	91	19
Cincinnati – Hamilton, OH – KY – IN CMSA	88	20
Raleigh – Durham, NC MSA	88	20
Milwaukee – Racine, WI CMSA	86	21
Columbus, OH MSA	85	22
Augusta, GA – SC MSA	78	23

Source: U.S. Department of Commerce, Bureau of the Census, Data User Services Division, *1990 Census of Population and Housing, Equal Employment Opportunity File, CD-90-EE0-1, January 1993,* CD-ROM.

★1187★

Occupations, By Race/Sex

Top 25 MSAs For Employment As Dressmakers, 1990: Whites

MSA/CMSA	Employees per 100,000 pop.	Rank
Pittsburgh – Beaver Valley, PA CMSA	4,843	1
Los Angeles – Anaheim – Riverside, CA CMSA	3,519	2
Chicago – Gary – Lake County, IL – IN – WI CMSA	2,051	3
Miami – Fort Lauderdale, FL CMSA	1,859	4
Philadelphia – Wilmington – Trenton, PA – NJ – DE – MD CMSA	1,265	5
Detroit – Ann Arbor, MI CMSA	1,227	6
San Francisco – Oakland – San Jose, CA CMSA	1,177	7
Dallas – Fort Worth, TX CMSA	1,014	8
Minneapolis – St. Paul, MN – WI MSA	892	9
Boston – Lawrence – Salem, MA – NH CMSA	833	10
Washington, DC – MD – VA MSA	802	11
Atlanta, GA MSA	777	12
Cleveland – Akron – Lorain, OH CMSA	763	13
Pittsburgh – Beaver Valley, PA CMSA	721	14
Denver – Boulder, CO CMSA	720	15
St. Louis, MO – IL MSA	697	16
Tampa – St. Petersburg – Clearwater, FL MSA	697	16
Houston – Galveston – Brazoria, TX CMSA	680	17
Seattle – Tacoma, WA CMSA	550	18
San Diego, CA MSA	544	19
Kansas City, MO – KS MSA	509	20
Milwaukee – Racine, WI CMSA	489	21

[Continued]

★1187★

Top 25 MSAs For Employment As Dressmakers, 1990: Whites

[Continued]

MSA/CMSA	Employees per 100,000 pop.	Rank
Cincinnati – Hamilton, OH – KY – IN CMSA	489	21
Phoenix, AZ MSA	472	22
Charlotte – Gastonia – Rock Hill, NC – SC MSA	422	23

Source: U.S. Department of Commerce, Bureau of the Census, Data User Services Division, *1990 Census of Population and Housing, Equal Employment Opportunity File, CD-90-EE0-1, January 1993,* CD-ROM.

★1188★

Occupations, By Race/Sex

Top 25 MSAs For Employment As Early Childhood Teacher's Assistants, 1990: Blacks

MSA/CMSA	Employees per 100,000 pop.	Rank
Columbus, OH MSA	6,399	1
Philadelphia – Wilmington – Trenton, PA – NJ – DE – MD CMSA	2,302	2
Washington, DC – MD – VA MSA	1,910	3
Chicago – Gary – Lake County, IL – IN – WI CMSA	1,674	4
Atlanta, GA MSA	1,509	5
Los Angeles – Anaheim – Riverside, CA CMSA	1,416	6
Houston – Galveston – Brazoria, TX CMSA	1,328	7
Miami – Fort Lauderdale, FL CMSA	1,278	8
Detroit – Ann Arbor, MI CMSA	1,240	9
Dallas – Fort Worth, TX CMSA	1,144	10
San Francisco – Oakland – San Jose, CA CMSA	1,046	11
Baltimore, MD MSA	1,007	12
St. Louis, MO – IL MSA	754	13
Cleveland – Akron – Lorain, OH CMSA	590	14
Jacksonville, FL MSA	581	15
Charlotte – Gastonia – Rock Hill, NC – SC MSA	580	16
Memphis, TN – AR – MS MSA	564	17
New Orleans, LA MSA	530	18
Norfolk – Virginia Beach – Newport News, VA MSA	528	19
Boston – Lawrence – Salem, MA – NH CMSA	456	20
Birmingham, AL MSA	450	21
Tampa – St. Petersburg – Clearwater, FL MSA	448	22
Greensboro – Winston-Salem – High Point, NC MSA	439	23

[Continued]

★1188★

Top 25 MSAs For Employment As Early Childhood Teacher's Assistants, 1990: Blacks

[Continued]

MSA/CMSA	Employees per 100,000 pop.	Rank
Orlando, FL MSA	408	24
Raleigh – Durham, NC MSA	394	25

Source: U.S. Department of Commerce, Bureau of the Census, Data User Services Division, 1990 Census of Population and Housing, Equal Employment Opportunity File, CD-90-EE0-1, January 1993, CD-ROM.

★1189★

Occupations, By Race/Sex

Top 25 MSAs For Employment As Early Childhood Teacher's Assistants, 1990: Whites

MSA/CMSA	Employees per 100,000 pop.	Rank
Cincinnati – Hamilton, OH – KY – IN CMSA	11,317	1
Los Angeles – Anaheim – Riverside, CA CMSA	9,511	2
Philadelphia – Wilmington – Trenton, PA – NJ – DE – MD CMSA	6,666	3
San Francisco – Oakland – San Jose, CA CMSA	5,911	4
Dallas – Fort Worth, TX CMSA	5,464	5
Chicago – Gary – Lake County, IL – IN – WI CMSA	5,356	6
Boston – Lawrence – Salem, MA – NH CMSA	5,352	7
Detroit – Ann Arbor, MI CMSA	4,730	8
Minneapolis – St. Paul, MN – WI MSA	4,711	9
Washington, DC – MD – VA MSA	4,625	10
Houston – Galveston – Brazoria, TX CMSA	4,004	11
Seattle – Tacoma, WA CMSA	3,873	12
Atlanta, GA MSA	3,819	13
Denver – Boulder, CO CMSA	3,236	14
Miami – Fort Lauderdale, FL CMSA	2,813	15
St. Louis, MO – IL MSA	2,594	16
San Diego, CA MSA	2,451	17
Phoenix, AZ MSA	2,331	18
Tampa – St. Petersburg – Clearwater, FL MSA	2,166	19
Cleveland – Akron – Lorain, OH CMSA	2,142	20
Baltimore, MD MSA	2,141	21
Kansas City, MO – KS MSA	2,036	22
Pittsburgh – Beaver Valley, PA CMSA	1,985	23
Charlotte – Gastonia – Rock Hill, NC – SC MSA	1,947	24
San Antonio, TX MSA	1,909	25

Source: U.S. Department of Commerce, Bureau of the Census, Data User Services Division, 1990 Census of Population and Housing, Equal Employment Opportunity File, CD-90-EE0-1, January 1993, CD-ROM.

★1190★

Occupations, By Race/Sex

Top 25 MSAs For Employment As Earth, Environmental, and Marine Science Teachers, 1990: Blacks

MSA/CMSA	Employees per 100,000 pop.	Rank
Columbus, GA – AL MSA	0	1
Ocala, FL MSA	0	1
Nashville, TN MSA	0	1
Owensboro, KY MSA	0	1
Omaha, NE – IA MSA	0	1
Oklahoma City, OK MSA	0	1
Orlando, FL MSA	0	1
Panama City, FL MSA	0	1
Parkersburg – Marietta, WV – OH MSA	0	1
New London – Norwich, CT – RI MSA	0	1
Odessa, TX MSA	0	1
New Bedford, MA MSA	0	1
Norfolk – Virginia Beach – Newport News, VA MSA	0	1
Pittsfield, MA MSA	0	1
Muncie, IN MSA	0	1
New York – Northern New Jersey – Long Island, NY – NJ – CT CMSA	0	1
Olympia, WA MSA	0	1
Redding, CA MSA	0	1
Poughkeepsie, NY MSA	0	1
Lynchburg, VA MSA	0	1
Muskegon, MI MSA	0	1
Pueblo, CO MSA	0	1
Raleigh – Durham, NC MSA	0	1
Portland, ME MSA	0	1
Provo – Orem, UT MSA	0	1

Source: U.S. Department of Commerce, Bureau of the Census, Data User Services Division, 1990 Census of Population and Housing, Equal Employment Opportunity File, CD-90-EE0-1, January 1993, CD-ROM.

★1191★

Occupations, By Race/Sex

Top 25 MSAs For Employment As Earth, Environmental, and Marine Science Teachers, 1990: Whites

MSA/CMSA	Employees per 100,000 pop.	Rank
Charlotte – Gastonia – Rock Hill, NC – SC MSA	73	1
New York – Northern New Jersey – Long Island, NY – NJ – CT CMSA	60	2
Dallas – Fort Worth, TX CMSA	55	3
Columbus, OH MSA	46	4
Washington, DC – MD – VA MSA	39	5
San Francisco – Oakland – San Jose, CA CMSA	38	6
Philadelphia – Wilmington – Trenton, PA – NJ – DE – MD CMSA	27	7

[Continued]

★1191★

Top 25 MSAs For Employment As Earth, Environmental, and Marine Science Teachers, 1990: Whites
[Continued]

MSA/CMSA	Employees per 100,000 pop.	Rank
Norfolk – Virginia Beach – Newport News, VA MSA	23	8
Houston – Galveston – Brazoria, TX CMSA	23	8
Cincinnati – Hamilton, OH – KY – IN CMSA	21	9
Grand Forks, ND MSA	20	10
Cleveland – Akron – Lorain, OH CMSA	17	11
Boston – Lawrence – Salem, MA – NH CMSA	17	11
Lafayette – West Lafayette, IN MSA	17	11
Lawrence, KS MSA	16	12
Sacramento, CA MSA	16	12
Syracuse, NY MSA	16	12
Bellingham, WA MSA	15	13
Denver – Boulder, CO CMSA	15	13
Omaha, NE – IA MSA	14	14
Raleigh – Durham, NC MSA	14	14
Athens, GA MSA	13	15
Abilene, TX MSA	12	16
Fort Collins – Loveland, CO MSA	12	16
Lubbock, TX MSA	11	17

Source: U.S. Department of Commerce, Bureau of the Census, Data User Services Division, *1990 Census of Population and Housing, Equal Employment Opportunity File, CD-90-EE0-1, January 1993*, CD-ROM.

★1192★

Occupations, By Race/Sex

Top 25 MSAs For Employment As Economics Teachers, 1990: Blacks

MSA/CMSA	Employees per 100,000 pop.	Rank
Panama City, FL MSA	16	1
New Orleans, LA MSA	13	2
Cincinnati – Hamilton, OH – KY – IN CMSA	12	3
Atlanta, GA MSA	10	4
Miami – Fort Lauderdale, FL CMSA	9	5
Lubbock, TX MSA	7	6
Raleigh – Durham, NC MSA	5	7
New Bedford, MA MSA	0	8
New London – Norwich, CT – RI MSA	0	8
Oklahoma City, OK MSA	0	8
Ocala, FL MSA	0	8
Owensboro, KY MSA	0	8
New Haven – Meriden, CT MSA	0	8
New York – Northern New Jersey – Long Island, NY – NJ – CT CMSA	0	8

[Continued]

★1192★

Top 25 MSAs For Employment As Economics Teachers, 1990: Blacks
[Continued]

MSA/CMSA	Employees per 100,000 pop.	Rank
Nashville, TN MSA	0	8
Muskegon, MI MSA	0	8
Muncie, IN MSA	0	8
Peoria, IL MSA	0	8
Norfolk – Virginia Beach – Newport News, VA MSA	0	8
Pascagoula, MS MSA	0	8
Naples, FL MSA	0	8
Pine Bluff, AR MSA	0	8
Pittsburgh – Beaver Valley, PA CMSA	0	8
Pittsfield, MA MSA	0	8
Phoenix, AZ MSA	0	8

Source: U.S. Department of Commerce, Bureau of the Census, Data User Services Division, *1990 Census of Population and Housing, Equal Employment Opportunity File, CD-90-EE0-1, January 1993*, CD-ROM.

★1193★

Occupations, By Race/Sex

Top 25 MSAs For Employment As Economics Teachers, 1990: Whites

MSA/CMSA	Employees per 100,000 pop.	Rank
Athens, GA MSA	191	1
Washington, DC – MD – VA MSA	145	2
Boston – Lawrence – Salem, MA – NH CMSA	141	3
Los Angeles – Anaheim – Riverside, CA CMSA	139	4
Philadelphia – Wilmington – Trenton, PA – NJ – DE – MD CMSA	98	5
Chicago – Gary – Lake County, IL – IN – WI CMSA	77	6
Miami – Fort Lauderdale, FL CMSA	63	7
San Francisco – Oakland – San Jose, CA CMSA	62	8
San Diego, CA MSA	61	9
Detroit – Ann Arbor, MI CMSA	50	10
Houston – Galveston – Brazoria, TX CMSA	48	11
St. Louis, MO – IL MSA	47	12
Seattle – Tacoma, WA CMSA	47	12
Hartford – New Britain – Middletown, CT CMSA	43	13
Phoenix, AZ MSA	35	14
Minneapolis – St. Paul, MN – WI MSA	34	15
Cleveland – Akron – Lorain, OH CMSA	30	16
Champaign – Urbana – Rantoul, IL MSA	30	16

[Continued]

★1193★

Top 25 MSAs For Employment As Economics Teachers, 1990: Whites

[Continued]

MSA/CMSA	Employees per 100,000 pop.	Rank
Portland – Vancouver, OR – WA CMSA	28	17
Toledo, OH MSA	28	17
Pittsburgh – Beaver Valley, PA CMSA	27	18
Albany – Schenectady – Troy, NY MSA	27	18
Cincinnati – Hamilton, OH – KY – IN CMSA	26	19
Bryan – College Station, TX MSA	26	19
Denver – Boulder, CO CMSA	25	20

Source: U.S. Department of Commerce, Bureau of the Census, Data User Services Division, *1990 Census of Population and Housing, Equal Employment Opportunity File,* CD-90-EE0-1, January 1993, CD-ROM.

★1194★

Occupations, By Race/Sex

Top 25 MSAs For Employment As Economists, 1990: Blacks

MSA/CMSA	Employees per 100,000 pop.	Rank
Springfield, MA MSA	1,229	1
New York – Northern New Jersey – Long Island, NY – NJ – CT CMSA	1,083	2
Chicago – Gary – Lake County, IL – IN – WI CMSA	422	3
Los Angeles – Anaheim – Riverside, CA CMSA	397	4
San Francisco – Oakland – San Jose, CA CMSA	327	5
Detroit – Ann Arbor, MI CMSA	283	6
Atlanta, GA MSA	268	7
Baltimore, MD MSA	208	8
Philadelphia – Wilmington – Trenton, PA – NJ – DE – MD CMSA	183	9
Houston – Galveston – Brazoria, TX CMSA	179	10
Dallas – Fort Worth, TX CMSA	168	11
St. Louis, MO – IL MSA	111	12
Norfolk – Virginia Beach – Newport News, VA MSA	111	12
Seattle – Tacoma, WA CMSA	87	13
Boston – Lawrence – Salem, MA – NH CMSA	84	14
Denver – Boulder, CO CMSA	76	15
Cincinnati – Hamilton, OH – KY – IN CMSA	74	16
Cleveland – Akron – Lorain, OH CMSA	73	17
Milwaukee – Racine, WI CMSA	72	18
Richmond – Petersburg, VA MSA	71	19

[Continued]

★1194★

Top 25 MSAs For Employment As Economists, 1990: Blacks

[Continued]

MSA/CMSA	Employees per 100,000 pop.	Rank
New Haven – Meriden, CT MSA	64	20
Charlotte – Gastonia – Rock Hill, NC – SC MSA	56	21
Raleigh – Durham, NC MSA	51	22
Miami – Fort Lauderdale, FL CMSA	50	23
Sacramento, CA MSA	48	24

Source: U.S. Department of Commerce, Bureau of the Census, Data User Services Division, *1990 Census of Population and Housing, Equal Employment Opportunity File,* CD-90-EE0-1, January 1993, CD-ROM.

★1195★

Occupations, By Race/Sex

Top 25 MSAs For Employment As Economists, 1990: Whites

MSA/CMSA	Employees per 100,000 pop.	Rank
Norfolk – Virginia Beach – Newport News, VA MSA	17,346	1
Washington, DC – MD – VA MSA	12,299	2
Chicago – Gary – Lake County, IL – IN – WI CMSA	7,741	3
Los Angeles – Anaheim – Riverside, CA CMSA	6,972	4
San Francisco – Oakland – San Jose, CA CMSA	6,489	5
Boston – Lawrence – Salem, MA – NH CMSA	5,932	6
Philadelphia – Wilmington – Trenton, PA – NJ – DE – MD CMSA	3,911	7
Dallas – Fort Worth, TX CMSA	3,205	8
Atlanta, GA MSA	2,970	9
Detroit – Ann Arbor, MI CMSA	2,573	10
Houston – Galveston – Brazoria, TX CMSA	2,540	11
Minneapolis – St. Paul, MN – WI MSA	2,524	12
Denver – Boulder, CO CMSA	2,190	13
Seattle – Tacoma, WA CMSA	2,155	14
Cleveland – Akron – Lorain, OH CMSA	1,611	15
Baltimore, MD MSA	1,610	16
Miami – Fort Lauderdale, FL CMSA	1,456	17
Phoenix, AZ MSA	1,454	18
St. Louis, MO – IL MSA	1,426	19
Pittsburgh – Beaver Valley, PA CMSA	1,294	20
Kansas City, MO – KS MSA	1,287	21
Cincinnati – Hamilton, OH – KY – IN CMSA	1,283	22
Portland – Vancouver, OR – WA CMSA	1,245	23

[Continued]

★1195★

Top 25 MSAs For Employment As Economists, 1990: Whites
[Continued]

MSA/CMSA	Employees per 100,000 pop.	Rank
San Diego, CA MSA	1,237	24
Columbus, OH MSA	1,092	25

Source: U.S. Department of Commerce, Bureau of the Census, Data User Services Division, *1990 Census of Population and Housing, Equal Employment Opportunity File, CD-90-EE0-1, January 1993,* CD-ROM.

★1196★

Occupations, By Race/Sex

Top 25 MSAs For Employment As Editors and Reporters, 1990: Blacks

MSA/CMSA	Employees per 100,000 pop.	Rank
Oklahoma City, OK MSA	2,854	1
Washington, DC – MD – VA MSA	1,627	2
Chicago – Gary – Lake County, IL – IN – WI CMSA	786	3
Los Angeles – Anaheim – Riverside, CA CMSA	771	4
Philadelphia – Wilmington – Trenton, PA – NJ – DE – MD CMSA	522	5
Detroit – Ann Arbor, MI CMSA	392	6
San Francisco – Oakland – San Jose, CA CMSA	352	7
Atlanta, GA MSA	323	8
Baltimore, MD MSA	226	9
Boston – Lawrence – Salem, MA – NH CMSA	210	10
Cleveland – Akron – Lorain, OH CMSA	203	11
Norfolk – Virginia Beach – Newport News, VA MSA	166	12
Miami – Fort Lauderdale, FL CMSA	158	13
Cincinnati – Hamilton, OH – KY – IN CMSA	150	14
St. Louis, MO – IL MSA	149	15
Dayton – Springfield, OH MSA	132	16
Houston – Galveston – Brazoria, TX CMSA	131	17
Dallas – Fort Worth, TX CMSA	121	18
Denver – Boulder, CO CMSA	115	19
Pittsburgh – Beaver Valley, PA CMSA	114	20
New Orleans, LA MSA	111	21
Champaign – Urbana – Rantoul, IL MSA	105	22
Greensboro – Winston-Salem – High Point, NC MSA	102	23
Raleigh – Durham, NC MSA	101	24
Milwaukee – Racine, WI CMSA	99	25

Source: U.S. Department of Commerce, Bureau of the Census, Data User Services Division, *1990 Census of Population and Housing, Equal Employment Opportunity File, CD-90-EE0-1, January 1993,* CD-ROM.

★1197★

Occupations, By Race/Sex

Top 25 MSAs For Employment As Editors and Reporters, 1990: Whites

MSA/CMSA	Employees per 100,000 pop.	Rank
Denver – Boulder, CO CMSA	39,861	1
Los Angeles – Anaheim – Riverside, CA CMSA	15,728	2
Washington, DC – MD – VA MSA	14,023	3
Chicago – Gary – Lake County, IL – IN – WI CMSA	10,511	4
Boston – Lawrence – Salem, MA – NH CMSA	8,073	5
San Francisco – Oakland – San Jose, CA CMSA	7,883	6
Philadelphia – Wilmington – Trenton, PA – NJ – DE – MD CMSA	6,538	7
Detroit – Ann Arbor, MI CMSA	3,799	8
Dallas – Fort Worth, TX CMSA	3,435	9
Minneapolis – St. Paul, MN – WI MSA	3,004	10
Atlanta, GA MSA	2,818	11
Seattle – Tacoma, WA CMSA	2,544	12
Cleveland – Akron – Lorain, OH CMSA	2,453	13
Miami – Fort Lauderdale, FL CMSA	2,452	14
San Diego, CA MSA	2,314	15
Denver – Boulder, CO CMSA	2,309	16
Baltimore, MD MSA	2,277	17
Houston – Galveston – Brazoria, TX CMSA	2,119	18
St. Louis, MO – IL MSA	1,866	19
Kansas City, MO – KS MSA	1,768	20
Phoenix, AZ MSA	1,603	21
Columbus, OH MSA	1,552	22
Pittsburgh – Beaver Valley, PA CMSA	1,525	23
Cincinnati – Hamilton, OH – KY – IN CMSA	1,411	24
Nashville, TN MSA	1,343	25

Source: U.S. Department of Commerce, Bureau of the Census, Data User Services Division, *1990 Census of Population and Housing, Equal Employment Opportunity File, CD-90-EE0-1, January 1993,* CD-ROM.

★1198★

Occupations, By Race/Sex

Top 25 MSAs For Employment As Education Teachers, 1990: Blacks

MSA/CMSA	Employees per 100,000 pop.	Rank
Fargo – Moorhead, ND – MN MSA	40	1
Atlanta, GA MSA	15	2
Houston – Galveston – Brazoria, TX CMSA	15	2
Detroit – Ann Arbor, MI CMSA	13	3
Baton Rouge, LA MSA	13	3

[Continued]

★1198★

Top 25 MSAs For Employment As Education Teachers, 1990: Blacks

[Continued]

MSA/CMSA	Employees per 100,000 pop.	Rank
Washington, DC – MD – VA MSA	11	4
Atlantic City, NJ MSA	8	5
Dallas – Fort Worth, TX CMSA	7	6
Charlotte – Gastonia – Rock Hill, NC – SC MSA	7	6
Chicago – Gary – Lake County, IL – IN – WI CMSA	6	7
Flint, MI MSA	6	7
Portland – Vancouver, OR – WA CMSA	5	8
Owensboro, KY MSA	0	9
Parkersburg – Marietta, WV – OH MSA	0	9
Odessa, TX MSA	0	9
Oklahoma City, OK MSA	0	9
Panama City, FL MSA	0	9
Orlando, FL MSA	0	9
Olympia, WA MSA	0	9
Norfolk – Virginia Beach – Newport News, VA MSA	0	9
Ocala, FL MSA	0	9
Muskegon, MI MSA	0	9
Omaha, NE – IA MSA	0	9
Raleigh – Durham, NC MSA	0	9
Poughkeepsie, NY MSA	0	9

Source: U.S. Department of Commerce, Bureau of the Census, Data User Services Division, *1990 Census of Population and Housing, Equal Employment Opportunity File, CD-90-EE0-1, January 1993,* CD-ROM.

★1199★

Occupations, By Race/Sex

Top 25 MSAs For Employment As Education Teachers, 1990: Whites

MSA/CMSA	Employees per 100,000 pop.	Rank
Charlotte – Gastonia – Rock Hill, NC – SC MSA	252	1
Los Angeles – Anaheim – Riverside, CA CMSA	58	2
Chicago – Gary – Lake County, IL – IN – WI CMSA	47	3
San Francisco – Oakland – San Jose, CA CMSA	34	4
New Haven – Meriden, CT MSA	31	5
Washington, DC – MD – VA MSA	29	6
Detroit – Ann Arbor, MI CMSA	23	7
Seattle – Tacoma, WA CMSA	22	8
Wichita, KS MSA	21	9
New Orleans, LA MSA	20	10
Phoenix, AZ MSA	18	11
Buffalo – Niagara Falls, NY CMSA	14	12
Boston – Lawrence – Salem, MA – NH CMSA	14	12

[Continued]

★1199★

Top 25 MSAs For Employment As Education Teachers, 1990: Whites

[Continued]

MSA/CMSA	Employees per 100,000 pop.	Rank
Mobile, AL MSA	14	12
Portland – Vancouver, OR – WA CMSA	14	12
Hartford – New Britain – Middletown, CT CMSA	13	13
Providence – Pawtucket – Fall River, RI – MA CMSA	13	13
Columbus, OH MSA	12	14
Indianapolis, IN MSA	12	14
Anchorage, AK MSA	12	14
Gainesville, FL MSA	12	14
Denver – Boulder, CO CMSA	12	14
Atlanta, GA MSA	11	15
Sharon, PA MSA	11	15
Iowa City, IA MSA	11	15

Source: U.S. Department of Commerce, Bureau of the Census, Data User Services Division, *1990 Census of Population and Housing, Equal Employment Opportunity File, CD-90-EE0-1, January 1993,* CD-ROM.

★1200★

Occupations, By Race/Sex

Top 25 MSAs For Employment As Elevator Operators, 1990: Blacks

MSA/CMSA	Employees per 100,000 pop.	Rank
Raleigh – Durham, NC MSA	1,325 ·	1
Chicago – Gary – Lake County, IL – IN – WI CMSA	276	2
Washington, DC – MD – VA MSA	211	3
Philadelphia – Wilmington – Trenton, PA – NJ – DE – MD CMSA	167	4
Detroit – Ann Arbor, MI CMSA	82	5
New Orleans, LA MSA	78	6
Los Angeles – Anaheim – Riverside, CA CMSA	57	7
St. Louis, MO – IL MSA	42	8
Pittsburgh – Beaver Valley, PA CMSA	36	9
Cleveland – Akron – Lorain, OH CMSA	36	9
Atlanta, GA MSA	32	10
Cincinnati – Hamilton, OH – KY – IN CMSA	29	11
Dallas – Fort Worth, TX CMSA	26	12
Houston – Galveston – Brazoria, TX CMSA	25	13
Sacramento, CA MSA	24	14
Richmond – Petersburg, VA MSA	24	14
San Francisco – Oakland – San Jose, CA CMSA	20	15
Greensboro – Winston-Salem – High Point, NC MSA	17	16

[Continued]

★1200★

Top 25 MSAs For Employment As Elevator Operators, 1990: Blacks
[Continued]

MSA/CMSA	Employees per 100,000 pop.	Rank
Baltimore, MD MSA	17	16
Rochester, NY MSA	17	16
Norfolk – Virginia Beach – Newport News, VA MSA	16	17
Oklahoma City, OK MSA	15	18
Kansas City, MO – KS MSA	14	19
Jackson, MS MSA	14	19
Greenville – Spartanburg, SC MSA	14	19

Source: U.S. Department of Commerce, Bureau of the Census, Data User Services Division, *1990 Census of Population and Housing, Equal Employment Opportunity File, CD-90-EE0-1, January 1993,* CD-ROM.

★1201★

Occupations, By Race/Sex

Top 25 MSAs For Employment As Elevator Operators, 1990: Whites

MSA/CMSA	Employees per 100,000 pop.	Rank
Sacramento, CA MSA	2,795	1
Chicago – Gary – Lake County, IL – IN – WI CMSA	304	2
Philadelphia – Wilmington – Trenton, PA – NJ – DE – MD CMSA	136	3
Los Angeles – Anaheim – Riverside, CA CMSA	117	4
Pittsburgh – Beaver Valley, PA CMSA	111	5
Boston – Lawrence – Salem, MA – NH CMSA	108	6
Minneapolis – St. Paul, MN – WI MSA	65	7
Albany – Schenectady – Troy, NY MSA	62	8
Cincinnati – Hamilton, OH – KY – IN CMSA	56	9
Kansas City, MO – KS MSA	52	10
Oklahoma City, OK MSA	49	11
St. Louis, MO – IL MSA	48	12
San Francisco – Oakland – San Jose, CA CMSA	41	13
Dallas – Fort Worth, TX CMSA	39	14
Miami – Fort Lauderdale, FL CMSA	37	15
New Orleans, LA MSA	36	16
Charlotte – Gastonia – Rock Hill, NC – SC MSA	35	17
Baton Rouge, LA MSA	34	18
Louisville, KY – IN MSA	33	19
Denver – Boulder, CO CMSA	30	20
Columbus, OH MSA	30	20
Omaha, NE – IA MSA	30	20

[Continued]

★1201★

Top 25 MSAs For Employment As Elevator Operators, 1990: Whites
[Continued]

MSA/CMSA	Employees per 100,000 pop.	Rank
Jackson, MS MSA	30	20
Sacramento, CA MSA	28	21
Enid, OK MSA	27	22

Source: U.S. Department of Commerce, Bureau of the Census, Data User Services Division, *1990 Census of Population and Housing, Equal Employment Opportunity File, CD-90-EE0-1, January 1993,* CD-ROM.

★1202★

Occupations, By Race/Sex

Top 25 MSAs For Employment As English Teachers, 1990: Blacks

MSA/CMSA	Employees per 100,000 pop.	Rank
Redding, CA MSA	182	1
Los Angeles – Anaheim – Riverside, CA CMSA	87	2
Washington, DC – MD – VA MSA	71	3
San Francisco – Oakland – San Jose, CA CMSA	44	4
Philadelphia – Wilmington – Trenton, PA – NJ – DE – MD CMSA	38	5
Baltimore, MD MSA	29	6
New Haven – Meriden, CT MSA	26	7
Miami – Fort Lauderdale, FL CMSA	25	8
Little Rock – North Little Rock, AR MSA	25	8
Chicago – Gary – Lake County, IL – IN – WI CMSA	23	9
Boston – Lawrence – Salem, MA – NH CMSA	21	10
Raleigh – Durham, NC MSA	21	10
Houston – Galveston – Brazoria, TX CMSA	19	11
Detroit – Ann Arbor, MI CMSA	18	12
Albany, GA MSA	17	13
New Orleans, LA MSA	15	14
Birmingham, AL MSA	15	14
Charlotte – Gastonia – Rock Hill, NC – SC MSA	15	14
Montgomery, AL MSA	15	14
Columbia, SC MSA	15	14
Macon – Warner Robins, GA MSA	15	14
St. Louis, MO – IL MSA	14	15
Atlanta, GA MSA	13	16
Sacramento, CA MSA	13	16
Cincinnati – Hamilton, OH – KY – IN CMSA	12	17

Source: U.S. Department of Commerce, Bureau of the Census, Data User Services Division, *1990 Census of Population and Housing, Equal Employment Opportunity File, CD-90-EE0-1, January 1993,* CD-ROM.

Occupations, By Race/Sex

Top 25 MSAs For Employment As English Teachers, 1990: Whites

MSA/CMSA	Employees per 100,000 pop.	Rank
Philadelphia – Wilmington – Trenton, PA – NJ – DE – MD CMSA	1,840	1
Los Angeles – Anaheim – Riverside, CA CMSA	938	2
San Francisco – Oakland – San Jose, CA CMSA	934	3
Chicago – Gary – Lake County, IL – IN – WI CMSA	695	4
Boston – Lawrence – Salem, MA – NH CMSA	579	5
Philadelphia – Wilmington – Trenton, PA – NJ – DE – MD CMSA	456	6
Washington, DC – MD – VA MSA	410	7
Detroit – Ann Arbor, MI CMSA	322	8
Dallas – Fort Worth, TX CMSA	273	9
San Diego, CA MSA	250	10
Seattle – Tacoma, WA CMSA	250	10
Cleveland – Akron – Lorain, OH CMSA	242	11
Pittsburgh – Beaver Valley, PA CMSA	219	12
Miami – Fort Lauderdale, FL CMSA	215	13
Houston – Galveston – Brazoria, TX CMSA	212	14
Buffalo – Niagara Falls, NY CMSA	198	15
Minneapolis – St. Paul, MN – WI MSA	195	16
Denver – Boulder, CO CMSA	193	17
Cincinnati – Hamilton, OH – KY – IN CMSA	189	18
Phoenix, AZ MSA	188	19
St. Louis, MO – IL MSA	174	20
Baltimore, MD MSA	170	21
Raleigh – Durham, NC MSA	153	22
Atlanta, GA MSA	153	22
Columbus, OH MSA	147	23

Source: U.S. Department of Commerce, Bureau of the Census, Data User Services Division, *1990 Census of Population and Housing, Equal Employment Opportunity File, CD-90-EE0-1,* January 1993, CD-ROM.

Occupations, By Race/Sex

Top 25 MSAs For Employment As Explosives Workers, 1990: Blacks

MSA/CMSA	Employees per 100,000 pop.	Rank
Cleveland – Akron – Lorain, OH CMSA	85	1
Houston – Galveston – Brazoria, TX CMSA	64	2
Birmingham, AL MSA	44	3
Chicago – Gary – Lake County, IL – IN – WI CMSA	37	4
Houma – Thibodaux, LA MSA	30	5
Milwaukee – Racine, WI CMSA	25	6
Baton Rouge, LA MSA	23	7
Norfolk – Virginia Beach – Newport News, VA MSA	21	8
Waterbury, CT MSA	19	9
New Orleans, LA MSA	19	9
Oklahoma City, OK MSA	18	10
San Francisco – Oakland – San Jose, CA CMSA	18	10
Miami – Fort Lauderdale, FL CMSA	17	11
San Diego, CA MSA	15	12
Baltimore, MD MSA	15	12
Pine Bluff, AR MSA	14	13
Greenville – Spartanburg, SC MSA	14	13
Beaumont – Port Arthur, TX MSA	13	14
Wichita Falls, TX MSA	13	14
Kankakee, IL MSA	12	15
Bryan – College Station, TX MSA	11	16
Allentown – Bethlehem – Easton, PA – NJ MSA	10	17
Cincinnati – Hamilton, OH – KY – IN CMSA	9	18
New York – Northern New Jersey – Long Island, NY – NJ – CT CMSA	9	18
Mobile, AL MSA	9	18

Source: U.S. Department of Commerce, Bureau of the Census, Data User Services Division, *1990 Census of Population and Housing, Equal Employment Opportunity File, CD-90-EE0-1,* January 1993, CD-ROM.

Occupations, By Race/Sex

Top 25 MSAs For Employment As Explosives Workers, 1990: Whites

MSA/CMSA	Employees per 100,000 pop.	Rank
Columbus, OH MSA	166	1
Birmingham, AL MSA	114	2
Houston – Galveston – Brazoria, TX CMSA	111	3
Chicago – Gary – Lake County, IL – IN – WI CMSA	107	4
Los Angeles – Anaheim – Riverside, CA CMSA	102	5

[Continued]

★ 1205 ★

Top 25 MSAs For Employment As Explosives Workers, 1990: Whites
[Continued]

MSA/CMSA	Employees per 100,000 pop.	Rank
Milwaukee – Racine, WI CMSA	92	6
Nashville, TN MSA	85	7
San Francisco – Oakland – San Jose, CA CMSA	81	8
Pittsburgh – Beaver Valley, PA CMSA	77	9
Hartford – New Britain – Middletown, CT CMSA	68	10
Philadelphia – Wilmington – Trenton, PA – NJ – DE – MD CMSA	65	11
Salt Lake City – Ogden, UT MSA	59	12
Houma – Thibodaux, LA MSA	53	13
St. Louis, MO – IL MSA	53	13
Parkersburg – Marietta, WV – OH MSA	51	14
Detroit – Ann Arbor, MI CMSA	48	15
Bremerton, WA MSA	48	15
Phoenix, AZ MSA	47	16
Scranton – Wilkes-Barre, PA MSA	47	16
Altoona, PA MSA	47	16
Boston – Lawrence – Salem, MA – NH CMSA	47	16
Baltimore, MD MSA	47	16
Appleton – Oshkosh – Neenah, WI MSA	46	17
Worcester, MA MSA	45	18
Louisville, KY – IN MSA	45	18

Source: U.S. Department of Commerce, Bureau of the Census, Data User Services Division, *1990 Census of Population and Housing, Equal Employment Opportunity File, CD-90-EE0-1, January 1993*, CD-ROM.

★ 1206 ★

Occupations, By Race/Sex

Top 25 MSAs For Employment As Family Child Care Providers, 1990: Blacks

MSA/CMSA	Employees per 100,000 pop.	Rank
Rochester, NY MSA	3,873	1
Washington, DC – MD – VA MSA	1,730	2
Chicago – Gary – Lake County, IL – IN – WI CMSA	1,248	3
Baltimore, MD MSA	1,137	4
Los Angeles – Anaheim – Riverside, CA CMSA	1,091	5
San Francisco – Oakland – San Jose, CA CMSA	1,008	6
Philadelphia – Wilmington – Trenton, PA – NJ – DE – MD CMSA	881	7
Houston – Galveston – Brazoria, TX CMSA	877	8
Atlanta, GA MSA	754	9

[Continued]

★ 1206 ★

Top 25 MSAs For Employment As Family Child Care Providers, 1990: Blacks
[Continued]

MSA/CMSA	Employees per 100,000 pop.	Rank
Norfolk – Virginia Beach – Newport News, VA MSA	710	10
Detroit – Ann Arbor, MI CMSA	652	11
Boston – Lawrence – Salem, MA – NH CMSA	476	12
Miami – Fort Lauderdale, FL CMSA	470	13
Richmond – Petersburg, VA MSA	458	14
Dallas – Fort Worth, TX CMSA	435	15
St. Louis, MO – IL MSA	397	16
Cleveland – Akron – Lorain, OH CMSA	387	17
San Diego, CA MSA	354	18
Cincinnati – Hamilton, OH – KY – IN CMSA	271	19
Nashville, TN MSA	254	20
Tampa – St. Petersburg – Clearwater, FL MSA	249	21
Charlotte – Gastonia – Rock Hill, NC – SC MSA	234	22
Jacksonville, FL MSA	215	23
Raleigh – Durham, NC MSA	210	24
Denver – Boulder, CO CMSA	201	25

Source: U.S. Department of Commerce, Bureau of the Census, Data User Services Division, *1990 Census of Population and Housing, Equal Employment Opportunity File, CD-90-EE0-1, January 1993*, CD-ROM.

★ 1207 ★

Occupations, By Race/Sex

Top 25 MSAs For Employment As Family Child Care Providers, 1990: Whites

MSA/CMSA	Employees per 100,000 pop.	Rank
St. Louis, MO – IL MSA	14,898	1
San Francisco – Oakland – San Jose, CA CMSA	10,035	2
Minneapolis – St. Paul, MN – WI MSA	9,358	3
New York – Northern New Jersey – Long Island, NY – NJ – CT CMSA	9,017	4
Washington, DC – MD – VA MSA	7,323	5
Chicago – Gary – Lake County, IL – IN – WI CMSA	6,775	6
Dallas – Fort Worth, TX CMSA	6,209	7
Seattle – Tacoma, WA CMSA	5,482	8
Denver – Boulder, CO CMSA	5,395	9
Boston – Lawrence – Salem, MA – NH CMSA	5,317	10
Portland – Vancouver, OR – WA CMSA	4,581	11
Kansas City, MO – KS MSA	4,446	12
Detroit – Ann Arbor, MI CMSA	4,391	13

[Continued]

★ 1207 ★

Top 25 MSAs For Employment As Family Child Care Providers, 1990: Whites

[Continued]

MSA/CMSA	Employees per 100,000 pop.	Rank
Phoenix, AZ MSA	4,226	14
Houston – Galveston – Brazoria, TX CMSA	4,225	15
San Diego, CA MSA	4,020	16
St. Louis, MO – IL MSA	4,019	17
Philadelphia – Wilmington – Trenton, PA – NJ – DE – MD CMSA	3,942	18
Baltimore, MD MSA	3,564	19
Sacramento, CA MSA	3,163	20
Atlanta, GA MSA	3,158	21
Salt Lake City – Ogden, UT MSA	2,827	22
Columbus, OH MSA	2,798	23
Indianapolis, IN MSA	2,663	24
Norfolk – Virginia Beach – Newport News, VA MSA	2,588	25

Source: U.S. Department of Commerce, Bureau of the Census, Data User Services Division, *1990 Census of Population and Housing, Equal Employment Opportunity File, CD-90-EE0-1, January 1993,* CD-ROM.

★ 1208 ★

Occupations, By Race/Sex

Top 25 MSAs For Employment As Farm Workers, 1990: Blacks

MSA/CMSA	Employees per 100,000 pop.	Rank
Pittsburgh – Beaver Valley, PA CMSA	1,544	1
Miami – Fort Lauderdale, FL CMSA	1,430	2
Lakeland – Winter Haven, FL MSA	852	3
Fort Pierce, FL MSA	814	4
Memphis, TN – AR – MS MSA	723	5
Orlando, FL MSA	623	6
New York – Northern New Jersey – Long Island, NY – NJ – CT CMSA	585	7
Jackson, MS MSA	540	8
Los Angeles – Anaheim – Riverside, CA CMSA	512	9
Atlanta, GA MSA	506	10
Raleigh – Durham, NC MSA	498	11
Philadelphia – Wilmington – Trenton, PA – NJ – DE – MD CMSA	467	12
Florence, SC MSA	409	13
Tampa – St. Petersburg – Clearwater, FL MSA	367	14
Naples, FL MSA	349	15
Columbia, SC MSA	274	16
Shreveport, LA MSA	273	17
Houston – Galveston – Brazoria, TX CMSA	272	18

[Continued]

★ 1208 ★

Top 25 MSAs For Employment As Farm Workers, 1990: Blacks

[Continued]

MSA/CMSA	Employees per 100,000 pop.	Rank
Baltimore, MD MSA	241	19
New Orleans, LA MSA	241	19
Dothan, AL MSA	237	20
Jacksonville, FL MSA	236	21
Ocala, FL MSA	234	22
Washington, DC – MD – VA MSA	223	23
Albany, GA MSA	214	24

Source: U.S. Department of Commerce, Bureau of the Census, Data User Services Division, *1990 Census of Population and Housing, Equal Employment Opportunity File, CD-90-EE0-1, January 1993,* CD-ROM.

★ 1209 ★

Occupations, By Race/Sex

Top 25 MSAs For Employment As Farm Workers, 1990: Whites

MSA/CMSA	Employees per 100,000 pop.	Rank
Portland – Vancouver, OR – WA CMSA	14,980	1
San Francisco – Oakland – San Jose, CA CMSA	7,234	2
Fresno, CA MSA	6,916	3
Visalia – Tulare – Porterville, CA MSA	5,361	4
Mcallen – Edinburg – Mission, TX MSA	5,313	5
Stockton, CA MSA	5,057	6
Tampa – St. Petersburg – Clearwater, FL MSA	3,974	7
New York – Northern New Jersey – Long Island, NY – NJ – CT CMSA	3,604	8
Salinas – Seaside – Monterey, CA MSA	3,534	9
Philadelphia – Wilmington – Trenton, PA – NJ – DE – MD CMSA	3,400	10
Merced, CA MSA	2,983	11
Bakersfield, CA MSA	2,971	12
San Diego, CA MSA	2,873	13
Modesto, CA MSA	2,766	14
Lexington-Fayette, KY MSA	2,709	15
Portland – Vancouver, OR – WA CMSA	2,440	16
Miami – Fort Lauderdale, FL CMSA	2,410	17
Lancaster, PA MSA	2,401	18
Chicago – Gary – Lake County, IL – IN – WI CMSA	2,323	19
Phoenix, AZ MSA	2,291	20
Minneapolis – St. Paul, MN – WI MSA	2,207	21
Detroit – Ann Arbor, MI CMSA	2,035	22

[Continued]

★1209★

Top 25 MSAs For Employment As Farm Workers, 1990: Whites

[Continued]

MSA/CMSA	Employees per 100,000 pop.	Rank
West Palm Beach – Boca Raton – Delray Beach, FL MSA	2,000	23
Dallas – Fort Worth, TX CMSA	1,991	24
Yakima, WA MSA	1,978	25

Source: U.S. Department of Commerce, Bureau of the Census, Data User Services Division, *1990 Census of Population and Housing, Equal Employment Opportunity File, CD-90-EE0-1, January 1993*, CD-ROM.

★1210★

Occupations, By Race/Sex

Top 25 MSAs For Employment As Fire Inspection and Fire Prevention Occupations, 1990: Blacks

MSA/CMSA	Employees per 100,000 pop.	Rank
Cleveland – Akron – Lorain, OH CMSA	270	1
Los Angeles – Anaheim – Riverside, CA CMSA	199	2
Norfolk – Virginia Beach – Newport News, VA MSA	171	3
New York – Northern New Jersey – Long Island, NY – NJ – CT CMSA	141	4
Washington, DC – MD – VA MSA	82	5
Detroit – Ann Arbor, MI CMSA	76	6
Miami – Fort Lauderdale, FL CMSA	36	7
San Diego, CA MSA	31	8
Beaumont – Port Arthur, TX MSA	26	9
Baltimore, MD MSA	25	10
Memphis, TN – AR – MS MSA	23	11
Jacksonville, FL MSA	21	12
New Orleans, LA MSA	19	13
Atlanta, GA MSA	19	13
Charlotte – Gastonia – Rock Hill, NC – SC MSA	19	13
Augusta, GA – SC MSA	19	13
Denver – Boulder, CO CMSA	17	14
Wilmington, NC MSA	17	14
Pascagoula, MS MSA	17	14
Savannah, GA MSA	15	15
San Francisco – Oakland – San Jose, CA CMSA	14	16
Dallas – Fort Worth, TX CMSA	14	16
Peoria, IL MSA	13	17
Buffalo – Niagara Falls, NY CMSA	13	17
Chicago – Gary – Lake County, IL – IN – WI CMSA	12	18

Source: U.S. Department of Commerce, Bureau of the Census, Data User Services Division, *1990 Census of Population and Housing, Equal Employment Opportunity File, CD-90-EE0-1, January 1993*, CD-ROM.

★1211★

Occupations, By Race/Sex

Top 25 MSAs For Employment As Fire Inspection and Fire Prevention Occupations, 1990: Whites

MSA/CMSA	Employees per 100,000 pop.	Rank
Atlanta, GA MSA	1,020	1
New York – Northern New Jersey – Long Island, NY – NJ – CT CMSA	843	2
San Francisco – Oakland – San Jose, CA CMSA	452	3
Chicago – Gary – Lake County, IL – IN – WI CMSA	386	4
Philadelphia – Wilmington – Trenton, PA – NJ – DE – MD CMSA	338	5
San Diego, CA MSA	258	6
Detroit – Ann Arbor, MI CMSA	172	7
Miami – Fort Lauderdale, FL CMSA	150	8
Houston – Galveston – Brazoria, TX CMSA	147	9
Boston – Lawrence – Salem, MA – NH CMSA	147	9
Phoenix, AZ MSA	145	10
Dallas – Fort Worth, TX CMSA	143	11
St. Louis, MO – IL MSA	125	12
Cleveland – Akron – Lorain, OH CMSA	125	12
Washington, DC – MD – VA MSA	125	12
Seattle – Tacoma, WA CMSA	118	13
Cincinnati – Hamilton, OH – KY – IN CMSA	116	14
Baltimore, MD MSA	112	15
Louisville, KY – IN MSA	104	16
Norfolk – Virginia Beach – Newport News, VA MSA	99	17
Reno, NV MSA	96	18
Minneapolis – St. Paul, MN – WI MSA	94	19
Columbus, OH MSA	92	20
Greensboro – Winston-Salem – High Point, NC MSA	91	21
West Palm Beach – Boca Raton – Delray Beach, FL MSA	90	22

Source: U.S. Department of Commerce, Bureau of the Census, Data User Services Division, *1990 Census of Population and Housing, Equal Employment Opportunity File, CD-90-EE0-1, January 1993*, CD-ROM.

★1212★

Occupations, By Race/Sex

Top 25 MSAs For Employment As Firefighting Occupations, 1990: Blacks

MSA/CMSA	Employees per 100,000 pop.	Rank
Atlantic City, NJ MSA	1,353	1
New York – Northern New Jersey – Long Island, NY – NJ – CT CMSA	1,325	2
Washington, DC – MD – VA MSA	932	3
Los Angeles – Anaheim – Riverside, CA CMSA	809	4
Philadelphia – Wilmington – Trenton, PA – NJ – DE – MD CMSA	767	5
Detroit – Ann Arbor, MI CMSA	657	6
Atlanta, GA MSA	612	7
Baltimore, MD MSA	502	8
San Francisco – Oakland – San Jose, CA CMSA	477	9
Boston – Lawrence – Salem, MA – NH CMSA	466	10
Houston – Galveston – Brazoria, TX CMSA	465	11
Memphis, TN – AR – MS MSA	434	12
St. Louis, MO – IL MSA	421	13
Dallas – Fort Worth, TX CMSA	321	14
Greensboro – Winston-Salem – High Point, NC MSA	278	15
Norfolk – Virginia Beach – Newport News, VA MSA	278	15
Miami – Fort Lauderdale, FL CMSA	270	16
Birmingham, AL MSA	258	17
Richmond – Petersburg, VA MSA	253	18
Cincinnati – Hamilton, OH – KY – IN CMSA	211	19
Milwaukee – Racine, WI CMSA	184	20
Jackson, MS MSA	180	21
Jacksonville, FL MSA	180	21
Kansas City, MO – KS MSA	175	22
Buffalo – Niagara Falls, NY CMSA	174	23

Source: U.S. Department of Commerce, Bureau of the Census, Data User Services Division, *1990 Census of Population and Housing, Equal Employment Opportunity File, CD-90-EE0-1, January 1993,* CD-ROM.

★1213★

Occupations, By Race/Sex

Top 25 MSAs For Employment As Firefighting Occupations, 1990: Whites

MSA/CMSA	Employees per 100,000 pop.	Rank
Las Vegas, NV MSA	17,799	1
Los Angeles – Anaheim – Riverside, CA CMSA	9,099	2
Boston – Lawrence – Salem, MA – NH CMSA	7,632	3
Chicago – Gary – Lake County, IL – IN – WI CMSA	7,312	4

[Continued]

★1213★

Top 25 MSAs For Employment As Firefighting Occupations, 1990: Whites
[Continued]

MSA/CMSA	Employees per 100,000 pop.	Rank
San Francisco – Oakland – San Jose, CA CMSA	5,186	5
Miami – Fort Lauderdale, FL CMSA	3,203	6
Dallas – Fort Worth, TX CMSA	3,166	7
Detroit – Ann Arbor, MI CMSA	3,072	8
Philadelphia – Wilmington – Trenton, PA – NJ – DE – MD CMSA	2,902	9
Cleveland – Akron – Lorain, OH CMSA	2,788	10
Atlanta, GA MSA	2,440	11
Seattle – Tacoma, WA CMSA	2,424	12
Baltimore, MD MSA	2,393	13
Washington, DC – MD – VA MSA	2,351	14
Houston – Galveston – Brazoria, TX CMSA	2,330	15
Providence – Pawtucket – Fall River, RI – MA CMSA	2,297	16
San Diego, CA MSA	2,018	17
St. Louis, MO – IL MSA	1,783	18
Norfolk – Virginia Beach – Newport News, VA MSA	1,611	19
Tampa – St. Petersburg – Clearwater, FL MSA	1,611	19
Denver – Boulder, CO CMSA	1,586	20
Milwaukee – Racine, WI CMSA	1,554	21
Columbus, OH MSA	1,537	22
Kansas City, MO – KS MSA	1,514	23
Sacramento, CA MSA	1,511	24

Source: U.S. Department of Commerce, Bureau of the Census, Data User Services Division, *1990 Census of Population and Housing, Equal Employment Opportunity File, CD-90-EE0-1, January 1993,* CD-ROM.

★1214★

Occupations, By Race/Sex

Top 25 MSAs For Employment As Fishers, 1990: Blacks

MSA/CMSA	Employees per 100,000 pop.	Rank
New Orleans, LA MSA	94	1
New York – Northern New Jersey – Long Island, NY – NJ – CT CMSA	73	2
Houston – Galveston – Brazoria, TX CMSA	64	3
Seattle – Tacoma, WA CMSA	54	4
Beaumont – Port Arthur, TX MSA	53	5
Pascagoula, MS MSA	50	6
New Orleans, LA MSA	49	7
Baltimore, MD MSA	39	8
Norfolk – Virginia Beach – Newport News, VA MSA	34	9

[Continued]

★1214★

Top 25 MSAs For Employment As Fishers, 1990: Blacks

[Continued]

MSA/CMSA	Employees per 100,000 pop.	Rank
Miami – Fort Lauderdale, FL CMSA	33	10
Detroit – Ann Arbor, MI CMSA	33	10
Los Angeles – Anaheim – Riverside, CA CMSA	30	11
Lafayette, LA MSA	29	12
Charleston, SC MSA	27	13
Lake Charles, LA MSA	26	14
San Francisco – Oakland – San Jose, CA CMSA	25	15
Fort Myers – Cape CoraL, Fl MSA	24	16
Jacksonville, FL MSA	23	17
Philadelphia – Wilmington – Trenton, PA – NJ – DE – MD CMSA	23	17
Tampa – St. Petersburg – Clearwater, FL MSA	21	18
Atlanta, GA MSA	15	19
Atlantic City, NJ MSA	14	20
Washington, DC – MD – VA MSA	13	21
Kansas City, MO – KS MSA	12	22
Corpus Christi, TX MSA	10	23

Source: U.S. Department of Commerce, Bureau of the Census, Data User Services Division, *1990 Census of Population and Housing, Equal Employment Opportunity File, CD-90-EE0-1, January 1993,* CD-ROM.

★1215★

Occupations, By Race/Sex

Top 25 MSAs For Employment As Fishers, 1990: Whites

MSA/CMSA	Employees per 100,000 pop.	Rank
Fort Pierce, FL MSA	1,797	1
Boston – Lawrence – Salem, MA – NH CMSA	1,324	2
New York – Northern New Jersey – Long Island, NY – NJ – CT CMSA	1,283	3
Providence – Pawtucket – Fall River, RI – MA CMSA	1,203	4
New Orleans, LA MSA	919	5
Houma – Thibodaux, LA MSA	843	6
Los Angeles – Anaheim – Riverside, CA CMSA	829	7
New Bedford, MA MSA	816	8
Mobile, AL MSA	661	9
Norfolk – Virginia Beach – Newport News, VA MSA	655	10
San Diego, CA MSA	568	11
Tampa – St. Petersburg – Clearwater, FL MSA	561	12
Miami – Fort Lauderdale, FL CMSA	532	13

[Continued]

★1215★

Top 25 MSAs For Employment As Fishers, 1990: Whites

[Continued]

MSA/CMSA	Employees per 100,000 pop.	Rank
San Francisco – Oakland – San Jose, CA CMSA	528	14
Houston – Galveston – Brazoria, TX CMSA	490	15
Bellingham, WA MSA	482	16
Anchorage, AK MSA	430	17
Jacksonville, FL MSA	402	18
Portland, ME MSA	352	19
Brownsville – Harlingen, TX MSA	339	20
Atlantic City, NJ MSA	328	21
Fort Myers – Cape CoraL, Fl MSA	312	22
Portsmouth – Dover – Rochester, NH – ME MSA	281	23
Panama City, FL MSA	272	24
Baltimore, MD MSA	269	25

Source: U.S. Department of Commerce, Bureau of the Census, Data User Services Division, *1990 Census of Population and Housing, Equal Employment Opportunity File, CD-90-EE0-1, January 1993,* CD-ROM.

★1216★

Occupations, By Race/Sex

Top 25 MSAs For Employment As Foreign Language Teachers, 1990: Blacks

MSA/CMSA	Employees per 100,000 pop.	Rank
Lafayette – West Lafayette, IN MSA	29	1
Philadelphia – Wilmington – Trenton, PA – NJ – DE – MD CMSA	29	1
Boston – Lawrence – Salem, MA – NH CMSA	19	2
Baltimore, MD MSA	15	3
State College, PA MSA	14	4
Charlotte – Gastonia – Rock Hill, NC – SC MSA	13	5
Miami – Fort Lauderdale, FL CMSA	11	6
Atlanta, GA MSA	9	7
Norfolk – Virginia Beach – Newport News, VA MSA	8	8
Little Rock – North Little Rock, AR MSA	7	9
Minneapolis – St. Paul, MN – WI MSA	7	9
Dallas – Fort Worth, TX CMSA	7	9
Cleveland – Akron – Lorain, OH CMSA	7	9
Athens, GA MSA	7	9
San Francisco – Oakland – San Jose, CA CMSA	6	10
Jackson, MS MSA	6	10
Fayetteville, NC MSA	6	10

[Continued]

★1216★

Top 25 MSAs For Employment As Foreign Language Teachers, 1990: Blacks

[Continued]

MSA/CMSA	Employees per 100,000 pop.	Rank
Washington, DC – MD – VA MSA	6	10
New Haven – Meriden, CT MSA	5	11
Columbia, SC MSA	4	12
Gainesville, FL MSA	0	13
Houma – Thibodaux, LA MSA	0	13
Hartford – New Britain – Middletown, CT CMSA	0	13
Houston – Galveston – Brazoria, TX CMSA	0	13
Honolulu, HI MSA	0	13

Source: U.S. Department of Commerce, Bureau of the Census, Data User Services Division, *1990 Census of Population and Housing, Equal Employment Opportunity File, CD-90-EE0-1, January 1993,* CD-ROM.

★1217★

Occupations, By Race/Sex

Top 25 MSAs For Employment As Foreign Language Teachers, 1990: Whites

MSA/CMSA	Employees per 100,000 pop.	Rank
Providence – Pawtucket – Fall River, RI – MA CMSA	427	1
Washington, DC – MD – VA MSA	281	2
Los Angeles – Anaheim – Riverside, CA CMSA	277	3
San Francisco – Oakland – San Jose, CA CMSA	271	4
Boston – Lawrence – Salem, MA – NH CMSA	254	5
Salinas – Seaside – Monterey, CA MSA	233	6
Austin, TX MSA	231	7
Provo – Orem, UT MSA	222	8
Minneapolis – St. Paul, MN – WI MSA	160	9
Philadelphia – Wilmington – Trenton, PA – NJ – DE – MD CMSA	159	10
Chicago – Gary – Lake County, IL – IN – WI CMSA	152	11
Detroit – Ann Arbor, MI CMSA	149	12
San Diego, CA MSA	141	13
Cincinnati – Hamilton, OH – KY – IN CMSA	116	14
Raleigh – Durham, NC MSA	113	15
Pittsburgh – Beaver Valley, PA CMSA	111	16
Champaign – Urbana – Rantoul, IL MSA	111	16
Seattle – Tacoma, WA CMSA	105	17
Eugene – Springfield, OR MSA	98	18
Baltimore, MD MSA	95	19
Madison, WI MSA	92	20

[Continued]

★1217★

Top 25 MSAs For Employment As Foreign Language Teachers, 1990: Whites

[Continued]

MSA/CMSA	Employees per 100,000 pop.	Rank
Dallas – Fort Worth, TX CMSA	91	21
Columbus, OH MSA	86	22
Buffalo – Niagara Falls, NY CMSA	80	23
Norfolk – Virginia Beach – Newport News, VA MSA	80	23

Source: U.S. Department of Commerce, Bureau of the Census, Data User Services Division, *1990 Census of Population and Housing, Equal Employment Opportunity File, CD-90-EE0-1, January 1993,* CD-ROM.

★1218★

Occupations, By Race/Sex

Top 25 MSAs For Employment As Forestry and Conservation Scientists, 1990: Blacks

MSA/CMSA	Employees per 100,000 pop.	Rank
Norfolk – Virginia Beach – Newport News, VA MSA	87	1
San Diego, CA MSA	52	2
Detroit – Ann Arbor, MI CMSA	50	3
San Francisco – Oakland – San Jose, CA CMSA	27	4
Greensboro – Winston-Salem – High Point, NC MSA	21	5
Santa Barbara – Santa Maria – Lompoc, CA MSA	20	6
Fresno, CA MSA	19	7
Dallas – Fort Worth, TX CMSA	18	8
Atlanta, GA MSA	18	8
Baltimore, MD MSA	16	9
Chicago – Gary – Lake County, IL – IN – WI CMSA	15	10
Jackson, TN MSA	15	10
Portland – Vancouver, OR – WA CMSA	14	11
Jacksonville, FL MSA	14	11
Birmingham, AL MSA	13	12
Milwaukee – Racine, WI CMSA	13	12
Jackson, MS MSA	11	13
Raleigh – Durham, NC MSA	10	14
Terre Haute, IN MSA	10	14
Miami – Fort Lauderdale, FL CMSA	9	15
Nashville, TN MSA	8	16
Memphis, TN – AR – MS MSA	8	16
Toledo, OH MSA	8	16
Fort Pierce, FL MSA	8	16
Alexandria, LA MSA	8	16

Source: U.S. Department of Commerce, Bureau of the Census, Data User Services Division, *1990 Census of Population and Housing, Equal Employment Opportunity File, CD-90-EE0-1, January 1993,* CD-ROM.

★1219★

Occupations, By Race/Sex

Top 25 MSAs For Employment As Forestry and Conservation Scientists, 1990: Whites

MSA/CMSA	Employees per 100,000 pop.	Rank
Tampa – St. Petersburg – Clearwater, FL MSA	522	1
Seattle – Tacoma, WA CMSA	427	2
Los Angeles – Anaheim – Riverside, CA CMSA	380	3
Washington, DC – MD – VA MSA	372	4
San Francisco – Oakland – San Jose, CA CMSA	340	5
Sacramento, CA MSA	323	6
New York – Northern New Jersey – Long Island, NY – NJ – CT CMSA	322	7
Eugene – Springfield, OR MSA	261	8
Philadelphia – Wilmington – Trenton, PA – NJ – DE – MD CMSA	253	9
Minneapolis – St. Paul, MN – WI MSA	230	10
Medford, OR MSA	216	11
Boston – Lawrence – Salem, MA – NH CMSA	192	12
Chicago – Gary – Lake County, IL – IN – WI CMSA	191	13
Atlanta, GA MSA	185	14
Duluth, MN – WI MSA	179	15
Denver – Boulder, CO CMSA	164	16
Olympia, WA MSA	162	17
Fresno, CA MSA	149	18
Baltimore, MD MSA	144	19
Salt Lake City – Ogden, UT MSA	129	20
Milwaukee – Racine, WI CMSA	124	21
Fort Collins – Loveland, CO MSA	120	22
Houston – Galveston – Brazoria, TX CMSA	117	23
Redding, CA MSA	113	24
Richmond – Petersburg, VA MSA	107	25

Source: U.S. Department of Commerce, Bureau of the Census, Data User Services Division, 1990 Census of Population and Housing, Equal Employment Opportunity File, CD-90-EEO-1, January 1993, CD-ROM.

★1220★

Occupations, By Race/Sex

Top 25 MSAs For Employment As Funeral Directors, 1990: Blacks

MSA/CMSA	Employees per 100,000 pop.	Rank
San Diego, CA MSA	458	1
Philadelphia – Wilmington – Trenton, PA – NJ – DE – MD CMSA	211	2
Chicago – Gary – Lake County, IL – IN – WI CMSA	169	3
Houston – Galveston – Brazoria, TX CMSA	160	4

[Continued]

★1220★

Top 25 MSAs For Employment As Funeral Directors, 1990: Blacks

[Continued]

MSA/CMSA	Employees per 100,000 pop.	Rank
Memphis, TN – AR – MS MSA	127	5
Detroit – Ann Arbor, MI CMSA	123	6
Atlanta, GA MSA	119	7
St. Louis, MO – IL MSA	114	8
Washington, DC – MD – VA MSA	88	9
San Francisco – Oakland – San Jose, CA CMSA	74	10
Baltimore, MD MSA	65	11
Los Angeles – Anaheim – Riverside, CA CMSA	64	12
Richmond – Petersburg, VA MSA	60	13
Dallas – Fort Worth, TX CMSA	55	14
Beaumont – Port Arthur, TX MSA	55	14
Cleveland – Akron – Lorain, OH CMSA	53	15
Charlotte – Gastonia – Rock Hill, NC – SC MSA	52	16
Kansas City, MO – KS MSA	48	17
Norfolk – Virginia Beach – Newport News, VA MSA	43	18
Greenville – Spartanburg, SC MSA	41	19
Miami – Fort Lauderdale, FL CMSA	40	20
Montgomery, AL MSA	40	20
Macon – Warner Robins, GA MSA	39	21
Toledo, OH MSA	35	22
Omaha, NE – IA MSA	35	22

Source: U.S. Department of Commerce, Bureau of the Census, Data User Services Division, 1990 Census of Population and Housing, Equal Employment Opportunity File, CD-90-EEO-1, January 1993, CD-ROM.

★1221★

Occupations, By Race/Sex

Top 25 MSAs For Employment As Funeral Directors, 1990: Whites

MSA/CMSA	Employees per 100,000 pop.	Rank
Milwaukee – Racine, WI CMSA	2,643	1
Chicago – Gary – Lake County, IL – IN – WI CMSA	1,151	2
Boston – Lawrence – Salem, MA – NH CMSA	815	3
Philadelphia – Wilmington – Trenton, PA – NJ – DE – MD CMSA	812	4
Los Angeles – Anaheim – Riverside, CA CMSA	763	5
Detroit – Ann Arbor, MI CMSA	632	6
Cleveland – Akron – Lorain, OH CMSA	577	7
San Francisco – Oakland – San Jose, CA CMSA	558	8

[Continued]

★1221★

Top 25 MSAs For Employment As Funeral Directors, 1990: Whites
[Continued]

MSA/CMSA	Employees per 100,000 pop.	Rank
Pittsburgh – Beaver Valley, PA CMSA	533	9
Dallas – Fort Worth, TX CMSA	498	10
Milwaukee – Racine, WI CMSA	418	11
St. Louis, MO – IL MSA	353	12
Tampa – St. Petersburg – Clearwater, FL MSA	327	13
Washington, DC – MD – VA MSA	312	14
Houston – Galveston – Brazoria, TX CMSA	310	15
Kansas City, MO – KS MSA	306	16
Scranton – Wilkes-Barre, PA MSA	301	17
Louisville, KY – IN MSA	282	18
Miami – Fort Lauderdale, FL CMSA	281	19
Cincinnati – Hamilton, OH – KY – IN CMSA	277	20
Baltimore, MD MSA	276	21
Minneapolis – St. Paul, MN – WI MSA	265	22
Buffalo – Niagara Falls, NY CMSA	261	23
Atlanta, GA MSA	254	24
Seattle – Tacoma, WA CMSA	239	25

Source: U.S. Department of Commerce, Bureau of the Census, Data User Services Division, *1990 Census of Population and Housing, Equal Employment Opportunity File, CD-90-EE0-1,* January 1993, CD-ROM.

★1222★
Occupations, By Race/Sex

Top 25 MSAs For Employment As Garbage Collectors, 1990: Blacks

MSA/CMSA	Employees per 100,000 pop.	Rank
Jackson, MS MSA	2,602	1
Philadelphia – Wilmington – Trenton, PA – NJ – DE – MD CMSA	1,029	2
Miami – Fort Lauderdale, FL CMSA	793	3
Washington, DC – MD – VA MSA	718	4
Chicago – Gary – Lake County, IL – IN – WI CMSA	584	5
Atlanta, GA MSA	486	6
Houston – Galveston – Brazoria, TX CMSA	462	7
Baltimore, MD MSA	394	8
Charlotte – Gastonia – Rock Hill, NC – SC MSA	378	9
Memphis, TN – AR – MS MSA	311	10
Norfolk – Virginia Beach – Newport News, VA MSA	288	11
Jacksonville, FL MSA	276	12
Cleveland – Akron – Lorain, OH CMSA	268	13

[Continued]

★1222★

Top 25 MSAs For Employment As Garbage Collectors, 1990: Blacks
[Continued]

MSA/CMSA	Employees per 100,000 pop.	Rank
Dallas – Fort Worth, TX CMSA	248	14
Birmingham, AL MSA	241	15
San Francisco – Oakland – San Jose, CA CMSA	232	16
Detroit – Ann Arbor, MI CMSA	192	17
Los Angeles – Anaheim – Riverside, CA CMSA	184	18
New Orleans, LA MSA	169	19
Louisville, KY – IN MSA	167	20
Raleigh – Durham, NC MSA	149	21
Baton Rouge, LA MSA	142	22
Pittsburgh – Beaver Valley, PA CMSA	138	23
Richmond – Petersburg, VA MSA	128	24
West Palm Beach – Boca Raton – Delray Beach, FL MSA	124	25

Source: U.S. Department of Commerce, Bureau of the Census, Data User Services Division, *1990 Census of Population and Housing, Equal Employment Opportunity File, CD-90-EE0-1,* January 1993, CD-ROM.

★1223★
Occupations, By Race/Sex

Top 25 MSAs For Employment As Garbage Collectors, 1990: Whites

MSA/CMSA	Employees per 100,000 pop.	Rank
Brownsville – Harlingen, TX MSA	6,150	1
Chicago – Gary – Lake County, IL – IN – WI CMSA	1,238	2
San Francisco – Oakland – San Jose, CA CMSA	966	3
Los Angeles – Anaheim – Riverside, CA CMSA	953	4
Philadelphia – Wilmington – Trenton, PA – NJ – DE – MD CMSA	706	5
Boston – Lawrence – Salem, MA – NH CMSA	594	6
Pittsburgh – Beaver Valley, PA CMSA	494	7
Portland – Vancouver, OR – WA CMSA	425	8
Detroit – Ann Arbor, MI CMSA	392	9
Cleveland – Akron – Lorain, OH CMSA	388	10
Minneapolis – St. Paul, MN – WI MSA	351	11
Buffalo – Niagara Falls, NY CMSA	350	12
Milwaukee – Racine, WI CMSA	326	13
Providence – Pawtucket – Fall River, RI – MA CMSA	254	14
Baltimore, MD MSA	251	15
Houston – Galveston – Brazoria, TX CMSA	249	16

[Continued]

★1223★

Top 25 MSAs For Employment As Garbage Collectors, 1990: Whites

[Continued]

MSA/CMSA	Employees per 100,000 pop.	Rank
Cincinnati – Hamilton, OH – KY – IN CMSA	235	17
El Paso, TX MSA	229	18
Dallas – Fort Worth, TX CMSA	227	19
Albany – Schenectady – Troy, NY MSA	220	20
Atlanta, GA MSA	213	21
Seattle – Tacoma, WA CMSA	208	22
Miami – Fort Lauderdale, FL CMSA	207	23
Scranton – Wilkes-Barre, PA MSA	189	24
San Antonio, TX MSA	178	25

Source: U.S. Department of Commerce, Bureau of the Census, Data User Services Division, 1990 Census of Population and Housing, Equal Employment Opportunity File, CD-90-EE0-1, January 1993, CD-ROM.

★1224★

Occupations, By Race/Sex

Top 25 MSAs For Employment As Geologists and Geodesists, 1990: Blacks

MSA/CMSA	Employees per 100,000 pop.	Rank
Rochester, NY MSA	119	1
Washington, DC – MD – VA MSA	59	2
Dallas – Fort Worth, TX CMSA	38	3
Chicago – Gary – Lake County, IL – IN – WI CMSA	30	4
New Orleans, LA MSA	24	5
Austin, TX MSA	21	6
Denver – Boulder, CO CMSA	16	7
New York – Northern New Jersey – Long Island, NY – NJ – CT CMSA	16	7
Raleigh – Durham, NC MSA	16	7
Los Angeles – Anaheim – Riverside, CA CMSA	15	8
Tulsa, OK MSA	15	8
Toledo, OH MSA	15	8
Atlanta, GA MSA	14	9
Charlotte – Gastonia – Rock Hill, NC – SC MSA	13	10
San Francisco – Oakland – San Jose, CA CMSA	12	11
Jackson, MS MSA	11	12
Albany – Schenectady – Troy, NY MSA	11	12
Seattle – Tacoma, WA CMSA	11	12
Midland, TX MSA	10	13
Tucson, AZ MSA	10	13
St. Louis, MO – IL MSA	10	13
Jackson, TN MSA	10	13
Shreveport, LA MSA	9	14

[Continued]

★1224★

Top 25 MSAs For Employment As Geologists and Geodesists, 1990: Blacks

[Continued]

MSA/CMSA	Employees per 100,000 pop.	Rank
Birmingham, AL MSA	9	14
Lafayette, LA MSA	8	15

Source: U.S. Department of Commerce, Bureau of the Census, Data User Services Division, 1990 Census of Population and Housing, Equal Employment Opportunity File, CD-90-EE0-1, January 1993, CD-ROM.

★1225★

Occupations, By Race/Sex

Top 25 MSAs For Employment As Geologists and Geodesists, 1990: Whites

MSA/CMSA	Employees per 100,000 pop.	Rank
Seattle – Tacoma, WA CMSA	6,930	1
Denver – Boulder, CO CMSA	3,522	2
Los Angeles – Anaheim – Riverside, CA CMSA	2,449	3
Dallas – Fort Worth, TX CMSA	2,226	4
San Francisco – Oakland – San Jose, CA CMSA	1,987	5
New Orleans, LA MSA	1,594	6
Washington, DC – MD – VA MSA	1,236	7
New York – Northern New Jersey – Long Island, NY – NJ – CT CMSA	1,183	8
Midland, TX MSA	1,135	9
Oklahoma City, OK MSA	1,005	10
Philadelphia – Wilmington – Trenton, PA – NJ – DE – MD CMSA	786	11
Boston – Lawrence – Salem, MA – NH CMSA	644	12
San Diego, CA MSA	641	13
Seattle – Tacoma, WA CMSA	596	14
Tulsa, OK MSA	569	15
Atlanta, GA MSA	540	16
Reno, NV MSA	533	17
Austin, TX MSA	531	18
Lafayette, LA MSA	523	19
Sacramento, CA MSA	513	20
Anchorage, AK MSA	432	21
Minneapolis – St. Paul, MN – WI MSA	419	22
Corpus Christi, TX MSA	401	23
Baltimore, MD MSA	360	24
Phoenix, AZ MSA	338	25

Source: U.S. Department of Commerce, Bureau of the Census, Data User Services Division, 1990 Census of Population and Housing, Equal Employment Opportunity File, CD-90-EE0-1, January 1993, CD-ROM.

★1226★

Occupations, By Race/Sex

Top 25 MSAs For Employment As Hairdressers and Cosmetologists, 1990: Blacks

MSA/CMSA	Employees per 100,000 pop.	Rank
Milwaukee – Racine, WI CMSA	5,290	1
Los Angeles – Anaheim – Riverside, CA CMSA	3,455	2
Chicago – Gary – Lake County, IL – IN – WI CMSA	3,202	3
Washington, DC – MD – VA MSA	2,957	4
Houston – Galveston – Brazoria, TX CMSA	2,179	5
Atlanta, GA MSA	2,124	6
Detroit – Ann Arbor, MI CMSA	1,936	7
Dallas – Fort Worth, TX CMSA	1,928	8
Philadelphia – Wilmington – Trenton, PA – NJ – DE – MD CMSA	1,833	9
Baltimore, MD MSA	1,462	10
Miami – Fort Lauderdale, FL CMSA	1,437	11
San Francisco – Oakland – San Jose, CA CMSA	1,352	12
Cleveland – Akron – Lorain, OH CMSA	1,054	13
Norfolk – Virginia Beach – Newport News, VA MSA	1,046	14
Memphis, TN – AR – MS MSA	998	15
St. Louis, MO – IL MSA	822	16
Richmond – Petersburg, VA MSA	807	17
Birmingham, AL MSA	660	18
New Orleans, LA MSA	617	19
Charlotte – Gastonia – Rock Hill, NC – SC MSA	544	20
Boston – Lawrence – Salem, MA – NH CMSA	514	21
Raleigh – Durham, NC MSA	487	22
Kansas City, MO – KS MSA	476	23
Cincinnati – Hamilton, OH – KY – IN CMSA	461	24
Jacksonville, FL MSA	454	25

Source: U.S. Department of Commerce, Bureau of the Census, Data User Services Division, *1990 Census of Population and Housing, Equal Employment Opportunity File, CD-90-EE0-1, January 1993,* CD-ROM.

★1227★

Occupations, By Race/Sex

Top 25 MSAs For Employment As Hairdressers and Cosmetologists, 1990: Whites

MSA/CMSA	Employees per 100,000 pop.	Rank
Oklahoma City, OK MSA	36,856	1
Los Angeles – Anaheim – Riverside, CA CMSA	31,242	2
Chicago – Gary – Lake County, IL – IN – WI CMSA	18,159	3
Philadelphia – Wilmington – Trenton, PA – NJ – DE – MD CMSA	13,208	4

[Continued]

★1227★

Top 25 MSAs For Employment As Hairdressers and Cosmetologists, 1990: Whites

[Continued]

MSA/CMSA	Employees per 100,000 pop.	Rank
San Francisco – Oakland – San Jose, CA CMSA	12,930	5
Detroit – Ann Arbor, MI CMSA	11,540	6
Boston – Lawrence – Salem, MA – NH CMSA	11,121	7
Miami – Fort Lauderdale, FL CMSA	9,936	8
Dallas – Fort Worth, TX CMSA	9,382	9
Minneapolis – St. Paul, MN – WI MSA	7,029	10
Pittsburgh – Beaver Valley, PA CMSA	6,964	11
Washington, DC – MD – VA MSA	6,939	12
St. Louis, MO – IL MSA	6,774	13
Seattle – Tacoma, WA CMSA	6,743	14
Houston – Galveston – Brazoria, TX CMSA	6,403	15
Phoenix, AZ MSA	6,387	16
Cleveland – Akron – Lorain, OH CMSA	6,334	17
Tampa – St. Petersburg – Clearwater, FL MSA	6,323	18
Atlanta, GA MSA	6,268	19
San Diego, CA MSA	6,061	20
Baltimore, MD MSA	5,223	21
Denver – Boulder, CO CMSA	4,977	22
Portland – Vancouver, OR – WA CMSA	4,574	23
Cincinnati – Hamilton, OH – KY – IN CMSA	4,201	24
Kansas City, MO – KS MSA	4,160	25

Source: U.S. Department of Commerce, Bureau of the Census, Data User Services Division, *1990 Census of Population and Housing, Equal Employment Opportunity File, CD-90-EE0-1, January 1993,* CD-ROM.

★1228★

Occupations, By Race/Sex

Top 25 MSAs For Employment As History Teachers, 1990: Blacks

MSA/CMSA	Employees per 100,000 pop.	Rank
Odessa, TX MSA	18	1
Champaign – Urbana – Rantoul, IL MSA	14	2
Hartford – New Britain – Middletown, CT CMSA	12	3
New Orleans, LA MSA	11	4
Raleigh – Durham, NC MSA	11	4
Houston – Galveston – Brazoria, TX CMSA	10	5
Cleveland – Akron – Lorain, OH CMSA	8	6
Atlanta, GA MSA	8	6

[Continued]

★1228★

Top 25 MSAs For Employment As History Teachers, 1990: Blacks
[Continued]

MSA/CMSA	Employees per 100,000 pop.	Rank
Philadelphia – Wilmington – Trenton, PA – NJ – DE – MD CMSA	8	6
Rochester, NY MSA	7	7
Macon – Warner Robins, GA MSA	7	7
San Diego, CA MSA	6	8
Boston – Lawrence – Salem, MA – NH CMSA	5	9
San Francisco – Oakland – San Jose, CA CMSA	3	10
Orlando, FL MSA	0	11
Parkersburg – Marietta, WV – OH MSA	0	11
Panama City, FL MSA	0	11
Oklahoma City, OK MSA	0	11
Ocala, FL MSA	0	11
Nashville, TN MSA	0	11
Norfolk – Virginia Beach – Newport News, VA MSA	0	11
Naples, FL MSA	0	11
New Bedford, MA MSA	0	11
Owensboro, KY MSA	0	11
Pensacola, FL MSA	0	11

Source: U.S. Department of Commerce, Bureau of the Census, Data User Services Division, *1990 Census of Population and Housing, Equal Employment Opportunity File, CD-90-EE0-1, January 1993,* CD-ROM.

★1229★
Occupations, By Race/Sex

Top 25 MSAs For Employment As History Teachers, 1990: Whites

MSA/CMSA	Employees per 100,000 pop.	Rank
Rochester, NY MSA	227	1
San Francisco – Oakland – San Jose, CA CMSA	149	2
Los Angeles – Anaheim – Riverside, CA CMSA	148	3
Philadelphia – Wilmington – Trenton, PA – NJ – DE – MD CMSA	100	4
Boston – Lawrence – Salem, MA – NH CMSA	97	5
Houston – Galveston – Brazoria, TX CMSA	85	6
Chicago – Gary – Lake County, IL – IN – WI CMSA	73	7
Washington, DC – MD – VA MSA	72	8
Cleveland – Akron – Lorain, OH CMSA	67	9
Milwaukee – Racine, WI CMSA	62	10
Dallas – Fort Worth, TX CMSA	56	11
St. Louis, MO – IL MSA	54	12

[Continued]

★1229★

Top 25 MSAs For Employment As History Teachers, 1990: Whites
[Continued]

MSA/CMSA	Employees per 100,000 pop.	Rank
San Diego, CA MSA	47	13
Nashville, TN MSA	46	14
Minneapolis – St. Paul, MN – WI MSA	46	14
Columbus, OH MSA	44	15
Muncie, IN MSA	37	16
Detroit – Ann Arbor, MI CMSA	37	16
Norfolk – Virginia Beach – Newport News, VA MSA	36	17
Iowa City, IA MSA	31	18
Worcester, MA MSA	30	19
Madison, WI MSA	30	19
Richmond – Petersburg, VA MSA	29	20
Albuquerque, NM MSA	29	20
Portland – Vancouver, OR – WA CMSA	29	20

Source: U.S. Department of Commerce, Bureau of the Census, Data User Services Division, *1990 Census of Population and Housing, Equal Employment Opportunity File, CD-90-EE0-1, January 1993,* CD-ROM.

★1230★
Occupations, By Race/Sex

Top 25 MSAs For Employment As Home Economics Teachers, 1990: Blacks

MSA/CMSA	Employees per 100,000 pop.	Rank
Honolulu, HI MSA	22	1
Philadelphia – Wilmington – Trenton, PA – NJ – DE – MD CMSA	20	2
New York – Northern New Jersey – Long Island, NY – NJ – CT CMSA	13	3
Los Angeles – Anaheim – Riverside, CA CMSA	12	4
Detroit – Ann Arbor, MI CMSA	10	5
Louisville, KY – IN MSA	9	6
Lake Charles, LA MSA	9	6
Cleveland – Akron – Lorain, OH CMSA	6	7
Portsmouth – Dover – Rochester, NH – ME MSA	0	8
Panama City, FL MSA	0	8
Ocala, FL MSA	0	8
Oklahoma City, OK MSA	0	8
Pittsfield, MA MSA	0	8
Owensboro, KY MSA	0	8
Orlando, FL MSA	0	8
Odessa, TX MSA	0	8
Olympia, WA MSA	0	8
Omaha, NE – IA MSA	0	8
Naples, FL MSA	0	8
Nashville, TN MSA	0	8

[Continued]

★1230★

Top 25 MSAs For Employment As Home Economics Teachers, 1990: Blacks

[Continued]

MSA/CMSA	Employees per 100,000 pop.	Rank
New Orleans, LA MSA	0	8
Parkersburg – Marietta, WV – OH MSA	0	8
Poughkeepsie, NY MSA	0	8
Reno, NV MSA	0	8
Pittsburgh – Beaver Valley, PA CMSA	0	8

Source: U.S. Department of Commerce, Bureau of the Census, Data User Services Division, *1990 Census of Population and Housing, Equal Employment Opportunity File, CD-90-EE0-1, January 1993,* CD-ROM.

★1231★

Occupations, By Race/Sex

Top 25 MSAs For Employment As Home Economics Teachers, 1990: Whites

MSA/CMSA	Employees per 100,000 pop.	Rank
Spokane, WA MSA	40	1
San Antonio, TX MSA	28	2
Cincinnati – Hamilton, OH – KY – IN CMSA	14	3
Philadelphia – Wilmington – Trenton, PA – NJ – DE – MD CMSA	12	4
Champaign – Urbana – Rantoul, IL MSA	11	5
St. Joseph, MO MSA	11	5
Tucson, AZ MSA	10	6
Greeley, CO MSA	10	6
Duluth, MN – WI MSA	10	6
Los Angeles – Anaheim – Riverside, CA CMSA	8	7
Knoxville, TN MSA	8	7
Detroit – Ann Arbor, MI CMSA	8	7
Johnstown, PA MSA	8	7
Anchorage, AK MSA	8	7
Austin, TX MSA	7	8
Sacramento, CA MSA	7	8
Greenville – Spartanburg, SC MSA	7	8
Rochester, MN MSA	7	8
Clarksville – Hopkinsville, TN – KY MSA	7	8
Allentown – Bethlehem – Easton, PA – NJ MSA	7	8
Nashville, TN MSA	6	9
Lafayette – West Lafayette, IN MSA	6	9
Appleton – Oshkosh – Neenah, WI MSA	5	10
Longview – Marshall, TX MSA	2	11
Springfield, IL MSA	1	12

Source: U.S. Department of Commerce, Bureau of the Census, Data User Services Division, *1990 Census of Population and Housing, Equal Employment Opportunity File, CD-90-EE0-1, January 1993,* CD-ROM.

★1232★

Occupations, By Race/Sex

Top 25 MSAs For Employment As Housekeepers and Butlers, 1990: Blacks

MSA/CMSA	Employees per 100,000 pop.	Rank
Shreveport, LA MSA	2,411	1
Philadelphia – Wilmington – Trenton, PA – NJ – DE – MD CMSA	401	2
Washington, DC – MD – VA MSA	401	2
Houston – Galveston – Brazoria, TX CMSA	322	3
Miami – Fort Lauderdale, FL CMSA	299	4
Los Angeles – Anaheim – Riverside, CA CMSA	275	5
Atlanta, GA MSA	265	6
New Orleans, LA MSA	260	7
Baltimore, MD MSA	259	8
Chicago – Gary – Lake County, IL – IN – WI CMSA	254	9
Memphis, TN – AR – MS MSA	199	10
Dallas – Fort Worth, TX CMSA	156	11
St. Louis, MO – IL MSA	145	12
West Palm Beach – Boca Raton – Delray Beach, FL MSA	141	13
San Francisco – Oakland – San Jose, CA CMSA	139	14
Charleston, SC MSA	139	14
Norfolk – Virginia Beach – Newport News, VA MSA	137	15
Detroit – Ann Arbor, MI CMSA	114	16
Richmond – Petersburg, VA MSA	102	17
Jacksonville, FL MSA	96	18
Mobile, AL MSA	95	19
Greenville – Spartanburg, SC MSA	94	20
Tampa – St. Petersburg – Clearwater, FL MSA	83	21
Columbia, SC MSA	81	22
Columbus, GA – AL MSA	72	23

Source: U.S. Department of Commerce, Bureau of the Census, Data User Services Division, *1990 Census of Population and Housing, Equal Employment Opportunity File, CD-90-EE0-1, January 1993,* CD-ROM.

★1233★

Occupations, By Race/Sex

Top 25 MSAs For Employment As Housekeepers and Butlers, 1990: Whites

MSA/CMSA	Employees per 100,000 pop.	Rank
Reno, NV MSA	2,115	1
Los Angeles – Anaheim – Riverside, CA CMSA	1,934	2
San Francisco – Oakland – San Jose, CA CMSA	625	3
Miami – Fort Lauderdale, FL CMSA	473	4

[Continued]

★1233★

Top 25 MSAs For Employment As Housekeepers and Butlers, 1990: Whites

[Continued]

MSA/CMSA	Employees per 100,000 pop.	Rank
Washington, DC – MD – VA MSA	462	5
San Diego, CA MSA	358	6
Houston – Galveston – Brazoria, TX CMSA	348	7
Dallas – Fort Worth, TX CMSA	247	8
Chicago – Gary – Lake County, IL – IN – WI CMSA	228	9
Philadelphia – Wilmington – Trenton, PA – NJ – DE – MD CMSA	210	10
Boston – Lawrence – Salem, MA – NH CMSA	198	11
Detroit – Ann Arbor, MI CMSA	160	12
Portland – Vancouver, OR – WA CMSA	143	13
West Palm Beach – Boca Raton – Delray Beach, FL MSA	139	14
Phoenix, AZ MSA	135	15
Denver – Boulder, CO CMSA	107	16
San Antonio, TX MSA	106	17
Providence – Pawtucket – Fall River, RI – MA CMSA	96	18
Indianapolis, IN MSA	96	18
Corpus Christi, TX MSA	94	19
Seattle – Tacoma, WA CMSA	93	20
Mcallen – Edinburg – Mission, TX MSA	93	20
Albany – Schenectady – Troy, NY MSA	90	21
Tampa – St. Petersburg – Clearwater, FL MSA	84	22
Visalia – Tulare – Porterville, CA MSA	78	23

Source: U.S. Department of Commerce, Bureau of the Census, Data User Services Division, *1990 Census of Population and Housing, Equal Employment Opportunity File, CD-90-EE0-1, January 1993,* CD-ROM.

★1234★

Occupations, By Race/Sex

Top 25 MSAs For Employment As Hunters and Trappers, 1990: Blacks

MSA/CMSA	Employees per 100,000 pop.	Rank
Chicago – Gary – Lake County, IL – IN – WI CMSA	22	1
Cleveland – Akron – Lorain, OH CMSA	13	2
Los Angeles – Anaheim – Riverside, CA CMSA	11	3
Tampa – St. Petersburg – Clearwater, FL MSA	10	4
Charleston, SC MSA	8	5
Norfolk – Virginia Beach – Newport News, VA MSA	8	5

[Continued]

★1234★

Top 25 MSAs For Employment As Hunters and Trappers, 1990: Blacks

[Continued]

MSA/CMSA	Employees per 100,000 pop.	Rank
Orlando, FL MSA	7	6
Ocala, FL MSA	0	7
Panama City, FL MSA	0	7
Olympia, WA MSA	0	7
Omaha, NE – IA MSA	0	7
Parkersburg – Marietta, WV – OH MSA	0	7
Oklahoma City, OK MSA	0	7
New Haven – Meriden, CT MSA	0	7
New London – Norwich, CT – RI MSA	0	7
New Orleans, LA MSA	0	7
Owensboro, KY MSA	0	7
Montgomery, AL MSA	0	7
Phoenix, AZ MSA	0	7
Poughkeepsie, NY MSA	0	7
Reading, PA MSA	0	7
Provo – Orem, UT MSA	0	7
Rapid City, SD MSA	0	7
Redding, CA MSA	0	7
Raleigh – Durham, NC MSA	0	7

Source: U.S. Department of Commerce, Bureau of the Census, Data User Services Division, *1990 Census of Population and Housing, Equal Employment Opportunity File, CD-90-EE0-1, January 1993,* CD-ROM.

★1235★

Occupations, By Race/Sex

Top 25 MSAs For Employment As Hunters and Trappers, 1990: Whites

MSA/CMSA	Employees per 100,000 pop.	Rank
Corpus Christi, TX MSA	123	1
New York – Northern New Jersey – Long Island, NY – NJ – CT CMSA	59	2
Dallas – Fort Worth, TX CMSA	51	3
Chicago – Gary – Lake County, IL – IN – WI CMSA	32	4
Seattle – Tacoma, WA CMSA	30	5
San Francisco – Oakland – San Jose, CA CMSA	29	6
San Diego, CA MSA	29	6
Denver – Boulder, CO CMSA	24	7
Orlando, FL MSA	24	7
Philadelphia – Wilmington – Trenton, PA – NJ – DE – MD CMSA	21	8
Minneapolis – St. Paul, MN – WI MSA	19	9
Olympia, WA MSA	19	9
Milwaukee – Racine, WI CMSA	18	10
Atlanta, GA MSA	18	10
Houston – Galveston – Brazoria, TX CMSA	18	10

[Continued]

★1235★

Top 25 MSAs For Employment As Hunters and Trappers, 1990: Whites
[Continued]

MSA/CMSA	Employees per 100,000 pop.	Rank
Salt Lake City – Ogden, UT MSA	16	11
Eugene – Springfield, OR MSA	15	12
Dayton – Springfield, OH MSA	15	12
Cincinnati – Hamilton, OH – KY – IN CMSA	15	12
Augusta, GA – SC MSA	14	13
Miami – Fort Lauderdale, FL CMSA	14	13
Albany – Schenectady – Troy, NY MSA	13	14
Fort Pierce, FL MSA	13	14
New London – Norwich, CT – RI MSA	13	14
Anchorage, AK MSA	12	15

Source: U.S. Department of Commerce, Bureau of the Census, Data User Services Division, *1990 Census of Population and Housing, Equal Employment Opportunity File, CD-90-EE0-1,* January 1993, CD-ROM.

★1236★
Occupations, By Race/Sex

Top 25 MSAs For Employment As Insurance Adjusters, Examiners, and Investigators, 1990: Blacks

MSA/CMSA	Employees per 100,000 pop.	Rank
Kansas City, MO – KS MSA	5,031	1
Los Angeles – Anaheim – Riverside, CA CMSA	2,692	2
Philadelphia – Wilmington – Trenton, PA – NJ – DE – MD CMSA	2,391	3
Chicago – Gary – Lake County, IL – IN – WI CMSA	2,372	4
Washington, DC – MD – VA MSA	2,135	5
Detroit – Ann Arbor, MI CMSA	1,924	6
Atlanta, GA MSA	1,654	7
Dallas – Fort Worth, TX CMSA	1,455	8
Jacksonville, FL MSA	1,140	9
Baltimore, MD MSA	1,135	10
San Francisco – Oakland – San Jose, CA CMSA	1,100	11
Houston – Galveston – Brazoria, TX CMSA	852	12
Columbus, OH MSA	845	13
St. Louis, MO – IL MSA	789	14
Hartford – New Britain – Middletown, CT CMSA	727	15
Birmingham, AL MSA	707	16
Boston – Lawrence – Salem, MA – NH CMSA	608	17
Cleveland – Akron – Lorain, OH CMSA	601	18

[Continued]

★1236★

Top 25 MSAs For Employment As Insurance Adjusters, Examiners, and Investigators, 1990: Blacks
[Continued]

MSA/CMSA	Employees per 100,000 pop.	Rank
Richmond – Petersburg, VA MSA	598	19
Indianapolis, IN MSA	551	20
Kansas City, MO – KS MSA	516	21
Tampa – St. Petersburg – Clearwater, FL MSA	413	22
Pittsburgh – Beaver Valley, PA CMSA	404	23
Milwaukee – Racine, WI CMSA	403	24
Louisville, KY – IN MSA	388	25

Source: U.S. Department of Commerce, Bureau of the Census, Data User Services Division, *1990 Census of Population and Housing, Equal Employment Opportunity File, CD-90-EE0-1,* January 1993, CD-ROM.

★1237★
Occupations, By Race/Sex

Top 25 MSAs For Employment As Insurance Adjusters, Examiners, and Investigators, 1990: Whites

MSA/CMSA	Employees per 100,000 pop.	Rank
Cincinnati – Hamilton, OH – KY – IN CMSA	21,891	1
Los Angeles – Anaheim – Riverside, CA CMSA	14,652	2
Philadelphia – Wilmington – Trenton, PA – NJ – DE – MD CMSA	10,946	3
Chicago – Gary – Lake County, IL – IN – WI CMSA	10,802	4
Dallas – Fort Worth, TX CMSA	7,667	5
Boston – Lawrence – Salem, MA – NH CMSA	7,645	6
San Francisco – Oakland – San Jose, CA CMSA	6,260	7
Hartford – New Britain – Middletown, CT CMSA	5,936	8
Minneapolis – St. Paul, MN – WI MSA	5,932	9
Detroit – Ann Arbor, MI CMSA	5,042	10
Seattle – Tacoma, WA CMSA	4,473	11
Atlanta, GA MSA	4,419	12
Tampa – St. Petersburg – Clearwater, FL MSA	4,121	13
Columbus, OH MSA	3,635	14
Washington, DC – MD – VA MSA	3,526	15
St. Louis, MO – IL MSA	3,457	16
Milwaukee – Racine, WI CMSA	3,363	17
Phoenix, AZ MSA	3,353	18
Pittsburgh – Beaver Valley, PA CMSA	3,309	19
Kansas City, MO – KS MSA	3,308	20

[Continued]

★1237★

Top 25 MSAs For Employment As Insurance Adjusters, Examiners, and Investigators, 1990: Whites

[Continued]

MSA/CMSA	Employees per 100,000 pop.	Rank
Houston – Galveston – Brazoria, TX CMSA	3,264	21
Baltimore, MD MSA	3,250	22
Cleveland – Akron – Lorain, OH CMSA	2,886	23
Indianapolis, IN MSA	2,871	24
Miami – Fort Lauderdale, FL CMSA	2,803	25

Source: U.S. Department of Commerce, Bureau of the Census, Data User Services Division, *1990 Census of Population and Housing, Equal Employment Opportunity File, CD-90-EE0-1, January 1993,* CD-ROM.

★1238★

Occupations, By Race/Sex

Top 25 MSAs For Employment As Interviewers, 1990: Blacks

MSA/CMSA	Employees per 100,000 pop.	Rank
Baton Rouge, LA MSA	4,884	1
Los Angeles – Anaheim – Riverside, CA CMSA	2,098	2
Chicago – Gary – Lake County, IL – IN – WI CMSA	1,944	3
Philadelphia – Wilmington – Trenton, PA – NJ – DE – MD CMSA	1,405	4
Washington, DC – MD – VA MSA	928	5
Detroit – Ann Arbor, MI CMSA	855	6
Atlanta, GA MSA	847	7
Houston – Galveston – Brazoria, TX CMSA	803	8
Baltimore, MD MSA	760	9
Dallas – Fort Worth, TX CMSA	577	10
San Francisco – Oakland – San Jose, CA CMSA	561	11
Miami – Fort Lauderdale, FL CMSA	505	12
Cleveland – Akron – Lorain, OH CMSA	465	13
St. Louis, MO – IL MSA	448	14
New Orleans, LA MSA	406	15
Cincinnati – Hamilton, OH – KY – IN CMSA	382	16
Boston – Lawrence – Salem, MA – NH CMSA	353	17
Jacksonville, FL MSA	308	18
Norfolk – Virginia Beach – Newport News, VA MSA	304	19
Memphis, TN – AR – MS MSA	285	20
Kansas City, MO – KS MSA	285	20
Birmingham, AL MSA	250	21

[Continued]

★1238★

Top 25 MSAs For Employment As Interviewers, 1990: Blacks

[Continued]

MSA/CMSA	Employees per 100,000 pop.	Rank
Pittsburgh – Beaver Valley, PA CMSA	249	22
Baton Rouge, LA MSA	222	23
Jackson, MS MSA	212	24

Source: U.S. Department of Commerce, Bureau of the Census, Data User Services Division, *1990 Census of Population and Housing, Equal Employment Opportunity File, CD-90-EE0-1, January 1993,* CD-ROM.

★1239★

Occupations, By Race/Sex

Top 25 MSAs For Employment As Interviewers, 1990: Whites

MSA/CMSA	Employees per 100,000 pop.	Rank
Kansas City, MO – KS MSA	8,922	1
Los Angeles – Anaheim – Riverside, CA CMSA	8,068	2
Chicago – Gary – Lake County, IL – IN – WI CMSA	4,417	3
Philadelphia – Wilmington – Trenton, PA – NJ – DE – MD CMSA	3,887	4
San Francisco – Oakland – San Jose, CA CMSA	3,845	5
Boston – Lawrence – Salem, MA – NH CMSA	2,583	6
Dallas – Fort Worth, TX CMSA	2,474	7
Detroit – Ann Arbor, MI CMSA	2,286	8
Minneapolis – St. Paul, MN – WI MSA	2,167	9
Miami – Fort Lauderdale, FL CMSA	1,928	10
Phoenix, AZ MSA	1,844	11
Houston – Galveston – Brazoria, TX CMSA	1,841	12
Seattle – Tacoma, WA CMSA	1,839	13
San Diego, CA MSA	1,633	14
Pittsburgh – Beaver Valley, PA CMSA	1,613	15
Washington, DC – MD – VA MSA	1,539	16
St. Louis, MO – IL MSA	1,514	17
Tampa – St. Petersburg – Clearwater, FL MSA	1,427	18
Portland – Vancouver, OR – WA CMSA	1,364	19
Cincinnati – Hamilton, OH – KY – IN CMSA	1,333	20
Cleveland – Akron – Lorain, OH CMSA	1,330	21
Denver – Boulder, CO CMSA	1,259	22
Baltimore, MD MSA	1,212	23

[Continued]

★1239★

Top 25 MSAs For Employment As Interviewers, 1990: Whites

[Continued]

MSA/CMSA	Employees per 100,000 pop.	Rank
Atlanta, GA MSA	1,209	24
Milwaukee – Racine, WI CMSA	1,151	25

Source: U.S. Department of Commerce, Bureau of the Census, Data User Services Division, *1990 Census of Population and Housing, Equal Employment Opportunity File, CD-90-EE0-1, January 1993,* CD-ROM.

★1240★

Occupations, By Race/Sex

Top 25 MSAs For Employment As Judges, 1990: Blacks

MSA/CMSA	Employees per 100,000 pop.	Rank
Kansas City, MO – KS MSA	362	1
Los Angeles – Anaheim – Riverside, CA CMSA	197	2
Chicago – Gary – Lake County, IL – IN – WI CMSA	186	3
Washington, DC – MD – VA MSA	165	4
Baltimore, MD MSA	88	5
Atlanta, GA MSA	83	6
Detroit – Ann Arbor, MI CMSA	81	7
Miami – Fort Lauderdale, FL CMSA	67	8
Cleveland – Akron – Lorain, OH CMSA	65	9
Philadelphia – Wilmington – Trenton, PA – NJ – DE – MD CMSA	50	10
Boston – Lawrence – Salem, MA – NH CMSA	43	11
Sacramento, CA MSA	42	12
New Orleans, LA MSA	35	13
Nashville, TN MSA	31	14
Houston – Galveston – Brazoria, TX CMSA	30	15
Dallas – Fort Worth, TX CMSA	30	15
Norfolk – Virginia Beach – Newport News, VA MSA	26	16
San Francisco – Oakland – San Jose, CA CMSA	24	17
St. Louis, MO – IL MSA	23	18
Columbus, OH MSA	22	19
Raleigh – Durham, NC MSA	21	20
Gainesville, FL MSA	21	20
Seattle – Tacoma, WA CMSA	20	21
Tampa – St. Petersburg – Clearwater, FL MSA	17	22
Fayetteville, NC MSA	16	23

Source: U.S. Department of Commerce, Bureau of the Census, Data User Services Division, *1990 Census of Population and Housing, Equal Employment Opportunity File, CD-90-EE0-1, January 1993,* CD-ROM.

★1241★

Occupations, By Race/Sex

Top 25 MSAs For Employment As Judges, 1990: Whites

MSA/CMSA	Employees per 100,000 pop.	Rank
Portland – Vancouver, OR – WA CMSA	2,330	1
Los Angeles – Anaheim – Riverside, CA CMSA	1,060	2
Chicago – Gary – Lake County, IL – IN – WI CMSA	756	3
San Francisco – Oakland – San Jose, CA CMSA	755	4
Washington, DC – MD – VA MSA	735	5
Philadelphia – Wilmington – Trenton, PA – NJ – DE – MD CMSA	711	6
Detroit – Ann Arbor, MI CMSA	542	7
Boston – Lawrence – Salem, MA – NH CMSA	534	8
Baltimore, MD MSA	385	9
Dallas – Fort Worth, TX CMSA	375	10
Phoenix, AZ MSA	317	11
Seattle – Tacoma, WA CMSA	296	12
Minneapolis – St. Paul, MN – WI MSA	294	13
Pittsburgh – Beaver Valley, PA CMSA	292	14
Cleveland – Akron – Lorain, OH CMSA	290	15
Tampa – St. Petersburg – Clearwater, FL MSA	285	16
Miami – Fort Lauderdale, FL CMSA	273	17
Atlanta, GA MSA	247	18
Denver – Boulder, CO CMSA	241	19
San Diego, CA MSA	235	20
Kansas City, MO – KS MSA	220	21
St. Louis, MO – IL MSA	218	22
Sacramento, CA MSA	200	23
Norfolk – Virginia Beach – Newport News, VA MSA	188	24
Indianapolis, IN MSA	187	25

Source: U.S. Department of Commerce, Bureau of the Census, Data User Services Division, *1990 Census of Population and Housing, Equal Employment Opportunity File, CD-90-EE0-1, January 1993,* CD-ROM.

★1242★

Occupations, By Race/Sex

Top 25 MSAs For Employment As Launderers and Ironers, 1990: Blacks

MSA/CMSA	Employees per 100,000 pop.	Rank
Charlotte – Gastonia – Rock Hill, NC – SC MSA	50	1
St. Louis, MO – IL MSA	25	2
Cleveland – Akron – Lorain, OH CMSA	17	3
Baltimore, MD MSA	15	4
West Palm Beach – Boca Raton – Delray Beach, FL MSA	14	5
Philadelphia – Wilmington – Trenton, PA – NJ – DE – MD CMSA	14	5
Dallas – Fort Worth, TX CMSA	11	6
Rochester, NY MSA	11	6
Memphis, TN – AR – MS MSA	11	6
Buffalo – Niagara Falls, NY CMSA	11	6
Detroit – Ann Arbor, MI CMSA	10	7
Columbus, GA – AL MSA	8	8
Shreveport, LA MSA	7	9
Indianapolis, IN MSA	7	9
Atlanta, GA MSA	7	9
Cincinnati – Hamilton, OH – KY – IN CMSA	6	10
Melbourne – Titusville – Palm Bay, FL MSA	5	11
Chicago – Gary – Lake County, IL – IN – WI CMSA	5	11
Miami – Fort Lauderdale, FL CMSA	5	11
Louisville, KY – IN MSA	1	12
Wichita, KS MSA	0	13
Norfolk – Virginia Beach – Newport News, VA MSA	0	13
Sioux City, IA – NE MSA	0	13
Ocala, FL MSA	0	13
Oklahoma City, OK MSA	0	13

Source: U.S. Department of Commerce, Bureau of the Census, Data User Services Division, *1990 Census of Population and Housing, Equal Employment Opportunity File, CD-90-EE0-1,* January 1993, CD-ROM.

★1243★

Occupations, By Race/Sex

Top 25 MSAs For Employment As Launderers and Ironers, 1990: Whites

MSA/CMSA	Employees per 100,000 pop.	Rank
San Diego, CA MSA	82	1
San Francisco – Oakland – San Jose, CA CMSA	58	2
New York – Northern New Jersey – Long Island, NY – NJ – CT CMSA	36	3
Chicago – Gary – Lake County, IL – IN – WI CMSA	35	4

[Continued]

★1243★

Top 25 MSAs For Employment As Launderers and Ironers, 1990: Whites

[Continued]

MSA/CMSA	Employees per 100,000 pop.	Rank
Washington, DC – MD – VA MSA	24	5
Provo – Orem, UT MSA	24	5
Eugene – Springfield, OR MSA	21	6
Enid, OK MSA	21	6
Minneapolis – St. Paul, MN – WI MSA	20	7
Cleveland – Akron – Lorain, OH CMSA	18	8
Tampa – St. Petersburg – Clearwater, FL MSA	18	8
Youngstown – Warren, OH MSA	18	8
Detroit – Ann Arbor, MI CMSA	16	9
Seattle – Tacoma, WA CMSA	16	9
Colorado Springs, CO MSA	15	10
St. Louis, MO – IL MSA	14	11
Oklahoma City, OK MSA	14	11
Dallas – Fort Worth, TX CMSA	13	12
Boston – Lawrence – Salem, MA – NH CMSA	13	12
Pittsburgh – Beaver Valley, PA CMSA	12	13
Midland, TX MSA	11	14
Memphis, TN – AR – MS MSA	11	14
Boise City, ID MSA	11	14
Jackson, MI MSA	10	15
San Diego, CA MSA	10	15

Source: U.S. Department of Commerce, Bureau of the Census, Data User Services Division, *1990 Census of Population and Housing, Equal Employment Opportunity File, CD-90-EE0-1,* January 1993, CD-ROM.

★1244★

Occupations, By Race/Sex

Top 25 MSAs For Employment As Law Teachers, 1990: Blacks

MSA/CMSA	Employees per 100,000 pop.	Rank
Harrisburg – Lebanon – Carlisle, PA MSA	43	1
New York – Northern New Jersey – Long Island, NY – NJ – CT CMSA	41	2
Houston – Galveston – Brazoria, TX CMSA	27	3
San Francisco – Oakland – San Jose, CA CMSA	19	4
Philadelphia – Wilmington – Trenton, PA – NJ – DE – MD CMSA	16	5
Los Angeles – Anaheim – Riverside, CA CMSA	15	6
Little Rock – North Little Rock, AR MSA	12	7
Baltimore, MD MSA	10	8

[Continued]

★1244★

Top 25 MSAs For Employment As Law Teachers, 1990: Blacks

[Continued]

MSA/CMSA	Employees per 100,000 pop.	Rank
Baton Rouge, LA MSA	8	9
San Diego, CA MSA	8	9
Columbus, OH MSA	7	10
Cleveland – Akron – Lorain, OH CMSA	7	10
Detroit – Ann Arbor, MI CMSA	6	11
Madison, WI MSA	6	11
Pine Bluff, AR MSA	0	12
Phoenix, AZ MSA	0	12
Norfolk – Virginia Beach – Newport News, VA MSA	0	12
Pascagoula, MS MSA	0	12
Owensboro, KY MSA	0	12
Orlando, FL MSA	0	12
Omaha, NE – IA MSA	0	12
Olympia, WA MSA	0	12
Odessa, TX MSA	0	12
Ocala, FL MSA	0	12
Pueblo, CO MSA	0	12

Source: U.S. Department of Commerce, Bureau of the Census, Data User Services Division, *1990 Census of Population and Housing, Equal Employment Opportunity File,* CD-90-EE0-1, January 1993, CD-ROM.

★1245★

Occupations, By Race/Sex

Top 25 MSAs For Employment As Law Teachers, 1990: Whites

MSA/CMSA	Employees per 100,000 pop.	Rank
Bloomington, IN MSA	459	1
Chicago – Gary – Lake County, IL – IN – WI CMSA	254	2
Boston – Lawrence – Salem, MA – NH CMSA	245	3
Washington, DC – MD – VA MSA	205	4
Los Angeles – Anaheim – Riverside, CA CMSA	154	5
San Francisco – Oakland – San Jose, CA CMSA	136	6
Philadelphia – Wilmington – Trenton, PA – NJ – DE – MD CMSA	120	7
San Diego, CA MSA	78	8
Cleveland – Akron – Lorain, OH CMSA	73	9
Tallahassee, FL MSA	71	10
Minneapolis – St. Paul, MN – WI MSA	67	11
Detroit – Ann Arbor, MI CMSA	66	12
New Orleans, LA MSA	65	13
New Haven – Meriden, CT MSA	59	14
St. Louis, MO – IL MSA	51	15
Miami – Fort Lauderdale, FL CMSA	51	15

[Continued]

★1245★

Top 25 MSAs For Employment As Law Teachers, 1990: Whites

[Continued]

MSA/CMSA	Employees per 100,000 pop.	Rank
Columbia, SC MSA	51	15
Raleigh – Durham, NC MSA	49	16
Cincinnati – Hamilton, OH – KY – IN CMSA	47	17
Pittsburgh – Beaver Valley, PA CMSA	44	18
Madison, WI MSA	44	18
Houston – Galveston – Brazoria, TX CMSA	44	18
Oklahoma City, OK MSA	42	19
Seattle – Tacoma, WA CMSA	42	19
Denver – Boulder, CO CMSA	41	20

Source: U.S. Department of Commerce, Bureau of the Census, Data User Services Division, *1990 Census of Population and Housing, Equal Employment Opportunity File,* CD-90-EE0-1, January 1993, CD-ROM.

★1246★

Occupations, By Race/Sex

Top 25 MSAs For Employment As Lawyers, 1990: Blacks

MSA/CMSA	Employees per 100,000 pop.	Rank
New Orleans, LA MSA	4,341	1
Washington, DC – MD – VA MSA	3,361	2
Los Angeles – Anaheim – Riverside, CA CMSA	1,924	3
Chicago – Gary – Lake County, IL – IN – WI CMSA	1,259	4
Philadelphia – Wilmington – Trenton, PA – NJ – DE – MD CMSA	1,089	5
Detroit – Ann Arbor, MI CMSA	1,037	6
San Francisco – Oakland – San Jose, CA CMSA	885	7
Atlanta, GA MSA	866	8
Baltimore, MD MSA	687	9
Houston – Galveston – Brazoria, TX CMSA	673	10
Boston – Lawrence – Salem, MA – NH CMSA	481	11
New Orleans, LA MSA	461	12
Cleveland – Akron – Lorain, OH CMSA	434	13
Dallas – Fort Worth, TX CMSA	389	14
Miami – Fort Lauderdale, FL CMSA	369	15
Columbus, OH MSA	252	16
Baton Rouge, LA MSA	206	17
Nashville, TN MSA	202	18
St. Louis, MO – IL MSA	192	19
West Palm Beach – Boca Raton – Delray Beach, FL MSA	165	20
Greensboro – Winston-Salem – High Point, NC MSA	163	21

[Continued]

★1246★

Top 25 MSAs For Employment As Lawyers, 1990: Blacks
[Continued]

MSA/CMSA	Employees per 100,000 pop.	Rank
Seattle – Tacoma, WA CMSA	155	22
Pittsburgh – Beaver Valley, PA CMSA	149	23
Austin, TX MSA	147	24
Indianapolis, IN MSA	147	24

Source: U.S. Department of Commerce, Bureau of the Census, Data User Services Division, *1990 Census of Population and Housing, Equal Employment Opportunity File, CD-90-EE0-1, January 1993,* CD-ROM.

★1247★

Occupations, By Race/Sex

Top 25 MSAs For Employment As Lawyers, 1990: Whites

MSA/CMSA	Employees per 100,000 pop.	Rank
Portland – Vancouver, OR – WA CMSA	97,275	1
Los Angeles – Anaheim – Riverside, CA CMSA	46,311	2
Washington, DC – MD – VA MSA	39,117	3
Chicago – Gary – Lake County, IL – IN – WI CMSA	33,895	4
San Francisco – Oakland – San Jose, CA CMSA	27,592	5
Philadelphia – Wilmington – Trenton, PA – NJ – DE – MD CMSA	21,840	6
Boston – Lawrence – Salem, MA – NH CMSA	20,680	7
Houston – Galveston – Brazoria, TX CMSA	13,961	8
Miami – Fort Lauderdale, FL CMSA	13,449	9
Detroit – Ann Arbor, MI CMSA	12,583	10
Dallas – Fort Worth, TX CMSA	12,155	11
Atlanta, GA MSA	10,665	12
Minneapolis – St. Paul, MN – WI MSA	9,872	13
Denver – Boulder, CO CMSA	9,537	14
San Diego, CA MSA	8,830	15
Cleveland – Akron – Lorain, OH CMSA	8,660	16
Seattle – Tacoma, WA CMSA	8,625	17
Baltimore, MD MSA	8,309	18
St. Louis, MO – IL MSA	6,799	19
Pittsburgh – Beaver Valley, PA CMSA	6,448	20
Phoenix, AZ MSA	6,351	21
New Orleans, LA MSA	6,025	22
Kansas City, MO – KS MSA	5,591	23

[Continued]

★1247★

Top 25 MSAs For Employment As Lawyers, 1990: Whites
[Continued]

MSA/CMSA	Employees per 100,000 pop.	Rank
Tampa – St. Petersburg – Clearwater, FL MSA	5,288	24
Sacramento, CA MSA	5,225	25

Source: U.S. Department of Commerce, Bureau of the Census, Data User Services Division, *1990 Census of Population and Housing, Equal Employment Opportunity File, CD-90-EE0-1, January 1993,* CD-ROM.

★1248★

Occupations, By Race/Sex

Top 25 MSAs For Employment As Legal Assistants, 1990: Blacks

MSA/CMSA	Employees per 100,000 pop.	Rank
Memphis, TN – AR – MS MSA	3,850	1
Washington, DC – MD – VA MSA	3,064	2
Los Angeles – Anaheim – Riverside, CA CMSA	1,486	3
Chicago – Gary – Lake County, IL – IN – WI CMSA	1,160	4
Philadelphia – Wilmington – Trenton, PA – NJ – DE – MD CMSA	800	5
San Francisco – Oakland – San Jose, CA CMSA	693	6
Atlanta, GA MSA	622	7
Houston – Galveston – Brazoria, TX CMSA	607	8
Baltimore, MD MSA	524	9
Dallas – Fort Worth, TX CMSA	516	10
Detroit – Ann Arbor, MI CMSA	381	11
Miami – Fort Lauderdale, FL CMSA	344	12
Cleveland – Akron – Lorain, OH CMSA	248	13
Boston – Lawrence – Salem, MA – NH CMSA	226	14
New Orleans, LA MSA	225	15
San Diego, CA MSA	183	16
St. Louis, MO – IL MSA	151	17
Pittsburgh – Beaver Valley, PA CMSA	128	18
Seattle – Tacoma, WA CMSA	127	19
Memphis, TN – AR – MS MSA	124	20
Denver – Boulder, CO CMSA	113	21
Tampa – St. Petersburg – Clearwater, FL MSA	112	22
West Palm Beach – Boca Raton – Delray Beach, FL MSA	111	23
Richmond – Petersburg, VA MSA	111	23
Hartford – New Britain – Middletown, CT CMSA	108	24

Source: U.S. Department of Commerce, Bureau of the Census, Data User Services Division, *1990 Census of Population and Housing, Equal Employment Opportunity File, CD-90-EE0-1, January 1993,* CD-ROM.

★1249★

Occupations, By Race/Sex

Top 25 MSAs For Employment As Legal Assistants, 1990: Whites

MSA/CMSA	Employees per 100,000 pop.	Rank
Austin, TX MSA	19,792	1
Los Angeles – Anaheim – Riverside, CA CMSA	15,599	2
Washington, DC – MD – VA MSA	10,394	3
San Francisco – Oakland – San Jose, CA CMSA	9,301	4
Philadelphia – Wilmington – Trenton, PA – NJ – DE – MD CMSA	6,773	5
Chicago – Gary – Lake County, IL – IN – WI CMSA	6,471	6
Dallas – Fort Worth, TX CMSA	5,608	7
Boston – Lawrence – Salem, MA – NH CMSA	5,068	8
Houston – Galveston – Brazoria, TX CMSA	4,541	9
Miami – Fort Lauderdale, FL CMSA	3,815	10
Seattle – Tacoma, WA CMSA	3,572	11
Denver – Boulder, CO CMSA	3,443	12
Minneapolis – St. Paul, MN – WI MSA	3,374	13
Phoenix, AZ MSA	3,247	14
Atlanta, GA MSA	3,209	15
San Diego, CA MSA	3,073	16
Detroit – Ann Arbor, MI CMSA	2,804	17
Baltimore, MD MSA	2,634	18
Sacramento, CA MSA	2,440	19
Cleveland – Akron – Lorain, OH CMSA	2,423	20
Tampa – St. Petersburg – Clearwater, FL MSA	2,161	21
Pittsburgh – Beaver Valley, PA CMSA	1,924	22
Kansas City, MO – KS MSA	1,775	23
Austin, TX MSA	1,747	24
Portland – Vancouver, OR – WA CMSA	1,713	25

Source: U.S. Department of Commerce, Bureau of the Census, Data User Services Division, *1990 Census of Population and Housing, Equal Employment Opportunity File, CD-90-EE0-1, January 1993,* CD-ROM.

★1250★

Occupations, By Race/Sex

Top 25 MSAs For Employment As Legislators, 1990: Blacks

MSA/CMSA	Employees per 100,000 pop.	Rank
Washington, DC – MD – VA MSA	210	1
Chicago – Gary – Lake County, IL – IN – WI CMSA	127	2
New York – Northern New Jersey – Long Island, NY – NJ – CT CMSA	118	3
Los Angeles – Anaheim – Riverside, CA CMSA	78	4
Buffalo – Niagara Falls, NY CMSA	43	5
San Francisco – Oakland – San Jose, CA CMSA	38	6
Houston – Galveston – Brazoria, TX CMSA	36	7
Atlanta, GA MSA	33	8
Baltimore, MD MSA	30	9
Jackson, MS MSA	30	9
Dallas – Fort Worth, TX CMSA	29	10
Detroit – Ann Arbor, MI CMSA	27	11
Philadelphia – Wilmington – Trenton, PA – NJ – DE – MD CMSA	25	12
Columbia, SC MSA	22	13
Sacramento, CA MSA	19	14
Denver – Boulder, CO CMSA	19	14
Richmond – Petersburg, VA MSA	17	15
Cleveland – Akron – Lorain, OH CMSA	17	15
St. Louis, MO – IL MSA	16	16
Indianapolis, IN MSA	15	17
Milwaukee – Racine, WI CMSA	15	17
Albany – Schenectady – Troy, NY MSA	14	18
Atlantic City, NJ MSA	13	19
Charleston, WV MSA	11	20
Tulsa, OK MSA	10	21

Source: U.S. Department of Commerce, Bureau of the Census, Data User Services Division, *1990 Census of Population and Housing, Equal Employment Opportunity File, CD-90-EE0-1, January 1993,* CD-ROM.

★1251★

Occupations, By Race/Sex

Top 25 MSAs For Employment As Legislators, 1990: Whites

MSA/CMSA	Employees per 100,000 pop.	Rank
Washington, DC – MD – VA MSA	1,404	1
New York – Northern New Jersey – Long Island, NY – NJ – CT CMSA	535	2
Los Angeles – Anaheim – Riverside, CA CMSA	436	3
Chicago – Gary – Lake County, IL – IN – WI CMSA	346	4

[Continued]

★1251★

Top 25 MSAs For Employment As Legislators, 1990: Whites

[Continued]

MSA/CMSA	Employees per 100,000 pop.	Rank
Boston – Lawrence – Salem, MA – NH CMSA	287	5
Albany – Schenectady – Troy, NY MSA	197	6
Minneapolis – St. Paul, MN – WI MSA	194	7
Sacramento, CA MSA	171	8
San Francisco – Oakland – San Jose, CA CMSA	164	9
Pittsburgh – Beaver Valley, PA CMSA	159	10
Cleveland – Akron – Lorain, OH CMSA	154	11
Philadelphia – Wilmington – Trenton, PA – NJ – DE – MD CMSA	126	12
St. Louis, MO – IL MSA	124	13
Dallas – Fort Worth, TX CMSA	124	13
Lansing – East Lansing, MI MSA	118	14
Hartford – New Britain – Middletown, CT CMSA	113	15
Denver – Boulder, CO CMSA	108	16
Baltimore, MD MSA	101	17
Detroit – Ann Arbor, MI CMSA	101	17
Seattle – Tacoma, WA CMSA	99	18
Phoenix, AZ MSA	90	19
Providence – Pawtucket – Fall River, RI – MA CMSA	85	20
Kansas City, MO – KS MSA	80	21
Tallahassee, FL MSA	71	22
Buffalo – Niagara Falls, NY CMSA	70	23

Source: U.S. Department of Commerce, Bureau of the Census, Data User Services Division, *1990 Census of Population and Housing, Equal Employment Opportunity File, CD-90-EE0-1, January 1993,* CD-ROM.

★1252★

Occupations, By Race/Sex

Top 25 MSAs For Employment As Librarians, 1990: Blacks

MSA/CMSA	Employees per 100,000 pop.	Rank
Seattle – Tacoma, WA CMSA	1,764	1
Washington, DC – MD – VA MSA	1,309	2
Philadelphia – Wilmington – Trenton, PA – NJ – DE – MD CMSA	840	3
Los Angeles – Anaheim – Riverside, CA CMSA	656	4
Chicago – Gary – Lake County, IL – IN – WI CMSA	587	5
Atlanta, GA MSA	532	6
Houston – Galveston – Brazoria, TX CMSA	422	7

[Continued]

★1252★

Top 25 MSAs For Employment As Librarians, 1990: Blacks

[Continued]

MSA/CMSA	Employees per 100,000 pop.	Rank
Baltimore, MD MSA	402	8
Detroit – Ann Arbor, MI CMSA	384	9
San Francisco – Oakland – San Jose, CA CMSA	377	10
St. Louis, MO – IL MSA	330	11
Cleveland – Akron – Lorain, OH CMSA	274	12
Miami – Fort Lauderdale, FL CMSA	262	13
Boston – Lawrence – Salem, MA – NH CMSA	235	14
Norfolk – Virginia Beach – Newport News, VA MSA	226	15
New Orleans, LA MSA	196	16
Nashville, TN MSA	192	17
Seattle – Tacoma, WA CMSA	180	18
Tallahassee, FL MSA	155	19
Birmingham, AL MSA	154	20
Memphis, TN – AR – MS MSA	153	21
Baton Rouge, LA MSA	140	22
Dallas – Fort Worth, TX CMSA	140	22
Raleigh – Durham, NC MSA	134	23
Richmond – Petersburg, VA MSA	131	24

Source: U.S. Department of Commerce, Bureau of the Census, Data User Services Division, *1990 Census of Population and Housing, Equal Employment Opportunity File, CD-90-EE0-1, January 1993,* CD-ROM.

★1253★

Occupations, By Race/Sex

Top 25 MSAs For Employment As Librarians, 1990: Whites

MSA/CMSA	Employees per 100,000 pop.	Rank
Sacramento, CA MSA	14,314	1
Los Angeles – Anaheim – Riverside, CA CMSA	7,153	2
Chicago – Gary – Lake County, IL – IN – WI CMSA	5,627	3
Washington, DC – MD – VA MSA	5,576	4
Boston – Lawrence – Salem, MA – NH CMSA	5,482	5
San Francisco – Oakland – San Jose, CA CMSA	4,794	6
Philadelphia – Wilmington – Trenton, PA – NJ – DE – MD CMSA	4,698	7
Detroit – Ann Arbor, MI CMSA	2,818	8
Dallas – Fort Worth, TX CMSA	2,485	9
Cleveland – Akron – Lorain, OH CMSA	2,280	10
Houston – Galveston – Brazoria, TX CMSA	2,036	11
Seattle – Tacoma, WA CMSA	1,924	12

[Continued]

★1253★

Top 25 MSAs For Employment As Librarians, 1990: Whites
[Continued]

MSA/CMSA	Employees per 100,000 pop.	Rank
Minneapolis – St. Paul, MN – WI MSA	1,908	13
Baltimore, MD MSA	1,847	14
St. Louis, MO – IL MSA	1,688	15
Atlanta, GA MSA	1,502	16
Denver – Boulder, CO CMSA	1,412	17
San Diego, CA MSA	1,346	18
Columbus, OH MSA	1,342	19
Hartford – New Britain – Middletown, CT CMSA	1,292	20
Cincinnati – Hamilton, OH – KY – IN CMSA	1,283	21
Pittsburgh – Beaver Valley, PA CMSA	1,212	22
Miami – Fort Lauderdale, FL CMSA	1,153	23
Milwaukee – Racine, WI CMSA	1,132	24
Providence – Pawtucket – Fall River, RI – MA CMSA	1,029	25

Source: U.S. Department of Commerce, Bureau of the Census, Data User Services Division, *1990 Census of Population and Housing, Equal Employment Opportunity File, CD-90-EE0-1,* January 1993, CD-ROM.

★1254★
Occupations, By Race/Sex

Top 25 MSAs For Employment As Library Clerks, 1990: Blacks

MSA/CMSA	Employees per 100,000 pop.	Rank
Raleigh – Durham, NC MSA	2,330	1
Chicago – Gary – Lake County, IL – IN – WI CMSA	980	2
Washington, DC – MD – VA MSA	844	3
Los Angeles – Anaheim – Riverside, CA CMSA	622	4
Philadelphia – Wilmington – Trenton, PA – NJ – DE – MD CMSA	499	5
Atlanta, GA MSA	490	6
Cleveland – Akron – Lorain, OH CMSA	440	7
Detroit – Ann Arbor, MI CMSA	422	8
Houston – Galveston – Brazoria, TX CMSA	303	9
San Francisco – Oakland – San Jose, CA CMSA	299	10
Dallas – Fort Worth, TX CMSA	292	11
Boston – Lawrence – Salem, MA – NH CMSA	279	12
Raleigh – Durham, NC MSA	270	13
Norfolk – Virginia Beach – Newport News, VA MSA	245	14
Miami – Fort Lauderdale, FL CMSA	241	15

[Continued]

★1254★

Top 25 MSAs For Employment As Library Clerks, 1990: Blacks
[Continued]

MSA/CMSA	Employees per 100,000 pop.	Rank
St. Louis, MO – IL MSA	228	16
Baltimore, MD MSA	216	17
Birmingham, AL MSA	177	18
New Orleans, LA MSA	169	19
Greensboro – Winston-Salem – High Point, NC MSA	167	20
Richmond – Petersburg, VA MSA	148	21
Memphis, TN – AR – MS MSA	139	22
Cincinnati – Hamilton, OH – KY – IN CMSA	138	23
Buffalo – Niagara Falls, NY CMSA	138	23
Jacksonville, FL MSA	132	24

Source: U.S. Department of Commerce, Bureau of the Census, Data User Services Division, *1990 Census of Population and Housing, Equal Employment Opportunity File, CD-90-EE0-1,* January 1993, CD-ROM.

★1255★
Occupations, By Race/Sex

Top 25 MSAs For Employment As Library Clerks, 1990: Whites

MSA/CMSA	Employees per 100,000 pop.	Rank
Sacramento, CA MSA	9,476	1
Los Angeles – Anaheim – Riverside, CA CMSA	5,007	2
Chicago – Gary – Lake County, IL – IN – WI CMSA	4,183	3
San Francisco – Oakland – San Jose, CA CMSA	3,402	4
Boston – Lawrence – Salem, MA – NH CMSA	3,400	5
Philadelphia – Wilmington – Trenton, PA – NJ – DE – MD CMSA	3,003	6
Washington, DC – MD – VA MSA	2,417	7
Cleveland – Akron – Lorain, OH CMSA	2,036	8
Detroit – Ann Arbor, MI CMSA	1,984	9
Minneapolis – St. Paul, MN – WI MSA	1,746	10
Seattle – Tacoma, WA CMSA	1,425	11
Dallas – Fort Worth, TX CMSA	1,317	12
Pittsburgh – Beaver Valley, PA CMSA	1,195	13
Rochester, NY MSA	1,125	14
St. Louis, MO – IL MSA	1,043	15
Phoenix, AZ MSA	1,023	16
San Diego, CA MSA	1,007	17
Columbus, OH MSA	999	18
Albany – Schenectady – Troy, NY MSA	988	19
Cincinnati – Hamilton, OH – KY – IN CMSA	984	20

[Continued]

★ 1255 ★

Top 25 MSAs For Employment As Library Clerks, 1990: Whites
[Continued]

MSA/CMSA	Employees per 100,000 pop.	Rank
Hartford – New Britain – Middletown, CT CMSA	960	21
Portland – Vancouver, OR – WA CMSA	939	22
Baltimore, MD MSA	935	23
Kansas City, MO – KS MSA	898	24
Atlanta, GA MSA	879	25

Source: U.S. Department of Commerce, Bureau of the Census, Data User Services Division, *1990 Census of Population and Housing, Equal Employment Opportunity File, CD-90-EE0-1, January 1993*, CD-ROM.

★ 1256 ★
Occupations, By Race/Sex

Top 25 MSAs For Employment As Licensed Practical Nurses, 1990: Blacks

MSA/CMSA	Employees per 100,000 pop.	Rank
Richmond – Petersburg, VA MSA	9,233	1
Chicago – Gary – Lake County, IL – IN – WI CMSA	3,578	2
Los Angeles – Anaheim – Riverside, CA CMSA	3,355	3
Philadelphia – Wilmington – Trenton, PA – NJ – DE – MD CMSA	2,935	4
Detroit – Ann Arbor, MI CMSA	2,572	5
Houston – Galveston – Brazoria, TX CMSA	2,281	6
Baltimore, MD MSA	2,044	7
Washington, DC – MD – VA MSA	1,938	8
Miami – Fort Lauderdale, FL CMSA	1,870	9
Atlanta, GA MSA	1,729	10
St. Louis, MO – IL MSA	1,480	11
Cleveland – Akron – Lorain, OH CMSA	1,420	12
Dallas – Fort Worth, TX CMSA	1,292	13
San Francisco – Oakland – San Jose, CA CMSA	1,131	14
New Orleans, LA MSA	1,103	15
Norfolk – Virginia Beach – Newport News, VA MSA	1,063	16
Birmingham, AL MSA	1,048	17
Memphis, TN – AR – MS MSA	1,035	18
Richmond – Petersburg, VA MSA	978	19
Cincinnati – Hamilton, OH – KY – IN CMSA	747	20
Jackson, MS MSA	684	21
Nashville, TN MSA	645	22
Columbia, SC MSA	642	23
San Antonio, TX MSA	636	24
Augusta, GA – SC MSA	627	25

Source: U.S. Department of Commerce, Bureau of the Census, Data User Services Division, *1990 Census of Population and Housing, Equal Employment Opportunity File, CD-90-EE0-1, January 1993*, CD-ROM.

★ 1257 ★
Occupations, By Race/Sex

Top 25 MSAs For Employment As Licensed Practical Nurses, 1990: Whites

MSA/CMSA	Employees per 100,000 pop.	Rank
Columbus, OH MSA	10,982	1
Los Angeles – Anaheim – Riverside, CA CMSA	8,042	2
Philadelphia – Wilmington – Trenton, PA – NJ – DE – MD CMSA	6,519	3
Boston – Lawrence – Salem, MA – NH CMSA	5,603	4
Cleveland – Akron – Lorain, OH CMSA	4,993	5
Detroit – Ann Arbor, MI CMSA	4,472	6
Chicago – Gary – Lake County, IL – IN – WI CMSA	4,388	7
Minneapolis – St. Paul, MN – WI MSA	4,164	8
Tampa – St. Petersburg – Clearwater, FL MSA	4,001	9
San Francisco – Oakland – San Jose, CA CMSA	3,536	10
Pittsburgh – Beaver Valley, PA CMSA	3,263	11
Dallas – Fort Worth, TX CMSA	3,164	12
Cincinnati – Hamilton, OH – KY – IN CMSA	3,074	13
St. Louis, MO – IL MSA	2,935	14
Houston – Galveston – Brazoria, TX CMSA	2,661	15
Seattle – Tacoma, WA CMSA	2,583	16
Miami – Fort Lauderdale, FL CMSA	2,508	17
Milwaukee – Racine, WI CMSA	2,501	18
Buffalo – Niagara Falls, NY CMSA	2,367	19
Indianapolis, IN MSA	2,082	20
Providence – Pawtucket – Fall River, RI – MA CMSA	2,078	21
San Antonio, TX MSA	2,060	22
San Diego, CA MSA	2,004	23
Scranton – Wilkes-Barre, PA MSA	1,994	24
Kansas City, MO – KS MSA	1,969	25

Source: U.S. Department of Commerce, Bureau of the Census, Data User Services Division, *1990 Census of Population and Housing, Equal Employment Opportunity File, CD-90-EE0-1, January 1993*, CD-ROM.

★ 1258 ★

Occupations, By Race/Sex

Top 25 MSAs For Employment As Locksmiths and Safe Repairers, 1990: Blacks

MSA/CMSA	Employees per 100,000 pop.	Rank
Killeen – Temple, TX MSA	220	1
Los Angeles – Anaheim – Riverside, CA CMSA	154	2
Washington, DC – MD – VA MSA	123	3
Philadelphia – Wilmington – Trenton, PA – NJ – DE – MD CMSA	96	4
Detroit – Ann Arbor, MI CMSA	73	5
Baltimore, MD MSA	56	6
Chicago – Gary – Lake County, IL – IN – WI CMSA	43	7
Boston – Lawrence – Salem, MA – NH CMSA	43	7
Indianapolis, IN MSA	34	8
San Francisco – Oakland – San Jose, CA CMSA	28	9
Lexington-Fayette, KY MSA	28	9
Augusta, GA – SC MSA	21	10
Denver – Boulder, CO CMSA	20	11
San Diego, CA MSA	19	12
Kansas City, MO – KS MSA	19	12
Killeen – Temple, TX MSA	18	13
Syracuse, NY MSA	18	13
Jackson, MS MSA	16	14
Las Vegas, NV MSA	16	14
Atlanta, GA MSA	14	15
Fayetteville, NC MSA	13	16
Greensboro – Winston-Salem – High Point, NC MSA	12	17
New Orleans, LA MSA	12	17
Gainesville, FL MSA	10	18
Miami – Fort Lauderdale, FL CMSA	10	18

Source: U.S. Department of Commerce, Bureau of the Census, Data User Services Division, *1990 Census of Population and Housing, Equal Employment Opportunity File, CD-90-EE0-1, January 1993*, CD-ROM.

★ 1259 ★

Occupations, By Race/Sex

Top 25 MSAs For Employment As Locksmiths and Safe Repairers, 1990: Whites

MSA/CMSA	Employees per 100,000 pop.	Rank
Boston – Lawrence – Salem, MA – NH CMSA	2,172	1
Los Angeles – Anaheim – Riverside, CA CMSA	1,723	2
San Francisco – Oakland – San Jose, CA CMSA	788	3
Philadelphia – Wilmington – Trenton, PA – NJ – DE – MD CMSA	713	4
Chicago – Gary – Lake County, IL – IN – WI CMSA	672	5

[Continued]

★ 1259 ★

Top 25 MSAs For Employment As Locksmiths and Safe Repairers, 1990: Whites

[Continued]

MSA/CMSA	Employees per 100,000 pop.	Rank
Washington, DC – MD – VA MSA	593	6
Boston – Lawrence – Salem, MA – NH CMSA	491	7
Dallas – Fort Worth, TX CMSA	479	8
Detroit – Ann Arbor, MI CMSA	403	9
Miami – Fort Lauderdale, FL CMSA	392	10
Seattle – Tacoma, WA CMSA	357	11
Phoenix, AZ MSA	352	12
Houston – Galveston – Brazoria, TX CMSA	351	13
Tampa – St. Petersburg – Clearwater, FL MSA	334	14
Minneapolis – St. Paul, MN – WI MSA	327	15
Atlanta, GA MSA	324	16
San Diego, CA MSA	284	17
St. Louis, MO – IL MSA	268	18
Cleveland – Akron – Lorain, OH CMSA	260	19
Denver – Boulder, CO CMSA	226	20
Baltimore, MD MSA	225	21
West Palm Beach – Boca Raton – Delray Beach, FL MSA	186	22
Las Vegas, NV MSA	178	23
Orlando, FL MSA	178	23
Cincinnati – Hamilton, OH – KY – IN CMSA	172	24

Source: U.S. Department of Commerce, Bureau of the Census, Data User Services Division, *1990 Census of Population and Housing, Equal Employment Opportunity File, CD-90-EE0-1, January 1993*, CD-ROM.

★ 1260 ★

Occupations, By Race/Sex

Top 25 MSAs For Employment As Locomotive Operating Occupations, 1990: Blacks

MSA/CMSA	Employees per 100,000 pop.	Rank
Macon – Warner Robins, GA MSA	1,607	1
Chicago – Gary – Lake County, IL – IN – WI CMSA	464	2
Philadelphia – Wilmington – Trenton, PA – NJ – DE – MD CMSA	214	3
Houston – Galveston – Brazoria, TX CMSA	134	4
Baltimore, MD MSA	125	5
Atlanta, GA MSA	121	6
Washington, DC – MD – VA MSA	118	7
Miami – Fort Lauderdale, FL CMSA	107	8
San Francisco – Oakland – San Jose, CA CMSA	105	9

[Continued]

★ 1260 ★

Top 25 MSAs For Employment As Locomotive Operating Occupations, 1990: Blacks
[Continued]

MSA/CMSA	Employees per 100,000 pop.	Rank
Birmingham, AL MSA	105	9
Boston – Lawrence – Salem, MA – NH CMSA	83	10
Kansas City, MO – KS MSA	79	11
Dallas – Fort Worth, TX CMSA	74	12
Los Angeles – Anaheim – Riverside, CA CMSA	73	13
New Orleans, LA MSA	61	14
Shreveport, LA MSA	61	14
Detroit – Ann Arbor, MI CMSA	49	15
Norfolk – Virginia Beach – Newport News, VA MSA	45	16
Lakeland – Winter Haven, FL MSA	45	16
Little Rock – North Little Rock, AR MSA	40	17
Pittsburgh – Beaver Valley, PA CMSA	40	17
St. Louis, MO – IL MSA	38	18
Roanoke, VA MSA	37	19
Memphis, TN – AR – MS MSA	33	20
Cleveland – Akron – Lorain, OH CMSA	32	21

Source: U.S. Department of Commerce, Bureau of the Census, Data User Services Division, *1990 Census of Population and Housing, Equal Employment Opportunity File, CD-90-EE0-1, January 1993*, CD-ROM.

★ 1261 ★

Occupations, By Race/Sex

Top 25 MSAs For Employment As Locomotive Operating Occupations, 1990: Whites

MSA/CMSA	Employees per 100,000 pop.	Rank
Phoenix, AZ MSA	2,069	1
Chicago – Gary – Lake County, IL – IN – WI CMSA	1,495	2
Los Angeles – Anaheim – Riverside, CA CMSA	859	3
Pittsburgh – Beaver Valley, PA CMSA	815	4
Philadelphia – Wilmington – Trenton, PA – NJ – DE – MD CMSA	632	5
Kansas City, MO – KS MSA	543	6
Houston – Galveston – Brazoria, TX CMSA	505	7
St. Louis, MO – IL MSA	443	8
Boston – Lawrence – Salem, MA – NH CMSA	431	9
Detroit – Ann Arbor, MI CMSA	394	10
San Francisco – Oakland – San Jose, CA CMSA	391	11
Cleveland – Akron – Lorain, OH CMSA	383	12

[Continued]

★ 1261 ★

Top 25 MSAs For Employment As Locomotive Operating Occupations, 1990: Whites
[Continued]

MSA/CMSA	Employees per 100,000 pop.	Rank
Cincinnati – Hamilton, OH – KY – IN CMSA	375	13
Minneapolis – St. Paul, MN – WI MSA	341	14
Denver – Boulder, CO CMSA	322	15
Dallas – Fort Worth, TX CMSA	320	16
Atlanta, GA MSA	317	17
Buffalo – Niagara Falls, NY CMSA	308	18
Salt Lake City – Ogden, UT MSA	305	19
Seattle – Tacoma, WA CMSA	303	20
Toledo, OH MSA	271	21
Birmingham, AL MSA	269	22
Harrisburg – Lebanon – Carlisle, PA MSA	262	23
Portland – Vancouver, OR – WA CMSA	262	23
Louisville, KY – IN MSA	262	23

Source: U.S. Department of Commerce, Bureau of the Census, Data User Services Division, *1990 Census of Population and Housing, Equal Employment Opportunity File, CD-90-EE0-1, January 1993*, CD-ROM.

★ 1262 ★

Occupations, By Race/Sex

Top 25 MSAs For Employment As Longshore Equipment Operators, 1990: Blacks

MSA/CMSA	Employees per 100,000 pop.	Rank
Houma – Thibodaux, LA MSA	188	1
Baltimore, MD MSA	106	2
Norfolk – Virginia Beach – Newport News, VA MSA	103	3
Houston – Galveston – Brazoria, TX CMSA	90	4
San Francisco – Oakland – San Jose, CA CMSA	88	5
Charleston, SC MSA	69	6
New York – Northern New Jersey – Long Island, NY – NJ – CT CMSA	68	7
Savannah, GA MSA	46	8
Chicago – Gary – Lake County, IL – IN – WI CMSA	45	9
Los Angeles – Anaheim – Riverside, CA CMSA	38	10
Beaumont – Port Arthur, TX MSA	37	11
Lake Charles, LA MSA	35	12
Mobile, AL MSA	28	13
Seattle – Tacoma, WA CMSA	26	14
Pensacola, FL MSA	24	15
Philadelphia – Wilmington – Trenton, PA – NJ – DE – MD CMSA	23	16
Miami – Fort Lauderdale, FL CMSA	22	17

[Continued]

★1262★

Top 25 MSAs For Employment As Longshore Equipment Operators, 1990: Blacks
[Continued]

MSA/CMSA	Employees per 100,000 pop.	Rank
Biloxi – Gulfport, MS MSA	16	18
Washington, DC – MD – VA MSA	14	19
Pascagoula, MS MSA	14	19
Jacksonville, FL MSA	12	20
Milwaukee – Racine, WI CMSA	12	20
Birmingham, AL MSA	11	21
Tampa – St. Petersburg – Clearwater, FL MSA	10	22
Modesto, CA MSA	10	22

Source: U.S. Department of Commerce, Bureau of the Census, Data User Services Division, *1990 Census of Population and Housing, Equal Employment Opportunity File, CD-90-EE0-1, January 1993,* CD-ROM.

★1263★

Occupations, By Race/Sex

Top 25 MSAs For Employment As Longshore Equipment Operators, 1990: Whites

MSA/CMSA	Employees per 100,000 pop.	Rank
Houston – Galveston – Brazoria, TX CMSA	399	1
Los Angeles – Anaheim – Riverside, CA CMSA	323	2
Seattle – Tacoma, WA CMSA	263	3
Portland – Vancouver, OR – WA CMSA	204	4
Baltimore, MD MSA	139	5
Philadelphia – Wilmington – Trenton, PA – NJ – DE – MD CMSA	135	6
Houston – Galveston – Brazoria, TX CMSA	92	7
Norfolk – Virginia Beach – Newport News, VA MSA	91	8
San Francisco – Oakland – San Jose, CA CMSA	80	9
Boston – Lawrence – Salem, MA – NH CMSA	49	10
Olympia, WA MSA	45	11
Mobile, AL MSA	41	12
Baton Rouge, LA MSA	35	13
New Orleans, LA MSA	35	13
Corpus Christi, TX MSA	33	14
Stockton, CA MSA	30	15
Savannah, GA MSA	27	16
Biloxi – Gulfport, MS MSA	27	16
Bremerton, WA MSA	22	17
Panama City, FL MSA	22	17
Houma – Thibodaux, LA MSA	21	18
San Diego, CA MSA	18	19
Melbourne – Titusville – Palm Bay, FL MSA	18	19

[Continued]

★1263★

Top 25 MSAs For Employment As Longshore Equipment Operators, 1990: Whites
[Continued]

MSA/CMSA	Employees per 100,000 pop.	Rank
Chicago – Gary – Lake County, IL – IN – WI CMSA	17	20
St. Louis, MO – IL MSA	15	21

Source: U.S. Department of Commerce, Bureau of the Census, Data User Services Division, *1990 Census of Population and Housing, Equal Employment Opportunity File, CD-90-EE0-1, January 1993,* CD-ROM.

★1264★

Occupations, By Race/Sex

Top 25 MSAs For Employment As Maids and Housemen, 1990: Blacks

MSA/CMSA	Employees per 100,000 pop.	Rank
Columbia, SC MSA	17,952	1
Chicago – Gary – Lake County, IL – IN – WI CMSA	7,558	2
Miami – Fort Lauderdale, FL CMSA	7,086	3
Philadelphia – Wilmington – Trenton, PA – NJ – DE – MD CMSA	6,244	4
Atlanta, GA MSA	5,457	5
Washington, DC – MD – VA MSA	5,410	6
Baltimore, MD MSA	4,352	7
Detroit – Ann Arbor, MI CMSA	4,350	8
New Orleans, LA MSA	4,214	9
Dallas – Fort Worth, TX CMSA	3,873	10
Houston – Galveston – Brazoria, TX CMSA	3,761	11
St. Louis, MO – IL MSA	3,450	12
Norfolk – Virginia Beach – Newport News, VA MSA	3,356	13
Las Vegas, NV MSA	3,118	14
Memphis, TN – AR – MS MSA	2,929	15
Los Angeles – Anaheim – Riverside, CA CMSA	2,630	16
Cleveland – Akron – Lorain, OH CMSA	2,512	17
Orlando, FL MSA	2,287	18
Boston – Lawrence – Salem, MA – NH CMSA	2,261	19
Tampa – St. Petersburg – Clearwater, FL MSA	2,234	20
Richmond – Petersburg, VA MSA	2,190	21
Charlotte – Gastonia – Rock Hill, NC – SC MSA	2,087	22
Birmingham, AL MSA	1,918	23
San Francisco – Oakland – San Jose, CA CMSA	1,886	24
Indianapolis, IN MSA	1,865	25

Source: U.S. Department of Commerce, Bureau of the Census, Data User Services Division, *1990 Census of Population and Housing, Equal Employment Opportunity File, CD-90-EE0-1, January 1993,* CD-ROM.

★1265★

Occupations, By Race/Sex

Top 25 MSAs For Employment As Maids and Housemen, 1990: Whites

MSA/CMSA	Employees per 100,000 pop.	Rank
Cincinnati – Hamilton, OH – KY – IN CMSA	16,820	1
New York – Northern New Jersey – Long Island, NY – NJ – CT CMSA	16,762	2
Chicago – Gary – Lake County, IL – IN – WI CMSA	7,933	3
San Francisco – Oakland – San Jose, CA CMSA	7,335	4
Boston – Lawrence – Salem, MA – NH CMSA	6,673	5
Detroit – Ann Arbor, MI CMSA	6,023	6
Miami – Fort Lauderdale, FL CMSA	5,493	7
Philadelphia – Wilmington – Trenton, PA – NJ – DE – MD CMSA	5,125	8
Las Vegas, NV MSA	4,774	9
Minneapolis – St. Paul, MN – WI MSA	4,752	10
Phoenix, AZ MSA	4,388	11
Pittsburgh – Beaver Valley, PA CMSA	4,150	12
Dallas – Fort Worth, TX CMSA	4,052	13
Seattle – Tacoma, WA CMSA	3,890	14
Tampa – St. Petersburg – Clearwater, FL MSA	3,843	15
St. Louis, MO – IL MSA	3,632	16
Cleveland – Akron – Lorain, OH CMSA	3,523	17
Washington, DC – MD – VA MSA	3,508	18
San Diego, CA MSA	3,475	19
Houston – Galveston – Brazoria, TX CMSA	3,392	20
Orlando, FL MSA	3,096	21
Portland – Vancouver, OR – WA CMSA	2,837	22
San Antonio, TX MSA	2,819	23
Denver – Boulder, CO CMSA	2,754	24
Kansas City, MO – KS MSA	2,592	25

Source: U.S. Department of Commerce, Bureau of the Census, Data User Services Division, *1990 Census of Population and Housing, Equal Employment Opportunity File, CD-90-EE0-1, January 1993,* CD-ROM.

★1266★

Occupations, By Race/Sex

Top 25 MSAs For Employment As Mail Carriers, Postal Service, 1990: Blacks

MSA/CMSA	Employees per 100,000 pop.	Rank
Dayton – Springfield, OH MSA	6,109	1
Chicago – Gary – Lake County, IL – IN – WI CMSA	4,510	2
Los Angeles – Anaheim – Riverside, CA CMSA	3,554	3
Washington, DC – MD – VA MSA	3,107	4
Detroit – Ann Arbor, MI CMSA	1,866	5
Houston – Galveston – Brazoria, TX CMSA	1,761	6
Atlanta, GA MSA	1,607	7
Philadelphia – Wilmington – Trenton, PA – NJ – DE – MD CMSA	1,514	8
Miami – Fort Lauderdale, FL CMSA	1,368	9
Dallas – Fort Worth, TX CMSA	1,292	10
San Francisco – Oakland – San Jose, CA CMSA	1,213	11
Baltimore, MD MSA	1,096	12
Cleveland – Akron – Lorain, OH CMSA	1,025	13
St. Louis, MO – IL MSA	934	14
New Orleans, LA MSA	882	15
Memphis, TN – AR – MS MSA	821	16
Norfolk – Virginia Beach – Newport News, VA MSA	770	17
Richmond – Petersburg, VA MSA	532	18
Baton Rouge, LA MSA	361	19
Birmingham, AL MSA	351	20
Dayton – Springfield, OH MSA	325	21
Columbus, OH MSA	316	22
Cincinnati – Hamilton, OH – KY – IN CMSA	308	23
Indianapolis, IN MSA	286	24
San Diego, CA MSA	284	25

Source: U.S. Department of Commerce, Bureau of the Census, Data User Services Division, *1990 Census of Population and Housing, Equal Employment Opportunity File, CD-90-EE0-1, January 1993,* CD-ROM.

★1267★

Occupations, By Race/Sex

Top 25 MSAs For Employment As Mail Carriers, Postal Service, 1990: Whites

MSA/CMSA	Employees per 100,000 pop.	Rank
Houston – Galveston – Brazoria, TX CMSA	21,075	1
Los Angeles – Anaheim – Riverside, CA CMSA	10,391	2
Philadelphia – Wilmington – Trenton, PA – NJ – DE – MD CMSA	7,177	3
Chicago – Gary – Lake County, IL – IN – WI CMSA	6,401	4

[Continued]

★ 1267 ★

Top 25 MSAs For Employment As Mail Carriers, Postal Service, 1990: Whites
[Continued]

MSA/CMSA	Employees per 100,000 pop.	Rank
Boston – Lawrence – Salem, MA – NH CMSA	6,395	5
San Francisco – Oakland – San Jose, CA CMSA	4,910	6
Detroit – Ann Arbor, MI CMSA	4,839	7
Dallas – Fort Worth, TX CMSA	4,034	8
Minneapolis – St. Paul, MN – WI MSA	3,371	9
Miami – Fort Lauderdale, FL CMSA	3,309	10
St. Louis, MO – IL MSA	3,189	11
Washington, DC – MD – VA MSA	3,139	12
Pittsburgh – Beaver Valley, PA CMSA	2,999	13
Cleveland – Akron – Lorain, OH CMSA	2,953	14
Tampa – St. Petersburg – Clearwater, FL MSA	2,755	15
Seattle – Tacoma, WA CMSA	2,587	16
Atlanta, GA MSA	2,565	17
Denver – Boulder, CO CMSA	2,519	18
Phoenix, AZ MSA	2,490	19
San Diego, CA MSA	2,369	20
Houston – Galveston – Brazoria, TX CMSA	2,325	21
Baltimore, MD MSA	2,302	22
Milwaukee – Racine, WI CMSA	1,988	23
Kansas City, MO – KS MSA	1,959	24
Portland – Vancouver, OR – WA CMSA	1,950	25

Source: U.S. Department of Commerce, Bureau of the Census, Data User Services Division, *1990 Census of Population and Housing, Equal Employment Opportunity File, CD-90-EE0-1,* January 1993, CD-ROM.

★ 1268 ★
Occupations, By Race/Sex

Top 25 MSAs For Employment As Marine and Naval Architects, 1990: Blacks

MSA/CMSA	Employees per 100,000 pop.	Rank
Jackson, TN MSA	112	1
Washington, DC – MD – VA MSA	38	2
Los Angeles – Anaheim – Riverside, CA CMSA	29	3
San Diego, CA MSA	24	4
New Orleans, LA MSA	16	5
Seattle – Tacoma, WA CMSA	15	6
Pascagoula, MS MSA	14	7
New London – Norwich, CT – RI MSA	12	8
Lafayette, LA MSA	11	9
Charleston, SC MSA	10	10
Philadelphia – Wilmington – Trenton, PA – NJ – DE – MD CMSA	10	10

[Continued]

★ 1268 ★

Top 25 MSAs For Employment As Marine and Naval Architects, 1990: Blacks
[Continued]

MSA/CMSA	Employees per 100,000 pop.	Rank
Jacksonville, FL MSA	9	11
Honolulu, HI MSA	9	11
Greensboro – Winston-Salem – High Point, NC MSA	9	11
Baltimore, MD MSA	8	12
Miami – Fort Lauderdale, FL CMSA	7	13
Salt Lake City – Ogden, UT MSA	6	14
San Francisco – Oakland – San Jose, CA CMSA	6	14
Mobile, AL MSA	5	15
Charlottesville, VA MSA	4	16
Portland – Vancouver, OR – WA CMSA	4	16
York, PA MSA	2	17
Owensboro, KY MSA	0	18
Muskegon, MI MSA	0	18
Parkersburg – Marietta, WV – OH MSA	0	18

Source: U.S. Department of Commerce, Bureau of the Census, Data User Services Division, *1990 Census of Population and Housing, Equal Employment Opportunity File, CD-90-EE0-1,* January 1993, CD-ROM.

★ 1269 ★
Occupations, By Race/Sex

Top 25 MSAs For Employment As Marine and Naval Architects, 1990: Whites

MSA/CMSA	Employees per 100,000 pop.	Rank
Raleigh – Durham, NC MSA	1,593	1
New London – Norwich, CT – RI MSA	680	2
New York – Northern New Jersey – Long Island, NY – NJ – CT CMSA	644	3
Washington, DC – MD – VA MSA	510	4
San Francisco – Oakland – San Jose, CA CMSA	496	5
Seattle – Tacoma, WA CMSA	416	6
New Orleans, LA MSA	380	7
Charleston, SC MSA	299	8
Bremerton, WA MSA	294	9
Baltimore, MD MSA	266	10
Pascagoula, MS MSA	266	10
Portsmouth – Dover – Rochester, NH – ME MSA	260	11
Boston – Lawrence – Salem, MA – NH CMSA	257	12
San Diego, CA MSA	254	13
Los Angeles – Anaheim – Riverside, CA CMSA	246	14
Houston – Galveston – Brazoria, TX CMSA	223	15

[Continued]

★1269★

Top 25 MSAs For Employment As Marine and Naval Architects, 1990: Whites

[Continued]

MSA/CMSA	Employees per 100,000 pop.	Rank
Philadelphia – Wilmington – Trenton, PA – NJ – DE – MD CMSA	222	16
Miami – Fort Lauderdale, FL CMSA	164	17
Tampa – St. Petersburg – Clearwater, FL MSA	161	18
Mobile, AL MSA	128 ·	19
Portland, ME MSA	122	20
Providence – Pawtucket – Fall River, RI – MA CMSA	110	21
Honolulu, HI MSA	110	21
Houma – Thibodaux, LA MSA	102	22
Jacksonville, FL MSA	98	23

Source: U.S. Department of Commerce, Bureau of the Census, Data User Services Division, *1990 Census of Population and Housing, Equal Employment Opportunity File, CD-90-EE0-1, January 1993,* CD-ROM.

★1270★

Occupations, By Race/Sex

Top 25 MSAs For Employment As Marine Life Cultivation Workers, 1990: Blacks

MSA/CMSA	Employees per 100,000 pop.	Rank
Tallahassee, FL MSA	13	1
Spokane, WA MSA	13	1
Cleveland – Akron – Lorain, OH CMSA	9	2
Baton Rouge, LA MSA	9	2
Muskegon, MI MSA	0	3
Orlando, FL MSA	0	3
Ocala, FL MSA	0	3
Oklahoma City, OK MSA	0	3
Panama City, FL MSA	0	3
New Haven – Meriden, CT MSA	0	3
Owensboro, KY MSA	0	3
Parkersburg – Marietta, WV – OH MSA	0	3
Norfolk – Virginia Beach – Newport News, VA MSA	0	3
Odessa, TX MSA	0	3
Olympia, WA MSA	0	3
Nashville, TN MSA	0	3
New Bedford, MA MSA	0	3
Raleigh – Durham, NC MSA	0	3
Omaha, NE – IA MSA	0	3
Pueblo, CO MSA	0	3
Las Cruces, NM MSA	0	3
Montgomery, AL MSA	0	3
Portsmouth – Dover – Rochester, NH – ME MSA	0	3

[Continued]

★1270★

Top 25 MSAs For Employment As Marine Life Cultivation Workers, 1990: Blacks

[Continued]

MSA/CMSA	Employees per 100,000 pop.	Rank
Rapid City, SD MSA	0	3
Provo – Orem, UT MSA	0	3

Source: U.S. Department of Commerce, Bureau of the Census, Data User Services Division, *1990 Census of Population and Housing, Equal Employment Opportunity File, CD-90-EE0-1, January 1993,* CD-ROM.

★1271★

Occupations, By Race/Sex

Top 25 MSAs For Employment As Marine Life Cultivation Workers, 1990: Whites

MSA/CMSA	Employees per 100,000 pop.	Rank
Seattle – Tacoma, WA CMSA	42	1
Portland – Vancouver, OR – WA CMSA	38	2
Fort Wayne, IN MSA	36	3
Tampa – St. Petersburg – Clearwater, FL MSA	29	4
Houston – Galveston – Brazoria, TX CMSA	17	5
Sacramento, CA MSA	16	6
Lancaster, PA MSA	15	7
Los Angeles – Anaheim – Riverside, CA CMSA	14	8
Baltimore, MD MSA	13	9
Richland – Kennewick – Pasco, WA MSA	13	9
Lafayette, LA MSA	13	9
Miami – Fort Lauderdale, FL CMSA	12	10
Lincoln, NE MSA	12	10
Dallas – Fort Worth, TX CMSA	12	10
Atlanta, GA MSA	10	11
Oklahoma City, OK MSA	10	11
Jacksonville, FL MSA	9	12
Grand Rapids, MI MSA	9	12
Tallahassee, FL MSA	8	13
Sherman – Denison, TX MSA	8	13
New York – Northern New Jersey – Long Island, NY – NJ – CT CMSA	8	13
Little Rock – North Little Rock, AR MSA	8	13
Eugene – Springfield, OR MSA	8	13
Pueblo, CO MSA	8	13
Indianapolis, IN MSA	8	13

Source: U.S. Department of Commerce, Bureau of the Census, Data User Services Division, *1990 Census of Population and Housing, Equal Employment Opportunity File, CD-90-EE0-1, January 1993,* CD-ROM.

★1272★

Occupations, By Race/Sex

Top 25 MSAs For Employment As Mathematical Science Teachers, 1990: Blacks

MSA/CMSA	Employees per 100,000 pop.	Rank
Redding, CA MSA	96	1
Baton Rouge, LA MSA	49	2
Miami – Fort Lauderdale, FL CMSA	42	3
San Francisco – Oakland – San Jose, CA CMSA	38	4
New Orleans, LA MSA	37	5
Tallahassee, FL MSA	36	6
Atlanta, GA MSA	35	7
Montgomery, AL MSA	32	8
Dallas – Fort Worth, TX CMSA	28	9
Cleveland – Akron – Lorain, OH CMSA	27	10
Phoenix, AZ MSA	21	11
Jackson, MS MSA	21	11
Fayetteville, NC MSA	21	11
Huntsville, AL MSA	20	12
Greensboro – Winston-Salem – High Point, NC MSA	18	13
Washington, DC – MD – VA MSA	17	14
Richmond – Petersburg, VA MSA	17	14
Chicago – Gary – Lake County, IL – IN – WI CMSA	16	15
St. Louis, MO – IL MSA	15	16
Los Angeles – Anaheim – Riverside, CA CMSA	14	17
Dayton – Springfield, OH MSA	14	17
Charlotte – Gastonia – Rock Hill, NC – SC MSA	13	18
Youngstown – Warren, OH MSA	12	19
Detroit – Ann Arbor, MI CMSA	11	20
Sacramento, CA MSA	11	20

Source: U.S. Department of Commerce, Bureau of the Census, Data User Services Division, *1990 Census of Population and Housing, Equal Employment Opportunity File, CD-90-EE0-1,* January 1993, CD-ROM.

★1273★

Occupations, By Race/Sex

Top 25 MSAs For Employment As Mathematical Science Teachers, 1990: Whites

MSA/CMSA	Employees per 100,000 pop.	Rank
Gainesville, FL MSA	949	1
Los Angeles – Anaheim – Riverside, CA CMSA	522	2
San Francisco – Oakland – San Jose, CA CMSA	469	3
Chicago – Gary – Lake County, IL – IN – WI CMSA	346	4
Philadelphia – Wilmington – Trenton, PA – NJ – DE – MD CMSA	339	5
Boston – Lawrence – Salem, MA – NH CMSA	293	6

[Continued]

★1273★

Top 25 MSAs For Employment As Mathematical Science Teachers, 1990: Whites
[Continued]

MSA/CMSA	Employees per 100,000 pop.	Rank
Washington, DC – MD – VA MSA	260	7
Detroit – Ann Arbor, MI CMSA	256	8
San Diego, CA MSA	245	9
Cleveland – Akron – Lorain, OH CMSA	191	10
Columbus, OH MSA	179	11
Seattle – Tacoma, WA CMSA	167	12
Austin, TX MSA	157	13
Atlanta, GA MSA	155	14
Minneapolis – St. Paul, MN – WI MSA	152	15
Houston – Galveston – Brazoria, TX CMSA	143	16
Dallas – Fort Worth, TX CMSA	130	17
Rochester, NY MSA	128	18
St. Louis, MO – IL MSA	125	19
Phoenix, AZ MSA	124	20
Santa Barbara – Santa Maria – Lompoc, CA MSA	111	21
Pittsburgh – Beaver Valley, PA CMSA	110	22
Tampa – St. Petersburg – Clearwater, FL MSA	107	23
Sacramento, CA MSA	104	24
Toledo, OH MSA	103	25

Source: U.S. Department of Commerce, Bureau of the Census, Data User Services Division, *1990 Census of Population and Housing, Equal Employment Opportunity File, CD-90-EE0-1,* January 1993, CD-ROM.

★1274★

Occupations, By Race/Sex

Top 25 MSAs For Employment As Medical Science Teachers, 1990: Blacks

MSA/CMSA	Employees per 100,000 pop.	Rank
New London – Norwich, CT – RI MSA	37	1
Washington, DC – MD – VA MSA	20	2
New Orleans, LA MSA	18	3
Columbia, SC MSA	16	4
San Diego, CA MSA	9	5
Houston – Galveston – Brazoria, TX CMSA	6	6
Odessa, TX MSA	0	7
Ocala, FL MSA	0	7
Omaha, NE – IA MSA	0	7
Oklahoma City, OK MSA	0	7
Nashville, TN MSA	0	7
Olympia, WA MSA	0	7
Orlando, FL MSA	0	7
Panama City, FL MSA	0	7
Owensboro, KY MSA	0	7
Naples, FL MSA	0	7

[Continued]

★1274★

Top 25 MSAs For Employment As Medical Science Teachers, 1990: Blacks
[Continued]

MSA/CMSA	Employees per 100,000 pop.	Rank
New London – Norwich, CT – RI MSA	0	7
Raleigh – Durham, NC MSA	0	7
Philadelphia – Wilmington – Trenton, PA – NJ – DE – MD CMSA	0	7
Muskegon, MI MSA	0	7
Las Vegas, NV MSA	0	7
Poughkeepsie, NY MSA	0	7
Provo – Orem, UT MSA	0	7
Reno, NV MSA	0	7
Rapid City, SD MSA	0	7

Source: U.S. Department of Commerce, Bureau of the Census, Data User Services Division, *1990 Census of Population and Housing, Equal Employment Opportunity File, CD-90-EE0-1, January 1993,* CD-ROM.

★1275★

Occupations, By Race/Sex

Top 25 MSAs For Employment As Medical Science Teachers, 1990: Whites

MSA/CMSA	Employees per 100,000 pop.	Rank
Syracuse, NY MSA	228	1
Los Angeles – Anaheim – Riverside, CA CMSA	110	2
Chicago – Gary – Lake County, IL – IN – WI CMSA	108	3
Houston – Galveston – Brazoria, TX CMSA	106	4
Dallas – Fort Worth, TX CMSA	72	5
Philadelphia – Wilmington – Trenton, PA – NJ – DE – MD CMSA	67	6
New Orleans, LA MSA	58	7
San Francisco – Oakland – San Jose, CA CMSA	53	8
Raleigh – Durham, NC MSA	51	9
Detroit – Ann Arbor, MI CMSA	49	10
Washington, DC – MD – VA MSA	46	11
St. Louis, MO – IL MSA	46	11
Charleston, SC MSA	44	12
Birmingham, AL MSA	41	13
Honolulu, HI MSA	40	14
Indianapolis, IN MSA	38	15
Columbia, SC MSA	37	16
Seattle – Tacoma, WA CMSA	34	17
Boston – Lawrence – Salem, MA – NH CMSA	33	18
Richmond – Petersburg, VA MSA	32	19
Syracuse, NY MSA	31	20
New Haven – Meriden, CT MSA	31	20
Memphis, TN – AR – MS MSA	31	20

[Continued]

★1275★

Top 25 MSAs For Employment As Medical Science Teachers, 1990: Whites
[Continued]

MSA/CMSA	Employees per 100,000 pop.	Rank
San Diego, CA MSA	30	21
Greensboro – Winston-Salem – High Point, NC MSA	30	21

Source: U.S. Department of Commerce, Bureau of the Census, Data User Services Division, *1990 Census of Population and Housing, Equal Employment Opportunity File, CD-90-EE0-1, January 1993,* CD-ROM.

★1276★

Occupations, By Race/Sex

Top 25 MSAs For Employment As Mining Engineers, 1990: Blacks

MSA/CMSA	Employees per 100,000 pop.	Rank
Boston – Lawrence – Salem, MA – NH CMSA	11	1
New York – Northern New Jersey – Long Island, NY – NJ – CT CMSA	11	1
Houma – Thibodaux, LA MSA	9	2
Los Angeles – Anaheim – Riverside, CA CMSA	8	3
Houston – Galveston – Brazoria, TX CMSA	5	4
El Paso, TX MSA	0	5
Eau Claire, WI MSA	0	5
Elmira, NY MSA	0	5
Enid, OK MSA	0	5
Erie, PA MSA	0	5
Eugene – Springfield, OR MSA	0	5
Fort Smith, AR – OK MSA	0	5
Fitchburg – Leominster, MA MSA	0	5
Flint, MI MSA	0	5
Florence, AL MSA	0	5
Fort Pierce, FL MSA	0	5
Florence, SC MSA	0	5
Dothan, AL MSA	0	5
Fort Collins – Loveland, CO MSA	0	5
Columbia, MO MSA	0	5
Des Moines, IA MSA	0	5
Dayton – Springfield, OH MSA	0	5
Daytona Beach, FL MSA	0	5
Duluth, MN – WI MSA	0	5
Fargo – Moorhead, ND – MN MSA	0	5

Source: U.S. Department of Commerce, Bureau of the Census, Data User Services Division, *1990 Census of Population and Housing, Equal Employment Opportunity File, CD-90-EE0-1, January 1993,* CD-ROM.

★1277★

Occupations, By Race/Sex

Top 25 MSAs For Employment As Mining Engineers, 1990: Whites

MSA/CMSA	Employees per 100,000 pop.	Rank
Sacramento, CA MSA	253	1
Pittsburgh – Beaver Valley, PA CMSA	238	2
Houston – Galveston – Brazoria, TX CMSA	188	3
Tucson, AZ MSA	127	4
Salt Lake City – Ogden, UT MSA	115	5
Phoenix, AZ MSA	84	6
Duluth, MN – WI MSA	71	7
New Orleans, LA MSA	70	8
New York – Northern New Jersey – Long Island, NY – NJ – CT CMSA	64	9
Reno, NV MSA	62	10
Washington, DC – MD – VA MSA	54	11
Lexington-Fayette, KY MSA	49	12
Tuscaloosa, AL MSA	49	12
Knoxville, TN MSA	49	12
Los Angeles – Anaheim – Riverside, CA CMSA	47	13
Johnson City – Kingsport – Bristol, TN – VA MSA	47	13
Spokane, WA MSA	44	14
Birmingham, AL MSA	40	15
Johnstown, PA MSA	39	16
St. Louis, MO – IL MSA	39	16
Cleveland – Akron – Lorain, OH CMSA	39	16
Las Vegas, NV MSA	37	17
Chicago – Gary – Lake County, IL – IN – WI CMSA	36	18
Huntington – Ashland, WV – KY – OH MSA	35	19
Longview – Marshall, TX MSA	34	20

Source: U.S. Department of Commerce, Bureau of the Census, Data User Services Division, *1990 Census of Population and Housing, Equal Employment Opportunity File, CD-90-EE0-1, January 1993,* CD-ROM.

★1278★

Occupations, By Race/Sex

Top 25 MSAs For Employment As Motion Picture Projectionists, 1990: Blacks

MSA/CMSA	Employees per 100,000 pop.	Rank
Cleveland – Akron – Lorain, OH CMSA	90	1
New York – Northern New Jersey – Long Island, NY – NJ – CT CMSA	89	2
Chicago – Gary – Lake County, IL – IN – WI CMSA	43	3
Washington, DC – MD – VA MSA	25	4
Atlanta, GA MSA	19	5

[Continued]

★1278★

Top 25 MSAs For Employment As Motion Picture Projectionists, 1990: Blacks

[Continued]

MSA/CMSA	Employees per 100,000 pop.	Rank
Dallas – Fort Worth, TX CMSA	19	5
Little Rock – North Little Rock, AR MSA	14	6
Abilene, TX MSA	13	7
Charleston, SC MSA	13	7
Miami – Fort Lauderdale, FL CMSA	13	7
San Francisco – Oakland – San Jose, CA CMSA	9	8
Hartford – New Britain – Middletown, CT CMSA	9	8
Huntsville, AL MSA	9	8
Indianapolis, IN MSA	9	8
Houston – Galveston – Brazoria, TX CMSA	9	8
Tuscaloosa, AL MSA	8	9
Kansas City, MO – KS MSA	7	10
Albany – Schenectady – Troy, NY MSA	7	10
Cincinnati – Hamilton, OH – KY – IN CMSA	6	11
Lakeland – Winter Haven, FL MSA	6	11
El Paso, TX MSA	5	12
St. Louis, MO – IL MSA	4	13
Boston – Lawrence – Salem, MA – NH CMSA	3	14
Panama City, FL MSA	0	15
Olympia, WA MSA	0	15

Source: U.S. Department of Commerce, Bureau of the Census, Data User Services Division, *1990 Census of Population and Housing, Equal Employment Opportunity File, CD-90-EE0-1, January 1993,* CD-ROM.

★1279★

Occupations, By Race/Sex

Top 25 MSAs For Employment As Motion Picture Projectionists, 1990: Whites

MSA/CMSA	Employees per 100,000 pop.	Rank
Nashville, TN MSA	1,285	1
New York – Northern New Jersey – Long Island, NY – NJ – CT CMSA	741	2
Chicago – Gary – Lake County, IL – IN – WI CMSA	330	3
San Francisco – Oakland – San Jose, CA CMSA	250	4
Dallas – Fort Worth, TX CMSA	201	5
Seattle – Tacoma, WA CMSA	164	6
Washington, DC – MD – VA MSA	163	7
Atlanta, GA MSA	151	8
Houston – Galveston – Brazoria, TX CMSA	135	9
Boston – Lawrence – Salem, MA – NH CMSA	129	10

[Continued]

★1279★

Top 25 MSAs For Employment As Motion Picture Projectionists, 1990: Whites
[Continued]

MSA/CMSA	Employees per 100,000 pop.	Rank
Philadelphia – Wilmington – Trenton, PA – NJ – DE – MD CMSA	115	11
Miami – Fort Lauderdale, FL CMSA	112	12
San Diego, CA MSA	112	12
Portland – Vancouver, OR – WA CMSA	96	13
New Orleans, LA MSA	94	14
Detroit – Ann Arbor, MI CMSA	90	15
Baltimore, MD MSA	88	16
Minneapolis – St. Paul, MN – WI MSA	85	17
Tampa – St. Petersburg – Clearwater, FL MSA	83	18
Rochester, NY MSA	82	19
Denver – Boulder, CO CMSA	80	20
Cleveland – Akron – Lorain, OH CMSA	73	21
Scranton – Wilkes-Barre, PA MSA	70	22
Raleigh – Durham, NC MSA	68	23
Pittsburgh – Beaver Valley, PA CMSA	66	24

Source: U.S. Department of Commerce, Bureau of the Census, Data User Services Division, *1990 Census of Population and Housing, Equal Employment Opportunity File, CD-90-EE0-1, January 1993*, CD-ROM.

★1280★

Occupations, By Race/Sex

Top 25 MSAs For Employment As Musicians and Composers, 1990: Blacks

MSA/CMSA	Employees per 100,000 pop.	Rank
Albany – Schenectady – Troy, NY MSA	1,830	1
Los Angeles – Anaheim – Riverside, CA CMSA	1,222	2
Chicago – Gary – Lake County, IL – IN – WI CMSA	605	3
Washington, DC – MD – VA MSA	539	4
Detroit – Ann Arbor, MI CMSA	413	5
San Francisco – Oakland – San Jose, CA CMSA	403	6
Philadelphia – Wilmington – Trenton, PA – NJ – DE – MD CMSA	393	7
Atlanta, GA MSA	254	8
Dallas – Fort Worth, TX CMSA	246	9
Miami – Fort Lauderdale, FL CMSA	244	10
Boston – Lawrence – Salem, MA – NH CMSA	206	11
New Orleans, LA MSA	190	12

[Continued]

★1280★

Top 25 MSAs For Employment As Musicians and Composers, 1990: Blacks
[Continued]

MSA/CMSA	Employees per 100,000 pop.	Rank
St. Louis, MO – IL MSA	185	13
Cleveland – Akron – Lorain, OH CMSA	172	14
Raleigh – Durham, NC MSA	140	15
Baltimore, MD MSA	139	16
Houston – Galveston – Brazoria, TX CMSA	118	17
Orlando, FL MSA	110	18
Las Vegas, NV MSA	104	19
Tampa – St. Petersburg – Clearwater, FL MSA	98	20
Minneapolis – St. Paul, MN – WI MSA	96	21
Richmond – Petersburg, VA MSA	95	22
Charlotte – Gastonia – Rock Hill, NC – SC MSA	92	23
Greensboro – Winston-Salem – High Point, NC MSA	91	24
Cincinnati – Hamilton, OH – KY – IN CMSA	87	25

Source: U.S. Department of Commerce, Bureau of the Census, Data User Services Division, *1990 Census of Population and Housing, Equal Employment Opportunity File, CD-90-EE0-1, January 1993*, CD-ROM.

★1281★

Occupations, By Race/Sex

Top 25 MSAs For Employment As Musicians and Composers, 1990: Whites

MSA/CMSA	Employees per 100,000 pop.	Rank
Cleveland – Akron – Lorain, OH CMSA	14,473	1
Los Angeles – Anaheim – Riverside, CA CMSA	11,619	2
San Francisco – Oakland – San Jose, CA CMSA	4,275	3
Chicago – Gary – Lake County, IL – IN – WI CMSA	3,770	4
Nashville, TN MSA	3,204	5
Boston – Lawrence – Salem, MA – NH CMSA	2,794	6
Philadelphia – Wilmington – Trenton, PA – NJ – DE – MD CMSA	2,505	7
Miami – Fort Lauderdale, FL CMSA	2,288	8
Detroit – Ann Arbor, MI CMSA	2,174	9
Dallas – Fort Worth, TX CMSA	2,084	10
Minneapolis – St. Paul, MN – WI MSA	1,985	11
Washington, DC – MD – VA MSA	1,911	12
Seattle – Tacoma, WA CMSA	1,789	13
Houston – Galveston – Brazoria, TX CMSA	1,605	14

[Continued]

★1281★

Top 25 MSAs For Employment As Musicians and Composers, 1990: Whites
[Continued]

MSA/CMSA	Employees per 100,000 pop.	Rank
San Diego, CA MSA	1,575	15
Atlanta, GA MSA	1,523	16
Cleveland – Akron – Lorain, OH CMSA	1,454	17
Denver – Boulder, CO CMSA	1,261	18
Phoenix, AZ MSA	1,245	19
Tampa – St. Petersburg – Clearwater, FL MSA	1,165	20
St. Louis, MO – IL MSA	1,144	21
Pittsburgh – Beaver Valley, PA CMSA	1,129	22
Orlando, FL MSA	1,123	23
Portland – Vancouver, OR – WA CMSA	1,067	24
Las Vegas, NV MSA	1,011	25

Source: U.S. Department of Commerce, Bureau of the Census, Data User Services Division, *1990 Census of Population and Housing, Equal Employment Opportunity File,* CD-90-EE0-1, January 1993, CD-ROM.

★1282★

Occupations, By Race/Sex

Top 25 MSAs For Employment As Nuclear Engineers, 1990: Blacks

MSA/CMSA	Employees per 100,000 pop.	Rank
Providence – Pawtucket – Fall River, RI – MA CMSA	29	1
San Francisco – Oakland – San Jose, CA CMSA	29	1
Charleston, SC MSA	24	2
Norfolk – Virginia Beach – Newport News, VA MSA	23	3
Orlando, FL MSA	11	4
Washington, DC – MD – VA MSA	9	5
New London – Norwich, CT – RI MSA	9	5
Pittsburgh – Beaver Valley, PA CMSA	7	6
Bremerton, WA MSA	5	7
New Orleans, LA MSA	5	7
Hickory – Morganton, NC MSA	0	8
Houston – Galveston – Brazoria, TX CMSA	0	8
Honolulu, HI MSA	0	8
Greenville – Spartanburg, SC MSA	0	8
Hartford – New Britain – Middletown, CT CMSA	0	8
Iowa City, IA MSA	0	8
Huntsville, AL MSA	0	8
Jacksonville, FL MSA	0	8
Indianapolis, IN MSA	0	8
Jacksonville, NC MSA	0	8

[Continued]

★1282★

Top 25 MSAs For Employment As Nuclear Engineers, 1990: Blacks
[Continued]

MSA/CMSA	Employees per 100,000 pop.	Rank
Jackson, MS MSA	0	8
Jamestown – Dunkirk, NY	0	8
Jackson, MI MSA	0	8
Hagerstown, MD MSA	0	8
Gadsden, AL MSA	0	8

Source: U.S. Department of Commerce, Bureau of the Census, Data User Services Division, *1990 Census of Population and Housing, Equal Employment Opportunity File,* CD-90-EE0-1, January 1993, CD-ROM.

★1283★

Occupations, By Race/Sex

Top 25 MSAs For Employment As Nuclear Engineers, 1990: Whites

MSA/CMSA	Employees per 100,000 pop.	Rank
Washington, DC – MD – VA MSA	518	1
San Francisco – Oakland – San Jose, CA CMSA	511	2
Washington, DC – MD – VA MSA	429	3
Norfolk – Virginia Beach – Newport News, VA MSA	412	4
Bremerton, WA MSA	351	5
Charleston, SC MSA	295	6
New York – Northern New Jersey – Long Island, NY – NJ – CT CMSA	285	7
Chicago – Gary – Lake County, IL – IN – WI CMSA	282	8
Philadelphia – Wilmington – Trenton, PA – NJ – DE – MD CMSA	280	9
Augusta, GA – SC MSA	269	10
Richland – Kennewick – Pasco, WA MSA	256	11
Charlotte – Gastonia – Rock Hill, NC – SC MSA	254	12
Portsmouth – Dover – Rochester, NH – ME MSA	239	13
Albany – Schenectady – Troy, NY MSA	220	14
Boston – Lawrence – Salem, MA – NH CMSA	215	15
Hartford – New Britain – Middletown, CT CMSA	195	16
Knoxville, TN MSA	176	17
Los Angeles – Anaheim – Riverside, CA CMSA	158	18
New London – Norwich, CT – RI MSA	145	19
Phoenix, AZ MSA	126	20
Seattle – Tacoma, WA CMSA	126	20
San Diego, CA MSA	122	21
Atlanta, GA MSA	110	22

[Continued]

★1283★

Top 25 MSAs For Employment As Nuclear Engineers, 1990: Whites

[Continued]

MSA/CMSA	Employees per 100,000 pop.	Rank
Chattanooga, TN–GA MSA	110	22
Albuquerque, NM MSA	95	23

Source: U.S. Department of Commerce, Bureau of the Census, Data User Services Division, *1990 Census of Population and Housing, Equal Employment Opportunity File,* CD-90-EEO-1, January 1993, CD-ROM.

★1284★

Occupations, By Race/Sex

Top 25 MSAs For Employment As Nursery Workers, 1990: Blacks

MSA/CMSA	Employees per 100,000 pop.	Rank
Portland–Vancouver, OR–WA CMSA	194	1
Orlando, FL MSA	161	2
Mobile, AL MSA	97	3
West Palm Beach–Boca Raton–Delray Beach, FL MSA	92	4
New York–Northern New Jersey–Long Island, NY–NJ–CT CMSA	69	5
Tallahassee, FL MSA	69	5
Birmingham, AL MSA	67	6
Raleigh–Durham, NC MSA	54	7
Philadelphia–Wilmington–Trenton, PA–NJ–DE–MD CMSA	45	8
Richmond–Petersburg, VA MSA	37	9
Augusta, GA–SC MSA	36	10
Cleveland–Akron–Lorain, OH CMSA	33	11
Chicago–Gary–Lake County, IL–IN–WI CMSA	33	11
Los Angeles–Anaheim–Riverside, CA CMSA	29	12
Dallas–Fort Worth, TX CMSA	29	12
Naples, FL MSA	28	13
New London–Norwich, CT–RI MSA	26	14
Fayetteville, NC MSA	25	15
Tyler, TX MSA	25	15
Atlanta, GA MSA	24	16
Seattle–Tacoma, WA CMSA	23	17
Daytona Beach, FL MSA	22	18
Memphis, TN–AR–MS MSA	19	19
Anderson, SC MSA	19	19
New Orleans, LA MSA	18	20

Source: U.S. Department of Commerce, Bureau of the Census, Data User Services Division, *1990 Census of Population and Housing, Equal Employment Opportunity File,* CD-90-EEO-1, January 1993, CD-ROM.

★1285★

Occupations, By Race/Sex

Top 25 MSAs For Employment As Nursery Workers, 1990: Whites

MSA/CMSA	Employees per 100,000 pop.	Rank
Medford, OR MSA	1,200	1
Los Angeles–Anaheim–Riverside, CA CMSA	916	2
San Francisco–Oakland–San Jose, CA CMSA	787	3
New York–Northern New Jersey–Long Island, NY–NJ–CT CMSA	709	4
San Diego, CA MSA	479	5
Portland–Vancouver, OR–WA CMSA	423	6
Detroit–Ann Arbor, MI CMSA	388	7
Orlando, FL MSA	367	8
Miami–Fort Lauderdale, FL CMSA	346	9
Cleveland–Akron–Lorain, OH CMSA	343	10
Seattle–Tacoma, WA CMSA	341	11
Boston–Lawrence–Salem, MA–NH CMSA	340	12
Tampa–St. Petersburg–Clearwater, FL MSA	332	13
Grand Rapids, MI MSA	319	14
Chicago–Gary–Lake County, IL–IN–WI CMSA	283	15
Kalamazoo, MI MSA	255	16
Minneapolis–St. Paul, MN–WI MSA	249	17
Denver–Boulder, CO CMSA	248	18
Buffalo–Niagara Falls, NY CMSA	242	19
Pittsburgh–Beaver Valley, PA CMSA	229	20
Atlanta, GA MSA	216	21
Washington, DC–MD–VA MSA	203	22
St. Louis, MO–IL MSA	198	23
Dallas–Fort Worth, TX CMSA	184	24
Houston–Galveston–Brazoria, TX CMSA	180	25

Source: U.S. Department of Commerce, Bureau of the Census, Data User Services Division, *1990 Census of Population and Housing, Equal Employment Opportunity File,* CD-90-EEO-1, January 1993, CD-ROM.

★1286★

Occupations, By Race/Sex

Top 25 MSAs For Employment As Occupational Therapists, 1990: Blacks

MSA/CMSA	Employees per 100,000 pop.	Rank
Greensboro – Winston-Salem – High Point, NC MSA	452	1
Detroit – Ann Arbor, MI CMSA	149	2
Chicago – Gary – Lake County, IL – IN – WI CMSA	131	3
Washington, DC – MD – VA MSA	127	4
Philadelphia – Wilmington – Trenton, PA – NJ – DE – MD CMSA	103	5
Miami – Fort Lauderdale, FL CMSA	89	6
Birmingham, AL MSA	85	7
Houston – Galveston – Brazoria, TX CMSA	68	8
Los Angeles – Anaheim – Riverside, CA CMSA	68	8
Dallas – Fort Worth, TX CMSA	44	9
San Francisco – Oakland – San Jose, CA CMSA	40	10
Memphis, TN – AR – MS MSA	37	11
Cleveland – Akron – Lorain, OH CMSA	32	12
Norfolk – Virginia Beach – Newport News, VA MSA	25	13
St. Louis, MO – IL MSA	23	14
Orlando, FL MSA	23	14
Jacksonville, FL MSA	22	15
Nashville, TN MSA	22	15
San Diego, CA MSA	19	16
Sherman – Denison, TX MSA	18	17
Baltimore, MD MSA	17	18
Cincinnati – Hamilton, OH – KY – IN CMSA	16	19
Waco, TX MSA	15	20
Montgomery, AL MSA	15	20
Huntsville, AL MSA	14	21

Source: U.S. Department of Commerce, Bureau of the Census, Data User Services Division, *1990 Census of Population and Housing, Equal Employment Opportunity File, CD-90-EE0-1,* January 1993, CD-ROM.

★1287★

Occupations, By Race/Sex

Top 25 MSAs For Employment As Occupational Therapists, 1990: Whites

MSA/CMSA	Employees per 100,000 pop.	Rank
New Orleans, LA MSA	2,817	1
Boston – Lawrence – Salem, MA – NH CMSA	1,346	2
Los Angeles – Anaheim – Riverside, CA CMSA	1,203	3
Chicago – Gary – Lake County, IL – IN – WI CMSA	1,176	4

[Continued]

★1287★

Top 25 MSAs For Employment As Occupational Therapists, 1990: Whites
[Continued]

MSA/CMSA	Employees per 100,000 pop.	Rank
Philadelphia – Wilmington – Trenton, PA – NJ – DE – MD CMSA	985	5
San Francisco – Oakland – San Jose, CA CMSA	945	6
Minneapolis – St. Paul, MN – WI MSA	943	7
Milwaukee – Racine, WI CMSA	847	8
Detroit – Ann Arbor, MI CMSA	783	9
Seattle – Tacoma, WA CMSA	645	10
Denver – Boulder, CO CMSA	538	11
Dallas – Fort Worth, TX CMSA	528	12
Baltimore, MD MSA	515	13
Houston – Galveston – Brazoria, TX CMSA	464	14
Pittsburgh – Beaver Valley, PA CMSA	460	15
Buffalo – Niagara Falls, NY CMSA	450	16
Washington, DC – MD – VA MSA	445	17
St. Louis, MO – IL MSA	426	18
Cleveland – Akron – Lorain, OH CMSA	425	19
Kansas City, MO – KS MSA	408	20
Columbus, OH MSA	355	21
Miami – Fort Lauderdale, FL CMSA	350	22
Phoenix, AZ MSA	340	23
San Diego, CA MSA	303	24
Grand Rapids, MI MSA	299	25

Source: U.S. Department of Commerce, Bureau of the Census, Data User Services Division, *1990 Census of Population and Housing, Equal Employment Opportunity File, CD-90-EE0-1,* January 1993, CD-ROM.

★1288★

Occupations, By Race/Sex

Top 25 MSAs For Employment As Optometrists, 1990: Blacks

MSA/CMSA	Employees per 100,000 pop.	Rank
Pensacola, FL MSA	70	1
New York – Northern New Jersey – Long Island, NY – NJ – CT CMSA	61	2
Dallas – Fort Worth, TX CMSA	49	3
San Francisco – Oakland – San Jose, CA CMSA	30	4
Cincinnati – Hamilton, OH – KY – IN CMSA	19	5
Philadelphia – Wilmington – Trenton, PA – NJ – DE – MD CMSA	18	6
Richmond – Petersburg, VA MSA	16	7
Washington, DC – MD – VA MSA	12	8

[Continued]

★1288★

Top 25 MSAs For Employment As Optometrists, 1990: Blacks
[Continued]

MSA/CMSA	Employees per 100,000 pop.	Rank
Memphis, TN–AR–MS MSA	11	9
Birmingham, AL MSA	10	10
Jackson, TN MSA	10	10
Indianapolis, IN MSA	9	11
Columbia, SC MSA	9	11
Baltimore, MD MSA	8	12
Mobile, AL MSA	8	12
Norfolk–Virginia Beach–Newport News, VA MSA	8	12
Charleston, SC MSA	7	13
Little Rock–North Little Rock, AR MSA	7	13
Portland–Vancouver, OR–WA CMSA	7	13
New Orleans, LA MSA	6	14
Toledo, OH MSA	5	15
Peoria, IL MSA	4	16
Bryan–College Station, TX MSA	0	17
Charleston, WV MSA	0	17
Buffalo–Niagara Falls, NY CMSA	0	17

Source: U.S. Department of Commerce, Bureau of the Census, Data User Services Division, 1990 Census of Population and Housing, Equal Employment Opportunity File, CD-90-EEO-1, January 1993, CD-ROM.

★1289★

Occupations, By Race/Sex

Top 25 MSAs For Employment As Optometrists, 1990: Whites

MSA/CMSA	Employees per 100,000 pop.	Rank
Milwaukee–Racine, WI CMSA	1,881	1
Los Angeles–Anaheim–Riverside, CA CMSA	1,484	2
Chicago–Gary–Lake County, IL–IN–WI CMSA	923	3
San Francisco–Oakland–San Jose, CA CMSA	659	4
Philadelphia–Wilmington–Trenton, PA–NJ–DE–MD CMSA	648	5
Boston–Lawrence–Salem, MA–NH CMSA	501	6
Detroit–Ann Arbor, MI CMSA	433	7
Washington, DC–MD–VA MSA	367	8
Pittsburgh–Beaver Valley, PA CMSA	363	9
Houston–Galveston–Brazoria, TX CMSA	363	9
San Diego, CA MSA	359	10
Cleveland–Akron–Lorain, OH CMSA	342	11
Miami–Fort Lauderdale, FL CMSA	342	11

[Continued]

★1289★

Top 25 MSAs For Employment As Optometrists, 1990: Whites
[Continued]

MSA/CMSA	Employees per 100,000 pop.	Rank
Dallas–Fort Worth, TX CMSA	299	12
St. Louis, MO–IL MSA	284	13
Baltimore, MD MSA	260	14
Denver–Boulder, CO CMSA	258	15
Minneapolis–St. Paul, MN–WI MSA	243	16
Portland–Vancouver, OR–WA CMSA	235	17
Phoenix, AZ MSA	223	18
Atlanta, GA MSA	193	19
Seattle–Tacoma, WA CMSA	193	19
Sacramento, CA MSA	189	20
Columbus, OH MSA	183	21
Indianapolis, IN MSA	180	22

Source: U.S. Department of Commerce, Bureau of the Census, Data User Services Division, 1990 Census of Population and Housing, Equal Employment Opportunity File, CD-90-EEO-1, January 1993, CD-ROM.

★1290★

Occupations, By Race/Sex

Top 25 MSAs For Employment As Painters, Sculptors, Craft-artists, and Artist Printmakers, 1990: Blacks

MSA/CMSA	Employees per 100,000 pop.	Rank
Greensboro–Winston-Salem–High Point, NC MSA	1,569	1
Washington, DC–MD–VA MSA	621	2
Los Angeles–Anaheim–Riverside, CA CMSA	599	3
Philadelphia–Wilmington–Trenton, PA–NJ–DE–MD CMSA	451	4
Atlanta, GA MSA	308	5
Chicago–Gary–Lake County, IL–IN–WI CMSA	306	6
Baltimore, MD MSA	245	7
Detroit–Ann Arbor, MI CMSA	196	8
San Francisco–Oakland–San Jose, CA CMSA	178	9
Miami–Fort Lauderdale, FL CMSA	167	10
Dallas–Fort Worth, TX CMSA	140	11
Richmond–Petersburg, VA MSA	113	12
Norfolk–Virginia Beach–Newport News, VA MSA	91	13
St. Louis, MO–IL MSA	89	14
Greensboro–Winston-Salem–High Point, NC MSA	85	15
Cleveland–Akron–Lorain, OH CMSA	81	16
Houston–Galveston–Brazoria, TX CMSA	79	17

[Continued]

★1290★

Top 25 MSAs For Employment As Painters, Sculptors, Craft-artists, and Artist Printmakers, 1990: Blacks

[Continued]

MSA/CMSA	Employees per 100,000 pop.	Rank
Denver – Boulder, CO CMSA	78	18
Boston – Lawrence – Salem, MA – NH CMSA	77	19
Seattle – Tacoma, WA CMSA	75	20
Nashville, TN MSA	63	21
Kansas City, MO – KS MSA	62	22
Charlotte – Gastonia – Rock Hill, NC – SC MSA	57	23
Memphis, TN – AR – MS MSA	54	24
Buffalo – Niagara Falls, NY CMSA	53	25

Source: U.S. Department of Commerce, Bureau of the Census, Data User Services Division, *1990 Census of Population and Housing, Equal Employment Opportunity File, CD-90-EE0-1,* January 1993, CD-ROM.

★1291★

Occupations, By Race/Sex

Top 25 MSAs For Employment As Painters, Sculptors, Craft-artists, and Artist Printmakers, 1990: Whites

MSA/CMSA	Employees per 100,000 pop.	Rank
Kansas City, MO – KS MSA	22,181	1
Los Angeles – Anaheim – Riverside, CA CMSA	14,022	2
Chicago – Gary – Lake County, IL – IN – WI CMSA	7,510	3
San Francisco – Oakland – San Jose, CA CMSA	7,025	4
Philadelphia – Wilmington – Trenton, PA – NJ – DE – MD CMSA	5,029	5
Boston – Lawrence – Salem, MA – NH CMSA	4,794	6
Washington, DC – MD – VA MSA	4,417	7
Dallas – Fort Worth, TX CMSA	3,603	8
Seattle – Tacoma, WA CMSA	3,246	9
Detroit – Ann Arbor, MI CMSA	3,197	10
Minneapolis – St. Paul, MN – WI MSA	2,923	11
Atlanta, GA MSA	2,790	12
San Diego, CA MSA	2,553	13
Houston – Galveston – Brazoria, TX CMSA	2,457	14
Denver – Boulder, CO CMSA	2,409	15
Miami – Fort Lauderdale, FL CMSA	2,407	16
St. Louis, MO – IL MSA	2,092	17
Cleveland – Akron – Lorain, OH CMSA	2,057	18
Baltimore, MD MSA	2,019	19
Kansas City, MO – KS MSA	1,907	20

[Continued]

★1291★

Top 25 MSAs For Employment As Painters, Sculptors, Craft-artists, and Artist Printmakers, 1990: Whites

[Continued]

MSA/CMSA	Employees per 100,000 pop.	Rank
Phoenix, AZ MSA	1,903	21
Tampa – St. Petersburg – Clearwater, FL MSA	1,833	22
Portland – Vancouver, OR – WA CMSA	1,641	23
Milwaukee – Racine, WI CMSA	1,600	24
Cincinnati – Hamilton, OH – KY – IN CMSA	1,423	25

Source: U.S. Department of Commerce, Bureau of the Census, Data User Services Division, *1990 Census of Population and Housing, Equal Employment Opportunity File, CD-90-EE0-1,* January 1993, CD-ROM.

★1292★

Occupations, By Race/Sex

Top 25 MSAs For Employment As Personnel and Labor Relations Managers, 1990: Blacks

MSA/CMSA	Employees per 100,000 pop.	Rank
Oklahoma City, OK MSA	3,572	1
Washington, DC – MD – VA MSA	2,627	2
Los Angeles – Anaheim – Riverside, CA CMSA	1,468	3
Chicago – Gary – Lake County, IL – IN – WI CMSA	1,316	4
Philadelphia – Wilmington – Trenton, PA – NJ – DE – MD CMSA	1,019	5
San Francisco – Oakland – San Jose, CA CMSA	821	6
Atlanta, GA MSA	757	7
Detroit – Ann Arbor, MI CMSA	733	8
Baltimore, MD MSA	485	9
Dallas – Fort Worth, TX CMSA	466	10
Houston – Galveston – Brazoria, TX CMSA	441	11
Miami – Fort Lauderdale, FL CMSA	362	12
New Orleans, LA MSA	297	13
Norfolk – Virginia Beach – Newport News, VA MSA	295	14
Boston – Lawrence – Salem, MA – NH CMSA	294	15
Cleveland – Akron – Lorain, OH CMSA	272	16
Richmond – Petersburg, VA MSA	261	17
Columbia, SC MSA	186	18
Memphis, TN – AR – MS MSA	186	18
Kansas City, MO – KS MSA	176	19
St. Louis, MO – IL MSA	172	20
Raleigh – Durham, NC MSA	161	21
Denver – Boulder, CO CMSA	161	21

[Continued]

★1292★

Top 25 MSAs For Employment As Personnel and Labor Relations Managers, 1990: Blacks

[Continued]

MSA/CMSA	Employees per 100,000 pop.	Rank
Milwaukee – Racine, WI CMSA	155	22
Charlotte – Gastonia – Rock Hill, NC – SC MSA	154	23

Source: U.S. Department of Commerce, Bureau of the Census, Data User Services Division, *1990 Census of Population and Housing, Equal Employment Opportunity File, CD-90-EE0-1, January 1993,* CD-ROM.

★1293★

Occupations, By Race/Sex

Top 25 MSAs For Employment As Personnel and Labor Relations Managers, 1990: Whites

MSA/CMSA	Employees per 100,000 pop.	Rank
Indianapolis, IN MSA	20,512	1
Los Angeles – Anaheim – Riverside, CA CMSA	13,442	2
Chicago – Gary – Lake County, IL – IN – WI CMSA	7,614	3
Washington, DC – MD – VA MSA	6,656	4
San Francisco – Oakland – San Jose, CA CMSA	6,556	5
Boston – Lawrence – Salem, MA – NH CMSA	6,021	6
Philadelphia – Wilmington – Trenton, PA – NJ – DE – MD CMSA	5,855	7
Dallas – Fort Worth, TX CMSA	4,583	8
Detroit – Ann Arbor, MI CMSA	4,278	9
Houston – Galveston – Brazoria, TX CMSA	3,579	10
Miami – Fort Lauderdale, FL CMSA	3,544	11
Atlanta, GA MSA	3,236	12
Minneapolis – St. Paul, MN – WI MSA	3,116	13
Seattle – Tacoma, WA CMSA	3,104	14
Baltimore, MD MSA	2,829	15
Denver – Boulder, CO CMSA	2,650	16
San Diego, CA MSA	2,601	17
Cleveland – Akron – Lorain, OH CMSA	2,447	18
St. Louis, MO – IL MSA	2,271	19
Phoenix, AZ MSA	2,100	20
Cincinnati – Hamilton, OH – KY – IN CMSA	1,987	21
Pittsburgh – Beaver Valley, PA CMSA	1,933	22
Tampa – St. Petersburg – Clearwater, FL MSA	1,848	23
Kansas City, MO – KS MSA	1,687	24
Columbus, OH MSA	1,637	25

Source: U.S. Department of Commerce, Bureau of the Census, Data User Services Division, *1990 Census of Population and Housing, Equal Employment Opportunity File, CD-90-EE0-1, January 1993,* CD-ROM.

★1294★

Occupations, By Race/Sex

Top 25 MSAs For Employment As Petroleum Engineers, 1990: Blacks

MSA/CMSA	Employees per 100,000 pop.	Rank
Dubuque, IA MSA	125	1
Los Angeles – Anaheim – Riverside, CA CMSA	85	2
New Orleans, LA MSA	70	3
Beaumont – Port Arthur, TX MSA	38	4
Lafayette, LA MSA	18	5
Jackson, MS MSA	14	6
Alexandria, LA MSA	13	7
Tulsa, OK MSA	12	8
Topeka, KS MSA	12	8
Rochester, NY MSA	9	9
Midland, TX MSA	9	9
Dallas – Fort Worth, TX CMSA	8	10
Tuscaloosa, AL MSA	8	10
Denver – Boulder, CO CMSA	8	10
Chicago – Gary – Lake County, IL – IN – WI CMSA	8	10
Austin, TX MSA	7	11
Toledo, OH MSA	7	11
Oklahoma City, OK MSA	6	12
Bakersfield, CA MSA	6	12
Cincinnati – Hamilton, OH – KY – IN CMSA	6	12
Houma – Thibodaux, LA MSA	6	12
Corpus Christi, TX MSA	5	13
Johnstown, PA MSA	4	14
Anchorage, AK MSA	3	15
Phoenix, AZ MSA	0	16

Source: U.S. Department of Commerce, Bureau of the Census, Data User Services Division, *1990 Census of Population and Housing, Equal Employment Opportunity File, CD-90-EE0-1, January 1993,* CD-ROM.

★1295★

Occupations, By Race/Sex

Top 25 MSAs For Employment As Petroleum Engineers, 1990: Whites

MSA/CMSA	Employees per 100,000 pop.	Rank
Dallas – Fort Worth, TX CMSA	4,696	1
Dallas – Fort Worth, TX CMSA	1,471	2
New Orleans, LA MSA	1,428	3
Midland, TX MSA	1,042	4
Lafayette, LA MSA	900	5
Denver – Boulder, CO CMSA	841	6
Anchorage, AK MSA	815	7
Los Angeles – Anaheim – Riverside, CA CMSA	735	8
Bakersfield, CA MSA	731	9
Oklahoma City, OK MSA	714	10
Tulsa, OK MSA	605	11
San Francisco – Oakland – San Jose, CA CMSA	339	12
Corpus Christi, TX MSA	255	13

[Continued]

★1295★

Top 25 MSAs For Employment As Petroleum Engineers, 1990: Whites
[Continued]

MSA/CMSA	Employees per 100,000 pop.	Rank
New York – Northern New Jersey – Long Island, NY – NJ – CT CMSA	204	14
Houma – Thibodaux, LA MSA	182	15
Baton Rouge, LA MSA	166	16
Tyler, TX MSA	159	17
Odessa, TX MSA	135	18
Casper, WY MSA	132	19
Wichita, KS MSA	123	20
Longview – Marshall, TX MSA	121	21
Beaumont – Port Arthur, TX MSA	118	22
Shreveport, LA MSA	111	23
Austin, TX MSA	105	24
Victoria, TX MSA	99	25

Source: U.S. Department of Commerce, Bureau of the Census, Data User Services Division, *1990 Census of Population and Housing, Equal Employment Opportunity File, CD-90-EE0-1, January 1993,* CD-ROM.

★1296★

Occupations, By Race/Sex

Top 25 MSAs For Employment As Pharmacists, 1990: Blacks

MSA/CMSA	Employees per 100,000 pop.	Rank
Pittsburgh – Beaver Valley, PA CMSA	879	1
Washington, DC – MD – VA MSA	599	2
Houston – Galveston – Brazoria, TX CMSA	510	3
Chicago – Gary – Lake County, IL – IN – WI CMSA	505	4
Philadelphia – Wilmington – Trenton, PA – NJ – DE – MD CMSA	367	5
Los Angeles – Anaheim – Riverside, CA CMSA	329	6
Miami – Fort Lauderdale, FL CMSA	284	7
Atlanta, GA MSA	278	8
New Orleans, LA MSA	266	9
Dallas – Fort Worth, TX CMSA	258	10
Detroit – Ann Arbor, MI CMSA	185	11
Baltimore, MD MSA	138	12
San Francisco – Oakland – San Jose, CA CMSA	130	13
Tampa – St. Petersburg – Clearwater, FL MSA	124	14
Norfolk – Virginia Beach – Newport News, VA MSA	119	15
Kansas City, MO – KS MSA	107	16
Cleveland – Akron – Lorain, OH CMSA	102	17
St. Louis, MO – IL MSA	99	18

[Continued]

★1296★

Top 25 MSAs For Employment As Pharmacists, 1990: Blacks
[Continued]

MSA/CMSA	Employees per 100,000 pop.	Rank
Columbus, OH MSA	90	19
Cincinnati – Hamilton, OH – KY – IN CMSA	66	20
West Palm Beach – Boca Raton – Delray Beach, FL MSA	64	21
Baton Rouge, LA MSA	63	22
Raleigh – Durham, NC MSA	63	22
Richmond – Petersburg, VA MSA	59	23
Tallahassee, FL MSA	56	24

Source: U.S. Department of Commerce, Bureau of the Census, Data User Services Division, *1990 Census of Population and Housing, Equal Employment Opportunity File, CD-90-EE0-1, January 1993,* CD-ROM.

★1297★

Occupations, By Race/Sex

Top 25 MSAs For Employment As Pharmacists, 1990: Whites

MSA/CMSA	Employees per 100,000 pop.	Rank
Kansas City, MO – KS MSA	10,900	1
Los Angeles – Anaheim – Riverside, CA CMSA	4,976	2
Chicago – Gary – Lake County, IL – IN – WI CMSA	4,703	3
Philadelphia – Wilmington – Trenton, PA – NJ – DE – MD CMSA	4,534	4
Detroit – Ann Arbor, MI CMSA	3,154	5
Boston – Lawrence – Salem, MA – NH CMSA	3,137	6
San Francisco – Oakland – San Jose, CA CMSA	2,460	7
Pittsburgh – Beaver Valley, PA CMSA	2,448	8
Dallas – Fort Worth, TX CMSA	2,230	9
Miami – Fort Lauderdale, FL CMSA	2,145	10
Atlanta, GA MSA	1,975	11
Houston – Galveston – Brazoria, TX CMSA	1,940	12
Minneapolis – St. Paul, MN – WI MSA	1,909	13
Cleveland – Akron – Lorain, OH CMSA	1,763	14
St. Louis, MO – IL MSA	1,757	15
Seattle – Tacoma, WA CMSA	1,729	16
Cincinnati – Hamilton, OH – KY – IN CMSA	1,728	17
Tampa – St. Petersburg – Clearwater, FL MSA	1,625	18
Washington, DC – MD – VA MSA	1,462	19
Phoenix, AZ MSA	1,458	20
Baltimore, MD MSA	1,445	21

[Continued]

★1297★

Top 25 MSAs For Employment As Pharmacists, 1990: Whites

[Continued]

MSA/CMSA	Employees per 100,000 pop.	Rank
Columbus, OH MSA	1,389	22
Kansas City, MO – KS MSA	1,385	23
Denver – Boulder, CO CMSA	1,216	24
Milwaukee – Racine, WI CMSA	1,203	25

Source: U.S. Department of Commerce, Bureau of the Census, Data User Services Division, *1990 Census of Population and Housing, Equal Employment Opportunity File, CD-90-EE0-1,* January 1993, CD-ROM.

★1298★

Occupations, By Race/Sex

Top 25 MSAs For Employment As Photographers, 1990: Blacks

MSA/CMSA	Employees per 100,000 pop.	Rank
Indianapolis, IN MSA	1,141	1
Los Angeles – Anaheim – Riverside, CA CMSA	627	2
Chicago – Gary – Lake County, IL – IN – WI CMSA	575	3
Washington, DC – MD – VA MSA	540	4
Detroit – Ann Arbor, MI CMSA	299	5
Philadelphia – Wilmington – Trenton, PA – NJ – DE – MD CMSA	297	6
San Francisco – Oakland – San Jose, CA CMSA	238	7
Atlanta, GA MSA	234	8
Houston – Galveston – Brazoria, TX CMSA	214	9
Baltimore, MD MSA	211	10
Dallas – Fort Worth, TX CMSA	186	11
St. Louis, MO – IL MSA	146	12
Memphis, TN – AR – MS MSA	137	13
Boston – Lawrence – Salem, MA – NH CMSA	130	14
New Orleans, LA MSA	129	15
Kansas City, MO – KS MSA	127	16
San Diego, CA MSA	110	17
Charlotte – Gastonia – Rock Hill, NC – SC MSA	98	18
Greensboro – Winston-Salem – High Point, NC MSA	92	19
Miami – Fort Lauderdale, FL CMSA	91	20
Norfolk – Virginia Beach – Newport News, VA MSA	81	21
Nashville, TN MSA	78	22
Cleveland – Akron – Lorain, OH CMSA	76	23
Cincinnati – Hamilton, OH – KY – IN CMSA	75	24
Seattle – Tacoma, WA CMSA	66	25

Source: U.S. Department of Commerce, Bureau of the Census, Data User Services Division, *1990 Census of Population and Housing, Equal Employment Opportunity File, CD-90-EE0-1,* January 1993, CD-ROM.

★1299★

Occupations, By Race/Sex

Top 25 MSAs For Employment As Photographers, 1990: Whites

MSA/CMSA	Employees per 100,000 pop.	Rank
Pittsburgh – Beaver Valley, PA CMSA	13,533	1
Los Angeles – Anaheim – Riverside, CA CMSA	10,141	2
Chicago – Gary – Lake County, IL – IN – WI CMSA	4,346	3
San Francisco – Oakland – San Jose, CA CMSA	4,341	4
Boston – Lawrence – Salem, MA – NH CMSA	3,319	5
Philadelphia – Wilmington – Trenton, PA – NJ – DE – MD CMSA	3,261	6
Washington, DC – MD – VA MSA	2,693	7
Dallas – Fort Worth, TX CMSA	2,650	8
Detroit – Ann Arbor, MI CMSA	2,261	9
Miami – Fort Lauderdale, FL CMSA	1,796	10
Atlanta, GA MSA	1,778	11
Minneapolis – St. Paul, MN – WI MSA	1,693	12
Houston – Galveston – Brazoria, TX CMSA	1,674	13
San Diego, CA MSA	1,547	14
Seattle – Tacoma, WA CMSA	1,546	15
Denver – Boulder, CO CMSA	1,418	16
Cleveland – Akron – Lorain, OH CMSA	1,326	17
Phoenix, AZ MSA	1,324	18
Tampa – St. Petersburg – Clearwater, FL MSA	1,258	19
St. Louis, MO – IL MSA	1,180	20
Pittsburgh – Beaver Valley, PA CMSA	1,162	21
Portland – Vancouver, OR – WA CMSA	1,044	22
Baltimore, MD MSA	1,038	23
Kansas City, MO – KS MSA	977	24
Cincinnati – Hamilton, OH – KY – IN CMSA	912	25

Source: U.S. Department of Commerce, Bureau of the Census, Data User Services Division, *1990 Census of Population and Housing, Equal Employment Opportunity File, CD-90-EE0-1,* January 1993, CD-ROM.

★1300★

Occupations, By Race/Sex

Top 25 MSAs For Employment As Physical Education Teachers, 1990: Blacks

MSA/CMSA	Employees per 100,000 pop.	Rank
Seattle – Tacoma, WA CMSA	111	1
Miami – Fort Lauderdale, FL CMSA	43	2
Greensboro – Winston-Salem – High Point, NC MSA	19	3
Dayton – Springfield, OH MSA	16	4
Bloomington, IN MSA	13	5
San Francisco – Oakland – San Jose, CA CMSA	13	5
Modesto, CA MSA	12	6
Cumberland, MD – WV MSA	11	7
Cincinnati – Hamilton, OH – KY – IN CMSA	11	7
Savannah, GA MSA	11	7
New York – Northern New Jersey – Long Island, NY – NJ – CT CMSA	11	7
Atlanta, GA MSA	10	8
Baton Rouge, LA MSA	9	9
Lafayette, LA MSA	9	9
Syracuse, NY MSA	9	9
Albany – Schenectady – Troy, NY MSA	8	10
Dallas – Fort Worth, TX CMSA	8	10
Salinas – Seaside – Monterey, CA MSA	8	10
Memphis, TN – AR – MS MSA	7	11
Detroit – Ann Arbor, MI CMSA	6	12
Canton, OH MSA	6	12
Boston – Lawrence – Salem, MA – NH CMSA	6	12
Merced, CA MSA	5	13
St. Louis, MO – IL MSA	2	14
Eugene – Springfield, OR MSA	0	15

Source: U.S. Department of Commerce, Bureau of the Census, Data User Services Division, *1990 Census of Population and Housing, Equal Employment Opportunity File, CD-90-EE0-1,* January 1993, CD-ROM.

★1301★

Occupations, By Race/Sex

Top 25 MSAs For Employment As Physical Education Teachers, 1990: Whites

MSA/CMSA	Employees per 100,000 pop.	Rank
Columbus, OH MSA	163	1
New York – Northern New Jersey – Long Island, NY – NJ – CT CMSA	142	2
San Francisco – Oakland – San Jose, CA CMSA	138	3
Chicago – Gary – Lake County, IL – IN – WI CMSA	104	4
Baltimore, MD MSA	92	5

[Continued]

★1301★

Top 25 MSAs For Employment As Physical Education Teachers, 1990: Whites
[Continued]

MSA/CMSA	Employees per 100,000 pop.	Rank
Boston – Lawrence – Salem, MA – NH CMSA	90	6
Philadelphia – Wilmington – Trenton, PA – NJ – DE – MD CMSA	82	7
Pittsburgh – Beaver Valley, PA CMSA	54	8
Albany – Schenectady – Troy, NY MSA	50	9
Cincinnati – Hamilton, OH – KY – IN CMSA	49	10
Cleveland – Akron – Lorain, OH CMSA	47	11
Detroit – Ann Arbor, MI CMSA	38	12
Salt Lake City – Ogden, UT MSA	33	13
Sacramento, CA MSA	33	13
Dallas – Fort Worth, TX CMSA	31	14
Salem, OR MSA	31	14
Washington, DC – MD – VA MSA	30	15
Seattle – Tacoma, WA CMSA	29	16
San Diego, CA MSA	27	17
Bryan – College Station, TX MSA	26	18
Harrisburg – Lebanon – Carlisle, PA MSA	25	19
Houston – Galveston – Brazoria, TX CMSA	25	19
State College, PA MSA	24	20
San Antonio, TX MSA	24	20
Buffalo – Niagara Falls, NY CMSA	23	21

Source: U.S. Department of Commerce, Bureau of the Census, Data User Services Division, *1990 Census of Population and Housing, Equal Employment Opportunity File, CD-90-EE0-1,* January 1993, CD-ROM.

★1302★

Occupations, By Race/Sex

Top 25 MSAs For Employment As Physical Therapists, 1990: Blacks

MSA/CMSA	Employees per 100,000 pop.	Rank
Alexandria, LA MSA	675	1
Washington, DC – MD – VA MSA	353	2
Philadelphia – Wilmington – Trenton, PA – NJ – DE – MD CMSA	292	3
Los Angeles – Anaheim – Riverside, CA CMSA	277	4
Chicago – Gary – Lake County, IL – IN – WI CMSA	248	5
Atlanta, GA MSA	192	6
Houston – Galveston – Brazoria, TX CMSA	182	7
Detroit – Ann Arbor, MI CMSA	139	8
Cleveland – Akron – Lorain, OH CMSA	103	9

[Continued]

★1302★

Top 25 MSAs For Employment As Physical Therapists, 1990: Blacks
[Continued]

MSA/CMSA	Employees per 100,000 pop.	Rank
Nashville, TN MSA	94	10
Miami – Fort Lauderdale, FL CMSA	92	11
Dallas – Fort Worth, TX CMSA	92	11
Baltimore, MD MSA	87	12
Norfolk – Virginia Beach – Newport News, VA MSA	82	13
New Orleans, LA MSA	80	14
Indianapolis, IN MSA	79	15
Memphis, TN – AR – MS MSA	78	16
Pittsburgh – Beaver Valley, PA CMSA	71	17
San Francisco – Oakland – San Jose, CA CMSA	67	18
Austin, TX MSA	50	19
San Antonio, TX MSA	50	19
Boston – Lawrence – Salem, MA – NH CMSA	47	20
Jacksonville, FL MSA	45	21
Greensboro – Winston-Salem – High Point, NC MSA	45	21
Richmond – Petersburg, VA MSA	42	22

Source: U.S. Department of Commerce, Bureau of the Census, Data User Services Division, *1990 Census of Population and Housing, Equal Employment Opportunity File, CD-90-EE0-1*, January 1993, CD-ROM.

★1303★

Occupations, By Race/Sex

Top 25 MSAs For Employment As Physical Therapists, 1990: Whites

MSA/CMSA	Employees per 100,000 pop.	Rank
Atlanta, GA MSA	5,738	1
Los Angeles – Anaheim – Riverside, CA CMSA	5,087	2
San Francisco – Oakland – San Jose, CA CMSA	2,837	3
Boston – Lawrence – Salem, MA – NH CMSA	2,566	4
Chicago – Gary – Lake County, IL – IN – WI CMSA	2,466	5
Philadelphia – Wilmington – Trenton, PA – NJ – DE – MD CMSA	2,432	6
Seattle – Tacoma, WA CMSA	1,444	7
Detroit – Ann Arbor, MI CMSA	1,411	8
Dallas – Fort Worth, TX CMSA	1,304	9
Washington, DC – MD – VA MSA	1,268	10
Denver – Boulder, CO CMSA	1,238	11
Minneapolis – St. Paul, MN – WI MSA	1,181	12
Miami – Fort Lauderdale, FL CMSA	1,074	13

[Continued]

★1303★

Top 25 MSAs For Employment As Physical Therapists, 1990: Whites
[Continued]

MSA/CMSA	Employees per 100,000 pop.	Rank
St. Louis, MO – IL MSA	1,073	14
San Diego, CA MSA	965	15
Houston – Galveston – Brazoria, TX CMSA	945	16
Baltimore, MD MSA	942	17
Atlanta, GA MSA	893	18
Cleveland – Akron – Lorain, OH CMSA	875	19
Milwaukee – Racine, WI CMSA	856	20
Pittsburgh – Beaver Valley, PA CMSA	818	21
Phoenix, AZ MSA	797	22
Tampa – St. Petersburg – Clearwater, FL MSA	768	23
Portland – Vancouver, OR – WA CMSA	717	24
Hartford – New Britain – Middletown, CT CMSA	661	25

Source: U.S. Department of Commerce, Bureau of the Census, Data User Services Division, *1990 Census of Population and Housing, Equal Employment Opportunity File, CD-90-EE0-1*, January 1993, CD-ROM.

★1304★

Occupations, By Race/Sex

Top 25 MSAs For Employment As Physicians' Assistants, 1990: Blacks

MSA/CMSA	Employees per 100,000 pop.	Rank
Greenville – Spartanburg, SC MSA	510	1
Atlanta, GA MSA	108	2
Chicago – Gary – Lake County, IL – IN – WI CMSA	99	3
Los Angeles – Anaheim – Riverside, CA CMSA	99	3
Washington, DC – MD – VA MSA	95	4
Philadelphia – Wilmington – Trenton, PA – NJ – DE – MD CMSA	85	5
Hartford – New Britain – Middletown, CT CMSA	76	6
Baltimore, MD MSA	75	7
Cleveland – Akron – Lorain, OH CMSA	62	8
Miami – Fort Lauderdale, FL CMSA	47	9
Boston – Lawrence – Salem, MA – NH CMSA	44	10
San Francisco – Oakland – San Jose, CA CMSA	40	11
Houston – Galveston – Brazoria, TX CMSA	39	12
Seattle – Tacoma, WA CMSA	35	13

[Continued]

★ 1304 ★

Top 25 MSAs For Employment As Physicians' Assistants, 1990: Blacks

[Continued]

MSA/CMSA	Employees per 100,000 pop.	Rank
Detroit – Ann Arbor, MI CMSA	32	14
Norfolk – Virginia Beach – Newport News, VA MSA	29	15
Columbus, OH MSA	29	15
Columbia, SC MSA	27	16
New Haven – Meriden, CT MSA	27	16
Nashville, TN MSA	26	17
Las Vegas, NV MSA	26	17
Memphis, TN – AR – MS MSA	25	18
Pittsburgh – Beaver Valley, PA CMSA	25	18
Beaumont – Port Arthur, TX MSA	22	19
Orlando, FL MSA	20	20

Source: U.S. Department of Commerce, Bureau of the Census, Data User Services Division, *1990 Census of Population and Housing, Equal Employment Opportunity File, CD-90-EE0-1, January 1993,* CD-ROM.

★ 1305 ★

Occupations, By Race/Sex

Top 25 MSAs For Employment As Physicians' Assistants, 1990: Whites

MSA/CMSA	Employees per 100,000 pop.	Rank
Kansas City, MO – KS MSA	1,686	1
Los Angeles – Anaheim – Riverside, CA CMSA	966	2
Philadelphia – Wilmington – Trenton, PA – NJ – DE – MD CMSA	658	3
San Francisco – Oakland – San Jose, CA CMSA	475	4
Chicago – Gary – Lake County, IL – IN – WI CMSA	470	5
Cleveland – Akron – Lorain, OH CMSA	403	6
Houston – Galveston – Brazoria, TX CMSA	379	7
Detroit – Ann Arbor, MI CMSA	369	8
Pittsburgh – Beaver Valley, PA CMSA	363	9
Minneapolis – St. Paul, MN – WI MSA	324	10
Washington, DC – MD – VA MSA	323	11
Miami – Fort Lauderdale, FL CMSA	288	12
Boston – Lawrence – Salem, MA – NH CMSA	287	13
Atlanta, GA MSA	256	14
Tampa – St. Petersburg – Clearwater, FL MSA	255	15
Dallas – Fort Worth, TX CMSA	232	16
Kansas City, MO – KS MSA	203	17
Seattle – Tacoma, WA CMSA	202	18

[Continued]

★ 1305 ★

Top 25 MSAs For Employment As Physicians' Assistants, 1990: Whites

[Continued]

MSA/CMSA	Employees per 100,000 pop.	Rank
St. Louis, MO – IL MSA	194	19
Indianapolis, IN MSA	193	20
Denver – Boulder, CO CMSA	193	20
Baltimore, MD MSA	175	21
San Diego, CA MSA	168	22
Phoenix, AZ MSA	154	23
Portland – Vancouver, OR – WA CMSA	146	24

Source: U.S. Department of Commerce, Bureau of the Census, Data User Services Division, *1990 Census of Population and Housing, Equal Employment Opportunity File, CD-90-EE0-1, January 1993,* CD-ROM.

★ 1306 ★

Occupations, By Race/Sex

Top 25 MSAs For Employment As Physicians, 1990: Blacks

MSA/CMSA	Employees per 100,000 pop.	Rank
Greenville – Spartanburg, SC MSA	4,028	1
Los Angeles – Anaheim – Riverside, CA CMSA	1,705	2
Washington, DC – MD – VA MSA	1,482	3
Chicago – Gary – Lake County, IL – IN – WI CMSA	1,126	4
Detroit – Ann Arbor, MI CMSA	935	5
Philadelphia – Wilmington – Trenton, PA – NJ – DE – MD CMSA	887	6
Atlanta, GA MSA	732	7
San Francisco – Oakland – San Jose, CA CMSA	672	8
Baltimore, MD MSA	620	9
Cleveland – Akron – Lorain, OH CMSA	504	10
Houston – Galveston – Brazoria, TX CMSA	448	11
Miami – Fort Lauderdale, FL CMSA	370	12
Norfolk – Virginia Beach – Newport News, VA MSA	298	13
Dallas – Fort Worth, TX CMSA	286	14
Boston – Lawrence – Salem, MA – NH CMSA	274	15
St. Louis, MO – IL MSA	264	16
Nashville, TN MSA	238	17
Memphis, TN – AR – MS MSA	237	18
New Orleans, LA MSA	217	19
Cincinnati – Hamilton, OH – KY – IN CMSA	177	20
Raleigh – Durham, NC MSA	160	21
Buffalo – Niagara Falls, NY CMSA	151	22
Richmond – Petersburg, VA MSA	149	23

[Continued]

★ 1306 ★

Top 25 MSAs For Employment As Physicians, 1990: Blacks

[Continued]

MSA/CMSA	Employees per 100,000 pop.	Rank
Birmingham, AL MSA	143	24
Charlotte – Gastonia – Rock Hill, NC – SC MSA	130	25

Source: U.S. Department of Commerce, Bureau of the Census, Data User Services Division, *1990 Census of Population and Housing, Equal Employment Opportunity File, CD-90-EE0-1, January 1993,* CD-ROM.

★ 1307 ★

Occupations, By Race/Sex

Top 25 MSAs For Employment As Physicians, 1990: Whites

MSA/CMSA	Employees per 100,000 pop.	Rank
Mobile, AL MSA	52,053	1
Los Angeles – Anaheim – Riverside, CA CMSA	27,160	2
Philadelphia – Wilmington – Trenton, PA – NJ – DE – MD CMSA	17,622	3
Chicago – Gary – Lake County, IL – IN – WI CMSA	16,625	4
San Francisco – Oakland – San Jose, CA CMSA	16,559	5
Boston – Lawrence – Salem, MA – NH CMSA	14,112	6
Washington, DC – MD – VA MSA	10,662	7
Detroit – Ann Arbor, MI CMSA	10,429	8
Miami – Fort Lauderdale, FL CMSA	8,606	9
Dallas – Fort Worth, TX CMSA	7,863	10
Houston – Galveston – Brazoria, TX CMSA	7,775	11
Baltimore, MD MSA	7,115	12
Cleveland – Akron – Lorain, OH CMSA	6,757	13
Seattle – Tacoma, WA CMSA	6,698	14
San Diego, CA MSA	5,871	15
Minneapolis – St. Paul, MN – WI MSA	5,761	16
Pittsburgh – Beaver Valley, PA CMSA	5,742	17
Atlanta, GA MSA	5,388	18
Denver – Boulder, CO CMSA	5,267	19
St. Louis, MO – IL MSA	5,244	20
Tampa – St. Petersburg – Clearwater, FL MSA	4,555	21
Phoenix, AZ MSA	4,500	22
Kansas City, MO – KS MSA	3,924	23
Portland – Vancouver, OR – WA CMSA	3,820	24
Milwaukee – Racine, WI CMSA	3,594	25

Source: U.S. Department of Commerce, Bureau of the Census, Data User Services Division, *1990 Census of Population and Housing, Equal Employment Opportunity File, CD-90-EE0-1, January 1993,* CD-ROM.

★ 1308 ★

Occupations, By Race/Sex

Top 25 MSAs For Employment As Physicists and Astronomers, 1990: Blacks

MSA/CMSA	Employees per 100,000 pop.	Rank
San Francisco – Oakland – San Jose, CA CMSA	70	1
Philadelphia – Wilmington – Trenton, PA – NJ – DE – MD CMSA	49	2
Augusta, GA – SC MSA	37	3
San Francisco – Oakland – San Jose, CA CMSA	35	4
Baltimore, MD MSA	32	5
Washington, DC – MD – VA MSA	30	6
Chicago – Gary – Lake County, IL – IN – WI CMSA	27	7
Miami – Fort Lauderdale, FL CMSA	25	8
Los Angeles – Anaheim – Riverside, CA CMSA	22	9
Huntsville, AL MSA	21	10
Houston – Galveston – Brazoria, TX CMSA	20	11
Richland – Kennewick – Pasco, WA MSA	17	12
Chattanooga, TN – GA MSA	16	13
Birmingham, AL MSA	16	13
Columbia, SC MSA	14	14
Pittsburgh – Beaver Valley, PA CMSA	12	15
Sacramento, CA MSA	12	15
Hartford – New Britain – Middletown, CT CMSA	12	15
Jackson, MS MSA	10	16
Boston – Lawrence – Salem, MA – NH CMSA	10	16
Tampa – St. Petersburg – Clearwater, FL MSA	10	16
Providence – Pawtucket – Fall River, RI – MA CMSA	10	16
Tallahassee, FL MSA	9	17
Little Rock – North Little Rock, AR MSA	9	17
Bakersfield, CA MSA	9	17

Source: U.S. Department of Commerce, Bureau of the Census, Data User Services Division, *1990 Census of Population and Housing, Equal Employment Opportunity File, CD-90-EE0-1, January 1993,* CD-ROM.

★1309★
Occupations, By Race/Sex

Top 25 MSAs For Employment As Physicists and Astronomers, 1990: Whites

MSA/CMSA	Employees per 100,000 pop.	Rank
Phoenix, AZ MSA	2,462	1
Washington, DC – MD – VA MSA	2,400	2
New York – Northern New Jersey – Long Island, NY – NJ – CT CMSA	1,608	3
Los Angeles – Anaheim – Riverside, CA CMSA	1,428	4
Boston – Lawrence – Salem, MA – NH CMSA	1,276	5
Chicago – Gary – Lake County, IL – IN – WI CMSA	861	6
Santa Fe, NM MSA	809	7
Philadelphia – Wilmington – Trenton, PA – NJ – DE – MD CMSA	656	8
Baltimore, MD MSA	551	9
Denver – Boulder, CO CMSA	544	10
San Diego, CA MSA	512	11
Albuquerque, NM MSA	361	12
Knoxville, TN MSA	356	13
Detroit – Ann Arbor, MI CMSA	326	14
Seattle – Tacoma, WA CMSA	309	15
Pittsburgh – Beaver Valley, PA CMSA	264	16
Dallas – Fort Worth, TX CMSA	262	17
Richland – Kennewick – Pasco, WA MSA	245	18
Raleigh – Durham, NC MSA	232	19
Santa Barbara – Santa Maria – Lompoc, CA MSA	222	20
Huntsville, AL MSA	217	21
Houston – Galveston – Brazoria, TX CMSA	215	22
Norfolk – Virginia Beach – Newport News, VA MSA	201	23
Cleveland – Akron – Lorain, OH CMSA	201	23
Albany – Schenectady – Troy, NY MSA	183	24

Source: U.S. Department of Commerce, Bureau of the Census, Data User Services Division, *1990 Census of Population and Housing, Equal Employment Opportunity File, CD-90-EE0-1, January 1993,* CD-ROM.

★1310★
Occupations, By Race/Sex

Top 25 MSAs For Employment As Physics Teachers, 1990: Blacks

MSA/CMSA	Employees per 100,000 pop.	Rank
Louisville, KY – IN MSA	44	1
Norfolk – Virginia Beach – Newport News, VA MSA	19	2
Boston – Lawrence – Salem, MA – NH CMSA	16	3
Waco, TX MSA	14	4
Greensboro – Winston-Salem – High Point, NC MSA	13	5
Austin, TX MSA	12	6
Richmond – Petersburg, VA MSA	7	7
Raleigh – Durham, NC MSA	6	8
Washington, DC – MD – VA MSA	5	9
Charleston, SC MSA	4	10
Lubbock, TX MSA	3	11
Orlando, FL MSA	0	12
Parkersburg – Marietta, WV – OH MSA	0	12
Owensboro, KY MSA	0	12
Ocala, FL MSA	0	12
Portsmouth – Dover – Rochester, NH – ME MSA	0	12
Rapid City, SD MSA	0	12
Provo – Orem, UT MSA	0	12
Oklahoma City, OK MSA	0	12
New Bedford, MA MSA	0	12
Redding, CA MSA	0	12
Muskegon, MI MSA	0	12
New London – Norwich, CT – RI MSA	0	12
Nashville, TN MSA	0	12
Muncie, IN MSA	0	12

Source: U.S. Department of Commerce, Bureau of the Census, Data User Services Division, *1990 Census of Population and Housing, Equal Employment Opportunity File, CD-90-EE0-1, January 1993,* CD-ROM.

★1311★
Occupations, By Race/Sex

Top 25 MSAs For Employment As Physics Teachers, 1990: Whites

MSA/CMSA	Employees per 100,000 pop.	Rank
Gainesville, FL MSA	195	1
Boston – Lawrence – Salem, MA – NH CMSA	144	2
Los Angeles – Anaheim – Riverside, CA CMSA	114	3
Chicago – Gary – Lake County, IL – IN – WI CMSA	109	4
San Francisco – Oakland – San Jose, CA CMSA	102	5
St. Louis, MO – IL MSA	78	6
Philadelphia – Wilmington – Trenton, PA – NJ – DE – MD CMSA	74	7

[Continued]

★1311★

Top 25 MSAs For Employment As Physics Teachers, 1990: Whites
[Continued]

MSA/CMSA	Employees per 100,000 pop.	Rank
Washington, DC – MD – VA MSA	71	8
Sacramento, CA MSA	70	9
Lafayette – West Lafayette, IN MSA	66	10
Baltimore, MD MSA	64	11
Dallas – Fort Worth, TX CMSA	62	12
Seattle – Tacoma, WA CMSA	60	13
Gainesville, FL MSA	59	14
Detroit – Ann Arbor, MI CMSA	56	15
Providence – Pawtucket – Fall River, RI – MA CMSA	52	16
Pittsburgh – Beaver Valley, PA CMSA	50	17
Minneapolis – St. Paul, MN – WI MSA	48	18
Tucson, AZ MSA	46	19
San Diego, CA MSA	38	20
Cincinnati – Hamilton, OH – KY – IN CMSA	38	20
Melbourne – Titusville – Palm Bay, FL MSA	37	21
Norfolk – Virginia Beach – Newport News, VA MSA	36	22
Cleveland – Akron – Lorain, OH CMSA	36	22
Salt Lake City – Ogden, UT MSA	36	22

Source: U.S. Department of Commerce, Bureau of the Census, Data User Services Division, *1990 Census of Population and Housing, Equal Employment Opportunity File, CD-90-EE0-1, January 1993*, CD-ROM.

★1312★

Occupations, By Race/Sex

Top 25 MSAs For Employment As Podiatrists, 1990: Blacks

MSA/CMSA	Employees per 100,000 pop.	Rank
Boston – Lawrence – Salem, MA – NH CMSA	76	1
San Francisco – Oakland – San Jose, CA CMSA	27	2
Chicago – Gary – Lake County, IL – IN – WI CMSA	22	3
Philadelphia – Wilmington – Trenton, PA – NJ – DE – MD CMSA	21	4
Washington, DC – MD – VA MSA	15	5
Boston – Lawrence – Salem, MA – NH CMSA	15	5
Dallas – Fort Worth, TX CMSA	14	6
Los Angeles – Anaheim – Riverside, CA CMSA	13	7
Nashville, TN MSA	12	8
Cleveland – Akron – Lorain, OH CMSA	12	8

[Continued]

★1312★

Top 25 MSAs For Employment As Podiatrists, 1990: Blacks
[Continued]

MSA/CMSA	Employees per 100,000 pop.	Rank
Pittsburgh – Beaver Valley, PA CMSA	12	8
Youngstown – Warren, OH MSA	11	9
Pine Bluff, AR MSA	7	10
Baton Rouge, LA MSA	6	11
San Antonio, TX MSA	6	11
Detroit – Ann Arbor, MI CMSA	6	11
Greenville – Spartanburg, SC MSA	5	12
Pittsfield, MA MSA	0	13
Muncie, IN MSA	0	13
Reading, PA MSA	0	13
Redding, CA MSA	0	13
New London – Norwich, CT – RI MSA	0	13
Norfolk – Virginia Beach – Newport News, VA MSA	0	13
Olympia, WA MSA	0	13
Odessa, TX MSA	0	13

Source: U.S. Department of Commerce, Bureau of the Census, Data User Services Division, *1990 Census of Population and Housing, Equal Employment Opportunity File, CD-90-EE0-1, January 1993*, CD-ROM.

★1313★

Occupations, By Race/Sex

Top 25 MSAs For Employment As Podiatrists, 1990: Whites

MSA/CMSA	Employees per 100,000 pop.	Rank
Oklahoma City, OK MSA	1,424	1
Philadelphia – Wilmington – Trenton, PA – NJ – DE – MD CMSA	587	2
Chicago – Gary – Lake County, IL – IN – WI CMSA	481	3
San Francisco – Oakland – San Jose, CA CMSA	341	4
Los Angeles – Anaheim – Riverside, CA CMSA	333	5
Boston – Lawrence – Salem, MA – NH CMSA	241	6
Detroit – Ann Arbor, MI CMSA	223	7
Cleveland – Akron – Lorain, OH CMSA	201	8
Baltimore, MD MSA	160	9
Miami – Fort Lauderdale, FL CMSA	142	10
Pittsburgh – Beaver Valley, PA CMSA	137	11
Phoenix, AZ MSA	106	12
West Palm Beach – Boca Raton – Delray Beach, FL MSA	102	13
Washington, DC – MD – VA MSA	97	14

[Continued]

★1313★

Top 25 MSAs For Employment As Podiatrists, 1990: Whites
[Continued]

MSA/CMSA	Employees per 100,000 pop.	Rank
Denver – Boulder, CO CMSA	87	15
Seattle – Tacoma, WA CMSA	87	15
Tampa – St. Petersburg – Clearwater, FL MSA	87	15
Scranton – Wilkes-Barre, PA MSA	84	16
St. Louis, MO – IL MSA	76	17
Dallas – Fort Worth, TX CMSA	69	18
San Diego, CA MSA	68	19
Buffalo – Niagara Falls, NY CMSA	67	20
Columbus, OH MSA	65	21
San Antonio, TX MSA	58	22
Atlanta, GA MSA	54	23

Source: U.S. Department of Commerce, Bureau of the Census, Data User Services Division, *1990 Census of Population and Housing, Equal Employment Opportunity File, CD-90-EE0-1, January 1993,* CD-ROM.

★1314★

Occupations, By Race/Sex

Top 25 MSAs For Employment As Police and Detectives, Public Service, 1990: Blacks

MSA/CMSA	Employees per 100,000 pop.	Rank
Raleigh – Durham, NC MSA	9,732	1
Washington, DC – MD – VA MSA	4,846	2
Chicago – Gary – Lake County, IL – IN – WI CMSA	4,259	3
Philadelphia – Wilmington – Trenton, PA – NJ – DE – MD CMSA	3,090	4
Detroit – Ann Arbor, MI CMSA	2,971	5
Los Angeles – Anaheim – Riverside, CA CMSA	2,964	6
Baltimore, MD MSA	1,832	7
Atlanta, GA MSA	1,467	8
Miami – Fort Lauderdale, FL CMSA	1,339	9
Houston – Galveston – Brazoria, TX CMSA	999	10
San Francisco – Oakland – San Jose, CA CMSA	855	11
St. Louis, MO – IL MSA	825	12
Dallas – Fort Worth, TX CMSA	796	13
New Orleans, LA MSA	738	14
Cleveland – Akron – Lorain, OH CMSA	717	15
Memphis, TN – AR – MS MSA	702	16
Boston – Lawrence – Salem, MA – NH CMSA	698	17
Norfolk – Virginia Beach – Newport News, VA MSA	459	18
Kansas City, MO – KS MSA	405	19
Birmingham, AL MSA	404	20
Buffalo – Niagara Falls, NY CMSA	399	21

[Continued]

★1314★

Top 25 MSAs For Employment As Police and Detectives, Public Service, 1990: Blacks
[Continued]

MSA/CMSA	Employees per 100,000 pop.	Rank
Charlotte – Gastonia – Rock Hill, NC – SC MSA	396	22
Raleigh – Durham, NC MSA	388	23
Pittsburgh – Beaver Valley, PA CMSA	377	24
Richmond – Petersburg, VA MSA	368	25

Source: U.S. Department of Commerce, Bureau of the Census, Data User Services Division, *1990 Census of Population and Housing, Equal Employment Opportunity File, CD-90-EE0-1, January 1993,* CD-ROM.

★1315★

Occupations, By Race/Sex

Top 25 MSAs For Employment As Police and Detectives, Public Service, 1990: Whites

MSA/CMSA	Employees per 100,000 pop.	Rank
Phoenix, AZ MSA	53,946	1
Los Angeles – Anaheim – Riverside, CA CMSA	19,450	2
Chicago – Gary – Lake County, IL – IN – WI CMSA	17,980	3
Philadelphia – Wilmington – Trenton, PA – NJ – DE – MD CMSA	13,305	4
Boston – Lawrence – Salem, MA – NH CMSA	9,589	5
Washington, DC – MD – VA MSA	8,876	6
San Francisco – Oakland – San Jose, CA CMSA	8,795	7
Miami – Fort Lauderdale, FL CMSA	8,283	8
Detroit – Ann Arbor, MI CMSA	7,604	9
Dallas – Fort Worth, TX CMSA	6,743	10
Houston – Galveston – Brazoria, TX CMSA	6,299	11
Baltimore, MD MSA	6,038	12
Cleveland – Akron – Lorain, OH CMSA	4,508	13
St. Louis, MO – IL MSA	4,388	14
San Diego, CA MSA	4,386	15
Atlanta, GA MSA	4,286	16
Seattle – Tacoma, WA CMSA	4,109	17
Phoenix, AZ MSA	3,726	18
Tampa – St. Petersburg – Clearwater, FL MSA	3,432	19
Denver – Boulder, CO CMSA	3,293	20
Pittsburgh – Beaver Valley, PA CMSA	3,245	21
Minneapolis – St. Paul, MN – WI MSA	3,229	22
Buffalo – Niagara Falls, NY CMSA	3,033	23

[Continued]

★1315★

Top 25 MSAs For Employment As Police and Detectives, Public Service, 1990: Whites
[Continued]

MSA/CMSA	Employees per 100,000 pop.	Rank
Milwaukee – Racine, WI CMSA	2,969	24
Kansas City, MO – KS MSA	2,904	25

Source: U.S. Department of Commerce, Bureau of the Census, Data User Services Division, *1990 Census of Population and Housing, Equal Employment Opportunity File, CD-90-EE0-1, January 1993, CD-ROM.*

★1316★

Occupations, By Race/Sex

Top 25 MSAs For Employment As Political Science Teachers, 1990: Blacks

MSA/CMSA	Employees per 100,000 pop.	Rank
Reno, NV MSA	15	1
Miami – Fort Lauderdale, FL CMSA	7	2
San Antonio, TX MSA	7	2
Syracuse, NY MSA	6	3
Baltimore, MD MSA	6	3
Philadelphia – Wilmington – Trenton, PA – NJ – DE – MD CMSA	5	4
Odessa, TX MSA	0	5
Oklahoma City, OK MSA	0	5
Parkersburg – Marietta, WV – OH MSA	0	5
Owensboro, KY MSA	0	5
Ocala, FL MSA	0	5
Panama City, FL MSA	0	5
New London – Norwich, CT – RI MSA	0	5
New Bedford, MA MSA	0	5
Omaha, NE – IA MSA	0	5
Nashville, TN MSA	0	5
Pascagoula, MS MSA	0	5
Norfolk – Virginia Beach – Newport News, VA MSA	0	5
New Haven – Meriden, CT MSA	0	5
Pittsfield, MA MSA	0	5
Rapid City, SD MSA	0	5
Provo – Orem, UT MSA	0	5
Raleigh – Durham, NC MSA	0	5
Macon – Warner Robins, GA MSA	0	5
Naples, FL MSA	0	5

Source: U.S. Department of Commerce, Bureau of the Census, Data User Services Division, *1990 Census of Population and Housing, Equal Employment Opportunity File, CD-90-EE0-1, January 1993, CD-ROM.*

★1317★

Occupations, By Race/Sex

Top 25 MSAs For Employment As Political Science Teachers, 1990: Whites

MSA/CMSA	Employees per 100,000 pop.	Rank
Raleigh – Durham, NC MSA	58	1
Boston – Lawrence – Salem, MA – NH CMSA	42	2
San Francisco – Oakland – San Jose, CA CMSA	40	3
Washington, DC – MD – VA MSA	36	4
Raleigh – Durham, NC MSA	33	5
Pittsburgh – Beaver Valley, PA CMSA	28	6
Baltimore, MD MSA	27	7
Los Angeles – Anaheim – Riverside, CA CMSA	27	7
New Haven – Meriden, CT MSA	25	8
Houston – Galveston – Brazoria, TX CMSA	23	9
St. Louis, MO – IL MSA	17	10
Greenville – Spartanburg, SC MSA	15	11
Santa Barbara – Santa Maria – Lompoc, CA MSA	15	11
Chicago – Gary – Lake County, IL – IN – WI CMSA	15	11
Springfield, MA MSA	14	12
Syracuse, NY MSA	13	13
San Diego, CA MSA	13	13
Mcallen – Edinburg – Mission, TX MSA	12	14
Jacksonville, FL MSA	11	15
New Orleans, LA MSA	11	15
Providence – Pawtucket – Fall River, RI – MA CMSA	10	16
Albuquerque, NM MSA	10	16
Enid, OK MSA	10	16
Bangor, ME MSA	10	16
Chico, CA MSA	10	16

Source: U.S. Department of Commerce, Bureau of the Census, Data User Services Division, *1990 Census of Population and Housing, Equal Employment Opportunity File, CD-90-EE0-1, January 1993, CD-ROM.*

★1318★

Occupations, By Race/Sex

Top 25 MSAs For Employment As Power Plant Operators, 1990: Blacks

MSA/CMSA	Employees per 100,000 pop.	Rank
Charlotte – Gastonia – Rock Hill, NC – SC MSA	177	1
Los Angeles – Anaheim – Riverside, CA CMSA	163	2
Detroit – Ann Arbor, MI CMSA	129	3
Augusta, GA – SC MSA	116	4
Philadelphia – Wilmington – Trenton, PA – NJ – DE – MD CMSA	107	5

[Continued]

★1318★

Top 25 MSAs For Employment As Power Plant Operators, 1990: Blacks

[Continued]

MSA/CMSA	Employees per 100,000 pop.	Rank
Memphis, TN–AR–MS MSA	83	6
Houston–Galveston–Brazoria, TX CMSA	69	7
St. Louis, MO–IL MSA	69	7
Washington, DC–MD–VA MSA	65	8
Charlotte–Gastonia–Rock Hill, NC–SC MSA	54	9
Baltimore, MD MSA	54	9
Chicago–Gary–Lake County, IL–IN–WI CMSA	51	10
Atlantic City, NJ MSA	45	11
Cleveland–Akron–Lorain, OH CMSA	43	12
Norfolk–Virginia Beach–Newport News, VA MSA	39	13
Beaumont–Port Arthur, TX MSA	39	13
San Diego, CA MSA	38	14
San Francisco–Oakland–San Jose, CA CMSA	38	14
Jacksonville, FL MSA	38	14
Charleston, SC MSA	34	15
Dallas–Fort Worth, TX CMSA	33	16
New Orleans, LA MSA	33	16
Cincinnati–Hamilton, OH–KY–IN CMSA	30	17
Baton Rouge, LA MSA	29	18
Milwaukee–Racine, WI CMSA	28	19

Source: U.S. Department of Commerce, Bureau of the Census, Data User Services Division, *1990 Census of Population and Housing, Equal Employment Opportunity File, CD-90-EE0-1, January 1993,* CD-ROM.

★1319★

Occupations, By Race/Sex

Top 25 MSAs For Employment As Power Plant Operators, 1990: Whites

MSA/CMSA	Employees per 100,000 pop.	Rank
Orlando, FL MSA	1,086	1
Chicago–Gary–Lake County, IL–IN–WI CMSA	917	2
Los Angeles–Anaheim–Riverside, CA CMSA	741	3
Philadelphia–Wilmington–Trenton, PA–NJ–DE–MD CMSA	609	4
Detroit–Ann Arbor, MI CMSA	594	5
Houston–Galveston–Brazoria, TX CMSA	377	6
Phoenix, AZ MSA	355	7
San Francisco–Oakland–San Jose, CA CMSA	340	8
Charlotte–Gastonia–Rock Hill, NC–SC MSA	339	9

[Continued]

★1319★

Top 25 MSAs For Employment As Power Plant Operators, 1990: Whites

[Continued]

MSA/CMSA	Employees per 100,000 pop.	Rank
Cleveland–Akron–Lorain, OH CMSA	310	10
Pittsburgh–Beaver Valley, PA CMSA	310	10
Baltimore, MD MSA	291	11
Boston–Lawrence–Salem, MA–NH CMSA	269	12
Washington, DC–MD–VA MSA	236	13
Miami–Fort Lauderdale, FL CMSA	234	14
Tampa–St. Petersburg–Clearwater, FL MSA	230	15
Syracuse, NY MSA	216	16
San Diego, CA MSA	208	17
Dallas–Fort Worth, TX CMSA	207	18
Jacksonville, FL MSA	207	18
Bakersfield, CA MSA	201	19
Cincinnati–Hamilton, OH–KY–IN CMSA	201	19
Birmingham, AL MSA	199	20
Augusta, GA–SC MSA	195	21
St. Louis, MO–IL MSA	194	22

Source: U.S. Department of Commerce, Bureau of the Census, Data User Services Division, *1990 Census of Population and Housing, Equal Employment Opportunity File, CD-90-EE0-1, January 1993,* CD-ROM.

★1320★

Occupations, By Race/Sex

Top 25 MSAs For Employment As Precious Stones and Metals Workers, 1990: Blacks

MSA/CMSA	Employees per 100,000 pop.	Rank
Atlanta, GA MSA	881	1
Providence–Pawtucket–Fall River, RI–MA CMSA	228	2
Miami–Fort Lauderdale, FL CMSA	141	3
Los Angeles–Anaheim–Riverside, CA CMSA	89	4
Detroit–Ann Arbor, MI CMSA	87	5
Chicago–Gary–Lake County, IL–IN–WI CMSA	68	6
Atlanta, GA MSA	54	7
Baltimore, MD MSA	53	8
Washington, DC–MD–VA MSA	48	9
Buffalo–Niagara Falls, NY CMSA	44	10
Fort Pierce, FL MSA	43	11
Philadelphia–Wilmington–Trenton, PA–NJ–DE–MD CMSA	39	12
Indianapolis, IN MSA	36	13
San Diego, CA MSA	28	14
Boston–Lawrence–Salem, MA–NH CMSA	27	15

[Continued]

★ 1320 ★

Top 25 MSAs For Employment As Precious Stones and Metals Workers, 1990: Blacks

[Continued]

MSA/CMSA	Employees per 100,000 pop.	Rank
Louisville, KY – IN MSA	21	16
Dallas – Fort Worth, TX CMSA	20	17
Birmingham, AL MSA	20	17
Cleveland – Akron – Lorain, OH CMSA	19	18
Tuscaloosa, AL MSA	18	19
Columbia, MO MSA	18	19
Cincinnati – Hamilton, OH – KY – IN CMSA	17	20
Houston – Galveston – Brazoria, TX CMSA	16	21
St. Louis, MO – IL MSA	15	22
Rochester, NY MSA	15	22

Source: U.S. Department of Commerce, Bureau of the Census, Data User Services Division, *1990 Census of Population and Housing, Equal Employment Opportunity File, CD-90-EE0-1, January 1993,* CD-ROM.

★ 1321 ★

Occupations, By Race/Sex

Top 25 MSAs For Employment As Precious Stones and Metals Workers, 1990: Whites

MSA/CMSA	Employees per 100,000 pop.	Rank
Tulsa, OK MSA	7,037	1
Providence – Pawtucket – Fall River, RI – MA CMSA	3,717	2
Los Angeles – Anaheim – Riverside, CA CMSA	3,335	3
Miami – Fort Lauderdale, FL CMSA	1,489	4
San Francisco – Oakland – San Jose, CA CMSA	1,134	5
Chicago – Gary – Lake County, IL – IN – WI CMSA	1,003	6
Dallas – Fort Worth, TX CMSA	980	7
Philadelphia – Wilmington – Trenton, PA – NJ – DE – MD CMSA	885	8
Boston – Lawrence – Salem, MA – NH CMSA	822	9
Detroit – Ann Arbor, MI CMSA	750	10
St. Louis, MO – IL MSA	436	11
Houston – Galveston – Brazoria, TX CMSA	430	12
Minneapolis – St. Paul, MN – WI MSA	429	13
Seattle – Tacoma, WA CMSA	424	14
Phoenix, AZ MSA	405	15
Albuquerque, NM MSA	382	16
Tampa – St. Petersburg – Clearwater, FL MSA	382	16
Washington, DC – MD – VA MSA	374	17
Atlanta, GA MSA	356	18

[Continued]

★ 1321 ★

Top 25 MSAs For Employment As Precious Stones and Metals Workers, 1990: Whites

[Continued]

MSA/CMSA	Employees per 100,000 pop.	Rank
Pittsburgh – Beaver Valley, PA CMSA	341	19
Cincinnati – Hamilton, OH – KY – IN CMSA	323	20
San Diego, CA MSA	298	21
Denver – Boulder, CO CMSA	295	22
Cleveland – Akron – Lorain, OH CMSA	295	22
Baltimore, MD MSA	284	23

Source: U.S. Department of Commerce, Bureau of the Census, Data User Services Division, *1990 Census of Population and Housing, Equal Employment Opportunity File, CD-90-EE0-1, January 1993,* CD-ROM.

★ 1322 ★

Occupations, By Race/Sex

Top 25 MSAs For Employment As Printing Press Operators, 1990: Blacks

MSA/CMSA	Employees per 100,000 pop.	Rank
Dayton – Springfield, OH MSA	4,498	1
Washington, DC – MD – VA MSA	2,595	2
Chicago – Gary – Lake County, IL – IN – WI CMSA	1,825	3
Los Angeles – Anaheim – Riverside, CA CMSA	1,412	4
Atlanta, GA MSA	1,306	5
Philadelphia – Wilmington – Trenton, PA – NJ – DE – MD CMSA	1,036	6
Baltimore, MD MSA	931	7
Dallas – Fort Worth, TX CMSA	813	8
Miami – Fort Lauderdale, FL CMSA	710	9
Memphis, TN – AR – MS MSA	604	10
Houston – Galveston – Brazoria, TX CMSA	562	11
San Francisco – Oakland – San Jose, CA CMSA	539	12
Cleveland – Akron – Lorain, OH CMSA	444	13
St. Louis, MO – IL MSA	423	14
Boston – Lawrence – Salem, MA – NH CMSA	401	15
Kansas City, MO – KS MSA	398	16
Richmond – Petersburg, VA MSA	348	17
Detroit – Ann Arbor, MI CMSA	348	17
New Orleans, LA MSA	322	18
Hartford – New Britain – Middletown, CT CMSA	315	19
Greensboro – Winston-Salem – High Point, NC MSA	306	20
Raleigh – Durham, NC MSA	299	21
Charlotte – Gastonia – Rock Hill, NC – SC MSA	298	22

[Continued]

★1322★

Top 25 MSAs For Employment As Printing Press Operators, 1990: Blacks
[Continued]

MSA/CMSA	Employees per 100,000 pop.	Rank
Nashville, TN MSA	293	23
Tampa – St. Petersburg – Clearwater, FL MSA	287	24

Source: U.S. Department of Commerce, Bureau of the Census, Data User Services Division, *1990 Census of Population and Housing, Equal Employment Opportunity File, CD-90-EE0-1, January 1993,* CD-ROM.

★1323★

Occupations, By Race/Sex

Top 25 MSAs For Employment As Printing Press Operators, 1990: Whites

MSA/CMSA	Employees per 100,000 pop.	Rank
Richland – Kennewick – Pasco, WA MSA	19,772	1
Los Angeles – Anaheim – Riverside, CA CMSA	13,975	2
Chicago – Gary – Lake County, IL – IN – WI CMSA	13,591	3
Philadelphia – Wilmington – Trenton, PA – NJ – DE – MD CMSA	8,926	4
San Francisco – Oakland – San Jose, CA CMSA	6,524	5
Boston – Lawrence – Salem, MA – NH CMSA	6,334	6
Minneapolis – St. Paul, MN – WI MSA	6,310	7
Dallas – Fort Worth, TX CMSA	5,354	8
Detroit – Ann Arbor, MI CMSA	4,903	9
Atlanta, GA MSA	4,167	10
Washington, DC – MD – VA MSA	4,113	11
Milwaukee – Racine, WI CMSA	3,807	12
St. Louis, MO – IL MSA	3,704	13
Cleveland – Akron – Lorain, OH CMSA	3,644	14
Miami – Fort Lauderdale, FL CMSA	3,339	15
Kansas City, MO – KS MSA	3,316	16
Cincinnati – Hamilton, OH – KY – IN CMSA	3,303	17
Seattle – Tacoma, WA CMSA	3,152	18
Baltimore, MD MSA	3,043	19
Houston – Galveston – Brazoria, TX CMSA	2,898	20
Portland – Vancouver, OR – WA CMSA	2,822	21
Phoenix, AZ MSA	2,616	22
Denver – Boulder, CO CMSA	2,611	23

[Continued]

★1323★

Top 25 MSAs For Employment As Printing Press Operators, 1990: Whites
[Continued]

MSA/CMSA	Employees per 100,000 pop.	Rank
Tampa – St. Petersburg – Clearwater, FL MSA	2,606	24
Pittsburgh – Beaver Valley, PA CMSA	2,519	25

Source: U.S. Department of Commerce, Bureau of the Census, Data User Services Division, *1990 Census of Population and Housing, Equal Employment Opportunity File, CD-90-EE0-1, January 1993,* CD-ROM.

★1324★

Occupations, By Race/Sex

Top 25 MSAs For Employment As Private Household Cleaners and Servants, 1990: Blacks

MSA/CMSA	Employees per 100,000 pop.	Rank
Indianapolis, IN MSA	12,174	1
Miami – Fort Lauderdale, FL CMSA	4,100	2
Houston – Galveston – Brazoria, TX CMSA	3,788	3
Washington, DC – MD – VA MSA	3,329	4
Dallas – Fort Worth, TX CMSA	3,269	5
Atlanta, GA MSA	3,255	6
Philadelphia – Wilmington – Trenton, PA – NJ – DE – MD CMSA	2,558	7
Los Angeles – Anaheim – Riverside, CA CMSA	2,452	8
Memphis, TN – AR – MS MSA	2,416	9
Chicago – Gary – Lake County, IL – IN – WI CMSA	2,287	10
New Orleans, LA MSA	2,027	11
Baltimore, MD MSA	1,722	12
Detroit – Ann Arbor, MI CMSA	1,679	13
St. Louis, MO – IL MSA	1,408	14
Birmingham, AL MSA	1,402	15
Norfolk – Virginia Beach – Newport News, VA MSA	1,309	16
Shreveport, LA MSA	1,300	17
Richmond – Petersburg, VA MSA	1,154	18
Jackson, MS MSA	1,083	19
San Francisco – Oakland – San Jose, CA CMSA	1,063	20
Charlotte – Gastonia – Rock Hill, NC – SC MSA	1,059	21
West Palm Beach – Boca Raton – Delray Beach, FL MSA	1,009	22
Jacksonville, FL MSA	997	23
Tampa – St. Petersburg – Clearwater, FL MSA	973	24
Mobile, AL MSA	891	25

Source: U.S. Department of Commerce, Bureau of the Census, Data User Services Division, *1990 Census of Population and Housing, Equal Employment Opportunity File, CD-90-EE0-1, January 1993,* CD-ROM.

★ 1325 ★
Occupations, By Race/Sex

Top 25 MSAs For Employment As Private Household Cleaners and Servants, 1990: Whites

MSA/CMSA	Employees per 100,000 pop.	Rank
Indianapolis, IN MSA	20,997	1
New York – Northern New Jersey – Long Island, NY – NJ – CT CMSA	13,258	2
San Francisco – Oakland – San Jose, CA CMSA	6,174	3
Miami – Fort Lauderdale, FL CMSA	5,304	4
Chicago – Gary – Lake County, IL – IN – WI CMSA	3,841	5
Washington, DC – MD – VA MSA	3,391	6
Houston – Galveston – Brazoria, TX CMSA	3,267	7
San Diego, CA MSA	2,901	8
Dallas – Fort Worth, TX CMSA	2,761	9
Philadelphia – Wilmington – Trenton, PA – NJ – DE – MD CMSA	2,550	10
Boston – Lawrence – Salem, MA – NH CMSA	2,460	11
Detroit – Ann Arbor, MI CMSA	2,001	12
Seattle – Tacoma, WA CMSA	1,894	13
Phoenix, AZ MSA	1,641	14
Denver – Boulder, CO CMSA	1,641	14
San Antonio, TX MSA	1,567	15
Tampa – St. Petersburg – Clearwater, FL MSA	1,565	16
West Palm Beach – Boca Raton – Delray Beach, FL MSA	1,411	17
Minneapolis – St. Paul, MN – WI MSA	1,399	18
Cleveland – Akron – Lorain, OH CMSA	1,286	19
Sacramento, CA MSA	1,276	20
El Paso, TX MSA	1,273	21
Pittsburgh – Beaver Valley, PA CMSA	1,207	22
Portland – Vancouver, OR – WA CMSA	1,193	23
St. Louis, MO – IL MSA	1,141	24

Source: U.S. Department of Commerce, Bureau of the Census, Data User Services Division, *1990 Census of Population and Housing, Equal Employment Opportunity File, CD-90-EE0-1, January 1993,* CD-ROM.

★ 1326 ★
Occupations, By Race/Sex

Top 25 MSAs For Employment As Proofreaders, 1990: Blacks

MSA/CMSA	Employees per 100,000 pop.	Rank
Cincinnati – Hamilton, OH – KY – IN CMSA	553	1
Washington, DC – MD – VA MSA	244	2
Chicago – Gary – Lake County, IL – IN – WI CMSA	231	3
Detroit – Ann Arbor, MI CMSA	103	4
Philadelphia – Wilmington – Trenton, PA – NJ – DE – MD CMSA	103	4
Atlanta, GA MSA	83	5
Miami – Fort Lauderdale, FL CMSA	77	6
Los Angeles – Anaheim – Riverside, CA CMSA	76	7
Dallas – Fort Worth, TX CMSA	74	8
Charlotte – Gastonia – Rock Hill, NC – SC MSA	44	9
Indianapolis, IN MSA	43	10
Tampa – St. Petersburg – Clearwater, FL MSA	42	11
Baltimore, MD MSA	40	12
Milwaukee – Racine, WI CMSA	35	13
Nashville, TN MSA	35	13
San Francisco – Oakland – San Jose, CA CMSA	30	14
Columbia, SC MSA	30	14
Columbus, OH MSA	28	15
Hartford – New Britain – Middletown, CT CMSA	28	15
Tallahassee, FL MSA	27	16
St. Louis, MO – IL MSA	25	17
Pittsburgh – Beaver Valley, PA CMSA	24	18
Greensboro – Winston-Salem – High Point, NC MSA	23	19
Orlando, FL MSA	22	20
Anderson, IN MSA	21	21

Source: U.S. Department of Commerce, Bureau of the Census, Data User Services Division, *1990 Census of Population and Housing, Equal Employment Opportunity File, CD-90-EE0-1, January 1993,* CD-ROM.

★ 1327 ★
Occupations, By Race/Sex

Top 25 MSAs For Employment As Proofreaders, 1990: Whites

MSA/CMSA	Employees per 100,000 pop.	Rank
Portland – Vancouver, OR – WA CMSA	4,421	1
Chicago – Gary – Lake County, IL – IN – WI CMSA	1,395	2
Los Angeles – Anaheim – Riverside, CA CMSA	1,168	3
Philadelphia – Wilmington – Trenton, PA – NJ – DE – MD CMSA	1,027	4
Washington, DC – MD – VA MSA	831	5
Minneapolis – St. Paul, MN – WI MSA	766	6
Boston – Lawrence – Salem, MA – NH CMSA	663	7
Detroit – Ann Arbor, MI CMSA	512	8
Dallas – Fort Worth, TX CMSA	486	9
San Francisco – Oakland – San Jose, CA CMSA	483	10
Baltimore, MD MSA	362	11
Atlanta, GA MSA	323	12
Houston – Galveston – Brazoria, TX CMSA	306	13
Lancaster, PA MSA	303	14
St. Louis, MO – IL MSA	281	15
Pittsburgh – Beaver Valley, PA CMSA	256	16
Tampa – St. Petersburg – Clearwater, FL MSA	242	17
Columbus, OH MSA	236	18
Milwaukee – Racine, WI CMSA	224	19
Kansas City, MO – KS MSA	215	20
San Diego, CA MSA	214	21
Cleveland – Akron – Lorain, OH CMSA	196	22
Phoenix, AZ MSA	188	23
Denver – Boulder, CO CMSA	180	24
Nashville, TN MSA	177	25

Source: U.S. Department of Commerce, Bureau of the Census, Data User Services Division, *1990 Census of Population and Housing, Equal Employment Opportunity File, CD-90-EE0-1,* January 1993, CD-ROM.

★ 1328 ★
Occupations, By Race/Sex

Top 25 MSAs For Employment As Psychologists, 1990: Blacks

MSA/CMSA	Employees per 100,000 pop.	Rank
Memphis, TN – AR – MS MSA	2,007	1
Chicago – Gary – Lake County, IL – IN – WI CMSA	755	2
Los Angeles – Anaheim – Riverside, CA CMSA	718	3
Washington, DC – MD – VA MSA	713	4

[Continued]

★ 1328 ★
Top 25 MSAs For Employment As Psychologists, 1990: Blacks
[Continued]

MSA/CMSA	Employees per 100,000 pop.	Rank
Philadelphia – Wilmington – Trenton, PA – NJ – DE – MD CMSA	506	5
San Francisco – Oakland – San Jose, CA CMSA	446	6
Detroit – Ann Arbor, MI CMSA	375	7
Baltimore, MD MSA	357	8
Miami – Fort Lauderdale, FL CMSA	326	9
Atlanta, GA MSA	222	10
Boston – Lawrence – Salem, MA – NH CMSA	208	11
Houston – Galveston – Brazoria, TX CMSA	201	12
Norfolk – Virginia Beach – Newport News, VA MSA	188	13
St. Louis, MO – IL MSA	167	14
Memphis, TN – AR – MS MSA	155	15
Pittsburgh – Beaver Valley, PA CMSA	144	16
Columbia, SC MSA	129	17
Dallas – Fort Worth, TX CMSA	108	18
Tampa – St. Petersburg – Clearwater, FL MSA	108	18
Greensboro – Winston-Salem – High Point, NC MSA	96	19
Richmond – Petersburg, VA MSA	96	19
Jacksonville, FL MSA	94	20
San Diego, CA MSA	86	21
New Orleans, LA MSA	86	21
Albany – Schenectady – Troy, NY MSA	83	22

Source: U.S. Department of Commerce, Bureau of the Census, Data User Services Division, *1990 Census of Population and Housing, Equal Employment Opportunity File, CD-90-EE0-1,* January 1993, CD-ROM.

★ 1329 ★
Occupations, By Race/Sex

Top 25 MSAs For Employment As Psychologists, 1990: Whites

MSA/CMSA	Employees per 100,000 pop.	Rank
Tampa – St. Petersburg – Clearwater, FL MSA	19,416	1
Los Angeles – Anaheim – Riverside, CA CMSA	11,527	2
San Francisco – Oakland – San Jose, CA CMSA	7,912	3
Boston – Lawrence – Salem, MA – NH CMSA	6,966	4
Chicago – Gary – Lake County, IL – IN – WI CMSA	5,286	5
Philadelphia – Wilmington – Trenton, PA – NJ – DE – MD CMSA	5,094	6

[Continued]

★1329★

Top 25 MSAs For Employment As Psychologists, 1990: Whites

[Continued]

MSA/CMSA	Employees per 100,000 pop.	Rank
Washington, DC–MD–VA MSA	4,106	7
Detroit–Ann Arbor, MI CMSA	3,112	8
Minneapolis–St. Paul, MN–WI MSA	2,974	9
Denver–Boulder, CO CMSA	2,742	10
Seattle–Tacoma, WA CMSA	2,706	11
San Diego, CA MSA	2,546	12
Dallas–Fort Worth, TX CMSA	2,275	13
Houston–Galveston–Brazoria, TX CMSA	2,209	14
Baltimore, MD MSA	1,841	15
Atlanta, GA MSA	1,824	16
Miami–Fort Lauderdale, FL CMSA	1,792	17
Pittsburgh–Beaver Valley, PA CMSA	1,557	18
Cleveland–Akron–Lorain, OH CMSA	1,555	19
Phoenix, AZ MSA	1,523	20
Tampa–St. Petersburg–Clearwater, FL MSA	1,409	21
St. Louis, MO–IL MSA	1,294	22
Hartford–New Britain–Middletown, CT CMSA	1,233	23
Milwaukee–Racine, WI CMSA	1,208	24
Sacramento, CA MSA	1,141	25

Source: U.S. Department of Commerce, Bureau of the Census, Data User Services Division, *1990 Census of Population and Housing, Equal Employment Opportunity File, CD-90-EE0-1,* January 1993, CD-ROM.

★1330★

Occupations, By Race/Sex

Top 25 MSAs For Employment As Psychology Teachers, 1990: Blacks

MSA/CMSA	Employees per 100,000 pop.	Rank
Olympia, WA MSA	41	1
San Francisco–Oakland–San Jose, CA CMSA	19	2
Huntsville, AL MSA	16	3
New Orleans, LA MSA	12	4
Tallahassee, FL MSA	11	5
Chicago–Gary–Lake County, IL–IN–WI CMSA	9	6
Jackson, MS MSA	8	7
San Diego, CA MSA	8	7
Houston–Galveston–Brazoria, TX CMSA	7	8
Raleigh–Durham, NC MSA	7	8
Champaign–Urbana–Rantoul, IL MSA	7	8
Detroit–Ann Arbor, MI CMSA	6	9
Clarksville–Hopkinsville, TN–KY MSA	6	9

[Continued]

★1330★

Top 25 MSAs For Employment As Psychology Teachers, 1990: Blacks

[Continued]

MSA/CMSA	Employees per 100,000 pop.	Rank
Decatur, AL MSA	5	10
Minneapolis–St. Paul, MN–WI MSA	5	10
Springfield, IL MSA	4	11
Dallas–Fort Worth, TX CMSA	4	11
Olympia, WA MSA	0	12
Orlando, FL MSA	0	12
Omaha, NE–IA MSA	0	12
Odessa, TX MSA	0	12
Oklahoma City, OK MSA	0	12
Ocala, FL MSA	0	12
Parkersburg–Marietta, WV–OH MSA	0	12
Phoenix, AZ MSA	0	12

Source: U.S. Department of Commerce, Bureau of the Census, Data User Services Division, *1990 Census of Population and Housing, Equal Employment Opportunity File, CD-90-EE0-1,* January 1993, CD-ROM.

★1331★

Occupations, By Race/Sex

Top 25 MSAs For Employment As Psychology Teachers, 1990: Whites

MSA/CMSA	Employees per 100,000 pop.	Rank
Portland–Vancouver, OR–WA CMSA	418	1
Los Angeles–Anaheim–Riverside, CA CMSA	162	2
Boston–Lawrence–Salem, MA–NH CMSA	112	3
San Francisco–Oakland–San Jose, CA CMSA	91	4
Philadelphia–Wilmington–Trenton, PA–NJ–DE–MD CMSA	83	5
Chicago–Gary–Lake County, IL–IN–WI CMSA	78	6
Seattle–Tacoma, WA CMSA	66	7
Baltimore, MD MSA	58	8
Pittsburgh–Beaver Valley, PA CMSA	49	9
Cincinnati–Hamilton, OH–KY–IN CMSA	48	10
Lubbock, TX MSA	47	11
Albuquerque, NM MSA	44	12
Washington, DC–MD–VA MSA	44	12
Milwaukee–Racine, WI CMSA	43	13
Austin, TX MSA	40	14
Lansing–East Lansing, MI MSA	40	14
Dallas–Fort Worth, TX CMSA	39	15
Cleveland–Akron–Lorain, OH CMSA	38	16
San Diego, CA MSA	38	16

[Continued]

★1331★

Top 25 MSAs For Employment As Psychology Teachers, 1990: Whites
[Continued]

MSA/CMSA	Employees per 100,000 pop.	Rank
Atlanta, GA MSA	38	16
Minneapolis – St. Paul, MN – WI MSA	37	17
San Antonio, TX MSA	35	18
Houston – Galveston – Brazoria, TX CMSA	35	18
Raleigh – Durham, NC MSA	34	19
Sacramento, CA MSA	34	19

Source: U.S. Department of Commerce, Bureau of the Census, Data User Services Division, *1990 Census of Population and Housing, Equal Employment Opportunity File, CD-90-EE0-1, January 1993,* CD-ROM.

★1332★

Occupations, By Race/Sex

Top 25 MSAs For Employment As Railroad Brake, Signal, and Switch Operators, 1990: Blacks

MSA/CMSA	Employees per 100,000 pop.	Rank
Charlotte – Gastonia – Rock Hill, NC – SC MSA	457	1
Houston – Galveston – Brazoria, TX CMSA	227	2
Atlanta, GA MSA	143	3
St. Louis, MO – IL MSA	119	4
Birmingham, AL MSA	108	5
Norfolk – Virginia Beach – Newport News, VA MSA	82	6
Kansas City, MO – KS MSA	77	7
Los Angeles – Anaheim – Riverside, CA CMSA	70	8
Savannah, GA MSA	70	8
Shreveport, LA MSA	68	9
Baton Rouge, LA MSA	60	10
San Francisco – Oakland – San Jose, CA CMSA	60	10
New Orleans, LA MSA	52	11
New York – Northern New Jersey – Long Island, NY – NJ – CT CMSA	51	12
Macon – Warner Robins, GA MSA	46	13
Roanoke, VA MSA	45	14
Memphis, TN – AR – MS MSA	45	14
El Paso, TX MSA	44	15
Little Rock – North Little Rock, AR MSA	43	16
Columbia, SC MSA	40	17
Portland – Vancouver, OR – WA CMSA	38	18
Longview – Marshall, TX MSA	35	19
Baltimore, MD MSA	34	20

[Continued]

★1332★

Top 25 MSAs For Employment As Railroad Brake, Signal, and Switch Operators, 1990: Blacks
[Continued]

MSA/CMSA	Employees per 100,000 pop.	Rank
Dallas – Fort Worth, TX CMSA	34	20
Washington, DC – MD – VA MSA	34	20

Source: U.S. Department of Commerce, Bureau of the Census, Data User Services Division, *1990 Census of Population and Housing, Equal Employment Opportunity File, CD-90-EE0-1, January 1993,* CD-ROM.

★1333★

Occupations, By Race/Sex

Top 25 MSAs For Employment As Railroad Brake, Signal, and Switch Operators, 1990: Whites

MSA/CMSA	Employees per 100,000 pop.	Rank
Amarillo, TX MSA	1,245	1
Kansas City, MO – KS MSA	713	2
Houston – Galveston – Brazoria, TX CMSA	535	3
St. Louis, MO – IL MSA	525	4
Los Angeles – Anaheim – Riverside, CA CMSA	492	5
Detroit – Ann Arbor, MI CMSA	480	6
Minneapolis – St. Paul, MN – WI MSA	443	7
Dallas – Fort Worth, TX CMSA	389	8
Seattle – Tacoma, WA CMSA	361	9
Salt Lake City – Ogden, UT MSA	333	10
Cincinnati – Hamilton, OH – KY – IN CMSA	321	11
Spokane, WA MSA	282	12
Cleveland – Akron – Lorain, OH CMSA	272	13
Portland – Vancouver, OR – WA CMSA	271	14
Denver – Boulder, CO CMSA	270	15
New Orleans, LA MSA	254	16
Duluth, MN – WI MSA	253	17
Roanoke, VA MSA	247	18
Stockton, CA MSA	229	19
Louisville, KY – IN MSA	219	20
Birmingham, AL MSA	208	21
Huntington – Ashland, WV – KY – OH MSA	201	22
Little Rock – North Little Rock, AR MSA	200	23
Amarillo, TX MSA	195	24
Baltimore, MD MSA	193	25

Source: U.S. Department of Commerce, Bureau of the Census, Data User Services Division, *1990 Census of Population and Housing, Equal Employment Opportunity File, CD-90-EE0-1, January 1993,* CD-ROM.

★ 1334 ★
Occupations, By Race/Sex

Top 25 MSAs For Employment As Railroad Conductors and Yardmasters, 1990: Blacks

MSA/CMSA	Employees per 100,000 pop.	Rank
Jacksonville, FL MSA	646	1
Philadelphia – Wilmington – Trenton, PA – NJ – DE – MD CMSA	254	2
Chicago – Gary – Lake County, IL – IN – WI CMSA	212	3
Atlanta, GA MSA	101	4
San Francisco – Oakland – San Jose, CA CMSA	90	5
Los Angeles – Anaheim – Riverside, CA CMSA	88	6
Dallas – Fort Worth, TX CMSA	82	7
Houston – Galveston – Brazoria, TX CMSA	76	8
Washington, DC – MD – VA MSA	71	9
Jacksonville, FL MSA	62	10
Baltimore, MD MSA	61	11
Sacramento, CA MSA	56	12
Birmingham, AL MSA	48	13
Augusta, GA – SC MSA	40	14
Norfolk – Virginia Beach – Newport News, VA MSA	39	15
Cincinnati – Hamilton, OH – KY – IN CMSA	39	15
Kansas City, MO – KS MSA	33	16
St. Louis, MO – IL MSA	31	17
Miami – Fort Lauderdale, FL CMSA	31	17
Cleveland – Akron – Lorain, OH CMSA	29	18
Denver – Boulder, CO CMSA	29	18
Little Rock – North Little Rock, AR MSA	27	19
Richmond – Petersburg, VA MSA	25	20
New Orleans, LA MSA	24	21
Detroit – Ann Arbor, MI CMSA	21	22

Source: U.S. Department of Commerce, Bureau of the Census, Data User Services Division, *1990 Census of Population and Housing, Equal Employment Opportunity File, CD-90-EE0-1, January 1993,* CD-ROM.

★ 1335 ★
Occupations, By Race/Sex

Top 25 MSAs For Employment As Railroad Conductors and Yardmasters, 1990: Whites

MSA/CMSA	Employees per 100,000 pop.	Rank
New Orleans, LA MSA	2,415	1
Chicago – Gary – Lake County, IL – IN – WI CMSA	1,177	2
Philadelphia – Wilmington – Trenton, PA – NJ – DE – MD CMSA	881	3
Los Angeles – Anaheim – Riverside, CA CMSA	761	4

[Continued]

★ 1335 ★

Top 25 MSAs For Employment As Railroad Conductors and Yardmasters, 1990: Whites
[Continued]

MSA/CMSA	Employees per 100,000 pop.	Rank
Detroit – Ann Arbor, MI CMSA	504	5
Pittsburgh – Beaver Valley, PA CMSA	474	6
San Francisco – Oakland – San Jose, CA CMSA	439	7
Portland – Vancouver, OR – WA CMSA	430	8
Houston – Galveston – Brazoria, TX CMSA	429	9
Boston – Lawrence – Salem, MA – NH CMSA	399	10
Dallas – Fort Worth, TX CMSA	394	11
Kansas City, MO – KS MSA	369	12
Cleveland – Akron – Lorain, OH CMSA	352	13
Salt Lake City – Ogden, UT MSA	339	14
Minneapolis – St. Paul, MN – WI MSA	326	15
Toledo, OH MSA	300	16
Baltimore, MD MSA	295	17
Sacramento, CA MSA	280	18
Jacksonville, FL MSA	280	18
Atlanta, GA MSA	256	19
Buffalo – Niagara Falls, NY CMSA	251	20
Cincinnati – Hamilton, OH – KY – IN CMSA	244	21
Seattle – Tacoma, WA CMSA	242	22
St. Louis, MO – IL MSA	236	23
Albany – Schenectady – Troy, NY MSA	236	23

Source: U.S. Department of Commerce, Bureau of the Census, Data User Services Division, *1990 Census of Population and Housing, Equal Employment Opportunity File, CD-90-EE0-1, January 1993,* CD-ROM.

★ 1336 ★
Occupations, By Race/Sex

Top 25 MSAs For Employment As Registered Nurses, 1990: Blacks

MSA/CMSA	Employees per 100,000 pop.	Rank
Owensboro, KY MSA	33,496	1
Los Angeles – Anaheim – Riverside, CA CMSA	9,317	2
Chicago – Gary – Lake County, IL – IN – WI CMSA	8,451	3
Washington, DC – MD – VA MSA	7,552	4
Philadelphia – Wilmington – Trenton, PA – NJ – DE – MD CMSA	6,549	5
Miami – Fort Lauderdale, FL CMSA	5,896	6
Houston – Galveston – Brazoria, TX CMSA	5,284	7

[Continued]

★ 1336 ★

Top 25 MSAs For Employment As Registered Nurses, 1990: Blacks
[Continued]

MSA/CMSA	Employees per 100,000 pop.	Rank
Detroit – Ann Arbor, MI CMSA	4,560	8
Atlanta, GA MSA	4,042	9
Baltimore, MD MSA	3,899	10
San Francisco – Oakland – San Jose, CA CMSA	3,484	11
Dallas – Fort Worth, TX CMSA	2,773	12
St. Louis, MO – IL MSA	2,712	13
Cleveland – Akron – Lorain, OH CMSA	2,130	14
Norfolk – Virginia Beach – Newport News, VA MSA	2,031	15
Birmingham, AL MSA	1,965	16
New Orleans, LA MSA	1,943	17
Memphis, TN – AR – MS MSA	1,912	18
Boston – Lawrence – Salem, MA – NH CMSA	1,465	19
Raleigh – Durham, NC MSA	1,413	20
Richmond – Petersburg, VA MSA	1,346	21
Nashville, TN MSA	1,270	22
Cincinnati – Hamilton, OH – KY – IN CMSA	1,172	23
Greensboro – Winston-Salem – High Point, NC MSA	1,058	24
Kansas City, MO – KS MSA	1,004	25

Source: U.S. Department of Commerce, Bureau of the Census, Data User Services Division, *1990 Census of Population and Housing, Equal Employment Opportunity File, CD-90-EE0-1,* January 1993, CD-ROM.

★ 1337 ★

Occupations, By Race/Sex

Top 25 MSAs For Employment As Registered Nurses, 1990: Whites

MSA/CMSA	Employees per 100,000 pop.	Rank
Houston – Galveston – Brazoria, TX CMSA	100,721	1
Los Angeles – Anaheim – Riverside, CA CMSA	59,404	2
Chicago – Gary – Lake County, IL – IN – WI CMSA	50,460	3
Philadelphia – Wilmington – Trenton, PA – NJ – DE – MD CMSA	48,627	4
Boston – Lawrence – Salem, MA – NH CMSA	43,249	5
San Francisco – Oakland – San Jose, CA CMSA	37,044	6
Detroit – Ann Arbor, MI CMSA	29,905	7
Minneapolis – St. Paul, MN – WI MSA	23,751	8
Pittsburgh – Beaver Valley, PA CMSA	23,349	9
Cleveland – Akron – Lorain, OH CMSA	22,930	10

[Continued]

★ 1337 ★

Top 25 MSAs For Employment As Registered Nurses, 1990: Whites
[Continued]

MSA/CMSA	Employees per 100,000 pop.	Rank
Washington, DC – MD – VA MSA	22,171	11
Dallas – Fort Worth, TX CMSA	20,102	12
St. Louis, MO – IL MSA	18,941	13
Seattle – Tacoma, WA CMSA	18,783	14
Baltimore, MD MSA	18,382	15
Houston – Galveston – Brazoria, TX CMSA	16,482	16
Atlanta, GA MSA	16,307	17
Miami – Fort Lauderdale, FL CMSA	16,103	18
Phoenix, AZ MSA	15,805	19
Tampa – St. Petersburg – Clearwater, FL MSA	15,397	20
Cincinnati – Hamilton, OH – KY – IN CMSA	14,806	21
Denver – Boulder, CO CMSA	14,415	22
Milwaukee – Racine, WI CMSA	14,083	23
San Diego, CA MSA	13,194	24
Portland – Vancouver, OR – WA CMSA	12,714	25

Source: U.S. Department of Commerce, Bureau of the Census, Data User Services Division, *1990 Census of Population and Housing, Equal Employment Opportunity File, CD-90-EE0-1,* January 1993, CD-ROM.

★ 1338 ★

Occupations, By Race/Sex

Top 25 MSAs For Employment As Respiratory Therapists, 1990: Blacks

MSA/CMSA	Employees per 100,000 pop.	Rank
Columbia, SC MSA	697	1
Chicago – Gary – Lake County, IL – IN – WI CMSA	588	2
Los Angeles – Anaheim – Riverside, CA CMSA	464	3
Washington, DC – MD – VA MSA	322	4
Philadelphia – Wilmington – Trenton, PA – NJ – DE – MD CMSA	309	5
Detroit – Ann Arbor, MI CMSA	302	6
Houston – Galveston – Brazoria, TX CMSA	300	7
Miami – Fort Lauderdale, FL CMSA	274	8
Atlanta, GA MSA	223	9
Dallas – Fort Worth, TX CMSA	197	10
Baltimore, MD MSA	194	11
San Francisco – Oakland – San Jose, CA CMSA	153	12
Memphis, TN – AR – MS MSA	132	13
New Orleans, LA MSA	130	14
Cleveland – Akron – Lorain, OH CMSA	126	15

[Continued]

★1338★

Top 25 MSAs For Employment As Respiratory Therapists, 1990: Blacks

[Continued]

MSA/CMSA	Employees per 100,000 pop.	Rank
St. Louis, MO – IL MSA	126	15
Indianapolis, IN MSA	105	16
Birmingham, AL MSA	84	17
Jackson, MS MSA	78	18
Boston – Lawrence – Salem, MA – NH CMSA	60	19
Kansas City, MO – KS MSA	60	19
Cincinnati – Hamilton, OH – KY – IN CMSA	55	20
Phoenix, AZ MSA	54	21
San Diego, CA MSA	49	22
Little Rock – North Little Rock, AR MSA	48	23

Source: U.S. Department of Commerce, Bureau of the Census, Data User Services Division, *1990 Census of Population and Housing, Equal Employment Opportunity File, CD-90-EE0-1, January 1993,* CD-ROM.

★1339★
Occupations, By Race/Sex

Top 25 MSAs For Employment As Respiratory Therapists, 1990: Whites

MSA/CMSA	Employees per 100,000 pop.	Rank
Denver – Boulder, CO CMSA	2,609	1
New York – Northern New Jersey – Long Island, NY – NJ – CT CMSA	1,848	2
Detroit – Ann Arbor, MI CMSA	1,357	3
Chicago – Gary – Lake County, IL – IN – WI CMSA	1,236	4
San Francisco – Oakland – San Jose, CA CMSA	1,141	5
Philadelphia – Wilmington – Trenton, PA – NJ – DE – MD CMSA	1,099	6
Miami – Fort Lauderdale, FL CMSA	1,031	7
Boston – Lawrence – Salem, MA – NH CMSA	898	8
Dallas – Fort Worth, TX CMSA	859	9
Atlanta, GA MSA	785	10
Tampa – St. Petersburg – Clearwater, FL MSA	784	11
Phoenix, AZ MSA	750	12
Cleveland – Akron – Lorain, OH CMSA	748	13
St. Louis, MO – IL MSA	645	14
Pittsburgh – Beaver Valley, PA CMSA	629	15
San Diego, CA MSA	605	16
Houston – Galveston – Brazoria, TX CMSA	524	17
Minneapolis – St. Paul, MN – WI MSA	522	18

[Continued]

★1339★

Top 25 MSAs For Employment As Respiratory Therapists, 1990: Whites

[Continued]

MSA/CMSA	Employees per 100,000 pop.	Rank
Kansas City, MO – KS MSA	512	19
Indianapolis, IN MSA	506	20
Seattle – Tacoma, WA CMSA	494	21
Denver – Boulder, CO CMSA	493	22
Washington, DC – MD – VA MSA	471	23
Dayton – Springfield, OH MSA	455	24
Milwaukee – Racine, WI CMSA	398	25

Source: U.S. Department of Commerce, Bureau of the Census, Data User Services Division, *1990 Census of Population and Housing, Equal Employment Opportunity File, CD-90-EE0-1, January 1993,* CD-ROM.

★1340★
Occupations, By Race/Sex

Top 25 MSAs For Employment As Roofers, 1990: Blacks

MSA/CMSA	Employees per 100,000 pop.	Rank
Albany, GA MSA	1,072	1
Miami – Fort Lauderdale, FL CMSA	952	2
Washington, DC – MD – VA MSA	554	3
Atlanta, GA MSA	519	4
Philadelphia – Wilmington – Trenton, PA – NJ – DE – MD CMSA	501	5
Los Angeles – Anaheim – Riverside, CA CMSA	489	6
Baltimore, MD MSA	486	7
Houston – Galveston – Brazoria, TX CMSA	469	8
Dallas – Fort Worth, TX CMSA	416	9
Chicago – Gary – Lake County, IL – IN – WI CMSA	403	10
Detroit – Ann Arbor, MI CMSA	398	11
Norfolk – Virginia Beach – Newport News, VA MSA	369	12
Charlotte – Gastonia – Rock Hill, NC – SC MSA	354	13
New Orleans, LA MSA	351	14
Tampa – St. Petersburg – Clearwater, FL MSA	349	15
Memphis, TN – AR – MS MSA	330	16
San Francisco – Oakland – San Jose, CA CMSA	328	17
Baton Rouge, LA MSA	248	18
Charleston, SC MSA	235	19
Columbia, SC MSA	228	20
Jackson, MS MSA	197	21
Mobile, AL MSA	196	22
Raleigh – Durham, NC MSA	194	23
Shreveport, LA MSA	191	24
Orlando, FL MSA	183	25

Source: U.S. Department of Commerce, Bureau of the Census, Data User Services Division, *1990 Census of Population and Housing, Equal Employment Opportunity File, CD-90-EE0-1, January 1993,* CD-ROM.

★1341★

Occupations, By Race/Sex

Top 25 MSAs For Employment As Roofers, 1990: Whites

MSA/CMSA	Employees per 100,000 pop.	Rank
New Orleans, LA MSA	7,116	1
New York – Northern New Jersey – Long Island, NY – NJ – CT CMSA	6,833	2
Philadelphia – Wilmington – Trenton, PA – NJ – DE – MD CMSA	4,460	3
Chicago – Gary – Lake County, IL – IN – WI CMSA	4,279	4
San Francisco – Oakland – San Jose, CA CMSA	3,332	5
Dallas – Fort Worth, TX CMSA	3,038	6
Detroit – Ann Arbor, MI CMSA	3,017	7
Cleveland – Akron – Lorain, OH CMSA	2,164	8
Miami – Fort Lauderdale, FL CMSA	2,047	9
Boston – Lawrence – Salem, MA – NH CMSA	2,037	10
Atlanta, GA MSA	1,918	11
Seattle – Tacoma, WA CMSA	1,741	12
Washington, DC – MD – VA MSA	1,699	13
Houston – Galveston – Brazoria, TX CMSA	1,689	14
Indianapolis, IN MSA	1,621	15
Phoenix, AZ MSA	1,590	16
Pittsburgh – Beaver Valley, PA CMSA	1,565	17
St. Louis, MO – IL MSA	1,564	18
Tampa – St. Petersburg – Clearwater, FL MSA	1,533	19
San Diego, CA MSA	1,433	20
Baltimore, MD MSA	1,355	21
Cincinnati – Hamilton, OH – KY – IN CMSA	1,325	22
Minneapolis – St. Paul, MN – WI MSA	1,296	23
Charlotte – Gastonia – Rock Hill, NC – SC MSA	1,185	24
Sacramento, CA MSA	1,184	25

Source: U.S. Department of Commerce, Bureau of the Census, Data User Services Division, *1990 Census of Population and Housing, Equal Employment Opportunity File,* CD-90-EE0-1, January 1993, CD-ROM.

★1342★

Occupations, By Race/Sex

Top 25 MSAs For Employment As Sailors and Deckhands, 1990: Blacks

MSA/CMSA	Employees per 100,000 pop.	Rank
Charleston, SC MSA	376	1
New York – Northern New Jersey – Long Island, NY – NJ – CT CMSA	173	2
San Francisco – Oakland – San Jose, CA CMSA	171	3
Norfolk – Virginia Beach – Newport News, VA MSA	155	4
Houston – Galveston – Brazoria, TX CMSA	151	5
Mobile, AL MSA	135	6
Los Angeles – Anaheim – Riverside, CA CMSA	125	7
Miami – Fort Lauderdale, FL CMSA	109	8
Jacksonville, FL MSA	105	9
Boston – Lawrence – Salem, MA – NH CMSA	78	10
Beaumont – Port Arthur, TX MSA	71	11
Charleston, SC MSA	67	12
Seattle – Tacoma, WA CMSA	58	13
Baton Rouge, LA MSA	46	14
West Palm Beach – Boca Raton – Delray Beach, FL MSA	39	15
Cleveland – Akron – Lorain, OH CMSA	37	16
Baltimore, MD MSA	31	17
Lake Charles, LA MSA	28	18
Philadelphia – Wilmington – Trenton, PA – NJ – DE – MD CMSA	26	19
Memphis, TN – AR – MS MSA	26	19
Washington, DC – MD – VA MSA	25	20
Chicago – Gary – Lake County, IL – IN – WI CMSA	21	21
Clarksville – Hopkinsville, TN – KY MSA	21	21
San Diego, CA MSA	20	22
Houma – Thibodaux, LA MSA	19	23

Source: U.S. Department of Commerce, Bureau of the Census, Data User Services Division, *1990 Census of Population and Housing, Equal Employment Opportunity File,* CD-90-EE0-1, January 1993, CD-ROM.

★1343★

Occupations, By Race/Sex

Top 25 MSAs For Employment As Sailors and Deckhands, 1990: Whites

MSA/CMSA	Employees per 100,000 pop.	Rank
Pittsburgh – Beaver Valley, PA CMSA	1,143	1
New Orleans, LA MSA	1,025	2
Los Angeles – Anaheim – Riverside, CA CMSA	877	3
Seattle – Tacoma, WA CMSA	855	4
Houma – Thibodaux, LA MSA	826	5
Houston – Galveston – Brazoria, TX CMSA	807	6
San Francisco – Oakland – San Jose, CA CMSA	686	7
Tampa – St. Petersburg – Clearwater, FL MSA	391	8
Norfolk – Virginia Beach – Newport News, VA MSA	378	9
Miami – Fort Lauderdale, FL CMSA	377	10
Mobile, AL MSA	341	11
Jacksonville, FL MSA	336	12
St. Louis, MO – IL MSA	330	13
San Diego, CA MSA	251	14
Pittsburgh – Beaver Valley, PA CMSA	242	15
Baltimore, MD MSA	227	16
Lake Charles, LA MSA	215	17
Philadelphia – Wilmington – Trenton, PA – NJ – DE – MD CMSA	210	18
Detroit – Ann Arbor, MI CMSA	195	19
Biloxi – Gulfport, MS MSA	185	20
Portland – Vancouver, OR – WA CMSA	179	21
Beaumont – Port Arthur, TX MSA	178	22
Boston – Lawrence – Salem, MA – NH CMSA	170	23
Baton Rouge, LA MSA	167	24
Bremerton, WA MSA	136	25

Source: U.S. Department of Commerce, Bureau of the Census, Data User Services Division, *1990 Census of Population and Housing, Equal Employment Opportunity File, CD-90-EEO-1, January 1993,* CD-ROM.

★1344★

Occupations, By Race/Sex

Top 25 MSAs For Employment As Sheriffs, Bailiffs, and Other Law Enforcement Officers, 1990: Blacks

MSA/CMSA	Employees per 100,000 pop.	Rank
San Diego, CA MSA	1,057	1
Los Angeles – Anaheim – Riverside, CA CMSA	1,021	2
Washington, DC – MD – VA MSA	892	3
Chicago – Gary – Lake County, IL – IN – WI CMSA	835	4

[Continued]

★1344★

Top 25 MSAs For Employment As Sheriffs, Bailiffs, and Other Law Enforcement Officers, 1990: Blacks
[Continued]

MSA/CMSA	Employees per 100,000 pop.	Rank
Atlanta, GA MSA	554	5
Detroit – Ann Arbor, MI CMSA	519	6
New Orleans, LA MSA	500	7
Philadelphia – Wilmington – Trenton, PA – NJ – DE – MD CMSA	442	8
Memphis, TN – AR – MS MSA	382	9
San Francisco – Oakland – San Jose, CA CMSA	374	10
Richmond – Petersburg, VA MSA	339	11
Houston – Galveston – Brazoria, TX CMSA	326	12
Norfolk – Virginia Beach – Newport News, VA MSA	301	13
Tampa – St. Petersburg – Clearwater, FL MSA	294	14
Baltimore, MD MSA	267	15
Miami – Fort Lauderdale, FL CMSA	257	16
Cleveland – Akron – Lorain, OH CMSA	205	17
Dallas – Fort Worth, TX CMSA	192	18
Birmingham, AL MSA	187	19
St. Louis, MO – IL MSA	128	20
Boston – Lawrence – Salem, MA – NH CMSA	121	21
San Diego, CA MSA	116	22
Columbia, SC MSA	112	23
Raleigh – Durham, NC MSA	110	24
Milwaukee – Racine, WI CMSA	102	25

Source: U.S. Department of Commerce, Bureau of the Census, Data User Services Division, *1990 Census of Population and Housing, Equal Employment Opportunity File, CD-90-EEO-1, January 1993,* CD-ROM.

★1345★

Occupations, By Race/Sex

Top 25 MSAs For Employment As Sheriffs, Bailiffs, and Other Law Enforcement Officers, 1990: Whites

MSA/CMSA	Employees per 100,000 pop.	Rank
Sacramento, CA MSA	6,643	1
New York – Northern New Jersey – Long Island, NY – NJ – CT CMSA	4,132	2
San Francisco – Oakland – San Jose, CA CMSA	2,797	3
Chicago – Gary – Lake County, IL – IN – WI CMSA	1,933	4
Washington, DC – MD – VA MSA	1,853	5
Tampa – St. Petersburg – Clearwater, FL MSA	1,608	6

[Continued]

★1345★

Top 25 MSAs For Employment As Sheriffs, Bailiffs, and Other Law Enforcement Officers, 1990: Whites

[Continued]

MSA/CMSA	Employees per 100,000 pop.	Rank
Atlanta, GA MSA	1,307	7
Philadelphia – Wilmington – Trenton, PA – NJ – DE – MD CMSA	1,297	8
Miami – Fort Lauderdale, FL CMSA	1,294	9
Houston – Galveston – Brazoria, TX CMSA	1,227	10
Dallas – Fort Worth, TX CMSA	1,205	11
Sacramento, CA MSA	1,103	12
Boston – Lawrence – Salem, MA – NH CMSA	1,091	13
San Diego, CA MSA	1,051	14
Denver – Boulder, CO CMSA	990	15
Detroit – Ann Arbor, MI CMSA	988	16
Minneapolis – St. Paul, MN – WI MSA	899	17
Phoenix, AZ MSA	869	18
New Orleans, LA MSA	861	19
Baltimore, MD MSA	791	20
Cincinnati – Hamilton, OH – KY – IN CMSA	768	21
West Palm Beach – Boca Raton – Delray Beach, FL MSA	768	21
Cleveland – Akron – Lorain, OH CMSA	762	22
Milwaukee – Racine, WI CMSA	692	23
Portland – Vancouver, OR – WA CMSA	651	24

Source: U.S. Department of Commerce, Bureau of the Census, Data User Services Division, *1990 Census of Population and Housing, Equal Employment Opportunity File, CD-90-EE0-1,* January 1993, CD-ROM.

★1346★

Occupations, By Race/Sex

Top 25 MSAs For Employment As Social Work Teachers, 1990: Blacks

MSA/CMSA	Employees per 100,000 pop.	Rank
Panama City, FL MSA	11	1
New York – Northern New Jersey – Long Island, NY – NJ – CT CMSA	7	2
Chicago – Gary – Lake County, IL – IN – WI CMSA	6	3
Owensboro, KY MSA	0	4
Ocala, FL MSA	0	4
Panama City, FL MSA	0	4
Nashville, TN MSA	0	4
Odessa, TX MSA	0	4
Parkersburg – Marietta, WV – OH MSA	0	4

[Continued]

★1346★

Top 25 MSAs For Employment As Social Work Teachers, 1990: Blacks

[Continued]

MSA/CMSA	Employees per 100,000 pop.	Rank
Olympia, WA MSA	0	4
Omaha, NE – IA MSA	0	4
Orlando, FL MSA	0	4
Norfolk – Virginia Beach – Newport News, VA MSA	0	4
Oklahoma City, OK MSA	0	4
New Bedford, MA MSA	0	4
Pascagoula, MS MSA	0	4
Muskegon, MI MSA	0	4
New London – Norwich, CT – RI MSA	0	4
Providence – Pawtucket – Fall River, RI – MA CMSA	0	4
Rapid City, SD MSA	0	4
Pueblo, CO MSA	0	4
Poughkeepsie, NY MSA	0	4
Melbourne – Titusville – Palm Bay, FL MSA	0	4
Raleigh – Durham, NC MSA	0	4
Pine Bluff, AR MSA	0	4

Source: U.S. Department of Commerce, Bureau of the Census, Data User Services Division, *1990 Census of Population and Housing, Equal Employment Opportunity File, CD-90-EE0-1,* January 1993, CD-ROM.

★1347★

Occupations, By Race/Sex

Top 25 MSAs For Employment As Social Work Teachers, 1990: Whites

MSA/CMSA	Employees per 100,000 pop.	Rank
Athens, GA MSA	34	1
Boston – Lawrence – Salem, MA – NH CMSA	31	2
Philadelphia – Wilmington – Trenton, PA – NJ – DE – MD CMSA	20	3
Buffalo – Niagara Falls, NY CMSA	17	4
Springfield, MA MSA	14	5
Chicago – Gary – Lake County, IL – IN – WI CMSA	13	6
Modesto, CA MSA	11	7
Seattle – Tacoma, WA CMSA	8	8
Reading, PA MSA	8	8
Los Angeles – Anaheim – Riverside, CA CMSA	7	9
Harrisburg – Lebanon – Carlisle, PA MSA	7	9
Nashville, TN MSA	7	9
Richmond – Petersburg, VA MSA	7	9
Lawrence, KS MSA	7	9
Portland, ME MSA	7	9
Charlotte – Gastonia – Rock Hill, NC – SC MSA	7	9

[Continued]

★1347★

Top 25 MSAs For Employment As Social Work Teachers, 1990: Whites
[Continued]

MSA/CMSA	Employees per 100,000 pop.	Rank
Baton Rouge, LA MSA	6	10
Knoxville, TN MSA	6	10
Anchorage, AK MSA	6	10
Columbus, OH MSA	5	11
Hartford – New Britain – Middletown, CT CMSA	5	11
Melbourne – Titusville – Palm Bay, FL MSA	5	11
Minneapolis – St. Paul, MN – WI MSA	2	12
Lewiston – Auburn, ME MSA	0	13
Longview – Marshall, TX MSA	0	13

Source: U.S. Department of Commerce, Bureau of the Census, Data User Services Division, *1990 Census of Population and Housing, Equal Employment Opportunity File, CD-90-EE0-1, January 1993,* CD-ROM.

★1348★

Occupations, By Race/Sex

Top 25 MSAs For Employment As Social Workers, 1990: Blacks

MSA/CMSA	Employees per 100,000 pop.	Rank
Sacramento, CA MSA	25,580	1
Chicago – Gary – Lake County, IL – IN – WI CMSA	8,635	2
Philadelphia – Wilmington – Trenton, PA – NJ – DE – MD CMSA	7,714	3
Los Angeles – Anaheim – Riverside, CA CMSA	6,749	4
Detroit – Ann Arbor, MI CMSA	5,505	5
Washington, DC – MD – VA MSA	4,252	6
Baltimore, MD MSA	3,901	7
Atlanta, GA MSA	2,520	8
St. Louis, MO – IL MSA	2,470	9
San Francisco – Oakland – San Jose, CA CMSA	2,368	10
Cleveland – Akron – Lorain, OH CMSA	2,307	11
Houston – Galveston – Brazoria, TX CMSA	2,276	12
Miami – Fort Lauderdale, FL CMSA	2,088	13
Boston – Lawrence – Salem, MA – NH CMSA	1,718	14
Dallas – Fort Worth, TX CMSA	1,572	15
New Orleans, LA MSA	1,456	16
Norfolk – Virginia Beach – Newport News, VA MSA	1,311	17
Pittsburgh – Beaver Valley, PA CMSA	1,145	18
Cincinnati – Hamilton, OH – KY – IN CMSA	1,133	19

[Continued]

★1348★

Top 25 MSAs For Employment As Social Workers, 1990: Blacks
[Continued]

MSA/CMSA	Employees per 100,000 pop.	Rank
Columbus, OH MSA	1,054	20
Memphis, TN – AR – MS MSA	1,022	21
Jacksonville, FL MSA	950	22
Richmond – Petersburg, VA MSA	943	23
Tampa – St. Petersburg – Clearwater, FL MSA	940	24
Columbia, SC MSA	863	25

Source: U.S. Department of Commerce, Bureau of the Census, Data User Services Division, *1990 Census of Population and Housing, Equal Employment Opportunity File, CD-90-EE0-1, January 1993,* CD-ROM.

★1349★

Occupations, By Race/Sex

Top 25 MSAs For Employment As Social Workers, 1990: Whites

MSA/CMSA	Employees per 100,000 pop.	Rank
Albany – Schenectady – Troy, NY MSA	42,168	1
Los Angeles – Anaheim – Riverside, CA CMSA	18,514	2
Boston – Lawrence – Salem, MA – NH CMSA	13,440	3
Chicago – Gary – Lake County, IL – IN – WI CMSA	12,648	4
Philadelphia – Wilmington – Trenton, PA – NJ – DE – MD CMSA	12,060	5
San Francisco – Oakland – San Jose, CA CMSA	11,831	6
Detroit – Ann Arbor, MI CMSA	8,460	7
Minneapolis – St. Paul, MN – WI MSA	8,053	8
Washington, DC – MD – VA MSA	6,637	9
Seattle – Tacoma, WA CMSA	5,866	10
Pittsburgh – Beaver Valley, PA CMSA	5,546	11
Cleveland – Akron – Lorain, OH CMSA	5,085	12
Dallas – Fort Worth, TX CMSA	4,920	13
San Diego, CA MSA	4,870	14
Baltimore, MD MSA	4,648	15
Denver – Boulder, CO CMSA	4,222	16
Miami – Fort Lauderdale, FL CMSA	4,161	17
St. Louis, MO – IL MSA	4,156	18
Phoenix, AZ MSA	3,884	19
Buffalo – Niagara Falls, NY CMSA	3,699	20
Tampa – St. Petersburg – Clearwater, FL MSA	3,674	21
Providence – Pawtucket – Fall River, RI – MA CMSA	3,658	22
Portland – Vancouver, OR – WA CMSA	3,577	23

[Continued]

★1349★

Top 25 MSAs For Employment As Social Workers, 1990: Whites
[Continued]

MSA/CMSA	Employees per 100,000 pop.	Rank
Cincinnati – Hamilton, OH – KY – IN CMSA	3,522	24
Houston – Galveston – Brazoria, TX CMSA	3,456	25

Source: U.S. Department of Commerce, Bureau of the Census, Data User Services Division, *1990 Census of Population and Housing, Equal Employment Opportunity File, CD-90-EE0-1, January 1993,* CD-ROM.

★1350★
Occupations, By Race/Sex

Top 25 MSAs For Employment As Sociologists, 1990: Blacks

MSA/CMSA	Employees per 100,000 pop.	Rank
Charleston, SC MSA	33	1
Baltimore, MD MSA	14	2
Rochester, NY MSA	14	2
Tallahassee, FL MSA	12	3
Denver – Boulder, CO CMSA	10	4
Dayton – Springfield, OH MSA	10	4
Raleigh – Durham, NC MSA	10	4
Janesville – Beloit, WI MSA	9	5
San Antonio, TX MSA	9	5
Miami – Fort Lauderdale, FL CMSA	8	6
Lynchburg, VA MSA	7	7
Washington, DC – MD – VA MSA	6	8
Sacramento, CA MSA	6	8
Beaumont – Port Arthur, TX MSA	6	8
San Francisco – Oakland – San Jose, CA CMSA	6	8
Pensacola, FL MSA	5	9
San Diego, CA MSA	5	9
Orlando, FL MSA	0	10
Parkersburg – Marietta, WV – OH MSA	0	10
Oklahoma City, OK MSA	0	10
Reno, NV MSA	0	10
Lawton, OK MSA	0	10
Rapid City, SD MSA	0	10
Norfolk – Virginia Beach – Newport News, VA MSA	0	10
Reading, PA MSA	0	10

Source: U.S. Department of Commerce, Bureau of the Census, Data User Services Division, *1990 Census of Population and Housing, Equal Employment Opportunity File, CD-90-EE0-1, January 1993,* CD-ROM.

★1351★
Occupations, By Race/Sex

Top 25 MSAs For Employment As Sociologists, 1990: Whites

MSA/CMSA	Employees per 100,000 pop.	Rank
Providence – Pawtucket – Fall River, RI – MA CMSA	136	1
Los Angeles – Anaheim – Riverside, CA CMSA	126	2
New York – Northern New Jersey – Long Island, NY – NJ – CT CMSA	114	3
Boston – Lawrence – Salem, MA – NH CMSA	86	4
Chicago – Gary – Lake County, IL – IN – WI CMSA	63	5
Rochester, NY MSA	48	6
Baltimore, MD MSA	45	7
Denver – Boulder, CO CMSA	40	8
Philadelphia – Wilmington – Trenton, PA – NJ – DE – MD CMSA	39	9
San Francisco – Oakland – San Jose, CA CMSA	36	10
Columbia, SC MSA	35	11
Salt Lake City – Ogden, UT MSA	34	12
Raleigh – Durham, NC MSA	32	13
Madison, WI MSA	31	14
Phoenix, AZ MSA	30	15
Tucson, AZ MSA	26	16
Seattle – Tacoma, WA CMSA	25	17
Sacramento, CA MSA	23	18
Kansas City, MO – KS MSA	23	18
Salinas – Seaside – Monterey, CA MSA	22	19
Minneapolis – St. Paul, MN – WI MSA	21	20
Charlottesville, VA MSA	21	20
Detroit – Ann Arbor, MI CMSA	21	20
Providence – Pawtucket – Fall River, RI – MA CMSA	20	21
Santa Barbara – Santa Maria – Lompoc, CA MSA	19	22

Source: U.S. Department of Commerce, Bureau of the Census, Data User Services Division, *1990 Census of Population and Housing, Equal Employment Opportunity File, CD-90-EE0-1, January 1993,* CD-ROM.

★1352★
Occupations, By Race/Sex

Top 25 MSAs For Employment As Sociology Teachers, 1990: Blacks

MSA/CMSA	Employees per 100,000 pop.	Rank
Redding, CA MSA	12	1
Columbia, SC MSA	10	2
Providence – Pawtucket – Fall River, RI – MA CMSA	8	3
Albany – Schenectady – Troy, NY MSA	8	3

[Continued]

★1352★

Top 25 MSAs For Employment As Sociology Teachers, 1990: Blacks

[Continued]

MSA/CMSA	Employees per 100,000 pop.	Rank
Detroit – Ann Arbor, MI CMSA	7	4
Cleveland – Akron – Lorain, OH CMSA	7	4
Lansing – East Lansing, MI MSA	4	5
Parkersburg – Marietta, WV – OH MSA	0	6
Pensacola, FL MSA	0	6
Panama City, FL MSA	0	6
Pittsburgh – Beaver Valley, PA CMSA	0	6
Owensboro, KY MSA	0	6
Muskegon, MI MSA	0	6
Orlando, FL MSA	0	6
Olympia, WA MSA	0	6
Ocala, FL MSA	0	6
Norfolk – Virginia Beach – Newport News, VA MSA	0	6
Odessa, TX MSA	0	6
Oklahoma City, OK MSA	0	6
Omaha, NE – IA MSA	0	6
Pascagoula, MS MSA	0	6
Rapid City, SD MSA	0	6
Little Rock – North Little Rock, AR MSA	0	6
Naples, FL MSA	0	6
Raleigh – Durham, NC MSA	0	6

Source: U.S. Department of Commerce, Bureau of the Census, Data User Services Division, *1990 Census of Population and Housing, Equal Employment Opportunity File, CD-90-EE0-1, January 1993,* CD-ROM.

★1353★

Occupations, By Race/Sex

Top 25 MSAs For Employment As Sociology Teachers, 1990: Whites

MSA/CMSA	Employees per 100,000 pop.	Rank
Sacramento, CA MSA	64	1
New York – Northern New Jersey – Long Island, NY – NJ – CT CMSA	61	2
Philadelphia – Wilmington – Trenton, PA – NJ – DE – MD CMSA	58	3
San Diego, CA MSA	32	4
San Francisco – Oakland – San Jose, CA CMSA	28	5
Boston – Lawrence – Salem, MA – NH CMSA	27	6
Minneapolis – St. Paul, MN – WI MSA	27	6
Atlanta, GA MSA	24	7
Washington, DC – MD – VA MSA	22	8
West Palm Beach – Boca Raton – Delray Beach, FL MSA	21	9

[Continued]

★1353★

Top 25 MSAs For Employment As Sociology Teachers, 1990: Whites

[Continued]

MSA/CMSA	Employees per 100,000 pop.	Rank
Sacramento, CA MSA	21	9
Syracuse, NY MSA	19	10
Johnson City – Kingsport – Bristol, TN – VA MSA	17	11
Reno, NV MSA	17	11
Columbia, SC MSA	16	12
Melbourne – Titusville – Palm Bay, FL MSA	16	12
Greenville – Spartanburg, SC MSA	13	13
Baltimore, MD MSA	12	14
Harrisburg – Lebanon – Carlisle, PA MSA	11	15
Bakersfield, CA MSA	11	15
Eau Claire, WI MSA	10	16
Seattle – Tacoma, WA CMSA	10	16
Raleigh – Durham, NC MSA	10	16
Rochester, NY MSA	9	17
Cleveland – Akron – Lorain, OH CMSA	9	17

Source: U.S. Department of Commerce, Bureau of the Census, Data User Services Division, *1990 Census of Population and Housing, Equal Employment Opportunity File, CD-90-EE0-1, January 1993,* CD-ROM.

★1354★

Occupations, By Race/Sex

Top 25 MSAs For Employment As Solderers and Brazers, 1990: Blacks

MSA/CMSA	Employees per 100,000 pop.	Rank
Columbia, SC MSA	290	1
New York – Northern New Jersey – Long Island, NY – NJ – CT CMSA	211	2
Philadelphia – Wilmington – Trenton, PA – NJ – DE – MD CMSA	141	3
Los Angeles – Anaheim – Riverside, CA CMSA	116	4
Dallas – Fort Worth, TX CMSA	112	5
Cleveland – Akron – Lorain, OH CMSA	82	6
Boston – Lawrence – Salem, MA – NH CMSA	81	7
Huntsville, AL MSA	72	8
Milwaukee – Racine, WI CMSA	57	9
Baltimore, MD MSA	57	9
Atlanta, GA MSA	49	10
Miami – Fort Lauderdale, FL CMSA	40	11
Tampa – St. Petersburg – Clearwater, FL MSA	38	12
Greenville – Spartanburg, SC MSA	36	13

[Continued]

★1354★

Top 25 MSAs For Employment As Solderers and Brazers, 1990: Blacks
[Continued]

MSA/CMSA	Employees per 100,000 pop.	Rank
Orlando, FL MSA	32	14
San Francisco – Oakland – San Jose, CA CMSA	30	15
St. Louis, MO – IL MSA	29	16
Phoenix, AZ MSA	29	16
Providence – Pawtucket – Fall River, RI – MA CMSA	28	17
Portland – Vancouver, OR – WA CMSA	27	18
Elkhart – Goshen, IN MSA	27	18
Fort Wayne, IN MSA	24	19
Columbus, OH MSA	23	20
Washington, DC – MD – VA MSA	22	21
New Bedford, MA MSA	18	22

Source: U.S. Department of Commerce, Bureau of the Census, Data User Services Division, *1990 Census of Population and Housing, Equal Employment Opportunity File, CD-90-EE0-1, January 1993,* CD-ROM.

★1355★

Occupations, By Race/Sex

Top 25 MSAs For Employment As Solderers and Brazers, 1990: Whites

MSA/CMSA	Employees per 100,000 pop.	Rank
Providence – Pawtucket – Fall River, RI – MA CMSA	1,503	1
New York – Northern New Jersey – Long Island, NY – NJ – CT CMSA	1,222	2
Boston – Lawrence – Salem, MA – NH CMSA	1,071	3
Chicago – Gary – Lake County, IL – IN – WI CMSA	795	4
Philadelphia – Wilmington – Trenton, PA – NJ – DE – MD CMSA	527	5
Tampa – St. Petersburg – Clearwater, FL MSA	357	6
Providence – Pawtucket – Fall River, RI – MA CMSA	337	7
Minneapolis – St. Paul, MN – WI MSA	310	8
Binghamton, NY MSA	289	9
Miami – Fort Lauderdale, FL CMSA	275	10
Detroit – Ann Arbor, MI CMSA	269	11
Fort Wayne, IN MSA	262	12
San Francisco – Oakland – San Jose, CA CMSA	260	13
Phoenix, AZ MSA	257	14
Cleveland – Akron – Lorain, OH CMSA	230	15
Hartford – New Britain – Middletown, CT CMSA	210	16

[Continued]

★1355★

Top 25 MSAs For Employment As Solderers and Brazers, 1990: Whites
[Continued]

MSA/CMSA	Employees per 100,000 pop.	Rank
Rochester, NY MSA	191	17
Lancaster, PA MSA	173	18
Columbus, OH MSA	168	19
Cincinnati – Hamilton, OH – KY – IN CMSA	165	20
Dallas – Fort Worth, TX CMSA	164	21
Seattle – Tacoma, WA CMSA	146	22
Huntsville, AL MSA	146	22
Milwaukee – Racine, WI CMSA	146	22
St. Louis, MO – IL MSA	132	23

Source: U.S. Department of Commerce, Bureau of the Census, Data User Services Division, *1990 Census of Population and Housing, Equal Employment Opportunity File, CD-90-EE0-1, January 1993,* CD-ROM.

★1356★

Occupations, By Race/Sex

Top 25 MSAs For Employment As Speech Therapists, 1990: Blacks

MSA/CMSA	Employees per 100,000 pop.	Rank
Dayton – Springfield, OH MSA	267	1
New York – Northern New Jersey – Long Island, NY – NJ – CT CMSA	223	2
Chicago – Gary – Lake County, IL – IN – WI CMSA	172	3
Philadelphia – Wilmington – Trenton, PA – NJ – DE – MD CMSA	133	4
Detroit – Ann Arbor, MI CMSA	110	5
New Orleans, LA MSA	86	6
Los Angeles – Anaheim – Riverside, CA CMSA	82	7
Nashville, TN MSA	79	8
Cleveland – Akron – Lorain, OH CMSA	71	9
St. Louis, MO – IL MSA	66	10
Dallas – Fort Worth, TX CMSA	64	11
Atlanta, GA MSA	63	12
Baton Rouge, LA MSA	62	13
Norfolk – Virginia Beach – Newport News, VA MSA	60	14
Houston – Galveston – Brazoria, TX CMSA	57	15
Baltimore, MD MSA	55	16
Richmond – Petersburg, VA MSA	55	16
Memphis, TN – AR – MS MSA	54	17
Charlotte – Gastonia – Rock Hill, NC – SC MSA	40	18
Kansas City, MO – KS MSA	34	19
Cincinnati – Hamilton, OH – KY – IN CMSA	32	20
Charleston, SC MSA	31	21

[Continued]

★1356★

Top 25 MSAs For Employment As Speech Therapists, 1990: Blacks
[Continued]

MSA/CMSA	Employees per 100,000 pop.	Rank
Miami – Fort Lauderdale, FL CMSA	27	22
Little Rock – North Little Rock, AR MSA	27	22
West Palm Beach – Boca Raton – Delray Beach, FL MSA	26	23

Source: U.S. Department of Commerce, Bureau of the Census, Data User Services Division, *1990 Census of Population and Housing, Equal Employment Opportunity File, CD-90-EE0-1, January 1993,* CD-ROM.

★1357★

Occupations, By Race/Sex

Top 25 MSAs For Employment As Speech Therapists, 1990: Whites

MSA/CMSA	Employees per 100,000 pop.	Rank
Kansas City, MO – KS MSA	5,305	1
Los Angeles – Anaheim – Riverside, CA CMSA	2,409	2
Chicago – Gary – Lake County, IL – IN – WI CMSA	2,202	3
Philadelphia – Wilmington – Trenton, PA – NJ – DE – MD CMSA	1,778	4
Boston – Lawrence – Salem, MA – NH CMSA	1,419	5
San Francisco – Oakland – San Jose, CA CMSA	1,358	6
Washington, DC – MD – VA MSA	967	7
Detroit – Ann Arbor, MI CMSA	953	8
Dallas – Fort Worth, TX CMSA	908	9
Minneapolis – St. Paul, MN – WI MSA	893	10
Houston – Galveston – Brazoria, TX CMSA	775	11
Pittsburgh – Beaver Valley, PA CMSA	745	12
Cleveland – Akron – Lorain, OH CMSA	707	13
St. Louis, MO – IL MSA	683	14
Baltimore, MD MSA	675	15
Seattle – Tacoma, WA CMSA	653	16
Milwaukee – Racine, WI CMSA	650	17
Denver – Boulder, CO CMSA	636	18
San Diego, CA MSA	623	19
Cincinnati – Hamilton, OH – KY – IN CMSA	599	20
Miami – Fort Lauderdale, FL CMSA	576	21
Buffalo – Niagara Falls, NY CMSA	564	22
Atlanta, GA MSA	530	23

[Continued]

★1357★

Top 25 MSAs For Employment As Speech Therapists, 1990: Whites
[Continued]

MSA/CMSA	Employees per 100,000 pop.	Rank
Phoenix, AZ MSA	524	24
Albany – Schenectady – Troy, NY MSA	459	25

Source: U.S. Department of Commerce, Bureau of the Census, Data User Services Division, *1990 Census of Population and Housing, Equal Employment Opportunity File, CD-90-EE0-1, January 1993,* CD-ROM.

★1358★

Occupations, By Race/Sex

Top 25 MSAs For Employment As Statisticians, 1990: Blacks

MSA/CMSA	Employees per 100,000 pop.	Rank
Charlotte – Gastonia – Rock Hill, NC – SC MSA	571	1
New York – Northern New Jersey – Long Island, NY – NJ – CT CMSA	469	2
Philadelphia – Wilmington – Trenton, PA – NJ – DE – MD CMSA	143	3
Chicago – Gary – Lake County, IL – IN – WI CMSA	113	4
Detroit – Ann Arbor, MI CMSA	74	5
Dallas – Fort Worth, TX CMSA	73	6
Baltimore, MD MSA	70	7
Atlanta, GA MSA	69	8
Raleigh – Durham, NC MSA	65	9
Hartford – New Britain – Middletown, CT CMSA	62	10
Miami – Fort Lauderdale, FL CMSA	57	11
Los Angeles – Anaheim – Riverside, CA CMSA	57	11
Richmond – Petersburg, VA MSA	53	12
Denver – Boulder, CO CMSA	42	13
Nashville, TN MSA	41	14
Columbus, OH MSA	40	15
Austin, TX MSA	37	16
New Haven – Meriden, CT MSA	37	16
San Diego, CA MSA	33	17
Indianapolis, IN MSA	31	18
Seattle – Tacoma, WA CMSA	31	18
Boston – Lawrence – Salem, MA – NH CMSA	30	19
Birmingham, AL MSA	27	20
Albany – Schenectady – Troy, NY MSA	24	21
Kalamazoo, MI MSA	24	21

Source: U.S. Department of Commerce, Bureau of the Census, Data User Services Division, *1990 Census of Population and Housing, Equal Employment Opportunity File, CD-90-EE0-1, January 1993,* CD-ROM.

★1359★

Occupations, By Race/Sex

Top 25 MSAs For Employment As Statisticians, 1990: Whites

MSA/CMSA	Employees per 100,000 pop.	Rank
Milwaukee – Racine, WI CMSA	2,539	1
New York – Northern New Jersey – Long Island, NY – NJ – CT CMSA	2,502	2
Chicago – Gary – Lake County, IL – IN – WI CMSA	1,053	3
Philadelphia – Wilmington – Trenton, PA – NJ – DE – MD CMSA	997	4
Boston – Lawrence – Salem, MA – NH CMSA	878	5
Los Angeles – Anaheim – Riverside, CA CMSA	821	6
San Francisco – Oakland – San Jose, CA CMSA	808	7
Detroit – Ann Arbor, MI CMSA	745	8
Baltimore, MD MSA	706	9
Dallas – Fort Worth, TX CMSA	523	10
Hartford – New Britain – Middletown, CT CMSA	501	11
Raleigh – Durham, NC MSA	407	12
Denver – Boulder, CO CMSA	378	13
Atlanta, GA MSA	339	14
Seattle – Tacoma, WA CMSA	330	15
Minneapolis – St. Paul, MN – WI MSA	321	16
St. Louis, MO – IL MSA	298	17
Houston – Galveston – Brazoria, TX CMSA	286	18
Columbus, OH MSA	247	19
Cincinnati – Hamilton, OH – KY – IN CMSA	236	20
Indianapolis, IN MSA	234	21
Albany – Schenectady – Troy, NY MSA	233	22
Kansas City, MO – KS MSA	220	23
San Diego, CA MSA	211	24
Cleveland – Akron – Lorain, OH CMSA	207	25

Source: U.S. Department of Commerce, Bureau of the Census, Data User Services Division, *1990 Census of Population and Housing, Equal Employment Opportunity File, CD-90-EE0-1, January 1993*, CD-ROM.

★1360★

Occupations, By Race/Sex

Top 25 MSAs For Employment As Stevedores, 1990: Blacks

MSA/CMSA	Employees per 100,000 pop.	Rank
Cincinnati – Hamilton, OH – KY – IN CMSA	316	1
Miami – Fort Lauderdale, FL CMSA	304	2
New Orleans, LA MSA	295	3
Philadelphia – Wilmington – Trenton, PA – NJ – DE – MD CMSA	254	4
New York – Northern New Jersey – Long Island, NY – NJ – CT CMSA	236	5
Houston – Galveston – Brazoria, TX CMSA	196	6
Los Angeles – Anaheim – Riverside, CA CMSA	176	7
San Francisco – Oakland – San Jose, CA CMSA	162	8
Baltimore, MD MSA	162	8
Savannah, GA MSA	153	9
Charleston, SC MSA	145	10
Chicago – Gary – Lake County, IL – IN – WI CMSA	101	11
Jacksonville, FL MSA	96	12
Lake Charles, LA MSA	94	13
Fort Pierce, FL MSA	72	14
Mobile, AL MSA	42	15
Seattle – Tacoma, WA CMSA	40	16
Beaumont – Port Arthur, TX MSA	39	17
Wilmington, NC MSA	36	18
Tampa – St. Petersburg – Clearwater, FL MSA	32	19
Pensacola, FL MSA	26	20
Richmond – Petersburg, VA MSA	25	21
New Haven – Meriden, CT MSA	24	22
Baton Rouge, LA MSA	23	23
Sacramento, CA MSA	22	24

Source: U.S. Department of Commerce, Bureau of the Census, Data User Services Division, *1990 Census of Population and Housing, Equal Employment Opportunity File, CD-90-EE0-1, January 1993*, CD-ROM.

★1361★

Occupations, By Race/Sex

Top 25 MSAs For Employment As Stevedores, 1990: Whites

MSA/CMSA	Employees per 100,000 pop.	Rank
Phoenix, AZ MSA	1,176	1
New York – Northern New Jersey – Long Island, NY – NJ – CT CMSA	1,157	2
Seattle – Tacoma, WA CMSA	641	3
Houston – Galveston – Brazoria, TX CMSA	306	4

[Continued]

★ 1361 ★

Top 25 MSAs For Employment As Stevedores, 1990: Whites
[Continued]

MSA/CMSA	Employees per 100,000 pop.	Rank
Baltimore, MD MSA	301	5
Portland – Vancouver, OR – WA CMSA	282	6
San Francisco – Oakland – San Jose, CA CMSA	247	7
Philadelphia – Wilmington – Trenton, PA – NJ – DE – MD CMSA	245	8
Norfolk – Virginia Beach – Newport News, VA MSA	104	9
New Orleans, LA MSA	97	10
San Diego, CA MSA	92	11
Boston – Lawrence – Salem, MA – NH CMSA	83	12
Beaumont – Port Arthur, TX MSA	79	13
Miami – Fort Lauderdale, FL CMSA	68	14
Baton Rouge, LA MSA	64	15
Lake Charles, LA MSA	64	15
New Haven – Meriden, CT MSA	52	16
Providence – Pawtucket – Fall River, RI – MA CMSA	51	17
Tampa – St. Petersburg – Clearwater, FL MSA	45	18
Chicago – Gary – Lake County, IL – IN – WI CMSA	44	19
Toledo, OH MSA	42	20
Cleveland – Akron – Lorain, OH CMSA	41	21
Albany – Schenectady – Troy, NY MSA	36	22
Savannah, GA MSA	35	23
Duluth, MN – WI MSA	34	24

Source: U.S. Department of Commerce, Bureau of the Census, Data User Services Division, *1990 Census of Population and Housing, Equal Employment Opportunity File, CD-90-EE0-1, January 1993,* CD-ROM.

★ 1362 ★
Occupations, By Race/Sex

Top 25 MSAs For Employment As Surveyors and Mapping Scientists, 1990: Blacks

MSA/CMSA	Employees per 100,000 pop.	Rank
Orlando, FL MSA	30	1
Washington, DC – MD – VA MSA	29	2
Detroit – Ann Arbor, MI CMSA	24	3
San Francisco – Oakland – San Jose, CA CMSA	20	4
Atlanta, GA MSA	18	5
New York – Northern New Jersey – Long Island, NY – NJ – CT CMSA	18	5
Dallas – Fort Worth, TX CMSA	17	6

[Continued]

★ 1362 ★

Top 25 MSAs For Employment As Surveyors and Mapping Scientists, 1990: Blacks
[Continued]

MSA/CMSA	Employees per 100,000 pop.	Rank
Los Angeles – Anaheim – Riverside, CA CMSA	12	7
Philadelphia – Wilmington – Trenton, PA – NJ – DE – MD CMSA	9	8
Flint, MI MSA	7	9
Oklahoma City, OK MSA	6	10
Providence – Pawtucket – Fall River, RI – MA CMSA	6	10
Tampa – St. Petersburg – Clearwater, FL MSA	5	11
Omaha, NE – IA MSA	0	12
Orlando, FL MSA	0	12
Pittsfield, MA MSA	0	12
Odessa, TX MSA	0	12
Peoria, IL MSA	0	12
Olympia, WA MSA	0	12
Panama City, FL MSA	0	12
New London – Norwich, CT – RI MSA	0	12
Nashville, TN MSA	0	12
Naples, FL MSA	0	12
Muskegon, MI MSA	0	12
Parkersburg – Marietta, WV – OH MSA	0	12

Source: U.S. Department of Commerce, Bureau of the Census, Data User Services Division, *1990 Census of Population and Housing, Equal Employment Opportunity File, CD-90-EE0-1, January 1993,* CD-ROM.

★ 1363 ★
Occupations, By Race/Sex

Top 25 MSAs For Employment As Surveyors and Mapping Scientists, 1990: Whites

MSA/CMSA	Employees per 100,000 pop.	Rank
Pensacola, FL MSA	488	1
Los Angeles – Anaheim – Riverside, CA CMSA	355	2
Philadelphia – Wilmington – Trenton, PA – NJ – DE – MD CMSA	256	3
San Francisco – Oakland – San Jose, CA CMSA	236	4
Miami – Fort Lauderdale, FL CMSA	221	5
Houston – Galveston – Brazoria, TX CMSA	198	6
Boston – Lawrence – Salem, MA – NH CMSA	167	7
Chicago – Gary – Lake County, IL – IN – WI CMSA	164	8
Portland – Vancouver, OR – WA CMSA	156	9

[Continued]

★1363★

Top 25 MSAs For Employment As Surveyors and Mapping Scientists, 1990: Whites
[Continued]

MSA/CMSA	Employees per 100,000 pop.	Rank
Denver – Boulder, CO CMSA	156	9
Dallas – Fort Worth, TX CMSA	151	10
Seattle – Tacoma, WA CMSA	148	11
Detroit – Ann Arbor, MI CMSA	140	12
Atlanta, GA MSA	137	13
San Diego, CA MSA	128	14
Sacramento, CA MSA	126	15
Washington, DC – MD – VA MSA	124	16
Albany – Schenectady – Troy, NY MSA	99	17
Minneapolis – St. Paul, MN – WI MSA	99	17
Raleigh – Durham, NC MSA	94	18
Cleveland – Akron – Lorain, OH CMSA	86	19
New Orleans, LA MSA	81	20
St. Louis, MO – IL MSA	81	20
Anchorage, AK MSA	72	21
Tampa – St. Petersburg – Clearwater, FL MSA	70	22

Source: U.S. Department of Commerce, Bureau of the Census, Data User Services Division, *1990 Census of Population and Housing, Equal Employment Opportunity File, CD-90-EE0-1,* January 1993, CD-ROM.

★1364★

Occupations, By Race/Sex

Top 25 MSAs For Employment As Tailors, 1990: Blacks

MSA/CMSA	Employees per 100,000 pop.	Rank
Pittsburgh – Beaver Valley, PA CMSA	1,378	1
Philadelphia – Wilmington – Trenton, PA – NJ – DE – MD CMSA	291	2
Miami – Fort Lauderdale, FL CMSA	223	3
Dallas – Fort Worth, TX CMSA	203	4
Baltimore, MD MSA	185	5
Atlanta, GA MSA	171	6
Chicago – Gary – Lake County, IL – IN – WI CMSA	164	7
Los Angeles – Anaheim – Riverside, CA CMSA	132	8
Greensboro – Winston-Salem – High Point, NC MSA	118	9
Washington, DC – MD – VA MSA	116	10
Cleveland – Akron – Lorain, OH CMSA	105	11
Jacksonville, FL MSA	103	12
Columbia, SC MSA	93	13
Cincinnati – Hamilton, OH – KY – IN CMSA	80	14

[Continued]

★1364★

Top 25 MSAs For Employment As Tailors, 1990: Blacks
[Continued]

MSA/CMSA	Employees per 100,000 pop.	Rank
San Francisco – Oakland – San Jose, CA CMSA	74	15
Memphis, TN – AR – MS MSA	74	15
Detroit – Ann Arbor, MI CMSA	69	16
Raleigh – Durham, NC MSA	61	17
Boston – Lawrence – Salem, MA – NH CMSA	55	18
Houston – Galveston – Brazoria, TX CMSA	53	19
Charlotte – Gastonia – Rock Hill, NC – SC MSA	48	20
Birmingham, AL MSA	45	21
Pittsburgh – Beaver Valley, PA CMSA	44	22
Buffalo – Niagara Falls, NY CMSA	41	23
St. Louis, MO – IL MSA	40	24

Source: U.S. Department of Commerce, Bureau of the Census, Data User Services Division, *1990 Census of Population and Housing, Equal Employment Opportunity File, CD-90-EE0-1,* January 1993, CD-ROM.

★1365★

Occupations, By Race/Sex

Top 25 MSAs For Employment As Tailors, 1990: Whites

MSA/CMSA	Employees per 100,000 pop.	Rank
Salt Lake City – Ogden, UT MSA	5,205	1
Los Angeles – Anaheim – Riverside, CA CMSA	2,999	2
Chicago – Gary – Lake County, IL – IN – WI CMSA	1,453	3
Philadelphia – Wilmington – Trenton, PA – NJ – DE – MD CMSA	1,370	4
Miami – Fort Lauderdale, FL CMSA	989	5
Boston – Lawrence – Salem, MA – NH CMSA	981	6
San Francisco – Oakland – San Jose, CA CMSA	748	7
Detroit – Ann Arbor, MI CMSA	579	8
Dallas – Fort Worth, TX CMSA	492	9
Allentown – Bethlehem – Easton, PA – NJ MSA	412	10
Cleveland – Akron – Lorain, OH CMSA	376	11
Minneapolis – St. Paul, MN – WI MSA	353	12
Houston – Galveston – Brazoria, TX CMSA	339	13
Rochester, NY MSA	338	14
Pittsburgh – Beaver Valley, PA CMSA	335	15

[Continued]

★1365★
Top 25 MSAs For Employment As Tailors, 1990: Whites
[Continued]

MSA/CMSA	Employees per 100,000 pop.	Rank
Seattle – Tacoma, WA CMSA	332	16
Scranton – Wilkes-Barre, PA MSA	313	17
Washington, DC – MD – VA MSA	303	18
Baltimore, MD MSA	301	19
Tampa – St. Petersburg – Clearwater, FL MSA	292	20
Denver – Boulder, CO CMSA	289	21
Knoxville, TN MSA	289	21
Greensboro – Winston-Salem – High Point, NC MSA	266	22
St. Louis, MO – IL MSA	258	23
San Diego, CA MSA	252	24

Source: U.S. Department of Commerce, Bureau of the Census, Data User Services Division, *1990 Census of Population and Housing, Equal Employment Opportunity File, CD-90-EE0-1, January 1993,* CD-ROM.

★1366★
Occupations, By Race/Sex
Top 25 MSAs For Employment As Taxicab Drivers and Chauffeurs, 1990: Blacks

MSA/CMSA	Employees per 100,000 pop.	Rank
Indianapolis, IN MSA	14,223	1
Washington, DC – MD – VA MSA	4,880	2
Chicago – Gary – Lake County, IL – IN – WI CMSA	3,060	3
Los Angeles – Anaheim – Riverside, CA CMSA	1,743	4
Philadelphia – Wilmington – Trenton, PA – NJ – DE – MD CMSA	1,589	5
Miami – Fort Lauderdale, FL CMSA	1,505	6
Atlanta, GA MSA	1,408	7
Houston – Galveston – Brazoria, TX CMSA	1,366	8
Baltimore, MD MSA	1,308	9
Detroit – Ann Arbor, MI CMSA	1,139	10
Dallas – Fort Worth, TX CMSA	1,072	11
Boston – Lawrence – Salem, MA – NH CMSA	888	12
San Francisco – Oakland – San Jose, CA CMSA	887	13
New Orleans, LA MSA	652	14
St. Louis, MO – IL MSA	420	15
Norfolk – Virginia Beach – Newport News, VA MSA	385	16
Cleveland – Akron – Lorain, OH CMSA	382	17
Raleigh – Durham, NC MSA	362	18
Memphis, TN – AR – MS MSA	340	19
Denver – Boulder, CO CMSA	313	20
Pittsburgh – Beaver Valley, PA CMSA	300	21

[Continued]

★1366★
Top 25 MSAs For Employment As Taxicab Drivers and Chauffeurs, 1990: Blacks
[Continued]

MSA/CMSA	Employees per 100,000 pop.	Rank
Orlando, FL MSA	281	22
Tampa – St. Petersburg – Clearwater, FL MSA	229	23
Charlotte – Gastonia – Rock Hill, NC – SC MSA	225	24
Richmond – Petersburg, VA MSA	218	25

Source: U.S. Department of Commerce, Bureau of the Census, Data User Services Division, *1990 Census of Population and Housing, Equal Employment Opportunity File, CD-90-EE0-1, January 1993,* CD-ROM.

★1367★
Occupations, By Race/Sex
Top 25 MSAs For Employment As Taxicab Drivers and Chauffeurs, 1990: Whites

MSA/CMSA	Employees per 100,000 pop.	Rank
San Diego, CA MSA	25,936	1
Los Angeles – Anaheim – Riverside, CA CMSA	7,588	2
Chicago – Gary – Lake County, IL – IN – WI CMSA	5,282	3
Boston – Lawrence – Salem, MA – NH CMSA	3,861	4
San Francisco – Oakland – San Jose, CA CMSA	3,794	5
Miami – Fort Lauderdale, FL CMSA	3,483	6
Philadelphia – Wilmington – Trenton, PA – NJ – DE – MD CMSA	2,925	7
Washington, DC – MD – VA MSA	2,296	8
Las Vegas, NV MSA	2,015	9
Detroit – Ann Arbor, MI CMSA	1,965	10
San Diego, CA MSA	1,914	11
Orlando, FL MSA	1,759	12
Minneapolis – St. Paul, MN – WI MSA	1,703	13
Tampa – St. Petersburg – Clearwater, FL MSA	1,543	14
Phoenix, AZ MSA	1,471	15
Baltimore, MD MSA	1,448	16
Pittsburgh – Beaver Valley, PA CMSA	1,382	17
Seattle – Tacoma, WA CMSA	1,373	18
Houston – Galveston – Brazoria, TX CMSA	1,370	19
Dallas – Fort Worth, TX CMSA	1,295	20
St. Louis, MO – IL MSA	1,238	21
Cleveland – Akron – Lorain, OH CMSA	1,132	22
Denver – Boulder, CO CMSA	1,045	23

[Continued]

★ 1367 ★

Top 25 MSAs For Employment As Taxicab Drivers and Chauffeurs, 1990: Whites
[Continued]

MSA/CMSA	Employees per 100,000 pop.	Rank
Portland – Vancouver, OR – WA CMSA	924	24
Cincinnati – Hamilton, OH – KY – IN CMSA	902	25

Source: U.S. Department of Commerce, Bureau of the Census, Data User Services Division, *1990 Census of Population and Housing, Equal Employment Opportunity File, CD-90-EE0-1, January 1993,* CD-ROM.

★ 1368 ★
Occupations, By Race/Sex

Top 25 MSAs For Employment As Teachers, Elementary School, 1990: Blacks

MSA/CMSA	Employees per 100,000 pop.	Rank
Jacksonville, FL MSA	32,026	1
Chicago – Gary – Lake County, IL – IN – WI CMSA	19,214	2
Los Angeles – Anaheim – Riverside, CA CMSA	14,446	3
Philadelphia – Wilmington – Trenton, PA – NJ – DE – MD CMSA	13,034	4
Washington, DC – MD – VA MSA	11,404	5
Detroit – Ann Arbor, MI CMSA	9,337	6
Houston – Galveston – Brazoria, TX CMSA	8,677	7
Atlanta, GA MSA	8,422	8
Miami – Fort Lauderdale, FL CMSA	7,530	9
Baltimore, MD MSA	6,920	10
New Orleans, LA MSA	6,792	11
Dallas – Fort Worth, TX CMSA	5,966	12
St. Louis, MO – IL MSA	5,313	13
Memphis, TN – AR – MS MSA	5,096	14
Norfolk – Virginia Beach – Newport News, VA MSA	4,817	15
San Francisco – Oakland – San Jose, CA CMSA	4,367	16
Cleveland – Akron – Lorain, OH CMSA	3,512	17
Richmond – Petersburg, VA MSA	3,152	18
Birmingham, AL MSA	3,117	19
Jackson, MS MSA	2,903	20
Baton Rouge, LA MSA	2,507	21
Jacksonville, FL MSA	2,503	22
Tampa – St. Petersburg – Clearwater, FL MSA	2,458	23
Kansas City, MO – KS MSA	2,390	24
Charlotte – Gastonia – Rock Hill, NC – SC MSA	2,236	25

Source: U.S. Department of Commerce, Bureau of the Census, Data User Services Division, *1990 Census of Population and Housing, Equal Employment Opportunity File, CD-90-EE0-1, January 1993,* CD-ROM.

★ 1369 ★
Occupations, By Race/Sex

Top 25 MSAs For Employment As Teachers, Elementary School, 1990: Whites

MSA/CMSA	Employees per 100,000 pop.	Rank
Milwaukee – Racine, WI CMSA	201,263	1
Los Angeles – Anaheim – Riverside, CA CMSA	117,556	2
Chicago – Gary – Lake County, IL – IN – WI CMSA	68,378	3
Philadelphia – Wilmington – Trenton, PA – NJ – DE – MD CMSA	59,169	4
San Francisco – Oakland – San Jose, CA CMSA	53,862	5
Boston – Lawrence – Salem, MA – NH CMSA	46,715	6
Detroit – Ann Arbor, MI CMSA	44,011	7
Dallas – Fort Worth, TX CMSA	40,155	8
Houston – Galveston – Brazoria, TX CMSA	38,937	9
Washington, DC – MD – VA MSA	34,160	10
Minneapolis – St. Paul, MN – WI MSA	28,682	11
Atlanta, GA MSA	27,750	12
Cleveland – Akron – Lorain, OH CMSA	27,005	13
Miami – Fort Lauderdale, FL CMSA	26,382	14
Seattle – Tacoma, WA CMSA	25,785	15
St. Louis, MO – IL MSA	24,505	16
San Diego, CA MSA	23,142	17
Pittsburgh – Beaver Valley, PA CMSA	22,458	18
Denver – Boulder, CO CMSA	21,821	19
Baltimore, MD MSA	21,743	20
Phoenix, AZ MSA	21,110	21
Tampa – St. Petersburg – Clearwater, FL MSA	18,625	22
Milwaukee – Racine, WI CMSA	18,574	23
Kansas City, MO – KS MSA	18,149	24
Portland – Vancouver, OR – WA CMSA	17,312	25

Source: U.S. Department of Commerce, Bureau of the Census, Data User Services Division, *1990 Census of Population and Housing, Equal Employment Opportunity File, CD-90-EE0-1, January 1993,* CD-ROM.

★1370★

Occupations, By Race/Sex

Top 25 MSAs For Employment As Teachers, Prekindergarten and Kindergarten, 1990: Blacks

MSA/CMSA	Employees per 100,000 pop.	Rank
Providence – Pawtucket – Fall River, RI – MA CMSA	3,524	1
Los Angeles – Anaheim – Riverside, CA CMSA	1,494	2
Chicago – Gary – Lake County, IL – IN – WI CMSA	1,368	3
Atlanta, GA MSA	1,297	4
Washington, DC – MD – VA MSA	1,263	5
Philadelphia – Wilmington – Trenton, PA – NJ – DE – MD CMSA	1,166	6
Houston – Galveston – Brazoria, TX CMSA	965	7
Dallas – Fort Worth, TX CMSA	833	8
Miami – Fort Lauderdale, FL CMSA	752	9
San Francisco – Oakland – San Jose, CA CMSA	603	10
St. Louis, MO – IL MSA	570	11
Birmingham, AL MSA	535	12
Greensboro – Winston-Salem – High Point, NC MSA	517	13
Cleveland – Akron – Lorain, OH CMSA	492	14
Tampa – St. Petersburg – Clearwater, FL MSA	482	15
Memphis, TN – AR – MS MSA	481	16
Detroit – Ann Arbor, MI CMSA	455	17
Baltimore, MD MSA	447	18
Raleigh – Durham, NC MSA	446	19
Charlotte – Gastonia – Rock Hill, NC – SC MSA	441	20
Nashville, TN MSA	428	21
New Orleans, LA MSA	416	22
Boston – Lawrence – Salem, MA – NH CMSA	415	23
Norfolk – Virginia Beach – Newport News, VA MSA	391	24
Charleston, SC MSA	357	25

Source: U.S. Department of Commerce, Bureau of the Census, Data User Services Division, *1990 Census of Population and Housing, Equal Employment Opportunity File, CD-90-EE0-1, January 1993,* CD-ROM.

★1371★

Occupations, By Race/Sex

Top 25 MSAs For Employment As Teachers, Prekindergarten and Kindergarten, 1990: Whites

MSA/CMSA	Employees per 100,000 pop.	Rank
Providence – Pawtucket – Fall River, RI – MA CMSA	12,329	1
Los Angeles – Anaheim – Riverside, CA CMSA	10,539	2
Chicago – Gary – Lake County, IL – IN – WI CMSA	6,591	3
San Francisco – Oakland – San Jose, CA CMSA	6,473	4
Boston – Lawrence – Salem, MA – NH CMSA	6,473	4
Philadelphia – Wilmington – Trenton, PA – NJ – DE – MD CMSA	5,786	5
Dallas – Fort Worth, TX CMSA	5,474	6
Atlanta, GA MSA	4,442	7
Washington, DC – MD – VA MSA	4,043	8
Houston – Galveston – Brazoria, TX CMSA	3,773	9
Seattle – Tacoma, WA CMSA	2,987	10
Minneapolis – St. Paul, MN – WI MSA	2,934	11
St. Louis, MO – IL MSA	2,810	12
Miami – Fort Lauderdale, FL CMSA	2,668	13
Detroit – Ann Arbor, MI CMSA	2,596	14
Phoenix, AZ MSA	2,412	15
Denver – Boulder, CO CMSA	2,224	16
Kansas City, MO – KS MSA	2,224	16
San Diego, CA MSA	2,152	17
Tampa – St. Petersburg – Clearwater, FL MSA	2,132	18
Cleveland – Akron – Lorain, OH CMSA	2,050	19
Baltimore, MD MSA	1,881	20
Cincinnati – Hamilton, OH – KY – IN CMSA	1,784	21
Charlotte – Gastonia – Rock Hill, NC – SC MSA	1,701	22
Pittsburgh – Beaver Valley, PA CMSA	1,580	23

Source: U.S. Department of Commerce, Bureau of the Census, Data User Services Division, *1990 Census of Population and Housing, Equal Employment Opportunity File, CD-90-EE0-1, January 1993,* CD-ROM.

★1372★

Occupations, By Race/Sex

Top 25 MSAs For Employment As Teachers, Secondary School, 1990: Blacks

MSA/CMSA	Employees per 100,000 pop.	Rank
Raleigh – Durham, NC MSA	4,289	1
Chicago – Gary – Lake County, IL – IN – WI CMSA	2,083	2
Philadelphia – Wilmington – Trenton, PA – NJ – DE – MD CMSA	1,584	3
Los Angeles – Anaheim – Riverside, CA CMSA	1,576	4
Washington, DC – MD – VA MSA	1,324	5
Houston – Galveston – Brazoria, TX CMSA	1,034	6
Detroit – Ann Arbor, MI CMSA	892	7
Atlanta, GA MSA	884	8
New Orleans, LA MSA	801	9
Miami – Fort Lauderdale, FL CMSA	757	10
St. Louis, MO – IL MSA	729	11
Norfolk – Virginia Beach – Newport News, VA MSA	719	12
Dallas – Fort Worth, TX CMSA	701	13
Memphis, TN – AR – MS MSA	662	14
Baltimore, MD MSA	548	15
San Francisco – Oakland – San Jose, CA CMSA	527	16
Jackson, MS MSA	459	17
Charlotte – Gastonia – Rock Hill, NC – SC MSA	439	18
Cleveland – Akron – Lorain, OH CMSA	346	19
Richmond – Petersburg, VA MSA	326	20
Baton Rouge, LA MSA	323	21
Birmingham, AL MSA	313	22
Greensboro – Winston-Salem – High Point, NC MSA	292	23
Nashville, TN MSA	276	24
Boston – Lawrence – Salem, MA – NH CMSA	259	25

Source: U.S. Department of Commerce, Bureau of the Census, Data User Services Division, *1990 Census of Population and Housing, Equal Employment Opportunity File, CD-90-EEO-1, January 1993,* CD-ROM.

★1373★

Occupations, By Race/Sex

Top 25 MSAs For Employment As Teachers, Secondary School, 1990: Whites

MSA/CMSA	Employees per 100,000 pop.	Rank
Cincinnati – Hamilton, OH – KY – IN CMSA	44,265	1
Los Angeles – Anaheim – Riverside, CA CMSA	21,877	2
Chicago – Gary – Lake County, IL – IN – WI CMSA	20,430	3
Philadelphia – Wilmington – Trenton, PA – NJ – DE – MD CMSA	13,517	4
San Francisco – Oakland – San Jose, CA CMSA	11,864	5
Boston – Lawrence – Salem, MA – NH CMSA	11,658	6
Detroit – Ann Arbor, MI CMSA	7,576	7
Dallas – Fort Worth, TX CMSA	7,350	8
Houston – Galveston – Brazoria, TX CMSA	6,698	9
Rochester, NY MSA	6,469	10
Washington, DC – MD – VA MSA	6,212	11
St. Louis, MO – IL MSA	5,728	12
Cleveland – Akron – Lorain, OH CMSA	5,629	13
Minneapolis – St. Paul, MN – WI MSA	5,367	14
Buffalo – Niagara Falls, NY CMSA	5,259	15
Pittsburgh – Beaver Valley, PA CMSA	4,903	16
Albany – Schenectady – Troy, NY MSA	4,693	17
San Diego, CA MSA	4,683	18
Atlanta, GA MSA	4,577	19
Seattle – Tacoma, WA CMSA	4,374	20
Miami – Fort Lauderdale, FL CMSA	4,263	21
Phoenix, AZ MSA	4,197	22
Baltimore, MD MSA	4,149	23
Cincinnati – Hamilton, OH – KY – IN CMSA	3,990	24
Syracuse, NY MSA	3,841	25

Source: U.S. Department of Commerce, Bureau of the Census, Data User Services Division, *1990 Census of Population and Housing, Equal Employment Opportunity File, CD-90-EEO-1, January 1993,* CD-ROM.

★1374★
Occupations, By Race/Sex

Top 25 MSAs For Employment As Teachers, Special Education, 1990: Blacks

MSA/CMSA	Employees per 100,000 pop.	Rank
Charleston, SC MSA	906	1
Los Angeles – Anaheim – Riverside, CA CMSA	428	2
Philadelphia – Wilmington – Trenton, PA – NJ – DE – MD CMSA	372	3
Chicago – Gary – Lake County, IL – IN – WI CMSA	321	4
Detroit – Ann Arbor, MI CMSA	255	5
Washington, DC – MD – VA MSA	190	6
Baltimore, MD MSA	184	7
Houston – Galveston – Brazoria, TX CMSA	140	8
Dallas – Fort Worth, TX CMSA	129	9
Atlanta, GA MSA	101	10
Cleveland – Akron – Lorain, OH CMSA	97	11
San Francisco – Oakland – San Jose, CA CMSA	86	12
St. Louis, MO – IL MSA	80	13
Norfolk – Virginia Beach – Newport News, VA MSA	77	14
Hartford – New Britain – Middletown, CT CMSA	58	15
Raleigh – Durham, NC MSA	57	16
Shreveport, LA MSA	57	16
Boston – Lawrence – Salem, MA – NH CMSA	55	17
New Orleans, LA MSA	51	18
Alexandria, LA MSA	50	19
Little Rock – North Little Rock, AR MSA	48	20
San Antonio, TX MSA	47	21
Baton Rouge, LA MSA	46	22
Charleston, SC MSA	45	23
Cincinnati – Hamilton, OH – KY – IN CMSA	42	24

Source: U.S. Department of Commerce, Bureau of the Census, Data User Services Division, *1990 Census of Population and Housing, Equal Employment Opportunity File, CD-90-EE0-1*, January 1993, CD-ROM.

★1375★
Occupations, By Race/Sex

Top 25 MSAs For Employment As Teachers, Special Education, 1990: Whites

MSA/CMSA	Employees per 100,000 pop.	Rank
Providence – Pawtucket – Fall River, RI – MA CMSA	4,934	1
Los Angeles – Anaheim – Riverside, CA CMSA	2,231	2
Philadelphia – Wilmington – Trenton, PA – NJ – DE – MD CMSA	1,617	3
Boston – Lawrence – Salem, MA – NH CMSA	1,409	4
Chicago – Gary – Lake County, IL – IN – WI CMSA	1,386	5
San Francisco – Oakland – San Jose, CA CMSA	1,010	6
Detroit – Ann Arbor, MI CMSA	779	7
Washington, DC – MD – VA MSA	693	8
Pittsburgh – Beaver Valley, PA CMSA	693	8
Minneapolis – St. Paul, MN – WI MSA	657	9
Albany – Schenectady – Troy, NY MSA	626	10
Dallas – Fort Worth, TX CMSA	609	11
Buffalo – Niagara Falls, NY CMSA	572	12
Cleveland – Akron – Lorain, OH CMSA	525	13
Houston – Galveston – Brazoria, TX CMSA	524	14
St. Louis, MO – IL MSA	510	15
San Diego, CA MSA	487	16
Hartford – New Britain – Middletown, CT CMSA	439	17
Salt Lake City – Ogden, UT MSA	432	18
Portland – Vancouver, OR – WA CMSA	419	19
Providence – Pawtucket – Fall River, RI – MA CMSA	418	20
Phoenix, AZ MSA	397	21
Rochester, NY MSA	395	22
Seattle – Tacoma, WA CMSA	390	23
Kansas City, MO – KS MSA	377	24

Source: U.S. Department of Commerce, Bureau of the Census, Data User Services Division, *1990 Census of Population and Housing, Equal Employment Opportunity File, CD-90-EE0-1*, January 1993, CD-ROM.

★ 1376 ★

Occupations, By Race/Sex

Top 25 MSAs For Employment As Technical Writers, 1990: Blacks

MSA/CMSA	Employees per 100,000 pop.	Rank
Mobile, AL MSA	426	1
Washington, DC – MD – VA MSA	408	2
Los Angeles – Anaheim – Riverside, CA CMSA	400	3
Chicago – Gary – Lake County, IL – IN – WI CMSA	208	4
Atlanta, GA MSA	168	5
San Francisco – Oakland – San Jose, CA CMSA	154	6
Boston – Lawrence – Salem, MA – NH CMSA	124	7
Detroit – Ann Arbor, MI CMSA	98	8
Baltimore, MD MSA	76	9
Houston – Galveston – Brazoria, TX CMSA	70	10
Dallas – Fort Worth, TX CMSA	66	11
Philadelphia – Wilmington – Trenton, PA – NJ – DE – MD CMSA	65	12
St. Louis, MO – IL MSA	58	13
Raleigh – Durham, NC MSA	46	14
Norfolk – Virginia Beach – Newport News, VA MSA	41	15
Huntsville, AL MSA	41	15
Minneapolis – St. Paul, MN – WI MSA	34	16
Richmond – Petersburg, VA MSA	33	17
Portland – Vancouver, OR – WA CMSA	27	18
West Palm Beach – Boca Raton – Delray Beach, FL MSA	27	18
Hartford – New Britain – Middletown, CT CMSA	26	19
Dayton – Springfield, OH MSA	25	20
Charlotte – Gastonia – Rock Hill, NC – SC MSA	24	21
Austin, TX MSA	24	21
El Paso, TX MSA	23	22

Source: U.S. Department of Commerce, Bureau of the Census, Data User Services Division, *1990 Census of Population and Housing, Equal Employment Opportunity File, CD-90-EE0-1, January 1993,* CD-ROM.

★ 1377 ★

Occupations, By Race/Sex

Top 25 MSAs For Employment As Technical Writers, 1990: Whites

MSA/CMSA	Employees per 100,000 pop.	Rank
Kansas City, MO – KS MSA	5,279	1
San Francisco – Oakland – San Jose, CA CMSA	4,874	2
Los Angeles – Anaheim – Riverside, CA CMSA	4,417	3
Boston – Lawrence – Salem, MA – NH CMSA	3,857	4
Washington, DC – MD – VA MSA	3,295	5
Dallas – Fort Worth, TX CMSA	2,148	6
Chicago – Gary – Lake County, IL – IN – WI CMSA	2,081	7
Philadelphia – Wilmington – Trenton, PA – NJ – DE – MD CMSA	1,952	8
Detroit – Ann Arbor, MI CMSA	1,593	9
Seattle – Tacoma, WA CMSA	1,449	10
Minneapolis – St. Paul, MN – WI MSA	1,356	11
San Diego, CA MSA	1,192	12
Baltimore, MD MSA	1,125	13
Portland – Vancouver, OR – WA CMSA	1,028	14
Atlanta, GA MSA	1,007	15
Denver – Boulder, CO CMSA	999	16
Houston – Galveston – Brazoria, TX CMSA	900	17
St. Louis, MO – IL MSA	841	18
Phoenix, AZ MSA	780	19
Cincinnati – Hamilton, OH – KY – IN CMSA	711	20
Pittsburgh – Beaver Valley, PA CMSA	658	21
Raleigh – Durham, NC MSA	608	22
Hartford – New Britain – Middletown, CT CMSA	597	23
Rochester, NY MSA	589	24
Milwaukee – Racine, WI CMSA	577	25

Source: U.S. Department of Commerce, Bureau of the Census, Data User Services Division, *1990 Census of Population and Housing, Equal Employment Opportunity File, CD-90-EE0-1, January 1993,* CD-ROM.

★ 1378 ★

Occupations, By Race/Sex

Top 25 MSAs For Employment As Theology Teachers, 1990: Blacks

MSA/CMSA	Employees per 100,000 pop.	Rank
Reading, PA MSA	11	1
Richmond – Petersburg, VA MSA	11	1
Oklahoma City, OK MSA	10	2
Huntsville, AL MSA	8	3
Baltimore, MD MSA	7	4
Hartford – New Britain – Middletown, CT CMSA	7	4

[Continued]

★1378★

Top 25 MSAs For Employment As Theology Teachers, 1990: Blacks
[Continued]

MSA/CMSA	Employees per 100,000 pop.	Rank
Lubbock, TX MSA	6	5
Portsmouth – Dover – Rochester, NH – ME MSA	6	5
Dallas – Fort Worth, TX CMSA	6	5
Washington, DC – MD – VA MSA	5	6
Lancaster, PA MSA	0	7
La Crosse, WI MSA	0	7
Lakeland – Winter Haven, FL MSA	0	7
Kansas City, MO – KS MSA	0	7
Janesville – Beloit, WI MSA	0	7
Knoxville, TN MSA	0	7
Killeen – Temple, TX MSA	0	7
Lake Charles, LA MSA	0	7
Lansing – East Lansing, MI MSA	0	7
Laredo, TX MSA	0	7
Lafayette – West Lafayette, IN MSA	0	7
Lafayette, LA MSA	0	7
Lima, OH MSA	0	7
Las Vegas, NV MSA	0	7
Johnstown, PA MSA	0	7

Source: U.S. Department of Commerce, Bureau of the Census, Data User Services Division, *1990 Census of Population and Housing, Equal Employment Opportunity File, CD-90-EE0-1, January 1993*, CD-ROM.

★1379★

Occupations, By Race/Sex

Top 25 MSAs For Employment As Theology Teachers, 1990: Whites

MSA/CMSA	Employees per 100,000 pop.	Rank
Pascagoula, MS MSA	209	1
San Francisco – Oakland – San Jose, CA CMSA	147	2
Philadelphia – Wilmington – Trenton, PA – NJ – DE – MD CMSA	146	3
Los Angeles – Anaheim – Riverside, CA CMSA	118	4
Chicago – Gary – Lake County, IL – IN – WI CMSA	116	5
Boston – Lawrence – Salem, MA – NH CMSA	115	6
Pittsburgh – Beaver Valley, PA CMSA	52	7
Minneapolis – St. Paul, MN – WI MSA	46	8
San Antonio, TX MSA	44	9
Dallas – Fort Worth, TX CMSA	41	10
Phoenix, AZ MSA	40	11
Greenville – Spartanburg, SC MSA	35	12
Lexington-Fayette, KY MSA	34	13

[Continued]

★1379★

Top 25 MSAs For Employment As Theology Teachers, 1990: Whites
[Continued]

MSA/CMSA	Employees per 100,000 pop.	Rank
Birmingham, AL MSA	28	14
Kansas City, MO – KS MSA	27	15
St. Louis, MO – IL MSA	27	15
Nashville, TN MSA	26	16
Champaign – Urbana – Rantoul, IL MSA	24	17
Detroit – Ann Arbor, MI CMSA	23	18
Washington, DC – MD – VA MSA	23	18
Albany – Schenectady – Troy, NY MSA	22	19
Raleigh – Durham, NC MSA	22	19
Charleston, SC MSA	21	20
Scranton – Wilkes-Barre, PA MSA	20	21
Seattle – Tacoma, WA CMSA	20	21

Source: U.S. Department of Commerce, Bureau of the Census, Data User Services Division, *1990 Census of Population and Housing, Equal Employment Opportunity File, CD-90-EE0-1, January 1993*, CD-ROM.

★1380★

Occupations, By Race/Sex

Top 25 MSAs For Employment As Truck Drivers, 1990: Blacks

MSA/CMSA	Employees per 100,000 pop.	Rank
Detroit – Ann Arbor, MI CMSA	37,009	1
Los Angeles – Anaheim – Riverside, CA CMSA	15,039	2
Chicago – Gary – Lake County, IL – IN – WI CMSA	14,921	3
Washington, DC – MD – VA MSA	14,687	4
Houston – Galveston – Brazoria, TX CMSA	13,718	5
Atlanta, GA MSA	12,625	6
Philadelphia – Wilmington – Trenton, PA – NJ – DE – MD CMSA	11,661	7
Dallas – Fort Worth, TX CMSA	9,852	8
Baltimore, MD MSA	8,844	9
Miami – Fort Lauderdale, FL CMSA	8,654	10
Detroit – Ann Arbor, MI CMSA	7,445	11
Memphis, TN – AR – MS MSA	6,023	12
San Francisco – Oakland – San Jose, CA CMSA	5,928	13
New Orleans, LA MSA	5,910	14
Norfolk – Virginia Beach – Newport News, VA MSA	5,329	15
Richmond – Petersburg, VA MSA	4,234	16
Charlotte – Gastonia – Rock Hill, NC – SC MSA	4,211	17
Cleveland – Akron – Lorain, OH CMSA	4,164	18
St. Louis, MO – IL MSA	3,524	19

[Continued]

★1380★

Top 25 MSAs For Employment As Truck Drivers, 1990: Blacks
[Continued]

MSA/CMSA	Employees per 100,000 pop.	Rank
Birmingham, AL MSA	3,068	20
Jacksonville, FL MSA	2,954	21
Greensboro – Winston-Salem – High Point, NC MSA	2,824	22
Baton Rouge, LA MSA	2,812	23
Raleigh – Durham, NC MSA	2,726	24
Jackson, MS MSA	2,528	25

Source: U.S. Department of Commerce, Bureau of the Census, Data User Services Division, *1990 Census of Population and Housing, Equal Employment Opportunity File,* CD-90-EE0-1, January 1993, CD-ROM.

★1381★
Occupations, By Race/Sex

Top 25 MSAs For Employment As Truck Drivers, 1990: Whites

MSA/CMSA	Employees per 100,000 pop.	Rank
York, PA MSA	111,194	1
Los Angeles – Anaheim – Riverside, CA CMSA	100,000	2
Chicago – Gary – Lake County, IL – IN – WI CMSA	64,987	3
Philadelphia – Wilmington – Trenton, PA – NJ – DE – MD CMSA	47,181	4
San Francisco – Oakland – San Jose, CA CMSA	39,837	5
Detroit – Ann Arbor, MI CMSA	38,751	6
Boston – Lawrence – Salem, MA – NH CMSA	34,100	7
Dallas – Fort Worth, TX CMSA	32,679	8
Houston – Galveston – Brazoria, TX CMSA	25,418	9
Minneapolis – St. Paul, MN – WI MSA	25,259	10
Cleveland – Akron – Lorain, OH CMSA	25,025	11
Miami – Fort Lauderdale, FL CMSA	24,603	12
Seattle – Tacoma, WA CMSA	24,382	13
St. Louis, MO – IL MSA	23,983	14
Atlanta, GA MSA	22,526	15
Pittsburgh – Beaver Valley, PA CMSA	21,345	16
Phoenix, AZ MSA	19,493	17
Tampa – St. Petersburg – Clearwater, FL MSA	19,193	18
Cincinnati – Hamilton, OH – KY – IN CMSA	18,514	19
Denver – Boulder, CO CMSA	18,289	20
Portland – Vancouver, OR – WA CMSA	18,081	21
Baltimore, MD MSA	18,077	22

[Continued]

★1381★

Top 25 MSAs For Employment As Truck Drivers, 1990: Whites
[Continued]

MSA/CMSA	Employees per 100,000 pop.	Rank
Kansas City, MO – KS MSA	16,059	23
Milwaukee – Racine, WI CMSA	15,843	24
Columbus, OH MSA	15,326	25

Source: U.S. Department of Commerce, Bureau of the Census, Data User Services Division, *1990 Census of Population and Housing, Equal Employment Opportunity File,* CD-90-EE0-1, January 1993, CD-ROM.

★1382★
Occupations, By Race/Sex

Top 25 MSAs For Employment As Typesetters and Compositors, 1990: Blacks

MSA/CMSA	Employees per 100,000 pop.	Rank
Norfolk – Virginia Beach – Newport News, VA MSA	521	1
Chicago – Gary – Lake County, IL – IN – WI CMSA	379	2
Washington, DC – MD – VA MSA	194	3
Los Angeles – Anaheim – Riverside, CA CMSA	166	4
Atlanta, GA MSA	163	5
Philadelphia – Wilmington – Trenton, PA – NJ – DE – MD CMSA	140	6
Detroit – Ann Arbor, MI CMSA	118	7
Baltimore, MD MSA	95	8
Memphis, TN – AR – MS MSA	78	9
San Francisco – Oakland – San Jose, CA CMSA	60	10
Charlotte – Gastonia – Rock Hill, NC – SC MSA	59	11
Miami – Fort Lauderdale, FL CMSA	56	12
Greensboro – Winston-Salem – High Point, NC MSA	55	13
Dallas – Fort Worth, TX CMSA	53	14
Houston – Galveston – Brazoria, TX CMSA	40	15
Montgomery, AL MSA	32	16
Mobile, AL MSA	29	17
Jackson, MS MSA	29	17
South Bend – Mishawaka, IN MSA	29	17
Orlando, FL MSA	26	18
Little Rock – North Little Rock, AR MSA	23	19
Milwaukee – Racine, WI CMSA	23	19
Nashville, TN MSA	19	20
Tallahassee, FL MSA	19	20
St. Louis, MO – IL MSA	19	20

Source: U.S. Department of Commerce, Bureau of the Census, Data User Services Division, *1990 Census of Population and Housing, Equal Employment Opportunity File,* CD-90-EE0-1, January 1993, CD-ROM.

★1383★
Occupations, By Race/Sex

Top 25 MSAs For Employment As Typesetters and Compositors, 1990: Whites

MSA/CMSA	Employees per 100,000 pop.	Rank
San Diego, CA MSA	5,127	1
Los Angeles – Anaheim – Riverside, CA CMSA	3,097	2
Chicago – Gary – Lake County, IL – IN – WI CMSA	2,850	3
Philadelphia – Wilmington – Trenton, PA – NJ – DE – MD CMSA	1,804	4
Boston – Lawrence – Salem, MA – NH CMSA	1,486	5
San Francisco – Oakland – San Jose, CA CMSA	1,473	6
Detroit – Ann Arbor, MI CMSA	1,313	7
Minneapolis – St. Paul, MN – WI MSA	1,295	8
Dallas – Fort Worth, TX CMSA	1,150	9
Washington, DC – MD – VA MSA	969	10
St. Louis, MO – IL MSA	883	11
Seattle – Tacoma, WA CMSA	781	12
Atlanta, GA MSA	758	13
Cleveland – Akron – Lorain, OH CMSA	733	14
Miami – Fort Lauderdale, FL CMSA	723	15
Denver – Boulder, CO CMSA	690	16
Cincinnati – Hamilton, OH – KY – IN CMSA	649	17
Kansas City, MO – KS MSA	647	18
Houston – Galveston – Brazoria, TX CMSA	620	19
Phoenix, AZ MSA	594	20
Baltimore, MD MSA	587	21
Indianapolis, IN MSA	565	22
Milwaukee – Racine, WI CMSA	561	23
Tampa – St. Petersburg – Clearwater, FL MSA	485	24
Portland – Vancouver, OR – WA CMSA	479	25

Source: U.S. Department of Commerce, Bureau of the Census, Data User Services Division, *1990 Census of Population and Housing, Equal Employment Opportunity File, CD-90-EEO-1, January 1993,* CD-ROM.

★1384★
Occupations, By Race/Sex

Top 25 MSAs For Employment As Typists, 1990: Blacks

MSA/CMSA	Employees per 100,000 pop.	Rank
Hartford – New Britain – Middletown, CT CMSA	20,593	1
Washington, DC – MD – VA MSA	10,656	2
Chicago – Gary – Lake County, IL – IN – WI CMSA	7,588	3
Los Angeles – Anaheim – Riverside, CA CMSA	7,278	4
Philadelphia – Wilmington – Trenton, PA – NJ – DE – MD CMSA	5,846	5
Detroit – Ann Arbor, MI CMSA	4,321	6
Atlanta, GA MSA	3,285	7
Baltimore, MD MSA	3,102	8
San Francisco – Oakland – San Jose, CA CMSA	2,755	9
Houston – Galveston – Brazoria, TX CMSA	2,736	10
St. Louis, MO – IL MSA	2,059	11
Miami – Fort Lauderdale, FL CMSA	1,993	12
Dallas – Fort Worth, TX CMSA	1,810	13
Cleveland – Akron – Lorain, OH CMSA	1,751	14
New Orleans, LA MSA	1,466	15
Norfolk – Virginia Beach – Newport News, VA MSA	1,288	16
Boston – Lawrence – Salem, MA – NH CMSA	1,163	17
Richmond – Petersburg, VA MSA	1,132	18
Columbus, OH MSA	991	19
Memphis, TN – AR – MS MSA	972	20
Kansas City, MO – KS MSA	968	21
Raleigh – Durham, NC MSA	781	22
Tampa – St. Petersburg – Clearwater, FL MSA	745	23
Jacksonville, FL MSA	743	24
Cincinnati – Hamilton, OH – KY – IN CMSA	736	25

Source: U.S. Department of Commerce, Bureau of the Census, Data User Services Division, *1990 Census of Population and Housing, Equal Employment Opportunity File, CD-90-EEO-1, January 1993,* CD-ROM.

★ 1385 ★

Occupations, By Race/Sex

Top 25 MSAs For Employment As Typists, 1990: Whites

MSA/CMSA	Employees per 100,000 pop.	Rank
San Diego, CA MSA	48,721	1
Los Angeles – Anaheim – Riverside, CA CMSA	26,842	2
Chicago – Gary – Lake County, IL – IN – WI CMSA	16,714	3
Philadelphia – Wilmington – Trenton, PA – NJ – DE – MD CMSA	16,487	4
San Francisco – Oakland – San Jose, CA CMSA	12,557	5
Boston – Lawrence – Salem, MA – NH CMSA	11,017	6
Detroit – Ann Arbor, MI CMSA	9,844	7
Washington, DC – MD – VA MSA	9,795	8
Minneapolis – St. Paul, MN – WI MSA	8,542	9
Dallas – Fort Worth, TX CMSA	8,022	10
Seattle – Tacoma, WA CMSA	6,179	11
Houston – Galveston – Brazoria, TX CMSA	5,839	12
Atlanta, GA MSA	5,780	13
Pittsburgh – Beaver Valley, PA CMSA	5,738	14
Cleveland – Akron – Lorain, OH CMSA	5,678	15
St. Louis, MO – IL MSA	5,644	16
Miami – Fort Lauderdale, FL CMSA	5,393	17
Baltimore, MD MSA	5,298	18
Denver – Boulder, CO CMSA	4,916	19
San Diego, CA MSA	4,883	20
Phoenix, AZ MSA	4,726	21
Milwaukee – Racine, WI CMSA	4,628	22
Tampa – St. Petersburg – Clearwater, FL MSA	4,372	23
Cincinnati – Hamilton, OH – KY – IN CMSA	4,357	24
Sacramento, CA MSA	4,085	25

Source: U.S. Department of Commerce, Bureau of the Census, Data User Services Division, *1990 Census of Population and Housing, Equal Employment Opportunity File, CD-90-EE0-1, January 1993,* CD-ROM.

★ 1386 ★

Occupations, By Race/Sex

Top 25 MSAs For Employment As Urban Planners, 1990: Blacks

MSA/CMSA	Employees per 100,000 pop.	Rank
Omaha, NE – IA MSA	163	1
Los Angeles – Anaheim – Riverside, CA CMSA	98	2
Washington, DC – MD – VA MSA	70	3
Houston – Galveston – Brazoria, TX CMSA	67	4

[Continued]

★ 1386 ★

Top 25 MSAs For Employment As Urban Planners, 1990: Blacks

[Continued]

MSA/CMSA	Employees per 100,000 pop.	Rank
Detroit – Ann Arbor, MI CMSA	58	5
Chicago – Gary – Lake County, IL – IN – WI CMSA	55	6
Cleveland – Akron – Lorain, OH CMSA	55	6
Dallas – Fort Worth, TX CMSA	48	7
Atlanta, GA MSA	47	8
Philadelphia – Wilmington – Trenton, PA – NJ – DE – MD CMSA	45	9
St. Louis, MO – IL MSA	37	10
Baltimore, MD MSA	35	11
San Francisco – Oakland – San Jose, CA CMSA	30	12
Seattle – Tacoma, WA CMSA	25	13
Atlantic City, NJ MSA	25	13
Cincinnati – Hamilton, OH – KY – IN CMSA	24	14
Albany, GA MSA	22	15
Tampa – St. Petersburg – Clearwater, FL MSA	21	16
Memphis, TN – AR – MS MSA	20	17
Milwaukee – Racine, WI CMSA	20	17
Dayton – Springfield, OH MSA	20	17
New Orleans, LA MSA	19	18
Rochester, NY MSA	19	18
Jacksonville, FL MSA	18	19
West Palm Beach – Boca Raton – Delray Beach, FL MSA	17	20

Source: U.S. Department of Commerce, Bureau of the Census, Data User Services Division, *1990 Census of Population and Housing, Equal Employment Opportunity File, CD-90-EE0-1, January 1993,* CD-ROM.

★ 1387 ★

Occupations, By Race/Sex

Top 25 MSAs For Employment As Urban Planners, 1990: Whites

MSA/CMSA	Employees per 100,000 pop.	Rank
Albany – Schenectady – Troy, NY MSA	1,443	1
New York – Northern New Jersey – Long Island, NY – NJ – CT CMSA	1,182	2
San Francisco – Oakland – San Jose, CA CMSA	986	3
Chicago – Gary – Lake County, IL – IN – WI CMSA	548	4
Boston – Lawrence – Salem, MA – NH CMSA	532	5
Washington, DC – MD – VA MSA	441	6
Minneapolis – St. Paul, MN – WI MSA	356	7

[Continued]

★1387★

Top 25 MSAs For Employment As Urban Planners, 1990: Whites
[Continued]

MSA/CMSA	Employees per 100,000 pop.	Rank
Seattle – Tacoma, WA CMSA	349	8
Philadelphia – Wilmington – Trenton, PA – NJ – DE – MD CMSA	346	9
San Diego, CA MSA	315	10
Baltimore, MD MSA	309	11
Phoenix, AZ MSA	275	12
Detroit – Ann Arbor, MI CMSA	248	13
Dallas – Fort Worth, TX CMSA	242	14
Miami – Fort Lauderdale, FL CMSA	220	15
Denver – Boulder, CO CMSA	186	16
Portland – Vancouver, OR – WA CMSA	179	17
Tampa – St. Petersburg – Clearwater, FL MSA	155	18
Hartford – New Britain – Middletown, CT CMSA	135	19
Kansas City, MO – KS MSA	120	20
Orlando, FL MSA	120	20
West Palm Beach – Boca Raton – Delray Beach, FL MSA	117	21
Houston – Galveston – Brazoria, TX CMSA	110	22
Albuquerque, NM MSA	109	23
Sacramento, CA MSA	106	24

Source: U.S. Department of Commerce, Bureau of the Census, Data User Services Division, *1990 Census of Population and Housing, Equal Employment Opportunity File, CD-90-EEO-1,* January 1993, CD-ROM.

★1388★

Occupations, By Race/Sex

Top 25 MSAs For Employment As Veterinarians, 1990: Blacks

MSA/CMSA	Employees per 100,000 pop.	Rank
Denver – Boulder, CO CMSA	113	1
Washington, DC – MD – VA MSA	98	2
Atlanta, GA MSA	55	3
Los Angeles – Anaheim – Riverside, CA CMSA	49	4
Philadelphia – Wilmington – Trenton, PA – NJ – DE – MD CMSA	48	5
San Francisco – Oakland – San Jose, CA CMSA	39	6
Boston – Lawrence – Salem, MA – NH CMSA	36	7
Miami – Fort Lauderdale, FL CMSA	28	8
Detroit – Ann Arbor, MI CMSA	28	8
Houston – Galveston – Brazoria, TX CMSA	22	9

[Continued]

★1388★

Top 25 MSAs For Employment As Veterinarians, 1990: Blacks
[Continued]

MSA/CMSA	Employees per 100,000 pop.	Rank
Kansas City, MO – KS MSA	20	10
Fresno, CA MSA	16	11
New Orleans, LA MSA	15	12
Cleveland – Akron – Lorain, OH CMSA	14	13
Indianapolis, IN MSA	14	13
Bryan – College Station, TX MSA	13	14
Dallas – Fort Worth, TX CMSA	13	14
Raleigh – Durham, NC MSA	12	15
Chicago – Gary – Lake County, IL – IN – WI CMSA	10	16
Orlando, FL MSA	10	16
Cincinnati – Hamilton, OH – KY – IN CMSA	10	16
Greenville – Spartanburg, SC MSA	9	17
Lansing – East Lansing, MI MSA	8	18
Sacramento, CA MSA	8	18
Omaha, NE – IA MSA	8	18

Source: U.S. Department of Commerce, Bureau of the Census, Data User Services Division, *1990 Census of Population and Housing, Equal Employment Opportunity File, CD-90-EEO-1,* January 1993, CD-ROM.

★1389★

Occupations, By Race/Sex

Top 25 MSAs For Employment As Veterinarians, 1990: Whites

MSA/CMSA	Employees per 100,000 pop.	Rank
Hartford – New Britain – Middletown, CT CMSA	1,888	1
Los Angeles – Anaheim – Riverside, CA CMSA	1,684	2
Philadelphia – Wilmington – Trenton, PA – NJ – DE – MD CMSA	1,232	3
San Francisco – Oakland – San Jose, CA CMSA	1,072	4
Washington, DC – MD – VA MSA	913	5
Chicago – Gary – Lake County, IL – IN – WI CMSA	904	6
Houston – Galveston – Brazoria, TX CMSA	757	7
Dallas – Fort Worth, TX CMSA	737	8
Boston – Lawrence – Salem, MA – NH CMSA	722	9
Minneapolis – St. Paul, MN – WI MSA	669	10
Detroit – Ann Arbor, MI CMSA	664	11
Miami – Fort Lauderdale, FL CMSA	646	12
Atlanta, GA MSA	567	13
Seattle – Tacoma, WA CMSA	547	14

[Continued]

★ 1389 ★

Top 25 MSAs For Employment As Veterinarians, 1990: Whites

[Continued]

MSA/CMSA	Employees per 100,000 pop.	Rank
Denver – Boulder, CO CMSA	504	15
St. Louis, MO – IL MSA	489	16
San Diego, CA MSA	443	17
Baltimore, MD MSA	443	17
Columbus, OH MSA	443	17
Sacramento, CA MSA	440	18
Kansas City, MO – KS MSA	402	19
Cleveland – Akron – Lorain, OH CMSA	376	20
Tampa – St. Petersburg – Clearwater, FL MSA	370	21
Portland – Vancouver, OR – WA CMSA	346	22
Phoenix, AZ MSA	335	23

Source: U.S. Department of Commerce, Bureau of the Census, Data User Services Division, *1990 Census of Population and Housing, Equal Employment Opportunity File, CD-90-EE0-1, January 1993,* CD-ROM.

★ 1390 ★

Occupations, By Race/Sex

Top 25 MSAs For Employment As Water and Sewage Treatment Plant Operators, 1990: Blacks

MSA/CMSA	Employees per 100,000 pop.	Rank
Cincinnati – Hamilton, OH – KY – IN CMSA	370	1
Washington, DC – MD – VA MSA	335	2
Detroit – Ann Arbor, MI CMSA	323	3
Houston – Galveston – Brazoria, TX CMSA	263	4
Miami – Fort Lauderdale, FL CMSA	210	5
Philadelphia – Wilmington – Trenton, PA – NJ – DE – MD CMSA	206	6
Atlanta, GA MSA	184	7
Chicago – Gary – Lake County, IL – IN – WI CMSA	181	8
Los Angeles – Anaheim – Riverside, CA CMSA	161	9
New Orleans, LA MSA	157	10
Baltimore, MD MSA	141	11
Cleveland – Akron – Lorain, OH CMSA	108	12
Tampa – St. Petersburg – Clearwater, FL MSA	105	13
Baton Rouge, LA MSA	77	14
Dallas – Fort Worth, TX CMSA	76	15
Macon – Warner Robins, GA MSA	67	16
San Diego, CA MSA	65	17
Beaumont – Port Arthur, TX MSA	62	18
Charleston, SC MSA	57	19
Raleigh – Durham, NC MSA	56	20

[Continued]

★ 1390 ★

Top 25 MSAs For Employment As Water and Sewage Treatment Plant Operators, 1990: Blacks

[Continued]

MSA/CMSA	Employees per 100,000 pop.	Rank
Pittsburgh – Beaver Valley, PA CMSA	48	21
Norfolk – Virginia Beach – Newport News, VA MSA	46	22
Birmingham, AL MSA	44	23
San Francisco – Oakland – San Jose, CA CMSA	42	24
Austin, TX MSA	39	25

Source: U.S. Department of Commerce, Bureau of the Census, Data User Services Division, *1990 Census of Population and Housing, Equal Employment Opportunity File, CD-90-EE0-1, January 1993,* CD-ROM.

★ 1391 ★

Occupations, By Race/Sex

Top 25 MSAs For Employment As Water and Sewage Treatment Plant Operators, 1990: Whites

MSA/CMSA	Employees per 100,000 pop.	Rank
Sacramento, CA MSA	1,937	1
Los Angeles – Anaheim – Riverside, CA CMSA	1,337	2
Philadelphia – Wilmington – Trenton, PA – NJ – DE – MD CMSA	1,210	3
Chicago – Gary – Lake County, IL – IN – WI CMSA	1,081	4
San Francisco – Oakland – San Jose, CA CMSA	878	5
Boston – Lawrence – Salem, MA – NH CMSA	822	6
Houston – Galveston – Brazoria, TX CMSA	723	7
Detroit – Ann Arbor, MI CMSA	649	8
Dallas – Fort Worth, TX CMSA	630	9
Cleveland – Akron – Lorain, OH CMSA	624	10
Miami – Fort Lauderdale, FL CMSA	584	11
Tampa – St. Petersburg – Clearwater, FL MSA	583	12
Pittsburgh – Beaver Valley, PA CMSA	577	13
Atlanta, GA MSA	493	14
Phoenix, AZ MSA	440	15
St. Louis, MO – IL MSA	439	16
Cincinnati – Hamilton, OH – KY – IN CMSA	415	17
Baltimore, MD MSA	408	18
Denver – Boulder, CO CMSA	397	19
Seattle – Tacoma, WA CMSA	376	20
Minneapolis – St. Paul, MN – WI MSA	362	21
Washington, DC – MD – VA MSA	351	22

[Continued]

★1391★
Top 25 MSAs For Employment As Water and Sewage Treatment Plant Operators, 1990: Whites
[Continued]

MSA/CMSA	Employees per 100,000 pop.	Rank
Jacksonville, FL MSA	333	23
Kansas City, MO–KS MSA	328	24
Buffalo–Niagara Falls, NY CMSA	322	25

Source: U.S. Department of Commerce, Bureau of the Census, Data User Services Division, *1990 Census of Population and Housing, Equal Employment Opportunity File, CD-90-EE0-1, January 1993,* CD-ROM.

★1392★
Occupations, By Race/Sex
Top 25 MSAs For Employment As Welders and Cutters, 1990: Blacks

MSA/CMSA	Employees per 100,000 pop.	Rank
Orlando, FL MSA	4,441	1
Detroit–Ann Arbor, MI CMSA	3,172	2
Chicago–Gary–Lake County, IL–IN–WI CMSA	2,462	3
Norfolk–Virginia Beach–Newport News, VA MSA	1,976	4
Houston–Galveston–Brazoria, TX CMSA	1,794	5
Philadelphia–Wilmington–Trenton, PA–NJ–DE–MD CMSA	1,648	6
Los Angeles–Anaheim–Riverside, CA CMSA	1,506	7
Cleveland–Akron–Lorain, OH CMSA	1,260	8
New Orleans, LA MSA	1,176	9
Baltimore, MD MSA	1,078	10
Birmingham, AL MSA	1,025	11
Atlanta, GA MSA	1,012	12
Miami–Fort Lauderdale, FL CMSA	825	13
Dallas–Fort Worth, TX CMSA	811	14
St. Louis, MO–IL MSA	793	15
Milwaukee–Racine, WI CMSA	784	16
Memphis, TN–AR–MS MSA	696	17
Washington, DC–MD–VA MSA	603	18
San Francisco–Oakland–San Jose, CA CMSA	508	19
Charlotte–Gastonia–Rock Hill, NC–SC MSA	497	20
Baton Rouge, LA MSA	489	21
Charleston, SC MSA	484	22
Mobile, AL MSA	473	23
Pascagoula, MS MSA	439	24
Flint, MI MSA	423	25

Source: U.S. Department of Commerce, Bureau of the Census, Data User Services Division, *1990 Census of Population and Housing, Equal Employment Opportunity File, CD-90-EE0-1, January 1993,* CD-ROM.

★1393★
Occupations, By Race/Sex
Top 25 MSAs For Employment As Welders and Cutters, 1990: Whites

MSA/CMSA	Employees per 100,000 pop.	Rank
Colorado Springs, CO MSA	15,769	1
Chicago–Gary–Lake County, IL–IN–WI CMSA	11,452	2
Detroit–Ann Arbor, MI CMSA	10,879	3
New York–Northern New Jersey–Long Island, NY–NJ–CT CMSA	10,789	4
Houston–Galveston–Brazoria, TX CMSA	9,563	5
Philadelphia–Wilmington–Trenton, PA–NJ–DE–MD CMSA	7,771	6
Cleveland–Akron–Lorain, OH CMSA	6,832	7
Dallas–Fort Worth, TX CMSA	5,976	8
Pittsburgh–Beaver Valley, PA CMSA	5,897	9
San Francisco–Oakland–San Jose, CA CMSA	5,413	10
St. Louis, MO–IL MSA	4,912	11
Minneapolis–St. Paul, MN–WI MSA	4,887	12
Seattle–Tacoma, WA CMSA	4,677	13
Milwaukee–Racine, WI CMSA	4,550	14
Boston–Lawrence–Salem, MA–NH CMSA	4,542	15
Cincinnati–Hamilton, OH–KY–IN CMSA	4,309	16
Portland–Vancouver, OR–WA CMSA	4,197	17
Tulsa, OK MSA	3,358	18
Miami–Fort Lauderdale, FL CMSA	3,300	19
Tampa–St. Petersburg–Clearwater, FL MSA	3,292	20
New Orleans, LA MSA	3,275	21
Atlanta, GA MSA	3,244	22
Birmingham, AL MSA	2,973	23
Baltimore, MD MSA	2,970	24
San Diego, CA MSA	2,951	25

Source: U.S. Department of Commerce, Bureau of the Census, Data User Services Division, *1990 Census of Population and Housing, Equal Employment Opportunity File, CD-90-EE0-1, January 1993,* CD-ROM.

★1394★

Occupations, By Race/Sex

Top 25 MSAs For Employment As Welfare Service Aides, 1990: Blacks

MSA/CMSA	Employees per 100,000 pop.	Rank
Indianapolis, IN MSA	2,952	1
Chicago – Gary – Lake County, IL – IN – WI CMSA	975	2
Los Angeles – Anaheim – Riverside, CA CMSA	531	3
Washington, DC – MD – VA MSA	418	4
Philadelphia – Wilmington – Trenton, PA – NJ – DE – MD CMSA	351	5
Detroit – Ann Arbor, MI CMSA	308	6
Baltimore, MD MSA	307	7
Boston – Lawrence – Salem, MA – NH CMSA	234	8
Cleveland – Akron – Lorain, OH CMSA	219	9
St. Louis, MO – IL MSA	183	10
Buffalo – Niagara Falls, NY CMSA	177	11
San Francisco – Oakland – San Jose, CA CMSA	168	12
Houston – Galveston – Brazoria, TX CMSA	163	13
New Orleans, LA MSA	143	14
Cincinnati – Hamilton, OH – KY – IN CMSA	135	15
Norfolk – Virginia Beach – Newport News, VA MSA	133	16
Miami – Fort Lauderdale, FL CMSA	117	17
San Diego, CA MSA	111	18
Atlanta, GA MSA	102	19
Seattle – Tacoma, WA CMSA	99	20
Tampa – St. Petersburg – Clearwater, FL MSA	92	21
Dallas – Fort Worth, TX CMSA	89	22
Dayton – Springfield, OH MSA	85	23
Memphis, TN – AR – MS MSA	82	24
Kansas City, MO – KS MSA	80	25

Source: U.S. Department of Commerce, Bureau of the Census, Data User Services Division, *1990 Census of Population and Housing, Equal Employment Opportunity File, CD-90-EE0-1, January 1993,* CD-ROM.

★1395★

Occupations, By Race/Sex

Top 25 MSAs For Employment As Welfare Service Aides, 1990: Whites

MSA/CMSA	Employees per 100,000 pop.	Rank
Cincinnati – Hamilton, OH – KY – IN CMSA	1,930	1
Los Angeles – Anaheim – Riverside, CA CMSA	1,609	2
Boston – Lawrence – Salem, MA – NH CMSA	1,077	3
San Francisco – Oakland – San Jose, CA CMSA	732	4
San Diego, CA MSA	652	5
Chicago – Gary – Lake County, IL – IN – WI CMSA	577	6
Detroit – Ann Arbor, MI CMSA	548	7
Seattle – Tacoma, WA CMSA	450	8
Philadelphia – Wilmington – Trenton, PA – NJ – DE – MD CMSA	353	9
Buffalo – Niagara Falls, NY CMSA	346	10
Providence – Pawtucket – Fall River, RI – MA CMSA	332	11
Sacramento, CA MSA	321	12
Minneapolis – St. Paul, MN – WI MSA	294	13
Washington, DC – MD – VA MSA	276	14
Portland – Vancouver, OR – WA CMSA	238	15
Baltimore, MD MSA	231	16
Denver – Boulder, CO CMSA	222	17
Kansas City, MO – KS MSA	219	18
Rochester, NY MSA	215	19
Albany – Schenectady – Troy, NY MSA	214	20
Cleveland – Akron – Lorain, OH CMSA	208	21
Dallas – Fort Worth, TX CMSA	206	22
Pittsburgh – Beaver Valley, PA CMSA	204	23
Milwaukee – Racine, WI CMSA	201	24
Phoenix, AZ MSA	201	24

Source: U.S. Department of Commerce, Bureau of the Census, Data User Services Division, *1990 Census of Population and Housing, Equal Employment Opportunity File, CD-90-EE0-1, January 1993,* CD-ROM.

★1396★

Occupations, By Race/Sex

Top 25 MSAs For Employment As Accountants and Auditors, 1990: Men

MSA/CMSA	Employees per 100,000 pop.	Rank
Seattle – Tacoma, WA CMSA	100,859	1
Los Angeles – Anaheim – Riverside, CA CMSA	48,198	2
Chicago – Gary – Lake County, IL – IN – WI CMSA	34,197	3
San Francisco – Oakland – San Jose, CA CMSA	27,376	4
Philadelphia – Wilmington – Trenton, PA – NJ – DE – MD CMSA	25,147	5
Washington, DC – MD – VA MSA	23,679	6
Boston – Lawrence – Salem, MA – NH CMSA	22,208	7
Dallas – Fort Worth, TX CMSA	19,019	8
Houston – Galveston – Brazoria, TX CMSA	16,648	9
Detroit – Ann Arbor, MI CMSA	13,963	10
Atlanta, GA MSA	12,521	11
Minneapolis – St. Paul, MN – WI MSA	11,850	12
Miami – Fort Lauderdale, FL CMSA	11,547	13
Cleveland – Akron – Lorain, OH CMSA	9,911	14
Baltimore, MD MSA	8,866	15
Seattle – Tacoma, WA CMSA	8,792	16
St. Louis, MO – IL MSA	8,707	17
Denver – Boulder, CO CMSA	8,693	18
Pittsburgh – Beaver Valley, PA CMSA	7,356	19
San Diego, CA MSA	6,762	20
Phoenix, AZ MSA	6,470	21
Cincinnati – Hamilton, OH – KY – IN CMSA	6,442	22
Tampa – St. Petersburg – Clearwater, FL MSA	5,960	23
Columbus, OH MSA	5,742	24
Kansas City, MO – KS MSA	5,700	25

Source: U.S. Department of Commerce, Bureau of the Census, Data User Services Division, *1990 Census of Population and Housing, Equal Employment Opportunity File, CD-90-EE0-1, January 1993,* CD-ROM.

★1397★

Occupations, By Race/Sex

Top 25 MSAs For Employment As Accountants and Auditors, 1990: Women

MSA/CMSA	Employees per 100,000 pop.	Rank
Cincinnati – Hamilton, OH – KY – IN CMSA	74,459	1
Los Angeles – Anaheim – Riverside, CA CMSA	57,905	2
San Francisco – Oakland – San Jose, CA CMSA	35,166	3
Chicago – Gary – Lake County, IL – IN – WI CMSA	34,489	4
Washington, DC – MD – VA MSA	25,907	5
Boston – Lawrence – Salem, MA – NH CMSA	22,334	6
Philadelphia – Wilmington – Trenton, PA – NJ – DE – MD CMSA	21,911	7
Dallas – Fort Worth, TX CMSA	21,853	8
Houston – Galveston – Brazoria, TX CMSA	19,503	9
Atlanta, GA MSA	17,141	10
Detroit – Ann Arbor, MI CMSA	15,929	11
Minneapolis – St. Paul, MN – WI MSA	12,529	12
Seattle – Tacoma, WA CMSA	12,210	13
Miami – Fort Lauderdale, FL CMSA	11,117	14
Denver – Boulder, CO CMSA	10,523	15
San Diego, CA MSA	9,614	16
St. Louis, MO – IL MSA	9,518	17
Baltimore, MD MSA	9,123	18
Cleveland – Akron – Lorain, OH CMSA	8,904	19
Phoenix, AZ MSA	8,484	20
Kansas City, MO – KS MSA	7,532	21
Cincinnati – Hamilton, OH – KY – IN CMSA	6,947	22
Tampa – St. Petersburg – Clearwater, FL MSA	6,835	23
Sacramento, CA MSA	6,599	24
Pittsburgh – Beaver Valley, PA CMSA	6,424	25

Source: U.S. Department of Commerce, Bureau of the Census, Data User Services Division, *1990 Census of Population and Housing, Equal Employment Opportunity File, CD-90-EE0-1, January 1993,* CD-ROM.

★1398★

Occupations, By Race/Sex

Top 25 MSAs For Employment As Actors and Directors, 1990: Men

MSA/CMSA	Employees per 100,000 pop.	Rank
New Orleans, LA MSA	16,531	1
New York – Northern New Jersey – Long Island, NY – NJ – CT CMSA	12,178	2
Chicago – Gary – Lake County, IL – IN – WI CMSA	2,343	3
San Francisco – Oakland – San Jose, CA CMSA	1,883	4
Washington, DC – MD – VA MSA	1,774	5
Boston – Lawrence – Salem, MA – NH CMSA	1,362	6
Miami – Fort Lauderdale, FL CMSA	1,242	7
Philadelphia – Wilmington – Trenton, PA – NJ – DE – MD CMSA	1,109	8
Dallas – Fort Worth, TX CMSA	937	9
Detroit – Ann Arbor, MI CMSA	846	10
Atlanta, GA MSA	841	11
Minneapolis – St. Paul, MN – WI MSA	817	12
Seattle – Tacoma, WA CMSA	674	13
San Diego, CA MSA	590	14
Denver – Boulder, CO CMSA	581	15
Houston – Galveston – Brazoria, TX CMSA	565	16
Baltimore, MD MSA	562	17
Portland – Vancouver, OR – WA CMSA	543	18
Orlando, FL MSA	496	19
Nashville, TN MSA	420	20
Phoenix, AZ MSA	400	21
Tampa – St. Petersburg – Clearwater, FL MSA	399	22
Pittsburgh – Beaver Valley, PA CMSA	348	23
Indianapolis, IN MSA	331	24
St. Louis, MO – IL MSA	329	25

Source: U.S. Department of Commerce, Bureau of the Census, Data User Services Division, *1990 Census of Population and Housing, Equal Employment Opportunity File, CD-90-EE0-1, January 1993*, CD-ROM.

★1399★

Occupations, By Race/Sex

Top 25 MSAs For Employment As Actors and Directors, 1990: Women

MSA/CMSA	Employees per 100,000 pop.	Rank
Rochester, NY MSA	9,669	1
New York – Northern New Jersey – Long Island, NY – NJ – CT CMSA	9,442	2
Chicago – Gary – Lake County, IL – IN – WI CMSA	1,545	3
San Francisco – Oakland – San Jose, CA CMSA	1,437	4
Washington, DC – MD – VA MSA	1,343	5
Boston – Lawrence – Salem, MA – NH CMSA	1,094	6
Philadelphia – Wilmington – Trenton, PA – NJ – DE – MD CMSA	689	7
Seattle – Tacoma, WA CMSA	626	8
Atlanta, GA MSA	568	9
Detroit – Ann Arbor, MI CMSA	553	10
Dallas – Fort Worth, TX CMSA	433	11
Minneapolis – St. Paul, MN – WI MSA	424	12
Miami – Fort Lauderdale, FL CMSA	411	13
Denver – Boulder, CO CMSA	400	14
Houston – Galveston – Brazoria, TX CMSA	376	15
Baltimore, MD MSA	369	16
Orlando, FL MSA	319	17
Pittsburgh – Beaver Valley, PA CMSA	290	18
San Diego, CA MSA	280	19
St. Louis, MO – IL MSA	258	20
Portland – Vancouver, OR – WA CMSA	245	21
Phoenix, AZ MSA	239	22
Cleveland – Akron – Lorain, OH CMSA	229	23
Nashville, TN MSA	218	24
Kansas City, MO – KS MSA	195	25

Source: U.S. Department of Commerce, Bureau of the Census, Data User Services Division, *1990 Census of Population and Housing, Equal Employment Opportunity File, CD-90-EE0-1, January 1993*, CD-ROM.

★1400★

Occupations, By Race/Sex

Top 25 MSAs For Employment As Administrators, Protective Services, 1990: Men

MSA/CMSA	Employees per 100,000 pop.	Rank
Albany – Schenectady – Troy, NY MSA	1,933	1
Los Angeles – Anaheim – Riverside, CA CMSA	1,208	2
Chicago – Gary – Lake County, IL – IN – WI CMSA	866	3
San Francisco – Oakland – San Jose, CA CMSA	758	4
Philadelphia – Wilmington – Trenton, PA – NJ – DE – MD CMSA	756	5
Boston – Lawrence – Salem, MA – NH CMSA	720	6
Washington, DC – MD – VA MSA	692	7
Detroit – Ann Arbor, MI CMSA	458	8
Baltimore, MD MSA	430	9
Dallas – Fort Worth, TX CMSA	356	10
Sacramento, CA MSA	356	10
Seattle – Tacoma, WA CMSA	340	11
St. Louis, MO – IL MSA	321	12
Cleveland – Akron – Lorain, OH CMSA	297	13
Atlanta, GA MSA	294	14
Denver – Boulder, CO CMSA	288	15
Miami – Fort Lauderdale, FL CMSA	286	16
Cincinnati – Hamilton, OH – KY – IN CMSA	266	17
San Diego, CA MSA	260	18
Pittsburgh – Beaver Valley, PA CMSA	253	19
Houston – Galveston – Brazoria, TX CMSA	252	20
Minneapolis – St. Paul, MN – WI MSA	250	21
Phoenix, AZ MSA	250	21
Columbus, OH MSA	246	22
Tampa – St. Petersburg – Clearwater, FL MSA	229	23

Source: U.S. Department of Commerce, Bureau of the Census, Data User Services Division, *1990 Census of Population and Housing, Equal Employment Opportunity File, CD-90-EEO-1, January 1993,* CD-ROM.

★1401★

Occupations, By Race/Sex

Top 25 MSAs For Employment As Administrators, Protective Services, 1990: Women

MSA/CMSA	Employees per 100,000 pop.	Rank
Orlando, FL MSA	788	1
Los Angeles – Anaheim – Riverside, CA CMSA	581	2
Washington, DC – MD – VA MSA	456	3
Philadelphia – Wilmington – Trenton, PA – NJ – DE – MD CMSA	342	4
Miami – Fort Lauderdale, FL CMSA	327	5
Chicago – Gary – Lake County, IL – IN – WI CMSA	320	6
Baltimore, MD MSA	310	7
Boston – Lawrence – Salem, MA – NH CMSA	275	8
Detroit – Ann Arbor, MI CMSA	260	9
San Francisco – Oakland – San Jose, CA CMSA	249	10
Sacramento, CA MSA	194	11
St. Louis, MO – IL MSA	192	12
Seattle – Tacoma, WA CMSA	161	13
Atlanta, GA MSA	157	14
Phoenix, AZ MSA	155	15
Columbus, OH MSA	152	16
Tampa – St. Petersburg – Clearwater, FL MSA	146	17
Dallas – Fort Worth, TX CMSA	130	18
Austin, TX MSA	121	19
Houston – Galveston – Brazoria, TX CMSA	115	20
West Palm Beach – Boca Raton – Delray Beach, FL MSA	112	21
Denver – Boulder, CO CMSA	107	22
San Diego, CA MSA	106	23
Cleveland – Akron – Lorain, OH CMSA	105	24
Orlando, FL MSA	104	25

Source: U.S. Department of Commerce, Bureau of the Census, Data User Services Division, *1990 Census of Population and Housing, Equal Employment Opportunity File, CD-90-EEO-1, January 1993,* CD-ROM.

★1402★

Occupations, By Race/Sex

Top 25 MSAs For Employment As Aerospace Engineers, 1990: Whites

MSA/CMSA	Employees per 100,000 pop.	Rank
Cincinnati – Hamilton, OH – KY – IN CMSA	30,365	1
Seattle – Tacoma, WA CMSA	12,321	2
Dallas – Fort Worth, TX CMSA	7,093	3
San Francisco – Oakland – San Jose, CA CMSA	5,765	4

[Continued]

★1402★

Top 25 MSAs For Employment As Aerospace Engineers, 1990: Whites
[Continued]

MSA/CMSA	Employees per 100,000 pop.	Rank
St. Louis, MO–IL MSA	5,467	5
New York–Northern New Jersey–Long Island, NY–NJ–CT CMSA	4,928	6
San Diego, CA MSA	3,470	7
Denver–Boulder, CO CMSA	3,451	8
Phoenix, AZ MSA	3,175	9
Houston–Galveston–Brazoria, TX CMSA	2,942	10
Hartford–New Britain–Middletown, CT CMSA	2,702	11
Melbourne–Titusville–Palm Bay, FL MSA	2,397	12
Wichita, KS MSA	2,192	13
Philadelphia–Wilmington–Trenton, PA–NJ–DE–MD CMSA	2,187	14
Cincinnati–Hamilton, OH–KY–IN CMSA	2,116	15
West Palm Beach–Boca Raton–Delray Beach, FL MSA	1,943	16
Huntsville, AL MSA	1,890	17
Washington, DC–MD–VA MSA	1,812	18
Boston–Lawrence–Salem, MA–NH CMSA	1,613	19
Orlando, FL MSA	1,526	20
Salt Lake City–Ogden, UT MSA	1,104	21
Albany–Schenectady–Troy, NY MSA	1,078	22
Atlanta, GA MSA	1,013	23
Cleveland–Akron–Lorain, OH CMSA	977	24
Baltimore, MD MSA	840	25

Source: U.S. Department of Commerce, Bureau of the Census, Data User Services Division, 1990 Census of Population and Housing, Equal Employment Opportunity File, CD-90-EE0-1, January 1993, CD-ROM.

★1403★

Occupations, By Race/Sex

Top 25 MSAs For Employment As Agriculture and Forestry Teachers, 1990: Blacks

MSA/CMSA	Employees per 100,000 pop.	Rank
Burlington, VT MSA	11	1
Richmond–Petersburg, VA MSA	8	2
Buffalo–Niagara Falls, NY CMSA	5	3
Washington, DC–MD–VA MSA	2	4
Ocala, FL MSA	0	5
Oklahoma City, OK MSA	0	5
Panama City, FL MSA	0	5
Muskegon, MI MSA	0	5
Orlando, FL MSA	0	5
New Haven–Meriden, CT MSA	0	5

[Continued]

★1403★

Top 25 MSAs For Employment As Agriculture and Forestry Teachers, 1990: Blacks
[Continued]

MSA/CMSA	Employees per 100,000 pop.	Rank
Muncie, IN MSA	0	5
Owensboro, KY MSA	0	5
Phoenix, AZ MSA	0	5
Nashville, TN MSA	0	5
New Orleans, LA MSA	0	5
New London–Norwich, CT–RI MSA	0	5
Omaha, NE–IA MSA	0	5
Pine Bluff, AR MSA	0	5
Redding, CA MSA	0	5
Poughkeepsie, NY MSA	0	5
Rapid City, SD MSA	0	5
Provo–Orem, UT MSA	0	5
Macon–Warner Robins, GA MSA	0	5
Raleigh–Durham, NC MSA	0	5
Pittsfield, MA MSA	0	5

Source: U.S. Department of Commerce, Bureau of the Census, Data User Services Division, 1990 Census of Population and Housing, Equal Employment Opportunity File, CD-90-EE0-1, January 1993, CD-ROM.

★1404★

Occupations, By Race/Sex

Top 25 MSAs For Employment As Agriculture and Forestry Teachers, 1990: Whites

MSA/CMSA	Employees per 100,000 pop.	Rank
Portland–Vancouver, OR–WA CMSA	33	1
State College, PA MSA	27	2
Springfield, MO MSA	22	3
Raleigh–Durham, NC MSA	19	4
San Diego, CA MSA	15	5
Kansas City, MO–KS MSA	15	5
Miami–Fort Lauderdale, FL CMSA	15	5
Rochester, NY MSA	14	6
Burlington, VT MSA	14	6
Boston–Lawrence–Salem, MA–NH CMSA	13	7
Modesto, CA MSA	13	7
Honolulu, HI MSA	13	7
Baton Rouge, LA MSA	13	7
Columbia, MO MSA	13	7
Appleton–Oshkosh–Neenah, WI MSA	13	7
Chicago–Gary–Lake County, IL–IN–WI CMSA	12	8
Lafayette–West Lafayette, IN MSA	11	9
Davenport–Rock Island–Moline, IA–IL MSA	11	9
Lansing–East Lansing, MI MSA	10	10
Bryan–College Station, TX MSA	10	10

[Continued]

★1404★

Top 25 MSAs For Employment As Agriculture and Forestry Teachers, 1990: Whites
[Continued]

MSA/CMSA	Employees per 100,000 pop.	Rank
Syracuse, NY MSA	10	10
Boise City, ID MSA	10	10
Detroit – Ann Arbor, MI CMSA	9	11
Wausau, WI MSA	9	11
Athens, GA MSA	9	11

Source: U.S. Department of Commerce, Bureau of the Census, Data User Services Division, *1990 Census of Population and Housing, Equal Employment Opportunity File, CD-90-EE0-1, January 1993,* CD-ROM.

★1405★
Occupations, By Race/Sex

Top 25 MSAs For Employment As Air Traffic Controllers, 1990: Blacks

MSA/CMSA	Employees per 100,000 pop.	Rank
Shreveport, LA MSA	590	1
Washington, DC – MD – VA MSA	382	2
Los Angeles – Anaheim – Riverside, CA CMSA	268	3
Atlanta, GA MSA	186	4
Houston – Galveston – Brazoria, TX CMSA	178	5
Miami – Fort Lauderdale, FL CMSA	167	6
Dallas – Fort Worth, TX CMSA	155	7
San Francisco – Oakland – San Jose, CA CMSA	124	8
Chicago – Gary – Lake County, IL – IN – WI CMSA	113	9
Norfolk – Virginia Beach – Newport News, VA MSA	104	10
Jacksonville, FL MSA	101	11
St. Louis, MO – IL MSA	101	11
Baltimore, MD MSA	83	12
Kansas City, MO – KS MSA	82	13
Philadelphia – Wilmington – Trenton, PA – NJ – DE – MD CMSA	80	14
Detroit – Ann Arbor, MI CMSA	60	15
San Diego, CA MSA	57	16
Cleveland – Akron – Lorain, OH CMSA	49	17
New Orleans, LA MSA	48	18
Memphis, TN – AR – MS MSA	45	19
Macon – Warner Robins, GA MSA	44	20
Dothan, AL MSA	41	21
Montgomery, AL MSA	40	22
Columbus, GA – AL MSA	38	23
Richmond – Petersburg, VA MSA	37	24

Source: U.S. Department of Commerce, Bureau of the Census, Data User Services Division, *1990 Census of Population and Housing, Equal Employment Opportunity File, CD-90-EE0-1, January 1993,* CD-ROM.

★1406★
Occupations, By Race/Sex

Top 25 MSAs For Employment As Air Traffic Controllers, 1990: Whites

MSA/CMSA	Employees per 100,000 pop.	Rank
Norfolk – Virginia Beach – Newport News, VA MSA	1,919	1
Los Angeles – Anaheim – Riverside, CA CMSA	1,437	2
Dallas – Fort Worth, TX CMSA	1,374	3
Chicago – Gary – Lake County, IL – IN – WI CMSA	1,269	4
Miami – Fort Lauderdale, FL CMSA	1,117	5
San Francisco – Oakland – San Jose, CA CMSA	1,046	6
Washington, DC – MD – VA MSA	982	7
Atlanta, GA MSA	951	8
Seattle – Tacoma, WA CMSA	892	9
Houston – Galveston – Brazoria, TX CMSA	889	10
Minneapolis – St. Paul, MN – WI MSA	782	11
Denver – Boulder, CO CMSA	692	12
Boston – Lawrence – Salem, MA – NH CMSA	682	13
Cleveland – Akron – Lorain, OH CMSA	649	14
Memphis, TN – AR – MS MSA	606	15
Kansas City, MO – KS MSA	586	16
San Diego, CA MSA	582	17
Phoenix, AZ MSA	557	18
Jacksonville, FL MSA	540	19
Salt Lake City – Ogden, UT MSA	500	20
Detroit – Ann Arbor, MI CMSA	446	21
Philadelphia – Wilmington – Trenton, PA – NJ – DE – MD CMSA	430	22
Indianapolis, IN MSA	411	23
Pittsburgh – Beaver Valley, PA CMSA	396	24
Baltimore, MD MSA	383	25

Source: U.S. Department of Commerce, Bureau of the Census, Data User Services Division, *1990 Census of Population and Housing, Equal Employment Opportunity File, CD-90-EE0-1, January 1993,* CD-ROM.

★1407★

Occupations, By Race/Sex

Top 25 MSAs For Employment As Aircraft Engine Mechanics, 1990: Blacks

MSA/CMSA	Employees per 100,000 pop.	Rank
Portsmouth – Dover – Rochester, NH – ME MSA	1,375	1
San Francisco – Oakland – San Jose, CA CMSA	896	2
New York – Northern New Jersey – Long Island, NY – NJ – CT CMSA	849	3
Miami – Fort Lauderdale, FL CMSA	532	4
Dallas – Fort Worth, TX CMSA	444	5
Atlanta, GA MSA	384	6
San Diego, CA MSA	307	7
Norfolk – Virginia Beach – Newport News, VA MSA	303	8
Philadelphia – Wilmington – Trenton, PA – NJ – DE – MD CMSA	246	9
Chicago – Gary – Lake County, IL – IN – WI CMSA	199	10
Lake Charles, LA MSA	173	11
Tulsa, OK MSA	166	12
Jacksonville, FL MSA	155	13
Pensacola, FL MSA	154	14
St. Louis, MO – IL MSA	146	15
Washington, DC – MD – VA MSA	142	16
Seattle – Tacoma, WA CMSA	137	17
San Antonio, TX MSA	133	18
Macon – Warner Robins, GA MSA	131	19
Oklahoma City, OK MSA	120	20
Sacramento, CA MSA	118	21
Houston – Galveston – Brazoria, TX CMSA	114	22
Phoenix, AZ MSA	107	23
Dothan, AL MSA	101	24
Kansas City, MO – KS MSA	99	25

Source: U.S. Department of Commerce, Bureau of the Census, Data User Services Division, *1990 Census of Population and Housing, Equal Employment Opportunity File, CD-90-EE0-1, January 1993,* CD-ROM.

★1408★

Occupations, By Race/Sex

Top 25 MSAs For Employment As Aircraft Engine Mechanics, 1990: Whites

MSA/CMSA	Employees per 100,000 pop.	Rank
Houma – Thibodaux, LA MSA	6,811	1
San Francisco – Oakland – San Jose, CA CMSA	5,276	2
New York – Northern New Jersey – Long Island, NY – NJ – CT CMSA	4,870	3
Atlanta, GA MSA	4,403	4
Seattle – Tacoma, WA CMSA	4,274	5

[Continued]

★1408★

Top 25 MSAs For Employment As Aircraft Engine Mechanics, 1990: Whites
[Continued]

MSA/CMSA	Employees per 100,000 pop.	Rank
Miami – Fort Lauderdale, FL CMSA	3,907	6
Dallas – Fort Worth, TX CMSA	3,380	7
Tulsa, OK MSA	2,941	8
Minneapolis – St. Paul, MN – WI MSA	2,612	9
Chicago – Gary – Lake County, IL – IN – WI CMSA	2,235	10
San Diego, CA MSA	2,185	11
Phoenix, AZ MSA	2,025	12
Oklahoma City, OK MSA	1,948	13
Denver – Boulder, CO CMSA	1,715	14
Kansas City, MO – KS MSA	1,658	15
San Antonio, TX MSA	1,649	16
Salt Lake City – Ogden, UT MSA	1,518	17
Philadelphia – Wilmington – Trenton, PA – NJ – DE – MD CMSA	1,492	18
St. Louis, MO – IL MSA	1,490	19
Houston – Galveston – Brazoria, TX CMSA	1,448	20
Detroit – Ann Arbor, MI CMSA	1,413	21
Pittsburgh – Beaver Valley, PA CMSA	1,381	22
Jacksonville, FL MSA	1,355	23
Norfolk – Virginia Beach – Newport News, VA MSA	1,249	24
Wichita, KS MSA	1,218	25

Source: U.S. Department of Commerce, Bureau of the Census, Data User Services Division, *1990 Census of Population and Housing, Equal Employment Opportunity File, CD-90-EE0-1, January 1993,* CD-ROM.

★1409★

Occupations, By Race/Sex

Top 25 MSAs For Employment As Airplane Pilots and Navigators, 1990: Men

MSA/CMSA	Employees per 100,000 pop.	Rank
Pittsburgh – Beaver Valley, PA CMSA	5,556	1
Los Angeles – Anaheim – Riverside, CA CMSA	4,673	2
Atlanta, GA MSA	4,443	3
New York – Northern New Jersey – Long Island, NY – NJ – CT CMSA	4,116	4
Chicago – Gary – Lake County, IL – IN – WI CMSA	3,432	5
Miami – Fort Lauderdale, FL CMSA	3,098	6
San Francisco – Oakland – San Jose, CA CMSA	3,078	7
Seattle – Tacoma, WA CMSA	2,826	8

[Continued]

★1409★

Top 25 MSAs For Employment As Airplane Pilots and Navigators, 1990: Men
[Continued]

MSA/CMSA	Employees per 100,000 pop.	Rank
Denver – Boulder, CO CMSA	2,589	9
Houston – Galveston – Brazoria, TX CMSA	2,408	10
Minneapolis – St. Paul, MN – WI MSA	2,383	11
San Diego, CA MSA	2,128	12
Phoenix, AZ MSA	1,969	13
Memphis, TN – AR – MS MSA	1,547	14
Philadelphia – Wilmington – Trenton, PA – NJ – DE – MD CMSA	1,535	15
Washington, DC – MD – VA MSA	1,479	16
St. Louis, MO – IL MSA	1,290	17
Detroit – Ann Arbor, MI CMSA	1,269	18
Pittsburgh – Beaver Valley, PA CMSA	1,191	19
Charlotte – Gastonia – Rock Hill, NC – SC MSA	1,135	20
Honolulu, HI MSA	1,080	21
Boston – Lawrence – Salem, MA – NH CMSA	889	22
Portland – Vancouver, OR – WA CMSA	888	23
Las Vegas, NV MSA	868	24
Kansas City, MO – KS MSA	864	25

Source: U.S. Department of Commerce, Bureau of the Census, Data User Services Division, *1990 Census of Population and Housing, Equal Employment Opportunity File, CD-90-EE0-1,* January 1993, CD-ROM.

★1410★

Occupations, By Race/Sex

Top 25 MSAs For Employment As Airplane Pilots and Navigators, 1990: Women

MSA/CMSA	Employees per 100,000 pop.	Rank
Indianapolis, IN MSA	192	1
New York – Northern New Jersey – Long Island, NY – NJ – CT CMSA	184	2
Los Angeles – Anaheim – Riverside, CA CMSA	176	3
Chicago – Gary – Lake County, IL – IN – WI CMSA	174	4
Denver – Boulder, CO CMSA	146	5
Phoenix, AZ MSA	119	6
San Francisco – Oakland – San Jose, CA CMSA	108	7
Seattle – Tacoma, WA CMSA	106	8
Washington, DC – MD – VA MSA	94	9
Philadelphia – Wilmington – Trenton, PA – NJ – DE – MD CMSA	91	10
Minneapolis – St. Paul, MN – WI MSA	90	11

[Continued]

★1410★

Top 25 MSAs For Employment As Airplane Pilots and Navigators, 1990: Women
[Continued]

MSA/CMSA	Employees per 100,000 pop.	Rank
Memphis, TN – AR – MS MSA	72	12
Cincinnati – Hamilton, OH – KY – IN CMSA	68	13
Atlanta, GA MSA	63	14
San Diego, CA MSA	60	15
Houston – Galveston – Brazoria, TX CMSA	58	16
Baltimore, MD MSA	55	17
Norfolk – Virginia Beach – Newport News, VA MSA	55	17
Boston – Lawrence – Salem, MA – NH CMSA	53	18
Louisville, KY – IN MSA	52	19
Miami – Fort Lauderdale, FL CMSA	47	20
Pittsburgh – Beaver Valley, PA CMSA	47	20
Honolulu, HI MSA	45	21
Milwaukee – Racine, WI CMSA	41	22
Anchorage, AK MSA	38	23

Source: U.S. Department of Commerce, Bureau of the Census, Data User Services Division, *1990 Census of Population and Housing, Equal Employment Opportunity File, CD-90-EE0-1,* January 1993, CD-ROM.

★1411★

Occupations, By Race/Sex

Top 25 MSAs For Employment As Announcers, 1990: Men

MSA/CMSA	Employees per 100,000 pop.	Rank
Columbus, OH MSA	2,258	1
Los Angeles – Anaheim – Riverside, CA CMSA	2,011	2
Chicago – Gary – Lake County, IL – IN – WI CMSA	1,119	3
Washington, DC – MD – VA MSA	978	4
Philadelphia – Wilmington – Trenton, PA – NJ – DE – MD CMSA	803	5
Dallas – Fort Worth, TX CMSA	768	6
Boston – Lawrence – Salem, MA – NH CMSA	712	7
San Francisco – Oakland – San Jose, CA CMSA	670	8
Houston – Galveston – Brazoria, TX CMSA	660	9
Detroit – Ann Arbor, MI CMSA	643	10
Miami – Fort Lauderdale, FL CMSA	582	11
Atlanta, GA MSA	529	12
Seattle – Tacoma, WA CMSA	442	13
Minneapolis – St. Paul, MN – WI MSA	437	14

[Continued]

★1411★

Top 25 MSAs For Employment As Announcers, 1990: Men
[Continued]

MSA/CMSA	Employees per 100,000 pop.	Rank
St. Louis, MO – IL MSA	420	15
Phoenix, AZ MSA	409	16
Cincinnati – Hamilton, OH – KY – IN CMSA	402	17
Pittsburgh – Beaver Valley, PA CMSA	397	18
Cleveland – Akron – Lorain, OH CMSA	387	19
San Diego, CA MSA	361	20
Denver – Boulder, CO CMSA	360	21
Baltimore, MD MSA	345	22
Tampa – St. Petersburg – Clearwater, FL MSA	324	23
New Orleans, LA MSA	303	24
Milwaukee – Racine, WI CMSA	297	25

Source: U.S. Department of Commerce, Bureau of the Census, Data User Services Division, *1990 Census of Population and Housing, Equal Employment Opportunity File, CD-90-EE0-1, January 1993,* CD-ROM.

★1412★

Occupations, By Race/Sex

Top 25 MSAs For Employment As Announcers, 1990: Women

MSA/CMSA	Employees per 100,000 pop.	Rank
Tampa – St. Petersburg – Clearwater, FL MSA	864	1
Los Angeles – Anaheim – Riverside, CA CMSA	551	2
Washington, DC – MD – VA MSA	310	3
San Francisco – Oakland – San Jose, CA CMSA	267	4
Philadelphia – Wilmington – Trenton, PA – NJ – DE – MD CMSA	218	5
Chicago – Gary – Lake County, IL – IN – WI CMSA	208	6
Atlanta, GA MSA	196	7
Boston – Lawrence – Salem, MA – NH CMSA	171	8
Dallas – Fort Worth, TX CMSA	167	9
Detroit – Ann Arbor, MI CMSA	164	10
Norfolk – Virginia Beach – Newport News, VA MSA	135	11
Cleveland – Akron – Lorain, OH CMSA	118	12
Denver – Boulder, CO CMSA	111	13
Tampa – St. Petersburg – Clearwater, FL MSA	111	13
St. Louis, MO – IL MSA	102	14
Baton Rouge, LA MSA	97	15
San Diego, CA MSA	97	15
San Antonio, TX MSA	97	15

[Continued]

★1412★

Top 25 MSAs For Employment As Announcers, 1990: Women
[Continued]

MSA/CMSA	Employees per 100,000 pop.	Rank
Memphis, TN – AR – MS MSA	96	16
Pittsburgh – Beaver Valley, PA CMSA	88	17
Houston – Galveston – Brazoria, TX CMSA	87	18
Miami – Fort Lauderdale, FL CMSA	86	19
Oklahoma City, OK MSA	77	20
Indianapolis, IN MSA	73	21
Milwaukee – Racine, WI CMSA	73	21

Source: U.S. Department of Commerce, Bureau of the Census, Data User Services Division, *1990 Census of Population and Housing, Equal Employment Opportunity File, CD-90-EE0-1, January 1993,* CD-ROM.

★1413★

Occupations, By Race/Sex

Top 25 MSAs For Employment As Architects, 1990: Men

MSA/CMSA	Employees per 100,000 pop.	Rank
Tampa – St. Petersburg – Clearwater, FL MSA	14,749	1
Los Angeles – Anaheim – Riverside, CA CMSA	10,363	2
San Francisco – Oakland – San Jose, CA CMSA	7,028	3
Chicago – Gary – Lake County, IL – IN – WI CMSA	5,900	4
Washington, DC – MD – VA MSA	4,843	5
Boston – Lawrence – Salem, MA – NH CMSA	4,664	6
Philadelphia – Wilmington – Trenton, PA – NJ – DE – MD CMSA	4,070	7
Seattle – Tacoma, WA CMSA	2,860	8
Dallas – Fort Worth, TX CMSA	2,721	9
Atlanta, GA MSA	2,696	10
Houston – Galveston – Brazoria, TX CMSA	2,522	11
San Diego, CA MSA	2,506	12
Miami – Fort Lauderdale, FL CMSA	2,369	13
Detroit – Ann Arbor, MI CMSA	2,073	14
Minneapolis – St. Paul, MN – WI MSA	1,938	15
Denver – Boulder, CO CMSA	1,783	16
Phoenix, AZ MSA	1,559	17
Baltimore, MD MSA	1,529	18
St. Louis, MO – IL MSA	1,462	19
Sacramento, CA MSA	1,397	20
Cleveland – Akron – Lorain, OH CMSA	1,341	21
Portland – Vancouver, OR – WA CMSA	1,209	22

[Continued]

★1413★

Top 25 MSAs For Employment As Architects, 1990: Men
[Continued]

MSA/CMSA	Employees per 100,000 pop.	Rank
Tampa – St. Petersburg – Clearwater, FL MSA	1,188	23
Honolulu, HI MSA	1,065	24
Kansas City, MO – KS MSA	1,045	25

Source: U.S. Department of Commerce, Bureau of the Census, Data User Services Division, *1990 Census of Population and Housing, Equal Employment Opportunity File, CD-90-EE0-1, January 1993,* CD-ROM.

★1414★

Occupations, By Race/Sex

Top 25 MSAs For Employment As Architects, 1990: Women

MSA/CMSA	Employees per 100,000 pop.	Rank
Pittsburgh – Beaver Valley, PA CMSA	3,151	1
Los Angeles – Anaheim – Riverside, CA CMSA	2,131	2
San Francisco – Oakland – San Jose, CA CMSA	1,742	3
Washington, DC – MD – VA MSA	1,552	4
Boston – Lawrence – Salem, MA – NH CMSA	1,093	5
Chicago – Gary – Lake County, IL – IN – WI CMSA	1,037	6
Philadelphia – Wilmington – Trenton, PA – NJ – DE – MD CMSA	749	7
Seattle – Tacoma, WA CMSA	684	8
San Diego, CA MSA	464	9
Atlanta, GA MSA	383	10
Miami – Fort Lauderdale, FL CMSA	380	11
Minneapolis – St. Paul, MN – WI MSA	377	12
Baltimore, MD MSA	366	13
Denver – Boulder, CO CMSA	321	14
Dallas – Fort Worth, TX CMSA	311	15
Detroit – Ann Arbor, MI CMSA	311	15
Houston – Galveston – Brazoria, TX CMSA	310	16
St. Louis, MO – IL MSA	270	17
Sacramento, CA MSA	241	18
Columbus, OH MSA	218	19
Portland – Vancouver, OR – WA CMSA	201	20
Honolulu, HI MSA	179	21
New Haven – Meriden, CT MSA	171	22
Pittsburgh – Beaver Valley, PA CMSA	163	23
Cleveland – Akron – Lorain, OH CMSA	158	24

Source: U.S. Department of Commerce, Bureau of the Census, Data User Services Division, *1990 Census of Population and Housing, Equal Employment Opportunity File, CD-90-EE0-1, January 1993,* CD-ROM.

★1415★

Occupations, By Race/Sex

Top 25 MSAs For Employment As Archivists and Curators, 1990: Men

MSA/CMSA	Employees per 100,000 pop.	Rank
Hartford – New Britain – Middletown, CT CMSA	1,371	1
Washington, DC – MD – VA MSA	883	2
Los Angeles – Anaheim – Riverside, CA CMSA	687	3
Chicago – Gary – Lake County, IL – IN – WI CMSA	446	4
San Francisco – Oakland – San Jose, CA CMSA	349	5
Boston – Lawrence – Salem, MA – NH CMSA	345	6
Philadelphia – Wilmington – Trenton, PA – NJ – DE – MD CMSA	336	7
Detroit – Ann Arbor, MI CMSA	188	8
Minneapolis – St. Paul, MN – WI MSA	158	9
Miami – Fort Lauderdale, FL CMSA	156	10
Baltimore, MD MSA	145	11
St. Louis, MO – IL MSA	132	12
Denver – Boulder, CO CMSA	130	13
Kansas City, MO – KS MSA	127	14
Cleveland – Akron – Lorain, OH CMSA	125	15
San Diego, CA MSA	119	16
Indianapolis, IN MSA	117	17
New Haven – Meriden, CT MSA	112	18
Houston – Galveston – Brazoria, TX CMSA	111	19
Dallas – Fort Worth, TX CMSA	104	20
Norfolk – Virginia Beach – Newport News, VA MSA	101	21
Seattle – Tacoma, WA CMSA	97	22
Milwaukee – Racine, WI CMSA	95	23
New Orleans, LA MSA	94	24
Atlanta, GA MSA	94	24

Source: U.S. Department of Commerce, Bureau of the Census, Data User Services Division, *1990 Census of Population and Housing, Equal Employment Opportunity File, CD-90-EE0-1, January 1993,* CD-ROM.

★1416★

Occupations, By Race/Sex

Top 25 MSAs For Employment As Archivists and Curators, 1990: Women

MSA/CMSA	Employees per 100,000 pop.	Rank
Phoenix, AZ MSA	2,124	1
Washington, DC – MD – VA MSA	1,116	2
Boston – Lawrence – Salem, MA – NH CMSA	622	3
Los Angeles – Anaheim – Riverside, CA CMSA	620	4

[Continued]

★1416★

Top 25 MSAs For Employment As Archivists and Curators, 1990: Women

[Continued]

MSA/CMSA	Employees per 100,000 pop.	Rank
San Francisco – Oakland – San Jose, CA CMSA	594	5
Philadelphia – Wilmington – Trenton, PA – NJ – DE – MD CMSA	566	6
Chicago – Gary – Lake County, IL – IN – WI CMSA	523	7
St. Louis, MO – IL MSA	269	8
Baltimore, MD MSA	256	9
Detroit – Ann Arbor, MI CMSA	251	10
Minneapolis – St. Paul, MN – WI MSA	181	11
Seattle – Tacoma, WA CMSA	147	12
Houston – Galveston – Brazoria, TX CMSA	146	13
Kansas City, MO – KS MSA	146	13
Pittsburgh – Beaver Valley, PA CMSA	146	13
Albany – Schenectady – Troy, NY MSA	141	14
Cleveland – Akron – Lorain, OH CMSA	140	15
Dallas – Fort Worth, TX CMSA	138	16
New Haven – Meriden, CT MSA	112	17
San Diego, CA MSA	109	18
Austin, TX MSA	106	19
Atlanta, GA MSA	106	19
Portland – Vancouver, OR – WA CMSA	104	20
Norfolk – Virginia Beach – Newport News, VA MSA	99	21
Hartford – New Britain – Middletown, CT CMSA	92	22

Source: U.S. Department of Commerce, Bureau of the Census, Data User Services Division, *1990 Census of Population and Housing, Equal Employment Opportunity File, CD-90-EE0-1, January 1993,* CD-ROM.

★1417★

Occupations, By Race/Sex

Top 25 MSAs For Employment As Art, Drama, and Music Teachers, 1990: Men

MSA/CMSA	Employees per 100,000 pop.	Rank
Champaign – Urbana – Rantoul, IL MSA	690	1
Los Angeles – Anaheim – Riverside, CA CMSA	557	2
Chicago – Gary – Lake County, IL – IN – WI CMSA	309	3
San Francisco – Oakland – San Jose, CA CMSA	307	4
Boston – Lawrence – Salem, MA – NH CMSA	255	5

[Continued]

★1417★

Top 25 MSAs For Employment As Art, Drama, and Music Teachers, 1990: Men

[Continued]

MSA/CMSA	Employees per 100,000 pop.	Rank
Philadelphia – Wilmington – Trenton, PA – NJ – DE – MD CMSA	215	6
Detroit – Ann Arbor, MI CMSA	154	7
Cincinnati – Hamilton, OH – KY – IN CMSA	144	8
Minneapolis – St. Paul, MN – WI MSA	138	9
Cleveland – Akron – Lorain, OH CMSA	130	10
Washington, DC – MD – VA MSA	125	11
Dallas – Fort Worth, TX CMSA	124	12
Phoenix, AZ MSA	114	13
Bloomington, IN MSA	109	14
Columbus, OH MSA	103	15
Houston – Galveston – Brazoria, TX CMSA	100	16
San Diego, CA MSA	100	16
Kansas City, MO – KS MSA	96	17
Austin, TX MSA	93	18
Raleigh – Durham, NC MSA	86	19
Baltimore, MD MSA	81	20
Rochester, NY MSA	74	21
St. Louis, MO – IL MSA	71	22
Atlanta, GA MSA	69	23
Toledo, OH MSA	69	23

Source: U.S. Department of Commerce, Bureau of the Census, Data User Services Division, *1990 Census of Population and Housing, Equal Employment Opportunity File, CD-90-EE0-1, January 1993,* CD-ROM.

★1418★

Occupations, By Race/Sex

Top 25 MSAs For Employment As Art, Drama, and Music Teachers, 1990: Women

MSA/CMSA	Employees per 100,000 pop.	Rank
Sharon, PA MSA	659	1
Los Angeles – Anaheim – Riverside, CA CMSA	489	2
Chicago – Gary – Lake County, IL – IN – WI CMSA	406	3
San Francisco – Oakland – San Jose, CA CMSA	322	4
Washington, DC – MD – VA MSA	316	5
Boston – Lawrence – Salem, MA – NH CMSA	264	6
Philadelphia – Wilmington – Trenton, PA – NJ – DE – MD CMSA	242	7
Seattle – Tacoma, WA CMSA	191	8
Dallas – Fort Worth, TX CMSA	171	9
Detroit – Ann Arbor, MI CMSA	168	10
Baltimore, MD MSA	158	11

[Continued]

★ 1418 ★

Top 25 MSAs For Employment As Art, Drama, and Music Teachers, 1990: Women

[Continued]

MSA/CMSA	Employees per 100,000 pop.	Rank
Pittsburgh – Beaver Valley, PA CMSA	156	12
Minneapolis – St. Paul, MN – WI MSA	154	13
Cleveland – Akron – Lorain, OH CMSA	146	14
Houston – Galveston – Brazoria, TX CMSA	145	15
Cincinnati – Hamilton, OH – KY – IN CMSA	105	16
San Diego, CA MSA	98	17
St. Louis, MO – IL MSA	96	18
Portland – Vancouver, OR – WA CMSA	95	19
Greenville – Spartanburg, SC MSA	91	20
Austin, TX MSA	88	21
Buffalo – Niagara Falls, NY CMSA	85	22
San Antonio, TX MSA	85	22
Greensboro – Winston-Salem – High Point, NC MSA	84	23
Raleigh – Durham, NC MSA	82	24

Source: U.S. Department of Commerce, Bureau of the Census, Data User Services Division, *1990 Census of Population and Housing, Equal Employment Opportunity File, CD-90-EE0-1,* January 1993, CD-ROM.

★ 1419 ★

Occupations, By Race/Sex

Top 25 MSAs For Employment As Athletes, 1990: Men

MSA/CMSA	Employees per 100,000 pop.	Rank
Buffalo – Niagara Falls, NY CMSA	3,633	1
New York – Northern New Jersey – Long Island, NY – NJ – CT CMSA	3,149	2
San Francisco – Oakland – San Jose, CA CMSA	1,766	3
Miami – Fort Lauderdale, FL CMSA	1,251	4
Boston – Lawrence – Salem, MA – NH CMSA	1,251	4
Chicago – Gary – Lake County, IL – IN – WI CMSA	1,211	5
Philadelphia – Wilmington – Trenton, PA – NJ – DE – MD CMSA	1,204	6
San Diego, CA MSA	1,041	7
Dallas – Fort Worth, TX CMSA	966	8
Detroit – Ann Arbor, MI CMSA	911	9
Washington, DC – MD – VA MSA	847	10
Houston – Galveston – Brazoria, TX CMSA	783	11

[Continued]

★ 1419 ★

Top 25 MSAs For Employment As Athletes, 1990: Men

[Continued]

MSA/CMSA	Employees per 100,000 pop.	Rank
Phoenix, AZ MSA	771	12
Tampa – St. Petersburg – Clearwater, FL MSA	770	13
St. Louis, MO – IL MSA	713	14
Baltimore, MD MSA	675	15
Seattle – Tacoma, WA CMSA	652	16
Atlanta, GA MSA	628	17
Cleveland – Akron – Lorain, OH CMSA	594	18
Minneapolis – St. Paul, MN – WI MSA	565	19
Pittsburgh – Beaver Valley, PA CMSA	548	20
Cincinnati – Hamilton, OH – KY – IN CMSA	519	21
Denver – Boulder, CO CMSA	497	22
Austin, TX MSA	479	23
Oklahoma City, OK MSA	470	24

Source: U.S. Department of Commerce, Bureau of the Census, Data User Services Division, *1990 Census of Population and Housing, Equal Employment Opportunity File, CD-90-EE0-1,* January 1993, CD-ROM.

★ 1420 ★

Occupations, By Race/Sex

Top 25 MSAs For Employment As Athletes, 1990: Women

MSA/CMSA	Employees per 100,000 pop.	Rank
Seattle – Tacoma, WA CMSA	1,516	1
Los Angeles – Anaheim – Riverside, CA CMSA	1,094	2
Philadelphia – Wilmington – Trenton, PA – NJ – DE – MD CMSA	675	3
Chicago – Gary – Lake County, IL – IN – WI CMSA	672	4
San Francisco – Oakland – San Jose, CA CMSA	548	5
Boston – Lawrence – Salem, MA – NH CMSA	488	6
Detroit – Ann Arbor, MI CMSA	440	7
Washington, DC – MD – VA MSA	384	8
Seattle – Tacoma, WA CMSA	343	9
Miami – Fort Lauderdale, FL CMSA	333	10
Baltimore, MD MSA	288	11
Minneapolis – St. Paul, MN – WI MSA	283	12
Dallas – Fort Worth, TX CMSA	279	13
San Diego, CA MSA	273	14
Cleveland – Akron – Lorain, OH CMSA	269	15
Atlanta, GA MSA	253	16

[Continued]

★1420★

Top 25 MSAs For Employment As Athletes, 1990: Women

[Continued]

MSA/CMSA	Employees per 100,000 pop.	Rank
Houston – Galveston – Brazoria, TX CMSA	233	17
St. Louis, MO – IL MSA	224	18
Tampa – St. Petersburg – Clearwater, FL MSA	208	19
Milwaukee – Racine, WI CMSA	186	20
Denver – Boulder, CO CMSA	185	21
Cincinnati – Hamilton, OH – KY – IN CMSA	183	22
Portland – Vancouver, OR – WA CMSA	171	23
Rochester, NY MSA	171	23
Orlando, FL MSA	163	24

Source: U.S. Department of Commerce, Bureau of the Census, Data User Services Division, *1990 Census of Population and Housing, Equal Employment Opportunity File, CD-90-EE0-1, January 1993,* CD-ROM.

★1421★

Occupations, By Race/Sex

Top 25 MSAs For Employment As Auctioneers, 1990: Men

MSA/CMSA	Employees per 100,000 pop.	Rank
Portland – Vancouver, OR – WA CMSA	212	1
New York – Northern New Jersey – Long Island, NY – NJ – CT CMSA	160	2
Philadelphia – Wilmington – Trenton, PA – NJ – DE – MD CMSA	149	3
Lancaster, PA MSA	112	4
Houston – Galveston – Brazoria, TX CMSA	105	5
Dallas – Fort Worth, TX CMSA	103	6
Tampa – St. Petersburg – Clearwater, FL MSA	80	7
San Francisco – Oakland – San Jose, CA CMSA	74	8
Chicago – Gary – Lake County, IL – IN – WI CMSA	73	9
Miami – Fort Lauderdale, FL CMSA	70	10
Phoenix, AZ MSA	66	11
Detroit – Ann Arbor, MI CMSA	64	12
Boston – Lawrence – Salem, MA – NH CMSA	62	13
Oklahoma City, OK MSA	61	14
Sharon, PA MSA	58	15
Baltimore, MD MSA	57	16
Columbia, MO MSA	57	16
Fort Wayne, IN MSA	53	17
Columbus, OH MSA	50	18

[Continued]

★1421★

Top 25 MSAs For Employment As Auctioneers, 1990: Men

[Continued]

MSA/CMSA	Employees per 100,000 pop.	Rank
Kansas City, MO – KS MSA	50	18
Cleveland – Akron – Lorain, OH CMSA	49	19
Pittsburgh – Beaver Valley, PA CMSA	48	20
St. Louis, MO – IL MSA	47	21
Salt Lake City – Ogden, UT MSA	47	21
Cincinnati – Hamilton, OH – KY – IN CMSA	46	22

Source: U.S. Department of Commerce, Bureau of the Census, Data User Services Division, *1990 Census of Population and Housing, Equal Employment Opportunity File, CD-90-EE0-1, January 1993,* CD-ROM.

★1422★

Occupations, By Race/Sex

Top 25 MSAs For Employment As Auctioneers, 1990: Women

MSA/CMSA	Employees per 100,000 pop.	Rank
Austin, TX MSA	90	1
Washington, DC – MD – VA MSA	53	2
San Francisco – Oakland – San Jose, CA CMSA	46	3
Los Angeles – Anaheim – Riverside, CA CMSA	30	4
Chicago – Gary – Lake County, IL – IN – WI CMSA	25	5
Miami – Fort Lauderdale, FL CMSA	19	6
Reading, PA MSA	19	6
Boston – Lawrence – Salem, MA – NH CMSA	18	7
Indianapolis, IN MSA	18	7
Pittsburgh – Beaver Valley, PA CMSA	18	7
Billings, MT MSA	17	8
Detroit – Ann Arbor, MI CMSA	17	8
Davenport – Rock Island – Moline, IA – IL MSA	17	8
Orlando, FL MSA	16	9
Philadelphia – Wilmington – Trenton, PA – NJ – DE – MD CMSA	15	10
San Antonio, TX MSA	13	11
Sharon, PA MSA	13	11
Atlanta, GA MSA	12	12
Canton, OH MSA	11	13
Youngstown – Warren, OH MSA	11	13
Allentown – Bethlehem – Easton, PA – NJ MSA	10	14
Bradenton, FL MSA	10	14
Greensboro – Winston-Salem – High Point, NC MSA	10	14

[Continued]

★1422★

Top 25 MSAs For Employment As Auctioneers, 1990: Women

[Continued]

MSA/CMSA	Employees per 100,000 pop.	Rank
Knoxville, TN MSA	10	14
Lancaster, PA MSA	10	14

Source: U.S. Department of Commerce, Bureau of the Census, Data User Services Division, *1990 Census of Population and Housing, Equal Employment Opportunity File, CD-90-EE0-1, January 1993,* CD-ROM.

★1423★

Occupations, By Race/Sex

Top 25 MSAs For Employment As Authors, 1990: Men

MSA/CMSA	Employees per 100,000 pop.	Rank
Indianapolis, IN MSA	8,469	1
New York – Northern New Jersey – Long Island, NY – NJ – CT CMSA	8,109	2
San Francisco – Oakland – San Jose, CA CMSA	3,235	3
Washington, DC – MD – VA MSA	2,996	4
Chicago – Gary – Lake County, IL – IN – WI CMSA	1,572	5
Boston – Lawrence – Salem, MA – NH CMSA	1,449	6
Philadelphia – Wilmington – Trenton, PA – NJ – DE – MD CMSA	1,091	7
Minneapolis – St. Paul, MN – WI MSA	921	8
Seattle – Tacoma, WA CMSA	870	9
Dallas – Fort Worth, TX CMSA	801	10
San Diego, CA MSA	670	11
Detroit – Ann Arbor, MI CMSA	643	12
Atlanta, GA MSA	625	13
Denver – Boulder, CO CMSA	581	14
Phoenix, AZ MSA	560	15
Houston – Galveston – Brazoria, TX CMSA	509	16
Miami – Fort Lauderdale, FL CMSA	485	17
Austin, TX MSA	416	18
Portland – Vancouver, OR – WA CMSA	388	19
Pittsburgh – Beaver Valley, PA CMSA	350	20
Raleigh – Durham, NC MSA	337	21
Tampa – St. Petersburg – Clearwater, FL MSA	297	22
Baltimore, MD MSA	295	23
St. Louis, MO – IL MSA	291	24
Cleveland – Akron – Lorain, OH CMSA	272	25

Source: U.S. Department of Commerce, Bureau of the Census, Data User Services Division, *1990 Census of Population and Housing, Equal Employment Opportunity File, CD-90-EE0-1, January 1993,* CD-ROM.

★1424★

Occupations, By Race/Sex

Top 25 MSAs For Employment As Authors, 1990: Women

MSA/CMSA	Employees per 100,000 pop.	Rank
Indianapolis, IN MSA	7,887	1
Los Angeles – Anaheim – Riverside, CA CMSA	5,063	2
San Francisco – Oakland – San Jose, CA CMSA	2,953	3
Washington, DC – MD – VA MSA	2,861	4
Chicago – Gary – Lake County, IL – IN – WI CMSA	2,045	5
Boston – Lawrence – Salem, MA – NH CMSA	1,629	6
Philadelphia – Wilmington – Trenton, PA – NJ – DE – MD CMSA	1,380	7
Seattle – Tacoma, WA CMSA	940	8
Minneapolis – St. Paul, MN – WI MSA	914	9
Dallas – Fort Worth, TX CMSA	872	10
Denver – Boulder, CO CMSA	834	11
San Diego, CA MSA	764	12
Atlanta, GA MSA	637	13
Detroit – Ann Arbor, MI CMSA	582	14
Houston – Galveston – Brazoria, TX CMSA	548	15
Miami – Fort Lauderdale, FL CMSA	487	16
St. Louis, MO – IL MSA	481	17
Sacramento, CA MSA	445	18
Portland – Vancouver, OR – WA CMSA	437	19
Baltimore, MD MSA	420	20
Phoenix, AZ MSA	406	21
Kansas City, MO – KS MSA	398	22
Cleveland – Akron – Lorain, OH CMSA	382	23
Austin, TX MSA	319	24
Cincinnati – Hamilton, OH – KY – IN CMSA	317	25

Source: U.S. Department of Commerce, Bureau of the Census, Data User Services Division, *1990 Census of Population and Housing, Equal Employment Opportunity File, CD-90-EE0-1, January 1993,* CD-ROM.

★1425★

Occupations, By Race/Sex

Top 25 MSAs For Employment As Baggage Porters and Bellhops, 1990: Men

MSA/CMSA	Employees per 100,000 pop.	Rank
Sacramento, CA MSA	3,051	1
Los Angeles – Anaheim – Riverside, CA CMSA	2,283	2
Miami – Fort Lauderdale, FL CMSA	1,716	3
Chicago – Gary – Lake County, IL – IN – WI CMSA	1,438	4

[Continued]

★1425★
Top 25 MSAs For Employment As Baggage Porters and Bellhops, 1990: Men
[Continued]

MSA/CMSA	Employees per 100,000 pop.	Rank
Dallas – Fort Worth, TX CMSA	1,372	5
Las Vegas, NV MSA	1,332	6
San Francisco – Oakland – San Jose, CA CMSA	1,255	7
Washington, DC – MD – VA MSA	961	8
Orlando, FL MSA	923	9
Honolulu, HI MSA	871	10
Atlanta, GA MSA	825	11
Phoenix, AZ MSA	790	12
Philadelphia – Wilmington – Trenton, PA – NJ – DE – MD CMSA	667	13
Detroit – Ann Arbor, MI CMSA	640	14
Houston – Galveston – Brazoria, TX CMSA	626	15
Denver – Boulder, CO CMSA	583	16
Minneapolis – St. Paul, MN – WI MSA	503	17
Pittsburgh – Beaver Valley, PA CMSA	491	18
St. Louis, MO – IL MSA	478	19
Tampa – St. Petersburg – Clearwater, FL MSA	450	20
San Diego, CA MSA	405	21
Boston – Lawrence – Salem, MA – NH CMSA	398	22
Seattle – Tacoma, WA CMSA	390	23
Salt Lake City – Ogden, UT MSA	381	24
New Orleans, LA MSA	379	25

Source: U.S. Department of Commerce, Bureau of the Census, Data User Services Division, *1990 Census of Population and Housing, Equal Employment Opportunity File, CD-90-EE0-1, January 1993,* CD-ROM.

★1426★
Occupations, By Race/Sex
Top 25 MSAs For Employment As Baggage Porters and Bellhops, 1990: Women

MSA/CMSA	Employees per 100,000 pop.	Rank
Milwaukee – Racine, WI CMSA	420	1
Los Angeles – Anaheim – Riverside, CA CMSA	278	2
Chicago – Gary – Lake County, IL – IN – WI CMSA	210	3
Las Vegas, NV MSA	178	4
Dallas – Fort Worth, TX CMSA	154	5
Atlanta, GA MSA	149	6
San Francisco – Oakland – San Jose, CA CMSA	137	7
Detroit – Ann Arbor, MI CMSA	114	8
Boston – Lawrence – Salem, MA – NH CMSA	112	9
Miami – Fort Lauderdale, FL CMSA	110	10

[Continued]

★1426★
Top 25 MSAs For Employment As Baggage Porters and Bellhops, 1990: Women
[Continued]

MSA/CMSA	Employees per 100,000 pop.	Rank
Seattle – Tacoma, WA CMSA	102	11
Orlando, FL MSA	93	12
Washington, DC – MD – VA MSA	90	13
Baltimore, MD MSA	81	14
Philadelphia – Wilmington – Trenton, PA – NJ – DE – MD CMSA	81	14
Honolulu, HI MSA	73	15
Atlantic City, NJ MSA	69	16
Nashville, TN MSA	60	17
Pittsburgh – Beaver Valley, PA CMSA	60	17
San Diego, CA MSA	58	18
Minneapolis – St. Paul, MN – WI MSA	57	19
Denver – Boulder, CO CMSA	56	20
Tampa – St. Petersburg – Clearwater, FL MSA	53	21
Houston – Galveston – Brazoria, TX CMSA	52	22
Kansas City, MO – KS MSA	50	23

Source: U.S. Department of Commerce, Bureau of the Census, Data User Services Division, *1990 Census of Population and Housing, Equal Employment Opportunity File, CD-90-EE0-1, January 1993,* CD-ROM.

★1427★
Occupations, By Race/Sex
Top 25 MSAs For Employment As Bakers, 1990: Men

MSA/CMSA	Employees per 100,000 pop.	Rank
Milwaukee – Racine, WI CMSA	10,177	1
Los Angeles – Anaheim – Riverside, CA CMSA	8,292	2
San Francisco – Oakland – San Jose, CA CMSA	3,601	3
Chicago – Gary – Lake County, IL – IN – WI CMSA	3,436	4
Philadelphia – Wilmington – Trenton, PA – NJ – DE – MD CMSA	2,814	5
Boston – Lawrence – Salem, MA – NH CMSA	2,028	6
Detroit – Ann Arbor, MI CMSA	1,779	7
Miami – Fort Lauderdale, FL CMSA	1,669	8
Houston – Galveston – Brazoria, TX CMSA	1,444	9
Seattle – Tacoma, WA CMSA	1,210	10
Washington, DC – MD – VA MSA	1,193	11
Dallas – Fort Worth, TX CMSA	1,134	12
Minneapolis – St. Paul, MN – WI MSA	1,130	13

[Continued]

★1427★

Top 25 MSAs For Employment As Bakers, 1990: Men
[Continued]

MSA/CMSA	Employees per 100,000 pop.	Rank
San Diego, CA MSA	947	14
Pittsburgh – Beaver Valley, PA CMSA	943	15
St. Louis, MO – IL MSA	938	16
Cleveland – Akron – Lorain, OH CMSA	927	17
Providence – Pawtucket – Fall River, RI – MA CMSA	806	18
Baltimore, MD MSA	693	19
Phoenix, AZ MSA	647	20
Atlanta, GA MSA	637	21
Denver – Boulder, CO CMSA	635	22
Portland – Vancouver, OR – WA CMSA	628	23
San Antonio, TX MSA	617	24
Buffalo – Niagara Falls, NY CMSA	611	25

Source: U.S. Department of Commerce, Bureau of the Census, Data User Services Division, 1990 Census of Population and Housing, Equal Employment Opportunity File, CD-90-EE0-1, January 1993, CD-ROM.

★1428★

Occupations, By Race/Sex

Top 25 MSAs For Employment As Bakers, 1990: Women

MSA/CMSA	Employees per 100,000 pop.	Rank
Cincinnati – Hamilton, OH – KY – IN CMSA	3,304	1
Los Angeles – Anaheim – Riverside, CA CMSA	3,256	2
Chicago – Gary – Lake County, IL – IN – WI CMSA	2,828	3
San Francisco – Oakland – San Jose, CA CMSA	1,725	4
Philadelphia – Wilmington – Trenton, PA – NJ – DE – MD CMSA	1,509	5
Detroit – Ann Arbor, MI CMSA	1,428	6
Boston – Lawrence – Salem, MA – NH CMSA	1,243	7
Houston – Galveston – Brazoria, TX CMSA	1,232	8
Pittsburgh – Beaver Valley, PA CMSA	1,020	9
Dallas – Fort Worth, TX CMSA	913	10
Atlanta, GA MSA	908	11
St. Louis, MO – IL MSA	837	12
Cleveland – Akron – Lorain, OH CMSA	821	13
Baltimore, MD MSA	791	14
Washington, DC – MD – VA MSA	789	15
Seattle – Tacoma, WA CMSA	756	16
Miami – Fort Lauderdale, FL CMSA	610	17

[Continued]

★1428★

Top 25 MSAs For Employment As Bakers, 1990: Women
[Continued]

MSA/CMSA	Employees per 100,000 pop.	Rank
Buffalo – Niagara Falls, NY CMSA	577	18
Denver – Boulder, CO CMSA	576	19
San Diego, CA MSA	571	20
Phoenix, AZ MSA	565	21
Portland – Vancouver, OR – WA CMSA	546	22
Minneapolis – St. Paul, MN – WI MSA	513	23
Sacramento, CA MSA	480	24
Rochester, NY MSA	475	25

Source: U.S. Department of Commerce, Bureau of the Census, Data User Services Division, 1990 Census of Population and Housing, Equal Employment Opportunity File, CD-90-EE0-1, January 1993, CD-ROM.

★1429★

Occupations, By Race/Sex

Top 25 MSAs For Employment As Barbers, 1990: Men

MSA/CMSA	Employees per 100,000 pop.	Rank
Jackson, MS MSA	4,498	1
Los Angeles – Anaheim – Riverside, CA CMSA	2,524	2
Chicago – Gary – Lake County, IL – IN – WI CMSA	2,088	3
Philadelphia – Wilmington – Trenton, PA – NJ – DE – MD CMSA	1,968	4
San Francisco – Oakland – San Jose, CA CMSA	1,450	5
Washington, DC – MD – VA MSA	1,187	6
Detroit – Ann Arbor, MI CMSA	1,088	7
Miami – Fort Lauderdale, FL CMSA	1,021	8
Houston – Galveston – Brazoria, TX CMSA	924	9
Boston – Lawrence – Salem, MA – NH CMSA	902	10
St. Louis, MO – IL MSA	859	11
Dallas – Fort Worth, TX CMSA	800	12
Atlanta, GA MSA	711	13
Pittsburgh – Beaver Valley, PA CMSA	694	14
Minneapolis – St. Paul, MN – WI MSA	667	15
Baltimore, MD MSA	645	16
Cleveland – Akron – Lorain, OH CMSA	633	17
Seattle – Tacoma, WA CMSA	616	18
Phoenix, AZ MSA	611	19
Cincinnati – Hamilton, OH – KY – IN CMSA	610	20
San Diego, CA MSA	533	21

[Continued]

★1429★

Top 25 MSAs For Employment As Barbers, 1990: Men
[Continued]

MSA/CMSA	Employees per 100,000 pop.	Rank
Kansas City, MO – KS MSA	519	22
Tampa – St. Petersburg – Clearwater, FL MSA	513	23
Denver – Boulder, CO CMSA	500	24
Columbus, OH MSA	457	25

Source: U.S. Department of Commerce, Bureau of the Census, Data User Services Division, *1990 Census of Population and Housing, Equal Employment Opportunity File, CD-90-EE0-1, January 1993,* CD-ROM.

★1430★
Occupations, By Race/Sex

Top 25 MSAs For Employment As Barbers, 1990: Women

MSA/CMSA	Employees per 100,000 pop.	Rank
Sarasota, FL MSA	926	1
New York – Northern New Jersey – Long Island, NY – NJ – CT CMSA	634	2
Dallas – Fort Worth, TX CMSA	487	3
San Francisco – Oakland – San Jose, CA CMSA	472	4
Chicago – Gary – Lake County, IL – IN – WI CMSA	430	5
Houston – Galveston – Brazoria, TX CMSA	337	6
Boston – Lawrence – Salem, MA – NH CMSA	310	7
Philadelphia – Wilmington – Trenton, PA – NJ – DE – MD CMSA	280	8
Honolulu, HI MSA	275	9
Oklahoma City, OK MSA	253	10
Miami – Fort Lauderdale, FL CMSA	250	11
Washington, DC – MD – VA MSA	250	11
Atlanta, GA MSA	244	12
Cleveland – Akron – Lorain, OH CMSA	242	13
Detroit – Ann Arbor, MI CMSA	240	14
Minneapolis – St. Paul, MN – WI MSA	238	15
Cincinnati – Hamilton, OH – KY – IN CMSA	217	16
Tampa – St. Petersburg – Clearwater, FL MSA	195	17
Seattle – Tacoma, WA CMSA	179	18
San Diego, CA MSA	175	19
Baltimore, MD MSA	156	20
Denver – Boulder, CO CMSA	152	21
Phoenix, AZ MSA	152	21

[Continued]

★1430★

Top 25 MSAs For Employment As Barbers, 1990: Women
[Continued]

MSA/CMSA	Employees per 100,000 pop.	Rank
Milwaukee – Racine, WI CMSA	148	22
Nashville, TN MSA	142	23

Source: U.S. Department of Commerce, Bureau of the Census, Data User Services Division, *1990 Census of Population and Housing, Equal Employment Opportunity File, CD-90-EE0-1, January 1993,* CD-ROM.

★1431★
Occupations, By Race/Sex

Top 25 MSAs For Employment As Bartenders, 1990: Men

MSA/CMSA	Employees per 100,000 pop.	Rank
Tucson, AZ MSA	13,448	1
Los Angeles – Anaheim – Riverside, CA CMSA	9,377	2
Chicago – Gary – Lake County, IL – IN – WI CMSA	6,155	3
San Francisco – Oakland – San Jose, CA CMSA	5,556	4
Philadelphia – Wilmington – Trenton, PA – NJ – DE – MD CMSA	4,437	5
Boston – Lawrence – Salem, MA – NH CMSA	4,146	6
Las Vegas, NV MSA	2,858	7
Miami – Fort Lauderdale, FL CMSA	2,813	8
Pittsburgh – Beaver Valley, PA CMSA	2,724	9
Dallas – Fort Worth, TX CMSA	2,536	10
San Diego, CA MSA	2,409	11
Milwaukee – Racine, WI CMSA	2,387	12
Minneapolis – St. Paul, MN – WI MSA	2,358	13
Washington, DC – MD – VA MSA	2,273	14
Detroit – Ann Arbor, MI CMSA	2,175	15
Houston – Galveston – Brazoria, TX CMSA	2,171	16
Seattle – Tacoma, WA CMSA	1,708	17
Atlanta, GA MSA	1,679	18
Phoenix, AZ MSA	1,620	19
Cleveland – Akron – Lorain, OH CMSA	1,572	20
St. Louis, MO – IL MSA	1,519	21
Tampa – St. Petersburg – Clearwater, FL MSA	1,478	22
Baltimore, MD MSA	1,367	23
New Orleans, LA MSA	1,312	24
Sacramento, CA MSA	1,306	25

Source: U.S. Department of Commerce, Bureau of the Census, Data User Services Division, *1990 Census of Population and Housing, Equal Employment Opportunity File, CD-90-EE0-1, January 1993,* CD-ROM.

★1432★
Occupations, By Race/Sex

Top 25 MSAs For Employment As Bartenders, 1990: Women

MSA/CMSA	Employees per 100,000 pop.	Rank
Tampa – St. Petersburg – Clearwater, FL MSA	5,992	1
New York – Northern New Jersey – Long Island, NY – NJ – CT CMSA	5,685	2
Chicago – Gary – Lake County, IL – IN – WI CMSA	5,440	3
Detroit – Ann Arbor, MI CMSA	3,097	4
San Francisco – Oakland – San Jose, CA CMSA	2,908	5
Seattle – Tacoma, WA CMSA	2,860	6
Philadelphia – Wilmington – Trenton, PA – NJ – DE – MD CMSA	2,722	7
Boston – Lawrence – Salem, MA – NH CMSA	2,390	8
Miami – Fort Lauderdale, FL CMSA	2,139	9
Dallas – Fort Worth, TX CMSA	2,085	10
Tampa – St. Petersburg – Clearwater, FL MSA	2,023	11
Milwaukee – Racine, WI CMSA	1,909	12
Houston – Galveston – Brazoria, TX CMSA	1,804	13
Cleveland – Akron – Lorain, OH CMSA	1,801	14
St. Louis, MO – IL MSA	1,775	15
Pittsburgh – Beaver Valley, PA CMSA	1,741	16
Phoenix, AZ MSA	1,734	17
Denver – Boulder, CO CMSA	1,711	18
Portland – Vancouver, OR – WA CMSA	1,710	19
Washington, DC – MD – VA MSA	1,572	20
San Diego, CA MSA	1,523	21
Minneapolis – St. Paul, MN – WI MSA	1,431	22
Baltimore, MD MSA	1,304	23
Atlanta, GA MSA	1,232	24
Orlando, FL MSA	1,196	25

Source: U.S. Department of Commerce, Bureau of the Census, Data User Services Division, *1990 Census of Population and Housing, Equal Employment Opportunity File, CD-90-EE0-1, January 1993,* CD-ROM.

★1433★
Occupations, By Race/Sex

Top 25 MSAs For Employment As Biological and Life Scientists, 1990: Men

MSA/CMSA	Employees per 100,000 pop.	Rank
Shreveport, LA MSA	2,141	1
San Francisco – Oakland – San Jose, CA CMSA	2,033	2
Washington, DC – MD – VA MSA	1,741	3
Los Angeles – Anaheim – Riverside, CA CMSA	1,470	4
Philadelphia – Wilmington – Trenton, PA – NJ – DE – MD CMSA	1,391	5
Boston – Lawrence – Salem, MA – NH CMSA	1,127	6
Chicago – Gary – Lake County, IL – IN – WI CMSA	1,006	7
San Diego, CA MSA	727	8
Seattle – Tacoma, WA CMSA	710	9
Baltimore, MD MSA	556	10
Raleigh – Durham, NC MSA	472	11
Denver – Boulder, CO CMSA	463	12
Sacramento, CA MSA	435	13
Atlanta, GA MSA	430	14
Portland – Vancouver, OR – WA CMSA	407	15
Detroit – Ann Arbor, MI CMSA	404	16
St. Louis, MO – IL MSA	379	17
Madison, WI MSA	361	18
Houston – Galveston – Brazoria, TX CMSA	358	19
Minneapolis – St. Paul, MN – WI MSA	324	20
Gainesville, FL MSA	321	21
Indianapolis, IN MSA	300	22
Dallas – Fort Worth, TX CMSA	251	23
Albany – Schenectady – Troy, NY MSA	239	24
Cincinnati – Hamilton, OH – KY – IN CMSA	238	25

Source: U.S. Department of Commerce, Bureau of the Census, Data User Services Division, *1990 Census of Population and Housing, Equal Employment Opportunity File, CD-90-EE0-1, January 1993,* CD-ROM.

★1434★
Occupations, By Race/Sex

Top 25 MSAs For Employment As Biological and Life Scientists, 1990: Women

MSA/CMSA	Employees per 100,000 pop.	Rank
Kansas City, MO – KS MSA	2,101	1
San Francisco – Oakland – San Jose, CA CMSA	1,575	2
Washington, DC – MD – VA MSA	1,412	3
Los Angeles – Anaheim – Riverside, CA CMSA	1,218	4
Philadelphia – Wilmington – Trenton, PA – NJ – DE – MD CMSA	1,173	5

[Continued]

★1434★

Top 25 MSAs For Employment As Biological and Life Scientists, 1990: Women
[Continued]

MSA/CMSA	Employees per 100,000 pop.	Rank
Boston – Lawrence – Salem, MA – NH CMSA	1,087	6
Chicago – Gary – Lake County, IL – IN – WI CMSA	825	7
Seattle – Tacoma, WA CMSA	611	8
San Diego, CA MSA	529	9
Detroit – Ann Arbor, MI CMSA	490	10
Baltimore, MD MSA	439	11
Raleigh – Durham, NC MSA	425	12
St. Louis, MO – IL MSA	363	13
Minneapolis – St. Paul, MN – WI MSA	339	14
Madison, WI MSA	331	15
Dallas – Fort Worth, TX CMSA	318	16
Sacramento, CA MSA	294	17
Atlanta, GA MSA	287	18
Portland – Vancouver, OR – WA CMSA	268	19
Miami – Fort Lauderdale, FL CMSA	265	20
Houston – Galveston – Brazoria, TX CMSA	263	21
Denver – Boulder, CO CMSA	261	22
Cincinnati – Hamilton, OH – KY – IN CMSA	220	23
Gainesville, FL MSA	214	24
Providence – Pawtucket – Fall River, RI – MA CMSA	183	25

Source: U.S. Department of Commerce, Bureau of the Census, Data User Services Division, *1990 Census of Population and Housing, Equal Employment Opportunity File, CD-90-EE0-1, January 1993,* CD-ROM.

★1435★

Occupations, By Race/Sex

Top 25 MSAs For Employment As Biological Science Teachers, 1990: Men

MSA/CMSA	Employees per 100,000 pop.	Rank
State College, PA MSA	256	1
Los Angeles – Anaheim – Riverside, CA CMSA	169	2
Boston – Lawrence – Salem, MA – NH CMSA	119	3
Columbus, OH MSA	108	4
San Francisco – Oakland – San Jose, CA CMSA	81	5
Philadelphia – Wilmington – Trenton, PA – NJ – DE – MD CMSA	70	6
Dallas – Fort Worth, TX CMSA	70	6
Austin, TX MSA	69	7
Raleigh – Durham, NC MSA	68	8
San Diego, CA MSA	63	9

[Continued]

★1435★

Top 25 MSAs For Employment As Biological Science Teachers, 1990: Men
[Continued]

MSA/CMSA	Employees per 100,000 pop.	Rank
Washington, DC – MD – VA MSA	56	10
Sacramento, CA MSA	49	11
Baltimore, MD MSA	47	12
Jackson, MS MSA	42	13
Providence – Pawtucket – Fall River, RI – MA CMSA	41	14
Rochester, NY MSA	39	15
St. Louis, MO – IL MSA	37	16
Minneapolis – St. Paul, MN – WI MSA	36	17
Louisville, KY – IN MSA	34	18
Omaha, NE – IA MSA	34	18
Santa Barbara – Santa Maria – Lompoc, CA MSA	33	19
Tucson, AZ MSA	33	19
Memphis, TN – AR – MS MSA	31	20
Milwaukee – Racine, WI CMSA	31	20
Portsmouth – Dover – Rochester, NH – ME MSA	31	20

Source: U.S. Department of Commerce, Bureau of the Census, Data User Services Division, *1990 Census of Population and Housing, Equal Employment Opportunity File, CD-90-EE0-1, January 1993,* CD-ROM.

★1436★

Occupations, By Race/Sex

Top 25 MSAs For Employment As Biological Science Teachers, 1990: Women

MSA/CMSA	Employees per 100,000 pop.	Rank
Alexandria, LA MSA	137	1
Boston – Lawrence – Salem, MA – NH CMSA	75	2
Los Angeles – Anaheim – Riverside, CA CMSA	74	3
Washington, DC – MD – VA MSA	71	4
Philadelphia – Wilmington – Trenton, PA – NJ – DE – MD CMSA	55	5
Columbus, OH MSA	49	6
Detroit – Ann Arbor, MI CMSA	47	7
Madison, WI MSA	47	7
Chicago – Gary – Lake County, IL – IN – WI CMSA	36	8
Baltimore, MD MSA	35	9
San Francisco – Oakland – San Jose, CA CMSA	35	9
Providence – Pawtucket – Fall River, RI – MA CMSA	33	10
New Orleans, LA MSA	32	11
Columbia, SC MSA	30	12
Raleigh – Durham, NC MSA	29	13
New Haven – Meriden, CT MSA	28	14
San Diego, CA MSA	28	14

[Continued]

★1436★

Top 25 MSAs For Employment As Biological Science Teachers, 1990: Women

[Continued]

MSA/CMSA	Employees per 100,000 pop.	Rank
Tulsa, OK MSA	28	14
Dallas – Fort Worth, TX CMSA	24	15
Seattle – Tacoma, WA CMSA	24	15
Cleveland – Akron – Lorain, OH CMSA	23	16
Jacksonville, FL MSA	23	16
Oklahoma City, OK MSA	23	16
Provo – Orem, UT MSA	21	17
Tallahassee, FL MSA	21	17

Source: U.S. Department of Commerce, Bureau of the Census, Data User Services Division, *1990 Census of Population and Housing, Equal Employment Opportunity File, CD-90-EE0-1, January 1993,* CD-ROM.

★1437★

Occupations, By Race/Sex

Top 25 MSAs For Employment As Bridge, Lock, and Lighthouse Tenders, 1990: Men

MSA/CMSA	Employees per 100,000 pop.	Rank
Honolulu, HI MSA	515	1
Chicago – Gary – Lake County, IL – IN – WI CMSA	146	2
Miami – Fort Lauderdale, FL CMSA	122	3
Norfolk – Virginia Beach – Newport News, VA MSA	117	4
Tampa – St. Petersburg – Clearwater, FL MSA	104	5
Houma – Thibodaux, LA MSA	91	6
Jacksonville, FL MSA	90	7
Pittsburgh – Beaver Valley, PA CMSA	85	8
Detroit – Ann Arbor, MI CMSA	77	9
New Orleans, LA MSA	65	10
Cleveland – Akron – Lorain, OH CMSA	60	11
Huntington – Ashland, WV – KY – OH MSA	60	11
San Francisco – Oakland – San Jose, CA CMSA	52	12
West Palm Beach – Boca Raton – Delray Beach, FL MSA	50	13
Minneapolis – St. Paul, MN – WI MSA	50	13
Portland – Vancouver, OR – WA CMSA	50	13
Atlantic City, NJ MSA	49	14
Seattle – Tacoma, WA CMSA	49	14
Milwaukee – Racine, WI CMSA	47	15
Sarasota, FL MSA	46	16
Cincinnati – Hamilton, OH – KY – IN CMSA	41	17
Fort Myers – Cape CoraL, Fl MSA	40	18

[Continued]

★1437★

Top 25 MSAs For Employment As Bridge, Lock, and Lighthouse Tenders, 1990: Men

[Continued]

MSA/CMSA	Employees per 100,000 pop.	Rank
Melbourne – Titusville – Palm Bay, FL MSA	40	18
Boston – Lawrence – Salem, MA – NH CMSA	39	19
Albany – Schenectady – Troy, NY MSA	35	20

Source: U.S. Department of Commerce, Bureau of the Census, Data User Services Division, *1990 Census of Population and Housing, Equal Employment Opportunity File, CD-90-EE0-1, January 1993,* CD-ROM.

★1438★

Occupations, By Race/Sex

Top 25 MSAs For Employment As Bridge, Lock, and Lighthouse Tenders, 1990: Women

MSA/CMSA	Employees per 100,000 pop.	Rank
Philadelphia – Wilmington – Trenton, PA – NJ – DE – MD CMSA	47	1
New Orleans, LA MSA	45	2
Miami – Fort Lauderdale, FL CMSA	34	3
Houma – Thibodaux, LA MSA	27	4
Pittsburgh – Beaver Valley, PA CMSA	25	5
Chicago – Gary – Lake County, IL – IN – WI CMSA	24	6
Dallas – Fort Worth, TX CMSA	21	7
Jacksonville, FL MSA	19	8
Wilmington, NC MSA	19	8
Detroit – Ann Arbor, MI CMSA	18	9
Fort Pierce, FL MSA	16	10
Cleveland – Akron – Lorain, OH CMSA	15	11
Houston – Galveston – Brazoria, TX CMSA	15	11
Tampa – St. Petersburg – Clearwater, FL MSA	15	11
Greensboro – Winston-Salem – High Point, NC MSA	14	12
Rochester, NY MSA	13	13
Atlanta, GA MSA	12	14
Charleston, SC MSA	12	14
Milwaukee – Racine, WI CMSA	12	14
Melbourne – Titusville – Palm Bay, FL MSA	12	14
New London – Norwich, CT – RI MSA	12	14
San Francisco – Oakland – San Jose, CA CMSA	12	14
Biloxi – Gulfport, MS MSA	11	15

[Continued]

★1438★

Top 25 MSAs For Employment As Bridge, Lock, and Lighthouse Tenders, 1990: Women
[Continued]

MSA/CMSA	Employees per 100,000 pop.	Rank
Panama City, FL MSA	11	15
Boston – Lawrence – Salem, MA – NH CMSA	10	16

Source: U.S. Department of Commerce, Bureau of the Census, Data User Services Division, *1990 Census of Population and Housing, Equal Employment Opportunity File, CD-90-EE0-1, January 1993,* CD-ROM.

★1439★
Occupations, By Race/Sex

Top 25 MSAs For Employment As Bus Drivers, 1990: Men

MSA/CMSA	Employees per 100,000 pop.	Rank
Milwaukee – Racine, WI CMSA	29,735	1
Los Angeles – Anaheim – Riverside, CA CMSA	11,088	2
Chicago – Gary – Lake County, IL – IN – WI CMSA	9,742	3
Philadelphia – Wilmington – Trenton, PA – NJ – DE – MD CMSA	7,159	4
San Francisco – Oakland – San Jose, CA CMSA	4,943	5
Washington, DC – MD – VA MSA	4,904	6
Boston – Lawrence – Salem, MA – NH CMSA	3,874	7
Minneapolis – St. Paul, MN – WI MSA	3,806	8
Pittsburgh – Beaver Valley, PA CMSA	3,249	9
Seattle – Tacoma, WA CMSA	2,975	10
Dallas – Fort Worth, TX CMSA	2,734	11
Detroit – Ann Arbor, MI CMSA	2,669	12
Houston – Galveston – Brazoria, TX CMSA	2,519	13
Baltimore, MD MSA	2,371	14
Cleveland – Akron – Lorain, OH CMSA	2,365	15
St. Louis, MO – IL MSA	2,327	16
Miami – Fort Lauderdale, FL CMSA	2,237	17
Atlanta, GA MSA	2,196	18
Milwaukee – Racine, WI CMSA	2,108	19
San Diego, CA MSA	2,012	20
Phoenix, AZ MSA	1,884	21
Denver – Boulder, CO CMSA	1,872	22
Portland – Vancouver, OR – WA CMSA	1,582	23
Kansas City, MO – KS MSA	1,566	24
New Orleans, LA MSA	1,564	25

Source: U.S. Department of Commerce, Bureau of the Census, Data User Services Division, *1990 Census of Population and Housing, Equal Employment Opportunity File, CD-90-EE0-1, January 1993,* CD-ROM.

★1440★
Occupations, By Race/Sex

Top 25 MSAs For Employment As Bus Drivers, 1990: Women

MSA/CMSA	Employees per 100,000 pop.	Rank
Indianapolis, IN MSA	14,048	1
Los Angeles – Anaheim – Riverside, CA CMSA	6,792	2
Chicago – Gary – Lake County, IL – IN – WI CMSA	5,967	3
Philadelphia – Wilmington – Trenton, PA – NJ – DE – MD CMSA	5,716	4
Washington, DC – MD – VA MSA	4,566	5
Detroit – Ann Arbor, MI CMSA	4,331	6
Houston – Galveston – Brazoria, TX CMSA	3,789	7
San Francisco – Oakland – San Jose, CA CMSA	3,455	8
Boston – Lawrence – Salem, MA – NH CMSA	3,310	9
Atlanta, GA MSA	3,230	10
Cleveland – Akron – Lorain, OH CMSA	2,917	11
St. Louis, MO – IL MSA	2,609	12
Seattle – Tacoma, WA CMSA	2,552	13
Norfolk – Virginia Beach – Newport News, VA MSA	2,327	14
Baltimore, MD MSA	2,127	15
Miami – Fort Lauderdale, FL CMSA	2,000	16
Dallas – Fort Worth, TX CMSA	1,979	17
Pittsburgh – Beaver Valley, PA CMSA	1,803	18
Cincinnati – Hamilton, OH – KY – IN CMSA	1,713	19
Minneapolis – St. Paul, MN – WI MSA	1,675	20
Columbus, OH MSA	1,619	21
Portland – Vancouver, OR – WA CMSA	1,517	22
Buffalo – Niagara Falls, NY CMSA	1,485	23
Rochester, NY MSA	1,479	24
Tampa – St. Petersburg – Clearwater, FL MSA	1,446	25

Source: U.S. Department of Commerce, Bureau of the Census, Data User Services Division, *1990 Census of Population and Housing, Equal Employment Opportunity File, CD-90-EE0-1, January 1993,* CD-ROM.

★1441★

Occupations, By Race/Sex

Top 25 MSAs For Employment As Business and Promotion Agents, 1990: Men

MSA/CMSA	Employees per 100,000 pop.	Rank
Milwaukee – Racine, WI CMSA	2,629	1
New York – Northern New Jersey – Long Island, NY – NJ – CT CMSA	2,301	2
Chicago – Gary – Lake County, IL – IN – WI CMSA	726	3
San Francisco – Oakland – San Jose, CA CMSA	686	4
Washington, DC – MD – VA MSA	398	5
Miami – Fort Lauderdale, FL CMSA	394	6
Boston – Lawrence – Salem, MA – NH CMSA	364	7
Dallas – Fort Worth, TX CMSA	351	8
San Diego, CA MSA	331	9
Nashville, TN MSA	273	10
Philadelphia – Wilmington – Trenton, PA – NJ – DE – MD CMSA	263	11
Atlanta, GA MSA	248	12
Detroit – Ann Arbor, MI CMSA	235	13
Houston – Galveston – Brazoria, TX CMSA	234	14
Denver – Boulder, CO CMSA	233	15
Minneapolis – St. Paul, MN – WI MSA	232	16
Phoenix, AZ MSA	229	17
Cleveland – Akron – Lorain, OH CMSA	215	18
Seattle – Tacoma, WA CMSA	197	19
Cincinnati – Hamilton, OH – KY – IN CMSA	193	20
Sacramento, CA MSA	188	21
Portland – Vancouver, OR – WA CMSA	173	22
Baltimore, MD MSA	159	23
Kansas City, MO – KS MSA	147	24
Orlando, FL MSA	140	25

Source: U.S. Department of Commerce, Bureau of the Census, Data User Services Division, 1990 Census of Population and Housing, Equal Employment Opportunity File, CD-90-EE0-1, January 1993, CD-ROM.

★1442★

Occupations, By Race/Sex

Top 25 MSAs For Employment As Business and Promotion Agents, 1990: Women

MSA/CMSA	Employees per 100,000 pop.	Rank
Milwaukee – Racine, WI CMSA	2,746	1
Los Angeles – Anaheim – Riverside, CA CMSA	1,809	2
Chicago – Gary – Lake County, IL – IN – WI CMSA	836	3
San Francisco – Oakland – San Jose, CA CMSA	619	4
Washington, DC – MD – VA MSA	611	5
Boston – Lawrence – Salem, MA – NH CMSA	372	6
Philadelphia – Wilmington – Trenton, PA – NJ – DE – MD CMSA	336	7
Dallas – Fort Worth, TX CMSA	328	8
Atlanta, GA MSA	322	9
Houston – Galveston – Brazoria, TX CMSA	309	10
Seattle – Tacoma, WA CMSA	273	11
Miami – Fort Lauderdale, FL CMSA	259	12
Detroit – Ann Arbor, MI CMSA	235	13
Denver – Boulder, CO CMSA	210	14
Minneapolis – St. Paul, MN – WI MSA	198	15
Phoenix, AZ MSA	188	16
San Diego, CA MSA	176	17
Las Vegas, NV MSA	160	18
Indianapolis, IN MSA	140	19
Portland – Vancouver, OR – WA CMSA	135	20
Baltimore, MD MSA	133	21
Kansas City, MO – KS MSA	132	22
Nashville, TN MSA	127	23
Norfolk – Virginia Beach – Newport News, VA MSA	116	24
Milwaukee – Racine, WI CMSA	114	25

Source: U.S. Department of Commerce, Bureau of the Census, Data User Services Division, 1990 Census of Population and Housing, Equal Employment Opportunity File, CD-90-EE0-1, January 1993, CD-ROM.

★1443★

Occupations, By Race/Sex

Top 25 MSAs For Employment As Business, Commerce, and Marketing Teachers, 1990: Men

MSA/CMSA	Employees per 100,000 pop.	Rank
Charleston, SC MSA	117	1
Washington, DC – MD – VA MSA	91	2
Philadelphia – Wilmington – Trenton, PA – NJ – DE – MD CMSA	85	3
Boston – Lawrence – Salem, MA – NH CMSA	55	4

[Continued]

★1443★

Top 25 MSAs For Employment As Business, Commerce, and Marketing Teachers, 1990: Men
[Continued]

MSA/CMSA	Employees per 100,000 pop.	Rank
San Francisco – Oakland – San Jose, CA CMSA	51	5
Detroit – Ann Arbor, MI CMSA	45	6
Rochester, NY MSA	36	7
Toledo, OH MSA	36	7
Los Angeles – Anaheim – Riverside, CA CMSA	36	7
Mobile, AL MSA	32	8
Chicago – Gary – Lake County, IL – IN – WI CMSA	31	9
Columbus, OH MSA	30	10
Atlanta, GA MSA	29	11
Dallas – Fort Worth, TX CMSA	26	12
San Antonio, TX MSA	26	12
St. Louis, MO – IL MSA	25	13
Houston – Galveston – Brazoria, TX CMSA	24	14
Seattle – Tacoma, WA CMSA	24	14
Omaha, NE – IA MSA	23	15
Phoenix, AZ MSA	23	15
West Palm Beach – Boca Raton – Delray Beach, FL MSA	22	16
Buffalo – Niagara Falls, NY CMSA	21	17
Champaign – Urbana – Rantoul, IL MSA	20	18
South Bend – Mishawaka, IN MSA	19	19
Oklahoma City, OK MSA	19	19

Source: U.S. Department of Commerce, Bureau of the Census, Data User Services Division, *1990 Census of Population and Housing, Equal Employment Opportunity File, CD-90-EE0-1, January 1993*, CD-ROM.

★1444★
Occupations, By Race/Sex

Top 25 MSAs For Employment As Business, Commerce, and Marketing Teachers, 1990: Women

MSA/CMSA	Employees per 100,000 pop.	Rank
Columbia, SC MSA	116	1
Los Angeles – Anaheim – Riverside, CA CMSA	96	2
Houston – Galveston – Brazoria, TX CMSA	75	3
Chicago – Gary – Lake County, IL – IN – WI CMSA	73	4
Washington, DC – MD – VA MSA	67	5
Philadelphia – Wilmington – Trenton, PA – NJ – DE – MD CMSA	65	6
San Francisco – Oakland – San Jose, CA CMSA	59	7
Dallas – Fort Worth, TX CMSA	46	8

[Continued]

★1444★

Top 25 MSAs For Employment As Business, Commerce, and Marketing Teachers, 1990: Women
[Continued]

MSA/CMSA	Employees per 100,000 pop.	Rank
Boston – Lawrence – Salem, MA – NH CMSA	44	9
San Antonio, TX MSA	37	10
Cleveland – Akron – Lorain, OH CMSA	36	11
Columbus, OH MSA	35	12
Detroit – Ann Arbor, MI CMSA	35	12
Atlanta, GA MSA	34	13
Pittsburgh – Beaver Valley, PA CMSA	33	14
Seattle – Tacoma, WA CMSA	33	14
Birmingham, AL MSA	32	15
Tampa – St. Petersburg – Clearwater, FL MSA	32	15
San Diego, CA MSA	30	16
Tucson, AZ MSA	29	17
Rochester, NY MSA	28	18
Sacramento, CA MSA	27	19
Milwaukee – Racine, WI CMSA	26	20
Erie, PA MSA	25	21
Baltimore, MD MSA	23	22

Source: U.S. Department of Commerce, Bureau of the Census, Data User Services Division, *1990 Census of Population and Housing, Equal Employment Opportunity File, CD-90-EE0-1, January 1993*, CD-ROM.

★1445★
Occupations, By Race/Sex

Top 25 MSAs For Employment As Butchers and Meat Cutters, 1990: Men

MSA/CMSA	Employees per 100,000 pop.	Rank
Knoxville, TN MSA	13,539	1
Los Angeles – Anaheim – Riverside, CA CMSA	10,719	2
Chicago – Gary – Lake County, IL – IN – WI CMSA	7,224	3
San Francisco – Oakland – San Jose, CA CMSA	4,649	4
Philadelphia – Wilmington – Trenton, PA – NJ – DE – MD CMSA	4,514	5
Detroit – Ann Arbor, MI CMSA	3,493	6
Miami – Fort Lauderdale, FL CMSA	2,923	7
Boston – Lawrence – Salem, MA – NH CMSA	2,703	8
Houston – Galveston – Brazoria, TX CMSA	2,698	9
Dallas – Fort Worth, TX CMSA	2,340	10
Washington, DC – MD – VA MSA	1,958	11
Minneapolis – St. Paul, MN – WI MSA	1,898	12

[Continued]

★1445★

Top 25 MSAs For Employment As Butchers and Meat Cutters, 1990: Men

[Continued]

MSA/CMSA	Employees per 100,000 pop.	Rank
St. Louis, MO – IL MSA	1,855	13
Cleveland – Akron – Lorain, OH CMSA	1,816	14
Baltimore, MD MSA	1,804	15
Pittsburgh – Beaver Valley, PA CMSA	1,752	16
Atlanta, GA MSA	1,619	17
Tampa – St. Petersburg – Clearwater, FL MSA	1,610	18
Seattle – Tacoma, WA CMSA	1,575	19
Phoenix, AZ MSA	1,539	20
Cincinnati – Hamilton, OH – KY – IN CMSA	1,534	21
Denver – Boulder, CO CMSA	1,513	22
Omaha, NE – IA MSA	1,503	23
San Antonio, TX MSA	1,482	24
Sioux City, IA – NE MSA	1,481	25

Source: U.S. Department of Commerce, Bureau of the Census, Data User Services Division, 1990 Census of Population and Housing, Equal Employment Opportunity File, CD-90-EE0-1, January 1993, CD-ROM.

★1446★

Occupations, By Race/Sex

Top 25 MSAs For Employment As Butchers and Meat Cutters, 1990: Women

MSA/CMSA	Employees per 100,000 pop.	Rank
Portland – Vancouver, OR – WA CMSA	1,183	1
Chicago – Gary – Lake County, IL – IN – WI CMSA	1,146	2
Los Angeles – Anaheim – Riverside, CA CMSA	896	3
New York – Northern New Jersey – Long Island, NY – NJ – CT CMSA	854	4
Sioux City, IA – NE MSA	621	5
Detroit – Ann Arbor, MI CMSA	599	6
Atlanta, GA MSA	530	7
San Francisco – Oakland – San Jose, CA CMSA	417	8
Birmingham, AL MSA	412	9
Fort Smith, AR – OK MSA	411	10
Pittsburgh – Beaver Valley, PA CMSA	400	11
Greeley, CO MSA	394	12
Seattle – Tacoma, WA CMSA	393	13
Amarillo, TX MSA	381	14
Houston – Galveston – Brazoria, TX CMSA	375	15
Jackson, MS MSA	375	15
Baltimore, MD MSA	357	16
Cleveland – Akron – Lorain, OH CMSA	348	17

[Continued]

★1446★

Top 25 MSAs For Employment As Butchers and Meat Cutters, 1990: Women

[Continued]

MSA/CMSA	Employees per 100,000 pop.	Rank
Modesto, CA MSA	326	18
Davenport – Rock Island – Moline, IA – IL MSA	316	19
New Orleans, LA MSA	316	19
Dallas – Fort Worth, TX CMSA	311	20
Miami – Fort Lauderdale, FL CMSA	308	21
St. Louis, MO – IL MSA	286	22
Boston – Lawrence – Salem, MA – NH CMSA	280	23

Source: U.S. Department of Commerce, Bureau of the Census, Data User Services Division, 1990 Census of Population and Housing, Equal Employment Opportunity File, CD-90-EE0-1, January 1993, CD-ROM.

★1447★

Occupations, By Race/Sex

Top 25 MSAs For Employment As Cabinet Makers and Bench Carpenters, 1990: Men

MSA/CMSA	Employees per 100,000 pop.	Rank
Denver – Boulder, CO CMSA	4,575	1
New York – Northern New Jersey – Long Island, NY – NJ – CT CMSA	4,394	2
San Francisco – Oakland – San Jose, CA CMSA	1,923	3
Chicago – Gary – Lake County, IL – IN – WI CMSA	1,728	4
Minneapolis – St. Paul, MN – WI MSA	1,268	5
Miami – Fort Lauderdale, FL CMSA	1,153	6
Philadelphia – Wilmington – Trenton, PA – NJ – DE – MD CMSA	1,147	7
Seattle – Tacoma, WA CMSA	1,082	8
Atlanta, GA MSA	1,052	9
Dallas – Fort Worth, TX CMSA	1,044	10
Sacramento, CA MSA	1,024	11
Detroit – Ann Arbor, MI CMSA	844	12
Washington, DC – MD – VA MSA	808	13
Tampa – St. Petersburg – Clearwater, FL MSA	778	14
Phoenix, AZ MSA	740	15
Boston – Lawrence – Salem, MA – NH CMSA	739	16
Portland – Vancouver, OR – WA CMSA	701	17
San Diego, CA MSA	698	18
Baltimore, MD MSA	612	19
Cleveland – Akron – Lorain, OH CMSA	561	20
Milwaukee – Racine, WI CMSA	539	21

[Continued]

★1447★

Top 25 MSAs For Employment As Cabinet Makers and Bench Carpenters, 1990: Men

[Continued]

MSA/CMSA	Employees per 100,000 pop.	Rank
Kansas City, MO – KS MSA	523	22
Houston – Galveston – Brazoria, TX CMSA	458	23
Columbus, OH MSA	429	24
Salt Lake City – Ogden, UT MSA	421	25

Source: U.S. Department of Commerce, Bureau of the Census, Data User Services Division, *1990 Census of Population and Housing, Equal Employment Opportunity File, CD-90-EE0-1, January 1993,* CD-ROM.

★1448★

Occupations, By Race/Sex

Top 25 MSAs For Employment As Cabinet Makers and Bench Carpenters, 1990: Women

MSA/CMSA	Employees per 100,000 pop.	Rank
Baltimore, MD MSA	111	1
Greensboro – Winston-Salem – High Point, NC MSA	109	2
Atlanta, GA MSA	93	3
Los Angeles – Anaheim – Riverside, CA CMSA	86	4
San Francisco – Oakland – San Jose, CA CMSA	85	5
Sacramento, CA MSA	79	6
Dallas – Fort Worth, TX CMSA	73	7
Portland – Vancouver, OR – WA CMSA	66	8
Seattle – Tacoma, WA CMSA	66	8
Tampa – St. Petersburg – Clearwater, FL MSA	65	9
Minneapolis – St. Paul, MN – WI MSA	59	10
Chicago – Gary – Lake County, IL – IN – WI CMSA	57	11
Fort Myers – Cape CoraL, Fl MSA	52	12
Elkhart – Goshen, IN MSA	51	13
Lakeland – Winter Haven, FL MSA	50	14
Charlotte – Gastonia – Rock Hill, NC – SC MSA	47	15
Indianapolis, IN MSA	47	15
Little Rock – North Little Rock, AR MSA	45	16
Richmond – Petersburg, VA MSA	43	17
Knoxville, TN MSA	39	18
San Antonio, TX MSA	39	18
Miami – Fort Lauderdale, FL CMSA	37	19
Ocala, FL MSA	34	20
St. Cloud, MN MSA	34	20
Cleveland – Akron – Lorain, OH CMSA	33	21

Source: U.S. Department of Commerce, Bureau of the Census, Data User Services Division, *1990 Census of Population and Housing, Equal Employment Opportunity File, CD-90-EE0-1, January 1993,* CD-ROM.

★1449★

Occupations, By Race/Sex

Top 25 MSAs For Employment As Captains and Other Officers, Fishing Vessels, 1990: Men

MSA/CMSA	Employees per 100,000 pop.	Rank
St. Louis, MO – IL MSA	400	1
New York – Northern New Jersey – Long Island, NY – NJ – CT CMSA	300	2
San Diego, CA MSA	201	3
Houma – Thibodaux, LA MSA	200	4
Miami – Fort Lauderdale, FL CMSA	153	5
Providence – Pawtucket – Fall River, RI – MA CMSA	153	5
New Bedford, MA MSA	142	6
Tampa – St. Petersburg – Clearwater, FL MSA	133	7
Boston – Lawrence – Salem, MA – NH CMSA	118	8
Mobile, AL MSA	118	8
Portland, ME MSA	112	9
West Palm Beach – Boca Raton – Delray Beach, FL MSA	111	10
Los Angeles – Anaheim – Riverside, CA CMSA	98	11
Brownsville – Harlingen, TX MSA	97	12
Fort Myers – Cape CoraL, Fl MSA	92	13
Atlantic City, NJ MSA	90	14
New Orleans, LA MSA	86	15
Houston – Galveston – Brazoria, TX CMSA	78	16
San Francisco – Oakland – San Jose, CA CMSA	68	17
Fort Walton Beach, FL MSA	63	18
Anchorage, AK MSA	55	19
Jacksonville, FL MSA	51	20
Corpus Christi, TX MSA	47	21
Norfolk – Virginia Beach – Newport News, VA MSA	43	22
Panama City, FL MSA	42	23

Source: U.S. Department of Commerce, Bureau of the Census, Data User Services Division, *1990 Census of Population and Housing, Equal Employment Opportunity File, CD-90-EE0-1, January 1993,* CD-ROM.

★1450★

Occupations, By Race/Sex

Top 25 MSAs For Employment As Captains and Other Officers, Fishing Vessels, 1990: Women

MSA/CMSA	Employees per 100,000 pop.	Rank
Dayton – Springfield, OH MSA	20	1
Miami – Fort Lauderdale, FL CMSA	16	2
Baltimore, MD MSA	10	3
Jacksonville, FL MSA	10	3
Charleston, SC MSA	7	4
Fresno, CA MSA	7	4

[Continued]

★1450★

Top 25 MSAs For Employment As Captains and Other Officers, Fishing Vessels, 1990: Women

[Continued]

MSA/CMSA	Employees per 100,000 pop.	Rank
Seattle – Tacoma, WA CMSA	7	4
Toledo, OH MSA	7	4
Boston – Lawrence – Salem, MA – NH CMSA	6	5
Mobile, AL MSA	6	5
Naples, FL MSA	5	6
Philadelphia – Wilmington – Trenton, PA – NJ – DE – MD CMSA	5	6
Pittsburgh – Beaver Valley, PA CMSA	4	7
Corpus Christi, TX MSA	3	8
Greensboro – Winston-Salem – High Point, NC MSA	3	8
Scranton – Wilkes-Barre, PA MSA	1	9
Albuquerque, NM MSA	0	10
Albany – Schenectady – Troy, NY MSA	0	10
Amarillo, TX MSA	0	10
Altoona, PA MSA	0	10
Albany, GA MSA	0	10
Alexandria, LA MSA	0	10
Allentown – Bethlehem – Easton, PA – NJ MSA	0	10
Abilene, TX MSA	0	10
Anchorage, AK MSA	0	10

Source: U.S. Department of Commerce, Bureau of the Census, Data User Services Division, 1990 Census of Population and Housing, Equal Employment Opportunity File, CD-90-EE0-1, January 1993, CD-ROM.

★1451★

Occupations, By Race/Sex

Top 25 MSAs For Employment As Chemical Engineers, 1990: Men

MSA/CMSA	Employees per 100,000 pop.	Rank
Austin, TX MSA	5,143	1
New York – Northern New Jersey – Long Island, NY – NJ – CT CMSA	4,666	2
Philadelphia – Wilmington – Trenton, PA – NJ – DE – MD CMSA	3,618	3
Chicago – Gary – Lake County, IL – IN – WI CMSA	2,729	4
Los Angeles – Anaheim – Riverside, CA CMSA	1,659	5
San Francisco – Oakland – San Jose, CA CMSA	1,508	6
Cleveland – Akron – Lorain, OH CMSA	1,377	7
Minneapolis – St. Paul, MN – WI MSA	1,220	8

[Continued]

★1451★

Top 25 MSAs For Employment As Chemical Engineers, 1990: Men

[Continued]

MSA/CMSA	Employees per 100,000 pop.	Rank
Cincinnati – Hamilton, OH – KY – IN CMSA	1,101	9
Baton Rouge, LA MSA	1,062	10
Saginaw – Bay City – Midland, MI MSA	984	11
Boston – Lawrence – Salem, MA – NH CMSA	846	12
Detroit – Ann Arbor, MI CMSA	840	13
St. Louis, MO – IL MSA	785	14
Beaumont – Port Arthur, TX MSA	678	15
Allentown – Bethlehem – Easton, PA – NJ MSA	624	16
New Orleans, LA MSA	614	17
Johnson City – Kingsport – Bristol, TN – VA MSA	556	18
Pittsburgh – Beaver Valley, PA CMSA	553	19
Buffalo – Niagara Falls, NY CMSA	551	20
Charleston, WV MSA	551	20
Augusta, GA – SC MSA	533	21
Baltimore, MD MSA	527	22
Knoxville, TN MSA	508	23
Richmond – Petersburg, VA MSA	447	24

Source: U.S. Department of Commerce, Bureau of the Census, Data User Services Division, 1990 Census of Population and Housing, Equal Employment Opportunity File, CD-90-EE0-1, January 1993, CD-ROM.

★1452★

Occupations, By Race/Sex

Top 25 MSAs For Employment As Chemical Engineers, 1990: Women

MSA/CMSA	Employees per 100,000 pop.	Rank
San Antonio, TX MSA	722	1
New York – Northern New Jersey – Long Island, NY – NJ – CT CMSA	566	2
Philadelphia – Wilmington – Trenton, PA – NJ – DE – MD CMSA	518	3
Chicago – Gary – Lake County, IL – IN – WI CMSA	394	4
San Francisco – Oakland – San Jose, CA CMSA	296	5
Minneapolis – St. Paul, MN – WI MSA	232	6
Los Angeles – Anaheim – Riverside, CA CMSA	227	7
Cincinnati – Hamilton, OH – KY – IN CMSA	184	8
Saginaw – Bay City – Midland, MI MSA	177	9
Washington, DC – MD – VA MSA	135	10

[Continued]

★1452★

Top 25 MSAs For Employment As Chemical Engineers, 1990: Women

[Continued]

MSA/CMSA	Employees per 100,000 pop.	Rank
Boston – Lawrence – Salem, MA – NH CMSA	124	11
St. Louis, MO – IL MSA	123	12
Baton Rouge, LA MSA	114	13
Allentown – Bethlehem – Easton, PA – NJ MSA	113	14
Beaumont – Port Arthur, TX MSA	109	15
Rochester, NY MSA	92	16
Baltimore, MD MSA	87	17
New Orleans, LA MSA	87	17
Pittsburgh – Beaver Valley, PA CMSA	82	18
Johnson City – Kingsport – Bristol, TN – VA MSA	76	19
Knoxville, TN MSA	71	20
Augusta, GA – SC MSA	69	21
Cleveland – Akron – Lorain, OH CMSA	61	22
Indianapolis, IN MSA	61	22
Seattle – Tacoma, WA CMSA	58	23

Source: U.S. Department of Commerce, Bureau of the Census, Data User Services Division, *1990 Census of Population and Housing, Equal Employment Opportunity File,* CD-90-EE0-1, January 1993, CD-ROM.

★1453★

Occupations, By Race/Sex

Top 25 MSAs For Employment As Chemistry Teachers, 1990: Men

MSA/CMSA	Employees per 100,000 pop.	Rank
Salt Lake City – Ogden, UT MSA	172	1
Chicago – Gary – Lake County, IL – IN – WI CMSA	144	2
Los Angeles – Anaheim – Riverside, CA CMSA	131	3
Boston – Lawrence – Salem, MA – NH CMSA	125	4
San Francisco – Oakland – San Jose, CA CMSA	117	5
Houston – Galveston – Brazoria, TX CMSA	79	6
Detroit – Ann Arbor, MI CMSA	66	7
Philadelphia – Wilmington – Trenton, PA – NJ – DE – MD CMSA	66	7
Baltimore, MD MSA	62	8
Hartford – New Britain – Middletown, CT CMSA	61	9
Dallas – Fort Worth, TX CMSA	54	10
Madison, WI MSA	54	10
New Orleans, LA MSA	49	11
Denver – Boulder, CO CMSA	48	12
Cleveland – Akron – Lorain, OH CMSA	46	13

[Continued]

★1453★

Top 25 MSAs For Employment As Chemistry Teachers, 1990: Men

[Continued]

MSA/CMSA	Employees per 100,000 pop.	Rank
State College, PA MSA	43	14
Lawrence, KS MSA	42	15
Raleigh – Durham, NC MSA	42	15
Austin, TX MSA	41	16
Washington, DC – MD – VA MSA	41	16
Gainesville, FL MSA	40	17
Scranton – Wilkes-Barre, PA MSA	40	17
Providence – Pawtucket – Fall River, RI – MA CMSA	40	17
Sacramento, CA MSA	39	18
Indianapolis, IN MSA	38	19

Source: U.S. Department of Commerce, Bureau of the Census, Data User Services Division, *1990 Census of Population and Housing, Equal Employment Opportunity File,* CD-90-EE-1, January 1993, CD-ROM.

★1454★

Occupations, By Race/Sex

Top 25 MSAs For Employment As Chemistry Teachers, 1990: Women

MSA/CMSA	Employees per 100,000 pop.	Rank
Bloomington, IN MSA	83	1
New York – Northern New Jersey – Long Island, NY – NJ – CT CMSA	72	2
Chicago – Gary – Lake County, IL – IN – WI CMSA	64	3
Los Angeles – Anaheim – Riverside, CA CMSA	51	4
Boston – Lawrence – Salem, MA – NH CMSA	45	5
Madison, WI MSA	45	5
San Francisco – Oakland – San Jose, CA CMSA	37	6
Norfolk – Virginia Beach – Newport News, VA MSA	32	7
Denver – Boulder, CO CMSA	28	8
Houston – Galveston – Brazoria, TX CMSA	26	9
Raleigh – Durham, NC MSA	25	10
Minneapolis – St. Paul, MN – WI MSA	23	11
Dallas – Fort Worth, TX CMSA	20	12
Richmond – Petersburg, VA MSA	20	12
San Diego, CA MSA	19	13
Syracuse, NY MSA	19	13
Baltimore, MD MSA	17	14
Lubbock, TX MSA	17	14
Melbourne – Titusville – Palm Bay, FL MSA	16	15
New Haven – Meriden, CT MSA	16	15
Pittsburgh – Beaver Valley, PA CMSA	16	15

[Continued]

★1454★

Top 25 MSAs For Employment As Chemistry Teachers, 1990: Women
[Continued]

MSA/CMSA	Employees per 100,000 pop.	Rank
Atlanta, GA MSA	15	16
Champaign – Urbana – Rantoul, IL MSA	15	16
Kalamazoo, MI MSA	14	17
Oklahoma City, OK MSA	14	17

Source: U.S. Department of Commerce, Bureau of the Census, Data User Services Division, *1990 Census of Population and Housing, Equal Employment Opportunity File, CD-90-EE0-1, January 1993,* CD-ROM.

★1455★

Occupations, By Race/Sex

Top 25 MSAs For Employment As Chemists, Except Biochemists, 1990: Men

MSA/CMSA	Employees per 100,000 pop.	Rank
Albany – Schenectady – Troy, NY MSA	9,573	1
Philadelphia – Wilmington – Trenton, PA – NJ – DE – MD CMSA	5,666	2
Chicago – Gary – Lake County, IL – IN – WI CMSA	4,995	3
San Francisco – Oakland – San Jose, CA CMSA	4,680	4
Los Angeles – Anaheim – Riverside, CA CMSA	4,028	5
Houston – Galveston – Brazoria, TX CMSA	3,079	6
Washington, DC – MD – VA MSA	2,651	7
Boston – Lawrence – Salem, MA – NH CMSA	2,115	8
Cleveland – Akron – Lorain, OH CMSA	1,863	9
St. Louis, MO – IL MSA	1,787	10
Detroit – Ann Arbor, MI CMSA	1,712	11
Minneapolis – St. Paul, MN – WI MSA	1,456	12
Cincinnati – Hamilton, OH – KY – IN CMSA	1,454	13
Pittsburgh – Beaver Valley, PA CMSA	1,396	14
Baltimore, MD MSA	1,323	15
Dallas – Fort Worth, TX CMSA	1,307	16
Denver – Boulder, CO CMSA	1,227	17
Raleigh – Durham, NC MSA	1,156	18
Indianapolis, IN MSA	1,111	19
San Diego, CA MSA	1,081	20
Rochester, NY MSA	1,024	21
Atlanta, GA MSA	978	22
Columbus, OH MSA	860	23

[Continued]

★1455★

Top 25 MSAs For Employment As Chemists, Except Biochemists, 1990: Men
[Continued]

MSA/CMSA	Employees per 100,000 pop.	Rank
Saginaw – Bay City – Midland, MI MSA	833	24
Baton Rouge, LA MSA	777	25

Source: U.S. Department of Commerce, Bureau of the Census, Data User Services Division, *1990 Census of Population and Housing, Equal Employment Opportunity File, CD-90-EE0-1, January 1993,* CD-ROM.

★1456★

Occupations, By Race/Sex

Top 25 MSAs For Employment As Chemists, Except Biochemists, 1990: Women

MSA/CMSA	Employees per 100,000 pop.	Rank
Augusta, GA – SC MSA	4,035	1
Philadelphia – Wilmington – Trenton, PA – NJ – DE – MD CMSA	2,017	2
San Francisco – Oakland – San Jose, CA CMSA	1,962	3
Chicago – Gary – Lake County, IL – IN – WI CMSA	1,854	4
Los Angeles – Anaheim – Riverside, CA CMSA	1,848	5
Washington, DC – MD – VA MSA	1,183	6
Houston – Galveston – Brazoria, TX CMSA	1,151	7
Boston – Lawrence – Salem, MA – NH CMSA	1,133	8
Dallas – Fort Worth, TX CMSA	672	9
Cleveland – Akron – Lorain, OH CMSA	650	10
Raleigh – Durham, NC MSA	643	11
Detroit – Ann Arbor, MI CMSA	637	12
Denver – Boulder, CO CMSA	597	13
Baltimore, MD MSA	595	14
Minneapolis – St. Paul, MN – WI MSA	585	15
St. Louis, MO – IL MSA	571	16
San Diego, CA MSA	474	17
Pittsburgh – Beaver Valley, PA CMSA	453	18
Atlanta, GA MSA	401	19
Cincinnati – Hamilton, OH – KY – IN CMSA	401	19
Rochester, NY MSA	370	20
Indianapolis, IN MSA	309	21
Columbus, OH MSA	308	22
Kansas City, MO – KS MSA	308	22
Miami – Fort Lauderdale, FL CMSA	305	23

Source: U.S. Department of Commerce, Bureau of the Census, Data User Services Division, *1990 Census of Population and Housing, Equal Employment Opportunity File, CD-90-EE0-1, January 1993,* CD-ROM.

★ 1457 ★
Occupations, By Race/Sex

Top 25 MSAs For Employment As Chief Executives and General Administrators, Public Administration, 1990: Men

MSA/CMSA	Employees per 100,000 pop.	Rank
Kansas City, MO – KS MSA	1,022	1
Los Angeles – Anaheim – Riverside, CA CMSA	553	2
Philadelphia – Wilmington – Trenton, PA – NJ – DE – MD CMSA	386	3
Chicago – Gary – Lake County, IL – IN – WI CMSA	379	4
Detroit – Ann Arbor, MI CMSA	345	5
San Francisco – Oakland – San Jose, CA CMSA	304	6
Washington, DC – MD – VA MSA	267	7
Houston – Galveston – Brazoria, TX CMSA	200	8
Cleveland – Akron – Lorain, OH CMSA	186	9
Dallas – Fort Worth, TX CMSA	183	10
St. Louis, MO – IL MSA	170	11
Miami – Fort Lauderdale, FL CMSA	156	12
San Diego, CA MSA	149	13
Boston – Lawrence – Salem, MA – NH CMSA	141	14
Baltimore, MD MSA	140	15
Tampa – St. Petersburg – Clearwater, FL MSA	126	16
Pittsburgh – Beaver Valley, PA CMSA	126	16
Norfolk – Virginia Beach – Newport News, VA MSA	122	17
Phoenix, AZ MSA	107	18
Denver – Boulder, CO CMSA	103	19
Buffalo – Niagara Falls, NY CMSA	101	20
Sacramento, CA MSA	93	21
Minneapolis – St. Paul, MN – WI MSA	92	22
Seattle – Tacoma, WA CMSA	90	23
Milwaukee – Racine, WI CMSA	90	23

Source: U.S. Department of Commerce, Bureau of the Census, Data User Services Division, *1990 Census of Population and Housing, Equal Employment Opportunity File, CD-90-EE0-1, January 1993,* CD-ROM.

★ 1458 ★
Occupations, By Race/Sex

Top 25 MSAs For Employment As Chief Executives and General Administrators, Public Administration, 1990: Women

MSA/CMSA	Employees per 100,000 pop.	Rank
Columbia, SC MSA	570	1
Los Angeles – Anaheim – Riverside, CA CMSA	412	2
Chicago – Gary – Lake County, IL – IN – WI CMSA	219	3
Washington, DC – MD – VA MSA	204	4
San Francisco – Oakland – San Jose, CA CMSA	188	5
Boston – Lawrence – Salem, MA – NH CMSA	117	6
Detroit – Ann Arbor, MI CMSA	97	7
Baltimore, MD MSA	89	8
Philadelphia – Wilmington – Trenton, PA – NJ – DE – MD CMSA	89	8
Houston – Galveston – Brazoria, TX CMSA	83	9
Minneapolis – St. Paul, MN – WI MSA	60	10
Dallas – Fort Worth, TX CMSA	58	11
Miami – Fort Lauderdale, FL CMSA	56	12
Tampa – St. Petersburg – Clearwater, FL MSA	54	13
Denver – Boulder, CO CMSA	52	14
Sacramento, CA MSA	51	15
Seattle – Tacoma, WA CMSA	51	15
Columbus, OH MSA	49	16
Hartford – New Britain – Middletown, CT CMSA	49	16
Austin, TX MSA	44	17
Dayton – Springfield, OH MSA	43	18
Cleveland – Akron – Lorain, OH CMSA	37	19
Daytona Beach, FL MSA	35	20
Milwaukee – Racine, WI CMSA	35	20
Allentown – Bethlehem – Easton, PA – NJ MSA	31	21

Source: U.S. Department of Commerce, Bureau of the Census, Data User Services Division, *1990 Census of Population and Housing, Equal Employment Opportunity File, CD-90-EE0-1, January 1993,* CD-ROM.

★1459★
Occupations, By Race/Sex

Top 25 MSAs For Employment As Child Care Workers, Private Household, 1990: Men

MSA/CMSA	Employees per 100,000 pop.	Rank
Charlottesville, VA MSA	405	1
San Francisco – Oakland – San Jose, CA CMSA	213	2
New York – Northern New Jersey – Long Island, NY – NJ – CT CMSA	174	3
Chicago – Gary – Lake County, IL – IN – WI CMSA	157	4
Boston – Lawrence – Salem, MA – NH CMSA	102	5
San Diego, CA MSA	92	6
Baltimore, MD MSA	86	7
Detroit – Ann Arbor, MI CMSA	85	8
Houston – Galveston – Brazoria, TX CMSA	83	9
Portland – Vancouver, OR – WA CMSA	78	10
Denver – Boulder, CO CMSA	63	11
Philadelphia – Wilmington – Trenton, PA – NJ – DE – MD CMSA	63	11
Milwaukee – Racine, WI CMSA	62	12
Phoenix, AZ MSA	54	13
Albany – Schenectady – Troy, NY MSA	53	14
Atlanta, GA MSA	53	14
Washington, DC – MD – VA MSA	52	15
Sacramento, CA MSA	49	16
Miami – Fort Lauderdale, FL CMSA	47	17
Dallas – Fort Worth, TX CMSA	45	18
St. Louis, MO – IL MSA	42	19
Pittsburgh – Beaver Valley, PA CMSA	37	20
Seattle – Tacoma, WA CMSA	36	21
Shreveport, LA MSA	36	21
Providence – Pawtucket – Fall River, RI – MA CMSA	35	22

Source: U.S. Department of Commerce, Bureau of the Census, Data User Services Division, 1990 Census of Population and Housing, Equal Employment Opportunity File, CD-90-EE0-1, January 1993, CD-ROM.

★1460★
Occupations, By Race/Sex

Top 25 MSAs For Employment As Child Care Workers, Private Household, 1990: Women

MSA/CMSA	Employees per 100,000 pop.	Rank
Phoenix, AZ MSA	12,620	1
New York – Northern New Jersey – Long Island, NY – NJ – CT CMSA	11,955	2
San Francisco – Oakland – San Jose, CA CMSA	4,904	3
Washington, DC – MD – VA MSA	4,763	4
Chicago – Gary – Lake County, IL – IN – WI CMSA	4,404	5
Houston – Galveston – Brazoria, TX CMSA	3,012	6
Boston – Lawrence – Salem, MA – NH CMSA	2,754	7
Philadelphia – Wilmington – Trenton, PA – NJ – DE – MD CMSA	2,513	8
Detroit – Ann Arbor, MI CMSA	2,467	9
Dallas – Fort Worth, TX CMSA	2,401	10
Seattle – Tacoma, WA CMSA	2,282	11
San Diego, CA MSA	2,028	12
Miami – Fort Lauderdale, FL CMSA	1,668	13
Minneapolis – St. Paul, MN – WI MSA	1,648	14
Atlanta, GA MSA	1,625	15
Denver – Boulder, CO CMSA	1,623	16
Baltimore, MD MSA	1,516	17
Phoenix, AZ MSA	1,498	18
Cleveland – Akron – Lorain, OH CMSA	1,458	19
Portland – Vancouver, OR – WA CMSA	1,346	20
St. Louis, MO – IL MSA	1,300	21
Norfolk – Virginia Beach – Newport News, VA MSA	1,180	22
Pittsburgh – Beaver Valley, PA CMSA	1,150	23
Sacramento, CA MSA	1,084	24
Kansas City, MO – KS MSA	986	25

Source: U.S. Department of Commerce, Bureau of the Census, Data User Services Division, 1990 Census of Population and Housing, Equal Employment Opportunity File, CD-90-EE0-1, January 1993, CD-ROM.

★1461★
Occupations, By Race/Sex

Top 25 MSAs For Employment As Clergy, 1990: Men

MSA/CMSA	Employees per 100,000 pop.	Rank
Columbus, OH MSA	13,326	1
Los Angeles – Anaheim – Riverside, CA CMSA	11,637	2
Chicago – Gary – Lake County, IL – IN – WI CMSA	7,094	3
Philadelphia – Wilmington – Trenton, PA – NJ – DE – MD CMSA	5,448	4
Dallas – Fort Worth, TX CMSA	5,388	5
San Francisco – Oakland – San Jose, CA CMSA	5,005	6
Detroit – Ann Arbor, MI CMSA	3,731	7
Boston – Lawrence – Salem, MA – NH CMSA	3,710	8
Washington, DC – MD – VA MSA	3,656	9
Atlanta, GA MSA	3,502	10
Houston – Galveston – Brazoria, TX CMSA	3,347	11
St. Louis, MO – IL MSA	2,895	12
Seattle – Tacoma, WA CMSA	2,806	13
Cleveland – Akron – Lorain, OH CMSA	2,697	14
Minneapolis – St. Paul, MN – WI MSA	2,681	15
Pittsburgh – Beaver Valley, PA CMSA	2,557	16
Tampa – St. Petersburg – Clearwater, FL MSA	2,253	17
Baltimore, MD MSA	2,125	18
Cincinnati – Hamilton, OH – KY – IN CMSA	2,078	19
San Diego, CA MSA	2,054	20
Charlotte – Gastonia – Rock Hill, NC – SC MSA	2,020	21
Phoenix, AZ MSA	1,978	22
Miami – Fort Lauderdale, FL CMSA	1,955	23
Kansas City, MO – KS MSA	1,847	24
Denver – Boulder, CO CMSA	1,811	25

Source: U.S. Department of Commerce, Bureau of the Census, Data User Services Division, *1990 Census of Population and Housing, Equal Employment Opportunity File, CD-90-EE0-1, January 1993,* CD-ROM.

★1462★
Occupations, By Race/Sex

Top 25 MSAs For Employment As Clergy, 1990: Women

MSA/CMSA	Employees per 100,000 pop.	Rank
Milwaukee – Racine, WI CMSA	2,122	1
Los Angeles – Anaheim – Riverside, CA CMSA	1,986	2
Chicago – Gary – Lake County, IL – IN – WI CMSA	1,251	3
San Francisco – Oakland – San Jose, CA CMSA	891	4
Philadelphia – Wilmington – Trenton, PA – NJ – DE – MD CMSA	839	5
Dallas – Fort Worth, TX CMSA	680	6
Minneapolis – St. Paul, MN – WI MSA	595	7
Boston – Lawrence – Salem, MA – NH CMSA	553	8
Detroit – Ann Arbor, MI CMSA	553	8
Washington, DC – MD – VA MSA	513	9
Seattle – Tacoma, WA CMSA	454	10
Kansas City, MO – KS MSA	409	11
Cleveland – Akron – Lorain, OH CMSA	384	12
Atlanta, GA MSA	360	13
Pittsburgh – Beaver Valley, PA CMSA	337	14
Houston – Galveston – Brazoria, TX CMSA	323	15
St. Louis, MO – IL MSA	308	16
San Diego, CA MSA	306	17
Denver – Boulder, CO CMSA	304	18
Miami – Fort Lauderdale, FL CMSA	280	19
Baltimore, MD MSA	265	20
Cincinnati – Hamilton, OH – KY – IN CMSA	258	21
Raleigh – Durham, NC MSA	242	22
Indianapolis, IN MSA	240	23
Milwaukee – Racine, WI CMSA	236	24

Source: U.S. Department of Commerce, Bureau of the Census, Data User Services Division, *1990 Census of Population and Housing, Equal Employment Opportunity File, CD-90-EE0-1, January 1993,* CD-ROM.

★1463★
Occupations, By Race/Sex

Top 25 MSAs For Employment As Computer Operators, 1990: Men

MSA/CMSA	Employees per 100,000 pop.	Rank
Tulsa, OK MSA	27,274	1
Los Angeles – Anaheim – Riverside, CA CMSA	16,298	2
Chicago – Gary – Lake County, IL – IN – WI CMSA	11,073	3
Philadelphia – Wilmington – Trenton, PA – NJ – DE – MD CMSA	8,790	4

[Continued]

★1463★

Top 25 MSAs For Employment As Computer Operators, 1990: Men
[Continued]

MSA/CMSA	Employees per 100,000 pop.	Rank
San Francisco – Oakland – San Jose, CA CMSA	8,087	5
Dallas – Fort Worth, TX CMSA	6,969	6
Washington, DC – MD – VA MSA	6,830	7
Boston – Lawrence – Salem, MA – NH CMSA	6,133	8
Houston – Galveston – Brazoria, TX CMSA	5,166	9
Detroit – Ann Arbor, MI CMSA	4,906	10
Atlanta, GA MSA	4,204	11
St. Louis, MO – IL MSA	3,378	12
Minneapolis – St. Paul, MN – WI MSA	3,293	13
Denver – Boulder, CO CMSA	3,168	14
Baltimore, MD MSA	3,038	15
Cleveland – Akron – Lorain, OH CMSA	3,021	16
Seattle – Tacoma, WA CMSA	2,816	17
Miami – Fort Lauderdale, FL CMSA	2,767	18
Kansas City, MO – KS MSA	2,402	19
San Diego, CA MSA	2,398	20
Pittsburgh – Beaver Valley, PA CMSA	2,314	21
Columbus, OH MSA	2,296	22
Phoenix, AZ MSA	2,185	23
Hartford – New Britain – Middletown, CT CMSA	2,144	24
Sacramento, CA MSA	1,772	25

Source: U.S. Department of Commerce, Bureau of the Census, Data User Services Division, *1990 Census of Population and Housing, Equal Employment Opportunity File, CD-90-EE0-1, January 1993,* CD-ROM.

★1464★

Occupations, By Race/Sex

Top 25 MSAs For Employment As Computer Operators, 1990: Women

MSA/CMSA	Employees per 100,000 pop.	Rank
Baltimore, MD MSA	36,384	1
Los Angeles – Anaheim – Riverside, CA CMSA	20,644	2
Chicago – Gary – Lake County, IL – IN – WI CMSA	15,977	3
Philadelphia – Wilmington – Trenton, PA – NJ – DE – MD CMSA	11,235	4
San Francisco – Oakland – San Jose, CA CMSA	9,419	5
Dallas – Fort Worth, TX CMSA	8,644	6
Detroit – Ann Arbor, MI CMSA	8,144	7
Washington, DC – MD – VA MSA	7,544	8
Boston – Lawrence – Salem, MA – NH CMSA	7,395	9

[Continued]

★1464★

Top 25 MSAs For Employment As Computer Operators, 1990: Women
[Continued]

MSA/CMSA	Employees per 100,000 pop.	Rank
Atlanta, GA MSA	6,642	10
Houston – Galveston – Brazoria, TX CMSA	6,322	11
Miami – Fort Lauderdale, FL CMSA	5,404	12
Baltimore, MD MSA	5,081	13
Cleveland – Akron – Lorain, OH CMSA	4,981	14
St. Louis, MO – IL MSA	4,903	15
Minneapolis – St. Paul, MN – WI MSA	4,716	16
Seattle – Tacoma, WA CMSA	4,511	17
Kansas City, MO – KS MSA	3,776	18
Cincinnati – Hamilton, OH – KY – IN CMSA	3,644	19
Denver – Boulder, CO CMSA	3,616	20
Phoenix, AZ MSA	3,504	21
Tampa – St. Petersburg – Clearwater, FL MSA	3,501	22
Columbus, OH MSA	3,314	23
San Diego, CA MSA	3,150	24
Pittsburgh – Beaver Valley, PA CMSA	3,036	25

Source: U.S. Department of Commerce, Bureau of the Census, Data User Services Division, *1990 Census of Population and Housing, Equal Employment Opportunity File, CD-90-EE0-1, January 1993,* CD-ROM.

★1465★

Occupations, By Race/Sex

Top 25 MSAs For Employment As Computer Programmers, 1990: Men

MSA/CMSA	Employees per 100,000 pop.	Rank
Norfolk – Virginia Beach – Newport News, VA MSA	45,107	1
Los Angeles – Anaheim – Riverside, CA CMSA	28,625	2
San Francisco – Oakland – San Jose, CA CMSA	23,748	3
Chicago – Gary – Lake County, IL – IN – WI CMSA	18,667	4
Washington, DC – MD – VA MSA	18,316	5
Dallas – Fort Worth, TX CMSA	13,780	6
Philadelphia – Wilmington – Trenton, PA – NJ – DE – MD CMSA	13,664	7
Boston – Lawrence – Salem, MA – NH CMSA	12,997	8
Minneapolis – St. Paul, MN – WI MSA	9,476	9
Detroit – Ann Arbor, MI CMSA	9,023	10
Atlanta, GA MSA	8,743	11
Houston – Galveston – Brazoria, TX CMSA	8,433	12

[Continued]

★1465★

Top 25 MSAs For Employment As Computer Programmers, 1990: Men
[Continued]

MSA/CMSA	Employees per 100,000 pop.	Rank
Denver – Boulder, CO CMSA	7,969	13
Seattle – Tacoma, WA CMSA	6,862	14
Baltimore, MD MSA	6,081	15
San Diego, CA MSA	5,817	16
St. Louis, MO – IL MSA	5,222	17
Raleigh – Durham, NC MSA	4,849	18
Cleveland – Akron – Lorain, OH CMSA	4,692	19
Phoenix, AZ MSA	4,623	20
Miami – Fort Lauderdale, FL CMSA	4,491	21
Austin, TX MSA	4,280	22
Kansas City, MO – KS MSA	4,016	23
Columbus, OH MSA	4,001	24
Hartford – New Britain – Middletown, CT CMSA	3,935	25

Source: U.S. Department of Commerce, Bureau of the Census, Data User Services Division, *1990 Census of Population and Housing, Equal Employment Opportunity File*, CD-90-EE0-1, January 1993, CD-ROM.

★1466★

Occupations, By Race/Sex

Top 25 MSAs For Employment As Computer Programmers, 1990: Women

MSA/CMSA	Employees per 100,000 pop.	Rank
Portland – Vancouver, OR – WA CMSA	22,576	1
Los Angeles – Anaheim – Riverside, CA CMSA	11,307	2
Washington, DC – MD – VA MSA	10,865	3
San Francisco – Oakland – San Jose, CA CMSA	10,126	4
Chicago – Gary – Lake County, IL – IN – WI CMSA	8,850	5
Philadelphia – Wilmington – Trenton, PA – NJ – DE – MD CMSA	7,187	6
Boston – Lawrence – Salem, MA – NH CMSA	7,015	7
Dallas – Fort Worth, TX CMSA	6,030	8
Atlanta, GA MSA	4,263	9
Houston – Galveston – Brazoria, TX CMSA	4,254	10
Minneapolis – St. Paul, MN – WI MSA	4,054	11
Detroit – Ann Arbor, MI CMSA	4,031	12
Baltimore, MD MSA	3,420	13
Denver – Boulder, CO CMSA	3,334	14
St. Louis, MO – IL MSA	2,945	15
Seattle – Tacoma, WA CMSA	2,834	16
Hartford – New Britain – Middletown, CT CMSA	2,496	17

[Continued]

★1466★

Top 25 MSAs For Employment As Computer Programmers, 1990: Women
[Continued]

MSA/CMSA	Employees per 100,000 pop.	Rank
Cleveland – Akron – Lorain, OH CMSA	2,267	18
San Diego, CA MSA	2,136	19
Miami – Fort Lauderdale, FL CMSA	2,096	20
Raleigh – Durham, NC MSA	2,043	21
Phoenix, AZ MSA	2,041	22
Kansas City, MO – KS MSA	1,912	23
Columbus, OH MSA	1,724	24
Austin, TX MSA	1,613	25

Source: U.S. Department of Commerce, Bureau of the Census, Data User Services Division, *1990 Census of Population and Housing, Equal Employment Opportunity File*, CD-90-EE0-1, January 1993, CD-ROM.

★1467★

Occupations, By Race/Sex

Top 25 MSAs For Employment As Computer Science Teachers, 1990: Men

MSA/CMSA	Employees per 100,000 pop.	Rank
Rochester, NY MSA	166	1
New York – Northern New Jersey – Long Island, NY – NJ – CT CMSA	92	2
Miami – Fort Lauderdale, FL CMSA	81	3
San Francisco – Oakland – San Jose, CA CMSA	81	3
Philadelphia – Wilmington – Trenton, PA – NJ – DE – MD CMSA	67	4
Chicago – Gary – Lake County, IL – IN – WI CMSA	64	5
Pittsburgh – Beaver Valley, PA CMSA	60	6
Boston – Lawrence – Salem, MA – NH CMSA	60	6
Dallas – Fort Worth, TX CMSA	53	7
Portland – Vancouver, OR – WA CMSA	49	8
Washington, DC – MD – VA MSA	41	9
Salt Lake City – Ogden, UT MSA	34	10
Phoenix, AZ MSA	33	11
Raleigh – Durham, NC MSA	32	12
Denver – Boulder, CO CMSA	32	12
Madison, WI MSA	30	13
Sacramento, CA MSA	30	13
Atlanta, GA MSA	29	14
Lynchburg, VA MSA	28	15
Albany – Schenectady – Troy, NY MSA	27	16
Charlotte – Gastonia – Rock Hill, NC – SC MSA	27	16

[Continued]

★1467★

Top 25 MSAs For Employment As Computer Science Teachers, 1990: Men
[Continued]

MSA/CMSA	Employees per 100,000 pop.	Rank
Eugene – Springfield, OR MSA	26	17
Houston – Galveston – Brazoria, TX CMSA	26	17
Lincoln, NE MSA	25	18
Milwaukee – Racine, WI CMSA	24	19

Source: U.S. Department of Commerce, Bureau of the Census, Data User Services Division, *1990 Census of Population and Housing, Equal Employment Opportunity File, CD-90-EE0-1, January 1993,* CD-ROM.

★1468★

Occupations, By Race/Sex

Top 25 MSAs For Employment As Computer Science Teachers, 1990: Women

MSA/CMSA	Employees per 100,000 pop.	Rank
Santa Barbara – Santa Maria – Lompoc, CA MSA	146	1
New York – Northern New Jersey – Long Island, NY – NJ – CT CMSA	90	2
San Francisco – Oakland – San Jose, CA CMSA	76	3
Boston – Lawrence – Salem, MA – NH CMSA	62	4
Chicago – Gary – Lake County, IL – IN – WI CMSA	43	5
Philadelphia – Wilmington – Trenton, PA – NJ – DE – MD CMSA	35	6
Seattle – Tacoma, WA CMSA	32	7
Kansas City, MO – KS MSA	28	8
Miami – Fort Lauderdale, FL CMSA	28	8
Providence – Pawtucket – Fall River, RI – MA CMSA	24	9
Pittsburgh – Beaver Valley, PA CMSA	22	10
Raleigh – Durham, NC MSA	22	10
Nashville, TN MSA	21	11
Spokane, WA MSA	21	11
Houston – Galveston – Brazoria, TX CMSA	19	12
Madison, WI MSA	19	12
Orlando, FL MSA	18	13
Phoenix, AZ MSA	18	13
Stockton, CA MSA	18	13
Syracuse, NY MSA	18	13
Washington, DC – MD – VA MSA	18	13
Pensacola, FL MSA	17	14
Memphis, TN – AR – MS MSA	16	15
Springfield, MA MSA	16	15
New Haven – Meriden, CT MSA	15	16

Source: U.S. Department of Commerce, Bureau of the Census, Data User Services Division, *1990 Census of Population and Housing, Equal Employment Opportunity File, CD-90-EE0-1, January 1993,* CD-ROM.

★1469★

Occupations, By Race/Sex

Top 25 MSAs For Employment As Computer Systems Analysts and Scientists, 1990: Men

MSA/CMSA	Employees per 100,000 pop.	Rank
Hartford – New Britain – Middletown, CT CMSA	29,611	1
San Francisco – Oakland – San Jose, CA CMSA	23,426	2
Washington, DC – MD – VA MSA	19,415	3
Los Angeles – Anaheim – Riverside, CA CMSA	19,364	4
Boston – Lawrence – Salem, MA – NH CMSA	16,458	5
Chicago – Gary – Lake County, IL – IN – WI CMSA	13,748	6
Dallas – Fort Worth, TX CMSA	10,023	7
Philadelphia – Wilmington – Trenton, PA – NJ – DE – MD CMSA	10,000	8
Seattle – Tacoma, WA CMSA	8,320	9
Houston – Galveston – Brazoria, TX CMSA	6,395	10
Atlanta, GA MSA	6,282	11
Minneapolis – St. Paul, MN – WI MSA	6,248	12
Baltimore, MD MSA	6,204	13
Detroit – Ann Arbor, MI CMSA	6,036	14
Denver – Boulder, CO CMSA	5,432	15
San Diego, CA MSA	5,096	16
Phoenix, AZ MSA	4,155	17
St. Louis, MO – IL MSA	3,683	18
Cleveland – Akron – Lorain, OH CMSA	3,347	19
Portland – Vancouver, OR – WA CMSA	3,074	20
Columbus, OH MSA	2,833	21
Pittsburgh – Beaver Valley, PA CMSA	2,745	22
Hartford – New Britain – Middletown, CT CMSA	2,715	23
Raleigh – Durham, NC MSA	2,591	24
Cincinnati – Hamilton, OH – KY – IN CMSA	2,445	25

Source: U.S. Department of Commerce, Bureau of the Census, Data User Services Division, *1990 Census of Population and Housing, Equal Employment Opportunity File, CD-90-EE0-1, January 1993,* CD-ROM.

★1470★
Occupations, By Race/Sex

Top 25 MSAs For Employment As Computer Systems Analysts and Scientists, 1990: Women

MSA/CMSA	Employees per 100,000 pop.	Rank
Savannah, GA MSA	13,545	1
Washington, DC – MD – VA MSA	10,275	2
Los Angeles – Anaheim – Riverside, CA CMSA	8,808	3
San Francisco – Oakland – San Jose, CA CMSA	8,271	4
Boston – Lawrence – Salem, MA – NH CMSA	6,634	5
Chicago – Gary – Lake County, IL – IN – WI CMSA	6,071	6
Philadelphia – Wilmington – Trenton, PA – NJ – DE – MD CMSA	5,009	7
Dallas – Fort Worth, TX CMSA	3,945	8
Seattle – Tacoma, WA CMSA	3,339	9
Baltimore, MD MSA	3,292	10
Atlanta, GA MSA	3,013	11
Detroit – Ann Arbor, MI CMSA	3,008	12
Minneapolis – St. Paul, MN – WI MSA	2,703	13
Houston – Galveston – Brazoria, TX CMSA	2,523	14
Denver – Boulder, CO CMSA	2,455	15
San Diego, CA MSA	1,957	16
St. Louis, MO – IL MSA	1,846	17
Hartford – New Britain – Middletown, CT CMSA	1,698	18
Phoenix, AZ MSA	1,596	19
Cleveland – Akron – Lorain, OH CMSA	1,498	20
Cincinnati – Hamilton, OH – KY – IN CMSA	1,169	21
Raleigh – Durham, NC MSA	1,162	22
Pittsburgh – Beaver Valley, PA CMSA	1,109	23
Kansas City, MO – KS MSA	1,097	24
Columbus, OH MSA	1,049	25

Source: U.S. Department of Commerce, Bureau of the Census, Data User Services Division, *1990 Census of Population and Housing, Equal Employment Opportunity File,* CD-90-EE0-1, January 1993, CD-ROM.

★1471★
Occupations, By Race/Sex

Top 25 MSAs For Employment As Cooks, 1990: Men

MSA/CMSA	Employees per 100,000 pop.	Rank
Buffalo – Niagara Falls, NY CMSA	78,700	1
Los Angeles – Anaheim – Riverside, CA CMSA	76,813	2
Chicago – Gary – Lake County, IL – IN – WI CMSA	38,053	3
San Francisco – Oakland – San Jose, CA CMSA	31,315	4

[Continued]

★1471★
Top 25 MSAs For Employment As Cooks, 1990: Men
[Continued]

MSA/CMSA	Employees per 100,000 pop.	Rank
Philadelphia – Wilmington – Trenton, PA – NJ – DE – MD CMSA	24,002	5
Detroit – Ann Arbor, MI CMSA	21,855	6
Dallas – Fort Worth, TX CMSA	20,370	7
Boston – Lawrence – Salem, MA – NH CMSA	19,843	8
Washington, DC – MD – VA MSA	16,801	9
Houston – Galveston – Brazoria, TX CMSA	16,641	10
Miami – Fort Lauderdale, FL CMSA	16,356	11
San Diego, CA MSA	14,567	12
Atlanta, GA MSA	12,832	13
St. Louis, MO – IL MSA	12,330	14
Seattle – Tacoma, WA CMSA	11,935	15
Minneapolis – St. Paul, MN – WI MSA	11,791	16
Cleveland – Akron – Lorain, OH CMSA	10,993	17
Phoenix, AZ MSA	10,532	18
Baltimore, MD MSA	9,725	19
Denver – Boulder, CO CMSA	9,633	20
Tampa – St. Petersburg – Clearwater, FL MSA	9,421	21
Pittsburgh – Beaver Valley, PA CMSA	9,119	22
Cincinnati – Hamilton, OH – KY – IN CMSA	7,890	23
Kansas City, MO – KS MSA	7,795	24
Orlando, FL MSA	7,221	25

Source: U.S. Department of Commerce, Bureau of the Census, Data User Services Division, *1990 Census of Population and Housing, Equal Employment Opportunity File,* CD-90-EE0-1, January 1993, CD-ROM.

★1472★
Occupations, By Race/Sex

Top 25 MSAs For Employment As Cooks, 1990: Women

MSA/CMSA	Employees per 100,000 pop.	Rank
Las Vegas, NV MSA	32,030	1
New York – Northern New Jersey – Long Island, NY – NJ – CT CMSA	27,758	2
Chicago – Gary – Lake County, IL – IN – WI CMSA	20,668	3
San Francisco – Oakland – San Jose, CA CMSA	16,686	4
Detroit – Ann Arbor, MI CMSA	16,211	5
Houston – Galveston – Brazoria, TX CMSA	13,862	6
Philadelphia – Wilmington – Trenton, PA – NJ – DE – MD CMSA	13,829	7

[Continued]

★1472★

Top 25 MSAs For Employment As Cooks, 1990: Women
[Continued]

MSA/CMSA	Employees per 100,000 pop.	Rank
Dallas – Fort Worth, TX CMSA	12,545	8
Washington, DC – MD – VA MSA	10,968	9
Atlanta, GA MSA	10,831	10
Cleveland – Akron – Lorain, OH CMSA	10,375	11
St. Louis, MO – IL MSA	9,971	12
Boston – Lawrence – Salem, MA – NH CMSA	9,487	13
Pittsburgh – Beaver Valley, PA CMSA	8,839	14
Minneapolis – St. Paul, MN – WI MSA	8,812	15
Seattle – Tacoma, WA CMSA	8,082	16
Miami – Fort Lauderdale, FL CMSA	7,527	17
Baltimore, MD MSA	7,067	18
Cincinnati – Hamilton, OH – KY – IN CMSA	6,661	19
Milwaukee – Racine, WI CMSA	5,958	20
Tampa – St. Petersburg – Clearwater, FL MSA	5,927	21
Portland – Vancouver, OR – WA CMSA	5,679	22
Norfolk – Virginia Beach – Newport News, VA MSA	5,659	23
San Diego, CA MSA	5,629	24
Indianapolis, IN MSA	5,592	25

Source: U.S. Department of Commerce, Bureau of the Census, Data User Services Division, *1990 Census of Population and Housing, Equal Employment Opportunity File, CD-90-EE0-1, January 1993,* CD-ROM.

★1473★

Occupations, By Race/Sex

Top 25 MSAs For Employment As Cooks, Private Household, 1990: Men

MSA/CMSA	Employees per 100,000 pop.	Rank
Las Vegas, NV MSA	173	1
Los Angeles – Anaheim – Riverside, CA CMSA	82	2
Phoenix, AZ MSA	45	3
Miami – Fort Lauderdale, FL CMSA	44	4
Detroit – Ann Arbor, MI CMSA	30	5
Houston – Galveston – Brazoria, TX CMSA	29	6
San Diego, CA MSA	24	7
New Orleans, LA MSA	24	7
San Francisco – Oakland – San Jose, CA CMSA	22	8
Honolulu, HI MSA	21	9
San Antonio, TX MSA	21	9
Pittsburgh – Beaver Valley, PA CMSA	21	9

[Continued]

★1473★

Top 25 MSAs For Employment As Cooks, Private Household, 1990: Men
[Continued]

MSA/CMSA	Employees per 100,000 pop.	Rank
Grand Rapids, MI MSA	20	10
Atlanta, GA MSA	19	11
Chicago – Gary – Lake County, IL – IN – WI CMSA	18	12
Fort Pierce, FL MSA	15	13
Baton Rouge, LA MSA	14	14
Washington, DC – MD – VA MSA	13	15
West Palm Beach – Boca Raton – Delray Beach, FL MSA	13	15
Minneapolis – St. Paul, MN – WI MSA	13	15
Charleston, WV MSA	12	16
Seattle – Tacoma, WA CMSA	11	17
Richmond – Petersburg, VA MSA	10	18
Sarasota, FL MSA	10	18
Waterloo – Cedar Falls, IA MSA	10	18

Source: U.S. Department of Commerce, Bureau of the Census, Data User Services Division, *1990 Census of Population and Housing, Equal Employment Opportunity File, CD-90-EE0-1, January 1993,* CD-ROM.

★1474★

Occupations, By Race/Sex

Top 25 MSAs For Employment As Cooks, Private Household, 1990: Women

MSA/CMSA	Employees per 100,000 pop.	Rank
Cincinnati – Hamilton, OH – KY – IN CMSA	869	1
Los Angeles – Anaheim – Riverside, CA CMSA	618	2
San Francisco – Oakland – San Jose, CA CMSA	340	3
Philadelphia – Wilmington – Trenton, PA – NJ – DE – MD CMSA	164	4
Washington, DC – MD – VA MSA	161	5
Dallas – Fort Worth, TX CMSA	154	6
Chicago – Gary – Lake County, IL – IN – WI CMSA	148	7
Boston – Lawrence – Salem, MA – NH CMSA	147	8
Miami – Fort Lauderdale, FL CMSA	143	9
Houston – Galveston – Brazoria, TX CMSA	127	10
West Palm Beach – Boca Raton – Delray Beach, FL MSA	104	11
Detroit – Ann Arbor, MI CMSA	92	12
New Orleans, LA MSA	82	13
Cincinnati – Hamilton, OH – KY – IN CMSA	77	14
Baltimore, MD MSA	76	15
Birmingham, AL MSA	66	16

[Continued]

★1474★

Top 25 MSAs For Employment As Cooks, Private Household, 1990: Women

[Continued]

MSA/CMSA	Employees per 100,000 pop.	Rank
Santa Barbara – Santa Maria – Lompoc, CA MSA	66	16
Tulsa, OK MSA	61	17
Fort Pierce, FL MSA	57	18
Fresno, CA MSA	57	18
Pittsburgh – Beaver Valley, PA CMSA	57	18
Louisville, KY – IN MSA	55	19
Memphis, TN – AR – MS MSA	55	19
Indianapolis, IN MSA	50	20
San Diego, CA MSA	47	21

Source: U.S. Department of Commerce, Bureau of the Census, Data User Services Division, *1990 Census of Population and Housing, Equal Employment Opportunity File, CD-90-EE0-1, January 1993,* CD-ROM.

★1475★

Occupations, By Race/Sex

Top 25 MSAs For Employment As Correctional Institution Officers, 1990: Men

MSA/CMSA	Employees per 100,000 pop.	Rank
San Antonio, TX MSA	10,885	1
Philadelphia – Wilmington – Trenton, PA – NJ – DE – MD CMSA	4,726	2
Los Angeles – Anaheim – Riverside, CA CMSA	2,513	3
Houston – Galveston – Brazoria, TX CMSA	2,365	4
Baltimore, MD MSA	2,180	5
San Francisco – Oakland – San Jose, CA CMSA	2,026	6
Chicago – Gary – Lake County, IL – IN – WI CMSA	1,975	7
Washington, DC – MD – VA MSA	1,740	8
Buffalo – Niagara Falls, NY CMSA	1,653	9
Boston – Lawrence – Salem, MA – NH CMSA	1,554	10
Sacramento, CA MSA	1,408	11
Miami – Fort Lauderdale, FL CMSA	1,279	12
Seattle – Tacoma, WA CMSA	1,166	13
Atlanta, GA MSA	1,019	14
Utica – Rome, NY MSA	993	15
Albany – Schenectady – Troy, NY MSA	958	16
Hagerstown, MD MSA	945	17
Providence – Pawtucket – Fall River, RI – MA CMSA	934	18
Columbia, SC MSA	911	19
Kansas City, MO – KS MSA	895	20
Bakersfield, CA MSA	878	21
Phoenix, AZ MSA	848	22

[Continued]

★1475★

Top 25 MSAs For Employment As Correctional Institution Officers, 1990: Men

[Continued]

MSA/CMSA	Employees per 100,000 pop.	Rank
Dallas – Fort Worth, TX CMSA	808	23
Elmira, NY MSA	783	24
Killeen – Temple, TX MSA	772	25

Source: U.S. Department of Commerce, Bureau of the Census, Data User Services Division, *1990 Census of Population and Housing, Equal Employment Opportunity File, CD-90-EE0-1, January 1993,* CD-ROM.

★1476★

Occupations, By Race/Sex

Top 25 MSAs For Employment As Correctional Institution Officers, 1990: Women

MSA/CMSA	Employees per 100,000 pop.	Rank
Indianapolis, IN MSA	2,359	1
Philadelphia – Wilmington – Trenton, PA – NJ – DE – MD CMSA	1,076	2
Los Angeles – Anaheim – Riverside, CA CMSA	934	3
Baltimore, MD MSA	814	4
Miami – Fort Lauderdale, FL CMSA	792	5
Chicago – Gary – Lake County, IL – IN – WI CMSA	666	6
Washington, DC – MD – VA MSA	629	7
San Francisco – Oakland – San Jose, CA CMSA	498	8
Detroit – Ann Arbor, MI CMSA	495	9
Houston – Galveston – Brazoria, TX CMSA	472	10
Columbia, SC MSA	450	11
Killeen – Temple, TX MSA	379	12
Boston – Lawrence – Salem, MA – NH CMSA	331	13
Indianapolis, IN MSA	328	14
Memphis, TN – AR – MS MSA	311	15
San Diego, CA MSA	295	16
Seattle – Tacoma, WA CMSA	290	17
Columbus, OH MSA	254	18
Phoenix, AZ MSA	246	19
Dallas – Fort Worth, TX CMSA	231	20
Sacramento, CA MSA	224	21
Lansing – East Lansing, MI MSA	218	22
Buffalo – Niagara Falls, NY CMSA	212	23
Montgomery, AL MSA	212	23
Kansas City, MO – KS MSA	202	24

Source: U.S. Department of Commerce, Bureau of the Census, Data User Services Division, *1990 Census of Population and Housing, Equal Employment Opportunity File, CD-90-EE0-1, January 1993,* CD-ROM.

★1477★

Occupations, By Race/Sex

Top 25 MSAs For Employment As Counselors, Educational and Vocational, 1990: Men

MSA/CMSA	Employees per 100,000 pop.	Rank
Cincinnati – Hamilton, OH – KY – IN CMSA	7,280	1
Los Angeles – Anaheim – Riverside, CA CMSA	4,517	2
Chicago – Gary – Lake County, IL – IN – WI CMSA	2,427	3
San Francisco – Oakland – San Jose, CA CMSA	2,331	4
Philadelphia – Wilmington – Trenton, PA – NJ – DE – MD CMSA	2,262	5
Boston – Lawrence – Salem, MA – NH CMSA	1,909	6
Washington, DC – MD – VA MSA	1,725	7
Detroit – Ann Arbor, MI CMSA	1,412	8
Pittsburgh – Beaver Valley, PA CMSA	1,153	9
Minneapolis – St. Paul, MN – WI MSA	1,097	10
Seattle – Tacoma, WA CMSA	1,080	11
Dallas – Fort Worth, TX CMSA	954	12
Baltimore, MD MSA	915	13
Cleveland – Akron – Lorain, OH CMSA	894	14
Houston – Galveston – Brazoria, TX CMSA	843	15
San Diego, CA MSA	841	16
Miami – Fort Lauderdale, FL CMSA	826	17
Providence – Pawtucket – Fall River, RI – MA CMSA	782	18
St. Louis, MO – IL MSA	778	19
Denver – Boulder, CO CMSA	751	20
Sacramento, CA MSA	744	21
Phoenix, AZ MSA	718	22
Buffalo – Niagara Falls, NY CMSA	664	23
Portland – Vancouver, OR – WA CMSA	626	24
Rochester, NY MSA	625	25

Source: U.S. Department of Commerce, Bureau of the Census, Data User Services Division, *1990 Census of Population and Housing, Equal Employment Opportunity File, CD-90-EE0-1, January 1993,* CD-ROM.

★1478★

Occupations, By Race/Sex

Top 25 MSAs For Employment As Counselors, Educational and Vocational, 1990: Women

MSA/CMSA	Employees per 100,000 pop.	Rank
Portland – Vancouver, OR – WA CMSA	12,415	1
Los Angeles – Anaheim – Riverside, CA CMSA	7,197	2
San Francisco – Oakland – San Jose, CA CMSA	3,949	3
Philadelphia – Wilmington – Trenton, PA – NJ – DE – MD CMSA	3,929	4
Chicago – Gary – Lake County, IL – IN – WI CMSA	3,605	5
Boston – Lawrence – Salem, MA – NH CMSA	3,374	6
Washington, DC – MD – VA MSA	3,214	7
Detroit – Ann Arbor, MI CMSA	2,373	8
Dallas – Fort Worth, TX CMSA	2,154	9
Houston – Galveston – Brazoria, TX CMSA	1,996	10
Seattle – Tacoma, WA CMSA	1,873	11
Miami – Fort Lauderdale, FL CMSA	1,853	12
Baltimore, MD MSA	1,721	13
San Diego, CA MSA	1,707	14
Cleveland – Akron – Lorain, OH CMSA	1,540	15
St. Louis, MO – IL MSA	1,500	16
Atlanta, GA MSA	1,489	17
Minneapolis – St. Paul, MN – WI MSA	1,466	18
Pittsburgh – Beaver Valley, PA CMSA	1,193	19
Cincinnati – Hamilton, OH – KY – IN CMSA	1,163	20
Denver – Boulder, CO CMSA	1,163	20
Sacramento, CA MSA	1,141	21
Portland – Vancouver, OR – WA CMSA	1,077	22
Tampa – St. Petersburg – Clearwater, FL MSA	1,015	23
Columbus, OH MSA	970	24

Source: U.S. Department of Commerce, Bureau of the Census, Data User Services Division, *1990 Census of Population and Housing, Equal Employment Opportunity File, CD-90-EE0-1, January 1993,* CD-ROM.

★1479★

Occupations, By Race/Sex

Top 25 MSAs For Employment As Dancers, 1990: Men

MSA/CMSA	Employees per 100,000 pop.	Rank
Sacramento, CA MSA	1,057	1
Los Angeles – Anaheim – Riverside, CA CMSA	595	2
San Francisco – Oakland – San Jose, CA CMSA	225	3
Las Vegas, NV MSA	192	4
Chicago – Gary – Lake County, IL – IN – WI CMSA	187	5
Miami – Fort Lauderdale, FL CMSA	148	6
Dallas – Fort Worth, TX CMSA	144	7
Orlando, FL MSA	135	8
Houston – Galveston – Brazoria, TX CMSA	110	9
Washington, DC – MD – VA MSA	101	10
Philadelphia – Wilmington – Trenton, PA – NJ – DE – MD CMSA	95	11
Detroit – Ann Arbor, MI CMSA	86	12
Cleveland – Akron – Lorain, OH CMSA	82	13
Honolulu, HI MSA	69	14
Milwaukee – Racine, WI CMSA	67	15
Boston – Lawrence – Salem, MA – NH CMSA	66	16
Seattle – Tacoma, WA CMSA	60	17
Tampa – St. Petersburg – Clearwater, FL MSA	60	17
Atlanta, GA MSA	53	18
Austin, TX MSA	47	19
Baltimore, MD MSA	45	20
Sacramento, CA MSA	40	21
Oklahoma City, OK MSA	39	22
Denver – Boulder, CO CMSA	38	23
St. Louis, MO – IL MSA	38	23

Source: U.S. Department of Commerce, Bureau of the Census, Data User Services Division, *1990 Census of Population and Housing, Equal Employment Opportunity File, CD-90-EE0-1, January 1993,* CD-ROM.

★1480★

Occupations, By Race/Sex

Top 25 MSAs For Employment As Dancers, 1990: Women

MSA/CMSA	Employees per 100,000 pop.	Rank
Cincinnati – Hamilton, OH – KY – IN CMSA	1,868	1
Los Angeles – Anaheim – Riverside, CA CMSA	1,188	2
Las Vegas, NV MSA	580	3
Philadelphia – Wilmington – Trenton, PA – NJ – DE – MD CMSA	531	4

[Continued]

★1480★

Top 25 MSAs For Employment As Dancers, 1990: Women
[Continued]

MSA/CMSA	Employees per 100,000 pop.	Rank
Houston – Galveston – Brazoria, TX CMSA	456	5
Detroit – Ann Arbor, MI CMSA	410	6
Dallas – Fort Worth, TX CMSA	389	7
Honolulu, HI MSA	382	8
Miami – Fort Lauderdale, FL CMSA	378	9
Atlanta, GA MSA	355	10
Washington, DC – MD – VA MSA	355	10
Chicago – Gary – Lake County, IL – IN – WI CMSA	314	11
San Francisco – Oakland – San Jose, CA CMSA	312	12
Orlando, FL MSA	287	13
Seattle – Tacoma, WA CMSA	286	14
Tampa – St. Petersburg – Clearwater, FL MSA	251	15
Phoenix, AZ MSA	244	16
Boston – Lawrence – Salem, MA – NH CMSA	236	17
Minneapolis – St. Paul, MN – WI MSA	230	18
San Diego, CA MSA	223	19
Norfolk – Virginia Beach – Newport News, VA MSA	200	20
Austin, TX MSA	190	21
Cleveland – Akron – Lorain, OH CMSA	185	22
Denver – Boulder, CO CMSA	184	23
Indianapolis, IN MSA	181	24

Source: U.S. Department of Commerce, Bureau of the Census, Data User Services Division, *1990 Census of Population and Housing, Equal Employment Opportunity File, CD-90-EE0-1, January 1993,* CD-ROM.

★1481★

Occupations, By Race/Sex

Top 25 MSAs For Employment As Data-entry Keyers, 1990: Men

MSA/CMSA	Employees per 100,000 pop.	Rank
Kansas City, MO – KS MSA	10,297	1
Los Angeles – Anaheim – Riverside, CA CMSA	7,737	2
San Francisco – Oakland – San Jose, CA CMSA	3,793	3
Chicago – Gary – Lake County, IL – IN – WI CMSA	3,508	4
Washington, DC – MD – VA MSA	2,417	5
Philadelphia – Wilmington – Trenton, PA – NJ – DE – MD CMSA	2,289	6
Dallas – Fort Worth, TX CMSA	2,017	7
Boston – Lawrence – Salem, MA – NH CMSA	1,828	8

[Continued]

★1481★

Top 25 MSAs For Employment As Data-entry Keyers, 1990: Men
[Continued]

MSA/CMSA	Employees per 100,000 pop.	Rank
Minneapolis – St. Paul, MN – WI MSA	1,527	9
Atlanta, GA MSA	1,451	10
Detroit – Ann Arbor, MI CMSA	1,255	11
San Diego, CA MSA	1,210	12
Seattle – Tacoma, WA CMSA	1,186	13
Houston – Galveston – Brazoria, TX CMSA	1,179	14
Miami – Fort Lauderdale, FL CMSA	1,175	15
Denver – Boulder, CO CMSA	1,089	16
Phoenix, AZ MSA	1,063	17
Baltimore, MD MSA	1,042	18
Austin, TX MSA	877	19
Kansas City, MO – KS MSA	799	20
St. Louis, MO – IL MSA	790	21
Pittsburgh – Beaver Valley, PA CMSA	723	22
Sacramento, CA MSA	714	23
Cincinnati – Hamilton, OH – KY – IN CMSA	690	24
Columbus, OH MSA	661	25

Source: U.S. Department of Commerce, Bureau of the Census, Data User Services Division, *1990 Census of Population and Housing, Equal Employment Opportunity File, CD-90-EE0-1, January 1993,* CD-ROM.

★1482★
Occupations, By Race/Sex

Top 25 MSAs For Employment As Data-entry Keyers, 1990: Women

MSA/CMSA	Employees per 100,000 pop.	Rank
Kansas City, MO – KS MSA	49,562	1
Los Angeles – Anaheim – Riverside, CA CMSA	35,331	2
Chicago – Gary – Lake County, IL – IN – WI CMSA	25,507	3
Philadelphia – Wilmington – Trenton, PA – NJ – DE – MD CMSA	18,090	4
San Francisco – Oakland – San Jose, CA CMSA	15,826	5
Dallas – Fort Worth, TX CMSA	13,515	6
Boston – Lawrence – Salem, MA – NH CMSA	12,742	7
Washington, DC – MD – VA MSA	11,403	8
Minneapolis – St. Paul, MN – WI MSA	10,251	9
Atlanta, GA MSA	9,825	10
Detroit – Ann Arbor, MI CMSA	9,760	11
Houston – Galveston – Brazoria, TX CMSA	9,025	12
Miami – Fort Lauderdale, FL CMSA	7,698	13

[Continued]

★1482★

Top 25 MSAs For Employment As Data-entry Keyers, 1990: Women
[Continued]

MSA/CMSA	Employees per 100,000 pop.	Rank
Baltimore, MD MSA	7,363	14
Seattle – Tacoma, WA CMSA	6,955	15
Cleveland – Akron – Lorain, OH CMSA	6,919	16
St. Louis, MO – IL MSA	6,613	17
Kansas City, MO – KS MSA	6,557	18
Phoenix, AZ MSA	6,364	19
Columbus, OH MSA	6,235	20
Denver – Boulder, CO CMSA	5,908	21
Cincinnati – Hamilton, OH – KY – IN CMSA	5,374	22
Tampa – St. Petersburg – Clearwater, FL MSA	5,240	23
San Diego, CA MSA	5,237	24
Milwaukee – Racine, WI CMSA	4,992	25

Source: U.S. Department of Commerce, Bureau of the Census, Data User Services Division, *1990 Census of Population and Housing, Equal Employment Opportunity File, CD-90-EE0-1, January 1993,* CD-ROM.

★1483★
Occupations, By Race/Sex

Top 25 MSAs For Employment As Dental Assistants, 1990: Men

MSA/CMSA	Employees per 100,000 pop.	Rank
Sacramento, CA MSA	834	1
Los Angeles – Anaheim – Riverside, CA CMSA	645	2
Chicago – Gary – Lake County, IL – IN – WI CMSA	239	3
Boston – Lawrence – Salem, MA – NH CMSA	163	4
San Francisco – Oakland – San Jose, CA CMSA	145	5
Detroit – Ann Arbor, MI CMSA	103	6
Baltimore, MD MSA	87	7
Miami – Fort Lauderdale, FL CMSA	80	8
Houston – Galveston – Brazoria, TX CMSA	76	9
Washington, DC – MD – VA MSA	73	10
Portland – Vancouver, OR – WA CMSA	63	11
Indianapolis, IN MSA	62	12
Atlanta, GA MSA	62	12
Seattle – Tacoma, WA CMSA	58	13
St. Louis, MO – IL MSA	57	14
Pittsburgh – Beaver Valley, PA CMSA	56	15
Philadelphia – Wilmington – Trenton, PA – NJ – DE – MD CMSA	52	16
Cleveland – Akron – Lorain, OH CMSA	51	17

[Continued]

★1483★

Top 25 MSAs For Employment As Dental Assistants, 1990: Men
[Continued]

MSA/CMSA	Employees per 100,000 pop.	Rank
Dallas – Fort Worth, TX CMSA	51	17
San Antonio, TX MSA	49	18
Great Falls, MT MSA	45	19
San Diego, CA MSA	42	20
Reno, NV MSA	38	21
Sacramento, CA MSA	36	22
El Paso, TX MSA	36	22

Source: U.S. Department of Commerce, Bureau of the Census, Data User Services Division, *1990 Census of Population and Housing, Equal Employment Opportunity File,* CD-90-EE0-1, January 1993, CD-ROM.

★1484★

Occupations, By Race/Sex

Top 25 MSAs For Employment As Dental Assistants, 1990: Women

MSA/CMSA	Employees per 100,000 pop.	Rank
New Orleans, LA MSA	15,067	1
Los Angeles – Anaheim – Riverside, CA CMSA	10,868	2
Chicago – Gary – Lake County, IL – IN – WI CMSA	6,082	3
San Francisco – Oakland – San Jose, CA CMSA	5,537	4
Philadelphia – Wilmington – Trenton, PA – NJ – DE – MD CMSA	4,351	5
Detroit – Ann Arbor, MI CMSA	3,930	6
Boston – Lawrence – Salem, MA – NH CMSA	3,361	7
Washington, DC – MD – VA MSA	2,576	8
Dallas – Fort Worth, TX CMSA	2,567	9
Seattle – Tacoma, WA CMSA	2,519	10
Houston – Galveston – Brazoria, TX CMSA	2,287	11
Minneapolis – St. Paul, MN – WI MSA	2,170	12
San Diego, CA MSA	2,145	13
Cleveland – Akron – Lorain, OH CMSA	2,087	14
Miami – Fort Lauderdale, FL CMSA	1,897	15
St. Louis, MO – IL MSA	1,797	16
Denver – Boulder, CO CMSA	1,737	17
Atlanta, GA MSA	1,652	18
Baltimore, MD MSA	1,558	19
Portland – Vancouver, OR – WA CMSA	1,475	20
Phoenix, AZ MSA	1,458	21
Pittsburgh – Beaver Valley, PA CMSA	1,448	22
Sacramento, CA MSA	1,413	23

[Continued]

★1484★

Top 25 MSAs For Employment As Dental Assistants, 1990: Women
[Continued]

MSA/CMSA	Employees per 100,000 pop.	Rank
Milwaukee – Racine, WI CMSA	1,399	24
Tampa – St. Petersburg – Clearwater, FL MSA	1,300	25

Source: U.S. Department of Commerce, Bureau of the Census, Data User Services Division, *1990 Census of Population and Housing, Equal Employment Opportunity File,* CD-90-EE0-1, January 1993, CD-ROM.

★1485★

Occupations, By Race/Sex

Top 25 MSAs For Employment As Dental Hygienists, 1990: Men

MSA/CMSA	Employees per 100,000 pop.	Rank
Orlando, FL MSA	107	1
San Francisco – Oakland – San Jose, CA CMSA	60	2
Philadelphia – Wilmington – Trenton, PA – NJ – DE – MD CMSA	55	3
Los Angeles – Anaheim – Riverside, CA CMSA	43	4
Boston – Lawrence – Salem, MA – NH CMSA	41	5
Chicago – Gary – Lake County, IL – IN – WI CMSA	39	6
Phoenix, AZ MSA	32	7
San Diego, CA MSA	29	8
Seattle – Tacoma, WA CMSA	27	9
Sacramento, CA MSA	26	10
Modesto, CA MSA	24	11
Killeen – Temple, TX MSA	22	12
Chattanooga, TN – GA MSA	20	13
Miami – Fort Lauderdale, FL CMSA	18	14
Abilene, TX MSA	18	14
Anniston, AL MSA	18	14
Portland – Vancouver, OR – WA CMSA	17	15
Kansas City, MO – KS MSA	16	16
Detroit – Ann Arbor, MI CMSA	15	17
Houston – Galveston – Brazoria, TX CMSA	14	18
Cleveland – Akron – Lorain, OH CMSA	14	18
Youngstown – Warren, OH MSA	13	19
Alexandria, LA MSA	13	19
Fresno, CA MSA	12	20
Grand Rapids, MI MSA	12	20

Source: U.S. Department of Commerce, Bureau of the Census, Data User Services Division, *1990 Census of Population and Housing, Equal Employment Opportunity File,* CD-90-EE0-1, January 1993, CD-ROM.

★1486★

Occupations, By Race/Sex

Top 25 MSAs For Employment As Dental Hygienists, 1990: Women

MSA/CMSA	Employees per 100,000 pop.	Rank
Providence – Pawtucket – Fall River, RI – MA CMSA	5,181	1
Los Angeles – Anaheim – Riverside, CA CMSA	2,954	2
San Francisco – Oakland – San Jose, CA CMSA	2,633	3
Chicago – Gary – Lake County, IL – IN – WI CMSA	2,269	4
Detroit – Ann Arbor, MI CMSA	2,005	5
Boston – Lawrence – Salem, MA – NH CMSA	1,873	6
Philadelphia – Wilmington – Trenton, PA – NJ – DE – MD CMSA	1,617	7
Minneapolis – St. Paul, MN – WI MSA	1,407	8
Washington, DC – MD – VA MSA	1,262	9
Seattle – Tacoma, WA CMSA	1,227	10
Miami – Fort Lauderdale, FL CMSA	1,195	11
Atlanta, GA MSA	1,148	12
Dallas – Fort Worth, TX CMSA	1,050	13
Portland – Vancouver, OR – WA CMSA	811	14
Houston – Galveston – Brazoria, TX CMSA	805	15
Cleveland – Akron – Lorain, OH CMSA	768	16
Phoenix, AZ MSA	705	17
Baltimore, MD MSA	681	18
Denver – Boulder, CO CMSA	680	19
Buffalo – Niagara Falls, NY CMSA	640	20
Milwaukee – Racine, WI CMSA	610	21
San Diego, CA MSA	579	22
Cincinnati – Hamilton, OH – KY – IN CMSA	578	23
Rochester, NY MSA	532	24
Columbus, OH MSA	529	25

Source: U.S. Department of Commerce, Bureau of the Census, Data User Services Division, *1990 Census of Population and Housing, Equal Employment Opportunity File, CD-90-EE0-1,* January 1993, CD-ROM.

★1487★

Occupations, By Race/Sex

Top 25 MSAs For Employment As Dentists, 1990: Men

MSA/CMSA	Employees per 100,000 pop.	Rank
San Antonio, TX MSA	14,680	1
Los Angeles – Anaheim – Riverside, CA CMSA	7,994	2
San Francisco – Oakland – San Jose, CA CMSA	5,007	3
Chicago – Gary – Lake County, IL – IN – WI CMSA	4,976	4
Philadelphia – Wilmington – Trenton, PA – NJ – DE – MD CMSA	3,538	5
Detroit – Ann Arbor, MI CMSA	3,040	6
Boston – Lawrence – Salem, MA – NH CMSA	2,980	7
Washington, DC – MD – VA MSA	2,658	8
Dallas – Fort Worth, TX CMSA	2,087	9
Seattle – Tacoma, WA CMSA	1,879	10
Houston – Galveston – Brazoria, TX CMSA	1,807	11
Miami – Fort Lauderdale, FL CMSA	1,795	12
Pittsburgh – Beaver Valley, PA CMSA	1,718	13
Minneapolis – St. Paul, MN – WI MSA	1,641	14
Cleveland – Akron – Lorain, OH CMSA	1,635	15
Atlanta, GA MSA	1,547	16
Baltimore, MD MSA	1,429	17
San Diego, CA MSA	1,309	18
Denver – Boulder, CO CMSA	1,279	19
St. Louis, MO – IL MSA	1,270	20
Kansas City, MO – KS MSA	1,225	21
Phoenix, AZ MSA	1,116	22
Milwaukee – Racine, WI CMSA	1,043	23
Sacramento, CA MSA	1,002	24
Portland – Vancouver, OR – WA CMSA	999	25

Source: U.S. Department of Commerce, Bureau of the Census, Data User Services Division, *1990 Census of Population and Housing, Equal Employment Opportunity File, CD-90-EE0-1,* January 1993, CD-ROM.

★1488★

Occupations, By Race/Sex

Top 25 MSAs For Employment As Dentists, 1990: Women

MSA/CMSA	Employees per 100,000 pop.	Rank
Indianapolis, IN MSA	2,377	1
Los Angeles – Anaheim – Riverside, CA CMSA	2,028	2
Chicago – Gary – Lake County, IL – IN – WI CMSA	947	3
San Francisco – Oakland – San Jose, CA CMSA	939	4

[Continued]

★1488★

Top 25 MSAs For Employment As Dentists, 1990: Women

[Continued]

MSA/CMSA	Employees per 100,000 pop.	Rank
Washington, DC – MD – VA MSA	590	5
Philadelphia – Wilmington – Trenton, PA – NJ – DE – MD CMSA	556	6
Boston – Lawrence – Salem, MA – NH CMSA	490	7
Dallas – Fort Worth, TX CMSA	418	8
Houston – Galveston – Brazoria, TX CMSA	400	9
Detroit – Ann Arbor, MI CMSA	390	10
Miami – Fort Lauderdale, FL CMSA	326	11
Minneapolis – St. Paul, MN – WI MSA	314	12
San Diego, CA MSA	313	13
Seattle – Tacoma, WA CMSA	267	14
Atlanta, GA MSA	255	15
Denver – Boulder, CO CMSA	225	16
Baltimore, MD MSA	224	17
Cleveland – Akron – Lorain, OH CMSA	210	18
Pittsburgh – Beaver Valley, PA CMSA	196	19
St. Louis, MO – IL MSA	183	20
Sacramento, CA MSA	163	21
Tampa – St. Petersburg – Clearwater, FL MSA	157	22
Raleigh – Durham, NC MSA	148	23
New Orleans, LA MSA	143	24
Memphis, TN – AR – MS MSA	141	25

Source: U.S. Department of Commerce, Bureau of the Census, Data User Services Division, *1990 Census of Population and Housing, Equal Employment Opportunity File, CD-90-EE0-1, January 1993,* CD-ROM.

★1489★

Occupations, By Race/Sex

Top 25 MSAs For Employment As Dietitians, 1990: Men

MSA/CMSA	Employees per 100,000 pop.	Rank
Columbus, OH MSA	805	1
Los Angeles – Anaheim – Riverside, CA CMSA	778	2
Chicago – Gary – Lake County, IL – IN – WI CMSA	444	3
Boston – Lawrence – Salem, MA – NH CMSA	307	4
San Francisco – Oakland – San Jose, CA CMSA	280	5
Philadelphia – Wilmington – Trenton, PA – NJ – DE – MD CMSA	221	6
Washington, DC – MD – VA MSA	211	7

[Continued]

★1489★

Top 25 MSAs For Employment As Dietitians, 1990: Men

[Continued]

MSA/CMSA	Employees per 100,000 pop.	Rank
Dallas – Fort Worth, TX CMSA	158	8
St. Louis, MO – IL MSA	146	9
Detroit – Ann Arbor, MI CMSA	140	10
Baltimore, MD MSA	130	11
Tampa – St. Petersburg – Clearwater, FL MSA	129	12
Miami – Fort Lauderdale, FL CMSA	127	13
Minneapolis – St. Paul, MN – WI MSA	116	14
Pittsburgh – Beaver Valley, PA CMSA	108	15
Atlanta, GA MSA	100	16
Seattle – Tacoma, WA CMSA	99	17
Memphis, TN – AR – MS MSA	97	18
Buffalo – Niagara Falls, NY CMSA	95	19
Dayton – Springfield, OH MSA	94	20
Hartford – New Britain – Middletown, CT CMSA	86	21
Cleveland – Akron – Lorain, OH CMSA	82	22
Houston – Galveston – Brazoria, TX CMSA	74	23
Albuquerque, NM MSA	71	24
Columbus, OH MSA	68	25

Source: U.S. Department of Commerce, Bureau of the Census, Data User Services Division, *1990 Census of Population and Housing, Equal Employment Opportunity File, CD-90-EE0-1, January 1993,* CD-ROM.

★1490★

Occupations, By Race/Sex

Top 25 MSAs For Employment As Dietitians, 1990: Women

MSA/CMSA	Employees per 100,000 pop.	Rank
Raleigh – Durham, NC MSA	6,520	1
Los Angeles – Anaheim – Riverside, CA CMSA	3,430	2
Chicago – Gary – Lake County, IL – IN – WI CMSA	2,438	3
Philadelphia – Wilmington – Trenton, PA – NJ – DE – MD CMSA	2,186	4
San Francisco – Oakland – San Jose, CA CMSA	1,877	5
Boston – Lawrence – Salem, MA – NH CMSA	1,847	6
Detroit – Ann Arbor, MI CMSA	1,674	7
Washington, DC – MD – VA MSA	1,483	8
Dallas – Fort Worth, TX CMSA	1,274	9
Houston – Galveston – Brazoria, TX CMSA	1,107	10
Cleveland – Akron – Lorain, OH CMSA	1,075	11

[Continued]

★1490★

Top 25 MSAs For Employment As Dietitians, 1990: Women

[Continued]

MSA/CMSA	Employees per 100,000 pop.	Rank
St. Louis, MO – IL MSA	996	12
Seattle – Tacoma, WA CMSA	980	13
Miami – Fort Lauderdale, FL CMSA	943	14
Atlanta, GA MSA	925	15
Baltimore, MD MSA	894	16
Minneapolis – St. Paul, MN – WI MSA	826	17
Pittsburgh – Beaver Valley, PA CMSA	776	18
Cincinnati – Hamilton, OH – KY – IN CMSA	709	19
Columbus, OH MSA	658	20
Buffalo – Niagara Falls, NY CMSA	644	21
Milwaukee – Racine, WI CMSA	633	22
San Diego, CA MSA	620	23
Kansas City, MO – KS MSA	602	24
Indianapolis, IN MSA	578	25

Source: U.S. Department of Commerce, Bureau of the Census, Data User Services Division, 1990 Census of Population and Housing, Equal Employment Opportunity File, CD-90-EE0-1, January 1993, CD-ROM.

★1491★

Occupations, By Race/Sex

Top 25 MSAs For Employment As Dressmakers, 1990: Men

MSA/CMSA	Employees per 100,000 pop.	Rank
Providence – Pawtucket – Fall River, RI – MA CMSA	1,404	1
New York – Northern New Jersey – Long Island, NY – NJ – CT CMSA	738	2
Chicago – Gary – Lake County, IL – IN – WI CMSA	213	3
Dallas – Fort Worth, TX CMSA	191	4
San Francisco – Oakland – San Jose, CA CMSA	187	5
San Diego, CA MSA	140	6
Philadelphia – Wilmington – Trenton, PA – NJ – DE – MD CMSA	126	7
Miami – Fort Lauderdale, FL CMSA	118	8
Atlanta, GA MSA	71	9
Seattle – Tacoma, WA CMSA	71	9
Washington, DC – MD – VA MSA	71	9
Houston – Galveston – Brazoria, TX CMSA	69	10
Phoenix, AZ MSA	67	11
Tampa – St. Petersburg – Clearwater, FL MSA	62	12
Honolulu, HI MSA	59	13

[Continued]

★1491★

Top 25 MSAs For Employment As Dressmakers, 1990: Men

[Continued]

MSA/CMSA	Employees per 100,000 pop.	Rank
El Paso, TX MSA	56	14
Baltimore, MD MSA	53	15
Denver – Boulder, CO CMSA	53	15
Decatur, AL MSA	52	16
Detroit – Ann Arbor, MI CMSA	49	17
Minneapolis – St. Paul, MN – WI MSA	48	18
Augusta, GA – SC MSA	46	19
West Palm Beach – Boca Raton – Delray Beach, FL MSA	46	19
Pittsburgh – Beaver Valley, PA CMSA	44	20
Boston – Lawrence – Salem, MA – NH CMSA	43	21

Source: U.S. Department of Commerce, Bureau of the Census, Data User Services Division, 1990 Census of Population and Housing, Equal Employment Opportunity File, CD-90-EE0-1, January 1993, CD-ROM.

★1492★

Occupations, By Race/Sex

Top 25 MSAs For Employment As Dressmakers, 1990: Women

MSA/CMSA	Employees per 100,000 pop.	Rank
Washington, DC – MD – VA MSA	8,447	1
Los Angeles – Anaheim – Riverside, CA CMSA	6,045	2
Chicago – Gary – Lake County, IL – IN – WI CMSA	2,737	3
San Francisco – Oakland – San Jose, CA CMSA	2,241	4
Miami – Fort Lauderdale, FL CMSA	2,236	5
Dallas – Fort Worth, TX CMSA	2,026	6
Philadelphia – Wilmington – Trenton, PA – NJ – DE – MD CMSA	1,887	7
Detroit – Ann Arbor, MI CMSA	1,436	8
Washington, DC – MD – VA MSA	1,390	9
Houston – Galveston – Brazoria, TX CMSA	1,150	10
Atlanta, GA MSA	1,146	11
San Diego, CA MSA	973	12
Cleveland – Akron – Lorain, OH CMSA	957	13
St. Louis, MO – IL MSA	942	14
Boston – Lawrence – Salem, MA – NH CMSA	941	15
Seattle – Tacoma, WA CMSA	935	16
Minneapolis – St. Paul, MN – WI MSA	932	17
Denver – Boulder, CO CMSA	838	18
Honolulu, HI MSA	768	19

[Continued]

★1492★
Top 25 MSAs For Employment As Dressmakers, 1990: Women
[Continued]

MSA/CMSA	Employees per 100,000 pop.	Rank
Tampa – St. Petersburg – Clearwater, FL MSA	768	19
Pittsburgh – Beaver Valley, PA CMSA	750	20
Kansas City, MO – KS MSA	641	21
Milwaukee – Racine, WI CMSA	621	22
Phoenix, AZ MSA	592	23
Cincinnati – Hamilton, OH – KY – IN CMSA	558	24

Source: U.S. Department of Commerce, Bureau of the Census, Data User Services Division, *1990 Census of Population and Housing, Equal Employment Opportunity File, CD-90-EE0-1, January 1993,* CD-ROM.

★1493★
Occupations, By Race/Sex
Top 25 MSAs For Employment As Early Childhood Teacher's Assistants, 1990: Men

MSA/CMSA	Employees per 100,000 pop.	Rank
Grand Rapids, MI MSA	1,240	1
Los Angeles – Anaheim – Riverside, CA CMSA	963	2
Chicago – Gary – Lake County, IL – IN – WI CMSA	590	3
San Francisco – Oakland – San Jose, CA CMSA	532	4
Washington, DC – MD – VA MSA	317	5
Boston – Lawrence – Salem, MA – NH CMSA	293	6
Miami – Fort Lauderdale, FL CMSA	289	7
Philadelphia – Wilmington – Trenton, PA – NJ – DE – MD CMSA	279	8
Detroit – Ann Arbor, MI CMSA	257	9
Minneapolis – St. Paul, MN – WI MSA	220	10
Albany – Schenectady – Troy, NY MSA	189	11
Atlanta, GA MSA	183	12
Houston – Galveston – Brazoria, TX CMSA	177	13
Dallas – Fort Worth, TX CMSA	176	14
Seattle – Tacoma, WA CMSA	164	15
St. Louis, MO – IL MSA	155	16
Cleveland – Akron – Lorain, OH CMSA	134	17
Baltimore, MD MSA	131	18
San Antonio, TX MSA	129	19
Denver – Boulder, CO CMSA	119	20
Hartford – New Britain – Middletown, CT CMSA	111	21
San Diego, CA MSA	109	22

[Continued]

★1493★
Top 25 MSAs For Employment As Early Childhood Teacher's Assistants, 1990: Men
[Continued]

MSA/CMSA	Employees per 100,000 pop.	Rank
Tampa – St. Petersburg – Clearwater, FL MSA	98	23
Milwaukee – Racine, WI CMSA	94	24
Cincinnati – Hamilton, OH – KY – IN CMSA	94	24

Source: U.S. Department of Commerce, Bureau of the Census, Data User Services Division, *1990 Census of Population and Housing, Equal Employment Opportunity File, CD-90-EE0-1, January 1993,* CD-ROM.

★1494★
Occupations, By Race/Sex
Top 25 MSAs For Employment As Early Childhood Teacher's Assistants, 1990: Women

MSA/CMSA	Employees per 100,000 pop.	Rank
Cleveland – Akron – Lorain, OH CMSA	18,155	1
Los Angeles – Anaheim – Riverside, CA CMSA	12,670	2
Philadelphia – Wilmington – Trenton, PA – NJ – DE – MD CMSA	8,955	3
San Francisco – Oakland – San Jose, CA CMSA	7,805	4
Dallas – Fort Worth, TX CMSA	6,972	5
Chicago – Gary – Lake County, IL – IN – WI CMSA	6,843	6
Washington, DC – MD – VA MSA	6,729	7
Detroit – Ann Arbor, MI CMSA	5,746	8
Boston – Lawrence – Salem, MA – NH CMSA	5,734	9
Houston – Galveston – Brazoria, TX CMSA	5,656	10
Atlanta, GA MSA	5,239	11
Minneapolis – St. Paul, MN – WI MSA	4,768	12
Seattle – Tacoma, WA CMSA	4,384	13
Miami – Fort Lauderdale, FL CMSA	3,954	14
Denver – Boulder, CO CMSA	3,592	15
St. Louis, MO – IL MSA	3,247	16
San Diego, CA MSA	3,203	17
Baltimore, MD MSA	3,084	18
Cleveland – Akron – Lorain, OH CMSA	2,628	19
Phoenix, AZ MSA	2,614	20
Tampa – St. Petersburg – Clearwater, FL MSA	2,594	21
San Antonio, TX MSA	2,558	22
Charlotte – Gastonia – Rock Hill, NC – SC MSA	2,472	23

[Continued]

★1494★

Top 25 MSAs For Employment As Early Childhood Teacher's Assistants, 1990: Women

[Continued]

MSA/CMSA	Employees per 100,000 pop.	Rank
Kansas City, MO – KS MSA	2,314	24
Pittsburgh – Beaver Valley, PA CMSA	2,296	25

Source: U.S. Department of Commerce, Bureau of the Census, Data User Services Division, 1990 Census of Population and Housing, Equal Employment Opportunity File, CD-90-EE0-1, January 1993, CD-ROM.

★1495★

Occupations, By Race/Sex

Top 25 MSAs For Employment As Earth, Environmental, and Marine Science Teachers, 1990: Men

MSA/CMSA	Employees per 100,000 pop.	Rank
Oklahoma City, OK MSA	70	1
New York – Northern New Jersey – Long Island, NY – NJ – CT CMSA	54	2
Dallas – Fort Worth, TX CMSA	49	3
Columbus, OH MSA	46	4
Washington, DC – MD – VA MSA	34	5
San Francisco – Oakland – San Jose, CA CMSA	22	6
Cincinnati – Hamilton, OH – KY – IN CMSA	21	7
Philadelphia – Wilmington – Trenton, PA – NJ – DE – MD CMSA	19	8
Houston – Galveston – Brazoria, TX CMSA	18	9
Cleveland – Akron – Lorain, OH CMSA	17	10
Lawrence, KS MSA	16	11
Denver – Boulder, CO CMSA	15	12
Omaha, NE – IA MSA	14	13
Raleigh – Durham, NC MSA	14	13
Grand Forks, ND MSA	13	14
Abilene, TX MSA	12	15
Albany – Schenectady – Troy, NY MSA	11	16
Casper, WY MSA	10	17
Bryan – College Station, TX MSA	9	18
Seattle – Tacoma, WA CMSA	9	18
Lincoln, NE MSA	9	18
Madison, WI MSA	9	18
Baltimore, MD MSA	8	19
Battle Creek, MI MSA	8	19
St. Louis, MO – IL MSA	8	19

Source: U.S. Department of Commerce, Bureau of the Census, Data User Services Division, 1990 Census of Population and Housing, Equal Employment Opportunity File, CD-90-EE0-1, January 1993, CD-ROM.

★1496★

Occupations, By Race/Sex

Top 25 MSAs For Employment As Earth, Environmental, and Marine Science Teachers, 1990: Women

MSA/CMSA	Employees per 100,000 pop.	Rank
Raleigh – Durham, NC MSA	32	1
Norfolk – Virginia Beach – Newport News, VA MSA	23	2
Lafayette – West Lafayette, IN MSA	17	3
New York – Northern New Jersey – Long Island, NY – NJ – CT CMSA	17	3
Sacramento, CA MSA	16	4
San Francisco – Oakland – San Jose, CA CMSA	16	4
Bellingham, WA MSA	15	5
Houston – Galveston – Brazoria, TX CMSA	14	6
Syracuse, NY MSA	13	7
Fort Collins – Loveland, CO MSA	12	8
Gainesville, FL MSA	11	9
Lubbock, TX MSA	11	9
Boston – Lawrence – Salem, MA – NH CMSA	10	10
Lancaster, PA MSA	9	11
Philadelphia – Wilmington – Trenton, PA – NJ – DE – MD CMSA	8	12
Rochester, NY MSA	8	12
Grand Forks, ND MSA	7	13
Athens, GA MSA	6	14
Dallas – Fort Worth, TX CMSA	6	14
Knoxville, TN MSA	6	14
San Diego, CA MSA	6	14
Washington, DC – MD – VA MSA	5	15
Bremerton, WA MSA	4	16
Scranton – Wilkes-Barre, PA MSA	4	16
Appleton – Oshkosh – Neenah, WI MSA	2	17

Source: U.S. Department of Commerce, Bureau of the Census, Data User Services Division, 1990 Census of Population and Housing, Equal Employment Opportunity File, CD-90-EE0-1, January 1993, CD-ROM.

★1497★

Occupations, By Race/Sex

Top 25 MSAs For Employment As Economics Teachers, 1990: Men

MSA/CMSA	Employees per 100,000 pop.	Rank
West Palm Beach – Boca Raton – Delray Beach, FL MSA	175	1
Boston – Lawrence – Salem, MA – NH CMSA	160	2
Los Angeles – Anaheim – Riverside, CA CMSA	114	3
Washington, DC – MD – VA MSA	107	4

[Continued]

★1497★

Top 25 MSAs For Employment As Economics Teachers, 1990: Men
[Continued]

MSA/CMSA	Employees per 100,000 pop.	Rank
Chicago – Gary – Lake County, IL – IN – WI CMSA	77	5
San Francisco – Oakland – San Jose, CA CMSA	72	6
Philadelphia – Wilmington – Trenton, PA – NJ – DE – MD CMSA	72	6
Miami – Fort Lauderdale, FL CMSA	53	7
Houston – Galveston – Brazoria, TX CMSA	48	8
Detroit – Ann Arbor, MI CMSA	43	9
Cincinnati – Hamilton, OH – KY – IN CMSA	38	10
San Diego, CA MSA	37	11
Seattle – Tacoma, WA CMSA	37	11
Hartford – New Britain – Middletown, CT CMSA	36	12
Albany – Schenectady – Troy, NY MSA	32	13
Bryan – College Station, TX MSA	32	13
Gainesville, FL MSA	30	14
Buffalo – Niagara Falls, NY CMSA	29	15
Phoenix, AZ MSA	29	15
Raleigh – Durham, NC MSA	27	16
New Orleans, LA MSA	25	17
St. Louis, MO – IL MSA	24	18
Minneapolis – St. Paul, MN – WI MSA	23	19
Cleveland – Akron – Lorain, OH CMSA	22	20
State College, PA MSA	22	20

Source: U.S. Department of Commerce, Bureau of the Census, Data User Services Division, *1990 Census of Population and Housing, Equal Employment Opportunity File, CD-90-EE0-1,* January 1993, CD-ROM.

★1498★
Occupations, By Race/Sex

Top 25 MSAs For Employment As Economics Teachers, 1990: Women

MSA/CMSA	Employees per 100,000 pop.	Rank
Sacramento, CA MSA	46	1
New York – Northern New Jersey – Long Island, NY – NJ – CT CMSA	39	2
Washington, DC – MD – VA MSA	38	3
Los Angeles – Anaheim – Riverside, CA CMSA	36	4
San Diego, CA MSA	24	5
St. Louis, MO – IL MSA	23	6
Boston – Lawrence – Salem, MA – NH CMSA	22	7

[Continued]

★1498★

Top 25 MSAs For Employment As Economics Teachers, 1990: Women
[Continued]

MSA/CMSA	Employees per 100,000 pop.	Rank
Pittsburgh – Beaver Valley, PA CMSA	21	8
Atlanta, GA MSA	19	9
Miami – Fort Lauderdale, FL CMSA	19	9
Albany – Schenectady – Troy, NY MSA	15	10
Flint, MI MSA	15	10
Portland – Vancouver, OR – WA CMSA	15	10
Detroit – Ann Arbor, MI CMSA	14	11
Minneapolis – St. Paul, MN – WI MSA	11	12
Syracuse, NY MSA	11	12
Burlington, VT MSA	10	13
Columbus, OH MSA	10	13
Denver – Boulder, CO CMSA	10	13
Knoxville, TN MSA	10	13
Montgomery, AL MSA	10	13
Nashville, TN MSA	10	13
Seattle – Tacoma, WA CMSA	10	13
Champaign – Urbana – Rantoul, IL MSA	9	14
Chattanooga, TN – GA MSA	9	14

Source: U.S. Department of Commerce, Bureau of the Census, Data User Services Division, *1990 Census of Population and Housing, Equal Employment Opportunity File, CD-90-EE0-1,* January 1993, CD-ROM.

★1499★
Occupations, By Race/Sex

Top 25 MSAs For Employment As Economists, 1990: Men

MSA/CMSA	Employees per 100,000 pop.	Rank
Nashville, TN MSA	10,197	1
Washington, DC – MD – VA MSA	9,707	2
Chicago – Gary – Lake County, IL – IN – WI CMSA	4,550	3
Los Angeles – Anaheim – Riverside, CA CMSA	4,499	4
San Francisco – Oakland – San Jose, CA CMSA	4,199	5
Boston – Lawrence – Salem, MA – NH CMSA	3,002	6
Philadelphia – Wilmington – Trenton, PA – NJ – DE – MD CMSA	2,379	7
Dallas – Fort Worth, TX CMSA	1,918	8
Atlanta, GA MSA	1,822	9
Detroit – Ann Arbor, MI CMSA	1,659	10
Houston – Galveston – Brazoria, TX CMSA	1,586	11
Minneapolis – St. Paul, MN – WI MSA	1,295	12

[Continued]

★1499★

Top 25 MSAs For Employment As Economists, 1990: Men
[Continued]

MSA/CMSA	Employees per 100,000 pop.	Rank
Denver – Boulder, CO CMSA	1,232	13
Seattle – Tacoma, WA CMSA	1,162	14
Cleveland – Akron – Lorain, OH CMSA	1,045	15
Baltimore, MD MSA	1,015	16
St. Louis, MO – IL MSA	888	17
Phoenix, AZ MSA	845	18
Miami – Fort Lauderdale, FL CMSA	816	19
San Diego, CA MSA	807	20
Portland – Vancouver, OR – WA CMSA	805	21
Pittsburgh – Beaver Valley, PA CMSA	771	22
Cincinnati – Hamilton, OH – KY – IN CMSA	735	23
Kansas City, MO – KS MSA	712	24
Columbus, OH MSA	663	25

Source: U.S. Department of Commerce, Bureau of the Census, Data User Services Division, *1990 Census of Population and Housing, Equal Employment Opportunity File, CD-90-EE0-1, January 1993*, CD-ROM.

★1500★

Occupations, By Race/Sex

Top 25 MSAs For Employment As Economists, 1990: Women

MSA/CMSA	Employees per 100,000 pop.	Rank
Tucson, AZ MSA	9,177	1
Washington, DC – MD – VA MSA	4,771	2
Chicago – Gary – Lake County, IL – IN – WI CMSA	3,797	3
Los Angeles – Anaheim – Riverside, CA CMSA	3,709	4
San Francisco – Oakland – San Jose, CA CMSA	3,519	5
Boston – Lawrence – Salem, MA – NH CMSA	3,158	6
Philadelphia – Wilmington – Trenton, PA – NJ – DE – MD CMSA	1,815	7
Dallas – Fort Worth, TX CMSA	1,565	8
Atlanta, GA MSA	1,484	9
Minneapolis – St. Paul, MN – WI MSA	1,281	10
Detroit – Ann Arbor, MI CMSA	1,239	11
Houston – Galveston – Brazoria, TX CMSA	1,206	12
Seattle – Tacoma, WA CMSA	1,173	13
Denver – Boulder, CO CMSA	1,070	14
Baltimore, MD MSA	803	15
Miami – Fort Lauderdale, FL CMSA	738	16

[Continued]

★1500★

Top 25 MSAs For Employment As Economists, 1990: Women
[Continued]

MSA/CMSA	Employees per 100,000 pop.	Rank
Phoenix, AZ MSA	729	17
Cleveland – Akron – Lorain, OH CMSA	680	18
Cincinnati – Hamilton, OH – KY – IN CMSA	672	19
St. Louis, MO – IL MSA	661	20
Kansas City, MO – KS MSA	658	21
Pittsburgh – Beaver Valley, PA CMSA	572	22
Milwaukee – Racine, WI CMSA	546	23
San Diego, CA MSA	544	24
Tampa – St. Petersburg – Clearwater, FL MSA	474	25

Source: U.S. Department of Commerce, Bureau of the Census, Data User Services Division, *1990 Census of Population and Housing, Equal Employment Opportunity File, CD-90-EE0-1, January 1993*, CD-ROM.

★1501★

Occupations, By Race/Sex

Top 25 MSAs For Employment As Editors and Reporters, 1990: Men

MSA/CMSA	Employees per 100,000 pop.	Rank
San Diego, CA MSA	20,944	1
Los Angeles – Anaheim – Riverside, CA CMSA	10,703	2
Washington, DC – MD – VA MSA	7,387	3
Chicago – Gary – Lake County, IL – IN – WI CMSA	5,644	4
San Francisco – Oakland – San Jose, CA CMSA	4,535	5
Boston – Lawrence – Salem, MA – NH CMSA	3,462	6
Philadelphia – Wilmington – Trenton, PA – NJ – DE – MD CMSA	3,382	7
Detroit – Ann Arbor, MI CMSA	2,122	8
Dallas – Fort Worth, TX CMSA	1,956	9
Atlanta, GA MSA	1,670	10
Miami – Fort Lauderdale, FL CMSA	1,581	11
Minneapolis – St. Paul, MN – WI MSA	1,507	12
San Diego, CA MSA	1,368	13
Seattle – Tacoma, WA CMSA	1,326	14
Cleveland – Akron – Lorain, OH CMSA	1,299	15
Houston – Galveston – Brazoria, TX CMSA	1,253	16
Denver – Boulder, CO CMSA	1,195	17
Baltimore, MD MSA	1,089	18
Pittsburgh – Beaver Valley, PA CMSA	943	19

[Continued]

★1501★

Top 25 MSAs For Employment As Editors and Reporters, 1990: Men

[Continued]

MSA/CMSA	Employees per 100,000 pop.	Rank
St. Louis, MO – IL MSA	911	20
Phoenix, AZ MSA	903	21
Portland – Vancouver, OR – WA CMSA	800	22
Sacramento, CA MSA	789	23
Cincinnati – Hamilton, OH – KY – IN CMSA	776	24
Kansas City, MO – KS MSA	757	25

Source: U.S. Department of Commerce, Bureau of the Census, Data User Services Division, *1990 Census of Population and Housing, Equal Employment Opportunity File, CD-90-EE0-1*, January 1993, CD-ROM.

★1502★

Occupations, By Race/Sex

Top 25 MSAs For Employment As Editors and Reporters, 1990: Women

MSA/CMSA	Employees per 100,000 pop.	Rank
Portland – Vancouver, OR – WA CMSA	23,590	1
Washington, DC – MD – VA MSA	8,894	2
Los Angeles – Anaheim – Riverside, CA CMSA	7,511	3
Chicago – Gary – Lake County, IL – IN – WI CMSA	6,004	4
Boston – Lawrence – Salem, MA – NH CMSA	5,018	5
San Francisco – Oakland – San Jose, CA CMSA	4,347	6
Philadelphia – Wilmington – Trenton, PA – NJ – DE – MD CMSA	3,773	7
Detroit – Ann Arbor, MI CMSA	2,127	8
Dallas – Fort Worth, TX CMSA	1,704	9
Minneapolis – St. Paul, MN – WI MSA	1,576	10
Atlanta, GA MSA	1,519	11
Baltimore, MD MSA	1,475	12
Cleveland – Akron – Lorain, OH CMSA	1,382	13
Seattle – Tacoma, WA CMSA	1,361	14
Denver – Boulder, CO CMSA	1,291	15
San Diego, CA MSA	1,186	16
Houston – Galveston – Brazoria, TX CMSA	1,168	17
St. Louis, MO – IL MSA	1,119	18
Kansas City, MO – KS MSA	1,106	19
Miami – Fort Lauderdale, FL CMSA	1,081	20
Columbus, OH MSA	975	21
Austin, TX MSA	828	22
Nashville, TN MSA	807	23

[Continued]

★1502★

Top 25 MSAs For Employment As Editors and Reporters, 1990: Women

[Continued]

MSA/CMSA	Employees per 100,000 pop.	Rank
Phoenix, AZ MSA	804	24
Cincinnati – Hamilton, OH – KY – IN CMSA	796	25

Source: U.S. Department of Commerce, Bureau of the Census, Data User Services Division, *1990 Census of Population and Housing, Equal Employment Opportunity File, CD-90-EE0-1*, January 1993, CD-ROM.

★1503★

Occupations, By Race/Sex

Top 25 MSAs For Employment As Education Teachers, 1990: Men

MSA/CMSA	Employees per 100,000 pop.	Rank
Sioux City, IA – NE MSA	162	1
Los Angeles – Anaheim – Riverside, CA CMSA	30	2
Atlanta, GA MSA	22	3
San Francisco – Oakland – San Jose, CA CMSA	19	4
Phoenix, AZ MSA	18	5
Seattle – Tacoma, WA CMSA	16	6
Houston – Galveston – Brazoria, TX CMSA	15	7
New Haven – Meriden, CT MSA	14	8
Washington, DC – MD – VA MSA	13	9
Providence – Pawtucket – Fall River, RI – MA CMSA	13	9
Denver – Boulder, CO CMSA	12	10
Gainesville, FL MSA	12	10
Indianapolis, IN MSA	12	10
Greensboro – Winston-Salem – High Point, NC MSA	11	11
Richmond – Petersburg, VA MSA	11	11
Wichita, KS MSA	10	12
Anniston, AL MSA	9	13
Iowa City, IA MSA	9	13
Raleigh – Durham, NC MSA	9	13
Hartford – New Britain – Middletown, CT CMSA	8	14
San Diego, CA MSA	8	14
Sharon, PA MSA	8	14
Spokane, WA MSA	8	14
Springfield, MA MSA	8	14
Tampa – St. Petersburg – Clearwater, FL MSA	8	14

Source: U.S. Department of Commerce, Bureau of the Census, Data User Services Division, *1990 Census of Population and Housing, Equal Employment Opportunity File, CD-90-EE0-1*, January 1993, CD-ROM.

★1504★

Occupations, By Race/Sex

Top 25 MSAs For Employment As Education Teachers, 1990: Women

MSA/CMSA	Employees per 100,000 pop.	Rank
Dayton – Springfield, OH MSA	130	1
Chicago – Gary – Lake County, IL – IN – WI CMSA	53	2
Los Angeles – Anaheim – Riverside, CA CMSA	38	3
Detroit – Ann Arbor, MI CMSA	36	4
Washington, DC – MD – VA MSA	27	5
New Haven – Meriden, CT MSA	17	6
San Francisco – Oakland – San Jose, CA CMSA	15	7
New Orleans, LA MSA	14	8
Portland – Vancouver, OR – WA CMSA	14	8
Baton Rouge, LA MSA	13	9
Charlotte – Gastonia – Rock Hill, NC – SC MSA	13	9
Minneapolis – St. Paul, MN – WI MSA	13	9
Anchorage, AK MSA	12	10
Wichita, KS MSA	11	11
Des Moines, IA MSA	10	12
Boston – Lawrence – Salem, MA – NH CMSA	9	13
Buffalo – Niagara Falls, NY CMSA	9	13
Columbia, SC MSA	9	13
Greeley, CO MSA	9	13
San Antonio, TX MSA	9	13
Seattle – Tacoma, WA CMSA	9	13
Worcester, MA MSA	9	13
Atlantic City, NJ MSA	8	14
Madison, WI MSA	8	14
Nashville, TN MSA	8	14

Source: U.S. Department of Commerce, Bureau of the Census, Data User Services Division, *1990 Census of Population and Housing, Equal Employment Opportunity File, CD-90-EE0-1, January 1993*, CD-ROM.

★1505★

Occupations, By Race/Sex

Top 25 MSAs For Employment As Elevator Operators, 1990: Men

MSA/CMSA	Employees per 100,000 pop.	Rank
Kansas City, MO – KS MSA	4,901	1
Chicago – Gary – Lake County, IL – IN – WI CMSA	535	2
Philadelphia – Wilmington – Trenton, PA – NJ – DE – MD CMSA	210	3
Los Angeles – Anaheim – Riverside, CA CMSA	160	4
Washington, DC – MD – VA MSA	104	5
Pittsburgh – Beaver Valley, PA CMSA	103	6

[Continued]

★1505★

Top 25 MSAs For Employment As Elevator Operators, 1990: Men
[Continued]

MSA/CMSA	Employees per 100,000 pop.	Rank
Boston – Lawrence – Salem, MA – NH CMSA	100	7
St. Louis, MO – IL MSA	81	8
Detroit – Ann Arbor, MI CMSA	79	9
San Francisco – Oakland – San Jose, CA CMSA	73	10
Minneapolis – St. Paul, MN – WI MSA	66	11
New Orleans, LA MSA	65	12
Dallas – Fort Worth, TX CMSA	65	12
Kansas City, MO – KS MSA	61	13
Cincinnati – Hamilton, OH – KY – IN CMSA	51	14
Miami – Fort Lauderdale, FL CMSA	45	15
Oklahoma City, OK MSA	45	15
Louisville, KY – IN MSA	41	16
San Diego, CA MSA	40	17
Albany – Schenectady – Troy, NY MSA	37	18
Baltimore, MD MSA	37	18
San Antonio, TX MSA	32	19
Atlanta, GA MSA	32	19
Rochester, NY MSA	30	20
Denver – Boulder, CO CMSA	30	20

Source: U.S. Department of Commerce, Bureau of the Census, Data User Services Division, *1990 Census of Population and Housing, Equal Employment Opportunity File, CD-90-EE0-1, January 1993*, CD-ROM.

★1506★

Occupations, By Race/Sex

Top 25 MSAs For Employment As Elevator Operators, 1990: Women

MSA/CMSA	Employees per 100,000 pop.	Rank
Norfolk – Virginia Beach – Newport News, VA MSA	266	1
Washington, DC – MD – VA MSA	145	2
Chicago – Gary – Lake County, IL – IN – WI CMSA	102	3
Philadelphia – Wilmington – Trenton, PA – NJ – DE – MD CMSA	101	4
Los Angeles – Anaheim – Riverside, CA CMSA	98	5
New Orleans, LA MSA	49	6
Pittsburgh – Beaver Valley, PA CMSA	44	7
Sacramento, CA MSA	44	7
Baton Rouge, LA MSA	34	8
Cincinnati – Hamilton, OH – KY – IN CMSA	34	8
Detroit – Ann Arbor, MI CMSA	31	9

[Continued]

★1506★

Top 25 MSAs For Employment As Elevator Operators, 1990: Women

[Continued]

MSA/CMSA	Employees per 100,000 pop.	Rank
Cleveland – Akron – Lorain, OH CMSA	28	10
Albany – Schenectady – Troy, NY MSA	25	11
Richmond – Petersburg, VA MSA	24	12
Boston – Lawrence – Salem, MA – NH CMSA	23	13
Buffalo – Niagara Falls, NY CMSA	21	14
Oklahoma City, OK MSA	19	15
Omaha, NE – IA MSA	15	16
Jackson, MS MSA	14	17
Rochester, NY MSA	14	17
Charleston, WV MSA	13	18
Enid, OK MSA	13	18
Raleigh – Durham, NC MSA	13	18
Youngstown – Warren, OH MSA	13	18
Abilene, TX MSA	12	19

Source: U.S. Department of Commerce, Bureau of the Census, Data User Services Division, *1990 Census of Population and Housing, Equal Employment Opportunity File, CD-90-EE0-1, January 1993,* CD-ROM.

★1507★

Occupations, By Race/Sex

Top 25 MSAs For Employment As English Teachers, 1990: Men

MSA/CMSA	Employees per 100,000 pop.	Rank
Dallas – Fort Worth, TX CMSA	998	1
Los Angeles – Anaheim – Riverside, CA CMSA	431	2
San Francisco – Oakland – San Jose, CA CMSA	426	3
Chicago – Gary – Lake County, IL – IN – WI CMSA	273	4
Boston – Lawrence – Salem, MA – NH CMSA	221	5
Washington, DC – MD – VA MSA	211	6
Philadelphia – Wilmington – Trenton, PA – NJ – DE – MD CMSA	203	7
Detroit – Ann Arbor, MI CMSA	146	8
Miami – Fort Lauderdale, FL CMSA	122	9
Cincinnati – Hamilton, OH – KY – IN CMSA	115	10
San Diego, CA MSA	110	11
Dallas – Fort Worth, TX CMSA	110	11
Denver – Boulder, CO CMSA	107	12
Buffalo – Niagara Falls, NY CMSA	104	13
Pittsburgh – Beaver Valley, PA CMSA	99	14
Seattle – Tacoma, WA CMSA	87	15
Houston – Galveston – Brazoria, TX CMSA	85	16

[Continued]

★1507★

Top 25 MSAs For Employment As English Teachers, 1990: Men

[Continued]

MSA/CMSA	Employees per 100,000 pop.	Rank
St. Louis, MO – IL MSA	84	17
Baton Rouge, LA MSA	79	18
Baltimore, MD MSA	78	19
Atlanta, GA MSA	76	20
Cleveland – Akron – Lorain, OH CMSA	76	20
Austin, TX MSA	75	21
Nashville, TN MSA	72	22
Lafayette – West Lafayette, IN MSA	72	22

Source: U.S. Department of Commerce, Bureau of the Census, Data User Services Division, *1990 Census of Population and Housing, Equal Employment Opportunity File, CD-90-EE0-1, January 1993,* CD-ROM.

★1508★

Occupations, By Race/Sex

Top 25 MSAs For Employment As English Teachers, 1990: Women

MSA/CMSA	Employees per 100,000 pop.	Rank
Mobile, AL MSA	1,052	1
Los Angeles – Anaheim – Riverside, CA CMSA	740	2
San Francisco – Oakland – San Jose, CA CMSA	652	3
Chicago – Gary – Lake County, IL – IN – WI CMSA	465	4
Boston – Lawrence – Salem, MA – NH CMSA	412	5
Philadelphia – Wilmington – Trenton, PA – NJ – DE – MD CMSA	310	6
Washington, DC – MD – VA MSA	284	7
Detroit – Ann Arbor, MI CMSA	201	8
Cleveland – Akron – Lorain, OH CMSA	187	9
Seattle – Tacoma, WA CMSA	185	10
Dallas – Fort Worth, TX CMSA	179	11
Houston – Galveston – Brazoria, TX CMSA	169	12
Minneapolis – St. Paul, MN – WI MSA	155	13
Phoenix, AZ MSA	155	13
San Diego, CA MSA	149	14
Raleigh – Durham, NC MSA	128	15
Pittsburgh – Beaver Valley, PA CMSA	126	16
Baltimore, MD MSA	121	17
Miami – Fort Lauderdale, FL CMSA	118	18
Sacramento, CA MSA	115	19
St. Louis, MO – IL MSA	104	20
Buffalo – Niagara Falls, NY CMSA	102	21

[Continued]

★1508★

Top 25 MSAs For Employment As English Teachers, 1990: Women

[Continued]

MSA/CMSA	Employees per 100,000 pop.	Rank
Atlanta, GA MSA	96	22
Denver – Boulder, CO CMSA	95	23
Columbus, OH MSA	87	24

Source: U.S. Department of Commerce, Bureau of the Census, Data User Services Division, *1990 Census of Population and Housing, Equal Employment Opportunity File, CD-90-EE0-1, January 1993,* CD-ROM.

★1509★

Occupations, By Race/Sex

Top 25 MSAs For Employment As Explosives Workers, 1990: Men

MSA/CMSA	Employees per 100,000 pop.	Rank
Norfolk – Virginia Beach – Newport News, VA MSA	200	1
New York – Northern New Jersey – Long Island, NY – NJ – CT CMSA	183	2
Birmingham, AL MSA	157	3
Los Angeles – Anaheim – Riverside, CA CMSA	151	4
Chicago – Gary – Lake County, IL – IN – WI CMSA	144	5
Milwaukee – Racine, WI CMSA	125	6
San Francisco – Oakland – San Jose, CA CMSA	108	7
Houma – Thibodaux, LA MSA	96	8
Tucson, AZ MSA	93	9
Nashville, TN MSA	85	10
Pittsburgh – Beaver Valley, PA CMSA	77	11
Hartford – New Britain – Middletown, CT CMSA	68	12
Philadelphia – Wilmington – Trenton, PA – NJ – DE – MD CMSA	68	12
Washington, DC – MD – VA MSA	67	13
Salt Lake City – Ogden, UT MSA	59	14
Baltimore, MD MSA	55	15
St. Louis, MO – IL MSA	53	16
Tulsa, OK MSA	53	16
Miami – Fort Lauderdale, FL CMSA	53	16
Parkersburg – Marietta, WV – OH MSA	51	17
Bremerton, WA MSA	48	18
Detroit – Ann Arbor, MI CMSA	48	18
Altoona, PA MSA	47	19
Boston – Lawrence – Salem, MA – NH CMSA	47	19
Scranton – Wilkes-Barre, PA MSA	47	19

Source: U.S. Department of Commerce, Bureau of the Census, Data User Services Division, *1990 Census of Population and Housing, Equal Employment Opportunity File, CD-90-EE0-1, January 1993,* CD-ROM.

★1510★

Occupations, By Race/Sex

Top 25 MSAs For Employment As Explosives Workers, 1990: Women

MSA/CMSA	Employees per 100,000 pop.	Rank
Oklahoma City, OK MSA	45	1
Los Angeles – Anaheim – Riverside, CA CMSA	30	2
Dallas – Fort Worth, TX CMSA	26	3
Louisville, KY – IN MSA	20	4
Bakersfield, CA MSA	16	5
San Antonio, TX MSA	14	6
Portland, ME MSA	12	7
San Francisco – Oakland – San Jose, CA CMSA	11	8
Allentown – Bethlehem – Easton, PA – NJ MSA	10	9
Kansas City, MO – KS MSA	10	9
Mobile, AL MSA	9	10
Phoenix, AZ MSA	9	10
Charleston, SC MSA	8	11
El Paso, TX MSA	8	11
New York – Northern New Jersey – Long Island, NY – NJ – CT CMSA	8	11
Philadelphia – Wilmington – Trenton, PA – NJ – DE – MD CMSA	8	11
Baltimore, MD MSA	7	12
Hagerstown, MD MSA	7	12
Johnson City – Kingsport – Bristol, TN – VA MSA	7	12
Cleveland – Akron – Lorain, OH CMSA	6	13
Norfolk – Virginia Beach – Newport News, VA MSA	6	13
Owensboro, KY MSA	6	13
Sacramento, CA MSA	6	13
Chicago – Gary – Lake County, IL – IN – WI CMSA	5	14
Detroit – Ann Arbor, MI CMSA	4	15

Source: U.S. Department of Commerce, Bureau of the Census, Data User Services Division, *1990 Census of Population and Housing, Equal Employment Opportunity File, CD-90-EE0-1, January 1993,* CD-ROM.

★1511★
Occupations, By Race/Sex

Top 25 MSAs For Employment As Family Child Care Providers, 1990: Men

MSA/CMSA	Employees per 100,000 pop.	Rank
Albany – Schenectady – Troy, NY MSA	411	1
New York – Northern New Jersey – Long Island, NY – NJ – CT CMSA	390	2
San Francisco – Oakland – San Jose, CA CMSA	371	3
Chicago – Gary – Lake County, IL – IN – WI CMSA	152	4
Seattle – Tacoma, WA CMSA	109	5
Houston – Galveston – Brazoria, TX CMSA	107	6
Dallas – Fort Worth, TX CMSA	101	7
Portland – Vancouver, OR – WA CMSA	100	8
Washington, DC – MD – VA MSA	94	9
San Diego, CA MSA	92	10
Minneapolis – St. Paul, MN – WI MSA	92	10
Denver – Boulder, CO CMSA	90	11
Philadelphia – Wilmington – Trenton, PA – NJ – DE – MD CMSA	87	12
Boston – Lawrence – Salem, MA – NH CMSA	82	13
Phoenix, AZ MSA	73	14
Sacramento, CA MSA	68	15
Tulsa, OK MSA	65	16
Richmond – Petersburg, VA MSA	56	17
Atlanta, GA MSA	52	18
Cincinnati – Hamilton, OH – KY – IN CMSA	52	18
Kansas City, MO – KS MSA	48	19
St. Louis, MO – IL MSA	47	20
Oklahoma City, OK MSA	47	20
Cleveland – Akron – Lorain, OH CMSA	44	21
Detroit – Ann Arbor, MI CMSA	44	21

Source: U.S. Department of Commerce, Bureau of the Census, Data User Services Division, *1990 Census of Population and Housing, Equal Employment Opportunity File, CD-90-EE0-1, January 1993*, CD-ROM.

★1512★
Occupations, By Race/Sex

Top 25 MSAs For Employment As Family Child Care Providers, 1990: Women

MSA/CMSA	Employees per 100,000 pop.	Rank
Phoenix, AZ MSA	22,216	1
New York – Northern New Jersey – Long Island, NY – NJ – CT CMSA	14,690	2
San Francisco – Oakland – San Jose, CA CMSA	13,013	3
Washington, DC – MD – VA MSA	10,336	4
Minneapolis – St. Paul, MN – WI MSA	9,563	5
Chicago – Gary – Lake County, IL – IN – WI CMSA	8,504	6
Dallas – Fort Worth, TX CMSA	7,063	7
Boston – Lawrence – Salem, MA – NH CMSA	5,969	8
Denver – Boulder, CO CMSA	5,841	9
Seattle – Tacoma, WA CMSA	5,822	10
Houston – Galveston – Brazoria, TX CMSA	5,791	11
San Diego, CA MSA	5,140	12
Detroit – Ann Arbor, MI CMSA	5,068	13
Philadelphia – Wilmington – Trenton, PA – NJ – DE – MD CMSA	4,891	14
Baltimore, MD MSA	4,759	15
Kansas City, MO – KS MSA	4,732	16
Portland – Vancouver, OR – WA CMSA	4,714	17
Phoenix, AZ MSA	4,555	18
St. Louis, MO – IL MSA	4,419	19
Atlanta, GA MSA	3,901	20
Sacramento, CA MSA	3,623	21
Norfolk – Virginia Beach – Newport News, VA MSA	3,398	22
Columbus, OH MSA	3,024	23
Salt Lake City – Ogden, UT MSA	2,913	24
Indianapolis, IN MSA	2,862	25

Source: U.S. Department of Commerce, Bureau of the Census, Data User Services Division, *1990 Census of Population and Housing, Equal Employment Opportunity File, CD-90-EE0-1, January 1993*, CD-ROM.

★1513★
Occupations, By Race/Sex

Top 25 MSAs For Employment As Farm Workers, 1990: Men

MSA/CMSA	Employees per 100,000 pop.	Rank
Kansas City, MO – KS MSA	22,049	1
Fresno, CA MSA	16,706	2
Visalia – Tulare – Porterville, CA MSA	12,737	3
Bakersfield, CA MSA	11,033	4
San Francisco – Oakland – San Jose, CA CMSA	10,011	5

[Continued]

★1513★

Top 25 MSAs For Employment As Farm Workers, 1990: Men

[Continued]

MSA/CMSA	Employees per 100,000 pop.	Rank
Salinas – Seaside – Monterey, CA MSA	9,933	6
Stockton, CA MSA	6,556	7
Yakima, WA MSA	5,759	8
Mcallen – Edinburg – Mission, TX MSA	5,569	9
Merced, CA MSA	5,417	10
Modesto, CA MSA	4,590	11
Santa Barbara – Santa Maria – Lompoc, CA MSA	4,287	12
Phoenix, AZ MSA	4,113	13
Tampa – St. Petersburg – Clearwater, FL MSA	4,004	14
San Diego, CA MSA	3,823	15
New York – Northern New Jersey – Long Island, NY – NJ – CT CMSA	3,434	16
Philadelphia – Wilmington – Trenton, PA – NJ – DE – MD CMSA	3,362	17
Miami – Fort Lauderdale, FL CMSA	3,207	18
West Palm Beach – Boca Raton – Delray Beach, FL MSA	3,104	19
Portland – Vancouver, OR – WA CMSA	3,020	20
Sacramento, CA MSA	2,786	21
Richland – Kennewick – Pasco, WA MSA	2,652	22
Dallas – Fort Worth, TX CMSA	2,562	23
Chicago – Gary – Lake County, IL – IN – WI CMSA	2,406	24
Lexington-Fayette, KY MSA	2,399	25

Source: U.S. Department of Commerce, Bureau of the Census, Data User Services Division, *1990 Census of Population and Housing, Equal Employment Opportunity File, CD-90-EE0-1, January 1993,* CD-ROM.

★1514★

Occupations, By Race/Sex

Top 25 MSAs For Employment As Farm Workers, 1990: Women

MSA/CMSA	Employees per 100,000 pop.	Rank
Cincinnati – Hamilton, OH – KY – IN CMSA	7,269	1
Bakersfield, CA MSA	3,928	2
Salinas – Seaside – Monterey, CA MSA	3,504	3
Visalia – Tulare – Porterville, CA MSA	2,872	4
Fresno, CA MSA	2,849	5
San Francisco – Oakland – San Jose, CA CMSA	2,848	6

[Continued]

★1514★

Top 25 MSAs For Employment As Farm Workers, 1990: Women

[Continued]

MSA/CMSA	Employees per 100,000 pop.	Rank
Mcallen – Edinburg – Mission, TX MSA	2,324	7
Tampa – St. Petersburg – Clearwater, FL MSA	1,787	8
New York – Northern New Jersey – Long Island, NY – NJ – CT CMSA	1,455	9
Miami – Fort Lauderdale, FL CMSA	1,450	10
Santa Barbara – Santa Maria – Lompoc, CA MSA	1,277	11
Yakima, WA MSA	1,221	12
Stockton, CA MSA	1,043	13
Philadelphia – Wilmington – Trenton, PA – NJ – DE – MD CMSA	1,037	14
Modesto, CA MSA	1,002	15
Merced, CA MSA	951	16
West Palm Beach – Boca Raton – Delray Beach, FL MSA	906	17
Seattle – Tacoma, WA CMSA	831	18
Sacramento, CA MSA	750	19
Detroit – Ann Arbor, MI CMSA	743	20
San Diego, CA MSA	725	21
Lancaster, PA MSA	716	22
Richland – Kennewick – Pasco, WA MSA	703	23
Chicago – Gary – Lake County, IL – IN – WI CMSA	669	24
Yuma, AZ MSA	657	25

Source: U.S. Department of Commerce, Bureau of the Census, Data User Services Division, *1990 Census of Population and Housing, Equal Employment Opportunity File, CD-90-EE0-1, January 1993,* CD-ROM.

★1515★

Occupations, By Race/Sex

Top 25 MSAs For Employment As Fire Inspection and Fire Prevention Occupations, 1990: Men

MSA/CMSA	Employees per 100,000 pop.	Rank
Minneapolis – St. Paul, MN – WI MSA	1,262	1
New York – Northern New Jersey – Long Island, NY – NJ – CT CMSA	979	2
Philadelphia – Wilmington – Trenton, PA – NJ – DE – MD CMSA	515	3
San Francisco – Oakland – San Jose, CA CMSA	423	4
Chicago – Gary – Lake County, IL – IN – WI CMSA	361	5
San Diego, CA MSA	236	6

[Continued]

★1515★

Top 25 MSAs For Employment As Fire Inspection and Fire Prevention Occupations, 1990: Men

[Continued]

MSA/CMSA	Employees per 100,000 pop.	Rank
Detroit – Ann Arbor, MI CMSA	207	7
Washington, DC – MD – VA MSA	181	8
Miami – Fort Lauderdale, FL CMSA	168	9
Phoenix, AZ MSA	159	10
Dallas – Fort Worth, TX CMSA	157	11
Boston – Lawrence – Salem, MA – NH CMSA	154	12
Norfolk – Virginia Beach – Newport News, VA MSA	152	13
Cleveland – Akron – Lorain, OH CMSA	136	14
Baltimore, MD MSA	130	15
Houston – Galveston – Brazoria, TX CMSA	128	16
St. Louis, MO – IL MSA	125	17
Seattle – Tacoma, WA CMSA	120	18
Louisville, KY – IN MSA	107	19
Cincinnati – Hamilton, OH – KY – IN CMSA	105	20
New Orleans, LA MSA	102	21
Beaumont – Port Arthur, TX MSA	97	22
Honolulu, HI MSA	96	23
Greensboro – Winston-Salem – High Point, NC MSA	91	24
West Palm Beach – Boca Raton – Delray Beach, FL MSA	90	25

Source: U.S. Department of Commerce, Bureau of the Census, Data User Services Division, *1990 Census of Population and Housing, Equal Employment Opportunity File, CD-90-EE0-1, January 1993,* CD-ROM.

★1516★

Occupations, By Race/Sex

Top 25 MSAs For Employment As Fire Inspection and Fire Prevention Occupations, 1990: Women

MSA/CMSA	Employees per 100,000 pop.	Rank
Sacramento, CA MSA	141	1
Norfolk – Virginia Beach – Newport News, VA MSA	118	2
San Francisco – Oakland – San Jose, CA CMSA	103	3
Philadelphia – Wilmington – Trenton, PA – NJ – DE – MD CMSA	101	4
San Diego, CA MSA	68	5
Detroit – Ann Arbor, MI CMSA	41	6
Augusta, GA – SC MSA	40	7
Chicago – Gary – Lake County, IL – IN – WI CMSA	37	8
New York – Northern New Jersey – Long Island, NY – NJ – CT CMSA	36	9

[Continued]

★1516★

Top 25 MSAs For Employment As Fire Inspection and Fire Prevention Occupations, 1990: Women

[Continued]

MSA/CMSA	Employees per 100,000 pop.	Rank
Las Vegas, NV MSA	32	10
Washington, DC – MD – VA MSA	31	11
Redding, CA MSA	27	12
Fresno, CA MSA	26	13
Reno, NV MSA	24	14
Pine Bluff, AR MSA	23	15
Tampa – St. Petersburg – Clearwater, FL MSA	23	15
Houston – Galveston – Brazoria, TX CMSA	19	16
Texarkana, TX – Texarkana, AR MSA	19	16
Miami – Fort Lauderdale, FL CMSA	18	17
Charleston, SC MSA	17	18
Salinas – Seaside – Monterey, CA MSA	17	18
Fort Walton Beach, FL MSA	16	19
Beaumont – Port Arthur, TX MSA	15	20
Daytona Beach, FL MSA	15	20
Savannah, GA MSA	15	20

Source: U.S. Department of Commerce, Bureau of the Census, Data User Services Division, *1990 Census of Population and Housing, Equal Employment Opportunity File, CD-90-EE0-1, January 1993,* CD-ROM.

★1517★

Occupations, By Race/Sex

Top 25 MSAs For Employment As Firefighting Occupations, 1990: Men

MSA/CMSA	Employees per 100,000 pop.	Rank
Minneapolis – St. Paul, MN – WI MSA	19,205	1
Los Angeles – Anaheim – Riverside, CA CMSA	10,575	2
Chicago – Gary – Lake County, IL – IN – WI CMSA	8,594	3
Boston – Lawrence – Salem, MA – NH CMSA	8,111	4
San Francisco – Oakland – San Jose, CA CMSA	5,850	5
Philadelphia – Wilmington – Trenton, PA – NJ – DE – MD CMSA	3,723	6
Detroit – Ann Arbor, MI CMSA	3,679	7
Dallas – Fort Worth, TX CMSA	3,563	8
Miami – Fort Lauderdale, FL CMSA	3,385	9
Washington, DC – MD – VA MSA	3,227	10
Atlanta, GA MSA	3,024	11
Cleveland – Akron – Lorain, OH CMSA	2,922	12
Houston – Galveston – Brazoria, TX CMSA	2,910	13

[Continued]

★1517★

Top 25 MSAs For Employment As Firefighting Occupations, 1990: Men

[Continued]

MSA/CMSA	Employees per 100,000 pop.	Rank
Baltimore, MD MSA	2,823	14
Seattle – Tacoma, WA CMSA	2,528	15
Providence – Pawtucket – Fall River, RI – MA CMSA	2,296	16
San Diego, CA MSA	2,196	17
St. Louis, MO – IL MSA	2,174	18
Norfolk – Virginia Beach – Newport News, VA MSA	1,858	19
Kansas City, MO – KS MSA	1,740	20
Milwaukee – Racine, WI CMSA	1,726	21
Denver – Boulder, CO CMSA	1,684	22
Tampa – St. Petersburg – Clearwater, FL MSA	1,656	23
Columbus, OH MSA	1,653	24
Sacramento, CA MSA	1,579	25

Source: U.S. Department of Commerce, Bureau of the Census, Data User Services Division, 1990 Census of Population and Housing, Equal Employment Opportunity File, CD-90-EE0-1, January 1993, CD-ROM.

★1518★

Occupations, By Race/Sex

Top 25 MSAs For Employment As Firefighting Occupations, 1990: Women

MSA/CMSA	Employees per 100,000 pop.	Rank
Richland – Kennewick – Pasco, WA MSA	346	1
San Francisco – Oakland – San Jose, CA CMSA	226	2
Chicago – Gary – Lake County, IL – IN – WI CMSA	200	3
Miami – Fort Lauderdale, FL CMSA	187	4
Sacramento, CA MSA	128	5
New York – Northern New Jersey – Long Island, NY – NJ – CT CMSA	125	6
San Diego, CA MSA	117	7
Washington, DC – MD – VA MSA	111	8
Houston – Galveston – Brazoria, TX CMSA	95	9
Detroit – Ann Arbor, MI CMSA	86	10
Baltimore, MD MSA	82	11
Seattle – Tacoma, WA CMSA	78	12
Dallas – Fort Worth, TX CMSA	76	13
Orlando, FL MSA	73	14
Boston – Lawrence – Salem, MA – NH CMSA	71	15
Phoenix, AZ MSA	70	16
Tampa – St. Petersburg – Clearwater, FL MSA	68	17
Cleveland – Akron – Lorain, OH CMSA	65	18

[Continued]

★1518★

Top 25 MSAs For Employment As Firefighting Occupations, 1990: Women

[Continued]

MSA/CMSA	Employees per 100,000 pop.	Rank
Denver – Boulder, CO CMSA	59	19
Milwaukee – Racine, WI CMSA	58	20
Atlanta, GA MSA	57	21
Visalia – Tulare – Porterville, CA MSA	54	22
Indianapolis, IN MSA	45	23
Charlotte – Gastonia – Rock Hill, NC – SC MSA	44	24
Norfolk – Virginia Beach – Newport News, VA MSA	44	24

Source: U.S. Department of Commerce, Bureau of the Census, Data User Services Division, 1990 Census of Population and Housing, Equal Employment Opportunity File, CD-90-EE0-1, January 1993, CD-ROM.

★1519★

Occupations, By Race/Sex

Top 25 MSAs For Employment As Fishers, 1990: Men

MSA/CMSA	Employees per 100,000 pop.	Rank
Fort Pierce, FL MSA	1,901	1
New York – Northern New Jersey – Long Island, NY – NJ – CT CMSA	1,354	2
Boston – Lawrence – Salem, MA – NH CMSA	1,312	3
Houma – Thibodaux, LA MSA	1,198	4
Providence – Pawtucket – Fall River, RI – MA CMSA	1,168	5
New Orleans, LA MSA	1,134	6
Los Angeles – Anaheim – Riverside, CA CMSA	923	7
New Bedford, MA MSA	853	8
Norfolk – Virginia Beach – Newport News, VA MSA	698	9
Mobile, AL MSA	696	10
Houston – Galveston – Brazoria, TX CMSA	688	11
San Francisco – Oakland – San Jose, CA CMSA	630	12
San Diego, CA MSA	590	13
Tampa – St. Petersburg – Clearwater, FL MSA	575	14
Miami – Fort Lauderdale, FL CMSA	553	15
Anchorage, AK MSA	514	16
Bellingham, WA MSA	508	17
Biloxi – Gulfport, MS MSA	420	18
Brownsville – Harlingen, TX MSA	385	19
Jacksonville, FL MSA	361	20
Beaumont – Port Arthur, TX MSA	357	21
Fort Myers – Cape CoraL, Fl MSA	336	22
Portland, ME MSA	334	23

[Continued]

★1519★

Top 25 MSAs For Employment As Fishers, 1990: Men

[Continued]

MSA/CMSA	Employees per 100,000 pop.	Rank
Atlantic City, NJ MSA	331	24
Corpus Christi, TX MSA	302	25

Source: U.S. Department of Commerce, Bureau of the Census, Data User Services Division, *1990 Census of Population and Housing, Equal Employment Opportunity File, CD-90-EEO-1, January 1993,* CD-ROM.

★1520★

Occupations, By Race/Sex

Top 25 MSAs For Employment As Fishers, 1990: Women

MSA/CMSA	Employees per 100,000 pop.	Rank
Austin, TX MSA	177	1
Bellingham, WA MSA	91	2
Houma – Thibodaux, LA MSA	72	3
New Orleans, LA MSA	68	4
Los Angeles – Anaheim – Riverside, CA CMSA	67	5
Jacksonville, FL MSA	64	6
Providence – Pawtucket – Fall River, RI – MA CMSA	61	7
Houston – Galveston – Brazoria, TX CMSA	51	8
Tampa – St. Petersburg – Clearwater, FL MSA	45	9
Miami – Fort Lauderdale, FL CMSA	42	10
Boston – Lawrence – Salem, MA – NH CMSA	38	11
Mobile, AL MSA	38	11
Lafayette, LA MSA	36	12
Jacksonville, NC MSA	35	13
Honolulu, HI MSA	33	14
Chico, CA MSA	32	15
Fort Pierce, FL MSA	32	15
New York – Northern New Jersey – Long Island, NY – NJ – CT CMSA	29	16
Anchorage, AK MSA	28	17
Norfolk – Virginia Beach – Newport News, VA MSA	28	17
Birmingham, AL MSA	27	18
New London – Norwich, CT – RI MSA	26	19
San Diego, CA MSA	23	20
Baltimore, MD MSA	20	21
Fort Smith, AR – OK MSA	20	21

Source: U.S. Department of Commerce, Bureau of the Census, Data User Services Division, *1990 Census of Population and Housing, Equal Employment Opportunity File, CD-90-EEO-1, January 1993,* CD-ROM.

★1521★

Occupations, By Race/Sex

Top 25 MSAs For Employment As Foreign Language Teachers, 1990: Men

MSA/CMSA	Employees per 100,000 pop.	Rank
Providence – Pawtucket – Fall River, RI – MA CMSA	147	1
New York – Northern New Jersey – Long Island, NY – NJ – CT CMSA	134	2
Salinas – Seaside – Monterey, CA MSA	115	3
Austin, TX MSA	111	4
Los Angeles – Anaheim – Riverside, CA CMSA	110	5
San Francisco – Oakland – San Jose, CA CMSA	105	6
Boston – Lawrence – Salem, MA – NH CMSA	90	7
San Diego, CA MSA	73	8
Champaign – Urbana – Rantoul, IL MSA	71	9
Minneapolis – St. Paul, MN – WI MSA	70	10
Chicago – Gary – Lake County, IL – IN – WI CMSA	69	11
Raleigh – Durham, NC MSA	64	12
Philadelphia – Wilmington – Trenton, PA – NJ – DE – MD CMSA	62	13
Buffalo – Niagara Falls, NY CMSA	56	14
Cincinnati – Hamilton, OH – KY – IN CMSA	44	15
Norfolk – Virginia Beach – Newport News, VA MSA	35	16
Baltimore, MD MSA	33	17
Tucson, AZ MSA	32	18
Washington, DC – MD – VA MSA	32	18
Fayetteville, NC MSA	31	19
Honolulu, HI MSA	30	20
Tallahassee, FL MSA	29	21
Kansas City, MO – KS MSA	28	22
Battle Creek, MI MSA	27	23
Bellingham, WA MSA	25	24

Source: U.S. Department of Commerce, Bureau of the Census, Data User Services Division, *1990 Census of Population and Housing, Equal Employment Opportunity File, CD-90-EEO-1, January 1993,* CD-ROM.

★1522★

Occupations, By Race/Sex

Top 25 MSAs For Employment As Foreign Language Teachers, 1990: Women

MSA/CMSA	Employees per 100,000 pop.	Rank
Greenville – Spartanburg, SC MSA	414	1
Washington, DC – MD – VA MSA	255	2
Boston – Lawrence – Salem, MA – NH CMSA	248	3
Los Angeles – Anaheim – Riverside, CA CMSA	230	4
San Francisco – Oakland – San Jose, CA CMSA	224	5
Chicago – Gary – Lake County, IL – IN – WI CMSA	149	6
Philadelphia – Wilmington – Trenton, PA – NJ – DE – MD CMSA	149	6
Detroit – Ann Arbor, MI CMSA	147	7
Salinas – Seaside – Monterey, CA MSA	146	8
Austin, TX MSA	132	9
Seattle – Tacoma, WA CMSA	120	10
Minneapolis – St. Paul, MN – WI MSA	108	11
Provo – Orem, UT MSA	106	12
Pittsburgh – Beaver Valley, PA CMSA	103	13
Eugene – Springfield, OR MSA	100	14
Dallas – Fort Worth, TX CMSA	93	15
San Diego, CA MSA	92	16
Columbus, OH MSA	91	17
Baltimore, MD MSA	82	18
Denver – Boulder, CO CMSA	81	19
Raleigh – Durham, NC MSA	79	20
Madison, WI MSA	75	21
Cincinnati – Hamilton, OH – KY – IN CMSA	74	22
St. Louis, MO – IL MSA	73	23
Bloomington, IN MSA	66	24

Source: U.S. Department of Commerce, Bureau of the Census, Data User Services Division, *1990 Census of Population and Housing, Equal Employment Opportunity File, CD-90-EE0-1, January 1993,* CD-ROM.

★1523★

Occupations, By Race/Sex

Top 25 MSAs For Employment As Forestry and Conservation Scientists, 1990: Men

MSA/CMSA	Employees per 100,000 pop.	Rank
Tampa – St. Petersburg – Clearwater, FL MSA	460	1
Los Angeles – Anaheim – Riverside, CA CMSA	439	2
Seattle – Tacoma, WA CMSA	386	3
Sacramento, CA MSA	296	4
San Francisco – Oakland – San Jose, CA CMSA	280	5

[Continued]

★1523★

Top 25 MSAs For Employment As Forestry and Conservation Scientists, 1990: Men
[Continued]

MSA/CMSA	Employees per 100,000 pop.	Rank
New York – Northern New Jersey – Long Island, NY – NJ – CT CMSA	263	6
Washington, DC – MD – VA MSA	236	7
Eugene – Springfield, OR MSA	205	8
Medford, OR MSA	196	9
Philadelphia – Wilmington – Trenton, PA – NJ – DE – MD CMSA	196	9
Minneapolis – St. Paul, MN – WI MSA	194	10
Duluth, MN – WI MSA	178	11
Atlanta, GA MSA	172	12
Boston – Lawrence – Salem, MA – NH CMSA	171	13
Chicago – Gary – Lake County, IL – IN – WI CMSA	170	14
Olympia, WA MSA	148	15
Baltimore, MD MSA	144	16
Fresno, CA MSA	142	17
Denver – Boulder, CO CMSA	135	18
Salt Lake City – Ogden, UT MSA	119	19
Milwaukee – Racine, WI CMSA	114	20
Salem, OR MSA	109	21
San Diego, CA MSA	104	22
Mobile, AL MSA	103	23
Redding, CA MSA	97	24

Source: U.S. Department of Commerce, Bureau of the Census, Data User Services Division, *1990 Census of Population and Housing, Equal Employment Opportunity File, CD-90-EE0-1, January 1993,* CD-ROM.

★1524★

Occupations, By Race/Sex

Top 25 MSAs For Employment As Forestry and Conservation Scientists, 1990: Women

MSA/CMSA	Employees per 100,000 pop.	Rank
Pittsburgh – Beaver Valley, PA CMSA	142	1
San Francisco – Oakland – San Jose, CA CMSA	93	2
Los Angeles – Anaheim – Riverside, CA CMSA	92	3
Portland – Vancouver, OR – WA CMSA	86	4
Seattle – Tacoma, WA CMSA	78	5
New York – Northern New Jersey – Long Island, NY – NJ – CT CMSA	68	6
Philadelphia – Wilmington – Trenton, PA – NJ – DE – MD CMSA	65	7
San Diego, CA MSA	62	8

[Continued]

★1524★

Top 25 MSAs For Employment As Forestry and Conservation Scientists, 1990: Women
[Continued]

MSA/CMSA	Employees per 100,000 pop.	Rank
Eugene – Springfield, OR MSA	61	9
Medford, OR MSA	51	10
Tampa – St. Petersburg – Clearwater, FL MSA	47	11
Chicago – Gary – Lake County, IL – IN – WI CMSA	46	12
Minneapolis – St. Paul, MN – WI MSA	44	13
Sacramento, CA MSA	42	14
Fort Collins – Loveland, CO MSA	41	15
Boston – Lawrence – Salem, MA – NH CMSA	37	16
Detroit – Ann Arbor, MI CMSA	37	16
Richmond – Petersburg, VA MSA	34	17
Denver – Boulder, CO CMSA	33	18
Olympia, WA MSA	32	19
St. Louis, MO – IL MSA	32	19
Atlanta, GA MSA	31	20
Indianapolis, IN MSA	31	20
Raleigh – Durham, NC MSA	31	20
Fresno, CA MSA	30	21

Source: U.S. Department of Commerce, Bureau of the Census, Data User Services Division, *1990 Census of Population and Housing, Equal Employment Opportunity File, CD-90-EE0-1,* January 1993, CD-ROM.

★1525★

Occupations, By Race/Sex

Top 25 MSAs For Employment As Funeral Directors, 1990: Men

MSA/CMSA	Employees per 100,000 pop.	Rank
Portland – Vancouver, OR – WA CMSA	2,619	1
Chicago – Gary – Lake County, IL – IN – WI CMSA	1,151	2
Philadelphia – Wilmington – Trenton, PA – NJ – DE – MD CMSA	884	3
Los Angeles – Anaheim – Riverside, CA CMSA	743	4
Boston – Lawrence – Salem, MA – NH CMSA	736	5
Detroit – Ann Arbor, MI CMSA	597	6
San Francisco – Oakland – San Jose, CA CMSA	557	7
Cleveland – Akron – Lorain, OH CMSA	533	8
Dallas – Fort Worth, TX CMSA	482	9
Pittsburgh – Beaver Valley, PA CMSA	475	10
Houston – Galveston – Brazoria, TX CMSA	420	11
St. Louis, MO – IL MSA	414	12

[Continued]

★1525★

Top 25 MSAs For Employment As Funeral Directors, 1990: Men
[Continued]

MSA/CMSA	Employees per 100,000 pop.	Rank
Milwaukee – Racine, WI CMSA	371	13
Atlanta, GA MSA	338	14
Washington, DC – MD – VA MSA	337	15
Baltimore, MD MSA	283	16
Tampa – St. Petersburg – Clearwater, FL MSA	280	17
Cincinnati – Hamilton, OH – KY – IN CMSA	259	18
Kansas City, MO – KS MSA	248	19
Minneapolis – St. Paul, MN – WI MSA	245	20
Louisville, KY – IN MSA	242	21
Miami – Fort Lauderdale, FL CMSA	241	22
Scranton – Wilkes-Barre, PA MSA	233	23
Memphis, TN – AR – MS MSA	233	23
Buffalo – Niagara Falls, NY CMSA	231	24

Source: U.S. Department of Commerce, Bureau of the Census, Data User Services Division, *1990 Census of Population and Housing, Equal Employment Opportunity File, CD-90-EE0-1,* January 1993, CD-ROM.

★1526★

Occupations, By Race/Sex

Top 25 MSAs For Employment As Funeral Directors, 1990: Women

MSA/CMSA	Employees per 100,000 pop.	Rank
Kansas City, MO – KS MSA	513	1
Chicago – Gary – Lake County, IL – IN – WI CMSA	189	2
Detroit – Ann Arbor, MI CMSA	163	3
Los Angeles – Anaheim – Riverside, CA CMSA	155	4
Philadelphia – Wilmington – Trenton, PA – NJ – DE – MD CMSA	139	5
San Francisco – Oakland – San Jose, CA CMSA	110	6
Kansas City, MO – KS MSA	106	7
Boston – Lawrence – Salem, MA – NH CMSA	103	8
Cleveland – Akron – Lorain, OH CMSA	97	9
Miami – Fort Lauderdale, FL CMSA	96	10
Dallas – Fort Worth, TX CMSA	93	11
Houston – Galveston – Brazoria, TX CMSA	89	12
Pittsburgh – Beaver Valley, PA CMSA	87	13
Scranton – Wilkes-Barre, PA MSA	68	14
Tampa – St. Petersburg – Clearwater, FL MSA	66	15

[Continued]

★1526★

Top 25 MSAs For Employment As Funeral Directors, 1990: Women

[Continued]

MSA/CMSA	Employees per 100,000 pop.	Rank
Washington, DC–MD–VA MSA	63	16
Buffalo–Niagara Falls, NY CMSA	61	17
Memphis, TN–AR–MS MSA	61	17
Baltimore, MD MSA	58	18
St. Louis, MO–IL MSA	53	19
Milwaukee–Racine, WI CMSA	49	20
Denver–Boulder, CO CMSA	44	21
Louisville, KY–IN MSA	44	21
Omaha, NE–IA MSA	40	22
Nashville, TN MSA	38	23

Source: U.S. Department of Commerce, Bureau of the Census, Data User Services Division, *1990 Census of Population and Housing, Equal Employment Opportunity File, CD-90-EE0-1, January 1993,* CD-ROM.

★1527★

Occupations, By Race/Sex

Top 25 MSAs For Employment As Garbage Collectors, 1990: Men

MSA/CMSA	Employees per 100,000 pop.	Rank
Milwaukee–Racine, WI CMSA	9,220	1
Chicago–Gary–Lake County, IL–IN–WI CMSA	1,943	2
Philadelphia–Wilmington–Trenton, PA–NJ–DE–MD CMSA	1,715	3
San Francisco–Oakland–San Jose, CA CMSA	1,493	4
Los Angeles–Anaheim–Riverside, CA CMSA	1,472	5
Miami–Fort Lauderdale, FL CMSA	908	6
Houston–Galveston–Brazoria, TX CMSA	756	7
Washington, DC–MD–VA MSA	753	8
Atlanta, GA MSA	680	9
Boston–Lawrence–Salem, MA–NH CMSA	632	10
Cleveland–Akron–Lorain, OH CMSA	620	11
Pittsburgh–Beaver Valley, PA CMSA	617	12
Baltimore, MD MSA	598	13
Detroit–Ann Arbor, MI CMSA	554	14
Dallas–Fort Worth, TX CMSA	547	15
Charlotte–Gastonia–Rock Hill, NC–SC MSA	500	16
Portland–Vancouver, OR–WA CMSA	452	17
Buffalo–Niagara Falls, NY CMSA	370	18
Minneapolis–St. Paul, MN–WI MSA	364	19
Milwaukee–Racine, WI CMSA	360	20

[Continued]

★1527★

Top 25 MSAs For Employment As Garbage Collectors, 1990: Men

[Continued]

MSA/CMSA	Employees per 100,000 pop.	Rank
San Antonio, TX MSA	347	21
Norfolk–Virginia Beach–Newport News, VA MSA	342	22
Cincinnati–Hamilton, OH–KY–IN CMSA	335	23
Memphis, TN–AR–MS MSA	314	24
Louisville, KY–IN MSA	306	25

Source: U.S. Department of Commerce, Bureau of the Census, Data User Services Division, *1990 Census of Population and Housing, Equal Employment Opportunity File, CD-90-EE0-1, January 1993,* CD-ROM.

★1528★

Occupations, By Race/Sex

Top 25 MSAs For Employment As Garbage Collectors, 1990: Women

MSA/CMSA	Employees per 100,000 pop.	Rank
Bangor, ME MSA	180	1
Washington, DC–MD–VA MSA	135	2
Los Angeles–Anaheim–Riverside, CA CMSA	127	3
Miami–Fort Lauderdale, FL CMSA	95	4
Philadelphia–Wilmington–Trenton, PA–NJ–DE–MD CMSA	74	5
San Francisco–Oakland–San Jose, CA CMSA	61	6
Houston–Galveston–Brazoria, TX CMSA	58	7
Sacramento, CA MSA	58	7
Baltimore, MD MSA	47	8
Chicago–Gary–Lake County, IL–IN–WI CMSA	44	9
Milwaukee–Racine, WI CMSA	43	10
Detroit–Ann Arbor, MI CMSA	42	11
Cleveland–Akron–Lorain, OH CMSA	41	12
Memphis, TN–AR–MS MSA	32	13
Phoenix, AZ MSA	31	14
Dallas–Fort Worth, TX CMSA	29	15
San Diego, CA MSA	29	15
Norfolk–Virginia Beach–Newport News, VA MSA	25	16
Little Rock–North Little Rock, AR MSA	20	17
Atlanta, GA MSA	19	18
Las Vegas, NV MSA	19	18
Portland–Vancouver, OR–WA CMSA	19	18
Raleigh–Durham, NC MSA	19	18

[Continued]

★ 1528 ★

Top 25 MSAs For Employment As Garbage Collectors, 1990: Women

[Continued]

MSA/CMSA	Employees per 100,000 pop.	Rank
Cincinnati – Hamilton, OH – KY – IN CMSA	17	19
Davenport – Rock Island – Moline, IA – IL MSA	17	19

Source: U.S. Department of Commerce, Bureau of the Census, Data User Services Division, *1990 Census of Population and Housing, Equal Employment Opportunity File, CD-90-EE0-1, January 1993,* CD-ROM.

★ 1529 ★

Occupations, By Race/Sex

Top 25 MSAs For Employment As Geologists and Geodesists, 1990: Men

MSA/CMSA	Employees per 100,000 pop.	Rank
Milwaukee – Racine, WI CMSA	6,219	1
Denver – Boulder, CO CMSA	3,048	2
Los Angeles – Anaheim – Riverside, CA CMSA	2,331	3
Dallas – Fort Worth, TX CMSA	2,081	4
San Francisco – Oakland – San Jose, CA CMSA	1,801	5
New Orleans, LA MSA	1,408	6
Washington, DC – MD – VA MSA	1,101	7
Midland, TX MSA	1,013	8
New York – Northern New Jersey – Long Island, NY – NJ – CT CMSA	988	9
Oklahoma City, OK MSA	947	10
Philadelphia – Wilmington – Trenton, PA – NJ – DE – MD CMSA	598	11
San Diego, CA MSA	572	12
Tulsa, OK MSA	560	13
Reno, NV MSA	512	14
Boston – Lawrence – Salem, MA – NH CMSA	501	15
Seattle – Tacoma, WA CMSA	497	16
Lafayette, LA MSA	495	17
Atlanta, GA MSA	433	18
Austin, TX MSA	428	19
Sacramento, CA MSA	412	20
Anchorage, AK MSA	396	21
Minneapolis – St. Paul, MN – WI MSA	369	22
Corpus Christi, TX MSA	365	23
Baltimore, MD MSA	334	24
Chicago – Gary – Lake County, IL – IN – WI CMSA	299	25

Source: U.S. Department of Commerce, Bureau of the Census, Data User Services Division, *1990 Census of Population and Housing, Equal Employment Opportunity File, CD-90-EE0-1, January 1993,* CD-ROM.

★ 1530 ★

Occupations, By Race/Sex

Top 25 MSAs For Employment As Geologists and Geodesists, 1990: Women

MSA/CMSA	Employees per 100,000 pop.	Rank
Seattle – Tacoma, WA CMSA	1,134	1
Denver – Boulder, CO CMSA	524	2
Los Angeles – Anaheim – Riverside, CA CMSA	366	3
San Francisco – Oakland – San Jose, CA CMSA	305	4
New Orleans, LA MSA	254	5
Dallas – Fort Worth, TX CMSA	250	6
Washington, DC – MD – VA MSA	247	7
New York – Northern New Jersey – Long Island, NY – NJ – CT CMSA	236	8
Philadelphia – Wilmington – Trenton, PA – NJ – DE – MD CMSA	203	9
Boston – Lawrence – Salem, MA – NH CMSA	164	10
Midland, TX MSA	140	11
Austin, TX MSA	131	12
Atlanta, GA MSA	130	13
Seattle – Tacoma, WA CMSA	122	14
Sacramento, CA MSA	116	15
San Diego, CA MSA	108	16
Oklahoma City, OK MSA	86	17
Tucson, AZ MSA	86	17
Chicago – Gary – Lake County, IL – IN – WI CMSA	68	18
Anchorage, AK MSA	65	19
Minneapolis – St. Paul, MN – WI MSA	61	20
Portland – Vancouver, OR – WA CMSA	59	21
Miami – Fort Lauderdale, FL CMSA	58	22
Tulsa, OK MSA	55	23
Phoenix, AZ MSA	52	24

Source: U.S. Department of Commerce, Bureau of the Census, Data User Services Division, *1990 Census of Population and Housing, Equal Employment Opportunity File, CD-90-EE0-1, January 1993,* CD-ROM.

★ 1531 ★

Occupations, By Race/Sex

Top 25 MSAs For Employment As Hairdressers and Cosmetologists, 1990: Men

MSA/CMSA	Employees per 100,000 pop.	Rank
Norfolk – Virginia Beach – Newport News, VA MSA	8,732	1
Los Angeles – Anaheim – Riverside, CA CMSA	7,021	2
San Francisco – Oakland – San Jose, CA CMSA	2,778	3
Chicago – Gary – Lake County, IL – IN – WI CMSA	2,655	4

[Continued]

★ 1531 ★

Top 25 MSAs For Employment As Hairdressers and Cosmetologists, 1990: Men
[Continued]

MSA/CMSA	Employees per 100,000 pop.	Rank
Miami – Fort Lauderdale, FL CMSA	2,398	5
Boston – Lawrence – Salem, MA – NH CMSA	2,252	6
Philadelphia – Wilmington – Trenton, PA – NJ – DE – MD CMSA	2,007	7
Dallas – Fort Worth, TX CMSA	1,550	8
Detroit – Ann Arbor, MI CMSA	1,424	9
Washington, DC – MD – VA MSA	1,387	10
Atlanta, GA MSA	1,235	11
Houston – Galveston – Brazoria, TX CMSA	1,101	12
San Diego, CA MSA	1,007	13
Phoenix, AZ MSA	936	14
Pittsburgh – Beaver Valley, PA CMSA	865	15
Tampa – St. Petersburg – Clearwater, FL MSA	838	16
Seattle – Tacoma, WA CMSA	738	17
St. Louis, MO – IL MSA	737	18
Baltimore, MD MSA	684	19
Cleveland – Akron – Lorain, OH CMSA	664	20
Minneapolis – St. Paul, MN – WI MSA	660	21
Denver – Boulder, CO CMSA	553	22
West Palm Beach – Boca Raton – Delray Beach, FL MSA	551	23
New Orleans, LA MSA	499	24
Providence – Pawtucket – Fall River, RI – MA CMSA	486	25

Source: U.S. Department of Commerce, Bureau of the Census, Data User Services Division, *1990 Census of Population and Housing, Equal Employment Opportunity File, CD-90-EE0-1,* January 1993, CD-ROM.

★ 1532 ★
Occupations, By Race/Sex

Top 25 MSAs For Employment As Hairdressers and Cosmetologists, 1990: Women

MSA/CMSA	Employees per 100,000 pop.	Rank
Charlotte – Gastonia – Rock Hill, NC – SC MSA	39,313	1
New York – Northern New Jersey – Long Island, NY – NJ – CT CMSA	38,744	2
Chicago – Gary – Lake County, IL – IN – WI CMSA	20,072	3
San Francisco – Oakland – San Jose, CA CMSA	16,277	4
Philadelphia – Wilmington – Trenton, PA – NJ – DE – MD CMSA	13,541	5

[Continued]

★ 1532 ★

Top 25 MSAs For Employment As Hairdressers and Cosmetologists, 1990: Women
[Continued]

MSA/CMSA	Employees per 100,000 pop.	Rank
Detroit – Ann Arbor, MI CMSA	12,306	6
Dallas – Fort Worth, TX CMSA	10,636	7
Washington, DC – MD – VA MSA	9,946	8
Boston – Lawrence – Salem, MA – NH CMSA	9,868	9
Miami – Fort Lauderdale, FL CMSA	9,656	10
Houston – Galveston – Brazoria, TX CMSA	9,051	11
Atlanta, GA MSA	7,445	12
Seattle – Tacoma, WA CMSA	6,932	13
St. Louis, MO – IL MSA	6,918	14
Cleveland – Akron – Lorain, OH CMSA	6,824	15
San Diego, CA MSA	6,695	16
Minneapolis – St. Paul, MN – WI MSA	6,682	17
Pittsburgh – Beaver Valley, PA CMSA	6,440	18
Baltimore, MD MSA	6,234	19
Phoenix, AZ MSA	6,218	20
Tampa – St. Petersburg – Clearwater, FL MSA	5,977	21
Denver – Boulder, CO CMSA	5,225	22
Portland – Vancouver, OR – WA CMSA	4,450	23
Kansas City, MO – KS MSA	4,296	24
Cincinnati – Hamilton, OH – KY – IN CMSA	4,235	25

Source: U.S. Department of Commerce, Bureau of the Census, Data User Services Division, *1990 Census of Population and Housing, Equal Employment Opportunity File, CD-90-EE0-1,* January 1993, CD-ROM.

★ 1533 ★
Occupations, By Race/Sex

Top 25 MSAs For Employment As History Teachers, 1990: Men

MSA/CMSA	Employees per 100,000 pop.	Rank
Champaign – Urbana – Rantoul, IL MSA	174	1
Los Angeles – Anaheim – Riverside, CA CMSA	133	2
San Francisco – Oakland – San Jose, CA CMSA	105	3
Houston – Galveston – Brazoria, TX CMSA	75	4
Boston – Lawrence – Salem, MA – NH CMSA	61	5
Milwaukee – Racine, WI CMSA	53	6
Chicago – Gary – Lake County, IL – IN – WI CMSA	53	6
Washington, DC – MD – VA MSA	52	7

[Continued]

★ 1533 ★

Top 25 MSAs For Employment As History Teachers, 1990: Men

[Continued]

MSA/CMSA	Employees per 100,000 pop.	Rank
Philadelphia – Wilmington – Trenton, PA – NJ – DE – MD CMSA	51	8
Cleveland – Akron – Lorain, OH CMSA	49	9
Minneapolis – St. Paul, MN – WI MSA	46	10
San Diego, CA MSA	46	10
Columbus, OH MSA	44	11
Madison, WI MSA	42	12
Muncie, IN MSA	37	13
Dallas – Fort Worth, TX CMSA	36	14
Nashville, TN MSA	34	15
Norfolk – Virginia Beach – Newport News, VA MSA	29	16
St. Louis, MO – IL MSA	27	17
Louisville, KY – IN MSA	26	18
Davenport – Rock Island – Moline, IA – IL MSA	25	19
Portland – Vancouver, OR – WA CMSA	24	20
Detroit – Ann Arbor, MI CMSA	24	20
Iowa City, IA MSA	24	20
Albany – Schenectady – Troy, NY MSA	23	21

Source: U.S. Department of Commerce, Bureau of the Census, Data User Services Division, *1990 Census of Population and Housing, Equal Employment Opportunity File, CD-90-EE0-1, January 1993,* CD-ROM.

★ 1534 ★

Occupations, By Race/Sex

Top 25 MSAs For Employment As History Teachers, 1990: Women

MSA/CMSA	Employees per 100,000 pop.	Rank
San Francisco – Oakland – San Jose, CA CMSA	71	1
Philadelphia – Wilmington – Trenton, PA – NJ – DE – MD CMSA	57	2
San Francisco – Oakland – San Jose, CA CMSA	47	3
Boston – Lawrence – Salem, MA – NH CMSA	41	4
St. Louis, MO – IL MSA	27	5
Cleveland – Akron – Lorain, OH CMSA	26	6
Chicago – Gary – Lake County, IL – IN – WI CMSA	25	7
Raleigh – Durham, NC MSA	24	8
Los Angeles – Anaheim – Riverside, CA CMSA	22	9
Dallas – Fort Worth, TX CMSA	20	10

[Continued]

★ 1534 ★

Top 25 MSAs For Employment As History Teachers, 1990: Women

[Continued]

MSA/CMSA	Employees per 100,000 pop.	Rank
Houston – Galveston – Brazoria, TX CMSA	20	10
Washington, DC – MD – VA MSA	20	10
Champaign – Urbana – Rantoul, IL MSA	19	11
Atlanta, GA MSA	18	12
Hartford – New Britain – Middletown, CT CMSA	18	12
Albuquerque, NM MSA	14	13
Columbia, SC MSA	14	13
Sacramento, CA MSA	14	13
Cincinnati – Hamilton, OH – KY – IN CMSA	13	14
Detroit – Ann Arbor, MI CMSA	13	14
Tampa – St. Petersburg – Clearwater, FL MSA	13	14
Wilmington, NC MSA	13	14
Austin, TX MSA	12	15
Nashville, TN MSA	12	15
Mobile, AL MSA	12	15

Source: U.S. Department of Commerce, Bureau of the Census, Data User Services Division, *1990 Census of Population and Housing, Equal Employment Opportunity File, CD-90-EE0-1, January 1993,* CD-ROM.

★ 1535 ★

Occupations, By Race/Sex

Top 25 MSAs For Employment As Home Economics Teachers, 1990: Men

MSA/CMSA	Employees per 100,000 pop.	Rank
Salt Lake City – Ogden, UT MSA	11	1
Detroit – Ann Arbor, MI CMSA	10	2
Washington, DC – MD – VA MSA	9	3
Rochester, MN MSA	7	4
Sacramento, CA MSA	7	4
Cincinnati – Hamilton, OH – KY – IN CMSA	7	4
Philadelphia – Wilmington – Trenton, PA – NJ – DE – MD CMSA	5	5
Duluth, MN – WI MSA	2	6
Lancaster, PA MSA	0	7
Lansing – East Lansing, MI MSA	0	7
Laredo, TX MSA	0	7
Las Cruces, NM MSA	0	7
Las Vegas, NV MSA	0	7
Lawrence, KS MSA	0	7
Lawton, OK MSA	0	7
Lewiston – Auburn, ME MSA	0	7
Lexington-Fayette, KY MSA	0	7
Lima, OH MSA	0	7
Lincoln, NE MSA	0	7
Little Rock – North Little Rock, AR MSA	0	7

[Continued]

★1535★

Top 25 MSAs For Employment As Home Economics Teachers, 1990: Men
[Continued]

MSA/CMSA	Employees per 100,000 pop.	Rank
Longview – Marshall, TX MSA	0	7
Los Angeles – Anaheim – Riverside, CA CMSA	0	7
Louisville, KY – IN MSA	0	7
Lubbock, TX MSA	0	7
Lynchburg, VA MSA	0	7

Source: U.S. Department of Commerce, Bureau of the Census, Data User Services Division, *1990 Census of Population and Housing, Equal Employment Opportunity File, CD-90-EE0-1, January 1993*, CD-ROM.

★1536★

Occupations, By Race/Sex

Top 25 MSAs For Employment As Home Economics Teachers, 1990: Women

MSA/CMSA	Employees per 100,000 pop.	Rank
Albany – Schenectady – Troy, NY MSA	53	1
San Antonio, TX MSA	28	2
Philadelphia – Wilmington – Trenton, PA – NJ – DE – MD CMSA	27	3
Los Angeles – Anaheim – Riverside, CA CMSA	20	4
Washington, DC – MD – VA MSA	13	5
Champaign – Urbana – Rantoul, IL MSA	11	6
Greeley, CO MSA	10	7
Tucson, AZ MSA	10	7
Lake Charles, LA MSA	9	8
Louisville, KY – IN MSA	9	8
Anchorage, AK MSA	8	9
Detroit – Ann Arbor, MI CMSA	8	9
Duluth, MN – WI MSA	8	9
Johnstown, PA MSA	8	9
Knoxville, TN MSA	8	9
Allentown – Bethlehem – Easton, PA – NJ MSA	7	10
Austin, TX MSA	7	10
Cincinnati – Hamilton, OH – KY – IN CMSA	7	10
Clarksville – Hopkinsville, TN – KY MSA	7	10
Greenville – Spartanburg, SC MSA	7	10
Cleveland – Akron – Lorain, OH CMSA	6	11
Lafayette – West Lafayette, IN MSA	6	11
Nashville, TN MSA	6	11

[Continued]

★1536★

Top 25 MSAs For Employment As Home Economics Teachers, 1990: Women
[Continued]

MSA/CMSA	Employees per 100,000 pop.	Rank
Appleton – Oshkosh – Neenah, WI MSA	5	12
Longview – Marshall, TX MSA	2	13

Source: U.S. Department of Commerce, Bureau of the Census, Data User Services Division, *1990 Census of Population and Housing, Equal Employment Opportunity File, CD-90-EE0-1, January 1993*, CD-ROM.

★1537★

Occupations, By Race/Sex

Top 25 MSAs For Employment As Housekeepers and Butlers, 1990: Men

MSA/CMSA	Employees per 100,000 pop.	Rank
Lubbock, TX MSA	366	1
Los Angeles – Anaheim – Riverside, CA CMSA	317	2
Philadelphia – Wilmington – Trenton, PA – NJ – DE – MD CMSA	75	3
Boston – Lawrence – Salem, MA – NH CMSA	73	4
Washington, DC – MD – VA MSA	66	5
Baltimore, MD MSA	63	6
Atlanta, GA MSA	62	7
Phoenix, AZ MSA	58	8
San Francisco – Oakland – San Jose, CA CMSA	57	9
San Diego, CA MSA	46	10
West Palm Beach – Boca Raton – Delray Beach, FL MSA	45	11
Miami – Fort Lauderdale, FL CMSA	36	12
Cincinnati – Hamilton, OH – KY – IN CMSA	31	13
Dallas – Fort Worth, TX CMSA	30	14
Memphis, TN – AR – MS MSA	26	15
Houston – Galveston – Brazoria, TX CMSA	23	16
Sacramento, CA MSA	22	17
Detroit – Ann Arbor, MI CMSA	22	17
Chicago – Gary – Lake County, IL – IN – WI CMSA	21	18
Cleveland – Akron – Lorain, OH CMSA	20	19
Tampa – St. Petersburg – Clearwater, FL MSA	17	20
New Orleans, LA MSA	16	21
Richmond – Petersburg, VA MSA	16	21
Seattle – Tacoma, WA CMSA	16	21
Raleigh – Durham, NC MSA	15	22

Source: U.S. Department of Commerce, Bureau of the Census, Data User Services Division, *1990 Census of Population and Housing, Equal Employment Opportunity File, CD-90-EE0-1, January 1993*, CD-ROM.

★1538★

Occupations, By Race/Sex

Top 25 MSAs For Employment As Housekeepers and Butlers, 1990: Women

MSA/CMSA	Employees per 100,000 pop.	Rank
San Antonio, TX MSA	5,454	1
Los Angeles – Anaheim – Riverside, CA CMSA	4,198	2
Washington, DC – MD – VA MSA	1,266	3
Houston – Galveston – Brazoria, TX CMSA	1,175	4
San Francisco – Oakland – San Jose, CA CMSA	1,034	5
Miami – Fort Lauderdale, FL CMSA	833	6
San Diego, CA MSA	709	7
Dallas – Fort Worth, TX CMSA	607	8
Philadelphia – Wilmington – Trenton, PA – NJ – DE – MD CMSA	583	9
Chicago – Gary – Lake County, IL – IN – WI CMSA	517	10
New Orleans, LA MSA	311	11
Baltimore, MD MSA	280	12
Atlanta, GA MSA	272	13
Detroit – Ann Arbor, MI CMSA	252	14
West Palm Beach – Boca Raton – Delray Beach, FL MSA	250	15
San Antonio, TX MSA	246	16
Boston – Lawrence – Salem, MA – NH CMSA	190	17
St. Louis, MO – IL MSA	176	18
Memphis, TN – AR – MS MSA	173	19
Norfolk – Virginia Beach – Newport News, VA MSA	164	20
Portland – Vancouver, OR – WA CMSA	160	21
Tampa – St. Petersburg – Clearwater, FL MSA	160	21
Denver – Boulder, CO CMSA	157	22
Corpus Christi, TX MSA	156	23
Indianapolis, IN MSA	145	24

Source: U.S. Department of Commerce, Bureau of the Census, Data User Services Division, *1990 Census of Population and Housing, Equal Employment Opportunity File, CD-90-EE0-1, January 1993*, CD-ROM.

★1539★

Occupations, By Race/Sex

Top 25 MSAs For Employment As Hunters and Trappers, 1990: Men

MSA/CMSA	Employees per 100,000 pop.	Rank
Panama City, FL MSA	99	1
New York – Northern New Jersey – Long Island, NY – NJ – CT CMSA	50	2
Dallas – Fort Worth, TX CMSA	43	3
San Diego, CA MSA	32	4

[Continued]

★1539★

Top 25 MSAs For Employment As Hunters and Trappers, 1990: Men

[Continued]

MSA/CMSA	Employees per 100,000 pop.	Rank
Cleveland – Akron – Lorain, OH CMSA	24	5
Chicago – Gary – Lake County, IL – IN – WI CMSA	22	6
San Francisco – Oakland – San Jose, CA CMSA	21	7
Denver – Boulder, CO CMSA	19	8
Minneapolis – St. Paul, MN – WI MSA	19	8
Olympia, WA MSA	19	8
Houston – Galveston – Brazoria, TX CMSA	18	9
Milwaukee – Racine, WI CMSA	18	9
Atlanta, GA MSA	16	10
Salt Lake City – Ogden, UT MSA	16	10
Cincinnati – Hamilton, OH – KY – IN CMSA	15	11
Eugene – Springfield, OR MSA	15	11
Orlando, FL MSA	15	11
Augusta, GA – SC MSA	14	12
Philadelphia – Wilmington – Trenton, PA – NJ – DE – MD CMSA	14	12
Albany – Schenectady – Troy, NY MSA	13	13
Fort Pierce, FL MSA	13	13
New London – Norwich, CT – RI MSA	13	13
Brownsville – Harlingen, TX MSA	12	14
Seattle – Tacoma, WA CMSA	12	14
Poughkeepsie, NY MSA	12	14

Source: U.S. Department of Commerce, Bureau of the Census, Data User Services Division, *1990 Census of Population and Housing, Equal Employment Opportunity File, CD-90-EE0-1, January 1993*, CD-ROM.

★1540★

Occupations, By Race/Sex

Top 25 MSAs For Employment As Hunters and Trappers, 1990: Women

MSA/CMSA	Employees per 100,000 pop.	Rank
Brownsville – Harlingen, TX MSA	43	1
Los Angeles – Anaheim – Riverside, CA CMSA	38	2
Seattle – Tacoma, WA CMSA	22	3
Anchorage, AK MSA	19	4
Orlando, FL MSA	16	5
San Francisco – Oakland – San Jose, CA CMSA	16	5
Norfolk – Virginia Beach – Newport News, VA MSA	13	6
Chicago – Gary – Lake County, IL – IN – WI CMSA	10	7

[Continued]

★1540★

Top 25 MSAs For Employment As Hunters and Trappers, 1990: Women
[Continued]

MSA/CMSA	Employees per 100,000 pop.	Rank
Tampa – St. Petersburg – Clearwater, FL MSA	10	7
Chico, CA MSA	8	8
Dallas – Fort Worth, TX CMSA	8	8
Miami – Fort Lauderdale, FL CMSA	8	8
Memphis, TN – AR – MS MSA	8	8
Dayton – Springfield, OH MSA	7	9
Philadelphia – Wilmington – Trenton, PA – NJ – DE – MD CMSA	7	9
San Diego, CA MSA	7	9
Sioux Falls, SD MSA	7	9
Pensacola, FL MSA	6	10
Denver – Boulder, CO CMSA	5	11
Houma – Thibodaux, LA MSA	5	11
Atlanta, GA MSA	2	12
Amarillo, TX MSA	0	13
Albany – Schenectady – Troy, NY MSA	0	13
Altoona, PA MSA	0	13
Albany, GA MSA	0	13

Source: U.S. Department of Commerce, Bureau of the Census, Data User Services Division, *1990 Census of Population and Housing, Equal Employment Opportunity File, CD-90-EE0-1, January 1993,* CD-ROM.

★1541★
Occupations, By Race/Sex

Top 25 MSAs For Employment As Insurance Adjusters, Examiners, and Investigators, 1990: Men

MSA/CMSA	Employees per 100,000 pop.	Rank
Portland – Vancouver, OR – WA CMSA	9,384	1
Los Angeles – Anaheim – Riverside, CA CMSA	6,917	2
Chicago – Gary – Lake County, IL – IN – WI CMSA	3,986	3
Philadelphia – Wilmington – Trenton, PA – NJ – DE – MD CMSA	3,984	4
San Francisco – Oakland – San Jose, CA CMSA	2,851	5
Dallas – Fort Worth, TX CMSA	2,666	6
Boston – Lawrence – Salem, MA – NH CMSA	2,496	7
Washington, DC – MD – VA MSA	1,908	8
Hartford – New Britain – Middletown, CT CMSA	1,675	9
Atlanta, GA MSA	1,656	10
Minneapolis – St. Paul, MN – WI MSA	1,641	11

[Continued]

★1541★

Top 25 MSAs For Employment As Insurance Adjusters, Examiners, and Investigators, 1990: Men
[Continued]

MSA/CMSA	Employees per 100,000 pop.	Rank
Detroit – Ann Arbor, MI CMSA	1,611	12
Houston – Galveston – Brazoria, TX CMSA	1,481	13
Seattle – Tacoma, WA CMSA	1,339	14
Miami – Fort Lauderdale, FL CMSA	1,307	15
Baltimore, MD MSA	1,238	16
Tampa – St. Petersburg – Clearwater, FL MSA	1,152	17
St. Louis, MO – IL MSA	1,132	18
Kansas City, MO – KS MSA	1,073	19
Sacramento, CA MSA	1,038	20
San Antonio, TX MSA	1,037	21
Phoenix, AZ MSA	1,034	22
Columbus, OH MSA	1,001	23
Denver – Boulder, CO CMSA	992	24
Pittsburgh – Beaver Valley, PA CMSA	934	25

Source: U.S. Department of Commerce, Bureau of the Census, Data User Services Division, *1990 Census of Population and Housing, Equal Employment Opportunity File, CD-90-EE0-1, January 1993,* CD-ROM.

★1542★
Occupations, By Race/Sex

Top 25 MSAs For Employment As Insurance Adjusters, Examiners, and Investigators, 1990: Women

MSA/CMSA	Employees per 100,000 pop.	Rank
Milwaukee – Racine, WI CMSA	19,073	1
Los Angeles – Anaheim – Riverside, CA CMSA	14,155	2
Chicago – Gary – Lake County, IL – IN – WI CMSA	9,659	3
Philadelphia – Wilmington – Trenton, PA – NJ – DE – MD CMSA	9,584	4
Dallas – Fort Worth, TX CMSA	6,908	5
San Francisco – Oakland – San Jose, CA CMSA	5,950	6
Boston – Lawrence – Salem, MA – NH CMSA	5,898	7
Detroit – Ann Arbor, MI CMSA	5,499	8
Hartford – New Britain – Middletown, CT CMSA	5,188	9
Minneapolis – St. Paul, MN – WI MSA	4,595	10
Atlanta, GA MSA	4,490	11
Washington, DC – MD – VA MSA	4,068	12
Seattle – Tacoma, WA CMSA	3,713	13
Columbus, OH MSA	3,583	14

[Continued]

★1542★

Top 25 MSAs For Employment As Insurance Adjusters, Examiners, and Investigators, 1990: Women
[Continued]

MSA/CMSA	Employees per 100,000 pop.	Rank
Tampa–St. Petersburg–Clearwater, FL MSA	3,489	15
Baltimore, MD MSA	3,224	16
Jacksonville, FL MSA	3,155	17
St. Louis, MO–IL MSA	3,148	18
Milwaukee–Racine, WI CMSA	3,092	19
Houston–Galveston–Brazoria, TX CMSA	2,891	20
Kansas City, MO–KS MSA	2,845	21
Pittsburgh–Beaver Valley, PA CMSA	2,788	22
Indianapolis, IN MSA	2,694	23
Phoenix, AZ MSA	2,661	24
Cleveland–Akron–Lorain, OH CMSA	2,599	25

Source: U.S. Department of Commerce, Bureau of the Census, Data User Services Division, *1990 Census of Population and Housing, Equal Employment Opportunity File, CD-90-EE0-1, January 1993,* CD-ROM.

★1543★

Occupations, By Race/Sex

Top 25 MSAs For Employment As Interviewers, 1990: Men

MSA/CMSA	Employees per 100,000 pop.	Rank
Milwaukee–Racine, WI CMSA	4,445	1
Los Angeles–Anaheim–Riverside, CA CMSA	3,323	2
Chicago–Gary–Lake County, IL–IN–WI CMSA	1,580	3
San Francisco–Oakland–San Jose, CA CMSA	1,507	4
Philadelphia–Wilmington–Trenton, PA–NJ–DE–MD CMSA	1,359	5
Boston–Lawrence–Salem, MA–NH CMSA	923	6
Washington, DC–MD–VA MSA	856	7
Dallas–Fort Worth, TX CMSA	818	8
Miami–Fort Lauderdale, FL CMSA	720	9
Phoenix, AZ MSA	665	10
Seattle–Tacoma, WA CMSA	652	11
Houston–Galveston–Brazoria, TX CMSA	632	12
Detroit–Ann Arbor, MI CMSA	604	13
Atlanta, GA MSA	541	14
San Diego, CA MSA	536	15
Baltimore, MD MSA	495	16
Cincinnati–Hamilton, OH–KY–IN CMSA	461	17

[Continued]

★1543★

Top 25 MSAs For Employment As Interviewers, 1990: Men
[Continued]

MSA/CMSA	Employees per 100,000 pop.	Rank
Minneapolis–St. Paul, MN–WI MSA	442	18
Denver–Boulder, CO CMSA	416	19
St. Louis, MO–IL MSA	415	20
Sacramento, CA MSA	363	21
Portland–Vancouver, OR–WA CMSA	361	22
Tampa–St. Petersburg–Clearwater, FL MSA	332	23
Kansas City, MO–KS MSA	327	24
Cleveland–Akron–Lorain, OH CMSA	321	25

Source: U.S. Department of Commerce, Bureau of the Census, Data User Services Division, *1990 Census of Population and Housing, Equal Employment Opportunity File, CD-90-EE0-1, January 1993,* CD-ROM.

★1544★

Occupations, By Race/Sex

Top 25 MSAs For Employment As Interviewers, 1990: Women

MSA/CMSA	Employees per 100,000 pop.	Rank
Kansas City, MO–KS MSA	10,621	1
Los Angeles–Anaheim–Riverside, CA CMSA	9,580	2
Chicago–Gary–Lake County, IL–IN–WI CMSA	5,262	3
Philadelphia–Wilmington–Trenton, PA–NJ–DE–MD CMSA	4,082	4
San Francisco–Oakland–San Jose, CA CMSA	3,983	5
Detroit–Ann Arbor, MI CMSA	2,574	6
Dallas–Fort Worth, TX CMSA	2,337	7
Houston–Galveston–Brazoria, TX CMSA	2,209	8
Boston–Lawrence–Salem, MA–NH CMSA	2,148	9
Minneapolis–St. Paul, MN–WI MSA	1,912	10
Washington, DC–MD–VA MSA	1,815	11
Miami–Fort Lauderdale, FL CMSA	1,793	12
Phoenix, AZ MSA	1,588	13
Atlanta, GA MSA	1,579	14
St. Louis, MO–IL MSA	1,571	15
Pittsburgh–Beaver Valley, PA CMSA	1,557	16
Cleveland–Akron–Lorain, OH CMSA	1,537	17
Baltimore, MD MSA	1,511	18
San Diego, CA MSA	1,494	19
Seattle–Tacoma, WA CMSA	1,450	20

[Continued]

★1544★

Top 25 MSAs For Employment As Interviewers, 1990: Women
[Continued]

MSA/CMSA	Employees per 100,000 pop.	Rank
Tampa – St. Petersburg – Clearwater, FL MSA	1,266	21
Cincinnati – Hamilton, OH – KY – IN CMSA	1,260	22
Portland – Vancouver, OR – WA CMSA	1,135	23
Kansas City, MO – KS MSA	1,123	24
Denver – Boulder, CO CMSA	1,109	25

Source: U.S. Department of Commerce, Bureau of the Census, Data User Services Division, *1990 Census of Population and Housing, Equal Employment Opportunity File, CD-90-EE0-1, January 1993*, CD-ROM.

★1545★

Occupations, By Race/Sex

Top 25 MSAs For Employment As Judges, 1990: Men

MSA/CMSA	Employees per 100,000 pop.	Rank
Portland – Vancouver, OR – WA CMSA	2,110	1
Los Angeles – Anaheim – Riverside, CA CMSA	903	2
Chicago – Gary – Lake County, IL – IN – WI CMSA	770	3
Washington, DC – MD – VA MSA	719	4
San Francisco – Oakland – San Jose, CA CMSA	637	5
Philadelphia – Wilmington – Trenton, PA – NJ – DE – MD CMSA	587	6
Detroit – Ann Arbor, MI CMSA	502	7
Boston – Lawrence – Salem, MA – NH CMSA	464	8
Baltimore, MD MSA	367	9
Dallas – Fort Worth, TX CMSA	344	10
Phoenix, AZ MSA	283	11
Cleveland – Akron – Lorain, OH CMSA	252	12
Minneapolis – St. Paul, MN – WI MSA	230	13
Pittsburgh – Beaver Valley, PA CMSA	220	14
Atlanta, GA MSA	219	15
St. Louis, MO – IL MSA	217	16
Miami – Fort Lauderdale, FL CMSA	215	17
Seattle – Tacoma, WA CMSA	208	18
Kansas City, MO – KS MSA	203	19
Sacramento, CA MSA	196	20
Denver – Boulder, CO CMSA	188	21
Norfolk – Virginia Beach – Newport News, VA MSA	184	22
Tampa – St. Petersburg – Clearwater, FL MSA	179	23

[Continued]

★1545★

Top 25 MSAs For Employment As Judges, 1990: Men
[Continued]

MSA/CMSA	Employees per 100,000 pop.	Rank
Houston – Galveston – Brazoria, TX CMSA	173	24
San Diego, CA MSA	166	25

Source: U.S. Department of Commerce, Bureau of the Census, Data User Services Division, *1990 Census of Population and Housing, Equal Employment Opportunity File, CD-90-EE0-1, January 1993*, CD-ROM.

★1546★

Occupations, By Race/Sex

Top 25 MSAs For Employment As Judges, 1990: Women

MSA/CMSA	Employees per 100,000 pop.	Rank
Columbus, OH MSA	652	1
Los Angeles – Anaheim – Riverside, CA CMSA	440	2
Chicago – Gary – Lake County, IL – IN – WI CMSA	201	3
Washington, DC – MD – VA MSA	193	4
Philadelphia – Wilmington – Trenton, PA – NJ – DE – MD CMSA	179	5
San Francisco – Oakland – San Jose, CA CMSA	173	6
Seattle – Tacoma, WA CMSA	133	7
Miami – Fort Lauderdale, FL CMSA	125	8
Tampa – St. Petersburg – Clearwater, FL MSA	123	9
Detroit – Ann Arbor, MI CMSA	121	10
Baltimore, MD MSA	119	11
Boston – Lawrence – Salem, MA – NH CMSA	113	12
Atlanta, GA MSA	111	13
Cleveland – Akron – Lorain, OH CMSA	103	14
San Diego, CA MSA	90	15
Minneapolis – St. Paul, MN – WI MSA	78	16
Pittsburgh – Beaver Valley, PA CMSA	72	17
Denver – Boulder, CO CMSA	69	18
Sacramento, CA MSA	67	19
New Orleans, LA MSA	62	20
Phoenix, AZ MSA	62	20
Dallas – Fort Worth, TX CMSA	61	21
Raleigh – Durham, NC MSA	59	22
Harrisburg – Lebanon – Carlisle, PA MSA	57	23
Milwaukee – Racine, WI CMSA	51	24

Source: U.S. Department of Commerce, Bureau of the Census, Data User Services Division, *1990 Census of Population and Housing, Equal Employment Opportunity File, CD-90-EE0-1, January 1993*, CD-ROM.

★1547★

Occupations, By Race/Sex

Top 25 MSAs For Employment As Launderers and Ironers, 1990: Men

MSA/CMSA	Employees per 100,000 pop.	Rank
Milwaukee – Racine, WI CMSA	32	1
Los Angeles – Anaheim – Riverside, CA CMSA	26	2
Detroit – Ann Arbor, MI CMSA	19	3
Washington, DC – MD – VA MSA	17	4
New York – Northern New Jersey – Long Island, NY – NJ – CT CMSA	15	5
Youngstown – Warren, OH MSA	12	6
Chicago – Gary – Lake County, IL – IN – WI CMSA	12	6
Cleveland – Akron – Lorain, OH CMSA	12	6
Orlando, FL MSA	10	7
Baltimore, MD MSA	7	8
Boston – Lawrence – Salem, MA – NH CMSA	7	8
Chattanooga, TN – GA MSA	7	8
Allentown – Bethlehem – Easton, PA – NJ MSA	6	9
Philadelphia – Wilmington – Trenton, PA – NJ – DE – MD CMSA	5	10
Houston – Galveston – Brazoria, TX CMSA	5	10
Charlotte – Gastonia – Rock Hill, NC – SC MSA	5	10
Columbus, OH MSA	5	10
Grand Rapids, MI MSA	4	11
Sioux Falls, SD MSA	3	12
Lansing – East Lansing, MI MSA	2	13
Salem, OR MSA	2	13
Kankakee, IL MSA	2	13
Lancaster, PA MSA	0	14
Laredo, TX MSA	0	14
Las Cruces, NM MSA	0	14

Source: U.S. Department of Commerce, Bureau of the Census, Data User Services Division, *1990 Census of Population and Housing, Equal Employment Opportunity File, CD-90-EE0-1,* January 1993, CD-ROM.

★1548★

Occupations, By Race/Sex

Top 25 MSAs For Employment As Launderers and Ironers, 1990: Women

MSA/CMSA	Employees per 100,000 pop.	Rank
Sacramento, CA MSA	97	1
Los Angeles – Anaheim – Riverside, CA CMSA	80	2
St. Louis, MO – IL MSA	39	3
San Francisco – Oakland – San Jose, CA CMSA	36	4
Chicago – Gary – Lake County, IL – IN – WI CMSA	34	5

[Continued]

★1548★

Top 25 MSAs For Employment As Launderers and Ironers, 1990: Women

[Continued]

MSA/CMSA	Employees per 100,000 pop.	Rank
Baltimore, MD MSA	29	6
San Diego, CA MSA	29	6
Seattle – Tacoma, WA CMSA	27	7
Dallas – Fort Worth, TX CMSA	24	8
Provo – Orem, UT MSA	24	8
Cleveland – Akron – Lorain, OH CMSA	23	9
Memphis, TN – AR – MS MSA	22	10
Detroit – Ann Arbor, MI CMSA	21	11
Enid, OK MSA	21	11
Eugene – Springfield, OR MSA	21	11
Minneapolis – St. Paul, MN – WI MSA	20	12
Houston – Galveston – Brazoria, TX CMSA	18	13
Tampa – St. Petersburg – Clearwater, FL MSA	18	13
Colorado Springs, CO MSA	15	14
San Antonio, TX MSA	15	14
Indianapolis, IN MSA	14	15
Oklahoma City, OK MSA	14	15
West Palm Beach – Boca Raton – Delray Beach, FL MSA	14	15
Albuquerque, NM MSA	13	16
Washington, DC – MD – VA MSA	13	16

Source: U.S. Department of Commerce, Bureau of the Census, Data User Services Division, *1990 Census of Population and Housing, Equal Employment Opportunity File, CD-90-EE0-1,* January 1993, CD-ROM.

★1549★

Occupations, By Race/Sex

Top 25 MSAs For Employment As Law Teachers, 1990: Men

MSA/CMSA	Employees per 100,000 pop.	Rank
Knoxville, TN MSA	366	1
Washington, DC – MD – VA MSA	200	2
Chicago – Gary – Lake County, IL – IN – WI CMSA	185	3
Boston – Lawrence – Salem, MA – NH CMSA	163	4
San Francisco – Oakland – San Jose, CA CMSA	154	5
Los Angeles – Anaheim – Riverside, CA CMSA	97	6
Philadelphia – Wilmington – Trenton, PA – NJ – DE – MD CMSA	88	7
Cleveland – Akron – Lorain, OH CMSA	63	8
San Diego, CA MSA	55	9
Houston – Galveston – Brazoria, TX CMSA	45	10

[Continued]

★1549★

Top 25 MSAs For Employment As Law Teachers, 1990: Men
[Continued]

MSA/CMSA	Employees per 100,000 pop.	Rank
New Orleans, LA MSA	44	11
St. Louis, MO – IL MSA	43	12
Tallahassee, FL MSA	43	12
Columbia, SC MSA	43	12
Detroit – Ann Arbor, MI CMSA	41	13
Denver – Boulder, CO CMSA	35	14
Atlanta, GA MSA	35	14
Baton Rouge, LA MSA	35	14
Lubbock, TX MSA	34	15
Oklahoma City, OK MSA	34	15
Cincinnati – Hamilton, OH – KY – IN CMSA	32	16
Minneapolis – St. Paul, MN – WI MSA	31	17
Raleigh – Durham, NC MSA	30	18
Miami – Fort Lauderdale, FL CMSA	29	19
Austin, TX MSA	28	20

Source: U.S. Department of Commerce, Bureau of the Census, Data User Services Division, *1990 Census of Population and Housing, Equal Employment Opportunity File, CD-90-EE0-1, January 1993,* CD-ROM.

★1550★
Occupations, By Race/Sex

Top 25 MSAs For Employment As Law Teachers, 1990: Women

MSA/CMSA	Employees per 100,000 pop.	Rank
Norfolk – Virginia Beach – Newport News, VA MSA	149	1
Boston – Lawrence – Salem, MA – NH CMSA	95	2
Los Angeles – Anaheim – Riverside, CA CMSA	72	3
Chicago – Gary – Lake County, IL – IN – WI CMSA	69	4
New Haven – Meriden, CT MSA	55	5
Philadelphia – Wilmington – Trenton, PA – NJ – DE – MD CMSA	48	6
Washington, DC – MD – VA MSA	48	6
Minneapolis – St. Paul, MN – WI MSA	36	7
Detroit – Ann Arbor, MI CMSA	31	8
San Diego, CA MSA	31	8
Madison, WI MSA	29	9
Tallahassee, FL MSA	28	10
Seattle – Tacoma, WA CMSA	27	11
Houston – Galveston – Brazoria, TX CMSA	26	12
Nashville, TN MSA	26	12
Birmingham, AL MSA	24	13
Pittsburgh – Beaver Valley, PA CMSA	24	13

[Continued]

★1550★

Top 25 MSAs For Employment As Law Teachers, 1990: Women
[Continued]

MSA/CMSA	Employees per 100,000 pop.	Rank
Miami – Fort Lauderdale, FL CMSA	22	14
New Orleans, LA MSA	21	15
Raleigh – Durham, NC MSA	19	16
Sacramento, CA MSA	19	16
Lansing – East Lansing, MI MSA	18	17
San Francisco – Oakland – San Jose, CA CMSA	18	17
Cleveland – Akron – Lorain, OH CMSA	17	18
Buffalo – Niagara Falls, NY CMSA	16	19

Source: U.S. Department of Commerce, Bureau of the Census, Data User Services Division, *1990 Census of Population and Housing, Equal Employment Opportunity File, CD-90-EE0-1, January 1993,* CD-ROM.

★1551★
Occupations, By Race/Sex

Top 25 MSAs For Employment As Lawyers, 1990: Men

MSA/CMSA	Employees per 100,000 pop.	Rank
Indianapolis, IN MSA	75,527	1
Los Angeles – Anaheim – Riverside, CA CMSA	37,536	2
Washington, DC – MD – VA MSA	30,220	3
Chicago – Gary – Lake County, IL – IN – WI CMSA	27,180	4
San Francisco – Oakland – San Jose, CA CMSA	21,051	5
Philadelphia – Wilmington – Trenton, PA – NJ – DE – MD CMSA	16,892	6
Boston – Lawrence – Salem, MA – NH CMSA	14,722	7
Houston – Galveston – Brazoria, TX CMSA	10,946	8
Detroit – Ann Arbor, MI CMSA	10,728	9
Miami – Fort Lauderdale, FL CMSA	10,635	10
Dallas – Fort Worth, TX CMSA	9,798	11
Atlanta, GA MSA	8,793	12
Minneapolis – St. Paul, MN – WI MSA	7,468	13
Cleveland – Akron – Lorain, OH CMSA	7,160	14
Denver – Boulder, CO CMSA	7,126	15
San Diego, CA MSA	6,875	16
Seattle – Tacoma, WA CMSA	6,689	17
Baltimore, MD MSA	6,409	18
St. Louis, MO – IL MSA	5,532	19
Pittsburgh – Beaver Valley, PA CMSA	5,127	20
Phoenix, AZ MSA	5,032	21

[Continued]

★1551★

Top 25 MSAs For Employment As Lawyers, 1990: Men

[Continued]

MSA/CMSA	Employees per 100,000 pop.	Rank
New Orleans, LA MSA	4,875	22
Kansas City, MO – KS MSA	4,579	23
Tampa – St. Petersburg – Clearwater, FL MSA	4,212	24
Sacramento, CA MSA	4,116	25

Source: U.S. Department of Commerce, Bureau of the Census, Data User Services Division, *1990 Census of Population and Housing, Equal Employment Opportunity File, CD-90-EE0-1, January 1993*, CD-ROM.

★1552★

Occupations, By Race/Sex

Top 25 MSAs For Employment As Lawyers, 1990: Women

MSA/CMSA	Employees per 100,000 pop.	Rank
Charlotte – Gastonia – Rock Hill, NC – SC MSA	28,282	1
Los Angeles – Anaheim – Riverside, CA CMSA	13,665	2
Washington, DC – MD – VA MSA	13,360	3
San Francisco – Oakland – San Jose, CA CMSA	9,229	4
Chicago – Gary – Lake County, IL – IN – WI CMSA	8,612	5
Boston – Lawrence – Salem, MA – NH CMSA	6,782	6
Philadelphia – Wilmington – Trenton, PA – NJ – DE – MD CMSA	6,185	7
Houston – Galveston – Brazoria, TX CMSA	3,982	8
Miami – Fort Lauderdale, FL CMSA	3,315	9
Dallas – Fort Worth, TX CMSA	2,952	10
Detroit – Ann Arbor, MI CMSA	2,948	11
Atlanta, GA MSA	2,822	12
Denver – Boulder, CO CMSA	2,718	13
Minneapolis – St. Paul, MN – WI MSA	2,653	14
Baltimore, MD MSA	2,637	15
San Diego, CA MSA	2,461	16
Seattle – Tacoma, WA CMSA	2,461	16
Cleveland – Akron – Lorain, OH CMSA	1,983	17
New Orleans, LA MSA	1,630	18
Phoenix, AZ MSA	1,576	19
Pittsburgh – Beaver Valley, PA CMSA	1,530	20
St. Louis, MO – IL MSA	1,477	21
Austin, TX MSA	1,450	22

[Continued]

★1552★

Top 25 MSAs For Employment As Lawyers, 1990: Women

[Continued]

MSA/CMSA	Employees per 100,000 pop.	Rank
Sacramento, CA MSA	1,446	23
Hartford – New Britain – Middletown, CT CMSA	1,390	24

Source: U.S. Department of Commerce, Bureau of the Census, Data User Services Division, *1990 Census of Population and Housing, Equal Employment Opportunity File, CD-90-EE0-1, January 1993*, CD-ROM.

★1553★

Occupations, By Race/Sex

Top 25 MSAs For Employment As Legal Assistants, 1990: Men

MSA/CMSA	Employees per 100,000 pop.	Rank
Pittsburgh – Beaver Valley, PA CMSA	7,674	1
Los Angeles – Anaheim – Riverside, CA CMSA	5,983	2
Washington, DC – MD – VA MSA	4,929	3
San Francisco – Oakland – San Jose, CA CMSA	3,245	4
Chicago – Gary – Lake County, IL – IN – WI CMSA	2,451	5
Philadelphia – Wilmington – Trenton, PA – NJ – DE – MD CMSA	1,716	6
Houston – Galveston – Brazoria, TX CMSA	1,573	7
Boston – Lawrence – Salem, MA – NH CMSA	1,403	8
Dallas – Fort Worth, TX CMSA	1,236	9
Atlanta, GA MSA	865	10
Detroit – Ann Arbor, MI CMSA	845	11
Miami – Fort Lauderdale, FL CMSA	794	12
Denver – Boulder, CO CMSA	775	13
San Diego, CA MSA	754	14
Phoenix, AZ MSA	749	15
Minneapolis – St. Paul, MN – WI MSA	743	16
Sacramento, CA MSA	727	17
Seattle – Tacoma, WA CMSA	721	18
Cleveland – Akron – Lorain, OH CMSA	663	19
Baltimore, MD MSA	632	20
Austin, TX MSA	605	21
Columbus, OH MSA	475	22
Pittsburgh – Beaver Valley, PA CMSA	438	23
Albany – Schenectady – Troy, NY MSA	414	24
Oklahoma City, OK MSA	412	25

Source: U.S. Department of Commerce, Bureau of the Census, Data User Services Division, *1990 Census of Population and Housing, Equal Employment Opportunity File, CD-90-EE0-1, January 1993*, CD-ROM.

★1554★

Occupations, By Race/Sex

Top 25 MSAs For Employment As Legal Assistants, 1990: Women

MSA/CMSA	Employees per 100,000 pop.	Rank
Pittsburgh – Beaver Valley, PA CMSA	17,657	1
Los Angeles – Anaheim – Riverside, CA CMSA	14,602	2
Washington, DC – MD – VA MSA	8,978	3
San Francisco – Oakland – San Jose, CA CMSA	8,211	4
Philadelphia – Wilmington – Trenton, PA – NJ – DE – MD CMSA	5,976	5
Chicago – Gary – Lake County, IL – IN – WI CMSA	5,493	6
Dallas – Fort Worth, TX CMSA	5,150	7
Houston – Galveston – Brazoria, TX CMSA	4,029	8
Boston – Lawrence – Salem, MA – NH CMSA	4,019	9
Miami – Fort Lauderdale, FL CMSA	3,563	10
Seattle – Tacoma, WA CMSA	3,116	11
Atlanta, GA MSA	2,989	12
Denver – Boulder, CO CMSA	2,956	13
San Diego, CA MSA	2,767	14
Minneapolis – St. Paul, MN – WI MSA	2,740	15
Phoenix, AZ MSA	2,740	15
Baltimore, MD MSA	2,554	16
Detroit – Ann Arbor, MI CMSA	2,384	17
Cleveland – Akron – Lorain, OH CMSA	2,030	18
Tampa – St. Petersburg – Clearwater, FL MSA	2,019	19
Sacramento, CA MSA	1,959	20
Kansas City, MO – KS MSA	1,635	21
Pittsburgh – Beaver Valley, PA CMSA	1,630	22
Portland – Vancouver, OR – WA CMSA	1,466	23
New Orleans, LA MSA	1,423	24

Source: U.S. Department of Commerce, Bureau of the Census, Data User Services Division, *1990 Census of Population and Housing, Equal Employment Opportunity File, CD-90-EE0-1, January 1993,* CD-ROM.

★1555★

Occupations, By Race/Sex

Top 25 MSAs For Employment As Legislators, 1990: Men

MSA/CMSA	Employees per 100,000 pop.	Rank
Washington, DC – MD – VA MSA	962	1
New York – Northern New Jersey – Long Island, NY – NJ – CT CMSA	359	2
Los Angeles – Anaheim – Riverside, CA CMSA	274	3
Chicago – Gary – Lake County, IL – IN – WI CMSA	246	4
Boston – Lawrence – Salem, MA – NH CMSA	188	5
Sacramento, CA MSA	140	6
Albany – Schenectady – Troy, NY MSA	106	7
Cleveland – Akron – Lorain, OH CMSA	105	8
Pittsburgh – Beaver Valley, PA CMSA	104	9
Minneapolis – St. Paul, MN – WI MSA	98	10
Buffalo – Niagara Falls, NY CMSA	97	11
St. Louis, MO – IL MSA	95	12
Philadelphia – Wilmington – Trenton, PA – NJ – DE – MD CMSA	83	13
Denver – Boulder, CO CMSA	77	14
Detroit – Ann Arbor, MI CMSA	74	15
Baltimore, MD MSA	70	16
San Francisco – Oakland – San Jose, CA CMSA	66	17
Dallas – Fort Worth, TX CMSA	66	17
Hartford – New Britain – Middletown, CT CMSA	63	18
Lansing – East Lansing, MI MSA	58	19
Providence – Pawtucket – Fall River, RI – MA CMSA	51	20
Seattle – Tacoma, WA CMSA	50	21
Houston – Galveston – Brazoria, TX CMSA	50	21
Phoenix, AZ MSA	49	22
New Orleans, LA MSA	48	23

Source: U.S. Department of Commerce, Bureau of the Census, Data User Services Division, *1990 Census of Population and Housing, Equal Employment Opportunity File, CD-90-EE0-1, January 1993,* CD-ROM.

★ 1556 ★

Occupations, By Race/Sex

Top 25 MSAs For Employment As Legislators, 1990: Women

MSA/CMSA	Employees per 100,000 pop.	Rank
Washington, DC – MD – VA MSA	697	1
New York – Northern New Jersey – Long Island, NY – NJ – CT CMSA	310	2
Los Angeles – Anaheim – Riverside, CA CMSA	286	3
Chicago – Gary – Lake County, IL – IN – WI CMSA	227	4
San Francisco – Oakland – San Jose, CA CMSA	146	5
Albany – Schenectady – Troy, NY MSA	105	6
Boston – Lawrence – Salem, MA – NH CMSA	103	7
Minneapolis – St. Paul, MN – WI MSA	96	8
Dallas – Fort Worth, TX CMSA	87	9
Denver – Boulder, CO CMSA	79	10
Philadelphia – Wilmington – Trenton, PA – NJ – DE – MD CMSA	68	11
Lansing – East Lansing, MI MSA	67	12
Sacramento, CA MSA	67	12
Cleveland – Akron – Lorain, OH CMSA	66	13
Baltimore, MD MSA	61	14
Hartford – New Britain – Middletown, CT CMSA	61	14
Seattle – Tacoma, WA CMSA	59	15
Atlanta, GA MSA	55	16
Pittsburgh – Beaver Valley, PA CMSA	55	16
Detroit – Ann Arbor, MI CMSA	54	17
Phoenix, AZ MSA	54	17
Tallahassee, FL MSA	52	18
Houston – Galveston – Brazoria, TX CMSA	45	19
Miami – Fort Lauderdale, FL CMSA	45	19
St. Louis, MO – IL MSA	45	19

Source: U.S. Department of Commerce, Bureau of the Census, Data User Services Division, *1990 Census of Population and Housing, Equal Employment Opportunity File, CD-90-EE0-1, January 1993*, CD-ROM.

★ 1557 ★

Occupations, By Race/Sex

Top 25 MSAs For Employment As Librarians, 1990: Men

MSA/CMSA	Employees per 100,000 pop.	Rank
Tampa – St. Petersburg – Clearwater, FL MSA	4,315	1
Los Angeles – Anaheim – Riverside, CA CMSA	2,066	2
Washington, DC – MD – VA MSA	1,812	3
Boston – Lawrence – Salem, MA – NH CMSA	1,425	4
Chicago – Gary – Lake County, IL – IN – WI CMSA	1,412	5
San Francisco – Oakland – San Jose, CA CMSA	1,317	6
Philadelphia – Wilmington – Trenton, PA – NJ – DE – MD CMSA	1,291	7
Detroit – Ann Arbor, MI CMSA	561	8
Cleveland – Akron – Lorain, OH CMSA	546	9
Dallas – Fort Worth, TX CMSA	520	10
Houston – Galveston – Brazoria, TX CMSA	448	11
St. Louis, MO – IL MSA	445	12
Baltimore, MD MSA	426	13
Austin, TX MSA	382	14
Columbus, OH MSA	347	15
Seattle – Tacoma, WA CMSA	342	16
San Diego, CA MSA	334	17
Denver – Boulder, CO CMSA	322	18
Minneapolis – St. Paul, MN – WI MSA	310	19
Pittsburgh – Beaver Valley, PA CMSA	300	20
Atlanta, GA MSA	296	21
Providence – Pawtucket – Fall River, RI – MA CMSA	289	22
Raleigh – Durham, NC MSA	284	23
Miami – Fort Lauderdale, FL CMSA	253	24
Tampa – St. Petersburg – Clearwater, FL MSA	240	25

Source: U.S. Department of Commerce, Bureau of the Census, Data User Services Division, *1990 Census of Population and Housing, Equal Employment Opportunity File, CD-90-EE0-1, January 1993*, CD-ROM.

★1558★
Occupations, By Race/Sex

Top 25 MSAs For Employment As Librarians, 1990: Women

MSA/CMSA	Employees per 100,000 pop.	Rank
Phoenix, AZ MSA	12,866	1
Los Angeles – Anaheim – Riverside, CA CMSA	6,999	2
Washington, DC – MD – VA MSA	5,455	3
Chicago – Gary – Lake County, IL – IN – WI CMSA	5,198	4
San Francisco – Oakland – San Jose, CA CMSA	4,549	5
Boston – Lawrence – Salem, MA – NH CMSA	4,540	6
Philadelphia – Wilmington – Trenton, PA – NJ – DE – MD CMSA	4,419	7
Detroit – Ann Arbor, MI CMSA	2,855	8
Dallas – Fort Worth, TX CMSA	2,254	9
Houston – Galveston – Brazoria, TX CMSA	2,198	10
Cleveland – Akron – Lorain, OH CMSA	2,073	11
Seattle – Tacoma, WA CMSA	1,896	12
Baltimore, MD MSA	1,876	13
Atlanta, GA MSA	1,795	14
Minneapolis – St. Paul, MN – WI MSA	1,675	15
St. Louis, MO – IL MSA	1,627	16
San Diego, CA MSA	1,266	17
Cincinnati – Hamilton, OH – KY – IN CMSA	1,257	18
Miami – Fort Lauderdale, FL CMSA	1,238	19
Denver – Boulder, CO CMSA	1,209	20
Hartford – New Britain – Middletown, CT CMSA	1,164	21
Columbus, OH MSA	1,157	22
Pittsburgh – Beaver Valley, PA CMSA	1,047	23
Milwaukee – Racine, WI CMSA	1,002	24
Norfolk – Virginia Beach – Newport News, VA MSA	975	25

Source: U.S. Department of Commerce, Bureau of the Census, Data User Services Division, *1990 Census of Population and Housing, Equal Employment Opportunity File,* CD-90-EE0-1, January 1993, CD-ROM.

★1559★
Occupations, By Race/Sex

Top 25 MSAs For Employment As Library Clerks, 1990: Men

MSA/CMSA	Employees per 100,000 pop.	Rank
Pittsburgh – Beaver Valley, PA CMSA	2,895	1
Los Angeles – Anaheim – Riverside, CA CMSA	2,306	2
San Francisco – Oakland – San Jose, CA CMSA	1,308	3
Chicago – Gary – Lake County, IL – IN – WI CMSA	1,192	4
Washington, DC – MD – VA MSA	1,033	5
Boston – Lawrence – Salem, MA – NH CMSA	1,030	6
Philadelphia – Wilmington – Trenton, PA – NJ – DE – MD CMSA	675	7
Detroit – Ann Arbor, MI CMSA	636	8
Cleveland – Akron – Lorain, OH CMSA	518	9
Dallas – Fort Worth, TX CMSA	485	10
San Diego, CA MSA	405	11
Miami – Fort Lauderdale, FL CMSA	371	12
Minneapolis – St. Paul, MN – WI MSA	359	13
Pittsburgh – Beaver Valley, PA CMSA	337	14
Baltimore, MD MSA	328	15
Atlanta, GA MSA	326	16
Columbus, OH MSA	321	17
Seattle – Tacoma, WA CMSA	303	18
Houston – Galveston – Brazoria, TX CMSA	302	19
Cincinnati – Hamilton, OH – KY – IN CMSA	265	20
Raleigh – Durham, NC MSA	259	21
Austin, TX MSA	252	22
Phoenix, AZ MSA	244	23
St. Louis, MO – IL MSA	243	24
Denver – Boulder, CO CMSA	236	25

Source: U.S. Department of Commerce, Bureau of the Census, Data User Services Division, *1990 Census of Population and Housing, Equal Employment Opportunity File,* CD-90-EE0-1, January 1993, CD-ROM.

★1560★

Occupations, By Race/Sex

Top 25 MSAs For Employment As Library Clerks, 1990: Women

MSA/CMSA	Employees per 100,000 pop.	Rank
Milwaukee – Racine, WI CMSA	10,314	1
Los Angeles – Anaheim – Riverside, CA CMSA	5,404	2
Chicago – Gary – Lake County, IL – IN – WI CMSA	4,376	3
San Francisco – Oakland – San Jose, CA CMSA	3,473	4
Boston – Lawrence – Salem, MA – NH CMSA	3,035	5
Philadelphia – Wilmington – Trenton, PA – NJ – DE – MD CMSA	2,995	6
Washington, DC – MD – VA MSA	2,641	7
Cleveland – Akron – Lorain, OH CMSA	2,052	8
Detroit – Ann Arbor, MI CMSA	1,912	9
Minneapolis – St. Paul, MN – WI MSA	1,518	10
Dallas – Fort Worth, TX CMSA	1,349	11
Seattle – Tacoma, WA CMSA	1,335	12
Atlanta, GA MSA	1,119	13
St. Louis, MO – IL MSA	1,049	14
Houston – Galveston – Brazoria, TX CMSA	1,030	15
Phoenix, AZ MSA	1,004	16
Pittsburgh – Beaver Valley, PA CMSA	988	17
Rochester, NY MSA	953	18
San Diego, CA MSA	950	19
Cincinnati – Hamilton, OH – KY – IN CMSA	913	20
Baltimore, MD MSA	897	21
Albany – Schenectady – Troy, NY MSA	874	22
Hartford – New Britain – Middletown, CT CMSA	864	23
Portland – Vancouver, OR – WA CMSA	853	24
Milwaukee – Racine, WI CMSA	850	25

Source: U.S. Department of Commerce, Bureau of the Census, Data User Services Division, *1990 Census of Population and Housing, Equal Employment Opportunity File, CD-90-EEO-1, January 1993,* CD-ROM.

★1561★

Occupations, By Race/Sex

Top 25 MSAs For Employment As Licensed Practical Nurses, 1990: Men

MSA/CMSA	Employees per 100,000 pop.	Rank
Dallas – Fort Worth, TX CMSA	2,123	1
Los Angeles – Anaheim – Riverside, CA CMSA	1,803	2
San Francisco – Oakland – San Jose, CA CMSA	747	3
Chicago – Gary – Lake County, IL – IN – WI CMSA	682	4
Philadelphia – Wilmington – Trenton, PA – NJ – DE – MD CMSA	606	5
San Antonio, TX MSA	569	6
Detroit – Ann Arbor, MI CMSA	458	7
Boston – Lawrence – Salem, MA – NH CMSA	433	8
Washington, DC – MD – VA MSA	422	9
Miami – Fort Lauderdale, FL CMSA	421	10
San Diego, CA MSA	415	11
Baltimore, MD MSA	406	12
Dallas – Fort Worth, TX CMSA	378	13
Tampa – St. Petersburg – Clearwater, FL MSA	358	14
Seattle – Tacoma, WA CMSA	343	15
Cleveland – Akron – Lorain, OH CMSA	342	16
Houston – Galveston – Brazoria, TX CMSA	311	17
Kansas City, MO – KS MSA	291	18
Cincinnati – Hamilton, OH – KY – IN CMSA	253	19
Denver – Boulder, CO CMSA	248	20
Sacramento, CA MSA	247	21
Minneapolis – St. Paul, MN – WI MSA	233	22
St. Louis, MO – IL MSA	232	23
Atlanta, GA MSA	208	24
Phoenix, AZ MSA	174	25

Source: U.S. Department of Commerce, Bureau of the Census, Data User Services Division, *1990 Census of Population and Housing, Equal Employment Opportunity File, CD-90-EEO-1, January 1993,* CD-ROM.

★1562★

Occupations, By Race/Sex

Top 25 MSAs For Employment As Licensed Practical Nurses, 1990: Women

MSA/CMSA	Employees per 100,000 pop.	Rank
Pittsburgh – Beaver Valley, PA CMSA	20,336	1
Los Angeles – Anaheim – Riverside, CA CMSA	14,069	2
Philadelphia – Wilmington – Trenton, PA – NJ – DE – MD CMSA	9,010	3
Chicago – Gary – Lake County, IL – IN – WI CMSA	7,824	4
Detroit – Ann Arbor, MI CMSA	6,768	5
Cleveland – Akron – Lorain, OH CMSA	6,146	6
Boston – Lawrence – Salem, MA – NH CMSA	5,855	7
San Francisco – Oakland – San Jose, CA CMSA	5,684	8
Houston – Galveston – Brazoria, TX CMSA	5,170	9
Dallas – Fort Worth, TX CMSA	4,422	10
Tampa – St. Petersburg – Clearwater, FL MSA	4,344	11
St. Louis, MO – IL MSA	4,232	12
Minneapolis – St. Paul, MN – WI MSA	4,169	13
Miami – Fort Lauderdale, FL CMSA	4,111	14
Pittsburgh – Beaver Valley, PA CMSA	3,724	15
Cincinnati – Hamilton, OH – KY – IN CMSA	3,574	16
Baltimore, MD MSA	3,564	17
Washington, DC – MD – VA MSA	3,260	18
Atlanta, GA MSA	3,236	19
Milwaukee – Racine, WI CMSA	2,867	20
Seattle – Tacoma, WA CMSA	2,743	21
San Antonio, TX MSA	2,708	22
Buffalo – Niagara Falls, NY CMSA	2,673	23
San Diego, CA MSA	2,584	24
Norfolk – Virginia Beach – Newport News, VA MSA	2,513	25

Source: U.S. Department of Commerce, Bureau of the Census, Data User Services Division, *1990 Census of Population and Housing, Equal Employment Opportunity File, CD-90-EE0-1, January 1993,* CD-ROM.

★1563★

Occupations, By Race/Sex

Top 25 MSAs For Employment As Locksmiths and Safe Repairers, 1990: Men

MSA/CMSA	Employees per 100,000 pop.	Rank
Sacramento, CA MSA	2,463	1
Los Angeles – Anaheim – Riverside, CA CMSA	2,017	2
San Francisco – Oakland – San Jose, CA CMSA	863	3
Philadelphia – Wilmington – Trenton, PA – NJ – DE – MD CMSA	800	4
Washington, DC – MD – VA MSA	736	5
Chicago – Gary – Lake County, IL – IN – WI CMSA	672	6
Boston – Lawrence – Salem, MA – NH CMSA	563	7
Dallas – Fort Worth, TX CMSA	485	8
Detroit – Ann Arbor, MI CMSA	446	9
Miami – Fort Lauderdale, FL CMSA	406	10
Houston – Galveston – Brazoria, TX CMSA	367	11
Phoenix, AZ MSA	366	12
Seattle – Tacoma, WA CMSA	312	13
San Diego, CA MSA	311	14
Atlanta, GA MSA	308	15
Minneapolis – St. Paul, MN – WI MSA	293	16
Tampa – St. Petersburg – Clearwater, FL MSA	280	17
Baltimore, MD MSA	271	18
Cleveland – Akron – Lorain, OH CMSA	252	19
Denver – Boulder, CO CMSA	249	20
St. Louis, MO – IL MSA	248	21
Las Vegas, NV MSA	194	22
Sacramento, CA MSA	181	23
Kansas City, MO – KS MSA	175	24
West Palm Beach – Boca Raton – Delray Beach, FL MSA	172	25

Source: U.S. Department of Commerce, Bureau of the Census, Data User Services Division, *1990 Census of Population and Housing, Equal Employment Opportunity File, CD-90-EE0-1, January 1993,* CD-ROM.

★1564★

Occupations, By Race/Sex

Top 25 MSAs For Employment As Locksmiths and Safe Repairers, 1990: Women

MSA/CMSA	Employees per 100,000 pop.	Rank
Houston – Galveston – Brazoria, TX CMSA	172	1
Houston – Galveston – Brazoria, TX CMSA	81	2
Tampa – St. Petersburg – Clearwater, FL MSA	71	3
Chicago – Gary – Lake County, IL – IN – WI CMSA	67	4
San Francisco – Oakland – San Jose, CA CMSA	59	5
New York – Northern New Jersey – Long Island, NY – NJ – CT CMSA	50	6
Seattle – Tacoma, WA CMSA	45	7
Atlanta, GA MSA	38	8
Detroit – Ann Arbor, MI CMSA	38	8
Minneapolis – St. Paul, MN – WI MSA	34	9
Milwaukee – Racine, WI CMSA	32	10
Miami – Fort Lauderdale, FL CMSA	31	11
Portland – Vancouver, OR – WA CMSA	31	11
Philadelphia – Wilmington – Trenton, PA – NJ – DE – MD CMSA	27	12
St. Louis, MO – IL MSA	26	13
Charlotte – Gastonia – Rock Hill, NC – SC MSA	25	14
Phoenix, AZ MSA	25	14
Oklahoma City, OK MSA	24	15
Orlando, FL MSA	22	16
Indianapolis, IN MSA	20	17
New Orleans, LA MSA	20	17
Providence – Pawtucket – Fall River, RI – MA CMSA	18	18
Albany, GA MSA	17	19
Nashville, TN MSA	15	20
Muncie, IN MSA	15	20

Source: U.S. Department of Commerce, Bureau of the Census, Data User Services Division, *1990 Census of Population and Housing, Equal Employment Opportunity File, CD-90-EE0-1, January 1993,* CD-ROM.

★1565★

Occupations, By Race/Sex

Top 25 MSAs For Employment As Locomotive Operating Occupations, 1990: Men

MSA/CMSA	Employees per 100,000 pop.	Rank
Buffalo – Niagara Falls, NY CMSA	3,740	1
Chicago – Gary – Lake County, IL – IN – WI CMSA	1,955	2
Los Angeles – Anaheim – Riverside, CA CMSA	929	3
Pittsburgh – Beaver Valley, PA CMSA	848	4
Philadelphia – Wilmington – Trenton, PA – NJ – DE – MD CMSA	811	5
Houston – Galveston – Brazoria, TX CMSA	656	6
Kansas City, MO – KS MSA	622	7
San Francisco – Oakland – San Jose, CA CMSA	486	8
Boston – Lawrence – Salem, MA – NH CMSA	466	9
St. Louis, MO – IL MSA	459	10
Detroit – Ann Arbor, MI CMSA	458	11
Atlanta, GA MSA	432	12
Cleveland – Akron – Lorain, OH CMSA	398	13
Cincinnati – Hamilton, OH – KY – IN CMSA	386	14
Birmingham, AL MSA	381	15
Dallas – Fort Worth, TX CMSA	376	16
Minneapolis – St. Paul, MN – WI MSA	356	17
Baltimore, MD MSA	329	18
Seattle – Tacoma, WA CMSA	327	19
Denver – Boulder, CO CMSA	316	20
Buffalo – Niagara Falls, NY CMSA	308	21
Salt Lake City – Ogden, UT MSA	306	22
Louisville, KY – IN MSA	284	23
Portland – Vancouver, OR – WA CMSA	281	24
Toledo, OH MSA	271	25

Source: U.S. Department of Commerce, Bureau of the Census, Data User Services Division, *1990 Census of Population and Housing, Equal Employment Opportunity File, CD-90-EE0-1, January 1993,* CD-ROM.

★1566★

Occupations, By Race/Sex

Top 25 MSAs For Employment As Locomotive Operating Occupations, 1990: Women

MSA/CMSA	Employees per 100,000 pop.	Rank
Tucson, AZ MSA	130	1
Los Angeles – Anaheim – Riverside, CA CMSA	79	2
San Francisco – Oakland – San Jose, CA CMSA	78	3
Boston – Lawrence – Salem, MA – NH CMSA	54	4

[Continued]

★1566★

Top 25 MSAs For Employment As Locomotive Operating Occupations, 1990: Women

[Continued]

MSA/CMSA	Employees per 100,000 pop.	Rank
Chicago – Gary – Lake County, IL – IN – WI CMSA	54	4
Philadelphia – Wilmington – Trenton, PA – NJ – DE – MD CMSA	35	5
Washington, DC – MD – VA MSA	33	6
Reno, NV MSA	28	7
Baltimore, MD MSA	23	8
Dallas – Fort Worth, TX CMSA	23	8
Denver – Boulder, CO CMSA	23	8
St. Louis, MO – IL MSA	22	9
Houston – Galveston – Brazoria, TX CMSA	18	10
Albuquerque, NM MSA	17	11
Cleveland – Akron – Lorain, OH CMSA	17	11
Eugene – Springfield, OR MSA	15	12
Salt Lake City – Ogden, UT MSA	15	12
Tucson, AZ MSA	15	12
Pittsburgh – Beaver Valley, PA CMSA	14	13
Atlanta, GA MSA	13	14
Knoxville, TN MSA	10	15
Louisville, KY – IN MSA	10	15
San Diego, CA MSA	10	15
Charleston, SC MSA	9	16
Fort Myers – Cape CoraL, Fl MSA	9	16

Source: U.S. Department of Commerce, Bureau of the Census, Data User Services Division, *1990 Census of Population and Housing, Equal Employment Opportunity File, CD-90-EE0-1, January 1993,* CD-ROM.

★1567★

Occupations, By Race/Sex

Top 25 MSAs For Employment As Longshore Equipment Operators, 1990: Men

MSA/CMSA	Employees per 100,000 pop.	Rank
Los Angeles – Anaheim – Riverside, CA CMSA	467	1
Los Angeles – Anaheim – Riverside, CA CMSA	418	2
Seattle – Tacoma, WA CMSA	296	3
Baltimore, MD MSA	245	4
New Orleans, LA MSA	225	5
Portland – Vancouver, OR – WA CMSA	204	6
Houston – Galveston – Brazoria, TX CMSA	193	7
Norfolk – Virginia Beach – Newport News, VA MSA	186	8
San Francisco – Oakland – San Jose, CA CMSA	177	9
Philadelphia – Wilmington – Trenton, PA – NJ – DE – MD CMSA	158	10

[Continued]

★1567★

Top 25 MSAs For Employment As Longshore Equipment Operators, 1990: Men

[Continued]

MSA/CMSA	Employees per 100,000 pop.	Rank
Honolulu, HI MSA	89	11
Savannah, GA MSA	73	12
Chicago – Gary – Lake County, IL – IN – WI CMSA	70	13
Mobile, AL MSA	69	14
Charleston, SC MSA	69	14
Boston – Lawrence – Salem, MA – NH CMSA	49	15
Olympia, WA MSA	45	16
Corpus Christi, TX MSA	44	17
Biloxi – Gulfport, MS MSA	43	18
Beaumont – Port Arthur, TX MSA	39	19
Stockton, CA MSA	38	20
Lake Charles, LA MSA	35	21
Baton Rouge, LA MSA	35	21
Miami – Fort Lauderdale, FL CMSA	31	22
Pensacola, FL MSA	30	23

Source: U.S. Department of Commerce, Bureau of the Census, Data User Services Division, *1990 Census of Population and Housing, Equal Employment Opportunity File, CD-90-EE0-1, January 1993,* CD-ROM.

★1568★

Occupations, By Race/Sex

Top 25 MSAs For Employment As Longshore Equipment Operators, 1990: Women

MSA/CMSA	Employees per 100,000 pop.	Rank
Norfolk – Virginia Beach – Newport News, VA MSA	33	1
Seattle – Tacoma, WA CMSA	9	2
Norfolk – Virginia Beach – Newport News, VA MSA	8	3
Sacramento, CA MSA	6	4
New York – Northern New Jersey – Long Island, NY – NJ – CT CMSA	5	5
Beaumont – Port Arthur, TX MSA	4	6
Albany, GA MSA	0	7
Alexandria, LA MSA	0	7
Abilene, TX MSA	0	7
Anchorage, AK MSA	0	7
Amarillo, TX MSA	0	7
Allentown – Bethlehem – Easton, PA – NJ MSA	0	7
Altoona, PA MSA	0	7
Albuquerque, NM MSA	0	7
Albany – Schenectady – Troy, NY MSA	0	7
Atlanta, GA MSA	0	7
Appleton – Oshkosh – Neenah, WI MSA	0	7
Asheville, NC MSA	0	7

[Continued]

★1568★

Top 25 MSAs For Employment As Longshore Equipment Operators, 1990: Women
[Continued]

MSA/CMSA	Employees per 100,000 pop.	Rank
Atlantic City, NJ MSA	0	7
Anderson, SC MSA	0	7
Anniston, AL MSA	0	7
Augusta, GA – SC MSA	0	7
Austin, TX MSA	0	7
Anderson, IN MSA	0	7
Athens, GA MSA	0	7

Source: U.S. Department of Commerce, Bureau of the Census, Data User Services Division, *1990 Census of Population and Housing, Equal Employment Opportunity File, CD-90-EE0-1, January 1993,* CD-ROM.

★1569★

Occupations, By Race/Sex

Top 25 MSAs For Employment As Maids and Housemen, 1990: Men

MSA/CMSA	Employees per 100,000 pop.	Rank
Kansas City, MO – KS MSA	15,117	1
Los Angeles – Anaheim – Riverside, CA CMSA	8,321	2
Chicago – Gary – Lake County, IL – IN – WI CMSA	4,780	3
San Francisco – Oakland – San Jose, CA CMSA	4,006	4
Boston – Lawrence – Salem, MA – NH CMSA	3,424	5
Philadelphia – Wilmington – Trenton, PA – NJ – DE – MD CMSA	3,386	6
Miami – Fort Lauderdale, FL CMSA	2,948	7
Las Vegas, NV MSA	2,923	8
Washington, DC – MD – VA MSA	2,867	9
Dallas – Fort Worth, TX CMSA	2,176	10
Detroit – Ann Arbor, MI CMSA	2,063	11
Houston – Galveston – Brazoria, TX CMSA	1,905	12
St. Louis, MO – IL MSA	1,736	13
Honolulu, HI MSA	1,627	14
Cleveland – Akron – Lorain, OH CMSA	1,531	15
Baltimore, MD MSA	1,407	16
Orlando, FL MSA	1,373	17
San Diego, CA MSA	1,363	18
Phoenix, AZ MSA	1,354	19
Pittsburgh – Beaver Valley, PA CMSA	1,340	20
Atlanta, GA MSA	1,295	21
Tampa – St. Petersburg – Clearwater, FL MSA	1,294	22
Minneapolis – St. Paul, MN – WI MSA	1,141	23

[Continued]

★1569★

Top 25 MSAs For Employment As Maids and Housemen, 1990: Men
[Continued]

MSA/CMSA	Employees per 100,000 pop.	Rank
Seattle – Tacoma, WA CMSA	1,066	24
New Orleans, LA MSA	1,027	25

Source: U.S. Department of Commerce, Bureau of the Census, Data User Services Division, *1990 Census of Population and Housing, Equal Employment Opportunity File, CD-90-EE0-1, January 1993,* CD-ROM.

★1570★

Occupations, By Race/Sex

Top 25 MSAs For Employment As Maids and Housemen, 1990: Women

MSA/CMSA	Employees per 100,000 pop.	Rank
Cincinnati – Hamilton, OH – KY – IN CMSA	28,063	1
New York – Northern New Jersey – Long Island, NY – NJ – CT CMSA	28,005	2
Chicago – Gary – Lake County, IL – IN – WI CMSA	14,092	3
San Francisco – Oakland – San Jose, CA CMSA	13,645	4
Miami – Fort Lauderdale, FL CMSA	10,514	5
Washington, DC – MD – VA MSA	9,039	6
Philadelphia – Wilmington – Trenton, PA – NJ – DE – MD CMSA	8,837	7
Dallas – Fort Worth, TX CMSA	8,765	8
Detroit – Ann Arbor, MI CMSA	8,586	9
Houston – Galveston – Brazoria, TX CMSA	8,397	10
Las Vegas, NV MSA	7,842	11
Boston – Lawrence – Salem, MA – NH CMSA	6,882	12
Atlanta, GA MSA	6,226	13
San Diego, CA MSA	5,889	14
Phoenix, AZ MSA	5,502	15
St. Louis, MO – IL MSA	5,417	16
Tampa – St. Petersburg – Clearwater, FL MSA	5,114	17
Seattle – Tacoma, WA CMSA	4,870	18
Baltimore, MD MSA	4,806	19
Orlando, FL MSA	4,728	20
Cleveland – Akron – Lorain, OH CMSA	4,608	21
Minneapolis – St. Paul, MN – WI MSA	4,496	22
Honolulu, HI MSA	4,128	23
New Orleans, LA MSA	4,119	24
Pittsburgh – Beaver Valley, PA CMSA	3,949	25

Source: U.S. Department of Commerce, Bureau of the Census, Data User Services Division, *1990 Census of Population and Housing, Equal Employment Opportunity File, CD-90-EE0-1, January 1993,* CD-ROM.

★1571★

Occupations, By Race/Sex

Top 25 MSAs For Employment As Mail Carriers, Postal Service, 1990: Men

MSA/CMSA	Employees per 100,000 pop.	Rank
Madison, WI MSA	24,663	1
Los Angeles – Anaheim – Riverside, CA CMSA	13,340	2
Chicago – Gary – Lake County, IL – IN – WI CMSA	8,175	3
San Francisco – Oakland – San Jose, CA CMSA	7,395	4
Philadelphia – Wilmington – Trenton, PA – NJ – DE – MD CMSA	7,067	5
Boston – Lawrence – Salem, MA – NH CMSA	5,465	6
Washington, DC – MD – VA MSA	5,220	7
Dallas – Fort Worth, TX CMSA	4,216	8
Detroit – Ann Arbor, MI CMSA	3,746	9
Miami – Fort Lauderdale, FL CMSA	3,218	10
Cleveland – Akron – Lorain, OH CMSA	3,113	11
St. Louis, MO – IL MSA	3,078	12
Houston – Galveston – Brazoria, TX CMSA	2,991	13
Atlanta, GA MSA	2,700	14
Pittsburgh – Beaver Valley, PA CMSA	2,601	15
Minneapolis – St. Paul, MN – WI MSA	2,583	16
Baltimore, MD MSA	2,390	17
San Diego, CA MSA	2,333	18
Denver – Boulder, CO CMSA	2,285	19
Tampa – St. Petersburg – Clearwater, FL MSA	2,253	20
Phoenix, AZ MSA	2,150	21
Seattle – Tacoma, WA CMSA	2,142	22
Kansas City, MO – KS MSA	1,800	23
Cincinnati – Hamilton, OH – KY – IN CMSA	1,676	24
Milwaukee – Racine, WI CMSA	1,571	25

Source: U.S. Department of Commerce, Bureau of the Census, Data User Services Division, *1990 Census of Population and Housing, Equal Employment Opportunity File, CD-90-EE0-1, January 1993*, CD-ROM.

★1572★

Occupations, By Race/Sex

Top 25 MSAs For Employment As Mail Carriers, Postal Service, 1990: Women

MSA/CMSA	Employees per 100,000 pop.	Rank
Columbus, OH MSA	5,053	1
New York – Northern New Jersey – Long Island, NY – NJ – CT CMSA	4,999	2
Chicago – Gary – Lake County, IL – IN – WI CMSA	3,190	3
Detroit – Ann Arbor, MI CMSA	3,034	4
San Francisco – Oakland – San Jose, CA CMSA	2,599	5
Philadelphia – Wilmington – Trenton, PA – NJ – DE – MD CMSA	1,819	6
Miami – Fort Lauderdale, FL CMSA	1,575	7
Houston – Galveston – Brazoria, TX CMSA	1,541	8
Atlanta, GA MSA	1,485	9
Dallas – Fort Worth, TX CMSA	1,414	10
Washington, DC – MD – VA MSA	1,354	11
Boston – Lawrence – Salem, MA – NH CMSA	1,222	12
St. Louis, MO – IL MSA	1,063	13
Baltimore, MD MSA	1,051	14
Seattle – Tacoma, WA CMSA	938	15
Cleveland – Akron – Lorain, OH CMSA	910	16
San Diego, CA MSA	894	17
Minneapolis – St. Paul, MN – WI MSA	856	18
Phoenix, AZ MSA	763	19
Denver – Boulder, CO CMSA	726	20
Tampa – St. Petersburg – Clearwater, FL MSA	713	21
Pittsburgh – Beaver Valley, PA CMSA	625	22
Indianapolis, IN MSA	591	23
Sacramento, CA MSA	574	24
Cincinnati – Hamilton, OH – KY – IN CMSA	546	25

Source: U.S. Department of Commerce, Bureau of the Census, Data User Services Division, *1990 Census of Population and Housing, Equal Employment Opportunity File, CD-90-EE0-1, January 1993*, CD-ROM.

★1573★

Occupations, By Race/Sex

Top 25 MSAs For Employment As Marine and Naval Architects, 1990: Men

MSA/CMSA	Employees per 100,000 pop.	Rank
Detroit – Ann Arbor, MI CMSA	1,603	1
New York – Northern New Jersey – Long Island, NY – NJ – CT CMSA	659	2
New London – Norwich, CT – RI MSA	653	3
Washington, DC – MD – VA MSA	552	4
San Francisco – Oakland – San Jose, CA CMSA	540	5
Seattle – Tacoma, WA CMSA	478	6
New Orleans, LA MSA	411	7
San Diego, CA MSA	355	8
Honolulu, HI MSA	303	9
Los Angeles – Anaheim – Riverside, CA CMSA	300	10
Charleston, SC MSA	294	11
Bremerton, WA MSA	283	12
Philadelphia – Wilmington – Trenton, PA – NJ – DE – MD CMSA	280	13
Baltimore, MD MSA	279	14
Portsmouth – Dover – Rochester, NH – ME MSA	260	15
Pascagoula, MS MSA	257	16
Boston – Lawrence – Salem, MA – NH CMSA	243	17
Houston – Galveston – Brazoria, TX CMSA	223	18
Miami – Fort Lauderdale, FL CMSA	171	19
Tampa – St. Petersburg – Clearwater, FL MSA	161	20
Mobile, AL MSA	122	21
Portland, ME MSA	122	21
Jacksonville, FL MSA	114	22
Providence – Pawtucket – Fall River, RI – MA CMSA	110	23
Houma – Thibodaux, LA MSA	102	24

Source: U.S. Department of Commerce, Bureau of the Census, Data User Services Division, *1990 Census of Population and Housing, Equal Employment Opportunity File, CD-90-EE0-1, January 1993*, CD-ROM.

★1574★

Occupations, By Race/Sex

Top 25 MSAs For Employment As Marine and Naval Architects, 1990: Women

MSA/CMSA	Employees per 100,000 pop.	Rank
Augusta, GA – SC MSA	121	1
New London – Norwich, CT – RI MSA	45	2
San Francisco – Oakland – San Jose, CA CMSA	31	3
Washington, DC – MD – VA MSA	28	4
New York – Northern New Jersey – Long Island, NY – NJ – CT CMSA	26	5
Los Angeles – Anaheim – Riverside, CA CMSA	25	6
Bremerton, WA MSA	23	7
Pascagoula, MS MSA	23	7
Charleston, SC MSA	15	8
Boston – Lawrence – Salem, MA – NH CMSA	14	9
Mobile, AL MSA	11	10
Olympia, WA MSA	10	11
Hartford – New Britain – Middletown, CT CMSA	8	12
Houston – Galveston – Brazoria, TX CMSA	8	12
Wilmington, NC MSA	8	12
Baltimore, MD MSA	7	13
Cleveland – Akron – Lorain, OH CMSA	7	13
Philadelphia – Wilmington – Trenton, PA – NJ – DE – MD CMSA	7	13
Fresno, CA MSA	6	14
Anderson, SC MSA	5	15
San Diego, CA MSA	3	16
Green Bay, WI MSA	2	17
Anchorage, AK MSA	0	18
Albany, GA MSA	0	18
Altoona, PA MSA	0	18

Source: U.S. Department of Commerce, Bureau of the Census, Data User Services Division, *1990 Census of Population and Housing, Equal Employment Opportunity File, CD-90-EE0-1, January 1993*, CD-ROM.

★1575★

Occupations, By Race/Sex

Top 25 MSAs For Employment As Marine Life Cultivation Workers, 1990: Men

MSA/CMSA	Employees per 100,000 pop.	Rank
Lakeland – Winter Haven, FL MSA	64	1
Tampa – St. Petersburg – Clearwater, FL MSA	29	2
Portland – Vancouver, OR – WA CMSA	27	3
Los Angeles – Anaheim – Riverside, CA CMSA	21	4

[Continued]

★1575★

Top 25 MSAs For Employment As Marine Life Cultivation Workers, 1990: Men
[Continued]

MSA/CMSA	Employees per 100,000 pop.	Rank
Sacramento, CA MSA	16	5
Baltimore, MD MSA	13	6
Spokane, WA MSA	13	6
Houston – Galveston – Brazoria, TX CMSA	12	7
Lincoln, NE MSA	12	7
Atlanta, GA MSA	10	8
Brownsville – Harlingen, TX MSA	10	8
Salem, OR MSA	10	8
Oklahoma City, OK MSA	10	8
Fresno, CA MSA	9	9
Yakima, WA MSA	9	9
Eugene – Springfield, OR MSA	8	10
Indianapolis, IN MSA	8	10
Sherman – Denison, TX MSA	8	10
Tallahassee, FL MSA	8	10
Little Rock – North Little Rock, AR MSA	8	10
New York – Northern New Jersey – Long Island, NY – NJ – CT CMSA	8	10
Orlando, FL MSA	8	10
Portsmouth – Dover – Rochester, NH – ME MSA	8	10
Pueblo, CO MSA	8	10
El Paso, TX MSA	7	11

Source: U.S. Department of Commerce, Bureau of the Census, Data User Services Division, *1990 Census of Population and Housing, Equal Employment Opportunity File, CD-90-EE0-1, January 1993*, CD-ROM.

★1576★
Occupations, By Race/Sex

Top 25 MSAs For Employment As Marine Life Cultivation Workers, 1990: Women

MSA/CMSA	Employees per 100,000 pop.	Rank
Portland – Vancouver, OR – WA CMSA	36	1
Lancaster, PA MSA	15	2
Dallas – Fort Worth, TX CMSA	12	3
Miami – Fort Lauderdale, FL CMSA	12	3
Portland – Vancouver, OR – WA CMSA	11	4
Richland – Kennewick – Pasco, WA MSA	10	5
Baton Rouge, LA MSA	9	6
Cleveland – Akron – Lorain, OH CMSA	9	6
Grand Rapids, MI MSA	9	6
Jacksonville, FL MSA	9	6
Los Angeles – Anaheim – Riverside, CA CMSA	9	6

[Continued]

★1576★

Top 25 MSAs For Employment As Marine Life Cultivation Workers, 1990: Women
[Continued]

MSA/CMSA	Employees per 100,000 pop.	Rank
Seattle – Tacoma, WA CMSA	9	6
Albany – Schenectady – Troy, NY MSA	8	7
Chico, CA MSA	7	8
Lafayette, LA MSA	7	8
Springfield, MO MSA	7	8
Portland, ME MSA	6	9
Houston – Galveston – Brazoria, TX CMSA	5	10
Salem, OR MSA	3	11
Mcallen – Edinburg – Mission, TX MSA	2	12
Medford, OR MSA	2	12
Albany, GA MSA	0	13
Amarillo, TX MSA	0	13
Alexandria, LA MSA	0	13
Altoona, PA MSA	0	13

Source: U.S. Department of Commerce, Bureau of the Census, Data User Services Division, *1990 Census of Population and Housing, Equal Employment Opportunity File, CD-90-EE0-1, January 1993*, CD-ROM.

★1577★
Occupations, By Race/Sex

Top 25 MSAs For Employment As Mathematical Science Teachers, 1990: Men

MSA/CMSA	Employees per 100,000 pop.	Rank
Mansfield, OH MSA	682	1
Los Angeles – Anaheim – Riverside, CA CMSA	491	2
San Francisco – Oakland – San Jose, CA CMSA	370	3
Chicago – Gary – Lake County, IL – IN – WI CMSA	238	4
Philadelphia – Wilmington – Trenton, PA – NJ – DE – MD CMSA	217	5
Detroit – Ann Arbor, MI CMSA	196	6
Boston – Lawrence – Salem, MA – NH CMSA	185	7
San Diego, CA MSA	171	8
Washington, DC – MD – VA MSA	165	9
Columbus, OH MSA	164	10
Sacramento, CA MSA	117	11
Phoenix, AZ MSA	117	11
Austin, TX MSA	111	12
Houston – Galveston – Brazoria, TX CMSA	107	13
Minneapolis – St. Paul, MN – WI MSA	107	13
Seattle – Tacoma, WA CMSA	101	14
Lansing – East Lansing, MI MSA	101	14
Tampa – St. Petersburg – Clearwater, FL MSA	99	15

[Continued]

★1577★

Top 25 MSAs For Employment As Mathematical Science Teachers, 1990: Men
[Continued]

MSA/CMSA	Employees per 100,000 pop.	Rank
Champaign – Urbana – Rantoul, IL MSA	95	16
Atlanta, GA MSA	91	17
Dallas – Fort Worth, TX CMSA	91	17
New Orleans, LA MSA	88	18
Tallahassee, FL MSA	86	19
Cleveland – Akron – Lorain, OH CMSA	86	19
Pittsburgh – Beaver Valley, PA CMSA	84	20

Source: U.S. Department of Commerce, Bureau of the Census, Data User Services Division, *1990 Census of Population and Housing, Equal Employment Opportunity File, CD-90-EE0-1, January 1993,* CD-ROM.

★1578★

Occupations, By Race/Sex

Top 25 MSAs For Employment As Mathematical Science Teachers, 1990: Women

MSA/CMSA	Employees per 100,000 pop.	Rank
Jackson, MS MSA	476	1
Chicago – Gary – Lake County, IL – IN – WI CMSA	199	2
San Francisco – Oakland – San Jose, CA CMSA	170	3
Los Angeles – Anaheim – Riverside, CA CMSA	160	4
Philadelphia – Wilmington – Trenton, PA – NJ – DE – MD CMSA	154	5
Cleveland – Akron – Lorain, OH CMSA	147	6
Washington, DC – MD – VA MSA	133	7
Boston – Lawrence – Salem, MA – NH CMSA	108	8
Atlanta, GA MSA	106	9
San Diego, CA MSA	86	10
Dallas – Fort Worth, TX CMSA	84	11
St. Louis, MO – IL MSA	81	12
Denver – Boulder, CO CMSA	78	13
Seattle – Tacoma, WA CMSA	72	14
Detroit – Ann Arbor, MI CMSA	71	15
Minneapolis – St. Paul, MN – WI MSA	68	16
Baltimore, MD MSA	63	17
Phoenix, AZ MSA	62	18
Houston – Galveston – Brazoria, TX CMSA	61	19
Raleigh – Durham, NC MSA	57	20
Rochester, NY MSA	56	21
Pittsburgh – Beaver Valley, PA CMSA	50	22
Knoxville, TN MSA	47	23

[Continued]

★1578★

Top 25 MSAs For Employment As Mathematical Science Teachers, 1990: Women
[Continued]

MSA/CMSA	Employees per 100,000 pop.	Rank
Austin, TX MSA	46	24
Sacramento, CA MSA	46	24

Source: U.S. Department of Commerce, Bureau of the Census, Data User Services Division, *1990 Census of Population and Housing, Equal Employment Opportunity File, CD-90-EE0-1, January 1993,* CD-ROM.

★1579★

Occupations, By Race/Sex

Top 25 MSAs For Employment As Medical Science Teachers, 1990: Men

MSA/CMSA	Employees per 100,000 pop.	Rank
Memphis, TN – AR – MS MSA	186	1
Chicago – Gary – Lake County, IL – IN – WI CMSA	105	2
Houston – Galveston – Brazoria, TX CMSA	99	3
New Orleans, LA MSA	69	4
Los Angeles – Anaheim – Riverside, CA CMSA	67	5
Dallas – Fort Worth, TX CMSA	63	6
Philadelphia – Wilmington – Trenton, PA – NJ – DE – MD CMSA	55	7
San Francisco – Oakland – San Jose, CA CMSA	46	8
Washington, DC – MD – VA MSA	46	8
Columbia, SC MSA	44	9
Indianapolis, IN MSA	38	10
Birmingham, AL MSA	36	11
Raleigh – Durham, NC MSA	36	11
Seattle – Tacoma, WA CMSA	34	12
Honolulu, HI MSA	33	13
Richmond – Petersburg, VA MSA	32	14
New Haven – Meriden, CT MSA	31	15
Greensboro – Winston-Salem – High Point, NC MSA	30	16
San Diego, CA MSA	30	16
Baltimore, MD MSA	27	17
Detroit – Ann Arbor, MI CMSA	27	17
Springfield, IL MSA	26	18
Mobile, AL MSA	26	18
Cleveland – Akron – Lorain, OH CMSA	23	19
Miami – Fort Lauderdale, FL CMSA	22	20

Source: U.S. Department of Commerce, Bureau of the Census, Data User Services Division, *1990 Census of Population and Housing, Equal Employment Opportunity File, CD-90-EE0-1, January 1993,* CD-ROM.

★1580★
Occupations, By Race/Sex
Top 25 MSAs For Employment As Medical Science Teachers, 1990: Women

MSA/CMSA	Employees per 100,000 pop.	Rank
Boise City, ID MSA	89	1
Los Angeles – Anaheim – Riverside, CA CMSA	55	2
St. Louis, MO – IL MSA	26	3
Chicago – Gary – Lake County, IL – IN – WI CMSA	25	4
Charleston, SC MSA	23	5
Detroit – Ann Arbor, MI CMSA	22	6
Washington, DC – MD – VA MSA	20	7
Dallas – Fort Worth, TX CMSA	19	8
Sacramento, CA MSA	17	9
Syracuse, NY MSA	17	9
Charlotte – Gastonia – Rock Hill, NC – SC MSA	16	10
Pittsburgh – Beaver Valley, PA CMSA	16	10
Raleigh – Durham, NC MSA	15	11
Birmingham, AL MSA	14	12
Boston – Lawrence – Salem, MA – NH CMSA	14	12
Des Moines, IA MSA	14	12
Memphis, TN – AR – MS MSA	14	12
Houston – Galveston – Brazoria, TX CMSA	13	13
Tampa – St. Petersburg – Clearwater, FL MSA	13	13
Jacksonville, FL MSA	12	14
Philadelphia – Wilmington – Trenton, PA – NJ – DE – MD CMSA	12	14
Portland – Vancouver, OR – WA CMSA	11	15
Cleveland – Akron – Lorain, OH CMSA	10	16
San Antonio, TX MSA	10	16
Wichita, KS MSA	10	16

Source: U.S. Department of Commerce, Bureau of the Census, Data User Services Division, *1990 Census of Population and Housing, Equal Employment Opportunity File, CD-90-EE0-1,* January 1993, CD-ROM.

★1581★
Occupations, By Race/Sex
Top 25 MSAs For Employment As Mining Engineers, 1990: Men

MSA/CMSA	Employees per 100,000 pop.	Rank
Sacramento, CA MSA	269	1
Pittsburgh – Beaver Valley, PA CMSA	215	2
Houston – Galveston – Brazoria, TX CMSA	158	3
Tucson, AZ MSA	126	4
Salt Lake City – Ogden, UT MSA	120	5

[Continued]

★1581★
Top 25 MSAs For Employment As Mining Engineers, 1990: Men
[Continued]

MSA/CMSA	Employees per 100,000 pop.	Rank
Phoenix, AZ MSA	80	6
Duluth, MN – WI MSA	71	7
Los Angeles – Anaheim – Riverside, CA CMSA	70	8
New Orleans, LA MSA	70	8
New York – Northern New Jersey – Long Island, NY – NJ – CT CMSA	64	9
Washington, DC – MD – VA MSA	54	10
Tuscaloosa, AL MSA	52	11
Lexington-Fayette, KY MSA	49	12
Knoxville, TN MSA	49	12
Johnson City – Kingsport – Bristol, TN – VA MSA	47	13
Huntington – Ashland, WV – KY – OH MSA	46	14
Spokane, WA MSA	44	15
Reno, NV MSA	40	16
Birmingham, AL MSA	40	16
St. Louis, MO – IL MSA	39	17
Johnstown, PA MSA	39	17
Cleveland – Akron – Lorain, OH CMSA	39	17
Las Vegas, NV MSA	37	18
San Francisco – Oakland – San Jose, CA CMSA	37	18
Longview – Marshall, TX MSA	34	19

Source: U.S. Department of Commerce, Bureau of the Census, Data User Services Division, *1990 Census of Population and Housing, Equal Employment Opportunity File, CD-90-EE0-1,* January 1993, CD-ROM.

★1582★
Occupations, By Race/Sex
Top 25 MSAs For Employment As Mining Engineers, 1990: Women

MSA/CMSA	Employees per 100,000 pop.	Rank
Oklahoma City, OK MSA	43	1
Pittsburgh – Beaver Valley, PA CMSA	23	2
New York – Northern New Jersey – Long Island, NY – NJ – CT CMSA	22	3
Reno, NV MSA	22	3
Tucson, AZ MSA	20	4
Seattle – Tacoma, WA CMSA	19	5
Los Angeles – Anaheim – Riverside, CA CMSA	14	6
Phoenix, AZ MSA	14	6
El Paso, TX MSA	9	7
Philadelphia – Wilmington – Trenton, PA – NJ – DE – MD CMSA	9	7

[Continued]

★1582★

Top 25 MSAs For Employment As Mining Engineers, 1990: Women
[Continued]

MSA/CMSA	Employees per 100,000 pop.	Rank
Lawrence, KS MSA	8	8
New Orleans, LA MSA	7	9
San Francisco – Oakland – San Jose, CA CMSA	7	9
State College, PA MSA	7	9
Kansas City, MO – KS MSA	6	10
Midland, TX MSA	6	10
Chicago – Gary – Lake County, IL – IN – WI CMSA	5	11
Columbus, OH MSA	5	11
Greensboro – Winston-Salem – High Point, NC MSA	3	12
Santa Fe, NM MSA	2	13
Amarillo, TX MSA	0	14
Allentown – Bethlehem – Easton, PA – NJ MSA	0	14
Abilene, TX MSA	0	14
Albuquerque, NM MSA	0	14
Alexandria, LA MSA	0	14

Source: U.S. Department of Commerce, Bureau of the Census, Data User Services Division, *1990 Census of Population and Housing, Equal Employment Opportunity File,* CD-90-EE0-1, January 1993, CD-ROM.

★1583★
Occupations, By Race/Sex

Top 25 MSAs For Employment As Motion Picture Projectionists, 1990: Men

MSA/CMSA	Employees per 100,000 pop.	Rank
Kansas City, MO – KS MSA	1,280	1
New York – Northern New Jersey – Long Island, NY – NJ – CT CMSA	748	2
Chicago – Gary – Lake County, IL – IN – WI CMSA	345	3
San Francisco – Oakland – San Jose, CA CMSA	217	4
Dallas – Fort Worth, TX CMSA	204	5
Washington, DC – MD – VA MSA	162	6
Atlanta, GA MSA	152	7
Houston – Galveston – Brazoria, TX CMSA	144	8
Seattle – Tacoma, WA CMSA	142	9
Miami – Fort Lauderdale, FL CMSA	118	10
Philadelphia – Wilmington – Trenton, PA – NJ – DE – MD CMSA	110	11
San Diego, CA MSA	99	12
New Orleans, LA MSA	94	13
Portland – Vancouver, OR – WA CMSA	90	14
Tampa – St. Petersburg – Clearwater, FL MSA	88	15

[Continued]

★1583★

Top 25 MSAs For Employment As Motion Picture Projectionists, 1990: Men
[Continued]

MSA/CMSA	Employees per 100,000 pop.	Rank
Boston – Lawrence – Salem, MA – NH CMSA	82	16
Detroit – Ann Arbor, MI CMSA	82	16
Denver – Boulder, CO CMSA	74	17
Minneapolis – St. Paul, MN – WI MSA	71	18
Raleigh – Durham, NC MSA	68	19
Pittsburgh – Beaver Valley, PA CMSA	66	20
Rochester, NY MSA	62	21
Baltimore, MD MSA	61	22
Cleveland – Akron – Lorain, OH CMSA	61	22
St. Louis, MO – IL MSA	61	22

Source: U.S. Department of Commerce, Bureau of the Census, Data User Services Division, *1990 Census of Population and Housing, Equal Employment Opportunity File,* CD-90-EE0-1, January 1993, CD-ROM.

★1584★
Occupations, By Race/Sex

Top 25 MSAs For Employment As Motion Picture Projectionists, 1990: Women

MSA/CMSA	Employees per 100,000 pop.	Rank
Charlotte – Gastonia – Rock Hill, NC – SC MSA	225	1
New York – Northern New Jersey – Long Island, NY – NJ – CT CMSA	126	2
San Francisco – Oakland – San Jose, CA CMSA	74	3
Boston – Lawrence – Salem, MA – NH CMSA	50	4
Dallas – Fort Worth, TX CMSA	36	5
Seattle – Tacoma, WA CMSA	35	6
Chicago – Gary – Lake County, IL – IN – WI CMSA	34	7
Cincinnati – Hamilton, OH – KY – IN CMSA	28	8
Baltimore, MD MSA	27	9
Scranton – Wilkes-Barre, PA MSA	27	9
Washington, DC – MD – VA MSA	26	10
Charlotte – Gastonia – Rock Hill, NC – SC MSA	25	11
Atlanta, GA MSA	24	12
Denver – Boulder, CO CMSA	23	13
San Diego, CA MSA	21	14
Rochester, NY MSA	20	15
Fort Myers – Cape Coral, Fl MSA	18	16
Memphis, TN – AR – MS MSA	18	16
Las Vegas, NV MSA	16	17
Milwaukee – Racine, WI CMSA	16	17
San Antonio, TX MSA	16	17

[Continued]

★1584★

Top 25 MSAs For Employment As Motion Picture Projectionists, 1990: Women
[Continued]

MSA/CMSA	Employees per 100,000 pop.	Rank
Tulsa, OK MSA	15	18
Albany – Schenectady – Troy, NY MSA	14	19
Colorado Springs, CO MSA	14	19
Fort Collins – Loveland, CO MSA	14	19

Source: U.S. Department of Commerce, Bureau of the Census, Data User Services Division, *1990 Census of Population and Housing, Equal Employment Opportunity File, CD-90-EE0-1, January 1993,* CD-ROM.

★1585★

Occupations, By Race/Sex

Top 25 MSAs For Employment As Musicians and Composers, 1990: Men

MSA/CMSA	Employees per 100,000 pop.	Rank
Cleveland – Akron – Lorain, OH CMSA	12,207	1
Los Angeles – Anaheim – Riverside, CA CMSA	11,517	2
San Francisco – Oakland – San Jose, CA CMSA	3,612	3
Chicago – Gary – Lake County, IL – IN – WI CMSA	3,308	4
Nashville, TN MSA	2,661	5
Miami – Fort Lauderdale, FL CMSA	2,258	6
Boston – Lawrence – Salem, MA – NH CMSA	1,976	7
Philadelphia – Wilmington – Trenton, PA – NJ – DE – MD CMSA	1,928	8
Dallas – Fort Worth, TX CMSA	1,837	9
Detroit – Ann Arbor, MI CMSA	1,678	10
Washington, DC – MD – VA MSA	1,656	11
Minneapolis – St. Paul, MN – WI MSA	1,354	12
Houston – Galveston – Brazoria, TX CMSA	1,333	13
San Diego, CA MSA	1,306	14
Seattle – Tacoma, WA CMSA	1,298	15
Atlanta, GA MSA	1,186	16
Phoenix, AZ MSA	1,068	17
Cleveland – Akron – Lorain, OH CMSA	1,013	18
Denver – Boulder, CO CMSA	987	19
Orlando, FL MSA	979	20
Las Vegas, NV MSA	970	21
Tampa – St. Petersburg – Clearwater, FL MSA	968	22
St. Louis, MO – IL MSA	846	23

[Continued]

★1585★

Top 25 MSAs For Employment As Musicians and Composers, 1990: Men
[Continued]

MSA/CMSA	Employees per 100,000 pop.	Rank
Portland – Vancouver, OR – WA CMSA	776	24
Baltimore, MD MSA	738	25

Source: U.S. Department of Commerce, Bureau of the Census, Data User Services Division, *1990 Census of Population and Housing, Equal Employment Opportunity File, CD-90-EE0-1, January 1993,* CD-ROM.

★1586★

Occupations, By Race/Sex

Top 25 MSAs For Employment As Musicians and Composers, 1990: Women

MSA/CMSA	Employees per 100,000 pop.	Rank
Cleveland – Akron – Lorain, OH CMSA	4,797	1
Los Angeles – Anaheim – Riverside, CA CMSA	3,206	2
San Francisco – Oakland – San Jose, CA CMSA	1,525	3
Chicago – Gary – Lake County, IL – IN – WI CMSA	1,432	4
Boston – Lawrence – Salem, MA – NH CMSA	1,119	5
Philadelphia – Wilmington – Trenton, PA – NJ – DE – MD CMSA	1,016	6
Detroit – Ann Arbor, MI CMSA	945	7
Washington, DC – MD – VA MSA	913	8
Minneapolis – St. Paul, MN – WI MSA	741	9
Nashville, TN MSA	690	10
Dallas – Fort Worth, TX CMSA	658	11
Seattle – Tacoma, WA CMSA	654	12
Cleveland – Akron – Lorain, OH CMSA	642	13
Atlanta, GA MSA	623	14
Pittsburgh – Beaver Valley, PA CMSA	579	15
Houston – Galveston – Brazoria, TX CMSA	571	16
St. Louis, MO – IL MSA	520	17
Denver – Boulder, CO CMSA	456	18
Miami – Fort Lauderdale, FL CMSA	446	19
San Diego, CA MSA	444	20
Phoenix, AZ MSA	413	21
Baltimore, MD MSA	394	22
Milwaukee – Racine, WI CMSA	388	23
Portland – Vancouver, OR – WA CMSA	378	24
Tampa – St. Petersburg – Clearwater, FL MSA	333	25

Source: U.S. Department of Commerce, Bureau of the Census, Data User Services Division, *1990 Census of Population and Housing, Equal Employment Opportunity File, CD-90-EE0-1, January 1993,* CD-ROM.

★ 1587 ★

Occupations, By Race/Sex

Top 25 MSAs For Employment As Nuclear Engineers, 1990: Men

MSA/CMSA	Employees per 100,000 pop.	Rank
Atlanta, GA MSA	541	1
Pittsburgh – Beaver Valley, PA CMSA	512	2
Washington, DC – MD – VA MSA	467	3
Norfolk – Virginia Beach – Newport News, VA MSA	411	4
Bremerton, WA MSA	359	5
Charleston, SC MSA	319	6
Augusta, GA – SC MSA	318	7
Chicago – Gary – Lake County, IL – IN – WI CMSA	307	8
Philadelphia – Wilmington – Trenton, PA – NJ – DE – MD CMSA	290	9
New York – Northern New Jersey – Long Island, NY – NJ – CT CMSA	284	10
Richland – Kennewick – Pasco, WA MSA	246	11
Charlotte – Gastonia – Rock Hill, NC – SC MSA	230	12
Boston – Lawrence – Salem, MA – NH CMSA	222	13
Honolulu, HI MSA	213	14
Portsmouth – Dover – Rochester, NH – ME MSA	210	15
Hartford – New Britain – Middletown, CT CMSA	205	16
Albany – Schenectady – Troy, NY MSA	199	17
Knoxville, TN MSA	178	18
Los Angeles – Anaheim – Riverside, CA CMSA	166	19
New London – Norwich, CT – RI MSA	138	20
Phoenix, AZ MSA	133	21
Seattle – Tacoma, WA CMSA	132	22
Chattanooga, TN – GA MSA	115	23
Atlanta, GA MSA	110	24
San Diego, CA MSA	110	24

Source: U.S. Department of Commerce, Bureau of the Census, Data User Services Division, *1990 Census of Population and Housing, Equal Employment Opportunity File, CD-90-EE0-1, January 1993*, CD-ROM.

★ 1588 ★

Occupations, By Race/Sex

Top 25 MSAs For Employment As Nuclear Engineers, 1990: Women

MSA/CMSA	Employees per 100,000 pop.	Rank
Detroit – Ann Arbor, MI CMSA	81	1
Washington, DC – MD – VA MSA	56	2
Pittsburgh – Beaver Valley, PA CMSA	46	3
Portsmouth – Dover – Rochester, NH – ME MSA	35	4
Knoxville, TN MSA	34	5
Charlotte – Gastonia – Rock Hill, NC – SC MSA	26	6
Bremerton, WA MSA	24	7
Norfolk – Virginia Beach – Newport News, VA MSA	24	7
Albany – Schenectady – Troy, NY MSA	21	8
New York – Northern New Jersey – Long Island, NY – NJ – CT CMSA	19	9
Baton Rouge, LA MSA	17	10
Chattanooga, TN – GA MSA	17	10
New London – Norwich, CT – RI MSA	16	11
Richland – Kennewick – Pasco, WA MSA	14	12
Santa Fe, NM MSA	14	12
San Diego, CA MSA	12	13
Harrisburg – Lebanon – Carlisle, PA MSA	10	14
Phoenix, AZ MSA	10	14
Tucson, AZ MSA	10	14
Albuquerque, NM MSA	9	15
Baltimore, MD MSA	9	15
Decatur, AL MSA	9	15
Honolulu, HI MSA	8	16
Richmond – Petersburg, VA MSA	8	16
Syracuse, NY MSA	7	17

Source: U.S. Department of Commerce, Bureau of the Census, Data User Services Division, *1990 Census of Population and Housing, Equal Employment Opportunity File, CD-90-EE0-1, January 1993*, CD-ROM.

★ 1589 ★

Occupations, By Race/Sex

Top 25 MSAs For Employment As Nursery Workers, 1990: Men

MSA/CMSA	Employees per 100,000 pop.	Rank
State College, PA MSA	1,282	1
Los Angeles – Anaheim – Riverside, CA CMSA	1,214	2
San Francisco – Oakland – San Jose, CA CMSA	1,036	3
San Diego, CA MSA	729	4
New York – Northern New Jersey – Long Island, NY – NJ – CT CMSA	426	5

[Continued]

★ 1589 ★

Top 25 MSAs For Employment As Nursery Workers, 1990: Men

[Continued]

MSA/CMSA	Employees per 100,000 pop.	Rank
Miami – Fort Lauderdale, FL CMSA	384	6
Portland – Vancouver, OR – WA CMSA	378	7
Chicago – Gary – Lake County, IL – IN – WI CMSA	351	8
Santa Barbara – Santa Maria – Lompoc, CA MSA	277	9
Tampa – St. Petersburg – Clearwater, FL MSA	254	10
Salem, OR MSA	248	11
Salinas – Seaside – Monterey, CA MSA	229	12
West Palm Beach – Boca Raton – Delray Beach, FL MSA	218	13
Reading, PA MSA	216	14
Phoenix, AZ MSA	205	15
Orlando, FL MSA	204	16
Boston – Lawrence – Salem, MA – NH CMSA	202	17
Seattle – Tacoma, WA CMSA	184	18
Dallas – Fort Worth, TX CMSA	175	19
Detroit – Ann Arbor, MI CMSA	151	20
Houston – Galveston – Brazoria, TX CMSA	151	20
Cleveland – Akron – Lorain, OH CMSA	137	21
Bakersfield, CA MSA	136	22
Pittsburgh – Beaver Valley, PA CMSA	116	23
Grand Rapids, MI MSA	111	24

Source: U.S. Department of Commerce, Bureau of the Census, Data User Services Division, *1990 Census of Population and Housing, Equal Employment Opportunity File, CD-90-EE0-1, January 1993,* CD-ROM.

★ 1590 ★

Occupations, By Race/Sex

Top 25 MSAs For Employment As Nursery Workers, 1990: Women

MSA/CMSA	Employees per 100,000 pop.	Rank
Allentown – Bethlehem – Easton, PA – NJ MSA	552	1
New York – Northern New Jersey – Long Island, NY – NJ – CT CMSA	460	2
Philadelphia – Wilmington – Trenton, PA – NJ – DE – MD CMSA	389	3
San Francisco – Oakland – San Jose, CA CMSA	381	4
Portland – Vancouver, OR – WA CMSA	377	5

[Continued]

★ 1590 ★

Top 25 MSAs For Employment As Nursery Workers, 1990: Women

[Continued]

MSA/CMSA	Employees per 100,000 pop.	Rank
Orlando, FL MSA	370	6
Detroit – Ann Arbor, MI CMSA	259	7
Grand Rapids, MI MSA	259	7
Cleveland – Akron – Lorain, OH CMSA	253	8
Seattle – Tacoma, WA CMSA	247	9
Miami – Fort Lauderdale, FL CMSA	244	10
San Diego, CA MSA	217	11
Denver – Boulder, CO CMSA	208	12
Kalamazoo, MI MSA	198	13
Chicago – Gary – Lake County, IL – IN – WI CMSA	194	14
Salem, OR MSA	175	15
Minneapolis – St. Paul, MN – WI MSA	171	16
Buffalo – Niagara Falls, NY CMSA	167	17
Boston – Lawrence – Salem, MA – NH CMSA	160	18
Tampa – St. Petersburg – Clearwater, FL MSA	158	19
Washington, DC – MD – VA MSA	155	20
Houston – Galveston – Brazoria, TX CMSA	146	21
Salinas – Seaside – Monterey, CA MSA	146	21
Honolulu, HI MSA	138	22
Atlanta, GA MSA	132	23

Source: U.S. Department of Commerce, Bureau of the Census, Data User Services Division, *1990 Census of Population and Housing, Equal Employment Opportunity File, CD-90-EE0-1, January 1993,* CD-ROM.

★ 1591 ★

Occupations, By Race/Sex

Top 25 MSAs For Employment As Occupational Therapists, 1990: Men

MSA/CMSA	Employees per 100,000 pop.	Rank
Dayton – Springfield, OH MSA	280	1
Los Angeles – Anaheim – Riverside, CA CMSA	206	2
Chicago – Gary – Lake County, IL – IN – WI CMSA	131	3
Seattle – Tacoma, WA CMSA	117	4
Boston – Lawrence – Salem, MA – NH CMSA	117	4
Pittsburgh – Beaver Valley, PA CMSA	109	5
Miami – Fort Lauderdale, FL CMSA	108	6
Buffalo – Niagara Falls, NY CMSA	93	7
San Francisco – Oakland – San Jose, CA CMSA	89	8

[Continued]

★1591★

Top 25 MSAs For Employment As Occupational Therapists, 1990: Men

[Continued]

MSA/CMSA	Employees per 100,000 pop.	Rank
Houston – Galveston – Brazoria, TX CMSA	87	9
Milwaukee – Racine, WI CMSA	71	10
Washington, DC – MD – VA MSA	65	11
Philadelphia – Wilmington – Trenton, PA – NJ – DE – MD CMSA	63	12
Cleveland – Akron – Lorain, OH CMSA	62	13
Detroit – Ann Arbor, MI CMSA	42	14
Austin, TX MSA	42	14
Little Rock – North Little Rock, AR MSA	41	15
Portland – Vancouver, OR – WA CMSA	41	15
San Diego, CA MSA	39	16
Atlanta, GA MSA	38	17
Minneapolis – St. Paul, MN – WI MSA	33	18
Honolulu, HI MSA	33	18
New Orleans, LA MSA	32	19
Lincoln, NE MSA	31	20
Phoenix, AZ MSA	30	21

Source: U.S. Department of Commerce, Bureau of the Census, Data User Services Division, *1990 Census of Population and Housing, Equal Employment Opportunity File, CD-90-EE0-1, January 1993,* CD-ROM.

★1592★

Occupations, By Race/Sex

Top 25 MSAs For Employment As Occupational Therapists, 1990: Women

MSA/CMSA	Employees per 100,000 pop.	Rank
Baltimore, MD MSA	3,295	1
Los Angeles – Anaheim – Riverside, CA CMSA	1,457	2
Boston – Lawrence – Salem, MA – NH CMSA	1,240	3
Chicago – Gary – Lake County, IL – IN – WI CMSA	1,240	3
San Francisco – Oakland – San Jose, CA CMSA	1,097	4
Philadelphia – Wilmington – Trenton, PA – NJ – DE – MD CMSA	1,078	5
Minneapolis – St. Paul, MN – WI MSA	931	6
Detroit – Ann Arbor, MI CMSA	906	7
Milwaukee – Racine, WI CMSA	783	8
Seattle – Tacoma, WA CMSA	579	9
Dallas – Fort Worth, TX CMSA	571	10
Washington, DC – MD – VA MSA	542	11
Denver – Boulder, CO CMSA	524	12

[Continued]

★1592★

Top 25 MSAs For Employment As Occupational Therapists, 1990: Women

[Continued]

MSA/CMSA	Employees per 100,000 pop.	Rank
Houston – Galveston – Brazoria, TX CMSA	519	13
Baltimore, MD MSA	511	14
St. Louis, MO – IL MSA	419	15
Kansas City, MO – KS MSA	411	16
Cleveland – Akron – Lorain, OH CMSA	407	17
Miami – Fort Lauderdale, FL CMSA	382	18
Buffalo – Niagara Falls, NY CMSA	369	19
Pittsburgh – Beaver Valley, PA CMSA	360	20
Columbus, OH MSA	357	21
Phoenix, AZ MSA	318	22
San Diego, CA MSA	310	23
Atlanta, GA MSA	293	24

Source: U.S. Department of Commerce, Bureau of the Census, Data User Services Division, *1990 Census of Population and Housing, Equal Employment Opportunity File, CD-90-EE0-1, January 1993,* CD-ROM.

★1593★

Occupations, By Race/Sex

Top 25 MSAs For Employment As Optometrists, 1990: Men

MSA/CMSA	Employees per 100,000 pop.	Rank
Phoenix, AZ MSA	1,530	1
Los Angeles – Anaheim – Riverside, CA CMSA	1,462	2
Chicago – Gary – Lake County, IL – IN – WI CMSA	853	3
San Francisco – Oakland – San Jose, CA CMSA	775	4
Philadelphia – Wilmington – Trenton, PA – NJ – DE – MD CMSA	553	5
Boston – Lawrence – Salem, MA – NH CMSA	386	6
Detroit – Ann Arbor, MI CMSA	383	7
Pittsburgh – Beaver Valley, PA CMSA	325	8
Miami – Fort Lauderdale, FL CMSA	314	9
Houston – Galveston – Brazoria, TX CMSA	305	10
San Diego, CA MSA	286	11
Cleveland – Akron – Lorain, OH CMSA	279	12
Dallas – Fort Worth, TX CMSA	263	13
Washington, DC – MD – VA MSA	256	14
Sacramento, CA MSA	237	15
St. Louis, MO – IL MSA	229	16
Seattle – Tacoma, WA CMSA	227	17

[Continued]

★1593★

Top 25 MSAs For Employment As Optometrists, 1990: Men
[Continued]

MSA/CMSA	Employees per 100,000 pop.	Rank
Denver – Boulder, CO CMSA	220	18
Baltimore, MD MSA	212	19
Minneapolis – St. Paul, MN – WI MSA	207	20
Phoenix, AZ MSA	194	21
Portland – Vancouver, OR – WA CMSA	192	22
Atlanta, GA MSA	183	23
Honolulu, HI MSA	177	24
Indianapolis, IN MSA	162	25

Source: U.S. Department of Commerce, Bureau of the Census, Data User Services Division, *1990 Census of Population and Housing, Equal Employment Opportunity File, CD-90-EE0-1, January 1993*, CD-ROM.

★1594★
Occupations, By Race/Sex

Top 25 MSAs For Employment As Optometrists, 1990: Women

MSA/CMSA	Employees per 100,000 pop.	Rank
Bryan – College Station, TX MSA	423	1
Los Angeles – Anaheim – Riverside, CA CMSA	271	2
San Francisco – Oakland – San Jose, CA CMSA	225	3
Chicago – Gary – Lake County, IL – IN – WI CMSA	184	4
Washington, DC – MD – VA MSA	134	5
Boston – Lawrence – Salem, MA – NH CMSA	131	6
Philadelphia – Wilmington – Trenton, PA – NJ – DE – MD CMSA	113	7
San Diego, CA MSA	93	8
Dallas – Fort Worth, TX CMSA	85	9
Houston – Galveston – Brazoria, TX CMSA	81	10
Cleveland – Akron – Lorain, OH CMSA	71	11
Birmingham, AL MSA	66	12
Detroit – Ann Arbor, MI CMSA	62	13
Baltimore, MD MSA	56	14
St. Louis, MO – IL MSA	55	15
Portland – Vancouver, OR – WA CMSA	50	16
Denver – Boulder, CO CMSA	43	17
Honolulu, HI MSA	43	17
Sacramento, CA MSA	41	18
Indianapolis, IN MSA	40	19
Pittsburgh – Beaver Valley, PA CMSA	38	20
Minneapolis – St. Paul, MN – WI MSA	36	21

[Continued]

★1594★

Top 25 MSAs For Employment As Optometrists, 1990: Women
[Continued]

MSA/CMSA	Employees per 100,000 pop.	Rank
San Antonio, TX MSA	36	21
Columbus, OH MSA	34	22
Phoenix, AZ MSA	34	22

Source: U.S. Department of Commerce, Bureau of the Census, Data User Services Division, *1990 Census of Population and Housing, Equal Employment Opportunity File, CD-90-EE0-1, January 1993*, CD-ROM.

★1595★
Occupations, By Race/Sex

Top 25 MSAs For Employment As Painters, Sculptors, Craft-artists, and Artist Printmakers, 1990: Men

MSA/CMSA	Employees per 100,000 pop.	Rank
Columbus, OH MSA	13,800	1
Los Angeles – Anaheim – Riverside, CA CMSA	9,305	2
Chicago – Gary – Lake County, IL – IN – WI CMSA	4,482	3
San Francisco – Oakland – San Jose, CA CMSA	3,892	4
Philadelphia – Wilmington – Trenton, PA – NJ – DE – MD CMSA	2,725	5
Washington, DC – MD – VA MSA	2,263	6
Boston – Lawrence – Salem, MA – NH CMSA	2,096	7
Dallas – Fort Worth, TX CMSA	1,995	8
Detroit – Ann Arbor, MI CMSA	1,837	9
Minneapolis – St. Paul, MN – WI MSA	1,616	10
Seattle – Tacoma, WA CMSA	1,567	11
Atlanta, GA MSA	1,469	12
Miami – Fort Lauderdale, FL CMSA	1,349	13
San Diego, CA MSA	1,198	14
Houston – Galveston – Brazoria, TX CMSA	1,193	15
Denver – Boulder, CO CMSA	1,169	16
Baltimore, MD MSA	1,049	17
St. Louis, MO – IL MSA	1,047	18
Cleveland – Akron – Lorain, OH CMSA	1,006	19
Tampa – St. Petersburg – Clearwater, FL MSA	995	20
Phoenix, AZ MSA	994	21
Milwaukee – Racine, WI CMSA	902	22
Kansas City, MO – KS MSA	899	23
Portland – Vancouver, OR – WA CMSA	765	24
Sacramento, CA MSA	747	25

Source: U.S. Department of Commerce, Bureau of the Census, Data User Services Division, *1990 Census of Population and Housing, Equal Employment Opportunity File, CD-90-EE0-1, January 1993*, CD-ROM.

★1596★

Occupations, By Race/Sex

Top 25 MSAs For Employment As Painters, Sculptors, Craft-artists, and Artist Printmakers, 1990: Women

MSA/CMSA	Employees per 100,000 pop.	Rank
Milwaukee – Racine, WI CMSA	11,791	1
Los Angeles – Anaheim – Riverside, CA CMSA	7,687	2
San Francisco – Oakland – San Jose, CA CMSA	4,201	3
Chicago – Gary – Lake County, IL – IN – WI CMSA	3,933	4
Washington, DC – MD – VA MSA	3,013	5
Philadelphia – Wilmington – Trenton, PA – NJ – DE – MD CMSA	2,905	6
Boston – Lawrence – Salem, MA – NH CMSA	2,842	7
Dallas – Fort Worth, TX CMSA	1,950	8
Seattle – Tacoma, WA CMSA	1,942	9
Atlanta, GA MSA	1,721	10
San Diego, CA MSA	1,649	11
Detroit – Ann Arbor, MI CMSA	1,616	12
Houston – Galveston – Brazoria, TX CMSA	1,569	13
Denver – Boulder, CO CMSA	1,436	14
Minneapolis – St. Paul, MN – WI MSA	1,400	15
Miami – Fort Lauderdale, FL CMSA	1,348	16
Baltimore, MD MSA	1,265	17
Cleveland – Akron – Lorain, OH CMSA	1,173	18
St. Louis, MO – IL MSA	1,172	19
Kansas City, MO – KS MSA	1,149	20
Phoenix, AZ MSA	1,032	21
Portland – Vancouver, OR – WA CMSA	994	22
Tampa – St. Petersburg – Clearwater, FL MSA	915	23
Cincinnati – Hamilton, OH – KY – IN CMSA	790	24
Milwaukee – Racine, WI CMSA	771	25

Source: U.S. Department of Commerce, Bureau of the Census, Data User Services Division, *1990 Census of Population and Housing, Equal Employment Opportunity File, CD-90-EE0-1, January 1993,* CD-ROM.

★1597★

Occupations, By Race/Sex

Top 25 MSAs For Employment As Personnel and Labor Relations Managers, 1990: Men

MSA/CMSA	Employees per 100,000 pop.	Rank
Kansas City, MO – KS MSA	13,127	1
Los Angeles – Anaheim – Riverside, CA CMSA	10,039	2
Chicago – Gary – Lake County, IL – IN – WI CMSA	4,622	3
Washington, DC – MD – VA MSA	4,432	4
San Francisco – Oakland – San Jose, CA CMSA	3,969	5
Philadelphia – Wilmington – Trenton, PA – NJ – DE – MD CMSA	3,498	6
Boston – Lawrence – Salem, MA – NH CMSA	3,006	7
Dallas – Fort Worth, TX CMSA	2,780	8
Detroit – Ann Arbor, MI CMSA	2,766	9
Houston – Galveston – Brazoria, TX CMSA	2,379	10
Miami – Fort Lauderdale, FL CMSA	2,322	11
Atlanta, GA MSA	1,880	12
Seattle – Tacoma, WA CMSA	1,719	13
Baltimore, MD MSA	1,670	14
Cleveland – Akron – Lorain, OH CMSA	1,589	15
Denver – Boulder, CO CMSA	1,412	16
San Diego, CA MSA	1,390	17
Minneapolis – St. Paul, MN – WI MSA	1,328	18
St. Louis, MO – IL MSA	1,247	19
Pittsburgh – Beaver Valley, PA CMSA	1,189	20
Phoenix, AZ MSA	1,139	21
Cincinnati – Hamilton, OH – KY – IN CMSA	1,054	22
Kansas City, MO – KS MSA	968	23
Columbus, OH MSA	940	24
Milwaukee – Racine, WI CMSA	920	25

Source: U.S. Department of Commerce, Bureau of the Census, Data User Services Division, *1990 Census of Population and Housing, Equal Employment Opportunity File, CD-90-EE0-1, January 1993,* CD-ROM.

★1598★

Occupations, By Race/Sex

Top 25 MSAs For Employment As Personnel and Labor Relations Managers, 1990: Women

MSA/CMSA	Employees per 100,000 pop.	Rank
Columbia, SC MSA	13,486	1
Los Angeles – Anaheim – Riverside, CA CMSA	9,305	2
Washington, DC – MD – VA MSA	5,318	3
Chicago – Gary – Lake County, IL – IN – WI CMSA	4,988	4

[Continued]

★1598★

Top 25 MSAs For Employment As Personnel and Labor Relations Managers, 1990: Women
[Continued]

MSA/CMSA	Employees per 100,000 pop.	Rank
San Francisco – Oakland – San Jose, CA CMSA	4,609	5
Philadelphia – Wilmington – Trenton, PA – NJ – DE – MD CMSA	3,624	6
Boston – Lawrence – Salem, MA – NH CMSA	3,432	7
Dallas – Fort Worth, TX CMSA	2,607	8
Detroit – Ann Arbor, MI CMSA	2,367	9
Atlanta, GA MSA	2,213	10
Houston – Galveston – Brazoria, TX CMSA	2,121	11
Minneapolis – St. Paul, MN – WI MSA	1,865	12
Miami – Fort Lauderdale, FL CMSA	1,799	13
Baltimore, MD MSA	1,766	14
San Diego, CA MSA	1,753	15
Seattle – Tacoma, WA CMSA	1,697	16
Denver – Boulder, CO CMSA	1,510	17
Phoenix, AZ MSA	1,329	18
St. Louis, MO – IL MSA	1,249	19
Tampa – St. Petersburg – Clearwater, FL MSA	1,169	20
Cleveland – Akron – Lorain, OH CMSA	1,154	21
Cincinnati – Hamilton, OH – KY – IN CMSA	1,060	22
Sacramento, CA MSA	1,052	23
Norfolk – Virginia Beach – Newport News, VA MSA	951	24
Milwaukee – Racine, WI CMSA	928	25

Source: U.S. Department of Commerce, Bureau of the Census, Data User Services Division, *1990 Census of Population and Housing, Equal Employment Opportunity File, CD-90-EE0-1, January 1993*, CD-ROM.

★1599★

Occupations, By Race/Sex

Top 25 MSAs For Employment As Petroleum Engineers, 1990: Men

MSA/CMSA	Employees per 100,000 pop.	Rank
San Diego, CA MSA	4,807	1
New Orleans, LA MSA	1,411	2
Dallas – Fort Worth, TX CMSA	1,407	3
Midland, TX MSA	1,008	4
Lafayette, LA MSA	878	5
Los Angeles – Anaheim – Riverside, CA CMSA	859	6
Anchorage, AK MSA	787	7
Denver – Boulder, CO CMSA	782	8
Bakersfield, CA MSA	713	9
Oklahoma City, OK MSA	711	10

[Continued]

★1599★

Top 25 MSAs For Employment As Petroleum Engineers, 1990: Men
[Continued]

MSA/CMSA	Employees per 100,000 pop.	Rank
Tulsa, OK MSA	636	11
San Francisco – Oakland – San Jose, CA CMSA	375	12
Corpus Christi, TX MSA	252	13
Houma – Thibodaux, LA MSA	198	14
New York – Northern New Jersey – Long Island, NY – NJ – CT CMSA	184	15
Tyler, TX MSA	167	16
Baton Rouge, LA MSA	166	17
Beaumont – Port Arthur, TX MSA	139	18
Casper, WY MSA	125	19
Wichita, KS MSA	116	20
Odessa, TX MSA	116	20
Longview – Marshall, TX MSA	113	21
Shreveport, LA MSA	111	22
Victoria, TX MSA	107	23
Chicago – Gary – Lake County, IL – IN – WI CMSA	106	24

Source: U.S. Department of Commerce, Bureau of the Census, Data User Services Division, *1990 Census of Population and Housing, Equal Employment Opportunity File, CD-90-EE0-1, January 1993*, CD-ROM.

★1600★

Occupations, By Race/Sex

Top 25 MSAs For Employment As Petroleum Engineers, 1990: Women

MSA/CMSA	Employees per 100,000 pop.	Rank
Albany, GA MSA	325	1
New Orleans, LA MSA	127	2
Dallas – Fort Worth, TX CMSA	124	3
Los Angeles – Anaheim – Riverside, CA CMSA	118	4
Denver – Boulder, CO CMSA	82	5
Midland, TX MSA	77	6
Lafayette, LA MSA	70	7
Anchorage, AK MSA	66	8
Bakersfield, CA MSA	50	9
Tulsa, OK MSA	49	10
Oklahoma City, OK MSA	31	11
New York – Northern New Jersey – Long Island, NY – NJ – CT CMSA	29	12
San Francisco – Oakland – San Jose, CA CMSA	23	13
Austin, TX MSA	19	14
Corpus Christi, TX MSA	19	14
Odessa, TX MSA	19	14
Beaumont – Port Arthur, TX MSA	17	15
Cleveland – Akron – Lorain, OH CMSA	16	16
Johnson City – Kingsport – Bristol, TN – VA MSA	15	17

[Continued]

★1600★

Top 25 MSAs For Employment As Petroleum Engineers, 1990: Women
[Continued]

MSA/CMSA	Employees per 100,000 pop.	Rank
Topeka, KS MSA	12	18
Boston–Lawrence–Salem, MA–NH CMSA	11	19
Little Rock–North Little Rock, AR MSA	8	20
Longview–Marshall, TX MSA	8	20
Sacramento, CA MSA	8	20
Seattle–Tacoma, WA CMSA	8	20

Source: U.S. Department of Commerce, Bureau of the Census, Data User Services Division, *1990 Census of Population and Housing, Equal Employment Opportunity File, CD-90-EE0-1, January 1993,* CD-ROM.

★1601★
Occupations, By Race/Sex

Top 25 MSAs For Employment As Pharmacists, 1990: Men

MSA/CMSA	Employees per 100,000 pop.	Rank
Cincinnati–Hamilton, OH–KY–IN CMSA	9,739	1
Los Angeles–Anaheim–Riverside, CA CMSA	5,140	2
Chicago–Gary–Lake County, IL–IN–WI CMSA	3,496	3
Philadelphia–Wilmington–Trenton, PA–NJ–DE–MD CMSA	3,262	4
San Francisco–Oakland–San Jose, CA CMSA	2,545	5
Boston–Lawrence–Salem, MA–NH CMSA	2,047	6
Detroit–Ann Arbor, MI CMSA	1,931	7
Dallas–Fort Worth, TX CMSA	1,577	8
Houston–Galveston–Brazoria, TX CMSA	1,528	9
Pittsburgh–Beaver Valley, PA CMSA	1,356	10
Miami–Fort Lauderdale, FL CMSA	1,350	11
Atlanta, GA MSA	1,308	12
Cleveland–Akron–Lorain, OH CMSA	1,198	13
Cincinnati–Hamilton, OH–KY–IN CMSA	1,174	14
Minneapolis–St. Paul, MN–WI MSA	1,156	15
St. Louis, MO–IL MSA	1,142	16
Tampa–St. Petersburg–Clearwater, FL MSA	1,108	17
Seattle–Tacoma, WA CMSA	1,087	18
Washington, DC–MD–VA MSA	1,082	19
Baltimore, MD MSA	1,053	20
Phoenix, AZ MSA	1,001	21

[Continued]

★1601★

Top 25 MSAs For Employment As Pharmacists, 1990: Men
[Continued]

MSA/CMSA	Employees per 100,000 pop.	Rank
San Diego, CA MSA	939	22
Kansas City, MO–KS MSA	922	23
Milwaukee–Racine, WI CMSA	897	24
Denver–Boulder, CO CMSA	809	25

Source: U.S. Department of Commerce, Bureau of the Census, Data User Services Division, *1990 Census of Population and Housing, Equal Employment Opportunity File, CD-90-EE0-1, January 1993,* CD-ROM.

★1602★
Occupations, By Race/Sex

Top 25 MSAs For Employment As Pharmacists, 1990: Women

MSA/CMSA	Employees per 100,000 pop.	Rank
Portland–Vancouver, OR–WA CMSA	4,519	1
Los Angeles–Anaheim–Riverside, CA CMSA	2,944	2
Chicago–Gary–Lake County, IL–IN–WI CMSA	2,494	3
Philadelphia–Wilmington–Trenton, PA–NJ–DE–MD CMSA	2,110	4
San Francisco–Oakland–San Jose, CA CMSA	1,591	5
Detroit–Ann Arbor, MI CMSA	1,520	6
Boston–Lawrence–Salem, MA–NH CMSA	1,357	7
Houston–Galveston–Brazoria, TX CMSA	1,272	8
Washington, DC–MD–VA MSA	1,217	9
Miami–Fort Lauderdale, FL CMSA	1,165	10
Dallas–Fort Worth, TX CMSA	1,158	11
Pittsburgh–Beaver Valley, PA CMSA	1,131	12
Atlanta, GA MSA	1,040	13
Seattle–Tacoma, WA CMSA	956	14
Minneapolis–St. Paul, MN–WI MSA	838	15
Columbus, OH MSA	777	16
Cleveland–Akron–Lorain, OH CMSA	739	17
St. Louis, MO–IL MSA	732	18
Tampa–St. Petersburg–Clearwater, FL MSA	727	19
Indianapolis, IN MSA	638	20
Cincinnati–Hamilton, OH–KY–IN CMSA	637	21
Baltimore, MD MSA	631	22
Kansas City, MO–KS MSA	612	23

[Continued]

★1602★

Top 25 MSAs For Employment As Pharmacists, 1990: Women
[Continued]

MSA/CMSA	Employees per 100,000 pop.	Rank
Phoenix, AZ MSA	544	24
Buffalo – Niagara Falls, NY CMSA	513	25

Source: U.S. Department of Commerce, Bureau of the Census, Data User Services Division, *1990 Census of Population and Housing, Equal Employment Opportunity File, CD-90-EE0-1, January 1993,* CD-ROM.

★1603★

Occupations, By Race/Sex

Top 25 MSAs For Employment As Photographers, 1990: Men

MSA/CMSA	Employees per 100,000 pop.	Rank
Pittsburgh – Beaver Valley, PA CMSA	11,798	1
Los Angeles – Anaheim – Riverside, CA CMSA	9,805	2
Chicago – Gary – Lake County, IL – IN – WI CMSA	3,861	3
San Francisco – Oakland – San Jose, CA CMSA	3,512	4
Washington, DC – MD – VA MSA	2,576	5
Boston – Lawrence – Salem, MA – NH CMSA	2,458	6
Philadelphia – Wilmington – Trenton, PA – NJ – DE – MD CMSA	2,360	7
Dallas – Fort Worth, TX CMSA	2,085	8
Detroit – Ann Arbor, MI CMSA	1,887	9
Miami – Fort Lauderdale, FL CMSA	1,570	10
Houston – Galveston – Brazoria, TX CMSA	1,380	11
San Diego, CA MSA	1,362	12
Atlanta, GA MSA	1,354	13
Minneapolis – St. Paul, MN – WI MSA	1,311	14
Seattle – Tacoma, WA CMSA	1,213	15
Denver – Boulder, CO CMSA	1,171	16
Cleveland – Akron – Lorain, OH CMSA	993	17
Phoenix, AZ MSA	955	18
Pittsburgh – Beaver Valley, PA CMSA	938	19
St. Louis, MO – IL MSA	935	20
Tampa – St. Petersburg – Clearwater, FL MSA	877	21
Portland – Vancouver, OR – WA CMSA	853	22
Baltimore, MD MSA	820	23
Kansas City, MO – KS MSA	743	24
Cincinnati – Hamilton, OH – KY – IN CMSA	700	25

Source: U.S. Department of Commerce, Bureau of the Census, Data User Services Division, *1990 Census of Population and Housing, Equal Employment Opportunity File, CD-90-EE0-1, January 1993,* CD-ROM.

★1604★

Occupations, By Race/Sex

Top 25 MSAs For Employment As Photographers, 1990: Women

MSA/CMSA	Employees per 100,000 pop.	Rank
Pittsburgh – Beaver Valley, PA CMSA	3,958	1
Los Angeles – Anaheim – Riverside, CA CMSA	2,888	2
San Francisco – Oakland – San Jose, CA CMSA	1,681	3
Chicago – Gary – Lake County, IL – IN – WI CMSA	1,331	4
Philadelphia – Wilmington – Trenton, PA – NJ – DE – MD CMSA	1,270	5
Boston – Lawrence – Salem, MA – NH CMSA	1,125	6
Dallas – Fort Worth, TX CMSA	911	7
Washington, DC – MD – VA MSA	858	8
Detroit – Ann Arbor, MI CMSA	725	9
Houston – Galveston – Brazoria, TX CMSA	722	10
Atlanta, GA MSA	673	11
Seattle – Tacoma, WA CMSA	525	12
San Diego, CA MSA	496	13
Minneapolis – St. Paul, MN – WI MSA	492	14
Baltimore, MD MSA	456	15
Cleveland – Akron – Lorain, OH CMSA	427	16
Phoenix, AZ MSA	406	17
Tampa – St. Petersburg – Clearwater, FL MSA	398	18
St. Louis, MO – IL MSA	394	19
Charlotte – Gastonia – Rock Hill, NC – SC MSA	382	20
Sacramento, CA MSA	381	21
Kansas City, MO – KS MSA	372	22
Miami – Fort Lauderdale, FL CMSA	365	23
Denver – Boulder, CO CMSA	335	24
New Orleans, LA MSA	292	25

Source: U.S. Department of Commerce, Bureau of the Census, Data User Services Division, *1990 Census of Population and Housing, Equal Employment Opportunity File, CD-90-EE0-1, January 1993,* CD-ROM.

★1605★

Occupations, By Race/Sex

Top 25 MSAs For Employment As Physical Education Teachers, 1990: Men

MSA/CMSA	Employees per 100,000 pop.	Rank
Greenville – Spartanburg, SC MSA	114	1
Los Angeles – Anaheim – Riverside, CA CMSA	86	2
San Francisco – Oakland – San Jose, CA CMSA	73	3
Chicago – Gary – Lake County, IL – IN – WI CMSA	50	4
Springfield, MA MSA	46	5
Miami – Fort Lauderdale, FL CMSA	44	6
Philadelphia – Wilmington – Trenton, PA – NJ – DE – MD CMSA	41	7
Cincinnati – Hamilton, OH – KY – IN CMSA	37	8
Albany – Schenectady – Troy, NY MSA	31	9
Boston – Lawrence – Salem, MA – NH CMSA	31	9
Pittsburgh – Beaver Valley, PA CMSA	29	10
San Antonio, TX MSA	24	11
Baltimore, MD MSA	24	11
Cumberland, MD – WV MSA	23	12
Modesto, CA MSA	21	13
Lafayette, LA MSA	21	13
Phoenix, AZ MSA	20	14
Salem, OR MSA	20	14
Minneapolis – St. Paul, MN – WI MSA	17	15
State College, PA MSA	17	15
Fargo – Moorhead, ND – MN MSA	17	15
Houston – Galveston – Brazoria, TX CMSA	17	15
Detroit – Ann Arbor, MI CMSA	16	16
New Orleans, LA MSA	15	17
Sacramento, CA MSA	15	17

Source: U.S. Department of Commerce, Bureau of the Census, Data User Services Division, *1990 Census of Population and Housing, Equal Employment Opportunity File, CD-90-EE0-1, January 1993,* CD-ROM.

★1606★

Occupations, By Race/Sex

Top 25 MSAs For Employment As Physical Education Teachers, 1990: Women

MSA/CMSA	Employees per 100,000 pop.	Rank
Phoenix, AZ MSA	165	1
San Francisco – Oakland – San Jose, CA CMSA	103	2
Los Angeles – Anaheim – Riverside, CA CMSA	90	3
Baltimore, MD MSA	68	4
Boston – Lawrence – Salem, MA – NH CMSA	65	5
Philadelphia – Wilmington – Trenton, PA – NJ – DE – MD CMSA	56	6
New York – Northern New Jersey – Long Island, NY – NJ – CT CMSA	53	7
Dallas – Fort Worth, TX CMSA	39	8
Greensboro – Winston-Salem – High Point, NC MSA	36	9
Cleveland – Akron – Lorain, OH CMSA	34	10
Salt Lake City – Ogden, UT MSA	33	11
Detroit – Ann Arbor, MI CMSA	28	12
Albany – Schenectady – Troy, NY MSA	27	13
Pittsburgh – Beaver Valley, PA CMSA	25	14
Washington, DC – MD – VA MSA	24	15
Buffalo – Niagara Falls, NY CMSA	23	16
Cincinnati – Hamilton, OH – KY – IN CMSA	23	16
Canton, OH MSA	22	17
Austin, TX MSA	21	18
Tampa – St. Petersburg – Clearwater, FL MSA	21	18
San Diego, CA MSA	20	19
Harrisburg – Lebanon – Carlisle, PA MSA	18	20
Sacramento, CA MSA	18	20
Seattle – Tacoma, WA CMSA	18	20
Miami – Fort Lauderdale, FL CMSA	17	21

Source: U.S. Department of Commerce, Bureau of the Census, Data User Services Division, *1990 Census of Population and Housing, Equal Employment Opportunity File, CD-90-EE0-1, January 1993,* CD-ROM.

★1607★
Occupations, By Race/Sex

Top 25 MSAs For Employment As Physical Therapists, 1990: Men

MSA/CMSA	Employees per 100,000 pop.	Rank
St. Louis, MO–IL MSA	1,969	1
New York–Northern New Jersey–Long Island, NY–NJ–CT CMSA	1,739	2
San Francisco–Oakland–San Jose, CA CMSA	925	3
Chicago–Gary–Lake County, IL–IN–WI CMSA	679	4
Philadelphia–Wilmington–Trenton, PA–NJ–DE–MD CMSA	578	5
Miami–Fort Lauderdale, FL CMSA	357	6
Boston–Lawrence–Salem, MA–NH CMSA	355	7
Detroit–Ann Arbor, MI CMSA	335	8
Dallas–Fort Worth, TX CMSA	329	9
San Diego, CA MSA	286	10
Houston–Galveston–Brazoria, TX CMSA	284	11
Washington, DC–MD–VA MSA	284	11
Minneapolis–St. Paul, MN–WI MSA	274	12
Seattle–Tacoma, WA CMSA	272	13
Denver–Boulder, CO CMSA	261	14
Phoenix, AZ MSA	258	15
Baltimore, MD MSA	247	16
Cleveland–Akron–Lorain, OH CMSA	238	17
Pittsburgh–Beaver Valley, PA CMSA	232	18
Atlanta, GA MSA	226	19
Salt Lake City–Ogden, UT MSA	215	20
Nashville, TN MSA	185	21
St. Louis, MO–IL MSA	184	22
Sacramento, CA MSA	179	23
Tampa–St. Petersburg–Clearwater, FL MSA	172	24

Source: U.S. Department of Commerce, Bureau of the Census, Data User Services Division, *1990 Census of Population and Housing, Equal Employment Opportunity File,* CD-90-EE0-1, January 1993, CD-ROM.

★1608★
Occupations, By Race/Sex

Top 25 MSAs For Employment As Physical Therapists, 1990: Women

MSA/CMSA	Employees per 100,000 pop.	Rank
Grand Rapids, MI MSA	5,162	1
Los Angeles–Anaheim–Riverside, CA CMSA	4,412	2
Boston–Lawrence–Salem, MA–NH CMSA	2,277	3
Chicago–Gary–Lake County, IL–IN–WI CMSA	2,220	4
Philadelphia–Wilmington–Trenton, PA–NJ–DE–MD CMSA	2,196	5
San Francisco–Oakland–San Jose, CA CMSA	2,180	6
Washington, DC–MD–VA MSA	1,365	7
Detroit–Ann Arbor, MI CMSA	1,304	8
Seattle–Tacoma, WA CMSA	1,217	9
Dallas–Fort Worth, TX CMSA	1,207	10
Houston–Galveston–Brazoria, TX CMSA	1,053	11
Denver–Boulder, CO CMSA	1,020	12
Minneapolis–St. Paul, MN–WI MSA	938	13
St. Louis, MO–IL MSA	930	14
Miami–Fort Lauderdale, FL CMSA	888	15
Atlanta, GA MSA	859	16
Baltimore, MD MSA	799	17
Cleveland–Akron–Lorain, OH CMSA	754	18
Milwaukee–Racine, WI CMSA	749	19
San Diego, CA MSA	744	20
Pittsburgh–Beaver Valley, PA CMSA	678	21
Tampa–St. Petersburg–Clearwater, FL MSA	664	22
Phoenix, AZ MSA	612	23
Portland–Vancouver, OR–WA CMSA	582	24
Hartford–New Britain–Middletown, CT CMSA	573	25

Source: U.S. Department of Commerce, Bureau of the Census, Data User Services Division, *1990 Census of Population and Housing, Equal Employment Opportunity File,* CD-90-EE0-1, January 1993, CD-ROM.

★1609★

Occupations, By Race/Sex

Top 25 MSAs For Employment As Physicians' Assistants, 1990: Men

MSA/CMSA	Employees per 100,000 pop.	Rank
Dayton – Springfield, OH MSA	1,235	1
Los Angeles – Anaheim – Riverside, CA CMSA	611	2
Philadelphia – Wilmington – Trenton, PA – NJ – DE – MD CMSA	491	3
Chicago – Gary – Lake County, IL – IN – WI CMSA	357	4
San Francisco – Oakland – San Jose, CA CMSA	293	5
Minneapolis – St. Paul, MN – WI MSA	270	6
Detroit – Ann Arbor, MI CMSA	219	7
Pittsburgh – Beaver Valley, PA CMSA	215	8
Cleveland – Akron – Lorain, OH CMSA	205	9
Miami – Fort Lauderdale, FL CMSA	193	10
Washington, DC – MD – VA MSA	191	11
Houston – Galveston – Brazoria, TX CMSA	170	12
San Diego, CA MSA	145	13
Atlanta, GA MSA	140	14
Indianapolis, IN MSA	138	15
Dallas – Fort Worth, TX CMSA	136	16
Baltimore, MD MSA	126	17
Seattle – Tacoma, WA CMSA	120	18
Kansas City, MO – KS MSA	120	18
Portland – Vancouver, OR – WA CMSA	117	19
Boston – Lawrence – Salem, MA – NH CMSA	111	20
Tampa – St. Petersburg – Clearwater, FL MSA	105	21
Denver – Boulder, CO CMSA	98	22
Honolulu, HI MSA	96	23
Buffalo – Niagara Falls, NY CMSA	87	24

Source: U.S. Department of Commerce, Bureau of the Census, Data User Services Division, *1990 Census of Population and Housing, Equal Employment Opportunity File, CD-90-EE0-1, January 1993,* CD-ROM.

★1610★

Occupations, By Race/Sex

Top 25 MSAs For Employment As Physicians' Assistants, 1990: Women

MSA/CMSA	Employees per 100,000 pop.	Rank
Albany – Schenectady – Troy, NY MSA	1,178	1
Los Angeles – Anaheim – Riverside, CA CMSA	740	2
Philadelphia – Wilmington – Trenton, PA – NJ – DE – MD CMSA	336	3
Chicago – Gary – Lake County, IL – IN – WI CMSA	322	4
Houston – Galveston – Brazoria, TX CMSA	310	5
Washington, DC – MD – VA MSA	278	6
Cleveland – Akron – Lorain, OH CMSA	260	7
San Francisco – Oakland – San Jose, CA CMSA	258	8
Atlanta, GA MSA	234	9
Boston – Lawrence – Salem, MA – NH CMSA	228	10
Detroit – Ann Arbor, MI CMSA	205	11
Seattle – Tacoma, WA CMSA	177	12
Pittsburgh – Beaver Valley, PA CMSA	173	13
Tampa – St. Petersburg – Clearwater, FL MSA	162	14
Phoenix, AZ MSA	152	15
Miami – Fort Lauderdale, FL CMSA	148	16
St. Louis, MO – IL MSA	137	17
Baltimore, MD MSA	124	18
Dallas – Fort Worth, TX CMSA	116	19
Charlotte – Gastonia – Rock Hill, NC – SC MSA	112	20
Denver – Boulder, CO CMSA	108	21
Memphis, TN – AR – MS MSA	97	22
Kansas City, MO – KS MSA	95	23
Nashville, TN MSA	88	24
Honolulu, HI MSA	86	25

Source: U.S. Department of Commerce, Bureau of the Census, Data User Services Division, *1990 Census of Population and Housing, Equal Employment Opportunity File, CD-90-EE0-1, January 1993,* CD-ROM.

★1611★

Occupations, By Race/Sex

Top 25 MSAs For Employment As Physicians, 1990: Men

MSA/CMSA	Employees per 100,000 pop.	Rank
Macon – Warner Robins, GA MSA	50,918	1
Los Angeles – Anaheim – Riverside, CA CMSA	28,775	2
Chicago – Gary – Lake County, IL – IN – WI CMSA	16,810	3
Philadelphia – Wilmington – Trenton, PA – NJ – DE – MD CMSA	15,771	4
San Francisco – Oakland – San Jose, CA CMSA	15,136	5
Boston – Lawrence – Salem, MA – NH CMSA	11,393	6
Detroit – Ann Arbor, MI CMSA	10,545	7
Washington, DC – MD – VA MSA	10,187	8
Miami – Fort Lauderdale, FL CMSA	8,113	9
Houston – Galveston – Brazoria, TX CMSA	7,299	10
Dallas – Fort Worth, TX CMSA	7,003	11
Baltimore, MD MSA	6,919	12
Cleveland – Akron – Lorain, OH CMSA	6,643	13
Seattle – Tacoma, WA CMSA	5,649	14
San Diego, CA MSA	5,395	15
St. Louis, MO – IL MSA	5,167	16
Atlanta, GA MSA	5,116	17
Pittsburgh – Beaver Valley, PA CMSA	4,974	18
Minneapolis – St. Paul, MN – WI MSA	4,785	19
Tampa – St. Petersburg – Clearwater, FL MSA	4,374	20
Denver – Boulder, CO CMSA	4,274	21
Phoenix, AZ MSA	4,103	22
Kansas City, MO – KS MSA	3,483	23
Milwaukee – Racine, WI CMSA	3,419	24
New Orleans, LA MSA	3,272	25

Source: U.S. Department of Commerce, Bureau of the Census, Data User Services Division, *1990 Census of Population and Housing, Equal Employment Opportunity File, CD-90-EEO-1, January 1993,* CD-ROM.

★1612★

Occupations, By Race/Sex

Top 25 MSAs For Employment As Physicians, 1990: Women

MSA/CMSA	Employees per 100,000 pop.	Rank
Greensboro – Winston-Salem – High Point, NC MSA	17,138	1
Los Angeles – Anaheim – Riverside, CA CMSA	7,881	2
Chicago – Gary – Lake County, IL – IN – WI CMSA	5,719	3
Philadelphia – Wilmington – Trenton, PA – NJ – DE – MD CMSA	4,868	4
San Francisco – Oakland – San Jose, CA CMSA	4,835	5
Boston – Lawrence – Salem, MA – NH CMSA	4,274	6
Washington, DC – MD – VA MSA	3,856	7
Detroit – Ann Arbor, MI CMSA	3,304	8
Baltimore, MD MSA	2,297	9
Houston – Galveston – Brazoria, TX CMSA	2,178	10
Cleveland – Akron – Lorain, OH CMSA	2,064	11
Dallas – Fort Worth, TX CMSA	1,755	12
Seattle – Tacoma, WA CMSA	1,711	13
Miami – Fort Lauderdale, FL CMSA	1,582	14
Pittsburgh – Beaver Valley, PA CMSA	1,548	15
Atlanta, GA MSA	1,424	16
Minneapolis – St. Paul, MN – WI MSA	1,419	17
St. Louis, MO – IL MSA	1,339	18
Denver – Boulder, CO CMSA	1,266	19
San Diego, CA MSA	1,131	20
Cincinnati – Hamilton, OH – KY – IN CMSA	1,007	21
Kansas City, MO – KS MSA	998	22
Raleigh – Durham, NC MSA	926	23
Portland – Vancouver, OR – WA CMSA	883	24
Tampa – St. Petersburg – Clearwater, FL MSA	829	25

Source: U.S. Department of Commerce, Bureau of the Census, Data User Services Division, *1990 Census of Population and Housing, Equal Employment Opportunity File, CD-90-EEO-1, January 1993,* CD-ROM.

★1613★

Occupations, By Race/Sex

Top 25 MSAs For Employment As Physicists and Astronomers, 1990: Men

MSA/CMSA	Employees per 100,000 pop.	Rank
Miami – Fort Lauderdale, FL CMSA	2,554	1
Washington, DC – MD – VA MSA	2,345	2
New York – Northern New Jersey – Long Island, NY – NJ – CT CMSA	1,590	3
Los Angeles – Anaheim – Riverside, CA CMSA	1,415	4
Boston – Lawrence – Salem, MA – NH CMSA	1,119	5
Chicago – Gary – Lake County, IL – IN – WI CMSA	862	6
Santa Fe, NM MSA	793	7
Philadelphia – Wilmington – Trenton, PA – NJ – DE – MD CMSA	665	8
Baltimore, MD MSA	529	9
Denver – Boulder, CO CMSA	522	10
San Diego, CA MSA	514	11
Albuquerque, NM MSA	393	12
Knoxville, TN MSA	333	13
Detroit – Ann Arbor, MI CMSA	293	14
Seattle – Tacoma, WA CMSA	273	15
Pittsburgh – Beaver Valley, PA CMSA	265	16
Richland – Kennewick – Pasco, WA MSA	239	17
Huntsville, AL MSA	228	18
Dallas – Fort Worth, TX CMSA	226	19
Raleigh – Durham, NC MSA	226	19
Santa Barbara – Santa Maria – Lompoc, CA MSA	222	20
Houston – Galveston – Brazoria, TX CMSA	211	21
Cleveland – Akron – Lorain, OH CMSA	206	22
Norfolk – Virginia Beach – Newport News, VA MSA	196	23
Augusta, GA – SC MSA	191	24

Source: U.S. Department of Commerce, Bureau of the Census, Data User Services Division, *1990 Census of Population and Housing, Equal Employment Opportunity File, CD-90-EE0-1, January 1993,* CD-ROM.

★1614★

Occupations, By Race/Sex

Top 25 MSAs For Employment As Physicists and Astronomers, 1990: Women

MSA/CMSA	Employees per 100,000 pop.	Rank
Sacramento, CA MSA	291	1
Washington, DC – MD – VA MSA	270	2
New York – Northern New Jersey – Long Island, NY – NJ – CT CMSA	255	3
Boston – Lawrence – Salem, MA – NH CMSA	230	4
Los Angeles – Anaheim – Riverside, CA CMSA	161	5
Philadelphia – Wilmington – Trenton, PA – NJ – DE – MD CMSA	134	6
Chicago – Gary – Lake County, IL – IN – WI CMSA	132	7
Baltimore, MD MSA	96	8
Seattle – Tacoma, WA CMSA	73	9
San Diego, CA MSA	67	10
Dallas – Fort Worth, TX CMSA	62	11
Santa Fe, NM MSA	57	12
Detroit – Ann Arbor, MI CMSA	50	13
St. Louis, MO – IL MSA	48	14
Knoxville, TN MSA	46	15
Raleigh – Durham, NC MSA	41	16
Chattanooga, TN – GA MSA	39	17
Houston – Galveston – Brazoria, TX CMSA	39	17
Huntsville, AL MSA	34	18
Minneapolis – St. Paul, MN – WI MSA	32	19
Denver – Boulder, CO CMSA	30	20
Miami – Fort Lauderdale, FL CMSA	30	20
Richland – Kennewick – Pasco, WA MSA	30	20
Bakersfield, CA MSA	26	21
Sacramento, CA MSA	26	21

Source: U.S. Department of Commerce, Bureau of the Census, Data User Services Division, *1990 Census of Population and Housing, Equal Employment Opportunity File, CD-90-EE0-1, January 1993,* CD-ROM.

★1615★

Occupations, By Race/Sex

Top 25 MSAs For Employment As Physics Teachers, 1990: Men

MSA/CMSA	Employees per 100,000 pop.	Rank
Milwaukee – Racine, WI CMSA	247	1
Boston – Lawrence – Salem, MA – NH CMSA	162	2
San Francisco – Oakland – San Jose, CA CMSA	143	3
Los Angeles – Anaheim – Riverside, CA CMSA	136	4

[Continued]

★1615★

Top 25 MSAs For Employment As Physics Teachers, 1990: Men
[Continued]

MSA/CMSA	Employees per 100,000 pop.	Rank
Chicago – Gary – Lake County, IL – IN – WI CMSA	105	5
Baltimore, MD MSA	83	6
St. Louis, MO – IL MSA	77	7
Gainesville, FL MSA	70	8
Washington, DC – MD – VA MSA	68	9
Philadelphia – Wilmington – Trenton, PA – NJ – DE – MD CMSA	63	10
Sacramento, CA MSA	63	10
Dallas – Fort Worth, TX CMSA	62	11
Seattle – Tacoma, WA CMSA	58	12
Lafayette – West Lafayette, IN MSA	53	13
Pittsburgh – Beaver Valley, PA CMSA	50	14
Detroit – Ann Arbor, MI CMSA	50	14
Norfolk – Virginia Beach – Newport News, VA MSA	46	15
Portland – Vancouver, OR – WA CMSA	46	15
Providence – Pawtucket – Fall River, RI – MA CMSA	46	15
Cincinnati – Hamilton, OH – KY – IN CMSA	42	16
Austin, TX MSA	41	17
Raleigh – Durham, NC MSA	37	18
Tucson, AZ MSA	37	18
Cleveland – Akron – Lorain, OH CMSA	37	18
Minneapolis – St. Paul, MN – WI MSA	33	19

Source: U.S. Department of Commerce, Bureau of the Census, Data User Services Division, *1990 Census of Population and Housing, Equal Employment Opportunity File, CD-90-EE0-1, January 1993,* CD-ROM.

★1616★
Occupations, By Race/Sex

Top 25 MSAs For Employment As Physics Teachers, 1990: Women

MSA/CMSA	Employees per 100,000 pop.	Rank
Spokane, WA MSA	29	1
Chicago – Gary – Lake County, IL – IN – WI CMSA	19	2
Philadelphia – Wilmington – Trenton, PA – NJ – DE – MD CMSA	18	3
Greenville – Spartanburg, SC MSA	16	4
Salt Lake City – Ogden, UT MSA	15	5
Albuquerque, NM MSA	14	6
Detroit – Ann Arbor, MI CMSA	14	6

[Continued]

★1616★

Top 25 MSAs For Employment As Physics Teachers, 1990: Women
[Continued]

MSA/CMSA	Employees per 100,000 pop.	Rank
Washington, DC – MD – VA MSA	14	6
Lafayette – West Lafayette, IN MSA	13	7
New Orleans, LA MSA	13	7
Austin, TX MSA	12	8
West Palm Beach – Boca Raton – Delray Beach, FL MSA	12	8
Amarillo, TX MSA	10	9
Boston – Lawrence – Salem, MA – NH CMSA	10	9
Los Angeles – Anaheim – Riverside, CA CMSA	10	9
Cincinnati – Hamilton, OH – KY – IN CMSA	9	10
Kansas City, MO – KS MSA	9	10
Oklahoma City, OK MSA	9	10
Norfolk – Virginia Beach – Newport News, VA MSA	9	10
Santa Barbara – Santa Maria – Lompoc, CA MSA	9	10
Tucson, AZ MSA	9	10
Cleveland – Akron – Lorain, OH CMSA	8	11
Hartford – New Britain – Middletown, CT CMSA	8	11
Knoxville, TN MSA	8	11
San Diego, CA MSA	8	11

Source: U.S. Department of Commerce, Bureau of the Census, Data User Services Division, *1990 Census of Population and Housing, Equal Employment Opportunity File, CD-90-EE0-1, January 1993,* CD-ROM.

★1617★
Occupations, By Race/Sex

Top 25 MSAs For Employment As Podiatrists, 1990: Men

MSA/CMSA	Employees per 100,000 pop.	Rank
Cincinnati – Hamilton, OH – KY – IN CMSA	1,284	1
Philadelphia – Wilmington – Trenton, PA – NJ – DE – MD CMSA	523	2
Chicago – Gary – Lake County, IL – IN – WI CMSA	456	3
San Francisco – Oakland – San Jose, CA CMSA	370	4
Los Angeles – Anaheim – Riverside, CA CMSA	332	5
Boston – Lawrence – Salem, MA – NH CMSA	223	6
Cleveland – Akron – Lorain, OH CMSA	205	7
Detroit – Ann Arbor, MI CMSA	204	8

[Continued]

★1617★

Top 25 MSAs For Employment As Podiatrists, 1990: Men

[Continued]

MSA/CMSA	Employees per 100,000 pop.	Rank
Miami – Fort Lauderdale, FL CMSA	164	9
Baltimore, MD MSA	160	10
Pittsburgh – Beaver Valley, PA CMSA	145	11
Seattle – Tacoma, WA CMSA	101	12
West Palm Beach – Boca Raton – Delray Beach, FL MSA	93	13
Phoenix, AZ MSA	89	14
Washington, DC – MD – VA MSA	87	15
Scranton – Wilkes-Barre, PA MSA	84	16
Tampa – St. Petersburg – Clearwater, FL MSA	78	17
Denver – Boulder, CO CMSA	74	18
St. Louis, MO – IL MSA	67	19
Dallas – Fort Worth, TX CMSA	67	19
San Diego, CA MSA	60	20
Buffalo – Niagara Falls, NY CMSA	60	20
Columbus, OH MSA	57	21
Atlanta, GA MSA	54	22
San Antonio, TX MSA	51	23

Source: U.S. Department of Commerce, Bureau of the Census, Data User Services Division, *1990 Census of Population and Housing, Equal Employment Opportunity File, CD-90-EE0-1, January 1993,* CD-ROM.

★1618★

Occupations, By Race/Sex

Top 25 MSAs For Employment As Podiatrists, 1990: Women

MSA/CMSA	Employees per 100,000 pop.	Rank
Miami – Fort Lauderdale, FL CMSA	231	1
Los Angeles – Anaheim – Riverside, CA CMSA	85	2
Philadelphia – Wilmington – Trenton, PA – NJ – DE – MD CMSA	85	2
San Francisco – Oakland – San Jose, CA CMSA	74	3
Chicago – Gary – Lake County, IL – IN – WI CMSA	47	4
Boston – Lawrence – Salem, MA – NH CMSA	39	5
Washington, DC – MD – VA MSA	30	6
Detroit – Ann Arbor, MI CMSA	25	7
Providence – Pawtucket – Fall River, RI – MA CMSA	21	8
Miami – Fort Lauderdale, FL CMSA	20	9
Tampa – St. Petersburg – Clearwater, FL MSA	18	10
Tucson, AZ MSA	18	10

[Continued]

★1618★

Top 25 MSAs For Employment As Podiatrists, 1990: Women

[Continued]

MSA/CMSA	Employees per 100,000 pop.	Rank
Phoenix, AZ MSA	17	11
Spokane, WA MSA	17	11
Dallas – Fort Worth, TX CMSA	16	12
Des Moines, IA MSA	13	13
Denver – Boulder, CO CMSA	13	13
San Diego, CA MSA	13	13
San Antonio, TX MSA	13	13
Syracuse, NY MSA	13	13
Gainesville, FL MSA	9	14
St. Louis, MO – IL MSA	9	14
West Palm Beach – Boca Raton – Delray Beach, FL MSA	9	14
Columbus, OH MSA	8	15
Cleveland – Akron – Lorain, OH CMSA	8	15

Source: U.S. Department of Commerce, Bureau of the Census, Data User Services Division, *1990 Census of Population and Housing, Equal Employment Opportunity File, CD-90-EE0-1, January 1993,* CD-ROM.

★1619★

Occupations, By Race/Sex

Top 25 MSAs For Employment As Police and Detectives, Public Service, 1990: Men

MSA/CMSA	Employees per 100,000 pop.	Rank
Phoenix, AZ MSA	58,952	1
Los Angeles – Anaheim – Riverside, CA CMSA	21,710	2
Chicago – Gary – Lake County, IL – IN – WI CMSA	20,076	3
Philadelphia – Wilmington – Trenton, PA – NJ – DE – MD CMSA	14,900	4
Washington, DC – MD – VA MSA	11,374	5
Boston – Lawrence – Salem, MA – NH CMSA	9,503	6
San Francisco – Oakland – San Jose, CA CMSA	9,231	7
Detroit – Ann Arbor, MI CMSA	9,092	8
Miami – Fort Lauderdale, FL CMSA	8,022	9
Houston – Galveston – Brazoria, TX CMSA	6,811	10
Dallas – Fort Worth, TX CMSA	6,768	11
Baltimore, MD MSA	6,705	12
Atlanta, GA MSA	5,005	13
St. Louis, MO – IL MSA	4,848	14
Cleveland – Akron – Lorain, OH CMSA	4,726	15
San Diego, CA MSA	4,477	16
Seattle – Tacoma, WA CMSA	4,028	17
Phoenix, AZ MSA	3,779	18
Tampa – St. Petersburg – Clearwater, FL MSA	3,300	19

[Continued]

★1619★
Top 25 MSAs For Employment As Police and Detectives, Public Service, 1990: Men
[Continued]

MSA/CMSA	Employees per 100,000 pop.	Rank
Pittsburgh – Beaver Valley, PA CMSA	3,262	20
Buffalo – Niagara Falls, NY CMSA	3,127	21
Denver – Boulder, CO CMSA	3,039	22
Minneapolis – St. Paul, MN – WI MSA	2,989	23
Milwaukee – Racine, WI CMSA	2,949	24
Kansas City, MO – KS MSA	2,889	25

Source: U.S. Department of Commerce, Bureau of the Census, Data User Services Division, *1990 Census of Population and Housing, Equal Employment Opportunity File, CD-90-EE0-1,* January 1993, CD-ROM.

★1620★
Occupations, By Race/Sex
Top 25 MSAs For Employment As Police and Detectives, Public Service, 1990: Women

MSA/CMSA	Employees per 100,000 pop.	Rank
West Palm Beach – Boca Raton – Delray Beach, FL MSA	7,971	1
Los Angeles – Anaheim – Riverside, CA CMSA	4,013	2
Chicago – Gary – Lake County, IL – IN – WI CMSA	2,725	3
Washington, DC – MD – VA MSA	2,630	4
Philadelphia – Wilmington – Trenton, PA – NJ – DE – MD CMSA	1,865	5
Miami – Fort Lauderdale, FL CMSA	1,838	6
San Francisco – Oakland – San Jose, CA CMSA	1,814	7
Detroit – Ann Arbor, MI CMSA	1,646	8
Baltimore, MD MSA	1,222	9
Dallas – Fort Worth, TX CMSA	1,056	10
Houston – Galveston – Brazoria, TX CMSA	965	11
Boston – Lawrence – Salem, MA – NH CMSA	922	12
San Diego, CA MSA	878	13
Atlanta, GA MSA	773	14
Cleveland – Akron – Lorain, OH CMSA	641	15
Denver – Boulder, CO CMSA	614	16
Seattle – Tacoma, WA CMSA	581	17
Phoenix, AZ MSA	559	18
Tampa – St. Petersburg – Clearwater, FL MSA	540	19
Sacramento, CA MSA	498	20
Kansas City, MO – KS MSA	481	21
Norfolk – Virginia Beach – Newport News, VA MSA	426	22
St. Louis, MO – IL MSA	400	23

[Continued]

★1620★
Top 25 MSAs For Employment As Police and Detectives, Public Service, 1990: Women
[Continued]

MSA/CMSA	Employees per 100,000 pop.	Rank
Minneapolis – St. Paul, MN – WI MSA	399	24
Indianapolis, IN MSA	378	25

Source: U.S. Department of Commerce, Bureau of the Census, Data User Services Division, *1990 Census of Population and Housing, Equal Employment Opportunity File, CD-90-EE0-1,* January 1993, CD-ROM.

★1621★
Occupations, By Race/Sex
Top 25 MSAs For Employment As Political Science Teachers, 1990: Men

MSA/CMSA	Employees per 100,000 pop.	Rank
Richmond – Petersburg, VA MSA	44	1
San Francisco – Oakland – San Jose, CA CMSA	40	2
Washington, DC – MD – VA MSA	36	3
Boston – Lawrence – Salem, MA – NH CMSA	32	4
New Haven – Meriden, CT MSA	25	5
Raleigh – Durham, NC MSA	25	5
Houston – Galveston – Brazoria, TX CMSA	23	6
Pittsburgh – Beaver Valley, PA CMSA	23	6
Syracuse, NY MSA	19	7
Los Angeles – Anaheim – Riverside, CA CMSA	19	7
Baltimore, MD MSA	17	8
St. Louis, MO – IL MSA	17	8
San Antonio, TX MSA	15	9
Santa Barbara – Santa Maria – Lompoc, CA MSA	15	9
Bangor, ME MSA	14	10
Springfield, MA MSA	14	10
Mcallen – Edinburg – Mission, TX MSA	12	11
Jacksonville, FL MSA	11	12
Albuquerque, NM MSA	10	13
Chico, CA MSA	10	13
Sacramento, CA MSA	10	13
Providence – Pawtucket – Fall River, RI – MA CMSA	10	13
Knoxville, TN MSA	9	14
Greenville – Spartanburg, SC MSA	8	15
Hartford – New Britain – Middletown, CT CMSA	8	15

Source: U.S. Department of Commerce, Bureau of the Census, Data User Services Division, *1990 Census of Population and Housing, Equal Employment Opportunity File, CD-90-EE0-1,* January 1993, CD-ROM.

★1622★

Occupations, By Race/Sex

Top 25 MSAs For Employment As Political Science Teachers, 1990: Women

MSA/CMSA	Employees per 100,000 pop.	Rank
Baton Rouge, LA MSA	29	1
Baltimore, MD MSA	16	2
Chicago – Gary – Lake County, IL – IN – WI CMSA	15	3
Los Angeles – Anaheim – Riverside, CA CMSA	14	4
San Diego, CA MSA	13	5
Bakersfield, CA MSA	10	6
Boston – Lawrence – Salem, MA – NH CMSA	10	6
Enid, OK MSA	10	6
Allentown – Bethlehem – Easton, PA – NJ MSA	8	7
Las Vegas, NV MSA	8	7
Philadelphia – Wilmington – Trenton, PA – NJ – DE – MD CMSA	8	7
Raleigh – Durham, NC MSA	8	7
Greenville – Spartanburg, SC MSA	7	8
Phoenix, AZ MSA	7	8
Santa Fe, NM MSA	7	8
Detroit – Ann Arbor, MI CMSA	6	9
Columbus, OH MSA	5	10
New Orleans, LA MSA	5	10
Pittsburgh – Beaver Valley, PA CMSA	5	10
Albuquerque, NM MSA	0	11
Anderson, IN MSA	0	11
Amarillo, TX MSA	0	11
Albany – Schenectady – Troy, NY MSA	0	11
Anchorage, AK MSA	0	11
Albany, GA MSA	0	11

Source: U.S. Department of Commerce, Bureau of the Census, Data User Services Division, *1990 Census of Population and Housing, Equal Employment Opportunity File, CD-90-EE0-1, January 1993*, CD-ROM.

★1623★

Occupations, By Race/Sex

Top 25 MSAs For Employment As Power Plant Operators, 1990: Men

MSA/CMSA	Employees per 100,000 pop.	Rank
Orlando, FL MSA	1,268	1
Los Angeles – Anaheim – Riverside, CA CMSA	1,037	2
Chicago – Gary – Lake County, IL – IN – WI CMSA	1,001	3
Philadelphia – Wilmington – Trenton, PA – NJ – DE – MD CMSA	700	4
Detroit – Ann Arbor, MI CMSA	653	5

[Continued]

★1623★

Top 25 MSAs For Employment As Power Plant Operators, 1990: Men

[Continued]

MSA/CMSA	Employees per 100,000 pop.	Rank
Houston – Galveston – Brazoria, TX CMSA	493	6
San Francisco – Oakland – San Jose, CA CMSA	375	7
Charlotte – Gastonia – Rock Hill, NC – SC MSA	366	8
Phoenix, AZ MSA	340	9
Cleveland – Akron – Lorain, OH CMSA	336	10
Pittsburgh – Beaver Valley, PA CMSA	303	11
Baltimore, MD MSA	300	12
St. Louis, MO – IL MSA	263	13
Washington, DC – MD – VA MSA	262	14
Boston – Lawrence – Salem, MA – NH CMSA	253	15
Miami – Fort Lauderdale, FL CMSA	253	15
Jacksonville, FL MSA	252	16
Augusta, GA – SC MSA	245	17
Tampa – St. Petersburg – Clearwater, FL MSA	242	18
San Diego, CA MSA	241	19
Dallas – Fort Worth, TX CMSA	238	20
Birmingham, AL MSA	214	21
Bakersfield, CA MSA	213	22
Cincinnati – Hamilton, OH – KY – IN CMSA	202	23
Richland – Kennewick – Pasco, WA MSA	191	24

Source: U.S. Department of Commerce, Bureau of the Census, Data User Services Division, *1990 Census of Population and Housing, Equal Employment Opportunity File, CD-90-EE0-1, January 1993,* CD-ROM.

★1624★

Occupations, By Race/Sex

Top 25 MSAs For Employment As Power Plant Operators, 1990: Women

MSA/CMSA	Employees per 100,000 pop.	Rank
Bakersfield, CA MSA	81	1
San Francisco – Oakland – San Jose, CA CMSA	75	2
Augusta, GA – SC MSA	66	3
New York – Northern New Jersey – Long Island, NY – NJ – CT CMSA	64	4
Baltimore, MD MSA	45	5
Washington, DC – MD – VA MSA	39	6
Memphis, TN – AR – MS MSA	36	7
Richland – Kennewick – Pasco, WA MSA	35	8
Cincinnati – Hamilton, OH – KY – IN CMSA	31	9

[Continued]

★ 1625 ★

Top 25 MSAs For Employment As Power Plant Operators, 1990: Women
[Continued]

MSA/CMSA	Employees per 100,000 pop.	Rank
Charlotte – Gastonia – Rock Hill, NC – SC MSA	27	10
Syracuse, NY MSA	27	10
Lansing – East Lansing, MI MSA	26	11
Phoenix, AZ MSA	26	11
San Diego, CA MSA	26	11
Beaumont – Port Arthur, TX MSA	25	12
West Palm Beach – Boca Raton – Delray Beach, FL MSA	25	12
Boston – Lawrence – Salem, MA – NH CMSA	24	13
Minneapolis – St. Paul, MN – WI MSA	24	13
Gainesville, FL MSA	23	14
Houston – Galveston – Brazoria, TX CMSA	21	15
Los Angeles – Anaheim – Riverside, CA CMSA	21	15
Seattle – Tacoma, WA CMSA	21	15
Chicago – Gary – Lake County, IL – IN – WI CMSA	20	16
Denver – Boulder, CO CMSA	19	17
Pittsburgh – Beaver Valley, PA CMSA	19	17

Source: U.S. Department of Commerce, Bureau of the Census, Data User Services Division, *1990 Census of Population and Housing, Equal Employment Opportunity File, CD-90-EEO-1, January 1993,* CD-ROM.

★ 1625 ★

Occupations, By Race/Sex

Top 25 MSAs For Employment As Precious Stones and Metals Workers, 1990: Men

MSA/CMSA	Employees per 100,000 pop.	Rank
Appleton – Oshkosh – Neenah, WI MSA	8,031	1
Los Angeles – Anaheim – Riverside, CA CMSA	4,415	2
Providence – Pawtucket – Fall River, RI – MA CMSA	1,658	3
Miami – Fort Lauderdale, FL CMSA	1,330	4
Chicago – Gary – Lake County, IL – IN – WI CMSA	1,022	5
San Francisco – Oakland – San Jose, CA CMSA	975	6
Dallas – Fort Worth, TX CMSA	736	7
Philadelphia – Wilmington – Trenton, PA – NJ – DE – MD CMSA	710	8
Boston – Lawrence – Salem, MA – NH CMSA	649	9
Detroit – Ann Arbor, MI CMSA	582	10

[Continued]

★ 1625 ★

Top 25 MSAs For Employment As Precious Stones and Metals Workers, 1990: Men
[Continued]

MSA/CMSA	Employees per 100,000 pop.	Rank
Albuquerque, NM MSA	523	11
Houston – Galveston – Brazoria, TX CMSA	500	12
Phoenix, AZ MSA	436	13
Washington, DC – MD – VA MSA	421	14
Seattle – Tacoma, WA CMSA	375	15
Tampa – St. Petersburg – Clearwater, FL MSA	321	16
Atlanta, GA MSA	305	17
San Diego, CA MSA	298	18
St. Louis, MO – IL MSA	274	19
Minneapolis – St. Paul, MN – WI MSA	271	20
Pittsburgh – Beaver Valley, PA CMSA	260	21
Cincinnati – Hamilton, OH – KY – IN CMSA	258	22
Baltimore, MD MSA	254	23
San Antonio, TX MSA	244	24
West Palm Beach – Boca Raton – Delray Beach, FL MSA	230	25

Source: U.S. Department of Commerce, Bureau of the Census, Data User Services Division, *1990 Census of Population and Housing, Equal Employment Opportunity File, CD-90-EEO-1, January 1993,* CD-ROM.

★ 1626 ★

Occupations, By Race/Sex

Top 25 MSAs For Employment As Precious Stones and Metals Workers, 1990: Women

MSA/CMSA	Employees per 100,000 pop.	Rank
Utica – Rome, NY MSA	2,929	1
New York – Northern New Jersey – Long Island, NY – NJ – CT CMSA	2,751	2
Los Angeles – Anaheim – Riverside, CA CMSA	1,099	3
San Francisco – Oakland – San Jose, CA CMSA	554	4
Miami – Fort Lauderdale, FL CMSA	433	5
Dallas – Fort Worth, TX CMSA	400	6
Albuquerque, NM MSA	359	7
Chicago – Gary – Lake County, IL – IN – WI CMSA	356	8
Detroit – Ann Arbor, MI CMSA	298	9
Boston – Lawrence – Salem, MA – NH CMSA	277	10
Philadelphia – Wilmington – Trenton, PA – NJ – DE – MD CMSA	269	11
Honolulu, HI MSA	194	12
Rapid City, SD MSA	193	13

[Continued]

★1626★

Top 25 MSAs For Employment As Precious Stones and Metals Workers, 1990: Women

[Continued]

MSA/CMSA	Employees per 100,000 pop.	Rank
Houston – Galveston – Brazoria, TX CMSA	180	14
St. Louis, MO – IL MSA	177	15
San Diego, CA MSA	175	16
Minneapolis – St. Paul, MN – WI MSA	173	17
Atlanta, GA MSA	166	18
Seattle – Tacoma, WA CMSA	163	19
Tucson, AZ MSA	155	20
Denver – Boulder, CO CMSA	152	21
Buffalo – Niagara Falls, NY CMSA	133	22
Washington, DC – MD – VA MSA	133	22
Austin, TX MSA	126	23
Milwaukee – Racine, WI CMSA	123	24

Source: U.S. Department of Commerce, Bureau of the Census, Data User Services Division, *1990 Census of Population and Housing, Equal Employment Opportunity File, CD-90-EE0-1, January 1993,* CD-ROM.

★1627★

Occupations, By Race/Sex

Top 25 MSAs For Employment As Printing Press Operators, 1990: Men

MSA/CMSA	Employees per 100,000 pop.	Rank
Syracuse, NY MSA	24,595	1
Los Angeles – Anaheim – Riverside, CA CMSA	18,996	2
Chicago – Gary – Lake County, IL – IN – WI CMSA	14,815	3
Philadelphia – Wilmington – Trenton, PA – NJ – DE – MD CMSA	8,950	4
San Francisco – Oakland – San Jose, CA CMSA	7,866	5
Washington, DC – MD – VA MSA	6,222	6
Boston – Lawrence – Salem, MA – NH CMSA	6,041	7
Dallas – Fort Worth, TX CMSA	5,898	8
Minneapolis – St. Paul, MN – WI MSA	5,470	9
Atlanta, GA MSA	4,644	10
Detroit – Ann Arbor, MI CMSA	4,439	11
Miami – Fort Lauderdale, FL CMSA	3,643	12
Milwaukee – Racine, WI CMSA	3,427	13
St. Louis, MO – IL MSA	3,423	14
Cleveland – Akron – Lorain, OH CMSA	3,414	15
Houston – Galveston – Brazoria, TX CMSA	3,396	16
Baltimore, MD MSA	3,310	17
Kansas City, MO – KS MSA	3,208	18
Cincinnati – Hamilton, OH – KY – IN CMSA	3,050	19

[Continued]

★1627★

Top 25 MSAs For Employment As Printing Press Operators, 1990: Men

[Continued]

MSA/CMSA	Employees per 100,000 pop.	Rank
Seattle – Tacoma, WA CMSA	2,908	20
Tampa – St. Petersburg – Clearwater, FL MSA	2,509	21
Denver – Boulder, CO CMSA	2,493	22
San Diego, CA MSA	2,476	23
Portland – Vancouver, OR – WA CMSA	2,439	24
Phoenix, AZ MSA	2,405	25

Source: U.S. Department of Commerce, Bureau of the Census, Data User Services Division, *1990 Census of Population and Housing, Equal Employment Opportunity File, CD-90-EE0-1, January 1993,* CD-ROM.

★1628★

Occupations, By Race/Sex

Top 25 MSAs For Employment As Printing Press Operators, 1990: Women

MSA/CMSA	Employees per 100,000 pop.	Rank
Portsmouth – Dover – Rochester, NH – ME MSA	3,419	1
Los Angeles – Anaheim – Riverside, CA CMSA	3,382	2
Chicago – Gary – Lake County, IL – IN – WI CMSA	2,378	3
Philadelphia – Wilmington – Trenton, PA – NJ – DE – MD CMSA	1,366	4
San Francisco – Oakland – San Jose, CA CMSA	1,344	5
Dallas – Fort Worth, TX CMSA	1,264	6
Minneapolis – St. Paul, MN – WI MSA	1,107	7
Atlanta, GA MSA	973	8
Washington, DC – MD – VA MSA	923	9
Boston – Lawrence – Salem, MA – NH CMSA	911	10
Detroit – Ann Arbor, MI CMSA	888	11
Houston – Galveston – Brazoria, TX CMSA	764	12
Miami – Fort Lauderdale, FL CMSA	751	13
St. Louis, MO – IL MSA	745	14
Baltimore, MD MSA	714	15
Seattle – Tacoma, WA CMSA	702	16
Cleveland – Akron – Lorain, OH CMSA	693	17
Charlotte – Gastonia – Rock Hill, NC – SC MSA	686	18
Kansas City, MO – KS MSA	664	19
Milwaukee – Racine, WI CMSA	618	20
Portland – Vancouver, OR – WA CMSA	571	21
Phoenix, AZ MSA	570	22

[Continued]

★1628★

Top 25 MSAs For Employment As Printing Press Operators, 1990: Women
[Continued]

MSA/CMSA	Employees per 100,000 pop.	Rank
Greensboro – Winston-Salem – High Point, NC MSA	548	23
San Diego, CA MSA	536	24
Denver – Boulder, CO CMSA	524	25

Source: U.S. Department of Commerce, Bureau of the Census, Data User Services Division, *1990 Census of Population and Housing, Equal Employment Opportunity File, CD-90-EE0-1, January 1993*, CD-ROM.

★1629★

Occupations, By Race/Sex

Top 25 MSAs For Employment As Private Household Cleaners and Servants, 1990: Men

MSA/CMSA	Employees per 100,000 pop.	Rank
Kansas City, MO – KS MSA	2,841	1
New York – Northern New Jersey – Long Island, NY – NJ – CT CMSA	2,320	2
San Francisco – Oakland – San Jose, CA CMSA	1,098	3
Miami – Fort Lauderdale, FL CMSA	571	4
Chicago – Gary – Lake County, IL – IN – WI CMSA	529	5
Houston – Galveston – Brazoria, TX CMSA	474	6
Washington, DC – MD – VA MSA	465	7
Boston – Lawrence – Salem, MA – NH CMSA	443	8
Philadelphia – Wilmington – Trenton, PA – NJ – DE – MD CMSA	419	9
San Diego, CA MSA	407	10
Dallas – Fort Worth, TX CMSA	380	11
Detroit – Ann Arbor, MI CMSA	296	12
Atlanta, GA MSA	273	13
Baltimore, MD MSA	255	14
Seattle – Tacoma, WA CMSA	215	15
West Palm Beach – Boca Raton – Delray Beach, FL MSA	171	16
Tampa – St. Petersburg – Clearwater, FL MSA	170	17
Phoenix, AZ MSA	169	18
St. Louis, MO – IL MSA	159	19
New Orleans, LA MSA	147	20
Portland – Vancouver, OR – WA CMSA	140	21
Denver – Boulder, CO CMSA	140	21
Sacramento, CA MSA	136	22

[Continued]

★1629★

Top 25 MSAs For Employment As Private Household Cleaners and Servants, 1990: Men
[Continued]

MSA/CMSA	Employees per 100,000 pop.	Rank
Cleveland – Akron – Lorain, OH CMSA	135	23
Pittsburgh – Beaver Valley, PA CMSA	132	24

Source: U.S. Department of Commerce, Bureau of the Census, Data User Services Division, *1990 Census of Population and Housing, Equal Employment Opportunity File, CD-90-EE0-1, January 1993*, CD-ROM.

★1630★

Occupations, By Race/Sex

Top 25 MSAs For Employment As Private Household Cleaners and Servants, 1990: Women

MSA/CMSA	Employees per 100,000 pop.	Rank
Indianapolis, IN MSA	41,950	1
New York – Northern New Jersey – Long Island, NY – NJ – CT CMSA	29,156	2
Miami – Fort Lauderdale, FL CMSA	9,804	3
San Francisco – Oakland – San Jose, CA CMSA	9,406	4
Houston – Galveston – Brazoria, TX CMSA	9,345	5
Washington, DC – MD – VA MSA	8,779	6
Dallas – Fort Worth, TX CMSA	7,142	7
Chicago – Gary – Lake County, IL – IN – WI CMSA	6,330	8
Philadelphia – Wilmington – Trenton, PA – NJ – DE – MD CMSA	4,851	9
San Diego, CA MSA	4,820	10
Atlanta, GA MSA	4,199	11
Detroit – Ann Arbor, MI CMSA	3,484	12
Boston – Lawrence – Salem, MA – NH CMSA	2,643	13
San Antonio, TX MSA	2,596	14
New Orleans, LA MSA	2,568	15
Memphis, TN – AR – MS MSA	2,548	16
Tampa – St. Petersburg – Clearwater, FL MSA	2,449	17
Baltimore, MD MSA	2,435	18
St. Louis, MO – IL MSA	2,424	19
West Palm Beach – Boca Raton – Delray Beach, FL MSA	2,409	20
Cleveland – Akron – Lorain, OH CMSA	2,053	21
Phoenix, AZ MSA	1,997	22
Seattle – Tacoma, WA CMSA	1,928	23
Denver – Boulder, CO CMSA	1,864	24
Norfolk – Virginia Beach – Newport News, VA MSA	1,776	25

Source: U.S. Department of Commerce, Bureau of the Census, Data User Services Division, *1990 Census of Population and Housing, Equal Employment Opportunity File, CD-90-EE0-1, January 1993*, CD-ROM.

★1631★

Occupations, By Race/Sex

Top 25 MSAs For Employment As Proofreaders, 1990: Men

MSA/CMSA	Employees per 100,000 pop.	Rank
Cleveland – Akron – Lorain, OH CMSA	2,194	1
Los Angeles – Anaheim – Riverside, CA CMSA	465	2
Chicago – Gary – Lake County, IL – IN – WI CMSA	458	3
Philadelphia – Wilmington – Trenton, PA – NJ – DE – MD CMSA	381	4
Washington, DC – MD – VA MSA	347	5
Detroit – Ann Arbor, MI CMSA	171	6
Boston – Lawrence – Salem, MA – NH CMSA	141	7
San Francisco – Oakland – San Jose, CA CMSA	134	8
Baltimore, MD MSA	133	9
Dallas – Fort Worth, TX CMSA	104	10
Lancaster, PA MSA	96	11
Minneapolis – St. Paul, MN – WI MSA	91	12
Pittsburgh – Beaver Valley, PA CMSA	90	13
Atlanta, GA MSA	77	14
Houston – Galveston – Brazoria, TX CMSA	77	14
St. Louis, MO – IL MSA	71	15
Hartford – New Britain – Middletown, CT CMSA	66	16
Columbus, OH MSA	65	17
Milwaukee – Racine, WI CMSA	61	18
Miami – Fort Lauderdale, FL CMSA	60	19
San Diego, CA MSA	59	20
Portland – Vancouver, OR – WA CMSA	58	21
Denver – Boulder, CO CMSA	55	22
Tallahassee, FL MSA	55	22
Tampa – St. Petersburg – Clearwater, FL MSA	53	23

Source: U.S. Department of Commerce, Bureau of the Census, Data User Services Division, *1990 Census of Population and Housing, Equal Employment Opportunity File, CD-90-EE0-1, January 1993,* CD-ROM.

★1632★

Occupations, By Race/Sex

Top 25 MSAs For Employment As Proofreaders, 1990: Women

MSA/CMSA	Employees per 100,000 pop.	Rank
Cincinnati – Hamilton, OH – KY – IN CMSA	3,016	1
Chicago – Gary – Lake County, IL – IN – WI CMSA	1,217	2
Los Angeles – Anaheim – Riverside, CA CMSA	1,024	3
Philadelphia – Wilmington – Trenton, PA – NJ – DE – MD CMSA	765	4
Washington, DC – MD – VA MSA	762	5
Minneapolis – St. Paul, MN – WI MSA	704	6
Boston – Lawrence – Salem, MA – NH CMSA	551	7
San Francisco – Oakland – San Jose, CA CMSA	496	8
Dallas – Fort Worth, TX CMSA	472	9
Detroit – Ann Arbor, MI CMSA	450	10
Atlanta, GA MSA	329	11
Baltimore, MD MSA	290	12
Houston – Galveston – Brazoria, TX CMSA	266	13
St. Louis, MO – IL MSA	241	14
Tampa – St. Petersburg – Clearwater, FL MSA	231	15
Columbus, OH MSA	208	16
Lancaster, PA MSA	207	17
Milwaukee – Racine, WI CMSA	198	18
Pittsburgh – Beaver Valley, PA CMSA	196	19
Phoenix, AZ MSA	189	20
Nashville, TN MSA	183	21
Miami – Fort Lauderdale, FL CMSA	178	22
Sacramento, CA MSA	176	23
Cincinnati – Hamilton, OH – KY – IN CMSA	170	24
Indianapolis, IN MSA	168	25

Source: U.S. Department of Commerce, Bureau of the Census, Data User Services Division, *1990 Census of Population and Housing, Equal Employment Opportunity File, CD-90-EE0-1, January 1993,* CD-ROM.

★1633★
Occupations, By Race/Sex

Top 25 MSAs For Employment As Psychologists, 1990: Men

MSA/CMSA	Employees per 100,000 pop.	Rank
Sacramento, CA MSA	8,493	1
Los Angeles – Anaheim – Riverside, CA CMSA	4,925	2
San Francisco – Oakland – San Jose, CA CMSA	3,214	3
Boston – Lawrence – Salem, MA – NH CMSA	2,643	4
Chicago – Gary – Lake County, IL – IN – WI CMSA	2,599	5
Philadelphia – Wilmington – Trenton, PA – NJ – DE – MD CMSA	2,437	6
Washington, DC – MD – VA MSA	1,639	7
Detroit – Ann Arbor, MI CMSA	1,584	8
Seattle – Tacoma, WA CMSA	1,245	9
Minneapolis – St. Paul, MN – WI MSA	1,237	10
Dallas – Fort Worth, TX CMSA	1,052	11
San Diego, CA MSA	1,028	12
Denver – Boulder, CO CMSA	987	13
Baltimore, MD MSA	905	14
Miami – Fort Lauderdale, FL CMSA	903	15
Houston – Galveston – Brazoria, TX CMSA	819	16
Atlanta, GA MSA	712	17
Pittsburgh – Beaver Valley, PA CMSA	683	18
Cleveland – Akron – Lorain, OH CMSA	676	19
Tampa – St. Petersburg – Clearwater, FL MSA	660	20
Phoenix, AZ MSA	645	21
Milwaukee – Racine, WI CMSA	637	22
St. Louis, MO – IL MSA	582	23
Norfolk – Virginia Beach – Newport News, VA MSA	546	24
Sacramento, CA MSA	543	25

Source: U.S. Department of Commerce, Bureau of the Census, Data User Services Division, *1990 Census of Population and Housing, Equal Employment Opportunity File, CD-90-EE0-1, January 1993*, CD-ROM.

★1634★
Occupations, By Race/Sex

Top 25 MSAs For Employment As Psychologists, 1990: Women

MSA/CMSA	Employees per 100,000 pop.	Rank
Hartford – New Britain – Middletown, CT CMSA	13,538	1
Los Angeles – Anaheim – Riverside, CA CMSA	8,173	2
San Francisco – Oakland – San Jose, CA CMSA	5,691	3
Boston – Lawrence – Salem, MA – NH CMSA	4,673	4
Chicago – Gary – Lake County, IL – IN – WI CMSA	3,607	5
Philadelphia – Wilmington – Trenton, PA – NJ – DE – MD CMSA	3,336	6
Washington, DC – MD – VA MSA	3,242	7
Detroit – Ann Arbor, MI CMSA	1,994	8
Denver – Boulder, CO CMSA	1,950	9
Minneapolis – St. Paul, MN – WI MSA	1,835	10
San Diego, CA MSA	1,737	11
Houston – Galveston – Brazoria, TX CMSA	1,697	12
Seattle – Tacoma, WA CMSA	1,689	13
Dallas – Fort Worth, TX CMSA	1,390	14
Atlanta, GA MSA	1,354	15
Baltimore, MD MSA	1,306	16
Miami – Fort Lauderdale, FL CMSA	1,266	17
Pittsburgh – Beaver Valley, PA CMSA	1,027	18
Cleveland – Akron – Lorain, OH CMSA	1,001	19
Phoenix, AZ MSA	995	20
St. Louis, MO – IL MSA	902	21
Tampa – St. Petersburg – Clearwater, FL MSA	885	22
Sacramento, CA MSA	795	23
Hartford – New Britain – Middletown, CT CMSA	749	24
Norfolk – Virginia Beach – Newport News, VA MSA	726	25

Source: U.S. Department of Commerce, Bureau of the Census, Data User Services Division, *1990 Census of Population and Housing, Equal Employment Opportunity File, CD-90-EE0-1, January 1993*, CD-ROM.

★1635★

Occupations, By Race/Sex

Top 25 MSAs For Employment As Psychology Teachers, 1990: Men

MSA/CMSA	Employees per 100,000 pop.	Rank
Greensboro – Winston-Salem – High Point, NC MSA	240	1
Los Angeles – Anaheim – Riverside, CA CMSA	100	2
Philadelphia – Wilmington – Trenton, PA – NJ – DE – MD CMSA	48	3
Chicago – Gary – Lake County, IL – IN – WI CMSA	48	3
San Francisco – Oakland – San Jose, CA CMSA	47	4
Baltimore, MD MSA	45	5
Boston – Lawrence – Salem, MA – NH CMSA	45	5
Lawrence, KS MSA	34	6
Pittsburgh – Beaver Valley, PA CMSA	34	6
Washington, DC – MD – VA MSA	32	7
Seattle – Tacoma, WA CMSA	28	8
Binghamton, NY MSA	28	8
Lansing – East Lansing, MI MSA	26	9
Detroit – Ann Arbor, MI CMSA	26	9
Cincinnati – Hamilton, OH – KY – IN CMSA	26	9
New Orleans, LA MSA	25	10
Toledo, OH MSA	25	10
Dallas – Fort Worth, TX CMSA	25	10
Muncie, IN MSA	23	11
Sacramento, CA MSA	22	12
Madison, WI MSA	21	13
Fayetteville – Springdale, AR MSA	21	13
Albuquerque, NM MSA	21	13
Austin, TX MSA	21	13
Tampa – St. Petersburg – Clearwater, FL MSA	20	14

Source: U.S. Department of Commerce, Bureau of the Census, Data User Services Division, *1990 Census of Population and Housing, Equal Employment Opportunity File, CD-90-EE0-1, January 1993,* CD-ROM.

★1636★

Occupations, By Race/Sex

Top 25 MSAs For Employment As Psychology Teachers, 1990: Women

MSA/CMSA	Employees per 100,000 pop.	Rank
Seattle – Tacoma, WA CMSA	224	1
San Francisco – Oakland – San Jose, CA CMSA	85	2
Boston – Lawrence – Salem, MA – NH CMSA	83	3
Los Angeles – Anaheim – Riverside, CA CMSA	81	4
Chicago – Gary – Lake County, IL – IN – WI CMSA	39	5

[Continued]

★1636★

Top 25 MSAs For Employment As Psychology Teachers, 1990: Women

[Continued]

MSA/CMSA	Employees per 100,000 pop.	Rank
Seattle – Tacoma, WA CMSA	38	6
San Diego, CA MSA	36	7
Houston – Galveston – Brazoria, TX CMSA	35	8
Philadelphia – Wilmington – Trenton, PA – NJ – DE – MD CMSA	35	8
Lubbock, TX MSA	30	9
Atlanta, GA MSA	26	10
Cleveland – Akron – Lorain, OH CMSA	25	11
Milwaukee – Racine, WI CMSA	25	11
Minneapolis – St. Paul, MN – WI MSA	24	12
Albuquerque, NM MSA	23	13
Cincinnati – Hamilton, OH – KY – IN CMSA	22	14
Denver – Boulder, CO CMSA	22	14
Raleigh – Durham, NC MSA	22	14
Eugene – Springfield, OR MSA	21	15
Montgomery, AL MSA	21	15
Pittsburgh – Beaver Valley, PA CMSA	21	15
Springfield, MA MSA	21	15
Chattanooga, TN – GA MSA	20	16
Jackson, MS MSA	20	16
Austin, TX MSA	19	17

Source: U.S. Department of Commerce, Bureau of the Census, Data User Services Division, *1990 Census of Population and Housing, Equal Employment Opportunity File, CD-90-EE0-1, January 1993,* CD-ROM.

★1637★

Occupations, By Race/Sex

Top 25 MSAs For Employment As Railroad Brake, Signal, and Switch Operators, 1990: Men

MSA/CMSA	Employees per 100,000 pop.	Rank
Sacramento, CA MSA	1,733	1
Kansas City, MO – KS MSA	815	2
Houston – Galveston – Brazoria, TX CMSA	748	3
St. Louis, MO – IL MSA	631	4
Los Angeles – Anaheim – Riverside, CA CMSA	600	5
Detroit – Ann Arbor, MI CMSA	489	6
Minneapolis – St. Paul, MN – WI MSA	466	7
Dallas – Fort Worth, TX CMSA	439	8
Seattle – Tacoma, WA CMSA	365	9
Salt Lake City – Ogden, UT MSA	343	10
Cincinnati – Hamilton, OH – KY – IN CMSA	341	11
Birmingham, AL MSA	316	12

[Continued]

★1637★

Top 25 MSAs For Employment As Railroad Brake, Signal, and Switch Operators, 1990: Men
[Continued]

MSA/CMSA	Employees per 100,000 pop.	Rank
Portland – Vancouver, OR – WA CMSA	315	13
New Orleans, LA MSA	306	14
Cleveland – Akron – Lorain, OH CMSA	288	15
Denver – Boulder, CO CMSA	286	16
Atlanta, GA MSA	283	17
Spokane, WA MSA	281	18
Roanoke, VA MSA	277	19
San Francisco – Oakland – San Jose, CA CMSA	276	20
Duluth, MN – WI MSA	253	21
El Paso, TX MSA	250	22
Little Rock – North Little Rock, AR MSA	245	23
New York – Northern New Jersey – Long Island, NY – NJ – CT CMSA	232	24
Stockton, CA MSA	229	25

Source: U.S. Department of Commerce, Bureau of the Census, Data User Services Division, *1990 Census of Population and Housing, Equal Employment Opportunity File, CD-90-EE0-1, January 1993*, CD-ROM.

★1638★

Occupations, By Race/Sex

Top 25 MSAs For Employment As Railroad Brake, Signal, and Switch Operators, 1990: Women

MSA/CMSA	Employees per 100,000 pop.	Rank
Pueblo, CO MSA	36	1
Chicago – Gary – Lake County, IL – IN – WI CMSA	33	2
New York – Northern New Jersey – Long Island, NY – NJ – CT CMSA	24	3
St. Louis, MO – IL MSA	24	3
Detroit – Ann Arbor, MI CMSA	17	4
Los Angeles – Anaheim – Riverside, CA CMSA	16	5
Roanoke, VA MSA	15	6
Des Moines, IA MSA	14	7
Baltimore, MD MSA	13	8
Boston – Lawrence – Salem, MA – NH CMSA	13	8
Montgomery, AL MSA	13	8
Atlanta, GA MSA	12	9
Pittsburgh – Beaver Valley, PA CMSA	11	10
Grand Forks, ND MSA	10	11
Oklahoma City, OK MSA	10	11
Spokane, WA MSA	10	11

[Continued]

★1638★

Top 25 MSAs For Employment As Railroad Brake, Signal, and Switch Operators, 1990: Women
[Continued]

MSA/CMSA	Employees per 100,000 pop.	Rank
Pueblo, CO MSA	9	12
Fargo – Moorhead, ND – MN MSA	8	13
Jacksonville, FL MSA	8	13
Kansas City, MO – KS MSA	8	13
Memphis, TN – AR – MS MSA	8	13
Beaumont – Port Arthur, TX MSA	7	14
Jackson, MI MSA	7	14
St. Joseph, MO MSA	7	14
Tulsa, OK MSA	7	14

Source: U.S. Department of Commerce, Bureau of the Census, Data User Services Division, *1990 Census of Population and Housing, Equal Employment Opportunity File, CD-90-EE0-1, January 1993*, CD-ROM.

★1639★

Occupations, By Race/Sex

Top 25 MSAs For Employment As Railroad Conductors and Yardmasters, 1990: Men

MSA/CMSA	Employees per 100,000 pop.	Rank
Denver – Boulder, CO CMSA	2,737	1
Chicago – Gary – Lake County, IL – IN – WI CMSA	1,298	2
Philadelphia – Wilmington – Trenton, PA – NJ – DE – MD CMSA	1,096	3
Los Angeles – Anaheim – Riverside, CA CMSA	852	4
Houston – Galveston – Brazoria, TX CMSA	515	5
Detroit – Ann Arbor, MI CMSA	505	6
Pittsburgh – Beaver Valley, PA CMSA	453	7
Dallas – Fort Worth, TX CMSA	443	8
San Francisco – Oakland – San Jose, CA CMSA	440	9
Portland – Vancouver, OR – WA CMSA	402	10
Kansas City, MO – KS MSA	385	11
Cleveland – Akron – Lorain, OH CMSA	385	11
Boston – Lawrence – Salem, MA – NH CMSA	360	12
Salt Lake City – Ogden, UT MSA	344	13
Baltimore, MD MSA	340	14
Minneapolis – St. Paul, MN – WI MSA	319	15
Jacksonville, FL MSA	312	16
Atlanta, GA MSA	302	17
Toledo, OH MSA	300	18
Sacramento, CA MSA	299	19
Cincinnati – Hamilton, OH – KY – IN CMSA	274	20

[Continued]

★ 1639 ★

Top 25 MSAs For Employment As Railroad Conductors and Yardmasters, 1990: Men

[Continued]

MSA/CMSA	Employees per 100,000 pop.	Rank
St. Louis, MO – IL MSA	261	21
Seattle – Tacoma, WA CMSA	250	22
Albany – Schenectady – Troy, NY MSA	246	23
Phoenix, AZ MSA	242	24

Source: U.S. Department of Commerce, Bureau of the Census, Data User Services Division, *1990 Census of Population and Housing, Equal Employment Opportunity File, CD-90-EE0-1, January 1993,* CD-ROM.

★ 1640 ★

Occupations, By Race/Sex

Top 25 MSAs For Employment As Railroad Conductors and Yardmasters, 1990: Women

MSA/CMSA	Employees per 100,000 pop.	Rank
Jacksonville, FL MSA	397	1
San Francisco – Oakland – San Jose, CA CMSA	252	2
Chicago – Gary – Lake County, IL – IN – WI CMSA	129	3
Los Angeles – Anaheim – Riverside, CA CMSA	98	4
Phoenix, AZ MSA	97	5
Sacramento, CA MSA	61	6
Boston – Lawrence – Salem, MA – NH CMSA	58	7
Atlanta, GA MSA	55	8
Dallas – Fort Worth, TX CMSA	54	9
Portland – Vancouver, OR – WA CMSA	51	10
Philadelphia – Wilmington – Trenton, PA – NJ – DE – MD CMSA	49	11
Washington, DC – MD – VA MSA	40	12
Kansas City, MO – KS MSA	39	13
Houston – Galveston – Brazoria, TX CMSA	35	14
Denver – Boulder, CO CMSA	31	15
Jacksonville, FL MSA	30	16
Norfolk – Virginia Beach – Newport News, VA MSA	29	17
Providence – Pawtucket – Fall River, RI – MA CMSA	28	18
Detroit – Ann Arbor, MI CMSA	25	19
Pittsburgh – Beaver Valley, PA CMSA	25	19
Provo – Orem, UT MSA	21	20
Albuquerque, NM MSA	19	21
Las Vegas, NV MSA	19	21
Billings, MT MSA	18	22
Rochester, NY MSA	18	22

Source: U.S. Department of Commerce, Bureau of the Census, Data User Services Division, *1990 Census of Population and Housing, Equal Employment Opportunity File, CD-90-EE0-1, January 1993,* CD-ROM.

★ 1641 ★

Occupations, By Race/Sex

Top 25 MSAs For Employment As Registered Nurses, 1990: Men

MSA/CMSA	Employees per 100,000 pop.	Rank
Houston – Galveston – Brazoria, TX CMSA	7,641	1
Los Angeles – Anaheim – Riverside, CA CMSA	6,097	2
San Francisco – Oakland – San Jose, CA CMSA	3,636	3
Philadelphia – Wilmington – Trenton, PA – NJ – DE – MD CMSA	3,241	4
Chicago – Gary – Lake County, IL – IN – WI CMSA	3,010	5
Boston – Lawrence – Salem, MA – NH CMSA	2,280	6
Miami – Fort Lauderdale, FL CMSA	1,744	7
Detroit – Ann Arbor, MI CMSA	1,651	8
Washington, DC – MD – VA MSA	1,505	9
Houston – Galveston – Brazoria, TX CMSA	1,423	10
St. Louis, MO – IL MSA	1,421	11
Seattle – Tacoma, WA CMSA	1,396	12
Dallas – Fort Worth, TX CMSA	1,378	13
Phoenix, AZ MSA	1,338	14
Cleveland – Akron – Lorain, OH CMSA	1,331	15
Minneapolis – St. Paul, MN – WI MSA	1,240	16
Baltimore, MD MSA	1,225	17
Tampa – St. Petersburg – Clearwater, FL MSA	1,152	18
San Diego, CA MSA	1,139	19
Pittsburgh – Beaver Valley, PA CMSA	1,094	20
Portland – Vancouver, OR – WA CMSA	978	21
Atlanta, GA MSA	964	22
Sacramento, CA MSA	943	23
San Antonio, TX MSA	933	24
Denver – Boulder, CO CMSA	921	25

Source: U.S. Department of Commerce, Bureau of the Census, Data User Services Division, *1990 Census of Population and Housing, Equal Employment Opportunity File, CD-90-EE0-1, January 1993,* CD-ROM.

★1642★

Occupations, By Race/Sex

Top 25 MSAs For Employment As Registered Nurses, 1990: Women

MSA/CMSA	Employees per 100,000 pop.	Rank
Seattle – Tacoma, WA CMSA	146,947	1
Los Angeles – Anaheim – Riverside, CA CMSA	84,756	2
Chicago – Gary – Lake County, IL – IN – WI CMSA	64,341	3
Philadelphia – Wilmington – Trenton, PA – NJ – DE – MD CMSA	54,536	4
San Francisco – Oakland – San Jose, CA CMSA	46,271	5
Boston – Lawrence – Salem, MA – NH CMSA	43,509	6
Detroit – Ann Arbor, MI CMSA	34,573	7
Washington, DC – MD – VA MSA	30,234	8
Cleveland – Akron – Lorain, OH CMSA	24,166	9
Houston – Galveston – Brazoria, TX CMSA	23,905	10
Dallas – Fort Worth, TX CMSA	23,384	11
Pittsburgh – Beaver Valley, PA CMSA	23,361	12
Minneapolis – St. Paul, MN – WI MSA	23,065	13
Miami – Fort Lauderdale, FL CMSA	21,871	14
Baltimore, MD MSA	21,639	15
St. Louis, MO – IL MSA	20,545	16
Atlanta, GA MSA	19,815	17
Seattle – Tacoma, WA CMSA	19,409	18
San Diego, CA MSA	15,845	19
Phoenix, AZ MSA	15,723	20
Tampa – St. Petersburg – Clearwater, FL MSA	15,593	21
Cincinnati – Hamilton, OH – KY – IN CMSA	15,291	22
Denver – Boulder, CO CMSA	14,441	23
Milwaukee – Racine, WI CMSA	14,419	24
Kansas City, MO – KS MSA	12,510	25

Source: U.S. Department of Commerce, Bureau of the Census, Data User Services Division, *1990 Census of Population and Housing, Equal Employment Opportunity File, CD-90-EE0-1, January 1993,* CD-ROM.

★1643★

Occupations, By Race/Sex

Top 25 MSAs For Employment As Respiratory Therapists, 1990: Men

MSA/CMSA	Employees per 100,000 pop.	Rank
Rochester, NY MSA	2,098	1
New York – Northern New Jersey – Long Island, NY – NJ – CT CMSA	1,642	2
Chicago – Gary – Lake County, IL – IN – WI CMSA	721	3
Miami – Fort Lauderdale, FL CMSA	661	4
Detroit – Ann Arbor, MI CMSA	638	5
San Francisco – Oakland – San Jose, CA CMSA	598	6
Philadelphia – Wilmington – Trenton, PA – NJ – DE – MD CMSA	537	7
Dallas – Fort Worth, TX CMSA	480	8
Boston – Lawrence – Salem, MA – NH CMSA	441	9
Tampa – St. Petersburg – Clearwater, FL MSA	417	10
Atlanta, GA MSA	415	11
Phoenix, AZ MSA	410	12
Houston – Galveston – Brazoria, TX CMSA	369	13
Pittsburgh – Beaver Valley, PA CMSA	358	14
Baltimore, MD MSA	332	15
Cleveland – Akron – Lorain, OH CMSA	325	16
Washington, DC – MD – VA MSA	296	17
San Diego, CA MSA	270	18
Seattle – Tacoma, WA CMSA	248	19
Indianapolis, IN MSA	239	20
Kansas City, MO – KS MSA	231	21
St. Louis, MO – IL MSA	220	22
Nashville, TN MSA	201	23
New Orleans, LA MSA	200	24
Portland – Vancouver, OR – WA CMSA	192	25

Source: U.S. Department of Commerce, Bureau of the Census, Data User Services Division, *1990 Census of Population and Housing, Equal Employment Opportunity File, CD-90-EE0-1, January 1993,* CD-ROM.

★1644★

Occupations, By Race/Sex

Top 25 MSAs For Employment As Respiratory Therapists, 1990: Women

MSA/CMSA	Employees per 100,000 pop.	Rank
Tampa – St. Petersburg – Clearwater, FL MSA	1,767	1
Chicago – Gary – Lake County, IL – IN – WI CMSA	1,465	2
New York – Northern New Jersey – Long Island, NY – NJ – CT CMSA	1,418	3
Detroit – Ann Arbor, MI CMSA	1,072	4
Philadelphia – Wilmington – Trenton, PA – NJ – DE – MD CMSA	954	5
San Francisco – Oakland – San Jose, CA CMSA	846	6
Miami – Fort Lauderdale, FL CMSA	784	7
Dallas – Fort Worth, TX CMSA	671	8
Atlanta, GA MSA	640	9
Houston – Galveston – Brazoria, TX CMSA	577	10
St. Louis, MO – IL MSA	563	11
Cleveland – Akron – Lorain, OH CMSA	562	12
Washington, DC – MD – VA MSA	554	13
Boston – Lawrence – Salem, MA – NH CMSA	550	14
San Diego, CA MSA	480	15
Phoenix, AZ MSA	458	16
Tampa – St. Petersburg – Clearwater, FL MSA	424	17
Minneapolis – St. Paul, MN – WI MSA	385	18
Denver – Boulder, CO CMSA	373	19
Indianapolis, IN MSA	372	20
Kansas City, MO – KS MSA	357	21
New Orleans, LA MSA	354	22
Seattle – Tacoma, WA CMSA	329	23
Pittsburgh – Beaver Valley, PA CMSA	324	24
Milwaukee – Racine, WI CMSA	300	25

Source: U.S. Department of Commerce, Bureau of the Census, Data User Services Division, *1990 Census of Population and Housing, Equal Employment Opportunity File, CD-90-EE0-1, January 1993,* CD-ROM.

★1645★

Occupations, By Race/Sex

Top 25 MSAs For Employment As Roofers, 1990: Men

MSA/CMSA	Employees per 100,000 pop.	Rank
Indianapolis, IN MSA	11,395	1
New York – Northern New Jersey – Long Island, NY – NJ – CT CMSA	8,227	2
Chicago – Gary – Lake County, IL – IN – WI CMSA	5,601	3
Philadelphia – Wilmington – Trenton, PA – NJ – DE – MD CMSA	4,987	4
San Francisco – Oakland – San Jose, CA CMSA	4,825	5
Dallas – Fort Worth, TX CMSA	4,577	6
Detroit – Ann Arbor, MI CMSA	3,497	7
Houston – Galveston – Brazoria, TX CMSA	3,203	8
Miami – Fort Lauderdale, FL CMSA	3,093	9
Atlanta, GA MSA	2,495	10
Washington, DC – MD – VA MSA	2,482	11
Cleveland – Akron – Lorain, OH CMSA	2,317	12
Boston – Lawrence – Salem, MA – NH CMSA	2,064	13
Phoenix, AZ MSA	2,035	14
San Diego, CA MSA	2,026	15
Tampa – St. Petersburg – Clearwater, FL MSA	1,907	16
Seattle – Tacoma, WA CMSA	1,879	17
Baltimore, MD MSA	1,845	18
Indianapolis, IN MSA	1,698	19
Pittsburgh – Beaver Valley, PA CMSA	1,658	20
St. Louis, MO – IL MSA	1,628	21
Charlotte – Gastonia – Rock Hill, NC – SC MSA	1,602	22
Minneapolis – St. Paul, MN – WI MSA	1,397	23
Cincinnati – Hamilton, OH – KY – IN CMSA	1,361	24
Sacramento, CA MSA	1,311	25

Source: U.S. Department of Commerce, Bureau of the Census, Data User Services Division, *1990 Census of Population and Housing, Equal Employment Opportunity File, CD-90-EE0-1, January 1993,* CD-ROM.

★1646★

Occupations, By Race/Sex

Top 25 MSAs For Employment As Roofers, 1990: Women

MSA/CMSA	Employees per 100,000 pop.	Rank
Tulsa, OK MSA	151	1
Dallas – Fort Worth, TX CMSA	117	2
Miami – Fort Lauderdale, FL CMSA	103	3
Houston – Galveston – Brazoria, TX CMSA	102	4
Philadelphia – Wilmington – Trenton, PA – NJ – DE – MD CMSA	97	5
New York – Northern New Jersey – Long Island, NY – NJ – CT CMSA	88	6
Cleveland – Akron – Lorain, OH CMSA	67	7
Atlanta, GA MSA	60	8
Boston – Lawrence – Salem, MA – NH CMSA	54	9
Chicago – Gary – Lake County, IL – IN – WI CMSA	54	9
Detroit – Ann Arbor, MI CMSA	54	9
Charleston, SC MSA	50	10
San Diego, CA MSA	44	11
San Francisco – Oakland – San Jose, CA CMSA	41	12
Washington, DC – MD – VA MSA	40	13
Tampa – St. Petersburg – Clearwater, FL MSA	36	14
Charlotte – Gastonia – Rock Hill, NC – SC MSA	32	15
Raleigh – Durham, NC MSA	30	16
Orlando, FL MSA	29	17
Baton Rouge, LA MSA	26	18
Kansas City, MO – KS MSA	26	18
Birmingham, AL MSA	25	19
Austin, TX MSA	24	20
Columbus, OH MSA	24	20
Indianapolis, IN MSA	24	20

Source: U.S. Department of Commerce, Bureau of the Census, Data User Services Division, *1990 Census of Population and Housing, Equal Employment Opportunity File,* CD-90-EE0-1, January 1993, CD-ROM.

★1647★

Occupations, By Race/Sex

Top 25 MSAs For Employment As Sailors and Deckhands, 1990: Men

MSA/CMSA	Employees per 100,000 pop.	Rank
Louisville, KY – IN MSA	1,449	1
New York – Northern New Jersey – Long Island, NY – NJ – CT CMSA	1,376	2
Los Angeles – Anaheim – Riverside, CA CMSA	1,053	3
Houston – Galveston – Brazoria, TX CMSA	984	4
San Francisco – Oakland – San Jose, CA CMSA	895	5
Houma – Thibodaux, LA MSA	878	6
Seattle – Tacoma, WA CMSA	868	7
Norfolk – Virginia Beach – Newport News, VA MSA	558	8
Miami – Fort Lauderdale, FL CMSA	499	9
Mobile, AL MSA	469	10
Jacksonville, FL MSA	416	11
Tampa – St. Petersburg – Clearwater, FL MSA	396	12
St. Louis, MO – IL MSA	344	13
San Diego, CA MSA	281	14
Beaumont – Port Arthur, TX MSA	272	15
Baltimore, MD MSA	263	16
Boston – Lawrence – Salem, MA – NH CMSA	251	17
Lake Charles, LA MSA	243	18
Pittsburgh – Beaver Valley, PA CMSA	240	19
Philadelphia – Wilmington – Trenton, PA – NJ – DE – MD CMSA	235	20
Biloxi – Gulfport, MS MSA	226	21
Baton Rouge, LA MSA	213	22
Detroit – Ann Arbor, MI CMSA	213	22
Portland – Vancouver, OR – WA CMSA	194	23
Charleston, SC MSA	186	24

Source: U.S. Department of Commerce, Bureau of the Census, Data User Services Division, *1990 Census of Population and Housing, Equal Employment Opportunity File,* CD-90-EE0-1, January 1993, CD-ROM.

★1648★

Occupations, By Race/Sex

Top 25 MSAs For Employment As Sailors and Deckhands, 1990: Women

MSA/CMSA	Employees per 100,000 pop.	Rank
Amarillo, TX MSA	92	1
Los Angeles – Anaheim – Riverside, CA CMSA	88	2
Houston – Galveston – Brazoria, TX CMSA	56	3
New York – Northern New Jersey – Long Island, NY – NJ – CT CMSA	54	4
San Francisco – Oakland – San Jose, CA CMSA	38	5
Tampa – St. Petersburg – Clearwater, FL MSA	30	6
New Orleans, LA MSA	28	7
Mobile, AL MSA	27	8
Jacksonville, FL MSA	25	9
Houma – Thibodaux, LA MSA	20	10
Miami – Fort Lauderdale, FL CMSA	19	11
Chicago – Gary – Lake County, IL – IN – WI CMSA	17	12
Louisville, KY – IN MSA	16	13
Norfolk – Virginia Beach – Newport News, VA MSA	16	13
San Diego, CA MSA	16	13
Pensacola, FL MSA	13	14
St. Louis, MO – IL MSA	12	15
Baltimore, MD MSA	10	16
Fort Myers – Cape CoraL, Fl MSA	10	16
Daytona Beach, FL MSA	9	17
Greenville – Spartanburg, SC MSA	9	17
Portland – Vancouver, OR – WA CMSA	9	17
Topeka, KS MSA	9	17
Atlantic City, NJ MSA	8	18
Boston – Lawrence – Salem, MA – NH CMSA	8	18

Source: U.S. Department of Commerce, Bureau of the Census, Data User Services Division, *1990 Census of Population and Housing, Equal Employment Opportunity File, CD-90-EE0-1, January 1993,* CD-ROM.

★1649★

Occupations, By Race/Sex

Top 25 MSAs For Employment As Sheriffs, Bailiffs, and Other Law Enforcement Officers, 1990: Men

MSA/CMSA	Employees per 100,000 pop.	Rank
Sacramento, CA MSA	6,905	1
New York – Northern New Jersey – Long Island, NY – NJ – CT CMSA	4,286	2
San Francisco – Oakland – San Jose, CA CMSA	2,653	3
Chicago – Gary – Lake County, IL – IN – WI CMSA	2,091	4
Washington, DC – MD – VA MSA	2,075	5
Tampa – St. Petersburg – Clearwater, FL MSA	1,592	6
Atlanta, GA MSA	1,494	7
Houston – Galveston – Brazoria, TX CMSA	1,389	8
Philadelphia – Wilmington – Trenton, PA – NJ – DE – MD CMSA	1,354	9
Detroit – Ann Arbor, MI CMSA	1,157	10
Dallas – Fort Worth, TX CMSA	1,147	11
Miami – Fort Lauderdale, FL CMSA	1,117	12
New Orleans, LA MSA	1,111	13
Sacramento, CA MSA	1,077	14
Boston – Lawrence – Salem, MA – NH CMSA	1,033	15
San Diego, CA MSA	980	16
Denver – Boulder, CO CMSA	929	17
Baltimore, MD MSA	858	18
Cleveland – Akron – Lorain, OH CMSA	812	19
West Palm Beach – Boca Raton – Delray Beach, FL MSA	757	20
Minneapolis – St. Paul, MN – WI MSA	737	21
Cincinnati – Hamilton, OH – KY – IN CMSA	731	22
Phoenix, AZ MSA	705	23
Milwaukee – Racine, WI CMSA	673	24
Norfolk – Virginia Beach – Newport News, VA MSA	672	25

Source: U.S. Department of Commerce, Bureau of the Census, Data User Services Division, *1990 Census of Population and Housing, Equal Employment Opportunity File, CD-90-EE0-1, January 1993,* CD-ROM.

★1650★
Occupations, By Race/Sex

Top 25 MSAs For Employment As Sheriffs, Bailiffs, and Other Law Enforcement Officers, 1990: Women

MSA/CMSA	Employees per 100,000 pop.	Rank
Pittsburgh – Beaver Valley, PA CMSA	1,778	1
New York – Northern New Jersey – Long Island, NY – NJ – CT CMSA	1,163	2
San Francisco – Oakland – San Jose, CA CMSA	876	3
Chicago – Gary – Lake County, IL – IN – WI CMSA	752	4
Washington, DC – MD – VA MSA	725	5
Miami – Fort Lauderdale, FL CMSA	464	6
Philadelphia – Wilmington – Trenton, PA – NJ – DE – MD CMSA	429	7
Atlanta, GA MSA	380	8
Detroit – Ann Arbor, MI CMSA	366	9
Tampa – St. Petersburg – Clearwater, FL MSA	345	10
Dallas – Fort Worth, TX CMSA	320	11
San Diego, CA MSA	306	12
Houston – Galveston – Brazoria, TX CMSA	289	13
New Orleans, LA MSA	263	14
Portland – Vancouver, OR – WA CMSA	245	15
Phoenix, AZ MSA	236	16
Denver – Boulder, CO CMSA	216	17
Baltimore, MD MSA	209	18
Sacramento, CA MSA	208	19
Norfolk – Virginia Beach – Newport News, VA MSA	206	20
Memphis, TN – AR – MS MSA	204	21
Boston – Lawrence – Salem, MA – NH CMSA	190	22
Cleveland – Akron – Lorain, OH CMSA	184	23
Minneapolis – St. Paul, MN – WI MSA	182	24
Seattle – Tacoma, WA CMSA	174	25

Source: U.S. Department of Commerce, Bureau of the Census, Data User Services Division, *1990 Census of Population and Housing, Equal Employment Opportunity File, CD-90-EE0-1, January 1993,* CD-ROM.

★1651★
Occupations, By Race/Sex

Top 25 MSAs For Employment As Social Work Teachers, 1990: Men

MSA/CMSA	Employees per 100,000 pop.	Rank
Tampa – St. Petersburg – Clearwater, FL MSA	20	1
New York – Northern New Jersey – Long Island, NY – NJ – CT CMSA	12	2
Washington, DC – MD – VA MSA	10	3
Baltimore, MD MSA	8	4
Boston – Lawrence – Salem, MA – NH CMSA	8	4
Charlotte – Gastonia – Rock Hill, NC – SC MSA	7	5
Richmond – Petersburg, VA MSA	7	5
Springfield, MA MSA	7	5
Lawrence, KS MSA	7	5
Los Angeles – Anaheim – Riverside, CA CMSA	7	5
Hartford – New Britain – Middletown, CT CMSA	5	6
Melbourne – Titusville – Palm Bay, FL MSA	5	6
Abilene, TX MSA	0	7
Albany, GA MSA	0	7
Albany – Schenectady – Troy, NY MSA	0	7
Albuquerque, NM MSA	0	7
Alexandria, LA MSA	0	7
Allentown – Bethlehem – Easton, PA – NJ MSA	0	7
Altoona, PA MSA	0	7
Amarillo, TX MSA	0	7
Anchorage, AK MSA	0	7
Anderson, IN MSA	0	7
Anderson, SC MSA	0	7
Anniston, AL MSA	0	7
Appleton – Oshkosh – Neenah, WI MSA	0	7

Source: U.S. Department of Commerce, Bureau of the Census, Data User Services Division, *1990 Census of Population and Housing, Equal Employment Opportunity File, CD-90-EE0-1, January 1993,* CD-ROM.

★1652★
Occupations, By Race/Sex

Top 25 MSAs For Employment As Social Work Teachers, 1990: Women

MSA/CMSA	Employees per 100,000 pop.	Rank
Cincinnati – Hamilton, OH – KY – IN CMSA	29	1
Boston – Lawrence – Salem, MA – NH CMSA	23	2
Chicago – Gary – Lake County, IL – IN – WI CMSA	19	3
Buffalo – Niagara Falls, NY CMSA	17	4

[Continued]

★1652★

Top 25 MSAs For Employment As Social Work Teachers, 1990: Women
[Continued]

704X

Employees per	100,000 pop.	Rank
Modesto, CA MSA	11	5
Washington, DC – MD – VA MSA	11	5
Reading, PA MSA	8	6
Seattle – Tacoma, WA CMSA	8	6
Harrisburg – Lebanon – Carlisle, PA MSA	7	7
Nashville, TN MSA	7	7
Portland, ME MSA	7	7
Springfield, MA MSA	7	7
Anchorage, AK MSA	6	8
Baton Rouge, LA MSA	6	8
Knoxville, TN MSA	6	8
Columbus, OH MSA	5	9
Minneapolis – St. Paul, MN – WI MSA	2	10
Albany – Schenectady – Troy, NY MSA	0	11
Alexandria, LA MSA	0	11
Allentown – Bethlehem – Easton, PA – NJ MSA	0	11
Albuquerque, NM MSA	0	11
Anderson, IN MSA	0	11
Amarillo, TX MSA	0	11
Albany, GA MSA	0	11
Abilene, TX MSA	0	11

Source: U.S. Department of Commerce, Bureau of the Census, Data User Services Division, *1990 Census of Population and Housing, Equal Employment Opportunity File, CD-90-EE0-1,* January 1993, CD-ROM.

★1653★

Occupations, By Race/Sex

Top 25 MSAs For Employment As Social Workers, 1990: Men

MSA/CMSA	Employees per 100,000 pop.	Rank
Dayton – Springfield, OH MSA	22,786	1
Los Angeles – Anaheim – Riverside, CA CMSA	10,906	2
Chicago – Gary – Lake County, IL – IN – WI CMSA	6,578	3
San Francisco – Oakland – San Jose, CA CMSA	6,145	4
Philadelphia – Wilmington – Trenton, PA – NJ – DE – MD CMSA	6,121	5
Boston – Lawrence – Salem, MA – NH CMSA	4,386	6
Detroit – Ann Arbor, MI CMSA	3,910	7
Washington, DC – MD – VA MSA	3,146	8
Minneapolis – St. Paul, MN – WI MSA	2,806	9
Seattle – Tacoma, WA CMSA	2,421	10
Dallas – Fort Worth, TX CMSA	2,413	11

[Continued]

★1653★

Top 25 MSAs For Employment As Social Workers, 1990: Men
[Continued]

MSA/CMSA	Employees per 100,000 pop.	Rank
Miami – Fort Lauderdale, FL CMSA	2,253	12
Pittsburgh – Beaver Valley, PA CMSA	2,228	13
Cleveland – Akron – Lorain, OH CMSA	2,137	14
Baltimore, MD MSA	2,115	15
San Diego, CA MSA	2,077	16
St. Louis, MO – IL MSA	1,927	17
Houston – Galveston – Brazoria, TX CMSA	1,910	18
Atlanta, GA MSA	1,731	19
Tampa – St. Petersburg – Clearwater, FL MSA	1,702	20
Phoenix, AZ MSA	1,691	21
Sacramento, CA MSA	1,687	22
Buffalo – Niagara Falls, NY CMSA	1,525	23
Milwaukee – Racine, WI CMSA	1,521	24
Denver – Boulder, CO CMSA	1,468	25

Source: U.S. Department of Commerce, Bureau of the Census, Data User Services Division, *1990 Census of Population and Housing, Equal Employment Opportunity File, CD-90-EE0-1,* January 1993, CD-ROM.

★1654★

Occupations, By Race/Sex

Top 25 MSAs For Employment As Social Workers, 1990: Women

MSA/CMSA	Employees per 100,000 pop.	Rank
Raleigh – Durham, NC MSA	50,805	1
Los Angeles – Anaheim – Riverside, CA CMSA	19,655	2
Chicago – Gary – Lake County, IL – IN – WI CMSA	16,021	3
Philadelphia – Wilmington – Trenton, PA – NJ – DE – MD CMSA	14,317	4
Boston – Lawrence – Salem, MA – NH CMSA	11,340	5
San Francisco – Oakland – San Jose, CA CMSA	10,475	6
Detroit – Ann Arbor, MI CMSA	10,283	7
Washington, DC – MD – VA MSA	8,150	8
Baltimore, MD MSA	6,563	9
Minneapolis – St. Paul, MN – WI MSA	6,179	10
Cleveland – Akron – Lorain, OH CMSA	5,387	11
St. Louis, MO – IL MSA	4,800	12
Seattle – Tacoma, WA CMSA	4,670	13
Pittsburgh – Beaver Valley, PA CMSA	4,507	14
Dallas – Fort Worth, TX CMSA	4,398	15

[Continued]

★1654★

Top 25 MSAs For Employment As Social Workers, 1990: Women
[Continued]

MSA/CMSA	Employees per 100,000 pop.	Rank
Houston – Galveston – Brazoria, TX CMSA	4,261	16
Atlanta, GA MSA	4,249	17
San Diego, CA MSA	4,246	18
Miami – Fort Lauderdale, FL CMSA	4,230	19
Denver – Boulder, CO CMSA	3,555	20
Cincinnati – Hamilton, OH – KY – IN CMSA	3,473	21
Phoenix, AZ MSA	3,111	22
Tampa – St. Petersburg – Clearwater, FL MSA	3,066	23
Buffalo – Niagara Falls, NY CMSA	3,064	24
Kansas City, MO – KS MSA	2,913	25

Source: U.S. Department of Commerce, Bureau of the Census, Data User Services Division, *1990 Census of Population and Housing, Equal Employment Opportunity File, CD-90-EE0-1, January 1993,* CD-ROM.

★1655★

Occupations, By Race/Sex

Top 25 MSAs For Employment As Sociologists, 1990: Men

MSA/CMSA	Employees per 100,000 pop.	Rank
Kansas City, MO – KS MSA	97	1
Los Angeles – Anaheim – Riverside, CA CMSA	86	2
New York – Northern New Jersey – Long Island, NY – NJ – CT CMSA	73	3
Boston – Lawrence – Salem, MA – NH CMSA	50	4
Raleigh – Durham, NC MSA	38	5
Columbia, SC MSA	35	6
Tucson, AZ MSA	29	7
Detroit – Ann Arbor, MI CMSA	26	8
Sacramento, CA MSA	23	9
Madison, WI MSA	23	9
Baltimore, MD MSA	21	10
Philadelphia – Wilmington – Trenton, PA – NJ – DE – MD CMSA	21	10
Phoenix, AZ MSA	21	10
Honolulu, HI MSA	20	11
Providence – Pawtucket – Fall River, RI – MA CMSA	20	11
Santa Barbara – Santa Maria – Lompoc, CA MSA	19	12
San Francisco – Oakland – San Jose, CA CMSA	18	13
Denver – Boulder, CO CMSA	17	14
Miami – Fort Lauderdale, FL CMSA	17	14

[Continued]

★1655★

Top 25 MSAs For Employment As Sociologists, 1990: Men
[Continued]

MSA/CMSA	Employees per 100,000 pop.	Rank
Salinas – Seaside – Monterey, CA MSA	16	15
Salt Lake City – Ogden, UT MSA	15	16
Binghamton, NY MSA	14	17
Louisville, KY – IN MSA	14	17
Charlottesville, VA MSA	13	18
Chicago – Gary – Lake County, IL – IN – WI CMSA	13	18

Source: U.S. Department of Commerce, Bureau of the Census, Data User Services Division, *1990 Census of Population and Housing, Equal Employment Opportunity File, CD-90-EE0-1, January 1993,* CD-ROM.

★1656★

Occupations, By Race/Sex

Top 25 MSAs For Employment As Sociologists, 1990: Women

MSA/CMSA	Employees per 100,000 pop.	Rank
Providence – Pawtucket – Fall River, RI – MA CMSA	82	1
Los Angeles – Anaheim – Riverside, CA CMSA	78	2
Rochester, NY MSA	57	3
Washington, DC – MD – VA MSA	56	4
Chicago – Gary – Lake County, IL – IN – WI CMSA	50	5
Boston – Lawrence – Salem, MA – NH CMSA	42	6
Baltimore, MD MSA	38	7
Denver – Boulder, CO CMSA	33	8
San Francisco – Oakland – San Jose, CA CMSA	32	9
Philadelphia – Wilmington – Trenton, PA – NJ – DE – MD CMSA	22	10
Minneapolis – St. Paul, MN – WI MSA	21	11
Tucson, AZ MSA	20	12
Salt Lake City – Ogden, UT MSA	19	13
Kansas City, MO – KS MSA	18	14
Raleigh – Durham, NC MSA	18	14
San Diego, CA MSA	18	14
Seattle – Tacoma, WA CMSA	18	14
Augusta, GA – SC MSA	17	15
Dallas – Fort Worth, TX CMSA	15	16
Dayton – Springfield, OH MSA	15	16
Phoenix, AZ MSA	15	16
Bakersfield, CA MSA	14	17
Columbus, OH MSA	14	17
Lawrence, KS MSA	13	18
Norfolk – Virginia Beach – Newport News, VA MSA	12	19

Source: U.S. Department of Commerce, Bureau of the Census, Data User Services Division, *1990 Census of Population and Housing, Equal Employment Opportunity File, CD-90-EE0-1, January 1993,* CD-ROM.

★1657★

Occupations, By Race/Sex

Top 25 MSAs For Employment As Sociology Teachers, 1990: Men

MSA/CMSA	Employees per 100,000 pop.	Rank
Jamestown – Dunkirk, NY	53	1
New York – Northern New Jersey – Long Island, NY – NJ – CT CMSA	44	2
San Diego, CA MSA	24	3
Los Angeles – Anaheim – Riverside, CA CMSA	20	4
Chicago – Gary – Lake County, IL – IN – WI CMSA	18	5
Reno, NV MSA	17	6
Providence – Pawtucket – Fall River, RI – MA CMSA	16	7
Columbia, SC MSA	16	7
Boston – Lawrence – Salem, MA – NH CMSA	15	8
Minneapolis – St. Paul, MN – WI MSA	14	9
Sacramento, CA MSA	14	9
Syracuse, NY MSA	13	10
Toledo, OH MSA	13	10
Atlanta, GA MSA	13	10
Harrisburg – Lebanon – Carlisle, PA MSA	11	11
Bakersfield, CA MSA	11	11
Melbourne – Titusville – Palm Bay, FL MSA	10	12
Johnson City – Kingsport – Bristol, TN – VA MSA	10	12
Raleigh – Durham, NC MSA	9	13
Rochester, NY MSA	9	13
Salt Lake City – Ogden, UT MSA	9	13
Springfield, MA MSA	9	13
Gainesville, FL MSA	9	13
Burlington, NC MSA	9	13
Cleveland – Akron – Lorain, OH CMSA	9	13

Source: U.S. Department of Commerce, Bureau of the Census, Data User Services Division, *1990 Census of Population and Housing, Equal Employment Opportunity File, CD-90-EE0-1, January 1993*, CD-ROM.

★1658★

Occupations, By Race/Sex

Top 25 MSAs For Employment As Sociology Teachers, 1990: Women

MSA/CMSA	Employees per 100,000 pop.	Rank
Abilene, TX MSA	44	1
New York – Northern New Jersey – Long Island, NY – NJ – CT CMSA	29	2
San Francisco – Oakland – San Jose, CA CMSA	23	3
West Palm Beach – Boca Raton – Delray Beach, FL MSA	21	4

[Continued]

★1658★

Top 25 MSAs For Employment As Sociology Teachers, 1990: Women
[Continued]

MSA/CMSA	Employees per 100,000 pop.	Rank
Washington, DC – MD – VA MSA	15	5
Greenville – Spartanburg, SC MSA	13	6
Minneapolis – St. Paul, MN – WI MSA	13	6
Boston – Lawrence – Salem, MA – NH CMSA	12	7
Atlanta, GA MSA	11	8
Columbia, SC MSA	10	9
Eau Claire, WI MSA	10	9
Raleigh – Durham, NC MSA	10	9
Seattle – Tacoma, WA CMSA	10	9
Albany – Schenectady – Troy, NY MSA	8	10
Denver – Boulder, CO CMSA	8	10
Huntington – Ashland, WV – KY – OH MSA	8	10
Lawrence, KS MSA	8	10
San Diego, CA MSA	8	10
Tallahassee, FL MSA	8	10
Worcester, MA MSA	8	10
Baltimore, MD MSA	7	11
Champaign – Urbana – Rantoul, IL MSA	7	11
Cleveland – Akron – Lorain, OH CMSA	7	11
Detroit – Ann Arbor, MI CMSA	7	11
Grand Forks, ND MSA	7	11

Source: U.S. Department of Commerce, Bureau of the Census, Data User Services Division, *1990 Census of Population and Housing, Equal Employment Opportunity File, CD-90-EE0-1, January 1993*, CD-ROM.

★1659★

Occupations, By Race/Sex

Top 25 MSAs For Employment As Solderers and Brazers, 1990: Men

MSA/CMSA	Employees per 100,000 pop.	Rank
Tampa – St. Petersburg – Clearwater, FL MSA	1,746	1
New York – Northern New Jersey – Long Island, NY – NJ – CT CMSA	664	2
Chicago – Gary – Lake County, IL – IN – WI CMSA	499	3
Boston – Lawrence – Salem, MA – NH CMSA	296	4
San Francisco – Oakland – San Jose, CA CMSA	243	5
Dallas – Fort Worth, TX CMSA	209	6
Phoenix, AZ MSA	191	7
Miami – Fort Lauderdale, FL CMSA	149	8

[Continued]

★1659★

Top 25 MSAs For Employment As Solderers and Brazers, 1990: Men
[Continued]

MSA/CMSA	Employees per 100,000 pop.	Rank
Cleveland – Akron – Lorain, OH CMSA	142	9
Philadelphia – Wilmington – Trenton, PA – NJ – DE – MD CMSA	135	10
Columbus, OH MSA	133	11
Providence – Pawtucket – Fall River, RI – MA CMSA	120	12
Detroit – Ann Arbor, MI CMSA	114	13
Houston – Galveston – Brazoria, TX CMSA	112	14
San Diego, CA MSA	104	15
Minneapolis – St. Paul, MN – WI MSA	102	16
Milwaukee – Racine, WI CMSA	94	17
Seattle – Tacoma, WA CMSA	92	18
Tampa – St. Petersburg – Clearwater, FL MSA	91	19
Fort Wayne, IN MSA	88	20
Austin, TX MSA	65	21
Portland – Vancouver, OR – WA CMSA	63	22
Oklahoma City, OK MSA	60	23
Binghamton, NY MSA	60	23
Rochester, NY MSA	59	24

Source: U.S. Department of Commerce, Bureau of the Census, Data User Services Division, *1990 Census of Population and Housing, Equal Employment Opportunity File, CD-90-EE0-1, January 1993*, CD-ROM.

★1660★
Occupations, By Race/Sex

Top 25 MSAs For Employment As Solderers and Brazers, 1990: Women

MSA/CMSA	Employees per 100,000 pop.	Rank
Houston – Galveston – Brazoria, TX CMSA	1,356	1
New York – Northern New Jersey – Long Island, NY – NJ – CT CMSA	1,191	2
Chicago – Gary – Lake County, IL – IN – WI CMSA	964	3
Boston – Lawrence – Salem, MA – NH CMSA	956	4
Philadelphia – Wilmington – Trenton, PA – NJ – DE – MD CMSA	612	5
San Francisco – Oakland – San Jose, CA CMSA	462	6
Tampa – St. Petersburg – Clearwater, FL MSA	363	7
Dallas – Fort Worth, TX CMSA	334	8
Minneapolis – St. Paul, MN – WI MSA	286	9

[Continued]

★1660★

Top 25 MSAs For Employment As Solderers and Brazers, 1990: Women
[Continued]

MSA/CMSA	Employees per 100,000 pop.	Rank
Binghamton, NY MSA	271	10
Providence – Pawtucket – Fall River, RI – MA CMSA	267	11
Phoenix, AZ MSA	220	12
Huntsville, AL MSA	201	13
Fort Wayne, IN MSA	198	14
Cleveland – Akron – Lorain, OH CMSA	196	15
Hartford – New Britain – Middletown, CT CMSA	182	16
Lancaster, PA MSA	179	17
Detroit – Ann Arbor, MI CMSA	175	18
Miami – Fort Lauderdale, FL CMSA	169	19
Rochester, NY MSA	161	20
Orlando, FL MSA	154	21
Cincinnati – Hamilton, OH – KY – IN CMSA	142	22
San Diego, CA MSA	134	23
Milwaukee – Racine, WI CMSA	129	24
Denver – Boulder, CO CMSA	120	25

Source: U.S. Department of Commerce, Bureau of the Census, Data User Services Division, *1990 Census of Population and Housing, Equal Employment Opportunity File, CD-90-EE0-1, January 1993*, CD-ROM.

★1661★
Occupations, By Race/Sex

Top 25 MSAs For Employment As Speech Therapists, 1990: Men

MSA/CMSA	Employees per 100,000 pop.	Rank
Cincinnati – Hamilton, OH – KY – IN CMSA	393	1
Los Angeles – Anaheim – Riverside, CA CMSA	265	2
Chicago – Gary – Lake County, IL – IN – WI CMSA	181	3
San Francisco – Oakland – San Jose, CA CMSA	145	4
Philadelphia – Wilmington – Trenton, PA – NJ – DE – MD CMSA	113	5
Dallas – Fort Worth, TX CMSA	111	6
Minneapolis – St. Paul, MN – WI MSA	110	7
Portland – Vancouver, OR – WA CMSA	98	8
Salt Lake City – Ogden, UT MSA	95	9
Boston – Lawrence – Salem, MA – NH CMSA	93	10
Milwaukee – Racine, WI CMSA	80	11
San Diego, CA MSA	76	12
Seattle – Tacoma, WA CMSA	68	13

[Continued]

★1661★

Top 25 MSAs For Employment As Speech Therapists, 1990: Men

[Continued]

MSA/CMSA	Employees per 100,000 pop.	Rank
Houston – Galveston – Brazoria, TX CMSA	68	13
St. Louis, MO – IL MSA	66	14
Pittsburgh – Beaver Valley, PA CMSA	61	15
Miami – Fort Lauderdale, FL CMSA	60	16
Detroit – Ann Arbor, MI CMSA	58	17
Phoenix, AZ MSA	56	18
Denver – Boulder, CO CMSA	55	19
Nashville, TN MSA	52	20
Cleveland – Akron – Lorain, OH CMSA	52	20
San Antonio, TX MSA	50	21
Norfolk – Virginia Beach – Newport News, VA MSA	47	22
Jacksonville, FL MSA	44	23

Source: U.S. Department of Commerce, Bureau of the Census, Data User Services Division, *1990 Census of Population and Housing, Equal Employment Opportunity File,* CD-90-EE0-1, January 1993, CD-ROM.

★1662★

Occupations, By Race/Sex

Top 25 MSAs For Employment As Speech Therapists, 1990: Women

MSA/CMSA	Employees per 100,000 pop.	Rank
Kansas City, MO – KS MSA	5,223	1
Los Angeles – Anaheim – Riverside, CA CMSA	2,340	2
Chicago – Gary – Lake County, IL – IN – WI CMSA	2,241	3
Philadelphia – Wilmington – Trenton, PA – NJ – DE – MD CMSA	1,805	4
Boston – Lawrence – Salem, MA – NH CMSA	1,395	5
San Francisco – Oakland – San Jose, CA CMSA	1,357	6
Washington, DC – MD – VA MSA	1,238	7
Detroit – Ann Arbor, MI CMSA	1,005	8
Dallas – Fort Worth, TX CMSA	901	9
Houston – Galveston – Brazoria, TX CMSA	784	10
Minneapolis – St. Paul, MN – WI MSA	783	11
Cleveland – Akron – Lorain, OH CMSA	726	12
Pittsburgh – Beaver Valley, PA CMSA	700	13
Baltimore, MD MSA	694	14
St. Louis, MO – IL MSA	683	15
Seattle – Tacoma, WA CMSA	629	16

[Continued]

★1662★

Top 25 MSAs For Employment As Speech Therapists, 1990: Women

[Continued]

MSA/CMSA	Employees per 100,000 pop.	Rank
Cincinnati – Hamilton, OH – KY – IN CMSA	603	17
San Diego, CA MSA	596	18
Atlanta, GA MSA	595	19
Denver – Boulder, CO CMSA	591	20
Milwaukee – Racine, WI CMSA	577	21
Miami – Fort Lauderdale, FL CMSA	577	21
Buffalo – Niagara Falls, NY CMSA	549	22
Phoenix, AZ MSA	491	23
Kansas City, MO – KS MSA	464	24

Source: U.S. Department of Commerce, Bureau of the Census, Data User Services Division, *1990 Census of Population and Housing, Equal Employment Opportunity File,* CD-90-EE0-1, January 1993, CD-ROM.

★1663★

Occupations, By Race/Sex

Top 25 MSAs For Employment As Statisticians, 1990: Men

MSA/CMSA	Employees per 100,000 pop.	Rank
Rochester, NY MSA	1,880	1
New York – Northern New Jersey – Long Island, NY – NJ – CT CMSA	1,684	2
Chicago – Gary – Lake County, IL – IN – WI CMSA	693	3
Philadelphia – Wilmington – Trenton, PA – NJ – DE – MD CMSA	643	4
San Francisco – Oakland – San Jose, CA CMSA	509	5
Boston – Lawrence – Salem, MA – NH CMSA	495	6
Detroit – Ann Arbor, MI CMSA	472	7
Los Angeles – Anaheim – Riverside, CA CMSA	471	8
Baltimore, MD MSA	467	9
Raleigh – Durham, NC MSA	274	10
Atlanta, GA MSA	237	11
Seattle – Tacoma, WA CMSA	235	12
Denver – Boulder, CO CMSA	187	13
Dallas – Fort Worth, TX CMSA	183	14
Albany – Schenectady – Troy, NY MSA	170	15
Minneapolis – St. Paul, MN – WI MSA	168	16
Hartford – New Britain – Middletown, CT CMSA	166	17
St. Louis, MO – IL MSA	166	17
Kansas City, MO – KS MSA	157	18
Harrisburg – Lebanon – Carlisle, PA MSA	142	19

[Continued]

★ 1663 ★

Top 25 MSAs For Employment As Statisticians, 1990: Men
[Continued]

MSA/CMSA	Employees per 100,000 pop.	Rank
Cincinnati – Hamilton, OH – KY – IN CMSA	133	20
Indianapolis, IN MSA	133	20
Houston – Galveston – Brazoria, TX CMSA	132	21
Buffalo – Niagara Falls, NY CMSA	126	22
Cleveland – Akron – Lorain, OH CMSA	121	23

Source: U.S. Department of Commerce, Bureau of the Census, Data User Services Division, *1990 Census of Population and Housing, Equal Employment Opportunity File, CD-90-EE0-1, January 1993,* CD-ROM.

★ 1664 ★
Occupations, By Race/Sex

Top 25 MSAs For Employment As Statisticians, 1990: Women

MSA/CMSA	Employees per 100,000 pop.	Rank
Milwaukee – Racine, WI CMSA	1,679	1
Washington, DC – MD – VA MSA	1,499	2
Los Angeles – Anaheim – Riverside, CA CMSA	626	3
Philadelphia – Wilmington – Trenton, PA – NJ – DE – MD CMSA	612	4
Chicago – Gary – Lake County, IL – IN – WI CMSA	594	5
San Francisco – Oakland – San Jose, CA CMSA	539	6
Boston – Lawrence – Salem, MA – NH CMSA	464	7
Dallas – Fort Worth, TX CMSA	441	8
Hartford – New Britain – Middletown, CT CMSA	404	9
Detroit – Ann Arbor, MI CMSA	373	10
Baltimore, MD MSA	366	11
Denver – Boulder, CO CMSA	262	12
Raleigh – Durham, NC MSA	248	13
Columbus, OH MSA	204	14
Houston – Galveston – Brazoria, TX CMSA	195	15
Minneapolis – St. Paul, MN – WI MSA	191	16
Atlanta, GA MSA	188	17
San Diego, CA MSA	182	18
Seattle – Tacoma, WA CMSA	175	19
Richmond – Petersburg, VA MSA	156	20
St. Louis, MO – IL MSA	149	21
Indianapolis, IN MSA	138	22
Miami – Fort Lauderdale, FL CMSA	135	23

[Continued]

★ 1664 ★

Top 25 MSAs For Employment As Statisticians, 1990: Women
[Continued]

MSA/CMSA	Employees per 100,000 pop.	Rank
Austin, TX MSA	129	24
Pittsburgh – Beaver Valley, PA CMSA	128	25

Source: U.S. Department of Commerce, Bureau of the Census, Data User Services Division, *1990 Census of Population and Housing, Equal Employment Opportunity File, CD-90-EE0-1, January 1993,* CD-ROM.

★ 1665 ★
Occupations, By Race/Sex

Top 25 MSAs For Employment As Stevedores, 1990: Men

MSA/CMSA	Employees per 100,000 pop.	Rank
Honolulu, HI MSA	1,583	1
New York – Northern New Jersey – Long Island, NY – NJ – CT CMSA	1,466	2
Seattle – Tacoma, WA CMSA	736	3
Houston – Galveston – Brazoria, TX CMSA	558	4
Philadelphia – Wilmington – Trenton, PA – NJ – DE – MD CMSA	490	5
Baltimore, MD MSA	432	6
San Francisco – Oakland – San Jose, CA CMSA	430	7
Norfolk – Virginia Beach – Newport News, VA MSA	420	8
New Orleans, LA MSA	385	9
Miami – Fort Lauderdale, FL CMSA	380	10
Portland – Vancouver, OR – WA CMSA	287	11
Savannah, GA MSA	188	12
Charleston, SC MSA	162	13
Lake Charles, LA MSA	158	14
Chicago – Gary – Lake County, IL – IN – WI CMSA	154	15
Honolulu, HI MSA	137	16
San Diego, CA MSA	127	17
Beaumont – Port Arthur, TX MSA	125	18
Jacksonville, FL MSA	118	19
Baton Rouge, LA MSA	87	20
Boston – Lawrence – Salem, MA – NH CMSA	83	21
Tampa – St. Petersburg – Clearwater, FL MSA	77	22
New Haven – Meriden, CT MSA	76	23
Mobile, AL MSA	70	24
Fort Pierce, FL MSA	59	25

Source: U.S. Department of Commerce, Bureau of the Census, Data User Services Division, *1990 Census of Population and Housing, Equal Employment Opportunity File, CD-90-EE0-1, January 1993,* CD-ROM.

★ 1666 ★

Occupations, By Race/Sex

Top 25 MSAs For Employment As Stevedores, 1990: Women

MSA/CMSA	Employees per 100,000 pop.	Rank
Mansfield, OH MSA	94	1
New York – Northern New Jersey – Long Island, NY – NJ – CT CMSA	38	2
Baltimore, MD MSA	31	3
San Francisco – Oakland – San Jose, CA CMSA	15	4
Fort Pierce, FL MSA	13	5
Houston – Galveston – Brazoria, TX CMSA	13	5
Miami – Fort Lauderdale, FL CMSA	13	5
Anchorage, AK MSA	12	6
New Orleans, LA MSA	12	6
Jacksonville, FL MSA	10	7
Providence – Pawtucket – Fall River, RI – MA CMSA	10	7
Philadelphia – Wilmington – Trenton, PA – NJ – DE – MD CMSA	9	8
Pittsburgh – Beaver Valley, PA CMSA	7	9
Knoxville, TN MSA	6	10
Norfolk – Virginia Beach – Newport News, VA MSA	6	10
Salinas – Seaside – Monterey, CA MSA	6	10
Seattle – Tacoma, WA CMSA	6	10
St. Louis, MO – IL MSA	5	11
Greeley, CO MSA	3	12
Brownsville – Harlingen, TX MSA	2	13
Altoona, PA MSA	0	14
Amarillo, TX MSA	0	14
Albany – Schenectady – Troy, NY MSA	0	14
Abilene, TX MSA	0	14
Alexandria, LA MSA	0	14

Source: U.S. Department of Commerce, Bureau of the Census, Data User Services Division, *1990 Census of Population and Housing, Equal Employment Opportunity File, CD-90-EE0-1*, January 1993, CD-ROM.

★ 1667 ★

Occupations, By Race/Sex

Top 25 MSAs For Employment As Surveyors and Mapping Scientists, 1990: Men

MSA/CMSA	Employees per 100,000 pop.	Rank
Pensacola, FL MSA	518	1
Los Angeles – Anaheim – Riverside, CA CMSA	365	2
San Francisco – Oakland – San Jose, CA CMSA	259	3
Philadelphia – Wilmington – Trenton, PA – NJ – DE – MD CMSA	243	4

[Continued]

★ 1667 ★

Top 25 MSAs For Employment As Surveyors and Mapping Scientists, 1990: Men

[Continued]

MSA/CMSA	Employees per 100,000 pop.	Rank
Miami – Fort Lauderdale, FL CMSA	201	5
Houston – Galveston – Brazoria, TX CMSA	181	6
Dallas – Fort Worth, TX CMSA	170	7
Boston – Lawrence – Salem, MA – NH CMSA	161	8
Seattle – Tacoma, WA CMSA	156	9
Chicago – Gary – Lake County, IL – IN – WI CMSA	155	10
Denver – Boulder, CO CMSA	153	11
Portland – Vancouver, OR – WA CMSA	145	12
Atlanta, GA MSA	142	13
Detroit – Ann Arbor, MI CMSA	139	14
Washington, DC – MD – VA MSA	134	15
San Diego, CA MSA	127	16
Sacramento, CA MSA	97	17
Cleveland – Akron – Lorain, OH CMSA	81	18
St. Louis, MO – IL MSA	81	18
Tampa – St. Petersburg – Clearwater, FL MSA	79	19
Minneapolis – St. Paul, MN – WI MSA	79	19
Raleigh – Durham, NC MSA	76	20
Albany – Schenectady – Troy, NY MSA	73	21
New Orleans, LA MSA	70	22
Anchorage, AK MSA	64	23

Source: U.S. Department of Commerce, Bureau of the Census, Data User Services Division, *1990 Census of Population and Housing, Equal Employment Opportunity File, CD-90-EE0-1*, January 1993, CD-ROM.

★ 1668 ★

Occupations, By Race/Sex

Top 25 MSAs For Employment As Surveyors and Mapping Scientists, 1990: Women

MSA/CMSA	Employees per 100,000 pop.	Rank
Alexandria, LA MSA	46	1
Sacramento, CA MSA	29	2
Albany – Schenectady – Troy, NY MSA	26	3
Detroit – Ann Arbor, MI CMSA	25	4
Oklahoma City, OK MSA	22	5
Philadelphia – Wilmington – Trenton, PA – NJ – DE – MD CMSA	22	5
Portland – Vancouver, OR – WA CMSA	22	5
Tallahassee, FL MSA	22	5
Miami – Fort Lauderdale, FL CMSA	20	6

[Continued]

★ 1668 ★

Top 25 MSAs For Employment As Surveyors and Mapping Scientists, 1990: Women
[Continued]

MSA/CMSA	Employees per 100,000 pop.	Rank
Minneapolis – St. Paul, MN – WI MSA	20	6
San Francisco – Oakland – San Jose, CA CMSA	19	7
Seattle – Tacoma, WA CMSA	19	7
Washington, DC – MD – VA MSA	19	7
New York – Northern New Jersey – Long Island, NY – NJ – CT CMSA	18	8
Raleigh – Durham, NC MSA	18	8
San Diego, CA MSA	18	8
Houston – Galveston – Brazoria, TX CMSA	17	9
Tulsa, OK MSA	17	9
Baltimore, MD MSA	16	10
Milwaukee – Racine, WI CMSA	15	11
Atlanta, GA MSA	13	12
Redding, CA MSA	12	13
New Orleans, LA MSA	11	14
Ocala, FL MSA	11	14
Jackson, MS MSA	10	15

Source: U.S. Department of Commerce, Bureau of the Census, Data User Services Division, *1990 Census of Population and Housing, Equal Employment Opportunity File, CD-90-EE0-1,* January 1993, CD-ROM.

★ 1669 ★
Occupations, By Race/Sex

Top 25 MSAs For Employment As Tailors, 1990: Men

MSA/CMSA	Employees per 100,000 pop.	Rank
New Orleans, LA MSA	6,403	1
Los Angeles – Anaheim – Riverside, CA CMSA	4,043	2
Philadelphia – Wilmington – Trenton, PA – NJ – DE – MD CMSA	1,165	3
Chicago – Gary – Lake County, IL – IN – WI CMSA	1,096	4
San Francisco – Oakland – San Jose, CA CMSA	974	5
Miami – Fort Lauderdale, FL CMSA	814	6
Boston – Lawrence – Salem, MA – NH CMSA	638	7
Dallas – Fort Worth, TX CMSA	509	8
Houston – Galveston – Brazoria, TX CMSA	365	9
Washington, DC – MD – VA MSA	349	10
Allentown – Bethlehem – Easton, PA – NJ MSA	298	11
Detroit – Ann Arbor, MI CMSA	297	12
Baltimore, MD MSA	282	13

[Continued]

★ 1669 ★

Top 25 MSAs For Employment As Tailors, 1990: Men
[Continued]

MSA/CMSA	Employees per 100,000 pop.	Rank
Cleveland – Akron – Lorain, OH CMSA	277	14
Pittsburgh – Beaver Valley, PA CMSA	265	15
Scranton – Wilkes-Barre, PA MSA	247	16
San Diego, CA MSA	236	17
Atlanta, GA MSA	231	18
Seattle – Tacoma, WA CMSA	218	19
Rochester, NY MSA	217	20
El Paso, TX MSA	204	21
Denver – Boulder, CO CMSA	185	22
Phoenix, AZ MSA	181	23
Greensboro – Winston-Salem – High Point, NC MSA	170	24
Tampa – St. Petersburg – Clearwater, FL MSA	155	25

Source: U.S. Department of Commerce, Bureau of the Census, Data User Services Division, *1990 Census of Population and Housing, Equal Employment Opportunity File, CD-90-EE0-1,* January 1993, CD-ROM.

★ 1670 ★
Occupations, By Race/Sex

Top 25 MSAs For Employment As Tailors, 1990: Women

MSA/CMSA	Employees per 100,000 pop.	Rank
Charlotte – Gastonia – Rock Hill, NC – SC MSA	2,923	1
Los Angeles – Anaheim – Riverside, CA CMSA	2,322	2
Chicago – Gary – Lake County, IL – IN – WI CMSA	967	3
San Francisco – Oakland – San Jose, CA CMSA	723	4
Philadelphia – Wilmington – Trenton, PA – NJ – DE – MD CMSA	661	5
Dallas – Fort Worth, TX CMSA	635	6
Boston – Lawrence – Salem, MA – NH CMSA	507	7
Miami – Fort Lauderdale, FL CMSA	488	8
Washington, DC – MD – VA MSA	445	9
Detroit – Ann Arbor, MI CMSA	405	10
Houston – Galveston – Brazoria, TX CMSA	398	11
Minneapolis – St. Paul, MN – WI MSA	349	12
Seattle – Tacoma, WA CMSA	331	13
Baltimore, MD MSA	294	14
Atlanta, GA MSA	266	15
San Diego, CA MSA	246	16
Denver – Boulder, CO CMSA	237	17

[Continued]

★1670★

Top 25 MSAs For Employment As Tailors, 1990: Women
[Continued]

MSA/CMSA	Employees per 100,000 pop.	Rank
Cleveland – Akron – Lorain, OH CMSA	226	18
Honolulu, HI MSA	218	19
St. Louis, MO – IL MSA	218	19
Greensboro – Winston-Salem – High Point, NC MSA	214	20
Sacramento, CA MSA	208	21
Tampa – St. Petersburg – Clearwater, FL MSA	194	22
Charlotte – Gastonia – Rock Hill, NC – SC MSA	176	23
Phoenix, AZ MSA	173	24

Source: U.S. Department of Commerce, Bureau of the Census, Data User Services Division, *1990 Census of Population and Housing, Equal Employment Opportunity File, CD-90-EE0-1,* January 1993, CD-ROM.

★1671★
Occupations, By Race/Sex

Top 25 MSAs For Employment As Taxicab Drivers and Chauffeurs, 1990: Men

MSA/CMSA	Employees per 100,000 pop.	Rank
Buffalo – Niagara Falls, NY CMSA	49,542	1
Los Angeles – Anaheim – Riverside, CA CMSA	11,236	2
Chicago – Gary – Lake County, IL – IN – WI CMSA	9,520	3
Washington, DC – MD – VA MSA	7,559	4
San Francisco – Oakland – San Jose, CA CMSA	5,132	5
Miami – Fort Lauderdale, FL CMSA	4,836	6
Boston – Lawrence – Salem, MA – NH CMSA	4,433	7
Philadelphia – Wilmington – Trenton, PA – NJ – DE – MD CMSA	4,149	8
Detroit – Ann Arbor, MI CMSA	2,707	9
Houston – Galveston – Brazoria, TX CMSA	2,639	10
Baltimore, MD MSA	2,566	11
Dallas – Fort Worth, TX CMSA	2,461	12
San Diego, CA MSA	2,140	13
Las Vegas, NV MSA	2,122	14
Atlanta, GA MSA	1,935	15
Minneapolis – St. Paul, MN – WI MSA	1,812	16
Orlando, FL MSA	1,715	17
Tampa – St. Petersburg – Clearwater, FL MSA	1,579	18
Honolulu, HI MSA	1,570	19
Pittsburgh – Beaver Valley, PA CMSA	1,562	20

[Continued]

★1671★

Top 25 MSAs For Employment As Taxicab Drivers and Chauffeurs, 1990: Men
[Continued]

MSA/CMSA	Employees per 100,000 pop.	Rank
New Orleans, LA MSA	1,534	21
Seattle – Tacoma, WA CMSA	1,479	22
Phoenix, AZ MSA	1,474	23
St. Louis, MO – IL MSA	1,443	24
Cleveland – Akron – Lorain, OH CMSA	1,275	25

Source: U.S. Department of Commerce, Bureau of the Census, Data User Services Division, *1990 Census of Population and Housing, Equal Employment Opportunity File, CD-90-EE0-1,* January 1993, CD-ROM.

★1672★
Occupations, By Race/Sex

Top 25 MSAs For Employment As Taxicab Drivers and Chauffeurs, 1990: Women

MSA/CMSA	Employees per 100,000 pop.	Rank
Kansas City, MO – KS MSA	2,689	1
Los Angeles – Anaheim – Riverside, CA CMSA	1,149	2
San Francisco – Oakland – San Jose, CA CMSA	612	3
Chicago – Gary – Lake County, IL – IN – WI CMSA	565	4
Detroit – Ann Arbor, MI CMSA	512	5
Philadelphia – Wilmington – Trenton, PA – NJ – DE – MD CMSA	499	6
Boston – Lawrence – Salem, MA – NH CMSA	496	7
Washington, DC – MD – VA MSA	491	8
Houston – Galveston – Brazoria, TX CMSA	391	9
Orlando, FL MSA	390	10
Miami – Fort Lauderdale, FL CMSA	375	11
Baltimore, MD MSA	274	12
Cleveland – Akron – Lorain, OH CMSA	254	13
Atlanta, GA MSA	247	14
San Diego, CA MSA	244	15
Phoenix, AZ MSA	243	16
Dallas – Fort Worth, TX CMSA	241	17
Tampa – St. Petersburg – Clearwater, FL MSA	222	18
St. Louis, MO – IL MSA	215	19
Seattle – Tacoma, WA CMSA	201	20
San Antonio, TX MSA	183	21
Denver – Boulder, CO CMSA	171	22
Las Vegas, NV MSA	169	23
Norfolk – Virginia Beach – Newport News, VA MSA	157	24
Sacramento, CA MSA	152	25

Source: U.S. Department of Commerce, Bureau of the Census, Data User Services Division, *1990 Census of Population and Housing, Equal Employment Opportunity File, CD-90-EE0-1,* January 1993, CD-ROM.

★1673★

Occupations, By Race/Sex

Top 25 MSAs For Employment As Teachers, Elementary School, 1990: Men

MSA/CMSA	Employees per 100,000 pop.	Rank
Phoenix, AZ MSA	59,892	1
Los Angeles – Anaheim – Riverside, CA CMSA	33,756	2
Chicago – Gary – Lake County, IL – IN – WI CMSA	18,331	3
Philadelphia – Wilmington – Trenton, PA – NJ – DE – MD CMSA	16,956	4
San Francisco – Oakland – San Jose, CA CMSA	14,287	5
Detroit – Ann Arbor, MI CMSA	12,546	6
Boston – Lawrence – Salem, MA – NH CMSA	11,698	7
Houston – Galveston – Brazoria, TX CMSA	8,249	8
Minneapolis – St. Paul, MN – WI MSA	7,839	9
Washington, DC – MD – VA MSA	7,768	10
Dallas – Fort Worth, TX CMSA	7,503	11
Pittsburgh – Beaver Valley, PA CMSA	7,232	12
Seattle – Tacoma, WA CMSA	7,117	13
Miami – Fort Lauderdale, FL CMSA	6,972	14
Cleveland – Akron – Lorain, OH CMSA	6,846	15
Baltimore, MD MSA	6,089	16
St. Louis, MO – IL MSA	5,793	17
San Diego, CA MSA	5,466	18
Denver – Boulder, CO CMSA	5,280	19
Atlanta, GA MSA	4,964	20
Phoenix, AZ MSA	4,937	21
Milwaukee – Racine, WI CMSA	4,811	22
Portland – Vancouver, OR – WA CMSA	4,400	23
Tampa – St. Petersburg – Clearwater, FL MSA	4,261	24
Sacramento, CA MSA	3,890	25

Source: U.S. Department of Commerce, Bureau of the Census, Data User Services Division, *1990 Census of Population and Housing, Equal Employment Opportunity File, CD-90-EEO-1, January 1993,* CD-ROM.

★1674★

Occupations, By Race/Sex

Top 25 MSAs For Employment As Teachers, Elementary School, 1990: Women

MSA/CMSA	Employees per 100,000 pop.	Rank
Greensboro – Winston-Salem – High Point, NC MSA	182,433	1
Los Angeles – Anaheim – Riverside, CA CMSA	116,107	2
Chicago – Gary – Lake County, IL – IN – WI CMSA	71,831	3
Philadelphia – Wilmington – Trenton, PA – NJ – DE – MD CMSA	56,135	4
San Francisco – Oakland – San Jose, CA CMSA	50,398	5
Detroit – Ann Arbor, MI CMSA	41,360	6
Houston – Galveston – Brazoria, TX CMSA	41,071	7
Dallas – Fort Worth, TX CMSA	39,922	8
Washington, DC – MD – VA MSA	38,841	9
Boston – Lawrence – Salem, MA – NH CMSA	37,996	10
Atlanta, GA MSA	31,384	11
Miami – Fort Lauderdale, FL CMSA	27,694	12
St. Louis, MO – IL MSA	24,152	13
Cleveland – Akron – Lorain, OH CMSA	23,886	14
Baltimore, MD MSA	22,814	15
Minneapolis – St. Paul, MN – WI MSA	21,802	16
San Diego, CA MSA	21,024	17
Seattle – Tacoma, WA CMSA	20,783	18
Denver – Boulder, CO CMSA	18,371	19
Phoenix, AZ MSA	17,944	20
Kansas City, MO – KS MSA	17,035	21
Tampa – St. Petersburg – Clearwater, FL MSA	17,026	22
Pittsburgh – Beaver Valley, PA CMSA	16,484	23
Milwaukee – Racine, WI CMSA	15,662	24
Cincinnati – Hamilton, OH – KY – IN CMSA	15,360	25

Source: U.S. Department of Commerce, Bureau of the Census, Data User Services Division, *1990 Census of Population and Housing, Equal Employment Opportunity File, CD-90-EEO-1, January 1993,* CD-ROM.

★1675★
Occupations, By Race/Sex
Top 25 MSAs For Employment As Teachers, Prekindergarten and Kindergarten, 1990: Men

MSA/CMSA	Employees per 100,000 pop.	Rank
Macon – Warner Robins, GA MSA	567	1
Los Angeles – Anaheim – Riverside, CA CMSA	352	2
San Francisco – Oakland – San Jose, CA CMSA	322	3
Philadelphia – Wilmington – Trenton, PA – NJ – DE – MD CMSA	279	4
Chicago – Gary – Lake County, IL – IN – WI CMSA	209	5
Dallas – Fort Worth, TX CMSA	148	6
Seattle – Tacoma, WA CMSA	148	6
Boston – Lawrence – Salem, MA – NH CMSA	135	7
Washington, DC – MD – VA MSA	130	8
Minneapolis – St. Paul, MN – WI MSA	107	9
Houston – Galveston – Brazoria, TX CMSA	84	10
Denver – Boulder, CO CMSA	82	11
Atlanta, GA MSA	78	12
Miami – Fort Lauderdale, FL CMSA	71	13
Kansas City, MO – KS MSA	67	14
San Diego, CA MSA	66	15
Sacramento, CA MSA	58	16
Detroit – Ann Arbor, MI CMSA	57	17
Greensboro – Winston-Salem – High Point, NC MSA	57	17
Baltimore, MD MSA	55	18
Nashville, TN MSA	53	19
Raleigh – Durham, NC MSA	50	20
Portland – Vancouver, OR – WA CMSA	49	21
Milwaukee – Racine, WI CMSA	48	22
Portland, ME MSA	46	23

Source: U.S. Department of Commerce, Bureau of the Census, Data User Services Division, *1990 Census of Population and Housing, Equal Employment Opportunity File, CD-90-EE0-1, January 1993,* CD-ROM.

★1676★
Occupations, By Race/Sex
Top 25 MSAs For Employment As Teachers, Prekindergarten and Kindergarten, 1990: Women

MSA/CMSA	Employees per 100,000 pop.	Rank
Springfield, IL MSA	16,346	1
Los Angeles – Anaheim – Riverside, CA CMSA	13,669	2
Chicago – Gary – Lake County, IL – IN – WI CMSA	8,049	3
San Francisco – Oakland – San Jose, CA CMSA	7,906	4

[Continued]

★1676★
Top 25 MSAs For Employment As Teachers, Prekindergarten and Kindergarten, 1990: Women
[Continued]

MSA/CMSA	Employees per 100,000 pop.	Rank
Boston – Lawrence – Salem, MA – NH CMSA	7,076	5
Philadelphia – Wilmington – Trenton, PA – NJ – DE – MD CMSA	6,853	6
Dallas – Fort Worth, TX CMSA	6,548	7
Atlanta, GA MSA	5,739	8
Washington, DC – MD – VA MSA	5,439	9
Houston – Galveston – Brazoria, TX CMSA	5,175	10
Miami – Fort Lauderdale, FL CMSA	3,465	11
St. Louis, MO – IL MSA	3,402	12
Seattle – Tacoma, WA CMSA	3,155	13
Detroit – Ann Arbor, MI CMSA	3,065	14
Minneapolis – St. Paul, MN – WI MSA	3,059	15
Phoenix, AZ MSA	2,651	16
Tampa – St. Petersburg – Clearwater, FL MSA	2,632	17
Cleveland – Akron – Lorain, OH CMSA	2,543	18
Kansas City, MO – KS MSA	2,537	19
San Diego, CA MSA	2,462	20
Denver – Boulder, CO CMSA	2,398	21
Baltimore, MD MSA	2,309	22
Charlotte – Gastonia – Rock Hill, NC – SC MSA	2,123	23
Cincinnati – Hamilton, OH – KY – IN CMSA	1,960	24
Nashville, TN MSA	1,918	25

Source: U.S. Department of Commerce, Bureau of the Census, Data User Services Division, *1990 Census of Population and Housing, Equal Employment Opportunity File, CD-90-EE0-1, January 1993,* CD-ROM.

★1677★
Occupations, By Race/Sex
Top 25 MSAs For Employment As Teachers, Secondary School, 1990: Men

MSA/CMSA	Employees per 100,000 pop.	Rank
Kansas City, MO – KS MSA	20,910	1
Los Angeles – Anaheim – Riverside, CA CMSA	11,700	2
Chicago – Gary – Lake County, IL – IN – WI CMSA	10,390	3
Philadelphia – Wilmington – Trenton, PA – NJ – DE – MD CMSA	6,943	4
San Francisco – Oakland – San Jose, CA CMSA	6,233	5
Boston – Lawrence – Salem, MA – NH CMSA	5,201	6

[Continued]

★ 1677 ★

Top 25 MSAs For Employment As Teachers, Secondary School, 1990: Men
[Continued]

MSA/CMSA	Employees per 100,000 pop.	Rank
Detroit – Ann Arbor, MI CMSA	3,835	7
St. Louis, MO – IL MSA	2,910	8
Minneapolis – St. Paul, MN – WI MSA	2,814	9
Cleveland – Akron – Lorain, OH CMSA	2,726	10
Washington, DC – MD – VA MSA	2,707	11
Houston – Galveston – Brazoria, TX CMSA	2,700	12
Dallas – Fort Worth, TX CMSA	2,681	13
Seattle – Tacoma, WA CMSA	2,509	14
San Diego, CA MSA	2,443	15
Pittsburgh – Beaver Valley, PA CMSA	2,310	16
Rochester, NY MSA	2,265	17
Miami – Fort Lauderdale, FL CMSA	2,243	18
Phoenix, AZ MSA	2,054	19
Milwaukee – Racine, WI CMSA	2,049	20
Buffalo – Niagara Falls, NY CMSA	2,048	21
Cincinnati – Hamilton, OH – KY – IN CMSA	1,936	22
Baltimore, MD MSA	1,858	23
Atlanta, GA MSA	1,795	24
Providence – Pawtucket – Fall River, RI – MA CMSA	1,770	25

Source: U.S. Department of Commerce, Bureau of the Census, Data User Services Division, *1990 Census of Population and Housing, Equal Employment Opportunity File, CD-90-EE0-1, January 1993*, CD-ROM.

★ 1678 ★
Occupations, By Race/Sex

Top 25 MSAs For Employment As Teachers, Secondary School, 1990: Women

MSA/CMSA	Employees per 100,000 pop.	Rank
Norfolk – Virginia Beach – Newport News, VA MSA	29,118	1
Los Angeles – Anaheim – Riverside, CA CMSA	14,252	2
Chicago – Gary – Lake County, IL – IN – WI CMSA	12,570	3
Philadelphia – Wilmington – Trenton, PA – NJ – DE – MD CMSA	8,361	4
San Francisco – Oakland – San Jose, CA CMSA	7,137	5
Boston – Lawrence – Salem, MA – NH CMSA	6,854	6
Dallas – Fort Worth, TX CMSA	5,627	7
Houston – Galveston – Brazoria, TX CMSA	5,263	8
Washington, DC – MD – VA MSA	5,071	9

[Continued]

★ 1678 ★

Top 25 MSAs For Employment As Teachers, Secondary School, 1990: Women
[Continued]

MSA/CMSA	Employees per 100,000 pop.	Rank
Detroit – Ann Arbor, MI CMSA	4,715	10
Rochester, NY MSA	4,378	11
Atlanta, GA MSA	3,698	12
St. Louis, MO – IL MSA	3,621	13
Buffalo – Niagara Falls, NY CMSA	3,347	14
Cleveland – Akron – Lorain, OH CMSA	3,324	15
Albany – Schenectady – Troy, NY MSA	3,033	16
Miami – Fort Lauderdale, FL CMSA	2,917	17
Baltimore, MD MSA	2,906	18
Pittsburgh – Beaver Valley, PA CMSA	2,796	19
San Diego, CA MSA	2,764	20
Minneapolis – St. Paul, MN – WI MSA	2,751	21
Syracuse, NY MSA	2,609	22
Phoenix, AZ MSA	2,392	23
Tampa – St. Petersburg – Clearwater, FL MSA	2,350	24
Cincinnati – Hamilton, OH – KY – IN CMSA	2,328	25

Source: U.S. Department of Commerce, Bureau of the Census, Data User Services Division, *1990 Census of Population and Housing, Equal Employment Opportunity File, CD-90-EE0-1, January 1993*, CD-ROM.

★ 1679 ★
Occupations, By Race/Sex

Top 25 MSAs For Employment As Teachers, Special Education, 1990: Men

MSA/CMSA	Employees per 100,000 pop.	Rank
Portland – Vancouver, OR – WA CMSA	1,032	1
Los Angeles – Anaheim – Riverside, CA CMSA	502	2
Philadelphia – Wilmington – Trenton, PA – NJ – DE – MD CMSA	361	3
Chicago – Gary – Lake County, IL – IN – WI CMSA	319	4
Boston – Lawrence – Salem, MA – NH CMSA	275	5
San Francisco – Oakland – San Jose, CA CMSA	239	6
Pittsburgh – Beaver Valley, PA CMSA	217	7
Detroit – Ann Arbor, MI CMSA	152	8
Washington, DC – MD – VA MSA	145	9
Albany – Schenectady – Troy, NY MSA	143	10
Phoenix, AZ MSA	129	11

[Continued]

★1679★
Top 25 MSAs For Employment As Teachers, Special Education, 1990: Men
[Continued]

MSA/CMSA	Employees per 100,000 pop.	Rank
Baltimore, MD MSA	114	12
Dallas–Fort Worth, TX CMSA	113	13
Portland–Vancouver, OR–WA CMSA	111	14
Houston–Galveston–Brazoria, TX CMSA	110	15
Buffalo–Niagara Falls, NY CMSA	109	16
Cleveland–Akron–Lorain, OH CMSA	104	17
Minneapolis–St. Paul, MN–WI MSA	102	18
Salt Lake City–Ogden, UT MSA	85	19
San Diego, CA MSA	84	20
Tampa–St. Petersburg–Clearwater, FL MSA	81	21
Austin, TX MSA	78	22
Atlanta, GA MSA	77	23
St. Louis, MO–IL MSA	75	24
Denver–Boulder, CO CMSA	74	25

Source: U.S. Department of Commerce, Bureau of the Census, Data User Services Division, *1990 Census of Population and Housing, Equal Employment Opportunity File, CD-90-EE0-1, January 1993,* CD-ROM.

★1680★
Occupations, By Race/Sex
Top 25 MSAs For Employment As Teachers, Special Education, 1990: Women

MSA/CMSA	Employees per 100,000 pop.	Rank
Seattle–Tacoma, WA CMSA	5,047	1
Los Angeles–Anaheim–Riverside, CA CMSA	2,468	2
Philadelphia–Wilmington–Trenton, PA–NJ–DE–MD CMSA	1,696	3
Chicago–Gary–Lake County, IL–IN–WI CMSA	1,420	4
Boston–Lawrence–Salem, MA–NH CMSA	1,222	5
Detroit–Ann Arbor, MI CMSA	907	6
San Francisco–Oakland–San Jose, CA CMSA	901	7
Washington, DC–MD–VA MSA	748	8
Dallas–Fort Worth, TX CMSA	634	9
Houston–Galveston–Brazoria, TX CMSA	577	10
Minneapolis–St. Paul, MN–WI MSA	562	11
Cleveland–Akron–Lorain, OH CMSA	518	12
St. Louis, MO–IL MSA	515	13
Buffalo–Niagara Falls, NY CMSA	505	14
Pittsburgh–Beaver Valley, PA CMSA	500	15

[Continued]

★1680★
Top 25 MSAs For Employment As Teachers, Special Education, 1990: Women
[Continued]

MSA/CMSA	Employees per 100,000 pop.	Rank
Albany–Schenectady–Troy, NY MSA	492	16
San Diego, CA MSA	476	17
Hartford–New Britain–Middletown, CT CMSA	435	18
Providence–Pawtucket–Fall River, RI–MA CMSA	394	19
Baltimore, MD MSA	376	20
Kansas City, MO–KS MSA	365	21
Salt Lake City–Ogden, UT MSA	360	22
Atlanta, GA MSA	359	23
Rochester, NY MSA	342	24
Seattle–Tacoma, WA CMSA	334	25

Source: U.S. Department of Commerce, Bureau of the Census, Data User Services Division, *1990 Census of Population and Housing, Equal Employment Opportunity File, CD-90-EE0-1, January 1993,* CD-ROM.

★1681★
Occupations, By Race/Sex
Top 25 MSAs For Employment As Technical Writers, 1990: Men

MSA/CMSA	Employees per 100,000 pop.	Rank
Sacramento, CA MSA	3,068	1
New York–Northern New Jersey–Long Island, NY–NJ–CT CMSA	2,901	2
San Francisco–Oakland–San Jose, CA CMSA	2,414	3
Boston–Lawrence–Salem, MA–NH CMSA	1,996	4
Washington, DC–MD–VA MSA	1,575	5
Dallas–Fort Worth, TX CMSA	1,219	6
Chicago–Gary–Lake County, IL–IN–WI CMSA	1,096	7
Philadelphia–Wilmington–Trenton, PA–NJ–DE–MD CMSA	993	8
Detroit–Ann Arbor, MI CMSA	884	9
Minneapolis–St. Paul, MN–WI MSA	746	10
Seattle–Tacoma, WA CMSA	717	11
Baltimore, MD MSA	660	12
San Diego, CA MSA	655	13
Portland–Vancouver, OR–WA CMSA	555	14
Atlanta, GA MSA	544	15
St. Louis, MO–IL MSA	534	16
Phoenix, AZ MSA	476	17
Houston–Galveston–Brazoria, TX CMSA	447	18
Denver–Boulder, CO CMSA	440	19
Cincinnati–Hamilton, OH–KY–IN CMSA	425	20

[Continued]

★1681★
Top 25 MSAs For Employment As Technical Writers, 1990: Men
[Continued]

MSA/CMSA	Employees per 100,000 pop.	Rank
Rochester, NY MSA	373	21
Norfolk – Virginia Beach – Newport News, VA MSA	336	22
Pittsburgh – Beaver Valley, PA CMSA	313	23
Milwaukee – Racine, WI CMSA	307	24
Hartford – New Britain – Middletown, CT CMSA	306	25

Source: U.S. Department of Commerce, Bureau of the Census, Data User Services Division, *1990 Census of Population and Housing, Equal Employment Opportunity File, CD-90-EE0-1, January 1993,* CD-ROM.

★1682★
Occupations, By Race/Sex
Top 25 MSAs For Employment As Technical Writers, 1990: Women

MSA/CMSA	Employees per 100,000 pop.	Rank
Tampa – St. Petersburg – Clearwater, FL MSA	3,093	1
San Francisco – Oakland – San Jose, CA CMSA	2,995	2
Los Angeles – Anaheim – Riverside, CA CMSA	2,209	3
Washington, DC – MD – VA MSA	2,205	4
Boston – Lawrence – Salem, MA – NH CMSA	2,082	5
Chicago – Gary – Lake County, IL – IN – WI CMSA	1,252	6
Philadelphia – Wilmington – Trenton, PA – NJ – DE – MD CMSA	1,059	7
Dallas – Fort Worth, TX CMSA	1,054	8
Seattle – Tacoma, WA CMSA	844	9
Detroit – Ann Arbor, MI CMSA	817	10
Minneapolis – St. Paul, MN – WI MSA	652	11
Atlanta, GA MSA	631	12
San Diego, CA MSA	630	13
Denver – Boulder, CO CMSA	603	14
Houston – Galveston – Brazoria, TX CMSA	563	15
Baltimore, MD MSA	541	16
Portland – Vancouver, OR – WA CMSA	528	17
Raleigh – Durham, NC MSA	417	18
Pittsburgh – Beaver Valley, PA CMSA	365	19
St. Louis, MO – IL MSA	365	19
Phoenix, AZ MSA	341	20
Hartford – New Britain – Middletown, CT CMSA	324	21
Cincinnati – Hamilton, OH – KY – IN CMSA	311	22

[Continued]

★1682★
Top 25 MSAs For Employment As Technical Writers, 1990: Women
[Continued]

MSA/CMSA	Employees per 100,000 pop.	Rank
Orlando, FL MSA	305	23
Columbus, OH MSA	297	24

Source: U.S. Department of Commerce, Bureau of the Census, Data User Services Division, *1990 Census of Population and Housing, Equal Employment Opportunity File, CD-90-EE0-1, January 1993,* CD-ROM.

★1683★
Occupations, By Race/Sex
Top 25 MSAs For Employment As Theology Teachers, 1990: Men

MSA/CMSA	Employees per 100,000 pop.	Rank
Asheville, NC MSA	167	1
San Francisco – Oakland – San Jose, CA CMSA	121	2
Philadelphia – Wilmington – Trenton, PA – NJ – DE – MD CMSA	106	3
Los Angeles – Anaheim – Riverside, CA CMSA	93	4
Chicago – Gary – Lake County, IL – IN – WI CMSA	92	5
Boston – Lawrence – Salem, MA – NH CMSA	86	6
Pittsburgh – Beaver Valley, PA CMSA	42	7
Dallas – Fort Worth, TX CMSA	36	8
Lexington-Fayette, KY MSA	34	9
Phoenix, AZ MSA	32	10
Minneapolis – St. Paul, MN – WI MSA	31	11
Greenville – Spartanburg, SC MSA	28	12
St. Louis, MO – IL MSA	27	13
San Antonio, TX MSA	27	13
Kansas City, MO – KS MSA	27	13
Nashville, TN MSA	26	14
Washington, DC – MD – VA MSA	23	15
Raleigh – Durham, NC MSA	22	16
Charleston, SC MSA	21	17
Richmond – Petersburg, VA MSA	20	18
Scranton – Wilkes-Barre, PA MSA	20	18
Seattle – Tacoma, WA CMSA	20	18
Miami – Fort Lauderdale, FL CMSA	19	19
Tucson, AZ MSA	19	19
Oklahoma City, OK MSA	18	20

Source: U.S. Department of Commerce, Bureau of the Census, Data User Services Division, *1990 Census of Population and Housing, Equal Employment Opportunity File, CD-90-EE0-1, January 1993,* CD-ROM.

★1684★

Occupations, By Race/Sex

Top 25 MSAs For Employment As Theology Teachers, 1990: Women

MSA/CMSA	Employees per 100,000 pop.	Rank
Altoona, PA MSA	61	1
Philadelphia – Wilmington – Trenton, PA – NJ – DE – MD CMSA	53	2
Boston – Lawrence – Salem, MA – NH CMSA	29	3
San Francisco – Oakland – San Jose, CA CMSA	26	4
Los Angeles – Anaheim – Riverside, CA CMSA	25	5
Chicago – Gary – Lake County, IL – IN – WI CMSA	24	6
Minneapolis – St. Paul, MN – WI MSA	20	7
Detroit – Ann Arbor, MI CMSA	17	8
San Antonio, TX MSA	17	8
Daytona Beach, FL MSA	15	9
Worcester, MA MSA	14	10
Dallas – Fort Worth, TX CMSA	11	11
Birmingham, AL MSA	10	12
Pittsburgh – Beaver Valley, PA CMSA	10	12
Spokane, WA MSA	10	12
Salem, OR MSA	9	13
Champaign – Urbana – Rantoul, IL MSA	8	14
Dayton – Springfield, OH MSA	8	14
Jacksonville, NC MSA	8	14
Phoenix, AZ MSA	8	14
Saginaw – Bay City – Midland, MI MSA	8	14
Tallahassee, FL MSA	8	14
Baltimore, MD MSA	7	15
Greenville – Spartanburg, SC MSA	7	15
Memphis, TN – AR – MS MSA	7	15

Source: U.S. Department of Commerce, Bureau of the Census, Data User Services Division, *1990 Census of Population and Housing, Equal Employment Opportunity File, CD-90-EE0-1, January 1993,* CD-ROM.

★1685★

Occupations, By Race/Sex

Top 25 MSAs For Employment As Truck Drivers, 1990: Men

MSA/CMSA	Employees per 100,000 pop.	Rank
Denver – Boulder, CO CMSA	159,470	1
Los Angeles – Anaheim – Riverside, CA CMSA	148,527	2
Chicago – Gary – Lake County, IL – IN – WI CMSA	81,589	3
Philadelphia – Wilmington – Trenton, PA – NJ – DE – MD CMSA	57,733	4

[Continued]

★1685★

Top 25 MSAs For Employment As Truck Drivers, 1990: Men

[Continued]

MSA/CMSA	Employees per 100,000 pop.	Rank
San Francisco – Oakland – San Jose, CA CMSA	50,734	5
Detroit – Ann Arbor, MI CMSA	43,725	6
Dallas – Fort Worth, TX CMSA	43,512	7
Houston – Galveston – Brazoria, TX CMSA	41,253	8
Boston – Lawrence – Salem, MA – NH CMSA	34,414	9
Miami – Fort Lauderdale, FL CMSA	33,271	10
Atlanta, GA MSA	33,228	11
Washington, DC – MD – VA MSA	29,184	12
Cleveland – Akron – Lorain, OH CMSA	27,797	13
St. Louis, MO – IL MSA	26,093	14
Baltimore, MD MSA	25,757	15
Minneapolis – St. Paul, MN – WI MSA	24,848	16
Seattle – Tacoma, WA CMSA	24,036	17
Pittsburgh – Beaver Valley, PA CMSA	21,939	18
Phoenix, AZ MSA	20,973	19
Tampa – St. Petersburg – Clearwater, FL MSA	20,504	20
Denver – Boulder, CO CMSA	19,448	21
Cincinnati – Hamilton, OH – KY – IN CMSA	19,130	22
Portland – Vancouver, OR – WA CMSA	17,747	23
San Diego, CA MSA	17,674	24
Kansas City, MO – KS MSA	17,276	25

Source: U.S. Department of Commerce, Bureau of the Census, Data User Services Division, *1990 Census of Population and Housing, Equal Employment Opportunity File, CD-90-EE0-1, January 1993,* CD-ROM.

★1686★

Occupations, By Race/Sex

Top 25 MSAs For Employment As Truck Drivers, 1990: Women

MSA/CMSA	Employees per 100,000 pop.	Rank
Seattle – Tacoma, WA CMSA	9,831	1
New York – Northern New Jersey – Long Island, NY – NJ – CT CMSA	6,660	2
San Francisco – Oakland – San Jose, CA CMSA	4,176	3
Chicago – Gary – Lake County, IL – IN – WI CMSA	3,637	4
Houston – Galveston – Brazoria, TX CMSA	3,452	5
Detroit – Ann Arbor, MI CMSA	3,159	6
Philadelphia – Wilmington – Trenton, PA – NJ – DE – MD CMSA	2,768	7

[Continued]

★1686★

Top 25 MSAs For Employment As Truck Drivers, 1990: Women
[Continued]

MSA/CMSA	Employees per 100,000 pop.	Rank
Dallas – Fort Worth, TX CMSA	2,441	8
Seattle – Tacoma, WA CMSA	2,384	9
Atlanta, GA MSA	2,351	10
Boston – Lawrence – Salem, MA – NH CMSA	2,335	11
Miami – Fort Lauderdale, FL CMSA	2,111	12
Washington, DC – MD – VA MSA	2,064	13
Phoenix, AZ MSA	1,826	14
Tampa – St. Petersburg – Clearwater, FL MSA	1,793	15
San Diego, CA MSA	1,784	16
Cleveland – Akron – Lorain, OH CMSA	1,743	17
Denver – Boulder, CO CMSA	1,712	18
St. Louis, MO – IL MSA	1,649	19
Baltimore, MD MSA	1,430	20
Minneapolis – St. Paul, MN – WI MSA	1,375	21
Portland – Vancouver, OR – WA CMSA	1,341	22
Sacramento, CA MSA	1,330	23
Norfolk – Virginia Beach – Newport News, VA MSA	1,317	24
Kansas City, MO – KS MSA	1,201	25

Source: U.S. Department of Commerce, Bureau of the Census, Data User Services Division, *1990 Census of Population and Housing, Equal Employment Opportunity File, CD-90-EE0-1, January 1993,* CD-ROM.

★1687★
Occupations, By Race/Sex

Top 25 MSAs For Employment As Typesetters and Compositors, 1990: Men

MSA/CMSA	Employees per 100,000 pop.	Rank
Pittsburgh – Beaver Valley, PA CMSA	2,580	1
Los Angeles – Anaheim – Riverside, CA CMSA	1,845	2
Chicago – Gary – Lake County, IL – IN – WI CMSA	1,386	3
Philadelphia – Wilmington – Trenton, PA – NJ – DE – MD CMSA	837	4
San Francisco – Oakland – San Jose, CA CMSA	769	5
Boston – Lawrence – Salem, MA – NH CMSA	647	6
Dallas – Fort Worth, TX CMSA	464	7
Washington, DC – MD – VA MSA	438	8
Detroit – Ann Arbor, MI CMSA	411	9
Minneapolis – St. Paul, MN – WI MSA	397	10

[Continued]

★1687★

Top 25 MSAs For Employment As Typesetters and Compositors, 1990: Men
[Continued]

MSA/CMSA	Employees per 100,000 pop.	Rank
Seattle – Tacoma, WA CMSA	239	11
Atlanta, GA MSA	236	12
Miami – Fort Lauderdale, FL CMSA	230	13
St. Louis, MO – IL MSA	225	14
Phoenix, AZ MSA	212	15
Portland – Vancouver, OR – WA CMSA	202	16
Baltimore, MD MSA	199	17
Cleveland – Akron – Lorain, OH CMSA	195	18
Indianapolis, IN MSA	181	19
Cincinnati – Hamilton, OH – KY – IN CMSA	180	20
Houston – Galveston – Brazoria, TX CMSA	177	21
Nashville, TN MSA	176	22
Milwaukee – Racine, WI CMSA	166	23
Denver – Boulder, CO CMSA	160	24
Buffalo – Niagara Falls, NY CMSA	149	25

Source: U.S. Department of Commerce, Bureau of the Census, Data User Services Division, *1990 Census of Population and Housing, Equal Employment Opportunity File, CD-90-EE0-1, January 1993,* CD-ROM.

★1688★
Occupations, By Race/Sex

Top 25 MSAs For Employment As Typesetters and Compositors, 1990: Women

MSA/CMSA	Employees per 100,000 pop.	Rank
Cincinnati – Hamilton, OH – KY – IN CMSA	3,459	1
Los Angeles – Anaheim – Riverside, CA CMSA	2,139	2
Chicago – Gary – Lake County, IL – IN – WI CMSA	2,042	3
Philadelphia – Wilmington – Trenton, PA – NJ – DE – MD CMSA	1,133	4
San Francisco – Oakland – San Jose, CA CMSA	1,114	5
Detroit – Ann Arbor, MI CMSA	1,035	6
Minneapolis – St. Paul, MN – WI MSA	913	7
Boston – Lawrence – Salem, MA – NH CMSA	890	8
Dallas – Fort Worth, TX CMSA	840	9
Washington, DC – MD – VA MSA	765	10
Atlanta, GA MSA	693	11
St. Louis, MO – IL MSA	677	12
Miami – Fort Lauderdale, FL CMSA	623	13
Denver – Boulder, CO CMSA	598	14

[Continued]

★1688★

Top 25 MSAs For Employment As Typesetters and Compositors, 1990: Women
[Continued]

MSA/CMSA	Employees per 100,000 pop.	Rank
Seattle – Tacoma, WA CMSA	564	15
Cleveland – Akron – Lorain, OH CMSA	556	16
Houston – Galveston – Brazoria, TX CMSA	546	17
Kansas City, MO – KS MSA	510	18
Cincinnati – Hamilton, OH – KY – IN CMSA	500	19
Baltimore, MD MSA	483	20
Indianapolis, IN MSA	421	21
Milwaukee – Racine, WI CMSA	418	22
Tampa – St. Petersburg – Clearwater, FL MSA	399	23
Phoenix, AZ MSA	388	24
Hartford – New Britain – Middletown, CT CMSA	368	25

Source: U.S. Department of Commerce, Bureau of the Census, Data User Services Division, *1990 Census of Population and Housing, Equal Employment Opportunity File, CD-90-EE0-1, January 1993,* CD-ROM.

★1689★

Occupations, By Race/Sex

Top 25 MSAs For Employment As Typists, 1990: Men

MSA/CMSA	Employees per 100,000 pop.	Rank
Tampa – St. Petersburg – Clearwater, FL MSA	6,769	1
Los Angeles – Anaheim – Riverside, CA CMSA	4,360	2
San Francisco – Oakland – San Jose, CA CMSA	2,442	3
Washington, DC – MD – VA MSA	2,195	4
Chicago – Gary – Lake County, IL – IN – WI CMSA	1,199	5
Boston – Lawrence – Salem, MA – NH CMSA	978	6
Philadelphia – Wilmington – Trenton, PA – NJ – DE – MD CMSA	778	7
Detroit – Ann Arbor, MI CMSA	648	8
Seattle – Tacoma, WA CMSA	609	9
San Diego, CA MSA	553	10
Dallas – Fort Worth, TX CMSA	529	11
Minneapolis – St. Paul, MN – WI MSA	462	12
Sacramento, CA MSA	403	13
Atlanta, GA MSA	393	14
Baltimore, MD MSA	387	15
St. Louis, MO – IL MSA	372	16
Miami – Fort Lauderdale, FL CMSA	353	17
Denver – Boulder, CO CMSA	351	18

[Continued]

★1689★

Top 25 MSAs For Employment As Typists, 1990: Men
[Continued]

MSA/CMSA	Employees per 100,000 pop.	Rank
Cleveland – Akron – Lorain, OH CMSA	298	19
Columbus, OH MSA	273	20
Honolulu, HI MSA	255	21
Tampa – St. Petersburg – Clearwater, FL MSA	243	22
Pittsburgh – Beaver Valley, PA CMSA	237	23
Houston – Galveston – Brazoria, TX CMSA	234	24
San Antonio, TX MSA	219	25

Source: U.S. Department of Commerce, Bureau of the Census, Data User Services Division, *1990 Census of Population and Housing, Equal Employment Opportunity File, CD-90-EE0-1, January 1993,* CD-ROM.

★1690★

Occupations, By Race/Sex

Top 25 MSAs For Employment As Typists, 1990: Women

MSA/CMSA	Employees per 100,000 pop.	Rank
Milwaukee – Racine, WI CMSA	68,535	1
Los Angeles – Anaheim – Riverside, CA CMSA	39,853	2
Chicago – Gary – Lake County, IL – IN – WI CMSA	24,678	3
Philadelphia – Wilmington – Trenton, PA – NJ – DE – MD CMSA	21,985	4
Washington, DC – MD – VA MSA	19,417	5
San Francisco – Oakland – San Jose, CA CMSA	17,606	6
Detroit – Ann Arbor, MI CMSA	13,658	7
Boston – Lawrence – Salem, MA – NH CMSA	11,567	8
Dallas – Fort Worth, TX CMSA	9,747	9
Houston – Galveston – Brazoria, TX CMSA	8,983	10
Atlanta, GA MSA	8,792	11
Minneapolis – St. Paul, MN – WI MSA	8,750	12
Baltimore, MD MSA	8,092	13
St. Louis, MO – IL MSA	7,423	14
Miami – Fort Lauderdale, FL CMSA	7,262	15
Cleveland – Akron – Lorain, OH CMSA	7,235	16
Seattle – Tacoma, WA CMSA	6,666	17
Pittsburgh – Beaver Valley, PA CMSA	6,206	18
San Diego, CA MSA	6,076	19
Phoenix, AZ MSA	5,682	20
Denver – Boulder, CO CMSA	5,497	21

[Continued]

★1690★

Top 25 MSAs For Employment As Typists, 1990: Women
[Continued]

MSA/CMSA	Employees per 100,000 pop.	Rank
Milwaukee – Racine, WI CMSA	5,271	22
Sacramento, CA MSA	5,233	23
Tampa – St. Petersburg – Clearwater, FL MSA	5,027	24
Cincinnati – Hamilton, OH – KY – IN CMSA	4,989	25

Source: U.S. Department of Commerce, Bureau of the Census, Data User Services Division, *1990 Census of Population and Housing, Equal Employment Opportunity File, CD-90-EE0-1, January 1993,* CD-ROM.

★1691★

Occupations, By Race/Sex

Top 25 MSAs For Employment As Urban Planners, 1990: Men

MSA/CMSA	Employees per 100,000 pop.	Rank
Cleveland – Akron – Lorain, OH CMSA	1,117	1
New York – Northern New Jersey – Long Island, NY – NJ – CT CMSA	967	2
San Francisco – Oakland – San Jose, CA CMSA	698	3
Chicago – Gary – Lake County, IL – IN – WI CMSA	382	4
Washington, DC – MD – VA MSA	329	5
Philadelphia – Wilmington – Trenton, PA – NJ – DE – MD CMSA	297	6
Boston – Lawrence – Salem, MA – NH CMSA	288	7
San Diego, CA MSA	257	8
Minneapolis – St. Paul, MN – WI MSA	256	9
Baltimore, MD MSA	245	10
Detroit – Ann Arbor, MI CMSA	217	11
Dallas – Fort Worth, TX CMSA	216	12
Seattle – Tacoma, WA CMSA	213	13
Phoenix, AZ MSA	193	14
Houston – Galveston – Brazoria, TX CMSA	157	15
Honolulu, HI MSA	148	16
Miami – Fort Lauderdale, FL CMSA	147	17
Denver – Boulder, CO CMSA	137	18
Portland – Vancouver, OR – WA CMSA	120	19
Tampa – St. Petersburg – Clearwater, FL MSA	116	20
West Palm Beach – Boca Raton – Delray Beach, FL MSA	110	21
Albuquerque, NM MSA	106	22
St. Louis, MO – IL MSA	102	23

[Continued]

★1691★

Top 25 MSAs For Employment As Urban Planners, 1990: Men
[Continued]

MSA/CMSA	Employees per 100,000 pop.	Rank
Sacramento, CA MSA	99	24
Kansas City, MO – KS MSA	93	25

Source: U.S. Department of Commerce, Bureau of the Census, Data User Services Division, *1990 Census of Population and Housing, Equal Employment Opportunity File, CD-90-EE0-1, January 1993,* CD-ROM.

★1692★

Occupations, By Race/Sex

Top 25 MSAs For Employment As Urban Planners, 1990: Women

MSA/CMSA	Employees per 100,000 pop.	Rank
Tallahassee, FL MSA	626	1
New York – Northern New Jersey – Long Island, NY – NJ – CT CMSA	472	2
San Francisco – Oakland – San Jose, CA CMSA	408	3
Boston – Lawrence – Salem, MA – NH CMSA	263	4
Chicago – Gary – Lake County, IL – IN – WI CMSA	239	5
Washington, DC – MD – VA MSA	219	6
Seattle – Tacoma, WA CMSA	167	7
Minneapolis – St. Paul, MN – WI MSA	108	8
Baltimore, MD MSA	107	9
San Diego, CA MSA	95	10
Philadelphia – Wilmington – Trenton, PA – NJ – DE – MD CMSA	94	11
Atlanta, GA MSA	92	12
Phoenix, AZ MSA	90	13
Detroit – Ann Arbor, MI CMSA	89	14
Miami – Fort Lauderdale, FL CMSA	89	14
Dallas – Fort Worth, TX CMSA	87	15
Cleveland – Akron – Lorain, OH CMSA	72	16
Tampa – St. Petersburg – Clearwater, FL MSA	71	17
Portland – Vancouver, OR – WA CMSA	62	18
Denver – Boulder, CO CMSA	57	19
Hartford – New Britain – Middletown, CT CMSA	57	19
Orlando, FL MSA	56	20
Providence – Pawtucket – Fall River, RI – MA CMSA	53	21
Greensboro – Winston-Salem – High Point, NC MSA	46	22
New Orleans, LA MSA	46	22

Source: U.S. Department of Commerce, Bureau of the Census, Data User Services Division, *1990 Census of Population and Housing, Equal Employment Opportunity File, CD-90-EE0-1, January 1993,* CD-ROM.

★1693★

Occupations, By Race/Sex

Top 25 MSAs For Employment As Veterinarians, 1990: Men

MSA/CMSA	Employees per 100,000 pop.	Rank
Columbus, OH MSA	1,458	1
Los Angeles – Anaheim – Riverside, CA CMSA	1,376	2
San Francisco – Oakland – San Jose, CA CMSA	892	3
Philadelphia – Wilmington – Trenton, PA – NJ – DE – MD CMSA	766	4
Chicago – Gary – Lake County, IL – IN – WI CMSA	697	5
Washington, DC – MD – VA MSA	653	6
Dallas – Fort Worth, TX CMSA	620	7
Houston – Galveston – Brazoria, TX CMSA	592	8
Miami – Fort Lauderdale, FL CMSA	538	9
Atlanta, GA MSA	486	10
Minneapolis – St. Paul, MN – WI MSA	472	11
Boston – Lawrence – Salem, MA – NH CMSA	463	12
Detroit – Ann Arbor, MI CMSA	431	13
St. Louis, MO – IL MSA	395	14
Denver – Boulder, CO CMSA	391	15
Seattle – Tacoma, WA CMSA	386	16
Kansas City, MO – KS MSA	358	17
San Diego, CA MSA	333	18
Tampa – St. Petersburg – Clearwater, FL MSA	317	19
Sacramento, CA MSA	312	20
Columbus, OH MSA	312	20
Baltimore, MD MSA	287	21
Portland – Vancouver, OR – WA CMSA	278	22
Cincinnati – Hamilton, OH – KY – IN CMSA	275	23
Cleveland – Akron – Lorain, OH CMSA	242	24

Source: U.S. Department of Commerce, Bureau of the Census, Data User Services Division, *1990 Census of Population and Housing, Equal Employment Opportunity File, CD-90-EE0-1, January 1993,* CD-ROM.

★1694★

Occupations, By Race/Sex

Top 25 MSAs For Employment As Veterinarians, 1990: Women

MSA/CMSA	Employees per 100,000 pop.	Rank
Portland – Vancouver, OR – WA CMSA	729	1
Los Angeles – Anaheim – Riverside, CA CMSA	575	2
Philadelphia – Wilmington – Trenton, PA – NJ – DE – MD CMSA	542	3
Washington, DC – MD – VA MSA	432	4
San Francisco – Oakland – San Jose, CA CMSA	366	5
Boston – Lawrence – Salem, MA – NH CMSA	329	6
Detroit – Ann Arbor, MI CMSA	280	7
Chicago – Gary – Lake County, IL – IN – WI CMSA	258	8
Seattle – Tacoma, WA CMSA	215	9
Houston – Galveston – Brazoria, TX CMSA	214	10
Minneapolis – St. Paul, MN – WI MSA	197	11
Dallas – Fort Worth, TX CMSA	189	12
San Diego, CA MSA	170	13
Cleveland – Akron – Lorain, OH CMSA	163	14
Baltimore, MD MSA	160	15
Sacramento, CA MSA	158	16
Miami – Fort Lauderdale, FL CMSA	153	17
Atlanta, GA MSA	136	18
Denver – Boulder, CO CMSA	132	19
Columbus, OH MSA	131	20
Raleigh – Durham, NC MSA	119	21
Phoenix, AZ MSA	113	22
Greensboro – Winston-Salem – High Point, NC MSA	108	23
St. Louis, MO – IL MSA	102	24
Rochester, NY MSA	96	25

Source: U.S. Department of Commerce, Bureau of the Census, Data User Services Division, *1990 Census of Population and Housing, Equal Employment Opportunity File, CD-90-EE0-1, January 1993,* CD-ROM.

★1695★

Occupations, By Race/Sex

Top 25 MSAs For Employment As Water and Sewage Treatment Plant Operators, 1990: Men

MSA/CMSA	Employees per 100,000 pop.	Rank
Honolulu, HI MSA	2,231	1
Los Angeles – Anaheim – Riverside, CA CMSA	1,684	2
Philadelphia – Wilmington – Trenton, PA – NJ – DE – MD CMSA	1,423	3
Chicago – Gary – Lake County, IL – IN – WI CMSA	1,236	4
Houston – Galveston – Brazoria, TX CMSA	1,069	5
San Francisco – Oakland – San Jose, CA CMSA	1,035	6
Detroit – Ann Arbor, MI CMSA	866	7
Boston – Lawrence – Salem, MA – NH CMSA	821	8
Miami – Fort Lauderdale, FL CMSA	792	9
Cleveland – Akron – Lorain, OH CMSA	720	10
Dallas – Fort Worth, TX CMSA	702	11
Tampa – St. Petersburg – Clearwater, FL MSA	664	12
Washington, DC – MD – VA MSA	649	13
Atlanta, GA MSA	618	14
Pittsburgh – Beaver Valley, PA CMSA	604	15
Baltimore, MD MSA	525	16
St. Louis, MO – IL MSA	462	17
Denver – Boulder, CO CMSA	420	18
Phoenix, AZ MSA	418	19
Cincinnati – Hamilton, OH – KY – IN CMSA	417	20
New Orleans, LA MSA	372	21
Seattle – Tacoma, WA CMSA	363	22
San Diego, CA MSA	358	23
Minneapolis – St. Paul, MN – WI MSA	344	24
Kansas City, MO – KS MSA	330	25

Source: U.S. Department of Commerce, Bureau of the Census, Data User Services Division, *1990 Census of Population and Housing, Equal Employment Opportunity File, CD-90-EE0-1, January 1993,* CD-ROM.

★1696★

Occupations, By Race/Sex

Top 25 MSAs For Employment As Water and Sewage Treatment Plant Operators, 1990: Women

MSA/CMSA	Employees per 100,000 pop.	Rank
Kansas City, MO – KS MSA	149	1
Detroit – Ann Arbor, MI CMSA	115	2
New York – Northern New Jersey – Long Island, NY – NJ – CT CMSA	109	3
Atlanta, GA MSA	80	4
San Francisco – Oakland – San Jose, CA CMSA	76	5
New Orleans, LA MSA	70	6
Chicago – Gary – Lake County, IL – IN – WI CMSA	62	7
Jacksonville, FL MSA	51	8
Washington, DC – MD – VA MSA	49	9
Phoenix, AZ MSA	44	10
Melbourne – Titusville – Palm Bay, FL MSA	38	11
Kansas City, MO – KS MSA	37	12
Philadelphia – Wilmington – Trenton, PA – NJ – DE – MD CMSA	35	13
Boston – Lawrence – Salem, MA – NH CMSA	32	14
Baltimore, MD MSA	31	15
Dallas – Fort Worth, TX CMSA	31	15
Tampa – St. Petersburg – Clearwater, FL MSA	30	16
Minneapolis – St. Paul, MN – WI MSA	28	17
Seattle – Tacoma, WA CMSA	27	18
Austin, TX MSA	26	19
Birmingham, AL MSA	26	19
Houston – Galveston – Brazoria, TX CMSA	26	19
Mansfield, OH MSA	26	19
Portland – Vancouver, OR – WA CMSA	25	20
Miami – Fort Lauderdale, FL CMSA	24	21

Source: U.S. Department of Commerce, Bureau of the Census, Data User Services Division, *1990 Census of Population and Housing, Equal Employment Opportunity File, CD-90-EE0-1, January 1993,* CD-ROM.

★1697★

Occupations, By Race/Sex

Top 25 MSAs For Employment As Welders and Cutters, 1990: Men

MSA/CMSA	Employees per 100,000 pop.	Rank
Honolulu, HI MSA	27,486	1
New York – Northern New Jersey – Long Island, NY – NJ – CT CMSA	16,686	2
Chicago – Gary – Lake County, IL – IN – WI CMSA	15,986	3
Houston – Galveston – Brazoria, TX CMSA	15,082	4
Detroit – Ann Arbor, MI CMSA	13,491	5
Philadelphia – Wilmington – Trenton, PA – NJ – DE – MD CMSA	9,287	6
Dallas – Fort Worth, TX CMSA	8,698	7
San Francisco – Oakland – San Jose, CA CMSA	7,885	8
Cleveland – Akron – Lorain, OH CMSA	7,661	9
Pittsburgh – Beaver Valley, PA CMSA	5,866	10
St. Louis, MO – IL MSA	5,510	11
Milwaukee – Racine, WI CMSA	5,418	12
Seattle – Tacoma, WA CMSA	5,205	13
Minneapolis – St. Paul, MN – WI MSA	4,887	14
Boston – Lawrence – Salem, MA – NH CMSA	4,820	15
Norfolk – Virginia Beach – Newport News, VA MSA	4,615	16
New Orleans, LA MSA	4,576	17
Cincinnati – Hamilton, OH – KY – IN CMSA	4,446	18
Portland – Vancouver, OR – WA CMSA	4,402	19
Atlanta, GA MSA	4,398	20
San Diego, CA MSA	4,174	21
Miami – Fort Lauderdale, FL CMSA	4,151	22
Tulsa, OK MSA	3,923	23
Baltimore, MD MSA	3,910	24
Birmingham, AL MSA	3,881	25

Source: U.S. Department of Commerce, Bureau of the Census, Data User Services Division, *1990 Census of Population and Housing, Equal Employment Opportunity File, CD-90-EE0-1, January 1993,* CD-ROM.

★1698★

Occupations, By Race/Sex

Top 25 MSAs For Employment As Welders and Cutters, 1990: Women

MSA/CMSA	Employees per 100,000 pop.	Rank
Minneapolis – St. Paul, MN – WI MSA	1,576	1
New York – Northern New Jersey – Long Island, NY – NJ – CT CMSA	1,038	2
Detroit – Ann Arbor, MI CMSA	992	3
Chicago – Gary – Lake County, IL – IN – WI CMSA	979	4
Cleveland – Akron – Lorain, OH CMSA	691	5
Philadelphia – Wilmington – Trenton, PA – NJ – DE – MD CMSA	515	6
Dallas – Fort Worth, TX CMSA	384	7
Grand Rapids, MI MSA	362	8
Miami – Fort Lauderdale, FL CMSA	331	9
Providence – Pawtucket – Fall River, RI – MA CMSA	328	10
Boston – Lawrence – Salem, MA – NH CMSA	320	11
Norfolk – Virginia Beach – Newport News, VA MSA	309	12
Nashville, TN MSA	292	13
San Francisco – Oakland – San Jose, CA CMSA	286	14
Flint, MI MSA	274	15
Pittsburgh – Beaver Valley, PA CMSA	244	16
St. Louis, MO – IL MSA	242	17
Milwaukee – Racine, WI CMSA	240	18
Minneapolis – St. Paul, MN – WI MSA	239	19
Hartford – New Britain – Middletown, CT CMSA	225	20
Charlotte – Gastonia – Rock Hill, NC – SC MSA	220	21
San Diego, CA MSA	220	21
Seattle – Tacoma, WA CMSA	210	22
Baltimore, MD MSA	200	23
Dayton – Springfield, OH MSA	198	24

Source: U.S. Department of Commerce, Bureau of the Census, Data User Services Division, *1990 Census of Population and Housing, Equal Employment Opportunity File, CD-90-EE0-1, January 1993,* CD-ROM.

★1699★

Occupations, By Race/Sex

Top 25 MSAs For Employment As Welfare Service Aides, 1990: Men

MSA/CMSA	Employees per 100,000 pop.	Rank
Baltimore, MD MSA	694	1
Los Angeles – Anaheim – Riverside, CA CMSA	629	2
San Francisco – Oakland – San Jose, CA CMSA	327	3
Chicago – Gary – Lake County, IL – IN – WI CMSA	295	4
Washington, DC – MD – VA MSA	245	5
San Diego, CA MSA	179	6
Detroit – Ann Arbor, MI CMSA	159	7
Seattle – Tacoma, WA CMSA	150	8
Sacramento, CA MSA	132	9
Boston – Lawrence – Salem, MA – NH CMSA	120	10
Philadelphia – Wilmington – Trenton, PA – NJ – DE – MD CMSA	108	11
Baltimore, MD MSA	89	12
Minneapolis – St. Paul, MN – WI MSA	88	13
Providence – Pawtucket – Fall River, RI – MA CMSA	84	14
Cleveland – Akron – Lorain, OH CMSA	68	15
St. Louis, MO – IL MSA	67	16
Kansas City, MO – KS MSA	67	16
Houston – Galveston – Brazoria, TX CMSA	66	17
Rochester, NY MSA	65	18
Dallas – Fort Worth, TX CMSA	61	19
Phoenix, AZ MSA	60	20
Tucson, AZ MSA	60	20
Denver – Boulder, CO CMSA	60	20
Buffalo – Niagara Falls, NY CMSA	59	21
Pittsburgh – Beaver Valley, PA CMSA	56	22

Source: U.S. Department of Commerce, Bureau of the Census, Data User Services Division, *1990 Census of Population and Housing, Equal Employment Opportunity File, CD-90-EE0-1, January 1993,* CD-ROM.

★1700★

Occupations, By Race/Sex

Top 25 MSAs For Employment As Welfare Service Aides, 1990: Women

MSA/CMSA	Employees per 100,000 pop.	Rank
Buffalo – Niagara Falls, NY CMSA	4,852	1
Los Angeles – Anaheim – Riverside, CA CMSA	2,134	2
Chicago – Gary – Lake County, IL – IN – WI CMSA	1,336	3
Boston – Lawrence – Salem, MA – NH CMSA	1,238	4

[Continued]

★1700★

Top 25 MSAs For Employment As Welfare Service Aides, 1990: Women

[Continued]

MSA/CMSA	Employees per 100,000 pop.	Rank
San Francisco – Oakland – San Jose, CA CMSA	886	5
San Diego, CA MSA	826	6
Detroit – Ann Arbor, MI CMSA	721	7
Philadelphia – Wilmington – Trenton, PA – NJ – DE – MD CMSA	622	8
Buffalo – Niagara Falls, NY CMSA	516	9
Washington, DC – MD – VA MSA	508	10
Seattle – Tacoma, WA CMSA	457	11
Baltimore, MD MSA	449	12
Sacramento, CA MSA	397	13
Cleveland – Akron – Lorain, OH CMSA	385	14
Providence – Pawtucket – Fall River, RI – MA CMSA	333	15
St. Louis, MO – IL MSA	323	16
Houston – Galveston – Brazoria, TX CMSA	299	17
Miami – Fort Lauderdale, FL CMSA	276	18
Minneapolis – St. Paul, MN – WI MSA	264	19
Cincinnati – Hamilton, OH – KY – IN CMSA	251	20
Dallas – Fort Worth, TX CMSA	251	20
Fresno, CA MSA	248	21
Kansas City, MO – KS MSA	244	22
Rochester, NY MSA	236	23
Atlanta, GA MSA	221	24

Source: U.S. Department of Commerce, Bureau of the Census, Data User Services Division, *1990 Census of Population and Housing, Equal Employment Opportunity File, CD-90-EE0-1, January 1993,* CD-ROM.

Chapter 14

INCOME

Topics Covered

Family and Household Income
Income By Race and Ethnicity
Personal Income
Personal Income Projections

★1701★

Family and Household Income

Aggregate Household Income of Less Than $150,000, 1989

[Table shows the top 50 areas]

	Mil. $	Rank
New York – Northern New Jersey – Long Island, NY – NJ – CT	272,208	1
Los Angeles – Anaheim – Riverside, CA	197,223	2
Chicago – Gary – Lake County, IL – IN – WI	112,511	3
San Francisco – Oakland – San Jose, CA	102,696	4
Philadelphia – Wilmington – Trenton, PA – NJ – DE – MD	83,579	5
Washington, DC – MD – VA	70,753	6
Boston – Lawrence – Salem, MA – NH	66,515	7
Detroit – Ann Arbor, MI	65,494	8
Dallas – Fort Worth, TX	53,492	9
Houston – Galveston – Brazoria, TX	47,722	10
Atlanta, GA	41,352	11
Miami – Fort Lauderdale, FL	40,411	12
Seattle – Tacoma, WA	38,292	13
Minneapolis – Saint Paul, MN – WI	36,610	14
Cleveland – Akron – Lorain, OH	35,898	15
Baltimore, MD	34,894	16
San Diego, CA	34,436	17
Saint Louis, MO – IL	32,526	18
Phoenix, AZ	28,109	19
Pittsburgh – Beaver Valley, PA	27,576	20
Denver – Boulder, CO	27,368	21
Tampa – Saint Petersburg – Clearwater, FL	26,697	22
Cincinnati – Hamilton, OH – KY – IN	22,519	23
Milwaukee – Racine, WI	21,300	24
Kansas City, MO – KS	21,178	25
Sacramento, CA	20,570	26
Portland – Vancouver, OR – WA	19,918	27
Columbus, OH	17,998	28
Hartford – New Britain – Middletown, CT	17,910	29
Norfolk – Virginia Beach – Newport News, VA	16,981	30
Indianapolis, IN	16,916	31
Charlotte – Gastonia – Rock Hill, NC – SC	15,297	32
Providence – Pawtucket – Fall River, RI – MA	15,152	33
Buffalo – Niagara Falls, NY	14,736	34
Orlando, FL	14,143	35
Rochester, NY	14,126	36
San Antonio, TX	13,794	37
West Palm Beach – Boca Raton – Delray Beach, FL	13,310	38
New Orleans, LA	13,240	39
Nashville, TN	12,618	40
Dayton – Springfield, OH	12,318	41
Greensboro – Winston-Salem – High Point, NC	12,278	42

[Continued]

★1701★

Aggregate Household Income of Less Than $150,000, 1989

[Continued]

	Mil. $	Rank
Richmond – Petersburg, VA	12,211	43
Albany – Schenectady – Troy, NY	12,198	44
Salt Lake City – Ogden, UT	11,868	45
Honolulu, HI	11,631	46
Louisville, KY – IN	11,615	47
Oklahoma City, OK	11,378	48
Jacksonville, FL	11,332	49
Memphis, TN – AR – MS	11,157	50

Source: U.S. Bureau of the Census, Data User Services Division, *1990 Census of Population and Housing*, Summary Tape File 3C, United States Summary, CD-ROM, February 1992.

★1702★

Family and Household Income

Aggregate Household Income of $150,000 or More, 1989

[Table shows the top 50 areas]

	Mil. $	Rank
New York – Northern New Jersey – Long Island, NY – NJ – CT	66,819	1
Los Angeles – Anaheim – Riverside, CA	38,922	2
San Francisco – Oakland – San Jose, CA	18,477	3
Chicago – Gary – Lake County, IL – IN – WI	18,421	4
Washington, DC – MD – VA	12,219	5
Philadelphia – Wilmington – Trenton, PA – NJ – DE – MD	12,131	6
Boston – Lawrence – Salem, MA – NH	10,200	7
Dallas – Fort Worth, TX	7,806	8
Detroit – Ann Arbor, MI	7,625	9
Houston – Galveston – Brazoria, TX	7,303	10
Miami – Fort Lauderdale, FL	6,848	11
Atlanta, GA	6,176	12
San Diego, CA	4,956	13
Minneapolis – Saint Paul, MN – WI	4,510	14
Seattle – Tacoma, WA	4,353	15
Baltimore, MD	4,181	16
Cleveland – Akron – Lorain, OH	4,018	17
West Palm Beach – Boca Raton – Delray Beach, FL	3,774	18
Saint Louis, MO – IL	3,601	19
Phoenix, AZ	3,407	20
Pittsburgh – Beaver Valley, PA	3,171	21
Denver – Boulder, CO	3,059	22
Tampa – Saint Petersburg – Clearwater, FL	2,642	23
Cincinnati – Hamilton, OH – KY – IN	2,517	24
Hartford – New Britain – Middletown, CT	2,393	25
Portland – Vancouver, OR – WA	2,149	26

[Continued]

★1702★

Aggregate Household Income of $150,000 or More, 1989

[Continued]

	Mil. $	Rank
Kansas City, MO–KS	2,140	27
Milwaukee–Racine, WI	2,098	28
Sacramento, CA	1,994	29
Indianapolis, IN	1,870	30
Columbus, OH	1,714	31
Honolulu, HI	1,640	32
Nashville, TN	1,593	33
Orlando, FL	1,583	34
New Orleans, LA	1,560	35
Charlotte–Gastonia–Rock Hill, NC–SC	1,535	36
San Antonio, TX	1,405	37
Memphis, TN–AR–MS	1,394	38
Providence–Pawtucket–Fall River, RI–MA	1,361	39
Greensboro–Winston-Salem–High Point, NC	1,340	40
Richmond–Petersburg, VA	1,320	41
Jacksonville, FL	1,271	42
Birmingham, AL	1,248	43
Las Vegas, NV	1,241	44
Louisville, KY–IN	1,207	45
Norfolk–Virginia Beach–Newport News, VA	1,200	46
Oklahoma City, OK	1,194	47
New Haven–Meriden, CT	1,187	48
Austin, TX	1,159	49
Rochester, NY	1,076	50

Source: U.S. Bureau of the Census, Data User Services Division, *1990 Census of Population and Housing,* Summary Tape File 3C, United States Summary, CD-ROM, February 1992.

★1703★

Family and Household Income

Aggregate Income of Institutionalized Persons 15 Years Old and Older, 1989

[Table shows the top 50 areas]

	Mil. $	Rank
Los Angeles–Anaheim–Riverside, CA	1,130	1
New York–Northern New Jersey–Long Island, NY–NJ–CT	1,072	2
Philadelphia–Wilmington–Trenton, PA–NJ–DE–MD	603	3
Chicago–Gary–Lake County, IL–IN–WI	493	4
San Francisco–Oakland–San Jose, CA	484	5
Washington, DC–MD–VA	338	6
Boston–Lawrence–Salem, MA–NH	292	7
Seattle–Tacoma, WA	280	8
Dallas–Fort Worth, TX	267	9
Tampa–Saint Petersburg–Clearwater, FL	240	10

[Continued]

★1703★

Aggregate Income of Institutionalized Persons 15 Years Old and Older, 1989

[Continued]

	Mil. $	Rank
Minneapolis–Saint Paul, MN–WI	230	11
Houston–Galveston–Brazoria, TX	218	12
Detroit–Ann Arbor, MI	217	13
San Diego, CA	205	14
Denver–Boulder, CO	195	15
Pittsburgh–Beaver Valley, PA	192	16
Miami–Fort Lauderdale, FL	190	17
Baltimore, MD	182	18
Atlanta, GA	168	19
Columbus, OH	166	20
Saint Louis, MO–IL	161	21
Cleveland–Akron–Lorain, OH	159	22
Salinas–Seaside–Monterey, CA	138	23
Kansas City, MO–KS	136	24
Sacramento, CA	136	25
Cincinnati–Hamilton, OH–KY–IN	133	26
Milwaukee–Racine, WI	128	27
Portland–Vancouver, OR–WA	108	28
Santa Barbara–Santa Maria–Lompoc, CA	107	29
Richmond–Petersburg, VA	106	30
Indianapolis, IN	103	31
Hartford–New Britain–Middletown, CT	102	32
Stockton, CA	99	33
Norfolk–Virginia Beach–Newport News, VA	97	34
Phoenix, AZ	96	35
Rochester, NY	92	36
Providence–Pawtucket–Fall River, RI–MA	92	37
Harrisburg–Lebanon–Carlisle, PA	86	38
Oklahoma City, OK	85	39
Orlando, FL	85	40
Raleigh–Durham, NC	84	41
Grand Rapids, MI	80	42
Charleston, SC	78	43
Louisville, KY–IN	78	44
Poughkeepsie, NY	77	45
Scranton–Wilkes-Barre, PA	74	46
Bakersfield, CA	73	47
Buffalo–Niagara Falls, NY	72	48
Charlotte–Gastonia–Rock Hill, NC–SC	71	49
Glens Falls, NY	70	50

Source: U.S. Bureau of the Census, Data User Services Division, *1990 Census of Population and Housing,* Summary Tape File 3C, United States Summary, CD-ROM, February 1992.

★1704★
Family and Household Income
Families With Income of Less Than $5,000, 1989
[Table shows the top 50 areas]

MSA	% of all families	Rank
McAllen–Edinburg–Mission, TX	12.2	1
Brownsville–Harlingen, TX	11.8	2
Laredo, TX	11.3	3
Albany, GA	9.8	4
Pine Bluff, AR	9.7	5
New Orleans, LA	9.0	6
Monroe, LA	8.9	7
Houma–Thibodaux, LA	8.7	8
Alexandria, LA	7.9	9
Lafayette, LA	7.9	9
Shreveport, LA	7.8	10
Corpus Christi, TX	7.7	11
Mobile, AL	7.7	11
El Paso, TX	7.5	12
Odessa, TX	7.4	13
Lake Charles, LA	7.2	14
Pueblo, CO	7.2	14
Baton Rouge, LA	7.1	15
Huntington–Ashland, WV–KY–OH	7.1	15
Biloxi–Gulfport, MS	7.0	16
Columbus, GA–AL	7.0	16
Texarkana, TX–Texarkana, AR	7.0	16
Beaumont–Port Arthur, TX	6.8	17
Las Cruces, NM	6.6	18
Memphis, TN–AR–MS	6.6	18
Pascagoula, MS	6.6	18
San Antonio, TX	6.6	18
Bryan–College Station, TX	6.5	19
Tuscaloosa, AL	6.5	19
Jackson, MS	6.4	20
Macon–Warner Robins, GA	6.4	20
Florence, SC	6.3	21
Longview–Marshall, TX	6.2	22
Gainesville, FL	6.1	23
Jackson, TN	6.1	23
Wheeling, WV–OH	6.0	24
Montgomery, AL	5.8	25
Savannah, GA	5.8	25
Steubenville–Weirton, OH–WV	5.7	26
Victoria, TX	5.7	26
Waco, TX	5.7	26
Lawton, OK	5.6	27
Saint Joseph, MO	5.6	27
Augusta, GA–SC	5.5	28
Charleston, SC	5.5	28
Owensboro, KY	5.4	29
Clarksville–Hopkinsville, TN–KY	5.3	30
Toledo, OH	5.3	30
Tyler, TX	5.3	30
Youngstown–Warren, OH	5.3	30

Source: U.S. Bureau of the Census, Data User Services Division, *1990 Census of Population and Housing,* Summary Tape File 3C, United States Summary, CD- ROM, February 1992.

★1705★
Family and Household Income
Families With Income of $25,000 to $27,499, 1989
[Table shows the top 50 areas]

MSA	% of all families	Rank
Jacksonville, NC	7.0	1
Enid, OK	6.6	2
Grand Forks, ND	6.4	3
Joplin, MO	6.3	4
Great Falls, MT	6.2	5
Johnstown, PA	6.2	5
Fort Smith, AR–OK	6.1	6
Anniston, AL	6.0	7
Fayetteville–Springdale, AR	6.0	7
Springfield, MO	6.0	7
Abilene, TX	5.9	8
Elmira, NY	5.9	8
Bradenton, FL	5.8	9
Fort Walton Beach, FL	5.8	9
Hickory–Morganton, NC	5.8	9
Jamestown–Dunkirk, NY	5.8	9
Killeen–Temple, TX	5.8	9
Sherman–Denison, TX	5.8	9
Williamsport, PA	5.8	9
Clarksville–Hopkinsville, TN–KY	5.7	10
Fort Pierce, FL	5.7	10
Gadsden, AL	5.7	10
Lakeland–Winter Haven, FL	5.7	10
Medford, OR	5.7	10
Ocala, FL	5.7	10
Panama City, FL	5.7	10
Pueblo, CO	5.7	10
Sharon, PA	5.7	10
Burlington, NC	5.6	11
Erie, PA	5.6	11
Fayetteville, NC	5.6	11
Muskegon, MI	5.6	11
Provo–Orem, UT	5.6	11
Rapid City, SD	5.6	11
Saint Joseph, MO	5.6	11
Altoona, PA	5.5	12
Billings, MT	5.5	12
Daytona Beach, FL	5.5	12
Lawton, OK	5.5	12
Lewiston–Auburn, ME	5.5	12
Longview–Marshall, TX	5.5	12
Sioux Falls, SD	5.5	12
State College, PA	5.5	12
Steubenville–Weirton, OH–WV	5.5	12
Yuma, AZ	5.5	12
Eau Claire, WI	5.4	13
Elkhart–Goshen, IN	5.4	13
Glens Falls, NY	5.4	13
Pittsfield, MA	5.4	13
Sioux City, IA–NE	5.4	13

Source: U.S. Bureau of the Census, Data User Services Division, *1990 Census of Population and Housing,* Summary Tape File 3C, United States Summary, CD- ROM, February 1992.

★1706★

Family and Household Income

Families With Income of $50,000 to $54,999, 1989

[Table shows the top 50 areas]

MSA	% of all families	Rank
Poughkeepsie, NY	7.9	1
Rochester, MN	7.5	2
Waterbury, CT	7.5	2
Burlington, VT	7.2	3
Cedar Rapids, IA	7.1	4
Madison, WI	7.1	4
Minneapolis – Saint Paul, MN – WI	7.1	4
New London – Norwich, CT – RI	7.1	4
Worcester, MA	7.1	4
Hartford – New Britain – Middletown, CT	6.9	5
Manchester, NH	6.9	5
Pittsfield, MA	6.7	6
Portsmouth – Dover – Rochester, NH – ME	6.7	6
Grand Rapids, MI	6.6	7
Iowa City, IA	6.6	7
Milwaukee – Racine, WI	6.6	7
New Haven – Meriden, CT	6.6	7
Seattle – Tacoma, WA	6.6	7
Sheboygan, WI	6.6	7
Boston – Lawrence – Salem, MA – NH	6.5	8
Fort Wayne, IN	6.5	8
Lancaster, PA	6.5	8
Raleigh – Durham, NC	6.5	8
Richmond – Petersburg, VA	6.5	8
Washington, DC – MD – VA	6.5	8
Allentown – Bethlehem – Easton, PA – NJ	6.4	9
Chicago – Gary – Lake County, IL – IN – WI	6.4	9
Des Moines, IA	6.4	9
Rochester, NY	6.4	9
Rockford, IL	6.4	9
Albany – Schenectady – Troy, NY	6.3	10
Baltimore, MD	6.3	10
Bloomington – Normal, IL	6.3	10
Fort Collins – Loveland, CO	6.3	10
Kansas City, MO – KS	6.3	10
Philadelphia – Wilmington – Trenton, PA – NJ – DE – MD	6.3	10
Portland, ME	6.3	10
Reading, PA	6.3	10
Denver – Boulder, CO	6.2	11
Detroit – Ann Arbor, MI	6.2	11
Fitchburg – Leominster, MA	6.2	11
Harrisburg – Lebanon – Carlisle, PA	6.2	11
Huntsville, AL	6.2	11
Indianapolis, IN	6.2	11
Peoria, IL	6.2	11
Providence – Pawtucket – Fall River, RI – MA	6.2	11
Richland – Kennewick – Pasco, WA	6.2	11

[Continued]

★1706★

Families With Income of $50,000 to $54,999, 1989

[Continued]

MSA	% of all families	Rank
Sacramento, CA	6.2	11
San Francisco – Oakland – San Jose, CA	6.2	11
Syracuse, NY	6.1	12

Source: U.S. Bureau of the Census, Data User Services Division, *1990 Census of Population and Housing,* Summary Tape File 3C, United States Summary, CD- ROM, February 1992.

★1707★

Family and Household Income

Families With Income of $75,000 to $99,999, 1989

[Table shows the top 50 areas]

MSA	% of all families	Rank
Washington, DC – MD – VA	14.8	1
Anchorage, AK	14.6	2
Poughkeepsie, NY	12.4	3
San Francisco – Oakland – San Jose, CA	12.1	4
Boston – Lawrence – Salem, MA – NH	11.9	5
Hartford – New Britain – Middletown, CT	11.7	6
Honolulu, HI	11.2	7
New York – Northern New Jersey – Long Island, NY – NJ – CT	11.1	8
New Haven – Meriden, CT	10.8	9
Waterbury, CT	10.0	10
Baltimore, MD	9.4	11
Los Angeles – Anaheim – Riverside, CA	9.4	11
Burlington, VT	9.3	12
Detroit – Ann Arbor, MI	9.0	13
Philadelphia – Wilmington – Trenton, PA – NJ – DE – MD	9.0	13
Atlanta, GA	8.7	14
Chicago – Gary – Lake County, IL – IN – WI	8.7	14
Worcester, MA	8.7	14
Huntsville, AL	8.6	15
Raleigh – Durham, NC	8.3	16
San Diego, CA	8.3	16
Santa Barbara – Santa Maria – Lompoc, CA	8.3	16
Minneapolis – Saint Paul, MN – WI	8.1	17
New London – Norwich, CT – RI	8.1	17
Rochester, NY	8.1	17
Denver – Boulder, CO	7.9	18
Seattle – Tacoma, WA	7.9	18
Dallas – Fort Worth, TX	7.7	19
Santa Fe, NM	7.7	19
Manchester, NH	7.6	20

[Continued]

★1707★

Families With Income of $75,000 to $99,999, 1989
[Continued]

MSA	% of all families	Rank
Albany – Schenectady – Troy, NY	7.5	21
Houston – Galveston – Brazoria, TX	7.4	22
Richmond – Petersburg, VA	7.4	22
Sacramento, CA	7.4	22
West Palm Beach – Boca Raton – Delray Beach, FL	7.4	22
Flint, MI	7.2	23
Lansing – East Lansing, MI	7.2	23
Kokomo, IN	7.1	24
Madison, WI	7.1	24
Atlantic City, NJ	7.0	25
Bloomington – Normal, IL	7.0	25
Providence – Pawtucket – Fall River, RI – MA	7.0	25
Rochester, MN	7.0	25
Austin, TX	6.9	26
Kalamazoo, MI	6.9	26
Portsmouth – Dover – Rochester, NH – ME	6.9	26
Iowa City, IA	6.8	27
Pittsfield, MA	6.8	27
Reno, NV	6.8	27
Springfield, MA	6.7	28

Source: U.S. Bureau of the Census, Data User Services Division, *1990 Census of Population and Housing,* Summary Tape File 3C, United States Summary, CD- ROM, February 1992.

★1708★

Family and Household Income

Families With Income of $100,000 to $124,999, 1989

[Table shows the top 50 areas]

MSA	% of all families	Rank
Washington, DC – MD – VA	6.71	1
Anchorage, AK	6.05	2
San Francisco – Oakland – San Jose, CA	5.25	3
New York – Northern New Jersey – Long Island, NY – NJ – CT	5.17	4
Boston – Lawrence – Salem, MA – NH	5.15	5
Honolulu, HI	4.56	6
New Haven – Meriden, CT	4.47	7
Hartford – New Britain – Middletown, CT	4.44	8
Poughkeepsie, NY	4.16	9
Los Angeles – Anaheim – Riverside, CA	4.09	10
Santa Barbara – Santa Maria – Lompoc, CA	3.73	11
Philadelphia – Wilmington – Trenton, PA – NJ – DE – MD	3.50	12

[Continued]

★1708★

Families With Income of $100,000 to $124,999, 1989
[Continued]

MSA	% of all families	Rank
West Palm Beach – Boca Raton – Delray Beach, FL	3.46	13
Baltimore, MD	3.40	14
Chicago – Gary – Lake County, IL – IN – WI	3.38	15
Naples, FL	3.36	16
Atlanta, GA	3.29	17
Waterbury, CT	3.28	18
San Diego, CA	3.25	19
Detroit – Ann Arbor, MI	3.23	20
Iowa City, IA	3.22	21
New London – Norwich, CT – RI	3.20	22
Santa Fe, NM	3.20	22
Worcester, MA	3.10	23
Raleigh – Durham, NC	3.08	24
Minneapolis – Saint Paul, MN – WI	3.05	25
Denver – Boulder, CO	3.03	26
Houston – Galveston – Brazoria, TX	2.97	27
Rochester, NY	2.93	28
Dallas – Fort Worth, TX	2.89	29
Charlottesville, VA	2.88	30
Burlington, VT	2.86	31
Huntsville, AL	2.86	31
Seattle – Tacoma, WA	2.75	32
Atlantic City, NJ	2.72	33
Portland, ME	2.66	34
Midland, TX	2.60	35
Sacramento, CA	2.59	36
Reno, NV	2.56	37
Richmond – Petersburg, VA	2.56	37
Austin, TX	2.55	38
Miami – Fort Lauderdale, FL	2.52	39
Salinas – Seaside – Monterey, CA	2.50	40
Sarasota, FL	2.49	41
Albany – Schenectady – Troy, NY	2.47	42
Kalamazoo, MI	2.47	42
Manchester, NH	2.46	43
Bloomington – Normal, IL	2.42	44
Phoenix, AZ	2.42	44
Rochester, MN	2.42	44

Source: U.S. Bureau of the Census, Data User Services Division, *1990 Census of Population and Housing,* Summary Tape File 3C, United States Summary, CD- ROM, February 1992.

★1709★
Family and Household Income
Families With Income of $125,000 to $149,999, 1989

[Table shows the top 50 areas]

MSA	% of all families	Rank
Washington, DC – MD – VA	2.69	1
Anchorage, AK	2.31	2
New York – Northern New Jersey – Long Island, NY – NJ-CT	2.31	2
San Francisco – Oakland – San Jose, CA	2.25	3
Boston – Lawrence – Salem, MA – NH	2.13	4
Naples, FL	1.91	5
Hartford – New Britain – Middletown, CT	1.80	6
New Haven – Meriden, CT	1.76	7
Rochester, MN	1.76	7
Honolulu, HI	1.75	8
Los Angeles – Anaheim – Riverside, CA	1.75	8
Santa Barbara – Santa Maria – Lompoc, CA	1.62	9
Poughkeepsie, NY	1.59	10
West Palm Beach – Boca Raton – Delray Beach, FL	1.58	11
Iowa City, IA	1.51	12
Chicago – Gary – Lake County, IL – IN – WI	1.46	13
San Diego, CA	1.45	14
Philadelphia – Wilmington – Trenton, PA – NJ – DE-MD	1.41	15
Atlanta, GA	1.35	16
Santa Fe, NM	1.34	17
Baltimore, MD	1.33	18
Charlottesville, VA	1.33	18
Raleigh – Durham, NC	1.33	18
Sarasota, FL	1.33	18
Dallas – Fort Worth, TX	1.29	19
Houston – Galveston – Brazoria, TX	1.25	20
Manchester, NH	1.25	20
Detroit – Ann Arbor, MI	1.24	21
Burlington, VT	1.23	22
Portland, ME	1.23	22
Minneapolis – Saint Paul, MN – WI	1.22	23
Seattle – Tacoma, WA	1.22	23
Denver – Boulder, CO	1.21	24
Madison, WI	1.21	24
Salinas – Seaside – Monterey, CA	1.17	25
Midland, TX	1.15	26
Worcester, MA	1.14	27
Atlantic City, NJ	1.10	28
State College, PA	1.10	28
Miami – Fort Lauderdale, FL	1.09	29
Reno, NV	1.09	29
Sacramento, CA	1.05	30
Albany – Schenectady – Troy, NY	1.04	31
Kalamazoo, MI	1.04	31
Roanoke, VA	1.01	32

[Continued]

★1709★
Families With Income of $125,000 to $149,999, 1989
[Continued]

MSA	% of all families	Rank
Pittsfield, MA	0.99	33
Lexington-Fayette, KY	0.98	34
Orlando, FL	0.98	34
Rochester, NY	0.97	35
Austin, TX	0.96	36

Source: U.S. Bureau of the Census, Data User Services Division, *1990 Census of Population and Housing*, Summary Tape File 3C, United States Summary, CD- ROM, February 1992.

★1710★
Family and Household Income
Families With Income of $150,000 or More, 1989
[Table shows the top 50 areas]

MSA	% of all families	Rank
Naples, FL	5.66	1
New York – Northern New Jersey – Long Island, NY – NJ – CT	4.45	2
West Palm Beach – Boca Raton – Delray Beach, FL	4.25	3
Washington, DC – MD – VA	4.17	4
San Francisco – Oakland – San Jose, CA	3.80	5
Santa Barbara – Santa Maria – Lompoc, CA	3.65	6
Boston – Lawrence – Salem, MA – NH	3.40	7
Los Angeles – Anaheim – Riverside, CA	3.38	8
Anchorage, AK	3.19	9
Sarasota, FL	3.08	10
New Haven – Meriden, CT	2.98	11
Chicago – Gary – Lake County, IL – IN – WI	2.90	12
Hartford – New Britain – Middletown, CT	2.77	13
Midland, TX	2.77	13
Atlanta, GA	2.71	14
Honolulu, HI	2.69	15
Philadelphia – Wilmington – Trenton, PA – NJ – DE – MD	2.63	16
Charlottesville, VA	2.62	17
Fort Pierce, FL	2.57	18
Iowa City, IA	2.57	18
San Diego, CA	2.55	19
Rochester, MN	2.54	20
Dallas – Fort Worth, TX	2.52	21
Santa Fe, NM	2.49	22
Miami – Fort Lauderdale, FL	2.45	23
Salinas – Seaside – Monterey, CA	2.45	23
Minneapolis – Saint Paul, MN – WI	2.44	24
Houston – Galveston – Brazoria, TX	2.43	25

[Continued]

★1710★

Families With Income of $150,000 or More, 1989

[Continued]

MSA	% of all families	Rank
Baltimore, MD	2.21	26
Portland, ME	2.20	27
Seattle – Tacoma, WA	2.18	28
Denver – Boulder, CO	2.15	29
Reno, NV	2.15	29
Fort Myers – Cape Coral, Fl	2.11	30
Pittsfield, MA	2.11	30
Detroit – Ann Arbor, MI	2.10	31
Atlantic City, NJ	2.05	32
Madison, WI	2.02	33
Austin, TX	1.98	34
Nashville, TN	1.96	35
Manchester, NH	1.95	36
Phoenix, AZ	1.95	36
Burlington, VT	1.94	37
Kalamazoo, MI	1.93	38
Richmond – Petersburg, VA	1.93	38
Raleigh – Durham, NC	1.91	39
Waterbury, CT	1.89	40
Saint Louis, MO – IL	1.87	41
Indianapolis, IN	1.86	42
Cincinnati – Hamilton, OH – KY – IN	1.85	43

Source: U.S. Bureau of the Census, Data User Services Division, *1990 Census of Population and Housing,* Summary Tape File 3C, United States Summary, CD- ROM, February 1992.

★1711★

Family and Household Income

Household Income, 1996: Leading Metropolitan Areas in Median Income

City	Income	Rank
Anchorage, AK	54,577	10
Bergen-Passaic, NJ	59,934	5
Middlesex-Somerset, NJ	61,447	3
Nassau-Suffolk, NY	70,091	1
New Haven-Stamford-Danbury, CT	59,763	7
Newark, NJ	56,742	9
Orange County, CA	59,821	6
San Jose, CA	62,407	2
Ventura, CA	57,362	8
Washington, DC-MD-VA	61,243	4

Source: "Private Properties: Moneyed Metros," *Wall Street Journal,* 29, March 1996, p. B8. Primary source: Equifax National Decisions Systems.

★1712★

Family and Household Income

Households With Earnings, 1989

[Table shows the top 50 areas]

MSA	% of all households	Rank
Anchorage, AK	93.6	1
Jacksonville, NC	89.6	2
Iowa City, IA	89.4	3
Washington, DC – MD – VA	89.1	4
Austin, TX	88.7	5
Dallas – Fort Worth, TX	88.4	6
Bryan – College Station, TX	88.1	7
Atlanta, GA	87.9	8
Raleigh – Durham, NC	87.8	9
Champaign – Urbana – Rantoul, IL	87.6	10
Houston – Galveston – Brazoria, TX	87.5	11
Honolulu, HI	87.4	12
Madison, WI	87.3	13
Burlington, VT	87.2	14
Fayetteville, NC	87.2	14
Grand Forks, ND	87.2	14
Lawrence, KS	87.1	15
Colorado Springs, CO	86.8	16
Columbia, MO	86.8	16
Provo – Orem, UT	86.6	17
Midland, TX	86.5	18
Reno, NV	86.5	18
Denver – Boulder, CO	86.4	19
Rochester, MN	86.4	19
Fort Collins – Loveland, CO	86.3	20
Santa Fe, NM	86.2	21
Tallahassee, FL	86.2	21
Bloomington – Normal, IL	86.1	22
Columbia, SC	86.1	22
Lafayette – West Lafayette, IN	86.1	22
Bloomington, IN	86.0	23
Huntsville, AL	85.8	24
Elkhart – Goshen, IN	85.7	25
Salt Lake City – Ogden, UT	85.6	26
Lincoln, NE	85.5	27
Minneapolis – Saint Paul, MN – WI	85.5	27
Boise, ID	85.3	28
Orlando, FL	85.3	28
Charlottesville, VA	85.2	29
Killeen – Temple, TX	85.2	29
Charleston, SC	85.1	30
Fargo – Moorhead, ND – MN	85.1	30
Norfolk – Virginia Beach – Newport News, VA	85.1	30
State College, PA	85.1	30
Charlotte – Gastonia – Rock Hill, NC – SC	85.0	31
Lubbock, TX	84.9	32
Las Vegas, NV	84.8	33
Grand Rapids, MI	84.6	34
Nashville, TN	84.6	34
Salinas – Seaside – Monterey, CA	84.6	34

Source: U.S. Bureau of the Census, Data User Services Division, *1990 Census of Population and Housing,* Summary Tape File 3C, United States Summary, CD- ROM, February 1992.

★1713★

Family and Household Income

Households With Farm Self-Employment Income, 1989

[Table shows the top 50 areas]

MSA	% of all households	Rank
Bismarck, ND	7.75	1
Wausau, WI	7.18	2
Saint Cloud, MN	6.70	3
Dubuque, IA	6.18	4
Greeley, CO	6.03	5
Fargo – Moorhead, ND – MN	5.49	6
Yakima, WA	5.45	7
Fayetteville – Springdale, AR	5.25	8
Eau Claire, WI	5.18	9
Grand Forks, ND	5.00	10
Merced, CA	4.86	11
Enid, OK	4.84	12
Owensboro, KY	4.77	13
Waterloo – Cedar Falls, IA	4.68	14
Bloomington – Normal, IL	4.65	15
Sioux City, IA – NE	4.55	16
Iowa City, IA	4.47	17
Lima, OH	4.45	18
Lexington-Fayette, KY	4.29	19
Visalia – Tulare – Porterville, CA	4.23	20
Lawrence, KS	4.16	21
Sioux Falls, SD	4.15	22
Rochester, MN	4.04	23
Joplin, MO	4.02	24
Johnson City – Kingsport – Bristol, TN – VA	3.94	25
Salem, OR	3.94	25
Yuba City, CA	3.82	26
San Angelo, TX	3.71	27
Richland – Kennewick – Pasco, WA	3.64	28
Champaign – Urbana – Rantoul, IL	3.58	29
Victoria, TX	3.56	30
Kokomo, IN	3.52	31
Billings, MT	3.50	32
Clarksville – Hopkinsville, TN – KY	3.50	32
Columbia, MO	3.45	33
Danville, VA	3.44	34
Kankakee, IL	3.43	35
Cedar Rapids, IA	3.40	36
Modesto, CA	3.37	37
Great Falls, MT	3.36	38
Rapid City, SD	3.33	39
Sherman – Denison, TX	3.33	39
Peoria, IL	3.18	40
Saint Joseph, MO	3.15	41
Jamestown – Dunkirk, NY	3.12	42
Bellingham, WA	3.09	43
Lancaster, PA	3.09	43
Lincoln, NE	3.07	44
Des Moines, IA	3.06	45
Springfield, IL	3.06	45

Source: U.S. Bureau of the Census, Data User Services Division, *1990 Census of Population and Housing*, Summary Tape File 3C, United States Summary, CD- ROM, February 1992.

★1714★

Family and Household Income

Households With Income of Less Than $5,000, 1989

Includes the income of the householder and all other persons 15 years old and over in the household, whether related to the householder or not. Because many households consist of only one person, average household income is usually less than average family income.

[Table shows the top 50 areas]

MSA	% of all households	Rank
McAllen – Edinburg – Mission, TX	14.7	1
Brownsville – Harlingen, TX	14.6	2
Bryan – College Station, TX	14.5	3
Laredo, TX	14.5	3
Pine Bluff, AR	13.9	4
Tuscaloosa, AL	12.7	5
Monroe, LA	12.3	6
Albany, GA	11.8	7
Lafayette, LA	11.6	8
New Orleans, LA	11.6	8
Gainesville, FL	11.5	9
Houma – Thibodaux, LA	11.5	9
Alexandria, LA	11.4	10
Texarkana, TX – Texarkana, AR	11.0	11
Waco, TX	11.0	11
Athens, GA	10.9	12
Huntington – Ashland, WV – KY – OH	10.9	12
Shreveport, LA	10.9	12
Mobile, AL	10.7	13
Baton Rouge, LA	10.3	14
Lake Charles, LA	10.3	14
Florence, SC	10.2	15
Jackson, TN	10.2	15
Longview – Marshall, TX	10.1	16
Columbus, GA – AL	10.0	17
Biloxi – Gulfport, MS	9.9	18
Corpus Christi, TX	9.9	18
Gadsden, AL	9.9	18
Beaumont – Port Arthur, TX	9.7	19
Lubbock, TX	9.7	19
Pueblo, CO	9.7	19
Tallahassee, FL	9.5	20
Las Cruces, NM	9.4	21
Memphis, TN – AR – MS	9.4	21
Lawrence, KS	9.3	22
Bloomington, IN	9.2	23
Florence, AL	9.2	23
Jackson, MS	9.2	23
Owensboro, KY	9.2	23
El Paso, TX	9.1	24
Macon – Warner Robins, GA	9.1	24
Anniston, AL	9.0	25
Johnson City – Kingsport – Bristol, TN – VA	9.0	25
Dothan, AL	8.9	26
Odessa, TX	8.9	26
Savannah, GA	8.9	26
Wheeling, WV – OH	8.9	26
Birmingham, AL	8.8	27

[Continued]

★1714★

Households With Income of Less Than $5,000, 1989
[Continued]

MSA	% of all households	Rank
Montgomery, AL	8.8	27
Victoria, TX	8.8	27

Source: U.S. Bureau of the Census, Data User Services Division, *1990 Census of Population and Housing*, Summary Tape File 3C, United States Summary, CD- ROM, February 1992.

★1715★
Family and Household Income

Households With Income of $5,000 to $9,999, 1989
[Table shows the top 50 areas]

MSA	% of all households	Rank
McAllen – Edinburg – Mission, TX	16.5	1
Brownsville – Harlingen, TX	15.4	2
Duluth, MN – WI	14.9	3
Huntington – Ashland, WV – KY – OH	14.9	3
Laredo, TX	14.5	4
New Bedford, MA	14.4	5
Cumberland, MD – WV	14.3	6
Pueblo, CO	13.9	7
Wheeling, WV – OH	13.7	8
Johnstown, PA	13.6	9
Chico, CA	13.5	10
Jamestown – Dunkirk, NY	13.5	10
Monroe, LA	13.5	10
Altoona, PA	13.4	11
Joplin, MO	13.4	11
Saint Joseph, MO	13.4	11
Alexandria, LA	13.3	12
Muncie, IN	13.3	12
Redding, CA	13.3	12
Danville, VA	13.2	13
Gadsden, AL	13.1	14
Johnson City – Kingsport – Bristol, TN – VA	13.1	14
Las Cruces, NM	13.1	14
Bryan – College Station, TX	13.0	15
Lawrence, KS	13.0	15
Pine Bluff, AR	13.0	15
Yuba City, CA	13.0	15
Scranton – Wilkes-Barre, PA	12.9	16
Terre Haute, IN	12.9	16
Muskegon, MI	12.8	17
Visalia – Tulare – Porterville, CA	12.8	17
Houma – Thibodaux, LA	12.6	18
Waco, TX	12.6	18
Anderson, SC	12.5	19
Fort Smith, AR – OK	12.5	19
Elmira, NY	12.4	20
Yakima, WA	12.4	20
Eau Claire, WI	12.3	21

[Continued]

★1715★

Households With Income of $5,000 to $9,999, 1989
[Continued]

MSA	% of all households	Rank
Florence, SC	12.3	21
Gainesville, FL	12.3	21
La Crosse, WI	12.3	21
Steubenville – Weirton, OH – WV	12.3	21
Shreveport, LA	12.1	22
Utica – Rome, NY	12.1	22
Waterloo – Cedar Falls, IA	12.1	22
Sharon, PA	12.0	23
Fresno, CA	11.9	24
Lake Charles, LA	11.9	24
Lewiston – Auburn, ME	11.9	24
Anniston, AL	11.8	25

Source: U.S. Bureau of the Census, Data User Services Division, *1990 Census of Population and Housing*, Summary Tape File 3C, United States Summary, CD- ROM, February 1992.

★1716★
Family and Household Income

Households With Income of $10,000 to $12,499, 1989
[Table shows the top 50 areas]

MSA	% of all households	Rank
McAllen – Edinburg – Mission, TX	8.1	1
Laredo, TX	7.8	2
Brownsville – Harlingen, TX	7.7	3
Bryan – College Station, TX	7.4	4
Las Cruces, NM	7.2	5
Houma – Thibodaux, LA	7.1	6
Ocala, FL	7.1	6
Alexandria, LA	6.8	7
El Paso, TX	6.8	7
Fort Smith, AR – OK	6.8	7
Johnstown, PA	6.8	7
Joplin, MO	6.8	7
Owensboro, KY	6.8	7
Chico, CA	6.7	8
Biloxi – Gulfport, MS	6.6	9
Cumberland, MD – WV	6.6	9
Medford, OR	6.6	9
Altoona, PA	6.5	10
Florence, AL	6.5	10
Gadsden, AL	6.5	10
Gainesville, FL	6.5	10
Huntington – Ashland, WV – KY – OH	6.5	10
Jamestown – Dunkirk, NY	6.5	10
Odessa, TX	6.5	10
Jacksonville, NC	6.4	11
Pueblo, CO	6.4	11
Wheeling, WV – OH	6.4	11
Abilene, TX	6.3	12
Fayetteville – Springdale, AR	6.3	12

[Continued]

★1716★

Households With Income of $10,000 to $12,499, 1989
[Continued]

MSA	% of all households	Rank
Great Falls, MT	6.3	12
Johnson City – Kingsport – Bristol, TN – VA	6.3	12
Killeen – Temple, TX	6.3	12
Scranton – Wilkes-Barre, PA	6.3	12
Springfield, MO	6.3	12
State College, PA	6.3	12
Texarkana, TX – Texarkana, AR	6.3	12
Waco, TX	6.3	12
Wichita Falls, TX	6.3	12
Athens, GA	6.2	13
Lafayette, LA	6.2	13
Sherman – Denison, TX	6.2	13
Yuma, AZ	6.2	13
Anniston, AL	6.1	14
Bloomington, IN	6.1	14
Charleston, WV	6.1	14
Danville, VA	6.1	14
Duluth, MN – WI	6.1	14
Redding, CA	6.1	14
Visalia – Tulare – Porterville, CA	6.1	14
Yuba City, CA	6.1	14

Source: U.S. Bureau of the Census, Data User Services Division, 1990 Census of Population and Housing, Summary Tape File 3C, United States Summary, CD- ROM, February 1992.

★1717★

Family and Household Income

Households With Income of $12,500 to $14,999, 1989
[Table shows the top 50 areas]

MSA	% of all households	Rank
Yuba City, CA	6.8	1
Brownsville – Harlingen, TX	6.7	2
McAllen – Edinburg – Mission, TX	6.5	3
Chico, CA	6.4	4
Jacksonville, NC	6.2	5
Visalia – Tulare – Porterville, CA	6.2	5
Laredo, TX	6.1	6
Biloxi – Gulfport, MS	6.0	7
Johnstown, PA	6.0	7
Las Cruces, NM	6.0	7
Fayetteville – Springdale, AR	5.9	8
Killeen – Temple, TX	5.9	8
Wheeling, WV – OH	5.9	8
Enid, OK	5.8	9
Grand Forks, ND	5.8	9
Joplin, MO	5.8	9
Merced, CA	5.8	9
Redding, CA	5.8	9
Yuma, AZ	5.8	9
Danville, VA	5.7	10

[Continued]

★1717★

Households With Income of $12,500 to $14,999, 1989
[Continued]

MSA	% of all households	Rank
Daytona Beach, FL	5.7	10
El Paso, TX	5.7	10
Jamestown – Dunkirk, NY	5.7	10
Ocala, FL	5.7	10
Gadsden, AL	5.6	11
Johnson City – Kingsport – Bristol, TN – VA	5.6	11
Rapid City, SD	5.6	11
Alexandria, LA	5.5	12
Clarksville – Hopkinsville, TN – KY	5.5	12
Florence, AL	5.5	12
Wichita Falls, TX	5.5	12
Altoona, PA	5.4	13
Cumberland, MD – WV	5.4	13
Fort Smith, AR – OK	5.4	13
Great Falls, MT	5.4	13
Greeley, CO	5.4	13
Huntington – Ashland, WV – KY – OH	5.4	13
Monroe, LA	5.4	13
Panama City, FL	5.4	13
Texarkana, TX – Texarkana, AR	5.4	13
Columbus, GA – AL	5.3	14
Fresno, CA	5.3	14
Lakeland – Winter Haven, FL	5.3	14
Medford, OR	5.3	14
Parkersburg – Marietta, WV – OH	5.3	14
Saint Joseph, MO	5.3	14
Sharon, PA	5.3	14
Waterloo – Cedar Falls, IA	5.3	14
Duluth, MN – WI	5.2	15
Provo – Orem, UT	5.2	15

Source: U.S. Bureau of the Census, Data User Services Division, 1990 Census of Population and Housing, Summary Tape File 3C, United States Summary, CD- ROM, February 1992.

★1718★

Family and Household Income

Households With Income of $15,000 to $17,999, 1989
[Table shows the top 50 areas]

MSA	% of all households	Rank
Jacksonville, NC	8.0	1
Clarksville – Hopkinsville, TN – KY	7.3	2
Killeen – Temple, TX	6.8	3
Enid, OK	6.6	4
Joplin, MO	6.6	4
Ocala, FL	6.6	4
Yuma, AZ	6.6	4
Daytona Beach, FL	6.4	5
Fayetteville, NC	6.4	5
Yuba City, CA	6.4	5
Bradenton, FL	6.3	6

[Continued]

★1718★

Households With Income of $15,000 to $17,999, 1989

[Continued]

MSA	% of all households	Rank
Cumberland, MD–WV	6.3	6
Fayetteville–Springdale, AR	6.3	6
Johnstown, PA	6.3	6
Pueblo, CO	6.3	6
Sharon, PA	6.3	6
Visalia–Tulare–Porterville, CA	6.3	6
Lawton, OK	6.2	7
Merced, CA	6.2	7
Alexandria, LA	6.1	8
Anderson, SC	6.1	8
Billings, MT	6.1	8
Biloxi–Gulfport, MS	6.1	8
Fort Smith, AR–OK	6.1	8
Jackson, TN	6.1	8
Laredo, TX	6.1	8
Rapid City, SD	6.1	8
Brownsville–Harlingen, TX	6.0	9
El Paso, TX	6.0	9
McAllen–Edinburg–Mission, TX	6.0	9
Monroe, LA	6.0	9
Terre Haute, IN	6.0	9
Altoona, PA	5.9	10
Charleston, WV	5.9	10
Chico, CA	5.9	10
Duluth, MN–WI	5.9	10
Gainesville, FL	5.9	10
Grand Forks, ND	5.9	10
Lakeland–Winter Haven, FL	5.9	10
Yakima, WA	5.9	10
Abilene, TX	5.8	11
Danville, VA	5.8	11
Fort Walton Beach, FL	5.8	11
Medford, OR	5.8	11
Panama City, FL	5.8	11
Sioux City, IA–NE	5.8	11
Tampa–Saint Petersburg–Clearwater, FL	5.8	11
Tyler, TX	5.8	11
Victoria, TX	5.8	11
Williamsport, PA	5.8	11

Source: U.S. Bureau of the Census, Data User Services Division, *1990 Census of Population and Housing*, Summary Tape File 3C, United States Summary, CD-ROM, February 1992.

★1719★

Family and Household Income

Households With Income of $17,500 to $19,999, 1989

[Table shows the top 50 areas]

MSA	% of all households	Rank
Rapid City, SD	6.8	1
Jacksonville, NC	6.6	2
Killeen–Temple, TX	6.6	2
Lawton, OK	6.6	2
Ocala, FL	6.4	3
Clarksville–Hopkinsville, TN–KY	6.3	4
Great Falls, MT	6.0	5
Johnstown, PA	5.9	6
Joplin, MO	5.8	7
Fayetteville, NC	5.7	8
Fort Walton Beach, FL	5.7	8
Bradenton, FL	5.6	9
Dubuque, IA	5.6	9
Merced, CA	5.6	9
Altoona, PA	5.5	10
Grand Forks, ND	5.5	10
San Angelo, TX	5.5	10
Yuma, AZ	5.5	10
Chico, CA	5.4	11
Daytona Beach, FL	5.4	11
McAllen–Edinburg–Mission, TX	5.4	11
Yakima, WA	5.4	11
El Paso, TX	5.3	12
Fort Smith, AR–OK	5.3	12
Lakeland–Winter Haven, FL	5.3	12
Pueblo, CO	5.3	12
Salem, OR	5.3	12
Sharon, PA	5.3	12
Tampa–Saint Petersburg–Clearwater, FL	5.3	12
Wheeling, WV–OH	5.3	12
Yuba City, CA	5.3	12
Abilene, TX	5.2	13
Alexandria, LA	5.2	13
Biloxi–Gulfport, MS	5.2	13
Fort Myers–Cape Coral, Fl	5.2	13
Springfield, MO	5.2	13
Brownsville–Harlingen, TX	5.1	14
Charleston, WV	5.1	14
Colorado Springs, CO	5.1	14
Columbus, GA–AL	5.1	14
Cumberland, MD–WV	5.1	14
Fayetteville–Springdale, AR	5.1	14
Johnson City–Kingsport–Bristol, TN–VA	5.1	14
Las Cruces, NM	5.1	14
Mansfield, OH	5.1	14
Panama City, FL	5.1	14
Pensacola, FL	5.1	14
Sioux City, IA–NE	5.1	14
Florence, AL	5.0	15
Steubenville–Weirton, OH–WV	5.0	15

Source: U.S. Bureau of the Census, Data User Services Division, *1990 Census of Population and Housing*, Summary Tape File 3C, United States Summary, CD-ROM, February 1992.

★1720★
Family and Household Income
Households With Income of $20,000 to $22,499, 1989

[Table shows the top 50 areas]

MSA	% of all households	Rank
Jacksonville, NC	8.1	1
Enid, OK	6.5	2
Ocala, FL	6.5	2
Bismarck, ND	6.4	3
Killeen – Temple, TX	6.4	3
Rapid City, SD	6.4	3
Bradenton, FL	6.2	4
Cheyenne, WY	6.2	4
Clarksville – Hopkinsville, TN – KY	6.2	4
Cumberland, MD – WV	6.2	4
Fayetteville, NC	6.2	4
Fayetteville – Springdale, AR	6.2	4
Fort Walton Beach, FL	6.2	4
Johnstown, PA	6.2	4
Panama City, FL	6.1	5
Great Falls, MT	6.0	6
Medford, OR	6.0	6
Sarasota, FL	6.0	6
Abilene, TX	5.9	7
Biloxi – Gulfport, MS	5.9	7
Daytona Beach, FL	5.9	7
Fort Smith, AR – OK	5.9	7
Lakeland – Winter Haven, FL	5.9	7
Lawton, OK	5.9	7
Salem, OR	5.9	7
Sioux City, IA – NE	5.9	7
Wichita Falls, TX	5.9	7
Williamsport, PA	5.9	7
Yuma, AZ	5.9	7
Asheville, NC	5.8	8
Chico, CA	5.8	8
Columbus, GA – AL	5.8	8
Joplin, MO	5.8	8
Sioux Falls, SD	5.8	8
Springfield, MO	5.8	8
Tampa – Saint Petersburg – Clearwater, FL	5.8	8
Yakima, WA	5.8	8
Colorado Springs, CO	5.7	9
Elkhart – Goshen, IN	5.7	9
Elmira, NY	5.7	9
Fort Myers – Cape Coral, Fl	5.7	9
Grand Forks, ND	5.7	9
Jackson, TN	5.7	9
Owensboro, KY	5.7	9
Pensacola, FL	5.7	9
Provo – Orem, UT	5.7	9
San Angelo, TX	5.7	9
Jamestown – Dunkirk, NY	5.6	10
Lewiston – Auburn, ME	5.6	10
Terre Haute, IN	5.6	10

Source: U.S. Bureau of the Census, Data User Services Division, *1990 Census of Population and Housing,* Summary Tape File 3C, United States Summary, CD- ROM, February 1992.

★1721★
Family and Household Income
Households With Income of $22,500 to $24,999, 1989

[Table shows the top 50 areas]

MSA	% of all households	Rank
Ocala, FL	5.6	1
Bradenton, FL	5.4	2
Fort Myers – Cape Coral, Fl	5.2	3
Sarasota, FL	5.2	3
Great Falls, MT	5.1	4
Johnstown, PA	5.1	4
Daytona Beach, FL	5.0	5
Pueblo, CO	5.0	5
Cumberland, MD – WV	4.7	6
Altoona, PA	4.6	7
Chico, CA	4.6	7
Fort Pierce, FL	4.6	7
Joplin, MO	4.6	7
Lakeland – Winter Haven, FL	4.6	7
Tampa – Saint Petersburg – Clearwater, FL	4.6	7
Fort Smith, AR – OK	4.5	8
Houma – Thibodaux, LA	4.5	8
Odessa, TX	4.5	8
Sharon, PA	4.5	8
Williamsport, PA	4.5	8
Muskegon, MI	4.4	9
Wheeling, WV – OH	4.4	9
Eugene – Springfield, OR	4.3	10
Jamestown – Dunkirk, NY	4.3	10
Yuma, AZ	4.3	10
Parkersburg – Marietta, WV – OH	4.2	11
Salem, OR	4.2	11
Steubenville – Weirton, OH – WV	4.2	11
Youngstown – Warren, OH	4.2	11
Fayetteville – Springdale, AR	4.1	12
Mansfield, OH	4.1	12
Saint Joseph, MO	4.1	12
Spokane, WA	4.1	12
Lima, OH	4.0	13
Panama City, FL	4.0	13
Redding, CA	4.0	13
Springfield, MO	4.0	13
Terre Haute, IN	4.0	13
Yakima, WA	4.0	13
Burlington, NC	3.9	14
Enid, OK	3.9	14
Fort Walton Beach, FL	3.9	14
Huntington – Ashland, WV – KY – OH	3.9	14
Las Cruces, NM	3.9	14
Longview – Marshall, TX	3.9	14
Melbourne – Titusville – Palm Bay, FL	3.9	14
Sherman – Denison, TX	3.9	14
Shreveport, LA	3.9	14
Texarkana, TX – Texarkana, AR	3.9	14
Yuba City, CA	3.9	14

Source: U.S. Bureau of the Census, Data User Services Division, *1990 Census of Population and Housing,* Summary Tape File 3C, United States Summary, CD- ROM, February 1992.

★1722★

Family and Household Income

Households With Income of $25,000 to $27,499, 1989

[Table shows the top 50 areas]

MSA	% of all households	Rank
Jacksonville, NC	6.6	1
Grand Forks, ND	5.9	2
Fort Walton Beach, FL	5.7	3
Lawton, OK	5.7	3
Clarksville – Hopkinsville, TN – KY	5.6	4
Enid, OK	5.6	4
Fayetteville – Springdale, AR	5.6	4
Hickory – Morganton, NC	5.6	4
Anniston, AL	5.5	5
Bradenton, FL	5.5	5
Fort Pierce, FL	5.5	5
Fort Smith, AR – OK	5.5	5
Great Falls, MT	5.5	5
Killeen – Temple, TX	5.5	5
Sioux Falls, SD	5.5	5
Yuma, AZ	5.5	5
Canton, OH	5.4	6
Elkhart – Goshen, IN	5.4	6
Elmira, NY	5.4	6
Erie, PA	5.4	6
Fayetteville, NC	5.4	6
Fort Myers – Cape Coral, Fl	5.4	6
Lakeland – Winter Haven, FL	5.4	6
Provo – Orem, UT	5.4	6
Rapid City, SD	5.4	6
Saint Cloud, MN	5.4	6
Sherman – Denison, TX	5.4	6
Springfield, MO	5.4	6
Williamsport, PA	5.4	6
Abilene, TX	5.3	7
Hagerstown, MD	5.3	7
Johnstown, PA	5.3	7
Lewiston – Auburn, ME	5.3	7
Saint Joseph, MO	5.3	7
Salt Lake City – Ogden, UT	5.3	7
Sharon, PA	5.3	7
State College, PA	5.3	7
Amarillo, TX	5.2	8
Daytona Beach, FL	5.2	8
Eau Claire, WI	5.2	8
Joplin, MO	5.2	8
Panama City, FL	5.2	8
Billings, MT	5.1	9
Charleston, SC	5.1	9
Jamestown – Dunkirk, NY	5.1	9
Lima, OH	5.1	9
Naples, FL	5.1	9
Ocala, FL	5.1	9
Olympia, WA	5.1	9
Orlando, FL	5.1	9

Source: U.S. Bureau of the Census, Data User Services Division, *1990 Census of Population and Housing,* Summary Tape File 3C, United States Summary, CD- ROM, February 1992.

★1723★

Family and Household Income

Households With Income of $27,500 to $29,999, 1989

[Table shows the top 50 areas]

MSA	% of all households	Rank
Sharon, PA	4.9	1
Altoona, PA	4.7	2
Hickory – Morganton, NC	4.7	2
Anniston, AL	4.6	3
Clarksville – Hopkinsville, TN – KY	4.6	3
Dubuque, IA	4.6	3
Enid, OK	4.6	3
Jacksonville, NC	4.6	3
La Crosse, WI	4.6	3
Rapid City, SD	4.6	3
Saint Cloud, MN	4.6	3
Bremerton, WA	4.5	4
Eau Claire, WI	4.5	4
Elkhart – Goshen, IN	4.5	4
Grand Forks, ND	4.5	4
Lakeland – Winter Haven, FL	4.5	4
Lewiston – Auburn, ME	4.5	4
Ocala, FL	4.5	4
Panama City, FL	4.5	4
Salem, OR	4.5	4
San Angelo, TX	4.5	4
Sarasota, FL	4.5	4
Billings, MT	4.4	5
Boise, ID	4.4	5
Fayetteville – Springdale, AR	4.4	5
Fort Myers – Cape Coral, Fl	4.4	5
Fort Walton Beach, FL	4.4	5
Johnstown, PA	4.4	5
Lancaster, PA	4.4	5
Sioux Falls, SD	4.4	5
Springfield, MO	4.4	5
Wausau, WI	4.4	5
Williamsport, PA	4.4	5
Asheville, NC	4.3	6
Biloxi – Gulfport, MS	4.3	6
Canton, OH	4.3	6
Casper, WY	4.3	6
Charlottesville, VA	4.3	6
Fayetteville, NC	4.3	6
Green Bay, WI	4.3	6
Hagerstown, MD	4.3	6
Harrisburg – Lebanon – Carlisle, PA	4.3	6
Joplin, MO	4.3	6
Killeen – Temple, TX	4.3	6
Lima, OH	4.3	6
Mansfield, OH	4.3	6
Provo – Orem, UT	4.3	6
Salt Lake City – Ogden, UT	4.3	6
Wichita Falls, TX	4.3	6
York, PA	4.3	6

Source: U.S. Bureau of the Census, Data User Services Division, *1990 Census of Population and Housing,* Summary Tape File 3C, United States Summary, CD- ROM, February 1992.

★1724★

Family and Household Income

Households With Income of $30,000 to $32,499, 1989

[Table shows the top 50 areas]

MSA	% of all households	Rank
Asheville, NC	5.6	1
Rapid City, SD	5.6	1
Elkhart – Goshen, IN	5.5	2
Salinas – Seaside – Monterey, CA	5.5	2
Hickory – Morganton, NC	5.4	3
York, PA	5.4	3
Altoona, PA	5.3	4
Appleton – Oshkosh – Neenah, WI	5.3	4
Bremerton, WA	5.3	4
Glens Falls, NY	5.3	4
Lancaster, PA	5.3	4
Lewiston – Auburn, ME	5.3	4
Sharon, PA	5.3	4
Topeka, KS	5.3	4
Williamsport, PA	5.3	4
Anniston, AL	5.2	5
Benton Harbor, MI	5.2	5
Canton, OH	5.2	5
Clarksville – Hopkinsville, TN – KY	5.2	5
Hagerstown, MD	5.2	5
Las Vegas, NV	5.2	5
Muskegon, MI	5.2	5
Orlando, FL	5.2	5
Owensboro, KY	5.2	5
Salt Lake City – Ogden, UT	5.2	5
Boise, ID	5.1	6
Burlington, NC	5.1	6
Des Moines, IA	5.1	6
Dubuque, IA	5.1	6
Erie, PA	5.1	6
Fargo – Moorhead, ND – MN	5.1	6
Grand Forks, ND	5.1	6
Green Bay, WI	5.1	6
Harrisburg – Lebanon – Carlisle, PA	5.1	6
Jacksonville, NC	5.1	6
Kankakee, IL	5.1	6
Lawton, OK	5.1	6
Olympia, WA	5.1	6
Provo – Orem, UT	5.1	6
Terre Haute, IN	5.1	6
Wausau, WI	5.1	6
Wichita, KS	5.1	6
Bellingham, WA	5.0	7
Daytona Beach, FL	5.0	7
Fayetteville, NC	5.0	7
Fort Myers – Cape Coral, Fl	5.0	7
Fort Wayne, IN	5.0	7
Lakeland – Winter Haven, FL	5.0	7
Roanoke, VA	5.0	7
Saint Cloud, MN	5.0	7

Source: U.S. Bureau of the Census, Data User Services Division, *1990 Census of Population and Housing*, Summary Tape File 3C, United States Summary, CD- ROM, February 1992.

★1725★

Family and Household Income

Households With Income of $32,500 to $34,999, 1989

[Table shows the top 50 areas]

MSA	% of all households	Rank
Sioux Falls, SD	4.7	1
Casper, WY	4.6	2
Appleton – Oshkosh – Neenah, WI	4.4	3
Cedar Rapids, IA	4.3	4
Elkhart – Goshen, IN	4.3	4
Glens Falls, NY	4.3	4
Lancaster, PA	4.3	4
Sheboygan, WI	4.3	4
Wausau, WI	4.3	4
York, PA	4.3	4
Dubuque, IA	4.2	5
Bremerton, WA	4.1	6
Fort Myers – Cape Coral, Fl	4.1	6
Harrisburg – Lebanon – Carlisle, PA	4.1	6
Hickory – Morganton, NC	4.1	6
Janesville – Beloit, WI	4.1	6
Medford, OR	4.1	6
Rochester, MN	4.1	6
Topeka, KS	4.1	6
Colorado Springs, CO	4.0	7
Eau Claire, WI	4.0	7
Green Bay, WI	4.0	7
Olympia, WA	4.0	7
Salt Lake City – Ogden, UT	4.0	7
Williamsport, PA	4.0	7
Canton, OH	3.9	8
Erie, PA	3.9	8
Fort Wayne, IN	3.9	8
Grand Rapids, MI	3.9	8
Kokomo, IN	3.9	8
Lewiston – Auburn, ME	3.9	8
Omaha, NE – IA	3.9	8
Saint Cloud, MN	3.9	8
Yakima, WA	3.9	8
Bradenton, FL	3.8	9
Burlington, NC	3.8	9
Columbia, SC	3.8	9
Des Moines, IA	3.8	9
Fort Pierce, FL	3.8	9
Fort Walton Beach, FL	3.8	9
La Crosse, WI	3.8	9
Lakeland – Winter Haven, FL	3.8	9
Lincoln, NE	3.8	9
Mansfield, OH	3.8	9
Portland – Vancouver, OR – WA	3.8	9
Provo – Orem, UT	3.8	9
Salinas – Seaside – Monterey, CA	3.8	9
Sioux City, IA – NE	3.8	9
Wichita, KS	3.8	9
Wilmington, NC	3.8	9

Source: U.S. Bureau of the Census, Data User Services Division, *1990 Census of Population and Housing*, Summary Tape File 3C, United States Summary, CD- ROM, February 1992.

★1726★
Family and Household Income
Households With Income of $35,000 to $37,499, 1989

[Table shows the top 50 areas]

MSA	% of all households	Rank
Sheboygan, WI	5.0	1
Green Bay, WI	4.8	2
Lancaster, PA	4.8	2
Appleton – Oshkosh – Neenah, WI	4.7	3
Elkhart – Goshen, IN	4.7	3
Hickory – Morganton, NC	4.7	3
Olympia, WA	4.7	3
Provo – Orem, UT	4.7	3
Wausau, WI	4.7	3
York, PA	4.7	3
Fort Wayne, IN	4.6	4
Grand Rapids, MI	4.6	4
Hagerstown, MD	4.6	4
Portsmouth – Dover – Rochester, NH – ME	4.6	4
Saint Cloud, MN	4.6	4
Bremerton, WA	4.5	5
Casper, WY	4.5	5
Cheyenne, WY	4.5	5
Jackson, MI	4.5	5
Kokomo, IN	4.5	5
Richland – Kennewick – Pasco, WA	4.5	5
Rochester, MN	4.5	5
Billings, MT	4.4	6
Burlington, VT	4.4	6
Des Moines, IA	4.4	6
Fort Walton Beach, FL	4.4	6
Harrisburg – Lebanon – Carlisle, PA	4.4	6
La Crosse, WI	4.4	6
Medford, OR	4.4	6
Norfolk – Virginia Beach – Newport News, VA	4.4	6
Orlando, FL	4.4	6
Reading, PA	4.4	6
Rockford, IL	4.4	6
Burlington, NC	4.3	7
Cedar Rapids, IA	4.3	7
Charlottesville, VA	4.3	7
Janesville – Beloit, WI	4.3	7
Manchester, NH	4.3	7
Omaha, NE – IA	4.3	7
Portland, ME	4.3	7
Salt Lake City – Ogden, UT	4.3	7
Seattle – Tacoma, WA	4.3	7
Dubuque, IA	4.2	8
Las Vegas, NV	4.2	8
Melbourne – Titusville – Palm Bay, FL	4.2	8
Pascagoula, MS	4.2	8
Portland – Vancouver, OR – WA	4.2	8
Reno, NV	4.2	8
Salem, OR	4.2	8
Salinas – Seaside – Monterey, CA	4.2	8

Source: U.S. Bureau of the Census, Data User Services Division, *1990 Census of Population and Housing*, Summary Tape File 3C, United States Summary, CD- ROM, February 1992.

★1727★
Family and Household Income
Households With Income of $37,500 to $39,999, 1989

[Table shows the top 50 areas]

MSA	% of all households	Rank
Appleton – Oshkosh – Neenah, WI	4.2	1
Sheboygan, WI	4.2	1
Manchester, NH	4.1	2
Glens Falls, NY	3.9	3
Green Bay, WI	3.9	3
Sioux Falls, SD	3.9	3
Elkhart – Goshen, IN	3.8	4
Olympia, WA	3.8	4
Wausau, WI	3.8	4
Boise, ID	3.7	5
Cedar Rapids, IA	3.7	5
Fort Wayne, IN	3.7	5
Grand Rapids, MI	3.7	5
Hagerstown, MD	3.7	5
Lancaster, PA	3.7	5
Rockford, IL	3.7	5
York, PA	3.7	5
Bismarck, ND	3.6	6
Bloomington – Normal, IL	3.6	6
Eau Claire, WI	3.6	6
Fort Walton Beach, FL	3.6	6
Harrisburg – Lebanon – Carlisle, PA	3.6	6
Janesville – Beloit, WI	3.6	6
Portsmouth – Dover – Rochester, NH – ME	3.6	6
Saint Cloud, MN	3.6	6
Salt Lake City – Ogden, UT	3.6	6
Sarasota, FL	3.6	6
Springfield, IL	3.6	6
Bremerton, WA	3.5	7
Fitchburg – Leominster, MA	3.5	7
Hickory – Morganton, NC	3.5	7
Kankakee, IL	3.5	7
Madison, WI	3.5	7
Minneapolis – Saint Paul, MN – WI	3.5	7
New London – Norwich, CT – RI	3.5	7
Provo – Orem, UT	3.5	7
Seattle – Tacoma, WA	3.5	7
Allentown – Bethlehem – Easton, PA – NJ	3.4	8
Bangor, ME	3.4	8
Des Moines, IA	3.4	8
Fort Myers – Cape Coral, Fl	3.4	8
La Crosse, WI	3.4	8
Milwaukee – Racine, WI	3.4	8
Norfolk – Virginia Beach – Newport News, VA	3.4	8
Pascagoula, MS	3.4	8
Portland – Vancouver, OR – WA	3.4	8
Reading, PA	3.4	8
Rochester, NY	3.4	8
Naples, FL	3.3	9
Peoria, IL	3.3	9

Source: U.S. Bureau of the Census, Data User Services Division, *1990 Census of Population and Housing*, Summary Tape File 3C, United States Summary, CD- ROM, February 1992.

★1728★

Family and Household Income

Households With Income of $40,000 to $42,999, 1989

[Table shows the top 50 areas]

MSA	% of all households	Rank
Sheboygan, WI	5.0	1
Janesville – Beloit, WI	4.6	2
Portland, ME	4.6	2
Lancaster, PA	4.5	3
Appleton – Oshkosh – Neenah, WI	4.4	4
York, PA	4.4	4
Bremerton, WA	4.3	5
Elkhart – Goshen, IN	4.3	5
Fitchburg – Leominster, MA	4.3	5
Grand Rapids, MI	4.3	5
Burlington, VT	4.2	6
Hagerstown, MD	4.2	6
Poughkeepsie, NY	4.2	6
Reading, PA	4.2	6
Salt Lake City – Ogden, UT	4.2	6
Allentown – Bethlehem – Easton, PA – NJ	4.1	7
Atlantic City, NJ	4.1	7
Cedar Rapids, IA	4.1	7
Des Moines, IA	4.1	7
Fort Wayne, IN	4.1	7
Green Bay, WI	4.1	7
Huntsville, AL	4.1	7
Kankakee, IL	4.1	7
Kokomo, IN	4.1	7
La Crosse, WI	4.1	7
Las Vegas, NV	4.1	7
Minneapolis – Saint Paul, MN – WI	4.1	7
New London – Norwich, CT – RI	4.1	7
Portsmouth – Dover – Rochester, NH – ME	4.1	7
Williamsport, PA	4.1	7
Bloomington – Normal, IL	4.0	8
Harrisburg – Lebanon – Carlisle, PA	4.0	8
Lewiston – Auburn, ME	4.0	8
Lima, OH	4.0	8
Milwaukee – Racine, WI	4.0	8
Olympia, WA	4.0	8
Omaha, NE – IA	4.0	8
Saint Cloud, MN	4.0	8
Salinas – Seaside – Monterey, CA	4.0	8
Seattle – Tacoma, WA	4.0	8
Springfield, MA	4.0	8
Victoria, TX	4.0	8
Worcester, MA	4.0	8
Flint, MI	3.9	9
Kalamazoo, MI	3.9	9
Manchester, NH	3.9	9
Reno, NV	3.9	9
Sacramento, CA	3.9	9
South Bend – Mishawaka, IN	3.9	9
Stockton, CA	3.9	9

Source: U.S. Bureau of the Census, Data User Services Division, *1990 Census of Population and Housing*, Summary Tape File 3C, United States Summary, CD- ROM, February 1992.

★1729★

Family and Household Income

Households With Income of $42,500 to $44,999, 1989

[Table shows the top 50 areas]

MSA	% of all households	Rank
Sheboygan, WI	3.5	1
Appleton – Oshkosh – Neenah, WI	3.4	2
Cedar Rapids, IA	3.4	2
Grand Rapids, MI	3.4	2
Green Bay, WI	3.4	2
Lima, OH	3.4	2
York, PA	3.4	2
Lancaster, PA	3.3	3
Minneapolis – Saint Paul, MN – WI	3.3	3
Wausau, WI	3.3	3
Bloomington – Normal, IL	3.2	4
Bremerton, WA	3.2	4
Hagerstown, MD	3.2	4
Harrisburg – Lebanon – Carlisle, PA	3.2	4
Madison, WI	3.2	4
Manchester, NH	3.2	4
Portsmouth – Dover – Rochester, NH – ME	3.2	4
Reading, PA	3.2	4
Richmond – Petersburg, VA	3.2	4
Rochester, MN	3.2	4
Rockford, IL	3.2	4
Albany – Schenectady – Troy, NY	3.1	5
Burlington, VT	3.1	5
Cheyenne, WY	3.1	5
Dayton – Springfield, OH	3.1	5
Elkhart – Goshen, IN	3.1	5
Janesville – Beloit, WI	3.1	5
Milwaukee – Racine, WI	3.1	5
Saint Cloud, MN	3.1	5
Springfield, IL	3.1	5
Allentown – Bethlehem – Easton, PA – NJ	3.0	6
Anderson, IN	3.0	6
Charlottesville, VA	3.0	6
Decatur, IL	3.0	6
Dubuque, IA	3.0	6
Hartford – New Britain – Middletown, CT	3.0	6
Kokomo, IN	3.0	6
Lincoln, NE	3.0	6
Olympia, WA	3.0	6
Peoria, IL	3.0	6
Rochester, NY	3.0	6
Salt Lake City – Ogden, UT	3.0	6
Seattle – Tacoma, WA	3.0	6
Sioux City, IA – NE	3.0	6
Casper, WY	2.9	7
Colorado Springs, CO	2.9	7
New London – Norwich, CT – RI	2.9	7
Pittsfield, MA	2.9	7

[Continued]

★1729★

Households With Income of $42,500 to $44,999, 1989
[Continued]

MSA	% of all households	Rank
Providence – Pawtucket – Fall River, RI – MA	2.9	7
Sioux Falls, SD	2.9	7

Source: U.S. Bureau of the Census, Data User Services Division, *1990 Census of Population and Housing*, Summary Tape File 3C, United States Summary, CD- ROM, February 1992.

★1730★
Family and Household Income

Households With Income of $45,000 to $47,499, 1989
[Table shows the top 50 areas]

MSA	% of all households	Rank
Portsmouth – Dover – Rochester, NH – ME	4.0	1
Burlington, VT	3.8	2
Cedar Rapids, IA	3.7	3
York, PA	3.7	3
Elkhart – Goshen, IN	3.6	4
Fitchburg – Leominster, MA	3.6	4
Lancaster, PA	3.6	4
Minneapolis – Saint Paul, MN – WI	3.6	4
New London – Norwich, CT – RI	3.6	4
Sheboygan, WI	3.6	4
Fort Wayne, IN	3.5	5
Grand Rapids, MI	3.5	5
Manchester, NH	3.5	5
Waterbury, CT	3.5	5
Worcester, MA	3.5	5
Allentown – Bethlehem – Easton, PA – NJ	3.4	6
Appleton – Oshkosh – Neenah, WI	3.4	6
Hartford – New Britain – Middletown, CT	3.4	6
Poughkeepsie, NY	3.4	6
Rockford, IL	3.4	6
Atlanta, GA	3.3	7
Bismarck, ND	3.3	7
Bremerton, WA	3.3	7
Janesville – Beloit, WI	3.3	7
Madison, WI	3.3	7
Milwaukee – Racine, WI	3.3	7
Reading, PA	3.3	7
Rochester, MN	3.3	7
Seattle – Tacoma, WA	3.3	7
Stockton, CA	3.3	7
Washington, DC – MD – VA	3.3	7
Wausau, WI	3.3	7
Baltimore, MD	3.2	8
Chicago – Gary – Lake County, IL – IN – WI	3.2	8
Dubuque, IA	3.2	8

[Continued]

★1730★

Households With Income of $45,000 to $47,499, 1989
[Continued]

MSA	% of all households	Rank
Green Bay, WI	3.2	8
Harrisburg – Lebanon – Carlisle, PA	3.2	8
Lima, OH	3.2	8
Lincoln, NE	3.2	8
Olympia, WA	3.2	8
Pascagoula, MS	3.2	8
Philadelphia – Wilmington – Trenton, PA – NJ – DE – MD	3.2	8
Portland, ME	3.2	8
Providence – Pawtucket – Fall River, RI – MA	3.2	8
Raleigh – Durham, NC	3.2	8
Richland – Kennewick – Pasco, WA	3.2	8
Sacramento, CA	3.2	8
Salinas – Seaside – Monterey, CA	3.2	8
Springfield, MA	3.2	8
Topeka, KS	3.2	8

Source: U.S. Bureau of the Census, Data User Services Division, *1990 Census of Population and Housing*, Summary Tape File 3C, United States Summary, CD- ROM, February 1992.

★1731★
Family and Household Income

Households With Income of $47,500 to $49,999, 1989
[Table shows the top 50 areas]

MSA	% of all households	Rank
Manchester, NH	3.2	1
Reading, PA	3.2	1
Sheboygan, WI	3.2	1
Burlington, VT	3.1	2
Appleton – Oshkosh – Neenah, WI	3.0	3
Grand Rapids, MI	2.9	4
Hartford – New Britain – Middletown, CT	2.9	4
Lancaster, PA	2.9	4
Minneapolis – Saint Paul, MN – WI	2.9	4
Portsmouth – Dover – Rochester, NH – ME	2.9	4
Poughkeepsie, NY	2.9	4
Rochester, MN	2.9	4
York, PA	2.9	4
Allentown – Bethlehem – Easton, PA – NJ	2.8	5
Anchorage, AK	2.8	5
Cedar Rapids, IA	2.8	5
Charlottesville, VA	2.8	5
Des Moines, IA	2.8	5
Fitchburg – Leominster, MA	2.8	5
Harrisburg – Lebanon – Carlisle, PA	2.8	5

[Continued]

★1731★

Households With Income of $47,500 to $49,999, 1989

[Continued]

MSA	% of all households	Rank
Madison, WI	2.8	5
New Haven – Meriden, CT	2.8	5
New London – Norwich, CT – RI	2.8	5
Waterbury, CT	2.8	5
Elmira, NY	2.7	6
Green Bay, WI	2.7	6
Janesville – Beloit, WI	2.7	6
Milwaukee – Racine, WI	2.7	6
Portland, ME	2.7	6
Rochester, NY	2.7	6
Seattle – Tacoma, WA	2.7	6
Washington, DC – MD – VA	2.7	6
Worcester, MA	2.7	6
Albany – Schenectady – Troy, NY	2.6	7
Atlanta, GA	2.6	7
Baltimore, MD	2.6	7
Binghamton, NY	2.6	7
Chicago – Gary – Lake County, IL – IN – WI	2.6	7
Fort Wayne, IN	2.6	7
Glens Falls, NY	2.6	7
Kankakee, IL	2.6	7
Lansing – East Lansing, MI	2.6	7
Lima, OH	2.6	7
Reno, NV	2.6	7
Richmond – Petersburg, VA	2.6	7
Syracuse, NY	2.6	7
Wausau, WI	2.6	7
Wichita, KS	2.6	7
Flint, MI	2.5	8
Philadelphia – Wilmington – Trenton, PA – NJ – DE – MD	2.5	8

Source: U.S. Bureau of the Census, Data User Services Division, *1990 Census of Population and Housing*, Summary Tape File 3C, United States Summary, CD- ROM, February 1992.

★1732★

Family and Household Income

Households With Income of $50,000 to $54,999, 1989

[Table shows the top 50 areas]

MSA	% of all households	Rank
Poughkeepsie, NY	6.8	1
Rochester, MN	6.2	2
Burlington, VT	6.1	3
Waterbury, CT	6.1	3
Hartford – New Britain – Middletown, CT	6.0	4
New London – Norwich, CT – RI	6.0	4
Washington, DC – MD – VA	6.0	4
Minneapolis – Saint Paul, MN – WI	5.8	5
Worcester, MA	5.7	6

[Continued]

★1732★

Households With Income of $50,000 to $54,999, 1989

[Continued]

MSA	% of all households	Rank
Honolulu, HI	5.6	7
Manchester, NH	5.6	7
Portsmouth – Dover – Rochester, NH – ME	5.6	7
Boston – Lawrence – Salem, MA – NH	5.5	8
Cedar Rapids, IA	5.5	8
Grand Rapids, MI	5.5	8
New Haven – Meriden, CT	5.5	8
San Francisco – Oakland – San Jose, CA	5.5	8
Baltimore, MD	5.4	9
Lancaster, PA	5.4	9
Pittsfield, MA	5.4	9
Allentown – Bethlehem – Easton, PA – NJ	5.3	10
Anchorage, AK	5.3	10
Chicago – Gary – Lake County, IL – IN – WI	5.3	10
Reading, PA	5.3	10
Richmond – Petersburg, VA	5.3	10
Seattle – Tacoma, WA	5.3	10
Atlanta, GA	5.2	11
Detroit – Ann Arbor, MI	5.2	11
Madison, WI	5.2	11
Milwaukee – Racine, WI	5.2	11
Philadelphia – Wilmington – Trenton, PA – NJ – DE – MD	5.2	11
Portland, ME	5.2	11
Rochester, NY	5.2	11
Rockford, IL	5.2	11
Sacramento, CA	5.2	11
Sheboygan, WI	5.2	11
Bremerton, WA	5.1	12
Fort Wayne, IN	5.1	12
Kansas City, MO – KS	5.1	12
Los Angeles – Anaheim – Riverside, CA	5.1	12
Raleigh – Durham, NC	5.1	12
San Diego, CA	5.1	12
Santa Barbara – Santa Maria – Lompoc, CA	5.1	12
York, PA	5.1	12
Albany – Schenectady – Troy, NY	5.0	13
Denver – Boulder, CO	5.0	13
Des Moines, IA	5.0	13
Fitchburg – Leominster, MA	5.0	13
Flint, MI	5.0	13
Indianapolis, IN	5.0	13

Source: U.S. Bureau of the Census, Data User Services Division, *1990 Census of Population and Housing*, Summary Tape File 3C, United States Summary, CD- ROM, February 1992.

★1733★

Family and Household Income

Households With Income of $55,000 to $59,999, 1989

[Table shows the top 50 areas]

MSA	% of all households	Rank
Fitchburg – Leominster, MA	5.3	1
Hartford – New Britain – Middletown, CT	5.2	2
Poughkeepsie, NY	5.2	2
Washington, DC – MD – VA	5.1	3
New Haven – Meriden, CT	4.9	4
Honolulu, HI	4.7	5
Waterbury, CT	4.7	5
Boston – Lawrence – Salem, MA – NH	4.6	6
Minneapolis – Saint Paul, MN – WI	4.6	6
New London – Norwich, CT – RI	4.6	6
Rochester, MN	4.6	6
San Francisco – Oakland – San Jose, CA	4.6	6
Baltimore, MD	4.5	7
Worcester, MA	4.5	7
Atlanta, GA	4.4	8
Anchorage, AK	4.3	9
Chicago – Gary – Lake County, IL – IN – WI	4.3	9
Manchester, NH	4.3	9
Pittsfield, MA	4.3	9
Portsmouth – Dover – Rochester, NH – ME	4.3	9
Burlington, VT	4.2	10
Detroit – Ann Arbor, MI	4.2	10
Huntsville, AL	4.2	10
Madison, WI	4.2	10
Philadelphia – Wilmington – Trenton, PA – NJ – DE – MD	4.2	10
Raleigh – Durham, NC	4.2	10
Richmond – Petersburg, VA	4.2	10
Rochester, NY	4.2	10
Grand Rapids, MI	4.1	11
Lansing – East Lansing, MI	4.1	11
New York – Northern New Jersey – Long Island, NY – NJ – CT	4.1	11
Sacramento, CA	4.1	11
Seattle – Tacoma, WA	4.1	11
Albany – Schenectady – Troy, NY	4.0	12
Denver – Boulder, CO	4.0	12
Los Angeles – Anaheim – Riverside, CA	4.0	12
Milwaukee – Racine, WI	4.0	12
San Diego, CA	4.0	12
Santa Barbara – Santa Maria – Lompoc, CA	4.0	12
Santa Fe, NM	4.0	12
Allentown – Bethlehem – Easton, PA – NJ	3.9	13
Bloomington – Normal, IL	3.9	13
Kalamazoo, MI	3.9	13
Lancaster, PA	3.9	13
Peoria, IL	3.9	13

[Continued]

★1733★

Households With Income of $55,000 to $59,999, 1989

[Continued]

MSA	% of all households	Rank
Providence – Pawtucket – Fall River, RI – MA	3.9	13
Rockford, IL	3.9	13
Salinas – Seaside – Monterey, CA	3.9	13
Springfield, MA	3.9	13
Syracuse, NY	3.9	13

Source: U.S. Bureau of the Census, Data User Services Division, *1990 Census of Population and Housing*, Summary Tape File 3C, United States Summary, CD- ROM, February 1992.

★1734★

Family and Household Income

Households With Income of $60,000 to $74,999, 1989

[Table shows the top 50 areas]

MSA	% of all households	Rank
Washington, DC – MD – VA	12.6	1
Poughkeepsie, NY	12.3	2
Anchorage, AK	11.8	3
Hartford – New Britain – Middletown, CT	11.7	4
Boston – Lawrence – Salem, MA – NH	11.2	5
Honolulu, HI	11.2	5
San Francisco – Oakland – San Jose, CA	11.1	6
New Haven – Meriden, CT	10.4	7
Waterbury, CT	10.3	8
New London – Norwich, CT – RI	10.2	9
New York – Northern New Jersey – Long Island, NY – NJ – CT	9.9	10
Worcester, MA	9.8	11
Baltimore, MD	9.7	12
Burlington, VT	9.6	13
Los Angeles – Anaheim – Riverside, CA	9.5	14
Atlanta, GA	9.4	15
Philadelphia – Wilmington – Trenton, PA – NJ – DE – MD	9.4	15
Chicago – Gary – Lake County, IL – IN – WI	9.3	16
Detroit – Ann Arbor, MI	9.3	16
Minneapolis – Saint Paul, MN – WI	9.3	16
Rochester, MN	9.2	17
Fitchburg – Leominster, MA	9.1	18
Rochester, NY	9.1	18
San Diego, CA	9.1	18
Santa Barbara – Santa Maria – Lompoc, CA	9.1	18
Manchester, NH	9.0	19
Seattle – Tacoma, WA	9.0	19
Atlantic City, NJ	8.7	20

[Continued]

★1734★

Households With Income of $60,000 to $74,999, 1989

[Continued]

MSA	% of all households	Rank
Pittsfield, MA	8.6	21
Richmond – Petersburg, VA	8.6	21
Raleigh – Durham, NC	8.5	22
Sacramento, CA	8.5	22
Flint, MI	8.4	23
Huntsville, AL	8.4	23
Kokomo, IN	8.4	23
Denver – Boulder, CO	8.3	24
Lansing – East Lansing, MI	8.3	24
Portsmouth – Dover – Rochester, NH – ME	8.3	24
Dallas – Fort Worth, TX	8.2	25
Salinas – Seaside – Monterey, CA	8.2	25
Santa Fe, NM	8.2	25
Albany – Schenectady – Troy, NY	8.0	26
Allentown – Bethlehem – Easton, PA – NJ	8.0	26
Houston – Galveston – Brazoria, TX	8.0	26
Midland, TX	8.0	26
Milwaukee – Racine, WI	7.9	27
Portland, ME	7.9	27
Saint Louis, MO – IL	7.9	27
Providence – Pawtucket – Fall River, RI – MA	7.8	28
Richland – Kennewick – Pasco, WA	7.8	28

Source: U.S. Bureau of the Census, Data User Services Division, *1990 Census of Population and Housing,* Summary Tape File 3C, United States Summary, CD- ROM, February 1992.

★1735★

Family and Household Income

Households With Income of $75,000 to $99,999, 1989

[Table shows the top 50 areas]

MSA	% of all households	Rank
Anchorage, AK	12.2	1
Washington, DC – MD – VA	12.0	2
Poughkeepsie, NY	10.0	3
San Francisco – Oakland – San Jose, CA	9.8	4
Boston – Lawrence – Salem, MA – NH	9.5	5
Honolulu, HI	9.5	5
Hartford – New Britain – Middletown, CT	9.3	6
New York – Northern New Jersey – Long Island, NY – NJ – CT	8.9	7
New Haven – Meriden, CT	8.4	8
Los Angeles – Anaheim – Riverside, CA	8.0	9
Baltimore, MD	7.6	10

[Continued]

★1735★

Households With Income of $75,000 to $99,999, 1989

[Continued]

MSA	% of all households	Rank
Waterbury, CT	7.6	10
Detroit – Ann Arbor, MI	7.1	11
Philadelphia – Wilmington – Trenton, PA – NJ – DE – MD	7.1	11
San Diego, CA	7.0	12
Santa Barbara – Santa Maria – Lompoc, CA	7.0	12
Atlanta, GA	6.9	13
Burlington, VT	6.9	13
Chicago – Gary – Lake County, IL – IN – WI	6.9	13
Worcester, MA	6.9	13
Huntsville, AL	6.7	14
New London – Norwich, CT – RI	6.5	15
Santa Fe, NM	6.4	16
Minneapolis – Saint Paul, MN – WI	6.3	17
Rochester, NY	6.2	18
Manchester, NH	6.1	19
Seattle – Tacoma, WA	6.1	19
Dallas – Fort Worth, TX	6.0	20
Raleigh – Durham, NC	6.0	20
Sacramento, CA	6.0	20
West Palm Beach – Boca Raton – Delray Beach, FL	6.0	20
Denver – Boulder, CO	5.9	21
Houston – Galveston – Brazoria, TX	5.9	21
Salinas – Seaside – Monterey, CA	5.9	21
Midland, TX	5.7	22
Richmond – Petersburg, VA	5.7	22
Albany – Schenectady – Troy, NY	5.6	23
Flint, MI	5.6	23
Portsmouth – Dover – Rochester, NH – ME	5.6	23
Atlantic City, NJ	5.5	24
Kokomo, IN	5.5	24
Lansing – East Lansing, MI	5.5	24
Naples, FL	5.4	25
Providence – Pawtucket – Fall River, RI – MA	5.4	25
Fitchburg – Leominster, MA	5.3	26
Pittsfield, MA	5.2	27
Rochester, MN	5.2	27
Springfield, MA	5.2	27
Allentown – Bethlehem – Easton, PA – NJ	5.1	28
Madison, WI	5.1	28

Source: U.S. Bureau of the Census, Data User Services Division, *1990 Census of Population and Housing,* Summary Tape File 3C, United States Summary, CD- ROM, February 1992.

★1736★

Family and Household Income

Households With Income of $100,000 to $124,999, 1989

[Table shows the top 50 areas]

MSA	% of all households	Rank
Washington, DC – MD – VA	5.32	1
Anchorage, AK	4.87	2
San Francisco – Oakland – San Jose, CA	4.25	3
New York – Northern New Jersey – Long Island, NY – NJ – CT	4.19	4
Boston – Lawrence – Salem, MA – NH	4.03	5
Honolulu, HI	3.97	6
Los Angeles – Anaheim – Riverside, CA	3.51	7
Hartford – New Britain – Middletown, CT	3.46	8
New Haven – Meriden, CT	3.46	8
Poughkeepsie, NY	3.36	9
Santa Barbara – Santa Maria – Lompoc, CA	3.02	10
Naples, FL	2.95	11
Baltimore, MD	2.76	12
Philadelphia – Wilmington – Trenton, PA – NY – DE – MD	2.75	13
San Diego, CA	2.73	14
West Palm Beach – Boca Raton – Delray Beach, FL	2.73	14
Chicago – Gary – Lake County, IL – IN – WI	2.70	15
Atlanta, GA	2.67	16
Waterbury, CT	2.61	17
Santa Fe, NM	2.60	18
Detroit – Ann Arbor, MI	2.54	19
New London – Norwich, CT – RI	2.54	19
Worcester, MA	2.39	20
Houston – Galveston – Brazoria, TX	2.34	21
Minneapolis – Saint Paul, MN – WI	2.33	22
Dallas – Fort Worth, TX	2.28	23
Denver – Boulder, CO	2.27	24
Rochester, NY	2.26	25
Raleigh – Durham, NC	2.22	26
Seattle – Tacoma, WA	2.20	27
Huntsville, AL	2.19	28
Burlington, VT	2.17	29
Salinas – Seaside – Monterey, CA	2.16	30
Atlantic City, NJ	2.12	31
Midland, TX	2.10	32
Sacramento, CA	2.08	33
Charlottesville, VA	2.05	34
Iowa City, IA	2.01	35
Miami – Fort Lauderdale, FL	2.00	36
Reno, NV	1.97	37
Richmond – Petersburg, VA	1.97	37
Portsmouth – Dover – Rochester, NH – ME	1.96	38
Phoenix, AZ	1.94	39
Sarasota, FL	1.93	40

[Continued]

★1736★

Households With Income of $100,000 to $124,999, 1989

[Continued]

MSA	% of all households	Rank
Portland, ME	1.92	41
Albany – Schenectady – Troy, NY	1.89	42
Manchester, NH	1.89	42
Austin, TX	1.86	43
Saint Louis, MO – IL	1.82	44
Stockton, CA	1.82	44

Source: U.S. Bureau of the Census, Data User Services Division, *1990 Census of Population and Housing*, Summary Tape File 3C, United States Summary, CD- ROM, February 1992.

★1737★

Family and Household Income

Households With Income of $125,000 to $149,999, 1989

[Table shows the top 50 areas]

MSA	% of all households	Rank
Washington, DC – MD – VA	2.149	1
Anchorage, AK	1.889	2
New York – Northern New Jersey – Long Island, NY – NJ – CT	1.859	3
San Francisco – Oakland – San Jose, CA	1.808	4
Boston – Lawrence – Salem, MA – NH	1.667	5
Honolulu, HI	1.540	6
Naples, FL	1.530	7
Los Angeles – Anaheim – Riverside, CA	1.476	8
Santa Barbara – Santa Maria – Lompoc, CA	1.411	9
Hartford – New Britain – Middletown, CT	1.407	10
Rochester, MN	1.397	11
New Haven – Meriden, CT	1.381	12
Poughkeepsie, NY	1.283	13
West Palm Beach – Boca Raton – Delray Beach, FL	1.214	14
Chicago – Gary – Lake County, IL – IN – WI	1.158	15
San Diego, CA	1.154	16
Philadelphia – Wilmington – Trenton, PA – NJ – DE – MD	1.114	17
Atlanta, GA	1.087	18
Salinas – Seaside – Monterey, CA	1.052	19
Baltimore, MD	1.049	20
Houston – Galveston – Brazoria, TX	1.003	21
Santa Fe, NM	1.002	22
Dallas – Fort Worth, TX	0.999	23
Sarasota, FL	0.999	23
Charlottesville, VA	0.998	24
Detroit – Ann Arbor, MI	0.982	25

[Continued]

★1737★

Households With Income of $125,000 to $149,999, 1989
[Continued]

MSA	% of all households	Rank
Raleigh – Durham, NC	0.965	26
Minneapolis – Saint Paul, MN – WI	0.934	27
Iowa City, IA	0.933	28
Seattle – Tacoma, WA	0.924	29
Denver – Boulder, CO	0.891	30
Portland, ME	0.890	31
Worcester, MA	0.889	32
Burlington, VT	0.884	33
Miami – Fort Lauderdale, FL	0.880	34
Midland, TX	0.875	35
Madison, WI	0.864	36
Reno, NV	0.841	37
Manchester, NH	0.833	38
Atlantic City, NJ	0.829	39
Sacramento, CA	0.810	40
Waterbury, CT	0.801	41
Fort Pierce, FL	0.761	42
Orlando, FL	0.760	43
Providence – Pawtucket – Fall River, RI – MA	0.760	43
Albany – Schenectady – Troy, NY	0.756	44
Lexington-Fayette, KY	0.751	45
Kalamazoo, MI	0.744	46
State College, PA	0.743	47
Rochester, NY	0.739	48

Source: U.S. Bureau of the Census, Data User Services Division, *1990 Census of Population and Housing*, Summary Tape File 3C, United States Summary, CD-ROM, February 1992.

★1738★

Family and Household Income

Households With Income of $150,000 or More, 1989
[Table shows the top 50 areas]

MSA	% of all households	Rank
Naples, FL	4.65	1
New York – Northern New Jersey – Long Island, NY – NJ – CT	3.58	2
West Palm Beach – Boca Raton – Delray Beach, FL	3.27	3
Washington, DC – MD – VA	3.25	4
San Francisco – Oakland – San Jose, CA	2.99	5
Santa Barbara – Santa Maria – Lompoc, CA	2.89	6
Los Angeles – Anaheim – Riverside, CA	2.86	7
Boston – Lawrence – Salem, MA – NH	2.59	8
Anchorage, AK	2.55	9
Honolulu, HI	2.39	10
New Haven – Meriden, CT	2.33	11

[Continued]

★1738★

Households With Income of $150,000 or More, 1989
[Continued]

MSA	% of all households	Rank
Sarasota, FL	2.32	12
Chicago – Gary – Lake County, IL – IN – WI	2.28	13
Midland, TX	2.20	14
Hartford – New Britain – Middletown, CT	2.17	15
Atlanta, GA	2.16	16
Fort Pierce, FL	2.10	17
Salinas – Seaside – Monterey, CA	2.09	18
San Diego, CA	2.09	18
Philadelphia – Wilmington – Trenton, PA – NJ – DE – MD	2.06	19
Santa Fe, NM	2.02	20
Dallas – Fort Worth, TX	1.98	21
Houston – Galveston – Brazoria, TX	1.94	22
Rochester, MN	1.94	22
Miami – Fort Lauderdale, FL	1.93	23
Minneapolis – Saint Paul, MN – WI	1.86	24
Charlottesville, VA	1.83	25
Baltimore, MD	1.78	26
Fort Myers – Cape Coral, Fl	1.68	27
Reno, NV	1.68	27
Seattle – Tacoma, WA	1.68	27
Iowa City, IA	1.67	28
Detroit – Ann Arbor, MI	1.66	29
Portland, ME	1.63	30
Denver – Boulder, CO	1.60	31
Nashville, TN	1.55	32
Atlantic City, NJ	1.54	33
Phoenix, AZ	1.54	33
Pittsfield, MA	1.54	33
Las Vegas, NV	1.49	34
Manchester, NH	1.48	35
Waterbury, CT	1.48	35
Poughkeepsie, NY	1.47	36
Saint Louis, MO – IL	1.47	36
Memphis, TN – AR – MS	1.46	37
Richmond – Petersburg, VA	1.46	37
Indianapolis, IN	1.45	38
Portsmouth – Dover – Rochester, NH – ME	1.45	38
Cincinnati – Hamilton, OH – KY – IN	1.44	39
Raleigh – Durham, NC	1.44	39

Source: U.S. Bureau of the Census, Data User Services Division, *1990 Census of Population and Housing*, Summary Tape File 3C, United States Summary, CD-ROM, February 1992.

★1739★

Income By Race and Ethnicity

Highest Medium Income, 1993: Black Families

City	Wages	Rank
Washington, DC	39,896	1
Newark, NJ	32,401	2
Los Angles, CA	30,141	3
Baltimore, MD	28,924	4
Atlanta, GA	27,498	5
New York, NY	27,053	6
Philadelphia, PA	26,980	7
Chicago, IL	24,756	8
Dallas, TX	23,881	9
Detroit, MI	23,764	10

Source: "Today's Debate: Million Man March—Message of Today's March is Self-Help, Not Racism," *USA TODAY*, 16 October 1995, p. 12A. Primary source: U.S. Bureau of the Census.

★1740★

Income By Race and Ethnicity

Total Aggregate Household Income of American Indians, Eskimos, and Aleuts, 1989

[Table shows the top 50 areas]

	Mil. $	Rank
Los Angeles – Anaheim – Riverside, CA	1,154	1
San Francisco – Oakland – San Jose, CA	568	2
New York – Northern New Jersey – Long Island, NY – NJ – CT	471	3
Tulsa, OK	432	4
Oklahoma City, OK	400	5
Seattle – Tacoma, WA	318	6
Phoenix, AZ	255	7
San Diego, CA	248	8
Dallas – Fort Worth, TX	248	9
Sacramento, CA	219	10
Detroit – Ann Arbor, MI	211	11
Chicago – Gary – Lake County, IL – IN – WI	205	12
Washington, DC – MD – VA	189	13
Minneapolis – Saint Paul, MN – WI	183	14
Houston – Galveston – Brazoria, TX	160	15
Philadelphia – Wilmington – Trenton, PA – NJ – DE – MD	157	16
Anchorage, AK	152	17
Portland – Vancouver, OR – WA	146	18
Albuquerque, NM	126	19
Denver – Boulder, CO	125	20
Tucson, AZ	104	21
Kansas City, MO – KS	100	22
Boston – Lawrence – Salem, MA – NH	97	23
Baltimore, MD	89	24
Miami – Fort Lauderdale, FL	83	25
Las Vegas, NV	80	26
Atlanta, GA	80	27
Tampa – Saint Petersburg – Clearwater, FL	78	28

[Continued]

★1740★

Total Aggregate Household Income of American Indians, Eskimos, and Aleuts, 1989

[Continued]

	Mil. $	Rank
Bakersfield, CA	78	29
Milwaukee – Racine, WI	70	30
Saint Louis, MO – IL	68	31
Fresno, CA	67	32
Norfolk – Virginia Beach – Newport News, VA	64	33
Stockton, CA	63	34
Buffalo – Niagara Falls, NY	62	35
Fort Smith, AR – OK	57	36
Cleveland – Akron – Lorain, OH	57	37
Salt Lake City – Ogden, UT	53	38
San Antonio, TX	52	39
Wichita, KS	51	40
Modesto, CA	50	41
Yakima, WA	47	42
Charlotte – Gastonia – Rock Hill, NC – SC	47	43
Honolulu, HI	47	44
Reno, NV	45	45
Orlando, FL	40	46
Santa Barbara – Santa Maria – Lompoc, CA	40	47
Greensboro – Winston-Salem – High Point, NC	37	48
Richmond – Petersburg, VA	37	49
Columbus, OH	37	50

Source: U.S. Bureau of the Census, Data User Services Division, *1990 Census of Population and Housing*, Summary Tape File 3C, United States Summary, CD-ROM, February 1992.

★1741★

Income By Race and Ethnicity

Total Aggregate Household Income of Asians and Pacific Islanders, 1989

[Table shows the top 50 areas]

	Mil. $	Rank
Los Angeles – Anaheim – Riverside, CA	18,777	1
San Francisco – Oakland – San Jose, CA	13,329	2
New York – Northern New Jersey – Long Island, NY – NJ – CT	13,096	3
Honolulu, HI	7,910	4
Chicago – Gary – Lake County, IL – IN – WI	3,757	5
Washington, DC – MD – VA	3,101	6
San Diego, CA	2,045	7
Seattle – Tacoma, WA	1,826	8
Houston – Galveston – Brazoria, TX	1,663	9
Philadelphia – Wilmington – Trenton, PA – NJ – DE – MD	1,586	10
Boston – Lawrence – Salem, MA – NH	1,506	11

[Continued]

★1741★

Total Aggregate Household Income of Asians and Pacific Islanders, 1989

[Continued]

	Mil. $	Rank
Sacramento, CA	1,232	12
Dallas – Fort Worth, TX	1,148	13
Detroit – Ann Arbor, MI	1,079	14
Baltimore, MD	667	15
Atlanta, GA	613	16
Portland – Vancouver, OR – WA	542	17
Miami – Fort Lauderdale, FL	516	18
Minneapolis – Saint Paul, MN – WI	511	19
Stockton, CA	473	20
Cleveland – Akron – Lorain, OH	459	21
Denver – Boulder, CO	456	22
Phoenix, AZ	415	23
Fresno, CA	398	24
Saint Louis, MO – IL	328	25
Norfolk – Virginia Beach – Newport News, VA	321	26
Salinas – Seaside – Monterey, CA	315	27
Las Vegas, NV	279	28
Tampa – Saint Petersburg – Clearwater, FL	254	29
Pittsburgh – Beaver Valley, PA	247	30
Hartford – New Britain – Middletown, CT	247	31
Columbus, OH	246	32
Orlando, FL	220	33
Salt Lake City – Ogden, UT	219	34
Cincinnati – Hamilton, OH – KY – IN	210	35
Milwaukee – Racine, WI	199	36
Jacksonville, FL	199	37
Kansas City, MO – KS	186	38
New Orleans, LA	185	39
Bakersfield, CA	185	40
Santa Barbara – Santa Maria – Lompoc, CA	180	41
Buffalo – Niagara Falls, NY	171	42
Raleigh – Durham, NC	168	43
Austin, TX	166	44
Providence – Pawtucket – Fall River, RI – MA	166	45
Oklahoma City, OK	165	46
Rochester, NY	164	47
Dayton – Springfield, OH	156	48
Richmond – Petersburg, VA	154	49
San Antonio, TX	146	50

Source: U.S. Bureau of the Census, Data User Services Division, *1990 Census of Population and Housing*, Summary Tape File 3C, United States Summary, CD-ROM, February 1992.

★1742★

Income By Race and Ethnicity

Total Aggregate Household Income of Blacks, 1989

[Table shows the top 50 areas]

	Mil. $	Rank
New York – Northern New Jersey – Long Island, NY – NJ – CT	35,562	1
Washington, DC – MD – VA	14,431	2
Los Angeles – Anaheim – Riverside, CA	14,368	3
Chicago – Gary – Lake County, IL – IN – WI	13,949	4
Philadelphia – Wilmington – Trenton, PA – NJ – DE – MD	10,562	5
Detroit – Ann Arbor, MI	9,185	6
Atlanta, GA	7,295	7
San Francisco – Oakland – San Jose, CA	6,383	8
Baltimore, MD	6,176	9
Houston – Galveston – Brazoria, TX	5,741	10
Dallas – Fort Worth, TX	4,878	11
Miami – Fort Lauderdale, FL	4,664	12
Cleveland – Akron – Lorain, OH	3,874	13
Saint Louis, MO – IL	3,529	14
Norfolk – Virginia Beach – Newport News, VA	3,327	15
Memphis, TN – AR – MS	2,780	16
New Orleans, LA	2,776	17
Boston – Lawrence – Salem, MA – NH	2,554	18
Richmond – Petersburg, VA	2,417	19
Charlotte – Gastonia – Rock Hill, NC – SC	1,996	20
Birmingham, AL	1,790	21
Raleigh – Durham, NC	1,724	22
Kansas City, MO – KS	1,721	23
Cincinnati – Hamilton, OH – KY – IN	1,691	24
Greensboro – Winston-Salem – High Point, NC	1,638	25
Indianapolis, IN	1,561	26
San Diego, CA	1,507	27
Milwaukee – Racine, WI	1,477	28
Columbus, OH	1,454	29
Pittsburgh – Beaver Valley, PA	1,424	30
Jacksonville, FL	1,399	31
Tampa – Saint Petersburg – Clearwater, FL	1,380	32
Nashville, TN	1,283	33
Seattle – Tacoma, WA	1,256	34
Dayton – Springfield, OH	1,150	35
Columbia, SC	1,072	36
Sacramento, CA	1,069	37
Hartford – New Britain – Middletown, CT	1,057	38
Jackson, MS	1,056	39
Orlando, FL	1,047	40
Denver – Boulder, CO	1,046	41
Charleston, SC	1,035	42
Baton Rouge, LA	1,020	43
Louisville, KY – IN	990	44

[Continued]

★1742★

Total Aggregate Household Income of Blacks, 1989

[Continued]

	Mil. $	Rank
Buffalo – Niagara Falls, NY	967	45
Augusta, GA – SC	909	46
Greenville – Spartanburg, SC	871	47
Rochester, NY	818	48
Oklahoma City, OK	787	49
West Palm Beach – Boca Raton – Delray Beach, FL	781	50

Source: U.S. Bureau of the Census, Data User Services Division, *1990 Census of Population and Housing*, Summary Tape File 3C, United States Summary, CD- ROM, February 1992.

★1743★

Income By Race and Ethnicity

Total Aggregate Household Income of Hispanics, 1989

[Table shows the top 50 areas]

	Mil. $	Rank
Los Angeles – Anaheim – Riverside, CA	37,986	1
New York – Northern New Jersey – Long Island, NY – NJ – CT1	25,183	2
Miami – Fort Lauderdale, FL	11,525	3
San Francisco – Oakland – San Jose, CA	10,143	4
Chicago – Gary – Lake County, IL – IN – WI	7,175	5
Houston – Galveston – Brazoria, TX	5,663	6
San Antonio, TX	4,397	7
San Diego, CA	3,987	8
Dallas – Fort Worth, TX	3,908	9
Washington, DC – MD – VA	2,726	10
El Paso, TX	2,516	11
Phoenix, AZ	2,511	12
Denver – Boulder, CO	2,019	13
Philadelphia – Wilmington – Trenton, PA – NJ – DE-MD	1,657	14
Sacramento, CA	1,622	15
McAllen – Edinburg – Mission, TX	1,612	16
Boston – Lawrence – Salem, MA – NH	1,548	17
Albuquerque, NM	1,536	18
Fresno, CA	1,475	19
Tampa – Saint Petersburg – Clearwater, FL	1,407	20
Corpus Christi, TX	1,223	21
Austin, TX	1,220	22
Tucson, AZ	1,192	23
Brownsville – Harlingen, TX	1,086	24
Bakersfield, CA	991	25
Detroit – Ann Arbor, MI	904	26
Orlando, FL	885	27
Stockton, CA	842	28

[Continued]

★1743★

Total Aggregate Household Income of Hispanics, 1989

[Continued]

	Mil. $	Rank
Salinas – Seaside – Monterey, CA	825	29
Seattle – Tacoma, WA	801	30
Santa Barbara – Santa Maria – Lompoc, CA	762	31
Laredo, TX	755	32
Las Vegas, NV	726	33
West Palm Beach – Boca Raton – Delray Beach, FL	683	34
Atlanta, GA	668	35
Visalia – Tulare – Porterville, CA	642	36
Modesto, CA	601	37
Hartford – New Britain – Middletown, CT	578	38
New Orleans, LA	535	39
Honolulu, HI	518	40
Santa Fe, NM	503	41
Salt Lake City – Ogden, UT	457	42
Las Cruces, NM	451	43
Cleveland – Akron – Lorain, OH	444	44
Kansas City, MO – KS	419	45
Milwaukee – Racine, WI	401	46
Baltimore, MD	387	47
Portland – Vancouver, OR – WA	363	48
Merced, CA	349	49
Providence – Pawtucket – Fall River, RI – MA	338	50

Source: U.S. Bureau of the Census, Data User Services Division, *1990 Census of Population and Housing*, Summary Tape File 3C, United States Summary, CD- ROM, February 1992.

★1744★

Income By Race and Ethnicity

Total Aggregate Household Income of Whites, 1989

[Table shows the top 50 areas]

	Mil. $	Rank
New York – Northern New Jersey – Long Island, NY – NJ – CT	280,809	1
Los Angeles – Anaheim – Riverside, CA	183,739	2
Chicago – Gary – Lake County, IL – IN – WI	109,485	3
San Francisco – Oakland – San Jose, CA	96,884	4
Philadelphia – Wilmington – Trenton, PA – NJ – DE – MD	82,638	5
Boston – Lawrence – Salem, MA – NH	71,910	6
Washington, DC – MD – VA	64,364	7
Detroit – Ann Arbor, MI	62,342	8
Dallas – Fort Worth, TX	52,981	9
Houston – Galveston – Brazoria, TX	44,815	10
Miami – Fort Lauderdale, FL	41,034	11

[Continued]

★1744★

Total Aggregate Household Income of Whites, 1989

[Continued]

	Mil. $	Rank
Minneapolis – Saint Paul, MN – WI	39,550	12
Atlanta, GA	39,364	13
Seattle – Tacoma, WA	38,975	14
Cleveland – Akron – Lorain, OH	35,362	15
San Diego, CA	33,824	16
Saint Louis, MO – IL	32,128	17
Baltimore, MD	32,056	18
Pittsburgh – Beaver Valley, PA	29,028	19
Phoenix, AZ	28,956	20
Denver – Boulder, CO	28,005	21
Tampa – Saint Petersburg – Clearwater, FL	27,426	22
Cincinnati – Hamilton, OH – KY – IN	23,083	23
Milwaukee – Racine, WI	21,465	24
Kansas City, MO – KS	21,130	25
Portland – Vancouver, OR – WA	20,892	26
Sacramento, CA	19,362	27
Hartford – New Britain – Middletown, CT	18,728	28
Columbus, OH	17,946	29
Indianapolis, IN	17,020	30
West Palm Beach – Boca Raton – Delray Beach, FL	16,016	31
Providence – Pawtucket – Fall River, RI – MA	15,832	32
Charlotte – Gastonia – Rock Hill, NC – SC	14,639	33
Buffalo – Niagara Falls, NY	14,512	34
Norfolk – Virginia Beach – Newport News, VA	14,386	35
Orlando, FL	14,193	36
Rochester, NY	14,096	37
San Antonio, TX	12,859	38
Nashville, TN	12,775	39
Albany – Schenectady – Troy, NY	12,507	40
Salt Lake City – Ogden, UT	12,228	41
Dayton – Springfield, OH	11,931	42
Greensboro – Winston-Salem – High Point, NC	11,857	43
Louisville, KY – IN	11,712	44
New Orleans, LA	11,691	45
Oklahoma City, OK	11,107	46
Jacksonville, FL	10,924	47
Richmond – Petersburg, VA	10,897	48
Birmingham, AL	9,937	49
Allentown – Bethlehem – Easton, PA – NJ	9,833	50

Source: U.S. Bureau of the Census, Data User Services Division, *1990 Census of Population and Housing,* Summary Tape File 3C, United States Summary, CD- ROM, February 1992.

★1745★

Income By Race and Ethnicity

Total Aggregate Income of American Indians, Eskimos, and Aleuts in 1989

[Table shows the top 50 areas]

	Mil. $	Rank
Los Angeles – Anaheim – Riverside, CA	1,166	1
San Francisco – Oakland – San Jose, CA	573	2
New York – Northern New Jersey – Long Island, NY – NJ – CT	489	3
Tulsa, OK	429	4
Oklahoma City, OK	401	5
Seattle – Tacoma, WA	347	6
Phoenix, AZ	255	7
San Diego, CA	254	8
Dallas – Fort Worth, TX	243	9
Detroit – Ann Arbor, MI	219	10
Sacramento, CA	212	11
Washington, DC – MD – VA	202	12
Chicago – Gary – Lake County, IL – IN – WI	199	13
Minneapolis – Saint Paul, MN – WI	192	14
Philadelphia – Wilmington – Trenton, PA – NJ – DE – MD	169	15
Anchorage, AK	160	16
Houston – Galveston – Brazoria, TX	156	17
Portland – Vancouver, OR – WA	151	18
Denver – Boulder, CO	142	19
Albuquerque, NM	128	20
Tucson, AZ	102	21
Kansas City, MO – KS	101	22
Boston – Lawrence – Salem, MA – NH	98	23
Baltimore, MD	87	24
Atlanta, GA	84	25
Miami – Fort Lauderdale, FL	83	26
Las Vegas, NV	82	27
Tampa – Saint Petersburg – Clearwater, FL	82	28
Bakersfield, CA	78	29
Milwaukee – Racine, WI	75	30
Norfolk – Virginia Beach – Newport News, VA	68	31
Fresno, CA	67	32
Saint Louis, MO – IL	65	33
Buffalo – Niagara Falls, NY	63	34
Cleveland – Akron – Lorain, OH	59	35
Stockton, CA	58	36
Fort Smith, AR – OK	58	37
Salt Lake City – Ogden, UT	57	38
Honolulu, HI	52	39
San Antonio, TX	51	40
Wichita, KS	50	41
Modesto, CA	50	42
Yakima, WA	48	43
Charlotte – Gastonia – Rock Hill, NC – SC	47	44
Reno, NV	46	45
Santa Barbara – Santa Maria – Lompoc, CA	45	46

[Continued]

★1745★

Total Aggregate Income of American Indians, Eskimos, and Aleuts in 1989

[Continued]

	Mil. $	Rank
Orlando, FL	42	47
Fayetteville, NC	41	48
Syracuse, NY	39	49
Richmond – Petersburg, VA	37	50

Source: U.S. Bureau of the Census, Data User Services Division, *1990 Census of Population and Housing*, Summary Tape File 3C, United States Summary, CD-ROM, February 1992.

★1746★

Income By Race and Ethnicity

Total Aggregate Income of Asians and Pacific Islanders in 1989

[Table shows the top 50 areas]

	Mil. $	Rank
Los Angeles – Anaheim – Riverside, CA	19,460	1
San Francisco – Oakland – San Jose, CA	13,802	2
New York – Northern New Jersey – Long Island, NY – NJ – CT	13,406	3
Honolulu, HI	8,047	4
Chicago – Gary – Lake County, IL – IN – WI	3,854	5
Washington, DC – MD – VA	3,240	6
San Diego, CA	2,213	7
Seattle – Tacoma, WA	2,011	8
Houston – Galveston – Brazoria, TX	1,699	9
Philadelphia – Wilmington – Trenton, PA – NJ – DE – MD	1,670	10
Boston – Lawrence – Salem, MA – NH	1,586	11
Sacramento, CA	1,286	12
Dallas – Fort Worth, TX	1,196	13
Detroit – Ann Arbor, MI	1,123	14
Baltimore, MD	692	15
Atlanta, GA	655	16
Portland – Vancouver, OR – WA	565	17
Miami – Fort Lauderdale, FL	562	18
Minneapolis – Saint Paul, MN – WI	537	19
Stockton, CA	486	20
Denver – Boulder, CO	484	21
Cleveland – Akron – Lorain, OH	477	22
Phoenix, AZ	440	23
Fresno, CA	426	24
Norfolk – Virginia Beach – Newport News, VA	359	25
Saint Louis, MO – IL	344	26
Salinas – Seaside – Monterey, CA	339	27
Las Vegas, NV	321	28
Tampa – Saint Petersburg – Clearwater, FL	271	29
Columbus, OH	259	30
Hartford – New Britain – Middletown, CT	259	31

[Continued]

★1746★

Total Aggregate Income of Asians and Pacific Islanders in 1989

[Continued]

	Mil. $	Rank
Pittsburgh – Beaver Valley, PA	254	32
Orlando, FL	240	33
Salt Lake City – Ogden, UT	226	34
Cincinnati – Hamilton, OH – KY – IN	216	35
Milwaukee – Racine, WI	210	36
Jacksonville, FL	206	37
Santa Barbara – Santa Maria – Lompoc, CA	204	38
Kansas City, MO – KS	198	39
Bakersfield, CA	190	40
New Orleans, LA	187	41
Raleigh – Durham, NC	181	42
Austin, TX	179	43
Providence – Pawtucket – Fall River, RI – MA	178	44
Oklahoma City, OK	177	45
Rochester, NY	176	46
Buffalo – Niagara Falls, NY	175	47
San Antonio, TX	169	48
Dayton – Springfield, OH	167	49
Richmond – Petersburg, VA	160	50

Source: U.S. Bureau of the Census, Data User Services Division, *1990 Census of Population and Housing*, Summary Tape File 3C, United States Summary, CD- ROM, February 1992.

★1747★

Income By Race and Ethnicity

Total Aggregate Income of Blacks in 1989

[Table shows the top 50 areas]

	Mil. $	Rank
New York – Northern New Jersey – Long Island, NY – NJ – CT	36,647	1
Washington, DC – MD – VA	14,732	2
Los Angeles – Anaheim – Riverside, CA	14,689	3
Chicago – Gary – Lake County, IL – IN – WI	14,238	4
Philadelphia – Wilmington – Trenton, PA – NJ – DE – MD	10,875	5
Detroit – Ann Arbor, MI	9,310	6
Atlanta, GA	7,408	7
San Francisco – Oakland – San Jose, CA	6,546	8
Baltimore, MD	6,325	9
Houston – Galveston – Brazoria, TX	5,847	10
Dallas – Fort Worth, TX	4,942	11
Miami – Fort Lauderdale, FL	4,770	12
Cleveland – Akron – Lorain, OH	3,943	13
Saint Louis, MO – IL	3,587	14
Norfolk – Virginia Beach – Newport News, VA	3,504	15
New Orleans, LA	2,828	16
Memphis, TN – AR – MS	2,821	17

[Continued]

★1747★

Total Aggregate Income of Blacks in 1989
[Continued]

	Mil. $	Rank
Boston – Lawrence – Salem, MA – NH	2,655	18
Richmond – Petersburg, VA	2,503	19
Charlotte – Gastonia – Rock Hill, NC – SC	2,025	20
Birmingham, AL	1,817	21
Raleigh – Durham, NC	1,794	22
Kansas City, MO – KS	1,762	23
Cincinnati – Hamilton, OH – KY – IN	1,713	24
Greensboro – Winston-Salem – High Point, NC	1,671	25
San Diego, CA	1,636	26
Indianapolis, IN	1,579	27
Columbus, OH	1,515	28
Milwaukee – Racine, WI	1,494	29
Pittsburgh – Beaver Valley, PA	1,468	30
Jacksonville, FL	1,452	31
Tampa – Saint Petersburg – Clearwater, FL	1,405	32
Nashville, TN	1,312	33
Seattle – Tacoma, WA	1,307	34
Dayton – Springfield, OH	1,166	35
Columbia, SC	1,138	36
Hartford – New Britain – Middletown, CT	1,091	37
Orlando, FL	1,086	38
Charleston, SC	1,084	39
Jackson, MS	1,078	40
Denver – Boulder, CO	1,077	41
Sacramento, CA	1,071	42
Baton Rouge, LA	1,040	43
Louisville, KY – IN	1,005	44
Buffalo – Niagara Falls, NY	985	45
Augusta, GA – SC	944	46
Greenville – Spartanburg, SC	885	47
Rochester, NY	832	48
San Antonio, TX	816	49
West Palm Beach – Boca Raton – Delray Beach, FL	805	50

Source: U.S. Bureau of the Census, Data User Services Division, *1990 Census of Population and Housing,* Summary Tape File 3C, United States Summary, CD- ROM, February 1992.

★1748★

Income By Race and Ethnicity

Total Aggregate Income of Hispanics in 1989
[Table shows the top 50 areas]

	Mil. $	Rank
Los Angeles – Anaheim – Riverside, CA	39,120	1
New York – Northern New Jersey – Long Island, NY – NJ – CT	25,757	2
Miami – Fort Lauderdale, FL	11,574	3
San Francisco – Oakland – San Jose, CA	10,524	4

[Continued]

★1748★

Total Aggregate Income of Hispanics in 1989
[Continued]

	Mil. $	Rank
Chicago – Gary – Lake County, IL – IN – WI	7,296	5
Houston – Galveston – Brazoria, TX	5,789	6
San Antonio, TX	4,482	7
San Diego, CA	4,225	8
Dallas – Fort Worth, TX	3,999	9
Washington, DC – MD – VA	2,844	10
Phoenix, AZ	2,587	11
El Paso, TX	2,571	12
Denver – Boulder, CO	2,055	13
Philadelphia – Wilmington – Trenton, PA – NJ – DE – MD	1,766	14
Sacramento, CA	1,675	15
McAllen – Edinburg – Mission, TX	1,637	16
Boston – Lawrence – Salem, MA – NH	1,613	17
Albuquerque, NM	1,560	18
Fresno, CA	1,529	19
Tampa – Saint Petersburg – Clearwater, FL	1,444	20
Austin, TX	1,267	21
Corpus Christi, TX	1,257	22
Tucson, AZ	1,230	23
Brownsville – Harlingen, TX	1,104	24
Bakersfield, CA	1,017	25
Detroit – Ann Arbor, MI	957	26
Salinas – Seaside – Monterey, CA	916	27
Orlando, FL	895	28
Stockton, CA	894	29
Seattle – Tacoma, WA	858	30
Santa Barbara – Santa Maria – Lompoc, CA	817	31
Laredo, TX	766	32
Las Vegas, NV	759	33
West Palm Beach – Boca Raton – Delray Beach, FL	724	34
Atlanta, GA	704	35
Visalia – Tulare – Porterville, CA	662	36
Hartford – New Britain – Middletown, CT	620	37
Modesto, CA	616	38
Honolulu, HI	567	39
New Orleans, LA	555	40
Santa Fe, NM	510	41
Salt Lake City – Ogden, UT	477	42
Las Cruces, NM	462	43
Cleveland – Akron – Lorain, OH	453	44
Kansas City, MO – KS	439	45
Baltimore, MD	412	46
Milwaukee – Racine, WI	402	47
Portland – Vancouver, OR – WA	400	48
Merced, CA	361	49
Providence – Pawtucket – Fall River, RI – MA	348	50

Source: U.S. Bureau of the Census, Data User Services Division, *1990 Census of Population and Housing,* Summary Tape File 3C, United States Summary, CD- ROM, February 1992.

★1749★
Income By Race and Ethnicity
Total Aggregate Income of Whites in 1989

[Table shows the top 50 areas]

	Mil. $	Rank
New York – Northern New Jersey – Long Island, NY – NJ – CT	283,080	1
Los Angeles – Anaheim – Riverside, CA	185,112	2
Chicago – Gary – Lake County, IL – IN – WI	110,459	3
San Francisco – Oakland – San Jose, CA	97,756	4
Philadelphia – Wilmington – Trenton, PA – NJ – DE – MD	83,623	5
Boston – Lawrence – Salem, MA – NH	72,802	6
Washington, DC – MD – VA	64,940	7
Detroit – Ann Arbor, MI	62,661	8
Dallas – Fort Worth, TX	53,348	9
Houston – Galveston – Brazoria, TX	45,059	10
Miami – Fort Lauderdale, FL	41,344	11
Minneapolis – Saint Paul, MN – WI	39,874	12
Atlanta, GA	39,543	13
Seattle – Tacoma, WA	39,287	14
Cleveland – Akron – Lorain, OH	35,626	15
San Diego, CA	34,555	16
Saint Louis, MO – IL	32,392	17
Baltimore, MD	32,344	18
Pittsburgh – Beaver Valley, PA	29,304	19
Phoenix, AZ	29,153	20
Denver – Boulder, CO	28,263	21
Tampa – Saint Petersburg – Clearwater, FL	27,765	22
Cincinnati – Hamilton, OH – KY – IN	23,302	23
Milwaukee – Racine, WI	21,666	24
Kansas City, MO – KS	21,353	25
Portland – Vancouver, OR – WA	21,063	26
Sacramento, CA	19,558	27
Hartford – New Britain – Middletown, CT	18,911	28
Columbus, OH	18,153	29
Indianapolis, IN	17,146	30
West Palm Beach – Boca Raton – Delray Beach, FL	16,117	31
Providence – Pawtucket – Fall River, RI – MA	16,027	32
Norfolk – Virginia Beach – Newport News, VA	14,811	33
Charlotte – Gastonia – Rock Hill, NC – SC	14,747	34
Buffalo – Niagara Falls, NY	14,654	35
Orlando, FL	14,384	36
Rochester, NY	14,257	37
San Antonio, TX	13,022	38
Nashville, TN	12,880	39
Albany – Schenectady – Troy, NY	12,667	40
Salt Lake City – Ogden, UT	12,313	41
Dayton – Springfield, OH	12,025	42
Greensboro – Winston-Salem – High Point, NC	11,948	43

[Continued]

★1749★
Total Aggregate Income of Whites in 1989
[Continued]

	Mil. $	Rank
Louisville, KY – IN	11,824	44
New Orleans, LA	11,821	45
Oklahoma City, OK	11,228	46
Jacksonville, FL	11,078	47
Richmond – Petersburg, VA	10,991	48
Birmingham, AL	9,978	49
Allentown – Bethlehem – Easton, PA – NJ	9,947	50

Source: U.S. Bureau of the Census, Data User Services Division, *1990 Census of Population and Housing*, Summary Tape File 3C, United States Summary, CD- ROM, February 1992.

★1750★
Personal Income
Personal Income Per Capita, 1993

[In dollars]

City	Dollars	Rank
Atlanta, GA MSA	22,675	14
Boston-Brockton-Nashua, MA- NH NECMA	24,861	6
Buffalo-Niagara Falls, NY MSA	20,013	40
Charlotte-Gastonia-Rock Hill, NC-SC MSA	20,856	32
Chicago-Gary-Kenosha, IL-In-WI CMSA	24,251	7
Cincinnati-Salem, OR-WA CMSA	20,744	34
Cleveland-Akron, OH CMSA	21,595	24
Columbus, OH MSA	20,717	35
Dallas-Fort Worth, TX CMSA	22,702	13
Dayton-Springfield, OH MSA	20,093	38
Denver-Boulder-Greeley, CO CMSA	23,463	11
Detroit-Ann Arbor-Flint, MI CMSA	22,600	15
Grand Rapids-Muskegon- Holland, MI MSA	20,062	39
Greensboro-Winston-Salem- High Point, NC MSA	20,772	33
Hartford, CT NECMA	26,147	4
Houston-Galveston-Brazoria, TX CMSA	22,028	17
Indianapolis, IN MSA	22,019	18
Jacksonville, FL MSA	20,102	37
Kansas City, MO-KS MSA	21,639	21
Los Angeles-Riverside-Orange County, CA CMSA	21,388	25
Louisville, KY-IN MSA	21,092	28
Memphis, TN-AR-MS MSA	20,386	36
Miami-Fort Lauderdale, FL CMSA	21,108	27
Milwaukee-Racine, WI CMSA	21,600	23
Minneapolis-St. Paul, MN-WI MSA	24,145	8
Nashville, TN MSA	21,634	22
New Orleans, LA MSA	18,882	44
New York-Northern New Jersey- Long Island,		49

[Continued]

★1750★

Personal Income Per Capita, 1993
[Continued]

City	Dollars	Rank
Norfolk-Virginia Beach-Newport News, VA-NC MSA	18,485	45
Oklahoma City, OK MSA	18,328	46
Orlando, FL MSA	19,224	43
Philadelphia-Wilmington-Atlanta City,		49
Phoenix-Mesa, AZ MSA	19,853	42
Pittsburgh, PA MSA	21,825	19
Portland-Salem, OR-WA CMSA	21,001	29
Providence-Warwick, RI NECMA	21,189	26
Richmond-Petersburg, VA MSA	23,262	12
Rochester, NY MSA	21,719	20
Sacramento-Yolo, CA CMSA	20,969	30
Salt Lake City-Ogden, UT MSA	17,481	48
San Antonio, TX MSA	17,889	47
San Diego, CA MSA	20,950	31
San Francisco-Oakland-San Jose, CA CMSA	27,293	3
Seattle-Tacoma-Bremerton, WA CMSA	23,873	10
St. Louis, MO-IL MSA	22,521	16
Tampa-St. Petersburg-Clearwater, FL MSA	20,004	41
Washington-Baltimore, DC-MD-VA-WV CMSA	25,956	5
West Palm Beach-Boca Raton, FL MSA	32,230	1
NY-NJ-CT-PA CMSA	28,122	2
PA-NJ-DE-MD CMSA	24,064	9

Source: U.S. Bureau of the Census, *Statistical Abstract of the United States: 1995,* (115th edition), Washington, DC: U.S. Government Printing Office, 1995, p. 463. Primary source: U.S. Bureau of Economic Analysis, *Survey of Current Business,* April issues; and unpublished data.

★1751★
Personal Income

Personal Income Per Capita, 1993: Percent of National Average

City	Percent	Rank
Atlanta, GA MSA	109.0	14
Boston-Brockton-Nashua, MA-NH NECMA	119.5	6
Buffalo-Niagara Falls, NY MSA	96.2	36
Charlotte-Gastonia-Rock Hill, NC-SC MSA	100.3	29
Chicago-Gary-Kenosha, IL-In-WI CMSA	116.6	7
Cincinnati-Salem, OR-WA CMSA	99.7	31
Cleveland-Akron, OH CMSA	103.8	21
Columbus, OH MSA	99.6	32
Dallas-Fort Worth, TX CMSA	109.1	13
Dayton-Springfield, OH MSA	96.6	34
Denver-Boulder-Greeley, CO CMSA	112.8	11
Detroit-Ann Arbor-Flint, MI CMSA	108.7	15

[Continued]

★1751★

Personal Income Per Capita, 1993: Percent of National Average
[Continued]

City	Percent	Rank
Grand Rapids-Muskegon-Holland, MI MSA	96.5	35
Greensboro-Winston-Salem-High Point, NC MSA	99.9	30
Hartford, CT NECMA	125.7	4
Houston-Galveston-Brazoria, TX CMSA	105.9	17
Indianapolis, IN MSA	105.9	17
Jacksonville, FL MSA	96.6	34
Kansas City, MO-KS MSA	104.0	20
Los Angeles-Riverside-Orange County, CA CMSA	102.8	22
Louisville, KY-IN MSA	101.4	25
Memphis, TN-AR-MS MSA	98.0	33
Miami-Fort Lauderdale, FL CMSA	101.5	24
Milwaukee-Racine, WI CMSA	108.7	15
Minneapolis-St. Paul, MN-WI MSA	116.1	8
Nashville, TN MSA	104.0	20
New Orleans, LA MSA	90.8	39
New York-Northern New Jersey-Long Island,		44
Norfolk-Virginia Beach-Newport News, VA-NC MSA	88.9	40
Oklahoma City, OK MSA	88.1	41
Orlando, FL MSA	92.4	38
Philadelphia-Wilmington-Atlanta City,		44
Phoenix-Mesa, AZ MSA	95.4	37
Pittsburgh, PA MSA	104.9	18
Portland-Salem, OR-WA CMSA	101.0	26
Providence-Warwick, RI NECMA	101.9	23
Richmond-Petersburg, VA MSA	111.8	12
Rochester, NY MSA	104.4	19
Sacramento-Yolo, CA CMSA	100.8	27
Salt Lake City-Ogden, UT MSA	84.0	43
San Antonio, TX MSA	86.0	42
San Diego, CA MSA	100.7	28
San Francisco-Oakland-San Jose, CA CMSA	131.2	3
Seattle-Tacoma-Bremerton, WA CMSA	114.8	10
St. Louis, MO-IL MSA	108.3	16
Tampa-St. Petersburg-Clearwater, FL MSA	96.2	36
Washington-Baltimore, DC-MD-VA-WV CMSA	124.8	5
West Palm Beach-Boca Raton, FL MSA	155.0	1
NY-NJ-CT-PA CMSA	135.2	2
PA-NJ-DE-MD CMSA	115.7	9

Source: U.S. Bureau of the Census, *Statistical Abstract of the United States: 1995,* (115th edition), Washington, DC: U.S. Government Printing Office, 1995, p. 463. Primary source: U.S. Bureau of Economic Analysis, *Survey of Current Business,* April issues; and unpublished data.

★1752★
Personal Income
Personal Income, 1993: Total

[In millions of dollars]

City	Millions	Rank
Atlanta, GA MSA	73,206	12
Boston-Brockton-Nashua, MA-NH NECMA	141,698	7
Buffalo-Niagara Falls, NY MSA	23,863	36
Charlotte-Gastonia-Rock Hill, NC-SC MSA	25,726	32
Chicago-Gary-Kenosha, IL-In-WI CMSA	205,307	3
Cincinnati-Hamilton, OH-KY-IN CMSA	39,025	23
Cleveland-Akron, OH CMSA	62,495	15
Columbus, OH MSA	29,195	30
Dallas-Fort Worth, TX CMSA	97,146	9
Dayton-Springfield, OH MSA	19,267	47
Denver-Boulder-Greeley, CO CMSA	50,359	19
Detroit-Ann Arbor-Flint, MI CMSA	118,551	8
Grand Rapids-Muskegon-Holland, MI MSA	19,545	44
Greensboro-Winston-Salem-High Point, NC MSA	22,682	38
Hartford, CT NECMA	29,275	29
Houston-Galveston-Brazoria, TX CMSA	88,727	10
Indianapolis, IN MSA	31,775	27
Jacksonville, FL MSA	19,346	46
Kansas City, MO-KS MSA	35,291	25
Los Angeles-Riverside-Orange County, CA CMSA	325,310	2
Louisville, KY-IN MSA	20,543	42
Memphis, TN-AR-MS MSA	21,247	40
Miami-Fort Lauderdale, FL CMSA	70,793	13
Milwaukee-Racine, WI CMSA	36,935	24
Minneapolis-St. Paul, MN-WI MSA	64,093	14
Nashville, TN MSA	22,597	39
New Orleans, LA MSA	24,623	35
New York-Northern New Jersey-Long Island,		49
Norfolk-Virginia Beach-Newport News, VA-NC MSA	27,984	31
Oklahoma City, OK MSA	18,250	48
Orlando, FL MSA	25,641	33
Philadelphia-Wilmington-Atlanta City,		49
Phoenix-Mesa, AZ MSA	47,490	20
Pittsburgh, PA MSA	52,531	18
Portland-Salem, OR-WA CMSA	40,832	22
Providence-Warwick, RI NECMA	19,369	45
Richmond-Petersburg, VA MSA	21,074	41
Rochester, NY MSA	23,657	37
Sacramento-Yolo, CA CMSA	33,052	26
Salt Lake City-Ogden, UT MSA	20,181	43
San Antonio, TX MSA	25,172	34
San Diego, CA MSA	54,719	17
San Francisco-Oakland-San Jose, CA CMSA	176,570	5

[Continued]

★1752★
Personal Income, 1993: Total
[Continued]

City	Millions	Rank
Seattle-Tacoma-Bremerton, WA CMSA	76,128	11
St. Louis, MO-IL MSA	56,936	16
Tampa-St. Petersburg-Clearwater, FL MSA	42,742	21
Washington-Baltimore, DC-MD-VA-WV CMSA	181,313	4
West Palm Beach-Boca Raton, FL MSA	30,031	28
NY-NJ-CT-PA CMSA	552,496	1
PA-NJ-DE-MD CMSA	142,974	6

Source: U.S. Bureau of the Census, *Statistical Abstract of the United States: 1995,* (115th edition), Washington, DC: U.S. Government Printing Office, 1995, p. 463. Primary source: U.S. Bureau of Economic Analysis, *Survey of Current Business,* April issues; and unpublished data.

★1753★
Personal Income Projections
Per Capita Income Projections, 2005: Leading Metropolitan Areas

City	Projected per capita income	Rank
San Francisco, CA	27,888	1
Bergen-Passaic, NJ	27,362	2
West Palm Beach-Boca Raton, FL	26,938	3
New Haven-Bridgeport-Stamford-Danbury-Waterbury, CT	26,853	4
Middlesex-Somerset-Hunterdon, NJ	26,760	5
Nassau-Suffolk, NY	26,504	6
Newark, NJ	25,803	7
New York, NY	25,332	8
Trenton, NJ	25,118	9
Washington, DC-MD-VA-WV	24,851	

Source: "The Good Life," *American Nurseryman,* 15 November, 1995, p. 8. Primary source: *American Demographics.*

★1754★
Personal Income Projections
Personal Income Per Capita, 1993, CMSAs: Total
[In 1987 dollars]

City/MSA	1987 dollars	Rank
Chicago-Gary-Kenosha, IL-IN-WI CMSA	18,931	4
Cincinnati-Hamilton, OH-KY-IN CMSA	16,194	16
Cleveland-Akron, OH CMSA	16,858	11
Dallas-Fort Worth, TX CMSA	17,722	8
Denver-Boulder-Greeley, CO CMSA	18,316	7
Detroit-Ann Arbor-Flint, MI CMSA	17,643	9
Houston-Galveston-Brazoria, TX CMSA	17,196	10

[Continued]

★1754★

Personal Income Per Capita, 1993, CMSAs: Total
[Continued]

City/MSA	1987 dollars	Rank
Los Angeles-Riverside-Orange County, CA CMSA	16,696	12
Miami-Fort Lauderdale, FL CMSA	16,478	13
Milwaukee-Racine, WI CMSA	17,643	9
New York-Northern New Jersey-Long Island, NY-NJ-CT-PA CMSA	21,953	1
Philadelphia-Wilmington-Atlantic City, PA-NJ-DE-MD CMSA	18,785	5
Portland-Salem, OR-WA CMSA	16,395	14
Sacramento-Yolo, CA CMSA	16,369	15
San Francisco-Oakland-San Jose, CA CMSA	21,306	2
Seattle-Tacoma-Bremerton, WA CMSA	18,636	6
Washington-Baltimore, DC-MD-VA-WV CMSA	20,262	3

Source: U.S. Department of Commerce, Economics and Statistics Administration, Bureau of Economic Analysis, *Survey of Current Business,* vol. 76, no. 6, Washington, D.C.: U.S. Government Printing Office, (June 1996), p. 67. *Note:* "CMSA" stands for "Consolidated Metropolitan Statistical Area."

★1755★

Personal Income Projections

Personal Income Per Capita, 2000, CMSAs: Total
[In 1987 dollars]

City/MSA	1987 dollars	Rank
Chicago-Gary-Kenosha, IL-IN-WI CMSA	20,578	4
Cincinnati-Hamilton, OH-KY-IN CMSA	17,820	17
Cleveland-Akron, OH CMSA	18,497	12
Dallas-Fort Worth, TX CMSA	19,404	9
Denver-Boulder-Greeley, CO CMSA	19,981	7
Detroit-Ann Arbor-Flint, MI CMSA	19,250	10
Houston-Galveston-Brazoria, TX CMSA	18,569	11
Los Angeles-Riverside-Orange County, CA CMSA	18,025	13
Miami-Fort Lauderdale, FL CMSA	17,926	15
Milwaukee-Racine, WI CMSA	19,495	8
New York-Northern New Jersey-Long Island, NY-NJ-CT-PA CMSA	23,791	1
Philadelphia-Wilmington-Atlantic City, PA-NJ-DE-MD CMSA	20,393	5
Portland-Salem, OR-WA CMSA	17,901	16
Sacramento-Yolo, CA CMSA	17,995	14
San Francisco-Oakland-San Jose, CA CMSA	23,163	2

[Continued]

★1755★

Personal Income Per Capita, 2000, CMSAs: Total
[Continued]

City/MSA	1987 dollars	Rank
Seattle-Tacoma-Bremerton, WA CMSA	20,051	6
Washington-Baltimore, DC-MD-VA-WV CMSA	21,910	3

Source: U.S. Department of Commerce, Economics and Statistics Administration, Bureau of Economic Analysis, *Survey of Current Business,* vol. 76, no. 6, Washington, D.C.: U.S. Government Printing Office, (June 1996), p. 67. *Note:* "CMSA" stands for "Consolidated Metropolitan Statistical Area."

★1756★

Personal Income Projections

Personal Income Per Capita, 2005, CMSAs: Total
[In 1987 dollars]

City/MSA	1987 dollars	Rank
Chicago-Gary-Kenosha, IL-IN-WI CMSA	21,745	4
Cincinnati-Hamilton, OH-KY-IN CMSA	18,882	17
Cleveland-Akron, OH CMSA	19,647	11
Dallas-Fort Worth, TX CMSA	20,535	9
Denver-Boulder-Greeley, CO CMSA	21,126	6
Detroit-Ann Arbor-Flint, MI CMSA	20,379	10
Houston-Galveston-Brazoria, TX CMSA	19,545	12
Los Angeles-Riverside-Orange County, CA CMSA	19,039	14
Miami-Fort Lauderdale, FL CMSA	18,945	15
Milwaukee-Racine, WI CMSA	20,738	8
New York-Northern New Jersey-Long Island, NY-NJ-CT-PA CMSA	25,148	1
Philadelphia-Wilmington-Atlantic City, PA-NJ-DE-MD CMSA	21,549	5
Portland-Salem, OR-WA CMSA	18,907	16
Sacramento-Yolo, CA CMSA	19,098	13
San Francisco-Oakland-San Jose, CA CMSA	24,501	2
Seattle-Tacoma-Bremerton, WA CMSA	21,093	7
Washington-Baltimore, DC-MD-VA-WV CMSA	23,041	3

Source: U.S. Department of Commerce, Economics and Statistics Administration, Bureau of Economic Analysis, *Survey of Current Business,* vol. 76, no. 6, Washington, D.C.: U.S. Government Printing Office, (June 1996), p. 67. *Note:* "CMSA" stands for "Consolidated Metropolitan Statistical Area."

★1757★
Personal Income Projections
Personal Income Projections, 2000, CMSAs: Total

[In millions of 1987 dollars]

City/MSA	Millions of 1987 dollars	Rank
Chicago-Gary-Kenosha, IL-IN-WI CMSA	183,262	3
Cincinnati-Hamilton, OH-KY-IN CMSA	35,320	15
Cleveland-Akron, OH CMSA	54,016	12
Dallas-Fort Worth, TX CMSA	92,360	8
Denver-Boulder-Greeley, CO CMSA	48,039	13
Detroit-Ann Arbor-Flint, MI CMSA	102,322	7
Houston-Galveston-Brazoria, TX CMSA	83,477	9
Los Angeles-Riverside-Orange County, CA CMSA	301,602	2
Miami-Fort Lauderdale, FL CMSA	66,291	11
Milwaukee-Racine, WI CMSA	32,855	17
New York-Northern New Jersey-Long Island, NY-NJ-CT-PA CMSA	479,982	1
Philadelphia-Wilmington-Atlantic City, PA-NJ-DE-MD CMSA	126,811	6
Portland-Salem, OR-WA CMSA	38,672	14
Sacramento-Yolo, CA CMSA	32,858	16
San Francisco-Oakland-San Jose, CA CMSA	161,812	5
Seattle-Tacoma-Bremerton, WA CMSA	71,791	10
Washington-Baltimore, DC-MD-VA-WV CMSA	166,382	4

Source: U.S. Department of Commerce, Economics and Statistics Administration, Bureau of Economic Analysis, *Survey of Current Business,* vol. 76, no. 6, Washington, D.C.: U.S. Government Printing Office, (June 1996), p. 67. *Note:* "CMSA" stands for "Consolidated Metropolitan Statistical Area."

★1758★
Personal Income Projections
Personal Income Projections, 2005, CMSAs: Total

[In millions of 1987 dollars]

City/MSA	Millions of 1987 dollars	Rank
Chicago-Gary-Kenosha, IL-IN-WI CMSA	200,468	3
Cincinnati-Hamilton, OH-KY-IN CMSA	38,671	15
Cleveland-Akron, OH CMSA	57,863	12
Dallas-Fort Worth, TX CMSA	103,833	8
Denver-Boulder-Greeley, CO CMSA	54,310	13
Detroit-Ann Arbor-Flint, MI CMSA	109,357	7
Houston-Galveston-Brazoria, TX CMSA	92,984	9

[Continued]

★1758★
Personal Income Projections, 2005, CMSAs: Total
[Continued]

City/MSA	Millions of 1987 dollars	Rank
Los Angeles-Riverside-Orange County, CA CMSA	337,862	2
Miami-Fort Lauderdale, FL CMSA	74,204	11
Milwaukee-Racine, WI CMSA	35,852	17
New York-Northern New Jersey-Long Island, NY-NJ-CT-PA CMSA	515,923	1
Philadelphia-Wilmington-Atlantic City, PA-NJ-DE-MD CMSA	137,662	6
Portland-Salem, OR-WA CMSA	43,480	14
Sacramento-Yolo, CA CMSA	38,139	16
San Francisco-Oakland-San Jose, CA CMSA	180,019	5
Seattle-Tacoma-Bremerton, WA CMSA	81,441	10
Washington-Baltimore, DC-MD-VA-WV CMSA	184,234	4

Source: U.S. Department of Commerce, Economics and Statistics Administration, Bureau of Economic Analysis, *Survey of Current Business,* vol. 76, no. 6, Washington, D.C.: U.S. Government Printing Office, (June 1996), p. 67. *Note:* "CMSA" stands for "Consolidated Metropolitan Statistical Area."

★1759★
Personal Income Projections
Personal Income, 1993, CMSAs: Total

[In millions of 1987 dollars]

City/MSA	Millions of 1987 dollars	Rank
Chicago-Gary-Kenosha, IL-IN-WI CMSA	160,271	3
Cincinnati-Hamilton, OH-KY-IN CMSA	30,465	15
Cleveland-Akron, OH CMSA	48,786	12
Dallas-Fort Worth, TX CMSA	75,836	8
Denver-Boulder-Greeley, CO CMSA	39,313	13
Detroit-Ann Arbor-Flint, MI CMSA	92,546	7
Houston-Galveston-Brazoria, TX CMSA	69,264	9
Los Angeles-Riverside-Orange County, CA CMSA	253,950	2
Miami-Fort Lauderdale, FL CMSA	55,264	11
Milwaukee-Racine, WI CMSA	28,833	16
New York-Northern New Jersey-Long Island, NY-NJ-CT-PA CMSA	431,300	1
Philadelphia-Wilmington-Atlantic City, PA-NJ-DE-MD CMSA	111,611	6
Portland-Salem, OR-WA CMSA	31,875	14

[Continued]

★1759★

Personal Income, 1993, CMSAs: Total
[Continued]

City/MSA	Millions of 1987 dollars	Rank
Sacramento-Yolo, CA CMSA	25,802	17
San Francisco-Oakland-San Jose, CA CMSA	137,837	5
Seattle-Tacoma-Bremerton, WA CMSA	59,429	10
Washington-Baltimore, DC-MD-VA-WV CMSA	141,541	4

Source: U.S. Department of Commerce, Economics and Statistics Administration, Bureau of Economic Analysis, *Survey of Current Business,* vol. 76, no. 6, Washington, D.C.: U.S. Government Printing Office, (June 1996), p. 67. *Note:* "CMSA" stands for "Consolidated Metropolitan Statistical Area."

Chapter 15

POVERTY

Topics Covered

General Poverty Rates
Persons Living Above Poverty Level
Persons Living Below Poverty Level
Poverty Status By Age, Race, and Ethnicity
Poverty Status of Families With Children
Poverty Status of Families Without Children
Ratios of Income to Poverty Level

★1760★
General Poverty Rates
Poverty Rates, 1989: All Families

[In percent; top 25 of selected cities only]

City	Families	Rank
Detroit, MI	29.0	1
New Orleans, LA	27.3	2
Cleveland, OH	25.2	3
Atlanta, GA	24.6	4
El Paso, TX	21.2	5
St. Louis, MO	20.6	6
Baton Rouge, LA	20.3	7
Memphis, TN	18.7	8
San Antonio, TX	18.7	8
Milwaukee, WI	18.5	9
Chicago, IL	18.3	10
Baltimore, MD	17.8	11
Houston, TX	17.2	12
Oakland, CA	16.7	13
New York, NY	16.3	14
Philadelphia, PA	16.1	15
Boston, MA	15.0	16
Los Angeles, CA	14.9	17
Dallas, TX	14.7	18
Tucson, AZ	14.4	19
Fort Worth, TX	13.6	20
Long Beach, CA	13.5	21
Washington, DC	13.3	22
Denver, CO	13.1	23
Columbus, OH	12.6	24

Source: Bureau of the Census, *Statistical Abstract of the United States 1993*, (113th edition), p. 472, Washington, DC: U.S. Government Printing Office.

★1761★
General Poverty Rates
Poverty Rates, 1989: All Persons

[In percent]

City	All persons	Rank
Detroit, MI	32.4	1
New Orleans, LA	31.6	2
Atlanta, GA	27.3	3
Baton Rouge, LA	26.2	4
El Paso, TX	25.3	5
St. Louis, MO	24.6	6
Memphis, TN	23.0	7
San Antonio, TX	22.6	8
Milwaukee, WI	22.2	9
Baltimore, MD	21.9	10
Chicago, IL	21.6	11
Houston, TX	20.7	12
Philadelphia, PA	20.3	13
Tucson, AZ	20.2	14
New York, NY	19.3	15
Los Angeles, CA	18.9	16
Oakland, CA	18.8	17
Boston, MA	18.7	18
Dallas, TX	18.0	19
Austin, TX	17.9	20
Fort Worth, TX	17.4	21

[Continued]

★1761★
Poverty Rates, 1989: All Persons

[Continued]

City	All persons	Rank
Columbus, OH	17.2	22
Denver, CO	17.1	23
Washington, DC	16.9	24
Long Beach, CA	16.8	25
Oklahoma City, OK	15.9	26
Kansas City, MO	15.3	27
Portland, OR	14.5	28
Phoenix, AZ	14.2	29
Albuquerque, NM	14.0	30
Nashville-Davidson, TN	13.4	31
San Diego, CA	13.4	31
Jacksonville, FL	13.0	32
San Francisco, CA	12.7	33
Indianapolis, IN	12.5	34
Seattle, WA	12.4	35
Charlotte, NC	10.8	36
San Jose, CA	9.3	37
Cleveland, OH	8.5	38
Virginia Beach, VA	5.9	39

Source: Bureau of the Census, *Statistical Abstract of the United States 1993* (113th edition), p. 472, Washington, DC: U.S. Government Printing Office.

★1762★
General Poverty Rates
Poverty Rates, 1990: Highest

From the source: *"Poor Cities: An Analysis of Poverty in U.S. Cities Over 50,000*, issued by the Greater Washington Research Center, finds that the 25 largest cities contain 43 percent of all poor city dwellers; 57 percent live in smaller cities. The report finds that poverty increased in seven out of ten cities during the 1980s and that poverty is becoming more concentrated in the cities where poverty rates were already the highest. Contrary to perceptions, the report says that 16 of the 25 cities with the highest poverty rates have populations under 100,000."

[In percent; top 25 cities only]

City	Poverty rate	Rank
Brownsville, TX	43.9	1
College Station, TX	38.0	2
Monroe, TX	37.8	3
Laredo, TX	37.3	4
Camden, NJ	36.6	5
East Lansing, MI	33.8	6
McAllen, TX	32.7	7
Detroit, MI	32.4	8
Saginaw, MI	31.7	9
New Orleans, LA	31.6	10
Bloomington, IN	31.5	11
Miami, FL	31.2	12
Flint, MI	30.6	13
Provo, UT	29.6	14
Gary, IN	29.4	15
Youngstown, OH	29.0	16
Cleveland, OH	28.7	17
Waco, TX	28.7	17

[Continued]

★1762★

Poverty Rates, 1990: Highest

[Continued]

City	Poverty rate	Rank
Port Arthur, TX	28.1	18
Pine Bluff, AZ	27.7	19
Albany, GA	27.5	20
Compton, CA	27.5	20
Hartford, CT	27.5	20
Lawrence, MA	27.5	20
Atlanta, GA	27.3	21

Source: Advisory Committee on Intergovernmental Relations, Washington, DC: *Intergovernmental Perspective*, Spring 1993, Vol. 19, No. 1, p. 22.

★1763★

General Poverty Rates

Poverty Rates, By Age, 1989: Children Under Age 6

[In percent; top 25 of selected cities only]

City	Children under age 6	Rank
Detroit, MI	52.4	1
New Orleans, LA	48.7	2
Atlanta, GA	47.3	3
Cleveland, OH	46.2	4
Milwaukee, WI	41.5	5
St. Louis, MO	41.2	6
Baton Rouge, LA	39.0	7
Memphis, TN	37.7	8
El Paso, TX	36.7	9
Chicago, IL	35.8	10
San Antonio, TX	35.6	11
Baltimore, MD	34.3	12
Oakland, CA	32.2	13
Philadelphia, PA	31.9	14
Houston, TX	31.3	15
New York, NY	30.9	16
Tucson, AZ	29.6	17
Denver, CO	29.3	18
Long Beach, CA	28.1	19
Boston, MA	27.9	20
Dallas, TX	27.9	20
Los Angeles, CA	27.7	21
Washington, DC	26.8	22
Oklahoma City, OK	26.7	23
Fort Worth, TX	26.3	24

Source: Bureau of the Census, *Statistical Abstract of the United States 1993* (113th edition), p. 472 Washington, DC: U.S. Government Printing Office.

★1764★

General Poverty Rates

Poverty Rates, By Age, 1989: Children Under Age 18

From the source: "... child poverty became more pervasive around the nation and less concentrated in a few large cities. For example, the 40 counties with the highest child poverty rates in the nation in 1989 were all rural (non-metropolitan). The overall poverty rate for children who did not live in cities with populations over 100,000 rose from 13.8 percent in 1979 to 15.4 percent in 1989."

[Population younger than 18 years old; top 20 counties only]

City	Rate	Rank
Detroit, MI	46.6	1
Laredo, TX	46.4	2
New Orleans, LA	46.3	3
Flint, MI	44.6	4
Miami, FL	44.1	5
Hartford, CT	43.8	6
Cleveland, OH	43.0	7
Gary, IN	43.0	7
Atlanta, GA	42.9	8
Dayton, OH	40.9	9
St. Louis, MO	39.7	10
Buffalo, NY	38.8	11
Rochester, NY	38.4	12
Milwaukee, WI	37.8	13
Newark, NJ	37.6	14
Cincinnati, OH	37.4	15
Fresno, CA	36.9	16
Shreveport, LA	36.7	17
Waco, TX	36.6	18
Macon, GA	36.1	19

Source: "Report finds poverty afflicts children in communities of all sizes," *Nation's Cities Weekly*, Vol. 15, No. 33, p. 2, August 17, 1992, Washington, DC: National League of Cities. Primary source: Children's Defense Fund.

★1765★

General Poverty Rates

Poverty Rates, By Age, 1989: Persons Over Age 65

[In percent; top 25 of selected cities only]

City	Persons over age 65	Rank
Atlanta, GA	25.1	1
New Orleans, LA	24.6	2
Memphis, TN	21.8	3
El Paso, TX	20.6	4
Detroit, MI	20.1	5
Baltimore, MD	19.3	6
Cleveland, OH	19.2	7
San Antonio, TX	19.1	8
St. Louis, MO	18.7	9
Baton Rouge, LA	18.2	10
Houston, TX	17.8	11
Washington, DC	17.2	12
New York, NY	16.5	13
Philadelphia, PA	16.3	14
Jacksonville, FL	16.1	15
Chicago, IL	15.9	16

[Continued]

★1766★

Poverty Rates, By Age, 1989: Persons Over Age 65

[Continued]

City	Persons over age 65	Rank
Boston, MA	15.3	17
Nashville-Davidson, TN	15.1	18
Dallas, TX	14.6	19
Kansas City, MO	14.6	19
Fort Worth, TX	14.4	20
Charlotte, NC	13.8	21
Oklahoma City, OK	13.1	22
Columbus, OH	13.0	23
Denver, CO	12.7	24

Source: Bureau of the Census, *Statistical Abstract of the United States 1993* (113th edition), p. 472, Washington, DC: U.S. Government Printing Office.

★1766★

Persons Living Above Poverty Level

Persons Under 5 Years Old Living Above Poverty Level in 1989

[Table shows the top 50 areas]

MSA	% of population	Rank
Provo – Orem, UT	8.8	1
Salt Lake City – Ogden, UT	8.3	2
Anchorage, AK	8.2	3
Rochester, MN	7.9	4
Midland, TX	7.6	5
Grand Rapids, MI	7.5	6
Elkhart – Goshen, IN	7.4	7
Jacksonville, NC	7.4	7
Killeen – Temple, TX	7.2	8
Fayetteville, NC	7.1	9
Grand Forks, ND	7.1	9
Rapid City, SD	7.1	9
Saint Cloud, MN	7.1	9
Salinas – Seaside – Monterey, CA	7.1	9
Sioux Falls, SD	7.1	9
Dallas – Fort Worth, TX	6.9	10
Minneapolis – Saint Paul, MN – WI	6.9	10
Modesto, CA	6.9	10
Bakersfield, CA	6.8	11
Bremerton, WA	6.8	11
Colorado Springs, CO	6.8	11
Fort Wayne, IN	6.8	11
Wichita, KS	6.8	11
Appleton – Oshkosh – Neenah, WI	6.7	12
Lancaster, PA	6.7	12
Merced, CA	6.7	12
Norfolk – Virginia Beach – Newport News, VA	6.7	12
Poughkeepsie, NY	6.7	12
Boise, ID	6.6	13
Charleston, SC	6.6	13
Clarksville – Hopkinsville, TN – KY	6.6	13
Houston – Galveston – Brazoria, TX	6.6	13

[Continued]

★1766★

Persons Under 5 Years Old Living Above Poverty Level in 1989

[Continued]

MSA	% of population	Rank
Manchester, NH	6.6	13
Omaha, NE – IA	6.6	13
Portsmouth – Dover – Rochester, NH – ME	6.6	13
Burlington, VT	6.5	14
Cheyenne, WY	6.5	14
Fitchburg – Leominster, MA	6.5	14
Los Angeles – Anaheim – Riverside, CA	6.5	14
Washington, DC – MD – VA	6.5	14
Atlanta, GA	6.4	15
Denver – Boulder, CO	6.4	15
Green Bay, WI	6.4	15
Honolulu, HI	6.4	15
Indianapolis, IN	6.4	15
Kansas City, MO – KS	6.4	15
New London – Norwich, CT – RI	6.4	15
Richland – Kennewick – Pasco, WA	6.4	15
Seattle – Tacoma, WA	6.4	15
Stockton, CA	6.3	16

Source: U.S. Bureau of the Census, Data User Services Division, *1990 Census of Population and Housing*, Summary Tape File 3C, United States Summary, CD-ROM, February 1992.

★1767★

Persons Living Above Poverty Level

Persons 5 Years Old Living Above Poverty Level in 1989

[Table shows the top 50 areas]

MSA	% of population	Rank
Casper, WY	1.79	1
Provo – Orem, UT	1.74	2
Salt Lake City – Ogden, UT	1.72	3
Anchorage, AK	1.67	4
Grand Rapids, MI	1.56	5
Richland – Kennewick – Pasco, WA	1.55	6
Rochester, MN	1.55	6
Fort Wayne, IN	1.54	7
Bremerton, WA	1.52	8
Saint Cloud, MN	1.52	8
Appleton – Oshkosh – Neenah, WI	1.51	9
Midland, TX	1.50	10
Boise, ID	1.47	11
Green Bay, WI	1.47	11
Sheboygan, WI	1.47	11
Sioux Falls, SD	1.46	12
Bakersfield, CA	1.45	13
Rapid City, SD	1.44	14
Merced, CA	1.42	15
Victoria, TX	1.42	15
Bismarck, ND	1.41	16
Greeley, CO	1.41	16

[Continued]

★1767★

Persons 5 Years Old Living Above Poverty Level in 1989

[Continued]

MSA	% of population	Rank
Yuba City, CA	1.40	17
Minneapolis – Saint Paul, MN – WI	1.39	18
Omaha, NE – IA	1.38	19
Elkhart – Goshen, IN	1.37	20
Fargo – Moorhead, ND – MN	1.37	20
Modesto, CA	1.37	20
Odessa, TX	1.37	20
Salinas – Seaside – Monterey, CA	1.37	20
Sioux City, IA – NE	1.37	20
Wausau, WI	1.37	20
Colorado Springs, CO	1.36	21
Grand Forks, ND	1.36	21
Lafayette, LA	1.36	21
Glens Falls, NY	1.34	22
Muskegon, MI	1.34	22
Topeka, KS	1.34	22
Wichita, KS	1.34	22
Dallas – Fort Worth, TX	1.33	23
Houston – Galveston – Brazoria, TX	1.33	23
Kankakee, IL	1.33	23
Baton Rouge, LA	1.32	24
Burlington, VT	1.32	24
Olympia, WA	1.32	24
Cedar Rapids, IA	1.31	25
Kokomo, IN	1.31	25
New London – Norwich, CT – RI	1.31	25
Honolulu, HI	1.30	26
Indianapolis, IN	1.30	26

Source: U.S. Bureau of the Census, Data User Services Division, *1990 Census of Population and Housing*, Summary Tape File 3C, United States Summary, CD-ROM, February 1992.

★1768★

Persons Living Above Poverty Level

Persons 6 to 11 Years Old Living Above Poverty Level in 1989

[Table shows the top 50 areas]

MSA	% of population	Rank
Provo – Orem, UT	11.6	1
Salt Lake City – Ogden, UT	11.4	2
Saint Cloud, MN	9.2	3
Midland, TX	9.0	4
Wausau, WI	9.0	4
Anchorage, AK	8.8	5
Bismarck, ND	8.8	5
Richland – Kennewick – Pasco, WA	8.8	5
Rochester, MN	8.8	5
Boise, ID	8.7	6
Grand Rapids, MI	8.7	6
Casper, WY	8.6	7
Dubuque, IA	8.5	8

[Continued]

★1768★

Persons 6 to 11 Years Old Living Above Poverty Level in 1989

[Continued]

MSA	% of population	Rank
Odessa, TX	8.5	8
Sioux Falls, SD	8.5	8
Appleton – Oshkosh – Neenah, WI	8.4	9
Elkhart – Goshen, IN	8.4	9
Fort Wayne, IN	8.4	9
Sioux City, IA – NE	8.3	10
Modesto, CA	8.2	11
Omaha, NE – IA	8.2	11
Bakersfield, CA	8.1	12
Bremerton, WA	8.1	12
Cheyenne, WY	8.1	12
Great Falls, MT	8.1	12
Green Bay, WI	8.1	12
Lake Charles, LA	8.1	12
Merced, CA	8.1	12
Olympia, WA	8.1	12
Sheboygan, WI	8.1	12
Victoria, TX	8.1	12
Wichita, KS	8.1	12
Lima, OH	8.0	13
Pascagoula, MS	8.0	13
Rapid City, SD	8.0	13
Billings, MT	7.9	14
Colorado Springs, CO	7.9	14
Minneapolis – Saint Paul, MN – WI	7.9	14
Baton Rouge, LA	7.8	15
Des Moines, IA	7.8	15
Houston – Galveston – Brazoria, TX	7.8	15
Visalia – Tulare – Porterville, CA	7.8	15
Cedar Rapids, IA	7.7	16
Fort Collins – Loveland, CO	7.7	16
Greeley, CO	7.7	16
Kansas City, MO – KS	7.7	16
Lancaster, PA	7.7	16
Portland – Vancouver, OR – WA	7.7	16
Salem, OR	7.7	16
Stockton, CA	7.7	16

Source: U.S. Bureau of the Census, Data User Services Division, *1990 Census of Population and Housing*, Summary Tape File 3C, United States Summary, CD-ROM, February 1992.

★1769★

Persons Living Above Poverty Level

Persons 12 to 17 Years Old Living Above Poverty Level in 1989

[Table shows the top 50 areas]

MSA	% of population	Rank
Provo – Orem, UT	10.5	1
Salt Lake City – Ogden, UT	9.9	2
Bismarck, ND	8.4	3
Pascagoula, MS	8.3	4

[Continued]

★1769★

Persons 12 to 17 Years Old Living Above Poverty Level in 1989
[Continued]

MSA	% of population	Rank
Sheboygan, WI	8.3	4
Wausau, WI	8.3	4
Kokomo, IN	8.2	5
Saint Cloud, MN	8.2	5
Elkhart–Goshen, IN	8.1	6
Lima, OH	8.1	6
Casper, WY	8.0	7
Dubuque, IA	8.0	7
Fort Wayne, IN	8.0	7
Kankakee, IL	8.0	7
Boise, ID	7.9	8
Richland–Kennewick–Pasco, WA	7.8	9
Peoria, IL	7.7	10
Billings, MT	7.6	11
Cheyenne, WY	7.6	11
Olympia, WA	7.6	11
Omaha, NE–IA	7.6	11
Anderson, SC	7.5	12
Appleton–Oshkosh–Neenah, WI	7.5	12
Bremerton, WA	7.5	12
Davenport–Rock Island–Moline, IA–IL	7.5	12
Decatur, AL	7.5	12
Decatur, IL	7.5	12
Grand Rapids, MI	7.5	12
Lake Charles, LA	7.5	12
Mansfield, OH	7.5	12
Saginaw–Bay City–Midland, MI	7.5	12
Sherman–Denison, TX	7.5	12
Texarkana, TX–Texarkana, AR	7.5	12
Victoria, TX	7.5	12
Anniston, AL	7.4	13
Fort Smith, AR–OK	7.4	13
Glens Falls, NY	7.4	13
Green Bay, WI	7.4	13
Hickory–Morganton, NC	7.4	13
Janesville–Beloit, WI	7.4	13
Anchorage, AK	7.3	14
Augusta, GA–SC	7.3	14
Corpus Christi, TX	7.3	14
Dothan, AL	7.3	14
Flint, MI	7.3	14
Gadsden, AL	7.3	14
Johnstown, PA	7.3	14
Lancaster, PA	7.3	14
Rockford, IL	7.3	14
Sioux Falls, SD	7.3	14

Source: U.S. Bureau of the Census, Data User Services Division, *1990 Census of Population and Housing,* Summary Tape File 3C, United States Summary, CD-ROM, February 1992.

★1770★

Persons Living Above Poverty Level

Persons 18 to 24 Years Old Living Above Poverty Level in 1989

[Table shows the top 50 areas]

MSA	% of population	Rank
Provo–Orem, UT	10.5	1
Jacksonville, NC	10.4	2
Bryan–College Station, TX	10.2	3
Fayetteville, NC	9.6	4
Killeen–Temple, TX	9.3	5
Grand Forks, ND	9.1	6
Boston–Lawrence–Salem, MA–NH	9.0	7
Los Angeles–Anaheim–Riverside, CA	9.0	7
Clarksville–Hopkinsville, TN–KY	8.9	8
Hickory–Morganton, NC	8.9	8
Manchester, NH	8.9	8
Norfolk–Virginia Beach–Newport News, VA	8.8	9
Saint Cloud, MN	8.8	9
Atlanta, GA	8.7	10
Burlington, VT	8.7	10
Charleston, SC	8.7	10
Elkhart–Goshen, IN	8.7	10
Lincoln, NE	8.7	10
Salinas–Seaside–Monterey, CA	8.7	10
San Diego, CA	8.7	10
Washington, DC–MD–VA	8.7	10
Waterbury, CT	8.7	10
Charlotte–Gastonia–Rock Hill, NC–SC	8.6	11
Fitchburg–Leominster, MA	8.6	11
Orlando, FL	8.6	11
Providence–Pawtucket–Fall River, RI–MA	8.6	11
Burlington, NC	8.5	12
Grand Rapids, MI	8.5	12
Honolulu, HI	8.5	12
Lafayette–West Lafayette, IN	8.5	12
Dallas–Fort Worth, TX	8.4	13
Fayetteville–Springdale, AR	8.4	13
New London–Norwich, CT–RI	8.4	13
Salt Lake City–Ogden, UT	8.4	13
Tallahassee, FL	8.4	13
Athens, GA	8.3	14
Austin, TX	8.3	14
Columbus, OH	8.3	14
Detroit–Ann Arbor, MI	8.3	14
Fort Wayne, IN	8.3	14
Greensboro–Winston-Salem–High Point, NC	8.3	14
Hartford–New Britain–Middletown, CT	8.3	14
Huntsville, AL	8.3	14
Portland, ME	8.3	14
Portsmouth–Dover–Rochester, NH–ME	8.3	14
Reno, NV	8.3	14
Santa Barbara–Santa Maria–Lompoc, CA	8.3	14

[Continued]

★1770★

Persons 18 to 24 Years Old Living Above Poverty Level in 1989
[Continued]

MSA	% of population	Rank
Worcester, MA	8.3	14
York, PA	8.3	14
Lubbock, TX	8.2	15

Source: U.S. Bureau of the Census, Data User Services Division, *1990 Census of Population and Housing*, Summary Tape File 3C, United States Summary, CD-ROM, February 1992.

★1771★
Persons Living Above Poverty Level

Persons 25 to 34 Years Old Living Above Poverty Level in 1989
[Table shows the top 50 areas]

MSA	% of population	Rank
Anchorage, AK	19.7	1
Raleigh – Durham, NC	19.0	2
Washington, DC – MD – VA	19.0	2
Dallas – Fort Worth, TX	18.9	3
Austin, TX	18.8	4
Minneapolis – Saint Paul, MN – WI	18.8	4
Rochester, MN	18.8	4
Atlanta, GA	18.4	5
Manchester, NH	18.4	5
Huntsville, AL	18.2	6
Burlington, VT	18.0	7
Madison, WI	17.9	8
Denver – Boulder, CO	17.8	9
Norfolk – Virginia Beach – Newport News, VA	17.8	9
Orlando, FL	17.8	9
Portsmouth – Dover – Rochester, NH – ME	17.8	9
San Francisco – Oakland – San Jose, CA	17.8	9
Boston – Lawrence – Salem, MA – NH	17.7	10
Grand Forks, ND	17.7	10
Seattle – Tacoma, WA	17.7	10
Colorado Springs, CO	17.5	11
Iowa City, IA	17.5	11
San Diego, CA	17.5	11
Sioux Falls, SD	17.5	11
Portland, ME	17.3	12
Fitchburg – Leominster, MA	17.2	13
Indianapolis, IN	17.2	13
New London – Norwich, CT – RI	17.2	13
Reno, NV	17.2	13
Fort Walton Beach, FL	17.1	14
Grand Rapids, MI	17.1	14
Houston – Galveston – Brazoria, TX	17.1	14
Los Angeles – Anaheim – Riverside, CA	17.1	14

[Continued]

★1771★

Persons 25 to 34 Years Old Living Above Poverty Level in 1989
[Continued]

MSA	% of population	Rank
Charleston, SC	17.0	15
Fayetteville, NC	17.0	15
Hartford – New Britain – Middletown, CT	17.0	15
Honolulu, HI	17.0	15
Charlotte – Gastonia – Rock Hill, NC – SC	16.9	16
Charlottesville, VA	16.8	17
Columbus, OH	16.8	17
Las Vegas, NV	16.8	17
Nashville, TN	16.8	17
Omaha, NE – IA	16.8	17
Baltimore, MD	16.7	18
Des Moines, IA	16.7	18
Green Bay, WI	16.7	18
Richmond – Petersburg, VA	16.7	18
Appleton – Oshkosh – Neenah, WI	16.6	19
Jacksonville, FL	16.6	19
Waterbury, CT	16.5	20

Source: U.S. Bureau of the Census, Data User Services Division, *1990 Census of Population and Housing*, Summary Tape File 3C, United States Summary, CD-ROM, February 1992.

★1772★
Persons Living Above Poverty Level

Persons 35 to 44 Years Old Living Above Poverty Level in 1989
[Table shows the top 50 areas]

MSA	% of population	Rank
Anchorage, AK	18.1	1
Santa Fe, NM	17.4	2
Denver – Boulder, CO	17.0	3
Washington, DC – MD – VA	16.8	4
Olympia, WA	16.6	5
Portland – Vancouver, OR – WA	16.6	5
Atlanta, GA	16.3	6
Reno, NV	16.2	7
San Francisco – Oakland – San Jose, CA	16.2	7
Seattle – Tacoma, WA	16.2	7
Boise, ID	16.1	8
Fort Collins – Loveland, CO	16.0	9
Portland, ME	15.9	10
Madison, WI	15.8	11
Raleigh – Durham, NC	15.8	11
Burlington, VT	15.6	12
Minneapolis – Saint Paul, MN – WI	15.6	12
Richmond – Petersburg, VA	15.6	12
Bremerton, WA	15.5	13
Casper, WY	15.4	14
Eugene – Springfield, OR	15.4	14
Springfield, IL	15.2	15

[Continued]

★1772★

Persons 35 to 44 Years Old Living Above Poverty Level in 1989
[Continued]

MSA	% of population	Rank
York, PA	15.2	15
Austin, TX	15.1	16
Fort Wayne, IN	15.1	16
Charlotte – Gastonia – Rock Hill, NC – SC	15.0	17
Cheyenne, WY	15.0	17
Houston – Galveston – Brazoria, TX	15.0	17
Nashville, TN	15.0	17
Sacramento, CA	15.0	17
Bellingham, WA	14.9	18
Bismarck, ND	14.9	18
Colorado Springs, CO	14.9	18
Greensboro – Winston-Salem – High Point, NC	14.9	18
Hartford – New Britain – Middletown, CT	14.9	18
Manchester, NH	14.9	18
Baltimore, MD	14.8	19
Dallas – Fort Worth, TX	14.8	19
Des Moines, IA	14.8	19
Green Bay, WI	14.8	19
Harrisburg – Lebanon – Carlisle, PA	14.8	19
Poughkeepsie, NY	14.8	19
Roanoke, VA	14.8	19
Asheville, NC	14.7	20
Boston – Lawrence – Salem, MA – NH	14.7	20
Hickory – Morganton, NC	14.7	20
Kansas City, MO – KS	14.7	20
Portsmouth – Dover – Rochester, NH – ME	14.7	20
Omaha, NE – IA	14.6	21
Wausau, WI	14.6	21

Source: U.S. Bureau of the Census, Data User Services Division, *1990 Census of Population and Housing,* Summary Tape File 3C, United States Summary, CD-ROM, February 1992.

★1773★
Persons Living Above Poverty Level

Persons 45 to 54 Years Old Living Above Poverty Level in 1989
[Table shows the top 50 areas]

MSA	% of population	Rank
Santa Fe, NM	11.7	1
Kokomo, IN	11.4	2
Hickory – Morganton, NC	11.3	3
Johnson City – Kingsport – Bristol, TN – VA	11.2	4
Washington, DC – MD – VA	11.1	5
Mansfield, OH	11.0	6

[Continued]

★1773★

Persons 45 to 54 Years Old Living Above Poverty Level in 1989
[Continued]

MSA	% of population	Rank
Anderson, SC	10.8	7
Burlington, NC	10.8	7
Reno, NV	10.8	7
Decatur, AL	10.7	8
Huntsville, AL	10.7	8
Las Vegas, NV	10.7	8
Anderson, IN	10.6	9
Florence, AL	10.6	9
Greensboro – Winston-Salem – High Point, NC	10.6	9
Poughkeepsie, NY	10.5	10
San Francisco – Oakland – San Jose, CA	10.5	10
Anchorage, AK	10.4	11
Cedar Rapids, IA	10.4	11
Chattanooga, TN – GA	10.4	11
Greenville – Spartanburg, SC	10.4	11
Hartford – New Britain – Middletown, CT	10.4	11
New York – Northern New Jersey – Long Island, NY – NJ – CT	10.4	11
Pascagoula, MS	10.4	11
Roanoke, VA	10.4	11
York, PA	10.4	11
Asheville, NC	10.3	12
Charlotte – Gastonia – Rock Hill, NC – SC	10.3	12
Parkersburg – Marietta, WV – OH	10.3	12
Atlanta, GA	10.2	13
Baltimore, MD	10.2	13
Charleston, WV	10.2	13
Danville, VA	10.2	13
Dayton – Springfield, OH	10.2	13
Harrisburg – Lebanon – Carlisle, PA	10.2	13
Janesville – Beloit, WI	10.2	13
Knoxville, TN	10.2	13
Olympia, WA	10.2	13
Flint, MI	10.1	14
Medford, OR	10.1	14
Panama City, FL	10.1	14
Rochester, MN	10.1	14
Rockford, IL	10.1	14
Saginaw – Bay City – Midland, MI	10.1	14
Denver – Boulder, CO	10.0	15
New Haven – Meriden, CT	10.0	15
Redding, CA	10.0	15
Seattle – Tacoma, WA	10.0	15
Steubenville – Weirton, OH – WV	10.0	15
Tulsa, OK	10.0	15

Source: U.S. Bureau of the Census, Data User Services Division, *1990 Census of Population and Housing,* Summary Tape File 3C, United States Summary, CD-ROM, February 1992.

★1774★
Persons Living Above Poverty Level

Persons 55 to 59 Years Old Living Above Poverty Level in 1989

[Table shows the top 50 areas]

MSA	% of population	Rank
Melbourne – Titusville – Palm Bay, FL	5.0	1
Steubenville – Weirton, OH – WV	5.0	1
Fort Myers – Cape Coral, Fl	4.8	2
Naples, FL	4.8	2
Pittsfield, MA	4.8	2
Sarasota, FL	4.8	2
Fort Walton Beach, FL	4.7	3
Burlington, NC	4.6	4
Florence, AL	4.6	4
Hickory – Morganton, NC	4.6	4
Kokomo, IN	4.6	4
Mansfield, OH	4.6	4
Ocala, FL	4.6	4
Reading, PA	4.6	4
Altoona, PA	4.5	5
Anderson, SC	4.5	5
Decatur, IL	4.5	5
Huntsville, AL	4.5	5
Roanoke, VA	4.5	5
Williamsport, PA	4.5	5
Allentown – Bethlehem – Easton, PA – NJ	4.4	6
Buffalo – Niagara Falls, NY	4.4	6
Charleston, WV	4.4	6
Chattanooga, TN – GA	4.4	6
Danville, VA	4.4	6
Enid, OK	4.4	6
Fort Pierce, FL	4.4	6
Harrisburg – Lebanon – Carlisle, PA	4.4	6
Pittsburgh – Beaver Valley, PA	4.4	6
Sharon, PA	4.4	6
Sherman – Denison, TX	4.4	6
Topeka, KS	4.4	6
Wheeling, WV – OH	4.4	6
York, PA	4.4	6
Youngstown – Warren, OH	4.4	6
Anderson, IN	4.3	7
Atlantic City, NJ	4.3	7
Dayton – Springfield, OH	4.3	7
Daytona Beach, FL	4.3	7
Flint, MI	4.3	7
Gadsden, AL	4.3	7
Greensboro – Winston-Salem – High Point, NC	4.3	7
Hagerstown, MD	4.3	7
Janesville – Beloit, WI	4.3	7
Johnson City – Kingsport – Bristol, TN – VA	4.3	7
Johnstown, PA	4.3	7
New York – Northern New Jersey – Long Island, NY – NJ – CT	4.3	7
Pueblo, CO	4.3	7

[Continued]

★1774★

Persons 55 to 59 Years Old Living Above Poverty Level in 1989
[Continued]

MSA	% of population	Rank
Scranton – Wilkes-Barre, PA	4.3	7
Pascagoula, MS	4.2	8

Source: U.S. Bureau of the Census, Data User Services Division, *1990 Census of Population and Housing*, Summary Tape File 3C, United States Summary, CD-ROM, February 1992.

★1775★
Persons Living Above Poverty Level

Persons 60 to 64 Years Old Living Above Poverty Level in 1989

[Table shows the top 50 areas]

MSA	% of population	Rank
Sarasota, FL	6.8	1
Naples, FL	6.6	2
Fort Myers – Cape Coral, Fl	6.5	3
Fort Pierce, FL	6.3	4
Ocala, FL	6.1	5
Bradenton, FL	6.0	6
Daytona Beach, FL	5.6	7
Pittsburgh – Beaver Valley, PA	5.3	8
Sharon, PA	5.3	8
Steubenville – Weirton, OH – WV	5.3	8
Cumberland, MD – WV	5.2	9
Melbourne – Titusville – Palm Bay, FL	5.2	9
West Palm Beach – Boca Raton – Delray Beach, FL	5.2	9
Johnstown, PA	5.1	10
Lakeland – Winter Haven, FL	5.1	10
Scranton – Wilkes-Barre, PA	5.0	11
Tampa – Saint Petersburg – Clearwater, FL	5.0	11
Wheeling, WV – OH	5.0	11
Youngstown – Warren, OH	5.0	11
Burlington, NC	4.8	12
Charleston, WV	4.8	12
Reading, PA	4.8	12
Allentown – Bethlehem – Easton, PA – NJ	4.7	13
Altoona, PA	4.7	13
Danville, VA	4.7	13
Roanoke, VA	4.7	13
Atlantic City, NJ	4.6	14
Buffalo – Niagara Falls, NY	4.6	14
Asheville, NC	4.5	15
Canton, OH	4.5	15
Elmira, NY	4.5	15
Jamestown – Dunkirk, NY	4.5	15
Parkersburg – Marietta, WV – OH	4.5	15
Pueblo, CO	4.5	15
Anderson, IN	4.4	16
Benton Harbor, MI	4.4	16

[Continued]

★1775★

Persons 60 to 64 Years Old Living Above Poverty Level in 1989

[Continued]

MSA	% of population	Rank
Binghamton, NY	4.4	16
Cleveland – Akron – Lorain, OH	4.4	16
Gadsden, AL	4.4	16
Harrisburg – Lebanon – Carlisle, PA	4.4	16
Huntington – Ashland, WV – KY – OH	4.4	16
New Bedford, MA	4.4	16
Panama City, FL	4.4	16
Pittsfield, MA	4.4	16
Utica – Rome, NY	4.4	16
Williamsport, PA	4.4	16
Decatur, IL	4.3	17
Erie, PA	4.3	17
Florence, AL	4.3	17
Peoria, IL	4.3	17

Source: U.S. Bureau of the Census, Data User Services Division, *1990 Census of Population and Housing,* Summary Tape File 3C, United States Summary, CD-ROM, February 1992.

★1776★

Persons Living Above Poverty Level

Persons 65 to 74 Years Old Living Above Poverty Level in 1989

[Table shows the top 50 areas]

MSA	% of population	Rank
Sarasota, FL	17.1	1
Bradenton, FL	14.7	2
Fort Myers – Cape Coral, Fl	14.5	3
Fort Pierce, FL	14.1	4
Naples, FL	13.8	5
Ocala, FL	13.1	6
West Palm Beach – Boca Raton – Delray Beach, FL	12.7	7
Daytona Beach, FL	12.3	8
Tampa – Saint Petersburg – Clearwater, FL	11.1	9
Lakeland – Winter Haven, FL	10.1	10
Melbourne – Titusville – Palm Bay, FL	10.1	10
Chico, CA	9.6	11
Johnstown, PA	9.6	11
Pittsburgh – Beaver Valley, PA	9.4	12
Scranton – Wilkes-Barre, PA	9.4	12
Sharon, PA	9.1	13
Steubenville – Weirton, OH – WV	9.1	13
Wheeling, WV – OH	9.1	13
Cumberland, MD – WV	8.9	14
Youngstown – Warren, OH	8.9	14
Medford, OR	8.7	15
Altoona, PA	8.6	16
Pittsfield, MA	8.6	16

[Continued]

★1776★

Persons 65 to 74 Years Old Living Above Poverty Level in 1989

[Continued]

MSA	% of population	Rank
Atlantic City, NJ	8.4	17
Allentown – Bethlehem – Easton, PA – NJ	8.3	18
Buffalo – Niagara Falls, NY	8.2	19
Duluth, MN – WI	8.2	19
New Bedford, MA	8.2	19
Reading, PA	8.2	19
Elmira, NY	8.1	20
Redding, CA	8.1	20
Asheville, NC	8.0	21
Utica – Rome, NY	8.0	21
Waterbury, CT	8.0	21
Williamsport, PA	8.0	21
Charleston, WV	7.9	22
Danville, VA	7.9	22
Canton, OH	7.8	23
Jamestown – Dunkirk, NY	7.8	23
Burlington, NC	7.7	24
Erie, PA	7.7	24
Gadsden, AL	7.7	24
Providence – Pawtucket – Fall River, RI – MA	7.7	24
Pueblo, CO	7.7	24
Springfield, MA	7.7	24
Yuma, AZ	7.7	24
Cleveland – Akron – Lorain, OH	7.6	25
Miami – Fort Lauderdale, FL	7.6	25
Sherman – Denison, TX	7.6	25
Terre Haute, IN	7.6	25

Source: U.S. Bureau of the Census, Data User Services Division, *1990 Census of Population and Housing,* Summary Tape File 3C, United States Summary, CD-ROM, February 1992.

★1777★

Persons Living Above Poverty Level

Persons 75 Years Old and Older Living Above Poverty Level in 1989

[Table shows the top 50 areas]

MSA	% of population	Rank
Sarasota, FL	12.39	1
Bradenton, FL	10.60	2
West Palm Beach – Boca Raton – Delray Beach, FL	9.34	3
Fort Myers – Cape Coral, Fl	8.29	4
Daytona Beach, FL	7.77	5
Tampa – Saint Petersburg – Clearwater, FL	7.58	6
Fort Pierce, FL	7.39	7
Naples, FL	7.38	8
Miami – Fort Lauderdale, FL	6.26	9
Ocala, FL	6.19	10
Chico, CA	5.94	11

[Continued]

★1777★

Persons 75 Years Old and Older Living Above Poverty Level in 1989

[Continued]

MSA	% of population	Rank
Scranton – Wilkes-Barre, PA	5.92	12
Lakeland – Winter Haven, FL	5.73	13
Saint Joseph, MO	5.67	14
Duluth, MN – WI	5.65	15
Pittsfield, MA	5.59	16
Wheeling, WV – OH	5.57	17
Johnstown, PA	5.55	18
Cumberland, MD – WV	5.54	19
Enid, OK	5.51	20
Sharon, PA	5.50	21
Pittsburgh – Beaver Valley, PA	5.48	22
Jamestown – Dunkirk, NY	5.47	23
Waterbury, CT	5.47	23
Altoona, PA	5.43	24
Medford, OR	5.42	25
New Bedford, MA	5.31	26
Reading, PA	5.30	27
Atlantic City, NJ	5.29	28
Steubenville – Weirton, OH – WV	5.09	29
Salem, OR	5.08	30
Sioux City, IA – NE	4.98	31
Asheville, NC	4.90	32
Williamsport, PA	4.90	32
Melbourne – Titusville – Palm Bay, FL	4.89	33
Sheboygan, WI	4.88	34
Sherman – Denison, TX	4.88	34
Allentown – Bethlehem – Easton, PA – NJ	4.87	35
Springfield, IL	4.87	35
Terre Haute, IN	4.87	35
Elmira, NY	4.82	36
Utica – Rome, NY	4.79	37
Roanoke, VA	4.78	38
Albany – Schenectady – Troy, NY	4.77	39
Buffalo – Niagara Falls, NY	4.75	40
Providence – Pawtucket – Fall River, RI – MA	4.71	41
New Haven – Meriden, CT	4.70	42
Pueblo, CO	4.70	42
South Bend – Mishawaka, IN	4.70	42
Binghamton, NY	4.69	43

Source: U.S. Bureau of the Census, Data User Services Division, *1990 Census of Population and Housing*, Summary Tape File 3C, United States Summary, CD-ROM, February 1992.

★1778★

Persons Living Below Poverty Level

Persons Under 5 Years Old Living Below Poverty Level in 1989

[Table shows the top 50 areas]

MSA	% of population	Rank
McAllen – Edinburg – Mission, TX	4.70	1
Laredo, TX	4.57	2
Brownsville – Harlingen, TX	4.46	3
Visalia – Tulare – Porterville, CA	3.36	4
El Paso, TX	3.35	5
Fresno, CA	3.26	6
Merced, CA	3.19	7
Monroe, LA	3.07	8
Yakima, WA	3.04	9
Albany, GA	3.03	10
Las Cruces, NM	2.96	11
Odessa, TX	2.85	12
Shreveport, LA	2.79	13
Yuba City, CA	2.77	14
Houma – Thibodaux, LA	2.76	15
Corpus Christi, TX	2.62	16
Bakersfield, CA	2.61	17
Pine Bluff, AR	2.56	18
Pueblo, CO	2.54	19
Alexandria, LA	2.47	20
San Antonio, TX	2.47	20
Flint, MI	2.42	21
New Orleans, LA	2.40	22
Columbus, GA – AL	2.36	23
Memphis, TN – AR – MS	2.36	23
Biloxi – Gulfport, MS	2.29	24
Lafayette, LA	2.29	24
Mobile, AL	2.28	25
Jackson, MS	2.21	26
Muskegon, MI	2.18	27
Yuma, AZ	2.16	28
Florence, SC	2.15	29
Waco, TX	2.11	30
Lake Charles, LA	2.10	31
Stockton, CA	2.09	32
Texarkana, TX – Texarkana, AR	2.07	33
Jackson, TN	2.06	34
Modesto, CA	2.05	35
Baton Rouge, LA	2.02	36
Benton Harbor, MI	2.02	36
Pensacola, FL	2.02	36
Amarillo, TX	2.01	37
Longview – Marshall, TX	2.01	37
Rapid City, SD	2.00	38
Macon – Warner Robins, GA	1.99	39
Beaumont – Port Arthur, TX	1.98	40
Huntington – Ashland, WV – KY – OH	1.98	40
San Angelo, TX	1.98	40
Lawton, OK	1.97	41
Savannah, GA	1.97	41

Source: U.S. Bureau of the Census, Data User Services Division, *1990 Census of Population and Housing*, Summary Tape File 3C, United States Summary, CD-ROM, February 1992.

★1779★

Persons Living Below Poverty Level

Persons 5 Years Old Living Below Poverty Level in 1989

[Table shows the top 50 areas]

MSA	% of population	Rank
McAllen – Edinburg – Mission, TX	1.042	1
Brownsville – Harlingen, TX	0.950	2
Laredo, TX	0.890	3
Merced, CA	0.701	4
Fresno, CA	0.695	5
Visalia – Tulare – Porterville, CA	0.695	5
El Paso, TX	0.654	6
Odessa, TX	0.645	7
Monroe, LA	0.644	8
Las Cruces, NM	0.611	9
Shreveport, LA	0.572	10
San Antonio, TX	0.544	11
Albany, GA	0.542	12
New Orleans, LA	0.541	13
Houma – Thibodaux, LA	0.537	14
Yuba City, CA	0.520	15
Yakima, WA	0.516	16
Alexandria, LA	0.515	17
Corpus Christi, TX	0.512	18
Pine Bluff, AR	0.505	19
Mobile, AL	0.501	20
Yuma, AZ	0.498	21
Bakersfield, CA	0.484	22
Jackson, MS	0.482	23
Lafayette, LA	0.477	24
Modesto, CA	0.464	25
San Angelo, TX	0.461	26
Stockton, CA	0.461	26
Cumberland, MD – WV	0.459	27
Lake Charles, LA	0.457	28
Pensacola, FL	0.457	28
Pueblo, CO	0.453	29
Owensboro, KY	0.448	30
Midland, TX	0.443	31
Beaumont – Port Arthur, TX	0.438	32
Texarkana, TX – Texarkana, AR	0.438	32
Baton Rouge, LA	0.437	33
Saint Joseph, MO	0.435	34
Victoria, TX	0.432	35
Muskegon, MI	0.426	36
Lawton, OK	0.425	37
Flint, MI	0.424	38
Jackson, TN	0.424	38
Waco, TX	0.421	39
Biloxi – Gulfport, MS	0.419	40
Memphis, TN – AR – MS	0.411	41
Rapid City, SD	0.411	41
Casper, WY	0.408	42
Chico, CA	0.399	43
Longview – Marshall, TX	0.399	43

Source: U.S. Bureau of the Census, Data User Services Division, *1990 Census of Population and Housing,* Summary Tape File 3C, United States Summary, CD-ROM, February 1992.

★1780★

Persons Living Below Poverty Level

Persons 6 to 11 Years Old Living Below Poverty Level in 1989

[Table shows the top 50 areas]

MSA	% of population	Rank
McAllen – Edinburg – Mission, TX	6.64	1
Brownsville – Harlingen, TX	5.93	2
Laredo, TX	5.79	3
El Paso, TX	3.92	4
Visalia – Tulare – Porterville, CA	3.84	5
Las Cruces, NM	3.61	6
Merced, CA	3.57	7
Houma – Thibodaux, LA	3.48	8
Fresno, CA	3.47	9
Monroe, LA	3.34	10
Albany, GA	3.25	11
Alexandria, LA	3.24	12
Pine Bluff, AR	3.07	13
Corpus Christi, TX	3.05	14
Shreveport, LA	3.05	14
Odessa, TX	3.04	15
Mobile, AL	2.80	16
New Orleans, LA	2.80	16
Lafayette, LA	2.74	17
Yakima, WA	2.74	17
Pueblo, CO	2.73	18
Yuma, AZ	2.73	18
San Antonio, TX	2.70	19
Yuba City, CA	2.65	20
Bakersfield, CA	2.60	21
Biloxi – Gulfport, MS	2.53	22
Jackson, MS	2.51	23
Beaumont – Port Arthur, TX	2.47	24
Florence, SC	2.47	24
Stockton, CA	2.46	25
Memphis, TN – AR – MS	2.42	26
Columbus, GA – AL	2.41	27
Victoria, TX	2.39	28
Flint, MI	2.36	29
Longview – Marshall, TX	2.32	30
Texarkana, TX – Texarkana, AR	2.32	30
Baton Rouge, LA	2.29	31
Pascagoula, MS	2.29	31
Savannah, GA	2.25	32
Lake Charles, LA	2.21	33
Modesto, CA	2.21	33
Huntington – Ashland, WV – KY – OH	2.18	34
Muskegon, MI	2.17	35
Montgomery, AL	2.16	36
Richland – Kennewick – Pasco, WA	2.15	37
Waco, TX	2.12	38
Tyler, TX	2.11	39
Benton Harbor, MI	2.09	40
Amarillo, TX	2.08	41
Dothan, AL	2.07	42

Source: U.S. Bureau of the Census, Data User Services Division, *1990 Census of Population and Housing,* Summary Tape File 3C, United States Summary, CD-ROM, February 1992.

★1781★

Persons Living Below Poverty Level

Persons 12 to 17 Years Old Living Below Poverty Level in 1989

[Table shows the top 50 areas]

MSA	% of population	Rank
McAllen – Edinburg – Mission, TX	6.77	1
Brownsville – Harlingen, TX	6.33	2
Laredo, TX	6.03	3
El Paso, TX	3.70	4
Las Cruces, NM	3.26	5
Albany, GA	3.00	6
Visalia – Tulare – Porterville, CA	2.92	7
Yuma, AZ	2.85	8
Houma – Thibodaux, LA	2.84	9
Monroe, LA	2.81	10
Pine Bluff, AR	2.70	11
Corpus Christi, TX	2.65	12
New Orleans, LA	2.63	13
Merced, CA	2.54	14
Fresno, CA	2.53	15
Florence, SC	2.51	16
Shreveport, LA	2.48	17
Alexandria, LA	2.43	18
Victoria, TX	2.41	19
Mobile, AL	2.33	20
Lafayette, LA	2.31	21
San Antonio, TX	2.24	22
Texarkana, TX – Texarkana, AR	2.24	22
Yakima, WA	2.23	23
Jackson, MS	2.22	24
Pascagoula, MS	2.21	25
Biloxi – Gulfport, MS	2.20	26
Odessa, TX	2.20	26
Huntington – Ashland, WV – KY – OH	2.16	27
Memphis, TN – AR – MS	2.12	28
Lake Charles, LA	2.10	29
Columbus, GA – AL	2.07	30
Montgomery, AL	2.06	31
Beaumont – Port Arthur, TX	1.98	32
Pueblo, CO	1.98	32
Baton Rouge, LA	1.96	33
Bakersfield, CA	1.93	34
Longview – Marshall, TX	1.90	35
Yuba City, CA	1.85	36
Savannah, GA	1.82	37
Jackson, TN	1.81	38
Macon – Warner Robins, GA	1.81	38
Waco, TX	1.80	39
Dothan, AL	1.79	40
Stockton, CA	1.79	40
Flint, MI	1.78	41
Pensacola, FL	1.72	42
Tuscaloosa, AL	1.71	43
Fort Smith, AR – OK	1.67	44
Augusta, GA – SC	1.65	45

Source: U.S. Bureau of the Census, Data User Services Division, *1990 Census of Population and Housing,* Summary Tape File 3C, United States Summary, CD-ROM, February 1992.

★1782★

Persons Living Below Poverty Level

Persons 18 to 24 Years Old Living Below Poverty Level in 1989

[Table shows the top 50 areas]

MSA	% of population	Rank
Bryan – College Station, TX	12.78	1
Lawrence, KS	10.39	2
State College, PA	10.09	3
Bloomington, IN	9.08	4
Gainesville, FL	8.65	5
Iowa City, IA	8.65	5
Athens, GA	7.49	6
Lafayette – West Lafayette, IN	6.71	7
Tallahassee, FL	6.58	8
Champaign – Urbana – Rantoul, IL	6.56	9
Columbia, MO	6.17	10
Provo – Orem, UT	5.85	11
Chico, CA	5.68	12
Tuscaloosa, AL	5.53	13
Muncie, IN	5.47	14
Waco, TX	5.23	15
Bloomington – Normal, IL	5.10	16
Las Cruces, NM	4.88	17
Fargo – Moorhead, ND – MN	4.85	18
Madison, WI	4.80	19
McAllen – Edinburg – Mission, TX	4.80	19
Lubbock, TX	4.76	20
La Crosse, WI	4.75	21
Charlottesville, VA	4.70	22
Brownsville – Harlingen, TX	4.53	23
Laredo, TX	4.52	24
Austin, TX	4.51	25
Fort Collins – Loveland, CO	4.46	26
Santa Barbara – Santa Maria – Lompoc, CA	4.11	27
Eau Claire, WI	4.10	28
Kalamazoo, MI	4.04	29
Fayetteville – Springdale, AR	3.86	30
Grand Forks, ND	3.85	31
Lincoln, NE	3.67	32
Lansing – East Lansing, MI	3.65	33
Baton Rouge, LA	3.54	34
Eugene – Springfield, OR	3.49	35
Saint Cloud, MN	3.47	36
Tucson, AZ	3.46	37
Greeley, CO	3.44	38
Monroe, LA	3.44	38
Bellingham, WA	3.38	39
Waterloo – Cedar Falls, IA	3.34	40
El Paso, TX	3.27	41
Springfield, MO	3.24	42
Albany, GA	3.12	43
Wilmington, NC	3.03	44
Lafayette, LA	3.02	45
Fresno, CA	2.99	46
Burlington, VT	2.97	47

Source: U.S. Bureau of the Census, Data User Services Division, *1990 Census of Population and Housing,* Summary Tape File 3C, United States Summary, CD-ROM, February 1992.

★1783★

Persons Living Below Poverty Level

Persons 25 to 34 Years Old Living Below Poverty Level in 1989

[Table shows the top 50 areas]

MSA	% of population	Rank
McAllen – Edinburg – Mission, TX	5.31	1
Brownsville – Harlingen, TX	4.97	2
Laredo, TX	4.84	3
El Paso, TX	4.00	4
Las Cruces, NM	3.77	5
Visalia – Tulare – Porterville, CA	3.53	6
Houma – Thibodaux, LA	3.45	7
Fresno, CA	3.40	8
Monroe, LA	3.39	9
Lafayette, LA	3.37	10
Odessa, TX	3.35	11
Pueblo, CO	3.29	12
Bryan – College Station, TX	3.26	13
Merced, CA	3.25	14
Huntington – Ashland, WV – KY – OH	3.18	15
Yakima, WA	3.17	16
Shreveport, LA	3.15	17
Gainesville, FL	3.10	18
New Orleans, LA	3.10	18
Corpus Christi, TX	3.05	19
Albany, GA	2.98	20
Flint, MI	2.98	20
Mobile, AL	2.96	21
San Antonio, TX	2.95	22
Alexandria, LA	2.93	23
Chico, CA	2.92	24
Yuba City, CA	2.92	24
Biloxi – Gulfport, MS	2.91	25
Columbia, MO	2.88	26
Pine Bluff, AR	2.88	26
Jackson, MS	2.86	27
Lake Charles, LA	2.85	28
Lawrence, KS	2.82	29
Lubbock, TX	2.82	29
Baton Rouge, LA	2.80	30
Tucson, AZ	2.76	31
Iowa City, IA	2.68	32
Bakersfield, CA	2.64	33
Eugene – Springfield, OR	2.64	33
Waco, TX	2.63	34
Memphis, TN – AR – MS	2.62	35
Pascagoula, MS	2.62	35
Amarillo, TX	2.61	36
Albuquerque, NM	2.59	37
Houston – Galveston – Brazoria, TX	2.59	37
Beaumont – Port Arthur, TX	2.56	38
Columbus, GA – AL	2.56	38
Pensacola, FL	2.56	38
Austin, TX	2.52	39
Longview – Marshall, TX	2.51	40

Source: U.S. Bureau of the Census, Data User Services Division, *1990 Census of Population and Housing*, Summary Tape File 3C, United States Summary, CD-ROM, February 1992.

★1784★

Persons Living Below Poverty Level

Persons 35 to 44 Years Old Living Below Poverty Level in 1989

[Table shows the top 50 areas]

MSA	% of population	Rank
McAllen – Edinburg – Mission, TX	4.86	1
Brownsville – Harlingen, TX	4.36	2
Laredo, TX	3.99	3
El Paso, TX	2.85	4
Las Cruces, NM	2.69	5
Houma – Thibodaux, LA	2.53	6
Visalia – Tulare – Porterville, CA	2.30	7
Yuma, AZ	2.30	7
Corpus Christi, TX	2.26	8
New Orleans, LA	2.21	9
Alexandria, LA	2.13	10
Lafayette, LA	2.13	10
Fresno, CA	2.04	11
Odessa, TX	2.03	12
Shreveport, LA	2.02	13
Pueblo, CO	2.01	14
Huntington – Ashland, WV – KY – OH	2.00	15
Mobile, AL	2.00	15
Monroe, LA	1.99	16
Pine Bluff, AR	1.98	17
Albany, GA	1.96	18
San Antonio, TX	1.92	19
Florence, SC	1.90	20
Yakima, WA	1.85	21
Lake Charles, LA	1.84	22
Biloxi – Gulfport, MS	1.83	23
Albuquerque, NM	1.81	24
Merced, CA	1.81	24
Tucson, AZ	1.81	24
Beaumont – Port Arthur, TX	1.79	25
Victoria, TX	1.74	26
Wheeling, WV – OH	1.74	26
Longview – Marshall, TX	1.71	27
Texarkana, TX – Texarkana, AR	1.71	27
Bakersfield, CA	1.70	28
Columbus, GA – AL	1.70	28
Yuba City, CA	1.69	29
Baton Rouge, LA	1.68	30
Miami – Fort Lauderdale, FL	1.67	31
Jackson, MS	1.65	32
Pascagoula, MS	1.64	33
Chico, CA	1.63	34
Houston – Galveston – Brazoria, TX	1.61	35
Memphis, TN – AR – MS	1.61	35
Redding, CA	1.61	35
Stockton, CA	1.61	35
Pensacola, FL	1.60	36
Charleston, WV	1.58	37
Eugene – Springfield, OR	1.57	38
Flint, MI	1.57	38

Source: U.S. Bureau of the Census, Data User Services Division, *1990 Census of Population and Housing*, Summary Tape File 3C, United States Summary, CD-ROM, February 1992.

★1785★

Persons Living Below Poverty Level

Persons 45 to 54 Years Old Living Below Poverty Level in 1989

[Table shows the top 50 areas]

MSA	% of population	Rank
McAllen – Edinburg – Mission, TX	2.65	1
Brownsville – Harlingen, TX	2.52	2
Laredo, TX	2.49	3
El Paso, TX	1.59	4
Huntington – Ashland, WV – KY – OH	1.48	5
Houma – Thibodaux, LA	1.47	6
Lafayette, LA	1.47	6
Yuma, AZ	1.36	7
Florence, SC	1.35	8
New Orleans, LA	1.34	9
Corpus Christi, TX	1.30	10
Alexandria, LA	1.29	11
Monroe, LA	1.29	11
Las Cruces, NM	1.24	12
Shreveport, LA	1.24	12
Johnson City – Kingsport – Bristol, TN – VA	1.23	13
Beaumont – Port Arthur, TX	1.21	14
Biloxi – Gulfport, MS	1.21	14
Odessa, TX	1.21	14
Gadsden, AL	1.19	15
Pine Bluff, AR	1.18	16
Pueblo, CO	1.17	17
Texarkana, TX – Texarkana, AR	1.17	17
Fort Smith, AR – OK	1.16	18
Victoria, TX	1.16	18
Yakima, WA	1.13	19
Miami – Fort Lauderdale, FL	1.12	20
Longview – Marshall, TX	1.11	21
Danville, VA	1.10	22
Mobile, AL	1.10	22
San Antonio, TX	1.09	23
Baton Rouge, LA	1.05	24
Visalia – Tulare – Porterville, CA	1.05	24
Albany, GA	1.04	25
Parkersburg – Marietta, WV – OH	1.04	25
Wheeling, WV – OH	1.04	25
Montgomery, AL	1.03	26
Florence, AL	1.02	27
Jackson, MS	1.02	27
Fresno, CA	1.01	28
Savannah, GA	1.00	29
Steubenville – Weirton, OH – WV	1.00	29
Altoona, PA	0.99	30
Lake Charles, LA	0.99	30
Yuba City, CA	0.99	30
Anniston, AL	0.98	31
Knoxville, TN	0.98	31
Birmingham, AL	0.97	32
Charleston, WV	0.97	32
Memphis, TN – AR – MS	0.97	32

Source: U.S. Bureau of the Census, Data User Services Division, *1990 Census of Population and Housing,* Summary Tape File 3C, United States Summary, CD-ROM, February 1992.

★1786★

Persons Living Below Poverty Level

Persons 55 to 59 Years Old Living Below Poverty Level in 1989

[Table shows the top 50 areas]

MSA	% of population	Rank
Brownsville – Harlingen, TX	1.03	1
McAllen – Edinburg – Mission, TX	0.99	2
Laredo, TX	0.91	3
Houma – Thibodaux, LA	0.74	4
Alexandria, LA	0.67	5
Huntington – Ashland, WV – KY – OH	0.67	5
Johnson City – Kingsport – Bristol, TN – VA	0.67	5
Texarkana, TX – Texarkana, AR	0.67	5
Corpus Christi, TX	0.64	6
Monroe, LA	0.63	7
Beaumont – Port Arthur, TX	0.62	8
Florence, SC	0.62	8
Gadsden, AL	0.62	8
El Paso, TX	0.61	9
Fort Smith, AR – OK	0.61	9
Las Cruces, NM	0.61	9
Pine Bluff, AR	0.61	9
Biloxi – Gulfport, MS	0.60	10
Lafayette, LA	0.60	10
Decatur, AL	0.59	11
Lake Charles, LA	0.59	11
New Orleans, LA	0.59	11
Pueblo, CO	0.59	11
Anniston, AL	0.58	12
Charleston, WV	0.58	12
Shreveport, LA	0.58	12
Enid, OK	0.57	13
Johnstown, PA	0.57	13
Wheeling, WV – OH	0.57	13
Mobile, AL	0.56	14
Florence, AL	0.55	15
Jackson, MS	0.55	15
Owensboro, KY	0.55	15
Victoria, TX	0.55	15
Cumberland, MD – WV	0.54	16
Longview – Marshall, TX	0.54	16
Midland, TX	0.54	16
Savannah, GA	0.53	17
Chattanooga, TN – GA	0.52	18
Albany, GA	0.50	19
Birmingham, AL	0.50	19
Great Falls, MT	0.50	19
Odessa, TX	0.50	19
San Antonio, TX	0.50	19
Amarillo, TX	0.49	20
Danville, VA	0.49	20
Miami – Fort Lauderdale, FL	0.49	20
Pascagoula, MS	0.49	20
Wichita Falls, TX	0.49	20
Yuma, AZ	0.49	20

Source: U.S. Bureau of the Census, Data User Services Division, *1990 Census of Population and Housing,* Summary Tape File 3C, United States Summary, CD-ROM, February 1992.

★1787★
Persons Living Below Poverty Level

Persons 60 to 64 Years Old Living Below Poverty Level in 1989

[Table shows the top 50 areas]

MSA	% of population	Rank
Brownsville – Harlingen, TX	1.139	1
McAllen – Edinburg – Mission, TX	1.012	2
Laredo, TX	0.953	3
Pine Bluff, AR	0.852	4
Gadsden, AL	0.836	5
Houma – Thibodaux, LA	0.819	6
Danville, VA	0.813	7
Ocala, FL	0.785	8
Huntington – Ashland, WV – KY – OH	0.768	9
Alexandria, LA	0.759	10
Johnson City – Kingsport – Bristol, TN – VA	0.757	11
Lafayette, LA	0.731	12
Beaumont – Port Arthur, TX	0.730	13
Corpus Christi, TX	0.702	14
Jackson, TN	0.700	15
Texarkana, TX – Texarkana, AR	0.695	16
Florence, SC	0.689	17
Shreveport, LA	0.679	18
Monroe, LA	0.673	19
Tyler, TX	0.669	20
New Orleans, LA	0.666	21
Odessa, TX	0.660	22
Victoria, TX	0.658	23
Longview – Marshall, TX	0.656	24
Mobile, AL	0.656	24
Birmingham, AL	0.650	25
Cumberland, MD – WV	0.641	26
Florence, AL	0.637	27
Jackson, MS	0.636	28
Columbus, GA – AL	0.631	29
Biloxi – Gulfport, MS	0.630	30
El Paso, TX	0.627	31
San Angelo, TX	0.627	31
Lake Charles, LA	0.621	32
Enid, OK	0.620	33
Wheeling, WV – OH	0.620	33
Pueblo, CO	0.615	34
Fort Smith, AR – OK	0.608	35
Las Cruces, NM	0.607	36
Yuma, AZ	0.601	37
Decatur, AL	0.597	38
Saint Joseph, MO	0.589	39
Miami – Fort Lauderdale, FL	0.586	40
Charleston, WV	0.584	41
Memphis, TN – AR – MS	0.576	42
Dothan, AL	0.574	43
Joplin, MO	0.574	43
Johnstown, PA	0.572	44
Panama City, FL	0.572	44
Daytona Beach, FL	0.560	45

Source: U.S. Bureau of the Census, Data User Services Division, 1990 Census of Population and Housing, Summary Tape File 3C, United States Summary, CD-ROM, February 1992.

★1788★
Persons Living Below Poverty Level

Persons 65 to 74 Years Old Living Below Poverty Level in 1989

[Table shows the top 50 areas]

MSA	% of population	Rank
Pine Bluff, AR	1.799	1
Florence, SC	1.731	2
Gadsden, AL	1.688	3
Danville, VA	1.628	4
McAllen – Edinburg – Mission, TX	1.619	5
Laredo, TX	1.586	6
Brownsville – Harlingen, TX	1.552	7
Johnson City – Kingsport – Bristol, TN – VA	1.467	8
Anniston, AL	1.462	9
Alexandria, LA	1.422	10
Decatur, AL	1.402	11
Texarkana, TX – Texarkana, AR	1.323	12
Dothan, AL	1.316	13
Florence, AL	1.298	14
Ocala, FL	1.292	15
Longview – Marshall, TX	1.269	16
Jackson, TN	1.266	17
Shreveport, LA	1.239	18
Monroe, LA	1.230	19
Sherman – Denison, TX	1.216	20
Anderson, SC	1.198	21
Huntington – Ashland, WV – KY – OH	1.173	22
Albany, GA	1.169	23
Cumberland, MD – WV	1.164	24
Lake Charles, LA	1.160	25
Asheville, NC	1.153	26
Miami – Fort Lauderdale, FL	1.143	27
Wheeling, WV – OH	1.143	27
Birmingham, AL	1.129	28
Chattanooga, TN – GA	1.126	29
Jackson, MS	1.120	30
Mobile, AL	1.116	31
Biloxi – Gulfport, MS	1.114	32
Johnstown, PA	1.113	33
Montgomery, AL	1.113	33
New Orleans, LA	1.106	34
Houma – Thibodaux, LA	1.092	35
Fort Smith, AR – OK	1.088	36
Memphis, TN – AR – MS	1.086	37
Lafayette, LA	1.082	38
Lynchburg, VA	1.074	39
Burlington, NC	1.065	40
Beaumont – Port Arthur, TX	1.063	41
Macon – Warner Robins, GA	1.047	42
Columbus, GA – AL	1.043	43
Savannah, GA	1.043	43
Knoxville, TN	1.038	44
Corpus Christi, TX	1.035	45
Lakeland – Winter Haven, FL	1.022	46
Panama City, FL	1.008	47

Source: U.S. Bureau of the Census, Data User Services Division, 1990 Census of Population and Housing, Summary Tape File 3C, United States Summary, CD-ROM, February 1992.

★1789★

Persons Living Below Poverty Level

Persons 75 Years Old and Older Living Below Poverty Level in 1989

[Table shows the top 50 areas]

MSA	% of population	Rank
Pine Bluff, AR	1.791	1
Joplin, MO	1.653	2
Texarkana, TX – Texarkana, AR	1.652	3
Jackson, TN	1.635	4
Danville, VA	1.605	5
Sherman – Denison, TX	1.581	6
Florence, AL	1.501	7
Gadsden, AL	1.482	8
Dothan, AL	1.438	9
Decatur, AL	1.433	10
Johnson City – Kingsport – Bristol, TN – VA	1.389	11
Alexandria, LA	1.369	12
Anderson, SC	1.324	13
Tyler, TX	1.288	14
Asheville, NC	1.274	15
Fort Smith, AR – OK	1.264	16
Cumberland, MD – WV	1.245	17
Monroe, LA	1.243	18
Montgomery, AL	1.233	19
Longview – Marshall, TX	1.230	20
Wheeling, WV – OH	1.230	20
Miami – Fort Lauderdale, FL	1.228	21
Florence, SC	1.223	22
Shreveport, LA	1.223	22
Enid, OK	1.221	23
Jackson, MS	1.204	24
Brownsville – Harlingen, TX	1.193	25
Parkersburg – Marietta, WV – OH	1.193	25
Anniston, AL	1.183	26
Birmingham, AL	1.182	27
Lewiston – Auburn, ME	1.175	28
Huntington – Ashland, WV – KY – OH	1.157	29
Waco, TX	1.156	30
Burlington, NC	1.153	31
McAllen – Edinburg – Mission, TX	1.134	32
Tuscaloosa, AL	1.125	33
Lynchburg, VA	1.113	34
Ocala, FL	1.098	35
Scranton – Wilkes-Barre, PA	1.096	36
Owensboro, KY	1.082	37
Saint Joseph, MO	1.072	38
Laredo, TX	1.057	39
Springfield, MO	1.049	40
Fayetteville – Springdale, AR	1.047	41
Dubuque, IA	1.032	42
Bradenton, FL	1.031	43
Chattanooga, TN – GA	1.031	43
Lakeland – Winter Haven, FL	1.031	43
Mobile, AL	1.026	44
Albany, GA	1.021	45

Source: U.S. Bureau of the Census, Data User Services Division, *1990 Census of Population and Housing,* Summary Tape File 3C, United States Summary, CD-ROM, February 1992.

★1790★

Poverty Status By Age, Race, and Ethnicity

American Indians, Eskimos, and Aleuts Under 5 Years Old Living Below Poverty Level in 1989

[Table shows the top 50 areas]

MSA	% of population	Rank
Rapid City, SD	0.63927	1
Great Falls, MT	0.36941	2
Yakima, WA	0.31882	3
Houma – Thibodaux, LA	0.26908	4
Billings, MT	0.24511	5
Anchorage, AK	0.21737	6
Tucson, AZ	0.20169	7
Lawton, OK	0.20092	8
Bellingham, WA	0.19408	9
Tulsa, OK	0.18958	10
Fort Smith, AR – OK	0.18077	11
Sioux City, IA – NE	0.16867	12
Oklahoma City, OK	0.15853	13
Bismarck, ND	0.15030	14
Green Bay, WI	0.14903	15
Grand Forks, ND	0.14289	16
Albuquerque, NM	0.13234	17
Duluth, MN – WI	0.13043	18
Phoenix, AZ	0.10278	19
Redding, CA	0.10202	20
Sioux Falls, SD	0.09854	21
Fargo – Moorhead, ND – MN	0.08415	22
Yuma, AZ	0.08326	23
Chico, CA	0.08017	24
Bremerton, WA	0.07063	25
Minneapolis – Saint Paul, MN – WI	0.06915	26
Reno, NV	0.06793	27
Enid, OK	0.06698	28
Bangor, ME	0.05749	29
Santa Fe, NM	0.05724	30
Cheyenne, WY	0.05606	31
Yuba City, CA	0.05300	32
Salt Lake City – Ogden, UT	0.05185	33
Spokane, WA	0.05036	34
Salem, OR	0.04928	35
Medford, OR	0.04850	36
Seattle – Tacoma, WA	0.04826	37
Visalia – Tulare – Porterville, CA	0.04777	38
Fresno, CA	0.04494	39
Appleton – Oshkosh – Neenah, WI	0.04252	40
Olympia, WA	0.04217	41
Stockton, CA	0.03766	42
Omaha, NE – IA	0.03720	43
Fayetteville, NC	0.03569	44
Lawrence, KS	0.03545	45
Wichita, KS	0.03483	46
Buffalo – Niagara Falls, NY	0.03431	47
Sheboygan, WI	0.03369	48
Pueblo, CO	0.03251	49
Fayetteville – Springdale, AR	0.03174	50

Source: U.S. Bureau of the Census, Data User Services Division, *1990 Census of Population and Housing,* Summary Tape File 3C, United States Summary, CD-ROM, February 1992.

★1791★
Poverty Status By Age, Race, and Ethnicity
American Indians, Eskimos, and Aleuts 5 Years Old Living Below Poverty Level in 1989
[Table shows the top 50 areas]

MSA	% of population	Rank
Rapid City, SD	0.13646	1
Great Falls, MT	0.08495	2
Houma – Thibodaux, LA	0.08094	3
Lawton, OK	0.07804	4
Grand Forks, ND	0.07781	5
Billings, MT	0.07671	6
Tucson, AZ	0.05428	7
Tulsa, OK	0.04697	8
Bellingham, WA	0.03756	9
Oklahoma City, OK	0.03035	10
Anchorage, AK	0.03004	11
Cheyenne, WY	0.02871	12
Bismarck, ND	0.02863	13
Sioux City, IA – NE	0.02782	14
Albuquerque, NM	0.02622	15
Fort Smith, AR – OK	0.02160	16
Yakima, WA	0.02118	17
Green Bay, WI	0.02056	18
Muskegon, MI	0.02013	19
Casper, WY	0.01960	20
Minneapolis – Saint Paul, MN – WI	0.01709	21
Phoenix, AZ	0.01626	22
Sioux Falls, SD	0.01615	23
Fayetteville, NC	0.01603	24
Santa Fe, NM	0.01538	25
Reno, NV	0.01531	26
Bremerton, WA	0.01476	27
La Crosse, WI	0.01430	28
Chico, CA	0.01428	29
Lawrence, KS	0.01345	30
Modesto, CA	0.01295	31
Olympia, WA	0.01240	32
Provo – Orem, UT	0.01176	33
Seattle – Tacoma, WA	0.01051	34
Joplin, MO	0.01038	35
Duluth, MN – WI	0.01000	36
Richland – Kennewick – Pasco, WA	0.01000	36
Naples, FL	0.00986	37
Appleton – Oshkosh – Neenah, WI	0.00984	38
Mobile, AL	0.00965	39
Medford, OR	0.00956	40
Yuma, AZ	0.00935	41
Topeka, KS	0.00932	42
Merced, CA	0.00897	43
Stockton, CA	0.00895	44
Cedar Rapids, IA	0.00889	45
Sheboygan, WI	0.00866	46
Saint Cloud, MN	0.00838	47
Fort Myers – Cape Coral, Fl	0.00836	48
Corpus Christi, TX	0.00829	49

Source: U.S. Bureau of the Census, Data User Services Division, *1990 Census of Population and Housing*, Summary Tape File 3C, United States Summary, CD-ROM, February 1992.

★1792★
Poverty Status By Age, Race, and Ethnicity
American Indians, Eskimos, and Aleuts 6 to 11 Years Old Living Below Poverty Level in 1989
[Table shows the top 50 areas]

MSA	% of population	Rank
Rapid City, SD	0.54338	1
Houma – Thibodaux, LA	0.33690	2
Yakima, WA	0.32623	3
Great Falls, MT	0.32307	4
Fort Smith, AR – OK	0.26491	5
Lawton, OK	0.25923	6
Tucson, AZ	0.22403	7
Tulsa, OK	0.20185	8
Billings, MT	0.18604	9
Bellingham, WA	0.17608	10
Anchorage, AK	0.17010	11
Oklahoma City, OK	0.16666	12
Bismarck, ND	0.13957	13
Albuquerque, NM	0.12901	14
Sioux City, IA – NE	0.12694	15
Green Bay, WI	0.10586	16
Duluth, MN – WI	0.09543	17
Phoenix, AZ	0.09236	18
Redding, CA	0.08909	19
Sioux Falls, SD	0.08642	20
Yuma, AZ	0.07484	21
Olympia, WA	0.07194	22
Lawrence, KS	0.07091	23
Visalia – Tulare – Porterville, CA	0.06957	24
Fayetteville, NC	0.06082	25
Enid, OK	0.05817	26
Fargo – Moorhead, ND – MN	0.05806	27
Minneapolis – Saint Paul, MN – WI	0.05787	28
Decatur, AL	0.05473	29
Bremerton, WA	0.05429	30
Medford, OR	0.05328	31
Salem, OR	0.05323	32
La Crosse, WI	0.05209	33
Spokane, WA	0.05147	34
Chico, CA	0.05052	35
Stockton, CA	0.05035	36
Richland – Kennewick – Pasco, WA	0.04999	37
Fresno, CA	0.04839	38
Cheyenne, WY	0.04648	39
Eugene – Springfield, OR	0.04630	40
Lincoln, NE	0.04494	41
Bangor, ME	0.04397	42
Yuba City, CA	0.04321	43
Merced, CA	0.04260	44
Appleton – Oshkosh – Neenah, WI	0.04221	45
Reno, NV	0.04162	46
Topeka, KS	0.04162	46
Pueblo, CO	0.03982	47
Bakersfield, CA	0.03735	48
Modesto, CA	0.03617	49

Source: U.S. Bureau of the Census, Data User Services Division, *1990 Census of Population and Housing*, Summary Tape File 3C, United States Summary, CD-ROM, February 1992.

★1793★

Poverty Status By Age, Race, and Ethnicity

American Indians, Eskimos, and Aleuts 12 to 17 Years Old Living Below Poverty Level in 1989

[Table shows the top 50 areas]

MSA	% of population	Rank
Rapid City, SD	0.32824	1
Houma – Thibodaux, LA	0.30518	2
Great Falls, MT	0.27416	3
Fort Smith, AR – OK	0.20181	4
Yakima, WA	0.19171	5
Bismarck, ND	0.17655	6
Tulsa, OK	0.17053	7
Tucson, AZ	0.14935	8
Lawton, OK	0.14890	9
Anchorage, AK	0.14624	10
Bellingham, WA	0.11974	11
Oklahoma City, OK	0.11086	12
Sioux City, IA – NE	0.10781	13
Duluth, MN – WI	0.10668	14
Yuma, AZ	0.09916	15
Albuquerque, NM	0.07949	16
Enid, OK	0.07227	17
Medford, OR	0.06968	18
Chico, CA	0.06919	19
Grand Forks, ND	0.06791	20
Spokane, WA	0.06752	21
Fayetteville, NC	0.06665	22
Redding, CA	0.06529	23
Billings, MT	0.06084	24
Phoenix, AZ	0.06008	25
Lawrence, KS	0.05501	26
Green Bay, WI	0.05344	27
Joplin, MO	0.04818	28
Visalia – Tulare – Porterville, CA	0.04649	29
Olympia, WA	0.04403	30
Modesto, CA	0.04237	31
McAllen – Edinburg – Mission, TX	0.04224	32
Salem, OR	0.03885	33
Minneapolis – Saint Paul, MN – WI	0.03863	34
Muskegon, MI	0.03711	35
Fresno, CA	0.03641	36
Provo – Orem, UT	0.03604	37
Fayetteville – Springdale, AR	0.03527	38
Yuba City, CA	0.03506	39
Colorado Springs, CO	0.03476	40
Sherman – Denison, TX	0.03473	41
Amarillo, TX	0.03466	42
Salt Lake City – Ogden, UT	0.03348	43
Sioux Falls, SD	0.03312	44
Stockton, CA	0.03225	45
Seattle – Tacoma, WA	0.03181	46
Cheyenne, WY	0.03145	47
Topeka, KS	0.03106	48
Casper, WY	0.03103	49
Lansing – East Lansing, MI	0.03005	50

Source: U.S. Bureau of the Census, Data User Services Division, *1990 Census of Population and Housing*, Summary Tape File 3C, United States Summary, CD-ROM, February 1992.

★1794★

Poverty Status By Age, Race, and Ethnicity

American Indians, Eskimos, and Aleuts 18 to 64 Years Old Living Below Poverty Level in 1989

[Table shows the top 50 areas]

MSA	% of population	Rank
Rapid City, SD	1.3879	1
Houma – Thibodaux, LA	0.9117	2
Great Falls, MT	0.8856	3
Yakima, WA	0.8781	4
Tucson, AZ	0.8090	5
Fort Smith, AR – OK	0.8015	6
Anchorage, AK	0.7873	7
Lawton, OK	0.6961	8
Tulsa, OK	0.6393	9
Billings, MT	0.6189	10
Oklahoma City, OK	0.5736	11
Albuquerque, NM	0.5691	12
Bellingham, WA	0.4602	13
Duluth, MN – WI	0.3767	14
Grand Forks, ND	0.3509	15
Bismarck, ND	0.3471	16
Sioux City, IA – NE	0.3408	17
Redding, CA	0.3278	18
Phoenix, AZ	0.3208	19
Green Bay, WI	0.3063	20
Sioux Falls, SD	0.2948	21
Chico, CA	0.2855	22
Medford, OR	0.2828	23
Spokane, WA	0.2632	24
Enid, OK	0.2626	25
Reno, NV	0.2588	26
Santa Fe, NM	0.2555	27
Lawrence, KS	0.2506	28
Yuma, AZ	0.2442	29
Olympia, WA	0.2351	30
Fargo – Moorhead, ND – MN	0.2316	31
Joplin, MO	0.2268	32
Salem, OR	0.2097	33
Yuba City, CA	0.2079	34
Fayetteville, NC	0.2029	35
Bremerton, WA	0.2024	36
Cheyenne, WY	0.1941	37
Pueblo, CO	0.1829	38
Stockton, CA	0.1733	39
Minneapolis – Saint Paul, MN – WI	0.1726	40
Bangor, ME	0.1714	41
Seattle – Tacoma, WA	0.1703	42
Eugene – Springfield, OR	0.1633	43
Salt Lake City – Ogden, UT	0.1576	44
Las Cruces, NM	0.1564	45
Visalia – Tulare – Porterville, CA	0.1529	46
Pensacola, FL	0.1437	47
Sherman – Denison, TX	0.1410	48
Fayetteville – Springdale, AR	0.1402	49
Bakersfield, CA	0.1345	50

Source: U.S. Bureau of the Census, Data User Services Division, *1990 Census of Population and Housing*, Summary Tape File 3C, United States Summary, CD-ROM, February 1992.

★1795★

Poverty Status By Age, Race, and Ethnicity

American Indians, Eskimos, and Aleuts 65 to 74 Years Old Living Below Poverty Level in 1989

[Table shows the top 50 areas]

MSA	% of population	Rank
Fort Smith, AR – OK	0.10744	1
Tucson, AZ	0.06433	2
Rapid City, SD	0.05655	3
Houma – Thibodaux, LA	0.05633	4
Bellingham, WA	0.04930	5
Tulsa, OK	0.04796	6
Lawton, OK	0.04664	7
Yakima, WA	0.04396	8
Yuma, AZ	0.03836	9
Great Falls, MT	0.02832	10
Joplin, MO	0.02743	11
Oklahoma City, OK	0.02659	12
Cheyenne, WY	0.02598	13
Green Bay, WI	0.02313	14
Redding, CA	0.02040	15
Pine Bluff, AR	0.01989	16
Topeka, KS	0.01988	17
Medford, OR	0.01913	18
Duluth, MN – WI	0.01834	19
Sioux City, IA – NE	0.01826	20
Alexandria, LA	0.01596	21
Fayetteville, NC	0.01530	22
Abilene, TX	0.01421	23
Albany, GA	0.01333	24
Albuquerque, NM	0.01332	25
Reno, NV	0.01257	26
Battle Creek, MI	0.01250	27
Bryan – College Station, TX	0.01231	28
Midland, TX	0.01126	29
Chico, CA	0.01098	30
Providence – Pawtucket – Fall River, RI – MA	0.01095	31
Jacksonville, NC	0.01001	32
Decatur, AL	0.00988	33
Phoenix, AZ	0.00985	34
Mobile, AL	0.00965	35
Sherman – Denison, TX	0.00947	36
Santa Fe, NM	0.00854	37
Dothan, AL	0.00840	38
Visalia – Tulare – Porterville, CA	0.00834	39
Kankakee, IL	0.00831	40
Columbus, GA – AL	0.00782	41
Eugene – Springfield, OR	0.00778	42
Spokane, WA	0.00775	43
Bakersfield, CA	0.00754	44
Anchorage, AK	0.00751	45
Burlington, NC	0.00739	46
Fresno, CA	0.00734	47
Seattle – Tacoma, WA	0.00715	48
Pensacola, FL	0.00697	49
Evansville, IN – KY	0.00681	50

Source: U.S. Bureau of the Census, Data User Services Division, *1990 Census of Population and Housing,* Summary Tape File 3C, United States Summary, CD-ROM, February 1992.

★1796★

Poverty Status By Age, Race, and Ethnicity

American Indians, Eskimos, and Aleuts 75 Years Old and Older Living Below Poverty Level in 1989

[Table shows the top 50 areas]

MSA	% of population	Rank
Great Falls, MT	0.06564	1
Rapid City, SD	0.05040	2
Tulsa, OK	0.04937	3
Yuma, AZ	0.04210	4
Fort Smith, AR – OK	0.03979	5
Yakima, WA	0.03548	6
Tucson, AZ	0.03254	7
Oklahoma City, OK	0.02878	8
Casper, WY	0.02613	9
Houma – Thibodaux, LA	0.02571	10
Bellingham, WA	0.01956	11
Bryan – College Station, TX	0.01805	12
Lawrence, KS	0.01712	13
Joplin, MO	0.01557	14
Fayetteville – Springdale, AR	0.01499	15
Green Bay, WI	0.01439	16
Lawton, OK	0.01435	17
Albuquerque, NM	0.01415	18
Enid, OK	0.01410	19
Redding, CA	0.01360	20
Lynchburg, VA	0.01336	21
Reno, NV	0.01296	22
Alexandria, LA	0.01292	23
Decatur, AL	0.01140	24
Duluth, MN – WI	0.01125	25
Santa Fe, NM	0.01111	26
Chico, CA	0.01098	27
Florence, AL	0.01066	28
Anchorage, AK	0.01060	29
Owensboro, KY	0.01032	30
Waco, TX	0.01005	31
Medford, OR	0.00956	32
Richland – Kennewick – Pasco, WA	0.00933	33
New London – Norwich, CT – RI	0.00899	34
Fayetteville, NC	0.00874	35
Benton Harbor, MI	0.00868	36
Shreveport, LA	0.00867	37
Janesville – Beloit, WI	0.00860	38
Mobile, AL	0.00860	38
Sherman – Denison, TX	0.00842	39
Dothan, AL	0.00840	40
La Crosse, WI	0.00817	41
Modesto, CA	0.00783	42
Phoenix, AZ	0.00773	43
Burlington, NC	0.00739	44
Providence – Pawtucket – Fall River, RI – MA	0.00701	45
Atlantic City, NJ	0.00689	46
Santa Barbara – Santa Maria – Lompoc, CA	0.00649	47
Cedar Rapids, IA	0.00593	48
Youngstown – Warren, OH	0.00589	49

Source: U.S. Bureau of the Census, Data User Services Division, *1990 Census of Population and Housing,* Summary Tape File 3C, United States Summary, CD-ROM, February 1992.

★ 1797 ★

Poverty Status By Age, Race, and Ethnicity

Asians and Pacific Islanders Under 5 Years Old Living Below Poverty Level in 1989

[Table shows the top 50 areas]

MSA	% of population	Rank
Merced, CA	0.8329	1
Fresno, CA	0.7074	2
Stockton, CA	0.6516	3
Yuba City, CA	0.5903	4
Honolulu, HI	0.5577	5
La Crosse, WI	0.4433	6
Wausau, WI	0.3709	7
Visalia – Tulare – Porterville, CA	0.2978	8
Eau Claire, WI	0.2937	9
Sheboygan, WI	0.2724	10
Modesto, CA	0.2486	11
Sacramento, CA	0.2256	12
Rochester, MN	0.1982	13
Green Bay, WI	0.1907	14
Chico, CA	0.1774	15
Redding, CA	0.1734	16
Minneapolis – Saint Paul, MN – WI	0.1595	17
Iowa City, IA	0.1561	18
Biloxi – Gulfport, MS	0.1486	19
San Francisco – Oakland – San Jose, CA	0.1276	20
Appleton – Oshkosh – Neenah, WI	0.1161	21
Madison, WI	0.1133	22
Columbia, MO	0.1112	23
Champaign – Urbana – Rantoul, IL	0.1104	24
Seattle – Tacoma, WA	0.1059	25
San Diego, CA	0.1043	26
Fitchburg – Leominster, MA	0.0983	27
Los Angeles – Anaheim – Riverside, CA	0.0935	28
Olympia, WA	0.0850	29
Gainesville, FL	0.0833	30
Bryan – College Station, TX	0.0821	31
Santa Barbara – Santa Maria – Lompoc, CA	0.0817	32
State College, PA	0.0727	33
Lafayette – West Lafayette, IN	0.0697	34
Salinas – Seaside – Monterey, CA	0.0694	35
Beaumont – Port Arthur, TX	0.0689	36
Milwaukee – Racine, WI	0.0669	37
Providence – Pawtucket – Fall River, RI – MA	0.0643	38
Bloomington, IN	0.0642	39
Salt Lake City – Ogden, UT	0.0636	40
Lansing – East Lansing, MI	0.0619	41
Lawton, OK	0.0592	42
Athens, GA	0.0570	43
Boston – Lawrence – Salem, MA – NH	0.0570	43
Wichita, KS	0.0561	44
Colorado Springs, CO	0.0559	45
Lincoln, NE	0.0557	46
Houma – Thibodaux, LA	0.0547	47

[Continued]

★ 1797 ★

Asians and Pacific Islanders Under 5 Years Old Living Below Poverty Level in 1989

[Continued]

MSA	% of population	Rank
Bakersfield, CA	0.0535	48
Anchorage, AK	0.0526	49

Source: U.S. Bureau of the Census, Data User Services Division, 1990 Census of Population and Housing, Summary Tape File 3C, United States Summary, CD-ROM, February 1992.

★ 1798 ★

Poverty Status By Age, Race, and Ethnicity

Asians and Pacific Islanders 5 Years Old Living Below Poverty Level in 1989

[Table shows the top 50 areas]

MSA	% of population	Rank
Merced, CA	0.18497	1
Fresno, CA	0.16270	2
Stockton, CA	0.14481	3
Honolulu, HI	0.11444	4
Yuba City, CA	0.11415	5
Wausau, WI	0.09965	6
Modesto, CA	0.08555	7
Visalia – Tulare – Porterville, CA	0.08207	8
Sheboygan, WI	0.06739	9
La Crosse, WI	0.06639	10
Chico, CA	0.05656	11
Rochester, MN	0.05448	12
Sacramento, CA	0.04983	13
Eau Claire, WI	0.04871	14
Lawrence, KS	0.04401	15
Minneapolis – Saint Paul, MN – WI	0.03644	16
Green Bay, WI	0.03392	17
Houma – Thibodaux, LA	0.03117	18
San Francisco – Oakland – San Jose, CA	0.02719	19
San Diego, CA	0.02662	20
Appleton – Oshkosh – Neenah, WI	0.02444	21
Seattle – Tacoma, WA	0.02321	22
Bryan – College Station, TX	0.02216	23
Los Angeles – Anaheim – Riverside, CA	0.02147	24
Alexandria, LA	0.02052	25
Biloxi – Gulfport, MS	0.02029	26
Salinas – Seaside – Monterey, CA	0.02024	27
Madison, WI	0.01907	28
Providence – Pawtucket – Fall River, RI – MA	0.01840	29
Pascagoula, MS	0.01822	30
Santa Barbara – Santa Maria – Lompoc, CA	0.01732	31
Beaumont – Port Arthur, TX	0.01633	32
Redding, CA	0.01632	33
Columbia, MO	0.01602	34
Colorado Springs, CO	0.01562	35
Olympia, WA	0.01551	36

[Continued]

★1798★

Asians and Pacific Islanders 5 Years Old Living Below Poverty Level in 1989

[Continued]

MSA	% of population	Rank
Anchorage, AK	0.01414	37
Boston – Lawrence – Salem, MA – NH	0.01359	38
Fort Smith, AR – OK	0.01307	39
Milwaukee – Racine, WI	0.01288	40
Springfield, MO	0.01288	40
Champaign – Urbana – Rantoul, IL	0.01271	41
Lansing – East Lansing, MI	0.01248	42
Eugene – Springfield, OR	0.01237	43
Portland – Vancouver, OR – WA	0.01116	44
Hickory – Morganton, NC	0.01083	45
Altoona, PA	0.01072	46
Gainesville, FL	0.01029	47
Lawton, OK	0.00987	48
Lincoln, NE	0.00983	49

Source: U.S. Bureau of the Census, Data User Services Division, *1990 Census of Population and Housing,* Summary Tape File 3C, United States Summary, CD-ROM, February 1992.

★1799★

Poverty Status By Age, Race, and Ethnicity

Asians and Pacific Islanders 6 to 11 Years Old Living Below Poverty Level in 1989

[Table shows the top 50 areas]

MSA	% of population	Rank
Stockton, CA	0.89321	1
Fresno, CA	0.85065	2
Merced, CA	0.84079	3
Honolulu, HI	0.61418	4
Yuba City, CA	0.59767	5
Modesto, CA	0.39917	6
La Crosse, WI	0.37384	7
Visalia – Tulare – Porterville, CA	0.36772	8
Sacramento, CA	0.33360	9
Chico, CA	0.23501	10
Wausau, WI	0.22964	11
Eau Claire, WI	0.22684	12
Sheboygan, WI	0.22334	13
Biloxi – Gulfport, MS	0.19784	14
Green Bay, WI	0.18295	15
Rochester, MN	0.17000	16
San Francisco – Oakland – San Jose, CA	0.15945	17
Minneapolis – Saint Paul, MN – WI	0.15210	18
Los Angeles – Anaheim – Riverside, CA	0.14248	19
San Diego, CA	0.14159	20
Seattle – Tacoma, WA	0.12664	21
Beaumont – Port Arthur, TX	0.11184	22
Appleton – Oshkosh – Neenah, WI	0.10282	23
Redding, CA	0.09930	24
Iowa City, IA	0.09155	25

[Continued]

★1799★

Asians and Pacific Islanders 6 to 11 Years Old Living Below Poverty Level in 1989

[Continued]

MSA	% of population	Rank
Olympia, WA	0.08621	26
Columbia, MO	0.08454	27
Houma – Thibodaux, LA	0.08313	28
Champaign – Urbana – Rantoul, IL	0.07745	29
Salinas – Seaside – Monterey, CA	0.07676	30
Providence – Pawtucket – Fall River, RI – MA	0.07656	31
Madison, WI	0.07546	32
Bakersfield, CA	0.07323	33
New Orleans, LA	0.07305	34
Bremerton, WA	0.07063	35
Panama City, FL	0.06693	36
Boston – Lawrence – Salem, MA – NH	0.06645	37
Portland – Vancouver, OR – WA	0.06536	38
Santa Barbara – Santa Maria – Lompoc, CA	0.05898	39
Bloomington, IN	0.05873	40
Pensacola, FL	0.05836	41
Killeen – Temple, TX	0.05797	42
Lansing – East Lansing, MI	0.05593	43
Milwaukee – Racine, WI	0.05475	44
Wichita, KS	0.05440	45
Worcester, MA	0.05127	46
Amarillo, TX	0.05065	47
Lawton, OK	0.04933	48
Anchorage, AK	0.04860	49
New York – Northern New Jersey – Long Island, NY – NJ – CT	0.04808	50

Source: U.S. Bureau of the Census, Data User Services Division, *1990 Census of Population and Housing,* Summary Tape File 3C, United States Summary, CD-ROM, February 1992.

★1800★

Poverty Status By Age, Race, and Ethnicity

Asians and Pacific Islanders 12 to 17 Years Old Living Below Poverty Level in 1989

[Table shows the top 50 areas]

MSA	% of population	Rank
Honolulu, HI	0.52593	1
Stockton, CA	0.52515	2
Merced, CA	0.50335	3
Fresno, CA	0.47192	4
Yuba City, CA	0.34572	5
Modesto, CA	0.28203	6
Visalia – Tulare – Porterville, CA	0.27443	7
Biloxi – Gulfport, MS	0.23386	8
Sacramento, CA	0.23347	9
San Francisco – Oakland – San Jose, CA	0.16970	10
Eau Claire, WI	0.16431	11
La Crosse, WI	0.15015	12

[Continued]

Asians and Pacific Islanders 12 to 17 Years Old Living Below Poverty Level in 1989
[Continued]

MSA	% of population	Rank
Chico, CA	0.14551	13
Los Angeles – Anaheim – Riverside, CA	0.14253	14
Beaumont – Port Arthur, TX	0.13759	15
San Diego, CA	0.12610	16
Rochester, MN	0.12398	17
Seattle – Tacoma, WA	0.11594	18
Sheboygan, WI	0.10878	19
Minneapolis – Saint Paul, MN – WI	0.10811	20
Wausau, WI	0.09879	21
Salinas – Seaside – Monterey, CA	0.09869	22
Olympia, WA	0.09179	23
Redding, CA	0.08977	24
Green Bay, WI	0.08890	25
Pensacola, FL	0.08856	26
New Orleans, LA	0.07435	27
Richland – Kennewick – Pasco, WA	0.07132	28
Portland – Vancouver, OR – WA	0.07091	29
Wichita, KS	0.06821	30
Appleton – Oshkosh – Neenah, WI	0.06410	31
Houston – Galveston – Brazoria, TX	0.06023	32
Bakersfield, CA	0.06017	33
Lawton, OK	0.05651	34
Killeen – Temple, TX	0.05640	35
Bremerton, WA	0.05481	36
Pascagoula, MS	0.05380	37
Salt Lake City – Ogden, UT	0.05325	38
Hickory – Morganton, NC	0.05232	39
Sioux City, IA – NE	0.05217	40
New York – Northern New Jersey – Long Island, NY – NJ – CT	0.05170	41
Fitchburg – Leominster, MA	0.04961	42
Fort Smith, AR – OK	0.04605	43
Wichita Falls, TX	0.04576	44
Las Vegas, NV	0.04572	45
Santa Barbara – Santa Maria – Lompoc, CA	0.04491	46
Panama City, FL	0.04488	47
Lansing – East Lansing, MI	0.04414	48
Iowa City, IA	0.04370	49
Denver – Boulder, CO	0.04307	50

Source: U.S. Bureau of the Census, Data User Services Division, *1990 Census of Population and Housing*, Summary Tape File 3C, United States Summary, CD-ROM, February 1992.

Poverty Status By Age, Race, and Ethnicity
Asians and Pacific Islanders 18 to 64 Years Old Living Below Poverty Level in 1989
[Table shows the top 50 areas]

MSA	% of population	Rank
Honolulu, HI	2.50613	1
Stockton, CA	1.59541	2
Fresno, CA	1.47673	3
Merced, CA	1.35592	4
Yuba City, CA	1.17822	5
Iowa City, IA	1.12153	6
Champaign – Urbana – Rantoul, IL	1.09348	7
Lawrence, KS	1.05993	8
Bryan – College Station, TX	1.03149	9
Columbia, MO	0.98150	10
Sacramento, CA	0.93349	11
San Francisco – Oakland – San Jose, CA	0.89781	12
Chico, CA	0.84779	13
Bloomington, IN	0.80383	14
Modesto, CA	0.74193	15
Los Angeles – Anaheim – Riverside, CA	0.73278	16
Gainesville, FL	0.69962	17
Lafayette – West Lafayette, IN	0.69679	18
Visalia – Tulare – Porterville, CA	0.69377	19
State College, PA	0.67132	20
Madison, WI	0.64563	21
La Crosse, WI	0.62714	22
San Diego, CA	0.58526	23
Santa Barbara – Santa Maria – Lompoc, CA	0.57115	24
Seattle – Tacoma, WA	0.56530	25
Biloxi – Gulfport, MS	0.49157	26
Rochester, MN	0.48558	27
Eugene – Springfield, OR	0.47259	28
Austin, TX	0.46163	29
Eau Claire, WI	0.45368	30
Beaumont – Port Arthur, TX	0.44266	31
Lansing – East Lansing, MI	0.43705	32
Wausau, WI	0.43501	33
Salinas – Seaside – Monterey, CA	0.42653	34
Athens, GA	0.40380	35
Sheboygan, WI	0.37833	36
New York – Northern New Jersey – Long Island, NY – NJ – CT	0.37184	37
Charlottesville, VA	0.35849	38
Minneapolis – Saint Paul, MN – WI	0.35664	39
Reno, NV	0.34751	40
Binghamton, NY	0.33989	41
Portland – Vancouver, OR – WA	0.32316	42
Green Bay, WI	0.31347	43
Provo – Orem, UT	0.31033	44
Boston – Lawrence – Salem, MA – NH	0.30711	45
Fort Collins – Loveland, CO	0.29817	46
Houston – Galveston – Brazoria, TX	0.29795	47
Olympia, WA	0.29646	48

[Continued]

★1801★

Asians and Pacific Islanders 18 to 64 Years Old Living Below Poverty Level in 1989

[Continued]

MSA	% of population	Rank
Lubbock, TX	0.29241	49
Tucson, AZ	0.28626	50

Source: U.S. Bureau of the Census, Data User Services Division, *1990 Census of Population and Housing*, Summary Tape File 3C, United States Summary, CD-ROM, February 1992.

★1802★

Poverty Status By Age, Race, and Ethnicity

Asians and Pacific Islanders 65 to 74 Years Old Living Below Poverty Level in 1989

[Table shows the top 50 areas]

MSA	% of population	Rank
Honolulu, HI	0.35122	1
Fresno, CA	0.07611	2
San Francisco – Oakland – San Jose, CA	0.07450	3
Benton Harbor, MI	0.05019	4
Yuba City, CA	0.04892	5
Stockton, CA	0.04182	6
Los Angeles – Anaheim – Riverside, CA	0.04021	7
Seattle – Tacoma, WA	0.03865	8
Visalia – Tulare – Porterville, CA	0.03366	9
Salinas – Seaside – Monterey, CA	0.03346	10
Merced, CA	0.03139	11
Eau Claire, WI	0.03054	12
Sacramento, CA	0.02903	13
New York – Northern New Jersey – Long Island, NY – NJ – CT	0.02674	14
Biloxi – Gulfport, MS	0.02638	15
San Diego, CA	0.02590	16
Portland – Vancouver, OR – WA	0.02470	17
Bryan – College Station, TX	0.02462	18
Sheboygan, WI	0.02310	19
Anchorage, AK	0.02297	20
Rochester, MN	0.02160	21
Killeen – Temple, TX	0.01998	22
Washington, DC – MD – VA	0.01998	22
Chicago – Gary – Lake County, IL – IN – WI	0.01992	23
Pensacola, FL	0.01916	24
Beaumont – Port Arthur, TX	0.01882	25
Modesto, CA	0.01835	26
Boston – Lawrence – Salem, MA – NH	0.01819	27
Reno, NV	0.01767	28
Colorado Springs, CO	0.01763	29
Greeley, CO	0.01745	30
Wausau, WI	0.01733	31
Olympia, WA	0.01675	32
Bakersfield, CA	0.01656	33
Lincoln, NE	0.01638	34

[Continued]

★1802★

Asians and Pacific Islanders 65 to 74 Years Old Living Below Poverty Level in 1989

[Continued]

MSA	% of population	Rank
La Crosse, WI	0.01634	35
Victoria, TX	0.01614	36
Houston – Galveston – Brazoria, TX	0.01541	37
Panama City, FL	0.01496	38
Santa Barbara – Santa Maria – Lompoc, CA	0.01407	39
Minneapolis – Saint Paul, MN – WI	0.01388	40
Las Vegas, NV	0.01349	41
Wichita, KS	0.01319	42
Chico, CA	0.01318	43
Topeka, KS	0.01305	44
Sioux City, IA – NE	0.01304	45
Bremerton, WA	0.01265	46
Hickory – Morganton, NC	0.01263	47
Salt Lake City – Ogden, UT	0.01128	48
Denver – Boulder, CO	0.01087	49

Source: U.S. Bureau of the Census, Data User Services Division, *1990 Census of Population and Housing*, Summary Tape File 3C, United States Summary, CD-ROM, February 1992.

★1803★

Poverty Status By Age, Race, and Ethnicity

Asians and Pacific Islanders 75 Years Old and Older Living Below Poverty Level in 1989

[Table shows the top 50 areas]

MSA	% of population	Rank
Honolulu, HI	0.262607	1
Stockton, CA	0.060546	2
Merced, CA	0.044842	3
San Francisco – Oakland – San Jose, CA	0.040139	4
Fresno, CA	0.033409	5
Yuba City, CA	0.032615	6
Seattle – Tacoma, WA	0.025633	7
Sacramento, CA	0.022956	8
Salinas – Seaside – Monterey, CA	0.021650	9
Visalia – Tulare – Porterville, CA	0.020197	10
Los Angeles – Anaheim – Riverside, CA	0.019344	11
La Crosse, WI	0.018385	12
Olympia, WA	0.017986	13
Biloxi – Gulfport, MS	0.017755	14
New York – Northern New Jersey – Long Island, NY – NJ – CT	0.017421	15
Victoria, TX	0.016137	16
Terre Haute, IN	0.016054	17
Bakersfield, CA	0.015456	18
Huntsville, AL	0.014231	19
Yuma, AZ	0.013097	20
Sioux City, IA – NE	0.013041	21
Bremerton, WA	0.012649	22

[Continued]

★1803★

Asians and Pacific Islanders 75 Years Old and Older Living Below Poverty Level in 1989
[Continued]

MSA	% of population	Rank
Fitchburg – Leominster, MA	0.011673	23
Chicago – Gary – Lake County, IL – IN – WI	0.011406	24
Greeley, CO	0.011379	25
Washington, DC – MD – VA	0.010985	26
Appleton – Oshkosh – Neenah, WI	0.010472	27
San Diego, CA	0.010328	28
Modesto, CA	0.009716	29
Beaumont – Port Arthur, TX	0.009689	30
Battle Creek, MI	0.008825	31
Houston – Galveston – Brazoria, TX	0.008704	32
Poughkeepsie, NY	0.008479	33
Fort Pierce, FL	0.008364	34
New Orleans, LA	0.008314	35
Boise, ID	0.008261	36
Boston – Lawrence – Salem, MA – NH	0.008222	37
State College, PA	0.008078	38
Bloomington – Normal, IL	0.007741	39
Steubenville – Weirton, OH – WV	0.007718	40
Spokane, WA	0.007472	41
Pine Bluff, AR	0.007019	42
Portland – Vancouver, OR – WA	0.006902	43
El Paso, TX	0.006761	44
Orlando, FL	0.006712	45
Eau Claire, WI	0.006543	46
Wichita, KS	0.006182	47
Worcester, MA	0.006179	48
Montgomery, AL	0.006153	49
Des Moines, IA	0.006108	50

Source: U.S. Bureau of the Census, Data User Services Division, *1990 Census of Population and Housing*, Summary Tape File 3C, United States Summary, CD-ROM, February 1992.

★1804★

Poverty Status By Age, Race, and Ethnicity

Blacks Under 5 Years Old Living Below Poverty Level in 1989

[Table shows the top 50 areas]

MSA	% of population	Rank
Albany, GA	2.6066	1
Monroe, LA	2.4601	2
Shreveport, LA	2.2250	3
Pine Bluff, AR	2.1079	4
Memphis, TN – AR – MS	2.0137	5
Jackson, MS	1.9016	6
New Orleans, LA	1.8693	7
Florence, SC	1.7981	8
Columbus, GA – AL	1.7715	9
Alexandria, LA	1.6677	10
Jackson, TN	1.5927	11

[Continued]

★1804★

Blacks Under 5 Years Old Living Below Poverty Level in 1989
[Continued]

MSA	% of population	Rank
Montgomery, AL	1.5623	12
Savannah, GA	1.5530	13
Macon – Warner Robins, GA	1.5446	14
Mobile, AL	1.4835	15
Baton Rouge, LA	1.4729	16
Lafayette, LA	1.4233	17
Charleston, SC	1.2699	18
Augusta, GA – SC	1.2585	19
Texarkana, TX – Texarkana, AR	1.2012	20
Benton Harbor, MI	1.1904	21
Lake Charles, LA	1.1747	22
Fayetteville, NC	1.1680	23
Flint, MI	1.1560	24
Houma – Thibodaux, LA	1.1524	25
Tuscaloosa, AL	1.1341	26
Beaumont – Port Arthur, TX	1.1215	27
Danville, VA	1.1112	28
Tallahassee, FL	1.0480	29
Longview – Marshall, TX	1.0201	30
Norfolk – Virginia Beach – Newport News, VA	1.0087	31
Gainesville, FL	1.0044	32
Milwaukee – Racine, WI	1.0012	33
Detroit – Ann Arbor, MI	0.9944	34
Birmingham, AL	0.9897	35
Kankakee, IL	0.9631	36
Dothan, AL	0.9598	37
Muskegon, MI	0.9586	38
Pensacola, FL	0.9567	39
Pascagoula, MS	0.9493	40
Tyler, TX	0.9484	41
Biloxi – Gulfport, MS	0.9263	42
Wilmington, NC	0.8995	43
Athens, GA	0.8850	44
Richmond – Petersburg, VA	0.8703	45
Waco, TX	0.8576	46
Clarksville – Hopkinsville, TN – KY	0.8487	47
Jacksonville, FL	0.8377	48
Columbia, SC	0.8197	49
Little Rock – North Little Rock, AR	0.8088	50

Source: U.S. Bureau of the Census, Data User Services Division, *1990 Census of Population and Housing*, Summary Tape File 3C, United States Summary, CD-ROM, February 1992.

★1805★

Poverty Status By Age, Race, and Ethnicity

Blacks 5 Years Old Living Below Poverty Level in 1989

[Table shows the top 50 areas]

MSA	% of population	Rank
Monroe, LA	0.5169	1
Shreveport, LA	0.4612	2
Albany, GA	0.4415	3
Jackson, MS	0.4251	4
New Orleans, LA	0.4153	5
Pine Bluff, AR	0.3813	6
Jackson, TN	0.3706	7
Mobile, AL	0.3495	8
Memphis, TN–AR–MS	0.3472	9
Lafayette, LA	0.3315	10
Alexandria, LA	0.3193	11
Savannah, GA	0.3145	12
Baton Rouge, LA	0.3065	13
Charleston, SC	0.2985	14
Florence, SC	0.2965	15
Lake Charles, LA	0.2914	16
Montgomery, AL	0.2892	17
Columbus, GA–AL	0.2839	18
Macon–Warner Robins, GA	0.2807	19
Augusta, GA–SC	0.2583	20
Tuscaloosa, AL	0.2378	21
Texarkana, TX–Texarkana, AR	0.2297	22
Houma–Thibodaux, LA	0.2253	23
Pensacola, FL	0.2207	24
Beaumont–Port Arthur, TX	0.2154	25
Birmingham, AL	0.2130	26
Gainesville, FL	0.2121	27
Kankakee, IL	0.2078	28
Fayetteville, NC	0.1989	29
Milwaukee–Racine, WI	0.1980	30
Longview–Marshall, TX	0.1952	31
Benton Harbor, MI	0.1940	32
Norfolk–Virginia Beach–Newport News, VA	0.1903	33
Tyler, TX	0.1864	34
Flint, MI	0.1854	35
Dothan, AL	0.1840	36
Muskegon, MI	0.1812	37
Danville, VA	0.1785	38
Tallahassee, FL	0.1768	39
Detroit–Ann Arbor, MI	0.1746	40
Richmond–Petersburg, VA	0.1728	41
Jacksonville, FL	0.1713	42
Little Rock–North Little Rock, AR	0.1680	43
Fort Pierce, FL	0.1633	44
Biloxi–Gulfport, MS	0.1598	45
Chicago–Gary–Lake County, IL–IN–WI	0.1594	46
Atlanta, GA	0.1587	47
Miami–Fort Lauderdale, FL	0.1549	48
Baltimore, MD	0.1548	49
Pascagoula, MS	0.1527	50

Source: U.S. Bureau of the Census, Data User Services Division, 1990 Census of Population and Housing, Summary Tape File 3C, United States Summary, CD-ROM, February 1992.

★1806★

Poverty Status By Age, Race, and Ethnicity

Blacks 6 to 11 Years Old Living Below Poverty Level in 1989

[Table shows the top 50 areas]

MSA	% of population	Rank
Albany, GA	2.9131	1
Monroe, LA	2.5529	2
Pine Bluff, AR	2.5442	3
Shreveport, LA	2.4493	4
Jackson, MS	2.1631	5
Alexandria, LA	2.1314	6
New Orleans, LA	2.1292	7
Memphis, TN–AR–MS	2.0948	8
Florence, SC	2.0132	9
Mobile, AL	1.8871	10
Lafayette, LA	1.7510	11
Savannah, GA	1.7402	12
Columbus, GA–AL	1.7316	13
Baton Rouge, LA	1.7264	14
Montgomery, AL	1.7185	15
Macon–Warner Robins, GA	1.6524	16
Tuscaloosa, AL	1.4636	17
Charleston, SC	1.4546	18
Houma–Thibodaux, LA	1.4247	19
Beaumont–Port Arthur, TX	1.4182	20
Texarkana, TX–Texarkana, AR	1.3985	21
Tallahassee, FL	1.3635	22
Augusta, GA–SC	1.3583	23
Jackson, TN	1.3554	24
Longview–Marshall, TX	1.3218	25
Dothan, AL	1.3194	26
Lake Charles, LA	1.3103	27
Pascagoula, MS	1.2261	28
Kankakee, IL	1.2103	29
Fayetteville, NC	1.2012	30
Benton Harbor, MI	1.1817	31
Birmingham, AL	1.1713	32
Gainesville, FL	1.1690	33
Flint, MI	1.1309	34
Danville, VA	1.1057	35
Norfolk–Virginia Beach–Newport News, VA	1.0549	36
Tyler, TX	1.0528	37
Milwaukee–Racine, WI	1.0461	38
Biloxi–Gulfport, MS	1.0369	39
Pensacola, FL	1.0096	40
Decatur, IL	0.9923	41
Muskegon, MI	0.9825	42
Little Rock–North Little Rock, AR	0.9655	43
Athens, GA	0.8946	44
Clarksville–Hopkinsville, TN–KY	0.8935	45
Detroit–Ann Arbor, MI	0.8903	46
Waco, TX	0.8836	47
Columbia, SC	0.8691	48
Jacksonville, FL	0.8615	49
Saint Louis, MO–IL	0.8536	50

Source: U.S. Bureau of the Census, Data User Services Division, 1990 Census of Population and Housing, Summary Tape File 3C, United States Summary, CD-ROM, February 1992.

★1807★
Poverty Status By Age, Race, and Ethnicity

Blacks 12 to 17 Years Old Living Below Poverty Level in 1989

[Table shows the top 50 areas]

MSA	% of population	Rank
Albany, GA	2.5622	1
Pine Bluff, AR	2.3349	2
Monroe, LA	2.0353	3
Shreveport, LA	2.0291	4
Florence, SC	2.0246	5
New Orleans, LA	1.9881	6
Jackson, MS	1.9613	7
Memphis, TN–AR–MS	1.8123	8
Montgomery, AL	1.7127	9
Mobile, AL	1.6070	10
Alexandria, LA	1.5674	11
Columbus, GA–AL	1.5518	12
Baton Rouge, LA	1.4411	13
Lafayette, LA	1.4324	14
Savannah, GA	1.4286	15
Macon–Warner Robins, GA	1.4247	16
Jackson, TN	1.3965	17
Texarkana, TX–Texarkana, AR	1.3469	18
Tuscaloosa, AL	1.2211	19
Lake Charles, LA	1.1943	20
Pascagoula, MS	1.1845	21
Tallahassee, FL	1.1520	22
Longview–Marshall, TX	1.1482	23
Augusta, GA–SC	1.1398	24
Charleston, SC	1.1285	25
Dothan, AL	1.1156	26
Beaumont–Port Arthur, TX	1.0896	27
Houma–Thibodaux, LA	1.0474	28
Fayetteville, NC	1.0409	29
Birmingham, AL	1.0078	30
Flint, MI	0.9697	31
Benton Harbor, MI	0.9580	32
Biloxi–Gulfport, MS	0.9542	33
Danville, VA	0.9088	34
Detroit–Ann Arbor, MI	0.8492	35
Columbia, SC	0.8369	36
Wilmington, NC	0.8322	37
Little Rock–North Little Rock, AR	0.8098	38
Kankakee, IL	0.8083	39
Pensacola, FL	0.8069	40
Waco, TX	0.8064	41
Norfolk–Virginia Beach–Newport News, VA	0.7856	42
Tyler, TX	0.7832	43
Chicago–Gary–Lake County, IL–IN–WI	0.7497	44
Gainesville, FL	0.7432	45
Milwaukee–Racine, WI	0.7398	46
Athens, GA	0.7148	47
Saint Louis, MO–IL	0.7131	48
Anniston, AL	0.7007	49
Clarksville–Hopkinsville, TN–KY	0.6976	50

Source: U.S. Bureau of the Census, Data User Services Division, *1990 Census of Population and Housing*, Summary Tape File 3C, United States Summary, CD-ROM, February 1992.

★1808★
Poverty Status By Age, Race, and Ethnicity

Blacks 18 to 64 Years Old Living Below Poverty Level in 1989

[Table shows the top 50 areas]

MSA	Number	Rank
New York–Northern New Jersey–Long Island, NY–NJ–CT	373,496	1
Chicago–Gary–Lake County, IL–IN–WI	213,211	2
Detroit–Ann Arbor, MI	155,447	3
Philadelphia–Wilmington–Trenton, PA–NJ–DE–MD	128,093	4
Los Angeles–Anaheim–Riverside, CA	121,778	5
Houston–Galveston–Brazoria, TX	90,796	6
Miami–Fort Lauderdale, FL	81,513	7
New Orleans, LA	79,958	8
Atlanta, GA	78,234	9
Dallas–Fort Worth, TX	71,727	10
Baltimore, MD	68,441	11
Cleveland–Akron–Lorain, OH	66,537	12
Washington, DC–MD–VA	66,397	13
Memphis, TN–AR–MS	60,650	14
Saint Louis, MO–IL	58,038	15
San Francisco–Oakland–San Jose, CA	51,604	16
Norfolk–Virginia Beach–Newport News, VA	42,967	17
Milwaukee–Racine, WI	36,081	18
Birmingham, AL	35,814	19
Pittsburgh–Beaver Valley, PA	30,645	20
Cincinnati–Hamilton, OH–KY–IN	29,967	21
Baton Rouge, LA	29,237	22
Jackson, MS	27,090	23
Tampa–Saint Petersburg–Clearwater, FL	25,810	24
Boston–Lawrence–Salem, MA–NH	25,549	25
Mobile, AL	24,994	26
Kansas City, MO–KS	24,491	27
Richmond–Petersburg, VA	23,522	28
Charlotte–Gastonia–Rock Hill, NC–SC	23,362	29
Shreveport, LA	23,156	30
Jacksonville, FL	22,402	31
Charleston, SC	21,323	32
Buffalo–Niagara Falls, NY	21,315	33
Columbus, OH	20,885	34
Indianapolis, IN	20,184	35
Louisville, KY–IN	18,482	36
Greensboro–Winston-Salem–High Point, NC	18,012	37
Raleigh–Durham, NC	17,602	38
Nashville, TN	17,471	39
Dayton–Springfield, OH	16,857	40
Montgomery, AL	15,820	41
Augusta, GA–SC	15,679	42
San Diego, CA	14,708	43
Beaumont–Port Arthur, TX	14,626	44

[Continued]

★1808★

Blacks 18 to 64 Years Old Living Below Poverty Level in 1989

[Continued]

MSA	Number	Rank
Flint, MI	14,566	45
Orlando, FL	14,511	46
Minneapolis – Saint Paul, MN – WI	14,380	47
West Palm Beach – Boca Raton – Delray Beach, FL	14,189	48
Macon – Warner Robins, GA	13,932	49
Oklahoma City, OK	13,651	50

Source: U.S. Bureau of the Census, Data User Services Division, *1990 Census of Population and Housing,* Summary Tape File 3C, United States Summary, CD- ROM, February 1992.

★1809★

Poverty Status By Age, Race, and Ethnicity

Blacks 65 to 74 Years Old Living Below Poverty Level in 1989

[Table shows the top 50 areas]

MSA	Number	Rank
New York – Northern New Jersey – Long Island, NY – NJ – CT	36,708	1
Chicago – Gary – Lake County, IL – IN – WI	19,262	2
Philadelphia – Wilmington – Trenton, PA – NJ – DE – MD	14,846	3
Detroit – Ann Arbor, MI	11,829	4
Los Angeles – Anaheim – Riverside, CA	8,964	5
Houston – Galveston – Brazoria, TX	8,780	6
Washington, DC – MD – VA	8,177	7
Baltimore, MD	7,479	8
New Orleans, LA	7,318	9
Memphis, TN – AR – MS	7,119	10
Atlanta, GA	7,061	11
Miami – Fort Lauderdale, FL	6,833	12
Cleveland – Akron – Lorain, OH	6,174	13
Dallas – Fort Worth, TX	6,120	14
Saint Louis, MO – IL	5,689	15
Norfolk – Virginia Beach – Newport News, VA	5,255	16
Birmingham, AL	4,570	17
San Francisco – Oakland – San Jose, CA	4,086	18
Charlotte – Gastonia – Rock Hill, NC – SC	3,209	19
Richmond – Petersburg, VA	3,165	20
Jackson, MS	3,128	21
Cincinnati – Hamilton, OH – KY – IN	3,115	22
Jacksonville, FL	3,066	23
Charleston, SC	3,052	24
Pittsburgh – Beaver Valley, PA	2,991	25
Tampa – Saint Petersburg – Clearwater, FL	2,831	26

[Continued]

★1809★

Blacks 65 to 74 Years Old Living Below Poverty Level in 1989

[Continued]

MSA	Number	Rank
Kansas City, MO – KS	2,606	27
Baton Rouge, LA	2,523	28
Raleigh – Durham, NC	2,487	29
Shreveport, LA	2,470	30
Mobile, AL	2,452	31
Nashville, TN	2,301	32
Greensboro – Winston-Salem – High Point, NC	2,292	33
Indianapolis, IN	2,093	34
Louisville, KY – IN	1,931	35
Augusta, GA – SC	1,899	36
Montgomery, AL	1,866	37
Columbia, SC	1,809	38
Macon – Warner Robins, GA	1,794	39
Buffalo – Niagara Falls, NY	1,782	40
Orlando, FL	1,769	41
Beaumont – Port Arthur, TX	1,739	42
Greenville – Spartanburg, SC	1,696	43
Savannah, GA	1,680	44
Boston – Lawrence – Salem, MA – NH	1,661	45
Dayton – Springfield, OH	1,655	46
Columbus, OH	1,628	47
Little Rock – North Little Rock, AR	1,563	48
Columbus, GA – AL	1,426	49
San Antonio, TX	1,384	50

Source: U.S. Bureau of the Census, Data User Services Division, *1990 Census of Population and Housing,* Summary Tape File 3C, United States Summary, CD- ROM, February 1992.

★1810★

Poverty Status By Age, Race, and Ethnicity

Blacks 75 Years Old and Older Living Below Poverty Level in 1989

[Table shows the top 50 areas]

MSA	% of population	Rank
Pine Bluff, AR	1.08438	1
Shreveport, LA	0.74206	2
Jackson, MS	0.73091	3
Albany, GA	0.72672	4
Montgomery, AL	0.69876	5
Jackson, TN	0.69119	6
Florence, SC	0.64979	7
Memphis, TN – AR – MS	0.62766	8
Monroe, LA	0.57669	9
Texarkana, TX – Texarkana, AR	0.57270	10
Savannah, GA	0.53004	11
Columbus, GA – AL	0.51836	12
Alexandria, LA	0.51689	13
Danville, VA	0.50869	14
Tuscaloosa, AL	0.49494	15
Longview – Marshall, TX	0.49129	16

[Continued]

★1810★

Blacks 75 Years Old and Older Living Below Poverty Level in 1989
[Continued]

MSA	% of population	Rank
Birmingham, AL	0.47653	17
Macon – Warner Robins, GA	0.46993	18
Tyler, TX	0.44875	19
Mobile, AL	0.44619	20
Tallahassee, FL	0.44521	21
Augusta, GA – SC	0.43295	22
Dothan, AL	0.42073	23
New Orleans, LA	0.41297	24
Charleston, SC	0.36656	25
Lynchburg, VA	0.35514	26
Beaumont – Port Arthur, TX	0.34300	27
Baton Rouge, LA	0.33506	28
Gainesville, FL	0.32727	29
Lake Charles, LA	0.32058	30
Lafayette, LA	0.31762	31
Wilmington, NC	0.29680	32
Waco, TX	0.29505	33
Anderson, SC	0.29409	34
Little Rock – North Little Rock, AR	0.29019	35
Jacksonville, FL	0.28851	36
Raleigh – Durham, NC	0.28702	37
Florence, AL	0.28555	38
Richmond – Petersburg, VA	0.27101	39
Burlington, NC	0.26984	40
Anniston, AL	0.25768	41
Gadsden, AL	0.25741	42
Pensacola, FL	0.24883	43
Greenville – Spartanburg, SC	0.24436	44
Ocala, FL	0.24123	45
Charlottesville, VA	0.24026	46
Norfolk – Virginia Beach – Newport News, VA	0.23924	47
Decatur, AL	0.23792	48
Baltimore, MD	0.23437	49
Atlantic City, NJ	0.23355	50

Source: U.S. Bureau of the Census, Data User Services Division, *1990 Census of Population and Housing,* Summary Tape File 3C, United States Summary, CD-ROM, February 1992.

★1811★

Poverty Status By Age, Race, and Ethnicity

Hispanics Under 5 Years Old Living Below Poverty Level in 1989

[Table shows the top 50 areas]

MSA	% of population	Rank
McAllen – Edinburg – Mission, TX	4.59372	1
Laredo, TX	4.46491	2
Brownsville – Harlingen, TX	4.30225	3
El Paso, TX	3.00722	4
Las Cruces, NM	2.50461	5
Visalia – Tulare – Porterville, CA	2.20088	6
Corpus Christi, TX	2.02833	7

[Continued]

★1811★

Hispanics Under 5 Years Old Living Below Poverty Level in 1989
[Continued]

MSA	% of population	Rank
San Antonio, TX	1.92336	8
Odessa, TX	1.84808	9
Fresno, CA	1.78340	10
Yakima, WA	1.76356	11
Pueblo, CO	1.68629	12
Yuma, AZ	1.58941	13
Bakersfield, CA	1.46317	14
Merced, CA	1.45794	15
Victoria, TX	1.27083	16
San Angelo, TX	1.13754	17
Lubbock, TX	1.10539	18
Tucson, AZ	1.07291	19
Albuquerque, NM	1.05457	20
Greeley, CO	1.03929	21
Midland, TX	1.02804	22
Salinas – Seaside – Monterey, CA	1.01614	23
Los Angeles – Anaheim – Riverside, CA	0.96547	24
Santa Fe, NM	0.96033	25
Richland – Kennewick – Pasco, WA	0.90447	26
Modesto, CA	0.85015	27
Springfield, MA	0.84913	28
Santa Barbara – Santa Maria – Lompoc, CA	0.77271	29
Houston – Galveston – Brazoria, TX	0.77175	30
Amarillo, TX	0.76674	31
Phoenix, AZ	0.74520	32
Austin, TX	0.74158	33
Stockton, CA	0.74007	34
Abilene, TX	0.70703	35
Yuba City, CA	0.70285	36
San Diego, CA	0.60892	37
Waco, TX	0.58639	38
Bryan – College Station, TX	0.54324	39
Naples, FL	0.53321	40
New York – Northern New Jersey – Long Island, NY – NJ – CT	0.50611	41
Dallas – Fort Worth, TX	0.47683	42
Miami – Fort Lauderdale, FL	0.46123	43
Denver – Boulder, CO	0.45712	44
Salem, OR	0.43953	45
Fitchburg – Leominster, MA	0.40955	46
Hartford – New Britain – Middletown, CT	0.40280	47
Reading, PA	0.39552	48
Waterbury, CT	0.37991	49
Sacramento, CA	0.36135	50

Source: U.S. Bureau of the Census, Data User Services Division, *1990 Census of Population and Housing,* Summary Tape File 3C, United States Summary, CD-ROM, February 1992.

★1812★
Poverty Status By Age, Race, and Ethnicity

Hispanics 5 Years Old Living Below Poverty Level in 1989

[Table shows the top 50 areas]

MSA	% of population	Rank
McAllen – Edinburg – Mission, TX	1.01944	1
Brownsville – Harlingen, TX	0.92611	2
Laredo, TX	0.87587	3
El Paso, TX	0.58535	4
Las Cruces, NM	0.52395	5
Odessa, TX	0.48682	6
Visalia – Tulare – Porterville, CA	0.44050	7
San Antonio, TX	0.42600	8
Corpus Christi, TX	0.40870	9
Yuma, AZ	0.39291	10
Fresno, CA	0.36884	11
San Angelo, TX	0.35548	12
Yakima, WA	0.35059	13
Merced, CA	0.33520	14
Victoria, TX	0.28375	15
Pueblo, CO	0.27062	16
Bakersfield, CA	0.26662	17
Midland, TX	0.26170	18
Albuquerque, NM	0.22702	19
Lubbock, TX	0.21380	20
Modesto, CA	0.20835	21
Tucson, AZ	0.20438	22
Los Angeles – Anaheim – Riverside, CA	0.18413	23
Santa Fe, NM	0.18369	24
Salinas – Seaside – Monterey, CA	0.18276	25
Greeley, CO	0.17827	26
Stockton, CA	0.17207	27
Yuba City, CA	0.16634	28
Richland – Kennewick – Pasco, WA	0.15930	29
Springfield, MA	0.15487	30
Santa Barbara – Santa Maria – Lompoc, CA	0.14989	31
Phoenix, AZ	0.14618	32
Houston – Galveston – Brazoria, TX	0.14392	33
Abilene, TX	0.14040	34
Austin, TX	0.13793	35
Waco, TX	0.13483	36
Amarillo, TX	0.13170	37
Fitchburg – Leominster, MA	0.12549	38
San Diego, CA	0.11757	39
Bryan – College Station, TX	0.11324	40
New York – Northern New Jersey – Long Island, NY – NJ – CT	0.10819	41
Miami – Fort Lauderdale, FL	0.10803	42
Naples, FL	0.10782	43
Tyler, TX	0.09583	44
Dallas – Fort Worth, TX	0.08818	45
Reading, PA	0.08736	46
Denver – Boulder, CO	0.08500	47
Wichita Falls, TX	0.08335	48

[Continued]

★1812★

Hispanics 5 Years Old Living Below Poverty Level in 1989

[Continued]

MSA	% of population	Rank
Hartford – New Britain – Middletown, CT	0.07947	49
New Bedford, MA	0.07854	50

Source: U.S. Bureau of the Census, Data User Services Division, 1990 Census of Population and Housing, Summary Tape File 3C, United States Summary, CD-ROM, February 1992.

★1813★
Poverty Status By Age, Race, and Ethnicity

Hispanics 6 to 11 Years Old Living Below Poverty Level in 1989

[Table shows the top 50 areas]

MSA	% of population	Rank
McAllen – Edinburg – Mission, TX	6.4944	1
Brownsville – Harlingen, TX	5.7462	2
Laredo, TX	5.6748	3
El Paso, TX	3.6061	4
Las Cruces, NM	3.0728	5
Visalia – Tulare – Porterville, CA	2.4692	6
Corpus Christi, TX	2.4199	7
Yuma, AZ	2.2059	8
San Antonio, TX	2.1438	9
Odessa, TX	1.9952	10
Fresno, CA	1.8382	11
Victoria, TX	1.7751	12
Merced, CA	1.7354	13
Pueblo, CO	1.7009	14
Yakima, WA	1.4580	15
Bakersfield, CA	1.4083	16
Albuquerque, NM	1.2100	17
Midland, TX	1.1791	18
Lubbock, TX	1.1611	19
San Angelo, TX	1.1040	20
Greeley, CO	1.0772	21
Salinas – Seaside – Monterey, CA	1.0369	22
Santa Fe, NM	1.0159	23
Richland – Kennewick – Pasco, WA	0.9831	24
Los Angeles – Anaheim – Riverside, CA	0.9821	25
Tucson, AZ	0.9684	26
Springfield, MA	0.8497	27
Modesto, CA	0.8394	28
Houston – Galveston – Brazoria, TX	0.8343	29
Stockton, CA	0.7915	30
Santa Barbara – Santa Maria – Lompoc, CA	0.7703	31
Austin, TX	0.7681	32
Abilene, TX	0.7455	33
Amarillo, TX	0.7124	34
Phoenix, AZ	0.7082	35
Yuba City, CA	0.6678	36

[Continued]

★1813★

Hispanics 6 to 11 Years Old Living Below Poverty Level in 1989

[Continued]

MSA	% of population	Rank
Waco, TX	0.6414	37
San Diego, CA	0.6408	38
Naples, FL	0.6167	39
New York – Northern New Jersey – Long Island, NY – NJ – CT	0.5719	40
Miami – Fort Lauderdale, FL	0.5616	41
Hartford – New Britain – Middletown, CT	0.4841	42
Bryan – College Station, TX	0.4743	43
Fitchburg – Leominster, MA	0.4640	44
Dallas – Fort Worth, TX	0.4416	45
Waterbury, CT	0.4345	46
Denver – Boulder, CO	0.4227	47
Wichita Falls, TX	0.4225	48
Tyler, TX	0.3972	49
Salem, OR	0.3960	50

Source: U.S. Bureau of the Census, Data User Services Division, *1990 Census of Population and Housing*, Summary Tape File 3C, United States Summary, CD-ROM, February 1992.

★1814★

Poverty Status By Age, Race, and Ethnicity

Hispanics 12 to 17 Years Old Living Below Poverty Level in 1989

[Table shows the top 50 areas]

MSA	% of population	Rank
McAllen – Edinburg – Mission, TX	6.5979	1
Brownsville – Harlingen, TX	6.1933	2
Laredo, TX	5.9112	3
El Paso, TX	3.4687	4
Las Cruces, NM	2.9644	5
Yuma, AZ	2.4744	6
Corpus Christi, TX	2.1004	7
Visalia – Tulare – Porterville, CA	1.8392	8
San Antonio, TX	1.7746	9
Victoria, TX	1.6568	10
Fresno, CA	1.4823	11
Odessa, TX	1.4025	12
Pueblo, CO	1.3620	13
Merced, CA	1.3419	14
Yakima, WA	1.2864	15
Bakersfield, CA	1.1018	16
Salinas – Seaside – Monterey, CA	0.9554	17
San Angelo, TX	0.9182	18
Albuquerque, NM	0.9127	19
Greeley, CO	0.8648	20
Los Angeles – Anaheim – Riverside, CA	0.8627	21
Midland, TX	0.8583	22
Lubbock, TX	0.8534	23
Tucson, AZ	0.8351	24
Richland – Kennewick – Pasco, WA	0.6732	25

[Continued]

★1814★

Hispanics 12 to 17 Years Old Living Below Poverty Level in 1989

[Continued]

MSA	% of population	Rank
Naples, FL	0.6555	26
Houston – Galveston – Brazoria, TX	0.6458	27
Santa Fe, NM	0.6408	28
Modesto, CA	0.6210	29
Springfield, MA	0.6130	30
Stockton, CA	0.6075	31
Santa Barbara – Santa Maria – Lompoc, CA	0.6033	32
Miami – Fort Lauderdale, FL	0.5804	33
Austin, TX	0.5732	34
Yuba City, CA	0.5602	35
San Diego, CA	0.5560	36
Abilene, TX	0.5374	37
Phoenix, AZ	0.5233	38
New York – Northern New Jersey – Long Island, NY – NJ – CT	0.5061	39
Waco, TX	0.4928	40
Amarillo, TX	0.4767	41
Hartford – New Britain – Middletown, CT	0.3384	42
Dallas – Fort Worth, TX	0.3379	43
Waterbury, CT	0.3280	44
Fitchburg – Leominster, MA	0.3171	45
Bryan – College Station, TX	0.3077	46
Wichita Falls, TX	0.3007	47
Denver – Boulder, CO	0.2786	48
Killeen – Temple, TX	0.2726	49
Chicago – Gary – Lake County, IL – IN – WI	0.2712	50

Source: U.S. Bureau of the Census, Data User Services Division, *1990 Census of Population and Housing*, Summary Tape File 3C, United States Summary, CD-ROM, February 1992.

★1815★

Poverty Status By Age, Race, and Ethnicity

Hispanics 18 to 64 Years Old Living Below Poverty Level in 1989

[Table shows the top 50 areas]

MSA	% of population	Rank
McAllen – Edinburg – Mission, TX	18.833	1
Brownsville – Harlingen, TX	17.475	2
Laredo, TX	17.253	3
El Paso, TX	11.348	4
Las Cruces, NM	9.543	5
Corpus Christi, TX	7.355	6
Yuma, AZ	6.547	7
San Antonio, TX	6.467	8
Visalia – Tulare – Porterville, CA	6.059	9
Pueblo, CO	5.400	10
Odessa, TX	5.373	11
Fresno, CA	5.333	12

[Continued]

★1815★

Hispanics 18 to 64 Years Old Living Below Poverty Level in 1989

[Continued]

MSA	% of population	Rank
Victoria, TX	4.970	13
Yakima, WA	4.289	14
Merced, CA	4.164	15
Albuquerque, NM	4.114	16
San Angelo, TX	3.850	17
Los Angeles – Anaheim – Riverside, CA	3.732	18
Lubbock, TX	3.517	19
Bakersfield, CA	3.509	20
Midland, TX	3.449	21
Miami – Fort Lauderdale, FL	3.395	22
Santa Fe, NM	3.330	23
Tucson, AZ	3.297	24
Salinas – Seaside – Monterey, CA	3.261	25
Santa Barbara – Santa Maria – Lompoc, CA	3.025	26
Greeley, CO	2.834	27
Austin, TX	2.756	28
Houston – Galveston – Brazoria, TX	2.721	29
Bryan – College Station, TX	2.636	30
Stockton, CA	2.539	31
Naples, FL	2.510	32
San Diego, CA	2.375	33
Richland – Kennewick – Pasco, WA	2.364	34
Modesto, CA	2.121	35
New York – Northern New Jersey – Long Island, NY – NJ – CT	2.108	36
Abilene, TX	2.094	37
Phoenix, AZ	2.086	38
Amarillo, TX	1.951	39
Yuba City, CA	1.933	40
Springfield, MA	1.863	41
Waco, TX	1.823	42
Dallas – Fort Worth, TX	1.601	43
Fitchburg – Leominster, MA	1.310	44
Denver – Boulder, CO	1.295	45
San Francisco – Oakland – San Jose, CA	1.181	46
Salem, OR	1.133	47
Chico, CA	1.103	48
Reno, NV	1.074	49
Chicago – Gary – Lake County, IL – IN – WI	1.073	50

Source: U.S. Bureau of the Census, Data User Services Division, *1990 Census of Population and Housing*, Summary Tape File 3C, United States Summary, CD-ROM, February 1992.

★1816★

Poverty Status By Age, Race, and Ethnicity

Hispanics 65 to 74 Years Old Living Below Poverty Level in 1989

[Table shows the top 50 areas]

MSA	% of population	Rank
Laredo, TX	1.50181	1
McAllen – Edinburg – Mission, TX	1.38211	2
Brownsville – Harlingen, TX	1.29363	3
El Paso, TX	0.80053	4
Corpus Christi, TX	0.68849	5
Las Cruces, NM	0.56970	6
Miami – Fort Lauderdale, FL	0.56822	7
San Antonio, TX	0.51509	8
Victoria, TX	0.43975	9
Pueblo, CO	0.38277	10
Santa Fe, NM	0.33407	11
Albuquerque, NM	0.29048	12
Odessa, TX	0.28251	13
San Angelo, TX	0.27524	14
Yuma, AZ	0.25165	15
Lubbock, TX	0.21740	16
Tucson, AZ	0.17844	17
Visalia – Tulare – Porterville, CA	0.17601	18
Abilene, TX	0.15712	19
Yakima, WA	0.14405	20
Fresno, CA	0.14307	21
Merced, CA	0.13621	22
New York – Northern New Jersey – Long Island, NY – NJ – CT	0.13587	23
Greeley, CO	0.11910	24
Houston – Galveston – Brazoria, TX	0.10814	25
Austin, TX	0.10632	26
Killeen – Temple, TX	0.09792	27
Los Angeles – Anaheim – Riverside, CA	0.09660	28
Waco, TX	0.08936	29
Phoenix, AZ	0.08916	30
Midland, TX	0.08630	31
Santa Barbara – Santa Maria – Lompoc, CA	0.08523	32
Stockton, CA	0.08510	33
Bakersfield, CA	0.07930	34
Amarillo, TX	0.07411	35
San Diego, CA	0.06857	36
Wichita Falls, TX	0.06782	37
Naples, FL	0.06640	38
Salinas – Seaside – Monterey, CA	0.06636	39
Tampa – Saint Petersburg – Clearwater, FL	0.06543	40
Denver – Boulder, CO	0.06087	41
Bryan – College Station, TX	0.06072	42
Orlando, FL	0.06031	43
Sherman – Denison, TX	0.04631	44
Cheyenne, WY	0.04238	45
Colorado Springs, CO	0.04156	46
San Francisco – Oakland – San Jose, CA	0.03899	47
Chicago – Gary – Lake County, IL – IN – WI	0.03871	48

[Continued]

★1816★

Hispanics 65 to 74 Years Old Living Below
Poverty Level in 1989
[Continued]

MSA	% of population	Rank
Dallas – Fort Worth, TX	0.03858	49
Las Vegas, NV	0.03830	50

Source: U.S. Bureau of the Census, Data User Services Division, *1990 Census of Population and Housing*, Summary Tape File 3C, United States Summary, CD-ROM, February 1992.

★1817★
Poverty Status By Age, Race, and Ethnicity

Hispanics 75 Years Old and Older Living Below
Poverty Level in 1989
[Table shows the top 50 areas]

MSA	% of population	Rank
Laredo, TX	0.98695	1
Brownsville – Harlingen, TX	0.90343	2
McAllen – Edinburg – Mission, TX	0.88673	3
El Paso, TX	0.57808	4
Corpus Christi, TX	0.53816	5
Miami – Fort Lauderdale, FL	0.51009	6
Santa Fe, NM	0.43574	7
San Antonio, TX	0.41763	8
Las Cruces, NM	0.38816	9
Victoria, TX	0.29720	10
Albuquerque, NM	0.25116	11
Pueblo, CO	0.23242	12
Yuma, AZ	0.20207	13
San Angelo, TX	0.15641	14
Midland, TX	0.15289	15
Tucson, AZ	0.13766	16
Odessa, TX	0.11939	17
Greeley, CO	0.11910	18
Abilene, TX	0.09026	19
Austin, TX	0.08713	20
Visalia – Tulare – Porterville, CA	0.08496	21
New York – Northern New Jersey – Long Island, NY – NJ – CT	0.08154	22
Lubbock, TX	0.08130	23
Tampa – Saint Petersburg – Clearwater, FL	0.07036	24
Fresno, CA	0.06981	25
Santa Barbara – Santa Maria – Lompoc, CA	0.06169	26
Yakima, WA	0.05984	27
Los Angeles – Anaheim – Riverside, CA	0.05724	28
Houston – Galveston – Brazoria, TX	0.05524	29
Bakersfield, CA	0.04913	30
West Palm Beach – Boca Raton – Delray Beach, FL	0.04702	31
Fort Collins – Loveland, CO	0.04567	32
Merced, CA	0.04540	33
Denver – Boulder, CO	0.04496	34

[Continued]

★1817★

Hispanics 75 Years Old and Older Living Below
Poverty Level in 1989
[Continued]

MSA	% of population	Rank
Waco, TX	0.04336	35
Phoenix, AZ	0.04316	36
Killeen – Temple, TX	0.04309	37
Stockton, CA	0.04182	38
Topeka, KS	0.04038	39
San Diego, CA	0.03899	40
Ocala, FL	0.03336	41
Salinas – Seaside – Monterey, CA	0.03233	42
San Francisco – Oakland – San Jose, CA	0.03093	43
Dallas – Fort Worth, TX	0.03034	44
Cheyenne, WY	0.03008	45
Richland – Kennewick – Pasco, WA	0.02933	46
New Orleans, LA	0.02914	47
Bryan – College Station, TX	0.02872	48
Orlando, FL	0.02871	49
Modesto, CA	0.02726	50

Source: U.S. Bureau of the Census, Data User Services Division, *1990 Census of Population and Housing*, Summary Tape File 3C, United States Summary, CD-ROM, February 1992.

★1818★
Poverty Status By Age, Race, and Ethnicity

Hispanics Under 5 Years Old Living Above
Poverty Level in 1989
[Table shows the top 50 areas]

MSA	% of population	Rank
Laredo, TX	5.1374	1
McAllen – Edinburg – Mission, TX	3.8757	2
El Paso, TX	3.7597	3
Brownsville – Harlingen, TX	3.5822	4
Las Cruces, NM	3.2839	5
Yuma, AZ	2.8645	6
Corpus Christi, TX	2.8163	7
Salinas – Seaside – Monterey, CA	2.7754	8
San Antonio, TX	2.7505	9
Santa Fe, NM	2.7238	10
Los Angeles – Anaheim – Riverside, CA	2.6084	11
Visalia – Tulare – Porterville, CA	2.5555	12
Merced, CA	2.4461	13
Albuquerque, NM	2.4131	14
Fresno, CA	2.2697	15
Odessa, TX	2.1676	16
Bakersfield, CA	2.1513	17
Victoria, TX	2.1382	18
Santa Barbara – Santa Maria – Lompoc, CA	1.9981	19
Modesto, CA	1.8531	20
Midland, TX	1.7559	21
Stockton, CA	1.7375	22
Yakima, WA	1.6635	23

[Continued]

★1818★

Hispanics Under 5 Years Old Living Above Poverty Level in 1989

[Continued]

MSA	% of population	Rank
Pueblo, CO	1.5920	24
Tucson, AZ	1.5764	25
Miami – Fort Lauderdale, FL	1.5665	26
San Angelo, TX	1.5529	27
San Diego, CA	1.5311	28
Houston – Galveston – Brazoria, TX	1.5248	29
Greeley, CO	1.5142	30
Lubbock, TX	1.4468	31
Austin, TX	1.4374	32
Phoenix, AZ	1.2529	33
San Francisco – Oakland – San Jose, CA	1.2093	34
Killeen – Temple, TX	1.1030	35
Dallas – Fort Worth, TX	1.0987	36
Amarillo, TX	0.9955	37
Yuba City, CA	0.9825	38
Abilene, TX	0.9101	39
Richland – Kennewick – Pasco, WA	0.9058	40
Las Vegas, NV	0.8766	41
Chicago – Gary – Lake County, IL – IN – WI	0.8749	42
Waco, TX	0.8624	43
Denver – Boulder, CO	0.8557	44
Sacramento, CA	0.8551	45
New York – Northern New Jersey – Long Island, NY – NJ – CT	0.8112	46
Naples, FL	0.7469	47
Reno, NV	0.7343	48
Cheyenne, WY	0.7274	49
Bryan – College Station, TX	0.7156	50

Source: U.S. Bureau of the Census, Data User Services Division, *1990 Census of Population and Housing*, Summary Tape File 3C, United States Summary, CD-ROM, February 1992.

★1819★

Poverty Status By Age, Race, and Ethnicity

Hispanics 5 Years Old Living Above Poverty Level in 1989

[Table shows the top 50 areas]

MSA	% of population	Rank
Laredo, TX	0.96969	1
El Paso, TX	0.83231	2
Brownsville – Harlingen, TX	0.78810	3
McAllen – Edinburg – Mission, TX	0.78009	4
Las Cruces, NM	0.72910	5
Corpus Christi, TX	0.64391	6
San Antonio, TX	0.61002	7
Santa Fe, NM	0.58098	8
Salinas – Seaside – Monterey, CA	0.56430	9
Yuma, AZ	0.55381	10
Merced, CA	0.51625	11

[Continued]

★1819★

Hispanics 5 Years Old Living Above Poverty Level in 1989

[Continued]

MSA	% of population	Rank
Bakersfield, CA	0.49772	12
Albuquerque, NM	0.49628	13
Los Angeles – Anaheim – Riverside, CA	0.48879	14
Victoria, TX	0.47606	15
Visalia – Tulare – Porterville, CA	0.46614	16
Fresno, CA	0.43386	17
Odessa, TX	0.43217	18
Pueblo, CO	0.42259	19
Yakima, WA	0.38502	20
Santa Barbara – Santa Maria – Lompoc, CA	0.38013	21
San Angelo, TX	0.37072	22
Greeley, CO	0.36792	23
Modesto, CA	0.34546	24
Stockton, CA	0.33435	25
Lubbock, TX	0.32699	26
Tucson, AZ	0.32210	27
Houston – Galveston – Brazoria, TX	0.31121	28
Miami – Fort Lauderdale, FL	0.29525	29
Richland – Kennewick – Pasco, WA	0.28927	30
San Diego, CA	0.28278	31
Austin, TX	0.27291	32
Midland, TX	0.26170	33
San Francisco – Oakland – San Jose, CA	0.24601	34
Phoenix, AZ	0.23434	35
Amarillo, TX	0.23194	36
Killeen – Temple, TX	0.22013	37
Yuba City, CA	0.21934	38
Dallas – Fort Worth, TX	0.19313	39
Abilene, TX	0.18386	40
Sacramento, CA	0.17919	41
Naples, FL	0.17817	42
Denver – Boulder, CO	0.17605	43
Chicago – Gary – Lake County, IL – IN – WI	0.17193	44
Bryan – College Station, TX	0.16166	45
Las Vegas, NV	0.16049	46
New York – Northern New Jersey – Long Island, NY – NJ – CT	0.14767	47
Colorado Springs, CO	0.14559	48
Waco, TX	0.14488	49
Cheyenne, WY	0.12442	50

Source: U.S. Bureau of the Census, Data User Services Division, *1990 Census of Population and Housing*, Summary Tape File 3C, United States Summary, CD-ROM, February 1992.

★1820★

Poverty Status By Age, Race, and Ethnicity

Hispanics 6 to 11 Years Old Living Above Poverty Level in 1989

[Table shows the top 50 areas]

MSA	% of population	Rank
Laredo, TX	6.097	1
McAllen – Edinburg – Mission, TX	4.874	2
Brownsville – Harlingen, TX	4.731	3
El Paso, TX	4.637	4
Corpus Christi, TX	4.051	5
Las Cruces, NM	3.935	6
Santa Fe, NM	3.450	7
San Antonio, TX	3.437	8
Yuma, AZ	3.395	9
Visalia – Tulare – Porterville, CA	3.293	10
Salinas – Seaside – Monterey, CA	3.104	11
Albuquerque, NM	2.936	12
Odessa, TX	2.807	13
Fresno, CA	2.776	14
Merced, CA	2.737	15
Victoria, TX	2.649	16
Pueblo, CO	2.643	17
Los Angeles – Anaheim – Riverside, CA	2.636	18
Bakersfield, CA	2.459	19
San Angelo, TX	2.282	20
Santa Barbara – Santa Maria – Lompoc, CA	2.276	21
Modesto, CA	2.162	22
Midland, TX	2.013	23
Stockton, CA	1.983	24
Lubbock, TX	1.954	25
Yakima, WA	1.891	26
Tucson, AZ	1.829	27
Miami – Fort Lauderdale, FL	1.769	28
Houston – Galveston – Brazoria, TX	1.755	29
Greeley, CO	1.710	30
San Diego, CA	1.603	31
Austin, TX	1.563	32
Phoenix, AZ	1.328	33
Abilene, TX	1.311	34
San Francisco – Oakland – San Jose, CA	1.273	35
Amarillo, TX	1.200	36
Dallas – Fort Worth, TX	1.132	37
Killeen – Temple, TX	1.124	38
Waco, TX	1.050	39
Richland – Kennewick – Pasco, WA	1.012	40
Sacramento, CA	1.004	41
Denver – Boulder, CO	1.003	42
Bryan – College Station, TX	0.995	43
Chicago – Gary – Lake County, IL – IN – WI	0.973	44
Yuba City, CA	0.960	45
Las Vegas, NV	0.884	46
New York – Northern New Jersey – Long Island, NY – NJ – CT	0.866	47
Naples, FL	0.858	48

[Continued]

★1820★

Hispanics 6 to 11 Years Old Living Above Poverty Level in 1989

[Continued]

MSA	% of population	Rank
Cheyenne, WY	0.796	49
Wichita Falls, TX	0.726	50

Source: U.S. Bureau of the Census, Data User Services Division, *1990 Census of Population and Housing*, Summary Tape File 3C, United States Summary, CD-ROM, February 1992.

★1821★

Poverty Status By Age, Race, and Ethnicity

Hispanics 12 to 17 Years Old Living Above Poverty Level in 1989

[Table shows the top 50 areas]

MSA	% of population	Rank
Laredo, TX	5.8767	1
McAllen – Edinburg – Mission, TX	5.4291	2
Brownsville – Harlingen, TX	5.2572	3
El Paso, TX	5.1899	4
Corpus Christi, TX	3.9726	5
Las Cruces, NM	3.7931	6
Santa Fe, NM	3.6816	7
San Antonio, TX	3.4735	8
Yuma, AZ	3.0553	9
Visalia – Tulare – Porterville, CA	2.7036	10
Albuquerque, NM	2.6951	11
Salinas – Seaside – Monterey, CA	2.6233	12
Merced, CA	2.5431	13
Pueblo, CO	2.5128	14
Los Angeles – Anaheim – Riverside, CA	2.4967	15
Victoria, TX	2.4959	16
Odessa, TX	2.4299	17
Fresno, CA	2.3642	18
Miami – Fort Lauderdale, FL	1.9989	19
San Angelo, TX	1.9064	20
Bakersfield, CA	1.9039	21
Tucson, AZ	1.8772	22
Modesto, CA	1.8725	23
Santa Barbara – Santa Maria – Lompoc, CA	1.7803	24
Lubbock, TX	1.7257	25
Stockton, CA	1.6272	26
Houston – Galveston – Brazoria, TX	1.5537	27
Greeley, CO	1.5407	28
Yakima, WA	1.4860	29
San Diego, CA	1.4851	30
Midland, TX	1.4314	31
Austin, TX	1.3541	32
Phoenix, AZ	1.2775	33
San Francisco – Oakland – San Jose, CA	1.1327	34
Yuba City, CA	1.0722	35
Abilene, TX	1.0455	36

[Continued]

★1821★

Hispanics 12 to 17 Years Old Living Above Poverty Level in 1989

[Continued]

MSA	% of population	Rank
Dallas – Fort Worth, TX	0.9719	37
Richland – Kennewick – Pasco, WA	0.9545	38
Denver – Boulder, CO	0.9450	39
Chicago – Gary – Lake County, IL – IN – WI	0.9327	40
Amarillo, TX	0.9224	41
Cheyenne, WY	0.9119	42
New York – Northern New Jersey – Long Island, NY – NJ – CT	0.9116	43
Sacramento, CA	0.8791	44
Naples, FL	0.8587	45
Killeen – Temple, TX	0.8327	46
Las Vegas, NV	0.8085	47
Waco, TX	0.8053	48
Bryan – College Station, TX	0.7984	49
Orlando, FL	0.7295	50

Source: U.S. Bureau of the Census, Data User Services Division, 1990 Census of Population and Housing, Summary Tape File 3C, United States Summary, CD-ROM, February 1992.

★1822★

Poverty Status By Age, Race, and Ethnicity

Hispanics 18 to 64 Years Old Living Above Poverty Level in 1989

[Table shows the top 50 areas]

MSA	% of population	Rank
Laredo, TX	33.473	1
El Paso, TX	28.051	2
McAllen – Edinburg – Mission, TX	27.114	3
Brownsville – Harlingen, TX	26.149	4
Santa Fe, NM	22.188	5
Las Cruces, NM	21.756	6
Corpus Christi, TX	21.665	7
San Antonio, TX	20.640	8
Albuquerque, NM	17.900	9
Miami – Fort Lauderdale, FL	17.877	10
Yuma, AZ	16.007	11
Los Angeles – Anaheim – Riverside, CA	15.773	12
Salinas – Seaside – Monterey, CA	15.097	13
Pueblo, CO	14.687	14
Visalia – Tulare – Porterville, CA	14.243	15
Fresno, CA	14.115	16
Victoria, TX	13.867	17
Merced, CA	13.051	18
Santa Barbara – Santa Maria – Lompoc, CA	12.735	19
Odessa, TX	11.308	20
Bakersfield, CA	11.053	21
Tucson, AZ	10.391	22
Stockton, CA	10.382	23
San Angelo, TX	10.188	24

[Continued]

★1822★

Hispanics 18 to 64 Years Old Living Above Poverty Level in 1989

[Continued]

MSA	% of population	Rank
Modesto, CA	9.691	25
Houston – Galveston – Brazoria, TX	9.379	26
Austin, TX	9.348	27
San Diego, CA	9.348	27
Lubbock, TX	9.191	28
Greeley, CO	8.593	29
San Francisco – Oakland – San Jose, CA	8.133	30
Yakima, WA	8.021	31
Midland, TX	7.862	32
New York – Northern New Jersey – Long Island, NY – NJ – CT	7.387	33
Phoenix, AZ	6.902	34
Dallas – Fort Worth, TX	6.214	35
Denver – Boulder, CO	5.836	36
Las Vegas, NV	5.769	37
Sacramento, CA	5.555	38
Naples, FL	5.429	39
Chicago – Gary – Lake County, IL – IN – WI	5.368	40
Abilene, TX	5.360	41
Yuba City, CA	5.317	42
Amarillo, TX	5.299	43
Killeen – Temple, TX	5.148	44
Bryan – College Station, TX	5.089	45
Waco, TX	4.829	46
Orlando, FL	4.715	47
Cheyenne, WY	4.666	48
Richland – Kennewick – Pasco, WA	4.656	49

Source: U.S. Bureau of the Census, Data User Services Division, 1990 Census of Population and Housing, Summary Tape File 3C, United States Summary, CD-ROM, February 1992.

★1823★

Poverty Status By Age, Race, and Ethnicity

Hispanics 65 to 74 Years Old Living Above Poverty Level in 1989

[Table shows the top 50 areas]

MSA	% of population	Rank
Laredo, TX	2.7905	1
El Paso, TX	1.9707	2
Brownsville – Harlingen, TX	1.9218	3
Miami – Fort Lauderdale, FL	1.8333	4
Santa Fe, NM	1.7993	5
McAllen – Edinburg – Mission, TX	1.7471	6
Pueblo, CO	1.5270	7
Corpus Christi, TX	1.5007	8
San Antonio, TX	1.4607	9
Las Cruces, NM	1.4014	10
Albuquerque, NM	1.2687	11
Yuma, AZ	1.0038	12

[Continued]

★1823★

Hispanics 65 to 74 Years Old Living Above Poverty Level in 1989
[Continued]

MSA	% of population	Rank
Victoria, TX	0.9010	13
Tucson, AZ	0.7307	14
Fresno, CA	0.7262	15
Visalia – Tulare – Porterville, CA	0.6999	16
Merced, CA	0.6648	17
Stockton, CA	0.6400	18
Los Angeles – Anaheim – Riverside, CA	0.6389	19
San Angelo, TX	0.6378	20
Salinas – Seaside – Monterey, CA	0.6009	21
Santa Barbara – Santa Maria – Lompoc, CA	0.5763	22
Bakersfield, CA	0.5301	23
Modesto, CA	0.4602	24
San Diego, CA	0.4416	25
San Francisco – Oakland – San Jose, CA	0.4111	26
Yuba City, CA	0.3767	27
Odessa, TX	0.3758	28
New York – Northern New Jersey – Long Island, NY – NJ – CT	0.3646	29
Tampa – Saint Petersburg – Clearwater, FL	0.3602	30
Greeley, CO	0.3399	31
Austin, TX	0.3305	32
Orlando, FL	0.3272	33
Cheyenne, WY	0.3240	34
West Palm Beach – Boca Raton – Delray Beach, FL	0.3087	35
Chico, CA	0.3042	36
Lubbock, TX	0.3032	37
Naples, FL	0.2998	38
Sacramento, CA	0.2989	39
Houston – Galveston – Brazoria, TX	0.2873	40
Phoenix, AZ	0.2862	41
Midland, TX	0.2861	42
Las Vegas, NV	0.2705	43
Denver – Boulder, CO	0.2551	44
Abilene, TX	0.2282	45
Yakima, WA	0.2272	46
Waco, TX	0.2258	47
Ocala, FL	0.2156	48
Bryan – College Station, TX	0.2134	49
Amarillo, TX	0.1872	50

Source: U.S. Bureau of the Census, Data User Services Division, *1990 Census of Population and Housing,* Summary Tape File 3C, United States Summary, CD-ROM, February 1992.

★1824★

Poverty Status By Age, Race, and Ethnicity

Hispanics 75 Years Old and Older Living Above Poverty Level in 1989

[Table shows the top 50 areas]

MSA	% of population	Rank
Laredo, TX	1.54759	1
Miami – Fort Lauderdale, FL	1.17886	2
Brownsville – Harlingen, TX	0.95379	3
McAllen – Edinburg – Mission, TX	0.95373	4
El Paso, TX	0.92189	5
Santa Fe, NM	0.91590	6
Las Cruces, NM	0.72836	7
Corpus Christi, TX	0.69078	8
Pueblo, CO	0.67370	9
San Antonio, TX	0.65563	10
Albuquerque, NM	0.61385	11
Yuma, AZ	0.39852	12
Fresno, CA	0.38562	13
Merced, CA	0.37443	14
Victoria, TX	0.35234	15
Visalia – Tulare – Porterville, CA	0.33951	16
Los Angeles – Anaheim – Riverside, CA	0.32208	17
Tucson, AZ	0.28941	18
Bakersfield, CA	0.27195	19
San Angelo, TX	0.26306	20
Santa Barbara – Santa Maria – Lompoc, CA	0.25730	21
Stockton, CA	0.24343	22
Salinas – Seaside – Monterey, CA	0.23534	23
San Diego, CA	0.22758	24
San Francisco – Oakland – San Jose, CA	0.22451	25
Tampa – Saint Petersburg – Clearwater, FL	0.21263	26
Modesto, CA	0.19540	27
New York – Northern New Jersey – Long Island, NY – NJ – CT	0.18505	28
Lubbock, TX	0.17293	29
Austin, TX	0.16812	30
Greeley, CO	0.16538	31
Odessa, TX	0.16059	32
Cheyenne, WY	0.15039	33
Phoenix, AZ	0.14302	34
Waco, TX	0.14276	35
Orlando, FL	0.14039	36
Sacramento, CA	0.13544	37
Yuba City, CA	0.13454	38
Naples, FL	0.13149	39
Midland, TX	0.13038	40
Houston – Galveston – Brazoria, TX	0.12320	41
Denver – Boulder, CO	0.12244	42
Yakima, WA	0.12181	43
Abilene, TX	0.11700	44
Las Vegas, NV	0.11127	45
Fitchburg – Leominster, MA	0.10993	46
Daytona Beach, FL	0.10790	47
West Palm Beach – Boca Raton – Delray Beach, FL	0.10376	48

[Continued]

★1824★

Hispanics 75 Years Old and Older Living Above Poverty Level in 1989

[Continued]

MSA	% of population	Rank
New Orleans, LA	0.10268	49
Sarasota, FL	0.09864	50

Source: U.S. Bureau of the Census, Data User Services Division, *1990 Census of Population and Housing*, Summary Tape File 3C, United States Summary, CD-ROM, February 1992.

★1825★

Poverty Status By Age, Race, and Ethnicity

White Female Heads of Households Living In Slums, 1994: Number

City	Number	Rank
Baltimore, MD	512	3
Boston, MA	453	6
Columbus, OH	640	1
Detroit, MI	321	13
Duluth, MN	370	9
Flint, MI	387	7
Jackson, MI	500	4
Jamestown, NY	306	15
Minneapolis, MN	330	11
Newport, KY	356	10
Portland, ME	383	8
Rockford, IL	317	14
Syracuse, NY	491	5
Toledo, OH	593	2
Waterloo, IA	324	12

Source: "Where the White Underclass Lives," *U.S. News & World Report*, 12 October, 1994, p. 41. Primary source: U.S. News & World Report; the Urban Institute; U.S. Census Bureau's data user services division. *Notes:* Data pertain to non-Hispanic whites and may include only parts of neighborhoods, depending on census tract boundaries.

★1826★

Poverty Status By Age, Race, and Ethnicity

White Female Heads of Households Living In Slums, 1994: Rate

City	Rate	Rank
Baltimore, MD	51.0	8
Boston, MA	73.0	1
Columbus, OH	40.0	13
Detroit, MI	59.0	5
Duluth, MN	60.0	4
Flint, MI	56.0	6
Jackson, MI	50.0	9
Jamestown, NY	45.0	12
Minneapolis, MN	65.0	3
Newport, KY	65.0	3
Portland, ME	70.0	2
Rockford, IL	51.0	8
Syracuse, NY	49.0	10

[Continued]

★1826★

White Female Heads of Households Living In Slums, 1994: Rate

[Continued]

City	Rate	Rank
Toledo, OH	46.0	11
Waterloo, IA	54.0	7

Source: "Where the White Underclass Lives," *U.S. News & World Report*, 12 October, 1994, p. 41. Primary source: *U.S. News & World Report*; the Urban Institute; U.S. Census Bureau's data user services division. *Notes:* Data pertain to non-Hispanic whites and may include only parts of neighborhoods, depending on census tract boundaries.

★1827★

Poverty Status By Age, Race, and Ethnicity

Whites 18 to 64 Years Old Living Below Poverty Level in 1989

[Table shows the top 50 areas]

MSA	% of population	Rank
Brownsville – Harlingen, TX	14.8	1
McAllen – Edinburg – Mission, TX	13.7	2
Bryan – College Station, TX	13.3	3
Lawrence, KS	12.4	4
Las Cruces, NM	12.3	5
State College, PA	12.2	6
Bloomington, IN	12.0	7
Laredo, TX	11.4	8
Iowa City, IA	11.1	9
Gainesville, FL	10.6	10
Huntington – Ashland, WV – KY – OH	10.5	11
Athens, GA	9.8	12
Chico, CA	9.6	13
El Paso, TX	9.4	14
Muncie, IN	9.1	15
Provo – Orem, UT	8.9	16
Columbia, MO	8.8	17
Lafayette – West Lafayette, IN	8.4	18
Eugene – Springfield, OR	8.2	19
Wheeling, WV – OH	7.9	20
Fargo – Moorhead, ND – MN	7.8	21
Johnson City – Kingsport – Bristol, TN – VA	7.7	22
Champaign – Urbana – Rantoul, IL	7.6	23
Cumberland, MD – WV	7.6	23
Fayetteville – Springdale, AR	7.6	23
Pueblo, CO	7.5	24
Houma – Thibodaux, LA	7.4	25
Duluth, MN – WI	7.3	26
La Crosse, WI	7.3	26
Waco, TX	7.3	26
Eau Claire, WI	7.1	27
Fort Collins – Loveland, CO	7.1	27
Lubbock, TX	7.1	27
Springfield, MO	7.1	27
Bloomington – Normal, IL	7.0	28
Altoona, PA	6.9	29
Charleston, WV	6.9	29

[Continued]

★1827★
Whites 18 to 64 Years Old Living Below Poverty Level in 1989
[Continued]

MSA	% of population	Rank
Saint Joseph, MO	6.9	29
Greeley, CO	6.8	30
Joplin, MO	6.8	30
Parkersburg – Marietta, WV – OH	6.8	30
Spokane, WA	6.8	30
Corpus Christi, TX	6.7	31
Grand Forks, ND	6.7	31
Owensboro, KY	6.7	31
Steubenville – Weirton, OH – WV	6.7	31
Tuscaloosa, AL	6.7	31
Waterloo – Cedar Falls, IA	6.7	31
Bangor, ME	6.6	32
Bellingham, WA	6.6	32

Source: U.S. Bureau of the Census, Data User Services Division, *1990 Census of Population and Housing,* Summary Tape File 3C, United States Summary, CD-ROM, February 1992.

★1828★
Poverty Status By Age, Race, and Ethnicity
Whites 65 to 74 Years Old Living Below Poverty Level in 1989
[Table shows the top 50 areas]

MSA	% of population	Rank
Johnson City – Kingsport – Bristol, TN – VA	1.420	1
Gadsden, AL	1.407	2
Brownsville – Harlingen, TX	1.262	3
McAllen – Edinburg – Mission, TX	1.246	4
Decatur, AL	1.171	5
Huntington – Ashland, WV – KY – OH	1.153	6
Laredo, TX	1.139	7
Cumberland, MD – WV	1.131	8
Wheeling, WV – OH	1.101	9
Johnstown, PA	1.096	10
Sherman – Denison, TX	1.080	11
Florence, AL	1.055	12
Anniston, AL	1.048	13
Ocala, FL	1.015	14
Asheville, NC	0.967	15
Joplin, MO	0.939	16
Danville, VA	0.936	17
Knoxville, TN	0.935	18
Saint Joseph, MO	0.928	19
Owensboro, KY	0.924	20
Scranton – Wilkes-Barre, PA	0.920	21
Parkersburg – Marietta, WV – OH	0.911	22
Anderson, SC	0.907	23
Enid, OK	0.906	24
Steubenville – Weirton, OH – WV	0.904	25
Fort Smith, AR – OK	0.885	26
Miami – Fort Lauderdale, FL	0.884	27

[Continued]

★1828★
Whites 65 to 74 Years Old Living Below Poverty Level in 1989
[Continued]

MSA	% of population	Rank
Altoona, PA	0.877	28
Hagerstown, MD	0.872	29
Chattanooga, TN – GA	0.862	30
Terre Haute, IN	0.862	30
Pueblo, CO	0.850	31
Charleston, WV	0.845	32
New Bedford, MA	0.832	33
Texarkana, TX – Texarkana, AR	0.832	33
Utica – Rome, NY	0.820	34
Hickory – Morganton, NC	0.819	35
Alexandria, LA	0.816	36
Dothan, AL	0.815	37
Lakeland – Winter Haven, FL	0.806	38
El Paso, TX	0.798	39
Lewiston – Auburn, ME	0.796	40
Houma – Thibodaux, LA	0.789	41
Biloxi – Gulfport, MS	0.787	42
Panama City, FL	0.786	43
Tampa – Saint Petersburg – Clearwater, FL	0.771	44
Corpus Christi, TX	0.753	45
Florence, SC	0.750	46
Pine Bluff, AR	0.744	47
Pittsburgh – Beaver Valley, PA	0.742	48

Source: U.S. Bureau of the Census, Data User Services Division, *1990 Census of Population and Housing,* Summary Tape File 3C, United States Summary, CD-ROM, February 1992.

★1829★
Poverty Status By Age, Race, and Ethnicity
Whites 75 Years Old and Older Living Below Poverty Level in 1989
[Table shows the top 50 areas]

MSA	% of population	Rank
Joplin, MO	1.614	1
Sherman – Denison, TX	1.423	2
Johnson City – Kingsport – Bristol, TN – VA	1.355	3
Cumberland, MD – WV	1.226	4
Gadsden, AL	1.225	5
Florence, AL	1.205	6
Wheeling, WV – OH	1.193	7
Parkersburg – Marietta, WV – OH	1.186	8
Decatur, AL	1.184	9
Lewiston – Auburn, ME	1.175	10
Enid, OK	1.154	11
Fort Smith, AR – OK	1.152	12
Huntington – Ashland, WV – KY – OH	1.115	13
Asheville, NC	1.103	14
Danville, VA	1.094	15
Scranton – Wilkes-Barre, PA	1.094	15

[Continued]

★1829★

Whites 75 Years Old and Older Living Below Poverty Level in 1989

[Continued]

MSA	% of population	Rank
Texarkana, TX–Texarkana, AR	1.074	16
Miami–Fort Lauderdale, FL	1.061	17
Saint Joseph, MO	1.053	18
Dubuque, IA	1.032	19
Fayetteville–Springdale, AR	1.032	19
Brownsville–Harlingen, TX	1.028	20
Anderson, SC	1.026	21
Springfield, MO	1.015	22
Dothan, AL	1.009	23
Owensboro, KY	0.994	24
Duluth, MN–WI	0.989	25
Johnstown, PA	0.979	26
Bradenton, FL	0.960	27
Bismarck, ND	0.959	28
Jackson, TN	0.944	29
New Bedford, MA	0.925	30
Anniston, AL	0.922	31
Saint Cloud, MN	0.919	32
McAllen–Edinburg–Mission, TX	0.909	33
Tampa–Saint Petersburg–Clearwater, FL	0.907	34
Altoona, PA	0.897	35
Knoxville, TN	0.891	36
Yakima, WA	0.883	37
Terre Haute, IN	0.882	38
Daytona Beach, FL	0.880	39
Burlington, NC	0.876	40
Pueblo, CO	0.868	41
Medford, OR	0.857	42
Abilene, TX	0.851	43
Ocala, FL	0.850	44
Waco, TX	0.845	45
Providence–Pawtucket–Fall River, RI–MA	0.844	46
Alexandria, LA	0.839	47
Steubenville–Weirton, OH–WV	0.836	48

Source: U.S. Bureau of the Census, Data User Services Division, *1990 Census of Population and Housing*, Summary Tape File 3C, United States Summary, CD-ROM, February 1992.

★1830★

Poverty Status of Families With Children

American Indian, Eskimo, or Aleut Female Householder, No Spouse Present, With Children Under 5 Years Old, Living Below Poverty, 1989

[Table shows the top 50 areas]

MSA	% of population	Rank
Rapid City, SD	0.103266	1
Anchorage, AK	0.075109	2
Great Falls, MT	0.061783	3
Yakima, WA	0.049782	4
Grand Forks, ND	0.049517	5

[Continued]

★1830★

American Indian, Eskimo, or Aleut Female Householder, No Spouse Present, With Children Under 5 Years Old, Living Below Poverty, 1989

[Continued]

MSA	% of population	Rank
Billings, MT	0.043203	6
Green Bay, WI	0.039570	7
Lawton, OK	0.034085	8
Sioux City, IA–NE	0.031299	9
Oklahoma City, OK	0.027012	10
Duluth, MN–WI	0.025836	11
Tucson, AZ	0.023842	12
Albuquerque, NM	0.021433	13
Fort Smith, AR–OK	0.020465	14
Reno, NV	0.018848	15
Sioux Falls, SD	0.018577	16
Chico, CA	0.018120	17
Santa Fe, NM	0.017942	18
Wichita, KS	0.017104	19
Bellingham, WA	0.016434	20
Enid, OK	0.015863	21
Salem, OR	0.015466	22
Saint Cloud, MN	0.015190	23
Saint Joseph, MO	0.014443	24
Panama City, FL	0.014174	25
Tulsa, OK	0.013823	26
Yuma, AZ	0.013097	27
Medford, OR	0.012979	28
Bangor, ME	0.012401	29
Minneapolis–Saint Paul, MN–WI	0.012337	30
Muskegon, MI	0.011951	31
Bismarck, ND	0.011929	32
Redding, CA	0.010882	33
Lincoln, NE	0.010766	34
Buffalo–Niagara Falls, NY	0.010426	35
Owensboro, KY	0.010322	36
Ocala, FL	0.010265	37
Flint, MI	0.010222	38
Bremerton, WA	0.010014	39
Seattle–Tacoma, WA	0.009847	40
Phoenix, AZ	0.009472	41
Spokane, WA	0.009409	42
Modesto, CA	0.009176	43
Sacramento, CA	0.008710	44
Eugene–Springfield, OR	0.008483	45
Visalia–Tulare–Porterville, CA	0.008335	46
Salt Lake City–Ogden, UT	0.008021	47
Salinas–Seaside–Monterey, CA	0.007592	48
Pittsfield, MA	0.007569	49
Fayetteville, NC	0.007284	50

Source: U.S. Bureau of the Census, Data User Services Division, *1990 Census of Population and Housing*, Summary Tape File 3C, United States Summary, CD-ROM, February 1992.

★1831★
Poverty Status of Families With Children

American Indian, Eskimo, or Aleut Female Householder, No Spouse Present, With Children Under 5 and 5 to 17 Years Old, Living Below Poverty, 1989

[Table shows the top 50 areas]

MSA	% of population	Rank
Yakima, WA	0.10433	1
Rapid City, SD	0.09589	2
Great Falls, MT	0.09396	3
Anchorage, AK	0.05876	4
Sioux City, IA–NE	0.05477	5
Houma–Thibodaux, LA	0.05305	6
Billings, MT	0.04497	7
Bellingham, WA	0.04461	8
Bismarck, ND	0.04294	9
Tucson, AZ	0.03794	10
Fort Smith, AR–OK	0.03695	11
Grand Forks, ND	0.03537	12
Tulsa, OK	0.03399	13
Green Bay, WI	0.03238	14
Santa Fe, NM	0.02990	15
Oklahoma City, OK	0.02847	16
Fargo–Moorhead, ND–MN	0.02740	17
Cheyenne, WY	0.02734	18
Medford, OR	0.02732	19
Lawton, OK	0.02691	20
Redding, CA	0.02312	21
Albuquerque, NM	0.02289	22
Minneapolis–Saint Paul, MN–WI	0.02289	22
La Crosse, WI	0.02247	23
Phoenix, AZ	0.01979	24
Casper, WY	0.01960	25
Duluth, MN–WI	0.01959	26
Yuma, AZ	0.01871	27
Bremerton, WA	0.01634	28
Merced, CA	0.01626	29
Fayetteville, NC	0.01530	30
Seattle–Tacoma, WA	0.01442	31
Topeka, KS	0.01429	32
Salem, OR	0.01403	33
Spokane, WA	0.01384	34
Appleton–Oshkosh–Neenah, WI	0.01333	35
Wichita Falls, TX	0.01307	36
Richland–Kennewick–Pasco, WA	0.01266	37
Omaha, NE–IA	0.01262	38
Visalia–Tulare–Porterville, CA	0.01250	39
Yuba City, CA	0.01223	40
Reno, NV	0.01217	41
Odessa, TX	0.01177	42
Corpus Christi, TX	0.01057	43
Sioux Falls, SD	0.01050	44
Sacramento, CA	0.01026	45
Manchester, NH	0.01014	46
Flint, MI	0.00999	47
Salt Lake City–Ogden, UT	0.00998	48
Fresno, CA	0.00989	49

Source: U.S. Bureau of the Census, Data User Services Division, *1990 Census of Population and Housing*, Summary Tape File 3C, United States Summary, CD-ROM, February 1992.

★1832★
Poverty Status of Families With Children

American Indian, Eskimo, or Aleut Female Householder, No Spouse Present, With Children 5 to 17 Years Old, Living Below Poverty, 1989

[Table shows the top 50 areas]

MSA	% of population	Rank
Rapid City, SD	0.17826	1
Lawton, OK	0.07445	2
Tucson, AZ	0.07303	3
Anchorage, AK	0.06671	4
Fort Smith, AR–OK	0.06651	5
Billings, MT	0.06613	6
Tulsa, OK	0.06347	7
Yakima, WA	0.06037	8
Great Falls, MT	0.05921	9
Lawrence, KS	0.05135	10
Oklahoma City, OK	0.04839	11
Green Bay, WI	0.04574	12
Houma–Thibodaux, LA	0.04430	13
Enid, OK	0.04230	14
Bismarck, ND	0.03698	15
Albuquerque, NM	0.03600	16
Casper, WY	0.03593	17
Duluth, MN–WI	0.03417	18
Fayetteville, NC	0.03023	19
Sioux City, IA–NE	0.02956	20
Bellingham, WA	0.02817	21
Burlington, VT	0.02739	22
Medford, OR	0.02732	23
Bremerton, WA	0.02688	24
Stockton, CA	0.02601	25
Redding, CA	0.02584	26
Chico, CA	0.02526	27
Flint, MI	0.02486	28
Lincoln, NE	0.02481	29
Merced, CA	0.02410	30
Minneapolis–Saint Paul, MN–WI	0.02358	31
Spokane, WA	0.02325	32
Grand Forks, ND	0.02122	33
Phoenix, AZ	0.02064	34
Eugene–Springfield, OR	0.02050	35
Fresno, CA	0.01918	36
Santa Fe, NM	0.01880	37
Wichita Falls, TX	0.01879	38
Sioux Falls, SD	0.01858	39
Kokomo, IN	0.01857	40
Amarillo, TX	0.01813	41
Richland–Kennewick–Pasco, WA	0.01800	42
Pueblo, CO	0.01788	43
Colorado Springs, CO	0.01763	44
Muskegon, MI	0.01698	45
La Crosse, WI	0.01634	46
Augusta, GA–SC	0.01613	47
Bakersfield, CA	0.01601	48
Olympia, WA	0.01551	49
Reno, NV	0.01531	50

Source: U.S. Bureau of the Census, Data User Services Division, *1990 Census of Population and Housing*, Summary Tape File 3C, United States Summary, CD-ROM, February 1992.

★1833★
Poverty Status of Families With Children

American Indian, Eskimo, or Aleut Female Householder, No Spouse Present, With Children Under 5 Years Old, Living Above Poverty, 1989

[Table shows the top 50 areas]

MSA	% of population	Rank
Anchorage, AK	0.04462	1
Lawrence, KS	0.03179	2
Yakima, WA	0.02489	3
Tulsa, OK	0.01904	4
Oklahoma City, OK	0.01846	5
Tucson, AZ	0.01814	6
Reno, NV	0.01492	7
Albuquerque, NM	0.01477	8
Sioux City, IA-NE	0.01391	9
Spokane, WA	0.01245	10
Rapid City, SD	0.01229	11
La Crosse, WI	0.01226	12
Redding, CA	0.01224	13
Pueblo, CO	0.01219	14
Bellingham, WA	0.01174	15
Duluth, MN-WI	0.01083	16
Phoenix, AZ	0.01041	17
Santa Fe, NM	0.00854	18
Decatur, IL	0.00853	19
Bangor, ME	0.00789	20
Boise, ID	0.00778	21
Great Falls, MT	0.00772	22
Longview-Marshall, TX	0.00739	23
Salt Lake City-Ogden, UT	0.00681	24
Minneapolis-Saint Paul, MN-WI	0.00674	25
Yuba City, CA	0.00652	26
Tallahassee, FL	0.00642	27
Muskegon, MI	0.00629	28
Syracuse, NY	0.00621	29
Alexandria, LA	0.00608	30
Battle Creek, MI	0.00588	31
Fort Smith, AR-OK	0.00568	32
Sacramento, CA	0.00567	33
Stockton, CA	0.00562	34
Merced, CA	0.00561	35
Pensacola, FL	0.00552	36
Chico, CA	0.00549	37
Fargo-Moorhead, ND-MN	0.00522	38
Joplin, MO	0.00519	39
Bakersfield, CA	0.00515	40
Visalia-Tulare-Porterville, CA	0.00481	41
Medford, OR	0.00478	42
Denver-Boulder, CO	0.00471	43
Salem, OR	0.00468	44
Portland-Vancouver, OR-WA	0.00460	45
Provo-Orem, UT	0.00455	46
Seattle-Tacoma, WA	0.00453	47
Elkhart-Goshen, IN	0.00448	48
Killeen-Temple, TX	0.00431	49
Steubenville-Weirton, OH-WV	0.00421	50

Source: U.S. Bureau of the Census, Data User Services Division, *1990 Census of Population and Housing,* Summary Tape File 3C, United States Summary, CD-ROM, February 1992.

★1834★
Poverty Status of Families With Children

American Indian, Eskimo, or Aleut Female Householder, No Spouse Present, With Children Under 5 and 5 to 17 Years Old, Living Above Poverty, 1989

[Table shows the top 50 areas]

MSA	% of population	Rank
Anchorage, AK	0.06009	1
Lawton, OK	0.04036	2
Yakima, WA	0.03019	3
Rapid City, SD	0.02828	4
Billings, MT	0.02292	5
Joplin, MO	0.01853	6
Fort Smith, AR-OK	0.01762	7
Albuquerque, NM	0.01644	8
Santa Fe, NM	0.01452	9
Tucson, AZ	0.01395	10
Yuba City, CA	0.01386	11
Spokane, WA	0.01328	12
Bellingham, WA	0.01252	13
Santa Barbara-Santa Maria-Lompoc, CA	0.01136	14
Salem, OR	0.01043	15
Tulsa, OK	0.01016	16
Phoenix, AZ	0.01013	17
Chico, CA	0.00933	18
Olympia, WA	0.00930	19
Lubbock, TX	0.00898	20
Redding, CA	0.00816	21
Benton Harbor, MI	0.00806	22
Green Bay, WI	0.00771	23
Oklahoma City, OK	0.00761	24
Stockton, CA	0.00728	25
Fargo-Moorhead, ND-MN	0.00718	26
Minneapolis-Saint Paul, MN-WI	0.00702	27
Eau Claire, WI	0.00654	28
Lynchburg, VA	0.00633	29
Salinas-Seaside-Monterey, CA	0.00619	30
Fayetteville-Springdale, AR	0.00617	31
San Angelo, TX	0.00609	32
Seattle-Tacoma, WA	0.00567	33
Merced, CA	0.00504	34
Visalia-Tulare-Porterville, CA	0.00481	35
Parkersburg-Marietta, WV-OH	0.00469	36
Modesto, CA	0.00459	37
Milwaukee-Racine, WI	0.00436	38
Waco, TX	0.00423	39
Bremerton, WA	0.00422	40
Pueblo, CO	0.00406	41
Champaign-Urbana-Rantoul, IL	0.00405	42
Fresno, CA	0.00390	43
Rockford, IL	0.00388	44
Greeley, CO	0.00379	45
Yuma, AZ	0.00374	46
Las Vegas, NV	0.00364	47
Sacramento, CA	0.00358	48
Enid, OK	0.00353	49
Grand Rapids, MI	0.00349	50

Source: U.S. Bureau of the Census, Data User Services Division, *1990 Census of Population and Housing,* Summary Tape File 3C, United States Summary, CD-ROM, February 1992.

★1835★
Poverty Status of Families With Children

American Indian, Eskimo, or Aleut Female Householder, No Spouse Present, With Children 5 to 17 Years Old, Living Above Poverty, 1989

[Table shows the top 50 areas]

MSA	% of population	Rank
Rapid City, SD	0.15121	1
Anchorage, AK	0.10339	2
Yakima, WA	0.07097	3
Tulsa, OK	0.06771	4
Oklahoma City, OK	0.06591	5
Albuquerque, NM	0.05639	6
Great Falls, MT	0.05535	7
Tucson, AZ	0.05068	8
Reno, NV	0.04908	9
Lawton, OK	0.04575	10
Santa Fe, NM	0.04528	11
Salem, OR	0.04496	12
Yuba City, CA	0.04485	13
Bismarck, ND	0.04175	14
Olympia, WA	0.04093	15
Enid, OK	0.03878	16
Yuma, AZ	0.03742	17
Fort Smith, AR – OK	0.03468	18
Lawrence, KS	0.03423	19
Topeka, KS	0.03230	20
Sioux City, IA – NE	0.03217	21
Merced, CA	0.03139	22
Fayetteville, NC	0.03023	23
Billings, MT	0.02821	24
Redding, CA	0.02788	25
Sacramento, CA	0.02701	26
Visalia – Tulare – Porterville, CA	0.02661	27
Decatur, AL	0.02584	28
Bremerton, WA	0.02424	29
Green Bay, WI	0.02364	30
Santa Barbara – Santa Maria – Lompoc, CA	0.02300	31
Phoenix, AZ	0.02285	32
Medford, OR	0.02254	33
Chico, CA	0.02251	34
Duluth, MN – WI	0.02209	35
Pueblo, CO	0.02194	36
Bellingham, WA	0.02191	37
Bangor, ME	0.02142	38
Bakersfield, CA	0.02116	39
Seattle – Tacoma, WA	0.02091	40
Portland – Vancouver, OR – WA	0.01942	41
Sioux Falls, SD	0.01858	42
Joplin, MO	0.01853	43
Tyler, TX	0.01784	44
Las Vegas, NV	0.01699	45
Muskegon, MI	0.01698	46
Fayetteville – Springdale, AR	0.01675	47
Wichita, KS	0.01669	48
Syracuse, NY	0.01652	49
Cheyenne, WY	0.01641	50

Source: U.S. Bureau of the Census, Data User Services Division, *1990 Census of Population and Housing*, Summary Tape File 3C, United States Summary, CD-ROM, February 1992.

★1836★
Poverty Status of Families With Children

American Indian, Eskimo, or Aleut Male Householder, No Spouse Present, With Children Under 5 Years Old, Living Below Poverty, 1989

[Table shows the top 50 areas]

MSA	% of population	Rank
Enid, OK	0.026439	1
Duluth, MN – WI	0.016252	2
Fayetteville – Springdale, AR	0.012345	3
Yakima, WA	0.011122	4
Tucson, AZ	0.010946	5
Pueblo, CO	0.009752	6
Albuquerque, NM	0.009364	7
Great Falls, MT	0.009010	8
Olympia, WA	0.008683	9
Bismarck, ND	0.008350	10
Grand Forks, ND	0.007074	11
Fort Smith, AR – OK	0.006822	12
Anchorage, AK	0.006627	13
Yuma, AZ	0.006548	14
Elkhart – Goshen, IN	0.005762	15
Green Bay, WI	0.005653	16
Panama City, FL	0.005512	17
Fort Pierce, FL	0.004780	18
Salinas – Seaside – Monterey, CA	0.004780	18
Bellingham, WA	0.004696	19
Battle Creek, MI	0.004412	20
Fort Collins – Loveland, CO	0.004298	21
Bryan – College Station, TX	0.004103	22
Redding, CA	0.004081	23
Yuba City, CA	0.004077	24
Oklahoma City, OK	0.003755	25
Salt Lake City – Ogden, UT	0.003451	26
Phoenix, AZ	0.003440	27
Bradenton, FL	0.003306	28
Chico, CA	0.003295	29
Wichita Falls, TX	0.003269	30
Lansing – East Lansing, MI	0.003236	31
Reno, NV	0.002749	32
Houma – Thibodaux, LA	0.002735	33
Santa Barbara – Santa Maria – Lompoc, CA	0.002706	34
Las Vegas, NV	0.002563	35
Santa Fe, NM	0.002563	35
Denver – Boulder, CO	0.002272	36
Springfield, MA	0.002266	37
Spokane, WA	0.002214	38
Tulsa, OK	0.002116	39
Des Moines, IA	0.002036	40
Minneapolis – Saint Paul, MN – WI	0.001989	41
Cumberland, MD – WV	0.001968	42
Buffalo – Niagara Falls, NY	0.001682	43
Wichita, KS	0.001649	44
Colorado Springs, CO	0.001511	45
Fresno, CA	0.001498	46
Portland – Vancouver, OR – WA	0.001489	47
Bakersfield, CA	0.001288	48

Source: U.S. Bureau of the Census, Data User Services Division, *1990 Census of Population and Housing*, Summary Tape File 3C, United States Summary, CD-ROM, February 1992.

★ 1837 ★

Poverty Status of Families With Children

American Indian, Eskimo, or Aleut Male Householder, No Spouse Present, With Children Under 5 and 5 to 17 Years Old, Living Below Poverty, 1989

[Table shows the top 50 areas]

MSA	% of population	Rank
Houma – Thibodaux, LA	0.022971	1
Rapid City, SD	0.015982	2
Saint Cloud, MN	0.010999	3
Yakima, WA	0.010592	4
Sioux Falls, SD	0.010500	5
Tucson, AZ	0.009447	6
Enid, OK	0.008813	7
Anchorage, AK	0.008395	8
Panama City, FL	0.007874	9
Sioux City, IA – NE	0.006955	10
Waco, TX	0.006345	11
Fort Smith, AR – OK	0.006253	12
Albuquerque, NM	0.006242	13
Phoenix, AZ	0.004759	14
Duluth, MN – WI	0.004584	15
Merced, CA	0.004484	16
Billings, MT	0.004408	17
Tulsa, OK	0.004232	18
Ocala, FL	0.004106	19
Yuma, AZ	0.003742	20
Eau Claire, WI	0.003635	21
Fort Myers – Cape Coral, Fl	0.002984	22
Flint, MI	0.002555	23
Melbourne – Titusville – Palm Bay, FL	0.002506	24
Oklahoma City, OK	0.002503	25
Bellingham, WA	0.002348	26
Salem, OR	0.001798	27
Rockford, IL	0.001762	28
Salinas – Seaside – Monterey, CA	0.001687	29
Bakersfield, CA	0.001656	30
Visalia – Tulare – Porterville, CA	0.001603	31
Spokane, WA	0.001384	32
Minneapolis – Saint Paul, MN – WI	0.001299	33
Olympia, WA	0.001240	34
Salt Lake City – Ogden, UT	0.001212	35
Reno, NV	0.001178	36
Cincinnati – Hamilton, OH – KY – IN	0.001089	37
Green Bay, WI	0.001028	38
Appleton – Oshkosh – Neenah, WI	0.000952	39
Syracuse, NY	0.000909	40
El Paso, TX	0.000845	41
Springfield, MO	0.000831	42
Wichita, KS	0.000824	43
Denver – Boulder, CO	0.000757	44
Los Angeles – Anaheim – Riverside, CA	0.000688	45
San Diego, CA	0.000560	46
New Orleans, LA	0.000484	47
Sacramento, CA	0.000405	48
Milwaukee – Racine, WI	0.000373	49
Atlanta, GA	0.000353	50

Source: U.S. Bureau of the Census, Data User Services Division, *1990 Census of Population and Housing*, Summary Tape File 3C, United States Summary, CD-ROM, February 1992.

★ 1838 ★

Poverty Status of Families With Children

American Indian, Eskimo, or Aleut Male Householder, No Spouse Present, With Children 5 to 17 Years Old, Living Below Poverty, 1989

[Table shows the top 50 areas]

MSA	% of population	Rank
Tucson, AZ	0.015295	1
Fort Smith, AR – OK	0.011938	2
Houma – Thibodaux, LA	0.011485	3
Decatur, AL	0.011402	4
Lawton, OK	0.010764	5
Albuquerque, NM	0.008115	6
Yakima, WA	0.007944	7
Panama City, FL	0.007874	8
Greeley, CO	0.007586	9
Redding, CA	0.007481	10
Fort Collins – Loveland, CO	0.006984	11
Medford, OR	0.006831	12
Joplin, MO	0.006671	13
Chico, CA	0.006589	14
Bellingham, WA	0.006261	15
Billings, MT	0.006172	16
Rapid City, SD	0.006147	17
Santa Fe, NM	0.005981	18
Fargo – Moorhead, ND – MN	0.005871	19
Bangor, ME	0.005637	20
Jackson, MI	0.005342	21
Anchorage, AK	0.005302	22
Enid, OK	0.005288	23
Monroe, LA	0.004923	24
Oklahoma City, OK	0.004797	25
Stockton, CA	0.004785	26
Bremerton, WA	0.004744	27
Spokane, WA	0.004704	28
Salem, OR	0.004676	29
Tulsa, OK	0.004655	30
Burlington, NC	0.004621	31
Olympia, WA	0.004341	32
Muncie, IN	0.004179	33
Portland, ME	0.004177	34
Sioux Falls, SD	0.004038	35
Dothan, AL	0.003818	36
Phoenix, AZ	0.003770	37
Yuma, AZ	0.003742	38
Topeka, KS	0.003727	39
South Bend – Mishawaka, IN	0.003643	40
Kalamazoo, MI	0.003581	41
Salt Lake City – Ogden, UT	0.003264	42
Lansing – East Lansing, MI	0.003236	43
Montgomery, AL	0.003077	44
Portland – Vancouver, OR – WA	0.003045	45
Modesto, CA	0.002969	46
Battle Creek, MI	0.002942	47
Seattle – Tacoma, WA	0.002852	48
Bakersfield, CA	0.002760	49
Roanoke, VA	0.002673	50

Source: U.S. Bureau of the Census, Data User Services Division, *1990 Census of Population and Housing*, Summary Tape File 3C, United States Summary, CD-ROM, February 1992.

★1839★
Poverty Status of Families With Children

American Indian, Eskimo, or Aleut Male Householder, No Spouse Present, With Children Under 5 Years Old, Living Above Poverty, 1989

[Table shows the top 50 areas]

MSA	% of population	Rank
Anchorage, AK	0.03137	1
Great Falls, MT	0.03089	2
Redding, CA	0.01564	3
Albuquerque, NM	0.01269	4
Enid, OK	0.01234	5
Rapid City, SD	0.01229	6
La Crosse, WI	0.01226	7
Bellingham, WA	0.01096	8
Lafayette – West Lafayette, IN	0.01072	9
San Angelo, TX	0.01016	10
Bakersfield, CA	0.01012	11
Gadsden, AL	0.01002	12
Fargo – Moorhead, ND – MN	0.00978	13
Elmira, NY	0.00945	14
Houma – Thibodaux, LA	0.00875	15
Benton Harbor, MI	0.00868	16
Phoenix, AZ	0.00844	17
Olympia, WA	0.00806	18
Mansfield, OH	0.00793	19
Panama City, FL	0.00787	20
Santa Fe, NM	0.00769	21
Lawton, OK	0.00718	22
Richland – Kennewick – Pasco, WA	0.00667	23
Sioux Falls, SD	0.00646	24
Janesville – Beloit, WI	0.00645	25
Champaign – Urbana – Rantoul, IL	0.00636	26
Appleton – Oshkosh – Neenah, WI	0.00571	27
Tulsa, OK	0.00564	28
Biloxi – Gulfport, MS	0.00507	29
Seattle – Tacoma, WA	0.00504	30
Waterbury, CT	0.00496	31
Salt Lake City – Ogden, UT	0.00457	32
Fresno, CA	0.00449	33
Las Vegas, NV	0.00445	34
Billings, MT	0.00441	35
Flint, MI	0.00441	35
Des Moines, IA	0.00433	36
Salem, OR	0.00432	37
Tucson, AZ	0.00390	38
Greeley, CO	0.00379	39
Baton Rouge, LA	0.00360	40
Charleston, WV	0.00359	41
Brownsville – Harlingen, TX	0.00346	42
Provo – Orem, UT	0.00341	43
Modesto, CA	0.00324	44
Oklahoma City, OK	0.00302	45
Peoria, IL	0.00295	46
Yakima, WA	0.00265	47
Sacramento, CA	0.00257	48
Lansing – East Lansing, MI	0.00254	49

Source: U.S. Bureau of the Census, Data User Services Division, *1990 Census of Population and Housing,* Summary Tape File 3C, United States Summary, CD-ROM, February 1992.

★1840★
Poverty Status of Families With Children

American Indian, Eskimo, or Aleut Male Householder, No Spouse Present, With Children Under 5 and 5 to 17 Years Old, Living Above Poverty, 1989

[Table shows the top 50 areas]

MSA	% of population	Rank
Pittsfield, MA	0.013876	1
Albuquerque, NM	0.012901	2
Reno, NV	0.011387	3
Green Bay, WI	0.010278	4
Eugene – Springfield, OR	0.010251	5
Lawton, OK	0.009867	6
Yakima, WA	0.009533	7
Wichita Falls, TX	0.008989	8
Great Falls, MT	0.007723	9
Chico, CA	0.007687	10
Visalia – Tulare – Porterville, CA	0.007053	11
Santa Fe, NM	0.006835	12
Tucson, AZ	0.006748	13
Monroe, LA	0.006330	14
Redding, CA	0.006121	15
Wilmington, NC	0.005820	16
Anchorage, AK	0.005302	17
Tulsa, OK	0.004937	18
Salem, OR	0.004676	19
Phoenix, AZ	0.003911	20
Bakersfield, CA	0.003864	21
Columbus, GA – AL	0.003703	22
Yuba City, CA	0.003261	23
Bremerton, WA	0.003162	24
Portsmouth – Dover – Rochester, NH – ME	0.003129	25
Savannah, GA	0.002885	26
Appleton – Oshkosh – Neenah, WI	0.002856	27
Lansing – East Lansing, MI	0.002773	28
Medford, OR	0.002732	29
Fort Myers – Cape Coral, Fl	0.002686	30
Fayetteville, NC	0.002549	31
Olympia, WA	0.002481	32
Minneapolis – Saint Paul, MN – WI	0.002435	33
Bellingham, WA	0.002348	34
Battle Creek, MI	0.002206	35
Portland – Vancouver, OR – WA	0.002165	36
Seattle – Tacoma, WA	0.002071	37
Salt Lake City – Ogden, UT	0.002052	38
Las Vegas, NV	0.001888	39
Fresno, CA	0.001798	40
San Diego, CA	0.001761	41
Little Rock – North Little Rock, AR	0.001754	42
Grand Rapids, MI	0.001598	43
Columbia, SC	0.001544	44
Pensacola, FL	0.001452	45
Lancaster, PA	0.001419	46
Sacramento, CA	0.001418	47
Modesto, CA	0.001349	48
Longview – Marshall, TX	0.001231	49
Bismarck, ND	0.001193	50

Source: U.S. Bureau of the Census, Data User Services Division, *1990 Census of Population and Housing,* Summary Tape File 3C, United States Summary, CD-ROM, February 1992.

★1841★

Poverty Status of Families With Children

American Indian, Eskimo, or Aleut Male Householder, No Spouse Present, With Children 5 to 17 Years Old, Living Above Poverty, 1989

[Table shows the top 50 areas]

MSA	% of population	Rank
Bellingham, WA	0.02739	1
Great Falls, MT	0.02446	2
Fort Smith, AR–OK	0.02388	3
Tucson, AZ	0.02369	4
Tulsa, OK	0.02341	5
Rapid City, SD	0.02336	6
Yakima, WA	0.02118	7
Albuquerque, NM	0.02060	8
Oklahoma City, OK	0.01909	9
Bangor, ME	0.01804	10
Spokane, WA	0.01799	11
Kokomo, IN	0.01650	12
Tuscaloosa, AL	0.01528	13
Burlington, NC	0.01479	14
Richland–Kennewick–Pasco, WA	0.01466	15
Santa Fe, NM	0.01452	16
Salem, OR	0.01403	17
Sioux City, IA–NE	0.01391	18
Chico, CA	0.01373	19
Yuma, AZ	0.01310	20
Modesto, CA	0.01268	21
Muskegon, MI	0.01258	22
Duluth, MN–WI	0.01250	23
Santa Barbara–Santa Maria–Lompoc, CA	0.01245	24
Anchorage, AK	0.01237	25
Enid, OK	0.01234	26
Yuba City, CA	0.01223	27
Bremerton, WA	0.01212	28
Pine Bluff, AR	0.01053	29
Fort Collins–Loveland, CO	0.01021	30
Redding, CA	0.01020	31
Cheyenne, WY	0.00957	32
Olympia, WA	0.00930	33
Fargo–Moorhead, ND–MN	0.00913	34
Medford, OR	0.00888	35
Jamestown–Dunkirk, NY	0.00846	36
Las Vegas, NV	0.00836	37
Billings, MT	0.00794	38
Green Bay, WI	0.00771	39
Seattle–Tacoma, WA	0.00762	40
Gainesville, FL	0.00735	41
Elkhart–Goshen, IN	0.00704	42
Jackson, MI	0.00668	43
El Paso, TX	0.00659	44
Pueblo, CO	0.00650	45
Janesville–Beloit, WI	0.00645	46
Davenport–Rock Island–Moline, IA–IL	0.00627	47
Phoenix, AZ	0.00622	48
Decatur, AL	0.00608	49
Colorado Springs, CO	0.00605	50

Source: U.S. Bureau of the Census, Data User Services Division, *1990 Census of Population and Housing,* Summary Tape File 3C, United States Summary, CD-ROM, February 1992.

★1842★

Poverty Status of Families With Children

American Indian, Eskimo, or Aleut Married Couples With Children Under 5 Years Old, Living Below Poverty, 1989

[Table shows the top 50 areas]

MSA	% of population	Rank
Rapid City, SD	0.051633	1
Tulsa, OK	0.035686	2
Yuba City, CA	0.035061	3
Great Falls, MT	0.025743	4
Fort Smith, AR–OK	0.022739	5
Houma–Thibodaux, LA	0.021330	6
Billings, MT	0.015870	7
Tucson, AZ	0.014695	8
Oklahoma City, OK	0.014392	9
Lawrence, KS	0.013448	10
Anchorage, AK	0.013255	11
Chico, CA	0.013178	12
Fort Collins–Loveland, CO	0.012357	13
Sherman–Denison, TX	0.011576	14
Springfield, IL	0.011079	15
Albuquerque, NM	0.009988	16
Bellingham, WA	0.009391	17
Pensacola, FL	0.009291	18
Phoenix, AZ	0.008105	19
Colorado Springs, CO	0.008060	20
Bangor, ME	0.007891	21
Naples, FL	0.007890	22
Reno, NV	0.007853	23
Visalia–Tulare–Porterville, CA	0.007694	24
Longview–Marshall, TX	0.007388	25
Jacksonville, NC	0.007341	26
Bismarck, ND	0.007157	27
Bryan–College Station, TX	0.006565	28
Amarillo, TX	0.006398	29
Lawton, OK	0.006279	30
Duluth, MN–WI	0.006251	31
Stockton, CA	0.006242	32
Green Bay, WI	0.006167	33
Texarkana, TX–Texarkana, AR	0.005827	34
Provo–Orem, UT	0.005691	35
Pueblo, CO	0.005689	36
Terre Haute, IN	0.005351	37
Yakima, WA	0.005296	38
Fargo–Moorhead, ND–MN	0.005219	39
Sioux City, IA–NE	0.005217	40
San Angelo, TX	0.005078	41
Binghamton, NY	0.004915	42
Sheboygan, WI	0.004813	43
Albany, GA	0.004442	44
Modesto, CA	0.004318	45
Austin, TX	0.004222	46
Bremerton, WA	0.004216	47
Elmira, NY	0.004202	48
Clarksville–Hopkinsville, TN–KY	0.004131	49
Killeen–Temple, TX	0.003917	50

Source: U.S. Bureau of the Census, Data User Services Division, *1990 Census of Population and Housing,* Summary Tape File 3C, United States Summary, CD-ROM, February 1992.

★1843★

Poverty Status of Families With Children

American Indian, Eskimo, or Aleut Married Couples With Children Under 5 and 5 to 17 Years Old, Living Below Poverty, 1989

[Table shows the top 50 areas]

MSA	% of population	Rank
Houma – Thibodaux, LA	0.11431	1
Yakima, WA	0.06355	2
Great Falls, MT	0.05149	3
Fort Smith, AR – OK	0.04207	4
Tucson, AZ	0.03554	5
Tulsa, OK	0.03216	6
Bismarck, ND	0.02982	7
Billings, MT	0.02910	8
Albuquerque, NM	0.02830	9
Las Cruces, NM	0.02509	10
Cheyenne, WY	0.02461	11
Bellingham, WA	0.02426	12
Grand Forks, ND	0.02264	13
Oklahoma City, OK	0.02180	14
Saint Joseph, MO	0.02167	15
Rapid City, SD	0.01967	16
Anchorage, AK	0.01767	17
Sioux City, IA – NE	0.01652	18
Lawton, OK	0.01615	19
Phoenix, AZ	0.01423	20
Midland, TX	0.01407	21
Duluth, MN – WI	0.01333	22
Chico, CA	0.01318	23
Enid, OK	0.01234	24
Redding, CA	0.01224	25
Appleton – Oshkosh – Neenah, WI	0.01111	26
Green Bay, WI	0.01079	27
Sherman – Denison, TX	0.01052	28
Bremerton, WA	0.01001	29
Wichita, KS	0.00969	30
Alexandria, LA	0.00912	31
Bangor, ME	0.00902	32
Sioux Falls, SD	0.00888	33
Rochester, MN	0.00845	34
Odessa, TX	0.00841	35
Yuba City, CA	0.00815	36
Pensacola, FL	0.00813	37
Columbia, MO	0.00801	38
Panama City, FL	0.00787	39
Amarillo, TX	0.00746	40
Olympia, WA	0.00744	41
Naples, FL	0.00723	42
Fort Collins – Loveland, CO	0.00698	43
Owensboro, KY	0.00688	44
Boise, ID	0.00680	45
Joplin, MO	0.00667	46
Stockton, CA	0.00666	47
Fargo – Moorhead, ND – MN	0.00652	48
Lima, OH	0.00648	49
Visalia – Tulare – Porterville, CA	0.00641	50

Source: U.S. Bureau of the Census, Data User Services Division, *1990 Census of Population and Housing,* Summary Tape File 3C, United States Summary, CD-ROM, February 1992.

★1844★

Poverty Status of Families With Children

American Indian, Eskimo, or Aleut Married Couples With Children 5 to 17 Years Old, Living Below Poverty, 1989

[Table shows the top 50 areas]

MSA	% of population	Rank
Houma – Thibodaux, LA	0.07329	1
Fort Smith, AR – OK	0.06765	2
Lawton, OK	0.04664	3
Tulsa, OK	0.04344	4
Bellingham, WA	0.03130	5
Oklahoma City, OK	0.03077	6
Tucson, AZ	0.03014	7
Great Falls, MT	0.02960	8
Yakima, WA	0.02913	9
Grand Forks, ND	0.02547	10
Duluth, MN – WI	0.02084	11
Lawrence, KS	0.02078	12
Billings, MT	0.02028	13
Bismarck, ND	0.02028	13
Longview – Marshall, TX	0.01909	14
Decatur, AL	0.01748	15
Albuquerque, NM	0.01727	16
Florence, AL	0.01599	17
Odessa, TX	0.01598	18
Alexandria, LA	0.01596	19
Medford, OR	0.01503	20
Yuma, AZ	0.01497	21
Rapid City, SD	0.01475	22
Springfield, MO	0.01413	23
Pensacola, FL	0.01394	24
Visalia – Tulare – Porterville, CA	0.01379	25
Tyler, TX	0.01322	26
Chico, CA	0.01318	27
Fayetteville, NC	0.01275	28
Fayetteville – Springdale, AR	0.01234	29
Sioux Falls, SD	0.01212	30
McAllen – Edinburg – Mission, TX	0.01173	31
Abilene, TX	0.01170	32
Pine Bluff, AR	0.01170	32
Pueblo, CO	0.01138	33
Dothan, AL	0.01069	34
Provo – Orem, UT	0.01024	35
Anchorage, AK	0.01016	36
Bangor, ME	0.00902	37
Boise, ID	0.00826	38
Bremerton, WA	0.00791	39
Panama City, FL	0.00787	40
Pascagoula, MS	0.00781	41
Phoenix, AZ	0.00768	42
Muskegon, MI	0.00755	43
Reno, NV	0.00746	44
Battle Creek, MI	0.00735	45
Jackson, MI	0.00735	45
Fresno, CA	0.00719	46
San Angelo, TX	0.00711	47

Source: U.S. Bureau of the Census, Data User Services Division, *1990 Census of Population and Housing,* Summary Tape File 3C, United States Summary, CD-ROM, February 1992.

★1845★

Poverty Status of Families With Children

American Indian, Eskimo, or Aleut Married Couples With Children Under 5 Years Old, Living Above Poverty, 1989

[Table shows the top 50 areas]

MSA	% of population	Rank
Tulsa, OK	0.1144	1
Anchorage, AK	0.1012	2
Fort Smith, AR–OK	0.0938	3
Oklahoma City, OK	0.0701	4
Rapid City, SD	0.0664	5
Lawton, OK	0.0646	6
Redding, CA	0.0510	7
Grand Forks, ND	0.0439	8
Jacksonville, NC	0.0414	9
Medford, OR	0.0410	10
Lawrence, KS	0.0391	11
Houma–Thibodaux, LA	0.0377	12
Chico, CA	0.0368	13
Joplin, MO	0.0363	14
Casper, WY	0.0359	15
Midland, TX	0.0356	16
Bellingham, WA	0.0352	17
Sherman–Denison, TX	0.0347	18
Yuba City, CA	0.0334	19
Reno, NV	0.0326	20
Albuquerque, NM	0.0308	21
Salinas–Seaside–Monterey, CA	0.0292	22
Greeley, CO	0.0288	23
Panama City, FL	0.0283	24
Fayetteville, NC	0.0280	25
Bremerton, WA	0.0274	26
Spokane, WA	0.0271	27
Bakersfield, CA	0.0265	28
Santa Fe, NM	0.0265	28
Yakima, WA	0.0260	29
Killeen–Temple, TX	0.0255	30
Tucson, AZ	0.0253	31
Phoenix, AZ	0.0245	32
Las Vegas, NV	0.0244	33
Billings, MT	0.0238	34
Green Bay, WI	0.0226	35
Muskegon, MI	0.0226	35
San Angelo, TX	0.0223	36
Colorado Springs, CO	0.0214	37
Seattle–Tacoma, WA	0.0213	38
Enid, OK	0.0212	39
Fayetteville–Springdale, AR	0.0212	39
Alexandria, LA	0.0205	40
Melbourne–Titusville–Palm Bay, FL	0.0203	41
Salem, OR	0.0201	42
Merced, CA	0.0196	43
Yuma, AZ	0.0196	43
Jackson, MI	0.0194	44
Lakeland–Winter Haven, FL	0.0190	45
Modesto, CA	0.0189	46

Source: U.S. Bureau of the Census, Data User Services Division, *1990 Census of Population and Housing,* Summary Tape File 3C, United States Summary, CD-ROM, February 1992.

★1846★

Poverty Status of Families With Children

American Indian, Eskimo, or Aleut Married Couples With Children 5 to 17 Years Old, Living Above Poverty, 1989

[Table shows the top 50 areas]

MSA	% of population	Rank
Tulsa, OK	0.3511	1
Fort Smith, AR–OK	0.2450	2
Oklahoma City, OK	0.2350	3
Decatur, AL	0.2318	4
Anchorage, AK	0.2068	5
Lawton, OK	0.2027	6
Houma–Thibodaux, LA	0.1592	7
Albuquerque, NM	0.1577	8
Rapid City, SD	0.1451	9
Yakima, WA	0.1425	10
Great Falls, MT	0.1326	11
Lawrence, KS	0.1235	12
Billings, MT	0.1234	13
Redding, CA	0.1183	14
Grand Forks, ND	0.1160	15
Bremerton, WA	0.1001	16
Yuba City, CA	0.0978	17
Fayetteville–Springdale, AR	0.0961	18
Joplin, MO	0.0912	19
Enid, OK	0.0899	20
Olympia, WA	0.0899	20
Bellingham, WA	0.0869	21
Cheyenne, WY	0.0793	22
Bakersfield, CA	0.0771	23
Reno, NV	0.0762	24
Santa Fe, NM	0.0760	25
Sherman–Denison, TX	0.0747	26
Pensacola, FL	0.0720	27
Colorado Springs, CO	0.0690	28
Medford, OR	0.0676	29
Stockton, CA	0.0649	30
Tucson, AZ	0.0628	31
Sacramento, CA	0.0623	32
Eugene–Springfield, OR	0.0622	33
Panama City, FL	0.0591	34
Chico, CA	0.0582	35
Bangor, ME	0.0575	36
Amarillo, TX	0.0565	37
Topeka, KS	0.0565	37
Fayetteville, NC	0.0557	38
Modesto, CA	0.0540	39
Huntsville, AL	0.0536	40
Springfield, MO	0.0532	41
Fresno, CA	0.0529	42
Salem, OR	0.0529	42
Salinas–Seaside–Monterey, CA	0.0529	42
Texarkana, TX–Texarkana, AR	0.0524	43
Mobile, AL	0.0522	44
Phoenix, AZ	0.0510	45
Wichita, KS	0.0507	46

Source: U.S. Bureau of the Census, Data User Services Division, *1990 Census of Population and Housing,* Summary Tape File 3C, United States Summary, CD-ROM, February 1992.

★1847★
Poverty Status of Families With Children
American Indian, Eskimo, or Aleut Married Couples With Children Under 5 and 5 to 17 Years Old, Living Above Poverty, 1989

[Table shows the top 50 areas]

MSA	% of population	Rank
Tulsa, OK	0.12159	1
Rapid City, SD	0.11925	2
Anchorage, AK	0.11311	3
Oklahoma City, OK	0.08938	4
Enid, OK	0.08284	5
Albuquerque, NM	0.06700	6
Fort Smith, AR–OK	0.05969	7
Houma–Thibodaux, LA	0.05907	8
Lawton, OK	0.05830	9
Santa Fe, NM	0.05724	10
Yakima, WA	0.05720	11
Redding, CA	0.05373	12
Bellingham, WA	0.05165	13
Decatur, AL	0.05093	14
Billings, MT	0.04761	15
Reno, NV	0.04751	16
Fayetteville, NC	0.04625	17
Great Falls, MT	0.04119	18
Olympia, WA	0.04093	19
Visalia–Tulare–Porterville, CA	0.03943	20
Medford, OR	0.03894	21
Fayetteville–Springdale, AR	0.03880	22
Duluth, MN–WI	0.03875	23
Amarillo, TX	0.03679	24
Sherman–Denison, TX	0.03368	25
Phoenix, AZ	0.03214	26
Abilene, TX	0.03176	27
Bismarck, ND	0.02982	28
Fresno, CA	0.02876	29
Salem, OR	0.02734	30
Sioux City, IA–NE	0.02695	31
Lawrence, KS	0.02690	32
Wichita, KS	0.02638	33
Bangor, ME	0.02593	34
Sacramento, CA	0.02532	35
Topeka, KS	0.02485	36
La Crosse, WI	0.02451	37
Green Bay, WI	0.02415	38
Tucson, AZ	0.02414	39
Bakersfield, CA	0.02392	40
Eugene–Springfield, OR	0.02368	41
Provo–Orem, UT	0.02352	42
Las Vegas, NV	0.02212	43
Chico, CA	0.02196	44
Joplin, MO	0.02150	45
Salt Lake City–Ogden, UT	0.02126	46
Appleton–Oshkosh–Neenah, WI	0.02094	47
Stockton, CA	0.02081	48
Bremerton, WA	0.02056	49
Florence, AL	0.02056	49

Source: U.S. Bureau of the Census, Data User Services Division, *1990 Census of Population and Housing*, Summary Tape File 3C, United States Summary, CD-ROM, February 1992.

★1848★
Poverty Status of Families With Children
Asian or Pacific Islander Female Householder With Children Under 5 Years Old, Living Below Poverty, 1989

[Table shows the top 50 areas]

MSA	% of population	Rank
Honolulu, HI	0.07067	1
Stockton, CA	0.03558	2
Yuba City, CA	0.02283	3
Merced, CA	0.02130	4
Olympia, WA	0.01861	5
Jacksonville, NC	0.01802	6
Rapid City, SD	0.01598	7
Sioux Falls, SD	0.01292	8
San Francisco–Oakland–San Jose, CA	0.01262	9
Lawton, OK	0.01256	10
Sacramento, CA	0.01249	11
Rochester, MN	0.01221	12
Seattle–Tacoma, WA	0.01219	13
Panama City, FL	0.01181	14
San Diego, CA	0.01181	14
Clarksville–Hopkinsville, TN–KY	0.01180	15
Fresno, CA	0.01109	16
Bremerton, WA	0.01107	17
Redding, CA	0.01088	18
La Crosse, WI	0.01021	19
Colorado Springs, CO	0.00957	20
Santa Fe, NM	0.00940	21
Santa Barbara–Santa Maria–Lompoc, CA	0.00866	22
Danville, VA	0.00828	23
Providence–Pawtucket–Fall River, RI–MA	0.00815	24
San Angelo, TX	0.00813	25
Bloomington–Normal, IL	0.00774	26
Los Angeles–Anaheim–Riverside, CA	0.00761	27
Chico, CA	0.00714	28
Charlottesville, VA	0.00686	29
Medford, OR	0.00683	30
Fitchburg–Leominster, MA	0.00681	31
Joplin, MO	0.00667	32
Iowa City, IA	0.00624	33
Reading, PA	0.00624	33
Fayetteville, NC	0.00619	34
Greeley, CO	0.00607	35
Portland–Vancouver, OR–WA	0.00582	36
State College, PA	0.00565	37
Minneapolis–Saint Paul, MN–WI	0.00560	38
Fort Walton Beach, FL	0.00556	39
Tucson, AZ	0.00525	40
Modesto, CA	0.00513	41
Bakersfield, CA	0.00497	42
Bloomington, IN	0.00459	43
Wichita, KS	0.00453	44
Worcester, MA	0.00435	45
Boston–Lawrence–Salem, MA–NH	0.00434	46

[Continued]

★1848★

Asian or Pacific Islander Female Householder With Children Under 5 Years Old, Living Below Poverty, 1989

[Continued]

MSA	% of population	Rank
Las Vegas, NV	0.00432	47
Beaumont – Port Arthur, TX	0.00415	48

Source: U.S. Bureau of the Census, Data User Services Division, *1990 Census of Population and Housing,* Summary Tape File 3C, United States Summary, CD-ROM, February 1992.

★1849★

Poverty Status of Families With Children

Asian or Pacific Islander Female Householder, No Spouse Present, With Children Under 5 and 5 to 17, Living Below Poverty, 1989

[Table shows the top 50 areas]

MSA	% of population	Rank
Honolulu, HI	0.123052	1
Fresno, CA	0.042547	2
Stockton, CA	0.039115	3
Rochester, MN	0.032873	4
Modesto, CA	0.023210	5
Seattle – Tacoma, WA	0.021570	6
Merced, CA	0.020179	7
San Francisco – Oakland – San Jose, CA	0.017527	8
Yuba City, CA	0.017123	9
Sacramento, CA	0.016677	10
Green Bay, WI	0.016444	11
Chico, CA	0.015924	12
San Diego, CA	0.015692	13
Minneapolis – Saint Paul, MN – WI	0.015137	14
Eau Claire, WI	0.014541	15
Richland – Kennewick – Pasco, WA	0.012664	16
Boston – Lawrence – Salem, MA – NH	0.011602	17
Wausau, WI	0.011265	18
Worcester, MA	0.010985	19
Houma – Thibodaux, LA	0.010938	20
Portland – Vancouver, OR – WA	0.010894	21
Providence – Pawtucket – Fall River, RI – MA	0.010600	22
Visalia – Tulare – Porterville, CA	0.010259	23
La Crosse, WI	0.010214	24
Los Angeles – Anaheim – Riverside, CA	0.010033	25
Lawton, OK	0.009867	26
Fort Walton Beach, FL	0.009042	27
Great Falls, MT	0.009010	28
Bakersfield, CA	0.008832	29
Champaign – Urbana – Rantoul, IL	0.008669	30
Panama City, FL	0.008662	31
Jacksonville, NC	0.008009	32
Lancaster, PA	0.007332	33

[Continued]

★1849★

Asian or Pacific Islander Female Householder, No Spouse Present, With Children Under 5 and 5 to 17, Living Below Poverty, 1989

[Continued]

MSA	% of population	Rank
Lubbock, TX	0.007187	34
Mobile, AL	0.007129	35
Olympia, WA	0.006822	36
Salinas – Seaside – Monterey, CA	0.006748	37
Wichita Falls, TX	0.006537	38
Wichita, KS	0.006182	39
Pensacola, FL	0.006097	40
Houston – Galveston – Brazoria, TX	0.005578	41
Lake Charles, LA	0.005353	42
Dothan, AL	0.005345	43
Madison, WI	0.005176	44
Killeen – Temple, TX	0.005092	45
Topeka, KS	0.004970	46
Fitchburg – Leominster, MA	0.004864	47
Anderson, IN	0.004592	48
Biloxi – Gulfport, MS	0.004566	49
Columbia, MO	0.004449	50

Source: U.S. Bureau of the Census, Data User Services Division, *1990 Census of Population and Housing,* Summary Tape File 3C, United States Summary, CD-ROM, February 1992.

★1850★

Poverty Status of Families With Children

Asian or Pacific Islander Female Householder, No Spouse Present, With Children 5 to 17 Years Old, Living Below Poverty, 1989

[Table shows the top 50 areas]

MSA	% of population	Rank
Honolulu, HI	0.14709	1
Stockton, CA	0.05056	2
Killeen – Temple, TX	0.04818	3
Fresno, CA	0.04659	4
Merced, CA	0.04484	5
Jacksonville, NC	0.03671	6
Sioux City, IA – NE	0.03652	7
Cheyenne, WY	0.03555	8
Seattle – Tacoma, WA	0.03513	9
Chico, CA	0.03459	10
Yuba City, CA	0.03425	11
Modesto, CA	0.03104	12
San Francisco – Oakland – San Jose, CA	0.03098	13
San Diego, CA	0.02978	14
Grand Forks, ND	0.02971	15
Lawton, OK	0.02960	16
Biloxi – Gulfport, MS	0.02892	17
Sacramento, CA	0.02788	18
Bryan – College Station, TX	0.02708	19
Visalia – Tulare – Porterville, CA	0.02661	20

[Continued]

★1850★

Asian or Pacific Islander Female Householder, No Spouse Present, With Children 5 to 17 Years Old, Living Below Poverty, 1989
[Continued]

MSA	% of population	Rank
Green Bay, WI	0.02621	21
Los Angeles – Anaheim – Riverside, CA	0.02430	22
Olympia, WA	0.02357	23
Sheboygan, WI	0.02310	24
Salinas – Seaside – Monterey, CA	0.02221	25
Bremerton, WA	0.02056	26
Eau Claire, WI	0.02036	27
Providence – Pawtucket – Fall River, RI – MA	0.02032	28
Pensacola, FL	0.02003	29
Pascagoula, MS	0.01996	30
Columbia, MO	0.01958	31
Rochester, MN	0.01878	32
Bakersfield, CA	0.01822	33
Wichita, KS	0.01793	34
Salem, OR	0.01762	35
Colorado Springs, CO	0.01738	36
Minneapolis – Saint Paul, MN – WI	0.01725	37
Yakima, WA	0.01695	38
Fitchburg – Leominster, MA	0.01654	39
Fayetteville, NC	0.01639	40
Wichita Falls, TX	0.01634	41
Beaumont – Port Arthur, TX	0.01633	42
Portland – Vancouver, OR – WA	0.01610	43
Portland, ME	0.01578	44
Hagerstown, MD	0.01565	45
Sherman – Denison, TX	0.01368	46
Fort Collins – Loveland, CO	0.01343	47
Panama City, FL	0.01339	48
Reading, PA	0.01278	49
Appleton – Oshkosh – Neenah, WI	0.01269	50

Source: U.S. Bureau of the Census, Data User Services Division, *1990 Census of Population and Housing,* Summary Tape File 3C, United States Summary, CD-ROM, February 1992.

★1851★

Poverty Status of Families With Children

Asian or Pacific Islander Female Householder, No Spouse Present, With Children Under 5 Years Old, Living Above Poverty, 1989
[Table shows the top 50 areas]

MSA	% of population	Rank
Honolulu, HI	0.14697	1
San Francisco – Oakland – San Jose, CA	0.02703	2
Salinas – Seaside – Monterey, CA	0.02165	3
San Diego, CA	0.01841	4
Great Falls, MT	0.01802	5
Charlottesville, VA	0.01754	6

[Continued]

★1851★

Asian or Pacific Islander Female Householder, No Spouse Present, With Children Under 5 Years Old, Living Above Poverty, 1989
[Continued]

MSA	% of population	Rank
Stockton, CA	0.01623	7
Anchorage, AK	0.01502	8
Los Angeles – Anaheim – Riverside, CA	0.01461	9
Bremerton, WA	0.01423	10
Cheyenne, WY	0.01367	11
Las Vegas, NV	0.01079	12
Reno, NV	0.01060	13
Santa Barbara – Santa Maria – Lompoc, CA	0.00974	14
Seattle – Tacoma, WA	0.00934	15
Hagerstown, MD	0.00906	16
Fitchburg – Leominster, MA	0.00778	17
Sacramento, CA	0.00763	18
Fresno, CA	0.00734	19
Yuba City, CA	0.00734	19
New York – Northern New Jersey – Long Island, NY – NJ – CT	0.00684	20
Sheboygan, WI	0.00674	21
Sarasota, FL	0.00648	22
New Haven – Meriden, CT	0.00641	23
Merced, CA	0.00617	24
Omaha, NE – IA	0.00582	25
Sioux Falls, SD	0.00565	26
Mansfield, OH	0.00555	27
Bloomington – Normal, IL	0.00542	28
Washington, DC – MD – VA	0.00538	29
Amarillo, TX	0.00533	30
Elmira, NY	0.00525	31
Pascagoula, MS	0.00521	32
Denver – Boulder, CO	0.00519	33
Corpus Christi, TX	0.00486	34
Bloomington, IN	0.00459	35
Austin, TX	0.00448	36
Elkhart – Goshen, IN	0.00448	36
Wausau, WI	0.00433	37
San Antonio, TX	0.00415	38
Savannah, GA	0.00412	39
Montgomery, AL	0.00410	40
Madison, WI	0.00409	41
Houston – Galveston – Brazoria, TX	0.00393	42
Poughkeepsie, NY	0.00385	43
New Orleans, LA	0.00379	44
Modesto, CA	0.00378	45
Olympia, WA	0.00372	46
Bakersfield, CA	0.00368	47
Nashville, TN	0.00365	48

Source: U.S. Bureau of the Census, Data User Services Division, *1990 Census of Population and Housing,* Summary Tape File 3C, United States Summary, CD-ROM, February 1992.

★1852★

Poverty Status of Families With Children

Asian or Pacific Islander Female Householder, No Spouse Present, With Children Under 5 and 5 to 17 Years Old, Living Above Poverty, 1989

[Table shows the top 50 areas]

MSA	% of population	Rank
Honolulu, HI	0.12748	1
Stockton, CA	0.03163	2
Salinas – Seaside – Monterey, CA	0.02221	3
Fresno, CA	0.02112	4
San Francisco – Oakland – San Jose, CA	0.02033	5
San Diego, CA	0.01533	6
Bellingham, WA	0.01174	7
Yuba City, CA	0.01142	8
Los Angeles – Anaheim – Riverside, CA	0.01107	9
Anchorage, AK	0.01105	10
Fort Smith, AR – OK	0.01080	11
Pueblo, CO	0.01056	12
Lynchburg, VA	0.01055	13
Owensboro, KY	0.01032	14
Sacramento, CA	0.00993	15
Bremerton, WA	0.00896	16
Killeen – Temple, TX	0.00862	17
Las Vegas, NV	0.00715	18
Reno, NV	0.00707	19
Seattle – Tacoma, WA	0.00676	20
Ocala, FL	0.00667	21
Springfield, MO	0.00665	22
Bakersfield, CA	0.00662	23
Brownsville – Harlingen, TX	0.00654	24
Worcester, MA	0.00641	25
Panama City, FL	0.00630	26
Madison, WI	0.00599	27
Modesto, CA	0.00594	28
Providence – Pawtucket – Fall River, RI – MA	0.00587	29
Portland – Vancouver, OR – WA	0.00555	30
Lafayette – West Lafayette, IN	0.00536	31
Washington, DC – MD – VA	0.00487	32
Austin, TX	0.00473	33
Bloomington, IN	0.00459	34
Des Moines, IA	0.00458	35
Waterbury, CT	0.00451	36
Lincoln, NE	0.00421	37
Anderson, SC	0.00413	38
Wichita, KS	0.00412	39
Waterloo – Cedar Falls, IA	0.00409	40
Flint, MI	0.00395	41
Richmond – Petersburg, VA	0.00393	42
Charlottesville, VA	0.00381	43
Minneapolis – Saint Paul, MN – WI	0.00369	44
Boston – Lawrence – Salem, MA – NH	0.00362	45
Houston – Galveston – Brazoria, TX	0.00356	46
Biloxi – Gulfport, MS	0.00355	47
Boise, ID	0.00340	48

[Continued]

★1852★

Asian or Pacific Islander Female Householder, No Spouse Present, With Children Under 5 and 5 to 17 Years Old, Living Above Poverty, 1989

[Continued]

MSA	% of population	Rank
Redding, CA	0.00340	48
Portland, ME	0.00325	49

Source: U.S. Bureau of the Census, Data User Services Division, *1990 Census of Population and Housing*, Summary Tape File 3C, United States Summary, CD-ROM, February 1992.

★1853★

Poverty Status of Families With Children

Asian or Pacific Islander Female Householder, No Spouse Present, With Children 5 to 17 Years Old, Living Above Poverty, 1989

[Table shows the top 50 areas]

MSA	% of population	Rank
Honolulu, HI	0.55762	1
San Francisco – Oakland – San Jose, CA	0.10671	2
Salinas – Seaside – Monterey, CA	0.08266	3
Anchorage, AK	0.07511	4
San Diego, CA	0.07410	5
Los Angeles – Anaheim – Riverside, CA	0.06792	6
Stockton, CA	0.06596	7
Sacramento, CA	0.06252	8
Lawton, OK	0.06189	9
Merced, CA	0.05661	10
Seattle – Tacoma, WA	0.05283	11
Colorado Springs, CO	0.04987	12
Fresno, CA	0.04764	13
Killeen – Temple, TX	0.04661	14
Las Vegas, NV	0.04478	15
Fort Walton Beach, FL	0.04312	16
Washington, DC – MD – VA	0.04254	17
Reno, NV	0.03927	18
Cheyenne, WY	0.03691	19
Bremerton, WA	0.03426	20
Olympia, WA	0.03287	21
Portland – Vancouver, OR – WA	0.03092	22
Anniston, AL	0.02844	23
New York – Northern New Jersey – Long Island, NY – NJ – CT	0.02747	24
Yuba City, CA	0.02691	25
Modesto, CA	0.02510	26
Santa Barbara – Santa Maria – Lompoc, CA	0.02462	27
Jacksonville, NC	0.02403	28
Rochester, MN	0.02348	29
Fitchburg – Leominster, MA	0.02237	30
San Angelo, TX	0.02234	31
Fayetteville, NC	0.02222	32
Salt Lake City – Ogden, UT	0.02210	33

[Continued]

★1853★

Asian or Pacific Islander Female Householder, No Spouse Present, With Children 5 to 17 Years Old, Living Above Poverty, 1989

[Continued]

MSA	% of population	Rank
Bakersfield, CA	0.02208	34
Eugene – Springfield, OR	0.02191	35
Iowa City, IA	0.02185	36
Chicago – Gary – Lake County, IL – IN – WI	0.02164	37
Houston – Galveston – Brazoria, TX	0.02129	38
Orlando, FL	0.02088	39
Kokomo, IN	0.02063	40
Denver – Boulder, CO	0.02013	41
Clarksville – Hopkinsville, TN – KY	0.02007	42
San Antonio, TX	0.01997	43
Spokane, WA	0.01992	44
Salem, OR	0.01942	45
Visalia – Tulare – Porterville, CA	0.01924	46
Redding, CA	0.01904	47
Richland – Kennewick – Pasco, WA	0.01866	48
Jacksonville, FL	0.01864	49
Lubbock, TX	0.01797	50

Source: U.S. Bureau of the Census, Data User Services Division, *1990 Census of Population and Housing*, Summary Tape File 3C, United States Summary, CD-ROM, February 1992.

★1854★

Poverty Status of Families With Children

Asian or Pacific Islander Male Householder, No Spouse Present, With Children Under 5 Years Old, Living Below, 1989

[Table shows the top 50 areas]

MSA	% of population	Rank
Honolulu, HI	0.01363	1
Fitchburg – Leominster, MA	0.01070	2
Killeen – Temple, TX	0.01018	3
Monroe, LA	0.00844	4
Yuba City, CA	0.00815	5
Sioux City, IA – NE	0.00782	6
Biloxi – Gulfport, MS	0.00710	7
Pueblo, CO	0.00569	8
Dothan, AL	0.00534	9
Rochester, MN	0.00470	10
Fayetteville, NC	0.00437	11
Reno, NV	0.00432	12
Waterloo – Cedar Falls, IA	0.00409	13
Merced, CA	0.00392	14
Stockton, CA	0.00375	15
Worcester, MA	0.00366	16
Fort Smith, AR – OK	0.00341	17
Salem, OR	0.00324	18
Green Bay, WI	0.00308	19
Beaumont – Port Arthur, TX	0.00277	20

[Continued]

★1854★

Asian or Pacific Islander Male Householder, No Spouse Present, With Children Under 5 Years Old, Living Below, 1989

[Continued]

MSA	% of population	Rank
Yakima, WA	0.00265	21
Fresno, CA	0.00255	22
Atlantic City, NJ	0.00250	23
San Francisco – Oakland – San Jose, CA	0.00222	24
Albuquerque, NM	0.00208	25
West Palm Beach – Boca Raton – Delray Beach, FL	0.00208	25
Seattle – Tacoma, WA	0.00188	26
Sacramento, CA	0.00182	27
Salt Lake City – Ogden, UT	0.00168	28
Los Angeles – Anaheim – Riverside, CA	0.00166	29
Bremerton, WA	0.00158	30
Minneapolis – Saint Paul, MN – WI	0.00154	31
Mobile, AL	0.00147	32
Lansing – East Lansing, MI	0.00139	33
Madison, WI	0.00136	34
Grand Rapids, MI	0.00131	35
Oklahoma City, OK	0.00115	36
Baton Rouge, LA	0.00114	37
Allentown – Bethlehem – Easton, PA – NJ	0.00102	38
Rochester, NY	0.00100	39
Boston – Lawrence – Salem, MA – NH	0.00086	40
Norfolk – Virginia Beach – Newport News, VA	0.00086	40
Youngstown – Warren, OH	0.00081	41
Providence – Pawtucket – Fall River, RI – MA	0.00079	42
New York – Northern New Jersey – Long Island, NY – NJ – CT	0.00078	43
San Diego, CA	0.00076	44
Portland – Vancouver, OR – WA	0.00074	45
El Paso, TX	0.00068	46
Scranton – Wilkes-Barre, PA	0.00068	46
Memphis, TN – AR – MS	0.00061	47

Source: U.S. Bureau of the Census, Data User Services Division, *1990 Census of Population and Housing*, Summary Tape File 3C, United States Summary, CD-ROM, February 1992.

★1855★

Poverty Status of Families With Children

Asian or Pacific Islander Male Householder, No Spouse Present, With Children Under 5 and 5 to 17 Years Old, Living Below Poverty, 1989

[Table shows the top 50 areas]

MSA	% of population	Rank
Honolulu, HI	0.013752	1
Green Bay, WI	0.008222	2
San Angelo, TX	0.008125	3
Fresno, CA	0.007341	4
Chico, CA	0.004942	5
Killeen – Temple, TX	0.003917	6
New Orleans, LA	0.003552	7
Stockton, CA	0.003537	8
Tucson, AZ	0.003299	9
Iowa City, IA	0.003121	10
Santa Barbara – Santa Maria – Lompoc, CA	0.002976	11
Sheboygan, WI	0.002888	12
Yuma, AZ	0.002806	13
Merced, CA	0.002803	14
Des Moines, IA	0.002799	15
Saint Cloud, MN	0.002619	16
Sacramento, CA	0.002498	17
Joplin, MO	0.002224	18
Wichita, KS	0.002061	19
Modesto, CA	0.001889	20
Bakersfield, CA	0.001656	21
Los Angeles – Anaheim – Riverside, CA	0.001652	22
Visalia – Tulare – Porterville, CA	0.001603	23
Baton Rouge, LA	0.001514	24
San Diego, CA	0.001281	25
Binghamton, NY	0.001134	26
San Francisco – Oakland – San Jose, CA	0.001039	27
Columbus, OH	0.000944	28
Salt Lake City – Ogden, UT	0.000933	29
Tampa – Saint Petersburg – Clearwater, FL	0.000822	30
Minneapolis – Saint Paul, MN – WI	0.000812	31
Brownsville – Harlingen, TX	0.000769	32
Seattle – Tacoma, WA	0.000742	33
Houston – Galveston – Brazoria, TX	0.000701	34
Raleigh – Durham, NC	0.000680	35
Phoenix, AZ	0.000660	36
Buffalo – Niagara Falls, NY	0.000589	37
Madison, WI	0.000545	38
Las Vegas, NV	0.000539	39
Boston – Lawrence – Salem, MA – NH	0.000527	40
New York – Northern New Jersey – Long Island, NY – NJ – CT	0.000448	41
Milwaukee – Racine, WI	0.000373	42
Washington, DC – MD – VA	0.000357	43
Portland – Vancouver, OR – WA	0.000338	44
Chicago – Gary – Lake County, IL – IN – WI	0.000335	45
Denver – Boulder, CO	0.000325	46

[Continued]

★1855★

Asian or Pacific Islander Male Householder, No Spouse Present, With Children Under 5 and 5 to 17 Years Old, Living Below Poverty, 1989

[Continued]

MSA	% of population	Rank
Philadelphia – Wilmington – Trenton, PA – NJ – DE – MD	0.000305	47
Baltimore, MD	0.000252	48
Pittsburgh – Beaver Valley, PA	0.000089	49
Dallas – Fort Worth, TX	0.000051	50

Source: U.S. Bureau of the Census, Data User Services Division, *1990 Census of Population and Housing,* Summary Tape File 3C, United States Summary, CD-ROM, February 1992.

★1856★

Poverty Status of Families With Children

Asian or Pacific Islander Male Householder, No Spouse Present, With Children 5 to 17 Years Old, Living Below Poverty, 1989

[Table shows the top 50 areas]

MSA	% of population	Rank
Honolulu, HI	0.03360	1
Enid, OK	0.02115	2
Stockton, CA	0.01873	3
Biloxi – Gulfport, MS	0.01471	4
Rochester, MN	0.01315	5
Yuba City, CA	0.00978	6
Fresno, CA	0.00974	7
Modesto, CA	0.00945	8
San Francisco – Oakland – San Jose, CA	0.00876	9
Eau Claire, WI	0.00872	10
Fort Collins – Loveland, CO	0.00860	11
San Diego, CA	0.00821	12
State College, PA	0.00808	13
Olympia, WA	0.00806	14
Merced, CA	0.00785	15
Los Angeles – Anaheim – Riverside, CA	0.00771	16
Sacramento, CA	0.00756	17
Amarillo, TX	0.00746	18
Seattle – Tacoma, WA	0.00742	19
Visalia – Tulare – Porterville, CA	0.00737	20
Springfield, MO	0.00707	21
Champaign – Urbana – Rantoul, IL	0.00694	22
Salinas – Seaside – Monterey, CA	0.00590	23
Killeen – Temple, TX	0.00548	24
Muncie, IN	0.00501	25
Gainesville, FL	0.00490	26
Bakersfield, CA	0.00442	27
Davenport – Rock Island – Moline, IA – IL	0.00428	28
Austin, TX	0.00422	29
Iowa City, IA	0.00416	30
Green Bay, WI	0.00411	31

[Continued]

★1856★

Asian or Pacific Islander Male Householder, No Spouse Present, With Children 5 to 17 Years Old, Living Below Poverty, 1989
[Continued]

MSA	% of population	Rank
Asheville, NC	0.00400	32
Boston – Lawrence – Salem, MA – NH	0.00388	33
Kalamazoo, MI	0.00358	34
Denver – Boulder, CO	0.00357	35
Augusta, GA – SC	0.00353	36
Eugene – Springfield, OR	0.00353	36
Minneapolis – Saint Paul, MN – WI	0.00349	37
Beaumont – Port Arthur, TX	0.00332	38
Shreveport, LA	0.00329	39
Salt Lake City – Ogden, UT	0.00326	40
Santa Barbara – Santa Maria – Lompoc, CA	0.00325	41
Providence – Pawtucket – Fall River, RI – MA	0.00315	42
Topeka, KS	0.00311	43
Lancaster, PA	0.00307	44
Portland – Vancouver, OR – WA	0.00304	45
New York – Northern New Jersey – Long Island, NY – NJ – CT	0.00295	46
Sheboygan, WI	0.00289	47
Lincoln, NE	0.00281	48
Chico, CA	0.00275	49

Source: U.S. Bureau of the Census, Data User Services Division, *1990 Census of Population and Housing*, Summary Tape File 3C, United States Summary, CD-ROM, February 1992.

★1857★
Poverty Status of Families With Children

Asian or Pacific Islander Male Householder, No Spouse Present, With Children Under 5 Years Old, Living Above Poverty, 1989
[Table shows the top 50 areas]

MSA	% of population	Rank
Honolulu, HI	0.08431	1
Merced, CA	0.02074	2
Stockton, CA	0.01394	3
Anchorage, AK	0.01370	4
San Francisco – Oakland – San Jose, CA	0.01369	5
Fitchburg – Leominster, MA	0.01265	6
Los Angeles – Anaheim – Riverside, CA	0.01023	7
Joplin, MO	0.00815	8
San Diego, CA	0.00789	9
Salinas – Seaside – Monterey, CA	0.00787	10
Wichita Falls, TX	0.00735	11
Yuba City, CA	0.00734	12
Portland, ME	0.00696	13
Lafayette – West Lafayette, IN	0.00689	14

[Continued]

★1857★

Asian or Pacific Islander Male Householder, No Spouse Present, With Children Under 5 Years Old, Living Above Poverty, 1989
[Continued]

MSA	% of population	Rank
Visalia – Tulare – Porterville, CA	0.00641	15
Fayetteville – Springdale, AR	0.00617	16
Sioux City, IA – NE	0.00609	17
Lincoln, NE	0.00608	18
Pine Bluff, AR	0.00585	19
Bryan – College Station, TX	0.00574	20
Santa Barbara – Santa Maria – Lompoc, CA	0.00568	21
Seattle – Tacoma, WA	0.00535	22
Champaign – Urbana – Rantoul, IL	0.00520	23
Las Vegas, NV	0.00513	24
Sacramento, CA	0.00513	24
Decatur, IL	0.00512	25
Medford, OR	0.00478	26
Des Moines, IA	0.00458	27
Fort Wayne, IN	0.00440	28
Fayetteville, NC	0.00437	29
Pascagoula, MS	0.00434	30
New York – Northern New Jersey – Long Island, NY – NJ – CT	0.00415	31
Portland – Vancouver, OR – WA	0.00413	32
West Palm Beach – Boca Raton – Delray Beach, FL	0.00405	33
Lubbock, TX	0.00404	34
Killeen – Temple, TX	0.00392	35
Fresno, CA	0.00390	36
Washington, DC – MD – VA	0.00390	36
Shreveport, LA	0.00389	37
Chico, CA	0.00384	38
Raleigh – Durham, NC	0.00381	39
Atlantic City, NJ	0.00376	40
Rochester, MN	0.00376	40
Duluth, MN – WI	0.00375	41
Laredo, TX	0.00375	41
Kalamazoo, MI	0.00358	42
Houston – Galveston – Brazoria, TX	0.00350	43
Redding, CA	0.00340	44
Evansville, IN – KY	0.00323	45
Lancaster, PA	0.00307	46

Source: U.S. Bureau of the Census, Data User Services Division, *1990 Census of Population and Housing*, Summary Tape File 3C, United States Summary, CD-ROM, February 1992.

★1858★

Poverty Status of Families With Children

Asian or Pacific Islander Male Householder, No Spouse Present, With Children Under 5 and 5 to 17 Years Old, Living Above Poverty, 1989

[Table shows the top 50 areas]

MSA	% of population	Rank
Honolulu, HI	0.05549	1
Merced, CA	0.01345	2
Sioux City, IA–NE	0.01217	3
Panama City, FL	0.01024	4
San Francisco – Oakland – San Jose, CA	0.00707	5
Alexandria, LA	0.00684	6
Midland, TX	0.00657	7
Great Falls, MT	0.00644	8
San Diego, CA	0.00616	9
Los Angeles – Anaheim – Riverside, CA	0.00566	10
Olympia, WA	0.00558	11
Visalia – Tulare – Porterville, CA	0.00545	12
Reading, PA	0.00535	13
Anchorage, AK	0.00530	14
Stockton, CA	0.00520	15
Fort Smith, AR–OK	0.00455	16
Portland – Vancouver, OR–WA	0.00453	17
Boise, ID	0.00437	18
Sacramento, CA	0.00432	19
Salem, OR	0.00396	20
Tallahassee, FL	0.00385	21
Battle Creek, MI	0.00368	22
Fort Walton Beach, FL	0.00348	23
Austin, TX	0.00345	24
Columbus, GA–AL	0.00329	25
Evansville, IN–KY	0.00287	26
Fresno, CA	0.00285	27
Seattle – Tacoma, WA	0.00285	27
Provo – Orem, UT	0.00266	28
Salt Lake City – Ogden, UT	0.00261	29
Washington, DC – MD – VA	0.00250	30
Jacksonville, FL	0.00232	31
Salinas – Seaside – Monterey, CA	0.00225	32
Atlantic City, NJ	0.00219	33
Santa Barbara – Santa Maria – Lompoc, CA	0.00216	34
Modesto, CA	0.00189	35
New Haven – Meriden, CT	0.00189	35
Yuma, AZ	0.00187	36
Minneapolis – Saint Paul, MN – WI	0.00183	37
Phoenix, AZ	0.00179	38
Canton, OH	0.00178	39
Denver – Boulder, CO	0.00168	40
Daytona Beach, FL	0.00162	41
Dallas – Fort Worth, TX	0.00160	42
Worcester, MA	0.00160	42
Baton Rouge, LA	0.00151	43
Lakeland – Winter Haven, FL	0.00148	44
Corpus Christi, TX	0.00143	45

[Continued]

★1858★

Asian or Pacific Islander Male Householder, No Spouse Present, With Children Under 5 and 5 to 17 Years Old, Living Above Poverty, 1989

[Continued]

MSA	% of population	Rank
New York – Northern New Jersey – Long Island, NY – NJ – CT	0.00143	45
Las Vegas, NV	0.00135	46

Source: U.S. Bureau of the Census, Data User Services Division, *1990 Census of Population and Housing*, Summary Tape File 3C, United States Summary, CD-ROM, February 1992.

★1859★

Poverty Status of Families With Children

Asian or Pacific Islander Male Householder, No Spouse Present, With Children 5 to 17 Years Old, Living Above Poverty, 1989

[Table shows the top 50 areas]

MSA	% of population	Rank
Honolulu, HI	0.20413	1
San Francisco – Oakland – San Jose, CA	0.04777	2
Stockton, CA	0.03454	3
Los Angeles – Anaheim – Riverside, CA	0.03110	4
Salinas – Seaside – Monterey, CA	0.02924	5
Santa Barbara – Santa Maria – Lompoc, CA	0.02624	6
Reno, NV	0.02474	7
San Diego, CA	0.02254	8
Sacramento, CA	0.01958	9
Anchorage, AK	0.01767	10
Fresno, CA	0.01723	11
Washington, DC – MD – VA	0.01664	12
Seattle – Tacoma, WA	0.01657	13
Rochester, MN	0.01597	14
Olympia, WA	0.01551	15
Yuba City, CA	0.01468	16
Waterloo – Cedar Falls, IA	0.01432	17
Bremerton, WA	0.01423	18
Pueblo, CO	0.01382	19
Modesto, CA	0.01322	20
Casper, WY	0.01307	21
Fort Smith, AR–OK	0.01307	21
Houston – Galveston – Brazoria, TX	0.01275	22
Panama City, FL	0.01181	23
New York – Northern New Jersey – Long Island, NY – NJ – CT	0.01156	24
Bakersfield, CA	0.01141	25
Merced, CA	0.01121	26
Biloxi – Gulfport, MS	0.01116	27
Alexandria, LA	0.01064	28
Sherman – Denison, TX	0.01052	29
Dallas – Fort Worth, TX	0.01042	30

[Continued]

★1859★

Asian or Pacific Islander Male Householder, No Spouse Present, With Children 5 to 17 Years Old, Living Above Poverty, 1989

[Continued]

MSA	% of population	Rank
Manchester, NH	0.01014	31
Huntsville, AL	0.01005	32
Atlantic City, NJ	0.01002	33
Visalia – Tulare – Porterville, CA	0.00994	34
Portland – Vancouver, OR – WA	0.00988	35
Norfolk – Virginia Beach – Newport News, VA	0.00967	36
Bismarck, ND	0.00954	37
Bellingham, WA	0.00939	38
Chico, CA	0.00933	39
South Bend – Mishawaka, IN	0.00931	40
Orlando, FL	0.00820	41
Las Vegas, NV	0.00782	42
Eugene – Springfield, OR	0.00778	43
Fort Walton Beach, FL	0.00765	44
Salt Lake City – Ogden, UT	0.00765	44
Roanoke, VA	0.00757	45
Pensacola, FL	0.00755	46
Grand Forks, ND	0.00707	47
Atlanta, GA	0.00699	48

Source: U.S. Bureau of the Census, Data User Services Division, *1990 Census of Population and Housing,* Summary Tape File 3C, United States Summary, CD-ROM, February 1992.

★1860★

Poverty Status of Families With Children

Asian or Pacific Islander Married Couples With Children Under 5 Years Old, Living Below Poverty, 1989

[Table shows the top 50 areas]

MSA	% of population	Rank
Champaign – Urbana – Rantoul, IL	0.0867	1
La Crosse, WI	0.0695	2
Iowa City, IA	0.0687	3
Gainesville, FL	0.0657	4
Columbia, MO	0.0641	5
Lafayette – West Lafayette, IN	0.0574	6
Bryan – College Station, TX	0.0566	7
Yuba City, CA	0.0506	8
Honolulu, HI	0.0493	9
Fresno, CA	0.0472	10
Athens, GA	0.0429	11
State College, PA	0.0388	12
Stockton, CA	0.0377	13
Merced, CA	0.0364	14
Lawrence, KS	0.0355	15
Sheboygan, WI	0.0347	16
Wausau, WI	0.0303	17
Rochester, MN	0.0301	18
Lincoln, NE	0.0281	19

[Continued]

★1860★

Asian or Pacific Islander Married Couples With Children Under 5 Years Old, Living Below Poverty, 1989

[Continued]

MSA	% of population	Rank
Madison, WI	0.0278	20
Huntsville, AL	0.0230	21
Eugene – Springfield, OR	0.0212	22
Beaumont – Port Arthur, TX	0.0205	23
Sacramento, CA	0.0201	24
San Francisco – Oakland – San Jose, CA	0.0194	25
Bloomington, IN	0.0193	26
Terre Haute, IN	0.0183	27
Los Angeles – Anaheim – Riverside, CA	0.0179	28
Lansing – East Lansing, MI	0.0176	29
Salt Lake City – Ogden, UT	0.0173	30
Tuscaloosa, AL	0.0173	30
San Diego, CA	0.0169	31
Jacksonville, NC	0.0167	32
Fargo – Moorhead, ND – MN	0.0163	33
Santa Barbara – Santa Maria – Lompoc, CA	0.0162	34
Green Bay, WI	0.0159	35
Seattle – Tacoma, WA	0.0156	36
New York – Northern New Jersey – Long Island, NY – NJ – CT	0.0145	37
Tucson, AZ	0.0142	38
Eau Claire, WI	0.0138	39
Minneapolis – Saint Paul, MN – WI	0.0138	39
Tallahassee, FL	0.0137	40
Spokane, WA	0.0133	41
Modesto, CA	0.0132	42
Appleton – Oshkosh – Neenah, WI	0.0127	43
Austin, TX	0.0127	43
Hickory – Morganton, NC	0.0126	44
Raleigh – Durham, NC	0.0122	45
Wichita, KS	0.0122	45
Chico, CA	0.0121	46

Source: U.S. Bureau of the Census, Data User Services Division, *1990 Census of Population and Housing,* Summary Tape File 3C, United States Summary, CD-ROM, February 1992.

★1861★

Poverty Status of Families With Children

Asian or Pacific Islander Married Couples With Children Under 5 and 5 to 17 Years Old, Living Below Poverty, 1989

[Table shows the top 50 areas]

MSA	% of population	Rank
Merced, CA	0.28195	1
Fresno, CA	0.25858	2
Stockton, CA	0.23532	3
Yuba City, CA	0.19977	4

[Continued]

★1861★

Asian or Pacific Islander Married Couples With Children Under 5 and 5 to 17 Years Old, Living Below Poverty, 1989

[Continued]

MSA	% of population	Rank
La Crosse, WI	0.18079	5
Visalia – Tulare – Porterville, CA	0.13978	6
Wausau, WI	0.12478	7
Honolulu, HI	0.12473	8
Modesto, CA	0.10877	9
Sacramento, CA	0.09047	10
Sheboygan, WI	0.07798	11
Eau Claire, WI	0.07561	12
Chico, CA	0.07413	13
Biloxi – Gulfport, MS	0.07204	14
Rochester, MN	0.06481	15
Redding, CA	0.05849	16
Green Bay, WI	0.05807	17
Minneapolis – Saint Paul, MN – WI	0.04915	18
Madison, WI	0.04658	19
Appleton – Oshkosh – Neenah, WI	0.04474	20
Columbia, MO	0.04360	21
San Francisco – Oakland – San Jose, CA	0.04212	22
Bloomington, IN	0.04038	23
Olympia, WA	0.04031	24
Iowa City, IA	0.03537	25
Beaumont – Port Arthur, TX	0.03516	26
Bryan – College Station, TX	0.03364	27
Los Angeles – Anaheim – Riverside, CA	0.03301	28
Lafayette – West Lafayette, IN	0.02833	29
Lansing – East Lansing, MI	0.02820	30
San Diego, CA	0.02586	31
Santa Barbara – Santa Maria – Lompoc, CA	0.02543	32
New Orleans, LA	0.02535	33
Seattle – Tacoma, WA	0.02442	34
Bakersfield, CA	0.02337	35
Bremerton, WA	0.02214	36
Salinas – Seaside – Monterey, CA	0.02193	37
Fayetteville – Springdale, AR	0.02028	38
Providence – Pawtucket – Fall River, RI – MA	0.02015	39
Milwaukee – Racine, WI	0.01972	40
Houma – Thibodaux, LA	0.01750	41
Lawton, OK	0.01615	42
Boston – Lawrence – Salem, MA – NH	0.01577	43
Fort Smith, AR – OK	0.01535	44
Des Moines, IA	0.01502	45
Portland – Vancouver, OR – WA	0.01414	46
Pensacola, FL	0.01365	47
Salt Lake City – Ogden, UT	0.01315	48
Raleigh – Durham, NC	0.01305	49
Worcester, MA	0.01236	50

Source: U.S. Bureau of the Census, Data User Services Division, *1990 Census of Population and Housing*, Summary Tape File 3C, United States Summary, CD-ROM, February 1992.

★1862★

Poverty Status of Families With Children

Asian or Pacific Islander Married Couples With Children 5 to 17 Years Old, Living Below Poverty, 1989

[Table shows the top 50 areas]

MSA	% of population	Rank
Stockton, CA	0.15896	1
Fresno, CA	0.13229	2
Honolulu, HI	0.12365	3
Yuba City, CA	0.10844	4
Merced, CA	0.10033	5
Modesto, CA	0.09662	6
Biloxi – Gulfport, MS	0.07102	7
Sacramento, CA	0.06826	8
San Francisco – Oakland – San Jose, CA	0.06328	9
Visalia – Tulare – Porterville, CA	0.06284	10
Los Angeles – Anaheim – Riverside, CA	0.06215	11
Beaumont – Port Arthur, TX	0.05758	12
Columbia, MO	0.04805	13
San Diego, CA	0.04552	14
Rochester, MN	0.04133	15
Iowa City, IA	0.04057	16
Chico, CA	0.04008	17
Eau Claire, WI	0.03853	18
Lawrence, KS	0.03668	19
New York – Northern New Jersey – Long Island, NY – NJ – CT	0.03361	20
Seattle – Tacoma, WA	0.03173	21
Houston – Galveston – Brazoria, TX	0.03085	22
Salinas – Seaside – Monterey, CA	0.02840	23
Champaign – Urbana – Rantoul, IL	0.02832	24
La Crosse, WI	0.02758	25
Panama City, FL	0.02756	26
Pensacola, FL	0.02671	27
Hickory – Morganton, NC	0.02616	28
Olympia, WA	0.02605	29
Portland – Vancouver, OR – WA	0.02470	30
Anchorage, AK	0.02253	31
Lafayette, LA	0.02204	32
Green Bay, WI	0.02158	33
Bakersfield, CA	0.02116	34
Sioux City, IA – NE	0.02087	35
Minneapolis – Saint Paul, MN – WI	0.02045	36
Redding, CA	0.02040	37
Wichita, KS	0.02019	38
Bellingham, WA	0.01956	39
Lincoln, NE	0.01919	40
Binghamton, NY	0.01853	41
Washington, DC – MD – VA	0.01802	42
New Orleans, LA	0.01800	43
Fort Collins – Loveland, CO	0.01773	44
Lexington-Fayette, KY	0.01751	45
Sheboygan, WI	0.01733	46
Des Moines, IA	0.01731	47
Philadelphia – Wilmington – Trenton, PA – NJ – DE – MD	0.01698	48

[Continued]

★1862★

Asian or Pacific Islander Married Couples With Children 5 to 17 Years Old, Living Below Poverty, 1989

[Continued]

MSA	% of population	Rank
Las Vegas, NV	0.01686	49
Reno, NV	0.01649	50

Source: U.S. Bureau of the Census, Data User Services Division, *1990 Census of Population and Housing*, Summary Tape File 3C, United States Summary, CD-ROM, February 1992.

★1863★

Poverty Status of Families With Children

Asian or Pacific Islander Married Couples With Children Under 5 Years Old, Living Above Poverty, 1989

[Table shows the top 50 areas]

MSA	% of population	Rank
Honolulu, HI	1.0522	1
San Francisco – Oakland – San Jose, CA	0.3679	2
Los Angeles – Anaheim – Riverside, CA	0.2232	3
Stockton, CA	0.1696	4
Salinas – Seaside – Monterey, CA	0.1650	5
Bryan – College Station, TX	0.1617	6
San Diego, CA	0.1597	7
Iowa City, IA	0.1592	8
Sacramento, CA	0.1536	9
Champaign – Urbana – Rantoul, IL	0.1520	10
Seattle – Tacoma, WA	0.1505	11
Washington, DC – MD – VA	0.1481	12
Anchorage, AK	0.1467	13
New York – Northern New Jersey – Long Island, NY – NJ – CT	0.1391	14
Poughkeepsie, NY	0.1280	15
Yuba City, CA	0.1272	16
Lafayette – West Lafayette, IN	0.1141	17
State College, PA	0.0977	18
Houston – Galveston – Brazoria, TX	0.0943	19
Merced, CA	0.0925	20
Chicago – Gary – Lake County, IL – IN – WI	0.0876	21
Fresno, CA	0.0863	22
Reno, NV	0.0860	23
Las Vegas, NV	0.0831	24
Modesto, CA	0.0826	25
Santa Barbara – Santa Maria – Lompoc, CA	0.0812	26
Portland – Vancouver, OR – WA	0.0809	27
Dallas – Fort Worth, TX	0.0797	28
Boston – Lawrence – Salem, MA – NH	0.0711	29
Fort Smith, AR – OK	0.0699	30

[Continued]

★1863★

Asian or Pacific Islander Married Couples With Children Under 5 Years Old, Living Above Poverty, 1989

[Continued]

MSA	% of population	Rank
Bakersfield, CA	0.0661	31
Athens, GA	0.0621	32
Austin, TX	0.0612	33
Denver – Boulder, CO	0.0592	34
Atlanta, GA	0.0591	35
Olympia, WA	0.0577	36
Bremerton, WA	0.0574	37
Huntsville, AL	0.0565	38
Norfolk – Virginia Beach – Newport News, VA	0.0554	39
Raleigh – Durham, NC	0.0548	40
Minneapolis – Saint Paul, MN – WI	0.0547	41
Salt Lake City – Ogden, UT	0.0534	42
Salem, OR	0.0532	43
Madison, WI	0.0523	44
Atlantic City, NJ	0.0513	45
Lawrence, KS	0.0513	45
New Haven – Meriden, CT	0.0513	45
Philadelphia – Wilmington – Trenton, PA – NJ – DE – MD	0.0512	46
Kalamazoo, MI	0.0506	47
Worcester, MA	0.0499	48

Source: U.S. Bureau of the Census, Data User Services Division, *1990 Census of Population and Housing*, Summary Tape File 3C, United States Summary, CD-ROM, February 1992.

★1864★

Poverty Status of Families With Children

Asian or Pacific Islander Married Couples With Children Under 5 and 5 to 17 Years Old, Living Above Poverty, 1989

[Table shows the top 50 areas]

MSA	% of population	Rank
Honolulu, HI	1.30287	1
San Francisco – Oakland – San Jose, CA	0.34503	2
Stockton, CA	0.32021	3
Los Angeles – Anaheim – Riverside, CA	0.19439	4
Merced, CA	0.19338	5
San Diego, CA	0.18715	6
Yuba City, CA	0.18591	7
Fresno, CA	0.16255	8
Modesto, CA	0.15896	9
Sacramento, CA	0.15448	10
Anchorage, AK	0.13961	11
Salinas – Seaside – Monterey, CA	0.13890	12
Seattle – Tacoma, WA	0.13020	13
Washington, DC – MD – VA	0.11747	14
New York – Northern New Jersey – Long Island, NY – NJ – CT	0.10141	15

[Continued]

★1864★

Asian or Pacific Islander Married Couples With Children Under 5 and 5 to 17 Years Old, Living Above Poverty, 1989

[Continued]

MSA	% of population	Rank
Bremerton, WA	0.09645	16
Houston – Galveston – Brazoria, TX	0.09326	17
Santa Barbara – Santa Maria – Lompoc, CA	0.09307	18
Salt Lake City – Ogden, UT	0.07937	19
Chicago – Gary – Lake County, IL – IN – WI	0.07890	20
Amarillo, TX	0.07731	21
Las Vegas, NV	0.07539	22
Dallas – Fort Worth, TX	0.07495	23
Reno, NV	0.07382	24
Olympia, WA	0.07318	25
Visalia – Tulare – Porterville, CA	0.07021	26
Portland – Vancouver, OR – WA	0.06902	27
Poughkeepsie, NY	0.06668	28
Fitchburg – Leominster, MA	0.06518	29
Bakersfield, CA	0.06293	30
Richland – Kennewick – Pasco, WA	0.06132	31
Norfolk – Virginia Beach – Newport News, VA	0.05644	32
Minneapolis – Saint Paul, MN – WI	0.05641	33
Lafayette – West Lafayette, IN	0.05513	34
Boston – Lawrence – Salem, MA – NH	0.05506	35
Fort Smith, AR – OK	0.05287	36
Kalamazoo, MI	0.05192	37
Wausau, WI	0.05113	38
Sheboygan, WI	0.05102	39
Denver – Boulder, CO	0.05032	40
Wichita Falls, TX	0.04903	41
Albuquerque, NM	0.04807	42
Fayetteville, NC	0.04735	43
New Orleans, LA	0.04722	44
Rockford, IL	0.04688	45
Chico, CA	0.04667	46
Champaign – Urbana – Rantoul, IL	0.04624	47
Austin, TX	0.04593	48
Killeen – Temple, TX	0.04504	49
Philadelphia – Wilmington – Trenton, PA – NJ – DE – MD	0.04472	50

Source: U.S. Bureau of the Census, Data User Services Division, *1990 Census of Population and Housing,* Summary Tape File 3C, United States Summary, CD-ROM, February 1992.

★1865★

Poverty Status of Families With Children

Asian or Pacific Islander Married Couples With Children 5 to 17 Years Old, Living Above Poverty, 1989

[Table shows the top 50 areas]

MSA	% of population	Rank
Honolulu, HI	3.3415	1
San Francisco – Oakland – San Jose, CA	0.8392	2
Los Angeles – Anaheim – Riverside, CA	0.5561	3
Stockton, CA	0.5160	4
San Diego, CA	0.4388	5
Salinas – Seaside – Monterey, CA	0.4293	6
Yuba City, CA	0.3596	7
Washington, DC – MD – VA	0.3515	8
New York – Northern New Jersey – Long Island, NY – NJ – CT	0.3289	9
Sacramento, CA	0.3289	9
Seattle – Tacoma, WA	0.3234	10
Anchorage, AK	0.2894	11
Houston – Galveston – Brazoria, TX	0.2749	12
Fresno, CA	0.2649	13
Chicago – Gary – Lake County, IL – IN – WI	0.2469	14
Olympia, WA	0.2313	15
Modesto, CA	0.2310	16
Bremerton, WA	0.2298	17
Merced, CA	0.2119	18
Santa Barbara – Santa Maria – Lompoc, CA	0.2105	19
Visalia – Tulare – Porterville, CA	0.2013	20
Portland – Vancouver, OR – WA	0.1997	21
Reno, NV	0.1979	22
Bakersfield, CA	0.1969	23
Fort Smith, AR – OK	0.1751	24
Las Vegas, NV	0.1658	25
Dallas – Fort Worth, TX	0.1645	26
Norfolk – Virginia Beach – Newport News, VA	0.1612	27
Boston – Lawrence – Salem, MA – NH	0.1517	28
Poughkeepsie, NY	0.1484	29
Lafayette – West Lafayette, IN	0.1409	30
Jacksonville, FL	0.1381	31
Rochester, MN	0.1381	31
Raleigh – Durham, NC	0.1360	32
Orlando, FL	0.1354	33
Philadelphia – Wilmington – Trenton, PA – NJ – DE – MD	0.1349	34
Atlanta, GA	0.1322	35
Bryan – College Station, TX	0.1321	36
Huntsville, AL	0.1310	37
Lawrence, KS	0.1284	38
Richland – Kennewick – Pasco, WA	0.1253	39
Iowa City, IA	0.1248	40
Baltimore, MD	0.1237	41
Atlantic City, NJ	0.1215	42
State College, PA	0.1212	43

[Continued]

★1865★

Asian or Pacific Islander Married Couples With Children 5 to 17 Years Old, Living Above Poverty, 1989

[Continued]

MSA	% of population	Rank
Denver – Boulder, CO	0.1203	44
Champaign – Urbana – Rantoul, IL	0.1202	45
Amarillo, TX	0.1189	46
Bellingham, WA	0.1158	47
Oklahoma City, OK	0.1145	48

Source: U.S. Bureau of the Census, Data User Services Division, 1990 Census of Population and Housing, Summary Tape File 3C, United States Summary, CD-ROM, February 1992.

★1866★

Poverty Status of Families With Children

Black Female Householder, No Spouse Present, With Children Under 5 Years Old, Living Below Poverty, 1989

[Table shows the top 50 areas]

MSA	% of population	Rank
Albany, GA	0.50106	1
Jackson, TN	0.41933	2
Macon – Warner Robins, GA	0.37780	3
Columbus, GA – AL	0.36697	4
New Orleans, LA	0.34799	5
Shreveport, LA	0.33409	6
Memphis, TN – AR – MS	0.33186	7
Pine Bluff, AR	0.32754	8
Florence, SC	0.32533	9
Benton Harbor, MI	0.29930	10
Monroe, LA	0.28975	11
Flint, MI	0.28551	12
Montgomery, AL	0.28135	13
Alexandria, LA	0.27669	14
Baton Rouge, LA	0.25006	15
Mobile, AL	0.24952	16
Savannah, GA	0.24853	17
Jackson, MS	0.24634	18
Wilmington, NC	0.24525	19
Muskegon, MI	0.24028	20
Detroit – Ann Arbor, MI	0.23300	21
Gainesville, FL	0.22194	22
Augusta, GA – SC	0.21396	23
Kalamazoo, MI	0.21351	24
Tallahassee, FL	0.20933	25
Richmond – Petersburg, VA	0.20470	26
Fayetteville, NC	0.20359	27
Norfolk – Virginia Beach – Newport News, VA	0.20328	28
Tuscaloosa, AL	0.19997	29
Lafayette, LA	0.19833	30
Athens, GA	0.19582	31
Pascagoula, MS	0.19264	32
Biloxi – Gulfport, MS	0.19176	33

[Continued]

★1866★

Black Female Householder, No Spouse Present, With Children Under 5 Years Old, Living Below Poverty, 1989

[Continued]

MSA	% of population	Rank
Danville, VA	0.18949	34
Beaumont – Port Arthur, TX	0.18576	35
Dothan, AL	0.18173	36
Lake Charles, LA	0.18140	37
Ocala, FL	0.17810	38
Birmingham, AL	0.17735	39
Milwaukee – Racine, WI	0.17285	40
Pensacola, FL	0.17102	41
Lynchburg, VA	0.16948	42
Charleston, SC	0.16927	43
Waco, TX	0.16814	44
Cincinnati – Hamilton, OH – KY – IN	0.16564	45
Cleveland – Akron – Lorain, OH	0.16331	46
Raleigh – Durham, NC	0.16316	47
Atlanta, GA	0.16188	48
Longview – Marshall, TX	0.16007	49
Jacksonville, FL	0.15572	50

Source: U.S. Bureau of the Census, Data User Services Division, 1990 Census of Population and Housing, Summary Tape File 3C, United States Summary, CD-ROM, February 1992.

★1867★

Poverty Status of Families With Children

Black Female Householder, No Spouse Present, With Children Under 5 and 5 to 17 Years Old, Living Below Poverty, 1989

[Table shows the top 50 areas]

MSA	% of population	Rank
Albany, GA	0.9115	1
Monroe, LA	0.8833	2
Pine Bluff, AR	0.8048	3
Shreveport, LA	0.7588	4
Memphis, TN – AR – MS	0.7460	5
New Orleans, LA	0.6857	6
Jackson, MS	0.6763	7
Mobile, AL	0.6091	8
Columbus, GA – AL	0.6023	9
Savannah, GA	0.5968	10
Florence, SC	0.5790	11
Alexandria, LA	0.5693	12
Jackson, TN	0.5527	13
Montgomery, AL	0.5483	14
Baton Rouge, LA	0.5367	15
Macon – Warner Robins, GA	0.5276	16
Lafayette, LA	0.5193	17
Texarkana, TX – Texarkana, AR	0.4895	18
Tallahassee, FL	0.4730	19
Tuscaloosa, AL	0.4724	20
Charleston, SC	0.4632	21
Augusta, GA – SC	0.4592	22

[Continued]

★ 1867 ★

Black Female Householder, No Spouse Present, With Children Under 5 and 5 to 17 Years Old, Living Below Poverty, 1989

[Continued]

MSA	% of population	Rank
Gainesville, FL	0.4380	23
Lake Charles, LA	0.4211	24
Longview – Marshall, TX	0.4199	25
Fayetteville, NC	0.4090	26
Houma – Thibodaux, LA	0.4047	27
Dothan, AL	0.3925	28
Benton Harbor, MI	0.3916	29
Pascagoula, MS	0.3913	30
Birmingham, AL	0.3852	31
Detroit – Ann Arbor, MI	0.3748	32
Milwaukee – Racine, WI	0.3745	33
Beaumont – Port Arthur, TX	0.3674	34
Norfolk – Virginia Beach – Newport News, VA	0.3634	35
Danville, VA	0.3587	36
Muskegon, MI	0.3497	37
Athens, GA	0.3462	38
Flint, MI	0.3389	39
Baltimore, MD	0.3362	40
Pensacola, FL	0.3284	41
Richmond – Petersburg, VA	0.3185	42
Chicago – Gary – Lake County, IL – IN – WI	0.3170	43
Jacksonville, FL	0.3154	44
Kankakee, IL	0.3117	45
Wilmington, NC	0.3084	46
Saint Louis, MO – IL	0.2994	47
Anniston, AL	0.2973	48
Biloxi – Gulfport, MS	0.2952	49
Atlanta, GA	0.2895	50

Source: U.S. Bureau of the Census, Data User Services Division, *1990 Census of Population and Housing,* Summary Tape File 3C, United States Summary, CD-ROM, February 1992.

★ 1868 ★

Poverty Status of Families With Children

Black Female Householder, No Spouse Present, With Children 5 to 17 Years Old, Living Below Poverty, 1989

[Table shows the top 50 areas]

MSA	% of population	Rank
Albany, GA	1.2944	1
Shreveport, LA	1.0624	2
New Orleans, LA	1.0519	3
Pine Bluff, AR	0.9779	4
Monroe, LA	0.9740	5
Jackson, TN	0.9297	6
Jackson, MS	0.9193	7
Florence, SC	0.9087	8
Memphis, TN – AR – MS	0.9070	9

[Continued]

★ 1868 ★

Black Female Householder, No Spouse Present, With Children 5 to 17 Years Old, Living Below Poverty, 1989

[Continued]

MSA	% of population	Rank
Macon – Warner Robins, GA	0.8972	10
Columbus, GA – AL	0.8771	11
Mobile, AL	0.8557	12
Savannah, GA	0.8355	13
Alexandria, LA	0.8141	14
Montgomery, AL	0.7883	15
Baton Rouge, LA	0.7708	16
Tuscaloosa, AL	0.7547	17
Augusta, GA – SC	0.7031	18
Lafayette, LA	0.6530	19
Texarkana, TX – Texarkana, AR	0.6401	20
Flint, MI	0.6293	21
Lake Charles, LA	0.6096	22
Charleston, SC	0.6078	23
Dothan, AL	0.5986	24
Beaumont – Port Arthur, TX	0.5971	25
Birmingham, AL	0.5948	26
Fayetteville, NC	0.5820	27
Houma – Thibodaux, LA	0.5754	28
Wilmington, NC	0.5736	29
Pascagoula, MS	0.5710	30
Longview – Marshall, TX	0.5658	31
Tallahassee, FL	0.5522	32
Benton Harbor, MI	0.5509	33
Norfolk – Virginia Beach – Newport News, VA	0.5086	34
Danville, VA	0.4949	35
Detroit – Ann Arbor, MI	0.4838	36
Biloxi – Gulfport, MS	0.4703	37
Waco, TX	0.4526	38
Milwaukee – Racine, WI	0.4465	39
Kankakee, IL	0.4426	40
Pensacola, FL	0.4405	41
Richmond – Petersburg, VA	0.4372	42
Columbia, SC	0.4343	43
Athens, GA	0.4326	44
Muskegon, MI	0.4246	45
Tyler, TX	0.4197	46
Little Rock – North Little Rock, AR	0.4147	47
Clarksville – Hopkinsville, TN – KY	0.4102	48
Gainesville, FL	0.4096	49
Atlanta, GA	0.3975	50

Source: U.S. Bureau of the Census, Data User Services Division, *1990 Census of Population and Housing,* Summary Tape File 3C, United States Summary, CD-ROM, February 1992.

★1869★

Poverty Status of Families With Children

Black Female Householder, No Spouse Present, With Children Under 5 Years Old, Living Above Poverty, 1989

[Table shows the top 50 areas]

MSA	% of population	Rank
Washington, DC–MD–VA	0.24776	1
Memphis, TN–AR–MS	0.23346	2
Florence, SC	0.22301	3
Baltimore, MD	0.22152	4
Savannah, GA	0.22010	5
Jackson, MS	0.20233	6
Montgomery, AL	0.19213	7
Atlanta, GA	0.18758	8
Richmond–Petersburg, VA	0.18449	9
Macon–Warner Robins, GA	0.17929	10
Columbia, SC	0.17912	11
Danville, VA	0.17662	12
Augusta, GA–SC	0.16885	13
Raleigh–Durham, NC	0.16656	14
Norfolk–Virginia Beach– Newport News, VA	0.15987	15
Lynchburg, VA	0.15682	16
Tallahassee, FL	0.14940	17
Columbus, GA–AL	0.14934	18
Fayetteville, NC	0.14787	19
Greensboro–Winston-Salem– High Point, NC	0.14585	20
New Orleans, LA	0.14207	21
Jacksonville, FL	0.13918	22
New York–Northern New Jersey–Long Island, NY– NJ–CT	0.13612	23
Charleston, SC	0.13573	24
Burlington, NC	0.13492	25
Philadelphia–Wilmington– Trenton, PA–NJ–DE–MD	0.13461	26
Birmingham, AL	0.13208	27
Pine Bluff, AR	0.12750	28
Detroit–Ann Arbor, MI	0.12467	29
Albany, GA	0.12349	30
Athens, GA	0.12287	31
Baton Rouge, LA	0.12134	32
Mobile, AL	0.12077	33
Charlotte–Gastonia–Rock Hill, NC–SC	0.11910	34
Shreveport, LA	0.11844	35
Greenville–Spartanburg, SC	0.11781	36
Atlantic City, NJ	0.11709	37
Tuscaloosa, AL	0.11626	38
Chicago–Gary–Lake County, IL–IN–WI	0.11150	39
Dothan, AL	0.11148	40
Clarksville–Hopkinsville, TN–KY	0.10918	41
Saint Louis, MO–IL	0.10847	42
Little Rock–North Little Rock, AR	0.10680	43
Miami–Fort Lauderdale, FL	0.10459	44
Houston–Galveston–Brazoria, TX	0.10434	45
Indianapolis, IN	0.10433	46
Kankakee, IL	0.10389	47

[Continued]

★1869★

Black Female Householder, No Spouse Present, With Children Under 5 Years Old, Living Above Poverty, 1989

[Continued]

MSA	% of population	Rank
Dallas–Fort Worth, TX	0.10259	48
Cleveland–Akron–Lorain, OH	0.10127	49
Charlottesville, VA	0.09992	50

Source: U.S. Bureau of the Census, Data User Services Division, *1990 Census of Population and Housing,* Summary Tape File 3C, United States Summary, CD-ROM, February 1992.

★1870★

Poverty Status of Families With Children

Black Female Householder, No Spouse Present, With Children Under 5 and 5 to 17 Years Old, Living Above Poverty, 1989

[Table shows the top 50 areas]

MSA	Number	Rank
New York–Northern New Jersey–Long Island, NY– NJ–CT	28,125	1
Chicago–Gary–Lake County, IL–IN–WI	12,852	2
Philadelphia–Wilmington– Trenton, PA–NJ–DE–MD	9,626	3
Los Angeles–Anaheim– Riverside, CA	9,381	4
Washington, DC–MD–VA	8,755	5
Detroit–Ann Arbor, MI	6,821	6
Baltimore, MD	5,589	7
Atlanta, GA	5,361	8
Miami–Fort Lauderdale, FL	4,727	9
San Francisco–Oakland–San Jose, CA	4,244	10
Houston–Galveston–Brazoria, TX	4,158	11
Dallas–Fort Worth, TX	4,142	12
Saint Louis, MO–IL	3,079	13
Cleveland–Akron–Lorain, OH	2,897	14
Memphis, TN–AR–MS	2,796	15
New Orleans, LA	2,168	16
Boston–Lawrence–Salem, MA–NH	2,062	17
Norfolk–Virginia Beach– Newport News, VA	1,998	18
Milwaukee–Racine, WI	1,705	19
Charlotte–Gastonia–Rock Hill, NC–SC	1,597	20
Kansas City, MO–KS	1,514	21
Cincinnati–Hamilton, OH–KY– IN	1,378	22
Jacksonville, FL	1,329	23
Tampa–Saint Petersburg– Clearwater, FL	1,298	24
Richmond–Petersburg, VA	1,270	25
Birmingham, AL	1,254	26
Indianapolis, IN	1,180	27

[Continued]

★1870★

Black Female Householder, No Spouse Present, With Children Under 5 and 5 to 17 Years Old, Living Above Poverty, 1989

[Continued]

MSA	Number	Rank
Greensboro – Winston-Salem – High Point, NC	1,050	28
Jackson, MS	1,014	29
Orlando, FL	1,011	30
Nashville, TN	978	31
Columbus, OH	947	32
West Palm Beach – Boca Raton – Delray Beach, FL	925	33
San Diego, CA	924	34
Hartford – New Britain – Middletown, CT	918	35
Raleigh – Durham, NC	909	36
Rochester, NY	865	37
Sacramento, CA	827	38
Columbia, SC	803	39
Pittsburgh – Beaver Valley, PA	789	40
Greenville – Spartanburg, SC	781	41
Seattle – Tacoma, WA	767	42
Charleston, SC	738	43
Buffalo – Niagara Falls, NY	728	44
Augusta, GA – SC	681	45
Dayton – Springfield, OH	674	46
Montgomery, AL	660	47
Baton Rouge, LA	650	48
Little Rock – North Little Rock, AR	624	49
Mobile, AL	621	50

Source: U.S. Bureau of the Census, Data User Services Division, *1990 Census of Population and Housing,* Summary Tape File 3C, United States Summary, CD- ROM, February 1992.

★1871★

Poverty Status of Families With Children

Black Female Householder, No Spouse Present, With Children 5 to 17 Years Old, Living Above Poverty, 1989

[Table shows the top 50 areas]

MSA	% of population	Rank
Albany, GA	1.0750	1
Memphis, TN – AR – MS	1.0009	2
Jackson, MS	0.9112	3
Jackson, TN	0.8797	4
Savannah, GA	0.8041	5
Montgomery, AL	0.8030	6
Washington, DC – MD – VA	0.8004	7
Macon – Warner Robins, GA	0.7865	8
Baltimore, MD	0.7753	9
Columbia, SC	0.7668	10
Columbus, GA – AL	0.7553	11
New Orleans, LA	0.7422	12
Richmond – Petersburg, VA	0.7418	13
Atlanta, GA	0.7394	14

[Continued]

★1871★

Black Female Householder, No Spouse Present, With Children 5 to 17 Years Old, Living Above Poverty, 1989

[Continued]

MSA	% of population	Rank
Tallahassee, FL	0.7333	15
Florence, SC	0.7119	16
Augusta, GA – SC	0.6950	17
Raleigh – Durham, NC	0.6673	18
Birmingham, AL	0.6513	19
Shreveport, LA	0.6398	20
Danville, VA	0.6338	21
Fayetteville, NC	0.6057	22
Pine Bluff, AR	0.6036	23
Flint, MI	0.5947	24
Norfolk – Virginia Beach – Newport News, VA	0.5707	25
Charlotte – Gastonia – Rock Hill, NC – SC	0.5629	26
Detroit – Ann Arbor, MI	0.5526	27
Greensboro – Winston-Salem – High Point, NC	0.5486	28
Wilmington, NC	0.5396	29
Monroe, LA	0.5387	30
Lynchburg, VA	0.5359	31
Baton Rouge, LA	0.5291	32
Charleston, SC	0.5169	33
New York – Northern New Jersey – Long Island, NY – NJ – CT	0.5161	34
Philadelphia – Wilmington – Trenton, PA – NJ – DE – MD	0.5066	35
Jacksonville, FL	0.5018	36
Chicago – Gary – Lake County, IL – IN – WI	0.4900	37
Little Rock – North Little Rock, AR	0.4839	38
Tuscaloosa, AL	0.4810	39
Saint Louis, MO – IL	0.4794	40
Mobile, AL	0.4791	41
Tyler, TX	0.4679	42
Alexandria, LA	0.4652	43
Greenville – Spartanburg, SC	0.4642	44
Athens, GA	0.4563	45
Houston – Galveston – Brazoria, TX	0.4448	46
Burlington, NC	0.4417	47
Nashville, TN	0.4391	48
Miami – Fort Lauderdale, FL	0.4382	49
Anderson, SC	0.4339	50

Source: U.S. Bureau of the Census, Data User Services Division, *1990 Census of Population and Housing,* Summary Tape File 3C, United States Summary, CD-ROM, February 1992.

★1872★

Poverty Status of Families With Children

Black Male Householder, No Spouse Present, With Children Under 5 Years Old, Living Below Poverty, 1989

[Table shows the top 50 areas]

MSA	% of population	Rank
Alexandria, LA	0.05777	1
Jackson, MS	0.03743	2
Pine Bluff, AR	0.03626	3
Monroe, LA	0.03516	4
Naples, FL	0.02893	5
Montgomery, AL	0.02701	6
Memphis, TN–AR–MS	0.02699	7
Baton Rouge, LA	0.02556	8
Tallahassee, FL	0.02397	9
Lafayette, LA	0.02347	10
New Orleans, LA	0.02284	11
Flint, MI	0.02230	12
Pascagoula, MS	0.02169	13
Bloomington–Normal, IL	0.02013	14
Savannah, GA	0.01978	15
Lynchburg, VA	0.01828	16
Saginaw–Bay City–Midland, MI	0.01803	17
Springfield, IL	0.01794	18
Champaign–Urbana–Rantoul, IL	0.01792	19
Anderson, SC	0.01791	20
Sherman–Denison, TX	0.01789	21
Biloxi–Gulfport, MS	0.01776	22
Burlington, NC	0.01756	23
Shreveport, LA	0.01735	24
Miami–Fort Lauderdale, FL	0.01695	25
Raleigh–Durham, NC	0.01659	26
Houma–Thibodaux, LA	0.01641	27
Huntsville, AL	0.01632	28
Charleston, SC	0.01598	29
Lawrence, KS	0.01589	30
Florence, SC	0.01574	31
Merced, CA	0.01569	32
Birmingham, AL	0.01531	33
Indianapolis, IN	0.01512	34
Cleveland–Akron–Lorain, OH	0.01489	35
Little Rock–North Little Rock, AR	0.01481	36
Danville, VA	0.01472	37
Mobile, AL	0.01426	38
West Palm Beach–Boca Raton–Delray Beach, FL	0.01413	39
Columbus, GA–AL	0.01399	40
Lake Charles, LA	0.01368	41
Lima, OH	0.01361	42
New Haven–Meriden, CT	0.01339	43
Wilmington, NC	0.01330	44
Detroit–Ann Arbor, MI	0.01320	45
Atlanta, GA	0.01313	46
Reading, PA	0.01307	47
Houston–Galveston–Brazoria, TX	0.01302	48
Jackson, TN	0.01282	49
Pensacola, FL	0.01278	50

Source: U.S. Bureau of the Census, Data User Services Division, *1990 Census of Population and Housing*, Summary Tape File 3C, United States Summary, CD-ROM, February 1992.

★1873★

Poverty Status of Families With Children

Black Male Householder, No Spouse Present, With Children Under 5 and 5 to 17 Years Old, Living Below Poverty, 1989

[Table shows the top 50 areas]

MSA	% of population	Rank
Monroe, LA	0.08228	1
Albany, GA	0.04886	2
Shreveport, LA	0.04546	3
Florence, SC	0.04110	4
New Orleans, LA	0.03907	5
Lafayette, LA	0.03785	6
Jackson, MS	0.03693	7
Memphis, TN–AR–MS	0.03524	8
Houma–Thibodaux, LA	0.03500	9
Baton Rouge, LA	0.03313	10
Alexandria, LA	0.03117	11
Tallahassee, FL	0.02611	12
Danville, VA	0.02576	13
Montgomery, AL	0.02564	14
West Palm Beach–Boca Raton–Delray Beach, FL	0.02443	15
Miami–Fort Lauderdale, FL	0.02368	16
Beaumont–Port Arthur, TX	0.02298	17
Enid, OK	0.02291	18
Burlington, NC	0.02125	19
Biloxi–Gulfport, MS	0.02080	20
Kankakee, IL	0.02078	21
Waterloo–Cedar Falls, IA	0.01978	22
Mobile, AL	0.01782	23
Flint, MI	0.01766	24
Gadsden, AL	0.01703	25
Kalamazoo, MI	0.01656	26
Columbus, OH	0.01619	27
Houston–Galveston–Brazoria, TX	0.01584	28
Birmingham, AL	0.01564	29
Columbia, SC	0.01544	30
Jackson, TN	0.01539	31
Bradenton, FL	0.01512	32
Baltimore, MD	0.01511	33
Clarksville–Hopkinsville, TN–KY	0.01475	34
Atlanta, GA	0.01472	35
Gainesville, FL	0.01470	36
Little Rock–North Little Rock, AR	0.01462	37
Saint Joseph, MO	0.01444	38
Pine Bluff, AR	0.01404	39
Lake Charles, LA	0.01368	40
Philadelphia–Wilmington–Trenton, PA–NJ–DE–MD	0.01358	41
Jacksonville, NC	0.01335	42
Tuscaloosa, AL	0.01329	43
Anderson, IN	0.01301	44
Detroit–Ann Arbor, MI	0.01288	45
Macon–Warner Robins, GA	0.01281	46
Savannah, GA	0.01278	47
Huntsville, AL	0.01256	48
Fort Myers–Cape Coral, Fl	0.01253	49
Anderson, SC	0.01240	50

Source: U.S. Bureau of the Census, Data User Services Division, *1990 Census of Population and Housing*, Summary Tape File 3C, United States Summary, CD-ROM, February 1992.

★1874★

Poverty Status of Families With Children

Black Male Householder, No Spouse Present, With Children Under 5 Years Old, Living Above Poverty, 1989

[Table shows the top 50 areas]

MSA	% of population	Rank
Albany, GA	0.10039	1
Atlantic City, NJ	0.07451	2
Richmond – Petersburg, VA	0.06146	3
Tallahassee, FL	0.06079	4
Columbus, GA – AL	0.06006	5
Washington, DC – MD – VA	0.05786	6
Memphis, TN – AR – MS	0.05714	7
Atlanta, GA	0.05520	8
Baltimore, MD	0.05520	8
Biloxi – Gulfport, MS	0.05225	9
Columbia, SC	0.04985	10
New Orleans, LA	0.04948	11
Miami – Fort Lauderdale, FL	0.04758	12
Jackson, MS	0.04755	13
Montgomery, AL	0.04752	14
Las Vegas, NV	0.04720	15
Battle Creek, MI	0.04707	16
Baton Rouge, LA	0.04638	17
Macon – Warner Robins, GA	0.04518	18
Raleigh – Durham, NC	0.04378	19
Norfolk – Virginia Beach – Newport News, VA	0.04312	20
West Palm Beach – Boca Raton – Delray Beach, FL	0.04192	21
Charlotte – Gastonia – Rock Hill, NC – SC	0.03976	22
Fayetteville, NC	0.03897	23
Florence, SC	0.03848	24
Augusta, GA – SC	0.03805	25
Jacksonville, NC	0.03804	26
Burlington, NC	0.03789	27
Philadelphia – Wilmington – Trenton, PA – NJ – DE – MD	0.03763	28
Midland, TX	0.03658	29
Houma – Thibodaux, LA	0.03610	30
Charleston, SC	0.03433	31
Detroit – Ann Arbor, MI	0.03361	32
Greensboro – Winston-Salem – High Point, NC	0.03354	33
Athens, GA	0.03328	34
Jacksonville, FL	0.03320	35
Houston – Galveston – Brazoria, TX	0.03279	36
Pine Bluff, AR	0.03275	37
New York – Northern New Jersey – Long Island, NY – NJ – CT	0.03195	38
Lynchburg, VA	0.03165	39
Anderson, SC	0.03099	40
Wilmington, NC	0.03076	41
Indianapolis, IN	0.03048	42
Roanoke, VA	0.02940	43
Dallas – Fort Worth, TX	0.02939	44
Greenville – Spartanburg, SC	0.02887	45
Monroe, LA	0.02883	46

[Continued]

★1874★

Black Male Householder, No Spouse Present, With Children Under 5 Years Old, Living Above Poverty, 1989
[Continued]

MSA	% of population	Rank
Flint, MI	0.02857	47
Fort Wayne, IN	0.02749	48
Saint Louis, MO – IL	0.02709	49

Source: U.S. Bureau of the Census, Data User Services Division, *1990 Census of Population and Housing*, Summary Tape File 3C, United States Summary, CD-ROM, February 1992.

★1875★

Poverty Status of Families With Children

Black Male Householder, No Spouse Present, With Children 5 to 17 Years Old, Living Below Poverty, 1989

[Table shows the top 50 areas]

MSA	% of population	Rank
Lafayette, LA	0.09533	1
Florence, SC	0.07171	2
Shreveport, LA	0.07059	3
Macon – Warner Robins, GA	0.06581	4
Jackson, MS	0.06045	5
New Orleans, LA	0.05788	6
Savannah, GA	0.05770	7
Monroe, LA	0.05697	8
Pascagoula, MS	0.05640	9
Albany, GA	0.05508	10
Longview – Marshall, TX	0.05233	11
Alexandria, LA	0.05169	12
Jackson, TN	0.05129	13
Memphis, TN – AR – MS	0.04828	14
Biloxi – Gulfport, MS	0.04819	15
Pine Bluff, AR	0.04679	16
Tallahassee, FL	0.04623	17
Mobile, AL	0.04571	18
Montgomery, AL	0.04547	19
Cheyenne, WY	0.04102	20
Columbia, MO	0.04093	21
Charleston, SC	0.03926	22
Augusta, GA – SC	0.03906	23
Columbus, GA – AL	0.03785	24
Miami – Fort Lauderdale, FL	0.03696	25
Baton Rouge, LA	0.03540	26
Tuscaloosa, AL	0.03189	27
Lake Charles, LA	0.03093	28
Houma – Thibodaux, LA	0.03008	29
Detroit – Ann Arbor, MI	0.02902	30
Atlanta, GA	0.02862	31
Baltimore, MD	0.02804	32
Tyler, TX	0.02776	33
Huntsville, AL	0.02763	34
Beaumont – Port Arthur, TX	0.02713	35
West Palm Beach – Boca Raton – Delray Beach, FL	0.02710	36

[Continued]

★1875★

Black Male Householder, No Spouse Present, With Children 5 to 17 Years Old, Living Below Poverty, 1989

[Continued]

MSA	% of population	Rank
Texarkana, TX – Texarkana, AR	0.02664	37
Houston – Galveston – Brazoria, TX	0.02654	38
Saginaw – Bay City – Midland, MI	0.02629	39
Panama City, FL	0.02599	40
Cleveland – Akron – Lorain, OH	0.02591	41
Pensacola, FL	0.02584	42
Fort Pierce, FL	0.02549	43
Chattanooga, TN – GA	0.02539	44
Gadsden, AL	0.02504	45
Youngstown – Warren, OH	0.02395	46
Columbia, SC	0.02382	47
Lakeland – Winter Haven, FL	0.02368	48
Birmingham, AL	0.02335	49
Flint, MI	0.02323	50

Source: U.S. Bureau of the Census, Data User Services Division, 1990 Census of Population and Housing, Summary Tape File 3C, United States Summary, CD-ROM, February 1992.

★1876★

Poverty Status of Families With Children

Black Male Householder, No Spouse Present, With Children Under 5 and 5 to 17 Years Old, Living Above Poverty, 1989

[Table shows the top 50 areas]

MSA	% of population	Rank
Florence, SC	0.05247	1
Shreveport, LA	0.04696	2
Savannah, GA	0.04657	3
Pine Bluff, AR	0.04562	4
Macon – Warner Robins, GA	0.04091	5
Miami – Fort Lauderdale, FL	0.04066	6
Gadsden, AL	0.04006	7
Montgomery, AL	0.03760	8
Biloxi – Gulfport, MS	0.03703	9
Benton Harbor, MI	0.03594	10
Washington, DC – MD – VA	0.03459	11
Baltimore, MD	0.03451	12
New Orleans, LA	0.03398	13
Atlanta, GA	0.03328	14
Jackson, MS	0.03313	15
Tallahassee, FL	0.03296	16
Burlington, NC	0.03234	17
Charlottesville, VA	0.03203	18
Richmond – Petersburg, VA	0.03131	19
Memphis, TN – AR – MS	0.03076	20
Philadelphia – Wilmington – Trenton, PA – NJ – DE – MD	0.03027	21
Baton Rouge, LA	0.02972	22
Athens, GA	0.02944	23

[Continued]

★1876★

Black Male Householder, No Spouse Present, With Children Under 5 and 5 to 17 Years Old, Living Above Poverty, 1989

[Continued]

MSA	% of population	Rank
Charleston, SC	0.02723	24
Tyler, TX	0.02710	25
Columbia, SC	0.02625	26
Fayetteville, NC	0.02586	27
New York – Northern New Jersey – Long Island, NY – NJ – CT	0.02539	28
Charlotte – Gastonia – Rock Hill, NC – SC	0.02513	29
Norfolk – Virginia Beach – Newport News, VA	0.02500	30
Anderson, SC	0.02479	31
Gainesville, FL	0.02450	32
Augusta, GA – SC	0.02369	33
Chicago – Gary – Lake County, IL – IN – WI	0.02354	34
Pascagoula, MS	0.02343	35
Danville, VA	0.02300	36
Atlantic City, NJ	0.02285	37
Springfield, IL	0.02269	38
Topeka, KS	0.02236	39
Flint, MI	0.02230	40
Detroit – Ann Arbor, MI	0.02191	41
Jacksonville, FL	0.02184	42
Monroe, LA	0.02180	43
Lawton, OK	0.02153	44
Greenville – Spartanburg, SC	0.02107	45
Dothan, AL	0.02062	46
Lafayette, LA	0.02012	47
West Palm Beach – Boca Raton – Delray Beach, FL	0.01992	48
Houston – Galveston – Brazoria, TX	0.01991	49
Birmingham, AL	0.01950	50

Source: U.S. Bureau of the Census, Data User Services Division, 1990 Census of Population and Housing, Summary Tape File 3C, United States Summary, CD-ROM, February 1992.

★1877★

Poverty Status of Families With Children

Black Male Householder, No Spouse Present, With Children 5 to 17 Years Old, Living Above Poverty, 1989

[Table shows the top 50 areas]

MSA	% of population	Rank
Memphis, TN – AR – MS	0.15513	1
Columbus, GA – AL	0.13741	2
Washington, DC – MD – VA	0.13528	3
Florence, SC	0.13293	4
Pine Bluff, AR	0.13101	5
Albany, GA	0.12082	6

[Continued]

★1877★

Black Male Householder, No Spouse Present, With Children 5 to 17 Years Old, Living Above Poverty, 1989

[Continued]

MSA	% of population	Rank
Baltimore, MD	0.11817	7
Columbia, SC	0.11802	8
Richmond – Petersburg, VA	0.11529	9
Macon – Warner Robins, GA	0.11419	10
Savannah, GA	0.11376	11
Shreveport, LA	0.11186	12
Atlanta, GA	0.11106	13
New Orleans, LA	0.10954	14
Baton Rouge, LA	0.10771	15
Montgomery, AL	0.10563	16
Augusta, GA – SC	0.10206	17
Birmingham, AL	0.10189	18
Fayetteville, NC	0.09834	19
Miami – Fort Lauderdale, FL	0.09419	20
Huntsville, AL	0.09418	21
Alexandria, LA	0.09350	22
Pascagoula, MS	0.09285	23
Lafayette, LA	0.09246	24
Danville, VA	0.09107	25
Jackson, MS	0.08978	26
Raleigh – Durham, NC	0.08811	27
Norfolk – Virginia Beach – Newport News, VA	0.08767	28
Greenville – Spartanburg, SC	0.08645	29
Atlantic City, NJ	0.08641	30
Philadelphia – Wilmington – Trenton, PA – NJ – DE – MD	0.08370	31
Beaumont – Port Arthur, TX	0.08001	32
Monroe, LA	0.07947	33
Charleston, SC	0.07911	34
Decatur, AL	0.07905	35
Detroit – Ann Arbor, MI	0.07895	36
New York – Northern New Jersey – Long Island, NY – NJ – CT	0.07776	37
Gadsden, AL	0.07712	38
Chicago – Gary – Lake County, IL – IN – WI	0.07665	39
Texarkana, TX – Texarkana, AR	0.07658	40
Jacksonville, FL	0.07422	41
Saint Louis, MO – IL	0.07402	42
Houston – Galveston – Brazoria, TX	0.07332	43
Mobile, AL	0.07318	44
Roanoke, VA	0.07083	45
Lakeland – Winter Haven, FL	0.07055	46
Charlotte – Gastonia – Rock Hill, NC – SC	0.06919	47
Tallahassee, FL	0.06678	48
Flint, MI	0.06598	49
Little Rock – North Little Rock, AR	0.06587	50

Source: U.S. Bureau of the Census, Data User Services Division, *1990 Census of Population and Housing,* Summary Tape File 3C, United States Summary, CD-ROM, February 1992.

★1878★

Poverty Status of Families With Children

Black Married Couples With Children Under 5 Years Old, Living Below Poverty, 1989

[Table shows the top 50 areas]

MSA	% of population	Rank
Jackson, TN	0.1141	1
Pine Bluff, AR	0.0994	2
Baton Rouge, LA	0.0835	3
Alexandria, LA	0.0806	4
Jackson, MS	0.0787	5
Killeen – Temple, TX	0.0752	6
Lafayette, LA	0.0747	7
Montgomery, AL	0.0714	8
Monroe, LA	0.0710	9
Lawton, OK	0.0691	10
Clarksville – Hopkinsville, TN – KY	0.0685	11
Fayetteville, NC	0.0656	12
Memphis, TN – AR – MS	0.0633	13
Tyler, TX	0.0628	14
Danville, VA	0.0598	15
Savannah, GA	0.0598	15
Waco, TX	0.0597	16
New Orleans, LA	0.0584	17
Macon – Warner Robins, GA	0.0576	18
Columbus, GA – AL	0.0564	19
Albany, GA	0.0551	20
Mobile, AL	0.0549	21
Beaumont – Port Arthur, TX	0.0548	22
Houma – Thibodaux, LA	0.0547	23
Charleston, SC	0.0533	24
Shreveport, LA	0.0523	25
Biloxi – Gulfport, MS	0.0517	26
Norfolk – Virginia Beach – Newport News, VA	0.0510	27
Little Rock – North Little Rock, AR	0.0499	28
Jacksonville, NC	0.0454	29
Huntsville, AL	0.0448	30
Midland, TX	0.0441	31
Pensacola, FL	0.0438	32
Augusta, GA – SC	0.0433	33
Birmingham, AL	0.0413	34
Columbia, SC	0.0413	34
Lubbock, TX	0.0400	35
Texarkana, TX – Texarkana, AR	0.0400	35
Columbia, MO	0.0374	36
Lake Charles, LA	0.0345	37
Florence, SC	0.0341	38
Houston – Galveston – Brazoria, TX	0.0332	39
Jacksonville, FL	0.0332	39
Odessa, TX	0.0320	40
Dothan, AL	0.0313	41
Decatur, IL	0.0307	42
Lakeland – Winter Haven, FL	0.0303	43
Las Cruces, NM	0.0303	43
Lynchburg, VA	0.0302	44
Gadsden, AL	0.0300	45

Source: U.S. Bureau of the Census, Data User Services Division, *1990 Census of Population and Housing,* Summary Tape File 3C, United States Summary, CD-ROM, February 1992.

★1879★

Poverty Status of Families With Children

Black Married Couples With Children Under 5 and 5 to 17 Years Old, Living Below Poverty, 1989

[Table shows the top 50 areas]

MSA	% of population	Rank
Jackson, MS	0.22054	1
Alexandria, LA	0.19839	2
Pine Bluff, AR	0.19652	3
Monroe, LA	0.19200	4
Charleston, SC	0.18821	5
Shreveport, LA	0.17736	6
Lafayette, LA	0.17007	7
Savannah, GA	0.16569	8
Memphis, TN–AR–MS	0.16012	9
Albany, GA	0.15814	10
Houma–Thibodaux, LA	0.15150	11
New Orleans, LA	0.14570	12
Lake Charles, LA	0.14512	13
Florence, SC	0.14343	14
Beaumont–Port Arthur, TX	0.14229	15
Tyler, TX	0.14209	16
Mobile, AL	0.14048	17
Baton Rouge, LA	0.13951	18
Kankakee, IL	0.13714	19
Columbus, GA–AL	0.13535	20
Montgomery, AL	0.12751	21
Fayetteville, NC	0.12055	22
Dothan, AL	0.11988	23
Augusta, GA–SC	0.11290	24
Jacksonville, NC	0.11212	25
Pensacola, FL	0.10714	26
Killeen–Temple, TX	0.10693	27
Macon–Warner Robins, GA	0.10530	28
Jackson, TN	0.10387	29
Birmingham, AL	0.10288	30
Lawton, OK	0.10136	31
Longview–Marshall, TX	0.09727	32
Anderson, SC	0.09229	33
Tuscaloosa, AL	0.09168	34
Biloxi–Gulfport, MS	0.08878	35
Texarkana, TX–Texarkana, AR	0.08824	36
Burlington, NC	0.08594	37
Clarksville–Hopkinsville, TN–KY	0.08440	38
Columbia, SC	0.08427	39
Little Rock–North Little Rock, AR	0.08185	40
Pascagoula, MS	0.08157	41
Jacksonville, FL	0.08007	42
Fort Pierce, FL	0.07807	43
Tallahassee, FL	0.07406	44
Miami–Fort Lauderdale, FL	0.07048	45
Anniston, AL	0.06895	46
Danville, VA	0.06807	47
Norfolk–Virginia Beach–Newport News, VA	0.06525	48
Florence, AL	0.06320	49
Gainesville, FL	0.06320	49

Source: U.S. Bureau of the Census, Data User Services Division, *1990 Census of Population and Housing,* Summary Tape File 3C, United States Summary, CD-ROM, February 1992.

★1880★

Poverty Status of Families With Children

Black Married Couples With Children 5 to 17 Years Old, Living Below Poverty, 1989

[Table shows the top 50 areas]

MSA	% of population	Rank
Pine Bluff, AR	0.30999	1
Florence, SC	0.29298	2
Lafayette, LA	0.26636	3
Jackson, MS	0.26328	4
Mobile, AL	0.23379	5
New Orleans, LA	0.22909	6
Baton Rouge, LA	0.22848	7
Albany, GA	0.22743	8
Shreveport, LA	0.22701	9
Montgomery, AL	0.22597	10
Monroe, LA	0.22224	11
Alexandria, LA	0.20828	12
Danville, VA	0.19409	13
Longview–Marshall, TX	0.19393	14
Memphis, TN–AR–MS	0.19384	15
Beaumont–Port Arthur, TX	0.19323	16
Macon–Warner Robins, GA	0.17396	17
Charleston, SC	0.16612	18
Lake Charles, LA	0.15345	19
Columbus, GA–AL	0.15263	20
Tuscaloosa, AL	0.15014	21
Texarkana, TX–Texarkana, AR	0.14984	22
Houma–Thibodaux, LA	0.14548	23
Birmingham, AL	0.14320	24
Savannah, GA	0.14178	25
Pascagoula, MS	0.13970	26
Columbia, SC	0.13743	27
Tyler, TX	0.13482	28
Biloxi–Gulfport, MS	0.12632	29
Fayetteville, NC	0.11946	30
Augusta, GA–SC	0.11063	31
Dothan, AL	0.10995	32
Little Rock–North Little Rock, AR	0.10777	33
Tallahassee, FL	0.10702	34
Anniston, AL	0.10514	35
Waco, TX	0.10311	36
Ocala, FL	0.09906	37
Pensacola, FL	0.09233	38
Gadsden, AL	0.09115	39
Miami–Fort Lauderdale, FL	0.08748	40
Huntsville, AL	0.08664	41
Houston–Galveston–Brazoria, TX	0.08537	42
Norfolk–Virginia Beach–Newport News, VA	0.08509	43
Bryan–College Station, TX	0.08370	44
Jacksonville, FL	0.08150	45
Jackson, TN	0.08079	46
Atlanta, GA	0.07941	47
Anderson, SC	0.07783	48
Wichita Falls, TX	0.07763	49
Clarksville–Hopkinsville, TN–KY	0.07613	50

Source: U.S. Bureau of the Census, Data User Services Division, *1990 Census of Population and Housing,* Summary Tape File 3C, United States Summary, CD-ROM, February 1992.

★1881★

Poverty Status of Families With Children

Black Married Couples With Children Under 5 Years Old, Living Above Poverty, 1989

[Table only shows the top 50 areas]

MSA	% of population	Rank
Fayetteville, NC	0.72514	1
Killeen – Temple, TX	0.64904	2
Jacksonville, NC	0.59064	3
Columbus, GA – AL	0.51219	4
Norfolk – Virginia Beach – Newport News, VA	0.50455	5
Jackson, MS	0.49368	6
Clarksville – Hopkinsville, TN – KY	0.49221	7
Albany, GA	0.44598	8
Savannah, GA	0.44596	9
Columbia, SC	0.44338	10
Florence, SC	0.42766	11
Charleston, SC	0.42417	12
Richmond – Petersburg, VA	0.42350	13
Memphis, TN – AR – MS	0.40896	14
Raleigh – Durham, NC	0.40830	15
Washington, DC – MD – VA	0.40738	16
Augusta, GA – SC	0.40422	17
Atlanta, GA	0.39516	18
Lawton, OK	0.37404	19
Macon – Warner Robins, GA	0.36677	20
Jackson, TN	0.35906	21
Tallahassee, FL	0.35788	22
New Orleans, LA	0.35381	23
Baton Rouge, LA	0.34263	24
Birmingham, AL	0.33752	25
Montgomery, AL	0.33229	26
Huntsville, AL	0.32481	27
Dothan, AL	0.31001	28
Alexandria, LA	0.29341	29
Baltimore, MD	0.29305	30
Burlington, NC	0.28462	31
Shreveport, LA	0.27696	32
Danville, VA	0.27320	33
Jacksonville, FL	0.27153	34
Lynchburg, VA	0.27004	35
Greensboro – Winston-Salem – High Point, NC	0.26547	36
Pine Bluff, AR	0.25969	37
Charlotte – Gastonia – Rock Hill, NC – SC	0.25170	38
Pascagoula, MS	0.24644	39
Beaumont – Port Arthur, TX	0.24638	40
Athens, GA	0.24509	41
Houston – Galveston – Brazoria, TX	0.24322	42
Lafayette, LA	0.24049	43
Anniston, AL	0.24045	44
Miami – Fort Lauderdale, FL	0.23317	45
Mobile, AL	0.23148	46
Biloxi – Gulfport, MS	0.22879	47
Lake Charles, LA	0.22542	48
Dallas – Fort Worth, TX	0.21967	49
Salinas – Seaside – Monterey, CA	0.21931	50

Source: U.S. Bureau of the Census, Data User Services Division, *1990 Census of Population and Housing,* Summary Tape File 3C, United States Summary, CD-ROM, February 1992.

★1882★

Poverty Status of Families With Children

Black Married Couples With Children Under 5 and 5 to 17 Years Old, Living Above Poverty, 1989

[Table shows the top 50 areas]

MSA	% of population	Rank
Fayetteville, NC	0.7157	1
Jackson, MS	0.6841	2
Albany, GA	0.6272	3
Pine Bluff, AR	0.6118	4
Memphis, TN – AR – MS	0.6046	5
Florence, SC	0.6008	6
Savannah, GA	0.5807	7
Columbia, SC	0.5782	8
Columbus, GA – AL	0.5772	9
Augusta, GA – SC	0.5678	10
Charleston, SC	0.5664	11
Montgomery, AL	0.5384	12
Norfolk – Virginia Beach – Newport News, VA	0.5333	13
Danville, VA	0.5133	14
Killeen – Temple, TX	0.5092	15
Baton Rouge, LA	0.4895	16
Jackson, TN	0.4719	17
New Orleans, LA	0.4687	18
Jacksonville, NC	0.4685	19
Lawton, OK	0.4673	20
Atlanta, GA	0.4519	21
Macon – Warner Robins, GA	0.4415	22
Shreveport, LA	0.4298	23
Richmond – Petersburg, VA	0.4293	24
Mobile, AL	0.4277	25
Washington, DC – MD – VA	0.4196	26
Tallahassee, FL	0.4118	27
Birmingham, AL	0.4079	28
Lafayette, LA	0.4048	29
Little Rock – North Little Rock, AR	0.4017	30
Beaumont – Port Arthur, TX	0.3948	31
Pascagoula, MS	0.3940	32
Raleigh – Durham, NC	0.3894	33
Huntsville, AL	0.3838	34
Tuscaloosa, AL	0.3747	35
Lake Charles, LA	0.3699	36
Charlotte – Gastonia – Rock Hill, NC – SC	0.3534	37
Anniston, AL	0.3404	38
Texarkana, TX – Texarkana, AR	0.3388	39
Jacksonville, FL	0.3352	40
Baltimore, MD	0.3319	41
Miami – Fort Lauderdale, FL	0.3311	42
Longview – Marshall, TX	0.3300	43
Lynchburg, VA	0.3263	44
Tyler, TX	0.3245	45
Dothan, AL	0.3184	46
Alexandria, LA	0.3170	47
Burlington, NC	0.3123	48
Houston – Galveston – Brazoria, TX	0.3119	49
Monroe, LA	0.3080	50

Source: U.S. Bureau of the Census, Data User Services Division, *1990 Census of Population and Housing,* Summary Tape File 3C, United States Summary, CD-ROM, February 1992.

Poverty Status of Families With Children

Black Married Couples With Children 5 to 17 Years Old, Living Above Poverty, 1989

[Table shows the top 50 areas]

MSA	% of population	Rank
Albany, GA	1.6826	1
Jackson, MS	1.6108	2
Florence, SC	1.5961	3
Columbus, GA–AL	1.5769	4
Pine Bluff, AR	1.5616	5
Fayetteville, NC	1.4146	6
Memphis, TN–AR–MS	1.4095	7
Macon–Warner Robins, GA	1.3981	8
Augusta, GA–SC	1.3460	9
Columbia, SC	1.3445	10
Danville, VA	1.3173	11
Montgomery, AL	1.3097	12
Charleston, SC	1.2674	13
Shreveport, LA	1.2365	14
Savannah, GA	1.2081	15
Richmond–Petersburg, VA	1.2041	16
Jackson, TN	1.1900	17
New Orleans, LA	1.1358	18
Norfolk–Virginia Beach–Newport News, VA	1.1320	19
Baton Rouge, LA	1.1210	20
Tallahassee, FL	1.1135	21
Birmingham, AL	1.0553	22
Washington, DC–MD–VA	1.0522	23
Tuscaloosa, AL	1.0331	24
Atlanta, GA	1.0236	25
Raleigh–Durham, NC	1.0234	26
Lake Charles, LA	1.0194	27
Burlington, NC	1.0184	28
Beaumont–Port Arthur, TX	0.9941	29
Lynchburg, VA	0.9571	30
Lawton, OK	0.9490	31
Huntsville, AL	0.9489	32
Alexandria, LA	0.9448	33
Lafayette, LA	0.9241	34
Pascagoula, MS	0.9215	35
Tyler, TX	0.8995	36
Monroe, LA	0.8981	37
Clarksville–Hopkinsville, TN–KY	0.8770	38
Killeen–Temple, TX	0.8766	39
Texarkana, TX–Texarkana, AR	0.8715	40
Longview–Marshall, TX	0.8674	41
Little Rock–North Little Rock, AR	0.8672	42
Anniston, AL	0.8635	43
Charlotte–Gastonia–Rock Hill, NC–SC	0.8487	44
Mobile, AL	0.8442	45
Baltimore, MD	0.8427	46
Greensboro–Winston-Salem–High Point, NC	0.8152	47
Dothan, AL	0.8017	48
Jacksonville, FL	0.7701	49
Wilmington, NC	0.7698	50

Source: U.S. Bureau of the Census, Data User Services Division, *1990 Census of Population and Housing,* Summary Tape File 3C, United States Summary, CD-ROM, February 1992.

Poverty Status of Families With Children

Hispanic Female Householder, No Spouse Present, With Children Under 5 Years Old, Living Below Poverty, 1989

[Table shows the top 50 areas]

MSA	% of population	Rank
Pueblo, CO	0.33970	1
Laredo, TX	0.22891	2
Brownsville–Harlingen, TX	0.21951	3
Springfield, MA	0.21757	4
McAllen–Edinburg–Mission, TX	0.20676	5
Las Cruces, NM	0.19925	6
Visalia–Tulare–Porterville, CA	0.18723	7
Corpus Christi, TX	0.17348	8
Fresno, CA	0.16435	9
San Antonio, TX	0.16135	10
El Paso, TX	0.16075	11
Albuquerque, NM	0.15502	12
Greeley, CO	0.13958	13
Yuma, AZ	0.13097	14
Victoria, TX	0.13044	15
Yakima, WA	0.13028	16
Bakersfield, CA	0.11886	17
Tucson, AZ	0.11321	18
Odessa, TX	0.11099	19
Merced, CA	0.10986	20
Fitchburg–Leominster, MA	0.09922	21
New Bedford, MA	0.09732	22
New York–Northern New Jersey–Long Island, NY–NJ–CT	0.09112	23
Hartford–New Britain–Middletown, CT	0.09062	24
San Angelo, TX	0.08735	25
Santa Fe, NM	0.08544	26
Richland–Kennewick–Pasco, WA	0.08531	27
Waterbury, CT	0.08438	28
Lubbock, TX	0.08310	29
Yuba City, CA	0.07909	30
Santa Barbara–Santa Maria–Lompoc, CA	0.07873	31
Denver–Boulder, CO	0.07553	32
Reading, PA	0.07102	33
Worcester, MA	0.06889	34
Midland, TX	0.06754	35
Los Angeles–Anaheim–Riverside, CA	0.06450	36
Jamestown–Dunkirk, NY	0.06413	37
Colorado Springs, CO	0.06347	38
Miami–Fort Lauderdale, FL	0.06296	39
Stockton, CA	0.06242	40
New Haven–Meriden, CT	0.05865	41
Salinas–Seaside–Monterey, CA	0.05651	42
Phoenix, AZ	0.05579	43
San Diego, CA	0.05528	44
Rochester, NY	0.05517	45
Modesto, CA	0.05398	46
Providence–Pawtucket–Fall River, RI–MA	0.05309	47
Boston–Lawrence–Salem, MA–NH	0.05214	48

[Continued]

★1884★

Hispanic Female Householder, No Spouse Present, With Children Under 5 Years Old, Living Below Poverty, 1989
[Continued]

MSA	% of population	Rank
Sacramento, CA	0.05023	49
Salem, OR	0.04928	50

Source: U.S. Bureau of the Census, Data User Services Division, *1990 Census of Population and Housing*, Summary Tape File 3C, United States Summary, CD-ROM, February 1992.

★1885★
Poverty Status of Families With Children

Hispanic Female Householder, No Spouse Present, With Children Under 5 and Children 5 to 17 Years Old, Living Below Poverty, 1989
[Table shows the top 50 areas]

MSA	% of population	Rank
Laredo, TX	0.62294	1
Brownsville – Harlingen, TX	0.58781	2
McAllen – Edinburg – Mission, TX	0.56604	3
El Paso, TX	0.52163	4
Las Cruces, NM	0.42137	5
Pueblo, CO	0.41609	6
Visalia – Tulare – Porterville, CA	0.40908	7
Corpus Christi, TX	0.40041	8
San Antonio, TX	0.39936	9
Fresno, CA	0.34922	10
Yuma, AZ	0.30591	11
Springfield, MA	0.26573	12
Bakersfield, CA	0.25852	13
Odessa, TX	0.24551	14
Merced, CA	0.24103	15
Victoria, TX	0.23399	16
Greeley, CO	0.21848	17
San Angelo, TX	0.20212	18
New York – Northern New Jersey – Long Island, NY – NJ – CT	0.19456	19
Santa Fe, NM	0.19138	20
Salinas – Seaside – Monterey, CA	0.19007	21
Albuquerque, NM	0.18166	22
Yakima, WA	0.18165	23
Lubbock, TX	0.17877	24
Tucson, AZ	0.17649	25
Stockton, CA	0.16125	26
Los Angeles – Anaheim – Riverside, CA	0.16111	27
Modesto, CA	0.15950	28
Hartford – New Britain – Middletown, CT	0.15287	29
Abilene, TX	0.13372	30
Midland, TX	0.12850	31
Reading, PA	0.12718	32
Fitchburg – Leominster, MA	0.12646	33
Phoenix, AZ	0.12502	34

[Continued]

★1885★

Hispanic Female Householder, No Spouse Present, With Children Under 5 and Children 5 to 17 Years Old, Living Below Poverty, 1989
[Continued]

MSA	% of population	Rank
San Diego, CA	0.12490	35
Waterbury, CT	0.12228	36
Santa Barbara – Santa Maria – Lompoc, CA	0.12202	37
Austin, TX	0.10722	38
Denver – Boulder, CO	0.10620	39
Richland – Kennewick – Pasco, WA	0.10531	40
Worcester, MA	0.10505	41
Cheyenne, WY	0.10254	42
New Haven – Meriden, CT	0.10127	43
Miami – Fort Lauderdale, FL	0.09384	44
Yuba City, CA	0.09377	45
Houston – Galveston – Brazoria, TX	0.09202	46
Amarillo, TX	0.09011	47
Waco, TX	0.08619	48
Sacramento, CA	0.08568	49
Allentown – Bethlehem – Easton, PA – NJ	0.08155	50

Source: U.S. Bureau of the Census, Data User Services Division, *1990 Census of Population and Housing*, Summary Tape File 3C, United States Summary, CD-ROM, February 1992.

★1886★
Poverty Status of Families With Children

Hispanic Female Householder, No Spouse Present, With Children 5 to 17 Years Old, Living Below Poverty, 1989
[Table shows the top 50 areas]

MSA	% of population	Rank
Brownsville – Harlingen, TX	1.1475	1
McAllen – Edinburg – Mission, TX	1.0515	2
Laredo, TX	0.9847	3
El Paso, TX	0.8213	4
Pueblo, CO	0.7403	5
Las Cruces, NM	0.6701	6
Corpus Christi, TX	0.6573	7
San Antonio, TX	0.5335	8
Yuma, AZ	0.4621	9
Victoria, TX	0.3631	10
Fresno, CA	0.3521	11
Albuquerque, NM	0.3419	12
Visalia – Tulare – Porterville, CA	0.3276	13
Springfield, MA	0.3124	14
Odessa, TX	0.3103	15
Greeley, CO	0.2966	16
Merced, CA	0.2898	17
New York – Northern New Jersey – Long Island, NY – NJ – CT	0.2837	18
Santa Fe, NM	0.2563	19

[Continued]

★ 1886 ★

Hispanic Female Householder, No Spouse Present, With Children 5 to 17 Years Old, Living Below Poverty, 1989

[Continued]

MSA	% of population	Rank
Miami – Fort Lauderdale, FL	0.2298	20
Bakersfield, CA	0.2243	21
Yakima, WA	0.2219	22
San Angelo, TX	0.2163	23
Hartford – New Britain – Middletown, CT	0.2110	24
Tucson, AZ	0.2087	25
Fitchburg – Leominster, MA	0.2082	26
Salinas – Seaside – Monterey, CA	0.2019	27
Lubbock, TX	0.1976	28
Waterbury, CT	0.1895	29
Stockton, CA	0.1831	30
Los Angeles – Anaheim – Riverside, CA	0.1724	31
Cheyenne, WY	0.1477	32
San Diego, CA	0.1471	33
Richland – Kennewick – Pasco, WA	0.1406	34
Santa Barbara – Santa Maria – Lompoc, CA	0.1383	35
Midland, TX	0.1379	36
Reading, PA	0.1355	37
Worcester, MA	0.1330	38
Modesto, CA	0.1309	39
Austin, TX	0.1294	40
New Haven – Meriden, CT	0.1230	41
Houston – Galveston – Brazoria, TX	0.1217	42
Denver – Boulder, CO	0.1195	43
Phoenix, AZ	0.1151	44
Amarillo, TX	0.1093	45
Abilene, TX	0.1070	46
New Bedford, MA	0.1019	47
Colorado Springs, CO	0.0990	48
Yuba City, CA	0.0938	49
Killeen – Temple, TX	0.0905	50

Source: U.S. Bureau of the Census, Data User Services Division, *1990 Census of Population and Housing*, Summary Tape File 3C, United States Summary, CD-ROM, February 1992.

★ 1887 ★

Poverty Status of Families With Children

Hispanic Female Householder, No Spouse Present, With Children Under 5 Years Old, Living Above Poverty, 1989

[Table shows the top 50 areas]

MSA	% of population	Rank
Laredo, TX	0.17637	1
El Paso, TX	0.16633	2
Brownsville – Harlingen, TX	0.15647	3
McAllen – Edinburg – Mission, TX	0.13532	4

[Continued]

★ 1887 ★

Hispanic Female Householder, No Spouse Present, With Children Under 5 Years Old, Living Above Poverty, 1989

[Continued]

MSA	% of population	Rank
Albuquerque, NM	0.13442	5
San Antonio, TX	0.11481	6
Santa Fe, NM	0.11192	7
Corpus Christi, TX	0.09889	8
Las Cruces, NM	0.09741	9
Salinas – Seaside – Monterey, CA	0.08519	10
Visalia – Tulare – Porterville, CA	0.08207	11
Miami – Fort Lauderdale, FL	0.07940	12
Pueblo, CO	0.07883	13
Los Angeles – Anaheim – Riverside, CA	0.07770	14
Fresno, CA	0.07596	15
Stockton, CA	0.06512	16
Tucson, AZ	0.06253	17
Yuma, AZ	0.06174	18
New York – Northern New Jersey – Long Island, NY – NJ – CT	0.06145	19
Austin, TX	0.05591	20
Bakersfield, CA	0.05557	21
San Diego, CA	0.05200	22
Springfield, MA	0.04835	23
Fitchburg – Leominster, MA	0.04572	24
San Angelo, TX	0.04469	25
San Francisco – Oakland – San Jose, CA	0.04297	26
Merced, CA	0.04092	27
Lubbock, TX	0.04087	28
Phoenix, AZ	0.04043	29
Santa Barbara – Santa Maria – Lompoc, CA	0.03977	30
Denver – Boulder, CO	0.03950	31
Modesto, CA	0.03913	32
Victoria, TX	0.03900	33
Odessa, TX	0.03868	34
Greeley, CO	0.03490	35
Houston – Galveston – Brazoria, TX	0.03444	36
Cheyenne, WY	0.03281	37
Sacramento, CA	0.03281	37
Wichita Falls, TX	0.03269	38
Orlando, FL	0.03253	39
Waterbury, CT	0.03249	40
Midland, TX	0.03189	41
Hartford – New Britain – Middletown, CT	0.03048	42
Waco, TX	0.02908	43
Atlantic City, NJ	0.02818	44
Yakima, WA	0.02754	45
Anchorage, AK	0.02739	46
Las Vegas, NV	0.02738	47
Dallas – Fort Worth, TX	0.02702	48
Boston – Lawrence – Salem, MA – NH	0.02666	49

Source: U.S. Bureau of the Census, Data User Services Division, *1990 Census of Population and Housing*, Summary Tape File 3C, United States Summary, CD-ROM, February 1992.

★1888★

Poverty Status of Families With Children

Hispanic Female Householder, No Spouse Present, With Children Under 5 and 5 to 17 Years Old, Living Above Poverty, 1989

[Table shows the top 50 areas]

MSA	% of population	Rank
El Paso, TX	0.19709	1
Brownsville – Harlingen, TX	0.19337	2
Laredo, TX	0.17562	3
Santa Fe, NM	0.14012	4
Corpus Christi, TX	0.13404	5
McAllen – Edinburg – Mission, TX	0.12828	6
San Antonio, TX	0.12280	7
San Angelo, TX	0.11680	8
Las Cruces, NM	0.11438	9
Victoria, TX	0.11431	10
Los Angeles – Anaheim – Riverside, CA	0.11182	11
Fresno, CA	0.10951	12
Albuquerque, NM	0.10196	13
Salinas – Seaside – Monterey, CA	0.09813	14
Bakersfield, CA	0.09623	15
Visalia – Tulare – Porterville, CA	0.08752	16
Odessa, TX	0.08660	17
Stockton, CA	0.08510	18
Merced, CA	0.08072	19
Santa Barbara – Santa Maria – Lompoc, CA	0.07467	20
Austin, TX	0.07012	21
Lubbock, TX	0.06872	22
San Diego, CA	0.06825	23
Tucson, AZ	0.06718	24
Miami – Fort Lauderdale, FL	0.06227	25
New York – Northern New Jersey – Long Island, NY – NJ – CT	0.06142	26
Phoenix, AZ	0.06102	27
Pueblo, CO	0.06095	28
Greeley, CO	0.05993	29
Yuma, AZ	0.05987	30
San Francisco – Oakland – San Jose, CA	0.04861	31
Amarillo, TX	0.04745	32
Modesto, CA	0.04372	33
Bryan – College Station, TX	0.04349	34
Midland, TX	0.04315	35
Houston – Galveston – Brazoria, TX	0.04131	36
Killeen – Temple, TX	0.04034	37
Denver – Boulder, CO	0.03971	38
Yakima, WA	0.03919	39
Sacramento, CA	0.03713	40
Abilene, TX	0.03677	41
Hartford – New Britain – Middletown, CT	0.03490	42
Springfield, MA	0.03456	43
Dallas – Fort Worth, TX	0.03346	44
Rockford, IL	0.03207	45
Wichita Falls, TX	0.03105	46
Chicago – Gary – Lake County, IL – IN – WI	0.02912	47

[Continued]

★1888★

Hispanic Female Householder, No Spouse Present, With Children Under 5 and 5 to 17 Years Old, Living Above Poverty, 1989

[Continued]

MSA	% of population	Rank
Cheyenne, WY	0.02734	48
Las Vegas, NV	0.02643	49
Richland – Kennewick – Pasco, WA	0.02599	50

Source: U.S. Bureau of the Census, Data User Services Division, *1990 Census of Population and Housing,* Summary Tape File 3C, United States Summary, CD-ROM, February 1992.

★1889★

Poverty Status of Families With Children

Hispanic Female Householder, No Spouse Present, With Children 5 to 17 Years Old, Living Above Poverty, 1989

[Table shows the top 50 areas]

MSA	% of population	Rank
El Paso, TX	0.8083	1
Laredo, TX	0.7700	2
Santa Fe, NM	0.7143	3
Brownsville – Harlingen, TX	0.6493	4
McAllen – Edinburg – Mission, TX	0.6080	5
San Antonio, TX	0.5635	6
Las Cruces, NM	0.5557	7
Corpus Christi, TX	0.5233	8
Albuquerque, NM	0.4792	9
Pueblo, CO	0.4145	10
Miami – Fort Lauderdale, FL	0.3856	11
Fresno, CA	0.3157	12
Victoria, TX	0.3106	13
Tucson, AZ	0.3068	14
Los Angeles – Anaheim – Riverside, CA	0.3040	15
Odessa, TX	0.2842	16
Salinas – Seaside – Monterey, CA	0.2789	17
Visalia – Tulare – Porterville, CA	0.2703	18
Yuma, AZ	0.2657	19
Stockton, CA	0.2459	20
Bakersfield, CA	0.2434	21
New York – Northern New Jersey – Long Island, NY – NJ – CT	0.2413	22
San Angelo, TX	0.2377	23
Santa Barbara – Santa Maria – Lompoc, CA	0.2305	24
Austin, TX	0.2245	25
Merced, CA	0.2220	26
San Diego, CA	0.2182	27
Lubbock, TX	0.1918	28
Greeley, CO	0.1813	29
Modesto, CA	0.1808	30
San Francisco – Oakland – San Jose, CA	0.1751	31
Springfield, MA	0.1728	32

[Continued]

★1889★

Hispanic Female Householder, No Spouse Present, With Children 5 to 17 Years Old, Living Above Poverty, 1989

[Continued]

MSA	% of population	Rank
Denver – Boulder, CO	0.1725	33
Houston – Galveston – Brazoria, TX	0.1721	34
Phoenix, AZ	0.1717	35
Sacramento, CA	0.1551	36
Amarillo, TX	0.1466	37
Hartford – New Britain – Middletown, CT	0.1380	38
Midland, TX	0.1304	39
Yakima, WA	0.1239	40
Abilene, TX	0.1237	41
Orlando, FL	0.1206	42
Las Vegas, NV	0.1167	43
Yuba City, CA	0.1117	44
Richland – Kennewick – Pasco, WA	0.1113	45
Naples, FL	0.1072	46
Colorado Springs, CO	0.1070	47
Dallas – Fort Worth, TX	0.1064	48
Chicago – Gary – Lake County, IL – IN – WI	0.1036	49
New Haven – Meriden, CT	0.1030	50

Source: U.S. Bureau of the Census, Data User Services Division, *1990 Census of Population and Housing*, Summary Tape File 3C, United States Summary, CD-ROM, February 1992.

★1890★

Poverty Status of Families With Children

Hispanic Male Householder, No Spouse Present, With Children Under 5 Years Old, Living Below Poverty, 1989

[Table shows the top 50 areas]

MSA	% of population	Rank
McAllen – Edinburg – Mission, TX	0.07379	1
Fresno, CA	0.07206	2
Las Cruces, NM	0.05977	3
Yakima, WA	0.05667	4
Tucson, AZ	0.05158	5
Visalia – Tulare – Porterville, CA	0.05065	6
Bakersfield, CA	0.05060	7
Albuquerque, NM	0.04973	8
Brownsville – Harlingen, TX	0.04921	9
El Paso, TX	0.04834	10
Laredo, TX	0.03828	11
San Antonio, TX	0.03617	12
Santa Barbara – Santa Maria – Lompoc, CA	0.03463	13
Santa Fe, NM	0.03332	14
Richland – Kennewick – Pasco, WA	0.03266	15
San Angelo, TX	0.03149	16
Los Angeles – Anaheim – Riverside, CA	0.03053	17

[Continued]

★1890★

Hispanic Male Householder, No Spouse Present, With Children Under 5 Years Old, Living Below Poverty, 1989

[Continued]

MSA	% of population	Rank
Merced, CA	0.02859	18
Pueblo, CO	0.02844	19
Abilene, TX	0.02340	20
Odessa, TX	0.02270	21
Phoenix, AZ	0.02201	22
Springfield, MA	0.02172	23
Naples, FL	0.02170	24
Miami – Fort Lauderdale, FL	0.02121	25
Greeley, CO	0.02048	26
San Diego, CA	0.01982	27
Austin, TX	0.01970	28
Casper, WY	0.01960	29
Waco, TX	0.01956	30
Fitchburg – Leominster, MA	0.01946	31
Amarillo, TX	0.01920	32
Sioux City, IA – NE	0.01913	33
Wichita Falls, TX	0.01798	34
Modesto, CA	0.01754	35
Houston – Galveston – Brazoria, TX	0.01741	36
Bradenton, FL	0.01700	37
Jamestown – Dunkirk, NY	0.01691	38
Corpus Christi, TX	0.01686	39
Chico, CA	0.01647	40
Salinas – Seaside – Monterey, CA	0.01631	41
Yuma, AZ	0.01590	42
Billings, MT	0.01587	43
Enid, OK	0.01586	44
Lubbock, TX	0.01527	45
Dallas – Fort Worth, TX	0.01431	46
Reading, PA	0.01367	47
Fort Pierce, FL	0.01314	48
Midland, TX	0.01313	49
Denver – Boulder, CO	0.01261	50

Source: U.S. Bureau of the Census, Data User Services Division, *1990 Census of Population and Housing*, Summary Tape File 3C, United States Summary, CD-ROM, February 1992.

★1891★

Poverty Status of Families With Children

Hispanic Male Householder, No Spouse Present, With Children Under 5 and 5 to 17 Years Old, Living Below Poverty, 1989

[Table shows the top 50 areas]

MSA	% of population	Rank
Visalia – Tulare – Porterville, CA	0.10355	1
McAllen – Edinburg – Mission, TX	0.09934	2
Las Cruces, NM	0.08708	3
Fresno, CA	0.08045	4
Brownsville – Harlingen, TX	0.07689	5

[Continued]

★1891★

Hispanic Male Householder, No Spouse Present, With Children Under 5 and 5 to 17 Years Old, Living Below Poverty, 1989
[Continued]

MSA	% of population	Rank
Bakersfield, CA	0.07158	6
Laredo, TX	0.06830	7
Santa Fe, NM	0.06237	8
El Paso, TX	0.05848	9
Yakima, WA	0.05084	10
Yuma, AZ	0.05052	11
Corpus Christi, TX	0.05002	12
Merced, CA	0.04877	13
Naples, FL	0.04734	14
Los Angeles – Anaheim – Riverside, CA	0.04505	15
San Antonio, TX	0.04408	16
Pueblo, CO	0.04145	17
Richland – Kennewick – Pasco, WA	0.04066	18
Albuquerque, NM	0.04037	19
Salinas – Seaside – Monterey, CA	0.03993	20
Tucson, AZ	0.03644	21
Midland, TX	0.02908	22
Phoenix, AZ	0.02846	23
Greeley, CO	0.02655	24
Lubbock, TX	0.02605	25
Victoria, TX	0.02555	26
Miami – Fort Lauderdale, FL	0.02515	27
Odessa, TX	0.02438	28
Houston – Galveston – Brazoria, TX	0.02223	29
Stockton, CA	0.02185	30
Bryan – College Station, TX	0.02134	31
San Angelo, TX	0.02133	32
Salem, OR	0.02050	33
Abilene, TX	0.02006	34
San Diego, CA	0.02002	35
Austin, TX	0.01855	36
Santa Barbara – Santa Maria – Lompoc, CA	0.01813	37
Tyler, TX	0.01652	38
Waco, TX	0.01586	39
Fort Collins – Loveland, CO	0.01504	40
Modesto, CA	0.01322	41
Amarillo, TX	0.01280	42
Denver – Boulder, CO	0.01223	43
West Palm Beach – Boca Raton – Delray Beach, FL	0.01181	44
Dallas – Fort Worth, TX	0.01148	45
New York – Northern New Jersey – Long Island, NY – NJ – CT	0.01057	46
Sacramento, CA	0.01006	47
Chicago – Gary – Lake County, IL – IN – WI	0.00927	48
Atlantic City, NJ	0.00908	49
Yuba City, CA	0.00897	50

Source: U.S. Bureau of the Census, Data User Services Division, *1990 Census of Population and Housing*, Summary Tape File 3C, United States Summary, CD-ROM, February 1992.

★1892★

Poverty Status of Families With Children

Hispanic Male Householder, No Spouse Present, With Children 5 to 17 Years Old, Living Below Poverty, 1989

[Table shows the top 50 areas]

MSA	% of population	Rank
McAllen – Edinburg – Mission, TX	0.12749	1
Brownsville – Harlingen, TX	0.12533	2
Laredo, TX	0.10507	3
Corpus Christi, TX	0.09689	4
Yuma, AZ	0.08232	5
El Paso, TX	0.08130	6
Las Cruces, NM	0.08117	7
Fresno, CA	0.06847	8
Visalia – Tulare – Porterville, CA	0.06444	9
Odessa, TX	0.06306	10
San Antonio, TX	0.06136	11
Pueblo, CO	0.06014	12
Albuquerque, NM	0.04932	13
Santa Fe, NM	0.04272	14
Miami – Fort Lauderdale, FL	0.03947	15
Merced, CA	0.03924	16
Los Angeles – Anaheim – Riverside, CA	0.03830	17
Midland, TX	0.03564	18
Tucson, AZ	0.03494	19
Bakersfield, CA	0.03275	20
Salinas – Seaside – Monterey, CA	0.03177	21
Greeley, CO	0.03110	22
Phoenix, AZ	0.03110	22
Cheyenne, WY	0.03008	23
San Angelo, TX	0.02844	24
Richland – Kennewick – Pasco, WA	0.02799	25
Houston – Galveston – Brazoria, TX	0.02509	26
Yuba City, CA	0.02446	27
Modesto, CA	0.02294	28
Santa Barbara – Santa Maria – Lompoc, CA	0.02192	29
Springfield, MA	0.02172	30
Naples, FL	0.02170	31
Lubbock, TX	0.02156	32
Austin, TX	0.02150	33
Yakima, WA	0.02065	34
Victoria, TX	0.02017	35
Reno, NV	0.01924	36
Chico, CA	0.01922	37
San Diego, CA	0.01898	38
New York – Northern New Jersey – Long Island, NY – NJ – CT	0.01863	39
Amarillo, TX	0.01813	40
Jamestown – Dunkirk, NY	0.01762	41
Dallas – Fort Worth, TX	0.01748	42
Fitchburg – Leominster, MA	0.01654	43
New Bedford, MA	0.01594	44
Denver – Boulder, CO	0.01574	45
Bradenton, FL	0.01512	46
Beaumont – Port Arthur, TX	0.01495	47

[Continued]

★1892★

Hispanic Male Householder, No Spouse Present, With Children 5 to 17 Years Old, Living Below Poverty, 1989

[Continued]

MSA	% of population	Rank
Wichita Falls, TX	0.01471	48
Abilene, TX	0.01337	49

Source: U.S. Bureau of the Census, Data User Services Division, *1990 Census of Population and Housing,* Summary Tape File 3C, United States Summary, CD-ROM, February 1992.

★1893★

Poverty Status of Families With Children

Hispanic Male Householder, No Spouse Present, With Children Under 5 Years Old, Living Above Poverty Level, 1989

[Table shows the top 50 areas]

MSA	% of population	Rank
Santa Fe, NM	0.14525	1
Yuma, AZ	0.13191	2
Los Angeles – Anaheim – Riverside, CA	0.10170	3
Albuquerque, NM	0.09946	4
Fresno, CA	0.09109	5
Merced, CA	0.08968	6
Bakersfield, CA	0.07599	7
Santa Barbara – Santa Maria – Lompoc, CA	0.07413	8
Las Cruces, NM	0.07158	9
Visalia – Tulare – Porterville, CA	0.07085	10
Salinas – Seaside – Monterey, CA	0.06495	11
Stockton, CA	0.06450	12
Corpus Christi, TX	0.05887	13
Brownsville – Harlingen, TX	0.05843	14
Victoria, TX	0.05783	15
El Paso, TX	0.05747	16
Phoenix, AZ	0.05721	17
Richland – Kennewick – Pasco, WA	0.05665	18
Modesto, CA	0.05614	19
Miami – Fort Lauderdale, FL	0.05328	20
Fitchburg – Leominster, MA	0.05156	21
McAllen – Edinburg – Mission, TX	0.05136	22
San Diego, CA	0.04992	23
Yakima, WA	0.04925	24
San Antonio, TX	0.04900	25
Tucson, AZ	0.04813	26
Odessa, TX	0.04624	27
San Francisco – Oakland – San Jose, CA	0.04180	28
Greeley, CO	0.04096	29
Laredo, TX	0.03978	30
Atlantic City, NJ	0.03882	31
New York – Northern New Jersey – Long Island, NY – NJ – CT	0.03817	32
Las Vegas, NV	0.03722	33

[Continued]

★1893★

Hispanic Male Householder, No Spouse Present, With Children Under 5 Years Old, Living Above Poverty Level, 1989

[Continued]

MSA	% of population	Rank
Houston – Galveston – Brazoria, TX	0.03676	34
Austin, TX	0.03672	35
Yuba City, CA	0.03588	36
Casper, WY	0.03430	37
Dallas – Fort Worth, TX	0.03168	38
Salem, OR	0.03129	39
San Angelo, TX	0.03047	40
Colorado Springs, CO	0.02972	41
Medford, OR	0.02937	42
West Palm Beach – Boca Raton – Delray Beach, FL	0.02884	43
Chicago – Gary – Lake County, IL – IN – WI	0.02817	44
Elkhart – Goshen, IN	0.02753	45
Lubbock, TX	0.02740	46
Sacramento, CA	0.02653	47
Reno, NV	0.02592	48
Naples, FL	0.02564	49
Denver – Boulder, CO	0.02337	50

Source: U.S. Bureau of the Census, Data User Services Division, *1990 Census of Population and Housing,* Summary Tape File 3C, United States Summary, CD-ROM, February 1992.

★1894★

Poverty Status of Families With Children

Hispanic Male Householder, No Spouse Present, With Children Under 5 and 5 to 17 Years Old, Living Above Poverty, 1989

[Table shows the top 50 areas]

MSA	% of population	Rank
Santa Fe, NM	0.09057	1
Merced, CA	0.08912	2
Laredo, TX	0.08406	3
Los Angeles – Anaheim – Riverside, CA	0.08029	4
Yakima, WA	0.07838	5
Fresno, CA	0.07551	6
Salinas – Seaside – Monterey, CA	0.06748	7
Bakersfield, CA	0.06035	8
Visalia – Tulare – Porterville, CA	0.05739	9
Santa Barbara – Santa Maria – Lompoc, CA	0.05303	10
Las Cruces, NM	0.05239	11
Yuma, AZ	0.05145	12
McAllen – Edinburg – Mission, TX	0.05084	13
Naples, FL	0.04997	14
Cheyenne, WY	0.04785	15
Albuquerque, NM	0.04682	16
Stockton, CA	0.04577	17

[Continued]

★1894★

Hispanic Male Householder, No Spouse Present, With Children Under 5 and 5 to 17 Years Old, Living Above Poverty, 1989

[Continued]

MSA	% of population	Rank
Modesto, CA	0.04399	18
Miami – Fort Lauderdale, FL	0.03981	19
Odessa, TX	0.03700	20
San Antonio, TX	0.03617	21
El Paso, TX	0.03465	22
Corpus Christi, TX	0.03258	23
Brownsville – Harlingen, TX	0.03229	24
San Diego, CA	0.03159	25
Pueblo, CO	0.03088	26
Houston – Galveston – Brazoria, TX	0.02924	27
Phoenix, AZ	0.02912	28
San Francisco – Oakland – San Jose, CA	0.02784	29
New York – Northern New Jersey – Long Island, NY – NJ – CT	0.02498	30
Tucson, AZ	0.02429	31
Victoria, TX	0.02286	32
Chicago – Gary – Lake County, IL – IN – WI	0.02044	33
Austin, TX	0.02022	34
Dallas – Fort Worth, TX	0.01933	35
Abilene, TX	0.01922	36
Waco, TX	0.01851	37
Las Vegas, NV	0.01699	38
Salem, OR	0.01655	39
Colorado Springs, CO	0.01637	40
Yuba City, CA	0.01631	41
Denver – Boulder, CO	0.01580	42
Worcester, MA	0.01556	43
Sacramento, CA	0.01553	44
San Angelo, TX	0.01523	45
Fort Pierce, FL	0.01474	46
Waterbury, CT	0.01444	47
Greeley, CO	0.01441	48
Atlantic City, NJ	0.01440	49
Richland – Kennewick – Pasco, WA	0.01400	50

Source: U.S. Bureau of the Census, Data User Services Division, *1990 Census of Population and Housing,* Summary Tape File 3C, United States Summary, CD-ROM, February 1992.

★1895★

Poverty Status of Families With Children

Hispanic Male Householder, No Spouse Present, With Children 5 to 17 Years Old, Living Above Poverty, 1989

[Table shows the top 50 areas]

MSA	% of population	Rank
Santa Fe, NM	0.24863	1
Albuquerque, NM	0.20642	2
El Paso, TX	0.18948	3
Fresno, CA	0.15581	4
Pueblo, CO	0.15522	5
San Antonio, TX	0.15337	6
Las Cruces, NM	0.15054	7
Visalia – Tulare – Porterville, CA	0.14972	8
Laredo, TX	0.14485	9
Los Angeles – Anaheim – Riverside, CA	0.14466	10
McAllen – Edinburg – Mission, TX	0.14418	11
Corpus Christi, TX	0.14404	12
Merced, CA	0.14293	13
Miami – Fort Lauderdale, FL	0.13109	14
Brownsville – Harlingen, TX	0.12686	15
Yuma, AZ	0.12349	16
Bakersfield, CA	0.11574	17
Salinas – Seaside – Monterey, CA	0.10909	18
Stockton, CA	0.10112	19
Yakima, WA	0.09215	20
Santa Barbara – Santa Maria – Lompoc, CA	0.09064	21
Lubbock, TX	0.08175	22
Modesto, CA	0.08151	23
Houston – Galveston – Brazoria, TX	0.07936	24
San Diego, CA	0.07790	25
San Angelo, TX	0.07719	26
Tucson, AZ	0.07678	27
Las Vegas, NV	0.07539	28
San Francisco – Oakland – San Jose, CA	0.07524	29
Greeley, CO	0.07358	30
Amarillo, TX	0.06932	31
Austin, TX	0.06909	32
New York – Northern New Jersey – Long Island, NY – NJ – CT	0.06693	33
Phoenix, AZ	0.06461	34
Richland – Kennewick – Pasco, WA	0.06399	35
Odessa, TX	0.06306	36
Yuba City, CA	0.06197	37
Sacramento, CA	0.05894	38
Denver – Boulder, CO	0.05638	39
Cheyenne, WY	0.05606	40
Reno, NV	0.05380	41
Victoria, TX	0.05245	42
Dallas – Fort Worth, TX	0.05119	43
Naples, FL	0.05062	44
Chicago – Gary – Lake County, IL – IN – WI	0.05044	45
Midland, TX	0.04971	46
Abilene, TX	0.04764	47
Wichita Falls, TX	0.04739	48

[Continued]

★1895★

Hispanic Male Householder, No Spouse Present, With Children 5 to 17 Years Old, Living Above Poverty, 1989

[Continued]

MSA	% of population	Rank
Colorado Springs, CO	0.04458	49
Waco, TX	0.04283	50

Source: U.S. Bureau of the Census, Data User Services Division, *1990 Census of Population and Housing*, Summary Tape File 3C, United States Summary, CD-ROM, February 1992.

★1896★

Poverty Status of Families With Children

Hispanic Married Couples With Children Under 5 Years Old, Living Below Poverty, 1989

Table only shows the top 50 areas.

MSA	% of population	Rank
McAllen – Edinburg – Mission, TX	0.58090	1
Laredo, TX	0.55764	2
Brownsville – Harlingen, TX	0.53437	3
Las Cruces, NM	0.39997	4
El Paso, TX	0.35226	5
Odessa, TX	0.24636	6
San Antonio, TX	0.20682	7
Corpus Christi, TX	0.19034	8
Visalia – Tulare – Porterville, CA	0.18210	9
Midland, TX	0.16321	10
Yuma, AZ	0.15997	11
Fresno, CA	0.15581	12
Yakima, WA	0.15199	13
Victoria, TX	0.15196	14
Pueblo, CO	0.13409	15
Houston – Galveston – Brazoria, TX	0.13376	16
Merced, CA	0.13172	17
Lubbock, TX	0.12577	18
Santa Fe, NM	0.12559	19
Austin, TX	0.11694	20
San Angelo, TX	0.11579	21
Amarillo, TX	0.11144	22
Tucson, AZ	0.10692	23
Abilene, TX	0.10447	24
Albuquerque, NM	0.09697	25
Los Angeles – Anaheim – Riverside, CA	0.09420	26
Bakersfield, CA	0.09016	27
Greeley, CO	0.08800	28
Salinas – Seaside – Monterey, CA	0.08576	29
Santa Barbara – Santa Maria – Lompoc, CA	0.08441	30
Dallas – Fort Worth, TX	0.08233	31
Yuba City, CA	0.08072	32
Modesto, CA	0.07935	33
Richland – Kennewick – Pasco, WA	0.07865	34
Waco, TX	0.07826	35

[Continued]

★1896★

Hispanic Married Couples With Children Under 5 Years Old, Living Below Poverty, 1989

[Continued]

MSA	% of population	Rank
Miami – Fort Lauderdale, FL	0.07712	36
Naples, FL	0.07692	37
Stockton, CA	0.07428	38
Phoenix, AZ	0.06984	39
Reno, NV	0.06911	40
Bryan – College Station, TX	0.06647	41
San Diego, CA	0.05861	42
Wichita Falls, TX	0.05557	43
Fitchburg – Leominster, MA	0.05253	44
Killeen – Temple, TX	0.05014	45
Salem, OR	0.04640	46
Longview – Marshall, TX	0.04063	47
Lawrence, KS	0.03790	48
Fort Collins – Loveland, CO	0.03707	49
Lawton, OK	0.03588	50

Source: U.S. Bureau of the Census, Data User Services Division, *1990 Census of Population and Housing*, Summary Tape File 3C, United States Summary, CD-ROM, February 1992.

★1897★

Poverty Status of Families With Children

Hispanic Married Couples With Children Under 5 and 5 to 17 Years Old, Living Below Poverty, 1989

[Table shows the top 50 areas]

MSA	% of population	Rank
McAllen – Edinburg – Mission, TX	1.86080	1
Laredo, TX	1.61289	2
Brownsville – Harlingen, TX	1.59696	3
El Paso, TX	1.00979	4
Las Cruces, NM	0.72172	5
Odessa, TX	0.61042	6
Visalia – Tulare – Porterville, CA	0.53347	7
Corpus Christi, TX	0.51959	8
San Antonio, TX	0.47723	9
Yuma, AZ	0.45933	10
Merced, CA	0.45010	11
Yakima, WA	0.39455	12
Victoria, TX	0.38864	13
Fresno, CA	0.38398	14
Bakersfield, CA	0.35310	15
Midland, TX	0.32267	16
Lubbock, TX	0.32160	17
Salinas – Seaside – Monterey, CA	0.28032	18
San Angelo, TX	0.27829	19
Los Angeles – Anaheim – Riverside, CA	0.26788	20
Pueblo, CO	0.24868	21
Houston – Galveston – Brazoria, TX	0.23883	22
Modesto, CA	0.23777	23
Richland – Kennewick – Pasco, WA	0.23728	24

[Continued]

★1897★

Hispanic Married Couples With Children Under 5 and 5 to 17 Years Old, Living Below Poverty, 1989

[Continued]

MSA	% of population	Rank
Albuquerque, NM	0.23160	25
Tucson, AZ	0.21248	26
Austin, TX	0.20740	27
Amarillo, TX	0.20475	28
Santa Barbara – Santa Maria – Lompoc, CA	0.19507	29
Greeley, CO	0.19344	30
Yuba City, CA	0.18754	31
Santa Fe, NM	0.17515	32
Naples, FL	0.17160	33
Bryan – College Station, TX	0.17068	34
Waco, TX	0.17026	35
Phoenix, AZ	0.16422	36
Tyler, TX	0.16126	37
Dallas – Fort Worth, TX	0.15754	38
San Diego, CA	0.15448	39
Abilene, TX	0.15210	40
Stockton, CA	0.15105	41
Miami – Fort Lauderdale, FL	0.13415	42
Killeen – Temple, TX	0.10772	43
Wichita Falls, TX	0.07681	44
Longview – Marshall, TX	0.07388	45
Salem, OR	0.07337	46
Chicago – Gary – Lake County, IL – IN – WI	0.07293	47
Denver – Boulder, CO	0.07163	48
Chico, CA	0.07138	49
Medford, OR	0.07036	50

Source: U.S. Bureau of the Census, Data User Services Division, *1990 Census of Population and Housing,* Summary Tape File 3C, United States Summary, CD-ROM, February 1992.

★1898★

Poverty Status of Families With Children

Hispanic Married Couples With Children 5 to 17 Years Old, Living Below Poverty, 1989

[Table shows the top 50 areas]

MSA	% of population	Rank
McAllen – Edinburg – Mission, TX	2.19244	1
Brownsville – Harlingen, TX	1.88721	2
Laredo, TX	1.77801	3
El Paso, TX	1.07875	4
Las Cruces, NM	0.93868	5
Yuma, AZ	0.92240	6
Corpus Christi, TX	0.64877	7
Victoria, TX	0.57692	8
Odessa, TX	0.53475	9
San Antonio, TX	0.49689	10
Visalia – Tulare – Porterville, CA	0.44178	11
Midland, TX	0.37051	12
San Angelo, TX	0.34532	13

[Continued]

★1898★

Hispanic Married Couples With Children 5 to 17 Years Old, Living Below Poverty, 1989

[Continued]

MSA	% of population	Rank
Merced, CA	0.32903	14
Pueblo, CO	0.32507	15
Fresno, CA	0.31326	16
Albuquerque, NM	0.29007	17
Lubbock, TX	0.28252	18
Yakima, WA	0.26798	19
Santa Fe, NM	0.25632	20
Miami – Fort Lauderdale, FL	0.22530	21
Tucson, AZ	0.22193	22
Bakersfield, CA	0.21694	23
Houston – Galveston – Brazoria, TX	0.21388	24
Naples, FL	0.20579	25
Waco, TX	0.18401	26
Greeley, CO	0.18282	27
Los Angeles – Anaheim – Riverside, CA	0.18123	28
Abilene, TX	0.17968	29
Salinas – Seaside – Monterey, CA	0.16476	30
Austin, TX	0.16275	31
Santa Barbara – Santa Maria – Lompoc, CA	0.15232	32
Stockton, CA	0.14335	33
Richland – Kennewick – Pasco, WA	0.13530	34
Wichita Falls, TX	0.12993	35
Phoenix, AZ	0.12931	36
Yuba City, CA	0.12638	37
Modesto, CA	0.12361	38
Bryan – College Station, TX	0.11981	39
San Diego, CA	0.11309	40
Dallas – Fort Worth, TX	0.10002	41
Tyler, TX	0.09980	42
Amarillo, TX	0.09758	43
Springfield, MA	0.09594	44
New York – Northern New Jersey – Long Island, NY – NJ – CT	0.07699	45
Chico, CA	0.07577	46
Fitchburg – Leominster, MA	0.06615	47
Orlando, FL	0.06507	48
Killeen – Temple, TX	0.06189	49
Denver – Boulder, CO	0.06130	50

Source: U.S. Bureau of the Census, Data User Services Division, *1990 Census of Population and Housing,* Summary Tape File 3C, United States Summary, CD-ROM, February 1992.

★1899★

Poverty Status of Families With Children

Hispanic Married Couples With Children 5 to 17 Years Old, Living Above Poverty, 1989

[Table shows the top 50 areas]

MSA	% of population	Rank
Laredo, TX	3.8682	1
Brownsville – Harlingen, TX	3.3561	2
McAllen – Edinburg – Mission, TX	3.3029	3
El Paso, TX	3.2540	4
Corpus Christi, TX	2.8171	5
Las Cruces, NM	2.5290	6
Santa Fe, NM	2.4863	7
San Antonio, TX	2.2706	8
Pueblo, CO	1.8830	9
Victoria, TX	1.8814	10
Albuquerque, NM	1.8422	11
Yuma, AZ	1.7980	12
Miami – Fort Lauderdale, FL	1.6972	13
Visalia – Tulare – Porterville, CA	1.6196	14
Odessa, TX	1.5858	15
San Angelo, TX	1.5062	16
Fresno, CA	1.3973	17
Merced, CA	1.3879	18
Salinas – Seaside – Monterey, CA	1.3842	19
Los Angeles – Anaheim – Riverside, CA	1.2970	20
Lubbock, TX	1.2321	21
Greeley, CO	1.1463	22
Bakersfield, CA	1.1449	23
Tucson, AZ	1.1116	24
Santa Barbara – Santa Maria – Lompoc, CA	1.0998	25
Modesto, CA	1.0658	26
Houston – Galveston – Brazoria, TX	1.0105	27
Midland, TX	0.9990	28
Stockton, CA	0.9696	29
Austin, TX	0.8795	30
Yakima, WA	0.8786	31
San Diego, CA	0.7945	32
Abilene, TX	0.7229	33
Phoenix, AZ	0.6923	34
San Francisco – Oakland – San Jose, CA	0.6397	35
Cheyenne, WY	0.6166	36
Amarillo, TX	0.6158	37
Dallas – Fort Worth, TX	0.6075	38
New York – Northern New Jersey – Long Island, NY – NJ – CT	0.5991	39
Bryan – College Station, TX	0.5949	40
Denver – Boulder, CO	0.5885	41
Naples, FL	0.5799	42
Killeen – Temple, TX	0.5703	43
Orlando, FL	0.5480	44
Yuba City, CA	0.5447	45
Chicago – Gary – Lake County, IL – IN – WI	0.5361	46
Waco, TX	0.5203	47
Sacramento, CA	0.5025	48

[Continued]

★1899★

Hispanic Married Couples With Children 5 to 17 Years Old, Living Above Poverty, 1989
[Continued]

MSA	% of population	Rank
Richland – Kennewick – Pasco, WA	0.4552	49
Las Vegas, NV	0.4540	50

Source: U.S. Bureau of the Census, Data User Services Division, *1990 Census of Population and Housing*, Summary Tape File 3C, United States Summary, CD-ROM, February 1992.

★1900★

Poverty Status of Families With Children

Hispanic Married Couples With Children Under 5 Years Old, Living Above Poverty Level, 1989

[Table shows the top 50 areas]

MSA	% of population	Rank
Laredo, TX	1.5904	1
El Paso, TX	1.0546	2
McAllen – Edinburg – Mission, TX	1.0421	3
Las Cruces, NM	0.9224	4
Brownsville – Harlingen, TX	0.9150	5
Corpus Christi, TX	0.8022	6
San Antonio, TX	0.7796	7
Santa Fe, NM	0.7296	8
Yuma, AZ	0.7044	9
Miami – Fort Lauderdale, FL	0.6995	10
Victoria, TX	0.6684	11
Albuquerque, NM	0.6484	12
Salinas – Seaside – Monterey, CA	0.6343	13
Los Angeles – Anaheim – Riverside, CA	0.6097	14
Midland, TX	0.5787	15
Merced, CA	0.5779	16
Santa Barbara – Santa Maria – Lompoc, CA	0.5744	17
Odessa, TX	0.5701	18
San Angelo, TX	0.5312	19
Fresno, CA	0.5278	20
Visalia – Tulare – Porterville, CA	0.5232	21
Pueblo, CO	0.4616	22
Houston – Galveston – Brazoria, TX	0.4471	23
Bakersfield, CA	0.4412	24
Modesto, CA	0.4218	25
Austin, TX	0.4099	26
Tucson, AZ	0.4037	27
Stockton, CA	0.3972	28
Lubbock, TX	0.3957	29
San Diego, CA	0.3900	30
Yakima, WA	0.3871	31
Amarillo, TX	0.3604	32
Killeen – Temple, TX	0.3435	33
Greeley, CO	0.3262	34
San Francisco – Oakland – San Jose, CA	0.3176	35
Dallas – Fort Worth, TX	0.3152	36

[Continued]

★1900★

Hispanic Married Couples With Children Under 5 Years Old, Living Above Poverty Level, 1989

[Continued]

MSA	% of population	Rank
Abilene, TX	0.3034	37
Phoenix, AZ	0.2952	38
New York – Northern New Jersey – Long Island, NY – NJ – CT	0.2672	39
Yuba City, CA	0.2658	40
Las Vegas, NV	0.2505	41
Waco, TX	0.2490	42
Naples, FL	0.2419	43
Reno, NV	0.2384	44
Orlando, FL	0.2327	45
Sacramento, CA	0.2312	46
Chicago – Gary – Lake County, IL – IN – WI	0.2283	47
Jacksonville, NC	0.2229	48
Denver – Boulder, CO	0.2186	49
Fayetteville, NC	0.2182	50

Source: U.S. Bureau of the Census, Data User Services Division, *1990 Census of Population and Housing,* Summary Tape File 3C, United States Summary, CD-ROM, February 1992.

★1901★

Poverty Status of Families With Children

Hispanic Married Couples With Children Under 5 and 5 to 17 Years Old, Living Above Poverty, 1989

[Table shows the top 50 areas]

MSA	% of population	Rank
Laredo, TX	1.9191	1
McAllen – Edinburg – Mission, TX	1.6673	2
Brownsville – Harlingen, TX	1.5162	3
El Paso, TX	1.4234	4
Las Cruces, NM	1.2730	5
Yuma, AZ	1.1993	6
Corpus Christi, TX	1.1161	7
Salinas – Seaside – Monterey, CA	1.0977	8
San Antonio, TX	1.0882	9
Visalia – Tulare – Porterville, CA	0.9958	10
Merced, CA	0.9753	11
Los Angeles – Anaheim – Riverside, CA	0.9644	12
Odessa, TX	0.9341	13
Victoria, TX	0.9024	14
Santa Fe, NM	0.8834	15
Fresno, CA	0.8544	16
Bakersfield, CA	0.8504	17
Modesto, CA	0.7395	18
Santa Barbara – Santa Maria – Lompoc, CA	0.7218	19
Albuquerque, NM	0.7193	20
Miami – Fort Lauderdale, FL	0.6305	21
Yakima, WA	0.6159	22
Houston – Galveston – Brazoria, TX	0.6059	23

[Continued]

★1901★

Hispanic Married Couples With Children Under 5 and 5 to 17 Years Old, Living Above Poverty, 1989

[Continued]

MSA	% of population	Rank
San Angelo, TX	0.5972	24
Stockton, CA	0.5865	25
Pueblo, CO	0.5827	26
Lubbock, TX	0.5583	27
Greeley, CO	0.5492	28
Midland, TX	0.5328	29
Tucson, AZ	0.5052	30
San Diego, CA	0.5038	31
Austin, TX	0.4964	32
Phoenix, AZ	0.4083	33
Dallas – Fort Worth, TX	0.3971	34
San Francisco – Oakland – San Jose, CA	0.3966	35
Killeen – Temple, TX	0.3651	36
Waco, TX	0.3627	37
Abilene, TX	0.3560	38
Amarillo, TX	0.3444	39
Chicago – Gary – Lake County, IL – IN – WI	0.3405	40
Yuba City, CA	0.3066	41
Richland – Kennewick – Pasco, WA	0.3053	42
Bryan – College Station, TX	0.3003	43
Las Vegas, NV	0.2946	44
Naples, FL	0.2821	45
Denver – Boulder, CO	0.2739	46
Sacramento, CA	0.2657	47
New York – Northern New Jersey – Long Island, NY – NJ – CT	0.2518	48
Salem, OR	0.2237	49
Tyler, TX	0.2148	50

Source: U.S. Bureau of the Census, Data User Services Division, *1990 Census of Population and Housing,* Summary Tape File 3C, United States Summary, CD-ROM, February 1992.

★1902★

Poverty Status of Families With Children

White Female Householder, No Spouse Present, With Children Under 5 Years Old, Living Below Poverty, 1989

[Table shows the top 50 areas]

MSA	% of population	Rank
Lewiston – Auburn, ME	0.582	1
Saint Joseph, MO	0.373	2
New Bedford, MA	0.367	3
Bangor, ME	0.365	4
Pueblo, CO	0.362	5
Richland – Kennewick – Pasco, WA	0.351	6
Huntington – Ashland, WV – KY – OH	0.347	7
Redding, CA	0.343	8

[Continued]

★1902★

White Female Householder, No Spouse Present, With Children Under 5 Years Old, Living Below Poverty, 1989

[Continued]

MSA	% of population	Rank
Flint, MI	0.340	9
Jackson, MI	0.339	10
Spokane, WA	0.337	11
Pittsfield, MA	0.332	12
Kokomo, IN	0.331	13
Eau Claire, WI	0.329	14
Davenport – Rock Island – Moline, IA – IL	0.326	15
Rapid City, SD	0.326	15
Yuba City, CA	0.319	16
Casper, WY	0.315	17
Battle Creek, MI	0.313	18
Duluth, MN – WI	0.309	19
Medford, OR	0.304	20
Joplin, MO	0.302	21
Grand Forks, ND	0.294	22
Parkersburg – Marietta, WV – OH	0.291	23
Chico, CA	0.290	24
Janesville – Beloit, WI	0.288	25
Owensboro, KY	0.288	25
Muskegon, MI	0.287	26
Anderson, IN	0.280	27
Cumberland, MD – WV	0.276	28
Green Bay, WI	0.275	29
Saginaw – Bay City – Midland, MI	0.274	30
Elmira, NY	0.273	31
Dubuque, IA	0.271	32
Jamestown – Dunkirk, NY	0.269	33
Olympia, WA	0.269	33
Terre Haute, IN	0.263	34
Binghamton, NY	0.260	35
Decatur, IL	0.259	36
Altoona, PA	0.256	37
Waterloo – Cedar Falls, IA	0.255	38
Erie, PA	0.251	39
Muncie, IN	0.250	40
Sioux City, IA – NE	0.249	41
Springfield, MO	0.249	41
Yakima, WA	0.248	42
Las Cruces, NM	0.247	43
Bremerton, WA	0.246	44
Enid, OK	0.245	45
Wheeling, WV – OH	0.245	45

Source: U.S. Bureau of the Census, Data User Services Division, *1990 Census of Population and Housing,* Summary Tape File 3C, United States Summary, CD-ROM, February 1992.

★1903★

Poverty Status of Families With Children

White Female Householder, No Spouse Present, With Children Under 5 and 5 to 17 Years Old, Living Below Poverty, 1989

[Table shows the top 50 areas]

MSA	% of population	Rank
Brownsville – Harlingen, TX	0.484	1
McAllen – Edinburg – Mission, TX	0.429	2
Laredo, TX	0.418	3
Las Cruces, NM	0.410	4
El Paso, TX	0.403	5
Pueblo, CO	0.400	6
Wheeling, WV – OH	0.378	7
Elmira, NY	0.353	8
Altoona, PA	0.345	9
Lewiston – Auburn, ME	0.328	10
Medford, OR	0.325	11
Redding, CA	0.320	12
Saint Joseph, MO	0.308	13
Chico, CA	0.301	14
Great Falls, MT	0.296	15
Sioux City, IA – NE	0.293	16
Cumberland, MD – WV	0.287	17
Corpus Christi, TX	0.286	18
San Antonio, TX	0.286	18
Flint, MI	0.284	19
Merced, CA	0.277	20
Rapid City, SD	0.275	21
Kokomo, IN	0.272	22
Casper, WY	0.271	23
Visalia – Tulare – Porterville, CA	0.266	24
Yakima, WA	0.263	25
Modesto, CA	0.259	26
Jamestown – Dunkirk, NY	0.254	27
Huntington – Ashland, WV – KY – OH	0.253	28
Fitchburg – Leominster, MA	0.252	29
Muskegon, MI	0.250	30
Yuba City, CA	0.249	31
Eugene – Springfield, OR	0.247	32
Bangor, ME	0.244	33
Erie, PA	0.243	34
Greeley, CO	0.242	35
Odessa, TX	0.242	35
Spokane, WA	0.240	36
New Bedford, MA	0.238	37
Anderson, IN	0.236	38
Battle Creek, MI	0.236	38
Cheyenne, WY	0.234	39
Jackson, MI	0.234	39
Enid, OK	0.233	40
Salem, OR	0.232	41
Billings, MT	0.231	42
Springfield, MA	0.231	42
Steubenville – Weirton, OH – WV	0.229	43
Williamsport, PA	0.227	44
Bremerton, WA	0.224	45

Source: U.S. Bureau of the Census, Data User Services Division, *1990 Census of Population and Housing,* Summary Tape File 3C, United States Summary, CD-ROM, February 1992.

★1904★

Poverty Status of Families With Children

White Female Householder, No Spouse Present, With Children 5 to 17 Years Old, Living Below Poverty, 1989

[Table shows the top 50 areas]

MSA	% of population	Rank
Brownsville – Harlingen, TX	0.946	1
Huntington – Ashland, WV – KY – OH	0.800	2
Las Cruces, NM	0.797	3
McAllen – Edinburg – Mission, TX	0.789	4
Pueblo, CO	0.744	5
Wheeling, WV – OH	0.715	6
Steubenville – Weirton, OH – WV	0.696	7
Parkersburg – Marietta, WV – OH	0.682	8
Altoona, PA	0.676	9
Casper, WY	0.665	10
Redding, CA	0.658	11
Duluth, MN – WI	0.645	12
El Paso, TX	0.636	13
Laredo, TX	0.634	14
Charleston, WV	0.624	15
Anderson, IN	0.609	16
Yuba City, CA	0.600	17
Battle Creek, MI	0.593	18
Flint, MI	0.579	19
Spokane, WA	0.571	20
Cumberland, MD – WV	0.570	21
Bangor, ME	0.554	22
Richland – Kennewick – Pasco, WA	0.545	23
Great Falls, MT	0.544	24
Johnson City – Kingsport – Bristol, TN – VA	0.542	25
Saginaw – Bay City – Midland, MI	0.540	26
Saint Joseph, MO	0.538	27
Jamestown – Dunkirk, NY	0.530	28
Johnstown, PA	0.529	29
Lewiston – Auburn, ME	0.525	30
Owensboro, KY	0.524	31
Waterloo – Cedar Falls, IA	0.520	32
Chico, CA	0.518	33
Corpus Christi, TX	0.506	34
Muncie, IN	0.505	35
Fort Smith, AR – OK	0.501	36
Sioux City, IA – NE	0.501	36
Billings, MT	0.499	37
Erie, PA	0.496	38
Williamsport, PA	0.493	39
Canton, OH	0.489	40
Eugene – Springfield, OR	0.488	41
Kokomo, IN	0.481	42
Elmira, NY	0.476	43
Visalia – Tulare – Porterville, CA	0.476	43
Terre Haute, IN	0.475	44
Biloxi – Gulfport, MS	0.472	45
Joplin, MO	0.468	46
New Bedford, MA	0.464	47
Fargo – Moorhead, ND – MN	0.463	48

Source: U.S. Bureau of the Census, Data User Services Division, *1990 Census of Population and Housing,* Summary Tape File 3C, United States Summary, CD-ROM, February 1992.

★1905★

Poverty Status of Families With Children

White Female Householder, No Spouse Present, With Children Under 5 and Children 5 to 17 Years Old, Living Above Poverty, 1989

[Table shows the top 50 areas]

MSA	% of population	Rank
Battle Creek, MI	0.212	1
Reno, NV	0.188	2
Victoria, TX	0.188	2
El Paso, TX	0.186	3
Anchorage, AK	0.185	4
Las Vegas, NV	0.185	4
Jackson, MI	0.182	5
Redding, CA	0.182	5
Salt Lake City – Ogden, UT	0.180	6
Amarillo, TX	0.176	7
Glens Falls, NY	0.175	8
Manchester, NH	0.174	9
Brownsville – Harlingen, TX	0.173	10
Janesville – Beloit, WI	0.168	11
Chico, CA	0.164	12
South Bend – Mishawaka, IN	0.164	12
Odessa, TX	0.163	13
Cheyenne, WY	0.160	14
Modesto, CA	0.160	14
Wichita Falls, TX	0.160	14
Spokane, WA	0.158	15
Cedar Rapids, IA	0.157	16
Santa Fe, NM	0.157	16
Fort Walton Beach, FL	0.154	17
Las Cruces, NM	0.152	18
Sacramento, CA	0.152	18
Springfield, IL	0.150	19
Elkhart – Goshen, IN	0.149	20
Elmira, NY	0.149	20
New Bedford, MA	0.149	20
Rockford, IL	0.149	20
Stockton, CA	0.149	20
Yuba City, CA	0.149	20
Bremerton, WA	0.148	21
Burlington, VT	0.148	21
Mansfield, OH	0.148	21
Bakersfield, CA	0.147	22
Corpus Christi, TX	0.146	23
Casper, WY	0.144	24
Columbia, MO	0.144	24
Panama City, FL	0.144	24
Richland – Kennewick – Pasco, WA	0.144	24
Abilene, TX	0.143	25
Sioux Falls, SD	0.143	25
Austin, TX	0.142	26
Reading, PA	0.142	26
Rochester, MN	0.142	26
Albuquerque, NM	0.140	27
Fort Wayne, IN	0.140	27
San Antonio, TX	0.140	27

Source: U.S. Bureau of the Census, Data User Services Division, *1990 Census of Population and Housing,* Summary Tape File 3C, United States Summary, CD-ROM, February 1992.

★ 1906 ★

★ 1906 ★

Poverty Status of Families With Children

White Female Householder, No Spouse Present, With Children Under 5 Years Old, Living Above Poverty, 1989

[Table shows the top 50 areas]

MSA	% of population	Rank
Anchorage, AK	0.326	1
Reno, NV	0.300	2
Casper, WY	0.296	3
Billings, MT	0.287	4
Sioux Falls, SD	0.270	5
Atlantic City, NJ	0.257	6
Wichita Falls, TX	0.247	7
Saint Joseph, MO	0.243	8
Des Moines, IA	0.241	9
Cedar Rapids, IA	0.239	10
Worcester, MA	0.233	11
Portsmouth – Dover – Rochester, NH – ME	0.232	12
Spokane, WA	0.232	12
Albuquerque, NM	0.230	13
Pittsfield, MA	0.230	13
Olympia, WA	0.229	14
Glens Falls, NY	0.228	15
Las Vegas, NV	0.226	16
Rapid City, SD	0.226	16
Cheyenne, WY	0.224	17
Bloomington, IN	0.223	18
Phoenix, AZ	0.223	18
Orlando, FL	0.222	19
Denver – Boulder, CO	0.221	20
Sherman – Denison, TX	0.220	21
Jackson, MI	0.218	22
Manchester, NH	0.216	23
Redding, CA	0.216	23
Battle Creek, MI	0.215	24
Lincoln, NE	0.215	24
Sacramento, CA	0.215	24
Williamsport, PA	0.215	24
Fort Walton Beach, FL	0.213	25
Amarillo, TX	0.211	26
Fayetteville – Springdale, AR	0.211	26
Hickory – Morganton, NC	0.211	26
Seattle – Tacoma, WA	0.211	26
Elmira, NY	0.209	27
Fort Wayne, IN	0.209	27
Indianapolis, IN	0.209	27
Boise, ID	0.208	28
Portland – Vancouver, OR – WA	0.208	28
Binghamton, NY	0.207	29
La Crosse, WI	0.202	30
Columbus, OH	0.199	31
Eugene – Springfield, OR	0.199	31
Janesville – Beloit, WI	0.199	31
Utica – Rome, NY	0.199	31
Lansing – East Lansing, MI	0.198	32
Sioux City, IA – NE	0.198	32

Source: U.S. Bureau of the Census, Data User Services Division, *1990 Census of Population and Housing,* Summary Tape File 3C, United States Summary, CD-ROM, February 1992.

★ 1907 ★

Poverty Status of Families With Children

White Female Householder, No Spouse Present, With Children 5 to 17 Years Old, Living Above Poverty, 1989

[Table shows the top 50 areas]

MSA	% of population	Rank
Portland, ME	1.32	1
Boise, ID	1.24	2
Olympia, WA	1.24	2
Springfield, IL	1.23	3
Santa Fe, NM	1.20	4
Spokane, WA	1.16	5
Pittsfield, MA	1.15	6
Manchester, NH	1.12	7
Hickory – Morganton, NC	1.11	8
Portland – Vancouver, OR – WA	1.11	8
Saint Joseph, MO	1.11	8
Sioux Falls, SD	1.11	8
Bangor, ME	1.10	9
Denver – Boulder, CO	1.10	9
Lewiston – Auburn, ME	1.10	9
Sacramento, CA	1.10	9
Billings, MT	1.09	10
Enid, OK	1.09	10
Portsmouth – Dover – Rochester, NH – ME	1.09	10
Eugene – Springfield, OR	1.08	11
Medford, OR	1.08	11
Omaha, NE – IA	1.08	11
Bismarck, ND	1.07	12
Kokomo, IN	1.07	12
Redding, CA	1.07	12
Salem, OR	1.07	12
Amarillo, TX	1.06	13
Fitchburg – Leominster, MA	1.06	13
Asheville, NC	1.05	14
Des Moines, IA	1.05	14
Topeka, KS	1.05	14
Cheyenne, WY	1.04	15
Lincoln, NE	1.04	15
Louisville, KY – IN	1.04	15
Rochester, MN	1.04	15
Battle Creek, MI	1.03	16
Burlington, VT	1.03	16
Columbia, MO	1.03	16
Elkhart – Goshen, IN	1.03	16
La Crosse, WI	1.03	16
New Bedford, MA	1.03	16
Reno, NV	1.03	16
Sherman – Denison, TX	1.03	16
Davenport – Rock Island – Moline, IA – IL	1.02	17
Kansas City, MO – KS	1.02	17
Phoenix, AZ	1.02	17
Seattle – Tacoma, WA	1.02	17
Anchorage, AK	1.01	18
Minneapolis – Saint Paul, MN – WI	1.01	18
Roanoke, VA	1.01	18

Source: U.S. Bureau of the Census, Data User Services Division, *1990 Census of Population and Housing,* Summary Tape File 3C, United States Summary, CD-ROM, February 1992.

★ 1908 ★

Poverty Status of Families With Children

White Male Householder, No Spouse Present, With Children Under 5 Years Old, Living Below Poverty, 1989

[Table shows the top 50 areas]

MSA	% of population	Rank
Las Cruces, NM	0.0760	1
Altoona, PA	0.0712	2
Enid, OK	0.0705	3
Yakima, WA	0.0662	4
Jamestown – Dunkirk, NY	0.0627	5
Wheeling, WV – OH	0.0603	6
Sioux City, IA – NE	0.0548	7
Lima, OH	0.0531	8
Chico, CA	0.0527	9
Parkersburg – Marietta, WV – OH	0.0523	10
Duluth, MN – WI	0.0521	11
Terre Haute, IN	0.0520	12
McAllen – Edinburg – Mission, TX	0.0514	13
Medford, OR	0.0506	14
Manchester, NH	0.0500	15
Cheyenne, WY	0.0492	16
Modesto, CA	0.0491	17
Kankakee, IL	0.0488	18
Joplin, MO	0.0482	19
Brownsville – Harlingen, TX	0.0477	20
Redding, CA	0.0469	21
Great Falls, MT	0.0463	22
Cumberland, MD – WV	0.0462	23
Billings, MT	0.0432	24
Olympia, WA	0.0416	25
Spokane, WA	0.0412	26
El Paso, TX	0.0406	27
Fort Smith, AR – OK	0.0404	28
Bloomington – Normal, IL	0.0403	29
Bradenton, FL	0.0401	30
Biloxi – Gulfport, MS	0.0396	31
Erie, PA	0.0396	31
Fresno, CA	0.0394	32
Huntington – Ashland, WV – KY – OH	0.0390	33
Pueblo, CO	0.0390	33
Lafayette, LA	0.0388	34
Santa Fe, NM	0.0384	35
Houma – Thibodaux, LA	0.0377	36
Lakeland – Winter Haven, FL	0.0375	37
Davenport – Rock Island – Moline, IA – IL	0.0356	38
Glens Falls, NY	0.0354	39
Williamsport, PA	0.0354	39
Eugene – Springfield, OR	0.0353	40
Tucson, AZ	0.0352	41
Springfield, MO	0.0349	42
Binghamton, NY	0.0348	43
Visalia – Tulare – Porterville, CA	0.0346	44
San Angelo, TX	0.0345	45
Rapid City, SD	0.0344	46
Richland – Kennewick – Pasco, WA	0.0340	47

Source: U.S. Bureau of the Census, Data User Services Division, *1990 Census of Population and Housing,* Summary Tape File 3C, United States Summary, CD-ROM, February 1992.

★ 1909 ★

Poverty Status of Families With Children

White Male Householder, No Spouse Present, With Children Under 5 and 5 to 17 Years Old, Living Below Poverty, 1989

[Table shows the top 50 areas]

MSA	% of population	Rank
Las Cruces, NM	0.0908	1
Brownsville – Harlingen, TX	0.0673	2
McAllen – Edinburg – Mission, TX	0.0673	2
Santa Fe, NM	0.0624	3
Pueblo, CO	0.0553	4
Laredo, TX	0.0533	5
El Paso, TX	0.0524	6
Chico, CA	0.0511	7
Yuma, AZ	0.0505	8
Biloxi – Gulfport, MS	0.0477	9
Sharon, PA	0.0405	10
Merced, CA	0.0404	11
Visalia – Tulare – Porterville, CA	0.0401	12
Fresno, CA	0.0393	13
Corpus Christi, TX	0.0332	14
Greeley, CO	0.0326	15
Amarillo, TX	0.0320	16
San Angelo, TX	0.0305	17
Odessa, TX	0.0303	18
San Antonio, TX	0.0303	18
Naples, FL	0.0302	19
Spokane, WA	0.0302	19
Midland, TX	0.0300	20
Altoona, PA	0.0291	21
Yuba City, CA	0.0285	22
Pensacola, FL	0.0276	23
Lafayette, LA	0.0273	24
Olympia, WA	0.0267	25
La Crosse, WI	0.0266	26
Bakersfield, CA	0.0263	27
Elmira, NY	0.0263	27
Casper, WY	0.0261	28
Billings, MT	0.0256	29
Portland, ME	0.0255	30
Abilene, TX	0.0251	31
Manchester, NH	0.0250	32
Hagerstown, MD	0.0247	33
Muskegon, MI	0.0245	34
Tucson, AZ	0.0244	35
Duluth, MN – WI	0.0238	36
Waco, TX	0.0233	37
Albuquerque, NM	0.0231	38
Ocala, FL	0.0231	38
Miami – Fort Lauderdale, FL	0.0230	39
Eau Claire, WI	0.0225	40
Lubbock, TX	0.0225	40
Wichita Falls, TX	0.0221	41
Cheyenne, WY	0.0219	42
Great Falls, MT	0.0219	42
Stockton, CA	0.0218	43

Source: U.S. Bureau of the Census, Data User Services Division, *1990 Census of Population and Housing,* Summary Tape File 3C, United States Summary, CD-ROM, February 1992.

★1910★
Poverty Status of Families With Children

White Male Householder, No Spouse Present, With Children 5 to 17 Years Old, Living Below Poverty, 1989

[Table shows the top 50 areas]

MSA	% of population	Rank
Las Cruces, NM	0.1255	1
Brownsville – Harlingen, TX	0.1146	2
Altoona, PA	0.1042	3
McAllen – Edinburg – Mission, TX	0.0881	4
Huntington – Ashland, WV – KY – OH	0.0845	5
Jamestown – Dunkirk, NY	0.0839	6
Sioux City, IA – NE	0.0835	7
Terre Haute, IN	0.0795	8
Charleston, WV	0.0791	9
Parkersburg – Marietta, WV – OH	0.0778	10
Corpus Christi, TX	0.0763	11
Redding, CA	0.0762	12
Wheeling, WV – OH	0.0753	13
Casper, WY	0.0751	14
Hickory – Morganton, NC	0.0726	15
Saint Joseph, MO	0.0722	16
Battle Creek, MI	0.0721	17
Fort Smith, AR – OK	0.0711	18
Sherman – Denison, TX	0.0705	19
Joplin, MO	0.0704	20
Owensboro, KY	0.0688	21
Rapid City, SD	0.0688	21
Yakima, WA	0.0688	21
Johnson City – Kingsport – Bristol, TN – VA	0.0672	22
Elmira, NY	0.0662	23
Visalia – Tulare – Porterville, CA	0.0657	24
Clarksville – Hopkinsville, TN – KY	0.0655	25
Wichita Falls, TX	0.0654	26
Salem, OR	0.0647	27
Amarillo, TX	0.0635	28
Texarkana, TX – Texarkana, AR	0.0624	29
Odessa, TX	0.0605	30
Houma – Thibodaux, LA	0.0602	31
Decatur, AL	0.0601	32
Eugene – Springfield, OR	0.0601	32
Lewiston – Auburn, ME	0.0590	33
Spokane, WA	0.0589	34
Steubenville – Weirton, OH – WV	0.0589	34
Jackson, MI	0.0588	35
Merced, CA	0.0577	36
Tucson, AZ	0.0577	36
Albuquerque, NM	0.0570	37
Laredo, TX	0.0570	37
Medford, OR	0.0567	38
El Paso, TX	0.0561	39
Panama City, FL	0.0559	40
Utica – Rome, NY	0.0556	41
Billings, MT	0.0555	42
Lake Charles, LA	0.0547	43
Chico, CA	0.0533	44

Source: U.S. Bureau of the Census, Data User Services Division, *1990 Census of Population and Housing*, Summary Tape File 3C, United States Summary, CD-ROM, February 1992.

★1911★
Poverty Status of Families With Children

White Male Householder, No Spouse Present, With Children Under 5 Years Old, Living Above Poverty, 1989

[Table shows the top 50 areas]

MSA	% of population	Rank
Anchorage, AK	0.199	1
Lewiston – Auburn, ME	0.199	1
Reno, NV	0.183	2
Bangor, ME	0.175	3
Williamsport, PA	0.171	4
Manchester, NH	0.168	5
Elkhart – Goshen, IN	0.167	6
Santa Fe, NM	0.162	7
Bremerton, WA	0.159	8
Jackson, MI	0.156	9
Altoona, PA	0.152	10
Yuba City, CA	0.149	11
Modesto, CA	0.148	12
Syracuse, NY	0.147	13
Hickory – Morganton, NC	0.146	14
Anderson, IN	0.145	15
Redding, CA	0.144	16
Lancaster, PA	0.140	17
Las Vegas, NV	0.140	17
Spokane, WA	0.139	18
Bakersfield, CA	0.138	19
York, PA	0.138	19
Burlington, VT	0.136	20
Portland, ME	0.136	20
Sioux City, IA – NE	0.136	20
Wausau, WI	0.136	20
Stockton, CA	0.135	21
Yakima, WA	0.135	21
Fort Myers – Cape Coral, Fl	0.134	22
Springfield, IL	0.129	23
Bellingham, WA	0.128	24
Salem, OR	0.128	24
Merced, CA	0.127	25
Portland – Vancouver, OR – WA	0.126	26
Rockford, IL	0.126	26
Lincoln, NE	0.122	27
Phoenix, AZ	0.121	28
Sacramento, CA	0.121	28
Atlantic City, NJ	0.118	29
Albany – Schenectady – Troy, NY	0.117	30
Erie, PA	0.117	30
Pittsfield, MA	0.116	31
Rochester, NY	0.116	31
Greeley, CO	0.114	32
Portsmouth – Dover – Rochester, NH – ME	0.114	32
Chico, CA	0.113	33
Houma – Thibodaux, LA	0.113	33
Mansfield, OH	0.113	33
Roanoke, VA	0.113	33
Fort Pierce, FL	0.112	34

Source: U.S. Bureau of the Census, Data User Services Division, *1990 Census of Population and Housing*, Summary Tape File 3C, United States Summary, CD-ROM, February 1992.

★1912★

Poverty Status of Families With Children

White Male Householder, No Spouse Present, With Children Under 5 and 5 to 17 Years Old, Living Above Poverty, 1989

[Table shows the top 50 areas]

MSA	% of population	Rank
Yuba City, CA	0.1264	1
Merced, CA	0.0987	2
Bakersfield, CA	0.0782	3
Stockton, CA	0.0778	4
York, PA	0.0763	5
Janesville – Beloit, WI	0.0760	6
Naples, FL	0.0756	7
Redding, CA	0.0735	8
Laredo, TX	0.0728	9
Cheyenne, WY	0.0711	10
Great Falls, MT	0.0695	11
Syracuse, NY	0.0690	12
Lakeland – Winter Haven, FL	0.0688	13
Reno, NV	0.0683	14
Yakima, WA	0.0678	15
Las Vegas, NV	0.0677	16
Bradenton, FL	0.0675	17
Salem, OR	0.0669	18
Sheboygan, WI	0.0655	19
Las Cruces, NM	0.0649	20
Santa Fe, NM	0.0624	21
Fort Myers – Cape Coral, Fl	0.0618	22
Odessa, TX	0.0605	23
Albuquerque, NM	0.0603	24
Kankakee, IL	0.0603	24
Eugene – Springfield, OR	0.0597	25
Springfield, IL	0.0596	26
Modesto, CA	0.0594	27
Los Angeles – Anaheim – Riverside, CA	0.0586	28
Ocala, FL	0.0585	29
Asheville, NC	0.0583	30
Anchorage, AK	0.0579	31
Fayetteville – Springdale, AR	0.0564	32
Topeka, KS	0.0559	33
Elkhart – Goshen, IN	0.0557	34
Portland – Vancouver, OR – WA	0.0556	35
Pensacola, FL	0.0555	36
Santa Barbara – Santa Maria – Lompoc, CA	0.0555	36
Harrisburg – Lebanon – Carlisle, PA	0.0551	37
Fitchburg – Leominster, MA	0.0545	38
Fresno, CA	0.0545	38
Rockford, IL	0.0543	39
Utica – Rome, NY	0.0540	40
Chico, CA	0.0538	41
Glens Falls, NY	0.0531	42
Lake Charles, LA	0.0517	43
Kokomo, IN	0.0516	44
Biloxi – Gulfport, MS	0.0512	45
Fort Smith, AR – OK	0.0506	46
Amarillo, TX	0.0501	47

Source: U.S. Bureau of the Census, Data User Services Division, *1990 Census of Population and Housing*, Summary Tape File 3C, United States Summary, CD-ROM, February 1992.

★1913★

Poverty Status of Families With Children

White Male Householder, No Spouse Present, With Children 5 to 17 Years Old, Living Above Poverty, 1989

[Table shows the top 50 areas]

MSA	% of population	Rank
Casper, WY	0.46	1
Yuba City, CA	0.43	2
Cheyenne, WY	0.42	3
Eugene – Springfield, OR	0.42	3
Olympia, WA	0.42	3
Richland – Kennewick – Pasco, WA	0.40	4
Glens Falls, NY	0.39	5
Las Vegas, NV	0.39	5
Redding, CA	0.38	6
Boise, ID	0.37	7
Hickory – Morganton, NC	0.37	7
Reno, NV	0.37	7
Salem, OR	0.37	7
Santa Fe, NM	0.37	7
Anchorage, AK	0.36	8
Medford, OR	0.36	8
Portland – Vancouver, OR – WA	0.36	8
Billings, MT	0.35	9
Janesville – Beloit, WI	0.34	10
Merced, CA	0.34	10
Pascagoula, MS	0.34	10
Bremerton, WA	0.33	11
Chico, CA	0.33	11
Greeley, CO	0.33	11
Kokomo, IN	0.33	11
Sherman – Denison, TX	0.33	11
Wichita, KS	0.33	11
Albuquerque, NM	0.32	12
Burlington, VT	0.32	12
Columbia, MO	0.32	12
Denver – Boulder, CO	0.32	12
Reading, PA	0.32	12
Spokane, WA	0.32	12
Amarillo, TX	0.31	13
Anderson, IN	0.31	13
Appleton – Oshkosh – Neenah, WI	0.31	13
Bellingham, WA	0.31	13
Davenport – Rock Island – Moline, IA – IL	0.31	13
Elkhart – Goshen, IN	0.31	13
Evansville, IN – KY	0.31	13
Great Falls, MT	0.31	13
Lancaster, PA	0.31	13
Manchester, NH	0.31	13
Seattle – Tacoma, WA	0.31	13
Binghamton, NY	0.30	14
Charleston, WV	0.30	14
Jackson, MI	0.30	14
Sacramento, CA	0.30	14
Sheboygan, WI	0.30	14
South Bend – Mishawaka, IN	0.30	14

Source: U.S. Bureau of the Census, Data User Services Division, *1990 Census of Population and Housing*, Summary Tape File 3C, United States Summary, CD-ROM, February 1992.

★1914★
Poverty Status of Families With Children

White Married Couples With Children Under 5 Years Old, Living Below Poverty, 1989

[Table shows the top 50 areas]

MSA	% of population	Rank
Brownsville – Harlingen, TX	0.476	1
Las Cruces, NM	0.441	2
Provo – Orem, UT	0.425	3
McAllen – Edinburg – Mission, TX	0.422	4
Huntington – Ashland, WV – KY – OH	0.420	5
Laredo, TX	0.329	6
El Paso, TX	0.307	7
Johnson City – Kingsport – Bristol, TN – VA	0.286	8
Houma – Thibodaux, LA	0.276	9
Biloxi – Gulfport, MS	0.272	10
Jacksonville, NC	0.262	11
Fayetteville – Springdale, AR	0.260	12
Joplin, MO	0.254	13
Charleston, WV	0.246	14
Wheeling, WV – OH	0.244	15
Owensboro, KY	0.243	16
Victoria, TX	0.243	16
Gadsden, AL	0.242	17
Johnstown, PA	0.238	18
Abilene, TX	0.231	19
Killeen – Temple, TX	0.227	20
Steubenville – Weirton, OH – WV	0.225	21
Knoxville, TN	0.224	22
Parkersburg – Marietta, WV – OH	0.217	23
Grand Forks, ND	0.215	24
Decatur, AL	0.213	25
Lawton, OK	0.213	25
Cumberland, MD – WV	0.212	26
Bryan – College Station, TX	0.205	27
Fort Smith, AR – OK	0.202	28
Eugene – Springfield, OR	0.201	29
Lake Charles, LA	0.201	29
Springfield, MO	0.199	30
Cheyenne, WY	0.197	31
Florence, AL	0.197	31
Corpus Christi, TX	0.196	32
Terre Haute, IN	0.194	33
Sharon, PA	0.192	34
Bismarck, ND	0.191	35
Clarksville – Hopkinsville, TN – KY	0.189	36
Bloomington, IN	0.187	37
Amarillo, TX	0.186	38
Anniston, AL	0.186	38
Visalia – Tulare – Porterville, CA	0.185	39
Saint Joseph, MO	0.184	40
Altoona, PA	0.182	41
Texarkana, TX – Texarkana, AR	0.182	41
Odessa, TX	0.181	42
Alexandria, LA	0.180	43
Lafayette, LA	0.178	44

Source: U.S. Bureau of the Census, Data User Services Division, *1990 Census of Population and Housing,* Summary Tape File 3C, United States Summary, CD-ROM, February 1992.

★1915★
Poverty Status of Families With Children

White Married Couples With Children Under 5 Years Old and Children 5 to 17 Years Old, Living Above Poverty, 1989

[Table shows the top 50 areas]

MSA	% of population	Rank
Provo – Orem, UT	3.59	1
Salt Lake City – Ogden, UT	3.16	2
Saint Cloud, MN	2.63	3
Rapid City, SD	2.62	4
Bismarck, ND	2.55	5
Sioux Falls, SD	2.51	6
Grand Forks, ND	2.50	7
Rochester, MN	2.43	8
Dubuque, IA	2.42	9
Grand Rapids, MI	2.42	9
Casper, WY	2.40	10
Appleton – Oshkosh – Neenah, WI	2.39	11
Boise, ID	2.28	12
Midland, TX	2.28	12
Elkhart – Goshen, IN	2.26	13
Fort Wayne, IN	2.26	13
Bremerton, WA	2.25	14
Fargo – Moorhead, ND – MN	2.24	15
Wausau, WI	2.19	16
Anchorage, AK	2.18	17
Richland – Kennewick – Pasco, WA	2.17	18
Omaha, NE – IA	2.16	19
Sheboygan, WI	2.16	19
Green Bay, WI	2.15	20
Minneapolis – Saint Paul, MN – WI	2.15	20
Lancaster, PA	2.14	21
Sioux City, IA – NE	2.13	22
Cheyenne, WY	2.11	23
Wichita, KS	2.11	23
Des Moines, IA	2.09	24
Cedar Rapids, IA	2.08	25
Jamestown – Dunkirk, NY	2.06	26
Lima, OH	2.06	26
Fort Collins – Loveland, CO	2.05	27
Muskegon, MI	2.05	27
Eau Claire, WI	2.03	28
Houma – Thibodaux, LA	2.02	29
Great Falls, MT	2.01	30
Poughkeepsie, NY	2.01	30
Billings, MT	1.99	31
Enid, OK	1.99	31
Syracuse, NY	1.99	31
Portland, ME	1.98	32
York, PA	1.98	32
Cincinnati – Hamilton, OH – KY – IN	1.97	33
Burlington, VT	1.96	34
Kokomo, IN	1.96	34
Glens Falls, NY	1.95	35
Greeley, CO	1.95	35
Portsmouth – Dover – Rochester, NH – ME	1.94	36

Source: U.S. Bureau of the Census, Data User Services Division, *1990 Census of Population and Housing,* Summary Tape File 3C, United States Summary, CD-ROM, February 1992.

★1916★

Poverty Status of Families With Children

White Married Couples With Children Under 5 and 5 to 17 Years Old, Living Below Poverty, 1989

[Table shows the top 50 areas]

MSA	% of population	Rank
McAllen – Edinburg – Mission, TX	1.347	1
Brownsville – Harlingen, TX	1.322	2
Laredo, TX	1.034	3
El Paso, TX	0.817	4
Las Cruces, NM	0.731	5
Provo – Orem, UT	0.418	6
Odessa, TX	0.397	7
Corpus Christi, TX	0.394	8
Houma – Thibodaux, LA	0.392	9
Huntington – Ashland, WV – KY – OH	0.388	10
Owensboro, KY	0.383	11
San Antonio, TX	0.369	12
Fort Smith, AR – OK	0.358	13
Yuma, AZ	0.356	14
Joplin, MO	0.353	15
Johnson City – Kingsport – Bristol, TN – VA	0.326	16
Johnstown, PA	0.325	17
Gadsden, AL	0.324	18
Pueblo, CO	0.316	19
Yuba City, CA	0.304	20
San Angelo, TX	0.297	21
Abilene, TX	0.293	22
Steubenville – Weirton, OH – WV	0.289	23
Wheeling, WV – OH	0.289	23
Amarillo, TX	0.280	24
Richland – Kennewick – Pasco, WA	0.276	25
Chico, CA	0.273	26
Charleston, WV	0.262	27
Killeen – Temple, TX	0.262	27
Biloxi – Gulfport, MS	0.261	28
Fayetteville – Springdale, AR	0.261	28
Enid, OK	0.259	29
Lubbock, TX	0.257	30
Cumberland, MD – WV	0.253	31
Visalia – Tulare – Porterville, CA	0.252	32
Merced, CA	0.250	33
Redding, CA	0.250	33
Altoona, PA	0.248	34
Victoria, TX	0.246	35
Waco, TX	0.240	36
Saint Joseph, MO	0.238	37
Greeley, CO	0.237	38
Sharon, PA	0.237	38
Parkersburg – Marietta, WV – OH	0.235	39
Great Falls, MT	0.234	40
Jamestown – Dunkirk, NY	0.234	40
Utica – Rome, NY	0.234	40
Lafayette, LA	0.233	41
Knoxville, TN	0.232	42
Ocala, FL	0.231	43

Source: U.S. Bureau of the Census, Data User Services Division, *1990 Census of Population and Housing,* Summary Tape File 3C, United States Summary, CD-ROM, February 1992.

★1917★

Poverty Status of Families With Children

White Married Couples With Children 5 to 17 Years Old, Living Below Poverty, 1989

[Table shows the top 50 areas]

MSA	% of population	Rank
Brownsville – Harlingen, TX	1.494	1
McAllen – Edinburg – Mission, TX	1.491	2
Laredo, TX	1.223	3
Huntington – Ashland, WV – KY – OH	0.992	4
Las Cruces, NM	0.951	5
El Paso, TX	0.826	6
Yuma, AZ	0.720	7
Houma – Thibodaux, LA	0.697	8
Johnson City – Kingsport – Bristol, TN – VA	0.646	9
Wheeling, WV – OH	0.606	10
Steubenville – Weirton, OH – WV	0.601	11
Cumberland, MD – WV	0.578	12
Parkersburg – Marietta, WV – OH	0.574	13
Corpus Christi, TX	0.556	14
Charleston, WV	0.540	15
Johnstown, PA	0.537	16
Florence, AL	0.503	17
Altoona, PA	0.486	18
Knoxville, TN	0.470	19
Fort Smith, AR – OK	0.462	20
Joplin, MO	0.456	21
Victoria, TX	0.451	22
Pascagoula, MS	0.430	23
Saint Joseph, MO	0.426	24
Biloxi – Gulfport, MS	0.413	25
Gadsden, AL	0.413	25
Owensboro, KY	0.412	26
Odessa, TX	0.404	27
Sherman – Denison, TX	0.402	28
San Antonio, TX	0.398	29
Pueblo, CO	0.394	30
Fayetteville – Springdale, AR	0.376	31
Enid, OK	0.374	32
Midland, TX	0.364	33
Alexandria, LA	0.363	34
Redding, CA	0.358	35
Chattanooga, TN – GA	0.352	36
Decatur, AL	0.351	37
Wichita Falls, TX	0.347	38
Texarkana, TX – Texarkana, AR	0.344	39
Yuba City, CA	0.342	40
Battle Creek, MI	0.335	41
Lake Charles, LA	0.331	42
Lexington-Fayette, KY	0.329	43
Sharon, PA	0.327	44
Jamestown – Dunkirk, NY	0.326	45
Waco, TX	0.326	45
Lafayette, LA	0.324	46
Amarillo, TX	0.317	47
Dubuque, IA	0.316	48

Source: U.S. Bureau of the Census, Data User Services Division, *1990 Census of Population and Housing,* Summary Tape File 3C, United States Summary, CD-ROM, February 1992.

★1918★
Poverty Status of Families With Children

White Married Couples With Children Under 5 Years Old, Living Above Poverty, 1989

[Table shows the top 50 areas]

MSA	Number	Rank
New York – Northern New Jersey – Long Island, NY – NJ – CT	291,069	1
Los Angeles – Anaheim – Riverside, CA	208,905	2
Chicago – Gary – Lake County, IL – IN – WI	142,084	3
Philadelphia – Wilmington – Trenton, PA – NJ – DE – MD	110,237	4
San Francisco – Oakland – San Jose, CA	102,492	5
Boston – Lawrence – Salem, MA – NH	89,378	6
Detroit – Ann Arbor, MI	83,070	7
Dallas – Fort Worth, TX	80,941	8
Washington, DC – MD – VA	70,865	9
Houston – Galveston – Brazoria, TX	65,741	10
Minneapolis – Saint Paul, MN – WI	61,487	11
Seattle – Tacoma, WA	55,517	12
Atlanta, GA	55,492	13
Cleveland – Akron – Lorain, OH	50,111	14
Miami – Fort Lauderdale, FL	49,986	15
Saint Louis, MO – IL	47,846	16
Baltimore, MD	45,549	17
San Diego, CA	43,734	18
Denver – Boulder, CO	41,183	19
Pittsburgh – Beaver Valley, PA	40,776	20
Phoenix, AZ	40,612	21
Cincinnati – Hamilton, OH – KY – IN	35,926	22
Tampa – Saint Petersburg – Clearwater, FL	35,089	23
Kansas City, MO – KS	32,063	24
Portland – Vancouver, OR – WA	31,162	25
Milwaukee – Racine, WI	29,964	26
Columbus, OH	29,040	27
Norfolk – Virginia Beach – Newport News, VA	28,954	28
Indianapolis, IN	27,197	29
Sacramento, CA	27,131	30
Providence – Pawtucket – Fall River, RI – MA	24,328	31
Hartford – New Britain – Middletown, CT	23,628	32
Charlotte – Gastonia – Rock Hill, NC – SC	23,562	33
Salt Lake City – Ogden, UT	23,242	34
Buffalo – Niagara Falls, NY	21,849	35
Orlando, FL	21,739	36
Rochester, NY	20,985	37
Nashville, TN	20,746	38
San Antonio, TX	19,629	39
Jacksonville, FL	18,697	40
Albany – Schenectady – Troy, NY	18,632	41
Greensboro – Winston-Salem – High Point, NC	18,564	42

[Continued]

★1918★

White Married Couples With Children Under 5 Years Old, Living Above Poverty, 1989
[Continued]

MSA	Number	Rank
Louisville, KY – IN	17,736	43
Dayton – Springfield, OH	17,702	44
New Orleans, LA	17,653	45
Grand Rapids, MI	16,943	46
Oklahoma City, OK	16,759	47
Birmingham, AL	15,917	48
Richmond – Petersburg, VA	15,906	49
Austin, TX	14,851	50

Source: U.S. Bureau of the Census, Data User Services Division, *1990 Census of Population and Housing*, Summary Tape File 3C, United States Summary, CD- ROM, February 1992.

★1919★
Poverty Status of Families With Children

White Married Couples With Children 5 to 17 Years Old, Living Above Poverty, 1989

[Table shows the top 50 areas]

MSA	% of population	Rank
Wausau, WI	7.0	1
Bismarck, ND	6.6	2
Sheboygan, WI	6.6	2
Casper, WY	6.5	3
Parkersburg – Marietta, WV – OH	6.5	3
Green Bay, WI	6.3	4
Appleton – Oshkosh – Neenah, WI	6.2	5
Dubuque, IA	6.2	5
Huntington – Ashland, WV – KY – OH	6.2	5
Kokomo, IN	6.2	5
Saint Cloud, MN	6.2	5
York, PA	6.2	5
Hickory – Morganton, NC	6.1	6
Johnson City – Kingsport – Bristol, TN – VA	6.1	6
Lima, OH	6.1	6
Owensboro, KY	6.1	6
Steubenville – Weirton, OH – WV	6.1	6
Anderson, SC	6.0	7
Billings, MT	6.0	7
Elkhart – Goshen, IN	6.0	7
Evansville, IN – KY	6.0	7
Fayetteville – Springdale, AR	6.0	7
Fort Smith, AR – OK	6.0	7
Gadsden, AL	6.0	7
Glens Falls, NY	6.0	7
Joplin, MO	6.0	7
Rochester, MN	6.0	7
Boise, ID	5.9	8
Cedar Rapids, IA	5.9	8
Charleston, WV	5.9	8
Decatur, AL	5.9	8
Johnstown, PA	5.9	8

[Continued]

★1919★
White Married Couples With Children 5 to 17 Years Old, Living Above Poverty, 1989
[Continued]

MSA	% of population	Rank
Mansfield, OH	5.9	8
Sioux City, IA–NE	5.9	8
Williamsport, PA	5.9	8
Altoona, PA	5.8	9
Eau Claire, WI	5.8	9
Fort Wayne, IN	5.8	9
Great Falls, MT	5.8	9
Lewiston–Auburn, ME	5.8	9
Peoria, IL	5.8	9
Sioux Falls, SD	5.8	9
Canton, OH	5.7	10
Fort Collins–Loveland, CO	5.7	10
Fort Walton Beach, FL	5.7	10
Hagerstown, MD	5.7	10
Janesville–Beloit, WI	5.7	10
La Crosse, WI	5.7	10
Pascagoula, MS	5.7	10
Richland–Kennewick–Pasco, WA	5.7	10

Source: U.S. Bureau of the Census, Data User Services Division, *1990 Census of Population and Housing*, Summary Tape File 3C, United States Summary, CD-ROM, February 1992.

★1920★
Poverty Status of Families Without Children
American Indian, Eskimo, or Aleut Female Householder, No Spouse Present, No Children Under 18 Years Old, Living Below Poverty, 1989
[Table shows the top 50 areas]

MSA	% of population	Rank
Rapid City, SD	0.040569	1
Redding, CA	0.025164	2
Oklahoma City, OK	0.019711	3
Albuquerque, NM	0.019144	4
Tucson, AZ	0.018894	5
Yuma, AZ	0.016839	6
Sioux City, IA–NE	0.013911	7
Duluth, MN–WI	0.012502	8
Tulsa, OK	0.012131	9
Fort Smith, AR–OK	0.011938	10
Bismarck, ND	0.011929	11
Lawton, OK	0.011661	12
Great Falls, MT	0.011584	13
Yakima, WA	0.010062	14
Joplin, MO	0.008895	15
Clarksville–Hopkinsville, TN–KY	0.008853	16
Green Bay, WI	0.008736	17
Decatur, AL	0.008361	18
Wilmington, NC	0.008314	19
Pine Bluff, AR	0.008188	20
Saint Joseph, MO	0.007222	21
Phoenix, AZ	0.007116	22
Anchorage, AK	0.007069	23

[Continued]

★1920★
American Indian, Eskimo, or Aleut Female Householder, No Spouse Present, No Children Under 18 Years Old, Living Below Poverty, 1989
[Continued]

MSA	% of population	Rank
Alexandria, LA	0.006841	24
Santa Fe, NM	0.006835	25
Bremerton, WA	0.006325	26
Billings, MT	0.006172	27
Longview–Marshall, TX	0.006156	28
Columbus, GA–AL	0.005760	29
Burlington, NC	0.005545	30
Columbia, MO	0.005339	31
Elkhart–Goshen, IN	0.004481	32
South Bend–Mishawaka, IN	0.004453	33
Spokane, WA	0.004428	34
Olympia, WA	0.004341	35
Amarillo, TX	0.004266	36
Bellingham, WA	0.003913	37
Chico, CA	0.003844	38
Bakersfield, CA	0.003680	39
Lake Charles, LA	0.003569	40
Bangor, ME	0.003382	41
Muncie, IN	0.003343	42
Houma–Thibodaux, LA	0.003282	43
Yuba City, CA	0.003261	44
Chattanooga, TN–GA	0.003232	45
Minneapolis–Saint Paul, MN–WI	0.003084	46
Montgomery, AL	0.003077	47
Des Moines, IA	0.003054	48
Canton, OH	0.003045	49
Provo–Orem, UT	0.003035	50

Source: U.S. Bureau of the Census, Data User Services Division, *1990 Census of Population and Housing*, Summary Tape File 3C, United States Summary, CD-ROM, February 1992.

★1921★
Poverty Status of Families Without Children
American Indian, Eskimo, or Aleut Female Householder, No Spouse Present, No Children Under 18 Years Old, Living Above Poverty, 1989
[Table shows the top 50 areas]

MSA	% of population	Rank
Tulsa, OK	0.07490	1
Lawton, OK	0.07086	2
Anchorage, AK	0.06495	3
Oklahoma City, OK	0.05204	4
Bellingham, WA	0.04148	5
Yakima, WA	0.03919	6
Rapid City, SD	0.03688	7
Santa Fe, NM	0.03588	8
Fort Smith, AR–OK	0.03468	9
Green Bay, WI	0.03186	10
Tucson, AZ	0.03134	11
Albuquerque, NM	0.02747	12

[Continued]

★1921★

American Indian, Eskimo, or Aleut Female Householder, No Spouse Present, No Children Under 18 Years Old, Living Above Poverty, 1989

[Continued]

MSA	% of population	Rank
Joplin, MO	0.02446	13
Fresno, CA	0.02412	14
Reno, NV	0.02317	15
Modesto, CA	0.02213	16
Midland, TX	0.02157	17
Fayetteville, NC	0.02003	18
Topeka, KS	0.01926	19
Billings, MT	0.01852	20
Merced, CA	0.01850	21
Duluth, MN – WI	0.01834	22
Las Vegas, NV	0.01713	23
Santa Barbara – Santa Maria – Lompoc, CA	0.01705	24
Phoenix, AZ	0.01692	25
Salem, OR	0.01691	26
Pensacola, FL	0.01684	27
Spokane, WA	0.01577	28
Buffalo – Niagara Falls, NY	0.01556	29
Stockton, CA	0.01540	30
Salinas – Seaside – Monterey, CA	0.01518	31
Fayetteville – Springdale, AR	0.01499	32
Redding, CA	0.01428	33
New London – Norwich, CT – RI	0.01424	34
Bakersfield, CA	0.01398	35
Visalia – Tulare – Porterville, CA	0.01379	36
Seattle – Tacoma, WA	0.01336	37
Richland – Kennewick – Pasco, WA	0.01333	38
La Crosse, WI	0.01328	39
Bremerton, WA	0.01318	40
San Diego, CA	0.01309	41
Yuba City, CA	0.01305	42
Sacramento, CA	0.01296	43
Sherman – Denison, TX	0.01263	44
Cheyenne, WY	0.01230	45
Medford, OR	0.01230	45
Chico, CA	0.01208	46
Springfield, IL	0.01161	47
Parkersburg – Marietta, WV – OH	0.01140	48
Bloomington, IN	0.01101	49

Source: U.S. Bureau of the Census, Data User Services Division, *1990 Census of Population and Housing*, Summary Tape File 3C, United States Summary, CD-ROM, February 1992.

★1922★

Poverty Status of Families Without Children

American Indian, Eskimo, or Aleut Male Householder, No Children Under 18 Years Old, Living Below Poverty, 1989

[Table shows the top 50 areas]

MSA	% of population	Rank
Tucson, AZ	0.014845	1
Lawton, OK	0.011661	2
Albuquerque, NM	0.009572	3
Yakima, WA	0.009003	4
Sioux Falls, SD	0.008077	5
Mansfield, OH	0.007928	6
Las Cruces, NM	0.007380	7
Boise, ID	0.007290	8
Manchester, NH	0.005410	9
Jacksonville, NC	0.005339	10
Waco, TX	0.004759	11
Oklahoma City, OK	0.004693	12
Portland, ME	0.004641	13
Columbus, GA – AL	0.004525	14
Billings, MT	0.004408	15
Chico, CA	0.004393	16
Odessa, TX	0.004204	17
Parkersburg – Marietta, WV – OH	0.004022	18
Phoenix, AZ	0.003958	19
Bellingham, WA	0.003913	20
Santa Fe, NM	0.003418	21
Yuba City, CA	0.003261	22
Tulsa, OK	0.003103	23
Fort Smith, AR – OK	0.002842	24
Houma – Thibodaux, LA	0.002735	25
Visalia – Tulare – Porterville, CA	0.002565	26
Duluth, MN – WI	0.002500	27
Madison, WI	0.002452	28
Syracuse, NY	0.002425	29
Salt Lake City – Ogden, UT	0.002238	30
Fayetteville, NC	0.002185	31
Sherman – Denison, TX	0.002105	32
Colorado Springs, CO	0.002015	33
Killeen – Temple, TX	0.001958	34
Olympia, WA	0.001861	35
Worcester, MA	0.001831	36
Bakersfield, CA	0.001656	37
Saginaw – Bay City – Midland, MI	0.001503	38
Charlotte – Gastonia – Rock Hill, NC – SC	0.001463	39
Columbia, SC	0.001324	40
Naples, FL	0.001315	41
Raleigh – Durham, NC	0.001224	42
Johnson City – Kingsport – Bristol, TN – VA	0.000917	43
San Diego, CA	0.000841	44
Detroit – Ann Arbor, MI	0.000750	45
Tampa – Saint Petersburg – Clearwater, FL	0.000725	46
El Paso, TX	0.000676	47
Minneapolis – Saint Paul, MN – WI	0.000649	48
Appleton – Oshkosh – Neenah, WI	0.000635	49
Dayton – Springfield, OH	0.000631	50

Source: U.S. Bureau of the Census, Data User Services Division, *1990 Census of Population and Housing*, Summary Tape File 3C, United States Summary, CD-ROM, February 1992.

★ 1923 ★

Poverty Status of Families Without Children

American Indian, Eskimo, or Aleut Male Householder, No Spouse Present, No Children Under 18 Years Old, Living Above Poverty, 1989

[Table shows the top 50 areas]

MSA	% of population	Rank
Yakima, WA	0.03019	1
Anchorage, AK	0.02430	2
Tulsa, OK	0.02313	3
Albuquerque, NM	0.02185	4
Fort Smith, AR–OK	0.02103	5
Santa Fe, NM	0.01880	6
Redding, CA	0.01700	7
Oklahoma City, OK	0.01627	8
Stockton, CA	0.01477	9
Reno, NV	0.01414	10
Longview–Marshall, TX	0.01293	11
Burlington, VT	0.01217	12
Lynchburg, VA	0.01196	13
Bismarck, ND	0.01193	14
Lawton, OK	0.01166	15
Visalia–Tulare–Porterville, CA	0.01154	16
Las Vegas, NV	0.01146	17
Yuba City, CA	0.01142	18
Grand Forks, ND	0.01132	19
Jackson, MI	0.01068	20
Great Falls, MT	0.01030	21
Bangor, ME	0.01015	22
Bremerton, WA	0.01001	23
Rapid City, SD	0.00983	24
Tucson, AZ	0.00975	25
Modesto, CA	0.00972	26
Joplin, MO	0.00964	27
Bradenton, FL	0.00945	28
Victoria, TX	0.00941	29
Duluth, MN–WI	0.00917	30
Alexandria, LA	0.00912	31
Wichita, KS	0.00865	32
Santa Barbara–Santa Maria–Lompoc, CA	0.00839	33
Pueblo, CO	0.00813	34
Battle Creek, MI	0.00809	35
Phoenix, AZ	0.00801	36
Fort Wayne, IN	0.00797	37
Salem, OR	0.00791	38
Green Bay, WI	0.00771	39
Lawrence, KS	0.00734	40
Fargo–Moorhead, ND–MN	0.00718	41
Fayetteville, NC	0.00692	42
Medford, OR	0.00683	43
Knoxville, TN	0.00678	44
Abilene, TX	0.00669	45
Muncie, IN	0.00669	45
Richland–Kennewick–Pasco, WA	0.00667	46
Portland–Vancouver, OR–WA	0.00656	47
Kalamazoo, MI	0.00627	48
Fresno, CA	0.00614	49

Source: U.S. Bureau of the Census, Data User Services Division, *1990 Census of Population and Housing*, Summary Tape File 3C, United States Summary, CD-ROM, February 1992.

★ 1924 ★

Poverty Status of Families Without Children

American Indian, Eskimo, or Aleut Married Couples, No Children Under 18 Years Old, Living Below Poverty, 1989

[Table shows the top 50 areas]

MSA	% of population	Rank
Fort Smith, AR–OK	0.10801	1
Great Falls, MT	0.06822	2
Houma–Thibodaux, LA	0.06290	3
Tulsa, OK	0.03258	4
Yuma, AZ	0.03087	5
Fargo–Moorhead, ND–MN	0.03066	6
Tucson, AZ	0.02939	7
Cheyenne, WY	0.02871	8
Bellingham, WA	0.02817	9
Rapid City, SD	0.02336	10
Sherman–Denison, TX	0.02315	11
Lawrence, KS	0.02078	12
Medford, OR	0.01913	13
Yakima, WA	0.01801	14
Lawton, OK	0.01794	15
Oklahoma City, OK	0.01752	16
Yuba City, CA	0.01549	17
Redding, CA	0.01428	18
Jackson, TN	0.01411	19
Fayetteville, NC	0.01348	20
Reno, NV	0.01335	21
Eugene–Springfield, OR	0.01131	22
Las Cruces, NM	0.01107	23
Alexandria, LA	0.01064	24
Albuquerque, NM	0.01061	25
Beaumont–Port Arthur, TX	0.01024	26
Muncie, IN	0.01003	27
Pensacola, FL	0.00987	28
Wichita Falls, TX	0.00981	29
Duluth, MN–WI	0.00958	30
Biloxi–Gulfport, MS	0.00913	31
Fort Walton Beach, FL	0.00904	32
Fayetteville–Springdale, AR	0.00882	33
Sioux City, IA–NE	0.00869	34
Visalia–Tulare–Porterville, CA	0.00866	35
Shreveport, LA	0.00837	36
Bakersfield, CA	0.00828	37
Bryan–College Station, TX	0.00821	38
Pueblo, CO	0.00813	39
Decatur, AL	0.00760	40
Parkersburg–Marietta, WV–OH	0.00737	41
Ocala, FL	0.00719	42
Phoenix, AZ	0.00631	43
Waterbury, CT	0.00587	44
Huntsville, AL	0.00586	45
Mobile, AL	0.00545	46
Lakeland–Winter Haven, FL	0.00543	47
Davenport–Rock Island–Moline, IA–IL	0.00542	48
Fort Pierce, FL	0.00518	49
Modesto, CA	0.00513	50

Source: U.S. Bureau of the Census, Data User Services Division, *1990 Census of Population and Housing*, Summary Tape File 3C, United States Summary, CD-ROM, February 1992.

★1925★
Poverty Status of Families Without Children
American Indian, Eskimo, or Aleut Married Couples, No Children Under 18 Years Old, Living Above Poverty, 1989
[Table shows the top 50 areas]

MSA	% of population	Rank
Tulsa, OK	0.5435	1
Fort Smith, AR–OK	0.3843	2
Oklahoma City, OK	0.3157	3
Lawton, OK	0.2413	4
Anchorage, AK	0.2390	5
Joplin, MO	0.2298	6
Yuba City, CA	0.2096	7
Redding, CA	0.1836	8
Great Falls, MT	0.1454	9
Bellingham, WA	0.1354	10
Enid, OK	0.1269	11
Bakersfield, CA	0.1233	12
Houma–Thibodaux, LA	0.1209	13
Bremerton, WA	0.1202	14
Medford, OR	0.1195	15
Reno, NV	0.1162	16
Modesto, CA	0.1158	17
Yakima, WA	0.1155	18
Rapid City, SD	0.1119	19
Albuquerque, NM	0.1086	20
Yuma, AZ	0.1066	21
Fayetteville, NC	0.1020	22
Olympia, WA	0.0999	23
Santa Fe, NM	0.0991	24
Fayetteville–Springdale, AR	0.0988	25
Chico, CA	0.0961	26
Cheyenne, WY	0.0889	27
Visalia–Tulare–Porterville, CA	0.0885	28
Pensacola, FL	0.0874	29
Wichita, KS	0.0865	30
Eugene–Springfield, OR	0.0834	31
Topeka, KS	0.0826	32
Lawrence, KS	0.0819	33
Stockton, CA	0.0818	34
Fort Walton Beach, FL	0.0800	35
Duluth, MN–WI	0.0796	36
Sherman–Denison, TX	0.0779	37
Sacramento, CA	0.0775	38
Salem, OR	0.0770	39
Tucson, AZ	0.0762	40
Odessa, TX	0.0715	41
Seattle–Tacoma, WA	0.0707	42
Green Bay, WI	0.0699	43
Abilene, TX	0.0677	44
Billings, MT	0.0670	45
Amarillo, TX	0.0656	46
Salinas–Seaside–Monterey, CA	0.0652	47
Pueblo, CO	0.0650	48
Decatur, AL	0.0646	49
Longview–Marshall, TX	0.0640	50

Source: U.S. Bureau of the Census, Data User Services Division, *1990 Census of Population and Housing*, Summary Tape File 3C, United States Summary, CD-ROM, February 1992.

★1926★
Poverty Status of Families Without Children
Asian or Pacific Islander Female Householder, No Spouse Present, No Children Under 18 Years Old, Living Above Poverty, 1989
[Table shows the top 50 areas]

MSA	% of population	Rank
Honolulu, HI	0.98095	1
San Francisco–Oakland–San Jose, CA	0.17172	2
Salinas–Seaside–Monterey, CA	0.10769	3
Los Angeles–Anaheim–Riverside, CA	0.10307	4
Stockton, CA	0.07469	5
Sacramento, CA	0.07467	6
Reno, NV	0.06440	7
San Diego, CA	0.06261	8
Seattle–Tacoma, WA	0.06088	9
Yuba City, CA	0.05871	10
Lawton, OK	0.05741	11
Fresno, CA	0.05678	12
Washington, DC–MD–VA	0.05184	13
New York–Northern New Jersey–Long Island, NY–NJ–CT	0.04547	14
Las Vegas, NV	0.03291	15
Bremerton, WA	0.02741	16
Chicago–Gary–Lake County, IL–IN–WI	0.02591	17
Grand Forks, ND	0.02547	18
Portland–Vancouver, OR–WA	0.02524	19
Charlottesville, VA	0.02517	20
Modesto, CA	0.02483	21
Santa Barbara–Santa Maria–Lompoc, CA	0.02327	22
Anchorage, AK	0.02297	23
Boston–Lawrence–Salem, MA–NH	0.02114	24
Orlando, FL	0.02088	25
Colorado Springs, CO	0.02015	26
Bloomington, IN	0.01927	27
Baltimore, MD	0.01876	28
Houston–Galveston–Brazoria, TX	0.01803	29
Austin, TX	0.01778	30
Fort Walton Beach, FL	0.01600	31
Tucson, AZ	0.01560	32
Spokane, WA	0.01550	33
Topeka, KS	0.01491	34
Salem, OR	0.01475	35
Visalia–Tulare–Porterville, CA	0.01475	35
Bakersfield, CA	0.01472	36
Fayetteville, NC	0.01457	37
Dallas–Fort Worth, TX	0.01444	38
Greeley, CO	0.01441	39
Salt Lake City–Ogden, UT	0.01427	40
Wilmington, NC	0.01413	41
Norfolk–Virginia Beach–Newport News, VA	0.01382	42
Redding, CA	0.01360	43
Sheboygan, WI	0.01348	44
Denver–Boulder, CO	0.01320	45

[Continued]

★ 1926 ★

Asian or Pacific Islander Female Householder, No Spouse Present, No Children Under 18 Years Old, Living Above Poverty, 1989

[Continued]

MSA	% of population	Rank
Chico, CA	0.01318	46
Benton Harbor, MI	0.01239	47
West Palm Beach – Boca Raton – Delray Beach, FL	0.01239	47
Bryan – College Station, TX	0.01231	48

Source: U.S. Bureau of the Census, Data User Services Division, *1990 Census of Population and Housing,* Summary Tape File 3C, United States Summary, CD-ROM, February 1992.

★ 1927 ★

Poverty Status of Families Without Children

Asian or Pacific Islander Female Householder, No Spouse Present, No Children Under 18 Years Old, Living Below Poverty, 1989

[Table shows the top 50 areas]

MSA	% of population	Rank
Honolulu, HI	0.04269	1
Rochester, MN	0.02348	2
Yuba City, CA	0.02283	3
Iowa City, IA	0.02185	4
Lawrence, KS	0.02078	5
Rapid City, SD	0.01967	6
San Francisco – Oakland – San Jose, CA	0.01505	7
Fayetteville, NC	0.01420	8
Grand Forks, ND	0.01415	9
Gainesville, FL	0.01372	10
Stockton, CA	0.01311	11
Los Angeles – Anaheim – Riverside, CA	0.01208	12
Seattle – Tacoma, WA	0.01129	13
Panama City, FL	0.01024	14
Worcester, MA	0.00961	15
Bloomington, IN	0.00918	16
Monroe, LA	0.00914	17
Sacramento, CA	0.00911	18
Green Bay, WI	0.00874	19
Champaign – Urbana – Rantoul, IL	0.00867	20
Lafayette, LA	0.00814	21
Amarillo, TX	0.00800	22
Bryan – College Station, TX	0.00739	23
Fresno, CA	0.00734	24
Salem, OR	0.00719	25
Florence, SC	0.00700	26
Visalia – Tulare – Porterville, CA	0.00673	27
San Diego, CA	0.00669	28
State College, PA	0.00646	29
Danville, VA	0.00644	30
Fayetteville – Springdale, AR	0.00617	31
New York – Northern New Jersey – Long Island, NY – NJ – CT	0.00584	32

[Continued]

★ 1927 ★

Asian or Pacific Islander Female Householder, No Spouse Present, No Children Under 18 Years Old, Living Below Poverty, 1989

[Continued]

MSA	% of population	Rank
Portland – Vancouver, OR – WA	0.00548	33
Eugene – Springfield, OR	0.00530	34
Sioux City, IA – NE	0.00522	35
Richmond – Petersburg, VA	0.00520	36
Tallahassee, FL	0.00514	37
Lansing – East Lansing, MI	0.00508	38
Abilene, TX	0.00501	39
Oklahoma City, OK	0.00501	39
Chico, CA	0.00494	40
Longview – Marshall, TX	0.00493	41
Houma – Thibodaux, LA	0.00492	42
Fitchburg – Leominster, MA	0.00486	43
Colorado Springs, CO	0.00479	44
Salinas – Seaside – Monterey, CA	0.00478	45
Mansfield, OH	0.00476	46
Columbia, SC	0.00463	47
Washington, DC – MD – VA	0.00443	48
Houston – Galveston – Brazoria, TX	0.00442	49

Source: U.S. Bureau of the Census, Data User Services Division, *1990 Census of Population and Housing,* Summary Tape File 3C, United States Summary, CD-ROM, February 1992.

★ 1928 ★

Poverty Status of Families Without Children

Asian or Pacific Islander Male Householder, No Spouse Present, No Children Under 18 Years Old, Living Above Poverty, 1989

[Table shows the top 50 areas]

MSA	% of population	Rank
Honolulu, HI	0.48850	1
San Francisco – Oakland – San Jose, CA	0.12126	2
Los Angeles – Anaheim – Riverside, CA	0.07938	3
Stockton, CA	0.05181	4
Salinas – Seaside – Monterey, CA	0.04471	5
San Diego, CA	0.04420	6
New York – Northern New Jersey – Long Island, NY – NJ – CT	0.04346	7
Washington, DC – MD – VA	0.04068	8
Seattle – Tacoma, WA	0.03814	9
Sacramento, CA	0.03686	10
Sioux City, IA – NE	0.03478	11
Fresno, CA	0.03281	12
Olympia, WA	0.03039	13
Las Vegas, NV	0.03035	14
Rochester, MN	0.02912	15
Anchorage, AK	0.02872	16
Portland – Vancouver, OR – WA	0.02720	17

[Continued]

<table>
<tr><td colspan="3" align="center">★1928★

Asian or Pacific Islander Male Householder, No Spouse Present, No Children Under 18 Years Old, Living Above Poverty, 1989

[Continued]</td></tr>
</table>

MSA	% of population	Rank
Yuba City, CA	0.02691	18
Houston – Galveston – Brazoria, TX	0.02662	19
Poughkeepsie, NY	0.02467	20
Reno, NV	0.02395	21
Austin, TX	0.02341	22
Huntsville, AL	0.02260	23
Chicago – Gary – Lake County, IL – IN – WI	0.02227	24
Boston – Lawrence – Salem, MA – NH	0.02136	25
State College, PA	0.01858	26
Athens, GA	0.01856	27
Chico, CA	0.01812	28
Bremerton, WA	0.01792	29
Norfolk – Virginia Beach – Newport News, VA	0.01741	30
Modesto, CA	0.01727	31
Dallas – Fort Worth, TX	0.01678	32
Iowa City, IA	0.01665	33
Worcester, MA	0.01648	34
Salt Lake City – Ogden, UT	0.01641	35
Santa Barbara – Santa Maria – Lompoc, CA	0.01623	36
Gadsden, AL	0.01603	37
Orlando, FL	0.01575	38
Bakersfield, CA	0.01546	39
Denver – Boulder, CO	0.01526	40
Hartford – New Britain – Middletown, CT	0.01510	41
Visalia – Tulare – Porterville, CA	0.01411	42
Melbourne – Titusville – Palm Bay, FL	0.01379	43
Lafayette, LA	0.01341	44
Atlanta, GA	0.01331	45
Fort Smith, AR – OK	0.01251	46
New Orleans, LA	0.01243	47
Philadelphia – Wilmington – Trenton, PA – NJ – DE – MD	0.01229	48
Champaign – Urbana – Rantoul, IL	0.01214	49
Oklahoma City, OK	0.01179	50

Source: U.S. Bureau of the Census, Data User Services Division, *1990 Census of Population and Housing*, Summary Tape File 3C, United States Summary, CD-ROM, February 1992.

<table>
<tr><td colspan="3" align="center">★1929★

Poverty Status of Families Without Children

Asian or Pacific Islander Male Householder, No Spouse Present, No Children Under 18 Years Old, Living Below Poverty, 1989

[Table shows the top 50 areas]</td></tr>
</table>

MSA	% of population	Rank
Lawrence, KS	0.03668	1
Honolulu, HI	0.02033	2
Gainesville, FL	0.01911	3
Iowa City, IA	0.01561	4
Stockton, CA	0.01352	5
Chico, CA	0.01318	6
Mobile, AL	0.01300	7
Fresno, CA	0.01214	8
Austin, TX	0.01113	9
Lafayette, LA	0.01102	10
Los Angeles – Anaheim – Riverside, CA	0.01077	11
Lubbock, TX	0.01033	12
Visalia – Tulare – Porterville, CA	0.00994	13
Champaign – Urbana – Rantoul, IL	0.00925	14
Modesto, CA	0.00918	15
San Francisco – Oakland – San Jose, CA	0.00875	16
Sacramento, CA	0.00871	17
State College, PA	0.00808	18
Seattle – Tacoma, WA	0.00789	19
Steubenville – Weirton, OH – WV	0.00772	20
Waco, TX	0.00740	21
Springfield, MO	0.00707	22
Amarillo, TX	0.00693	23
Spokane, WA	0.00664	24
Santa Barbara – Santa Maria – Lompoc, CA	0.00649	25
Beaumont – Port Arthur, TX	0.00637	26
Kankakee, IL	0.00623	27
Salinas – Seaside – Monterey, CA	0.00619	28
Longview – Marshall, TX	0.00616	29
Las Vegas, NV	0.00593	30
Abilene, TX	0.00585	31
Bryan – College Station, TX	0.00574	32
Tucson, AZ	0.00555	33
Parkersburg – Marietta, WV – OH	0.00536	34
Anchorage, AK	0.00530	35
Omaha, NE – IA	0.00518	36
Lansing – East Lansing, MI	0.00508	37
Sharon, PA	0.00496	38
Baton Rouge, LA	0.00492	39
Kalamazoo, MI	0.00492	39
New York – Northern New Jersey – Long Island, NY – NJ – CT	0.00490	40
Waterloo – Cedar Falls, IA	0.00477	41
Yakima, WA	0.00477	41
Charlottesville, VA	0.00458	42
Fargo – Moorhead, ND – MN	0.00457	43
Oklahoma City, OK	0.00428	44
Houston – Galveston – Brazoria, TX	0.00426	45
Bremerton, WA	0.00422	46

[Continued]

★1929★

Asian or Pacific Islander Male Householder, No Spouse Present, No Children Under 18 Years Old, Living Below Poverty, 1989

[Continued]

MSA	% of population	Rank
Saint Cloud, MN	0.00419	47
Daytona Beach, FL	0.00405	48

Source: U.S. Bureau of the Census, Data User Services Division, *1990 Census of Population and Housing*, Summary Tape File 3C, United States Summary, CD-ROM, February 1992.

★1930★
Poverty Status of Families Without Children

Asian or Pacific Islander Married Couples, No Children Under 18 Years Old, Living Above Poverty, 1989

[Table shows the top 50 areas]

MSA	% of population	Rank
Honolulu, HI	5.3836	1
San Francisco – Oakland – San Jose, CA	0.9347	2
Los Angeles – Anaheim – Riverside, CA	0.5640	3
Stockton, CA	0.5572	4
Salinas – Seaside – Monterey, CA	0.5424	5
Sacramento, CA	0.4593	6
Seattle – Tacoma, WA	0.3727	7
San Diego, CA	0.3683	8
Yuba City, CA	0.3677	9
Fresno, CA	0.3377	10
Washington, DC – MD – VA	0.3059	11
New York – Northern New Jersey – Long Island, NY – NJ – CT	0.2985	12
Santa Barbara – Santa Maria – Lompoc, CA	0.2627	13
Reno, NV	0.2458	14
Bremerton, WA	0.2277	15
Anchorage, AK	0.2249	16
Lafayette – West Lafayette, IN	0.2182	17
Visalia – Tulare – Porterville, CA	0.2164	18
Bryan – College Station, TX	0.2060	19
State College, PA	0.2028	20
Iowa City, IA	0.1956	21
Champaign – Urbana – Rantoul, IL	0.1907	22
Las Vegas, NV	0.1850	23
Merced, CA	0.1833	24
Portland – Vancouver, OR – WA	0.1828	25
Chicago – Gary – Lake County, IL – IN – WI	0.1824	26
Houston – Galveston – Brazoria, TX	0.1690	27
Bakersfield, CA	0.1588	28
Bloomington, IN	0.1587	29
Boston – Lawrence – Salem, MA – NH	0.1578	30

[Continued]

★1930★

Asian or Pacific Islander Married Couples, No Children Under 18 Years Old, Living Above Poverty, 1989

[Continued]

MSA	% of population	Rank
Salt Lake City – Ogden, UT	0.1341	31
Modesto, CA	0.1312	32
Austin, TX	0.1290	33
Olympia, WA	0.1265	34
Denver – Boulder, CO	0.1254	35
Lawrence, KS	0.1235	36
Lawton, OK	0.1184	37
Poughkeepsie, NY	0.1176	38
Rochester, MN	0.1174	39
Richland – Kennewick – Pasco, WA	0.1160	40
Dallas – Fort Worth, TX	0.1153	41
Norfolk – Virginia Beach – Newport News, VA	0.1133	42
Madison, WI	0.1120	43
Charlottesville, VA	0.1106	44
Baltimore, MD	0.1105	45
Spokane, WA	0.1099	46
Colorado Springs, CO	0.1091	47
Gainesville, FL	0.1068	48
Philadelphia – Wilmington – Trenton, PA – NJ – DE – MD	0.1068	48
Huntsville, AL	0.1059	49

Source: U.S. Bureau of the Census, Data User Services Division, *1990 Census of Population and Housing*, Summary Tape File 3C, United States Summary, CD-ROM, February 1992.

★1931★
Poverty Status of Families Without Children

Asian or Pacific Islander Married Couples, No Children Under 18 Years Old, Living Below Poverty, 1989

[Table shows the top 50 areas]

MSA	% of population	Rank
Honolulu, HI	0.14864	1
Lawrence, KS	0.07580	2
Columbia, MO	0.07475	3
Bryan – College Station, TX	0.07139	4
Lafayette – West Lafayette, IN	0.06126	5
Champaign – Urbana – Rantoul, IL	0.05837	6
Bloomington, IN	0.05139	7
San Francisco – Oakland – San Jose, CA	0.04778	8
Gainesville, FL	0.04311	9
State College, PA	0.04039	10
Iowa City, IA	0.03745	11
Los Angeles – Anaheim – Riverside, CA	0.03346	12
Lansing – East Lansing, MI	0.02820	13
Madison, WI	0.02806	14
Reno, NV	0.02670	15

[Continued]

★1931★

Asian or Pacific Islander Married Couples, No Children Under 18 Years Old, Living Below Poverty, 1989

[Continued]

MSA	% of population	Rank
Athens, GA	0.02624	16
Sacramento, CA	0.02586	17
Provo – Orem, UT	0.02542	18
New York – Northern New Jersey – Long Island, NY – NJ – CT	0.02538	19
Biloxi – Gulfport, MS	0.02435	20
Chico, CA	0.02416	21
Seattle – Tacoma, WA	0.02305	22
Lincoln, NE	0.02247	23
Eugene – Springfield, OR	0.02227	24
Lubbock, TX	0.02111	25
Stockton, CA	0.02039	26
San Diego, CA	0.01962	27
New Orleans, LA	0.01937	28
Houston – Galveston – Brazoria, TX	0.01935	29
Fresno, CA	0.01933	30
Austin, TX	0.01881	31
Visalia – Tulare – Porterville, CA	0.01827	32
Pascagoula, MS	0.01822	33
Yuba City, CA	0.01794	34
Washington, DC – MD – VA	0.01769	35
Kalamazoo, MI	0.01746	36
Eau Claire, WI	0.01745	37
Greeley, CO	0.01745	37
Grand Forks, ND	0.01698	38
Chicago – Gary – Lake County, IL – IN – WI	0.01694	39
Beaumont – Port Arthur, TX	0.01633	40
Salinas – Seaside – Monterey, CA	0.01631	41
Tuscaloosa, AL	0.01594	42
Salt Lake City – Ogden, UT	0.01567	43
Santa Barbara – Santa Maria – Lompoc, CA	0.01515	44
Toledo, OH	0.01449	45
Oklahoma City, OK	0.01408	46
Melbourne – Titusville – Palm Bay, FL	0.01379	47
New Haven – Meriden, CT	0.01358	48
Portland – Vancouver, OR – WA	0.01340	49

Source: U.S. Bureau of the Census, Data User Services Division, *1990 Census of Population and Housing*, Summary Tape File 3C, United States Summary, CD-ROM, February 1992.

★1932★

Poverty Status of Families Without Children

Black Female Householder, No Spouse Present, No Children Under 18 Years Old, Living Above Poverty, 1989

[Table shows the top 50 areas]

MSA	Number	Rank
New York – Northern New Jersey – Long Island, NY – NJ – CT	84,112	1
Chicago – Gary – Lake County, IL – IN – WI	33,814	2
Philadelphia – Wilmington – Trenton, PA – NJ – DE – MD	27,936	3
Los Angeles – Anaheim – Riverside, CA	27,202	4
Washington, DC – MD – VA	26,389	5
Detroit – Ann Arbor, MI	21,498	6
Baltimore, MD	16,123	7
Atlanta, GA	15,968	8
Houston – Galveston – Brazoria, TX	11,782	9
San Francisco – Oakland – San Jose, CA	11,116	10
Cleveland – Akron – Lorain, OH	9,869	11
Saint Louis, MO – IL	9,382	12
Dallas – Fort Worth, TX	9,307	13
Miami – Fort Lauderdale, FL	8,884	14
Memphis, TN – AR – MS	8,129	15
New Orleans, LA	7,714	16
Norfolk – Virginia Beach – Newport News, VA	6,902	17
Richmond – Petersburg, VA	6,346	18
Birmingham, AL	5,748	19
Boston – Lawrence – Salem, MA – NH	5,386	20
Charlotte – Gastonia – Rock Hill, NC – SC	5,120	21
Greensboro – Winston-Salem – High Point, NC	4,406	22
Cincinnati – Hamilton, OH – KY – IN	4,250	23
Kansas City, MO – KS	4,219	24
Pittsburgh – Beaver Valley, PA	4,142	25
Raleigh – Durham, NC	4,105	26
Milwaukee – Racine, WI	3,579	27
Nashville, TN	3,364	28
Jacksonville, FL	3,345	29
Indianapolis, IN	3,330	30
Columbus, OH	3,196	31
Tampa – Saint Petersburg – Clearwater, FL	2,960	32
Jackson, MS	2,861	33
Buffalo – Niagara Falls, NY	2,810	34
Dayton – Springfield, OH	2,565	35
Greenville – Spartanburg, SC	2,549	36
Louisville, KY – IN	2,528	37
Charleston, SC	2,452	38
Columbia, SC	2,411	39
Baton Rouge, LA	2,330	40
Augusta, GA – SC	2,241	41
Mobile, AL	2,191	42
Hartford – New Britain – Middletown, CT	2,189	43

[Continued]

★1932★

Black Female Householder, No Spouse Present, No Children Under 18 Years Old, Living Above Poverty, 1989

[Continued]

MSA	Number	Rank
Macon – Warner Robins, GA	2,083	44
Shreveport, LA	1,911	45
Orlando, FL	1,891	46
San Diego, CA	1,854	47
Little Rock – North Little Rock, AR	1,744	48
Rochester, NY	1,740	49
Denver – Boulder, CO	1,714	50

Source: U.S. Bureau of the Census, Data User Services Division, *1990 Census of Population and Housing*, Summary Tape File 3C, United States Summary, CD- ROM, February 1992.

★1933★

Poverty Status of Families Without Children

Black Female Householder, No Spouse Present, No Children Under 18 Years Old, Living Below Poverty, 1989

[Table shows the top 50 areas]

MSA	% of population	Rank
Shreveport, LA	0.32243	1
Monroe, LA	0.31859	2
Pine Bluff, AR	0.30765	3
Albany, GA	0.28251	4
Jackson, MS	0.27087	5
New Orleans, LA	0.26590	6
Florence, SC	0.25537	7
Memphis, TN – AR – MS	0.25506	8
Jackson, TN	0.23210	9
Mobile, AL	0.22603	10
Montgomery, AL	0.22016	11
Beaumont – Port Arthur, TX	0.21787	12
Danville, VA	0.21709	13
Columbus, GA – AL	0.21599	14
Macon – Warner Robins, GA	0.21558	15
Savannah, GA	0.20649	16
Baton Rouge, LA	0.20558	17
Birmingham, AL	0.19718	18
Alexandria, LA	0.19307	19
Texarkana, TX – Texarkana, AR	0.18979	20
Anniston, AL	0.18357	21
Lake Charles, LA	0.17308	22
Lafayette, LA	0.17294	23
Tyler, TX	0.17117	24
Charleston, SC	0.16967	25
Tuscaloosa, AL	0.16875	26
Biloxi – Gulfport, MS	0.15726	27
Longview – Marshall, TX	0.15330	28
Tallahassee, FL	0.15283	29
Pascagoula, MS	0.14404	30
Augusta, GA – SC	0.13558	31
Flint, MI	0.12498	32
Norfolk – Virginia Beach – Newport News, VA	0.11926	33

[Continued]

★1933★

Black Female Householder, No Spouse Present, No Children Under 18 Years Old, Living Below Poverty, 1989

[Continued]

MSA	% of population	Rank
Fayetteville, NC	0.11764	34
Wilmington, NC	0.11722	35
Pensacola, FL	0.11701	36
Dothan, AL	0.10995	37
Detroit – Ann Arbor, MI	0.10908	38
Huntsville, AL	0.10799	39
Waco, TX	0.10628	40
Baltimore, MD	0.10323	41
Atlanta, GA	0.10224	42
Columbia, SC	0.10169	43
Richmond – Petersburg, VA	0.10108	44
Clarksville – Hopkinsville, TN – KY	0.10092	45
Kankakee, IL	0.09870	46
Little Rock – North Little Rock, AR	0.09842	47
Raleigh – Durham, NC	0.09463	48
Chattanooga, TN – GA	0.09280	49
Gainesville, FL	0.09162	50

Source: U.S. Bureau of the Census, Data User Services Division, *1990 Census of Population and Housing*, Summary Tape File 3C, United States Summary, CD-ROM, February 1992.

★1934★

Poverty Status of Families Without Children

Black Male Householder, No Spouse Present, No Children Under 18 Years Old, Living Above Poverty, 1989

[Table shows the top 50 areas]

MSA	% of population	Rank
Memphis, TN – AR – MS	0.2511	1
Danville, VA	0.2162	2
Washington, DC – MD – VA	0.2148	3
Macon – Warner Robins, GA	0.2017	4
Burlington, NC	0.1978	5
Montgomery, AL	0.1955	6
Richmond – Petersburg, VA	0.1938	7
Atlanta, GA	0.1899	8
Savannah, GA	0.1892	9
Baltimore, MD	0.1821	10
Columbus, GA – AL	0.1798	11
Jackson, MS	0.1783	12
New Orleans, LA	0.1766	13
Albany, GA	0.1741	14
Pine Bluff, AR	0.1708	15
Norfolk – Virginia Beach – Newport News, VA	0.1649	16
Augusta, GA – SC	0.1628	17
Tuscaloosa, AL	0.1614	18
Birmingham, AL	0.1604	19
Raleigh – Durham, NC	0.1603	20
Lynchburg, VA	0.1568	21

[Continued]

★ 1934 ★

Black Male Householder, No Spouse Present, No Children Under 18 Years Old, Living Above Poverty, 1989

[Continued]

MSA	% of population	Rank
Detroit – Ann Arbor, MI	0.1554	22
Florence, SC	0.1513	23
Jackson, TN	0.1475	24
Charleston, SC	0.1438	25
Tallahassee, FL	0.1434	26
Mobile, AL	0.1420	27
Philadelphia – Wilmington – Trenton, PA – NJ – DE – MD	0.1403	28
Beaumont – Port Arthur, TX	0.1376	29
Charlottesville, VA	0.1365	30
Greensboro – Winston-Salem – High Point, NC	0.1353	31
Charlotte – Gastonia – Rock Hill, NC – SC	0.1330	32
Columbia, SC	0.1330	32
New York – Northern New Jersey – Long Island, NY – NJ – CT	0.1278	33
Fayetteville, NC	0.1264	34
Miami – Fort Lauderdale, FL	0.1226	35
Nashville, TN	0.1161	36
Pascagoula, MS	0.1145	37
Chicago – Gary – Lake County, IL – IN – WI	0.1140	38
Baton Rouge, LA	0.1136	39
Shreveport, LA	0.1107	40
Atlantic City, NJ	0.1093	41
Monroe, LA	0.1090	42
Huntsville, AL	0.1080	43
Longview – Marshall, TX	0.1077	44
Lafayette, LA	0.1049	45
Greenville – Spartanburg, SC	0.1047	46
Cleveland – Akron – Lorain, OH	0.1023	47
Flint, MI	0.1018	48
Houston – Galveston – Brazoria, TX	0.1018	48

Source: U.S. Bureau of the Census, Data User Services Division, *1990 Census of Population and Housing*, Summary Tape File 3C, United States Summary, CD-ROM, February 1992.

★ 1935 ★

Poverty Status of Families Without Children

Black Male Householder, No Spouse Present, No Children Under 18 Years Old, Living Below Poverty, 1989

[Table shows the top 50 areas]

MSA	% of population	Rank
Pine Bluff, AR	0.0924	1
Albany, GA	0.0862	2
New Orleans, LA	0.0611	3
Monroe, LA	0.0584	4

[Continued]

★ 1935 ★

Black Male Householder, No Spouse Present, No Children Under 18 Years Old, Living Below Poverty, 1989

[Continued]

MSA	% of population	Rank
Montgomery, AL	0.0567	5
Florence, SC	0.0533	6
Memphis, TN – AR – MS	0.0498	7
Jackson, MS	0.0496	8
Shreveport, LA	0.0491	9
Columbus, GA – AL	0.0490	10
Augusta, GA – SC	0.0438	11
Jackson, TN	0.0423	12
Tallahassee, FL	0.0420	13
Baton Rouge, LA	0.0415	14
Danville, VA	0.0414	15
Longview – Marshall, TX	0.0412	16
Lake Charles, LA	0.0398	17
Mobile, AL	0.0398	17
Gadsden, AL	0.0391	18
Macon – Warner Robins, GA	0.0391	18
Wilmington, NC	0.0391	18
Savannah, GA	0.0383	19
Tuscaloosa, AL	0.0365	20
Columbia, SC	0.0357	21
Huntsville, AL	0.0356	22
Lafayette, LA	0.0345	23
Detroit – Ann Arbor, MI	0.0343	24
Charleston, SC	0.0341	25
Waco, TX	0.0338	26
Beaumont – Port Arthur, TX	0.0316	27
Tyler, TX	0.0311	28
Midland, TX	0.0272	29
Texarkana, TX – Texarkana, AR	0.0266	30
Norfolk – Virginia Beach – Newport News, VA	0.0258	31
Fayetteville, NC	0.0255	32
Houston – Galveston – Brazoria, TX	0.0255	32
Alexandria, LA	0.0243	33
Anderson, SC	0.0234	34
Birmingham, AL	0.0228	35
Richmond – Petersburg, VA	0.0228	35
Greensboro – Winston-Salem – High Point, NC	0.0213	36
Fort Pierce, FL	0.0211	37
Raleigh – Durham, NC	0.0208	38
Chicago – Gary – Lake County, IL – IN – WI	0.0206	39
Youngstown – Warren, OH	0.0205	40
Atlanta, GA	0.0199	41
Saint Louis, MO – IL	0.0194	42
Clarksville – Hopkinsville, TN – KY	0.0189	43
Biloxi – Gulfport, MS	0.0188	44
Miami – Fort Lauderdale, FL	0.0188	44

Source: U.S. Bureau of the Census, Data User Services Division, *1990 Census of Population and Housing*, Summary Tape File 3C, United States Summary, CD-ROM, February 1992.

★1936★
Poverty Status of Families Without Children

Black Married Couples, No Children Under 18 Years Old, Living Above Poverty, 1989

[Table shows the top 50 areas]

MSA	% of population	Rank
Danville, VA	1.8784	1
Columbus, GA–AL	1.6600	2
Fayetteville, NC	1.6102	3
Richmond–Petersburg, VA	1.5721	4
Savannah, GA	1.5283	5
Pine Bluff, AR	1.4973	6
Norfolk–Virginia Beach–Newport News, VA	1.4500	7
Memphis, TN–AR–MS	1.4216	8
Jackson, MS	1.4112	9
Albany, GA	1.3984	10
Washington, DC–MD–VA	1.3937	11
Macon–Warner Robins, GA	1.3468	12
Augusta, GA–SC	1.3210	13
Raleigh–Durham, NC	1.2778	14
New Orleans, LA	1.2555	15
Columbia, SC	1.2510	16
Charleston, SC	1.2370	17
Jackson, TN	1.2311	18
Birmingham, AL	1.2209	19
Montgomery, AL	1.2146	20
Florence, SC	1.2121	21
Baltimore, MD	1.2051	22
Shreveport, LA	1.1737	23
Burlington, NC	1.1570	24
Lynchburg, VA	1.1512	25
Mobile, AL	1.0985	26
Atlanta, GA	1.0821	27
Beaumont–Port Arthur, TX	1.0647	28
Baton Rouge, LA	1.0383	29
Longview–Marshall, TX	1.0287	30
Tuscaloosa, AL	1.0185	31
Tyler, TX	1.0145	32
Lake Charles, LA	1.0028	33
Tallahassee, FL	0.9893	34
Greensboro–Winston-Salem–High Point, NC	0.9805	35
Huntsville, AL	0.9468	36
Wilmington, NC	0.9461	37
Lawton, OK	0.9364	38
Alexandria, LA	0.9228	39
Clarksville–Hopkinsville, TN–KY	0.9183	40
Detroit–Ann Arbor, MI	0.9086	41
Killeen–Temple, TX	0.9072	42
Texarkana, TX–Texarkana, AR	0.8965	43
Jacksonville, NC	0.8830	44
Jacksonville, FL	0.8695	45
Philadelphia–Wilmington–Trenton, PA–NJ–DE–MD	0.8634	46
Charlotte–Gastonia–Rock Hill, NC–SC	0.8588	47
Anderson, SC	0.8492	48
Dothan, AL	0.8445	49
Cleveland–Akron–Lorain, OH	0.8138	50

Source: U.S. Bureau of the Census, Data User Services Division, *1990 Census of Population and Housing,* Summary Tape File 3C, United States Summary, CD-ROM, February 1992.

★1937★
Poverty Status of Families Without Children

Black Married Couples, No Children Under 18 Years Old, Living Below Poverty, 1989

[Table shows the top 50 areas]

MSA	% of population	Rank
Pine Bluff, AR	0.38017	1
Florence, SC	0.33146	2
Albany, GA	0.31005	3
Jackson, MS	0.30880	4
Danville, VA	0.27136	5
Shreveport, LA	0.27068	6
Lafayette, LA	0.24816	7
Jackson, TN	0.23852	8
Longview–Marshall, TX	0.22286	9
Monroe, LA	0.21591	10
Alexandria, LA	0.21436	11
Memphis, TN–AR–MS	0.21166	12
Montgomery, AL	0.21161	13
Lake Charles, LA	0.20757	14
Texarkana, TX–Texarkana, AR	0.20061	15
Charleston, SC	0.19314	16
New Orleans, LA	0.18744	17
Savannah, GA	0.18465	18
Dothan, AL	0.18173	19
Columbus, GA–AL	0.18102	20
Birmingham, AL	0.17316	21
Macon–Warner Robins, GA	0.16827	22
Baton Rouge, LA	0.16355	23
Beaumont–Port Arthur, TX	0.15973	24
Lynchburg, VA	0.14627	25
Tuscaloosa, AL	0.14616	26
Mobile, AL	0.13692	27
Tallahassee, FL	0.13656	28
Augusta, GA–SC	0.13432	29
Clarksville–Hopkinsville, TN–KY	0.12807	30
Fayetteville, NC	0.12456	31
Tyler, TX	0.11434	32
Gainesville, FL	0.11072	33
Gadsden, AL	0.11018	34
Anniston, AL	0.10773	35
Columbia, SC	0.10588	36
Raleigh–Durham, NC	0.10388	37
Huntsville, AL	0.10213	38
Pascagoula, MS	0.10152	39
Anderson, SC	0.10124	40
Athens, GA	0.10111	41
Norfolk–Virginia Beach–Newport News, VA	0.09691	42
Houston–Galveston–Brazoria, TX	0.09641	43
Waco, TX	0.09518	44
Kankakee, IL	0.09350	45
Richmond–Petersburg, VA	0.09311	46
Jacksonville, FL	0.09077	47
Biloxi–Gulfport, MS	0.08928	48
Burlington, NC	0.08871	49
Houma–Thibodaux, LA	0.08805	50

Source: U.S. Bureau of the Census, Data User Services Division, *1990 Census of Population and Housing,* Summary Tape File 3C, United States Summary, CD-ROM, February 1992.

★ 1938 ★
Poverty Status of Families Without Children
Hispanic Female Householder, No Spouse Present, No Children Under 18 Years Old, Living Above Poverty, 1989
[Continued]

★ 1938 ★

Poverty Status of Families Without Children

Hispanic Female Householder, No Spouse Present, No Children Under 18 Years Old, Living Above Poverty, 1989

[Table shows the top 50 areas]

MSA	% of population	Rank
Laredo, TX	0.9945	1
El Paso, TX	0.7508	2
McAllen – Edinburg – Mission, TX	0.6422	3
Brownsville – Harlingen, TX	0.6236	4
Miami – Fort Lauderdale, FL	0.5668	5
San Antonio, TX	0.5109	6
Santa Fe, NM	0.4921	7
Corpus Christi, TX	0.4793	8
Albuquerque, NM	0.4528	9
Las Cruces, NM	0.4435	10
Pueblo, CO	0.3893	11
Yuma, AZ	0.2891	12
Los Angeles – Anaheim – Riverside, CA	0.2581	13
Tucson, AZ	0.2500	14
Victoria, TX	0.2488	15
New York – Northern New Jersey – Long Island, NY – NJ – CT	0.2477	16
Fresno, CA	0.2472	17
Santa Barbara – Santa Maria – Lompoc, CA	0.1878	18
Salinas – Seaside – Monterey, CA	0.1830	19
Visalia – Tulare – Porterville, CA	0.1776	20
Stockton, CA	0.1741	21
San Diego, CA	0.1712	22
Austin, TX	0.1703	23
San Francisco – Oakland – San Jose, CA	0.1647	24
Bakersfield, CA	0.1625	25
Modesto, CA	0.1598	26
Merced, CA	0.1418	27
Lubbock, TX	0.1276	28
Denver – Boulder, CO	0.1251	29
Midland, TX	0.1210	30
Houston – Galveston – Brazoria, TX	0.1166	31
Phoenix, AZ	0.1133	32
Greeley, CO	0.1108	33
San Angelo, TX	0.1006	34
Sacramento, CA	0.0980	35
Yuba City, CA	0.0970	36
Las Vegas, NV	0.0901	37
Orlando, FL	0.0900	38
Tampa – Saint Petersburg – Clearwater, FL	0.0857	39
Wichita Falls, TX	0.0825	40
West Palm Beach – Boca Raton – Delray Beach, FL	0.0818	41
Naples, FL	0.0789	42
Odessa, TX	0.0774	43
Waterbury, CT	0.0767	44
Chicago – Gary – Lake County, IL – IN – WI	0.0766	45
Hartford – New Britain – Middletown, CT	0.0752	46

[Continued]

MSA	% of population	Rank
Cheyenne, WY	0.0711	47
Dallas – Fort Worth, TX	0.0705	48
Springfield, MA	0.0691	49
Killeen – Temple, TX	0.0658	50

Source: U.S. Bureau of the Census, Data User Services Division, *1990 Census of Population and Housing*, Summary Tape File 3C, United States Summary, CD-ROM, February 1992.

★ 1939 ★

Poverty Status of Families Without Children

Hispanic Female Householder, No Spouse Present, No Children Under 18 Years Old, Living Below Poverty, 1989

[Table shows the top 50 areas]

MSA	% of population	Rank
Laredo, TX	0.39103	1
Brownsville – Harlingen, TX	0.31678	2
McAllen – Edinburg – Mission, TX	0.27585	3
El Paso, TX	0.21467	4
Corpus Christi, TX	0.16319	5
San Antonio, TX	0.15421	6
Pueblo, CO	0.12921	7
Las Cruces, NM	0.11069	8
San Angelo, TX	0.09649	9
Miami – Fort Lauderdale, FL	0.09560	10
Santa Fe, NM	0.08629	11
Victoria, TX	0.08203	12
Albuquerque, NM	0.07970	13
New York – Northern New Jersey – Long Island, NY – NJ – CT	0.05790	14
Fresno, CA	0.05588	15
Yuma, AZ	0.05426	16
Tucson, AZ	0.05308	17
Visalia – Tulare – Porterville, CA	0.05194	18
Austin, TX	0.04632	19
Bryan – College Station, TX	0.04595	20
Lubbock, TX	0.04447	21
Odessa, TX	0.04288	22
Abilene, TX	0.04095	23
Midland, TX	0.04033	24
Stockton, CA	0.03974	25
Waco, TX	0.03701	26
Bakersfield, CA	0.03588	27
Greeley, CO	0.03414	28
Los Angeles – Anaheim – Riverside, CA	0.03364	29
Houston – Galveston – Brazoria, TX	0.02916	30
Lawton, OK	0.02781	31
Salinas – Seaside – Monterey, CA	0.02699	32

[Continued]

★1939★

Hispanic Female Householder, No Spouse Present, No Children Under 18 Years Old, Living Below Poverty, 1989

[Continued]

MSA	% of population	Rank
Santa Barbara – Santa Maria – Lompoc, CA	0.02543	33
Hartford – New Britain – Middletown, CT	0.02542	34
Yakima, WA	0.02542	34
Yuba City, CA	0.02446	35
Springfield, MA	0.02266	36
Denver – Boulder, CO	0.02207	37
Fort Collins – Loveland, CO	0.02203	38
Phoenix, AZ	0.02172	39
Fitchburg – Leominster, MA	0.02043	40
Amarillo, TX	0.01973	41
Casper, WY	0.01960	42
San Diego, CA	0.01938	43
Naples, FL	0.01907	44
Waterbury, CT	0.01805	45
Rapid City, SD	0.01721	46
Saint Joseph, MO	0.01685	47
New Bedford, MA	0.01594	48
Merced, CA	0.01569	49

Source: U.S. Bureau of the Census, Data User Services Division, *1990 Census of Population and Housing*, Summary Tape File 3C, United States Summary, CD-ROM, February 1992.

★1940★

Poverty Status of Families Without Children

Hispanic Male Householder, No Spouse Present, No Children Under 18 Years Old, Living Above Poverty, 1989

[Table shows the top 50 areas]

MSA	% of population	Rank
Miami – Fort Lauderdale, FL	0.28385	1
Laredo, TX	0.26419	2
Las Cruces, NM	0.26124	3
Los Angeles – Anaheim – Riverside, CA	0.24859	4
Corpus Christi, TX	0.23864	5
El Paso, TX	0.23022	6
Fresno, CA	0.22637	7
Albuquerque, NM	0.22556	8
San Antonio, TX	0.22072	9
Brownsville – Harlingen, TX	0.21144	10
Santa Fe, NM	0.20847	11
Pueblo, CO	0.20398	12
Merced, CA	0.19394	13
Visalia – Tulare – Porterville, CA	0.19332	14
Salinas – Seaside – Monterey, CA	0.18360	15
Santa Barbara – Santa Maria – Lompoc, CA	0.17667	16
McAllen – Edinburg – Mission, TX	0.17182	17

[Continued]

★1940★

Hispanic Male Householder, No Spouse Present, No Children Under 18 Years Old, Living Above Poverty, 1989

[Continued]

MSA	% of population	Rank
Bakersfield, CA	0.15990	18
Houston – Galveston – Brazoria, TX	0.15847	19
Greeley, CO	0.15703	20
Stockton, CA	0.15064	21
Austin, TX	0.13191	22
San Francisco – Oakland – San Jose, CA	0.12820	23
Modesto, CA	0.12523	24
Las Vegas, NV	0.12435	25
Lubbock, TX	0.12397	26
New York – Northern New Jersey – Long Island, NY – NJ – CT	0.12169	27
Bryan – College Station, TX	0.12063	28
San Diego, CA	0.12034	29
Tucson, AZ	0.11711	30
Yakima, WA	0.11704	31
Dallas – Fort Worth, TX	0.10725	32
Reno, NV	0.10641	33
Naples, FL	0.10519	34
Richland – Kennewick – Pasco, WA	0.09465	35
Yuba City, CA	0.09458	36
Chicago – Gary – Lake County, IL – IN – WI	0.09082	37
Yuma, AZ	0.09074	38
Victoria, TX	0.08607	39
Sacramento, CA	0.08359	40
Phoenix, AZ	0.08247	41
Odessa, TX	0.08156	42
West Palm Beach – Boca Raton – Delray Beach, FL	0.07608	43
Cheyenne, WY	0.07383	44
Denver – Boulder, CO	0.07012	45
Washington, DC – MD – VA	0.06950	46
Waco, TX	0.06715	47
Waterbury, CT	0.06588	48
Abilene, TX	0.06101	49
Longview – Marshall, TX	0.06033	50

Source: U.S. Bureau of the Census, Data User Services Division, *1990 Census of Population and Housing*, Summary Tape File 3C, United States Summary, CD-ROM, February 1992.

★1941★

Poverty Status of Families Without Children

Hispanic Male Householder, No Spouse Present, No Children Under 18 Years Old, Living Below Poverty, 1989

[Table shows the top 50 areas]

MSA	% of population	Rank
Brownsville – Harlingen, TX	0.07843	1
McAllen – Edinburg – Mission, TX	0.07431	2
Laredo, TX	0.07280	3
Richland – Kennewick – Pasco, WA	0.05066	4
Yakima, WA	0.05031	5
Corpus Christi, TX	0.04801	6
El Paso, TX	0.04344	7
San Antonio, TX	0.03878	8
Miami – Fort Lauderdale, FL	0.03856	9
Pueblo, CO	0.03657	10
Santa Fe, NM	0.03418	11
Las Cruces, NM	0.03395	12
Victoria, TX	0.03362	13
San Angelo, TX	0.02945	14
Fresno, CA	0.02921	15
Tucson, AZ	0.02834	16
Visalia – Tulare – Porterville, CA	0.02821	17
Los Angeles – Anaheim – Riverside, CA	0.02668	18
Albuquerque, NM	0.02580	19
Yuma, AZ	0.02245	20
Bryan – College Station, TX	0.02216	21
Waco, TX	0.02168	22
Austin, TX	0.02034	23
Lubbock, TX	0.02021	24
Houston – Galveston – Brazoria, TX	0.02016	25
Greeley, CO	0.01972	26
Reading, PA	0.01932	27
Abilene, TX	0.01671	28
Stockton, CA	0.01560	29
Wichita Falls, TX	0.01553	30
Chico, CA	0.01483	31
New York – Northern New Jersey – Long Island, NY – NJ – CT	0.01471	32
Phoenix, AZ	0.01428	33
Midland, TX	0.01313	34
Naples, FL	0.01249	35
Amarillo, TX	0.01226	36
San Diego, CA	0.01181	37
Fayetteville – Springdale, AR	0.01146	38
Dallas – Fort Worth, TX	0.01140	39
Santa Barbara – Santa Maria – Lompoc, CA	0.01136	40
Topeka, KS	0.01118	41
Bakersfield, CA	0.01104	42
Odessa, TX	0.01093	43
Enid, OK	0.01058	44
Denver – Boulder, CO	0.01055	45
Longview – Marshall, TX	0.01047	46
Merced, CA	0.00953	47
Billings, MT	0.00882	48

[Continued]

★1941★

Hispanic Male Householder, No Spouse Present, No Children Under 18 Years Old, Living Below Poverty, 1989

[Continued]

MSA	% of population	Rank
Salinas – Seaside – Monterey, CA	0.00872	49
San Francisco – Oakland – San Jose, CA	0.00870	50

Source: U.S. Bureau of the Census, Data User Services Division, *1990 Census of Population and Housing*, Summary Tape File 3C, United States Summary, CD-ROM, February 1992.

★1942★

Poverty Status of Families Without Children

Hispanic Married Couples, No Children Under 18 Years Old, Living Above Poverty, 1989

[Table shows the top 50 areas]

MSA	% of population	Rank
Laredo, TX	3.3151	1
Santa Fe, NM	3.0980	2
El Paso, TX	2.7653	3
Miami – Fort Lauderdale, FL	2.7035	4
McAllen – Edinburg – Mission, TX	2.5650	5
Brownsville – Harlingen, TX	2.5035	6
Las Cruces, NM	2.3172	7
Corpus Christi, TX	2.2738	8
Albuquerque, NM	2.2542	9
San Antonio, TX	2.2503	10
Pueblo, CO	2.1316	11
Yuma, AZ	1.5090	12
Victoria, TX	1.4241	13
Visalia – Tulare – Porterville, CA	1.1846	14
Fresno, CA	1.1479	15
San Angelo, TX	1.0939	16
Tucson, AZ	1.0854	17
Merced, CA	1.0790	18
Los Angeles – Anaheim – Riverside, CA	1.0447	19
Salinas – Seaside – Monterey, CA	0.9945	20
Santa Barbara – Santa Maria – Lompoc, CA	0.9337	21
Stockton, CA	0.9246	22
Odessa, TX	0.8795	23
Bakersfield, CA	0.8593	24
Austin, TX	0.8239	25
Greeley, CO	0.7685	26
Modesto, CA	0.7457	27
San Diego, CA	0.7453	28
Lubbock, TX	0.7209	29
San Francisco – Oakland – San Jose, CA	0.7067	30
Houston – Galveston – Brazoria, TX	0.7047	31
New York – Northern New Jersey – Long Island, NY – NJ – CT	0.6789	32
Cheyenne, WY	0.6453	33

[Continued]

★1942★

Hispanic Married Couples, No Children Under 18 Years Old, Living Above Poverty, 1989

[Continued]

MSA	% of population	Rank
Denver – Boulder, CO	0.6252	34
Orlando, FL	0.6058	35
Yuba City, CA	0.5977	36
Las Vegas, NV	0.5874	37
Sacramento, CA	0.5874	37
Killeen – Temple, TX	0.5762	38
Tampa – Saint Petersburg – Clearwater, FL	0.5711	39
Midland, TX	0.5459	40
Phoenix, AZ	0.5434	41
West Palm Beach – Boca Raton – Delray Beach, FL	0.5101	42
Yakima, WA	0.5063	43
Bryan – College Station, TX	0.4842	44
Reno, NV	0.4810	45
Colorado Springs, CO	0.4569	46
Dallas – Fort Worth, TX	0.4486	47
Amarillo, TX	0.4458	48
Waco, TX	0.4452	49

Source: U.S. Bureau of the Census, Data User Services Division, *1990 Census of Population and Housing*, Summary Tape File 3C, United States Summary, CD-ROM, February 1992.

★1943★

Poverty Status of Families Without Children

Hispanic Married Couples, No Children Under 18 Years Old, Living Below Poverty, 1989

[Table shows the top 50 areas]

MSA	% of population	Rank
McAllen – Edinburg – Mission, TX	0.91045	1
Brownsville – Harlingen, TX	0.78156	2
Laredo, TX	0.70250	3
El Paso, TX	0.44590	4
Corpus Christi, TX	0.39441	5
Victoria, TX	0.32813	6
Las Cruces, NM	0.32396	7
Miami – Fort Lauderdale, FL	0.30283	8
San Antonio, TX	0.27893	9
Odessa, TX	0.25560	10
Pueblo, CO	0.22592	11
Midland, TX	0.17916	12
San Angelo, TX	0.17774	13
Yuma, AZ	0.17120	14
Lubbock, TX	0.16664	15
Santa Fe, NM	0.16404	16
Albuquerque, NM	0.14087	17
Visalia – Tulare – Porterville, CA	0.12567	18
Yakima, WA	0.12181	19
Abilene, TX	0.11617	20
Tucson, AZ	0.11186	21
Fresno, CA	0.10802	22
Houston – Galveston – Brazoria, TX	0.07903	23

[Continued]

★1943★

Hispanic Married Couples, No Children Under 18 Years Old, Living Below Poverty, 1989

[Continued]

MSA	% of population	Rank
Austin, TX	0.07523	24
Bakersfield, CA	0.06624	25
Yuba City, CA	0.06441	26
Los Angeles – Anaheim – Riverside, CA	0.06230	27
Amarillo, TX	0.06185	28
Merced, CA	0.06166	29
Modesto, CA	0.05884	30
Phoenix, AZ	0.05782	31
Richland – Kennewick – Pasco, WA	0.05665	32
Greeley, CO	0.05614	33
Naples, FL	0.05523	34
New York – Northern New Jersey – Long Island, NY – NJ – CT	0.05279	35
Killeen – Temple, TX	0.04818	36
Bryan – College Station, TX	0.04759	37
Casper, WY	0.04573	38
Santa Barbara – Santa Maria – Lompoc, CA	0.04518	39
Stockton, CA	0.04369	40
Orlando, FL	0.04027	41
Tampa – Saint Petersburg – Clearwater, FL	0.04014	42
Cheyenne, WY	0.03965	43
Dallas – Fort Worth, TX	0.03750	44
Salinas – Seaside – Monterey, CA	0.03683	45
San Diego, CA	0.03575	46
Jamestown – Dunkirk, NY	0.03383	47
Denver – Boulder, CO	0.03203	48
Springfield, MA	0.03060	49
Fort Collins – Loveland, CO	0.03009	50

Source: U.S. Bureau of the Census, Data User Services Division, *1990 Census of Population and Housing*, Summary Tape File 3C, United States Summary, CD-ROM, February 1992.

★1944★

Poverty Status of Families Without Children

White Female Householder, No Spouse Present, No Children Under 18 Years Old, Living Above Poverty, 1989

[Table shows the top 50 areas]

MSA	% of population	Rank
Scranton – Wilkes-Barre, PA	1.95	1
Pittsfield, MA	1.71	2
Pittsburgh – Beaver Valley, PA	1.68	3
Boston – Lawrence – Salem, MA – NH	1.62	4
Waterbury, CT	1.60	5
Springfield, MA	1.56	6
Providence – Pawtucket – Fall River, RI – MA	1.55	7
Wheeling, WV – OH	1.52	8

[Continued]

★1944★

White Female Householder, No Spouse Present, No Children Under 18 Years Old, Living Above Poverty, 1989

[Continued]

MSA	% of population	Rank
New Bedford, MA	1.51	9
Worcester, MA	1.51	9
Buffalo – Niagara Falls, NY	1.50	10
Altoona, PA	1.49	11
Johnstown, PA	1.47	12
New Haven – Meriden, CT	1.47	12
Cumberland, MD – WV	1.46	13
Atlantic City, NJ	1.45	14
Utica – Rome, NY	1.45	14
Youngstown – Warren, OH	1.43	15
Roanoke, VA	1.42	16
Charleston, WV	1.41	17
Albany – Schenectady – Troy, NY	1.40	18
Allentown – Bethlehem – Easton, PA – NJ	1.40	18
Burlington, NC	1.37	19
Elmira, NY	1.35	20
Hartford – New Britain – Middletown, CT	1.35	20
Johnson City – Kingsport – Bristol, TN – VA	1.35	20
Steubenville – Weirton, OH – WV	1.35	20
Lewiston – Auburn, ME	1.33	21
Asheville, NC	1.32	22
Knoxville, TN	1.32	22
Binghamton, NY	1.31	23
New York – Northern New Jersey – Long Island, NY – NJ – CT	1.31	23
Owensboro, KY	1.31	23
Erie, PA	1.30	24
Hickory – Morganton, NC	1.29	25
Louisville, KY – IN	1.29	25
Sharon, PA	1.29	25
Philadelphia – Wilmington – Trenton, PA – NJ – DE – MD	1.28	26
Fitchburg – Leominster, MA	1.27	27
Miami – Fort Lauderdale, FL	1.27	27
Cleveland – Akron – Lorain, OH	1.26	28
Jamestown – Dunkirk, NY	1.26	28
Sarasota, FL	1.26	28
Syracuse, NY	1.26	28
Williamsport, PA	1.26	28
Portland, ME	1.25	29
Springfield, IL	1.25	29
Terre Haute, IN	1.24	30
Gadsden, AL	1.23	31
Tampa – Saint Petersburg – Clearwater, FL	1.22	32

Source: U.S. Bureau of the Census, Data User Services Division, *1990 Census of Population and Housing*, Summary Tape File 3C, United States Summary, CD-ROM, February 1992.

★1945★

Poverty Status of Families Without Children

White Female Householder, No Spouse Present, No Children Under 18 Years Old, Living Below Poverty, 1989

[Table shows the top 50 areas]

MSA	% of population	Rank
Huntington – Ashland, WV – KY – OH	0.2883	1
Brownsville – Harlingen, TX	0.2810	2
Laredo, TX	0.2754	3
Johnson City – Kingsport – Bristol, TN – VA	0.2708	4
Saint Joseph, MO	0.2359	5
Parkersburg – Marietta, WV – OH	0.2192	6
McAllen – Edinburg – Mission, TX	0.2154	7
Cumberland, MD – WV	0.2125	8
Gadsden, AL	0.2073	9
Wheeling, WV – OH	0.2040	10
Pueblo, CO	0.1975	11
Knoxville, TN	0.1923	12
Steubenville – Weirton, OH – WV	0.1908	13
Enid, OK	0.1904	14
El Paso, TX	0.1858	15
Charleston, WV	0.1813	16
Bryan – College Station, TX	0.1772	17
Johnstown, PA	0.1737	18
Terre Haute, IN	0.1720	19
Las Cruces, NM	0.1675	20
Owensboro, KY	0.1629	21
Altoona, PA	0.1593	22
Corpus Christi, TX	0.1589	23
San Angelo, TX	0.1564	24
Houma – Thibodaux, LA	0.1531	25
Gainesville, FL	0.1524	26
San Antonio, TX	0.1476	27
Joplin, MO	0.1453	28
Florence, AL	0.1439	29
Pittsburgh – Beaver Valley, PA	0.1405	30
Danville, VA	0.1352	31
Decatur, AL	0.1323	32
Waterloo – Cedar Falls, IA	0.1323	32
Chattanooga, TN – GA	0.1297	33
Muncie, IN	0.1287	34
Wichita Falls, TX	0.1267	35
Monroe, LA	0.1259	36
Fayetteville – Springdale, AR	0.1252	37
Panama City, FL	0.1244	38
Scranton – Wilkes-Barre, PA	0.1235	39
Wilmington, NC	0.1222	40
Amarillo, TX	0.1216	41
Springfield, MO	0.1214	42
Miami – Fort Lauderdale, FL	0.1196	43
Sherman – Denison, TX	0.1189	44
Youngstown – Warren, OH	0.1183	45
Lake Charles, LA	0.1166	46
Waco, TX	0.1158	47
Pascagoula, MS	0.1145	48
Fort Smith, AR – OK	0.1131	49

Source: U.S. Bureau of the Census, Data User Services Division, *1990 Census of Population and Housing*, Summary Tape File 3C, United States Summary, CD-ROM, February 1992.

★1946★
Poverty Status of Families Without Children

White Male Householder, No Spouse Present, No Children Under 18 Years Old, Living Above Poverty, 1989

[Table shows the top 50 areas]

MSA	% of population	Rank
Waterbury, CT	0.76	1
Scranton – Wilkes-Barre, PA	0.68	2
Atlantic City, NJ	0.66	3
Las Vegas, NV	0.66	3
Johnstown, PA	0.65	4
Boston – Lawrence – Salem, MA – NH	0.64	5
Providence – Pawtucket – Fall River, RI – MA	0.64	5
Pittsfield, MA	0.63	6
Worcester, MA	0.61	7
Pittsburgh – Beaver Valley, PA	0.59	8
Reno, NV	0.59	8
Utica – Rome, NY	0.59	8
Allentown – Bethlehem – Easton, PA – NJ	0.58	9
Hartford – New Britain – Middletown, CT	0.57	10
Steubenville – Weirton, OH – WV	0.57	10
Albany – Schenectady – Troy, NY	0.56	11
Buffalo – Niagara Falls, NY	0.56	11
Miami – Fort Lauderdale, FL	0.56	11
New Haven – Meriden, CT	0.56	11
Springfield, MA	0.56	11
Binghamton, NY	0.55	12
Glens Falls, NY	0.55	12
Manchester, NH	0.55	12
New York – Northern New Jersey – Long Island, NY – NJ – CT	0.54	13
Reading, PA	0.54	13
Youngstown – Warren, OH	0.53	14
Lewiston – Auburn, ME	0.52	15
Cleveland – Akron – Lorain, OH	0.50	16
Erie, PA	0.50	16
Fitchburg – Leominster, MA	0.50	16
Portsmouth – Dover – Rochester, NH – ME	0.50	16
Rochester, NY	0.50	16
Wausau, WI	0.50	16
Canton, OH	0.49	17
Dubuque, IA	0.49	17
Grand Forks, ND	0.49	17
Williamsport, PA	0.49	17
Altoona, PA	0.48	18
Burlington, VT	0.48	18
Chicago – Gary – Lake County, IL – IN – WI	0.48	18
Detroit – Ann Arbor, MI	0.48	18
Elmira, NY	0.48	18
Johnson City – Kingsport – Bristol, TN – VA	0.48	18
La Crosse, WI	0.48	18
Minneapolis – Saint Paul, MN – WI	0.48	18
Sharon, PA	0.48	18

[Continued]

★1946★

White Male Householder, No Spouse Present, No Children Under 18 Years Old, Living Above Poverty, 1989

[Continued]

MSA	% of population	Rank
Hagerstown, MD	0.47	19
Portland, ME	0.47	19
Sarasota, FL	0.47	19
Wheeling, WV – OH	0.47	19

Source: U.S. Bureau of the Census, Data User Services Division, *1990 Census of Population and Housing,* Summary Tape File 3C, United States Summary, CD-ROM, February 1992.

★1947★
Poverty Status of Families Without Children

White Male Householder, No Spouse Present, No Children Under 18 Years Old, Living Below Poverty, 1989

[Table shows the top 50 areas]

MSA	% of population	Rank
Bryan – College Station, TX	0.1592	1
Lawrence, KS	0.1235	2
Gainesville, FL	0.1107	3
Huntington – Ashland, WV – KY – OH	0.0899	4
Chico, CA	0.0873	5
Lubbock, TX	0.0768	6
Brownsville – Harlingen, TX	0.0742	7
Las Cruces, NM	0.0723	8
Athens, GA	0.0710	9
Bloomington, IN	0.0688	10
Johnson City – Kingsport – Bristol, TN – VA	0.0654	11
Saint Joseph, MO	0.0626	12
Laredo, TX	0.0600	13
Alexandria, LA	0.0585	14
Knoxville, TN	0.0585	14
Tuscaloosa, AL	0.0585	14
Fargo – Moorhead, ND – MN	0.0581	15
Wheeling, WV – OH	0.0565	16
Tucson, AZ	0.0547	17
Houma – Thibodaux, LA	0.0541	18
Corpus Christi, TX	0.0537	19
Bismarck, ND	0.0525	20
McAllen – Edinburg – Mission, TX	0.0524	21
Springfield, MO	0.0524	21
Miami – Fort Lauderdale, FL	0.0517	22
Waco, TX	0.0502	23
Charleston, WV	0.0499	24
Decatur, AL	0.0494	25
Fayetteville – Springdale, AR	0.0494	25
Cumberland, MD – WV	0.0492	26
Columbia, MO	0.0489	27
Pueblo, CO	0.0488	28
Charlottesville, VA	0.0481	29

[Continued]

★1947★

White Male Householder, No Spouse Present, No Children Under 18 Years Old, Living Below Poverty, 1989

[Continued]

MSA	% of population	Rank
San Angelo, TX	0.0477	30
Austin, TX	0.0475	31
Anniston, AL	0.0465	32
Eau Claire, WI	0.0465	32
Johnstown, PA	0.0464	33
El Paso, TX	0.0450	34
Scranton – Wilkes-Barre, PA	0.0448	35
Parkersburg – Marietta, WV – OH	0.0442	36
Billings, MT	0.0441	37
Asheville, NC	0.0440	38
Wilmington, NC	0.0424	39
Daytona Beach, FL	0.0421	40
Eugene – Springfield, OR	0.0421	40
Fort Smith, AR – OK	0.0421	40
Tallahassee, FL	0.0420	41
San Antonio, TX	0.0417	42
Iowa City, IA	0.0416	43

Source: U.S. Bureau of the Census, Data User Services Division, *1990 Census of Population and Housing*, Summary Tape File 3C, United States Summary, CD-ROM, February 1992.

★1948★

Poverty Status of Families Without Children

White Married Couples, No Children Under 18 Years Old, Living Above Poverty, 1989

[Table shows the top 50 areas]

MSA	% of population	Rank
Sarasota, FL	18.7	1
Fort Myers – Cape Coral, Fl	16.7	2
Naples, FL	16.5	3
Bradenton, FL	16.3	4
Fort Pierce, FL	15.8	5
West Palm Beach – Boca Raton – Delray Beach, FL	14.5	6
Ocala, FL	14.3	7
Daytona Beach, FL	14.1	8
Melbourne – Titusville – Palm Bay, FL	13.8	9
Tampa – Saint Petersburg – Clearwater, FL	13.5	10
Lakeland – Winter Haven, FL	12.7	11
Johnson City – Kingsport – Bristol, TN – VA	12.5	12
Medford, OR	12.5	12
Reading, PA	12.4	13
Sharon, PA	12.4	13
York, PA	12.4	13
Cumberland, MD – WV	12.3	14
Steubenville – Weirton, OH – WV	12.3	14
Asheville, NC	12.2	15
Allentown – Bethlehem – Easton, PA – NJ	12.1	16

[Continued]

★1948★

White Married Couples, No Children Under 18 Years Old, Living Above Poverty, 1989

[Continued]

MSA	% of population	Rank
Parkersburg – Marietta, WV – OH	11.9	17
Sheboygan, WI	11.9	17
Florence, AL	11.8	18
Hickory – Morganton, NC	11.8	18
Johnstown, PA	11.8	18
Pittsburgh – Beaver Valley, PA	11.8	18
Wheeling, WV – OH	11.8	18
Cedar Rapids, IA	11.7	19
Enid, OK	11.7	19
Knoxville, TN	11.7	19
Pittsfield, MA	11.7	19
Scranton – Wilkes-Barre, PA	11.7	19
Williamsport, PA	11.7	19
Altoona, PA	11.6	20
Charleston, WV	11.6	20
Harrisburg – Lebanon – Carlisle, PA	11.6	20
Kokomo, IN	11.6	20
Canton, OH	11.5	21
Duluth, MN – WI	11.5	21
Hagerstown, MD	11.5	21
Joplin, MO	11.5	21
Lancaster, PA	11.5	21
Mansfield, OH	11.5	21
Redding, CA	11.5	21
Chico, CA	11.4	22
Roanoke, VA	11.4	22
Springfield, MO	11.4	22
Anderson, IN	11.3	23
Janesville – Beloit, WI	11.3	23
Panama City, FL	11.3	23

Source: U.S. Bureau of the Census, Data User Services Division, *1990 Census of Population and Housing*, Summary Tape File 3C, United States Summary, CD-ROM, February 1992.

★1949★

Poverty Status of Families Without Children

White Married Couples, No Children Under 18 Years Old, Living Below Poverty, 1989

[Table shows the top 50 areas]

MSA	% of population	Rank
Johnson City – Kingsport – Bristol, TN – VA	0.908	1
Huntington – Ashland, WV – KY – OH	0.869	2
Gadsden, AL	0.844	3
McAllen – Edinburg – Mission, TX	0.843	4
Brownsville – Harlingen, TX	0.804	5
Enid, OK	0.781	6
Houma – Thibodaux, LA	0.742	7
Decatur, AL	0.730	8
Joplin, MO	0.715	9

[Continued]

★1949★

White Married Couples, No Children Under 18 Years Old, Living Below Poverty, 1989
[Continued]

MSA	% of population	Rank
Ocala, FL	0.699	10
Florence, AL	0.695	11
Fort Smith, AR–OK	0.663	12
Fayetteville–Springdale, AR	0.645	13
Johnstown, PA	0.633	14
Sherman–Denison, TX	0.617	15
Texarkana, TX–Texarkana, AR	0.613	16
Owensboro, KY	0.612	17
Cumberland, MD–WV	0.610	18
Wheeling, WV–OH	0.606	19
Anniston, AL	0.579	20
Knoxville, TN	0.575	21
Saint Joseph, MO	0.572	22
Alexandria, LA	0.566	23
Parkersburg–Marietta, WV–OH	0.565	24
Lafayette, LA	0.540	25
Charleston, WV	0.533	26
Chattanooga, TN–GA	0.515	27
Danville, VA	0.509	28
San Angelo, TX	0.506	29
Laredo, TX	0.504	30
Pueblo, CO	0.503	31
Steubenville–Weirton, OH–WV	0.502	32
Medford, OR	0.501	33
Lakeland–Winter Haven, FL	0.498	34
Tyler, TX	0.494	35
Victoria, TX	0.487	36
Pine Bluff, AR	0.485	37
Waterloo–Cedar Falls, IA	0.479	38
Asheville, NC	0.476	39
Lake Charles, LA	0.476	39
Fort Myers–Cape Coral, Fl	0.474	40
Miami–Fort Lauderdale, FL	0.471	41
Abilene, TX	0.470	42
Daytona Beach, FL	0.464	43
Biloxi–Gulfport, MS	0.461	44
Panama City, FL	0.458	45
Las Cruces, NM	0.454	46
Wichita Falls, TX	0.449	47
Terre Haute, IN	0.448	48
Odessa, TX	0.443	49

Source: U.S. Bureau of the Census, Data User Services Division, *1990 Census of Population and Housing*, Summary Tape File 3C, United States Summary, CD-ROM, February 1992.

★1950★

Ratios of Income to Poverty Level

Persons With Ratio of Income to Poverty Level of .50, 1989

[Table shows the top 50 areas]

MSA	% of population	Rank
McAllen–Edinburg–Mission, TX	19.1	1
Brownsville–Harlingen, TX	18.2	2
Laredo, TX	17.1	3
Bryan–College Station, TX	13.3	4
Albany, GA	12.6	5
Monroe, LA	11.8	6
Houma–Thibodaux, LA	11.4	7
Pine Bluff, AR	11.4	7
El Paso, TX	11.3	8
Gainesville, FL	11.2	9
Las Cruces, NM	11.2	9
New Orleans, LA	11.1	10
Shreveport, LA	10.8	11
Lafayette, LA	10.7	12
Corpus Christi, TX	10.3	13
Odessa, TX	10.3	13
Athens, GA	10.0	14
Alexandria, LA	9.9	15
Mobile, AL	9.9	15
Baton Rouge, LA	9.7	16
Tuscaloosa, AL	9.7	16
Bloomington, IN	9.5	17
Pueblo, CO	9.5	17
Lawrence, KS	9.4	18
Waco, TX	9.4	18
Tallahassee, FL	9.1	19
Lake Charles, LA	9.0	20
Jackson, MS	8.8	21
San Antonio, TX	8.8	21
Beaumont–Port Arthur, TX	8.7	22
Huntington–Ashland, WV–KY–OH	8.7	22
State College, PA	8.7	22
Florence, SC	8.6	23
Memphis, TN–AR–MS	8.6	23
Lubbock, TX	8.5	24
Columbus, GA–AL	8.4	25
Biloxi–Gulfport, MS	8.2	26
Texarkana, TX–Texarkana, AR	8.2	26
Victoria, TX	8.2	26
Yuma, AZ	8.2	26
Pascagoula, MS	8.0	27
Longview–Marshall, TX	7.9	28
Tucson, AZ	7.9	28
Fresno, CA	7.8	29
Yakima, WA	7.8	29
Visalia–Tulare–Porterville, CA	7.7	30
Savannah, GA	7.6	31
Amarillo, TX	7.5	32
Montgomery, AL	7.5	32
Muncie, IN	7.5	32

Source: U.S. Bureau of the Census, Data User Services Division, *1990 Census of Population and Housing*, Summary Tape File 3C, United States Summary, CD-ROM, February 1992.

Persons With Ratio of Income to Poverty Level of .50 to .74, 1989

[Table shows the top 50 areas]

MSA	% of population	Rank
McAllen – Edinburg – Mission, TX	11.4	1
Laredo, TX	10.6	2
Brownsville – Harlingen, TX	10.2	3
El Paso, TX	7.4	4
Las Cruces, NM	7.2	5
Visalia – Tulare – Porterville, CA	6.1	6
Houma – Thibodaux, LA	5.9	7
Monroe, LA	5.9	7
Fresno, CA	5.7	8
Bryan – College Station, TX	5.6	9
Pine Bluff, AR	5.6	9
Flint, MI	5.5	10
Merced, CA	5.5	10
Yakima, WA	5.4	11
Alexandria, LA	5.2	12
Florence, SC	5.2	12
Huntington – Ashland, WV – KY – OH	5.2	12
Shreveport, LA	5.2	12
Yuba City, CA	5.2	12
Biloxi – Gulfport, MS	5.1	13
Corpus Christi, TX	5.1	13
Duluth, MN – WI	5.1	13
Jackson, MS	5.0	14
Waco, TX	4.9	15
Muskegon, MI	4.8	16
Odessa, TX	4.8	16
Richland – Kennewick – Pasco, WA	4.8	16
Lafayette, LA	4.7	17
Mobile, AL	4.7	17
San Antonio, TX	4.7	17
Beaumont – Port Arthur, TX	4.6	18
Chico, CA	4.6	18
Johnson City – Kingsport – Bristol, TN – VA	4.6	18
New Orleans, LA	4.6	18
Pueblo, CO	4.6	18
Texarkana, TX – Texarkana, AR	4.6	18
Albany, GA	4.5	19
Gadsden, AL	4.5	19
Saginaw – Bay City – Midland, MI	4.5	19
Victoria, TX	4.5	19
Bakersfield, CA	4.4	20
Battle Creek, MI	4.4	20
Gainesville, FL	4.4	20
Lawrence, KS	4.4	20
Memphis, TN – AR – MS	4.4	20
New Bedford, MA	4.4	20
Fort Smith, AR – OK	4.3	21
Pensacola, FL	4.3	21
Springfield, MA	4.3	21
Tuscaloosa, AL	4.3	21

Source: U.S. Bureau of the Census, Data User Services Division, *1990 Census of Population and Housing*, Summary Tape File 3C, United States Summary, CD-ROM, February 1992.

Persons With Ratio of Income to Poverty Level of .75 to .99, 1989

[Table shows the top 50 areas]

MSA	% of population	Rank
McAllen – Edinburg – Mission, TX	11.1	1
Brownsville – Harlingen, TX	10.5	2
Laredo, TX	9.9	3
Visalia – Tulare – Porterville, CA	8.4	4
Merced, CA	7.8	5
El Paso, TX	7.6	6
Fresno, CA	7.6	6
Las Cruces, NM	7.2	7
Yuba City, CA	7.1	8
Chico, CA	7.0	9
Yuma, AZ	7.0	9
Yakima, WA	6.7	10
Alexandria, LA	6.4	11
Bakersfield, CA	6.1	12
Fort Smith, AR – OK	6.1	12
Huntington – Ashland, WV – KY – OH	6.1	12
Stockton, CA	6.1	12
Houma – Thibodaux, LA	6.0	13
Monroe, LA	6.0	13
Florence, SC	5.9	14
Redding, CA	5.9	14
Corpus Christi, TX	5.8	15
Danville, VA	5.8	15
Gadsden, AL	5.8	15
Lafayette, LA	5.8	15
Pine Bluff, AR	5.8	15
Lubbock, TX	5.7	16
Pueblo, CO	5.7	16
Longview – Marshall, TX	5.6	17
Modesto, CA	5.6	17
Shreveport, LA	5.6	17
Texarkana, TX – Texarkana, AR	5.6	17
Dothan, AL	5.5	18
Gainesville, FL	5.5	18
San Antonio, TX	5.5	18
Biloxi – Gulfport, MS	5.4	19
Decatur, AL	5.4	19
Jackson, TN	5.4	19
Johnson City – Kingsport – Bristol, TN – VA	5.4	19
San Angelo, TX	5.4	19
Waco, TX	5.4	19
Joplin, MO	5.3	20
Odessa, TX	5.2	21
Wichita Falls, TX	5.2	21
Abilene, TX	5.1	22
Athens, GA	5.1	22
Bryan – College Station, TX	5.1	22
New Orleans, LA	5.1	22
Sherman – Denison, TX	5.1	22
Tyler, TX	5.1	22

Source: U.S. Bureau of the Census, Data User Services Division, *1990 Census of Population and Housing*, Summary Tape File 3C, United States Summary, CD-ROM, February 1992.

★1953★

Ratios of Income to Poverty Level

Persons With Ratio of Income to Poverty Level of 1.00 to 1.24, 1989

[Table shows the top 50 areas]

MSA	% of population	Rank
McAllen – Edinburg – Mission, TX	9.4	1
Laredo, TX	9.2	2
Brownsville – Harlingen, TX	8.3	3
El Paso, TX	7.7	4
Las Cruces, NM	7.6	5
Merced, CA	7.6	5
Visalia – Tulare – Porterville, CA	7.6	5
Yuba City, CA	7.5	6
Yuma, AZ	7.2	7
Odessa, TX	6.8	8
Yakima, WA	6.7	9
Fresno, CA	6.6	10
Killeen – Temple, TX	6.6	10
Biloxi – Gulfport, MS	6.5	11
Alexandria, LA	6.4	12
Monroe, LA	6.3	13
Florence, SC	6.1	14
Houma – Thibodaux, LA	6.1	14
Bakersfield, CA	6.0	15
Clarksville – Hopkinsville, TN – KY	6.0	15
Jacksonville, NC	6.0	15
Joplin, MO	6.0	15
Redding, CA	6.0	15
Chico, CA	5.9	16
San Angelo, TX	5.9	16
Columbus, GA – AL	5.8	17
Corpus Christi, TX	5.8	17
Fort Smith, AR – OK	5.8	17
Johnson City – Kingsport – Bristol, TN – VA	5.8	17
Pascagoula, MS	5.8	17
Pine Bluff, AR	5.8	17
Ocala, FL	5.7	18
Provo – Orem, UT	5.7	18
Pueblo, CO	5.7	18
San Antonio, TX	5.7	18
Dothan, AL	5.6	19
Gadsden, AL	5.6	19
Great Falls, MT	5.6	19
Huntington – Ashland, WV – KY – OH	5.6	19
Lafayette, LA	5.6	19
Lubbock, TX	5.6	19
Danville, VA	5.5	20
Fayetteville, NC	5.5	20
Florence, AL	5.5	20
Medford, OR	5.5	20
Shreveport, LA	5.5	20
Stockton, CA	5.5	20
Waco, TX	5.5	20
Albany, GA	5.4	21
Greeley, CO	5.4	21

Source: U.S. Bureau of the Census, Data User Services Division, *1990 Census of Population and Housing,* Summary Tape File 3C, United States Summary, CD-ROM, February 1992.

★1954★

Ratios of Income to Poverty Level

Persons With Ratio of Income to Poverty Level of 1.25 to 1.49, 1989

[Table shows the top 50 areas]

MSA	% of population	Rank
Brownsville – Harlingen, TX	7.0	1
Laredo, TX	7.0	1
Visalia – Tulare – Porterville, CA	6.9	2
McAllen – Edinburg – Mission, TX	6.8	3
Merced, CA	6.8	3
Rapid City, SD	6.8	3
El Paso, TX	6.7	4
Killeen – Temple, TX	6.5	5
Yuma, AZ	6.5	5
Yuba City, CA	6.4	6
Clarksville – Hopkinsville, TN – KY	6.3	7
Joplin, MO	6.3	7
Johnstown, PA	6.2	8
Biloxi – Gulfport, MS	6.1	9
Corpus Christi, TX	6.1	9
Houma – Thibodaux, LA	6.1	9
Las Cruces, NM	6.1	9
Provo – Orem, UT	6.1	9
Fort Smith, AR – OK	6.0	10
Jacksonville, NC	6.0	10
Lawton, OK	5.9	11
Odessa, TX	5.9	11
Redding, CA	5.9	11
Abilene, TX	5.8	12
Florence, AL	5.8	12
Fresno, CA	5.8	12
Alexandria, LA	5.7	13
Bakersfield, CA	5.7	13
Chico, CA	5.7	13
Johnson City – Kingsport – Bristol, TN – VA	5.7	13
Longview – Marshall, TX	5.7	13
Modesto, CA	5.7	13
Ocala, FL	5.7	13
Wichita Falls, TX	5.7	13
Altoona, PA	5.6	14
Huntington – Ashland, WV – KY – OH	5.6	14
Yakima, WA	5.6	14
Danville, VA	5.5	15
Dothan, AL	5.5	15
Fayetteville, NC	5.5	15
Fayetteville – Springdale, AR	5.5	15
Gadsden, AL	5.5	15
San Antonio, TX	5.5	15
Enid, OK	5.4	16
Greeley, CO	5.4	16
Pascagoula, MS	5.4	16
Waco, TX	5.4	16
Anniston, AL	5.3	17
Mobile, AL	5.3	17
Salinas – Seaside – Monterey, CA	5.3	17

Source: U.S. Bureau of the Census, Data User Services Division, *1990 Census of Population and Housing,* Summary Tape File 3C, United States Summary, CD-ROM, February 1992.

Persons With Ratio of Income to Poverty Level of 1.50 to 1.74, 1989

[Table shows the top 50 areas]

MSA	% of population	Rank
Provo – Orem, UT	7.9	1
Jacksonville, NC	6.9	2
El Paso, TX	6.8	3
Houma – Thibodaux, LA	6.7	4
Johnstown, PA	6.7	4
Merced, CA	6.7	4
Yuba City, CA	6.7	4
Panama City, FL	6.6	5
Clarksville – Hopkinsville, TN – KY	6.5	6
Dothan, AL	6.5	6
Fort Smith, AR – OK	6.5	6
Lawton, OK	6.5	6
Visalia – Tulare – Porterville, CA	6.5	6
Fayetteville, NC	6.4	7
Killeen – Temple, TX	6.4	7
Sioux City, IA – NE	6.4	7
Jamestown – Dunkirk, NY	6.3	8
Victoria, TX	6.3	8
Biloxi – Gulfport, MS	6.2	9
Brownsville – Harlingen, TX	6.2	9
Joplin, MO	6.2	9
Lakeland – Winter Haven, FL	6.2	9
Laredo, TX	6.2	9
Pine Bluff, AR	6.2	9
Pueblo, CO	6.2	9
Yakima, WA	6.2	9
Yuma, AZ	6.2	9
Cheyenne, WY	6.1	10
Gadsden, AL	6.1	10
Alexandria, LA	6.0	11
Columbus, GA – AL	6.0	11
Cumberland, MD – WV	6.0	11
Eugene – Springfield, OR	6.0	11
Grand Forks, ND	6.0	11
Ocala, FL	6.0	11
Odessa, TX	6.0	11
Texarkana, TX – Texarkana, AR	6.0	11
Williamsport, PA	6.0	11
Abilene, TX	5.9	12
Corpus Christi, TX	5.9	12
Florence, AL	5.9	12
Fort Walton Beach, FL	5.9	12
Johnson City – Kingsport – Bristol, TN – VA	5.9	12
Las Cruces, NM	5.9	12
McAllen – Edinburg – Mission, TX	5.9	12
Saint Joseph, MO	5.9	12
Wichita Falls, TX	5.9	12
Medford, OR	5.8	13
Owensboro, KY	5.8	13
Sherman – Denison, TX	5.8	13

Source: U.S. Bureau of the Census, Data User Services Division, *1990 Census of Population and Housing*, Summary Tape File 3C, United States Summary, CD-ROM, February 1992.

Persons With Ratio of Income to Poverty Level of 1.75 to 1.84, 1989

[Table shows the top 50 areas]

MSA	% of population	Rank
Provo – Orem, UT	3.06	1
Great Falls, MT	2.88	2
Yuma, AZ	2.75	3
Johnstown, PA	2.61	4
Merced, CA	2.61	4
Casper, WY	2.52	5
El Paso, TX	2.52	5
Sherman – Denison, TX	2.52	5
Joplin, MO	2.50	6
Fort Smith, AR – OK	2.46	7
Owensboro, KY	2.45	8
Salt Lake City – Ogden, UT	2.44	9
Alexandria, LA	2.42	10
Wichita Falls, TX	2.42	10
Odessa, TX	2.41	11
Jacksonville, NC	2.39	12
Muskegon, MI	2.39	12
Williamsport, PA	2.37	13
Fayetteville, NC	2.36	14
Rapid City, SD	2.36	14
Florence, AL	2.35	15
Fayetteville – Springdale, AR	2.34	16
Anderson, SC	2.29	17
Salem, OR	2.28	18
Biloxi – Gulfport, MS	2.27	19
Columbus, GA – AL	2.27	19
Visalia – Tulare – Porterville, CA	2.26	20
Billings, MT	2.25	21
Fort Walton Beach, FL	2.25	21
Chico, CA	2.24	22
Jackson, TN	2.24	22
Chattanooga, TN – GA	2.21	23
Clarksville – Hopkinsville, TN – KY	2.21	23
Gadsden, AL	2.21	23
Anniston, AL	2.20	24
Danville, VA	2.20	24
Parkersburg – Marietta, WV – OH	2.20	24
Pascagoula, MS	2.19	25
Saint Joseph, MO	2.19	25
Sharon, PA	2.18	26
Sioux City, IA – NE	2.17	27
Cumberland, MD – WV	2.16	28
Wheeling, WV – OH	2.16	28
Altoona, PA	2.15	29
Killeen – Temple, TX	2.15	29
Lakeland – Winter Haven, FL	2.14	30
Lafayette, LA	2.13	31
Las Cruces, NM	2.12	32
San Angelo, TX	2.12	32
Tucson, AZ	2.12	32

Source: U.S. Bureau of the Census, Data User Services Division, *1990 Census of Population and Housing*, Summary Tape File 3C, United States Summary, CD-ROM, February 1992.

★1957★
Ratios of Income to Poverty Level

Persons With Ratio of Income to Poverty Level of 1.85 to 1.99, 1989

[Table shows the top 50 areas]

MSA	% of population	Rank
Joplin, MO	4.6	1
Great Falls, MT	4.3	2
Rapid City, SD	4.2	3
Enid, OK	4.1	4
Fort Smith, AR – OK	4.1	4
Johnstown, PA	4.1	4
Provo – Orem, UT	4.1	4
Casper, WY	3.9	5
Cumberland, MD – WV	3.9	5
Houma – Thibodaux, LA	3.9	5
Killeen – Temple, TX	3.8	6
Sioux Falls, SD	3.8	6
Anniston, AL	3.7	7
Fayetteville – Springdale, AR	3.7	7
Fort Walton Beach, FL	3.7	7
Greeley, CO	3.7	7
Lawton, OK	3.7	7
Medford, OR	3.7	7
Odessa, TX	3.7	7
Salt Lake City – Ogden, UT	3.7	7
Springfield, MO	3.7	7
Williamsport, PA	3.7	7
Amarillo, TX	3.6	8
Biloxi – Gulfport, MS	3.6	8
Longview – Marshall, TX	3.6	8
Ocala, FL	3.6	8
Owensboro, KY	3.6	8
Panama City, FL	3.6	8
Abilene, TX	3.5	9
Altoona, PA	3.5	9
Billings, MT	3.5	9
Burlington, NC	3.5	9
Daytona Beach, FL	3.5	9
El Paso, TX	3.5	9
Fayetteville, NC	3.5	9
Gadsden, AL	3.5	9
Muskegon, MI	3.5	9
Pensacola, FL	3.5	9
Sharon, PA	3.5	9
Victoria, TX	3.5	9
Yuma, AZ	3.5	9
Clarksville – Hopkinsville, TN – KY	3.4	10
Dubuque, IA	3.4	10
Duluth, MN – WI	3.4	10
Lakeland – Winter Haven, FL	3.4	10
Pueblo, CO	3.4	10
Salem, OR	3.4	10
San Angelo, TX	3.4	10
South Bend – Mishawaka, IN	3.4	10
Yakima, WA	3.4	10

Source: U.S. Bureau of the Census, Data User Services Division, *1990 Census of Population and Housing*, Summary Tape File 3C, United States Summary, CD-ROM, February 1992.

★1958★
Ratios of Income to Poverty Level

Persons With Ratio of Income to Poverty Level of 2.00 and Over, 1989

[Table shows the top 50 areas]

MSA	% of population	Rank
Washington, DC – MD – VA	82.4	1
Hartford – New Britain – Middletown, CT	81.7	2
Waterbury, CT	80.5	3
Rochester, MN	79.6	4
Minneapolis – Saint Paul, MN – WI	78.8	5
Poughkeepsie, NY	78.8	5
Boston – Lawrence – Salem, MA – NH	78.7	6
Anchorage, AK	78.5	7
Manchester, NH	78.4	8
New Haven – Meriden, CT	78.3	9
New London – Norwich, CT – RI	77.0	10
San Francisco – Oakland – San Jose, CA	76.9	11
York, PA	76.9	11
Allentown – Bethlehem – Easton, PA – NJ	76.8	12
Portsmouth – Dover – Rochester, NH – ME	76.7	13
Sarasota, FL	76.7	13
Pittsfield, MA	76.5	14
Portland, ME	76.3	15
Seattle – Tacoma, WA	76.2	16
Worcester, MA	76.2	16
Sheboygan, WI	76.0	17
Honolulu, HI	75.7	18
Harrisburg – Lebanon – Carlisle, PA	75.5	19
Baltimore, MD	75.3	20
Grand Rapids, MI	75.2	21
Reading, PA	75.2	21
Appleton – Oshkosh – Neenah, WI	75.1	22
Cedar Rapids, IA	75.1	22
Fort Wayne, IN	75.1	22
Atlanta, GA	75.0	23
Fitchburg – Leominster, MA	74.9	24
Philadelphia – Wilmington – Trenton, PA – NJ – DE – MD	74.9	24
Denver – Boulder, CO	74.5	25
Lancaster, PA	74.5	25
Albany – Schenectady – Troy, NY	74.4	26
New York – Northern New Jersey – Long Island, NY – NJ – CT	74.4	26
Atlantic City, NJ	74.3	27
Rochester, NY	74.3	27
West Palm Beach – Boca Raton – Delray Beach, FL	74.3	27
Burlington, VT	74.1	28
Des Moines, IA	74.1	28
Chicago – Gary – Lake County, IL – IN – WI	74.0	29
Rockford, IL	74.0	29
Richmond – Petersburg, VA	73.9	30
Green Bay, WI	73.8	31

[Continued]

★1958★

Persons With Ratio of Income to Poverty Level of 2.00 and Over, 1989

[Continued]

MSA	% of population	Rank
Elkhart–Goshen, IN	73.7	32
Springfield, IL	73.6	33
Naples, FL	73.3	34
Providence–Pawtucket–Fall River, RI–MA	73.1	35
Reno, NV	73.1	35

Source: U.S. Bureau of the Census, Data User Services Division, *1990 Census of Population and Housing*, Summary Tape File 3C, United States Summary, CD-ROM, February 1992.

PART V

ECONOMIC PROFILE

Contents

Chapter 16

GENERAL ECONOMIC PROFILE

Topics Covered

Charity
Cost of Living
Fortune 500 Companies
Imports and Exports: Sales
Imports and Exports: Value

★1959★

Charity

Donations to the Catholic Church, Selected Cities: 1993

[In annual dollars per household]

City	1993	Rank
Baltimore, MD	222.61	3
Chicago, IL	262.23	1
Cleveland, OH	240.07	2

Source: "Average Catholic Household Donation in the Sunday Collection, 1991-93," *America*, 15 July 1995, p. 19.

★1960★

Cost of Living

Average Price of Gasoline, 1996, Selected Local Areas: Price Per Gallon

The national city average price per gallon of gasoline in February 1996 was $1.181. Data refer to all types of gasoline.

[In dollars per gallon]

City/MSA	Price	Rank
Baltimore, MD	1.189	8
Boston-Lawrence-Salem, MA-NH	1.193	7
Chicago-Gary-Lake County, IL-IN-WI	1.257	3
Cleveland-Akron-Lorain, OH	1.097	14
Dallas-Fort Worth, TX	1.105	13
Detroit-Ann Arbor, MI	1.126	12
Houston-Galveston-Brazoria, TX	1.139	11
Los Angeles-Anaheim-Riverside, CA	1.250	4
Miami-Fort Lauderdale, FL	1.209	6
New York-Northern New Jersey-Long Island, NY-NJ-CT	1.289	1
Philadelphia-Wilmington-Trenton, PA-NJ-DE-MD	1.142	10
Pittsburgh-Beaver Valley, PA	1.216	5
Saint Louis-East Saint Louis, MO-IL	1.077	15
San Francisco-Oakland-San Jose, CA	1.288	2
Washington, DC-MD-VA	1.165	9

Source: U.S. Department of Labor, Bureau of Labor Statistics, *CPI Detailed Report: Data for February 1996*, Washington, D.C.: U.S. Government Printing Office, April 1996, p. 88.

★1961★

Cost of Living

Average Price of Gasoline, 1996, Selected Local Areas: Price Per Gallon (Unleaded Regular)

The national city average price per gallon of unleaded regular gasoline in February 1996 was $1.124.

[In dollars per gallon]

City/MSA	Price	Rank
Baltimore, MD	1.131	7
Boston-Lawrence-Salem, MA-NH	1.150	5
Chicago-Gary-Lake County, IL-IN-WI	1.198	4
Cleveland-Akron-Lorain, OH	1.062	13
Dallas-Fort Worth, TX	1.038	14
Detroit-Ann Arbor, MI	1.082	11
Houston-Galveston-Brazoria, TX	1.072	12
Los Angeles-Anaheim-Riverside, CA	1.208	2
Miami-Fort Lauderdale, FL	1.128	8
New York-Northern New Jersey-Long Island, NY-NJ-CT	1.204	3
Philadelphia-Wilmington-Trenton, PA-NJ-DE-MD	1.099	9
Pittsburgh-Beaver Valley, PA	1.147	6
Saint Louis-East Saint Louis, MO-IL	1.020	15
San Francisco-Oakland-San Jose, CA	1.224	1
Washington, DC-MD-VA	1.095	10

Source: U.S. Department of Labor, Bureau of Labor Statistics, *CPI Detailed Report: Data for February 1996*, Washington, D.C.: U.S. Government Printing Office, April 1996, p. 88.

★1962★

Cost of Living

Average Price of Gasoline, 1996, Selected Local Areas: Price Per Gallon (Unleaded Midgrade)

The national city average price per gallon of unleaded midgrade gasoline in February 1996 was $1.220.

[In dollars per gallon]

City/MSA	Price	Rank
Baltimore, MD	1.235	8
Boston-Lawrence-Salem, MA-NH	1.254	7
Chicago-Gary-Lake County, IL-IN-WI	1.324	3
Cleveland-Akron-Lorain, OH	1.154	14
Dallas-Fort Worth, TX	1.177	13
Detroit-Ann Arbor, MI	1.192	12
Houston-Galveston-Brazoria, TX	1.198	11
Los Angeles-Anaheim-Riverside, CA	1.288	4
Miami-Fort Lauderdale, FL	1.273	5
New York-Northern New Jersey-Long Island, NY-NJ-CT	1.339	2
Philadelphia-Wilmington-Trenton, PA-NJ-DE-MD	1.230	9
Pittsburgh-Beaver Valley, PA	1.255	6
Saint Louis-East Saint Louis, MO-IL	1.116	15

[Continued]

★1962★

Average Price of Gasoline, 1996, Selected Local Areas: Price Per Gallon (Unleaded Midgrade)
[Continued]

City/MSA	Price	Rank
San Francisco-Oakland-San Jose, CA	1.353	1
Washington, DC-MD-VA	1.205	10

Source: U.S. Department of Labor, Bureau of Labor Statistics, *CPI Detailed Report: Data for February 1996*, Washington, D.C.: U.S. Government Printing Office, April 1996, p. 88.

★1963★

Cost of Living

Average Price of Gasoline, 1996, Selected Local Areas: Price Per Gallon (Unleaded Premium)

The national city average price per gallon of unleaded premium gasoline in February 1996 was $1.311.

[In dollars per gallon]

City/MSA	Price	Rank
Baltimore, MD	1.289	8
Boston-Lawrence-Salem, MA-NH	1.345	5
Chicago-Gary-Lake County, IL-IN-WI	1.396	3
Cleveland-Akron-Lorain, OH	1.247	12
Dallas-Fort Worth, TX	1.234	14
Detroit-Ann Arbor, MI	1.284	10
Houston-Galveston-Brazoria, TX	1.256	11
Los Angeles-Anaheim-Riverside, CA	1.396	3
Miami-Fort Lauderdale, FL	1.331	6
New York-Northern New Jersey-Long Island, NY-NJ-CT	1.425	2
Philadelphia-Wilmington-Trenton, PA-NJ-DE-MD	1.297	7
Pittsburgh-Beaver Valley, PA	1.357	4
Saint Louis-East Saint Louis, MO-IL	1.243	13
San Francisco-Oakland-San Jose, CA	1.435	1
Washington, DC-MD-VA	1.288	9

Source: U.S. Department of Labor, Bureau of Labor Statistics, *CPI Detailed Report: Data for February 1996*, Washington, D.C.: U.S. Government Printing Office, April 1996, p. 88.

★1964★

Cost of Living

Average Residential Prices of Electricity, 1996, Selected Local Areas: Cost Per Kilowatt-Hour

The national city average price per kilowatt-hour of electricity for residential consumers in February 1996 was $0.091.

[In dollars per kilowatt-hour]

City/MSA	Price	Rank
Baltimore, MD	.076	11
Boston-Lawrence-Salem, MA-NH	.115	4
Chicago-Gary-Lake County, IL-IN-WI	.110	5
Cleveland-Akron-Lorain, OH	.107	6
Dallas-Fort Worth, TX	.062	14
Detroit-Ann Arbor, MI	.099	7
Houston-Galveston-Brazoria, TX	.078	10
Los Angeles-Anaheim-Riverside, CA	.127	2
Miami-Fort Lauderdale, FL	.087	9
New York-Northern New Jersey-Long Island, NY-NJ-CT	.139	1
Philadelphia-Wilmington-Trenton, PA-NJ-DE-MD	.117	3
Pittsburgh-Beaver Valley, PA	.095	8
Saint Louis-East Saint Louis, MO-IL	.071	12
San Francisco-Oakland-San Jose, CA	.127	2
Washington, DC-MD-VA	.070	13

Source: U.S. Department of Labor, Bureau of Labor Statistics, *CPI Detailed Report: Data for February 1996*, Washington, D.C.: U.S. Government Printing Office, April 1996, p. 88.

★1965★

Cost of Living

Average Residential Prices of Electricity, 1996, Selected Local Areas: Cost Per 500 Kilowatt-Hours

The national city average price of 500 kilowatt-hours of electricity for residential consumers in February 1996 was $48.542.

[In dollars per 500 kilowatt-hours]

City/MSA	Price	Rank
Baltimore, MD	47.840	10
Boston-Lawrence-Salem, MA-NH	61.207	4
Chicago-Gary-Lake County, IL-IN-WI	57.993	6
Cleveland-Akron-Lorain, OH	54.474	7
Dallas-Fort Worth, TX	40.110	13
Detroit-Ann Arbor, MI	48.303	9
Houston-Galveston-Brazoria, TX	39.925	14
Los Angeles-Anaheim-Riverside, CA	65.172	2
Miami-Fort Lauderdale, FL	44.047	11
New York-Northern New Jersey-Long Island, NY-NJ-CT	72.024	1
Philadelphia-Wilmington-Trenton, PA-NJ-DE-MD	62.084	3

[Continued]

★1965★

Average Residential Prices of Electricity, 1996, Selected Local Areas: Cost Per 500 Kilowatt-Hours

[Continued]

City/MSA	Price	Rank
Pittsburgh-Beaver Valley, PA	51.589	8
Saint Louis-East Saint Louis, MO-IL	37.405	15
San Francisco-Oakland-San Jose, CA	61.080	5
Washington, DC-MD-VA	40.352	12

Source: U.S. Department of Labor, Bureau of Labor Statistics, CPI Detailed Report: Data for February 1996, Washington, D.C.: U.S. Government Printing Office, April 1996, p. 87.

★1966★

Cost of Living

Average Residential Prices of Fuel Oil #2, 1996, Selected Local Areas: Cost Per Gallon

The national city average price of one gallon of fuel oil #2 for residential consumers in February 1996 was $1.001.

[In dollars per gallon]

City/MSA	Price	Rank
Baltimore, MD	1.285	1
Boston-Lawrence-Salem, MA-NH	1.019	5
Chicago-Gary-Lake County, IL-IN-WI	1.042	4
New York-Northern New Jersey-Long Island, NY-NJ-CT	1.108	3
Philadelphia-Wilmington-Trenton, PA-NJ-DE-MD	.975	6
Washington, DC-MD-VA	1.112	2

Source: U.S. Department of Labor, Bureau of Labor Statistics, CPI Detailed Report: Data for February 1996, Washington, D.C.: U.S. Government Printing Office, April 1996, p. 87.

★1967★

Cost of Living

Average Residential Prices of Piped (Utility) Gas, 1996, Selected Local Areas: Cost Per Therm

The national city average price of one therm of piped (utility) gas for residential consumers in February 1996 was $0.637.

[In dollars per therm]

City/MSA	Price	Rank
Baltimore, MD	.765	5
Boston-Lawrence-Salem, MA-NH	1.031	2
Chicago-Gary-Lake County, IL-IN-WI	.452	15
Cleveland-Akron-Lorain, OH	.507	13
Dallas-Fort Worth, TX	.590	10
Detroit-Ann Arbor, MI	.503	14
Houston-Galveston-Brazoria, TX	.533	12
Los Angeles-Anaheim-Riverside, CA	.656	7

[Continued]

★1967★

Average Residential Prices of Piped (Utility) Gas, 1996, Selected Local Areas: Cost Per Therm

[Continued]

City/MSA	Price	Rank
Miami-Fort Lauderdale, FL	1.212	1
New York-Northern New Jersey-Long Island, NY-NJ-CT	.913	4
Philadelphia-Wilmington-Trenton, PA-NJ-DE-MD	.701	6
Pittsburgh-Beaver Valley, PA	.647	8
Saint Louis-East Saint Louis, MO-IL	.537	11
San Francisco-Oakland-San Jose, CA	.598	9
Washington, DC-MD-VA	.970	3

Source: U.S. Department of Labor, Bureau of Labor Statistics, CPI Detailed Report: Data for February 1996, Washington, D.C.: U.S. Government Printing Office, April 1996, p. 88.

★1968★

Cost of Living

Average Residential Prices of Piped (Utility) Gas, 1996, Selected Local Areas: Cost Per 40 Therms

The national city average price of 40 therms of piped (utility) gas for residential consumers in February 1996 was $29.645.

[In dollars per 40 therms]

City/MSA	Price	Rank
Baltimore, MD	33.010	6
Boston-Lawrence-Salem, MA-NH	44.626	2
Chicago-Gary-Lake County, IL-IN-WI	31.568	8
Cleveland-Akron-Lorain, OH	23.375	13
Dallas-Fort Worth, TX	25.872	10
Detroit-Ann Arbor, MI	24.911	11
Houston-Galveston-Brazoria, TX	23.330	14
Los Angeles-Anaheim-Riverside, CA	24.864	12
Miami-Fort Lauderdale, FL	46.781	1
New York-Northern New Jersey-Long Island, NY-NJ-CT	42.834	3
Philadelphia-Wilmington-Trenton, PA-NJ-DE-MD	32.136	7
Pittsburgh-Beaver Valley, PA	36.167	5
Saint Louis-East Saint Louis, MO-IL	31.252	9
San Francisco-Oakland-San Jose, CA	21.090	15
Washington, DC-MD-VA	36.819	4

Source: U.S. Department of Labor, Bureau of Labor Statistics, CPI Detailed Report: Data for February 1996, Washington, D.C.: U.S. Government Printing Office, April 1996, p. 87.

★1969★

Cost of Living

Average Residential Prices of Piped (Utility) Gas, 1996, Selected Local Areas: Cost Per 100 Therms

The national city average price of 100 therms of piped (utility) gas for residential consumers in February 1996 was $63.975.

[In dollars per 100 therms]

City/MSA	Price	Rank
Baltimore, MD	71.350	5
Boston-Lawrence-Salem, MA-NH	97.828	2
Chicago-Gary-Lake County, IL-IN-WI	59.468	10
Cleveland-Akron-Lorain, OH	49.785	14
Dallas-Fort Worth, TX	56.776	12
Detroit-Ann Arbor, MI	49.879	13
Houston-Galveston-Brazoria, TX	43.780	15
Los Angeles-Anaheim-Riverside, CA	65.585	8
Miami-Fort Lauderdale, FL	103.300	1
New York-Northern New Jersey-Long Island, NY-NJ-CT	88.236	3
Philadelphia-Wilmington-Trenton, PA-NJ-DE-MD	70.807	6
Pittsburgh-Beaver Valley, PA	68.239	7
Saint Louis-East Saint Louis, MO-IL	59.035	11
San Francisco-Oakland-San Jose, CA	62.149	9
Washington, DC-MD-VA	73.484	4

Source: U.S. Department of Labor, Bureau of Labor Statistics, *CPI Detailed Report: Data for February 1996*, Washington, D.C.: U.S. Government Printing Office, April 1996, p. 87.

★1970★

Cost of Living

Electricity Prices, 1995: Cost Per Kilowatt-Hour (Selected Cities)

[In cents per kilowatt-hour]

City/MSA	Cents	Rank
Alton, IL	6.6	1
Burlington, NC	4.38	5
Findlay, OH	3.15	8
Fort Wayne, IN	4.44	4
Greenville, SC	4.06	6
Holly, MI	5.41	3
Lebanon, TN	6.25	2
Shelbyville, KY	3.34	7

Source: Pluta, Rick and Jennifer Bott, "Pondering A Power Shift," *Oakland Press* (Oakland County, Michigan), 11 February 1996, p. E-1. Primary source: PHH Fantus Consulting report for the Michigan Jobs Commission.

★1971★

Cost of Living

Residential Electricity Bills (Base Rate) Summer 1993: 250 KWH (Highest)

[In dollars per month]

City	Dollars	Rank
Binghamton, NY	31.10	25
Bridgeport, CT	37.16	7
Bridgeton, NJ	32.54	18
Cedar Rapids, IA	32.45	19
Chicago, IL	36.16	10
Claremont, NH	33.52	13
Decatur, IL	36.94	9
Elkton, MD	32.21	21
Essex, NJ	31.62	22
Gary, IN	31.14	23
Hartford, CT	33.50	14
Hilo, HI	42.64	1
Honolulu, HI	33.46	15
Jackson, MS	35.63	11
Lihue, HI	40.95	3
Long Beach, NY	41.49	2
Manchester, NH	32.63	17
Middleton, NY	37.57	5
New Castle, PA	34.78	12
New York City, NY	37.27	6
Philadelphia, PA	38.71	4
Pittsburgh, PA	38.71	4
Poughkeepsie, NY	31.13	24
Rock Island, IL	32.23	20
Springfield, MA	32.99	16
Wailuku, HI	36.99	8

Source: National Association of Regulatory Utility Commissioners, *Residential Electric Bills: Summer 1993*, Washington, D.C.: National Association of Regulatory Utility Commissioners, n.p., 1994. *Note:* KWH stands for kilowatt hour.

★1972★

Cost of Living

Residential Electricity Bills (Base Rate) Summer 1993: 250 KWH (Lowest)

[In dollars per month]

City	Dollars	Rank
Amarillo, TX	14.48	15
Bellevue, WA	16.40	24
Billings, MT	12.01	4
Burlington, IA	15.39	21
Canton, OH	12.17	5
Cincinnati, OH	15.08	19
Duluth, MN	13.22	13
Franklin, NC	14.26	14
Houston, TX	12.87	10
Jefferson Parish, LA	14.52	16
Kalispell, MT	11.99	3
Las Vegas, NV	12.76	9
Lexington, KY	14.91	18
Long Beach, CA	10.58	1
Marietta, OH	10.97	2
Medford, OR	15.86	23
Miami, FL	15.46	22
Norton, VA	13.16	12

[Continued]

★1972★

Residential Electricity Bills (Base Rate) Summer 1993: 250 KWH (Lowest)

[Continued]

City	Dollars	Rank
Ontario, OR	13.12	11
Portland, OR	14.67	17
San Diego, CA	16.44	25
Sault Sainte Marie, MI	15.20	20
Shreveport, LA	15.08	19
Spokane, WA	12.55	7
Washington, DC	12.34	6
Yakima, WA	12.74	8

Source: National Association of Regulatory Utility Commissioners, *Residential Electric Bills: Summer 1993*, Washington, D.C.: National Association of Regulatory Utility Commissioners, n.p., 1994. *Note:* KWH stands for kilowatt hour.

★1973★

Cost of Living

Residential Electricity Bills (Base Rate), Summer 1993: 1,000 KWH (Highest)

[In dollars per month]

City	Dollars	Rank
Akron, OH	108.08	25
Bangor, ME	109.93	23
Bridgeport, CT	137.32	6
Bridgeton, NJ	133.86	9
Chicago, IL	117.44	15
Claremont, NH	111.92	21
Cleveland, OH	114.60	17
Decatur, IL	110.90	22
Dover Township, NJ	130.30	12
Elkton, MD	114.18	18
Essex, NJ	132.51	10
Hartford, CT	108.51	24
Hilo, HI	146.55	4
Honolulu, HI	112.82	19
Jackson, MS	112.71	20
Lihue, HI	147.34	3
Long Beach, NY	158.41	1
Manchester, NH	131.03	11
Middleton, NY	136.84	7
Moultonboro, NH	126.84	14
New York City, NY	140.77	5
Philadelphia, PA	148.83	2
Pittsburgh, PA	134.33	8
Presque Isle, ME	115.44	16
Rock Island, IL	110.90	22
Wailuku, HI	129.96	13

Source: National Association of Regulatory Utility Commissioners, *Residential Electric Bills: Summer 1993*, Washington, D.C.: National Association of Regulatory Utility Commissioners, n.p., 1994. *Note:* KWH stands for kilowatt hour.

★1974★

Cost of Living

Residential Electricity Bills (Base Rate), Summer 1993: 1,000 KWH (Lowest)

[In dollars per month]

City	Dollars	Rank
Amarillo, TX	43.96	8
Billings, MT	48.04	17
Burlington, IA	45.31	11
Canton, OH	32.89	1
Franklin, NC	37.07	2
Kalispell, MT	43.56	6
Las Vegas, NV	51.05	23
Lexington, KY	47.54	15
Long Beach, CA	42.31	4
Marietta, OH	43.88	7
Medford, OR	51.83	25
Miami, FL	47.37	14
Norton, VA	38.48	3
Ontario, OR	46.84	12
Pensacola, FL	43.25	5
Roanoke, VA	47.16	13
Saint Petersburg, FL	47.93	16
Sault Sainte Marie, MI	50.60	22
Savannah, GA	51.46	24
Shreveport, LA	48.30	18
Slidell, LA	48.80	19
Spokane, WA	44.31	9
Tampa, FL	49.80	21
Yakima, WA	44.41	10

Source: National Association of Regulatory Utility Commissioners, *Residential Electric Bills: Summer 1993*, Washington, D.C.: National Association of Regulatory Utility Commissioners, n.p., 1994. *Note:* KWH stands for kilowatt hour.

★1975★

Cost of Living

Residential Electricity Bills (Base Rate), Summer 1993: 500 KWH (Highest)

[In dollars per month]

City	Dollars	Rank
Binghamton, NY	56.30	25
Bridgeport, CT	65.82	10
Bridgeton, NJ	65.08	11
Chicago, IL	63.25	13
Claremont, NH	59.65	18
Cleveland, OH	60.38	16
Decatur, IL	61.93	15
Dover Township, NJ	58.03	22
Elkton, MD	59.53	19
Essex, NJ	63.25	13
Hartford, CT	58.51	20
Hilo, HI	77.27	2
Honolulu, HI	59.91	17
Jackson, MS	64.85	12
Lihue, HI	76.41	3
Long Beach, NY	80.46	1
Manchester, NH	66.37	9
Middleton, NY	72.39	4
Moultonboro, NH	62.74	14
New Castle, PA	57.86	23

[Continued]

★1975★

Residential Electricity Bills (Base Rate), Summer 1993: 500 KWH (Highest)
[Continued]

City	Dollars	Rank
New York City, NY	71.77	6
Philadelphia, PA	72.33	5
Pittsburgh, PA	70.56	7
Rock Island, IL	58.45	21
Springfield, MA	56.47	24
Wailuku, HI	67.98	8

Source: National Association of Regulatory Utility Commissioners, *Residential Electric Bills: Summer 1993*, Washington, D.C.: National Association of Regulatory Utility Commissioners, n.p., 1994. *Note:* KWH stands for kilowatt hour.

★1976★

Cost of Living

Residential Electricity Bills (Base Rate), Summer 1993: 500 KWH (Lowest)
[In dollars per month]

City	Dollars	Rank
Amarillo, TX	24.31	10
Bellevue, WA	28.26	24
Billings, MT	24.02	8
Burlington, IA	25.40	13
Canton, OH	24.34	11
Duluth, MN	26.83	19
Franklin, NC	22.55	6
Kalispell, MT	23.98	7
Las Vegas, NV	25.53	14
Lexington, KY	26.20	18
Long Beach, CA	21.15	1
Marietta, OH	21.94	3
Medford, OR	27.69	20
Miami, FL	25.26	12
Norton, VA	21.95	4
Ontario, OR	24.05	9
Pensacola, FL	25.66	15
Portland, OR	25.94	16
Roanoke, VA	27.21	21
Sault Sainte Marie, MI	27.00	20
Savannah, GA	28.33	25
Shreveport, LA	26.15	17
Slidell, LA	27.90	23
Spokane, WA	22.10	5
Yakima, WA	21.73	2

Source: National Association of Regulatory Utility Commissioners, *Residential Electric Bills: Summer 1993*, Washington, D.C.: National Association of Regulatory Utility Commissioners, n.p., 1994. *Note:* KWH stands for kilowatt hour.

★1977★

Cost of Living

Residential Electricity Bills (Base Rate), Summer 1993: 750 KWH (Highest)
[In dollars per month]

City	Dollars	Rank
Bangor, ME	82.45	25
Bridgeport, CT	101.57	8
Bridgeton, NJ	97.62	11
Chicago, IL	90.35	15
Claremont, NH	85.79	21
Cleveland, OH	85.95	20
Decatur, IL	86.41	18
Dover Township, NJ	92.38	14
Elkton, MD	86.86	17
Essex, NJ	97.13	12
Hartford, CT	83.51	24
Hilo, HI	111.91	2
Honolulu, HI	86.37	19
Jackson, MS	88.78	16
Lihue, HI	111.88	3
Long Beach, NY	119.44	1
Manchester, NH	100.11	9
Middleton, NY	107.21	5
Moultonboro, NH	95.16	13
New York City, NY	106.27	6
Philadelphia, PA	110.58	4
Pittsburgh, PA	102.46	7
Presque Isle, ME	83.98	23
Rock Island, IL	84.68	22
Wailuku, HI	98.97	10

Source: National Association of Regulatory Utility Commissioners, *Residential Electric Bills: Summer 1993*, Washington, D.C.: National Association of Regulatory Utility Commissioners, n.p., 1994. *Note:* KWH stands for kilowatt hour.

★1978★

Cost of Living

Residential Electricity Bills (Base Rate), Summer 1993: 750 KWH (Lowest)
[In dollars per month]

City	Dollars	Rank
Amarillo, TX	34.13	7
Billings, MT	36.03	13
Burlington, IA	35.41	11
Canton, OH	36.50	14
Franklin, NC	30.08	1
Kalispell, MT	34.33	10
Las Vegas, NV	38.29	20
Lexington, KY	36.87	15
Long Beach, CA	31.73	3
Marietta, OH	32.91	6
Medford, OR	39.76	25
Miami, FL	35.07	10
Norton, VA	30.22	2
Ontario, OR	35.45	12
Pensacola, FL	34.46	9
Portland, OR	37.60	17
Roanoke, VA	37.72	18
Saint Petersburg, FL	38.16	20
Sault Sainte Marie, MI	38.80	23

[Continued]

★ 1978 ★

Residential Electricity Bills (Base Rate), Summer 1993: 750 KWH (Lowest)
[Continued]

City	Dollars	Rank
Shreveport, LA	37.23	16
Slidell, LA	38.35	22
Spokane, WA	32.81	5
Tampa, FL	39.48	24
Yakima, WA	32.48	4

Source: National Association of Regulatory Utility Commissioners, *Residential Electric Bills: Summer 1993,* Washington, D.C.: National Association of Regulatory Utility Commissioners, n.p., 1994. *Note:* KWH stands for kilowatt hour.

★ 1979 ★
Cost of Living

Residential Electricity Bills, Summer 1993: 1,000 KWH (Highest)

[In dollars per month]

City	Dollars	Rank
Akron, OH	125.94	19
Bangor, ME	119.30	25
Bridgeport, CT	137.04	8
Bridgeton, NJ	122.90	22
Cleveland, OH	128.75	16
Dover Township, NJ	131.46	11
Fitchburg, MA	123.17	21
Hilo, HI	165.47	2
Lihue, HI	131.01	15
Long Beach, CA	131.43	12
Long Beach, NY	170.21	1
Manchester, NH	131.03	14
Middleton, NY	149.52	5
Moultonboro, NH	128.12	17
Nantucket, MA	155.62	4
New Bedford, MA	137.36	7
New York City, NY	158.24	3
Newport, RI	126.38	18
Philadelphia, PA	140.95	6
Pittsburgh, PA	132.39	9
Portland, ME	122.70	23
San Diego, CA	120.94	24
San Jose, CA	131.64	10
Toledo, OH	123.76	20
Wailuku, HI	131.30	13

Source: National Association of Regulatory Utility Commissioners, *Residential Electric Bills: Summer 1993,* Washington, D.C.: National Association of Regulatory Utility Commissioners, n.p., 1994. *Note:* KWH stands for kilowatt hour.

★ 1980 ★
Cost of Living

Residential Electricity Bills, Summer 1993: 1,000 KWH (Lowest)

[In dollars per month]

City	Dollars	Rank
Ashland, KY	50.52	9
Bellevue, WA	51.70	13
Billings, MT	51.39	12
Boise, ID	47.50	5
Burlington, IA	56.61	19
Canton, OH	51.74	14
Casper, WY	54.56	18
Cheyenne, WY	51.20	11
Duluth, MN	54.45	17
Indianapolis, IN	59.22	22
Kalispell, MT	48.56	7
Kingsport, TN	54.26	16
Las Vegas, NV	57.06	20
Lewiston, ID	46.08	3
Lexington, KY	47.72	6
Medford, OR	51.83	15
Milwaukee, WI	59.93	23
Norton, VA	50.99	10
Ontario, OR	46.84	4
Portland, OR	49.27	8
Sault Sainte Marie, MI	58.60	21
Spokane, WA	45.74	2
Superior, WI	61.10	24
Terre Haute, IN	61.41	25
Yakima, WA	44.41	1

Source: National Association of Regulatory Utility Commissioners, *Residential Electric Bills: Summer 1993,* Washington, D.C.: National Association of Regulatory Utility Commissioners, n.p., 1994. *Note:* KWH stands for kilowatt hour.

★ 1981 ★
Cost of Living

Residential Electricity Bills, Summer 1993: 250 KWH (Highest)

[In dollars per month]

City	Dollars	Rank
Binghamton, NY	33.84	23
Bridgeport, CT	37.09	10
Cambridge, MA	34.50	20
Cedar Rapids, IA	36.83	12
Chicago, IL	35.72	16
Claremont, NH	34.67	17
Cleveland, OH	33.73	24
Decatur, IL	36.73	14
Fitchburg, MA	33.23	25
Hartford, CT	34.58	19
Hilo, HI	47.63	1
Honolulu, HI	34.64	18
Keokuk, IA	33.96	21
Lihue, HI	36.86	11
Long Beach, NY	44.59	3
Middleton, NY	41.09	5
Nantucket, MA	45.08	2
New Bedford, MA	37.52	8
New Castle, PA	38.04	7

[Continued]

★1981★

Residential Electricity Bills, Summer 1993: 250 KWH (Highest)

[Continued]

City	Dollars	Rank
New York City, NY	41.82	4
Philadelphia, PA	36.74	13
Pittsburgh, PA	38.29	6
Springfield, MA	36.41	15
Toledo, OH	33.91	22
Wailuku, HI	37.33	9

Source: National Association of Regulatory Utility Commissioners, *Residential Electric Bills: Summer 1993*, Washington, D.C.: National Association of Regulatory Utility Commissioners, n.p., 1994. *Note:* KWH stands for kilowatt hour.

★1982★

Cost of Living

Residential Electricity Bills, Summer 1993: 250 KWH (Lowest)

[In dollars per month]

City	Dollars	Rank
Ashland, KY	16.73	16
Bellevue, WA	15.95	14
Billings, MT	15.36	12
Boise, ID	11.88	2
Burlington, IA	18.22	25
Casper, WY	15.03	11
Cheyenne, WY	14.43	8
Duluth, MN	13.05	5
Grand Rapids, MI	17.74	19
Houston, TX	17.94	21
Kalispell, MT	16.99	17
Las Vegas, NV	18.03	23
Lewiston, ID	10.76	1
Lexington, KY	14.96	10
Marietta, OH	18.00	22
Medford, OR	15.86	13
Norton, VA	16.28	15
Ontario, OR	13.12	7
Portland, OR	14.67	9
Salt Lake City, UT	18.10	24
Sault Sainte Marie, MI	17.20	18
Spokane, WA	12.95	4
Superior, WI	17.75	20
Washington, DC	13.07	6
Yakima, WA	12.74	3

Source: National Association of Regulatory Utility Commissioners, *Residential Electric Bills: Summer 1993*, Washington, D.C.: National Association of Regulatory Utility Commissioners, n.p., 1994. *Note:* KWH stands for kilowatt hour.

★1983★

Cost of Living

Residential Electricity Bills, Summer 1993: 500 KWH (Highest)

[In dollars per month]

City	Dollars	Rank
Binghamton, NY	61.45	25
Bridgeport, CT	65.68	13
Cedar Rapids, IA	64.65	14
Chicago, IL	62.38	21
Claremont, NH	61.86	23
Cleveland, OH	67.46	11
Decatur, IL	61.51	24
Fitchburg, MA	63.22	17
Hilo, HI	86.91	1
Honolulu, HI	62.24	22
Lihue, HI	68.24	10
Long Beach, CA	62.38	21
Long Beach, NY	86.45	2
Manchester, NH	66.37	12
Middleton, NY	79.15	5
Moultonboro, NH	63.37	16
Nantucket, MA	81.94	3
New Bedford, MA	70.81	6
New York City, NY	80.63	4
Newport, RI	63.04	19
Philadelphia, PA	68.39	9
Pittsburgh, PA	69.65	7
San Jose, CA	62.85	20
Springfield, MA	63.10	18
Toledo, OH	63.86	15
Wailuku, HI	68.66	8

Source: National Association of Regulatory Utility Commissioners, *Residential Electric Bills: Summer 1993*, Washington, D.C.: National Association of Regulatory Utility Commissioners, n.p., 1994. *Note:* KWH stands for kilowatt hour.

★1984★

Cost of Living

Residential Electricity Bills, Summer 1993: 500 KWH (Lowest)

[In dollars per month]

City	Dollars	Rank
Ashland, KY	29.22	14
Bellevue, WA	27.37	9
Biloxi, MS	34.43	25
Boise, ID	23.75	4
Burlington, IA	31.05	18
Casper, WY	30.03	15
Cheyenne, WY	28.85	12
Duluth, MN	26.50	8
Janesville, WI	34.23	23
Kalispell, MT	28.98	13
Kingsport, TN	30.72	16
Lewiston, ID	21.51	1
Lexington, KY	26.29	7
Louisville, KY	34.37	24
Marietta, OH	32.69	21
Medford, OR	27.69	10
Norton, VA	28.21	11
Ontario, OR	24.05	5

[Continued]

★1984★

Residential Electricity Bills, Summer 1993: 500 KWH (Lowest)

[Continued]

City	Dollars	Rank
Portland, OR	25.94	6
Roswell, NM	33.89	22
Sault Sainte Marie, MI	31.00	17
Spokane, WA	22.81	3
Superior, WI	32.20	20
Washington, DC	31.78	19
Yakima, WA	21.73	2

Source: National Association of Regulatory Utility Commissioners, *Residential Electric Bills: Summer 1993*, Washington, D.C.: National Association of Regulatory Utility Commissioners, n.p., 1994. *Note:* KWH stands for kilowatt hour.

★1985★
Cost of Living

Residential Electricity Bills, Summer 1993: 750 KWH (Highest)

[In dollars per month]

City	Dollars	Rank
Akron, OH	95.46	17
Bridgeport, CT	101.36	8
Bridgeton, NJ	89.98	23
Cedar Rapids, IA	90.43	22
Cleveland, OH	96.56	15
Dover Township, NJ	93.82	19
Fitchburg, MA	93.19	21
Hilo, HI	126.18	2
Honolulu, HI	89.83	25
Lihue, HI	99.63	12
Long Beach, CA	97.48	13
Long Beach, NY	128.34	1
Manchester, NH	100.11	10
Middleton, NY	117.19	5
Moultonboro, NH	96.12	16
Nantucket, MA	118.78	4
New Bedford, MA	104.09	7
New York City, NY	119.44	3
Newport, RI	94.72	18
Pawtucket, RI	89.92	24
Philadelphia, PA	104.67	6
Pittsburgh, PA	101.03	9
San Jose, CA	97.24	14
Toledo, OH	93.81	20
Wailuku, HI	99.97	11

Source: National Association of Regulatory Utility Commissioners, *Residential Electric Bills: Summer 1993*, Washington, D.C.: National Association of Regulatory Utility Commissioners, n.p., 1994. *Note:* KWH stands for kilowatt hour.

★1986★
Cost of Living

Residential Electricity Bills, Summer 1993: 750 KWH (Lowest)

[In dollars per month]

City	Dollars	Rank
Ashland, KY	39.86	13
Bellevue, WA	39.34	9
Billings, MT	39.38	10
Biloxi, MS	48.78	23
Boise, ID	35.63	5
Burlington, IA	43.89	17
Casper, WY	41.93	15
Cheyenne, WY	39.60	11
Duluth, MN	41.13	14
Fort Wayne, IN	49.22	24
Janesville, WI	49.60	25
Kalispell, MT	39.33	8
Kingsport, TN	42.49	16
Las Vegas, NV	44.05	18
Lewiston, ID	33.41	2
Lexington, KY	37.01	6
Marietta, OH	47.39	21
Medford, OR	39.76	12
Ontario, OR	35.45	4
Portland, OR	37.60	7
Roswell, NM	48.34	22
Sault Sainte Marie, MI	44.80	19
Spokane, WA	33.87	3
Superior, WI	46.65	20
Yakima, WA	32.48	1

Source: National Association of Regulatory Utility Commissioners, *Residential Electric Bills: Summer 1993*, Washington, D.C.: National Association of Regulatory Utility Commissioners, n.p., 1994. *Note:* KWH stands for kilowatt hour.

★1987★
Cost of Living

Residential Gas Bills, Non-Space Heating Usage, Winter 1993: 50 Therms (Highest)

[In dollars per month]

City	Dollars	Rank
Allentown, PA	42.43	23
Barnstable, MA	76.21	2
Bridgeport, CT	55.91	8
Brooklyn, NY	56.40	6
Erie, PA	42.82	21
Fairfax County, VA	41.64	24
Fall River, MA	43.33	18
Grafton, WV	49.39	11
Hartford, CT	48.71	12
Haverhill, MA	61.15	5
Hempstead, NY	46.14	15
Honolulu, HI	78.80	1
Lowell, MA	62.91	4
Manchester, NH	41.39	25
New York City, NY	47.22	13
Pittsfield, MA	71.84	3
Portland, ME	50.13	10
Portsmouth, NH	42.78	22
Portsmouth, VA	43.30	19

[Continued]

★1987★

Residential Gas Bills, Non-Space Heating Usage, Winter 1993: 50 Therms (Highest)

[Continued]

City	Dollars	Rank
Poughkeepsie, NY	44.04	16
Providence, RI	43.70	17
Silver Spring, MD	42.90	20
Springfield, MA	47.00	14
Waterbury, CT	52.41	9
Worcester, MA	56.00	7

Source: National Association of Regulatory Utility Commissioners, *Residential Gas Bills: Winter 1993-94,* Washington, D.C.: National Association of Regulatory Utility Commissioners, n.p., 1994.

★1988★

Cost of Living

Residential Gas Bills, Non-Space Heating Usage, Winter 1993: 50 Therms (Lowest)

[In dollars per month]

City	Dollars	Rank
Alton, IL	11.91	158
Ames, IA	12.23	155
Baton Rouge, LA	9.09	170
Battle Creek, MI	11.93	157
Burlington, IA	10.16	167
Cleveland, OH	11.28	163
Dayton, OH	11.80	159
El Paso, TX	8.79	172
Flint, MI	12.62	151
Garden City, KS	11.55	161
Gulfport-Biloxi, MS	12.44	154
Holland, MI	11.18	164
Jefferson City, MO	11.59	160
Lawton, OK	12.07	156
Lima, OH	11.91	158
Louisville, KY	10.03	168
Monroe, MI	12.54	153
Montrose, CO	9.59	169
Owensboro, KY	9.06	171
Port Huron, MI	12.74	150
Rock Island, IL	11.29	162
Rockford, IL	11.02	165
Salt Lake City, UT	4.37	173
Texarkana, TX	12.50	152
Yuma, CO	10.80	166

Source: National Association of Regulatory Utility Commissioners, *Residential Gas Bills: Winter 1993-94,* Washington, D.C.: National Association of Regulatory Utility Commissioners, n.p., 1994.

★1989★

Cost of Living

Residential Gas Bills, Non-Space-Heating Usage, Winter 1993: 10 Therms (Highest)

[In dollars per month]

City	Dollars	Rank
Barnstable, MA	22.16	2
Bridgeport, CT	17.78	8
Brooklyn, NY	17.23	10
Buffalo, NY	14.67	19
Erie, PA	17.81	7
Fairfax County, VA	14.14	22
Grafton, WV	15.09	16
Hartford, CT	15.94	14
Haverhill, MA	20.06	4
Hempstead, NY	16.02	13
Honolulu, HI	20.56	3
Lake Charles, LA	14.90	18
Lowell, MA	18.00	6
Muncie, IN	14.08	23
New York City, NY	16.39	11
Parkersburg, WV	13.84	25
Pittsfield, MA	23.32	1
Portsmouth, NH	14.36	21
Portsmouth, VA	15.90	15
Providence, RI	14.45	20
Silver Spring, MD	15.08	17
Springfield, MA	16.35	12
Waterbury, CT	17.48	9
Winchester, IN	13.98	24
Worcester, MA	18.13	5

Source: National Association of Regulatory Utility Commissioners, *Residential Gas Bills: Winter 1993-94,* Washington, D.C.: National Association of Regulatory Utility Commissioners, n.p., 1994.

★1990★

Cost of Living

Residential Gas Bills, Non-Space-Heating Usage, Winter 1993: 10 Therms (Highest)

[In dollars per month]

City	Dollars	Rank
Barnstable, MA	22.32	3
Boston, MA	17.85	11
Bridgeport, CT	17.85	11
Buffalo, NY	17.12	13
Chicago, IL	14.97	24
Erie, PA	17.81	12
Grafton, WV	15.09	22
Hartford, CT	15.98	15
Haverhill, MA	20.79	4
Hempstead, NY	18.31	8
Honolulu, HI	22.38	2
Lowell, MA	18.47	7
Muncie, IN	15.41	19
New York City, NY	17.96	9
Norfolk, VA	15.30	20
Panama City, FL	14.73	25
Pittsburgh, PA	15.25	21
Pittsfield, MA	23.94	1
Portsmouth, NH	15.07	23

[Continued]

★1990★

Residential Gas Bills, Non-Space-Heating Usage, Winter 1993: 10 Therms (Highest)

[Continued]

City	Dollars	Rank
Portsmouth, VA	15.79	16
Poughkeepsie, NY	15.54	18
Providence, RI	15.58	17
Springfield, MA	17.01	14
Waterbury, CT	17.91	10
Worcester, MA	18.87	6

Source: National Association of Regulatory Utility Commissioners, *Residential Gas Bills: Winter 1993-94,* Washington, D.C.: National Association of Regulatory Utility Commissioners, n.p., 1994.

★1991★

Cost of Living

Residential Gas Bills, Non-Space-Heating Usage, Winter 1993: 10 Therms (Lowest)

[In dollars per month]

City	Dollars	Rank
Auburn, IN	4.85	158
Baton Rouge, LA	4.95	156
Battle Creek, MI	6.59	144
Bellingham, WA	6.51	145
Casper, WY	4.43	159
Cheyenne, WY	3.14	165
Cleveland, OH	5.68	150
Dayton, OH	5.56	152
Eau Claire, WI	6.21	147
El Paso, TX	5.76	149
Lawton, OK	6.63	143
Lima, OH	5.89	148
Louisville, KY	5.59	151
Montrose, CO	5.13	155
Owensboro, KY	5.29	154
Rock Springs, WY	4.23	162
Rockford, IL	5.40	153
Salt Lake City, UT	4.37	160
San Diego, CA	3.97	163
San Jose, CA	3.59	164
Seattle, WA	6.65	142
Sheridan, WY	4.30	161
Sioux Falls, SD	6.40	146
Spokane, WA	6.69	141
Yuma, CO	4.88	157

Source: National Association of Regulatory Utility Commissioners, *Residential Gas Bills: Winter 1993-94,* Washington, D.C.: National Association of Regulatory Utility Commissioners, n.p., 1994.

★1992★

Cost of Living

Residential Gas Bills, Non-Space-Heating Usage, Winter 1993: 10 Therms (Lowest)

[In dollars per month]

City	Dollars	Rank
Aberdeen, SD	7.14	166
Amarillo, TX	8.53	154
Anchorage, AK	7.88	162
Baton Rouge, LA	8.16	159
Bellingham, WA	6.60	169
Casper, WY	4.43	173
Cheyenne, WY	3.14	176
Cincinnati, OH	11.41	92
Coeur d'Alene, ID	8.27	157
El Paso, TX	8.09	161
Fargo, ND	4.91	172
Great Falls, MT	7.66	164
Jackson, MS	8.14	160
Lawrence, KS	8.67	152
Los Angeles, CA	8.38	156
Louisville, KY	8.41	155
Missoula, MT	8.26	158
Owensboro, KY	8.56	153
Rock Springs, WY	4.23	175
San Diego, CA	6.09	170
San Jose, CA	5.26	171
Seattle, WA	7.03	167
Sheridan, WY	4.30	174
Sioux Falls, SD	6.79	168
Spokane, WA	7.47	165
Yuma, CO	7.86	163

Source: National Association of Regulatory Utility Commissioners, *Residential Gas Bills: Winter 1993-94,* Washington, D.C.: National Association of Regulatory Utility Commissioners, n.p., 1994.

★1993★

Cost of Living

Residential Gas Bills, Non-Space-Heating Usage, Winter 1993: 30 Therms (Highest)

[In dollars per month]

City	Dollars	Rank
Allentown, PA	27.98	24
Barnstable, MA	51.57	1
Bridgeport, CT	36.85	8
Brooklyn, NY	37.22	7
Erie, PA	30.06	16
Fairfax County, VA	29.61	17
Fall River, MA	28.53	22
Grafton, WV	32.24	11
Hartford, CT	32.33	10
Haverhill, MA	42.15	5
Hempstead, NY	31.08	14
Honolulu, HI	49.68	2
Lowell, MA	42.41	4
Manchester, NH	27.52	25
New York City, NY	31.80	13
Pittsfield, MA	47.86	3
Portland, ME	30.82	15
Portsmouth, NH	28.72	21

[Continued]

★1993★

Residential Gas Bills, Non-Space-Heating Usage, Winter 1993: 30 Therms (Highest)
[Continued]

City	Dollars	Rank
Portsmouth, VA	29.60	18
Poughkeepsie, NY	28.26	23
Providence, RI	29.33	19
Silver Spring, MD	29.23	20
Springfield, MA	31.94	12
Waterbury, CT	34.94	9
Worcester, MA	38.37	6

Source: National Association of Regulatory Utility Commissioners, *Residential Gas Bills: Winter 1993-94,* Washington, D.C.: National Association of Regulatory Utility Commissioners, n.p., 1994.

★1994★
Cost of Living

Residential Gas Bills, Non-Space-Heating Usage, Winter 1993: 30 Therms (Highest)
[In dollars per month]

City	Dollars	Rank
Barnstable, MA	52.07	3
Boston, MA	35.25	13
Bridgeport, CT	37.06	9
Brooklyn, NY	41.82	7
Buffalo, NY	31.64	19
Erie, PA	30.06	22
Grafton, WV	32.24	18
Hartford, CT	32.44	17
Haverhill, MA	44.43	5
Hempstead, NY	36.67	10
Honolulu, HI	55.14	2
Lowell, MA	43.81	6
New York City, NY	35.05	14
Norfolk, VA	29.91	24
Panama City, FL	30.20	21
Pittsfield, MA	49.73	4
Portsmouth, NH	30.85	20
Portsmouth, VA	29.26	25
Poughkeepsie, NY	36.59	11
Providence, RI	32.73	16
Raleigh-Durham, NC	62.04	1
Springfield, MA	33.92	15
Waterbury, CT	36.23	12
Wellsboro, PA	29.94	23
Worcester, MA	40.58	8

Source: National Association of Regulatory Utility Commissioners, *Residential Gas Bills: Winter 1993-94,* Washington, D.C.: National Association of Regulatory Utility Commissioners, n.p., 1994.

★1995★
Cost of Living

Residential Gas Bills, Non-Space-Heating Usage, Winter 1993: 30 Therms (Lowest)
[In dollars per month]

City	Dollars	Rank
Alton, IL	9.86	152
Ames, IA	10.40	149
Baton Rouge, LA	6.33	171
Battle Creek, MI	9.26	159
Burlington, IA	8.69	162
Cheyenne, WY	9.42	156
Cleveland, OH	8.48	164
Dayton, OH	8.68	163
El Paso, TX	7.27	169
Flint, MI	10.17	150
Garden City, KS	9.33	158
Gulfport-Biloxi, MS	10.54	147
Holland, MI	9.51	155
Jefferson City, MO	9.39	157
Lawton, OK	9.85	153
Lima, OH	8.90	161
Louisville, KY	7.81	167
Monroe, MI	10.42	148
Montrose, CO	7.36	168
Owensboro, KY	7.18	170
Port Huron, MI	10.15	151
Rock Island, IL	9.17	160
Rockford, IL	8.21	165
Texarkana, TX	9.65	154
Yuma, CO	7.84	166

Source: National Association of Regulatory Utility Commissioners, *Residential Gas Bills: Winter 1993-94,* Washington, D.C.: National Association of Regulatory Utility Commissioners, n.p., 1994.

★1996★
Cost of Living

Residential Gas Bills, Non-Space-Heating Usage, Winter 1993: 30 Therms (Lowest)
[In dollars per month]

City	Dollars	Rank
Aberdeen, SD	16.91	164
Amarillo, TX	15.30	175
Anchorage, AK	14.61	178
Baton Rouge, LA	15.96	171
Bellingham, WA	16.63	166
Casper, WY	13.30	180
Cheyenne, WY	9.42	183
El Paso, TX	14.26	179
Evansville, IN	17.00	162
Fargo, ND	14.73	177
Fayetteville, AR	17.63	160
Fort Smith, AR	17.09	161
Garden City, KS	15.54	174
Great Falls, MT	14.98	176
Lawrence, KS	17.71	159
Louisville, KY	16.27	169
Missoula, MT	16.37	168
Owensboro, KY	16.98	163
Prairie Du Chien, WI	16.42	167

[Continued]

★ 1996 ★

Residential Gas Bills, Non-Space-Heating Usage, Winter 1993: 30 Therms (Lowest)
[Continued]

City	Dollars	Rank
Rock Springs, WY	12.70	182
San Jose, CA	15.79	172
Sheridan, WY	12.90	181
Sioux Falls, SD	16.18	170
Spokane, WA	15.57	173
Yuma, CO	16.82	165

Source: National Association of Regulatory Utility Commissioners, *Residential Gas Bills: Winter 1993-94,* Washington, D.C.: National Association of Regulatory Utility Commissioners, n.p., 1994.

★ 1997 ★
Cost of Living

Residential Gas Bills, Non-Space-Heating Usage, Winter 1993: 50 Therms (Highest)
[In dollars per month]

City	Dollars	Rank
Barnstable, MA	77.03	2
Boston, MA	48.71	16
Bridgeport, CT	56.27	9
Brooklyn, NY	63.61	6
Buffalo, NY	46.17	18
Fitchburg, MA	43.91	24
Grafton, WV	49.39	14
Hartford, CT	48.90	15
Haverhill, MA	64.81	5
Hempstead, NY	55.03	10
Honolulu, HI	87.90	1
Lowell, MA	65.25	4
Manchester, NH	44.17	21
Marietta, OH	35.44	65
New York City, NY	52.16	12
Norfolk, VA	44.14	22
Panama City, FL	45.66	20
Pawtucket, RI	42.93	25
Pittsfield, MA	74.95	3
Portland, ME	43.97	23
Portsmouth, NH	46.33	17
Poughkeepsie, NY	57.64	8
Springfield, MA	50.30	13
Syracuse, NY	42.93	25
Waterbury, CT	54.56	11
Wellsboro, PA	45.86	19
Worcester, MA	59.68	7

Source: National Association of Regulatory Utility Commissioners, *Residential Gas Bills: Winter 1993-94,* Washington, D.C.: National Association of Regulatory Utility Commissioners, n.p., 1994.

★ 1998 ★
Cost of Living

Residential Gas Bills, Non-Space-Heating Usage, Winter 1993: 50 Therms (Lowest)
[In dollars per month]

City	Dollars	Rank
Barnstable, MA	77.03	2
Boston, MA	48.71	16
Bridgeport, CT	56.27	9
Brooklyn, NY	63.61	6
Buffalo, NY	46.17	18
Fitchburg, MA	43.91	24
Grafton, WV	49.39	14
Hartford, CT	48.90	15
Haverhill, MA	64.81	5
Hempstead, NY	55.03	10
Honolulu, HI	87.90	1
Lowell, MA	65.25	4
Manchester, NH	44.17	21
New York City, NY	52.16	12
Norfolk, VA	44.14	22
Panama City, FL	45.66	20
Pawtucket, RI	42.93	25
Pittsfield, MA	74.95	3
Portland, ME	43.97	23
Portsmouth, NH	46.33	17
Poughkeepsie, NY	57.64	8
Springfield, MA	50.30	13
Syracuse, NY	42.93	25
Waterbury, CT	54.56	11
Wellsboro, PA	45.86	19
Worcester, MA	59.68	7

Source: National Association of Regulatory Utility Commissioners, *Residential Gas Bills: Winter 1993-94,* Washington, D.C.: National Association of Regulatory Utility Commissioners, n.p., 1994.

★ 1999 ★
Cost of Living

Residential Gas Bills, Space-Heating Usage, Winter 1993: 100 Therms (Highest)
[In dollars per month]

City	Dollars	Rank
Barnstable, MA	108.27	2
Bridgeport, CT	103.57	5
Brooklyn, NY	91.55	11
Erie, PA	71.38	25
Fairfax County, VA	76.32	21
Fall River, MA	80.58	17
Fitchburg, MA	73.23	24
Grafton, WV	92.26	9
Hartford, CT	89.67	13
Haverhill, MA	100.16	6
Hempstead, NY	81.11	16
Honolulu, HI	151.60	1
Lowell, MA	106.85	3
Manchester, NH	81.24	15
New York City, NY	77.69	19
Pittsfield, MA	104.27	4
Portland, ME	91.57	10
Portsmouth, NH	80.12	18

[Continued]

★ 1999 ★

Residential Gas Bills, Space-Heating Usage, Winter 1993: 100 Therms (Highest)
[Continued]

City	Dollars	Rank
Portsmouth, VA	77.55	20
Poughkeepsie, NY	74.83	22
Providence, RI	82.88	14
Silver Spring, MD	73.47	23
Springfield, MA	99.71	7
Waterbury, CT	96.06	8
Worcester, MA	91.02	12

Source: National Association of Regulatory Utility Commissioners, *Residential Gas Bills: Winter 1993-94,* Washington, D.C.: National Association of Regulatory Utility Commissioners, n.p., 1994.

★ 2000 ★
Cost of Living

Residential Gas Bills, Space-Heating Usage, Winter 1993: 100 Therms (Highest)

[In dollars per month]

City	Dollars	Rank
Allentown, PA	152.35	3
Barnstable, MA	109.92	7
Boston, MA	94.19	20
Bridgeport, CT	104.29	11
Brooklyn, NY	100.32	16
Butler, PA	107.62	8
Grafton, WV	92.26	21
Hartford, CT	90.04	22
Haverhill, MA	107.47	9
Hempstead, NY	98.04	18
Honolulu, HI	169.80	1
Lowell, MA	101.53	13
Manchester, NH	86.79	24
Montrose, CO	104.25	12
New York City, NY	86.14	25
Pittsburgh, PA	124.88	5
Pittsfield, MA	110.49	6
Portsmouth, NH	87.22	23
Poughkeepsie, NY	100.80	14
Providence, RI	94.22	19
Scranton, PA	154.57	2
Springfield, MA	106.30	10
Waterbury, CT	100.36	15
Wellsboro, PA	140.78	4
Worcester, MA	98.39	17

Source: National Association of Regulatory Utility Commissioners, *Residential Gas Bills: Winter 1993-94,* Washington, D.C.: National Association of Regulatory Utility Commissioners, n.p., 1994.

★ 2001 ★
Cost of Living

Residential Gas Bills, Space-Heating Usage, Winter 1993: 100 Therms (Lowest)

[In dollars per month]

City	Dollars	Rank
Alton, IL	17.01	152
Ames, IA	16.81	153
Baton Rouge, LA	15.98	155
Battle Creek, MI	18.61	144
Burlington, IA	13.81	159
Cedar Rapids, IA	17.20	148
Cleveland, OH	18.28	146
Council Bluffs, IA	18.48	145
Dayton, OH	19.60	140
El Paso, TX	12.57	162
Flint, MI	18.74	143
Garden City, KS	17.10	150
Great Falls, MT	3.40	164
Gulfport-Biloxi, MS	17.19	149
Holland, MI	15.36	158
Jefferson City, MO	17.08	151
Kansas City, MO	16.55	154
Lima, OH	19.45	141
Louisville, KY	15.58	157
Monroe, MI	17.82	147
Owensboro, KY	13.77	160
Port Huron, MI	19.23	142
Rock Island, IL	15.60	156
Rockford, IL	13.76	161
Salt Lake City, UT	4.37	163

Source: National Association of Regulatory Utility Commissioners, *Residential Gas Bills: Winter 1993-94,* Washington, D.C.: National Association of Regulatory Utility Commissioners, n.p., 1994.

★ 2002 ★
Cost of Living

Residential Gas Bills, Space-Heating Usage, Winter 1993: 100 Therms (Lowest)

[In dollars per month]

City	Dollars	Rank
Aberdeen, SD	46.08	174
Amarillo, TX	38.62	186
Anchorage, AK	38.18	187
Baton Rouge, LA	48.09	168
Casper, WY	44.30	179
Cheyenne, WY	31.41	191
Connersville, IN	44.73	178
El Paso, TX	35.87	189
Evansville, IN	43.54	182
Fargo, ND	45.60	175
Fayetteville, AR	47.24	172
Flint, MI	45.54	176
Fort Smith, AR	42.37	184
Garden City, KS	37.80	188
Great Falls, MT	34.00	190
Jefferson City, MO	47.85	170
Louisville, KY	43.81	181
Missoula, MT	44.74	177
Monroe, MI	47.65	171

[Continued]

★2002★

Residential Gas Bills, Space-Heating Usage, Winter 1993: 100 Therms (Lowest)

[Continued]

City	Dollars	Rank
Owensboro, KY	46.43	173
Rock Springs, WY	42.34	185
Rockford, IL	48.08	169
Sheridan, WY	42.99	183
Spokane, WA	43.93	180
Sullivan, IN	47.85	170

Source: National Association of Regulatory Utility Commissioners, *Residential Gas Bills: Winter 1993-94,* Washington, D.C.: National Association of Regulatory Utility Commissioners, n.p., 1994.

★2003★

Cost of Living

Residential Gas Bills, Space-Heating Usage, Winter 1993: Typical Bill (Highest)

[In dollars per month]

City	Dollars	Rank
Allentown, PA	152.35	18
Barnstable, MA	157.93	16
Bridgeport, CT	234.06	2
Brooklyn, NY	203.29	6
Clarkstown, NY	144.88	25
Dover, NJ	151.50	20
Elizabeth, NJ	153.12	17
Erie, PA	151.57	19
Fergus Falls, MN	148.98	21
Fitchburg, MA	148.40	22
Hartford, CT	215.83	4
Haverhill, MA	197.16	8
Hempstead, NY	205.58	5
Lowell, MA	200.59	7
New York City, NY	256.60	1
Newark, NJ	165.57	12
Pittsfield, MA	219.21	3
Portland, ME	162.84	13
Portsmouth, NH	145.13	24
Providence, RI	159.01	15
Rochester, NY	148.31	23
Springfield, MA	178.89	11
Syracuse, NY	160.35	14
Waterbury, CT	186.81	10
Worcester, MA	191.29	9

Source: National Association of Regulatory Utility Commissioners, *Residential Gas Bills: Winter 1993-94,* Washington, D.C.: National Association of Regulatory Utility Commissioners, n.p., 1994.

★2004★

Cost of Living

Residential Gas Bills, Space-Heating Usage, Winter 1993: Typical Bill (Highest)

[In dollars per month]

City	Dollars	Rank
Barnstable, MA	160.49	21
Boston, MA	220.81	6
Bridgeport, CT	235.77	3
Brooklyn, NY	223.36	5
Buffalo, NY	172.36	17
Clarkstown, NY	186.50	13
Dover, NJ	153.16	24
Elizabeth, NJ	153.07	25
Fitchburg, MA	167.99	20
Hartford, CT	216.77	7
Haverhill, MA	213.83	8
Hempstead, NY	251.17	2
Lowell, MA	210.65	9
New York City, NY	284.99	1
Pittsfield, MA	233.52	4
Portsmouth, NH	154.02	23
Providence, RI	184.18	14
Rochester, NY	173.78	16
Scranton, PA	154.57	22
Springfield, MA	193.92	12
Syracuse, NY	169.66	18
Washington, DC	177.50	15
Waterbury, CT	195.58	11
Waukegan, IL	168.06	19
Worcester, MA	209.27	10

Source: National Association of Regulatory Utility Commissioners, *Residential Gas Bills: Winter 1993-94,* Washington, D.C.: National Association of Regulatory Utility Commissioners, n.p., 1994.

★2005★

Cost of Living

Residential Gas Bills, Space-Heating Usage, Winter 1993: Typical Bill (Lowest)

[In dollars per month]

City	Dollars	Rank
Albuquerque, NM	38.69	188
Baton Rouge, LA	38.91	187
Bellingham, WA	58.47	170
Brownsville, TX	35.05	189
Chattanooga, TN	47.13	179
El Paso, TX	42.04	185
Fayetteville, AR	60.04	169
Flagstaff, AZ	54.08	175
Great Falls, MT	47.60	178
Gulfport-Biloxi, MS	45.56	180
Honolulu, HI	32.86	190
Houston, TX	57.83	171
Lafayette, LA	51.63	177
Lake Charles, LA	45.26	181
Las Vegas, NV	57.70	172
Los Angeles, CA	44.49	184
Metairie, LA	44.51	183
Miami, FL	23.55	193
Panama City, FL	54.17	173

[Continued]

★ 2005 ★

Residential Gas Bills, Space-Heating Usage, Winter 1993: Typical Bill (Lowest)

[Continued]

City	Dollars	Rank
Phoenix, AZ	53.84	176
San Diego, CA	39.30	186
San Jose, CA	45.07	182
Tampa, FL	29.09	192
Tucson, AZ	54.09	174
West Palm Beach, FL	29.60	191

Source: National Association of Regulatory Utility Commissioners, *Residential Gas Bills: Winter 1993-94*, Washington, D.C.: National Association of Regulatory Utility Commissioners, n.p., 1994.

★ 2006 ★

Cost of Living

Residential Gas Bills, Space-Heating Usage, Winter 1993: Typical Bill (Lowest)

[In dollars per month]

City	Dollars	Rank
Albuquerque, NM	19.31	167
Ames, IA	24.33	157
Baton Rouge, LA	13.22	172
Brownsville, TX	23.01	160
Burlington, IA	24.04	158
Cedar Rapids, IA	26.08	152
Columbus, GA	25.91	153
El Paso, TX	14.08	171
Great Falls, MT	3.40	173
Gulfport-Biloxi, MS	15.86	169
Holland, MI	23.29	159
Jefferson City, MO	24.88	155
Kansas City, MO	24.64	156
Lawton, OK	20.87	164
Louisville, KY	26.68	151
Metairie, LA	21.89	162
Miami, FL	14.97	170
Montrose, CO	22.80	161
Owensboro, KY	21.31	163
Rock Island, IL	25.16	154
Rockford, IL	20.66	165
San Diego, CA	26.78	150
Tampa, FL	20.16	166
Texarkana, TX	23.29	159
West Palm Beach, FL	18.34	168

Source: National Association of Regulatory Utility Commissioners, *Residential Gas Bills: Winter 1993-94*, Washington, D.C.: National Association of Regulatory Utility Commissioners, n.p., 1994.

★ 2007 ★

Cost of Living

Water Prices, 1994: Most Expensive Cities

Data refer to costs to industrial users.

[In dollars per month]

City	Cost	Rank
Nashville, TN	1,819.98	1
Newport, NH	1,748.39	2
San Francisco, CA	1,730.34	3
Boston, MA	1,650.82	4
Burlington, VT	1,636.31	5
Houston, TX	1,372.44	6
Seattle, WA	1,224.78	7
Los Angeles, CA	1,183.97	8
Portland, ME	1,151.81	9
Charleston, SC	1,093.05	10

Source: "The Cost of Industrial Water Use," *Water Environment & Technology*, (January 1995), p. 13.

★ 2008 ★

Fortune 500 Companies

Fortune 500 Company Headquarters, 1995: Cities With Seven or More

City	Total	Rank
New York, NY	47	1
Chicago, IL	17	2
Houston, TX	17	2
Atlanta, GA	11	3
Philadelphia, PA	10	4
San Francisco, CA	10	4
Saint Louis, MO	9	5
Pittsburgh, PA	8	6
Cleveland, OH	7	7
Dallas, TX	7	7
Minneapolis, MN	7	7
Richmond, VA	7	7
Stamford, CT	7	7

Source: "Top Cities," *Fortune*, 29 April 1996, F-31.

★ 2009 ★

Imports and Exports: Sales

Export Sales Changes Since 1993, By Industry Group: Apparel (Dollars)

[In dollars]

City	Dollars	Rank
Chicago, IL	-14,357,090	9
Detroit, MI	35,111,296	2
Houston, TX	168,181	5
Los Angeles-Long Beach, CA	59,770,687	1
Miami, FL	23,300,051	3
Minneapolis-Saint Paul, MN-WI	-4,403,491	7
New York, NY	-4,855,986	8
San Francisco, CA	-45,243,986	10

[Continued]

★2009★

Export Sales Changes Since 1993, By Industry Group: Apparel (Dollars)

[Continued]

City	Dollars	Rank
San Jose, CA	998,300	4
Seattle-Bellevue-Everett, WA	36,801	6

Source: U.S. Department of Commerce, International Trade Administration, *Metropolitan Area Exports: An Export Performance Report on Over 250 U.S. Cities,* Washington, D.C.: U.S. Government Printing Office, April 1996, p. 64. Primary source: Exporter Location Series, Census Bureau.

★2010★

Imports and Exports: Sales

Export Sales Changes Since 1993, By Industry Group: Apparel (Percent)

[In percent]

City	Percent	Rank
Chicago, IL	-19.6	10
Detroit, MI	73.2	1
Houston, TX	1.3	5
Los Angeles-Long Beach, CA	10.7	3
Miami, FL	6.4	4
Minneapolis-Saint Paul, MN-WI	-17.0	9
New York, NY	-0.9	7
San Francisco, CA	-14.5	8
San Jose, CA	26.4	2
Seattle-Bellevue-Everett, WA	0.1	6

Source: U.S. Department of Commerce, International Trade Administration, *Metropolitan Area Exports: An Export Performance Report on Over 250 U.S. Cities,* Washington, D.C.: U.S. Government Printing Office, April 1996, p. 64. Primary source: Exporter Location Series, Census Bureau.

★2011★

Imports and Exports: Sales

Export Sales Changes Since 1993, By Industry Group: Lumber and Wood Products (Dollars)

[In dollars]

City	Dollars	Rank
Chicago, IL	-6,089,877	8
Detroit, MI	-1,058,366	5
Houston, TX	-15,228,717	10
Los Angeles-Long Beach, CA	13,790,010	1
Miami, FL	7,368,855	3
Minneapolis-Saint Paul, MN-WI	-617,841	4
New York, NY	-2,600,397	7
San Francisco, CA	13,709,621	2
San Jose, CA	-1,647,905	6
Seattle-Bellevue-Everett, WA	-13,107,879	9

Source: U.S. Department of Commerce, International Trade Administration, *Metropolitan Area Exports: An Export Performance Report on Over 250 U.S. Cities,* Washington, D.C.: U.S. Government Printing Office, April 1996, p. 64. Primary source: Exporter Location Series, Census Bureau.

★2012★

Imports and Exports: Sales

Export Sales Changes Since 1993, By Industry Group: Lumber and Wood Products (Percent)

[In percent]

City	Percent	Rank
Chicago, IL	-20.6	8
Detroit, MI	-5.2	6
Houston, TX	-21.1	9
Los Angeles-Long Beach, CA	17.3	2
Miami, FL	8.5	3
Minneapolis-Saint Paul, MN-WI	-5.4	7
New York, NY	-2.5	5
San Francisco, CA	89.8	1
San Jose, CA	-29.7	10
Seattle-Bellevue-Everett, WA	-0.6	4

Source: U.S. Department of Commerce, International Trade Administration, *Metropolitan Area Exports: An Export Performance Report on Over 250 U.S. Cities,* Washington, D.C.: U.S. Government Printing Office, April 1996, p. 64. Primary source: Exporter Location Series, Census Bureau.

★2013★

Imports and Exports: Sales

Export Sales Changes Since 1993, By Industry Group: Non-Manufactured Commodities (Dollars)

[In dollars]

City	Dollars	Rank
Chicago, IL	317,448,004	1
Detroit, MI	57,553,900	5
Houston, TX	68,926,372	4
Los Angeles-Long Beach, CA	74,808,193	3
Miami, FL	152,472,541	2
Minneapolis-Saint Paul, MN-WI	-90,159,557	9
New York, NY	-646,324,221	10
San Francisco, CA	-25,442,056	8
San Jose, CA	22,989,029	7
Seattle-Bellevue-Everett, WA	44,307,762	6

Source: U.S. Department of Commerce, International Trade Administration, *Metropolitan Area Exports: An Export Performance Report on Over 250 U.S. Cities,* Washington, D.C.: U.S. Government Printing Office, April 1996, p. 64. Primary source: Exporter Location Series, Census Bureau.

★2014★

Imports and Exports: Sales

Export Sales Changes Since 1993, By Industry Group: Non-Manufactured Commodities (Percent)

[In percent]

City	Percent	Rank
Chicago, IL	28.4	1
Detroit, MI	19.8	3
Houston, TX	19.1	4
Los Angeles-Long Beach, CA	4.6	6
Miami, FL	28.1	2
Minneapolis-Saint Paul, MN-WI	-3.2	8
New York, NY	-12.5	10

[Continued]

★2014★

Export Sales Changes Since 1993, By Industry Group: Non-Manufactured Commodities (Percent)
[Continued]

City	Percent	Rank
San Francisco, CA	-4.6	9
San Jose, CA	10.9	5
Seattle-Bellevue-Everett, WA	2.2	7

Source: U.S. Department of Commerce, International Trade Administration, *Metropolitan Area Exports: An Export Performance Report on Over 250 U.S. Cities,* Washington, D.C.: U.S. Government Printing Office, April 1996, p. 64. Primary source: Exporter Location Series, Census Bureau.

★2015★
Imports and Exports: Sales

Export Sales Changes Since 1993, By Industry Group: Textile Mill Products (Dollars)
[In dollars]

City	Dollars	Rank
Chicago, IL	7,210,546	3
Detroit, MI	2,271,398	5
Houston, TX	2,195,198	7
Los Angeles-Long Beach, CA	16,464,015	2
Miami, FL	1,926,745	8
Minneapolis-Saint Paul, MN-WI	-9,991,004	9
New York, NY	-17,470,582	10
San Francisco, CA	29,883,380	1
San Jose, CA	2,262,327	6
Seattle-Bellevue-Everett, WA	2,448,182	4

Source: U.S. Department of Commerce, International Trade Administration, *Metropolitan Area Exports: An Export Performance Report on Over 250 U.S. Cities,* Washington, D.C.: U.S. Government Printing Office, April 1996, p. 64. Primary source: Exporter Location Series, Census Bureau.

★2016★
Imports and Exports: Sales

Export Sales Changes Since 1993, By Industry Group: Textile Mill Products (Percent)
[In percent]

City	Percent	Rank
Chicago, IL	16.7	5
Detroit, MI	3.3	7
Houston, TX	22.3	4
Los Angeles-Long Beach, CA	13.9	6
Miami, FL	1.6	8
Minneapolis-Saint Paul, MN-WI	-34.2	10
New York, NY	-2.8	9
San Francisco, CA	27.7	3
San Jose, CA	106.8	1
Seattle-Bellevue-Everett, WA	30.1	2

Source: U.S. Department of Commerce, International Trade Administration, *Metropolitan Area Exports: An Export Performance Report on Over 250 U.S. Cities,* Washington, D.C.: U.S. Government Printing Office, April 1996, p. 64. Primary source: Exporter Location Series, Census Bureau.

★2017★
Imports and Exports: Sales

Export Sales Changes Since 1993, By Industry Group: Tobacco Products (Dollars)
[In dollars]

City	Dollars	Rank
Chicago, IL	371,088	3
Detroit, MI	-566,407	7
Los Angeles-Long Beach, CA	-1,183,065	8
Miami, FL	28,553	4
Minneapolis-Saint Paul, MN-WI	-8,910	5
New York, NY	198,855,495	1
San Francisco, CA	32,637,050	2
Seattle-Bellevue-Everett, WA	-32,150	6

Source: U.S. Department of Commerce, International Trade Administration, *Metropolitan Area Exports: An Export Performance Report on Over 250 U.S. Cities,* Washington, D.C.: U.S. Government Printing Office, April 1996, p. 64. Primary source: Exporter Location Series, Census Bureau. *Notes:* Food sales are included in the figures shown for New York, New York, and San Francisco, California.

★2018★
Imports and Exports: Sales

Export Sales Changes Since 1993, By Industry Group: Tobacco Products (Percent)
[In percent]

City	Percent	Rank
Chicago, IL	23.9	1
Detroit, MI	-67.1	5
Los Angeles-Long Beach, CA	-70.1	6
Miami, FL	0.5	4
Minneapolis-Saint Paul, MN-WI	-100.0	8
New York, NY	11.4	2
San Francisco, CA	3.3	3
Seattle-Bellevue-Everett, WA	-74.0	7

Source: U.S. Department of Commerce, International Trade Administration, *Metropolitan Area Exports: An Export Performance Report on Over 250 U.S. Cities,* Washington, D.C.: U.S. Government Printing Office, April 1996, p. 64. Primary source: Exporter Location Series, Census Bureau. *Notes:* Sales of food products are included in figures shown for New York, New York, and San Francisco, California.

★2019★
Imports and Exports: Sales

Export Sales Changes Since 1993, By Region: Mid-Atlantic (Dollars)

Data refer to the 20 leading areas, ranked by dollar changes.

[In dollars]

MSA	Dollar	Rank
Albany-Schenectady-Troy, NY	155,160,117	13
Allentown-Bethlehem-Easton, PA	97,251,466	14
Bergen-Passaic, NJ	462,051,742	3
Binghamton, NY	158,648,572	12
Buffalo-Niagara Falls, NY	434,498,440	4
Dutchess County, NY	184,019,869	10
Harrisburg-Lebanon-Carlisle, PA	195,851,142	8
Jamestown, NY	52,439,724	19
Jersey City, NJ	365,021,659	5

[Continued]

★2019★

Export Sales Changes Since 1993, By Region: Mid-Atlantic (Dollars)

[Continued]

MSA	Dollar	Rank
Lancaster, PA	63,245,724	16
Middlesex-Somerset-Hunterdon, NJ	195,329,911	9
Nassau-Suffolk, NY	63,055,312	17
Newark, NJ	918,051,628	1
Philadelphia, PA-NJ	676,687,697	2
Pittsburgh, PA	160,864,429	11
Rochester, NY	52,133,057	20
Scranton-Wilkes-Barre-Hazleton, PA	61,532,780	18
Syracuse, NY	226,852,610	6
Utica-Rome, NY	81,012,435	15
York, PA	200,183,841	7

Source: U.S. Department of Commerce, International Trade Administration, *Metropolitan Area Exports: An Export Performance Report on Over 250 U.S. Cities,* p. 34. Primary source: Exporter Location Series, Census Bureau.

★2020★

Imports and Exports: Sales

Export Sales Changes Since 1993, By Region: Mid-Atlantic (Percent)

Data refer to the 20 leading areas, ranked by percent changes.

[In percent]

MSA	Percent	Rank
Albany-Schenectady-Troy, NY	22.9	10
Allentown-Bethlehem-Easton, PA	7.6	19
Altoona, PA	8.9	18
Bergen-Passaic, NJ	11.8	15
Binghamton, NY	50.2	3
Buffalo-Niagara Falls, NY	38.3	5
Dutchess County, NY	23.1	9
Elmira, NY	66.4	1
Harrisburg-Lebanon-Carlisle, PA	57.7	2
Jamestown, NY	33.4	7
Jersey City, NJ	37.0	6
Lancaster, PA	15.6	14
Monmouth-Ocean, NJ	9.9	17
Newark, NJ	21.4	11
Philadelphia, PA-NJ	11.5	16
Scranton-Wilkes-Barre-Hazleton, PA	23.1	9
Syracuse, NY	16.5	13
Utica-Rome, NY	43.0	4
Williamsport, PA	17.2	12
York, PA	26.6	8

Source: U.S. Department of Commerce, International Trade Administration, *Metropolitan Area Exports: An Export Performance Report on Over 250 U.S. Cities,* p. 35. Primary source: Exporter Location Series, Census Bureau.

★2021★

Imports and Exports: Sales

Export Sales Changes Since 1993, By Region: Mountain (Dollars)

[In dollars]

MSA	Dollars	Rank
Albuquerque, NM	78,792,275	8
Boise City, ID	267,074,612	2
Colorado Springs, CO	236,422,890	3
Denver, CO	158,852,551	5
Fort Collins-Loveland, CO	70,148,185	9
Greeley, CO	225,799,609	4
Las Vegas, NV-AZ	-21,767,639	12
Phoenix-Mesa, AZ	1,062,150,277	1
Provo-Orem, UT	29,795,246	10
Reno, NV	29,565,480	11
Salt Lake City-Ogden, UT	147,793,930	7
Tucson, AZ	150,994,892	6

Source: U.S. Department of Commerce, International Trade Administration, *Metropolitan Area Exports: An Export Performance Report on Over 250 U.S. Cities,* p. 55. Primary source: Exporter Location Series, Census Bureau.

★2022★

Imports and Exports: Sales

Export Sales Changes Since 1993, By Region: Mountain (Percent)

[In percent]

MSA	Percent	Rank
Albuquerque, NM	30.7	4
Boise City, ID	26.1	5
Colorado Springs, CO	35.6	2
Denver, CO	17.1	9
Fort Collins-Loveland, CO	24.7	6
Greeley, CO	81.8	1
Las Vegas, NV-AZ	-13.1	12
Phoenix-Mesa, AZ	23.6	7
Provo-Orem, UT	17.5	8
Reno, NV	16.1	10
Salt Lake City-Ogden, UT	8.9	11
Tucson, AZ	31.0	3

Source: U.S. Department of Commerce, International Trade Administration, *Metropolitan Area Exports: An Export Performance Report on Over 250 U.S. Cities,* p. 56. Primary source: Exporter Location Series, Census Bureau.

★2023★

Imports and Exports: Sales

Export Sales Changes Since 1993, By Region: New England (Dollars)

[In dollars]

MSA	Dollar	Rank
Boston, MA-NH	622,878,329	1
Bridgeport, CT	-207,023,485	19
Brockton, MA	6,105,243	12
Danbury, CT	76,256,719	4
Hartford, CT	40,956,276	6
Lawrence, MA-NH	-16,213,360	16
Lowell, MA-NH	22,624,104	9

[Continued]

★2023★
Export Sales Changes Since 1993, By Region: New England (Dollars)
[Continued]

MSA	Dollar	Rank
Manchester, NH	8,255,362	11
Nashua, NH	-54,792,144	18
New Bedford, MA	12,941,770	10
New Haven-Meriden, CT	39,927,666	7
New London-Norwich, CT-RI	4,915,760	14
Pittsfield, MA	35,072,273	8
Portland, ME	-35,675,105	17
Portsmouth-Rochester, NH-ME	5,182,341	13
Providence-Fall River-Warwick, RI-MA	104,337,095	2
Springfield, MA	45,017,843	5
Stamford-Norwalk, CT	86,133,815	3
Waterbury, CT	-7,939,230	15
Worcester, MA-CT	-414,089,996	20

Source: U.S. Department of Commerce, International Trade Administration, *Metropolitan Area Exports: An Export Performance Report on Over 250 U.S. Cities,* p. 31. Primary source: Exporter Location Series, Census Bureau.

★2024★
Imports and Exports: Sales
Export Sales Changes Since 1993, By Region: New England (Percent)
[In percent]

MSA	Percent	Rank
Boston, MA-NH	9.6	4
Bridgeport, CT	-18.4	16
Brockton, MA	5.7	7
Danbury, CT	24.1	2
Hartford, CT	2.1	11
Lawrence, MA-NH	-2.0	13
Lowell, MA-NH	2.6	10
Manchester, NH	7.7	6
Nashua, NH	-18.9	17
New Bedford, MA	9.1	5
New Haven-Meriden, CT	3.9	8
New London-Norwich, CT-RI	3.6	9
Pittsfield, MA	45.4	1
Portland, ME	-10.0	15
Portsmouth-Rochester, NH-ME	1.1	12
Providence-Fall River-Warwick, RI-MA	9.1	5
Springfield, MA	11.6	3
Stamford-Norwalk, CT	2.6	10
Waterbury, CT	-4.2	14
Worcester, MA-CT	-40.7	18

Source: U.S. Department of Commerce, International Trade Administration, *Metropolitan Area Exports: An Export Performance Report on Over 250 U.S. Cities,* p. 32. Primary source: Exporter Location Series, Census Bureau.

★2025★
Imports and Exports: Sales
Export Sales Changes Since 1993, By Region: North Central (Dollars)
Data refer to the 20 leading areas, ranked by dollar changes.

[In dollars]

MSA	Dollar	Rank
Akron, OH	171,347,263	12
Chicago, IL	2,887,027,329	2
Cincinnati, OH-KY-IN	158,354,764	13
Cleveland-Lorain-Elyria, OH	510,563,633	4
Columbus, OH	128,455,033	17
Dayton-Springfield, OH	191,442,286	10
Detroit, MI	10,688,766,405	1
Eau Claire, WI	175,992,055	11
Fort Wayne, IN	130,298,673	16
Grand Rapids-Muskegon-Holland, MI	288,534,513	7
Indianapolis, IN	377,208,492	5
Kalamazoo-Battle Creek, MI	218,619,872	9
Kansas City, MO-KS	352,659,278	6
Kokomo, IN	130,932,714	15
Milwaukee-Waukesha, WI	576,239,832	3
Omaha, NE-IA	93,472,331	20
Rockford, IL	94,531,294	19
St. Louis, MO-IL	273,339,978	8
Toledo, OH	150,854,867	14
Wichita, KS	96,579,399	18

Source: U.S. Department of Commerce, International Trade Administration, *Metropolitan Area Exports: An Export Performance Report on Over 250 U.S. Cities,* p. 44. Primary source: Exporter Location Series, Census Bureau.

★2026★
Imports and Exports: Sales
Export Sales Changes Since 1993, By Region: North Central (Percent)
Data refer to the 20 leading areas, ranked by dollar changes.

[In percent]

MSA	Percent	Rank
Canton-Massillon, OH	26.3	13
Chicago, IL	20.0	17
Detroit, MI	63.7	3
Dubuque, IA	90.8	1
Eau Claire, WI	60.7	4
Fargo-Moorhead, ND-MN	22.7	15
Fort Wayne, IN	20.3	16
Gary, IN	18.7	19
Green Bay, WI	39.7	6
Hamilton-Middletown, OH	34.4	8
Kalamazoo-Battle Creek, MI	33.6	9
Lawrence, KS	19.2	18
Milwaukee-Waukesha, WI	24.7	14
Muncie, IN	67.0	2
Omaha, NE-IA	31.2	11
Rochester, MN	37.1	7
Springfield, IL	24.7	14
Springfield, MO	28.0	12

[Continued]

★2026★

Export Sales Changes Since 1993, By Region: North Central (Percent)
[Continued]

MSA	Percent	Rank
Terre Haute, IN	31.9	10
Waterloo-Cedar Falls, IA	45.7	5

Source: U.S. Department of Commerce, International Trade Administration, *Metropolitan Area Exports: An Export Performance Report on Over 250 U.S. Cities,* p. 44. Primary source: Exporter Location Series, Census Bureau.

★2027★
Imports and Exports: Sales

Export Sales Changes Since 1993, By Region: Pacific (Dollars)

Data refer to the 20 leading areas, ranked by dollar changes.

[In dollars]

MSA	Dollar	Rank
Anchorage, AK	69,412,936	13
Bakersfield, CA	299,719,402	8
Fresno, CA	90,302,105	11
Honolulu, HI	27,727,979	19
Los Angeles-Long Beach, CA	2,211,254,127	2
Modesto, CA	35,627,680	17
Oakland, CA	931,766,515	4
Orange County, CA	1,062,613,900	3
Portland-Vancouver, OR-WA	750,304,713	5
Richland-Kennewick-Pasco, WA	51,230,383	15
Riverside-San Bernardino, CA	365,050,937	7
Salinas, CA	27,438,423	20
San Diego, CA	509,529,055	6
San Francisco, CA	38,917,326	16
San Jose, CA	3,771,110,126	1
Santa Cruz-Watsonville, CA	193,088,616	9
Santa Rosa, CA	76,084,303	12
Stockton-Lodi, CA	32,816,368	18
Vallejo-Fairfield-Napa, CA	92,244,551	10
Ventura, CA	58,379,706	14

Source: U.S. Department of Commerce, International Trade Administration, *Metropolitan Area Exports: An Export Performance Report on Over 250 U.S. Cities,* p. 58. Primary source: Exporter Location Series, Census Bureau.

★2028★
Imports and Exports: Sales

Export Sales Changes Since 1993, By Region: Pacific (Percent)

Data refer to the 20 leading areas, ranked by percent changes.

[In percent]

MSA	Percent	Rank
Anchorage, AK	53.9	2
Bakersfield, CA	62.4	1
Bremerton, WA	21.2	8
Eugene-Springfield, OR	9.6	19
Fresno, CA	13.4	13

[Continued]

★2028★

Export Sales Changes Since 1993, By Region: Pacific (Percent)
[Continued]

MSA	Percent	Rank
Honolulu, HI	14.8	12
Los Angeles-Long Beach, CA	11.0	17
Modesto, CA	17.7	11
Oakland, CA	22.3	7
Orange County, CA	18.8	9
Portland-Vancouver, OR-WA	13.2	14
Richland-Kennewick-Pasco, WA	23.3	6
Riverside-San Bernardino, CA	33.4	4
Salem, OR	10.0	18
San Diego, CA	11.7	15
San Jose, CA	23.3	6
Santa Cruz-Watsonville, CA	29.1	5
Santa Rosa, CA	18.6	10
Stockton-Lodi, CA	11.4	16
Vallejo-Fairfield-Napa, CA	53.7	3

Source: U.S. Department of Commerce, International Trade Administration, *Metropolitan Area Exports: An Export Performance Report on Over 250 U.S. Cities,* p. 58. Primary source: Exporter Location Series, Census Bureau.

★2029★
Imports and Exports: Sales

Export Sales Changes Since 1993, By Region: South Atlantic (Dollars)

Data refer to the 20 leading areas, ranked by dollar changes.

[In dollars]

MSA	Dollar	Rank
Atlanta, GA	868,534,844	3
Augusta-Aiken, GA-SC	98,870,173	13
Baltimore, MD	85,561,043	17
Charleston, WV	98,657,264	14
Charlotte-Gastonia-Rock Hill, NC-SC	219,102,426	9
Columbia, SC	87,474,831	16
Florence, SC	50,936,711	20
Fort Lauderdale, FL	185,214,204	10
Greensboro-Winston-Salem-High Point, NC	320,213,747	6
Greenville-Spartanburg-Anderson, SC	282,907,884	8
Hickory-Morganton, NC	62,671,084	19
Jacksonville, FL	95,542,321	15
Miami, FL	1,002,441,568	2
Norfolk-Virginia Beach-Newport News, VA-NC	130,514,003	12
Raleigh-Durham-Chapel Hill, NC	137,789,027	11
Richmond-Petersburg, VA	1,248,420,970	1
Tampa-St. Petersburg-Clearwater, FL	540,075,048	5
Washington, DC-MD-VA-WV	718,702,248	4
West Palm Beach-Boca Raton, FL	69,451,366	18
Wilmington-Newark, DE-MD	296,588,718	7

Source: U.S. Department of Commerce, International Trade Administration, *Metropolitan Area Exports: An Export Performance Report on Over 250 U.S. Cities,* p. 38. Primary source: Exporter Location Series, Census Bureau.

★2030★

Imports and Exports: Sales

Export Sales Changes Since 1993, By Region: South Atlantic (Percent)

Data refer to the 20 leading areas, ranked by percent changes.

[In percent]

MSA	Percent	Rank
Albany, GA	20.5	13
Atlanta, GA	22.4	12
Augusta-Aiken, GA-SC	43.5	4
Charleston, WV	55.1	2
Columbia, SC	41.1	6
Cumberland, MD-WV	17.1	19
Danville, VA	17.2	18
Florence, SC	76.8	1
Fort Pierce-Port St. Lucie, FL	25.6	9
Greenville-Spartanburg-Anderson, SC	19.3	15
Hickory-Morganton, NC	18.7	17
Huntington-Ashland, WV-KY-OH	18.9	16
Jacksonville, FL	23.6	10
Norfolk-Virginia Beach-Newport News, VA-NC	19.3	15
Panama City, FL	33.3	7
Richmond-Petersburg, VA	31.1	8
Roanoke, VA	19.4	14
Tampa-St. Petersburg-Clearwater, FL	41.7	5
Wheeling, WV-OH	46.0	3
Wilmington, NC	22.8	11

Source: U.S. Department of Commerce, International Trade Administration, *Metropolitan Area Exports: An Export Performance Report on Over 250 U.S. Cities,* p. 40. Primary source: Exporter Location Series, Census Bureau.

★2031★

Imports and Exports: Sales

Export Sales Changes Since 1993, By Region: South Central (Dollars)

Data refer to the 20 leading areas, ranked by dollar changes.

[In dollars]

MSA	Dollar	Rank
Austin-San Marcos, TX	407,259,978	7
Biloxi-Gulfport-Pascagoula, MS	173,467,256	15
Brazoria, TX	285,935,917	10
Brownsville-Harlingen-San Benito, TX	208,995,926	12
Dallas, TX	862,071,548	2
EL Paso, TX	594,236,516	4
Fayetteville-Springdale-Rogers, AR	183,471,659	14
Fort Worth-Arlington, TX	451,794,981	6
Houston, TX	1,103,604,099	1
Huntsville, AL	98,538,113	18
Johnson City-Kingsport-Bristol, TN-VA	224,117,230	11
Knoxville, TN	108,771,252	17
Laredo, TX	95,553,640	19

[Continued]

★2031★

Export Sales Changes Since 1993, By Region: South Central (Dollars)

[Continued]

MSA	Dollar	Rank
Lexington, KY	454,375,444	5
Louisville, KY-IN	124,998,528	16
McAllen-Edinburg-Mission, TX	316,236,439	8
Memphis, TN-AR-MS	674,407,387	3
Nashville, TN	206,391,250	13
New Orleans, LA	292,021,745	9
San Antonio, TX	92,348,035	20

Source: U.S. Department of Commerce, International Trade Administration, *Metropolitan Area Exports: An Export Performance Report on Over 250 U.S. Cities,* p. 50. Primary source: Exporter Location Series, Census Bureau.

★2032★

Imports and Exports: Sales

Export Sales Changes Since 1993, By Region: South Central (Percent)

Data refer to the 20 leading areas, ranked by dollar changes.

[In percent]

MSA	Percent	Rank
Austin-San Marcos, TX	23.7	14
Biloxi-Gulfport-Pascagoula, MS	160.4	1
Brazoria, TX	19.4	19
Decatur, AL	28.7	11
El Paso, TX	20.0	18
Fayetteville-Springdale-Rogers, AR	73.3	2
Fort Worth-Arlington, TX	28.2	12
Jackson, TN	22.7	15
Knoxville, TN	18.7	20
Lafayette, LA	58.8	5
Lexington, KY	72.8	3
Lubbock, TX	67.4	4
McAllen-Edinburg-Mission, TX	20.9	17
Memphis, TN-AR-MS	32.8	9
Monroe, LA	38.8	7
Montgomery, AL	46.4	6
Odessa-Midland, TX	36.5	8
Pine Bluff, AR	21.6	16
Shreveport-Bossier City, LA	24.2	13
Wichita Falls, TX	31.3	10

Source: U.S. Department of Commerce, International Trade Administration, *Metropolitan Area Exports: An Export Performance Report on Over 250 U.S. Cities,* p. 52. Primary source: Exporter Location Series, Census Bureau.

★2033★
Imports and Exports: Sales

Export Sales Changes Since 1993, By Selected Market: Caribbean and Central America (Dollar Changes)

[In dollars]

MSA	Dollar	Rank
Chicago, IL	42,530,579	4
Detroit, MI	12,359,502	5
Houston, TX	102,734,728	2
Los Angeles-Long Beach, CA	-944,106	7
Miami, FL	80,118,190	3
Minneapolis-Saint Paul, MN-WI	-50,432,938	10
New York, NY	152,944,581	1
San Francisco, CA	5,170,247	6
San Jose, CA	-4,452,774	8
Seattle-Bellevue-Everett, WA	-29,492,197	9

Source: U.S. Department of Commerce, International Trade Administration, *Metropolitan Area Exports: An Export Performance Report on Over 250 U.S. Cities,* p. 65. Primary source: Exporter Location Series, Census Bureau.

★2034★
Imports and Exports: Sales

Export Sales Changes Since 1993, By Selected Market: Caribbean and Central America (Percent Changes)

[In percent]

MSA	Percent	Rank
Chicago, IL	19.3	3
Detroit, MI	24.3	1
Houston, TX	16.5	4
Los Angeles-Long Beach, CA	-0.5	7
Miami, FL	3.2	5
Minneapolis-Saint Paul, MN-WI	-21.9	8
New York, NY	21.4	2
San Francisco, CA	2.2	6
San Jose, CA	-22.0	9
Seattle-Bellevue-Everett, WA	-22.4	10

Source: U.S. Department of Commerce, International Trade Administration, *Metropolitan Area Exports: An Export Performance Report on Over 250 U.S. Cities,* p. 65. Primary source: Exporter Location Series, Census Bureau.

★2035★
Imports and Exports: Sales

Export Sales Changes Since 1993, By Selected Market: European Union (Dollar Changes)

[In dollars]

MSA	Dollar	Rank
Chicago, IL	620,328,421	2
Detroit, MI	268,591,832	4
Houston, TX	122,147,999	5
Los Angeles-Long Beach, CA	1,079,424,543	1
Miami, FL	1,926,299	8
Minneapolis-Saint Paul, MN-WI	10,865,924	7
New York, NY	-3,308,233,845	10
San Francisco, CA	20,155,007	6

[Continued]

★2035★

Export Sales Changes Since 1993, By Selected Market: European Union (Dollar Changes)

[Continued]

MSA	Dollar	Rank
San Jose, CA	493,808,557	3
Seattle-Bellevue-Everett, WA	-643,728,664	9

Source: U.S. Department of Commerce, International Trade Administration, *Metropolitan Area Exports: An Export Performance Report on Over 250 U.S. Cities,* p. 65. Primary source: Exporter Location Series, Census Bureau.

★2036★
Imports and Exports: Sales

Export Sales Changes Since 1993, By Selected Market: European Union (Percent Changes)

[In percent]

MSA	Percent	Rank
Chicago, IL	19.8	2
Detroit, MI	15.6	3
Houston, TX	6.0	5
Los Angeles-Long Beach, CA	34.6	1
Miami, FL	0.4	7
Minneapolis-Saint Paul, MN-WI	0.4	7
New York, NY	-39.1	9
San Francisco, CA	1.0	6
San Jose, CA	12.5	4
Seattle-Bellevue-Everett, WA	-12.8	8

Source: U.S. Department of Commerce, International Trade Administration, *Metropolitan Area Exports: An Export Performance Report on Over 250 U.S. Cities,* p. 65. Primary source: Exporter Location Series, Census Bureau.

★2037★
Imports and Exports: Sales

Export Sales Changes Since 1993, By Selected Market: Former Soviet Republics (Dollar Changes)

[In dollars]

MSA	Dollar	Rank
Chicago, IL	-83,403,061	7
Detroit, MI	29,737,390	2
Houston, TX	-98,711,937	9
Los Angeles-Long Beach, CA	-4,285,754	5
Miami, FL	-257,811	4
Minneapolis-Saint Paul, MN-WI	-93,891,800	8
New York, NY	-166,741,805	10
San Francisco, CA	-13,280,465	6
San Jose, CA	5,806,712	3
Seattle-Bellevue-Everett, WA	403,588,832	1

Source: U.S. Department of Commerce, International Trade Administration, *Metropolitan Area Exports: An Export Performance Report on Over 250 U.S. Cities,* p. 65. Primary source: Exporter Location Series, Census Bureau.

★2038★

Imports and Exports: Sales

Export Sales Changes Since 1993, By Selected Market: Former Soviet Republics (Percent Changes)

[In percent]

MSA	Percent	Rank
Chicago, IL	-48.1	9
Detroit, MI	106.0	2
Houston, TX	-35.1	8
Los Angeles-Long Beach, CA	-4.6	5
Miami, FL	-2.3	4
Minneapolis-Saint Paul, MN-WI	-49.7	10
New York, NY	-27.8	7
San Francisco, CA	-18.7	6
San Jose, CA	14.4	3
Seattle-Bellevue-Everett, WA	1,429.5	1

Source: U.S. Department of Commerce, International Trade Administration, *Metropolitan Area Exports: An Export Performance Report on Over 250 U.S. Cities,* p. 65. Primary source: Exporter Location Series, Census Bureau.

★2039★

Imports and Exports: Sales

Export Sales Changes Since 1993, By Selected Market: Japan (Dollar Changes)

[In dollars]

City	Dollar	Rank
Chicago, IL	169,792,324	4
Detroit, MI	158,532,372	5
Houston, TX	1,318,902	8
Los Angeles-Long Beach, CA	1,493,702,432	1
Miami, FL	39,900,145	7
Minneapolis-Saint Paul, MN-WI	-106,431,215	10
New York, NY	277,707,934	3
San Francisco, CA	143,697,934	6
San Jose, CA	746,309,841	2
Seattle-Bellevue-Everett, WA	-38,866,361	9

Source: U.S. Department of Commerce, International Trade Administration, *Metropolitan Area Exports: An Export Performance Report on Over 250 U.S. Cities,* Washington, D.C.: U.S. Government Printing Office, April 1996, p. 65. Primary source: Exporter Location Series, Census Bureau.

★2040★

Imports and Exports: Sales

Export Sales Changes Since 1993, By Selected Market: Japan (Percent Changes)

[In percent]

City	Percent	Rank
Chicago, IL	10.6	5
Detroit, MI	31.5	4
Houston, TX	0.2	8
Los Angeles-Long Beach, CA	34.6	3
Miami, FL	49.3	1
Minneapolis-Saint Paul, MN-WI	-13.0	10
New York, NY	7.8	7
San Francisco, CA	8.6	6

[Continued]

★2040★

Export Sales Changes Since 1993, By Selected Market: Japan (Percent Changes)

[Continued]

City	Percent	Rank
San Jose, CA	35.6	2
Seattle-Bellevue-Everett, WA	-0.7	9

Source: U.S. Department of Commerce, International Trade Administration, *Metropolitan Area Exports: An Export Performance Report on Over 250 U.S. Cities,* Washington, D.C.: U.S. Government Printing Office, April 1996, p. 65. Primary source: Exporter Location Series, Census Bureau.

★2041★

Imports and Exports: Sales

Export Sales Changes Since 1993, By Selected Market: NAFTA Countries (Dollar Changes)

[In dollars]

MSA	Dollar	Rank
Chicago, IL	831,646,066	2
Detroit, MI	10,401,458,951	1
Houston, TX	504,409,733	4
Los Angeles-Long Beach, CA	299,627,261	5
Miami, FL	142,713,210	8
Minneapolis-Saint Paul, MN-WI	167,501,832	7
New York, NY	77,685,249	9
San Francisco, CA	-9,366,523	10
San Jose, CA	587,357,123	3
Seattle-Bellevue-Everett, WA	207,567,924	6

Source: U.S. Department of Commerce, International Trade Administration, *Metropolitan Area Exports: An Export Performance Report on Over 250 U.S. Cities,* p. 65. Primary source: Exporter Location Series, Census Bureau.

★2042★

Imports and Exports: Sales

Export Sales Changes Since 1993, By Selected Market: NAFTA Countries (Percent Changes)

[In percent]

MSA	Percent	Rank
Chicago, IL	20.8	4
Detroit, MI	91.8	1
Houston, TX	21.6	3
Los Angeles-Long Beach, CA	10.2	7
Miami, FL	17.1	6
Minneapolis-Saint Paul, MN-WI	10.2	7
New York, NY	3.2	8
San Francisco, CA	-1.2	9
San Jose, CA	26.6	2
Seattle-Bellevue-Everett, WA	18.3	5

Source: U.S. Department of Commerce, International Trade Administration, *Metropolitan Area Exports: An Export Performance Report on Over 250 U.S. Cities,* p. 65. Primary source: Exporter Location Series, Census Bureau.

★ 2043 ★

Imports and Exports: Sales

Export Sales Changes Since 1993, By Selected Market: South America (Dollar Changes)

[In dollars]

MSA	Dollar	Rank
Chicago, IL	307,094,932	3
Detroit, MI	35,940,048	5
Houston, TX	355,755,808	2
Los Angeles-Long Beach, CA	-113,307,343	10
Miami, FL	720,600,837	1
Minneapolis-Saint Paul, MN-WI	42,134,989	4
New York, NY	-40,946,764	8
San Francisco, CA	-94,929	7
San Jose, CA	33,471,283	6
Seattle-Bellevue-Everett, WA	-94,342,906	9

Source: U.S. Department of Commerce, International Trade Administration, *Metropolitan Area Exports: An Export Performance Report on Over 250 U.S. Cities,* p. 65. Primary source: Exporter Location Series, Census Bureau.

★ 2044 ★

Imports and Exports: Sales

Export Sales Changes Since 1993, By Selected Market: South America (Percent Changes)

[In percent]

MSA	Percent	Rank
Chicago, IL	39.2	1
Detroit, MI	8.7	6
Houston, TX	22.9	2
Los Angeles-Long Beach, CA	-11.3	9
Miami, FL	18.5	4
Minneapolis-Saint Paul, MN-WI	20.9	3
New York, NY	-2.9	8
San Francisco, CA	-0.0	7
San Jose, CA	14.1	5
Seattle-Bellevue-Everett, WA	-27.7	10

Source: U.S. Department of Commerce, International Trade Administration, *Metropolitan Area Exports: An Export Performance Report on Over 250 U.S. Cities,* p. 65. Primary source: Exporter Location Series, Census Bureau.

★ 2045 ★

Imports and Exports: Sales

Export Sales Changes, 1994, By Industry Group: Furniture and Fixtures (Dollars)

[In dollars]

City	Dollars	Rank
Chicago, IL	-2,969,973	8
Detroit, MI	-115,953,730	10
Houston, TX	456,755	6
Los Angeles-Long Beach, CA	-3,889,702	9
Miami, FL	10,702,939	1
Minneapolis-Saint Paul, MN-WI	3,701,453	4
New York, NY	2,956,377	5
San Francisco, CA	-481,706	7
San Jose, CA	5,212,858	2
Seattle-Bellevue-Everett, WA	4,661,410	3

Source: U.S. Department of Commerce, International Trade Administration, *Metropolitan Area Exports: An Export Performance Report on Over 250 U.S. Cities,* Washington, D.C.: U.S. Government Printing Office, April 1996, p. 64. Primary source: Exporter Location Series, Census Bureau.

★ 2046 ★

Imports and Exports: Sales

Export Sales Changes, 1994, By Industry Group: Furniture and Fixtures (Percent)

[In percent]

City	Percent	Rank
Chicago, IL	-4.8	9
Detroit, MI	-26.3	10
Houston, TX	2.8	6
Los Angeles-Long Beach, CA	-3.2	8
Miami, FL	16.2	4
Minneapolis-Saint Paul, MN-WI	27.2	3
New York, NY	5.5	5
San Francisco, CA	-3.0	7
San Jose, CA	81.6	1
Seattle-Bellevue-Everett, WA	45.6	2

Source: U.S. Department of Commerce, International Trade Administration, *Metropolitan Area Exports: An Export Performance Report on Over 250 U.S. Cities,* Washington, D.C.: U.S. Government Printing Office, April 1996, p. 64. Primary source: Exporter Location Series, Census Bureau.

★ 2047 ★

Imports and Exports: Sales

Export Sales Changes, 1994, By Industry Group: Leather Products (Dollars)

[In dollars]

City	Dollars	Rank
Chicago, IL	-2,887,546	10
Detroit, MI	8,360,380	3
Houston, TX	21,748	8
Los Angeles-Long Beach, CA	10,343,869	2
Miami, FL	-609,753	9
Minneapolis-Saint Paul, MN-WI	4,397,356	4
New York, NY	12,031,020	1
San Francisco, CA	4,284,617	5
San Jose, CA	237,060	7
Seattle-Bellevue-Everett, WA	1,329,253	6

Source: U.S. Department of Commerce, International Trade Administration, *Metropolitan Area Exports: An Export Performance Report on Over 250 U.S. Cities,* Washington, D.C.: U.S. Government Printing Office, April 1996, p. 64. Primary source: Exporter Location Series, Census Bureau.

★ 2048 ★

Imports and Exports: Sales

Export Sales Changes, 1994, By Industry Group: Leather Products (Percent)

[In percent]

City	Percent	Rank
Chicago, IL	-6.0	10
Detroit, MI	1.9	7
Houston, TX	0.4	8
Los Angeles-Long Beach, CA	8.9	6
Miami, FL	-1.4	9
Minneapolis-Saint Paul, MN-WI	177.3	1
New York, NY	14.7	5
San Francisco, CA	34.7	2

[Continued]

★2048★

Export Sales Changes, 1994, By Industry Group: Leather Products (Percent)

[Continued]

City	Percent	Rank
San Jose, CA	18.6	3
Seattle-Bellevue-Everett, WA	16.8	4

Source: U.S. Department of Commerce, International Trade Administration, *Metropolitan Area Exports: An Export Performance Report on Over 250 U.S. Cities,* Washington, D.C.: U.S. Government Printing Office, April 1996, p. 64. Primary source: Exporter Location Series, Census Bureau.

★2049★

Imports and Exports: Sales

Export Sales Changes Since 1993, By Industry Group: Chemical Products (Dollars)

[In dollars]

City	Dollars	Rank
Chicago, IL	501,110,916	2
Detroit, MI	-56,998,108	9
Houston, TX	632,899,389	1
Los Angeles-Long Beach, CA	34,569,725	4
Miami, FL	-16,593,239	7
Minneapolis-Saint Paul, MN-WI	-47,044,242	8
New York, NY	249,982,775	3
San Francisco, CA	-250,525,394	10
San Jose, CA	-3,747,408	6
Seattle-Bellevue-Everett, WA	9,141,189	5

Source: U.S. Department of Commerce, International Trade Administration, *Metropolitan Area Exports: An Export Performance Report on Over 250 U.S. Cities,* Washington, D.C.: U.S. Government Printing Office, April 1996, p. 64. Primary source: Exporter Location Series, Census Bureau.

★2050★

Imports and Exports: Sales

Export Sales Changes Since 1993, By Industry Group: Chemical Products (Percent)

[In percent]

City	Percent	Rank
Chicago, IL	19.4	2
Detroit, MI	-18.4	8
Houston, TX	21.1	1
Los Angeles-Long Beach, CA	3.9	5
Miami, FL	-3.5	7
Minneapolis-Saint Paul, MN-WI	-21.2	9
New York, NY	12.1	4
San Francisco, CA	-22.6	10
San Jose, CA	-1.8	6
Seattle-Bellevue-Everett, WA	14.8	3

Source: U.S. Department of Commerce, International Trade Administration, *Metropolitan Area Exports: An Export Performance Report on Over 250 U.S. Cities,* Washington, D.C.: U.S. Government Printing Office, April 1996, p. 64. Primary source: Exporter Location Series, Census Bureau.

★2051★

Imports and Exports: Sales

Export Sales Changes Since 1993, By Industry Group: Electrical and Electronics Equipment (Dollars)

[In dollars]

City	Dollars	Rank
Chicago, IL	982,263,129	2
Detroit, MI	147,859,934	8
Houston, TX	197,402,401	4
Los Angeles-Long Beach, CA	178,387,168	6
Miami, FL	271,385,265	3
Minneapolis-Saint Paul, MN-WI	103,104,728	9
New York, NY	-92,990,772	10
San Francisco, CA	166,278,012	7
San Jose, CA	2,307,879,596	1
Seattle-Bellevue-Everett, WA	179,887,920	5

Source: U.S. Department of Commerce, International Trade Administration, *Metropolitan Area Exports: An Export Performance Report on Over 250 U.S. Cities,* Washington, D.C.: U.S. Government Printing Office, April 1996, p. 64. Primary source: Exporter Location Series, Census Bureau.

★2052★

Imports and Exports: Sales

Export Sales Changes Since 1993, By Industry Group: Electrical and Electronics Equipment (Percent)

[In percent]

City	Percent	Rank
Chicago, IL	29.1	4
Detroit, MI	14.6	7
Houston, TX	56.1	1
Los Angeles-Long Beach, CA	7.8	9
Miami, FL	22.8	5
Minneapolis-Saint Paul, MN-WI	16.3	6
New York, NY	-8.3	10
San Francisco, CA	13.6	8
San Jose, CA	32.3	3
Seattle-Bellevue-Everett, WA	37.8	2

Source: U.S. Department of Commerce, International Trade Administration, *Metropolitan Area Exports: An Export Performance Report on Over 250 U.S. Cities,* Washington, D.C.: U.S. Government Printing Office, April 1996, p. 64. Primary source: Exporter Location Series, Census Bureau.

★2053★

Imports and Exports: Sales

Export Sales Changes Since 1993, By Industry Group: Food Products (Dollars)

[In dollars]

City	Dollars	Rank
Chicago, IL	-33,685,415	9
Detroit, MI	10,661,973	7
Houston, TX	28,126,345	6
Los Angeles-Long Beach, CA	176,536,161	2
Miami, FL	28,453,730	5
Minneapolis-Saint Paul, MN-WI	-115,927,381	10
New York, NY	198,855,495	1

[Continued]

★2053★

Export Sales Changes Since 1993, By Industry Group: Food Products (Dollars)

[Continued]

City	Dollars	Rank
San Francisco, CA	32,637,050	4
San Jose, CA	-9,101,710	8
Seattle-Bellevue-Everett, WA	55,219,917	3

Source: U.S. Department of Commerce, International Trade Administration, *Metropolitan Area Exports: An Export Performance Report on Over 250 U.S. Cities,* Washington, D.C.: U.S. Government Printing Office, April 1996, p. 64. Primary source: Exporter Location Series, Census Bureau. *Notes:* Sales of tobacco products are included in the figures shown for New York, New York, and San Francisco, California.

★2054★

Imports and Exports: Sales

Export Sales Changes Since 1993, By Industry Group: Food Products (Percent)

[In percent]

City	Percent	Rank
Chicago, IL	-5.0	8
Detroit, MI	12.1	2
Houston, TX	6.9	6
Los Angeles-Long Beach, CA	15.6	1
Miami, FL	8.1	5
Minneapolis-Saint Paul, MN-WI	-7.6	10
New York, NY	11.4	3
San Francisco, CA	3.3	7
San Jose, CA	-7.4	9
Seattle-Bellevue-Everett, WA	11.0	4

Source: U.S. Department of Commerce, International Trade Administration, *Metropolitan Area Exports: An Export Performance Report on Over 250 U.S. Cities,* Washington, D.C.: U.S. Government Printing Office, April 1996, p. 64. Primary source: Exporter Location Series, Census Bureau. *Notes:* Sales of tobacco products are included in the figures shown for New York, New York, and San Francisco, California.

★2055★

Imports and Exports: Sales

Export Sales Changes Since 1993, By Industry Group: Industrial Machinery and Equipment (Dollars)

[In dollars]

City	Dollars	Rank
Chicago, IL	348,889,853	3
Detroit, MI	589,397,852	2
Houston, TX	306,430,395	5
Los Angeles-Long Beach, CA	217,758,882	7
Miami, FL	313,618,127	4
Minneapolis-Saint Paul, MN-WI	-2,984,891	9
New York, NY	255,508,858	6
San Francisco, CA	-290,685,662	10
San Jose, CA	1,151,768,923	1
Seattle-Bellevue-Everett, WA	10,888,198	8

Source: U.S. Department of Commerce, International Trade Administration, *Metropolitan Area Exports: An Export Performance Report on Over 250 U.S. Cities,* Washington, D.C.: U.S. Government Printing Office, April 1996, p. 64. Primary source: Exporter Location Series, Census Bureau.

★2056★

Imports and Exports: Sales

Export Sales Changes Since 1993, By Industry Group: Industrial Machinery and Equipment (Percent)

[In percent]

City	Percent	Rank
Chicago, IL	14.0	4
Detroit, MI	37.3	1
Houston, TX	6.6	7
Los Angeles-Long Beach, CA	9.3	6
Miami, FL	17.6	3
Minneapolis-Saint Paul, MN-WI	-0.2	9
New York, NY	10.7	5
San Francisco, CA	-15.0	10
San Jose, CA	17.7	2
Seattle-Bellevue-Everett, WA	2.9	8

Source: U.S. Department of Commerce, International Trade Administration, *Metropolitan Area Exports: An Export Performance Report on Over 250 U.S. Cities,* Washington, D.C.: U.S. Government Printing Office, April 1996, p. 64. Primary source: Exporter Location Series, Census Bureau.

★2057★

Imports and Exports: Sales

Export Sales Changes Since 1993, By Industry Group: Paper Products (Dollars)

[In dollars]

City	Dollars	Rank
Chicago, IL	132,985,389	2
Detroit, MI	-553,791	9
Houston, TX	15,204,627	7
Los Angeles-Long Beach, CA	25,528,452	6
Miami, FL	33,492,773	5
Minneapolis-Saint Paul, MN-WI	-56,288,769	10
New York, NY	52,747,100	4
San Francisco, CA	52,986,689	3
San Jose, CA	1,902,772	8
Seattle-Bellevue-Everett, WA	301,024,364	1

Source: U.S. Department of Commerce, International Trade Administration, *Metropolitan Area Exports: An Export Performance Report on Over 250 U.S. Cities,* Washington, D.C.: U.S. Government Printing Office, April 1996, p. 64. Primary source: Exporter Location Series, Census Bureau. *Notes:* Sales in printing and publishing are included in the figure shown for Seattle-Bellevue-Everett, Washington.

★2058★

Imports and Exports: Sales

Export Sales Changes Since 1993, By Industry Group: Paper Products (Percent)

[In percent]

City	Percent	Rank
Chicago, IL	52.0	3
Detroit, MI	-0.9	9
Houston, TX	92.2	1
Los Angeles-Long Beach, CA	20.6	5
Miami, FL	15.3	6
Minneapolis-Saint Paul, MN-WI	-31.2	10
New York, NY	6.0	8

[Continued]

★ 2058 ★

Export Sales Changes Since 1993, By Industry Group: Paper Products (Percent)
[Continued]

City	Percent	Rank
San Francisco, CA	43.3	4
San Jose, CA	14.3	7
Seattle-Bellevue-Everett, WA	82.3	2

Source: U.S. Department of Commerce, International Trade Administration, *Metropolitan Area Exports: An Export Performance Report on Over 250 U.S. Cities,* Washington, D.C.: U.S. Government Printing Office, April 1996, p. 64. Primary source: Exporter Location Series, Census Bureau. *Notes:* Sales in printing and publishing are included in the figure shown for Seattle-Bellevue-Everett, Washington.

★ 2059 ★
Imports and Exports: Sales

Export Sales Changes Since 1993, By Industry Group: Primary Metals (Dollars)
[In dollars]

City	Dollars	Rank
Chicago, IL	55,735,465	3
Detroit, MI	104,433,346	1
Houston, TX	2,899,142	8
Los Angeles-Long Beach, CA	14,207,406	5
Miami, FL	62,273,629	2
Minneapolis-Saint Paul, MN-WI	5,140,672	7
New York, NY	-4,288,877,266	10
San Francisco, CA	-5,469,035	9
San Jose, CA	16,686,616	4
Seattle-Bellevue-Everett, WA	9,431,003	6

Source: U.S. Department of Commerce, International Trade Administration, *Metropolitan Area Exports: An Export Performance Report on Over 250 U.S. Cities,* Washington, D.C.: U.S. Government Printing Office, April 1996, p. 64. Primary source: Exporter Location Series, Census Bureau.

★ 2060 ★
Imports and Exports: Sales

Export Sales Changes Since 1993, By Industry Group: Primary Metals (Percent)
[In percent]

City	Percent	Rank
Chicago, IL	15.3	4
Detroit, MI	21.0	1
Houston, TX	1.0	7
Los Angeles-Long Beach, CA	4.9	6
Miami, FL	21.0	1
Minneapolis-Saint Paul, MN-WI	12.1	5
New York, NY	-65.0	9
San Francisco, CA	-3.1	8
San Jose, CA	18.3	2
Seattle-Bellevue-Everett, WA	18.0	3

Source: U.S. Department of Commerce, International Trade Administration, *Metropolitan Area Exports: An Export Performance Report on Over 250 U.S. Cities,* Washington, D.C.: U.S. Government Printing Office, April 1996, p. 64. Primary source: Exporter Location Series, Census Bureau.

★ 2061 ★
Imports and Exports: Sales

Export Sales Changes Since 1993, By Industry Group: Printing and Publishing (Dollars)
[In dollars]

City	Dollars	Rank
Chicago, IL	-6,414,914	9
Detroit, MI	8,827,911	4
Houston, TX	966,485	6
Los Angeles-Long Beach, CA	24,865,613	2
Miami, FL	14,902,451	3
Minneapolis-Saint Paul, MN-WI	-27,652	7
New York, NY	-9,043,696	10
San Francisco, CA	4,192,599	5
San Jose, CA	-1,078,911	8
Seattle-Bellevue-Everett, WA	301,024,364	1

Source: U.S. Department of Commerce, International Trade Administration, *Metropolitan Area Exports: An Export Performance Report on Over 250 U.S. Cities,* Washington, D.C.: U.S. Government Printing Office, April 1996, p. 64. Primary source: Exporter Location Series, Census Bureau. *Notes:* Sales of paper are included in the figure shown for Seattle-Bellevue-Everett, Washington.

★ 2062 ★
Imports and Exports: Sales

Export Sales Changes Since 1993, By Industry Group: Printing and Publishing (Percent)
[In percent]

City	Percent	Rank
Chicago, IL	-3.3	10
Detroit, MI	21.5	3
Houston, TX	7.5	6
Los Angeles-Long Beach, CA	17.4	4
Miami, FL	28.8	2
Minneapolis-Saint Paul, MN-WI	-0.1	7
New York, NY	-1.5	9
San Francisco, CA	14.1	5
San Jose, CA	-1.2	8
Seattle-Bellevue-Everett, WA	82.3	1

Source: U.S. Department of Commerce, International Trade Administration, *Metropolitan Area Exports: An Export Performance Report on Over 250 U.S. Cities,* Washington, D.C., U.S. Government Printing Office, April 1996, p. 64. Primary source: Exporter Location Series, Census Bureau. *Notes:* Sales of paper are included in the figure shown for Seattle-Bellevue-Everett, Washington.

★ 2063 ★
Imports and Exports: Sales

Export Sales Changes Since 1993, By Industry Group: Refined Petroleum Products (Dollars)
[In dollars]

City	Dollars	Rank
Chicago, IL	12,050,680	1
Detroit, MI	-4,780,601	5
Houston, TX	-142,515,353	8
Los Angeles-Long Beach, CA	-172,922,846	9
Miami, FL	-74,632,243	6
Minneapolis-Saint Paul, MN-WI	374,424	4
New York, NY	-142,009,033	7
San Francisco, CA	-250,525,394	10

[Continued]

★ 2063 ★

Export Sales Changes Since 1993, By Industry Group: Refined Petroleum Products (Dollars)

[Continued]

City	Dollars	Rank
San Jose, CA	2,259,819	3
Seattle-Bellevue-Everett, WA	2,451,230	2

Source: U.S. Department of Commerce, International Trade Administration, *Metropolitan Area Exports: An Export Performance Report on Over 250 U.S. Cities,* Washington, D.C.: U.S. Government Printing Office, April 1996, p. 64. Primary source: Exporter Location Series, Census Bureau. *Notes:* Sales of chemical products are included in the figure shown for San Francisco, California.

★ 2064 ★

Imports and Exports: Sales

Export Sales Changes Since 1993, By Industry Group: Refined Petroleum Products (Percent)

[In percent]

City	Percent	Rank
Chicago, IL	21.7	2
Detroit, MI	-9.7	6
Houston, TX	-8.9	5
Los Angeles-Long Beach, CA	-23.6	8
Miami, FL	-51.9	10
Minneapolis-Saint Paul, MN-WI	6.7	4
New York, NY	-34.8	9
San Francisco, CA	-22.6	7
San Jose, CA	120.9	1
Seattle-Bellevue-Everett, WA	12.0	3

Source: U.S. Department of Commerce, International Trade Administration, *Metropolitan Area Exports: An Export Performance Report on Over 250 U.S. Cities,* Washington, D.C.: U.S. Government Printing Office, April 1996, p. 64. Primary source: Exporter Location Series, Census Bureau. *Notes:* Sales of chemical products are included in the figure for San Francisco, California.

★ 2065 ★

Imports and Exports: Sales

Export Sales Changes Since 1993, By Industry Group: Rubber and Plastic Products (Dollars)

[In dollars]

City	Dollars	Rank
Chicago, IL	105,322,339	1
Detroit, MI	8,360,380	7
Houston, TX	31,358,005	2
Los Angeles-Long Beach, CA	10,021,781	6
Miami, FL	19,079,380	5
Minneapolis-Saint Paul, MN-WI	21,264,386	4
New York, NY	-4,015,744	9
San Francisco, CA	-10,404,450	10
San Jose, CA	24,380,850	3
Seattle-Bellevue-Everett, WA	1,854,334	8

Source: U.S. Department of Commerce, International Trade Administration, *Metropolitan Area Exports: An Export Performance Report on Over 250 U.S. Cities,* Washington, D.C.: U.S. Government Printing Office, April 1996, p. 64. Primary source: Exporter Location Series, Census Bureau. *Notes:* Sales of leather products are included in the figure shown for Detroit, Michigan.

★ 2066 ★

Imports and Exports: Sales

Export Sales Changes Since 1993, By Industry Group: Rubber and Plastic Products (Percent)

[In percent]

City	Percent	Rank
Chicago, IL	34.0	2
Detroit, MI	1.9	8
Houston, TX	27.9	3
Los Angeles-Long Beach, CA	3.7	7
Miami, FL	9.4	5
Minneapolis-Saint Paul, MN-WI	13.0	4
New York, NY	-2.5	9
San Francisco, CA	-9.8	10
San Jose, CA	63.9	1
Seattle-Bellevue-Everett, WA	3.9	6

Source: U.S. Department of Commerce, International Trade Administration, *Metropolitan Area Exports: An Export Performance Report on Over 250 U.S. Cities,* Washington, D.C.: U.S. Government Printing Office, April 1996, p. 64. Primary source: Exporter Location Series, Census Bureau. *Notes:* Sales of leather products are included in the figure shown for Detroit, Michigan.

★ 2067 ★

Imports and Exports: Sales

Export Sales Changes Since 1993, By Industry Group: Scientific and Measuring Instruments (Dollars)

[In dollars]

City	Dollars	Rank
Chicago, IL	166,750,318	2
Detroit, MI	104,474,288	4
Houston, TX	-34,253,421	10
Los Angeles-Long Beach, CA	136,523,893	3
Miami, FL	73,425,043	5
Minneapolis-Saint Paul, MN-WI	49,075,494	6
New York, NY	6,519,496	8
San Francisco, CA	-5,704,512	9
San Jose, CA	220,092,505	1
Seattle-Bellevue-Everett, WA	31,137,294	7

Source: U.S. Department of Commerce, International Trade Administration, *Metropolitan Area Exports: An Export Performance Report on Over 250 U.S. Cities,* Washington, D.C.: U.S. Government Printing Office, April 1996, p. 64. Primary source: Exporter Location Series, Census Bureau.

★ 2068 ★

Imports and Exports: Sales

Export Sales Changes Since 1993, By Industry Group: Scientific and Measuring Instruments (Percent)

[In percent]

City	Percent	Rank
Chicago, IL	19.4	2
Detroit, MI	36.2	1
Houston, TX	-7.7	10
Los Angeles-Long Beach, CA	13.8	4
Miami, FL	12.5	5
Minneapolis-Saint Paul, MN-WI	5.2	7
New York, NY	1.0	8

[Continued]

★ 2068 ★

Export Sales Changes Since 1993, By Industry Group: Scientific and Measuring Instruments (Percent)

[Continued]

City	Percent	Rank
San Francisco, CA	-1.5	9
San Jose, CA	15.3	3
Seattle-Bellevue-Everett, WA	7.9	6

Source: U.S. Department of Commerce, International Trade Administration, *Metropolitan Area Exports: An Export Performance Report on Over 250 U.S. Cities,* Washington, D.C.: U.S. Government Printing Office, April 1996, p. 64. Primary source: Exporter Location Series, Census Bureau.

★ 2069 ★

Imports and Exports: Sales

Export Sales Changes Since 1993, By Industry Group: Stone, Clay, and Glass Products (Dollars)

[In dollars]

City	Dollars	Rank
Chicago, IL	21,823,796	3
Detroit, MI	52,805,845	1
Houston, TX	4,702,595	5
Los Angeles-Long Beach, CA	4,307,542	6
Miami, FL	-7,902,611	10
Minneapolis-Saint Paul, MN-WI	32,954,054	2
New York, NY	10,217,560	4
San Francisco, CA	276,324	7
San Jose, CA	-965,891	9
Seattle-Bellevue-Everett, WA	-31,209	8

Source: U.S. Department of Commerce, International Trade Administration, *Metropolitan Area Exports: An Export Performance Report on Over 250 U.S. Cities,* Washington, D.C.: U.S. Government Printing Office, April 1996, p. 64. Primary source: Exporter Location Series, Census Bureau.

★ 2070 ★

Imports and Exports: Sales

Export Sales Changes Since 1993, By Industry Group: Stone, Clay, and Glass Products (Percent)

[In percent]

City	Percent	Rank
Chicago, IL	20.9	3
Detroit, MI	27.2	2
Houston, TX	7.8	5
Los Angeles-Long Beach, CA	4.8	6
Miami, FL	-9.0	10
Minneapolis-Saint Paul, MN-WI	30.8	1
New York, NY	10.7	4
San Francisco, CA	0.5	7
San Jose, CA	-5.4	9
Seattle-Bellevue-Everett, WA	-0.1	8

Source: U.S. Department of Commerce, International Trade Administration, *Metropolitan Area Exports: An Export Performance Report on Over 250 U.S. Cities,* Washington, D.C.: U.S. Government Printing Office, April 1996, p. 64. Primary source: Exporter Location Series, Census Bureau.

★ 2071 ★

Imports and Exports: Sales

Export Sales Changes Since 1993, By Industry Group: Transportation Equipment (Dollars)

[In dollars]

City	Dollars	Rank
Chicago, IL	279,646,774	4
Detroit, MI	9,917,560,222	1
Houston, TX	2,903,513	7
Los Angeles-Long Beach, CA	1,365,419,804	2
Miami, FL	46,100,137	5
Minneapolis-Saint Paul, MN-WI	-19,125,814	8
New York, NY	-395,399,835	9
San Francisco, CA	335,005,193	3
San Jose, CA	3,647,903	6
Seattle-Bellevue-Everett, WA	-2,750,542,642	10

Source: U.S. Department of Commerce, International Trade Administration, *Metropolitan Area Exports: An Export Performance Report on Over 250 U.S. Cities,* Washington, D.C., U.S. Government Printing Office, April 1996, p. 64. Primary source: Exporter Location Series, Census Bureau.

★ 2072 ★

Imports and Exports: Sales

Export Sales Changes Since 1993, By Industry Group: Transportation Equipment (Percent)

[In percent]

City	Percent	Rank
Chicago, IL	32.0	2
Detroit, MI	98.5	1
Houston, TX	0.7	7
Los Angeles-Long Beach, CA	19.6	3
Miami, FL	3.8	5
Minneapolis-Saint Paul, MN-WI	-10.2	8
New York, NY	-16.4	10
San Francisco, CA	19.1	4
San Jose, CA	3.0	6
Seattle-Bellevue-Everett, WA	-16.1	9

Source: U.S. Department of Commerce, International Trade Administration, *Metropolitan Area Exports: An Export Performance Report on Over 250 U.S. Cities,* Washington, D.C.: U.S. Government Printing Office, April 1996, p. 64. Primary source: Exporter Location Series, Census Bureau.

★ 2073 ★

Imports and Exports: Sales

Export Sales Changes Since 1993, By Industry: Fabricated Metal Products (Dollars)

[In dollars]

City	Dollars	Rank
Chicago, IL	59,203,866	1
Detroit, MI	-184,736,443	10
Houston, TX	-17,883,567	7
Los Angeles-Long Beach, CA	-1,679,622	5
Miami, FL	1,981,309	4
Minneapolis-Saint Paul, MN-WI	16,361,501	3
New York, NY	-60,531,140	9
San Francisco, CA	-25,516,390	8

[Continued]

★2073★

Export Sales Changes Since 1993, By Industry: Fabricated Metal Products (Dollars)

[Continued]

City	Dollars	Rank
San Jose, CA	-7,025,591	6
Seattle-Bellevue-Everett, WA	33,234,332	2

Source: U.S. Department of Commerce, International Trade Administration, *Metropolitan Area Exports: An Export Performance Report on Over 250 U.S. Cities*, Washington, D.C.: U.S. Government Printing Office, April 1996, p. 64. Primary source: Exporter Location Series, Census Bureau.

★2074★

Imports and Exports: Sales

Export Sales Changes Since 1993, By Industry: Fabricated Metal Products (Percent)

[In percent]

City	Percent	Rank
Chicago, IL	14.7	2
Detroit, MI	-15.2	9
Houston, TX	-4.6	6
Los Angeles-Long Beach, CA	-0.4	5
Miami, FL	1.0	4
Minneapolis-Saint Paul, MN-WI	9.8	3
New York, NY	-20.2	10
San Francisco, CA	-13.2	8
San Jose, CA	-11.0	7
Seattle-Bellevue-Everett, WA	61.8	1

Source: U.S. Department of Commerce, International Trade Administration, *Metropolitan Area Exports: An Export Performance Report on Over 250 U.S. Cities*, Washington, D.C.: U.S. Government Printing Office, April 1996, p. 64. Primary source: Exporter Location Series, Census Bureau.

★2075★

Imports and Exports: Sales

Export Sales, 1994, By Industry Group: Apparel

[In dollars]

City	Dollars	Rank
Chicago, IL	58,761,835	6
Detroit, MI	83,106,618	5
Houston, TX	12,953,802	9
Los Angeles-Long Beach, CA	619,416,319	1
Miami, FL	387,109,776	3
Minneapolis-Saint Paul, MN-WI	21,491,268	8
New York, NY	523,534,398	2
San Francisco, CA	266,804,258	4
San Jose, CA	4,772,768	10
Seattle-Bellevue-Everett, WA	33,258,698	7

Source: U.S. Department of Commerce, International Trade Administration, *Metropolitan Area Exports: An Export Performance Report on Over 250 U.S. Cities*, Washington, D.C.: U.S. Government Printing Office, April 1996, p. 64. Primary source: Exporter Location Series, Census Bureau.

★2076★

Imports and Exports: Sales

Export Sales, 1994, By Industry Group: Chemical Products

[In dollars]

City	Dollar	Rank
Chicago, IL	3,079,173,234	2
Detroit, MI	252,173,551	7
Houston, TX	3,626,773,182	1
Los Angeles-Long Beach, CA	930,209,203	4
Miami, FL	456,105,408	6
Minneapolis-Saint Paul, MN-WI	174,372,476	9
New York, NY	2,324,333,087	3
San Francisco, CA	859,543,040	5
San Jose, CA	205,971,680	8
Seattle-Bellevue-Everett, WA	71,030,303	10

Source: U.S. Department of Commerce, International Trade Administration, *Metropolitan Area Exports: An Export Performance Report on Over 250 U.S. Cities*, Washington, D.C.: U.S. Government Printing Office, April 1996, p. 64. Primary source: Exporter Location Series, Census Bureau.

★2077★

Imports and Exports: Sales

Export Sales, 1994, By Industry Group: Electrical and Electronics Equipment

[In dollars]

City	Dollars	Rank
Chicago, IL	4,357,784,717	2
Detroit, MI	1,161,185,570	6
Houston, TX	549,102,120	10
Los Angeles-Long Beach, CA	2,467,776,664	3
Miami, FL	1,461,502,206	4
Minneapolis-Saint Paul, MN-WI	736,701,858	8
New York, NY	1,026,310,209	7
San Francisco, CA	1,393,348,049	5
San Jose, CA	9,445,277,116	1
Seattle-Bellevue-Everett, WA	655,895,012	9

Source: U.S. Department of Commerce, International Trade Administration, *Metropolitan Area Exports: An Export Performance Report on Over 250 U.S. Cities*, Washington, D.C.: U.S. Government Printing Office, April 1996, p. 64. Primary source: Exporter Location Series, Census Bureau.

★2078★

Imports and Exports: Sales

Export Sales, 1994, By Industry Group: Fabricated Metal Products

[In dollars]

City	Dollars	Rank
Chicago, IL	462,951,435	2
Detroit, MI	1,031,836,210	1
Houston, TX	371,749,081	4
Los Angeles-Long Beach, CA	433,275,243	3
Miami, FL	203,104,426	6
Minneapolis-Saint Paul, MN-WI	182,665,411	7
New York, NY	239,251,181	5
San Francisco, CA	168,271,091	8

[Continued]

★2078★

Export Sales, 1994, By Industry Group: Fabricated Metal Products

[Continued]

City	Dollars	Rank
San Jose, CA	57,096,244	10
Seattle-Bellevue-Everett, WA	86,998,206	9

Source: U.S. Department of Commerce, International Trade Administration, *Metropolitan Area Exports: An Export Performance Report on Over 250 U.S. Cities,* Washington, D.C.: U.S. Government Printing Office, April 1996, p. 64. Primary source: Exporter Location Series, Census Bureau.

★2079★

Imports and Exports: Sales

Export Sales, 1994, By Industry Group: Food Products

[In dollars]

City	Dollars	Rank
Chicago, IL	644,879,357	5
Detroit, MI	99,039,281	10
Houston, TX	438,715,613	7
Los Angeles-Long Beach, CA	1,311,079,342	3
Miami, FL	380,054,692	8
Minneapolis-Saint Paul, MN-WI	1,414,822,759	2
New York, NY	1,947,436,155	1
San Francisco, CA	1,032,352,706	4
San Jose, CA	113,955,003	9
Seattle-Bellevue-Everett, WA	558,303,141	6

Source: U.S. Department of Commerce, International Trade Administration, *Metropolitan Area Exports: An Export Performance Report on Over 250 U.S. Cities,* Washington, D.C.: U.S. Government Printing Office, April 1996, p. 64. Primary source: Exporter Location Series, Census Bureau. *Notes:* Sales of tobacco products are included in the figures shown for New York, New York, and San Francisco, California.

★2080★

Imports and Exports: Sales

Export Sales, 1994, By Industry Group: Furniture and Fixtures

[In dollars]

City	Dollars	Rank
Chicago, IL	58,695,859	4
Detroit, MI	324,216,943	1
Houston, TX	16,754,597	7
Los Angeles-Long Beach, CA	118,256,734	2
Miami, FL	76,910,548	3
Minneapolis-Saint Paul, MN-WI	17,306,329	6
New York, NY	57,035,299	5
San Francisco, CA	15,427,506	8
San Jose, CA	11,599,092	10
Seattle-Bellevue-Everett, WA	14,888,257	9

Source: U.S. Department of Commerce, International Trade Administration, *Metropolitan Area Exports: An Export Performance Report on Over 250 U.S. Cities,* Washington, D.C.: U.S. Government Printing Office, April 1996, p. 64. Primary source: Exporter Location Series, Census Bureau.

★2081★

Imports and Exports: Sales

Export Sales, 1994, By Industry Group: Industrial Machinery and Computers

[In dollars]

City	Dollars	Rank
Chicago, IL	2,844,074,806	3
Detroit, MI	2,169,544,290	6
Houston, TX	4,973,190,746	2
Los Angeles-Long Beach, CA	2,553,794,700	5
Miami, FL	2,098,175,314	7
Minneapolis-Saint Paul, MN-WI	1,323,626,798	9
New York, NY	2,647,087,419	4
San Francisco, CA	1,651,971,318	8
San Jose, CA	7,659,519,609	1
Seattle-Bellevue-Everett, WA	385,282,778	10

Source: U.S. Department of Commerce, International Trade Administration, *Metropolitan Area Exports: An Export Performance Report on Over 250 U.S. Cities,* Washington, D.C.: U.S. Government Printing Office, April 1996, p. 64. Primary source: Exporter Location Series, Census Bureau.

★2082★

Imports and Exports: Sales

Export Sales, 1994, By Industry Group: Leather Products

[In dollars]

City	Dollars	Rank
Chicago, IL	44,916,749	4
Detroit, MI	451,402,323	1
Houston, TX	4,960,092	9
Los Angeles-Long Beach, CA	126,705,506	2
Miami, FL	44,204,279	5
Minneapolis-Saint Paul, MN-WI	6,877,422	8
New York, NY	94,091,234	3
San Francisco, CA	16,643,055	6
San Jose, CA	1,511,691	10
Seattle-Bellevue-Everett, WA	9,260,942	7

Source: U.S. Department of Commerce, International Trade Administration, *Metropolitan Area Exports: An Export Performance Report on Over 250 U.S. Cities,* Washington, D.C.: U.S. Government Printing Office, April 1996, p. 64. Primary source: Exporter Location Series, Census Bureau.

★2083★

Imports and Exports: Sales

Export Sales, 1994, By Industry Group: Lumber and Wood Products

[In dollars]

City	Dollars	Rank
Chicago, IL	23,533,069	7
Detroit, MI	19,420,291	8
Houston, TX	56,866,507	5
Los Angeles-Long Beach, CA	93,478,743	4
Miami, FL	93,687,627	3
Minneapolis-Saint Paul, MN-WI	10,900,081	9
New York, NY	102,145,260	2
San Francisco, CA	28,977,495	6

[Continued]

★2083★

Export Sales, 1994, By Industry Group: Lumber and Wood Products

[Continued]

City	Dollars	Rank
San Jose, CA	3,897,758	10
Seattle-Bellevue-Everett, WA	2,126,822,834	1

Source: U.S. Department of Commerce, International Trade Administration, *Metropolitan Area Exports: An Export Performance Report on Over 250 U.S. Cities,* Washington, D.C.: U.S. Government Printing Office, April 1996, p. 64. Primary source: Exporter Location Series, Census Bureau.

★2084★

Imports and Exports: Sales

Export Sales, 1994, By Industry Group: Non-Manufactured Commodities

[In dollars]

City	Dollars	Rank
Chicago, IL	1,435,903,671	5
Detroit, MI	347,620,487	9
Houston, TX	430,515,140	8
Los Angeles-Long Beach, CA	1,698,791,474	4
Miami, FL	694,545,369	6
Minneapolis-Saint Paul, MN-WI	2,712,676,580	2
New York, NY	4,505,463,198	1
San Francisco, CA	522,307,852	7
San Jose, CA	233,594,148	10
Seattle-Bellevue-Everett, WA	2,049,413,403	3

Source: U.S. Department of Commerce, International Trade Administration, *Metropolitan Area Exports: An Export Performance Report on Over 250 U.S. Cities,* Washington, D.C.: U.S. Government Printing Office, April 1996, p. 64. Primary source: Exporter Location Series, Census Bureau.

★2085★

Imports and Exports: Sales

Export Sales, 1994, By Industry Group: Paper Products

[In dollars]

City	Dollars	Rank
Chicago, IL	388,724,855	3
Detroit, MI	58,717,752	8
Houston, TX	31,695,184	9
Los Angeles-Long Beach, CA	149,250,220	6
Miami, FL	252,719,488	4
Minneapolis-Saint Paul, MN-WI	124,002,386	7
New York, NY	935,103,449	1
San Francisco, CA	175,453,073	5
San Jose, CA	15,176,790	10
Seattle-Bellevue-Everett, WA	666,977,729	2

Source: U.S. Department of Commerce, International Trade Administration, *Metropolitan Area Exports: An Export Performance Report on Over 250 U.S. Cities,* Washington, D.C.: U.S. Government Printing Office, April 1996, p. 64. Primary source: Exporter Location Series, Census Bureau. *Notes:* Sales in printing and publishing are included in the figure shown for Seattle-Bellevue-Everett, Washington.

★2086★

Imports and Exports: Sales

Export Sales, 1994, By Industry Group: Primary Metals

[In dollars]

City	Dollars	Rank
Chicago, IL	419,523,435	3
Detroit, MI	601,095,384	2
Houston, TX	287,898,183	6
Los Angeles-Long Beach, CA	302,502,279	5
Miami, FL	358,597,962	4
Minneapolis-Saint Paul, MN-WI	47,587,881	10
New York, NY	2,313,984,306	1
San Francisco, CA	171,453,797	7
San Jose, CA	107,828,952	8
Seattle-Bellevue-Everett, WA	61,831,730	9

Source: U.S. Department of Commerce, International Trade Administration, *Metropolitan Area Exports: An Export Performance Report on Over 250 U.S. Cities,* Washington, D.C.: U.S. Government Printing Office, April 1996, p. 64. Primary source: Exporter Location Series, Census Bureau.

★2087★

Imports and Exports: Sales

Export Sales, 1994, By Industry Group: Printing and Publishing

[In dollars]

City	Dollars	Rank
Chicago, IL	190,449,891	3
Detroit, MI	49,959,248	7
Houston, TX	13,893,217	10
Los Angeles-Long Beach, CA	167,875,346	4
Miami, FL	66,700,940	6
Minneapolis-Saint Paul, MN-WI	41,833,910	8
New York, NY	579,507,072	2
San Francisco, CA	33,980,340	9
San Jose, CA	86,074,704	5
Seattle-Bellevue-Everett, WA	666,977,729	1

Source: U.S. Department of Commerce, International Trade Administration, *Metropolitan Area Exports: An Export Performance Report on Over 250 U.S. Cities,* Washington, D.C.: U.S. Government Printing Office, April 1996, p. 64. Primary source: Exporter Location Series, Census Bureau. *Notes:* Sales of paper are included in the figure shown for Seattle-Bellevue-Everett, Washington.

★2088★

Imports and Exports: Sales

Export Sales, 1994, By Industry Group: Refined Petroleum Products

[In dollars]

City	Dollars	Rank
Chicago, IL	67,510,197	6
Detroit, MI	44,514,968	7
Houston, TX	1,460,646,556	1
Los Angeles-Long Beach, CA	559,614,776	3
Miami, FL	69,181,848	5
Minneapolis-Saint Paul, MN-WI	5,975,273	9
New York, NY	266,237,659	4
San Francisco, CA	859,543,040	2

[Continued]

★ 2088 ★

Export Sales, 1994, By Industry Group: Refined Petroleum Products

[Continued]

City	Dollars	Rank
San Jose, CA	4,129,464	10
Seattle-Bellevue-Everett, WA	22,857,919	8

Source: U.S. Department of Commerce, International Trade Administration, *Metropolitan Area Exports: An Export Performance Report on Over 250 U.S. Cities,* Washington, D.C.: U.S. Government Printing Office, April 1996, p. 64. Primary source: Exporter Location Series, Census Bureau. *Notes:* Sales of chemical products are included in the figure shown for San Francisco, California.

★ 2089 ★

Imports and Exports: Sales

Export Sales, 1994, By Industry Group: Rubber and Plastic Products

[In dollars]

City	Dollars	Rank
Chicago, IL	415,486,944	2
Detroit, MI	451,402,323	1
Houston, TX	143,868,004	7
Los Angeles-Long Beach, CA	278,778,177	3
Miami, FL	221,369,409	4
Minneapolis-Saint Paul, MN-WI	184,300,789	5
New York, NY	157,001,663	6
San Francisco, CA	95,574,184	8
San Jose, CA	62,557,953	9
Seattle-Bellevue-Everett, WA	49,650,614	10

Source: U.S. Department of Commerce, International Trade Administration, *Metropolitan Area Exports: An Export Performance Report on Over 250 U.S. Cities,* Washington, D.C.: U.S. Government Printing Office, April 1996, p. 64. Primary source: Exporter Location Series, Census Bureau. *Notes:* Sales of leather products are included in the figure shown for Detroit, Michigan.

★ 2090 ★

Imports and Exports: Sales

Export Sales, 1994, By Industry Group: Scientific and Measuring Instruments

[In dollars]

City	Dollars	Rank
Chicago, IL	1,028,454,762	3
Detroit, MI	392,967,445	9
Houston, TX	408,331,789	8
Los Angeles-Long Beach, CA	1,125,848,918	2
Miami, FL	659,323,699	5
Minneapolis-Saint Paul, MN-WI	984,609,610	4
New York, NY	635,323,529	6
San Francisco, CA	384,099,054	10
San Jose, CA	1,657,652,405	1
Seattle-Bellevue-Everett, WA	423,958,437	7

Source: U.S. Department of Commerce, International Trade Administration, *Metropolitan Area Exports: An Export Performance Report on Over 250 U.S. Cities,* Washington, D.C.: U.S. Government Printing Office, April 1996, p. 64. Primary source: Exporter Location Series, Census Bureau.

★ 2091 ★

Imports and Exports: Sales

Export Sales, 1994, By Industry Group: Stone, Clay, and Glass Products

[In dollars]

City	Dollars	Rank
Chicago, IL	126,414,819	3
Detroit, MI	246,886,294	1
Houston, TX	64,720,439	7
Los Angeles-Long Beach, CA	94,173,992	5
Miami, FL	80,316,920	6
Minneapolis-Saint Paul, MN-WI	139,951,214	2
New York, NY	105,813,972	4
San Francisco, CA	58,951,517	8
San Jose, CA	16,877,442	10
Seattle-Bellevue-Everett, WA	36,196,150	9

Source: U.S. Department of Commerce, International Trade Administration, *Metropolitan Area Exports: An Export Performance Report on Over 250 U.S. Cities,* Washington, D.C.: U.S. Government Printing Office, April 1996, p. 64. Primary source: Exporter Location Series, Census Bureau.

★ 2092 ★

Imports and Exports: Sales

Export Sales, 1994, By Industry Group: Textile Mill Products

[In dollars]

City	Dollars	Rank
Chicago, IL	50,483,533	6
Detroit, MI	70,412,914	5
Houston, TX	12,040,622	8
Los Angeles-Long Beach, CA	134,673,224	3
Miami, FL	123,134,223	4
Minneapolis-Saint Paul, MN-WI	19,246,887	7
New York, NY	605,745,853	1
San Francisco, CA	137,581,947	2
San Jose, CA	4,379,965	10
Seattle-Bellevue-Everett, WA	10,570,216	9

Source: U.S. Department of Commerce, International Trade Administration, *Metropolitan Area Exports: An Export Performance Report on Over 250 U.S. Cities,* Washington, D.C.: U.S. Government Printing Office, April 1996, p. 64. Primary source: Exporter Location Series, Census Bureau.

★ 2093 ★

Imports and Exports: Sales

Export Sales, 1994, By Industry Group: Tobacco Products

[In dollars]

City	Dollars	Rank
Chicago, IL	1,920,746	4
Detroit, MI	277,470	6
Los Angeles-Long Beach, CA	503,530	5
Miami, FL	5,570,948	3
Minneapolis-Saint Paul, MN-WI	0	8
New York, NY	1,947,436,155	1

[Continued]

★ 2093 ★

Export Sales, 1994, By Industry Group: Tobacco Products

[Continued]

City	Dollars	Rank
San Francisco, CA	1,032,352,706	2
Seattle-Bellevue-Everett, WA	11,308	7

Source: U.S. Department of Commerce, International Trade Administration, *Metropolitan Area Exports: An Export Performance Report on Over 250 U.S. Cities,* Washington, D.C.: U.S. Government Printing Office, April 1996, p. 64. Primary source: Exporter Location Series, Census Bureau. *Notes:* Food products sales are included in the figures shown for New York, New York, and San Francisco, California.

★ 2094 ★

Imports and Exports: Sales

Export Sales, 1994, By Industry Group: Transportation Equipment

[In dollars]

City	Dollars	Rank
Chicago, IL	1,154,510,400	7
Detroit, MI	19,985,638,716	1
Houston, TX	402,341,515	8
Los Angeles-Long Beach, CA	8,331,782,070	3
Miami, FL	1,271,411,810	6
Minneapolis-Saint Paul, MN-WI	169,160,420	9
New York, NY	2,017,227,071	5
San Francisco, CA	2,086,062,557	4
San Jose, CA	123,559,043	10
Seattle-Bellevue-Everett, WA	14,352,912,500	2

Source: U.S. Department of Commerce, International Trade Administration, *Metropolitan Area Exports: An Export Performance Report on Over 250 U.S. Cities,* Washington, D.C., U.S. Government Printing Office, April 1996, p. 64. Primary source: Exporter Location Series, Census Bureau.

★ 2095 ★

Imports and Exports: Sales

Export Sales, 1994, By Selected Market: Australia

[In dollars]

City	Dollar	Rank
Chicago, IL	492,097,397	2
Detroit, MI	152,921,322	8
Houston, TX	204,246,703	7
Los Angeles-Long Beach, CA	596,783,094	1
Miami, FL	24,434,810	10
Minneapolis-Saint Paul, MN-WI	145,195,056	9
New York, NY	221,059,858	6
San Francisco, CA	409,194,919	4
San Jose, CA	356,725,744	5
Seattle-Bellevue-Everett, WA	430,795,917	3

Source: U.S. Department of Commerce, International Trade Administration, *Metropolitan Area Exports: An Export Performance Report on Over 250 U.S. Cities,* Washington, D.C.: U.S. Government Printing Office, April 1996, p. 66. Primary source: Exporter Location Series, Census Bureau.

★ 2096 ★

Imports and Exports: Sales

Export Sales, 1994, By Selected Market: Australia (Dollar Changes)

[In dollars]

City	Dollar	Rank
Chicago, IL	75,598,127	4
Detroit, MI	15,355,435	8
Houston, TX	31,983,067	7
Los Angeles-Long Beach, CA	176,429,391	1
Miami, FL	-4,467,138	10
Minneapolis-Saint Paul, MN-WI	4,149,452	9
New York, NY	63,731,926	5
San Francisco, CA	143,867,402	3
San Jose, CA	47,238,756	6
Seattle-Bellevue-Everett, WA	164,450,209	2

Source: U.S. Department of Commerce, International Trade Administration, *Metropolitan Area Exports: An Export Performance Report on Over 250 U.S. Cities,* Washington, D.C.: U.S. Government Printing Office, April 1996, p. 66. Primary source: Exporter Location Series, Census Bureau.

★ 2097 ★

Imports and Exports: Sales

Export Sales, 1994, By Selected Market: Australia (Percent Changes)

[In percent]

City	Percent	Rank
Chicago, IL	18.2	6
Detroit, MI	11.2	8
Houston, TX	18.6	5
Los Angeles-Long Beach, CA	42.0	3
Miami, FL	-15.5	10
Minneapolis-Saint Paul, MN-WI	2.9	9
New York, NY	40.5	4
San Francisco, CA	54.2	2
San Jose, CA	15.3	7
Seattle-Bellevue-Everett, WA	61.7	1

Source: U.S. Department of Commerce, International Trade Administration, *Metropolitan Area Exports: An Export Performance Report on Over 250 U.S. Cities,* Washington, D.C.: U.S. Government Printing Office, April 1996, p. 66. Primary source: Exporter Location Series, Census Bureau.

★ 2098 ★

Imports and Exports: Sales

Export Sales, 1994, By Selected Market: Caribbean and Central America

[In dollars]

MSA	Dollar	Rank
Chicago, IL	262,415,098	4
Detroit, MI	63,128,658	9
Houston, TX	726,148,765	3
Los Angeles-Long Beach, CA	173,222,319	7
Miami, FL	2,608,168,922	1
Minneapolis-Saint Paul, MN-WI	180,056,367	6
New York, NY	868,600,832	2
San Francisco, CA	237,779,086	5

[Continued]

★2098★

Export Sales, 1994, By Selected Market: Caribbean and Central America
[Continued]

MSA	Dollar	Rank
San Jose, CA	15,769,491	10
Seattle-Bellevue-Everett, WA	102,075,659	8

Source: U.S. Department of Commerce, International Trade Administration, *Metropolitan Area Exports: An Export Performance Report on Over 250 U.S. Cities,* p. 65. Primary source: Exporter Location Series, Census Bureau.

★2099★

Imports and Exports: Sales

Export Sales, 1994, By Selected Market: China
[In dollars]

City	Dollar	Rank
Chicago, IL	914,965,543	2
Detroit, MI	96,211,630	8
Houston, TX	270,396,235	5
Los Angeles-Long Beach, CA	522,699,581	3
Miami, FL	10,070,591	10
Minneapolis-Saint Paul, MN-WI	89,217,740	9
New York, NY	461,259,482	4
San Francisco, CA	241,372,890	6
San Jose, CA	228,298,975	7
Seattle-Bellevue-Everett, WA	1,852,846,987	1

Source: U.S. Department of Commerce, International Trade Administration, *Metropolitan Area Exports: An Export Performance Report on Over 250 U.S. Cities,* Washington, D.C.: U.S. Government Printing Office, April 1996, p. 65. Primary source: Exporter Location Series, Census Bureau.

★2100★

Imports and Exports: Sales

Export Sales, 1994, By Selected Market: China (Dollar Changes)
[In dollars]

City	Dollar	Rank
Chicago, IL	258,785,521	1
Detroit, MI	-65,366,447	8
Houston, TX	-13,587,533	4
Los Angeles-Long Beach, CA	-189,068,855	10
Miami, FL	-2,128,903	2
Minneapolis-Saint Paul, MN-WI	-25,062,389	6
New York, NY	-42,893,466	7
San Francisco, CA	-148,011,752	9
San Jose, CA	-19,080,667	5
Seattle-Bellevue-Everett, WA	-4,981,036	3

Source: U.S. Department of Commerce, International Trade Administration, *Metropolitan Area Exports: An Export Performance Report on Over 250 U.S. Cities,* Washington, D.C., U.S. Government Printing Office, April 1996, p. 65. Primary source: Exporter Location Series, Census Bureau.

★2101★

Imports and Exports: Sales

Export Sales, 1994, By Selected Market: China (Percent Changes)
[In percent]

City	Percent	Rank
Chicago, IL	39.4	1
Detroit, MI	-40.5	10
Houston, TX	-4.8	3
Los Angeles-Long Beach, CA	-26.6	8
Miami, FL	-17.5	6
Minneapolis-Saint Paul, MN-WI	-21.9	7
New York, NY	-8.5	5
San Francisco, CA	-38.0	9
San Jose, CA	-7.7	4
Seattle-Bellevue-Everett, WA	-0.3	2

Source: U.S. Department of Commerce, International Trade Administration, *Metropolitan Area Exports: An Export Performance Report on Over 250 U.S. Cities,* Washington, D.C.: U.S. Government Printing Office, April 1996, p. 65. Primary source: Exporter Location Series, Census Bureau.

★2102★

Imports and Exports: Sales

Export Sales, 1994, By Selected Market: East Asian
[In dollars]

City	Dollar	Rank
Chicago, IL	1,861,263,319	7
Detroit, MI	318,508,161	9
Houston, TX	2,020,701,671	5
Los Angeles-Long Beach, CA	4,763,056,848	2
Miami, FL	138,277,094	10
Minneapolis-Saint Paul, MN-WI	806,509,860	8
New York, NY	3,264,610,701	4
San Francisco, CA	1,924,942,579	6
San Jose, CA	4,940,260,413	1
Seattle-Bellevue-Everett, WA	3,596,711,193	3

Source: U.S. Department of Commerce, International Trade Administration, *Metropolitan Area Exports: An Export Performance Report on Over 250 U.S. Cities,* Washington, D.C.: U.S. Government Printing Office, April 1996, p. 66. Primary source: Exporter Location Series, Census Bureau.

★2103★

Imports and Exports: Sales

Export Sales, 1994, By Selected Market: East Asian (Dollar Changes)
[In dollars]

City	Dollar	Rank
Chicago, IL	405,289,940	3
Detroit, MI	-26,708,477	7
Houston, TX	446,921,350	2
Los Angeles-Long Beach, CA	-39,012,800	8
Miami, FL	48,545,458	6
Minneapolis-Saint Paul, MN-WI	135,784,427	4
New York, NY	117,120,357	5
San Francisco, CA	-148,011,752	9

[Continued]

★2103★

Export Sales, 1994, By Selected Market: East Asian (Dollar Changes)
[Continued]

City	Dollar	Rank
San Jose, CA	632,435,161	1
Seattle-Bellevue-Everett, WA	-332,559,085	10

Source: U.S. Department of Commerce, International Trade Administration, *Metropolitan Area Exports: An Export Performance Report on Over 250 U.S. Cities,* Washington, D.C.: U.S. Government Printing Office, April 1996, p. 66. Primary source: Exporter Location Series, Census Bureau.

★2104★

Imports and Exports: Sales

Export Sales, 1994, By Selected Market: East Asian (Percent Changes)
[In percent]

City	Percent	Rank
Chicago, IL	27.8	3
Detroit, MI	-7.7	8
Houston, TX	28.4	2
Los Angeles-Long Beach, CA	-0.8	7
Miami, FL	54.1	1
Minneapolis-Saint Paul, MN-WI	20.2	4
New York, NY	3.7	6
San Francisco, CA	-38.0	10
San Jose, CA	14.7	5
Seattle-Bellevue-Everett, WA	-8.5	9

Source: U.S. Department of Commerce, International Trade Administration, *Metropolitan Area Exports: An Export Performance Report on Over 250 U.S. Cities,* Washington, D.C.: U.S. Government Printing Office, April 1996, p. 66. Primary source: Exporter Location Series, Census Bureau.

★2105★

Imports and Exports: Sales

Export Sales, 1994, By Selected Market: European Union
[In dollars]

MSA	Dollar	Rank
Chicago, IL	3,747,019,671	5
Detroit, MI	1,993,436,157	9
Houston, TX	2,148,168,095	7
Los Angeles-Long Beach, CA	4,202,476,407	4
Miami, FL	549,274,386	10
Minneapolis-Saint Paul, MN-WI	3,105,676,373	6
New York, NY	5,152,743,115	1
San Francisco, CA	2,138,907,611	8
San Jose, CA	4,449,467,870	2
Seattle-Bellevue-Everett, WA	4,400,196,916	3

Source: U.S. Department of Commerce, International Trade Administration, *Metropolitan Area Exports: An Export Performance Report on Over 250 U.S. Cities,* p. 65. Primary source: Exporter Location Series, Census Bureau.

★2106★

Imports and Exports: Sales

Export Sales, 1994, By Selected Market: Former Soviet Republics
[In dollars]

MSA	Dollar	Rank
Chicago, IL	89,999,944	5
Detroit, MI	57,782,855	7
Houston, TX	182,156,725	3
Los Angeles-Long Beach, CA	89,412,873	6
Miami, FL	10,952,675	10
Minneapolis-Saint Paul, MN-WI	95,044,566	4
New York, NY	432,045,518	1
San Francisco, CA	57,772,367	8
San Jose, CA	46,096,633	9
Seattle-Bellevue-Everett, WA	431,821,330	2

Source: U.S. Department of Commerce, International Trade Administration, *Metropolitan Area Exports: An Export Performance Report on Over 250 U.S. Cities,* p. 65. Primary source: Exporter Location Series, Census Bureau.

★2107★

Imports and Exports: Sales

Export Sales, 1994, By Selected Market: Japan
[In dollars]

City	Dollar	Rank
Chicago, IL	1,777,848,920	6
Detroit, MI	661,417,541	8
Houston, TX	617,408,983	9
Los Angeles-Long Beach, CA	5,806,930,880	1
Miami, FL	120,850,394	10
Minneapolis-Saint Paul, MN-WI	709,630,971	7
New York, NY	3,832,310,844	3
San Francisco, CA	1,817,968,094	5
San Jose, CA	2,843,441,849	4
Seattle-Bellevue-Everett, WA	5,568,633,700	2

Source: U.S. Department of Commerce, International Trade Administration, *Metropolitan Area Exports: An Export Performance Report on Over 250 U.S. Cities,* Washington, D.C.: U.S. Government Printing Office, April 1996, p. 65. Primary source: Exporter Location Series, Census Bureau.

★2108★

Imports and Exports: Sales

Export Sales, 1994, By Selected Market: Middle East
[In dollars]

City	Dollar	Rank
Chicago, IL	483,011,862	5
Detroit, MI	1,124,875,897	2
Houston, TX	844,954,949	3
Los Angeles-Long Beach, CA	283,393,252	7
Miami, FL	50,881,999	10
Minneapolis-Saint Paul, MN-WI	373,933,304	6
New York, NY	1,605,677,254	1
San Francisco, CA	273,023,937	8
San Jose, CA	165,106,472	9
Seattle-Bellevue-Everett, WA	727,802,535	4

Source: U.S. Department of Commerce, International Trade Administration, *Metropolitan Area Exports: An Export Performance Report on Over 250 U.S. Cities,* Washington, D.C.: U.S. Government Printing Office, April 1996, p. 66. Primary source: Exporter Location Series, Census Bureau.

★2109★
Imports and Exports: Sales

Export Sales, 1994, By Selected Market: Middle East (Dollar Changes)

[In dollars]

City	Dollar	Rank
Chicago, IL	87,928,681	2
Detroit, MI	-198,035,002	9
Houston, TX	-407,048,185	10
Los Angeles-Long Beach, CA	-14,416,534	4
Miami, FL	-16,464,304	5
Minneapolis-Saint Paul, MN-WI	-37,801,951	7
New York, NY	-98,937,463	8
San Francisco, CA	-18,327,714	6
San Jose, CA	-12,592,535	3
Seattle-Bellevue-Everett, WA	169,419,956	1

Source: U.S. Department of Commerce, International Trade Administration, *Metropolitan Area Exports: An Export Performance Report on Over 250 U.S. Cities,* Washington, D.C.: U.S. Government Printing Office, April 1996, p. 66. Primary source: Exporter Location Series, Census Bureau.

★2110★
Imports and Exports: Sales

Export Sales, 1994, By Selected Market: Middle East (Percent Changes)

[In percent]

City	Percent	Rank
Chicago, IL	22.3	2
Detroit, MI	-15.0	8
Houston, TX	-32.5	10
Los Angeles-Long Beach, CA	-4.8	3
Miami, FL	-24.4	9
Minneapolis-Saint Paul, MN-WI	-9.2	7
New York, NY	-5.8	4
San Francisco, CA	-6.3	5
San Jose, CA	-7.1	6
Seattle-Bellevue-Everett, WA	30.3	1

Source: U.S. Department of Commerce, International Trade Administration, *Metropolitan Area Exports: An Export Performance Report on Over 250 U.S. Cities,* Washington, D.C.: U.S. Government Printing Office, April 1996, p. 66. Primary source: Exporter Location Series, Census Bureau.

★2111★
Imports and Exports: Sales

Export Sales, 1994, By Selected Market: NAFTA Countries

[In dollars]

MSA	Dollar	Rank
Chicago, IL	4,830,890,516	2
Detroit, MI	21,734,220,342	1
Houston, TX	2,839,658,301	4
Los Angeles-Long Beach, CA	3,232,558,991	3
Miami, FL	976,650,481	9
Minneapolis-Saint Paul, MN-WI	1,805,429,187	7
New York, NY	2,493,404,176	6
San Francisco, CA	788,867,784	10

[Continued]

★2111★

Export Sales, 1994, By Selected Market: NAFTA Countries

[Continued]

MSA	Dollar	Rank
San Jose, CA	2,796,516,695	5
Seattle-Bellevue-Everett, WA	1,344,745,613	8

Source: U.S. Department of Commerce, International Trade Administration, *Metropolitan Area Exports: An Export Performance Report on Over 250 U.S. Cities,* p. 65. Primary source: Exporter Location Series, Census Bureau.

★2112★
Imports and Exports: Sales

Export Sales, 1994, By Selected Market: South Africa

[In dollars]

City	Dollar	Rank
Chicago, IL	104,891,157	2
Detroit, MI	15,241,290	9
Houston, TX	88,296,243	3
Los Angeles-Long Beach, CA	38,343,571	7
Miami, FL	12,829,045	10
Minneapolis-Saint Paul, MN-WI	55,930,886	5
New York, NY	130,369,937	1
San Francisco, CA	25,799,477	8
San Jose, CA	68,700,883	4
Seattle-Bellevue-Everett, WA	43,278,675	6

Source: U.S. Department of Commerce, International Trade Administration, *Metropolitan Area Exports: An Export Performance Report on Over 250 U.S. Cities,* Washington, D.C.: U.S. Government Printing Office, April 1996, p. 66. Primary source: Exporter Location Series, Census Bureau.

★2113★
Imports and Exports: Sales

Export Sales, 1994, By Selected Market: South Africa (Dollar Changes)

[In dollars]

City	Dollar	Rank
Chicago, IL	30,967,466	1
Detroit, MI	7,920,546	4
Houston, TX	19,805,885	2
Los Angeles-Long Beach, CA	1,501,021	5
Miami, FL	-1,770,407	8
Minneapolis-Saint Paul, MN-WI	-20,729,879	9
New York, NY	9,128,854	3
San Francisco, CA	-1,653,365	7
San Jose, CA	111,966	6
Seattle-Bellevue-Everett, WA	-225,132,305	10

Source: U.S. Department of Commerce, International Trade Administration, *Metropolitan Area Exports: An Export Performance Report on Over 250 U.S. Cities,* Washington, D.C.: U.S. Government Printing Office, April 1996, p. 66. Primary source: Exporter Location Series, Census Bureau.

★2114★
Imports and Exports: Sales

Export Sales, 1994, By Selected Market: South Africa (Percent Changes)

[In percent]

City	Percent	Rank
Chicago, IL	41.9	2
Detroit, MI	108.2	1
Houston, TX	28.9	3
Los Angeles-Long Beach, CA	4.1	5
Miami, FL	-12.1	8
Minneapolis-Saint Paul, MN-WI	-27.0	9
New York, NY	7.5	4
San Francisco, CA	-6.0	7
San Jose, CA	0.2	6
Seattle-Bellevue-Everett, WA	-83.9	10

Source: U.S. Department of Commerce, International Trade Administration, *Metropolitan Area Exports: An Export Performance Report on Over 250 U.S. Cities,* Washington, D.C.: U.S. Government Printing Office, April 1996, p. 66. Primary source: Exporter Location Series, Census Bureau.

★2115★
Imports and Exports: Sales

Export Sales, 1994, By Selected Market: South America

[In dollars]

MSA	Dollar	Rank
Chicago, IL	1,091,387,536	4
Detroit, MI	448,980,832	7
Houston, TX	1,907,988,659	2
Los Angeles-Long Beach, CA	885,490,012	5
Miami, FL	4,620,082,108	1
Minneapolis-Saint Paul, MN-WI	244,135,360	10
New York, NY	1,349,196,617	3
San Francisco, CA	486,762,699	6
San Jose, CA	270,805,194	8
Seattle-Bellevue-Everett, WA	245,712,053	9

Source: U.S. Department of Commerce, International Trade Administration, *Metropolitan Area Exports: An Export Performance Report on Over 250 U.S. Cities,* p. 65. Primary source: Exporter Location Series, Census Bureau.

★2116★
Imports and Exports: Sales

Export Sales, 1994, By Selected Market: Total to World

[In dollars]

City	Dollar	Rank
Chicago, IL	17,333,603,392	6
Detroit, MI	27,469,655,137	1
Houston, TX	13,388,170,043	7
Los Angeles-Long Beach, CA	22,224,814,589	3
Miami, FL	9,266,745,514	9
Minneapolis-Saint Paul, MN-WI	8,863,530,759	10
New York, NY	23,543,749,240	2
San Francisco, CA	9,303,816,205	8

[Continued]

★2116★

Export Sales, 1994, By Selected Market: Total to World

[Continued]

City	Dollar	Rank
San Jose, CA	19,942,678,387	5
Seattle-Bellevue-Everett, WA	21,752,981,626	4

Source: U.S. Department of Commerce, International Trade Administration, *Metropolitan Area Exports: An Export Performance Report on Over 250 U.S. Cities,* Washington, D.C.: U.S. Government Printing Office, April 1996, p. 66. Primary source: Exporter Location Series, Census Bureau.

★2117★
Imports and Exports: Sales

Export Sales, 1994, By Selected Market: Total to World (Dollar Changes)

[In dollars]

City	Dollar	Rank
Chicago, IL	2,887,027,329	3
Detroit, MI	10,688,766,405	1
Houston, TX	1,103,604,099	5
Los Angeles-Long Beach, CA	2,211,254,127	4
Miami, FL	1,002,441,568	6
Minneapolis-Saint Paul, MN-WI	-140,287,262	8
New York, NY	-4,649,072,678	10
San Francisco, CA	38,917,326	7
San Jose, CA	3,771,110,126	2
Seattle-Bellevue-Everett, WA	-2,062,667,103	9

Source: U.S. Department of Commerce, International Trade Administration, *Metropolitan Area Exports: An Export Performance Report on Over 250 U.S. Cities,* Washington, D.C.: U.S. Government Printing Office, April 1996, p. 66. Primary source: Exporter Location Series, Census Bureau.

★2118★
Imports and Exports: Sales

Export Sales, 1994, By Selected Market: Total to World (Percent Changes)

[In percent]

City	Percent	Rank
Chicago, IL	20.0	3
Detroit, MI	63.7	1
Houston, TX	9.0	6
Los Angeles-Long Beach, CA	11.0	5
Miami, FL	12.1	4
Minneapolis-Saint Paul, MN-WI	-1.6	8
New York, NY	-16.5	10
San Francisco, CA	0.4	7
San Jose, CA	23.3	2
Seattle-Bellevue-Everett, WA	-8.7	9

Source: U.S. Department of Commerce, International Trade Administration, *Metropolitan Area Exports: An Export Performance Report on Over 250 U.S. Cities,* Washington, D.C.: U.S. Government Printing Office, April 1996, p. 66. Primary source: Exporter Location Series, Census Bureau.

★2119★
Imports and Exports: Sales
Exporters, 1994: Cities Growing the Fastest

Data refer to the percentage growth in exports from 1993 to 1994.

[In percentages]

City/MSA	Percentage	Rank
Biloxi-Gulfport-Pascagoula, MS	160.4	1
Dubuque, IA	90.8	2
Greeley, CO	81.8	3
Florence, SC	76.8	4
Fayetteville-Springdale-Rogers, AR	73.3	5
Lexington, KY	72.8	6
Lubbock, TX	67.4	7
Muncie, IN	67.0	8
Elmira, NY	66.4	9
Detroit, MI	63.7	10

Source: "Breaking Down Exports By Metro Area," *USA TODAY,* 30 May 1996, p. 6B. Primary source: U.S. Department of Commerce.

★2120★
Imports and Exports: Sales
Exporters, 1994: Leading Areas in Dollar Value of Exports

[In billions of dollars]

Metropolitan area	Dollars	Rank
Atlanta, GA	4.7	21
Bergen-Passaic, NJ	4.4	22
Boston, MA-NH	7.1	11
Chicago, IL	17.3	6
Cleveland-Lorain-Elyria, OH	4.1	24
Dallas, TX	5.7	15
Detroit, MI	27.5	1
Houston, TX	13.4	7
Laredo, TX	4.2	23
Los Angeles-Long Beach, CA	22.2	3
Miami, FL	9.3	8
Minneapolis-Saint Paul, MN-WI	8.9	9
New York, NY	23.5	2
Newark, NJ	5.2	18
Oakland, CA	5.1	19
Orange County, CA	6.7	12
Philadelphia, PA-NJ	6.5	13
Phoenix-Mesa, AZ	5.6	16
Portland-Vancouver, OR-WA	6.4	14
Richmond-Petersburg, VA	5.3	17
San Diego, CA	4.9	20
San Francisco, CA	9.3	8
San Jose, CA	19.9	5
Seattle-Bellevue-Everett, WA	21.8	4
Washington, DC-MD-VA-WV	8.0	10

Source: U.S. Department of Commerce, International Trade Administration, *Metropolitan Area Exports: An Export Performance Report on Over 250 U.S. Cities,* Washington, D.C.: U.S. Government Printing Office, April 1996, p. 10. Primary source: Exporter Location Series, Census Bureau.

★2121★
Imports and Exports: Sales
Exports From Major Customs Districts, 1994

[In billions of dollars]

City	Exports	Rank
Anchorage, AK	5.3	22
Baltimore, MD	8.2	15
Boston, MA	4.7	24
Buffalo, NY	21.3	7
Charleston, SC[1]	7.9	17
Chicago, IL	15.2	11
Cleveland, OH	5.4	21
Dallas-Fort Worth, TX	4.1	25
Detroit, MI	53.7	3
Duluth, MN	1.1	32
El Paso, TX	7.4	18
Great Falls, MT	3.2	27
Honolulu, HI	1.0	33
Houston-Galveston, TX	21.2	8
Laredo, TX	28.3	6
Los Angeles, CA	55.8	2
Miami, FL	19.5	10
Milwaukee, WI	0.1	36
Minneapolis, MN	1.3	31
Mobile, AL[1]	2.7	28
New Orleans, LA	20.7	9
New York, NY	56.5	1
Nogales, AZ	4.1	25
Norfolk, VA[1]	12.4	12
Ogdensburg, NY	9.1	14
Pembina, ND	5.9	19
Philadelphia, PA	5.0	23
Port Arthur, TX	0.9	34
Portland, ME	1.9	30
Portland, OR	8.1	16
Providence, RI	0.1	36
Saint Albans, VT	4.1	25
Saint Louis, MO	0.3	35
San Diego, CA	5.6	20
San Francisco, CA	34.2	4
Savannah, GA	9.3	13
Seattle, WA	33.1	5
Tampa, FL	5.6	20
Washington, DC	2.0	29
Wilmington, NC	3.9	26

Source: U.S. Bureau of the Census, *Statistical Abstract of the United States: 1995,* (115th edition), Washington, D.C.: U.S. Government Printing Office, 1995, p. 815. Primary source: U.S. Bureau of the Census, *U.S. Merchandise Trade: Selected Highlights,* series FT920, monthly. *Note:* 1. Beginning 1990, excludes exports of bituminous coal.

★2122★
Imports and Exports: Sales
Exports, 1994: Areas With Lowest Amounts in Dollar Value of Exports

[In millions of dollars]

City	Dollars	Rank
Albany, GA	31,809,840	17
Alexandria, LA	16,932,546	23
Altoona, PA	46,387,634	11
Bremerton, WA	54,582,146	7

[Continued]

★2122★

Exports, 1994: Areas With Lowest Amounts in Dollar Value of Exports

[Continued]

City	Dollars	Rank
Columbia, MO	50,173,690	10
Cumberland, MD-WV	64,260,954	2
Decatur, AL	54,467,829	8
Fayetteville, NC	57,909,024	4
Florence, AL	25,747,647	20
Houma, LA	53,768,325	9
Joplin, MO	44,601,213	12
Lake Charles, LA	55,910,699	6
Lawrence, KS	6,243,631	25
Naples, FL	55,984,555	5
Pensacola, FL	34,047,544	16
Redding, CA	28,625,590	19
Saint Joseph, MO	39,198,221	14
Sharon, PA	40,417,455	13
Sherman-Denison, TX	36,149,343	15
Springfield, IL	29,803,555	18
Tallahassee, FL	18,726,647	22
Texarkana, TX-AR	24,643,159	21
Wheeling, WV-OH	10,755,481	24
Wichita Falls, TX	65,093,442	1
Yuba City, CA	61,460,656	3

Source: U.S. Department of Commerce, International Trade Administration, *Metropolitan Area Exports: An Export Performance Report on Over 250 U.S. Cities,* Washington, D.C.: U.S. Government Printing Office, April 1996, p. 5. Primary source: Exporter Location Series, Census Bureau.

★2123★

Imports and Exports: Sales

Exports, 1994: Leading Areas in Dollars Gained Since 1993

[In millions of dollars]

Detroit	Dollars	Rank
Atlanta, GA	869	12
Bergen-Passaic, NJ	462	24
Boston, MA-NH	623	18
Chicago, IL	2,887	3
Cleveland-Lorain-Elyria, OH	511	22
Dallas, TX	862	13
Detroit, MI	10,689	1
El Paso, TX	594	19
Houston, TX	1,104	6
Lexington, KY	454	25
Los Angeles-Long Beach, CA	2,211	4
Memphis, TN-AR-MS	674	17
Miami, FL	1,002	9
Milwaukee-Waukesha, WI	576	20
Newark, NJ	918	11
Oakland, CA	932	10
Orange County, CA	1,063	7
Philadelphia, PA-NJ	677	16
Phoenix-Mesa, AZ	1,062	8
Portland-Vancouver, OR-WA	750	14
Richmond-Petersburg, VA	1,248	5
San Diego, CA	510	23

[Continued]

★2123★

Exports, 1994: Leading Areas in Dollars Gained Since 1993

[Continued]

Detroit	Dollars	Rank
San Jose, CA	3,771	2
Tampa-Saint Petersburg-Clearwater, FL	540	21
Washington, DC-MD-VA-WV	719	15

Source: U.S. Department of Commerce, International Trade Administration, *Metropolitan Area Exports: An Export Performance Report on Over 250 U.S. Cities,* Washington, D.C.: U.S. Government Printing Office, April 1996, p. 11. Primary source: Exporter Location Series, Census Bureau.

★2124★

Imports and Exports: Sales

Exports, 1994: Leading Areas in Percent Growth in Merchandise Exports Since 1993

[In percentages]

City	Percent growth	Rank
Anchorage, AK	53.9	16
Augusta-Aiken, GA-SC	43.5	23
Bakersfield, CA	62.4	11
Biloxi-Gulfport-Pascagoula, MS	160.4	1
Binghamton, NY	50.2	18
Charleston, WV	55.1	15
Detroit, MI	63.7	10
Dubuque, IA	90.8	2
Eau Claire, WI	60.7	12
Elmira, NY	66.4	9
Fayetteville-Springdale-Rogers, AR	73.3	5
Florence, SC	76.8	4
Greeley, CO	81.8	3
Harrisburg-Lebanon-Carlisle, PA	57.7	14
Lafayette, LA	58.8	13
Lexington, KY	72.8	6
Lubbock, TX	67.4	7
Montgomery, NY	46.4	19
Muncie, IN	67.0	8
Pittsfield, MA	45.4	22
Tampa-Saint Petersburg-Clearwater, FL	41.7	25
Utica-Rome, NY	43.0	24
Vallejo-Fairfield-Napa, CA	53.7	17
Waterloo-Cedar Falls, IA	45.7	21
Wheeling, WV	46.0	20

Source: U.S. Department of Commerce, International Trade Administration, *Metropolitan Area Exports: An Export Performance Report on Over 250 U.S. Cities,* Washington, D.C.: U.S. Government Printing Office, April 1996, p. 12. Primary source: Exporter Location Series, Census Bureau.

★2125★

Imports and Exports: Sales

Imports for Consumption, Major Customs Districts, 1994

[In billions of dollars]

City	Imports	Rank
Anchorage, AK	7.0	21
Baltimore, MD	11.8	14
Boston, MA	7.3	20
Buffalo, NY	26.4	6
Charleston, SC[1]	9.4	18
Chicago, IL	18.8	9
Cleveland, OH	6.4	22
Dallas-Fort Worth, TX	2.8	31
Detroit, MI	55.4	3
Duluth, MN	4.9	26
El Paso, TX	11.0	16
Great Falls, MT	5.3	25
Honolulu, HI	3.2	30
Houston-Galveston, TX	21.1	8
Laredo, TX	18.7	10
Los Angeles, CA	130.5	1
Miami, FL	12.7	12
Milwaukee, WI	0.5	37
Minneapolis, MN	1.0	34
Mobile, AL[1]	3.3	29
New Orleans, LA	24.3	7
New York, NY	78.4	2
Nogales, AZ	5.3	25
Norfolk, VA[1]	10.5	17
Ogdensburg, NY	12.5	13
Pembina, ND	6.2	23
Philadelphia, PA	13.4	11
Port Arthur, TX	4.0	28
Portland, ME	4.1	27
Portland, OR	5.8	24
Providence, RI	0.6	36
Saint Albans, VT	6.2	23
Saint Louis, MO	0.9	35
San Diego, CA	7.0	21
San Francisco, CA	47.4	4
Savannah, GA	11.3	15
Seattle, WA	45.4	5
Tampa, FL	8.5	19
Washington, DC	1.3	33
Wilmington, NC	1.9	32

Source: U.S. Bureau of the Census, *Statistical Abstract of the United States: 1995,* (115th edition), Washington, D.C.: U.S. Government Printing Office, 1995, p. 815. Primary source: U.S. Bureau of the Census, *U.S. Merchandise Trade: Selected Highlights,* series FT920, monthly. *Note:* 1. Beginning 1990, excludes exports of bituminous coal.

★2126★

Imports and Exports: Sales

Imports of Iron and Steel, 1993

[In short tons]

City/Customs District	Short tons	Rank
Baltimore, MD	618,258	9
Boston, MA	357,695	11
Chicago, IL	1,893,001	2
Cleveland, OH	952,727	5
Detroit, MI	848,413	6
Houston-Galveston, TX	1,144,926	4
Los Angeles, CA	1,857,718	3
Mobile, AL	561,436	10
New Orleans, LA	4,684,588	1
Philadelphia, PA	711,573	8
San Francisco, CA	746,637	7

Source: Plume, Janet, "New Rules Expected to Hurt Record Steel Trade," *Traffic World,* 10 June, 1996, p. 19.

★2127★

Imports and Exports: Sales

Imports of Iron and Steel, 1994

[In short tons]

City/Customs District	Short tons	Rank
Baltimore, MD	824,050	9
Boston, MA	668,546	11
Chicago, IL	2,929,722	2
Cleveland, OH	1,113,506	8
Detroit, MI	1,480,842	5
Houston-Galveston, TX	2,209,696	4
Los Angeles, CA	2,635,824	3
Mobile, AL	797,518	10
New Orleans, LA	10,002,160	1
Philadelphia, PA	1,411,707	6
San Francisco, CA	1,141,394	7

Source: Plume, Janet, "New Rules Expected to Hurt Record Steel Trade," *Traffic World,* 10 June, 1996, p. 19.

★2128★

Imports and Exports: Sales

Imports of Iron and Steel, 1995

[In short tons]

City/Customs District	Short tons
Baltimore, MD	640,748
Boston, MA	591,393
Chicago, IL	1,451,180
Cleveland, OH	812,080
Detroit, MI	675,243
Houston-Galveston, TX	2,142,694
Los Angeles, CA	2,228,916
Mobile, AL	479,957
New Orleans, LA	8,759,378
Philadelphia, PA	1,249,351
San Francisco, CA	1,143,029

Source: Plume, Janet, "New Rules Expected to Hurt Record Steel Trade," *Traffic World,* 10 June, 1996, p. 19.

★2129★

Imports and Exports: Value

Export Value, 1994, By Region: Mid-Atlantic

Data refer to the 20 leading areas, ranked by value of exports.

[In dollars]

MSA	Dollar	Rank
Albany-Schenectady-Troy, NY	831,365,928	15
Allentown-Bethlehem-Easton, PA	1,371,116,128	11
Bergen-Passaic, NJ	4,387,000,116	4
Binghamton, NY	474,877,881	17
Buffalo-Niagara Falls, NY	1,569,651,215	10
Dutchess County, NY	980,569,435	13
Harrisburg-Lebanon-Carlisle, PA	535,012,238	16
Jersey City, NJ	1,351,240,038	12
Lancaster, PA	469,339,181	18
Middlesex-Somerset-Hunterdon, NJ	3,035,890,854	7
Monmouth-Ocean, NJ	410,212,800	19
Nassau-Suffolk, NY	2,866,271,135	8
New York, NY	23,543,749,240	1
Newark, NJ	5,205,487,112	3
Philadelphia, PA-NJ	6,545,835,785	2
Pittsburgh, PA	3,150,609,651	5
Rochester, NY	3,143,661,788	6
Scranton-Wilkes-Barre-Hazleton, PA	328,151,069	20
Syracuse, NY	1,600,939,522	9
York, PA	952,004,973	14

Source: U.S. Department of Commerce, International Trade Administration, *Metropolitan Area Exports: An Export Performance Report on Over 250 U.S. Cities,* p. 33. Primary source: Exporter Location Series, Census Bureau.

★2130★

Imports and Exports: Value

Export Value, 1994, By Region: Mountain

[In dollars]

MSA	Dollars	Rank
Albuquerque, NM	335,480,983	9
Boise City, ID	1,289,820,030	3
Colorado Springs, CO	900,712,044	5
Denver, CO	1,089,812,265	4
Fort Collins-Loveland, CO	354,461,962	8
Greeley, CO	501,822,972	7
Las Vegas, NV-AZ	144,836,836	12
Phoenix-Mesa, AZ	5,561,093,693	1
Provo-Orem, UT	200,188,228	11
Reno, NV	213,652,355	10
Salt Lake City-Ogden, UT	1,808,673,252	2
Tucson, AZ	638,117,582	6

Source: U.S. Department of Commerce, International Trade Administration, *Metropolitan Area Exports: An Export Performance Report on Over 250 U.S. Cities,* p. 54. Primary source: Exporter Location Series, Census Bureau.

★2131★

Imports and Exports: Value

Export Value, 1994, By Region: New England

[In dollars]

MSA	Dollars	Rank
Boston, MA-NH	7,095,349,390	1
Bridgeport, CT	918,846,699	6
Brockton, MA	113,104,954	19
Danbury, CT	392,955,842	12
Hartford, CT	1,967,053,061	3
Lawrence, MA-NH	806,416,721	8
Lowell, MA-NH	890,090,652	7
Manchester, NH	115,302,567	18
Nashua, NH	235,398,399	14
New Bedford, MA	154,502,826	16
New Haven-Meriden, CT	1,075,478,242	5
New London-Norwich, CT-RI	141,454,049	17
Pittsfield, MA	112,240,264	20
Portland, ME	319,515,535	13
Portsmouth-Rochester, NH-ME	470,164,517	10
Providence-Fall River-Warwick, RI-MA	1,246,010,092	4
Springfield, MA	434,774,121	11
Stamford-Norwalk, CT	3,452,702,492	2
Waterbury, CT	179,607,116	15
Worcester, MA-CT	603,792,520	9

Source: U.S. Department of Commerce, International Trade Administration, *Metropolitan Area Exports: An Export Performance Report on Over 250 U.S. Cities,* Washington, D.C.: U.S. Government Printing Office, April 1996, p. 30. Primary source: Exporter Location Series, Census Bureau.

★2132★

Imports and Exports: Value

Export Value, 1994, By Region: North Central

Data refer to the 20 leading areas, ranked by dollar value of exports.

[In dollars]

MSA	Dollar	Rank
Akron, OH	1,606,289,098	14
Ann Arbor, MI	2,075,768,978	11
Chicago, IL	17,333,603,392	2
Cincinnati, OH-KY-IN	4,056,505,886	5
Cleveland-Lorain-Elyria, OH	4,093,322,966	4
Columbus, OH	1,295,467,590	16
Davenport-Rock Island-Moline-IA-IL	1,098,869,468	17
Dayton-Springfield, OH	2,671,308,908	9
Detroit, MI	27,469,655,137	1
Flint, MI	1,032,050,028	18
Grand Rapids-Muskegon-Holland, MI	1,993,494,017	12
Indianapolis, IN	3,003,834,284	7
Kalamazoo-Battle Creek, MI	868,950,604	20
Kansas City, MO-Ks	2,578,559,820	10
Kokomo, IN	1,858,412,518	13
Milwaukee-Waukesha, WI	2,913,544,707	8
Minneapolis-St. Paul, MN-WI	8,863,530,759	3
St. Louis, MO-IL	3,673,337,340	6

[Continued]

★2132★

Export Value, 1994, By Region: North Central
[Continued]

MSA	Dollar	Rank
Toledo, OH	986,928,080	19
Wichita, KS	1,504,557,637	15

Source: U.S. Department of Commerce, International Trade Administration, *Metropolitan Area Exports: An Export Performance Report on Over 250 U.S. Cities*, p. 42. Primary source: Exporter Location Series, Census Bureau.

★2133★

Imports and Exports: Value

Export Value, 1994, By Region: Pacific

Data refer to the 20 leading areas, ranked by dollar value of exports.

[In dollars]

MSA	Dollars	Rank
Bakersfield, CA	780,376,616	12
Fresno, CA	763,407,316	14
Los Angeles-Long Beach, CA	22,224,814,589	1
Oakland, CA	5,113,244,018	7
Orange County, CA	6,715,981,650	5
Portland-Vancouver, OR-WA	6,448,826,945	6
Richland-Kennewick-Pasco, WA	271,566,682	20
Riverside-San Bernardino, CA	1,458,849,995	9
Sacramento, CA	1,087,946,958	10
Salinas, CA	321,950,186	18
San Diego, CA	4,867,278,411	8
San Francisco, CA	9,303,816,205	4
San Jose, CA	19,942,678,387	3
Santa Barbara-Santa Maria-Lompoc, CA	420,154,380	17
Santa Cruz-Watsonville, CA	857,420,329	11
Santa Rosa, CA	485,151,372	16
Seattle-Bellevue-Everett, WA	21,752,981,626	2
Stockton-Lodi, CA	320,346,532	19
Tacoma, WA	774,869,018	13
Ventura, CA	698,677,973	15

Source: U.S. Department of Commerce, International Trade Administration, *Metropolitan Area Exports: An Export Performance Report on Over 250 U.S. Cities*, p. 57. Primary source: Exporter Location Series, Census Bureau.

★2134★

Imports and Exports: Value

Export Value, 1994, By Region: South Atlantic

Data refer to the 20 leading areas, ranked by value of exports.

[In dollars]

MSA	Dollar	Rank
Atlanta, GA	4,739,123,635	4
Augusta-Aiken, GA-SC	326,301,958	20
Baltimore, MD	1,868,967,765	7
Charleston-North Charleston, SC	388,467,350	19
Charlotte-Gastonia-Rock Hill, NC-SC	1,782,827,269	9
Fort Lauderdale, FL	1,506,662,094	12
Greensboro-Winston-Salem-High Point, NC	2,773,310,009	6

[Continued]

★2134★

Export Value, 1994, By Region: South Atlantic
[Continued]

MSA	Dollar	Rank
Greenville-Spartanburg-Anderson, SC	1,745,019,520	11
Hickory-Morganton, NC	397,915,417	18
Jacksonville, FL	500,395,802	16
Miami, FL	9,266,745,514	1
Norfolk-Virginia Beach-Newport News, VA-NC	807,674,367	15
Orlando, FL	848,511,709	13
Raleigh-Durham-Chapel Hill, NC	1,758,672,814	10
Richmond-Petersburg, VA	5,260,571,495	3
Savannah, GA	423,262,228	17
Tampa-St. Petersburg-Clearwater, FL	1,835,814,338	8
Washington, DC-MD-VA-WV	7,969,302,661	2
West Palm Beach-Boca Raton, FL	834,284,026	14
Wilmington-Newark, DE-MD	3,720,373,054	5

Source: U.S. Department of Commerce, International Trade Administration, *Metropolitan Area Exports: An Export Performance Report on Over 250 U.S. Cities*, p. 36. Primary source: Exporter Location Series, Census Bureau.

★2135★

Imports and Exports: Value

Export Value, 1994, By Region: South Central

Data refer to the 20 leading areas, ranked by dollar value of exports.

[In dollars]

MSA	Dollar	Rank
Austin-San Marcos, TX	2,128,773,530	7
Brazoria, TX	1,760,999,069	12
Brownsville-Harlingen-San Benito, TX	2,113,361,920	8
Dallas, TX	5,679,710,931	2
El Paso, TX	3,561,263,422	4
Fort Worth-Arlington, TX	2,052,001,428	9
Houston, TX	13,388,170,043	1
Huntsville, AL	672,092,188	18
Johnson City-Kingsport-Bristol, TN-VA	1,580,777,613	13
Knoxville, TN	689,179,313	17
Laredo, TX	4,157,377,819	3
Lexington, KY	1,078,565,940	16
Louisville, KY-IN	1,798,846,995	11
McAllen-Edinburg-Mission, TX	1,826,431,295	10
Memphis, TN-AR-MS	2,729,489,435	5
Nashville, TN	1,310,492,235	14
New Orleans, LA	2,326,231,047	6
Oklahoma City, OK	488,563,315	20
San Antonio, TX	656,275,677	19
Tulsa, OK	1,240,953,373	15

Source: U.S. Department of Commerce, International Trade Administration, *Metropolitan Area Exports: An Export Performance Report on Over 250 U.S. Cities*, p. 48. Primary source: Exporter Location Series, Census Bureau.

★2136★

Imports and Exports: Value

Export Value, 1994: Leading Metropolitan Areas

[In billions of dollars]

City/MSA	Value	Rank
Detroit, MI	27.5	1
New York, NY	23.5	2
Los Angeles-Long Beach, CA	22.2	3
Seattle-Bellevue-Everett, WA	21.8	4
San Jose, CA	19.9	5
Chicago, IL	17.3	6
Houston, TX	13.4	7
San Francisco, CA	9.3	8
Miami, FL	9.3	8
Minneapolis-Saint Paul, MN	8.9	9

Source: "Breaking Down Exports By Metro Area," *USA TODAY*, 30 May 1996, p. 6B.
Primary source: U.S. Department of Commerce.

Chapter 17

BUSINESS

Topics Covered

Home-Based Businesses
New Ventures
Offices
Travel

★2137★
Home-Based Businesses
Where the Electronic Cottages Are, 1996

"Electronic cottages" are defined as home-based businesses.

[In percentage of persons who work at home]

City	Percent	Rank
Austin, TX	6.0	5
Berkeley, CA	5.5	6
Bethesda-Chevy Chase, MD	6.1	4
Calabasas-101 Freeway, CA	5.2	7
Century City-Beverly Hills, CA	6.4	3
Greenwich, CT	5.5	6
Manhattan, NY	7.0	2
San Diego, CA	9.4	1
Santa Monica, CA	5.2	7

Source: Kotkin, Joel, "Still the Best Places to Do Business," *Inc.,* (July 1996), p. 46. Primary source: *The Edge City News,* the Edge City Group, Broad Run, Va., 1996.

★2138★
New Ventures
Broadcasting Industry, 1996

Data refers to number of stations which will be owned by Westinghouse after its purchase of Infinity.

City	Number of stations	Rank
Atlanta, GA	3	8
Boston, MA	6	5
Chicago, IL	10	2
Dallas-Forth Worth, TX	11	1
Detroit, MI	6	5
Houston, TX	5	6
Los Angeles, CA	6	5
New York, NY	7	4
Philadelphia, PA	6	5
San Francisco, CA	8	3
Washington, DC	4	7

Source: Norton, Erle, and Elizabeth Jensen, "Westinghouse Acquisition May Speed Company's Split," *Wall Street Journal,* 21 June, 1996, p. B4. Primary source: Westinghouse, Infinity (companies).

★2139★
New Ventures
Initial Public Offering Gains, 1996

[In percentages]

City	Gain	Rank
Atlanta, GA	51.5	8
Beaverton, OR	42.2	10
Boston, MA	37.0	11
Cambridge, MA	36.9	12
Chicago, IL	70.0	2
Columbus, OH	4.5	20
Dallas, TX	48.7	9
Houston, TX	57.3	6
Irvine, CA	33.4	13
Los Angeles, CA	61.8	4

[Continued]

★2139★
Initial Public Offering Gains, 1996
[Continued]

City	Gain	Rank
Menlo Park, CA	26.9	17
Minneapolis, MN	55.3	7
Mountain View, CA	32.3	15
New York, NY	33.2	14
Palo Alto, CA	16.5	19
San Diego, CA	102.7	1
San Jose, CA	25.0	18
Santa Clara, CA	63.8	3
Seattle, WA	28.5	16
Sunnyvale, CA	58.8	5

Source: Isa, Margaret, "When It Comes to I.P.O.'s, Is Geography Part of Destiny?" *New York Times,* 23 June, 1996, p. 4F. Primary source: Securities Data Company. *Note:* "I.P.O." stands for "Initial Public Offering."

★2140★
Offices
Cities With the Most Office Space Available, 1995
[In percentages]

City	Percentage	Rank
Dallas, TX	37	1
Westchester County, NY	31	2
New Haven, CT	30	3
Hartford, CT	26	4
Miami, FL	25	5

Source: "Glutted Office Markets," USA SNAPSHOTS, *USA TODAY,* 30 June 1995, p. 1B.

★2141★
Offices
Office-Space Costs, 1995: Exterior

Data refer to an unfurnished office space of approximately 150 square feet, with a window.

City	Price	Rank
Atlanta, GA	775	9
Chicago, IL	1,595	3
Cleveland, OH	825	7
Dallas, TX	650	12
Denver, CO	800	8
Indianapolis, IN	850	6
Los Angeles, CA	750	10
Miami, FL	1,148	5
New York City, NY	2,600	1
San Francisco, CA	1,300	4
Seattle, WA	747	11
Washington, DC	1,650	2

Source: "Suite Deals," *Entrepreneur,* (April 1996), p. 28. Primary source: HQ Business Centers. *Notes:* The figure provided for New York City, New York, is for a furnished office space.

★2142★

Offices

Office-Space Costs, 1995: Interior

Data refer to an unfurnished office space of approximately 150 square feet, with no window.

City	Price	Rank
Atlanta, GA	650	7
Chicago, IL	1,095	3
Cleveland, OH	625	9
Dallas, TX	550	10
Denver, CO	650	7
Indianapolis, IN	675	6
Los Angeles, CA	525	11
Miami, FL	873	5
New York City, NY	1,400	1
San Francisco, CA	950	4
Seattle, WA	637	8
Washington, DC	1,150	2

Source: "Suite Deals" *Entrepreneur,* (April 1996), p. 28. Primary source: HQ Business Centers. *Notes:* The figure provided for New York City, New York, is for a furnished office space.

★2143★

Offices

Office Space Rental Costs, 1995: Highest Amounts

[In annual dollars per square foot]

City	Rent	Rank
Boston, MA	33.00	2
New York, NY	32.46	4
Washington, DC	32.50	3
West Palm Beach, FL	33.07	1

Source: "Expensive Office Space," USA SNAPSHOTS, *USA TODAY,* 23 January 1996, p. 1B. Primary source: ONCOR International.

★2144★

Offices

Office Space Rental Costs, 1995: Lowest Amounts

[In annual dollars per square foot]

City	Rent	Rank
Denver, CO	14.50	2
Houston, TX	15.00	4
Saint Louis, MO	17.00	5
Saint Paul, MN	14.98	3
Tampa-Saint Petersburg, FL	13.78	1

Source: "Cheapest Office Space," USA SNAPSHOTS, *USA TODAY,* 24 January 1996, p. 1B. Primary source: ONCOR International.

★2145★

Offices

Office Vacancy Rates, 1995: Downtown Areas

[In percentages]

City	Rate	Rank
Atlanta, GA	17.3	4
Boston, MA	11.1	7
Chicago, IL	17.8	3
Dallas, TX	37.2	1
Denver, CO	15.0	5
Los Angeles, CA	23.0	2
New York, NY	13.1	6

Source: "A Brighter Real Estate Picture," *Business Week,* 4 September 1995, p. 95. Primary source: *Business Week,* Cushman & Wakefield Inc.

★2146★

Offices

Rental Rates for Office Space, 1994: Highest

[In dollars per square foot]

City	Highest	Rank
Boston, MA	26.30	2
New York, NY	25.56	3
Washington, DC	32.43	1

Source: "U.S. Office Rents," USA SNAPSHOTS, *USA TODAY,* 10 January 1995, p. 1B. Primary source: Colliers International.

★2147★

Offices

Rental Rates for Office Space, 1994: Lowest

[In dollars per square foot]

City	Lowest	Rank
Houston, TX	13.15	1
Louisville, KY	13.58	3
Memphis, TN	13.21	2

Source: "U.S. Office Rents," USA Snapshots, *USA TODAY,* 10 January 1995, p. 1B. Primary source: Colliers International.

★2148★

Offices

Where the Most New Facilities and Expansions are Located: 1994

[In number of facilities]

City	Number of expansions	Rank
Atlanta, GA	82	10
Charlotte-Gastonia-Rock Hill, NC-SC	142	2
Cincinnati, OH	93	8
Cleveland-Lorain-Elyria, OH	141	3
Columbus, OH	119	4
Dallas, TX	166	1
Fort Worth-Arlington, TX	92	9
Greensboro-Winston-Salem-High Point, NC	96	7

[Continued]

★2148★

Where the Most New Facilities and Expansions are Located: 1994

[Continued]

City	Number of expansions	Rank
Houston, TX	115	5
Phoenix-Mesa, AZ	112	6

Source: Venable, Tim, "Dallas Wins Again: Still the Hottest U.S. Metro Area for Corporate Facilities," *Site Selection,* (February 1995), p. 74.

★2149★
Travel

Reimbursable Per Diem Expenses for Federal Government Workers, 1996, By Type of Expense: Lodging

Data refer to rates set by the General Services Administration (GSA), and are effective as of April 1, 1996.

[In dollars]

City/MSA	Rate	Rank
Atlanta, GA	85	11
Boston, MA	116	4
Chicago, IL	119	3
Cincinnati, OH	69	16
Dallas, TX	84	12
Denver, CO	92	9
Los Angeles, CA	97	7
Miami, FL	77	14
Milwaukee, WI	70	15
Nashville, TN	69	16
New Orleans, LA	70	15
New York, NY	142	1
Norfolk-Virginia Beach, VA	108	6
Omaha, NE	63	17
Philadelphia, PA	90	10
Phoenix, AZ	96	8
San Francisco, CA	114	5
Seattle, WA	83	13
Washington, DC	124	2

Source: Durbin, Fran, "GSA Revises Allowable Daily Expenses for Federal Workers," *Travel Weekly,* 1 April 1996, p. 45. Primary source: General Services Administration (GSA).

★2150★
Travel

Reimbursable Per Diem Expenses for Federal Government Workers, 1996, By Type of Expense: Meals

Data refer to rates set by the General Services Administration (GSA), and are effective as of April 1, 1996.

[In dollars]

City/MSA	Rate	Rank
Atlanta, GA	34	2
Boston, MA	38	1
Chicago, IL	38	1
Cincinnati, OH	30	3
Dallas, TX	38	1
Denver, CO	34	2
Los Angeles, CA	38	1
Miami, FL	38	1
Milwaukee, WI	30	3
Nashville, TN	34	2
New Orleans, LA	34	2
New York, NY	38	1
Norfolk-Virginia Beach, VA	34	2
Omaha, NE	30	3
Philadelphia, PA	34	2
Phoenix, AZ	34	2
San Francisco, CA	38	1
Seattle, WA	34	2
Washington, DC	38	1

Source: Durbin, Fran, "GSA Revises Allowable Daily Expenses for Federal Workers," *Travel Weekly,* 1 April 1996, p. 45. Primary source: General Services Administration (GSA).

★2151★
Travel

Reimbursable Per Diem Expenses for Federal Government Workers, 1996, By Type of Expense: Total

Data refer to rates set by the General Services Administration (GSA), and are effective as of April 1, 1996.

[In dollars]

City/MSA	Rate	Rank
Atlanta, GA	119	11
Boston, MA	154	4
Chicago, IL	157	3
Cincinnati, OH	99	14
Dallas, TX	122	10
Denver, CO	126	8
Los Angeles, CA	135	6
Miami, FL	115	13
Milwaukee, WI	100	17
Nashville, TN	103	16
New Orleans, LA	104	15
New York, NY	180	1
Norfolk-Virginia Beach, VA	142	6
Omaha, NE	93	18
Philadelphia, PA	124	9
Phoenix, AZ	130	7

[Continued]

★2151★

**Reimbursable Per Diem Expenses for Federal
Government Workers, 1996, By Type of Expense:
Total**
[Continued]

City/MSA	Rate	Rank
San Francisco, CA	152	5
Seattle, WA	117	12
Washington, DC	162	2

Source: Durbin, Fran, "GSA Revises Allowable Daily Expenses for Federal Workers," *Travel Weekly*, 1 April 1996, p. 45. Primary source: General Services Administration (GSA).

Chapter 18

CONSTRUCTION INDUSTRY

Topics Covered

Costs
New Construction

★2152★
Costs
Hotel Construction Costs, 1996: 4 to 7 Stories
[In dollars per square foot]

City	Price	Rank
Atlanta, GA	73.10	24
Baltimore, MD	77.26	18
Boston, MA	100.27	3
Chicago, IL	91.69	8
Cleveland, OH	85.83	13
Dallas, TX	73.18	23
Denver, CO	79.04	17
Detroit, MI	89.48	11
Houston, TX	76.33	20
Kansas City, MO	80.40	16
Los Angeles, CA	95.43	4
Miami, FL	74.20	21
Minneapolis, MN	93.81	5
New Orleans, LA	73.27	22
New York City, NY	115.38	1
Philadelphia, PA	93.14	6
Phoenix, AZ	76.58	19
Pittsburgh, PA	86.34	12
Portland, OR	89.99	9
Saint Louis, MO	85.49	14
San Diego, CA	92.29	7
San Francisco, CA	106.63	2
Seattle, WA	89.92	10
Washington, DC	82.18	15
Winston-Salem, NC	66.90	25

Source: "Cost Trends: 6/96," *Building Design & Construction,* (June 1996), p. 29.

★2153★
Costs
Hotel Construction Costs, 1996: 8 to 24 Stories
[In dollars per square foot]

City	Price	Rank
Atlanta, GA	69.87	24
Baltimore, MD	73.85	18
Boston, MA	95.84	3
Chicago, IL	87.64	8
Cleveland, OH	82.04	13
Dallas, TX	69.95	23
Denver, CO	75.55	17
Detroit, MI	85.53	11
Houston, TX	72.95	20
Kansas City, MO	76.85	16
Los Angeles, CA	91.21	4
Miami, FL	70.93	21
Minneapolis, MN	89.67	5
New Orleans, LA	70.03	22
New York City, NY	110.28	1
Philadelphia, PA	89.02	6
Phoenix, AZ	73.20	19
Pittsburgh, PA	82.53	12
Portland, OR	86.02	9
Saint Louis, MO	81.72	14
San Diego, CA	88.21	7
San Francisco, CA	101.92	2
Seattle, WA	85.86	10

[Continued]

★2153★
Hotel Construction Costs, 1996: 8 to 24 Stories
[Continued]

City	Price	Rank
Washington, DC	78.55	15
Winston-Salem, NC	63.95	25

Source: "Cost Trends: 6/96," *Building Design & Construction,* (June 1996), p. 29.

★2154★
Costs
Motel Construction Costs, 1996: 3 to 4 Stories
[In dollars per square foot]

City	Price	Rank
Atlanta, GA	62.77	24
Baltimore, MD	66.34	18
Boston, MA	86.09	3
Chicago, IL	78.73	8
Cleveland, OH	73.70	13
Dallas, TX	62.84	23
Denver, CO	67.87	17
Detroit, MI	76.84	11
Houston, TX	65.54	20
Kansas City, MO	69.04	16
Los Angeles, CA	81.94	4
Miami, FL	63.71	21
Minneapolis, MN	80.55	5
New Orleans, LA	62.91	22
New York City, NY	99.07	1
Philadelphia, PA	79.97	6
Phoenix, AZ	65.76	19
Pittsburgh, PA	74.14	12
Portland, OR	77.27	9
Saint Louis, MO	73.41	14
San Diego, CA	79.24	7
San Francisco, CA	91.56	2
Seattle, WA	77.13	10
Washington, DC	70.57	15
Winston-Salem, NC	57.45	25

Source: "Cost Trends: 6/96," *Building Design & Construction,* (June 1996), p. 29.

★2155★
Costs
Apartment Construct Costs, 1996: 4 to 7 Stories
[In dollars per square foot]

City	Prices	Rank
Atlanta, GA	74.09	24
Baltimore, MD	78.31	18
Boston, MA	101.63	3
Chicago, IL	92.93	8
Cleveland, OH	87.00	13
Dallas, TX	74.18	23
Denver, CO	80.11	17
Detroit, MI	90.70	11
Houston, TX	77.36	20
Kansas City, MO	81.49	16

[Continued]

★2155★

Apartment Construct Costs, 1996: 4 to 7 Stories

[Continued]

City	Prices	Rank
Los Angeles, CA	96.72	4
Miami, FL	75.21	21
Minneapolis, MN	95.09	5
New Orleans, LA	74.26	22
New York City, NY	116.94	1
Philadelphia, PA	94.40	6
Phoenix, AZ	77.62	19
Pittsburgh, PA	87.51	12
Portland, OR	91.21	9
Saint Louis, MO	86.65	14
San Diego, CA	93.54	7
San Francisco, CA	108.08	2
Seattle, WA	91.04	10
Washington, DC	83.30	15
Winston-Salem, NC	67.81	25

Source: "Cost Trends: 6/96," *Building Design & Construction,* (June 1996), p. 29.

★2156★

Costs

Heat Pump Costs, 1996, By Type: Gas-Fired Heat Pump

City	Gas-fired heat pump	Rank
Atlanta, GA	9,000	1
Burlington, VT	7,000	3
Chicago, IL	8,000	2
New York, NY	8,000	2
Phoenix, AZ	9,000	1
Portland, OR	9,000	1

Source: Johnson, Arthur, "Shoptalk: The New Heat Pumps," *Builder,* (June 1996), p. 144.

★2157★

Costs

Heat Pump Costs, 1996, By Type: Ground Source Heat Pump

City	Ground source heat pump	Rank
Atlanta, GA	7,520	3
Burlington, VT	9,335	1
Chicago, IL	8,425	2
New York, NY	8,425	2
Phoenix, AZ	7,520	3
Portland, OR	7,520	3

Source: Johnson, Arthur, "Shoptalk: The New Heat Pumps," *Builder,* (June 1996), p. 144.

★2158★

New Construction

Distribution Facilities, 1990-95: New and Expanded Facilities

City	Number	Rank
Atlanta, GA	58	11
Charlotte-Gastonia-Rock Hill, NC-SC	111	5
Chicago, IL	114	4
Cincinnati, OH	70	7
Cleveland-Lorain-Elyria, OH	57	12
Columbus, OH	111	5
Dallas, TX	199	1
Dayton-Springfield, OH	39	17
Fort Lauderdale-Hollywood-Pompano Beach, FL	51	14
Fort Worth-Arlington, TX	119	3
Greensboro-Winston-Salem-High Point, NC	68	8
Houston, TX	51	14
Jacksonville, FL	42	15
Lakeland-Winter Haven, FL	39	17
Los Angeles-Long Beach, CA	52	13
Memphis, TN-AR-MS	61	10
Norfolk-Virginia Beach-Newport News, VA-NC	41	16
Orlando, FL	128	2
Phoenix-Mesa, AZ	74	6
Riverside-San Bernardino, CA	64	9

Source: "Top 20 U.S. Metro Areas, 1990-95 New and Expanded Distribution Facilities," *Site Selection,* (June 1996), p. 532. Primary source: Conway Data's New Plant database.

★2159★

New Construction

Laboratory Construction, 1996: Costs of New Construction

[In dollars per square foot; minimum prices]

City/MSA	Cost	Rank
Atlanta, GA	167	5
Boston, MA	188	3
Chicago, IL	188	3
Dallas, TX	167	5
Los Angeles, CA	209	2
New York, NY	230	1
Phoenix, AZ	157	6
San Francisco, CA	230	1
Seattle, WA	178	4

Source: "Cost Figures on Lab Construction Available," *R&D Magazine,* (March 1996), p. 9. Primary source: Survey conducted by *R&D Magazine* and Haines Lundberg Waehler (HLW), an architectural/engineering company.

★2160★

New Construction

Office-Space Construction, 1996: Number of Buildings (Selected Cities)

City	Buildings under way	Rank
Atlanta, GA	18	1
Washington, DC	9	2
Miami, FL	3	5
Richmond, VA	6	3
Charlotte, NC	8	4

Source: "Olympic City Build-Up," USA SNAPSHOTS, *USA TODAY,* 16 February 1996, p. 1B. Primary source: ONCOR International.

★2161★

New Construction

Office-Space Construction, 1996: Total Square Feet of Construction

City	Total square feet	Rank
Atlanta, GA	2,107,802	1
Charlotte, NC	654,000	5
Miami, FL	724,307	3
Richmond, VA	683,000	4
Washington, DC	1,676,517	2

Source: "Olympic City Build-Up," USA SNAPSHOTS, *USA TODAY,* 16 February 1996, p. 1B. Primary source: ONCOR International.

Chapter 19

FINANCE, INSURANCE, AND REAL ESTATE

Topic Covered

Establishments and Employment

★2162★

Establishments and Employment

Accident and Health Insurance

The U.S. total number of employees is 53,599; total number of establishments is 1,100.

MSA	Estab-lish-ments	Rank	Emp-loy-ment	Rank
Boston – Worcester – Lawrence, MA – NH – ME – CT CMSA	20	7	0[1]	2
Chicago – Gary – Kenosha, IL – IN – WI CMSA	29	5	0[2]	2
Dallas – Fort Worth, TX CMSA	52	1	2,911	1
Los Angeles – Riverside – Orange County, CA CMSA	33	4	0[3]	2
Miami – Fort Lauderdale, FL CMSA	12	8	0[4]	2
New York – Northern New Jersey – Long Island, NY – NJ – CT-CMSA	42	2	0[1]	2
Philadelphia – Wilmington – Atlantic City, PA – NJ – DE – MD CMSA	34	3	0[5]	2
San Francisco – Oakland – San Jose, CA CMSA	10	9	0[6]	2
Washington – Baltimore, DC – MD – VA – WV CMSA	27	6	0[4]	2

Source: U.S. Department of Commerce, Bureau of the Census, Data User Services Division, *1992 Economic Census, Volume 1F, Reports Series, Release 1F,* September 1995, CD-ROM. *Notes:* 1. 500-999 employees. 2. 5,000-9,999 employees. 3. 1,000-2,499 employees. 4. 250-499 employees. 5. 2,500-4,999 employees. 6. 100-249 employees.

★2163★

Establishments and Employment

Business Credit Institutions

The U.S. total number of employees is 86,526; total number of establishments is 5,038.

MSA	Estab-lish-ments	Rank	Emp-loy-ment	Rank
Atlanta, GA MSA	178	6	3,383	3
Boston – Worcester – Lawrence, MA – NH – ME – CT CMSA	133	9	0[1]	10
Chicago – Gary – Kenosha, IL – IN – WI CMSA	288	3	0[2]	10
Cincinnati – Hamilton, OH – KY – IN CMSA	41	23	0[1]	10
Cleveland – Akron, OH CMSA	60	17	0[3]	10
Columbus, OH MSA	35	25	0[3]	10
Dallas – Fort Worth, TX CMSA	206	5	0[4]	10
Denver – Boulder – Greeley, CO CMSA	102	11	0[1]	10
Detroit – Ann Arbor – Flint, MI CMSA	89	13	1,719	5
Houston – Galveston – Brazoria, TX CMSA	97	12	0[3]	10
Indianapolis, IN MSA	27	27	0[5]	10
Kansas City, MO – KS MSA	59	18	0[4]	10
Los Angeles – Riverside – Orange County, CA CMSA	416	2	5,576	1

[Continued]

★2163★

Business Credit Institutions

[Continued]

MSA	Estab-lish-ments	Rank	Emp-loy-ment	Rank
Miami – Fort Lauderdale, FL CMSA	112	10	0[1]	10
Milwaukee – Racine, WI CMSA	55	21	401	8
Minneapolis – St. Paul, MN – WI MSA	87	14	0[1]	10
New York – Northern New Jersey – Long Island, NY – NJ – CT-CMSA	631	1	0[6]	10
Norfolk – Virginia Beach – Newport News, VA – NC MSA	15	30	0[7]	10
Orlando, FL MSA	23	29	0[5]	10
Philadelphia – Wilmington – Atlantic City, PA – NJ – DE – MD CMSA	158	8	2,639	4
Phoenix – Mesa, AZ MSA	69	16	0[3]	10
Pittsburgh, PA MSA	40	24	702	7
Portland – Salem, OR – WA CMSA	58	19	0[1]	10
Sacramento – Yolo, CA CMSA	29	26	0[5]	10
San Diego, CA MSA	47	22	0[7]	10
San Francisco – Oakland – San Jose, CA CMSA	212	4	4,054	2
Seattle – Tacoma – Bremerton, WA CMSA	86	15	804	6
St. Louis, MO – IL MSA	55	21	0[3]	10
Tampa – St. Petersburg – Clearwater, FL MSA	56	20	0[3]	10
Washington – Baltimore, DC – MD – VA – WV CMSA	159	7	0[4]	10
West Palm Beach – Boca Raton, FL MSA	25	28	141	9

Source: U.S. Department of Commerce, Bureau of the Census, Data User Services Division, *1992 Economic Census, Volume 1F, Reports Series, Release 1F,* September 1995, CD-ROM. *Notes:* 1. 1,000-2,499 employees. 2. 5,000-9,999 employees. 3. 500-999 employees. 4. 2,500-4,999 employees. 5. 100-249 employees. 6. 10,000-24,999 employees. 7. 250-499 employees.

★2164★

Establishments and Employment

Cemetery Subdividers and Developers

The U.S. total number of employees is 40,102; total number of establishments is 6,490.

MSA	Estab-lish-ments	Rank	Emp-loy-ment	Rank
Atlanta, GA MSA	67	9	531	6
Boston – Worcester – Lawrence, MA – NH – ME – CT CMSA	111	7	0[1]	18
Chicago – Gary – Kenosha, IL – IN – WI CMSA	174	2	1,360	1
Cincinnati – Hamilton, OH – KY – IN CMSA	50	14	0[2]	18
Cleveland – Akron, OH CMSA	52	13	556	5
Columbus, OH MSA	33	22	195	14
Dallas – Fort Worth, TX CMSA	55	12	775	2

[Continued]

★2164★

Cemetery Subdividers and Developers
[Continued]

MSA	Estab-lish-ments	Rank	Emp-ploy-ment	Rank
Denver – Boulder – Greeley, CO CMSA	27	24	0[2]	18
Detroit – Ann Arbor – Flint, MI CMSA	76	8	0[1]	18
Houston – Galveston – Brazoria, TX CMSA	43	17	0[1]	18
Indianapolis, IN MSA	45	15	410	9
Kansas City, MO – KS MSA	39	20	296	11
Los Angeles – Riverside – Orange County, CA CMSA	114	6	0[3]	18
Miami – Fort Lauderdale, FL CMSA	41	18	736	3
Milwaukee – Racine, WI CMSA	36	21	0[4]	18
Minneapolis – St. Paul, MN – WI MSA	44	16	194	15
New York – Northern New Jersey – Long Island, NY – NJ – CT-CMSA	386	1	0[5]	18
Norfolk – Virginia Beach – Newport News, VA – NC MSA	26	25	16	
Orlando, FL MSA	22	27	262	13
Philadelphia – Wilmington – Atlantic City, PA – NJ – DE – MD CMSA	161	3	0[3]	18
Phoenix – Mesa, AZ MSA	16	29	274	12
Pittsburgh, PA MSA	125	4	0[1]	18
Portland – Salem, OR – WA CMSA	24	26	0[4]	18
Sacramento – Yolo, CA CMSA	19	28	0[4]	18
San Diego, CA MSA	22	27	430	8
San Francisco – Oakland – San Jose, CA CMSA	65	10	0[1]	18
Seattle – Tacoma – Bremerton, WA CMSA	40	19	432	7
St. Louis, MO – IL MSA	59	11	314	10
Tampa – St. Petersburg – Clearwater, FL MSA	32	23	680	4
Washington – Baltimore, DC – MD – VA – WV CMSA	124	5	0[3]	18
West Palm Beach – Boca Raton, FL MSA	10	30	120	17

Source: U.S. Department of Commerce, Bureau of the Census, Data User Services Division, *1992 Economic Census, Volume 1F, Reports Series, Release 1F,* September 1995, CD-ROM. *Notes:* 1. 500-999 employees. 2. 250-499 employees. 3. 1,000-2,499 employees. 4. 100-249 employees. 5. 2,500-4,999 employees.

★2165★
Establishments and Employment
Central Reserve Depository Institutions

The U.S. total number of employees is 26,334; total number of establishments is 67.

MSA	Estab-lish-ments	Rank	Emp-ploy-ment	Rank
Boston – Worcester – Lawrence, MA – NH – ME – CT CMSA	2	2	1,686	4
Chicago – Gary – Kenosha, IL – IN – WI CMSA	2	2	1,994	2
Dallas – Fort Worth, TX CMSA	2	2	1,293	6
Los Angeles – Riverside – Orange County, CA CMSA	1	3	733	7
Miami – Fort Lauderdale, FL CMSA	1	3	344	9
New York – Northern New Jersey – Long Island, NY – NJ – CT-CMSA	3	1	4,092	1
Philadelphia – Wilmington – Atlantic City, PA – NJ – DE – MD CMSA	2	2	1,796	3
San Francisco – Oakland – San Jose, CA CMSA	2	2	1,527	5
Washington – Baltimore, DC – MD – VA – WV CMSA	3	1	466	8

Source: U.S. Department of Commerce, Bureau of the Census, Data User Services Division, *1992 Economic Census, Volume 1F, Reports Series, Release 1F,* September 1995, CD-ROM.

★2166★
Establishments and Employment
Commercial Banks

The U.S. total number of employees is 1,506,055; total number of establishments is 62,761.

MSA	Estab-lish-ments	Rank	Emp-ploy-ment	Rank
New York – Northern New Jersey – Long Island, NY – NJ – CT-CMSA	4,259	1	164,795	1
Chicago – Gary – Kenosha, IL – IN – WI CMSA	1,031	7	63,669	2
Los Angeles – Riverside – Orange County, CA CMSA	2,310	2	60,244	3
San Francisco – Oakland – San Jose, CA CMSA	1,718	4	50,086	4
Philadelphia – Wilmington – Atlantic City, PA – NJ – DE – MD CMSA	1,630	5	49,359	5
Washington – Baltimore, DC – MD – VA – WV CMSA	2,037	3	41,515	6
Boston – Worcester – Lawrence, MA – NH – ME – CT CMSA	963	8	39,298	7
Detroit – Ann Arbor – Flint, MI CMSA	1,185	6	30,391	8
Dallas – Fort Worth, TX CMSA	680	11	26,530	9
Atlanta, GA MSA	821	9	24,679	10
Pittsburgh, PA MSA	634	14	21,107	11

[Continued]

★2166★
Commercial Banks
[Continued]

MSA	Establishments	Rank	Employment	Rank
Houston – Galveston – Brazoria, TX CMSA	599	15	19,700	12
Miami – Fort Lauderdale, FL CMSA	655	13	18,686	13
Cleveland – Akron, OH CMSA	679	12	18,420	14
Phoenix – Mesa, AZ MSA	539	18	16,707	15
Seattle – Tacoma – Bremerton, WA CMSA	688	10	16,333	16
Minneapolis – St. Paul, MN – WI MSA	461	20	15,968	17
St. Louis, MO – IL MSA	495	19	15,281	18
Tampa – St. Petersburg – Clearwater, FL MSA	540	17	12,947	19
Charlotte – Gastonia – Rock Hill, NC – SC MSA	394	25	12,613	20
Kansas City, MO – KS MSA	364	27	11,898	21
San Diego, CA MSA	448	21	11,244	22
Portland – Salem, OR – WA CMSA	435	22	10,694	23
Buffalo – Niagara Falls, NY MSA	247	40	10,646	24
Columbus, OH MSA	384	26	10,447	25

Source: U.S. Department of Commerce, Bureau of the Census, Data User Services Division, *1992 Economic Census, Volume 1F, Reports Series, Release 1F,* September 1995, CD-ROM. *Note:* Data are shown only for the top 25 areas.

★2167★
Establishments and Employment
Credit Unions

The U.S. total number of employees is 139,762; total number of establishments is 15,665.

MSA	Establishments	Rank	Employment	Rank
Los Angeles – Riverside – Orange County, CA CMSA	519	2	6,813	1
New York – Northern New Jersey – Long Island, NY – NJ – CT-CMSA	705	1	4,901	2
Detroit – Ann Arbor – Flint, MI CMSA	346	6	4,471	3
San Francisco – Oakland – San Jose, CA CMSA	333	7	3,725	4
Dallas – Fort Worth, TX CMSA	221	11	2,179	5
San Diego, CA MSA	115	22	2,002	6
Salt Lake City – Ogden, UT MSA	158	14	1,707	7
Denver – Boulder – Greeley, CO CMSA	154	15	1,683	8
Sacramento – Yolo, CA CMSA	95	29	1,533	9
San Antonio, TX MSA	76	35	1,497	10
Norfolk – Virginia Beach – Newport News, VA – NC MSA	115	22	1,430	11
Cleveland – Akron, OH CMSA	263	9	1,348	12
Miami – Fort Lauderdale, FL CMSA	96	28	1,291	13

[Continued]

★2167★
Credit Unions
[Continued]

MSA	Establishments	Rank	Employment	Rank
Tampa – St. Petersburg – Clearwater, FL MSA	85	32	1,197	14
Providence – Fall River – Warwick, RI – MA MSA	105	25	1,141	15
Atlanta, GA MSA	135	19	1,066	16
Pittsburgh, PA MSA	246	10	1,061	17
Indianapolis, IN MSA	98	27	1,031	18
Phoenix – Mesa, AZ MSA	84	33	1,022	19
Jacksonville, FL MSA	76	35	889	20
Oklahoma City, OK MSA	48	49	856	21
Honolulu, HI MSA	91	30	850	22
Austin – San Marcos, TX MSA	61	41	823	23
El Paso, TX MSA	38	58	808	24
Raleigh – Durham – Chapel Hill, NC MSA	47	50	778	25

Source: U.S. Department of Commerce, Bureau of the Census, Data User Services Division, *1992 Economic Census, Volume 1F, Reports Series, Release 1F,* September 1995, CD-ROM. *Note:* Data are shown only for the top 25 areas.

★2168★
Establishments and Employment
Depository Institutions

The U.S. total number of employees is 2,100,089; total number of establishments is 104,505.

MSA	Establishments	Rank	Employment	Rank
New York – Northern New Jersey – Long Island, NY – NJ – CT-CMSA	8,119	1	256,740	1
Los Angeles – Riverside – Orange County, CA CMSA	4,847	2	108,047	2
Chicago – Gary – Kenosha, IL – IN – WI CMSA	2,911	5	92,338	3
San Francisco – Oakland – San Jose, CA CMSA	3,075	4	70,687	4
Boston – Worcester – Lawrence, MA – NH – ME – CT CMSA	2,333	7	64,085	5
Philadelphia – Wilmington – Atlantic City, PA – NJ – DE – MD CMSA	2,700	6	63,166	6
Washington – Baltimore, DC – MD – VA – WV CMSA	3,293	3	61,530	7
Detroit – Ann Arbor – Flint, MI CMSA	1,879	8	41,123	8
Dallas – Fort Worth, TX CMSA	1,231	13	34,717	9
Atlanta, GA MSA	1,275	11	31,639	10
Miami – Fort Lauderdale, FL CMSA	1,331	10	30,848	11
Cleveland – Akron, OH CMSA	1,392	9	27,057	12
Pittsburgh, PA MSA	1,150	14	25,915	13
Seattle – Tacoma – Bremerton, WA CMSA	1,245	12	25,327	14

[Continued]

★2168★

Depository Institutions
[Continued]

MSA	Establishments	Rank	Employment	Rank
Houston – Galveston – Brazoria, TX CMSA	1,131	15	25,093	15
St. Louis, MO – IL MSA	863	19	22,711	16
Minneapolis – St. Paul, MN – WI MSA	752	21	22,253	17
San Diego, CA MSA	911	17	18,750	18
Phoenix – Mesa, AZ MSA	728	22	18,550	19
Tampa – St. Petersburg – Clearwater, FL MSA	875	18	17,720	20
Kansas City, MO – KS MSA	618	26	15,685	21
Hartford, CT MSA	617	27	15,631	22
Denver – Boulder – Greeley, CO CMSA	638	23	15,602	23
Milwaukee – Racine, WI CMSA	636	24	14,783	24
Portland – Salem, OR – WA CMSA	784	20	14,699	25

Source: U.S. Department of Commerce, Bureau of the Census, Data User Services Division, *1992 Economic Census, Volume 1F, Reports Series, Release 1F,* September 1995, CD-ROM. *Note:* Data are shown only for the top 25 areas.

★2169★

Establishments and Employment

Federal and Federally-sponsored Credit Agencies

The U.S. total number of employees is 21,298; total number of establishments is 1,349.

MSA	Establishments	Rank	Employment	Rank
Atlanta, GA MSA	9	3	0[1]	3
Boston – Worcester – Lawrence, MA – NH – ME – CT CMSA	4	7	0[2]	3
Chicago – Gary – Kenosha, IL – IN – WI CMSA	9	3	0[1]	3
Cincinnati – Hamilton, OH – KY – IN CMSA	2	9	0[3]	3
Cleveland – Akron, OH CMSA	4	7	0[3]	3
Columbus, OH MSA	5	6	0[2]	3
Dallas – Fort Worth, TX CMSA	7	4	0[1]	3
Denver – Boulder – Greeley, CO CMSA	4	7	0[1]	3
Detroit – Ann Arbor – Flint, MI CMSA	6	5	0[2]	3
Houston – Galveston – Brazoria, TX CMSA	3	8	17	2
Indianapolis, IN MSA	5	6	0[2]	3
Kansas City, MO – KS MSA	2	9	0[3]	3
Los Angeles – Riverside – Orange County, CA CMSA	10	2	0[1]	3
Miami – Fort Lauderdale, FL CMSA	1	10	0[3]	3
Milwaukee – Racine, WI CMSA	1	10	0[3]	3
Minneapolis – St. Paul, MN – WI MSA	7	4	0[4]	3

[Continued]

★2169★

Federal and Federally-sponsored Credit Agencies
[Continued]

MSA	Establishments	Rank	Employment	Rank
New York – Northern New Jersey – Long Island, NY – NJ – CT-CMSA	5	6	0[5]	3
Norfolk – Virginia Beach – Newport News, VA – NC MSA	2	9	0[3]	3
Orlando, FL MSA	3	8	0[3]	3
Philadelphia – Wilmington – Atlantic City, PA – NJ – DE – MD CMSA	9	3	0[5]	3
Phoenix – Mesa, AZ MSA	1	10	0[2]	3
Pittsburgh, PA MSA	4	7	0[2]	3
Portland – Salem, OR – WA CMSA	2	9	0[2]	3
Sacramento – Yolo, CA CMSA	4	7	0[1]	3
San Diego, CA MSA	1	10	0[3]	3
San Francisco – Oakland – San Jose, CA CMSA	5	6	0[2]	3
Seattle – Tacoma – Bremerton, WA CMSA	1	10	0[3]	3
St. Louis, MO – IL MSA	7	4	0[1]	3
Tampa – St. Petersburg – Clearwater, FL MSA	5	6	0[5]	3
Washington – Baltimore, DC – MD – VA – WV CMSA	25	1	6,336	1
West Palm Beach – Boca Raton, FL MSA	1	10	0[2]	3

Source: U.S. Department of Commerce, Bureau of the Census, Data User Services Division, *1992 Economic Census, Volume 1F, Reports Series, Release 1F,* September 1995, CD-ROM. *Notes:* 1. 250-499 employees. 2. 20-99 employees. 3. 0-19 employees. 4. 500-999 employees. 5. 100-249 employees.

★2170★

Establishments and Employment

Federal Reserve Banks

The U.S. total number of employees is 23,819; total number of establishments is 42.

MSA	Establishments	Rank	Employment	Rank
Boston – Worcester – Lawrence, MA – NH – ME – CT CMSA	1	1	1,569	4
Chicago – Gary – Kenosha, IL – IN – WI CMSA	1	1	1,883	2
Dallas – Fort Worth, TX CMSA	1	1	1,148	6
Los Angeles – Riverside – Orange County, CA CMSA	1	1	733	7
Miami – Fort Lauderdale, FL CMSA	1	1	344	9
New York – Northern New Jersey – Long Island, NY – NJ – CT-CMSA	1	1	3,722	1
Philadelphia – Wilmington – Atlantic City, PA – NJ – DE – MD CMSA	1	1	1,696	3

[Continued]

★2170★

Federal Reserve Banks

[Continued]

MSA	Estab-lish-ments	Rank	Emp-loy-ment	Rank
San Francisco – Oakland – San Jose, CA CMSA	1	1	1,335	5
Washington – Baltimore, DC – MD – VA – WV CMSA	1	1	433	8

Source: U.S. Department of Commerce, Bureau of the Census, Data User Services Division, *1992 Economic Census, Volume 1F, Reports Series, Release 1F,* September 1995, CD-ROM.

★2171★

Establishments and Employment

Fire, Marine, and Casualty Insurance

The U.S. total number of employees is 588,333; total number of establishments is 19,002.

MSA	Estab-lish-ments	Rank	Emp-loy-ment	Rank
Los Angeles – Riverside – Orange County, CA CMSA	1,044	2	38,029	1
San Francisco – Oakland – San Jose, CA CMSA	580	4	21,263	2
Hartford, CT MSA	155	27	18,533	3
Dallas – Fort Worth, TX CMSA	425	6	14,809	4
Columbus, OH MSA	158	25	13,259	5
Atlanta, GA MSA	357	8	12,675	6
Minneapolis – St. Paul, MN – WI MSA	230	15	11,479	7
San Antonio, TX MSA	110	36	9,934	8
Indianapolis, IN MSA	175	22	8,349	9
Cleveland – Akron, OH CMSA	253	14	7,613	10
Portland – Salem, OR – WA CMSA	220	18	7,106	11
Tampa – St. Petersburg – Clearwater, FL MSA	255	13	6,977	12
Cincinnati – Hamilton, OH – KY – IN CMSA	157	26	6,800	13
Kansas City, MO – KS MSA	190	20	6,112	14
Austin – San Marcos, TX MSA	105	38	6,096	15
Sacramento – Yolo, CA CMSA	159	24	5,846	16
Charlotte – Gastonia – Rock Hill, NC – SC MSA	135	30	5,381	17
St. Louis, MO – IL MSA	223	17	5,290	18
Nashville, TN MSA	135	30	4,991	19
Providence – Fall River – Warwick, RI – MA MSA	64	54	4,525	20
Madison, WI MSA	51	63	4,256	21
San Diego, CA MSA	184	21	4,082	22
Pittsburgh, PA MSA	165	23	3,914	23
Syracuse, NY MSA	80	46	3,877	24
Harrisburg – Lebanon – Carlisle, PA MSA	58	58	3,648	25

Source: U.S. Department of Commerce, Bureau of the Census, Data User Services Division, *1992 Economic Census, Volume 1F, Reports Series, Release 1F,* September 1995, CD-ROM. *Note:* Data are shown only for the top 25 areas.

★2172★

Establishments and Employment

Foreign Banking and Branches and Agencies of Foreign Banks

The U.S. total number of employees is 34,310; total number of establishments is 632.

MSA	Estab-lish-ments	Rank	Emp-loy-ment	Rank
Boston – Worcester – Lawrence, MA – NH – ME – CT CMSA	8	6	0[1]	3
Chicago – Gary – Kenosha, IL – IN – WI CMSA	55	4	2,011	1
Dallas – Fort Worth, TX CMSA	4	9	0[2]	3
Los Angeles – Riverside – Orange County, CA CMSA	93	2	0[3]	3
Miami – Fort Lauderdale, FL CMSA	57	3	0[4]	3
New York – Northern New Jersey – Long Island, NY – NJ – CT-CMSA	309	1	0[5]	3
Philadelphia – Wilmington – Atlantic City, PA – NJ – DE – MD CMSA	5	8	0[6]	3
San Francisco – Oakland – San Jose, CA CMSA	30	5	629	2
Washington – Baltimore, DC – MD – VA – WV CMSA	6	7	0[2]	3

Source: U.S. Department of Commerce, Bureau of the Census, Data User Services Division, *1992 Economic Census, Volume 1F, Reports Series, Release 1F,* September 1995, CD-ROM. *Notes:* 1. 100-249 employees. 2. 20-99 employees. 3. 2,500-4,999 employees. 4. 1,000-2,499 employees. 5. 25,000-49,999 employees. 6. 250-499 employees.

★2173★

Establishments and Employment

Foreign Trade and International Banking Institutions

The U.S. total number of employees is 3,250; total number of establishments is 71.

MSA	Estab-lish-ments	Rank	Emp-loy-ment	Rank
Boston – Worcester – Lawrence, MA – NH – ME – CT CMSA	1	6	0[1]	1
Chicago – Gary – Kenosha, IL – IN – WI CMSA	4	3	0[2]	1
Dallas – Fort Worth, TX CMSA	0	7	0	1
Los Angeles – Riverside – Orange County, CA CMSA	4	3	0[3]	1
Miami – Fort Lauderdale, FL CMSA	19	2	0[4]	1
New York – Northern New Jersey – Long Island, NY – NJ – CT-CMSA	23	1	0[4]	1
Philadelphia – Wilmington – Atlantic City, PA – NJ – DE – MD CMSA	2	5	0[1]	1

[Continued]

★2173★

Foreign Trade and International Banking Institutions
[Continued]

MSA	Estab-lish-ments	Rank	Emp-ploy-ment	Rank
San Francisco – Oakland – San Jose, CA CMSA	1	6	0[2]	1
Washington – Baltimore, DC – MD – VA – WV CMSA	3	4	0[1]	1

Source: U.S. Department of Commerce, Bureau of the Census, Data User Services Division, *1992 Economic Census, Volume 1F, Reports Series, Release 1F,* September 1995, CD-ROM. *Notes:* 1. 0-19 employees. 2. 20-99 employees. 3. 100-249 employees. 4. 1,000-2,499 employees.

★2174★

Establishments and Employment

Holding Offices

The U.S. total number of employees is 108,235; total number of establishments is 10,381.

MSA	Estab-lish-ments	Rank	Emp-ploy-ment	Rank
Atlanta, GA MSA	164	10	1,329	11
Boston – Worcester – Lawrence, MA – NH – ME – CT CMSA	228	8	0[1]	19
Chicago – Gary – Kenosha, IL – IN – WI CMSA	436	3	4,851	1
Cincinnati – Hamilton, OH – KY – IN CMSA	83	20	0[2]	19
Cleveland – Akron, OH CMSA	130	14	0[2]	19
Columbus, OH MSA	52	27	0[2]	19
Dallas – Fort Worth, TX CMSA	267	5	0[1]	19
Denver – Boulder – Greeley, CO CMSA	110	16	0[2]	19
Detroit – Ann Arbor – Flint, MI CMSA	145	13	1,075	13
Houston – Galveston – Brazoria, TX CMSA	252	6	3,010	3
Indianapolis, IN MSA	61	25	996	14
Kansas City, MO – KS MSA	103	18	1,551	8
Los Angeles – Riverside – Orange County, CA CMSA	420	4	0[3]	19
Miami – Fort Lauderdale, FL CMSA	157	11	1,822	6
Milwaukee – Racine, WI CMSA	116	15	0[2]	19
Minneapolis – St. Paul, MN – WI MSA	153	12	1,635	7
New York – Northern New Jersey – Long Island, NY – NJ – CT-CMSA	1,096	2	0[4]	19
Norfolk – Virginia Beach – Newport News, VA – NC MSA	34	29	0[5]	19
Orlando, FL MSA	46	28	339	18
Philadelphia – Wilmington – Atlantic City, PA – NJ – DE – MD CMSA	1,148	1	3,673	2
Phoenix – Mesa, AZ MSA	74	22	914	16

[Continued]

★2174★

Holding Offices
[Continued]

MSA	Estab-lish-ments	Rank	Emp-ploy-ment	Rank
Pittsburgh, PA MSA	82	21	2,243	5
Portland – Salem, OR – WA CMSA	63	24	0[2]	19
Sacramento – Yolo, CA CMSA	15	30	0[5]	19
San Diego, CA MSA	85	19	369	17
San Francisco – Oakland – San Jose, CA CMSA	217	9	2,899	4
Seattle – Tacoma – Bremerton, WA CMSA	105	17	1,478	9
St. Louis, MO – IL MSA	157	11	1,407	10
Tampa – St. Petersburg – Clearwater, FL MSA	72	23	963	15
Washington – Baltimore, DC – MD – VA – WV CMSA	230	7	0[3]	19
West Palm Beach – Boca Raton, FL MSA	57	26	1,097	12

Source: U.S. Department of Commerce, Bureau of the Census, Data User Services Division, *1992 Economic Census, Volume 1F, Reports Series, Release 1F,* September 1995, CD-ROM. *Notes:* 1. 2,500-4,999 employees. 2. 1,000-2,499 employees. 3. 5,000-9,999 employees. 4. 10,000-24,999 employees. 5. 100-249 employees.

★2175★

Establishments and Employment

Hospital and Medical Service Plans

The U.S. total number of employees is 196,637; total number of establishments is 1,746.

MSA	Estab-lish-ments	Rank	Emp-ploy-ment	Rank
Boston – Worcester – Lawrence, MA – NH – ME – CT CMSA	45	6	7,467	1
Chicago – Gary – Kenosha, IL – IN – WI CMSA	63	3	0[1]	3
Dallas – Fort Worth, TX CMSA	23	9	3,425	2
Los Angeles – Riverside – Orange County, CA CMSA	109	1	0[2]	3
Miami – Fort Lauderdale, FL CMSA	32	8	0[3]	3
New York – Northern New Jersey – Long Island, NY – NJ – CT-CMSA	97	2	0[2]	3
Philadelphia – Wilmington – Atlantic City, PA – NJ – DE – MD CMSA	34	7	0[1]	3
San Francisco – Oakland – San Jose, CA CMSA	47	5	0[3]	3
Washington – Baltimore, DC – MD – VA – WV CMSA	56	4	0[1]	3

Source: U.S. Department of Commerce, Bureau of the Census, Data User Services Division, *1992 Economic Census, Volume 1F, Reports Series, Release 1F,* September 1995, CD-ROM. *Notes:* 1. 5,000-9,999 employees. 2. 10,000-24,999 employees. 3. 2,500-4,999 employees.

★2176★

Establishments and Employment

Insurance Agents, Brokers, and Services

The U.S. total number of employees is 635,536; total number of establishments is 121,662.

MSA	Estab-lish-ments	Rank	Emp-loy-ment	Rank
New York – Northern New Jersey – Long Island, NY – NJ – CT-CMSA	7,737	1	63,801	1
Los Angeles – Riverside – Orange County, CA CMSA	5,583	2	34,027	2
Chicago – Gary – Kenosha, IL – IN – WI CMSA	3,982	3	26,303	3
Boston – Worcester – Lawrence, MA – NH – ME – CT CMSA	2,576	6	18,273	4
San Francisco – Oakland – San Jose, CA CMSA	2,868	4	17,926	5
Washington – Baltimore, DC – MD – VA – WV CMSA	2,719	5	17,505	6
Philadelphia – Wilmington – Atlantic City, PA – NJ – DE – MD CMSA	2,531	7	16,999	7
Dallas – Fort Worth, TX CMSA	2,411	8	15,147	8
Atlanta, GA MSA	1,687	12	12,467	9
Detroit – Ann Arbor – Flint, MI CMSA	1,912	10	12,134	10
Houston – Galveston – Brazoria, TX CMSA	1,854	11	11,082	11
Miami – Fort Lauderdale, FL CMSA	2,048	9	10,223	12
Seattle – Tacoma – Bremerton, WA CMSA	1,465	15	9,542	13
Minneapolis – St. Paul, MN – WI MSA	1,527	13	9,019	14
Tampa – St. Petersburg – Clearwater, FL MSA	1,255	19	7,573	15
Phoenix – Mesa, AZ MSA	1,295	18	7,284	16
Cleveland – Akron, OH CMSA	1,414	17	6,703	17
St. Louis, MO – IL MSA	1,493	14	6,533	18
Kansas City, MO – KS MSA	1,071	21	6,450	19
Denver – Boulder – Greeley, CO CMSA	1,424	16	6,039	20
Indianapolis, IN MSA	866	25	5,941	21
Pittsburgh, PA MSA	1,077	20	5,580	22
San Diego, CA MSA	1,046	22	5,562	23
Milwaukee – Racine, WI CMSA	1,009	23	5,002	24
Portland – Salem, OR – WA CMSA	991	24	4,951	25

Source: U.S. Department of Commerce, Bureau of the Census, Data User Services Division, *1992 Economic Census, Volume 1F, Reports Series, Release 1F,* September 1995, CD-ROM. *Note:* Data are shown only for the top 25 areas.

★2177★

Establishments and Employment

Insurance Carriers

The U.S. total number of employees is 1,516,643; total number of establishments is 38,977.

MSA	Estab-lish-ments	Rank	Emp-loy-ment	Rank
New York – Northern New Jersey – Long Island, NY – NJ – CT-CMSA	2,631	1	156,855	1
Los Angeles – Riverside – Orange County, CA CMSA	1,960	2	85,181	2
Hartford, CT MSA	287	31	61,997	3
San Francisco – Oakland – San Jose, CA CMSA	1,195	4	39,936	4
Dallas – Fort Worth, TX CMSA	928	6	35,377	5
Washington – Baltimore, DC – MD – VA – WV CMSA	1,092	5	34,360	6
Minneapolis – St. Paul, MN – WI MSA	483	17	31,509	7
Detroit – Ann Arbor – Flint, MI CMSA	688	9	29,627	8
Atlanta, GA MSA	727	8	29,512	9
Columbus, OH MSA	340	26	22,508	10
Seattle – Tacoma – Bremerton, WA CMSA	563	12	20,368	11
Des Moines, IA MSA	173	46	18,528	12
Jacksonville, FL MSA	278	33	17,802	13
Cleveland – Akron, OH CMSA	518	13	16,472	14
Kansas City, MO – KS MSA	421	20	16,360	15
Indianapolis, IN MSA	378	23	16,079	16
Springfield, MA MSA	58	84	15,807	17
Tampa – St. Petersburg – Clearwater, FL MSA	504	14	15,080	18
St. Louis, MO – IL MSA	475	18	15,038	19
Portland – Salem, OR – WA CMSA	416	21	14,819	20
Phoenix – Mesa, AZ MSA	472	19	14,444	21
Omaha, NE – IA MSA	157	47	14,076	22
San Antonio, TX MSA	246	36	13,656	23
Pittsburgh, PA MSA	405	22	13,430	24
Miami – Fort Lauderdale, FL CMSA	502	15	12,909	25

Source: U.S. Department of Commerce, Bureau of the Census, Data User Services Division, *1992 Economic Census, Volume 1F, Reports Series, Release 1F,* September 1995, CD-ROM. *Note:* Data are shown only for the top 25 areas.

★2178★

Establishments and Employment

Investment Advice

The U.S. total number of employees is 68,763; total number of establishments is 11,520.

MSA	Establishments	Rank	Employment	Rank
Boston – Worcester – Lawrence, MA – NH – ME – CT CMSA	482	5	0^1	7
Chicago – Gary – Kenosha, IL – IN – WI CMSA	529	4	3,369	3
Dallas – Fort Worth, TX CMSA	267	8	2,626	4
Los Angeles – Riverside – Orange County, CA CMSA	718	2	0^2	7
Miami – Fort Lauderdale, FL CMSA	181	9	631	6
New York – Northern New Jersey – Long Island, NY – NJ – CT-CMSA	1,742	1	17,513	1
Philadelphia – Wilmington – Atlantic City, PA – NJ – DE – MD CMSA	347	7	2,379	5
San Francisco – Oakland – San Jose, CA CMSA	610	3	4,411	2
Washington – Baltimore, DC – MD – VA – WV CMSA	427	6	0^3	7

Source: U.S. Department of Commerce, Bureau of the Census, Data User Services Division, *1992 Economic Census, Volume 1F, Reports Series, Release 1F,* September 1995, CD-ROM. *Notes:* 1. 5,000-9,999 employees. 2. 2,500-4,999 employees. 3. 1,000-2,499 employees.

★2179★

Establishments and Employment

Investment Offices

The U.S. total number of employees is 16,752; total number of establishments is 829.

MSA	Establishments	Rank	Employment	Rank
Atlanta, GA MSA	19	10	230	4
Boston – Worcester – Lawrence, MA – NH – ME – CT CMSA	44	5	5,465	1
Chicago – Gary – Kenosha, IL – IN – WI CMSA	29	6	0^1	10
Cincinnati – Hamilton, OH – KY – IN CMSA	1	21	0^2	10
Cleveland – Akron, OH CMSA	4	18	0^2	10
Columbus, OH MSA	6	16	11	8
Dallas – Fort Worth, TX CMSA	29	6	0^3	10
Denver – Boulder – Greeley, CO CMSA	17	11	197	5
Detroit – Ann Arbor – Flint, MI CMSA	9	14	0^4	10
Houston – Galveston – Brazoria, TX CMSA	23	7	0^1	10
Indianapolis, IN MSA	7	15	0^4	10
Kansas City, MO – KS MSA	5	17	0^5	10
Los Angeles – Riverside – Orange County, CA CMSA	48	3	0^3	10

[Continued]

★2179★

Investment Offices

[Continued]

MSA	Establishments	Rank	Employment	Rank
Miami – Fort Lauderdale, FL CMSA	20	9	0^4	10
Milwaukee – Racine, WI CMSA	3	19	0^2	10
Minneapolis – St. Paul, MN – WI MSA	20	9	0^5	10
New York – Northern New Jersey – Long Island, NY – NJ – CT-CMSA	117	1	0^5	10
Norfolk – Virginia Beach – Newport News, VA – NC MSA	1	21	0^2	10
Orlando, FL MSA	1	21	0^2	10
Philadelphia – Wilmington – Atlantic City, PA – NJ – DE – MD CMSA	67	2	2,872	2
Phoenix – Mesa, AZ MSA	7	15	0^2	10
Pittsburgh, PA MSA	1	21	0^2	10
Portland – Salem, OR – WA CMSA	5	17	0^4	10
Sacramento – Yolo, CA CMSA	1	21	0^2	10
San Diego, CA MSA	6	16	5	9
San Francisco – Oakland – San Jose, CA CMSA	46	4	316	3
Seattle – Tacoma – Bremerton, WA CMSA	13	12	24	7
St. Louis, MO – IL MSA	11	13	48	6
Tampa – St. Petersburg – Clearwater, FL MSA	2	20	0^2	10
Washington – Baltimore, DC – MD – VA – WV CMSA	22	8	0^6	10
West Palm Beach – Boca Raton, FL MSA	4	18	0^2	10

Source: U.S. Department of Commerce, Bureau of the Census, Data User Services Division, *1992 Economic Census, Volume 1F, Reports Series, Release 1F,* September 1995, CD-ROM. *Notes:* 1. 100-249 employees. 2. 0-19 employees. 3. 250-499 employees. 4. 20-99 employees. 5. 1,000-2,499 employees. 6. 500-999 employees.

★2180★

Establishments and Employment

Land Subdividers and Developers

The U.S. total number of employees is 88,604; total number of establishments is 15,338.

MSA	Establishments	Rank	Employment	Rank
New York – Northern New Jersey – Long Island, NY – NJ – CT-CMSA	857	1	6,163	1
Chicago – Gary – Kenosha, IL – IN – WI CMSA	432	4	2,665	2
Dallas – Fort Worth, TX CMSA	242	10	2,342	3
Atlanta, GA MSA	269	8	2,039	4
Miami – Fort Lauderdale, FL CMSA	249	9	2,005	5
Tampa – St. Petersburg – Clearwater, FL MSA	127	19	1,549	6

[Continued]

★2180★

Land Subdividers and Developers
[Continued]

MSA	Estab-lish-ments	Rank	Emp-loy-ment	Rank
Seattle – Tacoma – Bremerton, WA CMSA	240	11	1,315	7
San Diego, CA MSA	179	14	1,306	8
Cleveland – Akron, OH CMSA	109	25	1,179	9
Fort Myers – Cape Coral, FL MSA	35	52	1,013	10
Phoenix – Mesa, AZ MSA	128	18	912	11
West Palm Beach – Boca Raton, FL MSA	89	27	891	12
Orlando, FL MSA	124	20	874	13
Charlotte – Gastonia – Rock Hill, NC – SC MSA	74	31	738	14
Richmond – Petersburg, VA MSA	68	35	722	15
New Orleans, LA MSA	59	39	689	16
Indianapolis, IN MSA	105	26	653	17
St. Louis, MO – IL MSA	139	17	603	18
Minneapolis – St. Paul, MN – WI MSA	146	16	594	19
Kansas City, MO – KS MSA	111	23	578	20
Jacksonville, FL MSA	67	36	550	21
Columbus, OH MSA	73	32	507	22
Birmingham, AL MSA	54	42	393	23
San Antonio, TX MSA	67	36	375	24
Lakeland – Winter Haven, FL MSA	28	58	371	25

Source: U.S. Department of Commerce, Bureau of the Census, Data User Services Division, *1992 Economic Census, Volume 1F, Reports Series, Release 1F,* September 1995, CD-ROM. *Note:* Data are shown only for the top 25 areas.

★2181★

Establishments and Employment

Life Insurance

The U.S. total number of employees is 609,237; total number of establishments is 13,424.

MSA	Estab-lish-ments	Rank	Emp-loy-ment	Rank
New York – Northern New Jersey – Long Island, NY – NJ – CT-CMSA	996	1	75,688	1
Hartford, CT MSA	97	31	41,599	2
Minneapolis – St. Paul, MN – WI MSA	161	15	14,630	3
Springfield, MA MSA	31	65	13,162	4
Dallas – Fort Worth, TX CMSA	325	6	12,613	5
Des Moines, IA MSA	81	37	11,566	6
San Francisco – Oakland – San Jose, CA CMSA	271	9	8,632	7
Jacksonville, FL MSA	135	23	7,771	8
Denver – Boulder – Greeley, CO CMSA	160	16	7,023	9
Kansas City, MO – KS MSA	137	22	6,756	10
Tampa – St. Petersburg – Clearwater, FL MSA	157	18	6,471	11
St. Louis, MO – IL MSA	173	14	6,380	12

[Continued]

★2181★

Life Insurance
[Continued]

MSA	Estab-lish-ments	Rank	Emp-loy-ment	Rank
Miami – Fort Lauderdale, FL CMSA	142	20	6,004	13
Columbus, OH MSA	103	28	5,938	14
Indianapolis, IN MSA	139	21	5,297	15
Seattle – Tacoma – Bremerton, WA CMSA	148	19	5,142	16
Cleveland – Akron, OH CMSA	188	12	4,619	17
Greensboro – Winston-Salem – High Point, NC MSA	84	35	4,310	18
Portland, ME MSA	30	66	3,974	19
Syracuse, NY MSA	40	59	3,898	20
Madison, WI MSA	39	60	3,869	21
Charlotte – Gastonia – Rock Hill, NC – SC MSA	133	24	3,772	22
Orlando, FL MSA	106	26	3,602	23
Phoenix – Mesa, AZ MSA	159	17	3,492	24
Allentown – Bethlehem – Easton, PA MSA	39	60	3,201	25

Source: U.S. Department of Commerce, Bureau of the Census, Data User Services Division, *1992 Economic Census, Volume 1F, Reports Series, Release 1F,* September 1995, CD-ROM. *Note:* Data are shown only for the top 25 areas.

★2182★

Establishments and Employment

Loan Brokers

The U.S. total number of employees is 32,362; total number of establishments is 6,157.

MSA	Estab-lish-ments	Rank	Emp-loy-ment	Rank
Atlanta, GA MSA	169	7	0[1]	11
Boston – Worcester – Lawrence, MA – NH – ME – CT CMSA	107	10	502	4
Chicago – Gary – Kenosha, IL – IN – WI CMSA	205	5	0[2]	11
Cincinnati – Hamilton, OH – KY – IN CMSA	25	27	0[3]	11
Cleveland – Akron, OH CMSA	42	22	0[4]	11
Columbus, OH MSA	36	23	191	9
Dallas – Fort Worth, TX CMSA	105	11	0[4]	11
Denver – Boulder – Greeley, CO CMSA	92	12	488	5
Detroit – Ann Arbor – Flint, MI CMSA	85	13	0[1]	11
Houston – Galveston – Brazoria, TX CMSA	63	17	0[3]	11
Indianapolis, IN MSA	43	21	368	7
Kansas City, MO – KS MSA	33	25	174	10
Los Angeles – Riverside – Orange County, CA CMSA	1,119	1	0[5]	11
Miami – Fort Lauderdale, FL CMSA	169	7	550	3
Milwaukee – Racine, WI CMSA	34	24	0[3]	11

[Continued]

★2182★

Loan Brokers

[Continued]

MSA	Estab-lish-ments	Rank	Emp-ploy-ment	Rank
Minneapolis – St. Paul, MN – WI MSA	49	20	487	6
New York – Northern New Jersey – Long Island, NY – NJ – CT-CMSA	418	3	0^2	11
Norfolk – Virginia Beach – Newport News, VA – NC MSA	14	28	0^6	11
Orlando, FL MSA	50	19	0^3	11
Philadelphia – Wilmington – Atlantic City, PA – NJ – DE – MD CMSA	107	10	0^1	11
Phoenix – Mesa, AZ MSA	68	16	577	2
Pittsburgh, PA MSA	28	26	0^3	11
Portland – Salem, OR – WA CMSA	81	14	0^4	11
Sacramento – Yolo, CA CMSA	113	9	0^1	11
San Diego, CA MSA	209	4	892	1
San Francisco – Oakland – San Jose, CA CMSA	586	2	0^7	11
Seattle – Tacoma – Bremerton, WA CMSA	149	8	0^1	11
St. Louis, MO – IL MSA	33	25	274	8
Tampa – St. Petersburg – Clearwater, FL MSA	78	15	0^1	11
Washington – Baltimore, DC – MD – VA – WV CMSA	198	6	0^2	11
West Palm Beach – Boca Raton, FL MSA	51	18	0^3	11

Source: U.S. Department of Commerce, Bureau of the Census, Data User Services Division, *1992 Economic Census, Volume 1F, Reports Series, Release 1F,* September 1995, CD-ROM. *Notes:* 1. 500-999 employees. 2. 1,000-2,499 employees. 3. 100-249 employees. 4. 250-499 employees. 5. 5,000-9,999 employees. 6. 20-99 employees. 7. 2,500-4,999 employees.

★2183★

Establishments and Employment

Management Investment Offices, Open End

The U.S. total number of employees is 15,648; total number of establishments is 561.

MSA	Estab-lish-ments	Rank	Emp-ploy-ment	Rank
Boston – Worcester – Lawrence, MA – NH – ME – CT CMSA	34	4	0^1	4
Chicago – Gary – Kenosha, IL – IN – WI CMSA	21	7	0^2	4
Dallas – Fort Worth, TX CMSA	22	6	0^3	4
Los Angeles – Riverside – Orange County, CA CMSA	37	3	442	2
Miami – Fort Lauderdale, FL CMSA	14	8	18	3
New York – Northern New Jersey – Long Island, NY – NJ – CT-CMSA	79	1	1,136	1
Philadelphia – Wilmington – Atlantic City, PA – NJ – DE – MD CMSA	44	2	0^4	4

[Continued]

★2183★

Management Investment Offices, Open End

[Continued]

MSA	Estab-lish-ments	Rank	Emp-ploy-ment	Rank
San Francisco – Oakland – San Jose, CA CMSA	32	5	0^3	4
Washington – Baltimore, DC – MD – VA – WV CMSA	14	8	0^5	4

Source: U.S. Department of Commerce, Bureau of the Census, Data User Services Division, *1992 Economic Census, Volume 1F, Reports Series, Release 1F,* September 1995, CD-ROM. *Notes:* 1. 5,000-9,999 employees. 2. 20-99 employees. 3. 250-499 employees. 4. 2,500-4,999 employees. 5. 500-999 employees.

★2184★

Establishments and Employment

Mortgage Bankers and Brokers

The U.S. total number of employees is 178,976; total number of establishments is 16,152.

MSA	Estab-lish-ments	Rank	Emp-ploy-ment	Rank
Atlanta, GA MSA	390	8	0^1	12
Boston – Worcester – Lawrence, MA – NH – ME – CT CMSA	296	11	3,665	5
Chicago – Gary – Kenosha, IL – IN – WI CMSA	511	5	0^2	12
Cincinnati – Hamilton, OH – KY – IN CMSA	84	29	0^3	12
Cleveland – Akron, OH CMSA	128	21	0^4	12
Columbus, OH MSA	94	26	1,420	11
Dallas – Fort Worth, TX CMSA	343	10	0^2	12
Denver – Boulder – Greeley, CO CMSA	278	12	2,947	7
Detroit – Ann Arbor – Flint, MI CMSA	257	13	0^2	12
Houston – Galveston – Brazoria, TX CMSA	239	16	0^1	12
Indianapolis, IN MSA	119	22	2,060	9
Kansas City, MO – KS MSA	117	23	1,781	10
Los Angeles – Riverside – Orange County, CA CMSA	2,227	1	0^5	12
Miami – Fort Lauderdale, FL CMSA	438	6	4,640	2
Milwaukee – Racine, WI CMSA	89	28	0^4	12
Minneapolis – St. Paul, MN – WI MSA	181	19	4,498	4
New York – Northern New Jersey – Long Island, NY – NJ – CT-CMSA	1,110	2	11,453	1
Norfolk – Virginia Beach – Newport News, VA – NC MSA	90	27	0^3	12
Orlando, FL MSA	160	20	0^4	12
Philadelphia – Wilmington – Atlantic City, PA – NJ – DE – MD CMSA	350	9	0^2	12
Phoenix – Mesa, AZ MSA	247	14	2,808	8
Pittsburgh, PA MSA	78	30	0^3	12

[Continued]

★2184★
Mortgage Bankers and Brokers
[Continued]

MSA	Establishments	Rank	Employment	Rank
Portland – Salem, OR – WA CMSA	228	17	0[4]	12
Sacramento – Yolo, CA CMSA	241	15	0[4]	12
San Diego, CA MSA	398	7	4,609	3
San Francisco – Oakland – San Jose, CA CMSA	1,027	3	0[2]	12
Seattle – Tacoma – Bremerton, WA CMSA	398	7	0[1]	12
St. Louis, MO – IL MSA	102	25	3,468	6
Tampa – St. Petersburg – Clearwater, FL MSA	222	18	0[4]	12
Washington – Baltimore, DC – MD – VA – WV CMSA	674	4	0[2]	12
West Palm Beach – Boca Raton, FL MSA	115	24	0[3]	12

Source: U.S. Department of Commerce, Bureau of the Census, Data User Services Division, *1992 Economic Census, Volume 1F, Reports Series, Release 1F,* September 1995, CD-ROM. *Notes:* 1. 2,500-4,999 employees. 2. 5,000-9,999 employees. 3. 500-999 employees. 4. 1,000-2,499 employees. 5. 10,000-24,999 employees.

★2185★
Establishments and Employment
Mortgage Bankers and Loan Correspondents

The U.S. total number of employees is 146,614; total number of establishments is 9,995.

MSA	Establishments	Rank	Employment	Rank
Atlanta, GA MSA	221	10	3,148	9
Boston – Worcester – Lawrence, MA – NH – ME – CT CMSA	189	11	3,163	8
Chicago – Gary – Kenosha, IL – IN – WI CMSA	306	5	0[1]	21
Cincinnati – Hamilton, OH – KY – IN CMSA	59	26	0[2]	21
Cleveland – Akron, OH CMSA	86	21	899	17
Columbus, OH MSA	58	27	1,229	16
Dallas – Fort Worth, TX CMSA	238	9	0[1]	21
Denver – Boulder – Greeley, CO CMSA	186	12	2,459	11
Detroit – Ann Arbor – Flint, MI CMSA	172	15	0[3]	21
Houston – Galveston – Brazoria, TX CMSA	176	14	3,323	6
Indianapolis, IN MSA	76	23	1,692	14
Kansas City, MO – KS MSA	84	22	1,607	15
Los Angeles – Riverside – Orange County, CA CMSA	1,108	1	13,933	1
Miami – Fort Lauderdale, FL CMSA	269	6	4,090	3
Milwaukee – Racine, WI CMSA	55	28	774	18
Minneapolis – St. Paul, MN – WI MSA	132	18	4,011	4
New York – Northern New Jersey – Long Island, NY – NJ – CT-CMSA	692	2	0[1]	21

[Continued]

★2185★
Mortgage Bankers and Loan Correspondents
[Continued]

MSA	Establishments	Rank	Employment	Rank
Norfolk – Virginia Beach – Newport News, VA – NC MSA	76	23	0[2]	21
Orlando, FL MSA	110	20	0[2]	21
Philadelphia – Wilmington – Atlantic City, PA – NJ – DE – MD CMSA	243	8	0[1]	21
Phoenix – Mesa, AZ MSA	179	13	2,231	12
Pittsburgh, PA MSA	50	29	659	19
Portland – Salem, OR – WA CMSA	147	16	0[4]	21
Sacramento – Yolo, CA CMSA	128	19	0[4]	21
San Diego, CA MSA	189	11	3,717	5
San Francisco – Oakland – San Jose, CA CMSA	441	4	6,023	2
Seattle – Tacoma – Bremerton, WA CMSA	249	7	2,540	10
St. Louis, MO – IL MSA	69	24	3,194	7
Tampa – St. Petersburg – Clearwater, FL MSA	144	17	1,896	13
Washington – Baltimore, DC – MD – VA – WV CMSA	476	3	0[1]	21
West Palm Beach – Boca Raton, FL MSA	64	25	376	20

Source: U.S. Department of Commerce, Bureau of the Census, Data User Services Division, *1992 Economic Census, Volume 1F, Reports Series, Release 1F,* September 1995, CD-ROM. *Notes:* 1. 5,000-9,999 employees. 2. 500-999 employees. 3. 2,500-4,999 employees. 4. 1,000-2,499 employees.

★2186★
Establishments and Employment
National Commercial Banks

The U.S. total number of employees is 852,039; total number of establishments is 31,360.

MSA	Establishments	Rank	Employment	Rank
New York – Northern New Jersey – Long Island, NY – NJ – CT-CMSA	2,258	1	78,217	1
Chicago – Gary – Kenosha, IL – IN – WI CMSA	481	11	34,538	2
Los Angeles – Riverside – Orange County, CA CMSA	1,335	2	34,231	3
Philadelphia – Wilmington – Atlantic City, PA – NJ – DE – MD CMSA	1,088	4	30,559	4
Dallas – Fort Worth, TX CMSA	466	12	20,670	5
Boston – Worcester – Lawrence, MA – NH – ME – CT CMSA	489	9	18,307	6
Cleveland – Akron, OH CMSA	620	6	17,550	7
Atlanta, GA MSA	524	8	16,482	8
Miami – Fort Lauderdale, FL CMSA	483	10	14,934	9
Houston – Galveston – Brazoria, TX CMSA	424	13	13,521	10

[Continued]

★2186★

National Commercial Banks
[Continued]

MSA	Establishments	Rank	Employment	Rank
Seattle – Tacoma – Bremerton, WA CMSA	401	14	11,642	11
Minneapolis – St. Paul, MN – WI MSA	260	22	11,619	12
Charlotte – Gastonia – Rock Hill, NC – SC MSA	213	27	10,065	13
Columbus, OH MSA	299	17	9,194	14
St. Louis, MO – IL MSA	202	28	8,968	15
Tampa – St. Petersburg – Clearwater, FL MSA	282	18	8,265	16
Denver – Boulder – Greeley, CO CMSA	218	25	7,844	17
Indianapolis, IN MSA	263	20	7,444	18
Nashville, TN MSA	215	26	6,919	19
Kansas City, MO – KS MSA	143	38	6,487	20
Greensboro – Winston-Salem – High Point, NC MSA	165	31	6,343	21
New Orleans, LA MSA	145	37	5,482	22
San Antonio, TX MSA	152	33	5,373	23
Orlando, FL MSA	226	24	5,241	24
Memphis, TN – AR – MS MSA	167	30	4,836	25

Source: U.S. Department of Commerce, Bureau of the Census, Data User Services Division, *1992 Economic Census, Volume 1F, Reports Series, Release 1F,* September 1995, CD-ROM. *Note:* Data are shown only for the top 25 areas.

★2187★
Establishments and Employment

Nondeposit Trust Facilities

The U.S. total number of employees is 19,497; total number of establishments is 410.

MSA	Establishments	Rank	Employment	Rank
Boston – Worcester – Lawrence, MA – NH – ME – CT CMSA	9	6	0[1]	2
Chicago – Gary – Kenosha, IL – IN – WI CMSA	28	2	0[2]	2
Dallas – Fort Worth, TX CMSA	5	8	0[3]	2
Los Angeles – Riverside – Orange County, CA CMSA	22	3	0[2]	2
Miami – Fort Lauderdale, FL CMSA	9	6	0[3]	2
New York – Northern New Jersey – Long Island, NY – NJ – CT-CMSA	51	1	0[4]	2
Philadelphia – Wilmington – Atlantic City, PA – NJ – DE – MD CMSA	10	5	0[2]	2
San Francisco – Oakland – San Jose, CA CMSA	19	4	547	1
Washington – Baltimore, DC – MD – VA – WV CMSA	8	7	0[1]	2

Source: U.S. Department of Commerce, Bureau of the Census, Data User Services Division, *1992 Economic Census, Volume 1F, Reports Series, Release 1F,* September 1995, CD-ROM. *Notes:* 1. 250-499 employees. 2. 1,000-2,499 employees. 3. 20-99 employees. 4. 5,000-9,999 employees.

★2188★
Establishments and Employment

Nondepository Credit Institutions

The U.S. total number of employees is 445,590; total number of establishments is 39,439.

MSA	Establishments	Rank	Employment	Rank
Los Angeles – Riverside – Orange County, CA CMSA	3,536	1	36,005	1
Washington – Baltimore, DC – MD – VA – WV CMSA	1,218	4	21,168	2
Dallas – Fort Worth, TX CMSA	816	7	15,787	3
San Francisco – Oakland – San Jose, CA CMSA	1,592	3	15,491	4
Philadelphia – Wilmington – Atlantic City, PA – NJ – DE – MD CMSA	802	8	13,517	5
Phoenix – Mesa, AZ MSA	441	16	11,824	6
Detroit – Ann Arbor – Flint, MI CMSA	459	15	11,822	7
Miami – Fort Lauderdale, FL CMSA	715	9	11,488	8
Atlanta, GA MSA	963	6	10,917	9
Minneapolis – St. Paul, MN – WI MSA	439	17	8,643	10
San Diego, CA MSA	604	12	8,262	11
Boston – Worcester – Lawrence, MA – NH – ME – CT CMSA	608	11	8,245	12
Denver – Boulder – Greeley, CO CMSA	552	13	8,208	13
Jacksonville, FL MSA	209	39	7,049	14
Columbus, OH MSA	270	29	6,270	15
St. Louis, MO – IL MSA	322	23	5,752	16
Seattle – Tacoma – Bremerton, WA CMSA	660	10	5,414	17
Kansas City, MO – KS MSA	319	24	5,404	18
Tampa – St. Petersburg – Clearwater, FL MSA	422	18	4,863	19
Greensboro – Winston-Salem – High Point, NC MSA	218	37	4,634	20
Indianapolis, IN MSA	275	27	4,374	21
Charlotte – Gastonia – Rock Hill, NC – SC MSA	326	22	4,358	22
Portland – Salem, OR – WA CMSA	409	19	4,202	23
Salt Lake City – Ogden, UT MSA	216	38	3,790	24
Sacramento – Yolo, CA CMSA	380	20	3,518	25

Source: U.S. Department of Commerce, Bureau of the Census, Data User Services Division, *1992 Economic Census, Volume 1F, Reports Series, Release 1F,* September 1995, CD-ROM. *Note:* Data are shown only for the top 25 areas.

★2189★

Establishments and Employment

Offices of Bank Holding Companies

The U.S. total number of employees is 26,741; total number of establishments is 2,256.

MSA	Estab-lish-ments	Rank	Emp-loy-ment	Rank
Boston – Worcester – Lawrence, MA – NH – ME – CT CMSA	42	6	0[1]	3
Chicago – Gary – Kenosha, IL – IN – WI CMSA	104	1	0[2]	3
Dallas – Fort Worth, TX CMSA	34	7	0[3]	3
Los Angeles – Riverside – Orange County, CA CMSA	56	4	0[1]	3
Miami – Fort Lauderdale, FL CMSA	19	9	95	2
New York – Northern New Jersey – Long Island, NY – NJ – CT-CMSA	86	2	0[1]	3
Philadelphia – Wilmington – Atlantic City, PA – NJ – DE – MD CMSA	68	3	0[2]	3
San Francisco – Oakland – San Jose, CA CMSA	26	8	253	1
Washington – Baltimore, DC – MD – VA – WV CMSA	51	5	0[1]	3

Source: U.S. Department of Commerce, Bureau of the Census, Data User Services Division, *1992 Economic Census, Volume 1F, Reports Series, Release 1F*, September 1995, CD-ROM. *Notes:* 1. 1,000-2,499 employees. 2. 500-999 employees. 3. 100-249 employees.

★2190★

Establishments and Employment

Operators of Apartment Buildings

The U.S. total number of employees is 228,270; total number of establishments is 48,330.

MSA	Estab-lish-ments	Rank	Emp-loy-ment	Rank
New York – Northern New Jersey – Long Island, NY – NJ – CT-CMSA	10,426	1	39,364	1
Los Angeles – Riverside – Orange County, CA CMSA	3,713	2	15,358	2
Washington – Baltimore, DC – MD – VA – WV CMSA	1,332	5	11,770	3
Chicago – Gary – Kenosha, IL – IN – WI CMSA	1,764	4	8,765	4
San Francisco – Oakland – San Jose, CA CMSA	2,044	3	8,641	5
Philadelphia – Wilmington – Atlantic City, PA – NJ – DE – MD CMSA	764	10	6,331	6
Dallas – Fort Worth, TX CMSA	892	8	5,820	7
Miami – Fort Lauderdale, FL CMSA	979	7	4,162	8
Detroit – Ann Arbor – Flint, MI CMSA	739	11	4,073	9
Seattle – Tacoma – Bremerton, WA CMSA	1,045	6	4,014	10

[Continued]

★2190★

Operators of Apartment Buildings

[Continued]

MSA	Estab-lish-ments	Rank	Emp-loy-ment	Rank
Houston – Galveston – Brazoria, TX CMSA	701	12	3,774	11
San Diego, CA MSA	799	9	3,739	12
Minneapolis – St. Paul, MN – WI MSA	658	14	3,696	13
Atlanta, GA MSA	520	17	3,495	14
Denver – Boulder – Greeley, CO CMSA	617	15	2,724	15
St. Louis, MO – IL MSA	309	23	2,499	16
Tampa – St. Petersburg – Clearwater, FL MSA	366	20	2,496	17
Cleveland – Akron, OH CMSA	477	18	2,412	18
Phoenix – Mesa, AZ MSA	398	19	2,273	19
Portland – Salem, OR – WA CMSA	527	16	2,087	20
Cincinnati – Hamilton, OH – KY – IN CMSA	310	22	1,858	21
Milwaukee – Racine, WI CMSA	312	21	1,830	22
Indianapolis, IN MSA	228	31	1,708	23
Norfolk – Virginia Beach – Newport News, VA – NC MSA	257	27	1,608	24
Las Vegas, NV – AZ MSA	243	28	1,600	25

Source: U.S. Department of Commerce, Bureau of the Census, Data User Services Division, *1992 Economic Census, Volume 1F, Reports Series, Release 1F*, September 1995, CD-ROM. *Note:* Data are shown only for the top 25 areas.

★2191★

Establishments and Employment

Operators of Nonresidential Buildings

The U.S. total number of employees is 168,138; total number of establishments is 32,905.

MSA	Estab-lish-ments	Rank	Emp-loy-ment	Rank
New York – Northern New Jersey – Long Island, NY – NJ – CT-CMSA	5,181	1	26,013	1
Los Angeles – Riverside – Orange County, CA CMSA	2,263	2	14,121	2
Chicago – Gary – Kenosha, IL – IN – WI CMSA	1,028	4	6,879	3
San Francisco – Oakland – San Jose, CA CMSA	1,170	3	6,828	4
Washington – Baltimore, DC – MD – VA – WV CMSA	1,016	5	6,133	5
Dallas – Fort Worth, TX CMSA	601	9	4,230	6
Cleveland – Akron, OH CMSA	348	15	3,823	7
Philadelphia – Wilmington – Atlantic City, PA – NJ – DE – MD CMSA	641	8	3,731	8
Miami – Fort Lauderdale, FL CMSA	828	6	3,529	9
Boston – Worcester – Lawrence, MA – NH – ME – CT CMSA	778	7	3,505	10

[Continued]

★2191★

Operators of Nonresidential Buildings
[Continued]

MSA	Estab-lish-ments	Rank	Emp-ploy-ment	Rank
San Diego, CA MSA	366	13	2,584	11
Seattle – Tacoma – Bremerton, WA CMSA	483	11	2,195	12
St. Louis, MO – IL MSA	333	16	2,016	13
Denver – Boulder – Greeley, CO CMSA	312	17	1,933	14
Detroit – Ann Arbor – Flint, MI CMSA	427	12	1,899	15
Houston – Galveston – Brazoria, TX CMSA	489	10	1,882	16
Sacramento – Yolo, CA CMSA	169	31	1,743	17
Honolulu, HI MSA	265	21	1,702	18
Minneapolis – St. Paul, MN – WI MSA	280	19	1,693	19
Atlanta, GA MSA	362	14	1,692	20
Pittsburgh, PA MSA	312	17	1,630	21
Milwaukee – Racine, WI CMSA	184	27	1,480	22
Tampa – St. Petersburg – Clearwater, FL MSA	293	18	1,385	23
Kansas City, MO – KS MSA	210	25	1,310	24
West Palm Beach – Boca Raton, FL MSA	234	23	1,298	25

Source: U.S. Department of Commerce, Bureau of the Census, Data User Services Division, *1992 Economic Census, Volume 1F, Reports Series, Release 1F,* September 1995, CD-ROM. *Note:* Data are shown only for the top 25 areas.

★2192★

Establishments and Employment

Operators of Residential Mobile Home Sites

The U.S. total number of employees is 29,270; total number of establishments is 9,572.

MSA	Estab-lish-ments	Rank	Emp-ploy-ment	Rank
Boston – Worcester – Lawrence, MA – NH – ME – CT CMSA	112	7	292	6
Chicago – Gary – Kenosha, IL – IN – WI CMSA	152	5	527	5
Dallas – Fort Worth, TX CMSA	109	8	257	7
Los Angeles – Riverside – Orange County, CA CMSA	804	1	2,826	1
Miami – Fort Lauderdale, FL CMSA	198	4	701	3
New York – Northern New Jersey – Long Island, NY – NJ – CT-CMSA	675	2	0[1]	9
Philadelphia – Wilmington – Atlantic City, PA – NJ – DE – MD CMSA	126	6	542	4

[Continued]

★2192★

Operators of Residential Mobile Home Sites
[Continued]

MSA	Estab-lish-ments	Rank	Emp-ploy-ment	Rank
San Francisco – Oakland – San Jose, CA CMSA	337	3	1,323	2
Washington – Baltimore, DC – MD – VA – WV CMSA	90	9	245	8

Source: U.S. Department of Commerce, Bureau of the Census, Data User Services Division, *1992 Economic Census, Volume 1F, Reports Series, Release 1F,* September 1995, CD-ROM. *Note:* 1. 1,000-2,499 employees.

★2193★

Establishments and Employment

Patent Owners and Lessors

The U.S. total number of employees is 17,409; total number of establishments is 1,514.

MSA	Estab-lish-ments	Rank	Emp-ploy-ment	Rank
Boston – Worcester – Lawrence, MA – NH – ME – CT CMSA	18	9	0[1]	5
Chicago – Gary – Kenosha, IL – IN – WI CMSA	60	4	0[1]	5
Dallas – Fort Worth, TX CMSA	31	7	0[1]	5
Los Angeles – Riverside – Orange County, CA CMSA	144	3	1,923	2
Miami – Fort Lauderdale, FL CMSA	27	8	443	4
New York – Northern New Jersey – Long Island, NY – NJ – CT-CMSA	193	1	4,355	1
Philadelphia – Wilmington – Atlantic City, PA – NJ – DE – MD CMSA	161	2	591	3
San Francisco – Oakland – San Jose, CA CMSA	41	6	0[1]	5
Washington – Baltimore, DC – MD – VA – WV CMSA	49	5	0[1]	5

Source: U.S. Department of Commerce, Bureau of the Census, Data User Services Division, *1992 Economic Census, Volume 1F, Reports Series, Release 1F,* September 1995, CD-ROM. *Note:* 1. 250-499 employees.

★2194★

Establishments and Employment

Pension, Health and Welfare Funds

The U.S. total number of employees is 20,374; total number of establishments is 1,491.

MSA	Establishments	Rank	Employment	Rank
Boston – Worcester – Lawrence, MA – NH – ME – CT CMSA	42	6	0[1]	1
Chicago – Gary – Kenosha, IL – IN – WI CMSA	60	4	0[1]	1
Dallas – Fort Worth, TX CMSA	31	7	0[2]	1
Los Angeles – Riverside – Orange County, CA CMSA	105	2	0[3]	1
Miami – Fort Lauderdale, FL CMSA	21	8	0[4]	1
New York – Northern New Jersey – Long Island, NY – NJ – CT-CMSA	115	1	0[1]	1
Philadelphia – Wilmington – Atlantic City, PA – NJ – DE – MD CMSA	51	5	0[2]	1
San Francisco – Oakland – San Jose, CA CMSA	70	3	0[3]	1
Washington – Baltimore, DC – MD – VA – WV CMSA	51	5	0[1]	1

Source: U.S. Department of Commerce, Bureau of the Census, Data User Services Division, *1992 Economic Census, Volume 1F, Reports Series, Release 1F,* September 1995, CD-ROM. *Notes:* 1. 500-999 employees. 2. 250-499 employees. 3. 1,000-2,499 employees. 4. 100-249 employees.

★2195★

Establishments and Employment

Personal Credit Institutions

The U.S. total number of employees is 158,790; total number of establishments is 16,900.

MSA	Establishments	Rank	Employment	Rank
Los Angeles – Riverside – Orange County, CA CMSA	883	1	10,099	1
Phoenix – Mesa, AZ MSA	124	23	8,464	2
Miami – Fort Lauderdale, FL CMSA	164	13	5,637	3
Dallas – Fort Worth, TX CMSA	260	8	4,341	4
Columbus, OH MSA	136	21	4,196	5
Philadelphia – Wilmington – Atlantic City, PA – NJ – DE – MD CMSA	285	7	3,686	6
Greensboro – Winston-Salem – High Point, NC MSA	111	28	3,582	7
San Diego, CA MSA	158	14	3,197	8
Atlanta, GA MSA	386	4	3,059	9
Denver – Boulder – Greeley, CO CMSA	168	12	2,978	10
San Francisco – Oakland – San Jose, CA CMSA	348	6	2,723	11
Minneapolis – St. Paul, MN – WI MSA	164	13	2,375	12

[Continued]

★2195★

Personal Credit Institutions

[Continued]

MSA	Establishments	Rank	Employment	Rank
Salt Lake City – Ogden, UT MSA	89	33	2,195	13
Indianapolis, IN MSA	124	23	2,052	14
Jacksonville, FL MSA	83	36	2,039	15
Charlotte – Gastonia – Rock Hill, NC – SC MSA	150	16	1,536	16
Tampa – St. Petersburg – Clearwater, FL MSA	139	19	1,291	17
Cleveland – Akron, OH CMSA	169	11	1,193	18
Memphis, TN – AR – MS MSA	106	31	1,105	19
Seattle – Tacoma – Bremerton, WA CMSA	175	10	1,080	20
Pittsburgh, PA MSA	168	12	1,069	21
St. Louis, MO – IL MSA	158	14	1,041	22
Kansas City, MO – KS MSA	141	18	1,026	23
Nashville, TN MSA	125	22	995	24
Cincinnati – Hamilton, OH – KY – IN CMSA	117	25	951	25

Source: U.S. Department of Commerce, Bureau of the Census, Data User Services Division, *1992 Economic Census, Volume 1F, Reports Series, Release 1F,* September 1995, CD-ROM. *Note:* Data are shown only for the top 25 areas.

★2196★

Establishments and Employment

Real Estate

The U.S. total number of employees is 1,231,471; total number of establishments is 229,493.

MSA	Establishments	Rank	Employment	Rank
New York – Northern New Jersey – Long Island, NY – NJ – CT-CMSA	31,134	1	153,350	1
Los Angeles – Riverside – Orange County, CA CMSA	15,502	2	88,557	2
Washington – Baltimore, DC – MD – VA – WV CMSA	7,239	5	57,250	3
Chicago – Gary – Kenosha, IL – IN – WI CMSA	8,137	4	53,646	4
San Francisco – Oakland – San Jose, CA CMSA	8,256	3	45,556	5
Dallas – Fort Worth, TX CMSA	4,176	9	35,053	6
Miami – Fort Lauderdale, FL CMSA	5,352	6	29,896	7
Philadelphia – Wilmington – Atlantic City, PA – NJ – DE – MD CMSA	4,326	7	28,698	8
Boston – Worcester – Lawrence, MA – NH – ME – CT CMSA	4,322	8	27,540	9
Houston – Galveston – Brazoria, TX CMSA	3,620	11	25,770	10
Detroit – Ann Arbor – Flint, MI CMSA	3,387	12	20,887	11
Atlanta, GA MSA	2,950	14	20,776	12

[Continued]

★2196★

Real Estate
[Continued]

MSA	Estab-lish-ments	Rank	Emp-loy-ment	Rank
Seattle – Tacoma – Bremerton, WA CMSA	4,063	10	19,677	13
San Diego, CA MSA	3,331	13	18,510	14
Cleveland – Akron, OH CMSA	2,075	19	17,159	15
Denver – Boulder – Greeley, CO CMSA	2,855	15	16,147	16
Minneapolis – St. Paul, MN – WI MSA	2,552	16	16,109	17
Phoenix – Mesa, AZ MSA	2,452	18	14,950	18
Tampa – St. Petersburg – Clearwater, FL MSA	2,483	17	13,978	19
St. Louis, MO – IL MSA	1,993	20	12,043	20
West Palm Beach – Boca Raton, FL MSA	1,828	22	11,380	21
Portland – Salem, OR – WA CMSA	1,983	21	10,569	22
Orlando, FL MSA	1,584	26	10,559	23
Honolulu, HI MSA	1,796	23	10,380	24
Sacramento – Yolo, CA CMSA	1,622	24	9,669	25

Source: U.S. Department of Commerce, Bureau of the Census, Data User Services Division, *1992 Economic Census, Volume 1F, Reports Series, Release 1F,* September 1995, CD-ROM. *Note:* Data are shown only for the top 25 areas.

★2197★

Establishments and Employment

Real Estate Agents and Managers

The U.S. total number of employees is 646,561; total number of establishments is 106,552.

MSA	Estab-lish-ments	Rank	Emp-loy-ment	Rank
New York – Northern New Jersey – Long Island, NY – NJ – CT-CMSA	12,333	1	74,130	1
Los Angeles – Riverside – Orange County, CA CMSA	7,204	2	45,714	2
Chicago – Gary – Kenosha, IL – IN – WI CMSA	4,420	3	32,924	3
Washington – Baltimore, DC – MD – VA – WV CMSA	3,775	5	32,675	4
San Francisco – Oakland – San Jose, CA CMSA	3,935	4	24,813	5
Dallas – Fort Worth, TX CMSA	2,047	9	21,199	6
Miami – Fort Lauderdale, FL CMSA	2,832	6	18,131	7
Houston – Galveston – Brazoria, TX CMSA	1,908	11	16,933	8
Philadelphia – Wilmington – Atlantic City, PA – NJ – DE – MD CMSA	2,148	8	14,894	9
Atlanta, GA MSA	1,545	15	12,638	10
Detroit – Ann Arbor – Flint, MI CMSA	1,656	12	11,922	11
Seattle – Tacoma – Bremerton, WA CMSA	1,923	10	10,897	12

[Continued]

★2197★

Real Estate Agents and Managers
[Continued]

MSA	Estab-lish-ments	Rank	Emp-loy-ment	Rank
Phoenix – Mesa, AZ MSA	1,346	16	9,547	13
San Diego, CA MSA	1,635	13	9,495	14
Denver – Boulder – Greeley, CO CMSA	1,588	14	9,428	15
Cleveland – Akron, OH CMSA	891	22	8,499	16
Minneapolis – St. Paul, MN – WI MSA	1,171	19	8,295	17
West Palm Beach – Boca Raton, FL MSA	1,206	18	7,763	18
Tampa – St. Petersburg – Clearwater, FL MSA	1,277	17	7,000	19
Orlando, FL MSA	859	23	6,538	20
Honolulu, HI MSA	1,128	20	6,396	21
Portland – Salem, OR – WA CMSA	832	24	6,053	22
St. Louis, MO – IL MSA	929	21	5,810	23
Indianapolis, IN MSA	524	32	5,148	24
Kansas City, MO – KS MSA	589	28	4,920	25

Source: U.S. Department of Commerce, Bureau of the Census, Data User Services Division, *1992 Economic Census, Volume 1F, Reports Series, Release 1F,* September 1995, CD-ROM. *Note:* Data are shown only for the top 25 areas.

★2198★

Establishments and Employment

Real Estate Investment Trusts

The U.S. total number of employees is 4,771; total number of establishments is 655.

MSA	Estab-lish-ments	Rank	Emp-loy-ment	Rank
Boston – Worcester – Lawrence, MA – NH – ME – CT CMSA	46	3	0[1]	5
Chicago – Gary – Kenosha, IL – IN – WI CMSA	26	5	719	1
Dallas – Fort Worth, TX CMSA	17	8	0[2]	5
Los Angeles – Riverside – Orange County, CA CMSA	68	1	524	2
Miami – Fort Lauderdale, FL CMSA	20	7	0[3]	5
New York – Northern New Jersey – Long Island, NY – NJ – CT-CMSA	65	2	473	3
Philadelphia – Wilmington – Atlantic City, PA – NJ – DE – MD CMSA	22	6	0[2]	5
San Francisco – Oakland – San Jose, CA CMSA	30	4	93	4

Source: U.S. Department of Commerce, Bureau of the Census, Data User Services Division, *1992 Economic Census, Volume 1F, Reports Series, Release 1F,* September 1995, CD-ROM. *Notes:* 1. 250-499 employees. 2. 100-249 employees. 3. 20-99 employees.

★2199★

Establishments and Employment

Real Estate Operators (except Developers) and Lessors

The U.S. total number of employees is 462,564; total number of establishments is 102,887.

MSA	Estab-lish-ments	Rank	Emp-loy-ment	Rank
New York – Northern New Jersey – Long Island, NY – NJ – CT-CMSA	17,570	1	70,889	1
Los Angeles – Riverside – Orange County, CA CMSA	7,464	2	34,121	2
Washington – Baltimore, DC – MD – VA – WV CMSA	2,745	5	19,624	3
San Francisco – Oakland – San Jose, CA CMSA	3,907	3	17,772	4
Chicago – Gary – Kenosha, IL – IN – WI CMSA	3,186	4	17,037	5
Philadelphia – Wilmington – Atlantic City, PA – NJ – DE – MD CMSA	1,731	9	11,308	6
Dallas – Fort Worth, TX CMSA	1,816	8	10,945	7
Miami – Fort Lauderdale, FL CMSA	2,218	6	9,194	8
Boston – Worcester – Lawrence, MA – NH – ME – CT CMSA	1,713	10	8,327	9
San Diego, CA MSA	1,502	12	7,500	10
Seattle – Tacoma – Bremerton, WA CMSA	1,886	7	7,339	11
Detroit – Ann Arbor – Flint, MI CMSA	1,515	11	7,256	12
Cleveland – Akron, OH CMSA	987	19	6,656	13
Houston – Galveston – Brazoria, TX CMSA	1,461	13	6,650	14
Minneapolis – St. Paul, MN – WI MSA	1,144	14	6,077	15
Atlanta, GA MSA	1,108	16	5,915	16
Denver – Boulder – Greeley, CO CMSA	1,141	15	5,811	17
St. Louis, MO – IL MSA	887	21	5,205	18
Tampa – St. Petersburg – Clearwater, FL MSA	1,020	18	5,168	19
Phoenix – Mesa, AZ MSA	972	20	4,478	20
Portland – Salem, OR – WA CMSA	1,034	17	3,989	21
Sacramento – Yolo, CA CMSA	659	23	3,752	22
Milwaukee – Racine, WI CMSA	602	26	3,725	23
Pittsburgh, PA MSA	751	22	3,592	24
Cincinnati – Hamilton, OH – KY – IN CMSA	637	24	3,375	25

Source: U.S. Department of Commerce, Bureau of the Census, Data User Services Division, *1992 Economic Census, Volume 1F, Reports Series, Release 1F*, September 1995, CD-ROM. *Note:* Data are shown only for the top 25 areas.

★2200★

Establishments and Employment

Savings Institutions

The U.S. total number of employees is 341,920; total number of establishments is 20,544.

MSA	Estab-lish-ments	Rank	Emp-loy-ment	Rank
New York – Northern New Jersey – Long Island, NY – NJ – CT-CMSA	2,204	1	47,808	1
Los Angeles – Riverside – Orange County, CA CMSA	1,387	2	32,678	2
San Francisco – Oakland – San Jose, CA CMSA	813	4	13,500	3
Miami – Fort Lauderdale, FL CMSA	411	8	7,712	4
Hartford, CT MSA	287	12	6,714	5
Cleveland – Akron, OH CMSA	388	9	6,120	6
Seattle – Tacoma – Bremerton, WA CMSA	295	11	5,401	7
San Diego, CA MSA	251	13	4,983	8
Dallas – Fort Worth, TX CMSA	154	23	3,909	9
Atlanta, GA MSA	186	18	3,336	10
Pittsburgh, PA MSA	248	14	3,201	11
West Palm Beach – Boca Raton, FL MSA	214	16	2,868	12
Milwaukee – Racine, WI CMSA	178	19	2,816	13
Rochester, NY MSA	81	32	2,798	14
Tampa – St. Petersburg – Clearwater, FL MSA	203	17	2,746	15
Cincinnati – Hamilton, OH – KY – IN CMSA	234	15	2,481	16
St. Louis, MO – IL MSA	177	20	2,414	17
Providence – Fall River – Warwick, RI – MA MSA	103	27	2,275	18
Springfield, MA MSA	120	24	2,208	19
Albany – Schenectady – Troy, NY MSA	79	34	2,074	20
Honolulu, HI MSA	110	26	2,042	21
Portland – Salem, OR – WA CMSA	171	21	2,002	22
Greenville – Spartanburg – Anderson, SC MSA	80	33	1,882	23
Richmond – Petersburg, VA MSA	81	32	1,750	24
Orlando, FL MSA	101	28	1,427	25

Source: U.S. Department of Commerce, Bureau of the Census, Data User Services Division, *1992 Economic Census, Volume 1F, Reports Series, Release 1F*, September 1995, CD-ROM. *Note:* Data are shown only for the top 25 areas.

★ 2201 ★

Establishments and Employment

Security and Commodity Brokers, Dealers, and Flotation Companies

The U.S. total number of employees is 312,846; total number of establishments is 19,237.

MSA	Establishments	Rank	Employment	Rank
Chicago – Gary – Kenosha, IL – IN – WI CMSA	1,450	2	24,583	1
Los Angeles – Riverside – Orange County, CA CMSA	855	3	13,283	2
San Francisco – Oakland – San Jose, CA CMSA	560	4	11,464	3
Minneapolis – St. Paul, MN – WI MSA	237	14	5,768	4
Dallas – Fort Worth, TX CMSA	414	5	4,801	5
Houston – Galveston – Brazoria, TX CMSA	279	10	4,623	6
St. Louis, MO – IL MSA	210	16	4,424	7
Miami – Fort Lauderdale, FL CMSA	274	11	4,067	8
Atlanta, GA MSA	293	9	3,630	9
Seattle – Tacoma – Bremerton, WA CMSA	256	13	3,319	10
Detroit – Ann Arbor – Flint, MI CMSA	212	15	3,194	11
West Palm Beach – Boca Raton, FL MSA	167	20	2,537	12
San Diego, CA MSA	206	17	2,327	13
Tampa – St. Petersburg – Clearwater, FL MSA	180	18	2,197	14
Cleveland – Akron, OH CMSA	140	23	2,173	15
Milwaukee – Racine, WI CMSA	135	24	2,086	16
Phoenix – Mesa, AZ MSA	168	19	2,041	17
Memphis, TN – AR – MS MSA	86	30	1,595	18
Pittsburgh, PA MSA	115	25	1,580	19
Portland – Salem, OR – WA CMSA	144	22	1,527	20
Columbus, OH MSA	89	29	1,512	21
Kansas City, MO – KS MSA	145	21	1,510	22
Hartford, CT MSA	64	40	1,462	23
Richmond – Petersburg, VA MSA	58	43	1,459	24
Indianapolis, IN MSA	90	28	1,356	25

Source: U.S. Department of Commerce, Bureau of the Census, Data User Services Division, *1992 Economic Census, Volume 1F, Reports Series, Release 1F*, September 1995, CD-ROM. *Note:* Data are shown only for the top 25 areas.

★ 2202 ★

Establishments and Employment

Security and Commodity Brokers, Dealers, Exchanges, and Services

The U.S. total number of employees is 406,444; total number of establishments is 31,177.

MSA	Establishments	Rank	Employment	Rank
Chicago – Gary – Kenosha, IL – IN – WI CMSA	2,009	2	31,483	1
Los Angeles – Riverside – Orange County, CA CMSA	1,602	3	18,086	2
San Francisco – Oakland – San Jose, CA CMSA	1,193	4	16,811	3
Philadelphia – Wilmington – Atlantic City, PA – NJ – DE – MD CMSA	754	7	8,911	4
Dallas – Fort Worth, TX CMSA	695	8	7,479	5
Denver – Boulder – Greeley, CO CMSA	517	9	7,389	6
Minneapolis – St. Paul, MN – WI MSA	490	11	7,237	7
St. Louis, MO – IL MSA	364	16	5,095	8
Atlanta, GA MSA	506	10	4,759	9
Miami – Fort Lauderdale, FL CMSA	469	12	4,722	10
Kansas City, MO – KS MSA	233	21	4,537	11
Seattle – Tacoma – Bremerton, WA CMSA	450	13	4,186	12
Detroit – Ann Arbor – Flint, MI CMSA	420	14	3,918	13
Milwaukee – Racine, WI CMSA	228	23	3,129	14
San Diego, CA MSA	367	15	2,921	15
West Palm Beach – Boca Raton, FL MSA	271	20	2,907	16
Cleveland – Akron, OH CMSA	299	19	2,750	17
Tampa – St. Petersburg – Clearwater, FL MSA	300	18	2,646	18
Phoenix – Mesa, AZ MSA	314	17	2,427	19
Hartford, CT MSA	129	33	2,261	20
Pittsburgh, PA MSA	218	24	2,229	21
Portland – Salem, OR – WA CMSA	229	22	1,858	22
Columbus, OH MSA	159	25	1,853	23
Richmond – Petersburg, VA MSA	119	36	1,817	24
Memphis, TN – AR – MS MSA	124	35	1,774	25

Source: U.S. Department of Commerce, Bureau of the Census, Data User Services Division, *1992 Economic Census, Volume 1F, Reports Series, Release 1F*, September 1995, CD-ROM. *Note:* Data are shown only for the top 25 areas.

★ 2203 ★

Establishments and Employment

Security and Commodity Exchanges

The U.S. total number of employees is 6,739; total number of establishments is 35.

MSA	Estab- lish- ments	Rank	Emp- loy- ment	Rank
Boston – Worcester – Lawrence, MA – NH – ME – CT CMSA	1	5	0[1]	3
Chicago – Gary – Kenosha, IL – IN – WI CMSA	4	3	2,524	2
Dallas – Fort Worth, TX CMSA	0	6	0	3
Los Angeles – Riverside – Orange County, CA CMSA	1	5	0[1]	3
Miami – Fort Lauderdale, FL CMSA	0	6	0	3
New York – Northern New Jersey – Long Island, NY – NJ – CT-CMSA	13	1	3,436	1
Philadelphia – Wilmington – Atlantic City, PA – NJ – DE – MD CMSA	1	5	0[2]	3
San Francisco – Oakland – San Jose, CA CMSA	5	2	0[3]	3
Washington – Baltimore, DC – MD – VA – WV CMSA	3	4	0[4]	3

Source: U.S. Department of Commerce, Bureau of the Census, Data User Services Division, *1992 Economic Census, Volume 1F, Reports Series, Release 1F,* September 1995, CD-ROM. *Notes:* 1. 20-99 employees. 2. 100-249 employees. 3. 250-499 employees. 4. 0-19 employees.

★ 2204 ★

Establishments and Employment

Services Allied With the Exchange of Securities Or Commodities

The U.S. total number of employees is 86,859; total number of establishments is 11,905.

MSA	Estab- lish- ments	Rank	Emp- loy- ment	Rank
Boston – Worcester – Lawrence, MA – NH – ME – CT CMSA	496	5	0[1]	5
Chicago – Gary – Kenosha, IL – IN – WI CMSA	555	4	4,376	2
Dallas – Fort Worth, TX CMSA	281	8	2,678	3
Los Angeles – Riverside – Orange County, CA CMSA	746	2	0[2]	5
Miami – Fort Lauderdale, FL CMSA	195	9	655	4
New York – Northern New Jersey – Long Island, NY – NJ – CT-CMSA	1,847	1	23,775	1
Philadelphia – Wilmington – Atlantic City, PA – NJ – DE – MD CMSA	364	7	0[2]	5

[Continued]

★ 2204 ★

Services Allied With the Exchange of Securities Or Commodities

[Continued]

MSA -	Estab- lish- ments	Rank	Emp- loy- ment	Rank
San Francisco – Oakland – San Jose, CA CMSA	628	3	0[1]	5
Washington – Baltimore, DC – MD – VA – WV CMSA	433	6	0[2]	5

Source: U.S. Department of Commerce, Bureau of the Census, Data User Services Division, *1992 Economic Census, Volume 1F, Reports Series, Release 1F,* September 1995, CD-ROM. *Notes:* 1. 5,000-9,999 employees. 2. 2,500-4,999 employees.

★ 2205 ★

Establishments and Employment

Short-term Business Credit Institutions, Except Agricultural

The U.S. total number of employees is 54,847; total number of establishments is 2,370.

MSA	Estab- lish- ments	Rank	Emp- loy- ment	Rank
Boston – Worcester – Lawrence, MA – NH – ME – CT CMSA	52	9	0[1]	5
Chicago – Gary – Kenosha, IL – IN – WI CMSA	135	3	0[2]	5
Dallas – Fort Worth, TX CMSA	117	4	3,657	1
Los Angeles – Riverside – Orange County, CA CMSA	211	2	3,649	2
Miami – Fort Lauderdale, FL CMSA	67	8	0[3]	5
New York – Northern New Jersey – Long Island, NY – NJ – CT-CMSA	289	1	0[4]	5
Philadelphia – Wilmington – Atlantic City, PA – NJ – DE – MD CMSA	80	6	1,419	4
San Francisco – Oakland – San Jose, CA CMSA	73	7	1,665	3
Washington – Baltimore, DC – MD – VA – WV CMSA	98	5	0[3]	5

Source: U.S. Department of Commerce, Bureau of the Census, Data User Services Division, *1992 Economic Census, Volume 1F, Reports Series, Release 1F,* September 1995, CD-ROM. *Notes:* 1. 500-999 employees. 2. 5,000-9,999 employees. 3. 1,000-2,499 employees. 4. 10,000-24,999 employees.

★2206★

Establishments and Employment

State Commercial Banks

The U.S. total number of employees is 654,016; total number of establishments is 31,401.

MSA	Establish-ments	Rank	Emp-loy-ment	Rank
New York – Northern New Jersey – Long Island, NY – NJ – CT-CMSA	2,001	1	86,578	1
Chicago – Gary – Kenosha, IL – IN – WI CMSA	550	5	29,131	2
Los Angeles – Riverside – Orange County, CA CMSA	975	3	26,013	3
Boston – Worcester – Lawrence, MA – NH – ME – CT CMSA	474	8	20,991	4
Philadelphia – Wilmington – Atlantic City, PA – NJ – DE – MD CMSA	542	6	18,800	5
Atlanta, GA MSA	297	9	8,197	6
St. Louis, MO – IL MSA	293	10	6,313	7
Houston – Galveston – Brazoria, TX CMSA	175	22	6,179	8
Dallas – Fort Worth, TX CMSA	214	15	5,860	9
Kansas City, MO – KS MSA	221	14	5,411	10
Seattle – Tacoma – Bremerton, WA CMSA	287	12	4,691	11
Tampa – St. Petersburg – Clearwater, FL MSA	258	13	4,682	12
Minneapolis – St. Paul, MN – WI MSA	201	19	4,349	13
Grand Rapids – Muskegon – Holland, MI MSA	202	18	3,978	14
Albany – Schenectady – Troy, NY MSA	173	23	3,761	15
Miami – Fort Lauderdale, FL CMSA	172	24	3,752	16
Raleigh – Durham – Chapel Hill, NC MSA	202	18	3,489	17
Oklahoma City, OK MSA	90	41	3,184	18
Charlotte – Gastonia – Rock Hill, NC – SC MSA	181	21	2,548	19
Denver – Boulder – Greeley, CO CMSA	89	42	2,540	20
Rochester, NY MSA	129	33	2,454	21
Harrisburg – Lebanon – Carlisle, PA MSA	116	35	2,384	22
Allentown – Bethlehem – Easton, PA MSA	139	31	2,292	23
Salt Lake City – Ogden, UT MSA	126	34	2,224	24
Indianapolis, IN MSA	140	30	2,150	25

Source: U.S. Department of Commerce, Bureau of the Census, Data User Services Division, *1992 Economic Census, Volume 1F, Reports Series, Release 1F*, September 1995, CD-ROM. *Note:* Data are shown only for the top 25 areas.

★2207★

Establishments and Employment

Surety Insurance

The U.S. total number of employees is 11,167; total number of establishments is 548.

MSA	Establish-ments	Rank	Emp-loy-ment	Rank
Atlanta, GA MSA	16	8	0^1	8
Boston – Worcester – Lawrence, MA – NH – ME – CT CMSA	18	7	0^1	8
Chicago – Gary – Kenosha, IL – IN – WI CMSA	22	5	0^2	8
Cincinnati – Hamilton, OH – KY – IN CMSA	4	19	0^3	8
Cleveland – Akron, OH CMSA	5	18	21	7
Columbus, OH MSA	7	16	41	6
Dallas – Fort Worth, TX CMSA	16	8	0^2	8
Denver – Boulder – Greeley, CO CMSA	12	11	65	5
Detroit – Ann Arbor – Flint, MI CMSA	15	9	0^4	8
Houston – Galveston – Brazoria, TX CMSA	12	11	147	1
Indianapolis, IN MSA	6	17	0^4	8
Kansas City, MO – KS MSA	9	14	100	4
Los Angeles – Riverside – Orange County, CA CMSA	53	1	0^5	8
Miami – Fort Lauderdale, FL CMSA	14	10	0^2	8
Milwaukee – Racine, WI CMSA	8	15	0^6	8
Minneapolis – St. Paul, MN – WI MSA	10	13	0^4	8
New York – Northern New Jersey – Long Island, NY – NJ – CT-CMSA	38	2	0^5	8
Norfolk – Virginia Beach – Newport News, VA – NC MSA	0	21	0	8
Orlando, FL MSA	4	19	0^3	8
Philadelphia – Wilmington – Atlantic City, PA – NJ – DE – MD CMSA	20	6	0^1	8
Phoenix – Mesa, AZ MSA	12	11	0^4	8
Pittsburgh, PA MSA	9	14	0^4	8
Portland – Salem, OR – WA CMSA	4	19	21	7
Sacramento – Yolo, CA CMSA	6	17	0^4	8
San Diego, CA MSA	10	13	114	2
San Francisco – Oakland – San Jose, CA CMSA	28	3	0^6	8
Seattle – Tacoma – Bremerton, WA CMSA	9	14	113	3
St. Louis, MO – IL MSA	6	17	0^4	8
Tampa – St. Petersburg – Clearwater, FL MSA	11	12	0^4	8
Washington – Baltimore, DC – MD – VA – WV CMSA	26	4	0^5	8
West Palm Beach – Boca Raton, FL MSA	3	20	0^3	8

Source: U.S. Department of Commerce, Bureau of the Census, Data User Services Division, *1992 Economic Census, Volume 1F, Reports Series, Release 1F*, September 1995, CD-ROM. *Notes:* 1. 100-249 employees. 2. 250-499 employees. 3. 0-19 employees. 4. 20-99 employees. 5. 1,000-2,499 employees. 6. 500-999 employees.

★2208★

Establishments and Employment

Title Abstract Offices

The U.S. total number of employees is 33,742; total number of establishments is 4,716.

MSA	Estab-lish-ments	Rank	Emp-ploy-ment	Rank
New York – Northern New Jersey – Long Island, NY – NJ – CT-CMSA	374	1	2,168	1
Minneapolis – St. Paul, MN – WI MSA	91	5	1,143	2
Chicago – Gary – Kenosha, IL – IN – WI CMSA	99	4	1,020	3
Cleveland – Akron, OH CMSA	88	6	825	4
Dallas – Fort Worth, TX CMSA	71	8	567	5
Miami – Fort Lauderdale, FL CMSA	53	12	566	6
Oklahoma City, OK MSA	40	14	518	7
St. Louis, MO – IL MSA	38	15	425	8
Kansas City, MO – KS MSA	37	16	390	9
Indianapolis, IN MSA	28	18	296	10
Tulsa, OK MSA	20	23	281	11
Columbus, OH MSA	31	17	269	12
Milwaukee – Racine, WI CMSA	18	25	268	13
Tampa – St. Petersburg – Clearwater, FL MSA	59	10	261	14
Rochester, NY MSA	19	24	244	15
Orlando, FL MSA	37	16	239	16
San Antonio, TX MSA	19	24	230	17
San Diego, CA MSA	15	28	209	18
Salt Lake City – Ogden, UT MSA	22	21	205	19
New Orleans, LA MSA	20	23	194	20
Atlanta, GA MSA	28	18	184	21
Madison, WI MSA	7	36	180	22
Austin – San Marcos, TX MSA	15	28	158	23
Boise City, ID MSA	10	33	157	24
Albany – Schenectady – Troy, NY MSA	17	26	142	25

Source: U.S. Department of Commerce, Bureau of the Census, Data User Services Division, *1992 Economic Census, Volume 1F, Reports Series, Release 1F*, September 1995, CD-ROM. *Note:* Data are shown only for the top 25 areas.

★2209★

Establishments and Employment

Title Insurance

The U.S. total number of employees is 34,473; total number of establishments is 1,532.

MSA	Estab-lish-ments	Rank	Emp-ploy-ment	Rank
San Diego, CA MSA	10	22	939	1
Denver – Boulder – Greeley, CO CMSA	28	12	513	2
Tampa – St. Petersburg – Clearwater, FL MSA	37	9	378	3
Fresno, CA MSA	16	18	367	4
Las Vegas, NV – AZ MSA	13	21	308	5
St. Louis, MO – IL MSA	20	16	299	6

[Continued]

★2209★

Title Insurance
[Continued]

MSA	Estab-lish-ments	Rank	Emp-ploy-ment	Rank
Bakersfield, CA MSA	5	27	272	7
Salinas, CA MSA	13	21	238	8
Kansas City, MO – KS MSA	18	17	226	9
Indianapolis, IN MSA	9	23	166	10
Santa Barbara – Santa Maria – Lompoc, CA MSA	9	23	144	11
San Antonio, TX MSA	5	27	134	12
Albuquerque, NM MSA	6	26	130	13
Austin – San Marcos, TX MSA	6	26	114	14
Colorado Springs, CO MSA	7	25	114	14
Memphis, TN – AR – MS MSA	4	28	109	15
Lansing – East Lansing, MI MSA	5	27	108	16
Norfolk – Virginia Beach – Newport News, VA – NC MSA	6	26	85	17
Columbus, OH MSA	10	22	81	18
Melbourne – Titusville – Palm Bay, FL MSA	6	26	64	19
Fort Pierce – Port St. Lucie, FL MSA	8	24	62	20
Fort Myers – Cape Coral, FL MSA	4	28	48	21
Dayton – Springfield, OH MSA	4	28	44	22
Albany – Schenectady – Troy, NY MSA	5	27	43	23
Daytona Beach, FL MSA	4	28	39	24

Source: U.S. Department of Commerce, Bureau of the Census, Data User Services Division, *1992 Economic Census, Volume 1F, Reports Series, Release 1F*, September 1995, CD-ROM. *Note:* Data are shown only for the top 25 areas.

Chapter 20

WOMEN-OWNED BUSINESSES

Topics Covered

★2210★

Establishments and Employment

Women-Owned Businesses, 1992: Leading Metropolitan Areas

City	Total	Rank
Washington, DC	122,007	4
Philadelphia, PA	95,441	5
Los Angeles, CA	232,723	1
New York, NY	187,525	2
Chicago, IL	163,883	3

Source: "Women In Business," *Washington, Post,* 6 March 1992, p. D2. Primary source: U.S. Bureau of the Census.

★2211★

Establishments and Employment

Women-Owned Businesses, 1992: Sales

Data refer to sales in metropolitan areas with the most women-owned businesses.

[In billions of dollars]

City	Sales	Rank
Washington, DC	10.7	5
Philadelphia, PA	15.8	4
Los Angeles, CA	28.7	2
New York, NY	36.5	1
Chicago, IL	26.0	3

Source: "Women In Business," *Washington, Post,* 6 March 1992, p. D2. Primary source: U.S. Bureau of the Census.

Chapter 21

MANUFACTURING

Topic Covered

Market Shares

★2212★

Market Shares

Change in Manufacturing Market Share Sector Between 1994 and 1995

[In percentages]

City	Percent	Rank
Dallas, TX	14.36	7
Fort Wayne, IN	28.28	3
Fort Worth-Arlington, TX	16.07	6
Grand Rapids-Muskegon, MI	29.10	1
Greensboro-Winston-Salem, NC	27.91	4
Greenville-Spartanburg, SC	27.66	5
San Jose, CA	28.52	2

Source: Carroll, Rick, "Survey Ranks Dallas Area In the Middle In Blue-Collar Jobs," *Dallas Business Journal,* 23-29 February, 1996, p. 9.

★2213★

Market Shares

Manufacturing Market Share, 1995

City	October 1995	Rank
Dallas, TX	230,400	1
Fort Wayne, IN	74,700	7
Fort Worth-Arlington, TX	105,700	6
Grand Rapids-Muskegon, MI	149,700	4
Greensboro-Winston-Salem, NC	169,300	3
Greenville-Spartanburg, SC	123,300	5
San Jose, CA	228,400	2

Source: Carroll, Rick, "Survey Ranks Dallas Area In the Middle In Blue-Collar Jobs," *Dallas Business Journal,* 23-29 February, 1996, p. 9.

Chapter 22

SERVICE INDUSTRY

Topics Covered

Establishments and Employment
Tax-Exempt Establishments and Employment
Hotels and Motels
Restaurants

★2214★

Establishments and Employment

Accounting, Auditing, and Bookkeeping Services

The U.S. total number of employees is 520,603; total number of establishments is 79,097.

MSA	Estab-lish-ments	Rank	Emp-loy-ment	Rank
New York – Northern New Jersey – Long Island, NY – NJ – CT-CMSA	6,689	1	64,765	1
Los Angeles – Riverside – Orange County, CA CMSA	5,442	2	45,022	2
Chicago – Gary – Kenosha, IL – IN – WI CMSA	2,700	3	23,503	3
San Francisco – Oakland – San Jose, CA CMSA	2,575	4	16,808	4
Boston – Worcester – Lawrence, MA – NH – ME – CT CMSA	1,689	7	13,982	5
Dallas – Fort Worth, TX CMSA	1,663	8	11,082	6
Detroit – Ann Arbor – Flint, MI CMSA	1,489	10	10,121	7
Houston – Galveston – Brazoria, TX CMSA	1,438	11	10,058	8
Phoenix – Mesa, AZ MSA	956	15	9,571	9
Atlanta, GA MSA	1,211	12	8,494	10
Miami – Fort Lauderdale, FL CMSA	1,817	6	8,419	11
Minneapolis – St. Paul, MN – WI MSA	885	17	7,438	12
Denver – Boulder – Greeley, CO CMSA	1,147	14	6,749	13
Cleveland – Akron, OH CMSA	851	19	6,227	14
St. Louis, MO – IL MSA	764	21	6,052	15
San Antonio, TX MSA	428	30	5,466	16
Pittsburgh, PA MSA	577	22	4,693	17
Tampa – St. Petersburg – Clearwater, FL MSA	852	18	4,495	18
San Diego, CA MSA	888	16	4,395	19
Kansas City, MO – KS MSA	573	23	4,247	20
Portland – Salem, OR – WA CMSA	793	20	4,058	21
Hartford, CT MSA	335	40	3,854	22
Milwaukee – Racine, WI CMSA	482	28	3,815	23
Charlotte – Gastonia – Rock Hill, NC – SC MSA	408	31	3,669	24
Cincinnati – Hamilton, OH – KY – IN CMSA	487	27	3,619	25

Source: U.S. Department of Commerce, Bureau of the Census, Data User Services Division, *1992 Economic Census, Volume 1F, Reports Series, Release 1F,* September 1995, CD-ROM. *Note:* Data are shown only for the top 25 areas.

★2215★

Establishments and Employment

Advertising Agencies

The U.S. total number of employees is 132,042; total number of establishments is 13,879.

MSA	Estab-lish-ments	Rank	Emp-loy-ment	Rank
New York – Northern New Jersey – Long Island, NY – NJ – CT-CMSA	1,968	1	31,839	1
Los Angeles – Riverside – Orange County, CA CMSA	905	2	9,790	2
San Francisco – Oakland – San Jose, CA CMSA	400	5	4,284	3
Dallas – Fort Worth, TX CMSA	323	9	3,637	4
Minneapolis – St. Paul, MN – WI MSA	270	12	3,302	5
Boston – Worcester – Lawrence, MA – NH – ME – CT CMSA	376	6	3,140	6
Atlanta, GA MSA	296	10	2,562	7
Cleveland – Akron, OH CMSA	217	13	1,862	8
Miami – Fort Lauderdale, FL CMSA	353	8	1,777	9
St. Louis, MO – IL MSA	160	16	1,516	10
Houston – Galveston – Brazoria, TX CMSA	217	13	1,484	11
Seattle – Tacoma – Bremerton, WA CMSA	171	14	1,463	12
Kansas City, MO – KS MSA	148	19	1,406	13
Pittsburgh, PA MSA	126	22	1,252	14
San Diego, CA MSA	147	20	1,102	15
Portland – Salem, OR – WA CMSA	122	23	941	16
Tampa – St. Petersburg – Clearwater, FL MSA	162	15	878	17
Richmond – Petersburg, VA MSA	81	28	836	18
Rochester, NY MSA	72	32	827	19
Nashville, TN MSA	81	28	714	20
Memphis, TN – AR – MS MSA	68	35	664	21
Orlando, FL MSA	114	24	653	22
Raleigh – Durham – Chapel Hill, NC MSA	58	43	652	23
Phoenix – Mesa, AZ MSA	150	18	643	24
Louisville, KY – IN MSA	75	31	641	25

Source: U.S. Department of Commerce, Bureau of the Census, Data User Services Division, *1992 Economic Census, Volume 1F, Reports Series, Release 1F,* September 1995, CD-ROM. *Note:* Data are shown only for the top 25 areas.

★2216★

Establishments and Employment

Amusement Parks

The U.S. total number of employees is 80,745; total number of establishments is 825.

MSA	Estab- lish- ments	Rank	Emp- loy- ment	Rank
Los Angeles – Riverside – Orange County, CA CMSA	25	2	15,679	1
San Francisco – Oakland – San Jose, CA CMSA	13	9	3,972	2
Chicago – Gary – Kenosha, IL – IN – WI CMSA	24	3	1,035	3
New York – Northern New Jersey – Long Island, NY – NJ – CT-CMSA	39	1	688	4
Philadelphia – Wilmington – Atlantic City, PA – NJ – DE – MD CMSA	23	4	563	5
Boston – Worcester – Lawrence, MA – NH – ME – CT CMSA	13	9	378	6
Seattle – Tacoma – Bremerton, WA CMSA	5	16	292	7
Miami – Fort Lauderdale, FL CMSA	10	11	261	8
Oklahoma City, OK MSA	4	17	176	9
Phoenix – Mesa, AZ MSA	7	14	172	10
El Paso, TX MSA	3	18	155	11
Memphis, TN – AR – MS MSA	6	15	119	12
Colorado Springs, CO MSA	3	18	105	13
Detroit – Ann Arbor – Flint, MI CMSA	17	6	93	14
Grand Rapids – Muskegon – Holland, MI MSA	7	14	87	15
Indianapolis, IN MSA	9	12	70	16
New Orleans, LA MSA	4	17	52	17
Chattanooga, TN – GA MSA	4	17	48	18
Mobile, AL MSA	4	17	22	19
Albany – Schenectady – Troy, NY MSA	3	18	0[1]	20
Albuquerque, NM MSA	2	19	0[1]	20
Allentown – Bethlehem – Easton, PA MSA	3	18	0	2	0
Anchorage, AK MSA	0	21	0	20
Appleton – Oshkosh – Neenah, WI MSA	0	21	0	20
Atlanta, GA MSA	9	12	0	2	0

Source: U.S. Department of Commerce, Bureau of the Census, Data User Services Division, *1992 Economic Census, Volume 1F, Reports Series, Release 1F,* September 1995, CD-ROM. *Notes:* Data are shown only for the top 25 areas. 1. 0-19 employees.

★2217★

Establishments and Employment

Arboreta and Botanical Or Zoological Gardens

The U.S. total number of employees is 1,056; total number of establishments is 119.

MSA	Estab- lish- ments	Rank	Emp- loy- ment	Rank
Atlanta, GA MSA	1	7	0[1]	3
Boston – Worcester – Lawrence, MA – NH – ME – CT CMSA	6	2	0[1]	3
Chicago – Gary – Kenosha, IL – IN – WI CMSA	1	7	0[1]	3
Cincinnati – Hamilton, OH – KY – IN CMSA	0	8	0	3
Cleveland – Akron, OH CMSA	0	8	0	3
Dallas – Fort Worth, TX CMSA	3	5	0[1]	3
Denver – Boulder – Greeley, CO CMSA	1	7	0[1]	3
Detroit – Ann Arbor – Flint, MI CMSA	1	7	0[1]	3
Houston – Galveston – Brazoria, TX CMSA	0	8	0	3
Indianapolis, IN MSA	1	7	0[1]	3
Kansas City, MO – KS MSA	2	6	0[1]	3
Los Angeles – Riverside – Orange County, CA CMSA	6	2	15	2
Miami – Fort Lauderdale, FL CMSA	4	4	0[2]	3
Milwaukee – Racine, WI CMSA	1	7	0[1]	3
Minneapolis – St. Paul, MN – WI MSA	0	8	0	3
New York – Northern New Jersey – Long Island, NY – NJ – CT-CMSA	7	1	21	1
Orlando, FL MSA	1	7	0[1]	3
Philadelphia – Wilmington – Atlantic City, PA – NJ – DE – MD CMSA	0	8	0	3
Phoenix – Mesa, AZ MSA	2	6	0[3]	3
Pittsburgh, PA MSA	0	8	0	3
Portland – Salem, OR – WA CMSA	0	8	0	3
Sacramento – Yolo, CA CMSA	0	8	0	3
San Diego, CA MSA	4	4	0[1]	3
San Francisco – Oakland – San Jose, CA CMSA	5	3	0[1]	3
Seattle – Tacoma – Bremerton, WA CMSA	0	8	0	3
St. Louis, MO – IL MSA	0	8	0	3
Tampa – St. Petersburg – Clearwater, FL MSA	1	7	0[3]	3
Washington – Baltimore, DC – MD – VA – WV CMSA	2	6	0[1]	3
West Palm Beach – Boca Raton, FL MSA	3	5	0[3]	3

Source: U.S. Department of Commerce, Bureau of the Census, Data User Services Division, *1992 Economic Census, Volume 1F, Reports Series, Release 1F,* September 1995, CD-ROM. *Notes:* 1. 0-19 employees. 2. 100-249 employees. 3. 20-99 employees.

★2218★
Establishments and Employment
Architectural Services

The U.S. total number of employees is 121,675; total number of establishments is 17,875.

MSA	Estab- lish- ments	Rank	Emp- ploy- ment	Rank
Los Angeles – Riverside – Orange County, CA CMSA	1,223	2	9,230	1
San Francisco – Oakland – San Jose, CA CMSA	922	3	6,264	2
Chicago – Gary – Kenosha, IL – IN – WI CMSA	742	4	5,353	3
Boston – Worcester – Lawrence, MA – NH – ME – CT CMSA	530	6	5,197	4
Washington – Baltimore, DC – MD – VA – WV CMSA	655	5	5,092	5
Philadelphia – Wilmington – Atlantic City, PA – NJ – DE – MD CMSA	391	8	4,316	6
Seattle – Tacoma – Bremerton, WA CMSA	468	7	3,214	7
Dallas – Fort Worth, TX CMSA	348	10	2,729	8
Minneapolis – St. Paul, MN – WI MSA	243	16	2,623	9
Detroit – Ann Arbor – Flint, MI CMSA	333	11	2,499	10
Atlanta, GA MSA	321	12	2,375	11
Houston – Galveston – Brazoria, TX CMSA	305	13	2,317	12
St. Louis, MO – IL MSA	181	20	1,964	13
Denver – Boulder – Greeley, CO CMSA	283	14	1,945	14
Miami – Fort Lauderdale, FL CMSA	381	9	1,746	15
Phoenix – Mesa, AZ MSA	230	17	1,587	16
Honolulu, HI MSA	160	21	1,497	17
San Diego, CA MSA	268	15	1,470	18
Orlando, FL MSA	147	23	1,383	19
Columbus, OH MSA	127	27	1,273	20
Cleveland – Akron, OH CMSA	200	18	1,246	21
Pittsburgh, PA MSA	130	26	1,190	22
Portland – Salem, OR – WA CMSA	183	19	1,167	23
Indianapolis, IN MSA	113	30	1,096	24
Charlotte – Gastonia – Rock Hill, NC – SC MSA	103	33	929	25

Source: U.S. Department of Commerce, Bureau of the Census, Data User Services Division, *1992 Economic Census, Volume 1F, Reports Series, Release 1F,* September 1995, CD-ROM. *Note:* Data are shown only for the top 25 areas.

★2219★
Establishments and Employment
Armored Car Services

The U.S. total number of employees is 20,538; total number of establishments is 690.

MSA	Estab- lish- ments	Rank	Emp- ploy- ment	Rank
Atlanta, GA MSA	12	7	517	2
Boston – Worcester – Lawrence, MA – NH – ME – CT CMSA	17	4	552	1
Chicago – Gary – Kenosha, IL – IN – WI CMSA	11	8	0[1]	11
Cincinnati – Hamilton, OH – KY – IN CMSA	5	13	0[2]	11
Cleveland – Akron, OH CMSA	5	13	171	9
Dallas – Fort Worth, TX CMSA	13	6	443	3
Denver – Boulder – Greeley, CO CMSA	6	12	0[2]	11
Detroit – Ann Arbor – Flint, MI CMSA	10	9	0[3]	11
Houston – Galveston – Brazoria, TX CMSA	10	9	317	4
Indianapolis, IN MSA	4	14	0[2]	11
Kansas City, MO – KS MSA	5	13	0[2]	11
Los Angeles – Riverside – Orange County, CA CMSA	33	2	0[4]	11
Miami – Fort Lauderdale, FL CMSA	15	5	0[3]	11
Milwaukee – Racine, WI CMSA	4	14	155	10
Minneapolis – St. Paul, MN – WI MSA	4	14	0[2]	11
New York – Northern New Jersey – Long Island, NY – NJ – CT-CMSA	44	1	0[5]	11
Orlando, FL MSA	3	15	0[2]	11
Philadelphia – Wilmington – Atlantic City, PA – NJ – DE – MD CMSA	6	12	0[1]	11
Phoenix – Mesa, AZ MSA	5	13	0[2]	11
Pittsburgh, PA MSA	5	13	173	8
Portland – Salem, OR – WA CMSA	6	12	0[2]	11
Sacramento – Yolo, CA CMSA	4	14	211	7
San Diego, CA MSA	9	10	256	5
San Francisco – Oakland – San Jose, CA CMSA	21	3	0[1]	11
Seattle – Tacoma – Bremerton, WA CMSA	9	10	0[2]	11
St. Louis, MO – IL MSA	6	12	0[2]	11
Tampa – St. Petersburg – Clearwater, FL MSA	8	11	237	6
Washington – Baltimore, DC – MD – VA – WV CMSA	12	7	0[1]	11
West Palm Beach – Boca Raton, FL MSA	2	16	0[6]	11

Source: U.S. Department of Commerce, Bureau of the Census, Data User Services Division, *1992 Economic Census, Volume 1F, Reports Series, Release 1F,* September 1995, CD-ROM. *Notes:* 1. 500-999 employees. 2. 100-249 employees. 3. 250-499 employees. 4. 1,000-2,499 employees. 5. 2,500-4,999 employees. 6. 20-99 employees.

★ 2220 ★

Establishments and Employment

Authors, Composers, and Other Arts-related Services

The U.S. total number of employees is 6,735; total number of establishments is 3,054.

MSA	Establish-ments	Rank	Emp-loy-ment	Rank
Atlanta, GA MSA	30	12	97	7
Boston – Worcester – Lawrence, MA – NH – ME – CT CMSA	57	6	104	5
Chicago – Gary – Kenosha, IL – IN – WI CMSA	101	5	0[1]	19
Cincinnati – Hamilton, OH – KY – IN CMSA	16	20	0[2]	19
Cleveland – Akron, OH CMSA	30	12	58	11
Dallas – Fort Worth, TX CMSA	34	11	63	10
Denver – Boulder – Greeley, CO CMSA	34	11	88	8
Detroit – Ann Arbor – Flint, MI CMSA	39	10	136	4
Houston – Galveston – Brazoria, TX CMSA	29	13	0[2]	19
Indianapolis, IN MSA	11	23	20	17
Kansas City, MO – KS MSA	14	21	30	16
Los Angeles – Riverside – Orange County, CA CMSA	773	1	1,234	1
Miami – Fort Lauderdale, FL CMSA	57	6	100	6
Milwaukee – Racine, WI CMSA	14	21	31	15
Minneapolis – St. Paul, MN – WI MSA	54	7	146	3
New York – Northern New Jersey – Long Island, NY – NJ – CT-CMSA	501	2	0[3]	19
Orlando, FL MSA	19	19	35	14
Philadelphia – Wilmington – Atlantic City, PA – NJ – DE – MD CMSA	51	8	0[1]	19
Phoenix – Mesa, AZ MSA	28	14	38	12
Pittsburgh, PA MSA	11	23	12	18
Portland – Salem, OR – WA CMSA	25	16	0[2]	19
Sacramento – Yolo, CA CMSA	13	22	0[2]	19
San Diego, CA MSA	27	15	104	5
San Francisco – Oakland – San Jose, CA CMSA	106	4	255	2
Seattle – Tacoma – Bremerton, WA CMSA	41	9	65	9
St. Louis, MO – IL MSA	23	17	36	13
Tampa – St. Petersburg – Clearwater, FL MSA	22	18	31	15
Washington – Baltimore, DC – MD – VA – WV CMSA	140	3	0[4]	19

Source: U.S. Department of Commerce, Bureau of the Census, Data User Services Division, *1992 Economic Census, Volume 1F, Reports Series, Release 1F*, September 1995, CD-ROM. *Notes:* 1. 100-249 employees. 2. 20-99 employees. 3. 1,000-2,499 employees. 4. 250-499 employees.

★ 2221 ★

Establishments and Employment

Automobile Parking

The U.S. total number of employees is 51,563; total number of establishments is 10,171.

MSA	Estab-lish-ments	Rank	Emp-loy-ment	Rank
New York – Northern New Jersey – Long Island, NY – NJ – CT-CMSA	1,321	1	9,285	1
Los Angeles – Riverside – Orange County, CA CMSA	1,241	2	6,740	2
Atlanta, GA MSA	271	9	1,258	3
Minneapolis – St. Paul, MN – WI MSA	141	15	1,011	4
San Diego, CA MSA	286	7	943	5
New Orleans, LA MSA	140	16	863	6
Pittsburgh, PA MSA	103	24	855	7
Dallas – Fort Worth, TX CMSA	356	5	788	8
Honolulu, HI MSA	133	17	787	9
St. Louis, MO – IL MSA	122	20	758	10
Cincinnati – Hamilton, OH – KY – IN CMSA	102	25	507	11
Nashville, TN MSA	124	19	501	12
Denver – Boulder – Greeley, CO CMSA	205	13	489	13
Phoenix – Mesa, AZ MSA	85	28	438	14
Hartford, CT MSA	53	36	413	15
Columbus, OH MSA	121	21	378	16
Kansas City, MO – KS MSA	122	20	342	17
Buffalo – Niagara Falls, NY MSA	66	30	312	18
Milwaukee – Racine, WI CMSA	73	29	295	19
Richmond – Petersburg, VA MSA	92	26	252	20
Louisville, KY – IN MSA	64	31	233	21
Indianapolis, IN MSA	50	37	220	22
Dayton – Springfield, OH MSA	62	32	198	23
Memphis, TN – AR – MS MSA	92	26	179	24
San Antonio, TX MSA	88	27	176	25

Source: U.S. Department of Commerce, Bureau of the Census, Data User Services Division, *1992 Economic Census, Volume 1F, Reports Series, Release 1F*, September 1995, CD-ROM. *Note:* Data are shown only for the top 25 areas.

★ 2222 ★

Establishments and Employment

Automotive Exhaust System Repair Shops

The U.S. total number of employees is 23,277; total number of establishments is 5,521.

MSA	Estab-lish-ments	Rank	Emp-loy-ment	Rank
Detroit – Ann Arbor – Flint, MI CMSA	239	3	1,104	1
Los Angeles – Riverside – Orange County, CA CMSA	212	4	755	2
Washington – Baltimore, DC – MD – VA – WV CMSA	115	5	669	3
Boston – Worcester – Lawrence, MA – NH – ME – CT CMSA	101	8	537	4
Cleveland – Akron, OH CMSA	111	6	481	5

[Continued]

★2222★

Automotive Exhaust System Repair Shops
[Continued]

MSA	Estab-lish-ments	Rank	Emp-ploy-ment	Rank
Philadelphia – Wilmington – Atlantic City, PA – NJ – DE – MD CMSA	104	7	454	6
St. Louis, MO – IL MSA	80	12	418	7
Minneapolis – St. Paul, MN – WI MSA	61	15	366	8
Dallas – Fort Worth, TX CMSA	95	10	345	9
Miami – Fort Lauderdale, FL CMSA	52	16	317	10
Pittsburgh, PA MSA	69	13	286	11
Cincinnati – Hamilton, OH – KY – IN CMSA	49	18	283	12
Seattle – Tacoma – Bremerton, WA CMSA	65	14	282	13
Buffalo – Niagara Falls, NY MSA	51	17	272	14
Atlanta, GA MSA	61	15	263	15
Rochester, NY MSA	39	22	236	16
Tampa – St. Petersburg – Clearwater, FL MSA	46	19	229	17
Indianapolis, IN MSA	43	21	228	18
Kansas City, MO – KS MSA	46	19	204	19
San Diego, CA MSA	36	24	199	20
Columbus, OH MSA	43	21	193	21
Syracuse, NY MSA	32	27	180	22
Grand Rapids – Muskegon – Holland, MI MSA	38	23	176	23
Norfolk – Virginia Beach – Newport News, VA – NC MSA	34	25	174	24
Salt Lake City – Ogden, UT MSA	31	28	157	25

Source: U.S. Department of Commerce, Bureau of the Census, Data User Services Division, *1992 Economic Census, Volume 1F, Reports Series, Release 1F,* September 1995, CD-ROM. *Note:* Data are shown only for the top 25 areas.

★2223★

Establishments and Employment

Automotive Glass Replacement Shops

The U.S. total number of employees is 22,240; total number of establishments is 4,925.

MSA	Estab-lish-ments	Rank	Emp-ploy-ment	Rank
New York – Northern New Jersey – Long Island, NY – NJ – CT-CMSA	305	1	1,382	1
Los Angeles – Riverside – Orange County, CA CMSA	221	2	1,057	2
Detroit – Ann Arbor – Flint, MI CMSA	144	5	769	3
Washington – Baltimore, DC – MD – VA – WV CMSA	163	3	747	4
Boston – Worcester – Lawrence, MA – NH – ME – CT CMSA	159	4	591	5
Seattle – Tacoma – Bremerton, WA CMSA	117	6	538	6

[Continued]

★2223★

Automotive Glass Replacement Shops
[Continued]

MSA	Estab-lish-ments	Rank	Emp-ploy-ment	Rank
Dallas – Fort Worth, TX CMSA	84	9	421	7
Phoenix – Mesa, AZ MSA	55	15	387	8
Minneapolis – St. Paul, MN – WI MSA	77	11	383	9
Houston – Galveston – Brazoria, TX CMSA	73	12	381	10
Miami – Fort Lauderdale, FL CMSA	63	13	316	11
St. Louis, MO – IL MSA	58	14	275	12
San Diego, CA MSA	44	19	244	13
Cleveland – Akron, OH CMSA	44	19	221	14
Atlanta, GA MSA	45	18	213	15
Norfolk – Virginia Beach – Newport News, VA – NC MSA	38	22	192	16
Pittsburgh, PA MSA	49	17	188	17
Salt Lake City – Ogden, UT MSA	41	20	166	18
Tampa – St. Petersburg – Clearwater, FL MSA	40	21	165	19
Buffalo – Niagara Falls, NY MSA	34	24	159	20
Albuquerque, NM MSA	23	32	154	21
Kansas City, MO – KS MSA	37	23	151	22
Nashville, TN MSA	18	36	142	23
Richmond – Petersburg, VA MSA	31	26	131	24
San Antonio, TX MSA	24	31	130	25

Source: U.S. Department of Commerce, Bureau of the Census, Data User Services Division, *1992 Economic Census, Volume 1F, Reports Series, Release 1F,* September 1995, CD-ROM. *Note:* Data are shown only for the top 25 areas.

★2224★

Establishments and Employment

Automotive Rental and Leasing, Without Drivers

The U.S. total number of employees is 132,323; total number of establishments is 10,566.

MSA	Estab-lish-ments	Rank	Emp-ploy-ment	Rank
Los Angeles – Riverside – Orange County, CA CMSA	593	2	9,002	1
Chicago – Gary – Kenosha, IL – IN – WI CMSA	361	3	5,083	2
Miami – Fort Lauderdale, FL CMSA	201	9	4,094	3
Boston – Worcester – Lawrence, MA – NH – ME – CT CMSA	261	4	3,530	4
Atlanta, GA MSA	164	12	3,270	5
Dallas – Fort Worth, TX CMSA	238	7	3,125	6
Orlando, FL MSA	89	20	2,882	7
Phoenix – Mesa, AZ MSA	112	15	2,664	8
Denver – Boulder – Greeley, CO CMSA	104	18	1,993	9
Tampa – St. Petersburg – Clearwater, FL MSA	122	14	1,933	10
Cleveland – Akron, OH CMSA	177	11	1,825	11

[Continued]

★2224★

Automotive Rental and Leasing, Without Drivers

[Continued]

MSA	Establishments	Rank	Employment	Rank
Minneapolis – St. Paul, MN – WI MSA	106	17	1,740	12
Pittsburgh, PA MSA	94	19	1,665	13
Las Vegas, NV – AZ MSA	70	27	1,420	14
Cincinnati – Hamilton, OH – KY – IN CMSA	80	24	1,413	15
St. Louis, MO – IL MSA	88	21	1,397	16
Honolulu, HI MSA	36	43	1,337	17
Charlotte – Gastonia – Rock Hill, NC – SC MSA	76	25	1,291	18
San Diego, CA MSA	111	16	1,239	19
Indianapolis, IN MSA	72	26	1,221	20
Kansas City, MO – KS MSA	76	25	1,136	21
Nashville, TN MSA	65	29	1,118	22
New Orleans, LA MSA	52	34	1,083	23
San Antonio, TX MSA	65	29	968	24
Louisville, KY – IN MSA	48	36	959	25

Source: U.S. Department of Commerce, Bureau of the Census, Data User Services Division, *1992 Economic Census, Volume 1F, Reports Series, Release 1F,* September 1995, CD-ROM. *Note:* Data are shown only for the top 25 areas.

★2225★

Establishments and Employment

Automotive Repair Shops

The U.S. total number of employees is 519,503; total number of establishments is 128,738.

MSA	Establishments	Rank	Employment	Rank
New York – Northern New Jersey – Long Island, NY – NJ – CT-CMSA	9,741	1	35,725	1
Los Angeles – Riverside – Orange County, CA CMSA	7,680	2	34,614	2
Chicago – Gary – Kenosha, IL – IN – WI CMSA	3,944	3	20,071	3
San Francisco – Oakland – San Jose, CA CMSA	3,596	4	15,450	4
Washington – Baltimore, DC – MD – VA – WV CMSA	2,880	6	14,125	5
Philadelphia – Wilmington – Atlantic City, PA – NJ – DE – MD CMSA	3,088	5	12,413	6
Detroit – Ann Arbor – Flint, MI CMSA	2,476	8	11,842	7
Boston – Worcester – Lawrence, MA – NH – ME – CT CMSA	2,794	7	10,748	8
Dallas – Fort Worth, TX CMSA	2,075	9	9,489	9
Houston – Galveston – Brazoria, TX CMSA	1,937	11	8,692	10
Seattle – Tacoma – Bremerton, WA CMSA	1,653	12	7,706	11
Miami – Fort Lauderdale, FL CMSA	1,968	10	7,135	12

[Continued]

★2225★

Automotive Repair Shops

[Continued]

MSA	Establishments	Rank	Employment	Rank
Atlanta, GA MSA	1,579	13	6,752	13
St. Louis, MO – IL MSA	1,446	14	6,554	14
Cleveland – Akron, OH CMSA	1,407	15	6,322	15
San Diego, CA MSA	1,369	16	6,310	16
Phoenix – Mesa, AZ MSA	1,259	18	5,934	17
Denver – Boulder – Greeley, CO CMSA	1,283	17	5,921	18
Minneapolis – St. Paul, MN – WI MSA	1,182	21	5,873	19
Portland – Salem, OR – WA CMSA	1,012	22	4,708	20
Tampa – St. Petersburg – Clearwater, FL MSA	1,193	20	4,613	21
Pittsburgh, PA MSA	1,252	19	4,291	22
Sacramento – Yolo, CA CMSA	837	25	4,110	23
Kansas City, MO – KS MSA	869	23	3,884	24
Milwaukee – Racine, WI CMSA	786	26	3,803	25

Source: U.S. Department of Commerce, Bureau of the Census, Data User Services Division, *1992 Economic Census, Volume 1F, Reports Series, Release 1F,* September 1995, CD-ROM. *Note:* Data are shown only for the top 25 areas.

★2226★

Establishments and Employment

Automotive Repair, Services, and Parking

The U.S. total number of employees is 863,856; total number of establishments is 171,970.

MSA	Establishments	Rank	Employment	Rank
Los Angeles – Riverside – Orange County, CA CMSA	10,845	2	63,245	1
New York – Northern New Jersey – Long Island, NY – NJ – CT-CMSA	13,363	1	61,784	2
Chicago – Gary – Kenosha, IL – IN – WI CMSA	5,556	3	34,410	3
San Francisco – Oakland – San Jose, CA CMSA	4,718	4	27,484	4
Washington – Baltimore, DC – MD – VA – WV CMSA	4,326	5	25,467	5
Philadelphia – Wilmington – Atlantic City, PA – NJ – DE – MD CMSA	4,002	6	21,820	6
Detroit – Ann Arbor – Flint, MI CMSA	3,524	8	20,392	7
Boston – Worcester – Lawrence, MA – NH – ME – CT CMSA	3,721	7	18,119	8
Dallas – Fort Worth, TX CMSA	3,143	9	17,498	9
Houston – Galveston – Brazoria, TX CMSA	2,679	10	15,592	10
Miami – Fort Lauderdale, FL CMSA	2,587	11	14,513	11
Atlanta, GA MSA	2,340	13	14,074	12
Seattle – Tacoma – Bremerton, WA CMSA	2,429	12	12,636	13

[Continued]

★ 2226 ★

Automotive Repair, Services, and Parking

[Continued]

MSA	Estab-lish-ments	Rank	Emp-loy-ment	Rank
Phoenix – Mesa, AZ MSA	1,739	18	12,028	14
Minneapolis – St. Paul, MN – WI MSA	1,721	19	11,840	15
Cleveland – Akron, OH CMSA	2,106	14	11,672	16
St. Louis, MO – IL MSA	1,918	16	10,720	17
San Diego, CA MSA	2,033	15	10,636	18
Denver – Boulder – Greeley, CO CMSA	1,862	17	10,375	19
Tampa – St. Petersburg – Clearwater, FL MSA	1,581	21	8,136	20
Pittsburgh, PA MSA	1,625	20	7,993	21
Portland – Salem, OR – WA CMSA	1,445	22	7,637	22
Cincinnati – Hamilton, OH – KY – IN CMSA	1,208	24	7,293	23
Orlando, FL MSA	945	29	6,998	24
Kansas City, MO – KS MSA	1,248	23	6,698	25

Source: U.S. Department of Commerce, Bureau of the Census, Data User Services Division, *1992 Economic Census, Volume 1F, Reports Series, Release 1F,* September 1995, CD-ROM. *Note:* Data are shown only for the top 25 areas.

★ 2227 ★

Establishments and Employment

Automotive Services, Except Repair

The U.S. total number of employees is 160,467; total number of establishments is 22,495.

MSA	Estab-lish-ments	Rank	Emp-loy-ment	Rank
Los Angeles – Riverside – Orange County, CA CMSA	1,331	2	12,889	1
Detroit – Ann Arbor – Flint, MI CMSA	720	4	5,042	2
San Francisco – Oakland – San Jose, CA CMSA	557	5	4,804	3
Dallas – Fort Worth, TX CMSA	474	7	4,096	4
Washington – Baltimore, DC – MD – VA – WV CMSA	516	6	3,796	5
Minneapolis – St. Paul, MN – WI MSA	292	15	3,216	6
Houston – Galveston – Brazoria, TX CMSA	324	13	3,163	7
Phoenix – Mesa, AZ MSA	283	16	2,992	8
Atlanta, GA MSA	326	12	2,794	9
San Diego, CA MSA	267	18	2,144	10
Seattle – Tacoma – Bremerton, WA CMSA	349	11	2,074	11
St. Louis, MO – IL MSA	262	19	2,011	12
Denver – Boulder – Greeley, CO CMSA	270	17	1,972	13
Milwaukee – Racine, WI CMSA	170	26	1,717	14
Cincinnati – Hamilton, OH – KY – IN CMSA	175	25	1,572	15
Indianapolis, IN MSA	195	22	1,512	16

[Continued]

★ 2227 ★

Automotive Services, Except Repair

[Continued]

MSA	Estab-lish-ments	Rank	Emp-loy-ment	Rank
Tampa – St. Petersburg – Clearwater, FL MSA	211	21	1,453	17
Kansas City, MO – KS MSA	181	23	1,336	18
Columbus, OH MSA	149	28	1,335	19
Pittsburgh, PA MSA	176	24	1,182	20
Louisville, KY – IN MSA	115	35	1,153	21
Jacksonville, FL MSA	113	36	1,128	22
San Antonio, TX MSA	143	29	1,121	23
Dayton – Springfield, OH MSA	97	42	1,009	24
Charlotte – Gastonia – Rock Hill, NC – SC MSA	127	33	942	25

Source: U.S. Department of Commerce, Bureau of the Census, Data User Services Division, *1992 Economic Census, Volume 1F, Reports Series, Release 1F,* September 1995, CD-ROM. *Note:* Data are shown only for the top 25 areas.

★ 2228 ★

Establishments and Employment

Automotive Transmission Repair Shops

The U.S. total number of employees is 24,136; total number of establishments is 6,277.

MSA	Estab-lish-ments	Rank	Emp-loy-ment	Rank
Los Angeles – Riverside – Orange County, CA CMSA	415	2	1,495	1
San Francisco – Oakland – San Jose, CA CMSA	145	5	619	2
Dallas – Fort Worth, TX CMSA	125	8	606	3
Philadelphia – Wilmington – Atlantic City, PA – NJ – DE – MD CMSA	150	4	527	4
Detroit – Ann Arbor – Flint, MI CMSA	133	6	496	5
Houston – Galveston – Brazoria, TX CMSA	121	9	469	6
Boston – Worcester – Lawrence, MA – NH – ME – CT CMSA	102	12	432	7
Seattle – Tacoma – Bremerton, WA CMSA	101	13	430	8
Atlanta, GA MSA	105	11	416	9
San Diego, CA MSA	98	14	361	10
Phoenix – Mesa, AZ MSA	81	15	329	11
Miami – Fort Lauderdale, FL CMSA	111	10	321	12
Tampa – St. Petersburg – Clearwater, FL MSA	66	17	279	13
Charlotte – Gastonia – Rock Hill, NC – SC MSA	31	33	271	14
Denver – Boulder – Greeley, CO CMSA	70	16	263	15
Cleveland – Akron, OH CMSA	62	18	260	16
San Antonio, TX MSA	59	19	233	17
St. Louis, MO – IL MSA	66	17	229	18

[Continued]

★2228★

Automotive Transmission Repair Shops
[Continued]

MSA	Estab-lish-ments	Rank	Emp-ploy-ment	Rank
Portland – Salem, OR – WA CMSA	56	20	212	19
Minneapolis – St. Paul, MN – WI MSA	55	21	209	20
Salt Lake City – Ogden, UT MSA	35	30	183	21
Indianapolis, IN MSA	30	34	177	22
Orlando, FL MSA	51	23	174	23
Kansas City, MO – KS MSA	46	24	171	24
Pittsburgh, PA MSA	53	22	162	25

Source: U.S. Department of Commerce, Bureau of the Census, Data User Services Division, *1992 Economic Census, Volume 1F, Reports Series, Release 1F,* September 1995, CD-ROM. *Note:* Data are shown only for the top 25 areas.

★2229★

Establishments and Employment

Bands, Orchestras, Actors, and Other Entertainers and Entertainment Groups

The U.S. total number of employees is 30,038; total number of establishments is 5,831.

MSA	Estab-lish-ments	Rank	Emp-ploy-ment	Rank
Los Angeles – Riverside – Orange County, CA CMSA	1,912	1	7,082	1
Nashville, TN MSA	232	3	1,819	2
Las Vegas, NV – AZ MSA	73	9	623	3
Miami – Fort Lauderdale, FL CMSA	86	8	540	4
Minneapolis – St. Paul, MN – WI MSA	58	13	411	5
Dallas – Fort Worth, TX CMSA	57	14	387	6
St. Louis, MO – IL MSA	63	11	371	7
Norfolk – Virginia Beach – Newport News, VA – NC MSA	21	29	261	8
San Diego, CA MSA	42	16	261	8
Austin – San Marcos, TX MSA	35	21	242	9
Pittsburgh, PA MSA	20	30	221	10
Cleveland – Akron, OH CMSA	28	24	178	11
Phoenix – Mesa, AZ MSA	38	19	165	12
West Palm Beach – Boca Raton, FL MSA	21	29	162	13
San Antonio, TX MSA	22	28	161	14
Atlanta, GA MSA	41	17	120	15
Omaha, NE – IA MSA	17	31	113	16
Orlando, FL MSA	21	29	112	17
Knoxville, TN MSA	8	39	95	18
Kansas City, MO – KS MSA	24	27	87	19
Tampa – St. Petersburg – Clearwater, FL MSA	33	23	83	20
Columbus, OH MSA	17	31	80	21
Fort Wayne, IN MSA	3	44	62	22
Des Moines, IA MSA	10	37	57	23
Oklahoma City, OK MSA	12	35	54	24

Source: U.S. Department of Commerce, Bureau of the Census, Data User Services Division, *1992 Economic Census, Volume 1F, Reports Series, Release 1F,* September 1995, CD-ROM. *Note:* Data are shown only for the top 25 areas.

★2230★

Establishments and Employment

Barber Shops

The U.S. total number of employees is 14,504; total number of establishments is 4,902.

MSA	Estab-lish-ments	Rank	Emp-ploy-ment	Rank
Los Angeles – Riverside – Orange County, CA CMSA	244	2	702	1
San Francisco – Oakland – San Jose, CA CMSA	154	4	541	2
Philadelphia – Wilmington – Atlantic City, PA – NJ – DE – MD CMSA	210	3	503	3
Chicago – Gary – Kenosha, IL – IN – WI CMSA	115	7	416	4
Dallas – Fort Worth, TX CMSA	101	8	359	5
Boston – Worcester – Lawrence, MA – NH – ME – CT CMSA	119	6	333	6
Houston – Galveston – Brazoria, TX CMSA	67	13	243	7
San Antonio, TX MSA	42	22	229	8
Pittsburgh, PA MSA	77	9	210	9
San Diego, CA MSA	30	27	191	10
Miami – Fort Lauderdale, FL CMSA	74	10	176	11
Phoenix – Mesa, AZ MSA	58	15	169	12
Charlotte – Gastonia – Rock Hill, NC – SC MSA	53	17	167	13
Milwaukee – Racine, WI CMSA	61	14	160	14
Minneapolis – St. Paul, MN – WI MSA	39	23	159	15
Honolulu, HI MSA	32	25	156	16
Atlanta, GA MSA	53	17	142	17
Cleveland – Akron, OH CMSA	70	11	135	18
Hartford, CT MSA	57	16	134	19
Norfolk – Virginia Beach – Newport News, VA – NC MSA	32	25	132	20
Kansas City, MO – KS MSA	49	18	126	21
St. Louis, MO – IL MSA	43	21	123	22
Orlando, FL MSA	15	37	113	23
Tampa – St. Petersburg – Clearwater, FL MSA	21	32	111	24
Cincinnati – Hamilton, OH – KY – IN CMSA	45	20	108	25

Source: U.S. Department of Commerce, Bureau of the Census, Data User Services Division, *1992 Economic Census, Volume 1F, Reports Series, Release 1F,* September 1995, CD-ROM. *Note:* Data are shown only for the top 25 areas.

★ 2231 ★

Establishments and Employment

Beauty Shops

The U.S. total number of employees is 387,249; total number of establishments is 82,768.

MSA	Establish-ments	Rank	Emp-loy-ment	Rank
Los Angeles – Riverside – Orange County, CA CMSA	3,455	2	17,104	1
Chicago – Gary – Kenosha, IL – IN – WI CMSA	2,676	3	15,209	2
Philadelphia – Wilmington – Atlantic City, PA – NJ – DE – MD CMSA	2,405	6	11,954	3
Boston – Worcester – Lawrence, MA – NH – ME – CT CMSA	2,517	4	11,479	4
San Francisco – Oakland – San Jose, CA CMSA	1,959	7	8,932	5
Miami – Fort Lauderdale, FL CMSA	1,591	8	7,402	6
Minneapolis – St. Paul, MN – WI MSA	1,011	15	7,280	7
Cleveland – Akron, OH CMSA	1,147	12	6,957	8
Dallas – Fort Worth, TX CMSA	1,271	10	6,955	9
Houston – Galveston – Brazoria, TX CMSA	1,158	11	6,870	10
Atlanta, GA MSA	982	16	5,180	11
Phoenix – Mesa, AZ MSA	907	19	5,150	12
Pittsburgh, PA MSA	1,090	14	4,927	13
St. Louis, MO – IL MSA	949	17	4,839	14
Tampa – St. Petersburg – Clearwater, FL MSA	923	18	4,369	15
Milwaukee – Racine, WI CMSA	756	21	4,278	16
San Diego, CA MSA	616	25	3,377	17
Norfolk – Virginia Beach – Newport News, VA – NC MSA	636	22	3,267	18
Cincinnati – Hamilton, OH – KY – IN CMSA	620	24	3,222	19
Kansas City, MO – KS MSA	607	26	3,005	20
Portland – Salem, OR – WA CMSA	518	30	2,777	21
Orlando, FL MSA	519	29	2,775	22
West Palm Beach – Boca Raton, FL MSA	506	31	2,753	23
Columbus, OH MSA	485	32	2,667	24
San Antonio, TX MSA	525	28	2,577	25

Source: U.S. Department of Commerce, Bureau of the Census, Data User Services Division, *1992 Economic Census, Volume 1F, Reports Series, Release 1F,* September 1995, CD-ROM. *Note:* Data are shown only for the top 25 areas.

★ 2232 ★

Establishments and Employment

Bowling Centers

The U.S. total number of employees is 95,701; total number of establishments is 6,093.

MSA	Establish-ments	Rank	Emp-loy-ment	Rank
Los Angeles – Riverside – Orange County, CA CMSA	149	4	4,021	1
Detroit – Ann Arbor – Flint, MI CMSA	184	3	3,622	2
Chicago – Gary – Kenosha, IL – IN – WI CMSA	225	2	3,607	3
Seattle – Tacoma – Bremerton, WA CMSA	60	14	2,083	4
Minneapolis – St. Paul, MN – WI MSA	92	9	1,999	5
Milwaukee – Racine, WI CMSA	95	8	1,897	6
Cleveland – Akron, OH CMSA	107	6	1,726	7
St. Louis, MO – IL MSA	77	12	1,523	8
Denver – Boulder – Greeley, CO CMSA	50	16	1,144	9
Dallas – Fort Worth, TX CMSA	39	21	1,098	10
Buffalo – Niagara Falls, NY MSA	60	14	1,078	11
Grand Rapids – Muskegon – Holland, MI MSA	47	18	927	12
Pittsburgh, PA MSA	86	11	908	13
Phoenix – Mesa, AZ MSA	33	25	879	14
Cincinnati – Hamilton, OH – KY – IN CMSA	53	15	842	15
Atlanta, GA MSA	35	23	837	16
Miami – Fort Lauderdale, FL CMSA	37	22	837	16
Rochester, NY MSA	48	17	802	17
Portland – Salem, OR – WA CMSA	48	17	782	18
Kansas City, MO – KS MSA	44	19	780	19
Tampa – St. Petersburg – Clearwater, FL MSA	33	25	757	20
Columbus, OH MSA	35	23	640	21
San Diego, CA MSA	21	32	638	22
Norfolk – Virginia Beach – Newport News, VA – NC MSA	23	30	632	23
Dayton – Springfield, OH MSA	39	21	614	24

Source: U.S. Department of Commerce, Bureau of the Census, Data User Services Division, *1992 Economic Census, Volume 1F, Reports Series, Release 1F,* September 1995, CD-ROM. *Note:* Data are shown only for the top 25 areas.

★2233★

Establishments and Employment

Business and Secretarial Schools

The U.S. total number of employees is 17,552; total number of establishments is 863.

MSA	Establishments	Rank	Employment	Rank
Atlanta, GA MSA	17	8	287	6
Boston – Worcester – Lawrence, MA – NH – ME – CT CMSA	17	8	163	9
Chicago – Gary – Kenosha, IL – IN – WI CMSA	23	5	0[1]	16
Cincinnati – Hamilton, OH – KY – IN CMSA	4	17	56	14
Cleveland – Akron, OH CMSA	17	8	0[2]	16
Dallas – Fort Worth, TX CMSA	21	6	382	3
Denver – Boulder – Greeley, CO CMSA	15	9	375	4
Detroit – Ann Arbor – Flint, MI CMSA	27	3	0[1]	16
Houston – Galveston – Brazoria, TX CMSA	20	7	472	2
Indianapolis, IN MSA	1	19	0[3]	16
Kansas City, MO – KS MSA	5	16	0[4]	16
Los Angeles – Riverside – Orange County, CA CMSA	52	2	0[5]	16
Miami – Fort Lauderdale, FL CMSA	15	9	0[1]	16
Milwaukee – Racine, WI CMSA	2	18	0[6]	16
Minneapolis – St. Paul, MN – WI MSA	9	13	180	8
New York – Northern New Jersey – Long Island, NY – NJ – CT-CMSA	101	1	2,526	1
Orlando, FL MSA	2	18	0[4]	16
Philadelphia – Wilmington – Atlantic City, PA – NJ – DE – MD CMSA	15	9	0[1]	16
Phoenix – Mesa, AZ MSA	11	12	189	7
Pittsburgh, PA MSA	11	12	333	5
Portland – Salem, OR – WA CMSA	13	10	0[3]	16
Sacramento – Yolo, CA CMSA	4	17	132	11
San Diego, CA MSA	12	11	147	10
San Francisco – Oakland – San Jose, CA CMSA	23	5	0[1]	16
Seattle – Tacoma – Bremerton, WA CMSA	7	15	0[4]	16
St. Louis, MO – IL MSA	8	14	64	13
Tampa – St. Petersburg – Clearwater, FL MSA	9	13	90	12
Washington – Baltimore, DC – MD – VA – WV CMSA	24	4	0[2]	16
West Palm Beach – Boca Raton, FL MSA	4	17	28	15

Source: U.S. Department of Commerce, Bureau of the Census, Data User Services Division, *1992 Economic Census, Volume 1F, Reports Series, Release 1F,* September 1995, CD-ROM. *Notes:* 1. 250-499 employees. 2. 500-999 employees. 3. 100-249 employees. 4. 20-99 employees. 5. 1,000-2,499 employees. 6. 0-19 employees.

★2234★

Establishments and Employment

Business Services

The U.S. total number of employees is 5,542,417; total number of establishments is 306,551.

MSA	Establishments	Rank	Employment	Rank
New York – Northern New Jersey – Long Island, NY – NJ – CT-CMSA	32,413	1	557,877	1
Los Angeles – Riverside – Orange County, CA CMSA	20,093	2	396,092	2
Chicago – Gary – Kenosha, IL – IN – WI CMSA	12,921	3	252,429	3
Washington – Baltimore, DC – MD – VA – WV CMSA	11,834	5	250,704	4
San Francisco – Oakland – San Jose, CA CMSA	11,912	4	219,460	5
Boston – Worcester – Lawrence, MA – NH – ME – CT CMSA	8,104	6	175,040	6
Houston – Galveston – Brazoria, TX CMSA	5,760	12	163,409	7
Dallas – Fort Worth, TX CMSA	7,293	8	162,952	8
Philadelphia – Wilmington – Atlantic City, PA – NJ – DE – MD CMSA	7,869	7	150,612	9
Detroit – Ann Arbor – Flint, MI CMSA	5,990	11	127,408	10
Atlanta, GA MSA	6,372	10	121,239	11
Tampa – St. Petersburg – Clearwater, FL MSA	3,547	19	98,145	12
Minneapolis – St. Paul, MN – WI MSA	4,665	13	94,151	13
Miami – Fort Lauderdale, FL CMSA	6,635	9	87,436	14
Cleveland – Akron, OH CMSA	3,608	18	70,284	15
Denver – Boulder – Greeley, CO CMSA	4,214	15	70,082	16
St. Louis, MO – IL MSA	3,415	20	67,903	17
Seattle – Tacoma – Bremerton, WA CMSA	4,664	14	65,839	18
Phoenix – Mesa, AZ MSA	3,707	16	61,845	19
San Diego, CA MSA	3,634	17	61,548	20
Pittsburgh, PA MSA	2,577	22	50,558	21
Milwaukee – Racine, WI CMSA	2,262	25	46,979	22
Columbus, OH MSA	1,762	31	46,382	23
Cincinnati – Hamilton, OH – KY – IN CMSA	2,071	26	46,152	24
Kansas City, MO – KS MSA	2,413	23	44,098	25

Source: U.S. Department of Commerce, Bureau of the Census, Data User Services Division, *1992 Economic Census, Volume 1F, Reports Series, Release 1F,* September 1995, CD-ROM. *Note:* Data are shown only for the top 25 areas.

★ 2235 ★

Establishments and Employment

Camps and Recreational Vehicle Parks

The U.S. total number of employees is 25,078; total number of establishments is 5,315.

MSA	Estab- lish- ments	Rank	Emp- ploy- ment	Rank
San Francisco – Oakland – San Jose, CA CMSA	97	3	582	1
San Diego, CA MSA	43	10	531	2
Phoenix – Mesa, AZ MSA	46	9	464	3
Tampa – St. Petersburg – Clearwater, FL MSA	69	6	409	4
Tucson, AZ MSA	24	20	261	5
Boston – Worcester – Lawrence, MA – NH – ME – CT CMSA	72	5	216	6
Norfolk – Virginia Beach – Newport News, VA – NC MSA	38	12	215	7
Sacramento – Yolo, CA CMSA	33	14	193	8
Lakeland – Winter Haven, FL MSA	21	23	153	9
Fresno, CA MSA	27	17	149	10
Nashville, TN MSA	13	30	147	11
Minneapolis – St. Paul, MN – WI MSA	29	15	126	12
Portland – Salem, OR – WA CMSA	27	17	123	13
San Antonio, TX MSA	18	25	107	14
Knoxville, TN MSA	24	20	77	15
Miami – Fort Lauderdale, FL CMSA	18	25	73	16
Dallas – Fort Worth, TX CMSA	25	19	67	17
Jacksonville, FL MSA	13	30	65	18
Portland, ME MSA	23	21	65	18
Santa Barbara – Santa Maria – Lompoc, CA MSA	9	34	65	18
Syracuse, NY MSA	22	22	62	19
Austin – San Marcos, TX MSA	11	32	61	20
St. Louis, MO – IL MSA	22	22	57	21
Pittsburgh, PA MSA	16	27	51	22
Stockton – Lodi, CA MSA	12	31	46	23

Source: U.S. Department of Commerce, Bureau of the Census, Data User Services Division, *1992 Economic Census, Volume 1F, Reports Series, Release 1F,* September 1995, CD-ROM. *Note:* Data are shown only for the top 25 areas.

★ 2236 ★

Establishments and Employment

Carpet and Upholstery Cleaning

The U.S. total number of employees is 39,318; total number of establishments is 7,693.

MSA	Estab- lish- ments	Rank	Emp- ploy- ment	Rank
New York – Northern New Jersey – Long Island, NY – NJ – CT-CMSA	397	2	2,373	1
Los Angeles – Riverside – Orange County, CA CMSA	400	1	2,004	2
San Francisco – Oakland – San Jose, CA CMSA	222	4	1,246	3
Dallas – Fort Worth, TX CMSA	145	7	981	4

[Continued]

★ 2236 ★

Carpet and Upholstery Cleaning
[Continued]

MSA	Estab- lish- ments	Rank	Emp- ploy- ment	Rank
Philadelphia – Wilmington – Atlantic City, PA – NJ – DE – MD CMSA	143	8	760	5
Miami – Fort Lauderdale, FL CMSA	109	13	713	6
Detroit – Ann Arbor – Flint, MI CMSA	158	6	686	7
Phoenix – Mesa, AZ MSA	126	10	678	8
Atlanta, GA MSA	98	15	670	9
Kansas City, MO – KS MSA	86	16	631	10
St. Louis, MO – IL MSA	75	21	623	11
Denver – Boulder – Greeley, CO CMSA	118	11	590	12
Minneapolis – St. Paul, MN – WI MSA	77	20	580	13
Houston – Galveston – Brazoria, TX CMSA	81	17	570	14
San Diego, CA MSA	109	13	564	15
Boston – Worcester – Lawrence, MA – NH – ME – CT CMSA	128	9	547	16
Cleveland – Akron, OH CMSA	80	18	484	17
San Antonio, TX MSA	37	38	449	18
Tampa – St. Petersburg – Clearwater, FL MSA	103	14	429	19
Nashville, TN MSA	47	32	422	20
Portland – Salem, OR – WA CMSA	79	19	413	21
Orlando, FL MSA	63	24	411	22
Indianapolis, IN MSA	60	25	399	23
Cincinnati – Hamilton, OH – KY – IN CMSA	69	22	385	24
Louisville, KY – IN MSA	28	47	372	25

Source: U.S. Department of Commerce, Bureau of the Census, Data User Services Division, *1992 Economic Census, Volume 1F, Reports Series, Release 1F,* September 1995, CD-ROM. *Note:* Data are shown only for the top 25 areas.

★ 2237 ★

Establishments and Employment

Carwashes

The U.S. total number of employees is 93,081; total number of establishments is 11,589.

MSA	Estab- lish- ments	Rank	Emp- ploy- ment	Rank
Los Angeles – Riverside – Orange County, CA CMSA	720	2	8,535	1
Detroit – Ann Arbor – Flint, MI CMSA	383	4	2,906	2
San Francisco – Oakland – San Jose, CA CMSA	257	5	2,575	3
Phoenix – Mesa, AZ MSA	161	11	2,082	4
Dallas – Fort Worth, TX CMSA	164	10	2,025	5
Houston – Galveston – Brazoria, TX CMSA	140	15	1,982	6

[Continued]

★ 2237 ★

Carwashes
[Continued]

MSA	Estab-lish-ments	Rank	Emp-loy-ment	Rank
Minneapolis – St. Paul, MN – WI MSA	143	14	1,970	7
Washington – Baltimore, DC – MD – VA – WV CMSA	219	7	1,842	8
Atlanta, GA MSA	151	12	1,538	9
San Diego, CA MSA	132	16	1,153	10
Denver – Boulder – Greeley, CO CMSA	117	19	1,085	11
Milwaukee – Racine, WI CMSA	84	26	1,001	12
St. Louis, MO – IL MSA	123	17	974	13
Kansas City, MO – KS MSA	103	21	860	14
Tampa – St. Petersburg – Clearwater, FL MSA	102	22	834	15
Columbus, OH MSA	77	27	827	16
Indianapolis, IN MSA	94	23	741	17
San Antonio, TX MSA	63	31	733	18
Pittsburgh, PA MSA	92	24	723	19
Louisville, KY – IN MSA	61	32	722	20
Cincinnati – Hamilton, OH – KY – IN CMSA	89	25	691	21
Seattle – Tacoma – Bremerton, WA CMSA	150	13	685	22
Dayton – Springfield, OH MSA	45	42	649	23
Charlotte – Gastonia – Rock Hill, NC – SC MSA	65	30	567	24
Grand Rapids – Muskegon – Holland, MI MSA	61	32	547	25

Source: U.S. Department of Commerce, Bureau of the Census, Data User Services Division, *1992 Economic Census, Volume 1F, Reports Series, Release 1F,* September 1995, CD-ROM. *Note:* Data are shown only for the top 25 areas.

★ 2238 ★
Establishments and Employment

Child Day Care Services

The U.S. total number of employees is 282,675; total number of establishments is 35,327.

MSA	Estab-lish-ments	Rank	Emp-loy-ment	Rank
Los Angeles – Riverside – Orange County, CA CMSA	1,337	2	10,689	1
Dallas – Fort Worth, TX CMSA	789	7	9,487	2
Washington – Baltimore, DC – MD – VA – WV CMSA	883	4	8,882	3
Atlanta, GA MSA	727	10	8,624	4
San Francisco – Oakland – San Jose, CA CMSA	1,206	3	7,958	5
Chicago – Gary – Kenosha, IL – IN – WI CMSA	734	9	7,533	6
Boston – Worcester – Lawrence, MA – NH – ME – CT CMSA	840	5	6,044	7
Seattle – Tacoma – Bremerton, WA CMSA	713	11	5,501	8

[Continued]

★ 2238 ★

Child Day Care Services
[Continued]

MSA	Estab-lish-ments	Rank	Emp-loy-ment	Rank
Detroit – Ann Arbor – Flint, MI CMSA	666	12	5,229	9
Minneapolis – St. Paul, MN – WI MSA	570	13	4,489	10
Phoenix – Mesa, AZ MSA	312	19	4,055	11
Miami – Fort Lauderdale, FL CMSA	473	14	3,958	12
Denver – Boulder – Greeley, CO CMSA	331	17	3,945	13
St. Louis, MO – IL MSA	362	16	3,454	14
Tampa – St. Petersburg – Clearwater, FL MSA	389	15	3,162	15
Charlotte – Gastonia – Rock Hill, NC – SC MSA	292	21	2,549	16
Kansas City, MO – KS MSA	269	24	2,513	17
Indianapolis, IN MSA	229	30	2,503	18
Raleigh – Durham – Chapel Hill, NC MSA	232	29	2,501	19
Cleveland – Akron, OH CMSA	249	26	2,478	20
Cincinnati – Hamilton, OH – KY – IN CMSA	216	33	2,476	21
Oklahoma City, OK MSA	228	31	2,442	22
Portland – Salem, OR – WA CMSA	278	23	2,349	23
Orlando, FL MSA	258	25	2,315	24
Columbus, OH MSA	155	46	2,291	25

Source: U.S. Department of Commerce, Bureau of the Census, Data User Services Division, *1992 Economic Census, Volume 1F, Reports Series, Release 1F,* September 1995, CD-ROM. *Note:* Data are shown only for the top 25 areas.

★ 2239 ★
Establishments and Employment

Coin-operated Amusement Devices

The U.S. total number of employees is 28,084; total number of establishments is 4,932.

MSA	Estab-lish-ments	Rank	Emp-loy-ment	Rank
New York – Northern New Jersey – Long Island, NY – NJ – CT-CMSA	331	1	1,813	1
Las Vegas, NV – AZ MSA	62	10	1,698	2
Los Angeles – Riverside – Orange County, CA CMSA	181	2	1,086	3
Chicago – Gary – Kenosha, IL – IN – WI CMSA	148	3	840	4
Dallas – Fort Worth, TX CMSA	78	6	612	5
Boston – Worcester – Lawrence, MA – NH – ME – CT CMSA	78	6	547	6
Houston – Galveston – Brazoria, TX CMSA	54	13	411	7
Cleveland – Akron, OH CMSA	55	12	372	8
Detroit – Ann Arbor – Flint, MI CMSA	55	12	362	9

[Continued]

★2239★

Coin-operated Amusement Devices

[Continued]

MSA	Estab-lish-ments	Rank	Emp-loy-ment	Rank
Reno, NV MSA	15	37	360	10
San Antonio, TX MSA	41	17	343	11
Pittsburgh, PA MSA	71	8	342	12
Atlanta, GA MSA	58	11	330	13
Miami – Fort Lauderdale, FL CMSA	63	9	305	14
St. Louis, MO – IL MSA	50	15	302	15
Greenville – Spartanburg – Anderson, SC MSA	38	19	279	16
Minneapolis – St. Paul, MN – WI MSA	33	22	279	16
Norfolk – Virginia Beach – Newport News, VA – NC MSA	28	26	267	17
Orlando, FL MSA	40	18	264	18
Charlotte – Gastonia – Rock Hill, NC – SC MSA	35	21	256	19
Phoenix – Mesa, AZ MSA	36	20	248	20
San Diego, CA MSA	31	23	248	20
Portland – Salem, OR – WA CMSA	45	16	245	21
Honolulu, HI MSA	25	28	239	22
Seattle – Tacoma – Bremerton, WA CMSA	51	14	235	23

Source: U.S. Department of Commerce, Bureau of the Census, Data User Services Division, *1992 Economic Census, Volume 1F, Reports Series, Release 1F,* September 1995, CD-ROM. *Note:* Data are shown only for the top 25 areas.

★2240★

Establishments and Employment

Coin-operated Laundries and Drycleaning Stores

The U.S. total number of employees is 40,382; total number of establishments is 12,401.

MSA	Estab-lish-ments	Rank	Emp-loy-ment	Rank
Atlanta, GA MSA	151	13	459	6
Boston – Worcester – Lawrence, MA – NH – ME – CT CMSA	317	4	0[1]	11
Chicago – Gary – Kenosha, IL – IN – WI CMSA	489	3	0[1]	11
Cincinnati – Hamilton, OH – KY – IN CMSA	86	20	0[2]	11
Cleveland – Akron, OH CMSA	99	17	0[2]	11
Dallas – Fort Worth, TX CMSA	205	9	644	4
Denver – Boulder – Greeley, CO CMSA	83	21	0[2]	11
Detroit – Ann Arbor – Flint, MI CMSA	215	8	0[3]	11
Houston – Galveston – Brazoria, TX CMSA	154	12	0[3]	11
Indianapolis, IN MSA	94	18	0[2]	11
Kansas City, MO – KS MSA	81	22	0[4]	11
Los Angeles – Riverside – Orange County, CA CMSA	513	2	0[1]	11

[Continued]

★2240★

Coin-operated Laundries and Drycleaning Stores

[Continued]

MSA	Estab-lish-ments	Rank	Emp-loy-ment	Rank
Miami – Fort Lauderdale, FL CMSA	199	10	549	5
Milwaukee – Racine, WI CMSA	63	26	0[4]	11
Minneapolis – St. Paul, MN – WI MSA	60	27	309	8
New York – Northern New Jersey – Long Island, NY – NJ – CT-CMSA	1,536	1	3,301	1
Orlando, FL MSA	71	24	0[4]	11
Philadelphia – Wilmington – Atlantic City, PA – NJ – DE – MD CMSA	248	6	849	2
Phoenix – Mesa, AZ MSA	88	19	0[2]	11
Pittsburgh, PA MSA	79	23	293	9
Portland – Salem, OR – WA CMSA	55	28	0[4]	11
Sacramento – Yolo, CA CMSA	50	29	0[4]	11
San Diego, CA MSA	111	15	330	7
San Francisco – Oakland – San Jose, CA CMSA	242	7	823	3
Seattle – Tacoma – Bremerton, WA CMSA	122	14	0[2]	11
St. Louis, MO – IL MSA	170	11	0[3]	11
Tampa – St. Petersburg – Clearwater, FL MSA	108	16	288	10
Washington – Baltimore, DC – MD – VA – WV CMSA	311	5	0[1]	11
West Palm Beach – Boca Raton, FL MSA	67	25	0[4]	11

Source: U.S. Department of Commerce, Bureau of the Census, Data User Services Division, *1992 Economic Census, Volume 1F, Reports Series, Release 1F,* September 1995, CD-ROM. *Notes:* 1. 1,000-2,499 employees. 2. 250-499 employees. 3. 500-999 employees. 4. 100-249 employees.

★2241★

Establishments and Employment

Commercial Economic, Sociological, and Educational Research

The U.S. total number of employees is 100,729; total number of establishments is 5,165.

MSA	Estab-lish-ments	Rank	Emp-loy-ment	Rank
New York – Northern New Jersey – Long Island, NY – NJ – CT-CMSA	882	1	15,543	1
Philadelphia – Wilmington – Atlantic City, PA – NJ – DE – MD CMSA	168	7	5,492	2
Los Angeles – Riverside – Orange County, CA CMSA	346	3	5,439	3
Boston – Worcester – Lawrence, MA – NH – ME – CT CMSA	173	6	4,030	4
Tampa – St. Petersburg – Clearwater, FL MSA	41	22	2,360	5

[Continued]

★2241★

Commercial Economic, Sociological, and Educational Research

[Continued]

MSA	Establishments	Rank	Employment	Rank
Atlanta, GA MSA	101	9	2,092	6
Dallas – Fort Worth, TX CMSA	106	8	1,925	7
Minneapolis – St. Paul, MN – WI MSA	101	9	1,755	8
Phoenix – Mesa, AZ MSA	62	17	1,709	9
Denver – Boulder – Greeley, CO CMSA	100	10	1,675	10
Norfolk – Virginia Beach – Newport News, VA – NC MSA	15	37	1,335	11
Toledo, OH MSA	18	34	1,313	12
St. Louis, MO – IL MSA	57	18	1,173	13
Kansas City, MO – KS MSA	43	21	1,154	14
Seattle – Tacoma – Bremerton, WA CMSA	90	11	1,001	15
Omaha, NE – IA MSA	17	35	840	16
San Diego, CA MSA	74	14	755	17
Miami – Fort Lauderdale, FL CMSA	78	13	739	18
Austin – San Marcos, TX MSA	30	25	598	19
Greensboro – Winston-Salem – High Point, NC MSA	21	32	575	20
Indianapolis, IN MSA	27	28	557	21
Rochester, NY MSA	23	30	491	22
Salt Lake City – Ogden, UT MSA	19	33	437	23
Fort Wayne, IN MSA	4	47	406	24
Springfield, MA MSA	9	42	403	25

Source: U.S. Department of Commerce, Bureau of the Census, Data User Services Division, *1992 Economic Census, Volume 1F, Reports Series, Release 1F,* September 1995, CD-ROM. *Note:* Data are shown only for the top 25 areas.

★2242★

Establishments and Employment

Commercial Photography, Art, and Graphics

The U.S. total number of employees is 67,125; total number of establishments is 16,513.

MSA	Establishments	Rank	Employment	Rank
Los Angeles – Riverside – Orange County, CA CMSA	1,198	2	5,258	1
San Francisco – Oakland – San Jose, CA CMSA	718	4	2,631	2
Detroit – Ann Arbor – Flint, MI CMSA	363	11	2,450	3
Dallas – Fort Worth, TX CMSA	377	9	1,953	4
Boston – Worcester – Lawrence, MA – NH – ME – CT CMSA	467	6	1,757	5
Minneapolis – St. Paul, MN – WI MSA	400	7	1,690	6
Atlanta, GA MSA	371	10	1,449	7
Philadelphia – Wilmington – Atlantic City, PA – NJ – DE – MD CMSA	386	8	1,372	8

[Continued]

★2242★

Commercial Photography, Art, and Graphics

[Continued]

MSA	Establishments	Rank	Employment	Rank
Miami – Fort Lauderdale, FL CMSA	371	10	1,093	9
St. Louis, MO – IL MSA	217	15	1,063	10
Greensboro – Winston-Salem – High Point, NC MSA	100	26	940	11
Cleveland – Akron, OH CMSA	229	14	901	12
Houston – Galveston – Brazoria, TX CMSA	206	16	893	13
Denver – Boulder – Greeley, CO CMSA	253	12	882	14
Indianapolis, IN MSA	121	25	820	15
Seattle – Tacoma – Bremerton, WA CMSA	251	13	792	16
Phoenix – Mesa, AZ MSA	183	17	689	17
San Diego, CA MSA	171	18	631	18
Pittsburgh, PA MSA	129	23	551	19
Tampa – St. Petersburg – Clearwater, FL MSA	148	21	546	20
Honolulu, HI MSA	68	35	526	21
Kansas City, MO – KS MSA	122	24	480	22
Columbus, OH MSA	100	26	426	23
Dayton – Springfield, OH MSA	57	38	424	24
Louisville, KY – IN MSA	76	31	385	25

Source: U.S. Department of Commerce, Bureau of the Census, Data User Services Division, *1992 Economic Census, Volume 1F, Reports Series, Release 1F,* September 1995, CD-ROM. *Note:* Data are shown only for the top 25 areas.

★2243★

Establishments and Employment

Commercial Physical and Biological Research

The U.S. total number of employees is 111,124; total number of establishments is 3,826.

MSA	Establishments	Rank	Employment	Rank
Los Angeles – Riverside – Orange County, CA CMSA	242	5	6,766	1
San Diego, CA MSA	136	6	6,027	2
Boston – Worcester – Lawrence, MA – NH – ME – CT CMSA	257	4	5,972	3
Las Vegas, NV – AZ MSA	15	33	3,074	4
Dallas – Fort Worth, TX CMSA	37	17	2,194	5
Orlando, FL MSA	25	24	1,540	6
Huntsville, AL MSA	31	19	1,451	7
Dayton – Springfield, OH MSA	37	17	1,364	8
Albuquerque, NM MSA	40	15	1,332	9
Houston – Galveston – Brazoria, TX CMSA	62	12	1,306	10
Austin – San Marcos, TX MSA	42	14	1,104	11
Santa Barbara – Santa Maria – Lompoc, CA MSA	33	18	855	12
Colorado Springs, CO MSA	15	33	642	13
Norfolk – Virginia Beach – Newport News, VA – NC MSA	22	26	630	14

[Continued]

★2243★

Commercial Physical and Biological Research
[Continued]

MSA	Estab-lish-ments	Rank	Emp-loy-ment	Rank
Raleigh – Durham – Chapel Hill, NC MSA	39	16	523	15
Minneapolis – St. Paul, MN – WI MSA	59	13	513	16
Salt Lake City – Ogden, UT MSA	26	23	468	17
St. Louis, MO – IL MSA	27	22	337	18
Atlanta, GA MSA	33	18	290	19
Tucson, AZ MSA	20	28	266	20
Madison, WI MSA	13	34	254	21
Indianapolis, IN MSA	17	31	253	22
Melbourne – Titusville – Palm Bay, FL MSA	16	32	250	23
Springfield, MA MSA	8	39	242	24
Kansas City, MO – KS MSA	21	27	240	25

Source: U.S. Department of Commerce, Bureau of the Census, Data User Services Division, *1992 Economic Census, Volume 1F, Reports Series, Release 1F,* September 1995, CD-ROM. *Note:* Data are shown only for the top 25 areas.

★2244★

Establishments and Employment

Commercial Sports

The U.S. total number of employees is 90,439; total number of establishments is 3,751.

MSA	Estab-lish-ments	Rank	Emp-loy-ment	Rank
New York – Northern New Jersey – Long Island, NY – NJ – CT-CMSA	338	1	6,606	1
Los Angeles – Riverside – Orange County, CA CMSA	239	2	5,550	2
Miami – Fort Lauderdale, FL CMSA	135	4	3,925	3
Detroit – Ann Arbor – Flint, MI CMSA	58	9	2,788	4
Boston – Worcester – Lawrence, MA – NH – ME – CT CMSA	71	8	2,571	5
Minneapolis – St. Paul, MN – WI MSA	30	22	1,799	6
Tampa – St. Petersburg – Clearwater, FL MSA	48	13	1,708	7
New Orleans, LA MSA	23	26	1,698	8
Pittsburgh, PA MSA	38	19	1,598	9
Cleveland – Akron, OH CMSA	57	10	1,521	10
Phoenix – Mesa, AZ MSA	44	15	1,507	11
Oklahoma City, OK MSA	27	24	1,345	12
Kansas City, MO – KS MSA	18	31	1,343	13
Atlanta, GA MSA	29	23	1,325	14
Indianapolis, IN MSA	43	16	1,161	15
West Palm Beach – Boca Raton, FL MSA	33	21	1,052	16
Jacksonville, FL MSA	21	28	848	17
San Diego, CA MSA	38	19	811	18

[Continued]

★2244★

Commercial Sports
[Continued]

MSA	Estab-lish-ments	Rank	Emp-loy-ment	Rank
Denver – Boulder – Greeley, CO CMSA	44	15	772	19
St. Louis, MO – IL MSA	45	14	769	20
Daytona Beach, FL MSA	14	35	725	21
Charlotte – Gastonia – Rock Hill, NC – SC MSA	49	12	669	22
Omaha, NE – IA MSA	20	29	668	23
Louisville, KY – IN MSA	42	17	659	24
Orlando, FL MSA	35	20	649	25

Source: U.S. Department of Commerce, Bureau of the Census, Data User Services Division, *1992 Economic Census, Volume 1F, Reports Series, Release 1F,* September 1995, CD-ROM. *Note:* Data are shown only for the top 25 areas.

★2245★

Establishments and Employment

Computer Integrated Systems

The U.S. total number of employees is 97,602; total number of establishments is 5,011.

MSA	Estab-lish-ments	Rank	Emp-loy-ment	Rank
Boston – Worcester – Lawrence, MA – NH – ME – CT CMSA	172	6	4,925	1
Chicago – Gary – Kenosha, IL – IN – WI CMSA	186	5	4,258	2
San Francisco – Oakland – San Jose, CA CMSA	264	4	4,240	3
Los Angeles – Riverside – Orange County, CA CMSA	309	3	3,748	4
Atlanta, GA MSA	140	9	2,932	5
Dallas – Fort Worth, TX CMSA	145	7	2,755	6
Minneapolis – St. Paul, MN – WI MSA	101	13	2,245	7
Detroit – Ann Arbor – Flint, MI CMSA	112	11	1,783	8
St. Louis, MO – IL MSA	60	17	1,628	9
Norfolk – Virginia Beach – Newport News, VA – NC MSA	27	33	1,075	10
Dayton – Springfield, OH MSA	26	34	1,025	11
San Diego, CA MSA	65	16	938	12
Pittsburgh, PA MSA	59	18	922	13
Phoenix – Mesa, AZ MSA	46	22	859	14
Melbourne – Titusville – Palm Bay, FL MSA	21	39	849	15
Tampa – St. Petersburg – Clearwater, FL MSA	49	20	766	16
Kansas City, MO – KS MSA	42	24	711	17
Charlotte – Gastonia – Rock Hill, NC – SC MSA	32	30	700	18
Austin – San Marcos, TX MSA	32	30	693	19
Hartford, CT MSA	33	29	607	20
Columbus, OH MSA	38	26	556	21
Birmingham, AL MSA	24	36	533	22

[Continued]

★ 2245 ★

Computer Integrated Systems
[Continued]

MSA	Estab-lish-ments	Rank	Emp-loy-ment	Rank
Miami – Fort Lauderdale, FL CMSA	70	15	490	23
Jacksonville, FL MSA	26	34	486	24
Raleigh – Durham – Chapel Hill, NC MSA	34	28	436	25

Source: U.S. Department of Commerce, Bureau of the Census, Data User Services Division, *1992 Economic Census, Volume 1F, Reports Series, Release 1F,* September 1995, CD-ROM. *Note:* Data are shown only for the top 25 areas.

★ 2246 ★

Establishments and Employment

Computer Maintenance and Repair

The U.S. total number of employees is 63,064; total number of establishments is 5,041.

MSA	Estab-lish-ments	Rank	Emp-loy-ment	Rank
Boston – Worcester – Lawrence, MA – NH – ME – CT CMSA	160	6	6,496	1
Los Angeles – Riverside – Orange County, CA CMSA	362	2	5,601	2
New York – Northern New Jersey – Long Island, NY – NJ – CT-CMSA	438	1	5,515	3
Minneapolis – St. Paul, MN – WI MSA	77	15	2,693	4
Dallas – Fort Worth, TX CMSA	139	7	2,283	5
Atlanta, GA MSA	112	9	1,318	6
San Antonio, TX MSA	40	25	1,071	7
Cleveland – Akron, OH CMSA	57	18	802	8
Rochester, NY MSA	21	38	666	9
Tampa – St. Petersburg – Clearwater, FL MSA	51	20	596	10
Salt Lake City – Ogden, UT MSA	29	32	557	11
Oklahoma City, OK MSA	32	30	556	12
Miami – Fort Lauderdale, FL CMSA	80	13	554	13
St. Louis, MO – IL MSA	53	19	552	14
Memphis, TN – AR – MS MSA	32	30	545	15
Norfolk – Virginia Beach – Newport News, VA – NC MSA	24	36	480	16
Austin – San Marcos, TX MSA	33	29	476	17
San Diego, CA MSA	70	16	454	18
Pittsburgh, PA MSA	46	22	397	19
Indianapolis, IN MSA	34	28	384	20
Des Moines, IA MSA	17	41	321	21
Raleigh – Durham – Chapel Hill, NC MSA	32	30	318	22
Richmond – Petersburg, VA MSA	39	26	308	23
Columbus, OH MSA	35	27	272	24
Greensboro – Winston-Salem – High Point, NC MSA	18	40	267	25

Source: U.S. Department of Commerce, Bureau of the Census, Data User Services Division, *1992 Economic Census, Volume 1F, Reports Series, Release 1F,* September 1995, CD-ROM. *Note:* Data are shown only for the top 25 areas.

★ 2247 ★

Establishments and Employment

Computer Programming Services

The U.S. total number of employees is 242,707; total number of establishments is 23,265.

MSA	Estab-lish-ments	Rank	Emp-loy-ment	Rank
Washington – Baltimore, DC – MD – VA – WV CMSA	1,481	3	39,535	1
San Francisco – Oakland – San Jose, CA CMSA	1,550	2	15,089	2
Los Angeles – Riverside – Orange County, CA CMSA	1,319	4	13,027	3
Boston – Worcester – Lawrence, MA – NH – ME – CT CMSA	949	6	11,436	4
Chicago – Gary – Kenosha, IL – IN – WI CMSA	1,174	5	9,084	5
Dallas – Fort Worth, TX CMSA	621	9	6,303	6
Atlanta, GA MSA	664	8	6,243	7
Houston – Galveston – Brazoria, TX CMSA	462	11	6,045	8
Minneapolis – St. Paul, MN – WI MSA	544	10	5,446	9
San Diego, CA MSA	273	17	4,901	10
Detroit – Ann Arbor – Flint, MI CMSA	454	12	4,241	11
St. Louis, MO – IL MSA	313	16	2,900	12
Seattle – Tacoma – Bremerton, WA CMSA	408	14	2,713	13
Kansas City, MO – KS MSA	150	27	2,453	14
Norfolk – Virginia Beach – Newport News, VA – NC MSA	118	30	2,259	15
Cleveland – Akron, OH CMSA	267	18	2,256	16
Colorado Springs, CO MSA	71	41	2,110	17
Tampa – St. Petersburg – Clearwater, FL MSA	239	21	2,106	18
Raleigh – Durham – Chapel Hill, NC MSA	170	24	2,067	19
Pittsburgh, PA MSA	182	22	1,965	20
Dayton – Springfield, OH MSA	89	35	1,926	21
Phoenix – Mesa, AZ MSA	253	20	1,763	22
Orlando, FL MSA	181	23	1,660	23
Hartford, CT MSA	162	25	1,549	24
Miami – Fort Lauderdale, FL CMSA	352	15	1,492	25

Source: U.S. Department of Commerce, Bureau of the Census, Data User Services Division, *1992 Economic Census, Volume 1F, Reports Series, Release 1F,* September 1995, CD-ROM. *Note:* Data are shown only for the top 25 areas.

★2248★
Establishments and Employment
Computer Rental and Leasing

The U.S. total number of employees is 8,087; total number of establishments is 854.

MSA	Estab-lish-ments	Rank	Emp-ploy-ment	Rank
New York – Northern New Jersey – Long Island, NY – NJ – CT-CMSA	108	1	965	1
Boston – Worcester – Lawrence, MA – NH – ME – CT CMSA	32	7	360	2
Miami – Fort Lauderdale, FL CMSA	18	11	328	3
Houston – Galveston – Brazoria, TX CMSA	17	12	132	4
San Diego, CA MSA	13	14	108	5
St. Louis, MO – IL MSA	13	14	100	6
Minneapolis – St. Paul, MN – WI MSA	17	12	95	7
Pittsburgh, PA MSA	11	16	81	8
Kansas City, MO – KS MSA	10	17	80	9
Orlando, FL MSA	10	17	57	10
Austin – San Marcos, TX MSA	5	22	50	11
Charlotte – Gastonia – Rock Hill, NC – SC MSA	9	18	46	12
San Antonio, TX MSA	8	19	31	13
New Orleans, LA MSA	5	22	27	14
Jacksonville, FL MSA	4	23	26	15
Omaha, NE – IA MSA	6	21	19	16
Harrisburg – Lebanon – Carlisle, PA MSA	4	23	18	17
Sacramento – Yolo, CA CMSA	4	23	16	18
Honolulu, HI MSA	4	23	13	19
Las Vegas, NV – AZ MSA	3	24	10	20
Albany – Schenectady – Troy, NY MSA	3	24	0[1]	21
Albuquerque, NM MSA	1	26	0 2	1
Allentown – Bethlehem – Easton, PA MSA	0	27	0	21
Anchorage, AK MSA	0	27	0	21
Appleton – Oshkosh – Neenah, WI MSA	0	27	0	21

Source: U.S. Department of Commerce, Bureau of the Census, Data User Services Division, *1992 Economic Census, Volume 1F, Reports Series, Release 1F,* September 1995, CD-ROM. *Notes:* Data are shown only for the top 25 areas. 1. 20-99 employees.

★2249★
Establishments and Employment
Consumer Credit Reporting Agencies, Mercantile Reporting Agencies, and Adjustment and Collection Agencies

The U.S. total number of employees is 98,452; total number of establishments is 7,472.

MSA	Estab-lish-ments	Rank	Emp-ploy-ment	Rank
Los Angeles – Riverside – Orange County, CA CMSA	422	2	7,292	1
Philadelphia – Wilmington – Atlantic City, PA – NJ – DE – MD CMSA	189	4	3,725	2
Atlanta, GA MSA	165	8	3,201	3
San Francisco – Oakland – San Jose, CA CMSA	160	9	3,087	4
Minneapolis – St. Paul, MN – WI MSA	102	15	3,068	5
Dallas – Fort Worth, TX CMSA	171	7	3,043	6
Boston – Worcester – Lawrence, MA – NH – ME – CT CMSA	137	10	2,002	7
Phoenix – Mesa, AZ MSA	98	16	1,962	8
Miami – Fort Lauderdale, FL CMSA	172	6	1,815	9
Seattle – Tacoma – Bremerton, WA CMSA	108	14	1,732	10
St. Louis, MO – IL MSA	80	19	1,549	11
Columbus, OH MSA	59	24	1,512	12
Denver – Boulder – Greeley, CO CMSA	115	12	1,424	13
Tampa – St. Petersburg – Clearwater, FL MSA	88	17	1,301	14
Detroit – Ann Arbor – Flint, MI CMSA	110	13	1,209	15
Buffalo – Niagara Falls, NY MSA	40	35	1,142	16
New Orleans, LA MSA	63	21	1,131	17
Cleveland – Akron, OH CMSA	88	17	1,069	18
San Diego, CA MSA	83	18	1,014	19
Kansas City, MO – KS MSA	62	22	876	20
Nashville, TN MSA	57	26	805	21
Indianapolis, IN MSA	55	27	756	22
Louisville, KY – IN MSA	47	30	728	23
Salt Lake City – Ogden, UT MSA	60	23	726	24
Pittsburgh, PA MSA	58	25	715	25

Source: U.S. Department of Commerce, Bureau of the Census, Data User Services Division, *1992 Economic Census, Volume 1F, Reports Series, Release 1F,* September 1995, CD-ROM. *Note:* Data are shown only for the top 25 areas.

★2250★

Establishments and Employment

Dance Studios, Schools, and Halls

The U.S. total number of employees is 23,790; total number of establishments is 4,839.

MSA	Estab-lish-ments	Rank	Emp-ploy-ment	Rank
Los Angeles – Riverside – Orange County, CA CMSA	200	2	1,847	1
Washington – Baltimore, DC – MD – VA – WV CMSA	134	3	792	2
Boston – Worcester – Lawrence, MA – NH – ME – CT CMSA	117	4	530	3
Atlanta, GA MSA	74	9	429	4
Dallas – Fort Worth, TX CMSA	107	5	429	4
Detroit – Ann Arbor – Flint, MI CMSA	91	7	421	5
Minneapolis – St. Paul, MN – WI MSA	73	10	391	6
Tampa – St. Petersburg – Clearwater, FL MSA	58	13	388	7
St. Louis, MO – IL MSA	66	11	347	8
Seattle – Tacoma – Bremerton, WA CMSA	62	12	307	9
Phoenix – Mesa, AZ MSA	43	16	294	10
Miami – Fort Lauderdale, FL CMSA	81	8	281	11
Kansas City, MO – KS MSA	52	14	280	12
Pittsburgh, PA MSA	52	14	266	13
Indianapolis, IN MSA	41	18	228	14
Salt Lake City – Ogden, UT MSA	40	19	224	15
Cleveland – Akron, OH CMSA	52	14	200	16
Columbus, OH MSA	29	26	180	17
San Antonio, TX MSA	21	33	180	17
Jacksonville, FL MSA	25	29	174	18
Albany – Schenectady – Troy, NY MSA	18	35	170	19
Providence – Fall River – Warwick, RI – MA MSA	33	23	164	20
Charlotte – Gastonia – Rock Hill, NC – SC MSA	39	20	163	21
Norfolk – Virginia Beach – Newport News, VA – NC MSA	42	17	158	22
Birmingham, AL MSA	31	24	156	23

Source: U.S. Department of Commerce, Bureau of the Census, Data User Services Division, *1992 Economic Census, Volume 1F, Reports Series, Release 1F,* September 1995, CD-ROM. *Note:* Data are shown only for the top 25 areas.

★2251★

Establishments and Employment

Data Processing Schools

The U.S. total number of employees is 11,244; total number of establishments is 1,390.

MSA	Estab-lish-ments	Rank	Emp-ploy-ment	Rank
Atlanta, GA MSA	43	8	0[1]	20
Boston – Worcester – Lawrence, MA – NH – ME – CT CMSA	49	7	379	5
Chicago – Gary – Kenosha, IL – IN – WI CMSA	53	5	0[2]	20
Cincinnati – Hamilton, OH – KY – IN CMSA	12	17	128	12
Cleveland – Akron, OH CMSA	16	14	0[3]	20
Dallas – Fort Worth, TX CMSA	29	11	149	9
Denver – Boulder – Greeley, CO CMSA	39	9	122	13
Detroit – Ann Arbor – Flint, MI CMSA	51	6	950	2
Houston – Galveston – Brazoria, TX CMSA	19	12	189	8
Indianapolis, IN MSA	11	18	34	19
Kansas City, MO – KS MSA	13	16	110	15
Los Angeles – Riverside – Orange County, CA CMSA	97	2	914	4
Miami – Fort Lauderdale, FL CMSA	16	14	136	10
Milwaukee – Racine, WI CMSA	10	19	0[3]	20
Minneapolis – St. Paul, MN – WI MSA	19	12	233	7
New York – Northern New Jersey – Long Island, NY – NJ – CT-CMSA	173	1	1,589	1
Orlando, FL MSA	16	14	48	16
Philadelphia – Wilmington – Atlantic City, PA – NJ – DE – MD CMSA	35	10	0[4]	20
Phoenix – Mesa, AZ MSA	16	14	0[1]	20
Pittsburgh, PA MSA	13	16	116	14
Portland – Salem, OR – WA CMSA	14	15	0[3]	20
Sacramento – Yolo, CA CMSA	17	13	0[3]	20
San Diego, CA MSA	16	14	110	15
San Francisco – Oakland – San Jose, CA CMSA	71	4	0[2]	20
Seattle – Tacoma – Bremerton, WA CMSA	35	10	255	6
St. Louis, MO – IL MSA	14	15	135	11
Tampa – St. Petersburg – Clearwater, FL MSA	11	18	47	17
Washington – Baltimore, DC – MD – VA – WV CMSA	96	3	937	3
West Palm Beach – Boca Raton, FL MSA	12	17	36	18

Source: U.S. Department of Commerce, Bureau of the Census, Data User Services Division, *1992 Economic Census, Volume 1F, Reports Series, Release 1F,* September 1995, CD-ROM. *Notes:* 1. 100-249 employees. 2. 500-999 employees. 3. 20-99 employees. 4. 250-499 employees.

★2252★

Establishments and Employment

Data Processing Services

The U.S. total number of employees is 285,571; total number of establishments is 9,051.

MSA	Estab-lish-ments	Rank	Emp-ploy-ment	Rank
New York – Northern New Jersey – Long Island, NY – NJ – CT-CMSA	935	1	28,881	1
Dallas – Fort Worth, TX CMSA	306	6	20,496	2
Los Angeles – Riverside – Orange County, CA CMSA	590	2	18,398	3
Detroit – Ann Arbor – Flint, MI CMSA	258	9	13,788	4
San Francisco – Oakland – San Jose, CA CMSA	344	5	9,642	5
Boston – Worcester – Lawrence, MA – NH – ME – CT CMSA	267	8	9,372	6
Atlanta, GA MSA	174	12	8,535	7
St. Louis, MO – IL MSA	107	18	5,566	8
Omaha, NE – IA MSA	34	41	5,549	9
Minneapolis – St. Paul, MN – WI MSA	147	14	5,495	10
Dayton – Springfield, OH MSA	44	32	4,356	11
Denver – Boulder – Greeley, CO CMSA	176	11	4,058	12
Columbus, OH MSA	83	23	3,633	13
Cleveland – Akron, OH CMSA	128	16	3,501	14
San Diego, CA MSA	115	17	3,204	15
Seattle – Tacoma – Bremerton, WA CMSA	131	15	2,727	16
Des Moines, IA MSA	35	40	2,608	17
Milwaukee – Racine, WI CMSA	59	28	2,555	18
Charlotte – Gastonia – Rock Hill, NC – SC MSA	49	30	2,201	19
Pittsburgh, PA MSA	79	24	2,052	20
Huntsville, AL MSA	17	52	1,893	21
Jacksonville, FL MSA	42	34	1,876	22
Little Rock – North Little Rock, AR MSA	32	42	1,790	23
Hartford, CT MSA	51	29	1,585	24
Tucson, AZ MSA	15	54	1,385	25

Source: U.S. Department of Commerce, Bureau of the Census, Data User Services Division, *1992 Economic Census, Volume 1F, Reports Series, Release 1F,* September 1995, CD-ROM. *Note:* Data are shown only for the top 25 areas.

★2253★

Establishments and Employment

Dental Laboratories

The U.S. total number of employees is 39,106; total number of establishments is 7,527.

MSA	Estab-lish-ments	Rank	Emp-ploy-ment	Rank
Los Angeles – Riverside – Orange County, CA CMSA	484	2	2,196	1
San Francisco – Oakland – San Jose, CA CMSA	340	3	1,528	2
Detroit – Ann Arbor – Flint, MI CMSA	181	5	1,038	3
Minneapolis – St. Paul, MN – WI MSA	102	14	955	4
Atlanta, GA MSA	132	11	850	5
Boston – Worcester – Lawrence, MA – NH – ME – CT CMSA	137	10	694	6
Seattle – Tacoma – Bremerton, WA CMSA	149	9	676	7
St. Louis, MO – IL MSA	106	13	603	8
Dallas – Fort Worth, TX CMSA	128	12	583	9
Kansas City, MO – KS MSA	47	25	576	10
Tampa – St. Petersburg – Clearwater, FL MSA	91	17	568	11
Cleveland – Akron, OH CMSA	78	20	517	12
Miami – Fort Lauderdale, FL CMSA	152	8	512	13
Houston – Galveston – Brazoria, TX CMSA	86	18	476	14
Phoenix – Mesa, AZ MSA	100	15	432	15
Denver – Boulder – Greeley, CO CMSA	93	16	429	16
Milwaukee – Racine, WI CMSA	50	23	399	17
Indianapolis, IN MSA	39	30	390	18
San Diego, CA MSA	91	17	325	19
San Antonio, TX MSA	40	29	291	20
Buffalo – Niagara Falls, NY MSA	32	34	274	21
Harrisburg – Lebanon – Carlisle, PA MSA	19	46	266	22
Charlotte – Gastonia – Rock Hill, NC – SC MSA	32	34	260	23
Orlando, FL MSA	49	24	259	24
Columbus, OH MSA	39	30	242	25

Source: U.S. Department of Commerce, Bureau of the Census, Data User Services Division, *1992 Economic Census, Volume 1F, Reports Series, Release 1F,* September 1995, CD-ROM. *Note:* Data are shown only for the top 25 areas.

★2254★

Establishments and Employment

Detective Agencies and Protective Services

The U.S. total number of employees is 534,110; total number of establishments is 14,546.

MSA	Estab-lish-ments	Rank	Emp-loy-ment	Rank
Los Angeles – Riverside – Orange County, CA CMSA	1,158	2	47,546	1
Chicago – Gary – Kenosha, IL – IN – WI CMSA	494	4	25,872	2
Washington – Baltimore, DC – MD – VA – WV CMSA	482	5	21,051	3
San Francisco – Oakland – San Jose, CA CMSA	459	6	20,987	4
Boston – Worcester – Lawrence, MA – NH – ME – CT CMSA	349	7	15,656	5
Miami – Fort Lauderdale, FL CMSA	496	3	13,464	6
Dallas – Fort Worth, TX CMSA	332	9	12,405	7
Detroit – Ann Arbor – Flint, MI CMSA	284	11	11,212	8
Atlanta, GA MSA	266	12	10,760	9
Pittsburgh, PA MSA	122	21	7,255	10
Cleveland – Akron, OH CMSA	172	14	6,519	11
San Diego, CA MSA	174	13	6,309	12
Denver – Boulder – Greeley, CO CMSA	166	15	5,886	13
Tampa – St. Petersburg – Clearwater, FL MSA	163	16	5,768	14
Phoenix – Mesa, AZ MSA	160	17	5,442	15
New Orleans, LA MSA	113	24	5,263	16
Seattle – Tacoma – Bremerton, WA CMSA	155	18	5,052	17
Minneapolis – St. Paul, MN – WI MSA	121	22	5,015	18
St. Louis, MO – IL MSA	140	20	4,692	19
San Antonio, TX MSA	91	29	4,030	20
Honolulu, HI MSA	39	51	3,743	21
Milwaukee – Racine, WI CMSA	83	31	3,623	22
Indianapolis, IN MSA	96	26	3,607	23
Columbus, OH MSA	82	32	3,522	24
Las Vegas, NV – AZ MSA	78	34	3,513	25

Source: U.S. Department of Commerce, Bureau of the Census, Data User Services Division, *1992 Economic Census, Volume 1F, Reports Series, Release 1F,* September 1995, CD-ROM. *Note:* Data are shown only for the top 25 areas.

★2255★

Establishments and Employment

Diet and Weight Reducing Services

The U.S. total number of employees is 39,522; total number of establishments is 3,795.

MSA	Estab-lish-ments	Rank	Emp-loy-ment	Rank
Atlanta, GA MSA	51	13	729	8
Boston – Worcester – Lawrence, MA – NH – ME – CT CMSA	181	3	1,901	1
Chicago – Gary – Kenosha, IL – IN – WI CMSA	110	6	1,658	2
Cincinnati – Hamilton, OH – KY – IN CMSA	23	23	0[1]	19
Cleveland – Akron, OH CMSA	54	11	284	16
Dallas – Fort Worth, TX CMSA	70	9	874	4
Denver – Boulder – Greeley, CO CMSA	33	18	0[1]	19
Detroit – Ann Arbor – Flint, MI CMSA	71	8	339	15
Houston – Galveston – Brazoria, TX CMSA	16	25	0[2]	19
Indianapolis, IN MSA	34	17	759	7
Kansas City, MO – KS MSA	42	14	492	11
Los Angeles – Riverside – Orange County, CA CMSA	216	2	0[3]	19
Miami – Fort Lauderdale, FL CMSA	55	10	674	9
Milwaukee – Racine, WI CMSA	34	17	0[2]	19
Minneapolis – St. Paul, MN – WI MSA	32	19	1,094	3
New York – Northern New Jersey – Long Island, NY – NJ – CT-CMSA	258	1	0[4]	19
Orlando, FL MSA	28	21	670	10
Philadelphia – Wilmington – Atlantic City, PA – NJ – DE – MD CMSA	82	7	0[3]	19
Phoenix – Mesa, AZ MSA	24	22	379	14
Pittsburgh, PA MSA	37	15	262	17
Portland – Salem, OR – WA CMSA	28	21	0[5]	19
Sacramento – Yolo, CA CMSA	35	16	0[1]	19
San Diego, CA MSA	52	12	412	13
San Francisco – Oakland – San Jose, CA CMSA	131	4	801	6
Seattle – Tacoma – Bremerton, WA CMSA	51	13	0[2]	19
St. Louis, MO – IL MSA	42	14	803	5
Tampa – St. Petersburg – Clearwater, FL MSA	29	20	148	18
Washington – Baltimore, DC – MD – VA – WV CMSA	121	5	0[3]	19
West Palm Beach – Boca Raton, FL MSA	20	24	431	12

Source: U.S. Department of Commerce, Bureau of the Census, Data User Services Division, *1992 Economic Census, Volume 1F, Reports Series, Release 1F,* September 1995, CD-ROM. *Notes:* 1. 100-249 employees. 2. 500-999 employees. 3. 1,000-2,499 employees. 4. 2,500-4,999 employees. 5. 250-499 employees.

★2256★

Establishments and Employment

Drive-in Motion Picture Theaters

The U.S. total number of employees is 3,325; total number of establishments is 534.

MSA	Estab-lish-ments	Rank	Emp-loy-ment	Rank
Chicago – Gary – Kenosha, IL – IN – WI CMSA	15	2	104	1
San Diego, CA MSA	3	10	82	2
Kansas City, MO – KS MSA	6	7	54	3
Cleveland – Akron, OH CMSA	11	3	32	4
Boston – Worcester – Lawrence, MA – NH – ME – CT CMSA	6	7	30	5
Indianapolis, IN MSA	6	7	30	5
Salt Lake City – Ogden, UT MSA	4	9	26	6
Denver – Boulder – Greeley, CO CMSA	5	8	24	7
Louisville, KY – IN MSA	7	6	24	7
Harrisburg – Lebanon – Carlisle, PA MSA	3	10	16	8
Pittsburgh, PA MSA	11	3	14	9
Des Moines, IA MSA	3	10	6	10
Buffalo – Niagara Falls, NY MSA	4	9	4	11
Lexington, KY MSA	4	9	3	12
Allentown – Bethlehem – Easton, PA MSA	4	9	2	13
Scranton – Wilkes-Barre – Hazleton, PA MSA	3	10	2	13
Boise City, ID MSA	3	10	1	14
Minneapolis – St. Paul, MN – WI MSA	6	7	1	14
Albany – Schenectady – Troy, NY MSA	2	11	0[1]	15
Albuquerque, NM MSA	1	12	0[1]	15
Anchorage, AK MSA	0	13	0	15
Appleton – Oshkosh – Neenah, WI MSA	0	13	0	15
Atlanta, GA MSA	2	11	0 1	5
Augusta – Aiken, GA – SC MSA	0	13	0	15
Austin – San Marcos, TX MSA	1	12	0[1]	15

Source: U.S. Department of Commerce, Bureau of the Census, Data User Services Division, *1992 Economic Census, Volume 1F, Reports Series, Release 1F,* September 1995, CD-ROM. *Notes:* Data are shown only for the top 25 areas. 1. 0-19 employees.

★2257★

Establishments and Employment

Electrical Repair Shops

The U.S. total number of employees is 161,864; total number of establishments is 21,199.

MSA	Estab-lish-ments	Rank	Emp-loy-ment	Rank
Los Angeles – Riverside – Orange County, CA CMSA	1,013	2	10,462	1
Chicago – Gary – Kenosha, IL – IN – WI CMSA	702	3	8,065	2
Dallas – Fort Worth, TX CMSA	376	9	5,041	3
Washington – Baltimore, DC – MD – VA – WV CMSA	570	4	4,827	4
Philadelphia – Wilmington – Atlantic City, PA – NJ – DE – MD CMSA	483	7	4,529	5
Miami – Fort Lauderdale, FL CMSA	549	5	4,005	6
San Francisco – Oakland – San Jose, CA CMSA	492	6	3,995	7
Atlanta, GA MSA	290	11	3,626	8
Detroit – Ann Arbor – Flint, MI CMSA	376	9	3,209	9
Houston – Galveston – Brazoria, TX CMSA	359	10	2,867	10
Cleveland – Akron, OH CMSA	268	13	2,376	11
Seattle – Tacoma – Bremerton, WA CMSA	260	14	2,229	12
Tampa – St. Petersburg – Clearwater, FL MSA	277	12	2,212	13
St. Louis, MO – IL MSA	244	15	1,777	14
Phoenix – Mesa, AZ MSA	244	15	1,682	15
Norfolk – Virginia Beach – Newport News, VA – NC MSA	143	24	1,627	16
West Palm Beach – Boca Raton, FL MSA	136	27	1,624	17
Orlando, FL MSA	175	19	1,600	18
Denver – Boulder – Greeley, CO CMSA	236	16	1,533	19
San Diego, CA MSA	186	18	1,488	20
Minneapolis – St. Paul, MN – WI MSA	187	17	1,462	21
Pittsburgh, PA MSA	153	23	1,407	22
New Orleans, LA MSA	166	20	1,329	23
Kansas City, MO – KS MSA	165	21	1,267	24
Portland – Salem, OR – WA CMSA	155	22	1,223	25

Source: U.S. Department of Commerce, Bureau of the Census, Data User Services Division, *1992 Economic Census, Volume 1F, Reports Series, Release 1F,* September 1995, CD-ROM. *Note:* Data are shown only for the top 25 areas.

★2258★

Establishments and Employment

Employees of Federal Express, 1995: Number

City	Number	Rank
Anchorage, AK	330	7
Chicago, IL	600	6
Fort Worth, TX	600	6
Indianapolis, IN	1,830	2

[Continued]

★2258★

Employees of Federal Express, 1995: Number
[Continued]

City	Number	Rank
Los Angeles, CA	1,025	4
Memphis, TN	8,700	1
Newark, NJ	650	5
Oakland, CA	1,100	3

Source: "FedEx Reaches Deeper Into Asia From Strategic Subic Bay Hub," *Nikkei Weekly*, 27 November, 1995, p. 27. Primary source: *Nikkei Industrial Daily.*

★2259★
Establishments and Employment

Employment Agencies

The U.S. total number of employees is 132,811; total number of establishments is 12,146.

MSA	Establishments	Rank	Employment	Rank
Los Angeles – Riverside – Orange County, CA CMSA	859	2	15,002	1
San Francisco – Oakland – San Jose, CA CMSA	470	4	7,051	2
Boston – Worcester – Lawrence, MA – NH – ME – CT CMSA	366	6	5,231	3
Dallas – Fort Worth, TX CMSA	309	10	4,199	4
Atlanta, GA MSA	327	8	3,805	5
Houston – Galveston – Brazoria, TX CMSA	311	9	3,220	6
Philadelphia – Wilmington – Atlantic City, PA – NJ – DE – MD CMSA	359	7	2,992	7
San Diego, CA MSA	120	19	2,520	8
St. Louis, MO – IL MSA	140	17	2,336	9
Phoenix – Mesa, AZ MSA	127	18	2,030	10
Corpus Christi, TX MSA	12	62	1,695	11
New Orleans, LA MSA	56	34	1,488	12
Nashville, TN MSA	69	29	1,289	13
Charlotte – Gastonia – Rock Hill, NC – SC MSA	90	22	1,172	14
Detroit – Ann Arbor – Flint, MI CMSA	231	11	1,172	14
Cleveland – Akron, OH CMSA	174	13	1,170	15
El Paso, TX MSA	20	54	1,116	16
San Antonio, TX MSA	57	33	1,098	17
Pittsburgh, PA MSA	103	20	1,059	18
Tucson, AZ MSA	24	50	964	19
Providence – Fall River – Warwick, RI – MA MSA	73	27	930	20
Omaha, NE – IA MSA	50	35	861	21
Miami – Fort Lauderdale, FL CMSA	201	12	852	22
Kansas City, MO – KS MSA	97	21	776	23
Rockford, IL MSA	17	57	762	24

Source: U.S. Department of Commerce, Bureau of the Census, Data User Services Division, *1992 Economic Census, Volume 1F, Reports Series, Release 1F,* September 1995, CD-ROM. *Note:* Data are shown only for the top 25 areas.

★2260★
Establishments and Employment

Engineering Services

The U.S. total number of employees is 657,609; total number of establishments is 41,834.

MSA	Establishments	Rank	Employment	Rank
Washington – Baltimore, DC – MD – VA – WV CMSA	2,009	3	65,633	1
Los Angeles – Riverside – Orange County, CA CMSA	2,839	2	42,453	2
Houston – Galveston – Brazoria, TX CMSA	1,221	7	31,395	3
San Francisco – Oakland – San Jose, CA CMSA	1,983	4	30,998	4
Boston – Worcester – Lawrence, MA – NH – ME – CT CMSA	1,264	6	28,815	5
Detroit – Ann Arbor – Flint, MI CMSA	1,190	8	23,195	6
Philadelphia – Wilmington – Atlantic City, PA – NJ – DE – MD CMSA	1,141	9	21,737	7
Chicago – Gary – Kenosha, IL – IN – WI CMSA	1,339	5	21,238	8
Pittsburgh, PA MSA	506	17	14,359	9
Atlanta, GA MSA	718	13	12,807	10
Denver – Boulder – Greeley, CO CMSA	776	11	11,411	11
Seattle – Tacoma – Bremerton, WA CMSA	787	10	10,651	12
San Diego, CA MSA	667	14	8,153	13
Kansas City, MO – KS MSA	274	27	7,356	14
Dallas – Fort Worth, TX CMSA	764	12	7,322	15
Cleveland – Akron, OH CMSA	474	18	6,373	16
Norfolk – Virginia Beach – Newport News, VA – NC MSA	228	34	5,926	17
Minneapolis – St. Paul, MN – WI MSA	543	15	5,731	18
St. Louis, MO – IL MSA	387	22	5,603	19
Austin – San Marcos, TX MSA	256	29	5,577	20
Cincinnati – Hamilton, OH – KY – IN CMSA	318	24	5,222	21
Tampa – St. Petersburg – Clearwater, FL MSA	453	20	5,133	22
Phoenix – Mesa, AZ MSA	464	19	4,892	23
Miami – Fort Lauderdale, FL CMSA	537	16	4,557	24
Hartford, CT MSA	208	38	4,307	25

Source: U.S. Department of Commerce, Bureau of the Census, Data User Services Division, *1992 Economic Census, Volume 1F, Reports Series, Release 1F,* September 1995, CD-ROM. *Note:* Data are shown only for the top 25 areas.

★2261★

Establishments and Employment

Engineering, Accounting, Research, Management, and Related Services (except Noncommercial Research Organizations)

The U.S. total number of employees is 2,271,478; total number of establishments is 232,885.

MSA	Establishments	Rank	Employment	Rank
New York – Northern New Jersey – Long Island, NY – NJ – CT-CMSA	22,342	1	226,093	1
Los Angeles – Riverside – Orange County, CA CMSA	15,844	2	161,286	2
Washington – Baltimore, DC – MD – VA – WV CMSA	10,303	3	158,869	3
Chicago – Gary – Kenosha, IL – IN – WI CMSA	8,908	5	95,904	4
San Francisco – Oakland – San Jose, CA CMSA	9,256	4	91,103	5
Boston – Worcester – Lawrence, MA – NH – ME – CT CMSA	6,564	6	83,695	6
Philadelphia – Wilmington – Atlantic City, PA – NJ – DE – MD CMSA	5,710	7	71,077	7
Houston – Galveston – Brazoria, TX CMSA	4,907	9	67,114	8
Detroit – Ann Arbor – Flint, MI CMSA	4,741	10	58,560	9
Dallas – Fort Worth, TX CMSA	4,922	8	45,612	10
Atlanta, GA MSA	4,138	12	42,898	11
Denver – Boulder – Greeley, CO CMSA	3,785	14	33,199	12
Pittsburgh, PA MSA	1,987	22	32,428	13
Seattle – Tacoma – Bremerton, WA CMSA	3,911	13	31,528	14
Minneapolis – St. Paul, MN – WI MSA	3,190	15	28,296	15
San Diego, CA MSA	3,045	16	27,802	16
Miami – Fort Lauderdale, FL CMSA	4,590	11	27,715	17
Phoenix – Mesa, AZ MSA	2,710	17	25,027	18
Cleveland – Akron, OH CMSA	2,599	18	23,015	19
St. Louis, MO – IL MSA	2,256	20	22,558	20
Melbourne – Titusville – Palm Bay, FL MSA	432	72	19,672	21
Kansas City, MO – KS MSA	1,632	24	19,014	22
Tampa – St. Petersburg – Clearwater, FL MSA	2,394	19	18,770	23
Columbus, OH MSA	1,284	29	16,735	24
Cincinnati – Hamilton, OH – KY – IN CMSA	1,525	27	16,470	25

Source: U.S. Department of Commerce, Bureau of the Census, Data User Services Division, *1992 Economic Census, Volume 1F, Reports Series, Release 1F,* September 1995, CD-ROM. *Note:* Data are shown only for the top 25 areas.

★2262★

Establishments and Employment

Environmental Consulting

The U.S. total number of employees is 41,095; total number of establishments is 4,095.

MSA	Establishments	Rank	Employment	Rank
Atlanta, GA MSA	62	13	429	13
Boston – Worcester – Lawrence, MA – NH – ME – CT CMSA	123	6	1,481	3
Chicago – Gary – Kenosha, IL – IN – WI CMSA	105	9	0^1	21
Cincinnati – Hamilton, OH – KY – IN CMSA	32	22	0^2	21
Cleveland – Akron, OH CMSA	33	21	228	16
Dallas – Fort Worth, TX CMSA	67	12	873	5
Denver – Boulder – Greeley, CO CMSA	113	7	1,158	4
Detroit – Ann Arbor – Flint, MI CMSA	69	11	642	9
Houston – Galveston – Brazoria, TX CMSA	110	8	813	7
Indianapolis, IN MSA	22	25	170	19
Kansas City, MO – KS MSA	39	19	238	15
Los Angeles – Riverside – Orange County, CA CMSA	204	3	0^1	21
Miami – Fort Lauderdale, FL CMSA	39	19	244	14
Milwaukee – Racine, WI CMSA	20	26	0^3	21
Minneapolis – St. Paul, MN – WI MSA	40	18	856	6
New York – Northern New Jersey – Long Island, NY – NJ – CT-CMSA	286	1	2,380	2
Orlando, FL MSA	23	24	173	18
Philadelphia – Wilmington – Atlantic City, PA – NJ – DE – MD CMSA	158	5	0^1	21
Phoenix – Mesa, AZ MSA	37	20	221	17
Pittsburgh, PA MSA	39	19	519	11
Portland – Salem, OR – WA CMSA	41	17	0^2	21
Sacramento – Yolo, CA CMSA	58	14	0^4	21
San Diego, CA MSA	52	15	577	10
San Francisco – Oakland – San Jose, CA CMSA	168	4	3,429	1
Seattle – Tacoma – Bremerton, WA CMSA	79	10	703	8
St. Louis, MO – IL MSA	30	23	166	20
Tampa – St. Petersburg – Clearwater, FL MSA	47	16	487	12
Washington – Baltimore, DC – MD – VA – WV CMSA	225	2	0^5	21
West Palm Beach – Boca Raton, FL MSA	19	27	170	19

Source: U.S. Department of Commerce, Bureau of the Census, Data User Services Division, *1992 Economic Census, Volume 1F, Reports Series, Release 1F,* September 1995, CD-ROM. *Notes:* 1. 1,000-2,499 employees. 2. 250-499 employees. 3. 100-249 employees. 4. 500-999 employees. 5. 2,500-4,999 employees.

★2263★

Establishments and Employment

Equipment Rental

The U.S. total number of employees is 115,039; total number of establishments is 15,273.

MSA	Estab-lish-ments	Rank	Emp-loy-ment	Rank
Atlanta, GA MSA	274	9	2,170	3
Boston – Worcester – Lawrence, MA – NH – ME – CT CMSA	257	11	4,232	1
Chicago – Gary – Kenosha, IL – IN – WI CMSA	375	4	0[1]	20
Cincinnati – Hamilton, OH – KY – IN CMSA	130	22	0[2]	20
Cleveland – Akron, OH CMSA	156	18	1,265	11
Dallas – Fort Worth, TX CMSA	313	7	2,776	2
Denver – Boulder – Greeley, CO CMSA	185	14	1,511	10
Detroit – Ann Arbor – Flint, MI CMSA	251	12	1,983	5
Houston – Galveston – Brazoria, TX CMSA	339	6	0[1]	20
Indianapolis, IN MSA	109	25	792	16
Kansas City, MO – KS MSA	141	20	917	15
Los Angeles – Riverside – Orange County, CA CMSA	850	1	0[3]	20
Miami – Fort Lauderdale, FL CMSA	260	10	1,914	6
Milwaukee – Racine, WI CMSA	82	28	0[2]	20
Minneapolis – St. Paul, MN – WI MSA	150	19	1,681	8
New York – Northern New Jersey – Long Island, NY – NJ – CT-CMSA	822	2	0[3]	20
Orlando, FL MSA	118	24	777	17
Philadelphia – Wilmington – Atlantic City, PA – NJ – DE – MD CMSA	297	8	2,106	4
Phoenix – Mesa, AZ MSA	168	16	1,641	9
Pittsburgh, PA MSA	103	26	719	18
Portland – Salem, OR – WA CMSA	128	23	0[4]	20
Sacramento – Yolo, CA CMSA	90	27	587	19
San Diego, CA MSA	135	21	1,062	13
San Francisco – Oakland – San Jose, CA CMSA	367	5	0[1]	20
Seattle – Tacoma – Bremerton, WA CMSA	218	13	1,885	7
St. Louis, MO – IL MSA	161	17	1,257	12
Tampa – St. Petersburg – Clearwater, FL MSA	169	15	1,021	14
Washington – Baltimore, DC – MD – VA – WV CMSA	376	3	0[1]	20
West Palm Beach – Boca Raton, FL MSA	71	29	0[5]	20

Source: U.S. Department of Commerce, Bureau of the Census, Data User Services Division, *1992 Economic Census, Volume 1F, Reports Series, Release 1F,* September 1995, CD-ROM. *Notes:* 1. 2,500-4,999 employees. 2. 500-999 employees. 3. 5,000-9,999 employees. 4. 1,000-2,499 employees. 5. 250-499 employees.

★2264★

Establishments and Employment

Facilities Support Management Services

The U.S. total number of employees is 74,976; total number of establishments is 904.

MSA	Estab-lish-ments	Rank	Emp-loy-ment	Rank
Melbourne – Titusville – Palm Bay, FL MSA	17	10	15,064	1
Houston – Galveston – Brazoria, TX CMSA	32	4	1,493	2
Dallas – Fort Worth, TX CMSA	24	7	1,398	3
Norfolk – Virginia Beach – Newport News, VA – NC MSA	27	5	967	4
Memphis, TN – AR – MS MSA	10	13	595	5
Bakersfield, CA MSA	5	17	530	6
St. Louis, MO – IL MSA	8	14	391	7
El Paso, TX MSA	5	17	365	8
San Diego, CA MSA	15	12	339	9
Sacramento – Yolo, CA CMSA	5	17	336	10
Nashville, TN MSA	7	15	296	11
Oklahoma City, OK MSA	8	14	281	12
Miami – Fort Lauderdale, FL CMSA	10	13	236	13
San Antonio, TX MSA	7	15	181	14
Tampa – St. Petersburg – Clearwater, FL MSA	6	16	178	15
Kansas City, MO – KS MSA	4	18	170	16
Boston – Worcester – Lawrence, MA – NH – ME – CT CMSA	18	9	166	17
Raleigh – Durham – Chapel Hill, NC MSA	6	16	166	17
Jacksonville, FL MSA	4	18	157	18
Charlotte – Gastonia – Rock Hill, NC – SC MSA	4	18	101	19
New Orleans, LA MSA	7	15	79	20
Corpus Christi, TX MSA	4	18	72	21
Salt Lake City – Ogden, UT MSA	6	16	65	22
Austin – San Marcos, TX MSA	5	17	57	23
Sarasota – Bradenton, FL MSA	5	17	48	24

Source: U.S. Department of Commerce, Bureau of the Census, Data User Services Division, *1992 Economic Census, Volume 1F, Reports Series, Release 1F,* September 1995, CD-ROM. *Note:* Data are shown only for the top 25 areas.

★2265★

Establishments and Employment

Federal Express, 1995: Number of Parcels Handled Per Hour

City	Number	Rank
Anchorage, AK	1,800	6
Chicago, IL	32,000	5
Fort Worth, TX	67,000	3
Indianapolis, IN	96,000	2
Los Angeles, CA	32,000	5
Memphis, TN	325,000	1
Newark, NJ	64,000	4
Oakland, CA	32,000	5

Source: "FedEx Reaches Deeper Into Asia From Strategic Subic Bay Hub," *Nikkei Weekly,* 27 November, 1995, p. 27. Primary source: *Nikkei Industrial Daily.*

★2266★

Establishments and Employment

Formal Wear Rental

The U.S. total number of employees is 11,943; total number of establishments is 2,242.

MSA	Estab-lish-ments	Rank	Emp-loy-ment	Rank
Atlanta, GA MSA	21	18	138	11
Boston – Worcester – Lawrence, MA – NH – ME – CT CMSA	48	9	241	5
Chicago – Gary – Kenosha, IL – IN – WI CMSA	100	3	0[1]	21
Cincinnati – Hamilton, OH – KY – IN CMSA	18	21	52	19
Cleveland – Akron, OH CMSA	43	11	217	7
Dallas – Fort Worth, TX CMSA	44	10	268	3
Denver – Boulder – Greeley, CO CMSA	24	16	0[2]	21
Detroit – Ann Arbor – Flint, MI CMSA	54	8	253	4
Houston – Galveston – Brazoria, TX CMSA	60	7	399	2
Indianapolis, IN MSA	20	19	159	10
Kansas City, MO – KS MSA	12	26	84	14
Los Angeles – Riverside – Orange County, CA CMSA	151	2	0[1]	21
Miami – Fort Lauderdale, FL CMSA	34	13	169	9
Milwaukee – Racine, WI CMSA	17	22	0[2]	21
Minneapolis – St. Paul, MN – WI MSA	24	16	109	13
New York – Northern New Jersey – Long Island, NY – NJ – CT-CMSA	165	1	0[1]	21
Orlando, FL MSA	14	24	57	18
Philadelphia – Wilmington – Atlantic City, PA – NJ – DE – MD CMSA	62	6	0[3]	21
Phoenix – Mesa, AZ MSA	17	22	75	16
Pittsburgh, PA MSA	19	20	84	14
Portland – Salem, OR – WA CMSA	26	15	0[2]	21
Sacramento – Yolo, CA CMSA	13	25	33	20
San Diego, CA MSA	30	14	112	12
San Francisco – Oakland – San Jose, CA CMSA	64	5	406	1
Seattle – Tacoma – Bremerton, WA CMSA	40	12	221	6
St. Louis, MO – IL MSA	30	14	195	8
Tampa – St. Petersburg – Clearwater, FL MSA	23	17	76	15
Washington – Baltimore, DC – MD – VA – WV CMSA	69	4	0[3]	21
West Palm Beach – Boca Raton, FL MSA	15	23	72	17

Source: U.S. Department of Commerce, Bureau of the Census, Data User Services Division, *1992 Economic Census, Volume 1F, Reports Series, Release 1F*, September 1995, CD-ROM. *Notes:* 1. 500-999 employees. 2. 100-249 employees. 3. 250-499 employees.

★2267★

Establishments and Employment

Funeral Service and Crematories

The U.S. total number of employees is 88,328; total number of establishments is 15,647.

MSA	Estab-lish-ments	Rank	Emp-loy-ment	Rank
New York – Northern New Jersey – Long Island, NY – NJ – CT-CMSA	1,151	1	5,311	1
Los Angeles – Riverside – Orange County, CA CMSA	273	5	2,782	2
Houston – Galveston – Brazoria, TX CMSA	133	12	2,398	3
Chicago – Gary – Kenosha, IL – IN – WI CMSA	441	2	2,234	4
Detroit – Ann Arbor – Flint, MI CMSA	245	7	2,020	5
Philadelphia – Wilmington – Atlantic City, PA – NJ – DE – MD CMSA	350	4	1,414	6
Boston – Worcester – Lawrence, MA – NH – ME – CT CMSA	387	3	1,413	7
St. Louis, MO – IL MSA	163	10	1,383	8
Cleveland – Akron, OH CMSA	203	9	1,317	9
San Francisco – Oakland – San Jose, CA CMSA	161	11	1,257	10
Pittsburgh, PA MSA	258	6	1,141	11
Dallas – Fort Worth, TX CMSA	129	14	1,004	12
Miami – Fort Lauderdale, FL CMSA	90	20	939	13
Atlanta, GA MSA	112	16	854	14
Indianapolis, IN MSA	112	16	689	15
Minneapolis – St. Paul, MN – WI MSA	116	15	658	16
Tampa – St. Petersburg – Clearwater, FL MSA	86	21	647	17
Cincinnati – Hamilton, OH – KY – IN CMSA	132	13	639	18
Norfolk – Virginia Beach – Newport News, VA – NC MSA	71	26	594	19
Kansas City, MO – KS MSA	91	19	568	20
Milwaukee – Racine, WI CMSA	107	17	528	21
Seattle – Tacoma – Bremerton, WA CMSA	68	27	526	22
Providence – Fall River – Warwick, RI – MA MSA	105	18	522	23
San Antonio, TX MSA	35	43	502	24
Greensboro – Winston-Salem – High Point, NC MSA	63	30	498	25

Source: U.S. Department of Commerce, Bureau of the Census, Data User Services Division, *1992 Economic Census, Volume 1F, Reports Series, Release 1F*, September 1995, CD-ROM. *Note:* Data are shown only for the top 25 areas.

★2268★

Establishments and Employment

General Automotive Repair Shops

The U.S. total number of employees is 229,859; total number of establishments is 64,822.

MSA	Establishments	Rank	Employment	Rank
Los Angeles – Riverside – Orange County, CA CMSA	4,103	2	15,622	1
New York – Northern New Jersey – Long Island, NY – NJ – CT-CMSA	4,905	1	14,874	2
Chicago – Gary – Kenosha, IL – IN – WI CMSA	1,816	4	7,533	3
San Francisco – Oakland – San Jose, CA CMSA	1,918	3	7,104	4
Washington – Baltimore, DC – MD – VA – WV CMSA	1,579	6	6,912	5
Philadelphia – Wilmington – Atlantic City, PA – NJ – DE – MD CMSA	1,641	5	5,438	6
Houston – Galveston – Brazoria, TX CMSA	1,045	8	4,563	7
Boston – Worcester – Lawrence, MA – NH – ME – CT CMSA	1,321	7	4,428	8
Detroit – Ann Arbor – Flint, MI CMSA	970	11	4,098	9
Dallas – Fort Worth, TX CMSA	1,003	9	3,838	10
Miami – Fort Lauderdale, FL CMSA	972	10	3,177	11
Atlanta, GA MSA	809	12	3,141	12
Seattle – Tacoma – Bremerton, WA CMSA	789	13	3,086	13
San Diego, CA MSA	710	14	2,886	14
Phoenix – Mesa, AZ MSA	674	16	2,860	15
St. Louis, MO – IL MSA	700	15	2,823	16
Cleveland – Akron, OH CMSA	634	18	2,704	17
Minneapolis – St. Paul, MN – WI MSA	560	21	2,568	18
Denver – Boulder – Greeley, CO CMSA	654	17	2,524	19
Portland – Salem, OR – WA CMSA	517	22	2,218	20
Pittsburgh, PA MSA	632	19	2,047	21
Sacramento – Yolo, CA CMSA	417	24	2,024	22
Tampa – St. Petersburg – Clearwater, FL MSA	612	20	2,023	23
Cincinnati – Hamilton, OH – KY – IN CMSA	432	23	1,822	24
Milwaukee – Racine, WI CMSA	398	26	1,637	25

Source: U.S. Department of Commerce, Bureau of the Census, Data User Services Division, *1992 Economic Census, Volume 1F, Reports Series, Release 1F*, September 1995, CD-ROM. *Note:* Data are shown only for the top 25 areas.

★2269★

Establishments and Employment

Health Services

The U.S. total number of employees is 4,452,539; total number of establishments is 441,705.

MSA	Establishments	Rank	Employment	Rank
New York – Northern New Jersey – Long Island, NY – NJ – CT-CMSA	40,598	1	333,550	1
Los Angeles – Riverside – Orange County, CA CMSA	30,586	2	277,681	2
Chicago – Gary – Kenosha, IL – IN – WI CMSA	14,559	3	136,277	3
Boston – Worcester – Lawrence, MA – NH – ME – CT CMSA	9,768	7	115,133	4
San Francisco – Oakland – San Jose, CA CMSA	14,042	4	113,625	5
Washington – Baltimore, DC – MD – VA – WV CMSA	12,935	5	110,051	6
Philadelphia – Wilmington – Atlantic City, PA – NJ – DE – MD CMSA	11,596	6	99,845	7
Miami – Fort Lauderdale, FL CMSA	9,141	9	86,935	8
Dallas – Fort Worth, TX CMSA	8,319	10	86,093	9
Detroit – Ann Arbor – Flint, MI CMSA	9,421	8	84,065	10
Houston – Galveston – Brazoria, TX CMSA	7,063	11	74,702	11
Tampa – St. Petersburg – Clearwater, FL MSA	4,938	15	61,188	12
Atlanta, GA MSA	6,093	12	59,853	13
Seattle – Tacoma – Bremerton, WA CMSA	6,059	13	54,201	14
Cleveland – Akron, OH CMSA	5,370	14	51,319	15
Minneapolis – St. Paul, MN – WI MSA	3,723	21	49,923	16
St. Louis, MO – IL MSA	4,449	19	43,605	17
San Diego, CA MSA	4,929	16	41,651	18
Phoenix – Mesa, AZ MSA	4,809	17	38,536	19
Pittsburgh, PA MSA	4,764	18	38,143	20
Denver – Boulder – Greeley, CO CMSA	4,372	20	35,705	21
Cincinnati – Hamilton, OH – KY – IN CMSA	3,136	23	34,791	22
Milwaukee – Racine, WI CMSA	3,030	24	34,149	23
Kansas City, MO – KS MSA	2,855	26	33,776	24
Indianapolis, IN MSA	2,542	29	32,169	25

Source: U.S. Department of Commerce, Bureau of the Census, Data User Services Division, *1992 Economic Census, Volume 1F, Reports Series, Release 1F*, September 1995, CD-ROM. *Note:* Data are shown only for the top 25 areas.

★2270★
Establishments and Employment
Heavy Construction Equipment Rental and Leasing

The U.S. total number of employees is 34,704; total number of establishments is 3,853.

MSA	Establishments	Rank	Employment	Rank
Los Angeles – Riverside – Orange County, CA CMSA	430	1	3,685	1
New York – Northern New Jersey – Long Island, NY – NJ – CT-CMSA	234	2	2,348	2
Houston – Galveston – Brazoria, TX CMSA	108	5	1,646	3
Miami – Fort Lauderdale, FL CMSA	80	10	727	4
San Diego, CA MSA	97	8	698	5
Phoenix – Mesa, AZ MSA	54	13	680	6
Boston – Worcester – Lawrence, MA – NH – ME – CT CMSA	107	6	669	7
New Orleans, LA MSA	34	19	578	8
San Antonio, TX MSA	22	24	509	9
Cleveland – Akron, OH CMSA	28	22	486	10
Atlanta, GA MSA	60	12	449	11
Orlando, FL MSA	26	23	434	12
Las Vegas, NV – AZ MSA	43	15	421	13
Pittsburgh, PA MSA	35	18	378	14
Tampa – St. Petersburg – Clearwater, FL MSA	42	16	361	15
Dallas – Fort Worth, TX CMSA	46	14	350	16
Beaumont – Port Arthur, TX MSA	12	33	288	17
Lafayette, LA MSA	18	27	279	18
St. Louis, MO – IL MSA	28	22	263	19
Cincinnati – Hamilton, OH – KY – IN CMSA	20	26	253	20
Birmingham, AL MSA	14	31	251	21
Fresno, CA MSA	18	27	247	22
Jacksonville, FL MSA	20	26	225	23
Indianapolis, IN MSA	21	25	221	24
Buffalo – Niagara Falls, NY MSA	20	26	217	25

Source: U.S. Department of Commerce, Bureau of the Census, Data User Services Division, *1992 Economic Census, Volume 1F, Reports Series, Release 1F*, September 1995, CD-ROM. *Note:* Data are shown only for the top 25 areas.

★2271★
Establishments and Employment
Help Supply Services

The U.S. total number of employees is 1,841,921; total number of establishments is 19,020.

MSA	Establishments	Rank	Employment	Rank
Los Angeles – Riverside – Orange County, CA CMSA	1,307	2	137,790	1
Houston – Galveston – Brazoria, TX CMSA	488	9	80,146	2
Tampa – St. Petersburg – Clearwater, FL MSA	254	15	62,372	3
San Francisco – Oakland – San Jose, CA CMSA	705	4	62,344	4
Dallas – Fort Worth, TX CMSA	602	6	57,269	5
Boston – Worcester – Lawrence, MA – NH – ME – CT CMSA	551	7	49,923	6
Detroit – Ann Arbor – Flint, MI CMSA	488	9	42,989	7
Atlanta, GA MSA	512	8	40,973	8
Philadelphia – Wilmington – Atlantic City, PA – NJ – DE – MD CMSA	470	10	32,078	9
Miami – Fort Lauderdale, FL CMSA	333	11	30,139	10
Minneapolis – St. Paul, MN – WI MSA	287	13	29,596	11
Cleveland – Akron, OH CMSA	295	12	28,385	12
Phoenix – Mesa, AZ MSA	240	17	22,938	13
Columbus, OH MSA	141	26	21,133	14
St. Louis, MO – IL MSA	183	18	21,130	15
Seattle – Tacoma – Bremerton, WA CMSA	249	16	19,729	16
Denver – Boulder – Greeley, CO CMSA	274	14	19,368	17
San Diego, CA MSA	174	22	16,485	18
Kansas City, MO – KS MSA	165	24	16,185	19
Indianapolis, IN MSA	115	29	15,874	20
New Orleans, LA MSA	131	27	15,587	21
Raleigh – Durham – Chapel Hill, NC MSA	111	31	15,261	22
Greenville – Spartanburg – Anderson, SC MSA	83	42	14,822	23
Sarasota – Bradenton, FL MSA	62	51	14,752	24
Salt Lake City – Ogden, UT MSA	97	36	12,993	25

Source: U.S. Department of Commerce, Bureau of the Census, Data User Services Division, *1992 Economic Census, Volume 1F, Reports Series, Release 1F*, September 1995, CD-ROM. *Note:* Data are shown only for the top 25 areas.

★2272★

Establishments and Employment

Home Health Care Services

The U.S. total number of employees is 341,889; total number of establishments is 8,045.

MSA	Estab-lish-ments	Rank	Emp-ploy-ment	Rank
New York – Northern New Jersey – Long Island, NY – NJ – CT-CMSA	596	1	49,515	1
Miami – Fort Lauderdale, FL CMSA	329	2	9,586	2
Los Angeles – Riverside – Orange County, CA CMSA	329	2	9,377	3
Boston – Worcester – Lawrence, MA – NH – ME – CT CMSA	159	6	9,008	4
Dallas – Fort Worth, TX CMSA	151	8	7,504	5
Tampa – St. Petersburg – Clearwater, FL MSA	135	9	6,845	6
Buffalo – Niagara Falls, NY MSA	40	30	5,247	7
San Antonio, TX MSA	56	23	5,057	8
Detroit – Ann Arbor – Flint, MI CMSA	134	10	4,631	9
Minneapolis – St. Paul, MN – WI MSA	69	17	4,508	10
Atlanta, GA MSA	152	7	4,246	11
Cleveland – Akron, OH CMSA	96	12	3,591	12
Pittsburgh, PA MSA	86	14	3,419	13
St. Louis, MO – IL MSA	84	15	3,026	14
Seattle – Tacoma – Bremerton, WA CMSA	66	19	2,904	15
Orlando, FL MSA	66	19	2,895	16
Beaumont – Port Arthur, TX MSA	27	39	2,659	17
West Palm Beach – Boca Raton, FL MSA	67	18	2,558	18
Norfolk – Virginia Beach – Newport News, VA – NC MSA	42	29	2,468	19
Nashville, TN MSA	66	19	2,423	20
Kansas City, MO – KS MSA	59	22	2,344	21
New Orleans, LA MSA	90	13	2,275	22
Charlotte – Gastonia – Rock Hill, NC – SC MSA	43	28	2,247	23
Albany – Schenectady – Troy, NY MSA	36	33	2,132	24
Phoenix – Mesa, AZ MSA	64	20	2,082	25

Source: U.S. Department of Commerce, Bureau of the Census, Data User Services Division, *1992 Economic Census, Volume 1F, Reports Series, Release 1F,* September 1995, CD-ROM. *Note:* Data are shown only for the top 25 areas.

★2273★

Establishments and Employment

Hospitals

The U.S. total number of employees is 428,150; total number of establishments is 1,403.

MSA	Estab-lish-ments	Rank	Emp-ploy-ment	Rank
Los Angeles – Riverside – Orange County, CA CMSA	127	1	41,403	1
Miami – Fort Lauderdale, FL CMSA	41	4	19,781	2
Dallas – Fort Worth, TX CMSA	64	2	17,511	3
Tampa – St. Petersburg – Clearwater, FL MSA	32	5	13,556	4
New York – Northern New Jersey – Long Island, NY – NJ – CT-CMSA	28	7	13,493	5
Atlanta, GA MSA	25	9	8,186	6
New Orleans, LA MSA	30	6	8,056	7
Boston – Worcester – Lawrence, MA – NH – ME – CT CMSA	25	9	7,220	8
Richmond – Petersburg, VA MSA	11	14	6,896	9
Nashville, TN MSA	13	12	5,515	10
Las Vegas, NV – AZ MSA	10	15	5,339	11
San Antonio, TX MSA	17	10	5,087	12
West Palm Beach – Boca Raton, FL MSA	13	12	5,000	13
San Diego, CA MSA	13	12	3,773	14
Orlando, FL MSA	10	15	3,458	15
Austin – San Marcos, TX MSA	15	11	3,455	16
Phoenix – Mesa, AZ MSA	11	14	3,433	17
Albuquerque, NM MSA	6	19	3,377	18
Sarasota – Bradenton, FL MSA	7	18	3,160	19
Tucson, AZ MSA	10	15	3,014	20
Oklahoma City, OK MSA	6	19	2,488	21
Kansas City, MO – KS MSA	12	13	2,437	22
Chattanooga, TN – GA MSA	9	16	2,423	23
Beaumont – Port Arthur, TX MSA	6	19	2,293	24
Charleston – North Charleston, SC MSA	5	20	2,274	25

Source: U.S. Department of Commerce, Bureau of the Census, Data User Services Division, *1992 Economic Census, Volume 1F, Reports Series, Release 1F,* September 1995, CD-ROM. *Note:* Data are shown only for the top 25 areas.

★2274★

Establishments and Employment

Hotels

The U.S. total number of employees is 1,160,693; total number of establishments is 16,665.

MSA	Estab-lish-ments	Rank	Emp-ploy-ment	Rank
Las Vegas, NV – AZ MSA	160	14	106,301	1
Los Angeles – Riverside – Orange County, CA CMSA	911	1	65,375	2
New York – Northern New Jersey – Long Island, NY – NJ – CT-CMSA	708	2	62,343	3
Philadelphia – Wilmington – Atlantic City, PA – NJ – DE – MD CMSA	356	5	58,518	4

[Continued]

★2274★

Hotels
[Continued]

MSA	Establishments	Rank	Employment	Rank
San Francisco – Oakland – San Jose, CA CMSA	572	3	35,816	5
Orlando, FL MSA	198	12	30,835	6
Miami – Fort Lauderdale, FL CMSA	380	4	26,099	7
Dallas – Fort Worth, TX CMSA	215	10	23,935	8
Reno, NV MSA	68	35	22,894	9
Boston – Worcester – Lawrence, MA – NH – ME – CT CMSA	258	8	21,845	10
Phoenix – Mesa, AZ MSA	133	18	19,664	11
Honolulu, HI MSA	118	20	19,362	12
San Diego, CA MSA	210	11	19,031	13
Atlanta, GA MSA	228	9	18,770	14
New Orleans, LA MSA	109	21	12,257	15
Detroit – Ann Arbor – Flint, MI CMSA	167	13	11,320	16
Tampa – St. Petersburg – Clearwater, FL MSA	153	15	10,616	17
St. Louis, MO – IL MSA	123	19	9,282	18
Minneapolis – St. Paul, MN – WI MSA	89	25	8,858	19
Denver – Boulder – Greeley, CO CMSA	102	22	8,769	20
Pittsburgh, PA MSA	89	25	8,610	21
West Palm Beach – Boca Raton, FL MSA	74	33	8,299	22
Nashville, TN MSA	84	28	8,267	23
Cincinnati – Hamilton, OH – KY – IN CMSA	80	29	7,367	24
Cleveland – Akron, OH CMSA	86	27	7,076	25

Source: U.S. Department of Commerce, Bureau of the Census, Data User Services Division, *1992 Economic Census, Volume 1F, Reports Series, Release 1F,* September 1995, CD-ROM. *Note:* Data are shown only for the top 25 areas.

★2275★

Establishments and Employment

Hotels, Rooming Houses, Camps, and Other Lodging Places (except Membership Lodging)

The U.S. total number of employees is 1,489,058; total number of establishments is 48,619.

MSA	Establishments	Rank	Employment	Rank
Las Vegas, NV – AZ MSA	344	18	108,237	1
Los Angeles – Riverside – Orange County, CA CMSA	2,120	1	75,648	2
Washington – Baltimore, DC – MD – VA – WV CMSA	716	6	43,594	3
San Francisco – Oakland – San Jose, CA CMSA	1,202	3	42,201	4
Chicago – Gary – Kenosha, IL – IN – WI CMSA	656	7	36,513	5
Orlando, FL MSA	420	15	35,866	6

[Continued]

★2275★

Hotels, Rooming Houses, Camps, and Other Lodging Places (except Membership Lodging)
[Continued]

MSA	Establishments	Rank	Employment	Rank
Miami – Fort Lauderdale, FL CMSA	737	5	29,330	7
Dallas – Fort Worth, TX CMSA	467	12	26,833	8
Boston – Worcester – Lawrence, MA – NH – ME – CT CMSA	619	8	25,351	9
Reno, NV MSA	169	38	23,756	10
San Diego, CA MSA	484	9	22,186	11
Phoenix – Mesa, AZ MSA	311	19	21,988	12
Atlanta, GA MSA	450	13	21,864	13
Seattle – Tacoma – Bremerton, WA CMSA	444	14	14,585	14
Detroit – Ann Arbor – Flint, MI CMSA	473	11	14,372	15
Tampa – St. Petersburg – Clearwater, FL MSA	477	10	13,806	16
New Orleans, LA MSA	186	35	13,291	17
Minneapolis – St. Paul, MN – WI MSA	253	25	11,479	18
St. Louis, MO – IL MSA	274	23	10,922	19
Denver – Boulder – Greeley, CO CMSA	256	24	10,787	20
Norfolk – Virginia Beach – Newport News, VA – NC MSA	368	16	10,757	21
Pittsburgh, PA MSA	208	30	10,118	22
Nashville, TN MSA	206	31	10,044	23
West Palm Beach – Boca Raton, FL MSA	166	39	9,191	24
Cleveland – Akron, OH CMSA	248	26	9,177	25

Source: U.S. Department of Commerce, Bureau of the Census, Data User Services Division, *1992 Economic Census, Volume 1F, Reports Series, Release 1F,* September 1995, CD-ROM. *Note:* Data are shown only for the top 25 areas.

★2276★

Establishments and Employment

Individual and Family Social Services

The U.S. total number of employees is 42,550; total number of establishments is 7,373.

MSA	Establishments	Rank	Employment	Rank
Atlanta, GA MSA	97	15	366	14
Boston – Worcester – Lawrence, MA – NH – ME – CT CMSA	144	9	1,907	1
Chicago – Gary – Kenosha, IL – IN – WI CMSA	225	4	1,592	2
Cincinnati – Hamilton, OH – KY – IN CMSA	28	27	0[1]	21
Cleveland – Akron, OH CMSA	72	19	0[2]	21
Dallas – Fort Worth, TX CMSA	183	7	887	7
Denver – Boulder – Greeley, CO CMSA	99	14	450	11
Detroit – Ann Arbor – Flint, MI CMSA	169	8	0[3]	21

[Continued]

★2276★

Individual and Family Social Services
[Continued]

MSA	Estab-lish-ments	Rank	Emp-ploy-ment	Rank
Houston – Galveston – Brazoria, TX CMSA	86	16	0[1]	21
Indianapolis, IN MSA	48	24	194	19
Kansas City, MO – KS MSA	51	23	310	16
Los Angeles – Riverside – Orange County, CA CMSA	530	1	0[4]	21
Miami – Fort Lauderdale, FL CMSA	117	10	539	10
Milwaukee – Racine, WI CMSA	59	22	0[2]	21
Minneapolis – St. Paul, MN – WI MSA	112	12	1,170	5
New York – Northern New Jersey – Long Island, NY – NJ – CT-CMSA	480	2	0[4]	21
Orlando, FL MSA	60	21	196	18
Philadelphia – Wilmington – Atlantic City, PA – NJ – DE – MD CMSA	116	11	0[5]	21
Phoenix – Mesa, AZ MSA	97	15	647	8
Pittsburgh, PA MSA	32	26	191	20
Portland – Salem, OR – WA CMSA	105	13	0[2]	21
Sacramento – Yolo, CA CMSA	71	20	368	13
San Diego, CA MSA	86	16	356	15
San Francisco – Oakland – San Jose, CA CMSA	266	3	981	6
Seattle – Tacoma – Bremerton, WA CMSA	193	6	1,264	3
St. Louis, MO – IL MSA	74	18	632	9
Tampa – St. Petersburg – Clearwater, FL MSA	81	17	375	12
Washington – Baltimore, DC – MD – VA – WV CMSA	209	5	1,177	4
West Palm Beach – Boca Raton, FL MSA	44	25	264	17

Source: U.S. Department of Commerce, Bureau of the Census, Data User Services Division, *1992 Economic Census, Volume 1F, Reports Series, Release 1F,* September 1995, CD-ROM. *Notes:* 1. 100-249 employees. 2. 250-499 employees. 3. 500-999 employees. 4. 2,500-4,999 employees. 5. 1,000-2,499 employees.

★2277★

Establishments and Employment

Information Retrieval Services

The U.S. total number of employees is 31,869; total number of establishments is 1,090.

MSA	Estab-lish-ments	Rank	Emp-ploy-ment	Rank
Atlanta, GA MSA	22	11	0[1]	12
Boston – Worcester – Lawrence, MA – NH – ME – CT CMSA	42	6	897	3
Chicago – Gary – Kenosha, IL – IN – WI CMSA	42	6	2,107	1
Cincinnati – Hamilton, OH – KY – IN CMSA	5	19	99	8

[Continued]

★2277★

Information Retrieval Services
[Continued]

MSA	Estab-lish-ments	Rank	Emp-ploy-ment	Rank
Cleveland – Akron, OH CMSA	9	17	0[2]	12
Dallas – Fort Worth, TX CMSA	52	5	0[1]	12
Denver – Boulder – Greeley, CO CMSA	26	10	0[3]	12
Detroit – Ann Arbor – Flint, MI CMSA	16	13	0[3]	12
Houston – Galveston – Brazoria, TX CMSA	37	7	577	5
Indianapolis, IN MSA	9	17	0[2]	12
Kansas City, MO – KS MSA	8	18	65	10
Los Angeles – Riverside – Orange County, CA CMSA	74	2	0[1]	12
Miami – Fort Lauderdale, FL CMSA	27	9	609	4
Milwaukee – Racine, WI CMSA	5	19	0[2]	12
Minneapolis – St. Paul, MN – WI MSA	18	12	410	6
New York – Northern New Jersey – Long Island, NY – NJ – CT-CMSA	100	1	0[4]	12
Orlando, FL MSA	8	18	0[5]	12
Philadelphia – Wilmington – Atlantic City, PA – NJ – DE – MD CMSA	35	8	0[6]	12
Phoenix – Mesa, AZ MSA	11	15	0[2]	12
Pittsburgh, PA MSA	8	18	0[2]	12
Portland – Salem, OR – WA CMSA	11	15	0[5]	12
Sacramento – Yolo, CA CMSA	18	12	0[6]	12
San Diego, CA MSA	15	14	0[6]	12
San Francisco – Oakland – San Jose, CA CMSA	64	4	0[1]	12
Seattle – Tacoma – Bremerton, WA CMSA	18	12	0[3]	12
St. Louis, MO – IL MSA	8	18	79	9
Tampa – St. Petersburg – Clearwater, FL MSA	10	16	209	7
Washington – Baltimore, DC – MD – VA – WV CMSA	71	3	1,922	2
West Palm Beach – Boca Raton, FL MSA	8	18	39	11

Source: U.S. Department of Commerce, Bureau of the Census, Data User Services Division, *1992 Economic Census, Volume 1F, Reports Series, Release 1F,* September 1995, CD-ROM. *Notes:* 1. 1,000-2,499 employees. 2. 100-249 employees. 3. 250-499 employees. 4. 2,500-4,999 employees. 5. 20-99 employees. 6. 500-999 employees.

★2278★

Establishments and Employment

Interior Designing

The U.S. total number of employees is 20,648; total number of establishments is 6,202.

MSA	Estab-lish-ments	Rank	Emp-ploy-ment	Rank
Los Angeles – Riverside – Orange County, CA CMSA	514	2	2,265	1
Chicago – Gary – Kenosha, IL – IN – WI CMSA	298	3	970	2
San Francisco – Oakland – San Jose, CA CMSA	193	6	879	3
Miami – Fort Lauderdale, FL CMSA	270	4	692	4
Atlanta, GA MSA	162	8	678	5
Dallas – Fort Worth, TX CMSA	163	7	665	6
Philadelphia – Wilmington – Atlantic City, PA – NJ – DE – MD CMSA	151	9	576	7
West Palm Beach – Boca Raton, FL MSA	134	10	410	8
Detroit – Ann Arbor – Flint, MI CMSA	104	12	353	9
Boston – Worcester – Lawrence, MA – NH – ME – CT CMSA	105	11	299	10
Cleveland – Akron, OH CMSA	88	13	277	11
Seattle – Tacoma – Bremerton, WA CMSA	80	16	272	12
San Diego, CA MSA	83	15	253	13
Minneapolis – St. Paul, MN – WI MSA	79	17	232	14
St. Louis, MO – IL MSA	74	19	217	15
Tampa – St. Petersburg – Clearwater, FL MSA	86	14	215	16
Indianapolis, IN MSA	38	28	190	17
Pittsburgh, PA MSA	37	29	188	18
Orlando, FL MSA	41	26	186	19
Kansas City, MO – KS MSA	46	24	148	20
Syracuse, NY MSA	8	52	136	21
Honolulu, HI MSA	30	33	131	22
Sacramento – Yolo, CA CMSA	40	27	130	23
Charlotte – Gastonia – Rock Hill, NC – SC MSA	42	25	125	24
Greensboro – Winston-Salem – High Point, NC MSA	51	21	115	25

Source: U.S. Department of Commerce, Bureau of the Census, Data User Services Division, *1992 Economic Census, Volume 1F, Reports Series, Release 1F,* September 1995, CD-ROM. *Note:* Data are shown only for the top 25 areas.

★2279★

Establishments and Employment

Intermediate Care Facilities

The U.S. total number of employees is 164,704; total number of establishments is 3,375.

MSA	Estab-lish-ments	Rank	Emp-ploy-ment	Rank
Boston – Worcester – Lawrence, MA – NH – ME – CT CMSA	118	1	6,251	1
Washington – Baltimore, DC – MD – VA – WV CMSA	84	4	4,169	2
New York – Northern New Jersey – Long Island, NY – NJ – CT-CMSA	59	7	2,675	3
Oklahoma City, OK MSA	38	13	2,413	4
Indianapolis, IN MSA	68	5	2,277	5
Minneapolis – St. Paul, MN – WI MSA	110	2	2,117	6
St. Louis, MO – IL MSA	37	14	2,115	7
Tulsa, OK MSA	31	17	1,971	8
Dallas – Fort Worth, TX CMSA	44	9	1,923	9
Norfolk – Virginia Beach – Newport News, VA – NC MSA	16	24	1,877	10
Nashville, TN MSA	16	24	1,586	11
Houston – Galveston – Brazoria, TX CMSA	36	15	1,233	12
Portland, ME MSA	12	28	1,147	13
New Orleans, LA MSA	15	25	1,079	14
Columbus, OH MSA	32	16	1,026	15
Des Moines, IA MSA	17	23	968	16
Kansas City, MO – KS MSA	23	19	938	17
Scranton – Wilkes-Barre – Hazleton, PA MSA	8	32	605	18
Richmond – Petersburg, VA MSA	8	32	565	19
Tampa – St. Petersburg – Clearwater, FL MSA	8	32	565	19
Rockford, IL MSA	11	29	480	20
San Francisco – Oakland – San Jose, CA CMSA	21	21	466	21
Seattle – Tacoma – Bremerton, WA CMSA	14	26	462	22
Charlotte – Gastonia – Rock Hill, NC – SC MSA	15	25	426	23
Greensboro – Winston-Salem – High Point, NC MSA	9	31	378	24

Source: U.S. Department of Commerce, Bureau of the Census, Data User Services Division, *1992 Economic Census, Volume 1F, Reports Series, Release 1F,* September 1995, CD-ROM. *Note:* Data are shown only for the top 25 areas.

★2280★
Establishments and Employment

Job Training and Vocational Rehabilitation Services

The U.S. total number of employees is 32,078; total number of establishments is 2,643.

MSA	Establishments	Rank	Employment	Rank
Atlanta, GA MSA	46	10	606	8
Boston – Worcester – Lawrence, MA – NH – ME – CT CMSA	44	12	919	3
Chicago – Gary – Kenosha, IL – IN – WI CMSA	62	7	0[1]	21
Cincinnati – Hamilton, OH – KY – IN CMSA	9	26	0[2]	21
Cleveland – Akron, OH CMSA	21	21	0[3]	21
Dallas – Fort Worth, TX CMSA	35	15	747	5
Denver – Boulder – Greeley, CO CMSA	43	13	0[3]	21
Detroit – Ann Arbor – Flint, MI CMSA	48	9	693	6
Houston – Galveston – Brazoria, TX CMSA	24	19	0[2]	21
Indianapolis, IN MSA	8	27	256	14
Kansas City, MO – KS MSA	23	20	121	18
Los Angeles – Riverside – Orange County, CA CMSA	264	1	0[4]	21
Miami – Fort Lauderdale, FL CMSA	27	18	385	13
Milwaukee – Racine, WI CMSA	16	24	93	19
Minneapolis – St. Paul, MN – WI MSA	77	5	632	7
New York – Northern New Jersey – Long Island, NY – NJ – CT-CMSA	87	4	1,236	2
Orlando, FL MSA	18	23	158	17
Philadelphia – Wilmington – Atlantic City, PA – NJ – DE – MD CMSA	62	7	0[4]	21
Phoenix – Mesa, AZ MSA	36	14	472	12
Pittsburgh, PA MSA	20	22	566	10
Portland – Salem, OR – WA CMSA	55	8	0[3]	21
Sacramento – Yolo, CA CMSA	45	11	510	11
San Diego, CA MSA	34	16	572	9
San Francisco – Oakland – San Jose, CA CMSA	128	2	1,610	1
Seattle – Tacoma – Bremerton, WA CMSA	88	3	789	4
St. Louis, MO – IL MSA	16	24	160	16
Tampa – St. Petersburg – Clearwater, FL MSA	28	17	180	15
Washington – Baltimore, DC – MD – VA – WV CMSA	75	6	0[1]	21
West Palm Beach – Boca Raton, FL MSA	12	25	27	20

Source: U.S. Department of Commerce, Bureau of the Census, Data User Services Division, *1992 Economic Census, Volume 1F, Reports Series, Release 1F*, September 1995, CD-ROM. *Notes:* 1. 500-999 employees. 2. 100-249 employees. 3. 250-499 employees. 4. 1,000-2,499 employees.

★2281★
Establishments and Employment

Kidney Dialysis Centers

The U.S. total number of employees is 21,195; total number of establishments is 1,119.

MSA	Establishments	Rank	Employment	Rank
Los Angeles – Riverside – Orange County, CA CMSA	101	1	2,062	1
New York – Northern New Jersey – Long Island, NY – NJ – CT-CMSA	39	4	1,331	2
Washington – Baltimore, DC – MD – VA – WV CMSA	58	2	987	3
Miami – Fort Lauderdale, FL CMSA	33	6	639	4
Chicago – Gary – Kenosha, IL – IN – WI CMSA	30	7	636	5
San Antonio, TX MSA	16	11	363	6
New Orleans, LA MSA	20	10	319	7
San Diego, CA MSA	13	13	273	8
Tampa – St. Petersburg – Clearwater, FL MSA	21	9	259	9
Atlanta, GA MSA	20	10	244	10
St. Louis, MO – IL MSA	13	13	162	11
Kansas City, MO – KS MSA	6	19	150	12
Greensboro – Winston-Salem – High Point, NC MSA	7	18	148	13
West Palm Beach – Boca Raton, FL MSA	12	14	141	14
Norfolk – Virginia Beach – Newport News, VA – NC MSA	5	20	130	15
Greenville – Spartanburg – Anderson, SC MSA	5	20	111	16
Corpus Christi, TX MSA	4	21	108	17
Orlando, FL MSA	9	16	100	18
Sarasota – Bradenton, FL MSA	6	19	86	19
Fresno, CA MSA	4	21	53	20
Daytona Beach, FL MSA	5	20	49	21
Beaumont – Port Arthur, TX MSA	3	22	38	22
Albany – Schenectady – Troy, NY MSA	3	22	0[1]	23
Albuquerque, NM MSA	3	22	0[1]	23
Allentown – Bethlehem – Easton, PA MSA	3	22	0[1]	23

Source: U.S. Department of Commerce, Bureau of the Census, Data User Services Division, *1992 Economic Census, Volume 1F, Reports Series, Release 1F*, September 1995, CD-ROM. *Notes:* Data are shown only for the top 25 areas. 1. 20-99 employees.

★2282★

Establishments and Employment

Laundry, Cleaning, and Garment Services

The U.S. total number of employees is 425,829; total number of establishments is 55,760.

MSA	Estab-lish-ments	Rank	Emp-ploy-ment	Rank
New York – Northern New Jersey – Long Island, NY – NJ – CT-CMSA	5,929	1	30,594	1
Los Angeles – Riverside – Orange County, CA CMSA	3,505	2	26,766	2
Chicago – Gary – Kenosha, IL – IN – WI CMSA	2,038	3	14,607	3
Washington – Baltimore, DC – MD – VA – WV CMSA	1,732	4	12,064	4
San Francisco – Oakland – San Jose, CA CMSA	1,614	5	11,118	5
Boston – Worcester – Lawrence, MA – NH – ME – CT CMSA	1,300	6	9,385	6
Dallas – Fort Worth, TX CMSA	1,190	8	9,291	7
Detroit – Ann Arbor – Flint, MI CMSA	1,139	9	9,011	8
Philadelphia – Wilmington – Atlantic City, PA – NJ – DE – MD CMSA	1,199	7	8,597	9
Houston – Galveston – Brazoria, TX CMSA	846	12	8,150	10
Atlanta, GA MSA	950	11	6,902	11
Miami – Fort Lauderdale, FL CMSA	960	10	6,640	12
Cleveland – Akron, OH CMSA	579	17	5,105	13
Minneapolis – St. Paul, MN – WI MSA	501	19	4,993	14
St. Louis, MO – IL MSA	648	14	4,874	15
Phoenix – Mesa, AZ MSA	523	18	4,619	16
San Diego, CA MSA	591	16	4,618	17
Seattle – Tacoma – Bremerton, WA CMSA	699	13	4,612	18
Denver – Boulder – Greeley, CO CMSA	619	15	4,420	19
Kansas City, MO – KS MSA	448	21	3,760	20
Pittsburgh, PA MSA	448	21	3,756	21
Cincinnati – Hamilton, OH – KY – IN CMSA	425	22	3,690	22
Indianapolis, IN MSA	418	23	3,494	23
Tampa – St. Petersburg – Clearwater, FL MSA	488	20	3,417	24
San Antonio, TX MSA	353	27	3,293	25

Source: U.S. Department of Commerce, Bureau of the Census, Data User Services Division, *1992 Economic Census, Volume 1F, Reports Series, Release 1F*, September 1995, CD-ROM. *Note:* Data are shown only for the top 25 areas.

★2283★

Establishments and Employment

Legal Services

The U.S. total number of employees is 923,617; total number of establishments is 151,737.

MSA	Estab-lish-ments	Rank	Emp-ploy-ment	Rank
New York – Northern New Jersey – Long Island, NY – NJ – CT-CMSA	14,978	1	120,798	1
Los Angeles – Riverside – Orange County, CA CMSA	10,504	2	69,401	2
Washington – Baltimore, DC – MD – VA – WV CMSA	5,261	4	50,318	3
Chicago – Gary – Kenosha, IL – IN – WI CMSA	5,386	3	39,966	4
San Francisco – Oakland – San Jose, CA CMSA	5,107	5	36,420	5
Philadelphia – Wilmington – Atlantic City, PA – NJ – DE – MD CMSA	3,836	8	32,975	6
Boston – Worcester – Lawrence, MA – NH – ME – CT CMSA	4,046	7	27,191	7
Miami – Fort Lauderdale, FL CMSA	4,064	6	19,549	8
Dallas – Fort Worth, TX CMSA	2,792	11	19,141	9
Houston – Galveston – Brazoria, TX CMSA	2,902	10	19,041	10
Detroit – Ann Arbor – Flint, MI CMSA	2,938	9	17,279	11
Atlanta, GA MSA	2,183	12	13,455	12
Seattle – Tacoma – Bremerton, WA CMSA	1,938	13	12,960	13
Minneapolis – St. Paul, MN – WI MSA	1,402	18	12,900	14
Denver – Boulder – Greeley, CO CMSA	1,804	15	10,974	15
San Diego, CA MSA	1,838	14	10,811	16
Cleveland – Akron, OH CMSA	1,538	16	10,595	17
Phoenix – Mesa, AZ MSA	1,396	19	9,831	18
Pittsburgh, PA MSA	1,130	23	8,924	19
Tampa – St. Petersburg – Clearwater, FL MSA	1,532	17	8,775	20
St. Louis, MO – IL MSA	1,276	21	8,607	21
New Orleans, LA MSA	1,390	20	8,176	22
Portland – Salem, OR – WA CMSA	1,181	22	6,969	23
Kansas City, MO – KS MSA	913	27	6,797	24
Milwaukee – Racine, WI CMSA	881	29	6,694	25

Source: U.S. Department of Commerce, Bureau of the Census, Data User Services Division, *1992 Economic Census, Volume 1F, Reports Series, Release 1F*, September 1995, CD-ROM. *Note:* Data are shown only for the top 25 areas.

★2284★
Establishments and Employment
Libraries

The U.S. total number of employees is 902; total number of establishments is 232.

MSA	Estab- lish- ments	Rank	Emp- ploy- ment	Rank
Houston – Galveston – Brazoria, TX CMSA	9	4	61	1
San Francisco – Oakland – San Jose, CA CMSA	9	4	50	2
Los Angeles – Riverside – Orange County, CA CMSA	12	2	36	3
Dallas – Fort Worth, TX CMSA	7	5	32	4
Miami – Fort Lauderdale, FL CMSA	3	8	20	5
Rochester, NY MSA	4	7	12	6
San Antonio, TX MSA	3	8	8	7
Kansas City, MO – KS MSA	4	7	5	8
Albuquerque, NM MSA	3	8	3	9
Lafayette, LA MSA	3	8	3	9
Albany – Schenectady – Troy, NY MSA	1	10	0[1]	10
Allentown – Bethlehem – Easton, PA MSA	0	11	0	10
Anchorage, AK MSA	0	11	0	10
Appleton – Oshkosh – Neenah, WI MSA	0	11	0	10
Atlanta, GA MSA	3	8	0[1]	10
Augusta – Aiken, GA – SC MSA	0	11	0	10
Austin – San Marcos, TX MSA	2	9	0[1]	10
Bakersfield, CA MSA	0	11	0	10
Baton Rouge, LA MSA	3	8	0[1]	10
Beaumont – Port Arthur, TX MSA	0	11	0	10
Birmingham, AL MSA	0	11	0	10
Boise City, ID MSA	1	10	0 1	0
Boston – Worcester – Lawrence, MA – NH – ME – CT CMSA	0	11	0	10
Buffalo – Niagara Falls, NY MSA	0	11	0	10
Canton – Massillon, OH MSA	0	11	0	10

Source: U.S. Department of Commerce, Bureau of the Census, Data User Services Division, *1992 Economic Census, Volume 1F, Reports Series, Release 1F,* September 1995, CD-ROM. *Notes:* Data are shown only for the top 25 areas. 1. 0-19 employees.

★2285★
Establishments and Employment
Mailing, Reproduction, Commercial Art and Photography, and Stenographic Services

The U.S. total number of employees is 234,595; total number of establishments is 32,086.

MSA	Estab- lish- ments	Rank	Emp- ploy- ment	Rank
New York – Northern New Jersey – Long Island, NY – NJ – CT-CMSA	4,390	1	35,210	1
Los Angeles – Riverside – Orange County, CA CMSA	2,452	2	21,544	2
Washington – Baltimore, DC – MD – VA – WV CMSA	1,282	5	11,649	3
San Francisco – Oakland – San Jose, CA CMSA	1,427	4	10,584	4
Dallas – Fort Worth, TX CMSA	781	7	7,025	5
Philadelphia – Wilmington – Atlantic City, PA – NJ – DE – MD CMSA	762	8	6,991	6
Boston – Worcester – Lawrence, MA – NH – ME – CT CMSA	842	6	6,075	7
Detroit – Ann Arbor – Flint, MI CMSA	665	11	5,741	8
Minneapolis – St. Paul, MN – WI MSA	673	10	4,974	9
Atlanta, GA MSA	658	12	4,673	10
Houston – Galveston – Brazoria, TX CMSA	523	14	4,506	11
Miami – Fort Lauderdale, FL CMSA	751	9	3,795	12
Seattle – Tacoma – Bremerton, WA CMSA	559	13	3,219	13
St. Louis, MO – IL MSA	364	19	3,208	14
Cleveland – Akron, OH CMSA	399	18	2,994	15
San Diego, CA MSA	439	16	2,616	16
Pittsburgh, PA MSA	237	25	2,595	17
Phoenix – Mesa, AZ MSA	411	17	2,554	18
Tampa – St. Petersburg – Clearwater, FL MSA	320	21	2,523	19
Cincinnati – Hamilton, OH – KY – IN CMSA	236	26	2,148	20
Milwaukee – Racine, WI CMSA	264	22	2,089	21
Portland – Salem, OR – WA CMSA	322	20	1,952	22
Kansas City, MO – KS MSA	252	23	1,903	23
Indianapolis, IN MSA	201	28	1,680	24
Sacramento – Yolo, CA CMSA	239	24	1,572	25

Source: U.S. Department of Commerce, Bureau of the Census, Data User Services Division, *1992 Economic Census, Volume 1F, Reports Series, Release 1F,* September 1995, CD-ROM. *Note:* Data are shown only for the top 25 areas.

★2286★

Establishments and Employment

Management and Public Relations Services

The U.S. total number of employees is 643,952; total number of establishments is 72,130.

MSA	Estab-lish-ments	Rank	Emp-ploy-ment	Rank
New York – Northern New Jersey – Long Island, NY – NJ – CT-CMSA	8,911	1	71,791	1
Washington – Baltimore, DC – MD – VA – WV CMSA	4,458	3	51,556	2
Los Angeles – Riverside – Orange County, CA CMSA	5,254	2	46,651	3
Chicago – Gary – Kenosha, IL – IN – WI CMSA	3,438	4	32,423	4
San Francisco – Oakland – San Jose, CA CMSA	2,906	5	23,267	5
Boston – Worcester – Lawrence, MA – NH – ME – CT CMSA	2,334	6	21,928	6
Philadelphia – Wilmington – Atlantic City, PA – NJ – DE – MD CMSA	2,081	7	21,533	7
Dallas – Fort Worth, TX CMSA	1,792	8	18,585	8
Houston – Galveston – Brazoria, TX CMSA	1,510	11	16,744	9
Melbourne – Titusville – Palm Bay, FL MSA	118	68	15,692	10
Atlanta, GA MSA	1,550	10	15,119	11
Detroit – Ann Arbor – Flint, MI CMSA	1,400	12	13,837	12
Miami – Fort Lauderdale, FL CMSA	1,578	9	10,550	13
Minneapolis – St. Paul, MN – WI MSA	1,249	13	9,001	14
Pittsburgh, PA MSA	582	23	6,680	15
Seattle – Tacoma – Bremerton, WA CMSA	1,158	15	6,554	16
St. Louis, MO – IL MSA	748	19	6,540	17
Cleveland – Akron, OH CMSA	883	17	6,447	18
San Diego, CA MSA	912	16	6,247	19
Phoenix – Mesa, AZ MSA	877	18	5,917	20
West Palm Beach – Boca Raton, FL MSA	591	22	5,166	21
Orlando, FL MSA	535	24	5,124	22
Sacramento – Yolo, CA CMSA	524	26	5,014	23
Columbus, OH MSA	430	29	4,775	24
Kansas City, MO – KS MSA	533	25	4,653	25

Source: U.S. Department of Commerce, Bureau of the Census, Data User Services Division, *1992 Economic Census, Volume 1F, Reports Series, Release 1F,* September 1995, CD-ROM. *Note:* Data are shown only for the top 25 areas.

★2287★

Establishments and Employment

Management Consulting Services

The U.S. total number of employees is 211,781; total number of establishments is 33,762.

MSA	Estab-lish-ments	Rank	Emp-ploy-ment	Rank
New York – Northern New Jersey – Long Island, NY – NJ – CT-CMSA	4,453	1	32,991	1
Chicago – Gary – Kenosha, IL – IN – WI CMSA	1,826	4	13,734	2
Los Angeles – Riverside – Orange County, CA CMSA	2,128	3	12,900	3
Boston – Worcester – Lawrence, MA – NH – ME – CT CMSA	1,331	6	11,667	4
San Francisco – Oakland – San Jose, CA CMSA	1,425	5	9,211	5
Philadelphia – Wilmington – Atlantic City, PA – NJ – DE – MD CMSA	1,028	7	6,665	6
Atlanta, GA MSA	824	8	6,236	7
Dallas – Fort Worth, TX CMSA	773	9	6,040	8
Detroit – Ann Arbor – Flint, MI CMSA	695	10	4,698	9
Houston – Galveston – Brazoria, TX CMSA	586	14	4,144	10
Minneapolis – St. Paul, MN – WI MSA	683	12	3,204	11
Miami – Fort Lauderdale, FL CMSA	690	11	3,148	12
Cleveland – Akron, OH CMSA	445	17	2,877	13
San Diego, CA MSA	408	18	2,259	14
Seattle – Tacoma – Bremerton, WA CMSA	557	15	2,242	15
Pittsburgh, PA MSA	282	22	1,855	16
St. Louis, MO – IL MSA	368	19	1,658	17
Phoenix – Mesa, AZ MSA	446	16	1,626	18
Tampa – St. Petersburg – Clearwater, FL MSA	352	20	1,608	19
Kansas City, MO – KS MSA	253	25	1,293	20
San Antonio, TX MSA	141	38	1,289	21
Hartford, CT MSA	128	39	1,272	22
Milwaukee – Racine, WI CMSA	270	24	1,252	23
Sacramento – Yolo, CA CMSA	195	29	1,226	24
Portland – Salem, OR – WA CMSA	312	21	1,190	25

Source: U.S. Department of Commerce, Bureau of the Census, Data User Services Division, *1992 Economic Census, Volume 1F, Reports Series, Release 1F,* September 1995, CD-ROM. *Note:* Data are shown only for the top 25 areas.

★2288★

Establishments and Employment

Management Services

The U.S. total number of employees is 277,718; total number of establishments is 19,733.

MSA	Estab-lish-ments	Rank	Emp-loy-ment	Rank
Los Angeles – Riverside – Orange County, CA CMSA	1,707	2	24,305	1
Chicago – Gary – Kenosha, IL – IN – WI CMSA	821	4	14,858	2
Philadelphia – Wilmington – Atlantic City, PA – NJ – DE – MD CMSA	598	6	12,482	3
Dallas – Fort Worth, TX CMSA	554	7	9,409	4
Houston – Galveston – Brazoria, TX CMSA	515	9	9,276	5
San Francisco – Oakland – San Jose, CA CMSA	644	5	7,972	6
Detroit – Ann Arbor – Flint, MI CMSA	395	11	7,239	7
Atlanta, GA MSA	355	12	7,120	8
Boston – Worcester – Lawrence, MA – NH – ME – CT CMSA	523	8	6,889	9
Miami – Fort Lauderdale, FL CMSA	492	10	5,795	10
Orlando, FL MSA	154	23	3,671	11
Pittsburgh, PA MSA	173	22	3,615	12
Minneapolis – St. Paul, MN – WI MSA	248	17	3,418	13
St. Louis, MO – IL MSA	186	20	3,389	14
Phoenix – Mesa, AZ MSA	243	18	3,096	15
San Diego, CA MSA	255	16	2,864	16
Cleveland – Akron, OH CMSA	259	15	2,850	17
West Palm Beach – Boca Raton, FL MSA	180	21	2,722	18
Grand Rapids – Muskegon – Holland, MI MSA	70	44	2,574	19
Columbus, OH MSA	120	30	2,534	20
Kansas City, MO – KS MSA	141	24	2,511	21
Seattle – Tacoma – Bremerton, WA CMSA	292	13	2,429	22
Jacksonville, FL MSA	71	43	2,313	23
Indianapolis, IN MSA	138	25	2,239	24
Austin – San Marcos, TX MSA	128	28	2,129	25

Source: U.S. Department of Commerce, Bureau of the Census, Data User Services Division, *1992 Economic Census, Volume 1F, Reports Series, Release 1F,* September 1995, CD-ROM. *Note:* Data are shown only for the top 25 areas.

★2289★

Establishments and Employment

Massage Parlors, Tanning Salons, and Saunas

The U.S. total number of employees is 16,252; total number of establishments is 4,354.

MSA	Estab-lish-ments	Rank	Emp-loy-ment	Rank
Atlanta, GA MSA	52	15	217	12
Boston – Worcester – Lawrence, MA – NH – ME – CT CMSA	78	10	284	8
Chicago – Gary – Kenosha, IL – IN – WI CMSA	171	3	523	5
Cincinnati – Hamilton, OH – KY – IN CMSA	42	17	0[1]	24
Cleveland – Akron, OH CMSA	59	14	158	14
Dallas – Fort Worth, TX CMSA	102	8	960	2
Denver – Boulder – Greeley, CO CMSA	69	12	235	11
Detroit – Ann Arbor – Flint, MI CMSA	131	6	441	6
Houston – Galveston – Brazoria, TX CMSA	42	17	235	11
Indianapolis, IN MSA	52	15	266	10
Kansas City, MO – KS MSA	36	18	126	15
Los Angeles – Riverside – Orange County, CA CMSA	244	1	1,076	1
Miami – Fort Lauderdale, FL CMSA	42	17	87	17
Milwaukee – Racine, WI CMSA	27	20	88	16
Minneapolis – St. Paul, MN – WI MSA	89	9	376	7
New York – Northern New Jersey – Long Island, NY – NJ – CT-CMSA	238	2	0[2]	24
Orlando, FL MSA	16	23	48	21
Philadelphia – Wilmington – Atlantic City, PA – NJ – DE – MD CMSA	76	11	0[3]	24
Phoenix – Mesa, AZ MSA	24	22	57	20
Pittsburgh, PA MSA	27	20	74	18
Portland – Salem, OR – WA CMSA	36	18	0[1]	24
Sacramento – Yolo, CA CMSA	25	21	71	19
San Diego, CA MSA	49	16	193	13
San Francisco – Oakland – San Jose, CA CMSA	139	4	810	3
Seattle – Tacoma – Bremerton, WA CMSA	134	5	529	4
St. Louis, MO – IL MSA	63	13	274	9
Tampa – St. Petersburg – Clearwater, FL MSA	31	19	38	23
Washington – Baltimore, DC – MD – VA – WV CMSA	114	7	0[2]	24
West Palm Beach – Boca Raton, FL MSA	13	24	41	22

Source: U.S. Department of Commerce, Bureau of the Census, Data User Services Division, *1992 Economic Census, Volume 1F, Reports Series, Release 1F,* September 1995, CD-ROM. *Notes:* 1. 100-249 employees. 2. 500-999 employees. 3. 250-499 employees.

Medical Equipment Rental and Leasing

The U.S. total number of employees is 31,062; total number of establishments is 3,276.

MSA	Establishments	Rank	Employment	Rank
Philadelphia – Wilmington – Atlantic City, PA – NJ – DE – MD CMSA	69	5	2,002	1
Los Angeles – Riverside – Orange County, CA CMSA	144	2	1,716	2
New York – Northern New Jersey – Long Island, NY – NJ – CT-CMSA	160	1	1,563	3
Pittsburgh, PA MSA	47	11	776	4
Dallas – Fort Worth, TX CMSA	56	7	672	5
Miami – Fort Lauderdale, FL CMSA	127	3	624	6
Houston – Galveston – Brazoria, TX CMSA	41	13	541	7
Denver – Boulder – Greeley, CO CMSA	31	17	513	8
St. Louis, MO – IL MSA	34	16	484	9
San Diego, CA MSA	21	22	451	10
Boston – Worcester – Lawrence, MA – NH – ME – CT CMSA	54	8	434	11
Cleveland – Akron, OH CMSA	35	15	404	12
Minneapolis – St. Paul, MN – WI MSA	21	22	401	13
Atlanta, GA MSA	38	14	366	14
Indianapolis, IN MSA	15	26	360	15
Cincinnati – Hamilton, OH – KY – IN CMSA	23	21	327	16
Tampa – St. Petersburg – Clearwater, FL MSA	43	12	324	17
Kansas City, MO – KS MSA	21	22	273	18
Phoenix – Mesa, AZ MSA	30	18	240	19
Orlando, FL MSA	29	19	232	20
Hartford, CT MSA	9	32	228	21
Louisville, KY – IN MSA	21	22	204	22
Buffalo – Niagara Falls, NY MSA	13	28	193	23
Jacksonville, FL MSA	17	24	192	24
Raleigh – Durham – Chapel Hill, NC MSA	8	33	190	25

Source: U.S. Department of Commerce, Bureau of the Census, Data User Services Division, *1992 Economic Census, Volume 1F, Reports Series, Release 1F,* September 1995, CD-ROM. *Note:* Data are shown only for the top 25 areas.

Medical Laboratories

The U.S. total number of employees is 138,760; total number of establishments is 8,434.

MSA	Establishments	Rank	Employment	Rank
New York – Northern New Jersey – Long Island, NY – NJ – CT-CMSA	829	1	15,625	1
Los Angeles – Riverside – Orange County, CA CMSA	658	2	11,762	2
Boston – Worcester – Lawrence, MA – NH – ME – CT CMSA	217	8	4,717	3
Detroit – Ann Arbor – Flint, MI CMSA	149	10	4,040	4
Chicago – Gary – Kenosha, IL – IN – WI CMSA	260	6	3,781	5
San Francisco – Oakland – San Jose, CA CMSA	285	5	3,595	6
Miami – Fort Lauderdale, FL CMSA	302	3	3,081	7
Dallas – Fort Worth, TX CMSA	165	9	2,723	8
Tampa – St. Petersburg – Clearwater, FL MSA	123	14	2,595	9
Columbus, OH MSA	41	30	2,481	10
Seattle – Tacoma – Bremerton, WA CMSA	130	12	2,325	11
Pittsburgh, PA MSA	124	13	2,318	12
San Diego, CA MSA	106	16	2,282	13
Houston – Galveston – Brazoria, TX CMSA	142	11	1,968	14
Atlanta, GA MSA	124	13	1,916	15
Kansas City, MO – KS MSA	57	24	1,793	16
Milwaukee – Racine, WI CMSA	42	29	1,590	17
Nashville, TN MSA	49	26	1,419	18
Phoenix – Mesa, AZ MSA	89	18	1,185	19
San Antonio, TX MSA	75	19	1,165	20
Cleveland – Akron, OH CMSA	107	15	1,154	21
Indianapolis, IN MSA	69	22	1,152	22
Denver – Boulder – Greeley, CO CMSA	69	22	1,082	23
Greensboro – Winston-Salem – High Point, NC MSA	34	33	1,077	24
Hartford, CT MSA	74	20	1,045	25

Source: U.S. Department of Commerce, Bureau of the Census, Data User Services Division, *1992 Economic Census, Volume 1F, Reports Series, Release 1F,* September 1995, CD-ROM. *Note:* Data are shown only for the top 25 areas.

★2292★

Establishments and Employment

Membership Sports and Recreation Clubs

The U.S. total number of employees is 124,632; total number of establishments is 7,275.

MSA	Estab-lish-ments	Rank	Emp-loy-ment	Rank
Los Angeles – Riverside – Orange County, CA CMSA	226	2	8,242	1
Chicago – Gary – Kenosha, IL – IN – WI CMSA	171	6	4,958	2
West Palm Beach – Boca Raton, FL MSA	62	16	3,857	3
Boston – Worcester – Lawrence, MA – NH – ME – CT CMSA	185	4	3,367	4
Minneapolis – St. Paul, MN – WI MSA	100	9	3,356	5
San Francisco – Oakland – San Jose, CA CMSA	132	7	3,064	6
Houston – Galveston – Brazoria, TX CMSA	88	11	2,879	7
Miami – Fort Lauderdale, FL CMSA	85	12	2,785	8
Dallas – Fort Worth, TX CMSA	91	10	2,733	9
Detroit – Ann Arbor – Flint, MI CMSA	118	8	2,549	10
Atlanta, GA MSA	76	15	2,220	11
Phoenix – Mesa, AZ MSA	42	25	1,623	12
Tampa – St. Petersburg – Clearwater, FL MSA	56	18	1,574	13
Orlando, FL MSA	45	23	1,566	14
St. Louis, MO – IL MSA	77	14	1,496	15
Cleveland – Akron, OH CMSA	82	13	1,180	16
Fort Pierce – Port St. Lucie, FL MSA	24	38	1,124	17
Sarasota – Bradenton, FL MSA	35	30	1,020	18
San Diego, CA MSA	45	23	1,007	19
Jacksonville, FL MSA	27	35	985	20
Pittsburgh, PA MSA	58	17	953	21
Tucson, AZ MSA	21	41	900	22
Fort Myers – Cape Coral, FL MSA	22	40	811	23
Las Vegas, NV – AZ MSA	23	39	764	24
Daytona Beach, FL MSA	25	37	755	25

Source: U.S. Department of Commerce, Bureau of the Census, Data User Services Division, *1992 Economic Census, Volume 1F, Reports Series, Release 1F,* September 1995, CD-ROM. *Note:* Data are shown only for the top 25 areas.

★2293★

Establishments and Employment

Motels, Motor Hotels, and Tourist Courts

The U.S. total number of employees is 295,231; total number of establishments is 25,019.

MSA	Estab-lish-ments	Rank	Emp-loy-ment	Rank
New York – Northern New Jersey – Long Island, NY – NJ – CT-CMSA	668	2	9,032	1
Los Angeles – Riverside – Orange County, CA CMSA	946	1	8,530	2
San Francisco – Oakland – San Jose, CA CMSA	445	4	5,432	3
Philadelphia – Wilmington – Atlantic City, PA – NJ – DE – MD CMSA	477	3	3,919	4
Orlando, FL MSA	167	17	3,832	5
Norfolk – Virginia Beach – Newport News, VA – NC MSA	237	11	3,583	6
Miami – Fort Lauderdale, FL CMSA	323	6	3,119	7
Boston – Worcester – Lawrence, MA – NH – ME – CT CMSA	245	10	3,085	8
Atlanta, GA MSA	206	15	3,016	9
Dallas – Fort Worth, TX CMSA	216	13	2,781	10
Detroit – Ann Arbor – Flint, MI CMSA	245	10	2,750	11
Tampa – St. Petersburg – Clearwater, FL MSA	232	12	2,640	12
San Diego, CA MSA	212	14	2,527	13
Myrtle Beach, SC MSA	247	8	2,494	14
Knoxville, TN MSA	206	15	2,360	15
Minneapolis – St. Paul, MN – WI MSA	119	24	2,352	16
Portland – Salem, OR – WA CMSA	133	20	2,111	17
Daytona Beach, FL MSA	146	19	2,015	18
Cleveland – Akron, OH CMSA	127	21	1,958	19
Jacksonville, FL MSA	118	25	1,912	20
Indianapolis, IN MSA	84	36	1,877	21
Denver – Boulder – Greeley, CO CMSA	124	22	1,833	22
Phoenix – Mesa, AZ MSA	122	23	1,809	23
Las Vegas, NV – AZ MSA	154	18	1,715	24
Nashville, TN MSA	105	26	1,621	25

Source: U.S. Department of Commerce, Bureau of the Census, Data User Services Division, *1992 Economic Census, Volume 1F, Reports Series, Release 1F,* September 1995, CD-ROM. *Note:* Data are shown only for the top 25 areas.

★2294★

Establishments and Employment

Motion Picture Production, Distribution, and Services

The U.S. total number of employees is 249,225; total number of establishments is 12,967.

MSA	Estab-lish-ments	Rank	Emp-loy-ment	Rank
Los Angeles – Riverside – Orange County, CA CMSA	4,869	1	143,966	1
New York – Northern New Jersey – Long Island, NY – NJ – CT-CMSA	2,173	2	32,230	2
Dallas – Fort Worth, TX CMSA	227	6	3,472	3
Atlanta, GA MSA	170	12	2,833	4
Miami – Fort Lauderdale, FL CMSA	215	7	1,576	5
Boston – Worcester – Lawrence, MA – NH – ME – CT CMSA	194	8	1,440	6
Minneapolis – St. Paul, MN – WI MSA	172	11	1,298	7
Pittsburgh, PA MSA	73	20	1,181	8
Orlando, FL MSA	67	22	863	9
Nashville, TN MSA	83	16	775	10
Salt Lake City – Ogden, UT MSA	61	24	764	11
St. Louis, MO – IL MSA	81	18	699	12
Phoenix – Mesa, AZ MSA	79	19	584	13
San Diego, CA MSA	82	17	542	14
Cleveland – Akron, OH CMSA	59	25	518	15
Charlotte – Gastonia – Rock Hill, NC – SC MSA	53	27	514	16
Tampa – St. Petersburg – Clearwater, FL MSA	66	23	364	17
Kansas City, MO – KS MSA	53	27	306	18
Memphis, TN – AR – MS MSA	31	34	292	19
Des Moines, IA MSA	24	40	283	20
Provo – Orem, UT MSA	24	40	228	21
Columbus, OH MSA	23	41	202	22
Richmond – Petersburg, VA MSA	27	37	192	23
Norfolk – Virginia Beach – Newport News, VA – NC MSA	27	37	184	24
Honolulu, HI MSA	42	28	177	25

Source: U.S. Department of Commerce, Bureau of the Census, Data User Services Division, *1992 Economic Census, Volume 1F, Reports Series, Release 1F,* September 1995, CD-ROM. *Note:* Data are shown only for the top 25 areas.

★2295★

Establishments and Employment

Motion Picture Theaters

The U.S. total number of employees is 105,188; total number of establishments is 6,892.

MSA	Estab-lish-ments	Rank	Emp-loy-ment	Rank
Los Angeles – Riverside – Orange County, CA CMSA	426	2	8,887	1
New York – Northern New Jersey – Long Island, NY – NJ – CT-CMSA	458	1	8,509	2
San Francisco – Oakland – San Jose, CA CMSA	186	3	4,096	3
Chicago – Gary – Kenosha, IL – IN – WI CMSA	162	4	3,036	4
Dallas – Fort Worth, TX CMSA	107	8	2,188	5
Boston – Worcester – Lawrence, MA – NH – ME – CT CMSA	116	6	2,099	6
Miami – Fort Lauderdale, FL CMSA	75	14	1,483	7
Cleveland – Akron, OH CMSA	78	13	1,424	8
San Diego, CA MSA	72	15	1,421	9
Houston – Galveston – Brazoria, TX CMSA	81	11	1,362	10
Phoenix – Mesa, AZ MSA	53	21	1,327	11
Minneapolis – St. Paul, MN – WI MSA	68	17	1,311	12
Atlanta, GA MSA	80	12	1,295	13
Denver – Boulder – Greeley, CO CMSA	59	18	1,133	14
St. Louis, MO – IL MSA	56	20	1,087	15
Kansas City, MO – KS MSA	47	23	994	16
Pittsburgh, PA MSA	57	19	827	17
Tampa – St. Petersburg – Clearwater, FL MSA	51	22	746	18
Salt Lake City – Ogden, UT MSA	47	23	730	19
Indianapolis, IN MSA	43	24	663	20
Buffalo – Niagara Falls, NY MSA	33	28	637	21
Orlando, FL MSA	41	25	630	22
Norfolk – Virginia Beach – Newport News, VA – NC MSA	31	30	605	23
Austin – San Marcos, TX MSA	28	32	595	24
Columbus, OH MSA	32	29	571	25

Source: U.S. Department of Commerce, Bureau of the Census, Data User Services Division, *1992 Economic Census, Volume 1F, Reports Series, Release 1F,* September 1995, CD-ROM. *Note:* Data are shown only for the top 25 areas.

★ 2296 ★

Establishments and Employment

Museums and Art Galleries

The U.S. total number of employees is 2,258; total number of establishments is 356.

MSA	Estab-lish-ments	Rank	Emp-ploy-ment	Rank
Atlanta, GA MSA	3	6	0[1]	3
Boston – Worcester – Lawrence, MA – NH – ME – CT CMSA	11	2	0[2]	3
Chicago – Gary – Kenosha, IL – IN – WI CMSA	10	3	0[2]	3
Cincinnati – Hamilton, OH – KY – IN CMSA	2	7	0[1]	3
Cleveland – Akron, OH CMSA	1	8	0[1]	3
Dallas – Fort Worth, TX CMSA	8	4	0[2]	3
Denver – Boulder – Greeley, CO CMSA	4	5	0[1]	3
Detroit – Ann Arbor – Flint, MI CMSA	2	7	0[1]	3
Houston – Galveston – Brazoria, TX CMSA	2	7	0[1]	3
Indianapolis, IN MSA	0	9	0	3
Kansas City, MO – KS MSA	2	7	0[2]	3
Los Angeles – Riverside – Orange County, CA CMSA	20	1	0[3]	3
Miami – Fort Lauderdale, FL CMSA	4	5	0[2]	3
Milwaukee – Racine, WI CMSA	0	9	0	3
Minneapolis – St. Paul, MN – WI MSA	2	7	0[2]	3
New York – Northern New Jersey – Long Island, NY – NJ – CT-CMSA	20	1	81	1
Orlando, FL MSA	4	5	0[2]	3
Philadelphia – Wilmington – Atlantic City, PA – NJ – DE – MD CMSA	2	7	0[1]	3
Phoenix – Mesa, AZ MSA	2	7	0[1]	3
Pittsburgh, PA MSA	1	8	0[1]	3
Portland – Salem, OR – WA CMSA	1	8	0[1]	3
Sacramento – Yolo, CA CMSA	0	9	0	3
San Diego, CA MSA	2	7	0[1]	3
San Francisco – Oakland – San Jose, CA CMSA	11	2	0[3]	3
Seattle – Tacoma – Bremerton, WA CMSA	1	8	0[1]	3
St. Louis, MO – IL MSA	3	6	0[1]	3
Tampa – St. Petersburg – Clearwater, FL MSA	2	7	0[1]	3
Washington – Baltimore, DC – MD – VA – WV CMSA	4	5	44	2
West Palm Beach – Boca Raton, FL MSA	1	8	0[1]	3

Source: U.S. Department of Commerce, Bureau of the Census, Data User Services Division, *1992 Economic Census, Volume 1F, Reports Series, Release 1F,* September 1995, CD-ROM. *Notes:* 1. 0-19 employees. 2. 20-99 employees. 3. 100-249 employees.

★ 2297 ★

Establishments and Employment

News Syndicates

The U.S. total number of employees is 8,209; total number of establishments is 598.

MSA	Estab-lish-ments	Rank	Emp-ploy-ment	Rank
Los Angeles – Riverside – Orange County, CA CMSA	36	3	346	1
Chicago – Gary – Kenosha, IL – IN – WI CMSA	28	4	290	2
San Francisco – Oakland – San Jose, CA CMSA	22	5	179	3
Dallas – Fort Worth, TX CMSA	5	14	137	4
San Diego, CA MSA	8	11	121	5
Boston – Worcester – Lawrence, MA – NH – ME – CT CMSA	17	6	118	6
Miami – Fort Lauderdale, FL CMSA	14	7	92	7
Raleigh – Durham – Chapel Hill, NC MSA	7	12	64	8
Detroit – Ann Arbor – Flint, MI CMSA	5	14	62	9
Minneapolis – St. Paul, MN – WI MSA	11	8	44	10
Pittsburgh, PA MSA	5	14	27	11
Honolulu, HI MSA	6	13	26	12
Providence – Fall River – Warwick, RI – MA MSA	4	15	18	13
Albany – Schenectady – Troy, NY MSA	5	14	0[1]	14
Albuquerque, NM MSA	2	17	0[1]	14
Allentown – Bethlehem – Easton, PA MSA	2	17	0	1	4
Anchorage, AK MSA	2	17	0	1	4
Appleton – Oshkosh – Neenah, WI MSA	0	19		0	14
Atlanta, GA MSA	7	12		0[1]	14
Augusta – Aiken, GA – SC MSA	0	19		0	14
Austin – San Marcos, TX MSA	1	18	0	1	4
Bakersfield, CA MSA	0	19		0	14
Baton Rouge, LA MSA	3	16	0	1	4
Beaumont – Port Arthur, TX MSA	1	18	0	1	4
Birmingham, AL MSA	2	17	0	1	4

Source: U.S. Department of Commerce, Bureau of the Census, Data User Services Division, *1992 Economic Census, Volume 1F, Reports Series, Release 1F,* September 1995, CD-ROM. *Notes:* Data are shown only for the top 25 areas. 1. 20-99 employees.

★ 2298 ★

Establishments and Employment

Nursing and Personal Care Facilities

The U.S. total number of employees is 1,134,929; total number of establishments is 14,954.

MSA	Estab- lish- ments	Rank	Emp- ploy- ment	Rank
New York – Northern New Jersey – Long Island, NY – NJ – CT-CMSA	566	2	67,484	1
Los Angeles – Riverside – Orange County, CA CMSA	711	1	47,712	2
Boston – Worcester – Lawrence, MA – NH – ME – CT CMSA	481	3	40,904	3
Chicago – Gary – Kenosha, IL – IN – WI CMSA	328	4	32,809	4
Washington – Baltimore, DC – MD – VA – WV CMSA	262	6	22,359	5
San Francisco – Oakland – San Jose, CA CMSA	292	5	19,630	6
Philadelphia – Wilmington – Atlantic City, PA – NJ – DE – MD CMSA	213	9	18,597	7
Detroit – Ann Arbor – Flint, MI CMSA	212	10	18,587	8
Cleveland – Akron, OH CMSA	187	12	18,580	9
Dallas – Fort Worth, TX CMSA	241	7	16,739	10
Minneapolis – St. Paul, MN – WI MSA	235	8	15,513	11
St. Louis, MO – IL MSA	183	13	13,838	12
Seattle – Tacoma – Bremerton, WA CMSA	147	16	13,354	13
Tampa – St. Petersburg – Clearwater, FL MSA	136	20	12,204	14
Indianapolis, IN MSA	188	11	12,173	15
Cincinnati – Hamilton, OH – KY – IN CMSA	161	15	11,451	16
Hartford, CT MSA	94	24	10,780	17
Atlanta, GA MSA	134	22	10,482	18
Houston – Galveston – Brazoria, TX CMSA	141	18	9,679	19
Miami – Fort Lauderdale, FL CMSA	179	14	9,618	20
Kansas City, MO – KS MSA	139	19	9,079	21
Milwaukee – Racine, WI CMSA	70	30	8,771	22
Columbus, OH MSA	93	25	8,081	23
Portland – Salem, OR – WA CMSA	135	21	8,032	24
Providence – Fall River – Warwick, RI – MA MSA	90	27	7,883	25

Source: U.S. Department of Commerce, Bureau of the Census, Data User Services Division, *1992 Economic Census, Volume 1F, Reports Series, Release 1F,* September 1995, CD-ROM. *Note:* Data are shown only for the top 25 areas.

★ 2299 ★

Establishments and Employment

Offices and Clinics of Chiropractors

The U.S. total number of employees is 84,730; total number of establishments is 27,329.

MSA	Estab- lish- ments	Rank	Emp- ploy- ment	Rank
New York – Northern New Jersey – Long Island, NY – NJ – CT-CMSA	2,555	1	7,807	1
Los Angeles – Riverside – Orange County, CA CMSA	1,873	2	5,603	2
San Francisco – Oakland – San Jose, CA CMSA	1,036	3	2,944	3
Chicago – Gary – Kenosha, IL – IN – WI CMSA	629	4	2,054	4
Philadelphia – Wilmington – Atlantic City, PA – NJ – DE – MD CMSA	584	5	2,021	5
Boston – Worcester – Lawrence, MA – NH – ME – CT CMSA	517	7	1,774	6
Minneapolis – St. Paul, MN – WI MSA	493	10	1,626	7
Miami – Fort Lauderdale, FL CMSA	465	11	1,582	8
Atlanta, GA MSA	510	8	1,539	9
Detroit – Ann Arbor – Flint, MI CMSA	525	6	1,526	10
Dallas – Fort Worth, TX CMSA	397	13	1,461	11
Washington – Baltimore, DC – MD – VA – WV CMSA	343	16	1,459	12
Seattle – Tacoma – Bremerton, WA CMSA	507	9	1,304	13
Phoenix – Mesa, AZ MSA	444	12	1,303	14
Houston – Galveston – Brazoria, TX CMSA	354	15	1,228	15
Pittsburgh, PA MSA	333	18	1,187	16
Tampa – St. Petersburg – Clearwater, FL MSA	325	19	1,147	17
San Diego, CA MSA	387	14	965	18
Denver – Boulder – Greeley, CO CMSA	341	17	914	19
St. Louis, MO – IL MSA	320	20	904	20
Cincinnati – Hamilton, OH – KY – IN CMSA	174	26	788	21
West Palm Beach – Boca Raton, FL MSA	195	23	686	22
Cleveland – Akron, OH CMSA	151	28	657	23
Portland – Salem, OR – WA CMSA	274	22	632	24
Milwaukee – Racine, WI CMSA	186	25	590	25

Source: U.S. Department of Commerce, Bureau of the Census, Data User Services Division, *1992 Economic Census, Volume 1F, Reports Series, Release 1F,* September 1995, CD-ROM. *Note:* Data are shown only for the top 25 areas.

★ 2300 ★

Establishments and Employment

Offices and Clinics of Dentists

The U.S. total number of employees is 554,589; total number of establishments is 108,804.

MSA	Establishments	Rank	Employment	Rank
New York – Northern New Jersey – Long Island, NY – NJ – CT-CMSA	10,503	1	46,789	1
Los Angeles – Riverside – Orange County, CA CMSA	6,655	2	34,474	2
San Francisco – Oakland – San Jose, CA CMSA	3,976	4	21,765	3
Chicago – Gary – Kenosha, IL – IN – WI CMSA	4,021	3	19,630	4
Washington – Baltimore, DC – MD – VA – WV CMSA	3,187	5	16,195	5
Detroit – Ann Arbor – Flint, MI CMSA	2,576	7	15,571	6
Boston – Worcester – Lawrence, MA – NH – ME – CT CMSA	2,717	6	14,516	7
Philadelphia – Wilmington – Atlantic City, PA – NJ – DE – MD CMSA	2,567	8	14,359	8
Seattle – Tacoma – Bremerton, WA CMSA	1,816	9	11,084	9
Dallas – Fort Worth, TX CMSA	1,796	10	8,600	10
Minneapolis – St. Paul, MN – WI MSA	1,203	17	7,437	11
Atlanta, GA MSA	1,340	14	7,351	12
Miami – Fort Lauderdale, FL CMSA	1,539	11	7,335	13
Houston – Galveston – Brazoria, TX CMSA	1,478	12	7,245	14
Cleveland – Akron, OH CMSA	1,423	13	7,012	15
San Diego, CA MSA	1,196	18	6,319	16
Portland – Salem, OR – WA CMSA	1,042	20	5,852	17
Denver – Boulder – Greeley, CO CMSA	1,213	16	5,618	18
St. Louis, MO – IL MSA	1,101	19	5,462	19
Pittsburgh, PA MSA	1,263	15	5,296	20
Phoenix – Mesa, AZ MSA	984	21	4,987	21
Milwaukee – Racine, WI CMSA	844	22	4,759	22
Tampa – St. Petersburg – Clearwater, FL MSA	806	24	4,640	23
Sacramento – Yolo, CA CMSA	837	23	4,513	24
Cincinnati – Hamilton, OH – KY – IN CMSA	742	26	4,133	25

Source: U.S. Department of Commerce, Bureau of the Census, Data User Services Division, *1992 Economic Census, Volume 1F, Reports Series, Release 1F,* September 1995, CD-ROM. *Note:* Data are shown only for the top 25 areas.

★ 2301 ★

Establishments and Employment

Offices and Clinics of Doctors of Medicine

The U.S. total number of employees is 1,356,685; total number of establishments is 197,701.

MSA	Establishments	Rank	Employment	Rank
New York – Northern New Jersey – Long Island, NY – NJ – CT-CMSA	19,988	1	103,711	1
Los Angeles – Riverside – Orange County, CA CMSA	15,439	2	102,828	2
San Francisco – Oakland – San Jose, CA CMSA	5,738	5	43,376	3
Chicago – Gary – Kenosha, IL – IN – WI CMSA	6,893	3	42,682	4
Washington – Baltimore, DC – MD – VA – WV CMSA	6,712	4	41,107	5
Philadelphia – Wilmington – Atlantic City, PA – NJ – DE – MD CMSA	5,057	6	33,323	6
Boston – Worcester – Lawrence, MA – NH – ME – CT CMSA	4,184	8	28,833	7
Miami – Fort Lauderdale, FL CMSA	4,637	7	27,320	8
Detroit – Ann Arbor – Flint, MI CMSA	3,634	10	23,222	9
Dallas – Fort Worth, TX CMSA	3,820	9	21,612	10
Houston – Galveston – Brazoria, TX CMSA	3,593	11	20,972	11
Atlanta, GA MSA	2,776	12	20,243	12
Seattle – Tacoma – Bremerton, WA CMSA	2,307	15	16,181	13
Cleveland – Akron, OH CMSA	2,436	14	14,939	14
Tampa – St. Petersburg – Clearwater, FL MSA	2,437	13	14,862	15
Minneapolis – St. Paul, MN – WI MSA	1,030	32	14,612	16
San Diego, CA MSA	2,197	16	14,606	17
Phoenix – Mesa, AZ MSA	2,190	17	14,417	18
Pittsburgh, PA MSA	2,111	18	13,752	19
St. Louis, MO – IL MSA	1,947	19	13,475	20
Cincinnati – Hamilton, OH – KY – IN CMSA	1,466	21	11,677	21
Denver – Boulder – Greeley, CO CMSA	1,712	20	11,315	22
Milwaukee – Racine, WI CMSA	1,315	24	10,942	23
Portland – Salem, OR – WA CMSA	1,363	22	10,041	24
Kansas City, MO – KS MSA	1,117	30	9,969	25

Source: U.S. Department of Commerce, Bureau of the Census, Data User Services Division, *1992 Economic Census, Volume 1F, Reports Series, Release 1F,* September 1995, CD-ROM. *Note:* Data are shown only for the top 25 areas.

★ 2302 ★

Establishments and Employment

Offices and Clinics of Doctors of Osteopathy

The U.S. total number of employees is 47,029; total number of establishments is 8,708.

MSA	Estab-lish-ments	Rank	Emp-loy-ment	Rank
Detroit – Ann Arbor – Flint, MI CMSA	736	2	5,554	1
Dallas – Fort Worth, TX CMSA	380	3	1,873	2
New York – Northern New Jersey – Long Island, NY – NJ – CT-CMSA	295	4	1,457	3
Columbus, OH MSA	134	13	1,205	4
Phoenix – Mesa, AZ MSA	220	5	1,149	5
Tampa – St. Petersburg – Clearwater, FL MSA	219	6	1,032	6
Miami – Fort Lauderdale, FL CMSA	207	7	1,020	7
Cleveland – Akron, OH CMSA	185	8	901	8
Youngstown – Warren, OH MSA	121	14	755	9
Grand Rapids – Muskegon – Holland, MI MSA	138	11	732	10
Los Angeles – Riverside – Orange County, CA CMSA	175	9	732	10
Dayton – Springfield, OH MSA	112	15	685	11
Kansas City, MO – KS MSA	109	16	661	12
Tulsa, OK MSA	135	12	611	13
St. Louis, MO – IL MSA	104	18	576	14
Denver – Boulder – Greeley, CO CMSA	106	17	488	15
West Palm Beach – Boca Raton, FL MSA	79	20	428	16
Oklahoma City, OK MSA	73	24	408	17
Orlando, FL MSA	71	25	383	18
Allentown – Bethlehem – Easton, PA MSA	69	26	376	19
Atlanta, GA MSA	78	21	364	20
Harrisburg – Lebanon – Carlisle, PA MSA	60	30	364	20
Des Moines, IA MSA	65	27	359	21
Canton – Massillon, OH MSA	33	42	352	22
Lancaster, PA MSA	46	34	341	23

Source: U.S. Department of Commerce, Bureau of the Census, Data User Services Division, *1992 Economic Census, Volume 1F, Reports Series, Release 1F,* September 1995, CD-ROM. *Note:* Data are shown only for the top 25 areas.

★ 2303 ★

Establishments and Employment

Offices and Clinics of Optometrists

The U.S. total number of employees is 68,596; total number of establishments is 17,135.

MSA	Estab-lish-ments	Rank	Emp-loy-ment	Rank
Los Angeles – Riverside – Orange County, CA CMSA	1,117	1	4,519	1
San Francisco – Oakland – San Jose, CA CMSA	512	3	1,908	2
Detroit – Ann Arbor – Flint, MI CMSA	293	8	1,499	3
Philadelphia – Wilmington – Atlantic City, PA – NJ – DE – MD CMSA	387	5	1,444	4
Boston – Worcester – Lawrence, MA – NH – ME – CT CMSA	325	7	1,214	5
Houston – Galveston – Brazoria, TX CMSA	238	11	1,067	6
Dallas – Fort Worth, TX CMSA	280	9	1,029	7
Cleveland – Akron, OH CMSA	180	14	726	8
Pittsburgh, PA MSA	185	13	720	9
San Diego, CA MSA	180	14	719	10
Seattle – Tacoma – Bremerton, WA CMSA	187	12	719	10
St. Louis, MO – IL MSA	132	17	690	11
Denver – Boulder – Greeley, CO CMSA	147	15	680	12
Atlanta, GA MSA	180	14	677	13
Miami – Fort Lauderdale, FL CMSA	239	10	666	14
Minneapolis – St. Paul, MN – WI MSA	129	18	509	15
Cincinnati – Hamilton, OH – KY – IN CMSA	115	21	466	16
Columbus, OH MSA	120	19	466	16
Portland – Salem, OR – WA CMSA	119	20	419	17
Milwaukee – Racine, WI CMSA	85	30	408	18
Indianapolis, IN MSA	102	23	394	19
Greensboro – Winston-Salem – High Point, NC MSA	80	32	388	20
Dayton – Springfield, OH MSA	83	31	373	21
Norfolk – Virginia Beach – Newport News, VA – NC MSA	98	25	350	22
Las Vegas, NV – AZ MSA	69	40	341	23

Source: U.S. Department of Commerce, Bureau of the Census, Data User Services Division, *1992 Economic Census, Volume 1F, Reports Series, Release 1F,* September 1995, CD-ROM. *Note:* Data are shown only for the top 25 areas.

★ 2304 ★

Establishments and Employment

Offices and Clinics of Podiatrists

The U.S. total number of employees is 26,429; total number of establishments is 7,948.

MSA	Estab-lish-ments	Rank	Emp-loy-ment	Rank
New York – Northern New Jersey – Long Island, NY – NJ – CT-CMSA	1,159	1	3,228	1
Detroit – Ann Arbor – Flint, MI CMSA	305	5	1,334	2
Los Angeles – Riverside – Orange County, CA CMSA	445	2	1,286	3
Philadelphia – Wilmington – Atlantic City, PA – NJ – DE – MD CMSA	351	3	1,169	4
Washington – Baltimore, DC – MD – VA – WV CMSA	296	6	1,075	5
San Francisco – Oakland – San Jose, CA CMSA	246	7	653	6
Miami – Fort Lauderdale, FL CMSA	178	10	607	7
Cleveland – Akron, OH CMSA	183	9	570	8
Boston – Worcester – Lawrence, MA – NH – ME – CT CMSA	186	8	549	9
Pittsburgh, PA MSA	114	12	377	10
Dallas – Fort Worth, TX CMSA	120	11	356	11
Houston – Galveston – Brazoria, TX CMSA	114	12	353	12
Atlanta, GA MSA	87	15	328	13
Tampa – St. Petersburg – Clearwater, FL MSA	92	14	313	14
Phoenix – Mesa, AZ MSA	82	16	291	15
Seattle – Tacoma – Bremerton, WA CMSA	97	13	280	16
St. Louis, MO – IL MSA	73	18	278	17
West Palm Beach – Boca Raton, FL MSA	74	17	261	18
Indianapolis, IN MSA	52	25	250	19
Buffalo – Niagara Falls, NY MSA	63	21	233	20
Columbus, OH MSA	61	23	232	21
Cincinnati – Hamilton, OH – KY – IN CMSA	66	20	230	22
Milwaukee – Racine, WI CMSA	61	23	206	23
Hartford, CT MSA	54	24	193	24
Orlando, FL MSA	45	27	187	25

Source: U.S. Department of Commerce, Bureau of the Census, Data User Services Division, *1992 Economic Census, Volume 1F, Reports Series, Release 1F*, September 1995, CD-ROM. *Note:* Data are shown only for the top 25 areas.

★ 2305 ★

Establishments and Employment

Outdoor Advertising Services

The U.S. total number of employees is 13,154; total number of establishments is 1,308.

MSA	Estab-lish-ments	Rank	Emp-loy-ment	Rank
Las Vegas, NV – AZ MSA	11	14	295	1
Dallas – Fort Worth, TX CMSA	37	4	281	2
Miami – Fort Lauderdale, FL CMSA	26	7	272	3
Atlanta, GA MSA	20	9	255	4
Tampa – St. Petersburg – Clearwater, FL MSA	16	11	173	5
Minneapolis – St. Paul, MN – WI MSA	15	12	165	6
St. Louis, MO – IL MSA	11	14	127	7
Boston – Worcester – Lawrence, MA – NH – ME – CT CMSA	11	14	124	8
San Antonio, TX MSA	11	14	107	9
Columbus, OH MSA	8	17	103	10
Nashville, TN MSA	9	16	101	11
Allentown – Bethlehem – Easton, PA MSA	5	20	89	12
Denver – Boulder – Greeley, CO CMSA	10	15	86	13
Greenville – Spartanburg – Anderson, SC MSA	6	19	83	14
Pensacola, FL MSA	6	19	83	14
Pittsburgh, PA MSA	8	17	80	15
Indianapolis, IN MSA	8	17	79	16
Kansas City, MO – KS MSA	9	16	70	17
Raleigh – Durham – Chapel Hill, NC MSA	8	17	64	18
Memphis, TN – AR – MS MSA	7	18	63	19
El Paso, TX MSA	7	18	62	20
Charlotte – Gastonia – Rock Hill, NC – SC MSA	5	20	61	21
Austin – San Marcos, TX MSA	5	20	57	22
Knoxville, TN MSA	6	19	57	22
Oklahoma City, OK MSA	8	17	57	22

Source: U.S. Department of Commerce, Bureau of the Census, Data User Services Division, *1992 Economic Census, Volume 1F, Reports Series, Release 1F*, September 1995, CD-ROM. *Note:* Data are shown only for the top 25 areas.

★ 2306 ★
Establishments and Employment
Passenger Car Leasing

The U.S. total number of employees is 6,936; total number of establishments is 919.

MSA	Estab-lish-ments	Rank	Emp-loy-ment	Rank
Chicago – Gary – Kenosha, IL – IN – WI CMSA	46	3	727	1
Boston – Worcester – Lawrence, MA – NH – ME – CT CMSA	29	5	499	2
Miami – Fort Lauderdale, FL CMSA	28	6	177	3
Milwaukee – Racine, WI CMSA	22	9	130	4
Kansas City, MO – KS MSA	8	18	109	5
Atlanta, GA MSA	17	12	103	6
Louisville, KY – IN MSA	6	20	98	7
Minneapolis – St. Paul, MN – WI MSA	16	13	84	8
San Francisco – Oakland – San Jose, CA CMSA	20	10	71	9
Memphis, TN – AR – MS MSA	6	20	53	10
Dayton – Springfield, OH MSA	8	18	40	11
Orlando, FL MSA	6	20	36	12
Santa Barbara – Santa Maria – Lompoc, CA MSA	6	20	30	13
Houston – Galveston – Brazoria, TX CMSA	12	14	29	14
San Diego, CA MSA	8	18	25	15
Richmond – Petersburg, VA MSA	8	18	20	16
San Antonio, TX MSA	3	23	13	17
Springfield, MA MSA	4	22	9	18
Buffalo – Niagara Falls, NY MSA	5	21	7	19
Honolulu, HI MSA	4	22	6	20
Albany – Schenectady – Troy, NY MSA	3	23	0[1]	21
Albuquerque, NM MSA	0	26	0	21
Allentown – Bethlehem – Easton, PA MSA	2	24	0	21
Anchorage, AK MSA	0	26	0	21
Appleton – Oshkosh – Neenah, WI MSA	1	25	0[1]	21

Source: U.S. Department of Commerce, Bureau of the Census, Data User Services Division, *1992 Economic Census, Volume 1F, Reports Series, Release 1F,* September 1995, CD-ROM. *Notes:* Data are shown only for the top 25 areas. 1. 0-19 employees.

★ 2307 ★
Establishments and Employment
Passenger Car Rental

The U.S. total number of employees is 81,170; total number of establishments is 4,894.

MSA	Estab-lish-ments	Rank	Emp-loy-ment	Rank
San Francisco – Oakland – San Jose, CA CMSA	129	5	3,823	1
Miami – Fort Lauderdale, FL CMSA	100	9	3,250	2
Washington – Baltimore, DC – MD – VA – WV CMSA	145	3	2,997	3
Chicago – Gary – Kenosha, IL – IN – WI CMSA	135	4	2,905	4
Orlando, FL MSA	44	18	2,408	5
Atlanta, GA MSA	66	15	2,271	6
Boston – Worcester – Lawrence, MA – NH – ME – CT CMSA	125	6	2,007	7
Houston – Galveston – Brazoria, TX CMSA	104	8	1,952	8
Honolulu, HI MSA	23	32	1,269	9
San Diego, CA MSA	72	13	1,041	10
Pittsburgh, PA MSA	37	23	973	11
Indianapolis, IN MSA	27	29	813	12
Minneapolis – St. Paul, MN – WI MSA	40	20	788	13
San Antonio, TX MSA	32	24	679	14
Kansas City, MO – KS MSA	30	26	626	15
Nashville, TN MSA	22	33	616	16
Sacramento – Yolo, CA CMSA	38	22	616	16
Louisville, KY – IN MSA	22	33	549	17
Buffalo – Niagara Falls, NY MSA	24	31	514	18
Columbus, OH MSA	23	32	505	19
Charleston – North Charleston, SC MSA	15	40	461	20
Oklahoma City, OK MSA	19	36	388	21
Memphis, TN – AR – MS MSA	21	34	350	22
Dayton – Springfield, OH MSA	24	31	333	23
Rochester, NY MSA	25	30	323	24

Source: U.S. Department of Commerce, Bureau of the Census, Data User Services Division, *1992 Economic Census, Volume 1F, Reports Series, Release 1F,* September 1995, CD-ROM. *Note:* Data are shown only for the top 25 areas.

★ 2308 ★

Establishments and Employment

Personnel Supply Services

The U.S. total number of employees is 1,974,732; total number of establishments is 31,166.

MSA	Establishments	Rank	Employment	Rank
Los Angeles – Riverside – Orange County, CA CMSA	2,166	2	152,792	1
New York – Northern New Jersey – Long Island, NY – NJ – CT-CMSA	3,557	1	150,415	2
Houston – Galveston – Brazoria, TX CMSA	799	10	83,366	3
San Francisco – Oakland – San Jose, CA CMSA	1,175	4	69,395	4
Tampa – St. Petersburg – Clearwater, FL MSA	415	15	63,109	5
Dallas – Fort Worth, TX CMSA	911	7	61,468	6
Boston – Worcester – Lawrence, MA – NH – ME – CT CMSA	917	6	55,154	7
Atlanta, GA MSA	839	8	44,778	8
Detroit – Ann Arbor – Flint, MI CMSA	719	11	44,161	9
Philadelphia – Wilmington – Atlantic City, PA – NJ – DE – MD CMSA	829	9	35,070	10
Miami – Fort Lauderdale, FL CMSA	534	12	30,991	11
Minneapolis – St. Paul, MN – WI MSA	460	14	30,355	12
Cleveland – Akron, OH CMSA	469	13	29,555	13
Phoenix – Mesa, AZ MSA	367	17	24,968	14
St. Louis, MO – IL MSA	323	18	23,466	15
Columbus, OH MSA	220	26	21,498	16
Seattle – Tacoma – Bremerton, WA CMSA	410	16	20,469	17
Denver – Boulder – Greeley, CO CMSA	415	15	20,117	18
San Diego, CA MSA	294	19	19,005	19
Milwaukee – Racine, WI CMSA	282	20	18,733	20
New Orleans, LA MSA	187	29	17,075	21
Kansas City, MO – KS MSA	262	23	16,961	22
Indianapolis, IN MSA	182	30	16,373	23
Raleigh – Durham – Chapel Hill, NC MSA	161	34	15,901	24
Portland – Salem, OR – WA CMSA	265	22	15,476	25

Source: U.S. Department of Commerce, Bureau of the Census, Data User Services Division, *1992 Economic Census, Volume 1F, Reports Series, Release 1F,* September 1995, CD-ROM. *Note:* Data are shown only for the top 25 areas.

★ 2309 ★

Establishments and Employment

Photocopying and Duplicating Services

The U.S. total number of employees is 58,149; total number of establishments is 4,949.

MSA	Establishments	Rank	Employment	Rank
Los Angeles – Riverside – Orange County, CA CMSA	517	1	7,183	1
New York – Northern New Jersey – Long Island, NY – NJ – CT-CMSA	464	2	7,126	2
Boston – Worcester – Lawrence, MA – NH – ME – CT CMSA	124	6	1,459	3
Atlanta, GA MSA	77	13	1,305	4
Dallas – Fort Worth, TX CMSA	115	7	1,292	5
Detroit – Ann Arbor – Flint, MI CMSA	96	11	1,225	6
San Diego, CA MSA	124	6	1,116	7
Seattle – Tacoma – Bremerton, WA CMSA	97	10	1,057	8
Cleveland – Akron, OH CMSA	52	18	881	9
Minneapolis – St. Paul, MN – WI MSA	59	16	868	10
Phoenix – Mesa, AZ MSA	62	15	787	11
Miami – Fort Lauderdale, FL CMSA	89	12	780	12
St. Louis, MO – IL MSA	56	17	540	13
Austin – San Marcos, TX MSA	38	22	513	14
Tampa – St. Petersburg – Clearwater, FL MSA	41	20	492	15
Orlando, FL MSA	37	23	477	16
New Orleans, LA MSA	40	21	464	17
Kansas City, MO – KS MSA	40	21	460	18
Salt Lake City – Ogden, UT MSA	41	20	427	19
Pittsburgh, PA MSA	36	24	402	20
Columbus, OH MSA	35	25	393	21
Honolulu, HI MSA	24	30	384	22
San Antonio, TX MSA	32	26	305	23
Nashville, TN MSA	29	27	304	24
Indianapolis, IN MSA	17	35	302	25

Source: U.S. Department of Commerce, Bureau of the Census, Data User Services Division, *1992 Economic Census, Volume 1F, Reports Series, Release 1F,* September 1995, CD-ROM. *Note:* Data are shown only for the top 25 areas.

★2310★

Establishments and Employment

Photographic Studios, Portrait

The U.S. total number of employees is 66,822; total number of establishments is 11,381.

MSA	Estab-lish-ments	Rank	Emp-ploy-ment	Rank
Los Angeles – Riverside – Orange County, CA CMSA	614	2	4,690	1
Minneapolis – St. Paul, MN – WI MSA	156	13	3,219	2
New York – Northern New Jersey – Long Island, NY – NJ – CT-CMSA	640	1	2,934	3
St. Louis, MO – IL MSA	140	15	2,657	4
Chicago – Gary – Kenosha, IL – IN – WI CMSA	348	3	2,087	5
Cleveland – Akron, OH CMSA	146	14	1,596	6
San Francisco – Oakland – San Jose, CA CMSA	300	4	1,533	7
Houston – Galveston – Brazoria, TX CMSA	182	10	1,498	8
Washington – Baltimore, DC – MD – VA – WV CMSA	238	6	1,428	9
Charlotte – Gastonia – Rock Hill, NC – SC MSA	87	23	1,406	10
Philadelphia – Wilmington – Atlantic City, PA – NJ – DE – MD CMSA	260	5	1,364	11
Dallas – Fort Worth, TX CMSA	225	7	1,290	12
Seattle – Tacoma – Bremerton, WA CMSA	177	11	1,165	13
Detroit – Ann Arbor – Flint, MI CMSA	224	8	1,152	14
Pittsburgh, PA MSA	112	19	1,049	15
Atlanta, GA MSA	159	12	926	16
Phoenix – Mesa, AZ MSA	110	20	858	17
Portland – Salem, OR – WA CMSA	120	18	709	18
Miami – Fort Lauderdale, FL CMSA	126	16	634	19
San Diego, CA MSA	110	20	614	20
Denver – Boulder – Greeley, CO CMSA	123	17	548	21
Tampa – St. Petersburg – Clearwater, FL MSA	85	24	547	22
Kansas City, MO – KS MSA	84	25	524	23
Oklahoma City, OK MSA	54	33	519	24
Cincinnati – Hamilton, OH – KY – IN CMSA	107	21	511	25

Source: U.S. Department of Commerce, Bureau of the Census, Data User Services Division, *1992 Economic Census, Volume 1F, Reports Series, Release 1F*, September 1995, CD-ROM. *Note:* Data are shown only for the top 25 areas.

★2311★

Establishments and Employment

Physical Fitness Facilities

The U.S. total number of employees is 129,925; total number of establishments is 9,216.

MSA	Estab-lish-ments	Rank	Emp-ploy-ment	Rank
Los Angeles – Riverside – Orange County, CA CMSA	502	2	10,586	1
San Francisco – Oakland – San Jose, CA CMSA	337	3	6,940	2
Chicago – Gary – Kenosha, IL – IN – WI CMSA	262	6	5,289	3
Boston – Worcester – Lawrence, MA – NH – ME – CT CMSA	284	5	4,102	4
Seattle – Tacoma – Bremerton, WA CMSA	164	8	3,133	5
Philadelphia – Wilmington – Atlantic City, PA – NJ – DE – MD CMSA	240	7	3,055	6
Denver – Boulder – Greeley, CO CMSA	119	13	3,049	7
Dallas – Fort Worth, TX CMSA	144	10	2,491	8
Houston – Galveston – Brazoria, TX CMSA	134	11	2,244	9
Atlanta, GA MSA	129	12	2,185	10
San Diego, CA MSA	110	14	2,179	11
Minneapolis – St. Paul, MN – WI MSA	86	17	2,105	12
Miami – Fort Lauderdale, FL CMSA	144	10	1,617	13
Detroit – Ann Arbor – Flint, MI CMSA	160	9	1,607	14
Cleveland – Akron, OH CMSA	83	18	1,366	15
St. Louis, MO – IL MSA	97	15	1,280	16
Sacramento – Yolo, CA CMSA	80	19	1,223	17
Phoenix – Mesa, AZ MSA	88	16	1,158	18
Norfolk – Virginia Beach – Newport News, VA – NC MSA	47	29	1,065	19
Kansas City, MO – KS MSA	54	25	946	20
Milwaukee – Racine, WI CMSA	45	30	920	21
Indianapolis, IN MSA	61	23	912	22
Oklahoma City, OK MSA	51	26	864	23
Columbus, OH MSA	45	30	833	24
Pittsburgh, PA MSA	66	22	799	25

Source: U.S. Department of Commerce, Bureau of the Census, Data User Services Division, *1992 Economic Census, Volume 1F, Reports Series, Release 1F*, September 1995, CD-ROM. *Note:* Data are shown only for the top 25 areas.

★2312★
Establishments and Employment
Prepackaged Software

The U.S. total number of employees is 131,020; total number of establishments is 7,108.

MSA	Estab- lish- ments	Rank	Emp- loy- ment	Rank
San Francisco – Oakland – San Jose, CA CMSA	689	1	23,495	1
Boston – Worcester – Lawrence, MA – NH – ME – CT CMSA	462	4	14,764	2
Los Angeles – Riverside – Orange County, CA CMSA	484	3	8,652	3
Atlanta, GA MSA	228	8	5,113	4
Seattle – Tacoma – Bremerton, WA CMSA	169	10	4,555	5
Dallas – Fort Worth, TX CMSA	234	7	3,239	6
Raleigh – Durham – Chapel Hill, NC MSA	55	24	2,819	7
San Diego, CA MSA	125	15	2,508	8
Detroit – Ann Arbor – Flint, MI CMSA	144	12	2,465	9
Minneapolis – St. Paul, MN – WI MSA	132	14	1,911	10
Cincinnati – Hamilton, OH – KY – IN CMSA	48	26	1,841	11
Phoenix – Mesa, AZ MSA	91	17	988	12
Pittsburgh, PA MSA	78	19	982	13
Orlando, FL MSA	57	23	885	14
Miami – Fort Lauderdale, FL CMSA	76	20	735	15
Omaha, NE – IA MSA	23	37	686	16
St. Louis, MO – IL MSA	57	23	678	17
Columbus, OH MSA	40	31	675	18
Austin – San Marcos, TX MSA	83	18	630	19
Indianapolis, IN MSA	43	29	616	20
Hartford, CT MSA	41	30	591	21
Des Moines, IA MSA	13	47	556	22
Tucson, AZ MSA	24	36	448	23
Santa Barbara – Santa Maria – Lompoc, CA MSA	17	43	439	24
Tampa – St. Petersburg – Clearwater, FL MSA	64	22	429	25

Source: U.S. Department of Commerce, Bureau of the Census, Data User Services Division, *1992 Economic Census, Volume 1F, Reports Series, Release 1F,* September 1995, CD-ROM. *Note:* Data are shown only for the top 25 areas.

★2313★
Establishments and Employment
Professional Sports Clubs, Managers, Promoters

The U.S. total number of employees is 34,154; total number of establishments is 1,085.

MSA	Estab- lish- ments	Rank	Emp- loy- ment	Rank
Houston – Galveston – Brazoria, TX CMSA	15	14	2,024	1
Los Angeles – Riverside – Orange County, CA CMSA	66	2	1,636	2
Chicago – Gary – Kenosha, IL – IN – WI CMSA	44	3	1,477	3
Minneapolis – St. Paul, MN – WI MSA	14	15	1,283	4
Atlanta, GA MSA	19	10	1,241	5
Miami – Fort Lauderdale, FL CMSA	24	7	991	6
Indianapolis, IN MSA	18	11	805	7
San Diego, CA MSA	18	11	565	8
West Palm Beach – Boca Raton, FL MSA	10	19	484	9
Tampa – St. Petersburg – Clearwater, FL MSA	17	12	476	10
St. Louis, MO – IL MSA	16	13	395	11
Portland – Salem, OR – WA CMSA	15	14	297	12
Orlando, FL MSA	11	18	290	13
Phoenix – Mesa, AZ MSA	19	10	285	14
Columbus, OH MSA	13	16	106	15
Louisville, KY – IN MSA	5	24	84	16
Nashville, TN MSA	4	25	60	17
Greensboro – Winston-Salem – High Point, NC MSA	3	26	56	18
Raleigh – Durham – Chapel Hill, NC MSA	10	19	54	19
Rochester, NY MSA	8	21	50	20
Birmingham, AL MSA	4	25	44	21
Memphis, TN – AR – MS MSA	7	22	37	22
Honolulu, HI MSA	6	23	25	23
Las Vegas, NV – AZ MSA	7	22	19	24
Columbia, SC MSA	3	26	17	25

Source: U.S. Department of Commerce, Bureau of the Census, Data User Services Division, *1992 Economic Census, Volume 1F, Reports Series, Release 1F,* September 1995, CD-ROM. *Note:* Data are shown only for the top 25 areas.

★2314★
Establishments and Employment
Public Golf Courses

The U.S. total number of employees is 42,348; total number of establishments is 3,780.

MSA	Estab- lish- ments	Rank	Emp- loy- ment	Rank
Los Angeles – Riverside – Orange County, CA CMSA	127	1	4,217	1
Phoenix – Mesa, AZ MSA	44	12	1,776	2
San Francisco – Oakland – San Jose, CA CMSA	66	7	1,522	3
Miami – Fort Lauderdale, FL CMSA	27	20	1,028	4

[Continued]

★2314★
Public Golf Courses
[Continued]

MSA	Estab-lish-ments	Rank	Emp-ploy-ment	Rank
Detroit – Ann Arbor – Flint, MI CMSA	117	2	994	5
San Diego, CA MSA	22	24	858	6
Seattle – Tacoma – Bremerton, WA CMSA	49	10	651	7
Honolulu, HI MSA	10	33	633	8
Orlando, FL MSA	20	26	600	9
Boston – Worcester – Lawrence, MA – NH – ME – CT CMSA	70	6	593	10
St. Louis, MO – IL MSA	41	13	582	11
Dallas – Fort Worth, TX CMSA	29	19	573	12
Las Vegas, NV – AZ MSA	14	30	552	13
Cleveland – Akron, OH CMSA	79	4	540	14
Pittsburgh, PA MSA	63	8	516	15
Atlanta, GA MSA	29	19	462	16
Tampa – St. Petersburg – Clearwater, FL MSA	26	21	410	17
Portland – Salem, OR – WA CMSA	36	15	355	18
Charlotte – Gastonia – Rock Hill, NC – SC MSA	26	21	321	19
West Palm Beach – Boca Raton, FL MSA	14	30	321	19
Kansas City, MO – KS MSA	20	26	314	20
Indianapolis, IN MSA	36	15	307	21
Columbus, OH MSA	35	16	288	22
Greensboro – Winston-Salem – High Point, NC MSA	34	17	269	23
Minneapolis – St. Paul, MN – WI MSA	45	11	259	24

Source: U.S. Department of Commerce, Bureau of the Census, Data User Services Division, *1992 Economic Census, Volume 1F, Reports Series, Release 1F,* September 1995, CD-ROM. *Note:* Data are shown only for the top 25 areas.

★2315★
Establishments and Employment
Public Relations Services

The U.S. total number of employees is 27,021; total number of establishments is 5,103.

MSA	Estab-lish-ments	Rank	Emp-ploy-ment	Rank
New York – Northern New Jersey – Long Island, NY – NJ – CT-CMSA	902	1	6,494	1
Boston – Worcester – Lawrence, MA – NH – ME – CT CMSA	133	6	778	2
Miami – Fort Lauderdale, FL CMSA	118	8	641	3
Dallas – Fort Worth, TX CMSA	125	7	521	4
St. Louis, MO – IL MSA	53	18	513	5
San Diego, CA MSA	67	16	268	6
Kansas City, MO – KS MSA	40	23	251	7
Cleveland – Akron, OH CMSA	47	20	226	8

[Continued]

★2315★
Public Relations Services
[Continued]

MSA	Estab-lish-ments	Rank	Emp-ploy-ment	Rank
Nashville, TN MSA	43	21	225	9
Columbus, OH MSA	47	20	207	10
Charlotte – Gastonia – Rock Hill, NC – SC MSA	24	29	188	11
Tampa – St. Petersburg – Clearwater, FL MSA	37	24	143	12
New Orleans, LA MSA	20	32	136	13
Lansing – East Lansing, MI MSA	11	40	92	14
Raleigh – Durham – Chapel Hill, NC MSA	26	27	87	15
Reno, NV MSA	14	37	85	16
Louisville, KY – IN MSA	12	39	80	17
Tallahassee, FL MSA	24	29	79	18
Austin – San Marcos, TX MSA	26	27	72	19
Las Vegas, NV – AZ MSA	14	37	72	19
San Antonio, TX MSA	19	33	70	20
Grand Rapids – Muskegon – Holland, MI MSA	12	39	68	21
Salt Lake City – Ogden, UT MSA	13	38	47	22
Harrisburg – Lebanon – Carlisle, PA MSA	12	39	40	23
Oklahoma City, OK MSA	20	32	40	23

Source: U.S. Department of Commerce, Bureau of the Census, Data User Services Division, *1992 Economic Census, Volume 1F, Reports Series, Release 1F,* September 1995, CD-ROM. *Note:* Data are shown only for the top 25 areas.

★2316★
Establishments and Employment
Racing, Including Track Operation

The U.S. total number of employees is 56,285; total number of establishments is 2,666.

MSA	Estab-lish-ments	Rank	Emp-ploy-ment	Rank
Los Angeles – Riverside – Orange County, CA CMSA	173	2	3,914	1
Miami – Fort Lauderdale, FL CMSA	111	3	2,934	2
Tampa – St. Petersburg – Clearwater, FL MSA	31	13	1,232	3
Phoenix – Mesa, AZ MSA	25	17	1,222	4
Louisville, KY – IN MSA	37	11	575	5
West Palm Beach – Boca Raton, FL MSA	23	19	568	6
Minneapolis – St. Paul, MN – WI MSA	16	24	516	7
Memphis, TN – AR – MS MSA	15	25	473	8
Columbus, OH MSA	22	20	448	9
St. Louis, MO – IL MSA	29	14	374	10
Orlando, FL MSA	24	18	359	11
Indianapolis, IN MSA	25	17	356	12
San Diego, CA MSA	20	21	246	13
Birmingham, AL MSA	10	28	242	14

[Continued]

★2316★

Racing, Including Track Operation
[Continued]

MSA	Estab-lish-ments	Rank	Emp-ploy-ment	Rank
Greensboro – Winston-Salem – High Point, NC MSA	22	20	147	15
Bakersfield, CA MSA	5	33	89	16
Atlanta, GA MSA	10	28	84	17
Nashville, TN MSA	12	27	60	18
Tulsa, OK MSA	9	29	39	19
Las Vegas, NV – AZ MSA	8	30	37	20
Peoria – Pekin, IL MSA	3	35	27	21
Raleigh – Durham – Chapel Hill, NC MSA	6	32	26	22
Fresno, CA MSA	5	33	18	23
Albany – Schenectady – Troy, NY MSA	16	24	0[1]	24
Albuquerque, NM MSA	9	29	0	2	4

Source: U.S. Department of Commerce, Bureau of the Census, Data User Services Division, *1992 Economic Census, Volume 1F, Reports Series, Release 1F,* September 1995, CD-ROM. *Notes:* Data are shown only for the top 25 areas. 1. 100-249 employees.

★2317★
Establishments and Employment

Research, Development, and Testing Services (except Noncommercial Research Organizations)

The U.S. total number of employees is 282,315; total number of establishments is 13,531.

MSA	Estab-lish-ments	Rank	Emp-ploy-ment	Rank
New York – Northern New Jersey – Long Island, NY – NJ – CT-CMSA	1,509	1	28,490	1
Los Angeles – Riverside – Orange County, CA CMSA	862	2	16,634	2
San Francisco – Oakland – San Jose, CA CMSA	742	4	12,892	3
Boston – Worcester – Lawrence, MA – NH – ME – CT CMSA	552	5	12,636	4
Chicago – Gary – Kenosha, IL – IN – WI CMSA	515	6	12,020	5
Detroit – Ann Arbor – Flint, MI CMSA	249	11	8,304	6
San Diego, CA MSA	251	10	7,281	7
Pittsburgh, PA MSA	124	19	5,145	8
Houston – Galveston – Brazoria, TX CMSA	275	8	5,128	9
Dallas – Fort Worth, TX CMSA	231	12	5,049	10
Las Vegas, NV – AZ MSA	28	53	3,179	11
Minneapolis – St. Paul, MN – WI MSA	207	14	3,157	12
Tampa – St. Petersburg – Clearwater, FL MSA	103	22	3,145	13
Atlanta, GA MSA	193	15	3,131	14

[Continued]

★2317★

Research, Development, and Testing Services (except Noncommercial Research Organizations)
[Continued]

MSA	Estab-lish-ments	Rank	Emp-ploy-ment	Rank
Phoenix – Mesa, AZ MSA	135	17	2,780	15
Cincinnati – Hamilton, OH – KY – IN CMSA	121	20	2,566	16
Orlando, FL MSA	86	25	2,486	17
Cleveland – Akron, OH CMSA	130	18	2,371	18
Norfolk – Virginia Beach – Newport News, VA – NC MSA	63	32	2,274	19
St. Louis, MO – IL MSA	120	21	2,119	20
Austin – San Marcos, TX MSA	97	24	2,052	21
Huntsville, AL MSA	47	38	2,035	22
Raleigh – Durham – Chapel Hill, NC MSA	98	23	1,983	23
Dayton – Springfield, OH MSA	61	33	1,808	24
Toledo, OH MSA	44	41	1,651	25

Source: U.S. Department of Commerce, Bureau of the Census, Data User Services Division, *1992 Economic Census, Volume 1F, Reports Series, Release 1F,* September 1995, CD-ROM. *Note:* Data are shown only for the top 25 areas.

★2318★
Establishments and Employment

Residential Care

The U.S. total number of employees is 138,707; total number of establishments is 12,121.

MSA	Estab-lish-ments	Rank	Emp-ploy-ment	Rank
Atlanta, GA MSA	71	18	695	19
Boston – Worcester – Lawrence, MA – NH – ME – CT CMSA	169	10	2,184	9
Chicago – Gary – Kenosha, IL – IN – WI CMSA	68	20	0[1]	24
Cincinnati – Hamilton, OH – KY – IN CMSA	47	24	0[2]	24
Cleveland – Akron, OH CMSA	64	22	0[2]	24
Dallas – Fort Worth, TX CMSA	86	16	1,301	14
Denver – Boulder – Greeley, CO CMSA	68	20	1,011	15
Detroit – Ann Arbor – Flint, MI CMSA	370	3	3,494	3
Houston – Galveston – Brazoria, TX CMSA	67	21	443	23
Indianapolis, IN MSA	45	25	644	21
Kansas City, MO – KS MSA	75	17	817	16
Los Angeles – Riverside – Orange County, CA CMSA	875	1	0[3]	24
Miami – Fort Lauderdale, FL CMSA	165	11	1,758	13
Milwaukee – Racine, WI CMSA	161	13	0[1]	24
Minneapolis – St. Paul, MN – WI MSA	214	6	3,210	4
New York – Northern New Jersey – Long Island, NY – NJ – CT-CMSA	367	4	7,112	1

[Continued]

★2318★

Residential Care

[Continued]

MSA	Estab-lish-ments	Rank	Emp-loy-ment	Rank
Orlando, FL MSA	59	23	680	20
Philadelphia – Wilmington – Atlantic City, PA – NJ – DE – MD CMSA	162	12	0[4]	24
Phoenix – Mesa, AZ MSA	119	15	1,893	11
Pittsburgh, PA MSA	170	9	2,623	7
Portland – Salem, OR – WA CMSA	289	5	2,871	6
Sacramento – Yolo, CA CMSA	147	14	779	17
San Diego, CA MSA	203	7	3,013	5
San Francisco – Oakland – San Jose, CA CMSA	681	2	4,042	2
Seattle – Tacoma – Bremerton, WA CMSA	202	8	2,513	8
St. Louis, MO – IL MSA	70	19	719	18
Tampa – St. Petersburg – Clearwater, FL MSA	162	12	1,881	12
Washington – Baltimore, DC – MD – VA – WV CMSA	162	12	2,162	10
West Palm Beach – Boca Raton, FL MSA	41	26	461	22

Source: U.S. Department of Commerce, Bureau of the Census, Data User Services Division, *1992 Economic Census, Volume 1F, Reports Series, Release 1F,* September 1995, CD-ROM. *Notes:* 1. 1,000-2,499 employees. 2. 500-999 employees. 3. 10,000-24,999 employees. 4. 2,500-4,999 employees.

★2319★

Establishments and Employment

Reupholstery and Furniture Repair

The U.S. total number of employees is 21,249; total number of establishments is 6,731.

MSA	Estab-lish-ments	Rank	Emp-loy-ment	Rank
New York – Northern New Jersey – Long Island, NY – NJ – CT-CMSA	488	1	1,794	1
Los Angeles – Riverside – Orange County, CA CMSA	384	2	1,623	2
Chicago – Gary – Kenosha, IL – IN – WI CMSA	217	3	875	3
San Francisco – Oakland – San Jose, CA CMSA	216	4	738	4
Detroit – Ann Arbor – Flint, MI CMSA	95	11	470	5
Miami – Fort Lauderdale, FL CMSA	157	5	416	6
Atlanta, GA MSA	100	10	407	7
Seattle – Tacoma – Bremerton, WA CMSA	106	8	378	8
Dallas – Fort Worth, TX CMSA	102	9	374	9
Phoenix – Mesa, AZ MSA	80	13	362	10
Philadelphia – Wilmington – Atlantic City, PA – NJ – DE – MD CMSA	135	6	327	11

[Continued]

★2319★

Reupholstery and Furniture Repair

[Continued]

MSA	Estab-lish-ments	Rank	Emp-loy-ment	Rank
Minneapolis – St. Paul, MN – WI MSA	79	14	281	12
Denver – Boulder – Greeley, CO CMSA	75	17	269	13
San Diego, CA MSA	77	16	266	14
Indianapolis, IN MSA	50	23	202	15
St. Louis, MO – IL MSA	78	15	202	15
Kansas City, MO – KS MSA	49	24	190	16
San Antonio, TX MSA	42	27	186	17
Tampa – St. Petersburg – Clearwater, FL MSA	71	18	175	18
Greensboro – Winston-Salem – High Point, NC MSA	49	24	171	19
Milwaukee – Racine, WI CMSA	53	21	171	19
Cincinnati – Hamilton, OH – KY – IN CMSA	64	19	167	20
Pittsburgh, PA MSA	54	20	162	21
Hickory – Morganton, NC MSA	18	40	159	22
Norfolk – Virginia Beach – Newport News, VA – NC MSA	50	23	149	23

Source: U.S. Department of Commerce, Bureau of the Census, Data User Services Division, *1992 Economic Census, Volume 1F, Reports Series, Release 1F,* September 1995, CD-ROM. *Note:* Data are shown only for the top 25 areas.

★2320★

Establishments and Employment

Secretarial and Court Reporting Services

The U.S. total number of employees is 30,245; total number of establishments is 6,746.

MSA	Estab-lish-ments	Rank	Emp-loy-ment	Rank
Los Angeles – Riverside – Orange County, CA CMSA	464	2	2,381	1
Miami – Fort Lauderdale, FL CMSA	225	5	888	2
Boston – Worcester – Lawrence, MA – NH – ME – CT CMSA	147	9	771	3
Atlanta, GA MSA	128	13	740	4
Dallas – Fort Worth, TX CMSA	164	7	728	5
Minneapolis – St. Paul, MN – WI MSA	126	14	540	6
Cleveland – Akron, OH CMSA	79	20	464	7
St. Louis, MO – IL MSA	56	25	429	8
San Diego, CA MSA	100	17	417	9
Tampa – St. Petersburg – Clearwater, FL MSA	95	18	359	10
Pittsburgh, PA MSA	41	31	327	11
Kansas City, MO – KS MSA	50	27	273	12
Baton Rouge, LA MSA	26	40	257	13
Orlando, FL MSA	58	24	222	14
West Palm Beach – Boca Raton, FL MSA	72	21	220	15

[Continued]

★2320★

Secretarial and Court Reporting Services
[Continued]

MSA	Estab-lish-ments	Rank	Emp-loy-ment	Rank
Providence – Fall River – Warwick, RI – MA MSA	28	38	209	16
Columbus, OH MSA	36	34	186	17
Austin – San Marcos, TX MSA	42	30	180	18
New Orleans, LA MSA	63	23	171	19
Beaumont – Port Arthur, TX MSA	12	52	165	20
Norfolk – Virginia Beach – Newport News, VA – NC MSA	29	37	154	21
Jacksonville, FL MSA	47	29	147	22
Charlotte – Gastonia – Rock Hill, NC – SC MSA	39	32	145	23
Indianapolis, IN MSA	47	29	139	24
Salt Lake City – Ogden, UT MSA	37	33	139	24

Source: U.S. Department of Commerce, Bureau of the Census, Data User Services Division, *1992 Economic Census, Volume 1F, Reports Series, Release 1F,* September 1995, CD-ROM. *Note:* Data are shown only for the top 25 areas.

★2321★

Establishments and Employment

Security Systems Services

The U.S. total number of employees is 51,755; total number of establishments is 2,968.

MSA	Estab-lish-ments	Rank	Emp-loy-ment	Rank
Dallas – Fort Worth, TX CMSA	71	8	2,649	1
Washington – Baltimore, DC – MD – VA – WV CMSA	122	3	2,209	2
San Francisco – Oakland – San Jose, CA CMSA	68	9	2,139	3
Chicago – Gary – Kenosha, IL – IN – WI CMSA	96	4	1,747	4
Miami – Fort Lauderdale, FL CMSA	94	5	1,368	5
Boston – Worcester – Lawrence, MA – NH – ME – CT CMSA	77	7	1,245	6
Atlanta, GA MSA	63	10	1,168	7
Seattle – Tacoma – Bremerton, WA CMSA	30	17	853	8
Phoenix – Mesa, AZ MSA	40	13	845	9
Cleveland – Akron, OH CMSA	39	14	626	10
Minneapolis – St. Paul, MN – WI MSA	23	21	557	11
Tampa – St. Petersburg – Clearwater, FL MSA	30	17	532	12
San Antonio, TX MSA	21	22	521	13
St. Louis, MO – IL MSA	30	17	488	14
Pittsburgh, PA MSA	29	18	469	15
Columbus, OH MSA	23	21	439	16
San Diego, CA MSA	29	18	407	17
Indianapolis, IN MSA	17	26	394	18
Charlotte – Gastonia – Rock Hill, NC – SC MSA	26	19	390	19

[Continued]

★2321★

Security Systems Services
[Continued]

MSA	Estab-lish-ments	Rank	Emp-loy-ment	Rank
Orlando, FL MSA	25	20	372	20
Richmond – Petersburg, VA MSA	14	29	346	21
Buffalo – Niagara Falls, NY MSA	16	27	344	22
Austin – San Marcos, TX MSA	15	28	329	23
Kansas City, MO – KS MSA	17	26	327	24
Milwaukee – Racine, WI CMSA	18	25	321	25

Source: U.S. Department of Commerce, Bureau of the Census, Data User Services Division, *1992 Economic Census, Volume 1F, Reports Series, Release 1F,* September 1995, CD-ROM. *Note:* Data are shown only for the top 25 areas.

★2322★

Establishments and Employment

Services Allied To Motion Picture Distribution

The U.S. total number of employees is 947; total number of establishments is 210.

MSA	Estab-lish-ments	Rank	Emp-loy-ment	Rank
Atlanta, GA MSA	1	9	0[1]	3
Boston – Worcester – Lawrence, MA – NH – ME – CT CMSA	9	4	0[1]	3
Chicago – Gary – Kenosha, IL – IN – WI CMSA	12	3	0[1]	3
Cincinnati – Hamilton, OH – KY – IN CMSA	4	6	23	2
Cleveland – Akron, OH CMSA	1	9	0[2]	3
Dallas – Fort Worth, TX CMSA	6	5	0[1]	3
Denver – Boulder – Greeley, CO CMSA	2	8	0[2]	3
Detroit – Ann Arbor – Flint, MI CMSA	3	7	0[1]	3
Houston – Galveston – Brazoria, TX CMSA	0	10	0	3
Indianapolis, IN MSA	1	9	0[2]	3
Kansas City, MO – KS MSA	1	9	0[2]	3
Los Angeles – Riverside – Orange County, CA CMSA	66	1	0[3]	3
Miami – Fort Lauderdale, FL CMSA	3	7	0[2]	3
Milwaukee – Racine, WI CMSA	2	8	0[2]	3
Minneapolis – St. Paul, MN – WI MSA	0	10	0	3
New York – Northern New Jersey – Long Island, NY – NJ – CT-CMSA	44	2	199	1
Orlando, FL MSA	0	10	0	3
Philadelphia – Wilmington – Atlantic City, PA – NJ – DE – MD CMSA	3	7	0[2]	3
Phoenix – Mesa, AZ MSA	1	9	0[2]	3
Pittsburgh, PA MSA	0	10	0	3
Portland – Salem, OR – WA CMSA	0	10	0	3
Sacramento – Yolo, CA CMSA	1	9	0[2]	3

[Continued]

★2322★

Services Allied To Motion Picture Distribution

[Continued]

MSA	Estab-lish-ments	Rank	Emp-loy-ment	Rank
San Diego, CA MSA	0	10	0	3
San Francisco – Oakland – San Jose, CA CMSA	3	7	0^1	3
Seattle – Tacoma – Bremerton, WA CMSA	3	7	0^1	3
St. Louis, MO – IL MSA	1	9	0^2	3
Tampa – St. Petersburg – Clearwater, FL MSA	0	10	0	3
Washington – Baltimore, DC – MD – VA – WV CMSA	4	6	0^2	3
West Palm Beach – Boca Raton, FL MSA	1	9	0^2	3

Source: U.S. Department of Commerce, Bureau of the Census, Data User Services Division, *1992 Economic Census, Volume 1F, Reports Series, Release 1F*, September 1995, CD-ROM. *Notes:* 1. 20-99 employees. 2. 0-19 employees. 3. 100-249 employees.

★2323★

Establishments and Employment

Services Allied To Motion Picture Production

The U.S. total number of employees is 162,216; total number of establishments is 3,895.

MSA	Estab-lish-ments	Rank	Emp-loy-ment	Rank
Atlanta, GA MSA	47	9	1,981	1
Boston – Worcester – Lawrence, MA – NH – ME – CT CMSA	41	10	0^1	16
Chicago – Gary – Kenosha, IL – IN – WI CMSA	110	3	0^2	16
Cincinnati – Hamilton, OH – KY – IN CMSA	18	18	0^1	16
Cleveland – Akron, OH CMSA	9	21	0^3	16
Dallas – Fort Worth, TX CMSA	54	7	0^4	16
Denver – Boulder – Greeley, CO CMSA	31	14	243	10
Detroit – Ann Arbor – Flint, MI CMSA	49	8	1,338	2
Houston – Galveston – Brazoria, TX CMSA	23	16	0^3	16
Indianapolis, IN MSA	18	18	0^3	16
Kansas City, MO – KS MSA	10	20	72	14
Los Angeles – Riverside – Orange County, CA CMSA	1,852	1	0^5	16
Miami – Fort Lauderdale, FL CMSA	63	6	708	4
Milwaukee – Racine, WI CMSA	9	21	47	15
Minneapolis – St. Paul, MN – WI MSA	34	13	0^1	16
New York – Northern New Jersey – Long Island, NY – NJ – CT-CMSA	631	2	0^6	16
Orlando, FL MSA	24	15	521	5

[Continued]

★2323★

Services Allied To Motion Picture Production

[Continued]

MSA	Estab-lish-ments	Rank	Emp-loy-ment	Rank
Philadelphia – Wilmington – Atlantic City, PA – NJ – DE – MD CMSA	39	12	0^1	16
Phoenix – Mesa, AZ MSA	20	17	262	9
Pittsburgh, PA MSA	24	15	511	6
Portland – Salem, OR – WA CMSA	17	19	125	13
Sacramento – Yolo, CA CMSA	6	22	0^7	16
San Diego, CA MSA	23	16	232	11
San Francisco – Oakland – San Jose, CA CMSA	103	4	0^4	16
Seattle – Tacoma – Bremerton, WA CMSA	40	11	346	8
St. Louis, MO – IL MSA	20	17	384	7
Tampa – St. Petersburg – Clearwater, FL MSA	20	17	129	12
Washington – Baltimore, DC – MD – VA – WV CMSA	102	5	930	3
West Palm Beach – Boca Raton, FL MSA	9	21	0^7	16

Source: U.S. Department of Commerce, Bureau of the Census, Data User Services Division, *1992 Economic Census, Volume 1F, Reports Series, Release 1F*, September 1995, CD-ROM. *Notes:* 1. 250-499 employees. 2. 25,000-49,999 employees. 3. 100-249 employees. 4. 1,000-2,499 employees. 5. 100,000 or more employees. 6. 10,000-24,999 employees. 7. 20-99 employees.

★2324★

Establishments and Employment

Services To Dwellings and Other Buildings

The U.S. total number of employees is 817,944; total number of establishments is 57,649.

MSA	Estab-lish-ments	Rank	Emp-loy-ment	Rank
New York – Northern New Jersey – Long Island, NY – NJ – CT-CMSA	4,156	1	88,419	1
Washington – Baltimore, DC – MD – VA – WV CMSA	2,095	3	47,365	2
Los Angeles – Riverside – Orange County, CA CMSA	2,688	2	38,200	3
Philadelphia – Wilmington – Atlantic City, PA – NJ – DE – MD CMSA	1,539	6	31,396	4
San Francisco – Oakland – San Jose, CA CMSA	1,702	5	25,323	5
Boston – Worcester – Lawrence, MA – NH – ME – CT CMSA	1,283	7	23,560	6
Houston – Galveston – Brazoria, TX CMSA	818	13	19,553	7
Detroit – Ann Arbor – Flint, MI CMSA	1,104	8	14,575	8
Dallas – Fort Worth, TX CMSA	989	10	14,537	9
Atlanta, GA MSA	863	12	13,682	10
Minneapolis – St. Paul, MN – WI MSA	682	17	13,137	11

[Continued]

★ 2324 ★

Services To Dwellings and Other Buildings

[Continued]

MSA	Estab-lish-ments	Rank	Emp-ploy-ment	Rank
St. Louis, MO – IL MSA	702	16	12,044	12
Miami – Fort Lauderdale, FL CMSA	1,101	9	11,981	13
Denver – Boulder – Greeley, CO CMSA	634	19	10,251	14
Cleveland – Akron, OH CMSA	675	18	9,696	15
Greenville – Spartanburg – Anderson, SC MSA	246	45	9,489	16
Pittsburgh, PA MSA	466	24	9,337	17
Cincinnati – Hamilton, OH – KY – IN CMSA	398	27	9,042	18
Phoenix – Mesa, AZ MSA	731	14	8,529	19
Seattle – Tacoma – Bremerton, WA CMSA	955	11	8,503	20
San Diego, CA MSA	564	20	7,675	21
Milwaukee – Racine, WI CMSA	496	23	7,535	22
Kansas City, MO – KS MSA	509	21	7,445	23
Tampa – St. Petersburg – Clearwater, FL MSA	728	15	7,263	24
Greensboro – Winston-Salem – High Point, NC MSA	339	32	6,390	25

Source: U.S. Department of Commerce, Bureau of the Census, Data User Services Division, *1992 Economic Census, Volume 1F, Reports Series, Release 1F,* September 1995, CD-ROM. *Note:* Data are shown only for the top 25 areas.

★ 2325 ★

Establishments and Employment

Shoe Repair Shops and Shoeshine Parlors

The U.S. total number of employees is 6,397; total number of establishments is 2,702.

MSA	Estab-lish-ments	Rank	Emp-ploy-ment	Rank
Los Angeles – Riverside – Orange County, CA CMSA	139	2	449	1
San Francisco – Oakland – San Jose, CA CMSA	89	3	215	2
Dallas – Fort Worth, TX CMSA	65	6	184	3
Grand Rapids – Muskegon – Holland, MI MSA	11	29	144	4
Detroit – Ann Arbor – Flint, MI CMSA	48	10	121	5
San Diego, CA MSA	36	13	110	6
St. Louis, MO – IL MSA	37	12	109	7
Philadelphia – Wilmington – Atlantic City, PA – NJ – DE – MD CMSA	61	7	105	8
Minneapolis – St. Paul, MN – WI MSA	39	11	103	9
Atlanta, GA MSA	53	9	83	10
San Antonio, TX MSA	24	17	70	11
Austin – San Marcos, TX MSA	19	21	69	12
Cleveland – Akron, OH CMSA	24	17	63	13

[Continued]

★ 2325 ★

Shoe Repair Shops and Shoeshine Parlors

[Continued]

MSA	Estab-lish-ments	Rank	Emp-ploy-ment	Rank
Kansas City, MO – KS MSA	23	18	63	13
New Orleans, LA MSA	25	16	54	14
Tampa – St. Petersburg – Clearwater, FL MSA	22	19	51	15
Pittsburgh, PA MSA	22	19	48	16
Indianapolis, IN MSA	25	16	46	17
Jacksonville, FL MSA	18	22	46	17
Oklahoma City, OK MSA	11	29	46	17
Phoenix – Mesa, AZ MSA	34	14	46	17
Salt Lake City – Ogden, UT MSA	15	25	45	18
Norfolk – Virginia Beach – Newport News, VA – NC MSA	21	20	43	19
Greensboro – Winston-Salem – High Point, NC MSA	21	20	42	20
Portland – Salem, OR – WA CMSA	27	15	42	20

Source: U.S. Department of Commerce, Bureau of the Census, Data User Services Division, *1992 Economic Census, Volume 1F, Reports Series, Release 1F,* September 1995, CD-ROM. *Note:* Data are shown only for the top 25 areas.

★ 2326 ★

Establishments and Employment

Sign Painting Shops

The U.S. total number of employees is 9,241; total number of establishments is 2,562.

MSA	Estab-lish-ments	Rank	Emp-ploy-ment	Rank
Los Angeles – Riverside – Orange County, CA CMSA	141	2	724	1
Dallas – Fort Worth, TX CMSA	40	12	234	2
Atlanta, GA MSA	50	7	195	3
Boston – Worcester – Lawrence, MA – NH – ME – CT CMSA	61	5	167	4
Philadelphia – Wilmington – Atlantic City, PA – NJ – DE – MD CMSA	52	6	154	5
Miami – Fort Lauderdale, FL CMSA	48	8	140	6
Minneapolis – St. Paul, MN – WI MSA	34	14	136	7
Jacksonville, FL MSA	20	21	121	8
Kansas City, MO – KS MSA	27	17	115	9
St. Louis, MO – IL MSA	29	15	109	10
Columbus, OH MSA	14	26	85	11
San Diego, CA MSA	28	16	82	12
Richmond – Petersburg, VA MSA	15	25	80	13
Charlotte – Gastonia – Rock Hill, NC – SC MSA	17	23	71	14
Cleveland – Akron, OH CMSA	17	23	62	15
Norfolk – Virginia Beach – Newport News, VA – NC MSA	16	24	59	16
Knoxville, TN MSA	12	28	57	17
Buffalo – Niagara Falls, NY MSA	14	26	53	18

[Continued]

★ 2326 ★

Sign Painting Shops
[Continued]

MSA	Estab-lish-ments	Rank	Emp-ploy-ment	Rank
Louisville, KY – IN MSA	13	27	51	19
Sarasota – Bradenton, FL MSA	9	31	44	20
Greenville – Spartanburg – Anderson, SC MSA	13	27	43	21
Dayton – Springfield, OH MSA	10	30	42	22
Hartford, CT MSA	9	31	42	22
Las Vegas, NV – AZ MSA	17	23	41	23
Lexington, KY MSA	11	29	41	23

Source: U.S. Department of Commerce, Bureau of the Census, Data User Services Division, *1992 Economic Census, Volume 1F, Reports Series, Release 1F*, September 1995, CD-ROM. *Note:* Data are shown only for the top 25 areas.

★ 2327 ★

Establishments and Employment

Skilled Nursing Care Facilities

The U.S. total number of employees is 937,907; total number of establishments is 10,242.

MSA	Estab-lish-ments	Rank	Emp-ploy-ment	Rank
New York – Northern New Jersey – Long Island, NY – NJ – CT-CMSA	457	2	62,457	1
Los Angeles – Riverside – Orange County, CA CMSA	557	1	44,440	2
Boston – Worcester – Lawrence, MA – NH – ME – CT CMSA	313	3	33,261	3
San Francisco – Oakland – San Jose, CA CMSA	251	4	18,769	4
Cleveland – Akron, OH CMSA	127	12	15,107	5
Dallas – Fort Worth, TX CMSA	181	6	14,139	6
Minneapolis – St. Paul, MN – WI MSA	108	16	13,195	7
St. Louis, MO – IL MSA	128	11	11,525	8
Tampa – St. Petersburg – Clearwater, FL MSA	115	14	11,147	9
Hartford, CT MSA	78	21	10,009	10
Indianapolis, IN MSA	108	16	9,704	11
Atlanta, GA MSA	99	18	9,343	12
Cincinnati – Hamilton, OH – KY – IN CMSA	114	15	9,247	13
Miami – Fort Lauderdale, FL CMSA	129	10	8,956	14
Houston – Galveston – Brazoria, TX CMSA	98	19	8,240	15
Kansas City, MO – KS MSA	106	17	7,848	16
Providence – Fall River – Warwick, RI – MA MSA	74	22	7,360	17
Columbus, OH MSA	55	25	6,918	18
San Diego, CA MSA	72	23	6,643	19
Pittsburgh, PA MSA	78	21	5,942	20
Phoenix – Mesa, AZ MSA	52	27	5,769	21
Springfield, MA MSA	41	33	4,838	22

[Continued]

★ 2327 ★

Skilled Nursing Care Facilities
[Continued]

MSA	Estab-lish-ments	Rank	Emp-ploy-ment	Rank
Louisville, KY – IN MSA	41	33	4,581	23
Youngstown – Warren, OH MSA	44	31	4,551	24
Charlotte – Gastonia – Rock Hill, NC – SC MSA	42	32	4,342	25

Source: U.S. Department of Commerce, Bureau of the Census, Data User Services Division, *1992 Economic Census, Volume 1F, Reports Series, Release 1F*, September 1995, CD-ROM. *Note:* Data are shown only for the top 25 areas.

★ 2328 ★

Establishments and Employment

Social Services

The U.S. total number of employees is 505,401; total number of establishments is 59,123.

MSA	Estab-lish-ments	Rank	Emp-ploy-ment	Rank
Los Angeles – Riverside – Orange County, CA CMSA	3,090	1	27,275	1
New York – Northern New Jersey – Long Island, NY – NJ – CT-CMSA	2,705	2	26,911	2
San Francisco – Oakland – San Jose, CA CMSA	2,328	3	14,928	3
Philadelphia – Wilmington – Atlantic City, PA – NJ – DE – MD CMSA	1,165	8	13,973	4
Washington – Baltimore, DC – MD – VA – WV CMSA	1,421	4	13,667	5
Dallas – Fort Worth, TX CMSA	1,124	10	12,605	6
Chicago – Gary – Kenosha, IL – IN – WI CMSA	1,132	9	11,429	7
Boston – Worcester – Lawrence, MA – NH – ME – CT CMSA	1,246	6	11,281	8
Atlanta, GA MSA	965	12	10,378	9
Detroit – Ann Arbor – Flint, MI CMSA	1,275	5	10,299	10
Seattle – Tacoma – Bremerton, WA CMSA	1,214	7	10,175	11
Minneapolis – St. Paul, MN – WI MSA	1,001	11	9,606	12
Houston – Galveston – Brazoria, TX CMSA	931	13	9,125	13
Phoenix – Mesa, AZ MSA	572	19	7,113	14
Miami – Fort Lauderdale, FL CMSA	805	14	6,738	15
Portland – Salem, OR – WA CMSA	742	15	6,268	16
San Diego, CA MSA	645	17	6,218	17
Denver – Boulder – Greeley, CO CMSA	560	20	5,929	18
Tampa – St. Petersburg – Clearwater, FL MSA	676	16	5,630	19
Pittsburgh, PA MSA	471	22	5,522	20
St. Louis, MO – IL MSA	541	21	4,996	21

[Continued]

★2328★
Social Services
[Continued]

MSA	Estab-lish-ments	Rank	Emp-loy-ment	Rank
Milwaukee – Racine, WI CMSA	452	23	4,642	22
Raleigh – Durham – Chapel Hill, NC MSA	332	30	3,986	23
Cleveland – Akron, OH CMSA	420	26	3,908	24
Kansas City, MO – KS MSA	432	25	3,832	25

Source: U.S. Department of Commerce, Bureau of the Census, Data User Services Division, *1992 Economic Census, Volume 1F, Reports Series, Release 1F*, September 1995, CD-ROM. *Note:* Data are shown only for the top 25 areas.

★2329★
Establishments and Employment
Sporting and Recreational Camps

The U.S. total number of employees is 9,659; total number of establishments is 1,840.

MSA	Estab-lish-ments	Rank	Emp-loy-ment	Rank
Atlanta, GA MSA	0	18	0	13
Boston – Worcester – Lawrence, MA – NH – ME – CT CMSA	20	4	52	9
Chicago – Gary – Kenosha, IL – IN – WI CMSA	19	5	0[1]	13
Cincinnati – Hamilton, OH – KY – IN CMSA	3	15	6	12
Cleveland – Akron, OH CMSA	1	17	0[2]	13
Dallas – Fort Worth, TX CMSA	13	7	0[1]	13
Denver – Boulder – Greeley, CO CMSA	10	9	0[3]	13
Detroit – Ann Arbor – Flint, MI CMSA	15	6	159	5
Houston – Galveston – Brazoria, TX CMSA	5	13	0[2]	13
Indianapolis, IN MSA	0	18	0	13
Kansas City, MO – KS MSA	4	14	11	11
Los Angeles – Riverside – Orange County, CA CMSA	36	2	0[3]	13
Miami – Fort Lauderdale, FL CMSA	6	12	0[2]	13
Milwaukee – Racine, WI CMSA	4	14	0[2]	13
Minneapolis – St. Paul, MN – WI MSA	9	10	95	8
New York – Northern New Jersey – Long Island, NY – NJ – CT-CMSA	69	1	391	1
Orlando, FL MSA	12	8	0[1]	13
Philadelphia – Wilmington – Atlantic City, PA – NJ – DE – MD CMSA	24	3	239	3
Phoenix – Mesa, AZ MSA	5	13	111	7
Pittsburgh, PA MSA	2	16	0[2]	13
Portland – Salem, OR – WA CMSA	8	11	6	12
Sacramento – Yolo, CA CMSA	6	12	0[1]	13
San Diego, CA MSA	9	10	262	2

[Continued]

★2329★
Sporting and Recreational Camps
[Continued]

MSA	Estab-lish-ments	Rank	Emp-loy-ment	Rank
San Francisco – Oakland – San Jose, CA CMSA	36	2	172	4
Seattle – Tacoma – Bremerton, WA CMSA	12	8	0[1]	13
St. Louis, MO – IL MSA	6	12	19	10
Tampa – St. Petersburg – Clearwater, FL MSA	8	11	132	6
Washington – Baltimore, DC – MD – VA – WV CMSA	24	3	0[1]	13
West Palm Beach – Boca Raton, FL MSA	2	16	0[2]	13

Source: U.S. Department of Commerce, Bureau of the Census, Data User Services Division, *1992 Economic Census, Volume 1F, Reports Series, Release 1F*, September 1995, CD-ROM. *Notes:* 1. 20-99 employees. 2. 0-19 employees. 3. 100-249 employees.

★2330★
Establishments and Employment
Surveying Services

The U.S. total number of employees is 45,324; total number of establishments is 8,418.

MSA	Estab-lish-ments	Rank	Emp-loy-ment	Rank
Washington – Baltimore, DC – MD – VA – WV CMSA	210	3	1,758	1
Houston – Galveston – Brazoria, TX CMSA	158	6	1,472	2
Chicago – Gary – Kenosha, IL – IN – WI CMSA	174	5	1,367	3
Los Angeles – Riverside – Orange County, CA CMSA	224	2	1,296	4
Boston – Worcester – Lawrence, MA – NH – ME – CT CMSA	195	4	1,137	5
Atlanta, GA MSA	145	7	972	6
Miami – Fort Lauderdale, FL CMSA	115	12	891	7
San Francisco – Oakland – San Jose, CA CMSA	128	8	874	8
Dallas – Fort Worth, TX CMSA	124	9	845	9
Philadelphia – Wilmington – Atlantic City, PA – NJ – DE – MD CMSA	117	11	804	10
Seattle – Tacoma – Bremerton, WA CMSA	122	10	745	11
Tampa – St. Petersburg – Clearwater, FL MSA	84	13	640	12
Detroit – Ann Arbor – Flint, MI CMSA	80	14	604	13
Charlotte – Gastonia – Rock Hill, NC – SC MSA	70	15	518	14
Lafayette, LA MSA	11	57	459	15
Orlando, FL MSA	57	21	443	16

[Continued]

★2330★

Surveying Services

[Continued]

MSA	Estab-lish-ments	Rank	Emp-loy-ment	Rank
New Orleans, LA MSA	41	30	411	17
Denver – Boulder – Greeley, CO CMSA	80	14	409	18
Jacksonville, FL MSA	52	25	405	19
Pittsburgh, PA MSA	68	16	361	20
Norfolk – Virginia Beach – Newport News, VA – NC MSA	53	24	355	21
Cleveland – Akron, OH CMSA	61	19	351	22
Minneapolis – St. Paul, MN – WI MSA	63	18	346	23
West Palm Beach – Boca Raton, FL MSA	51	26	338	24
Kansas City, MO – KS MSA	31	37	320	25

Source: U.S. Department of Commerce, Bureau of the Census, Data User Services Division, *1992 Economic Census, Volume 1F, Reports Series, Release 1F,* September 1995, CD-ROM. *Note:* Data are shown only for the top 25 areas.

★2331★

Establishments and Employment

Tax Return Preparation Services

The U.S. total number of employees is 122,954; total number of establishments is 7,924.

MSA	Estab-lish-ments	Rank	Emp-loy-ment	Rank
Los Angeles – Riverside – Orange County, CA CMSA	447	1	6,297	1
Chicago – Gary – Kenosha, IL – IN – WI CMSA	159	5	4,580	2
Washington – Baltimore, DC – MD – VA – WV CMSA	170	4	3,724	3
Detroit – Ann Arbor – Flint, MI CMSA	136	6	3,350	4
Boston – Worcester – Lawrence, MA – NH – ME – CT CMSA	113	7	3,347	5
San Francisco – Oakland – San Jose, CA CMSA	297	3	3,338	6
Philadelphia – Wilmington – Atlantic City, PA – NJ – DE – MD CMSA	92	11	2,697	7
Dallas – Fort Worth, TX CMSA	101	10	2,159	8
Atlanta, GA MSA	102	9	1,843	9
St. Louis, MO – IL MSA	71	14	1,723	10
Phoenix – Mesa, AZ MSA	63	15	1,521	11
Norfolk – Virginia Beach – Newport News, VA – NC MSA	52	20	1,473	12
Kansas City, MO – KS MSA	60	17	1,362	13
Cleveland – Akron, OH CMSA	53	19	1,340	14
San Diego, CA MSA	110	8	1,284	15
Minneapolis – St. Paul, MN – WI MSA	71	14	1,231	16
Seattle – Tacoma – Bremerton, WA CMSA	83	13	1,211	17

[Continued]

★2331★

Tax Return Preparation Services

[Continued]

MSA	Estab-lish-ments	Rank	Emp-loy-ment	Rank
Milwaukee – Racine, WI CMSA	53	19	1,161	18
Charlotte – Gastonia – Rock Hill, NC – SC MSA	61	16	1,131	19
Pittsburgh, PA MSA	43	24	1,120	20
Tampa – St. Petersburg – Clearwater, FL MSA	44	23	1,109	21
Indianapolis, IN MSA	34	30	1,059	22
Columbus, OH MSA	36	28	958	23
Raleigh – Durham – Chapel Hill, NC MSA	32	32	757	24
Louisville, KY – IN MSA	47	21	747	25

Source: U.S. Department of Commerce, Bureau of the Census, Data User Services Division, *1992 Economic Census, Volume 1F, Reports Series, Release 1F,* September 1995, CD-ROM. *Note:* Data are shown only for the top 25 areas.

★2332★

Establishments and Employment

Telephone Answering Services

The U.S. total number of employees is 37,914; total number of establishments is 3,191.

MSA	Estab-lish-ments	Rank	Emp-loy-ment	Rank
New York – Northern New Jersey – Long Island, NY – NJ – CT-CMSA	327	1	3,773	1
Los Angeles – Riverside – Orange County, CA CMSA	248	2	3,645	2
Chicago – Gary – Kenosha, IL – IN – WI CMSA	129	3	1,769	3
Philadelphia – Wilmington – Atlantic City, PA – NJ – DE – MD CMSA	68	9	1,426	4
Boston – Worcester – Lawrence, MA – NH – ME – CT CMSA	92	5	1,076	5
Dallas – Fort Worth, TX CMSA	76	6	942	6
Houston – Galveston – Brazoria, TX CMSA	69	8	712	7
Miami – Fort Lauderdale, FL CMSA	43	13	639	8
Atlanta, GA MSA	54	10	539	9
San Diego, CA MSA	37	15	492	10
Kansas City, MO – KS MSA	24	22	466	11
Phoenix – Mesa, AZ MSA	39	14	464	12
Pittsburgh, PA MSA	39	14	423	13
Seattle – Tacoma – Bremerton, WA CMSA	32	18	407	14
Allentown – Bethlehem – Easton, PA MSA	9	35	393	15
St. Louis, MO – IL MSA	30	19	379	16
Lancaster, PA MSA	6	38	377	17
Columbus, OH MSA	12	32	314	18
Las Vegas, NV – AZ MSA	17	27	303	19

[Continued]

★2332★

Telephone Answering Services

[Continued]

MSA	Estab-lish-ments	Rank	Emp-ploy-ment	Rank
Tampa – St. Petersburg – Clearwater, FL MSA	34	17	298	20
Salt Lake City – Ogden, UT MSA	14	30	288	21
Minneapolis – St. Paul, MN – WI MSA	36	16	287	22
Orlando, FL MSA	29	20	277	23
Indianapolis, IN MSA	15	29	260	24
Norfolk – Virginia Beach – Newport News, VA – NC MSA	15	29	257	25

Source: U.S. Department of Commerce, Bureau of the Census, Data User Services Division, *1992 Economic Census, Volume 1F, Reports Series, Release 1F*, September 1995, CD-ROM. *Note:* Data are shown only for the top 25 areas.

★2333★

Establishments and Employment

Temporary Help Supply

The U.S. total number of employees is 1,422,317; total number of establishments is 15,630.

MSA	Estab-lish-ments	Rank	Emp-ploy-ment	Rank
Los Angeles – Riverside – Orange County, CA CMSA	1,114	2	110,945	1
Boston – Worcester – Lawrence, MA – NH – ME – CT CMSA	481	6	39,857	2
Detroit – Ann Arbor – Flint, MI CMSA	387	10	36,438	3
Dallas – Fort Worth, TX CMSA	446	8	36,283	4
Atlanta, GA MSA	471	7	35,679	5
Houston – Galveston – Brazoria, TX CMSA	373	11	34,989	6
Minneapolis – St. Paul, MN – WI MSA	245	15	26,907	7
Miami – Fort Lauderdale, FL CMSA	273	12	24,274	8
Cleveland – Akron, OH CMSA	255	13	24,255	9
Tampa – St. Petersburg – Clearwater, FL MSA	207	17	19,963	10
Columbus, OH MSA	116	26	18,928	11
St. Louis, MO – IL MSA	146	23	18,341	12
Phoenix – Mesa, AZ MSA	191	18	15,808	13
San Diego, CA MSA	156	19	15,496	14
Raleigh – Durham – Chapel Hill, NC MSA	101	28	15,061	15
New Orleans, LA MSA	101	28	14,091	16
Kansas City, MO – KS MSA	132	24	14,044	17
Indianapolis, IN MSA	91	31	13,611	18
Greenville – Spartanburg – Anderson, SC MSA	65	41	13,192	19
Pittsburgh, PA MSA	149	21	11,198	20
Greensboro – Winston-Salem – High Point, NC MSA	113	27	9,658	21
Rochester, NY MSA	83	34	9,603	22

[Continued]

★2333★

Temporary Help Supply

[Continued]

MSA	Estab-lish-ments	Rank	Emp-ploy-ment	Rank
Salt Lake City – Ogden, UT MSA	62	42	9,207	23
Louisville, KY – IN MSA	66	40	9,086	24
Nashville, TN MSA	70	38	9,039	25

Source: U.S. Department of Commerce, Bureau of the Census, Data User Services Division, *1992 Economic Census, Volume 1F, Reports Series, Release 1F*, September 1995, CD-ROM. *Note:* Data are shown only for the top 25 areas.

★2334★

Establishments and Employment

Testing Laboratories

The U.S. total number of employees is 70,462; total number of establishments is 4,540.

MSA	Estab-lish-ments	Rank	Emp-ploy-ment	Rank
Los Angeles – Riverside – Orange County, CA CMSA	274	2	4,429	1
Boston – Worcester – Lawrence, MA – NH – ME – CT CMSA	122	7	2,634	2
Chicago – Gary – Kenosha, IL – IN – WI CMSA	134	5	2,171	3
Detroit – Ann Arbor – Flint, MI CMSA	92	9	1,525	4
Pittsburgh, PA MSA	47	18	1,247	5
Raleigh – Durham – Chapel Hill, NC MSA	29	26	1,132	6
Dallas – Fort Worth, TX CMSA	88	10	930	7
New Orleans, LA MSA	44	19	925	8
Minneapolis – St. Paul, MN – WI MSA	47	18	889	9
San Antonio, TX MSA	25	29	769	10
Atlanta, GA MSA	59	14	749	11
Memphis, TN – AR – MS MSA	17	36	661	12
Salt Lake City – Ogden, UT MSA	38	21	660	13
St. Louis, MO – IL MSA	36	23	609	14
Orlando, FL MSA	26	28	596	15
Miami – Fort Lauderdale, FL CMSA	54	15	574	16
West Palm Beach – Boca Raton, FL MSA	23	31	558	17
San Diego, CA MSA	41	20	499	18
Baton Rouge, LA MSA	25	29	498	19
Bakersfield, CA MSA	24	30	444	20
Tulsa, OK MSA	30	25	404	21
Austin – San Marcos, TX MSA	25	29	350	22
Dayton – Springfield, OH MSA	15	38	343	23
Albuquerque, NM MSA	17	36	327	24
Norfolk – Virginia Beach – Newport News, VA – NC MSA	26	28	309	25

Source: U.S. Department of Commerce, Bureau of the Census, Data User Services Division, *1992 Economic Census, Volume 1F, Reports Series, Release 1F*, September 1995, CD-ROM. *Note:* Data are shown only for the top 25 areas.

★2335★

Establishments and Employment

Theatrical Producers (except Motion Picture), Bands, Orchestras, and Entertainers

The U.S. total number of employees is 68,998; total number of establishments is 10,086.

MSA	Estab-lish-ments	Rank	Emp-loy-ment	Rank
Los Angeles – Riverside – Orange County, CA CMSA	2,812	1	15,336	1
Nashville, TN MSA	333	4	2,415	2
Honolulu, HI MSA	46	29	1,263	3
Miami – Fort Lauderdale, FL CMSA	178	7	1,160	4
Minneapolis – St. Paul, MN – WI MSA	123	12	1,145	5
Las Vegas, NV – AZ MSA	115	13	1,064	6
Dallas – Fort Worth, TX CMSA	128	10	994	7
St. Louis, MO – IL MSA	93	15	911	8
Pittsburgh, PA MSA	44	30	478	9
New Orleans, LA MSA	49	28	467	10
San Diego, CA MSA	75	18	466	11
Orlando, FL MSA	61	22	453	12
Phoenix – Mesa, AZ MSA	69	20	399	13
Atlanta, GA MSA	92	16	385	14
San Antonio, TX MSA	43	31	325	15
Kansas City, MO – KS MSA	50	27	309	16
Norfolk – Virginia Beach – Newport News, VA – NC MSA	37	34	308	17
Cleveland – Akron, OH CMSA	51	26	301	18
Austin – San Marcos, TX MSA	57	24	298	19
Tampa – St. Petersburg – Clearwater, FL MSA	56	25	277	20
Indianapolis, IN MSA	41	32	255	21
West Palm Beach – Boca Raton, FL MSA	39	33	216	22
Salt Lake City – Ogden, UT MSA	24	41	212	23
Oklahoma City, OK MSA	18	46	203	24
Omaha, NE – IA MSA	30	37	173	25

Source: U.S. Department of Commerce, Bureau of the Census, Data User Services Division, *1992 Economic Census, Volume 1F, Reports Series, Release 1F,* September 1995, CD-ROM. *Note:* Data are shown only for the top 25 areas.

★2336★

Establishments and Employment

Tire Retreading and Repair Shops

The U.S. total number of employees is 12,898; total number of establishments is 1,845.

MSA	Estab-lish-ments	Rank	Emp-loy-ment	Rank
Chicago – Gary – Kenosha, IL – IN – WI CMSA	48	3	417	1
St. Louis, MO – IL MSA	34	5	330	2
Atlanta, GA MSA	32	7	212	3
Detroit – Ann Arbor – Flint, MI CMSA	21	12	186	4
Miami – Fort Lauderdale, FL CMSA	48	3	169	5

[Continued]

★2336★

Tire Retreading and Repair Shops

[Continued]

MSA	Estab-lish-ments	Rank	Emp-loy-ment	Rank
Dallas – Fort Worth, TX CMSA	21	12	152	6
Phoenix – Mesa, AZ MSA	23	10	143	7
Greensboro – Winston-Salem – High Point, NC MSA	12	19	135	8
Cleveland – Akron, OH CMSA	26	9	128	9
Indianapolis, IN MSA	14	17	127	10
Washington – Baltimore, DC – MD – VA – WV CMSA	22	11	125	11
Kansas City, MO – KS MSA	11	20	124	12
San Antonio, TX MSA	22	11	114	13
Jacksonville, FL MSA	15	16	112	14
San Diego, CA MSA	8	22	110	15
Pittsburgh, PA MSA	22	11	103	16
Birmingham, AL MSA	11	20	92	17
Scranton – Wilkes-Barre – Hazleton, PA MSA	6	24	86	18
Columbus, OH MSA	9	21	85	19
Richmond – Petersburg, VA MSA	7	23	84	20
Tampa – St. Petersburg – Clearwater, FL MSA	14	17	82	21
Memphis, TN – AR – MS MSA	9	21	80	22
Greenville – Spartanburg – Anderson, SC MSA	17	15	78	23
Grand Rapids – Muskegon – Holland, MI MSA	7	23	77	24
Oklahoma City, OK MSA	9	21	77	24

Source: U.S. Department of Commerce, Bureau of the Census, Data User Services Division, *1992 Economic Census, Volume 1F, Reports Series, Release 1F,* September 1995, CD-ROM. *Note:* Data are shown only for the top 25 areas.

★2337★

Establishments and Employment

Total (taxable)

The U.S. total number of employees is 19,290,352; total number of establishments is 1,825,435.

MSA	Estab-lish-ments	Rank	Emp-loy-ment	Rank
New York – Northern New Jersey – Long Island, NY – NJ – CT-CMSA	166,296	1	1,660,996	1
Los Angeles – Riverside – Orange County, CA CMSA	120,694	2	1,421,224	2
Washington – Baltimore, DC – MD – VA – WV CMSA	58,300	5	750,541	3
Chicago – Gary – Kenosha, IL – IN – WI CMSA	62,176	3	740,211	4
San Francisco – Oakland – San Jose, CA CMSA	59,233	4	637,184	5
Boston – Worcester – Lawrence, MA – NH – ME – CT CMSA	43,733	7	523,959	6
Philadelphia – Wilmington – Atlantic City, PA – NJ – DE – MD CMSA	44,709	6	523,540	7

[Continued]

★2337★
Total (taxable)
[Continued]

MSA	Establishments	Rank	Employment	Rank
Dallas–Fort Worth, TX CMSA	34,948	10	433,890	8
Houston–Galveston–Brazoria, TX CMSA	30,550	11	425,178	9
Detroit–Ann Arbor–Flint, MI CMSA	36,085	8	395,674	10
Atlanta, GA MSA	27,879	12	328,291	11
Miami–Fort Lauderdale, FL CMSA	35,552	9	323,050	12
Minneapolis–St. Paul, MN–WI MSA	20,706	16	265,183	13
Seattle–Tacoma–Bremerton, WA CMSA	26,240	13	246,485	14
Tampa–St. Petersburg–Clearwater, FL MSA	18,869	19	244,024	15
Cleveland–Akron, OH CMSA	20,729	15	219,265	16
San Diego, CA MSA	20,257	17	212,512	17
Denver–Boulder–Greeley, CO CMSA	21,063	14	210,468	18
Phoenix–Mesa, AZ MSA	19,028	18	210,140	19
St. Louis, MO–IL MSA	18,540	20	205,420	20
Las Vegas, NV–AZ MSA	6,959	46	185,968	21
Pittsburgh, PA MSA	16,605	21	182,815	22
Orlando, FL MSA	11,790	26	169,046	23
Cincinnati–Hamilton, OH–KY–IN CMSA	12,212	24	149,242	24
Kansas City, MO–KS MSA	12,561	23	146,421	25

Source: U.S. Department of Commerce, Bureau of the Census, Data User Services Division, *1992 Economic Census, Volume 1F, Reports Series, Release 1F,* September 1995, CD-ROM. *Note:* Data are shown only for the top 25 areas.

★2338★
Establishments and Employment
Utility Trailer and Recreational Vehicle Rental

The U.S. total number of employees is 2,054; total number of establishments is 440.

MSA	Establishments	Rank	Employment	Rank
Los Angeles–Riverside–Orange County, CA CMSA	34	1	285	1
Chicago–Gary–Kenosha, IL–IN–WI CMSA	15	3	76	2
Orlando, FL MSA	7	8	52	3
St. Louis, MO–IL MSA	5	10	37	4
Phoenix–Mesa, AZ MSA	6	9	32	5
San Diego, CA MSA	7	8	28	6
Las Vegas, NV–AZ MSA	5	10	18	7
Boston–Worcester–Lawrence, MA–NH–ME–CT CMSA	6	9	11	8
Charlotte–Gastonia–Rock Hill, NC–SC MSA	4	11	8	9
Norfolk–Virginia Beach–Newport News, VA–NC MSA	3	12	8	9

[Continued]

★2338★
Utility Trailer and Recreational Vehicle Rental
[Continued]

MSA	Establishments	Rank	Employment	Rank
West Palm Beach–Boca Raton, FL MSA	4	11	8	9
Albany–Schenectady–Troy, NY MSA	1	14	0[1]	10
Albuquerque, NM MSA	3	12	0[1]	10
Allentown–Bethlehem–Easton, PA MSA	2	13	0[1]	10
Anchorage, AK MSA	7	8	0[1]	10
Appleton–Oshkosh–Neenah, WI MSA	0	15	0	10
Atlanta, GA MSA	5	10	0	1	0
Augusta–Aiken, GA–SC MSA	2	13	0[1]	10
Austin–San Marcos, TX MSA	2	13	0[1]	10
Bakersfield, CA MSA	1	14	0[1]	10
Baton Rouge, LA MSA	1	14	0[1]	10
Beaumont–Port Arthur, TX MSA	2	13	0[1]	10
Birmingham, AL MSA	0	15	0	10
Boise City, ID MSA	0	15	0	10
Buffalo–Niagara Falls, NY MSA	2	13	0[1]	10

Source: U.S. Department of Commerce, Bureau of the Census, Data User Services Division, *1992 Economic Census, Volume 1F, Reports Series, Release 1F,* September 1995, CD-ROM. *Notes:* Data are shown only for the top 25 areas. 1. 0-19 employees.

★2339★
Establishments and Employment
Video Tape Rental

The U.S. total number of employees is 123,671; total number of establishments is 21,998.

MSA	Establishments	Rank	Employment	Rank
New York–Northern New Jersey–Long Island, NY–NJ–CT-CMSA	1,420	1	6,730	1
Los Angeles–Riverside–Orange County, CA CMSA	1,038	2	4,889	2
Washington–Baltimore, DC–MD–VA–WV CMSA	633	4	4,487	3
San Francisco–Oakland–San Jose, CA CMSA	548	5	3,055	4
Detroit–Ann Arbor–Flint, MI CMSA	410	8	2,692	5
Dallas–Fort Worth, TX CMSA	329	10	2,391	6
Minneapolis–St. Paul, MN–WI MSA	307	11	2,184	7
Seattle–Tacoma–Bremerton, WA CMSA	336	9	1,979	8
Houston–Galveston–Brazoria, TX CMSA	302	12	1,934	9
Atlanta, GA MSA	239	15	1,525	10
Portland–Salem, OR–WA CMSA	209	16	1,406	11
Cleveland–Akron, OH CMSA	256	13	1,342	12

[Continued]

★2339★

Video Tape Rental
[Continued]

MSA	Estab-lish-ments	Rank	Emp-ploy-ment	Rank
Miami – Fort Lauderdale, FL CMSA	248	14	1,158	13
Sacramento – Yolo, CA CMSA	171	19	1,125	14
St. Louis, MO – IL MSA	203	17	1,084	15
San Diego, CA MSA	201	18	1,035	16
Denver – Boulder – Greeley, CO CMSA	155	21	996	17
Syracuse, NY MSA	60	46	970	18
Kansas City, MO – KS MSA	127	26	967	19
Phoenix – Mesa, AZ MSA	160	20	961	20
Indianapolis, IN MSA	131	24	895	21
Cincinnati – Hamilton, OH – KY – IN CMSA	148	23	878	22
Tampa – St. Petersburg – Clearwater, FL MSA	152	22	787	23
Las Vegas, NV – AZ MSA	90	33	780	24
Hartford, CT MSA	105	28	765	25

Source: U.S. Department of Commerce, Bureau of the Census, Data User Services Division, *1992 Economic Census, Volume 1F, Reports Series, Release 1F,* September 1995, CD-ROM. *Note:* Data are shown only for the top 25 areas.

★2340★

Establishments and Employment

Vocational Schools

The U.S. total number of employees is 63,224; total number of establishments is 4,615.

MSA	Estab-lish-ments	Rank	Emp-ploy-ment	Rank
New York – Northern New Jersey – Long Island, NY – NJ – CT-CMSA	482	1	6,685	1
Los Angeles – Riverside – Orange County, CA CMSA	379	2	5,689	2
Detroit – Ann Arbor – Flint, MI CMSA	149	5	2,221	3
San Francisco – Oakland – San Jose, CA CMSA	185	3	1,988	4
Dallas – Fort Worth, TX CMSA	100	8	1,693	5
Houston – Galveston – Brazoria, TX CMSA	88	11	1,498	6
Cleveland – Akron, OH CMSA	69	14	1,375	7
Miami – Fort Lauderdale, FL CMSA	85	12	1,326	8
Boston – Worcester – Lawrence, MA – NH – ME – CT CMSA	116	6	1,017	9
Minneapolis – St. Paul, MN – WI MSA	55	16	940	10
San Diego, CA MSA	66	15	914	11
Atlanta, GA MSA	91	10	913	12
Tampa – St. Petersburg – Clearwater, FL MSA	51	17	890	13
Kansas City, MO – KS MSA	41	20	735	14

[Continued]

★2340★

Vocational Schools
[Continued]

MSA	Estab-lish-ments	Rank	Emp-ploy-ment	Rank
St. Louis, MO – IL MSA	43	19	608	15
Pittsburgh, PA MSA	41	20	579	16
Norfolk – Virginia Beach – Newport News, VA – NC MSA	32	25	567	17
Portland – Salem, OR – WA CMSA	66	15	531	18
San Antonio, TX MSA	24	31	514	19
Hartford, CT MSA	26	30	510	20
Orlando, FL MSA	38	21	433	21
New Orleans, LA MSA	37	22	429	22
Tulsa, OK MSA	21	33	397	23
Columbus, OH MSA	28	28	394	24
Nashville, TN MSA	20	34	329	25

Source: U.S. Department of Commerce, Bureau of the Census, Data User Services Division, *1992 Economic Census, Volume 1F, Reports Series, Release 1F,* September 1995, CD-ROM. *Note:* Data are shown only for the top 25 areas.

★2341★

Establishments and Employment

Watch, Clock, and Jewelry Repair

The U.S. total number of employees is 5,141; total number of establishments is 1,662.

MSA	Estab-lish-ments	Rank	Emp-ploy-ment	Rank
Los Angeles – Riverside – Orange County, CA CMSA	110	2	416	1
Detroit – Ann Arbor – Flint, MI CMSA	54	6	145	2
Atlanta, GA MSA	32	13	142	3
San Francisco – Oakland – San Jose, CA CMSA	56	5	131	4
Philadelphia – Wilmington – Atlantic City, PA – NJ – DE – MD CMSA	40	9	120	5
San Diego, CA MSA	27	14	91	6
Pittsburgh, PA MSA	21	17	81	7
Miami – Fort Lauderdale, FL CMSA	46	7	80	8
Portland – Salem, OR – WA CMSA	18	19	68	9
St. Louis, MO – IL MSA	23	16	65	10
Minneapolis – St. Paul, MN – WI MSA	17	20	64	11
Dayton – Springfield, OH MSA	10	25	59	12
Providence – Fall River – Warwick, RI – MA MSA	18	19	56	13
Milwaukee – Racine, WI CMSA	12	23	55	14
San Antonio, TX MSA	19	18	54	15
Honolulu, HI MSA	9	26	53	16
Lancaster, PA MSA	5	30	52	17
Tampa – St. Petersburg – Clearwater, FL MSA	14	21	42	18
Kansas City, MO – KS MSA	14	21	41	19
Omaha, NE – IA MSA	9	26	40	20

[Continued]

★2341★

Watch, Clock, and Jewelry Repair
[Continued]

MSA	Estab-lish-ments	Rank	Emp-ploy-ment	Rank
Columbus, OH MSA	10	25	36	21
Grand Rapids – Muskegon – Holland, MI MSA	8	27	32	22
Sacramento – Yolo, CA CMSA	14	21	32	22
West Palm Beach – Boca Raton, FL MSA	13	22	31	23
Phoenix – Mesa, AZ MSA	12	23	26	24

Source: U.S. Department of Commerce, Bureau of the Census, Data User Services Division, *1992 Economic Census, Volume 1F, Reports Series, Release 1F,* September 1995, CD-ROM. *Note:* Data are shown only for the top 25 areas.

★2342★
Establishments and Employment

Welding Repair

The U.S. total number of employees is 22,247; total number of establishments is 5,383.

MSA	Estab-lish-ments	Rank	Emp-ploy-ment	Rank
Los Angeles – Riverside – Orange County, CA CMSA	218	2	1,015	1
Chicago – Gary – Kenosha, IL – IN – WI CMSA	115	3	589	2
New Orleans, LA MSA	20	29	404	3
Washington – Baltimore, DC – MD – VA – WV CMSA	90	5	393	4
Houston – Galveston – Brazoria, TX CMSA	68	9	385	5
Minneapolis – St. Paul, MN – WI MSA	52	13	355	6
Seattle – Tacoma – Bremerton, WA CMSA	65	10	303	7
Philadelphia – Wilmington – Atlantic City, PA – NJ – DE – MD CMSA	80	6	270	8
Cleveland – Akron, OH CMSA	57	12	269	9
Miami – Fort Lauderdale, FL CMSA	79	7	257	10
Jackson, MS MSA	17	32	243	11
Phoenix – Mesa, AZ MSA	32	19	215	12
Charlotte – Gastonia – Rock Hill, NC – SC MSA	36	15	199	13
Boston – Worcester – Lawrence, MA – NH – ME – CT CMSA	74	8	197	14
Dallas – Fort Worth, TX CMSA	61	11	194	15
Atlanta, GA MSA	38	14	179	16
Pittsburgh, PA MSA	34	17	165	17
Tulsa, OK MSA	23	27	148	18
Hartford, CT MSA	28	22	134	19
Kansas City, MO – KS MSA	26	24	129	20
Beaumont – Port Arthur, TX MSA	12	36	125	21
Salt Lake City – Ogden, UT MSA	20	29	115	22
Indianapolis, IN MSA	29	21	113	23

[Continued]

★2342★

Welding Repair
[Continued]

MSA	Estab-lish-ments	Rank	Emp-ploy-ment	Rank
Buffalo – Niagara Falls, NY MSA	20	29	109	24
Tampa – St. Petersburg – Clearwater, FL MSA	35	16	109	24

Source: U.S. Department of Commerce, Bureau of the Census, Data User Services Division, *1992 Economic Census, Volume 1F, Reports Series, Release 1F,* September 1995, CD-ROM. *Note:* Data are shown only for the top 25 areas.

★2343★
Tax-Exempt Establishments and Employment

Business and Secretarial Schools

The U.S. total number of employees is 552; total number of establishments is 38.

MSA	Estab-lish-ments	Rank	Emp-ploy-ment	Rank
Albany – Schenectady – Troy, NY MSA	0	5	0	1
Atlanta, GA MSA	0	5	0	1
Boston – Worcester – Lawrence, MA – NH – ME – CT CMSA	4	2	0[1]	1
Buffalo – Niagara Falls, NY MSA	0	5	0	1
Chicago – Gary – Kenosha, IL – IN – WI CMSA	0	5	0	1
Cincinnati – Hamilton, OH – KY – IN CMSA	0	5	0	1
Cleveland – Akron, OH CMSA	0	5	0	1
Columbus, OH MSA	0	5	0	1
Dallas – Fort Worth, TX CMSA	0	5	0	1
Denver – Boulder – Greeley, CO CMSA	2	3	0[2]	1
Detroit – Ann Arbor – Flint, MI CMSA	1	4	0[2]	1
Hartford, CT MSA	0	5	0	1
Houston – Galveston – Brazoria, TX CMSA	0	5	0	1
Indianapolis, IN MSA	0	5	0	1
Kansas City, MO – KS MSA	1	4	0[2]	1
Los Angeles – Riverside – Orange County, CA CMSA	0	5	0	1
Miami – Fort Lauderdale, FL CMSA	1	4	0[1]	1
Milwaukee – Racine, WI CMSA	0	5	0	1
Minneapolis – St. Paul, MN – WI MSA	1	4	0[1]	1
New York – Northern New Jersey – Long Island, NY – NJ – CT-CMSA	8	1	0[1]	1
Philadelphia – Wilmington – Atlantic City, PA – NJ – DE – MD CMSA	1	4	0[1]	1
Phoenix – Mesa, AZ MSA	4	2	0[1]	1
Pittsburgh, PA MSA	0	5	0	1
Portland – Salem, OR – WA CMSA	0	5	0	1

[Continued]

★2343★

Business and Secretarial Schools
[Continued]

MSA	Estab-lish-ments	Rank	Emp-loy-ment	Rank
Providence – Fall River – Warwick, RI – MA MSA	0	5	0	1
Sacramento – Yolo, CA CMSA	0	5	0	1
San Diego, CA MSA	0	5	0	1
San Francisco – Oakland – San Jose, CA CMSA	0	5	0	1
Seattle – Tacoma – Bremerton, WA CMSA	0	5	0	1
St. Louis, MO – IL MSA	2	3	0[1]	1
Tampa – St. Petersburg – Clearwater, FL MSA	0	5	0	1
Washington – Baltimore, DC – MD – VA – WV CMSA	0	5	0	1

Source: U.S. Department of Commerce, Bureau of the Census, Data User Services Division, 1992 Economic Census, Volume 1F, Reports Series, Release 1F, September 1995, CD-ROM. Notes: 1. 20-99 employees. 2. 0-19 employees.

★2344★

Tax-Exempt Establishments and Employment

Camps and Membership Lodging

The U.S. total number of employees is 17,634; total number of establishments is 3,198.

MSA	Estab-lish-ments	Rank	Emp-loy-ment	Rank
San Diego, CA MSA	15	27	557	1
San Francisco – Oakland – San Jose, CA CMSA	53	4	393	2
Bloomington, IN MSA	39	10	306	3
Austin – San Marcos, TX MSA	31	15	281	4
Columbus, OH MSA	48	6	231	5
Lawrence, KS MSA	28	18	199	6
Fort Collins – Loveland, CO MSA	14	28	186	7
Minneapolis – St. Paul, MN – WI MSA	35	12	185	8
Raleigh – Durham – Chapel Hill, NC MSA	34	13	176	9
Champaign – Urbana, IL MSA	39	10	169	10
Albany – Schenectady – Troy, NY MSA	16	26	166	11
Columbia, MO MSA	32	14	149	12
Grand Rapids – Muskegon – Holland, MI MSA	11	31	134	13
Cleveland – Akron, OH CMSA	27	19	111	14
Harrisburg – Lebanon – Carlisle, PA MSA	10	32	107	15
Pittsburgh, PA MSA	32	14	104	16
Gainesville, FL MSA	31	15	101	17
Lincoln, NE MSA	32	14	98	18
Lexington, KY MSA	19	24	96	19
Tuscaloosa, AL MSA	18	25	94	20
Indianapolis, IN MSA	38	11	93	21
Buffalo – Niagara Falls, NY MSA	8	34	84	22

[Continued]

★2344★

Camps and Membership Lodging
[Continued]

MSA	Estab-lish-ments	Rank	Emp-loy-ment	Rank
Cincinnati – Hamilton, OH – KY – IN CMSA	30	16	81	23
Providence – Fall River – Warwick, RI – MA MSA	22	21	80	24
Syracuse, NY MSA	32	14	76	25

Source: U.S. Department of Commerce, Bureau of the Census, Data User Services Division, 1992 Economic Census, Volume 1F, Reports Series, Release 1F, September 1995, CD-ROM. Note: Data are shown only for the top 25 areas.

★2345★

Tax-Exempt Establishments and Employment

Clinics of Doctors of Medicine and Dentists

The U.S. total number of employees is 157,758; total number of establishments is 3,302.

MSA	Estab-lish-ments	Rank	Emp-loy-ment	Rank
Minneapolis – St. Paul, MN – WI MSA	71	9	7,033	1
Washington – Baltimore, DC – MD – VA – WV CMSA	84	6	6,877	2
San Diego, CA MSA	65	10	5,262	3
Cleveland – Akron, OH CMSA	49	12	3,473	4
Chicago – Gary – Kenosha, IL – IN – WI CMSA	75	8	3,051	5
Kansas City, MO – KS MSA	31	17	1,322	6
Atlanta, GA MSA	25	20	1,091	7
Pittsburgh, PA MSA	43	14	1,064	8
Providence – Fall River – Warwick, RI – MA MSA	25	20	785	9
Scranton – Wilkes-Barre – Hazleton, PA MSA	30	18	730	10
St. Louis, MO – IL MSA	21	23	707	11
Rochester, NY MSA	14	28	701	12
Phoenix – Mesa, AZ MSA	26	19	676	13
Harrisburg – Lebanon – Carlisle, PA MSA	14	28	545	14
Hartford, CT MSA	13	29	488	15
Jacksonville, FL MSA	10	32	486	16
San Antonio, TX MSA	18	25	423	17
Kalamazoo – Battle Creek, MI MSA	10	32	371	18
Oklahoma City, OK MSA	12	30	350	19
Columbus, OH MSA	18	25	326	20
Fresno, CA MSA	13	29	320	21
Albuquerque, NM MSA	12	30	294	22
Orlando, FL MSA	12	30	217	23
Memphis, TN – AR – MS MSA	8	34	164	24
Tampa – St. Petersburg – Clearwater, FL MSA	11	31	149	25

Source: U.S. Department of Commerce, Bureau of the Census, Data User Services Division, 1992 Economic Census, Volume 1F, Reports Series, Release 1F, September 1995, CD-ROM. Note: Data are shown only for the top 25 areas.

★2346★
Tax-Exempt Establishments and Employment
Data Processing Schools

The U.S. total number of employees is 213; total number of establishments is 10.

MSA	Estab-lish-ments	Rank	Emp-loy-ment	Rank
Albany – Schenectady – Troy, NY MSA	0	2	0	1
Atlanta, GA MSA	0	2	0	1
Boston – Worcester – Lawrence, MA – NH – ME – CT CMSA	0	2	0	1
Buffalo – Niagara Falls, NY MSA	0	2	0	1
Chicago – Gary – Kenosha, IL – IN – WI CMSA	1	1	0^1	1
Cincinnati – Hamilton, OH – KY – IN CMSA	0	2	0	1
Cleveland – Akron, OH CMSA	0	2	0	1
Columbus, OH MSA	0	2	0	1
Dallas – Fort Worth, TX CMSA	1	1	0^2	1
Denver – Boulder – Greeley, CO CMSA	1	1	0^2	1
Detroit – Ann Arbor – Flint, MI CMSA	0	2	0	1
Hartford, CT MSA	0	2	0	1
Houston – Galveston – Brazoria, TX CMSA	0	2	0	1
Indianapolis, IN MSA	0	2	0	1
Kansas City, MO – KS MSA	0	2	0	1
Los Angeles – Riverside – Orange County, CA CMSA	0	2	0	1
Miami – Fort Lauderdale, FL CMSA	0	2	0	1
Milwaukee – Racine, WI CMSA	0	2	0	1
Minneapolis – St. Paul, MN – WI MSA	0	2	0	1
New York – Northern New Jersey – Long Island, NY – NJ – CT-CMSA	1	1	0^2	1
Philadelphia – Wilmington – Atlantic City, PA – NJ – DE – MD CMSA	0	2	0	1
Phoenix – Mesa, AZ MSA	0	2	0	1
Pittsburgh, PA MSA	0	2	0	1
Portland – Salem, OR – WA CMSA	1	1	0^1	1
Providence – Fall River – Warwick, RI – MA MSA	0	2	0	1
Sacramento – Yolo, CA CMSA	0	2	0	1
San Diego, CA MSA	0	2	0	1
San Francisco – Oakland – San Jose, CA CMSA	0	2	0	1
Seattle – Tacoma – Bremerton, WA CMSA	0	2	0	1
St. Louis, MO – IL MSA	0	2	0	1
Tampa – St. Petersburg – Clearwater, FL MSA	0	2	0	1
Washington – Baltimore, DC – MD – VA – WV CMSA	0	2	0	1

Source: U.S. Department of Commerce, Bureau of the Census, Data User Services Division, *1992 Economic Census, Volume 1F, Reports Series, Release 1F*, September 1995, CD-ROM. *Notes:* 1. 0-19 employees. 2. 20-99 employees.

★2347★
Tax-Exempt Establishments and Employment
Fairs

The U.S. total number of employees is 6,380; total number of establishments is 633.

MSA	Estab-lish-ments	Rank	Emp-loy-ment	Rank
Albany – Schenectady – Troy, NY MSA	6	4	143	1
Atlanta, GA MSA	2	8	0^1	6
Boston – Worcester – Lawrence, MA – NH – ME – CT CMSA	4	6	0^2	6
Buffalo – Niagara Falls, NY MSA	2	8	0^3	6
Chicago – Gary – Kenosha, IL – IN – WI CMSA	9	2	0^3	6
Cincinnati – Hamilton, OH – KY – IN CMSA	4	6	0^3	6
Cleveland – Akron, OH CMSA	7	3	0^3	6
Columbus, OH MSA	4	6	19	3
Dallas – Fort Worth, TX CMSA	7	3	0^2	6
Denver – Boulder – Greeley, CO CMSA	2	8	0^1	6
Detroit – Ann Arbor – Flint, MI CMSA	7	3	13	4
Hartford, CT MSA	1	9	0^1	6
Houston – Galveston – Brazoria, TX CMSA	5	5	0^2	6
Indianapolis, IN MSA	2	8	0^1	6
Kansas City, MO – KS MSA	3	7	0^3	6
Los Angeles – Riverside – Orange County, CA CMSA	2	8	0^2	6
Miami – Fort Lauderdale, FL CMSA	3	7	0^3	6
Milwaukee – Racine, WI CMSA	5	5	0^2	6
Minneapolis – St. Paul, MN – WI MSA	16	1	55	2
New York – Northern New Jersey – Long Island, NY – NJ – CT-CMSA	7	3	0^3	6
Philadelphia – Wilmington – Atlantic City, PA – NJ – DE – MD CMSA	3	7	0^1	6
Phoenix – Mesa, AZ MSA	2	8	0^2	6
Pittsburgh, PA MSA	4	6	7	5
Portland – Salem, OR – WA CMSA	2	8	0^1	6
Providence – Fall River – Warwick, RI – MA MSA	0	10	0	6
Sacramento – Yolo, CA CMSA	1	9	0^3	6
San Diego, CA MSA	0	10	0	6
San Francisco – Oakland – San Jose, CA CMSA	6	4	0^4	6
Seattle – Tacoma – Bremerton, WA CMSA	5	5	0^2	6
St. Louis, MO – IL MSA	4	6	0^3	6
Tampa – St. Petersburg – Clearwater, FL MSA	4	6	0^5	6
Washington – Baltimore, DC – MD – VA – WV CMSA	6	4	0^3	6

Source: U.S. Department of Commerce, Bureau of the Census, Data User Services Division, *1992 Economic Census, Volume 1F, Reports Series, Release 1F*, September 1995, CD-ROM. *Notes:* 1. 0-19 employees. 2. 100-249 employees. 3. 20-99 employees. 4. 500-999 employees. 5. 250-499 employees.

★ 2348 ★

Tax-Exempt Establishments and Employment

Gymnasiums, Athletic Clubs, and Membership Sports and Recreation Clubs

The U.S. total number of employees is 140,016; total number of establishments is 7,635.

MSA	Estab-lish-ments	Rank	Emp-ploy-ment	Rank
Albany – Schenectady – Troy, NY MSA	27	28	409	24
Atlanta, GA MSA	86	11	2,272	8
Boston – Worcester – Lawrence, MA – NH – ME – CT CMSA	215	5	0[1]	26
Buffalo – Niagara Falls, NY MSA	37	24	773	22
Chicago – Gary – Kenosha, IL – IN – WI CMSA	170	6	0[1]	26
Cincinnati – Hamilton, OH – KY – IN CMSA	82	12	0[2]	26
Cleveland – Akron, OH CMSA	70	13	2,367	6
Columbus, OH MSA	46	21	1,030	20
Dallas – Fort Worth, TX CMSA	69	14	2,317	7
Denver – Boulder – Greeley, CO CMSA	59	16	1,193	16
Detroit – Ann Arbor – Flint, MI CMSA	124	8	2,449	5
Hartford, CT MSA	35	25	603	23
Houston – Galveston – Brazoria, TX CMSA	61	15	1,850	10
Indianapolis, IN MSA	39	23	955	21
Kansas City, MO – KS MSA	56	18	1,051	19
Los Angeles – Riverside – Orange County, CA CMSA	166	7	0[3]	26
Miami – Fort Lauderdale, FL CMSA	28	27	1,231	15
Milwaukee – Racine, WI CMSA	53	19	1,268	14
Minneapolis – St. Paul, MN – WI MSA	57	17	1,677	11
New York – Northern New Jersey – Long Island, NY – NJ – CT-CMSA	602	1	11,827	1
Philadelphia – Wilmington – Atlantic City, PA – NJ – DE – MD CMSA	231	3	4,062	2
Phoenix – Mesa, AZ MSA	51	20	1,499	13
Pittsburgh, PA MSA	96	10	2,624	4
Portland – Salem, OR – WA CMSA	39	23	0[2]	26
Providence – Fall River – Warwick, RI – MA MSA	43	22	344	25
Sacramento – Yolo, CA CMSA	25	29	0[4]	26
San Diego, CA MSA	51	20	1,053	18
San Francisco – Oakland – San Jose, CA CMSA	216	4	3,114	3
Seattle – Tacoma – Bremerton, WA CMSA	119	9	1,863	9
St. Louis, MO – IL MSA	61	15	1,601	12
Tampa – St. Petersburg – Clearwater, FL MSA	32	26	1,152	17
Washington – Baltimore, DC – MD – VA – WV CMSA	242	2	0[1]	26

Source: U.S. Department of Commerce, Bureau of the Census, Data User Services Division, *1992 Economic Census, Volume 1F, Reports Series, Release 1F,* September 1995, CD-ROM. *Notes:* 1. 2,500-4,999 employees. 2. 1,000-2,499 employees. 3. 5,000-9,999 employees. 4. 250-499 employees.

★ 2349 ★

Tax-Exempt Establishments and Employment

Job Training and Vocational Rehabilitation Services

The U.S. total number of employees is 270,458; total number of establishments is 6,118.

MSA	Estab-lish-ments	Rank	Emp-ploy-ment	Rank
Los Angeles – Riverside – Orange County, CA CMSA	237	2	10,136	1
San Francisco – Oakland – San Jose, CA CMSA	176	5	7,161	2
Philadelphia – Wilmington – Atlantic City, PA – NJ – DE – MD CMSA	156	7	6,347	3
Cleveland – Akron, OH CMSA	62	13	5,433	4
Detroit – Ann Arbor – Flint, MI CMSA	102	8	4,739	5
Minneapolis – St. Paul, MN – WI MSA	92	9	4,040	6
Milwaukee – Racine, WI CMSA	47	18	3,725	7
Seattle – Tacoma – Bremerton, WA CMSA	69	11	3,067	8
St. Louis, MO – IL MSA	54	15	2,908	9
Columbus, OH MSA	34	27	2,677	10
Kansas City, MO – KS MSA	50	16	2,585	11
Tampa – St. Petersburg – Clearwater, FL MSA	32	28	2,467	12
Providence – Fall River – Warwick, RI – MA MSA	39	25	2,405	13
Raleigh – Durham – Chapel Hill, NC MSA	25	32	2,131	14
Cincinnati – Hamilton, OH – KY – IN CMSA	39	25	1,995	15
Miami – Fort Lauderdale, FL CMSA	58	14	1,960	16
Harrisburg – Lebanon – Carlisle, PA MSA	17	36	1,888	17
Pittsburgh, PA MSA	49	17	1,831	18
Dayton – Springfield, OH MSA	25	32	1,822	19
Denver – Boulder – Greeley, CO CMSA	49	17	1,813	20
Norfolk – Virginia Beach – Newport News, VA – NC MSA	15	38	1,704	21
Indianapolis, IN MSA	30	29	1,516	22
Jacksonville, FL MSA	17	36	1,499	23
Rochester, NY MSA	41	23	1,499	23
Buffalo – Niagara Falls, NY MSA	41	23	1,449	24

Source: U.S. Department of Commerce, Bureau of the Census, Data User Services Division, *1992 Economic Census, Volume 1F, Reports Series, Release 1F,* September 1995, CD-ROM. *Note:* Data are shown only for the top 25 areas.

★2350★

Tax-Exempt Establishments and Employment

Legal Aid Societies and Similar Legal Services

The U.S. total number of employees is 21,341; total number of establishments is 1,725.

MSA	Estab-lish-ments	Rank	Emp-loy-ment	Rank
New York – Northern New Jersey – Long Island, NY – NJ – CT-CMSA	135	1	3,956	1
Los Angeles – Riverside – Orange County, CA CMSA	63	3	1,665	2
San Francisco – Oakland – San Jose, CA CMSA	74	2	836	3
Chicago – Gary – Kenosha, IL – IN – WI CMSA	43	5	559	4
Minneapolis – St. Paul, MN – WI MSA	21	9	260	5
Columbus, OH MSA	7	20	203	6
Buffalo – Niagara Falls, NY MSA	11	16	198	7
San Diego, CA MSA	11	16	168	8
Rochester, NY MSA	9	18	140	9
Austin – San Marcos, TX MSA	9	18	138	10
St. Louis, MO – IL MSA	10	17	136	11
Pittsburgh, PA MSA	11	16	135	12
Kansas City, MO – KS MSA	11	16	133	13
Phoenix – Mesa, AZ MSA	13	14	128	14
Salt Lake City – Ogden, UT MSA	6	21	127	15
Toledo, OH MSA	6	21	123	16
Raleigh – Durham – Chapel Hill, NC MSA	11	16	115	17
Syracuse, NY MSA	4	23	96	18
Indianapolis, IN MSA	7	20	90	19
Albany – Schenectady – Troy, NY MSA	8	19	85	20
Charleston, WV MSA	4	23	85	20
New Orleans, LA MSA	9	18	79	21
Grand Rapids – Muskegon – Holland, MI MSA	7	20	73	22
Tallahassee, FL MSA	9	18	73	22
McAllen – Edinburg – Mission, TX MSA	5	22	69	23

Source: U.S. Department of Commerce, Bureau of the Census, Data User Services Division, *1992 Economic Census, Volume 1F, Reports Series, Release 1F,* September 1995, CD-ROM. *Note:* Data are shown only for the top 25 areas.

★2351★

Tax-Exempt Establishments and Employment

Management and Public Relations Services, Except Facilities Support Management Services

The U.S. total number of employees is 21,519; total number of establishments is 1,694.

MSA	Estab-lish-ments	Rank	Emp-loy-ment	Rank
New York – Northern New Jersey – Long Island, NY – NJ – CT-CMSA	133	1	4,597	1
San Francisco – Oakland – San Jose, CA CMSA	39	8	518	2
St. Louis, MO – IL MSA	11	19	342	3
Pittsburgh, PA MSA	20	12	312	4
Minneapolis – St. Paul, MN – WI MSA	37	9	303	5
Cincinnati – Hamilton, OH – KY – IN CMSA	14	16	255	6
Harrisburg – Lebanon – Carlisle, PA MSA	6	24	216	7
Dayton – Springfield, OH MSA	6	24	149	8
Albany – Schenectady – Troy, NY MSA	10	20	142	9
Kansas City, MO – KS MSA	18	13	137	10
San Diego, CA MSA	12	18	137	10
Milwaukee – Racine, WI CMSA	16	15	136	11
Phoenix – Mesa, AZ MSA	16	15	123	12
Grand Rapids – Muskegon – Holland, MI MSA	4	26	104	13
Sacramento – Yolo, CA CMSA	12	18	103	14
Houston – Galveston – Brazoria, TX CMSA	11	19	98	15
Buffalo – Niagara Falls, NY MSA	13	17	89	16
Orlando, FL MSA	7	23	74	17
Allentown – Bethlehem – Easton, PA MSA	5	25	64	18
Omaha, NE – IA MSA	6	24	62	19
Madison, WI MSA	10	20	58	20
Wichita, KS MSA	4	26	52	21
Richmond – Petersburg, VA MSA	7	23	47	22
Tampa – St. Petersburg – Clearwater, FL MSA	9	21	39	23
Columbus, OH MSA	9	21	32	24

Source: U.S. Department of Commerce, Bureau of the Census, Data User Services Division, *1992 Economic Census, Volume 1F, Reports Series, Release 1F,* September 1995, CD-ROM. *Note:* Data are shown only for the top 25 areas.

★ 2352 ★

Tax-Exempt Establishments and Employment

Research, Testing, and Consulting Services, Except Facilities Support Management Services

The U.S. total number of employees is 147,406; total number of establishments is 5,507.

MSA	Estab-lish-ments	Rank	Emp-loy-ment	Rank
New York – Northern New Jersey – Long Island, NY – NJ – CT-CMSA	527	2	21,246	1
San Francisco – Oakland – San Jose, CA CMSA	248	4	7,371	2
San Diego, CA MSA	80	9	4,368	3
Philadelphia – Wilmington – Atlantic City, PA – NJ – DE – MD CMSA	146	7	3,952	4
Raleigh – Durham – Chapel Hill, NC MSA	61	14	3,629	5
Buffalo – Niagara Falls, NY MSA	41	19	2,794	6
Albany – Schenectady – Troy, NY MSA	45	17	2,616	7
Seattle – Tacoma – Bremerton, WA CMSA	77	12	2,214	8
Detroit – Ann Arbor – Flint, MI CMSA	79	10	2,001	9
Atlanta, GA MSA	64	13	1,256	10
Syracuse, NY MSA	22	31	1,215	11
Norfolk – Virginia Beach – Newport News, VA – NC MSA	17	35	1,096	12
Pittsburgh, PA MSA	58	15	994	13
Birmingham, AL MSA	21	32	983	14
Minneapolis – St. Paul, MN – WI MSA	83	8	940	15
Houston – Galveston – Brazoria, TX CMSA	58	15	775	16
Kansas City, MO – KS MSA	36	22	664	17
Honolulu, HI MSA	28	26	644	18
St. Louis, MO – IL MSA	40	20	644	18
Tucson, AZ MSA	27	27	602	19
Albuquerque, NM MSA	26	28	435	20
Cincinnati – Hamilton, OH – KY – IN CMSA	38	21	428	21
Louisville, KY – IN MSA	14	38	393	22
Providence – Fall River – Warwick, RI – MA MSA	23	30	360	23
New Orleans, LA MSA	24	29	357	24

Source: U.S. Department of Commerce, Bureau of the Census, Data User Services Division, *1992 Economic Census, Volume 1F, Reports Series, Release 1F,* September 1995, CD-ROM. *Note:* Data are shown only for the top 25 areas.

★ 2353 ★

Tax-Exempt Establishments and Employment

Selected Amusement, Recreation, and Related Services

The U.S. total number of employees is 285,453; total number of establishments is 14,435.

MSA	Estab-lish-ments	Rank	Emp-loy-ment	Rank
Los Angeles – Riverside – Orange County, CA CMSA	377	5	11,665	1
San Francisco – Oakland – San Jose, CA CMSA	463	2	9,553	2
Minneapolis – St. Paul, MN – WI MSA	159	10	4,812	3
Seattle – Tacoma – Bremerton, WA CMSA	227	8	4,743	4
Cleveland – Akron, OH CMSA	141	13	4,722	5
Pittsburgh, PA MSA	148	12	4,669	6
Dallas – Fort Worth, TX CMSA	159	10	4,517	7
Detroit – Ann Arbor – Flint, MI CMSA	191	9	4,477	8
Houston – Galveston – Brazoria, TX CMSA	130	14	4,455	9
West Palm Beach – Boca Raton, FL MSA	73	33	4,353	10
Atlanta, GA MSA	156	11	3,847	11
San Diego, CA MSA	109	19	3,825	12
Milwaukee – Racine, WI CMSA	114	18	3,070	13
St. Louis, MO – IL MSA	115	17	2,908	14
Cincinnati – Hamilton, OH – KY – IN CMSA	126	15	2,851	15
Miami – Fort Lauderdale, FL CMSA	76	30	2,702	16
Norfolk – Virginia Beach – Newport News, VA – NC MSA	69	35	2,681	17
Phoenix – Mesa, AZ MSA	95	22	2,569	18
Honolulu, HI MSA	34	51	2,518	19
Columbus, OH MSA	86	24	2,358	20
Tampa – St. Petersburg – Clearwater, FL MSA	73	33	2,358	20
Portland – Salem, OR – WA CMSA	104	20	2,316	21
Indianapolis, IN MSA	80	26	2,254	22
Denver – Boulder – Greeley, CO CMSA	116	16	2,227	23
Kansas City, MO – KS MSA	87	23	2,038	24

Source: U.S. Department of Commerce, Bureau of the Census, Data User Services Division, *1992 Economic Census, Volume 1F, Reports Series, Release 1F,* September 1995, CD-ROM. *Note:* Data are shown only for the top 25 areas.

★2354★

Tax-Exempt Establishments and Employment

Selected Membership Organizations

The U.S. total number of employees is 602,527; total number of establishments is 72,386.

MSA	Estab-lish-ments	Rank	Emp-loy-ment	Rank
New York – Northern New Jersey – Long Island, NY – NJ – CT-CMSA	4,108	1	45,390	1
Los Angeles – Riverside – Orange County, CA CMSA	2,537	3	25,743	2
San Francisco – Oakland – San Jose, CA CMSA	1,781	5	17,185	3
Boston – Worcester – Lawrence, MA – NH – ME – CT CMSA	1,518	6	13,533	4
Philadelphia – Wilmington – Atlantic City, PA – NJ – DE – MD CMSA	1,423	7	13,446	5
Minneapolis – St. Paul, MN – WI MSA	985	10	10,794	6
Dallas – Fort Worth, TX CMSA	1,006	9	9,459	7
Detroit – Ann Arbor – Flint, MI CMSA	984	11	9,017	8
Seattle – Tacoma – Bremerton, WA CMSA	967	12	8,599	9
Pittsburgh, PA MSA	1,098	8	7,505	10
St. Louis, MO – IL MSA	643	17	7,224	11
Atlanta, GA MSA	663	16	6,572	12
Denver – Boulder – Greeley, CO CMSA	755	13	6,473	13
Houston – Galveston – Brazoria, TX CMSA	663	16	6,334	14
Cleveland – Akron, OH CMSA	724	14	5,775	15
Miami – Fort Lauderdale, FL CMSA	709	15	5,616	16
Phoenix – Mesa, AZ MSA	499	22	5,422	17
Columbus, OH MSA	497	23	5,346	18
Indianapolis, IN MSA	613	18	5,311	19
Milwaukee – Racine, WI CMSA	383	29	5,064	20
Tampa – St. Petersburg – Clearwater, FL MSA	517	20	4,813	21
San Diego, CA MSA	491	24	4,810	22
Portland – Salem, OR – WA CMSA	557	19	4,534	23
Austin – San Marcos, TX MSA	423	26	4,402	24
Cincinnati – Hamilton, OH – KY – IN CMSA	415	28	4,119	25

Source: U.S. Department of Commerce, Bureau of the Census, Data User Services Division, *1992 Economic Census, Volume 1F, Reports Series, Release 1F,* September 1995, CD-ROM. *Note:* Data are shown only for the top 25 areas.

★2355★

Tax-Exempt Establishments and Employment

Specialty Hospitals

The U.S. total number of employees is 478,431; total number of establishments is 797.

MSA	Estab-lish-ments	Rank	Emp-loy-ment	Rank
Boston – Worcester – Lawrence, MA – NH – ME – CT CMSA	36	2	26,051	1
Washington – Baltimore, DC – MD – VA – WV CMSA	24	4	19,461	2
San Francisco – Oakland – San Jose, CA CMSA	10	11	10,233	3
Atlanta, GA MSA	12	9	8,899	4
Seattle – Tacoma – Bremerton, WA CMSA	7	13	4,618	5
Kansas City, MO – KS MSA	6	14	3,997	6
San Diego, CA MSA	7	13	3,718	7
San Antonio, TX MSA	7	13	3,373	8
Miami – Fort Lauderdale, FL CMSA	4	16	3,312	9
Rochester, NY MSA	3	17	3,244	10
Tampa – St. Petersburg – Clearwater, FL MSA	5	15	3,211	11
Kalamazoo – Battle Creek, MI MSA	5	15	2,857	12
Dayton – Springfield, OH MSA	4	16	2,391	13
New Orleans, LA MSA	4	16	2,197	14
Charlotte – Gastonia – Rock Hill, NC – SC MSA	4	16	2,114	15
Springfield, MA MSA	5	15	2,111	16
Indianapolis, IN MSA	6	14	2,005	17
Omaha, NE – IA MSA	4	16	1,789	18
Grand Rapids – Muskegon – Holland, MI MSA	3	17	1,645	19
Raleigh – Durham – Chapel Hill, NC MSA	4	16	1,598	20
Baton Rouge, LA MSA	3	17	1,592	21
Scranton – Wilkes-Barre – Hazleton, PA MSA	6	14	1,525	22
Oklahoma City, OK MSA	5	15	1,445	23
Louisville, KY – IN MSA	3	17	1,418	24
Greensboro – Winston-Salem – High Point, NC MSA	6	14	1,291	25

Source: U.S. Department of Commerce, Bureau of the Census, Data User Services Division, *1992 Economic Census, Volume 1F, Reports Series, Release 1F,* September 1995, CD-ROM. *Note:* Data are shown only for the top 25 areas.

★ 2356 ★

Tax-Exempt Establishments and Employment

Total (tax-exempt)

The U.S. total number of employees is 8,108,944; total number of establishments is 208,911.

MSA	Establishments	Rank	Employment	Rank
New York – Northern New Jersey – Long Island, NY – NJ – CT-CMSA	15,008	1	869,864	1
Chicago – Gary – Kenosha, IL – IN – WI CMSA	5,523	6	301,454	2
Los Angeles – Riverside – Orange County, CA CMSA	7,204	3	300,370	3
Washington – Baltimore, DC – MD – VA – WV CMSA	7,627	2	295,750	4
Boston – Worcester – Lawrence, MA – NH – ME – CT CMSA	6,133	4	267,904	5
Philadelphia – Wilmington – Atlantic City, PA – NJ – DE – MD CMSA	4,950	7	254,178	6
San Francisco – Oakland – San Jose, CA CMSA	6,047	5	196,209	7
Detroit – Ann Arbor – Flint, MI CMSA	3,627	8	183,913	8
Cleveland – Akron, OH CMSA	2,241	13	118,272	9
Pittsburgh, PA MSA	2,574	11	113,452	10
Minneapolis – St. Paul, MN – WI MSA	2,711	10	110,776	11
Seattle – Tacoma – Bremerton, WA CMSA	2,958	9	108,628	12
St. Louis, MO – IL MSA	1,837	15	101,434	13
Dallas – Fort Worth, TX CMSA	2,282	12	87,046	14
Houston – Galveston – Brazoria, TX CMSA	1,701	18	82,448	15
Atlanta, GA MSA	1,745	16	72,634	16
Milwaukee – Racine, WI CMSA	1,415	22	69,687	17
Miami – Fort Lauderdale, FL CMSA	1,591	20	68,326	18
San Diego, CA MSA	1,610	19	66,842	19
Cincinnati – Hamilton, OH – KY – IN CMSA	1,498	21	65,911	20
Denver – Boulder – Greeley, CO CMSA	1,871	14	64,477	21
Kansas City, MO – KS MSA	1,279	28	61,499	22
Phoenix – Mesa, AZ MSA	1,396	23	58,762	23
Portland – Salem, OR – WA CMSA	1,742	17	58,165	24
Buffalo – Niagara Falls, NY MSA	1,044	32	56,725	25

Source: U.S. Department of Commerce, Bureau of the Census, Data User Services Division, *1992 Economic Census, Volume 1F, Reports Series, Release 1F,* September 1995, CD-ROM. *Note:* Data are shown only for the top 25 areas.

★ 2357 ★

Hotels and Motels

Cities With Highest Hotel Taxes

	Tax rate	Rank
New York, NY	21.25	1
Houston, TX	15.25	2
Chicago, IL	14.9	3
Los Angeles, CA	14	4
Atlanta, GA	13	5
Dallas, TX	13	5

Source: Brewer, Geoffrey, "Manager's Handbook: Travel and Entertainment—U.S. Cities With Highest Bed Taxes," *Sales & Marketing Management,* (October 1993), p. 75. Primary source: International Association of Convention and Visitors Bureaus.

★ 2358 ★

Hotels and Motels

Cities With the Greatest Number of Hotel Rooms, 1995: Number of Hotels

City/MSA	Number of hotels	Rank
Anaheim-Santa Ana, CA	351	5
Atlanta, GA	370	3
Chicago, IL	378	2
Las Vegas, NV	231	8
Los Angeles-Long Beach, CA	617	1
New York, NY	230	9
Orlando, FL	311	6
San Diego, CA	352	4
San Francisco, CA	294	7
Washington, DC	351	5

Source: "Where the Rooms Are," *Wall Street Journal,* 17 November 1995, p. B8. Primary source: Smith Travel Research; September 1995.

★ 2359 ★

Hotels and Motels

Cities With the Greatest Number of Hotel Rooms, 1995: Number of Rooms

City/MSA	Number of rooms	Rank
Anaheim-Santa Ana, CA	44,374	9
Atlanta, GA	58,445	7
Chicago, IL	68,793	4
Las Vegas, NV	93,719	1
Los Angeles-Long Beach, CA	78,597	3
New York, NY	61,512	6
Orlando, FL	84,982	2
San Diego, CA	44,655	8
San Francisco, CA	42,531	10
Washington, DC	66,505	5

Source: "Where the Rooms Are," *Wall Street Journal,* 17 November 1995, p. B8. Primary source: Smith Travel Research; September 1995.

★2360★

Hotels and Motels

Hotel and Motel Occupancy Rates, 1996: Leading Cities

[In percentages]

City	Percentage occupied	Rank
Honolulu, HI	80.6	1
New York, NY	77.5	2
Salt Lake City, UT	76.3	3
Austin, TX	75.9	4
San Jose, CA	75.3	5
Orlando, FL	74.3	6
San Francisco, CA	74.2	7
New Orleans, LA	73.8	8
Raleigh-Durham, NC	73.5	9
Seattle, WA	72.2	10

Source: Lomanno, Mark V., "Hot & Not," *H&MM (Hotel & Motel Management),* 4 March, 1996, p. 16.

★2361★

Hotels and Motels

Hotel and Motel Occupancy Rates, 1996: Lowest Rates

[In percentages]

City	Percentage occupied	Rank
Daytona Beach, FL	53.5	1
Riverside, CA	56.6	2
Knoxville, TN	57.6	3
Norfolk, VA	58.3	4
Tulsa, OK	58.7	5
Dayton, OH	59.8	6
Atlantic City, NJ	60.0	7
Louisville, KY	60.1	8
Melbourne, FL	60.8	9
Albany, NY	61.3	10

Source: Lomanno, Mark V., "Hot & Not," *H&MM (Hotel & Motel Management),* 4 March, 1996, p. 16.

★2362★

Hotels and Motels

Hotel and Motel Room Construction, 1995: Leading Cities

City	Number of rooms constructed	Rank
Philadelphia, PA	1,699	1
Houston, TX	1,185	2
San Antonio, TX	1,037	3
Knoxville, TN	897	4
Atlanta, GA	736	5

Source: "Secondary Market Drives New Construction In 1995," *Hotels,* (March 1996), p. 8.

★2363★

Hotels and Motels

Hotel Rooms, 1996: Top Cities

City	Number of rooms	Rank
Las Vegas, NV	87,267	1
Orlando, FL	85,924	2
Los Angeles, CA	78,984	3
Chicago, IL	68,365	4
Washington, DC	66,356	5
New York, NY	61,823	6

Source: "Cities With the Most Hotel Rooms," *USA TODAY,* 9 May 1996, p. 1B. Primary source: Smith Travel Research.

★2364★

Hotels and Motels

Hotels, 1995: Selected Cities

City	Hotels	Rank
Detroit, MI	24	7
Seattle, WA	58	4
Baltimore, MD	26	6
Chicago, IL	116	2
San Francisco, CA	163	1
Orlando, FL	45	5
Houston, TX	106	3

Source: Gray, Madison J., "Becoming 'World Class' City Requires New Amenities for Dining, Fun," *Detroit News,* 21 December 1995, p. 1K. Primary source: U.S. Department of Commerce 1992 Census of Retail Trade (Geographic Area Series), Bureau of the Census; U.S. Department of Commerce 1992 Census of Service Industries (Geographic Area Series), Bureau of the Census.

★2365★

Restaurants

Dining Out, 1995: Leading Cities

[In number of meals eaten out each week]

City	Times	Rank
Dallas/Fort Worth, TX	4.3	2
Houston, TX	4.7	1
Kansas City, KS-MO	3.9	4
Los Angeles, CA	4.0	3
New York, NY	3.8	5

Source: "Big Foodies," *Crain's New York Business,* 6 November 1995, p. 6. Primary source: *Zagat Restaurant Survey.*

★2366★

Restaurants

Dining Out, 1996: Highest Prices

[Average costs include drink, taxes, and tips]

City	Cost	Rank
Baltimore, MD	22.38	7
Boston, MA	21.83	9
Chicago, IL	21.87	8
Cleveland, OH	22.68	6
Los Angeles, CA	23.90	4

[Continued]

★ 2366 ★

Dining Out, 1996: Highest Prices
[Continued]

City	Cost	Rank
Miami, FL	21.80	10
New York, NY	29.81	1
Philadelphia, PA	25.17	2
San Francisco, CA	24.78	3
Washington, DC	23.88	5

Source: Rechin, Kevin, "The Heftiest Tabs," *USA TODAY*, 8 March, 1996. Primary source: Zagat Restaurant Surveys.

★ 2367 ★
Restaurants

Restaurants, 1995: Selected Cities

City	Restaurants	Rank
Detroit, MI	313	5
Seattle, WA	735	3
Baltimore, MD	335	4
Chicago, IL	1,631	1
San Francisco, CA	1,299	2
Orlando, FL	177	6
Houston, TX	1,229	2

Source: Gray, Madison J., "Becoming 'World Class' City Requires New Amenities for Dining, Fun," *Detroit News*, 21 December 1995, p. 1K. Primary source: U.S. Department of Commerce 1992 Census of Retail Trade (Geographic Area Series), Bureau of the Census; U.S. Department of Commerce 1992 Census of Service Industries (Geographic Area Series), Bureau of the Census.

★ 2368 ★
Restaurants

Tipping for Service, 1995: Persons Who Tip 15 Percent or Less

[In percentages of persons who say they tip 15 percent or less]

City/MSA	Percentage	Rank
Minneapolis, MN	61	1
San Francisco, CA	59	2
Los Angeles, CA	54	3
Detroit, MI	48	4
Saint Louis, MO	48	5
Atlanta, GA	46	6
Orlando, FL	45	7
Chicago, IL	44	8
New Orleans, LA	42	9
New York, NY	41	10
Boston, MA	39	11
Miami, FL	38	12
Philadelphia, PA	29	13

Source: Hamlin, Suzanne, "For Big Tips, Los Angeles Comes In Last," *New York Times*, 15 May 1996, p. B1. Primary source: Zagat (company) surveys of 35 cities.

★ 2369 ★
Restaurants

Tipping for Service, 1995: Persons Who Tip 16 to 19 Percent

[In percentages of persons who say they tip 16 to 19 percent]

City/MSA	Percentage	Rank
New York, NY	25	1
Philadelphia, PA	23	2
Miami, FL	21	3
Chicago, IL	20	4
Boston, MA	17	5
Los Angeles, CA	16	6
San Francisco, CA	15	7
Saint Louis, MO	14	8
Atlanta, GA	13	9
Detroit, MI	12	10
Orlando, FL	12	10
New Orleans, LA	11	11
Minneapolis, MN	8	12

Source: Hamlin, Suzanne, "For Big Tips, Los Angeles Comes In Last," *New York Times*, 15 May 1996, p. B1. Primary source: Zagat (company) surveys of 35 cities.

★ 2370 ★
Restaurants

Tipping for Service, 1995: Persons Who Tip 20 Percent or More

[In percentages of persons who say they tip 20 percent or more]

City/MSA	Percentage	Rank
Philadelphia, PA	48	1
New Orleans, LA	47	2
Boston, MA	44	3
Orlando, FL	43	4
Atlanta, GA	42	5
Miami, FL	41	6
Detroit, MI	40	7
Saint Louis, MO	38	8
Chicago, IL	36	9
New York, NY	34	10
Minneapolis, MN	32	11
San Francisco, CA	26	12
Los Angeles, CA	25	13

Source: Hamlin, Suzanne, "For Big Tips, Los Angeles Comes In Last," *New York Times*, 15 May 1996, p. B1. Primary source: Zagat (company) surveys of 35 cities.

Chapter 23

WHOLESALE TRADE

Topics Covered

General Summary
Establishments and Employment

★2371★
General Summary
Wholesale Trade, 1992: Establishments

City	Number	Rank
Atlanta, GA MSA	9,070	10
Boston-Worcester-Lawrence, MA-NH-ME-CT CMSA	10,733	7
Chicago-Gary-Kenosha, IL-IN-WI CMSA	18,573	3
Cincinnati-Hamilton, OH-KY-IN CMSA	3,546	20
Cleveland-Akron, OH CMSA	6,069	15
Dallas-Fort Worth, TX CMSA	10,567	8
Denver-Boulder-Greeley, CO CMSA	5,353	16
Detroit-Ann Arbor-Flint, MI CMSA	9,068	11
Houston-Galveston-Brazoria, TX CMSA	9,046	12
Kansas City, MO-KS MSA	4,016	19
Los Angeles-Riverside-Orange County, CA CMSA	31,250	2
Miami-Fort Lauderdale, FL CMSA	12,024	5
Minneapolis-St. Paul, MN-WI CMSA	6,436	14
New York-Northern New Jersey-Long Island,		21
Philadelphia-Wilmington-Atlantic City,		21
Portland-Salem, OR-WA CMSA	4,615	18
San Francisco-Oakland-San Jose, CA CMSA	13,550	4
Seattle-Tacoma-Bremerton, WA CMSA	7,101	13
St. Louis, MO-IL MSA	5,302	17
Washington-Baltimore, DC-MD-VA-WV CMSA	9,294	9
NY-NJ-CT-PA CMSA	50,178	1
PA-NJ-DE-MD CMSA	11,229	6

Source: U.S. Bureau of the Census, *Statistical Abstract of the United States: 1995,* (115th edition), Washington, DC: U.S. Government Printing Office, 1995, p. 792. Primary source: U.S. Bureau of the Census, *1992 Census of Wholesale Trade,* Geographic Area Series, WC92-A-52.

★2372★
General Summary
Wholesale Trade, 1992: Merchant Wholesaler Establishments
[In billions of dollars]

City	Number	Rank
Atlanta, GA MSA	6,546	12
Boston-Worcester-Lawrence, MA-NH-ME-CT CMSA	8,478	7
Chicago-Gary-Kenosha, IL-IN-WI CMSA	14,244	3
Cincinnati-Hamilton, OH-KY-IN CMSA	2,579	20
Cleveland-Akron, OH CMSA	4,653	15
Dallas-Fort Worth, TX CMSA	7,906	8
Denver-Boulder-Greeley, CO CMSA	4,069	17

[Continued]

★2372★
Wholesale Trade, 1992: Merchant Wholesaler Establishments
[Continued]

City	Number	Rank
Detroit-Ann Arbor-Flint, MI CMSA	6,864	11
Houston-Galveston-Brazoria, TX CMSA	7,408	10
Kansas City, MO-KS MSA	3,036	19
Los Angeles-Riverside-Orange County, CA CMSA	26,744	2
Miami-Fort Lauderdale, FL CMSA	10,556	5
Minneapolis-St. Paul, MN-WI CMSA	4,817	14
New York-Northern New Jersey-Long Island,		21
Philadelphia-Wilmington-Atlantic City,		21
Portland-Salem, OR-WA CMSA	3,723	18
San Francisco-Oakland-San Jose, CA CMSA	11,054	4
Seattle-Tacoma-Bremerton, WA CMSA	5,597	13
St. Louis, MO-IL MSA	4,075	16
Washington-Baltimore, DC-MD-VA-WV CMSA	7,521	9
NY-NJ-CT-PA CMSA	43,048	1
PA-NJ-DE-MD CMSA	8,966	6

Source: U.S. Bureau of the Census, *Statistical Abstract of the United States: 1995,* (115th edition), Washington, DC: U.S. Government Printing Office, 1995, p. 792. Primary source: U.S. Bureau of the Census, *1992 Census of Wholesale Trade,* Geographic Area Series, WC92-A-52.

★2373★
General Summary
Wholesale Trade, 1992: Merchant Wholesalers' Sales
[In billions of dollars]

City	Billions	Rank
Atlanta, GA MSA	34.4	11
Boston-Worcester-Lawrence, MA-NH-ME-CT CMSA	46.4	6
Chicago-Gary-Kenosha, IL-IN-WI CMSA	87.2	3
Cincinnati-Hamilton, OH-KY-IN CMSA	13.3	20
Cleveland-Akron, OH CMSA	18.3	18
Dallas-Fort Worth, TX CMSA	37.3	8
Denver-Boulder-Greeley, CO CMSA	18.2	19
Detroit-Ann Arbor-Flint, MI CMSA	31.3	12
Houston-Galveston-Brazoria, TX CMSA	64.3	4
Kansas City, MO-KS MSA	18.5	17
Los Angeles-Riverside-Orange County, CA CMSA	162.9	2
Miami-Fort Lauderdale, FL CMSA	35.0	10

[Continued]

★2373★

Wholesale Trade, 1992: Merchant Wholesalers' Sales
[Continued]

City	Billions	Rank
Minneapolis-St. Paul, MN-WI CMSA	28.4	13
New York-Northern New Jersey-Long Island,		21
Philadelphia-Wilmington-Atlantic City,		21
Portland-Salem, OR-WA CMSA	26.2	15
San Francisco-Oakland-San Jose, CA CMSA	61.2	5
Seattle-Tacoma-Bremerton, WA CMSA	28.3	14
St. Louis, MO-IL MSA	20.9	16
Washington-Baltimore, DC-MD-VA-WV CMSA	36.3	9
NY-NJ-CT-PA CMSA	301.4	1
PA-NJ-DE-MD CMSA	39.9	7

Source: U.S. Bureau of the Census, *Statistical Abstract of the United States: 1995,* (115th edition), Washington, DC: U.S. Government Printing Office, 1995, p. 792. Primary source: U.S. Bureau of the Census, *1992 Census of Wholesale Trade,* Geographic Area Series, WC92-A-52.

★2374★
General Summary

Wholesale Trade, 1992: Sales
[In billions of dollars]

City	Billions	Rank
Atlanta, GA MSA	93.4	8
Boston-Worcester-Lawrence, MA-NH-ME-CT CMSA	88.0	10
Chicago-Gary-Kenosha, IL-IN-WI CMSA	188.5	3
Cincinnati-Hamilton, OH-KY-IN CMSA	37.6	20
Cleveland-Akron, OH CMSA	40.0	16
Dallas-Fort Worth, TX CMSA	98.8	6
Denver-Boulder-Greeley, CO CMSA	41.9	15
Detroit-Ann Arbor-Flint, MI CMSA	95.7	7
Houston-Galveston-Brazoria, TX CMSA	117.3	5
Kansas City, MO-KS MSA	38.2	18
Los Angeles-Riverside-Orange County, CA CMSA	248.9	2
Miami-Fort Lauderdale, FL CMSA	48.6	14
Minneapolis-St. Paul, MN-WI CMSA	58.2	12
New York-Northern New Jersey-Long Island,		21
Philadelphia-Wilmington-Atlantic City,		21
Portland-Salem, OR-WA CMSA	38.1	19
San Francisco-Oakland-San Jose, CA CMSA	125.4	4

[Continued]

★2374★

Wholesale Trade, 1992: Sales
[Continued]

City	Billions	Rank
Seattle-Tacoma-Bremerton, WA CMSA	48.9	13
St. Louis, MO-IL MSA	38.7	17
Washington-Baltimore, DC-MD-VA-WV CMSA	71.5	11
NY-NJ-CT-PA CMSA	457.8	1
PA-NJ-DE-MD CMSA	90.6	9

Source: U.S. Bureau of the Census, *Statistical Abstract of the United States: 1995,* (115th edition), Washington, DC: U.S. Government Printing Office, 1995, p. 792. Primary source: U.S. Bureau of the Census, *1992 Census of Wholesale Trade,* Geographic Area Series, WC92-A-52.

★2375★
Establishments and Employment

Beer and Ale

The U.S. total number of employees is 91,086; total number of establishments is 3,403.

MSA	Establishments	Rank	Employment	Rank
Chicago-Gary-Kenosha, IL-IN-WI CMSA	65	4	2,664	1
San Francisco-Oakland-San Jose, CA CMSA	53	6	1,873	2
Dallas-Fort Worth, TX CMSA	25	13	1,377	3
Seattle-Tacoma-Bremerton, WA CMSA	28	11	1,317	4
St. Louis, MO-IL MSA	34	8	1,092	5
Cleveland-Akron, OH CMSA	21	14	1,023	6
Atlanta, GA MSA	16	18	981	7
Tampa-St. Petersburg-Clearwater, FL MSA	13	20	842	8
San Antonio, TX MSA	15	19	822	9
San Diego, CA MSA	10	23	794	10
Phoenix-Mesa, AZ MSA	10	23	692	11
Minneapolis-St. Paul, MN-WI MSA	31	9	657	12
Norfolk-Virginia Beach-Newport News, VA-NC MSA	6	27	641	13
New Orleans, LA MSA	9	24	621	14
Milwaukee-Racine, WI CMSA	16	18	616	15
Buffalo-Niagara Falls, NY MSA	10	23	548	16
Memphis, TN-AR-MS MSA	9	24	524	17
Birmingham, AL MSA	4	29	491	18
Kansas City, MO-KS MSA	11	22	487	19
Charlotte-Gastonia-Rock Hill, NC-SC MSA	13	20	486	20
Indianapolis, IN MSA	12	21	478	21
Orlando, FL MSA	4	29	461	22
Jacksonville, FL MSA	8	25	445	23
Hartford, CT MSA	7	26	442	24
Grand Rapids-Muskegon-Holland, MI MSA	13	20	424	25

Source: U.S. Department of Commerce, Bureau of the Census, Data User Services Division, *1992 Economic Census, Volume 1F, Reports Series, Release 1F,* September 1995, CD-ROM. *Note:* Data are shown only for the top 25 areas.

★2376★

Establishments and Employment

Beer, Wine, and Distilled Alcoholic Beverages

The U.S. total number of employees is 141,821; total number of establishments is 5,259.

MSA	Estab-lish-ments	Rank	Emp-loy-ment	Rank
Los Angeles – Riverside – Orange County, CA CMSA	145	3	7,719	1
Chicago – Gary – Kenosha, IL – IN – WI CMSA	124	5	5,049	2
San Francisco – Oakland – San Jose, CA CMSA	193	2	4,953	3
Washington – Baltimore, DC – MD – VA – WV CMSA	99	6	3,969	4
Detroit – Ann Arbor – Flint, MI CMSA	78	8	2,931	5
Dallas – Fort Worth, TX CMSA	56	12	2,767	6
Houston – Galveston – Brazoria, TX CMSA	62	11	2,732	7
Miami – Fort Lauderdale, FL CMSA	56	12	2,602	8
Atlanta, GA MSA	40	17	1,973	9
Seattle – Tacoma – Bremerton, WA CMSA	65	10	1,964	10
Tampa – St. Petersburg – Clearwater, FL MSA	27	22	1,697	11
St. Louis, MO – IL MSA	52	13	1,484	12
San Antonio, TX MSA	26	23	1,387	13
Phoenix – Mesa, AZ MSA	22	25	1,327	14
New Orleans, LA MSA	26	23	1,324	15
Minneapolis – St. Paul, MN – WI MSA	46	15	1,300	16
Indianapolis, IN MSA	19	28	1,223	17
Milwaukee – Racine, WI CMSA	32	20	1,113	18
Portland – Salem, OR – WA CMSA	42	16	1,106	19
Hartford, CT MSA	16	31	1,084	20
Kansas City, MO – KS MSA	20	27	1,071	21
San Diego, CA MSA	18	29	1,057	22
Orlando, FL MSA	10	37	981	23
Buffalo – Niagara Falls, NY MSA	16	31	951	24
Cincinnati – Hamilton, OH – KY – IN CMSA	39	18	944	25

Source: U.S. Department of Commerce, Bureau of the Census, Data User Services Division, *1992 Economic Census, Volume 1F, Reports Series, Release 1F*, September 1995, CD-ROM. *Note:* Data are shown only for the top 25 areas.

★2377★

Establishments and Employment

Books, Periodicals, and Newspapers

The U.S. total number of employees is 77,392; total number of establishments is 4,205.

MSA	Estab-lish-ments	Rank	Emp-loy-ment	Rank
New York – Northern New Jersey – Long Island, NY – NJ – CT-CMSA	634	1	13,525	1
Chicago – Gary – Kenosha, IL – IN – WI CMSA	195	3	5,195	2
Los Angeles – Riverside – Orange County, CA CMSA	289	2	3,908	3
Boston – Worcester – Lawrence, MA – NH – ME – CT CMSA	146	5	3,082	4
Philadelphia – Wilmington – Atlantic City, PA – NJ – DE – MD CMSA	108	7	2,542	5
San Francisco – Oakland – San Jose, CA CMSA	156	4	2,236	6
Dallas – Fort Worth, TX CMSA	96	8	1,875	7
Nashville, TN MSA	32	22	1,837	8
Atlanta, GA MSA	84	9	1,088	9
Minneapolis – St. Paul, MN – WI MSA	64	13	1,007	10
Houston – Galveston – Brazoria, TX CMSA	65	12	998	11
Cleveland – Akron, OH CMSA	47	17	932	12
Hartford, CT MSA	18	30	923	13
Miami – Fort Lauderdale, FL CMSA	83	10	893	14
St. Louis, MO – IL MSA	42	18	873	15
Portland – Salem, OR – WA CMSA	54	15	726	16
San Diego, CA MSA	51	16	656	17
Buffalo – Niagara Falls, NY MSA	17	31	611	18
Columbus, OH MSA	27	25	581	19
Phoenix – Mesa, AZ MSA	36	20	558	20
Richmond – Petersburg, VA MSA	16	32	525	21
Orlando, FL MSA	33	21	494	22
Kansas City, MO – KS MSA	37	19	450	23
Salt Lake City – Ogden, UT MSA	25	26	446	24
Charlotte – Gastonia – Rock Hill, NC – SC MSA	25	26	419	25

Source: U.S. Department of Commerce, Bureau of the Census, Data User Services Division, *1992 Economic Census, Volume 1F, Reports Series, Release 1F*, September 1995, CD-ROM. *Note:* Data are shown only for the top 25 areas.

★2378★

Establishments and Employment

Brick, Stone, and Related Construction Materials

The U.S. total number of employees is 32,062; total number of establishments is 4,285.

MSA	Establish-ments	Rank	Emp-loy-ment	Rank
Los Angeles – Riverside – Orange County, CA CMSA	268	2	2,481	1
New York – Northern New Jersey – Long Island, NY – NJ – CT-CMSA	360	1	2,474	2
Chicago – Gary – Kenosha, IL – IN – WI CMSA	146	3	1,289	3
Miami – Fort Lauderdale, FL CMSA	138	4	954	4
Dallas – Fort Worth, TX CMSA	95	8	724	5
San Francisco – Oakland – San Jose, CA CMSA	108	5	718	6
Atlanta, GA MSA	104	6	664	7
Minneapolis – St. Paul, MN – WI MSA	56	15	649	8
Washington – Baltimore, DC – MD – VA – WV CMSA	83	10	645	9
Cleveland – Akron, OH CMSA	53	17	466	10
Tampa – St. Petersburg – Clearwater, FL MSA	57	14	434	11
Phoenix – Mesa, AZ MSA	54	16	375	12
St. Louis, MO – IL MSA	47	18	355	13
Nashville, TN MSA	25	27	340	14
San Diego, CA MSA	45	19	316	15
San Antonio, TX MSA	25	27	291	16
Portland – Salem, OR – WA CMSA	37	21	280	17
Denver – Boulder – Greeley, CO CMSA	39	20	278	18
Kansas City, MO – KS MSA	30	23	275	19
New Orleans, LA MSA	25	27	266	20
Rochester, NY MSA	18	34	246	21
Memphis, TN – AR – MS MSA	18	34	227	22
Milwaukee – Racine, WI CMSA	24	28	227	22
Scranton – Wilkes-Barre – Hazleton, PA MSA	14	38	204	23
Pittsburgh, PA MSA	33	22	201	24

Source: U.S. Department of Commerce, Bureau of the Census, Data User Services Division, *1992 Economic Census, Volume 1F, Reports Series, Release 1F,* September 1995, CD-ROM. *Note:* Data are shown only for the top 25 areas.

★2379★

Establishments and Employment

Chemicals and Allied Products

The U.S. total number of employees is 147,010; total number of establishments is 14,193.

MSA	Establish-ments	Rank	Emp-loy-ment	Rank
Los Angeles – Riverside – Orange County, CA CMSA	797	2	8,927	1
Chicago – Gary – Kenosha, IL – IN – WI CMSA	690	3	8,066	2
Houston – Galveston – Brazoria, TX CMSA	521	4	6,249	3
Cleveland – Akron, OH CMSA	307	9	4,858	4
Atlanta, GA MSA	394	6	4,211	5
Dallas – Fort Worth, TX CMSA	297	11	4,083	6
Detroit – Ann Arbor – Flint, MI CMSA	339	7	3,408	7
San Francisco – Oakland – San Jose, CA CMSA	308	8	3,243	8
Charlotte – Gastonia – Rock Hill, NC – SC MSA	185	16	2,758	9
Minneapolis – St. Paul, MN – WI MSA	209	13	2,280	10
Cincinnati – Hamilton, OH – KY – IN CMSA	154	18	2,252	11
Miami – Fort Lauderdale, FL CMSA	258	12	2,002	12
St. Louis, MO – IL MSA	197	14	1,978	13
Milwaukee – Racine, WI CMSA	134	22	1,844	14
Pittsburgh, PA MSA	139	21	1,714	15
Indianapolis, IN MSA	113	25	1,620	16
Kansas City, MO – KS MSA	115	24	1,234	17
Tampa – St. Petersburg – Clearwater, FL MSA	151	19	1,182	18
Greensboro – Winston-Salem – High Point, NC MSA	80	32	1,032	19
Phoenix – Mesa, AZ MSA	116	23	946	20
Portland – Salem, OR – WA CMSA	108	26	939	21
Richmond – Petersburg, VA MSA	57	41	903	22
Orlando, FL MSA	79	33	874	23
Jacksonville, FL MSA	59	40	865	24
New Orleans, LA MSA	86	30	860	25

Source: U.S. Department of Commerce, Bureau of the Census, Data User Services Division, *1992 Economic Census, Volume 1F, Reports Series, Release 1F,* September 1995, CD-ROM. *Note:* Data are shown only for the top 25 areas.

★2380★

Establishments and Employment

Coal and Other Minerals and Ores

The U.S. total number of employees is 5,301; total number of establishments is 822.

MSA	Estab- lish- ments	Rank	Emp- ploy- ment	Rank
Chicago – Gary – Kenosha, IL – IN – WI CMSA	26	3	276	1
Pittsburgh, PA MSA	41	2	222	2
Nashville, TN MSA	7	14	144	3
Philadelphia – Wilmington – Atlantic City, PA – NJ – DE – MD CMSA	13	8	125	4
Johnson City – Kingsport – Bristol, TN – VA MSA	6	15	79	5
Charleston, WV MSA	11	10	64	6
St. Louis, MO – IL MSA	9	12	62	7
San Francisco – Oakland – San Jose, CA CMSA	10	11	59	8
Knoxville, TN MSA	14	7	55	9
Richmond – Petersburg, VA MSA	9	12	42	10
Lexington, KY MSA	12	9	28	11
Louisville, KY – IN MSA	5	16	24	12
Chattanooga, TN – GA MSA	6	15	17	13
West Palm Beach – Boca Raton, FL MSA	4	17	17	13
Buffalo – Niagara Falls, NY MSA	6	15	14	14
Harrisburg – Lebanon – Carlisle, PA MSA	4	17	13	15
Greenville – Spartanburg – Anderson, SC MSA	3	18	9	16
San Diego, CA MSA	3	18	8	17
Portland – Salem, OR – WA CMSA	3	18	7	18
Albany – Schenectady – Troy, NY MSA	0	21	0	19
Albuquerque, NM MSA	0	21	0	19
Allentown – Bethlehem – Easton, PA MSA	1	20	0[1]	19
Anchorage, AK MSA	1	20	0[1]	19
Appleton – Oshkosh – Neenah, WI MSA	0	21	0	19
Atlanta, GA MSA	9	12	0 1	9

Source: U.S. Department of Commerce, Bureau of the Census, Data User Services Division, *1992 Economic Census, Volume 1F, Reports Series, Release 1F,* September 1995, CD-ROM. *Notes:* Data are shown only for the top 25 areas. 1. 0-19 employees.

★2381★

Establishments and Employment

Computers and Computer Peripheral Equipment and Software

The U.S. total number of employees is 279,686; total number of establishments is 17,578.

MSA	Estab- lish- ments	Rank	Emp- ploy- ment	Rank
San Francisco – Oakland – San Jose, CA CMSA	1,178	3	31,212	1
Los Angeles – Riverside – Orange County, CA CMSA	1,556	1	24,987	2
New York – Northern New Jersey – Long Island, NY – NJ – CT-CMSA	1,401	2	24,302	3
Chicago – Gary – Kenosha, IL – IN – WI CMSA	642	6	15,432	4
Boston – Worcester – Lawrence, MA – NH – ME – CT CMSA	667	5	12,612	5
Dallas – Fort Worth, TX CMSA	553	7	10,986	6
Atlanta, GA MSA	508	8	8,515	7
Denver – Boulder – Greeley, CO CMSA	299	15	6,210	8
Detroit – Ann Arbor – Flint, MI CMSA	330	14	5,815	9
Minneapolis – St. Paul, MN – WI MSA	357	11	5,667	10
Houston – Galveston – Brazoria, TX CMSA	340	13	4,480	11
Miami – Fort Lauderdale, FL CMSA	462	9	3,913	12
San Diego, CA MSA	219	16	3,273	13
Cleveland – Akron, OH CMSA	214	17	3,080	14
Phoenix – Mesa, AZ MSA	212	18	3,076	15
Pittsburgh, PA MSA	131	24	2,304	16
Portland – Salem, OR – WA CMSA	180	19	2,288	17
St. Louis, MO – IL MSA	166	20	2,280	18
Orlando, FL MSA	146	21	2,105	19
Columbus, OH MSA	106	31	2,071	20
Sacramento – Yolo, CA CMSA	110	29	2,065	21
Tampa – St. Petersburg – Clearwater, FL MSA	145	22	2,055	22
Milwaukee – Racine, WI CMSA	108	30	2,025	23
Indianapolis, IN MSA	122	25	1,934	24
Kansas City, MO – KS MSA	132	23	1,926	25

Source: U.S. Department of Commerce, Bureau of the Census, Data User Services Division, *1992 Economic Census, Volume 1F, Reports Series, Release 1F,* September 1995, CD-ROM. *Note:* Data are shown only for the top 25 areas.

★2382★

Establishments and Employment

Confectionery

The U.S. total number of employees is 56,322; total number of establishments is 2,693.

MSA	Estab-lish-ments	Rank	Emp-loy-ment	Rank
New York – Northern New Jersey – Long Island, NY – NJ – CT-CMSA	303	1	4,160	1
Chicago – Gary – Kenosha, IL – IN – WI CMSA	93	3	3,773	2
Los Angeles – Riverside – Orange County, CA CMSA	132	2	3,026	3
Dallas – Fort Worth, TX CMSA	43	11	1,940	4
Houston – Galveston – Brazoria, TX CMSA	30	17	1,304	5
Boston – Worcester – Lawrence, MA – NH – ME – CT CMSA	56	5	1,136	6
St. Louis, MO – IL MSA	20	22	935	7
Atlanta, GA MSA	31	16	851	8
Cleveland – Akron, OH CMSA	36	14	802	9
San Diego, CA MSA	29	18	688	10
Kansas City, MO – KS MSA	22	20	674	11
Pittsburgh, PA MSA	39	12	644	12
Seattle – Tacoma – Bremerton, WA CMSA	46	10	621	13
Miami – Fort Lauderdale, FL CMSA	48	8	598	14
Columbus, OH MSA	19	23	558	15
Orlando, FL MSA	12	28	558	15
Buffalo – Niagara Falls, NY MSA	17	24	537	16
Minneapolis – St. Paul, MN – WI MSA	33	15	526	17
Tampa – St. Petersburg – Clearwater, FL MSA	22	20	516	18
Syracuse, NY MSA	9	31	496	19
El Paso, TX MSA	15	25	492	20
Memphis, TN – AR – MS MSA	17	24	485	21
Milwaukee – Racine, WI CMSA	22	20	476	22
Grand Rapids – Muskegon – Holland, MI MSA	20	22	470	23
Charlotte – Gastonia – Rock Hill, NC – SC MSA	13	27	456	24

Source: U.S. Department of Commerce, Bureau of the Census, Data User Services Division, *1992 Economic Census, Volume 1F, Reports Series, Release 1F,* September 1995, CD-ROM. *Note:* Data are shown only for the top 25 areas.

★2383★

Establishments and Employment

Construction and Mining (except Petroleum) Machinery and Equipment

The U.S. total number of employees is 73,518; total number of establishments is 5,157.

MSA	Estab-lish-ments	Rank	Emp-loy-ment	Rank
New York – Northern New Jersey – Long Island, NY – NJ – CT-CMSA	195	1	2,177	1
Los Angeles – Riverside – Orange County, CA CMSA	158	2	2,150	2
Pittsburgh, PA MSA	58	15	1,408	3
Denver – Boulder – Greeley, CO CMSA	68	11	1,374	4
Dallas – Fort Worth, TX CMSA	78	9	1,340	5
Washington – Baltimore, DC – MD – VA – WV CMSA	103	5	1,336	6
Minneapolis – St. Paul, MN – WI MSA	57	16	1,181	7
Miami – Fort Lauderdale, FL CMSA	116	4	1,134	8
Atlanta, GA MSA	93	7	1,122	9
Birmingham, AL MSA	40	22	1,045	10
Salt Lake City – Ogden, UT MSA	38	24	995	11
Kansas City, MO – KS MSA	51	18	994	12
Cleveland – Akron, OH CMSA	59	14	949	13
Portland – Salem, OR – WA CMSA	62	13	935	14
Phoenix – Mesa, AZ MSA	68	11	928	15
Louisville, KY – IN MSA	31	29	860	16
Charlotte – Gastonia – Rock Hill, NC – SC MSA	42	21	857	17
Boston – Worcester – Lawrence, MA – NH – ME – CT CMSA	71	10	852	18
St. Louis, MO – IL MSA	46	19	795	19
Milwaukee – Racine, WI CMSA	43	20	733	20
Charleston, WV MSA	29	31	714	21
Detroit – Ann Arbor – Flint, MI CMSA	56	17	688	22
Jacksonville, FL MSA	23	37	674	23
Raleigh – Durham – Chapel Hill, NC MSA	23	37	579	24
Columbus, OH MSA	31	29	565	25

Source: U.S. Department of Commerce, Bureau of the Census, Data User Services Division, *1992 Economic Census, Volume 1F, Reports Series, Release 1F,* September 1995, CD-ROM. *Note:* Data are shown only for the top 25 areas.

★2384★

Establishments and Employment

Dairy Products, Except Dried Or Canned

The U.S. total number of employees is 50,975; total number of establishments is 3,378.

MSA	Establish-ments	Rank	Employ-ment	Rank
New York – Northern New Jersey – Long Island, NY – NJ – CT-CMSA	426	1	5,604	1
Los Angeles – Riverside – Orange County, CA CMSA	147	3	3,342	2
San Francisco – Oakland – San Jose, CA CMSA	90	4	2,129	3
Chicago – Gary – Kenosha, IL – IN – WI CMSA	161	2	2,010	4
Detroit – Ann Arbor – Flint, MI CMSA	65	6	1,192	5
Seattle – Tacoma – Bremerton, WA CMSA	46	9	915	6
Miami – Fort Lauderdale, FL CMSA	60	7	910	7
Dallas – Fort Worth, TX CMSA	29	14	793	8
Boston – Worcester – Lawrence, MA – NH – ME – CT CMSA	50	8	758	9
Houston – Galveston – Brazoria, TX CMSA	28	15	731	10
Minneapolis – St. Paul, MN – WI MSA	36	11	632	11
Phoenix – Mesa, AZ MSA	34	12	608	12
Cleveland – Akron, OH CMSA	19	20	550	13
Atlanta, GA MSA	29	14	522	14
Grand Rapids – Muskegon – Holland, MI MSA	8	30	497	15
St. Louis, MO – IL MSA	31	13	466	16
Syracuse, NY MSA	16	23	463	17
Tampa – St. Petersburg – Clearwater, FL MSA	25	16	457	18
Harrisburg – Lebanon – Carlisle, PA MSA	11	27	439	19
Orlando, FL MSA	20	19	372	20
Nashville, TN MSA	11	27	349	21
Indianapolis, IN MSA	19	20	337	22
Kansas City, MO – KS MSA	17	22	313	23
Sacramento – Yolo, CA CMSA	28	15	307	24
New Orleans, LA MSA	16	23	305	25

Source: U.S. Department of Commerce, Bureau of the Census, Data User Services Division, *1992 Economic Census, Volume 1F, Reports Series, Release 1F,* September 1995, CD-ROM. *Note:* Data are shown only for the top 25 areas.

★2385★

Establishments and Employment

Drugs, Drug Proprietaries, and Druggists' Sundries

The U.S. total number of employees is 158,167; total number of establishments is 6,070.

MSA	Establish-ments	Rank	Employ-ment	Rank
New York – Northern New Jersey – Long Island, NY – NJ – CT-CMSA	1,001	1	34,664	1
Los Angeles – Riverside – Orange County, CA CMSA	582	2	10,940	2
Philadelphia – Wilmington – Atlantic City, PA – NJ – DE – MD CMSA	130	7	6,057	3
Miami – Fort Lauderdale, FL CMSA	294	3	4,109	4
Dallas – Fort Worth, TX CMSA	170	6	4,001	5
Boston – Worcester – Lawrence, MA – NH – ME – CT CMSA	111	8	3,937	6
Atlanta, GA MSA	108	9	3,883	7
Youngstown – Warren. OH MSA	19	38	2,741	8
Memphis, TN – AR – MS MSA	38	25	2,554	9
Cleveland – Akron, OH CMSA	60	18	2,298	10
Houston – Galveston – Brazoria, TX CMSA	99	11	2,289	11
Denver – Boulder – Greeley, CO CMSA	71	16	1,977	12
Minneapolis – St. Paul, MN – WI MSA	81	12	1,903	13
Detroit – Ann Arbor – Flint, MI CMSA	79	13	1,840	14
Seattle – Tacoma – Bremerton, WA CMSA	74	14	1,722	15
Pittsburgh, PA MSA	34	28	1,574	16
Hartford, CT MSA	25	32	1,470	17
St. Louis, MO – IL MSA	59	19	1,390	18
Tampa – St. Petersburg – Clearwater, FL MSA	74	14	1,277	19
Jacksonville, FL MSA	24	33	1,272	20
Phoenix – Mesa, AZ MSA	79	13	1,115	21
Charlotte – Gastonia – Rock Hill, NC – SC MSA	29	30	1,088	22
Kansas City, MO – KS MSA.	39	24	1,072	23
Harrisburg – Lebanon – Carlisle, PA MSA	16	41	830	24
Sacramento – Yolo, CA CMSA	24	33	821	25

Source: U.S. Department of Commerce, Bureau of the Census, Data User Services Division, *1992 Economic Census, Volume 1F, Reports Series, Release 1F,* September 1995, CD-ROM. *Note:* Data are shown only for the top 25 areas.

★ 2386 ★

Establishments and Employment

Durable Goods

The U.S. total number of employees is 3,349,064; total number of establishments is 313,464.

MSA	Estab- lish- ments	Rank	Emp- ploy- ment	Rank
New York – Northern New Jersey – Long Island, NY – NJ – CT-CMSA	26,947	1	298,239	1
Los Angeles – Riverside – Orange County, CA CMSA	19,831	2	242,210	2
Chicago – Gary – Kenosha, IL – IN – WI CMSA	12,376	3	168,611	3
San Francisco – Oakland – San Jose, CA CMSA	8,851	4	117,371	4
Dallas – Fort Worth, TX CMSA	7,290	7	90,616	5
Washington – Baltimore, DC – MD – VA – WV CMSA	6,392	11	85,290	6
Boston – Worcester – Lawrence, MA – NH – ME – CT CMSA	7,253	8	84,094	7
Philadelphia – Wilmington – Atlantic City, PA – NJ – DE – MD CMSA	7,447	6	82,992	8
Atlanta, GA MSA	6,239	12	79,310	9
Detroit – Ann Arbor – Flint, MI CMSA	6,598	9	74,018	10
Houston – Galveston – Brazoria, TX CMSA	6,422	10	68,662	11
Miami – Fort Lauderdale, FL CMSA	7,732	5	57,265	12
Minneapolis – St. Paul, MN – WI MSA	4,448	14	56,826	13
Cleveland – Akron, OH CMSA	4,427	15	52,265	14
Seattle – Tacoma – Bremerton, WA CMSA	4,852	13	51,801	15
Denver – Boulder – Greeley, CO CMSA	3,794	16	43,174	16
St. Louis, MO – IL MSA	3,544	17	39,721	17
Pittsburgh, PA MSA	3,124	20	36,826	18
Portland – Salem, OR – WA CMSA	3,231	18	34,922	19
Kansas City, MO – KS MSA	2,776	22	33,622	20
Phoenix – Mesa, AZ MSA	3,148	19	32,468	21
Cincinnati – Hamilton, OH – KY – IN CMSA	2,466	26	30,531	22
Milwaukee – Racine, WI CMSA	2,470	25	29,617	23
Charlotte – Gastonia – Rock Hill, NC – SC MSA	2,601	24	28,358	24
Tampa – St. Petersburg – Clearwater, FL MSA	2,852	21	28,162	25

Source: U.S. Department of Commerce, Bureau of the Census, Data User Services Division, *1992 Economic Census, Volume 1F, Reports Series, Release 1F,* September 1995, CD-ROM. *Note:* Data are shown only for the top 25 areas.

★ 2387 ★

Establishments and Employment

Electrical Apparatus and Equipment, Wiring Supplies, and Construction Materials

The U.S. total number of employees is 190,238; total number of establishments is 18,511.

MSA	Estab- lish- ments	Rank	Emp- ploy- ment	Rank
New York – Northern New Jersey – Long Island, NY – NJ – CT-CMSA	1,468	1	17,955	1
Los Angeles – Riverside – Orange County, CA CMSA	1,089	2	11,815	2
Chicago – Gary – Kenosha, IL – IN – WI CMSA	830	3	9,703	3
San Francisco – Oakland – San Jose, CA CMSA	570	4	7,022	4
Atlanta, GA MSA	384	10	5,499	5
Boston – Worcester – Lawrence, MA – NH – ME – CT CMSA	514	6	5,134	6
Dallas – Fort Worth, TX CMSA	435	7	4,710	7
Houston – Galveston – Brazoria, TX CMSA	360	11	4,075	8
Miami – Fort Lauderdale, FL CMSA	401	8	3,115	9
Minneapolis – St. Paul, MN – WI MSA	300	13	3,061	10
Cleveland – Akron, OH CMSA	294	14	3,051	11
St. Louis, MO – IL MSA	233	16	2,453	12
Pittsburgh, PA MSA	211	19	2,218	13
Milwaukee – Racine, WI CMSA	189	22	2,157	14
Portland – Salem, OR – WA CMSA	202	20	1,940	15
Cincinnati – Hamilton, OH – KY – IN CMSA	172	25	1,910	16
Charlotte – Gastonia – Rock Hill, NC – SC MSA	178	24	1,908	17
Phoenix – Mesa, AZ MSA	219	18	1,853	18
Columbus, OH MSA	125	30	1,674	19
Tampa – St. Petersburg – Clearwater, FL MSA	193	21	1,631	20
Indianapolis, IN MSA	157	27	1,583	21
Kansas City, MO – KS MSA	182	23	1,548	22
San Diego, CA MSA	162	26	1,515	23
Orlando, FL MSA	133	28	1,458	24
New Orleans, LA MSA	129	29	1,275	25

Source: U.S. Department of Commerce, Bureau of the Census, Data User Services Division, *1992 Economic Census, Volume 1F, Reports Series, Release 1F,* September 1995, CD-ROM. *Note:* Data are shown only for the top 25 areas.

★ 2388 ★

Establishments and Employment

Electrical Appliances, Television and Radio Sets

The U.S. total number of employees is 52,910; total number of establishments is 3,785.

MSA	Estab-lish-ments	Rank	Emp-loy-ment	Rank
New York – Northern New Jersey – Long Island, NY – NJ – CT-CMSA	504	1	9,770	1
Los Angeles – Riverside – Orange County, CA CMSA	390	2	6,832	2
Chicago – Gary – Kenosha, IL – IN – WI CMSA	171	4	4,579	3
Miami – Fort Lauderdale, FL CMSA	235	3	2,192	4
Dallas – Fort Worth, TX CMSA	114	5	1,674	5
Atlanta, GA MSA	82	9	1,466	6
San Francisco – Oakland – San Jose, CA CMSA	110	6	1,231	7
Boston – Worcester – Lawrence, MA – NH – ME – CT CMSA	100	7	1,183	8
Minneapolis – St. Paul, MN – WI MSA	70	10	929	9
Seattle – Tacoma – Bremerton, WA CMSA	64	12	918	10
Cleveland – Akron, OH CMSA	43	18	783	11
Tampa – St. Petersburg – Clearwater, FL MSA	37	19	664	12
St. Louis, MO – IL MSA	45	16	577	13
Kansas City, MO – KS MSA	47	15	545	14
Phoenix – Mesa, AZ MSA	44	17	460	15
Houston – Galveston – Brazoria, TX CMSA	51	14	452	16
Pittsburgh, PA MSA	29	22	369	17
San Diego, CA MSA	37	19	334	18
Salt Lake City – Ogden, UT MSA	30	21	301	19
New Orleans, LA MSA	22	26	300	20
Milwaukee – Racine, WI CMSA	22	26	296	21
Memphis, TN – AR – MS MSA	23	25	275	22
Jacksonville, FL MSA	10	37	268	23
Greensboro – Winston-Salem – High Point, NC MSA	19	28	256	24
San Antonio, TX MSA	23	25	249	25

Source: U.S. Department of Commerce, Bureau of the Census, Data User Services Division, *1992 Economic Census, Volume 1F, Reports Series, Release 1F*, September 1995, CD-ROM. *Note:* Data are shown only for the top 25 areas.

★ 2389 ★

Establishments and Employment

Electrical Goods

The U.S. total number of employees is 435,700; total number of establishments is 39,303.

MSA	Estab-lish-ments	Rank	Emp-loy-ment	Rank
Los Angeles – Riverside – Orange County, CA CMSA	3,031	2	37,754	1
San Francisco – Oakland – San Jose, CA CMSA	1,691	4	23,159	2
Dallas – Fort Worth, TX CMSA	1,182	6	15,066	3
Boston – Worcester – Lawrence, MA – NH – ME – CT CMSA	1,251	5	14,818	4
Washington – Baltimore, DC – MD – VA – WV CMSA	928	9	12,218	5
Atlanta, GA MSA	832	10	11,947	6
Philadelphia – Wilmington – Atlantic City, PA – NJ – DE – MD CMSA	1,040	8	10,961	7
Miami – Fort Lauderdale, FL CMSA	1,153	7	9,473	8
Detroit – Ann Arbor – Flint, MI CMSA	696	13	7,751	9
Houston – Galveston – Brazoria, TX CMSA	716	11	7,699	10
Minneapolis – St. Paul, MN – WI MSA	707	12	7,564	11
Denver – Boulder – Greeley, CO CMSA	616	15	6,770	12
San Diego, CA MSA	459	18	6,745	13
Seattle – Tacoma – Bremerton, WA CMSA	652	14	6,540	14
Cleveland – Akron, OH CMSA	565	16	6,296	15
St. Louis, MO – IL MSA	455	19	4,976	16
Phoenix – Mesa, AZ MSA	555	17	4,804	17
Kansas City, MO – KS MSA	395	22	4,679	18
Portland – Salem, OR – WA CMSA	413	20	4,113	19
Pittsburgh, PA MSA	352	24	3,732	20
Indianapolis, IN MSA	355	23	3,726	21
Tampa – St. Petersburg – Clearwater, FL MSA	412	21	3,700	22
Milwaukee – Racine, WI CMSA	327	26	3,611	23
Cincinnati – Hamilton, OH – KY – IN CMSA	293	27	3,528	24
Orlando, FL MSA	347	25	3,430	25

Source: U.S. Department of Commerce, Bureau of the Census, Data User Services Division, *1992 Economic Census, Volume 1F, Reports Series, Release 1F*, September 1995, CD-ROM. *Note:* Data are shown only for the top 25 areas.

★ 2390 ★

Establishments and Employment

Farm and Garden Machinery and Equipment

The U.S. total number of employees is 102,068; total number of establishments is 10,742.

MSA	Estab- lish- ments	Rank	Emp- loy- ment	Rank
Los Angeles – Riverside – Orange County, CA CMSA	178	2	1,763	1
Minneapolis – St. Paul, MN – WI MSA	97	7	1,441	2
Dallas – Fort Worth, TX CMSA	104	5	1,311	3
Atlanta, GA MSA	82	10	1,021	4
Washington – Baltimore, DC – MD – VA – WV CMSA	88	8	948	5
San Francisco – Oakland – San Jose, CA CMSA	102	6	856	6
Kansas City, MO – KS MSA	54	18	832	7
Columbus, OH MSA	46	20	824	8
Lancaster, PA MSA	38	26	802	9
St. Louis, MO – IL MSA	79	11	785	10
Memphis, TN – AR – MS MSA	60	15	773	11
Portland – Salem, OR – WA CMSA	63	13	704	12
Milwaukee – Racine, WI CMSA	35	29	689	13
Fresno, CA MSA	63	13	679	14
Bakersfield, CA MSA	36	28	644	15
Phoenix – Mesa, AZ MSA	57	16	544	16
Houston – Galveston – Brazoria, TX CMSA	62	14	532	17
Raleigh – Durham – Chapel Hill, NC MSA	24	36	479	18
Charlotte – Gastonia – Rock Hill, NC – SC MSA	38	26	469	19
Orlando, FL MSA	55	17	463	20
Seattle – Tacoma – Bremerton, WA CMSA	33	30	460	21
Sacramento – Yolo, CA CMSA	42	22	429	22
Cleveland – Akron, OH CMSA	47	19	425	23
Grand Rapids – Muskegon – Holland, MI MSA	35	29	424	24
Boston – Worcester – Lawrence, MA – NH – ME – CT CMSA	62	14	420	25

Source: U.S. Department of Commerce, Bureau of the Census, Data User Services Division, *1992 Economic Census, Volume 1F, Reports Series, Release 1F,* September 1995, CD-ROM. *Note:* Data are shown only for the top 25 areas.

★ 2391 ★

Establishments and Employment

Farm Supplies

The U.S. total number of employees is 137,387; total number of establishments is 17,469.

MSA	Estab- lish- ments	Rank	Emp- loy- ment	Rank
Los Angeles – Riverside – Orange County, CA CMSA	334	2	2,356	1
Minneapolis – St. Paul, MN – WI MSA	160	5	2,291	2
Philadelphia – Wilmington – Atlantic City, PA – NJ – DE – MD CMSA	143	9	1,293	3
Dallas – Fort Worth, TX CMSA	150	8	1,187	4
San Francisco – Oakland – San Jose, CA CMSA	158	6	1,184	5
Fresno, CA MSA	82	21	1,164	6
Portland – Salem, OR – WA CMSA	129	10	1,028	7
St. Louis, MO – IL MSA	112	12	1,009	8
Tampa – St. Petersburg – Clearwater, FL MSA	85	20	939	9
Omaha, NE – IA MSA	66	22	845	10
Lancaster, PA MSA	39	36	830	11
Miami – Fort Lauderdale, FL CMSA	165	4	830	11
Nashville, TN MSA	49	28	801	12
Salinas, CA MSA	34	41	795	13
Indianapolis, IN MSA	91	18	709	14
Kansas City, MO – KS MSA	94	17	674	15
Detroit – Ann Arbor – Flint, MI CMSA	98	15	665	16
Houston – Galveston – Brazoria, TX CMSA	119	11	616	17
Modesto, CA MSA	47	30	612	18
Atlanta, GA MSA	90	19	610	19
Phoenix – Mesa, AZ MSA	102	14	588	20
Lexington, KY MSA	47	30	534	21
Raleigh – Durham – Chapel Hill, NC MSA	51	27	526	22
Sacramento – Yolo, CA CMSA	60	24	517	23
Bakersfield, CA MSA	45	31	515	24

Source: U.S. Department of Commerce, Bureau of the Census, Data User Services Division, *1992 Economic Census, Volume 1F, Reports Series, Release 1F,* September 1995, CD-ROM. *Note:* Data are shown only for the top 25 areas.

★2392★

Establishments and Employment

Fish and Seafoods

The U.S. total number of employees is 29,651; total number of establishments is 3,100.

MSA	Establish-ments	Rank	Employ-ment	Rank
New York – Northern New Jersey – Long Island, NY – NJ – CT-CMSA	387	1	2,504	1
Seattle – Tacoma – Bremerton, WA CMSA	134	5	2,113	2
Philadelphia – Wilmington – Atlantic City, PA – NJ – DE – MD CMSA	54	10	1,103	3
Miami – Fort Lauderdale, FL CMSA	136	4	968	4
Tampa – St. Petersburg – Clearwater, FL MSA	42	14	854	5
Norfolk – Virginia Beach – Newport News, VA – NC MSA	48	12	849	6
Providence – Fall River – Warwick, RI – MA MSA	63	8	650	7
Portland, ME MSA	42	14	638	8
Mobile, AL MSA	47	13	571	9
New Orleans, LA MSA	72	7	507	10
Lafayette, LA MSA	15	21	421	11
Honolulu, HI MSA	31	16	364	12
Houston – Galveston – Brazoria, TX CMSA	41	15	287	13
San Diego, CA MSA	27	17	253	14
Dallas – Fort Worth, TX CMSA	13	23	212	15
Denver – Boulder – Greeley, CO CMSA	7	29	199	16
Beaumont – Port Arthur, TX MSA	10	26	179	17
Charleston – North Charleston, SC MSA	11	25	156	18
Jacksonville, FL MSA	16	20	154	19
Atlanta, GA MSA	15	21	153	20
Cleveland – Akron, OH CMSA	10	26	133	21
Rochester, NY MSA	7	29	114	22
St. Louis, MO – IL MSA	8	28	104	23
Austin – San Marcos, TX MSA	4	32	100	24
Orlando, FL MSA	12	24	84	25

Source: U.S. Department of Commerce, Bureau of the Census, Data User Services Division, *1992 Economic Census, Volume 1F, Reports Series, Release 1F,* September 1995, CD-ROM. *Note:* Data are shown only for the top 25 areas.

★2393★

Establishments and Employment

Flowers, Nursery Stock, and Florists' Supplies

The U.S. total number of employees is 46,096; total number of establishments is 4,322.

MSA	Establish-ments	Rank	Employ-ment	Rank
New York – Northern New Jersey – Long Island, NY – NJ – CT-CMSA	421	1	4,483	1
Miami – Fort Lauderdale, FL CMSA	206	3	2,850	2
Los Angeles – Riverside – Orange County, CA CMSA	306	2	2,804	3
San Francisco – Oakland – San Jose, CA CMSA	165	4	2,342	4
Dallas – Fort Worth, TX CMSA	94	7	1,394	5
Houston – Galveston – Brazoria, TX CMSA	80	11	813	6
Atlanta, GA MSA	73	13	765	7
San Diego, CA MSA	87	8	731	8
Orlando, FL MSA	76	12	648	9
Detroit – Ann Arbor – Flint, MI CMSA	60	14	633	10
Denver – Boulder – Greeley, CO CMSA	47	18	559	11
Cleveland – Akron, OH CMSA	49	16	547	12
Minneapolis – St. Paul, MN – WI MSA	43	20	538	13
Phoenix – Mesa, AZ MSA	48	17	462	14
Portland – Salem, OR – WA CMSA	46	19	462	14
St. Louis, MO – IL MSA	34	22	403	15
Montgomery, AL MSA	6	44	393	16
Pittsburgh, PA MSA	26	28	353	17
West Palm Beach – Boca Raton, FL MSA	40	21	353	17
Salt Lake City – Ogden, UT MSA	28	26	341	18
Milwaukee – Racine, WI CMSA	27	27	323	19
Tampa – St. Petersburg – Clearwater, FL MSA	51	15	306	20
Birmingham, AL MSA	22	30	295	21
Providence – Fall River – Warwick, RI – MA MSA	10	40	276	22
Sacramento – Yolo, CA CMSA	25	29	276	22

Source: U.S. Department of Commerce, Bureau of the Census, Data User Services Division, *1992 Economic Census, Volume 1F, Reports Series, Release 1F,* September 1995, CD-ROM. *Note:* Data are shown only for the top 25 areas.

★2394★

Establishments and Employment

Footwear

The U.S. total number of employees is 21,826; total number of establishments is 1,712.

MSA	Estab-lish-ments	Rank	Emp-loy-ment	Rank
New York – Northern New Jersey – Long Island, NY – NJ – CT-CMSA	485	1	5,374	1
Boston – Worcester – Lawrence, MA – NH – ME – CT CMSA	99	4	3,201	2
Miami – Fort Lauderdale, FL CMSA	120	3	802	3
St. Louis, MO – IL MSA	59	5	618	4
Dallas – Fort Worth, TX CMSA	29	8	281	5
Washington – Baltimore, DC – MD – VA – WV CMSA	28	9	231	6
San Diego, CA MSA	28	9	193	7
Minneapolis – St. Paul, MN – WI MSA	20	12	155	8
El Paso, TX MSA	15	15	144	9
Santa Barbara – Santa Maria – Lompoc, CA MSA	7	22	126	10
Atlanta, GA MSA	24	10	116	11
Indianapolis, IN MSA	5	23	101	12
Charlotte – Gastonia – Rock Hill, NC – SC MSA	11	19	86	13
Cincinnati – Hamilton, OH – KY – IN CMSA	13	17	69	14
Honolulu, HI MSA	12	18	54	15
Norfolk – Virginia Beach – Newport News, VA – NC MSA	4	24	50	16
Cleveland – Akron, OH CMSA	7	22	42	17
Buffalo – Niagara Falls, NY MSA	4	24	39	18
Phoenix – Mesa, AZ MSA	4	24	35	19
Allentown – Bethlehem – Easton, PA MSA	3	25	19	20
Chattanooga, TN – GA MSA	3	25	16	21
Tampa – St. Petersburg – Clearwater, FL MSA	8	21	15	22
Jacksonville, FL MSA	3	25	13	23
Kansas City, MO – KS MSA	4	24	13	23
Sacramento – Yolo, CA CMSA	4	24	9	24

Source: U.S. Department of Commerce, Bureau of the Census, Data User Services Division, *1992 Economic Census, Volume 1F, Reports Series, Release 1F,* September 1995, CD-ROM. *Note:* Data are shown only for the top 25 areas.

★2395★

Establishments and Employment

Fresh Fruits and Vegetables

The U.S. total number of employees is 101,372; total number of establishments is 6,003.

MSA	Estab-lish-ments	Rank	Emp-loy-ment	Rank
Los Angeles – Riverside – Orange County, CA CMSA	456	2	10,054	1
New York – Northern New Jersey – Long Island, NY – NJ – CT-CMSA	526	1	5,444	2
Miami – Fort Lauderdale, FL CMSA	231	3	2,632	3
Philadelphia – Wilmington – Atlantic City, PA – NJ – DE – MD CMSA	195	5	2,619	4
San Francisco – Oakland – San Jose, CA CMSA	224	4	2,577	5
McAllen – Edinburg – Mission, TX MSA	83	12	2,466	6
Lakeland – Winter Haven, FL MSA	48	24	2,279	7
Tampa – St. Petersburg – Clearwater, FL MSA	86	11	1,944	8
Dallas – Fort Worth, TX CMSA	77	14	1,772	9
Chicago – Gary – Kenosha, IL – IN – WI CMSA	168	6	1,641	10
Salinas, CA MSA	98	8	1,442	11
Atlanta, GA MSA	63	18	1,423	12
Fresno, CA MSA	80	13	1,291	13
Orlando, FL MSA	49	23	1,291	13
Bakersfield, CA MSA	44	26	1,105	14
San Antonio, TX MSA	55	20	1,075	15
Minneapolis – St. Paul, MN – WI MSA	60	19	1,034	16
Portland – Salem, OR – WA CMSA	54	21	961	17
Indianapolis, IN MSA	30	31	921	18
Seattle – Tacoma – Bremerton, WA CMSA	69	15	912	19
Kansas City, MO – KS MSA	33	29	906	20
San Diego, CA MSA	66	16	778	21
Pittsburgh, PA MSA	49	23	711	22
Phoenix – Mesa, AZ MSA	52	22	690	23
Grand Rapids – Muskegon – Holland, MI MSA	39	28	678	24

Source: U.S. Department of Commerce, Bureau of the Census, Data User Services Division, *1992 Economic Census, Volume 1F, Reports Series, Release 1F,* September 1995, CD-ROM. *Note:* Data are shown only for the top 25 areas.

★2396★

Establishments and Employment

Groceries and Related Products

The U.S. total number of employees is 811,902; total number of establishments is 42,874.

MSA	Establishments	Rank	Employment	Rank
New York – Northern New Jersey – Long Island, NY – NJ – CT-CMSA	5,741	1	64,999	1
Los Angeles – Riverside – Orange County, CA CMSA	2,736	2	53,228	2
Chicago – Gary – Kenosha, IL – IN – WI CMSA	1,591	3	29,974	3
San Francisco – Oakland – San Jose, CA CMSA	1,583	4	26,255	4
Boston – Worcester – Lawrence, MA – NH – ME – CT CMSA	1,150	5	20,038	5
Philadelphia – Wilmington – Atlantic City, PA – NJ – DE – MD CMSA	1,089	7	19,107	6
Washington – Baltimore, DC – MD – VA – WV CMSA	773	8	17,270	7
Detroit – Ann Arbor – Flint, MI CMSA	714	10	16,139	8
Dallas – Fort Worth, TX CMSA	559	11	15,892	9
Seattle – Tacoma – Bremerton, WA CMSA	769	9	15,108	10
Miami – Fort Lauderdale, FL CMSA	1,146	6	14,810	11
Atlanta, GA MSA	534	12	12,750	12
Houston – Galveston – Brazoria, TX CMSA	493	13	12,261	13
Minneapolis – St. Paul, MN – WI MSA	410	15	9,889	14
Tampa – St. Petersburg – Clearwater, FL MSA	444	14	8,934	15
Denver – Boulder – Greeley, CO CMSA	368	19	8,435	16
Phoenix – Mesa, AZ MSA	383	17	8,290	17
Pittsburgh, PA MSA	334	21	8,177	18
Kansas City, MO – KS MSA	278	23	8,145	19
Cleveland – Akron, OH CMSA	337	20	8,088	20
Milwaukee – Racine, WI CMSA	258	26	7,845	21
Portland – Salem, OR – WA CMSA	384	16	7,832	22
Cincinnati – Hamilton, OH – KY – IN CMSA	268	25	7,684	23
Grand Rapids – Muskegon – Holland, MI MSA	182	39	7,366	24
St. Louis, MO – IL MSA	377	18	7,233	25

Source: U.S. Department of Commerce, Bureau of the Census, Data User Services Division, *1992 Economic Census, Volume 1F, Reports Series, Release 1F,* September 1995, CD-ROM. *Note:* Data are shown only for the top 25 areas.

★2397★

Establishments and Employment

Hardware, and Plumbing and Heating Equipment and Supplies

The U.S. total number of employees is 241,043; total number of establishments is 24,674.

MSA	Establishments	Rank	Employment	Rank
Los Angeles – Riverside – Orange County, CA CMSA	1,365	2	15,513	1
Chicago – Gary – Kenosha, IL – IN – WI CMSA	1,038	3	11,173	2
Boston – Worcester – Lawrence, MA – NH – ME – CT CMSA	612	5	6,052	3
Dallas – Fort Worth, TX CMSA	603	6	5,937	4
Cleveland – Akron, OH CMSA	357	13	5,508	5
Houston – Galveston – Brazoria, TX CMSA	490	10	4,954	6
Detroit – Ann Arbor – Flint, MI CMSA	497	9	4,610	7
Atlanta, GA MSA	471	11	4,544	8
Minneapolis – St. Paul, MN – WI MSA	348	15	3,699	9
Miami – Fort Lauderdale, FL CMSA	439	12	3,676	10
Seattle – Tacoma – Bremerton, WA CMSA	353	14	3,471	11
St. Louis, MO – IL MSA	302	16	2,905	12
Portland – Salem, OR – WA CMSA	241	22	2,768	13
Denver – Boulder – Greeley, CO CMSA	285	17	2,631	14
Charlotte – Gastonia – Rock Hill, NC – SC MSA	233	23	2,583	15
Kansas City, MO – KS MSA	253	20	2,481	16
Phoenix – Mesa, AZ MSA	250	21	2,410	17
Pittsburgh, PA MSA	277	18	2,256	18
Indianapolis, IN MSA	198	25	2,240	19
Milwaukee – Racine, WI CMSA	190	26	2,130	20
Tampa – St. Petersburg – Clearwater, FL MSA	268	19	2,068	21
Memphis, TN – AR – MS MSA	137	34	1,953	22
Greensboro – Winston-Salem – High Point, NC MSA	156	30	1,932	23
San Diego, CA MSA	203	24	1,883	24
Grand Rapids – Muskegon – Holland, MI MSA	123	39	1,860	25

Source: U.S. Department of Commerce, Bureau of the Census, Data User Services Division, *1992 Economic Census, Volume 1F, Reports Series, Release 1F,* September 1995, CD-ROM. *Note:* Data are shown only for the top 25 areas.

★2398★

Establishments and Employment

Industrial and Personal Service Paper

The U.S. total number of employees is 63,567; total number of establishments is 5,293.

MSA	Estab-lish-ments	Rank	Emp-loy-ment	Rank
New York – Northern New Jersey – Long Island, NY – NJ – CT-CMSA	833	1	8,566	1
Los Angeles – Riverside – Orange County, CA CMSA	391	2	4,714	2
Boston – Worcester – Lawrence, MA – NH – ME – CT CMSA	165	5	2,552	3
San Francisco – Oakland – San Jose, CA CMSA	142	6	2,188	4
Atlanta, GA MSA	102	8	1,762	5
Miami – Fort Lauderdale, FL CMSA	142	6	1,589	6
Dallas – Fort Worth, TX CMSA	121	7	1,377	7
Cleveland – Akron, OH CMSA	76	13	1,374	8
St. Louis, MO – IL MSA	84	11	1,024	9
Minneapolis – St. Paul, MN – WI MSA	68	14	903	10
Charlotte – Gastonia – Rock Hill, NC – SC MSA	48	19	742	11
Buffalo – Niagara Falls, NY MSA	25	28	577	12
Kansas City, MO – KS MSA	48	19	560	13
Indianapolis, IN MSA	43	22	554	14
Honolulu, HI MSA	24	29	536	15
Columbus, OH MSA	25	28	493	16
Pittsburgh, PA MSA	44	21	482	17
Jacksonville, FL MSA	36	25	468	18
Memphis, TN – AR – MS MSA	31	26	465	19
Milwaukee – Racine, WI CMSA	47	20	429	20
Appleton – Oshkosh – Neenah, WI MSA	17	35	424	21
Tampa – St. Petersburg – Clearwater, FL MSA	58	17	397	22
Greensboro – Winston-Salem – High Point, NC MSA	42	23	378	23
San Antonio, TX MSA	24	29	353	24
Salt Lake City – Ogden, UT MSA	20	33	346	25

Source: U.S. Department of Commerce, Bureau of the Census, Data User Services Division, *1992 Economic Census, Volume 1F, Reports Series, Release 1F,* September 1995, CD-ROM. *Note:* Data are shown only for the top 25 areas.

★2399★

Establishments and Employment

Industrial Machinery and Equipment

The U.S. total number of employees is 259,024; total number of establishments is 30,322.

MSA	Estab-lish-ments	Rank	Emp-loy-ment	Rank
New York – Northern New Jersey – Long Island, NY – NJ – CT-CMSA	2,101	1	19,096	1
Chicago – Gary – Kenosha, IL – IN – WI CMSA	1,534	3	17,332	2
Los Angeles – Riverside – Orange County, CA CMSA	1,595	2	15,706	3
Houston – Galveston – Brazoria, TX CMSA	1,212	4	11,363	4
Detroit – Ann Arbor – Flint, MI CMSA	912	5	7,719	5
Atlanta, GA MSA	704	8	6,777	6
Philadelphia – Wilmington – Atlantic City, PA – NJ – DE – MD CMSA	756	6	5,958	7
Cleveland – Akron, OH CMSA	640	12	5,669	8
Minneapolis – St. Paul, MN – WI MSA	464	14	5,593	9
Dallas – Fort Worth, TX CMSA	653	9	5,574	10
Boston – Worcester – Lawrence, MA – NH – ME – CT CMSA	649	10	5,543	11
San Francisco – Oakland – San Jose, CA CMSA	727	7	5,491	12
Charlotte – Gastonia – Rock Hill, NC – SC MSA	537	13	5,454	13
Milwaukee – Racine, WI CMSA	389	15	3,661	14
Washington – Baltimore, DC – MD – VA – WV CMSA	370	18	3,381	15
Pittsburgh, PA MSA	370	18	3,373	16
St. Louis, MO – IL MSA	350	20	3,167	17
Miami – Fort Lauderdale, FL CMSA	647	11	3,108	18
Portland – Salem, OR – WA CMSA	307	21	2,750	19
Denver – Boulder – Greeley, CO CMSA	376	17	2,728	20
Kansas City, MO – KS MSA	271	23	2,478	21
Indianapolis, IN MSA	283	22	2,400	22
New Orleans, LA MSA	247	28	2,309	23
Greenville – Spartanburg – Anderson, SC MSA	236	29	2,269	24
Phoenix – Mesa, AZ MSA	257	24	2,151	25

Source: U.S. Department of Commerce, Bureau of the Census, Data User Services Division, *1992 Economic Census, Volume 1F, Reports Series, Release 1F,* September 1995, CD-ROM. *Note:* Data are shown only for the top 25 areas.

★2400★

Establishments and Employment

Industrial Supplies

The U.S. total number of employees is 152,661; total number of establishments is 16,199.

MSA	Estab- lish- ments	Rank	Emp- loy- ment	Rank
Los Angeles – Riverside – Orange County, CA CMSA	828	2	9,118	1
Chicago – Gary – Kenosha, IL – IN – WI CMSA	719	3	7,456	2
Houston – Galveston – Brazoria, TX CMSA	608	4	7,149	3
Philadelphia – Wilmington – Atlantic City, PA – NJ – DE – MD CMSA	407	5	4,309	4
Detroit – Ann Arbor – Flint, MI CMSA	401	6	4,033	5
Dallas – Fort Worth, TX CMSA	313	9	3,661	6
Cleveland – Akron, OH CMSA	342	8	3,485	7
San Francisco – Oakland – San Jose, CA CMSA	368	7	3,369	8
Minneapolis – St. Paul, MN – WI MSA	222	12	3,203	9
Atlanta, GA MSA	313	9	3,075	10
Boston – Worcester – Lawrence, MA – NH – ME – CT CMSA	313	9	2,831	11
St. Louis, MO – IL MSA	222	12	2,357	12
Pittsburgh, PA MSA	228	11	2,307	13
Cincinnati – Hamilton, OH – KY – IN CMSA	175	18	2,195	14
Milwaukee – Racine, WI CMSA	198	15	2,085	15
Charlotte – Gastonia – Rock Hill, NC – SC MSA	189	16	2,015	16
Portland – Salem, OR – WA CMSA	187	17	1,862	17
Kansas City, MO – KS MSA	158	20	1,574	18
Miami – Fort Lauderdale, FL CMSA	243	10	1,466	19
Baton Rouge, LA MSA	110	25	1,369	20
Denver – Boulder – Greeley, CO CMSA	164	19	1,320	21
Indianapolis, IN MSA	133	21	1,300	22
Columbus, OH MSA	99	31	1,107	23
Birmingham, AL MSA	118	23	1,059	24
Greensboro – Winston-Salem – High Point, NC MSA	102	29	1,056	25

Source: U.S. Department of Commerce, Bureau of the Census, Data User Services Division, *1992 Economic Census, Volume 1F, Reports Series, Release 1F*, September 1995, CD-ROM. *Note:* Data are shown only for the top 25 areas.

★2401★

Establishments and Employment

Jewelry, Watches, Precious Stones, and Precious Metals

The U.S. total number of employees is 50,452; total number of establishments is 7,421.

MSA	Estab- lish- ments	Rank	Emp- loy- ment	Rank
Los Angeles – Riverside – Orange County, CA CMSA	829	2	5,732	1
Providence – Fall River – Warwick, RI – MA MSA	181	7	3,053	2
Chicago – Gary – Kenosha, IL – IN – WI CMSA	284	4	2,813	3
Miami – Fort Lauderdale, FL CMSA	350	3	2,154	4
San Francisco – Oakland – San Jose, CA CMSA	237	5	1,755	5
Dallas – Fort Worth, TX CMSA	197	6	1,497	6
Boston – Worcester – Lawrence, MA – NH – ME – CT CMSA	124	9	860	7
Atlanta, GA MSA	141	8	697	8
Minneapolis – St. Paul, MN – WI MSA	68	17	616	9
Albuquerque, NM MSA	57	21	613	10
St. Louis, MO – IL MSA	61	20	532	11
Kansas City, MO – KS MSA	31	26	513	12
Seattle – Tacoma – Bremerton, WA CMSA	74	16	490	13
Honolulu, HI MSA	84	13	469	14
Houston – Galveston – Brazoria, TX CMSA	120	10	449	15
Cincinnati – Hamilton, OH – KY – IN CMSA	29	27	410	16
Salt Lake City – Ogden, UT MSA	24	30	395	17
Phoenix – Mesa, AZ MSA	62	19	325	18
San Diego, CA MSA	76	15	298	19
Tampa – St. Petersburg – Clearwater, FL MSA	47	22	287	20
Cleveland – Akron, OH CMSA	42	24	248	21
New Orleans, LA MSA	28	28	230	22
Pittsburgh, PA MSA	43	23	205	23
Chattanooga, TN – GA MSA	9	44	178	24
Memphis, TN – AR – MS MSA	23	31	169	25

Source: U.S. Department of Commerce, Bureau of the Census, Data User Services Division, *1992 Economic Census, Volume 1F, Reports Series, Release 1F*, September 1995, CD-ROM. *Note:* Data are shown only for the top 25 areas.

★2402★

Establishments and Employment

Lumber, Plywood, Millwork, and Wood Panels

The U.S. total number of employees is 111,626; total number of establishments is 8,364.

MSA	Estab-lish-ments	Rank	Emp-loy-ment	Rank
Los Angeles – Riverside – Orange County, CA CMSA	395	2	5,092	1
Washington – Baltimore, DC – MD – VA – WV CMSA	184	7	3,416	2
Portland – Salem, OR – WA CMSA	226	5	2,957	3
Chicago – Gary – Kenosha, IL – IN – WI CMSA	278	3	2,802	4
Atlanta, GA MSA	163	10	2,487	5
Dallas – Fort Worth, TX CMSA	142	11	2,329	6
San Francisco – Oakland – San Jose, CA CMSA	165	9	2,232	7
Minneapolis – St. Paul, MN – WI MSA	113	13	1,796	8
Pittsburgh, PA MSA	63	26	1,654	9
Houston – Galveston – Brazoria, TX CMSA	77	20	1,598	10
Greensboro – Winston-Salem – High Point, NC MSA	108	15	1,541	11
Detroit – Ann Arbor – Flint, MI CMSA	138	12	1,518	12
Kansas City, MO – KS MSA	66	23	1,363	13
Sacramento – Yolo, CA CMSA	78	19	1,269	14
Miami – Fort Lauderdale, FL CMSA	111	14	1,215	15
St. Louis, MO – IL MSA	88	17	1,003	16
Charlotte – Gastonia – Rock Hill, NC – SC MSA	56	29	994	17
Grand Rapids – Muskegon – Holland, MI MSA	49	33	939	18
Tampa – St. Petersburg – Clearwater, FL MSA	73	22	937	19
Phoenix – Mesa, AZ MSA	74	21	884	20
Louisville, KY – IN MSA	65	24	875	21
Memphis, TN – AR – MS MSA	52	31	856	22
San Diego, CA MSA	59	28	838	23
Cleveland – Akron, OH CMSA	83	18	803	24
Indianapolis, IN MSA	62	27	799	25

Source: U.S. Department of Commerce, Bureau of the Census, Data User Services Division, *1992 Economic Census, Volume 1F, Reports Series, Release 1F,* September 1995, CD-ROM. *Note:* Data are shown only for the top 25 areas.

★2403★

Establishments and Employment

Machinery, Equipment, and Supplies

The U.S. total number of employees is 689,680; total number of establishments is 73,865.

MSA	Estab-lish-ments	Rank	Emp-loy-ment	Rank
Los Angeles – Riverside – Orange County, CA CMSA	3,615	2	37,515	1
Chicago – Gary – Kenosha, IL – IN – WI CMSA	2,887	3	31,352	2
Houston – Galveston – Brazoria, TX CMSA	2,207	4	22,424	3
Dallas – Fort Worth, TX CMSA	1,512	9	15,124	4
Detroit – Ann Arbor – Flint, MI CMSA	1,654	5	14,774	5
Philadelphia – Wilmington – Atlantic City, PA – NJ – DE – MD CMSA	1,576	7	14,366	6
Atlanta, GA MSA	1,397	10	13,938	7
San Francisco – Oakland – San Jose, CA CMSA	1,560	8	12,990	8
Minneapolis – St. Paul, MN – WI MSA	957	15	12,742	9
Cleveland – Akron, OH CMSA	1,201	12	11,717	10
Boston – Worcester – Lawrence, MA – NH – ME – CT CMSA	1,305	11	11,602	11
Miami – Fort Lauderdale, FL CMSA	1,648	6	10,950	12
Washington – Baltimore, DC – MD – VA – WV CMSA	1,037	13	10,274	13
Charlotte – Gastonia – Rock Hill, NC – SC MSA	885	16	9,614	14
Seattle – Tacoma – Bremerton, WA CMSA	986	14	9,288	15
St. Louis, MO – IL MSA	845	17	8,211	16
Pittsburgh, PA MSA	786	19	8,179	17
Milwaukee – Racine, WI CMSA	749	20	7,805	18
Portland – Salem, OR – WA CMSA	733	21	7,337	19
Cincinnati – Hamilton, OH – KY – IN CMSA	690	22	7,261	20
Denver – Boulder – Greeley, CO CMSA	798	18	7,002	21
Phoenix – Mesa, AZ MSA	632	24	6,893	22
Kansas City, MO – KS MSA	648	23	6,863	23
Indianapolis, IN MSA	563	26	5,096	24
Columbus, OH MSA	374	38	4,970	25

Source: U.S. Department of Commerce, Bureau of the Census, Data User Services Division, *1992 Economic Census, Volume 1F, Reports Series, Release 1F,* September 1995, CD-ROM. *Note:* Data are shown only for the top 25 areas.

★ 2404 ★

Establishments and Employment

Meats and Meat Products

The U.S. total number of employees is 60,537; total number of establishments is 4,123.

MSA	Estab-lish-ments	Rank	Emp-loy-ment	Rank
New York – Northern New Jersey – Long Island, NY – NJ – CT-CMSA	737	1	7,165	1
Chicago – Gary – Kenosha, IL – IN – WI CMSA	263	3	4,337	2
Philadelphia – Wilmington – Atlantic City, PA – NJ – DE – MD CMSA	116	4	1,910	3
Boston – Worcester – Lawrence, MA – NH – ME – CT CMSA	97	7	1,449	4
Detroit – Ann Arbor – Flint, MI CMSA	86	8	1,435	5
Atlanta, GA MSA	55	11	1,415	6
Miami – Fort Lauderdale, FL CMSA	107	6	1,350	7
Omaha, NE – IA MSA	19	27	1,265	8
Dallas – Fort Worth, TX CMSA	59	10	1,081	9
Milwaukee – Racine, WI CMSA	34	18	991	10
San Antonio, TX MSA	29	23	658	11
Houston – Galveston – Brazoria, TX CMSA	44	15	623	12
Cleveland – Akron, OH CMSA	32	20	620	13
San Diego, CA MSA	25	24	612	14
Minneapolis – St. Paul, MN – WI MSA	37	17	595	15
Providence – Fall River – Warwick, RI – MA MSA	22	25	554	16
Kansas City, MO – KS MSA	31	21	549	17
Nashville, TN MSA	21	26	523	18
Phoenix – Mesa, AZ MSA	39	16	517	19
Portland – Salem, OR – WA CMSA	45	14	493	20
St. Louis, MO – IL MSA	30	22	492	21
Tampa – St. Petersburg – Clearwater, FL MSA	39	16	488	22
Honolulu, HI MSA	22	25	434	23
Pittsburgh, PA MSA	33	19	355	24
Oklahoma City, OK MSA	25	24	339	25

Source: U.S. Department of Commerce, Bureau of the Census, Data User Services Division, *1992 Economic Census, Volume 1F, Reports Series, Release 1F,* September 1995, CD-ROM. *Note:* Data are shown only for the top 25 areas.

★ 2405 ★

Establishments and Employment

Medical, Dental, and Hospital Equipment and Supplies

The U.S. total number of employees is 125,470; total number of establishments is 9,521.

MSA	Estab-lish-ments	Rank	Emp-loy-ment	Rank
Chicago – Gary – Kenosha, IL – IN – WI CMSA	395	3	8,514	1
Los Angeles – Riverside – Orange County, CA CMSA	590	2	8,390	2
Atlanta, GA MSA	233	9	4,455	3
Boston – Worcester – Lawrence, MA – NH – ME – CT CMSA	263	6	4,045	4
Dallas – Fort Worth, TX CMSA	246	8	3,612	5
San Francisco – Oakland – San Jose, CA CMSA	261	7	3,467	6
Minneapolis – St. Paul, MN – WI MSA	168	13	2,751	7
Miami – Fort Lauderdale, FL CMSA	340	4	2,749	8
Detroit – Ann Arbor – Flint, MI CMSA	205	11	2,676	9
St. Louis, MO – IL MSA	158	14	2,563	10
Tampa – St. Petersburg – Clearwater, FL MSA	148	16	2,535	11
Houston – Galveston – Brazoria, TX CMSA	181	12	1,986	12
Cleveland – Akron, OH CMSA	149	15	1,975	13
Pittsburgh, PA MSA	107	20	1,851	14
Indianapolis, IN MSA	78	26	1,756	15
Kansas City, MO – KS MSA	117	18	1,369	16
Phoenix – Mesa, AZ MSA	120	17	1,343	17
Milwaukee – Racine, WI CMSA	99	21	1,309	18
Columbus, OH MSA	85	25	1,223	19
San Diego, CA MSA	111	19	1,141	20
Cincinnati – Hamilton, OH – KY – IN CMSA	86	24	1,094	21
New Orleans, LA MSA	75	27	871	22
Birmingham, AL MSA	64	28	858	23
Memphis, TN – AR – MS MSA	59	30	856	24
Nashville, TN MSA	75	27	795	25

Source: U.S. Department of Commerce, Bureau of the Census, Data User Services Division, *1992 Economic Census, Volume 1F, Reports Series, Release 1F,* September 1995, CD-ROM. *Note:* Data are shown only for the top 25 areas.

★ 2406 ★

Establishments and Employment

Men's and Boys' Clothing and Furnishings

The U.S. total number of employees is 51,908; total number of establishments is 4,620.

MSA	Establishments	Rank	Employment	Rank
New York – Northern New Jersey – Long Island, NY – NJ – CT-CMSA	1,217	1	13,368	1
Chicago – Gary – Kenosha, IL – IN – WI CMSA	173	3	2,045	2
Boston – Worcester – Lawrence, MA – NH – ME – CT CMSA	97	8	1,884	3
Atlanta, GA MSA	105	7	1,131	4
Dallas – Fort Worth, TX CMSA	123	5	1,049	5
Reading, PA MSA	10	37	1,046	6
San Francisco – Oakland – San Jose, CA CMSA	113	6	1,010	7
Miami – Fort Lauderdale, FL CMSA	139	4	878	8
Kansas City, MO – KS MSA	32	19	629	9
Houston – Galveston – Brazoria, TX CMSA	48	14	605	10
Phoenix – Mesa, AZ MSA	29	20	536	11
New Orleans, LA MSA	16	31	533	12
Detroit – Ann Arbor – Flint, MI CMSA	42	15	528	13
Tampa – St. Petersburg – Clearwater, FL MSA	29	20	504	14
San Diego, CA MSA	42	15	462	15
Minneapolis – St. Paul, MN – WI MSA	61	12	456	16
Charlotte – Gastonia – Rock Hill, NC – SC MSA	42	15	409	17
Columbus, OH MSA	23	25	399	18
Nashville, TN MSA	16	31	394	19
San Antonio, TX MSA	22	26	374	20
St. Louis, MO – IL MSA	38	17	346	21
Pittsburgh, PA MSA	25	23	343	22
El Paso, TX MSA	21	27	320	23
Raleigh – Durham – Chapel Hill, NC MSA	15	32	297	24
Cleveland – Akron, OH CMSA	35	18	242	25

Source: U.S. Department of Commerce, Bureau of the Census, Data User Services Division, *1992 Economic Census, Volume 1F, Reports Series, Release 1F,* September 1995, CD-ROM. *Note:* Data are shown only for the top 25 areas.

★ 2407 ★

Establishments and Employment

Metals and Minerals, Except Petroleum

The U.S. total number of employees is 138,042; total number of establishments is 11,248.

MSA	Establishments	Rank	Employment	Rank
Chicago – Gary – Kenosha, IL – IN – WI CMSA	774	2	14,420	1
Houston – Galveston – Brazoria, TX CMSA	488	4	5,998	2
Detroit – Ann Arbor – Flint, MI CMSA	435	5	5,531	3
Cleveland – Akron, OH CMSA	348	7	4,468	4
Philadelphia – Wilmington – Atlantic City, PA – NJ – DE – MD CMSA	349	6	3,989	5
Pittsburgh, PA MSA	242	9	3,349	6
Dallas – Fort Worth, TX CMSA	262	8	3,122	7
Atlanta, GA MSA	236	10	2,970	8
San Francisco – Oakland – San Jose, CA CMSA	221	11	2,674	9
Minneapolis – St. Paul, MN – WI MSA	148	17	2,471	10
St. Louis, MO – IL MSA	194	13	2,468	11
Birmingham, AL MSA	116	19	2,370	12
Washington – Baltimore, DC – MD – VA – WV CMSA	149	16	1,988	13
Cincinnati – Hamilton, OH – KY – IN CMSA	141	18	1,966	14
Charlotte – Gastonia – Rock Hill, NC – SC MSA	105	22	1,234	15
Kansas City, MO – KS MSA	89	24	1,203	16
Milwaukee – Racine, WI CMSA	114	20	1,177	17
Indianapolis, IN MSA	82	26	1,148	18
Toledo, OH MSA	52	36	1,145	19
Nashville, TN MSA	63	32	1,127	20
Tulsa, OK MSA	81	27	1,107	21
Grand Rapids – Muskegon – Holland, MI MSA	66	30	1,090	22
Miami – Fort Lauderdale, FL CMSA	150	15	1,052	23
New Orleans, LA MSA	68	29	942	24
Phoenix – Mesa, AZ MSA	78	28	842	25

Source: U.S. Department of Commerce, Bureau of the Census, Data User Services Division, *1992 Economic Census, Volume 1F, Reports Series, Release 1F,* September 1995, CD-ROM. *Note:* Data are shown only for the top 25 areas.

★ 2408 ★

Establishments and Employment

Metals Service Centers and Offices

The U.S. total number of employees is 132,741; total number of establishments is 10,426.

MSA	Estab-lish-ments	Rank	Emp-loy-ment	Rank
Chicago – Gary – Kenosha, IL – IN – WI CMSA	748	2	14,144	1
New York – Northern New Jersey – Long Island, NY – NJ – CT-CMSA	945	1	10,045	2
Los Angeles – Riverside – Orange County, CA CMSA	690	3	9,149	3
Philadelphia – Wilmington – Atlantic City, PA – NJ – DE – MD CMSA	336	6	3,864	4
Pittsburgh, PA MSA	201	11	3,127	5
San Francisco – Oakland – San Jose, CA CMSA	211	10	2,615	6
St. Louis, MO – IL MSA	185	13	2,406	7
Boston – Worcester – Lawrence, MA – NH – ME – CT CMSA	189	12	2,144	8
Denver – Boulder – Greeley, CO CMSA	99	21	1,266	9
Toledo, OH MSA	52	34	1,145	10
Nashville, TN MSA	56	31	983	11
Louisville, KY – IN MSA	45	37	718	12
Buffalo – Niagara Falls, NY MSA	62	30	693	13
Richmond – Petersburg, VA MSA	39	41	600	14
Chattanooga, TN – GA MSA	17	56	564	15
San Antonio, TX MSA	43	39	448	16
Greenville – Spartanburg – Anderson, SC MSA	29	46	388	17
Knoxville, TN MSA	27	48	345	18
San Diego, CA MSA	51	35	332	19
Baton Rouge, LA MSA	28	47	331	20
Little Rock – North Little Rock, AR MSA	22	51	328	21
Rockford, IL MSA	19	54	318	22
Stockton – Lodi, CA MSA	11	61	300	23
Des Moines, IA MSA	19	54	278	24
Fort Wayne, IN MSA	19	54	270	25

Source: U.S. Department of Commerce, Bureau of the Census, Data User Services Division, *1992 Economic Census, Volume 1F, Reports Series, Release 1F,* September 1995, CD-ROM. *Note:* Data are shown only for the top 25 areas.

★ 2409 ★

Establishments and Employment

Nondurable Goods

The U.S. total number of employees is 2,442,337; total number of establishments is 181,993.

MSA	Estab-lish-ments	Rank	Emp-loy-ment	Rank
New York – Northern New Jersey – Long Island, NY – NJ – CT-CMSA	23,231	1	290,255	1
Los Angeles – Riverside – Orange County, CA CMSA	11,419	2	156,892	2
Chicago – Gary – Kenosha, IL – IN – WI CMSA	6,197	3	97,703	3
San Francisco – Oakland – San Jose, CA CMSA	4,699	4	65,694	4
Philadelphia – Wilmington – Atlantic City, PA – NJ – DE – MD CMSA	3,782	6	58,813	5
Boston – Worcester – Lawrence, MA – NH – ME – CT CMSA	3,480	7	56,795	6
Dallas – Fort Worth, TX CMSA	3,277	8	49,878	7
Washington – Baltimore, DC – MD – VA – WV CMSA	2,902	9	47,769	8
Atlanta, GA MSA	2,831	10	45,373	9
Miami – Fort Lauderdale, FL CMSA	4,292	5	42,867	10
Houston – Galveston – Brazoria, TX CMSA	2,624	11	38,579	11
Detroit – Ann Arbor – Flint, MI CMSA	2,470	12	37,501	12
Seattle – Tacoma – Bremerton, WA CMSA	2,249	13	33,782	13
Cleveland – Akron, OH CMSA	1,642	16	31,254	14
Minneapolis – St. Paul, MN – WI MSA	1,988	14	30,233	15
Cincinnati – Hamilton, OH – KY – IN CMSA	1,080	25	25,978	16
St. Louis, MO – IL MSA	1,758	15	24,565	17
Denver – Boulder – Greeley, CO CMSA	1,559	17	23,203	18
Kansas City, MO – KS MSA	1,240	22	20,114	19
Portland – Salem, OR – WA CMSA	1,384	19	19,967	20
Tampa – St. Petersburg – Clearwater, FL MSA	1,440	18	19,786	21
Phoenix – Mesa, AZ MSA	1,337	21	18,701	22
Pittsburgh, PA MSA	1,196	23	18,693	23
Charlotte – Gastonia – Rock Hill, NC – SC MSA	1,162	24	17,308	24
Milwaukee – Racine, WI CMSA	1,029	26	16,796	25

Source: U.S. Department of Commerce, Bureau of the Census, Data User Services Division, *1992 Economic Census, Volume 1F, Reports Series, Release 1F,* September 1995, CD-ROM. *Note:* Data are shown only for the top 25 areas.

★2410★
Establishments and Employment
Office Equipment

The U.S. total number of employees is 148,991; total number of establishments is 8,631.

MSA	Establishments	Rank	Employment	Rank
New York – Northern New Jersey – Long Island, NY – NJ – CT-CMSA	630	1	15,238	1
Los Angeles – Riverside – Orange County, CA CMSA	462	2	9,573	2
Chicago – Gary – Kenosha, IL – IN – WI CMSA	277	3	6,647	3
Washington – Baltimore, DC – MD – VA – WV CMSA	208	5	5,351	4
Boston – Worcester – Lawrence, MA – NH – ME – CT CMSA	186	7	5,327	5
Dallas – Fort Worth, TX CMSA	162	8	4,945	6
San Francisco – Oakland – San Jose, CA CMSA	224	4	4,430	7
Philadelphia – Wilmington – Atlantic City, PA – NJ – DE – MD CMSA	191	6	3,904	8
Atlanta, GA MSA	130	10	3,891	9
Minneapolis – St. Paul, MN – WI MSA	107	14	2,616	10
Detroit – Ann Arbor – Flint, MI CMSA	114	13	2,495	11
Miami – Fort Lauderdale, FL CMSA	141	9	2,253	12
Cleveland – Akron, OH CMSA	99	15	2,216	13
Seattle – Tacoma – Bremerton, WA CMSA	119	12	1,879	14
Denver – Boulder – Greeley, CO CMSA	92	16	1,867	15
Phoenix – Mesa, AZ MSA	87	18	1,863	16
St. Louis, MO – IL MSA	74	21	1,861	17
Pittsburgh, PA MSA	70	22	1,578	18
Hartford, CT MSA	67	23	1,515	19
Tampa – St. Petersburg – Clearwater, FL MSA	89	17	1,483	20
Kansas City, MO – KS MSA	76	20	1,311	21
Indianapolis, IN MSA	57	28	1,292	22
San Diego, CA MSA	80	19	1,291	23
Milwaukee – Racine, WI CMSA	64	26	1,174	24
Portland – Salem, OR – WA CMSA	66	24	1,155	25

Source: U.S. Department of Commerce, Bureau of the Census, Data User Services Division, *1992 Economic Census, Volume 1F, Reports Series, Release 1F,* September 1995, CD-ROM. *Note:* Data are shown only for the top 25 areas.

★2411★
Establishments and Employment
Ophthalmic Goods

The U.S. total number of employees is 25,561; total number of establishments is 1,783.

MSA	Establishments	Rank	Employment	Rank
Los Angeles – Riverside – Orange County, CA CMSA	162	2	2,702	1
Dallas – Fort Worth, TX CMSA	32	10	955	2
Miami – Fort Lauderdale, FL CMSA	73	3	648	3
Boston – Worcester – Lawrence, MA – NH – ME – CT CMSA	50	5	580	4
Minneapolis – St. Paul, MN – WI MSA	18	17	391	5
Tampa – St. Petersburg – Clearwater, FL MSA	27	11	388	6
Philadelphia – Wilmington – Atlantic City, PA – NJ – DE – MD CMSA	40	7	343	7
Pittsburgh, PA MSA	19	16	340	8
Cleveland – Akron, OH CMSA	16	19	325	9
Louisville, KY – IN MSA	14	20	319	10
Kansas City, MO – KS MSA	14	20	303	11
Phoenix – Mesa, AZ MSA	19	16	302	12
Indianapolis, IN MSA	13	21	261	13
Grand Rapids – Muskegon – Holland, MI MSA	7	27	260	14
Atlanta, GA MSA	38	8	248	15
Omaha, NE – IA MSA	11	23	247	16
Greensboro – Winston-Salem – High Point, NC MSA	8	26	238	17
Portland – Salem, OR – WA CMSA	25	13	225	18
Scranton – Wilkes-Barre – Hazleton, PA MSA	5	29	225	18
Nashville, TN MSA	6	28	218	19
San Diego, CA MSA	18	17	202	20
Houston – Galveston – Brazoria, TX CMSA	17	18	194	21
Buffalo – Niagara Falls, NY MSA	11	23	180	22
Green Bay, WI MSA	7	27	178	23
Memphis, TN – AR – MS MSA	11	23	176	24

Source: U.S. Department of Commerce, Bureau of the Census, Data User Services Division, *1992 Economic Census, Volume 1F, Reports Series, Release 1F,* September 1995, CD-ROM. *Note:* Data are shown only for the top 25 areas.

★2412★

Establishments and Employment

Paint, Varnishes, and Supplies

The U.S. total number of employees is 28,862; total number of establishments is 3,539.

MSA	Estab-lish-ments	Rank	Emp-ploy-ment	Rank
Cleveland – Akron, OH CMSA	57	14	1,726	1
Chicago – Gary – Kenosha, IL – IN – WI CMSA	146	3	1,209	2
Atlanta, GA MSA	128	5	981	3
Dallas – Fort Worth, TX CMSA	122	6	885	4
San Francisco – Oakland – San Jose, CA CMSA	83	10	877	5
Detroit – Ann Arbor – Flint, MI CMSA	69	11	769	6
Boston – Worcester – Lawrence, MA – NH – ME – CT CMSA	65	12	712	7
Houston – Galveston – Brazoria, TX CMSA	95	7	683	8
Seattle – Tacoma – Bremerton, WA CMSA	95	7	622	9
Miami – Fort Lauderdale, FL CMSA	94	8	512	10
Minneapolis – St. Paul, MN – WI MSA	49	16	489	11
Denver – Boulder – Greeley, CO CMSA	50	15	467	12
St. Louis, MO – IL MSA	61	13	391	13
Milwaukee – Racine, WI CMSA	38	20	362	14
Kansas City, MO – KS MSA	43	17	301	15
Orlando, FL MSA	43	17	296	16
Buffalo – Niagara Falls, NY MSA	20	28	295	17
Norfolk – Virginia Beach – Newport News, VA – NC MSA	39	19	289	18
Tampa – St. Petersburg – Clearwater, FL MSA	37	21	289	18
Phoenix – Mesa, AZ MSA	41	18	259	19
Pittsburgh, PA MSA	30	24	243	20
Louisville, KY – IN MSA	30	24	239	21
Grand Rapids – Muskegon – Holland, MI MSA	17	30	232	22
Greenville – Spartanburg – Anderson, SC MSA	18	29	203	23
San Diego, CA MSA	18	29	196	24

Source: U.S. Department of Commerce, Bureau of the Census, Data User Services Division, *1992 Economic Census, Volume 1F, Reports Series, Release 1F*, September 1995, CD-ROM. *Note:* Data are shown only for the top 25 areas.

★2413★

Establishments and Employment

Paper and Paper Products

The U.S. total number of employees is 269,038; total number of establishments is 19,661.

MSA	Estab-lish-ments	Rank	Emp-ploy-ment	Rank
Los Angeles – Riverside – Orange County, CA CMSA	1,258	2	22,954	1
Chicago – Gary – Kenosha, IL – IN – WI CMSA	1,035	3	16,768	2
Atlanta, GA MSA	418	9	11,358	3
San Francisco – Oakland – San Jose, CA CMSA	602	4	8,449	4
Dallas – Fort Worth, TX CMSA	514	7	8,441	5
Cincinnati – Hamilton, OH – KY – IN CMSA	187	19	8,316	6
Cleveland – Akron, OH CMSA	262	16	7,487	7
Washington – Baltimore, DC – MD – VA – WV CMSA	487	8	7,048	8
Detroit – Ann Arbor – Flint, MI CMSA	365	11	4,751	9
Miami – Fort Lauderdale, FL CMSA	393	10	4,490	10
Minneapolis – St. Paul, MN – WI MSA	267	14	4,253	11
Houston – Galveston – Brazoria, TX CMSA	306	12	3,611	12
St. Louis, MO – IL MSA	263	15	3,346	13
Kansas City, MO – KS MSA	188	18	3,174	14
Denver – Boulder – Greeley, CO CMSA	217	17	2,743	15
Portland – Salem, OR – WA CMSA	178	21	2,211	16
Pittsburgh, PA MSA	163	23	2,096	17
Indianapolis, IN MSA	137	26	1,958	18
Charlotte – Gastonia – Rock Hill, NC – SC MSA	136	27	1,886	19
Phoenix – Mesa, AZ MSA	165	22	1,841	20
Tampa – St. Petersburg – Clearwater, FL MSA	184	20	1,786	21
Hartford, CT MSA	89	37	1,776	22
Buffalo – Niagara Falls, NY MSA	89	37	1,673	23
Norfolk – Virginia Beach – Newport News, VA – NC MSA	86	38	1,637	24
Milwaukee – Racine, WI CMSA	152	25	1,622	25

Source: U.S. Department of Commerce, Bureau of the Census, Data User Services Division, *1992 Economic Census, Volume 1F, Reports Series, Release 1F*, September 1995, CD-ROM. *Note:* Data are shown only for the top 25 areas.

★2414★
Establishments and Employment
Petroleum and Petroleum Products

The U.S. total number of employees is 168,344; total number of establishments is 16,060.

MSA	Establishments	Rank	Employment	Rank
Los Angeles – Riverside – Orange County, CA CMSA	326	2	4,598	1
Washington – Baltimore, DC – MD – VA – WV CMSA	144	8	3,344	2
Chicago – Gary – Kenosha, IL – IN – WI CMSA	277	4	3,319	3
St. Louis, MO – IL MSA	125	11	2,621	4
Boston – Worcester – Lawrence, MA – NH – ME – CT CMSA	147	7	2,409	5
San Francisco – Oakland – San Jose, CA CMSA	143	9	1,910	6
Dallas – Fort Worth, TX CMSA	210	5	1,803	7
Detroit – Ann Arbor – Flint, MI CMSA	123	12	1,720	8
Seattle – Tacoma – Bremerton, WA CMSA	98	15	1,557	9
Miami – Fort Lauderdale, FL CMSA	116	13	1,440	10
Pittsburgh, PA MSA	84	20	1,249	11
Portland – Salem, OR – WA CMSA	98	15	1,186	12
Denver – Boulder – Greeley, CO CMSA	95	17	1,174	13
Atlanta, GA MSA	127	10	1,135	14
Minneapolis – St. Paul, MN – WI MSA	103	14	1,126	15
Phoenix – Mesa, AZ MSA	84	20	1,119	16
New Orleans, LA MSA	77	21	1,013	17
Cleveland – Akron, OH CMSA	96	16	994	18
Kansas City, MO – KS MSA	75	22	961	19
Tampa – St. Petersburg – Clearwater, FL MSA	87	18	928	20
Sacramento – Yolo, CA CMSA	59	28	865	21
Norfolk – Virginia Beach – Newport News, VA – NC MSA	63	25	844	22
Indianapolis, IN MSA	69	23	798	23
Nashville, TN MSA	60	27	776	24
Greensboro – Winston-Salem – High Point, NC MSA	59	28	772	25

Source: U.S. Department of Commerce, Bureau of the Census, Data User Services Division, *1992 Economic Census, Volume 1F, Reports Series, Release 1F,* September 1995, CD-ROM. *Note:* Data are shown only for the top 25 areas.

★2415★
Establishments and Employment
Petroleum Bulk Stations and Terminals

The U.S. total number of employees is 130,047; total number of establishments is 12,098.

MSA	Establishments	Rank	Employment	Rank
Los Angeles – Riverside – Orange County, CA CMSA	184	2	3,013	1
Houston – Galveston – Brazoria, TX CMSA	157	3	2,248	2
Chicago – Gary – Kenosha, IL – IN – WI CMSA	145	4	2,015	3
Philadelphia – Wilmington – Atlantic City, PA – NJ – DE – MD CMSA	101	7	1,852	4
Boston – Worcester – Lawrence, MA – NH – ME – CT CMSA	85	12	1,746	5
St. Louis, MO – IL MSA	87	10	1,333	6
Miami – Fort Lauderdale, FL CMSA	71	16	1,132	7
Pittsburgh, PA MSA	60	19	1,045	8
Dallas – Fort Worth, TX CMSA	126	5	1,031	9
Atlanta, GA MSA	90	9	870	10
Minneapolis – St. Paul, MN – WI MSA	75	14	849	11
Phoenix – Mesa, AZ MSA	61	18	849	11
Tampa – St. Petersburg – Clearwater, FL MSA	64	17	765	12
Denver – Boulder – Greeley, CO CMSA	54	21	756	13
Norfolk – Virginia Beach – Newport News, VA – NC MSA	49	23	729	14
Greensboro – Winston-Salem – High Point, NC MSA	47	24	677	15
New Orleans, LA MSA	47	24	671	16
Nashville, TN MSA	44	26	596	17
Charlotte – Gastonia – Rock Hill, NC – SC MSA	58	20	586	18
Kansas City, MO – KS MSA	51	22	514	19
Memphis, TN – AR – MS MSA	35	35	483	20
San Antonio, TX MSA	36	34	479	21
Albany – Schenectady – Troy, NY MSA	25	45	478	22
Shreveport – Bossier City, LA MSA	25	45	477	23
Sacramento – Yolo, CA CMSA	36	34	471	24

Source: U.S. Department of Commerce, Bureau of the Census, Data User Services Division, *1992 Economic Census, Volume 1F, Reports Series, Release 1F,* September 1995, CD-ROM. *Note:* Data are shown only for the top 25 areas.

★2416★
Establishments and Employment
Photographic Equipment and Supplies

The U.S. total number of employees is 27,372; total number of establishments is 1,461.

MSA	Estab-lish-ments	Rank	Emp-loy-ment	Rank
Los Angeles – Riverside – Orange County, CA CMSA	164	2	3,433	1
Chicago – Gary – Kenosha, IL – IN – WI CMSA	88	3	2,621	2
San Francisco – Oakland – San Jose, CA CMSA	44	5	1,169	3
Dallas – Fort Worth, TX CMSA	41	7	1,030	4
Boston – Worcester – Lawrence, MA – NH – ME – CT CMSA	45	4	1,020	5
Minneapolis – St. Paul, MN – WI MSA	31	10	577	6
Cleveland – Akron, OH CMSA	21	13	524	7
St. Louis, MO – IL MSA	17	16	390	8
Denver – Boulder – Greeley, CO CMSA	24	11	349	9
Tampa – St. Petersburg – Clearwater, FL MSA	13	19	310	10
Miami – Fort Lauderdale, FL CMSA	43	6	308	11
Kansas City, MO – KS MSA	19	15	300	12
Charlotte – Gastonia – Rock Hill, NC – SC MSA	12	20	270	13
Hartford, CT MSA	5	25	197	14
San Diego, CA MSA	16	17	150	15
Nashville, TN MSA	13	19	149	16
Memphis, TN – AR – MS MSA	5	25	146	17
Portland – Salem, OR – WA CMSA	12	20	123	18
Milwaukee – Racine, WI CMSA	15	18	121	19
Louisville, KY – IN MSA	4	26	86	20
Austin – San Marcos, TX MSA	6	24	81	21
Knoxville, TN MSA	6	24	79	22
Orlando, FL MSA	7	23	64	23
Oklahoma City, OK MSA	4	26	51	24
Columbus, OH MSA	8	22	45	25

Source: U.S. Department of Commerce, Bureau of the Census, Data User Services Division, *1992 Economic Census, Volume 1F, Reports Series, Release 1F,* September 1995, CD-ROM. *Note:* Data are shown only for the top 25 areas.

★2417★
Establishments and Employment
Plastics Materials and Basic Forms and Shapes

The U.S. total number of employees is 33,459; total number of establishments is 3,490.

MSA	Estab-lish-ments	Rank	Emp-loy-ment	Rank
Los Angeles – Riverside – Orange County, CA CMSA	291	2	3,165	1
Detroit – Ann Arbor – Flint, MI CMSA	124	5	1,192	2
Houston – Galveston – Brazoria, TX CMSA	117	6	1,145	3
Dallas – Fort Worth, TX CMSA	87	10	901	4
San Francisco – Oakland – San Jose, CA CMSA	97	9	835	5
Cleveland – Akron, OH CMSA	81	11	804	6
Minneapolis – St. Paul, MN – WI MSA	72	12	772	7
Atlanta, GA MSA	109	7	709	8
Milwaukee – Racine, WI CMSA	33	20	675	9
St. Louis, MO – IL MSA	45	15	508	10
Miami – Fort Lauderdale, FL CMSA	59	13	489	11
Cincinnati – Hamilton, OH – KY – IN CMSA	38	17	373	12
Phoenix – Mesa, AZ MSA	33	20	333	13
Charlotte – Gastonia – Rock Hill, NC – SC MSA	36	19	320	14
Denver – Boulder – Greeley, CO CMSA	39	16	317	15
Kansas City, MO – KS MSA	31	22	312	16
Tampa – St. Petersburg – Clearwater, FL MSA	32	21	305	17
San Diego, CA MSA	37	18	304	18
Greenville – Spartanburg – Anderson, SC MSA	22	26	298	19
Columbus, OH MSA	25	24	276	20
Pittsburgh, PA MSA	23	25	249	21
Rochester, NY MSA	22	26	226	22
Indianapolis, IN MSA	26	23	207	23
Greensboro – Winston-Salem – High Point, NC MSA	19	27	206	24
Rockford, IL MSA	11	34	185	25

Source: U.S. Department of Commerce, Bureau of the Census, Data User Services Division, *1992 Economic Census, Volume 1F, Reports Series, Release 1F,* September 1995, CD-ROM. *Note:* Data are shown only for the top 25 areas.

Poultry and Poultry Products

The U.S. total number of employees is 19,916; total number of establishments is 1,224.

MSA	Estab-lish-ments	Rank	Emp-ploy-ment	Rank
Washington–Baltimore, DC–MD–VA–WV CMSA	19	8	582	1
Lancaster, PA MSA	17	9	458	2
Atlanta, GA MSA	23	7	427	3
Philadelphia–Wilmington–Atlantic City, PA–NJ–DE–MD CMSA	32	5	421	4
Cleveland–Akron, OH CMSA	8	18	411	5
Miami–Fort Lauderdale, FL CMSA	24	6	336	6
Dallas–Fort Worth, TX CMSA	17	9	290	7
Tampa–St. Petersburg–Clearwater, FL MSA	15	11	210	8
Greensboro–Winston-Salem–High Point, NC MSA	10	16	196	9
Portland–Salem, OR–WA CMSA	5	21	168	10
Raleigh–Durham–Chapel Hill, NC MSA	13	13	143	11
Buffalo–Niagara Falls, NY MSA	5	21	133	12
New Orleans, LA MSA	4	22	132	13
Stockton–Lodi, CA MSA	6	20	132	13
St. Louis, MO–IL MSA	12	14	131	14
San Antonio, TX MSA	10	16	126	15
Phoenix–Mesa, AZ MSA	11	15	120	16
Kansas City, MO–KS MSA	12	14	108	17
Springfield, MO MSA	6	20	105	18
Columbus, OH MSA	8	18	95	19
Detroit–Ann Arbor–Flint, MI CMSA	14	12	93	20
Hartford, CT MSA	4	22	87	21
Scranton–Wilkes-Barre–Hazleton, PA MSA	5	21	87	21
Memphis, TN–AR–MS MSA	5	21	86	22
Nashville, TN MSA	5	21	73	23

Source: U.S. Department of Commerce, Bureau of the Census, Data User Services Division, *1992 Economic Census, Volume 1F, Reports Series, Release 1F,* September 1995, CD-ROM. *Note:* Data are shown only for the top 25 areas.

Printing and Writing Paper

The U.S. total number of employees is 36,646; total number of establishments is 2,561.

MSA	Estab-lish-ments	Rank	Emp-ploy-ment	Rank
Los Angeles–Riverside–Orange County, CA CMSA	171	2	2,855	1
Dallas–Fort Worth, TX CMSA	99	5	1,293	2
Minneapolis–St. Paul, MN–WI MSA	52	11	1,042	3
Miami–Fort Lauderdale, FL CMSA	46	12	629	4

[Continued]

MSA	Estab-lish-ments	Rank	Emp-ploy-ment	Rank
Cleveland–Akron, OH CMSA	36	14	551	5
Kansas City, MO–KS MSA	32	16	537	6
St. Louis, MO–IL MSA	35	15	494	7
Houston–Galveston–Brazoria, TX CMSA	41	13	422	8
Tampa–St. Petersburg–Clearwater, FL MSA	24	22	390	9
Milwaukee–Racine, WI CMSA	23	23	376	10
Greensboro–Winston-Salem–High Point, NC MSA	12	30	369	11
Columbus, OH MSA	27	19	355	12
Nashville, TN MSA	16	26	284	13
Indianapolis, IN MSA	18	25	277	14
Richmond–Petersburg, VA MSA	11	31	262	15
Orlando, FL MSA	16	26	254	16
Omaha, NE–IA MSA	10	32	245	17
Rochester, NY MSA	16	26	233	18
Birmingham, AL MSA	15	27	229	19
Louisville, KY–IN MSA	15	27	225	20
Pittsburgh, PA MSA	21	24	223	21
Des Moines, IA MSA	11	31	222	22
New Orleans, LA MSA	13	29	218	23
Buffalo–Niagara Falls, NY MSA	15	27	211	24
Austin–San Marcos, TX MSA	13	29	207	25

Source: U.S. Department of Commerce, Bureau of the Census, Data User Services Division, *1992 Economic Census, Volume 1F, Reports Series, Release 1F,* September 1995, CD-ROM. *Note:* Data are shown only for the top 25 areas.

Professional and Commercial Equipment and Supplies

The U.S. total number of employees is 685,092; total number of establishments is 46,792.

MSA	Estab-lish-ments	Rank	Emp-ploy-ment	Rank
Los Angeles–Riverside–Orange County, CA CMSA	3,390	2	54,054	1
San Francisco–Oakland–San Jose, CA CMSA	2,002	3	43,739	2
Chicago–Gary–Kenosha, IL–IN–WI CMSA	1,804	4	39,186	3
Washington–Baltimore, DC–MD–VA–WV CMSA	1,374	6	27,782	4
Boston–Worcester–Lawrence, MA–NH–ME–CT CMSA	1,425	5	26,254	5
Dallas–Fort Worth, TX CMSA	1,217	8	23,139	6
Atlanta, GA MSA	1,137	10	20,405	7
Philadelphia–Wilmington–Atlantic City, PA–NJ–DE–MD CMSA	1,195	9	17,417	8
Minneapolis–St. Paul, MN–WI MSA	806	13	13,716	9

[Continued]

★2420★

Professional and Commercial Equipment and Supplies
[Continued]

MSA	Estab- lish- ments	Rank	Emp- loy- ment	Rank
Detroit – Ann Arbor – Flint, MI CMSA	854	11	13,132	10
Denver – Boulder – Greeley, CO CMSA	702	15	11,858	11
Miami – Fort Lauderdale, FL CMSA	1,270	7	11,620	12
Houston – Galveston – Brazoria, TX CMSA	845	12	11,001	13
Seattle – Tacoma – Bremerton, WA CMSA	787	14	10,222	14
Cleveland – Akron, OH CMSA	613	16	9,372	15
St. Louis, MO – IL MSA	539	17	8,251	16
Tampa – St. Petersburg – Clearwater, FL MSA	506	19	7,524	17
Phoenix – Mesa, AZ MSA	539	17	7,314	18
Pittsburgh, PA MSA	417	22	7,069	19
San Diego, CA MSA	517	18	6,451	20
Kansas City, MO – KS MSA	432	21	6,217	21
Indianapolis, IN MSA	330	26	6,138	22
Cincinnati – Hamilton, OH – KY – IN CMSA	362	24	6,072	23
Portland – Salem, OR – WA CMSA	471	20	5,512	24
Milwaukee – Racine, WI CMSA	360	25	5,447	25

Source: U.S. Department of Commerce, Bureau of the Census, Data User Services Division, *1992 Economic Census, Volume 1F, Reports Series, Release 1F,* September 1995, CD-ROM. *Note:* Data are shown only for the top 25 areas.

★2421★
Establishments and Employment

Refrigeration Equipment and Supplies

The U.S. total number of employees is 11,928; total number of establishments is 1,455.

MSA	Estab- lish- ments	Rank	Emp- loy- ment	Rank
Chicago – Gary – Kenosha, IL – IN – WI CMSA	62	3	450	1
Indianapolis, IN MSA	12	16	371	2
Dallas – Fort Worth, TX CMSA	34	8	358	3
Atlanta, GA MSA	32	9	273	4
Philadelphia – Wilmington – Atlantic City, PA – NJ – DE – MD CMSA	37	6	262	5
Des Moines, IA MSA	7	21	229	6
St. Louis, MO – IL MSA	24	10	224	7
Minneapolis – St. Paul, MN – WI MSA	24	10	185	8
Miami – Fort Lauderdale, FL CMSA	44	5	179	9
Washington – Baltimore, DC – MD – VA – WV CMSA	19	12	174	10
Louisville, KY – IN MSA	15	13	164	11

[Continued]

★2421★

Refrigeration Equipment and Supplies
[Continued]

MSA	Estab- lish- ments	Rank	Emp- loy- ment	Rank
Kansas City, MO – KS MSA	15	13	149	12
Richmond – Petersburg, VA MSA	10	18	143	13
Phoenix – Mesa, AZ MSA	20	11	142	14
Omaha, NE – IA MSA	11	17	133	15
Tampa – St. Petersburg – Clearwater, FL MSA	13	15	133	15
Cleveland – Akron, OH CMSA	12	16	131	16
Birmingham, AL MSA	8	20	117	17
Columbus, OH MSA	14	14	111	18
Memphis, TN – AR – MS MSA	13	15	103	19
San Diego, CA MSA	19	12	96	20
Detroit – Ann Arbor – Flint, MI CMSA	15	13	88	21
Norfolk – Virginia Beach – Newport News, VA – NC MSA	10	18	85	22
New Orleans, LA MSA	11	17	79	23
Little Rock – North Little Rock, AR MSA	10	18	76	24

Source: U.S. Department of Commerce, Bureau of the Census, Data User Services Division, *1992 Economic Census, Volume 1F, Reports Series, Release 1F,* September 1995, CD-ROM. *Note:* Data are shown only for the top 25 areas.

★2422★
Establishments and Employment

Roofing, Siding, and Insulation Materials

The U.S. total number of employees is 30,060; total number of establishments is 2,848.

MSA	Estab- lish- ments	Rank	Emp- loy- ment	Rank
New York – Northern New Jersey – Long Island, NY – NJ – CT-CMSA	172	1	2,046	1
Dallas – Fort Worth, TX CMSA	68	7	908	2
Washington – Baltimore, DC – MD – VA – WV CMSA	76	5	815	3
San Francisco – Oakland – San Jose, CA CMSA	57	10	714	4
Minneapolis – St. Paul, MN – WI MSA	39	16	608	5
Atlanta, GA MSA	60	9	571	6
St. Louis, MO – IL MSA	46	13	570	7
Cleveland – Akron, OH CMSA	49	12	547	8
Detroit – Ann Arbor – Flint, MI CMSA	63	8	487	9
Miami – Fort Lauderdale, FL CMSA	40	15	465	10
Houston – Galveston – Brazoria, TX CMSA	33	17	441	11
Pittsburgh, PA MSA	28	22	409	12
Tampa – St. Petersburg – Clearwater, FL MSA	31	19	399	13
Phoenix – Mesa, AZ MSA	25	23	396	14

[Continued]

★2422★
Roofing, Siding, and Insulation Materials
[Continued]

MSA	Establishments	Rank	Employment	Rank
Milwaukee – Racine, WI CMSA	32	18	372	15
Indianapolis, IN MSA	31	19	366	16
Kansas City, MO – KS MSA	31	19	310	17
Richmond – Petersburg, VA MSA	29	21	297	18
Lancaster, PA MSA	7	40	279	19
Columbus, OH MSA	21	26	278	20
Grand Rapids – Muskegon – Holland, MI MSA	22	25	276	21
San Antonio, TX MSA	14	33	264	22
Charlotte – Gastonia – Rock Hill, NC – SC MSA	30	20	249	23
Green Bay, WI MSA	3	44	232	24
Salt Lake City – Ogden, UT MSA	21	26	232	24

Source: U.S. Department of Commerce, Bureau of the Census, Data User Services Division, *1992 Economic Census, Volume 1F, Reports Series, Release 1F,* September 1995, CD-ROM. *Note:* Data are shown only for the top 25 areas.

★2423★
Establishments and Employment
Scrap and Waste Materials

The U.S. total number of employees is 98,005; total number of establishments is 8,928.

MSA	Establishments	Rank	Employment	Rank
Los Angeles – Riverside – Orange County, CA CMSA	484	2	7,319	1
Chicago – Gary – Kenosha, IL – IN – WI CMSA	401	3	4,852	2
San Francisco – Oakland – San Jose, CA CMSA	201	6	2,697	3
Philadelphia – Wilmington – Atlantic City, PA – NJ – DE – MD CMSA	237	4	2,488	4
Detroit – Ann Arbor – Flint, MI CMSA	198	7	2,144	5
Dallas – Fort Worth, TX CMSA	136	13	1,860	6
Houston – Galveston – Brazoria, TX CMSA	153	9	1,830	7
Cleveland – Akron, OH CMSA	154	8	1,795	8
Washington – Baltimore, DC – MD – VA – WV CMSA	147	11	1,736	9
Pittsburgh, PA MSA	151	10	1,635	10
Atlanta, GA MSA	137	12	1,589	11
St. Louis, MO – IL MSA	106	15	1,552	12
Milwaukee – Racine, WI CMSA	66	20	1,097	13
Portland – Salem, OR – WA CMSA	84	18	1,017	14
Minneapolis – St. Paul, MN – WI MSA	95	17	987	15
Phoenix – Mesa, AZ MSA	62	22	967	16
Charlotte – Gastonia – Rock Hill, NC – SC MSA	74	19	958	17
Miami – Fort Lauderdale, FL CMSA	127	14	895	18

[Continued]

★2423★
Scrap and Waste Materials
[Continued]

MSA	Establishments	Rank	Employment	Rank
Denver – Boulder – Greeley, CO CMSA	63	21	820	19
Grand Rapids – Muskegon – Holland, MI MSA	41	31	710	20
Kansas City, MO – KS MSA	52	25	699	21
Birmingham, AL MSA	50	27	647	22
Tampa – St. Petersburg – Clearwater, FL MSA	59	24	593	23
Hartford, CT MSA	35	33	580	24
Indianapolis, IN MSA	44	30	576	25

Source: U.S. Department of Commerce, Bureau of the Census, Data User Services Division, *1992 Economic Census, Volume 1F, Reports Series, Release 1F,* September 1995, CD-ROM. *Note:* Data are shown only for the top 25 areas.

★2424★
Establishments and Employment
Service Establishment Equipment and Supplies

The U.S. total number of employees is 62,965; total number of establishments is 7,579.

MSA	Establishments	Rank	Employment	Rank
New York – Northern New Jersey – Long Island, NY – NJ – CT-CMSA	562	1	4,676	1
Los Angeles – Riverside – Orange County, CA CMSA	406	2	3,946	2
Boston – Worcester – Lawrence, MA – NH – ME – CT CMSA	163	7	1,470	3
San Francisco – Oakland – San Jose, CA CMSA	160	8	1,399	4
Atlanta, GA MSA	144	10	1,312	5
Dallas – Fort Worth, TX CMSA	194	4	1,311	6
Minneapolis – St. Paul, MN – WI MSA	82	17	1,030	7
Phoenix – Mesa, AZ MSA	81	18	1,025	8
Cleveland – Akron, OH CMSA	85	16	798	9
St. Louis, MO – IL MSA	105	13	772	10
Pittsburgh, PA MSA	82	17	721	11
Tampa – St. Petersburg – Clearwater, FL MSA	67	22	705	12
Charlotte – Gastonia – Rock Hill, NC – SC MSA	59	25	686	13
Kansas City, MO – KS MSA	74	20	624	14
Richmond – Petersburg, VA MSA	29	40	603	15
Salt Lake City – Ogden, UT MSA	64	23	594	16
San Diego, CA MSA	74	20	575	17
Omaha, NE – IA MSA	23	46	535	18
Greensboro – Winston-Salem – High Point, NC MSA	71	21	519	19
Nashville, TN MSA	44	29	513	20
Toledo, OH MSA	28	41	453	21
New Orleans, LA MSA	40	31	397	22

[Continued]

★2424★

Service Establishment Equipment and Supplies

[Continued]

MSA	Estab- lish- ments	Rank	Emp- ploy- ment	Rank
Indianapolis, IN MSA	58	26	395	23
Grand Rapids – Muskegon – Holland, MI MSA	36	35	394	24
Sacramento – Yolo, CA CMSA	51	27	357	25

Source: U.S. Department of Commerce, Bureau of the Census, Data User Services Division, *1992 Economic Census, Volume 1F, Reports Series, Release 1F,* September 1995, CD-ROM. *Note:* Data are shown only for the top 25 areas.

★2425★

Establishments and Employment

Sporting and Recreational Goods and Supplies

The U.S. total number of employees is 52,269; total number of establishments is 5,530.

MSA	Estab- lish- ments	Rank	Emp- ploy- ment	Rank
Los Angeles – Riverside – Orange County, CA CMSA	480	1	4,947	1
San Francisco – Oakland – San Jose, CA CMSA	153	4	1,526	2
Atlanta, GA MSA	104	12	1,241	3
Miami – Fort Lauderdale, FL CMSA	146	5	1,181	4
Kansas City, MO – KS MSA	62	19	1,152	5
Denver – Boulder – Greeley, CO CMSA	111	10	1,146	6
Minneapolis – St. Paul, MN – WI MSA	117	9	1,099	7
Detroit – Ann Arbor – Flint, MI CMSA	110	11	971	8
Dallas – Fort Worth, TX CMSA	131	8	893	9
Washington – Baltimore, DC – MD – VA – WV CMSA	91	15	824	10
Greenville – Spartanburg – Anderson, SC MSA	27	32	774	11
Portland – Salem, OR – WA CMSA	85	16	737	12
San Diego, CA MSA	95	14	727	13
Indianapolis, IN MSA	34	27	543	14
Orlando, FL MSA	46	22	524	15
Cleveland – Akron, OH CMSA	52	21	493	16
Milwaukee – Racine, WI CMSA	39	23	491	17
Houston – Galveston – Brazoria, TX CMSA	83	17	469	18
Columbus, OH MSA	38	24	466	19
St. Louis, MO – IL MSA	55	20	449	20
Austin – San Marcos, TX MSA	21	36	408	21
Providence – Fall River – Warwick, RI – MA MSA	20	37	397	22
Tampa – St. Petersburg – Clearwater, FL MSA	66	18	385	23
Columbia, SC MSA	13	44	382	24
Phoenix – Mesa, AZ MSA	52	21	382	24

Source: U.S. Department of Commerce, Bureau of the Census, Data User Services Division, *1992 Economic Census, Volume 1F, Reports Series, Release 1F,* September 1995, CD-ROM. *Note:* Data are shown only for the top 25 areas.

★2426★

Establishments and Employment

Stationery and Office Supplies

The U.S. total number of employees is 168,825; total number of establishments is 11,807.

MSA	Estab- lish- ments	Rank	Emp- ploy- ment	Rank
Los Angeles – Riverside – Orange County, CA CMSA	696	2	15,385	1
Dallas – Fort Worth, TX CMSA	294	6	5,771	2
Cleveland – Akron, OH CMSA	150	13	5,562	3
Minneapolis – St. Paul, MN – WI MSA	147	14	2,308	4
Miami – Fort Lauderdale, FL CMSA	205	10	2,272	5
Kansas City, MO – KS MSA	108	17	2,077	6
St. Louis, MO – IL MSA	144	15	1,828	7
Pittsburgh, PA MSA	98	20	1,391	8
Indianapolis, IN MSA	76	23	1,127	9
Norfolk – Virginia Beach – Newport News, VA – NC MSA	63	29	1,122	10
Sacramento – Yolo, CA CMSA	69	25	1,122	10
Phoenix – Mesa, AZ MSA	93	21	1,060	11
San Diego, CA MSA	98	20	1,057	12
Charlotte – Gastonia – Rock Hill, NC – SC MSA	76	23	999	13
Tampa – St. Petersburg – Clearwater, FL MSA	102	18	999	13
Buffalo – Niagara Falls, NY MSA	49	36	885	14
Nashville, TN MSA	59	30	860	15
Memphis, TN – AR – MS MSA	66	27	834	16
San Antonio, TX MSA	63	29	819	17
Milwaukee – Racine, WI CMSA	82	22	817	18
Orlando, FL MSA	70	24	775	19
Birmingham, AL MSA	59	30	697	20
Columbus, OH MSA	68	26	690	21
Grand Rapids – Muskegon – Holland, MI MSA	49	36	677	22
Des Moines, IA MSA	37	45	668	23

Source: U.S. Department of Commerce, Bureau of the Census, Data User Services Division, *1992 Economic Census, Volume 1F, Reports Series, Release 1F,* September 1995, CD-ROM. *Note:* Data are shown only for the top 25 areas.

★2427★

Establishments and Employment

Tobacco and Tobacco Products

The U.S. total number of employees is 50,345; total number of establishments is 1,702.

MSA	Estab- lish- ments	Rank	Emp- ploy- ment	Rank
New York – Northern New Jersey – Long Island, NY – NJ – CT-CMSA	246	1	3,478	1
Boston – Worcester – Lawrence, MA – NH – ME – CT CMSA	26	8	1,011	2
Washington – Baltimore, DC – MD – VA – WV CMSA	24	9	1,005	3
San Francisco – Oakland – San Jose, CA CMSA	29	6	892	4

[Continued]

★ 2427 ★

Tobacco and Tobacco Products

[Continued]

MSA	Estab-lish-ments	Rank	Emp-loy-ment	Rank
Minneapolis – St. Paul, MN – WI MSA	12	15	638	5
Atlanta, GA MSA	16	12	602	6
Syracuse, NY MSA	5	22	531	7
Seattle – Tacoma – Bremerton, WA CMSA	11	16	516	8
Orlando, FL MSA	5	22	493	9
Houston – Galveston – Brazoria, TX CMSA	16	12	490	10
St. Louis, MO – IL MSA	14	14	479	11
Buffalo – Niagara Falls, NY MSA	11	16	476	12
Tampa – St. Petersburg – Clearwater, FL MSA	15	13	437	13
Dayton – Springfield, OH MSA	4	23	417	14
New Orleans, LA MSA	11	16	416	15
Jacksonville, FL MSA	5	22	398	16
Pittsburgh, PA MSA	20	10	392	17
Columbus, OH MSA	11	16	377	18
Knoxville, TN MSA	10	17	324	19
Miami – Fort Lauderdale, FL CMSA	36	5	321	20
Sacramento – Yolo, CA CMSA	6	21	321	20
Dallas – Fort Worth, TX CMSA	17	11	297	21
Birmingham, AL MSA	5	22	283	22
Cleveland – Akron, OH CMSA	16	12	279	23
Columbia, SC MSA	7	20	271	24

Source: U.S. Department of Commerce, Bureau of the Census, Data User Services Division, *1992 Economic Census, Volume 1F, Reports Series, Release 1F*, September 1995, CD-ROM. *Note:* Data are shown only for the top 25 areas.

★ 2428 ★

Establishments and Employment

Toys and Hobby Goods and Supplies

The U.S. total number of employees is 31,685; total number of establishments is 2,738.

MSA	Estab-lish-ments	Rank	Emp-loy-ment	Rank
Los Angeles – Riverside – Orange County, CA CMSA	383	2	5,198	1
New York – Northern New Jersey – Long Island, NY – NJ – CT-CMSA	435	1	4,891	2
San Francisco – Oakland – San Jose, CA CMSA	114	4	1,542	3
Chicago – Gary – Kenosha, IL – IN – WI CMSA	123	3	1,312	4
Dallas – Fort Worth, TX CMSA	72	6	1,034	5
Atlanta, GA MSA	41	11	453	6
Minneapolis – St. Paul, MN – WI MSA	46	9	436	7
Miami – Fort Lauderdale, FL CMSA	75	5	414	8

[Continued]

★ 2428 ★

Toys and Hobby Goods and Supplies

[Continued]

MSA	Estab-lish-ments	Rank	Emp-loy-ment	Rank
Cleveland – Akron, OH CMSA	32	13	410	9
Tampa – St. Petersburg – Clearwater, FL MSA	27	17	343	10
St. Louis, MO – IL MSA	29	15	330	11
San Diego, CA MSA	29	15	297	12
Denver – Boulder – Greeley, CO CMSA	30	14	284	13
Houston – Galveston – Brazoria, TX CMSA	25	19	252	14
Portland – Salem, OR – WA CMSA	26	18	222	15
Las Vegas, NV – AZ MSA	11	26	201	16
Greensboro – Winston-Salem – High Point, NC MSA	9	27	194	17
Nashville, TN MSA	13	24	157	18
Kansas City, MO – KS MSA	28	16	143	19
Salt Lake City – Ogden, UT MSA	14	23	135	20
San Antonio, TX MSA	13	24	126	21
Orlando, FL MSA	18	21	115	22
Tucson, AZ MSA	6	30	112	23
Providence – Fall River – Warwick, RI – MA MSA	13	24	100	24
Springfield, MO MSA	7	29	96	25

Source: U.S. Department of Commerce, Bureau of the Census, Data User Services Division, *1992 Economic Census, Volume 1F, Reports Series, Release 1F*, September 1995, CD-ROM. *Note:* Data are shown only for the top 25 areas.

★ 2429 ★

Establishments and Employment

Transportation Equipment and Supplies, Except Motor Vehicles

The U.S. total number of employees is 39,444; total number of establishments is 3,866.

MSA	Estab-lish-ments	Rank	Emp-loy-ment	Rank
Los Angeles – Riverside – Orange County, CA CMSA	450	1	4,832	1
Miami – Fort Lauderdale, FL CMSA	385	2	3,720	2
New York – Northern New Jersey – Long Island, NY – NJ – CT-CMSA	347	3	3,370	3
Dallas – Fort Worth, TX CMSA	170	5	1,927	4
Wichita, KS MSA	45	15	1,398	5
Phoenix – Mesa, AZ MSA	51	13	1,328	6
Houston – Galveston – Brazoria, TX CMSA	89	9	957	7
Atlanta, GA MSA	61	11	631	8
New Orleans, LA MSA	51	13	596	9
San Antonio, TX MSA	47	14	565	10
Boston – Worcester – Lawrence, MA – NH – ME – CT CMSA	47	14	486	11
West Palm Beach – Boca Raton, FL MSA	28	21	478	12

[Continued]

★ 2429 ★

Transportation Equipment and Supplies, Except Motor Vehicles
[Continued]

MSA	Establish-ments	Rank	Emp-loy-ment	Rank
Cleveland – Akron, OH CMSA	28	21	391	13
Tampa – St. Petersburg – Clearwater, FL MSA	62	10	362	14
Kansas City, MO – KS MSA	40	17	361	15
St. Louis, MO – IL MSA	43	16	335	16
Memphis, TN – AR – MS MSA	25	22	311	17
Minneapolis – St. Paul, MN – WI MSA	35	20	294	18
San Diego, CA MSA	36	19	290	19
Norfolk – Virginia Beach – Newport News, VA – NC MSA	25	22	201	20
Tulsa, OK MSA	23	24	173	21
Mobile, AL MSA	14	29	166	22
Orlando, FL MSA	28	21	152	23
Oklahoma City, OK MSA	25	22	149	24
Jacksonville, FL MSA	22	25	140	25

Source: U.S. Department of Commerce, Bureau of the Census, Data User Services Division, *1992 Economic Census, Volume 1F, Reports Series, Release 1F*, September 1995, CD-ROM. *Note:* Data are shown only for the top 25 areas.

★ 2430 ★

Establishments and Employment

Warm Air Heating and Air-conditioning Equipment and Supplies

The U.S. total number of employees is 45,129; total number of establishments is 5,486.

MSA	Establish-ments	Rank	Emp-loy-ment	Rank
Dallas – Fort Worth, TX CMSA	148	5	2,088	1
Chicago – Gary – Kenosha, IL – IN – WI CMSA	173	3	1,688	2
Houston – Galveston – Brazoria, TX CMSA	136	6	1,115	3
Detroit – Ann Arbor – Flint, MI CMSA	112	8	1,058	4
Atlanta, GA MSA	112	8	1,054	5
Miami – Fort Lauderdale, FL CMSA	93	10	1,042	6
San Francisco – Oakland – San Jose, CA CMSA	79	11	745	7
Seattle – Tacoma – Bremerton, WA CMSA	65	15	647	8
St. Louis, MO – IL MSA	73	13	643	9
Syracuse, NY MSA	29	35	541	10
Cleveland – Akron, OH CMSA	68	14	483	11
Tampa – St. Petersburg – Clearwater, FL MSA	76	12	479	12
Phoenix – Mesa, AZ MSA	52	20	468	13
Columbus, OH MSA	48	23	464	14
Indianapolis, IN MSA	50	21	463	15
Minneapolis – St. Paul, MN – WI MSA	64	16	455	16

[Continued]

★ 2430 ★

Warm Air Heating and Air-conditioning Equipment and Supplies
[Continued]

MSA	Establish-ments	Rank	Emp-loy-ment	Rank
Charlotte – Gastonia – Rock Hill, NC – SC MSA	57	18	452	17
Pittsburgh, PA MSA	64	16	451	18
Cincinnati – Hamilton, OH – KY – IN CMSA	40	27	443	19
Kansas City, MO – KS MSA	46	24	438	20
Nashville, TN MSA	36	29	434	21
San Antonio, TX MSA	33	32	427	22
Birmingham, AL MSA	42	26	425	23
Greensboro – Winston-Salem – High Point, NC MSA	60	17	422	24
Milwaukee – Racine, WI CMSA	42	26	417	25

Source: U.S. Department of Commerce, Bureau of the Census, Data User Services Division, *1992 Economic Census, Volume 1F, Reports Series, Release 1F*, September 1995, CD-ROM. *Note:* Data are shown only for the top 25 areas.

★ 2431 ★

Establishments and Employment

Wholesale Trade, Total

The U.S. total number of employees is 5,791,401; total number of establishments is 495,457.

MSA	Establish-ments	Rank	Emp-loy-ment	Rank
New York – Northern New Jersey – Long Island, NY – NJ – CT-CMSA	50,178	1	588,494	1
Los Angeles – Riverside – Orange County, CA CMSA	31,250	2	399,102	2
Chicago – Gary – Kenosha, IL – IN – WI CMSA	18,573	3	266,314	3
San Francisco – Oakland – San Jose, CA CMSA	13,550	4	183,065	4
Philadelphia – Wilmington – Atlantic City, PA – NJ – DE – MD CMSA	11,229	6	141,805	5
Boston – Worcester – Lawrence, MA – NH – ME – CT CMSA	10,733	7	140,889	6
Dallas – Fort Worth, TX CMSA	10,567	8	140,494	7
Washington – Baltimore, DC – MD – VA – WV CMSA	9,294	9	133,059	8
Atlanta, GA MSA	9,070	10	124,683	9
Detroit – Ann Arbor – Flint, MI CMSA	9,068	11	111,519	10
Houston – Galveston – Brazoria, TX CMSA	9,046	12	107,241	11
Miami – Fort Lauderdale, FL CMSA	12,024	5	100,132	12
Minneapolis – St. Paul, MN – WI MSA	6,436	14	87,059	13
Seattle – Tacoma – Bremerton, WA CMSA	7,101	13	85,583	14

[Continued]

★2431★
Wholesale Trade, Total
[Continued]

MSA	Establishments	Rank	Employment	Rank
Cleveland – Akron, OH CMSA	6,069	15	83,519	15
Denver – Boulder – Greeley, CO CMSA	5,353	16	66,377	16
St. Louis, MO – IL MSA	5,302	17	64,286	17
Cincinnati – Hamilton, OH – KY – IN CMSA	3,546	25	56,509	18
Pittsburgh, PA MSA	4,320	20	55,519	19
Portland – Salem, OR – WA CMSA	4,615	18	54,889	20
Kansas City, MO – KS MSA	4,016	23	53,736	21
Phoenix – Mesa, AZ MSA	4,485	19	51,169	22
Tampa – St. Petersburg – Clearwater, FL MSA	4,292	21	47,948	23
Milwaukee – Racine, WI CMSA	3,499	26	46,413	24
Charlotte – Gastonia – Rock Hill, NC – SC MSA	3,763	24	45,666	25

Source: U.S. Department of Commerce, Bureau of the Census, Data User Services Division, *1992 Economic Census, Volume 1F, Reports Series, Release 1F,* September 1995, CD-ROM. *Note:* Data are shown only for the top 25 areas.

★2432★
Establishments and Employment
Wine and Distilled Alcoholic Beverages

The U.S. total number of employees is 50,735; total number of establishments is 1,856.

MSA	Establishments	Rank	Employment	Rank
New York – Northern New Jersey – Long Island, NY – NJ – CT-CMSA	203	1	6,450	1
San Francisco – Oakland – San Jose, CA CMSA	140	2	3,080	2
Chicago – Gary – Kenosha, IL – IN – WI CMSA	59	4	2,385	3
Dallas – Fort Worth, TX CMSA	31	11	1,390	4
Boston – Worcester – Lawrence, MA – NH – ME – CT CMSA	43	8	1,239	5
Atlanta, GA MSA	24	13	992	6
Tampa – St. Petersburg – Clearwater, FL MSA	14	21	855	7
Indianapolis, IN MSA	7	28	745	8
New Orleans, LA MSA	17	18	703	9
Seattle – Tacoma – Bremerton, WA CMSA	37	10	647	10
Minneapolis – St. Paul, MN – WI MSA	15	20	643	11
Hartford, CT MSA	9	26	642	12
Columbia, SC MSA	10	25	637	13
Phoenix – Mesa, AZ MSA	12	23	635	14
Kansas City, MO – KS MSA	9	26	584	15
San Antonio, TX MSA	11	24	565	16
Orlando, FL MSA	6	29	520	17
Milwaukee – Racine, WI CMSA	16	19	497	18

[Continued]

★2432★
Wine and Distilled Alcoholic Beverages
[Continued]

MSA	Establishments	Rank	Employment	Rank
Albany – Schenectady – Troy, NY MSA	8	27	458	19
Las Vegas, NV – AZ MSA	9	26	432	20
Buffalo – Niagara Falls, NY MSA	6	29	403	21
St. Louis, MO – IL MSA	18	17	392	22
Albuquerque, NM MSA	7	28	375	23
Syracuse, NY MSA	5	30	312	24
San Diego, CA MSA	8	27	263	25

Source: U.S. Department of Commerce, Bureau of the Census, Data User Services Division, *1992 Economic Census, Volume 1F, Reports Series, Release 1F,* September 1995, CD-ROM. *Note:* Data are shown only for the top 25 areas.

★2433★
Establishments and Employment
Women's, Children's, and Infants' Clothing and Accessories

The U.S. total number of employees is 72,485; total number of establishments is 7,581.

MSA	Establishments	Rank	Employment	Rank
New York – Northern New Jersey – Long Island, NY – NJ – CT-CMSA	3,006	1	37,687	1
Los Angeles – Riverside – Orange County, CA CMSA	1,207	2	9,239	2
San Francisco – Oakland – San Jose, CA CMSA	205	5	2,431	3
Miami – Fort Lauderdale, FL CMSA	363	3	2,246	4
Dallas – Fort Worth, TX CMSA	247	4	1,754	5
Boston – Worcester – Lawrence, MA – NH – ME – CT CMSA	129	8	1,245	6
San Diego, CA MSA	59	13	793	7
Atlanta, GA MSA	155	6	656	8
Minneapolis – St. Paul, MN – WI MSA	89	9	565	9
Allentown – Bethlehem – Easton, PA MSA	21	20	306	10
Charlotte – Gastonia – Rock Hill, NC – SC MSA	63	11	301	11
St. Louis, MO – IL MSA	33	18	234	12
El Paso, TX MSA	29	19	225	13
Phoenix – Mesa, AZ MSA	35	17	221	14
Harrisburg – Lebanon – Carlisle, PA MSA	4	35	141	15
Tampa – St. Petersburg – Clearwater, FL MSA	35	17	129	16
Providence – Fall River – Warwick, RI – MA MSA	17	23	94	17
Tulsa, OK MSA	11	28	87	18
Milwaukee – Racine, WI CMSA	13	26	83	19
Austin – San Marcos, TX MSA	14	25	78	20

[Continued]

★2433★

Women's, Children's, and Infants' Clothing and Accessories

[Continued]

MSA	Estab-lish-ments	Rank	Emp-ploy-ment	Rank
Santa Barbara – Santa Maria – Lompoc, CA MSA	10	29	77	21
West Palm Beach – Boca Raton, FL MSA	33	18	76	22
Birmingham, AL MSA	9	30	73	23
Kansas City, MO – KS MSA	29	19	70	24
Albuquerque, NM MSA	6	33	69	25

Source: U.S. Department of Commerce, Bureau of the Census, Data User Services Division, *1992 Economic Census, Volume 1F, Reports Series, Release 1F*, September 1995, CD-ROM. *Note:* Data are shown only for the top 25 areas.

Chapter 24

RETAIL TRADE

Topics Covered

General Summary
Apparel and Apparel Products
Establishments and Employment
Foods and Food Products
Home Furnishings and Equipment
Medicines

★ 2434 ★
General Summary
Retail Trade, 1992: Sales Per Capita

[In dollars]

City	Sales	Rank
Atlanta, GA MSA	8,461	8
Chicago-Gary-Kenosha, IL-IN-WI CMSA	7,721	20
Cincinnati-Hamilton, OH-KY-IN CMSA	7,379	23
Cleveland-Akron, OH CMSA	7,218	25
Columbus, OH MSA	8,787	3
Dallas-Fort Worth, TX CMSA	8,406	10
Denver-Boulder-Greeley, CO CMSA	8,499	7
Detroit-Ann Arbor-Flint, MI CMSA	7,952	14
Houston-Galveston-Brazoria, TX CMSA	7,740	19
Indianapolis, IN MSA	8,671	5
Kansas City, MO-KS MSA	7,840	17
Los Angeles-Riverside-Orange County, CA CMSA	7,141	26
Miami-Fort Lauderdale, FL CMSA	9,702	1
Milwaukee-Racine, WI CMSA	7,825	18
Minneapolis-St. Paul, MN-WI MSA	8,637	6
Orlando, FL MSA	9,470	2
Philadelphia-Wilmington-Atlantic City, PA-NJ-DE-MD CMSA	7,867	15
Phoenix-Mesa, AZ, MSA	8,027	13
Pittsburgh, PA MSA	7,309	24
Portland-Salem, OR-WA CMSA	8,183	12
San Diego, CA MSA	7,386	22
San Francisco-Oakland-San Jose, CA CMSA	8,226	11
Seattle-Tacoma-Bremerton, WA CMSA	8,440	9
St. Louis, MO-IL MSA	7,609	21
Tampa-St. Petersburg-Clearwater, FL MSA	8,734	4
Washington-Baltimore, DC-MD-VA-WV CMSA	7,849	16

Source: U.S. Bureau of the Census, *Statistical Abstract of the United States: 1995*, (115th edition), Washington, D.C.: U.S. Government Printing Office, 1995, p. 790. Primary source: U.S. Bureau of the Census, *1992 Census of Retail Trade*, RC92-A-52.

★ 2435 ★
General Summary
Retail Trade, 1992: Total Sales

[In millions of dollars]

City	Sales	Rank
Atlanta, GA MSA	26,525	12
Boston-Worcester-Lawrence, MA-NH-ME-CT CMSA	44,532	7
Chicago-Gary-Kenosha, IL-IN-Wi CMSA	64,858	3
Cincinnati-Hamilton, OH-KY-IN CMSA	13,739	23

[Continued]

★ 2435 ★
Retail Trade, 1992: Total Sales

[Continued]

City	Sales	Rank
Cleveland-Akron, OH CMSA	20,840	15
Columbus, OH MSA	12,224	28
Dallas-Fort Worth, TX CMSA	35,359	9
Denver-Boulder-Greeley, CO CMSA	17,743	20
Detroit-Ann Arbor-Flint, MI CMSA	41,636	8
Houston-Galveston-Brazoria, TX CMSA	30,576	11
Indianapolis, IN MSA	12,352	26
Kansas City, MO-KS MSA	12,655	25
Los Angeles-Riverside-Orange County, CA CMSA	107,567	2
Miami-Fort Lauderdale, FL CMSA	32,182	10
Milwaukee-Racine, WI CMSA	12,747	24
Minneapolis-St. Paul, MN-WI MSA	22,603	14
New York-Northern New Jersey-Long Island, Orlando, FL MSA	12,343	27
Philadelphia-Wilmington-Atlantic City, Phoenix-Mesa, AZ, MSA	18,724	18
Pittsburgh, PA MSA	17,575	21
Portland-Salem, OR-WA CMSA	15,542	22
San Diego, CA MSA	19,216	16
San Francisco-Oakland-San Jose, CA CMSA	52,731	5
Seattle-Tacoma-Bremerton, WA CMSA	26,436	13
St. Louis, MO-IL MSA	19,145	17
Tampa-St. Petersburg-Clearwater, FL MSA	18,487	19
Washington-Baltimore, DC-MD-VA-WV CMSA	54,251	4
NY-NJ-CT-PA CMSA	140,681	1
PA-NJ-DE-MD CMSA	46,633	6

Source: U.S. Bureau of the Census, *Statistical Abstract of the United States: 1995*, (115th edition), Washington, DC: U.S. Government Printing Office, 1995, p. 790. Primary source: U.S. Bureau of the Census, *1992 Census of Retail Trade*, RC92-A-52.

★ 2436 ★
Apparel and Apparel Products
Apparel Manufacturing Leaders, 1995: Employees

City	Number	Rank
Los Angeles, CA	101,000	1
New York, NY	100,000	2
Miami, FL	19,642	3
San Francisco, CA	15,000	4
Greenville, SC	13,700	5
Dallas, TX	9,766	6
Greensboro, NC	9,700	7

[Continued]

★2436★

Apparel Manufacturing Leaders, 1995: Employees
[Continued]

City	Number	Rank
LeHigh Valley, PA	8,400	8
Charlotte, NC	8,000	9

Source: Moore, Lila, "Home Is Where You Sew It," *Apparel Industry Magazine,* (September 1995), p. 38. Primary source: *Apparel Industry Magazine* survey. *Notes:* The state of Georgia claims 57607 employees, which figure gives it a ranking of third place in this category. However, it is not included in the actual table because the data were not detailed for cities or counties.

★2437★

Apparel and Apparel Products

Apparel Manufacturing Leaders, 1995: Facilities

City	Number	Rank
New York, NY	4,500	1
Los Angeles, CA	4,024	2
Miami, FL	670	3
Dallas, TX	460	4
San Francisco, CA	417	5
LeHigh Valley, PA	200	6
Greenville, SC	150	7
Greensboro, NC	140	8
Charlotte, NC	107	9

Source: Moore, Lila, "Home Is Where You Sew It," *Apparel Industry Magazine,* (September 1995), p. 38. Primary source: *Apparel Industry Magazine* survey. *Notes:* The state of Georgia claims 669 apparel manufacturing facilities, which figure gives it a ranking of third place in this category. However, it is not included in the actual table because the data were not detailed for cities or counties.

★2438★

Apparel and Apparel Products

Apparel Manufacturing Leaders, 1995: Hourly Earnings

City	Hourly earnings	Rank
San Francisco, CA	11.58	1
Los Angeles, CA	8.30	2
Charlotte, NC	7.96	3
Greensboro, NC	7.48	4
Dallas, TX	7.42	5
Miami, FL	7.25	6
Greenville, SC	7.23	7
New York, NY	7.00	8
LeHigh Valley, PA	6.48	9

Source: Moore, Lila, "Home Is Where You Sew It," *Apparel Industry Magazine,* (September 1995), p. 38. Primary source: *Apparel Industry Magazine* survey. *Notes:* Employees in the apparel manufacturing industry in the state of Georgia earned an average wage of $6.45 per hour in 1993. Georgia is not listed in the actual table, however, because data were not detailed for cities or counties.

★2439★

Apparel and Apparel Products

Clothing Costs, 1995: 501 Jeans

Price shown for New York, New York, refers to stores in mid-town Manhattan; for San Francisco, California, discount stores.

[In dollars per pair]

City/MSA	Price	Rank
New York, NY	50.00	1
San Francisco, CA	29.95	2

Source: Lenzner, Robert and Stephen S. Johnson, "A Few Yards of Denim and Five Copper Rivets," *Forbes,* 26 February 1996, p. 82.

★2440★

Establishments and Employment

Apparel and Accessory Stores

The U.S. total number of employees is 1,144,587; total number of establishments is 145,490.

MSA	Establishments	Rank	Employment	Rank
New York – Northern New Jersey – Long Island, NY – NJ – CT-CMSA	13,814	1	114,391	1
Los Angeles – Riverside – Orange County, CA CMSA	8,115	2	66,294	2
Chicago – Gary – Kenosha, IL – IN – WI CMSA	5,049	3	48,633	3
Washington – Baltimore, DC – MD – VA – WV CMSA	4,368	4	41,310	4
San Francisco – Oakland – San Jose, CA CMSA	3,736	6	34,287	5
Philadelphia – Wilmington – Atlantic City, PA – NJ – DE – MD CMSA	3,795	5	30,180	6
Detroit – Ann Arbor – Flint, MI CMSA	2,878	9	25,058	7
Miami – Fort Lauderdale, FL CMSA	3,087	8	22,739	8
Dallas – Fort Worth, TX CMSA	2,407	10	20,072	9
Houston – Galveston – Brazoria, TX CMSA	2,093	11	19,239	10
Atlanta, GA MSA	1,820	12	15,882	11
Seattle – Tacoma – Bremerton, WA CMSA	1,425	15	13,342	12
Minneapolis – St. Paul, MN – WI MSA	1,438	14	12,827	13
Cleveland – Akron, OH CMSA	1,580	13	12,597	14
St. Louis, MO – IL MSA	1,400	16	12,072	15
San Diego, CA MSA	1,398	17	11,809	16
Pittsburgh, PA MSA	1,377	18	10,754	17
Tampa – St. Petersburg – Clearwater, FL MSA	1,237	19	9,565	18
Phoenix – Mesa, AZ MSA	1,223	20	9,099	19
Denver – Boulder – Greeley, CO CMSA	1,106	21	8,312	20
Portland – Salem, OR – WA CMSA	801	27	8,089	21
Cincinnati – Hamilton, OH – KY – IN CMSA	986	22	7,956	22
Milwaukee – Racine, WI CMSA	870	24	7,555	23

[Continued]

★2440★

Apparel and Accessory Stores
[Continued]

MSA	Estab-lish-ments	Rank	Emp-loy-ment	Rank
Orlando, FL MSA	811	26	7,151	24
Sacramento – Yolo, CA CMSA	726	33	7,145	25

Source: U.S. Department of Commerce, Bureau of the Census, Data User Services Division, *1992 Economic Census, Volume 1F, Reports Series, Release 1F,* September 1995, CD-ROM. *Note:* Data are shown only for the top 25 areas.

★2441★

Establishments and Employment

Art Dealers

The U.S. total number of employees is 16,982; total number of establishments is 5,010.

MSA	Estab-lish-ments	Rank	Emp-loy-ment	Rank
Los Angeles – Riverside – Orange County, CA CMSA	312	2	1,092	1
Chicago – Gary – Kenosha, IL – IN – WI CMSA	176	4	700	2
Seattle – Tacoma – Bremerton, WA CMSA	109	6	444	3
Detroit – Ann Arbor – Flint, MI CMSA	96	9	407	4
Boston – Worcester – Lawrence, MA – NH – ME – CT CMSA	102	8	369	5
Philadelphia – Wilmington – Atlantic City, PA – NJ – DE – MD CMSA	91	10	314	6
Miami – Fort Lauderdale, FL CMSA	103	7	301	7
Minneapolis – St. Paul, MN – WI MSA	80	12	292	8
Atlanta, GA MSA	73	14	272	9
Dallas – Fort Worth, TX CMSA	82	11	259	10
Honolulu, HI MSA	20	32	228	11
San Diego, CA MSA	68	15	227	12
Phoenix – Mesa, AZ MSA	77	13	216	13
West Palm Beach – Boca Raton, FL MSA	68	15	203	14
Denver – Boulder – Greeley, CO CMSA	50	18	193	15
St. Louis, MO – IL MSA	55	17	192	16
New Orleans, LA MSA	46	20	184	17
Salinas, CA MSA	38	22	165	18
Houston – Galveston – Brazoria, TX CMSA	63	16	150	19
Cleveland – Akron, OH CMSA	40	21	148	20
Pittsburgh, PA MSA	33	24	143	21
Las Vegas, NV – AZ MSA	20	32	135	22
Tampa – St. Petersburg – Clearwater, FL MSA	48	19	122	23

[Continued]

★2441★

Art Dealers
[Continued]

MSA	Estab-lish-ments	Rank	Emp-loy-ment	Rank
Raleigh – Durham – Chapel Hill, NC MSA	24	28	105	24
Albany – Schenectady – Troy, NY MSA	17	34	95	25

Source: U.S. Department of Commerce, Bureau of the Census, Data User Services Division, *1992 Economic Census, Volume 1F, Reports Series, Release 1F,* September 1995, CD-ROM. *Note:* Data are shown only for the top 25 areas.

★2442★

Establishments and Employment

Auto and Home Supply Stores

The U.S. total number of employees is 269,069; total number of establishments is 41,308.

MSA	Estab-lish-ments	Rank	Emp-loy-ment	Rank
Los Angeles – Riverside – Orange County, CA CMSA	2,307	1	16,353	1
New York – Northern New Jersey – Long Island, NY – NJ – CT-CMSA	1,746	2	10,722	2
San Francisco – Oakland – San Jose, CA CMSA	837	4	6,352	3
Washington – Baltimore, DC – MD – VA – WV CMSA	754	6	6,282	4
Chicago – Gary – Kenosha, IL – IN – WI CMSA	840	3	6,274	5
Dallas – Fort Worth, TX CMSA	815	5	5,916	6
Detroit – Ann Arbor – Flint, MI CMSA	721	7	5,633	7
Houston – Galveston – Brazoria, TX CMSA	670	9	5,602	8
Philadelphia – Wilmington – Atlantic City, PA – NJ – DE – MD CMSA	576	10	4,608	9
Seattle – Tacoma – Bremerton, WA CMSA	546	12	4,117	10
Atlanta, GA MSA	566	11	3,884	11
Miami – Fort Lauderdale, FL CMSA	677	8	3,876	12
Boston – Worcester – Lawrence, MA – NH – ME – CT CMSA	517	13	3,227	13
Phoenix – Mesa, AZ MSA	367	18	3,216	14
San Diego, CA MSA	391	15	2,997	15
Cleveland – Akron, OH CMSA	416	14	2,881	16
St. Louis, MO – IL MSA	381	16	2,747	17
Minneapolis – St. Paul, MN – WI MSA	314	21	2,454	18
Tampa – St. Petersburg – Clearwater, FL MSA	351	19	2,389	19
Denver – Boulder – Greeley, CO CMSA	332	20	2,383	20
Pittsburgh, PA MSA	376	17	2,338	21

[Continued]

★2442★

Auto and Home Supply Stores
[Continued]

MSA	Establish-ments	Rank	Emp-ploy-ment	Rank
Sacramento – Yolo, CA CMSA	274	23	2,262	22
Portland – Salem, OR – WA CMSA	301	22	2,118	23
San Antonio, TX MSA	257	24	2,058	24
Indianapolis, IN MSA	234	28	1,895	25

Source: U.S. Department of Commerce, Bureau of the Census, Data User Services Division, *1992 Economic Census, Volume 1F, Reports Series, Release 1F,* September 1995, CD-ROM. *Note:* Data are shown only for the top 25 areas.

★2443★

Establishments and Employment

Automotive Dealers

The U.S. total number of employees is 1,267,533; total number of establishments is 96,373.

MSA	Establish-ments	Rank	Emp-ploy-ment	Rank
Los Angeles – Riverside – Orange County, CA CMSA	4,144	2	66,980	1
New York – Northern New Jersey – Long Island, NY – NJ – CT-CMSA	4,415	1	61,348	2
Chicago – Gary – Kenosha, IL – IN – WI CMSA	2,074	3	37,048	3
Washington – Baltimore, DC – MD – VA – WV CMSA	1,721	5	35,967	4
San Francisco – Oakland – San Jose, CA CMSA	1,728	4	27,175	5
Detroit – Ann Arbor – Flint, MI CMSA	1,507	8	27,075	6
Philadelphia – Wilmington – Atlantic City, PA – NJ – DE – MD CMSA	1,523	7	27,028	7
Dallas – Fort Worth, TX CMSA	1,613	6	24,431	8
Houston – Galveston – Brazoria, TX CMSA	1,325	11	22,634	9
Boston – Worcester – Lawrence, MA – NH – ME – CT CMSA	1,488	9	22,410	10
Miami – Fort Lauderdale, FL CMSA	1,460	10	19,939	11
Seattle – Tacoma – Bremerton, WA CMSA	1,209	12	17,810	12
Atlanta, GA MSA	1,102	13	17,356	13
Phoenix – Mesa, AZ MSA	761	19	14,512	14
Cleveland – Akron, OH CMSA	932	14	13,829	15
Pittsburgh, PA MSA	890	16	13,264	16
Minneapolis – St. Paul, MN – WI MSA	721	20	13,240	17
Tampa – St. Petersburg – Clearwater, FL MSA	854	17	13,070	18
St. Louis, MO – IL MSA	919	15	13,029	19
San Diego, CA MSA	777	18	13,003	20
Denver – Boulder – Greeley, CO CMSA	705	21	12,037	21

[Continued]

★2443★

Automotive Dealers
[Continued]

MSA	Establish-ments	Rank	Emp-ploy-ment	Rank
Portland – Salem, OR – WA CMSA	700	22	10,943	22
Kansas City, MO – KS MSA	581	25	9,015	23
Milwaukee – Racine, WI CMSA	449	34	8,963	24
Orlando, FL MSA	623	23	8,765	25

Source: U.S. Department of Commerce, Bureau of the Census, Data User Services Division, *1992 Economic Census, Volume 1F, Reports Series, Release 1F,* September 1995, CD-ROM. *Note:* Data are shown only for the top 25 areas.

★2444★

Establishments and Employment

Boat Dealers

The U.S. total number of employees is 27,282; total number of establishments is 4,773.

MSA	Establish-ments	Rank	Emp-ploy-ment	Rank
New York – Northern New Jersey – Long Island, NY – NJ – CT-CMSA	263	1	1,425	1
Miami – Fort Lauderdale, FL CMSA	194	2	1,233	2
Los Angeles – Riverside – Orange County, CA CMSA	142	3	804	3
Detroit – Ann Arbor – Flint, MI CMSA	88	6	753	4
Seattle – Tacoma – Bremerton, WA CMSA	104	5	717	5
Tampa – St. Petersburg – Clearwater, FL MSA	82	7	529	6
Houston – Galveston – Brazoria, TX CMSA	73	9	443	7
Minneapolis – St. Paul, MN – WI MSA	48	12	400	8
Dallas – Fort Worth, TX CMSA	41	15	315	9
Norfolk – Virginia Beach – Newport News, VA – NC MSA	48	12	287	10
Orlando, FL MSA	38	17	241	11
Las Vegas, NV – AZ MSA	21	27	223	12
Cleveland – Akron, OH CMSA	37	18	214	13
San Diego, CA MSA	40	16	210	14
Fort Myers – Cape Coral, FL MSA	33	20	205	15
Grand Rapids – Muskegon – Holland, MI MSA	30	22	199	16
Sarasota – Bradenton, FL MSA	26	24	197	17
St. Louis, MO – IL MSA	35	19	195	18
Milwaukee – Racine, WI CMSA	27	23	192	19
Jacksonville, FL MSA	25	25	177	20
Indianapolis, IN MSA	15	33	176	21
West Palm Beach – Boca Raton, FL MSA	43	13	166	22
New Orleans, LA MSA	32	21	153	23

[Continued]

★2444★

Boat Dealers
[Continued]

MSA	Estab-lish-ments	Rank	Emp-loy-ment	Rank
Charleston – North Charleston, SC MSA	24	26	148	24
Rochester, NY MSA	21	27	145	25

Source: U.S. Department of Commerce, Bureau of the Census, Data User Services Division, *1992 Economic Census, Volume 1F, Reports Series, Release 1F*, September 1995, CD-ROM. *Note:* Data are shown only for the top 25 areas.

★2445★

Establishments and Employment

Book Stores

The U.S. total number of employees is 92,480; total number of establishments is 12,887.

MSA	Estab-lish-ments	Rank	Emp-loy-ment	Rank
New York – Northern New Jersey – Long Island, NY – NJ – CT-CMSA	906	1	7,568	1
Los Angeles – Riverside – Orange County, CA CMSA	724	2	6,249	2
San Francisco – Oakland – San Jose, CA CMSA	460	3	4,582	3
Boston – Worcester – Lawrence, MA – NH – ME – CT CMSA	371	6	3,555	4
Washington – Baltimore, DC – MD – VA – WV CMSA	434	4	3,315	5
Chicago – Gary – Kenosha, IL – IN – WI CMSA	398	5	3,012	6
Philadelphia – Wilmington – Atlantic City, PA – NJ – DE – MD CMSA	331	7	2,129	7
Detroit – Ann Arbor – Flint, MI CMSA	222	9	2,017	8
Seattle – Tacoma – Bremerton, WA CMSA	245	8	1,807	9
Dallas – Fort Worth, TX CMSA	214	10	1,439	10
Atlanta, GA MSA	171	12	1,322	11
San Diego, CA MSA	175	11	1,264	12
Denver – Boulder – Greeley, CO CMSA	159	13	1,224	13
Houston – Galveston – Brazoria, TX CMSA	159	13	1,087	14
Portland – Salem, OR – WA CMSA	136	15	1,035	15
Cleveland – Akron, OH CMSA	122	18	1,014	16
Minneapolis – St. Paul, MN – WI MSA	134	16	1,003	17
Miami – Fort Lauderdale, FL CMSA	150	14	894	18
Phoenix – Mesa, AZ MSA	128	17	786	19
St. Louis, MO – IL MSA	117	19	780	20
Pittsburgh, PA MSA	115	20	744	21
Columbus, OH MSA	81	23	675	22
Kansas City, MO – KS MSA	101	21	669	23

[Continued]

★2445★

Book Stores
[Continued]

MSA	Estab-lish-ments	Rank	Emp-loy-ment	Rank
Hartford, CT MSA	74	25	665	24
Austin – San Marcos, TX MSA	68	28	659	25

Source: U.S. Department of Commerce, Bureau of the Census, Data User Services Division, *1992 Economic Census, Volume 1F, Reports Series, Release 1F*, September 1995, CD-ROM. *Note:* Data are shown only for the top 25 areas.

★2446★

Establishments and Employment

Building Materials and Garden Supplies Stores

The U.S. total number of employees is 665,747; total number of establishments is 69,483.

MSA	Estab-lish-ments	Rank	Emp-loy-ment	Rank
New York – Northern New Jersey – Long Island, NY – NJ – CT-CMSA	4,172	1	35,750	1
Los Angeles – Riverside – Orange County, CA CMSA	2,447	2	29,962	2
Chicago – Gary – Kenosha, IL – IN – WI CMSA	1,773	3	23,422	3
San Francisco – Oakland – San Jose, CA CMSA	1,336	5	17,070	4
Washington – Baltimore, DC – MD – VA – WV CMSA	1,247	7	15,644	5
Detroit – Ann Arbor – Flint, MI CMSA	1,285	6	13,459	6
Philadelphia – Wilmington – Atlantic City, PA – NJ – DE – MD CMSA	1,377	4	12,956	7
Boston – Worcester – Lawrence, MA – NH – ME – CT CMSA	1,239	8	12,678	8
Dallas – Fort Worth, TX CMSA	817	9	9,322	9
Minneapolis – St. Paul, MN – WI MSA	645	16	9,015	10
Seattle – Tacoma – Bremerton, WA CMSA	743	10	8,823	11
Atlanta, GA MSA	706	13	8,278	12
Houston – Galveston – Brazoria, TX CMSA	713	11	8,239	13
Cleveland – Akron, OH CMSA	709	12	7,644	14
Miami – Fort Lauderdale, FL CMSA	691	14	6,848	15
St. Louis, MO – IL MSA	639	17	6,646	16
Tampa – St. Petersburg – Clearwater, FL MSA	544	18	6,293	17
Pittsburgh, PA MSA	663	15	5,870	18
Cincinnati – Hamilton, OH – KY – IN CMSA	473	20	5,846	19
Milwaukee – Racine, WI CMSA	388	25	5,805	20
San Diego, CA MSA	388	25	5,667	21
Denver – Boulder – Greeley, CO CMSA	442	21	5,536	22

[Continued]

★2446★

Building Materials and Garden Supplies Stores

[Continued]

MSA	Estab-lish-ments	Rank	Emp-loy-ment	Rank
Phoenix – Mesa, AZ MSA	397	24	4,947	23
Portland – Salem, OR – WA CMSA	505	19	4,878	24
Sacramento – Yolo, CA CMSA	424	22	4,878	24

Source: U.S. Department of Commerce, Bureau of the Census, Data User Services Division, *1992 Economic Census, Volume 1F, Reports Series, Release 1F,* September 1995, CD-ROM. *Note:* Data are shown only for the top 25 areas.

★2447★

Establishments and Employment

Candy, Nut, and Confectionery Stores

The U.S. total number of employees is 25,504; total number of establishments is 5,029.

MSA	Estab-lish-ments	Rank	Emp-loy-ment	Rank
New York – Northern New Jersey – Long Island, NY – NJ – CT-CMSA	461	1	1,733	1
Los Angeles – Riverside – Orange County, CA CMSA	258	3	1,339	2
Philadelphia – Wilmington – Atlantic City, PA – NJ – DE – MD CMSA	195	4	922	3
San Francisco – Oakland – San Jose, CA CMSA	151	5	833	4
Cleveland – Akron, OH CMSA	106	9	707	5
Pittsburgh, PA MSA	78	11	515	6
Minneapolis – St. Paul, MN – WI MSA	84	10	421	7
Milwaukee – Racine, WI CMSA	59	13	306	8
St. Louis, MO – IL MSA	53	15	304	9
Columbus, OH MSA	44	19	271	10
San Diego, CA MSA	49	17	262	11
Miami – Fort Lauderdale, FL CMSA	55	14	255	12
Norfolk – Virginia Beach – Newport News, VA – NC MSA	32	26	249	13
Buffalo – Niagara Falls, NY MSA	45	18	241	14
Knoxville, TN MSA	29	27	220	15
Las Vegas, NV – AZ MSA	41	20	220	15
Indianapolis, IN MSA	39	22	211	16
Kansas City, MO – KS MSA	40	21	210	17
Honolulu, HI MSA	22	33	191	18
Youngstown – Warren, OH MSA	17	38	186	19
Phoenix – Mesa, AZ MSA	36	24	160	20
Sacramento – Yolo, CA CMSA	35	25	148	21
West Palm Beach – Boca Raton, FL MSA	22	33	148	21
Salt Lake City – Ogden, UT MSA	24	32	137	22
Harrisburg – Lebanon – Carlisle, PA MSA	22	33	133	23

Source: U.S. Department of Commerce, Bureau of the Census, Data User Services Division, *1992 Economic Census, Volume 1F, Reports Series, Release 1F,* September 1995, CD-ROM. *Note:* Data are shown only for the top 25 areas.

★2448★

Establishments and Employment

Children's and Infants' Wear Stores

The U.S. total number of employees is 38,509; total number of establishments is 5,637.

MSA	Estab-lish-ments	Rank	Emp-loy-ment	Rank
Los Angeles – Riverside – Orange County, CA CMSA	408	2	2,711	1
San Francisco – Oakland – San Jose, CA CMSA	155	6	1,199	2
Detroit – Ann Arbor – Flint, MI CMSA	94	9	874	3
Miami – Fort Lauderdale, FL CMSA	134	8	828	4
Dallas – Fort Worth, TX CMSA	90	10	647	5
Houston – Galveston – Brazoria, TX CMSA	72	11	479	6
Atlanta, GA MSA	61	13	448	7
Cleveland – Akron, OH CMSA	53	15	443	8
Minneapolis – St. Paul, MN – WI MSA	50	17	422	9
Pittsburgh, PA MSA	51	16	422	9
St. Louis, MO – IL MSA	49	18	379	10
San Diego, CA MSA	66	12	370	11
Phoenix – Mesa, AZ MSA	50	17	323	12
Buffalo – Niagara Falls, NY MSA	27	26	271	13
Orlando, FL MSA	27	26	262	14
Indianapolis, IN MSA	30	23	251	15
Honolulu, HI MSA	24	28	239	16
Richmond – Petersburg, VA MSA	25	27	236	17
Columbus, OH MSA	21	31	233	18
Sacramento – Yolo, CA CMSA	33	20	231	19
Norfolk – Virginia Beach – Newport News, VA – NC MSA	34	19	218	20
New Orleans, LA MSA	31	22	214	21
Salt Lake City – Ogden, UT MSA	21	31	208	22
Kansas City, MO – KS MSA	27	26	207	23
Providence – Fall River – Warwick, RI – MA MSA	28	25	202	24

Source: U.S. Department of Commerce, Bureau of the Census, Data User Services Division, *1992 Economic Census, Volume 1F, Reports Series, Release 1F,* September 1995, CD-ROM. *Note:* Data are shown only for the top 25 areas.

★2449★

Establishments and Employment

Dairy Products Stores

The U.S. total number of employees is 7,879; total number of establishments is 2,340.

MSA	Estab-lish-ments	Rank	Emp-loy-ment	Rank
Los Angeles – Riverside – Orange County, CA CMSA	185	2	630	1
San Francisco – Oakland – San Jose, CA CMSA	71	5	437	2
Pittsburgh, PA MSA	36	10	167	3
Cleveland – Akron, OH CMSA	40	9	137	4
Syracuse, NY MSA	29	12	137	4

[Continued]

★ 2449 ★

Dairy Products Stores
[Continued]

MSA	Establishments	Rank	Employment	Rank
Phoenix – Mesa, AZ MSA	15	21	95	5
Atlanta, GA MSA	19	17	92	6
Buffalo – Niagara Falls, NY MSA	20	16	70	7
Indianapolis, IN MSA	15	21	61	8
Sarasota – Bradenton, FL MSA	5	29	61	8
Rochester, NY MSA	17	19	50	9
San Diego, CA MSA	21	15	43	10
Minneapolis – St. Paul, MN – WI MSA	22	14	41	11
Allentown – Bethlehem – Easton, PA MSA	9	25	40	12
Providence – Fall River – Warwick, RI – MA MSA	17	19	34	13
Albany – Schenectady – Troy, NY MSA	16	20	33	14
Harrisburg – Lebanon – Carlisle, PA MSA	8	26	31	15
Columbus, OH MSA	10	24	30	16
Milwaukee – Racine, WI CMSA	12	23	29	17
Honolulu, HI MSA	5	29	28	18
Fresno, CA MSA	3	31	26	19
West Palm Beach – Boca Raton, FL MSA	8	26	25	20
Saginaw – Bay City – Midland, MI MSA	8	26	23	21
Louisville, KY – IN MSA	4	30	22	22
Sacramento – Yolo, CA CMSA	5	29	21	23

Source: U.S. Department of Commerce, Bureau of the Census, Data User Services Division, *1992 Economic Census, Volume 1F, Reports Series, Release 1F,* September 1995, CD-ROM. *Note:* Data are shown only for the top 25 areas.

★ 2450 ★

Establishments and Employment

Department Stores (excl. Leased Depts.)

The U.S. total number of employees is 1,719,276; total number of establishments is 11,001.

MSA	Establishments	Rank	Employment	Rank
Los Angeles – Riverside – Orange County, CA CMSA	423	1	83,523	1
Chicago – Gary – Kenosha, IL – IN – WI CMSA	279	3	55,619	2
Detroit – Ann Arbor – Flint, MI CMSA	205	7	49,840	3
Philadelphia – Wilmington – Atlantic City, PA – NJ – DE – MD CMSA	231	5	41,043	4
San Francisco – Oakland – San Jose, CA CMSA	171	9	38,194	5
Dallas – Fort Worth, TX CMSA	176	8	32,336	6
Boston – Worcester – Lawrence, MA – NH – ME – CT CMSA	224	6	29,869	7

[Continued]

★ 2450 ★

Department Stores (excl. Leased Depts.)
[Continued]

MSA	Establishments	Rank	Employment	Rank
Houston – Galveston – Brazoria, TX CMSA	152	10	27,930	8
Atlanta, GA MSA	138	11	27,363	9
Minneapolis – St. Paul, MN – WI MSA	110	15	25,019	10
Pittsburgh, PA MSA	124	12	21,668	11
St. Louis, MO – IL MSA	119	13	20,949	12
Miami – Fort Lauderdale, FL CMSA	93	18	19,332	13
Cleveland – Akron, OH CMSA	114	14	19,282	14
Phoenix – Mesa, AZ MSA	87	21	15,720	15
Kansas City, MO – KS MSA	88	20	15,501	16
Tampa – St. Petersburg – Clearwater, FL MSA	97	16	14,389	17
San Diego, CA MSA	75	26	14,290	18
Indianapolis, IN MSA	84	22	13,871	19
Portland – Salem, OR – WA CMSA	78	25	13,399	20
Columbus, OH MSA	65	27	12,571	21
Dayton – Springfield, OH MSA	57	31	10,641	22
Grand Rapids – Muskegon – Holland, MI MSA	43	40	10,356	23
Orlando, FL MSA	63	28	10,326	24
Buffalo – Niagara Falls, NY MSA	60	29	10,226	25

Source: U.S. Department of Commerce, Bureau of the Census, Data User Services Division, *1992 Economic Census, Volume 1F, Reports Series, Release 1F,* September 1995, CD-ROM. *Note:* Data are shown only for the top 25 areas.

★ 2451 ★

Establishments and Employment

Discount Or Mass Merchandising (excl. Leased Depts.)

The U.S. total number of employees is 899,398; total number of establishments is 6,737.

MSA	Establishments	Rank	Employment	Rank
Atlanta, GA MSA	86	9	0[1]	14
Boston – Worcester – Lawrence, MA – NH – ME – CT CMSA	163	2	0[1]	14
Chicago – Gary – Kenosha, IL – IN – WI CMSA	148	4	22,695	2
Cincinnati – Hamilton, OH – KY – IN CMSA	48	19	0[2]	14
Cleveland – Akron, OH CMSA	67	13	7,789	11
Dallas – Fort Worth, TX CMSA	88	8	15,483	3
Denver – Boulder – Greeley, CO CMSA	41	20	7,909	10
Detroit – Ann Arbor – Flint, MI CMSA	122	6	30,888	1
Houston – Galveston – Brazoria, TX CMSA	80	11	0[1]	14
Los Angeles – Riverside – Orange County, CA CMSA	161	3	0[3]	14

[Continued]

★ 2451 ★

Discount Or Mass Merchandising (excl. Leased Depts.)

[Continued]

MSA	Establishments	Rank	Employment	Rank
Miami – Fort Lauderdale, FL CMSA	35	22	0[2]	14
Minneapolis – St. Paul, MN – WI MSA	58	14	11,962	5
New York – Northern New Jersey – Long Island, NY – NJ – CT-CMSA	204	1	0[3]	14
Philadelphia – Wilmington – Atlantic City, PA – NJ – DE – MD CMSA	147	5	0[1]	14
Phoenix – Mesa, AZ MSA	40	21	0[2]	14
Pittsburgh, PA MSA	74	12	8,274	9
Portland – Salem, OR – WA CMSA	52	17	9,022	7
San Diego, CA MSA	28	23	5,142	13
San Francisco – Oakland – San Jose, CA CMSA	53	16	8,572	8
Seattle – Tacoma – Bremerton, WA CMSA	51	18	9,054	6
St. Louis, MO – IL MSA	84	10	11,971	4
Tampa – St. Petersburg – Clearwater, FL MSA	55	15	7,751	12
Washington – Baltimore, DC – MD – VA – WV CMSA	116	7	0[1]	14

Source: U.S. Department of Commerce, Bureau of the Census, Data User Services Division, *1992 Economic Census, Volume 1F, Reports Series, Release 1F,* September 1995, CD-ROM. *Notes:* 1. 10,000-24,999 employees. 2. 5,000-9,999 employees. 3. 25,000-49,999 employees.

★ 2452 ★

Establishments and Employment

Drug and Proprietary Stores

The U.S. total number of employees is 587,943; total number of establishments is 48,142.

MSA	Establishments	Rank	Employment	Rank
New York – Northern New Jersey – Long Island, NY – NJ – CT-CMSA	4,554	1	46,421	1
Los Angeles – Riverside – Orange County, CA CMSA	2,177	2	29,160	2
Chicago – Gary – Kenosha, IL – IN – WI CMSA	1,452	3	26,511	3
San Francisco – Oakland – San Jose, CA CMSA	843	8	16,811	4
Boston – Worcester – Lawrence, MA – NH – ME – CT CMSA	1,098	5	16,320	5
Philadelphia – Wilmington – Atlantic City, PA – NJ – DE – MD CMSA	1,388	4	16,151	6
Washington – Baltimore, DC – MD – VA – WV CMSA	1,029	6	15,411	7

[Continued]

★ 2452 ★

Drug and Proprietary Stores

[Continued]

MSA	Establishments	Rank	Employment	Rank
Detroit – Ann Arbor – Flint, MI CMSA	968	7	15,085	8
Miami – Fort Lauderdale, FL CMSA	795	9	10,811	9
Cleveland – Akron, OH CMSA	500	14	9,170	10
Dallas – Fort Worth, TX CMSA	588	11	7,984	11
Houston – Galveston – Brazoria, TX CMSA	532	13	7,679	12
Atlanta, GA MSA	617	10	7,272	13
Seattle – Tacoma – Bremerton, WA CMSA	468	15	7,231	14
Pittsburgh, PA MSA	577	12	7,054	15
Minneapolis – St. Paul, MN – WI MSA	376	16	6,255	16
Tampa – St. Petersburg – Clearwater, FL MSA	355	18	5,591	17
San Diego, CA MSA	331	20	4,976	18
St. Louis, MO – IL MSA	369	17	4,972	19
Phoenix – Mesa, AZ MSA	274	21	4,812	20
Milwaukee – Racine, WI CMSA	267	23	4,788	21
Cincinnati – Hamilton, OH – KY – IN CMSA	338	19	4,478	22
Buffalo – Niagara Falls, NY MSA	256	24	4,030	23
New Orleans, LA MSA	245	26	3,795	24
Indianapolis, IN MSA	245	26	3,595	25

Source: U.S. Department of Commerce, Bureau of the Census, Data User Services Division, *1992 Economic Census, Volume 1F, Reports Series, Release 1F,* September 1995, CD-ROM. *Note:* Data are shown only for the top 25 areas.

★ 2453 ★

Establishments and Employment

Eating and Drinking Places

The U.S. total number of employees is 6,547,908; total number of establishments is 433,608.

MSA	Establishments	Rank	Employment	Rank
Los Angeles – Riverside – Orange County, CA CMSA	22,449	2	375,055	1
New York – Northern New Jersey – Long Island, NY – NJ – CT-CMSA	33,648	1	358,575	2
Chicago – Gary – Kenosha, IL – IN – WI CMSA	14,361	3	221,253	3
Washington – Baltimore, DC – MD – VA – WV CMSA	11,229	5	187,619	4
San Francisco – Oakland – San Jose, CA CMSA	12,432	4	179,334	5
Boston – Worcester – Lawrence, MA – NH – ME – CT CMSA	10,152	6	148,896	6
Detroit – Ann Arbor – Flint, MI CMSA	8,335	8	146,506	7
Philadelphia – Wilmington – Atlantic City, PA – NJ – DE – MD CMSA	10,132	7	133,134	8

[Continued]

★2453★

Eating and Drinking Places
[Continued]

MSA	Estab-lish-ments	Rank	Emp-loy-ment	Rank
Dallas – Fort Worth, TX CMSA	6,675	9	119,090	9
Atlanta, GA MSA	5,600	13	104,837	10
Houston – Galveston – Brazoria, TX CMSA	5,677	11	103,932	11
Seattle – Tacoma – Bremerton, WA CMSA	5,981	10	92,990	12
Miami – Fort Lauderdale, FL CMSA	5,649	12	89,945	13
Minneapolis – St. Paul, MN – WI MSA	4,001	18	85,127	14
Cleveland – Akron, OH CMSA	5,311	14	82,366	15
St. Louis, MO – IL MSA	4,392	16	79,477	16
San Diego, CA MSA	4,245	17	72,231	17
Phoenix – Mesa, AZ MSA	3,978	19	69,395	18
Pittsburgh, PA MSA	4,449	15	66,083	19
Denver – Boulder – Greeley, CO CMSA	3,813	20	65,949	20
Tampa – St. Petersburg – Clearwater, FL MSA	3,445	22	60,323	21
Cincinnati – Hamilton, OH – KY – IN CMSA	3,236	23	59,545	22
Portland – Salem, OR – WA CMSA	3,515	21	55,645	23
Indianapolis, IN MSA	2,504	28	48,341	24
Orlando, FL MSA	2,192	32	48,161	25

Source: U.S. Department of Commerce, Bureau of the Census, Data User Services Division, *1992 Economic Census, Volume 1F, Reports Series, Release 1F,* September 1995, CD-ROM. *Note:* Data are shown only for the top 25 areas.

★2454★

Establishments and Employment

Family Clothing Stores

The U.S. total number of employees is 309,516; total number of establishments is 19,452.

MSA	Estab-lish-ments	Rank	Emp-loy-ment	Rank
Los Angeles – Riverside – Orange County, CA CMSA	932	2	17,358	1
Chicago – Gary – Kenosha, IL – IN – WI CMSA	591	3	12,218	2
San Francisco – Oakland – San Jose, CA CMSA	510	5	11,635	3
Boston – Worcester – Lawrence, MA – NH – ME – CT CMSA	478	6	10,787	4
Washington – Baltimore, DC – MD – VA – WV CMSA	552	4	10,709	5
Seattle – Tacoma – Bremerton, WA CMSA	221	12	6,648	6
Philadelphia – Wilmington – Atlantic City, PA – NJ – DE – MD CMSA	387	7	6,278	7
Miami – Fort Lauderdale, FL CMSA	354	8	5,527	8

[Continued]

★2454★

Family Clothing Stores
[Continued]

MSA	Estab-lish-ments	Rank	Emp-loy-ment	Rank
Houston – Galveston – Brazoria, TX CMSA	300	10	5,101	9
Dallas – Fort Worth, TX CMSA	305	9	5,035	10
Detroit – Ann Arbor – Flint, MI CMSA	286	11	4,690	11
Atlanta, GA MSA	194	14	4,321	12
San Diego, CA MSA	178	15	3,885	13
Portland – Salem, OR – WA CMSA	140	20	3,804	14
Minneapolis – St. Paul, MN – WI MSA	213	13	3,189	15
Sacramento – Yolo, CA CMSA	84	32	2,991	16
Tampa – St. Petersburg – Clearwater, FL MSA	164	16	2,929	17
St. Louis, MO – IL MSA	156	18	2,390	18
Phoenix – Mesa, AZ MSA	161	17	2,314	19
Cleveland – Akron, OH CMSA	149	19	2,269	20
San Antonio, TX MSA	108	25	2,195	21
Orlando, FL MSA	126	24	2,090	22
Hartford, CT MSA	85	31	2,084	23
Pittsburgh, PA MSA	138	21	2,052	24
Birmingham, AL MSA	59	45	1,884	25

Source: U.S. Department of Commerce, Bureau of the Census, Data User Services Division, *1992 Economic Census, Volume 1F, Reports Series, Release 1F,* September 1995, CD-ROM. *Note:* Data are shown only for the top 25 areas.

★2455★

Establishments and Employment

Florists

The U.S. total number of employees is 122,114; total number of establishments is 27,341.

MSA	Estab-lish-ments	Rank	Emp-loy-ment	Rank
New York – Northern New Jersey – Long Island, NY – NJ – CT-CMSA	2,015	1	7,631	1
Los Angeles – Riverside – Orange County, CA CMSA	1,245	2	5,931	2
Washington – Baltimore, DC – MD – VA – WV CMSA	653	4	4,006	3
Philadelphia – Wilmington – Atlantic City, PA – NJ – DE – MD CMSA	594	6	2,902	4
San Francisco – Oakland – San Jose, CA CMSA	598	5	2,789	5
Detroit – Ann Arbor – Flint, MI CMSA	492	8	2,630	6
Boston – Worcester – Lawrence, MA – NH – ME – CT CMSA	580	7	2,398	7
Seattle – Tacoma – Bremerton, WA CMSA	349	11	1,894	8
Dallas – Fort Worth, TX CMSA	388	9	1,838	9
Pittsburgh, PA MSA	344	12	1,758	10

[Continued]

★ 2455 ★

Florists
[Continued]

MSA	Estab-lish-ments	Rank	Emp-loy-ment	Rank
Minneapolis – St. Paul, MN – WI MSA	247	16	1,653	11
Atlanta, GA MSA	339	13	1,547	12
Houston – Galveston – Brazoria, TX CMSA	328	14	1,401	13
Cleveland – Akron, OH CMSA	293	15	1,340	14
Miami – Fort Lauderdale, FL CMSA	351	10	1,272	15
St. Louis, MO – IL MSA	239	17	1,134	16
San Diego, CA MSA	239	17	1,079	17
Phoenix – Mesa, AZ MSA	182	23	942	18
Denver – Boulder – Greeley, CO CMSA	207	19	932	19
Tampa – St. Petersburg – Clearwater, FL MSA	232	18	921	20
Portland – Salem, OR – WA CMSA	187	21	897	21
Indianapolis, IN MSA	170	24	878	22
Cincinnati – Hamilton, OH – KY – IN CMSA	189	20	862	23
Columbus, OH MSA	127	31	832	24
Kansas City, MO – KS MSA	186	22	817	25

Source: U.S. Department of Commerce, Bureau of the Census, Data User Services Division, *1992 Economic Census, Volume 1F, Reports Series, Release 1F,* September 1995, CD-ROM. *Note:* Data are shown only for the top 25 areas.

★ 2456 ★

Establishments and Employment

Food Stores

The U.S. total number of employees is 2,969,317; total number of establishments is 180,568.

MSA	Estab-lish-ments	Rank	Emp-loy-ment	Rank
New York – Northern New Jersey – Long Island, NY – NJ – CT-CMSA	18,120	1	206,005	1
Los Angeles – Riverside – Orange County, CA CMSA	7,791	2	128,529	2
Chicago – Gary – Kenosha, IL – IN – WI CMSA	4,821	3	92,410	3
Boston – Worcester – Lawrence, MA – NH – ME – CT CMSA	3,973	7	79,074	4
Washington – Baltimore, DC – MD – VA – WV CMSA	4,307	6	76,150	5
Philadelphia – Wilmington – Atlantic City, PA – NJ – DE – MD CMSA	4,433	4	69,832	6
San Francisco – Oakland – San Jose, CA CMSA	4,380	5	67,875	7
Houston – Galveston – Brazoria, TX CMSA	2,842	9	52,306	8
Detroit – Ann Arbor – Flint, MI CMSA	3,839	8	50,737	9

[Continued]

★ 2456 ★

Food Stores
[Continued]

MSA	Estab-lish-ments	Rank	Emp-loy-ment	Rank
Dallas – Fort Worth, TX CMSA	2,464	10	44,888	10
Miami – Fort Lauderdale, FL CMSA	2,392	11	44,423	11
Atlanta, GA MSA	1,764	14	39,940	12
Cleveland – Akron, OH CMSA	2,108	12	35,213	13
Seattle – Tacoma – Bremerton, WA CMSA	2,059	13	34,299	14
Pittsburgh, PA MSA	1,571	15	33,672	15
Phoenix – Mesa, AZ MSA	1,260	21	29,224	16
Tampa – St. Petersburg – Clearwater, FL MSA	1,433	17	28,348	17
Minneapolis – St. Paul, MN – WI MSA	1,316	20	28,177	18
St. Louis, MO – IL MSA	1,396	18	27,886	19
Denver – Boulder – Greeley, CO CMSA	915	25	24,406	20
Cincinnati – Hamilton, OH – KY – IN CMSA	1,317	19	23,727	21
San Diego, CA MSA	1,516	16	22,718	22
Buffalo – Niagara Falls, NY MSA	836	29	20,219	23
Portland – Salem, OR – WA CMSA	1,247	22	19,881	24
Milwaukee – Racine, WI CMSA	866	27	19,439	25

Source: U.S. Department of Commerce, Bureau of the Census, Data User Services Division, *1992 Economic Census, Volume 1F, Reports Series, Release 1F,* September 1995, CD-ROM. *Note:* Data are shown only for the top 25 areas.

★ 2457 ★

Establishments and Employment

Fruit and Vegetable Markets

The U.S. total number of employees is 16,258; total number of establishments is 2,971.

MSA	Estab-lish-ments	Rank	Emp-loy-ment	Rank
Detroit – Ann Arbor – Flint, MI CMSA	83	6	1,448	1
Chicago – Gary – Kenosha, IL – IN – WI CMSA	100	5	887	2
Boston – Worcester – Lawrence, MA – NH – ME – CT CMSA	79	7	790	3
Los Angeles – Riverside – Orange County, CA CMSA	122	3	755	4
San Francisco – Oakland – San Jose, CA CMSA	113	4	722	5
Tampa – St. Petersburg – Clearwater, FL MSA	38	10	433	6
Miami – Fort Lauderdale, FL CMSA	59	9	371	7
Cleveland – Akron, OH CMSA	32	14	262	8
Pittsburgh, PA MSA	37	11	225	9
Lancaster, PA MSA	23	17	213	10
West Palm Beach – Boca Raton, FL MSA	24	16	171	11

[Continued]

★ 2457 ★

Fruit and Vegetable Markets

[Continued]

MSA	Estab-lish-ments	Rank	Emp-loy-ment	Rank
St. Louis, MO – IL MSA	35	13	170	12
Houston – Galveston – Brazoria, TX CMSA	12	26	168	13
Milwaukee – Racine, WI CMSA	18	21	165	14
Memphis, TN – AR – MS MSA	14	24	145	15
Providence – Fall River – Warwick, RI – MA MSA	22	18	131	16
Atlanta, GA MSA	22	18	130	17
San Diego, CA MSA	26	15	128	18
Springfield, MA MSA	7	30	127	19
Seattle – Tacoma – Bremerton, WA CMSA	36	12	125	20
Saginaw – Bay City – Midland, MI MSA	11	27	104	21
Buffalo – Niagara Falls, NY MSA	16	22	88	22
Orlando, FL MSA	20	20	87	23
Albuquerque, NM MSA	10	28	81	24
Honolulu, HI MSA	15	23	72	25

Source: U.S. Department of Commerce, Bureau of the Census, Data User Services Division, *1992 Economic Census, Volume 1F, Reports Series, Release 1F,* September 1995, CD-ROM. *Note:* Data are shown only for the top 25 areas.

★ 2458 ★

Establishments and Employment

Fuel Dealers

The U.S. total number of employees is 81,506; total number of establishments is 10,973.

MSA	Estab-lish-ments	Rank	Emp-loy-ment	Rank
New York – Northern New Jersey – Long Island, NY – NJ – CT-CMSA	1,189	1	13,463	1
Boston – Worcester – Lawrence, MA – NH – ME – CT CMSA	620	2	5,088	2
Philadelphia – Wilmington – Atlantic City, PA – NJ – DE – MD CMSA	370	3	3,710	3
Washington – Baltimore, DC – MD – VA – WV CMSA	174	4	2,003	4
Hartford, CT MSA	151	6	1,240	5
Providence – Fall River – Warwick, RI – MA MSA	153	5	1,159	6
Albany – Schenectady – Troy, NY MSA	72	10	683	7
Detroit – Ann Arbor – Flint, MI CMSA	84	7	590	8
Allentown – Bethlehem – Easton, PA MSA	69	12	589	9
Harrisburg – Lebanon – Carlisle, PA MSA	66	14	566	10
Reading, PA MSA	32	31	556	11
Seattle – Tacoma – Bremerton, WA CMSA	59	16	555	12

[Continued]

★ 2458 ★

Fuel Dealers

[Continued]

MSA	Estab-lish-ments	Rank	Emp-loy-ment	Rank
Springfield, MA MSA	68	13	548	13
Richmond – Petersburg, VA MSA	44	26	493	14
Scranton – Wilkes-Barre – Hazleton, PA MSA	75	9	493	14
Lancaster, PA MSA	27	35	463	15
Dallas – Fort Worth, TX CMSA	71	11	448	16
Cincinnati – Hamilton, OH – KY – IN CMSA	60	15	438	17
New London – Norwich, CT – RI MSA	41	27	429	18
Norfolk – Virginia Beach – Newport News, VA – NC MSA	49	22	429	18
Atlanta, GA MSA	55	19	406	19
Portland, ME MSA	29	33	405	20
Greensboro – Winston-Salem – High Point, NC MSA	54	20	400	21
Jacksonville, FL MSA	48	23	337	22
St. Louis, MO – IL MSA	60	15	337	22

Source: U.S. Department of Commerce, Bureau of the Census, Data User Services Division, *1992 Economic Census, Volume 1F, Reports Series, Release 1F,* September 1995, CD-ROM. *Note:* Data are shown only for the top 25 areas.

★ 2459 ★

Establishments and Employment

Furniture and Homefurnishings Stores

The U.S. total number of employees is 702,164; total number of establishments is 110,073.

MSA	Estab-lish-ments	Rank	Emp-loy-ment	Rank
New York – Northern New Jersey – Long Island, NY – NJ – CT-CMSA	8,487	1	52,094	1
Los Angeles – Riverside – Orange County, CA CMSA	5,984	2	45,019	2
Chicago – Gary – Kenosha, IL – IN – WI CMSA	3,446	3	26,871	3
Washington – Baltimore, DC – MD – VA – WV CMSA	3,265	4	24,128	4
San Francisco – Oakland – San Jose, CA CMSA	3,211	5	22,923	5
Philadelphia – Wilmington – Atlantic City, PA – NJ – DE – MD CMSA	2,418	6	15,447	6
Detroit – Ann Arbor – Flint, MI CMSA	1,878	9	14,814	7
Boston – Worcester – Lawrence, MA – NH – ME – CT CMSA	2,299	7	14,502	8
Dallas – Fort Worth, TX CMSA	1,646	10	12,499	9
Miami – Fort Lauderdale, FL CMSA	1,884	8	11,363	10
Seattle – Tacoma – Bremerton, WA CMSA	1,631	11	10,861	11

[Continued]

★2459★

Furniture and Homefurnishings Stores
[Continued]

MSA	Estab-lish-ments	Rank	Emp-ploy-ment	Rank
Houston – Galveston – Brazoria, TX CMSA	1,380	13	10,507	12
Atlanta, GA MSA	1,442	12	9,263	13
Minneapolis – St. Paul, MN – WI MSA	1,107	16	8,507	14
San Diego, CA MSA	1,128	15	8,064	15
Cleveland – Akron, OH CMSA	1,211	14	7,834	16
St. Louis, MO – IL MSA	1,052	19	7,405	17
Denver – Boulder – Greeley, CO CMSA	1,062	18	6,943	18
Phoenix – Mesa, AZ MSA	1,046	20	6,652	19
Tampa – St. Petersburg – Clearwater, FL MSA	1,078	17	6,651	20
Pittsburgh, PA MSA	959	21	6,041	21
Portland – Salem, OR – WA CMSA	889	22	5,974	22
Milwaukee – Racine, WI CMSA	689	24	5,345	23
Sacramento – Yolo, CA CMSA	662	28	4,969	24
Norfolk – Virginia Beach – Newport News, VA – NC MSA	631	30	4,824	25

Source: U.S. Department of Commerce, Bureau of the Census, Data User Services Division, *1992 Economic Census, Volume 1F, Reports Series, Release 1F,* September 1995, CD-ROM. *Note:* Data are shown only for the top 25 areas.

★2460★

Establishments and Employment

Gasoline Service Stations

The U.S. total number of employees is 675,080; total number of establishments is 105,334.

MSA	Estab-lish-ments	Rank	Emp-ploy-ment	Rank
New York – Northern New Jersey – Long Island, NY – NJ – CT-CMSA	6,367	1	29,029	1
Los Angeles – Riverside – Orange County, CA CMSA	3,883	2	25,080	2
Chicago – Gary – Kenosha, IL – IN – WI CMSA	2,526	3	18,062	3
Washington – Baltimore, DC – MD – VA – WV CMSA	2,224	4	17,111	4
Detroit – Ann Arbor – Flint, MI CMSA	2,032	6	13,997	5
Philadelphia – Wilmington – Atlantic City, PA – NJ – DE – MD CMSA	1,994	7	12,227	6
Boston – Worcester – Lawrence, MA – NH – ME – CT CMSA	2,170	5	12,082	7
San Francisco – Oakland – San Jose, CA CMSA	1,700	8	12,032	8
Minneapolis – St. Paul, MN – WI MSA	1,090	15	11,032	9
Dallas – Fort Worth, TX CMSA	1,618	9	9,445	10
Atlanta, GA MSA	1,317	10	8,384	11

[Continued]

★2460★

Gasoline Service Stations
[Continued]

MSA	Estab-lish-ments	Rank	Emp-ploy-ment	Rank
Cleveland – Akron, OH CMSA	1,164	13	8,173	12
St. Louis, MO – IL MSA	1,101	14	7,872	13
Houston – Galveston – Brazoria, TX CMSA	1,272	11	6,730	14
Pittsburgh, PA MSA	938	16	6,461	15
Seattle – Tacoma – Bremerton, WA CMSA	856	17	6,409	16
Miami – Fort Lauderdale, FL CMSA	1,176	12	6,210	17
Phoenix – Mesa, AZ MSA	587	25	5,409	18
Denver – Boulder – Greeley, CO CMSA	739	19	5,112	19
Cincinnati – Hamilton, OH – KY – IN CMSA	705	20	5,106	20
Tampa – St. Petersburg – Clearwater, FL MSA	805	18	5,048	21
San Diego, CA MSA	598	24	4,974	22
Milwaukee – Racine, WI CMSA	615	23	4,623	23
Portland – Salem, OR – WA CMSA	544	28	4,556	24
Indianapolis, IN MSA	620	22	4,452	25

Source: U.S. Department of Commerce, Bureau of the Census, Data User Services Division, *1992 Economic Census, Volume 1F, Reports Series, Release 1F,* September 1995, CD-ROM. *Note:* Data are shown only for the top 25 areas.

★2461★

Establishments and Employment

General Merchandise Stores

The U.S. total number of employees is 2,078,530; total number of establishments is 34,606.

MSA	Estab-lish-ments	Rank	Emp-ploy-ment	Rank
New York – Northern New Jersey – Long Island, NY – NJ – CT-CMSA	2,238	1	120,076	1
Los Angeles – Riverside – Orange County, CA CMSA	1,097	2	102,722	2
Chicago – Gary – Kenosha, IL – IN – WI CMSA	833	3	64,897	3
Detroit – Ann Arbor – Flint, MI CMSA	512	7	55,775	4
Washington – Baltimore, DC – MD – VA – WV CMSA	718	5	50,671	5
Philadelphia – Wilmington – Atlantic City, PA – NJ – DE – MD CMSA	768	4	49,646	6
San Francisco – Oakland – San Jose, CA CMSA	454	9	47,553	7
Boston – Worcester – Lawrence, MA – NH – ME – CT CMSA	633	6	39,157	8
Dallas – Fort Worth, TX CMSA	504	8	37,994	9
Houston – Galveston – Brazoria, TX CMSA	387	10	32,398	10

[Continued]

★2461★

General Merchandise Stores
[Continued]

MSA	Establishments	Rank	Employment	Rank
Atlanta, GA MSA	376	11	31,871	11
Minneapolis–St. Paul, MN–WI MSA	253	16	27,791	12
Miami–Fort Lauderdale, FL CMSA	345	12	25,220	13
Pittsburgh, PA MSA	289	14	24,523	14
St. Louis, MO–IL MSA	281	15	23,720	15
Cleveland–Akron, OH CMSA	322	13	23,455	16
Seattle–Tacoma–Bremerton, WA CMSA	239	18	22,580	17
Phoenix–Mesa, AZ MSA	174	27	18,528	18
Denver–Boulder–Greeley, CO CMSA	180	26	18,348	19
Kansas City, MO–KS MSA	190	23	17,803	20
San Diego, CA MSA	192	22	17,382	21
Tampa–St. Petersburg–Clearwater, FL MSA	240	17	16,984	22
Cincinnati–Hamilton, OH–KY–IN CMSA	196	20	16,837	23
Portland–Salem, OR–WA CMSA	188	24	16,604	24
Milwaukee–Racine, WI CMSA	158	31	16,248	25

Source: U.S. Department of Commerce, Bureau of the Census, Data User Services Division, *1992 Economic Census, Volume 1F, Reports Series, Release 1F,* September 1995, CD-ROM. *Note:* Data are shown only for the top 25 areas.

★2462★

Establishments and Employment

Grocery Stores

The U.S. total number of employees is 2,682,153; total number of establishments is 133,263.

MSA	Establishments	Rank	Employment	Rank
New York–Northern New Jersey–Long Island, NY–NJ–CT-CMSA	11,490	1	171,896	1
Los Angeles–Riverside–Orange County, CA CMSA	4,593	2	109,843	2
Chicago–Gary–Kenosha, IL–IN–WI CMSA	3,013	4	78,861	3
Washington–Baltimore, DC–MD–VA–WV CMSA	3,143	3	68,143	4
Philadelphia–Wilmington–Atlantic City, PA–NJ–DE–MD CMSA	2,849	5	60,194	5
San Francisco–Oakland–San Jose, CA CMSA	2,652	7	55,559	6
Houston–Galveston–Brazoria, TX CMSA	2,280	9	49,272	7
Detroit–Ann Arbor–Flint, MI CMSA	2,707	6	42,605	8
Dallas–Fort Worth, TX CMSA	1,927	10	42,292	9
Miami–Fort Lauderdale, FL CMSA	1,636	11	40,096	10

[Continued]

★2462★

Grocery Stores
[Continued]

MSA	Establishments	Rank	Employment	Rank
Atlanta, GA MSA	1,385	14	37,650	11
Cleveland–Akron, OH CMSA	1,417	13	30,956	12
Seattle–Tacoma–Bremerton, WA CMSA	1,492	12	30,471	13
Pittsburgh, PA MSA	1,053	16	29,461	14
Phoenix–Mesa, AZ MSA	960	20	27,292	15
Tampa–St. Petersburg–Clearwater, FL MSA	1,099	15	26,240	16
St. Louis, MO–IL MSA	965	18	24,961	17
Minneapolis–St. Paul, MN–WI MSA	802	23	24,413	18
Denver–Boulder–Greeley, CO CMSA	590	33	22,037	19
Cincinnati–Hamilton, OH–KY–IN CMSA	918	21	20,621	20
San Diego, CA MSA	1,000	17	19,445	21
Buffalo–Niagara Falls, NY MSA	534	38	18,102	22
Portland–Salem, OR–WA CMSA	963	19	18,023	23
Orlando, FL MSA	657	25	17,047	24
San Antonio, TX MSA	648	27	16,927	25

Source: U.S. Department of Commerce, Bureau of the Census, Data User Services Division, *1992 Economic Census, Volume 1F, Reports Series, Release 1F,* September 1995, CD-ROM. *Note:* Data are shown only for the top 25 areas.

★2463★

Establishments and Employment

Hardware Stores

The U.S. total number of employees is 136,230; total number of establishments is 18,984.

MSA	Establishments	Rank	Employment	Rank
New York–Northern New Jersey–Long Island, NY–NJ–CT-CMSA	1,393	1	6,865	1
Chicago–Gary–Kenosha, IL–IN–WI CMSA	618	2	6,856	2
San Francisco–Oakland–San Jose, CA CMSA	332	7	5,211	3
Los Angeles–Riverside–Orange County, CA CMSA	542	3	3,945	4
Detroit–Ann Arbor–Flint, MI CMSA	414	4	3,495	5
St. Louis, MO–IL MSA	168	14	2,433	6
Seattle–Tacoma–Bremerton, WA CMSA	189	13	2,370	7
Minneapolis–St. Paul, MN–WI MSA	226	9	2,065	8
Milwaukee–Racine, WI CMSA	131	15	1,743	9
Cincinnati–Hamilton, OH–KY–IN CMSA	127	16	1,711	10
Atlanta, GA MSA	189	13	1,517	11
Houston–Galveston–Brazoria, TX CMSA	189	13	1,491	12

[Continued]

★2463★

Hardware Stores

[Continued]

MSA	Estab- lish- ments	Rank	Emp- ploy- ment	Rank
Cleveland – Akron, OH CMSA	197	12	1,449	13
Pittsburgh, PA MSA	217	10	1,418	14
Dallas – Fort Worth, TX CMSA	189	13	1,376	15
Indianapolis, IN MSA	102	19	1,273	16
Denver – Boulder – Greeley, CO CMSA	113	18	1,179	17
Columbus, OH MSA	73	30	1,028	18
Miami – Fort Lauderdale, FL CMSA	198	11	1,014	19
Kansas City, MO – KS MSA	117	17	1,002	20
Memphis, TN – AR – MS MSA	48	43	906	21
Portland – Salem, OR – WA CMSA	101	20	841	22
Phoenix – Mesa, AZ MSA	88	25	834	23
Tampa – St. Petersburg – Clearwater, FL MSA	117	17	772	24
Grand Rapids – Muskegon – Holland, MI MSA	89	24	740	25

Source: U.S. Department of Commerce, Bureau of the Census, Data User Services Division, *1992 Economic Census, Volume 1F, Reports Series, Release 1F,* September 1995, CD-ROM. *Note:* Data are shown only for the top 25 areas.

★2464★

Establishments and Employment

Home and Auto Supply Stores

The U.S. total number of employees is 13,308; total number of establishments is 2,154.

MSA	Estab- lish- ments	Rank	Emp- ploy- ment	Rank
New York – Northern New Jersey – Long Island, NY – NJ – CT-CMSA	49	2	184	1
Tampa – St. Petersburg – Clearwater, FL MSA	16	12	138	2
Houston – Galveston – Brazoria, TX CMSA	24	5	114	3
Washington – Baltimore, DC – MD – VA – WV CMSA	16	12	109	4
Phoenix – Mesa, AZ MSA	13	15	88	5
Miami – Fort Lauderdale, FL CMSA	25	4	87	6
Charlotte – Gastonia – Rock Hill, NC – SC MSA	13	15	85	7
Pittsburgh, PA MSA	20	9	81	8
Atlanta, GA MSA	25	4	79	9
Dallas – Fort Worth, TX CMSA	22	7	77	10
St. Louis, MO – IL MSA	18	11	76	11
Greenville – Spartanburg – Anderson, SC MSA	19	10	70	12
Philadelphia – Wilmington – Atlantic City, PA – NJ – DE – MD CMSA	8	20	69	13
Kansas City, MO – KS MSA	9	19	68	14

[Continued]

★2464★

Home and Auto Supply Stores

[Continued]

MSA	Estab- lish- ments	Rank	Emp- ploy- ment	Rank
New Orleans, LA MSA	15	13	66	15
San Francisco – Oakland – San Jose, CA CMSA	11	17	64	16
Greensboro – Winston-Salem – High Point, NC MSA	14	14	58	17
Indianapolis, IN MSA	7	21	55	18
San Antonio, TX MSA	12	16	53	19
Minneapolis – St. Paul, MN – WI MSA	8	20	48	20
Charleston – North Charleston, SC MSA	8	20	47	21
Memphis, TN – AR – MS MSA	11	17	46	22
Birmingham, AL MSA	7	21	45	23
San Diego, CA MSA	10	18	42	24
Lakeland – Winter Haven, FL MSA	5	23	39	25

Source: U.S. Department of Commerce, Bureau of the Census, Data User Services Division, *1992 Economic Census, Volume 1F, Reports Series, Release 1F,* September 1995, CD-ROM. *Note:* Data are shown only for the top 25 areas.

★2465★

Establishments and Employment

Household Appliance Stores

The U.S. total number of employees is 53,782; total number of establishments is 9,743.

MSA	Estab- lish- ments	Rank	Emp- ploy- ment	Rank
Los Angeles – Riverside – Orange County, CA CMSA	359	2	2,468	1
Chicago – Gary – Kenosha, IL – IN – WI CMSA	197	6	1,628	2
San Francisco – Oakland – San Jose, CA CMSA	204	4	1,072	3
Seattle – Tacoma – Bremerton, WA CMSA	151	8	990	4
Miami – Fort Lauderdale, FL CMSA	102	11	783	5
Detroit – Ann Arbor – Flint, MI CMSA	112	10	653	6
Tampa – St. Petersburg – Clearwater, FL MSA	77	17	608	7
Sacramento – Yolo, CA CMSA	57	24	552	8
Cleveland – Akron, OH CMSA	90	14	534	9
Dallas – Fort Worth, TX CMSA	120	9	530	10
Houston – Galveston – Brazoria, TX CMSA	101	12	525	11
Atlanta, GA MSA	88	16	498	12
San Diego, CA MSA	68	20	497	13
Portland – Salem, OR – WA CMSA	65	21	467	14
Phoenix – Mesa, AZ MSA	72	19	461	15
St. Louis, MO – IL MSA	94	13	449	16
Minneapolis – St. Paul, MN – WI MSA	89	15	389	17

[Continued]

★2465★

Household Appliance Stores

[Continued]

MSA	Estab-lish-ments	Rank	Emp-ploy-ment	Rank
Indianapolis, IN MSA	57	24	369	18
Pittsburgh, PA MSA	74	18	368	19
Buffalo – Niagara Falls, NY MSA	54	25	355	20
Grand Rapids – Muskegon – Holland, MI MSA	38	34	353	21
Charlotte – Gastonia – Rock Hill, NC – SC MSA	52	26	341	22
Nashville, TN MSA	50	27	320	23
Rochester, NY MSA	29	40	310	24
Kansas City, MO – KS MSA	54	25	287	25

Source: U.S. Department of Commerce, Bureau of the Census, Data User Services Division, *1992 Economic Census, Volume 1F, Reports Series, Release 1F,* September 1995, CD-ROM. *Note:* Data are shown only for the top 25 areas.

★2466★

Establishments and Employment

Jewelry Stores

The U.S. total number of employees is 147,888; total number of establishments is 28,077.

MSA	Estab-lish-ments	Rank	Emp-ploy-ment	Rank
New York – Northern New Jersey – Long Island, NY – NJ – CT-CMSA	2,622	1	12,261	1
Los Angeles – Riverside – Orange County, CA CMSA	1,485	2	7,358	2
Chicago – Gary – Kenosha, IL – IN – WI CMSA	819	3	4,928	3
Washington – Baltimore, DC – MD – VA – WV CMSA	801	4	4,730	4
San Francisco – Oakland – San Jose, CA CMSA	798	5	3,865	5
Boston – Worcester – Lawrence, MA – NH – ME – CT CMSA	614	8	3,661	6
Philadelphia – Wilmington – Atlantic City, PA – NJ – DE – MD CMSA	705	6	3,392	7
Detroit – Ann Arbor – Flint, MI CMSA	547	9	3,013	8
Dallas – Fort Worth, TX CMSA	471	10	2,586	9
Houston – Galveston – Brazoria, TX CMSA	423	11	2,550	10
Miami – Fort Lauderdale, FL CMSA	632	7	2,247	11
Atlanta, GA MSA	335	12	1,819	12
Cleveland – Akron, OH CMSA	298	13	1,734	13
Honolulu, HI MSA	272	16	1,713	14
St. Louis, MO – IL MSA	262	18	1,602	15
Seattle – Tacoma – Bremerton, WA CMSA	268	17	1,474	16
Minneapolis – St. Paul, MN – WI MSA	259	19	1,469	17

[Continued]

★2466★

Jewelry Stores

[Continued]

MSA	Estab-lish-ments	Rank	Emp-ploy-ment	Rank
Phoenix – Mesa, AZ MSA	268	17	1,449	18
San Diego, CA MSA	288	14	1,405	19
Tampa – St. Petersburg – Clearwater, FL MSA	281	15	1,383	20
Pittsburgh, PA MSA	247	20	1,272	21
Cincinnati – Hamilton, OH – KY – IN CMSA	201	22	1,226	22
Denver – Boulder – Greeley, CO CMSA	214	21	1,211	23
Milwaukee – Racine, WI CMSA	194	24	1,110	24
New Orleans, LA MSA	181	25	1,055	25

Source: U.S. Department of Commerce, Bureau of the Census, Data User Services Division, *1992 Economic Census, Volume 1F, Reports Series, Release 1F,* September 1995, CD-ROM. *Note:* Data are shown only for the top 25 areas.

★2467★

Establishments and Employment

Liquor Stores

The U.S. total number of employees is 132,989; total number of establishments is 31,386.

MSA	Estab-lish-ments	Rank	Emp-ploy-ment	Rank
New York – Northern New Jersey – Long Island, NY – NJ – CT-CMSA	3,269	1	11,901	1
Washington – Baltimore, DC – MD – VA – WV CMSA	1,263	3	7,441	2
Boston – Worcester – Lawrence, MA – NH – ME – CT CMSA	1,031	5	6,846	3
Los Angeles – Riverside – Orange County, CA CMSA	1,852	2	6,164	4
Philadelphia – Wilmington – Atlantic City, PA – NJ – DE – MD CMSA	921	6	4,962	5
Chicago – Gary – Kenosha, IL – IN – WI CMSA	1,041	4	4,851	6
Minneapolis – St. Paul, MN – WI MSA	407	11	3,128	7
San Francisco – Oakland – San Jose, CA CMSA	711	7	2,846	8
Detroit – Ann Arbor – Flint, MI CMSA	619	8	2,374	9
Dallas – Fort Worth, TX CMSA	418	10	2,255	10
Denver – Boulder – Greeley, CO CMSA	436	9	1,740	11
Atlanta, GA MSA	358	13	1,699	12
Cleveland – Akron, OH CMSA	322	15	1,538	13
Miami – Fort Lauderdale, FL CMSA	298	17	1,326	14
Indianapolis, IN MSA	252	20	1,309	15
Providence – Fall River – Warwick, RI – MA MSA	240	21	1,223	16

[Continued]

★2467★

Liquor Stores

[Continued]

MSA	Estab-lish-ments	Rank	Emp-loy-ment	Rank
Pittsburgh, PA MSA	328	14	1,104	17
San Diego, CA MSA	300	16	1,094	18
Houston – Galveston – Brazoria, TX CMSA	404	12	1,039	19
St. Louis, MO – IL MSA	228	22	1,030	20
Hartford, CT MSA	281	18	983	21
Cincinnati – Hamilton, OH – KY – IN CMSA	222	23	920	22
Milwaukee – Racine, WI CMSA	196	24	916	23
Springfield, MA MSA	136	32	916	23
Kansas City, MO – KS MSA	262	19	891	24

Source: U.S. Department of Commerce, Bureau of the Census, Data User Services Division, *1992 Economic Census, Volume 1F, Reports Series, Release 1F,* September 1995, CD-ROM. *Note:* Data are shown only for the top 25 areas.

★2468★

Establishments and Employment

Lumber and Other Building Materials Dealers

The U.S. total number of employees is 386,260; total number of establishments is 25,401.

MSA	Estab-lish-ments	Rank	Emp-loy-ment	Rank
Los Angeles – Riverside – Orange County, CA CMSA	928	2	19,635	1
Washington – Baltimore, DC – MD – VA – WV CMSA	435	7	9,396	2
San Francisco – Oakland – San Jose, CA CMSA	481	5	8,151	3
Philadelphia – Wilmington – Atlantic City, PA – NJ – DE – MD CMSA	488	4	7,611	4
Detroit – Ann Arbor – Flint, MI CMSA	413	8	6,765	5
Minneapolis – St. Paul, MN – WI MSA	209	15	5,442	6
Dallas – Fort Worth, TX CMSA	235	12	5,117	7
Miami – Fort Lauderdale, FL CMSA	222	13	4,697	8
Atlanta, GA MSA	201	17	4,687	9
Houston – Galveston – Brazoria, TX CMSA	203	16	4,641	10
Cleveland – Akron, OH CMSA	240	10	4,611	11
Seattle – Tacoma – Bremerton, WA CMSA	280	9	4,437	12
Tampa – St. Petersburg – Clearwater, FL MSA	156	21	4,190	13
San Diego, CA MSA	146	22	3,928	14
Denver – Boulder – Greeley, CO CMSA	158	20	3,319	15
Pittsburgh, PA MSA	219	14	3,225	16
Sacramento – Yolo, CA CMSA	173	19	3,039	17
Phoenix – Mesa, AZ MSA	123	27	2,930	18

[Continued]

★2468★

Lumber and Other Building Materials Dealers

[Continued]

MSA	Estab-lish-ments	Rank	Emp-loy-ment	Rank
St. Louis, MO – IL MSA	236	11	2,851	19
Milwaukee – Racine, WI CMSA	120	28	2,718	20
Orlando, FL MSA	118	29	2,628	21
Portland – Salem, OR – WA CMSA	182	18	2,606	22
Indianapolis, IN MSA	105	33	2,499	23
Kansas City, MO – KS MSA	128	26	2,398	24
Norfolk – Virginia Beach – Newport News, VA – NC MSA	99	35	2,396	25

Source: U.S. Department of Commerce, Bureau of the Census, Data User Services Division, *1992 Economic Census, Volume 1F, Reports Series, Release 1F,* September 1995, CD-ROM. *Note:* Data are shown only for the top 25 areas.

★2469★

Establishments and Employment

Manufactured (mobile) Home Dealers

The U.S. total number of employees is 22,814; total number of establishments is 4,053.

MSA	Estab-lish-ments	Rank	Emp-loy-ment	Rank
Pittsburgh, PA MSA	33	9	394	1
Seattle – Tacoma – Bremerton, WA CMSA	48	4	386	2
Portland – Salem, OR – WA CMSA	40	6	358	3
Los Angeles – Riverside – Orange County, CA CMSA	103	1	347	4
Detroit – Ann Arbor – Flint, MI CMSA	59	2	303	5
Greenville – Spartanburg – Anderson, SC MSA	40	6	255	6
Dallas – Fort Worth, TX CMSA	45	5	249	7
Tampa – St. Petersburg – Clearwater, FL MSA	51	3	240	8
Phoenix – Mesa, AZ MSA	39	7	235	9
Greensboro – Winston-Salem – High Point, NC MSA	40	6	206	10
Las Vegas, NV – AZ MSA	48	4	205	11
Grand Rapids – Muskegon – Holland, MI MSA	28	13	199	12
St. Louis, MO – IL MSA	39	7	198	13
Charlotte – Gastonia – Rock Hill, NC – SC MSA	34	8	196	14
Orlando, FL MSA	32	10	196	14
Atlanta, GA MSA	27	14	195	15
Knoxville, TN MSA	21	19	186	16
Houston – Galveston – Brazoria, TX CMSA	30	12	174	17
Fort Myers – Cape Coral, FL MSA	11	29	172	18
Dover, DE MSA	13	27	168	19
Lakeland – Winter Haven, FL MSA	23	17	145	20
Nashville, TN MSA	22	18	140	21
Columbus, OH MSA	17	23	137	22

[Continued]

★2469★

Manufactured (mobile) Home Dealers
[Continued]

MSA	Estab-lish-ments	Rank	Emp-loy-ment	Rank
Charleston – North Charleston, SC MSA	17	23	136	23
Augusta – Aiken, GA – SC MSA	25	15	131	24

Source: U.S. Department of Commerce, Bureau of the Census, Data User Services Division, *1992 Economic Census, Volume 1F, Reports Series, Release 1F,* September 1995, CD-ROM. *Note:* Data are shown only for the top 25 areas.

★2470★

Establishments and Employment

Men's and Boys' Clothing and Accessory Stores

The U.S. total number of employees is 104,520; total number of establishments is 15,566.

MSA	Estab-lish-ments	Rank	Emp-loy-ment	Rank
Los Angeles – Riverside – Orange County, CA CMSA	991	2	6,993	1
Chicago – Gary – Kenosha, IL – IN – WI CMSA	658	3	4,691	2
San Francisco – Oakland – San Jose, CA CMSA	468	5	3,328	3
Philadelphia – Wilmington – Atlantic City, PA – NJ – DE – MD CMSA	442	6	3,075	4
Detroit – Ann Arbor – Flint, MI CMSA	356	8	2,452	5
Miami – Fort Lauderdale, FL CMSA	349	9	1,990	6
Dallas – Fort Worth, TX CMSA	262	10	1,757	7
Houston – Galveston – Brazoria, TX CMSA	219	11	1,662	8
Atlanta, GA MSA	208	12	1,567	9
Cleveland – Akron, OH CMSA	190	13	1,446	10
San Diego, CA MSA	171	14	1,263	11
Seattle – Tacoma – Bremerton, WA CMSA	147	16	1,163	12
Minneapolis – St. Paul, MN – WI MSA	147	16	1,110	13
St. Louis, MO – IL MSA	159	15	1,093	14
Pittsburgh, PA MSA	145	17	989	15
Norfolk – Virginia Beach – Newport News, VA – NC MSA	118	18	891	16
Buffalo – Niagara Falls, NY MSA	80	30	799	17
New Orleans, LA MSA	97	22	768	18
Denver – Boulder – Greeley, CO CMSA	118	18	753	19
Milwaukee – Racine, WI CMSA	96	23	752	20
Memphis, TN – AR – MS MSA	87	25	720	21
Richmond – Petersburg, VA MSA	82	28	717	22
Phoenix – Mesa, AZ MSA	113	20	705	23

[Continued]

★2470★

Men's and Boys' Clothing and Accessory Stores
[Continued]

MSA	Estab-lish-ments	Rank	Emp-loy-ment	Rank
Cincinnati – Hamilton, OH – KY – IN CMSA	111	21	691	24
Columbus, OH MSA	70	34	674	25

Source: U.S. Department of Commerce, Bureau of the Census, Data User Services Division, *1992 Economic Census, Volume 1F, Reports Series, Release 1F,* September 1995, CD-ROM. *Note:* Data are shown only for the top 25 areas.

★2471★

Establishments and Employment

Musical Instrument Stores

The U.S. total number of employees is 23,605; total number of establishments is 4,149.

MSA	Estab-lish-ments	Rank	Emp-loy-ment	Rank
Los Angeles – Riverside – Orange County, CA CMSA	227	1	1,427	1
San Francisco – Oakland – San Jose, CA CMSA	126	4	714	2
Seattle – Tacoma – Bremerton, WA CMSA	91	6	514	3
Dallas – Fort Worth, TX CMSA	64	10	511	4
Detroit – Ann Arbor – Flint, MI CMSA	69	9	499	5
Minneapolis – St. Paul, MN – WI MSA	41	19	448	6
Houston – Galveston – Brazoria, TX CMSA	57	12	391	7
Miami – Fort Lauderdale, FL CMSA	53	13	308	8
Cleveland – Akron, OH CMSA	50	14	290	9
Atlanta, GA MSA	60	11	276	10
San Diego, CA MSA	49	15	262	11
Denver – Boulder – Greeley, CO CMSA	46	16	260	12
St. Louis, MO – IL MSA	32	23	227	13
Tampa – St. Petersburg – Clearwater, FL MSA	37	20	227	13
Kansas City, MO – KS MSA	32	23	210	14
Salt Lake City – Ogden, UT MSA	27	25	199	15
Pittsburgh, PA MSA	36	21	176	16
Nashville, TN MSA	27	25	170	17
Columbus, OH MSA	23	27	168	18
Phoenix – Mesa, AZ MSA	44	18	163	19
Louisville, KY – IN MSA	26	26	159	20
Indianapolis, IN MSA	27	25	156	21
Madison, WI MSA	10	40	150	22
Tucson, AZ MSA	19	31	147	23
Charlotte – Gastonia – Rock Hill, NC – SC MSA	23	27	143	24

Source: U.S. Department of Commerce, Bureau of the Census, Data User Services Division, *1992 Economic Census, Volume 1F, Reports Series, Release 1F,* September 1995, CD-ROM. *Note:* Data are shown only for the top 25 areas.

★2472★
Establishments and Employment
National Chain (excl. Leased Depts.)

The U.S. total number of employees is 335,216; total number of establishments is 1,876.

MSA	Establishments	Rank	Employment	Rank
Atlanta, GA MSA	13	18	0[1]	6
Boston–Worcester–Lawrence, MA–NH–ME–CT CMSA	28	10	0[2]	6
Chicago–Gary–Kenosha, IL–IN–WI CMSA	66	3	0[3]	6
Cincinnati–Hamilton, OH–KY–IN CMSA	11	19	0[4]	6
Cleveland–Akron, OH CMSA	18	14	0[1]	6
Dallas–Fort Worth, TX CMSA	38	6	6,597	2
Denver–Boulder–Greeley, CO CMSA	25	11	0[1]	6
Detroit–Ann Arbor–Flint, MI CMSA	36	7	0[2]	6
Houston–Galveston–Brazoria, TX CMSA	31	8	0[2]	6
Los Angeles–Riverside–Orange County, CA CMSA	93	1	0[3]	6
Miami–Fort Lauderdale, FL CMSA	25	11	0[2]	6
Minneapolis–St. Paul, MN–WI MSA	21	13	5,072	3
New York–Northern New Jersey–Long Island, NY–NJ–CT-CMSA	68	2	0[3]	6
Philadelphia–Wilmington–Atlantic City, PA–NJ–DE–MD CMSA	31	8	0[2]	6
Phoenix–Mesa, AZ MSA	18	14	0[1]	6
Pittsburgh, PA MSA	29	9	0[2]	6
Portland–Salem, OR–WA CMSA	14	17	0[4]	6
San Diego, CA MSA	15	16	3,272	5
San Francisco–Oakland–San Jose, CA CMSA	44	5	8,328	1
Seattle–Tacoma–Bremerton, WA CMSA	17	15	0[1]	6
St. Louis, MO–IL MSA	14	17	0[1]	6
Tampa–St. Petersburg–Clearwater, FL MSA	23	12	3,602	4
Washington–Baltimore, DC–MD–VA–WV CMSA	58	4	0[3]	6

Source: U.S. Department of Commerce, Bureau of the Census, Data User Services Division, *1992 Economic Census, Volume 1F, Reports Series, Release 1F*, September 1995, CD-ROM. *Notes:* 1. 2,500-4,999 employees. 2. 5,000-9,999 employees. 3. 10,000-24,999 employees. 4. 1,000-2,499 employees.

★2473★
Establishments and Employment
New and Used Car Dealers

The U.S. total number of employees is 860,139; total number of establishments is 24,380.

MSA	Establishments	Rank	Employment	Rank
New York–Northern New Jersey–Long Island, NY–NJ–CT-CMSA	1,448	1	46,155	1
Los Angeles–Riverside–Orange County, CA CMSA	886	2	44,584	2
Chicago–Gary–Kenosha, IL–IN–WI CMSA	656	3	27,801	3
Washington–Baltimore, DC–MD–VA–WV CMSA	482	6	27,098	4
Philadelphia–Wilmington–Atlantic City, PA–NJ–DE–MD CMSA	535	5	20,467	5
Detroit–Ann Arbor–Flint, MI CMSA	380	8	19,177	6
San Francisco–Oakland–San Jose, CA CMSA	463	7	18,532	7
Boston–Worcester–Lawrence, MA–NH–ME–CT CMSA	540	4	17,250	8
Dallas–Fort Worth, TX CMSA	247	12	16,101	9
Houston–Galveston–Brazoria, TX CMSA	212	16	14,889	10
Miami–Fort Lauderdale, FL CMSA	189	17	13,354	11
Atlanta, GA MSA	239	13	12,178	12
Seattle–Tacoma–Bremerton, WA CMSA	225	14	10,951	13
Pittsburgh, PA MSA	309	9	10,038	14
Cleveland–Akron, OH CMSA	257	11	9,838	15
Minneapolis–St. Paul, MN–WI MSA	219	15	9,562	16
Phoenix–Mesa, AZ MSA	138	23	9,456	17
St. Louis, MO–IL MSA	258	10	9,071	18
San Diego, CA MSA	164	19	8,695	19
Tampa–St. Petersburg–Clearwater, FL MSA	133	24	8,684	20
Denver–Boulder–Greeley, CO CMSA	138	23	8,255	21
Portland–Salem, OR–WA CMSA	146	21	7,290	22
Milwaukee–Racine, WI CMSA	139	22	6,905	23
Kansas City, MO–KS MSA	167	18	6,468	24
Cincinnati–Hamilton, OH–KY–IN CMSA	155	20	6,238	25

Source: U.S. Department of Commerce, Bureau of the Census, Data User Services Division, *1992 Economic Census, Volume 1F, Reports Series, Release 1F*, September 1995, CD-ROM. *Note:* Data are shown only for the top 25 areas.

★2474★

Establishments and Employment

Paint, Glass, and Wallpaper Stores

The U.S. total number of employees is 48,944; total number of establishments is 10,188.

MSA	Establishments	Rank	Employment	Rank
Los Angeles – Riverside – Orange County, CA CMSA	527	2	3,364	1
San Francisco – Oakland – San Jose, CA CMSA	265	4	1,671	2
Philadelphia – Wilmington – Atlantic City, PA – NJ – DE – MD CMSA	259	5	1,041	3
Washington – Baltimore, DC – MD – VA – WV CMSA	192	7	934	4
Detroit – Ann Arbor – Flint, MI CMSA	166	8	881	5
Dallas – Fort Worth, TX CMSA	152	10	702	6
Houston – Galveston – Brazoria, TX CMSA	146	11	671	7
Miami – Fort Lauderdale, FL CMSA	156	9	661	8
Atlanta, GA MSA	138	12	633	9
Seattle – Tacoma – Bremerton, WA CMSA	95	16	588	10
San Diego, CA MSA	96	15	581	11
Minneapolis – St. Paul, MN – WI MSA	78	23	558	12
Cleveland – Akron, OH CMSA	117	13	550	13
Sacramento – Yolo, CA CMSA	79	22	545	14
Portland – Salem, OR – WA CMSA	88	18	478	15
Denver – Boulder – Greeley, CO CMSA	90	17	444	16
Phoenix – Mesa, AZ MSA	73	25	419	17
Tampa – St. Petersburg – Clearwater, FL MSA	105	14	400	18
Pittsburgh, PA MSA	82	20	391	19
Indianapolis, IN MSA	76	24	387	20
Louisville, KY – IN MSA	60	27	367	21
Kansas City, MO – KS MSA	80	21	362	22
St. Louis, MO – IL MSA	82	20	354	23
Columbus, OH MSA	76	24	298	24
Milwaukee – Racine, WI CMSA	61	26	288	25

Source: U.S. Department of Commerce, Bureau of the Census, Data User Services Division, *1992 Economic Census, Volume 1F, Reports Series, Release 1F,* September 1995, CD-ROM. *Note:* Data are shown only for the top 25 areas.

★2475★

Establishments and Employment

Pet Shops

The U.S. total number of employees is 38,408; total number of establishments is 7,160.

MSA	Establishments	Rank	Employment	Rank
Los Angeles – Riverside – Orange County, CA CMSA	501	2	2,894	1
San Francisco – Oakland – San Jose, CA CMSA	265	4	1,329	2
Detroit – Ann Arbor – Flint, MI CMSA	192	6	1,232	3
Philadelphia – Wilmington – Atlantic City, PA – NJ – DE – MD CMSA	174	8	1,191	4
Boston – Worcester – Lawrence, MA – NH – ME – CT CMSA	177	7	1,037	5
Seattle – Tacoma – Bremerton, WA CMSA	137	9	896	6
Dallas – Fort Worth, TX CMSA	117	12	765	7
Minneapolis – St. Paul, MN – WI MSA	105	14	710	8
San Diego, CA MSA	121	11	620	9
Houston – Galveston – Brazoria, TX CMSA	102	15	546	10
Phoenix – Mesa, AZ MSA	60	23	523	11
Cleveland – Akron, OH CMSA	84	18	510	12
Miami – Fort Lauderdale, FL CMSA	123	10	495	13
St. Louis, MO – IL MSA	74	20	474	14
Columbus, OH MSA	48	29	448	15
Atlanta, GA MSA	89	16	428	16
Portland – Salem, OR – WA CMSA	83	19	426	17
Indianapolis, IN MSA	56	24	417	18
Tampa – St. Petersburg – Clearwater, FL MSA	87	17	414	19
Pittsburgh, PA MSA	61	22	407	20
Sacramento – Yolo, CA CMSA	63	21	338	21
Norfolk – Virginia Beach – Newport News, VA – NC MSA	50	28	326	22
Kansas City, MO – KS MSA	54	25	276	23
Dayton – Springfield, OH MSA	21	43	252	24
Orlando, FL MSA	54	25	225	25

Source: U.S. Department of Commerce, Bureau of the Census, Data User Services Division, *1992 Economic Census, Volume 1F, Reports Series, Release 1F,* September 1995, CD-ROM. *Note:* Data are shown only for the top 25 areas.

★2476★

Establishments and Employment

Radio, Television, Computer, and Music Stores

The U.S. total number of employees is 235,010; total number of establishments is 34,835.

MSA	Estab- lish- ments	Rank	Emp- ploy- ment	Rank
Los Angeles – Riverside – Orange County, CA CMSA	2,205	2	20,619	1
New York – Northern New Jersey – Long Island, NY – NJ – CT-CMSA	2,611	1	16,055	2
San Francisco – Oakland – San Jose, CA CMSA	1,167	4	11,010	3
Chicago – Gary – Kenosha, IL – IN – WI CMSA	1,238	3	9,807	4
Washington – Baltimore, DC – MD – VA – WV CMSA	1,125	5	8,739	5
Detroit – Ann Arbor – Flint, MI CMSA	660	8	5,205	6
Dallas – Fort Worth, TX CMSA	637	9	5,186	7
Philadelphia – Wilmington – Atlantic City, PA – NJ – DE – MD CMSA	765	6	5,064	8
Boston – Worcester – Lawrence, MA – NH – ME – CT CMSA	740	7	4,500	9
Miami – Fort Lauderdale, FL CMSA	624	10	4,106	10
Houston – Galveston – Brazoria, TX CMSA	519	12	4,084	11
Seattle – Tacoma – Bremerton, WA CMSA	540	11	3,710	12
San Diego, CA MSA	405	14	3,532	13
Minneapolis – St. Paul, MN – WI MSA	341	19	3,298	14
Atlanta, GA MSA	471	13	3,121	15
Denver – Boulder – Greeley, CO CMSA	399	15	3,043	16
St. Louis, MO – IL MSA	324	20	2,655	17
Cleveland – Akron, OH CMSA	368	16	2,502	18
Phoenix – Mesa, AZ MSA	351	17	2,472	19
Tampa – St. Petersburg – Clearwater, FL MSA	348	18	2,216	20
Milwaukee – Racine, WI CMSA	220	26	2,125	21
Pittsburgh, PA MSA	312	21	1,957	22
Sacramento – Yolo, CA CMSA	209	27	1,949	23
Kansas City, MO – KS MSA	240	24	1,825	24
Portland – Salem, OR – WA CMSA	294	22	1,742	25

Source: U.S. Department of Commerce, Bureau of the Census, Data User Services Division, *1992 Economic Census, Volume 1F, Reports Series, Release 1F*, September 1995, CD-ROM. *Note:* Data are shown only for the top 25 areas.

★2477★

Establishments and Employment

Recreational Vehicle Dealers

The U.S. total number of employees is 22,304; total number of establishments is 2,826.

MSA	Estab- lish- ments	Rank	Emp- ploy- ment	Rank
Los Angeles – Riverside – Orange County, CA CMSA	147	1	1,685	1
Seattle – Tacoma – Bremerton, WA CMSA	61	3	668	2
Portland – Salem, OR – WA CMSA	56	4	559	3
San Diego, CA MSA	39	8	481	4
Phoenix – Mesa, AZ MSA	50	5	477	5
Tampa – St. Petersburg – Clearwater, FL MSA	41	7	445	6
Dallas – Fort Worth, TX CMSA	47	6	370	7
Boston – Worcester – Lawrence, MA – NH – ME – CT CMSA	35	9	299	8
New York – Northern New Jersey – Long Island, NY – NJ – CT-CMSA	47	6	289	9
Philadelphia – Wilmington – Atlantic City, PA – NJ – DE – MD CMSA	32	11	273	10
Orlando, FL MSA	18	18	231	11
Las Vegas, NV – AZ MSA	18	18	230	12
Salt Lake City – Ogden, UT MSA	19	17	208	13
Knoxville, TN MSA	12	23	203	14
Houston – Galveston – Brazoria, TX CMSA	27	13	189	15
Grand Rapids – Muskegon – Holland, MI MSA	25	14	183	16
Cleveland – Akron, OH CMSA	24	15	175	17
Fresno, CA MSA	10	25	169	18
Albuquerque, NM MSA	12	23	165	19
Atlanta, GA MSA	15	20	161	20
St. Louis, MO – IL MSA	23	16	159	21
Minneapolis – St. Paul, MN – WI MSA	23	16	157	22
Oklahoma City, OK MSA	9	26	157	22
Indianapolis, IN MSA	10	25	151	23
Sarasota – Bradenton, FL MSA	15	20	144	24

Source: U.S. Department of Commerce, Bureau of the Census, Data User Services Division, *1992 Economic Census, Volume 1F, Reports Series, Release 1F*, September 1995, CD-ROM. *Note:* Data are shown only for the top 25 areas.

★2478★

Establishments and Employment

Retail Trade

The U.S. total number of employees is 18,407,453; total number of establishments is 1,526,215.

MSA	Estab-lish-ments	Rank	Emp-loy-ment	Rank
New York – Northern New Jersey – Long Island, NY – NJ – CT-CMSA	120,935	1	1,161,530	1
Los Angeles – Riverside – Orange County, CA CMSA	72,769	2	959,019	2
Chicago – Gary – Kenosha, IL – IN – WI CMSA	45,100	3	622,698	3
Washington – Baltimore, DC – MD – VA – WV CMSA	38,945	4	522,560	4
San Francisco – Oakland – San Jose, CA CMSA	38,002	5	476,338	5
Boston – Worcester – Lawrence, MA – NH – ME – CT CMSA	33,782	7	429,170	6
Philadelphia – Wilmington – Atlantic City, PA – NJ – DE – MD CMSA	35,113	6	417,777	7
Detroit – Ann Arbor – Flint, MI CMSA	28,695	8	397,173	8
Dallas – Fort Worth, TX CMSA	23,215	9	316,098	9
Houston – Galveston – Brazoria, TX CMSA	20,249	11	286,439	10
Atlanta, GA MSA	18,542	13	267,388	11
Miami – Fort Lauderdale, FL CMSA	22,380	10	262,885	12
Seattle – Tacoma – Bremerton, WA CMSA	18,764	12	241,092	13
Minneapolis – St. Paul, MN – WI MSA	14,398	17	228,203	14
Cleveland – Akron, OH CMSA	16,955	14	220,464	15
St. Louis, MO – IL MSA	14,400	16	200,277	16
Pittsburgh, PA MSA	14,551	15	191,305	17
Phoenix – Mesa, AZ MSA	12,380	20	180,472	18
San Diego, CA MSA	13,683	18	179,885	19
Tampa – St. Petersburg – Clearwater, FL MSA	12,736	19	170,989	20
Denver – Boulder – Greeley, CO CMSA	12,375	21	168,360	21
Cincinnati – Hamilton, OH – KY – IN CMSA	10,497	23	149,337	22
Portland – Salem, OR – WA CMSA	10,886	22	143,751	23
Milwaukee – Racine, WI CMSA	9,220	25	133,200	24
Kansas City, MO – KS MSA	9,233	24	130,446	25

Source: U.S. Department of Commerce, Bureau of the Census, Data User Services Division, *1992 Economic Census, Volume 1F, Reports Series, Release 1F,* September 1995, CD-ROM. *Note:* Data are shown only for the top 25 areas.

★2479★

Establishments and Employment

Shoe Stores

The U.S. total number of employees is 184,415; total number of establishments is 37,206.

MSA	Estab-lish-ments	Rank	Emp-loy-ment	Rank
New York – Northern New Jersey – Long Island, NY – NJ – CT-CMSA	3,297	1	16,548	1
Los Angeles – Riverside – Orange County, CA CMSA	2,024	2	10,580	2
Chicago – Gary – Kenosha, IL – IN – WI CMSA	1,286	3	7,534	3
Washington – Baltimore, DC – MD – VA – WV CMSA	1,195	4	6,708	4
Philadelphia – Wilmington – Atlantic City, PA – NJ – DE – MD CMSA	1,048	5	5,066	5
San Francisco – Oakland – San Jose, CA CMSA	865	7	4,350	6
Detroit – Ann Arbor – Flint, MI CMSA	796	8	4,200	7
Boston – Worcester – Lawrence, MA – NH – ME – CT CMSA	871	6	4,183	8
Miami – Fort Lauderdale, FL CMSA	753	9	3,795	9
Dallas – Fort Worth, TX CMSA	618	10	3,305	10
Houston – Galveston – Brazoria, TX CMSA	528	11	2,798	11
Atlanta, GA MSA	479	12	2,635	12
Cleveland – Akron, OH CMSA	468	13	2,372	13
St. Louis, MO – IL MSA	375	16	2,016	14
Pittsburgh, PA MSA	399	15	1,933	15
San Diego, CA MSA	358	17	1,871	16
Minneapolis – St. Paul, MN – WI MSA	339	19	1,813	17
Denver – Boulder – Greeley, CO CMSA	354	18	1,566	18
Tampa – St. Petersburg – Clearwater, FL MSA	303	21	1,515	19
Phoenix – Mesa, AZ MSA	331	20	1,510	20
Milwaukee – Racine, WI CMSA	240	25	1,471	21
Cincinnati – Hamilton, OH – KY – IN CMSA	291	22	1,460	22
Seattle – Tacoma – Bremerton, WA CMSA	405	14	1,460	22
Indianapolis, IN MSA	189	34	1,399	23
Charlotte – Gastonia – Rock Hill, NC – SC MSA	219	26	1,307	24

Source: U.S. Department of Commerce, Bureau of the Census, Data User Services Division, *1992 Economic Census, Volume 1F, Reports Series, Release 1F,* September 1995, CD-ROM. *Note:* Data are shown only for the top 25 areas.

★2480★

Establishments and Employment

Sporting Goods Stores and Bicycle Shops

The U.S. total number of employees is 137,417; total number of establishments is 23,314.

MSA	Estab-lish-ments	Rank	Emp-loy-ment	Rank
Los Angeles – Riverside – Orange County, CA CMSA	1,056	2	8,938	1
New York – Northern New Jersey – Long Island, NY – NJ – CT-CMSA	1,367	1	8,305	2
San Francisco – Oakland – San Jose, CA CMSA	703	3	5,251	3
Chicago – Gary – Kenosha, IL – IN – WI CMSA	632	5	4,503	4
Washington – Baltimore, DC – MD – VA – WV CMSA	634	4	4,309	5
Detroit – Ann Arbor – Flint, MI CMSA	471	8	3,311	6
Boston – Worcester – Lawrence, MA – NH – ME – CT CMSA	484	6	3,185	7
Philadelphia – Wilmington – Atlantic City, PA – NJ – DE – MD CMSA	478	7	3,091	8
Seattle – Tacoma – Bremerton, WA CMSA	397	9	3,078	9
Minneapolis – St. Paul, MN – WI MSA	332	11	2,731	10
Houston – Galveston – Brazoria, TX CMSA	319	13	2,471	11
Denver – Boulder – Greeley, CO CMSA	308	14	2,332	12
Miami – Fort Lauderdale, FL CMSA	349	10	2,244	13
Dallas – Fort Worth, TX CMSA	323	12	1,869	14
San Diego, CA MSA	277	15	1,869	14
Phoenix – Mesa, AZ MSA	232	17	1,545	15
Cleveland – Akron, OH CMSA	261	16	1,440	16
St. Louis, MO – IL MSA	218	20	1,432	17
Salt Lake City – Ogden, UT MSA	145	27	1,398	18
Sacramento – Yolo, CA CMSA	188	21	1,386	19
Pittsburgh, PA MSA	221	19	1,368	20
Atlanta, GA MSA	224	18	1,322	21
Portland – Salem, OR – WA CMSA	187	22	1,251	22
Milwaukee – Racine, WI CMSA	151	25	1,019	23
Indianapolis, IN MSA	128	29	956	24

Source: U.S. Department of Commerce, Bureau of the Census, Data User Services Division, *1992 Economic Census, Volume 1F, Reports Series, Release 1F*, September 1995, CD-ROM. *Note:* Data are shown only for the top 25 areas.

★2481★

Establishments and Employment

Used Car Dealers

The U.S. total number of employees is 62,793; total number of establishments is 18,672.

MSA	Estab-lish-ments	Rank	Emp-loy-ment	Rank
New York – Northern New Jersey – Long Island, NY – NJ – CT-CMSA	747	1	1,918	1
Los Angeles – Riverside – Orange County, CA CMSA	425	2	1,753	2
Chicago – Gary – Kenosha, IL – IN – WI CMSA	375	4	1,474	3
Dallas – Fort Worth, TX CMSA	390	3	1,372	4
Houston – Galveston – Brazoria, TX CMSA	287	6	1,166	5
Miami – Fort Lauderdale, FL CMSA	321	5	1,039	6
Seattle – Tacoma – Bremerton, WA CMSA	216	10	950	7
Phoenix – Mesa, AZ MSA	142	20	901	8
Washington – Baltimore, DC – MD – VA – WV CMSA	259	7	884	9
Philadelphia – Wilmington – Atlantic City, PA – NJ – DE – MD CMSA	256	9	870	10
Tampa – St. Petersburg – Clearwater, FL MSA	213	11	845	11
Orlando, FL MSA	174	14	728	12
Norfolk – Virginia Beach – Newport News, VA – NC MSA	132	23	721	13
Atlanta, GA MSA	209	12	690	14
Detroit – Ann Arbor – Flint, MI CMSA	213	11	666	15
St. Louis, MO – IL MSA	179	13	569	16
Louisville, KY – IN MSA	85	39	538	17
Cleveland – Akron, OH CMSA	165	15	516	18
Portland – Salem, OR – WA CMSA	114	28	509	19
Pittsburgh, PA MSA	135	22	508	20
San Antonio, TX MSA	107	29	499	21
Cincinnati – Hamilton, OH – KY – IN CMSA	144	19	491	22
San Francisco – Oakland – San Jose, CA CMSA	162	16	490	23
Jacksonville, FL MSA	105	31	481	24
Nashville, TN MSA	145	18	445	25

Source: U.S. Department of Commerce, Bureau of the Census, Data User Services Division, *1992 Economic Census, Volume 1F, Reports Series, Release 1F*, September 1995, CD-ROM. *Note:* Data are shown only for the top 25 areas.

★2482★

Establishments and Employment

Used Merchandise Stores

The U.S. total number of employees is 93,267; total number of establishments is 19,826.

MSA	Estab-lish-ments	Rank	Emp-ploy-ment	Rank
Los Angeles – Riverside – Orange County, CA CMSA	753	2	5,172	1
New York – Northern New Jersey – Long Island, NY – NJ-CT-CMSA	980	1	3,966	2
San Francisco – Oakland – San Jose, CA CMSA	530	3	3,365	3
Washington – Baltimore, DC – MD – VA – WV CMSA	504	4	2,725	4
Dallas – Fort Worth, TX CMSA	488	5	2,469	5
Seattle – Tacoma – Bremerton, WA CMSA	376	8	2,441	6
Houston – Galveston – Brazoria, TX CMSA	414	6	2,163	7
Detroit – Ann Arbor – Flint, MI CMSA	274	13	1,839	8
Philadelphia – Wilmington – Atlantic City, PA – NJ – DE – MD CMSA	286	12	1,534	9
Atlanta, GA MSA	366	9	1,505	10
Miami – Fort Lauderdale, FL CMSA	360	10	1,458	11
Phoenix – Mesa, AZ MSA	187	17	1,430	12
San Diego, CA MSA	180	20	1,428	13
Denver – Boulder – Greeley, CO CMSA	220	15	1,239	14
Boston – Worcester – Lawrence, MA – NH – ME – CT CMSA	310	11	1,200	15
Portland – Salem, OR – WA CMSA	203	16	1,158	16
New Orleans, LA MSA	132	28	1,146	17
San Antonio, TX MSA	182	19	942	18
Minneapolis – St. Paul, MN – WI MSA	149	22	896	19
Kansas City, MO – KS MSA	144	23	891	20
Cleveland – Akron, OH CMSA	143	24	889	21
Tampa – St. Petersburg – Clearwater, FL MSA	232	14	878	22
Norfolk – Virginia Beach – Newport News, VA – NC MSA	134	27	868	23
St. Louis, MO – IL MSA	184	18	858	24
Birmingham, AL MSA	84	39	852	25

Source: U.S. Department of Commerce, Bureau of the Census, Data User Services Division, *1992 Economic Census, Volume 1F, Reports Series, Release 1F,* September 1995, CD-ROM. *Note:* Data are shown only for the top 25 areas.

★2483★

Establishments and Employment

Variety Stores

The U.S. total number of employees is 115,861; total number of establishments is 12,561.

MSA	Estab-lish-ments	Rank	Emp-ploy-ment	Rank
Philadelphia – Wilmington – Atlantic City, PA – NJ – DE – MD CMSA	319	2	3,611	1
Los Angeles – Riverside – Orange County, CA CMSA	227	5	3,155	2
Detroit – Ann Arbor – Flint, MI CMSA	196	7	2,425	3
Miami – Fort Lauderdale, FL CMSA	115	13	1,730	4
Cleveland – Akron, OH CMSA	126	10	1,576	5
Pittsburgh, PA MSA	119	12	1,483	6
Atlanta, GA MSA	125	11	1,453	7
Dallas – Fort Worth, TX CMSA	193	8	1,308	8
Houston – Galveston – Brazoria, TX CMSA	131	9	1,184	9
St. Louis, MO – IL MSA	111	15	1,096	10
Columbus, OH MSA	67	22	915	11
Norfolk – Virginia Beach – Newport News, VA – NC MSA	91	17	857	12
San Antonio, TX MSA	73	19	786	13
Tampa – St. Petersburg – Clearwater, FL MSA	83	18	735	14
Buffalo – Niagara Falls, NY MSA	56	26	723	15
Greensboro – Winston-Salem – High Point, NC MSA	70	21	712	16
Charlotte – Gastonia – Rock Hill, NC – SC MSA	93	16	692	17
New Orleans, LA MSA	55	27	667	18
Scranton – Wilkes-Barre – Hazleton, PA MSA	33	45	617	19
Dayton – Springfield, OH MSA	45	34	583	20
Minneapolis – St. Paul, MN – WI MSA	55	27	562	21
Louisville, KY – IN MSA	58	25	532	22
Orlando, FL MSA	46	33	492	23
Rochester, NY MSA	35	43	486	24
Richmond – Petersburg, VA MSA	42	37	473	25

Source: U.S. Department of Commerce, Bureau of the Census, Data User Services Division, *1992 Economic Census, Volume 1F, Reports Series, Release 1F,* September 1995, CD-ROM. *Note:* Data are shown only for the top 25 areas.

★2484★

Establishments and Employment

Women's Clothing Stores

The U.S. total number of employees is 423,022; total number of establishments is 50,174.

MSA	Establishments	Rank	Employment	Rank
Los Angeles – Riverside – Orange County, CA CMSA	2,760	2	23,784	1
Chicago – Gary – Kenosha, IL – IN – WI CMSA	1,642	3	18,809	2
San Francisco – Oakland – San Jose, CA CMSA	1,252	6	11,240	3
Detroit – Ann Arbor – Flint, MI CMSA	1,005	9	10,989	4
Miami – Fort Lauderdale, FL CMSA	1,021	8	8,405	5
Houston – Galveston – Brazoria, TX CMSA	696	11	7,873	6
Dallas – Fort Worth, TX CMSA	836	10	7,719	7
Atlanta, GA MSA	638	12	5,734	8
Minneapolis – St. Paul, MN – WI MSA	521	14	5,399	9
Cleveland – Akron, OH CMSA	547	13	5,298	10
St. Louis, MO – IL MSA	483	15	5,250	11
Pittsburgh, PA MSA	471	16	4,617	12
San Diego, CA MSA	450	17	3,547	13
Cincinnati – Hamilton, OH – KY – IN CMSA	316	23	3,522	14
Tampa – St. Petersburg – Clearwater, FL MSA	425	19	3,468	15
Phoenix – Mesa, AZ MSA	365	20	3,318	16
West Palm Beach – Boca Raton, FL MSA	350	21	3,271	17
Milwaukee – Racine, WI CMSA	293	25	3,142	18
Indianapolis, IN MSA	266	28	2,825	19
Kansas City, MO – KS MSA	236	35	2,715	20
Columbus, OH MSA	215	40	2,534	21
New Orleans, LA MSA	247	30	2,485	22
Norfolk – Virginia Beach – Newport News, VA – NC MSA	287	26	2,432	23
Orlando, FL MSA	256	29	2,430	24
San Antonio, TX MSA	277	27	2,423	25

Source: U.S. Department of Commerce, Bureau of the Census, Data User Services Division, *1992 Economic Census, Volume 1F, Reports Series, Release 1F,* September 1995, CD-ROM. *Note:* Data are shown only for the top 25 areas.

★2485★

Establishments and Employment

Department Stores, 1995: Selected Cities

City	Department stores	Rank
Baltimore, MD	5	6
Chicago, IL	41	2
Detroit, MI	4	7
Houston, TX	71	1
Orlando, FL	11	3

[Continued]

★2485★

Department Stores, 1995: Selected Cities

[Continued]

City	Department stores	Rank
San Francisco, CA	6	5
Seattle, WA	10	4

Source: Gray, Madison J., "Becoming 'World Class' City Requires New Amenities for Dining, Fun," *Detroit News,* 21 December 1995, p. 1K. Primary source: U.S. Department of Commerce 1992 Census of Retail Trade (Geographic Area Series), Bureau of the Census; U.S. Department of Commerce 1992 Census of Service Industries (Geographic Area Series), Bureau of the Census.

★2486★

Establishments and Employment

Movie Theaters, 1995: Selected Cities

City	Movie theaters	Rank
Detroit, MI	6	7
Seattle, WA	26	4
Baltimore, MD	12	5
Chicago, IL	36	3
San Francisco, CA	61	1
Orlando, FL	8	6
Houston, TX	53	2

Source: Gray, Madison J., "Becoming 'World Class' City Requires New Amenities for Dining, Fun," *Detroit News,* 21 December 1995, p. 1K. Primary source: U.S. Department of Commerce 1992 Census of Retail Trade (Geographic Area Series), Bureau of the Census; U.S. Department of Commerce 1992 Census of Service Industries (Geographic Area Series), Bureau of the Census.

★2487★

Foods and Food Products

Liquid Teas, 1995: Percent Change in Sales Since 1994

[In percentages]

City/Location	Percent	Rank
Atlanta, GA	12.4	7
Baltimore-Washington, DC	3.1	10
Boston, MA	10.9	8
Chicago, IL	2.5	11
Dallas-Fort Worth, TX	35.9	2
Knoxville, TN	32.9	3
Los Angeles, CA	-0.7	12
Miami-Fort Lauderdale, FL	-13.6	13
Minneapolis-Saint Paul, MN	15.8	5
New Orleans-Mobile, LA	31.8	4
New York	4.7	9
Phoenix-Tucson, AZ	14.4	6
Providence, RI	64.2	1
Seattle-Tacoma, WA	2.5	11

Source: "Industry Issues," *BEVERAGE Industry,* (June 1996), p. 50.

★2488★

Foods and Food Products

Liquid Teas, 1995: Percent Change in Sales Volume Since 1994

[In percent]

City/Location	Percent	Rank
Atlanta, GA	19.4	7
Baltimore-Washington, DC	9.2	11
Boston, MA	10.6	10
Chicago, IL	11.4	9
Dallas-Fort Worth, TX	53.2	2
Knoxville, TN	51.2	3
Los Angeles, CA	8.8	12
Miami-Fort Lauderdale, FL	-16.3	14
Minneapolis-Saint Paul, MN	35.4	5
New Orleans-Mobile, LA	45.9	4
New York, NY	5.0	13
Phoenix-Tucson, AZ	30.1	6
Providence, RI	79.3	1
Seattle-Tacoma, WA	13.1	8

Source: "Industry Issues," *BEVERAGE Industry,* (June 1996), p. 50.

★2489★

Foods and Food Products

Liquid Teas, 1995: Sales

[In thousands]

City/Location	Sales	Rank
Atlanta, GA	1,934	12
Baltimore-Washington, DC	10,841	4
Boston, MA	6,154	6
Chicago, IL	12,946	3
Dallas-Fort Worth, TX	3,918	9
Knoxville, TN	865	14
Los Angeles, CA	29,290	2
Miami-Fort Lauderdale, FL	8,775	5
Minneapolis-Saint Paul, MN	3,416	10
New Orleans-Mobile, LA	3,094	11
New York, NY	50,056	1
Phoenix-Tucson, AZ	5,448	8
Providence, RI	1,118	13
Seattle-Tacoma, WA	6,116	7

Source: "Industry Issues," *BEVERAGE Industry,* (June 1996), p. 50.

★2490★

Foods and Food Products

Liquid Teas, 1995: Sales Volume

[In thousands]

City/Location	Sales	Rank
Atlanta, GA	4,670	12
Baltimore-Washington, DC	19,402	4
Boston, MA	11,907	6
Chicago, IL	24,800	3
Dallas-Fort Worth, TX	8,600	9
Knoxville, TN	2,325	13
Los Angeles, CA	50,264	2
Miami-Fort Lauderdale, FL	17,287	5
Minneapolis-Saint Paul, MN	8,013	10

[Continued]

★2490★

Liquid Teas, 1995: Sales Volume

[Continued]

City/Location	Sales	Rank
New Orleans-Mobile, LA	7,710	11
New York, NY	80,409	1
Phoenix-Tucson, AZ	10,892	7
Providence, RI	2,162	14
Seattle-Tacoma, WA	10,439	8

Source: "Industry Issues," *BEVERAGE Industry,* (June 1996), p. 50.

★2491★

Foods and Food Products

Meat Prices, 1995: Flank Steak

[In dollars per pound; represents wholesale costs].

[In dollars per pound; represents wholesale costs]

City	Cost	Rank
Chicago, IL	3.20	3
Dallas, TX	3.65	1
Los Angeles, CA	2.81	4
New York, NY	3.25	2

Source: "Price Check: Beef," *Restaurants & Institutions,* 1 September 1995, p. 38. Primary source: *Restaurants & Institutions* research.

★2492★

Foods and Food Products

Meat Prices, 1995: Top Sirloin

[In dollars per pound; represents wholesale costs]

City	Cost	Rank
Chicago, IL	2.30	4
Dallas, TX	2.80	1
Los Angeles, CA	2.35	3
New York, NY	2.40	2

Source: "Price Check: Beef," *Restaurants & Institutions,* 1 September 1995, p. 38. Primary source: *Restaurants & Institutions* research.

★2493★

Foods and Food Products

Pizza, 1995: Least Popular Cities

Data refer to the average amount spent on pizza, per person, annually.

City	Amount	Rank
McAllen, TX	30.43	1
Laredo, TX	30.66	2
Brownsville, TX	34.04	3
New York, NY	39.76	4
Jersey City, NJ	41.23	5

Source: "Home Delivery," *Wall Street Journal,* 28 June 1996, p. B8. Primary source: Equifax National Decision Systems, San Diego, and NPD/Crest, Chicago.

★2494★

Foods and Food Products

Pizza, 1995: Most Popular Cities

Data refer to the average amount spent on pizza, per person, annually.

City	Amount	Rank
Lawrence, KS	84.59	1
Bryan-College Station, TX	84.56	2
Iowa City, IA	83.54	3
Fort Collins, CO	83.24	4
Green Bay, WI	82.37	5

Source: "Home Delivery," *Wall Street Journal,* 28 June 1996, p. B8. Primary source: Equifax National Decision Systems, San Diego, and NPD/Crest, Chicago.

★2495★

Foods and Food Products

Salted Snacks Consumption, 1996: Top Cities

[In pounds per year]

City	Pounds of snacks consumed	Rank
Green Bay, WI	33.3	1
Spokane, WA	30.9	2
Grand Rapids, MI	30.8	3
Denver, CO	29.8	4
Milwaukee, WI	29.5	5

Source: "Worth Their Salt In Snacks," USA SNAPSHOTS, *USA TODAY,* 6 May 1996, p. 1B. Primary source: Snack Food Association.

★2496★

Foods and Food Products

Supermarkets, 1995: Annual Sales Per Capita

City	Sales	Rank
Albany, NY	1,317	13
Albuquerque, NM	1,154	35
Atlanta, GA	1,360	6
Baltimore-Washington, MD-DC	1,202	25
Billings, MT	1,254	19
Birmingham, AL	1,237	21
Boston, MA	1,234	22
Buffalo, NY	1,209	24
Charlotte, NC	1,295	16
Chicago, IL	1,038	42
Cincinnati, OH	1,180	29
Cleveland, OH	1,076	40
Columbia, SC	1,318	12
Dallas, TX	1,322	11
Denver, CO	1,332	9
Des Moines, IA	1,187	28
Detroit, MI	1,029	44
Fargo, ND	1,020	45
Fresno, CA	1,030	43
Grand Rapids, MI	1,159	34
Hartford, CT	1,343	8
Houston, TX	1,219	23
Indianapolis, IN	1,234	22
Jacksonville, FL	1,297	15
Kansas City, KS	1,178	30

[Continued]

★2496★

Supermarkets, 1995: Annual Sales Per Capita
[Continued]

City	Sales	Rank
Los Angeles, CA	1,089	39
Louisville, KY	1,127	37
Memphis, TN	1,172	32
Miami, FL	1,257	18
Milwaukee, WI	1,172	32
Minneapolis, MN	1,059	41
Nashville, TN	1,285	17
New Orleans, LA	1,247	20
New York, NY	987	46
Oklahoma City, OK	1,146	36
Omaha, NE	1,190	27
Philadelphia, PA	1,127	37
Phoenix, AZ	1,394	4
Pittsburgh, PA	1,160	33
Portland, OR	1,358	7
Richmond, VA	1,192	26
Saint Louis, MO	1,098	38
Salt Lake City, UT	1,366	5
San Antonio, TX	1,303	14
San Francisco, CA	1,177	31
Scranton-Harrisburg, PA	1,172	32
Seattle, WA	1,460	2
Spokane, WA	1,421	3
Springfield, MO	1,325	10
Tampa, FL	1,493	1

Source: "For the Record," *Progressive Grocer* Annual Report, *Progressive Grocer,* (April 1996), p. 55.

★2497★

Foods and Food Products

Supermarkets, 1995: Annual Sales Per Household

City	Sales	Rank
Albany, NY	3,542	10
Albuquerque, NM	3,273	22
Atlanta, GA	3,675	6
Baltimore-Washington, MD-DC	3,216	25
Billings, MT	3,260	23
Birmingham, AL	3,297	20
Boston, MA	3,279	21
Buffalo, NY	3,205	26
Charlotte, NC	3,377	18
Chicago, IL	2,852	43
Cincinnati, OH	3,122	33
Cleveland, OH	2,814	44
Columbia, SC	3,610	8
Dallas, TX	3,523	11
Denver, CO	3,412	15
Des Moines, IA	3,072	35
Detroit, MI	2,766	46
Fargo, ND	2,704	47
Fresno, CA	3,186	29
Grand Rapids, MI	3,175	31
Hartford, CT	3,569	9
Houston, TX	3,380	17

[Continued]

★2497★

Supermarkets, 1995: Annual Sales Per Household
[Continued]

City	Sales	Rank
Indianapolis, IN	3,279	21
Jacksonville, FL	3,454	14
Kansas City, KS	3,067	37
Los Angeles, CA	3,179	30
Louisville, KY	2,973	40
Memphis, TN	3,188	28
Miami, FL	3,191	27
Milwaukee, WI	3,122	33
Minneapolis, MN	2,801	45
Nashville, TN	3,356	19
New Orleans, LA	3,472	13
New York, NY	2,695	48
Oklahoma City, OK	2,979	39
Omaha, NE	3,118	34
Philadelphia, PA	3,064	38
Phoenix, AZ	3,711	5
Pittsburgh, PA	2,967	41
Portland, OR	3,504	12
Richmond, VA	3,244	24
Saint Louis, MO	2,861	42
Salt Lake City, UT	4,175	1
San Antonio, TX	3,839	2
San Francisco, CA	3,163	32
Scranton-Harrisburg, PA	3,068	36
Seattle, WA	3,767	3
Spokane, WA	3,719	4
Springfield, MO	3,405	16
Tampa, FL	3,652	7

Source: "For the Record," *Progressive Grocer* Annual Report, *Progressive Grocer*, (April 1996), p. 55.

★2498★

Foods and Food Products

Supermarkets, 1995: Sales
[In millions of dollars]

City	Sales	Rank
Albany, NY	5,571	25
Albuquerque, NM	4,393	36
Atlanta, GA	6,294	16
Baltimore-Washington, MD-DC	10,991	4
Billings, MT	1,014	50
Birmingham, AL	6,061	20
Boston, MA	10,697	5
Buffalo, NY	3,798	39
Charlotte, NC	10,608	6
Chicago, IL	10,200	7
Cincinnati, OH	9,614	8
Cleveland, OH	5,078	31
Columbia, SC	5,433	27
Dallas, TX	8,727	10
Denver, CO	5,302	28
Des Moines, IA	3,608	40
Detroit, MI	6,669	12
Fargo, ND	1,176	49

[Continued]

★2498★

Supermarkets, 1995: Sales
[Continued]

City	Sales	Rank
Fresno, CA	2,401	47
Grand Rapids, MI	3,159	42
Hartford, CT	5,540	26
Houston, TX	6,230	18
Indianapolis, IN	5,170	30
Jacksonville, FL	4,230	37
Kansas City, KS	4,963	32
Los Angeles, CA	22,117	1
Louisville, KY	2,569	44
Memphis, TN	6,646	14
Miami, FL	5,964	23
Milwaukee, WI	6,007	21
Minneapolis, MN	4,567	34
Nashville, TN	6,652	13
New Orleans, LA	5,997	22
New York, NY	17,542	2
Oklahoma City, OK	3,572	41
Omaha, NE	2,529	45
Philadelphia, PA	7,246	11
Phoenix, AZ	5,580	24
Pittsburgh, PA	4,819	33
Portland, OR	5,206	29
Richmond, VA	4,394	35
Saint Louis, MO	6,521	15
Salt Lake City, UT	4,087	38
San Antonio, TX	6,258	17
San Francisco, CA	11,606	3
Scranton-Harrisburg, PA	2,861	43
Seattle, WA	6,174	19
Spokane, WA	1,587	48
Springfield, MO	2,460	46
Tampa, FL	9,074	9

Source: "For the Record," *Progressive Grocer* Annual Report, *Progressive Grocer*, (April 1996), p. 54.

★2499★

Foods and Food Products

Supermarkets, 1995: Sales Per Checkout
[In dollars per week]

City	Sales	Rank
Albany, NY	24,506	16
Albuquerque, NM	23,389	25
Atlanta, GA	22,363	32
Baltimore-Washington, MD-DC	24,223	18
Billings, MT	22,459	30
Birmingham, AL	19,885	47
Boston, MA	26,022	9
Buffalo, NY	25,220	13
Charlotte, NC	19,968	46
Chicago, IL	26,281	6
Cincinnati, OH	24,120	20
Cleveland, OH	23,886	22
Columbia, SC	19,665	48
Dallas, TX	21,601	39
Denver, CO	26,678	5

[Continued]

★ 2499 ★

Supermarkets, 1995: Sales Per Checkout
[Continued]

City	Sales	Rank
Des Moines, IA	21,509	41
Detroit, MI	22,513	29
Fargo, ND	24,311	17
Fresno, CA	23,335	26
Grand Rapids, MI	21,588	40
Hartford, CT	25,443	11
Houston, TX	24,630	14
Indianapolis, IN	22,972	27
Jacksonville, FL	22,110	35
Kansas City, KS	22,405	31
Los Angeles, CA	28,037	1
Louisville, KY	22,273	33
Memphis, TN	19,368	49
Miami, FL	26,859	4
Milwaukee, WI	24,006	21
Minneapolis, MN	26,264	7
Nashville, TN	20,865	42
New Orleans, LA	20,039	45
New York, NY	23,739	23
Oklahoma City, OK	20,862	43
Omaha, NE	22,108	36
Philadelphia, PA	26,059	8
Phoenix, AZ	25,253	12
Pittsburgh, PA	24,561	15
Portland, OR	21,786	37
Richmond, VA	21,638	38
Saint Louis, MO	22,618	28
Salt Lake City, UT	25,772	10
San Antonio, TX	28,018	2
San Francisco, CA	27,500	3
Scranton-Harrisburg, PA	22,111	34
Seattle, WA	24,311	17
Spokane, WA	23,514	24
Springfield, MO	20,239	44
Tampa, FL	24,183	19

Source: "For the Record," *Progressive Grocer* Annual Report, *Progressive Grocer*, (April 1996), p. 55.

★ 2500 ★

Foods and Food Products

Supermarkets, 1995: Total Number

City	Number	Rank
Albany, NY	522	26
Albuquerque, NM	438	31
Atlanta, GA	584	19
Baltimore-Washington, MD-DC	959	6
Billings, MT	140	48
Birmingham, AL	707	14
Boston, MA	782	11
Buffalo, NY	280	44
Charlotte, NC	1,341	3
Chicago, IL	861	7
Cincinnati, OH	987	4
Cleveland, OH	489	28
Columbia, SC	661	17

[Continued]

★ 2500 ★

Supermarkets, 1995: Total Number
[Continued]

City	Number	Rank
Dallas, TX	800	10
Denver, CO	415	35
Des Moines, IA	405	36
Detroit, MI	678	15
Fargo, ND	146	47
Fresno, CA	265	45
Grand Rapids, MI	357	39
Hartford, CT	400	38
Houston, TX	528	25
Indianapolis, IN	551	23
Jacksonville, FL	417	34
Kansas City, KS	554	22
Los Angeles, CA	1,784	1
Louisville, KY	323	41
Memphis, TN	814	9
Miami, FL	422	33
Milwaukee, WI	670	16
Minneapolis, MN	423	32
Nashville, TN	823	8
New Orleans, LA	642	18
New York, NY	1,577	2
Oklahoma City, OK	401	37
Omaha, NE	265	45
Philadelphia, PA	556	21
Phoenix, AZ	462	30
Pittsburgh, PA	500	27
Portland, OR	558	20
Richmond, VA	475	29
Saint Louis, MO	746	12
Salt Lake City, UT	345	40
San Antonio, TX	438	31
San Francisco, CA	983	5
Scranton-Harrisburg, PA	320	42
Seattle, WA	550	24
Spokane, WA	188	46
Springfield, MO	306	43
Tampa, FL	745	13

Source: "For the Record," *Progressive Grocer* Annual Report, *Progressive Grocer*, (April 1996), p. 54.

★ 2501 ★

Foods and Food Products

Supermarkets, 1995: Total Number of Checkouts

City	Number	Rank
Albany, NY	4,372	24
Albuquerque, NM	3,612	36
Atlanta, GA	5,412	17
Baltimore-Washington, MD-DC	8,726	4
Billings, MT	868	50
Birmingham, AL	5,861	13
Boston, MA	7,905	6
Buffalo, NY	2,896	41
Charlotte, NC	10,216	3
Chicago, IL	7,464	9
Cincinnati, OH	7,665	8

[Continued]

★ 2501 ★

Supermarkets, 1995: Total Number of Checkouts
[Continued]

City	Number	Rank
Cleveland, OH	4,088	31
Columbia, SC	5,313	19
Dallas, TX	7,769	7
Denver, CO	3,822	33
Des Moines, IA	3,226	39
Detroit, MI	5,697	15
Fargo, ND	930	49
Fresno, CA	1,979	47
Grand Rapids, MI	2,814	42
Hartford, CT	4,187	30
Houston, TX	4,864	21
Indianapolis, IN	4,328	25
Jacksonville, FL	3,679	35
Kansas City, KS	4,260	28
Los Angeles, CA	15,170	1
Louisville, KY	2,218	45
Memphis, TN	6,599	11
Miami, FL	4,270	27
Milwaukee, WI	4,812	22
Minneapolis, MN	3,344	37
Nashville, TN	6,131	12
New Orleans, LA	5,755	14
New York, NY	14,211	2
Oklahoma City, OK	3,293	38
Omaha, NE	2,200	46
Philadelphia, PA	5,347	18
Phoenix, AZ	4,249	29
Pittsburgh, PA	3,773	34
Portland, OR	4,595	23
Richmond, VA	3,905	32
Saint Louis, MO	5,544	16
Salt Lake City, UT	3,050	40
San Antonio, TX	4,295	26
San Francisco, CA	8,116	5
Scranton-Harrisburg, PA	2,488	43
Seattle, WA	4,884	20
Spokane, WA	1,298	48
Springfield, MO	2,337	44
Tampa, FL	7,216	10

Source: "For the Record," *Progressive Grocer* Annual Report, *Progressive Grocer,* (April 1996), p. 55.

★ 2502 ★

Home Furnishings and Equipment

Spending on Home Furnishings and Equipment, 1995: Selected Cities

City	Spending	Rank
Anchorage, AK	1,734	4
Chicago, IL	1,536	5
Cincinnati, OH	1,364	9
Cleveland, OH	994	14
Detroit, MI	1,413	6
Honolulu, HI	1,324	10
Kansas City, KS-MO	1,789	2
Los Angeles, CA	1,205	12

[Continued]

★ 2502 ★

Spending on Home Furnishings and Equipment, 1995: Selected Cities
[Continued]

City	Spending	Rank
Milwaukee, Wi	1,408	8
Minneapolis-Saint Paul, MN	1,998	1
Portland, OR	1,205	12
Saint Louis, MO	1,017	13
San Diego, CA	1,262	11
San Francisco, CA	1,409	7
Seattle, WA	1,773	3

Source: 'Reaching Today's Consumer: "Consumer Spending by Region," *Furniture/Today,* 1996 Retail Planning Guide, 25 December 1995, p. 76.

★ 2503 ★

Medicines

Vitamin Costs Per Day, 1995, By Type: Calcium

Data are averages of 2 or more brands.

City/MSA	Price	Rank
Chicago, IL	0.23	2
Houston, TX	0.21	3
Miami, FL	0.11	4
Minneapolis, MN	0.29	1
New Orleans, LA	0.08	5
San Francisco, CA	0.08	5

Source: "*Money's* 20-City Price Guide," *Money,* (September 1995), p. 84.

★ 2504 ★

Medicines

Vitamin Costs Per Day, 1995, By Type: Multivitamins

Data are averages of 2 or more brands.

City/MSA	Price	Rank
Atlanta, GA	0.05	3
Dallas, TX	0.07	1
Denver, CO	0.05	3
Los Angeles, CA	0.06	2
Minneapolis, MN	0.07	1
New Orleans, LA	0.04	4
San Diego, CA	0.05	3
Saint Louis, MO	0.06	2
San Francisco, CA	0.06	2

Source: "*Money's* 20-City Price Guide," *Money,* (September 1995), p. 84.

★ 2505 ★

Medicines

Vitamin Costs Per Day, 1995, By Type: Vitamin C

Data are averages of 2 or more brands.

City/MSA	Price	Rank
Atlanta, GA	0.07	1
Charlotte, NC	0.04	4
Boston, MA	0.05	3
Honolulu, HI	0.02	6
Denver, CO	0.05	3
Houston, TX	0.03	5
Kansas City, KS	0.03	5
Miami, FL	0.04	4
Los Angeles, CA	0.04	4
Minneapolis, MN	0.05	3
New Orleans, LA	0.03	5
Phoenix, AZ	0.05	3
Portland, OR	0.04	4
Saint Louis, MO	0.06	2

Source: "Money's 20-City Price Guide," *Money,* (September 1995), p. 84.

★ 2506 ★

Medicines

Vitamin Costs Per Day, 1995, By Type: Vitamin E

Data are averages of 2 or more brands.

City/MSA	Price	Rank
Charlotte, NC	0.07	7
Boston, MA	0.10	4
Chicago, IL	0.08	6
Dallas, TX	0.09	5
Honolulu, HI	0.12	2
Houston, TX	0.08	6
Kansas City, KS	0.03	9
Miami, FL	0.11	3
Los Angeles, CA	0.08	6
Minneapolis, MN	0.06	8
New Orleans, LA	0.06	8
Phoenix, AZ	0.15	1
Pittsburgh, PA	0.06	8
San Diego, CA	0.07	7

Source: "Money's 20-City Price Guide," *Money,* (September 1995), p. 84.

★ 2507 ★

Medicines

Vitamin Prices, 1995, By Type: Calcium

Data are averages of 2 or more brands.

City/MSA	Price	Rank
Chicago, IL	6.99	2
Houston, TX	6.29	3
Miami, FL	5.34	4
Minneapolis, MN	8.79	1
New Orleans, LA	3.94	6
San Francisco, CA	4.04	5

Source: "Money's 20-City Price Guide," *Money,* (September 1995), p. 84.

★ 2508 ★

Medicines

Vitamin Prices, 1995, By Type: Multivitamins

Data are averages of 2 or more brands.

City/MSA	Price	Rank
Atlanta, GA	6.48	8
Dallas, TX	7.39	5
Denver, CO	6.60	7
Los Angeles, CA	7.68	4
Minneapolis, MN	9.66	1
New Orleans, LA	5.53	9
San Diego, CA	7.22	6
Saint Louis, MO	8.49	2
San Francisco, CA	7.77	3

Source: "Money's 20-City Price Guide," *Money,* (September 1995), p. 84.

★ 2509 ★

Medicines

Vitamin Prices, 1995, By Type: Vitamin C

Data are averages of 2 or more brands.

City/MSA	Price	Rank
Atlanta, GA	7.09	2
Charlotte, NC	4.25	10
Boston, MA	5.39	6
Honolulu, HI	11.00	1
Denver, CO	4.99	7
Houston, TX	3.45	12
Kansas City, KS	3.56	13
Miami, FL	4.11	11
Los Angeles, CA	4.75	8
Minneapolis, MN	5.53	5
New Orleans, LA	3.57	14
Phoenix, AZ	5.77	4
Portland, OR	4.29	9
Saint Louis, MO	6.29	3

Source: "Money's 20-City Price Guide," *Money,* (September 1995), p. 84.

★ 2510 ★

Medicines

Vitamin Prices, 1995, By Type: Vitamin E

Data are averages of 2 or more brands.

City/MSA	Price	Rank
Charlotte, NC	6.96	8
Boston, MA	10.74	2
Chicago, IL	7.86	5
Dallas, TX	9.27	3
Honolulu, HI	12.67	1
Houston, TX	7.86	5
Kansas City, KS	6.94	9
Miami, FL	6.24	11
Los Angeles, CA	8.16	4
Minneapolis, MN	6.23	12
New Orleans, LA	6.65	10
Phoenix, AZ	7.55	6

[Continued]

★2510★

Vitamin Prices, 1995, By Type: Vitamin E

[Continued]

City/MSA	Price	Rank
Pittsburgh, PA	5.93	13
San Diego, CA	7.01	7

Source: "Money's 20-City Price Guide," *Money,* (September 1995), p. 84.

Chapter 25

TRANSPORTATION SECTOR

Topics Covered

Airports
Bridges
Cab Drivers
Cost of Living
Shipping

★2511★

Airports

Noise Control, 1996: Airports With Neighbors Affected By Noise Pollution

Data refer to the number of neighbors hearing excessive airport noise (defined by the FAA—Federal Aviation Administration) as an average level of 65 decibels or more.

City	Number	Rank
Atlanta, GA	81,621	4
Chicago, IL[1]	93,860	3
Chicago, IL[2]	79,960	5
Los Angeles, CA	75,000	6
Miami, FL	163,234	2
Minneapolis-Saint Paul, MN	30,720	11
New York, NY[3]	194,972	1
New York, NY[4]	51,317	7
San Antonio, TX	37,268	9
San Diego, CA	40,000	8
Seattle-Tacoma, WA	31,800	10

Source: Skelton, Renee, "The Sky's the Limit?" *Amicus Journal,* (Summer 1996), p. 34. *Notes:* 1. O'Hare. 2. Midway. 3. LaGuardia. 4. Kennedy.

★2512★

Airports

Noise Control, 1996: Monthly Noise Complaints At Selected Airports

City	Number	Rank
Atlanta, GA	250	9
Boston, MA	275	7
Chicago, IL[1]	367	4
Cincinnati-Northern Kentucky, OH-KY	262	8
Denver, CO	2,500	1
Detroit, MI	626	3
Minneapolis-Saint Paul, MN	700	2
Saint Louis, MO	135	11
San Francisco, CA	300	6
San Jose, CA	250	9
Seattle-Tacoma, WA	350	5
Washington, DC[2]	225	10

Source: Skelton, Renee, "The Sky's the Limit?" *Amicus Journal,* (Summer 1996), p. 35. *Notes:* Figures may include repeat callers. 1. O'Hare. 2. National.

★2513★

Airports

On-Time Arrivals At Airports, 1995

According to the source, a flight is considered on time if it is within fifteen minutes of schedule. The U.S. average for on-time arrivals is 78.0%.

[In percentages]

City	Percentage	Rank
Atlanta, GA	74.6	19
Boston, MA	74.3	20
Charlotte, NC	81.7	2
Chicago, IL[1]	79.0	11
Cincinnati, OH	82.3	1

[Continued]

★2513★

On-Time Arrivals At Airports, 1995

[Continued]

City	Percentage	Rank
Dallas-Fort Worth, TX	80.7	6
Denver, CO	81.2	4
Detroit, MI	81.5	3
Houston, TX[2]	81.2	4
Las Vegas, NV	79.2	9
Los Angeles, CA	70.8	23
Miami, FL	76.1	15
Minneapolis, MN	81.7	2
New York, NY[3]	80.6	7
New York, NY[4]	75.3	17
New York, NY[5]	73.1	21
Orlando, FL	77.3	14
Philadelphia, PA	79.8	8
Phoenix, AZ	79.1	10
Pittsburgh, PA	81.0	5
Saint Louis, MO	75.9	16
Salt Lake City, UT	78.1	12
San Diego, CA	77.8	13
San Francisco, CA	71.2	22
Seattle, WA	75.0	18
Tampa, FL	75.9	16
Washington, DC[6]	79.8	8

Source: "On-Time Performance of Largest U.S. Airports," *Travel Weekly,* 13 May 1996, p. 59. Primary source: U.S. Department of Transportation. *Notes:* 1. O'Hare 2. Intercontinental. 3. LaGuardia. 4. Newark. 5. Kennedy. 6. National.

★2514★

Airports

On-Time Departures At Airports, 1995

According to the source, a flight is considered on time if it is within fifteen minutes of schedule. The U.S. average for on-time departures is 81.0%.

[In percentages]

City	Percentage	Rank
Atlanta, GA	77.6	21
Boston, MA	82.0	10
Charlotte, NC	81.0	15
Chicago, IL[1]	78.1	20
Cincinnati, OH	83.1	9
Dallas-Fort Worth, TX	80.9	16
Denver, CO	82.0	10
Detroit, MI	78.8	18
Houston, TX[2]	85.7	3
Las Vegas, NV	81.1	14
Los Angeles, CA	77.4	22
Miami, FL	83.1	9
Minneapolis, MN	83.3	8
New York, NY[3]	84.7	5
New York, NY[4]	81.6	11
New York, NY[5]	81.2	13
Orlando, FL	86.2	2
Philadelphia, PA	83.7	6
Phoenix, AZ	81.1	14
Pittsburgh, PA	81.4	12

[Continued]

★2514★
On-Time Departures At Airports, 1995
[Continued]

City	Percentage	Rank
Saint Louis, MO	78.2	19
Salt Lake City, UT	80.1	17
San Diego, CA	83.6	7
San Francisco, CA	78.1	20
Seattle, WA	83.7	6
Tampa, FL	85.2	4
Washington, DC[6]	86.5	1

Source: "On-Time Performance of Largest U.S. Airports," *Travel Weekly,* 13 May 1996, p. 59. Primary source: U.S. Department of Transportation. *Notes:* 1. O'Hare. 2. Intercontinental. 3. LaGuardia. 4. Newark. 5. Kennedy. 6. National.

★2515★
Airports
Airport Cargo, 1995: Top Airports in Volume

City/Airport	Cargo volume	Rank
Memphis, TN	1,712,006	1
Los Angeles, CA	1,597,219	2
Miami, FL	1,584,680	3
New York, NY	1,572,840	4
Louisville, KY	1,351,147	5
Chicago, IL	1,235,806	6
Anchorage, AK	987,484	7
Newark, NJ	905,966	8
Dallas-Fort Worth, TX	777,698	9
Atlanta, GA	771,389	10
San Francisco, CA	697,802	11
Dayton, OH	632,658	12
Oakland, CA	541,776	13
Indianapolis, IN	520,955	14
Philadelphia, PA	492,268	15
Honolulu, HI	412,866	16
Seattle-Tacoma, WA	407,473	17
Boston, MA	395,589	18

Source: "Top 30 ACI Airports/Cargo Volume," *International Business,* (April 1996), p. 24. Primary source: ACI.

★2516★
Airports
Airport Layovers, 1995: Most Popular Airports
[In percentages]

City	Percent	Rank
Atlanta, GA (Hartsfield International Airport)	15	1
San Francisco, CA (San Francisco International Airport)	14	2
Chicago, IL (O'Hare International Airport)	12	3

Source: Jones, Del, "Business Travel Today," *USA TODAY,* 11 September 1995, p. 1B. Primary source: PLUS ATM Network/*Travel Holiday* frequent travelers survey.

★2517★
Airports
Busiest Airports, 1995: Number of Passengers
[In millions]

City	Number	Rank
Atlanta, GA	57.7	2
Chicago, IL	67.2	1
Dallas-Fort Worth, TX	54.3	3
Denver, CO	31.0	7
Detroit, MI	29.0	9
Las Vegas, NV	28.0	10
Los Angeles, CA	53.9	4
Miami, FL	33.2	6
Minneapolis-Saint Paul, MN	26.7	12
New York, NY	30.3	8
Newark, NJ	26.5	13
Phoenix, AZ	27.6	11
San Francisco, CA	36.2	5

Source: "Fricker, Daniel G., "U.S. to Fund Airport Plans: It's A Deal: Transportation Chief Agrees to $150 Million For Metro," *Detroit Free Press,* 1 May, 1996, p. 1B. Primary source: Airports Council International, preliminary 1995 figures. *Notes:* Airport names: O'Hare International (Chicago); Hartsfield International (Atlanta); Dallas-Fort Worth Regional (Dallas-Fort Worth); Los Angeles International (Los Angeles); San Francisco International (San Francisco); Miami International (Miami); Denver International (Denver); John F. Kennedy International (New York); Detroit Metropolitan (Detroit); McCarran International (Las Vegas); Sky Harbor International (Phoenix); Minneapolis-Saint Paul International (Phoenix); Minneapolis-Saint Paul International (Minneapolis-Saint Paul); Newark International (Newark).

★2518★
Bridges
Traffic Volume on Bridges With Poor Safety Ratings
[In thousands of vehicles]

County	Traffic volume	Rank
Arlington, VA	56,185	8
Bristol, MA	53,184	12
Camden, NJ	54,200	11
Cuyahoga, OH	102,700	2
Essex, MA	48,150	14
Essex, NJ	54,700	10
Hudson, NJ	42,800	16
Middlesex, MA	71,200	4
Middlesex, NJ	56,415	7
Monroe, NY	44,582	15
New York, NY	82,867	3
Onondaga, NY	59,100	6
Queens, NY	63,904	5
San Francisco, CA	103,000	1
Union, NJ	50,300	13
Washtenaw, MI	55,000	9

Source: "The 25 Worst Bridges," *USA TODAY,* 29 August 1994, p. 2A. Primary source: Federal Highway Administration. *Notes:* Data for Middlesex, Massachusetts; New York, New York; Queens, New York; and Hudson, New Jersey, are averages of traffic volume on more than one bridge.

★2519★

Cab Drivers

Where Cabbies Know Their Cities, 1995

[In percentages]

City	Percentage	Rank
San Francisco, CA	26	1
New York, NY	21	2
Chicago, IL	12	3
Denver, CO	6	4
Atlanta, GA	5	5

Source: Ward, Sam, "Cities With the Most Knowledgeable Cab Drivers," *USA TODAY,* 31 August 1995, p. 1B. Primary source: Plus ATM Network/*Travel Holiday* frequent traveler survey.

★2520★

Cost of Living

Bus Fares, 1995: Cost of One-Way Ride

Data refer to prices in effect from April 1, 1995 through December 31, 1995.

City/MSA	Fare	Rank
Ridgecrest, CA	1.50	1
Philadelphia, PA	1.30	2
San Diego, CA	1.28	3
Baltimore, MD	1.25	4
Detroit, MI	1.25	4
Miami, FL	1.25	4
Richmond, VA	1.25	4
Sacramento, CA	1.25	4
Salinas, CA	1.25	4
Seaside, CA	1.25	4
Pittsburgh, PA	1.23	5
Chicago, IL	1.16	6
Nashville, TN	1.15	7
Wilmington, DE	1.15	7
Atlanta, GA	1.13	8
New York, NY	1.13	8
San Francisco, CA	1.12	9
Allentown, PA	1.10	10
Buffalo, NY	1.10	10
Harrisburg, PA	1.10	10
Memphis, TN	1.10	10
San Jose, CA	1.10	10
York, PA	1.10	10
Norfolk, VA	1.05	11
Saint Clair, PA	1.05	11

Source: American Public Transit Association (APTA), *1995 APTA Transit Fare Summary,* Washington, D.C.: American Public Transit Association (APTA), 1995. *Note:* Data are shown only for the top 25 areas.

★2521★

Cost of Living

Ferry Boat Fares, 1995: Cost of One-Way Ride

Data refer to prices in effect from April 1, 1995 through December 31, 1995.

City/MSA	Fare	Rank
Boston, MA	4.00	2
New York, NY	1.13	4
Norfolk, VA	0.75	5
San Francisco, CA	4.25	1
Seattle, WA	3.50	3

Source: American Public Transit Association (APTA), *1995 APTA Transit Fare Summary,* Washington, D.C.: American Public Transit Association (APTA), 1995.

★2522★

Cost of Living

Railway Fares (Commuter Rail), 1995: Cost of One-Way Ride

Data refer to prices in effect from April 1, 1995 through December 31, 1995.

City/MSA	Fare	Rank
Atlantic City, NJ	0.85	9
Baltimore, MD	3.00	3
Boston, MA	0.85	9
Chicago, IL	2.35	6
Los Angeles, CA	2.50	4
Miami, FL	3.00	3
New Haven, CT	2.25	7
New York, NY	2.40	5
Philadelphia, PA	3.25	2
San Diego, CA	2.50	4
San Francisco, CA	1.00	8
Washington, DC	3.30	1

Source: American Public Transit Association (APTA), *1995 APTA Transit Fare Summary,* Washington, D.C.: American Public Transit Association (APTA), 1995.

★2523★

Cost of Living

Railway Fares (Heavy Rail), 1995: Cost of One-Way Ride

Data refer to prices in effect from April 1, 1995 through December 31, 1995.

City/MSA	Fare	Rank
Atlanta, GA	1.25	2
Baltimore, MD	1.25	2
Boston, MA	0.85	5
Chicago, IL	1.50	1
Cleveland, OH	1.50	1
Los Angeles, CA	0.25	8
Miami, FL	1.25	2
New York, NY	0.75	6
Philadelphia, PA	0.68	7
San Francisco, CA	0.90	4
Washington, DC	1.00	3

Source: American Public Transit Association (APTA), *1995 APTA Transit Fare Summary,* Washington, D.C.: American Public Transit Association (APTA), 1995.

★ 2524 ★

Cost of Living

Railway Fares (Inclined Plane), 1995: Cost of One-Way Ride

Data refer to prices in effect from April 1, 1995 through December 31, 1995.

City/MSA	Fare	Rank
Chattanooga, TN	6.00	1
Johnstown, PA	1.25	2
Pittsburgh, PA	1.00	3

Source: American Public Transit Association (APTA), *1995 APTA Transit Fare Summary*, Washington, D.C.: American Public Transit Association (APTA), 1995.

★ 2525 ★

Cost of Living

Railway Fares (Light Rail), 1995: Cost of One-Way Ride

Data refer to prices in effect from April 1, 1995 through December 31, 1995.

City/MSA	Fare	Rank
Philadelphia, PA	1.60	1
Cleveland, OH	1.50	2
Los Angeles, CA	1.35	3
Baltimore, MD	1.25	4
Pittsburgh, PA	1.25	4
Sacramento, CA	1.25	4
Wilmington, DE	1.15	5
Buffalo, NY	1.10	6
San Jose, CA	1.10	6
York, PA	1.10	6
Visalia, CA	1.03	7
New Orleans, LA	1.00	8
New York, NY	1.00	8
Portland, OR	1.00	8
Saint Louis, MO	1.00	8
San Diego, CA	1.00	8
San Francisco, CA	1.00	8
Steubenville, OH	1.00	8
Syracuse, NY	1.00	8
Trenton, NJ	1.00	8
West Palm Beach, FL	1.00	8
Williamsport, PA	1.00	8
Stamford, CT	0.95	9
Tampa, FL	0.95	9
Shreveport, LA	0.90	10

Source: American Public Transit Association (APTA), *1995 APTA Transit Fare Summary*, Washington, D.C.: American Public Transit Association (APTA), 1995.
Note: Data are shown only for the top 25 areas.

★ 2526 ★

Cost of Living

Trolley Fares, 1995: Cost of One-Way Ride

Data refer to prices in effect from April 1, 1995 through December 31, 1995.

City/MSA	Fare	Rank
Boston, MA	0.60	5
Dayton, OH	0.90	3
Philadelphia, PA	1.60	1
San Francisco, CA	1.00	2
Seattle, WA	0.85	4

Source: American Public Transit Association (APTA), *1995 APTA Transit Fare Summary*, Washington, D.C.: American Public Transit Association (APTA), 1995.

★ 2527 ★

Cost of Living

Where Driving A Vehicle Is The Least Expensive, 1995: Leading 5 Cities

[In cents per mile]

City	Cost	Rank
Sioux Falls, SD	35.8	1
Bismarck, ND	36.3	2
Burlington, VT	36.4	3
Boise, ID	36.7	4
Nashville, TN	37.1	5

Source: "About Town," *Entrepreneur*, (September 1995), p. 63. Primary source: Runzheimer International.

★ 2528 ★

Cost of Living

Where Driving A Vehicle Is The Most Expensive, 1995: Leading 5 Cities

[In cents per mile]

City	Cost	Rank
Los Angeles, CA	55.8	1
Boston, MA	49.8	2
Philadelphia, PA	49.0	3
Providence, RI	48.5	4
Hartford, CT	48.0	5

Source: "About Town," *Entrepreneur*, (September 1995), p. 63. Primary source: Runzheimer International.

★ 2529 ★

Cost of Living

Automobile Rental Rates, 1995

Data are based on an economy car with unlimited mileage.

[In dollars per day]

City/MSA	Rent	Rank
Atlanta, GA	40	1
Washington, DC	39	2
New Orleans, LA	34	3
San Francisco, CA	33	4
Orlando, FL	32	5

[Continued]

★ 2529 ★

Automobile Rental Rates, 1995
[Continued]

City/MSA	Rent	Rank
Denver, CO	30	6
Chicago, IL	27	7
San Diego, CA	26	8
Los Angeles, CA	25	9
Miami, FL	22	10

Source: "The Cost of A Car," *Physicians' Travel & Meeting Guide,* (August 1995), p. 10. Primary source: *Travel News* survey.

★ 2530 ★
Cost of Living

Bus System Operating Costs Per Vehicle Mile: 1993

[In dollars per vehicle mile]

City	Costs	Rank
Boston, MA	7.92	3
Chicago, IL	6.76	6
Los Angeles, CA	7.33	5
New York, NY	11.19	1
Philadelphia, PA	8.23	2
Washington, DC	7.83	4

Source: Finder, Alan and Richard Perez-Pena, "For the M.T.A., Some Fiscal Successes," *New York Times,* 13 August 1995, p. 15. Primary source: Federal Transit Administration.

★ 2531 ★
Cost of Living

Commuter Rail System Operating Costs Per Vehicle Mile: 1993

[In dollars per vehicle mile]

City	Costs	Rank
Boston, MA	6.76	6
Chicago, IL	11.66	2
Chicago, IL	7.60	5
New Jersey, NY	8.62	4
New York, NY	11.49	3
Philadelphia, PA	12.96	1

Source: Finder, Alan and Richard Perez-Pena, "For the M.T.A., Some Fiscal Successes," *New York Times,* 13 August 1995, p. 15. Primary source: Federal Transit Administration.

★ 2532 ★
Cost of Living

Drivers' Costs, 1995: Highest

[In cents per mile]

City	Cost[1]	Rank
Boston, MA	49.8	2
Hartford, CT	48.0	5
Los Angeles, CA	55.8	1
Philadelphia, PA	49.0	3
Providence, RI	48.5	4

Source: "Costliest Big Cities for Driving," USA SNAPSHOTS, *USA TODAY,* 3 May 1995, p. 1A. Primary source: Runzheimer International. *Notes:* 1. Based on insurance, depreciation, license, fees, taxes, fuel, oil, tires, and maintenance to drive a 1995 Taurus GL 15,000 miles per year over four years.

★ 2533 ★
Cost of Living

Public Transportation Administrations, 1993

Table shows the percentage of public transportation systems operating costs allotted to administration in each location.

City	Percent	Rank
Boston, MA	17	3
Chicago, IL	13	6
Los Angeles, CA	15	4
New York, NY	14	5
Philadelphia, PA	19	2
Washington, DC	35	1

Source: Finder, Alan and Richard Perez-Pena, "For the M.T.A., Some Fiscal Successes," *New York Times,* 13 August 1995, p. 15. Primary source: Federal Transit Administration.

★ 2534 ★
Cost of Living

Subway System Operating Costs Per Vehicle Mile: 1993

[In dollars per vehicle mile]

City	Costs	Rank
Boston, MA	10.87	1
Chicago, IL	6.20	6
Miami, FL	7.99	3
New York, NY	7.22	4
Philadelphia, PA	7.16	5
Washington, DC	8.55	2

Source: Finder, Alan and Richard Perez-Pena, "For the M.T.A., Some Fiscal Successes," *New York Times,* 13 August 1995, p. 15. Primary source: Federal Transit Administration.

★ 2535 ★
Shipping

Container Ports in North America, 1995

[In 20-foot-equivalent units]

City	Number	Rank
Charleston, NC	1,023,903	7
Hampton Roads, VA	1,077,848	6
Honolulu, HI	805,036	8
Long Beach, CA	2,842,502	1

[Continued]

★ 2535 ★

Container Ports in North America, 1995

[Continued]

City	Number	Rank
Los Angeles, CA	2,555,344	2
Oakland, CA	1,549,886	3
Seattle, WA	1,479,076	4
Tacoma, WA	1,092,087	5

Source: Minahan, Tim, "A New Wave In Shipping," *Purchasing*, 6 June, 1996, p. 49.
Primary source: American Association of Port Authorities.

Chapter 26

TRANSPORTATION, COMMUNICATIONS, AND UTILITIES

Topic Covered

Establishments and Employment

★ 2536 ★

Establishments and Employment

Broadcasting & Cable Services, Radio & TV

The U.S. total number of employees is 350,718; total number of establishments is 13,017.

MSA	Estab-lish-ments	Rank	Emp-loy-ment	Rank
Los Angeles – Riverside – Orange County, CA CMSA	383	2	18,380	1
Washington – Baltimore, DC – MD – VA – WV CMSA	246	3	9,819	2
Chicago – Gary – Kenosha, IL – IN – WI CMSA	218	4	7,656	3
Philadelphia – Wilmington – Atlantic City, PA – NJ – DE – MD CMSA	148	7	5,456	4
Atlanta, GA MSA	118	10	5,429	5
Dallas – Fort Worth, TX CMSA	143	8	4,841	6
Detroit – Ann Arbor – Flint, MI CMSA	140	9	4,747	7
Seattle – Tacoma – Bremerton, WA CMSA	112	11	4,450	8
Miami – Fort Lauderdale, FL CMSA	112	11	4,260	9
Norfolk – Virginia Beach – Newport News, VA – NC MSA	61	23	3,552	10
San Diego, CA MSA	63	21	3,284	11
Minneapolis – St. Paul, MN – WI MSA	95	13	3,216	12
Cleveland – Akron, OH CMSA	83	17	3,192	13
Phoenix – Mesa, AZ MSA	78	18	3,101	14
St. Louis, MO – IL MSA	90	14	2,889	15
Tampa – St. Petersburg – Clearwater, FL MSA	84	16	2,771	16
Pittsburgh, PA MSA	85	15	2,763	17
Hartford, CT MSA	37	40	2,533	18
Cincinnati – Hamilton, OH – KY – IN CMSA	59	24	2,378	19
Portland – Salem, OR – WA CMSA	66	20	2,284	20
Indianapolis, IN MSA	58	25	2,266	21
Charlotte – Gastonia – Rock Hill, NC – SC MSA	58	25	2,207	22
Sacramento – Yolo, CA CMSA	56	26	2,195	23
San Antonio, TX MSA	52	29	2,070	24
Kansas City, MO – KS MSA	50	31	1,985	25

Source: U.S. Department of Commerce, Bureau of the Census, Data User Services Division, 1992 Economic Census, Volume 1F, Reports Series, Release 1F, September 1995, CD-ROM. Note: Data are shown only for the top 25 areas.

★ 2537 ★

Establishments and Employment

Bus Charter Service

The U.S. total number of employees is 24,604; total number of establishments is 1,307.

MSA	Estab-lish-ments	Rank	Emp-loy-ment	Rank
Boston – Worcester – Lawrence, MA – NH – ME – CT CMSA	27	7	0[1]	5
Chicago – Gary – Kenosha, IL – IN – WI CMSA	29	6	0[2]	5
Los Angeles – Riverside – Orange County, CA CMSA	70	2	1,383	1
New York – Northern New Jersey – Long Island, NY – NJ – CT-CMSA	155	1	0[3]	5
Philadelphia – Wilmington – Atlantic City, PA – NJ – DE – MD CMSA	40	4	665	4
San Francisco – Oakland – San Jose, CA CMSA	36	5	884	3
Washington – Baltimore, DC – MD – VA – WV CMSA	51	3	892	2

Source: U.S. Department of Commerce, Bureau of the Census, Data User Services Division, 1992 Economic Census, Volume 1F, Reports Series, Release 1F, September 1995, CD-ROM. Notes: 1. 250-499 employees. 2. 500-999 employees. 3. 2,500-4,999 employees.

★ 2538 ★

Establishments and Employment

Cable & Other Pay TV

The U.S. total number of employees is 128,963; total number of establishments is 4,468.

MSA	Estab-lish-ments	Rank	Emp-loy-ment	Rank
Los Angeles – Riverside – Orange County, CA CMSA	147	2	7,156	1
Atlanta, GA MSA	53	9	3,297	2
Philadelphia – Wilmington – Atlantic City, PA – NJ – DE – MD CMSA	61	7	2,521	3
San Diego, CA MSA	25	18	1,710	4
Hartford, CT MSA	7	34	1,556	5
Miami – Fort Lauderdale, FL CMSA	44	10	1,551	6
Phoenix – Mesa, AZ MSA	30	16	1,310	7
Tampa – St. Petersburg – Clearwater, FL MSA	25	18	1,184	8
St. Louis, MO – IL MSA	37	13	1,121	9
Minneapolis – St. Paul, MN – WI MSA	36	14	1,090	10
Cleveland – Akron, OH CMSA	27	17	1,087	11
Pittsburgh, PA MSA	34	15	1,014	12
Norfolk – Virginia Beach – Newport News, VA – NC MSA	14	27	945	13
Providence – Fall River – Warwick, RI – MA MSA	24	19	943	14
Portland – Salem, OR – WA CMSA	17	24	819	15

★ 2538 ★

Cable & Other Pay TV
[Continued]

MSA	Estab-lish-ments	Rank	Emp-loy-ment	Rank
Nashville, TN MSA	24	19	798	16
Orlando, FL MSA	17	24	772	17
Indianapolis, IN MSA	19	22	738	18
Kansas City, MO – KS MSA	17	24	727	19
Birmingham, AL MSA	25	18	689	20
West Palm Beach – Boca Raton, FL MSA	13	28	634	21
Charlotte – Gastonia – Rock Hill, NC – SC MSA	16	25	591	22
Austin – San Marcos, TX MSA	22	20	495	23
Sarasota – Bradenton, FL MSA	9	32	493	24
Syracuse, NY MSA	13	28	487	25

Source: U.S. Department of Commerce, Bureau of the Census, Data User Services Division, *1992 Economic Census, Volume 1F, Reports Series, Release 1F,* September 1995, CD-ROM. *Note:* Data are shown only for the top 25 areas.

★ 2539 ★

Establishments and Employment

Courier Services, Except By Air

The U.S. total number of employees is 307,061; total number of establishments is 5,966.

MSA	Estab-lish-ments	Rank	Emp-loy-ment	Rank
San Francisco – Oakland – San Jose, CA CMSA	196	4	14,215	1
Dallas – Fort Worth, TX CMSA	137	7	7,603	2
Atlanta, GA MSA	77	14	6,591	3
Minneapolis – St. Paul, MN – WI MSA	94	11	6,236	4
Miami – Fort Lauderdale, FL CMSA	190	5	5,635	5
St. Louis, MO – IL MSA	84	13	5,302	6
Seattle – Tacoma – Bremerton, WA CMSA	58	18	5,171	7
Jacksonville, FL MSA	31	29	4,138	8
Cleveland – Akron, OH CMSA	42	25	4,056	9
Pittsburgh, PA MSA	49	21	3,824	10
Phoenix – Mesa, AZ MSA	65	16	3,542	11
Omaha, NE – IA MSA	29	31	1,897	12
San Diego, CA MSA	62	17	1,112	13
Honolulu, HI MSA	31	29	697	14
Greensboro – Winston-Salem – High Point, NC MSA	27	33	587	15
Tampa – St. Petersburg – Clearwater, FL MSA	57	19	458	16
Memphis, TN – AR – MS MSA	32	28	412	17
Rochester, NY MSA	22	36	394	18
Chattanooga, TN – GA MSA	11	47	369	19
Norfolk – Virginia Beach – Newport News, VA – NC MSA	26	34	328	20
Pensacola, FL MSA	6	52	214	21
Fresno, CA MSA	20	38	213	22

[Continued]

★ 2539 ★

Courier Services, Except By Air
[Continued]

MSA	Estab-lish-ments	Rank	Emp-loy-ment	Rank
Tucson, AZ MSA	20	38	194	23
West Palm Beach – Boca Raton, FL MSA	22	36	179	24
Lexington, KY MSA	11	47	164	25

Source: U.S. Department of Commerce, Bureau of the Census, Data User Services Division, *1992 Economic Census, Volume 1F, Reports Series, Release 1F,* September 1995, CD-ROM. *Note:* Data are shown only for the top 25 areas.

★ 2540 ★

Establishments and Employment

Deep Sea Foreign & Domestic Freight

The U.S. total number of employees is 26,798; total number of establishments is 615.

MSA	Estab-lish-ments	Rank	Emp-loy-ment	Rank
Boston – Worcester – Lawrence, MA – NH – ME – CT CMSA	10	10	411	4
Chicago – Gary – Kenosha, IL – IN – WI CMSA	14	9	293	5
Houma, LA MSA	19	8	0[1]	6
Houston – Galveston – Brazoria, TX CMSA	39	2	0[2]	6
Los Angeles – Riverside – Orange County, CA CMSA	23	7	863	3
Miami – Fort Lauderdale, FL CMSA	37	3	0[2]	6
New Orleans, LA MSA	31	4	2,781	2
New York – Northern New Jersey – Long Island, NY – NJ – CT-CMSA	165	1	6,206	1
Norfolk – Virginia Beach – Newport News, VA – NC MSA	14	9	0[1]	6
Philadelphia – Wilmington – Atlantic City, PA – NJ – DE – MD CMSA	27	5	0[3]	6
San Francisco – Oakland – San Jose, CA CMSA	23	7	0[4]	6
Seattle – Tacoma – Bremerton, WA CMSA	24	6	0[2]	6
Tampa – St. Petersburg – Clearwater, FL MSA	2	11	0[5]	6
Washington – Baltimore, DC – MD – VA – WV CMSA	23	7	0[3]	6

Source: U.S. Department of Commerce, Bureau of the Census, Data User Services Division, *1992 Economic Census, Volume 1F, Reports Series, Release 1F,* September 1995, CD-ROM. *Notes:* 1. 250-499 employees. 2. 1,000-2,499 employees. 3. 500-999 employees. 4. 2,500-4,999 employees. 5. 100-249 employees.

★2541★

Establishments and Employment

Dump Trucking of Sand, Gravel, Dirt

The U.S. total number of employees is 66,956; total number of establishments is 13,383.

MSA	Estab-lish-ments	Rank	Emp-ploy-ment	Rank
Atlanta, GA MSA	118	13	595	10
Boston – Worcester – Lawrence, MA – NH – ME – CT CMSA	169	9	505	11
Chicago – Gary – Kenosha, IL – IN – WI CMSA	456	3	0[1]	15
Cleveland – Akron, OH CMSA	162	10	797	8
Dallas – Fort Worth, TX CMSA	136	11	599	9
Detroit – Ann Arbor – Flint, MI CMSA	173	8	856	6
Houston – Galveston – Brazoria, TX CMSA	123	12	0[2]	15
Los Angeles – Riverside – Orange County, CA CMSA	471	2	2,437	1
Miami – Fort Lauderdale, FL CMSA	55	16	385	14
Minneapolis – St. Paul, MN – WI MSA	97	15	421	12
New York – Northern New Jersey – Long Island, NY – NJ – CT-CMSA	539	1	1,823	2
Philadelphia – Wilmington – Atlantic City, PA – NJ – DE – MD CMSA	233	6	1,186	5
San Francisco – Oakland – San Jose, CA CMSA	297	5	1,452	4
Seattle – Tacoma – Bremerton, WA CMSA	106	14	418	13
St. Louis, MO – IL MSA	178	7	839	7
Washington – Baltimore, DC – MD – VA – WV CMSA	313	4	1,504	3

Source: U.S. Department of Commerce, Bureau of the Census, Data User Services Division, *1992 Economic Census, Volume 1F, Reports Series, Release 1F,* September 1995, CD-ROM. *Notes:* 1. 1,000-2,499 employees. 2. 500-999 employees.

★2542★

Establishments and Employment

Freight Forwarding

The U.S. total number of employees is 48,903; total number of establishments is 5,308.

MSA	Estab-lish-ments	Rank	Emp-ploy-ment	Rank
Atlanta, GA MSA	119	9	1,094	7
Boston – Worcester – Lawrence, MA – NH – ME – CT CMSA	117	10	0[1]	13
Chicago – Gary – Kenosha, IL – IN – WI CMSA	317	4	3,970	2
Dallas – Fort Worth, TX CMSA	102	11	985	9
Denver – Boulder – Greeley, CO CMSA	45	16	0[2]	13
Detroit – Ann Arbor – Flint, MI CMSA	78	13	0[1]	13

[Continued]

★2542★

Freight Forwarding

[Continued]

MSA	Estab-lish-ments	Rank	Emp-ploy-ment	Rank
Houston – Galveston – Brazoria, TX CMSA	184	6	1,914	5
Los Angeles – Riverside – Orange County, CA CMSA	572	2	0[3]	13
Miami – Fort Lauderdale, FL CMSA	423	3	3,184	3
Minneapolis – St. Paul, MN – WI MSA	69	14	635	10
New York – Northern New Jersey – Long Island, NY – NJ – CT-CMSA	876	1	8,245	1
Philadelphia – Wilmington – Atlantic City, PA – NJ – DE – MD CMSA	92	12	1,078	8
San Diego, CA MSA	58	15	309	11
San Francisco – Oakland – San Jose, CA CMSA	223	5	2,781	4
Seattle – Tacoma – Bremerton, WA CMSA	166	7	0[1]	13
Tampa – St. Petersburg – Clearwater, FL MSA	38	17	216	12
Washington – Baltimore, DC – MD – VA – WV CMSA	123	8	1,257	6

Source: U.S. Department of Commerce, Bureau of the Census, Data User Services Division, *1992 Economic Census, Volume 1F, Reports Series, Release 1F,* September 1995, CD-ROM. *Notes:* 1. 1,000-2,499 employees. 2. 250-499 employees. 3. 5,000-9,999 employees.

★2543★

Establishments and Employment

Freight Transportation Arrangement

The U.S. total number of employees is 106,979; total number of establishments is 12,553.

MSA	Estab-lish-ments	Rank	Emp-ploy-ment	Rank
New York – Northern New Jersey – Long Island, NY – NJ – CT-CMSA	1,973	1	19,480	1
Los Angeles – Riverside – Orange County, CA CMSA	1,017	2	11,471	2
Miami – Fort Lauderdale, FL CMSA	717	3	5,111	3
Houston – Galveston – Brazoria, TX CMSA	422	5	3,751	4
Laredo, TX MSA	335	7	3,603	5
Philadelphia – Wilmington – Atlantic City, PA – NJ – DE – MD CMSA	256	11	3,007	6
Atlanta, GA MSA	262	10	2,208	7
Detroit – Ann Arbor – Flint, MI CMSA	200	14	2,049	8
Dallas – Fort Worth, TX CMSA	221	13	1,646	9

[Continued]

★2543★

Freight Transportation Arrangement
[Continued]

MSA	Estab-lish-ments	Rank	Emp-loy-ment	Rank
New Orleans, LA MSA	187	15	1,449	10
Memphis, TN – AR – MS MSA	84	27	1,312	11
Minneapolis – St. Paul, MN – WI MSA	155	17	1,116	12
St. Louis, MO – IL MSA	148	18	1,015	13
Buffalo – Niagara Falls, NY MSA	71	30	905	14
Charlotte – Gastonia – Rock Hill, NC – SC MSA	108	23	780	15
San Diego, CA MSA	110	22	718	16
Charleston – North Charleston, SC MSA	64	32	663	17
Kansas City, MO – KS MSA	112	21	642	18
Pittsburgh, PA MSA	85	26	642	18
West Palm Beach – Boca Raton, FL MSA	32	45	636	19
Savannah, GA MSA	60	33	630	20
Providence – Fall River – Warwick, RI – MA MSA	25	49	524	21
El Paso, TX MSA	59	34	523	22
Columbus, OH MSA	56	36	511	23
Phoenix – Mesa, AZ MSA	90	24	503	24

Source: U.S. Department of Commerce, Bureau of the Census, Data User Services Division, *1992 Economic Census, Volume 1F, Reports Series, Release 1F,* September 1995, CD-ROM. *Note:* Data are shown only for the top 25 areas.

★2544★

Establishments and Employment

Garbage & Trash Collection

The U.S. total number of employees is 94,054; total number of establishments is 7,405.

MSA	Estab-lish-ments	Rank	Emp-loy-ment	Rank
Atlanta, GA MSA	75	11	960	13
Boston – Worcester – Lawrence, MA – NH – ME – CT CMSA	149	5	0[1]	14
Chicago – Gary – Kenosha, IL – IN – WI CMSA	165	4	3,332	3
Cleveland – Akron, OH CMSA	68	13	978	12
Dallas – Fort Worth, TX CMSA	42	16	1,511	9
Detroit – Ann Arbor – Flint, MI CMSA	118	8	1,551	7
Houston – Galveston – Brazoria, TX CMSA	72	12	0[1]	14
Los Angeles – Riverside – Orange County, CA CMSA	234	2	5,340	2
Miami – Fort Lauderdale, FL CMSA	55	14	1,240	10
Minneapolis – St. Paul, MN – WI MSA	142	7	1,913	6
New York – Northern New Jersey – Long Island, NY – NJ – CT-CMSA	913	1	9,959	1

[Continued]

★2544★

Garbage & Trash Collection
[Continued]

MSA	Estab-lish-ments	Rank	Emp-loy-ment	Rank
Philadelphia – Wilmington – Atlantic City, PA – NJ – DE – MD CMSA	143	6	2,375	5
San Francisco – Oakland – San Jose, CA CMSA	98	9	2,801	4
Seattle – Tacoma – Bremerton, WA CMSA	45	15	1,237	11
St. Louis, MO – IL MSA	81	10	1,529	8
Washington – Baltimore, DC – MD – VA – WV CMSA	230	3	0[2]	14

Source: U.S. Department of Commerce, Bureau of the Census, Data User Services Division, *1992 Economic Census, Volume 1F, Reports Series, Release 1F,* September 1995, CD-ROM. *Notes:* 1. 1,000-2,499 employees. 2. 2,500-4,999 employees.

★2545★

Establishments and Employment

General Freight

The U.S. total number of employees is 97,594; total number of establishments is 12,186.

MSA	Estab-lish-ments	Rank	Emp-loy-ment	Rank
Atlanta, GA MSA	122	15	1,710	8
Boston – Worcester – Lawrence, MA – NH – ME – CT CMSA	189	9	1,361	12
Chicago – Gary – Kenosha, IL – IN – WI CMSA	653	3	5,434	2
Cleveland – Akron, OH CMSA	142	12	801	14
Dallas – Fort Worth, TX CMSA	184	11	1,384	11
Detroit – Ann Arbor – Flint, MI CMSA	240	5	3,865	3
Houston – Galveston – Brazoria, TX CMSA	141	13	1,398	10
Los Angeles – Riverside – Orange County, CA CMSA	701	2	7,642	1
Miami – Fort Lauderdale, FL CMSA	125	14	784	15
Minneapolis – St. Paul, MN – WI MSA	188	10	1,990	5
New York – Northern New Jersey – Long Island, NY – NJ – CT-CMSA	1,194	1	0[1]	16
Philadelphia – Wilmington – Atlantic City, PA – NJ – DE – MD CMSA	215	6	1,789	7
San Francisco – Oakland – San Jose, CA CMSA	294	4	2,786	4
Seattle – Tacoma – Bremerton, WA CMSA	119	16	1,837	6

[Continued]

★2545★

General Freight

[Continued]

MSA	Estab-lish-ments	Rank	Emp-loy-ment	Rank
St. Louis, MO – IL MSA	205	7	1,513	9
Washington – Baltimore, DC – MD – VA – WV CMSA	194	8	1,256	13

Source: U.S. Department of Commerce, Bureau of the Census, Data User Services Division, *1992 Economic Census, Volume 1F, Reports Series, Release 1F,* September 1995, CD-ROM. *Note:* 1. 5,000-9,999 employees.

★2546★

Establishments and Employment

General Freight Trucking, Except Local

The U.S. total number of employees is 553,202; total number of establishments is 25,014.

MSA	Estab-lish-ments	Rank	Emp-loy-ment	Rank
Atlanta, GA MSA	323	6	15,737	4
Boston – Worcester – Lawrence, MA – NH – ME – CT CMSA	317	7	0[1]	16
Chicago – Gary – Kenosha, IL – IN – WI CMSA	635	2	19,781	2
Cleveland – Akron, OH CMSA	270	12	6,727	8
Dallas – Fort Worth, TX CMSA	313	8	13,187	5
Detroit – Ann Arbor – Flint, MI CMSA	298	10	8,711	7
Houston – Galveston – Brazoria, TX CMSA	199	15	6,027	11
Los Angeles – Riverside – Orange County, CA CMSA	625	3	16,352	3
Miami – Fort Lauderdale, FL CMSA	112	16	5,689	14
Minneapolis – St. Paul, MN – WI MSA	217	14	5,974	12
New York – Northern New Jersey – Long Island, NY – NJ – CT-CMSA	976	1	22,038	1
Philadelphia – Wilmington – Atlantic City, PA – NJ – DE – MD CMSA	388	4	8,923	6
San Francisco – Oakland – San Jose, CA CMSA	328	5	5,813	13
Seattle – Tacoma – Bremerton, WA CMSA	218	13	4,505	15
St. Louis, MO – IL MSA	290	11	6,060	10
Washington – Baltimore, DC – MD – VA – WV CMSA	300	9	6,691	9

Source: U.S. Department of Commerce, Bureau of the Census, Data User Services Division, *1992 Economic Census, Volume 1F, Reports Series, Release 1F,* September 1995, CD-ROM. *Note:* 1. 5,000-9,999 employees.

★2547★

Establishments and Employment

Household Goods Moving

The U.S. total number of employees is 13,237; total number of establishments is 2,566.

MSA	Estab-lish-ments	Rank	Emp-loy-ment	Rank
Atlanta, GA MSA	26	15	225	4
Boston – Worcester – Lawrence, MA – NH – ME – CT CMSA	85	6	0[1]	11
Chicago – Gary – Kenosha, IL – IN – WI CMSA	121	3	0[2]	11
Cleveland – Akron, OH CMSA	29	14	88	9
Dallas – Fort Worth, TX CMSA	33	12	114	8
Detroit – Ann Arbor – Flint, MI CMSA	52	8	285	3
Houston – Galveston – Brazoria, TX CMSA	31	13	0[3]	11
Los Angeles – Riverside – Orange County, CA CMSA	176	2	1,254	1
Miami – Fort Lauderdale, FL CMSA	45	9	209	6
Minneapolis – St. Paul, MN – WI MSA	34	11	127	7
New York – Northern New Jersey – Long Island, NY – NJ – CT-CMSA	314	1	0[4]	11
Philadelphia – Wilmington – Atlantic City, PA – NJ – DE – MD CMSA	55	7	0[3]	11
San Francisco – Oakland – San Jose, CA CMSA	118	4	589	2
Seattle – Tacoma – Bremerton, WA CMSA	16	16	80	10
St. Louis, MO – IL MSA	42	10	213	5
Washington – Baltimore, DC – MD – VA – WV CMSA	86	5	0[2]	11

Source: U.S. Department of Commerce, Bureau of the Census, Data User Services Division, *1992 Economic Census, Volume 1F, Reports Series, Release 1F,* September 1995, CD-ROM. *Notes:* 1. 250-499 employees. 2. 500-999 employees. 3. 100-249 employees. 4. 1,000-2,499 employees.

★2548★

Establishments and Employment

Household Goods Moving, Except Local

The U.S. total number of employees is 61,592; total number of establishments is 3,248.

MSA	Estab-lish-ments	Rank	Emp-loy-ment	Rank
Atlanta, GA MSA	50	8	826	8
Boston – Worcester – Lawrence, MA – NH – ME – CT CMSA	64	5	1,113	6
Chicago – Gary – Kenosha, IL – IN – WI CMSA	103	3	4,201	1
Cleveland – Akron, OH CMSA	32	14	740	11
Dallas – Fort Worth, TX CMSA	52	6	1,356	4
Detroit – Ann Arbor – Flint, MI CMSA	51	7	1,305	5

[Continued]

★ 2548 ★

Household Goods Moving, Except Local
[Continued]

MSA	Estab-lish-ments	Rank	Emp-loy-ment	Rank
Houston – Galveston – Brazoria, TX CMSA	33	13	0[1]	14
Los Angeles – Riverside – Orange County, CA CMSA	146	2	0[2]	14
Miami – Fort Lauderdale, FL CMSA	40	10	499	13
Minneapolis – St. Paul, MN – WI MSA	31	15	820	9
New York – Northern New Jersey – Long Island, NY – NJ – CT-CMSA	246	1	0[3]	14
Philadelphia – Wilmington – Atlantic City, PA – NJ – DE – MD CMSA	39	11	1,102	7
San Francisco – Oakland – San Jose, CA CMSA	64	5	748	10
Seattle – Tacoma – Bremerton, WA CMSA	42	9	715	12
St. Louis, MO – IL MSA	37	12	1,443	3
Washington – Baltimore, DC – MD – VA – WV CMSA	80	4	1,892	2

Source: U.S. Department of Commerce, Bureau of the Census, Data User Services Division, *1992 Economic Census, Volume 1F, Reports Series, Release 1F,* September 1995, CD-ROM. *Notes:* 1. 500-999 employees. 2. 1,000-2,499 employees. 3. 2,500-4,999 employees.

★ 2549 ★
Establishments and Employment

Household Goods Moving, With Storage

The U.S. total number of employees is 36,483; total number of establishments is 2,641.

MSA	Estab-lish-ments	Rank	Emp-loy-ment	Rank
Atlanta, GA MSA	24	15	403	4
Boston – Worcester – Lawrence, MA – NH – ME – CT CMSA	62	7	0[1]	8
Chicago – Gary – Kenosha, IL – IN – WI CMSA	79	5	0[2]	8
Cleveland – Akron, OH CMSA	27	14	242	6
Dallas – Fort Worth, TX CMSA	35	10	0[1]	8
Detroit – Ann Arbor – Flint, MI CMSA	34	11	0[3]	8
Houston – Galveston – Brazoria, TX CMSA	33	12	0[1]	8
Los Angeles – Riverside – Orange County, CA CMSA	195	2	0[4]	8
Miami – Fort Lauderdale, FL CMSA	44	9	469	3
Minneapolis – St. Paul, MN – WI MSA	20	16	230	7
New York – Northern New Jersey – Long Island, NY – NJ – CT-CMSA	246	1	0[4]	8

[Continued]

★ 2549 ★

Household Goods Moving, With Storage
[Continued]

MSA	Estab-lish-ments	Rank	Emp-loy-ment	Rank
Philadelphia – Wilmington – Atlantic City, PA – NJ – DE – MD CMSA	64	6	0[2]	8
San Francisco – Oakland – San Jose, CA CMSA	141	3	2,540	1
Seattle – Tacoma – Bremerton, WA CMSA	50	8	950	2
St. Louis, MO – IL MSA	28	13	265	5
Washington – Baltimore, DC – MD – VA – WV CMSA	90	4	0[2]	8

Source: U.S. Department of Commerce, Bureau of the Census, Data User Services Division, *1992 Economic Census, Volume 1F, Reports Series, Release 1F,* September 1995, CD-ROM. *Notes:* 1. 500-999 employees. 2. 1,000-2,499 employees. 3. 250-499 employees. 4. 2,500-4,999 employees.

★ 2550 ★
Establishments and Employment

Intercity & Rural Bus Transportation

The U.S. total number of employees is 20,404; total number of establishments is 607.

MSA	Estab-lish-ments	Rank	Emp-loy-ment	Rank
Boston – Worcester – Lawrence, MA – NH – ME – CT CMSA	11	5	0[1]	3
Chicago – Gary – Kenosha, IL – IN – WI CMSA	14	4	0[2]	3
Los Angeles – Riverside – Orange County, CA CMSA	26	2	1,281	2
New York – Northern New Jersey – Long Island, NY – NJ – CT-CMSA	80	1	7,359	1
Philadelphia – Wilmington – Atlantic City, PA – NJ – DE – MD CMSA	21	3	0[1]	3
San Francisco – Oakland – San Jose, CA CMSA	8	7	0[3]	3
Washington – Baltimore, DC – MD – VA – WV CMSA	10	6	0[1]	3

Source: U.S. Department of Commerce, Bureau of the Census, Data User Services Division, *1992 Economic Census, Volume 1F, Reports Series, Release 1F,* September 1995, CD-ROM. *Notes:* 1. 250-499 employees. 2. 500-999 employees. 3. 100-249 employees.

★2551★

Establishments and Employment

Local & Interurban Passenger Transit

The U.S. total number of employees is 354,913; total number of establishments is 17,805.

MSA	Estab-lish-ments	Rank	Emp-loy-ment	Rank
New York – Northern New Jersey – Long Island, NY – NJ – CT-CMSA	3,523	1	67,760	1
Los Angeles – Riverside – Orange County, CA CMSA	642	2	20,795	2
Boston – Worcester – Lawrence, MA – NH – ME – CT CMSA	616	4	15,208	3
Chicago – Gary – Kenosha, IL – IN – WI CMSA	525	5	15,048	4
Philadelphia – Wilmington – Atlantic City, PA – NJ – DE – MD CMSA	495	6	10,751	5
San Francisco – Oakland – San Jose, CA CMSA	358	7	8,596	6
Pittsburgh, PA MSA	241	8	7,882	7
Washington – Baltimore, DC – MD – VA – WV CMSA	638	3	7,716	8
Minneapolis – St. Paul, MN – WI MSA	185	10	6,433	9
Milwaukee – Racine, WI CMSA	150	13	5,171	10
St. Louis, MO – IL MSA	161	12	4,850	11
San Diego, CA MSA	98	24	4,453	12
Las Vegas, NV – AZ MSA	47	43	4,308	13
Kansas City, MO – KS MSA	127	16	4,101	14
Hartford, CT MSA	96	26	3,683	15
Detroit – Ann Arbor – Flint, MI CMSA	192	9	3,589	16
Honolulu, HI MSA	65	35	3,345	17
Buffalo – Niagara Falls, NY MSA	82	28	3,239	18
Seattle – Tacoma – Bremerton, WA CMSA	117	19	2,989	19
Portland – Salem, OR – WA CMSA	99	23	2,912	20
Cleveland – Akron, OH CMSA	118	18	2,898	21
Miami – Fort Lauderdale, FL CMSA	184	11	2,869	22
Dallas – Fort Worth, TX CMSA	121	17	2,707	23
Atlanta, GA MSA	130	15	2,312	24
Providence – Fall River – Warwick, RI – MA MSA	97	25	2,219	25

Source: U.S. Department of Commerce, Bureau of the Census, Data User Services Division, *1992 Economic Census, Volume 1F, Reports Series, Release 1F,* September 1995, CD-ROM. *Note:* Data are shown only for the top 25 areas.

★2552★

Establishments and Employment

Local Trucking With Storage

The U.S. total number of employees is 64,417; total number of establishments is 4,512.

MSA	Estab-lish-ments	Rank	Emp-loy-ment	Rank
San Francisco – Oakland – San Jose, CA CMSA	218	3	3,733	1
Seattle – Tacoma – Bremerton, WA CMSA	89	8	1,879	2
Dallas – Fort Worth, TX CMSA	65	11	1,321	3
Honolulu, HI MSA	20	28	1,118	4
Miami – Fort Lauderdale, FL CMSA	80	9	927	5
Phoenix – Mesa, AZ MSA	36	19	910	6
Atlanta, GA MSA	40	18	855	7
Norfolk – Virginia Beach – Newport News, VA – NC MSA	30	22	747	8
Pittsburgh, PA MSA	44	17	705	9
St. Louis, MO – IL MSA	49	16	654	10
San Diego, CA MSA	54	13	625	11
Minneapolis – St. Paul, MN – WI MSA	33	20	504	12
Cleveland – Akron, OH CMSA	53	14	414	13
Tampa – St. Petersburg – Clearwater, FL MSA	30	22	288	14
Jacksonville, FL MSA	21	27	258	15
El Paso, TX MSA	24	25	209	16
Memphis, TN – AR – MS MSA	14	32	209	16
Anchorage, AK MSA	10	36	176	17
Bakersfield, CA MSA	11	35	166	18
Savannah, GA MSA	10	36	163	19
Colorado Springs, CO MSA	12	34	160	20
Tucson, AZ MSA	10	36	158	21
Austin – San Marcos, TX MSA	16	30	155	22
Salinas, CA MSA	15	31	144	23
West Palm Beach – Boca Raton, FL MSA	20	28	144	23

Source: U.S. Department of Commerce, Bureau of the Census, Data User Services Division, *1992 Economic Census, Volume 1F, Reports Series, Release 1F,* September 1995, CD-ROM. *Note:* Data are shown only for the top 25 areas.

★2553★

Establishments and Employment

Marinas

The U.S. total number of employees is 17,913; total number of establishments is 3,348.

MSA	Estab-lish-ments	Rank	Emp-loy-ment	Rank
Miami – Fort Lauderdale, FL CMSA	88	3	541	1
Boston – Worcester – Lawrence, MA – NH – ME – CT CMSA	78	5	396	2
Tampa – St. Petersburg – Clearwater, FL MSA	44	10	301	3
Norfolk – Virginia Beach – Newport News, VA – NC MSA	39	12	281	4

[Continued]

★ 2553 ★

Marinas

[Continued]

MSA	Estab-lish-ments	Rank	Emp-loy-ment	Rank
Sarasota – Bradenton, FL MSA	22	20	273	5
Providence – Fall River – Warwick, RI – MA MSA	38	13	267	6
Jacksonville, FL MSA	24	18	189	7
Minneapolis – St. Paul, MN – WI MSA	28	15	162	8
Houma, LA MSA	10	31	159	9
San Diego, CA MSA	17	25	151	10
Charleston – North Charleston, SC MSA	18	24	146	11
Melbourne – Titusville – Palm Bay, FL MSA	20	22	138	12
New Orleans, LA MSA	25	17	125	13
Portland, ME MSA	16	26	110	14
Fort Pierce – Port St. Lucie, FL MSA	16	26	101	15
Savannah, GA MSA	13	28	95	16
Bellingham, WA MSA	6	35	52	17
Knoxville, TN MSA	8	33	38	18
Kansas City, MO – KS MSA	6	35	28	19
Kalamazoo – Battle Creek, MI MSA	3	38	26	20
Omaha, NE – IA MSA	6	35	25	21
Johnson City – Kingsport – Bristol, TN – VA MSA	7	34	21	22
Davenport – Moline – Rock Island, IA – IL MSA	5	36	13	23
Louisville, KY – IN MSA	4	37	12	24
Saginaw – Bay City – Midland, MI MSA	3	38	10	25

Source: U.S. Department of Commerce, Bureau of the Census, Data User Services Division, *1992 Economic Census, Volume 1F, Reports Series, Release 1F*, September 1995, CD-ROM. *Note:* Data are shown only for the top 25 areas.

★ 2554 ★

Establishments and Employment

Marine Cargo Handling

The U.S. total number of employees is 58,840; total number of establishments is 871.

MSA	Estab-lish-ments	Rank	Emp-loy-ment	Rank
Boston – Worcester – Lawrence, MA – NH – ME – CT CMSA	9	14	336	8
Chicago – Gary – Kenosha, IL – IN – WI CMSA	23	8	0[1]	10
Houma, LA MSA	21	10	247	9
Houston – Galveston – Brazoria, TX CMSA	60	1	4,528	2
Los Angeles – Riverside – Orange County, CA CMSA	38	5	0[2]	10
Miami – Fort Lauderdale, FL CMSA	47	4	5,033	1

[Continued]

★ 2554 ★

Marine Cargo Handling

[Continued]

MSA	Estab-lish-ments	Rank	Emp-loy-ment	Rank
New Orleans, LA MSA	56	2	3,009	3
New York – Northern New Jersey – Long Island, NY – NJ – CT-CMSA	49	3	3,001	4
Norfolk – Virginia Beach – Newport News, VA – NC MSA	17	13	0[3]	10
Philadelphia – Wilmington – Atlantic City, PA – NJ – DE – MD CMSA	29	7	0[3]	10
San Francisco – Oakland – San Jose, CA CMSA	34	6	2,016	5
Seattle – Tacoma – Bremerton, WA CMSA	22	9	0[4]	10
Tampa – St. Petersburg – Clearwater, FL MSA	18	12	912	7
Washington – Baltimore, DC – MD – VA – WV CMSA	19	11	1,906	6

Source: U.S. Department of Commerce, Bureau of the Census, Data User Services Division, *1992 Economic Census, Volume 1F, Reports Series, Release 1F*, September 1995, CD-ROM. *Notes:* 1. 250-499 employees. 2. 5,000-9,999 employees. 3. 2,500-4,999 employees. 4. 1,000-2,499 employees.

★ 2555 ★

Establishments and Employment

Passenger Transportation Arrangement

The U.S. total number of employees is 192,981; total number of establishments is 31,793.

MSA	Estab-lish-ments	Rank	Emp-loy-ment	Rank
New York – Northern New Jersey – Long Island, NY – NJ – CT-CMSA	3,971	1	21,365	1
Los Angeles – Riverside – Orange County, CA CMSA	2,374	2	14,617	2
Chicago – Gary – Kenosha, IL – IN – WI CMSA	1,481	3	11,387	3
Miami – Fort Lauderdale, FL CMSA	1,067	6	7,366	4
Philadelphia – Wilmington – Atlantic City, PA – NJ – DE – MD CMSA	817	8	5,472	5
Honolulu, HI MSA	438	16	5,300	6
Atlanta, GA MSA	538	12	4,326	7
Dallas – Fort Worth, TX CMSA	613	9	4,083	8
Minneapolis – St. Paul, MN – WI MSA	391	18	3,792	9
Detroit – Ann Arbor – Flint, MI CMSA	592	11	3,541	10
St. Louis, MO – IL MSA	282	23	3,232	11
Houston – Galveston – Brazoria, TX CMSA	516	13	2,751	12
Kansas City, MO – KS MSA	205	27	2,661	13

[Continued]

★2555★

Passenger Transportation Arrangement
[Continued]

MSA	Estab-lish-ments	Rank	Emp-loy-ment	Rank
Orlando, FL MSA	322	21	2,527	14
Tampa – St. Petersburg – Clearwater, FL MSA	404	17	2,428	15
Phoenix – Mesa, AZ MSA	379	19	2,393	16
San Diego, CA MSA	471	14	2,154	17
Milwaukee – Racine, WI CMSA	242	25	1,887	18
Cleveland – Akron, OH CMSA	324	20	1,806	19
Pittsburgh, PA MSA	273	24	1,487	20
Las Vegas, NV – AZ MSA	160	31	1,183	21
Salt Lake City – Ogden, UT MSA	124	38	1,158	22
Cincinnati – Hamilton, OH – KY – IN CMSA	141	34	1,122	23
Nashville, TN MSA	112	41	998	24
Hartford, CT MSA	183	28	989	25

Source: U.S. Department of Commerce, Bureau of the Census, Data User Services Division, *1992 Economic Census, Volume 1F, Reports Series, Release 1F,* September 1995, CD-ROM. *Note:* Data are shown only for the top 25 areas.

★2556★

Establishments and Employment

Public Warehousing & Storage

The U.S. total number of employees is 95,145; total number of establishments is 9,718.

MSA	Estab-lish-ments	Rank	Emp-loy-ment	Rank
Los Angeles – Riverside – Orange County, CA CMSA	734	1	6,534	1
Chicago – Gary – Kenosha, IL – IN – WI CMSA	324	4	4,672	2
San Francisco – Oakland – San Jose, CA CMSA	394	3	3,116	3
Houston – Galveston – Brazoria, TX CMSA	199	7	2,559	4
Atlanta, GA MSA	173	12	2,442	5
New Orleans, LA MSA	59	29	2,093	6
Dallas – Fort Worth, TX CMSA	236	5	2,092	7
Washington – Baltimore, DC – MD – VA – WV CMSA	197	8	1,602	8
Harrisburg – Lebanon – Carlisle, PA MSA	20	56	1,456	9
Columbus, OH MSA	53	32	1,417	10
Memphis, TN – AR – MS MSA	77	24	1,157	11
Kansas City, MO – KS MSA	92	20	1,132	12
Greensboro – Winston-Salem – High Point, NC MSA	46	36	1,005	13
Sacramento – Yolo, CA CMSA	88	21	898	14
St. Louis, MO – IL MSA	82	22	870	15
Tampa – St. Petersburg – Clearwater, FL MSA	95	19	833	16
Minneapolis – St. Paul, MN – WI MSA	80	23	808	17
Jacksonville, FL MSA	61	28	744	18

[Continued]

★2556★

Public Warehousing & Storage
[Continued]

MSA	Estab-lish-ments	Rank	Emp-loy-ment	Rank
Portland – Salem, OR – WA CMSA	101	17	712	19
Indianapolis, IN MSA	49	35	688	20
Phoenix – Mesa, AZ MSA	116	15	578	21
Louisville, KY – IN MSA	42	39	564	22
Charleston – North Charleston, SC MSA	37	43	554	23
San Diego, CA MSA	125	14	522	24
Norfolk – Virginia Beach – Newport News, VA – NC MSA	71	26	500	25

Source: U.S. Department of Commerce, Bureau of the Census, Data User Services Division, *1992 Economic Census, Volume 1F, Reports Series, Release 1F,* September 1995, CD-ROM. *Note:* Data are shown only for the top 25 areas.

★2557★

Establishments and Employment

Radio & TV Broadcasting

The U.S. total number of employees is 221,755; total number of establishments is 8,549.

MSA	Estab-lish-ments	Rank	Emp-loy-ment	Rank
New York – Northern New Jersey – Long Island, NY – NJ – CT-CMSA	261	1	25,140	1
Los Angeles – Riverside – Orange County, CA CMSA	236	2	11,224	2
Philadelphia – Wilmington – Atlantic City, PA – NJ – DE – MD CMSA	87	8	2,935	3
Miami – Fort Lauderdale, FL CMSA	68	12	2,709	4
Norfolk – Virginia Beach – Newport News, VA – NC MSA	47	21	2,607	5
Houston – Galveston – Brazoria, TX CMSA	70	10	2,414	6
Atlanta, GA MSA	65	13	2,132	7
Minneapolis – St. Paul, MN – WI MSA	59	14	2,126	8
Cleveland – Akron, OH CMSA	56	15	2,105	9
Denver – Boulder – Greeley, CO CMSA	55	16	1,846	10
Phoenix – Mesa, AZ MSA	48	20	1,791	11
St. Louis, MO – IL MSA	53	17	1,768	12
Pittsburgh, PA MSA	51	18	1,749	13
Charlotte – Gastonia – Rock Hill, NC – SC MSA	42	23	1,616	14
Tampa – St. Petersburg – Clearwater, FL MSA	59	14	1,587	15
San Diego, CA MSA	38	26	1,574	16
Indianapolis, IN MSA	39	25	1,528	17
Portland – Salem, OR – WA CMSA	49	19	1,465	18
Kansas City, MO – KS MSA	33	31	1,258	19
Salt Lake City – Ogden, UT MSA	31	33	1,156	20

[Continued]

★ 2557 ★

Radio & TV Broadcasting
[Continued]

MSA	Estab-lish-ments	Rank	Emp-loy-ment	Rank
Nashville, TN MSA	48	20	1,149	21
Orlando, FL MSA	37	27	1,118	22
Buffalo – Niagara Falls, NY MSA	26	38	1,022	23
Las Vegas, NV–AZ MSA	44	22	1,011	24
Louisville, KY–IN MSA	28	36	997	25

Source: U.S. Department of Commerce, Bureau of the Census, Data User Services Division, *1992 Economic Census, Volume 1F, Reports Series, Release 1F*, September 1995, CD-ROM. *Note:* Data are shown only for the top 25 areas.

★ 2558 ★

Establishments and Employment

Refrigerated Warehousing & Storage

The U.S. total number of employees is 18,963; total number of establishments is 929.

MSA	Estab-lish-ments	Rank	Emp-loy-ment	Rank
Atlanta, GA MSA	6	11	0[1]	5
Boston – Worcester – Lawrence, MA – NH – ME – CT CMSA	24	4	0[1]	5
Chicago – Gary – Kenosha, IL – IN – WI CMSA	17	6	0[2]	5
Cleveland – Akron, OH CMSA	3	12	0[3]	5
Dallas – Fort Worth, TX CMSA	10	8	0[2]	5
Detroit – Ann Arbor – Flint, MI CMSA	7	10	108	3
Houston – Galveston – Brazoria, TX CMSA	6	11	69	4
Los Angeles – Riverside – Orange County, CA CMSA	45	1	1,037	1
Miami – Fort Lauderdale, FL CMSA	13	7	0[4]	5
Minneapolis – St. Paul, MN – WI MSA	7	10	0[4]	5
New York – Northern New Jersey – Long Island, NY – NJ – CT-CMSA	33	3	0[5]	5
Philadelphia – Wilmington – Atlantic City, PA – NJ – DE – MD CMSA	39	2	0[2]	5
San Francisco – Oakland – San Jose, CA CMSA	33	3	578	2
Seattle – Tacoma – Bremerton, WA CMSA	18	5	0[2]	5
St. Louis, MO – IL MSA	6	11	0[4]	5
Washington – Baltimore, DC – MD – VA – WV CMSA	8	9	0[4]	5

Source: U.S. Department of Commerce, Bureau of the Census, Data User Services Division, *1992 Economic Census, Volume 1F, Reports Series, Release 1F*, September 1995, CD-ROM. *Notes:* 1. 250-499 employees. 2. 500-999 employees. 3. 20-99 employees. 4. 100-249 employees. 5. 1,000-2,499 employees.

★ 2559 ★

Establishments and Employment

Refuse Systems

The U.S. total number of employees is 80,917; total number of establishments is 3,317.

MSA	Estab-lish-ments	Rank	Emp-loy-ment	Rank
Boston – Worcester – Lawrence, MA – NH – ME – CT CMSA	89	5	2,684	5
Chicago – Gary – Kenosha, IL – IN – WI CMSA	107	3	3,223	3
Dallas – Fort Worth, TX CMSA	51	8	1,015	7
Houston – Galveston – Brazoria, TX CMSA	84	6	2,757	4
Los Angeles – Riverside – Orange County, CA CMSA	170	2	4,466	1
New York – Northern New Jersey – Long Island, NY – NJ – CT-CMSA	224	1	0[1]	8
Philadelphia – Wilmington – Atlantic City, PA – NJ – DE – MD CMSA	81	7	2,251	6
San Francisco – Oakland – San Jose, CA CMSA	96	4	4,346	2

Source: U.S. Department of Commerce, Bureau of the Census, Data User Services Division, *1992 Economic Census, Volume 1F, Reports Series, Release 1F*, September 1995, CD-ROM. *Note:* 1. 2,500-4,999 employees.

★ 2560 ★

Establishments and Employment

Sanitary Services

The U.S. total number of employees is 92,467; total number of establishments is 5,064.

MSA	Estab-lish-ments	Rank	Emp-loy-ment	Rank
New York – Northern New Jersey – Long Island, NY – NJ – CT-CMSA	322	1	5,680	1
Los Angeles – Riverside – Orange County, CA CMSA	265	2	5,332	2
Detroit – Ann Arbor – Flint, MI CMSA	122	7	2,900	3
Philadelphia – Wilmington – Atlantic City, PA – NJ – DE – MD CMSA	110	8	2,490	4
Columbus, OH MSA	20	34	1,553	5
Miami – Fort Lauderdale, FL CMSA	49	19	1,471	6
Las Vegas, NV – AZ MSA	28	29	1,412	7
Buffalo – Niagara Falls, NY MSA	39	22	1,278	8
Dallas – Fort Worth, TX CMSA	78	10	1,240	9
Pittsburgh, PA MSA	64	13	1,064	10
Knoxville, TN MSA	21	33	1,046	11
Cleveland – Akron, OH CMSA	46	20	1,014	12
Atlanta, GA MSA	61	16	1,006	13
Cincinnati – Hamilton, OH – KY – IN CMSA	29	28	992	14
St. Louis, MO – IL MSA	65	12	958	15

[Continued]

★ 2560 ★

Sanitary Services
[Continued]

MSA	Estab-lish-ments	Rank	Emp-ploy-ment	Rank
Minneapolis – St. Paul, MN – WI MSA	67	11	770	16
Tampa – St. Petersburg – Clearwater, FL MSA	38	23	759	17
Allentown – Bethlehem – Easton, PA MSA	11	43	740	18
Indianapolis, IN MSA	31	26	712	19
Jacksonville, FL MSA	33	25	646	20
Charlotte – Gastonia – Rock Hill, NC – SC MSA	25	30	642	21
Portland – Salem, OR – WA CMSA	50	18	614	22
San Diego, CA MSA	30	27	600	23
Providence – Fall River – Warwick, RI – MA MSA	31	26	521	24
Lake Charles, LA MSA	10	44	496	25

Source: U.S. Department of Commerce, Bureau of the Census, Data User Services Division, *1992 Economic Census, Volume 1F, Reports Series, Release 1F,* September 1995, CD-ROM. *Note:* Data are shown only for the top 25 areas.

★ 2561 ★

Establishments and Employment

School Buses

The U.S. total number of employees is 130,093; total number of establishments is 4,260.

MSA	Estab-lish-ments	Rank	Emp-ploy-ment	Rank
Boston – Worcester – Lawrence, MA – NH – ME – CT CMSA	163	3	0^1	3
Chicago – Gary – Kenosha, IL – IN – WI CMSA	108	4	0^1	3
Los Angeles – Riverside – Orange County, CA CMSA	52	6	8,443	2
New York – Northern New Jersey – Long Island, NY – NJ – CT-CMSA	549	1	27,591	1
Philadelphia – Wilmington – Atlantic City, PA – NJ – DE – MD CMSA	106	5	0^2	3
San Francisco – Oakland – San Jose, CA CMSA	13	7	0^3	3
Washington – Baltimore, DC – MD – VA – WV CMSA	293	2	0^2	3

Source: U.S. Department of Commerce, Bureau of the Census, Data User Services Division, *1992 Economic Census, Volume 1F, Reports Series, Release 1F,* September 1995, CD-ROM. *Notes:* 1. 5,000-9,999 employees. 2. 2,500-4,999 employees. 3. 500-999 employees.

★ 2562 ★

Establishments and Employment

Tour Operators

The U.S. total number of employees is 30,519; total number of establishments is 3,008.

MSA	Estab-lish-ments	Rank	Emp-ploy-ment	Rank
Atlanta, GA MSA	37	12	0^1	7
Boston – Worcester – Lawrence, MA – NH – ME – CT CMSA	67	8	900	5
Chicago – Gary – Kenosha, IL – IN – WI CMSA	114	5	0^2	7
Dallas – Fort Worth, TX CMSA	37	12	0^3	7
Denver – Boulder – Greeley, CO CMSA	33	14	0^1	7
Detroit – Ann Arbor – Flint, MI CMSA	34	13	0^1	7
Houston – Galveston – Brazoria, TX CMSA	34	13	0^1	7
Los Angeles – Riverside – Orange County, CA CMSA	274	2	0^4	7
Miami – Fort Lauderdale, FL CMSA	143	3	1,278	3
Minneapolis – St. Paul, MN – WI MSA	44	11	951	4
New York – Northern New Jersey – Long Island, NY – NJ – CT-CMSA	404	1	3,637	1
Philadelphia – Wilmington – Atlantic City, PA – NJ – DE – MD CMSA	85	6	0^5	7
San Diego, CA MSA	47	10	0^1	7
San Francisco – Oakland – San Jose, CA CMSA	140	4	1,933	2
Seattle – Tacoma – Bremerton, WA CMSA	70	7	0^2	7
Tampa – St. Petersburg – Clearwater, FL MSA	34	13	190	6
Washington – Baltimore, DC – MD – VA – WV CMSA	66	9	0^5	7

Source: U.S. Department of Commerce, Bureau of the Census, Data User Services Division, *1992 Economic Census, Volume 1F, Reports Series, Release 1F,* September 1995, CD-ROM. *Notes:* 1. 250-499 employees. 2. 1,000-2,499 employees. 3. 100-249 employees. 4. 2,500-4,999 employees. 5. 500-999 employees.

★2563★
Establishments and Employment
Towing & Tugboat Service

The U.S. total number of employees is 24,639; total number of establishments is 941.

MSA	Estab-lish-ments	Rank	Emp-loy-ment	Rank
Boston – Worcester – Lawrence, MA – NH – ME – CT CMSA	10	12	78	8
Chicago – Gary – Kenosha, IL – IN – WI CMSA	13	9	209	7
Houma, LA MSA	105	2	1,680	2
Houston – Galveston – Brazoria, TX CMSA	47	4	1,165	3
Los Angeles – Riverside – Orange County, CA CMSA	11	11	468	5
Miami – Fort Lauderdale, FL CMSA	12	10	0[1]	9
New Orleans, LA MSA	128	1	3,945	1
New York – Northern New Jersey – Long Island, NY – NJ – CT-CMSA	50	3	737	4
Norfolk – Virginia Beach – Newport News, VA – NC MSA	21	6	0[2]	9
Philadelphia – Wilmington – Atlantic City, PA – NJ – DE – MD CMSA	19	7	0[3]	9
San Francisco – Oakland – San Jose, CA CMSA	16	8	457	6
Seattle – Tacoma – Bremerton, WA CMSA	23	5	0[4]	9
Tampa – St. Petersburg – Clearwater, FL MSA	4	13	0[1]	9
Washington – Baltimore, DC – MD – VA – WV CMSA	10	12	0[1]	9

Source: U.S. Department of Commerce, Bureau of the Census, Data User Services Division, *1992 Economic Census, Volume 1F, Reports Series, Release 1F,* September 1995, CD-ROM. *Notes:* 1. 100-249 employees. 2. 500-999 employees. 3. 250-499 employees. 4. 1,000-2,499 employees.

★2564★
Establishments and Employment
Travel Agencies

The U.S. total number of employees is 149,140; total number of establishments is 27,688.

MSA	Estab-lish-ments	Rank	Emp-loy-ment	Rank
San Francisco – Oakland – San Jose, CA CMSA	1,205	4	6,528	1
Washington – Baltimore, DC – MD – VA – WV CMSA	990	5	5,445	2
Miami – Fort Lauderdale, FL CMSA	862	7	4,652	3
Dallas – Fort Worth, TX CMSA	558	9	3,755	4
Atlanta, GA MSA	489	12	3,288	5
Seattle – Tacoma – Bremerton, WA CMSA	510	11	2,752	6
Minneapolis – St. Paul, MN – WI MSA	337	17	2,362	7

[Continued]

★2564★
Travel Agencies
[Continued]

MSA	Estab-lish-ments	Rank	Emp-loy-ment	Rank
Honolulu, HI MSA	288	20	2,061	8
Phoenix – Mesa, AZ MSA	326	18	1,925	9
San Diego, CA MSA	410	14	1,770	10
Tampa – St. Petersburg – Clearwater, FL MSA	356	16	1,668	11
Cleveland – Akron, OH CMSA	297	19	1,657	12
Orlando, FL MSA	236	24	1,480	13
Pittsburgh, PA MSA	239	23	1,276	14
Milwaukee – Racine, WI CMSA	211	25	1,176	15
Salt Lake City – Ogden, UT MSA	103	40	1,015	16
Cincinnati – Hamilton, OH – KY – IN CMSA	129	32	1,005	17
Hartford, CT MSA	168	28	924	18
Las Vegas, NV – AZ MSA	129	32	881	19
Nashville, TN MSA	91	44	811	20
West Palm Beach – Boca Raton, FL MSA	202	26	784	21
Raleigh – Durham – Chapel Hill, NC MSA	94	42	666	22
Grand Rapids – Muskegon – Holland, MI MSA	79	50	644	23
New Orleans, LA MSA	147	30	629	24
Buffalo – Niagara Falls, NY MSA	126	33	579	25

Source: U.S. Department of Commerce, Bureau of the Census, Data User Services Division, *1992 Economic Census, Volume 1F, Reports Series, Release 1F,* September 1995, CD-ROM. *Note:* Data are shown only for the top 25 areas.

★2565★
Establishments and Employment
Trucking & Courier Services, Except Air

The U.S. total number of employees is 1,484,655; total number of establishments is 101,169.

MSA	Estab-lish-ments	Rank	Emp-loy-ment	Rank
New York – Northern New Jersey – Long Island, NY – NJ – CT-CMSA	6,699	1	98,332	1
Los Angeles – Riverside – Orange County, CA CMSA	3,908	2	76,839	2
Chicago – Gary – Kenosha, IL – IN – WI CMSA	3,104	3	60,060	3
San Francisco – Oakland – San Jose, CA CMSA	1,953	4	35,844	4
Washington – Baltimore, DC – MD – VA – WV CMSA	1,933	5	31,854	5
Dallas – Fort Worth, TX CMSA	1,224	10	31,279	6
Atlanta, GA MSA	996	14	30,007	7
Detroit – Ann Arbor – Flint, MI CMSA	1,386	8	26,231	8
Houston – Galveston – Brazoria, TX CMSA	1,034	12	21,653	9
Minneapolis – St. Paul, MN – WI MSA	1,043	11	20,068	10

[Continued]

★2565★

Trucking & Courier Services, Except Air
[Continued]

MSA	Estab-lish-ments	Rank	Emp-loy-ment	Rank
St. Louis, MO–IL MSA	1,226	9	19,559	11
Seattle–Tacoma–Bremerton, WA CMSA	929	15	18,252	12
Kansas City, MO–KS MSA	749	19	17,983	13
Miami–Fort Lauderdale, FL CMSA	867	16	16,856	14
Portland–Salem, OR–WA CMSA	846	17	16,681	15
Cleveland–Akron, OH CMSA	999	13	16,309	16
Charlotte–Gastonia–Rock Hill, NC–SC MSA	461	30	16,307	17
Indianapolis, IN MSA	605	24	16,148	18
Denver–Boulder–Greeley, CO CMSA	735	20	15,660	19
Phoenix–Mesa, AZ MSA	632	23	14,534	20
Pittsburgh, PA MSA	815	18	14,477	21
Nashville, TN MSA	411	35	12,944	22
Columbus, OH MSA	508	27	12,328	23
Cincinnati–Hamilton, OH–KY–IN CMSA	689	22	12,320	24
Salt Lake City–Ogden, UT MSA	358	39	12,245	25

Source: U.S. Department of Commerce, Bureau of the Census, Data User Services Division, *1992 Economic Census, Volume 1F, Reports Series, Release 1F,* September 1995, CD-ROM. *Note:* Data are shown only for the top 25 areas.

★2566★

Establishments and Employment

Trucking Terminal Facilities

The U.S. total number of employees is 295; total number of establishments is 21.

MSA	Estab-lish-ments	Rank	Emp-loy-ment	Rank
Albany–Schenectady–Troy, NY MSA	0	3	0	1
Albuquerque, NM MSA	0	3	0	1
Allentown–Bethlehem–Easton, PA MSA	0	3	0	1
Amarillo, TX MSA	0	3	0	1
Anchorage, AK MSA	0	3	0	1
Appleton–Oshkosh–Neenah, WI MSA	0	3	0	1
Asheville, NC MSA	0	3	0	1
Atlanta, GA MSA	0	3	0	1
Augusta–Aiken, GA–SC MSA	0	3	0	1
Austin–San Marcos, TX MSA	0	3	0	1
Bakersfield, CA MSA	0	3	0	1
Barnstable–Yarmouth, MA MSA	0	3	0	1
Baton Rouge, LA MSA	0	3	0	1
Beaumont–Port Arthur, TX MSA	0	3	0	1
Bellingham, WA MSA	0	3	0	1
Billings, MT MSA	0	3	0	1
Biloxi–Gulfport–Pascagoula, MS MSA	0	3	0	1

[Continued]

★2566★

Trucking Terminal Facilities
[Continued]

MSA	Estab-lish-ments	Rank	Emp-loy-ment	Rank
Binghamton, NY MSA	0	3	0	1
Birmingham, AL MSA	0	3	0	1
Bismarck, ND MSA	0	3	0	1
Boise City, ID MSA	0	3	0	1
Boston–Worcester–Lawrence, MA–NH–ME–CT CMSA	0	3	0	1
Brownsville–Harlingen–San Benito, TX MSA	0	3	0	1
Buffalo–Niagara Falls, NY MSA	0	3	0	1
Burlington, VT MSA	0	3	0	1

Source: U.S. Department of Commerce, Bureau of the Census, Data User Services Division, *1992 Economic Census, Volume 1F, Reports Series, Release 1F,* September 1995, CD-ROM. *Note:* Data are shown only for the top 25 areas.

★2567★

Establishments and Employment

Water Transportation

The U.S. total number of employees is 171,314; total number of establishments is 8,147.

MSA	Estab-lish-ments	Rank	Emp-loy-ment	Rank
Miami–Fort Lauderdale, FL CMSA	318	3	14,991	1
New York–Northern New Jersey–Long Island, NY–NJ–CT-CMSA	810	1	14,023	2
New Orleans, LA MSA	372	2	13,175	3
Los Angeles–Riverside–Orange County, CA CMSA	201	9	10,177	4
Houston–Galveston–Brazoria, TX CMSA	315	4	9,466	5
Seattle–Tacoma–Bremerton, WA CMSA	206	8	7,207	6
Charleston–North Charleston, SC MSA	60	22	4,032	7
Savannah, GA MSA	46	29	3,556	8
Jacksonville, FL MSA	99	15	3,405	9
Houma, LA MSA	225	5	3,084	10
Honolulu, HI MSA	50	26	3,020	11
Mobile, AL MSA	84	18	3,007	12
St. Louis, MO–IL MSA	86	17	2,035	13
Tampa–St. Petersburg–Clearwater, FL MSA	115	14	1,991	14
Baton Rouge, LA MSA	54	24	1,591	15
Boston–Worcester–Lawrence, MA–NH–ME–CT CMSA	147	12	1,561	16
Beaumont–Port Arthur, TX MSA	68	20	1,524	17
Pittsburgh, PA MSA	54	24	1,049	18
San Diego, CA MSA	47	28	782	19
Wilmington, NC MSA	42	31	731	20
Huntington–Ashland, WV–KY–OH MSA	24	42	721	21

[Continued]

★ 2567 ★

Water Transportation
[Continued]

MSA	Estab-lish-ments	Rank	Emp-ploy-ment	Rank
Biloxi – Gulfport – Pascagoula, MS MSA	34	35	698	22
Memphis, TN – AR – MS MSA	22	44	502	23
Providence – Fall River – Warwick, RI – MA MSA	56	23	450	24
New London – Norwich, CT – RI MSA	42	31	443	25

Source: U.S. Department of Commerce, Bureau of the Census, Data User Services Division, *1992 Economic Census, Volume 1F, Reports Series, Release 1F*, September 1995, CD-ROM. *Note:* Data are shown only for the top 25 areas.

★ 2568 ★
Establishments and Employment

Water Transportation of Freight

The U.S. total number of employees is 37,229; total number of establishments is 836.

MSA	Estab-lish-ments	Rank	Emp-ploy-ment	Rank
New York – Northern New Jersey – Long Island, NY – NJ – CT-CMSA	177	1	6,550	1
New Orleans, LA MSA	45	3	3,967	2
Miami – Fort Lauderdale, FL CMSA	38	4	1,065	3
Chicago – Gary – Kenosha, IL – IN – WI CMSA	23	7	795	4
Portland – Salem, OR – WA CMSA	13	10	555	5
Jacksonville, FL MSA	17	9	464	6
Boston – Worcester – Lawrence, MA – NH – ME – CT CMSA	10	12	411	7
Houma, LA MSA	30	5	408	8
Cleveland – Akron, OH CMSA	13	10	399	9
Charleston – North Charleston, SC MSA	8	14	165	10
Albany – Schenectady – Troy, NY MSA	0	22	0	11
Albuquerque, NM MSA	0	22	0	11
Allentown – Bethlehem – Easton, PA MSA	0	22	0	11
Amarillo, TX MSA	0	22	0	11
Anchorage, AK MSA	3	19	0[1]	11
Appleton – Oshkosh – Neenah, WI MSA	0	22	0	11
Asheville, NC MSA	0	22	0	11
Atlanta, GA MSA	9	13	0[1]	11
Augusta – Aiken, GA – SC MSA	0	22	0	11
Austin – San Marcos, TX MSA	0	22	0	11
Bakersfield, CA MSA	0	22	0	11
Barnstable – Yarmouth, MA MSA	0	22	0	11
Baton Rouge, LA MSA	3	19	0[1]	11

[Continued]

★ 2568 ★

Water Transportation of Freight
[Continued]

MSA	Estab-lish-ments	Rank	Emp-ploy-ment	Rank
Beaumont – Port Arthur, TX MSA	11	11	0[1]	11
Bellingham, WA MSA	1	21	0[1]	11

Source: U.S. Department of Commerce, Bureau of the Census, Data User Services Division, *1992 Economic Census, Volume 1F, Reports Series, Release 1F*, September 1995, CD-ROM. *Notes:* Data are shown only for the top 25 areas. 1. 20-99 employees.

★ 2569 ★
Establishments and Employment

Water Transportation of Passengers

The U.S. total number of employees is 23,308; total number of establishments is 1,033.

MSA	Estab-lish-ments	Rank	Emp-ploy-ment	Rank
Miami – Fort Lauderdale, FL CMSA	70	1	7,757	1
New Orleans, LA MSA	33	3	1,443	2
Boston – Worcester – Lawrence, MA – NH – ME – CT CMSA	25	6	268	3
Norfolk – Virginia Beach – Newport News, VA – NC MSA	14	11	254	4
Jacksonville, FL MSA	11	14	120	5
Houma, LA MSA	13	12	90	6
Charleston – North Charleston, SC MSA	4	19	78	7
Grand Rapids – Muskegon – Holland, MI MSA	6	17	15	8
Rochester, NY MSA	3	20	10	9
Milwaukee – Racine, WI CMSA	4	19	9	10
Fort Pierce – Port St. Lucie, FL MSA	4	19	5	11
Sarasota – Bradenton, FL MSA	4	19	3	12
Albany – Schenectady – Troy, NY MSA	1	22	0[1]	13
Albuquerque, NM MSA	0	23	0	13
Allentown – Bethlehem – Easton, PA MSA	1	22	0[1]	13
Amarillo, TX MSA	0	23	0	13
Anchorage, AK MSA	5	18	0[1]	13
Appleton – Oshkosh – Neenah, WI MSA	0	23	0	13
Asheville, NC MSA	0	23	0	13
Atlanta, GA MSA	1	22	0[1]	13
Augusta – Aiken, GA – SC MSA	1	22	0[1]	13
Austin – San Marcos, TX MSA	2	21	0[1]	13
Bakersfield, CA MSA	0	23	0	13
Barnstable – Yarmouth, MA MSA	5	18	0[1]	13
Baton Rouge, LA MSA	1	22	0[1]	13

Source: U.S. Department of Commerce, Bureau of the Census, Data User Services Division, *1992 Economic Census, Volume 1F, Reports Series, Release 1F*, September 1995, CD-ROM. *Notes:* Data are shown only for the top 25 areas. 1. 20-99 employees.

Chapter 27

UTILITIES SECTOR

Topics Covered

Energy Prices
Telephones
Utilities

★2570★

Energy Prices

Average Price of Energy, 1994, By Type: Electricity

The average for U.S. cities is $48.20 per 500 kilowatt-hours. Data refer to selected metropolitan areas.

[In dollars per 500 kilowatt-hours]

MSA	Dollars per unit	Rank
Baltimore, MD MSA	48.62	10
Boston-Lawrence-Salem, MA-NH CMSA	57.26	5
Chicago-Gary-Lake County, IL-IN-WI CMSA	45.07	11
Cleveland-Akron-Lorain, OH CMSA	54.24	7
Dallas-Fort Worth, TX CMSA	50.81	8
Detroit-Ann Arbor, MI CMSA	49.27	9
Houston-Galveston-Brazoria, TX CMSA	43.77	13
Los Angeles-Anaheim-Riverside, CA CMSA	61.5	3
Miami-Fort Lauderdale, FL CMSA	43.83	12
New York-Northern New Jersey-Long Island, NY-NJ-CT CMSA	72.47	1
Philadelphia-Wilmington-Trenton, PA-NJ-DE-MD CMSA	59.1	4
Pittsburgh-Beaver Valley, PA CMSA	54.82	6
Saint Louis-East Saint Louis, MO-IL CMSA	41.49	15
San Francisco-Oakland-San Jose, CA CMSA	62.98	2
Washington, DC-MD-VA MSA	42.52	14

Source: U.S. Bureau of the Census, *Statistical Abstract of the United States: 1995,* (115th edition), Washington, D.C.: U.S. Government Printing Office, 1995, p. 507. Primary source: U.S. Bureau of Labor Statistics, *CPI Detailed Report,* January 1994 issue. *Notes:* "CMSA" stands for "Consolidated Metropolitan Statistical Area." "MSA" stands for "Metropolitan Statistical Area."

★2571★

Energy Prices

Average Price of Energy, 1994, By Type: Fuel Oil No. 2

The average for U.S. cities is $0.92 per gallon. Data refer to selected metropolitan areas.

[In dollars per gallon]

MSA	Dollars per unit	Rank
Baltimore, MD MSA	1.01	2
Boston-Lawrence-Salem, MA-NH CMSA	0.92	5
Chicago-Gary-Lake County, IL-IN-WI CMSA	0.99	3
Detroit-Ann Arbor, MI CMSA	0.93	4
New York-Northern New Jersey-Long Island, NY-NJ-CT CMSA	1.01	2
Philadelphia-Wilmington-Trenton, PA-NJ-DE-MD CMSA	0.91	6
Washington, DC-MD-VA MSA	1.05	1

Source: U.S. Bureau of the Census, *Statistical Abstract of the United States: 1995,* (115th edition), Washington, D.C.: U.S. Government Printing Office, 1995, p. 507. Primary source: U.S. Bureau of Labor Statistics, *CPI Detailed Report,* January 1994 issue. *Notes:* "CMSA" stands for "Consolidated Metropolitan Statistical Area." "MSA" stands for "Metropolitan Statistical Area."

★2572★

Energy Prices

Average Price of Energy, 1994, By Type: Gasoline (All Types)

The average for U.S. cities is $1.11 per gallon. Data refer to selected metropolitan areas.

[In dollars per gallon]

MSA	Dollars per unit[1]	Rank
Baltimore, MD MSA	1.16	5
Boston-Lawrence-Salem, MA-NH CMSA	1.14	6
Chicago-Gary-Lake County, IL-IN-WI CMSA	1.11	7
Cleveland-Akron-Lorain, OH CMSA	1.03	11
Dallas-Fort Worth, TX CMSA	1.07	9
Detroit-Ann Arbor, MI CMSA	0.98	12
Houston-Galveston-Brazoria, TX CMSA	1.04	10
Los Angeles-Anaheim-Riverside, CA CMSA	1.20	3
Miami-Fort Lauderdale, FL CMSA	1.22	1
New York-Northern New Jersey-Long Island, NY-NJ-CT CMSA	1.21	2
Philadelphia-Wilmington-Trenton, PA-NJ-DE-MD CMSA	1.16	5

[Continued]

★2572★

Average Price of Energy, 1994, By Type: Gasoline (All Types)
[Continued]

MSA	Dollars per unit[1]	Rank
Pittsburgh-Beaver Valley, PA CMSA	1.09	8
Saint Louis-East Saint Louis, MO-IL CMSA	0.95	13
San Francisco-Oakland-San Jose, CA CMSA	1.21	2
Washington, DC-MD-VA MSA	1.18	4

Source: U.S. Bureau of the Census, *Statistical Abstract of the United States: 1995,* (115th edition), Washington, D.C.: U.S. Government Printing Office, 1995, p. 507. Primary source: U.S. Bureau of Labor Statistics, *CPI Detailed Report,* January 1994 issue. *Notes:* "CMSA" stands for "Consolidated Metropolitan Statistical Area." "MSA" stands for "Metropolitan Statistical Area." 1. Includes types of gasoline not shown separately.

★2573★
Energy Prices

Average Price of Energy, 1994, By Type: Gasoline (Unleaded Premium)

The average for U.S. cities is $1.24 per gallon. Data refer to selected metropolitan areas.

[In dollars per gallon]

MSA	Dollars per unit	Rank
Baltimore, MD MSA	1.26	7
Boston-Lawrence-Salem, MA-NH CMSA	1.30	4
Chicago-Gary-Lake County, IL-IN-WI CMSA	1.24	8
Cleveland-Akron-Lorain, OH CMSA	1.17	9
Dallas-Fort Worth, TX CMSA	1.17	9
Detroit-Ann Arbor, MI CMSA	1.12	10
Houston-Galveston-Brazoria, TX CMSA	1.17	9
Los Angeles-Anaheim-Riverside, CA CMSA	1.34	3
Miami-Fort Lauderdale, FL CMSA	1.35	2
New York-Northern New Jersey-Long Island, NY-NJ-CT CMSA	1.35	2
Philadelphia-Wilmington-Trenton, PA-NJ-DE-MD CMSA	1.27	6
Pittsburgh-Beaver Valley, PA CMSA	1.24	8
Saint Louis-East Saint Louis, MO-IL CMSA	1.09	11

[Continued]

★2573★

Average Price of Energy, 1994, By Type: Gasoline (Unleaded Premium)
[Continued]

MSA	Dollars per unit	Rank
San Francisco-Oakland-San Jose, CA CMSA	1.37	1
Washington, DC-MD-VA MSA	1.29	5

Source: U.S. Bureau of the Census, *Statistical Abstract of the United States: 1995,* (115th edition), Washington, D.C.: U.S. Government Printing Office, 1995, p. 507. Primary source: U.S. Bureau of Labor Statistics, *CPI Detailed Report,* January 1994 issue. *Notes:* "CMSA" stands for "Consolidated Metropolitan Statistical Area." "MSA" stands for "Metropolitan Statistical Area."

★2574★
Energy Prices

Average Price of Energy, 1994, By Type: Gasoline (Unleaded Regular)

The average for U.S. cities is $1.04 per gallon. Data refer to selected metropolitan areas.

[In dollars per gallon]

MSA	Dollars per unit	Rank
Baltimore, MD MSA	1.07	6
Boston-Lawrence-Salem, MA-NH CMSA	1.05	7
Chicago-Gary-Lake County, IL-IN-WI CMSA	1.05	7
Cleveland-Akron-Lorain, OH CMSA	1.00	10
Dallas-Fort Worth, TX CMSA	1.00	10
Detroit-Ann Arbor, MI CMSA	0.94	12
Houston-Galveston-Brazoria, TX CMSA	0.96	11
Los Angeles-Anaheim-Riverside, CA CMSA	1.13	3
Miami-Fort Lauderdale, FL CMSA	1.15	1
New York-Northern New Jersey-Long Island, NY-NJ-CT CMSA	1.11	4
Philadelphia-Wilmington-Trenton, PA-NJ-DE-MD CMSA	1.03	8
Pittsburgh-Beaver Valley, PA CMSA	1.01	9
Saint Louis-East Saint Louis, MO-IL CMSA	0.88	13
San Francisco-Oakland-San Jose, CA CMSA	1.14	2
Washington, DC-MD-VA MSA	1.09	5

Source: U.S. Bureau of the Census, *Statistical Abstract of the United States: 1995,* (115th edition), Washington, D.C.: U.S. Government Printing Office, 1995, p. 507. Primary source: U.S. Bureau of Labor Statistics, *CPI Detailed Report,* January 1994 issue. *Notes:* "CMSA" stands for "Consolidated Metropolitan Statistical Area." "MSA" stands for "Metropolitan Statistical Area."

★ 2575 ★

Energy Prices

Average Price of Energy, 1994, By Type: Piped (Utility) Gas

The average for U.S. cities is $66.47 per 100 therms. Data refer to selected metropolitan areas.

[In dollars per 100 therms]

MSA	Dollars per unit	Rank
Baltimore, MD MSA	64.44	9
Boston-Lawrence-Salem, MA-NH CMSA	94.34	2
Chicago-Gary-Lake County, IL-IN-WI CMSA	68.07	6
Cleveland-Akron-Lorain, OH CMSA	55.06	13
Dallas-Fort Worth, TX CMSA	57.21	12
Detroit-Ann Arbor, MI CMSA	52.91	14
Houston-Galveston-Brazoria, TX CMSA	52.19	15
Los Angeles-Anaheim-Riverside, CA CMSA	67.12	7
Miami-Fort Lauderdale, FL CMSA	90.39	3
New York-Northern New Jersey-Long Island, NY-NJ-CT CMSA	96.89	1
Philadelphia-Wilmington-Trenton, PA-NJ-DE-MD CMSA	74.92	5
Pittsburgh-Beaver Valley, PA CMSA	65.15	8
Saint Louis-East Saint Louis, MO-IL CMSA	60.99	11
San Francisco-Oakland-San Jose, CA CMSA	62.05	10
Washington, DC-MD-VA MSA	77.73	4

Source: U.S. Bureau of the Census, *Statistical Abstract of the United States: 1995*, (115th edition), Washington, D.C.: U.S. Government Printing Office, 1995, p. 507. Primary source: U.S. Bureau of Labor Statistics, *CPI Detailed Report*, January 1994 issue. *Notes:* "CMSA" stands for "Consolidated Metropolitan Statistical Area." "MSA" stands for "Metropolitan Statistical Area."

★ 2576 ★

Energy Prices

Average Residential Energy Prices, 1995, By Type: All Gasolines

Data refer to prices for unleaded regular, unleaded midgrade, and unleaded premium gasoline in selected areas. The average for U.S. cities is $1.185.

[In dollars per gallon; October 1995]

City/MSA	Dollars	Rank
Baltimore, MD	1.188	9
Boston-Lawrence-Salem, MA-NH	1.220	6
Chicago-Gary-Lake County, IL-IN-WI	1.247	4
Cleveland-Akron-Lorain, OH	1.096	13
Dallas-Fort Worth, TX	1.147	11

[Continued]

★ 2576 ★

Average Residential Energy Prices, 1995, By Type: All Gasolines

[Continued]

City/MSA	Dollars	Rank
Detroit-Ann Arbor, MI	1.086	14
Houston-Galveston-Brazoria, TX	1.138	12
Los Angeles-Anaheim-Riverside, CA	1.245	5
Miami-Fort Lauderdale, FL	1.212	7
New York-Northern New Jersey-Long Island, NY-NJ-CT	1.289	1
Philadelphia-Wilmington-Trenton, PA-NJ-DE-MD	1.169	10
Pittsburgh-Beaver Valley, PA	1.266	3
Saint Louis-East Saint Louis, MO-IL	1.005	15
San Francisco-Oakland-San Jose, CA	1.284	2
Washington, DC-MD-VA	1.192	8

Source: U.S. Department of Labor, Bureau of Labor Statistics, *CPI Detailed Report: Data for October 1995*, Washington, D.C.: U.S. Department of Labor, December 1995, p. 91.

★ 2577 ★

Energy Prices

Average Residential Energy Prices, 1995, By Type: Electricity

The average for U.S. cities is $49.472. Data refer to selected areas.

[In dollars per 500 kilowatt-hours; October 1995]

City/MSA	Dollars	Rank
Baltimore, MD	47.850	10
Boston-Lawrence-Salem, MA-NH	61.873	4
Chicago-Gary-Lake County, IL-IN-WI	59.444	6
Cleveland-Akron-Lorain, OH	55.497	7
Dallas-Fort Worth, TX	46.674	11
Detroit-Ann Arbor, MI	48.864	9
Houston-Galveston-Brazoria, TX	39.995	14
Los Angeles-Anaheim-Riverside, CA	64.752	2
Miami-Fort Lauderdale, FL	44.047	13
New York-Northern New Jersey-Long Island, NY-NJ-CT	70.321	1
Philadelphia-Wilmington-Trenton, PA-NJ-DE-MD	61.726	5
Pittsburgh-Beaver Valley, PA	51.589	8
Saint Louis-East Saint Louis, MO-IL	37.321	15
San Francisco-Oakland-San Jose, CA	63.294	3
Washington, DC-MD-VA	45.189	12

Source: U.S. Department of Labor, Bureau of Labor Statistics, *CPI Detailed Report: Data for October 1995*, Washington, D.C.: U.S. Department of Labor, December 1995, p. 89.

★ 2578 ★
Energy Prices
Average Residential Energy Prices, 1995, By Type: Fuel Oil No. 2

The average for U.S. cities is $0.873. Data refer to selected areas.

[In dollars per gallon; October 1995]

City/MSA	Dollars	Rank
Baltimore, MD	.989	3
Boston-Lawrence-Salem, MA-NH	.907	6
Chicago-Gary-Lake County, IL-IN-WI	1.038	1
Detroit-Ann Arbor, MI	.920	5
New York-Northern New Jersey-Long Island, NY-NJ-CT	.973	4
Philadelphia-Wilmington-Trenton, PA-NJ-DE-MD	.807	7
Washington, DC-MD-VA	1.033	2

Source: U.S. Department of Labor, Bureau of Labor Statistics, CPI Detailed Report: Data for December 1995, Washington, D.C.: U.S. Department of Labor, December 1995, p. 89. Note: NA Data not adequate for publication.

★ 2579 ★
Energy Prices
Average Residential Energy Prices, 1995, By Type: Gasoline (Unleaded Midgrade)

The average for U.S. cities is $1.221. Data refer to selected areas.

[In dollars per gallon; October 1995]

City/MSA	Dollars	Rank
Baltimore, MD	1.230	9
Boston-Lawrence-Salem, MA-NH	1.293	4
Chicago-Gary-Lake County, IL-IN-WI	1.308	3
Cleveland-Akron-Lorain, OH	1.142	14
Dallas-Fort Worth, TX	1.175	12
Detroit-Ann Arbor, MI	1.149	13
Houston-Galveston-Brazoria, TX	1.183	11
Los Angeles-Anaheim-Riverside, CA	1.283	6
Miami-Fort Lauderdale, FL	1.266	7
New York-Northern New Jersey-Long Island, NY-NJ-CT	1.342	2
Philadelphia-Wilmington-Trenton, PA-NJ-DE-MD	1.249	8
Pittsburgh-Beaver Valley, PA	1.292	5
Saint Louis-East Saint Louis, MO-IL	1.045	15
San Francisco-Oakland-San Jose, CA	1.356	1
Washington, DC-MD-VA	1.224	10

Source: U.S. Department of Labor, Bureau of Labor Statistics, CPI Detailed Report: Data for October 1995, Washington, D.C.: U.S. Department of Labor, December 1995, p. 91.

★ 2580 ★
Energy Prices
Average Residential Energy Prices, 1995, By Type: Gasoline (Unleaded Premium)

The average for U.S. cities is $1.315. Data refer to selected areas.

[In dollars per gallon; October 1995]

City/MSA	Dollars	Rank
Baltimore, MD	1.283	10
Boston-Lawrence-Salem, MA-NH	1.377	6
Chicago-Gary-Lake County, IL-IN-WI	1.384	5
Cleveland-Akron-Lorain, OH	1.228	13
Dallas-Fort Worth, TX	1.257	11
Detroit-Ann Arbor, MI	1.239	12
Houston-Galveston-Brazoria, TX	1.257	11
Los Angeles-Anaheim-Riverside, CA	1.389	4
Miami-Fort Lauderdale, FL	1.339	7
New York-Northern New Jersey-Long Island, NY-NJ-CT	1.423	2
Philadelphia-Wilmington-Trenton, PA-NJ-DE-MD	1.313	8
Pittsburgh-Beaver Valley, PA	1.392	3
Saint Louis-East Saint Louis, MO-IL	1.174	14
San Francisco-Oakland-San Jose, CA	1.439	1
Washington, DC-MD-VA	1.309	9

Source: U.S. Department of Labor, Bureau of Labor Statistics, CPI Detailed Report: Data for October 1995, Washington, D.C.: U.S. Department of Labor, December 1995, p. 91.

★ 2581 ★
Energy Prices
Average Residential Energy Prices, 1995, By Type: Gasoline (Unleaded Regular)

The average for U.S. cities is $1.127. Data refer to selected areas.

[In dollars per gallon; October 1995]

City/MSA	Dollars	Rank
Baltimore, MD	1.133	7
Boston-Lawrence-Salem, MA-NH	1.176	6
Chicago-Gary-Lake County, IL-IN-WI	1.191	4
Cleveland-Akron-Lorain, OH	1.063	12
Dallas-Fort Worth, TX	1.074	11
Detroit-Ann Arbor, MI	1.054	13
Houston-Galveston-Brazoria, TX	1.074	11
Los Angeles-Anaheim-Riverside, CA	1.201	3
Miami-Fort Lauderdale, FL	1.132	8
New York-Northern New Jersey-Long Island, NY-NJ-CT	1.204	2
Philadelphia-Wilmington-Trenton, PA-NJ-DE-MD	1.124	9
Pittsburgh-Beaver Valley, PA	1.184	5
Saint Louis-East Saint Louis, MO-IL	.947	14

[Continued]

★2581★

Average Residential Energy Prices, 1995, By Type: Gasoline (Unleaded Regular)

[Continued]

City/MSA	Dollars	Rank
San Francisco-Oakland-San Jose, CA	1.217	1
Washington, DC-MD-VA	1.119	10

Source: U.S. Department of Labor, Bureau of Labor Statistics, *CPI Detailed Report: Data for October 1995*, Washington, D.C.: U.S. Department of Labor, December 1995, p. 91.

★2582★

Energy Prices

Average Residential Energy Prices, 1995, By Type: Piped (Utility) Gas, 100 Therms

The average for U.S. cities is $59.917. Data refer to selected areas.

[In dollars per 100 therms; October 1995]

City/MSA	Dollars	Rank
Baltimore, MD	54.410	8
Boston-Lawrence-Salem, MA-NH	53.736	9
Chicago-Gary-Lake County, IL-IN-WI	49.665	12
Cleveland-Akron-Lorain, OH	50.026	11
Dallas-Fort Worth, TX	58.088	7
Detroit-Ann Arbor, MI	47.427	13
Houston-Galveston-Brazoria, TX	43.780	15
Los Angeles-Anaheim-Riverside, CA	74.449	5
Miami-Fort Lauderdale, FL	88.678	1
New York-Northern New Jersey-Long Island, NY-NJ-CT	83.326	2
Philadelphia-Wilmington-Trenton, PA-NJ-DE-MD	72.500	6
Pittsburgh-Beaver Valley, PA	50.860	10
Saint Louis-East Saint Louis, MO-IL	47.285	14
San Francisco-Oakland-San Jose, CA	76.946	3
Washington, DC-MD-VA	76.009	4

Source: U.S. Department of Labor, Bureau of Labor Statistics, *CPI Detailed Report: Data for October 1995*, Washington, D.C.: U.S. Department of Labor, December 1995, p. 89.

★2583★

Energy Prices

Average Residential Energy Prices, 1995, By Type: Piped (Utility) Gas, 40 Therms

The average for U.S. cities is $28.573. Data refer to selected areas.

[In dollars per 40 therms; October 1995]

City/MSA	Dollars	Rank
Baltimore, MD	26.960	11
Boston-Lawrence-Salem, MA-NH	28.892	7
Chicago-Gary-Lake County, IL-IN-WI	27.913	8
Cleveland-Akron-Lorain, OH	23.490	13
Dallas-Fort Worth, TX	27.413	10
Detroit-Ann Arbor, MI	22.914	15
Houston-Galveston-Brazoria, TX	23.330	14
Los Angeles-Anaheim-Riverside, CA	30.139	6
Miami-Fort Lauderdale, FL	39.987	2
New York-Northern New Jersey-Long Island, NY-NJ-CT	40.572	1
Philadelphia-Wilmington-Trenton, PA-NJ-DE-MD	33.353	4
Pittsburgh-Beaver Valley, PA	33.145	5
Saint Louis-East Saint Louis, MO-IL	26.753	12
San Francisco-Oakland-San Jose, CA	27.551	9
Washington, DC-MD-VA	36.322	3

Source: U.S. Department of Labor, Bureau of Labor Statistics, *CPI Detailed Report: Data for October 1995*, Washington, D.C.: U.S. Department of Labor, December 1995, p. 89.

★2584★

Energy Prices

Average Residential Energy Prices, 1995, By Type: Piped (Utility) Gas, Per Therm

The average for U.S. cities is $0.094. Data refer to selected areas.

[In dollars per kilowatt-hour; October 1995]

City/MSA	Dollars	Rank
Baltimore, MD	.076	12
Boston-Lawrence-Salem, MA-NH	.117	4
Chicago-Gary-Lake County, IL-IN-WI	.113	5
Cleveland-Akron-Lorain, OH	.108	6
Dallas-Fort Worth, TX	.086	11
Detroit-Ann Arbor, MI	.099	7
Houston-Galveston-Brazoria, TX	.090	9
Los Angeles-Anaheim-Riverside, CA	.126	3
Miami-Fort Lauderdale, FL	.087	10
New York-Northern New Jersey-Long Island, NY-NJ-CT	.134	1
Philadelphia-Wilmington-Trenton, PA-NJ-DE-MD	.117	4
Pittsburgh-Beaver Valley, PA	.095	8
Saint Louis-East Saint Louis, MO-IL	.072	13

[Continued]

★2584★

Average Residential Energy Prices, 1995, By Type: Piped (Utility) Gas, Per Therm

[Continued]

City/MSA	Dollars	Rank
San Francisco-Oakland-San Jose, CA	.131	2
Washington, DC-MD-VA	.095	8

Source: U.S. Department of Labor, Bureau of Labor Statistics, *CPI Detailed Report: Data for October 1995*, Washington, D.C.: U.S. Department of Labor, December 1995, p. 90.

★2585★

Energy Prices

Average Residential Energy Prices, 1995, By Type: Piped (Utility) Gas, Per Therm

The average for U.S. cities is $0.602. Data refer to selected areas.

[In dollars per therm; October 1995]

City/MSA	Dollars	Rank
Baltimore, MD	.595	9
Boston-Lawrence-Salem, MA-NH	.581	10
Chicago-Gary-Lake County, IL-IN-WI	.382	15
Cleveland-Akron-Lorain, OH	.506	12
Dallas-Fort Worth, TX	.752	4
Detroit-Ann Arbor, MI	.467	13
Houston-Galveston-Brazoria, TX	.533	11
Los Angeles-Anaheim-Riverside, CA	.747	5
Miami-Fort Lauderdale, FL	1.047	1
New York-Northern New Jersey-Long Island, NY-NJ-CT	.844	2
Philadelphia-Wilmington-Trenton, PA-NJ-DE-MD	.726	7
Pittsburgh-Beaver Valley, PA	.699	8
Saint Louis-East Saint Louis, MO-IL	.432	14
San Francisco-Oakland-San Jose, CA	.740	6
Washington, DC-MD-VA	.807	3

Source: U.S. Department of Labor, Bureau of Labor Statistics, *CPI Detailed Report: Data for October 1995*, Washington, D.C.: U.S. Department of Labor, December 1995, p. 90.

★2586★

Telephones

Telephone Lines (Local) Installed, 1994: Business

[In millions]

City	Lines	Rank
New York, NY	2.0	1
Chicago, IL	1.1	2
Los Angeles, CA	0.8	3
San Francisco, CA	0.5	4
Boston, MA	0.3	5

Source: Higgins, Steve, "Are Local Telephone Wars Much Ado Over Nothing?" *Investor's Business Daily*, 4 May 1995, p. A6. Primary source: Multimedia Telecommunications Association.

★2587★

Telephones

Telephone Lines (Local) Installed, 1994: Residential

[In millions]

City	Lines	Rank
New York, NY	4.5	1
Chicago, IL	2.2	2
Los Angeles, CA	1.7	3
San Francisco, CA	0.6	4
Boston, MA	0.4	5

Source: Higgins, Steve, "Are Local Telephone Wars Much Ado Over Nothing?" *Investor's Business Daily*, 4 May 1995, p. A6. Primary source: Multimedia Telecommunications Association.

★2588★

Utilities

Water and Sewerage Rates in the 20 Most Populous Cities

Data refer to prices based on 120,000 gallons of water usage and a water meter of 5/8 of an inch.

[In dollars per year]

City	Rate	Rank
Baltimore, MD	315.04	16
Boston, MA	868.66	1
Chicago, IL	214.08	20
Columbus, OH	482.04	9
Dallas, TX	548.88	7
Detroit, MI	274.00	18
Houston, TX	699.00	4
Indianapolis, IN	448.83	11
Jacksonville, FL	667.00	5
Los Angeles, CA	399.36	13
Memphis, TN	214.53	19
Milwaukee, WI	351.24	15
New York, NY	440.00	12
Philadelphia, PA	619.44	6
Phoenix, AZ	302.92	17
San Antonio, TX	376.86	14
San Diego, CA	706.00	3
San Francisco, CA	765.08	2

[Continued]

★2588★

Water and Sewerage Rates in the 20 Most Populous Cities
[Continued]

City	Rate	Rank
San Jose, CA	508.56	8
Washington, DC	458.88	10

Source: Oguntoyinbo, Lekan, "Detroit to Raise Water, Sewer Fees," *Detroit Free Press*, 22 February 1996, p. 1B. Primary source: Detroit (Michigan) Water and Sewerage Department.

PART VI

GOVERNMENT

Contents

Chapter 28

FEDERAL GOVERNMENT FINANCES

Topic Covered

Taxes and Tax Revenues

★ 2589 ★
Taxes and Tax Revenues

Taxes Paid By Family of Four, 1992, As Percent of Income, By Income Level: $25,000

City	Percentage	Rank
Albuquerque, NM	5.9	26
Atlanta, GA	11.4	9
Baltimore, MD	16.3	5
Bridgeport, CT	18.1	3
Burlington, VT	7.6	21
Charleston, WV	6.8	25
Charlotte, NC	8.3	17
Chicago, IL	11.8	8
Columbia, SC	7.9	20
Columbus, OH	8.6	14
Des Moines, IA	7.4	22
Detroit, MI	18.9	2
Honolulu, HI	7.4	22
Indianapolis, IN	8.1	19
Jackson, MS	5.8	27
Kansas City, MO	7.9	20
Louisville, KY	9.8	11
Memphis, TN	6.9	24
Milwaukee, WI	13.1	7
New York City, NY	10.4	10
Newark, NJ	23.4	1
Omaha, NE	8.6	14
Philadelphia, PA	15.8	6
Portland, ME	8.5	15
Portland, OR	9.7	12
Providence, RI	17.1	4
Salt Lake City, UT	8.2	18
Sioux Falls, SD	7.3	23
Virginia Beach, VA	8.4	16
Washington, DC	9.1	13

Source: U.S. Bureau of the Census, *Statistical Abstract of the United States: 1995*, (115th edition), Washington, D.C.: U.S. Government Printing Office, 1995, p. 313. Primary source: U.S. Government of the District of Columbia, Department of Finance and Revenue, *Tax Rates and Tax Burdens in the District of Columbia: A Nationwide Comparison*, annual.

★ 2590 ★
Taxes and Tax Revenues

Taxes Paid By Family of Four, 1992, As Percent of Income, By Income Level: $50,000

City	Percentage	Rank
Albuquerque, NM	6.9	25
Atlanta, GA	11.2	10
Baltimore, MD	16.5	5
Bridgeport, CT	18.8	3
Burlington, VT	8.3	21
Charleston, WV	7.1	24
Charlotte, NC	8.8	18
Chicago, IL	11.9	9
Columbia, SC	9.6	15
Columbus, OH	9.4	16
Des Moines, IA	8.2	22
Detroit, MI	19.4	2
Honolulu, HI	8.6	20
Indianapolis, IN	7.4	23

[Continued]

★ 2590 ★

Taxes Paid By Family of Four, 1992, As Percent of Income, By Income Level: $50,000

[Continued]

City	Percentage	Rank
Jackson, MS	6.8	26
Kansas City, MO	8.7	19
Louisville, KY	10.2	13
Memphis, TN	5.8	28
Milwaukee, WI	14.6	7
New York City, NY	13.2	8
Newark, NJ	22.9	1
Omaha, NE	9.1	17
Philadelphia, PA	15.2	6
Portland, ME	10.3	12
Portland, OR	10.7	11
Providence, RI	16.8	4
Salt Lake City, UT	9.4	16
Sioux Falls, SD	6.4	27
Virginia Beach, VA	8.8	18
Washington, DC	10.1	14

Source: U.S. Bureau of the Census, *Statistical Abstract of the United States: 1995*, (115th edition), Washington, D.C.: U.S. Government Printing Office, 1995, p. 313. Primary source: U.S. Government of the District of Columbia, Department of Finance and Revenue, *Tax Rates and Tax Burdens in the District of Columbia: A Nationwide Comparison*, annual.

★ 2591 ★
Taxes and Tax Revenues

Taxes Paid By Family of Four, 1992, As Percent of Income, By Income Level: $75,000

City	Percentage	Rank
Albuquerque, NM	7.9	27
Atlanta, GA	12.1	11
Baltimore, MD	17.1	5
Bridgeport, CT	21.7	2
Burlington, VT	9.6	21
Charleston, WV	8.5	24
Charlotte, NC	9.7	20
Chicago, IL	12.4	10
Columbia, SC	10.9	14
Columbus, OH	10.3	17
Des Moines, IA	9.0	23
Detroit, MI	19.7	3
Honolulu, HI	9.7	20
Indianapolis, IN	8.4	25
Jackson, MS	8.1	26
Kansas City, MO	9.4	22
Louisville, KY	10.8	15
Memphis, TN	6.0	29
Milwaukee, WI	15.2	6
New York City, NY	14.9	8
Newark, NJ	23.6	1
Omaha, NE	10.5	16
Philadelphia, PA	15.1	7
Portland, ME	12.5	9
Portland, OR	11.5	12
Providence, RI	18.1	4
Salt Lake City, UT	10.1	18

[Continued]

★2591★

Taxes Paid By Family of Four, 1992, As Percent of Income, By Income Level: $75,000

[Continued]

City	Percentage	Rank
Sioux Falls, SD	7.1	28
Virginia Beach, VA	10.0	19
Washington, DC	11.2	13

Source: U.S. Bureau of the Census, *Statistical Abstract of the United States: 1995,* (115th edition), Washington, D.C.: U.S. Government Printing Office, 1995, p. 313. Primary source: U.S. Government of the District of Columbia, Department of Finance and Revenue, *Tax Rates and Tax Burdens in the District of Columbia: A Nationwide Comparison,* annual.

★2592★

Taxes and Tax Revenues

Taxes Paid By Family of Four, 1992, As Percent of Income, By Income Level: $100,000

City	Percentage	Rank
Albuquerque, NM	8.5	24
Atlanta, GA	12.0	11
Baltimore, MD	16.7	5
Bridgeport, CT	21.2	2
Burlington, VT	10.1	17
Charleston, WV	8.8	23
Charlotte, NC	9.7	20
Chicago, IL	12.1	10
Columbia, SC	10.9	14
Columbus, OH	10.1	17
Des Moines, IA	9.1	22
Detroit, MI	19.3	3
Honolulu, HI	9.9	19
Indianapolis, IN	8.1	26
Jackson, MS	8.2	25
Kansas City, MO	9.2	21
Louisville, KY	10.8	15
Memphis, TN	5.7	28
Milwaukee, WI	15.1	7
New York City, NY	15.2	6
Newark, NJ	23.4	1
Omaha, NE	10.7	16
Philadelphia, PA	14.8	8
Portland, ME	12.8	9
Portland, OR	11.5	13
Providence, RI	17.9	4
Salt Lake City, UT	10.0	18
Sioux Falls, SD	6.7	27
Virginia Beach, VA	9.9	19
Washington, DC	11.6	12

Source: U.S. Bureau of the Census, *Statistical Abstract of the United States: 1995,* (115th edition), Washington, D.C.: U.S. Government Printing Office, 1995, p. 313. Primary source: U.S. Government of the District of Columbia, Department of Finance and Revenue, *Tax Rates and Tax Burdens in the District of Columbia: A Nationwide Comparison,* annual.

★2593★

Taxes and Tax Revenues

Taxes Paid By Family of Four, 1992, By Gross Family Income Level: $25,000

City	Taxes	Rank
Albuquerque, NM	1,478	29
Atlanta, GA	2,838	9
Baltimore, MD	4,068	5
Bridgeport, CT	4,519	3
Burlington, VT	1,909	23
Charleston, WV	1,691	28
Charlotte, NC	2,085	18
Chicago, IL	2,954	8
Columbia, SC	1,971	21
Columbus, OH	2,151	15
Des Moines, IA	1,844	25
Detroit, MI	4,723	2
Honolulu, HI	1,853	24
Indianapolis, IN	2,017	20
Jackson, MS	1,451	30
Kansas City, MO	1,965	22
Louisville, KY	2,439	11
Memphis, TN	1,718	27
Milwaukee, WI	3,274	7
New York City, NY	2,603	10
Newark, NJ	5,853	1
Omaha, NE	2,159	14
Philadelphia, PA	3,956	6
Portland, ME	2,132	16
Portland, OR	2,428	12
Providence, RI	4,271	4
Salt Lake City, UT	2,038	19
Sioux Falls, SD	1,837	26
Virginia Beach, VA	2,089	17
Washington, DC	2,278	13

Source: U.S. Bureau of the Census, *Statistical Abstract of the United States: 1995,* (115th edition), Washington, D.C.: U.S. Government Printing Office, 1995, p. 313. Primary source: U.S. Government of the District of Columbia, Department of Finance and Revenue, *Tax Rates and Tax Burdens in the District of Columbia: A Nationwide Comparison,* annual.

★2594★

Taxes and Tax Revenues

Taxes Paid By Family of Four, 1992, By Gross Family Income Level: $50,000

City	Taxes	Rank
Albuquerque, NM	3,434	27
Atlanta, GA	5,593	10
Baltimore, MD	8,246	5
Bridgeport, CT	9,416	3
Burlington, VT	4,132	23
Charleston, WV	3,542	26
Charlotte, NC	4,412	20
Chicago, IL	5,938	9
Columbia, SC	4,799	15
Columbus, OH	4,713	16
Des Moines, IA	4,120	24
Detroit, MI	9,680	2
Honolulu, HI	4,306	22
Indianapolis, IN	3,703	25

[Continued]

★2594★

Taxes Paid By Family of Four, 1992, By Gross Family Income Level: $50,000

[Continued]

City	Taxes	Rank
Jackson, MS	3,421	28
Kansas City, MO	4,358	21
Louisville, KY	5,100	13
Memphis, TN	2,896	30
Milwaukee, WI	7,288	7
New York City, NY	6,579	8
Newark, NJ	11,445	1
Omaha, NE	4,529	18
Philadelphia, PA	7,610	6
Portland, ME	5,144	12
Portland, OR	5,369	11
Providence, RI	8,396	4
Salt Lake City, UT	4,682	17
Sioux Falls, SD	3,180	29
Virginia Beach, VA	4,423	19
Washington, DC	5,041	14

Source: U.S. Bureau of the Census, *Statistical Abstract of the United States: 1995*, (115th edition), Washington, D.C.: U.S. Government Printing Office, 1995, p. 313. Primary source: U.S. Government of the District of Columbia, Department of Finance and Revenue, *Tax Rates and Tax Burdens in the District of Columbia: A Nationwide Comparison*, annual.

★2595★

Taxes and Tax Revenues

Taxes Paid By Family of Four, 1992, By Gross Family Income Level: $75,000

City	Taxes	Rank
Albuquerque, NM	5,943	28
Atlanta, GA	9,107	11
Baltimore, MD	12,791	5
Bridgeport, CT	16,270	2
Burlington, VT	7,197	22
Charleston, WV	6,373	25
Charlotte, NC	7,253	21
Chicago, IL	9,326	10
Columbia, SC	8,151	14
Columbus, OH	7,712	17
Des Moines, IA	6,770	24
Detroit, MI	14,773	3
Honolulu, HI	7,272	20
Indianapolis, IN	6,268	26
Jackson, MS	6,080	27
Kansas City, MO	7,024	23
Louisville, KY	8,099	15
Memphis, TN	4,506	30
Milwaukee, WI	11,425	6
New York City, NY	11,199	8
Newark, NJ	17,696	1
Omaha, NE	7,872	16
Philadelphia, PA	11,361	7
Portland, ME	9,361	9
Portland, OR	8,623	12
Providence, RI	13,542	4
Salt Lake City, UT	7,564	18

[Continued]

★2595★

Taxes Paid By Family of Four, 1992, By Gross Family Income Level: $75,000

[Continued]

City	Taxes	Rank
Sioux Falls, SD	5,312	29
Virginia Beach, VA	7,521	19
Washington, DC	8,416	13

Source: U.S. Bureau of the Census, *Statistical Abstract of the United States: 1995*, (115th edition), Washington, D.C.: U.S. Government Printing Office, 1995, p. 313. Primary source: U.S. Government of the District of Columbia, Department of Finance and Revenue, *Tax Rates and Tax Burdens in the District of Columbia: A Nationwide Comparison*, annual.

★2596★

Taxes and Tax Revenues

Taxes Paid By Family of Four, 1992, By Gross Family Income Level: $100,000

City	Taxes	Rank
Albuquerque, NM	8,461	26
Atlanta, GA	12,019	11
Baltimore, MD	16,659	5
Bridgeport, CT	21,285	2
Burlington, VT	10,134	18
Charleston, WV	8,836	25
Charlotte, NC	9,734	22
Chicago, IL	12,084	10
Columbia, SC	10,905	14
Columbus, OH	10,650	17
Des Moines, IA	9,109	24
Detroit, MI	19,290	3
Honolulu, HI	9,921	21
Indianapolis, IN	8,061	28
Jackson, MS	8,237	27
Kansas City, MO	9,224	23
Louisville, KY	10,777	15
Memphis, TN	5,702	30
Milwaukee, WI	15,071	7
New York City, NY	15,247	6
Newark, NJ	23,420	1
Omaha, NE	10,668	16
Philadelphia, PA	14,755	8
Portland, ME	12,759	9
Portland, OR	11,542	13
Providence, RI	17,945	4
Salt Lake City, UT	10,020	19
Sioux Falls, SD	6,701	29
Virginia Beach, VA	9,930	20
Washington, DC	11,556	12
Median[1]	9,921	21

Source: U.S. Bureau of the Census, *Statistical Abstract of the United States: 1995*, (115th edition), Washington, DC: U.S. Government Printing Office, 1995, p. 313. Primary source: U.S. Government of the District of Columbia, Department of Finance and Revenue, *Tax Rates and Tax Burdens in the District of Columbia: A Nationwide Comparison*, annual. *Note:* 1. Median of all 51 cities.

Chapter 29

COUNTY GOVERNMENT FINANCES

Topics Covered

County Government Expenditures
County Government Revenues

★ 2597 ★
County Government Expenditures

County Government Expenditures, 1991-92, By Function: All Education

[In thousands of dollars]

County	Total revenues	Rank
Allegheny, PA	21,826	30
Baltimore, MD	615,740	4
Bergen, NJ	118,080	11
Bexar, TX	0	53
Broward, FL	0	53
Bucks, PA	2,696	42
Camden, NJ	74,234	17
Clark, NV	0	53
Contra Costa, CA	25,728	29
Cook, IL	2,767	40
Cuyahoga, OH	0	53
Dade, FL	0	53
Dallas, TX	0	53
DeKalb, GA	21	52
Delaware, PA	0	53
DuPage, IL	353	47
El Paso, TX	66	50
Erie, NY	138,182	10
Essex, MA	4,729	37
Essex, NJ	82,064	13
Fairfax, VA	849,263	2
Franklin, OH	7,482	35
Fresno, CA	41,622	23
Fulton, GA	0	53
Hamilton, OH	18,552	31
Harris, TX	933	44
Hennepin, MN	0	53
Hillsborough, FL	301	48
Hudson, NJ	40,187	25
Jackson, MO	0	53
Jefferson, KY	755	45
Kern, CA	41,361	24
King, WA	458	46
Los Angeles, CA	312,169	5
Macomb, MI	0	53
Middlesex, MA	0	53
Middlesex, NJ	78,878	14
Milwaukee, WI	0	53
Monmouth, NJ	28,633	27
Monroe, NY	146,025	9
Montgomery, MD	874,683	1
Montgomery, OH	11,075	32
Montgomery, PA	6,283	36
Multnomah, OR	1,479	43
Nassau, NY	158,040	8
Norfolk, MA	2,763	41
Oakland, MI	3,719	39
Oklahoma, OK	9,479	33
Orange, CA	70,192	19
Orange, FL	0	53
Palm Beach, FL	3,743	38
Pierce, WA	0	53
Pinellas, FL	0	53
Prince Georges, MD	640,151	3

[Continued]

★ 2597 ★

County Government Expenditures, 1991-92, By Function: All Education

[Continued]

County	Total revenues	Rank
Riverside, CA	70,593	18
Sacramento, CA	40,028	26
Saint Louis, MO	0	53
Salt Lake, UT	0	53
San Bernardino, CA	60,383	20
San Diego, CA	76,409	16
San Mateo, CA	47,711	22
Santa Clara, CA	90,838	12
Shelby, TN	185,597	6
Suffolk, NY	177,506	7
Summit, OH	0	53
Tarrant, TX	44	51
Travis, TX	92	49
Tulsa, OK	9,091	34
Union, NJ	56,826	21
Ventura, CA	27,412	28
Wayne, MI	0	53
Westchester, NY	76,760	15
Worcester, MA	0	53

Source: U.S. Bureau of the Census, *Annual Survey of Government Finances 1992*, Washington, D.C.: U.S. Government Printing Office, 1995, n.p. Primary source: U.S. Bureau of the Census.

★ 2598 ★
County Government Expenditures

County Government Expenditures, 1991-92, By Function: Elemenentary and Secondary Education

[In thousands of dollars]

County	Total revenues	Rank
Allegheny, PA	2,792	38
Baltimore, MD	521,258	4
Bergen, NJ	69,816	14
Bexar, TX	0	47
Broward, FL	0	47
Bucks, PA	0	47
Camden, NJ	37,901	22
Clark, NV	0	47
Contra Costa, CA	35,728	24
Cook, IL	2,767	39
Cuyahoga, OH	0	47
Dade, FL	0	47
Dallas, TX	0	47
DeKalb, GA	0	47
Delaware, PA	0	47
DuPage, IL	353	44
El Paso, TX	0	47
Erie, NY	90,081	9

[Continued]

★2598★

County Government Expenditures, 1991-92, By Function: Elemenentary and Secondary Education

[Continued]

County	Total revenues	Rank
Essex, MA	4,729	35
Essex, NJ	40,112	20
Fairfax, VA	849,263	1
Franklin, OH	7,482	34
Fresno, CA	41,622	18
Fulton, GA	0	47
Hamilton, OH	18,552	30
Harris, TX	0	47
Hennepin, MN	0	47
Hillsborough, FL	301	45
Hudson, NJ	25,279	26
Jackson, MO	0	47
Jefferson, KY	755	42
Kern, CA	41,361	19
King, WA	458	43
Los Angeles, CA	312,169	5
Macomb, MI	0	47
Middlesex, MA	0	47
Middlesex, NJ	37,549	23
Milwaukee, WI	0	47
Monmouth, NJ	23,224	27
Monroe, NY	81,715	10
Montgomery, MD	779,367	2
Montgomery, OH	11,075	31
Montgomery, PA	0	47
Multnomah, OR	1,479	41
Nassau, NY	58,620	16
Norfolk, MA	2,763	40
Oakland, MI	3,719	37
Oklahoma, OK	9,479	32
Orange, CA	70,192	13
Orange, FL	0	47
Palm Beach, FL	3,743	36
Pierce, WA	0	47
Pinellas, FL	0	47
Prince Georges, MD	602,778	3
Riverside, CA	70,593	12
Sacramento, CA	40,028	21
Saint Louis, MO	201	46
Salt Lake, UT	0	47
San Bernardino, CA	60,383	15
San Diego, CA	76,409	11
San Mateo, CA	47,711	17
Santa Clara, CA	90,838	8
Shelby, TN	185,550	6
Suffolk, NY	99,779	7
Summit, OH	0	47
Tarrant, TX	0	47
Travis, TX	0	47
Tulsa, OK	9,091	33
Union, NJ	21,108	29
Ventura, CA	27,412	25
Wayne, MI	0	47

[Continued]

★2598★

County Government Expenditures, 1991-92, By Function: Elemenentary and Secondary Education

[Continued]

County	Total revenues	Rank
Westchester, NY	22,822	28
Worcester, MA	0	47

Source: U.S. Bureau of the Census, *Annual Survey of Government Finances 1992*, Washington, D.C.: U.S. Government Printing Office, 1995, n.p. Primary source: U.S. Bureau of the Census.

★2599★

County Government Expenditures

County Government Expenditures, 1991-92, By Function: Higher Education

[In thousands of dollars]

County	Total revenues	Rank
Allegheny, PA	19,034	16
Baltimore, MD	94,482	3
Bergen, NJ	69,816	6
Bucks, PA	2,696	23
Camden, NJ	37,901	9
DeKalb, GA	21	26
El Paso, TX	6,302	20
Erie, NY	90,081	4
Essex, NJ	40,112	8
Franklin, OH	7,482	19
Hamilton, OH	18,552	17
Hudson, NJ	25,279	12
Middlesex, NJ	37,549	10
Monmouth, NJ	23,224	13
Monroe, NY	81,715	5
Montgomery, MD	95,316	2
Montgomery, OH	11,075	18
Montgomery, PA	6,283	21
Nassau, NY	58,620	7
Oakland, MI	3,719	22
Prince Georges, MD	37,373	11
Saint Louis, MO	201	24
Shelby, TN	47	25
Suffolk, NY	99,779	1
Union, NJ	21,108	15
Westchester, NY	22,822	14

Source: U.S. Bureau of the Census, *Annual Survey of Government Finances 1992*, Washington, D.C.: U.S. Government Printing Office, 1995, n.p. Primary source: U.S. Bureau of the Census.

★2600★
County Government Expenditures
County Government Expenditures, 1991-92, By Function: Hospitals

[In thousands of dollars]

County	Total revenues	Rank	Amount per capita	Rank
Allegheny, PA	76,724	26	0.05750	35
Bergen, NJ	97,697	20	0.11700	18
Bexar, TX	158,430	15	0.12848	15
Camden, NJ	28,863	36	0.07259	31
Clark, NV	176,290	14	0.20847	7
Contra Costa, CA	81,817	24	0.09733	26
Cook, IL	510,378	3	0.09931	24
Dade, FL	534,250	2	0.26606	4
Dallas, TX	240,303	9	0.12559	16
DeKalb, GA	26,809	37	0.04757	37
El Paso, TX	60,259	30	0.09588	28
Erie, NY	142,446	16	0.14651	11
Essex, NJ	81,571	25	0.10547	23
Franklin, OH	205	50	0.00021	50
Fresno, CA	97,437	21	0.13809	12
Fulton, GA	87,595	23	0.13157	14
Hamilton, OH	50,306	31	0.05769	34
Harris, TX	327,206	4	0.11011	22
Hennepin, MN	210,727	11	0.20236	8
Hillsborough, FL	250,979	8	0.29233	1
Hudson, NJ	66,961	28	0.12066	17
Jackson, MO	10,123	44	0.01597	42
Jefferson, KY	3,994	46	0.00595	45
Kern, CA	93,695	22	0.15943	9
King, WA	4,287	45	0.00275	46
Los Angeles, CA	1,367,335	1	0.15103	10
Middlesex, MA	16,667	40	0.01195	43
Middlesex, NJ	47,461	32	0.06934	32
Milwaukee, WI	257,611	6	0.27063	3
Monmouth, NJ	13,634	41	0.02409	40
Monroe, NY	40,660	34	0.05613	36
Montgomery, PA	476	48	0.00069	48
Nassau, NY	277,668	5	0.21325	6
Norfolk, MA	17,851	39	0.02875	39
Oakland, MI	10,771	43	0.00963	44
Riverside, CA	141,884	17	0.11012	21
Sacramento, CA	285	49	0.00026	49
San Bernardino, CA	178,915	13	0.11661	19
San Diego, CA	3,728	47	0.00143	47
San Mateo, CA	74,914	27	0.11290	20
Santa Clara, CA	205,489	12	0.13444	13
Shelby, TN	212,629	10	0.25168	5
Summit, OH	18,989	38	0.03629	38
Tarrant, TX	118,187	19	0.09687	27
Tulsa, OK	44,588	33	0.08577	29
Union, NJ	40,122	35	0.08133	30
Ventura, CA	66,871	29	0.09740	25
Wayne, MI	128,429	18	0.06127	33
Westchester, NY	256,683	7	0.29108	2
Worcester, MA	11,784	42	0.01664	41

Source: U.S. Bureau of the Census, *Annual Survey of Government Finances 1992*, Washington, D.C.: U.S. Government Printing Office, 1995, n.p. Primary source: U.S. Bureau of the Census.

★2601★
County Government Expenditures
County Government Expenditures, 1991-92, By Function: Libraries

[In thousands of dollars]

County	Total revenues	Rank
Allegheny, PA	5,675	33
Baltimore, MD	25,256	4
Bexar, TX	839	44
Broward, FL	26,015	3
Bucks, PA	4,264	34
Camden, NJ	2,071	40
Contra Costa, CA	10,824	18
Dade, FL	30,855	2
Dallas, TX	224	47
DeKalb, GA	13,797	15
Delaware, PA	1,523	42
El Paso, TX	144	49
Erie, NY	21,074	8
Essex, NJ	4	51
Fairfax, VA	23,339	5
Fresno, CA	8,605	26
Fulton, GA	16,865	13
Harris, TX	8,298	27
Hennepin, MN	22,111	7
Hillsborough, FL	11,616	16
Jefferson, KY	3,390	35
Kern, CA	6,951	31
Los Angeles, CA	60,857	1
Macomb, MI	2,152	37
Middlesex, NJ	1	52
Monmouth, NJ	5,839	32
Monroe, NY	7,236	30
Montgomery, MD	19,363	9
Montgomery, PA	2,146	38
Multnomah, OR	18,508	10
Nassau, NY	186	48
Oakland, MI	1,267	43
Oklahoma, OK	7,833	29
Orange, CA	22,164	6
Orange, FL	10,853	17
Palm Beach, FL	17,265	12
Pierce, WA	11	50
Pinellas, FL	2,648	36
Prince Georges, MD	17,559	11
Riverside, CA	9,042	22
Sacramento, CA	10,623	19
Salt Lake, UT	8,935	24
San Bernardino, CA	9,153	21
San Diego, CA	8,880	25
San Mateo, CA	8,134	28
Santa Clara, CA	15,355	14
Shelby, TN	1,792	41
Suffolk, NY	252	45
Tulsa, OK	8,972	23
Ventura, CA	9,369	20
Wayne, MI	2,112	39
Westchester, NY	231	46

Source: U.S. Bureau of the Census, *Annual Survey of Government Finances 1992*, Washington, D.C.: U.S. Government Printing Office, 1995, n.p. Primary source: U.S. Bureau of the Census.

★2602★
County Government Expenditures

County Government Expenditures, 1991-92, By Function: Public Welfare

[In thousands of dollars]

County	Total revenues	Rank
Camden, NJ	747	24
Contra Costa, CA	17,707	10
Cuyahoga, OH	79,119	2
El Paso, TX	113	29
Erie, NY	41,638	5
Fairfax, VA	6,392	17
Franklin, OH	3,526	18
Fresno, CA	2,572	20
Hamilton, OH	11,368	15
Hennepin, MN	16,441	11
Kern, CA	2,317	21
King, WA	320	27
Los Angeles, CA	306,670	1
Macomb, MI	468	25
Milwaukee, WI	12,209	13
Monroe, NY	42,390	4
Montgomery, OH	9,272	16
Nassau, NY	14,858	12
Oakland, MI	403	26
Orange, CA	24,557	7
Riverside, CA	278	28
San Bernardino, CA	1,715	23
San Diego, CA	22,062	8
San Mateo, CA	2,759	19
Santa Clara, CA	20,165	9
Suffolk, NY	28,672	6
Summit, OH	11,389	14
Ventura, CA	1,762	22
Westchester, NY	48,150	3

Source: U.S. Bureau of the Census, *Annual Survey of Government Finances 1992,* Washington, D.C.: U.S. Government Printing Office, 1995, n.p. Primary source: U.S. Bureau of the Census.

★2603★
County Government Expenditures

County Government Expenditures, 1991-92, By Function: Public Welfare Medical Vendors

[In thousands of dollars]

County	Total revenues	Rank
Baltimore, MD	679	26
Clark, NV	13,301	12
Contra Costa, CA	24,322	7
Cuyahoga, OH	65,841	1
Dallas, TX	12	31
El Paso, TX	5	32
Erie, NY	5,512	18
Fairfax, VA	130	28
Franklin, OH	20,976	9
Fresno, CA	18,020	10
Hamilton, OH	7,882	14

[Continued]

★2603★

County Government Expenditures, 1991-92, By Function: Public Welfare Medical Vendors

[Continued]

County	Total revenues	Rank
Hennepin, MN	26,589	6
Jefferson, KY	3,152	22
Macomb, MI	1,745	23
Middlesex, NJ	3	33
Milwaukee, WI	710	25
Monroe, NY	7,003	16
Montgomery, OH	26,981	5
Oklahoma, OK	341	27
Orange, CA	31,114	4
Orange, FL	7,783	15
Palm Beach, FL	5,631	17
Pinellas, FL	15,514	11
Riverside, CA	863	24
Sacramento, CA	9,892	13
San Bernardino, CA	3,600	20
Santa Clara, CA	57,061	2
Shelby, TN	104	29
Summit, OH	22,112	8
Tarrant, TX	43	30
Travis, TX	3,281	21
Tulsa, OK	104	29
Ventura, CA	4,736	19
Wayne, MI	49,238	3

Source: U.S. Bureau of the Census, *Annual Survey of Government Finances 1992,* Washington, D.C.: U.S. Government Printing Office, 1995, n.p. Primary source: U.S. Bureau of the Census.

★2604★
County Government Expenditures

County Government Expenditures, 1991-92, By Function: Public Welfare Vendor Payments (Other Types)

[In thousands of dollars]

County	Total revenues	Rank
Allegheny, PA	374	19
Bergen, NJ	2,911	10
Bexar, TX	18	30
Camden, NJ	696	15
Contra Costa, CA	77	27
Cuyahoga, OH	14,318	1
Dade, FL	4,632	6
Dallas, TX	3,150	9
Delaware, PA	77	27
El Paso, TX	247	21
Erie, NY	6,078	4
Hamilton, OH	9,657	2
Hennepin, MN	239	22
Jefferson, KY	104	25

[Continued]

★ 2604 ★

County Government Expenditures, 1991-92, By Function: Public Welfare Vendor Payments (Other Types)

[Continued]

County	Total revenues	Rank
Macomb, MI	1,988	11
Middlesex, NJ	4,327	7
Milwaukee, WI	710	14
Monroe, NY	689	16
Montgomery, PA	79	26
Nassau, NY	5,404	5
Oakland, MI	190	24
Oklahoma, OK	310	20
Palm Beach, FL	596	18
Pinellas, FL	618	17
Prince Georges, MD	794	13
Salt Lake, UT	21	29
Suffolk, NY	6,297	3
Tarrant, TX	1,366	12
Travis, TX	54	28
Tulsa, OK	213	23
Union, NJ	3,287	8

Source: U.S. Bureau of the Census, *Annual Survey of Government Finances 1992*, Washington, D.C.: U.S. Government Printing Office, 1995, n.p. Primary source: U.S. Bureau of the Census.

★ 2605 ★
County Government Expenditures

County Government Expenditures, 1991-92, By Function: Public Welfare (Categorical Cash Assistance)

[In thousands of dollars]

County	Total revenues	Rank
Bergen, NJ	9,996	25
Camden, NJ	62,099	19
Contra Costa, CA	102,062	15
Erie, NY	114,511	12
Essex, NJ	165,405	9
Fairfax, VA	1,724	27
Fresno, CA	288,325	5
Hennepin, MN	63,682	17
Hudson, NJ	62,915	18
Jefferson, KY	243	28
Kern, CA	136,661	10
Los Angeles, CA	2,214,672	1
Middlesex, NJ	23,329	24
Monmouth, NJ	25,021	23
Monroe, NY	124,353	11
Nassau, NY	44,955	21
Orange, CA	224,881	6
Riverside, CA	201,029	7
Sacramento, CA	401,290	4
San Bernardino, CA	406,355	3

[Continued]

★ 2605 ★

County Government Expenditures, 1991-92, By Function: Public Welfare (Categorical Cash Assistance)

[Continued]

County	Total revenues	Rank
San Diego, CA	493,835	2
San Mateo, CA	48,375	20
Santa Clara, CA	188,573	8
Suffolk, NY	108,533	14
Tarrant, TX	4,898	26
Union, NJ	28,573	22
Ventura, CA	76,312	16
Westchester, NY	114,292	13

Source: U.S. Bureau of the Census, *Annual Survey of Government Finances 1992*, Washington, D.C.: U.S. Government Printing Office, 1995, n.p. Primary source: U.S. Bureau of the Census.

★ 2606 ★
County Government Expenditures

County Government Expenditures, 1991-92, By Function: Public Welfare (Welfare Institutions)

[In thousands of dollars]

County	Total revenues	Rank	Amount per capita	Rank
Bucks, PA	15,114	6	0.02717	5
Camden, NJ	18,610	5	0.04680	3
Dade, FL	19,078	4	0.00950	7
Delaware, PA	28,045	2	0.05104	1
Harris, TX	1,444	12	0.00049	12
Montgomery, OH	2,669	11	0.00461	10
Montgomery, PA	20,802	3	0.03015	4
Nassau, NY	65,438	1	0.05026	2
Orange, CA	7,690	9	0.00309	11
Orange, FL	3,898	10	0.00545	9
Palm Beach, FL	11,802	7	0.01310	6
Suffolk, NY	11,179	8	0.00835	8

Source: U.S. Bureau of the Census, *Annual Survey of Government Finances 1992*, Washington, D.C.: U.S. Government Printing Office, 1995, n.p. Primary source: U.S. Bureau of the Census.

★2607★
County Government Expenditures

County Government Expenditures, 1991-92, By Function: Transportation (Water Transportation and Terminals)

[In thousands of dollars]

County	Total revenues	Rank	Amount per capita	Rank
Dade, FL	86,901	1	0.043278	1
Harris, TX	4,132	3	0.001390	5
Hillsborough, FL	14,593	2	0.016997	2
Jefferson, KY	2,859	4	0.004262	3
Shelby, TN	1,898	5	0.002247	4
Ventura, CA	673	6	0.000980	6
Wayne, MI	151	7	0.000072	7

Source: U.S. Bureau of the Census, *Annual Survey of Government Finances 1992*, Washington, D.C.: U.S. Government Printing Office, 1995, n.p. Primary source: U.S. Bureau of the Census.

★2608★
County Government Expenditures

County Government Expenditures, 1991-92: Assistance and Subsidies

[In thousands of dollars]

County	Total revenues	Rank
Bergen, NJ	9,996	29
Camden, NJ	62,846	20
Contra Costa, CA	119,769	15
Cuyahoga, OH	79,119	17
El Paso, TX	113	38
Erie, NY	156,149	12
Essex, NJ	165,405	10
Fairfax, VA	8,116	31
Franklin, OH	3,526	33
Fresno, CA	290,897	5
Hamilton, OH	11,368	28
Hennepin, MN	80,123	16
Hudson, NJ	62,915	19
Jefferson, KY	243	37
Kern, CA	138,978	13
King, WA	320	36
Los Angeles, CA	2,521,342	1
Macomb, MI	468	34
Middlesex, NJ	23,329	25
Milwaukee, WI	12,209	26
Monmouth, NJ	25,021	24
Monroe, NY	166,743	9
Montgomery, OH	9,272	30
Nassau, NY	59,813	21
Oakland, MI	403	35
Orange, CA	249,438	6
Riverside, CA	201,307	8
Sacramento, CA	401,290	4
San Bernardino, CA	408,070	3
San Diego, CA	515,897	2
San Mateo, CA	51,134	22
Santa Clara, CA	208,738	7

[Continued]

★2608★

County Government Expenditures, 1991-92: Assistance and Subsidies

[Continued]

County	Total revenues	Rank
Suffolk, NY	137,205	14
Summit, OH	11,389	27
Tarrant, TX	4,898	32
Union, NJ	28,573	23
Ventura, CA	78,074	18
Westchester, NY	162,442	11

Source: U.S. Bureau of the Census, *Annual Survey of Government Finances 1992*, Washington, D.C.: U.S. Government Printing Office, 1995, n.p. Primary source: U.S. Bureau of the Census.

★2609★
County Government Expenditures

County Government Expenditures, 1991-92: Capital Outlay

[In thousands of dollars]

County	Total revenues	Rank
Allegheny, PA	305,369	4
Baltimore, MD	168,882	12
Bergen, NJ	27,283	57
Bexar, TX	34,751	51
Broward, FL	244,737	5
Bucks, PA	12,197	65
Camden, NJ	37,386	48
Clark, NV	239,821	7
Contra Costa, CA	51,576	38
Cook, IL	208,288	9
Cuyahoga, OH	57,361	34
Dade, FL	345,150	3
Dallas, TX	76,089	28
DeKalb, GA	47,034	40
Delaware, PA	17,321	61
DuPage, IL	83,115	25
El Paso, TX	33,333	53
Erie, NY	31,262	55
Essex, MA	77	72
Essex, NJ	13,447	63
Fairfax, VA	146,463	15
Franklin, OH	65,520	32
Fresno, CA	33,961	52
Fulton, GA	69,924	29
Hamilton, OH	32,613	54
Harris, TX	142,608	17
Hennepin, MN	43,098	43
Hillsborough, FL	174,759	11
Hudson, NJ	24,476	58
Jackson, MO	13,289	64
Jefferson, KY	65,484	33
Kern, CA	38,960	46
King, WA	118,100	22

[Continued]

★2609★
County Government Expenditures, 1991-92: Capital Outlay
[Continued]

County	Total revenues	Rank
Los Angeles, CA	554,977	1
Macomb, MI	35,813	50
Middlesex, NJ	11,707	66
Milwaukee, WI	145,348	16
Monmouth, NJ	41,658	44
Monroe, NY	131,786	19
Montgomery, MD	118,353	21
Montgomery, OH	51,829	36
Montgomery, PA	6,655	69
Multnomah, OR	9,973	67
Nassau, NY	242,155	6
Norfolk, MA	302	70
Oakland, MI	53,057	35
Oklahoma, OK	8,678	68
Orange, CA	451,592	2
Orange, FL	114,606	24
Palm Beach, FL	211,419	8
Pierce, WA	30,853	56
Pinellas, FL	68,007	31
Prince Georges, MD	142,429	18
Riverside, CA	81,419	26
Sacramento, CA	122,528	20
Saint Louis, MO	37,239	49
Salt Lake, UT	16,909	62
San Bernardino, CA	157,912	13
San Diego, CA	115,082	23
San Mateo, CA	51,621	37
Santa Clara, CA	79,558	27
Shelby, TN	69,527	30
Suffolk, NY	46,326	41
Summit, OH	17,406	60
Tarrant, TX	37,679	47
Travis, TX	39,444	45
Tulsa, OK	49,649	39
Union, NJ	18,237	59
Ventura, CA	44,589	42
Wayne, MI	177,948	10
Westchester, NY	153,313	14
Worcester, MA	121	71

Source: U.S. Bureau of the Census, *Annual Survey of Government Finances 1992,* Washington, D.C.: U.S. Government Printing Office, 1995, n.p. Primary source: U.S. Bureau of the Census.

★2610★
County Government Expenditures
County Government Expenditures, 1991-92: Capital Outlay (For Equipment)
[In thousands of dollars]

County	Total revenues	Rank
Allegheny, PA	7,736	40
Baltimore, MD	18,072	13
Bergen, NJ	2,848	57
Bexar, TX	12,562	22
Broward, FL	28,024	8
Bucks, PA	2,021	63
Camden, NJ	9,227	36
Clark, NV	17,963	15
Contra Costa, CA	9,429	34
Cook, IL	16,201	18
Cuyahoga, OH	10,262	30
Dade, FL	78,517	2
Dallas, TX	10,489	28
DeKalb, GA	2,011	64
Delaware, PA	403	69
DuPage, IL	9,163	37
El Paso, TX	7,956	39
Erie, NY	9,536	33
Essex, MA	71	71
Essex, NJ	3,466	53
Fairfax, VA	25,052	9
Franklin, OH	10,400	29
Fresno, CA	12,367	23
Fulton, GA	4,537	48
Hamilton, OH	4,601	47
Harris, TX	11,997	24
Hennepin, MN	6,416	42
Hillsborough, FL	18,002	14
Hudson, NJ	1,731	66
Jackson, MO	1,651	67
Jefferson, KY	1,606	68
Kern, CA	23,211	11
King, WA	31,088	6
Los Angeles, CA	198,837	1
Macomb, MI	4,144	50
Middlesex, NJ	2,192	59
Milwaukee, WI	9,619	32
Monmouth, NJ	2,971	55
Monroe, NY	9,083	38
Montgomery, MD	31,901	5
Montgomery, OH	7,144	41
Montgomery, PA	2,906	56
Multnomah, OR	1,763	65
Nassau, NY	24,431	10
Oakland, MI	2,150	61
Oklahoma, OK	2,044	62
Orange, CA	29,532	7
Orange, FL	16,693	17
Palm Beach, FL	11,542	26
Pierce, WA	3,279	54
Pinellas, FL	11,718	25
Prince Georges, MD	37,243	4
Riverside, CA	11,372	27
Sacramento, CA	21,578	12

[Continued]

★2610★

County Government Expenditures, 1991-92: Capital Outlay (For Equipment)
[Continued]

County	Total revenues	Rank
Saint Louis, MO	4,987	46
Salt Lake, UT	4,529	49
San Bernardino, CA	40,483	3
San Diego, CA	17,883	16
San Mateo, CA	5,977	43
Santa Clara, CA	15,744	19
Shelby, TN	9,757	31
Suffolk, NY	13,738	21
Summit, OH	2,740	58
Tarrant, TX	9,382	35
Travis, TX	3,633	52
Tulsa, OK	2,182	60
Union, NJ	5,777	45
Ventura, CA	14,064	20
Wayne, MI	3,884	51
Westchester, NY	5,824	44
Worcester, MA	121	70

Source: U.S. Bureau of the Census, *Annual Survey of Government Finances 1992*, Washington, D.C.: U.S. Government Printing Office, 1995, n.p. Primary source: U.S. Bureau of the Census.

★2611★
County Government Expenditures

County Government Expenditures, 1991-92: Capital Outlay (For Land and Existing Structures

[In thousands of dollars]

County	Total revenues	Rank
Allegheny, PA	23	57
Baltimore, MD	-1036	62
Bergen, NJ	4,988	24
Bexar, TX	56	54
Broward, FL	54,737	3
Bucks, PA	1,299	34
Clark, NV	25,077	7
Contra Costa, CA	5,839	23
Cook, IL	44	55
Cuyahoga, OH	537	41
Dade, FL	19,814	11
Dallas, TX	3,897	26
DeKalb, GA	2,199	30
DuPage, IL	20,178	10
El Paso, TX	6	58
Essex, NJ	34	56
Fairfax, VA	27,274	6
Franklin, OH	6,153	21
Fresno, CA	324	46
Fulton, GA	2,971	29
Hamilton, OH	3	59
Harris, TX	20,526	9

[Continued]

★2611★

County Government Expenditures, 1991-92: Capital Outlay (For Land and Existing Structures
[Continued]

County	Total revenues	Rank
Hennepin, MN	2,095	31
Hillsborough, FL	28,461	5
Jackson, MO	108	50
Jefferson, KY	-119	60
Kern, CA	145	49
King, WA	8,011	19
Los Angeles, CA	58,081	2
Macomb, MI	349	45
Middlesex, NJ	1,181	35
Milwaukee, WI	1,084	36
Monmouth, NJ	10,859	15
Montgomery, MD	16,485	12
Montgomery, OH	359	44
Montgomery, PA	102	51
Nassau, NY	497	42
Oklahoma, OK	76	52
Orange, CA	136,533	1
Orange, FL	780	40
Palm Beach, FL	24,869	8
Pierce, WA	1,729	33
Pinellas, FL	7,205	20
Prince Georges, MD	14,698	13
Riverside, CA	9,275	18
Sacramento, CA	3,545	27
Saint Louis, MO	9,325	17
Salt Lake, UT	867	38
San Bernardino, CA	49,571	4
San Diego, CA	13,761	14
San Mateo, CA	934	37
Santa Clara, CA	3,165	28
Shelby, TN	67	53
Suffolk, NY	3,943	25
Summit, OH	159	48
Tarrant, TX	806	39
Travis, TX	9,827	16
Tulsa, OK	452	43
Union, NJ	307	47
Ventura, CA	1,857	32
Wayne, MI	6,015	22
Westchester, NY	-723	61

Source: U.S. Bureau of the Census, *Annual Survey of Government Finances 1992*, Washington, D.C.: U.S. Government Printing Office, 1995, n.p. Primary source: U.S. Bureau of the Census.

★2612★
County Government Expenditures
County Government Expenditures, 1991-92: Capital Outlay (For Construction)
[In thousands of dollars]

County	Total revenues	Rank
Allegheny, PA	297,610	2
Baltimore, MD	151,846	11
Bergen, NJ	19,447	57
Bexar, TX	22,133	54
Broward, FL	161,976	10
Bucks, PA	8,877	65
Camden, NJ	28,159	45
Clark, NV	196,781	6
Contra Costa, CA	36,308	40
Cook, IL	192,043	7
Cuyahoga, OH	46,562	36
Dade, FL	246,819	4
Dallas, TX	61,703	27
DeKalb, GA	42,824	39
Delaware, PA	16,918	58
DuPage, IL	53,774	31
El Paso, TX	25,371	51
Erie, NY	21,726	55
Essex, MA	6	71
Essex, NJ	9,947	64
Fairfax, VA	94,137	19
Franklin, OH	48,967	34
Fresno, CA	21,270	56
Fulton, GA	62,416	26
Hamilton, OH	28,009	46
Harris, TX	110,085	16
Hennepin, MN	34,587	41
Hillsborough, FL	128,296	14
Hudson, NJ	22,745	53
Jackson, MO	11,530	62
Jefferson, KY	63,997	25
Kern, CA	15,604	59
King, WA	79,001	22
Los Angeles, CA	298,059	1
Macomb, MI	31,320	42
Middlesex, NJ	8,334	66
Milwaukee, WI	134,645	13
Monmouth, NJ	27,828	47
Monroe, NY	122,703	15
Montgomery, MD	69,967	23
Montgomery, OH	44,326	38
Montgomery, PA	3,647	69
Multnomah, OR	8,210	67
Nassau, NY	217,227	5
Norfolk, MA	302	70
Oakland, MI	50,907	32
Oklahoma, OK	6,558	68
Orange, CA	285,527	3
Orange, FL	97,133	18
Palm Beach, FL	175,008	8
Pierce, WA	25,845	50
Pinellas, FL	49,084	33
Prince Georges, MD	90,488	20
Riverside, CA	60,772	28

[Continued]

★2612★
County Government Expenditures, 1991-92: Capital Outlay (For Construction)
[Continued]

County	Total revenues	Rank
Sacramento, CA	97,405	17
Saint Louis, MO	22,927	52
Salt Lake, UT	11,513	63
San Bernardino, CA	67,858	24
San Diego, CA	83,438	21
San Mateo, CA	44,710	37
Santa Clara, CA	60,649	29
Shelby, TN	59,703	30
Suffolk, NY	28,645	44
Summit, OH	14,507	60
Tarrant, TX	27,491	48
Travis, TX	25,984	49
Tulsa, OK	47,015	35
Union, NJ	12,153	61
Ventura, CA	28,668	43
Wayne, MI	168,049	9
Westchester, NY	148,212	12

Source: U.S. Bureau of the Census, *Annual Survey of Government Finances 1992,* Washington, D.C.: U.S. Government Printing Office, 1995, n.p. Primary source: U.S. Bureau of the Census.

★2613★
County Government Expenditures
County Government Expenditures, 1991-92: Current Operations
[In thousands of dollars]

County	Total revenues	Rank
Allegheny, PA	565,166	26
Baltimore, MD	960,522	11
Bergen, NJ	396,903	39
Bexar, TX	311,999	45
Broward, FL	514,784	28
Bucks, PA	138,910	66
Camden, NJ	322,686	43
Clark, NV	669,229	21
Contra Costa, CA	604,270	24
Cook, IL	1,167,259	9
Cuyahoga, OH	863,611	15
Dade, FL	2,030,052	2
Dallas, TX	506,480	29
DeKalb, GA	263,933	51
Delaware, PA	210,518	56
DuPage, IL	152,364	62
El Paso, TX	144,765	65
Erie, NY	574,488	25
Essex, MA	22,998	73
Essex, NJ	414,896	36
Fairfax, VA	1,544,626	3
Franklin, OH	364,867	40

[Continued]

★2613★

County Government Expenditures, 1991-92: Current Operations

[Continued]

County	Total revenues	Rank
Fresno, CA	425,248	34
Fulton, GA	270,363	49
Hamilton, OH	336,908	42
Harris, TX	929,674	13
Hennepin, MN	816,083	18
Hillsborough, FL	677,891	20
Hudson, NJ	269,695	50
Jackson, MO	90,156	67
Jefferson, KY	150,442	63
Kern, CA	495,222	31
King, WA	498,808	30
Los Angeles, CA	6,500,214	1
Macomb, MI	165,475	61
Middlesex, MA	52,028	70
Middlesex, NJ	289,739	47
Milwaukee, WI	639,268	23
Monmouth, NJ	236,934	53
Monroe, NY	491,622	32
Montgomery, MD	1,334,311	5
Montgomery, OH	300,572	46
Montgomery, PA	176,341	60
Multnomah, OR	262,958	52
Nassau, NY	1,507,599	4
Norfolk, MA	37,186	72
Oakland, MI	346,541	41
Oklahoma, OK	63,299	69
Orange, CA	1,206,270	7
Orange, FL	405,823	37
Palm Beach, FL	422,652	35
Pierce, WA	180,522	59
Pinellas, FL	322,170	44
Prince Georges, MD	1,101,767	10
Riverside, CA	836,575	17
Sacramento, CA	745,302	19
Saint Louis, MO	206,219	57
Salt Lake, UT	204,731	58
San Bernardino, CA	930,082	12
San Diego, CA	1,310,712	6
San Mateo, CA	403,289	38
Santa Clara, CA	1,173,382	8
Shelby, TN	515,343	27
Suffolk, NY	924,500	14
Summit, OH	231,023	55
Tarrant, TX	271,384	48
Travis, TX	146,433	64
Tulsa, OK	67,128	68
Union, NJ	233,244	54
Ventura, CA	438,397	33
Wayne, MI	668,614	22
Westchester, NY	839,488	16
Worcester, MA	39,801	71

Source: U.S. Bureau of the Census, *Annual Survey of Government Finances 1992*, Washington, D.C.: U.S. Government Printing Office, 1995, n.p. Primary source: U.S. Bureau of the Census.

★2614★

County Government Expenditures

County Government Expenditures, 1991-92: Interest on General Debt

[In thousands of dollars]

County	Total revenues	Rank
Allegheny, PA	48,269	32
Baltimore, MD	91,065	16
Bergen, NJ	20,103	49
Bexar, TX	96,650	15
Broward, FL	170,690	5
Bucks, PA	7,893	61
Camden, NJ	7,870	62
Clark, NV	120,090	9
Contra Costa, CA	34,161	38
Cook, IL	83,257	18
Cuyahoga, OH	57,752	23
Dade, FL	304,973	1
Dallas, TX	63,492	22
DeKalb, GA	7,788	63
Delaware, PA	9,612	60
DuPage, IL	17,788	51
El Paso, TX	17,411	52
Erie, NY	55,329	24
Essex, NJ	24,134	44
Fairfax, VA	97,044	14
Franklin, OH	50,506	29
Fresno, CA	12,744	59
Fulton, GA	35,872	37
Hamilton, OH	20,366	48
Harris, TX	280,109	2
Hennepin, MN	22,540	46
Hillsborough, FL	128,504	7
Hudson, NJ	5,593	65
Jackson, MO	13,075	57
Jefferson, KY	131,709	6
Kern, CA	15,848	53
King, WA	53,328	27
Los Angeles, CA	270,225	3
Macomb, MI	3,897	68
Middlesex, MA	126	72
Middlesex, NJ	18,392	50
Milwaukee, WI	24,742	43
Monmouth, NJ	13,389	56
Monroe, NY	49,973	31
Montgomery, MD	117,688	10
Montgomery, OH	33,150	39
Montgomery, PA	55,155	25
Multnomah, OR	1,637	69
Nassau, NY	115,590	11
Norfolk, MA	685	70
Oakland, MI	21,564	47
Oklahoma, OK	53,580	26
Orange, CA	189,045	4
Orange, FL	120,701	8
Palm Beach, FL	74,806	21
Pierce, WA	6,010	64
Pinellas, FL	42,354	35
Prince Georges, MD	40,902	36
Riverside, CA	98,613	13

[Continued]

★2614★

County Government Expenditures, 1991-92: Interest on General Debt

[Continued]

County	Total revenues	Rank
Sacramento, CA	85,917	17
Saint Louis, MO	25,357	42
Salt Lake, UT	15,465	54
San Bernardino, CA	79,051	20
San Diego, CA	30,985	40
San Mateo, CA	5,032	66
Santa Clara, CA	23,617	45
Shelby, TN	83,236	19
Suffolk, NY	115,570	12
Summit, OH	14,489	55
Tarrant, TX	47,273	33
Travis, TX	42,410	34
Tulsa, OK	27,768	41
Union, NJ	4,483	67
Ventura, CA	13,062	58
Wayne, MI	51,805	28
Westchester, NY	50,284	30
Worcester, MA	415	71

Source: U.S. Bureau of the Census, *Annual Survey of Government Finances 1992*, Washington, D.C.: U.S. Government Printing Office, 1995, n.p. Primary source: U.S. Bureau of the Census.

★2615★

County Government Expenditures

County Government Expenditures, 1991-92: Public Welfare

[In thousands of dollars]

County	Total revenues	Rank
Allegheny, PA	72,535	30
Baltimore, MD	4,967	55
Bergen, NJ	62,517	32
Bexar, TX	16,416	45
Broward, FL	17,041	44
Bucks, PA	24,060	39
Camden, NJ	117,569	21
Contra Costa, CA	262,685	15
Cook, IL	434	65
Cuyahoga, OH	306,193	13
Dade, FL	33,175	37
Dallas, TX	14,287	48
DeKalb, GA	1,563	61
Delaware, PA	53,316	35
DuPage, IL	12,992	50
El Paso, TX	1,212	62
Erie, NY	387,341	7
Essex, NJ	210,683	17
Fairfax, VA	89,607	26
Franklin, OH	122,837	20
Fresno, CA	394,050	6

[Continued]

★2615★

County Government Expenditures, 1991-92: Public Welfare

[Continued]

County	Total revenues	Rank
Fulton, GA	9,316	51
Hamilton, OH	99,314	23
Harris, TX	15,150	47
Hennepin, MN	246,242	16
Hillsborough, FL	39,556	36
Hudson, NJ	91,135	25
Jackson, MO	3,519	56
Jefferson, KY	6,725	53
Kern, CA	196,534	18
King, WA	758	64
Los Angeles, CA	374,589	8
Macomb, MI	17,164	43
Middlesex, NJ	55,552	34
Milwaukee, WI	164,587	19
Monmouth, NJ	70,716	31
Monroe, NY	337,169	10
Montgomery, MD	15,214	46
Montgomery, OH	88,127	27
Montgomery, PA	31,755	38
Nassau, NY	298,213	14
Oakland, MI	2,650	57
Oklahoma, OK	2,476	58
Orange, CA	463,641	5
Orange, FL	23,700	40
Palm Beach, FL	22,220	41
Pierce, WA	2,413	59
Pinellas, FL	21,273	42
Prince Georges, MD	2,256	60
Riverside, CA	307,070	12
Sacramento, CA	518,426	3
Salt Lake, UT	21	66
San Bernardino, CA	596,106	2
San Diego, CA	827,774	1
San Mateo, CA	93,504	24
Santa Clara, CA	504,729	4
Shelby, TN	5,572	54
Suffolk, NY	317,511	11
Summit, OH	85,698	28
Tarrant, TX	7,690	52
Travis, TX	13,656	49
Tulsa, OK	838	63
Union, NJ	57,211	33
Ventura, CA	107,812	22
Wayne, MI	74,824	29
Westchester, NY	364,058	9

Source: U.S. Bureau of the Census, *Annual Survey of Government Finances 1992*, Washington, D.C.: U.S. Government Printing Office, 1995, n.p. Primary source: U.S. Bureau of the Census.

★2616★

County Government Revenues

County Government Revenues, 1991-92: Direct General Expenditures

[In thousands of dollars]

County	Total revenues	Rank
Allegheny, PA	918,804	23
Baltimore, MD	1,220,469	15
Bergen, NJ	454,285	40
Bexar, TX	443,400	41
Broward, FL	930,211	22
Bucks, PA	159,000	66
Camden, NJ	430,788	43
Clark, NV	1,029,140	19
Contra Costa, CA	809,776	28
Cook, IL	1,458,804	10
Cuyahoga, OH	1,057,843	18
Dade, FL	2,680,175	2
Dallas, TX	646,061	34
DeKalb, GA	318,755	52
Delaware, PA	237,451	60
DuPage, IL	253,267	58
El Paso, TX	195,622	65
Erie, NY	817,228	27
Essex, MA	23,075	73
Essex, NJ	617,882	36
Fairfax, VA	1,796,249	6
Franklin, OH	484,419	39
Fresno, CA	762,850	29
Fulton, GA	376,159	47
Hamilton, OH	401,255	45
Harris, TX	1,352,391	12
Hennepin, MN	961,844	21
Hillsborough, FL	981,154	20
Hudson, NJ	362,679	48
Jackson, MO	116,520	69
Jefferson, KY	347,878	50
Kern, CA	689,008	31
King, WA	670,556	32
Los Angeles, CA	9,846,758	1
Macomb, MI	205,653	64
Middlesex, MA	52,154	70
Middlesex, NJ	343,167	51
Milwaukee, WI	821,567	26
Monmouth, NJ	317,002	53
Monroe, NY	840,124	25
Montgomery, MD	1,570,352	8
Montgomery, OH	394,823	46
Montgomery, PA	238,151	59
Multnomah, OR	274,568	55
Nassau, NY	1,925,157	5
Norfolk, MA	38,173	72
Oakland, MI	421,565	44
Oklahoma, OK	125,557	68
Orange, CA	2,096,345	3
Orange, FL	641,130	35
Palm Beach, FL	708,877	30
Pierce, WA	217,385	63
Pinellas, FL	432,531	42
Prince Georges, MD	1,285,098	13

[Continued]

★2616★

County Government Revenues, 1991-92: Direct General Expenditures

[Continued]

County	Total revenues	Rank
Riverside, CA	1,217,914	16
Sacramento, CA	1,355,037	11
Saint Louis, MO	268,815	57
Salt Lake, UT	237,105	61
San Bernardino, CA	1,575,115	7
San Diego, CA	1,972,676	4
San Mateo, CA	511,076	38
Santa Clara, CA	1,485,295	9
Shelby, TN	668,106	33
Suffolk, NY	1,223,601	14
Summit, OH	274,307	56
Tarrant, TX	361,234	49
Travis, TX	228,287	62
Tulsa, OK	144,545	67
Union, NJ	284,537	54
Ventura, CA	574,122	37
Wayne, MI	898,367	24
Westchester, NY	1,205,527	17
Worcester, MA	40,337	71

Source: U.S. Bureau of the Census, *Annual Survey of Government Finances 1992*, Washington, D.C.: U.S. Government Printing Office, 1995, n.p. Primary source: U.S. Bureau of the Census.

★2617★

County Government Revenues

County Government Revenues, 1991-92: General Revenues From Charges and Miscellaneous General Revenues

[In thousands of dollars]

County	Total revenues	Rank
Allegheny, PA	128,716	38
Baltimore, MD	222,132	24
Bergen, NJ	139,746	36
Bexar, TX	187,393	29
Broward, FL	390,473	7
Bucks, PA	24,926	67
Camden, NJ	55,266	59
Clark, NV	482,871	4
Contra Costa, CA	152,493	34
Cook, IL	286,493	16
Cuyahoga, OH	304,272	12
Dade, FL	1,587,114	1
Dallas, TX	197,176	27
DeKalb, GA	103,945	42
Delaware, PA	67,658	54
DuPage, IL	76,639	49
El Paso, TX	58,582	57
Erie, NY	197,248	26

[Continued]

★2617★

County Government Revenues, 1991-92: General Revenues From Charges and Miscellaneous General Revenues

[Continued]

County	Total revenues	Rank
Essex, MA	4,642	73
Essex, NJ	44,914	64
Fairfax, VA	368,468	8
Franklin, OH	84,648	47
Fresno, CA	113,790	40
Fulton, GA	95,754	44
Hamilton, OH	51,437	61
Harris, TX	409,256	6
Hennepin, MN	322,225	11
Hillsborough, FL	446,881	5
Hudson, NJ	37,272	65
Jackson, MO	22,799	69
Jefferson, KY	169,699	32
Kern, CA	126,316	39
King, WA	183,577	30
Los Angeles, CA	1,033,310	2
Macomb, MI	23,785	68
Middlesex, MA	21,719	70
Middlesex, NJ	69,431	53
Milwaukee, WI	278,287	17
Monmouth, NJ	92,063	46
Monroe, NY	156,797	33
Montgomery, MD	228,549	23
Montgomery, OH	107,497	41
Montgomery, PA	83,308	48
Multnomah, OR	25,516	66
Nassau, NY	323,274	10
Norfolk, MA	13,643	72
Oakland, MI	74,850	50
Oklahoma, OK	72,985	51
Orange, CA	562,327	3
Orange, FL	258,461	19
Palm Beach, FL	270,456	18
Pierce, WA	50,812	62
Pinellas, FL	175,535	31
Prince Georges, MD	191,702	28
Riverside, CA	248,303	22
Sacramento, CA	365,438	9
Saint Louis, MO	63,773	55
Salt Lake, UT	54,785	60
San Bernardino, CA	298,087	13
San Diego, CA	249,385	21
San Mateo, CA	98,503	43
Santa Clara, CA	250,647	20
Shelby, TN	296,821	14
Suffolk, NY	146,512	35
Summit, OH	71,278	52
Tarrant, TX	92,080	45
Travis, TX	58,219	58
Tulsa, OK	62,440	56
Union, NJ	49,684	63
Ventura, CA	132,368	37

[Continued]

★2617★

County Government Revenues, 1991-92: General Revenues From Charges and Miscellaneous General Revenues

[Continued]

County	Total revenues	Rank
Wayne, MI	216,644	25
Westchester, NY	293,726	15
Worcester, MA	14,419	71

Source: U.S. Bureau of the Census, *Annual Survey of Government Finances 1992*, Washington, D.C.: U.S. Government Printing Office, 1995, n.p. Primary source: U.S. Bureau of the Census.

★2618★

County Government Revenues

County Government Revenues, 1991-92: General Revenues From Own Sources

[In thousands of dollars]

County	Total revenues	Rank
Allegheny, PA	430,291	33
Baltimore, MD	932,578	11
Bergen, NJ	341,884	39
Bexar, TX	379,302	37
Broward, FL	7,520,007	1
Bucks, PA	97,911	68
Camden, NJ	215,066	53
Clark, NV	755,967	15
Contra Costa, CA	410,742	35
Cook, IL	1,164,251	8
Cuyahoga, OH	641,471	22
Dade, FL	2,471,339	4
Dallas, TX	513,064	30
DeKalb, GA	382,631	36
Delaware, PA	147,627	62
DuPage, IL	209,818	55
El Paso, TX	136,577	64
Erie, NY	723,877	18
Essex, MA	13,428	73
Essex, NJ	277,937	43
Fairfax, VA	1,606,788	5
Franklin, OH	243,936	49
Fresno, CA	231,937	50
Fulton, GA	6,000,074	2
Hamilton, OH	251,833	48
Harris, TX	1,096,446	10
Hennepin, MN	622,679	23
Hillsborough, FL	745,007	17
Hudson, NJ	166,998	58
Jackson, MO	120,394	65
Jefferson, KY	293,731	42
Kern, CA	304,419	41
King, WA	522,603	29
Los Angeles, CA	3,840,435	3

[Continued]

★2618★

County Government Revenues, 1991-92: General Revenues From Own Sources
[Continued]

County	Total revenues	Rank
Macomb, MI	83,701	69
Middlesex, MA	46,044	70
Middlesex, NJ	255,061	47
Milwaukee, WI	436,547	32
Monmouth, NJ	274,417	44
Monroe, NY	562,947	27
Montgomery, MD	1,378,209	7
Montgomery, OH	211,484	54
Montgomery, PA	176,262	57
Multnomah, OR	154,465	61
Nassau, NY	1,390,524	6
Norfolk, MA	20,491	71
Oakland, MI	221,357	52
Oklahoma, OK	112,524	66
Orange, CA	1,105,203	9
Orange, FL	565,986	26
Palm Beach, FL	612,991	24
Pierce, WA	141,682	63
Pinellas, FL	438,574	31
Prince Georges, MD	898,964	13
Riverside, CA	538,244	28
Sacramento, CA	716,021	19
Saint Louis, MO	366,582	38
Salt Lake, UT	224,000	51
San Bernardino, CA	589,685	25
San Diego, CA	691,465	21
San Mateo, CA	272,566	45
Santa Clara, CA	748,629	16
Shelby, TN	713,707	20
Suffolk, NY	922,100	12
Summit, OH	163,848	59
Tarrant, TX	271,178	46
Travis, TX	156,890	60
Tulsa, OK	107,735	67
Union, NJ	183,038	56
Ventura, CA	337,585	40
Wayne, MI	426,727	34
Westchester, NY	867,074	14
Worcester, MA	17,740	72

Source: U.S. Bureau of the Census, *Annual Survey of Government Finances 1992,* Washington, D.C.: U.S. Government Printing Office, 1995, n.p. Primary source: U.S. Bureau of the Census.

★2619★
County Government Revenues

County Government Revenues, 1991-92: General Revenues From Own Sources (Alcoholic Beverages Sales)

[In thousands of dollars]

County	Total revenues	Rank
Cook, IL	32,304	1
DeKalb, GA	3,499	2
Fulton, GA	3,073	3
Shelby, TN	892	4

Source: U.S. Bureau of the Census, *Annual Survey of Government Finances 1992,* Washington, D.C.: U.S. Government Printing Office, 1995, n.p. Primary source: U.S. Bureau of the Census.

★2620★
County Government Revenues

County Government Revenues, 1991-92: General Revenues From Own Sources (General Sales Taxes)

[In thousands of dollars]

County	Total revenues	Rank
Contra Costa, CA	7,765	34
Cook, IL	4,546	36
Cuyahoga, OH	96,782	9
DeKalb, GA	62,756	14
DuPage, IL	23,916	23
El Paso, TX	14,727	29
Erie, NY	328,378	3
Fairfax, VA	71,548	12
Franklin, OH	43,927	15
Fresno, CA	8,257	33
Fulton, GA	195,523	5
Hamilton, OH	38,824	19
Jackson, MO	43,102	16
Kern, CA	18,442	27
King, WA	64,819	13
Los Angeles, CA	35,790	21
Milwaukee, WI	26,077	22
Monroe, NY	204,164	4
Montgomery, OH	42,079	17
Nassau, NY	502,149	1
Orange, CA	11,710	31
Pierce, WA	20,701	24
Pinellas, FL	38,525	20
Riverside, CA	19,741	25
Sacramento, CA	87,392	11
Saint Louis, MO	154,952	7
Salt Lake, UT	39,273	18
San Bernardino, CA	15,019	28
San Diego, CA	9,971	32
San Mateo, CA	13,802	30
Santa Clara, CA	88,644	10
Shelby, TN	158,508	6
Suffolk, NY	373,556	2

[Continued]

★2620★

County Government Revenues, 1991-92: General Revenues From Own Sources (General Sales Taxes)

[Continued]

County	Total revenues	Rank
Summit, OH	18,971	26
Travis, TX	1,895	37
Ventura, CA	4,813	35
Westchester, NY	153,195	8

Source: U.S. Bureau of the Census, *Annual Survey of Government Finances 1992*, Washington, D.C.: U.S. Government Printing Office, 1995, n.p. Primary source: U.S. Bureau of the Census.

★2621★
County Government Revenues

County Government Revenues, 1991-92: General Revenues From Own Sources (Motor Fuels Sales)

[In thousands of dollars]

County	Total revenues	Rank
Broward, FL	20,984	3
Clark, NV	16,930	4
Cook, IL	91,253	1
Dade, FL	34,844	2
DuPage, IL	14,766	8
Hillsborough, FL	4,428	10
Multnomah, OR	7,024	9
Orange, FL	15,130	7
Palm Beach, FL	16,209	6
Pinellas, FL	16,416	5

Source: U.S. Bureau of the Census, *Annual Survey of Government Finances 1992*, Washington, D.C.: U.S. Government Printing Office, 1995, n.p. Primary source: U.S. Bureau of the Census.

★2622★
County Government Revenues

County Government Revenues, 1991-92: General Revenues From Own Sources (Motor Vehicles Licenses)

Data refer to finances of individual county governments with 500,000 or more persons in 1991-92.

[In thousands of dollars]

County	Total revenues	Rank
Bexar, TX	11,735	6
Broward, FL	5,237	13
Cook, IL	545	29
Cuyahoga, OH	12,056	4
Dade, FL	7,901	8

[Continued]

★2622★

County Government Revenues, 1991-92: General Revenues From Own Sources (Motor Vehicles Licenses)

[Continued]

County	Total revenues	Rank
Dallas, TX	20,607	2
El Paso, TX	2,512	24
Erie, NY	2,091	25
Fairfax, VA	11,877	5
Franklin, OH	4,064	17
Fulton, GA	141	30
Hamilton, OH	5,534	10
Harris, TX	21,199	1
Hennepin, MN	1,149	28
Hillsborough, FL	3,934	18
King, WA	5,095	14
Monroe, NY	2,638	22
Montgomery, OH	5,465	11
Multnomah, OR	4,978	15
Nassau, NY	4,083	16
Orange, FL	3,319	20
Palm Beach, FL	3,297	21
Pierce, WA	1,871	26
Pinellas, FL	3,343	19
Shelby, TN	12,484	3
Suffolk, NY	5,270	12
Summit, OH	2,601	23
Tarrant, TX	11,018	7
Travis, TX	6,305	9
Westchester, NY	1,252	27

Source: U.S. Bureau of the Census, *Annual Survey of Government Finances 1992*, Washington, D.C.: U.S. Government Printing Office, 1995, n.p. Primary source: U.S. Bureau of the Census.

★2623★
County Government Revenues

County Government Revenues, 1991-92: General Revenues From Own Sources (Property Taxes)

Data refer to finances of individual county governments with 500,000 or more persons in 1991-92.

[In thousands of dollars]

County	Total revenues	Rank
Allegheny, PA	287,272	17
Baltimore, MD	387,194	13
Bergen, NJ	199,935	31
Bexar, TX	175,502	39
Broward, FL	311,018	14
Bucks, PA	72,472	59
Camden, NJ	159,800	41
Clark, NV	131,185	47
Contra Costa, CA	234,758	24
Cook, IL	696,740	3
Cuyahoga, OH	214,238	29

[Continued]

★2623★

County Government Revenues, 1991-92: General Revenues From Own Sources (Property Taxes)

[Continued]

County	Total revenues	Rank
Dade, FL	681,966	4
Dallas, TX	286,256	18
DeKalb, GA	182,243	37
Delaware, PA	79,966	58
DuPage, IL	91,016	56
El Paso, TX	58,957	62
Erie, NY	188,636	35
Essex, MA	5,448	71
Essex, NJ	233,023	25
Fairfax, VA	1,024,892	2
Franklin, OH	107,545	51
Fresno, CA	100,296	53
Fulton, GA	289,687	16
Hamilton, OH	143,898	44
Harris, TX	63,090	61
Hennepin, MN	298,130	15
Hillsborough, FL	263,893	20
Hudson, NJ	129,726	49
Jackson, MO	51,081	65
Jefferson, KY	47,852	67
Kern, CA	149,247	43
King, WA	231,206	26
Los Angeles, CA	2,666,153	1
Macomb, MI	56,981	63
Middlesex, MA	16,649	70
Middlesex, NJ	183,499	36
Milwaukee, WI	131,148	48
Monmouth, NJ	176,945	38
Monroe, NY	197,212	32
Montgomery, MD	679,363	5
Montgomery, OH	50,649	66
Montgomery, PA	92,392	54
Multnomah, OR	91,032	55
Nassau, NY	550,277	6
Norfolk, MA	3,236	72
Oakland, MI	139,163	45
Oklahoma, OK	39,296	69
Orange, CA	511,925	7
Orange, FL	236,054	23
Palm Beach, FL	268,038	19
Pierce, WA	55,194	64
Pinellas, FL	190,690	34
Prince Georges, MD	407,086	9
Riverside, CA	249,475	22
Sacramento, CA	226,180	27
Saint Louis, MO	102,006	52
Salt Lake, UT	116,949	50
San Bernardino, CA	259,147	21
San Diego, CA	397,606	10
San Mateo, CA	154,188	42
Santa Clara, CA	392,296	12
Shelby, TN	223,573	28
Suffolk, NY	394,303	11

[Continued]

★2623★

County Government Revenues, 1991-92: General Revenues From Own Sources (Property Taxes)

[Continued]

County	Total revenues	Rank
Summit, OH	65,707	60
Tarrant, TX	162,704	40
Travis, TX	89,672	57
Tulsa, OK	44,211	68
Union, NJ	132,290	46
Ventura, CA	190,937	33
Wayne, MI	205,999	30
Westchester, NY	415,078	8
Worcester, MA	765	73

Source: U.S. Bureau of the Census, *Annual Survey of Government Finances 1992,* Washington, D.C.: U.S. Government Printing Office, 1995, n.p. Primary source: U.S. Bureau of the Census.

★2624★

County Government Revenues

County Government Revenues, 1991-92: General Revenues From Own Sources (Public Utilities Sales)

[In thousands of dollars]

County	Total revenues	Rank
Baltimore, MD	29,389	7
Bexar, TX	174	31
Broward, FL	908	24
Clark, NV	2,424	14
Contra Costa, CA	1,224	21
Dade, FL	112,918	1
Dallas, TX	363	29
El Paso, TX	49	34
Fairfax, VA	53,540	2
Fresno, CA	1,944	18
Harris, TX	1,511	20
Hillsborough, FL	12,993	9
Jefferson, KY	816	25
Kern, CA	2,704	13
King, WA	2,020	17
Los Angeles, CA	42,785	4
Montgomery, MD	53,504	3
Multnomah, OR	657	28
Orange, CA	1,818	19
Orange, FL	2,116	16
Palm Beach, FL	37,420	5
Pierce, WA	710	27
Pinellas, FL	761	26
Prince Georges, MD	34,515	6
Riverside, CA	3,094	12
Sacramento, CA	9,296	10
Saint Louis, MO	24,578	8
San Bernardino, CA	3,411	11

[Continued]

★2624★

County Government Revenues, 1991-92: General Revenues From Own Sources (Public Utilities Sales)
[Continued]

County	Total revenues	Rank
San Diego, CA	2,141	15
San Mateo, CA	348	30
Santa Clara, CA	982	23
Tarrant, TX	128	32
Travis, TX	94	33
Ventura, CA	1,097	22

Source: U.S. Bureau of the Census, *Annual Survey of Government Finances 1992*, Washington, D.C.: U.S. Government Printing Office, 1995, n.p. Primary source: U.S. Bureau of the Census.

★2625★
County Government Revenues

County Government Revenues, 1991-92: General Revenues From Own Sources (Selective Sales Taxes)
[In thousands of dollars]

County	Total revenues	Rank
Allegheny, PA	12,516	21
Baltimore, MD	38,438	11
Bexar, TX	4,056	33
Broward, FL	32,523	12
Clark, NV	72,786	3
Contra Costa, CA	1,851	43
Cook, IL	166,778	1
Cuyahoga, OH	3,531	37
Dade, FL	161,602	2
Dallas, TX	8,672	24
DeKalb, GA	20,010	17
DuPage, IL	14,766	18
El Paso, TX	1,553	45
Erie, NY	5,477	29
Fairfax, VA	58,608	7
Fresno, CA	2,369	42
Fulton, GA	7,996	25
Hamilton, OH	4,291	32
Harris, TX	23,110	16
Hillsborough, FL	23,541	14
Jackson, MO	2,930	38
Jefferson, KY	13,227	20
Kern, CA	3,564	36
King, WA	23,369	15
Los Angeles, CA	48,313	8
Monroe, NY	532	49
Montgomery, MD	62,129	4
Montgomery, OH	1,673	44
Multnomah, OR	11,147	22
Nassau, NY	10,741	23
Orange, CA	2,717	39

[Continued]

★2625★

County Government Revenues, 1991-92: General Revenues From Own Sources (Selective Sales Taxes)
[Continued]

County	Total revenues	Rank
Orange, FL	60,044	6
Palm Beach, FL	60,625	5
Pierce, WA	5,904	27
Pinellas, FL	26,654	13
Prince Georges, MD	44,753	9
Riverside, CA	4,050	34
Sacramento, CA	13,566	19
Saint Louis, MO	39,287	10
Salt Lake, UT	6,537	26
San Bernardino, CA	4,452	31
San Diego, CA	3,903	35
San Mateo, CA	1,463	46
Santa Clara, CA	1,169	47
Shelby, TN	5,859	28
Suffolk, NY	2,459	41
Tarrant, TX	4,890	30
Travis, TX	290	50
Ventura, CA	1,152	48
Westchester, NY	2,631	40

Source: U.S. Bureau of the Census, *Annual Survey of Government Finances 1992*, Washington, D.C.: U.S. Government Printing Office, 1995, n.p. Primary source: U.S. Bureau of the Census.

★2626★
County Government Revenues

County Government Revenues, 1991-92: General Revenues From Own Sources (Taxes)
[In thousands of dollars]

County	Total revenues	Rank
Allegheny, PA	301,575	27
Baltimore, MD	710,446	8
Bergen, NJ	202,138	39
Bexar, TX	191,909	41
Broward, FL	361,534	19
Bucks, PA	72,985	66
Camden, NJ	159,800	48
Clark, NV	273,096	33
Contra Costa, CA	258,249	35
Cook, IL	877,758	6
Cuyahoga, OH	337,199	23
Dade, FL	884,225	5
Dallas, TX	315,888	24
DeKalb, GA	278,686	32
Delaware, PA	79,969	64
DuPage, IL	133,179	53
El Paso, TX	77,995	65
Erie, NY	526,629	13
Essex, MA	8,786	71
Essex, NJ	233,023	36

[Continued]

★2626★

County Government Revenues, 1991-92: General Revenues From Own Sources (Taxes)
[Continued]

County	Total revenues	Rank
Fairfax, VA	1,238,320	2
Franklin, OH	159,288	49
Fresno, CA	118,147	57
Fulton, GA	504,320	14
Hamilton, OH	200,396	40
Harris, TX	687,190	10
Hennepin, MN	300,454	28
Hillsborough, FL	298,126	29
Hudson, NJ	129,726	54
Jackson, MO	97,595	60
Jefferson, KY	124,032	56
Kern, CA	178,103	45
King, WA	339,026	22
Los Angeles, CA	2,807,125	1
Macomb, MI	59,916	67
Middlesex, MA	24,325	70
Middlesex, NJ	185,630	42
Milwaukee, WI	158,260	50
Monmouth, NJ	182,354	43
Monroe, NY	406,150	18
Montgomery, MD	1,149,660	3
Montgomery, OH	103,987	58
Montgomery, PA	92,954	61
Multnomah, OR	128,949	55
Nassau, NY	1,067,250	4
Norfolk, MA	6,848	72
Oakland, MI	146,507	51
Oklahoma, OK	39,539	69
Orange, CA	542,876	12
Orange, FL	307,525	25
Palm Beach, FL	342,535	21
Pierce, WA	90,870	63
Pinellas, FL	263,039	34
Prince Georges, MD	707,262	9
Riverside, CA	289,941	31
Sacramento, CA	350,583	20
Saint Louis, MO	302,809	26
Salt Lake, UT	169,215	47
San Bernardino, CA	291,598	30
San Diego, CA	442,080	16
San Mateo, CA	174,063	46
Santa Clara, CA	497,982	15
Shelby, TN	416,886	17
Suffolk, NY	775,588	7
Summit, OH	92,570	62
Tarrant, TX	179,098	44
Travis, TX	98,671	59
Tulsa, OK	45,295	68
Union, NJ	133,354	52
Ventura, CA	205,217	38
Wayne, MI	210,083	37

[Continued]

★2626★

County Government Revenues, 1991-92: General Revenues From Own Sources (Taxes)
[Continued]

County	Total revenues	Rank
Westchester, NY	573,348	11
Worcester, MA	3,321	73

Source: U.S. Bureau of the Census, *Annual Survey of Government Finances 1992*, Washington, D.C.: U.S. Government Printing Office, 1995, n.p. Primary source: U.S. Bureau of the Census.

★2627★
County Government Revenues

County Government Revenues, 1991-92: General Revenues From Own Sources (Tobacco Product Sales)
[In thousands of dollars]

County	Total revenues	Rank
Cook, IL	39,450	1
Fairfax, VA	2,176	4
Jackson, MO	2,930	3
Saint Louis, MO	4,700	2
Shelby, TN	15	5

Source: U.S. Bureau of the Census, *Annual Survey of Government Finances 1992*, Washington, D.C.: U.S. Government Printing Office, 1995, n.p. Primary source: U.S. Bureau of the Census.

★2628★
County Government Revenues

County Government Revenues, 1991-92: Intergovernmental Expenditures
[In thousands of dollars]

County	Total revenues	Rank
Allegheny, PA	51,211	20
Baltimore, MD	37,327	23
Bergen, NJ	26,618	27
Bexar, TX	10,849	53
Broward, FL	24,291	32
Bucks, PA	9,460	56
Camden, NJ	17,940	41
Clark, NV	1,060	61
Contra Costa, CA	25,232	30
Cook, IL	26,517	28
Cuyahoga, OH	9,086	57
Dade, FL	12,655	51
Dallas, TX	100	65
DeKalb, GA	98,158	11
Delaware, PA	16,637	44
El Paso, TX	9,464	55

[Continued]

★ 2628 ★

County Government Revenues, 1991-92: Intergovernmental Expenditures
[Continued]

County	Total revenues	Rank
Erie, NY	264,308	2
Essex, NJ	34,920	25
Fairfax, VA	54,934	19
Franklin, OH	24,231	33
Fresno, CA	43,320	22
Fulton, GA	247,629	3
Hamilton, OH	84,538	12
Hennepin, MN	8,304	58
Hillsborough, FL	23,985	34
Hudson, NJ	56,165	18
Jackson, MO	155	64
Jefferson, KY	17,188	43
Kern, CA	13,419	48
King, WA	46,511	21
Los Angeles, CA	573,368	1
Macomb, MI	13,087	49
Middlesex, NJ	21,506	37
Monmouth, NJ	25,646	29
Monroe, NY	190,600	5
Montgomery, MD	73,830	13
Montgomery, OH	16,002	45
Montgomery, PA	14,525	47
Multnomah, OR	17,699	42
Nassau, NY	192,373	4
Oakland, MI	22,194	36
Oklahoma, OK	11,039	52
Orange, CA	71,220	15
Orange, FL	12,768	50
Palm Beach, FL	15,268	46
Pierce, WA	561	62
Pinellas, FL	22,985	35
Prince Georges, MD	56,643	17
Riverside, CA	36,285	24
Sacramento, CA	24,623	31
Saint Louis, MO	120,515	10
Salt Lake, UT	19,347	39
San Bernardino, CA	58,358	16
San Diego, CA	21,353	38
San Mateo, CA	17,947	40
Santa Clara, CA	71,398	14
Shelby, TN	158,999	6
Suffolk, NY	148,181	9
Summit, OH	10,441	54
Tarrant, TX	176	63
Tulsa, OK	8,072	59
Union, NJ	28,339	26
Ventura, CA	4,787	60
Wayne, MI	156,527	7
Westchester, NY	152,970	8
Worcester, MA	50	66

Source: U.S. Bureau of the Census, *Annual Survey of Government Finances 1992*, Washington, D.C.: U.S. Government Printing Office, 1995, n.p. Primary source: U.S. Bureau of the Census.

★ 2629 ★

County Government Revenues

County Government Revenues, 1991-92: Intergovernmental Revenues

[In thousands of dollars]

County	Total revenues	Rank
Allegheny, PA	5,062	3
Bergen, NJ	70	13
Bucks, PA	1,928	5
Essex, NJ	368	7
Jefferson, KY	205	12
Los Angeles, CA	1,999	4
Monroe, NY	330	10
Montgomery, MD	6,278	2
Montgomery, PA	60	14
Palm Beach, FL	343	9
Prince Georges, MD	440	6
Sacramento, CA	6,882	1
San Diego, CA	17	15
Suffolk, NY	241	11
Wayne, MI	350	8

Source: U.S. Bureau of the Census, *Annual Survey of Government Finances 1992*, Washington, D.C.: U.S. Government Printing Office, 1995, n.p. Primary source: U.S. Bureau of the Census.

★ 2630 ★

County Government Revenues

County Government Revenues, 1991-92: Intergovernmental Revenues From Federal Government

[In thousands of dollars]

County	Total revenues	Rank
Allegheny, PA	14,756	19
Baltimore, MD	6,953	36
Bergen, NJ	21,491	15
Bexar, TX	1,575	59
Broward, FL	2,345	54
Bucks, PA	769	66
Camden, NJ	2,411	52
Clark, NV	38,338	5
Contra Costa, CA	13,315	20
Cook, IL	3,088	47
Cuyahoga, OH	7,758	31
Dade, FL	1,089	63
Dallas, TX	3,059	48
DeKalb, GA	4,334	44
DuPage, IL	1,022	64
El Paso, TX	1,819	58
Erie, NY	2,040	56
Essex, NJ	9,526	28
Fairfax, VA	30,917	9
Franklin, OH	2,396	53
Fresno, CA	6,542	39
Fulton, GA	2,662	50
Hamilton, OH	12,301	22
Harris, TX	16,017	18

[Continued]

★2630★

County Government Revenues, 1991-92: Intergovernmental Revenues From Federal Government

[Continued]

County	Total revenues	Rank
Hennepin, MN	17,271	16
Hillsborough, FL	32,068	8
Hudson, NJ	8,770	29
Jackson, MO	1,534	60
Jefferson, KY	1,868	57
Kern, CA	4,081	45
King, WA	13,304	21
Los Angeles, CA	174,045	1
Macomb, MI	5,665	42
Middlesex, NJ	4,896	43
Milwaukee, WI	33,274	7
Monmouth, NJ	7,430	34
Monroe, NY	11,500	24
Montgomery, MD	1,101	62
Montgomery, OH	11,049	25
Montgomery, PA	12	68
Multnomah, OR	24,916	14
Nassau, NY	57,443	3
Oakland, MI	6,729	38
Oklahoma, OK	673	67
Orange, CA	28,052	11
Orange, FL	3,056	49
Palm Beach, FL	7,393	35
Pierce, WA	7,652	32
Pinellas, FL	7,549	33
Prince Georges, MD	2,153	55
Riverside, CA	8,542	30
Sacramento, CA	11,522	23
Saint Louis, MO	10,123	27
Salt Lake, UT	5,796	41
San Bernardino, CA	35,436	6
San Diego, CA	47,907	4
San Mateo, CA	2,523	51
Santa Clara, CA	26,419	13
Shelby, TN	3,525	46
Suffolk, NY	16,902	17
Summit, OH	6,950	37
Tarrant, TX	5,799	40
Travis, TX	1,217	61
Tulsa, OK	844	65
Union, NJ	10,379	26
Ventura, CA	27,752	12
Wayne, MI	57,840	2
Westchester, NY	30,812	10

Source: U.S. Bureau of the Census, *Annual Survey of Government Finances 1992*, Washington, D.C.: U.S. Government Printing Office, 1995, n.p. Primary source: U.S. Bureau of the Census.

★2631★

County Government Revenues

County Government Revenues, 1991-92: Intergovernmental Revenues From Local Governments

[In thousands of dollars]

County	Total revenues	Rank
Allegheny, PA	266	66
Baltimore, MD	6,953	41
Bergen, NJ	6,130	43
Bexar, TX	10,280	28
Broward, FL	2,345	53
Camden, NJ	9,426	32
Clark, NV	38,260	9
Contra Costa, CA	33,609	12
Cook, IL	3,088	49
Cuyahoga, OH	3,696	47
Dade, FL	1,089	61
Dallas, TX	17,704	23
DeKalb, GA	4,334	45
Delaware, PA	60	68
DuPage, IL	1,022	62
El Paso, TX	10,111	30
Erie, NY	14,668	25
Essex, NJ	3,346	48
Fairfax, VA	23,311	17
Franklin, OH	20,626	20
Fresno, CA	7,092	40
Fulton, GA	2,662	51
Hamilton, OH	18,236	22
Harris, TX	48,291	7
Hennepin, MN	12,835	26
Hillsborough, FL	32,068	13
Hudson, NJ	1,972	56
Jackson, MO	6,492	42
Jefferson, KY	1,868	57
Kern, CA	19,649	21
King, WA	47,326	8
Los Angeles, CA	237,190	1
Macomb, MI	36,016	10
Middlesex, NJ	1,669	59
Milwaukee, WI	21,145	19
Monmouth, NJ	426	65
Monroe, NY	15,038	24
Montgomery, MD	1,011	63
Montgomery, OH	35,378	11
Montgomery, PA	708	64
Multnomah, OR	2,471	52
Nassau, NY	90	67
Oakland, MI	111,640	2
Oklahoma, OK	1,808	58
Orange, CA	57,622	4
Orange, FL	3,056	50
Palm Beach, FL	7,393	39
Pierce, WA	10,196	29
Pinellas, FL	7,549	37
Prince Georges, MD	2,153	54
Riverside, CA	50,571	6
Sacramento, CA	3,892	46
Saint Louis, MO	1,479	60

[Continued]

★2631★

County Government Revenues, 1991-92: Intergovernmental Revenues From Local Governments
[Continued]

County	Total revenues	Rank
Salt Lake, UT	2,060	55
San Bernardino, CA	56,279	5
San Diego, CA	59,795	3
San Mateo, CA	8,061	36
Santa Clara, CA	26,419	15
Shelby, TN	21,360	18
Suffolk, NY	7,511	38
Summit, OH	11,141	27
Tarrant, TX	8,687	34
Travis, TX	8,967	33
Tulsa, OK	4,731	44
Union, NJ	9,533	31
Ventura, CA	27,752	14
Wayne, MI	23,604	16
Westchester, NY	8,185	35

Source: U.S. Bureau of the Census, *Annual Survey of Government Finances 1992*, Washington, D.C.: U.S. Government Printing Office, 1995, n.p. Primary source: U.S. Bureau of the Census.

★2632★

County Government Revenues

County Government Revenues, 1991-92: Intergovernmental Revenues From Own Sources
[In thousands of dollars]

County	Total revenues	Rank
Allegheny, PA	148,440	4
Baltimore, MD	18,465	41
Bergen, NJ	2,988	58
Bexar, TX	19,160	38
Broward, FL	18,273	43
Bucks, PA	31,677	25
Camden, NJ	17,102	44
Clark, NV	1,771	60
Contra Costa, CA	56,143	13
Cuyahoga, OH	61,864	11
Dade, FL	282	63
Dallas, TX	26,429	30
DeKalb, GA	18,332	42
Delaware, PA	31,520	26
DuPage, IL	5,849	55
El Paso, TX	11,199	51
Erie, NY	25,011	33
Essex, NJ	55,690	14
Fairfax, VA	15,417	47
Franklin, OH	53,585	16
Fresno, CA	45,399	18
Fulton, GA	22,475	34
Hamilton, OH	33,324	23
Harris, TX	36,415	22

[Continued]

★2632★

County Government Revenues, 1991-92: Intergovernmental Revenues From Own Sources
[Continued]

County	Total revenues	Rank
Hennepin, MN	16,377	46
Hillsborough, FL	2,131	59
Hudson, NJ	33,077	24
Jackson, MO	418	62
Jefferson, KY	5,918	54
Kern, CA	67,308	9
King, WA	64,414	10
Los Angeles, CA	971,920	1
Macomb, MI	18,610	40
Middlesex, MA	0	66
Middlesex, NJ	18,894	39
Milwaukee, WI	89,034	7
Monmouth, NJ	11,977	49
Monroe, NY	25,831	31
Montgomery, MD	6,695	53
Montgomery, OH	22,023	35
Montgomery, PA	40,156	20
Multnomah, OR	0	66
Nassau, NY	55,061	15
Norfolk, MA	0	66
Oakland, MI	29,987	27
Oklahoma, OK	0	66
Orange, CA	146,850	5
Orange, FL	1,257	61
Palm Beach, FL	18	65
Pierce, WA	28,217	28
Pinellas, FL	45	64
Prince Georges, MD	5,594	56
Riverside, CA	60,625	12
Sacramento, CA	82,554	8
Saint Louis, MO	4,940	57
Salt Lake, UT	20,399	37
San Bernardino, CA	118,543	6
San Diego, CA	162,817	3
San Mateo, CA	36,509	21
Santa Clara, CA	50,713	17
Shelby, TN	7,166	52
Suffolk, NY	25,450	32
Summit, OH	17,069	45
Tarrant, TX	26,952	29
Travis, TX	15,396	48
Tulsa, OK	0	66
Union, NJ	20,476	36
Ventura, CA	43,936	19
Wayne, MI	254,302	2
Westchester, NY	11,598	50
Worcester, MA	0	66

Source: U.S. Bureau of the Census, *Annual Survey of Government Finances 1992*, Washington, D.C.: U.S. Government Printing Office, 1995, n.p. Primary source: U.S. Bureau of the Census.

★2633★

County Government Revenues

County Government Revenues, 1991-92: Intergovernmental Revenues From State Governments (For Education)

[In thousands of dollars]

County	Total revenues	Rank
Allegheny, PA	665	34
Baltimore, MD	153,438	4
Bergen, NJ	25,726	20
Camden, NJ	28,049	18
Contra Costa, CA	19,817	25
Erie, NY	29,474	16
Essex, MA	2,336	33
Essex, NJ	20,651	24
Fairfax, VA	191,665	3
Franklin, OH	5,588	32
Fresno, CA	28,944	17
Hamilton, OH	10,602	29
Hudson, NJ	13,204	28
Kern, CA	24,755	22
Los Angeles, CA	234,919	2
Middlesex, NJ	26,020	19
Monmouth, NJ	15,482	27
Monroe, NY	32,994	13
Montgomery, MD	115,338	5
Montgomery, OH	6,655	31
Multnomah, OR	222	35
Nassau, NY	54,632	8
Orange, CA	24,934	21
Prince Georges, MD	255,553	1
Riverside, CA	36,982	11
Sacramento, CA	29,814	14
San Bernardino, CA	41,875	9
San Diego, CA	41,267	10
San Mateo, CA	23,656	23
Santa Clara, CA	36,760	12
Shelby, TN	60,671	7
Suffolk, NY	77,128	6
Tulsa, OK	23	36
Union, NJ	10,219	30
Ventura, CA	16,694	26
Westchester, NY	29,618	15

Source: U.S. Bureau of the Census, *Annual Survey of Government Finances 1992*, Washington, D.C.: U.S. Government Printing Office, 1995, n.p. Primary source: U.S. Bureau of the Census.

★2634★

County Government Revenues

County Government (500,000 Population and More) Revenues, 1991-92: Intergovernmental Revenues from State Governments (For General Support of Local Governmet)

[In thousands of dollars]

County	Total revenues	Rank
Allegheny, PA	4,493	38
Baltimore, MD	14,298	30
Bexar, TX	2,046	42
Broward, FL	92,173	6
Bucks, PA	1,127	48
Clark, NV	171,934	3
Contra Costa, CA	37,174	19
Cuyahoga, OH	28,606	22
Dade, FL	28,206	25
Dallas, TX	5,367	37
DeKalb, GA	46,878	15
Delaware, PA	1,134	47
DuPage, IL	1,047	49
El Paso, TX	822	51
Essex, NJ	1,650	43
Fairfax, VA	11,372	31
Franklin, OH	31,867	21
Fresno, CA	50,146	13
Fulton, GA	33,956	20
Hamilton, OH	28,389	24
Harris, TX	6,471	36
Hennepin, MN	19,203	27
Hillsborough, FL	49,301	14
Jackson, MO	264	53
Jefferson, KY	37,987	17
Kern, CA	37,530	18
King, WA	3,021	39
Los Angeles, CA	425,988	1
Macomb, MI	10,513	33
Milwaukee, WI	55,104	11
Montgomery, MD	23,255	26
Montgomery, OH	15,475	29
Montgomery, PA	1,379	46
Multnomah, OR	2,992	40
Nassau, NY	144	54
Oakland, MI	16,286	28
Oklahoma, OK	995	50
Orange, CA	109,368	4
Orange, FL	178,258	2
Palm Beach, FL	52,412	12
Pierce, WA	1,632	44
Pinellas, FL	62,486	8
Prince Georges, MD	9,708	35
Riverside, CA	66,661	7
Sacramento, CA	56,851	10
Saint Louis, MO	794	52
San Bernardino, CA	60,897	9
San Diego, CA	100,464	5
San Mateo, CA	28,404	23
Santa Clara, CA	92,173	6
Shelby, TN	10,193	34
Summit, OH	10,712	32

[Continued]

★2634★

County Government (500,000 Population and More) Revenues, 1991-92: Intergovernmental Revenues from State Governments (For General Support of Local Governmet)
[Continued]

County	Total revenues	Rank
Tarrant, TX	2,277	41
Travis, TX	1,606	45
Tulsa, OK	127	55
Ventura, CA	28,206	25
Wayne, MI	38,897	16

Source: U.S. Bureau of the Census, *Annual Survey of Government Finances 1992,* Washington, D.C.: U.S. Government Printing Office, 1995, n.p. Primary source: U.S. Bureau of the Census.

★2635★

County Government Revenues

County Government Revenues, 1991-92: Intergovernmental Revenues From State Governments (For Highways)
[In thousands of dollars]

County	Total revenues	Rank
Allegheny, PA	7,212	40
Baltimore, MD	21,260	13
Bergen, NJ	0	63
Bexar, TX	141	57
Broward, FL	6,191	42
Bucks, PA	395	56
Camden, NJ	0	63
Clark, NV	12,072	27
Contra Costa, CA	11,969	28
Cook, IL	70,749	2
Cuyahoga, OH	14,454	22
Dade, FL	33,845	8
Dallas, TX	401	55
DeKalb, GA	639	54
Delaware, PA	833	52
DuPage, IL	9,120	34
El Paso, TX	66	60
Erie, NY	3,445	48
Essex, MA	0	63
Essex, NJ	41	62
Fairfax, VA	0	63
Franklin, OH	18,305	17
Fresno, CA	15,929	18
Fulton, GA	0	63
Hamilton, OH	12,256	25
Harris, TX	933	51
Hennepin, MN	8,461	35
Hillsborough, FL	25,231	9
Hudson, NJ	0	63
Jackson, MO	698	53
Jefferson, KY	2,077	49

[Continued]

★2635★

County Government Revenues, 1991-92: Intergovernmental Revenues From State Governments (For Highways)
[Continued]

County	Total revenues	Rank
Kern, CA	13,565	24
King, WA	24,240	10
Los Angeles, CA	106,406	1
Macomb, MI	34,446	7
Middlesex, MA	0	63
Middlesex, NJ	0	63
Milwaukee, WI	9,438	33
Monmouth, NJ	0	63
Monroe, NY	5,077	44
Montgomery, MD	15,443	20
Montgomery, OH	10,066	31
Montgomery, PA	1,021	50
Multnomah, OR	20,341	15
Nassau, NY	4,029	47
Norfolk, MA	0	63
Oakland, MI	52,507	4
Oklahoma, OK	6,912	41
Orange, CA	39,550	5
Orange, FL	9,867	32
Palm Beach, FL	8,256	36
Pierce, WA	11,628	29
Pinellas, FL	12,185	26
Prince Georges, MD	15,101	21
Riverside, CA	20,696	14
Sacramento, CA	19,998	16
Saint Louis, MO	15,856	19
Salt Lake, UT	4,598	46
San Bernardino, CA	22,846	12
San Diego, CA	36,559	6
San Mateo, CA	10,708	30
Santa Clara, CA	24,221	11
Shelby, TN	7,597	38
Suffolk, NY	4,839	45
Summit, OH	7,447	39
Tarrant, TX	44	61
Travis, TX	92	58
Tulsa, OK	6,123	43
Union, NJ	83	59
Ventura, CA	14,429	23
Wayne, MI	68,052	3
Westchester, NY	8,045	37
Worcester, MA	0	63

Source: U.S. Bureau of the Census, *Annual Survey of Government Finances 1992,* Washington, D.C.: U.S. Government Printing Office, 1995, n.p. Primary source: U.S. Bureau of the Census.

★2636★
County Government Revenues
County Government Revenues, 1991-92: Intergovernmental Revenues From State Governments (For Public Welfare)

[In thousands of dollars]

County	Total revenues	Rank
Allegheny, PA	69,735	26
Bergen, NJ	62,517	28
Bexar, TX	46,245	31
Broward, FL	78	59
Bucks, PA	23,626	42
Camden, NJ	117,569	20
Contra Costa, CA	249,691	13
Cook, IL	95,287	24
Cuyahoga, OH	290,418	10
Dade, FL	11,422	47
Dallas, TX	39,056	38
Delaware, PA	41,758	36
DuPage, IL	9,770	49
El Paso, TX	12,373	46
Erie, NY	272,457	12
Essex, NJ	168,283	18
Fairfax, VA	25,512	40
Franklin, OH	65,531	27
Fresno, CA	408,264	6
Fulton, GA	2,715	55
Hamilton, OH	77,740	25
Harris, TX	45,012	33
Hennepin, MN	282,221	11
Hillsborough, FL	25,231	41
Hudson, NJ	115,652	21
Jefferson, KY	154	57
Kern, CA	225,068	15
Los Angeles, CA	4,150,987	1
Macomb, MI	14,323	44
Middlesex, NJ	42,665	35
Milwaukee, WI	147,865	19
Monmouth, NJ	40,838	37
Monroe, NY	233,291	14
Montgomery, MD	2,635	56
Montgomery, OH	61,216	29
Montgomery, PA	31,734	39
Nassau, NY	219,280	16
Norfolk, MA	9,228	50
Oakland, MI	13,166	45
Oklahoma, OK	152	58
Orange, CA	379,112	8
Orange, FL	9,867	48
Palm Beach, FL	8,256	51
Riverside, CA	402,647	7
Sacramento, CA	425,399	5
Salt Lake, UT	7,964	52
San Bernardino, CA	635,304	3
San Diego, CA	803,911	2
San Mateo, CA	95,365	23
Santa Clara, CA	546,458	4
Shelby, TN	3,024	54
Suffolk, NY	192,294	17
Summit, OH	45,845	32

[Continued]

★2636★
County Government Revenues, 1991-92: Intergovernmental Revenues From State Governments (For Public Welfare)
[Continued]

County	Total revenues	Rank
Tarrant, TX	20,624	43
Travis, TX	5,596	53
Union, NJ	43,928	34
Ventura, CA	106,817	22
Wayne, MI	50,822	30
Westchester, NY	316,857	9

Source: U.S. Bureau of the Census, *Annual Survey of Government Finances 1992*, Washington, D.C.: U.S. Government Printing Office, 1995, n.p. Primary source: U.S. Bureau of the Census.

★2637★
County Government Revenues
County Government Revenues, 1991-92: Revenues From Current Charges

[In thousands of dollars]

County	Total revenues	Rank
Allegheny, PA	88,512	35
Baltimore, MD	131,097	24
Bergen, NJ	121,393	26
Bexar, TX	77,152	37
Broward, FL	174,337	16
Bucks, PA	17,057	64
Camden, NJ	38,589	52
Clark, NV	361,201	3
Contra Costa, CA	77,438	36
Cook, IL	215,205	12
Cuyahoga, OH	201,094	14
Dade, FL	1,234,404	1
Dallas, TX	135,093	23
DeKalb, GA	73,024	39
Delaware, PA	59,343	43
DuPage, IL	41,621	49
El Paso, TX	39,350	50
Erie, NY	135,929	22
Essex, MA	3,536	73
Essex, NJ	28,449	57
Fairfax, VA	232,498	10
Franklin, OH	22,223	58
Fresno, CA	61,177	42
Fulton, GA	51,759	44
Hamilton, OH	14,128	67
Harris, TX	186,313	15
Hennepin, MN	254,266	5
Hillsborough, FL	310,997	4
Hudson, NJ	18,796	61
Jackson, MO	8,054	72
Jefferson, KY	31,647	55

[Continued]

★2637★

County Government Revenues, 1991-92: Revenues From Current Charges

[Continued]

County	Total revenues	Rank
Kern, CA	90,705	33
King, WA	121,202	27
Los Angeles, CA	503,675	2
Macomb, MI	11,789	70
Middlesex, MA	21,614	59
Middlesex, NJ	47,997	46
Milwaukee, WI	250,565	6
Monmouth, NJ	75,862	38
Monroe, NY	106,662	31
Montgomery, MD	158,212	18
Montgomery, OH	48,322	45
Montgomery, PA	17,613	62
Multnomah, OR	14,586	66
Nassau, NY	240,033	8
Norfolk, MA	13,370	69
Oakland, MI	38,402	53
Oklahoma, OK	11,718	71
Orange, CA	231,545	11
Orange, FL	99,070	32
Palm Beach, FL	111,311	28
Pierce, WA	28,919	56
Pinellas, FL	108,610	30
Prince Georges, MD	122,132	25
Riverside, CA	110,514	29
Sacramento, CA	213,187	13
Saint Louis, MO	19,777	60
Salt Lake, UT	37,085	54
San Bernardino, CA	154,469	20
San Diego, CA	159,996	17
San Mateo, CA	67,640	41
Santa Clara, CA	141,850	21
Shelby, TN	235,469	9
Suffolk, NY	68,459	40
Summit, OH	38,692	51
Tarrant, TX	45,046	47
Travis, TX	16,172	65
Tulsa, OK	17,388	63
Union, NJ	44,720	48
Ventura, CA	90,092	34
Wayne, MI	155,049	19
Westchester, NY	243,831	7
Worcester, MA	13,749	68

Source: U.S. Bureau of the Census, *Annual Survey of Government Finances 1992,* Washington, D.C.: U.S. Government Printing Office, 1995, n.p. Primary source: U.S. Bureau of the Census.

★2638★

County Government Revenues

County Government Revenues, 1991-92: Revenues From Current Charges (Airports)

[In thousands of dollars]

County	Total revenues	Rank
Allegheny, PA	53,723	6
Broward, FL	58,271	4
Clark, NV	118,823	2
Contra Costa, CA	2,182	20
Cuyahoga, OH	538	29
Dade, FL	310,348	1
DeKalb, GA	1,663	24
Fulton, GA	900	27
Hillsborough, FL	58,033	5
Jefferson, KY	18,058	11
Kern, CA	1,681	23
King, WA	5,535	14
Los Angeles, CA	2,266	19
Milwaukee, WI	26,572	10
Monroe, NY	12,869	13
Oakland, MI	2,157	21
Orange, CA	53,371	7
Palm Beach, FL	44,819	8
Pierce, WA	133	31
Pinellas, FL	3,367	16
Riverside, CA	626	28
Sacramento, CA	30,902	9
Saint Louis, MO	4,783	15
San Bernardino, CA	1,818	22
San Diego, CA	3,345	17
San Mateo, CA	1,040	26
Santa Clara, CA	1,480	25
Suffolk, NY	448	30
Ventura, CA	2,284	18
Wayne, MI	79,928	3
Westchester, NY	16,232	12

Source: U.S. Bureau of the Census, *Annual Survey of Government Finances 1992,* Washington, D.C.: U.S. Government Printing Office, 1995, n.p. Primary source: U.S. Bureau of the Census.

★2639★

County Government Revenues

County Government Revenues, 1991-92: Revenues From Current Charges (Commercial Activity – Miscellaneous)

[In thousands of dollars]

County	Total revenues	Rank
Contra Costa, CA	14,011	3
Erie, NY	17,660	2
Monmouth, NJ	18,560	1
Oakland, MI	298	5
Union, NJ	5,895	4

Source: U.S. Bureau of the Census, *Annual Survey of Government Finances 1992,* Washington, D.C.: U.S. Government Printing Office, 1995, n.p. Primary source: U.S. Bureau of the Census.

★2640★
County Government Revenues

County Government Revenues, 1991-92: Revenues From Current Charges (Education)

[In thousands of dollars]

County	Total revenues	Rank
Baltimore, MD	55,171	2
Bergen, NJ	29,664	5
Camden, NJ	16,287	14
Contra Costa, CA	203	25
Erie, NY	17,875	13
Essex, MA	769	23
Essex, NJ	13,982	15
Fairfax, VA	28,351	6
Franklin, OH	949	22
Fresno, CA	111	29
Hamilton, OH	20	31
Hudson, NJ	4,026	17
Kern, CA	188	26
Los Angeles, CA	159	27
Middlesex, NJ	17,888	12
Monmouth, NJ	23,062	9
Monroe, NY	24,293	7
Montgomery, MD	61,164	1
Nassau, NY	34,406	4
Norfolk, MA	1,034	21
Orange, CA	1,645	20
Prince Georges, MD	47,191	3
Riverside, CA	356	24
Sacramento, CA	14	32
San Bernardino, CA	1,793	19
San Diego, CA	97	30
San Mateo, CA	1	34
Santa Clara, CA	3,588	18
Shelby, TN	4,698	16
Suffolk, NY	20,979	10
Tulsa, OK	2	33
Union, NJ	23,595	8
Ventura, CA	143	28
Westchester, NY	19,186	11

Source: U.S. Bureau of the Census, *Annual Survey of Government Finances 1992,* Washington, D.C.: U.S. Government Printing Office, 1995, n.p. Primary source: U.S. Bureau of the Census.

★2641★
County Government Revenues

County Government Revenues, 1991-92: Revenues From Current Charges (Education– School Lunch Gross Sales)

[In thousands of dollars]

County	Total revenues	Rank
Baltimore, MD	10,513	2
Bergen, NJ	42	9
Camden, NJ	530	7
Contra Costa, CA	8	10
Fairfax, VA	21,278	1

[Continued]

★2641★

County Government Revenues, 1991-92: Revenues From Current Charges (Education– School Lunch Gross Sales)
[Continued]

County	Total revenues	Rank
Montgomery, MD	10,383	4
Prince Georges, MD	10,489	3
Riverside, CA	312	8
Santa Clara, CA	8	10
Shelby, TN	4,698	6
Union, NJ	7,642	5

Source: U.S. Bureau of the Census, *Annual Survey of Government Finances 1992,* Washington, D.C.: U.S. Government Printing Office, 1995, n.p. Primary source: U.S. Bureau of the Census.

★2642★
County Government Revenues

County Government Revenues, 1991-92: Revenues From Current Charges (Higher Education)

[In thousands of dollars]

County	Total revenues	Rank
Baltimore, MD	34,358	2
Bergen, NJ	17,494	9
Camden, NJ	15,678	12
Erie, NY	17,875	8
Essex, NJ	13,562	14
Hudson, NJ	3,807	15
Middlesex, NJ	16,902	10
Monmouth, NJ	19,576	6
Monroe, NY	24,293	4
Montgomery, MD	31,278	3
Nassau, NY	34,406	1
Prince Georges, MD	16,565	11
Suffolk, NY	20,979	5
Union, NJ	15,380	13
Westchester, NY	19,186	7

Source: U.S. Bureau of the Census, *Annual Survey of Government Finances 1992,* Washington, D.C.: U.S. Government Printing Office, 1995, n.p. Primary source: U.S. Bureau of the Census.

★2643★

County Government Revenues

County Government Revenues, 1991-92: Revenues From Current Charges (Highways)

[In thousands of dollars]

County	Total revenues	Rank
Broward, FL	1,676	9
Clark, NV	889	17
Contra Costa, CA	105	27
Cook, IL	312	22
Dade, FL	4,582	7
Dallas, TX	48	30
Essex, NJ	92	29
Franklin, OH	7	31
Fresno, CA	519	18
Hamilton, OH	100	28
Harris, TX	62,000	1
Hillsborough, FL	8,125	3
Kern, CA	246	24
King, WA	1,050	12
Los Angeles, CA	6,563	6
Milwaukee, WI	6	32
Multnomah, OR	346	21
Nassau, NY	2,979	8
Oakland, MI	986	15
Orange, CA	7,556	4
Orange, FL	468	20
Pierce, WA	517	19
Pinellas, FL	971	16
Riverside, CA	6,631	5
Sacramento, CA	8,203	2
Saint Louis, MO	300	23
Salt Lake, UT	191	25
San Bernardino, CA	1,054	11
San Diego, CA	1,034	13
San Mateo, CA	1,261	10
Summit, OH	141	26
Tarrant, TX	3	33
Wayne, MI	1,027	14
Worcester, MA	1	34

Source: U.S. Bureau of the Census, *Annual Survey of Government Finances 1992*, Washington, D.C.: U.S. Government Printing Office, 1995, n.p. Primary source: U.S. Bureau of the Census.

★2644★

County Government Revenues

County Government Revenues, 1991-92: Revenues From Current Charges (Hospitals)

[In thousands of dollars]

County	Total revenues	Rank
Allegheny, PA	12,634	31
Bergen, NJ	76,966	15
Bexar, TX	66,083	17
Camden, NJ	14,443	29
Clark, NV	154,462	6
Contra Costa, CA	14,210	30

[Continued]

★2644★

County Government Revenues, 1991-92: Revenues From Current Charges (Hospitals)

[Continued]

County	Total revenues	Rank
Cook, IL	117,463	10
Cuyahoga, OH	184,144	5
Dade, FL	539,984	1
Dallas, TX	93,797	13
El Paso, TX	30,239	23
Erie, NY	95,890	11
Essex, NJ	1,164	39
Fresno, CA	43,699	20
Harris, TX	67,510	16
Hennepin, MN	132,528	9
Hillsborough, FL	207,268	2
Hudson, NJ	11,073	33
Jefferson, KY	1,974	37
Kern, CA	50,713	19
Los Angeles, CA	94,350	12
Middlesex, MA	16,540	28
Middlesex, NJ	22,064	25
Milwaukee, WI	186,790	4
Monroe, NY	12,601	32
Nassau, NY	147,489	8
Norfolk, MA	8,519	36
Oakland, MI	1,792	38
Riverside, CA	18,719	26
San Bernardino, CA	37,277	22
San Mateo, CA	39,456	21
Santa Clara, CA	93,379	14
Shelby, TN	195,661	3
Summit, OH	17,882	27
Tarrant, TX	25,903	24
Union, NJ	10,931	35
Ventura, CA	63,852	18
Westchester, NY	147,908	7
Worcester, MA	11,056	34

Source: U.S. Bureau of the Census, *Annual Survey of Government Finances 1992*, Washington, D.C.: U.S. Government Printing Office, 1995, n.p. Primary source: U.S. Bureau of the Census.

★2645★

County Government Revenues

County Government Revenues, 1991-92: Revenues From Current Charges (Housing and Community Development)

[In thousands of dollars]

County	Total revenues	Rank
Allegheny, PA	286	12
Bergen, NJ	2,051	8
Broward, FL	2,441	7
Bucks, PA	36	14

[Continued]

★2645★

County Government Revenues, 1991-92: Revenues From Current Charges (Housing and Community Development)

[Continued]

County	Total revenues	Rank
Contra Costa, CA	992	10
Dade, FL	11,379	5
Fairfax, VA	13,198	2
Los Angeles, CA	11,413	4
Middlesex, NJ	15	15
Montgomery, MD	15,045	1
Montgomery, PA	258	13
Norfolk, NY	13	16
Pinellas, FL	549	11
Prince Georges, MD	1,327	9
Riverside, CA	6,059	6
Sacramento, CA	12,208	3
Shelby, TN	1	18
Tarrant, TX	6	17

Source: U.S. Bureau of the Census, *Annual Survey of Government Finances 1992*, Washington, D.C.: U.S. Government Printing Office, 1995, n.p. Primary source: U.S. Bureau of the Census.

★2646★

County Government Revenues

County Government Revenues, 1991-92: Revenues From Current Charges (Local School Charges-Other)

[In thousands of dollars]

County	Total revenues	Rank
Baltimore, MD	10,300	4
Bergen, NJ	12,128	3
Camden, NJ	79	23
Contra Costa, CA	195	17
Essex, MA	769	13
Essex, NJ	420	15
Fairfax, VA	7,073	5
Franklin, OH	949	12
Fresno, CA	111	21
Hamilton, OH	20	25
Hudson, NJ	219	16
Kern, CA	188	18
Los Angeles, CA	159	19
Middlesex, NJ	986	11
Monmouth, NJ	3,486	7
Montgomery, MD	19,503	2
Norfolk, MA	1,034	10
Orange, CA	1,645	9
Prince Georges, MD	20,137	1
Riverside, CA	44	24
Sacramento, CA	14	26
San Bernardino, CA	1,793	8

[Continued]

★2646★

County Government Revenues, 1991-92: Revenues From Current Charges (Local School Charges-Other)

[Continued]

County	Total revenues	Rank
San Diego, CA	97	22
San Mateo, CA	1	28
Santa Clara, CA	3,580	6
Tulsa, OK	2	27
Union, NJ	573	14
Ventura, CA	143	20

Source: U.S. Bureau of the Census, *Annual Survey of Government Finances 1992*, Washington, D.C.: U.S. Government Printing Office, 1995, n.p. Primary source: U.S. Bureau of the Census.

★2647★

County Government Revenues

County Government Revenues, 1991-92: Revenues From Current Charges (Parking Facilities)

[In thousands of dollars]

County	Total revenues	Rank
Allegheny, PA	263	21
Baltimore, MD	3,436	3
Bexar, TX	303	20
Clark, NV	518	16
Cuyahoga, OH	1,457	9
Dade, FL	1,320	11
Dallas, TX	1,364	10
DeKalb, GA	174	23
El Paso, TX	178	22
Fairfax, VA	72	28
Franklin, OH	1,820	7
Fresno, CA	158	25
Harris, TX	482	17
Hennepin, MN	2,346	4
Hillsborough, FL	160	24
Hudson, NJ	28	29
Los Angeles, CA	19,098	1
Macomb, MI	132	27
Middlesex, NJ	570	15
Monroe, NY	1,566	8
Montgomery, MD	10,629	2
Montgomery, OH	394	18
Montgomery, PA	340	19
Oklahoma, OK	736	12
Orange, CA	601	14
Palm Beach, FL	695	13
Prince Georges, MD	1,898	6
Sacramento, CA	1,925	5
Tulsa, OK	142	26

Source: U.S. Bureau of the Census, *Annual Survey of Government Finances 1992*, Washington, D.C.: U.S. Government Printing Office, 1995, n.p. Primary source: U.S. Bureau of the Census.

★2648★
County Government Revenues
County Government Revenues, 1991-92: Revenues From Current Charges (Parks and Recreation)

[In thousands of dollars]

County	Total revenues	Rank
Allegheny, PA	3,087	25
Baltimore, MD	2,252	28
Bergen, NJ	3,749	24
Broward, FL	8,037	15
Bucks, PA	676	54
Clark, NV	12,244	10
Contra Costa, CA	25	61
Cook, IL	9,209	13
Dade, FL	21,055	3
DeKalb, GA	1,661	40
Delaware, PA	135	60
DuPage, IL	2,210	29
El Paso, TX	1,389	45
Erie, NY	1,245	46
Essex, NJ	4,753	21
Fairfax, VA	1,873	34
Franklin, OH	1,419	44
Fresno, CA	412	57
Fulton, GA	1,114	49
Harris, TX	1,458	43
Hillsborough, FL	1,813	38
Hudson, NJ	157	59
Jackson, MO	3,785	23
Jefferson, KY	872	50
Kern, CA	1,689	39
King, WA	12,868	9
Los Angeles, CA	54,475	1
Macomb, MI	269	58
Middlesex, NJ	1,619	41
Milwaukee, WI	25,986	2
Monmouth, NJ	5,872	19
Monroe, NY	2,069	32
Montgomery, MD	17,373	4
Montgomery, OH	581	55
Multnomah, OR	2,741	26
Nassau, NY	14,779	5
Norfolk, MA	687	52
Oakland, MI	4,965	20
Orange, CA	11,176	11
Orange, FL	8,829	14
Palm Beach, FL	1,842	37
Pierce, WA	1,488	42
Pinellas, FL	678	53
Prince Georges, MD	13,796	7
Riverside, CA	725	51
Sacramento, CA	7,970	16
Saint Louis, MO	2,131	31
Salt Lake, UT	9,394	12
San Bernardino, CA	6,384	17
San Diego, CA	1,159	48
San Mateo, CA	1,848	35
Santa Clara, CA	1,983	33
Shelby, TN	2,307	27

[Continued]

★2648★
County Government Revenues, 1991-92: Revenues From Current Charges (Parks and Recreation)
[Continued]

County	Total revenues	Rank
Suffolk, NY	5,874	18
Tarrant, TX	2,175	30
Travis, TX	535	56
Tulsa, OK	13,078	8
Union, NJ	4,249	22
Ventura, CA	1,162	47
Wayne, MI	1,846	36
Westchester, NY	14,560	6

Source: U.S. Bureau of the Census, *Annual Survey of Government Finances 1992*, Washington, D.C.: U.S. Government Printing Office, 1995, n.p. Primary source: U.S. Bureau of the Census.

★2649★
County Government Revenues
County Government Revenues, 1991-92: Revenues From Current Charges (Sewerage)

[In thousands of dollars]

County	Total revenues	Rank
Baltimore, MD	29,841	9
Broward, FL	34,717	7
Clark, NV	38,090	6
Contra Costa, CA	1,652	30
Cuyahoga, OH	1,670	29
Dade, FL	79,040	1
DeKalb, GA	32,896	8
DuPage, IL	9,715	20
Erie, NY	3,259	24
Fairfax, VA	66,428	3
Franklin, OH	1,392	31
Fresno, CA	181	32
Fulton, GA	26,864	11
Jackson, MO	172	33
Kern, CA	2,013	27
King, WA	16	35
Los Angeles, CA	14,883	15
Monroe, NY	27,149	10
Montgomery, OH	22,697	12
Multnomah, OR	118	34
Nassau, NY	4,444	23
Oakland, MI	10,038	19
Orange, FL	41,035	5
Palm Beach, FL	18,579	14
Pierce, WA	14,594	16
Pinellas, FL	20,897	13
Sacramento, CA	67,937	2
San Bernardino, CA	3,055	25
San Diego, CA	11,402	18
San Mateo, CA	2,844	26
Santa Clara, CA	6,802	22

[Continued]

★2649★

County Government Revenues, 1991-92: Revenues From Current Charges (Sewerage)

[Continued]

County	Total revenues	Rank
Suffolk, NY	7,775	21
Summit, OH	13,156	17
Ventura, CA	1,686	28
Wayne, MI	44,861	4

Source: U.S. Bureau of the Census, *Annual Survey of Government Finances 1992*, Washington, D.C.: U.S. Government Printing Office, 1995, n.p. Primary source: U.S. Bureau of the Census.

★2650★

County Government Revenues

County Government Revenues, 1991-92: Revenues From Current Charges (Solid Waste Management)

[In thousands of dollars]

County	Total revenues	Rank
Baltimore, MD	778	32
Broward, FL	6,833	26
Bucks, PA	120	39
Cuyahoga, OH	647	34
Dade, FL	161,029	1
DeKalb, GA	24,437	16
Delaware, PA	30,679	12
DuPage, IL	11,452	22
Essex, NJ	74	40
Fairfax, VA	82,386	2
Franklin, OH	1,615	31
Fresno, CA	1,857	30
Fulton, GA	7,603	25
Hamilton, OH	2,490	28
Hennepin, MN	57,727	4
Hillsborough, FL	9,798	24
Jefferson, KY	14	42
Kern, CA	14,564	20
King, WA	55,335	5
Los Angeles, CA	18,048	18
Middlesex, NJ	240	37
Monmouth, NJ	28,368	14
Monroe, NY	13,724	21
Montgomery, MD	37,528	10
Montgomery, OH	16,151	19
Oakland, MI	697	33
Orange, CA	80,453	3
Orange, FL	29,063	13
Pierce, WA	4,744	27
Pinellas, FL	43,871	8
Prince Georges, MD	45,307	7
Riverside, CA	27,943	15
Sacramento, CA	34,900	11

[Continued]

★2650★

County Government Revenues, 1991-92: Revenues From Current Charges (Solid Waste Management)

[Continued]

County	Total revenues	Rank
Salt Lake, UT	11,188	23
San Bernardino, CA	49,275	6
San Diego, CA	39,570	9
San Mateo, CA	2,090	29
Santa Clara, CA	265	36
Shelby, TN	9	43
Travis, TX	158	38
Union, NJ	50	41
Ventura, CA	404	35
Westchester, NY	18,430	17

Source: U.S. Bureau of the Census, *Annual Survey of Government Finances 1992*, Washington, D.C.: U.S. Government Printing Office, 1995, n.p. Primary source: U.S. Bureau of the Census.

★2651★

County Government Revenues

County Government Revenues, 1991-92: Revenues From Current Charges (Water Transportation and Terminals)

[In thousands of dollars]

County	Total revenues	Rank
Dade, FL	35,560	1
Hillsborough, FL	11,400	2
Jefferson, KY	2,035	4
Ventura, CA	4,293	3

Source: U.S. Bureau of the Census, *Annual Survey of Government Finances 1992*, Washington, D.C.: U.S. Government Printing Office, 1995, n.p. Primary source: U.S. Bureau of the Census.

★2652★

County Government Revenues

County Government Revenues, 1991-92: Revenues From Employee Retirement

[In thousands of dollars]

County	Total revenues	Rank
Allegheny, PA	32,333	18
Baltimore, MD	98,242	6
Bexar, TX	4,604	35
Bucks, PA	12,117	27
Contra Costa, CA	82,970	11
Cook, IL	176,430	4
Dallas, TX	8,951	31
DeKalb, GA	31,893	19
Delaware, PA	10,818	29

[Continued]

★2652★

County Government Revenues, 1991-92: Revenues From Employee Retirement
[Continued]

County	Total revenues	Rank
Essex, MA	9,325	30
Fairfax, VA	236,664	2
Fresno, CA	74,653	13
Fulton, GA	29,358	22
Jackson, MO	1,850	36
Kern, CA	60,553	15
Los Angeles, CA	1,353,081	1
Macomb, MI	23,825	23
Middlesex, MA	29,821	20
Milwaukee, WI	86,767	10
Montgomery, PA	11,089	28
Norfolk, MA	15,569	25
Oakland, MI	29,706	21
Oklahoma, OK	6,166	33
Orange, CA	201,117	3
Prince Georges, MD	66,632	14
Sacramento, CA	88,029	9
Saint Louis, MO	12,428	26
San Bernardino, CA	92,159	8
San Diego, CA	95,529	7
San Mateo, CA	55,845	16
Santa Clara, CA	6,436	32
Shelby, TN	34,299	17
Tulsa, OK	5,524	34
Ventura, CA	99,313	5
Wayne, MI	81,686	12
Worcester, MA	18,944	24

Source: U.S. Bureau of the Census, *Annual Survey of Government Finances 1992,* Washington, D.C.: U.S. Government Printing Office, 1995, n.p. Primary source: U.S. Bureau of the Census.

★2653★
County Government Revenues

County Government Revenues, 1991-92: Revenues From Fines and Forfeits
[In thousands of dollars]

County	Total revenues	Rank
Allegheny, PA	2,853	41
Baltimore, MD	1,763	51
Bergen, NJ	4,725	29
Bexar, TX	6,692	21
Broward, FL	10,967	9
Bucks, PA	1,883	48
Camden, NJ	2,000	47
Clark, NV	7,124	18
Contra Costa, CA	7,178	17
Cook, IL	8,339	13
Cuyahoga, OH	3,675	36
Dade, FL	38,912	2

[Continued]

★2653★

County Government Revenues, 1991-92: Revenues From Fines and Forfeits
[Continued]

County	Total revenues	Rank
Dallas, TX	8,083	16
DeKalb, GA	12,271	7
Delaware, PA	2,466	43
DuPage, IL	888	60
El Paso, TX	2,690	42
Erie, NY	597	61
Essex, NJ	2,358	45
Fairfax, VA	5,119	28
Franklin, OH	2,433	44
Fresno, CA	5,788	24
Fulton, GA	1,433	54
Hamilton, OH	5,316	27
Harris, TX	13,344	5
Hennepin, MN	889	59
Hillsborough, FL	3,824	34
Hudson, NJ	8,125	14
Jackson, MO	30	66
Kern, CA	5,486	25
King, WA	6,722	20
Los Angeles, CA	105,377	1
Macomb, MI	490	62
Middlesex, NJ	3,052	39
Milwaukee, WI	4,622	31
Monmouth, NJ	4,080	33
Monroe, NY	942	57
Montgomery, MD	1,590	52
Montgomery, OH	1,512	53
Montgomery, PA	3,712	35
Multnomah, OR	1,817	50
Nassau, NY	4,082	32
Oakland, MI	3,267	38
Oklahoma, OK	124	64
Orange, CA	26,597	3
Orange, FL	9,827	10
Palm Beach, FL	9,521	11
Pierce, WA	3,576	37
Pinellas, FL	5,409	26
Prince Georges, MD	1,833	49
Riverside, CA	6,045	23
Sacramento, CA	12,228	8
Saint Louis, MO	1,141	56
Salt Lake, UT	1,287	55
San Bernardino, CA	7,107	19
San Diego, CA	18,914	4
San Mateo, CA	4,673	30
Santa Clara, CA	12,948	6
Shelby, TN	1	68
Suffolk, NY	9,049	12
Summit, OH	6,372	22
Tarrant, TX	2,889	40
Travis, TX	2,139	46
Tulsa, OK	4	67
Union, NJ	469	63

[Continued]

★2653★

County Government Revenues, 1991-92: Revenues From Fines and Forfeits

[Continued]

County	Total revenues	Rank
Ventura, CA	8,087	15
Wayne, MI	904	58
Westchester, NY	109	65

Source: U.S. Bureau of the Census, *Annual Survey of Government Finances 1992*, Washington, D.C.: U.S. Government Printing Office, 1995, n.p. Primary source: U.S. Bureau of the Census.

★2654★

County Government Revenues

County Government Revenues, 1991-92: Revenues From Interest Earnings

[In thousands of dollars]

County	Total revenues	Rank
Allegheny, PA	27,013	43
Baltimore, MD	56,050	18
Bergen, NJ	6,092	63
Bexar, TX	99,684	9
Broward, FL	151,889	5
Bucks, PA	4,999	65
Camden, NJ	3,380	67
Clark, NV	84,241	15
Contra Costa, CA	48,033	28
Cook, IL	41,525	31
Cuyahoga, OH	86,968	14
Dade, FL	249,077	1
Dallas, TX	53,333	24
DeKalb, GA	13,642	53
Delaware, PA	5,613	64
DuPage, IL	22,008	46
El Paso, TX	13,407	55
Erie, NY	40,184	34
Essex, MA	384	70
Essex, NJ	2,640	69
Fairfax, VA	96,325	11
Franklin, OH	53,546	23
Fresno, CA	17,587	48
Fulton, GA	29,628	42
Hamilton, OH	24,761	44
Harris, TX	187,723	4
Hennepin, MN	37,760	38
Hillsborough, FL	101,823	8
Hudson, NJ	6,809	62
Jackson, MO	12,705	56
Jefferson, KY	124,223	6
Kern, CA	13,411	54
King, WA	46,577	29
Los Angeles, CA	220,882	3
Macomb, MI	8,141	61
Middlesex, MA	105	72

[Continued]

★2654★

County Government Revenues, 1991-92: Revenues From Interest Earnings

[Continued]

County	Total revenues	Rank
Middlesex, NJ	11,300	57
Milwaukee, WI	10,479	59
Monmouth, NJ	9,908	60
Monroe, NY	39,145	36
Montgomery, MD	51,660	25
Montgomery, OH	39,977	35
Montgomery, PA	54,519	20
Multnomah, OR	3,903	66
Nassau, NY	49,005	27
Norfolk, MA	114	71
Oakland, MI	24,710	45
Oklahoma, OK	60,555	17
Orange, CA	246,385	2
Orange, FL	122,781	7
Palm Beach, FL	83,888	16
Pierce, WA	10,529	58
Pinellas, FL	53,743	22
Prince Georges, MD	41,363	32
Riverside, CA	96,988	10
Sacramento, CA	95,360	12
Saint Louis, MO	34,993	39
Salt Lake, UT	14,361	52
San Bernardino, CA	87,066	13
San Diego, CA	38,910	37
San Mateo, CA	15,129	49
Santa Clara, CA	49,738	26
Shelby, TN	54,448	21
Suffolk, NY	55,451	19
Summit, OH	14,542	51
Tarrant, TX	43,549	30
Travis, TX	33,301	41
Tulsa, OK	21,996	47
Union, NJ	3,151	68
Ventura, CA	14,637	50
Wayne, MI	41,017	33
Westchester, NY	34,778	40
Worcester, MA	90	73

Source: U.S. Bureau of the Census, *Annual Survey of Government Finances 1992*, Washington, D.C.: U.S. Government Printing Office, 1995, n.p. Primary source: U.S. Bureau of the Census.

★ 2655 ★
County Government Revenues
County Government Revenues, 1991-92: Revenues From Sales of Property

[In thousands of dollars]

County	Total revenues	Rank
Allegheny, PA	21	35
Bexar, TX	2	41
Contra Costa, CA	580	13
DeKalb, GA	58	31
Essex, NJ	75	30
Fairfax, VA	51	32
Fulton, GA	8,480	3
Hamilton, OH	111	27
Harris, TX	92	28
Hennepin, MN	16	37
Hillsborough, FL	5,789	4
Jefferson, KY	364	16
Kern, CA	41	33
King, WA	275	17
Los Angeles, CA	5,528	5
Middlesex, NJ	170	23
Monmouth, NJ	3	40
Monroe, NY	39	34
Montgomery, MD	2,357	7
Montgomery, PA	251	19
Multnomah, OR	261	18
Nassau, NY	463	15
Oakland, MI	77	29
Oklahoma, OK	228	21
Orange, CA	243	20
Palm Beach, FL	2,489	6
Pierce, WA	688	12
Pinellas, FL	151	25
Prince Georges, MD	15,011	1
Riverside, CA	165	24
Sacramento, CA	492	14
Saint Louis, MO	5	39
Salt Lake, UT	151	25
San Bernardino, CA	1,718	8
San Diego, CA	855	11
Santa Clara, CA	1,050	10
Suffolk, NY	19	36
Travis, TX	134	26
Tulsa, OK	221	22
Ventura, CA	9	38
Wayne, MI	1,602	9
Westchester, NY	12,195	2

Source: U.S. Bureau of the Census, *Annual Survey of Government Finances 1992*, Washington, D.C.: U.S. Government Printing Office, 1995, n.p. Primary source: U.S. Bureau of the Census.

★ 2656 ★
County Government Revenues
County Government Revenues, 1991-92: Revenues From Special Assessments

[In thousands of dollars]

County	Total revenues	Rank
Baltimore, MD	22,017	6
Broward, FL	40,657	3
Clark, NV	18,099	9
Contra Costa, CA	3,594	20
Dade, FL	49,884	2
DeKalb, GA	3,400	21
DuPage, IL	399	30
Erie, NY	12,035	13
Fairfax, VA	6,547	15
Fresno, CA	1,767	23
Fulton, GA	536	29
Hamilton, OH	743	27
Hennepin, MN	7	36
Hillsborough, FL	15,232	10
Kern, CA	2,597	22
King, WA	653	28
Los Angeles, CA	127,595	1
Montgomery, MD	129	33
Montgomery, OH	1,020	25
Multnomah, OR	61	34
Oakland, MI	3,742	19
Orange, CA	13,835	11
Orange, FL	23,281	5
Palm Beach, FL	20,369	7
Pierce, WA	5,810	17
Pinellas, FL	5,111	18
Prince Georges, MD	161	32
Riverside, CA	19,110	8
Sacramento, CA	27,905	4
San Bernardino, CA	11,953	14
San Diego, CA	5,960	16
San Mateo, CA	15	35
Summit, OH	1,563	24
Tulsa, OK	317	31
Ventura, CA	785	26
Wayne, MI	13,126	12

Source: U.S. Bureau of the Census, *Annual Survey of Government Finances 1992*, Washington, D.C.: U.S. Government Printing Office, 1995, n.p. Primary source: U.S. Bureau of the Census.

★ 2657 ★
County Government Revenues
County Government Revenues, 1991-92: Revenues From Utilities

[In thousands of dollars]

County	Total revenues	Rank
Broward, FL	31,066	9
Clark, NV	85,127	3
Dade, FL	147,914	1
DeKalb, GA	25,200	13

[Continued]

★2657★

County Government Revenues, 1991-92: Revenues From Utilities

[Continued]

County	Total revenues	Rank
DuPage, IL	1,533	24
Erie, NY	29,791	10
Fairfax, VA	60,782	7
Franklin, OH	850	28
Fresno, CA	157	31
Fulton, GA	8,728	19
Hillsborough, FL	66,998	6
Los Angeles, CA	18,097	16
Milwaukee, WI	73,228	5
Monroe, NY	28,119	12
Montgomery, MD	114,966	2
Montgomery, OH	28,453	11
Oakland, MI	14,799	17
Oklahoma, OK	192	30
Orange, FL	12,381	18
Palm Beach, FL	21,591	14
Pinellas, FL	38,563	8
Riverside, CA	288	29
Sacramento, CA	3,024	23
San Bernardino, CA	4,312	22
San Diego, CA	1,116	27
San Mateo, CA	1,394	26
Santa Clara, CA	19,484	15
Suffolk, NY	75,137	4
Summit, OH	4,556	21
Ventura, CA	8,076	20
Westchester, NY	1,509	25

Source: U.S. Bureau of the Census, *Annual Survey of Government Finances 1992,* Washington, D.C.: U.S. Government Printing Office, 1995, n.p. Primary source: U.S. Bureau of the Census.

★2658★

County Government Revenues

County Government Revenues, 1991-92: Total Expenditures

[In thousands of dollars]

County	Total revenues	Rank
Allegheny, PA	996,522	25
Baltimore, MD	1,320,085	16
Bergen, NJ	480,903	43
Bexar, TX	454,845	46
Broward, FL	1,054,388	23
Bucks, PA	171,805	66
Camden, NJ	448,728	47
Clark, NV	1,172,793	18
Contra Costa, CA	883,782	28
Cook, IL	1,545,834	10
Cuyohoga, OH	1,066,929	22
Dade, FL	2,996,708	2

[Continued]

★2658★

County Government Revenues, 1991-92: Total Expenditures

[Continued]

County	Total revenues	Rank
Dallas, TX	648,174	36
DeKalb, GA	462,104	45
Delaware, PA	259,929	58
DuPage, IL	255,104	61
El Paso, TX	205,086	65
Erie, NY	1,118,424	21
Essex, MA	34,387	73
Essex, NJ	652,802	35
Fairfax, VA	2,018,077	6
Franklin, OH	509,109	40
Fresno, CA	836,914	30
Fulton, GA	644,557	37
Hamilton, OH	485,793	42

Source: U.S. Bureau of the Census, *Annual Survey of Government Finances 1992,* Washington, D.C.: U.S. Government Printing Office, 1995, n.p. Primary source: U.S. Bureau of the Census. *Note:* Data are shown only for the top 25 areas.

★2659★

County Government Revenues

County Government Revenues, 1991-92: Total General Expenditures

[In thousands of dollars]

County	Total revenues	Rank
Allegheny, PA	970,015	25
Baltimore, MD	1,257,796	16
Bergen, NJ	480,903	42
Bexar, TX	454,249	44
Broward, FL	954,502	26
Bucks, PA	168,460	66
Camden, NJ	448,728	45
Clark, NV	1,030,200	22
Contra Costa, CA	835,008	27
Cook, IL	1,485,321	10
Cuyohoga, OH	1,066,929	19
Dade, FL	2,692,830	2
Dallas, TX	646,161	36
DeKalb, GA	416,913	48
Delaware, PA	254,088	59
DuPage, IL	253,267	60
El Paso, TX	205,086	65
Erie, NY	1,081,536	18
Essex, MA	23,075	73
Essex, NJ	652,802	35
Fairfax, VA	1,851,183	6
Franklin, OH	508,650	40
Fresno, CA	806,170	30
Fulton, GA	623,788	37
Hamilton, OH	485,793	41

Source: U.S. Bureau of the Census, *Annual Survey of Government Finances 1992,* Washington, D.C.: U.S. Government Printing Office, 1995, n.p. Primary source: U.S. Bureau of the Census. *Note:* Data are shown only for the top 25 areas.

★2660★
County Government Revenues
County Government Revenues, 1991-92: Total General Revenues
[In thousands of dollars]

County	Total revenues	Rank
Orange, CA	20,212,752	1
Los Angeles, CA	10,639,193	2
Dade, FL	2,913,175	3
San Diego, CA	2,029,814	4
Fairfax, VA	1,931,185	5
Nassau, NY	1,845,882	6
Santa Clara, CA	1,663,145	7
Montgomery, MD	1,649,869	8
San Bernardino, CA	1,624,597	9
Cook, IL	1,437,921	10
Sacramento, CA	1,399,162	11
Westchester, NY	1,314,116	12
Suffolk, NY	1,297,282	13
Prince Georges, MD	1,296,071	14
Harris, TX	1,287,241	15
Riverside, CA	1,261,196	16
Baltimore, MD	1,188,804	17
Erie, NY	1,104,838	18
Cuyahoga, OH	1,070,094	19
Clark, NV	1,029,614	20
Hennepin, MN	1,001,249	21
Hillsborough, FL	958,002	22
Wayne, MI	935,781	23
Monroe, NY	906,750	24
Broward, FL	888,184	25

Source: U.S. Bureau of the Census, *Annual Survey of Government Finances 1992*, Washington, D.C.: U.S. Government Printing Office, 1995, n.p. Primary source: U.S. Bureau of the Census. *Note:* Data are shown only for the top 25 areas.

★2661★
County Government Revenues
County Government Revenues, 1991-92: Total Intergovernmental Revenues
[In thousands of dollars]

County	Total revenues	Rank
Los Angeles, CA	6,798,758	1
San Diego, CA	1,338,349	2
San Bernardino, CA	1,034,912	3
Santa Clara, CA	914,516	4
Orange, CA	907,549	5
Riverside, CA	722,952	6
Sacramento, CA	683,141	7
Fresno, CA	603,811	8
Wayne, MI	509,054	9
Contra Costa, CA	458,008	10
Nassau, NY	455,358	11
Westchester, NY	447,042	12
Dade, FL	441,836	13
Kern, CA	440,763	14
Cuyahoga, OH	428,623	15
Milwaukee, WI	407,950	16
Prince Georges, MD	397,107	17

[Continued]

★2661★
County Government Revenues, 1991-92: Total Intergovernmental Revenues
[Continued]

County	Total revenues	Rank
Erie, NY	380,961	18
Hennepin, MN	378,570	19
Suffolk, NY	375,182	20
Monroe, NY	343,803	21
Fairfax, VA	324,397	22
Allegheny, PA	323,331	23
Essex, NJ	282,516	24
Cook, IL	273,670	25

Source: U.S. Bureau of the Census, *Annual Survey of Government Finances 1992*, Washington, D.C.: U.S. Government Printing Office, 1995, n.p. Primary source: U.S. Bureau of the Census. *Note:* Data are shown only for the top 25 areas.

★2662★
County Government Revenues
County Government Revenues, 1991-92: Total Intergovernmental Revenues From State Governments
[In thousands of dollars]

County	Total revenues	Rank
Los Angeles, CA	6,387,523	1
San Diego, CA	1,230,647	2
San Bernardino, CA	943,197	3
Santa Clara, CA	845,719	4
Orange, CA	821,875	5
Sacramento, CA	667,727	6
Riverside, CA	663,839	7
Fresno, CA	590,177	8
Wayne, MI	427,610	9
Cuyahoga, OH	417,169	10
Kern, CA	417,033	11
Contra Costa, CA	411,084	12
Westchester, NY	408,045	13
Nassau, NY	397,825	14
Erie, NY	364,253	15
Prince Georges, MD	354,542	16
Milwaukee, WI	353,531	17
Suffolk, NY	350,769	18
Hennepin, MN	348,464	19
Monroe, NY	317,265	20
Allegheny, PA	308,309	21
Fairfax, VA	270,169	22
Essex, NJ	269,644	23
Cook, IL	255,331	24
Dade, FL	252,976	25

Source: U.S. Bureau of the Census, *Annual Survey of Government Finances 1992*, Washington, D.C.: U.S. Government Printing Office, 1995, n.p. Primary source: U.S. Bureau of the Census. *Note:* Data are shown only for the top 25 areas.

★2663★

County Government Revenues

County Government Revenues, 1991-92: Total Revenues

[In thousands of dollars]

County	Total revenues	Rank	Amount per capita	Rank
Allegheny, PA	785,955	30	0.589	39
Baltimore, MD	1,287,046	16	1.825	3
Bergen, NJ	485,728	41	0.582	40
Bexar, TX	469,711	43	0.381	54
Broward, FL	919,250	26	0.706	34
Bucks, PA	179,432	64	0.323	60
Camden, NJ	412,786	48	1.038	20
Clark, NV	1,114,741	19	1.318	11
Contra Costa, CA	95,172	69	0.113	68
Cook, IL	1,614,351	10	0.314	61
Dade, FL	3,061,089	2	1.524	5
Dallas, TX	651,279	36	0.340	58
DeKalb, GA	472,895	42	0.839	29
Delaware, PA	267,554	59	0.487	45
DuPage, IL	255,717	60	0.313	62
El Paso, TX	179,211	65	0.285	64
Erie, NY	1,134,629	18	1.167	14
Essex, MA	45,267	73	0.068	71
Essex, NJ	560,453	38	0.725	32
Fairfax, VA	2,228,631	3	2.600	1
Franklin, OH	454,187	45	0.458	49
Fresno, CA	910,558	28	1.290	13
Fulton, GA	681,215	34	1.023	22
Hamilton, OH	461,250	44	0.529	43
Harris, TX	1,287,241	15	0.433	51
Hennepin, MN	1,001,249	22	0.962	25
Hillsborough, FL	958,002	24	1.116	16
Hudson, NJ	356,179	52	0.642	36
Jackson, MO	137,713	66	0.217	67
Jefferson, KY	376,181	49	0.561	41
Kern, CA	805,735	29	1.371	8
King, WA	701,129	33	0.450	50
Los Angeles, CA	12,010,371	1	1.327	10
Macomb, MI	255,588	61	0.351	56
Middlesex, MA	91,533	70	0.066	72
Middlesex, NJ	366,707	51	0.536	42
Milwaukee, WI	962,438	23	1.011	23
Monmouth, NJ	366,774	50	0.648	35
Monroe, NY	934,869	25	1.291	12
Montgomery, MD	1,764,835	7	2.260	2
Montgomery, OH	415,699	47	0.718	33
Montgomery, PA	268,526	58	0.389	53
Multnomah, OR	281,077	56	0.468	48
Nassau, NY	1,845,882	6	1.418	7
Norfolk, MA	55,783	72	0.090	69
Oakland, MI	534,262	40	0.478	47
Oklahoma, OK	134,793	67	0.220	66
Orange, CA	2,213,869	4	0.891	27
Orange, FL	680,892	35	0.953	26
Palm Beach, FL	718,941	31	0.798	31
Pierce, WA	211,670	62	0.342	57
Pinellas, FL	544,698	39	0.637	37
Prince Georges, MD	1,362,703	13	1.815	4
Riverside, CA	1,261,484	17	0.979	24

[Continued]

★2663★

County Government Revenues, 1991-92: Total Revenues

[Continued]

County	Total revenues	Rank	Amount per capita	Rank
Sacramento, CA	1,490,215	11	1.363	9
Saint Louis, MO	422,505	46	0.422	52
Salt Lake, UT	283,488	55	0.371	55
San Bernardino, CA	1,721,068	8	1.122	15
San Diego, CA	2,126,459	5	0.818	30
San Mateo, CA	575,019	37	0.867	28
Santa Clara, CA	1,689,065	9	1.105	17
Shelby, TN	916,311	27	1.085	18
Suffolk, NY	1,372,419	12	1.026	21
Summit, OH	275,644	57	0.527	44
Tarrant, TX	351,796	53	0.288	63
Travis, TX	198,664	63	0.324	59
Tulsa, OK	128,466	68	0.247	65
Union, NJ	299,139	54	0.606	38
Ventura, CA	714,891	32	1.041	19
Wayne, MI	1,017,467	21	0.485	46
Westchester, NY	1,315,625	14	1.492	6
Worcester, MA	60,119	71	0.085	70

Source: U.S. Bureau of the Census, *Annual Survey of Government Finances 1992*, Washington, D.C.: U.S. Government Printing Office, 1995, n.p. Primary source: U.S. Bureau of the Census.

Chapter 30

CITY GOVERNMENT FINANCES

Topics Covered

City Government Debt
City Government Expenditures
City Government Revenues
City Government Expenditures, By Source
City Government Revenues, By Source
Taxes and Tax Revenues

★2664★

City Government Debt

City Government Debt, 1991-92, By Type: Education

[In thousands of dollars]

City	Total debt	Rank
Atlanta, GA	37,160	8
Baltimore, MD	61,586	6
Boston, MA	85,524	5
Buffalo, NY	30,685	10
Chicago, IL	8,750	11
Cincinnati, OH	4,565	12
Memphis, TN	32,062	9
Milwaukee, WI	1,260	13
Nashville-Davidson, TN	111,143	3
New York City, NY	3,127,455	1
Newark, NJ	41,553	7
Philadelphia, PA	593	14
San Francisco, CA	90,245	4
Toledo, OH	390	15
Virginia Beach, VA	146,664	2

Source: U.S. Bureau of the Census, *Annual Survey of Government Finances 1992,* Washington, D.C.: U.S. Government Printing Office, 1995, n.p. Primary source: U.S. Bureau of the Census.

★2665★

City Government Debt

City Government Debt, 1991-92, By Type: General Purpose

[In thousands of dollars]

City	Total debt	Rank
Albuquerque, NM	95,596	10
Atlanta, GA	8,000	39
Austin, TX	28,000	33
Baltimore, MD	37,285	29
Baton Rouge, LA	0	42
Boston, MA	70,715	17
Buffalo, NY	51,985	23
Charlotte, NC	76,445	15
Chicago, IL	405,585	2
Cincinnati, OH	34,485	30
Cleveland, OH	64,655	18
Columbus, OH	266,391	3
Dallas, TX	10,470	38
Denver, CO	84,460	12
Detroit, MI	39,565	27
El Paso, TX	24,240	35
Fort Worth, TX	29,950	32
Honolulu, HI	256,428	4
Houston, TX	115,300	8
Indianapolis, IN	56,586	20
Jacksonville, FL	25,070	34
Kansas City, MO	0	42
Los Angeles, CA	38,850	28
Memphis, TN	82,776	13
Miami, FL	56,285	21

[Continued]

★2665★

City Government Debt, 1991-92, By Type: General Purpose

[Continued]

City	Total debt	Rank
Milwaukee, WI	76,596	14
Minneapolis, MN	51,200	24
Nashville-Davidson, TN	1,381	40
New Orleans, LA	179,881	5
New York City, NY	3,401,164	1
Newark, NJ	0	42
Oakland, CA	0	42
Oklahoma City, OK	19,250	37
Omaha, NE	48,740	25
Philadelphia, PA	0	42
Pittsburgh, PA	45,000	26
Portland, OR	62,656	19
Sacramento, CA	0	42
Saint Louis, MO	0	42
San Antonio, TX	70,720	16
San Diego, CA	22,335	36
San Francisco, CA	155,560	7
San Jose, CA	173,865	6
Seattle, WA	31,303	31
Toledo, OH	190	41
Tulsa, OK	114,085	9
Virginia Beach, VA	89,019	11
Washington, DC	55,680	22

Source: U.S. Bureau of the Census, *Annual Survey of Government Finances 1992,* Washington, D.C.: U.S. Government Printing Office, 1995, n.p. Primary source: U.S. Bureau of the Census.

★2666★

City Government Debt

City Government Debt, 1991-92, By Type: Long Term (Full Faith and Credit)

[In thousands of dollars]

City	Total debt	Rank
Albuquerque, NM	95,596	14
Atlanta, GA	8,000	39
Austin, TX	28,000	33
Baltimore, MD	37,285	29
Baton Rouge, LA	0	42
Boston, MA	70,715	19
Buffalo, NY	52,890	24
Charlotte, NC	99,445	13
Chicago, IL	405,585	3
Cincinnati, OH	34,485	30
Cleveland, OH	64,655	20
Columbus, OH	317,689	4
Dallas, TX	10,470	38
Denver, CO	106,260	12
Detroit, MI	39,565	27
El Paso, TX	24,240	35
Fort Worth, TX	29,950	32

[Continued]

★ 2666 ★

City Government Debt, 1991-92, By Type: Long-Term (Full Faith and Credit)

[Continued]

City	Total debt	Rank
Honolulu, HI	256,428	5
Houston, TX	115,300	9
Indianapolis, IN	56,586	22
Jacksonville, FL	25,070	34
Kansas City, MO	0	42
Los Angeles, CA	38,850	28
Memphis, TN	82,776	15
Miami, FL	56,285	23
Milwaukee, WI	76,596	16
Minneapolis, MN	61,830	21
Nashville-Davidson, TN	1,381	40
New Orleans, LA	179,881	6
New York City, NY	4,312,695	1
Newark, NJ	0	42
Oakland, CA	0	42
Oklahoma City, OK	19,250	37
Omaha, NE	48,740	25
Philadelphia, PA	0	42
Pittsburgh, PA	45,000	26
Portland, OR	73,162	17
Sacramento, CA	0	42
Saint Louis, MO	0	42
San Antonio, TX	70,720	18
San Diego, CA	22,335	36
San Francisco, CA	155,560	8
San Jose, CA	173,865	7
Seattle, WA	31,303	31
Toledo, OH	190	41
Tulsa, OK	114,085	11
Virginia Beach, VA	114,524	10
Washington, DC	556,580	2

Source: U.S. Bureau of the Census, *Annual Survey of Government Finances 1992*, Washington, D.C.: U.S. Government Printing Office, 1995, n.p. Primary source: U.S. Bureau of the Census.

★ 2667 ★

City Government Debt

City Government Debt, 1991-92, By Type: Long-Term Debt Retired (General Purpose)

[In thousands of dollars]

City	Total debt	Rank
Albuquerque, NM	131,061	15
Atlanta, GA	34,792	41
Austin, TX	43,846	38
Baltimore, MD	66,768	25
Baton Rouge, LA	50,293	33
Boston, MA	55,363	28
Buffalo, NY	82,608	19
Charlotte, NC	24,642	44

[Continued]

★ 2667 ★

City Government Debt, 1991-92, By Type: Long-Term Debt Retired (General Purpose)

[Continued]

City	Total debt	Rank
Chicago, IL	429,304	4
Cincinnati, OH	20,674	45
Cleveland, OH	50,250	34
Columbus, OH	85,577	18
Dallas, TX	135,313	13
Denver, CO	65,238	26
Detroit, MI	47,441	36
El Paso, TX	100,416	17
Fort Worth, TX	43,947	37
Honolulu, HI	72,468	22
Houston, TX	529,762	2
Indianapolis, IN	120,897	16
Jacksonville, FL	145,872	12
Kansas City, MO	72,155	23
Los Angeles, CA	351,263	6
Memphis, TN	80,891	21
Miami, FL	68,011	24
Milwaukee, WI	55,300	29
Minneapolis, MN	169,372	10
Nashville-Davidson, TN	53,940	30
New Orleans, LA	192,420	8
New York City, NY	1,776,862	1
Newark, NJ	11,775	47
Oakland, CA	172,687	9
Oklahoma City, OK	52,888	31
Omaha, NE	42,570	39
Philadelphia, PA	149,220	11
Pittsburgh, PA	39,458	40
Portland, OR	131,650	14
Sacramento, CA	16,938	46
Saint Louis, MO	81,183	20
San Antonio, TX	26,697	43
San Diego, CA	51,811	32
San Francisco, CA	372,303	5
San Jose, CA	49,698	35
Seattle, WA	29,496	42
Toledo, OH	9,109	48
Tulsa, OK	197,446	7
Virginia Beach, VA	58,908	27
Washington, DC	462,095	3

Source: U.S. Bureau of the Census, *Annual Survey of Government Finances 1992*, Washington, D.C.: U.S. Government Printing Office, 1995, n.p. Primary source: U.S. Bureau of the Census.

★2668★
City Government Debt

City Government Debt, 1991-92, By Type: Long-Term Debt Issued (General Purpose)

[In thousands of dollars]

City	Total debt	Rank
Albuquerque, NM	1,790	36
Atlanta, GA	364,333	8
Austin, TX	32,005	28
Baltimore, MD	48,810	25
Baton Rouge, LA	20,000	32
Boston, MA	52,402	23
Buffalo, NY	24,276	30
Charlotte, NC	167,644	12
Chicago, IL	109,300	14
Cincinnati, OH	0	39
Cleveland, OH	0	39
Columbus, OH	0	39
Dallas, TX	599,443	5
Denver, CO	1,292,604	1
Detroit, MI	80,222	19
El Paso, TX	75,740	21
Fort Worth, TX	0	39
Honolulu, HI	0	39
Houston, TX	521,527	6
Indianapolis, IN	276,535	9
Jacksonville, FL	406,918	7
Kansas City, MO	239,276	10
Los Angeles, CA	696,413	3
Memphis, TN	0	39
Miami, FL	40,215	26
Milwaukee, WI	9,487	34
Minneapolis, MN	99,765	15
Nashville-Davidson, TN	23,540	31
New Orleans, LA	74,446	22
New York City, NY	1,214,530	2
Newark, NJ	0	39
Oakland, CA	205,338	11
Oklahoma City, OK	99,550	16
Omaha, NE	0	39
Philadelphia, PA	10,875	33
Pittsburgh, PA	33,015	27
Portland, OR	52,116	24
Sacramento, CA	156,739	13
Saint Louis, MO	91,945	17
San Antonio, TX	1,086	38
San Diego, CA	77,398	20
San Francisco, CA	626,581	4
San Jose, CA	31,210	29
Seattle, WA	0	39
Toledo, OH	6,689	35
Tulsa, OK	81,370	18
Virginia Beach, VA	1,745	37
Washington, DC	0	39

Source: U.S. Bureau of the Census, *Annual Survey of Government Finances 1992*, Washington, D.C.: U.S. Government Printing Office, 1995, n.p. Primary source: U.S. Bureau of the Census.

★2669★
City Government Debt

City Government Debt, 1991-92, By Type: Long-Term Debt Issued (Nonguaranteed)

[In thousands of dollars]

City	Total debt	Rank
Albuquerque, NM	61,320	30
Atlanta, GA	364,333	8
Austin, TX	132,306	16
Baltimore, MD	72,970	26
Baton Rouge, LA	20,000	38
Boston, MA	52,402	31
Buffalo, NY	24,276	36
Charlotte, NC	167,444	14
Chicago, IL	109,300	18
Cincinnati, OH	0	44
Cleveland, OH	66,930	29
Columbus, OH	72,695	27
Dallas, TX	625,641	6
Denver, CO	1,292,604	3
Detroit, MI	349,662	10
El Paso, TX	76,505	24
Fort Worth, TX	16,360	39
Honolulu, HI	0	44
Houston, TX	745,934	4
Indianapolis, IN	276,535	11
Jacksonville, FL	576,003	7
Kansas City, MO	259,276	12
Los Angeles, CA	1,369,778	2
Memphis, TN	70,000	28
Miami, FL	40,215	33
Milwaukee, WI	9,487	41
Minneapolis, MN	99,765	20
Nashville-Davidson, TN	23,540	37
New Orleans, LA	74,446	25
New York City, NY	2,329,826	1
Newark, NJ	0	44
Oakland, CA	205,338	13
Oklahoma City, OK	129,676	17
Omaha, NE	0	44
Philadelphia, PA	10,875	40
Pittsburgh, PA	33,015	34
Portland, OR	52,116	32
Sacramento, CA	156,739	15
Saint Louis, MO	91,945	21
San Antonio, TX	363,884	9
San Diego, CA	77,398	23
San Francisco, CA	733,761	5
San Jose, CA	31,210	35
Seattle, WA	104,000	19
Toledo, OH	6,689	42
Tulsa, OK	81,370	22
Virginia Beach, VA	1,745	43
Washington, DC	0	44

Source: U.S. Bureau of the Census, *Annual Survey of Government Finances 1992*, Washington, D.C.: U.S. Government Printing Office, 1995, n.p. Primary source: U.S. Bureau of the Census.

★ 2670 ★

City Government Debt

City Government Debt, 1991-92, By Type: Long-Term Debt Nonguaranteed (Utilities)

[In thousands of dollars]

City	Total debt	Rank
Albuquerque, NM	59,530	13
Atlanta, GA	0	20
Austin, TX	100,301	9
Baltimore, MD	24,160	16
Baton Rouge, LA	0	20
Boston, MA	0	20
Buffalo, NY	0	20
Charlotte, NC	0	20
Chicago, IL	0	20
Cincinnati, OH	0	20
Cleveland, OH	66,930	12
Columbus, OH	72,695	10
Dallas, TX	26,198	15
Denver, CO	0	20
Detroit, MI	269,440	4
El Paso, TX	765	19
Fort Worth, TX	16,360	18
Honolulu, HI	0	20
Houston, TX	224,407	5
Indianapolis, IN	0	20
Jacksonville, FL	169,085	6
Kansas City, MO	20,000	17
Los Angeles, CA	673,365	2
Memphis, TN	70,000	11
Miami, FL	0	20
Milwaukee, WI	0	20
Minneapolis, MN	0	20
Nashville-Davidson, TN	0	20
New Orleans, LA	0	20
New York City, NY	1,115,296	1
Newark, NJ	0	20
Oakland, CA	0	20
Oklahoma City, OK	30,126	14
Omaha, NE	0	20
Philadelphia, PA	0	20
Pittsburgh, PA	0	20
Portland, OR	0	20
Sacramento, CA	0	20
Saint Louis, MO	0	20
San Antonio, TX	362,798	3
San Diego, CA	0	20
San Francisco, CA	107,180	7
San Jose, CA	0	20
Seattle, WA	104,000	8
Toledo, OH	0	20
Tulsa, OK	0	20
Virginia Beach, VA	0	20
Washington, DC	0	20

Source: U.S. Bureau of the Census, *Annual Survey of Government Finances 1992*, Washington, D.C.: U.S. Government Printing Office, 1995, n.p. Primary source: U.S. Bureau of the Census.

★ 2671 ★

City Government Debt

City Government Debt, 1991-92, By Type: Long-Term Debt Retired (Utilities)

[In thousands of dollars]

City	Total debt	Rank
Albuquerque, NM	8,181	21
Atlanta, GA	1,860	32
Austin, TX	24,154	11
Baltimore, MD	3,385	26
Baton Rouge, LA	0	41
Boston, MA	2,025	30
Buffalo, NY	2,365	28
Charlotte, NC	5,179	24
Chicago, IL	12,330	17
Cincinnati, OH	6,040	23
Cleveland, OH	55,177	9
Columbus, OH	103,251	5
Dallas, TX	10,117	18
Denver, CO	16,420	15
Detroit, MI	191,069	4
El Paso, TX	2,610	27
Fort Worth, TX	7,725	22
Honolulu, HI	2,275	29
Houston, TX	251,702	2
Indianapolis, IN	1,313	36
Jacksonville, FL	32,493	10
Kansas City, MO	3,655	25
Los Angeles, CA	85,650	6
Memphis, TN	17,200	13
Miami, FL	0	41
Milwaukee, WI	0	41
Minneapolis, MN	1,465	35
Nashville-Davidson, TN	69,620	7
New Orleans, LA	1,860	32
New York City, NY	990,486	1
Newark, NJ	955	37
Oakland, CA	0	41
Oklahoma City, OK	8,853	20
Omaha, NE	0	41
Philadelphia, PA	55,449	8
Pittsburgh, PA	0	41
Portland, OR	17,191	14
Sacramento, CA	1,875	31
Saint Louis, MO	920	38
San Antonio, TX	203,554	3
San Diego, CA	0	41
San Francisco, CA	1,580	34
San Jose, CA	7	40
Seattle, WA	22,585	12
Toledo, OH	203	39
Tulsa, OK	1,795	33
Virginia Beach, VA	12,911	16
Washington, DC	8,867	19

Source: U.S. Bureau of the Census, *Annual Survey of Government Finances 1992*, Washington, D.C.: U.S. Government Printing Office, 1995, n.p. Primary source: U.S. Bureau of the Census.

★2672★

City Government Debt

City Government Debt, 1991-92, By Type: Long-Term Debt Issued (Utilities)

[In thousands of dollars]

City	Total debt	Rank
Buffalo, NY	905	8
Charlotte, NC	23,000	4
Columbus, OH	51,298	2
Denver, CO	21,800	5
Minneapolis, MN	10,630	6
New York City, NY	911,531	1
Portland, OR	10,506	7
Virginia Beach, VA	25,505	3

Source: U.S. Bureau of the Census, *Annual Survey of Government Finances 1992*, Washington, D.C.: U.S. Government Printing Office, 1995, n.p. Primary source: U.S. Bureau of the Census.

★2673★

City Government Debt

City Government Debt, 1991-92, By Type: Long-Term Debt Outstanding

[In thousands of dollars]

City	Total debt	Rank
Albuquerque, NM	156,916	24
Atlanta, GA	372,333	13
Austin, TX	160,306	23
Baltimore, MD	110,255	33
Baton Rouge, LA	20,000	45
Boston, MA	123,117	31
Buffalo, NY	77,166	40
Charlotte, NC	267,089	15
Chicago, IL	514,885	9
Cincinnati, OH	34,485	43
Cleveland, OH	131,585	29
Columbus, OH	390,384	11
Dallas, TX	636,111	6
Denver, CO	1,398,864	3
Detroit, MI	389,227	12
El Paso, TX	100,745	34
Fort Worth, TX	46,310	42
Honolulu, HI	256,428	17
Houston, TX	861,234	5
Indianapolis, IN	333,121	14
Jacksonville, FL	601,073	7
Kansas City, MO	259,276	16
Los Angeles, CA	1,408,628	2
Memphis, TN	152,776	26
Miami, FL	96,500	36
Milwaukee, WI	86,083	38
Minneapolis, MN	161,595	22
Nashville-Davidson, TN	24,921	44
New Orleans, LA	254,327	18
New York City, NY	6,642,521	1
Newark, NJ	0	48
Oakland, CA	205,338	19

[Continued]

★2673★

City Government Debt, 1991-92, By Type: Long-Term Debt Outstanding

[Continued]

City	Total debt	Rank
Oklahoma City, OK	148,926	27
Omaha, NE	48,740	41
Philadelphia, PA	10,875	46
Pittsburgh, PA	78,015	39
Portland, OR	125,278	30
Sacramento, CA	156,739	25
Saint Louis, MO	91,945	37
San Antonio, TX	434,604	10
San Diego, CA	99,733	35
San Francisco, CA	889,321	4
San Jose, CA	205,075	20
Seattle, WA	135,303	28
Toledo, OH	6,879	47
Tulsa, OK	195,455	21
Virginia Beach, VA	116,269	32
Washington, DC	556,580	8

Source: U.S. Bureau of the Census, *Annual Survey of Government Finances 1992*, Washington, D.C.: U.S. Government Printing Office, 1995, n.p. Primary source: U.S. Bureau of the Census.

★2674★

City Government Debt

City Government Debt, 1991-92, By Type: Long-Term Debt Retired

[In thousands of dollars]

City	Total debt	Rank
Albuquerque, NM	139,242	18
Atlanta, GA	36,652	43
Austin, TX	68,000	32
Baltimore, MD	70,153	30
Baton Rouge, LA	50,293	39
Boston, MA	57,388	34
Buffalo, NY	84,973	24
Charlotte, NC	29,821	44
Chicago, IL	441,634	4
Cincinnati, OH	26,714	45
Cleveland, OH	105,427	21
Columbus, OH	188,828	12
Dallas, TX	145,430	17
Denver, CO	81,658	26
Detroit, MI	238,510	7
El Paso, TX	103,026	22
Fort Worth, TX	51,672	38
Honolulu, HI	74,743	28
Houston, TX	781,464	2
Indianapolis, IN	122,210	20
Jacksonville, FL	178,365	13
Kansas City, MO	75,810	27
Los Angeles, CA	436,913	5

[Continued]

★2674★
City Government Debt, 1991-92, By Type: Long-Term Debt Retired
[Continued]

City	Total debt	Rank
Memphis, TN	98,091	23
Miami, FL	68,011	31
Milwaukee, WI	55,300	35
Minneapolis, MN	170,837	15
Nashville-Davidson, TN	123,560	19
New Orleans, LA	194,280	11
New York City, NY	2,767,348	1
Newark, NJ	12,730	47
Oakland, CA	172,687	14
Oklahoma City, OK	61,741	33
Omaha, NE	42,570	41
Philadelphia, PA	204,669	9
Pittsburgh, PA	39,458	42
Portland, OR	148,841	16
Sacramento, CA	18,813	46
Saint Louis, MO	82,103	25
San Antonio, TX	230,251	8
San Diego, CA	51,811	37
San Francisco, CA	373,883	6
San Jose, CA	49,705	40
Seattle, WA	52,081	36
Toledo, OH	9,312	48
Tulsa, OK	199,241	10
Virginia Beach, VA	71,819	29
Washington, DC	470,962	3

Source: U.S. Bureau of the Census, *Annual Survey of Government Finances 1992*, Washington, D.C.: U.S. Government Printing Office, 1995, n.p. Primary source: U.S. Bureau of the Census.

★2675★
City Government Debt
City Government Debt, 1991-92, By Type: Public Debt for Private Purposes
[In thousands of dollars]

City	Total debt	Rank
Albuquerque, NM	556,606	11
Atlanta, GA	284,729	17
Austin, TX	271,203	19
Baltimore, MD	618,054	10
Baton Rouge, LA	51,476	34
Boston, MA	0	39
Buffalo, NY	0	39
Charlotte, NC	15,210	37
Chicago, IL	2,159,561	3
Cincinnati, OH	0	39
Cleveland, OH	0	39
Columbus, OH	0	39
Dallas, TX	224,164	23
Denver, CO	68,105	31
Detroit, MI	30,565	35

[Continued]

★2675★
City Government Debt, 1991-92, By Type: Public Debt for Private Purposes
[Continued]

City	Total debt	Rank
El Paso, TX	239,203	21
Fort Worth, TX	295,413	15
Honolulu, HI	0	39
Houston, TX	550,375	12
Indianapolis, IN	52,238	33
Jacksonville, FL	1,346,996	5
Kansas City, MO	273,808	18
Los Angeles, CA	1,429,030	4
Memphis, TN	20,404	36
Miami, FL	135,389	27
Milwaukee, WI	118,061	28
Minneapolis, MN	11,156,654	1
Nashville-Davidson, TN	1,071,555	7
New Orleans, LA	331,743	14
New York City, NY	2,828,161	2
Newark, NJ	0	39
Oakland, CA	174,090	25
Oklahoma City, OK	61,365	32
Omaha, NE	0	39
Philadelphia, PA	166,720	26
Pittsburgh, PA	247,394	20
Portland, OR	291,501	16
Sacramento, CA	0	39
Saint Louis, MO	229,009	22
San Antonio, TX	68,230	30
San Diego, CA	1,066,240	8
San Francisco, CA	723,658	9
San Jose, CA	218,786	24
Seattle, WA	0	39
Toledo, OH	9,073	38
Tulsa, OK	1,129,571	6
Virginia Beach, VA	82,581	29
Washington, DC	519,909	13

Source: U.S. Bureau of the Census, *Annual Survey of Government Finances 1992*, Washington, D.C.: U.S. Government Printing Office, 1995, n.p. Primary source: U.S. Bureau of the Census.

★2676★
City Government Debt
City Government Debt, 1991-92, By Type: Refunding Issues of Long-Term Debt
[In thousands of dollars]

City	Total debt	Rank
Buffalo, NY	49,305	14
Chicago, IL	45,505	15
Cleveland, OH	80,068	8
Columbus, OH	131,575	6
Detroit, MI	53,524	13
El Paso, TX	70,240	10

[Continued]

★2676★

City Government Debt, 1991-92, By Type: Refunding Issues of Long-Term Debt

[Continued]

City	Total debt	Rank
Indianapolis, IN	59,900	11
Kansas City, MO	41,765	16
Los Angeles, CA	223,365	2
Miami, FL	54,135	12
Minneapolis, MN	25,590	18
New Orleans, LA	179,881	4
New York City, NY	1,516,155	1
Oakland, CA	152,298	5
San Antonio, TX	123,645	7
San Francisco, CA	222,620	3
San Jose, CA	21,090	19
Tulsa, OK	70,655	9
Virginia Beach, VA	37,590	17

Source: U.S. Bureau of the Census, *Annual Survey of Government Finances 1992*, Washington, D.C.: U.S. Government Printing Office, 1995, n.p. Primary source: U.S. Bureau of the Census.

★2677★

City Government Debt

City Government Debt, 1991-92, By Type: Short-Term Debt Outstanding

[In thousands of dollars]

City	Total debt	Rank
Albuquerque, NM	9,925	17
Atlanta, GA	0	26
Austin, TX	0	26
Baltimore, MD	51,554	10
Baton Rouge, LA	9,072	18
Boston, MA	0	26
Buffalo, NY	98,292	4
Charlotte, NC	0	26
Chicago, IL	0	26
Cincinnati, OH	5,000	19
Cleveland, OH	0	26
Columbus, OH	4,000	21
Dallas, TX	70,400	8
Denver, CO	0	26
Detroit, MI	76,397	7
El Paso, TX	0	26
Fort Worth, TX	36,000	11
Honolulu, HI	0	26
Houston, TX	0	26
Indianapolis, IN	30,171	13
Jacksonville, FL	0	26
Kansas City, MO	0	26
Los Angeles, CA	90,103	6
Memphis, TN	0	26
Miami, FL	0	26
Milwaukee, WI	716	25

[Continued]

★2677★

City Government Debt, 1991-92, By Type: Short-Term Debt Outstanding

[Continued]

City	Total debt	Rank
Minneapolis, MN	0	26
Nashville-Davidson, TN	25,410	15
New Orleans, LA	3,730	22
New York City, NY	1,716,114	1
Newark, NJ	29,324	14
Oakland, CA	35,000	12
Oklahoma City, OK	869	24
Omaha, NE	4,200	20
Philadelphia, PA	96,200	5
Pittsburgh, PA	0	26
Portland, OR	0	26
Sacramento, CA	1,835	23
Saint Louis, MO	0	26
San Antonio, TX	160,000	2
San Diego, CA	111,834	3
San Francisco, CA	0	26
San Jose, CA	18,000	16
Seattle, WA	0	26
Toledo, OH	57,184	9
Tulsa, OK	0	26
Virginia Beach, VA	0	26
Washington, DC	0	26

Source: U.S. Bureau of the Census, *Annual Survey of Government Finances 1992*, Washington, D.C.: U.S. Government Printing Office, 1995, n.p. Primary source: U.S. Bureau of the Census.

★2678★

City Government Debt

City Government Debt, 1991-92, By Type: Total Borrowing

[In thousands of dollars]

City	Total debt	Rank
Albuquerque, NM	156,916	20
Atlanta, GA	372,333	10
Austin, TX	160,306	19
Baltimore, MD	110,255	29
Baton Rouge, LA	20,000	45
Boston, MA	123,117	28
Buffalo, NY	80,153	33
Charlotte, NC	267,089	14
Chicago, IL	469,380	9
Cincinnati, OH	39,485	42
Cleveland, OH	51,517	39
Columbus, OH	258,809	15
Dallas, TX	663,311	6
Denver, CO	1,398,864	2
Detroit, MI	335,703	11
El Paso, TX	30,505	43
Fort Worth, TX	71,310	37

[Continued]

★2678★

City Government Debt, 1991-92, By Type: Total Borrowing
[Continued]

City	Total debt	Rank
Honolulu, HI	256,428	16
Houston, TX	861,234	4
Indianapolis, IN	273,221	13
Jacksonville, FL	601,073	7
Kansas City, MO	217,511	17
Los Angeles, CA	1,185,263	3
Memphis, TN	152,776	22
Miami, FL	42,365	41
Milwaukee, WI	86,083	32
Minneapolis, MN	136,005	24
Nashville-Davidson, TN	29,903	44
New Orleans, LA	74,929	36
New York City, NY	5,126,366	1
Newark, NJ	0	48
Oakland, CA	60,540	38
Oklahoma City, OK	148,926	23
Omaha, NE	48,740	40
Philadelphia, PA	10,875	46
Pittsburgh, PA	78,015	35
Portland, OR	125,278	26
Sacramento, CA	156,740	21
Saint Louis, MO	91,945	31
San Antonio, TX	310,959	12
San Diego, CA	99,733	30
San Francisco, CA	666,701	5
San Jose, CA	201,985	18
Seattle, WA	135,303	25
Toledo, OH	7,776	47
Tulsa, OK	124,800	27
Virginia Beach, VA	78,679	34
Washington, DC	556,580	8

Source: U.S. Bureau of the Census, *Annual Survey of Government Finances 1992,* Washington, D.C.: U.S. Government Printing Office, 1995, n.p. Primary source: U.S. Bureau of the Census.

★2679★
City Government Debt

City Government Debt, 1991-92, By Type: Total Debt Redemption

[In thousands of dollars]

City	Total debt	Rank
Albuquerque, NM	146,117	16
Atlanta, GA	36,652	38
Austin, TX	212,250	8
Baltimore, MD	452,621	4
Baton Rouge, LA	50,688	32
Boston, MA	57,388	28
Buffalo, NY	39,796	35
Charlotte, NC	29,821	40
Chicago, IL	396,129	5

[Continued]

★2679★

City Government Debt, 1991-92, By Type: Total Debt Redemption
[Continued]

City	Total debt	Rank
Cincinnati, OH	26,714	42
Cleveland, OH	25,359	44
Columbus, OH	169,134	12
Dallas, TX	145,430	17
Denver, CO	81,658	24
Detroit, MI	186,639	10
El Paso, TX	95,986	21
Fort Worth, TX	51,672	31
Honolulu, HI	74,743	25
Houston, TX	781,464	2
Indianapolis, IN	62,310	26
Jacksonville, FL	178,365	11
Kansas City, MO	34,045	39
Los Angeles, CA	213,558	7
Memphis, TN	98,091	20
Miami, FL	15,836	46
Milwaukee, WI	55,577	29
Minneapolis, MN	147,977	15
Nashville-Davidson, TN	123,560	19
New Orleans, LA	45,885	33
New York City, NY	1,372,427	1
Newark, NJ	12,730	47
Oakland, CA	25,467	43
Oklahoma City, OK	61,940	27
Omaha, NE	43,070	34
Philadelphia, PA	204,669	9
Pittsburgh, PA	39,458	36
Portland, OR	148,916	14
Sacramento, CA	18,813	45
Saint Louis, MO	82,103	23
San Antonio, TX	221,606	6
San Diego, CA	85,883	22
San Francisco, CA	158,423	13
San Jose, CA	28,615	41
Seattle, WA	52,081	30
Toledo, OH	9,312	48
Tulsa, OK	128,586	18
Virginia Beach, VA	37,915	37
Washington, DC	470,962	3

Source: U.S. Bureau of the Census, *Annual Survey of Government Finances 1992,* Washington, D.C.: U.S. Government Printing Office, 1995, n.p. Primary source: U.S. Bureau of the Census.

★2680★
City Government Debt
City Government Debt, 1991-92, By Type: Utility Debt

[In thousands of dollars]

City	Total debt	Rank
Albuquerque, NM	300,367	14
Atlanta, GA	73,210	27
Austin, TX	2,012,730	5
Baltimore, MD	96,495	22
Baton Rouge, LA	96	42
Boston, MA	5,920	39
Buffalo, NY	26,780	33
Charlotte, NC	108,385	20
Chicago, IL	225,145	18
Cincinnati, OH	68,855	28
Cleveland, OH	412,615	11
Columbus, OH	424,341	10
Dallas, TX	274,187	16
Denver, CO	250,617	17
Detroit, MI	338,529	12
El Paso, TX	102,580	21
Fort Worth, TX	174,070	19
Honolulu, HI	49,895	29
Houston, TX	624,932	8
Indianapolis, IN	8,192	37
Jacksonville, FL	2,731,758	4
Kansas City, MO	77,575	25
Los Angeles, CA	3,412,500	2
Memphis, TN	322,655	13
Miami, FL	0	43
Milwaukee, WI	0	43
Minneapolis, MN	15,540	36
Nashville-Davidson, TN	565,928	9
New Orleans, LA	20,645	34
New York City, NY	8,393,637	1
Newark, NJ	27,006	32
Oakland, CA	0	43
Oklahoma City, OK	73,978	26
Omaha, NE	0	43
Philadelphia, PA	1,311,505	6
Pittsburgh, PA	0	43
Portland, OR	85,520	24
Sacramento, CA	42,020	30
Saint Louis, MO	5,810	40
San Antonio, TX	2,927,737	3
San Diego, CA	0	43
San Francisco, CA	293,693	15
San Jose, CA	116	41
Seattle, WA	692,145	7
Toledo, OH	15,582	35
Tulsa, OK	36,295	31
Virginia Beach, VA	96,157	23
Washington, DC	7,403	38

Source: U.S. Bureau of the Census, *Annual Survey of Government Finances 1992*, Washington, D.C.: U.S. Government Printing Office, 1995, n.p. Primary source: U.S. Bureau of the Census.

★2681★
City Government Debt
City Government Debt, 1991-92, By Type: Utility Debt (Electric Power Systems)

[In thousands of dollars]

City	Total debt	Rank
Austin, TX	1,656,043	4
Cleveland, OH	67,650	9
Columbus, OH	206,856	7
Jacksonville, FL	2,731,758	1
Los Angeles, CA	2,662,140	2
Memphis, TN	254,675	6
Nashville-Davidson, TN	164,019	8
Portland, OR	43,920	10
San Antonio, TX	2,655,105	3
San Francisco, CA	22	11
Seattle, WA	515,045	5

Source: U.S. Bureau of the Census, *Annual Survey of Government Finances 1992*, Washington, D.C.: U.S. Government Printing Office, 1995, n.p. Primary source: U.S. Bureau of the Census.

★2682★
City Government Debt
City Government Debt, 1991-92, By Type: Utility Debt (Gas Supply Systems)

[In thousands of dollars]

City	Total debt	Rank
Baton Rouge, LA	96	3
Memphis, TN	3,995	2
Philadelphia, PA	700,638	1

Source: U.S. Bureau of the Census, *Annual Survey of Government Finances 1992*, Washington, D.C.: U.S. Government Printing Office, 1995, n.p. Primary source: U.S. Bureau of the Census.

★2683★
City Government Debt
City Government Debt, 1991-92, By Type: Utility Debt (Transit Systems)

[In thousands of dollars]

City	Total debt	Rank
Boston, MA	5,520	5
Charlotte, NC	3,423	6
Detroit, MI	75	7
Indianapolis, IN	8,192	4
New York, NY	3,256,620	1
Philadelphia, PA	127,856	2
Sacramento, CA	31,115	3

Source: U.S. Bureau of the Census, *Annual Survey of Government Finances 1992*, Washington, D.C.: U.S. Government Printing Office, 1995, n.p. Primary source: U.S. Bureau of the Census.

★ 2684 ★
City Government Debt

City Government Debt, 1991-92, By Type: Utility Debt (Water Supply Systems)

[In thousands of dollars]

City	Total debt	Rank
Albuquerque, NM	300,367	9
Atlanta, GA	73,210	25
Austin, TX	356,687	6
Baltimore, MD	96,495	20
Baton Rouge, LA	0	40
Boston, MA	400	38
Buffalo, NY	26,780	31
Charlotte, NC	104,962	18
Chicago, IL	225,145	14
Cincinnati, OH	68,855	26
Cleveland, OH	344,965	7
Columbus, OH	217,485	15
Dallas, TX	274,187	11
Denver, CO	250,617	13
Detroit, MI	338,454	8
El Paso, TX	102,580	19
Fort Worth, TX	174,070	17
Honolulu, HI	49,895	28
Houston, TX	624,932	3
Indianapolis, IN	0	40
Jacksonville, FL	0	40
Kansas City, MO	77,575	23
Los Angeles, CA	750,360	2
Memphis, TN	63,985	27
Miami, FL	0	40
Milwaukee, WI	0	40
Minneapolis, MN	15,540	34
Nashville-Davidson, TN	401,909	5
New Orleans, LA	20,645	32
New York City, NY	5,137,017	1
Newark, NJ	27,006	30
Oakland, CA	0	40
Oklahoma City, OK	73,978	24
Omaha, NE	0	40
Philadelphia, PA	483,011	4
Pittsburgh, PA	0	40
Portland, OR	85,520	22
Sacramento, CA	10,905	35
Saint Louis, MO	5,810	37
San Antonio, TX	272,632	12
San Diego, CA	0	40
San Francisco, CA	293,671	10
San Jose, CA	116	39
Seattle, WA	177,100	16
Toledo, OH	15,582	33
Tulsa, OK	36,295	29
Virginia Beach, VA	96,157	21
Washington, DC	7,403	36

Source: U.S. Bureau of the Census, *Annual Survey of Government Finances 1992*, Washington, D.C.: U.S. Government Printing Office, 1995, n.p. Primary source: U.S. Bureau of the Census.

★ 2685 ★
City Government Debt

City Government Debt, 1991-92: Debt Outstanding

[In thousands of dollars]

City	Total debt	Rank
Albuquerque, NM	1,269,435	20
Atlanta, GA	1,433,054	18
Austin, TX	3,189,676	11
Baltimore, MD	1,308,051	19
Baton Rouge, LA	754,188	36
Boston, MA	1,070,639	26
Buffalo, NY	500,125	42
Charlotte, NC	999,281	29
Chicago, IL	6,012,046	3
Cincinnati, OH	259,517	45
Cleveland, OH	761,241	34
Columbus, OH	1,246,835	22
Dallas, TX	3,586,357	8
Denver, CO	3,344,088	10
Detroit, MI	1,685,475	15
El Paso, TX	448,393	44
Fort Worth, TX	934,606	30
Honolulu, HI	1,051,090	27
Houston, TX	3,494,830	9
Indianapolis, In	1,232,421	23
Jacksonville, FL	4,653,803	4
Kansas City, MO	905,332	31
Los Angeles, CA	8,002,815	2
Memphis, TN	810,817	32
Miami, FL	564,770	41
Milwaukee, WI	600,382	38
Minneapolis, MN	2,289,852	13
Nashville-Davidson, TN	2,215,909	14
New Orleans, LA	1,125,844	25
New York City, NY	34,984,016	1
Newark, NJ	151,730	48
Oakland, CA	1,144,082	24
Oklahoma City, OK	571,114	39
Omaha, NE	194,849	46
Philadelphia, PA	3,834,710	7
Pittsburgh, PA	660,819	37
Portland, OR	758,688	35
Sacramento, CA	452,130	43
Saint Louis, MO	766,899	33
San Antonio, TX	4,238,892	5
San Diego, CA	1,646,069	16
San Francisco, CA	3,173,852	12
San Jose, CA	1,249,308	21
Seattle, WA	1,031,875	28
Toledo, OH	193,728	47
Tulsa, OK	1,584,973	17
Virginia Beach, VA	565,581	40
Washington, DC	3,941,839	6

Source: U.S. Bureau of the Census, *Annual Survey of Government Finances 1992*, Washington, D.C.: U.S. Government Printing Office, 1995, n.p. Primary source: U.S. Bureau of the Census.

★ 2686 ★

City Government Debt

City Government Debt, 1991-92: General Debt

[In thousands of dollars]

City	Total debt	Rank
Albuquerque, NM	959,143	26
Atlanta, GA	1,359,844	15
Austin, TX	1,176,946	19
Baltimore, MD	1,160,002	20
Baton Rouge, LA	745,020	31
Boston, MA	1,064,719	24
Buffalo, NY	375,053	41
Charlotte, NC	890,896	27
Chicago, IL	5,786,901	2
Cincinnati, OH	185,662	46
Cleveland, OH	348,626	42
Columbus, OH	818,494	29
Dallas, TX	3,241,770	5
Denver, CO	3,093,471	6
Detroit, MI	1,270,549	16
El Paso, TX	345,813	43
Fort Worth, TX	724,536	32
Honolulu, HI	1,001,195	25
Houston, TX	2,869,898	8
Indianapolis, IN	1,194,058	18
Jacksonville, FL	1,922,045	11
Kansas City, MO	827,757	28
Los Angeles, CA	4,500,212	3
Memphis, TN	488,162	38
Miami, FL	564,770	36
Milwaukee, WI	599,666	35
Minneapolis, MN	2,274,312	10
Nashville-Davidson, TN	1,624,571	12
New Orleans, LA	1,101,469	23
New York City, NY	24,874,265	1
Newark, NJ	95,400	48
Oakland, CA	1,109,082	22
Oklahoma City, OK	496,267	37
Omaha, NE	190,649	45
Philadelphia, PA	2,427,005	9
Pittsburgh, PA	660,819	33
Portland, OR	629,248	34
Sacramento, CA	408,275	40
Saint Louis, MO	761,089	30
San Antonio, TX	1,151,155	21
San Diego, CA	1,534,235	14
San Francisco, CA	2,880,159	7
San Jose, CA	1,231,192	17
Seattle, WA	339,730	44
Toledo, OH	120,962	47
Tulsa, OK	1,548,678	13
Virginia Beach, VA	469,424	39
Washington, DC	3,934,436	4

Source: U.S. Bureau of the Census, *Annual Survey of Government Finances 1992*, Washington, D.C.: U.S. Government Printing Office, 1995, n.p. Primary source: U.S. Bureau of the Census.

★ 2687 ★

City Government Debt

City Government Debt, 1991-92: Long-Term Debt Outstanding

[In thousands of dollars]

City	Total debt	Rank
Albuquerque, NM	1,259,510	19
Atlanta, GA	1,433,054	18
Austin, TX	3,189,676	11
Baltimore, MD	1,256,497	20
Baton Rouge, LA	745,116	36
Boston, MA	1,070,639	26
Buffalo, NY	401,833	44
Charlotte, NC	999,281	29
Chicago, IL	6,012,046	3
Cincinnati, OH	254,517	45
Cleveland, OH	761,241	34
Columbus, OH	1,242,835	21
Dallas, TX	3,515,957	8
Denver, CO	3,344,088	10
Detroit, MI	1,609,078	15
El Paso, TX	448,393	43
Fort Worth, TX	898,606	31
Honolulu, HI	1,051,090	27
Houston, TX	3,494,830	9
Indianapolis, In	1,202,250	23
Jacksonville, FL	4,653,803	4
Kansas City, MO	905,332	30
Los Angeles, CA	7,912,712	2
Memphis, TN	810,817	32
Miami, FL	564,770	41
Milwaukee, WI	599,666	38
Minneapolis, MN	2,289,852	13
Nashville-Davidson, TN	2,190,499	14
New Orleans, LA	1,122,114	24
New York City, NY	33,267,902	1
Newark, NJ	122,406	48
Oakland, CA	1,109,082	25
Oklahoma City, OK	570,245	39
Omaha, NE	190,649	46
Philadelphia, PA	3,738,510	7
Pittsburgh, PA	660,819	37
Portland, OR	758,688	35
Sacramento, CA	450,295	42
Saint Louis, MO	766,899	33
San Antonio, TX	4,078,892	5
San Diego, CA	1,534,235	17
San Francisco, CA	3,173,852	12
San Jose, CA	1,231,308	22
Seattle, WA	1,031,875	28
Toledo, OH	136,544	47
Tulsa, OK	1,584,973	16
Virginia Beach, VA	565,581	40
Washington, DC	3,941,839	6

Source: U.S. Bureau of the Census, *Annual Survey of Government Finances 1992*, Washington, D.C.: U.S. Government Printing Office, 1995, n.p. Primary source: U.S. Bureau of the Census.

★ 2688 ★
City Government Debt

City Government Debt; 1991-92, By Type: Long-Term Debt Refunded

[In thousands of dollars]

City	Total debt	Rank
Albuquerque, NM	0	20
Atlanta, GA	0	20
Austin, TX	0	20
Baltimore, MD	0	20
Baton Rouge, LA	0	20
Boston, MA	0	20
Buffalo, NY	45,177	14
Charlotte, NC	0	20
Chicago, IL	45,505	13
Cincinnati, OH	0	20
Cleveland, OH	80,068	8
Columbus, OH	131,575	6
Dallas, TX	0	20
Denver, CO	0	20
Detroit, MI	53,524	11
El Paso, TX	7,040	19
Fort Worth, TX	0	20
Honolulu, HI	0	20
Houston, TX	0	20
Indianapolis, IN	59,900	10
Jacksonville, FL	0	20
Kansas City, MO	41,765	15
Los Angeles, CA	223,365	2
Memphis, TN	0	20
Miami, FL	52,175	12
Milwaukee, WI	0	20
Minneapolis, MN	22,860	17
Nashville-Davidson, TN	0	20
New Orleans, LA	148,395	4
New York City, NY	1,446,615	1
Newark, NJ	0	20
Oakland, CA	147,220	5
Oklahoma City, OK	0	20
Omaha, NE	0	20
Philadelphia, PA	0	20
Pittsburgh, PA	0	20
Portland, OR	0	20
Sacramento, CA	0	20
Saint Louis, MO	0	20
San Antonio, TX	123,645	7
San Diego, CA	0	20
San Francisco, CA	215,460	3
San Jose, CA	21,090	18
Seattle, WA	0	20
Toledo, OH	0	20
Tulsa, OK	70,655	9
Virginia Beach, VA	33,904	16
Washington, DC	0	20

Source: U.S. Bureau of the Census, *Annual Survey of Government Finances 1992,* Washington, D.C.: U.S. Government Printing Office, 1995, n.p. Primary source: U.S. Bureau of the Census.

★ 2689 ★
City Government Debt

City Government Debt; 1991-92, By Type: Net Long-Term Debt Outstanding

[In thousands of dollars]

City	Total debt	Rank
Albuquerque, NM	602,221	27
Atlanta, GA	856,542	23
Austin, TX	2,644,018	10
Baltimore, MD	558,797	29
Baton Rouge, LA	222,432	44
Boston, MA	1,037,547	16
Buffalo, NY	387,209	40
Charlotte, NC	936,553	20
Chicago, IL	3,673,306	3
Cincinnati, OH	232,438	43
Cleveland, OH	534,875	31
Columbus, OH	1,173,355	14
Dallas, TX	2,896,666	8
Denver, CO	3,144,497	7
Detroit, MI	1,349,768	13
El Paso, TX	189,282	45
Fort Worth, TX	558,304	30
Honolulu, HI	1,048,817	15
Houston, TX	2,215,524	11
Indianapolis, IN	981,885	17
Jacksonville, FL	2,853,823	9
Kansas City, MO	575,988	28
Los Angeles, CA	6,113,442	2
Memphis, TN	750,422	25
Miami, FL	405,009	39
Milwaukee, WI	320,843	41
Minneapolis, MN	923,329	21
Nashville-Davidson, TN	950,095	18
New Orleans, LA	673,705	26
New York City, NY	28,913,224	1
Newark, NJ	122,406	48
Oakland, CA	767,345	24
Oklahoma City, OK	439,384	34
Omaha, NE	164,660	46
Philadelphia, PA	3,168,504	6
Pittsburgh, PA	412,015	38
Portland, OR	414,216	37
Sacramento, CA	287,289	42
Saint Louis, MO	480,627	32
San Antonio, TX	3,619,184	4
San Diego, CA	417,389	36
San Francisco, CA	2,199,715	12
San Jose, CA	882,630	22
Seattle, WA	940,248	19
Toledo, OH	124,361	47
Tulsa, OK	426,661	35
Virginia Beach, VA	475,064	33
Washington, DC	3,393,385	5

Source: U.S. Bureau of the Census, *Annual Survey of Government Finances 1992,* Washington, D.C.: U.S. Government Printing Office, 1995, n.p. Primary source: U.S. Bureau of the Census.

★2690★
City Government Debt
City Government Debt Outstanding, 1992

[In millions of dollars]

City	Millions	Rank
New York City, NY[1]	34,984	1
Los Angeles, CA	8,003	2
Chicago, IL	6,012	3
Jacksonville, FL	4,654	4
San Antonio, TX	4,239	5
Houston, TX	3,962	6
Washington, DC[1]	3,942	7
Philadelphia, PA[1]	3,835	8
Dallas, TX	3,586	9
Denver, CO[1]	3,344	10
Austin, TX	3,190	11
San Francisco, CA[1]	3,174	12
Phoenix, AZ	2,310	13
Minneapolis, MN	2,290	14
Nashville-Davidson, TN[1]	2,216	15
Detroit, MI	1,685	16
San Diego, CA	1,646	17
Tulsa, OK	1,585	18
Atlanta, GA	1,433	19
Baltimore, MD[1]	1,308	20
Albuquerque, NM	1,269	21
San Jose, CA	1,249	22
Columbus, OH	1,247	23
Indianapolis, IN[1]	1,232	24
Oakland, CA	1,144	25

Source: U.S. Bureau of the Census, *Statistical Abstract of the United States: 1995,* (115th edition), Washington, D.C.: U.S. Government Printing Office, 1995, p. 320. Primary source: U.S. Bureau of the Census, *City Government Finances,* series GF, no. 4, annual. *Notes:* Data are shown only for the top 25 areas. 1. Represents, in effect, city-county consolidated government.

★2691★
City Government Expenditures
City Government Expenditures, 1991-92: Total General Expenditures

[In thousands of dollars]

City	Total expenditures	Rank
Albuquerque, NM	476,482	37
Atlanta, GA	623,740	26
Austin, TX	611,379	27
Baltimore, MD	1,550,290	9
Baton Rouge, LA	395,362	41
Boston, MA	1,559,843	8
Buffalo, NY	757,363	19
Charlotte, NC	500,070	35
Chicago, IL	3,281,304	4
Cincinnati, OH	525,482	32
Cleveland, OH	551,671	31
Columbus, OH	599,649	28
Dallas, TX	1,372,621	12
Denver, CO	1,513,329	10
Detroit, MI	1,576,539	7
El Paso, TX	268,143	46
Fort Worth, TX	436,262	40

[Continued]

★2691★
City Government Expenditures, 1991-92: Total General Expenditures
[Continued]

City	Total expenditures	Rank
Honolulu, HI	891,715	14
Houston, TX	1,451,983	11
Indianapolis, IN	878,971	15
Jacksonville, FL	792,228	18
Kansas City, MO	569,973	30
Los Angeles, CA	3,534,442	3
Memphis, TN	878,561	16
Miami, FL	323,861	45
Milwaukee, WI	584,319	29
Minneapolis, MN	736,166	21
Nashville-Davidson, TN	856,958	17
New Orleans, LA	683,622	23
New York City, NY	34,330,524	1
Newark, NJ	449,669	38
Oakland, CA	507,867	34
Oklahoma City, OK	361,779	43
Omaha, NE	208,534	48
Philadelphia, PA	2,822,682	5
Pittsburgh, PA	378,625	42
Portland, OR	494,724	36
Sacramento, CA	352,414	44
Saint Louis, MO	516,991	33
San Antonio, TX	657,115	25
San Diego, CA	1,084,147	13
San Francisco, CA	2,302,375	6
San Jose, CA	710,036	22
Seattle, WA	737,177	20
Toledo, OH	234,149	47
Tulsa, OK	444,488	39
Virginia Beach, VA	681,905	24
Washington, DC	4,585,654	2

Source: U.S. Bureau of the Census, *Annual Survey of Government Finances 1992,* Washington, D.C.: U.S. Government Printing Office, 1995, n.p. Primary source: U.S. Bureau of the Census.

★2692★
City Government Expenditures
City Government Expenditures, 1991-92, By Function: All Education

[In thousands of dollars]

City	Total expenditures	Rank
Albuquerque, NM	0	22
Atlanta, GA	18,757	12
Austin, TX	0	22
Baltimore, MD	537,372	3
Baton Rouge, LA	0	22
Boston, MA	478,827	4
Buffalo, NY	362,439	6
Charlotte, NC	0	22

[Continued]

★2692★

City Government Expenditures, 1991-92, By Function: All Education

[Continued]

City	Total expenditures	Rank
Chicago, IL	35,092	10
Cincinnati, OH	0	22
Cleveland, OH	0	22
Columbus, OH	0	22
Dallas, TX	0	22
Denver, CO	0	22
Detroit, MI	6,165	16
El Paso, TX	0	22
Fort Worth, TX	0	22
Honolulu, HI	0	22
Houston, TX	0	22
Indianapolis, IN	0	22
Jacksonville, FL	0	22
Kansas City, MO	23,559	11
Los Angeles, CA	8,571	15
Memphis, TN	434,569	5
Miami, FL	0	22
Milwaukee, WI	0	22
Minneapolis, MN	0	22
Nashville-Davidson, TN	271,093	8
New Orleans, LA	0	22
New York City, NY	8,007,747	1
Newark, NJ	207	20
Oakland, CA	4,073	17
Oklahoma City, OK	0	22
Omaha, NE	294	19
Philadelphia, PA	16,597	13
Pittsburgh, PA	0	22
Portland, OR	0	22
Sacramento, CA	172	21
Saint Louis, MO	3,359	18
San Antonio, TX	9,229	14
San Diego, CA	0	22
San Francisco, CA	57,512	9
San Jose, CA	0	22
Seattle, WA	0	22
Toledo, OH	0	22
Tulsa, OK	0	22
Virginia Beach, VA	333,835	7
Washington, DC	742,892	2

Source: U.S. Bureau of the Census, *Annual Survey of Government Finances 1992,* Washington, D.C.: U.S. Government Printing Office, 1995, n.p. Primary source: U.S. Bureau of the Census.

★2693★

City Government Expenditures

City Government Expenditures, 1991-92, By Function: Elementary and Secondary Education

[In thousands of dollars]

City	Total expenditures	Rank
Albuquerque, NM	0	20
Atlanta, GA	18,757	12
Austin, TX	0	20
Baltimore, MD	537,372	3
Baton Rouge, LA	0	20
Boston, MA	478,827	4
Buffalo, NY	362,439	6
Charlotte, NC	0	20
Chicago, IL	35,092	10
Cincinnati, OH	0	20
Cleveland, OH	0	20
Columbus, OH	0	20
Dallas, TX	0	20
Denver, CO	0	20
Detroit, MI	6,165	15
El Paso, TX	0	20
Fort Worth, TX	0	20
Honolulu, HI	0	20
Houston, TX	0	20
Indianapolis, IN	0	20
Jacksonville, FL	0	20
Kansas City, MO	23,559	11
Los Angeles, CA	8,571	13
Memphis, TN	434,569	5
Miami, FL	0	20
Milwaukee, WI	0	20
Minneapolis, MN	0	20
Nashville-Davidson, TN	271,093	8
New Orleans, LA	0	20
New York City, NY	7,392,424	1
Newark, NJ	177	18
Oakland, CA	4,073	16
Oklahoma City, OK	0	20
Omaha, NE	0	20
Philadelphia, PA	0	20
Pittsburgh, PA	0	20
Portland, OR	0	20
Sacramento, CA	172	19
Saint Louis, MO	3,176	17
San Antonio, TX	8,366	14
San Diego, CA	0	20
San Francisco, CA	57,512	9
San Jose, CA	0	20
Seattle, WA	0	20
Toledo, OH	0	20
Tulsa, OK	0	20
Virginia Beach, VA	333,830	7
Washington, DC	623,749	2

Source: U.S. Bureau of the Census, *Annual Survey of Government Finances 1992,* Washington, D.C.: U.S. Government Printing Office, 1995, n.p. Primary source: U.S. Bureau of the Census.

★2694★

City Government Expenditures

City Government Expenditures, 1991-92, By Function: Employee Retirement Expenditures

[In thousands of dollars]

City	Total expenditures	Rank
Albuquerque, NM	0	42
Atlanta, GA	60,929	14
Austin, TX	22,975	31
Baltimore, MD	90,814	10
Baton Rouge, LA	21,438	33
Boston, MA	163,832	8
Buffalo, NY	0	42
Charlotte, NC	5,137	40
Chicago, IL	408,322	3
Cincinnati, OH	53,156	16
Cleveland, OH	0	42
Columbus, OH	0	42
Dallas, TX	101,319	9
Denver, CO	23,633	30
Detroit, MI	249,477	6
El Paso, TX	16,880	35
Fort Worth, TX	21,869	32
Honolulu, HI	0	42
Houston, TX	67,647	11
Indianapolis, IN	35,082	23
Jacksonville, FL	40,000	20
Kansas City, MO	30,310	28
Los Angeles, CA	632,004	2
Memphis, TN	64,797	12
Miami, FL	35,004	24
Milwaukee, WI	63,014	13
Minneapolis, MN	29,689	29
Nashville-Davidson, TN	39,648	21
New Orleans, LA	34,782	25
New York City, NY	3,479,030	1
Newark, NJ	6,814	38
Oakland, CA	45,635	19
Oklahoma City, OK	5,999	39
Omaha, NE	13,757	37
Philadelphia, PA	293,853	5
Pittsburgh, PA	33,864	26
Portland, OR	35,639	22
Sacramento, CA	19,179	34
Saint Louis, MO	58,053	15
San Antonio, TX	13,918	36
San Diego, CA	45,890	18
San Francisco, CA	231,715	7
San Jose, CA	33,149	27
Seattle, WA	51,636	17
Toledo, OH	0	42
Tulsa, OK	4,126	41
Virginia Beach, VA	0	42
Washington, DC	372,333	4

Source: U.S. Bureau of the Census, *Annual Survey of Government Finances 1992*, Washington, D.C.: U.S. Government Printing Office, 1995, n.p. Primary source: U.S. Bureau of the Census.

★2695★

City Government Expenditures

City Government Expenditures, 1991-92, By Function: Environment and Housing (Capital Outlay)

[In thousands of dollars]

City	Total expenditures	Rank
Albuquerque, NM	43,610	15
Atlanta, GA	19,844	28
Austin, TX	22,439	26
Baltimore, MD	58,811	9
Baton Rouge, LA	24,988	23
Boston, MA	12,773	37
Buffalo, NY	2,069	43
Charlotte, NC	22,309	27
Chicago, IL	47,781	14
Cincinnati, OH	34,832	19
Cleveland, OH	1,644	44
Columbus, OH	57,922	10
Dallas, TX	49,471	13
Denver, CO	1,184	45
Detroit, MI	88,173	6
El Paso, TX	31,859	20
Fort Worth, TX	74,434	7
Honolulu, HI	57,090	11
Houston, TX	124,850	3
Indianapolis, IN	13,749	35
Jacksonville, FL	15,470	31
Kansas City, MO	15,091	32
Los Angeles, CA	154,736	2
Memphis, TN	13,775	34
Miami, FL	12,962	36
Milwaukee, WI	14,525	33
Minneapolis, MN	8,167	38
Nashville-Davidson, TN	37,902	17
New Orleans, LA	28,559	21
New York City, NY	763,518	1
Newark, NJ	2	47
Oakland, CA	4,093	41
Oklahoma City, OK	27,877	22
Omaha, NE	7,958	39
Philadelphia, PA	49,809	12
Pittsburgh, PA	34	46
Portland, OR	60,259	8
Sacramento, CA	2,766	42
Saint Louis, MO	0	48
San Antonio, TX	22,792	25
San Diego, CA	112,428	4
San Francisco, CA	105,372	5
San Jose, CA	23,943	24
Seattle, WA	18,546	29
Toledo, OH	15,532	30
Tulsa, OK	36,835	18
Virginia Beach, VA	6,769	40
Washington, DC	41,393	16

Source: U.S. Bureau of the Census, *Annual Survey of Government Finances 1992*, Washington, D.C.: U.S. Government Printing Office, 1995, n.p. Primary source: U.S. Bureau of the Census.

★ 2696 ★
City Government Expenditures

City Government Expenditures, 1991-92, By Function: Environment and Housing (Housing and Community Development)

[In thousands of dollars]

City	Total expenditures	Rank
Albuquerque, NM	17,416	28
Atlanta, GA	14,677	30
Austin, TX	4,756	46
Baltimore, MD	63,087	15
Baton Rouge, LA	10,837	34
Boston, MA	44,907	22
Buffalo, NY	67,888	13
Charlotte, NC	12,320	33
Chicago, IL	127,844	5
Cincinnati, OH	53,568	16
Cleveland, OH	68,231	12
Columbus, OH	4,307	47
Dallas, TX	14,011	31
Denver, CO	10,638	35
Detroit, MI	51,402	17
El Paso, TX	6,212	41
Fort Worth, TX	5,702	42
Honolulu, HI	101,892	7
Houston, TX	21,062	25
Indianapolis, IN	30,039	23
Jacksonville, FL	49,548	18
Kansas City, MO	7,900	39
Los Angeles, CA	255,569	2
Memphis, TN	19,542	27
Miami, FL	17,276	29
Milwaukee, WI	46,349	20
Minneapolis, MN	130,628	4
Nashville-Davidson, TN	5,277	43
New Orleans, LA	82,027	10
New York City, NY	2,444,709	1
Newark, NJ	66,496	14
Oakland, CA	45,806	21
Oklahoma City, OK	6,437	40
Omaha, NE	10,335	36
Philadelphia, PA	89,476	9
Pittsburgh, PA	9,300	38
Portland, OR	19,933	26
Sacramento, CA	0	48
Saint Louis, MO	27,433	24
San Antonio, TX	12,887	32
San Diego, CA	89,860	8
San Francisco, CA	75,287	11
San Jose, CA	110,439	6
Seattle, WA	49,153	19
Toledo, OH	9,572	37
Tulsa, OK	5,135	45
Virginia Beach, VA	5,249	44
Washington, DC	218,913	3

Source: U.S. Bureau of the Census, *Annual Survey of Government Finances 1992*, Washington, D.C.: U.S. Government Printing Office, 1995, n.p. Primary source: U.S. Bureau of the Census.

★ 2697 ★
City Government Expenditures

City Government Expenditures, 1991-92, By Function: Environment and Housing (Natural Resources)

[In thousands of dollars]

City	Total expenditures	Rank
Albuquerque, NM	0	21
Atlanta, GA	1,223	13
Austin, TX	3,880	9
Baltimore, MD	0	21
Baton Rouge, LA	0	21
Boston, MA	14	20
Buffalo, NY	0	21
Charlotte, NC	2,918	10
Chicago, IL	0	21
Cincinnati, OH	1,133	14
Cleveland, OH	0	21
Columbus, OH	0	21
Dallas, TX	0	21
Denver, CO	4,982	7
Detroit, MI	0	21
El Paso, TX	9,969	2
Fort Worth, TX	0	21
Honolulu, HI	4,530	8
Houston, TX	0	21
Indianapolis, IN	7,357	6
Jacksonville, FL	867	15
Kansas City, MO	8,285	5
Los Angeles, CA	8,663	4
Memphis, TN	1,410	12
Miami, FL	109	19
Milwaukee, WI	9,987	1
Minneapolis, MN	0	21
Nashville-Davidson, TN	2,277	11
New Orleans, LA	0	21
New York City, NY	0	21
Newark, NJ	0	21
Oakland, CA	0	21
Oklahoma City, OK	0	21
Omaha, NE	0	21
Philadelphia, PA	0	21
Pittsburgh, PA	0	21
Portland, OR	0	21
Sacramento, CA	0	21
Saint Louis, MO	0	21
San Antonio, TX	9,789	3
San Diego, CA	493	17
San Francisco, CA	560	16
San Jose, CA	0	21
Seattle, WA	0	21
Toledo, OH	0	21
Tulsa, OK	0	21
Virginia Beach, VA	244	18
Washington, DC	0	21

Source: U.S. Bureau of the Census, *Annual Survey of Government Finances 1992*, Washington, D.C.: U.S. Government Printing Office, 1995, n.p. Primary source: U.S. Bureau of the Census.

★2698★

City Government Expenditures

City Government Expenditures, 1991-92, By Function: Environment and Housing (Parks and Recreation)

[In thousands of dollars]

City	Total expenditures	Rank
Albuquerque, NM	38,637	27
Atlanta, GA	52,545	21
Austin, TX	53,791	19
Baltimore, MD	48,930	22
Baton Rouge, LA	19,844	42
Boston, MA	23,427	40
Buffalo, NY	21,870	41
Charlotte, NC	99,018	6
Chicago, IL	44,082	24
Cincinnati, OH	41,269	25
Cleveland, OH	34,928	31
Columbus, OH	40,738	26
Dallas, TX	95,547	7
Denver, CO	77,973	10
Detroit, MI	93,525	8
El Paso, TX	17,688	44
Fort Worth, TX	24,560	39
Honolulu, HI	80,335	9
Houston, TX	67,758	15
Indianapolis, IN	37,016	28
Jacksonville, FL	32,409	33
Kansas City, MO	69,413	14
Los Angeles, CA	165,547	2
Memphis, TN	75,704	12
Miami, FL	33,695	32
Milwaukee, WI	12,247	46
Minneapolis, MN	61,271	17
Nashville-Davidson, TN	25,662	38
New Orleans, LA	27,578	36
New York City, NY	364,775	1
Newark, NJ	9,066	48
Oakland, CA	47,763	23
Oklahoma City, OK	28,985	34
Omaha, NE	16,585	45
Philadelphia, PA	74,551	13
Pittsburgh, PA	35,149	30
Portland, OR	36,344	29
Sacramento, CA	53,346	20
Saint Louis, MO	17,926	43
San Antonio, TX	76,071	11
San Diego, CA	117,088	4
San Francisco, CA	120,599	3
San Jose, CA	63,856	16
Seattle, WA	111,677	5
Toledo, OH	9,211	47
Tulsa, OK	26,953	37
Virginia Beach, VA	28,669	35
Washington, DC	59,896	18

Source: U.S. Bureau of the Census, *Annual Survey of Government Finances 1992,* Washington, D.C.: U.S. Government Printing Office, 1995, n.p. Primary source: U.S. Bureau of the Census.

★2699★

City Government Expenditures

City Government Expenditures, 1991-92, By Function: Environment and Housing (Sewerage)

[In thousands of dollars]

City	Total expenditures	Rank
Albuquerque, NM	59,550	25
Atlanta, GA	48,570	29
Austin, TX	103,011	13
Baltimore, MD	113,871	9
Baton Rouge, LA	43,374	33
Boston, MA	82,902	19
Buffalo, NY	30,484	39
Charlotte, NC	43,777	32
Chicago, IL	102,098	15
Cincinnati, OH	102,216	14
Cleveland, OH	9,029	46
Columbus, OH	96,212	17
Dallas, TX	106,950	11
Denver, CO	38,495	35
Detroit, MI	208,005	4
El Paso, TX	46,493	30
Fort Worth, TX	99,974	16
Honolulu, HI	105,442	12
Houston, TX	234,623	3
Indianapolis, IN	63,702	23
Jacksonville, FL	46,203	31
Kansas City, MO	33,125	38
Los Angeles, CA	249,789	2
Memphis, TN	35,718	37
Miami, FL	14,423	43
Milwaukee, WI	52,022	27
Minneapolis, MN	36,081	36
Nashville-Davidson, TN	66,654	22
New Orleans, LA	69,256	21
New York City, NY	932,961	1
Newark, NJ	27,677	40
Oakland, CA	11,687	44
Oklahoma City, OK	50,205	28
Omaha, NE	23,518	41
Philadelphia, PA	143,194	7
Pittsburgh, PA	3,878	47
Portland, OR	108,520	10
Sacramento, CA	10,069	45
Saint Louis, MO	3,615	48
San Antonio, TX	53,765	26
San Diego, CA	189,717	5
San Francisco, CA	157,455	6
San Jose, CA	86,051	18
Seattle, WA	78,660	20
Toledo, OH	39,361	34
Tulsa, OK	60,751	24
Virginia Beach, VA	16,391	42
Washington, DC	123,000	8

Source: U.S. Bureau of the Census, *Annual Survey of Government Finances 1992,* Washington, D.C.: U.S. Government Printing Office, 1995, n.p. Primary source: U.S. Bureau of the Census.

★2700★
City Government Expenditures

City Government Expenditures, 1991-92, By Function: Environment and Housing (Solid Waste Management)

[In thousands of dollars]

City	Total expenditures	Rank
Albuquerque, NM	21,725	28
Atlanta, GA	24,980	25
Austin, TX	13,603	39
Baltimore, MD	37,323	12
Baton Rouge, LA	21,083	29
Boston, MA	30,940	17
Buffalo, NY	31,247	16
Charlotte, NC	16,678	31
Chicago, IL	144,335	3
Cincinnati, OH	13,476	41
Cleveland, OH	28,866	21
Columbus, OH	24,013	27
Dallas, TX	31,476	15
Denver, CO	13,590	40
Detroit, MI	93,906	5
El Paso, TX	11,241	43
Fort Worth, TX	14,351	37
Honolulu, HI	91,248	6
Houston, TX	35,959	13
Indianapolis, IN	35,355	14
Jacksonville, FL	60,597	8
Kansas City, MO	9,799	45
Los Angeles, CA	179,015	2
Memphis, TN	27,344	22
Miami, FL	29,685	19
Milwaukee, WI	38,279	11
Minneapolis, MN	25,745	24
Nashville-Davidson, TN	14,472	36
New Orleans, LA	19,961	30
New York City, NY	709,946	1
Newark, NJ	30,680	18
Oakland, CA	4,191	48
Oklahoma City, OK	10,190	44
Omaha, NE	9,158	46
Philadelphia, PA	130,281	4
Pittsburgh, PA	16,205	33
Portland, OR	6,942	47
Sacramento, CA	24,705	26
Saint Louis, MO	11,543	42
San Antonio, TX	26,501	23
San Diego, CA	50,677	9
San Francisco, CA	14,665	35
San Jose, CA	16,297	32
Seattle, WA	63,916	7
Toledo, OH	13,916	38
Tulsa, OK	28,906	20
Virginia Beach, VA	15,435	34
Washington, DC	45,802	10

Source: U.S. Bureau of the Census, *Annual Survey of Government Finances 1992*, Washington, D.C.,: U.S. Government Printing Office, 1995, n.p. Primary source: U.S. Bureau of the Census.

★2701★
City Government Expenditures

City Government Expenditures, 1991-92, By Function: Exhibit – Salaries and Wages

[In thousands of dollars]

City	Total expenditures	Rank
Albuquerque, NM	143,694	43
Atlanta, GA	226,041	27
Austin, TX	279,459	23
Baltimore, MD	789,785	8
Baton Rouge, LA	125,973	46
Boston, MA	806,871	7
Buffalo, NY	369,783	16
Charlotte, NC	144,200	42
Chicago, IL	1,574,689	4
Cincinnati, OH	220,102	30
Cleveland, OH	285,330	22
Columbus, OH	223,200	28
Dallas, TX	431,139	13
Denver, CO	369,490	17
Detroit, MI	611,942	9
El Paso, TX	146,158	41
Fort Worth, TX	139,352	44
Honolulu, HI	304,346	21
Houston, TX	562,000	11
Indianapolis, IN	335,599	20
Jacksonville, FL	263,223	26
Kansas City, MO	219,416	31
Los Angeles, CA	2,126,188	2
Memphis, TN	563,361	10
Miami, FL	161,514	37
Milwaukee, WI	268,871	25
Minneapolis, MN	193,776	33
Nashville-Davidson, TN	463,975	12
New Orleans, LA	221,075	29
New York City, NY	15,276,602	1
Newark, NJ	164,364	36
Oakland, CA	169,802	35
Oklahoma City, OK	135,148	45
Omaha, NE	92,107	48
Philadelphia, PA	1,180,521	5
Pittsburgh, PA	157,273	38
Portland, OR	180,763	34
Sacramento, CA	151,500	40
Saint Louis, MO	207,822	32
San Antonio, TX	356,488	18
San Diego, CA	392,653	14
San Francisco, CA	1,171,430	6
San Jose, CA	277,745	24
Seattle, WA	389,800	15
Toledo, OH	103,163	47
Tulsa, OK	156,159	39
Virginia Beach, VA	340,745	19
Washington, DC	1,929,128	3

Source: U.S. Bureau of the Census, *Annual Survey of Government Finances 1992*, Washington, D.C.: U.S. Government Printing Office, 1995, n.p. Primary source: U.S. Bureau of the Census.

★2702★

City Government Expenditures

City Government Expenditures, 1991-92, By Function: General Expenditures, Not Elsewhere Classified

[In thousands of dollars]

City	Total expenditures	Rank
Albuquerque, NM	42,259	27
Atlanta, GA	45,530	25
Austin, TX	34,717	33
Baltimore, MD	79,723	11
Baton Rouge, LA	30,390	37
Boston, MA	124,557	7
Buffalo, NY	76,576	13
Charlotte, NC	67,625	19
Chicago, IL	343,722	5
Cincinnati, OH	40,783	28
Cleveland, OH	33,782	34
Columbus, OH	19,590	43
Dallas, TX	37,324	32
Denver, CO	85,372	10
Detroit, MI	273,981	6
El Paso, TX	7,836	48
Fort Worth, TX	25,809	40
Honolulu, HI	109,123	8
Houston, TX	75,517	15
Indianapolis, IN	48,359	23
Jacksonville, FL	38,581	31
Kansas City, MO	32,421	35
Los Angeles, CA	450,541	2
Memphis, TN	44,867	26
Miami, FL	16,899	45
Milwaukee, WI	68,564	17
Minneapolis, MN	48,600	22
Nashville-Davidson, TN	38,624	30
New Orleans, LA	24,673	41
New York City, NY	3,342,387	1
Newark, NJ	78,968	12
Oakland, CA	75,743	14
Oklahoma City, OK	26,919	39
Omaha, NE	23,551	42
Philadelphia, PA	373,171	4
Pittsburgh, PA	102,295	9
Portland, OR	46,699	24
Sacramento, CA	27,683	38
Saint Louis, MO	40,078	29
San Antonio, TX	52,095	21
San Diego, CA	67,941	18
San Francisco, CA	72,809	16
San Jose, CA	17,013	44
Seattle, WA	66,218	20
Toledo, OH	9,266	46
Tulsa, OK	32,405	36
Virginia Beach, VA	7,872	47
Washington, DC	441,497	3

Source: U.S. Bureau of the Census, *Annual Survey of Government Finances 1992*, Washington, D.C.: U.S. Government Printing Office, 1995, n.p. Primary source: U.S. Bureau of the Census.

★2703★

City Government Expenditures

City Government Expenditures, 1991-92, By Function: Governmental Administration (Financial)

[In thousands of dollars]

City	Total expenditures	Rank
Albuquerque, NM	11,724	29
Atlanta, GA	16,407	23
Austin, TX	6,408	45
Baltimore, MD	42,146	8
Baton Rouge, LA	10,061	36
Boston, MA	24,883	12
Buffalo, NY	9,411	38
Charlotte, NC	10,903	32
Chicago, IL	61,526	3
Cincinnati, OH	16,037	24
Cleveland, OH	11,937	28
Columbus, OH	12,812	26
Dallas, TX	17,925	19
Denver, CO	22,594	14
Detroit, MI	48,088	6
El Paso, TX	7,202	43
Fort Worth, TX	10,322	35
Honolulu, HI	39,970	9
Houston, TX	32,495	11
Indianapolis, IN	38,150	10
Jacksonville, FL	16,422	22
Kansas City, MO	20,141	17
Los Angeles, CA	101,972	2
Memphis, TN	7,856	42
Miami, FL	10,605	33
Milwaukee, WI	19,609	18
Minneapolis, MN	6,825	44
Nashville-Davidson, TN	11,141	31
New Orleans, LA	21,710	15
New York City, NY	255,473	1
Newark, NJ	8,786	41
Oakland, CA	10,577	34
Oklahoma City, OK	4,939	47
Omaha, NE	4,667	48
Philadelphia, PA	53,640	5
Pittsburgh, PA	11,627	30
Portland, OR	16,975	20
Sacramento, CA	9,248	39
Saint Louis, MO	16,920	21
San Antonio, TX	9,655	37
San Diego, CA	20,199	16
San Francisco, CA	43,039	7
San Jose, CA	14,404	25
Seattle, WA	23,778	13
Toledo, OH	5,450	46
Tulsa, OK	8,896	40
Virginia Beach, VA	12,800	27
Washington, DC	55,601	4

Source: U.S. Bureau of the Census, *Annual Survey of Government Finances 1992*, Washington, D.C.: U.S. Government Printing Office, 1995, n.p. Primary source: U.S. Bureau of the Census.

★2704★

City Government Expenditures

City Government Expenditures, 1991-92, By Function: Governmental Administration (Judicial and Legal)

[In thousands of dollars]

City	Total expenditures	Rank
Albuquerque, NM	2,783	43
Atlanta, GA	13,946	21
Austin, TX	6,724	28
Baltimore, MD	27,769	9
Baton Rouge, LA	20,477	16
Boston, MA	12,080	22
Buffalo, NY	2,846	42
Charlotte, NC	822	48
Chicago, IL	19,057	17
Cincinnati, OH	3,845	39
Cleveland, OH	21,895	14
Columbus, OH	17,868	18
Dallas, TX	11,427	23
Denver, CO	26,085	11
Detroit, MI	37,708	6
El Paso, TX	5,061	34
Fort Worth, TX	4,377	38
Honolulu, HI	21,573	15
Houston, TX	26,335	10
Indianapolis, IN	28,534	8
Jacksonville, FL	17,784	19
Kansas City, MO	7,118	26
Los Angeles, CA	49,665	5
Memphis, TN	4,647	37
Miami, FL	3,003	41
Milwaukee, WI	7,090	27
Minneapolis, MN	5,455	31
Nashville-Davidson, TN	25,682	12
New Orleans, LA	28,713	7
New York City, NY	438,970	1
Newark, NJ	5,339	33
Oakland, CA	4,789	36
Oklahoma City, OK	6,363	29
Omaha, NE	1,793	47
Philadelphia, PA	164,177	2
Pittsburgh, PA	2,766	44
Portland, OR	2,577	45
Sacramento, CA	2,109	46
Saint Louis, MO	5,464	30
San Antonio, TX	7,589	25
San Diego, CA	14,546	20
San Francisco, CA	91,151	4
San Jose, CA	4,843	35
Seattle, WA	24,748	13
Toledo, OH	8,058	24
Tulsa, OK	3,159	40
Virginia Beach, VA	5,398	32
Washington, DC	127,975	3

Source: U.S. Bureau of the Census, *Annual Survey of Government Finances 1992*, Washington, D.C.: U.S. Government Printing Office, 1995, n.p. Primary source: U.S. Bureau of the Census.

★2705★

City Government Expenditures

City Government Expenditures, 1991-92, By Function: Governmental Administration (Other Governmental Administration)

[In thousands of dollars]

City	Total expenditures	Rank
Albuquerque, NM	6,733	31
Atlanta, GA	8,642	23
Austin, TX	5,346	39
Baltimore, MD	11,949	16
Baton Rouge, LA	5,379	38
Boston, MA	8,074	25
Buffalo, NY	3,820	44
Charlotte, NC	7,503	29
Chicago, IL	37,757	3
Cincinnati, OH	5,714	36
Cleveland, OH	7,507	28
Columbus, OH	7,923	27
Dallas, TX	9,505	21
Denver, CO	11,403	17
Detroit, MI	29,823	6
El Paso, TX	3,460	45
Fort Worth, TX	3,944	43
Honolulu, HI	18,623	11
Houston, TX	20,373	9
Indianapolis, IN	17,262	12
Jacksonville, FL	9,234	22
Kansas City, MO	7,117	30
Los Angeles, CA	65,749	2
Memphis, TN	4,224	42
Miami, FL	8,053	26
Milwaukee, WI	6,497	33
Minneapolis, MN	8,550	24
Nashville-Davidson, TN	6,010	35
New Orleans, LA	13,949	15
New York City, NY	162,393	1
Newark, NJ	9,899	20
Oakland, CA	14,873	14
Oklahoma City, OK	4,397	41
Omaha, NE	2,780	47
Philadelphia, PA	32,496	5
Pittsburgh, PA	10,274	18
Portland, OR	9,948	19
Sacramento, CA	5,336	40
Saint Louis, MO	5,464	37
San Antonio, TX	6,597	32
San Diego, CA	22,350	8
San Francisco, CA	26,095	7
San Jose, CA	16,092	13
Seattle, WA	18,642	10
Toledo, OH	2,181	48
Tulsa, OK	3,205	46
Virginia Beach, VA	6,440	34
Washington, DC	36,471	4

Source: U.S. Bureau of the Census, *Annual Survey of Government Finances 1992*, Washington, D.C.: U.S. Government Printing Office, 1995, n.p. Primary source: U.S. Bureau of the Census.

★2706★
City Government Expenditures
City Government Expenditures, 1991-92, By Function: Health

[In thousands of dollars]

City	Total expenditures	Rank
Albuquerque, NM	7,066	33
Atlanta, GA	0	45
Austin, TX	37,211	10
Baltimore, MD	57,736	8
Baton Rouge, LA	6,145	35
Boston, MA	1,006	42
Buffalo, NY	1,876	39
Charlotte, NC	2,988	37
Chicago, IL	97,037	6
Cincinnati, OH	32,368	11
Cleveland, OH	10,448	29
Columbus, OH	22,543	13
Dallas, TX	18,616	16
Denver, CO	47,153	9
Detroit, MI	97,504	5
El Paso, TX	14,721	21
Fort Worth, TX	10,583	28
Honolulu, HI	8,817	31
Houston, TX	58,721	7
Indianapolis, IN	31,619	12
Jacksonville, FL	16,202	19
Kansas City, MO	12,024	26
Los Angeles, CA	10,943	27
Memphis, TN	6,967	34
Miami, FL	75	44
Milwaukee, WI	12,321	25
Minneapolis, MN	9,948	30
Nashville-Davidson, TN	21,589	14
New Orleans, LA	14,234	22
New York City, NY	473,263	1
Newark, NJ	12,721	24
Oakland, CA	0	45
Oklahoma City, OK	1,125	41
Omaha, NE	909	43
Philadelphia, PA	286,544	2
Pittsburgh, PA	7,117	32
Portland, OR	0	45
Sacramento, CA	2,082	38
Saint Louis, MO	15,306	20
San Antonio, TX	17,832	17
San Diego, CA	1,732	40
San Francisco, CA	240,020	3
San Jose, CA	0	45
Seattle, WA	13,509	23
Toledo, OH	5,486	36
Tulsa, OK	18,754	15
Virginia Beach, VA	16,812	18
Washington, DC	167,682	4

Source: U.S. Bureau of the Census, *Annual Survey of Government Finances 1992,* Washington, D.C.: U.S. Government Printing Office, 1995, n.p. Primary source: U.S. Bureau of the Census.

★2707★
City Government Expenditures
City Government Expenditures, 1991-92, By Function: Hospitals

[In thousands of dollars]

City	Total expenditures	Rank
Austin, TX	58,157	8
Baton Rouge, LA	24,570	11
Boston, MA	236,176	4
Charlotte, NC	3,172,256	1
Dallas, TX	104,834	6
Denver, CO	86,940	7
Indianapolis, IN	144,647	5
Jacksonville, FL	17,772	12
Kansas City, MO	29,175	10
Nashville-Davidson, TN	9,210	14
Pittsburgh, PA	48,540	9
Saint Louis, MO	15,400	13
San Francisco, CA	308,732	3
Washington, DC	367,468	2

Source: U.S. Bureau of the Census, *Annual Survey of Government Finances 1992,* Washington, D.C.: U.S. Government Printing Office, 1995, n.p. Primary source: U.S. Bureau of the Census.

★2708★
City Government Expenditures
City Government Expenditures, 1991-92, By Function: Interest on General Debt

[In thousands of dollars]

City	Total expenditures	Rank
Albuquerque, NM	85,350	20
Atlanta, GA	96,468	16
Austin, TX	99,995	14
Baltimore, MD	90,850	19
Baton Rouge, LA	58,931	27
Boston, MA	52,914	31
Buffalo, NY	25,182	40
Charlotte, NC	59,676	26
Chicago, IL	356,239	2
Cincinnati, OH	12,526	48
Cleveland, OH	21,735	44
Columbus, OH	58,155	28
Dallas, TX	201,619	6
Denver, CO	202,929	5
Detroit, MI	81,185	21
El Paso, TX	27,372	38
Fort Worth, TX	54,655	29
Honolulu, HI	61,610	25
Houston, TX	170,640	8
Indianapolis, IN	53,215	30
Jacksonville, FL	144,894	11
Kansas City, MO	45,672	32
Los Angeles, CA	298,295	3
Memphis, TN	23,344	41
Miami, FL	33,189	36
Milwaukee, WI	35,729	35

[Continued]

★2708★

City Government Expenditures, 1991-92, By Function: Interest on General Debt
[Continued]

City	Total expenditures	Rank
Minneapolis, MN	163,903	9
Nashville-Davidson, TN	115,288	13
New Orleans, LA	93,950	17
New York City, NY	1,696,710	1
Newark, NJ	13,038	47
Oakland, CA	73,861	23
Oklahoma City, OK	26,096	39
Omaha, NE	14,472	45
Philadelphia, PA	147,977	10
Pittsburgh, PA	44,618	33
Portland, OR	42,735	34
Sacramento, CA	21,921	43
Saint Louis, MO	66,304	24
San Antonio, TX	91,897	18
San Diego, CA	132,132	12
San Francisco, CA	183,077	7
San Jose, CA	81,179	22
Seattle, WA	22,206	42
Toledo, OH	13,228	46
Tulsa, OK	99,436	15
Virginia Beach, VA	31,764	37
Washington, DC	236,241	4

Source: U.S. Bureau of the Census, *Annual Survey of Government Finances 1992*, Washington, D.C.: U.S. Government Printing Office, 1995, n.p. Primary source: U.S. Bureau of the Census.

★2709★

City Government Expenditures

City Government Expenditures, 1991-92, By Function: Other Hospitals
[In thousands of dollars]

City	Total expenditures	Rank
Indianapolis, IN	2,634	9
Jacksonville, FL	17,772	5
Kansas City, MO	29,175	4
Memphis, TN	9,210	8
New York City, NY	463,303	1
Philadelphia, PA	48,540	2
Saint Louis, MO	15,400	6
San Francisco, CA	30,936	3
Washington, DC	10,151	7

Source: U.S. Bureau of the Census, *Annual Survey of Government Finances 1992*, Washington, D.C.: U.S. Government Printing Office, 1995, n.p. Primary source: U.S. Bureau of the Census.

★2710★

City Government Expenditures

City Government Expenditures, 1991-92, By Function: Other Social Services Functions
[In thousands of dollars]

City	Total expenditures	Rank
Albuquerque, NM	4,600	15
Atlanta, GA	422	24
Austin, TX	916	21
Baltimore, MD	1,829	17
Baton Rouge, LA	1,046	18
Boston, MA	774	22
Buffalo, NY	0	28
Charlotte, NC	525	23
Chicago, IL	109,556	5
Cincinnati, OH	0	28
Cleveland, OH	0	28
Columbus, OH	0	28
Dallas, TX	0	28
Denver, CO	52,317	6
Detroit, MI	0	28
El Paso, TX	222	25
Fort Worth, TX	0	28
Honolulu, HI	0	28
Houston, TX	0	28
Indianapolis, IN	25,479	8
Jacksonville, FL	12,481	11
Kansas City, MO	29,175	7
Los Angeles, CA	0	28
Memphis, TN	0	28
Miami, FL	1,043	19
Milwaukee, WI	0	28
Minneapolis, MN	0	28
Nashville-Davidson, TN	9,607	14
New Orleans, LA	3,655	16
New York City, NY	2,816,109	1
Newark, NJ	14,908	10
Oakland, CA	1,033	20
Oklahoma City, OK	0	28
Omaha, NE	0	28
Philadelphia, PA	208,154	2
Pittsburgh, PA	30	27
Portland, OR	0	28
Sacramento, CA	0	28
Saint Louis, MO	15,400	9
San Antonio, TX	12,074	12
San Diego, CA	153	26
San Francisco, CA	137,616	4
San Jose, CA	0	28
Seattle, WA	0	28
Toledo, OH	0	28
Tulsa, OK	0	28
Virginia Beach, VA	9,611	13
Washington, DC	191,886	3

Source: U.S. Bureau of the Census, *Annual Survey of Government Finances 1992*, Washington, D.C.: U.S. Government Printing Office, 1995, n.p. Primary source: U.S. Bureau of the Census.

★2711★
City Government Expenditures

City Government Expenditures, 1991-92, By Function: Public Safety (Corrections)

[In thousands of dollars]

City	Total expenditures	Rank
Albuquerque, NM	15,416	12
Atlanta, GA	12,574	14
Austin, TX	0	36
Baltimore, MD	4,919	22
Baton Rouge, LA	12,924	13
Boston, MA	42,216	6
Buffalo, NY	0	36
Charlotte, NC	0	36
Chicago, IL	0	36
Cincinnati, OH	287	33
Cleveland, OH	5,315	21
Columbus, OH	9,595	17
Dallas, TX	3,542	23
Denver, CO	32,773	8
Detroit, MI	656	31
El Paso, TX	50	34
Fort Worth, TX	0	36
Honolulu, HI	0	36
Houston, TX	12,299	15
Indianapolis, IN	26,690	10
Jacksonville, FL	40,412	7
Kansas City, MO	3,283	24
Los Angeles, CA	1,136	30
Memphis, TN	0	36
Miami, FL	0	36
Milwaukee, WI	0	36
Minneapolis, MN	2,291	25
Nashville-Davidson, TN	30,709	9
New Orleans, LA	44,173	5
New York City, NY	1,053,535	1
Newark, NJ	0	36
Oakland, CA	5,447	20
Oklahoma City, OK	1,676	27
Omaha, NE	2,063	26
Philadelphia, PA	140,329	3
Pittsburgh, PA	0	36
Portland, OR	0	36
Sacramento, CA	3	35
Saint Louis, MO	18,767	11
San Antonio, TX	1,188	29
San Diego, CA	1,357	28
San Francisco, CA	50,388	4
San Jose, CA	0	36
Seattle, WA	8,169	18
Toledo, OH	6,925	19
Tulsa, OK	302	32
Virginia Beach, VA	10,571	16
Washington, DC	318,316	2

Source: U.S. Bureau of the Census, *Annual Survey of Government Finances 1992,* Washington, D.C.: U.S. Government Printing Office, 1995, n.p. Primary source: U.S. Bureau of the Census.

★2712★
City Government Expenditures

City Government Expenditures, 1991-92, By Function: Public Safety (Fire Protection)

[In thousands of dollars]

City	Total expenditures	Rank
Albuquerque, NM	28,611	43
Atlanta, GA	38,809	34
Austin, TX	35,423	37
Baltimore, MD	83,634	10
Baton Rouge, LA	20,274	47
Boston, MA	86,289	9
Buffalo, NY	41,405	29
Charlotte, NC	33,175	39
Chicago, IL	230,546	3
Cincinnati, OH	49,855	22
Cleveland, OH	67,329	13
Columbus, OH	67,063	14
Dallas, TX	75,468	11
Denver, CO	53,118	21
Detroit, MI	92,644	8
El Paso, TX	22,514	46
Fort Worth, TX	32,046	40
Honolulu, HI	43,659	27
Houston, TX	147,467	4
Indianapolis, IN	37,872	35
Jacksonville, FL	55,505	18
Kansas City, MO	40,781	30
Los Angeles, CA	265,371	2
Memphis, TN	58,652	17
Miami, FL	45,545	25
Milwaukee, WI	53,718	20
Minneapolis, MN	29,419	42
Nashville-Davidson, TN	38,980	33
New Orleans, LA	37,388	36
New York City, NY	699,223	1
Newark, NJ	44,166	26
Oakland, CA	39,667	31
Oklahoma City, OK	47,982	23
Omaha, NE	25,201	45
Philadelphia, PA	123,300	5
Pittsburgh, PA	43,192	28
Portland, OR	47,663	24
Sacramento, CA	39,570	32
Saint Louis, MO	25,519	44
San Antonio, TX	65,622	15
San Diego, CA	74,907	12
San Francisco, CA	101,188	6
San Jose, CA	54,781	19
Seattle, WA	62,356	16
Toledo, OH	31,001	41
Tulsa, OK	34,361	38
Virginia Beach, VA	19,329	48
Washington, DC	96,841	7

Source: U.S. Bureau of the Census, *Annual Survey of Government Finances 1992,* Washington, D.C.: U.S. Government Printing Office, 1995, n.p. Primary source: U.S. Bureau of the Census.

★2713★

City Government Expenditures

City Government Expenditures, 1991-92, By Function: Public Safety (Police Protection)

[In thousands of dollars]

City	Total expenditures	Rank
Albuquerque, NM	55,453	38
Atlanta, GA	73,793	29
Austin, TX	51,824	41
Baltimore, MD	153,896	11
Baton Rouge, LA	39,178	47
Boston, MA	137,225	12
Buffalo, NY	55,102	39
Charlotte, NC	42,838	44
Chicago, IL	627,396	3
Cincinnati, OH	65,448	34
Cleveland, OH	122,576	14
Columbus, OH	126,938	13
Dallas, TX	168,012	9
Denver, CO	91,668	20
Detroit, MI	289,563	5
El Paso, TX	42,725	45
Fort Worth, TX	52,526	40
Honolulu, HI	114,062	16
Houston, TX	268,695	7
Indianapolis, IN	87,927	21
Jacksonville, FL	78,187	24
Kansas City, MO	78,107	25
Los Angeles, CA	650,386	2
Memphis, TN	73,907	28
Miami, FL	87,582	23
Milwaukee, WI	118,138	15
Minneapolis, MN	55,944	37
Nashville-Davidson, TN	63,629	35
New Orleans, LA	77,291	26
New York City, NY	1,872,326	1
Newark, NJ	65,865	33
Oakland, CA	74,531	27
Oklahoma City, OK	67,515	32
Omaha, NE	32,667	48
Philadelphia, PA	344,831	4
Pittsburgh, PA	57,567	36
Portland, OR	71,494	31
Sacramento, CA	73,201	30
Saint Louis, MO	87,808	22
San Antonio, TX	99,049	18
San Diego, CA	168,469	8
San Francisco, CA	164,092	10
San Jose, CA	110,401	17
Seattle, WA	94,670	19
Toledo, OH	46,131	43
Tulsa, OK	46,313	42
Virginia Beach, VA	41,138	46
Washington, DC	272,749	6

Source: U.S. Bureau of the Census, *Annual Survey of Government Finances 1992*, Washington, D.C.: U.S. Government Printing Office, 1995, n.p. Primary source: U.S. Bureau of the Census.

★2714★

City Government Expenditures

City Government Expenditures, 1991-92, By Function: Public Safety (Protective Inspections and Regulations)

[In thousands of dollars]

City	Total expenditures	Rank
Albuquerque, NM	4,688	27
Atlanta, GA	4,265	29
Austin, TX	1,320	45
Baltimore, MD	3,539	34
Baton Rouge, LA	2,840	37
Boston, MA	9,639	14
Buffalo, NY	3,716	32
Charlotte, NC	993	46
Chicago, IL	23,439	4
Cincinnati, OH	5,562	22
Cleveland, OH	271	48
Columbus, OH	6,096	20
Dallas, TX	6,117	19
Denver, CO	5,311	25
Detroit, MI	18,364	6
El Paso, TX	3,451	35
Fort Worth, TX	3,269	36
Honolulu, HI	5,387	24
Houston, TX	11,079	11
Indianapolis, IN	5,544	23
Jacksonville, FL	4,840	26
Kansas City, MO	3,743	31
Los Angeles, CA	71,742	2
Memphis, TN	2,777	38
Miami, FL	3,606	33
Milwaukee, WI	16,090	8
Minneapolis, MN	10,009	13
Nashville-Davidson, TN	3,979	30
New Orleans, LA	8,883	15
New York City, NY	116,333	1
Newark, NJ	721	47
Oakland, CA	6,535	18
Oklahoma City, OK	1,412	44
Omaha, NE	1,847	43
Philadelphia, PA	17,457	7
Pittsburgh, PA	2,051	41
Portland, OR	10,407	12
Sacramento, CA	5,739	21
Saint Louis, MO	7,682	16
San Antonio, TX	4,581	28
San Diego, CA	12,481	10
San Francisco, CA	14,050	9
San Jose, CA	6,828	17
Seattle, WA	19,435	5
Toledo, OH	1,930	42
Tulsa, OK	2,764	39
Virginia Beach, VA	2,491	40
Washington, DC	47,010	3

Source: U.S. Bureau of the Census, *Annual Survey of Government Finances 1992*, Washington, D.C.: U.S. Government Printing Office, 1995, n.p. Primary source: U.S. Bureau of the Census.

★2715★
City Government Expenditures
City Government Expenditures, 1991-92, By Function: Public Welfare

[In thousands of dollars]

City	Total expenditures	Rank
Albuquerque, NM	45,389	8
Atlanta, GA	437	22
Austin, TX	916	20
Baltimore, MD	1,829	16
Baton Rouge, LA	1,046	18
Boston, MA	26,453	9
Buffalo, NY	0	28
Charlotte, NC	525	21
Chicago, IL	109,556	6
Cincinnati, OH	0	28
Cleveland, OH	36	25
Columbus, OH	0	28
Dallas, TX	0	28
Denver, CO	133,074	5
Detroit, MI	0	28
El Paso, TX	222	23
Fort Worth, TX	0	28
Honolulu, HI	0	28
Houston, TX	0	28
Indianapolis, IN	76,932	7
Jacksonville, FL	16,544	10
Kansas City, MO	0	28
Los Angeles, CA	0	28
Memphis, TN	0	28
Miami, FL	1,050	17
Milwaukee, WI	0	28
Minneapolis, MN	0	28
Nashville-Davidson, TN	11,419	13
New Orleans, LA	5,689	14
New York City, NY	6,840,102	1
Newark, NJ	0	28
Oakland, CA	1,033	19
Oklahoma City, OK	0	28
Omaha, NE	3,896	15
Philadelphia, PA	212,551	4
Pittsburgh, PA	30	26
Portland, OR	0	28
Sacramento, CA	0	28
Saint Louis, MO	13	27
San Antonio, TX	12,074	12
San Diego, CA	153	24
San Francisco, CA	313,313	3
San Jose, CA	0	28
Seattle, WA	0	28
Toledo, OH	0	28
Tulsa, OK	0	28
Virginia Beach, VA	15,409	11
Washington, DC	872,042	2

Source: U.S. Bureau of the Census, *Annual Survey of Government Finances 1992,* Washington, D.C.: U.S. Government Printing Office, 1995, n.p. Primary source: U.S. Bureau of the Census.

★2716★
City Government Expenditures
City Government Expenditures, 1991-92, By Function: Public Welfare (Categorical Cash Assistance)

[In thousands of dollars]

City	Total expenditures	Rank
Boston, MA	24,000	6
Denver, CO	57,658	4
Indianapolis, IN	41,420	5
Nashville-Davidson, TN	381	7
New York City, NY	3,138,179	1
San Francisco, CA	90,539	3
Virginia Beach, VA	13	8
Washington, DC	110,765	2

Source: U.S. Bureau of the Census, *Annual Survey of Government Finances 1992,* Washington, D.C.: U.S. Government Printing Office, 1995, n.p. Primary source: U.S. Bureau of the Census.

★2717★
City Government Expenditures
City Government Expenditures, 1991-92, By Function: Public Welfare (Other Cash Assistance)

[In thousands of dollars]

City	Total expenditures	Rank
Boston, MA	1,679	6
Denver, CO	549	7
Jacksonville, FL	4,063	5
Miami, FL	7	9
New York City, NY	642,087	1
Newark, NJ	17,711	4
San Francisco, CA	47,148	2
Virginia Beach, VA	476	8
Washington, DC	18,870	3

Source: U.S. Bureau of the Census, *Annual Survey of Government Finances 1992,* Washington, D.C.: U.S. Government Printing Office, 1995, n.p. Primary source: U.S. Bureau of the Census.

★2718★
City Government Expenditures
City Government Expenditures, 1991-92, By Function: Public Welfare (Vendor Payments - Medical)

[In thousands of dollars]

City	Total expenditures	Rank
Denver, CO	19	6
Nashville-Davidson, TN	594	4
Newark, NJ	11,123	2
Saint Louis, MO	1,435	3

[Continued]

★2718★

City Government Expenditures, 1991-92, By Function: Public Welfare (Vendor Payments – Medical)

[Continued]

City	Total expenditures	Rank
Virginia Beach, VA	96	5
Washington, DC	514,987	1

Source: U.S. Bureau of the Census, *Annual Survey of Government Finances 1992*, Washington, D.C.: U.S. Government Printing Office, 1995, n.p. Primary source: U.S. Bureau of the Census.

★2719★

City Government Expenditures

City Government Expenditures, 1991-92, By Function: Public Welfare (Vendor Payments – Other)

[In thousands of dollars]

City	Total expenditures	Rank
Atlanta, GA	15	8
Indianapolis, IN	1,523	5
Nashville-Davidson, TN	837	6
New York City, NY	243,727	1
Newark, NJ	1,647	4
Philadelphia, PA	212	7
Virginia Beach, VA	5,213	3
Washington, DC	6,660	2

Source: U.S. Bureau of the Census, *Annual Survey of Government Finances 1992*, Washington, D.C.: U.S. Government Printing Office, 1995, n.p. Primary source: U.S. Bureau of the Census.

★2720★

City Government Expenditures

City Government Expenditures, 1991-92, By Function: Public Welfare (Welfare Institutions)

[In thousands of dollars]

City	Total expenditures	Rank
Cleveland, OH	36	5
Indianapolis, IN	8,510	2
New Orleans, LA	2,034	4
Philadelphia, PA	4,185	3
Washington, DC	28,874	1

Source: U.S. Bureau of the Census, *Annual Survey of Government Finances 1992*, Washington, D.C.: U.S. Government Printing Office, 1995, n.p. Primary source: U.S. Bureau of the Census.

★2721★

City Government Expenditures

City Government Expenditures, 1991-92, By Function: Transportation (Air Transportation)

[In thousands of dollars]

City	Total expenditures	Rank
Albuquerque, NM	22,770	22
Atlanta, GA	111,281	8
Austin, TX	15,331	24
Baltimore, MD	0	32
Baton Rouge, LA	11,388	25
Boston, MA	0	32
Buffalo, NY	0	32
Charlotte, NC	44,048	13
Chicago, IL	386,708	3
Cincinnati, OH	2,436	28
Cleveland, OH	45,912	12
Columbus, OH	22,382	23
Dallas, TX	476,418	1
Denver, CO	468,718	2
Detroit, MI	5,369	27
El Paso, TX	11,098	26
Fort Worth, TX	28,998	20
Honolulu, HI	0	32
Houston, TX	115,465	7
Indianapolis, IN	49,626	11
Jacksonville, FL	40,698	15
Kansas City, MO	53,766	10
Los Angeles, CA	223,418	4
Memphis, TN	0	32
Miami, FL	0	32
Milwaukee, WI	0	32
Minneapolis, MN	0	32
Nashville-Davidson, TN	178	30
New Orleans, LA	43,505	14
New York City, NY	0	32
Newark, NJ	0	32
Oakland, CA	29,983	19
Oklahoma City, OK	34,479	18
Omaha, NE	0	32
Philadelphia, PA	124,166	6
Pittsburgh, PA	0	32
Portland, OR	0	32
Sacramento, CA	82	31
Saint Louis, MO	87,062	9
San Antonio, TX	28,212	21
San Diego, CA	1,719	29
San Francisco, CA	126,215	5
San Jose, CA	38,348	16
Seattle, WA	0	32
Toledo, OH	0	32
Tulsa, OK	38,138	17
Virginia Beach, VA	0	32
Washington, DC	0	32

Source: U.S. Bureau of the Census, *Annual Survey of Government Finances 1992*, Washington, D.C.: U.S. Government Printing Office, 1995, n.p. Primary source: U.S. Bureau of the Census.

★2722★

City Government Expenditures

City Government Expenditures, 1991-92, By Function: Transportation (Highways)

[In thousands of dollars]

City	Total expenditures	Rank
Albuquerque, NM	37,738	34
Atlanta, GA	25,147	40
Austin, TX	21,950	42
Baltimore, MD	144,406	4
Baton Rouge, LA	41,218	31
Boston, MA	50,900	20
Buffalo, NY	20,524	45
Charlotte, NC	52,980	16
Chicago, IL	364,677	2
Cincinnati, OH	44,316	28
Cleveland, OH	48,181	25
Columbus, OH	52,943	17
Dallas, TX	63,404	13
Denver, CO	64,943	10
Detroit, MI	100,167	7
El Paso, TX	23,622	41
Fort Worth, TX	52,089	18
Honolulu, HI	43,925	29
Houston, TX	128,175	5
Indianapolis, IN	49,199	22
Jacksonville, FL	44,720	27
Kansas City, MO	50,693	21
Los Angeles, CA	153,393	3
Memphis, TN	36,547	35
Miami, FL	9,087	47
Milwaukee, WI	46,419	26
Minneapolis, MN	49,071	23
Nashville-Davidson, TN	35,156	36
New Orleans, LA	38,564	33
New York City, NY	795,275	1
Newark, NJ	5,780	48
Oakland, CA	16,533	46
Oklahoma City, OK	40,908	32
Omaha, NE	29,968	37
Philadelphia, PA	95,194	8
Pittsburgh, PA	21,694	43
Portland, OR	64,135	11
Sacramento, CA	48,782	24
Saint Louis, MO	20,869	44
San Antonio, TX	53,053	15
San Diego, CA	76,374	9
San Francisco, CA	42,036	30
San Jose, CA	63,949	12
Seattle, WA	51,173	19
Toledo, OH	27,833	38
Tulsa, OK	27,728	39
Virginia Beach, VA	55,843	14
Washington, DC	121,644	6

Source: U.S. Bureau of the Census, *Annual Survey of Government Finances 1992*, Washington, D.C.: U.S. Government Printing Office, 1995, n.p. Primary source: U.S. Bureau of the Census.

★2723★

City Government Expenditures

City Government Expenditures, 1991-92, By Function: Transportation (Parking Facilities)

[In thousands of dollars]

City	Total expenditures	Rank
Albuquerque, NM	1,617	27
Atlanta, GA	0	43
Austin, TX	0	43
Baltimore, MD	155,621	1
Baton Rouge, LA	415	37
Boston, MA	842	30
Buffalo, NY	5,968	10
Charlotte, NC	733	32
Chicago, IL	1,974	26
Cincinnati, OH	5,614	11
Cleveland, OH	3,869	19
Columbus, OH	470	35
Dallas, TX	2,297	22
Denver, CO	5,151	14
Detroit, MI	9,399	6
El Paso, TX	101	41
Fort Worth, TX	182	40
Honolulu, HI	2,044	25
Houston, TX	0	43
Indianapolis, IN	5,293	13
Jacksonville, FL	2,501	21
Kansas City, MO	6,678	9
Los Angeles, CA	7,952	7
Memphis, TN	55	42
Miami, FL	7,030	8
Milwaukee, WI	5,541	12
Minneapolis, MN	64,687	2
Nashville-Davidson, TN	338	38
New Orleans, LA	4,100	17
New York City, NY	24,994	3
Newark, NJ	0	43
Oakland, CA	4,064	18
Oklahoma City, OK	2,151	24
Omaha, NE	766	31
Philadelphia, PA	0	43
Pittsburgh, PA	0	43
Portland, OR	4,171	16
Sacramento, CA	18,345	4
Saint Louis, MO	3,661	20
San Antonio, TX	2,160	23
San Diego, CA	693	34
San Francisco, CA	14,149	5
San Jose, CA	4,410	15
Seattle, WA	445	36
Toledo, OH	728	33
Tulsa, OK	1,551	28
Virginia Beach, VA	252	39
Washington, DC	1,143	29

Source: U.S. Bureau of the Census, *Annual Survey of Government Finances 1992*, Washington, D.C.: U.S. Government Printing Office, 1995, n.p. Primary source: U.S. Bureau of the Census.

★2724★
City Government Expenditures

City Government Expenditures, 1991-92, By Function: Transportation (Transit Subsidies)

[In thousands of dollars]

City	Total expenditures	Rank
Boston, MA	50,244	5
Buffalo, NY	350	14
Chicago, IL	45,641	6
Cincinnati, OH	22,559	7
Jacksonville, FL	10,413	10
Kansas City, MO	21,052	8
Los Angeles, CA	82,169	3
New Orleans, LA	3,600	11
New York City, NY	504,916	1
Philadelphia, PA	50,347	4
Sacramento, CA	650	13
Saint Louis, MO	15,763	9
Virginia Beach, VA	956	12
Washington, DC	162,327	2

Source: U.S. Bureau of the Census, *Annual Survey of Government Finances 1992*, Washington, D.C.: U.S. Government Printing Office, 1995, n.p. Primary source: U.S. Bureau of the Census.

★2725★
City Government Expenditures

City Government Expenditures, 1991-92, By Function: Transportation (Water Transportation and Terminals)

[In thousands of dollars]

City	Total expenditures	Rank
Baltimore, MD	405	11
Cleveland, OH	50	14
Dallas, TX	34	15
Jacksonville, FL	29,434	2
Los Angeles, CA	117,769	1
Memphis, TN	1,102	8
Milwaukee, WI	3,402	6
Minneapolis, MN	1,481	7
New Orleans, LA	623	10
New York City, NY	14,290	5
Oakland, CA	21,954	4
Omaha, NE	82	13
Philadelphia, PA	4	16
Sacramento, CA	395	12
Saint Louis, MO	813	9
San Francisco, CA	25,736	3

Source: U.S. Bureau of the Census, *Annual Survey of Government Finances 1992*, Washington, D.C.: U.S. Government Printing Office, 1995, n.p. ????????? PS U.S. Bureau of the Census.

★2726★
City Government Expenditures

City Government Expenditures, 1991-92, By Function: Utility and Liquor Store Expenditures

[In thousands of dollars]

City	Total expenditures	Rank
Albuquerque, NM	69,815	24
Atlanta, GA	81,845	20
Austin, TX	478,325	9
Baltimore, MD	46,387	32
Baton Rouge, LA	5,967	45
Boston, MA	57,371	28
Buffalo, NY	17,006	42
Charlotte, NC	61,140	27
Chicago, IL	197,549	15
Cincinnati, OH	80,747	21
Cleveland, OH	251,600	12
Columbus, OH	128,952	18
Dallas, TX	145,657	17
Denver, CO	112,513	19
Detroit, MI	305,010	11
El Paso, TX	73,832	23
Fort Worth, TX	64,559	25
Honolulu, HI	208,934	14
Houston, TX	238,372	13
Indianapolis, IN	24,391	40
Jacksonville, FL	866,942	3
Kansas City, MO	62,030	26
Los Angeles, CA	2,410,819	2
Memphis, TN	818,992	5
Miami, FL	0	46
Milwaukee, WI	36,561	34
Minneapolis, MN	29,311	37
Nashville-Davidson, TN	628,504	6
New Orleans, LA	54,473	29
New York City, NY	4,689,509	1
Newark, NJ	34,332	35
Oakland, CA	0	46
Oklahoma City, OK	49,109	31
Omaha, NE	0	46
Philadelphia, PA	606,770	7
Pittsburgh, PA	16,232	44
Portland, OR	50,327	30
Sacramento, CA	27,575	39
Saint Louis, MO	28,223	38
San Antonio, TX	829,487	4
San Diego, CA	181,274	16
San Francisco, CA	559,913	8
San Jose, CA	17,004	43
Seattle, WA	383,794	10
Toledo, OH	23,853	41
Tulsa, OK	42,399	33
Virginia Beach, VA	34,172	36
Washington, DC	78,223	22

Source: U.S. Bureau of the Census, *Annual Survey of Government Finances 1992*, Washington, D.C.: U.S. Government Printing Office, 1995, n.p. Primary source: U.S. Bureau of the Census.

★2727★

City Government Expenditures

City Government Expenditures, 1991-92: Assistance and Subsidies

[In thousands of dollars]

City	Total expenditures	Rank
Boston, MA	1,679	8
Denver, CO	58,207	4
Indianapolis, IN	41,420	5
Jacksonville, FL	4,063	7
Miami, FL	7	11
Nashville-Davidson, TN	381	10
New York City, NY	2,274,629	1
Newark, NJ	17,711	6
San Francisco, CA	137,687	2
Virginia Beach, VA	489	9
Washington, DC	129,635	3

Source: U.S. Bureau of the Census, *Annual Survey of Government Finances 1992*, Washington, D.C.: U.S. Government Printing Office, 1995, n.p. Primary source: U.S. Bureau of the Census.

★2728★

City Government Expenditures

City Government Expenditures, 1991-92: Capital Outlay

[In thousands of dollars]

City	Total expenditures	Rank
Albuquerque, NM	109,491	31
Atlanta, GA	133,545	22
Austin, TX	88,020	34
Baltimore, MD	261,145	11
Baton Rouge, LA	55,298	42
Boston, MA	155,655	17
Buffalo, NY	47,491	43
Charlotte, NC	188,886	15
Chicago, IL	654,400	2
Cincinnati, OH	128,939	26
Cleveland, OH	73,595	39
Columbus, OH	137,534	20
Dallas, TX	508,270	5
Denver, CO	531,717	3
Detroit, MI	203,935	14
El Paso, TX	74,985	38
Fort Worth, TX	149,048	19
Honolulu, HI	215,696	13
Houston, TX	297,811	8
Indianapolis, IN	135,032	21
Jacksonville, FL	116,581	29
Kansas City, MO	150,142	18
Los Angeles, CA	525,468	4
Memphis, TN	133,346	24
Miami, FL	39,605	45
Milwaukee, WI	81,341	37
Minneapolis, MN	221,146	12
Nashville-Davidson, TN	83,091	36
New Orleans, LA	118,659	28

[Continued]

★2728★

City Government Expenditures, 1991-92: Capital Outlay

[Continued]

City	Total expenditures	Rank
New York City, NY	3,757,588	1
Newark, NJ	14,575	48
Oakland, CA	63,392	41
Oklahoma City, OK	109,998	30
Omaha, NE	31,564	47
Philadelphia, PA	283,930	9
Pittsburgh, PA	36,125	46
Portland, OR	105,545	32
Sacramento, CA	67,444	40
Saint Louis, MO	83,802	35
San Antonio, TX	133,511	23
San Diego, CA	277,835	10
San Francisco, CA	307,624	7
San Jose, CA	187,769	16
Seattle, WA	123,206	27
Toledo, OH	41,716	44
Tulsa, OK	102,898	33
Virginia Beach, VA	130,860	25
Washington, DC	472,242	6

Source: U.S. Bureau of the Census, *Annual Survey of Government Finances 1992*, Washington, D.C.: U.S. Government Printing Office, 1995, n.p. Primary source: U.S. Bureau of the Census.

★2729★

City Government Expenditures

City Government Expenditures, 1991-92: Capital Outlay (For Construction)

[In thousands of dollars]

City	Total expenditures	Rank
Albuquerque, NM	91,323	27
Atlanta, GA	80,740	31
Austin, TX	75,901	32
Baltimore, MD	229,626	10
Baton Rouge, LA	37,733	42
Boston, MA	127,322	19
Buffalo, NY	37,156	43
Charlotte, NC	164,356	14
Chicago, IL	609,332	2
Cincinnati, OH	95,383	25
Cleveland, OH	58,465	40
Columbus, OH	120,024	20
Dallas, TX	430,475	4
Denver, CO	487,591	3
Detroit, MI	147,248	15
El Paso, TX	67,455	35
Fort Worth, TX	143,857	16
Honolulu, HI	183,123	12
Houston, TX	253,111	8
Indianapolis, IN	88,146	28
Jacksonville, FL	66,286	36

[Continued]

★2729★

City Government Expenditures, 1991-92: Capital Outlay (For Construction)

[Continued]

City	Total expenditures	Rank
Kansas City, MO	135,401	18
Los Angeles, CA	425,771	5
Memphis, TN	110,271	22
Miami, FL	32,088	45
Milwaukee, WI	63,149	38
Minneapolis, MN	167,043	13
Nashville-Davidson, TN	63,886	37
New Orleans, LA	100,840	24
New York City, NY	3,378,091	1
Newark, NJ	11,735	48
Oakland, CA	55,386	41
Oklahoma City, OK	85,306	30
Omaha, NE	28,154	47
Philadelphia, PA	257,888	7
Pittsburgh, PA	31,921	46
Portland, OR	93,645	26
Sacramento, CA	59,780	39
Saint Louis, MO	74,448	34
San Antonio, TX	116,349	21
San Diego, CA	244,324	9
San Francisco, CA	260,328	6
San Jose, CA	137,799	17
Seattle, WA	87,964	29
Toledo, OH	33,265	44
Tulsa, OK	75,887	33
Virginia Beach, VA	109,981	23
Washington, DC	219,530	11

Source: U.S. Bureau of the Census, *Annual Survey of Government Finances 1992,* Washington, D.C.: U.S. Government Printing Office, 1995, n.p. Primary source: U.S. Bureau of the Census.

★2730★

City Government Expenditures

City Government Expenditures, 1991-92: Capital Outlay (For Equipment)

[In thousands of dollars]

City	Total expenditures	Rank
Albuquerque, NM	8,542	38
Atlanta, GA	21,845	15
Austin, TX	10,238	35
Baltimore, MD	26,345	11
Baton Rouge, LA	10,831	32
Boston, MA	28,018	10
Buffalo, NY	10,035	36
Charlotte, NC	15,871	26
Chicago, IL	39,416	6
Cincinnati, OH	15,593	27
Cleveland, OH	14,036	29
Columbus, OH	14,779	28

[Continued]

★2730★

City Government Expenditures, 1991-92: Capital Outlay (For Equipment)

[Continued]

City	Total expenditures	Rank
Dallas, TX	67,123	3
Denver, CO	20,053	20
Detroit, MI	30,034	8
El Paso, TX	7,449	40
Fort Worth, TX	5,191	43
Honolulu, HI	23,959	12
Houston, TX	39,915	5
Indianapolis, IN	39,111	7
Jacksonville, FL	18,926	21
Kansas City, MO	10,592	33
Los Angeles, CA	62,363	4
Memphis, TN	20,068	19
Miami, FL	6,668	41
Milwaukee, WI	17,835	24
Minneapolis, MN	9,584	37
Nashville-Davidson, TN	13,972	30
New Orleans, LA	12,135	31
New York City, NY	348,812	1
Newark, NJ	2,426	48
Oakland, CA	3,092	45
Oklahoma City, OK	20,932	17
Omaha, NE	3,057	46
Philadelphia, PA	21,211	16
Pittsburgh, PA	2,966	47
Portland, OR	10,413	34
Sacramento, CA	6,266	42
Saint Louis, MO	3,332	44
San Antonio, TX	16,188	25
San Diego, CA	18,671	22
San Francisco, CA	28,417	9
San Jose, CA	18,233	23
Seattle, WA	23,334	13
Toledo, OH	8,036	39
Tulsa, OK	22,202	14
Virginia Beach, VA	20,879	18
Washington, DC	71,878	2

Source: U.S. Bureau of the Census, *Annual Survey of Government Finances 1992,* Washington, D.C.: U.S. Government Printing Office, 1995, n.p. Primary source: U.S. Bureau of the Census.

★2731★

City Government Expenditures

City Government Expenditures, 1991-92: Capital Outlay (For Land and Existing Structures)

[In thousands of dollars]

City	Total expenditures	Rank
Albuquerque, NM	9,626	20
Atlanta, GA	30,960	6
Austin, TX	1,881	36
Baltimore, MD	5,174	30
Baton Rouge, LA	6,734	25
Boston, MA	315	44
Buffalo, NY	300	45
Charlotte, NC	8,659	21
Chicago, IL	5,652	28
Cincinnati, OH	17,963	13
Cleveland, OH	14,036	16
Columbus, OH	14,779	15
Dallas, TX	10,672	18
Denver, CO	25,073	9
Detroit, MI	26,653	8
El Paso, TX	81	46
Fort Worth, TX	0	47
Honolulu, HI	8,614	22
Houston, TX	4,785	33
Indianapolis, IN	7,775	24
Jacksonville, FL	31,369	5
Kansas City, MO	4,149	34
Los Angeles, CA	37,334	3
Memphis, TN	3,007	35
Miami, FL	849	40
Milwaukee, WI	357	42
Minneapolis, MN	44,519	2
Nashville-Davidson, TN	5,233	29
New Orleans, LA	5,684	27
New York City, NY	30,685	7
Newark, NJ	414	41
Oakland, CA	4,914	31
Oklahoma City, OK	20,932	11
Omaha, NE	353	43
Philadelphia, PA	4,831	32
Pittsburgh, PA	1,238	38
Portland, OR	10,413	19
Sacramento, CA	1,398	37
Saint Louis, MO	6,022	26
San Antonio, TX	974	39
San Diego, CA	14,840	14
San Francisco, CA	18,879	12
San Jose, CA	31,737	4
Seattle, WA	11,908	17
Toledo, OH	8,036	23
Tulsa, OK	22,202	10
Virginia Beach, VA	0	47
Washington, DC	180,834	1

Source: U.S. Bureau of the Census, *Annual Survey of Government Finances 1992*, Washington, D.C.: U.S. Government Printing Office, 1995, n.p. Primary source: U.S. Bureau of the Census.

★2732★

City Government Expenditures

City Government Expenditures, 1991-92: Current Operations

[In thousands of dollars]

City	Total expenditures	Rank
Albuquerque, NM	280,691	38
Atlanta, GA	359,071	31
Austin, TX	376,920	28
Baltimore, MD	1,196,832	9
Baton Rouge, LA	278,772	39
Boston, MA	1,224,912	7
Buffalo, NY	683,784	12
Charlotte, NC	250,067	41
Chicago, IL	2,193,149	5
Cincinnati, OH	339,025	34
Cleveland, OH	455,399	23
Columbus, OH	391,055	27
Dallas, TX	638,565	17
Denver, CO	643,056	16
Detroit, MI	1,217,806	8
El Paso, TX	161,522	47
Fort Worth, TX	231,414	44
Honolulu, HI	614,409	18
Houston, TX	980,188	10
Indianapolis, IN	644,515	15
Jacksonville, FL	513,101	21
Kansas City, MO	329,373	35
Los Angeles, CA	2,688,944	3
Memphis, TN	706,486	11
Miami, FL	249,139	42
Milwaukee, WI	440,744	24
Minneapolis, MN	326,630	36
Nashville-Davidson, TN	652,009	14
New Orleans, LA	469,431	22
New York City, NY	23,672,301	1
Newark, NJ	361,375	30
Oakland, CA	370,614	29
Oklahoma City, OK	224,515	45
Omaha, NE	159,504	48
Philadelphia, PA	2,305,965	4
Pittsburgh, PA	286,433	37
Portland, OR	346,344	32
Sacramento, CA	258,313	40
Saint Louis, MO	343,960	33
San Antonio, TX	425,571	25
San Diego, CA	665,420	13
San Francisco, CA	1,601,216	6
San Jose, CA	424,846	26
Seattle, WA	515,012	20
Toledo, OH	170,207	46
Tulsa, OK	238,235	43
Virginia Beach, VA	517,210	19
Washington, DC	3,585,209	2

Source: U.S. Bureau of the Census, *Annual Survey of Government Finances 1992*, Washington, D.C.: U.S. Government Printing Office, 1995, n.p. Primary source: U.S. Bureau of the Census.

★2733★
City Government Expenditures

City Government Expenditures, 1991-92: Direct General Expenditures

[In thousands of dollars]

City	Total expenditures	Rank
Albuquerque, NM	475,532	37
Atlanta, GA	589,084	26
Austin, TX	564,935	28
Baltimore, MD	1,548,827	7
Baton Rouge, LA	393,001	41
Boston, MA	1,435,160	11
Buffalo, NY	756,457	19
Charlotte, NC	498,629	33
Chicago, IL	3,203,788	4
Cincinnati, OH	480,490	36
Cleveland, OH	550,729	30
Columbus, OH	586,744	27
Dallas, TX	1,348,454	12
Denver, CO	1,436,909	10
Detroit, MI	1,502,926	8
El Paso, TX	263,879	46
Fort Worth, TX	435,117	39
Honolulu, HI	891,715	14
Houston, TX	1,448,639	9
Indianapolis, IN	874,182	15
Jacksonville, FL	778,639	18
Kansas City, MO	525,187	31
Los Angeles, CA	3,512,707	3
Memphis, TN	863,176	16
Miami, FL	321,940	45
Milwaukee, WI	557,814	29
Minneapolis, MN	711,679	20
Nashville-Davidson, TN	850,769	17
New Orleans, LA	682,040	22
New York City, NY	31,401,228	1
Newark, NJ	406,699	40
Oakland, CA	507,867	32
Oklahoma City, OK	360,609	43
Omaha, NE	205,540	48
Philadelphia, PA	2,737,872	5
Pittsburgh, PA	367,176	42
Portland, OR	494,624	34
Sacramento, CA	347,678	44
Saint Louis, MO	494,066	35
San Antonio, TX	650,979	25
San Diego, CA	1,075,387	13
San Francisco, CA	2,229,604	6
San Jose, CA	693,794	21
Seattle, WA	660,424	24
Toledo, OH	225,151	47
Tulsa, OK	440,569	38
Virginia Beach, VA	680,323	23
Washington, DC	4,423,327	2

Source: U.S. Bureau of the Census, *Annual Survey of Government Finances 1992*, Washington, D.C.: U.S. Government Printing Office, 1995, n.p. Primary source: U.S. Bureau of the Census.

★2734★
City Government Expenditures

City Government Expenditures, 1991-92: Interest on General Debt

[In thousands of dollars]

City	Total expenditures	Rank
Albuquerque, NM	85,350	20
Atlanta, GA	96,468	16
Austin, TX	99,995	14
Baltimore, MD	90,850	19
Baton Rouge, LA	58,931	27
Boston, MA	52,914	31
Buffalo, NY	25,182	40
Charlotte, NC	59,676	26
Chicago, IL	356,239	2
Cincinnati, OH	12,526	48
Cleveland, OH	21,735	44
Columbus, OH	58,155	28
Dallas, TX	201,619	6
Denver, CO	202,929	5
Detroit, MI	81,185	21
El Paso, TX	27,372	38
Fort Worth, TX	54,655	29
Honolulu, HI	61,610	25
Houston, TX	170,640	8
Indianapolis, IN	53,215	30
Jacksonville, FL	144,894	11
Kansas City, MO	45,672	32
Los Angeles, CA	298,295	3
Memphis, TN	23,344	41
Miami, FL	33,189	36
Milwaukee, WI	35,729	35
Minneapolis, MN	163,903	9
Nashville-Davidson, TN	115,288	13
New Orleans, LA	93,950	17
New York City, NY	1,696,710	1
Newark, NJ	13,038	47
Oakland, CA	73,861	23
Oklahoma City, OK	26,096	39
Omaha, NE	14,472	45
Philadelphia, PA	147,977	10
Pittsburgh, PA	44,618	33
Portland, OR	42,735	34
Sacramento, CA	21,921	43
Saint Louis, MO	66,304	24
San Antonio, TX	91,897	18
San Diego, CA	132,132	12
San Francisco, CA	183,077	7
San Jose, CA	81,179	22
Seattle, WA	22,206	42
Toledo, OH	13,228	46
Tulsa, OK	99,436	15
Virginia Beach, VA	31,764	37
Washington, DC	236,241	4

Source: U.S. Bureau of the Census, *Annual Survey of Government Finances 1992*, Washington, D.C.: U.S. Government Printing Office, 1995, n.p. Primary source: U.S. Bureau of the Census.

★ 2735 ★

City Government Expenditures

City Government Expenditures, 1991-92: Intergovernmental Expenditures

[In thousands of dollars]

City	Total expenditures	Rank
Albuquerque, NM	950	42
Atlanta, GA	34,656	14
Austin, TX	46,444	10
Baltimore, MD	1,463	38
Baton Rouge, LA	2,361	35
Boston, MA	124,683	3
Buffalo, NY	906	44
Charlotte, NC	1,441	39
Chicago, IL	77,516	5
Cincinnati, OH	44,992	11
Cleveland, OH	942	43
Columbus, OH	12,905	23
Dallas, TX	24,167	17
Denver, CO	76,420	7
Detroit, MI	73,613	8
El Paso, TX	4,264	31
Fort Worth, TX	1,145	41
Honolulu, HI	0	46
Houston, TX	3,344	33
Indianapolis, IN	4,789	29
Jacksonville, FL	13,589	22
Kansas City, MO	44,786	12
Los Angeles, CA	21,735	19
Memphis, TN	15,385	21
Miami, FL	1,921	36
Milwaukee, WI	26,505	15
Minneapolis, MN	24,487	16
Nashville, TN	6,189	27
New Orleans, LA	1,582	37
New York City, NY	2,929,296	1
Newark, NJ	42,970	13
Oakland, CA	0	46
Oklahoma City, OK	1,170	40
Omaha, NE	2,994	34
Philadelphia, PA	84,810	4
Pittsburgh, PA	11,449	24
Portland, OR	100	45
Sacramento, CA	4,736	30
Saint Louis, MO	22,925	18
San Antonio, TX	6,136	28
San Diego, CA	8,760	26
San Francisco, CA	72,771	9
San Jose, CA	16,242	20
Seattle, WA	76,753	6
Toledo, OH	8,998	25
Tulsa, OK	3,919	32
Virginia Beach, VA	1,582	37
Washington, DC	162,327	2

Source: U.S. Bureau of the Census, *Annual Survey of Government Finances 1992*, Washington, D.C.: U.S. Government Printing Office, 1995, n.p. Primary source: U.S. Bureau of the Census.

★ 2736 ★

City Government Expenditures

City Government Expenditures, 1991-92: Total Expenditures on All Functions

[In thousands of dollars]

City	Total expenditures	Rank
Albuquerque, NM	546,297	37
Atlanta, GA	766,514	26
Austin, TX	1,112,679	19
Baltimore, MD	1,687,491	12
Baton Rouge, LA	422,767	42
Boston, MA	1,781,046	8
Buffalo, NY	774,369	24
Charlotte, NC	566,347	35
Chicago, IL	3,887,175	4
Cincinnati, OH	659,385	32
Cleveland, OH	803,271	22
Columbus, OH	728,601	28
Dallas, TX	1,619,597	14
Denver, CO	1,649,475	13
Detroit, MI	2,131,026	7
El Paso, TX	358,855	46
Fort Worth, TX	522,690	38
Honolulu, HI	1,100,649	20
Houston, TX	1,758,002	10
Indianapolis, IN	938,444	21
Jacksonville, FL	1,699,170	11
Kansas City, MO	662,313	31
Los Angeles, CA	6,577,265	2
Memphis, TN	1,762,350	9
Miami, FL	358,865	45
Milwaukee, WI	683,894	30
Minneapolis, MN	795,166	23
Nashville-Davidson, TN	1,525,110	15
New Orleans, LA	772,877	25
New York City, NY	42,499,063	1
Newark, NJ	490,815	40
Oakland, CA	553,502	36
Oklahoma City, OK	416,887	43
Omaha, NE	222,291	48
Philadelphia, PA	3,723,305	5
Pittsburgh, PA	428,721	41
Portland, OR	580,690	34
Sacramento, CA	399,168	44
Saint Louis, MO	603,267	33
San Antonio, TX	1,500,520	16
San Diego, CA	1,311,311	17
San Francisco, CA	3,094,003	6
San Jose, CA	760,189	27
Seattle, WA	1,172,607	18
Toledo, OH	258,002	47
Tulsa, OK	491,013	39
Virginia Beach, VA	716,077	29
Washington, DC	5,036,210	3

Source: U.S. Bureau of the Census, *Annual Survey of Government Finances 1992*, Washington, D.C.: U.S. Government Printing Office, 1995, n.p. Primary source: U.S. Bureau of the Census.

★2737★

City Government Expenditures

City Government Expenditures, 1991-92, By Function: Governmental Administration (General Public Buildings)

[In thousands of dollars]

City	Total expenditures	Rank
Albuquerque, NM	5,730	32
Atlanta, GA	15,689	14
Austin, TX	2,151	41
Baltimore, MD	16,911	11
Baton Rouge, LA	6,842	23
Boston, MA	7,020	22
Buffalo, NY	6,488	26
Charlotte, NC	550	45
Chicago, IL	23,270	8
Cincinnati, OH	6,470	27
Cleveland, OH	9,774	18
Columbus, OH	10,001	17
Dallas, TX	18,146	10
Denver, CO	8,449	20
Detroit, MI	16,711	12
El Paso, TX	870	44
Fort Worth, TX	5,345	33
Honolulu, HI	39,002	6
Houston, TX	0	47
Indianapolis, IN	4,633	36
Jacksonville, FL	7,583	21
Kansas City, MO	6,108	30
Los Angeles, CA	69,705	3
Memphis, TN	1,137	43
Miami, FL	2,949	39
Milwaukee, WI	14,113	15
Minneapolis, MN	9,321	19
Nashville-Davidson, TN	1,702	42
New Orleans, LA	16,235	13
New York City, NY	180,228	1
Newark, NJ	11,172	16
Oakland, CA	6,435	28
Oklahoma City, OK	0	47
Omaha, NE	2,302	40
Philadelphia, PA	116,883	2
Pittsburgh, PA	5,154	35
Portland, OR	6,181	29
Sacramento, CA	35	46
Saint Louis, MO	5,174	34
San Antonio, TX	6,596	25
San Diego, CA	20,545	9
San Francisco, CA	33,160	7
San Jose, CA	3,964	37
Seattle, WA	6,744	24
Toledo, OH	3,872	38
Tulsa, OK	5,731	31
Virginia Beach, VA	47,476	5
Washington, DC	48,298	4

Source: U.S. Bureau of the Census, *Annual Survey of Government Finances 1992*, Washington, D.C.: U.S. Government Printing Office, 1995, n.p. Primary source: U.S. Bureau of the Census.

★2738★

City Government Expenditures

City Government Expenditures, 1991-92, By Function: Higher Education

[In thousands of dollars]

City	Total expenditures	Rank
New York City, NY	615,323	1
Newark, NJ	30	7
Omaha, NE	294	5
Philadelphia, PA	16,597	3
Saint Louis, MO	183	6
San Antonio, TX	863	4
Virginia Beach, VA	5	8
Washington, DC	119,143	2

Source: U.S. Bureau of the Census, *Annual Survey of Government Finances 1992*, Washington, D.C.: U.S. Government Printing Office, 1995, n.p. Primary source: U.S. Bureau of the Census.

★2739★

City Government Expenditures

City Government Expenditures, 1991-92, By Function: Libraries

[In thousands of dollars]

City	Total expenditures	Rank
Albuquerque, NM	6,616	30
Atlanta, GA	0	36
Austin, TX	8,188	25
Baltimore, MD	14,433	17
Baton Rouge, LA	8,146	26
Boston, MA	28,308	5
Buffalo, NY	71	35
Charlotte, NC	0	36
Chicago, IL	99,308	2
Cincinnati, OH	0	36
Cleveland, OH	0	36
Columbus, OH	0	36
Dallas, TX	14,783	16
Denver, CO	21,970	9
Detroit, MI	22,374	8
El Paso, TX	6,235	31
Fort Worth, TX	7,530	28
Honolulu, HI	473	34
Houston, TX	25,320	7
Indianapolis, IN	0	36
Jacksonville, FL	10,878	19
Kansas City, MO	0	36
Los Angeles, CA	47,082	3
Memphis, TN	8,982	21
Miami, FL	0	36
Milwaukee, WI	18,204	13
Minneapolis, MN	16,937	15
Nashville-Davidson, TN	8,942	22
New Orleans, LA	7,520	29
New York City, NY	227,712	1
Newark, NJ	13,699	18
Oakland, CA	8,322	24

[Continued]

★2739★

City Government Expenditures, 1991-92, By Function: Libraries

[Continued]

City	Total expenditures	Rank
Oklahoma City, OK	0	36
Omaha, NE	5,576	33
Philadelphia, PA	36,976	4
Pittsburgh, PA	5,708	32
Portland, OR	0	36
Sacramento, CA	8,941	23
Saint Louis, MO	0	36
San Antonio, TX	10,673	20
San Diego, CA	20,714	12
San Francisco, CA	27,047	6
San Jose, CA	17,181	14
Seattle, WA	21,678	11
Toledo, OH	0	36
Tulsa, OK	0	36
Virginia Beach, VA	7,531	27
Washington, DC	21,846	10

Source: U.S. Bureau of the Census, Annual Survey of Government Finances 1992, Washington, D.C.: U.S. Government Printing Office, 1995, n.p. Primary source: U.S. Bureau of the Census.

★2740★

City Government Expenditures

City Government Expenditures, 1991-92, By Function: Own Hospitals

[In thousands of dollars]

City	Total expenditures	Rank
Austin, TX	104,834	5
Baton Rouge, LA	24,570	9
Boston, MA	236,176	3
Denver, CO	86,940	6
Indianapolis, IN	142,013	4
Nashville-Davidson, TN	58,157	7
New York City, NY	2,708,953	1
San Francisco, CA	27,796	8
Washington, DC	357,317	2

Source: U.S. Bureau of the Census, Annual Survey of Government Finances 1992, Washington, D.C.: U.S. Government Printing Office, 1995, n.p. Primary source: U.S. Bureau of the Census.

★2741★

City Government Expenditures

City Government Expenditures, 1992, By Source: Education

[In millions of dollars]

City	Millions	Rank
New York City, NY[1]	8,008	1
Washington, DC[1]	743	2
Baltimore, MD[1]	537	3
Boston, MA[1]	479	4
Memphis, TN	435	5
Buffalo, NY	362	6
Virginia Beach, VA[1]	334	7
Rochester, NY	320	8
Anchorage, AK[1]	284	9
Nashville-Davidson, TN[1]	271	10
Norfolk, VA[1]	196	11
San Francisco, CA[1]	58	12
Chicago, IL	35	13
Kansas City, MO	24	14
Atlanta, GA	19	15
Philadelphia, PA[1]	17	16
Los Angeles, CA	9	17
San Antonio, TX	9	17
Detroit, MI	6	18
Oakland, CA	4	19
Birmingham, AL	3	20
St. Louis, MO[1]	3	20
Phoenix, AZ	1	21

Source: U.S. Bureau of the Census, Statistical Abstract of the United States: 1995, (115th edition), Washington, D.C.: U.S. Government Printing Office, 1995, p. 321. Primary source: U.S. Bureau of the Census, City Government Finances, series GF, no. 4, annual. Notes: Data are shown only for the top 25 areas. 1. Represents, in effect, city-county consolidated government.

★2742★

City Government Expenditures

General Expenditures of Largest Cities, 1992, Total Expenditures

[Total in millions of dollars]

City	Total (mil. dol.)	Rank
New York City, NY	34,331	1
Washington, DC	4,586	2
Los Angeles, CA	3,534	3
Chicago, IL	3,281	4
Philadelphia, PA	2,823	5
San Francisco, CA	2,302	6
Detroit, MI	1,577	7
Boston, MA	1,560	8
Baltimore, MD	1,550	9
Denver, CO	1,513	10
Houston, TX	1,452	11
Dallas, TX	1,373	12
San Diego, CA	1,084	13
Phoenix, AZ	924	14
Indianapolis, IN	895	15
Honolulu, HI	892	16
Memphis, TN	879	17

[Continued]

★2742★

General Expenditures of Largest Cities, 1992, Total Expenditures

[Continued]

City	Total (mil. dol.)	Rank
Nashville-Davidson, TX	857	18
Jacksonville, FL	779	19
Buffalo, NY	757	20
Seattle, WA	737	21
Minneapolis, MN	736	22
San Jose, CA	710	23
Anchorage, AK	699	24
New Orleans, LA	684	25

Source: U.S. Bureau of the Census, *Statistical Abstract of the United States: 1995,* (115th edition), Washington, DC: U.S. Government Printing Office, 1995, p. 318. Primary source: U.S. Bureau of the Census, *City Government Finances,* series GF, no. 4, annual. *Note:* Data are shown only for the top 25 areas.

★2743★

City Government Expenditures

Government Debt of Largest Cities, 1992: Total Outstanding Debt

[Total in millions of dollars]

City	Total (mil. dol.)	Rank
New York City, NY	34,984	1
Los Angeles, CA	8,003	2
Chicago, IL	6,012	3
Jacksonville, FL	4,654	4
San Antonio, TX	4,239	5
Houston, TX	3,962	6
Washington, DC	3,942	7
Philadelphia, PA	3,835	8
Dallas, TX	3,586	9
Denver, CO	3,344	10
Austin, TX	3,190	11
San Francisco, CA	3,174	12
Phoenix, AZ	2,310	13
Minneapolis, MN	2,290	14
Nashville-Davidson, TX	2,216	15
Detroit, MI	1,685	16
San Diego, CA	1,646	17
Tulsa, OK	1,585	18
Atlanta, GA	1,433	19
Baltimore, MD	1,308	20
Baton Rouge, LA	1,269	21
San Jose, CA	1,249	22
Columbus, OH	1,247	23
Indianapolis, IN	1,232	24
Oakland, CA	1,144	25

Source: U.S. Bureau of the Census, *Statistical Abstract of the United States: 1995,* (115th edition), Washington, DC: U.S. Government Printing Office, 1995, p. 318. Primary source: U.S. Bureau of the Census, *City Government Finances,* series GF, no. 4, annual. *Note:* Data are shown only for the top 25 areas.

★2744★

City Government Revenues

City Government Revenues, 1991-92: Intergovernmental Revenues From State Governments (For Housing and Community Development)

[In thousands of dollars]

City	Total revenues	Rank
Baltimore, MD	1,653	9
Boston, MA	219	13
Buffalo, NY	2,721	7
Chicago, IL	38,869	2
Detroit, MI	1	17
Fort Worth, TX	953	12
Memphis, TN	180	14
Milwaukee, WI	118	15
Minneapolis, MN	3,005	5
New York City, NY	60,690	1
Oakland, CA	7,737	4
Philadelphia, PA	10,903	3
San Diego, CA	1,674	8
San Francisco, CA	2,830	6
San Jose, CA	1,000	11
Seattle, WA	1,409	10
Virginia Beach, VA	9	16

Source: U.S. Bureau of the Census, *Annual Survey of Government Finances 1992,* Washington, D.C.: U.S. Government Printing Office, 1995, n.p. Primary source: U.S. Bureau of the Census.

★2745★

City Government Revenues

City Government Cash and Securities Holdings, 1991-92, By Purpose: Bond Funds

[In thousands of dollars]

City	Total holdings	Rank
Albuquerque, NM	117,391	31
Atlanta, GA	317,411	13
Austin, TX	318,064	12
Baltimore, MD	111,743	32
Baton Rouge, LA	50,724	39
Boston, MA	126,075	27
Buffalo, NY	73,543	37
Charlotte, NC	238,749	15
Chicago, IL	1,024,104	3
Cincinnati, OH	101,591	33
Cleveland, OH	77,621	36
Columbus, OH	131,732	26
Dallas, TX	656,552	5
Denver, CO	2,014,702	1
Detroit, MI	425,268	7
El Paso, TX	25,915	45
Fort Worth, TX	124,140	28
Honolulu, HI	91,686	34
Houston, TX	391,880	8
Indianapolis, IN	372,124	10

[Continued]

★2745★

City Government Cash and Securities Holdings, 1991-92, By Purpose: Bond Funds
[Continued]

City	Total holdings	Rank
Jacksonville, FL	456,637	6
Kansas City, MO	271,768	14
Los Angeles, CA	212,422	16
Memphis, TN	77,876	35
Miami, FL	69,786	38
Milwaukee, WI	25,705	46
Minneapolis, MN	173,428	21
Nashville-Davidson, TN	137,897	23
New Orleans, LA	135,476	25
New York City, NY	891,038	4
Newark, NJ	5,187	48
Oakland, CA	196,528	18
Oklahoma City, OK	122,613	30
Omaha, NE	16,460	47
Philadelphia, PA	327,463	11
Pittsburgh, PA	43,308	41
Portland, OR	50,268	40
Sacramento, CA	43,228	42
Saint Louis, MO	188,185	20
San Antonio, TX	390,693	9
San Diego, CA	34,146	43
San Francisco, CA	1,068,603	2
San Jose, CA	206,054	17
Seattle, WA	123,592	29
Toledo, OH	27,831	44
Tulsa, OK	188,368	19
Virginia Beach, VA	168,375	22
Washington, DC	137,635	24

Source: U.S. Bureau of the Census, *Annual Survey of Government Finances 1992,* Washington, D.C.: U.S. Government Printing Office, 1995, n.p. Primary source: U.S. Bureau of the Census.

★2746★

City Government Revenues

City Government Cash and Securities Holdings, 1991-92, By Purpose: Employee Retirement

[In thousands of dollars]

City	Total holdings	Rank
Albuquerque, NM	0	42
Atlanta, GA	598,999	22
Austin, TX	519,242	26
Baltimore, MD	1,084,610	13
Baton Rouge, LA	386,178	28
Boston, MA	1,079,636	14
Buffalo, NY	0	42
Charlotte, NC	94,488	37
Chicago, IL	4,811,212	4
Cincinnati, OH	912,067	17
Cleveland, OH	0	42

[Continued]

★2746★

City Government Cash and Securities Holdings, 1991-92, By Purpose: Employee Retirement
[Continued]

City	Total holdings	Rank
Columbus, OH	0	42
Dallas, TX	1,404,891	10
Denver, CO	568,275	23
Detroit, MI	3,655,583	5
El Paso, TX	294,213	31
Fort Worth, TX	464,502	27
Honolulu, HI	0	42
Houston, TX	1,849,781	6
Indianapolis, IN	66,386	38
Jacksonville, FL	792,013	19
Kansas City, MO	655,294	20
Los Angeles, CA	8,953,154	2
Memphis, TN	1,260,003	11
Miami, FL	639,287	21
Milwaukee, WI	1,536,010	9
Minneapolis, MN	1,127,109	12
Nashville-Davidson, TN	522,146	25
New Orleans, LA	308,426	30
New York City, NY	45,049,578	1
Newark, NJ	11,986	40
Oakland, CA	277,423	33
Oklahoma City, OK	106,782	35
Omaha, NE	245,924	34
Philadelphia, PA	1,833,022	7
Pittsburgh, PA	60,324	39
Portland, OR	7,260	41
Sacramento, CA	281,868	32
Saint Louis, MO	852,953	18
San Antonio, TX	314,469	29
San Diego, CA	998,192	16
San Francisco, CA	4,836,236	3
San Jose, CA	1,037,478	15
Seattle, WA	543,260	24
Toledo, OH	0	42
Tulsa, OK	104,347	36
Virginia Beach, VA	0	42
Washington, DC	1,814,043	8

Source: U.S. Bureau of the Census, *Annual Survey of Government Finances 1992,* Washington, D.C.: U.S. Government Printing Office, 1995, n.p. Primary source: U.S. Bureau of the Census.

★2747★

City Government Revenues

City Government Cash and Securities Holdings, 1991-92, By Purpose: Exhibit – Contribution to Own Retirement Systems

[In thousands of dollars]

City	Total holdings	Rank
Alburquerque, NM	0	42
Atlanta, GA	23,787	25
Austin, TX	16,395	30
Baltimore, MD	30,322	20
Baton Rouge, LA	11,350	34
Boston, MA	50,717	10
Buffalo, NY	0	42
Charlotte, NC	3,140	40
Chicago, IL	252,678	3
Cincinnati, OH	26,990	24
Cleveland, OH	0	42
Columbus, OH	0	42
Dallas, TX	76,640	8
Denver, CO	28,657	21
Detroit, MI	131,799	7
El Paso, TX	14,242	32
Fort Worth, TX	15,486	31
Honolulu, HI	0	42
Houston, TX	52,646	9
Indianapolis, IN	17,644	29
Jacksonville, FL	40,347	13
Kansas City, MO	23,630	26
Los Angeles, CA	623,645	2
Memphis, TN	34,428	15
Miami, FL	21,570	27
Milwaukee, WI	34,911	14
Minneapolis, MN	27,352	23
Nashville-Davidson, TN	50,560	11
New Orleans, LA	31,694	17
New York City, NY	1,645,840	1
Newark, NJ	6,444	37
Oakland, CA	30,536	19
Oklahoma City, OK	4,768	38
Omaha, NE	8,280	35
Philadelphia, PA	216,172	5
Pittsburgh, PA	13,554	33
Portland, OR	32,480	16
Sacramento, CA	2,985	41
Saint Louis, MO	7,817	36
San Antonio, TX	20,989	28
San Diego, CA	28,183	22
San Francisco, CA	200,797	6
San Jose, CA	41,080	12
Seattle, WA	31,185	18
Toledo, OH	0	42
Tulsa, OK	4,000	39
Virginia Beach, VA	0	42
Washington, DC	224,715	4

Source: U.S. Bureau of the Census, *Annual Survey of Government Finances 1992*, Washington, D.C.: U.S. Government Printing Office, 1995, n.p. Primary source: U.S. Bureau of the Census.

★2748★

City Government Revenues

City Government Cash and Securities Holdings, 1991-92, By Purpose: Offset of Debt

[In thousands of dollars]

City	Total holdings	Rank
Albuquerque, NM	657,289	12
Atlanta, GA	576,512	14
Austin, TX	545,658	17
Baltimore, MD	697,700	11
Baton Rouge, LA	522,684	18
Boston, MA	33,092	42
Buffalo, NY	14,624	45
Charlotte, NC	62,728	40
Chicago, IL	2,338,740	2
Cincinnati, OH	22,079	44
Cleveland, OH	226,366	31
Columbus, OH	69,480	39
Dallas, TX	619,291	13
Denver, CO	199,591	33
Detroit, MI	259,310	28
El Paso, TX	259,111	29
Fort Worth, TX	340,302	24
Honolulu, HI	2,273	47
Houston, TX	1,279,306	6
Indianapolis, IN	220,365	32
Jacksonville, FL	1,799,980	3
Kansas City, MO	329,344	25
Los Angeles, CA	1,799,270	4
Memphis, TN	60,395	41
Miami, FL	159,761	35
Milwaukee, WI	278,823	27
Minneapolis, MN	1,366,523	5
Nashville-Davidson, TN	1,240,404	7
New Orleans, LA	448,409	20
New York City, NY	4,354,678	1
Newark, NJ	0	48
Oakland, CA	341,737	23
Oklahoma City, OK	130,861	36
Omaha, NE	25,989	43
Philadelphia, PA	570,006	15
Pittsburgh, PA	248,804	30
Portland, OR	344,472	22
Sacramento, CA	163,006	34
Saint Louis, MO	286,272	26
San Antonio, TX	459,708	19
San Diego, CA	1,116,846	9
San Francisco, CA	974,137	10
San Jose, CA	348,678	21
Seattle, WA	91,627	37
Toledo, OH	12,183	46
Tulsa, OK	1,158,312	8
Virginia Beach, Va	90,517	38
Washington, DC	548,454	16

Source: U.S. Bureau of the Census, *Annual Survey of Government Finances 1992*, Washington, D.C.: U.S. Government Printing Office, 1995, n.p. Primary source: U.S. Bureau of the Census.

★2749★

City Government Revenues

City Government Cash and Securities Holdings: 1991-92

[In thousands of dollars]

City	Total holdings	Rank
Albuquerque, NM	827,797	34
Atlanta, GA	1,874,189	18
Austin, TX	1,541,196	23
Baltimore, MD	2,150,861	14
Baton Rouge, LA	1,053,018	29
Boston, MA	1,780,555	19
Buffalo, NY	195,617	46
Charlotte, NC	677,473	37
Chicago, IL	8,893,177	3
Cincinnati, OH	1,358,049	26
Cleveland, OH	430,631	41
Columbus, OH	332,189	44
Dallas, TX	2,827,233	12
Denver, CO	3,050,975	8
Detroit, MI	4,483,403	5
El Paso, TX	782,737	35
Fort Worth, TX	1,028,431	30
Honolulu, HI	732,136	36
Houston, TX	3,685,891	6
Indianapolis, IN	845,101	33
Jacksonville, FL	3,334,947	7
Kansas City, MO	1,542,753	22
Los Angeles, CA	13,439,640	2
Memphis, TN	1,605,143	20
Miami, FL	888,982	32
Milwaukee, WI	1,987,622	16
Minneapolis, MN	2,801,340	13
Nashville-Davidson, TN	2,084,832	15
New Orleans, LA	1,107,565	28
New York City, NY	54,380,986	1
Newark, NJ	109,872	47
Oakland, CA	1,156,249	27
Oklahoma City, OK	525,031	39
Omaha, NE	313,688	45
Philadelphia, PA	3,034,945	9
Pittsburgh, PA	399,269	42
Portland, OR	524,969	40
Sacramento, CA	629,194	38
Saint Louis, MO	1,446,300	24
San Antonio, TX	1,379,855	25
San Diego, CA	3,025,079	10
San Francisco, CA	7,598,751	4
San Jose, CA	1,925,142	17
Seattle, WA	918,687	31
Toledo, OH	65,679	48
Tulsa, OK	1,573,759	21
Virginia Beach, VA	388,226	43
Washington, DC	2,885,416	11

Source: U.S. Bureau of the Census, *Annual Survey of Government Finances 1992*, Washington, D.C.: U.S. Government Printing Office, 1995, n.p. Primary source: U.S. Bureau of the Census.

★2750★

City Government Revenues

City Government Expenditures, 1991-92: Total Revenues

[In thousands of dollars]

City	Total revenues	Rank
Albuquerque, NM	470,152	36
Atlanta, GA	810,963	23
Austin, TX	1,130,427	18
Baltimore, MD	1,997,098	8
Baton Rouge, LA	455,482	37
Boston, MA	1,829,833	10
Buffalo, NY	689,540	28
Charlotte, NC	427,577	39
Chicago, IL	4,514,395	4
Cincinnati, OH	523,095	34
Cleveland, OH	535,138	33
Columbus, OH	557,909	32
Dallas, TX	1,370,536	16
Denver, CO	1,171,128	17
Detroit, MI	2,052,675	7
El Paso, TX	359,143	45
Fort Worth, TX	500,619	35
Honolulu, HI	962,062	21
Houston, TX	1,801,795	11
Indianapolis, IN	964,779	20
Jacksonville, FL	1,598,629	13
Kansas City, MO	670,837	29
Los Angeles, CA	6,992,982	2
Memphis, TN	1,891,139	9
Miami, FL	380,926	44
Milwaukee, WI	832,601	22
Minneapolis, MN	750,435	26
Nashville-Davidson, TN	1,636,251	12
New Orleans, LA	746,656	27
New York City, NY	36,782,012	1
Newark, NJ	452,880	38
Oakland, CA	565,865	31
Oklahoma City, OK	354,765	46
Omaha, NE	227,702	48
Philadelphia, PA	3,470,794	5
Pittsburgh, PA	406,994	41
Portland, OR	402,451	42
Sacramento, CA	385,725	43
Saint Louis, MO	604,356	30
San Antonio, TX	1,427,054	15
San Diego, CA	1,427,264	14
San Francisco, CA	3,416,701	6
San Jose, CA	767,853	25
Seattle, WA	1,104,462	19
Toledo, OH	234,812	47
Tulsa, OK	416,219	40
Virginia Beach, VA	775,285	24
Washington, DC	4,753,635	3

Source: U.S. Bureau of the Census, *Annual Survey of Government Finances 1992*, Washington, D.C.: U.S. Government Printing Office, 1995, n.p. Primary source: U.S. Bureau of the Census.

★2751★
City Government Revenues

City Government Revenues, 1991-92: General Revenues From Own Sources

[In thousands of dollars]

City	Total revenues	Rank
Albuquerque, NM	319,232	38
Atlanta, GA	556,772	20
Austin, TX	526,074	23
Baltimore, MD	878,182	12
Baton Rouge, LA	357,858	34
Boston, MA	938,180	11
Buffalo, NY	222,115	45
Charlotte, NC	317,045	39
Chicago, IL	2,475,982	5
Cincinnati, OH	427,379	30
Cleveland, OH	402,726	32
Columbus, OH	452,948	26
Dallas, TX	1,025,195	9
Denver, CO	797,103	14
Detroit, MI	861,092	13
El Paso, TX	240,237	44
Fort Worth, TX	338,707	35
Honolulu, HI	747,982	15
Houston, TX	1,352,968	8
Indianapolis, IN	649,409	17
Jacksonville, FL	628,585	18
Kansas City, MO	484,794	24
Los Angeles, CA	3,366,750	2
Memphis, TN	308,906	40
Miami, FL	257,723	43
Milwaukee, WI	293,475	41
Minneapolis, MN	449,692	27
Nashville-Davidson, TN	731,297	16
New Orleans, LA	534,892	22
New York City, NY	22,301,834	1
Newark, NJ	187,884	48
Oakland, CA	438,171	28
Oklahoma City, OK	336,130	37
Omaha, NE	191,751	46
Philadelphia, PA	1,943,428	6
Pittsburgh, PA	282,609	42
Portland, OR	336,710	36
Sacramento, CA	3,000,102	3
Saint Louis, MO	420,593	31
San Antonio, TX	437,288	29
San Diego, CA	940,623	10
San Francisco, CA	1,740,716	7
San Jose, CA	546,855	21
Seattle, WA	615,083	19
Toledo, OH	190,121	47
Tulsa, OK	387,191	33
Virginia Beach, VA	465,188	25
Washington, DC	2,911,270	4

Source: U.S. Bureau of the Census, *Annual Survey of Government Finances 1992,* Washington, D.C.: U.S. Government Printing Office, 1995, n.p. Primary source: U.S. Bureau of the Census.

★2752★
City Government Revenues

City Government Revenues, 1991-92: General Revenues From Own Sources (Alcoholic Beverages Sales)

[In thousands of dollars]

City	Total revenues	Rank
Atlanta, GA	12,434	4
Baton Rouge, LA	381	7
Chicago, IL	12,541	3
Memphis, TN	13,328	2
Nashville-Davidson, TN	9,736	5
New York City, NY	22,418	1
Washington, DC	5,835	6

Source: U.S. Bureau of the Census, *Annual Survey of Government Finances 1992,* Washington, D.C.: U.S. Government Printing Office, 1995, n.p. Primary source: U.S. Bureau of the Census.

★2753★
City Government Revenues

City Government Revenues, 1991-92: General Revenues From Own Sources (General Sales Taxes)

[In thousands of dollars]

City	Total revenues	Rank
Albuquerque, NM	64,507	19
Atlanta, GA	0	30
Austin, TX	55,401	22
Baltimore, MD	0	30
Baton Rouge, LA	101,858	13
Boston, MA	0	30
Buffalo, NY	0	30
Charlotte, NC	0	30
Chicago, IL	298,282	3
Cincinnati, OH	0	30
Cleveland, OH	0	30
Columbus, OH	0	30
Dallas, TX	121,669	12
Denver, CO	209,574	5
Detroit, MI	0	30
El Paso, TX	46,437	25
Fort Worth, TX	39,809	26
Honolulu, HI	0	30
Houston, TX	203,773	6
Indianapolis, IN	0	30
Jacksonville, FL	36,199	28
Kansas City, MO	69,121	18
Los Angeles, CA	270,383	4
Memphis, TN	0	30
Miami, FL	0	30
Milwaukee, WI	0	30
Minneapolis, MN	0	30
Nashville-Davidson, TN	145,263	7
New Orleans, LA	88,445	14
New York City, NY	2,277,822	1

[Continued]

★2753★

City Government Revenues, 1991-92: General Revenues From Own Sources (General Sales Taxes)
[Continued]

City	Total revenues	Rank
Newark, NJ	0	30
Oakland, CA	30,440	29
Oklahoma City, OK	136,863	8
Omaha, NE	56,698	21
Philadelphia, PA	38,301	27
Pittsburgh, PA	0	30
Portland, OR	0	30
Sacramento, CA	47,458	24
Saint Louis, MO	50,526	23
San Antonio, TX	69,860	17
San Diego, CA	121,887	11
San Francisco, CA	125,779	10
San Jose, CA	72,022	16
Seattle, WA	82,842	15
Toledo, OH	0	30
Tulsa, OK	130,040	9
Virginia Beach, VA	59,072	20
Washington, DC	442,496	2

Source: U.S. Bureau of the Census, *Annual Survey of Government Finances 1992*, Washington, D.C.: U.S. Government Printing Office, 1995, n.p. Primary source: U.S. Bureau of the Census.

★2754★
City Government Revenues

City Government Revenues, 1991-92: General Revenues From Own Sources (Income Taxes)
[In thousands of dollars]

City	Total revenues	Rank
Baltimore, MD	119,842	8
Cincinnati, OH	175,002	7
Cleveland, OH	209,391	6
Columbus, OH	244,664	5
Detroit, MI	278,174	4
Indianapolis, IN	63,659	12
Kansas City, MO	103,750	11
New York City, NY	5,202,397	1
Philadelphia, PA	816,101	2
Pittsburgh, PA	36,625	13
Saint Louis, MO	113,908	9
Toledo, OH	104,870	10
Washington, DC	715,677	3

Source: U.S. Bureau of the Census, *Annual Survey of Government Finances 1992*, Washington, D.C.: U.S. Government Printing Office, 1995, n.p. Primary source: U.S. Bureau of the Census.

★2755★
City Government Revenues

City Government Revenues, 1991-92: General Revenues From Own Sources (Motor Fuels Sales)
[In thousands of dollars]

City	Total revenues	Rank
Chicago, IL	61,675	1
Honolulu, HI	44,165	2
Miami, FL	4,745	4
New York City, NY	8	6
Oklahoma City, OK	906	5
Washington, DC	28,586	3

Source: U.S. Bureau of the Census, *Annual Survey of Government Finances 1992*, Washington, D.C.: U.S. Government Printing Office, 1995, n.p. Primary source: U.S. Bureau of the Census.

★2756★
City Government Revenues

City Government Revenues, 1991-92: General Revenues From Own Sources (Property Taxes)
[In thousands of dollars]

City	Total revenues	Rank
Albuquerque, NM	47,234	42
Atlanta, GA	122,556	28
Austin, TX	98,147	34
Baltimore, MD	458,204	7
Baton Rouge, LA	53,655	39
Boston, MA	599,198	4
Buffalo, NY	121,984	29
Charlotte, NC	140,111	20
Chicago, IL	586,212	5
Cincinnati, OH	43,195	43
Cleveland, OH	49,030	41
Columbus, OH	22,926	46
Dallas, TX	295,144	12
Denver, CO	99,485	33
Detroit, MI	215,382	15
El Paso, TX	66,068	35
Fort Worth, TX	130,086	23
Honolulu, HI	388,537	9
Houston, TX	399,845	8
Indianapolis, IN	322,482	11
Jacksonville, FL	197,834	16
Kansas City, MO	62,233	37
Los Angeles, CA	774,409	3
Memphis, TN	117,976	31
Miami, FL	126,851	26
Milwaukee, WI	154,753	18
Minneapolis, MN	142,488	19
Nashville-Davidson, TN	263,324	13
New Orleans, LA	137,619	22
New York City, NY	7,898,700	1
Newark, NJ	61,649	38
Oakland, CA	112,760	32
Oklahoma City, OK	26,600	45

[Continued]

★2756★

City Government Revenues, 1991-92: General Revenues From Own Sources (Property Taxes)

[Continued]

City	Total revenues	Rank
Omaha, NE	66,047	36
Philadelphia, PA	330,016	10
Pittsburgh, PA	121,850	30
Portland, OR	138,450	21
Sacramento, CA	52,064	40
Saint Louis, MO	36,894	44
San Antonio, TX	123,604	27
San Diego, CA	156,402	17
San Francisco, CA	535,575	6
San Jose, CA	129,154	24
Seattle, WA	127,570	25
Toledo, OH	10,375	48
Tulsa, OK	19,059	47
Virginia Beach, VA	233,446	14
Washington, DC	903,319	2

Source: U.S. Bureau of the Census, *Annual Survey of Government Finances 1992,* Washington, D.C.: U.S. Government Printing Office, 1995, n.p. Primary source: U.S. Bureau of the Census.

★2757★

City Government Revenues

City Government Revenues, 1991-92: General Revenues From Own Sources (Public Utilities)

[In thousands of dollars]

City	Total revenues	Rank
Albuquerque, NM	9,771	33
Atlanta, GA	24,212	22
Austin, TX	9,228	35
Baltimore, MD	27,841	18
Baton Rouge, LA	34,816	13
Boston, MA	0	40
Buffalo, NY	14,427	28
Charlotte, NC	2,086	38
Chicago, IL	292,101	2
Cincinnati, OH	1,237	39
Cleveland, OH	0	40
Columbus, OH	0	40
Dallas, TX	60,675	7
Denver, CO	16,664	26
Detroit, MI	43,582	11
El Paso, TX	9,436	34
Fort Worth, TX	18,451	25
Honolulu, HI	14,616	27
Houston, TX	129,035	4
Indianapolis, IN	0	40
Jacksonville, FL	40,835	12
Kansas City, MO	59,230	8
Los Angeles, CA	420,989	1
Memphis, TN	10,224	32

[Continued]

★2757★

City Government Revenues, 1991-92: General Revenues From Own Sources (Public Utilities)

[Continued]

City	Total revenues	Rank
Miami, FL	29,936	17
Milwaukee, WI	0	40
Minneapolis, MN	14,245	29
Nashville-Davidson, TN	8,129	36
New Orleans, LA	26,291	20
New York City, NY	231,571	3
Newark, NJ	0	40
Oakland, CA	31,960	15
Oklahoma City, OK	21,812	24
Omaha, NE	11,090	30
Philadelphia, PA	0	40
Pittsburgh, PA	0	40
Portland, OR	24,077	23
Sacramento, CA	31,346	16
Saint Louis, MO	47,063	10
San Antonio, TX	7,028	37
San Diego, CA	27,237	19
San Francisco, CA	33,755	14
San Jose, CA	66,503	6
Seattle, WA	59,022	9
Toledo, OH	0	40
Tulsa, OK	10,979	31
Virginia Beach, VA	24,854	21
Washington, DC	115,297	5

Source: U.S. Bureau of the Census, *Annual Survey of Government Finances 1992,* Washington, D.C.: U.S. Government Printing Office, 1995, n.p. Primary source: U.S. Bureau of the Census.

★2758★

City Government Revenues

City Government Revenues, 1991-92: General Revenues From Own Sources (Selective Sales Taxes)

[In thousands of dollars]

City	Total revenues	Rank
Albuquerque, NM	15,404	37
Atlanta, GA	68,136	12
Austin, TX	18,466	36
Baltimore, MD	47,725	17
Baton Rouge, LA	35,197	24
Boston, MA	24,567	31
Buffalo, NY	15,032	38
Charlotte, NC	12,172	42
Chicago, IL	556,298	2
Cincinnati, OH	4,040	46
Cleveland, OH	3,627	47
Columbus, OH	5,702	44
Dallas, TX	79,503	7

[Continued]

★2759★

City Government Revenues, 1991-92: General Revenues From Own Sources (Taxes)
[Continued]

City	Total revenues	Rank
Baton Rouge, LA	202,523	32
Boston, MA	641,357	9
Buffalo, NY	142,920	44
Charlotte, NC	164,610	40
Chicago, IL	1,591,948	4
Cincinnati, OH	237,577	26
Cleveland, OH	272,756	25
Columbus, OH	286,749	23
Dallas, TX	505,253	11
Denver, CO	390,693	15
Detroit, MI	550,548	10
El Paso, TX	128,876	46
Fort Worth, TX	195,733	33
Honolulu, HI	482,457	12
Houston, TX	779,309	7
Indianapolis, IN	419,476	14
Jacksonville, FL	290,899	22
Kansas City, MO	329,992	19
Los Angeles, CA	1,932,580	3
Memphis, TN	158,825	41
Miami, FL	170,560	37
Milwaukee, WI	166,391	39
Minneapolis, MN	192,192	35
Nashville-Davidson, TN	478,741	13
New Orleans, LA	300,706	21
New York City, NY	17,140,573	1
Newark, NJ	97,186	48
Oakland, CA	221,924	30
Oklahoma City, OK	194,078	34
Omaha, NE	144,214	43
Philadelphia, PA	1,482,875	5
Pittsburgh, PA	236,715	27
Portland, OR	202,843	31
Sacramento, CA	154,059	42
Saint Louis, MO	277,009	24
San Antonio, TX	223,870	28
San Diego, CA	382,649	16
San Francisco, CA	976,884	6
San Jose, CA	327,647	20
Seattle, WA	370,448	18
Toledo, OH	127,708	47
Tulsa, OK	166,573	38
Virginia Beach, VA	373,566	17
Washington, DC	2,406,646	2

Source: U.S. Bureau of the Census, *Annual Survey of Government Finances 1992*, Washington, D.C.: U.S. Government Printing Office, 1995, n.p. Primary source: U.S. Bureau of the Census.

★2758★

City Government Revenues, 1991-92: General Revenues From Own Sources (Selective Sales Taxes)
[Continued]

City	Total revenues	Rank
Denver, CO	36,912	23
Detroit, MI	43,582	19
El Paso, TX	12,571	41
Fort Worth, TX	21,651	34
Honolulu, HI	58,781	13
Houston, TX	155,483	5
Indianapolis, IN	20,097	35
Jacksonville, FL	47,435	18
Kansas City, MO	77,908	8
Los Angeles, CA	487,209	3
Memphis, TN	30,472	28
Miami, FL	34,681	26
Milwaukee, WI	5,061	45
Minneapolis, MN	38,349	21
Nashville-Davidson, TN	27,793	30
New Orleans, LA	48,641	16
New York City, NY	1,154,332	1
Newark, NJ	8,227	43
Oakland, CA	37,347	22
Oklahoma City, OK	24,195	32
Omaha, NE	13,111	40
Philadelphia, PA	35,114	25
Pittsburgh, PA	29,155	29
Portland, OR	31,344	27
Sacramento, CA	42,560	20
Saint Louis, MO	58,460	14
San Antonio, TX	23,906	33
San Diego, CA	71,953	10
San Francisco, CA	106,823	6
San Jose, CA	73,723	9
Seattle, WA	71,249	11
Toledo, OH	0	48
Tulsa, OK	14,031	39
Virginia Beach, VA	54,026	15
Washington, DC	229,336	4

Source: U.S. Bureau of the Census, *Annual Survey of Government Finances 1992*, Washington, D.C.: U.S. Government Printing Office, 1995, n.p. Primary source: U.S. Bureau of the Census.

★2759★

City Government Revenues

City Government Revenues, 1991-92: General Revenues From Own Sources (Taxes)

[In thousands of dollars]

City	Total revenues	Rank
Albuquerque, NM	132,368	45
Atlanta, GA	222,877	29
Austin, TX	176,183	36
Baltimore, MD	664,387	8

[Continued]

★2760★
City Government Revenues

City Government Revenues, 1991-92: General Revenues From Own Sources (Tobacco Products)

[In thousands of dollars]

City	Total revenues	Rank
Albuquerque, NM	9,771	33
Atlanta, GA	24,212	22
Austin, TX	9,228	35
Baltimore, MD	27,841	18
Baton Rouge, LA	34,816	13
Boston, MA	0	40
Buffalo, NY	14,427	28
Charlotte, NC	2,086	38
Chicago, IL	292,101	2
Cincinnati, OH	1,237	39
Cleveland, OH	0	40
Columbus, OH	0	40
Dallas, TX	60,675	7
Denver, CO	16,664	26
Detroit, MI	43,582	11
El Paso, TX	9,436	34
Fort Worth, TX	18,451	25
Honolulu, HI	14,616	27
Houston, TX	129,035	4
Indianapolis, IN	0	40
Jacksonville, FL	40,835	12
Kansas City, MO	59,230	8
Los Angeles, CA	420,989	1
Memphis, TN	10,224	32
Miami, FL	29,936	17
Milwaukee, WI	0	40
Minneapolis, MN	14,245	29
Nashville-Davidson, TN	8,129	36
New Orleans, LA	26,291	20
New York City, NY	231,571	3
Newark, NJ	0	40
Oakland, CA	31,960	15
Oklahoma City, OK	21,812	24
Omaha, NE	11,090	30
Philadelphia, PA	0	40
Pittsburgh, PA	0	40
Portland, OR	24,077	23
Sacramento, CA	31,346	16
Saint Louis, MO	47,063	10
San Antonio, TX	7,028	37
San Diego, CA	27,237	19
San Francisco, CA	33,755	14
San Jose, CA	66,503	6
Seattle, WA	59,022	9
Toledo, OH	0	40
Tulsa, OK	10,979	31
Virginia Beach, VA	24,854	21
Washington, DC	115,297	5

Source: U.S. Bureau of the Census, *Annual Survey of Government Finances 1992*, Washington, D.C.: U.S. Government Printing Office, 1995, n.p. Primary source: U.S. Bureau of the Census.

★2761★
City Government Revenues

City Government Revenues, 1991-92: Intergovernmental Revenues From Federal Government

[In thousands of dollars]

City	Total revenues	Rank
Albuquerque, NM	29,372	24
Atlanta, GA	55,486	15
Austin, TX	8,470	46
Baltimore, MD	53,142	16
Baton Rouge, LA	24,188	31
Boston, MA	23,432	32
Buffalo, NY	45,033	19
Charlotte, NC	21,692	35
Chicago, IL	256,460	3
Cincinnati, OH	26,948	28
Cleveland, OH	63,270	11
Columbus, OH	47,364	18
Dallas, TX	41,774	20
Denver, CO	27,272	27
Detroit, MI	129,605	6
El Paso, TX	22,435	33
Fort Worth, TX	19,343	38
Honolulu, HI	61,289	13
Houston, TX	41,036	21
Indianapolis, IN	35,088	22
Jacksonville, FL	57,239	14
Kansas City, MO	27,663	26
Los Angeles, CA	137,364	5
Memphis, TN	26,740	29
Miami, FL	13,931	40
Milwaukee, WI	50,432	17
Minneapolis, MN	26,097	30
Nashville-Davidson, TN	12,614	42
New Orleans, LA	77,804	10
New York City, NY	1,149,685	2
Newark, NJ	61,593	12
Oakland, CA	29,072	25
Oklahoma City, OK	10,141	44
Omaha, NE	4,075	47
Philadelphia, PA	156,801	4
Pittsburgh, PA	20,818	37
Portland, OR	11,757	43
Sacramento, CA	906	48
Saint Louis, MO	32,477	23
San Antonio, TX	22,162	34
San Diego, CA	91,791	8
San Francisco, CA	121,575	7
San Jose, CA	9,435	45
Seattle, WA	21,392	36
Toledo, OH	13,415	41
Tulsa, OK	15,315	39
Virginia Beach, VA	91,232	9
Washington, DC	1,450,536	1

Source: U.S. Bureau of the Census, *Annual Survey of Government Finances 1992*, Washington, D.C.: U.S. Government Printing Office, 1995, n.p. Primary source: U.S. Bureau of the Census.

★2762★

City Government Revenues

City Government Revenues, 1991-92: Intergovernmental Revenues From Local Governments

[In thousands of dollars]

City	Total revenues	Rank
Albuquerque, NM	9,805	20
Atlanta, GA	72,714	5
Austin, TX	3,768	30
Baltimore, MD	86,288	3
Baton Rouge, LA	4,885	25
Boston, MA	1,570	37
Buffalo, NY	72,510	6
Charlotte, NC	39,337	13
Chicago, IL	5	47
Cincinnati, OH	18,636	17
Cleveland, OH	972	39
Columbus, OH	6,410	22
Dallas, TX	2,903	34
Denver, CO	585	41
Detroit, MI	43,348	11
El Paso, TX	2,636	35
Fort Worth, TX	3,652	31
Honolulu, HI	585	41
Houston, TX	11,487	19
Indianapolis, IN	1,402	38
Jacksonville, FL	257	44
Kansas City, MO	4,657	28
Los Angeles, CA	87,852	2
Memphis, TN	275,880	1
Miami, FL	6,608	21
Milwaukee, WI	417	42
Minneapolis, MN	14,917	18
Nashville-Davidson, TN	779	40
New Orleans, LA	10	46
New York City, NY	81,030	4
Newark, NJ	22,361	16
Oakland, CA	5,202	24
Oklahoma City, OK	111	45
Omaha, NE	4,210	29
Philadelphia, PA	71,270	7
Pittsburgh, PA	48,331	9
Portland, OR	26,387	15
Sacramento, CA	6,347	23
Saint Louis, MO	3,567	33
San Antonio, TX	42,483	12
San Diego, CA	45,144	10
San Francisco, CA	4,741	26
San Jose, CA	28,356	14
Seattle, WA	4,687	27
Toledo, OH	2,019	36
Tulsa, OK	351	43
Virginia Beach, VA	3,651	32
Washington, DC	57,604	8

Source: U.S. Bureau of the Census, *Annual Survey of Government Finances 1992,* Washington, D.C.: U.S. Government Printing Office, 1995, n.p. Primary source: U.S. Bureau of the Census.

★2763★

City Government Revenues

City Government Revenues, 1991-92: Intergovernmental Revenues From State Governments (For Education)

[In thousands of dollars]

City	Total revenues	Rank
Albuquerque, NM	9,890	9
Austin, TX	109,481	7
Boston, MA	356,293	2
Charlotte, NC	4,078,689	1
Detroit, MI	165,657	5
Indianapolis, IN	147	14
Nashville-Davidson, TN	198,017	4
New York City, NY	291,041	3
Newark, NJ	294	12
Oakland, CA	209	13
Pittsburgh, PA	2,465	11
Salt Lake, UT	8,405	10
San Jose, CA	50,345	8
Virginia Beach, VA	115,673	6

Source: U.S. Bureau of the Census, *Annual Survey of Government Finances 1992,* Washington, D.C.: U.S. Government Printing Office, 1995, n.p. Primary source: U.S. Bureau of the Census.

★2764★

City Government Revenues

City Government (300,000 Population and More) Revenues, 1991-92: Intergovernmental Revenues From State Governments (For General Support of Local Government

[In thousands of dollars]

City	Total revenues	Rank
Albuquerque, NM	95,129	8
Atlanta, GA	0	45
Austin, TX	1,555	39
Baltimore, MD	38,413	15
Baton Rouge, LA	6,971	32
Boston, MA	285,003	3
Buffalo, NY	27,543	21
Charlotte, NC	29,725	18
Chicago, IL	225,222	4
Cincinnati, OH	27,120	22
Cleveland, OH	45,946	13
Columbus, OH	29,419	19
Dallas, TX	3,129	36
Denver, CO	3,129	36
Detroit, MI	298,164	2
El Paso, TX	798	41
Fort Worth, TX	903	40
Honolulu, HI	33,833	17
Houston, TX	5,100	33
Indianapolis, IN	102,493	7
Jacksonville, FL	68,556	11
Kansas City, MO	0	45

[Continued]

★2764★

City Government (300,000 Population and More) Revenues, 1991-92: Intergovernmental Revenues From State Governments (For General Support of Local Government
[Continued]

City	Total revenues	Rank
Los Angeles, CA	141,006	6
Memphis, TN	36,828	16
Miami, FL	24,330	25
Milwaukee, WI	215,127	5
Minneapolis, MN	83,667	9
Nashville-Davidson, TN	24,945	24
New Orleans, LA	7,930	30
New York City, NY	647,997	1
Newark, NJ	70,552	10
Oakland, CA	14,982	28
Oklahoma City, OK	605	42
Omaha, NE	7,974	29
Philadelphia, PA	25,068	23
Pittsburgh, PA	4,131	35
Portland, OR	4,772	34
Sacramento, CA	15,095	27
Saint Louis, MO	570	43
San Antonio, TX	1,694	38
San Diego, CA	42,902	14
San Francisco, CA	66,074	12
San Jose, CA	28,961	20
Seattle, WA	7,136	31
Toledo, OH	15,142	26
Tulsa, OK	460	44
Virginia Beach, VA	1,750	37
Washington, DC	0	45

Source: U.S. Bureau of the Census, *Annual Survey of Government Finances 1992,* Washington, D.C.: U.S. Government Printing Office, 1995, n.p. Primary source: U.S. Bureau of the Census.

★2765★

City Government Revenues

City Government Revenues, 1991-92: Intergovernmental Revenues From State Governments (For Health and Hospitals)
[In thousands of dollars]

City	Total revenues	Rank
Albuquerque, NM	4,469	15
Atlanta, GA	0	33
Austin, TX	3,116	19
Baltimore, MD	104,797	4
Baton Rouge, LA	322	29
Boston, MA	0	33
Buffalo, NY	1,265	25
Charlotte, NC	0	33
Chicago, IL	36,083	6
Cincinnati, OH	7,555	9

[Continued]

★2765★

City Government Revenues, 1991-92: Intergovernmental Revenues From State Governments (For Health and Hospitals)
[Continued]

City	Total revenues	Rank
Cleveland, OH	638	28
Columbus, OH	709	27
Dallas, TX	3,325	18
Denver, CO	5,305	12
Detroit, MI	36,230	5
El Paso, TX	3,435	17
Fort Worth, TX	2,561	22
Honolulu, HI	0	33
Houston, TX	3,935	16
Indianapolis, IN	9,971	7
Jacksonville, FL	37	32
Kansas City, MO	4,725	13
Los Angeles, CA	63	31
Memphis, TN	0	33
Miami, FL	0	33
Milwaukee, WI	1,201	26
Minneapolis, MN	2,915	21
Nashville-Davidson, TN	6,283	10
New Orleans, LA	2,967	20
New York City, NY	283,287	1
Newark, NJ	2,144	23
Oakland, CA	0	33
Oklahoma City, OK	0	33
Omaha, NE	218	30
Philadelphia, PA	207,485	3
Pittsburgh, PA	0	33
Portland, OR	0	33
Sacramento, CA	0	33
Saint Louis, MO	8,349	8
San Antonio, TX	4,544	14
San Diego, CA	0	33
San Francisco, CA	224,198	2
San Jose, CA	0	33
Seattle, WA	0	33
Toledo, OH	1,547	24
Tulsa, OK	0	33
Virginia Beach, VA	6,020	11
Washington, DC	0	33

Source: U.S. Bureau of the Census, *Annual Survey of Government Finances 1992,* Washington, D.C.: U.S. Government Printing Office, 1995, n.p. Primary source: U.S. Bureau of the Census.

★2766★
City Government Revenues

City Government Revenues, 1991-92: Intergovernmental Revenues From State Governments (For Highways)

[In thousands of dollars]

City	Total revenues	Rank
Albuquerque, NM	7,645	27
Atlanta, GA	363	39
Austin, TX	1,845	37
Baltimore, MD	171,435	1
Baton Rouge, LA	3,819	33
Boston, MA	16,469	18
Buffalo, NY	0	42
Charlotte, NC	10,291	26
Chicago, IL	116,335	3
Cincinnati, OH	14,571	20
Cleveland, OH	18,256	16
Columbus, OH	14,426	22
Dallas, TX	79	40
Denver, CO	18,582	14
Detroit, MI	37,445	5
El Paso, TX	0	42
Fort Worth, TX	0	42
Hillsborough, FL	0	42
Honolulu, HI	0	42
Houston, TX	458	38
Indianapolis, IN	26,937	7
Jacksonville, FL	6,833	29
Kansas City, MO	10,333	25
Los Angeles, CA	70,676	4
Memphis, TN	19,134	11
Miami, FL	0	42
Milwaukee, WI	33,627	6
Minneapolis, MN	13,669	23
Nashville-Davidson, TN	16,425	19
New Orleans, LA	3,038	35
New York City, NY	134,416	2
Newark, NJ	3,222	34
Oakland, CA	6,481	31
Oklahoma City, OK	0	42
Omaha, NE	14,569	21
Philadelphia, PA	21,960	8
Pittsburgh, PA	4,246	32
Portland, OR	20,793	9
Sacramento, CA	6,814	30
Saint Louis, MO	11,990	24
San Antonio, TX	12	41
San Diego, CA	20,240	10
San Francisco, CA	18,614	13
San Jose, CA	18,650	12
Seattle, WA	18,372	15
Toledo, OH	6,907	28
Tulsa, OK	2,608	36
Virginia Beach, VA	17,507	17
Washington, DC	0	42

Source: U.S. Bureau of the Census, *Annual Survey of Government Finances 1992,* Washington, D.C.: U.S. Government Printing Office, 1995, n.p. Primary source: U.S. Bureau of the Census.

★2767★
City Government Revenues

City Government Revenues, 1991-92: Intergovernmental Revenues From State Governments (For Public Welfare)

[In thousands of dollars]

City	Total revenues	Rank
Austin, TX	10,673	11
Baton Rouge, LA	1,591	16
Boston, MA	111,001	5
Chicago, IL	29,598	9
Cleveland, OH	1,629	15
Denver, CO	167,000	3
Indianapolis, IN	89,755	6
Nashville-Davidson, TN	43,883	7
New Orleans, LA	2,117	14
New York City, NY	6,011,379	1
Newark, NJ	34,365	8
Oakland, CA	265	17
Philadelphia, PA	120,012	4
Saint Louis, MO	2,296	13
San Antonio, TX	7,207	12
San Francisco, CA	309,645	2
Virginia Beach, VA	11,152	10

Source: U.S. Bureau of the Census, *Annual Survey of Government Finances 1992,* Washington, D.C.: U.S. Government Printing Office, 1995, n.p. Primary source: U.S. Bureau of the Census.

★2768★
City Government Revenues

City Government Revenues, 1991-92: Revenues From Charges (Education)

[In thousands of dollars]

City	Total revenues	Rank
Baltimore, MD	5,492	6
Boston, MA	3,337	7
Buffalo, NY	1,596	8
Memphis, TN	8,492	4
Nashville-Davidson, TN	8,278	5
New York City, NY	165,042	1
Oakland, CA	2	9
Virginia Beach, VA	10,954	3
Washington, DC	13,804	2

Source: U.S. Bureau of the Census, *Annual Survey of Government Finances 1992,* Washington, D.C.: U.S. Government Printing Office, 1995, n.p. Primary source: U.S. Bureau of the Census.

★2769★

City Government Revenues

City Government Revenues, 1991-92: Revenues From Charges and General Miscellaneous Revenues

[In thousands of dollars]

City	Total revenues	Rank
Albuquerque, NM	186,864	28
Atlanta, GA	333,895	13
Austin, TX	349,891	11
Baltimore, MD	213,795	25
Baton Rouge, LA	155,335	30
Boston, MA	296,823	15
Buffalo, NY	79,195	45
Charlotte, NC	152,435	32
Chicago, IL	884,034	3
Cincinnati, OH	189,802	27
Cleveland, OH	129,970	39
Columbus, OH	166,199	29
Dallas, TX	519,942	7
Denver, CO	406,410	10
Detroit, MI	310,544	14
El Paso, TX	111,361	41
Fort Worth, TX	142,974	36
Honolulu, HI	265,525	16
Houston, TX	573,659	5
Indianapolis, IN	229,933	21
Jacksonville, FL	337,686	12
Kansas City, MO	154,802	31
Los Angeles, CA	1,434,170	2
Memphis, TN	150,081	33
Miami, FL	87,163	44
Milwaukee, WI	127,084	40
Minneapolis, MN	257,500	17
Nashville-Davidson, TN	252,556	18
New Orleans, LA	234,186	20
New York City, NY	5,161,261	1
Newark, NJ	90,698	43
Oakland, CA	216,247	24
Oklahoma City, OK	142,052	37
Omaha, NE	47,537	47
Philadelphia, PA	460,553	9
Pittsburgh, PA	45,894	48
Portland, OR	133,867	38
Sacramento, CA	146,043	34
Saint Louis, MO	143,584	35
San Antonio, TX	213,418	26
San Diego, CA	557,974	6
San Francisco, CA	763,832	4
San Jose, CA	219,208	23
Seattle, WA	244,635	19
Toledo, OH	62,413	46
Tulsa, OK	220,618	22
Virginia Beach, VA	91,622	42
Washington, DC	504,624	8

Source: U.S. Bureau of the Census, *Annual Survey of Government Finances 1992*, Washington, D.C.: U.S. Government Printing Office, 1995, n.p. Primary source: U.S. Bureau of the Census.

★2770★

City Government Revenues

City Government Revenues, 1991-92: Revenues From Current Charges

[In thousands of dollars]

City	Total revenues	Rank
Albuquerque, NM	100,417	28
Atlanta, GA	209,484	13
Austin, TX	232,264	10
Baltimore, MD	101,085	27
Baton Rouge, LA	91,130	35
Boston, MA	199,973	14
Buffalo, NY	56,518	42
Charlotte, NC	103,874	26
Chicago, IL	520,373	3
Cincinnati, OH	116,948	24
Cleveland, OH	68,688	39
Columbus, OH	123,483	23
Dallas, TX	383,312	6
Denver, CO	271,743	8
Detroit, MI	218,769	12
El Paso, TX	60,460	41
Fort Worth, TX	69,168	38
Honolulu, HI	174,075	17
Houston, TX	404,566	5
Indianapolis, IN	186,481	15
Jacksonville, FL	149,671	18
Kansas City, MO	83,447	36
Los Angeles, CA	922,370	2
Memphis, TN	99,221	29
Miami, FL	56,342	43
Milwaukee, WI	65,559	40
Minneapolis, MN	95,360	32
Nashville-Davidson, TN	135,850	22
New Orleans, LA	147,538	20
New York City, NY	3,575,377	1
Newark, NJ	47,544	45
Oakland, CA	148,042	19
Oklahoma City, OK	97,264	31
Omaha, NE	39,311	47
Philadelphia, PA	334,681	7
Pittsburgh, PA	12,361	48
Portland, OR	83,210	37
Sacramento, CA	92,480	34
Saint Louis, MO	93,024	33
San Antonio, TX	97,790	30
San Diego, CA	222,063	11
San Francisco, CA	467,729	4
San Jose, CA	142,064	21
Seattle, WA	177,670	16
Toledo, OH	47,773	44
Tulsa, OK	116,100	25
Virginia Beach, VA	45,759	46
Washington, DC	263,671	9

Source: U.S. Bureau of the Census, *Annual Survey of Government Finances 1992*, Washington, D.C.: U.S. Government Printing Office, 1995, n.p. Primary source: U.S. Bureau of the Census.

★2771★
City Government Revenues

City Government Revenues, 1991-92: Revenues From Current Charges (Airports)

[In thousands of dollars]

City	Total revenues	Rank
Albuquerque, NM	28,700	17
Atlanta, GA	126,032	7
Austin, TX	15,393	23
Baltimore, MD	0	30
Baton Rouge, LA	5,748	25
Boston, MA	0	30
Buffalo, NY	0	30
Charlotte, NC	49,149	12
Chicago, IL	328,036	1
Cincinnati, OH	1,093	29
Cleveland, OH	33,846	16
Columbus, OH	21,540	20
Dallas, TX	204,612	3
Denver, CO	135,823	5
Detroit, MI	2,137	26
El Paso, TX	12,162	24
Fort Worth, TX	1,104	28
Honolulu, HI	0	30
Houston, TX	128,912	6
Indianapolis, IN	41,109	14
Jacksonville, FL	17,065	22
Kansas City, MO	43,520	13
Los Angeles, CA	244,830	2
Memphis, TN	0	30
Miami, FL	0	30
Milwaukee, WI	0	30
Minneapolis, MN	0	30
Nashville-Davidson, TN	0	30
New Orleans, LA	39,327	15
New York City, NY	0	30
Newark, NJ	0	30
Oakland, CA	52,946	10
Oklahoma City, OK	24,195	19
Omaha, NE	0	30
Philadelphia, PA	105,502	8
Pittsburgh, PA	0	30
Portland, OR	0	30
Sacramento, CA	0	30
Saint Louis, MO	67,073	9
San Antonio, TX	27,114	18
San Diego, CA	1,680	27
San Francisco, CA	162,274	4
San Jose, CA	49,215	11
Seattle, WA	0	30
Toledo, OH	0	30
Tulsa, OK	18,482	21
Virginia Beach, VA	0	30
Washington, DC	0	30

Source: U.S. Bureau of the Census, *Annual Survey of Government Finances 1992*, Washington, D.C.: U.S. Government Printing Office, 1995, n.p. Primary source: U.S. Bureau of the Census.

★2772★
City Government Revenues

City Government Revenues, 1991-92: Revenues From Current Charges (Commercial Activity– Miscellaneous)

[In thousands of dollars]

City	Total revenues	Rank
Atlanta, GA	46	16
Baltimore, MD	6,046	4
Charlotte, NC	244	11
Cincinnati, OH	155	15
Cleveland, OH	2,326	5
Dallas, TX	6,166	3
Detroit, MI	727	7
Miami, FL	3	18
Minneapolis, MN	34	17
Nashville-Davidson, TN	444	10
New Orleans, LA	8,396	2
New York City, NY	61,494	1
Saint Louis, MO	195	14
San Antonio, TX	694	8
San Diego, CA	507	9
San Francisco, CA	210	12
Toledo, OH	205	13
Washington, DC	814	6

Source: U.S. Bureau of the Census, *Annual Survey of Government Finances 1992*, Washington, D.C.: U.S. Government Printing Office, 1995, n.p. Primary source: U.S. Bureau of the Census.

★2773★
City Government Revenues

City Government Revenues, 1991-92: Revenues From Current Charges (Education–Other Charges for Local Schools)

[In thousands of dollars]

City	Total revenues	Rank
Baltimore, MD	805	5
Boston, MA	617	6
Buffalo, NY	241	8
Memphis, TN	1,372	3
Nashville-Davidson, TN	1,049	4
New York City, NY	6,994	1
Oakland, CA	2	9
Virginia Beach, VA	2,786	2
Washington, DC	283	7

Source: U.S. Bureau of the Census, *Annual Survey of Government Finances 1992*, Washington, D.C.: U.S. Government Printing Office, 1995, n.p. Primary source: U.S. Bureau of the Census.

★2774★

City Government Revenues

City Government Revenues, 1991-92: Revenues From Current Charges (Education – School Lunch Gross Sales)

[In thousands of dollars]

City	Total revenues	Rank
Baltimore, MD	4,687	5
Boston, MA	2,720	6
Buffalo, NY	1,355	8
Memphis, TN	7,120	4
Nashville-Davidson, TN	7,229	3
New York City, NY	22,206	1
Virginia Beach, VA	8,168	2
Washington, DC	1,818	7

Source: U.S. Bureau of the Census, *Annual Survey of Government Finances 1992,* Washington, D.C.: U.S. Government Printing Office, 1995, n.p. Primary source: U.S. Bureau of the Census.

★2775★

City Government Revenues

City Government Revenues, 1991-92: Revenues From Current Charges (Higher Education)

[In thousands of dollars]

City	Total revenues	Rank
New York City, NY	135,842	1
Washington, DC	11,703	2

Source: U.S. Bureau of the Census, *Annual Survey of Government Finances 1992,* Washington, D.C.: U.S. Government Printing Office, 1995, n.p. Primary source: U.S. Bureau of the Census.

★2776★

City Government Revenues

City Government Revenues, 1991-92: Revenues From Current Charges (Highways)

[In thousands of dollars]

City	Total revenues	Rank
Albuquerque, NM	1,619	12
Atlanta, GA	0	36
Austin, TX	192	25
Baltimore, MD	847	18
Baton Rouge, LA	0	36
Boston, MA	0	36
Buffalo, NY	0	36
Charlotte, NC	0	36
Chicago, IL	22,754	2
Cincinnati, OH	4,204	5
Cleveland, OH	1,265	14
Columbus, OH	4,078	7
Dallas, TX	1,289	13
Denver, CO	178	26

[Continued]

★2776★

City Government Revenues, 1991-92: Revenues From Current Charges (Highways)

[Continued]

City	Total revenues	Rank
Detroit, MI	1,079	15
El Paso, TX	6,134	3
Fort Worth, TX	9	35
Honolulu, HI	884	16
Houston, TX	355	22
Indianapolis, IN	86	29
Jacksonville, FL	45	31
Kansas City, MO	0	36
Los Angeles, CA	4,199	6
Memphis, TN	0	36
Miami, FL	0	36
Milwaukee, WI	314	23
Minneapolis, MN	1,792	10
Nashville-Davidson, TN	0	36
New Orleans, LA	1,777	11
New York City, NY	696,235	1
Newark, NJ	61	30
Oakland, CA	17	34
Oklahoma City, OK	152	27
Omaha, NE	798	19
Philadelphia, PA	0	36
Pittsburgh, PA	311	24
Portland, OR	26	32
Sacramento, CA	22	33
Saint Louis, MO	709	21
San Antonio, TX	137	28
San Diego, CA	0	36
San Francisco, CA	725	20
San Jose, CA	2,470	9
Seattle, WA	870	17
Toledo, OH	5,820	4
Tulsa, OK	3,053	8
Virginia Beach, VA	0	36
Washington, DC	0	36

Source: U.S. Bureau of the Census, *Annual Survey of Government Finances 1992,* Washington, D.C.: U.S. Government Printing Office, 1995, n.p. Primary source: U.S. Bureau of the Census.

★2777★

City Government Revenues

City Government Revenues, 1991-92: Revenues From Current Charges (Hospitals)

[In thousands of dollars]

City	Total revenues	Rank
Austin, TX	100,870	2
Baton Rouge, LA	28,548	8
Boston, MA	82,915	4
Denver, CO	40,198	7
Indianapolis, IN	47,597	6

[Continued]

★2777★

City Government Revenues, 1991-92: Revenues From Current Charges (Hospitals)
[Continued]

City	Total revenues	Rank
Nashville-Davidson, TN	16,180	9
New York City, NY	1,123,841	1
San Francisco, CA	92,536	3
Washington, DC	69,822	5

Source: U.S. Bureau of the Census, *Annual Survey of Government Finances 1992,* Washington, D.C.: U.S. Government Printing Office, 1995, n.p. Primary source: U.S. Bureau of the Census.

★2778★
City Government Revenues

City Government Revenues, 1991-92: Revenues From Current Charges (Housing and Community Development)

[In thousands of dollars]

City	Total revenues	Rank
Albuquerque, NM	1,309	21
Atlanta, GA	1,850	19
Austin, TX	30	38
Baltimore, MD	0	41
Baton Rouge, LA	1,433	20
Boston, MA	10,430	7
Buffalo, NY	15,994	4
Charlotte, NC	327	31
Chicago, IL	0	41
Cincinnati, OH	334	30
Cleveland, OH	0	41
Columbus, OH	0	41
Dallas, TX	110	33
Denver, CO	2,159	18
Detroit, MI	7,978	11
El Paso, TX	0	41
Fort Worth, TX	82	35
Honolulu, HI	9,555	9
Houston, TX	90	34
Indianapolis, IN	3,083	15
Jacksonville, FL	3,490	14
Kansas City, MO	0	41
Los Angeles, CA	27,056	2
Memphis, TN	849	26
Miami, FL	28	39
Milwaukee, WI	14,777	6
Minneapolis, MN	2,534	17
Nashville-Davidson, TN	0	41
New Orleans, LA	10,364	8
New York City, NY	665,403	1
Newark, NJ	14,884	5
Oakland, CA	3,001	16
Oklahoma City, OK	402	29

[Continued]

★2778★

City Government Revenues, 1991-92: Revenues From Current Charges (Housing and Community Development)
[Continued]

City	Total revenues	Rank
Omaha, NE	854	25
Philadelphia, PA	1,182	22
Pittsburgh, PA	225	32
Portland, OR	8,165	10
Sacramento, CA	0	41
Saint Louis, MO	572	27
San Antonio, TX	493	28
San Diego, CA	7,678	12
San Francisco, CA	4,512	13
San Jose, CA	871	24
Seattle, WA	37	37
Toledo, OH	39	36
Tulsa, OK	943	23
Virginia Beach, VA	18	40
Washington, DC	19,579	3

Source: U.S. Bureau of the Census, *Annual Survey of Government Finances 1992,* Washington, D.C.: U.S. Government Printing Office, 1995, n.p. Primary source: U.S. Bureau of the Census.

★2779★
City Government Revenues

City Government Revenues, 1991-92: Revenues From Current Charges (Parking Facilities)

[In thousands of dollars]

City	Total revenues	Rank
Albuquerque, NM	2,109	34
Atlanta, GA	180	48
Austin, TX	1,262	39
Baltimore, MD	17,254	4
Baton Rouge, LA	828	42
Boston, MA	13,345	7
Buffalo, NY	5,302	19
Charlotte, NC	718	45
Chicago, IL	12,331	9
Cincinnati, OH	7,577	15
Cleveland, OH	2,864	27
Columbus, OH	2,614	31
Dallas, TX	2,725	29
Denver, CO	4,087	23
Detroit, MI	13,007	8
El Paso, TX	727	44
Fort Worth, TX	1,179	40
Honolulu, HI	5,729	18
Houston, TX	2,281	33
Indianapolis, IN	2,836	28
Jacksonville, FL	3,149	26
Kansas City, MO	1,950	35

[Continued]

★2779★

City Government Revenues, 1991-92: Revenues From Current Charges (Parking Facilities)
[Continued]

City	Total revenues	Rank
Los Angeles, CA	25,721	2
Memphis, TN	790	43
Miami, FL	10,493	14
Milwaukee, WI	7,524	16
Minneapolis, MN	18,063	3
Nashville-Davidson, TN	2,718	30
New Orleans, LA	2,590	32
New York City, NY	58,996	1
Newark, NJ	709	46
Oakland, CA	10,780	13
Oklahoma City, OK	4,944	20
Omaha, NE	1,887	36
Philadelphia, PA	1,590	38
Pittsburgh, PA	907	41
Portland, OR	10,890	12
Sacramento, CA	11,003	11
Saint Louis, MO	5,997	17
San Antonio, TX	3,877	24
San Diego, CA	4,811	21
San Francisco, CA	13,763	6
San Jose, CA	4,193	22
Seattle, WA	11,110	10
Toledo, OH	1,854	37
Tulsa, OK	3,703	25
Virginia Beach, VA	600	47
Washington, DC	14,080	5

Source: U.S. Bureau of the Census, *Annual Survey of Government Finances 1992*, Washington, D.C.: U.S. Government Printing Office, 1995, n.p. Primary source: U.S. Bureau of the Census.

★2780★

City Government Revenues

City Government Revenues, 1991-92: Revenues From Current Charges (Sewerage)
[In thousands of dollars]

City	Total revenues	Rank
Albuquerque, NM	28,857	34
Atlanta, GA	32,149	30
Austin, TX	84,672	10
Baltimore, MD	43,126	23
Baton Rouge, LA	21,139	42
Boston, MA	76,187	15
Buffalo, NY	26,672	37
Charlotte, NC	35,745	27
Chicago, IL	111,258	7
Cincinnati, OH	77,939	14
Cleveland, OH	14,329	45
Columbus, OH	79,432	11
Dallas, TX	105,252	8

[Continued]

★2780★

City Government Revenues, 1991-92: Revenues From Current Charges (Sewerage)
[Continued]

City	Total revenues	Rank
Denver, CO	43,472	22
Detroit, MI	159,161	5
El Paso, TX	22,130	40
Fort Worth, TX	42,655	24
Honolulu, HI	78,867	12
Houston, TX	237,172	3
Indianapolis, IN	45,981	21
Jacksonville, FL	50,196	20
Kansas City, MO	21,258	41
Los Angeles, CA	299,315	2
Memphis, TN	33,983	28
Miami, FL	5,757	46
Milwaukee, WI	28,800	35
Minneapolis, MN	32,094	31
Nashville-Davidson, TN	57,210	18
New Orleans, LA	39,161	26
New York City, NY	601,982	1
Newark, NJ	31,541	32
Oakland, CA	15,811	43
Oklahoma City, OK	39,428	25
Omaha, NE	27,947	36
Philadelphia, PA	181,707	4
Pittsburgh, PA	0	47
Portland, OR	50,378	19
Sacramento, CA	30,139	33
Saint Louis, MO	0	47
San Antonio, TX	15,085	44
San Diego, CA	125,210	6
San Francisco, CA	85,998	9
San Jose, CA	63,388	17
Seattle, WA	78,505	13
Toledo, OH	25,705	38
Tulsa, OK	32,816	29
Virginia Beach, VA	22,269	39
Washington, DC	70,777	16

Source: U.S. Bureau of the Census, *Annual Survey of Government Finances 1992*, Washington, D.C.: U.S. Government Printing Office, 1995, n.p. Primary source: U.S. Bureau of the Census.

★2781★

City Government Revenues

City Government Revenues, 1991-92: Revenues From Current Charges (Water Transportation and Terminals)

[In thousands of dollars]

City	Total revenues	Rank
Baltimore, MD	572	11
Jacksonville, FL	22,355	4
Los Angeles, CA	174,661	1
Memphis, TN	998	8
Milwaukee, WI	2,907	6
Minneapolis, MN	2,529	7
New Orleans, LA	898	9
New York City, NY	8,792	5
Oakland, CA	54,443	2
Omaha, NE	31	12
Saint Louis, MO	817	10
San Francisco, CA	33,982	3

Source: U.S. Bureau of the Census, *Annual Survey of Government Finances 1992,* Washington, D.C.: U.S. Government Printing Office, 1995, n.p. Primary source: U.S. Bureau of the Census.

★2782★

City Government Revenues

City Government Revenues, 1991-92: Revenues From Fines and Forfeits

[In thousands of dollars]

City	Total revenues	Rank
Albuquerque, NM	1,744	44
Atlanta, GA	13,078	14
Austin, TX	7,142	26
Baltimore, MD	16,062	10
Baton Rouge, LA	2,851	38
Boston, MA	46,855	6
Buffalo, NY	5,236	33
Charlotte, NC	1,024	46
Chicago, IL	83,257	2
Cincinnati, OH	2,609	40
Cleveland, OH	9,916	17
Columbus, OH	7,995	23
Dallas, TX	18,906	9
Denver, CO	14,340	12
Detroit, MI	20,215	8
El Paso, TX	8,214	22
Fort Worth, TX	4,258	35
Honolulu, HI	612	47
Houston, TX	34,862	7
Indianapolis, IN	2,551	41
Jacksonville, FL	6,014	29
Kansas City, MO	13,380	13
Los Angeles, CA	73,737	3
Memphis, TN	6,440	28
Miami, FL	1,175	45
Milwaukee, WI	9,120	20
Minneapolis, MN	7,264	25

[Continued]

★2782★

City Government Revenues, 1991-92: Revenues From Fines and Forfeits

[Continued]

City	Total revenues	Rank
Nashville-Davidson, TN	5,164	34
New Orleans, LA	10,471	16
New York City, NY	408,274	1
Newark, NJ	9,845	18
Oakland, CA	5,636	30
Oklahoma City, OK	9,478	19
Omaha, NE	157	48
Philadelphia, PA	8,813	21
Pittsburgh, PA	5,307	32
Portland, OR	3,813	36
Sacramento, CA	2,513	42
Saint Louis, MO	6,895	27
San Antonio, TX	7,493	24
San Diego, CA	15,370	11
San Francisco, CA	47,753	5
San Jose, CA	3,383	37
Seattle, WA	11,697	15
Toledo, OH	1,782	43
Tulsa, OK	5,351	31
Virginia Beach, VA	2,704	39
Washington, DC	51,860	4

Source: U.S. Bureau of the Census, *Annual Survey of Government Finances 1992,* Washington, D.C.: U.S. Government Printing Office, 1995, n.p. Primary source: U.S. Bureau of the Census.

★2783★

City Government Revenues

City Government Revenues, 1991-92: Revenues From Interest Earnings

[In thousands of dollars]

City	Total revenues	Rank
Albuquerque, NM	76,757	17
Atlanta, GA	92,403	12
Austin, TX	102,568	10
Baltimore, MD	76,298	18
Baton Rouge, LA	54,591	22
Boston, MA	18,509	43
Buffalo, NY	8,595	45
Charlotte, NC	35,099	33
Chicago, IL	272,399	3
Cincinnati, OH	36,565	32
Cleveland, OH	41,542	29
Columbus, OH	27,329	38
Dallas, TX	87,299	16
Denver, CO	89,488	14
Detroit, MI	47,883	25
El Paso, TX	39,457	30
Fort Worth, TX	53,495	23
Honolulu, HI	47,451	26

[Continued]

★2783★
City Government Revenues, 1991-92: Revenues From Interest Earnings
[Continued]

City	Total revenues	Rank
Houston, TX	119,865	8
Indianapolis, IN	31,357	36
Jacksonville, FL	175,562	5
Kansas City, MO	46,983	27
Los Angeles, CA	338,763	2
Memphis, TN	24,710	39
Miami, FL	18,431	44
Milwaukee, WI	44,956	28
Minneapolis, MN	136,970	7
Nashville-Davidson, TN	105,102	9
New Orleans, LA	63,471	20
New York City, NY	678,092	1
Newark, NJ	4,545	48
Oakland, CA	58,935	21
Oklahoma City, OK	24,196	40
Omaha, NE	6,237	47
Philadelphia, PA	88,024	15
Pittsburgh, PA	23,569	41
Portland, OR	33,062	35
Sacramento, CA	19,301	42
Saint Louis, MO	38,642	31
San Antonio, TX	91,333	13
San Diego, CA	178,059	4
San Francisco, CA	161,026	6
San Jose, CA	49,102	24
Seattle, WA	28,653	37
Toledo, OH	8,522	46
Tulsa, OK	96,405	11
Virginia Beach, VA	33,324	34
Washington, DC	67,838	19

Source: U.S. Bureau of the Census, *Annual Survey of Government Finances 1992*, Washington, D.C.: U.S. Government Printing Office, 1995, n.p. Primary source: U.S. Bureau of the Census.

★2784★
City Government Revenues
City Government Revenues, 1991-92: Revenues From Sales of Property

[In thousands of dollars]

City	Total revenues	Rank
Albuquerque, NM	196	34
Atlanta, GA	1,193	19
Austin, TX	90	38
Baltimore, MD	0	44
Baton Rouge, LA	112	37
Boston, MA	21,421	2
Buffalo, NY	460	27
Charlotte, NC	352	30
Chicago, IL	2,181	9

[Continued]

★2784★
City Government Revenues, 1991-92: Revenues From Sales of Property
[Continued]

City	Total revenues	Rank
Cincinnati, OH	1,817	14
Cleveland, OH	0	44
Columbus, OH	54	41
Dallas, TX	1,760	15
Denver, CO	722	22
Detroit, MI	1,486	17
El Paso, TX	15	42
Fort Worth, TX	412	28
Honolulu, HI	2,674	8
Houston, TX	683	23
Indianapolis, IN	77	39
Jacksonville, FL	191	35
Kansas City, MO	568	24
Los Angeles, CA	26,346	1
Memphis, TN	1,521	16
Miami, FL	278	31
Milwaukee, WI	1,300	18
Minneapolis, MN	1,118	20
Nashville-Davidson, TN	166	36
New Orleans, LA	225	33
New York City, NY	8,441	4
Newark, NJ	2,711	7
Oakland, CA	535	25
Oklahoma City, OK	518	26
Omaha, NE	1	43
Philadelphia, PA	1,970	12
Pittsburgh, PA	0	44
Portland, OR	822	21
Sacramento, CA	245	32
Saint Louis, MO	2,157	10
San Antonio, TX	1,979	11
San Diego, CA	15,593	3
San Francisco, CA	1,893	13
San Jose, CA	0	44
Seattle, WA	386	29
Toledo, OH	0	44
Tulsa, OK	62	40
Virginia Beach, VA	6,639	5
Washington, DC	3,874	6

Source: U.S. Bureau of the Census, *Annual Survey of Government Finances 1992*, Washington, D.C.: U.S. Government Printing Office, 1995, n.p. Primary source: U.S. Bureau of the Census.

★2785★

City Government Revenues

City Government Revenues, 1991-92: Revenues From Sales of Property (Housing and Community Development)

[In thousands of dollars]

City	Total revenues	Rank
Atlanta, GA	38	18
Boston, MA	8,905	2
Charlotte, NC	352	13
Detroit, MI	1,417	6
Honolulu, HI	1,680	5
Jacksonville, FL	171	14
Kansas City, MO	568	10
Los Angeles, CA	3,053	3
Memphis, TN	33	19
Miami, FL	61	17
Minneapolis, MN	663	9
Oklahoma City, OK	501	11
Philadelphia, PA	1,970	4
Portland, OR	395	12
Saint Louis, MO	789	8
San Antonio, TX	164	15
San Diego, CA	15,593	1
San Francisco, CA	895	7
Tulsa, OK	62	16

Source: U.S. Bureau of the Census, *Annual Survey of Government Finances 1992,* Washington, D.C.: U.S. Government Printing Office, 1995, n.p. Primary source: U.S. Bureau of the Census.

★2786★

City Government Revenues

City Government Revenues, 1991-92: Revenues From Special Assessments

[In thousands of dollars]

City	Total revenues	Rank
Albuquerque, NM	5,725	10
Atlanta, GA	359	30
Austin, TX	1,601	20
Baltimore, MD	0	39
Baton Rouge, LA	265	32
Boston, MA	0	39
Buffalo, NY	575	27
Charlotte, NC	0	39
Chicago, IL	2,993	15
Cincinnati, OH	1,668	18
Cleveland, OH	96	34
Columbus, OH	248	33
Dallas, TX	3,825	14
Denver, CO	10,377	6
Detroit, MI	1,327	22
El Paso, TX	0	39
Fort Worth, TX	1,627	19
Honolulu, HI	27,919	1
Houston, TX	1,092	23
Indianapolis, IN	2,248	17

[Continued]

★2786★

City Government Revenues, 1991-92: Revenues From Special Assessments

[Continued]

City	Total revenues	Rank
Jacksonville, FL	268	31
Kansas City, MO	2,370	16
Los Angeles, CA	11,109	5
Memphis, TN	0	39
Miami, FL	6,294	9
Milwaukee, WI	5,662	11
Minneapolis, MN	6,918	8
Nashville-Davidson, TN	0	39
New Orleans, LA	25	36
New York City, NY	0	39
Newark, NJ	0	39
Oakland, CA	490	29
Oklahoma City, OK	46	35
Omaha, NE	1,522	21
Philadelphia, PA	24	37
Pittsburgh, PA	0	39
Portland, OR	7,810	7
Sacramento, CA	12,013	4
Saint Louis, MO	566	28
San Antonio, TX	5,129	12
San Diego, CA	18,139	2
San Francisco, CA	0	39
San Jose, CA	15,886	3
Seattle, WA	1,040	25
Toledo, OH	1,057	24
Tulsa, OK	881	26
Virginia Beach, VA	5	38
Washington, DC	4,802	13

Source: U.S. Bureau of the Census, *Annual Survey of Government Finances 1992,* Washington, D.C.: U.S. Government Printing Office, 1995, n.p. Primary source: U.S. Bureau of the Census.

★2787★

City Government Revenues

City Government Revenues, 1991-92: Revenues From Utilities and Liquor Stores

[In thousands of dollars]

City	Total revenues	Rank
Albuquerque, NM	43,444	31
Atlanta, GA	60,911	23
Austin, TX	500,130	8
Baltimore, MD	51,525	27
Baton Rouge, LA	2,821	44
Boston, MA	68,931	20
Buffalo, NY	19,533	40
Charlotte, NC	34,061	35
Chicago, IL	228,370	11
Cincinnati, OH	64,154	22
Cleveland, OH	167,464	14

[Continued]

★2787★

City Government Revenues, 1991-92: Revenues From Utilities and Liquor Stores

[Continued]

City	Total revenues	Rank
Columbus, OH	88,692	18
Dallas, TX	121,938	16
Denver, CO	85,275	19
Detroit, MI	169,039	13
El Paso, TX	41,547	32
Fort Worth, TX	64,998	21
Honolulu, HI	91,095	17
Houston, TX	234,720	10
Indianapolis, IN	7,335	42
Jacksonville, FL	728,716	5
Kansas City, MO	46,960	29
Los Angeles, CA	2,141,337	1
Memphis, TN	843,888	3
Miami, FL	0	45
Milwaukee, WI	48,416	28
Minneapolis, MN	23,179	37
Nashville-Davidson, TN	604,657	6
New Orleans, LA	55,727	24
New York City, NY	1,993,472	2
Newark, NJ	3,668	43
Oakland, CA	0	45
Oklahoma City, OK	38,170	34
Omaha, NE	0	45
Philadelphia, PA	586,565	7
Pittsburgh, PA	0	45
Portland, OR	51,527	26
Sacramento, CA	20,311	39
Saint Louis, MO	30,186	36
San Antonio, TX	838,663	4
San Diego, CA	125,068	15
San Francisco, CA	224,835	12
San Jose, CA	8,278	41
Seattle, WA	332,192	9
Toledo, OH	20,659	38
Tulsa, OK	44,153	30
Virginia Beach, VA	39,372	33
Washington, DC	53,587	25

Source: U.S. Bureau of the Census, *Annual Survey of Government Finances 1992*, Washington, D.C.: U.S. Government Printing Office, 1995, n.p. Primary source: U.S. Bureau of the Census.

★2788★

City Government Revenues

City Government Revenues, 1991-92: Total General Revenues

[In thousands of dollars]

City	Total revenues	Rank
Albuquerque, NM	470,152	35
Atlanta, GA	694,655	21
Austin, TX	560,330	27
Baltimore, MD	1,759,692	7
Baton Rouge, LA	413,860	39
Boston, MA	1,595,277	8
Buffalo, NY	689,540	22
Charlotte, NC	427,577	37
Chicago, IL	3,297,561	4
Cincinnati, OH	523,095	33
Cleveland, OH	535,138	32
Columbus, OH	557,909	28
Dallas, TX	1,083,447	12
Denver, CO	1,045,692	13
Detroit, MI	1,566,596	9
El Paso, TX	270,827	46
Fort Worth, TX	380,720	41
Honolulu, HI	870,967	17
Houston, TX	1,416,573	10
Indianapolis, IN	932,989	15
Jacksonville, FL	773,882	18
Kansas City, MO	541,363	30
Los Angeles, CA	3,888,711	3
Memphis, TN	881,799	16
Miami, FL	306,183	45
Milwaukee, WI	600,973	26
Minneapolis, MN	619,694	25
Nashville-Davidson, TN	989,440	14
New Orleans, LA	657,674	23
New York City, NY	36,782,012	1
Newark, NJ	452,880	36
Oakland, CA	540,031	31
Oklahoma City, OK	354,765	43
Omaha, NE	227,702	48
Philadelphia, PA	2,817,666	5
Pittsburgh, PA	373,202	42
Portland, OR	402,451	40
Sacramento, CA	330,719	44
Saint Louis, MO	494,486	34
San Antonio, TX	555,096	29
San Diego, CA	1,174,030	11
San Francisco, CA	2,640,255	6
San Jose, CA	641,962	24
Seattle, WA	712,748	20
Toledo, OH	234,812	47
Tulsa, OK	416,219	38
Virginia Beach, VA	735,913	19
Washington, DC	4,419,410	2

Source: U.S. Bureau of the Census, *Annual Survey of Government Finances 1992*, Washington, D.C.: U.S. Government Printing Office, 1995, n.p. Primary source: U.S. Bureau of the Census.

★2789★

City Government Revenues

City Government Revenues, 1991-92: Total Intergovernmental Revenues From State Governments

[In thousands of dollars]

City	Total revenues	Rank
Albuquerque, NM	111,743	18
Atlanta, GA	9,683	45
Austin, TX	22,018	39
Baltimore, MD	742,080	3
Baton Rouge, LA	26,929	36
Boston, MA	632,095	5
Buffalo, NY	349,882	8
Charlotte, NC	49,503	29
Chicago, IL	565,114	6
Cincinnati, OH	50,132	28
Cleveland, OH	68,170	22
Columbus, OH	51,187	27
Dallas, TX	13,575	42
Denver, CO	220,732	14
Detroit, MI	532,551	7
El Paso, TX	5,519	47
Fort Worth, TX	19,018	41
Honolulu, HI	61,111	24
Houston, TX	11,082	44
Indianapolis, IN	247,090	12
Jacksonville, FL	87,801	20
Kansas City, MO	24,249	37
Los Angeles, CA	296,745	9
Memphis, TN	270,273	10
Miami, FL	27,921	33
Milwaukee, WI	256,649	11
Minneapolis, MN	128,988	17
Nashville-Davidson, TN	244,750	13
New Orleans, LA	44,968	30
New York City, NY	13,249,463	1
Newark, NJ	181,042	15
Oakland, CA	67,586	23
Oklahoma City, OK	8,383	46
Omaha, NE	27,666	34
Philadelphia, PA	646,167	4
Pittsburgh, PA	21,444	40
Portland, OR	27,597	35
Sacramento, CA	23,364	38
Saint Louis, MO	37,849	31
San Antonio, TX	53,163	26
San Diego, CA	96,472	19
San Francisco, CA	773,223	2
San Jose, CA	57,316	25
Seattle, WA	71,596	21
Toledo, OH	29,257	32
Tulsa, OK	13,362	43
Virginia Beach, VA	175,842	16
Washington, DC	0	48

Source: U.S. Bureau of the Census, *Annual Survey of Government Finances 1992*, Washington, D.C.: U.S. Government Printing Office, 1995, n.p. Primary source: U.S. Bureau of the Census.

★2790★

City Government Revenues

City Government Revenues, 1991-92: Revenues From Current Charges (Parks and Recreation)

[In thousands of dollars]

City	Total revenues	Rank
Albuquerque, NM	7,178	29
Atlanta, GA	17,767	10
Austin, TX	6,701	30
Baltimore, MD	9,155	26
Baton Rouge, LA	5,923	34
Boston, MA	61	46
Buffalo, NY	4,647	36
Charlotte, NC	15,851	11
Chicago, IL	0	47
Cincinnati, OH	20,824	7
Cleveland, OH	6,264	32
Columbus, OH	4,307	38
Dallas, TX	20,633	8
Denver, CO	22,613	5
Detroit, MI	14,689	13
El Paso, TX	3,089	43
Fort Worth, TX	6,325	31
Honolulu, HI	13,274	17
Houston, TX	14,132	14
Indianapolis, IN	13,601	16
Jacksonville, FL	3,966	40
Kansas City, MO	10,305	24
Los Angeles, CA	39,465	1
Memphis, TN	27,340	4
Miami, FL	13,939	15
Milwaukee, WI	4,196	39
Minneapolis, MN	12,930	19
Nashville-Davidson, TN	9,616	25
New Orleans, LA	2,268	44
New York City, NY	21,738	6
Newark, NJ	0	47
Oakland, CA	3,252	42
Oklahoma City, OK	12,160	20
Omaha, NE	5,941	33
Philadelphia, PA	10,840	21
Pittsburgh, PA	3,571	41
Portland, OR	8,868	27
Sacramento, CA	10,385	23
Saint Louis, MO	8,459	28
San Antonio, TX	13,112	18
San Diego, CA	33,473	2
San Francisco, CA	32,685	3
San Jose, CA	10,471	22
Seattle, WA	19,238	9
Toledo, OH	1,905	45
Tulsa, OK	4,445	37
Virginia Beach, VA	5,517	35
Washington, DC	15,844	12

Source: U.S. Bureau of the Census, *Annual Survey of Government Finances 1992*, Washington, D.C.: U.S. Government Printing Office, 1995, n.p. Primary source: U.S. Bureau of the Census.

★2791★
City Government Revenues

City Government Revenues, 1991-92: Revenues From Current Charges (Solid-Waste Management)

[In thousands of dollars]

City	Total revenues	Rank
Albuquerque, NM	23,568	11
Atlanta, GA	28,367	7
Austin, TX	17,131	17
Baltimore, MD	13,228	22
Baton Rouge, LA	14,397	19
Boston, MA	3	39
Buffalo, NY	439	34
Charlotte, NC	0	40
Chicago, IL	1,860	31
Cincinnati, OH	0	40
Cleveland, OH	211	36
Columbus, OH	0	40
Dallas, TX	29,913	5
Denver, CO	0	40
Detroit, MI	667	33
El Paso, TX	12,919	23
Fort Worth, TX	13,446	21
Honolulu, HI	63,090	1
Houston, TX	0	40
Indianapolis, IN	18,581	13
Jacksonville, FL	34,254	3
Kansas City, MO	0	40
Los Angeles, CA	22,308	12
Memphis, TN	18,573	14
Miami, FL	17,504	16
Milwaukee, WI	309	35
Minneapolis, MN	17,521	15
Nashville-Davidson, TN	25,561	10
New Orleans, LA	16,900	18
New York City, NY	14,159	20
Newark, NJ	0	40
Oakland, CA	4,214	28
Oklahoma City, OK	11,534	24
Omaha, NE	0	40
Philadelphia, PA	76	37
Pittsburgh, PA	0	40
Portland, OR	1,546	32
Sacramento, CA	27,170	9
Saint Louis, MO	56	38
San Antonio, TX	28,256	8
San Diego, CA	29,663	6
San Francisco, CA	1,880	30
San Jose, CA	8,603	26
Seattle, WA	52,858	2
Toledo, OH	9,293	25
Tulsa, OK	31,993	4
Virginia Beach, VA	2,200	29
Washington, DC	6,044	27

Source: U.S. Bureau of the Census, *Annual Survey of Government Finances 1992,* Washington, D.C.: U.S. Government Printing Office, 1995, n.p. Primary source: U.S. Bureau of the Census.

★2792★
City Government Revenues

City Government Revenues, 1991-92: Revenues From Employee Retirement Funds

[In thousands of dollars]

City	Total revenues	Rank
Albuquerque, NM	0	42
Atlanta, GA	55,397	24
Austin, TX	69,967	21
Baltimore, MD	185,881	8
Baton Rouge, LA	38,801	31
Boston, MA	165,625	10
Buffalo, NY	0	42
Charlotte, NC	34,061	34
Chicago, IL	988,464	2
Cincinnati, OH	64,154	22
Cleveland, OH	0	42
Columbus, OH	0	42
Dallas, TX	165,151	12
Denver, CO	40,161	30
Detroit, MI	307,040	5
El Paso, TX	46,769	27
Fort Worth, TX	54,901	25
Honolulu, HI	0	42
Houston, TX	150,502	13
Indianapolis, IN	24,455	40
Jacksonville, FL	96,031	17
Kansas City, MO	82,514	18
Los Angeles, CA	962,934	3
Memphis, TN	165,452	11
Miami, FL	74,743	20
Milwaukee, WI	183,212	9
Minneapolis, MN	107,562	16
Nashville-Davidson, TN	42,154	29
New Orleans, LA	33,255	37
New York City, NY	1,993,472	1
Newark, NJ	1,482	41
Oakland, CA	25,834	39
Oklahoma City, OK	38,170	32
Omaha, NE	31,671	38
Philadelphia, PA	260,536	7
Pittsburgh, PA	33,792	35
Portland, OR	51,527	26
Sacramento, CA	34,695	33
Saint Louis, MO	79,684	19
San Antonio, TX	33,295	36
San Diego, CA	128,166	14
San Francisco, CA	551,611	4
San Jose, CA	117,613	15
Seattle, WA	59,522	23
Toledo, OH	0	42
Tulsa, OK	44,153	28
Virginia Beach, VA	0	42
Washington, DC	280,638	6

Source: U.S. Bureau of the Census, *Annual Survey of Government Finances 1992,* Washington, D.C.: U.S. Government Printing Office, 1995, n.p. Primary source: U.S. Bureau of the Census.

★2793★

City Government Revenues

City Government (300,000 Population and More) Revenues, 1991-92: Total Intergovernmental Revenues

[In thousands of dollars]

City	Total revenues	Rank
Albuquerque, NM	150,920	20
Atlanta, GA	137,883	22
Austin, TX	34,256	44
Baltimore, MD	881,510	4
Baton Rouge, LA	56,002	39
Boston, MA	657,097	8
Buffalo, NY	467,425	11
Charlotte, NC	110,532	27
Chicago, IL	821,579	6
Cincinnati, OH	95,716	31
Cleveland, OH	132,412	23
Columbus, OH	104,961	28
Dallas, TX	58,252	37
Denver, CO	248,589	17
Detroit, MI	705,504	7
El Paso, TX	30,590	46
Fort Worth, TX	42,013	42
Honolulu, HI	122,985	24
Houston, TX	63,605	36
Indianapolis, IN	283,580	13
Jacksonville, FL	145,297	21
Kansas City, MO	56,569	38
Los Angeles, CA	521,961	10
Memphis, TN	572,893	9
Miami, FL	48,460	40
Milwaukee, WI	307,498	12
Minneapolis, MN	170,002	19
Nashville-Davidson, TN	258,143	16
New Orleans, LA	122,782	25
New York City, NY	14,480,178	1
Newark, NJ	264,996	15
Oakland, CA	101,860	29
Oklahoma City, OK	18,635	48
Omaha, NE	35,951	43
Philadelphia, PA	874,238	5
Pittsburgh, PA	90,593	33
Portland, OR	65,741	35
Sacramento, CA	30,617	45
Saint Louis, MO	73,893	34
San Antonio, TX	117,808	26
San Diego, CA	233,407	18
San Francisco, CA	899,539	3
San Jose, CA	95,107	32
Seattle, WA	97,665	30
Toledo, OH	44,691	41
Tulsa, OK	29,028	47
Virginia Beach, VA	270,725	14
Washington, DC	1,508,140	2

Source: U.S. Bureau of the Census, *Annual Survey of Government Finances 1992,* Washington, D.C.: U.S. Government Printing Office, 1995, n.p. Primary source: U.S. Bureau of the Census.

★2794★

City Government Revenues

General Revenues of Largest Cities, 1992: Total Revenues

[Total in millions of dollars]

City	Total (mil. dol.)	Rank
New York City, NY	36,782	1
Washington, DC	4,419	2
Los Angeles, CA	3,889	3
Chicago, IL	3,298	4
Philadelphia, PA	2,818	5
San Francisco, CA	2,640	6
Baltimore, MD	1,760	7
Boston, MA	1,595	8
Detroit, MI	1,567	9
Houston, TX	1,417	10
San Diego, CA	1,174	11
Dallas, TX	1,083	12
Denver, CO	1,046	13
Nashville-Davidson, TX	989	14
Phoenix, AZ	988	15
Indianapolis, IN	933	16
Memphis, TN	882	17
Honolulu, HI	871	18
Virginia Beach, VA	736	19
Jacksonville, FL	731	20
Seattle, WA	713	21
Anchorage, AK	696	22
Atlanta, GA	695	23
Buffalo, NY	690	24
New Orleans, LA	658	25

Source: U.S. Bureau of the Census, *Statistical Abstract of the United States: 1995,* (115th edition), Washington, DC: U.S. Government Printing Office, 1995, p. 318. Primary source: U.S. Bureau of the Census, *City Government Finances,* series GF, no. 4, annual. *Note:* Data are shown only for the top 25 areas.

★2795★

City Government Revenues

Intergovernmental Revenues of Largest Cities, 1992: Total Revenues

[Total in millions of dollars]

City	Total (mil. dol.)	Rank
New York City, NY	14,480	1
Washington, DC	1,508	2
San Francisco, CA	900	3
Baltimore, MD	882	4
Philadelphia, PA	874	5
Chicago, IL	822	6
Detroit, MI	706	7
Boston, MA	657	8
Memphis, TN	573	9
Los Angeles, CA	522	10
Buffalo, NY	467	11
Rochester, NY	362	12
Phoenix, AZ	312	13
Milwaukee, WI	307	14

[Continued]

★2795★

Intergovernmental Revenues of Largest Cities, 1992: Total Revenues

[Continued]

City	Total (mil. dol.)	Rank
Indianapolis, IN	284	15
Virginia Beach, VA	271	16
Anchorage, AK	270	17
Newark, NJ	265	18
Nashville-Davidson, TX	258	19
Denver, CO	249	20
San Diego, CA	233	21
Norfolk, VA	211	22
Minneapolis, MN	170	23
Albuquerque, NM	151	24
Jacksonville, FL	145	25

Source: U.S. Bureau of the Census, *Statistical Abstract of the United States: 1995,* (115th edition), Washington, DC: U.S. Government Printing Office, 1995, p. 318. Primary source: U.S. Bureau of the Census, *City Government Finances,* series GF, no. 4, annual. *Note:* Data are shown only for the top 25 areas.

★2796★

City Government Revenues

Tax Revenues of Largest Cities, 1992: Total Revenues

[Total in millions of dollars]

City	Total (mil. dol.)	Rank
New York City, NY	17,141	1
Washington, DC	2,407	2
Los Angeles, CA	1,933	3
Chicago, IL	1,592	4
Philadelphia, PA	1,483	5
San Francisco, CA	977	6
Houston, TX	779	7
Baltimore, MD	664	8
Boston, MA	641	9
Detroit, MI	551	10
Dallas, TX	505	11
Honolulu, HI	482	12
Nashville-Davidson, TX	479	13
Indianapolis, IN	419	14
Denver, CO	391	15
San Diego, CA	383	16
Virginia Beach, VA	374	17
Seattle, WA	370	18
Phoenix, AZ	334	19
Kansas City, MO	330	20
San Jose, CA	328	21
New Orleans, LA	301	22
Columbus, OH	287	23
St. Louis, MO	277	24
Cleveland, OH	273	25

Source: U.S. Bureau of the Census, *Statistical Abstract of the United States: 1995,* (115th edition), Washington, DC: U.S. Government Printing Office, 1995, p. 318. Primary source: U.S. Bureau of the Census, *City Government Finances,* series GF, no. 4, annual. *Note:* Data are shown only for the top 25 areas.

★2797★

City Government Expenditures, By Source

City Government Expenditures, 1992, By Source: Total From All Sources

[In millions of dollars]

City	Millions[1]	Rank
New York City, NY[2]	42,499	1
Los Angeles, CA	6,577	2
Boston, MA[2]	5,036	3
Chicago, IL	3,887	4
Philadelphia, PA[2]	3,723	5
San Diego, CA	3,723	5
Jacksonville, FL	3,024	6
Dallas, TX	2,131	7
Seattle, WA	1,781	8
Washington, DC[2]	1,762	9
Houston, TX	1,758	10
Indianapolis, IN[2]	1,687	11
Columbus, OH	1,686	12
Austin, TX	1,649	13
Phoenix, AZ	1,620	14
Denver, CO[1]	1,525	15
San Jose, CA	1,501	16
Detroit, MI	1,311	17
El Paso, TX	1,173	18
Fort Worth, TX	1,113	19
Cincinnati, OH	1,101	20
San Antonio, TX	1,091	21
San Francisco, CA[2]	954	22
Anchorage, AK[2]	868	23
New Orleans, LA[2]	803	24

Source: U.S. Bureau of the Census, *Statistical Abstract of the United States: 1995,* (115th edition), Washington, DC: U.S. Government Printing Office, 1995, p. 321. Primary source: U.S. Bureau of the Census, *City Government Finances,* series GF, no. 4, annual. *Notes:* Data are shown only for the top 25 areas. 1. Includes items not shown separately. 2. Represents, in effect, city-county consolidated government.

★2798★

City Government Expenditures, By Source

City Government Expenditures, 1992, By Source: Total General Expenditures

[In millions of dollars]

City	Millions[1]	Rank
New York City, NY[2]	34,331	1
Washington, DC[2]	4,586	2
Los Angeles, CA	3,534	3
Chicago, IL	3,281	4
Philadelphia, PA[2]	2,823	5
San Francisco, CA[2]	2,302	6
Detroit, MI	1,577	7
Boston, MA[2]	1,560	8
Baltimore, MD[2]	1,550	9
Denver, CO[1]	1,513	10
Houston, TX	1,452	11
Dallas, TX	1,373	12
San Diego, CA	1,084	13
Phoenix, AZ	924	14
Indianapolis, IN[2]	895	15
Honolulu, HI[2]	892	16
Memphis, TN	879	17

[Continued]

★2798★

City Government Expenditures, 1992, By Source: Total General Expenditures
[Continued]

City	Millions[1]	Rank
Nashville-Davidson, TN[2]	857	18
Jacksonville, FL	779	19
Buffalo, NY	757	20
Seattle, WA	737	21
Minneapolis, MN	736	22
San Jose, CA	710	23
Anchorage, AK[2]	699	24
New Orleans, LA[2]	684	25

Source: U.S. Bureau of the Census, *Statistical Abstract of the United States: 1995,* (115th edition), Washington, DC: U.S. Government Printing Office, 1995, p. 321. Primary source: U.S. Bureau of the Census, *City Government Finances,* series GF, no. 4, annual. *Notes:* Data are shown only for the top 25 areas. 1. Includes items not shown separately. 2. Represents, in effect, city-county consolidated government.

★2799★

City Government Expenditures, By Source

City Government Expenditures, 1992, By Source: Fire Protection
[In millions of dollars]

City	Millions	Rank
New York City, NY[1]	699	1
Los Angeles, CA	265	2
Chicago, IL	231	3
Houston, TX	147	4
Philadelphia, PA[1]	123	5
San Francisco, CA[1]	101	6
Washington, DC[1]	97	7
Detroit, MI	93	8
Boston, MA[1]	86	9
Baltimore, MD[1]	84	10
Phoenix, AZ	83	11
Dallas, TX	75	12
San Diego, CA	75	12
Cleveland, OH	67	13
Columbus, OH	67	13
San Antonio, TX	66	14
Seattle, WA	62	15
Memphis, TN	59	16
Jacksonville, FL	56	17
Long Beach, CA	56	17
San Jose, CA	55	18
Milwaukee, WI	54	19
Denver, CO[1]	53	20
Cincinnati, OH	50	21
Oklahoma City, OK	48	22

Source: U.S. Bureau of the Census, *Statistical Abstract of the United States: 1995,* (115th edition), Washington, DC: U.S. Government Printing Office, 1995, p. 321. Primary source: U.S. Bureau of the Census, *City Government Finances,* series GF, no. 4, annual. *Notes:* Data are shown only for the top 25 areas. 1. Represents, in effect, city-county consolidated government.

★2800★

City Government Expenditures, By Source

City Government Expenditures, 1992, By Source: Health and Hospitals
[In millions of dollars]

City	Millions	Rank
New York City, NY[1]	3,646	1
San Francisco, CA[1]	549	2
Washington, DC[1]	535	3
Philadelphia, PA[1]	335	4
Boston, MA[1]	237	5
Indianapolis, IN[1]	176	6
Austin, TX	142	7
Denver, CO[1]	134	8
Colorado Springs, CO	109	9
Detroit, MI	98	10
Chicago, IL	97	11
Nashville-Davidson, TN[1]	80	12
Houston, TX	59	13
Baltimore, MD[1]	58	14
Kansas City, MO	41	15
Cincinnati, OH	32	16
Baton Rouge, LA[1]	31	17
St. Louis, MO[1]	31	17
Norfolk, VA[1]	30	18
Anchorage, AK[1]	27	19
Long Beach, CA	25	20
Columbus, OH	23	21
Jacksonville, FL	21	22
Dallas, TX	19	23
Tulsa, OK	19	23

Source: U.S. Bureau of the Census, *Statistical Abstract of the United States: 1995,* (115th edition), Washington, DC: U.S. Government Printing Office, 1995, p. 321. Primary source: U.S. Bureau of the Census, *City Government Finances,* series GF, no. 4, annual. *Notes:* Data are shown only for the top 25 areas. 1. Represents, in effect, city-county consolidated government.

★2801★

City Government Expenditures, By Source

City Government Expenditures, 1992, By Source: Highways
[In millions of dollars]

City	Millions	Rank
New York City, NY[1]	795	1
Chicago, IL	365	2
Los Angeles, CA	153	3
Baltimore, MD[1]	144	4
Houston, TX	128	5
Washington, DC[1]	122	6
Detroit, MI	100	7
Philadelphia, PA[1]	95	8
San Diego, CA	76	9
Wichita, KS	69	10
Phoenix, AZ	68	11
Austin, TX	65	12
Kansas City, MO	64	13
San Jose, CA	64	13
Dallas, TX	63	14
Albuquerque, NM	56	15
St. Paul, MN	55	16

[Continued]

★2801★

City Government Expenditures, 1992, By Source: Highways

[Continued]

City	Millions	Rank
Colorado Springs, CO	54	17
Las Vegas, NV	54	17
Atlanta, GA	53	18
Columbus, OH	53	18
San Antonio, TX	53	18
Oklahoma City, OK	52	19
Boston, MA[1]	51	20
Long Beach, CA	51	20

Source: U.S. Bureau of the Census, *Statistical Abstract of the United States: 1995,* (115th edition), Washington, DC: U.S. Government Printing Office, 1995, p. 321. Primary source: U.S. Bureau of the Census, *City Government Finances,* series GF, no. 4, annual. *Notes:* Data are shown only for the top 25 areas. 1. Represents, in effect, city-county consolidated government.

★2802★

City Government Expenditures, By Source

City Government Expenditures, 1992, By Source: Housing and Community Development

[In millions of dollars]

City	Millions	Rank
New York City, NY[1]	2,445	1
Los Angeles, CA	256	2
Washington, DC[1]	219	3
Minneapolis, MN	131	4
Chicago, IL	128	5
San Jose, CA	110	6
Honolulu, HI[1]	102	7
Anaheim, CA	97	8
San Diego, CA	90	9
Philadelphia, PA[1]	89	10
New Orleans, LA[1]	82	11
San Francisco, CA[1]	75	12
Long Beach, CA	70	13
Buffalo, NY	68	14
Cleveland, OH	68	14
Newark, NJ	66	15
Norfolk, VA[1]	66	15
Baltimore, MD[1]	63	16
St. Paul, MN	59	17
Phoenix, AZ	57	18
Cincinnati, OH	54	19
Rochester, NY	54	19
Detroit, MI	51	20
Jacksonville, FL	50	21
Seattle, WA	49	22

Source: U.S. Bureau of the Census, *Statistical Abstract of the United States: 1995,* (115th edition), Washington, DC: U.S. Government Printing Office, 1995, p. 321. Primary source: U.S. Bureau of the Census, *City Government Finances,* series GF, no. 4, annual. *Notes:* Data are shown only for the top 25 areas. 1. Represents, in effect, city-county consolidated government.

★2803★

City Government Expenditures, By Source

City Government Expenditures, 1992, By Source: Police Protection

[In millions of dollars]

City	Millions	Rank
New York City, NY[1]	1,872	1
Los Angeles, CA	650	2
Chicago, IL	627	3
Philadelphia, PA[1]	345	4
Detroit, MI	290	5
Washington, DC[1]	273	6
Houston, TX	269	7
Dallas, TX	168	8
San Diego, CA	168	8
San Francisco, CA[1]	164	9
Phoenix, AZ	155	10
Baltimore, MD[1]	154	11
Boston, MA[1]	137	12
Columbus, OH	127	13
Cleveland, OH	123	14
Milwaukee, WI	118	15
Honolulu, HI[1]	114	16
San Jose, CA	110	17
San Antonio, TX	99	18
Seattle, WA	95	19
Long Beach, CA	94	20
Denver, CO[1]	92	21
Indianapolis, IN[1]	88	22
Miami, FL	88	22
St. Louis, MO[1]	88	22

Source: U.S. Bureau of the Census, *Statistical Abstract of the United States: 1995,* (115th edition), Washington, DC: U.S. Government Printing Office, 1995, p. 321. Primary source: U.S. Bureau of the Census, *City Government Finances,* series GF, no. 4, annual. *Notes:* Data are shown only for the top 25 areas. 1. Represents, in effect, city-county consolidated government.

★2804★

City Government Expenditures, By Source

City Government Expenditures, 1992, By Source: Public Welfare

[In millions of dollars]

City	Millions	Rank
New York City, NY[1]	6,840	1
Washington, DC[1]	872	2
San Francisco, CA[1]	313	3
Philadelphia, PA[1]	213	4
Denver, CO[1]	133	5
Chicago, IL	110	6
Indianapolis, IN[1]	77	7
Newark, NJ	45	8
Norfolk, VA[1]	32	9
Boston, MA[1]	26	10
Jacksonville, FL	17	11
Virginia Beach, VA[1]	15	12
San Antonio, TX	12	13
Louisville, KY	11	14
Nashville-Davidson, TN[1]	11	14
Anchorage, AK[1]	6	15
New Orleans, LA[1]	6	15

[Continued]

★ 2804 ★

City Government Expenditures, 1992, By Source: Public Welfare

[Continued]

City	Millions	Rank
Albuquerque, NM	5	16
Lexington-Fayette, KY[1]	5	16
St. Louis, MO[1]	4	17
Baltimore, MD[1]	2	18
Tucson, AZ	2	18
Wichita, KS	2	18
Austin, TX	1	19
Baton Rouge, LA[1]	1	19

Source: U.S. Bureau of the Census, *Statistical Abstract of the United States: 1995,* (115th edition), Washington, DC: U.S. Government Printing Office, 1995, p. 321. Primary source: U.S. Bureau of the Census, *City Government Finances,* series GF, no. 4, annual. *Notes:* Data are shown only for the top 25 areas. 1. Represents, in effect, city-county consolidated government.

★ 2805 ★

City Government Expenditures, By Source

City Government Expenditures, 1992, By Source: Utilities and Liquor Stores

[In millions of dollars]

City	Millions	Rank
New York City, NY[1]	4,690	1
Los Angeles, CA	2,411	2
Jacksonville, FL	867	3
San Antonio, TX	829	4
Memphis, TN	819	5
Nashville-Davidson, TN[1]	629	6
Philadelphia, PA[1]	607	7
San Francisco, CA[1]	490	8
Austin, TX	478	9
Seattle, WA	384	10
Detroit, MI	305	11
Colorado Springs, CO	284	12
Anaheim, CA	266	13
Cleveland, OH	252	14
Houston, TX	238	15
Honolulu, HI[1]	209	16
Chicago, IL	198	17
San Diego, CA	181	18
Riverside, CA	180	19
Anchorage, AK[1]	162	20
Dallas, TX	146	21
Phoenix, AZ	143	22
Long Beach, CA	137	23
Columbus, OH	129	24
Denver, CO[1]	113	25

Source: U.S. Bureau of the Census, *Statistical Abstract of the United States: 1995,* (115th edition), Washington, DC: U.S. Government Printing Office, 1995, p. 321. Primary source: U.S. Bureau of the Census, *City Government Finances,* series GF, no. 4, annual. *Notes:* Data are shown only for the top 25 areas. 1. Represents, in effect, city-county consolidated government.

★ 2806 ★

City Government Revenues, By Source

City Government Revenues, 1992: Total From All Sources

[In millions of dollars]

City	Millions	Rank
New York City, NY[1]	44,888	1
Los Angeles, CA	6,993	2
Washington, DC[1]	4,754	3
Chicago, IL	4,514	4
Philadelphia, PA[1]	3,471	5
San Francisco, CA[1]	3,417	6
Detroit, MI	2,043	7
Baltimore, MD[1]	1,997	8
Memphis, TN	1,891	9
Boston, MA[1]	1,830	10
Houston, TX	1,802	11
Nashville-Davidson, TN[1]	1,636	12
Jacksonville, FL	1,556	13
San Antonio, TX	1,427	14
San Diego, CA	1,427	14
Dallas, TX	1,371	15
Denver, CO[1]	1,171	16
Phoenix, AZ	1,152	17
Austin, TX	1,130	18
Seattle, WA	1,104	19
Indianapolis, IN[1]	965	20
Honolulu, HI[1]	962	21
Milwaukee, WI	833	22
Anchorage, AK[1]	815	23
Atlanta, GA	811	24

Source: U.S. Bureau of the Census, *Statistical Abstract of the United States: 1995,* (115th edition), Washington, DC: U.S. Government Printing Office, 1995, p. 320. Primary source: U.S. Bureau of the Census, *City Government Finances,* series GF, no. 4, annual. *Notes:* Data are shown only for the top 25 areas. 1. Represents, in effect, city-county consolidated government.

★ 2807 ★

City Government Revenues, By Source

City Government Revenues, 1992: Total General Revenues

[In millions of dollars]

City	Millions[1]	Rank
New York City, NY[2]	36,782	1
Washington, DC[2]	4,419	2
Los Angeles, CA	3,889	3
Chicago, IL	3,298	4
Philadelphia, PA[2]	2,818	5
San Francisco, CA[2]	2,640	6
Baltimore, MD[2]	1,760	7
Boston, MA[2]	1,595	8
Detroit, MI	1,567	9
Houston, TX	1,417	10
San Diego, CA	1,174	11
Dallas, TX	1,083	12
Denver, CO[2]	1,046	13
Nashville-Davidson, TN[2]	989	14
Phoenix, AZ	988	15
Indianapolis, IN[2]	933	16
Memphis, TN	882	17

[Continued]

★2807★

City Government Revenues, 1992: Total General Revenues

[Continued]

City	Millions[1]	Rank
Honolulu, HI[2]	871	18
Virginia Beach, VA[2]	736	19
Jacksonville, FL	731	20
Seattle, WA	713	21
Anchorage, AK[2]	696	22
Atlanta, GA	695	23
Buffalo, NY	690	24
New Orleans, LA[2]	658	25

Source: U.S. Bureau of the Census, *Statistical Abstract of the United States: 1995*, (115th edition), Washington, DC: U.S. Government Printing Office, 1995, p. 320. Primary source: U.S. Bureau of the Census, *City Government Finances*, series GF, no. 4, annual. *Notes:* Data are shown only for the top 25 areas. 1. Includes items not shown separately. 2. Represents, in effect, city-county consolidated government.

★2808★

City Government Revenues, By Source

City Government Revenues, 1992: From Federal Government

[In millions of dollars]

City	Millions	Rank
Washington, DC[1]	1,451	1
New York City, NY[1]	1,150	2
Chicago, IL	256	3
Philadelphia, PA[1]	157	4
Los Angeles, CA	137	5
Detroit, MI	130	6
San Francisco, CA[1]	122	7
San Diego, CA	92	8
Virginia Beach, VA[1]	91	9
Phoenix, AZ	82	10
New Orleans, LA[1]	78	11
Cleveland, OH	63	12
Newark, NJ	62	13
Honolulu, HI[1]	61	14
Jacksonville, FL	57	15
Atlanta, GA	55	16
Rochester, NY	54	17
Baltimore, MD[1]	53	18
Milwaukee, WI	50	19
Norfolk, VA[1]	48	20
Columbus, OH	47	21
Buffalo, NY	45	22
Dallas, TX	42	23
Long Beach, CA	42	23
Houston, TX	41	24

Source: U.S. Bureau of the Census, *Statistical Abstract of the United States: 1995*, (115th edition), Washington, DC: U.S. Government Printing Office, 1995, p. 320. Primary source: U.S. Bureau of the Census, *City Government Finances*, series GF, no. 4, annual. *Notes:* Data are shown only for the top 25 areas. 1. Represents, in effect, city-county consolidated government.

★2809★

City Government Revenues, By Source

City Government Revenues, 1992: From State and Local Governments

[In millions of dollars]

City	Millions	Rank
New York City, NY[1]	13,330	1
Baltimore, MD[1]	828	2
San Francisco, CA[1]	778	3
Philadelphia, PA[1]	717	4
Boston, MA[1]	634	5
Detroit, MI	576	6
Chicago, IL	565	7
Memphis, TN	546	8
Buffalo, NY	422	9
Los Angeles, CA	385	10
Rochester, NY	308	11
Anchorage, AK[1]	264	12
Milwaukee, WI	257	13
Indianapolis, IN[1]	248	14
Nashville-Davidson, TN[1]	246	15
Phoenix, AZ	230	16
Denver, CO[1]	221	17
Newark, NJ	203	18
Virginia Beach, VA[1]	179	19
Norfolk, VA[1]	163	20
Minneapolis, MN	144	21
San Diego, CA	142	22
Albuquerque, NM	122	23
St. Paul, MN	102	24
Las Vegas, NV	98	25

Source: U.S. Bureau of the Census, *Statistical Abstract of the United States: 1995*, (115th edition), Washington, DC: U.S. Government Printing Office, 1995, p. 320. Primary source: U.S. Bureau of the Census, *City Government Finances*, series GF, no. 4, annual. *Notes:* Data are shown only for the top 25 areas. 1. Represents, in effect, city-county consolidated government.

★2810★

Taxes and Tax Revenues

City Government Revenues, 1992, By Source: Total From All Sources

[In millions of dollars]

City	Millions	Rank
New York City, NY[1]	17,141	1
Washington, DC[1]	2,407	2
Los Angeles, CA	1,933	3
Chicago, IL	1,592	4
Philadelphia, PA[1]	1,483	5
San Francisco, CA[1]	977	6
Houston, TX	779	7
Baltimore, MD[1]	664	8
Boston, MA[1]	641	9
Detroit, MI	551	10
Dallas, TX	505	11
Honolulu, HI[1]	482	12
Nashville-Davidson, TN[1]	479	13
Indianapolis, IN[1]	419	14
Denver, CO[1]	391	15
San Diego, CA	383	16
Virginia Beach, VA[1]	374	17

[Continued]

★2810★

City Government Revenues, 1992, By Source: Total From All Sources

[Continued]

City	Millions	Rank
Seattle, WA	370	18
Phoenix, AZ	334	19
Kansas City, MO	330	20
San Jose, CA	328	21
New Orleans, LA[1]	301	22
Columbus, OH	287	23
St. Louis, MO[1]	277	24
Cleveland, OH	273	25

Source: U.S. Bureau of the Census, *Statistical Abstract of the United States: 1995*, (115th edition), Washington, DC: U.S. Government Printing Office, 1995, p. 320. Primary source: U.S. Bureau of the Census, *City Government Finances*, series GF, no. 4, annual. Notes: Data are shown only for the top 25 areas. 1. Represents, in effect, city-county consolidated government.

★2811★

Taxes and Tax Revenues

City Government Revenues, 1992, By Source: Utilities and Liquor Stores

[In millions of dollars]

City	Millions	Rank
Los Angeles, CA	2,141	1
New York City, NY[1]	1,993	2
Memphis, TN	844	3
San Antonio, TX	839	4
Jacksonville, FL	729	5
Nashville-Davidson, TN[1]	605	6
Philadelphia, PA[1]	587	7
Austin, TX	500	8
Seattle, WA	332	9
Colorado Springs, CO	260	10
Anaheim, CA	243	11
Houston, TX	235	12
Chicago, IL	228	13
San Francisco, CA[1]	225	14
Riverside, CA	197	15
Detroit, MI	169	16
Cleveland, OH	167	17
San Diego, CA	125	18
Dallas, TX	122	19
Long Beach, CA	120	20
Phoenix, AZ	103	21
Anchorage, AK[1]	94	22
Honolulu, HI[1]	91	23
Columbus, OH	89	24
Denver, CO[1]	85	25

Source: U.S. Bureau of the Census, *Statistical Abstract of the United States: 1995*, (115th edition), Washington, DC: U.S. Government Printing Office, 1995, p. 320. Primary source: U.S. Bureau of the Census, *City Government Finances*, series GF, no. 4, annual. Notes: Data are shown only for the top 25 areas. 1. Represents, in effect, city-county consolidated government.

★2812★

Taxes and Tax Revenues

City Government Tax Revenues, 1992, By Source: Property Taxes

[In millions of dollars]

City	Millions	Rank
New York City, NY[1]	7,899	1
Washington, DC[1]	903	2
Los Angeles, CA	774	3
Boston, MA[1]	599	4
Chicago, IL	596	5
San Francisco, CA[1]	536	6
Baltimore, MD[1]	458	7
Houston, TX	400	8
Honolulu, HI[1]	389	9
Philadelphia, PA[1]	330	10
Indianapolis, IN[1]	322	11
Dallas, TX	295	12
Nashville-Davidson, TN[1]	263	13
Virginia Beach, VA[1]	233	14
Detroit, MI	215	15
Jacksonville, FL	198	16
Anchorage, AK[1]	165	17
San Diego, CA	156	18
Milwaukee, WI	155	19
Minneapolis, MN	142	20
Charlotte, NC	140	21
New Orleans, LA[1]	138	22
Portland, OR	138	22
Fort Worth, TX	130	23
San Jose, CA	129	24

Source: U.S. Bureau of the Census, *Statistical Abstract of the United States: 1995*, (115th edition), Washington, DC: U.S. Government Printing Office, 1995, p. 320. Primary source: U.S. Bureau of the Census, *City Government Finances*, series GF, no. 4, annual. Notes: Data are shown only for the top 25 areas. 1. Represents, in effect, city-county consolidated government.

★2813★

Taxes and Tax Revenues

City Government Tax Revenues, 1992, By Source: Sales and Gross Receipts

[In millions of dollars]

City	Millions	Rank
New York City, NY[1]	3,432	1
Chicago, IL	855	2
Los Angeles, CA	758	3
Washington, DC[1]	672	4
Houston, TX	359	5
Denver, CO[1]	246	6
San Francisco, CA[1]	233	7
Dallas, TX	201	8
Phoenix, AZ	197	9
San Diego, CA	194	10
Nashville-Davidson, TN[1]	173	11
Oklahoma City, OK	161	12
Seattle, WA	154	13
Kansas City, MO	147	14
San Jose, CA	146	15
Tulsa, OK	144	16
Baton Rouge, LA[1]	137	17

[Continued]

★2813★

City Government Tax Revenues, 1992, By Source: Sales and Gross Receipts

[Continued]

City	Millions	Rank
New Orleans, LA[1]	137	17
Virginia Beach, VA[1]	113	18
St. Louis, MO[1]	109	19
Tucson, AZ	104	20
San Antonio, TX	94	21
Long Beach, CA	91	22
Sacramento, CA	90	23
Albuquerque, NM	80	24

Source: U.S. Bureau of the Census, *Statistical Abstract of the United States: 1995*, (115th edition), Washington, DC: U.S. Government Printing Office, 1995, p. 320. Primary source: U.S. Bureau of the Census, *City Government Finances*, series GF, no. 4, annual. *Notes:* Data are shown only for the top 25 areas. 1. Represents, in effect, city-county consolidated government.

★2814★

Taxes and Tax Revenues

City Sales Tax Rates (Selected Cities), 1993

[In cents]

City	Cents	Rank
Washington, DC	6.00	1
New York, NY	4.25	2
Juneau, AK	4.00	3
Mobile, AL	4.00	3
Aurora, CO	3.50	4
Denver, CO	3.50	4
Huntsville, AL	3.50	4
Birmingham, AL	3.00	5
Fort Collins, CO	3.00	5
Tulsa, OK	3.00	5
Oklahoma City, OK	2.875	6
Boulder, CO	2.86	7
Monroe, LA	2.50	8
Montgomery, AL	2.50	8
Shreveport, LA	2.50	8
Yonkers, NY	2.50	8
Colorado Springs, CO	2.40	9
Baton Rouge, LA	2.00	10
Rapid City, SD	2.00	10
Sioux Falls, SD	2.00	10
Sun Valley, ID	2.00	10
Tucson, AZ	2.00	10
Seattle, WA	1.70	11
Lincoln, NE	1.50	12
Omaha, NE	1.50	12

Source: Advisory Commission on Intergovernmental Relations, *Significant Features of Fiscal Federalism, vol. 1: Budget Processes and Tax Systems 1994*, Washington, D.C.: Advisory Commission on Intergovernmental Relations, June 1994, M-190, p. 108. *Note:* Data are shown only for the top 25 areas.

★2815★

Taxes and Tax Revenues

Residential Property Taxes, 1992, in Selected Cities: Effective Rate Per $100

City	Rate	Rank
Detroit, MI	4.53	1
Milwaukee, WI	3.83	2
Newark, NJ	3.14	3
Manchester, NH	2.75	4
Des Moines, IA	2.66	5
Philadelphia, PA	2.64	6
Providence, RI	2.55	7
Bridgeport, CT	2.49	8
Baltimore, MD	2.44	9
Sioux Falls, IA	2.36	10
Portland, OR	2.32	11
Omaha, NE	2.29	12
Jacksonville, FL	2.15	13
Houston, TX	2.00	14
Boise City, ID	1.98	15
Columbus, OH	1.80	16
Fargo, ND	1.78	17
Wichita, KS	1.76	18
Indianapolis, IN	1.75	19
Atlanta, GA	1.74	20
Portland, ME	1.74	20
Anchorage, AK	1.71	21
New Orleans, LA	1.61	22
Phoenix, AZ	1.53	23
Burlington, VT	1.51	24

Source: U.S. Bureau of the Census, *Statistical Abstract of the United States: 1995*, (115th edition), Washington, DC: U.S. Government Printing Office, 1995, p. 313. Primary source: U.S. Government of the District of Columbia, Department of Finance and Revenue, *Tax Rates and Tax Burdens in the District of Columbia: A Nationwide Comparison*, annual. *Note:* Data are shown only for the top 25 areas.

★2816★

Taxes and Tax Revenues

Residential Property Taxes, 1992, in Selected Cities: Nominal Rate Per $100

City	Rate	Rank
Fargo, ND	41.49	1
Billings, MT	38.21	2
Columbia, SC	31.36	3
Newark, NJ	19.96	4
New Orleans, LA	16.06	5
Phoenix, AZ	15.28	6
Jackson, MS	14.73	7
Wichita, KS	14.66	8
Indianapolis, IN	11.65	9
Minneapolis, MN	11.50	10
New York City, NY	10.89	11
Oklahoma City, OK	9.45	12
Chicago, IL	9.31	13
Detroit, MI	9.17	14
Philadelphia, PA	8.26	15
Cheyenne, WY	7.83	16
Birmingham, AL	6.95	17
Denver, CO	6.73	18
Bridgeport, CT	6.33	19

[Continued]

★2816★

Residential Property Taxes, 1992, in Selected Cities: Nominal Rate Per $100

[Continued]

City	Rate	Rank
Baltimore, MD	6.11	20
Kansas City, MO	6.03	21
Atlanta, GA	5.81	22
Columbus, OH	5.14	23
Little Rock, AR	5.08	24
Des Moines, IA	4.04	25

Source: U.S. Bureau of the Census, *Statistical Abstract of the United States: 1995,* (115th edition), Washington, DC: U.S. Government Printing Office, 1995, p. 313. Primary source: U.S. Government of the District of Columbia, Department of Finance and Revenue, *Tax Rates and Tax Burdens in the District of Columbia: A Nationwide Comparison,* annual. *Note:* Data are shown only for the top 25 areas.

★2817★

Taxes and Tax Revenues

Sales Tax Rates (Selected Cities), 1993: Combined State and Local Tax Rate

[In cents]

City	Cents	Rank
Shreveport, LA	9.50	1
Mobile, AL	9.00	2
New Orleans, LA	9.00	2
Chicago, IL	8.75	3
San Antonio, TX	8.52	4
Dallas, TX	8.25	5
Houston, TX	8.25	5
Knoxville, TN	8.25	5
Memphis, TN	8.25	5
Nashville, TN	8.25	5
New York, NY	8.25	5
Yonkers, NY	8.25	5
Seattle, WA	8.20	6
Albany, NY	8.00	7
Austin, TX	8.00	7
Baton Rouge, LA	8.00	7
Birmingham, AL	8.00	7
Buffalo, NY	8.00	7
Montgomery, AL	8.00	7
Rochester, NY	8.00	7
Spokane, WA	8.00	7
Tacoma, WA	7.80	8
Chattanooga, TN	7.75	9
Corpus Christi, TX	7.75	9
Fort Worth, TX	7.75	9

Source: Advisory Commission on Intergovernmental Relations, *Significant Features of Fiscal Federalism, vol. 1: Budget Processes and Tax Systems 1994,* Washington, D.C.: Advisory Commission on Intergovernmental Relations, June 1994, M-190, p. 108. *Note:* Data are shown only for the top 25 areas.

Chapter 31

CRIMINAL JUSTICE AND LAW ENFORCEMENT

Topics Covered

Crimes and Crime Rates
Drug Use and Abuse
Prisons and Prison Population
Tax Crime

★2818★
Crimes and Crime Rates
Aggravated Assault Rate, 1993
[Rate is per 100,000 persons]

City	Aggravated assault	Rank
Alexandria, LA MSA	1,668.2	1
Pueblo, CO MSA	1,189.5	2
Miami, FL MSA	1,151.8	3
Little Rock-North Little Rock, AR MSA	1,050.3	4
Tallahassee, FL MSA	1,042.0	5
Baton Rouge, LA MSA	1,038.5	6
Jackson, MI MSA	1,015.5	7
Anniston, AL MSA	973.0	8
Sioux City, IA-NE MSA	962.8	9
Albuquerque, NM MSA	945.5	10
Gainesville, FL MSA	932.0	11
Jacksonville, FL MSA	913.5	12
Gadsden, AL MSA	908.9	13
Los Angeles-Long Beach, CA MSA	899.3	14
Jackson, TN MSA	894.2	15
Sumter, SC MSA	883.4	16
Tampa St. Petersburg-Clearwater, FL MSA	854.1	17
Ocala, FL MSA	842.6	18
Greenville-Spartanburg-Anderson, SC MSA	837.9	19
Monroe, LA MSA	827.8	20
Orlando, FL MSA	811.6	21
Birmingham, AL MSA	802.8	22
Charlotte-Gastonia-Rock Hill, NC-SC MSA	798.2	23
Modesto, CA MSA	784.7	24
Barnstable-Yarmouth, MA MSA	775.2	25

Source: Federal Bureau of Investigation, Uniform Crime Reports series, *Crime in the United States, 1993*, Washington, D.C.: Federal Bureau of Investigation, 1994, pp. 79-107. *Note:* Data are shown only for the top 25 areas.

★2819★
Crimes and Crime Rates
Burglary Rate, 1993
[Rate is per 100,000 persons]

City	Burglary	Rank
Miami, FL MSA	2,595.3	1
Albany, GA MSA	2,573.9	2
Tallahassee, FL MSA	2,426.1	3
Gainesville, FL MSA	2,322.0	4
Pine Bluff, AR MSA	2,309.9	5
Greenville, NC MSA	2,196.3	6
Jackson, MS MSA	2,193.7	7
Lakeland-Winter Haven, FL MSA	2,160.6	8
Fayetteville, NC MSA	2,046.9	9
Baton Rouge, LA MSA	1,993.9	10
Stockton-Lodi, CA MSA	1,953.5	11
Riverside-San Bernardino, CA MSA	1,928.8	12
Myrtle Beach, SC MSA	1,918.1	13
Sumter, SC MSA	1,898.2	14

[Continued]

★2819★
Burglary Rate, 1993
[Continued]

City	Burglary	Rank
Jacksonville, FL MSA	1,897.0	15
McAllen-Edinburg-Mission, TX MSA	1,867.5	16
Jackson, TN MSA	1,862.2	17
Fresno, CA MSA	1,852.2	18
Orlando, FL MSA	1,833.5	19
Memphis, TN-AR-MS MSA	1,832.1	20
Little Rock-North Little Rock, AR MSA	1,798.5	21
Fort Lauderdale, FL MSA	1,781.6	22
Modesto, CA MSA	1,758.5	23
Yakima, WA MSA	1,753.1	24
Charlotte-Gastonia-Rock Hill, NC-SC MSA	1,746.3	25

Source: Federal Bureau of Investigation, Uniform Crime Reports series, *Crime in the United States, 1993*, Washington, D.C.: Federal Bureau of Investigation, 1994, pp. 79-107. *Note:* Data are shown only for the top 25 areas.

★2820★
Crimes and Crime Rates
Forcible Rapes, 1993: Rate for All Forcible Rapes
[Rate is per 100,000 persons]

City	Forcible rape	Rank
Rapid City, SD MSA	99.0	1
Killeen-Temple, TX MSA	95.8	2
Ocala, FL MSA	90.5	3
Gainesville, FL MSA	90.0	4
Tallahassee, FL MSA	88.0	5
Waco, TX MSA	86.0	6
Memphis, TN-AR-MS MSA	85.8	7
Jacksonville, FL MSA	85.3	8
Anchorage, AK MSA	84.6	9
Yakima, WA MSA	84.0	10
Vineland-Millville-Bridgeton, NJ MSA	80.3	11
Pine Bluff, AR MSA	79.9	12
Beaumont-Port Arthur, TX MSA	79.6	13
Tyler, TX MSA	78.1	14
Sioux Falls, SD MSA	77.5	15
Nashville, TN MSA	74.0	16
Oklahoma City, OK MSA	73.9	17
Little Rock-North Little Rock, AR MSA	73.3	18
Pueblo, CO MSA	72.2	19
Dubuque, IA MSA	70.8	20
Seattle-Bellevue-Everett, WA MSA	69.8	21
Fayetteville, NC MSA	69.2	22
Reno, NV MSA	68.4	23
Houston, TX MSA[1]	68.2	24
Toledo, OH MSA	68.0	25

Source: Federal Bureau of Investigation, Uniform Crime Reports series, *Crime in the United States, 1993*, Washington, D.C.: Federal Bureau of Investigation, 1994, pp. 79-107. *Notes:* Data are shown only for the top 25 areas. 1. Due to reporting changes figures are not comparable to previous years.

★2821★

Crimes and Crime Rates

Larceny-Theft Rate, 1993

[Rate is per 100,000 persons]

City	Larceny-theft	Rank
Yuba City, CA MSA	24,797.0	1
Miami, FL MSA	6,655.3	2
Tucson, AZ MSA	6,142.3	3
Atlanta City, NJ MSA	5,766.0	4
Gainesville, FL MSA	5,760.4	5
Tallahassee, FL MSA	5,664.7	6
Corpus Christi, TX MSA	5,629.5	7
Myrtle Beach, SC MSA	5,559.5	8
Tuscaloosa, AL MSA	5,549.6	9
Baton Rouge, LA MSA	5,420.2	10
San Antonio, TX MSA	5,297.9	11
Lincoln, NE MSA	5,149.2	12
Yakima, WA MSA	5,109.9	13
Fort Lauderdale, FL MSA	5,108.1	14
Austin-San Marcos, TX MSA	5,103.6	15
Panama City, FL MSA	5,081.9	16
Amarillo, TX MSA	5,072.0	17
Little Rock-North Little Rock, AR MSA	4,949.7	18
Shreveport-Bossier City, LA MSA	4,911.7	19
El Paso, TX MSA	4,895.6	20
Jackson, TN MSA	4,797.9	21
Lakeland-Winter Haven, FL MSA	4,749.4	22
Brownsville-Harlingen-San Benito, TX MSA	4,697.6	23
Albany, GA MSA	4,667.7	24
Yolo, CA MSA	4,618.9	25

Source: Federal Bureau of Investigation, Uniform Crime Reports series, *Crime in the United States, 1993*, Washington, D.C.: Federal Bureau of Investigation, 1994, pp. 79-107. *Note:* Data are shown only for the top 25 areas.

★2822★

Crimes and Crime Rates

Motor Vehicle Theft Rate: 1993

[Rate is per 100,000 persons]

City	Motor vehicle theft	Rank
Miami, FL MSA	2,113.6	1
Fresno, CA MSA	2,045.3	2
Memphis, TN-AR-MS MSA	1,424.1	3
Los Angeles-Long Beach, CA MSA	1,378.2	4
New York, NY MSA	1,368.8	5
Newark, NJ MSA	1,302.6	6
San Diego, CA MSA	1,263.4	7
Jersey City, NJ MSA	1,258.2	8
Sacramento, CA MSA	1,240.5	9
Lawrence, MA-NH MSA[1]	1,195.2	10
New Orleans, LA MSA	1,194.1	11
Bridgeport, CT MSA	1,191.1	12
Trenton, NJ MSA	1,154.9	13
Houston, TX MSA[1]	1,125.8	14
Tallahassee, FL MSA	1,119.6	15

[Continued]

★2822★

Motor Vehicle Theft Rate: 1993

[Continued]

City	Motor vehicle theft	Rank
Stockton-Lodi, CA MSA	1,112.8	16
Riverside-San Bernardino, CA MSA	1,088.1	17
Jackson, MS MSA	1,086.2	18
Springfield, MA MSA[1]	1,059.7	19
Brockton, MA MSA	1,054.3	20
Phoenix-Mesa AZ MSA	1,045.6	21
Detroit, MI MSA	1,041.9	22
Jacksonville, FL MSA	1,009.4	23
Fort Lauderdale, FL MSA	1,009.0	24
Gary-Hammond, IN MSA	1,002.5	25

Source: Federal Bureau of Investigation, Uniform Crime Reports series, *Crime in the United States, 1993*, Washington, D.C.: Federal Bureau of Investigation, 1994, pp. 79-107. *Notes:* Data are shown only for the top 25 areas. 1. Due to reporting changes figures are not comparable to previous years.

★2823★

Crimes and Crime Rates

Murders and Nonnegligent Manslaughters, 1993: Rates for All Murders and Nonnegligent Manslaughters

[Rate is per 100,000 persons]

City	Murder and nonnegligent manslaughter	Rank
New Orleans, LA MSA	37.7	1
Shreveport-Bossier City, LA MSA	25.8	2
Jackson, MS MSA	25.2	3
Jackson, TN MSA	23.3	4
New York, NY MSA	23.2	5
Memphis, TN-AR-MS MSA	21.9	6
Fayetteville, NC MSA	21.7	7
Los Angeles-Long Beach, CA MSA	21.3	8
Gary-Hammond, IN MSA	20.2	9
Little Rock-North Little Rock, AR MSA	20.1	10
Alexandria, LA MSA	19.8	11
Pine Bluff, AR MSA	19.7	12
Birmingham, AL MSA	19.3	13
Baton Rouge, LA MSA	19.1	14
Albany, GA MSA	18.7	15
San Antonio, TX MSA	18.6	16
Miami, FL MSA	18.1	17
Richmond-Petersburg, VA MSA	17.4	18
Baltimore, MD MSA	17.2	19
Texarkana, TX- Texarkana, AR MSA	17.1	20
Fresno, CA MSA	16.9	21
Charlotte-Gastonia-Rock Hill, NC-SC MSA	16.6	22
Waco, TX MSA	16.4	23

[Continued]

★2823★

Murders and Nonnegligent Manslaughters, 1993: Rates for All Murders and Nonnegligent Manslaughters
[Continued]

City	Murder and nonnegligent manslaughter	Rank
Houston, TX MSA[1]	15.9	24
Detroit, MI MSA	15.8	25

Source: Federal Bureau of Investigation, Uniform Crime Reports series, *Crime in the United States, 1993*, Washington, D.C.: Federal Bureau of Investigation, 1994, pp. 79-107. *Notes:* Data are shown only for the top 25 areas. 1. Due to reporting changes figures are not comparable to previous years.

★2824★
Crimes and Crime Rates

Murders Committed, 1995

City	Murders committed	Rank
Atlanta, GA	62	12
Boston, MA	37	15
Chicago, IL	388	2
Dallas, TX	147	8
Detroit, MI	271	4
Gary, IN	54	13
Houston, TX	138	9
Los Angeles, CA	352	3
Minneapolis, MN	51	14
New York, NY	563	1
New Orleans, LA	196	7
Philadelphia, PA	199	6
Phoenix, AZ	118	10
Saint Louis, MO	107	11
Washington, DC	208	5

Source: Butterfield, Fox, "Many Cities in U.S. Show Sharp Drop in Homicide Rate," *New York Times*, 13 August 1995, p. 1. Primary source: Local police departments.

★2825★
Crimes and Crime Rates

Murders Committed, 1995: Selected Cities

Data refer to murders committed in the first six months of 1995.

City	Number	Rank
Ann Arbor, MI	1	21
Atlanta, GA	82	9
Buffalo, NY	28	17
Chicago, IL	388	2
Cleveland, OH	69	12
Columbus, OH	32	16
Dallas, TX	148	8
Detroit, MI	234	4
Flint, MI	19	18
Grand Rapids, MI	10	19
Houston, TX	138	9
Lansing, MI	8	20

[Continued]

★2825★

Murders Committed, 1995: Selected Cities
[Continued]

City	Number	Rank
Las Vegas, NV	46	14
Livonia, MI	0	22
Los Angeles, CA	358	3
Miami, FL	48	13
New Orleans, LA	189	6
New York, NY	574	1
Philadelphia, PA	191	5
Phoenix, AZ	102	10
San Antonio, TX	78	11
San Diego, CA	39	15
Warren, MI	0	22
Washington, DC	151	7

Source: Sniffen, Michael J., "Homicides Drop Sharply Across Nation," *Detroit Free Press*, 18 December 1995, p. 5A. Primary source: FBI.

★2826★
Crimes and Crime Rates

Murders, 1995: Lowest Numbers

Data refer to murders per 100,000 residents in cities with more than 250,000 inhabitants.

[In number of incidents committed per 100,000 residents]

City/MSA	Number	Rank
Arlington, TX	3	1
Virginia Beach, VA	4	2
Honolulu, HI	5	3
Mesa, AZ	5	3
San Jose, CA	5	3

Source: "Crime Count," *U.S. News & World Report*, 13 May 1996, p. 13. Primary source: Federal Bureau of Investigation (FBI).

★2827★
Crimes and Crime Rates

Murders, 1995: Highest Numbers

Data refer to murders per 100,000 residents in cities with more than 250,000 inhabitants.

[In number of incidents committed per 100,000 persons]

City/MSA	Number	Rank
New Orleans, LA	73	1
Washington, DC	62	2
Saint Louis, MO	52	3
Oklahoma City, OK	49	4
Detroit, MI	46	5

Source: "Crime Count," *U.S. News & World Report*, 13 May 1996, p. 13. Primary source: Federal Bureau of Investigation (FBI).

★2828★

Crimes and Crime Rates

Murders, 1995: Percent Change in Cities With Lowest Rates

Data refer to crimes per 100,000 residents in cities with more than 250,000 inhabitants.

[In percentages]

City/MSA	Percent change	Rank
Virginia Beach, VA	-51.5	1
Arlington, TX	-50.0	2
San Jose, CA	+15.2	3
Honolulu, HI	+14.3	4
Mesa, AZ	0.0	5

Source: "Crime Count," *U.S. News & World Report,* 13 May 1996, p. 13. Primary source: Federal Bureau of Investigation (FBI).

★2829★

Crimes and Crime Rates

Murders, 1995: Percent Change in Cities With Highest Rates

Data refer to murders per 100,000 residents in cities with more than 250,000 inhabitants. Data for Oklahoma City, Oklahoma, include the 168 people who were killed in the bombing of the federal building on April 19, 1995.

[In percentages]

City/MSA	Percent change	Rank
Oklahoma City, OK	+249.2	1
Washington, DC	-11.8	2
Detroit, MI	-12.2	3
New Orleans, LA	-14.4	4
Saint Louis, MO	-17.7	5

Source: "Crime Count," *U.S. News & World Report,* 13 May 1996, p. 13. Primary source: Federal Bureau of Investigation (FBI).

★2830★

Crimes and Crime Rates

Property Crime Rates, 1993, By Type: Total Rate

[Rate is per 100,000 population]

City	Rates	Rank
Miami, FL	14,852	1
Atlanta, GA	13,313	2
Baton Rouge, LA	13,170	3
St. Louis, MO	12,773	4
Tampa, FL	12,460	5
Newark, NJ	10,483	6
Tucson, AZ	10,457	7
Seattle, WA	10,398	8
Kansas City, MO	10,152	9
Oklahoma City, OK	9,806	10
Rochester, NY	9,697	11
Austin, TX	9,652	12
Stockton, CA	9,622	13
Baltimore, MD	9,547	14

[Continued]

★2830★

Property Crime Rates, 1993, By Type: Total Rate
[Continued]

City	Rates	Rank
Portland, OR	9,523	15
Fresno, CA	9,494	16
Charlotte, NC	9,467	17
Birmingham, AL	9,338	18
Oakland, CA	9,314	19
Corpus Christi, TX	9,273	20
Minneapolis, MN	9,268	21
Fort Worth, TX	9,241	22
San Antonio, TX	9,229	23
Detroit, MI	9,212	24
Nashville-Davidson, TN	9,021	25

Source: U.S. Bureau of the Census, *Statistical Abstract of the United States: 1995,* (115th edition), Washington, D.C.: U.S. Government Printing Office, 1995, p. 201. Primary source: U.S. Federal Bureau of Investigation, *Crime in the United States,* annual. *Note:* Data are shown only for the top 25 areas.

★2831★

Crimes and Crime Rates

Property Crime Rates, 1993, By Type: Burglaries

[Rate is per 100,000 population]

City	Rates	Rank
Baton Rouge, LA	3,344	1
Miami, FL	3,296	2
Atlanta, GA	3,269	3
St. Louis, MO	3,204	4
Tampa, FL	3,111	5
Kansas City, MO	2,780	6
Rochester, NY	2,694	7
Minneapolis, MN	2,552	8
Newark, NJ	2,549	9
Charlotte, NC	2,528	10
Memphis, TN	2,474	11
Birmingham, AL	2,466	12
Baltimore, MD	2,442	13
Stockton, CA	2,417	14
Buffalo, NY	2,339	15
New Orleans, LA	2,275	16
Fort Worth, TX	2,267	17
Detroit, MI	2,264	18
Jacksonville, FL	2,250	19
Fresno, CA	2,230	20
Oakland, CA	2,216	21
Oklahoma City, OK	2,186	22
Sacramento, CA	2,089	23
Riverside, CA	2,064	24
St. Petersburg, FL	2,022	25

Source: U.S. Bureau of the Census, *Statistical Abstract of the United States: 1995,* (115th edition), Washington, D.C.: U.S. Government Printing Office, 1995, p. 201. Primary source: U.S. Federal Bureau of Investigation, *Crime in the United States,* annual. *Note:* Data are shown only for the top 25 areas.

★2832★
Crimes and Crime Rates
Property Crime Rates, 1993, By Type: Larceny-Thefts

[Rate is per 100,000 population]

City	Rates	Rank
Miami, FL	8,556	1
Baton Rouge, LA	8,050	2
Atlanta, GA	7,757	3
Tucson, AZ	7,524	4
Seattle, WA	7,374	5
Austin, TX	7,101	6
St. Louis, MO	6,969	7
Corpus Christi, TX	6,964	8
Tampa, FL	6,416	9
Oklahoma City, OK	6,409	10
Nashville-Davidson, TN	6,319	11
Charlotte, NC	6,236	12
San Antonio, TX	6,219	13
Portland, OR	5,939	14
Rochester, NY	5,747	15
Fort Worth, TX	5,678	16
Baltimore, MD	5,655	17
Birmingham, AL	5,554	18
Stockton, CA	5,540	19
Washington, DC	5,444	20
Minneapolis, MN	5,442	21
Kansas City, MO	5,423	22
El Paso, TX	5,309	23
Norfolk, VA	5,254	24
Dallas, TX	5,197	25

Source: U.S. Bureau of the Census, *Statistical Abstract of the United States: 1995,* (115th edition), Washington, D.C.: U.S. Government Printing Office, 1995, p. 201. Primary source: U.S. Federal Bureau of Investigation, *Crime in the United States,* annual. *Note:* Data are shown only for the top 25 areas.

★2833★
Crimes and Crime Rates
Property Crime Rates, 1993, By Type: Motor Vehicle Thefts

[Rate is per 100,000 population]

City	Rates	Rank
Newark, NJ	4,073	1
Fresno, CA	3,443	2
Miami, FL	3,001	3
Tampa, FL	2,933	4
Detroit, MI	2,751	5
St. Louis, MO	2,600	6
Atlanta, GA	2,288	7
Boston, MA	2,154	8
Memphis, TN	2,147	9
Oakland, CA	2,061	10
Sacramento, CA	2,039	11
Cleveland, OH	2,011	12
Kansas City, MO	1,949	13
New Orleans, LA	1,942	14
Portland, OR	1,860	15
Baton Rouge, LA	1,776	16
Pittsburgh, PA	1,766	17
Long Beach, CA	1,720	18

[Continued]

★2833★
Property Crime Rates, 1993, By Type: Motor Vehicle Thefts
[Continued]

City	Rates	Rank
Milwaukee, WI	1,704	19
Buffalo, NY	1,699	20
Los Angeles, CA	1,695	21
Dallas, TX	1,675	22
Stockton, CA	1,666	23
San Diego, CA	1,665	24
Houston, TX	1,596	25

Source: U.S. Bureau of the Census, *Statistical Abstract of the United States: 1995,* (115th edition), Washington, D.C.: U.S. Government Printing Office, 1995, p. 201. Primary source: U.S. Federal Bureau of Investigation, *Crime in the United States,* annual. *Note:* Data are shown only for the top 25 areas.

★2834★
Crimes and Crime Rates
Property Crimes, 1993: Rate for All Property Crimes

[Rate is per 100,000 persons]

City	Property crime[1]	Rank
Miami, FL MSA	11,364.2	1
Tallahassee, FL MSA	9,210.3	2
Gainesville, FL MSA	8,802.7	3
Tucson, AZ MSA	8,465.7	4
Baton Rouge, LA MSA	8,345.4	5
Fort Lauderdale, FL MSA	7,898.7	6
Lakeland-Winter Haven, FL MSA	7,836.5	7
San Antonio, TX MSA	7,821.3	8
Albany, GA MSA	7,713.3	9
Myrtle Beach, SC MSA	7,693.3	10
Corpus Christi, TX MSA	7,685.0	11
Atlantic City, NJ MSA	7,661.8	12
Stockton-Lodi, CA MSA	7,436.7	13
Little Rock-North Little Rock, AR MSA	7,431.6	14
Yakima, WA MSA	7,318.2	15
Fayetteville, NC MSA	7,201.0	16
New Orleans, LA MSA	7,199.1	17
Jacksonville, FL MSA	7,178.1	18
Panama City, FL MSA	7,121.5	19
Shreveport-Bossier City, LA MSA	7,110.5	20
Jackson, TN MSA	7,086.4	21
Austin-San Marcos, TX MSA	7,056.3	22
Jackson, MS MSA	7,033.8	23
Tuscaloosa, AL MSA	7,029.2	24
Fresno, CA MSA	7,015.0	25

Source: Federal Bureau of Investigation, Uniform Crime Reports series, *Crime in the United States, 1993,* Washington, D.C.: Federal Bureau of Investigation, 1994, pp. 79-107. *Notes:* Data are shown only for the top 25 areas. 1. Property crimes are offenses of burglary, larceny-theft, and motor vehicle theft. Data are not included for the property crime of arson.

★2835★
Crimes and Crime Rates
Robbery Rate, 1993

[Rate is per 100,000 persons]

City	Robbery rate	Rank
New York, NY MSA	1,047.7	1
Miami, FL MSA	913.3	2
Los Angeles-Long Beach, CA MSA	721.6	3
Baltimore, MD MSA	636.2	4
Jersey City, NJ MSA	598.3	5
San Francisco, CA MSA	593.8	6
Newark, NJ MSA	564.8	7
New Orleans, LA MSA	558.9	8
Memphis, TN-AR-MS MSA	548.9	9
Oakland, CA MSA	453.1	10
Fresno, CA MSA	427.7	11
Las Vegas, NV-AZ MSA	413.9	12
Albany, GA MSA	412.1	13
Tallahassee, FL MSA	408.7	14
Jackson, MS MSA	406.9	15
Jacksonville, FL MSA	406.0	16
Baton Rouge, LA MSA	402.0	17
Detroit, MI MSA	400.2	18
Bridgeport, CT MSA	392.6	19
Stockton-Lodi, CA MSA	379.4	20
Atlanta, GA MSA	369.1	21
Fort Lauderdale, FL MSA	366.5	22
Savannah, GA MSA	359.7	23
Fayetteville, NC MSA	350.3	24
Charlotte-Gastonia-Rock Hill, NC-SC MSA	343.0	25

Source: Federal Bureau of Investigation, Uniform Crime Reports series, *Crime in the United States, 1993*, Washington, D.C.: Federal Bureau of Investigation, 1994, pp. 79-107. *Note:* Data are shown only for the top 25 areas.

★2836★
Crimes and Crime Rates
Serious Crimes, 1995: Lowest Numbers

Data refer to crimes per 100,000 residents in cities with more than 250,000 inhabitants.

[In percentages]

City/MSA	Number	Rank
San Jose, CA	4,428	1
Virginia Beach, VA	4,744	2
Santa Ana, CA	5,184	3
San Diego, CA	5,496	4
Pittsburgh, PA	5,900	5

Source: "Crime Count," *U.S. News & World Report*, 13 May 1996, p. 13. Primary source: Federal Bureau of Investigation (FBI).

★2837★
Crimes and Crime Rates
Serious Crimes, 1995: Highest Numbers

Data refer to crimes per 100,000 residents in cities with more than 250,000 inhabitants.

[In number of incidents committed per 100,000 persons]

City/MSA	Number	Rank
Atlanta, GA	16,783	1
Miami, FL	15,607	2
Saint Louis, MO	15,300	3
Newark, NJ	14,894	4
Tampa, FL	13,943	5

Source: "Crime Count," *U.S. News & World Report*, 13 May 1996, p. 13. Primary source: Federal Bureau of Investigation (FBI).

★2838★
Crimes and Crime Rates
Serious Crimes, 1995: Percent Change in Cities With Lowest Rates

Data refer to crimes per 100,000 residents in cities with more than 250,000 inhabitants.

[In percentages]

City/MSA	Percent change	Rank
Pittsburgh, PA	-17.5	1
San Diego, CA	-16.3	2
Santa Ana, CA	-13.9	3
Virginia Beach, VA	-4.5	4
San Jose, CA	-1.3	5

Source: "Crime Count," *U.S. News & World Report*, 13 May 1996, p. 13. Primary source: Federal Bureau of Investigation (FBI).

★2839★
Crimes and Crime Rates
Serious Crimes, 1995: Percent Change in Cities With Highest Rates

Data refer to crimes per 100,000 residents in cities with more than 250,000 inhabitants.

[In percentages]

City/MSA	Percent change	Rank
Newark, NJ	+7.7	1
Atlanta, GA	+4.1	2
Saint Louis, MO	-6.4	3
Miami, FL	-9.1	4
Tampa, FL	-20.2	5

Source: "Crime Count," *U.S. News & World Report*, 13 May 1996, p. 13. Primary source: Federal Bureau of Investigation (FBI).

★2840★
Crimes and Crime Rates
Violent Crime Rates, 1993, By Type: Aggravated Assaults

[Rate is per 100,000 population]

City	Rates	Rank
Atlanta, GA	2,368	1
Tampa, FL	2,120	2
St. Louis, MO	2,116	3
Baton Rouge, LA	2,086	4
Miami, FL	1,903	5
Birmingham, AL	1,694	6
Washington, DC	1,558	7
Newark, NJ	1,474	8
Kansas City, MO	1,470	9
Aurora, CO	1,432	10
Chicago, IL	1,425	11
Charlotte, NC	1,424	12
St. Petersburg, FL	1,415	13
Detroit, MI	1,274	14
Oakland, CA	1,258	15
Portland, OR	1,232	16
Los Angeles, CA	1,204	17
Albuquerque, NM	1,187	18
Baltimore, MD	1,166	19
Nashville-Davidson, TN	1,127	20
Boston, MA	1,117	21
Riverside, CA	1,047	22
Jacksonville, FL	1,040	23
Indianapolis, IN	968	24
Oklahoma City, OK	910	25

Source: U.S. Bureau of the Census, *Statistical Abstract of the United States: 1995,* (115th edition), Washington, D.C.: U.S. Government Printing Office, 1995, p. 201. Primary source: U.S. Federal Bureau of Investigation, *Crime in the United States,* annual. *Note:* Data are shown only for the top 25 areas.

★2841★
Crimes and Crime Rates
Violent Crime Rates, 1993, By Type: Forcible Rapes

[Rate is per 100,000 population]

City	Rates	Rank
Cleveland, OH	164.9	1
Indianapolis, IN	136.9	2
Cincinnati, OH	123.6	3
Atlanta, GA	122.1	4
Kansas City, MO	118.3	5
Memphis, TN	117.1	6
Oklahoma City, OK	112.6	7
Nashville-Davidson, TN	112.3	8
Birmingham, AL	110.5	9
Fort Worth, TX	109.4	10
Toledo, OH	107.7	11
Portland, OR	105.3	12
Jacksonville, FL	104.0	13
Columbus, OH	101.7	14
Dallas, TX	95.9	15
Newark, NJ	95.2	16
Oakland, CA	93.6	17
Baltimore, MD	91.1	18

[Continued]

★2841★
Violent Crime Rates, 1993, By Type: Forcible Rapes
[Continued]

City	Rates	Rank
Buffalo, NY	90.8	19
Akron, OH	90.7	20
Tulsa, OK	89.6	21
Colorado Springs, CO	87.0	22
Boston, MA	86.7	23
Tampa, FL	85.5	24
Anchorage, AK	84.6	25

Source: U.S. Bureau of the Census, *Statistical Abstract of the United States: 1995,* (115th edition), Washington, D.C.: U.S. Government Printing Office, 1995, p. 201. Primary source: U.S. Federal Bureau of Investigation, *Crime in the United States,* annual. *Note:* Data are shown only for the top 25 areas.

★2842★
Crimes and Crime Rates
Violent Crime Rates, 1993, By Type: Murders

[Rate is per 100,000 population]

City	Rates per 100,000 population	Rank
New Orleans, LA	80.3	1
Washington, DC	78.5	2
St. Louis, MO	69.0	3
Detroit, MI	56.8	4
Atlanta, GA	50.4	5
Baltimore, MD	48.2	6
Birmingham, AL	45.0	7
Oakland, CA	40.8	8
Newark, NJ	35.6	9
Kansas City, MO	35.1	10
Miami, FL	34.1	11
Cleveland, OH	33.0	12
Baton Rouge, LA	32.8	13
Memphis, TN	32.0	14
Los Angeles, CA	30.5	15
Dallas, TX	30.4	16
Chicago, IL	30.3	17
Charlotte, NC	28.9	18
Fort Worth, TX	28.7	19
Long Beach, CA	28.4	20
Philadelphia, PA	28.1	21
Rochester, NY	27.2	22
Santa Ana, CA	26.8	23
New York, NY	26.5	24
Houston, TX	25.9	25

Source: U.S. Bureau of the Census, *Statistical Abstract of the United States: 1995,* (115th edition), Washington, D.C.: U.S. Government Printing Office, 1995, p. 201. Primary source: U.S. Federal Bureau of Investigation, *Crime in the United States,* annual. *Note:* Data are shown only for the top 25 areas.

★2843★
Crimes and Crime Rates

Violent Crime Rates, 1993, By Type: Robberies

[Rate is per 100,000 population]

City	Rates	Rank
Newark, NJ	2,183	1
Miami, FL	1,901	2
Baltimore, MD	1,689	3
St. Louis, MO	1,608	4
Atlanta, GA	1,501	5
Detroit, MI	1,332	6
Chicago, IL	1,262	7
Washington, DC	1,230	8
Oakland, CA	1,209	9
New York, NY	1,171	10
San Francisco, CA	1,148	11
Los Angeles, CA	1,090	12
Jersey City, NJ	1,086	13
New Orleans, LA	1,054	14
Tampa, FL	1,026	15
Kansas City, MO	894	16
Buffalo, NY	892	17
Memphis, TN	867	18
Minneapolis, MN	867	18
Cleveland, OH	850	19
Long Beach, CA	839	20
Baton Rouge, LA	827	21
Charlotte, NC	763	22
Fresno, CA	758	23
Pittsburgh, PA	756	24

Source: U.S. Bureau of the Census, *Statistical Abstract of the United States: 1995,* (115th edition), Washington, D.C.: U.S. Government Printing Office, 1995, p. 201. Primary source: U.S. Federal Bureau of Investigation, *Crime in the United States,* annual. *Note:* Data are shown only for the top 25 areas.

★2844★
Crimes and Crime Rates

Violent Crimes in Cities With 100,000 to 249,999 Persons, 1993: Aggravated Assault Rates

[Rate is per 100,000 population]

City	Rate	Rank
Little Rock, AR	2,497.1	1
San Bernardino, CA	2,184.1	2
Baton Rouge, LA	2,086.1	3
Flint, MI	1,791.2	4
Orlando, FL	1,558.7	5
Pueblo, CO	1,453.3	6
Aurora, CO	1,432.2	7
St. Petersburg, FL	1,415.4	8
Chattanooga, TN	1,373.6	9
Tallahassee, FL	1,326.3	10
Knoxville, TN	1,296.0	11
Tacoma, WA	1,173.0	12
Hartford, CT	1,114.4	13
Gary, IN	1,078.6	14
Winston-Salem, NC	1,064.6	15
Huntsville, AL	1,059.6	16
Lancaster, CA	1,053.9	17
Riverside, CA	1,047.1	18
Pasadena, TX	1,044.7	19

[Continued]

★2844★

Violent Crimes in Cities With 100,000 to 249,999 Persons, 1993: Aggravated Assault Rates

[Continued]

City	Rate	Rank
Waco, TX	983.6	20
Grand Rapids, MI	933.3	21
New Haven, CT	931.5	22
Pomano, CA	872.4	23
Lowell, MA	872.3	24
Jersey City, NJ	852.8	25

Source: Maguire, Kathleen, and Ann L. Pastore, eds., *Sourcebook of Criminal Justice Statistics 1994,* U.S. Department of Justice, Bureau of Justice Statistics, Washington, D.C.: U.S. Government Printing Office, 1995, p. 320. Primary source: National Rifle Association of America, Institute for Legislative Action; data were made available through the Federal Bureau of Investigation's Uniform Crime Reporting Program. *Note:* Data are shown only for the top 25 areas.

★2845★
Crimes and Crime Rates

Violent Crimes in Cities With 100,000 to 249,999 Persons, 1993: Homicide Rates

[Rate is per 100,000 population]

City	Rate	Rank
Gary, IN	89.1	1
Richmond, VA	54.5	2
San Bernardino, CA	47.1	3
Jackson, MS	41.9	4
Inglewood, CA	40.0	5
Shreveport, LA	38.5	6
Little Rock, AR	38.0	7
Flint, MI	34.3	8
Baton Rouge, LA	32.8	9
Portsmouth, VA	31.1	10
Pomano, CA	28.2	11
Waco, TX	27.3	12
Rochester, NY	27.2	13
Dayton, OH	26.6	14
Chattanooga, TN	24.5	15
Winston-Salem, NC	24.5	15
Savannah, GA	23.3	16
Hartford, CT	22.7	17
Fort Lauderdale, FL	20.6	18
Mobile, AL	20.6	18
Stockton, CA	20.3	19
Pasadena, CA	20.2	20
Montgomery, AL	20.1	21
Beaumont, TX	19.5	22
Waterbury, CT	18.7	23

Source: Maguire, Kathleen, and Ann L. Pastore, eds., *Sourcebook of Criminal Justice Statistics 1994,* U.S. Department of Justice, Bureau of Justice Statistics, Washington, D.C.: U.S. Government Printing Office, 1995, p. 320. Primary source: National Rifle Association of America, Institute for Legislative Action; data were made available through the Federal Bureau of Investigation's Uniform Crime Reporting Program. *Note:* Data are shown only for the top 25 areas.

★2846★
Crimes and Crime Rates

Violent Crimes in Cities With 100,000 to 249,999 Persons, 1993: Rape Rates

[Rate is per 100,000 population]

City	Rate	Rank
Beaumont, TX	169.8	1
Gary, IN	147.7	2
Dayton, OH	145.9	3
Waco, TX	133.0	4
Winston-Salem, NC	120.3	5
Little Rock, AR	120.2	6
Salt Lake City, UT	119.7	7
Orlando, FL	118.2	8
New Haven, CT	104.9	9
Tallahassee, FL	103.6	10
Tacoma, WA	101.7	11
Chattanooga, TN	99.3	12
South Bend, IN	97.2	13
Sioux Falls, SD	96.9	14
Macon, GA	93.1	15
Akron, OH	90.7	16
Reno, NV	88.7	17
Jackson, MS	87.3	18
Santa Rosa, CA	86.6	19
Pueblo, CO	85.8	20
Richmond, VA	84.7	21
Pasadena, TX	82.9	22
Baton Rouge, LA	78.5	23
Springfield, MA	77.9	24
Durham, NC	76.1	25

Source: Maguire, Kathleen, and Ann L. Pastore, eds., *Sourcebook of Criminal Justice Statistics 1994*, U.S. Department of Justice, Bureau of Justice Statistics, Washington, D.C.: U.S. Government Printing Office, 1995, p. 320. Primary source: National Rifle Association of America, Institute for Legislative Action; data were made available through the Federal Bureau of Investigation's Uniform Crime Reporting Program. *Note:* Data are shown only for the top 25 areas.

★2847★
Crimes and Crime Rates

Violent Crimes in Cities With 100,000 to 249,999 Persons, 1993: Rates

Violent crime includes homicide, rape, robbery, and aggravated assault.

[Rate is per 100,000 population]

City	Rate	Rank
Little Rock, AR	3,290.2	1
San Bernardino, CA	3,194.9	2
Baton Rouge, LA	3,024.7	3
Orlando, FL	2,342.3	4
St. Petersburg, FL	2,166.9	5
Hartford, CT	2,154.4	6
Gary, IN	2,108.0	7
New Haven, CT	2,053.4	8
Inglewood, CA	2,042.0	9
Tallahassee, FL	2,034.0	10
Jersey City, NJ	1,990.5	11
Chattanooga, TN	1,954.4	12
Winston-Salem, NC	1,925.2	13
Tacoma, WA	1,831.3	14

[Continued]

★2847★

Violent Crimes in Cities With 100,000 to 249,999 Persons, 1993: Rates

[Continued]

City	Rate	Rank
Aurora, CO	1,807.3	15
Knoxville, TN	1,715.5	16
Pueblo, CO	1,710.6	17
Pomano, CA	1,659.4	18
Riverside, CA	1,649.1	19
Berkeley, CA	1,596.6	20
Richmond, VA	1,595.0	21
Dayton, OH	1,585.0	22
Stockton, CA	1,577.5	23
Fort Lauderdale, FL	1,559.6	24
Paterson, NJ	1,555.5	25

Source: Maguire, Kathleen, and Ann L. Pastore, eds., *Sourcebook of Criminal Justice Statistics 1994*, U.S. Department of Justice, Bureau of Justice Statistics, Washington, D.C.: U.S. Government Printing Office, 1995, p. 320. Primary source: National Rifle Association of America, Institute for Legislative Action; data were made available through the Federal Bureau of Investigation's Uniform Crime Reporting Program. *Note:* Data are shown only for the top 25 areas.

★2848★
Crimes and Crime Rates

Violent Crimes in Cities With 100,000 to 249,999 Persons, 1993: Robbery Rates

[Rate is per 100,000 population]

City	Rate	Rank
Inglewood, CA	1,179.9	1
Jersey City, NJ	1,085.6	2
New Haven, CT	999.3	3
Hartford, CT	942.3	4
San Bernardino, CA	889.7	5
Fort Lauderdale, FL	842.8	6
Baton Rouge, LA	827.3	7
Elizabeth, NJ	804.5	8
Dayton, OH	800.1	9
Berkeley, CA	797.8	10
Gary, IN	792.6	11
Paterson, NJ	775.6	12
Richmond, VA	768.5	13
Jackson, MS	759.2	14
Flint, MI	724.4	15
Winston-Salem, NC	715.8	16
Portsmouth, VA	704.1	17
Pomano, CA	701.7	18
Stockton, CA	700.4	19
Rochester, NY	696.1	20
St. Petersburg, FL	669.8	21
Little Rock, AR	634.9	22
Orlando, FL	626.3	23
Pasadena, CA	622.6	24
Tallahassee, FL	597.3	25

Source: Maguire, Kathleen, and Ann L. Pastore, eds., *Sourcebook of Criminal Justice Statistics 1994*, U.S. Department of Justice, Bureau of Justice Statistics, Washington, D.C.: U.S. Government Printing Office, 1995, p. 320. Primary source: National Rifle Association of America, Institute for Legislative Action; data were made available through the Federal Bureau of Investigation's Uniform Crime Reporting Program. *Note:* Data are shown only for the top 25 areas.

★2849★

Crimes and Crime Rates

Violent Crimes in Cities With 250,000 or More Persons, 1993: Aggravated Assault Rates

[Rate is per 100,000 population]

City	Rate	Rank
Atlanta, GA	2,368.2	1
Tampa, FL	2,119.9	2
St. Louis, MO	2,115.7	3
Miami, FL	1,903.0	4
Birmingham, AL	1,694.4	5
Washington, DC	1,557.6	6
Newark, NJ	1,473.6	7
Kansas City, MO	1,470.3	8
Chicago, IL	1,425.4	9
Charlotte, NC	1,423.6	10
Detroit, MI	1,274.3	11
Oakland, CA	1,258.0	12
Portland, OR	1,231.7	13
Los Angeles, CA	1,203.8	14
Albuquerque, NM	1,187.1	15
Baltimore, MD	1,166.2	16
Nashville, TN	1,127.4	17
Boston, MA	1,116.5	18
Jacksonville, FL	1,039.6	19
Indianapolis, IN	968.2	20
Oklahoma City, OK	909.6	21
Dallas, TX	905.3	22
Tulsa, OK	894.7	23
New York, NY	854.4	24
Buffalo, NY	853.3	25

Source: Maguire, Kathleen, and Ann L. Pastore, eds., *Sourcebook of Criminal Justice Statistics 1994*, U.S. Department of Justice, Bureau of Justice Statistics, Washington, D.C.: U.S. Government Printing Office, 1995, p. 320. Primary source: National Rifle Association of America, Institute for Legislative Action; data were made available through the Federal Bureau of Investigation's Uniform Crime Reporting Program. *Note:* Data are shown only for the top 25 areas.

★2850★

Crimes and Crime Rates

Violent Crimes in Cities With 250,000 or More Persons, 1993: Homicide Rates

[Rate is per 100,000 population]

City	Rate	Rank
New Orleans, LA	80.3	1
Washington, DC	78.5	2
St. Louis, MO	69.0	3
Detroit, MI	56.8	4
Atlanta, GA	50.4	5
Baltimore, MD	48.2	6
Birmingham, AL	45.0	7
Oakland, CA	40.8	8
Newark, NJ	35.6	9
Kansas City, MO	35.1	10
Miami, FL	34.1	11
Cleveland, OH	33.0	12
Memphis, TN	32.0	13
Los Angeles, CA	30.5	14
Dallas, TX	30.4	15
Chicago, IL	30.3	16
Charlotte, NC	28.9	17

[Continued]

★2850★

Violent Crimes in Cities With 250,000 or More Persons, 1993: Homicide Rates

[Continued]

City	Rate	Rank
Fort Worth, TX	28.7	18
Long Beach, CA	28.4	19
Philadelphia, PA	28.1	20
Santa Ana, CA	26.8	21
New York, NY	26.5	22
Houston, TX	25.9	23
Milwaukee, WI	25.2	24
Norfolk, VA	24.1	25

Source: Maguire, Kathleen, and Ann L. Pastore, eds., *Sourcebook of Criminal Justice Statistics 1994*, U.S. Department of Justice, Bureau of Justice Statistics, Washington, D.C.: U.S. Government Printing Office, 1995, p. 320. Primary source: National Rifle Association of America, Institute for Legislative Action; data were made available through the Federal Bureau of Investigation's Uniform Crime Reporting Program. *Note:* Data are shown only for the top 25 areas.

★2851★

Crimes and Crime Rates

Violent Crimes in Cities With 250,000 or More Persons, 1993: Rape Rates

[Rate is per 100,000 population]

City	Rate	Rank
Cleveland, OH	164.9	1
Minneapolis, MN	141.3	2
Indianapolis, IN	136.9	3
Cincinnati, OH	122.5	4
Atlanta, GA	122.1	5
Kansas City, MO	118.3	6
Memphis, TN	117.1	7
Oklahoma City, OK	112.6	8
Nashville, TN	112.3	9
Birmingham, AL	110.5	10
Fort Worth, TX	109.4	11
Toledo, OH	107.7	12
Portland, OR	105.3	13
Jacksonville, FL	104.0	14
Columbus, OH	101.7	15
Dallas, TX	95.9	16
Newark, NJ	95.2	17
Oakland, CA	93.6	18
Baltimore, MD	91.1	19
Buffalo, NY	90.8	20
Charlotte, NC	90.8	20
Tulsa, OK	89.6	21
St. Paul, MN	89.2	22
Colorado Springs, CO	87.0	23
Boston, MA	86.7	24

Source: Maguire, Kathleen, and Ann L. Pastore, eds., *Sourcebook of Criminal Justice Statistics 1994*, U.S. Department of Justice, Bureau of Justice Statistics, Washington, D.C.: U.S. Government Printing Office, 1995, p. 320. Primary source: National Rifle Association of America, Institute for Legislative Action; data were made available through the Federal Bureau of Investigation's Uniform Crime Reporting Program. *Note:* Data are shown only for the top 25 areas.

★2852★
Crimes and Crime Rates
Violent Crimes in Cities With 250,000 or More Persons, 1993: Rates

Violent crime includes homicide, rape, robbery, and aggravated assault.

[Rate is per 100,000 population]

City	Rate	Rank
Atlanta, GA	4,041.2	1
Miami, FL	3,893.0	2
St. Louis, MO	3,874.9	3
Newark, NJ	3,787.4	4
Tampa, FL	3,246.7	5
Baltimore, MD	2,994.0	6
Washington, DC	2,921.8	7
Oakland, CA	2,601.6	8
Kansas City, MO	2,517.3	9
Birmingham, AL	2,484.7	10
Los Angeles, CA	2,374.3	11
Charlotte, NC	2,299.8	12
New York, NY	2,089.8	13
New Orleans, LA	2,039.0	14
Boston, MA	1,957.7	15
Buffalo, NY	1,859.6	16
Portland, OR	1,856.5	17
San Francisco, CA	1,815.0	18
Nashville, TN	1,784.1	19
Minneapolis, MN	1,767.7	20
Dallas, TX	1,743.3	21
Jacksonville, FL	1,698.2	22
Indianapolis, IN	1,665.8	23
Albuquerque, NM	1,644.1	24
Cleveland, OH	1,643.2	25

Source: Maguire, Kathleen, and Ann L. Pastore, eds., *Sourcebook of Criminal Justice Statistics 1994*, U.S. Department of Justice, Bureau of Justice Statistics, Washington, D.C.: U.S. Government Printing Office, 1995, p. 320. Primary source: National Rifle Association of America, Institute for Legislative Action; data were made available through the Federal Bureau of Investigation's Uniform Crime Reporting Program. *Note:* Data are shown only for the top 25 areas.

★2853★
Crimes and Crime Rates
Violent Crimes in Cities With 250,000 or More Persons, 1993: Robbery Rates

[Rate is per 100,000 population]

City	Rate	Rank
Newark, NJ	2,183.1	1
Miami, FL	1,901.1	2
Baltimore, MD	1,688.5	3
St. Louis, MO	1,607.8	4
Atlanta, GA	1,500.5	5
Detroit, MI	1,332.4	6
Chicago, IL	1,261.7	7
Washington, DC	1,229.6	8
Oakland, CA	1,209.2	9
New York, NY	1,170.5	10
San Francisco, CA	1,148.1	11
Los Angeles, CA	1,089.7	12
New Orleans, LA	1,053.5	13
Tampa, FL	1,026.4	14

[Continued]

★2853★
Violent Crimes in Cities With 250,000 or More Persons, 1993: Robbery Rates
[Continued]

City	Rate	Rank
Kansas City, MO	893.6	15
Buffalo, NY	892.1	16
Memphis, TN	866.9	17
Minneapolis, MN	866.8	18
Cleveland, OH	849.7	19
Long Beach, CA	838.6	20
Charlotte, NC	763.1	21
Fresno, CA	757.7	22
Pittsburgh, PA	755.6	23
Philadelphia, PA	739.4	24
Boston, MA	736.8	25

Source: Maguire, Kathleen, and Ann L. Pastore, eds., *Sourcebook of Criminal Justice Statistics 1994*, U.S. Department of Justice, Bureau of Justice Statistics, Washington, D.C.: U.S. Government Printing Office, 1995, p. 320. Primary source: National Rifle Association of America, Institute for Legislative Action; data were made available through the Federal Bureau of Investigation's Uniform Crime Reporting Program. *Note:* Data are shown only for the top 25 areas.

★2854★
Crimes and Crime Rates
Violent Crimes, 1993: Rate for All Violent Crimes
[Rate is per 100,000 persons]

City	Rate	Rank
Miami, FL MSA	2,136.2	1
New York, NY MSA	1,865.5	2
Alexandria, LA MSA	1,833.0	3
Los Angeles-Long Beach, CA MSA	1,682.4	4
Tallahassee, FL MSA	1,546.0	5
Baton Rouge, LA MSA	1,510.7	6
Little Rock-North Little Rock, AR MSA	1,453.1	7
Jersey City, NJ MSA	1,441.1	8
Jacksonville, FL MSA	1,419.9	9
Pueblo, CO MSA	1,403.9	10
Baltimore, MD MSA	1,356.1	11
Gainesville, FL MSA	1,328.6	12
New Orleans, LA MSA	1,312.6	13
Jackson, TN MSA	1,294.7	14
Albuquerque, NM MSA	1,273.6	15
Tampa St. Petersburg-Clearwater, FL MSA	1,223.4	16
Charlotte-Gastonia-Rock Hill, NC-SC MSA	1,204.4	17
Anniston, AL MSA	1,183.6	18
Sumter, SC MSA	1,179.1	19
Gadsden, AL MSA	1,177.5	20
Birmingham, AL MSA	1,146.8	21
Ocala, FL MSA	1,141.7	22
Oakland, CA MSA	1,137.5	23
Sioux City, IA-NE MSA	1,133.8	24
Columbia, SC MSA	1,129.1	25

Source: Federal Bureau of Investigation, Uniform Crime Reports series, *Crime in the United States, 1993*, Washington, D.C.: Federal Bureau of Investigation, 1994, pp. 79-107. *Note:* Data are shown only for the top 25 areas.

★ 2855 ★

Crimes and Crime Rates

Violent Crimes, 1993: Total Rate

Data refer to murders, forcible rapes, robberies, and aggravated assaults.

[Rate is per 100,000 population]

City	Rates per 100,000 population	Rank
Atlanta, GA	4,041	1
Miami, FL	3,893	2
Saint Louis, MO	3,875	3
Newark, NJ	3,787	4
Tampa, FL	3,247	5
Baton Rouge, LA	3,025	6
Baltimore, MD	2,994	7
Washington, DC	2,922	8
Oakland, CA	2,602	9
Kansas City, MO	2,517	10
Birmingham, AL	2,485	11
Los Angeles, CA	2,374	12
Charlotte, NC	2,300	13
St. Petersburg, FL	2,167	14
New York, NY	2,090	15
New Orleans, LA	2,039	16
Jersey City, NJ	1,991	17
Boston, MA	1,958	18
Buffalo, NY	1,860	19
Portland, OR	1,857	20
San Francisco, CA	1,815	21
Aurora, CO	1,807	22
Nashville-Davidson, TN	1,784	23
Dallas, TX	1,743	24
Jacksonville, FL	1,698	25

Source: U.S. Bureau of the Census, *Statistical Abstract of the United States: 1995*, (115th edition), Washington, D.C.: U.S. Government Printing Office, 1995, p. 201. Primary source: U.S. Federal Bureau of Investigation, *Crime in the United States*, annual. *Note:* Data are shown only for the top 25 areas.

★ 2856 ★

Drug Use and Abuse

Drug Use By Arrestees, 1993, By Type of Drug and Sex: Females Using Any Drug

Data refer to the use of cocaine, opiates, marijuana, phencyclidine (PCP), methadone, benzodiazepines, methaqualone, propoxyphene, barbiturates, and amphetamines. Data on drug use are obtained every quarter for approximately two weeks by trained local staff who obtain voluntary and anonymous urine specimens and interviews from a new sample of arrestees. The cities of Chicago, Miami, and Omaha, did not test or interview female arrestees.

[In percent testing positive for drug use]

City	Percent	Rank
Atlanta, GA	74	6
Birmingham, AL	55	14
Cleveland, OH	77	4
Dallas, TX	61	11
Denver, CO	66	9
Detroit, MI	76	5
Fort Lauderdale, FL	60	12

[Continued]

★ 2856 ★

Drug Use By Arrestees, 1993, By Type of Drug and Sex: Females Using Any Drug

[Continued]

City	Percent	Rank
Houston, TX	53	15
Indianapolis, IN	58	13
Los Angeles, CA	77	4
Manhattan, NY	83	1
New Orleans, LA	47	17
Philadelphia, PA	79	2
Phoenix, AZ	62	10
Portland, OR	74	6
Saint Louis, MO	69	8
San Antonio, TX	42	18
San Diego, CA	78	3
San Jose, CA	51	16
Washington, DC	71	7

Source: Maguire, Kathleen, and Ann L. Pastore, eds., *Sourcebook of Criminal Justice Statistics 1994*, U.S. Department of Justice, Bureau of Justice Statistics, Washington, D.C.: U.S. Government Printing Office, 1995, p. 415. Primary source: U.S. Department of Justice, National Institute of Justice, *Drug Use Forecasting 1993 Annual Report on Adult Arrestees: Drugs and Crime in America's Cities*, NCJ-147411, Washington, D.C.: U.S. Department of Justice, 1994, pp. 6-28.

★ 2857 ★

Drug Use and Abuse

Drug Use By Arrestees, 1993, By Type of Drug and Sex: Females Using Cocaine

Data on drug use are obtained every quarter for approximately two weeks by trained local staff who obtain voluntary and anonymous urine specimens and interviews from a new sample of arrestees. The cities of Chicago, Miami, and Omaha, did not test or interview female arrestees.

[In percent testing positive for drug use]

City	Percent	Rank
Atlanta, GA	68	3
Birmingham, AL	41	11
Cleveland, OH	69	2
Dallas, TX	43	10
Denver, CO	47	8
Detroit, MI	64	4
Fort Lauderdale, FL	45	9
Houston, TX	43	10
Indianapolis, IN	36	14
Los Angeles, CA	59	7
Manhattan, NY	70	1
New Orleans, LA	37	13
Philadelphia, PA	61	6
Phoenix, AZ	38	12
Portland, OR	47	8
Saint Louis, MO	62	5
San Antonio, TX	24	15
San Diego, CA	36	14
San Jose, CA	19	16
Washington, DC	62	5

Source: Maguire, Kathleen, and Ann L. Pastore, eds., *Sourcebook of Criminal Justice Statistics 1994*, U.S. Department of Justice, Bureau of Justice Statistics, Washington, D.C.: U.S. Government Printing Office, 1995, p. 415. Primary source: U.S. Department of Justice, National Institute of Justice, *Drug Use Forecasting 1993 Annual Report on Adult Arrestees: Drugs and Crime in America's Cities*, NCJ-147411, Washington, D.C.: U.S. Department of Justice, 1994, pp. 6-28.

★2858★
Drug Use and Abuse

Drug Use By Arrestees, 1993, By Type of Drug and Sex: Females Using Marijuana

Data on drug use are obtained every quarter for approximately two weeks by trained local staff who obtain voluntary and anonymous urine specimens and interviews from a new sample of arrestees. The cities of Chicago, Miami, and Omaha, did not test or interview female arrestees.

[In percent testing positive for drug use]

City	Percent	Rank
Atlanta, GA	16	6
Birmingham, AL	12	10
Cleveland, OH	13	9
Dallas, TX	19	4
Denver, CO	24	2
Detroit, MI	10	11
Fort Lauderdale, FL	20	3
Houston, TX	15	7
Indianapolis, IN	25	1
Los Angeles, CA	15	7
Manhattan, NY	19	4
New Orleans, LA	14	8
Philadelphia, PA	20	3
Phoenix, AZ	20	3
Portland, OR	17	5
Saint Louis, MO	15	7
San Antonio, TX	16	6
San Diego, CA	25	1
San Jose, CA	17	5
Washington, DC	9	12

Source: Maguire, Kathleen, and Ann L. Pastore, eds., *Sourcebook of Criminal Justice Statistics 1994*, U.S. Department of Justice, Bureau of Justice Statistics, Washington, D.C.: U.S. Government Printing Office, 1995, p. 415. Primary source: U.S. Department of Justice, National Institute of Justice, *Drug Use Forecasting 1993 Annual Report on Adult Arrestees: Drugs and Crime in America's Cities*, NCJ-147411, Washington, D.C.: U.S. Department of Justice, 1994, pp. 6-28.

★2859★
Drug Use and Abuse

Drug Use By Arrestees, 1993, By Type of Drug and Sex: Females Using Multiple Drugs

Data refer to the use of cocaine, opiates, marijuana, phencyclidine (PCP), methadone, benzodiazepines, methaqualone, propoxyphene, barbiturates, and amphetamines. Data on drug use are obtained every quarter for approximately two weeks by trained local staff who obtain voluntary and anonymous urine specimens and interviews from a new sample of arrestees. The cities of Chicago, Miami, and Omaha, did not test or interview female arrestees.

[In percent testing positive for drug use]

City	Percent	Rank
Atlanta, GA	16	12
Birmingham, AL	14	14
Cleveland, OH	15	13
Dallas, TX	21	8
Denver, CO	22	7
Detroit, MI	19	10
Fort Lauderdale, FL	20	9
Houston, TX	16	12
Indianapolis, IN	22	7

[Continued]

★2859★

Drug Use By Arrestees, 1993, By Type of Drug and Sex: Females Using Multiple Drugs

[Continued]

City	Percent	Rank
Los Angeles, CA	29	6
Manhattan, NY	34	2
New Orleans, LA	16	12
Philadelphia, PA	32	3
Phoenix, AZ	30	5
Portland, OR	30	5
Saint Louis, MO	18	11
San Antonio, TX	19	10
San Diego, CA	39	1
San Jose, CA	20	9
Washington, DC	31	4

Source: Maguire, Kathleen, and Ann L. Pastore, eds., *Sourcebook of Criminal Justice Statistics 1994*, U.S. Department of Justice, Bureau of Justice Statistics, Washington, D.C.: U.S. Government Printing Office, 1995, p. 415. Primary source: U.S. Department of Justice, National Institute of Justice, *Drug Use Forecasting 1993 Annual Report on Adult Arrestees: Drugs and Crime in America's Cities*, NCJ-147411, Washington, D.C.: U.S. Department of Justice, 1994, pp. 6-28.

★2860★
Drug Use and Abuse

Drug Use By Arrestees, 1993, By Type of Drug and Sex: Females Using Opiates

Data on drug use are obtained every quarter for approximately two weeks by trained local staff who obtain voluntary and anonymous urine specimens and interviews from a new sample of arrestees. The cities of Chicago, Miami, and Omaha, did not test or interview female arrestees.

[In percent testing positive for drug use]

City	Percent	Rank
Atlanta, GA	4	10
Birmingham, AL	4	10
Cleveland, OH	4	10
Dallas, TX	10	6
Denver, CO	6	8
Detroit, MI	14	5
Fort Lauderdale, FL	3	11
Houston, TX	4	10
Indianapolis, IN	4	10
Los Angeles, CA	14	5
Manhattan, NY	23	1
New Orleans, LA	5	9
Philadelphia, PA	14	5
Phoenix, AZ	14	5
Portland, OR	19	4
Saint Louis, MO	6	8
San Antonio, TX	14	5
San Diego, CA	20	3
San Jose, CA	8	7
Washington, DC	21	2

Source: Maguire, Kathleen, and Ann L. Pastore, eds., *Sourcebook of Criminal Justice Statistics 1994*, U.S. Department of Justice, Bureau of Justice Statistics, Washington, D.C.: U.S. Government Printing Office, 1995, p. 415. Primary source: U.S. Department of Justice, National Institute of Justice, *Drug Use Forecasting 1993 Annual Report on Adult Arrestees: Drugs and Crime in America's Cities*, NCJ-147411, Washington, D.C.: U.S. Department of Justice, 1994, pp. 6-28.

★2861★

Drug Use and Abuse

Drug Use By Arrestees, 1993, By Type of Drug and Sex: Males Using Any Drug

Data refer to the use of cocaine, opiates, marijuana, phencyclidine (PCP), methadone, benzodiazepines, methaqualone, propoxyphene, barbiturates, and amphetamines. Data on drug use are obtained every quarter for approximately two weeks by trained local staff who obtain voluntary and anonymous urine specimens and interviews from a new sample of arrestees.

[In percent testing positive for drug use]

City	Percent	Rank
Atlanta, GA	72	4
Birmingham, AL	68	6
Chicago, IL	81	1
Cleveland, OH	64	8
Dallas, TX	62	10
Denver, CO	64	8
Detroit, MI	63	9
Fort Lauderdale, FL	61	11
Houston, TX	59	13
Indianapolis, IN	60	12
Los Angeles, CA	66	7
Manhattan, NY	78	2
Miami, FL	70	5
New Orleans, LA	62	10
Omaha, NE	54	15
Philadelphia, PA	76	3
Phoenix, AZ	62	10
Portland, OR	63	9
Saint Louis, MO	68	6
San Antonio, TX	55	14
San Diego, CA	78	2
San Jose, CA	54	15
Washington, DC	60	12

Source: Maguire, Kathleen, and Ann L. Pastore, eds., *Sourcebook of Criminal Justice Statistics 1994*, U.S. Department of Justice, Bureau of Justice Statistics, Washington, D.C.: U.S. Government Printing Office, 1995, p. 415. Primary source: U.S. Department of Justice, National Institute of Justice, *Drug Use Forecasting 1993 Annual Report on Adult Arrestees: Drugs and Crime in America's Cities*, NCJ-147411, Washington, D.C.: U.S. Department of Justice, 1994, pp. 6-28.

★2862★

Drug Use and Abuse

Drug Use By Arrestees, 1993, By Type of Drug and Sex: Males Using Cocaine

Data on drug use are obtained every quarter for approximately two weeks by trained local staff who obtain voluntary and anonymous urine specimens and interviews from a new sample of arrestees.

[In percent testing positive for drug use]

City	Percent	Rank
Atlanta, GA	59	3
Birmingham, AL	51	6
Chicago, IL	53	5
Cleveland, OH	48	8
Dallas, TX	44	9
Denver, CO	41	11
Detroit, MI	34	13
Fort Lauderdale, FL	43	10

[Continued]

★2862★

Drug Use By Arrestees, 1993, By Type of Drug and Sex: Males Using Cocaine

[Continued]

City	Percent	Rank
Houston, TX	41	11
Indianapolis, IN	32	15
Los Angeles, CA	48	8
Manhattan, NY	66	1
Miami, FL	61	2
New Orleans, LA	48	8
Omaha, NE	19	19
Philadelphia, PA	56	4
Phoenix, AZ	30	17
Portland, OR	33	14
Saint Louis, MO	50	7
San Antonio, TX	31	16
San Diego, CA	37	12
San Jose, CA	23	18
Washington, DC	37	12

Source: Maguire, Kathleen, and Ann L. Pastore, eds., *Sourcebook of Criminal Justice Statistics 1994*, U.S. Department of Justice, Bureau of Justice Statistics, Washington, D.C.: U.S. Government Printing Office, 1995, p. 415. Primary source: U.S. Department of Justice, National Institute of Justice, *Drug Use Forecasting 1993 Annual Report on Adult Arrestees: Drugs and Crime in America's Cities*, NCJ-147411, Washington, D.C.: U.S. Department of Justice, 1994, pp. 6-28.

★2863★

Drug Use and Abuse

Drug Use By Arrestees, 1993, By Type of Drug and Sex: Males Using Marijuana

Data on drug use are obtained every quarter for approximately two weeks by trained local staff who obtain voluntary and anonymous urine specimens and interviews from a new sample of arrestees.

[In percent testing positive for drug use]

City	Percent	Rank
Atlanta, GA	26	10
Birmingham, AL	28	8
Chicago, IL	40	2
Cleveland, OH	23	13
Dallas, TX	28	8
Denver, CO	36	4
Detroit, MI	37	3
Fort Lauderdale, FL	30	7
Houston, TX	24	12
Indianapolis, IN	42	1
Los Angeles, CA	23	13
Manhattan, NY	21	14
Miami, FL	26	10
New Orleans, LA	25	11
Omaha, NE	42	1
Philadelphia, PA	32	5
Phoenix, AZ	31	6
Portland, OR	30	7
Saint Louis, MO	28	8
San Antonio, TX	32	5
San Diego, CA	40	2

[Continued]

★2863★

Drug Use By Arrestees, 1993, By Type of Drug and Sex: Males Using Marijuana

[Continued]

City	Percent	Rank
San Jose, CA	27	9
Washington, DC	26	10

Source: Maguire, Kathleen, and Ann L. Pastore, eds., *Sourcebook of Criminal Justice Statistics 1994*, U.S. Department of Justice, Bureau of Justice Statistics, Washington, D.C.: U.S. Government Printing Office, 1995, p. 415. Primary source: U.S. Department of Justice, National Institute of Justice, *Drug Use Forecasting 1993 Annual Report on Adult Arrestees: Drugs and Crime in America's Cities*, NCJ-147411, Washington, D.C.: U.S. Department of Justice, 1994, pp. 6-28.

★2864★

Drug Use and Abuse

Drug Use By Arrestees, 1993, By Type of Drug and Sex: Males Using Multiple Drugs

Data refer to the use of cocaine, opiates, marijuana, phencyclidine (PCP), methadone, benzodiazepines, methaqualone, propoxyphene, barbiturates, and amphetamines. Data on drug use are obtained every quarter for approximately two weeks by trained local staff who obtain voluntary and anonymous urine specimens and interviews from a new sample of arrestees.

[In percent testing positive for drug use]

City	Percent	Rank
Atlanta, GA	17	10
Birmingham, AL	19	9
Chicago, IL	38	2
Cleveland, OH	17	10
Dallas, TX	21	7
Denver, CO	19	9
Detroit, MI	15	12
Fort Lauderdale, FL	16	11
Houston, TX	16	11
Indianapolis, IN	23	5
Los Angeles, CA	27	4
Manhattan, NY	34	3
Miami, FL	21	7
New Orleans, LA	20	8
Omaha, NE	13	13
Philadelphia, PA	34	3
Phoenix, AZ	22	6
Portland, OR	23	5
Saint Louis, MO	22	6
San Antonio, TX	23	5
San Diego, CA	42	1
San Jose, CA	19	9
Washington, DC	20	8

Source: Maguire, Kathleen, and Ann L. Pastore, eds., *Sourcebook of Criminal Justice Statistics 1994*, U.S. Department of Justice, Bureau of Justice Statistics, Washington, D.C.: U.S. Government Printing Office, 1995, p. 415. Primary source: U.S. Department of Justice, National Institute of Justice, *Drug Use Forecasting 1993 Annual Report on Adult Arrestees: Drugs and Crime in America's Cities*, NCJ-147411, Washington, D.C.: U.S. Department of Justice, 1994, pp. 6-28.

★2865★

Drug Use and Abuse

Drug Use By Arrestees, 1993, By Type of Drug and Sex: Males Using Opiates

Data on drug use are obtained every quarter for approximately two weeks by trained local staff who obtain voluntary and anonymous urine specimens and interviews from a new sample of arrestees.

[In percent testing positive for drug use]

City	Percent	Rank
Atlanta, GA	3	12
Birmingham, AL	4	11
Chicago, IL	28	1
Cleveland, OH	4	11
Dallas, TX	4	11
Denver, CO	4	11
Detroit, MI	8	8
Fort Lauderdale, FL	1	14
Houston, TX	2	13
Indianapolis, IN	4	11
Los Angeles, CA	9	7
Manhattan, NY	20	2
Miami, FL	2	13
New Orleans, LA	5	10
Omaha, NE	2	13
Philadelphia, PA	11	5
Phoenix, AZ	6	9
Portland, OR	11	5
Saint Louis, MO	9	7
San Antonio, TX	14	4
San Diego, CA	16	3
San Jose, CA	6	9
Washington, DC	10	6

Source: Maguire, Kathleen, and Ann L. Pastore, eds., *Sourcebook of Criminal Justice Statistics 1994*, U.S. Department of Justice, Bureau of Justice Statistics, Washington, D.C.: U.S. Government Printing Office, 1995, p. 415. Primary source: U.S. Department of Justice, National Institute of Justice, *Drug Use Forecasting 1993 Annual Report on Adult Arrestees: Drugs and Crime in America's Cities*, NCJ-147411, Washington, D.C.: U.S. Department of Justice, 1994, pp. 6-28.

★2866★

Drug Use and Abuse

Drug Use By Arrestees, 1993, By Type of Drug, Age, and Sex: Females Age 15 to 20 Using Any Drug

Data refer to the use of cocaine, opiates, marijuana, phencyclidine (PCP), methadone, benzodiazepines, methaqualone, propoxyphene, barbiturates, and amphetamines. Data on drug use are obtained every quarter for approximately two weeks by trained local staff who obtain voluntary and anonymous urine specimens and interviews from a new sample of arrestees. The cities of Chicago, Miami, and Omaha, did not test or interview female arrestees.

[In percent testing positive for drug use]

City	Percent	Rank
Atlanta, GA	34	10
Birmingham, AL	31	12
Cleveland, OH	64	2
Dallas, TX	36	9
Denver, CO	62	4
Fort Lauderdale, FL	40	7

[Continued]

★2866★

Drug Use By Arrestees, 1993, By Type of Drug, Age, and Sex: Females Age 15 to 20 Using Any Drug

[Continued]

City	Percent	Rank
Houston, TX	33	11
Indianapolis, IN	38	8
Los Angeles, CA	62	4
Manhattan, NY	47	6
New Orleans, LA	20	14
Philadelphia, PA	64	2
Phoenix, AZ	51	5
Portland, OR	63	3
Saint Louis, MO	34	10
San Antonio, TX	34	10
San Diego, CA	70	1
San Jose, CA	31	12
Washington, DC	30	13

Source: Maguire, Kathleen, and Ann L. Pastore, eds., *Sourcebook of Criminal Justice Statistics 1994*, U.S. Department of Justice, Bureau of Justice Statistics, Washington, D.C.: U.S. Government Printing Office, 1995, p. 415. Primary source: U.S. Department of Justice, National Institute of Justice, *Drug Use Forecasting 1993 Annual Report on Adult Arrestees: Drugs and Crime in America's Cities*, NCJ-147411, Washington, D.C.: U.S. Department of Justice, 1994, pp. 6-28.

★2867★

Drug Use and Abuse

Drug Use By Arrestees, 1993, By Type of Drug, Age, and Sex: Females Age 15 to 20 Using Cocaine

Data on drug use are obtained every quarter for approximately two weeks by trained local staff who obtain voluntary and anonymous urine specimens and interviews from a new sample of arrestees. The cities of Chicago, Miami, and Omaha, did not test or interview female arrestees.

[In percent testing positive for drug use]

City	Percent	Rank
Atlanta, GA	25	7
Birmingham, AL	22	9
Cleveland, OH	36	2
Dallas, TX	11	15
Denver, CO	27	6
Fort Lauderdale, FL	23	8
Houston, TX	20	11
Indianapolis, IN	10	16
Los Angeles, CA	32	3
Manhattan, NY	31	4
New Orleans, LA	12	14
Philadelphia, PA	19	12
Phoenix, AZ	28	5
Portland, OR	42	1
Saint Louis, MO	23	8
San Antonio, TX	13	13
San Diego, CA	21	10

[Continued]

★2867★

Drug Use By Arrestees, 1993, By Type of Drug, Age, and Sex: Females Age 15 to 20 Using Cocaine

[Continued]

City	Percent	Rank
San Jose, CA	9	17
Washington, DC	9	17

Source: Maguire, Kathleen, and Ann L. Pastore, eds., *Sourcebook of Criminal Justice Statistics 1994*, U.S. Department of Justice, Bureau of Justice Statistics, Washington, D.C.: U.S. Government Printing Office, 1995, p. 415. Primary source: U.S. Department of Justice, National Institute of Justice, *Drug Use Forecasting 1993 Annual Report on Adult Arrestees: Drugs and Crime in America's Cities*, NCJ-147411, Washington, D.C.: U.S. Department of Justice, 1994, pp. 6-28.

★2868★

Drug Use and Abuse

Drug Use By Arrestees, 1993, By Type of Drug, Age, and Sex: Females Age 15 to 20 Using Marijuana

Data on drug use are obtained every quarter for approximately two weeks by trained local staff who obtain voluntary and anonymous urine specimens and interviews from a new sample of arrestees. The cities of Chicago, Miami, and Omaha, did not test or interview female arrestees.

[In percent testing positive for drug use]

City	Percent	Rank
Atlanta, GA	11	13
Birmingham, AL	3	16
Cleveland, OH	39	3
Dallas, TX	29	7
Denver, CO	43	2
Fort Lauderdale, FL	17	10
Houston, TX	15	12
Indianapolis, IN	30	6
Los Angeles, CA	34	4
Manhattan, NY	16	11
New Orleans, LA	10	14
Philadelphia, PA	33	5
Phoenix, AZ	26	8
Portland, OR	17	10
Saint Louis, MO	16	11
San Antonio, TX	17	10
San Diego, CA	48	1
San Jose, CA	6	15
Washington, DC	22	9

Source: Maguire, Kathleen, and Ann L. Pastore, eds., *Sourcebook of Criminal Justice Statistics 1994*, U.S. Department of Justice, Bureau of Justice Statistics, Washington, D.C.: U.S. Government Printing Office, 1995, p. 415. Primary source: U.S. Department of Justice, National Institute of Justice, *Drug Use Forecasting 1993 Annual Report on Adult Arrestees: Drugs and Crime in America's Cities*, NCJ-147411, Washington, D.C.: U.S. Department of Justice, 1994, pp. 6-28.

★2869★

Drug Use and Abuse

Drug Use By Arrestees, 1993, By Type of Drug, Age, and Sex: Females Age 15 to 20 Using Opiates

Data on drug use are obtained every quarter for approximately two weeks by trained local staff who obtain voluntary and anonymous urine specimens and interviews from a new sample of arrestees. The cities of Chicago, Miami, and Omaha, did not test or interview female arrestees.

[In percent testing positive for drug use]

City	Percent	Rank
Atlanta, GA	7	5
Birmingham, AL	3	9
Cleveland, OH	0	11
Dallas, TX	0	11
Denver, CO	0	11
Fort Lauderdale, FL	0	11
Houston, TX	5	7
Indianapolis, IN	2	10
Los Angeles, CA	2	10
Manhattan, NY	11	3
New Orleans, LA	2	10
Philadelphia, PA	12	2
Phoenix, AZ	0	11
Portland, OR	20	1
Saint Louis, MO	4	8
San Antonio, TX	10	4
San Diego, CA	6	6
San Jose, CA	3	9
Washington, DC	4	8

Source: Maguire, Kathleen, and Ann L. Pastore, eds., *Sourcebook of Criminal Justice Statistics 1994,* U.S. Department of Justice, Bureau of Justice Statistics, Washington, D.C.: U.S. Government Printing Office, 1995, p. 415. Primary source: U.S. Department of Justice, National Institute of Justice, *Drug Use Forecasting 1993 Annual Report on Adult Arrestees: Drugs and Crime in America's Cities,* NCJ-147411, Washington, D.C.: U.S. Department of Justice, 1994, pp. 6-28.

★2870★

Drug Use and Abuse

Drug Use By Arrestees, 1993, By Type of Drug, Age, and Sex: Females Age 21 to 25 Using Any Drug

Data refer to the use of cocaine, opiates, marijuana, phencyclidine (PCP), methadone, benzodiazepines, methaqualone, propoxyphene, barbiturates, and amphetamines. Data on drug use are obtained every quarter for approximately two weeks by trained local staff who obtain voluntary and anonymous urine specimens and interviews from a new sample of arrestees. The cities of Chicago, Miami, and Omaha, did not test or interview female arrestees.

[In percent testing positive for drug use]

City	Percent	Rank
Atlanta, GA	61	7
Birmingham, AL	40	16
Cleveland, OH	75	2
Dallas, TX	55	11
Denver, CO	62	6
Detroit, MI	61	7
Fort Lauderdale, FL	37	18
Houston, TX	40	16

[Continued]

★2870★

Drug Use By Arrestees, 1993, By Type of Drug, Age, and Sex: Females Age 21 to 25 Using Any Drug

[Continued]

City	Percent	Rank
Indianapolis, IN	51	12
Los Angeles, CA	70	4
Manhattan, NY	82	1
New Orleans, LA	42	15
Philadelphia, PA	67	5
Phoenix, AZ	57	9
Portland, OR	58	8
Saint Louis, MO	56	10
San Antonio, TX	39	17
San Diego, CA	71	3
San Jose, CA	45	14
Washington, DC	50	13

Source: Maguire, Kathleen, and Ann L. Pastore, eds., *Sourcebook of Criminal Justice Statistics 1994,* U.S. Department of Justice, Bureau of Justice Statistics, Washington, D.C.: U.S. Government Printing Office, 1995, p. 415. Primary source: U.S. Department of Justice, National Institute of Justice, *Drug Use Forecasting 1993 Annual Report on Adult Arrestees: Drugs and Crime in America's Cities,* NCJ-147411, Washington, D.C.: U.S. Department of Justice, 1994, pp. 6-28.

★2871★

Drug Use and Abuse

Drug Use By Arrestees, 1993, By Type of Drug, Age, and Sex: Females Age 21 to 25 Using Cocaine

Data on drug use are obtained every quarter for approximately two weeks by trained local staff who obtain voluntary and anonymous urine specimens and interviews from a new sample of arrestees. The cities of Chicago, Miami, and Omaha, did not test or interview female arrestees.

[In percent testing positive for drug use]

City	Percent	Rank
Atlanta, GA	54	3
Birmingham, AL	28	12
Cleveland, OH	68	1
Dallas, TX	36	9
Denver, CO	43	7
Detroit, MI	46	6
Fort Lauderdale, FL	26	13
Houston, TX	31	10
Indianapolis, IN	30	11
Los Angeles, CA	49	4
Manhattan, NY	61	2
New Orleans, LA	30	11
Philadelphia, PA	49	4
Phoenix, AZ	36	9
Portland, OR	36	9
Saint Louis, MO	48	5
San Antonio, TX	20	14
San Diego, CA	26	13

[Continued]

★2871★

Drug Use By Arrestees, 1993, By Type of Drug, Age, and Sex: Females Age 21 to 25 Using Cocaine

[Continued]

City	Percent	Rank
San Jose, CA	15	15
Washington, DC	41	8

Source: Maguire, Kathleen, and Ann L. Pastore, eds., *Sourcebook of Criminal Justice Statistics 1994*, U.S. Department of Justice, Bureau of Justice Statistics, Washington, D.C.: U.S. Government Printing Office, 1995, p. 415. Primary source: U.S. Department of Justice, National Institute of Justice, *Drug Use Forecasting 1993 Annual Report on Adult Arrestees: Drugs and Crime in America's Cities*, NCJ-147411, Washington, D.C.: U.S. Department of Justice, 1994, pp. 6-28.

★2872★

Drug Use and Abuse

Drug Use By Arrestees, 1993, By Type of Drug, Age, and Sex: Females Age 21 to 25 Using Marijuana

Data on drug use are obtained every quarter for approximately two weeks by trained local staff who obtain voluntary and anonymous urine specimens and interviews from a new sample of arrestees. The cities of Chicago, Miami, and Omaha, did not test or interview female arrestees.

[In percent testing positive for drug use]

City	Percent	Rank
Atlanta, GA	12	10
Birmingham, AL	12	10
Cleveland, OH	12	10
Dallas, TX	20	5
Denver, CO	23	3
Detroit, MI	18	7
Fort Lauderdale, FL	17	8
Houston, TX	17	8
Indianapolis, IN	27	2
Los Angeles, CA	16	9
Manhattan, NY	27	2
New Orleans, LA	19	6
Philadelphia, PA	22	4
Phoenix, AZ	23	3
Portland, OR	12	10
Saint Louis, MO	18	7
San Antonio, TX	20	5
San Diego, CA	30	1
San Jose, CA	18	7
Washington, DC	7	11

Source: Maguire, Kathleen, and Ann L. Pastore, eds., *Sourcebook of Criminal Justice Statistics 1994*, U.S. Department of Justice, Bureau of Justice Statistics, Washington, D.C.: U.S. Government Printing Office, 1995, p. 415. Primary source: U.S. Department of Justice, National Institute of Justice, *Drug Use Forecasting 1993 Annual Report on Adult Arrestees: Drugs and Crime in America's Cities*, NCJ-147411, Washington, D.C.: U.S. Department of Justice, 1994, pp. 6-28.

★2873★

Drug Use and Abuse

Drug Use By Arrestees, 1993, By Type of Drug, Age, and Sex: Females Age 21 to 25 Using Opiates

Data on drug use are obtained every quarter for approximately two weeks by trained local staff who obtain voluntary and anonymous urine specimens and interviews from a new sample of arrestees. The cities of Chicago, Miami, and Omaha, did not test or interview female arrestees.

[In percent testing positive for drug use]

City	Percent	Rank
Atlanta, GA	4	9
Birmingham, AL	2	11
Cleveland, OH	3	10
Dallas, TX	7	6
Denver, CO	4	9
Detroit, MI	4	9
Fort Lauderdale, FL	0	12
Houston, TX	2	11
Indianapolis, IN	4	9
Los Angeles, CA	10	4
Manhattan, NY	17	1
New Orleans, LA	3	10
Philadelphia, PA	13	3
Phoenix, AZ	6	7
Portland, OR	10	4
Saint Louis, MO	5	8
San Antonio, TX	10	4
San Diego, CA	14	2
San Jose, CA	10	4
Washington, DC	9	5

Source: Maguire, Kathleen, and Ann L. Pastore, eds., *Sourcebook of Criminal Justice Statistics 1994*, U.S. Department of Justice, Bureau of Justice Statistics, Washington, D.C.: U.S. Government Printing Office, 1995, p. 415. Primary source: U.S. Department of Justice, National Institute of Justice, *Drug Use Forecasting 1993 Annual Report on Adult Arrestees: Drugs and Crime in America's Cities*, NCJ-147411, Washington, D.C.: U.S. Department of Justice, 1994, pp. 6-28.

★2874★

Drug Use and Abuse

Drug Use By Arrestees, 1993, By Type of Drug, Age, and Sex: Females Age 26 to 30 Using Any Drug

Data refer to the use of cocaine, opiates, marijuana, phencyclidine (PCP), methadone, benzodiazepines, methaqualone, propoxyphene, barbiturates, and amphetamines. Data on drug use are obtained every quarter for approximately two weeks by trained local staff who obtain voluntary and anonymous urine specimens and interviews from a new sample of arrestees. The cities of Chicago, Miami, and Omaha, did not test or interview female arrestees.

[In percent testing positive for drug use]

City	Percent	Rank
Atlanta, GA	84	3
Birmingham, AL	66	12
Cleveland, OH	81	5
Dallas, TX	70	10
Denver, CO	64	13
Detroit, MI	79	6
Fort Lauderdale, FL	76	9

[Continued]

★2874★

Drug Use By Arrestees, 1993, By Type of Drug, Age, and Sex: Females Age 26 to 30 Using Any Drug

[Continued]

City	Percent	Rank
Houston, TX	54	15
Indianapolis, IN	68	11
Los Angeles, CA	77	8
Manhattan, NY	84	3
New Orleans, LA	53	16
Philadelphia, PA	87	2
Phoenix, AZ	66	12
Portland, OR	83	4
Saint Louis, MO	88	1
San Antonio, TX	46	17
San Diego, CA	78	7
San Jose, CA	58	14
Washington, DC	81	5

Source: Maguire, Kathleen, and Ann L. Pastore, eds., *Sourcebook of Criminal Justice Statistics 1994*, U.S. Department of Justice, Bureau of Justice Statistics, Washington, D.C.: U.S. Government Printing Office, 1995, p. 415. Primary source: U.S. Department of Justice, National Institute of Justice, *Drug Use Forecasting 1993 Annual Report on Adult Arrestees: Drugs and Crime in America's Cities*, NCJ-147411, Washington, D.C.: U.S. Department of Justice, 1994, pp. 6-28.

★2875★

Drug Use and Abuse

Drug Use By Arrestees, 1993, By Type of Drug, Age, and Sex: Females Age 26 to 30 Using Cocaine

Data on drug use are obtained every quarter for approximately two weeks by trained local staff who obtain voluntary and anonymous urine specimens and interviews from a new sample of arrestees. The cities of Chicago, Miami, and Omaha, did not test or interview female arrestees.

[In percent testing positive for drug use]

City	Percent	Rank
Atlanta, GA	76	3
Birmingham, AL	55	9
Cleveland, OH	76	3
Dallas, TX	54	10
Denver, CO	52	11
Detroit, MI	73	4
Fort Lauderdale, FL	60	8
Houston, TX	39	15
Indianapolis, IN	42	13
Los Angeles, CA	61	7
Manhattan, NY	71	5
New Orleans, LA	48	12
Philadelphia, PA	79	2
Phoenix, AZ	40	14
Portland, OR	62	6
Saint Louis, MO	82	1
San Antonio, TX	32	17
San Diego, CA	38	16

[Continued]

★2875★

Drug Use By Arrestees, 1993, By Type of Drug, Age, and Sex: Females Age 26 to 30 Using Cocaine

[Continued]

City	Percent	Rank
San Jose, CA	20	18
Washington, DC	71	5

Source: Maguire, Kathleen, and Ann L. Pastore, eds., *Sourcebook of Criminal Justice Statistics 1994*, U.S. Department of Justice, Bureau of Justice Statistics, Washington, D.C.: U.S. Government Printing Office, 1995, p. 415. Primary source: U.S. Department of Justice, National Institute of Justice, *Drug Use Forecasting 1993 Annual Report on Adult Arrestees: Drugs and Crime in America's Cities*, NCJ-147411, Washington, D.C.: U.S. Department of Justice, 1994, pp. 6-28.

★2876★

Drug Use and Abuse

Drug Use By Arrestees, 1993, By Type of Drug, Age, and Sex: Females Age 26 to 30 Using Marijuana

Data on drug use are obtained every quarter for approximately two weeks by trained local staff who obtain voluntary and anonymous urine specimens and interviews from a new sample of arrestees. The cities of Chicago, Miami, and Omaha, did not test or interview female arrestees.

[In percent testing positive for drug use]

City	Percent	Rank
Atlanta, GA	21	6
Birmingham, AL	17	9
Cleveland, OH	10	14
Dallas, TX	20	7
Denver, CO	27	3
Detroit, MI	12	13
Fort Lauderdale, FL	32	1
Houston, TX	16	10
Indianapolis, IN	31	2
Los Angeles, CA	18	8
Manhattan, NY	22	5
New Orleans, LA	15	11
Philadelphia, PA	22	5
Phoenix, AZ	20	7
Portland, OR	23	4
Saint Louis, MO	14	12
San Antonio, TX	12	13
San Diego, CA	23	4
San Jose, CA	17	9
Washington, DC	16	10

Source: Maguire, Kathleen, and Ann L. Pastore, eds., *Sourcebook of Criminal Justice Statistics 1994*, U.S. Department of Justice, Bureau of Justice Statistics, Washington, D.C.: U.S. Government Printing Office, 1995, p. 415. Primary source: U.S. Department of Justice, National Institute of Justice, *Drug Use Forecasting 1993 Annual Report on Adult Arrestees: Drugs and Crime in America's Cities*, NCJ-147411, Washington, D.C.: U.S. Department of Justice, 1994, pp. 6-28.

★2877★

Drug Use and Abuse

Drug Use By Arrestees, 1993, By Type of Drug, Age, and Sex: Females Age 26 to 30 Using Opiates

Data on drug use are obtained every quarter for approximately two weeks by trained local staff who obtain voluntary and anonymous urine specimens and interviews from a new sample of arrestees. The cities of Chicago, Miami, and Omaha, did not test or interview female arrestees.

[In percent testing positive for drug use]

City	Percent	Rank
Atlanta, GA	3	11
Birmingham, AL	2	12
Cleveland, OH	4	10
Dallas, TX	12	6
Denver, CO	2	12
Detroit, MI	8	7
Fort Lauderdale, FL	7	8
Houston, TX	3	11
Indianapolis, IN	3	11
Los Angeles, CA	13	5
Manhattan, NY	24	1
New Orleans, LA	2	12
Philadelphia, PA	13	5
Phoenix, AZ	13	5
Portland, OR	17	4
Saint Louis, MO	8	7
San Antonio, TX	18	3
San Diego, CA	20	2
San Jose, CA	5	9
Washington, DC	12	6

Source: Maguire, Kathleen, and Ann L. Pastore, eds., *Sourcebook of Criminal Justice Statistics 1994*, U.S. Department of Justice, Bureau of Justice Statistics, Washington, D.C.: U.S. Government Printing Office, 1995, p. 415. Primary source: U.S. Department of Justice, National Institute of Justice, *Drug Use Forecasting 1993 Annual Report on Adult Arrestees: Drugs and Crime in America's Cities*, NCJ-147411, Washington, D.C.: U.S. Department of Justice, 1994, pp. 6-28.

★2878★

Drug Use and Abuse

Drug Use By Arrestees, 1993, By Type of Drug, Age, and Sex: Females Age 31 to 35 Using Any Drug

Data refer to the use of cocaine, opiates, marijuana, phencyclidine (PCP), methadone, benzodiazepines, methaqualone, propoxyphene, barbiturates, and amphetamines. Data on drug use are obtained every quarter for approximately two weeks by trained local staff who obtain voluntary and anonymous urine specimens and interviews from a new sample of arrestees. The cities of Chicago, Miami, and Omaha, did not test or interview female arrestees.

[In percent testing positive for drug use]

City	Percent	Rank
Atlanta, GA	93	1
Birmingham, AL	66	13
Cleveland, OH	81	8
Dallas, TX	68	12
Denver, CO	78	9
Detroit, MI	82	7
Fort Lauderdale, FL	63	15

[Continued]

★2878★

Drug Use By Arrestees, 1993, By Type of Drug, Age, and Sex: Females Age 31 to 35 Using Any Drug

[Continued]

City	Percent	Rank
Houston, TX	64	14
Indianapolis, IN	72	10
Los Angeles, CA	86	4
Manhattan, NY	91	2
New Orleans, LA	58	16
Philadelphia, PA	90	3
Phoenix, AZ	69	11
Portland, OR	82	7
Saint Louis, MO	72	10
San Antonio, TX	48	17
San Diego, CA	85	5
San Jose, CA	58	16
Washington, DC	84	6

Source: Maguire, Kathleen, and Ann L. Pastore, eds., *Sourcebook of Criminal Justice Statistics 1994*, U.S. Department of Justice, Bureau of Justice Statistics, Washington, D.C.: U.S. Government Printing Office, 1995, p. 415. Primary source: U.S. Department of Justice, National Institute of Justice, *Drug Use Forecasting 1993 Annual Report on Adult Arrestees: Drugs and Crime in America's Cities*, NCJ-147411, Washington, D.C.: U.S. Department of Justice, 1994, pp. 6-28.

★2879★

Drug Use and Abuse

Drug Use By Arrestees, 1993, By Type of Drug, Age, and Sex: Females Age 31 to 35 Using Cocaine

Data on drug use are obtained every quarter for approximately two weeks by trained local staff who obtain voluntary and anonymous urine specimens and interviews from a new sample of arrestees. The cities of Chicago, Miami, and Omaha, did not test or interview female arrestees.

[In percent testing positive for drug use]

City	Percent	Rank
Atlanta, GA	90	1
Birmingham, AL	55	10
Cleveland, OH	76	5
Dallas, TX	51	13
Denver, CO	63	9
Detroit, MI	70	6
Fort Lauderdale, FL	54	11
Houston, TX	55	10
Indianapolis, IN	52	12
Los Angeles, CA	64	8
Manhattan, NY	82	3
New Orleans, LA	48	14
Philadelphia, PA	79	4
Phoenix, AZ	42	17
Portland, OR	46	15
Saint Louis, MO	69	7
San Antonio, TX	30	19
San Diego, CA	43	16

[Continued]

★2879★

Drug Use By Arrestees, 1993, By Type of Drug, Age, and Sex: Females Age 31 to 35 Using Cocaine
[Continued]

City	Percent	Rank
San Jose, CA	32	18
Washington, DC	83	2

Source: Maguire, Kathleen, and Ann L. Pastore, eds., *Sourcebook of Criminal Justice Statistics 1994,* U.S. Department of Justice, Bureau of Justice Statistics, Washington, D.C.: U.S. Government Printing Office, 1995, p. 415. Primary source: U.S. Department of Justice, National Institute of Justice, *Drug Use Forecasting 1993 Annual Report on Adult Arrestees: Drugs and Crime in America's Cities,* NCJ-147411, Washington, D.C.: U.S. Department of Justice, 1994, pp. 6-28.

★2880★
Drug Use and Abuse

Drug Use By Arrestees, 1993, By Type of Drug, Age, and Sex: Females Age 31 to 35 Using Marijuana

Data on drug use are obtained every quarter for approximately two weeks by trained local staff who obtain voluntary and anonymous urine specimens and interviews from a new sample of arrestees. The cities of Chicago, Miami, and Omaha, did not test or interview female arrestees.

[In percent testing positive for drug use]

City	Percent	Rank
Atlanta, GA	17	5
Birmingham, AL	11	9
Cleveland, OH	10	10
Dallas, TX	18	4
Denver, CO	18	4
Detroit, MI	2	12
Fort Lauderdale, FL	10	10
Houston, TX	16	6
Indianapolis, IN	28	2
Los Angeles, CA	14	7
Manhattan, NY	17	5
New Orleans, LA	13	8
Philadelphia, PA	16	6
Phoenix, AZ	19	3
Portland, OR	19	3
Saint Louis, MO	13	8
San Antonio, TX	17	5
San Diego, CA	28	2
San Jose, CA	29	1
Washington, DC	3	11

Source: Maguire, Kathleen, and Ann L. Pastore, eds., *Sourcebook of Criminal Justice Statistics 1994,* U.S. Department of Justice, Bureau of Justice Statistics, Washington, D.C.: U.S. Government Printing Office, 1995, p. 415. Primary source: U.S. Department of Justice, National Institute of Justice, *Drug Use Forecasting 1993 Annual Report on Adult Arrestees: Drugs and Crime in America's Cities,* NCJ-147411, Washington, D.C.: U.S. Department of Justice, 1994, pp. 6-28.

★2881★
Drug Use and Abuse

Drug Use By Arrestees, 1993, By Type of Drug, Age, and Sex: Females Age 31 to 35 Using Opiates

Data on drug use are obtained every quarter for approximately two weeks by trained local staff who obtain voluntary and anonymous urine specimens and interviews from a new sample of arrestees. The cities of Chicago, Miami, and Omaha, did not test or interview female arrestees.

[In percent testing positive for drug use]

City	Percent	Rank
Atlanta, GA	3	12
Birmingham, AL	3	12
Cleveland, OH	4	11
Dallas, TX	17	6
Denver, CO	12	8
Detroit, MI	20	5
Fort Lauderdale, FL	2	13
Houston, TX	5	10
Indianapolis, IN	4	11
Los Angeles, CA	17	6
Manhattan, NY	22	3
New Orleans, LA	10	9
Philadelphia, PA	14	7
Phoenix, AZ	21	4
Portland, OR	24	2
Saint Louis, MO	1	14
San Antonio, TX	17	6
San Diego, CA	28	1
San Jose, CA	2	13
Washington, DC	28	1

Source: Maguire, Kathleen, and Ann L. Pastore, eds., *Sourcebook of Criminal Justice Statistics 1994,* U.S. Department of Justice, Bureau of Justice Statistics, Washington, D.C.: U.S. Government Printing Office, 1995, p. 415. Primary source: U.S. Department of Justice, National Institute of Justice, *Drug Use Forecasting 1993 Annual Report on Adult Arrestees: Drugs and Crime in America's Cities,* NCJ-147411, Washington, D.C.: U.S. Department of Justice, 1994, pp. 6-28.

★2882★
Drug Use and Abuse

Drug Use By Arrestees, 1993, By Type of Drug, Age, and Sex: Females Age 36 and Older Using Any Drug

Data refer to the use of cocaine, opiates, marijuana, phencyclidine (PCP), methadone, benzodiazepines, methaqualone, propoxyphene, barbiturates, and amphetamines. Data on drug use are obtained every quarter for approximately two weeks by trained local staff who obtain voluntary and anonymous urine specimens and interviews from a new sample of arrestees. The cities of Chicago, Miami, and Omaha, did not test or interview female arrestees.

[In percent testing positive for drug use]

City	Percent	Rank
Atlanta, GA	74	6
Birmingham, AL	56	13
Cleveland, OH	76	5
Dallas, TX	66	9
Denver, CO	64	10
Detroit, MI	83	2
Fort Lauderdale, FL	62	11

[Continued]

★2882★

Drug Use By Arrestees, 1993, By Type of Drug, Age, and Sex: Females Age 36 and Older Using Any Drug
[Continued]

City	Percent	Rank
Houston, TX	68	8
Indianapolis, IN	57	12
Los Angeles, CA	79	4
Manhattan, NY	91	1
New Orleans, LA	52	14
Philadelphia, PA	80	3
Phoenix, AZ	56	13
Portland, OR	76	5
Saint Louis, MO	73	7
San Antonio, TX	44	16
San Diego, CA	79	4
San Jose, CA	50	15
Washington, DC	76	5

Source: Maguire, Kathleen, and Ann L. Pastore, eds., *Sourcebook of Criminal Justice Statistics 1994*, U.S. Department of Justice, Bureau of Justice Statistics, Washington, D.C.: U.S. Government Printing Office, 1995, p. 415. Primary source: U.S. Department of Justice, National Institute of Justice, *Drug Use Forecasting 1993 Annual Report on Adult Arrestees: Drugs and Crime in America's Cities*, NCJ-147411, Washington, D.C.: U.S. Department of Justice, 1994, pp. 6-28.

★2883★
Drug Use and Abuse

Drug Use By Arrestees, 1993, By Type of Drug, Age, and Sex: Females Age 36 and Older Using Cocaine

Data on drug use are obtained every quarter for approximately two weeks by trained local staff who obtain voluntary and anonymous urine specimens and interviews from a new sample of arrestees. The cities of Chicago, Miami, and Omaha, did not test or interview female arrestees.

[In percent testing positive for drug use]

City	Percent	Rank
Atlanta, GA	67	2
Birmingham, AL	35	13
Cleveland, OH	67	2
Dallas, TX	56	7
Denver, CO	39	10
Detroit, MI	67	2
Fort Lauderdale, FL	43	8
Houston, TX	60	5
Indianapolis, IN	36	12
Los Angeles, CA	66	3
Manhattan, NY	83	1
New Orleans, LA	38	11
Philadelphia, PA	57	6
Phoenix, AZ	31	14
Portland, OR	42	9
Saint Louis, MO	64	4
San Antonio, TX	26	15
San Diego, CA	36	12

[Continued]

★2883★

Drug Use By Arrestees, 1993, By Type of Drug, Age, and Sex: Females Age 36 and Older Using Cocaine
[Continued]

City	Percent	Rank
San Jose, CA	16	16
Washington, DC	66	3

Source: Maguire, Kathleen, and Ann L. Pastore, eds., *Sourcebook of Criminal Justice Statistics 1994*, U.S. Department of Justice, Bureau of Justice Statistics, Washington, D.C.: U.S. Government Printing Office, 1995, p. 415. Primary source: U.S. Department of Justice, National Institute of Justice, *Drug Use Forecasting 1993 Annual Report on Adult Arrestees: Drugs and Crime in America's Cities*, NCJ-147411, Washington, D.C.: U.S. Department of Justice, 1994, pp. 6-28.

★2884★
Drug Use and Abuse

Drug Use By Arrestees, 1993, By Type of Drug, Age, and Sex: Females Age 36 and Older Using Marijuana

Data on drug use are obtained every quarter for approximately two weeks by trained local staff who obtain voluntary and anonymous urine specimens and interviews from a new sample of arrestees. The cities of Chicago, Miami, and Omaha, did not test or interview female arrestees.

[In percent testing positive for drug use]

City	Percent	Rank
Atlanta, GA	13	6
Birmingham, AL	12	7
Cleveland, OH	8	10
Dallas, TX	12	7
Denver, CO	19	2
Detroit, MI	11	8
Fort Lauderdale, FL	23	1
Houston, TX	10	9
Indianapolis, IN	14	5
Los Angeles, CA	7	11
Manhattan, NY	14	5
New Orleans, LA	12	7
Philadelphia, PA	12	7
Phoenix, AZ	15	4
Portland, OR	13	6
Saint Louis, MO	14	5
San Antonio, TX	15	4
San Diego, CA	17	3
San Jose, CA	11	8
Washington, DC	8	10

Source: Maguire, Kathleen, and Ann L. Pastore, eds., *Sourcebook of Criminal Justice Statistics 1994*, U.S. Department of Justice, Bureau of Justice Statistics, Washington, D.C.: U.S. Government Printing Office, 1995, p. 415. Primary source: U.S. Department of Justice, National Institute of Justice, *Drug Use Forecasting 1993 Annual Report on Adult Arrestees: Drugs and Crime in America's Cities*, NCJ-147411, Washington, D.C.: U.S. Department of Justice, 1994, pp. 6-28.

★2885★
Drug Use and Abuse

Drug Use By Arrestees, 1993, By Type of Drug, Age, and Sex: Females Age 36 and Older Using Opiates

Data on drug use are obtained every quarter for approximately two weeks by trained local staff who obtain voluntary and anonymous urine specimens and interviews from a new sample of arrestees. The cities of Chicago, Miami, and Omaha, did not test or interview female arrestees.

[In percent testing positive for drug use]

City	Percent	Rank
Atlanta, GA	5	14
Birmingham, AL	7	12
Cleveland, OH	10	11
Dallas, TX	13	9
Denver, CO	11	10
Detroit, MI	17	7
Fort Lauderdale, FL	6	13
Houston, TX	6	13
Indianapolis, IN	7	12
Los Angeles, CA	20	5
Manhattan, NY	31	2
New Orleans, LA	6	13
Philadelphia, PA	17	7
Phoenix, AZ	23	4
Portland, OR	26	3
Saint Louis, MO	11	10
San Antonio, TX	19	6
San Diego, CA	20	5
San Jose, CA	15	8
Washington, DC	33	1

Source: Maguire, Kathleen, and Ann L. Pastore, eds., *Sourcebook of Criminal Justice Statistics 1994,* U.S. Department of Justice, Bureau of Justice Statistics, Washington, D.C.: U.S. Government Printing Office, 1995, p. 415. Primary source: U.S. Department of Justice, National Institute of Justice, *Drug Use Forecasting 1993 Annual Report on Adult Arrestees: Drugs and Crime in America's Cities,* NCJ-147411, Washington, D.C.: U.S. Department of Justice, 1994, pp. 6-28.

★2886★
Drug Use and Abuse

Drug Use By Arrestees, 1993, By Type of Drug, Age, and Sex: Males Age 15 to 20 Using Cocaine

Data on drug use are obtained every quarter for approximately two weeks by trained local staff who obtain voluntary and anonymous urine specimens and interviews from a new sample of arrestees.

[In percent testing positive for drug use]

City	Percent	Rank
Atlanta, GA	22	9
Birmingham, AL	23	8
Chicago, IL	44	1
Cleveland, OH	28	6
Dallas, TX	19	11
Denver, CO	17	13
Detroit, MI	9	18
Fort Lauderdale, FL	27	7
Houston, TX	27	7
Indianapolis, IN	16	14
Los Angeles, CA	30	4

[Continued]

★2886★

Drug Use By Arrestees, 1993, By Type of Drug, Age, and Sex: Males Age 15 to 20 Using Cocaine
[Continued]

City	Percent	Rank
Manhattan, NY	23	8
Miami, FL	32	3
New Orleans, LA	34	2
Omaha, NE	10	17
Philadelphia, PA	21	10
Phoenix, AZ	16	14
Portland, OR	29	5
Saint Louis, MO	30	4
San Antonio, TX	18	12
San Diego, CA	21	10
San Jose, CA	13	16
Washington, DC	15	15

Source: Maguire, Kathleen, and Ann L. Pastore, eds., *Sourcebook of Criminal Justice Statistics 1994,* U.S. Department of Justice, Bureau of Justice Statistics, Washington, D.C.: U.S. Government Printing Office, 1995, p. 415. Primary source: U.S. Department of Justice, National Institute of Justice, *Drug Use Forecasting 1993 Annual Report on Adult Arrestees: Drugs and Crime in America's Cities,* NCJ-147411, Washington, D.C.: U.S. Department of Justice, 1994, pp. 6-28.

★2887★
Drug Use and Abuse

Drug Use By Arrestees, 1993, By Type of Drug, Age, and Sex: Males Age 15 to 20 Using Marijuana

Data on drug use are obtained every quarter for approximately two weeks by trained local staff who obtain voluntary and anonymous urine specimens and interviews from a new sample of arrestees.

[In percent testing positive for drug use]

City	Percent	Rank
Atlanta, GA	52	6
Birmingham, AL	45	9
Chicago, IL	46	8
Cleveland, OH	39	12
Dallas, TX	34	13
Denver, CO	57	2
Detroit, MI	54	4
Fort Lauderdale, FL	46	8
Houston, TX	39	12
Indianapolis, IN	48	7
Los Angeles, CA	32	14
Manhattan, NY	46	8
Miami, FL	32	14
New Orleans, LA	34	13
Omaha, NE	60	1
Philadelphia, PA	56	3
Phoenix, AZ	31	15
Portland, OR	44	10
Saint Louis, MO	39	12
San Antonio, TX	42	11
San Diego, CA	44	10

[Continued]

★2887★

Drug Use By Arrestees, 1993, By Type of Drug, Age, and Sex: Males Age 15 to 20 Using Marijuana

[Continued]

City	Percent	Rank
San Jose, CA	30	16
Washington, DC	53	5

Source: Maguire, Kathleen, and Ann L. Pastore, eds., *Sourcebook of Criminal Justice Statistics 1994*, U.S. Department of Justice, Bureau of Justice Statistics, Washington, D.C.: U.S. Government Printing Office, 1995, p. 415. Primary source: U.S. Department of Justice, National Institute of Justice, *Drug Use Forecasting 1993 Annual Report on Adult Arrestees: Drugs and Crime in America's Cities*, NCJ-147411, Washington, D.C.: U.S. Department of Justice, 1994, pp. 6-28.

★2888★

Drug Use and Abuse

Drug Use By Arrestees, 1993, By Type of Drug, Age, and Sex: Males Age 15 to 20 Using Opiates

Data on drug use are obtained every quarter for approximately two weeks by trained local staff who obtain voluntary and anonymous urine specimens and interviews from a new sample of arrestees.

[In percent testing positive for drug use]

City	Percent	Rank
Birmingham, AL	4	5
Chicago, IL	20	1
Cleveland, OH	1	8
Denver, CO	0	9
Detroit, MI	1	8
Fort Lauderdale, FL	1	8
Houston, TX	1	8
Indianapolis, IN	0	9
Manhattan, NY	5	4
Miami, FL	0	9
New Orleans, LA	4	5
Omaha, NE	1	8
Philadelphia, PA	7	3
Portland, OR	7	3
Saint Louis, MO	9	2
San Antonio, TX	4	5
San Diego, CA	3	6
Washington, DC	2	7

Source: Maguire, Kathleen, and Ann L. Pastore, eds., *Sourcebook of Criminal Justice Statistics 1994*, U.S. Department of Justice, Bureau of Justice Statistics, Washington, D.C.: U.S. Government Printing Office, 1995, p. 415. Primary source: U.S. Department of Justice, National Institute of Justice, *Drug Use Forecasting 1993 Annual Report on Adult Arrestees: Drugs and Crime in America's Cities*, NCJ-147411, Washington, D.C.: U.S. Department of Justice, 1994, pp. 6-28.

★2889★

Drug Use and Abuse

Drug Use By Arrestees, 1993, By Type of Drug, Age, and Sex: Males Age 15-20 Using Any Drug

Data refer to the use of cocaine, opiates, marijuana, phencyclidine (PCP), methadone, benzodiazepines, methaqualone, propoxyphene, barbiturates, and amphetamines. Data on drug use are obtained every quarter for approximately two weeks by trained local staff who obtain voluntary and anonymous urine specimens and interviews from a new sample of arrestees.

[In percent testing positive for drug use]

City	Percent	Rank
Atlanta, GA	59	6
Birmingham, AL	53	12
Chicago, IL	76	1
Cleveland, OH	54	11
Dallas, TX	46	17
Denver, CO	62	4
Detroit, MI	56	9
Fort Lauderdale, FL	58	7
Houston, TX	55	10
Indianapolis, IN	52	13
Los Angeles, CA	51	14
Manhattan, NY	60	5
Miami, FL	42	19
New Orleans, LA	54	11
Omaha, NE	60	5
Philadelphia, PA	69	3
Phoenix, AZ	48	16
Portland, OR	62	4
Saint Louis, MO	57	8
San Antonio, TX	49	15
San Diego, CA	72	2
San Jose, CA	44	18
Washington, DC	58	7

Source: Maguire, Kathleen, and Ann L. Pastore, eds., *Sourcebook of Criminal Justice Statistics 1994*, U.S. Department of Justice, Bureau of Justice Statistics, Washington, D.C.: U.S. Government Printing Office, 1995, p. 415. Primary source: U.S. Department of Justice, National Institute of Justice, *Drug Use Forecasting 1993 Annual Report on Adult Arrestees: Drugs and Crime in America's Cities*, NCJ-147411, Washington, D.C.: U.S. Department of Justice, 1994, pp. 6-28.

★2890★

Drug Use and Abuse

Drug Use By Arrestees, 1993, By Type of Drug, Age, and Sex: Males Age 21 to 25 Using Any Drug

Data refer to the use of cocaine, opiates, marijuana, phencyclidine (PCP), methadone, benzodiazepines, methaqualone, propoxyphene, barbiturates, and amphetamines. Data on drug use are obtained every quarter for approximately two weeks by trained local staff who obtain voluntary and anonymous urine specimens and interviews from a new sample of arrestees.

[In percent testing positive for drug use]

City	Percent	Rank
Atlanta, GA	63	7
Birmingham, AL	66	4
Chicago, IL	76	1
Cleveland, OH	59	10

[Continued]

★2890★

Drug Use By Arrestees, 1993, By Type of Drug, Age, and Sex: Males Age 21 to 25 Using Any Drug

[Continued]

City	Percent	Rank
Dallas, TX	61	9
Denver, CO	65	5
Detroit, MI	62	8
Fort Lauderdale, FL	66	4
Houston, TX	58	11
Indianapolis, IN	63	7
Los Angeles, CA	56	13
Manhattan, NY	70	3
Miami, FL	64	6
New Orleans, LA	55	14
Omaha, NE	55	14
Philadelphia, PA	74	2
Phoenix, AZ	63	7
Portland, OR	57	12
Saint Louis, MO	63	7
San Antonio, TX	57	12
San Diego, CA	76	1
San Jose, CA	52	15
Washington, DC	49	16

Source: Maguire, Kathleen, and Ann L. Pastore, eds., *Sourcebook of Criminal Justice Statistics 1994,* U.S. Department of Justice, Bureau of Justice Statistics, Washington, D.C.: U.S. Government Printing Office, 1995, p. 415. Primary source: U.S. Department of Justice, National Institute of Justice, *Drug Use Forecasting 1993 Annual Report on Adult Arrestees: Drugs and Crime in America's Cities,* NCJ-147411, Washington, D.C.: U.S. Department of Justice, 1994, pp. 6-28.

★2891★

Drug Use and Abuse

Drug Use By Arrestees, 1993, By Type of Drug, Age, and Sex: Males Age 21 to 25 Using Cocaine

Data on drug use are obtained every quarter for approximately two weeks by trained local staff who obtain voluntary and anonymous urine specimens and interviews from a new sample of arrestees.

[In percent testing positive for drug use]

City	Percent	Rank
Atlanta, GA	46	5
Birmingham, AL	40	7
Chicago, IL	53	3
Cleveland, OH	39	8
Dallas, TX	38	9
Denver, CO	36	10
Detroit, MI	23	16
Fort Lauderdale, FL	41	6
Houston, TX	35	11
Indianapolis, IN	30	13
Los Angeles, CA	39	8
Manhattan, NY	58	1
Miami, FL	48	4
New Orleans, LA	40	7
Omaha, NE	17	18
Philadelphia, PA	55	2
Phoenix, AZ	27	14

[Continued]

★2891★

Drug Use By Arrestees, 1993, By Type of Drug, Age, and Sex: Males Age 21 to 25 Using Cocaine

[Continued]

City	Percent	Rank
Portland, OR	26	15
Saint Louis, MO	40	7
San Antonio, TX	36	10
San Diego, CA	32	12
San Jose, CA	23	16
Washington, DC	19	17

Source: Maguire, Kathleen, and Ann L. Pastore, eds., *Sourcebook of Criminal Justice Statistics 1994,* U.S. Department of Justice, Bureau of Justice Statistics, Washington, D.C.: U.S. Government Printing Office, 1995, p. 415. Primary source: U.S. Department of Justice, National Institute of Justice, *Drug Use Forecasting 1993 Annual Report on Adult Arrestees: Drugs and Crime in America's Cities,* NCJ-147411, Washington, D.C.: U.S. Department of Justice, 1994, pp. 6-28.

★2892★

Drug Use and Abuse

Drug Use By Arrestees, 1993, By Type of Drug, Age, and Sex: Males Age 21 to 25 Using Marijuana

Data on drug use are obtained every quarter for approximately two weeks by trained local staff who obtain voluntary and anonymous urine specimens and interviews from a new sample of arrestees.

[In percent testing positive for drug use]

City	Percent	Rank
Atlanta, GA	33	13
Birmingham, AL	39	8
Chicago, IL	40	7
Cleveland, OH	30	15
Dallas, TX	37	10
Denver, CO	43	6
Detroit, MI	50	3
Fort Lauderdale, FL	45	5
Houston, TX	38	9
Indianapolis, IN	53	1
Los Angeles, CA	30	15
Manhattan, NY	32	14
Miami, FL	40	7
New Orleans, LA	34	12
Omaha, NE	47	4
Philadelphia, PA	40	7
Phoenix, AZ	37	10
Portland, OR	34	12
Saint Louis, MO	35	11
San Antonio, TX	38	9
San Diego, CA	51	2
San Jose, CA	29	16
Washington, DC	33	13

Source: Maguire, Kathleen, and Ann L. Pastore, eds., *Sourcebook of Criminal Justice Statistics 1994,* U.S. Department of Justice, Bureau of Justice Statistics, Washington, D.C.: U.S. Government Printing Office, 1995, p. 415. Primary source: U.S. Department of Justice, National Institute of Justice, *Drug Use Forecasting 1993 Annual Report on Adult Arrestees: Drugs and Crime in America's Cities,* NCJ-147411, Washington, D.C.: U.S. Department of Justice, 1994, pp. 6-28.

★ 2893 ★

Drug Use and Abuse

Drug Use By Arrestees, 1993, By Type of Drug, Age, and Sex: Males Age 21 to 25 Using Opiates

Data on drug use are obtained every quarter for approximately two weeks by trained local staff who obtain voluntary and anonymous urine specimens and interviews from a new sample of arrestees.

[In percent testing positive for drug use]

City	Percent	Rank
Birmingham, AL	4	6
Chicago, IL	33	1
Dallas, TX	2	8
Denver, CO	2	8
Detroit, MI	2	8
Fort Lauderdale, FL	0	10
Houston, TX	3	7
Indianapolis, IN	1	9
Los Angeles, CA	6	5
Manhattan, NY	11	2
Miami, FL	2	8
New Orleans, LA	3	7
Omaha, NE	3	7
Philadelphia, PA	9	4
Phoenix, AZ	2	8
Portland, OR	11	2
Saint Louis, MO	9	4
San Antonio, TX	10	3
San Diego, CA	10	3
San Jose, CA	3	7
Washington, DC	1	9

Source: Maguire, Kathleen, and Ann L. Pastore, eds., *Sourcebook of Criminal Justice Statistics 1994*, U.S. Department of Justice, Bureau of Justice Statistics, Washington, D.C.: U.S. Government Printing Office, 1995, p. 415. Primary source: U.S. Department of Justice, National Institute of Justice, *Drug Use Forecasting 1993 Annual Report on Adult Arrestees: Drugs and Crime in America's Cities*, NCJ-147411, Washington, D.C.: U.S. Department of Justice, 1994, pp. 6-28.

★ 2894 ★

Drug Use and Abuse

Drug Use By Arrestees, 1993, By Type of Drug, Age, and Sex: Males Age 26 to 30 Using Any Drug

Data refer to the use of cocaine, opiates, marijuana, phencyclidine (PCP), methadone, benzodiazepines, methaqualone, propoxyphene, barbiturates, and amphetamines. Data on drug use are obtained every quarter for approximately two weeks by trained local staff who obtain voluntary and anonymous urine specimens and interviews from a new sample of arrestees.

[In percent testing positive for drug use]

City	Percent	Rank
Atlanta, GA	78	4
Birmingham, AL	69	10
Chicago, IL	80	3
Cleveland, OH	71	8
Dallas, TX	70	9
Denver, CO	76	5
Detroit, MI	54	19
Fort Lauderdale, FL	64	14
Houston, TX	60	16

[Continued]

★ 2894 ★

Drug Use By Arrestees, 1993, By Type of Drug, Age, and Sex: Males Age 26 to 30 Using Any Drug

[Continued]

City	Percent	Rank
Indianapolis, IN	65	13
Los Angeles, CA	68	11
Manhattan, NY	81	2
Miami, FL	76	5
New Orleans, LA	68	11
Omaha, NE	59	17
Philadelphia, PA	83	1
Phoenix, AZ	66	12
Portland, OR	74	7
Saint Louis, MO	75	6
San Antonio, TX	57	18
San Diego, CA	80	3
San Jose, CA	63	15
Washington, DC	65	13

Source: Maguire, Kathleen, and Ann L. Pastore, eds., *Sourcebook of Criminal Justice Statistics 1994*, U.S. Department of Justice, Bureau of Justice Statistics, Washington, D.C.: U.S. Government Printing Office, 1995, p. 415. Primary source: U.S. Department of Justice, National Institute of Justice, *Drug Use Forecasting 1993 Annual Report on Adult Arrestees: Drugs and Crime in America's Cities*, NCJ-147411, Washington, D.C.: U.S. Department of Justice, 1994, pp. 6-28.

★ 2895 ★

Drug Use and Abuse

Drug Use By Arrestees, 1993, By Type of Drug, Age, and Sex: Males Age 26 to 30 Using Cocaine

Data on drug use are obtained every quarter for approximately two weeks by trained local staff who obtain voluntary and anonymous urine specimens and interviews from a new sample of arrestees.

[In percent testing positive for drug use]

City	Percent	Rank
Atlanta, GA	68	3
Birmingham, AL	64	4
Chicago, IL	55	7
Cleveland, OH	56	6
Dallas, TX	56	6
Denver, CO	52	8
Detroit, MI	26	17
Fort Lauderdale, FL	50	9
Houston, TX	45	11
Indianapolis, IN	36	13
Los Angeles, CA	46	10
Manhattan, NY	73	1
Miami, FL	68	3
New Orleans, LA	56	6
Omaha, NE	23	18
Philadelphia, PA	72	2
Phoenix, AZ	26	17
Portland, OR	32	15
Saint Louis, MO	62	5
San Antonio, TX	35	14
San Diego, CA	36	13

[Continued]

★2895★

Drug Use By Arrestees, 1993, By Type of Drug, Age, and Sex: Males Age 26 to 30 Using Cocaine

[Continued]

City	Percent	Rank
San Jose, CA	27	16
Washington, DC	43	12

Source: Maguire, Kathleen, and Ann L. Pastore, eds., *Sourcebook of Criminal Justice Statistics 1994*, U.S. Department of Justice, Bureau of Justice Statistics, Washington, D.C.: U.S. Government Printing Office, 1995, p. 415. Primary source: U.S. Department of Justice, National Institute of Justice, *Drug Use Forecasting 1993 Annual Report on Adult Arrestees: Drugs and Crime in America's Cities*, NCJ-147411, Washington, D.C.: U.S. Department of Justice, 1994, pp. 6-28.

★2896★

Drug Use and Abuse

Drug Use By Arrestees, 1993, By Type of Drug, Age, and Sex: Males Age 26 to 30 Using Marijuana

Data on drug use are obtained every quarter for approximately two weeks by trained local staff who obtain voluntary and anonymous urine specimens and interviews from a new sample of arrestees.

[In percent testing positive for drug use]

City	Percent	Rank
Atlanta, GA	28	9
Birmingham, AL	27	10
Chicago, IL	34	7
Cleveland, OH	22	13
Dallas, TX	28	9
Denver, CO	39	4
Detroit, MI	34	7
Fort Lauderdale, FL	29	8
Houston, TX	24	12
Indianapolis, IN	46	1
Los Angeles, CA	25	11
Manhattan, NY	21	14
Miami, FL	28	9
New Orleans, LA	24	12
Omaha, NE	44	2
Philadelphia, PA	28	9
Phoenix, AZ	35	6
Portland, OR	38	5
Saint Louis, MO	25	11
San Antonio, TX	29	8
San Diego, CA	41	3
San Jose, CA	29	8
Washington, DC	20	15

Source: Maguire, Kathleen, and Ann L. Pastore, eds., *Sourcebook of Criminal Justice Statistics 1994*, U.S. Department of Justice, Bureau of Justice Statistics, Washington, D.C.: U.S. Government Printing Office, 1995, p. 415. Primary source: U.S. Department of Justice, National Institute of Justice, *Drug Use Forecasting 1993 Annual Report on Adult Arrestees: Drugs and Crime in America's Cities*, NCJ-147411, Washington, D.C.: U.S. Department of Justice, 1994, pp. 6-28.

★2897★

Drug Use and Abuse

Drug Use By Arrestees, 1993, By Type of Drug, Age, and Sex: Males Age 26 to 30 Using Opiates

Data on drug use are obtained every quarter for approximately two weeks by trained local staff who obtain voluntary and anonymous urine specimens and interviews from a new sample of arrestees.

[In percent testing positive for drug use]

City	Percent	Rank
Atlanta, GA	2	11
Birmingham, AL	2	11
Chicago, IL	30	1
Cleveland, OH	2	11
Dallas, TX	6	8
Denver, CO	4	9
Detroit, MI	4	9
Fort Lauderdale, FL	1	12
Indianapolis, IN	2	11
Los Angeles, CA	8	6
Manhattan, NY	21	2
Miami, FL	2	11
New Orleans, LA	3	10
Omaha, NE	2	11
Philadelphia, PA	8	6
Phoenix, AZ	4	9
Portland, OR	10	5
Saint Louis, MO	8	6
San Antonio, TX	14	4
San Diego, CA	15	3
San Jose, CA	3	10
Washington, DC	7	7

Source: Maguire, Kathleen, and Ann L. Pastore, eds., *Sourcebook of Criminal Justice Statistics 1994*, U.S. Department of Justice, Bureau of Justice Statistics, Washington, D.C.: U.S. Government Printing Office, 1995, p. 415. Primary source: U.S. Department of Justice, National Institute of Justice, *Drug Use Forecasting 1993 Annual Report on Adult Arrestees: Drugs and Crime in America's Cities*, NCJ-147411, Washington, D.C.: U.S. Department of Justice, 1994, pp. 6-28.

★2898★

Drug Use and Abuse

Drug Use By Arrestees, 1993, By Type of Drug, Age, and Sex: Males Age 31 to 35 Using Any Drug

Data refer to the use of cocaine, opiates, marijuana, phencyclidine (PCP), methadone, benzodiazepines, methaqualone, propoxyphene, barbiturates, and amphetamines. Data on drug use are obtained every quarter for approximately two weeks by trained local staff who obtain voluntary and anonymous urine specimens and interviews from a new sample of arrestees.

[In percent testing positive for drug use]

City	Percent	Rank
Atlanta, GA	80	4
Birmingham, AL	78	6
Chicago, IL	89	1
Cleveland, OH	71	8
Dallas, TX	68	10
Denver, CO	64	12
Detroit, MI	71	8
Fort Lauderdale, FL	63	13

[Continued]

★2898★

Drug Use By Arrestees, 1993, By Type of Drug, Age, and Sex: Males Age 31 to 35 Using Any Drug
[Continued]

City	Percent	Rank
Houston, TX	64	12
Indianapolis, IN	63	13
Los Angeles, CA	73	7
Manhattan, NY	87	2
Miami, FL	80	4
New Orleans, LA	70	9
Omaha, NE	59	14
Philadelphia, PA	79	5
Phoenix, AZ	70	9
Portland, OR	66	11
Saint Louis, MO	82	3
San Antonio, TX	64	12
San Diego, CA	80	4
San Jose, CA	58	15
Washington, DC	68	10

Source: Maguire, Kathleen, and Ann L. Pastore, eds., *Sourcebook of Criminal Justice Statistics 1994*, U.S. Department of Justice, Bureau of Justice Statistics, Washington, D.C.: U.S. Government Printing Office, 1995, p. 415. Primary source: U.S. Department of Justice, National Institute of Justice, *Drug Use Forecasting 1993 Annual Report on Adult Arrestees: Drugs and Crime in America's Cities*, NCJ-147411, Washington, D.C.: U.S. Department of Justice, 1994, pp. 6-28.

★2899★
Drug Use and Abuse

Drug Use By Arrestees, 1993, By Type of Drug, Age, and Sex: Males Age 31 to 35 Using Cocaine

Data on drug use are obtained every quarter for approximately two weeks by trained local staff who obtain voluntary and anonymous urine specimens and interviews from a new sample of arrestees.

[In percent testing positive for drug use]

City	Percent	Rank
Atlanta, GA	73	3
Birmingham, AL	66	5
Chicago, IL	58	8
Cleveland, OH	60	7
Dallas, TX	60	7
Denver, CO	49	12
Detroit, MI	55	9
Fort Lauderdale, FL	49	12
Houston, TX	51	11
Indianapolis, IN	35	16
Los Angeles, CA	60	7
Manhattan, NY	78	1
Miami, FL	74	2
New Orleans, LA	62	6
Omaha, NE	27	18
Philadelphia, PA	68	4
Phoenix, AZ	40	14
Portland, OR	42	13
Saint Louis, MO	74	2
San Antonio, TX	39	15
San Diego, CA	40	14

[Continued]

★2899★

Drug Use By Arrestees, 1993, By Type of Drug, Age, and Sex: Males Age 31 to 35 Using Cocaine
[Continued]

City	Percent	Rank
San Jose, CA	28	17
Washington, DC	53	10

Source: Maguire, Kathleen, and Ann L. Pastore, eds., *Sourcebook of Criminal Justice Statistics 1994*, U.S. Department of Justice, Bureau of Justice Statistics, Washington, D.C.: U.S. Government Printing Office, 1995, p. 415. Primary source: U.S. Department of Justice, National Institute of Justice, *Drug Use Forecasting 1993 Annual Report on Adult Arrestees: Drugs and Crime in America's Cities*, NCJ-147411, Washington, D.C.: U.S. Department of Justice, 1994, pp. 6-28.

★2900★
Drug Use and Abuse

Drug Use By Arrestees, 1993, By Type of Drug, Age, and Sex: Males Age 31 to 35 Using Marijuana

Data on drug use are obtained every quarter for approximately two weeks by trained local staff who obtain voluntary and anonymous urine specimens and interviews from a new sample of arrestees.

[In percent testing positive for drug use]

City	Percent	Rank
Atlanta, GA	17	15
Birmingham, AL	21	13
Chicago, IL	44	1
Cleveland, OH	14	17
Dallas, TX	22	12
Denver, CO	25	10
Detroit, MI	28	7
Fort Lauderdale, FL	24	11
Houston, TX	22	12
Indianapolis, IN	38	3
Los Angeles, CA	20	14
Manhattan, NY	14	17
Miami, FL	27	8
New Orleans, LA	17	15
Omaha, NE	40	2
Philadelphia, PA	21	13
Phoenix, AZ	31	5
Portland, OR	26	9
Saint Louis, MO	16	16
San Antonio, TX	34	4
San Diego, CA	38	3
San Jose, CA	29	6
Washington, DC	22	12

Source: Maguire, Kathleen, and Ann L. Pastore, eds., *Sourcebook of Criminal Justice Statistics 1994*, U.S. Department of Justice, Bureau of Justice Statistics, Washington, D.C.: U.S. Government Printing Office, 1995, p. 415. Primary source: U.S. Department of Justice, National Institute of Justice, *Drug Use Forecasting 1993 Annual Report on Adult Arrestees: Drugs and Crime in America's Cities*, NCJ-147411, Washington, D.C.: U.S. Department of Justice, 1994, pp. 6-28.

★2901★

Drug Use and Abuse

Drug Use By Arrestees, 1993, By Type of Drug, Age, and Sex: Males Age 31 to 35 Using Opiates

Data on drug use are obtained every quarter for approximately two weeks by trained local staff who obtain voluntary and anonymous urine specimens and interviews from a new sample of arrestees.

[In percent testing positive for drug use]

City	Percent	Rank
Atlanta, GA	2	14
Birmingham, AL	3	13
Chicago, IL	30	1
Cleveland, OH	4	12
Dallas, TX	4	12
Denver, CO	4	12
Detroit, MI	11	6
Fort Lauderdale, FL	1	15
Houston, TX	2	14
Indianapolis, IN	6	11
Los Angeles, CA	12	5
Manhattan, NY	27	2
Miami, FL	2	14
New Orleans, LA	6	11
Omaha, NE	3	13
Philadelphia, PA	9	8
Phoenix, AZ	7	10
Portland, OR	8	9
Saint Louis, MO	6	11
San Antonio, TX	18	3
San Diego, CA	13	4
San Jose, CA	10	7
Washington, DC	11	6

Source: Maguire, Kathleen, and Ann L. Pastore, eds., *Sourcebook of Criminal Justice Statistics 1994,* U.S. Department of Justice, Bureau of Justice Statistics, Washington, D.C.: U.S. Government Printing Office, 1995, p. 415. Primary source: U.S. Department of Justice, National Institute of Justice, *Drug Use Forecasting 1993 Annual Report on Adult Arrestees: Drugs and Crime in America's Cities,* NCJ-147411, Washington, D.C.: U.S. Department of Justice, 1994, pp. 6-28.

★2902★

Drug Use and Abuse

Drug Use By Arrestees, 1993, By Type of Drug, Age, and Sex: Males Age 36 and Older Using Any Drug

Data refer to the use of cocaine, opiates, marijuana, phencyclidine (PCP), methadone, benzodiazepines, methaqualone, propoxyphene, barbiturates, and amphetamines. Data on drug use are obtained every quarter for approximately two weeks by trained local staff who obtain voluntary and anonymous urine specimens and interviews from a new sample of arrestees.

[In percent testing positive for drug use]

City	Percent	Rank
Atlanta, GA	75	5
Birmingham, AL	69	9
Chicago, IL	83	1
Cleveland, OH	66	10
Dallas, TX	63	12
Denver, CO	56	14
Detroit, MI	71	8

[Continued]

★2902★

Drug Use By Arrestees, 1993, By Type of Drug, Age, and Sex: Males Age 36 and Older Using Any Drug

[Continued]

City	Percent	Rank
Fort Lauderdale, FL	56	14
Houston, TX	55	15
Indianapolis, IN	58	13
Los Angeles, CA	76	4
Manhattan, NY	80	3
Miami, FL	73	7
New Orleans, LA	63	12
Omaha, NE	41	18
Philadelphia, PA	74	6
Phoenix, AZ	56	14
Portland, OR	58	13
Saint Louis, MO	71	8
San Antonio, TX	53	17
San Diego, CA	82	2
San Jose, CA	54	16
Washington, DC	65	11

Source: Maguire, Kathleen, and Ann L. Pastore, eds., *Sourcebook of Criminal Justice Statistics 1994,* U.S. Department of Justice, Bureau of Justice Statistics, Washington, D.C.: U.S. Government Printing Office, 1995, p. 415. Primary source: U.S. Department of Justice, National Institute of Justice, *Drug Use Forecasting 1993 Annual Report on Adult Arrestees: Drugs and Crime in America's Cities,* NCJ-147411, Washington, D.C.: U.S. Department of Justice, 1994, pp. 6-28.

★2903★

Drug Use and Abuse

Drug Use By Arrestees, 1993, By Type of Drug, Age, and Sex: Males Age 36 and Older Using Cocaine

Data on drug use are obtained every quarter for approximately two weeks by trained local staff who obtain voluntary and anonymous urine specimens and interviews from a new sample of arrestees.

[In percent testing positive for drug use]

City	Percent	Rank
Atlanta, GA	68	3
Birmingham, AL	58	6
Chicago, IL	57	7
Cleveland, OH	57	7
Dallas, TX	52	8
Denver, CO	41	13
Detroit, MI	60	5
Fort Lauderdale, FL	44	12
Houston, TX	36	15
Indianapolis, IN	37	14
Los Angeles, CA	61	4
Manhattan, NY	73	1
Miami, FL	69	2
New Orleans, LA	51	9
Omaha, NE	19	19
Philadelphia, PA	61	4
Phoenix, AZ	33	16
Portland, OR	36	15
Saint Louis, MO	60	5

[Continued]

★2903★

Drug Use By Arrestees, 1993, By Type of Drug, Age, and Sex: Males Age 36 and Older Using Cocaine
[Continued]

City	Percent	Rank
San Antonio, TX	30	17
San Diego, CA	47	11
San Jose, CA	24	18
Washington, DC	50	10

Source: Maguire, Kathleen, and Ann L. Pastore, eds., *Sourcebook of Criminal Justice Statistics 1994*, U.S. Department of Justice, Bureau of Justice Statistics, Washington, D.C.: U.S. Government Printing Office, 1995, p. 415. Primary source: U.S. Department of Justice, National Institute of Justice, *Drug Use Forecasting 1993 Annual Report on Adult Arrestees: Drugs and Crime in America's Cities*, NCJ-147411, Washington, D.C.: U.S. Department of Justice, 1994, pp. 6-28.

★2904★
Drug Use and Abuse

Drug Use By Arrestees, 1993, By Type of Drug, Age, and Sex: Males Age 36 and Older Using Marijuana

Data on drug use are obtained every quarter for approximately two weeks by trained local staff who obtain voluntary and anonymous urine specimens and interviews from a new sample of arrestees.

[In percent testing positive for drug use]

City	Percent	Rank
Atlanta, GA	16	9
Birmingham, AL	12	13
Chicago, IL	36	1
Cleveland, OH	7	15
Dallas, TX	14	11
Denver, CO	25	3
Detroit, MI	15	10
Fort Lauderdale, FL	17	8
Houston, TX	11	14
Indianapolis, IN	24	4
Los Angeles, CA	11	14
Manhattan, NY	13	12
Miami, FL	13	12
New Orleans, LA	16	9
Omaha, NE	24	4
Philadelphia, PA	17	8
Phoenix, AZ	20	6
Portland, OR	18	7
Saint Louis, MO	17	8
San Antonio, TX	18	7
San Diego, CA	27	2
San Jose, CA	21	5
Washington, DC	12	13

Source: Maguire, Kathleen, and Ann L. Pastore, eds., *Sourcebook of Criminal Justice Statistics 1994*, U.S. Department of Justice, Bureau of Justice Statistics, Washington, D.C.: U.S. Government Printing Office, 1995, p. 415. Primary source: U.S. Department of Justice, National Institute of Justice, *Drug Use Forecasting 1993 Annual Report on Adult Arrestees: Drugs and Crime in America's Cities*, NCJ-147411, Washington, D.C.: U.S. Department of Justice, 1994, pp. 6-28.

★2905★
Drug Use and Abuse

Drug Use By Arrestees, 1993, By Type of Drug, Age, and Sex: Males Age 36 and Older Using Opiates

Data on drug use are obtained every quarter for approximately two weeks by trained local staff who obtain voluntary and anonymous urine specimens and interviews from a new sample of arrestees.

[In percent testing positive for drug use]

City	Percent	Rank
Atlanta, GA	5	14
Birmingham, AL	8	12
Chicago, IL	28	2
Cleveland, OH	10	10
Dallas, TX	9	11
Denver, CO	5	14
Detroit, MI	20	5
Fort Lauderdale, FL	3	16
Houston, TX	2	17
Indianapolis, IN	11	9
Los Angeles, CA	16	6
Manhattan, NY	23	4
Miami, FL	4	15
New Orleans, LA	6	13
Omaha, NE	2	17
Philadelphia, PA	20	5
Phoenix, AZ	14	8
Portland, OR	15	7
Saint Louis, MO	10	10
San Antonio, TX	24	3
San Diego, CA	29	1
San Jose, CA	10	10
Washington, DC	24	3

Source: Maguire, Kathleen, and Ann L. Pastore, eds., *Sourcebook of Criminal Justice Statistics 1994*, U.S. Department of Justice, Bureau of Justice Statistics, Washington, D.C.: U.S. Government Printing Office, 1995, p. 415. Primary source: U.S. Department of Justice, National Institute of Justice, *Drug Use Forecasting 1993 Annual Report on Adult Arrestees: Drugs and Crime in America's Cities*, NCJ-147411, Washington, D.C.: U.S. Department of Justice, 1994, pp. 6-28.

★2906★
Drug Use and Abuse

Drug Use By Arrestees, 1993, By Type of Drug, Race, Ethnicity, and Sex: Black Females Using Any Drug

Data refer to the use of cocaine, opiates, marijuana, phencyclidine (PCP), methadone, benzodiazepines, methaqualone, propoxyphene, barbiturates, and amphetamines. Data on drug use are obtained every quarter for approximately two weeks by trained local staff who obtain voluntary and anonymous urine specimens and interviews from a new sample of arrestees. The cities of Chicago, Miami, and Omaha, did not test or interview female arrestees.

[In percent testing positive for drug use]

City	Percent	Rank
Atlanta, GA	76	6
Birmingham, AL	52	16
Cleveland, OH	80	3
Dallas, TX	63	11
Denver, CO	79	4

[Continued]

★2906★

Drug Use By Arrestees, 1993, By Type of Drug, Race, Ethnicity, and Sex: Black Females Using Any Drug

[Continued]

City	Percent	Rank
Detroit, MI	74	7
Fort Lauderdale, FL	59	13
Houston, TX	54	15
Indianapolis, IN	67	10
Los Angeles, CA	81	2
Manhattan, NY	87	1
New Orleans, LA	46	17
Philadelphia, PA	81	2
Phoenix, AZ	73	8
Portland, OR	79	4
Saint Louis, MO	67	10
San Antonio, TX	58	14
San Diego, CA	78	5
San Jose, CA	60	12
Washington, DC	70	9

Source: Maguire, Kathleen, and Ann L. Pastore, eds., *Sourcebook of Criminal Justice Statistics 1994*, U.S. Department of Justice, Bureau of Justice Statistics, Washington, D.C.: U.S. Government Printing Office, 1995, p. 415. Primary source: U.S. Department of Justice, National Institute of Justice, *Drug Use Forecasting 1993 Annual Report on Adult Arrestees: Drugs and Crime in America's Cities*, NCJ-147411, Washington, D.C.: U.S. Department of Justice, 1994, pp. 6-28.

★2907★
Drug Use and Abuse

Drug Use By Arrestees, 1993, By Type of Drug, Race, Ethnicity, and Sex: Black Females Using Cocaine

Data on drug use are obtained every quarter for approximately two weeks by trained local staff who obtain voluntary and anonymous urine specimens and interviews from a new sample of arrestees. The cities of Chicago, Miami, and Omaha, did not test or interview female arrestees.

[In percent testing positive for drug use]

City	Percent	Rank
Atlanta, GA	70	3
Birmingham, AL	44	14
Cleveland, OH	72	2
Dallas, TX	48	11
Denver, CO	62	7
Detroit, MI	62	7
Fort Lauderdale, FL	46	13
Houston, TX	42	15
Indianapolis, IN	53	9
Los Angeles, CA	69	4
Manhattan, NY	78	1
New Orleans, LA	38	16
Philadelphia, PA	65	6
Phoenix, AZ	67	5
Portland, OR	70	3
Saint Louis, MO	62	7
San Antonio, TX	47	12
San Diego, CA	57	8

[Continued]

★2907★

Drug Use By Arrestees, 1993, By Type of Drug, Race, Ethnicity, and Sex: Black Females Using Cocaine

[Continued]

City	Percent	Rank
San Jose, CA	52	10
Washington, DC	62	7

Source: Maguire, Kathleen, and Ann L. Pastore, eds., *Sourcebook of Criminal Justice Statistics 1994*, U.S. Department of Justice, Bureau of Justice Statistics, Washington, D.C.: U.S. Government Printing Office, 1995, p. 415. Primary source: U.S. Department of Justice, National Institute of Justice, *Drug Use Forecasting 1993 Annual Report on Adult Arrestees: Drugs and Crime in America's Cities*, NCJ-147411, Washington, D.C.: U.S. Department of Justice, 1994, pp. 6-28.

★2908★
Drug Use and Abuse

Drug Use By Arrestees, 1993, By Type of Drug, Race, Ethnicity, and Sex: Black Females Using Marijuana

Data on drug use are obtained every quarter for approximately two weeks by trained local staff who obtain voluntary and anonymous urine specimens and interviews from a new sample of arrestees. The cities of Chicago, Miami, and Omaha, did not test or interview female arrestees.

[In percent testing positive for drug use]

City	Percent	Rank
Atlanta, GA	16	9
Birmingham, AL	10	14
Cleveland, OH	11	13
Dallas, TX	20	6
Denver, CO	26	1
Detroit, MI	10	14
Fort Lauderdale, FL	24	2
Houston, TX	15	10
Indianapolis, IN	22	4
Los Angeles, CA	17	8
Manhattan, NY	19	7
New Orleans, LA	12	12
Philadelphia, PA	21	5
Phoenix, AZ	15	10
Portland, OR	14	11
Saint Louis, MO	12	12
San Antonio, TX	23	3
San Diego, CA	26	1
San Jose, CA	17	8
Washington, DC	8	15

Source: Maguire, Kathleen, and Ann L. Pastore, eds., *Sourcebook of Criminal Justice Statistics 1994*, U.S. Department of Justice, Bureau of Justice Statistics, Washington, D.C.: U.S. Government Printing Office, 1995, p. 415. Primary source: U.S. Department of Justice, National Institute of Justice, *Drug Use Forecasting 1993 Annual Report on Adult Arrestees: Drugs and Crime in America's Cities*, NCJ-147411, Washington, D.C.: U.S. Department of Justice, 1994, pp. 6-28.

★2909★

Drug Use and Abuse

Drug Use By Arrestees, 1993, By Type of Drug, Race, Ethnicity, and Sex: Black Females Using Opiates

Data on drug use are obtained every quarter for approximately two weeks by trained local staff who obtain voluntary and anonymous urine specimens and interviews from a new sample of arrestees. The cities of Chicago, Miami, and Omaha, did not test or interview female arrestees.

[In percent testing positive for drug use]

City	Percent	Rank
Atlanta, GA	3	9
Birmingham, AL	1	11
Cleveland, OH	3	9
Dallas, TX	10	4
Denver, CO	2	10
Detroit, MI	10	4
Fort Lauderdale, FL	2	10
Houston, TX	6	6
Indianapolis, IN	3	9
Los Angeles, CA	6	6
Manhattan, NY	15	2
New Orleans, LA	4	8
Philadelphia, PA	10	4
Phoenix, AZ	8	5
Portland, OR	14	3
Saint Louis, MO	4	8
San Antonio, TX	6	6
San Diego, CA	14	3
San Jose, CA	5	7
Washington, DC	20	1

Source: Maguire, Kathleen, and Ann L. Pastore, eds., Sourcebook of Criminal Justice Statistics 1994, U.S. Department of Justice, Bureau of Justice Statistics, Washington, D.C.: U.S. Government Printing Office, 1995, p. 415. Primary source: U.S. Department of Justice, National Institute of Justice, Drug Use Forecasting 1993 Annual Report on Adult Arrestees: Drugs and Crime in America's Cities, NCJ-147411, Washington, D.C.: U.S. Department of Justice, 1994, pp. 6-28.

★2910★

Drug Use and Abuse

Drug Use By Arrestees, 1993, By Type of Drug, Race, Ethnicity, and Sex: Black Males Using Any Drug

Data refer to the use of cocaine, opiates, marijuana, phencyclidine (PCP), methadone, benzodiazepines, methaqualone, propoxyphene, barbiturates, and amphetamines. Data on drug use are obtained every quarter for approximately two weeks by trained local staff who obtain voluntary and anonymous urine specimens and interviews from a new sample of arrestees.

[In percent testing positive for drug use]

City	Percent	Rank
Atlanta, GA	74	7
Birmingham, AL	68	11
Chicago, IL	80	2
Cleveland, OH	68	11
Dallas, TX	68	11
Denver, CO	73	8
Detroit, MI	63	13
Houston, TX	68	11

[Continued]

★2910★

Drug Use By Arrestees, 1993, By Type of Drug, Race, Ethnicity, and Sex: Black Males Using Any Drug

[Continued]

City	Percent	Rank
Indianapolis, IN	63	13
Los Angeles, CA	78	4
Manhattan, NY	86	1
Miami, FL	77	5
New Orleans, LA	64	12
Omaha, NE	61	14
Philadelphia, PA	76	6
Phoenix, AZ	76	6
Port Lauderdale, FL	69	10
Portland, OR	70	9
Saint Louis, MO	69	10
San Antonio, TX	60	15
San Diego, CA	79	3
San Jose, CA	68	11
Washington, DC	61	14

Source: Maguire, Kathleen, and Ann L. Pastore, eds., Sourcebook of Criminal Justice Statistics 1994, U.S. Department of Justice, Bureau of Justice Statistics, Washington, D.C.: U.S. Government Printing Office, 1995, p. 415. Primary source: U.S. Department of Justice, National Institute of Justice, Drug Use Forecasting 1993 Annual Report on Adult Arrestees: Drugs and Crime in America's Cities, NCJ-147411, Washington, D.C.: U.S. Department of Justice, 1994, pp. 6-28.

★2911★

Drug Use and Abuse

Drug Use By Arrestees, 1993, By Type of Drug, Race, Ethnicity, and Sex: Black Males Using Cocaine

Data on drug use are obtained every quarter for approximately two weeks by trained local staff who obtain voluntary and anonymous urine specimens and interviews from a new sample of arrestees.

[In percent testing positive for drug use]

City	Percent	Rank
Atlanta, GA	61	4
Birmingham, AL	53	8
Chicago, IL	52	9
Cleveland, OH	53	8
Dallas, TX	51	10
Denver, CO	57	6
Detroit, MI	34	16
Fort Lauderdale, FL	54	7
Houston, TX	52	9
Indianapolis, IN	45	13
Los Angeles, CA	64	3
Manhattan, NY	77	1
Miami, FL	70	2
New Orleans, LA	51	10
Omaha, NE	32	17
Philadelphia, PA	59	5
Phoenix, AZ	61	4
Portland, OR	48	11
Saint Louis, MO	52	9
San Antonio, TX	40	14

[Continued]

★2911★

Drug Use By Arrestees, 1993, By Type of Drug, Race, Ethnicity, and Sex: Black Males Using Cocaine

[Continued]

City	Percent	Rank
San Diego, CA	57	6
San Jose, CA	47	12
Washington, DC	37	15

Source: Maguire, Kathleen, and Ann L. Pastore, eds., *Sourcebook of Criminal Justice Statistics 1994,* U.S. Department of Justice, Bureau of Justice Statistics, Washington, D.C.: U.S. Government Printing Office, 1995, p. 415. Primary source: U.S. Department of Justice, National Institute of Justice, *Drug Use Forecasting 1993 Annual Report on Adult Arrestees: Drugs and Crime in America's Cities,* NCJ-147411, Washington, D.C.: U.S. Department of Justice, 1994, pp. 6-28.

★2912★

Drug Use and Abuse

Drug Use By Arrestees, 1993, By Type of Drug, Race, Ethnicity, and Sex: Black Males Using Marijuana

Data on drug use are obtained every quarter for approximately two weeks by trained local staff who obtain voluntary and anonymous urine specimens and interviews from a new sample of arrestees.

[In percent testing positive for drug use]

City	Percent	Rank
Atlanta, GA	26	10
Birmingham, AL	26	10
Chicago, IL	39	2
Cleveland, OH	22	12
Dallas, TX	30	8
Denver, CO	32	6
Detroit, MI	37	3
Fort Lauderdale, FL	32	6
Houston, TX	26	10
Indianapolis, IN	39	2
Los Angeles, CA	22	12
Manhattan, NY	21	13
Miami, FL	31	7
New Orleans, LA	25	11
Omaha, NE	44	1
Philadelphia, PA	31	7
Phoenix, AZ	25	11
Portland, OR	27	9
Saint Louis, MO	26	10
San Antonio, TX	35	4
San Diego, CA	33	5
San Jose, CA	32	6
Washington, DC	27	9

Source: Maguire, Kathleen, and Ann L. Pastore, eds., *Sourcebook of Criminal Justice Statistics 1994,* U.S. Department of Justice, Bureau of Justice Statistics, Washington, D.C.: U.S. Government Printing Office, 1995, p. 415. Primary source: U.S. Department of Justice, National Institute of Justice, *Drug Use Forecasting 1993 Annual Report on Adult Arrestees: Drugs and Crime in America's Cities,* NCJ-147411, Washington, D.C.: U.S. Department of Justice, 1994, pp. 6-28.

★2913★

Drug Use and Abuse

Drug Use By Arrestees, 1993, By Type of Drug, Race, Ethnicity, and Sex: Black Males Using Opiates

Data on drug use are obtained every quarter for approximately two weeks by trained local staff who obtain voluntary and anonymous urine specimens and interviews from a new sample of arrestees.

[In percent testing positive for drug use]

City	Percent	Rank
Atlanta, GA	2	10
Birmingham, AL	4	8
Chicago, IL	28	1
Cleveland, OH	3	9
Dallas, TX	4	8
Denver, CO	2	10
Detroit, MI	7	6
Houston, TX	2	10
Indianapolis, IN	6	7
Los Angeles, CA	9	4
Manhattan, NY	17	2
Miami, FL	2	10
New Orleans, LA	4	8
Omaha, NE	2	10
Philadelphia, PA	10	3
Phoenix, AZ	4	8
Portland, OR	6	7
Saint Louis, MO	9	4
San Antonio, TX	8	5
San Diego, CA	6	7
San Jose, CA	7	6
Washington, DC	10	3

Source: Maguire, Kathleen, and Ann L. Pastore, eds., *Sourcebook of Criminal Justice Statistics 1994,* U.S. Department of Justice, Bureau of Justice Statistics, Washington, D.C.: U.S. Government Printing Office, 1995, p. 415. Primary source: U.S. Department of Justice, National Institute of Justice, *Drug Use Forecasting 1993 Annual Report on Adult Arrestees: Drugs and Crime in America's Cities,* NCJ-147411, Washington, D.C.: U.S. Department of Justice, 1994, pp. 6-28.

★2914★

Drug Use and Abuse

Drug Use By Arrestees, 1993, By Type of Drug, Race, Ethnicity, and Sex: Hispanic Females Using Any Drug

Data refer to the use of cocaine, opiates, marijuana, phencyclidine (PCP), methadone, benzodiazepines, methaqualone, propoxyphene, barbiturates, and amphetamines. Data on drug use are obtained every quarter for approximately two weeks by trained local staff who obtain voluntary and anonymous urine specimens and interviews from a new sample of arrestees. The cities of Chicago, Miami, and Omaha, did not test or interview female arrestees.

[In percent testing positive for drug use]

City	Percent	Rank
Dallas, TX	48	6
Denver, CO	64	3
Houston, TX	37	8
Los Angeles, CA	64	3
Manhattan, NY	80	1
Philadelphia, PA	58	4

[Continued]

★2914★

Drug Use By Arrestees, 1993, By Type of Drug, Race, Ethnicity, and Sex: Hispanic Females Using Any Drug

[Continued]

City	Percent	Rank
Phoenix, AZ	55	5
San Antonio, TX	35	9
San Diego, CA	68	2
San Jose, CA	45	7

Source: Maguire, Kathleen, and Ann L. Pastore, eds., *Sourcebook of Criminal Justice Statistics 1994*, U.S. Department of Justice, Bureau of Justice Statistics, Washington, D.C.: U.S. Government Printing Office, 1995, p. 415. Primary source: U.S. Department of Justice, National Institute of Justice, *Drug Use Forecasting 1993 Annual Report on Adult Arrestees: Drugs and Crime in America's Cities*, NCJ-147411, Washington, D.C.: U.S. Department of Justice, 1994, pp. 6-28.

★2915★

Drug Use and Abuse

Drug Use By Arrestees, 1993, By Type of Drug, Race, Ethnicity, and Sex: Hispanic Females Using Cocaine

Data on drug use are obtained every quarter for approximately two weeks by trained local staff who obtain voluntary and anonymous urine specimens and interviews from a new sample of arrestees. The cities of Chicago, Miami, and Omaha, did not test or interview female arrestees.

[In percent testing positive for drug use]

City	Percent	Rank
Dallas, TX	31	8
Denver, CO	49	3
Houston, TX	32	7
Los Angeles, CA	51	2
Manhattan, NY	64	1
Philadelphia, PA	45	4
Phoenix, AZ	40	6
San Antonio, TX	21	9
San Diego, CA	41	5
San Jose, CA	17	10

Source: Maguire, Kathleen, and Ann L. Pastore, eds., *Sourcebook of Criminal Justice Statistics 1994*, U.S. Department of Justice, Bureau of Justice Statistics, Washington, D.C.: U.S. Government Printing Office, 1995, p. 415. Primary source: U.S. Department of Justice, National Institute of Justice, *Drug Use Forecasting 1993 Annual Report on Adult Arrestees: Drugs and Crime in America's Cities*, NCJ-147411, Washington, D.C.: U.S. Department of Justice, 1994, pp. 6-28.

★2916★

Drug Use and Abuse

Drug Use By Arrestees, 1993, By Type of Drug, Race, Ethnicity, and Sex: Hispanic Females Using Marijuana

Data on drug use are obtained every quarter for approximately two weeks by trained local staff who obtain voluntary and anonymous urine specimens and interviews from a new sample of arrestees. The cities of Chicago, Miami, and Omaha, did not test or interview female arrestees.

[In percent testing positive for drug use]

City	Percent	Rank
Dallas, TX	12	6
Denver, CO	26	1
Houston, TX	7	8
Los Angeles, CA	8	7
Manhattan, NY	19	2
Philadelphia, PA	13	5
Phoenix, AZ	18	3
San Antonio, TX	12	6
San Diego, CA	15	4
San Jose, CA	13	5

Source: Maguire, Kathleen, and Ann L. Pastore, eds., *Sourcebook of Criminal Justice Statistics 1994*, U.S. Department of Justice, Bureau of Justice Statistics, Washington, D.C.: U.S. Government Printing Office, 1995, p. 415. Primary source: U.S. Department of Justice, National Institute of Justice, *Drug Use Forecasting 1993 Annual Report on Adult Arrestees: Drugs and Crime in America's Cities*, NCJ-147411, Washington, D.C.: U.S. Department of Justice, 1994, pp. 6-28.

★2917★

Drug Use and Abuse

Drug Use By Arrestees, 1993, By Type of Drug, Race, Ethnicity, and Sex: Hispanic Females Using Opiates

Data on drug use are obtained every quarter for approximately two weeks by trained local staff who obtain voluntary and anonymous urine specimens and interviews from a new sample of arrestees. The cities of Chicago, Miami, and Omaha, did not test or interview female arrestees.

[In percent testing positive for drug use]

City	Percent	Rank
Dallas, TX	10	7
Denver, CO	11	6
Houston, TX	0	9
Los Angeles, CA	19	3
Manhattan, NY	30	2
Philadelphia, PA	16	4
Phoenix, AZ	15	5
San Antonio, TX	15	5
San Diego, CA	32	1
San Jose, CA	8	8

Source: Maguire, Kathleen, and Ann L. Pastore, eds., *Sourcebook of Criminal Justice Statistics 1994*, U.S. Department of Justice, Bureau of Justice Statistics, Washington, D.C.: U.S. Government Printing Office, 1995, p. 415. Primary source: U.S. Department of Justice, National Institute of Justice, *Drug Use Forecasting 1993 Annual Report on Adult Arrestees: Drugs and Crime in America's Cities*, NCJ-147411, Washington, D.C.: U.S. Department of Justice, 1994, pp. 6-28.

★2918★
Drug Use and Abuse
Drug Use By Arrestees, 1993, By Type of Drug, Race, Ethnicity, and Sex: Hispanic Males Using Any Drug

Data refer to the use of cocaine, opiates, marijuana, phencyclidine (PCP), methadone, benzodiazepines, methaqualone, propoxyphene, barbiturates, and amphetamines. Data on drug use are obtained every quarter for approximately two weeks by trained local staff who obtain voluntary and anonymous urine specimens and interviews from a new sample of arrestees.

[In percent testing positive for drug use]

City	Percent	Rank
Chicago, IL	82	1
Cleveland, OH	64	5
Dallas, TX	47	13
Denver, CO	62	6
Fort Lauderdale, FL	49	11
Houston, TX	46	14
Los Angeles, CA	56	9
Manhattan, NY	70	3
Miami, FL	58	8
Omaha, NE	48	12
Philadelphia, PA	77	2
Phoenix, AZ	61	7
Portland, OR	69	4
San Antonio, TX	53	10
San Diego, CA	77	2
San Jose, CA	49	11

Source: Maguire, Kathleen, and Ann L. Pastore, eds., *Sourcebook of Criminal Justice Statistics 1994*, U.S. Department of Justice, Bureau of Justice Statistics, Washington, D.C.: U.S. Government Printing Office, 1995, p. 415. Primary source: U.S. Department of Justice, National Institute of Justice, *Drug Use Forecasting 1993 Annual Report on Adult Arrestees: Drugs and Crime in America's Cities*, NCJ-147411, Washington, D.C.: U.S. Department of Justice, 1994, pp. 6-28.

★2919★
Drug Use and Abuse
Drug Use By Arrestees, 1993, By Type of Drug, Race, Ethnicity, and Sex: Hispanic Males Using Cocaine

Data on drug use are obtained every quarter for approximately two weeks by trained local staff who obtain voluntary and anonymous urine specimens and interviews from a new sample of arrestees.

[In percent testing positive for drug use]

City	Percent	Rank
Chicago, IL	53	3
Cleveland, OH	42	7
Dallas, TX	36	9
Denver, CO	36	9
Fort Lauderdale, FL	39	8
Houston, TX	27	11
Los Angeles, CA	44	6
Manhattan, NY	55	2
Miami, FL	50	4
Omaha, NE	11	13
Philadelphia, PA	53	3
Phoenix, AZ	36	9

[Continued]

★2919★
Drug Use By Arrestees, 1993, By Type of Drug, Race, Ethnicity, and Sex: Hispanic Males Using Cocaine
[Continued]

City	Percent	Rank
Portland, OR	58	1
San Antonio, TX	30	10
San Diego, CA	46	5
San Jose, CA	22	12

Source: Maguire, Kathleen, and Ann L. Pastore, eds., *Sourcebook of Criminal Justice Statistics 1994*, U.S. Department of Justice, Bureau of Justice Statistics, Washington, D.C.: U.S. Government Printing Office, 1995, p. 415. Primary source: U.S. Department of Justice, National Institute of Justice, *Drug Use Forecasting 1993 Annual Report on Adult Arrestees: Drugs and Crime in America's Cities*, NCJ-147411, Washington, D.C.: U.S. Department of Justice, 1994, pp. 6-28.

★2920★
Drug Use and Abuse
Drug Use By Arrestees, 1993, By Type of Drug, Race, Ethnicity, and Sex: Hispanic Males Using Marijuana

Data on drug use are obtained every quarter for approximately two weeks by trained local staff who obtain voluntary and anonymous urine specimens and interviews from a new sample of arrestees.

[In percent testing positive for drug use]

City	Percent	Rank
Chicago, IL	48	1
Cleveland, OH	36	5
Dallas, TX	23	11
Denver, CO	43	2
Fort Lauderdale, FL	28	8
Houston, TX	19	14
Los Angeles, CA	22	12
Manhattan, NY	25	9
Miami, FL	20	13
Omaha, NE	37	4
Philadelphia, PA	39	3
Phoenix, AZ	35	6
Portland, OR	24	10
San Antonio, TX	30	7
San Diego, CA	39	3
San Jose, CA	24	10

Source: Maguire, Kathleen, and Ann L. Pastore, eds., *Sourcebook of Criminal Justice Statistics 1994*, U.S. Department of Justice, Bureau of Justice Statistics, Washington, D.C.: U.S. Government Printing Office, 1995, p. 415. Primary source: U.S. Department of Justice, National Institute of Justice, *Drug Use Forecasting 1993 Annual Report on Adult Arrestees: Drugs and Crime in America's Cities*, NCJ-147411, Washington, D.C.: U.S. Department of Justice, 1994, pp. 6-28.

★2921★

Drug Use and Abuse

Drug Use By Arrestees, 1993, By Type of Drug, Race, Ethnicity, and Sex: Hispanic Males Using Opiates

Data on drug use are obtained every quarter for approximately two weeks by trained local staff who obtain voluntary and anonymous urine specimens and interviews from a new sample of arrestees.

[In percent testing positive for drug use]

City	Percent	Rank
Chicago, IL	28	1
Cleveland, OH	16	6
Dallas, TX	4	11
Denver, CO	7	10
Fort Lauderdale, FL	0	14
Houston, TX	1	13
Los Angeles, CA	9	8
Manhattan, NY	24	3
Miami, FL	1	13
Omaha, NE	2	12
Philadelphia, PA	15	7
Phoenix, AZ	8	9
Portland, OR	23	4
San Antonio, TX	17	5
San Diego, CA	25	2
San Jose, CA	7	10

Source: Maguire, Kathleen, and Ann L. Pastore, eds., *Sourcebook of Criminal Justice Statistics 1994*, U.S. Department of Justice, Bureau of Justice Statistics, Washington, D.C.: U.S. Government Printing Office, 1995, p. 415. Primary source: U.S. Department of Justice, National Institute of Justice, *Drug Use Forecasting 1993 Annual Report on Adult Arrestees: Drugs and Crime in America's Cities*, NCJ-147411, Washington, D.C.: U.S. Department of Justice, 1994, pp. 6-28.

★2922★

Drug Use and Abuse

Drug Use By Arrestees, 1993, By Type of Drug, Race, Ethnicity, and Sex: White Females Using Any Drug

Data refer to the use of cocaine, opiates, marijuana, phencyclidine (PCP), methadone, benzodiazepines, methaqualone, propoxyphene, barbiturates, and amphetamines. Data on drug use are obtained every quarter for approximately two weeks by trained local staff who obtain voluntary and anonymous urine specimens and interviews from a new sample of arrestees. The cities of Chicago, Miami, and Omaha, did not test or interview female arrestees.

[In percent testing positive for drug use]

City	Percent	Rank
Atlanta, GA	70	8
Birmingham, AL	66	11
Cleveland, OH	68	10
Dallas, TX	61	13
Denver, CO	59	15
Detroit, MI	85	1
Fort Lauderdale, FL	61	13
Houston, TX	64	12
Indianapolis, IN	50	18
Los Angeles, CA	83	3
Manhattan, NY	76	6
New Orleans, LA	52	17

[Continued]

★2922★

Drug Use By Arrestees, 1993, By Type of Drug, Race, Ethnicity, and Sex: White Females Using Any Drug

[Continued]

City	Percent	Rank
Philadelphia, PA	82	4
Phoenix, AZ	60	14
Portland, OR	72	7
Saint Louis, MO	77	5
San Antonio, TX	49	19
San Diego, CA	84	2
San Jose, CA	55	16
Washington, DC	69	9

Source: Maguire, Kathleen, and Ann L. Pastore, eds., *Sourcebook of Criminal Justice Statistics 1994*, U.S. Department of Justice, Bureau of Justice Statistics, Washington, D.C.: U.S. Government Printing Office, 1995, p. 415. Primary source: U.S. Department of Justice, National Institute of Justice, *Drug Use Forecasting 1993 Annual Report on Adult Arrestees: Drugs and Crime in America's Cities*, NCJ-147411, Washington, D.C.: U.S. Department of Justice, 1994, pp. 6-28.

★2923★

Drug Use and Abuse

Drug Use By Arrestees, 1993, By Type of Drug, Race, Ethnicity, and Sex: White Females Using Cocaine

Data on drug use are obtained every quarter for approximately two weeks by trained local staff who obtain voluntary and anonymous urine specimens and interviews from a new sample of arrestees. The cities of Chicago, Miami, and Omaha, did not test or interview female arrestees.

[In percent testing positive for drug use]

City	Percent	Rank
Atlanta, GA	62	2
Birmingham, AL	34	11
Cleveland, OH	56	4
Dallas, TX	41	9
Denver, CO	36	10
Detroit, MI	70	1
Fort Lauderdale, FL	45	8
Houston, TX	51	7
Indianapolis, IN	17	15
Los Angeles, CA	52	6
Manhattan, NY	56	4
New Orleans, LA	34	11
Philadelphia, PA	54	5
Phoenix, AZ	27	12
Portland, OR	36	10
Saint Louis, MO	62	2
San Antonio, TX	19	14
San Diego, CA	24	13
San Jose, CA	12	16
Washington, DC	57	3

Source: Maguire, Kathleen, and Ann L. Pastore, eds., *Sourcebook of Criminal Justice Statistics 1994*, U.S. Department of Justice, Bureau of Justice Statistics, Washington, D.C.: U.S. Government Printing Office, 1995, p. 415. Primary source: U.S. Department of Justice, National Institute of Justice, *Drug Use Forecasting 1993 Annual Report on Adult Arrestees: Drugs and Crime in America's Cities*, NCJ-147411, Washington, D.C.: U.S. Department of Justice, 1994, pp. 6-28.

★2924★

Drug Use and Abuse

Drug Use By Arrestees, 1993, By Type of Drug, Race, Ethnicity, and Sex: White Females Using Marijuana

Data on drug use are obtained every quarter for approximately two weeks by trained local staff who obtain voluntary and anonymous urine specimens and interviews from a new sample of arrestees. The cities of Chicago, Miami, and Omaha, did not test or interview female arrestees.

[In percent testing positive for drug use]

City	Percent	Rank
Atlanta, GA	12	11
Birmingham, AL	19	6
Cleveland, OH	22	3
Dallas, TX	20	5
Denver, CO	22	3
Detroit, MI	13	10
Fort Lauderdale, FL	18	7
Houston, TX	21	4
Indianapolis, IN	30	1
Los Angeles, CA	19	6
Manhattan, NY	21	4
New Orleans, LA	24	2
Philadelphia, PA	17	8
Phoenix, AZ	21	4
Portland, OR	18	7
Saint Louis, MO	22	3
San Antonio, TX	21	4
San Diego, CA	30	1
San Jose, CA	22	3
Washington, DC	14	9

Source: Maguire, Kathleen, and Ann L. Pastore, eds., *Sourcebook of Criminal Justice Statistics 1994*, U.S. Department of Justice, Bureau of Justice Statistics, Washington, D.C.: U.S. Government Printing Office, 1995, p. 415. Primary source: U.S. Department of Justice, National Institute of Justice, *Drug Use Forecasting 1993 Annual Report on Adult Arrestees: Drugs and Crime in America's Cities*, NCJ-147411, Washington, D.C.: U.S. Department of Justice, 1994, pp. 6-28.

★2925★

Drug Use and Abuse

Drug Use By Arrestees, 1993, By Type of Drug, Race, Ethnicity, and Sex: White Females Using Opiates

Data on drug use are obtained every quarter for approximately two weeks by trained local staff who obtain voluntary and anonymous urine specimens and interviews from a new sample of arrestees. The cities of Chicago, Miami, and Omaha, did not test or interview female arrestees.

[In percent testing positive for drug use]

City	Percent	Rank
Atlanta, GA	7	14
Birmingham, AL	11	10
Cleveland, OH	10	11
Dallas, TX	11	10
Denver, CO	6	15
Detroit, MI	26	3
Fort Lauderdale, FL	4	16
Houston, TX	3	17
Indianapolis, IN	6	15

[Continued]

★2925★

Drug Use By Arrestees, 1993, By Type of Drug, Race, Ethnicity, and Sex: White Females Using Opiates

[Continued]

City	Percent	Rank
Los Angeles, CA	22	4
Manhattan, NY	35	1
New Orleans, LA	9	12
Philadelphia, PA	27	2
Phoenix, AZ	15	8
Portland, OR	19	6
Saint Louis, MO	12	9
San Antonio, TX	17	7
San Diego, CA	20	5
San Jose, CA	8	13
Washington, DC	26	3

Source: Maguire, Kathleen, and Ann L. Pastore, eds., *Sourcebook of Criminal Justice Statistics 1994*, U.S. Department of Justice, Bureau of Justice Statistics, Washington, D.C.: U.S. Government Printing Office, 1995, p. 415. Primary source: U.S. Department of Justice, National Institute of Justice, *Drug Use Forecasting 1993 Annual Report on Adult Arrestees: Drugs and Crime in America's Cities*, NCJ-147411, Washington, D.C.: U.S. Department of Justice, 1994, pp. 6-28.

★2926★

Drug Use and Abuse

Drug Use By Arrestees, 1993, By Type of Drug, Race, Ethnicity, and Sex: White Males Using Any Drug

Data refer to the use of cocaine, opiates, marijuana, phencyclidine (PCP), methadone, benzodiazepines, methaqualone, propoxyphene, barbiturates, and amphetamines. Data on drug use are obtained every quarter for approximately two weeks by trained local staff who obtain voluntary and anonymous urine specimens and interviews from a new sample of arrestees.

[In percent testing positive for drug use]

City	Percent	Rank
Atlanta, GA	58	12
Birmingham, AL	68	7
Chicago, IL	85	1
Cleveland, OH	50	15
Dallas, TX	56	13
Denver, CO	56	13
Detroit, MI	61	10
Fort Lauderdale, FL	56	13
Houston, TX	59	11
Indianapolis, IN	56	13
Los Angeles, CA	80	3
Manhattan, NY	69	6
Miami, FL	72	5
New Orleans, LA	54	14
Omaha, NE	49	16
Philadelphia, PA	75	4
Phoenix, AZ	61	10
Portland, OR	59	11
Saint Louis, MO	63	9
San Antonio, TX	58	12
San Diego, CA	82	2

[Continued]

★ 2926 ★

Drug Use By Arrestees, 1993, By Type of Drug, Race, Ethnicity, and Sex: White Males Using Any Drug

[Continued]

City	Percent	Rank
San Jose, CA	64	8
Washington, DC	48	17

Source: Maguire, Kathleen, and Ann L. Pastore, eds., *Sourcebook of Criminal Justice Statistics 1994*, U.S. Department of Justice, Bureau of Justice Statistics, Washington, D.C.: U.S. Government Printing Office, 1995, p. 415. Primary source: U.S. Department of Justice, National Institute of Justice, *Drug Use Forecasting 1993 Annual Report on Adult Arrestees: Drugs and Crime in America's Cities*, NCJ-147411, Washington, D.C.: U.S. Department of Justice, 1994, pp. 6-28.

★ 2927 ★

Drug Use and Abuse

Drug Use By Arrestees, 1993, By Type of Drug, Race, Ethnicity, and Sex: White Males Using Cocaine

Data on drug use are obtained every quarter for approximately two weeks by trained local staff who obtain voluntary and anonymous urine specimens and interviews from a new sample of arrestees.

[In percent testing positive for drug use]

City	Percent	Rank
Atlanta, GA	33	10
Birmingham, AL	40	5
Chicago, IL	59	1
Cleveland, OH	26	12
Dallas, TX	34	9
Denver, CO	23	13
Detroit, MI	35	8
Fort Lauderdale, FL	34	9
Houston, TX	36	7
Indianapolis, IN	12	17
Los Angeles, CA	34	9
Manhattan, NY	57	3
Miami, FL	58	2
New Orleans, LA	30	11
Omaha, NE	9	18
Philadelphia, PA	48	4
Phoenix, AZ	18	15
Portland, OR	21	14
Saint Louis, MO	38	6
San Antonio, TX	26	12
San Diego, CA	18	15
San Jose, CA	15	16
Washington, DC	35	8

Source: Maguire, Kathleen, and Ann L. Pastore, eds., *Sourcebook of Criminal Justice Statistics 1994*, U.S. Department of Justice, Bureau of Justice Statistics, Washington, D.C.: U.S. Government Printing Office, 1995, p. 415. Primary source: U.S. Department of Justice, National Institute of Justice, *Drug Use Forecasting 1993 Annual Report on Adult Arrestees: Drugs and Crime in America's Cities*, NCJ-147411, Washington, D.C.: U.S. Department of Justice, 1994, pp. 6-28.

★ 2928 ★

Drug Use and Abuse

Drug Use By Arrestees, 1993, By Type of Drug, Race, Ethnicity, and Sex: White Males Using Marijuana

Data on drug use are obtained every quarter for approximately two weeks by trained local staff who obtain voluntary and anonymous urine specimens and interviews from a new sample of arrestees.

[In percent testing positive for drug use]

City	Percent	Rank
Atlanta, GA	25	11
Birmingham, AL	33	6
Chicago, IL	39	4
Cleveland, OH	23	13
Dallas, TX	24	12
Denver, CO	33	6
Detroit, MI	35	5
Fort Lauderdale, FL	28	9
Houston, TX	27	10
Indianapolis, IN	45	2
Los Angeles, CA	32	7
Manhattan, NY	14	16
Miami, FL	21	14
New Orleans, LA	27	10
Omaha, NE	42	3
Philadelphia, PA	33	6
Phoenix, AZ	31	8
Portland, OR	33	6
Saint Louis, MO	42	3
San Antonio, TX	33	6
San Diego, CA	47	1
San Jose, CA	35	5
Washington, DC	15	15

Source: Maguire, Kathleen, and Ann L. Pastore, eds., *Sourcebook of Criminal Justice Statistics 1994*, U.S. Department of Justice, Bureau of Justice Statistics, Washington, D.C.: U.S. Government Printing Office, 1995, p. 415. Primary source: U.S. Department of Justice, National Institute of Justice, *Drug Use Forecasting 1993 Annual Report on Adult Arrestees: Drugs and Crime in America's Cities*, NCJ-147411, Washington, D.C.: U.S. Department of Justice, 1994, pp. 6-28.

★ 2929 ★

Drug Use and Abuse

Drug Use By Arrestees, 1993, By Type of Drug, Race, Ethnicity, and Sex: White Males Using Opiates

Data on drug use are obtained every quarter for approximately two weeks by trained local staff who obtain voluntary and anonymous urine specimens and interviews from a new sample of arrestees.

[In percent testing positive for drug use]

City	Percent	Rank
Atlanta, GA	4	11
Birmingham, AL	8	8
Chicago, IL	29	1
Cleveland, OH	5	10
Dallas, TX	6	9
Denver, CO	3	12
Detroit, MI	10	7
Fort Lauderdale, FL	2	13

[Continued]

★2929★

Drug Use By Arrestees, 1993, By Type of Drug, Race, Ethnicity, and Sex: White Males Using Opiates

[Continued]

City	Percent	Rank
Houston, TX	3	12
Indianapolis, IN	3	12
Los Angeles, CA	14	4
Manhattan, NY	24	2
Miami, FL	6	9
New Orleans, LA	8	8
Omaha, NE	2	13
Philadelphia, PA	15	3
Phoenix, AZ	6	9
Portland, OR	10	7
Saint Louis, MO	5	10
San Antonio, TX	11	6
San Diego, CA	15	3
San Jose, CA	5	10
Washington, DC	13	5

Source: Maguire, Kathleen, and Ann L. Pastore, eds., *Sourcebook of Criminal Justice Statistics 1994,* U.S. Department of Justice, Bureau of Justice Statistics, Washington, D.C.: U.S. Government Printing Office, 1995, p. 415. Primary source: U.S. Department of Justice, National Institute of Justice, *Drug Use Forecasting 1993 Annual Report on Adult Arrestees: Drugs and Crime in America's Cities,* NCJ-147411, Washington, D.C.: U.S. Department of Justice, 1994, pp. 6-28.

★2930★

Drug Use and Abuse

Drug Use By Female Arrestees, 1992: Any Drug

Data refer to percentage testing positive for drug use.

[In percentages]

City	Percentage[1]	Rank
Atlanta, GA	65	8
Birmingham, AL	59	12
Cleveland, OH	74	3
Dallas, TX	66	7
Denver, CO	61	11
Detroit, MI	72	5
Fort Lauderdale, FL	62	10
Houston, TX	54	14
Indianapolis, IN	50	16
Kansas City, MO	73	4
Los Angeles, CA	72	5
Manhattan, NY	85	1
New Orleans, LA	52	15
Philadelphia, PA	78	2
Phoenix, AZ	63	9
Portland, OR	73	4
San Antonio, TX	44	17
San Diego, CA	72	5
San Jose, CA	56	13
St. Louis, MO	70	6
Washington, DC	72	5

Source: U.S. Bureau of the Census, *Statistical Abstract of the United States: 1995,* (115th edition), Washington, D.C.: U.S. Government Printing Office, 1995, p. 207. Primary source: U.S. National Institute of Justice, *Drug Use Forecasting,* annual.
Note: 1. Includes other drugs not shown separately.

★2931★

Drug Use and Abuse

Drug Use By Female Arrestees, 1992: Cocaine

Data refer to percentage testing positive for cocaine use.

[In percentages]

City	Percentage	Rank
Atlanta, GA	58	6
Birmingham, AL	46	12
Cleveland, OH	66	3
Dallas, TX	48	10
Denver, CO	50	8
Detroit, MI	62	5
Fort Lauderdale, FL	47	11
Houston, TX	44	13
Indianapolis, IN	25	16
Kansas City, MO	62	5
Los Angeles, CA	58	6
Manhattan, NY	72	1
New Orleans, LA	44	13
Philadelphia, PA	67	2
Phoenix, AZ	49	9
Portland, OR	54	7
San Antonio, TX	25	16
San Diego, CA	37	14
San Jose, CA	32	15
St. Louis, MO	62	5
Washington, DC	64	4

Source: U.S. Bureau of the Census, *Statistical Abstract of the United States: 1995,* (115th edition), Washington, D.C.: U.S. Government Printing Office, 1995, p. 207. Primary source: U.S. National Institute of Justice, *Drug Use Forecasting,* annual.

★2932★

Drug Use and Abuse

Drug Use By Female Arrestees, 1992: Heroin

Data refer to percentage testing positive for heroin use.

[In percentages]

City	Percentage	Rank
Atlanta, GA	5	13
Birmingham, AL	4	14
Cleveland, OH	5	13
Dallas, TX	8	10
Denver, CO	5	13
Detroit, MI	15	5
Fort Lauderdale, FL	3	15
Houston, TX	4	14
Indianapolis, IN	7	11
Kansas City, MO	3	15
Los Angeles, CA	13	7
Manhattan, NY	24	1
New Orleans, LA	6	12
Philadelphia, PA	11	8
Phoenix, AZ	15	5
Portland, OR	22	2
San Antonio, TX	14	6
San Diego, CA	17	4
San Jose, CA	9	9

[Continued]

★2932★

Drug Use By Female Arrestees, 1992: Heroin
[Continued]

City	Percentage	Rank
St. Louis, MO	7	11
Washington, DC	19	3

Source: U.S. Bureau of the Census, *Statistical Abstract of the United States: 1995*, (115th edition), Washington, D.C.: U.S. Government Printing Office, 1995, p. 207. Primary source: U.S. National Institute of Justice, *Drug Use Forecasting*, annual.

★2933★

Drug Use and Abuse

Drug Use By Female Arrestees, 1992: Marijuana

Data refer to percentage testing positive for marijuana use.

[In percentages]

City	Percentage	Rank
Atlanta, GA	13	10
Birmingham, AL	13	10
Cleveland, OH	11	12
Dallas, TX	24	3
Denver, CO	19	5
Detroit, MI	11	12
Fort Lauderdale, FL	21	4
Houston, TX	12	11
Indianapolis, IN	26	1
Kansas City, MO	18	6
Los Angeles, CA	13	10
Manhattan, NY	12	11
New Orleans, LA	8	13
Philadelphia, PA	15	9
Phoenix, AZ	15	9
Portland, OR	17	7
San Antonio, TX	16	8
San Diego, CA	25	2
San Jose, CA	18	6
St. Louis, MO	11	12
Washington, DC	8	13

Source: U.S. Bureau of the Census, *Statistical Abstract of the United States: 1995*, (115th edition), Washington, D.C.: U.S. Government Printing Office, 1995, p. 207. Primary source: U.S. National Institute of Justice, *Drug Use Forecasting*, annual.

★2934★

Drug Use and Abuse

Drug Use By Male Arrestees, 1992: Any Drug

Data refer to percentage testing positive for drug use.

[In percentages]

City	Percentage[1]	Rank
Atlanta, GA	69	3
Birmingham, AL	64	6
Chicago, IL	69	3
Cleveland, OH	64	6
Dallas, TX	59	8
Denver, CO	60	7
Detroit, MI	58	9
Fort Lauderdale, FL	64	6

[Continued]

★2934★

Drug Use By Male Arrestees, 1992: Any Drug
[Continued]

City	Percentage[1]	Rank
Houston, TX	59	8
Indianapolis, IN	52	11
Kansas City, MO	60	7
Los Angeles, CA	67	5
Manhattan, NY	77	2
Miami, FL	68	4
New Orleans, LA	60	7
Omaha, NE	48	13
Philadelphia, PA	78	1
Phoenix, AZ	47	14
Portland, OR	60	7
San Antonio, TX	54	10
San Diego, CA	77	2
San Jose, CA	50	12
St. Louis, MO	64	6
Washington, DC	60	7

Source: U.S. Bureau of the Census, *Statistical Abstract of the United States: 1995*, (115th edition), Washington, D.C.: U.S. Government Printing Office, 1995, p. 207. Primary source: U.S. National Institute of Justice, *Drug Use Forecasting*, annual. *Note:* 1. Includes other drugs not shown separately.

★2935★

Drug Use and Abuse

Drug Use By Male Arrestees, 1992: Cocaine

Data refer to percentage testing positive for cocaine use.

[In percentages]

City	Percentage	Rank
Atlanta, GA	58	3
Birmingham, AL	49	8
Chicago, IL	56	4
Cleveland, OH	53	5
Dallas, TX	41	12
Denver, CO	38	13
Detroit, MI	37	14
Fort Lauderdale, FL	46	9
Houston, TX	41	12
Indianapolis, IN	23	19
Kansas City, MO	41	12
Los Angeles, CA	52	6
Manhattan, NY	62	2
Miami, FL	56	4
New Orleans, LA	49	8
Omaha, NE	16	20
Philadelphia, PA	63	1
Phoenix, AZ	26	18
Portland, OR	35	15
San Antonio, TX	32	16
San Diego, CA	45	10
San Jose, CA	28	17
St. Louis, MO	50	7
Washington, DC	44	11

Source: U.S. Bureau of the Census, *Statistical Abstract of the United States: 1995*, (115th edition), Washington, D.C.: U.S. Government Printing Office, 1995, p. 207. Primary source: U.S. National Institute of Justice, *Drug Use Forecasting*, annual.

★ 2936 ★

Drug Use and Abuse

Drug Use By Male Arrestees, 1992: Heroin

Data refer to percentage testing positive for heroin use.

[In percentages]

City	Percentage	Rank
Atlanta, GA	4	11
Birmingham, AL	3	12
Chicago, IL	19	1
Cleveland, OH	3	12
Dallas, TX	4	11
Denver, CO	2	13
Detroit, MI	8	8
Fort Lauderdale, FL	1	14
Houston, TX	3	12
Indianapolis, IN	4	11
Kansas City, MO	2	13
Los Angeles, CA	10	7
Manhattan, NY	18	2
Miami, FL	2	13
New Orleans, LA	4	11
Omaha, NE	2	13
Philadelphia, PA	12	5
Phoenix, AZ	5	10
Portland, OR	11	6
San Antonio, TX	15	4
San Diego, CA	16	3
San Jose, CA	4	11
St. Louis, MO	7	9
Washington, DC	11	6

Source: U.S. Bureau of the Census, *Statistical Abstract of the United States: 1995,* (115th edition), Washington, D.C.: U.S. Government Printing Office, 1995, p. 207. Primary source: U.S. National Institute of Justice, *Drug Use Forecasting,* annual.

★ 2937 ★

Drug Use and Abuse

Drug Use By Male Arrestees, 1992: Marijuana

Data refer to percentage testing positive for marijuana use.

[In percentages]

City	Percentage	Rank
Atlanta, GA	22	11
Birmingham, AL	22	11
Chicago, IL	26	8
Cleveland, OH	17	15
Dallas, TX	28	6
Denver, CO	34	3
Detroit, MI	27	7
Fort Lauderdale, FL	32	4
Houston, TX	24	9
Indianapolis, IN	35	2
Kansas City, MO	28	6
Los Angeles, CA	23	10
Manhattan, NY	22	11
Miami, FL	30	5
New Orleans, LA	19	14
Omaha, NE	38	1
Philadelphia, PA	26	8
Phoenix, AZ	22	11

[Continued]

★ 2937 ★

Drug Use By Male Arrestees, 1992: Marijuana

[Continued]

City	Percentage	Rank
Portland, OR	28	6
San Antonio, TX	28	6
San Diego, CA	35	2
San Jose, CA	24	9
St. Louis, MO	21	12
Washington, DC	20	13

Source: U.S. Bureau of the Census, *Statistical Abstract of the United States: 1995,* (115th edition), Washington, D.C.: U.S. Government Printing Office, 1995, p. 207. Primary source: U.S. National Institute of Justice, *Drug Use Forecasting,* annual.

★ 2938 ★

Drug Use and Abuse

Drug Use By Male Juvenile Arrestees, 1993, By Type of Drug and Age: Ages 13 to 14 Years Using Any Drug

Data refer to use of cocaine, opiates, marijuana, phencyclidine (PCP), methadone, benzodiazepines, barbiturates, and amphetamines. Data are collected at 12 Drug Use Forecasting (DUF) sites. There are no data presented for the "Age 9 to 12" category because 11 DUF sites reported less than 20 cases within each drug category.

[In percent testing positive for drug use]

City	Percent	Rank
Birmingham, AL	10	8
Cleveland, OH	18	6
Denver, CO	35	1
Indianapolis, IN	5	10
Los Angeles, CA	20	4
Phoenix, AZ	17	7
Portland, OR	6	9
Saint Louis, MO	10	8
San Antonio, TX	22	3
San Diego, CA	32	2
San Jose, CA	22	3
Washington, DC	19	5

Source: Maguire, Kathleen, and Ann L. Pastore, eds., *Sourcebook of Criminal Justice Statistics 1994,* U.S. Department of Justice, Bureau of Justice Statistics, Washington, D.C.: U.S. Government Printing Office, 1995, p. 419. Primary source: U.S. Department of Justice, National Institute of Justice, *Drug Use Forecasting 1993 Annual Report on Juvenile Arrestees/Detainees: Drugs and Crime in America's Cities,* NCJ-150709, Washington, D.C.: U.S. Department of Justice, 1994, pp. 5-16.

★ 2939 ★

Drug Use and Abuse

Drug Use By Male Juvenile Arrestees, 1993, By Type of Drug and Age: Ages 13 to 14 Years Using Cocaine

[In percent testing positive for drug use]

City	Percent	Rank
Birmingham, AL	3	5
Cleveland, OH	10	1
Denver, CO	4	4
Indianapolis, IN	0	8

[Continued]

★2939★

Drug Use By Male Juvenile Arrestees, 1993, By Type of Drug and Age: Ages 13 to 14 Years Using Cocaine

[Continued]

City	Percent	Rank
Los Angeles, CA	7	2
Phoenix, AZ	6	3
Portland, OR	0	8
Saint Louis, MO	2	6
San Antonio, TX	3	5
San Diego, CA	4	4
San Jose, CA	1	7
Washington, DC	0	8

Source: Maguire, Kathleen, and Ann L. Pastore, eds., *Sourcebook of Criminal Justice Statistics 1994*, U.S. Department of Justice, Bureau of Justice Statistics, Washington, D.C.: U.S. Government Printing Office, 1995, p. 419. Primary source: U.S. Department of Justice, National Institute of Justice, *Drug Use Forecasting 1993 Annual Report on Juvenile Arrestees/Detainees: Drugs and Crime in America's Cities*, NCJ-150709, Washington, D.C.: U.S. Department of Justice, 1994, pp. 5-16.

★2940★

Drug Use and Abuse

Drug Use By Male Juvenile Arrestees, 1993, By Type of Drug and Age: Ages 13 to 14 Years Using Marijuana

[In percent testing positive for drug use]

City	Percent	Rank
Birmingham, AL	8	8
Cleveland, OH	14	6
Denver, CO	35	1
Indianapolis, IN	5	9
Los Angeles, CA	14	6
Phoenix, AZ	12	7
Portland, OR	4	10
Saint Louis, MO	8	8
San Antonio, TX	22	3
San Diego, CA	29	2
San Jose, CA	21	4
Washington, DC	19	5

Source: Maguire, Kathleen, and Ann L. Pastore, eds., *Sourcebook of Criminal Justice Statistics 1994*, U.S. Department of Justice, Bureau of Justice Statistics, Washington, D.C.: U.S. Government Printing Office, 1995, p. 419. Primary source: U.S. Department of Justice, National Institute of Justice, *Drug Use Forecasting 1993 Annual Report on Juvenile Arrestees/Detainees: Drugs and Crime in America's Cities*, NCJ-150709, Washington, D.C.: U.S. Department of Justice, 1994, pp. 5-16.

★2941★

Drug Use and Abuse

Drug Use By Male Juvenile Arrestees, 1993, By Type of Drug and Age: Ages 13 to 14 Years Using Multiple Drugs

Data refer to use of cocaine, opiates, marijuana, phencyclidine (PCP), methadone, benzodiazepines, methaqualone, propoxyphene, barbiturates, and amphetamines.

[In percent testing positive for drug use]

City	Percent	Rank
Birmingham, AL	1	6
Cleveland, OH	7	1
Denver, CO	6	2
Indianapolis, IN	1	6
Los Angeles, CA	5	3
Phoenix, AZ	5	3
Portland, OR	0	7
Saint Louis, MO	1	6
San Antonio, TX	3	4
San Diego, CA	6	2
San Jose, CA	3	4
Washington, DC	2	5

Source: Maguire, Kathleen, and Ann L. Pastore, eds., *Sourcebook of Criminal Justice Statistics 1994*, U.S. Department of Justice, Bureau of Justice Statistics, Washington, D.C.: U.S. Government Printing Office, 1995, p. 419. Primary source: U.S. Department of Justice, National Institute of Justice, *Drug Use Forecasting 1993 Annual Report on Juvenile Arrestees/Detainees: Drugs and Crime in America's Cities*, NCJ-150709, Washington, D.C.: U.S. Department of Justice, 1994, pp. 5-16.

★2942★

Drug Use and Abuse

Drug Use By Male Juvenile Arrestees, 1993, By Type of Drug and Age: Ages 15 to 16 Years Using Any Drug

Data refer to use of cocaine, opiates, marijuana, phencyclidine (PCP), methadone, benzodiazepines, barbiturates, and amphetamines. Data are collected at 12 Drug Use Forecasting (DUF) sites. There are no data presented for the "Age 9 to 12" category because 11 DUF sites reported less than 20 cases within each drug category.

[In percent testing positive for drug use]

City	Percent	Rank
Birmingham, AL	19	9
Cleveland, OH	33	6
Denver, CO	57	1
Indianapolis, IN	18	10
Los Angeles, CA	35	5
Phoenix, AZ	36	4
Portland, OR	15	11
Saint Louis, MO	26	8
San Antonio, TX	37	3
San Diego, CA	47	2
San Jose, CA	31	7
Washington, DC	57	1

Source: Maguire, Kathleen, and Ann L. Pastore, eds., *Sourcebook of Criminal Justice Statistics 1994*, U.S. Department of Justice, Bureau of Justice Statistics, Washington, D.C.: U.S. Government Printing Office, 1995, p. 419. Primary source: U.S. Department of Justice, National Institute of Justice, *Drug Use Forecasting 1993 Annual Report on Juvenile Arrestees/Detainees: Drugs and Crime in America's Cities*, NCJ-150709, Washington, D.C.: U.S. Department of Justice, 1994, pp. 5-16.

★2943★

Drug Use and Abuse

Drug Use By Male Juvenile Arrestees, 1993, By Type of Drug and Age: Ages 15 to 16 Years Using Cocaine

[In percent testing positive for drug use]

City	Percent	Rank
Birmingham, AL	5	7
Cleveland, OH	13	1
Denver, CO	8	4
Indianapolis, IN	2	8
Los Angeles, CA	12	2
Phoenix, AZ	8	4
Portland, OR	2	8
Saint Louis, MO	8	4
San Antonio, TX	10	3
San Diego, CA	6	6
San Jose, CA	6	6
Washington, DC	7	5

Source: Maguire, Kathleen, and Ann L. Pastore, eds., *Sourcebook of Criminal Justice Statistics 1994*, U.S. Department of Justice, Bureau of Justice Statistics, Washington, D.C.: U.S. Government Printing Office, 1995, p. 419. Primary source: U.S. Department of Justice, National Institute of Justice, *Drug Use Forecasting 1993 Annual Report on Juvenile Arrestees/Detainees: Drugs and Crime in America's Cities*, NCJ-150709, Washington, D.C.: U.S. Department of Justice, 1994, pp. 5-16.

★2944★

Drug Use and Abuse

Drug Use By Male Juvenile Arrestees, 1993, By Type of Drug and Age: Ages 15 to 16 Years Using Marijuana

[In percent testing positive for drug use]

City	Percent	Rank
Birmingham, AL	16	10
Cleveland, OH	24	7
Denver, CO	54	1
Indianapolis, IN	16	10
Los Angeles, CA	26	6
Phoenix, AZ	30	5
Portland, OR	12	11
Saint Louis, MO	20	9
San Antonio, TX	33	4
San Diego, CA	37	3
San Jose, CA	23	8
Washington, DC	52	2

Source: Maguire, Kathleen, and Ann L. Pastore, eds., *Sourcebook of Criminal Justice Statistics 1994*, U.S. Department of Justice, Bureau of Justice Statistics, Washington, D.C.: U.S. Government Printing Office, 1995, p. 419. Primary source: U.S. Department of Justice, National Institute of Justice, *Drug Use Forecasting 1993 Annual Report on Juvenile Arrestees/Detainees: Drugs and Crime in America's Cities*, NCJ-150709, Washington, D.C.: U.S. Department of Justice, 1994, pp. 5-16.

★2945★

Drug Use and Abuse

Drug Use By Male Juvenile Arrestees, 1993, By Type of Drug and Age: Ages 15 to 16 Years Using Multiple Drugs

Data refer to use of cocaine, opiates, marijuana, phencyclidine (PCP), methadone, benzodiazepines, methaqualone, propoxyphene, barbiturates, and amphetamines.

[In percent testing positive for drug use]

City	Percent	Rank
Birmingham, AL	4	7
Cleveland, OH	6	5
Denver, CO	7	4
Indianapolis, IN	2	8
Los Angeles, CA	9	3
Phoenix, AZ	5	6
Portland, OR	1	9
Saint Louis, MO	4	7
San Antonio, TX	10	2
San Diego, CA	15	1
San Jose, CA	5	6
Washington, DC	15	1

Source: Maguire, Kathleen, and Ann L. Pastore, eds., *Sourcebook of Criminal Justice Statistics 1994*, U.S. Department of Justice, Bureau of Justice Statistics, Washington, D.C.: U.S. Government Printing Office, 1995, p. 419. Primary source: U.S. Department of Justice, National Institute of Justice, *Drug Use Forecasting 1993 Annual Report on Juvenile Arrestees/Detainees: Drugs and Crime in America's Cities*, NCJ-150709, Washington, D.C.: U.S. Department of Justice, 1994, pp. 5-16.

★2946★

Drug Use and Abuse

Drug Use By Male Juvenile Arrestees, 1993, By Type of Drug and Age: Ages 15 to 16 Years Using Opiates

[In percent testing positive for drug use]

City	Percent	Rank
Birmingham, AL	1	3
Cleveland, OH	0	4
Denver, CO	1	3
Indianapolis, IN	0	4
Los Angeles, CA	1	3
Phoenix, AZ	0	4
Portland, OR	0	4
Saint Louis, MO	2	2
San Antonio, TX	3	1
San Jose, CA	1	3
Washington, DC	1	3

Source: Maguire, Kathleen, and Ann L. Pastore, eds., *Sourcebook of Criminal Justice Statistics 1994*, U.S. Department of Justice, Bureau of Justice Statistics, Washington, D.C.: U.S. Government Printing Office, 1995, p. 419. Primary source: U.S. Department of Justice, National Institute of Justice, *Drug Use Forecasting 1993 Annual Report on Juvenile Arrestees/Detainees: Drugs and Crime in America's Cities*, NCJ-150709, Washington, D.C.: U.S. Department of Justice, 1994, pp. 5-16.

★2947★

Drug Use and Abuse

Drug Use By Male Juvenile Arrestees, 1993, By Type of Drug and Age: Ages 17 to 18 Years Using Any Drug

Data refer to use of cocaine, opiates, marijuana, phencyclidine (PCP), methadone, benzodiazepines, barbiturates, and amphetamines. Data are collected at 12 Drug Use Forecasting (DUF) sites. There are no data presented for the "Age 9 to 12" category because 11 DUF sites reported less than 20 cases within each drug category.

[In percent testing positive for drug use]

City	Percent	Rank
Birmingham, AL	39	6
Cleveland, OH	48	3
Denver, CO	66	1
Indianapolis, IN	42	5
Los Angeles, CA	39	6
Phoenix, AZ	47	4
Portland, OR	34	8
Saint Louis, MO	17	10
San Antonio, TX	33	9
San Diego, CA	48	3
San Jose, CA	37	7
Washington, DC	59	2

Source: Maguire, Kathleen, and Ann L. Pastore, eds., *Sourcebook of Criminal Justice Statistics 1994*, U.S. Department of Justice, Bureau of Justice Statistics, Washington, D.C.: U.S. Government Printing Office, 1995, p. 419. Primary source: U.S. Department of Justice, National Institute of Justice, *Drug Use Forecasting 1993 Annual Report on Juvenile Arrestees/Detainees: Drugs and Crime in America's Cities*, NCJ-150709, Washington, D.C.: U.S. Department of Justice, 1994, pp. 5-16.

★2948★

Drug Use and Abuse

Drug Use By Male Juvenile Arrestees, 1993, By Type of Drug and Age: Ages 17 to 18 Years Using Cocaine

[In percent testing positive for drug use]

City	Percent	Rank
Birmingham, AL	7	6
Cleveland, OH	26	1
Denver, CO	13	3
Indianapolis, IN	2	8
Los Angeles, CA	18	2
Phoenix, AZ	9	5
Portland, OR	11	4
Saint Louis, MO	0	9
San Antonio, TX	0	9
San Diego, CA	9	5
San Jose, CA	4	7
Washington, DC	13	3

Source: Maguire, Kathleen, and Ann L. Pastore, eds., *Sourcebook of Criminal Justice Statistics 1994*, U.S. Department of Justice, Bureau of Justice Statistics, Washington, D.C.: U.S. Government Printing Office, 1995, p. 419. Primary source: U.S. Department of Justice, National Institute of Justice, *Drug Use Forecasting 1993 Annual Report on Juvenile Arrestees/Detainees: Drugs and Crime in America's Cities*, NCJ-150709, Washington, D.C.: U.S. Department of Justice, 1994, pp. 5-16.

★2949★

Drug Use and Abuse

Drug Use By Male Juvenile Arrestees, 1993, By Type of Drug and Age: Ages 17 to 18 Years Using Marijuana

[In percent testing positive for drug use]

City	Percent	Rank
Birmingham, AL	36	6
Cleveland, OH	36	6
Denver, CO	62	1
Indianapolis, IN	39	4
Los Angeles, CA	26	9
Phoenix, AZ	44	3
Portland, OR	26	9
Saint Louis, MO	17	10
San Antonio, TX	33	7
San Diego, CA	38	5
San Jose, CA	32	8
Washington, DC	54	2

Source: Maguire, Kathleen, and Ann L. Pastore, eds., *Sourcebook of Criminal Justice Statistics 1994*, U.S. Department of Justice, Bureau of Justice Statistics, Washington, D.C.: U.S. Government Printing Office, 1995, p. 419. Primary source: U.S. Department of Justice, National Institute of Justice, *Drug Use Forecasting 1993 Annual Report on Juvenile Arrestees/Detainees: Drugs and Crime in America's Cities*, NCJ-150709, Washington, D.C.: U.S. Department of Justice, 1994, pp. 5-16.

★2950★

Drug Use and Abuse

Drug Use By Male Juvenile Arrestees, 1993, By Type of Drug and Age: Ages 17 to 18 Years Using Multiple Drugs

Data refer to use of cocaine, opiates, marijuana, phencyclidine (PCP), methadone, benzodiazepines, methaqualone, propoxyphene, barbiturates, and amphetamines.

[In percent testing positive for drug use]

City	Percent	Rank
Birmingham, AL	8	7
Cleveland, OH	19	1
Denver, CO	11	5
Indianapolis, IN	6	8
Los Angeles, CA	14	4
Phoenix, AZ	16	2
Portland, OR	6	8
Saint Louis, MO	0	10
San Antonio, TX	3	9
San Diego, CA	15	3
San Jose, CA	10	6
Washington, DC	19	1

Source: Maguire, Kathleen, and Ann L. Pastore, eds., *Sourcebook of Criminal Justice Statistics 1994*, U.S. Department of Justice, Bureau of Justice Statistics, Washington, D.C.: U.S. Government Printing Office, 1995, p. 419. Primary source: U.S. Department of Justice, National Institute of Justice, *Drug Use Forecasting 1993 Annual Report on Juvenile Arrestees/Detainees: Drugs and Crime in America's Cities*, NCJ-150709, Washington, D.C.: U.S. Department of Justice, 1994, pp. 5-16.

★2951★

Drug Use and Abuse

Drug Use By Male Juvenile Arrestees, 1993, By Type of Drug and Age: Ages 17 to 18 Years Using Opiates

[In percent testing positive for drug use]

City	Percent	Rank
Birmingham, AL	1	2
Cleveland, OH	0	3
Denver, CO	1	2
Indianapolis, IN	2	1
Portland, OR	1	2
Saint Louis, MO	0	3
San Antonio, TX	0	3
San Diego, CA	2	1
San Jose, CA	0	3
Washington, DC	2	1

Source: Maguire, Kathleen, and Ann L. Pastore, eds., *Sourcebook of Criminal Justice Statistics 1994*, U.S. Department of Justice, Bureau of Justice Statistics, Washington, D.C.: U.S. Government Printing Office, 1995, p. 419. Primary source: U.S. Department of Justice, National Institute of Justice, *Drug Use Forecasting 1993 Annual Report on Juvenile Arrestees/Detainees: Drugs and Crime in America's Cities*, NCJ-150709, Washington, D.C.: U.S. Department of Justice, 1994, pp. 5-16.

★2952★

Drug Use and Abuse

Drug Use By Male Juvenile Arrestees, 1993, By Type of Drug and Age: Total Number for Ages 13 to 18 Years Using Any Drug

Data refer to use of cocaine, opiates, marijuana, phencyclidine (PCP), methadone, benzodiazepines, barbiturates, and amphetamines. Data are collected at 12 Drug Use Forecasting (DUF) sites. There are no data presented for the "Age 9 to 12" category because 11 DUF sites reported less than 20 cases within each drug category.

[In percent testing positive for drug use]

City	Percent	Rank
Birmingham, AL	24	8
Cleveland, OH	36	4
Denver, CO	54	1
Indianapolis, IN	19	10
Los Angeles, CA	34	5
Phoenix, AZ	36	4
Portland, OR	18	11
Saint Louis, MO	20	9
San Antonio, TX	32	6
San Diego, CA	43	3
San Jose, CA	30	7
Washington, DC	51	2

Source: Maguire, Kathleen, and Ann L. Pastore, eds., *Sourcebook of Criminal Justice Statistics 1994*, U.S. Department of Justice, Bureau of Justice Statistics, Washington, D.C.: U.S. Government Printing Office, 1995, p. 419. Primary source: U.S. Department of Justice, National Institute of Justice, *Drug Use Forecasting 1993 Annual Report on Juvenile Arrestees/Detainees: Drugs and Crime in America's Cities*, NCJ-150709, Washington, D.C.: U.S. Department of Justice, 1994, pp. 5-16.

★2953★

Drug Use and Abuse

Drug Use By Male Juvenile Arrestees, 1993, By Type of Drug and Age: Total Number for Ages 13 to 18 Years Using Cocaine

[In percent testing positive for drug use]

City	Percent	Rank
Birmingham, AL	5	6
Cleveland, OH	18	1
Denver, CO	8	3
Indianapolis, IN	2	8
Los Angeles, CA	13	2
Phoenix, AZ	8	3
Portland, OR	4	7
Saint Louis, MO	6	5
San Antonio, TX	7	4
San Diego, CA	6	5
San Jose, CA	4	7
Washington, DC	7	4

Source: Maguire, Kathleen, and Ann L. Pastore, eds., *Sourcebook of Criminal Justice Statistics 1994*, U.S. Department of Justice, Bureau of Justice Statistics, Washington, D.C.: U.S. Government Printing Office, 1995, p. 419. Primary source: U.S. Department of Justice, National Institute of Justice, *Drug Use Forecasting 1993 Annual Report on Juvenile Arrestees/Detainees: Drugs and Crime in America's Cities*, NCJ-150709, Washington, D.C.: U.S. Department of Justice, 1994, pp. 5-16.

★2954★

Drug Use and Abuse

Drug Use By Male Juvenile Arrestees, 1993, By Type of Drug and Age: Total Number for Ages 13 to 18 Years Using Marijuana

[In percent testing positive for drug use]

City	Percent	Rank
Birmingham, AL	22	9
Cleveland, OH	27	6
Denver, CO	51	1
Indianapolis, IN	18	10
Los Angeles, CA	24	8
Phoenix, AZ	31	4
Portland, OR	14	12
Saint Louis, MO	16	11
San Antonio, TX	30	5
San Diego, CA	35	3
San Jose, CA	25	7
Washington, DC	47	2

Source: Maguire, Kathleen, and Ann L. Pastore, eds., *Sourcebook of Criminal Justice Statistics 1994*, U.S. Department of Justice, Bureau of Justice Statistics, Washington, D.C.: U.S. Government Printing Office, 1995, p. 419. Primary source: U.S. Department of Justice, National Institute of Justice, *Drug Use Forecasting 1993 Annual Report on Juvenile Arrestees/Detainees: Drugs and Crime in America's Cities*, NCJ-150709, Washington, D.C.: U.S. Department of Justice, 1994, pp. 5-16.

★2955★

Drug Use and Abuse

Drug Use By Male Juvenile Arrestees, 1993, By Type of Drug and Age: Total Number for Ages 13 to 18 Years Using Multiple Drugs

Data refer to use of cocaine, opiates, marijuana, phencyclidine (PCP), methadone, benzodiazepines, methaqualone, propoxyphene, barbiturates, and amphetamines.

[In percent testing positive for drug use]

City	Percent	Rank
Birmingham, AL	5	8
Cleveland, OH	11	3
Denver, CO	8	5
Indianapolis, IN	3	9
Los Angeles, CA	10	4
Phoenix, AZ	8	5
Portland, OR	2	10
Saint Louis, MO	2	10
San Antonio, TX	7	6
San Diego, CA	13	2
San Jose, CA	6	7
Washington, DC	14	1

Source: Maguire, Kathleen, and Ann L. Pastore, eds., *Sourcebook of Criminal Justice Statistics 1994*, U.S. Department of Justice, Bureau of Justice Statistics, Washington, D.C.: U.S. Government Printing Office, 1995, p. 419. Primary source: U.S. Department of Justice, National Institute of Justice, *Drug Use Forecasting 1993 Annual Report on Juvenile Arrestees/Detainees: Drugs and Crime in America's Cities*, NCJ-150709, Washington, D.C.: U.S. Department of Justice, 1994, pp. 5-16.

★2956★

Drug Use and Abuse

Drug Use By Male Juvenile Arrestees, 1993, By Type of Drug and Age: Total Number for Ages 13 to 18 Years Using Opiates

[In percent testing positive for drug use]

City	Percent	Rank
Birmingham, AL	1	2
Cleveland, OH	0	3
San Antonio, TX	2	1
San Diego, CA	1	2
Washington, DC	1	2

Source: Maguire, Kathleen, and Ann L. Pastore, eds., *Sourcebook of Criminal Justice Statistics 1994*, U.S. Department of Justice, Bureau of Justice Statistics, Washington, D.C.: U.S. Government Printing Office, 1995, p. 419. Primary source: U.S. Department of Justice, National Institute of Justice, *Drug Use Forecasting 1993 Annual Report on Juvenile Arrestees/Detainees: Drugs and Crime in America's Cities*, NCJ-150709, Washington, D.C.: U.S. Department of Justice, 1994, pp. 5-16.

★2957★

Prisons and Prison Population

Correctional Facilities (Private), 1994: Population

City/Location	Population	Rank
Clifton, TN	1,287	1
Kinder, LA	1,277	2
Winnfield, LA	1,277	2
Mineral Wells, TX	1,045	3
Venus, TX	1,000	4

[Continued]

★2957★

Correctional Facilities (Private), 1994: Population
[Continued]

City/Location	Population	Rank
Nashville, TN	993	5
Eloy, AZ	850	6
Newton County, TX	751	7
Eden, TX	700	8
Groesbeck, TX	664	9
San Antonio, TX	540	10
Cleveland, TX	520	11
Kyle, TX	518	12
Hinton, OK	502	13
Beattyville, KY	500	14
Saint Marys, KY	500	14
Lockhart, TX	498.5	15
Florence, AZ	466	16
Marana, AZ	448	17
Spur, TX	439	18
Desert Center, CA	434	19
Chattanooga, TN	414	20
Fort Worth, TX	401	21
Houston, TX	371	22
Bridgeport, TX	360	23

Source: Maguire, Kathleen, and Ann L. Pastore, eds., *Sourcebook of Criminal Justice Statistics 1994*, U.S. Department of Justice, Bureau of Justice Statistics, Washington, D.C.: U.S. Government Printing Office, 1995, p. 102. Primary source: Charles W. Thomas, *Private Adult Correctional Facility Census*, Eighth edition, Center for Studies in Criminology and Law (Gainesville, FL: University of Florida, 1995). Table adapted by *Sourcebook of Criminal Justice Statistics* staff. *Note:* Data are shown only for the top 25 areas.

★2958★

Prisons and Prison Population

Correctional Facilities (Private), 1994: Rated Capacity

City/Location	Capacity	Rank
Henderson County, TX	1,500	1
Clifton, TN	1,336	2
Palm Beach County, FL	1,318	3
Kinder, LA	1,282	4
Winnfield, LA	1,282	4
Mineral Wells, TX	1,100	5
Nashville, TN	1,092	6
Venus, TX	1,040	7
Greenwood, MS	1,019	8
Eloy, AZ	1,000	9
Holly Springs, MS	1,000	9
Jack County, TX	1,000	9
Travis County, TX	1,000	9
Willacy County, TX	1,000	9
Williamson County, TX	1,000	9
Holdenville, OK	960	10
Newton County, TX	872	11
Groesbeck, TX	836	12
Gretna, FL	768	13
Bay County, FL	750	14
Glades County, FL	750	14
Eden, TX	710	15
San Antonio, TX	623	16

[Continued]

★2958★

Correctional Facilities (Private), 1994: Rated Capacity
[Continued]

City/Location	Capacity	Rank
Cleveland, TX	520	17
Kyle, TX	520	17

Source: Maguire, Kathleen, and Ann L. Pastore, eds., *Sourcebook of Criminal Justice Statistics 1994,* U.S. Department of Justice, Bureau of Justice Statistics, Washington, D.C.: U.S. Government Printing Office, 1995, p. 102. Primary source: Charles W. Thomas, *Private Adult Correctional Facility Census,* Eighth edition, Center for Studies in Criminology and Law (Gainesville, FL: University of Florida, 1995). Table adapted by *Sourcebook of Criminal Justice Statistics* staff. *Note:* Data are shown only for the top 25 areas.

★2959★

Prisons and Prison Population

Federal Correctional Institutions, 1993: Average Daily Population

City/Location	Pop.	Rank
Allenwood, PA	741.5	37
Ashland, KY	1,041	21
Bastrop, TX	1,127	13
Big Spring, TX	1,013	24
Butner, NC	807	34
Danbury, CT	615	39
Dublin, CA	1,006	25
El Reno, OK	1,717	1
Englewood, CO	861	32
Estill, SC	198	41
Fairton, NJ	1,080	17
Florence, CO	931	31
Fort Dix, NJ	987	29
Fort Worth, TX	1,364	4
Jesup, GA	1,203	11
La Tuna, TX	995	28
Lompoc, CA	1,053	20
Loretto, PA	542	40
Manchester, KY	946	30
Marianna, FL	1,275	8
McKean, PA	1,116	14
Memphis, TN	1,304	6
Milan, MI	1,474	3
Morgantown, WV	781	35
Oakdale, LA	1,362	5
Otisville, NY	1,022	23
Oxford, WI	997	27
Petersburg, VA	1,059	19
Phoenix, AZ	1,282	7
Ray Brook, NY	1,001	26
Safford, AZ	696	38
Sandstone, MN	849	33
Schuylkill, PA	1,079	18
Seagoville, TX	1,112	16
Sheridan, OR	1,257	9
Talladega, AL	1,028	22
Tallahassee, FL	1,477	2
Terminal Island, CA	1,235	10
Texarkana, TX	1,113	15

[Continued]

★2959★

Federal Correctional Institutions, 1993: Average Daily Population
[Continued]

City/Location	Pop.	Rank
Three Rivers, TX	1,194	12
Tucson, AZ	753	36

Source: Maguire, Kathleen, and Ann L. Pastore, eds., *Sourcebook of Criminal Justice Statistics 1994,* U.S. Department of Justice, Bureau of Justice Statistics, Washington, D.C.: U.S. Government Printing Office, 1995, p. 110. Primary source: U.S. Department of Justice, Federal Bureau of Prisons, *State of the Bureau 1993: A Day in the Life,* Washington, D.C.: U.S. Department of Justice, 1995, pp. 45-59. Table constructed by *Sourcebook of Criminal Justice Statistics* staff.

★2960★

Prisons and Prison Population

Federal Correctional Institutions, 1993: Rated Capacity

City/Location	Capacity	Rank
Allenwood, PA	907	6
Ashland, KY	730	21
Bastrop, TX	971	4
Big Spring, TX	472	32
Butner, NC	513	29
Danbury, CT	520	28
Dublin, CA	634	24
El Reno, OK	931	5
Englewood, CO	506	30
Estill, SC	858	8
Fairton, NJ	733	20
Florence, CO	744	18
Fort Dix, NJ	1,872	1
Fort Worth, TX	1,056	3
Jesup, GA	744	18
La Tuna, TX	528	27
Lompoc, CA	472	32
Loretto, PA	477	31
Manchester, KY	756	16
Marianna, FL	805	12
McKean, PA	744	18
Memphis, TN	810	11
Milan, MI	1,116	2
Morgantown, WV	854	9
Oakdale, LA	850	10
Otisville, NY	631	25
Oxford, WI	586	26
Petersburg, VA	734	19
Phoenix, AZ	793	13
Ray Brook, NY	780	15
Safford, AZ	431	34
Sandstone, MN	452	33
Schuylkill, PA	729	22
Seagoville, TX	805	12
Sheridan, OR	749	17
Talladega, AL	699	23
Tallahassee, FL	886	7
Terminal Island, CA	452	33
Texarkana, TX	749	17

[Continued]

★2960★

Federal Correctional Institutions, 1993: Rated Capacity
[Continued]

City/Location	Capacity	Rank
Three Rivers, TX	784	14
Tucson, AZ	389	35

Source: Maguire, Kathleen, and Ann L. Pastore, eds., *Sourcebook of Criminal Justice Statistics 1994,* U.S. Department of Justice, Bureau of Justice Statistics, Washington, D.C.: U.S. Government Printing Office, 1995, p. 110. Primary source: U.S. Department of Justice, Federal Bureau of Prisons, *State of the Bureau 1993: A Day in the Life,* Washington, D.C.: U.S. Department of Justice, 1995, pp. 45-59. Table constructed by *Sourcebook of Criminal Justice Statistics* staff.

★2961★
Prisons and Prison Population

Federal Correctional Institutions, 1993: Staff (Number)

City/Location	Staff	Rank
Allenwood, PA	263	29
Ashland, KY	350	8
Bastrop, TX	251	32
Big Spring, TX	252	31
Butner, NC	390	4
Danbury, CT	300	24
Dublin, CA	290	26
El Reno, OK	488	1
Englewood, CO	329	17
Estill, SC	289	27
Fairton, NJ	341	12
Florence, CO	370	6
Fort Dix, NJ	370	6
Fort Worth, TX	395	3
Jesup, GA	323	20
La Tuna, TX	315	22
Lompoc, CA	186	36
Loretto, PA	227	34
Manchester, KY	326	18
Marianna, FL	366	7
McKean, PA	325	19
Memphis, TN	305	23
Milan, MI	418	2
Morgantown, WV	210	35
Oakdale, LA	299	25
Otisville, NY	334	15
Oxford, WI	336	14
Petersburg, VA	375	5
Phoenix, AZ	349	9
Ray Brook, NY	290	26
Safford, AZ	183	37
Sandstone, MN	253	30
Schuylkill, PA	348	10
Seagoville, TX	268	28
Sheridan, OR	325	19
Talladega, AL	339	13
Tallahassee, FL	346	11
Terminal Island, CA	331	16
Texarkana, TX	316	21

[Continued]

★2961★

Federal Correctional Institutions, 1993: Staff (Number)
[Continued]

City/Location	Staff	Rank
Three Rivers, TX	299	25
Tucson, AZ	243	33

Source: Maguire, Kathleen, and Ann L. Pastore, eds., *Sourcebook of Criminal Justice Statistics 1994,* U.S. Department of Justice, Bureau of Justice Statistics, Washington, D.C.: U.S. Government Printing Office, 1995, p. 110. Primary source: U.S. Department of Justice, Federal Bureau of Prisons, *State of the Bureau 1993: A Day in the Life,* Washington, D.C.: U.S. Department of Justice, 1995, pp. 45-59. Table constructed by *Sourcebook of Criminal Justice Statistics* staff.

★2962★
Prisons and Prison Population

Federal Prison Camps, 1993: Average Daily Population

City/Location	Pop.	Rank
Alderson, WV	975	1
Allenwood, PA	728	4
Boron, CA	568	7
Bryan, TX	703	5
Duluth, MN	610	6
Eglin, FL	901	2
El Paso, TX	470	12
Maxwell, AL	864	3
Millington, TN	420	13
Nellis, NV	476	11
Pensacola, FL	497	10
Seymour Johnson, NC	529	8
Yankton, SD	509	9

Source: Maguire, Kathleen, and Ann L. Pastore, eds., *Sourcebook of Criminal Justice Statistics 1994,* U.S. Department of Justice, Bureau of Justice Statistics, Washington, D.C.: U.S. Government Printing Office, 1995, p. 110. Primary source: U.S. Department of Justice, Federal Bureau of Prisons, *State of the Bureau 1993: A Day in the Life,* Washington, D.C.: U.S. Department of Justice, 1995, pp. 45-59. Table constructed by *Sourcebook of Criminal Justice Statistics* staff.

★2963★
Prisons and Prison Population

Federal Prison Camps, 1993: Rated Capacity

City/Location	Capacity	Rank
Alderson, WV	1,094	1
Allenwood, PA	534	6
Boron, CA	340	10
Bryan, TX	480	7
Duluth, MN	693	3
Eglin, FL	560	5
El Paso, TX	257	13
Maxwell, AL	960	2
Millington, TN	403	9
Nellis, NV	263	12
Pensacola, FL	312	11

[Continued]

★2963★

Federal Prison Camps, 1993: Rated Capacity
[Continued]

City/Location	Capacity	Rank
Seymour Johnson, NC	576	4
Yankton, SD	406	8

Source: Maguire, Kathleen, and Ann L. Pastore, eds., *Sourcebook of Criminal Justice Statistics 1994*, U.S. Department of Justice, Bureau of Justice Statistics, Washington, D.C.: U.S. Government Printing Office, 1995, p. 110. Primary source: U.S. Department of Justice, Federal Bureau of Prisons, *State of the Bureau 1993: A Day in the Life,* Washington, D.C.: U.S. Department of Justice, 1995, pp. 45-59. Table constructed by *Sourcebook of Criminal Justice Statistics* staff.

★2964★

Prisons and Prison Population

Federal Prison Camps, 1993: Staff (Number)

City/Location	Staff	Rank
Alderson, WV	350	1
Allenwood, PA	147	4
Boron, CA	248	2
Bryan, TX	143	6
Duluth, MN	152	3
Eglin, FL	144	5
El Paso, TX	103	9
Maxwell, AL	127	7
Millington, TN	83	11
Nellis, NV	67	12
Pensacola, FL	99	10
Seymour Johnson, NC	103	9
Yankton, SD	126	8

Source: Maguire, Kathleen, and Ann L. Pastore, eds., *Sourcebook of Criminal Justice Statistics 1994*, U.S. Department of Justice, Bureau of Justice Statistics, Washington, D.C.: U.S. Government Printing Office, 1995, p. 110. Primary source: U.S. Department of Justice, Federal Bureau of Prisons, *State of the Bureau 1993: A Day in the Life,* Washington, D.C.: U.S. Department of Justice, 1995, pp. 45-59. Table constructed by *Sourcebook of Criminal Justice Statistics* staff.

★2965★

Prisons and Prison Population

Federal Prison Satellite Camps, 1993: Average Daily Population

The source defines a satellite camp as a federal prison camp that is adjacent to the main federal prison camp.

City/Location	Pop.	Rank
Ashland, KY	273	15
Atlanta, GA	508	2
Bastrop, TX	25	31
Big Spring, TX	185	23
Bryan, TX	117	28
Butner, NC	261	18
Danbury, CT	179	24
Dublin, CA	227	21
El Reno, OK	272	16
Englewood, CO	122	27
Estill, SC	248	19
Fairton, NJ	74	30
Florence, CO	238	20
Jesup, GA	462	3

[Continued]

★2965★

Federal Prison Satellite Camps, 1993: Average Daily Population
[Continued]

City/Location	Pop.	Rank
La Tuna, TX	314	8
Leavenworth, KS	371	5
Lewisburg, PA	197.5	22
Lompoc, CA	292	11
Manchester, KY	375	4
Marianna, FL	295	10
Marion, IL	276	13
McKean, PA	265	17
Miami, FL	146	26
Oakdale, LA	84	29
Oxford, WI	158	25
Petersburg, VA	275	14
Phoenix, AZ	287	12
Schuylkill, PA	272	16
Sheridan, OR	514	1
Talladega, AL	307	9
Terre Haute, IN	370	6
Texarkana, TX	292	11
Three Rivers, TX	354	7

Source: Maguire, Kathleen, and Ann L. Pastore, eds., *Sourcebook of Criminal Justice Statistics 1994*, U.S. Department of Justice, Bureau of Justice Statistics, Washington, D.C.: U.S. Government Printing Office, 1995, p. 111. Primary source: U.S. Department of Justice, Federal Bureau of Prisons, *State of the Bureau 1993: A Day in the Life,* Washington, D.C.: U.S. Department of Justice, 1995, pp. 45-59. Table constructed by *Sourcebook of Criminal Justice Statistics* staff.

★2966★

Prisons and Prison Population

Federal Prison Satellite Camps, 1993: Rated Capacity

The source defines a satellite camp as a federal prison camp that is adjacent to the main federal prison camp.

City/Location	Capacity	Rank
Ashland, KY	296	6
Atlanta, GA	488	3
Bastrop, TX	94	23
Big Spring, TX	108	19
Bryan, TX	62	25
Butner, NC	296	6
Danbury, CT	96	22
Dublin, CA	225	12
El Reno, OK	144	18
Englewood, CO	74	24
Estill, SC	256	10
Fairton, NJ	49	26
Florence, CO	512	1
Jesup, GA	508	2
La Tuna, TX	164	15
Leavenworth, KS	324	5
Lewisburg, PA	266	9
Lompoc, CA	206	13
Manchester, KY	512	1
Marianna, FL	296	6
Marion, IL	255	11

[Continued]

★2966★

Federal Prison Satellite Camps, 1993: Rated Capacity
[Continued]

City/Location	Capacity	Rank
McKean, PA	296	6
Miami, FL	98	21
Oakdale, LA	94	23
Oxford, WI	106	20
Petersburg, VA	148	16
Phoenix, AZ	272	8
Schuylkill, PA	296	6
Sheridan, OR	384	4
Talladega, AL	296	6
Terre Haute, IN	284	7
Texarkana, TX	147	17
Three Rivers, TX	192	14

Source: Maguire, Kathleen, and Ann L. Pastore, eds., *Sourcebook of Criminal Justice Statistics 1994*, U.S. Department of Justice, Bureau of Justice Statistics, Washington, D.C.: U.S. Government Printing Office, 1995, p. 111. Primary source: U.S. Department of Justice, Federal Bureau of Prisons, *State of the Bureau 1993: A Day in the Life*, Washington, D.C.: U.S. Department of Justice, 1995, pp. 45-59. Table constructed by *Sourcebook of Criminal Justice Statistics* staff.

★2967★
Prisons and Prison Population

Metropolitan Correctional/Detention Centers, 1993: Average Daily Population

City/Location	Pop.	Rank
Chicago, IL	604	9
Lexington, KY	1,916	1
Los Angeles, CA	1,028	4
Miami, FL	729	7
New York, NY	814	6
Oakdale, LA	657	8
Rochester, MN	827	5
San Diego, CA	1,149	2
Springfield, MO	1,071	3

Source: Maguire, Kathleen, and Ann L. Pastore, eds., *Sourcebook of Criminal Justice Statistics 1994*, U.S. Department of Justice, Bureau of Justice Statistics, Washington, D.C.: U.S. Government Printing Office, 1995, p. 111. Primary source: U.S. Department of Justice, Federal Bureau of Prisons, *State of the Bureau 1993: A Day in the Life*, Washington, D.C.: U.S. Department of Justice, 1995, pp. 45-59. Table constructed by *Sourcebook of Criminal Justice Statistics* staff.

★2968★
Prisons and Prison Population

Metropolitan Correctional/Detention Centers, 1993: Rated Capacity

City/Location	Capacity	Rank
Chicago, IL	411	9
Lexington, KY	1,307	1
Los Angeles, CA	728	3
Miami, FL	496	8
New York, NY	523	7
Oakdale, LA	621	5
Rochester, MN	609	6

[Continued]

★2968★

Metropolitan Correctional/Detention Centers, 1993: Rated Capacity
[Continued]

City/Location	Capacity	Rank
San Diego, CA	622	4
Springfield, MO	1,014	2

Source: Maguire, Kathleen, and Ann L. Pastore, eds., *Sourcebook of Criminal Justice Statistics 1994*, U.S. Department of Justice, Bureau of Justice Statistics, Washington, D.C.: U.S. Government Printing Office, 1995, p. 111. Primary source: U.S. Department of Justice, Federal Bureau of Prisons, *State of the Bureau 1993: A Day in the Life*, Washington, D.C.: U.S. Department of Justice, 1995, pp. 45-59. Table constructed by *Sourcebook of Criminal Justice Statistics* staff.

★2969★
Prisons and Prison Population

Metropolitan Correctional/Detention Centers, 1993: Staff (Number)

City/Location	Staff	Rank
Chicago, IL	241	9
Lexington, KY	510	2
Los Angeles, CA	276	7
Miami, FL	342	4
New York, NY	312	5
Oakdale, LA	245	8
Rochester, MN	469	3
San Diego, CA	286	6
Springfield, MO	681	1

Source: Maguire, Kathleen, and Ann L. Pastore, eds., *Sourcebook of Criminal Justice Statistics 1994*, U.S. Department of Justice, Bureau of Justice Statistics, Washington, D.C.: U.S. Government Printing Office, 1995, p. 111. Primary source: U.S. Department of Justice, Federal Bureau of Prisons, *State of the Bureau 1993: A Day in the Life*, Washington, D.C.: U.S. Department of Justice, 1995, pp. 45-59. Table constructed by *Sourcebook of Criminal Justice Statistics* staff.

★2970★
Prisons and Prison Population

United States Penitentiaries, 1993: Average Daily Population

City/Location	Population	Rank
Allenwood, PA	56	7
Atlanta, GA	2,067	1
Leavenworth, KS	1,611	2
Lewisburg, PA	1,374	5
Lompoc, CA	1,683	3
Marion, IL	353	6
Terre Haute, IN	1,395	4

Source: Maguire, Kathleen, and Ann L. Pastore, eds., *Sourcebook of Criminal Justice Statistics 1994*, U.S. Department of Justice, Bureau of Justice Statistics, Washington, D.C.: U.S. Government Printing Office, 1995, p. 110. Primary source: U.S. Department of Justice, Federal Bureau of Prisons, *State of the Bureau 1993: A Day in the Life*, Washington, D.C.: U.S. Department of Justice, 1995, pp. 45-59. Table constructed by *Sourcebook of Criminal Justice Statistics* staff.

★2971★

Prisons and Prison Population

United States Penitentiaries, 1993: Rated Capacity

City/Location	Capacity	Rank
Allenwood, PA	640	6
Atlanta, GA	1,349	1
Leavenworth, KS	1,114	2
Lewisburg, PA	902	4
Lompoc, CA	1,099	3
Marion, IL	440	7
Terre Haute, IN	766	5

Source: Maguire, Kathleen, and Ann L. Pastore, eds., *Sourcebook of Criminal Justice Statistics 1994*, U.S. Department of Justice, Bureau of Justice Statistics, Washington, D.C.: U.S. Government Printing Office, 1995, p. 110. Primary source: U.S. Department of Justice, Federal Bureau of Prisons, *State of the Bureau 1993: A Day in the Life,* Washington, D.C.: U.S. Department of Justice, 1995, pp. 45-59. Table constructed by *Sourcebook of Criminal Justice Statistics* staff.

★2972★

Prisons and Prison Population

United States Penitentiaries, 1993: Staff (Number)

City/Location	Staff	Rank
Allenwood, PA	265	7
Atlanta, GA	721	1
Leavenworth, KS	543	3
Lewisburg, PA	622	2
Lompoc, CA	519	4
Marion, IL	361	6
Terre Haute, IN	513	5

Source: Maguire, Kathleen, and Ann L. Pastore, eds., *Sourcebook of Criminal Justice Statistics 1994*, U.S. Department of Justice, Bureau of Justice Statistics, Washington, D.C.: U.S. Government Printing Office, 1995, p. 110. Primary source: U.S. Department of Justice, Federal Bureau of Prisons, *State of the Bureau 1993: A Day in the Life,* Washington, D.C.: U.S. Department of Justice, 1995, pp. 45-59. Table constructed by *Sourcebook of Criminal Justice Statistics* staff.

★2973★

Tax Crime

Internal Revenue Service Agents and Criminal Investigators, 1995: Number Per Million Persons

City	Agents per million	Rank
Washington, DC	663	1
Manhattan, NY	230	2
Fort Worth, TX	147	3
Oklahoma City, OK	113	4
Anchorage, AK	109	5
Chicago, IL	106	6
San Francisco, CA	104	7
Atlanta, GA	103	8
New Haven, CT	102	9
Cheyenne, WY	101	10
Denver, CO	98	11
Saint Louis, MO	98	11
New Orleans, LA	97	12

[Continued]

★2973★

Internal Revenue Service Agents and Criminal Investigators, 1995: Number Per Million Persons

[Continued]

City	Agents per million	Rank
Tulsa, OK	95	13
Houston, TX	92	14
Philadelphia, PA	92	14
Las Vegas, NV	89	15
Providence, RI	89	15
Los Angeles, CA	86	16
Miami, FL	85	17
Wilmington, DE	85	17
Boston, MA	83	18
Fargo, ND	80	19
Nashville, TN	80	19
Topeka, KS	79	20

Source: Johnston, David Cay, "Where the IRS Aims the Prosecution Ax," *New York Times,* 14 April 1996, p. 9. *Note:* Data are shown only for the top 25 areas.

★2974★

Tax Crime

Tax-Crime Referrals to the Internal Revenue Service, 1995: Rate Per Million Persons

City	Referrals per million	Rank
Washington, DC	71	1
Tulsa, OK	65	2
Louisville, KY	60	3
Oklahoma City, OK	55	4
Charleston, WV	45	5
Roanoke, VA	43	6
Wheeling, WV	42	7
Manhattan, NY	39	8
Pittsburgh, PA	34	9
Las Vegas, NV	32	10
Honolulu, HI	31	11
Anchorage, AK	30	12
Fargo, ND	30	12
Miami, FL	30	12
Wilmington, DE	30	12
New York, NY	28	13
San Antonio, TX	27	14
Columbia, SC	26	15
Tampa, FL	25	16
Fort Worth, TX	23	17
Memphis, TN	23	17
Scranton, PA	23	17
Mobile, AL	22	18
Indianapolis, IN	20	19
New Orleans, LA	20	19

Source: Johnston, David Cay, "Where the IRS Aims the Prosecution Ax," *New York Times,* 14 April 1996, p. 9. *Note:* Data are shown only for the top 25 areas.

PART VII

LEISURE TIME

Contents

Chapter 32

ARTS AND LEISURE

Topics Covered

Finances and Expenditures
Parks and Recreation
Public Libraries
Sports Activities
Television Viewing
Travel and Tourism

★2975★
Finances and Expenditures

Cities With the Highest Grant Amounts Received From the National Endowment for the Arts, 1995

[In millions of dollars]

City	Amount	Rank
Atlanta, GA	2.6	6
Baltimore, MD	1.9	9
Boston, MA	2.3	8
Chicago, IL	3.6	3
Los Angeles, CA	3.4	4
Minneapolis, MN	2.9	5
New York, NY	23.9	1
Philadelphia, PA	2.5	7
San Francisco, CA	3.8	2
Sante Fe, NM	2.3	8

Source: "Grants to States, Other California Cities: *San Francisco Examiner,* 27 August 1995, p. A-10. Primary source: California Department of Education.

★2976★
Finances and Expenditures

Entertainment Spending, 1995-2000: Leading Counties

Data refer to purchases including movie, theater, theme park, and sporting events tickets; reading materials, and videos.

[In percentage of growth]

County	Growth percentage	Rank
Martin County, FL	57	1
Orange County, NC	55	2
Summit County, UT	54	3
Saint Lucie County, FL	54	3
Palm Beach County, FL	52	4
Wake County, NC	51	5
Williamsburg/James City, VA	51	5
Lee County, FL	50	6
Williamson County, TX	50	6
Putnam County, GA	50	6

Source: "Having Fun," *Wall Street Journal,* 5 April 1996, p. B8. Primary source: Equifax National Decision Systems, San Diego, California.

★2977★
Parks and Recreation

National Parks Acreage, 1991

The top 25 parks according to the number of visitors in April 1994 (represented in the table by the cities in which they are located), are ranked by their total acreage.

[In acres]

Cities	Acreage	Rank
Yellowstone National Park, WY	2,219,790.71	1
Boulder City, NV	1,495,665.52	2
Page, AZ	1,236,880	3
Grand Canyon, AZ	1,218,375.24	4
Port Angeles, WA	922,653.99	5
National Park, CA	761,170.20	6

[Continued]

★2977★

National Parks Acreage, 1991
[Continued]

Cities	Acreage	Rank
Gatlinburg, TN	520,269.44	7
Estes Park, CO	265,197.86	8
Asheville, NC	85,954.83	9
Gulf Breeze-Ocean Springs, FL-MS	73,958.82	10
San Francisco, CA[1]	73,121.82	11
Bushkill, PA	66,651.86	12
Tupelo, MS	51,742.09	13
South Wellfleet, MA	43,557.24	14
Bar Harbor, ME	41,888.01	15
Brooklyn, NY	26,310.93	16
Sharpsburg, MD	19,236.60	17
Dunwoody, GA	9,256.69	18
McLean, VA	7,159.46	19
Washington, DC[2]	6,467.85	20
New York, NY[3]	58.38	21
San Francisco, CA[4]	50	22
Philadelphia, PA	44.85	23
Washington, DC[5]	17.50	24
New York, NY[6]	1	25

Source: Department of the Interior, National Park Service, Office of Public Affairs and the Division of Publications: *The National Parks: Index 1991,* pp. 16-101, Washington, DC: U.S. Government Printing Office. *Notes:* 1. Golden Gate National Recreation Area. 2. National Capital Parks. 3. Statue of Liberty National Monument. 4. San Francisco Maritime National Historical Park. 5. John F. Kennedy Center for the Performing Arts. 6. Castle Clinton National Monument.

★2978★
Parks and Recreation

National Parks By Age, 1991

The top 25 parks according to the number of visitors in April 1994 (represented in the table by the cities in which they are located), are ranked by the years in which they were established or authorized (from oldest to youngest).

Cities	Established or authorized	Rank
Yellowstone National Park, WY	1872	1
National Park, CA	1890	2
Bar Harbor, ME	1919	3
Grand Canyon, AZ	1919	3
Estes Park, CO	1915	4
Washington, DC[1]	1923	5
New York, NY[2]	1924	6
McLean, VA	1930	7
Gatlinburg, TN	1934	8
Asheville, NC	1936	9
Port Angeles, WA	1938	10
Sharpsburg, MD	1938	10
Tupelo, MS	1938	10
New York, NY[3]	1946	11
Philadelphia, PA	1956	12
Washington, DC[4]	1958	13
Boulder City, NV	1964	14
Bushkill, PA	1965	15
South Wellfleet, MA	1966	16
Gulf Breeze-Ocean Springs, FL-MS	1971	17

[Continued]

★ 2978 ★

National Parks By Age, 1991

[Continued]

Cities	Established or authorized	Rank
Brooklyn, NY	1972	18
Page, AZ	1972	18
San Francisco, CA[5]	1972	18
Dunwoody, GA	1978	19
San Francisco, CA[6]	1988	20

Source: Department of the Interior, National Park Service, Office of Public Affairs and the Division of Publications: *The National Parks: Index 1991*, pp. 16-101, Washington, DC: U.S. Government Printing Office. *Notes:* National Parks established or authorized during the same year are ranked equally. 1. National Capital Parks. 2. Statue of Liberty National Monument. 3. Castle Clinton National Monument. 4. John F. Kennedy Center for the Performing Arts. 5. Golden Gate National Recreation Area. 6. San Francisco Maritime National Historical Park.

★ 2979 ★

Parks and Recreation

National Parks Cemetery Land Totals, 1991

National Parks (represented in the table by the cities in which they are located), are ranked according to their cemetery acreage.

[In acres]

Cities	Cemetery acreage	Rank
Vicksburg, MS	116.28	1
Gettysburg, PA	20.58	2
Murfreesboro, TN	20.09	3
Dover, TN	15.34	4
Fredericksburg, VA	12.0	5
Sharpsburg, MD	11.36	6
Shiloh, TN	10.05	7
Petersburg, VA	8.72	8
Yorktown, VA	2.91	9

Source: Department of the Interior, National Park Service, Office of Public Affairs and the Division of Publications: *The National Parks: Index 1991*, pp. 16-101, Washington, DC: U.S. Government Printing Office.

★ 2980 ★

Parks and Recreation

National Parks Federal Land Totals, 1991

The top 24 parks according to the number of visitors in April 1994 (represented in the table by the cities in which they are located), are ranked by their shares of federal acreage.

[In acres]

Cities	Acreage	Rank
Yellowstone National Park, WY	2,219,772.73	1
Boulder City, NV	1,468,952.15	2
Page, AZ	1,193,671	3
Grand Canyon, AZ	1,179,194.10	4
Port Angeles, WA	912,869.98	5
Gatlinburg, TN	520,003.78	6
National Park, CA	459,463.69	7
Estes Park, CO	264,747.10	8
Asheville, NC	78,837.76	9

[Continued]

★ 2980 ★

National Parks Federal Land Totals, 1991

[Continued]

Cities	Acreage	Rank
Gulf Breeze-Ocean Springs, FL-MS	69,150.03	10
Bushkill, PA	54,600.79	11
Tupelo, MS	51,651.13	12
Bar Harbor, ME	40,728.10	13
San Francisco, CA[1]	28,749.72	14
South Wellfleet, MA	27,386.39	15
Brooklyn, NY	20,375.87	16
Sharpsburg, MD	14,068.92	17
McLean, VA	7,088.61	18
Washington, DC[2]	6,467.85	19
Dunwoody, GA	4,005.03	20
New York, NY[3]	58.38	21
Philadelphia, PA	41.87	22
Washington, DC[4]	17.50	23
New York, NY[5]	1	24

Source: Department of the Interior, National Park Service, Office of Public Affairs and the Division of Publications: *The National Parks: Index 1991*, pp. 16-101, Washington, DC: U.S. Government Printing Office. *Notes:* 1. Golden Gate National Recreation Area. 2. National Capital Parks. 3. Statue of Liberty National Monument. 4. John F. Kennedy Center for the Performing Arts. 5. Castle Clinton National Monument.

★ 2981 ★

Parks and Recreation

National Parks Federal Reserve Land Totals, 1991

National Parks (represented in the table by the cities in which they are located), are ranked according to their federal reserve land acreage.

[In acres]

Cities	Acreage	Rank
Glennallen, AK	4,349,563.92	1
McKinley Park, AK	1,310,565	2
Anchorage, AK	1,288,259.61	3
Fairbanks, AK	948,504	4
King Salmon, AK[1]	454,151	5
King Salmon, AK[2]	374,000	6
Gustavus, AK	55,439	7

Source: Department of the Interior, National Park Service, Office of Public Affairs and the Division of Publications: *The National Parks: Index 1991*, pp. 16-101, Washington, DC: U.S. Government Printing Office. *Notes:* 1. Aniakchak National Monument and Preserve. 2. Katmai National Park and Preserve.

★2982★

Parks and Recreation

National Parks Land Area Totals, 1991

National Parks (represented in the table by the cities in which they are located), are ranked according to their land area acreage.

[In acres]

Cities	Land area	Rank
Boulder City, NV	1,348,075.70	1
International Falls, MN	138,266	2
Houghton, MI	133,781.87	3
Crescent City, CA	106,000	4
Munising, MI	63,122.08	5
Empire, MI	58,473	6
South Wellfleet, MA	27,004	7
Manteo, NC	26,326.24	8
St. Marys, GA	26,153.10	9
Bayfield, WI	16,321.90	10
Berlin, MD	15,977.67	11
Ocean Springs, MS	10,078.82	12
Morehead City, NC	8,741	13
Fritch, TX	7,768	14
St. Croix, VI	143	15

Source: Department of the Interior, National Park Service, Office of Public Affairs and the Division of Publications: *The National Parks: Index 1991*, pp. 16-101, Washington, DC: U.S. Government Printing Office.

★2983★

Parks and Recreation

National Parks Non-Federal Land Totals, 1991

The top parks according to the number of visitors in April 1994 (represented in the table by the cities in which they are located), are ranked by their shares of non-federal acreage.

[In acres]

Cities	Acreage	Rank
San Francisco, CA[1]	44,372.10	1
Page, AZ	43,209	2
Grand Canyon, AZ	39,181.24	3
Boulder City, NV	26,713.37	4
South Wellfleet, MA	16,171.40	5
Bushkill, PA	12,051.08	6
Port Angeles, WA	9,784.01	7
Asheville, NC	7,117.07	8
Brooklyn, NY	5,935.06	9
Dunwoody, GA	5,251.66	10
Sharpsburg, MD	5,167.68	11
Gulf Breeze-Ocean Springs, FL-MS	4,808.79	12
National Park, CA	1,706.51	13
Bar Harbor, ME	1,159.91	14
Estes Park, CO	450.76	15
Gatlinburg, TN	265.66	16
Tupelo, MS	90.96	17
McLean, VA	70.85	18
San Francisco, CA[2]	50	19
Yellowstone National Park, WY	17.98	20
Philadelphia, PA	2.98	21

Source: Department of the Interior, National Park Service, Office of Public Affairs and the Division of Publications: *The National Parks: Index 1991*, pp. 16-101, Washington, DC: U.S. Government Printing Office. *Notes:* 1. Golden Gate National Recreation Area. 2. San Francisco Maritime National Historical Park.

★2984★

Parks and Recreation

National Parks Non-Federal Reserve Land Totals, 1991

National Parks (represented in the table by the cities in which they are located), are ranked according to their non-federal reserve land acreage.

[In acres]

Cities	Acreage	Rank
Glennallen, AK	507,157.07	1
Anchorage, AK	119,033.39	2
King Salmon, AK[1]	11,452	3
Gustavus, AK	2,445	4
McKinley Park, AK	800	5
Fairbanks, AK	125	6

Source: Department of the Interior, National Park Service, Office of Public Affairs and the Division of Publications: *The National Parks: Index 1991*, pp. 16-101, Washington, DC: U.S. Government Printing Office. *Note:* 1. Aniakchak National Monument and Preserve.

★2985★

Parks and Recreation

National Parks Reserve Land Totals, 1991

National Parks (represented in the table by the cities in which they are located), are ranked according to their reserve land acreage.

[In acres]

Cities	Acreage	Rank
Glennallen, AK	4,856,720.99	1
Anchorage, AK	1,407,273	2
McKinley Park, AK	1,311,365	3
Fairbanks, AK	948,629	4
King Salmon, AK[1]	465,603	5
King Salmon, AK[2]	374,000	6
Gustavus, AK	57,884	7

Source: Department of the Interior, National Park Service, Office of Public Affairs and the Division of Publications: *The National Parks: Index 1991*, pp. 16-101, Washington, DC: U.S. Government Printing Office. *Notes:* 1. Aniakchak National Monument and Preserve. 2. Katmai National Park and Preserve.

★2986★

Parks and Recreation

National Parks Water Area Totals, 1991

National Parks (represented in the table by the cities in which they are located), are ranked according to their water areas.

[In acres]

Cities	Water area	Rank
Glennallen, AK	8,700,000	1
Homestead, FL	1,296,500	2
Port Angeles, WA	876,669	3
National Park, CA	677,600	4
Homestead, FL	625,000	5
Three Rivers, CA[3]	456,552	6
Twentynine Palms, CA	429,690	7
Ajo, AZ	312,600	8
Three Rivers, CA[4]	280,428	9
Ashford, WA	216,855	10

[Continued]

★ 2986 ★

National Parks Water Area Totals, 1991
[Continued]

Cities	Water area	Rank
Houghton, MI	132,018	11
Hawaii National Park, HI	123,100	12
International Falls, MN	83,789	13
Luray, VA	79,579	14
Mineral, CA	78,982	15
Tucson, AZ	71,400	16
Interior, SD	64,250	17
Petrified Forest National Park, AZ	50,260	18
Salt Flat, TX	46,850	19
Arco, ID	43,243	20
Mosca, CO	33,450	21
Carlsbad, NM	33,125	22
Medora, ND	29,920	23
Tulelake, CA	28,460	24
Point Reyes, CA	25,370	25
Los Alamos, NM	23,267	26
Berlin, MD	22,079	27
Makawao, HI	19,270	28
Hopkins, SC	15,000	29
Paicines, CA	12,952	30
Montrose, CO	11,180	31
Harrison, AR	10,529	32
Wilcox, AZ	9,440	33
St. Marys, GA	8,840	34
Park, CO	8,100	35
St. Thomas, VI	5,650	36
Estes Park, CO	2,917	37
Sulphur, OK	2,409	38
Kalaupapa, HI	2,000	39
Ocean Springs, MS	1,800	40
Patchogue, NY	1,363	41
Agana, GU	1,002	42

Source: Department of the Interior, National Park Service, Office of Public Affairs and the Division of Publications: *The National Parks: Index 1991*, pp. 16-101, Washington, DC: U.S. Government Printing Office.

★ 2987 ★

Parks and Recreation

National Parks Wilderness Lands Totals, 1991

National Parks (represented in the table by the cities in which they are located), are ranked according to their acreage of wilderness lands.

[In acres]

Cities	Acreage	Rank
Glennallen, AK	8,700,000	1
Fairbanks, AK	7,052,000	2
Kotzebue, AK[1]	5,800,000	3
King Salmon, AK	3,473,000	4
Gustavus, AK	2,770,000	5
Anchorage, AK	2,470,000	6
McKinley Park, AK	1,900,000	7
Homestead, FL	1,296,500	8
Port Angeles, WA	876,669	9
National Park, CA	677,600	10

[Continued]

★ 2987 ★

National Parks Wilderness Lands Totals, 1991
[Continued]

Cities	Acreage	Rank
Three Rivers, CA[2]	456,552	11
Twentynine Palms, CA	429,690	12
Ajo, AZ	312,600	13
Three Rivers, CA[3]	280,428	14
Ashford, WA	216,855	15
Kotzebue, AK[4]	190,000	16
Houghton, MI	132,018	17
Hawaii National Park, HI	123,100	18
Luray, VA	79,579	19
Mineral, CA	78,982	20
Tucson, AZ	71,400	21
Interior, SD	64,250	22
Petrified Forest National Park, AZ	50,260	23
Salt Flat, TX	46,850	24
Arco, ID	43,243	25
Mosca, CO	33,450	26
Carlsbad, NM	33,125	27
Medora, ND	29,920	28
Tulelake, CA	28,460	29
Point Reyes, CA	25,370	30
Los Alamos, NM	23,267	31
Makawao, HI	19,270	32
Hopkins, SC	15,000	33
Paicines, CA	12,952	34
Montrose, CO	11,180	35
Harrison, AR	10,529	36
Wilcox, AZ	9,440	37
St. Marys, GA	8,840	38
Park, CO	8,100	39
Estes Park, CO	2,917	40
Ocean Springs, MS	1,800	41
Patchogue, NY	1,363	42

Source: Department of the Interior, National Park Service, Office of Public Affairs and the Division of Publications: *The National Parks: Index 1991*, pp. 16-101, Washington, DC: U.S. Government Printing Office. *Notes:* 1. Noatak National Preserve. 2. Kings Canyon National Park. 3. Sequoia National Park. 4. Kobuk Valley National Park.

★ 2988 ★

Public Libraries

Library Holdings, 1995

Data shown are for public library systems serving one million or more people.

[In millions of holdings]

City	Holdings	Rank
New York, NY	10.5	1
Queens, NY	9.3	2
Philadelphia, PA	6.7	3
Pittsburgh, PA	6.4	4
Chicago, IL	6.0	5
Los Angeles County, CA	6.0	5
Brooklyn, NY	5.9	6
Los Angeles, CA	5.0	7
Houston, TX	4.0	8

[Continued]

★2988★
Library Holdings, 1995
[Continued]

City	Holdings	Rank
Miami-Dade County, FL	3.4	9
Detroit, MI	2.7	10
Dallas, TX	2.5	11
Orange County, CA	2.3	12
San Diego, CA	2.2	13
Broward County, FL	2.0	14
Sacramento, CA	1.7	15
Phoenix, AZ	1.7	15
San Antonio, TX	1.6	16
Riverside, CA	1.4	17
Providence, RI	1.4	17
San Bernardino County, CA	1.1	18
Maricopa County, AZ	0.5	19

Source: "Dallas Library Struggling to Make Do Despite Cuts," *Dallas Morning News,* 16 July 1995, p. 26A.

★2989★
Public Libraries
Library Materials Expenditure Per Capita, 1995

Data shown are for public library systems serving one million or more people.

[In dollars]

City	Expenditures per capita	Rank
Orange County, CA	4.31	1
Philadelphia, PA	3.47	2
Miami-Dade County, FL	3.14	3
Broward County, FL	3.04	4
Queens, NY	2.92	5
New York, NY	2.55	6
Detroit, MI	2.34	7
Houston, TX	2.33	8
Chicago, IL	2.29	9
Brooklyn, NY	2.07	10
Phoenix, AZ	2.06	11
San Antonio, TX	1.76	12
San Diego, CA	1.70	13
Dallas, TX	1.57	14
Los Angeles, CA	1.49	15
Riverside, CA	1.48	16
Sacramento, CA	1.29	17
Los Angeles County, CA	1.26	18
San Bernardino County, CA	1.26	19
Pittsburgh, PA	0.72	20
Maricopa County, AZ	0.55	21
Providence, RI	0.40	22

Source: "Dallas Library Struggling to Make Do Despite Cuts," *Dallas Morning News,* 16 July 1995, p. 26A. Primary source: Public Library Data Service, Dallas Public Library. *Notes:* Dallas comparisons number is different than in above stats because of accounting differences.

★2990★
Sports Activities
Boat Towing, 1995: Rates

[In dollars per hour; daytime rates]

City/Port	Cost	Rank
Baltimore, MD	125.00	4
Galveston, TX	100.00	6
Newport Beach, CA	130.00	3
Port Jefferson, NY	150.00	1
Sandusky, OH	120.00	5
Seattle, WA	135.00	2

Source: "Catch the Wave," *Motor Boating & Sailing,* (September 1995), p. 32.

★2991★
Sports Activities
Boating Costs, 1995: Prices of Marine Diesel

[In dollars per gallon]

City	Cost	Rank
Chicago, IL	1.65	1
Galveston, TX	1.60	2
Fort Lauderdale, FL	1.55	3
San Diego, CA	1.54	4
Boston, MA	1.45	5
Seattle, WA	1.28	6

Source: "What a Gallon of Marine Diesel Costs," *Motor Boating & Sailing,* (April 1996), p. 50.

★2992★
Sports Activities
Fishing, 1995: Most Popular Places

Data refer to fresh-water anglers who say they fish once a year.

[In percentages]

City/MSA	Percentage	Rank
Detroit, MI	18.7	1
Chicago, IL	18.6	2
Atlanta, GA	15.4	3
Houston, TX	14.6	4
Riverside-San Bernardino, CA	13.4	5

Source: "Check It Out: Top Fishing Cities," *Detroit News,* 29 May 1996, p. 1K. Primary source: National Sporting Goods Association survey.

★2993★
Sports Activities
Marina Service Prices, 1995, Selected Cities: Mechanics' Rates

[In dollars per hour]

City	Rate	Rank
Port Washington, NY	65.00	1
Fort Lauderdale, FL	60.00	2
Waukegan, IL	55.00	3
Seattle, WA	48.00	4
San Diego, CA	48.00	4

[Continued]

★ 2993 ★

Marina Service Prices, 1995, Selected Cities: Mechanics' Rates

[Continued]

City	Rate	Rank
Sausalito, CA	45.00	5
Galveston, TX	36.00	6

Source: "What It Costs," *Motor Boating & Sailing,* (May 1996), p. 30.

★ 2994 ★

Sports Activities

Metropolitan Areas With the Highest Numbers of Golf Courses, 1995

City/MSA	Number	Rank
New York-Newark, NY-NJ	411	1
Chicago, IL	311	2
Boston, MA	239	3
Detroit, MI	202	4
Minneapolis, MN	167	5
Philadelphia, PA	166	6
Pittsburgh, PA	150	7
Phoenix, AZ	142	8
Washington, DC	141	9
Atlanta, GA	140	10

Source: "Private Properties: Greening of America," *Wall Street Journal,* 22 September 1995, p. B8. Primary source: *Golf Digest. The Golf Company.*

★ 2995 ★

Sports Activities

Salt-Water Anglers, 1995: Leading Cities

[In percentage of population that fishes]

City/Port	Percentage	Rank
Houston, TX	15.4	1
Philadelphia, PA	11.3	2
Los Angeles-Long Beach, CA	5.3	3
Washington, DC	4.7	4
Boston, MA	4.6	5

Source: "Anglers Abound in Great Lakes Metropolitan Areas," *Lakeland Boating,* (July 1996), p. 18.

★ 2996 ★

Sports Activities

Ski-Lift Tickets, 1995: Selected Resorts

[In dollars per day's lift].

City	Costs	Rank
Aspen, CO	52	1
Big Sky, MT	43	6
Deer Valley, UT	49	2
Jackson Hole, WY	42	7
Park City, MT	47	4
Squaw Valley, CA	45	5
Snowmass, CO	52	1
Taos, NM	38	8

[Continued]

★ 2996 ★

Ski-Lift Tickets, 1995: Selected Resorts

[Continued]

City	Costs	Rank
Telluride, CO	45	5
Vail, CO	48	3

Source: Sloan, Gene, "Top Ski Lift Tickets Schuss Past $50," *USA TODAY,* 6 October 1995, p. 2D.

★ 2997 ★

Television Viewing

Television Ownership, 1995: Cities With the Highest Cable Percentage of Television Households

Data refer to cities that rank among the top ten of the fifty cities with the greatest number of television-owning households.

City/MSA	Cable percent of households	Rank
Boston, MA	77	5
Buffalo, NY	72	8
Harrisburg-Lancaster, PA	73	7
Hartford-New Haven, CT	85	1
New Orleans, LA	70	10
Norfolk-Portsmouth, VA	72	8
Orlando, FL	74	6
Philadelphia, PA	74	6
Pittsburgh, PA	77	5
Providence, RI	74	6
San Diego, CA	82	2
San Francisco, CA	70	10
Scranton–Wilkes Barre, PA	80	4
Seattle-Tacoma, WA	71	9
Tampa-Saint Petersburg, FL	70	10
West Palm Beach-Fort Pierce, FL	81	3

Source: "Top 50 Market Penetration Overview," *Cablevision,* 29 April 1996, p. 131.

★ 2998 ★

Television Viewing

Television Ownership, 1995: Ten Cities With the Most Cable Television Households

Data refer to the leading ten cities of the fifty cities with the greatest number of television-owning households.

City/MSA	Cable TV households	Rank
Atlanta, GA	1,014,950	10
Boston, MA	1,624,860	5
Chicago, IL	1,795,890	4
Detroit, MI	1,127,940	8
Los Angeles, CA	2,997,230	2
New York, NY	4,528,750	1
Philadelphia, PA	1,961,070	3
San Francisco, CA	1,577,580	6
Seattle-Tacoma, WA	1,040,250	9
Washington, DC	1,237,970	7

Source: "Top 50 Market Penetration Overview," *Cablevision,* 29 April 1996, p. 131.

★2999★
Television Viewing

Television Ownership, 1995: Ten Cities With the Most Television Households

City/MSA	Households	Rank
Atlanta, GA	1,583,520	10
Boston, MA	2,121,530	6
Chicago, IL	3,082,040	3
Dallas-Fort Worth, TX	1,821,900	8
Detroit, MI	1,736,910	9
Los Angeles, CA	4,917,550	2
New York, NY	6,695,140	1
Philadelphia, PA	2,645,690	4
San Francisco, CA	2,257,210	5
Washington, DC	1,883,590	7

Source: "Top 50 Market Penetration Overview," *Cablevision,* 29 April 1996, p. 131.

★3000★
Travel and Tourism

Hotel Taxes Slated for Tourism Promotion, 1995

Data refer to taxes collected from tourists and used to promote and improve tourism.

[In percentages]

City	Percentage	Rank
Reno, NV	90	1
Atlantic City, NJ	75	2
Las Vegas, NV	67	3
Boston, MA	65	4
Houston, TX	65	4

Source: "Top U.S. Cities for Reinvesting Travel Taxes," *Travel Weekly,* 1 February, 1996, p. 27. Primary source: Travel and Tourism Government Affairs Council study.

★3001★
Travel and Tourism

International Visitors, 1994: Leading Cities

[In millions of visitors]

City	International visitors	Rank
Boston, MA	0.9	9
Chicago, IL	1.0	8
Honolulu, HI	2.3	5
Las Vegas, NV	1.8	6
Los Angeles, CA	3.3	2
Miami, FL	2.8	3
New York, NY	4.1	1
Orlando, FL	2.3	5
San Francisco, CA	2.5	4
Washington, DC	1.2	7

Source: "Top 10 City Destinations in 1994," *Travel Weekly,* 27 November 1995, p. 51. Primary source: USTTA. *Note:* Travelers from Canada and Mexico are not included in the data.

★3002★
Travel and Tourism

International Visitors, 1994: Percent Change From 1993

City	Percent change 1994/1993	Rank
Boston, MA	4.9	5
Chicago, IL	2.8	6
Honolulu, HI	7.0	3
Las Vegas, NV	20.3	1
Los Angeles, CA	5.1	4
Miami, FL	-9.9	9
New York, NY	7.8	2
Orlando, FL	-12.3	10
San Francisco, CA	2.1	7
Washington, DC	-0.1	8

Source: "Top 10 City Destinations in 1994," *Travel Weekly,* 27 November 1995, p. 51. Primary source: USTTA. *Note:* Travelers from Canada and Mexico are not included in the data.

★3003★
Travel and Tourism

Most Likely Places of Origin for Tourists to Hawaii, 1995

City	Arrivals	Rank
Dallas, TX	55,300	3
Detroit, MI	38,950	6
Las Vegas, NV	24,540	8
Minneapolis, MN	50,080	4
Phoenix, AZ	47,070	5
Portland, OR	73,470	2
Salt Lake City, UT	31,070	7
Seattle, WA	157,160	1

Source: Bartlett, Tony, "Despite Flat Year, Arrivals Rise From Cities That Added Lift," *Travel Weekly,* 22 April, 1996, p. 71. Primary source: Hawaii Visitors Bureau.

★3004★
Travel and Tourism

Restaurant Taxes Slated for Tourism Promotion, 1995

Data refer to taxes collected from tourists and used to promote and improve tourism.

[In percentages]

City	Percentage	Rank
Kansas City, MO	21	1
Saint Louis, MO	18	2
Minneapolis, MN	14	3
Washington, DC	10	4
Denver, CO	6	5

Source: "Top U.S. Cities for Reinvesting Travel Taxes," *Travel Weekly,* 1 February, 1996, p. 27. Primary source: Travel and Tourism Government Affairs Council study.

★ 3005 ★

Travel and Tourism

Vacation Homes (Low-Range Prices), 1995: Average Price for Homes Considered Affordable

Data refer to prices of single-family vacation homes.

[In thousands of dollars]

City/MSA	Price	Rank
Cherokee Village, AR	20	1
Prescott, AZ	25	2
Au Gres, MI	25	2
Rye, NH	30	3
New Philadelphia, OH	30	3
Saint Augustine, FL	35	4
Cadillac, MI	35	4
Tomahawk, WI	35	4
Pine City, MN	40	5
Sunrise Beach, MO	40	6
Banner Elk, NC	40	6
Corpus Christi, TX	45	7
Lake Charles, LA	50	8
Colorado Springs, CO	55	9
Portsmouth, NH	55	9

Source: "Vacation Homes: Chic Is Not Cheap," *Trade & Culture,* (January 1996), p. 9. Primary source: Coldwell Banker (company) survey.

★ 3006 ★

Travel and Tourism

Vacation Homes (Low-Range Prices), 1995: Average Price for Homes Considered Expensive

Data refer to prices of single-family vacation homes.

[In thousands of dollars]

City/MSA	Price	Rank
Rancho Santa Fe, CA	275	1
Maui, Wailea, HI	250	2
Hamptons, NY	225	3
Orcas Island, WA	225	3
Aspen, CO	200	4
Carmel, CA	192	5
Monterey Basin, CA	192	5
Incline Village, NV	175	6
Stone Harbor, NJ	165	7
Jackson Hole, WY	150	8
Galena, IL	145	9
Key Biscayne, FL	135	10
Oahu, Kaneohe, HI	135	10
Martha's Vineyard Island, MA	135	10
Santa Fe, NM	125	11
Deer Valley, UT	125	11
Park City, UT	125	11

Source: "Vacation Homes: Chic Is Not Cheap," *Trade & Culture,* (January 1996), p. 9. Primary source: Coldwell Banker (company) survey.

Chapter 33

CONVENTIONS, EXHIBITIONS, AND TRADE SHOWS

Topics Covered

Political Conventions
Trade Shows

★3007★

Political Conventions

Most Popular Cities for Political Conventions: Democratic Party Conventions Hosted

City	Total	Rank
Baltimore, MD	9	2
Chicago, IL	10	1
New York, NY	5	3
Saint Louis, MO	4	4
Philadelphia, PA	2	5

Source: "Chicago: The Host With the Most," *USA TODAY,* 21 July 1994, p. 3A. Primary source: *Congressional Quarterly.*

★3008★

Political Conventions

Most Popular Cities for Political Conventions: Republican Party Conventions Hosted

City	Total	Rank
Baltimore, MD	1	3
Chicago, IL	14	1
New York, NY	0	4
Saint Louis, MO	1	3
Philadelphia, PA	5	2

Source: "Chicago: The Host With the Most," *USA TODAY,* 21 July 1994, p. 3A. Primary source: *Congressional Quarterly.*

★3009★

Political Conventions

Most Popular Cities for Political Conventions: Total Conventions Hosted

City	Total	Rank
Chicago, IL	24	1
Baltimore, MD	10	2
Philadelphia, PA	7	3
Saint Louis, MO	5	4
New York, NY	5	5

Source: "Chicago: The Host With the Most," *USA TODAY,* 21 July 1994, p. 3A. Primary source: *Congressional Quarterly.*

★3010★

Trade Shows

Popular Trade Show Sites, 1995

City	Shows booked in 1995	Rank
Chicago, IL	208	1
Atlanta, GA	207	2
New York, NY	173	3
Las Vegas, NV	163	4
Dallas, TX	144	5
San Francisco, CA	143	6
Orlando, FL	124	7

[Continued]

★3010★

Popular Trade Show Sites, 1995
[Continued]

City	Shows booked in 1995	Rank
Boston, MA	116	8
Washington, DC	115	9

Source: Faiola, Anthony and David Segal, "Convention Warfare," *Washington Post,* 15 August 1995, p. C1. Primary source: *Tradeshow Week.*

Listing of Sources

The listing below shows the 177 sources from which *Gale City & Metro Rankings Reporter,* 2nd Edition was drawn. Each item is followed by one or more refences to tables for which the citation is the source.

- "The 25 Worst Bridges," *USA TODAY,* 29 August 1994. Table: 2518

- "About Town," *Entrepreneur,* (September 1995). Tables: 2527-2528

- Advisory Committee on Intergovernmental Relations, *Intergovernmental Perspective,* (Spring 1993), vol. 19, no. 1, Washington, D.C.: Advisory Committee on Intergovernmental Relations. Table: 1762

- Advisory Committee on Intergovernmental Relations, *Significant Features of Fiscal Federalism, vol. 1: Budget Processes and Tax Systems 1994,* Washington, D.C.: Advisory Committee on Intergovernmental Relations, (June 1994), M-190. Tables: 2814, 2817

- Aeppel, Timothy, "Giant Sewage Storage Tank Shakes City," *Wall Street Journal,* 22 January 1996. Table: 15

- American Public Transit Association (APTA), *1995 APTA Transit Fare Summary,* Washington, D.C.: American Public Transit Association (APTA), 1995. Tables: 2520-2526

- "Anglers Abound in Great Lakes Metropolitan Areas," *Lakeland Boating,* (July 1996). Table: 2995

- Auerbach, Jonathan, "A Guide to What's Cooking In Kitchens," *Wall Street Journal,* 17 November 1995. Tables: 712-713

- "Average Catholic Household Donation in the Sunday Collection, 1991- 93," *America,* 15 July 1995. Table: 1959

- Bartlett, Tony, "Despite Flat Year, Arrivals Rise From Cities That Added Lift," *Travel Weekly,* 22 April 1996. Table: 3003

- "Big Foodies," *Crain's New York Business,* 6 November 1995. Table: 2365

- "Bogus Calls Keep EMS On Run," *Detroit Free Press,* 21 June 1996. Tables: 647-650

- "Border Apprehensions On the Rise," *USA TODAY,* 9 February 1996. Table: 396

- "Breaking Down Exports By Metro Area," *USA TODAY,* 30 May 1996. Tables: 2119, 2136

- Brewer, Geoffrey, "Manager's Handbook: Travel and Entertainment—U.S. Cities With Highest Bed Taxes," *Sales & Marketing Management,* (October 1993). Table: 2357

- "A Brighter Real Estate Picture," *Business Week,* 4 September 1995. Table: 2145

- Butterfield, Fox, "Many Cities in U.S. Show Sharp Drop in Homicide Rate," *New York Times,* 13 August 1995. Table: 2824

- Callis, Robert R., *Housing Vacancies and Home-ownership, Annual Statistics: 1993,* U.S. Bureau of the Census, Current Housing Reports, Series H111/93-A, Washington, D.C.: U.S. Government Printing Office, 1994. Tables: 699-700, 766-769

- Carroll, Rick, "Survey Ranks Dallas Area In the Middle In Blue-Collar Jobs," *Dallas Business Journal,* 23-29 February, 1996. Tables: 2212-2213

- Castaneda, Carol J., "Postal Service: 90% On-Time Record Is Something to Write Home About," *USA TODAY,* 5 June 1996. Table: 1079

- "Catch the Wave," *Motor Boating & Sailing,* (September 1995). Table: 2990

- Chang, Trina, "Back Surgery," *American Health,* (May 1996). Table: 643

- Chang, Trina, "Breast Cancer Surgery," *American Health,* (May 1996). Tables: 644-645

- Chang, Trina, "The Bill for Bypass Surgery," *American Health,* (April 1995). Table: 646

- "Cheapest Office Space," USA SNAPSHOTS, *USA TODAY,* 24 January 1996. Table: 2144

- "Check It Out: Top Fishing Cities," *Detroit News,* 29 May 1996. Table: 2992

- "Chemical Traffic," *Chemical Week,* 12 June 1996. Table: 7

- "Chicago: The Host With the Most," *USA TODAY,* 21 July 1994. Tables: 3007-3009

- "Child Care Fees Across the Nation," *Child Care Information Exchange,* (July 1996). Tables: 545-547

- "Cities With the Most Hotel Rooms," *USA TODAY,* 9 May 1996. Table: 2363

- "Cost Figures on Lab Construction Available," *R&D Magazine,* (March 1996). Table: 2159

- "The Cost of A Car," *Physicians' Travel & Meeting Guide,* (August 1995). Table: 2529

- "The Cost of Industrial Water Use," *Water Environment & Technology,* (January 1995). Table: 2007

- "Cost Trends: 6/96," *Building Design & Construction,* (June 1996). Tables: 2152-2155

- "Costliest Big Cities for Driving," USA SNAPSHOTS, *USA TODAY,* 3 May 1995. Table: 2532

- "Crime Count," *U.S. News & World Report,* 13 May 1996. Tables: 2826-2829, 2836-2839

- *Dairy Goat Journal,* (March 1996). Table: 13

- "Dallas Library Struggling to Make Do Despite Cuts," *Dallas Morning News,* 16 July 1995. Tables: 2988-2989

- "Dallas-Ft. Worth Area Tops Affordable Housing List," *American City & County,* (November 1995). Tables: 708-711, 715-716

- Davis, Robert, "'Meth' Use in the '90s" A Growing 'Epidemic,'" *USA TODAY,* 7 September 1995. Tables: 659-660

- "Dow Jones Real Estate Index: Vacation Home Prices," *Wall Street Journal,* 29 March 1996. Table: 703

- Durbin, Fran, "GSA Revises Allowable Daily Expenses for Federal Workers," *Travel Weekly,* 1 April 1996. Tables: 2149-2151

- "Employment Leaders," *Wall Street Journal,* 31 May 1996. Table: 834

- "Expensive Office Space," USA SNAPSHOTS, *USA TODAY,* 23 January 1996. Table: 2143

- Faiola, Anthony, and David Segal, "Convention Warfare," *Washington Post,* 15 August 1995. Table: 3010

- Fairly, Peter, "'Nowhere to Hide' from Chemical Hazard, Says Report," *Chemical Week,* 23 August 1995. Tables: 293-294

- Federal Bureau of Investigation, Uniform Crime Reports series, *Crime in the United States, 1993,* Washington, D.C.: Federal Bureau of Investigation, 1994. Tables: 2818-2823, 2834-2835, 2854

- "FedEx Reaches Deeper Into Asia From Strategic Subic Bay Hub," *Nikkei Weekly,* 27 November, 1995. Tables: 2258, 2265

- Finder, Alan, and Richard Perez-Pena, "For the M.T.A., Some Fiscal Successes," *New York Times,* 13 August 1995. Tables: 2530-2534

- "Fine Pollutants in Air Cause Many Deaths, Study Suggests," *New York Times,* 9 May 1996. Tables: 16-17

- "For the Record," *Progressive Grocer* Annual Report, *Progressive Grocer,* (April 1996). Tables: 2496-2501

- "Fricker, Daniel G., "It's A Deal: Transportation Chief Agrees to $150 Million For Metro," *Detroit Free Press,* 1 May 1996. Table: 2517

- "Funeral/Cremation Price Survey," *Consumers Digest,* (September/October 1995). Tables: 548-549

- "Glutted Office Markets," USA SNAPSHOTS, *USA TODAY,* 30 June 1995. Table: 2140

- "Go Midwest, Young Home Buyer," *Builder,* (January 1995). Tables: 706, 714

- "The Good Life," *American Nurseryman,* 15 November 1995. Table: 1753

- "Grants to States, Other California Cities," *San Francisco Examiner,* 27 August 1995. Table: 2975

- Gray, Madison J., "Becoming 'World Class' City Requires New Amenities for Dining, Fun," *Detroit News,* 21 December 1995. Tables: 358, 2364, 2367, 2485-2486

- Gunsch, Dawn, "For Your Information: A New Administration Means New Regulation," *Personnel Journal* (March 1993). Tables: 541-542

- Hamlin, Suzanne, "For Big Tips, Los Angeles Comes In Last," *New York Times,* 15 May 1996. Tables: 2368-2370

- Hansen, Kristin A., *Geographical Mobility: March 1993 to March 1994,* U.S. Bureau of the Census, *Current Population Reports* series, P20-485, Washington, D.C.: U.S. Government Printing Office, 1995. Tables: 502-516, 671-698

- "Having Fun," *Wall Street Journal,* 5 April 1996. Tables: 704, 2976

- "Health Care Fact: Largest Managed Care Markets," *AHA News,* 16 October 1995. Table: 665

- Henry, Tamara, "Urban Area Teacher Shortages," *USA TODAY,* 22 May 1996. Tables: 800-801

- "Heroin Use on the Increase," *Detroit Free Press,* 18 June 1996. Tables: 657-658

- Higgins, Steve, "Are Local Telephone Wars Much Ado Over Nothing?" *Investor's Business Daily,* 4 May 1995. Tables: 2586-2587

- "High-Rises Fall to HUD's New Plans," *ENR,* (The McGraw-Hill Construction Weekly), 11 September 1995. Tables: 666-668

- "Home Delivery," *Wall Street Journal,* 28 June 1996. Tables: 2493-2494

- Hostetler, Michele, "Area Rings Up Plethora of Telecom Work," *Business Journal,* 25-31 March, 1995. Table: 921

- "Industry Issues," *BEVERAGE Industry,* (June 1996). Tables: 2487- 2490

- Ingersoll, Bruce, "Rice Farmers in Arkansas are Raising Cain as They Would Lose Most if U.S. Ends Subsidies," *Wall Street Journal,* 12 September 1995. Tables: 9-10

- Isa, Margaret, "When It Comes to I.P.O.'s, Is Geography Part of Destiny?" *New York Times,* 23 June, 1996. Table: 2139

- Johnson, Arthur, "Shoptalk: The New Heat Pumps," *Builder,* (June 1996). Tables: 2156-2157

- Johnson, Kirk, and Thomas J. Lueck, "Economy in the New York Region Is Recovering, But Pace is Slow," *New York Times,* 19 February 1996. Table: 934

- Johnston, David Cay, "Where the IRS Aims the Prosecution Ax," *New York Times,* 14 April 1996. Tables: 2973-2974

- Jones, Del, "Business Travel Today," *USA TODAY,* 11 September 1995. Table: 2516

- Komarow, Steve, "Army Unveils Chemical Cache," *USA TODAY,* 23 January 1996. Table: 8

- Kotkin, Joel, "Still the Best Places to Do Business," *Inc.,* (July 1996). Table: 2137

- "Lawyers in the Minority," *Wall Street Journal,* 7 April 1995. Tables: 922-923

- Lenzner, Robert, and Stephen S. Johnson, "A Few Yards of Denim and Five Copper Rivets," *Forbes,* 26 February 1996. Table: 2439

- Loeb, Penny, "Fast Pucks: Waste, Fraud and Abuse," *U.S. News & World Report,* 27 March 1995. Tables: 669-670

- Lomanno, Mark V., "Hot & Not," *H&MM (Hotel & Motel Management),* 4 March 1996. Tables: 2360-2361

- "Lose Some, Win Some," *Business Week,* 11 September 1995. Table: 833

- Love, Jacqueline, "Ozone Levels Still Called Health Threat for Region," *Detroit Free Press,* 20 June 1996. Tables: 1-2, 5-6

- Maguire, Kathleen, and Ann L. Pastore, eds., *Sourcebook of Criminal Justice Statistics 1994,* U.S. Department of Justice, Bureau of Justice Statistics, Washington, D.C.: U.S. Government Printing Office, 1995. Tables: 356-357, 2844-2853, 2856-2929, 2938-2972

- McCarthy, Mike, "Buyers Still In Control of Residential Real Estate," *Business Journal,* 5 June 1995. Table: 705

- Minahan, Tim, "A New Wave In Shipping," *Purchasing,* 6 June 1996. Table: 2535

- Minzesheimer, Bob, "To Be NYC Cabbie, Fare's Not Cheap: Medallions Auctioned for $175,000," *USA TODAY,* 20 May 1996. Table: 919

- "Money For Nothing? Not Hardly!" *Traffic Management,* (April 1995). Table: 1078

- "*Money's* 20-City Price Guide," *Money,* (September 1995). Tables: 2503-2510

- Moore, Lila, "Home Is Where You Sew It," *Apparel Industry Magazine,* (September 1995). Tables: 2436-2438

- National Association of Regulatory Utility Commissioners, *Residential Electric Bills: Summer 1993,* Washington, D.C.: National Association of Regulatory Utility Commissioners. Tables: 1971-1986

- National Association of Regulatory Utility Commissioners, *Residential Gas Bills: Winter 1993-94,* Washington, D.C.: National Association of Regulatory Utility Commissioners. Tables: 1987-2006

- National Institutes of Health, Division of Epidemiology and Prevention Research, National Institute on Drug Abuse, *Epidemiologic Trends in Drug Abuse,* Community Epidemiology Work Group (CEWG), Rockville, Maryland: National Institutes of Health, (December 1994). Tables: 571, 663- 664

- *Nation's Cities Weekly,* vol 16, no. 8, 22 February 1993, Washington, DC: National League of Cities. Tables: 397-398

- "The Network Paycheck," *Network World,* 5 June 1995. Table: 1077

- "No Vacancies," *Wall Street Journal,* 21 June 1996. Table: 761

- Norton, Erle, and Elizabeth Jensen, "Westinghouse Acquisition May Speed Company's Split," *Wall Street Journal,* 21 June 1996. Table: 2138

- Oguntoyinbo, Lekan, "Detroit to Raise Water, Sewer Fees," *Detroit Free Press,* 22 February 1996. Table: 2588

- "Olympic City Build-Up," USA SNAPSHOTS, *USA TODAY,* 16 February 1996. Tables: 2160-2161

- "On-Time Performance of Largest U.S. Airports," *Travel Weekly,* 13 May 1996. Tables: 2513-2514

- "The Other NY," *Site Selection,* (October 1995). Table: 1066

- "Penthouse Prices," USA SNAPSHOTS, *USA TODAY,* 22 May 1996. Table: 707

- Plume, Janet, "New Rules Expected to Hurt Record Steel Trade," *Traffic World,* 10 June 1996. Tables: 2126-2128

- Pluta, Rick, and Jennifer Bott, "Pondering A Power Shift," *Oakland Press* (Oakland County, Michigan), 11 February 1996. Table: 1970

- "Population Rankings," *Crain's Small Business,* (January 1996). Table: 354

- "Price Check: Beef," *Restaurants & Institutions,* 1 September 1995. Tables: 2491-2492

- "Private Properties: Greening of America," *Wall Street Journal,* 22 September 1995. Table: 2994

- "Private Properties: Moneyed Metros," *Wall Street Journal,* 29 March 1996. Table: 1711

- "Reaching Today's Consumer: Consumer Spending by Region," *Furniture/Today,* 1996 Retail Planning Guide, 25 December 1995. Table: 2502

- Rechin, Kevin, "The Heftiest Tabs," *USA TODAY,* 8 March 1996. Table: 2366

- "Report Finds Poverty Afflicts Children in Communities of All Sizes," *Nation's Cities Weekly,* vol. 15, no. 33, 17 August 17 1992, Washington, DC: National League of Cities. Table: 1764

- Robichaux, Mark, "FCC's 'Social Contract' for Cable Companies Draws Ire," *Wall Street Journal,* 29 January 1996. Tables: 530-531

- Rousseau, Rita, "Immigration: the Reluctant Enforcers," *Restaurants & Institutions,* 1 October 1995. Table: 920

- Schmeltzer, John, "Mortgage Tide Shifts to Low Incomes: Banks Own Up to Reinvestment Mandate," *Chicago Tribune,* 8 May 1996. Tables: 701-702

- "Secondary Market Drives New Construction In 1995," *Hotels,* (March 1996). Table: 2362

- "Settling In the Sun," *Detroit Free Press,* 9 October 1995. Table: 517

- "Single Parents," *St. Louis Post-Dispatch,* 10 January 1995. Tables: 528-529

- Skelton, Renee, "The Sky's the Limit?" *Amicus Journal,* (Summer 1996). Tables: 2511-2512

- Sloan, Gene, "Top Ski Lift Tickets Schuss Past $50," *USA TODAY,* 6 October 1995. Table: 2996

- Sniffen, Michael J., "Homicides Drop Sharply Across Nation," *Detroit Free Press,* 18 December 1995. Table: 2825

- "Snowiest Cities in USA," *USA TODAY,* 2 February 1996. Table: 296

- "Speed Freaks," *U.S. News & World Report,* 13 November 1995. Table: 590

- *State Government News,* October 1991. Table: 301

- Stevens, Carol, "Vaccination Rate Embarrasses State: Michigan Ranks Worst in Nation for Getting Kids Immunized," *Detroit News and Free Press,* 19 May 1996. Tables: 661-662

- "Suite Deals," *Entrepreneur,* (April 1996). Table: 2141-2142

- Thompson, Garland L., "School Dropouts: Despite Progress, Minority Rates Still Exceed Whites," *Black Issues in Higher Education,* 15 June 1995. Tables: 798-799

- Tilove, Jonathan, "Demographic Balkanization?," *Detroit News,* 19 May 1996. Table: 399

- "Today's Debate: Million Man March—Message of Today's March is Self- Help, Not Racism," *USA TODAY,* 16 October 1995. Table: 1739

- "Top 10 City Destinations in 1994," *Travel Weekly,* 27 November 1995. Tables: 3001-3002

- "Top 10 Housing Markets: 1995," *Builder,* (January 1995). Table: 738-740

- "Top 20 U.S. Metro Areas, 1990-95 New and Expanded Distribution Facilities," *Site Selection,* (June 1996). Table: 2158

- "Top 30 ACI Airports/Cargo Volume," *International Business,* (April 1996). Table: 2515

- "Top 50 Market Penetration Overview," *Cablevision,* 29 April 1996. Tables: 2997-2999

- "Top Cities," *Fortune,* 29 April 1996, F-31. Table: 2008

- "Top U.S. Cities for Reinvesting Travel Taxes," *Travel Weekly,* 1 February 1996. Tables: 3000, 3004

- U.S. Department of Commerce, Economics and Statistics Administration, Bureau of the Census, *Annual Survey of Government Finances 1992,* Washington, D.C.: U.S. Government Printing Office, 1995. Tables: 2597- 2689, 2691-2740, 2744-2793

- U.S. Department of Commerce, Economics and Statistics Administration, Bureau of the Census, *County and City Data Book 1994: A Statistical Abstract Supplement,* Washington, D.C.: U.S. Government Printing Office, August 1994. Tables: 11-12, 307-308, 348-349, 351-353

- U.S. Department of Commerce, Economics and Statistics Administration, Bureau of the Census, Current Population Reports, Special Studies, P23-190, *65+ In the United States,* Washington, D.C.: U.S. Government Printing Office, 1996. Tables: 309-316

- U.S. Department of Commerce, Economics and Statistics Administration, Bureau of the Census, Data User Services Division, *1990 Census of Population and Housing,* Summary Tape File 3C, United States Summary, CD-ROM, February 1992. Tables: 297-300, 302-306, 317-347, 362-386, 437-445, 518-527, 802-832, 1701-1710, 1712-1738, 1740-1749, 1766-1824, 1827- 1958

Listing of Sources

- U.S. Department of Commerce, Economics and Statistics Administration, Bureau of the Census, Data User Services Division, *1990 Census of Population and Housing, Equal Employment Opportunity File, CD-90-EE0-1, January 1993,* CD-ROM. Tables: 1089-1700

- U.S. Department of Commerce, Economics and Statistics Administration, Bureau of the Census, Data User Services Division, *1992 Economic Census, Volume 1F, Reports Series, Release 1F,* September 1995, CD-ROM. Tables: 2162-2209, 2214-2257, 2259-2264, 2266-2356, 2375-2433, 2440-2484, 2536-2569

- U.S. Department of Commerce, Economics and Statistics Administration, Bureau of the Census, *New Residential Construction in Selected Metropolitan Areas, Fourth Quarter 1993,* Current Construction Reports, C21/93-Q4, Washington, D.C.: U.S. Government Printing Office, March 1994. Tables: 718-737, 741-760

- U.S. Department of Commerce, Economics and Statistics Administration, Bureau of the Census, *Statistical Abstract of the United States 1993* (113th edition), Washington, D.C.: U.S. Government Printing Office (1993), p. 472. Tables: 1760-1761, 1763, 1765

- U.S. Department of Commerce, Economics and Statistics Administration, Bureau of the Census, *Statistical Abstract of the United States 1995,* (115th edition), Washington, D.C.: U.S. Government Printing Office, 1995. Tables: 3-4, 350, 355, 532-540, 651-656, 835-838, 933, 1064-1065, 1076, 1750-1752, 2121, 2125, 2371-2374, 2434-2435, 2570-2575, 2589-2596, 2690, 2741-2743, 2794-2813, 2815-2816, 2830-2833, 2840-2843, 2855, 2930-2937

- U.S. Department of Commerce, Economics and Statistics Administration, Bureau of Economic Analysis, *Survey of Current Business,* vol. 76, no. 6, Washington, D.C.: U.S. Government Printing Office, (June 1996). Tables: 359-361, 839-900, 1073-1075, 1754-1759

- U.S. Department of Commerce, International Trade Administration, *Metropolitan Area Exports: An Export Performance Report on Over 250 U.S. Cities,* Washington, D.C.: U.S. Government Printing Office, April 1996. Tables: 2009-2118, 2120, 2122-2124, 2129-2135

- U.S. Department of Education, Office of Educational Research and Improvement, National Center for Education Statistics, *Digest of Education Statistics 1994,* NCES 94-115, Lanham, Maryland: Bernan, 1995. Tables: 770-779, 781-784, 785-792, 793-797

- U.S. Department of Health and Human Services, Public Health Service, Centers for Disease Control and Prevention (CDC), CDC Surveillance Summaries, MMWR: Morbidity and Mortality Weekly Report, 24 March 1995, vol. 44, no. SS-1, *Youth Risk Behavior Surveillance—United States, 1993,* Atlanta, GA: Centers for Disease Control and Prevention, 1995. Tables: 550-570, 572-589, 591-632

- U.S. Department of Health and Human Services, Public Health Service, Centers for Disease Control and Prevention (CDC), National Center for HIV, STD, and TB Prevention, *HIV/AIDS Surveillance Report,* Year-end edition, vol. 7, no. 2, Atlanta, Georgia: Centers for Disease Control and Prevention. Tables: 633-642

- U.S. Department of the Interior, National Park Service, Office of Public Affairs and the Division of Publications: *The National Parks: Index 1991,* pp. 16-101, Washington, D.C.: U.S. Government Printing Office, 1991. Tables: 2977-2987

- U.S. Department of the Interior, National Park Service, Office of Public Affairs and the Division of Publications: *The National Parks: Index 1995,* Washington, D.C.: U.S. Government Printing Office, 1995. Tables: 14, 295

- U.S. Department of Justice, Immigration and Naturalization Service, *Statistical Yearbook of the Immigration and Naturalization Service, 1994,* Washington, D.C.: U.S. Government Printing Office, 1996. Tables: 387-395, 400-436, 446-501

- U.S. Department of Labor, Bureau of Labor Statistics, *CPI Detailed Report: Data for December 1995,* Washington, D.C.: U.S. Government Printing Office, February 1996. Table: 2578

- U.S. Department of Labor, Bureau of Labor Statistics, *CPI Detailed Report: Data for February 1996,* Washington, D.C.: U.S. Government Printing Office, April 1996. Tables: 1960-1969

- U.S. Department of Labor, Bureau of Labor Statistics, *CPI Detailed Report: Data for October 1995,* Washington, D.C.: U.S. Government Printing Office, December 1995. Tables: 2576-2577, 2579-2585

- U.S. Department of Labor, Bureau of Labor Statistics, *Employment and Earnings,* Washington, D.C.: U.S. Government Printing Office, September 1995. Tables: 901-918, 1067-1072

- U.S. Department of Labor, Bureau of Labor Statistics, *Geographic Profile of Employment and Unemployment, 1993,* Washington, D.C.: U.S. Government Printing Office, September 1994. Tables: 924-932, 1055-1063, 1080-1088

- U.S. Department of Labor, Bureau of Labor Statistics, *Geographic Profile of Employment and Unemployment, 1994,* Washington, D.C.: U.S. Government Printing Office, December 1995. Tables: 935-1054

- U.S. Environmental Protection Agency, "Toxic Release Inventory, 1992." In *National Economic, Social, and Environmental Data Bank* [CD-ROM]. Prepared by U.S. Department of Commerce, Economics and Statistics Administration, Washington, D.C.: U.S. Department of Commerce, National Economic, Social, and Environmental Data Bank, Economics and Statistics Administration, Office of Business Analysis, February 1995. Tables: 18-292

- "U.S. Office Rents," USA SNAPSHOTS, *USA TODAY,* 10 January 1995. Table: 2146-2147

- "USA's Most Educational Places," USA SNAPSHOTS, *USA TODAY,* 26 December 1995. Table: 780

- "Vacation Homes: Chic Is Not Cheap," *Trade & Culture,* (January 1996). Tables: 3005-3006

- Venable, Tim, "Dallas Wins Again: Still the Hottest U.S. Metro Area for Corporate Facilities," *Site Selection,* (February 1995). Table: 2148

- Ward, Sam, "Cities With the Most Knowledgeable Cab Drivers," *USA TODAY,* 31 August 1995. Table: 2519

- "What a Gallon of Marine Diesel Costs," *Motor Boating & Sailing,* (April 1996). Table: 2991

- "What It Costs," *Motor Boating & Sailing,* (May 1996). Table: 2993

- "Where Daycare Is A Bargain," USA SNAPSHOTS, *USA TODAY,* 19 March 1996. Table: 544

- "Where Daycare Is No Bargain," USA SNAPSHOTS, *USA TODAY,* 18 March 1996. Table: 543

- "Where Rent Is A Killer," USA SNAPSHOTS, *USA TODAY,* 16 May 1996. Table: 717

- "Where the Rooms Are," *Wall Street Journal,* 17 November 1995. Tables: 2358-2359

- "Where the White Underclass Lives," *U.S. News & World Report,* 12 October 1994. Tables: 1825-1826

- "Will Virtual Vacancy Belie the Numbers?" *Chain Store Age* (May 1996). Tables: 762-765

- "Women In Business," *Washington Post,* 6 March 1992. Tables: 2210-2211

- "Worth Their Salt In Snacks," USA SNAPSHOTS, *USA TODAY,* 6 May 1996. Table: 2495

Location Index

The Location Index organizes in one alphabetic list all cities included in *Gale City & Metro Rankings Reporter,* 2nd Edition tables. Each citation is followed by page and table reference numbers. Page numbers are preceded by "p." or "pp." Page references do not necessarily identify the page on which a table begins. In cases where tables span two or more pages, references point to the page on which the index term actually appears, which may be the second or subsequent page of a table. Table reference numbers appear in brackets ([]).

Albany, NY continued:
— hotels and motels, p. 1011 [2361]
— revenues, p. 1220 [2817]
— toxic chemicals, pp. 36, 48, 54 [144, 196-197, 224]

Albany–Schenectady–Troy, NY MSA
— asian population, p. 94 [317]
— establishments and employment, pp. 932, 935-936, 943, 958-959, 962, 969, 973, 975, 981, 986, 991, 1001, 1018, 1035, 1043, 1048, 1052, 1056, 1098-1099 [2200, 2206, 2208-2209, 2216, 2248, 2250, 2256, 2272, 2281, 2284, 2297, 2306, 2316, 2338, 2380, 2415, 2432, 2441, 2449, 2458, 2566, 2568-2569]
— family and household income, pp. 706, 709-711, 721, 723-727 [1701, 1706-1709, 1729, 1731-1737]
— first ancestry, pp. 312, 314-315, 317-324, 326, 328, 330 [803, 805, 808, 811-812, 814, 816-818, 820, 822, 825, 828, 831]
— hours and earnings, p. 420 [1065-1066]
— immigrants admitted, p. 173 [445]
— imports and exports, pp. 877-878, 902 [2019-2020, 2129]
— income, pp. 731, 734 [1744, 1749]
— marital status, men, p. 211 [520-521]
— marital status, women, p. 214 [525]
— occupancy, pp. 435-436, 441, 452-453, 460, 462, 468-469, 478, 481, 491, 495-496, 502-504, 514-516, 524, 528, 536, 539, 545-546, 549-552, 556-557, 559, 562, 566, 569-570, 576, 583, 585, 591, 593, 595, 598, 602, 610-612, 615-616, 618, 628-631, 636-638, 640, 643, 647, 651-652, 660, 662, 668, 676, 681-682, 684, 686, 688, 693-694 [1096-1097, 1099, 1111, 1135, 1138, 1153, 1157, 1171, 1174, 1193, 1201, 1223-1224, 1233, 1235, 1250-1251, 1255, 1278, 1280, 1283, 1300-1301, 1309, 1328, 1335, 1349, 1352, 1357-1359, 1361, 1363, 1373, 1375, 1379, 1387, 1395, 1400, 1402, 1416, 1433, 1437, 1450, 1455, 1459, 1467, 1475, 1493, 1495, 1497-1498, 1505-1506, 1511, 1533, 1536, 1539-1540, 1553, 1555-1556, 1560, 1568, 1576, 1584, 1587-1588, 1605-1606, 1610, 1622, 1639, 1651-1652, 1658, 1663, 1666-1668, 1678-1680]
— population, pp. 74, 77, 80, 83, 85, 103, 106, 110, 113, 117, 132, 135-136, 140, 142 [297-300, 302, 333, 337, 345, 350, 355, 382-386]
— poverty, pp. 751, 827, 831, 847-848, 854 [1777, 1911, 1918, 1944, 1946, 1958]
— tax-exempt establishments and employment, pp. 1003-1008 [2343-2344, 2346-2348, 2350-2352]

Albany State College (Albany, GA)
— degrees conferred, pp. 286, 288, 290, 293, 295 [771, 773, 775, 777, 779]
— enrollment, pp. 296, 299 [781, 784]
— finances and expenditures, pp. 304, 307 [793, 796]

Albemarle, VA
— toxic chemicals, p. 14 [47]

Albuquerque, NM
— asian population, p. 99 [326]
— city government debt, pp. 1154-1166 [2665-2671, 2673-2675, 2677-2680, 2684-2690]
— city government expenditures, pp. 1166-1187, 1214, 1216

Albuquerque, NM continued:
[2691-2706, 2708, 2710-2715, 2721-2723, 2726, 2728-2737, 2739, 2801, 2804]
— city government revenues, pp. 1189-1213, 1217 [2745-2751, 2753, 2756-2766, 2769-2771, 2776, 2778-2780, 2782-2784, 2786-2793, 2795, 2809]
— cost of living, pp. 874-875 [2005-2006]
— crimes and crime rates, pp. 1228, 1231-1232 [2840, 2849, 2852]
— diseases, pp. 247-250 [634, 636-637, 640, 642]
— employment, pp. 336-338 [835-838]
— foods and food products, pp. 1071-1073 [2496-2501]
— hours and earnings, p. 423 [1076]
— immigrants admitted, p. 171 [441-442]
— imports and exports, pp. 878, 902 [2021-2022, 2130]
— income, pp. 728, 730-731, 733 [1740, 1743, 1745, 1748]
— marital status, men, p. 210 [518]
— marital status, women, p. 212 [523]
— population, pp. 74, 77, 81, 83, 85, 89, 99, 101-102, 104-105, 109-110, 125-127, 133, 136, 140, 143 [297-300, 302, 305, 327, 329-331, 334-336, 342, 344-345, 370-372, 383-386]
— poverty, pp. 754, 757-760, 769-777, 780-789, 793, 800, 811-822, 824-828, 832-835, 843-846 [1783-1784, 1790-1796, 1811-1824, 1830-1847, 1854, 1864, 1884-1901, 1905-1906, 1909-1910, 1912-1913, 1920-1925, 1938-1943]
— poverty rates, p. 742 [1761]
— revenues, pp. 1112-1114, 1219 [2589-2596, 2813]
— vacancies, pp. 280-281 [762-765]

Albuquerque, NM MSA
— crimes and crime rates, pp. 1222, 1232 [2818, 2854]
— establishments and employment, pp. 936, 943, 946, 955, 958, 962, 969, 973, 975, 981, 986, 991, 999, 1001, 1018, 1028, 1043-1044, 1056, 1065, 1098-1099 [2209, 2216, 2223, 2243, 2248, 2256, 2273, 2281, 2284, 2297, 2306, 2316, 2334, 2338, 2380, 2401, 2432-2433, 2457, 2477, 2566, 2568-2569]
— occupancy, pp. 493, 517, 528, 531, 533, 537, 563, 591, 608, 628, 634, 643, 650, 652, 664-665, 667-669, 674, 676, 681-682, 699 [1229, 1283, 1309, 1317, 1321, 1331, 1387, 1450, 1489, 1534, 1548, 1566, 1568, 1582, 1588, 1613, 1616, 1621-1622, 1625-1626, 1635-1636, 1640, 1651-1652, 1691]
— population, pp. 113, 117 [350, 355]
— tax-exempt establishments and employment, pp. 1004, 1008 [2345, 2352]

Alcorn, MS
— toxic chemicals, pp. 49, 65 [201, 274]

Alcorn State University (Alcorn, MS)
— degrees conferred, pp. 286, 288, 290, 293, 295 [771, 773, 775, 777, 779]
— enrollment, pp. 296, 299 [781, 784]
— finances and expenditures, pp. 304, 307 [793, 796]

Alderson, WV
— prisons and prison population, pp. 1269-1270 [2962-2964]

Alexandria, LA
— employment, p. 361 [908, 910]
— family and household income, pp. 708, 713-716 [1704, 1714-

Numbers following p. or pp. are page references. Numbers in [ ] are table references.

1296

Numbers following p. or pp. are page references. Numbers in [ ] are table references.

Location Index

1297

Numbers following p. or pp. are page references. Numbers in [ ] are table references.

Anderson, SC continued:
— toxic chemicals, p. 49 [201]

Androscoggin, ME
— toxic chemicals, p. 51 [211]

Angelina, TX
— toxic chemicals, pp. 33, 58, 63 [132, 244, 265]

Ann Arbor, MI
— crimes and crime rates, p. 1224 [2825]
— diseases, pp. 247-249 [634, 636-637, 640, 642]
— hours and earnings, pp. 420-421 [1065, 1067, 1069]
— imports and exports, p. 902 [2132]

Ann Arbor, MI PMSA
— population, pp. 113, 117 [350, 355]

Anne Arundel, MD
— toxic chemicals, p. 65 [274]

Anniston, AL
— asian population, p. 97 [323]
— chemical weapons, p. 6 [8]
— family and household income, pp. 708, 713-715, 718-719 [1705, 1714-1716, 1722-1724]
— first ancestry, p. 328 [829]
— marital status, women, p. 215 [527]
— population, pp. 76, 79-80, 83, 87, 90, 111, 122-123, 128, 134, 137, 139, 143 [297-300, 302, 306, 345, 364-366, 375, 383-386]
— poverty, pp. 746, 755-757, 767, 769, 779-780, 792, 802, 809-811, 829, 840, 842, 849-850, 852-854 [1769, 1785-1786, 1788-1789, 1807, 1810, 1828-1829, 1853, 1867, 1879-1883, 1914, 1933, 1937, 1947, 1949, 1954, 1956-1957]

Anniston, AL MSA
— crimes and crime rates, pp. 1222, 1232 [2818, 2854]
— occupancy, pp. 472, 606, 614, 644, 681 [1180, 1485, 1503, 1568, 1651]

Anson, NC
— toxic chemicals, p. 9 [22]

Appleton–Oshkosh–Neenah, WI MSA
— asian population, p. 96 [321]
— establishments and employment, pp. 943, 958, 962, 975, 981, 986, 1001, 1018, 1027, 1098-1099 [2216, 2248, 2256, 2284, 2297, 2306, 2338, 2380, 2398, 2566, 2568-2569]
— family and household income, pp. 719-722 [1724-1731]
— first ancestry, pp. 313-316, 318, 322-323 [804, 806, 808, 810, 813, 819-820]
— marital status, women, p. 213 [524]
— occupancy, pp. 436, 483, 494, 570, 611, 629, 643, 669, 681 [1098, 1205, 1231, 1404, 1496, 1536, 1568, 1625, 1651]
— population, pp. 75, 77, 81-82, 86, 88, 108, 113, 117, 122, 133, 137, 141 [297-300, 302-303, 341, 350, 355, 363, 383-386]
— poverty, pp. 744-747, 757-758, 761-763, 765, 781, 784-785, 787, 789, 791, 797-798, 828-829, 831, 833, 854 [1766-1769, 1771, 1790-1792, 1797-1800, 1803, 1831, 1837, 1839-1840, 1843, 1847, 1850, 1860-1861, 1913, 1915, 1919, 1922, 1958]

Aransas, TX
— toxic chemicals, pp. 29, 35 [116, 142]

Arapahoe, CO
— toxic chemicals, pp. 58, 67 [241, 284]

Arco, ID
— parks, p. 1279 [2986-2987]

Arizona State University (Tempe, AZ)
— degrees conferred, pp. 288, 291 [772, 776]
— enrollment, pp. 298, 300-301, 303-304 [782-783, 786-788, 790-792]

Arkansas Baptist College (Little Rock, AR)
— degrees conferred, pp. 286, 288, 290, 293, 295 [771, 773, 775, 777, 779]
— enrollment, pp. 296, 299 [781, 784]
— finances and expenditures, pp. 304, 307 [793, 796]

Arlington, TX
— crimes and crime rates, pp. 1224-1225 [2826, 2828]
— employment, pp. 336-338 [835-838]
— hours and earnings, p. 423 [1076]
— population, pp. 90, 112 [307, 348]

Arlington, VA
— bridges, p. 1079 [2518]

Ascension Parish, LA
— toxic chemicals, pp. 8-11, 14, 16-17, 20-21, 29, 31, 33, 36, 40-43, 48, 50, 52-55, 57, 59, 62-63, 65-66, 68-70 [19-21, 24, 26-28, 44-45, 58, 62, 75-78, 115, 123-124, 134, 146, 164-166, 173-174, 176, 178, 197-198, 209, 215, 218, 221, 226, 230, 239-240, 247, 259, 265, 274-276, 278, 287-288, 293-294]

Asheville, NC
— family and household income, pp. 717-719 [1720, 1723-1724]
— first ancestry, pp. 315-316, 325, 329 [808-809, 823-824, 829]
— hours and earnings, p. 421 [1068]
— marital status, men, pp. 210-212 [519, 521-522]
— marital status, women, p. 215 [527]
— parks, pp. 1276-1278 [2977-2978, 2980, 2983]
— population, pp. 75, 78-79, 84, 86, 88, 127-132, 134, 138-139, 142 [297-300, 302, 304, 372-374, 376-386]
— poverty, pp. 748-751, 756-757, 779, 795, 825, 828, 847, 849-850 [1772-1773, 1775-1777, 1788-1789, 1828-1829, 1856, 1907, 1912, 1944, 1947-1949]

Asheville, NC MSA
— establishments and employment, pp. 1098-1099 [2566, 2568-2569]
— occupancy, pp. 436, 442, 460, 643, 695 [1099, 1113, 1152, 1568, 1683]

Ashford, WA
— parks, pp. 1278-1279 [2986-2987]

Ashland, KY
— cost of living, pp. 866-868 [1980, 1982, 1984, 1986]
— prisons and prison population, pp. 1268-1270 [2959-2961, 2965-2966]

Ashland, OH
— toxic chemicals, p. 36 [145]

Ashtabula, OH
— toxic chemicals, pp. 30, 44, 48, 65, 68 [122, 179, 196, 273, 287]

Aspen, CO
— sports activities, p. 1281 [2996]
— travel, p. 1283 [3006]

Numbers following p. or pp. are page references. Numbers in [ ] are table references.

Numbers following p. or pp. are page references. Numbers in [ ] are table references.

Numbers following p. or pp. are page references. Numbers in [ ] are table references.

1301

Numbers following p. or pp. are page references. Numbers in [ ] are table references.

Numbers following p. or pp. are page references. Numbers in [ ] are table references.

Location Index

1303

Barry County, MO
—toxic chemicals, p. 51 [209]
Bartholomew County, IN
—toxic chemicals, pp. 61, 67 [256, 284]
Bartow County, GA
—toxic chemicals, pp. 12, 23 [37, 86]
Bastrop, TX
—prisons and prison population, pp. 1268-1270 [2959-2961, 2965-2966]
Baton Rouge, LA
—air quality, p. 5 [4]
—asian population, p. 99 [326]
—city government debt, pp. 1154-1165 [2665-2671, 2673-2675, 2677-2680, 2682, 2684-2689]
—city government expenditures, pp. 1166-1189, 1214, 1216 [2691-2708, 2710-2715, 2721-2723, 2726, 2728-2737, 2739-2740, 2743, 2800, 2804]
—city government revenues, pp. 1189-1212 [2745-2753, 2756-2762, 2764-2767, 2769-2771, 2776-2780, 2782-2784, 2786-2793]
—cost of living, pp. 869-871, 873-875 [1988, 1991-1992, 1995-1996, 2001-2002, 2005-2006]
—crimes and crime rates, pp. 1225-1226, 1228-1230, 1233 [2830-2833, 2840, 2842-2848, 2855]
—diseases, pp. 247-248 [634, 637]
—family and household income, pp. 708, 713 [1704, 1714]
—federal assistance, p. 258 [670]
—first ancestry, pp. 317, 327 [811-812, 826]
—hours and earnings, pp. 420-422 [1067, 1069, 1072]
—income, pp. 729, 733 [1742, 1747]
—land area, p. 6 [11]
—marital status, women, p. 215 [526]
—population, pp. 74, 77, 80, 83, 85, 90, 100-101, 119, 122, 135, 137-138, 143 [297-300, 302, 307, 328-329, 356, 363-364, 383-386]
—poverty, pp. 745, 751-755, 765-769, 785, 793-794, 796, 801-811, 837, 839-842, 850 [1767-1768, 1778-1785, 1804-1810, 1839, 1854-1855, 1858, 1866-1883, 1929, 1932-1937, 1950]
—poverty rates, pp. 742-743 [1760-1761, 1763, 1765]
—revenues, pp. 1218-1220 [2813-2814, 2817]
Baton Rouge, LA MSA
—crimes and crime rates, pp. 1222-1223, 1226-1227, 1232 [2818-2819, 2821, 2823, 2834-2835, 2854]
—establishments and employment, pp. 975, 981, 992, 999, 1001, 1028, 1032, 1098-1099 [2284, 2297, 2320, 2334, 2338, 2400, 2408, 2566-2569]
—occupancy, pp. 436, 439, 442, 445, 448, 453, 457, 459-460, 466-468, 479, 481-482, 490, 497, 500, 503, 508-509, 511-512, 522, 524, 529, 532, 538, 541-543, 545, 548, 550-551, 554, 556-557, 560, 564-565, 570, 574, 591-593, 601, 615-616, 635, 643, 647, 652, 657, 668, 679, 682, 687 [1098, 1106, 1112, 1120, 1126, 1138, 1146-1147, 1150, 1154, 1166, 1170, 1172, 1198, 1201, 1204, 1222, 1238, 1244, 1246, 1252, 1263, 1266, 1270, 1272, 1295-1296, 1300, 1312, 1318, 1332, 1340, 1342-1343, 1347, 1356, 1360-1361, 1368, 1372, 1374, 1380, 1390, 1392, 1404, 1412, 1451-1452, 1455, 1473, 1504,

Baton Rouge, LA MSA continued:
1506-1507, 1549, 1567, 1576, 1588, 1599, 1622, 1646-1647, 1652, 1665]
—population, pp. 113, 117 [350, 355]
—tax-exempt establishments and employment, p. 1009 [2355]
Battle Creek, MI
—asian population, p. 97 [322]
—cost of living, pp. 869-871, 873 [1988, 1991, 1995, 2001]
—first ancestry, pp. 313, 315-316 [804, 808-809]
—marital status, men, p. 210 [518]
—marital status, women, p. 213 [523]
—population, pp. 75, 78, 80, 83, 87, 90, 127, 130, 133, 137, 139, 142 [297-300, 302, 306, 372, 377, 383-386]
—poverty, pp. 760, 765, 782-785, 787, 796, 806, 823-825, 827, 830, 834, 851 [1795, 1803, 1833, 1836, 1838, 1840, 1844, 1858, 1874, 1902-1907, 1910, 1917, 1923, 1951]
Battle Creek, MI MSA
—occupancy, pp. 611, 622 [1495, 1521]
Baxter County, AR
—population, p. 91 [309-311]
—toxic chemicals, pp. 41, 58 [166, 242]
Bay County, FL
—prisons and prison population, p. 1267 [2958]
—toxic chemicals, pp. 29-30, 48 [117, 120-121, 198]
Bayfield, WI
—parks, p. 1278 [2982]
Beach, FL
—poverty, p. 777 [1823]
Beattyville, KY
—prisons and prison population, p. 1267 [2957]
Beaufort County, NC
—toxic chemicals, p. 57 [240]
Beaufort County, SC
—toxic chemicals, p. 31 [124]
Beaumont, TX
—chemicals, p. 5 [7]
—crimes and crime rates, pp. 1229-1230 [2845-2846]
Beaumont–Port Arthur, TX MSA
—air quality, p. 4 [3]
—asian population, p. 99 [326]
—crimes and crime rates, p. 1222 [2820]
—establishments and employment, pp. 968-969, 973, 975, 981, 993, 1001, 1003, 1024, 1098-1099 [2270, 2272-2273, 2281, 2284, 2297, 2320, 2338, 2342, 2392, 2566-2568]
—family and household income, pp. 708, 713 [1704, 1714]
—first ancestry, p. 317 [811-812]
—immigrants admitted, p. 171 [441]
—occupancy, pp. 457, 482, 485-486, 489, 507, 521-522, 526, 532, 542-543, 546, 550-551, 564, 591-592, 620-621, 643, 657, 669, 675, 679, 687 [1146-1147, 1204, 1210, 1214, 1220, 1262, 1294-1295, 1304, 1318, 1342-1343, 1350, 1360-1361, 1390, 1451-1452, 1515-1516, 1519, 1567-1568, 1599-1600, 1624, 1638, 1647, 1665]
—population, pp. 74, 77, 80, 83, 86, 90, 100-101, 113, 117, 128-130, 134, 136, 138, 143 [297-300, 302, 306, 328-329, 350, 355, 374, 376-377, 383-386]
—poverty, pp. 751-756, 761-769, 790-791, 793, 795, 797-798, 801-802, 805-806, 808-811, 816, 834, 837, 839-842, 850-851 [1778-1781, 1783-1788, 1797-1810, 1848,

Numbers following p. or pp. are page references. Numbers in [ ] are table references.

1304

Numbers following p. or pp. are page references. Numbers in [ ] are table references.

Bethune – Cookman College (Daytona Beach, FL)
— degrees conferred, pp. 286, 288, 290, 293, 295 [771, 773, 775, 777, 779]
— enrollment, pp. 296, 299 [781, 784]
— finances and expenditures, pp. 304, 307 [793, 796]
Bexar, TX
— county government expenditures, pp. 1116, 1118-1119, 1121-1126 [2597-2598, 2600-2601, 2604, 2609-2615]
— county government revenues, pp. 1127-1128, 1130-1139, 1142-1143, 1145-1149, 1151 [2616-2618, 2622-2626, 2628, 2630-2632, 2634-2637, 2644, 2647, 2652-2655, 2658-2659, 2663]
— county population, p. 116 [353]
— toxic chemicals, pp. 21, 24, 28, 37, 45 [80, 91-92, 113, 149, 186]
— vital statistics, p. 255 [662]
Bibb, AL
— toxic chemicals, p. 56 [236]
Bibb, GA
— toxic chemicals, p. 29 [117]
Big Bend National Park, TX
— water and water use, p. 70 [295]
Big Sky, MT
— sports activities, p. 1281 [2996]
Big Spring, TX
— prisons and prison population, pp. 1268-1270 [2959-2961, 2965-2966]
Billings, MT
— cost of living, pp. 863-868 [1972, 1974, 1976, 1978, 1980, 1982, 1986]
— establishments and employment, p. 1098 [2566]
— family and household income, pp. 708, 713, 715, 718, 720 [1705, 1713, 1717, 1722-1723, 1726]
— first ancestry, pp. 312-316, 318, 322, 326-327, 330 [803-804, 806-807, 810, 813, 819, 824, 827, 832]
— foods and food products, pp. 1071-1073 [2496-2501]
— marital status, women, p. 213 [523]
— occupancy, pp. 578, 676 [1422, 1640]
— population, pp. 76, 78, 80, 83, 87, 101, 109, 112, 126-127, 133, 138, 141 [297-300, 302, 329, 342-343, 347, 370-371, 373, 383-386]
— postal service, p. 425 [1079]
— poverty, pp. 745-746, 757-759, 780-789, 815, 823-829, 831-833, 835, 845, 849, 853-854 [1768-1769, 1790-1794, 1830-1832, 1834-1835, 1837-1839, 1841-1847, 1890, 1903-1904, 1906-1910, 1913, 1915, 1919-1922, 1925, 1941, 1947, 1956-1957]
— revenues, p. 1219 [2816]
Biloxi, MS
— cost of living, pp. 867-868 [1984, 1986]
Biloxi – Gulfport – Pascagoula, MS
— asian population, pp. 96, 99 [320, 326]
— establishments and employment, pp. 1098-1099 [2566-2567]
— family and household income, pp. 708, 713-718 [1704, 1714, 1716-1720, 1723]
— first ancestry, pp. 317-318, 330 [811-812, 832]
— imports and exports, pp. 881, 899-900 [2031-2032, 2119,

Biloxi – Gulfport – Pascagoula, MS continued:
2124]
— marital status, men, p. 210 [518]
— occupancy, pp. 451, 508, 543, 585, 621, 643, 679 [1133, 1262-1263, 1343, 1438, 1519, 1567, 1647]
— population, pp. 75, 78, 81-82, 86, 101, 108, 113, 117, 122, 134, 136, 139, 143 [297-300, 302, 330, 341, 350, 355, 364, 383-386]
— poverty, pp. 751-756, 761-767, 779, 785, 790, 792-794, 796, 798, 801-802, 805-810, 824, 826, 828-830, 834, 839-842, 850-854 [1778-1781, 1783-1788, 1797-1807, 1828, 1839, 1849-1850, 1852, 1854, 1856, 1859, 1861-1862, 1866-1868, 1872-1876, 1878-1881, 1904, 1908-1909, 1912, 1914, 1916-1917, 1924, 1931, 1933, 1935, 1937, 1949-1957]
Binghamton, NY
— asian population, pp. 95, 98 [319, 324]
— cost of living, pp. 863-864, 866-867 [1971, 1975, 1981, 1983]
— establishments and employment, p. 1098 [2566]
— family and household income, p. 723 [1731]
— first ancestry, pp. 312-313, 315-316, 320-321, 323-324, 326, 328-329 [802-803, 808-809, 815-818, 820, 822, 825, 828, 830]
— hours and earnings, pp. 420-421 [1066, 1068]
— imports and exports, pp. 877-878, 900, 902 [2019-2020, 2124, 2129]
— marital status, men, p. 212 [522]
— occupancy, pp. 548, 674, 683, 685 [1355, 1635, 1655, 1659-1660]
— population, pp. 75, 78, 80, 83, 86, 88, 103, 113, 117, 129, 131, 135-136, 140-141 [297-300, 302, 304, 333, 350, 355, 376, 380, 383-386]
— poverty, pp. 750-751, 763, 786, 794, 798, 823, 825-826, 828, 847-848 [1775, 1777, 1801, 1842, 1855, 1862, 1902, 1906, 1908, 1913, 1944, 1946]
Birmingham, AL
— city government expenditures, p. 1188 [2741]
— crimes and crime rates, pp. 1222-1223, 1225-1226, 1228, 1231-1233 [2818, 2823, 2830-2832, 2840-2842, 2849-2852, 2854-2855]
— degrees conferred, pp. 287, 289, 291, 293, 295 [771, 773, 775, 777, 779]
— diseases, p. 250 [646]
— drug use, pp. 1233-1254, 1257-1267 [2856-2913, 2922-2956]
— employment, pp. 336-338 [835-838]
— enrollment, pp. 297, 299 [781, 784]
— establishments and employment, pp. 924, 956, 959, 968, 975, 981, 989-990, 1000-1001, 1015, 1019, 1024, 1028, 1030-1031, 1037-1042, 1044, 1054, 1059, 1068, 1087, 1098 [2180, 2245, 2250, 2270, 2284, 2297, 2313, 2316, 2336, 2338, 2375, 2383, 2393, 2400, 2405, 2407, 2419, 2421, 2423, 2426-2427, 2430, 2433, 2454, 2464, 2482, 2538, 2566]
— family and household income, pp. 707, 713 [1702, 1714]
— finances and expenditures, pp. 305, 307 [793, 796]
— first ancestry, pp. 325, 328 [823, 829]
— foods and food products, pp. 1071-1073 [2496-2501]
— home ownership, p. 266 [699]
— hours and earnings, p. 423 [1076]

Numbers following p. or pp. are page references. Numbers in [ ] are table references.

1306

Numbers following p. or pp. are page references. Numbers in [ ] are table references.

Boise City, ID continued:
— population, pp. 75, 78, 81-82, 86, 104, 109, 111, 113, 117, 122, 126, 133, 137, 141 [297-300, 302, 334, 343, 346, 350, 355, 363, 371-372, 383-386]
— poverty, pp. 744-747, 765, 782, 787, 792, 796, 825, 828-829, 831, 833 [1766-1769, 1772, 1803, 1833, 1843-1844, 1852, 1858, 1906-1907, 1913, 1915, 1919, 1922]
— revenues, p. 1219 [2815]
— toxic chemicals, p. 8 [17]
Bolivar County, MS
— toxic chemicals, p. 41 [166]
Boone County, KY
— toxic chemicals, p. 50 [206]
Boron, CA
— prisons and prison population, pp. 1269-1270 [2962-2964]
Bosque County, TX
— population, p. 91 [309-310]
Boston, MA
— air quality, pp. 4-5 [3-4]
— airports, pp. 1078-1079 [2512-2515]
— alcohol use, pp. 226-229 [553-564]
— aliens, pp. 146-147 [388, 391, 394]
— asian population, pp. 93-95, 99 [317-319, 326]
— city government debt, pp. 1154-1165 [2664-2671, 2673-2675, 2677-2680, 2683-2689]
— city government expenditures, pp. 1166-1188, 1213-1215 [2691-2708, 2710-2717, 2721-2724, 2726-2737, 2739-2742, 2797-2801, 2803-2804]
— city government revenues, pp. 1189-1213, 1216-1217 [2744-2751, 2753, 2756-2771, 2773-2774, 2776-2780, 2782-2796, 2806-2807, 2809]
— cocaine and heroin use, pp. 229-231 [565-570, 572-574]
— construction, p. 913 [2159]
— consumer expenditures, pp. 218-222 [532-540]
— cost of living, pp. 860-863, 869, 871-875, 1080-1082 [1960-1969, 1990, 1994, 1997-1998, 2000, 2004, 2007, 2521-2523, 2526, 2528, 2530-2534]
— costs, p. 912 [2152-2155]
— crimes and crime rates, pp. 1224, 1226, 1228, 1231-1233 [2824, 2833, 2840-2841, 2849, 2851-2853, 2855]
— daycare, pp. 222-223 [541, 543, 545-547]
— diseases, pp. 246-250 [633, 635, 638, 641, 643-644, 646]
— distribution of employment, pp. 370-376, 378-382, 385-390, 393-398, 402-407, 411-416 [945-954, 965-974, 985-994, 1005-1014, 1025-1034, 1045-1054]
— drug use, pp. 226, 233 [550-552, 578-580]
— drug use, marijuana, pp. 233-235 [581-589]
— eating habits, pp. 237-239 [597-602]
— emergency medical services, p. 251 [647-650]
— employment, pp. 336-338, 359-365, 367 [833, 835-838, 901, 903, 905, 907, 911, 913, 915, 917, 922-923, 933]
— energy prices, pp. 1102-1107 [2570-2585]
— establishments and employment, pp. 916-932, 934-935, 942-1003, 1016, 1018-1023, 1025-1037, 1039-1043, 1048-1050, 1052-1057, 1060, 1063-1068, 1086-1093, 1095-1099 [2162-2166, 2168-2170, 2172-2176, 2178-2179, 2182-2189, 2191-2194, 2196, 2198-2199, 2203-2207, 2214-2220, 2222-2226,

Boston, MA continued:
2228, 2230-2231, 2233-2236, 2238-2256, 2259-2264, 2266-2280, 2282-2301, 2303-2309, 2311-2312, 2314-2315, 2317-2318, 2320-2324, 2326-2334, 2337-2338, 2340, 2342, 2377, 2381-2390, 2394, 2396-2401, 2403-2406, 2408-2412, 2414-2416, 2420, 2424, 2427, 2429, 2431-2433, 2441-2443, 2445-2446, 2450-2461, 2466-2467, 2472-2473, 2475-2480, 2482, 2537, 2540-2542, 2544-2551, 2553-2554, 2558-2559, 2561-2563, 2566-2569]
— exercise habits, pp. 239-242 [603-617]
— family and household income, pp. 706-707, 709-711, 723-727 [1701-1703, 1706-1710, 1732-1738]
— finances and expenditures, pp. 309, 1276 [798-799, 2975]
— first ancestry, pp. 312-313, 317-321, 323-326, 330 [802, 805, 810-812, 814, 816-818, 821-822, 824, 826, 831]
— foods and food products, pp. 1069-1073 [2487-2490, 2496-2501]
— funeral prices, p. 224 [548-549]
— general summary, pp. 1014-1015, 1046 [2371-2374, 2435]
— geographic mobility, pp. 204-207, 258-265 [502-517, 671-698]
— hours and earnings, pp. 420, 423-424 [1065, 1076-1078]
— housing, pp. 267-269, 275 [708, 710, 712-713, 715, 738-740]
— immigrants admitted, pp. 149-173 [401, 403, 405, 407, 409, 411, 413, 415-445]
— imports and exports, pp. 878-879, 899-902 [2023-2024, 2120-2121, 2123, 2125-2128, 2131]
— income, pp. 728-736 [1740-1752]
— land area, p. 6 [11]
— marital status, men, p. 211 [520]
— marital status, women, p. 214 [525]
— medical insurance, p. 255 [665]
— medicines, p. 1075 [2505-2506, 2509-2510]
— naturalized citizens, pp. 173-185 [446-464]
— occupancy, pp. 432-483, 485-493, 495-510, 512-537, 539-571, 573-618, 620-703 [1089-1094, 1096-1097, 1099-1115, 1117-1123, 1125-1129, 1131, 1133-1137, 1139, 1141, 1143, 1145, 1147, 1149-1161, 1163-1165, 1167, 1169, 1171-1173, 1175-1185, 1187-1189, 1191, 1193-1197, 1199, 1201-1203, 1205-1207, 1211-1213, 1215-1217, 1219, 1221, 1223, 1225-1229, 1233, 1236-1241, 1243, 1245-1249, 1251-1255, 1257-1261, 1263-1265, 1267, 1269, 1273, 1275-1276, 1278-1281, 1283, 1285, 1287, 1289-1293, 1297-1315, 1317, 1319-1323, 1325, 1327-1329, 1331, 1335-1339, 1341-1345, 1347-1349, 1351, 1353-1355, 1357-1359, 1361, 1363-1367, 1369-1377, 1379, 1381, 1383-1385, 1387-1389, 1391, 1393-1402, 1404, 1406, 1409-1447, 1449-1472, 1474-1494, 1496-1502, 1504-1509, 1511-1512, 1515, 1517-1527, 1529-1534, 1537-1538, 1541-1547, 1549-1563, 1565-1567, 1569-1574, 1577-1578, 1580, 1583-1587, 1589-1598, 1600-1636, 1638-1665, 1667, 1669-1700]
— offices, p. 907 [2143, 2145-2146]
— population, pp. 74, 76, 80, 84-85, 90, 99-100, 102-103, 105-107, 110, 115-116, 119, 124-125, 135-136, 140, 142 [297-300, 302, 308, 327-328, 331-333, 337-340, 345, 352, 354, 357, 368-370, 383-386]
— population, immigrants, p. 148 [399]
— poverty, pp. 746-748, 761-765, 767-768, 778, 789-790, 792-

Numbers following p. or pp. are page references. Numbers in [ ] are table references.

1308

Numbers following p. or pp. are page references. Numbers in [ ] are table references.

1309

Location Index

Numbers following p. or pp. are page references. Numbers in [ ] are table references.

Numbers following p. or pp. are page references. Numbers in [ ] are table references.

Burlington, NC continued:
    [297-300, 302, 372-378, 383-386]
— poverty, pp. 746, 748-750, 756-757, 760, 769, 780, 784, 786,
    803-807, 809-811, 832, 840, 842, 847, 854 [1770,
    1773-1776, 1788-1789, 1795-1796, 1810, 1829,
    1838, 1841, 1869, 1871-1874, 1876, 1879, 1881-
    1883, 1920, 1934, 1936-1937, 1944, 1957]

Burlington, NC MSA
— occupancy, p. 684 [1657]

Burlington, VT
— cost of living, pp. 875, 1081 [2007, 2527]
— costs, p. 913 [2156-2157]
— family and household income, pp. 709-712, 720-727 [1706-
    1710, 1712, 1726, 1728-1737]
— first ancestry, pp. 312, 314, 316-317, 320, 324-325 [802-803,
    805, 809, 811-812, 815-816, 821-822, 824]
— hours and earnings, p. 422 [1071]
— marital status, men, p. 211 [520]
— marital status, women, p. 214 [525]
— population, pp. 76, 78, 80, 83, 87, 106, 109, 122-126, 134,
    137, 141 [297-300, 302, 338, 343, 364-368, 370-
    371, 383-386]
— poverty, pp. 744-747, 753, 781, 824-825, 827-829, 834, 848,
    854 [1766-1767, 1770-1772, 1782, 1832, 1905,
    1907, 1911, 1913, 1915, 1923, 1946, 1958]
— revenues, pp. 1112-1114, 1219 [2589-2596, 2815]

Burlington, VT MSA
— establishments and employment, p. 1098 [2566]
— occupancy, pp. 436, 570, 612 [1098, 1403-1404, 1498]

Burlington County, NJ
— toxic chemicals, pp. 11, 24, 26, 32, 40, 60, 68 [29, 91, 99,
    127, 161, 249, 285, 287]

Bushkill, PA
— parks, pp. 1276-1278 [2977-2978, 2980, 2983]
— water and water use, p. 70 [295]

Butler County, KS
— toxic chemicals, pp. 13, 34-35, 52, 57 [42, 139-140, 214,
    238]

Butler County, KY
— toxic chemicals, p. 20 [73]

Butler County, OH
— toxic chemicals, pp. 19, 23, 44, 57, 67, 69 [73, 88, 179, 238,
    284, 291]

Butler County, PA
— cost of living, p. 873 [2000]
— toxic chemicals, p. 43 [177]

Butner, NC
— prisons and prison population, pp. 1268-1270 [2959-2961,
    2965-2966]

Butte County, CA
— toxic chemicals, p. 67 [283]

C.A. Fredd State Technical College (Tuscaloosa, AL)
— degrees conferred, pp. 286, 288, 290, 293, 295 [771, 773,
    775, 777, 779]
— enrollment, pp. 296, 299 [781, 784]
— finances and expenditures, pp. 304, 307 [793, 796]

Cabarrus County, NC
— toxic chemicals, p. 22 [82]

Cabell County, WV
— toxic chemicals, pp. 16, 21, 33, 51, 62 [58, 78, 132, 211, 261]

Caddo Parish, LA
— toxic chemicals, p. 20 [76]

Cadillac, MI
— travel, p. 1283 [3005]

Calabasas, CA
— home-based businesses, p. 906 [2137]

Calcasieu Parish, LA
— toxic chemicals, pp. 8-12, 20, 23, 25, 29, 31, 34-37, 39-40, 42-
    43, 48, 55, 57, 59, 64-68 [19-21, 24, 27-28, 30-31, 33,
    75, 88, 97, 115-116, 123-124, 126, 136, 138, 143, 146,
    149-150, 159, 164, 173-174, 176-177, 196, 226, 238-
    239, 247, 267, 273, 277, 281, 287-288]

Caldwell County, NC
— toxic chemicals, pp. 45, 52 [184, 213]

Calhoun, AL
— toxic chemicals, pp. 32, 34, 50, 58, 61, 67 [131, 139, 209, 241,
    257, 284]

Calhoun, AR
— toxic chemicals, p. 65 [273]

Calhoun, IA
— toxic chemicals, p. 61 [257]

Calhoun, MI
— toxic chemicals, p. 35 [140]

Calhoun, TX
— toxic chemicals, pp. 10, 17-18, 20-21, 32, 35, 40, 44, 51-52, 60,
    68 [27, 63, 65-69, 75, 79, 129, 142, 164, 180, 182, 211,
    216, 250, 285, 287]

California State University (Long Beach, CA)
— degrees conferred, p. 288 [772]

California State University (Northridge, CA)
— enrollment, p. 304 [792]

Callaway County, MO
— toxic chemicals, p. 33 [133]

Cambria County, PA
— toxic chemicals, pp. 32, 47, 52, 62 [131, 194, 217, 259]

Cambridge, MA
— cost of living, p. 866 [1981]
— ventures, p. 906 [2139]

Camden, NJ
— bridges, p. 1079 [2518]
— county government expenditures, pp. 1116-1122, 1124-1126
    [2597-2602, 2604-2606, 2608-2610, 2612-2615]
— county government revenues, pp. 1127-1128, 1130, 1132-
    1139, 1141-1143, 1146-1147, 1149, 1151 [2616-2618,
    2623, 2626, 2628, 2630-2633, 2635-2637, 2640-2642,
    2644, 2646, 2653-2654, 2658-2659, 2663]
— county population, p. 116 [353]
— poverty rates, p. 742 [1762]
— toxic chemicals, pp. 16, 19-20, 44, 59 [58, 73-74, 182, 248]

Camden County, GA
— toxic chemicals, pp. 30, 46 [120-121, 188]

Cameron County, PA
— toxic chemicals, p. 31 [124]

Canadian County, OK
— toxic chemicals, p. 37 [151]

Canton, OH
— cost of living, pp. 863-866 [1972, 1974, 1976, 1978, 1980]

Numbers following p. or pp. are page references. Numbers in [ ] are table references.

Location Index

Champaign–Urbana–Rantoul, IL MSA continued:
— marital status, women, p. 214 [525]
— occupancy, pp. 450, 464, 477, 479, 488, 492, 494, 537, 559, 576, 588, 593, 612, 622, 627-629, 648, 684, 696 [1131, 1163, 1193, 1196, 1217, 1228, 1231, 1330, 1379, 1417, 1443, 1454, 1498, 1521, 1533-1534, 1536, 1577, 1658, 1684]
— population, pp. 75, 78, 81-82, 86, 90, 101, 104, 107, 110, 122-125, 134, 136, 139, 143 [297-300, 302, 306, 330, 335, 340, 344, 364-369, 383-386]
— poverty, pp. 753, 761-763, 778, 782, 785, 790, 794-795, 797-801, 805, 836-838 [1782, 1797-1799, 1801, 1827, 1834, 1839, 1849, 1856-1857, 1860, 1862-1865, 1872, 1927-1931]
— tax-exempt establishments and employment, p. 1004 [2344]

Charles County, MD
— livestock, p. 7 [13]

Charleston, NC
— shipping, p. 1082 [2535]

Charleston, SC
— asian population, p. 95 [320]
— cost of living, p. 875 [2007]
— family and household income, pp. 707-708, 712, 718 [1703-1704, 1712, 1722]
— imports and exports, pp. 899, 901 [2121, 2125]
— income, pp. 729, 733 [1742, 1747]
— marital status, men, p. 211 [521]
— marital status, women, p. 214 [526]
— occupancy, pp. 445, 451, 456, 461, 467, 471, 473, 487, 494-495, 507, 510, 513-514, 516, 519, 528, 532, 541-542, 546, 548, 550, 555, 557, 559, 564-565, 585, 587, 590, 617, 620, 643, 646, 649, 652, 679, 687, 695 [1118, 1132, 1144, 1154, 1168, 1178, 1182, 1214, 1232, 1234, 1262, 1268-1269, 1275, 1278, 1282-1283, 1288, 1310, 1318, 1340, 1342, 1350, 1356, 1360, 1370, 1374, 1379, 1390, 1392, 1438, 1443, 1450, 1510, 1516, 1566-1567, 1573-1574, 1580, 1587, 1646-1647, 1665, 1683]
— population, pp. 74, 77, 81-82, 85, 100, 103, 121-122, 124-125, 134, 137-138, 143 [297-300, 302, 328, 333, 362-363, 367-370, 383-386]
— poverty, pp. 744, 746-747, 765-769, 801-811, 839-842 [1766, 1770-1771, 1804-1810, 1866-1872, 1874-1883, 1932-1937]
— toxic chemicals, pp. 10, 29, 31, 48, 65 [27, 117, 123, 126, 198, 273]
— vacancies, pp. 280-281 [762-765]

Charleston, WV
— establishments and employment, pp. 1018-1019 [2380, 2383]
— family and household income, pp. 715-716 [1716-1717, 1719]
— first ancestry, pp. 312, 316, 328 [802, 809, 829]
— hours and earnings, p. 422 [1072]
— imports and exports, pp. 880-881, 900 [2029-2030, 2124]
— marital status, men, p. 210 [519]
— marital status, women, pp. 213, 215 [524, 527]
— occupancy, pp. 447, 457, 502, 519, 591, 601, 616 [1124,

Charleston, WV continued:
1147, 1250, 1288, 1451, 1473, 1506]
— population, pp. 75, 78-79, 84, 86, 108, 113, 117, 126, 128-131, 135, 137, 140, 142 [297-300, 302, 341, 350, 355, 371, 374-380, 383-386]
— postal service, p. 425 [1079]
— poverty, pp. 748-750, 754-756, 778-779, 785, 824, 827-831, 847-850 [1773-1776, 1784-1787, 1827-1828, 1839, 1904, 1910, 1913-1914, 1916-1917, 1919, 1944-1945, 1947-1949]
— revenues, pp. 1112-1114 [2589-2596]
— tax crime, p. 1272 [2974]
— tax-exempt establishments and employment, p. 1007 [2350]

Charleston–North Charleston, SC MSA
— establishments and employment, pp. 969, 986, 1024, 1050, 1059, 1062, 1089, 1093-1094, 1098-1099 [2273, 2307, 2392, 2444, 2464, 2469, 2543, 2553, 2556, 2567-2569]
— imports and exports, p. 903 [2134]
— population, pp. 113, 117 [350, 355]

Charlotte, NC
— airports, p. 1078 [2513-2514]
— apparel and apparel products, p. 1047 [2436-2438]
— city government debt, pp. 1154-1165 [2665-2675, 2677-2680, 2683-2689]
— city government expenditures, pp. 1166-1187 [2691-2708, 2710-2715, 2721-2723, 2726, 2728-2737, 2739]
— city government revenues, pp. 1189-1212 [2745-2751, 2753, 2756-2766, 2769-2772, 2776, 2778-2780, 2782-2793]
— construction, p. 914 [2160-2161]
— crimes and crime rates, pp. 1225-1226, 1228-1229, 1231-1233 [2830-2832, 2840, 2842-2843, 2849-2853, 2855]
— demolitions, p. 258 [666-668]
— employment, pp. 336-338 [835-838]
— foods and food products, pp. 1071-1073 [2496-2501]
— geographic mobility, p. 207 [517]
— hours and earnings, p. 423 [1076]
— land area, p. 7 [12]
— medicines, p. 1075 [2505-2506, 2509-2510]
— population, pp. 112, 115 [348, 351]
— poverty rates, pp. 742, 744 [1761, 1765]
— revenues, pp. 1112-1114, 1218 [2589-2596, 2812]
— vacancies, pp. 280-281 [762-765]

Charlotte County, FL
— population, p. 91 [309-311]

Charlotte–Gastonia–Rock Hill, NC–SC MSA
— air quality, p. 5 [4]
— asian population, p. 94 [318]
— construction, p. 913 [2158]
— crimes and crime rates, pp. 1222-1223, 1227, 1232 [2818-2819, 2823, 2835, 2854]
— distribution of employment, pp. 370-376, 385-390, 393-398, 402-407, 411-416 [945-954, 985-994, 1005-1014, 1025-1034, 1045-1054]
— employment, pp. 361, 367, 428-429 [907, 931, 1082, 1087]
— establishments and employment, pp. 918, 920, 924, 927, 930, 935, 942, 944, 947-949, 953-954, 956, 958-960, 963, 965, 969, 972, 980, 985, 988, 990, 993, 995-998, 1001, 1003, 1015-1017, 1019-1021, 1023, 1025-1029, 1031-1032, 1034-1036, 1039-1040, 1042-1043, 1059-1062,

Numbers following p. or pp. are page references. Numbers in [ ] are table references.

Numbers following p. or pp. are page references. Numbers in [ ] are table references.

Location Index

Numbers following p. or pp. are page references. Numbers in [ ] are table references.

Numbers following p. or pp. are page references. Numbers in [ ] are table references.

Numbers following p. or pp. are page references. Numbers in [ ] are table references.

Clarke County, AL
— toxic chemicals, p. 30 [120]

Clarkstown, NY
— cost of living, p. 874 [2003-2004]

Clarksville–Hopkinsville, TN–KY MSA
— asian population, p. 97 [323]
— family and household income, pp. 708, 713, 715-719 [1704-1705, 1713, 1717-1720, 1722-1724]
— first ancestry, pp. 329-330 [829, 831]
— marital status, women, p. 213 [524]
— occupancy, pp. 494, 537, 542, 629 [1231, 1330, 1342, 1536]
— population, pp. 75, 78, 82, 86, 88-89, 100-101, 103-104, 106, 109-111, 121, 123-125, 133, 136, 139, 143 [297-300, 302-303, 306, 328, 330, 333, 335, 337, 343-344, 346-347, 362, 365-369, 383-386]
— poverty, pp. 744, 746, 765-767, 786, 789, 793, 802-803, 805, 808-811, 827, 829, 832, 840-842, 852-854 [1766, 1770, 1804, 1806-1807, 1842, 1848, 1853, 1868-1869, 1873, 1878-1881, 1883, 1910, 1914, 1920, 1933, 1935-1937, 1953-1957]

Clatsop County, OR
— toxic chemicals, pp. 29-31 [117, 121, 125]

Clay County, FL
— toxic chemicals, pp. 8-9, 54 [19-20, 221]

Clay County, MO
— toxic chemicals, pp. 16, 50, 52, 58, 69 [58, 206, 213, 242, 289]

Clay County, MS
— toxic chemicals, p. 52 [216]

Clayton County, GA
— toxic chemicals, p. 32 [130]

Clearfield County, PA
— toxic chemicals, p. 50 [206]

Cleveland, OH
— aliens, pp. 146-147 [388, 391, 394]
— charity, p. 860 [1959]
— city government debt, pp. 1154-1165 [2665-2671, 2673-2681, 2684-2689]
— city government expenditures, pp. 1166-1187, 1214-1216 [2691-2706, 2708, 2710-2715, 2720-2723, 2725-2726, 2728-2737, 2739, 2799, 2802-2803, 2805]
— city government revenues, pp. 1189-1213, 1217 [2745-2751, 2753-2754, 2756-2762, 2764-2767, 2769-2772, 2776, 2778-2780, 2782-2784, 2786-2793, 2796, 2808]
— CMSA population, p. 120 [361]
— construction, p. 913 [2158]
— consumer expenditures, pp. 218-222 [532-540]
— cost of living, pp. 860-871, 873, 1080-1081 [1960-1965, 1967-1969, 1973, 1975, 1977, 1979, 1981, 1983, 1985, 1988, 1991, 1995, 2001, 2523, 2525]
— costs, p. 912 [2152-2155]
— crimes and crime rates, pp. 1224, 1226, 1228-1229, 1231-1232 [2825, 2833, 2841-2843, 2850-2853]
— diseases, p. 250 [646]
— distribution of employment, pp. 368-376, 383-416 [935-954, 975-1054]
— drug use, pp. 1233-1254, 1256-1267 [2856-2892, 2894-

Cleveland, OH continued:
2913, 2918-2956]
— emergency medical services, p. 251 [647-650]
— employment, pp. 336-339, 344-348, 354-359, 361, 363, 365-367, 428-429 [835-840, 856-869, 885-901, 907, 915, 924, 927, 930, 932-933, 1080-1081, 1085]
— energy prices, pp. 1102-1107 [2570, 2572-2577, 2579-2585]
— establishments and employment, pp. 916, 918-926, 928, 930-933, 935-936, 942-985, 987-988, 990-1003, 1015-1043, 1047-1055, 1057-1069, 1086-1092, 1094-1095, 1097-1099 [2163-2164, 2166-2169, 2171, 2174, 2176-2177, 2179-2182, 2184-2186, 2190-2191, 2195-2197, 2199-2202, 2207-2208, 2214-2215, 2217-2220, 2222-2226, 2228-2234, 2236, 2238-2240, 2242, 2244, 2246-2247, 2249-2257, 2259-2263, 2266-2272, 2274-2278, 2280, 2282-2283, 2285-2296, 2298-2304, 2308-2311, 2314-2315, 2317-2318, 2320-2331, 2333, 2335-2337, 2339-2340, 2342, 2375, 2377-2379, 2381-2390, 2392-2394, 2396-2407, 2409-2414, 2416-2431, 2440-2457, 2459-2463, 2465-2468, 2470-2484, 2536, 2538-2539, 2541, 2544-2549, 2551-2552, 2555, 2557-2558, 2560, 2564-2565, 2568]
— family and household income, pp. 706-707 [1701-1703]
— federal assistance, p. 258 [669]
— first ancestry, pp. 312, 314, 319, 321-324, 326, 328, 330 [802-803, 806, 814-815, 817-818, 820, 822, 825, 828, 832]
— foods and food products, pp. 1071-1074 [2496-2501]
— fortune 500 companies, p. 875 [2008]
— general summary, pp. 1014-1015, 1046 [2371-2374, 2434-2435]
— home furnishings and equipment, p. 1074 [2502]
— hours and earnings, pp. 420, 422-424 [1065, 1073-1078]
— immigrants admitted, pp. 148, 150-167, 173 [400, 404, 406, 408, 410, 412, 414, 416-436, 445]
— imports and exports, pp. 879, 899-902 [2025, 2120-2121, 2123, 2125-2128, 2132]
— income, pp. 728-738 [1740-1752, 1754-1759]
— land area, p. 6 [11]
— marital status, men, p. 212 [522]
— naturalized citizens, pp. 174-185 [446-464]
— occupancy, pp. 432-437, 439-455, 457-466, 468-480, 482-483, 485-487, 489-490, 492-493, 495-512, 514-530, 532-545, 547-557, 559-571, 574-579, 581-583, 585-601, 603-614, 616-618, 620-621, 624-625, 627-630, 632-651, 653-668, 670-682, 684-694, 696-703 [1089-1090, 1092-1096, 1100-1101, 1106-1115, 1117-1120, 1122-1127, 1132, 1134-1137, 1139-1143, 1146-1147, 1149-1161, 1164-1167, 1172-1189, 1191, 1193-1197, 1200, 1203-1204, 1206, 1210-1211, 1213, 1216, 1220-1223, 1226-1230, 1234, 1236-1257, 1259-1261, 1264-1267, 1270, 1272-1273, 1277-1281, 1284-1287, 1289-1293, 1296-1299, 1301-1307, 1309, 1311-1315, 1318-1323, 1325, 1327, 1329, 1331, 1333-1339, 1341-1342, 1344-1345, 1348-1349, 1352-1357, 1359, 1361, 1363-1375, 1380-1381, 1383-1386, 1388-1397, 1399-1402, 1405-1406, 1411-1421, 1423-1424, 1427-1432, 1436-1441, 1444-1448, 1451-1453, 1455-1458, 1460-1466, 1469-1472, 1477-1480, 1482-1490, 1492-1495, 1497, 1499-1502, 1506-1508, 1510-1511, 1515, 1517-1518, 1525-

Numbers following p. or pp. are page references. Numbers in [ ] are table references.

1319

Location Index

Cleveland, OH continued:
> 1528, 1531-1534, 1536-1537, 1539, 1542-1563,
> 1565-1566, 1569-1572, 1574, 1576-1581, 1583,
> 1585-1586, 1589-1598, 1600-1604, 1606-1613,
> 1615-1620, 1623, 1627-1631, 1633-1634, 1636-
> 1637, 1639, 1641-1646, 1649-1650, 1653-1654,
> 1657-1663, 1667, 1669-1674, 1676-1680, 1685-
> 1695, 1697-1700]
— offices, pp. 906-907 [2141-2142, 2148]
— population, pp. 74, 76, 79, 84-85, 89-90, 106, 112-113, 115,
> 117, 119-120, 130, 135, 137, 139, 143 [297-300,
> 302, 305, 308, 337, 349-350, 352, 355, 357, 359-
> 360, 378, 383-386]
— postal service, p. 425 [1079]
— poverty, pp. 750, 767-768, 801, 803, 805, 807, 831, 839,
> 841-842, 847-848 [1775-1776, 1808-1809, 1866,
> 1869-1870, 1872, 1875, 1918, 1932, 1934, 1936,
> 1944, 1946]
— poverty rates, pp. 742-743 [1760-1765]
— refugees and asylees, pp. 189-200 [485-501]
— restaurants, p. 1011 [2366]
— revenues, p. 1218 [2810-2811]
— tax-exempt establishments and employment,
> 1003-1006, 1008-1010 [2343-2349, 2353-2354,
> 2356]
— toxic chemicals, p. 8 [16-17]
— unemployment, pp. 417-419 [1055-1057, 1064]
— vacancies, pp. 280-282 [762-765, 767]
— vital statistics, pp. 251-253 [651-656]
Cleveland, TX
— prisons and prison population, pp. 1267-1268 [2957-2958]
Cleveland County, NC
— toxic chemicals, pp. 22, 32 [81, 128]
Cleveland State University (Cleveland, OH)
— degrees conferred, p. 291 [776]
Clifton, TN
— prisons and prison population, p. 1267 [2957-2958]
Clifton Forge, VA
— population, p. 92 [312]
Clinton County, IA
— toxic chemicals, pp. 40, 47, 68 [164, 192, 285]
Clinton County, MI
— toxic chemicals, p. 57 [237]
Clinton County, NY
— toxic chemicals, p. 39 [158]
Clinton County, PA
— toxic chemicals, pp. 17, 26, 30, 39 [60, 102, 122, 158]
Clinton Junior College (Clinton, SC)
— degrees conferred, pp. 286, 288, 290, 293, 295 [771, 773,
> 775, 777, 779]
— enrollment, pp. 296, 299 [781, 784]
— finances and expenditures, pp. 304, 307 [793, 796]
Cloud County, KS
— population, pp. 91-92 [310, 312]
Coahoma Community College (Coahoma County, MS)
— degrees conferred, pp. 286, 288, 290, 293, 295 [771, 773,
> 775, 777, 779]
— enrollment, pp. 296, 299 [781, 784]
— finances and expenditures, pp. 304, 307 [793, 796]

Coahoma County, MS
— toxic chemicals, pp. 12, 28, 56 [37, 113, 235]
Cobb County, GA
— toxic chemicals, pp. 62, 67 [258, 281]
Cocke County, TN
— toxic chemicals, pp. 10, 19, 43, 57 [26, 71, 177, 239]
Cocoa, FL
— geographic mobility, p. 207 [517]
Coeur d'Alene, ID
— cost of living, p. 870 [1992]
Coffee County, GA
— toxic chemicals, p. 20 [74]
Colbert County, AL
— toxic chemicals, pp. 9, 29, 34, 43, 48-49 [23, 115, 139, 177,
> 196, 201, 204]
Coleman County, TX
— population, p. 91 [310]
Coles County, IL
— toxic chemicals, p. 64 [271]
College of Du Page (Du Page, IL)
— degrees conferred, p. 286 [770]
— enrollment, pp. 302-304 [789, 791-792]
College Station, TX
— poverty rates, p. 742 [1762]
Collin County, TX
— toxic chemicals, pp. 21-22, 33, 45 [80, 82, 135, 186]
Colonial Height County, VA
— toxic chemicals, p. 37 [148]
Colorado Springs, CO
— asian population, pp. 96-98 [320, 322-323, 325]
— city government expenditures, pp. 1214-1216 [2800-2801,
> 2805]
— crimes and crime rates, pp. 1228, 1231 [2841, 2851]
— employment, pp. 336-338 [835-838]
— family and household income, pp. 712, 716-717, 719, 721
> [1712, 1719-1720, 1725, 1729]
— first ancestry, pp. 312-313, 322, 329 [803-804, 819, 830]
— hours and earnings, p. 423 [1076]
— housing, p. 275 [742]
— immigrants admitted, p. 169 [438]
— imports and exports, pp. 878, 902 [2021-2022, 2130]
— land area, p. 7 [12]
— marital status, women, p. 213 [524]
— population, pp. 74, 77, 81-82, 86, 89-90, 101, 103-104, 108-
> 112, 115, 121, 125-126, 133, 136, 140, 142 [297-300,
> 302, 305, 307, 330, 333-335, 341, 343-344, 346-348,
> 351, 362, 369-371, 383-386]
— poverty, pp. 744-745, 747-748, 759, 761, 764, 772, 774, 781,
> 783, 786, 788-789, 791-792, 811, 813, 815, 817-819,
> 833, 835-836, 838, 846 [1766-1768, 1771-1772, 1793,
> 1797-1798, 1802, 1816, 1819, 1832, 1836, 1841-1842,
> 1845-1846, 1848, 1850, 1853, 1884, 1886, 1889, 1893-
> 1895, 1922, 1926-1927, 1930, 1942]
— revenues, pp. 1218-1219 [2811, 2814]
— travel, p. 1283 [3005]
Colorado Springs, CO MSA
— establishments and employment, pp. 936, 943, 955, 957, 1092
> [2209, 2216, 2243, 2247, 2552]
— housing, pp. 270-274, 276-279 [719, 723, 725, 727, 729, 732,

Numbers following p. or pp. are page references. Numbers in [ ] are table references.

1320

Columbus, OH continued:
  972, 976-978, 980, 982, 984-990, 993, 995-996,
  998-1000, 1002-1003, 1016, 1018-1019, 1021,
  1023, 1027-1031, 1036-1042, 1050-1052, 1055,
  1059, 1061-1062, 1064, 1068-1069, 1089, 1094-
  1095, 1098 [2163-2164, 2166, 2169, 2171, 2174,
  2177, 2179-2182, 2184-2186, 2188, 2195, 2201-
  2202, 2207-2209, 2218, 2221-2222, 2227, 2229,
  2231-2232, 2234, 2237-2238, 2242, 2245-2246,
  2249-2250, 2252-2254, 2261, 2271, 2279, 2286,
  2288, 2291, 2294-2295, 2298, 2302-2305, 2307-
  2309, 2311-2316, 2320-2321, 2326-2327, 2331-
  2333, 2336, 2340-2341, 2377, 2381-2383, 2387,
  2390, 2398, 2400, 2403, 2405-2406, 2416-2419,
  2421-2422, 2425-2427, 2430, 2445, 2447-2450,
  2455, 2463, 2469-2471, 2474-2475, 2483-2484,
  2543, 2556, 2560, 2565]
— family and household income, pp. 706-707 [1701-1703]
— finances and expenditures, p. 309 [798-799]
— first ancestry, pp. 320, 326-327, 329-330 [815, 825-826, 830,
  832]
— general summary, p. 1046 [2434-2435]
— geographic mobility, p. 207 [517]
— hours and earnings, p. 423 [1076]
— imports and exports, pp. 879, 902 [2025, 2132]
— income, pp. 728-729, 731-736 [1740-1742, 1744, 1746-
  1747, 1749-1752]
— land area, p. 7 [12]
— marital status, women, p. 213 [523]
— occupancy, pp. 432, 434, 441, 444, 448, 450, 453-456, 459-
  466, 470-472, 474-476, 479-482, 484-486, 488, 493,
  496, 498, 500, 504-505, 509, 512, 518-519, 521-
  524, 526, 530, 535-536, 545, 548-550, 560-561,
  564, 567, 569, 573, 575-576, 578, 582, 584, 586,
  588, 590, 593-594, 596-600, 602-603, 605, 607-609,
  611-614, 617-618, 621, 623, 628, 631, 633-634,
  636, 638-639, 645, 647, 650, 654-656, 658, 666,
  668, 672, 679, 682-683, 685, 687, 695, 698, 700
  [1089, 1093-1094, 1109, 1117, 1125-1126, 1130-
  1131, 1137, 1139, 1142-1143, 1151, 1153, 1156,
  1158-1161, 1164-1165, 1167, 1176-1177, 1182,
  1185-1186, 1188, 1191, 1195, 1197, 1199, 1201,
  1203, 1205, 1207, 1211, 1213, 1217, 1229, 1236-
  1237, 1240, 1244, 1246, 1253, 1255, 1257, 1266,
  1273, 1287, 1289, 1293, 1296-1297, 1301, 1304,
  1313, 1326-1327, 1347-1348, 1354-1355, 1358-
  1359, 1381, 1384, 1389, 1396, 1400-1401, 1411,
  1414, 1417, 1421, 1429, 1435-1436, 1440, 1443-
  1444, 1447, 1455-1456, 1458, 1461, 1463-1466,
  1469-1470, 1476, 1478, 1481-1482, 1486, 1489-
  1490, 1495, 1498-1499, 1502, 1508, 1512, 1517,
  1522, 1533, 1541-1542, 1546-1547, 1553, 1557-
  1559, 1572, 1577, 1582, 1592, 1594-1595, 1597,
  1602, 1617-1618, 1622, 1631-1632, 1646, 1652,
  1656, 1659, 1664, 1682, 1689, 1693-1694]
— offices, p. 907 [2148]
— population, pp. 74, 77, 81, 83, 85, 90, 113, 117, 119, 124-
  126, 134, 136, 139, 142 [297-300, 302, 308, 350,
  355, 357, 368-370, 383-386]

Columbus, OH continued:
— postal service, p. 425 [1079]
— poverty, pp. 746-747, 767-768, 778, 794, 804-805, 825, 831,
  839 [1770-1771, 1808-1809, 1825-1826, 1855, 1870,
  1873, 1906, 1918, 1932]
— poverty rates, pp. 742, 744 [1760-1761, 1765]
— refugees and asylees, pp. 190-200 [485-501]
— revenues, pp. 1112-1114, 1218-1220 [2589-2596, 2810-2811,
  2815-2816]
— tax-exempt establishments and employment, pp. 1003-1009
  [2343-2351, 2353-2354]
— unemployment, pp. 418-419 [1060-1061, 1063]
— utilities, p. 1107 [2588]
— ventures, p. 906 [2139]
Columbus County, NC
— toxic chemicals, pp. 30-31, 48 [121, 125, 196]
Comanche County, KS
— population, p. 92 [312]
Community College of Allegheny County (Pittsburgh, PA)
— degrees conferred, p. 286 [770]
Community College of Rhode Island (Warwick, RI)
— degrees conferred, p. 286 [770]
Community College of the Air Force (Montgomery, AL)
— degrees conferred, p. 286 [770]
— enrollment, pp. 298, 302-304 [782-783, 789, 791-792]
Compton, CA
— poverty rates, p. 743 [1762]
Concordia College (Selma, AL)
— degrees conferred, pp. 286, 288, 290, 293, 295 [771, 773, 775,
  777, 779]
— enrollment, pp. 296, 299 [781, 784]
— finances and expenditures, pp. 304, 307 [793, 796]
Connersville, IN
— cost of living, p. 873 [2002]
Contra Costa County, CA
— county government expenditures, pp. 1116, 1118-1126 [2597-
  2598, 2600-2605, 2608-2615]
— county government revenues, pp. 1127-1151 [2616-2618,
  2620, 2623-2626, 2628, 2630-2641, 2643-2646, 2648-
  2649, 2652-2656, 2658-2659, 2661-2663]
— county population, p. 116 [353]
— toxic chemicals, pp. 10-11, 28-29, 39, 43, 46, 51, 55-56, 59, 62,
  65 [25, 29, 32, 113, 115-116, 158, 174, 176, 191, 211,
  227, 234, 247, 259, 273]
Cook County, GA
— toxic chemicals, pp. 28, 38, 46, 56 [112-113, 153, 188, 235]
Cook County, IL
— county government expenditures, pp. 1116, 1118, 1121-1126
  [2597-2598, 2600, 2609-2615]
— county government revenues, pp. 1127-1130, 1132-1135,
  1138-1139, 1142, 1144-1147, 1149-1151 [2616-2623,
  2625-2628, 2630-2631, 2635-2637, 2643-2644, 2648,
  2652-2654, 2658-2663]
— county population, p. 116 [353]
— housing, p. 266 [701-702]
— population, p. 92 [313-314]
— toxic chemicals, pp. 8-9, 12, 15-16, 18, 21-22, 25-29, 31-39, 41-
  42, 44-47, 49, 51-55, 57-58, 60-70 [18, 20, 33, 37, 50,
  56, 67, 77-79, 82, 98, 101-103, 109-110, 114, 126, 128,

Numbers following p. or pp. are page references. Numbers in [ ] are table references.

Numbers following p. or pp. are page references. Numbers in [ ] are table references.

Dallas, TX continued:

1341, 1344-1345, 1348-1349, 1354-1359, 1362-1402, 1405-1408, 1411-1421, 1423-1436, 1438-1448, 1453-1467, 1469-1472, 1474-1484, 1486-1496, 1499-1502, 1505, 1507-1508, 1510-1513, 1515, 1517-1518, 1522, 1525-1534, 1537-1546, 1548, 1551-1563, 1565-1566, 1569-1572, 1576-1580, 1583-1586, 1589, 1592-1604, 1606-1615, 1617-1620, 1623, 1625-1635, 1637, 1639-1646, 1649-1650, 1653-1654, 1656, 1659-1664, 1667, 1669-1700]

— offices, pp. 906-907 [2140-2142, 2145, 2148]
— population, pp. 74, 76, 81-82, 85, 89-90, 92, 99-103, 105-106, 108, 110, 113, 116-117, 119-121, 125-126, 133, 136, 139, 143 [297-300, 302, 305, 308, 313-314, 327-329, 331-332, 336, 338, 340-341, 345, 350, 354-355, 357, 359-360, 362, 369-371, 383-386]
— population, immigrants, p. 148 [399]
— poverty, pp. 744-748, 767-776, 794, 796, 799-800, 803, 806, 810, 813-822, 831, 835, 837-839, 843-846 [1766-1767, 1770-1772, 1808-1809, 1811-1822, 1855, 1858-1859, 1863-1865, 1869-1870, 1874, 1881, 1887-1901, 1918, 1926, 1928, 1930, 1932, 1938, 1940-1943]
— poverty rates, pp. 742-744 [1760-1761, 1763, 1765]
— refugees and asylees, pp. 190-200 [485-501]
— restaurants, p. 1011 [2365]
— revenues, pp. 1217-1218, 1220 [2810-2813, 2817]
— self-image, pp. 243-244 [618-623]
— steroid use, p. 232 [575-577]
— tax-exempt establishments and employment, pp. 1003, 1005-1006, 1008-1010 [2343, 2346-2348, 2353-2354, 2356]
— teachers, pp. 309-310 [800-801]
— television viewing, p. 1282 [2999]
— tobacco use, pp. 236-237 [591-596]
— toxic chemicals, pp. 8, 21-23, 32, 37, 60, 66-67 [18, 80, 82, 85, 130, 149, 152, 249, 276, 283]
— trade shows, p. 1286 [3010]
— travel, pp. 908, 1282 [2149-2151, 3003]
— unemployment, pp. 417-418 [1055-1057]
— utilities, p. 1107 [2588]
— vacancies, pp. 280-282 [762-765, 768]
— ventures, p. 906 [2138-2139]
— vital statistics, pp. 251-253 [651-656]
— youth risk behavior, pp. 244-246 [624-632]

Dallas County, AL
— toxic chemicals, p. 30 [121]

Danbury, CT
— hours and earnings, p. 420 [1065]
— imports and exports, pp. 878-879, 902 [2023-2024, 2131]
— marital status, parents, p. 216 [529]
— prisons and prison population, pp. 1268-1270 [2959-2961, 2965-2966]

Dane County, WI
— livestock, p. 7 [13]
— toxic chemicals, pp. 26, 48, 52, 55 [103, 197, 214, 227]

Danville, VA
— employment, pp. 344-348, 354-360, 362-364 [856-864, 866-869, 885-893, 895-900, 902, 904, 906, 912, 914, 916, 918]
— family and household income, pp. 713-716 [1713, 1715-1718]
— first ancestry, pp. 316, 328 [809, 829]
— imports and exports, p. 881 [2030]
— marital status, men, pp. 211-212 [521-522]
— marital status, women, pp. 214-215 [526-527]
— population, pp. 76, 79, 84, 87-88, 127-132, 135, 138, 143 [297-300, 302-304, 373-386]
— poverty, pp. 748-750, 755-757, 765-768, 779, 789, 801-805, 807-811, 836, 840-842, 847, 850-853 [1773-1776, 1785-1789, 1804-1807, 1810, 1828-1829, 1848, 1866-1869, 1871-1873, 1876-1883, 1927, 1933-1937, 1945, 1949, 1952-1954, 1956]

Darke County, OH
— toxic chemicals, p. 54 [224]

Darlington County, SC
— toxic chemicals, pp. 12, 17, 25, 41 [34, 62, 95, 165]

Dauphin County, PA
— toxic chemicals, p. 26 [101]

Davenport – Moline – Rock Island, IA – IL MSA
— establishments and employment, p. 1093 [2553]
— first ancestry, pp. 313, 318, 327 [804, 813, 827]
— housing, pp. 267, 269 [706, 714]
— imports and exports, p. 902 [2132]
— occupancy, pp. 436, 570, 578, 589, 626, 628 [1098, 1404, 1422, 1446, 1528, 1533]
— population, pp. 75, 77, 80, 83, 86, 88, 112-113, 117, 132, 134, 137, 140, 142 [297-300, 302-303, 347, 350, 355, 382-386]
— poverty, pp. 746, 786, 794, 823, 825-826, 828, 834 [1769, 1841, 1856, 1902, 1907-1908, 1913, 1924]

Davidson County, NC
— toxic chemicals, p. 48 [196]

Davidson County, TN
— toxic chemicals, pp. 8, 12, 17, 26, 55-56, 58 [18, 34, 62, 101, 103, 227, 234, 240]

Davies County, KY
— toxic chemicals, pp. 11, 26, 40, 48, 68-69 [30, 102, 161, 200, 288, 290]

Dayton, OH
— airports, p. 1079 [2515]
— construction, p. 913 [2158]
— cost of living, pp. 869-871, 873, 1081 [1988, 1991, 1995, 2001, 2526]
— crimes and crime rates, pp. 1229-1230 [2845-2848]
— diseases, pp. 247-250 [634, 636-637, 640, 642]
— distribution of employment, pp. 370-376, 393-398, 402-407, 411-416 [945-954, 1005-1014, 1025-1034, 1045-1054]
— establishments and employment, pp. 936, 945, 948, 950, 953, 955-957, 960, 984, 986, 991, 996, 999, 1002, 1041, 1052, 1064, 1068 [2209, 2221, 2227, 2232, 2237, 2242-2243, 2245, 2247, 2252, 2302-2303, 2306-2307, 2317, 2326, 2334, 2341, 2427, 2450, 2475, 2483]
— family and household income, pp. 706, 721 [1701, 1729]
— first ancestry, pp. 320, 327 [815, 826]
— hotels and motels, p. 1011 [2361]

Numbers following p. or pp. are page references. Numbers in [ ] are table references.

Location Index

1325

Numbers following p. or pp. are page references. Numbers in [ ] are table references.

Numbers following p. or pp. are page references. Numbers in [ ] are table references.

Numbers following p. or pp. are page references. Numbers in [ ] are table references.

Numbers following p. or pp. are page references. Numbers in [ ] are table references.

Numbers following p. or pp. are page references. Numbers in [ ] are table references.

1330

Numbers following p. or pp. are page references. Numbers in [ ] are table references.

Location Index

1331

Numbers following p. or pp. are page references. Numbers in [ ] are table references.

Numbers following p. or pp. are page references. Numbers in [ ] are table references.

Numbers following p. or pp. are page references. Numbers in [ ] are table references.

1334

Numbers following p. or pp. are page references. Numbers in [ ] are table references.

Numbers following p. or pp. are page references. Numbers in [ ] are table references.

Numbers following p. or pp. are page references. Numbers in [ ] are table references.

Garland County, AR
— toxic chemicals, pp. 33, 53 [132, 218]

Gary, IN
— cost of living, p. 863 [1971]
— crimes and crime rates, pp. 1223-1224, 1229-1230 [2822-2824, 2844-2848]
— diseases, pp. 247-249 [634, 636-637, 640, 642]
— hours and earnings, pp. 420-421 [1067, 1069]
— imports and exports, p. 879 [2026]
— population, pp. 113, 117 [350, 355]
— poverty rates, pp. 742-743 [1762, 1764]

Gaston County, NC
— toxic chemicals, pp. 9, 16, 19, 25, 27, 30, 36, 39, 41, 54-55, 68 [22, 58, 72, 95, 106, 122, 144, 158, 168, 223, 230, 288]

Gatlinburg, TN
— parks, pp. 1276-1278 [2977-2978, 2980, 2983]

Geauga County, OH
— toxic chemicals, pp. 20, 28, 41, 48 [74, 110, 167, 197]

Genesee County, MI
— toxic chemicals, pp. 37-38, 40, 42, 49, 61, 69 [148, 154, 163, 170, 204, 256, 289]

Gentry County, MO
— population, p. 92 [312]

George County, MS
— toxic chemicals, p. 22 [82]

George Mason University (Fairfax, VA)
— degrees conferred, p. 291 [776]

George Washington University (Washington, DC)
— degrees conferred, p. 291 [776]
— enrollment, p. 303 [790]

Georgetown County, SC
— toxic chemicals, p. 10 [24]

Georgia State University (Atlanta, GA)
— degrees conferred, p. 291 [776]

Gering, NE
— parks, p. 7 [14]

Gettysburg, PA
— parks, p. 1277 [2979]

Gila County, AZ
— toxic chemicals, pp. 22-23, 28, 33-34, 45, 53, 59, 62, 66, 69 [81, 83, 86, 110, 132, 134, 136, 187, 218, 244, 258, 260, 278, 291]

Giles County, VA
— toxic chemicals, pp. 17-18, 23 [64-65, 88]

Gillespie County, TX
— population, p. 91 [309-310]

Glades County, FL
— prisons and prison population, p. 1267 [2958]

Glen Jean, WV
— water and water use, p. 70 [295]

Glenn County, CA
— toxic chemicals, pp. 60, 64 [248, 271]

Glennallen, AK
— parks, pp. 1277-1279 [2981, 2984-2987]

Glens Falls, NY
— employment, p. 363 [914]
— family and household income, pp. 707-708, 719-720, 723 [1703, 1705, 1724-1725, 1727, 1731]

Glens Falls, NY continued:
— first ancestry, pp. 314-318, 320-321, 325-326, 329 [805, 808-809, 811-812, 816-817, 824-825, 830]
— hours and earnings, p. 420 [1066]
— marital status, men, pp. 211-212 [521-522]
— population, pp. 76, 79, 81-82, 87-88, 101, 103, 130, 132, 135, 138, 140-141 [297-300, 302, 304, 330, 332-333, 377, 382-386]
— poverty, pp. 745-746, 824-826, 828-829, 831, 848 [1767, 1769, 1905-1906, 1908, 1912-1913, 1915, 1919, 1946]

Glens Falls, NY MSA
— occupancy, p. 448 [1127]

Gloucester County, NJ
— toxic chemicals, pp. 23-24, 26, 34-35, 52-53, 57-60, 67 [87, 92, 103, 139-140, 214, 219, 237, 242, 244, 248, 284]

Glynn County, GA
— toxic chemicals, pp. 19, 24, 31, 34, 39, 48-49 [71, 90, 125, 139, 160, 196, 204]

Gogebic County, MI
— population, p. 91 [309-310]

Goodhue County, MN
— toxic chemicals, p. 14 [47]

Gordon County, GA
— toxic chemicals, p. 25 [95, 98]

Grafton, WV
— cost of living, pp. 868-873 [1987, 1989-1990, 1993-1994, 1997-2000]

Grambling State University (Grambling, LA)
— degrees conferred, pp. 286, 288, 290, 293, 295 [771, 773, 775, 777, 779]
— enrollment, pp. 297, 299 [781, 784]
— finances and expenditures, pp. 304, 307 [793, 796]

Grand Canyon, AZ
— parks, pp. 1276-1278 [2977-2978, 2980, 2983]

Grand Forks, ND
— asian population, p. 96 [320-321]
— employment, pp. 359-361 [902, 906, 908]
— family and household income, pp. 708, 712-713, 715-719 [1705, 1712-1713, 1717-1720, 1722-1724]
— first ancestry, pp. 314-317, 322-323, 327-328 [806-807, 810-811, 819-820, 827-828]
— marital status, men, p. 211 [520]
— marital status, women, p. 214 [525]
— occupancy, pp. 477, 611, 675, 684 [1191, 1495-1496, 1638, 1658]
— population, pp. 76, 79, 82, 87, 90, 109, 111, 121-125, 133, 136, 140-141 [297-300, 302, 306, 342, 346, 362, 364-370, 383-386]
— poverty, pp. 744-747, 753, 757-759, 779-781, 783, 787-788, 790, 797, 823, 829, 834-836, 839, 848, 853 [1766-1767, 1770-1771, 1782, 1790-1791, 1793-1794, 1827, 1830-1832, 1836, 1843-1846, 1850, 1859, 1902, 1914-1915, 1923, 1926-1927, 1931, 1946, 1955]
— toxic chemicals, pp. 46-47 [188, 193]

Grand Rapids, MI
— air quality, p. 4 [3]
— asian population, p. 99 [326]
— cost of living, p. 867 [1982]
— crimes and crime rates, pp. 1224, 1229 [2825, 2844]

Numbers following p. or pp. are page references. Numbers in [ ] are table references.

1338

Numbers following p. or pp. are page references. Numbers in [ ] are table references.

Numbers following p. or pp. are page references. Numbers in [ ] are table references.

Numbers following p. or pp. are page references. Numbers in [ ] are table references.

Location Index

1341

Numbers following p. or pp. are page references. Numbers in [ ] are table references.

Location Index

Numbers following p. or pp. are page references. Numbers in [ ] are table references.

1344

Houston, TX continued:
— hours and earnings, pp. 420, 422-424 [1065, 1072, 1076, 1078]
— housing, pp. 268-269, 275-276 [709, 711, 716, 738-740, 744]
— immigrants admitted, pp. 149-167 [401, 403, 405, 407, 409, 411, 413, 415-436]
— imports and exports, pp. 875-877, 881-900, 903-904 [2009-2016, 2031, 2033-2092, 2094-2118, 2120, 2123, 2135-2136]
— land area, p. 6 [12]
— libraries, pp. 1279-1280 [2988-2989]
— medicines, pp. 1074-1075 [2503, 2505-2507, 2509-2510]
— naturalized citizens, pp. 174-185 [446-464]
— offices, pp. 907-908 [2144, 2147-2148]
— population, pp. 85, 90, 113, 117, 119-120 [301, 308, 350, 355, 357-358]
— population, immigrants, p. 148 [397-399]
— poverty rates, pp. 742-743 [1760-1761, 1763, 1765]
— prisons and prison population, p. 1267 [2957]
— refugees and asylees, pp. 190-200 [485-501]
— restaurants, pp. 1011-1012 [2365, 2367]
— revenues, pp. 1217-1220 [2810-2813, 2815, 2817]
— sports activities, pp. 1280-1281 [2992, 2995]
— tax crime, p. 1272 [2973]
— teachers, pp. 309-310 [800-801]
— toxic chemicals, p. 24 [92]
— travel, p. 1282 [3000]
— unemployment, pp. 417-419 [1055-1057, 1062, 1064]
— utilities, p. 1107 [2588]
— vacancies, pp. 280-282 [762-766, 768]
— ventures, p. 906 [2138-2139]
— vital statistics, p. 255 [662]
Houston Community College (Houston, TX)
— enrollment, pp. 298, 302-304 [782-783, 788-789, 791-792]
Houston–Galveston–Brazoria, TX CMSA
— air quality, p. 4 [3-4]
— asian population, pp. 93-95, 99 [317-320, 326]
— CMSA population, p. 120 [361]
— consumer expenditures, pp. 218-222 [532-540]
— cost of living, pp. 860-863 [1960-1965, 1967-1969]
— employment, p. 339 [839-840]
— energy prices, pp. 1102-1107 [2570, 2572-2577, 2579-2585]
— establishments and employment, pp. 916-919, 921-926, 928-933, 935, 942-955, 957-968, 971-989, 991, 993-994, 996-999, 1001-1003, 1016-1024, 1026-1042, 1047-1069, 1087-1091, 1093-1098 [2163-2164, 2166, 2168-2169, 2174, 2176, 2179, 2182, 2184-2186, 2190-2191, 2196-2197, 2199, 2201, 2206-2207, 2214-2215, 2217-2220, 2223, 2225-2228, 2230-2231, 2233-2234, 2236-2237, 2239-2240, 2242-2243, 2247-2248, 2251, 2253, 2255, 2257, 2259-2264, 2266-2271, 2276-2277, 2279-2280, 2282-2292, 2295-2296, 2298-2301, 2303-2304, 2306-2308, 2310-2311, 2313, 2317-2318, 2322-2324, 2327-2330, 2332-2333, 2337, 2339-2340, 2342, 2376-2377, 2379, 2381-2382, 2384-2393, 2396-2397, 2399-2407, 2409, 2411-2413, 2415, 2417, 2419-2420, 2422-2423, 2425,

Houston–Galveston–Brazoria, TX CMSA continued:
2427-2431, 2440-2446, 2448, 2450-2457, 2459-2484, 2540-2549, 2554-2559, 2562-2563, 2565, 2567]
— family and household income, pp. 706-707, 710-712, 725-727 [1701-1703, 1707-1710, 1712, 1734-1738]
— first ancestry, pp. 312, 314, 318, 327, 330 [802, 806, 812, 826, 831]
— general summary, pp. 1014-1015, 1046 [2371-2374, 2434-2435]
— geographic mobility, pp. 204-207, 258-265 [502-516, 671-698]
— hours and earnings, pp. 422-423 [1073-1075]
— housing, p. 276 [744]
— immigrants admitted, pp. 168-172 [437, 439-444]
— imports and exports, pp. 899, 901 [2121, 2125-2128]
— income, pp. 728-738 [1740-1752, 1754-1759]
— marital status, men, p. 212 [521]
— marital status, women, p. 214 [526]
— occupancy, pp. 432-437, 439-456, 458-490, 492-528, 530-546, 548-590, 592-614, 616, 618, 620-622, 624-625, 627-651, 653-664, 666-683, 685-703 [1089-1092, 1094-1097, 1100-1102, 1105-1115, 1117-1129, 1131, 1134-1141, 1143-1145, 1148-1161, 1163-1189, 1191, 1193-1198, 1200, 1202-1208, 1211-1216, 1219-1223, 1226-1229, 1232-1233, 1235-1240, 1244-1250, 1252-1254, 1256-1257, 1259-1267, 1269, 1271, 1273-1282, 1285-1287, 1289-1293, 1296-1299, 1301-1309, 1314-1315, 1317-1325, 1327-1345, 1348-1349, 1356-1357, 1359-1361, 1363-1377, 1380-1394, 1396-1402, 1405-1421, 1423-1434, 1438-1447, 1449, 1453-1497, 1499-1503, 1507-1508, 1511-1512, 1515-1520, 1525-1528, 1531-1534, 1537-1539, 1541-1545, 1547-1567, 1569-1581, 1583, 1585-1586, 1589-1598, 1601-1605, 1607-1614, 1619-1621, 1623-1634, 1636-1637, 1639-1650, 1653-1654, 1659-1682, 1685-1691, 1693-1697, 1699-1700]
— population, pp. 74, 76, 81-82, 85, 99-102, 104-107, 110, 113, 116-117, 120-122, 125-127, 134, 136, 139, 144 [297-300, 302, 327-329, 331-332, 335-336, 338-340, 345, 350, 354-355, 359-360, 362-363, 369-372, 383-386]
— poverty, pp. 744-745, 747-748, 754, 763-765, 767-777, 790-796, 798-800, 803-810, 812-822, 831, 835-839, 841-846 [1766-1768, 1771-1772, 1783-1784, 1800-1803, 1808-1809, 1811-1824, 1849, 1851-1853, 1855, 1857, 1859, 1862-1865, 1869-1878, 1880-1882, 1885-1901, 1918, 1926-1932, 1934-1935, 1937-1943]
— tax-exempt establishments and employment, pp. 1003, 1005-1010 [2343, 2346-2348, 2351-2354, 2356]
— vital statistics, pp. 251-253 [651-656]
Howard County, IN
— toxic chemicals, pp. 33, 38 [135, 154]
Howard County, TX
— toxic chemicals, pp. 29, 50, 59 [116, 207, 247]
Howard University (Washington, DC)
— degrees conferred, pp. 286, 288, 290, 293, 295 [771, 773, 775, 777, 779]
— enrollment, pp. 297, 299 [781, 784]
— finances and expenditures, pp. 304, 307 [793, 796]
Hudson County, NJ
— bridges, p. 1079 [2518]
— county government expenditures, pp. 1116-1118, 1120-1122,

Numbers following p. or pp. are page references. Numbers in [ ] are table references.

1345

Hudson County, NJ continued:
1124-1126 [2597-2600, 2605, 2608-2610, 2612-2615]
— county government revenues, pp. 1127-1128, 1131, 1133-1139, 1141-1144, 1146-1147, 1151 [2616-2618, 2623, 2626, 2628, 2630-2633, 2635-2637, 2640, 2642, 2644, 2646-2648, 2653-2654, 2663]
— county population, p. 116 [353]
— population, p. 92 [313]
— toxic chemicals, pp. 25, 36, 38, 55, 58, 65 [98, 145, 147, 155, 227, 242, 275]

Humacao County, PR
— toxic chemicals, p. 39 [160]

Humboldt County, CA
— toxic chemicals, pp. 29-30, 48 [117, 121, 198]

Humphreys County, TN
— toxic chemicals, pp. 21, 23, 29, 43, 47, 65-66 [77, 86, 116, 179, 195, 273, 278]

Huntingdon County, PA
— toxic chemicals, p. 39 [157]

Huntington–Ashland, WV–KY–OH MSA
— establishments and employment, p. 1098 [2567]
— family and household income, pp. 708, 713-714, 716-717 [1704, 1714-1716, 1718, 1721]
— first ancestry, pp. 316, 320, 328-329 [809, 816, 829-830]
— imports and exports, p. 881 [2030]
— marital status, men, p. 210 [519]
— marital status, women, pp. 213, 215 [524, 527]
— occupancy, pp. 451, 514, 538, 585, 649, 684 [1133, 1277, 1333, 1437, 1581, 1658]
— population, pp. 75, 77, 79, 84, 86, 88, 113, 117, 127-130, 135, 138, 140-141 [297-300, 302, 304, 350, 355, 373-378, 383-386]
— poverty, pp. 750-757, 778-779, 822-824, 826-827, 829-831, 847-852 [1775, 1778, 1780-1781, 1783-1789, 1827-1829, 1902-1904, 1908, 1910, 1914, 1916-1917, 1919, 1945, 1947, 1949-1954]

Huntington County, IN
— toxic chemicals, p. 15 [51]

Huntsville, AL
— asian population, pp. 93, 95, 97-98 [317, 319, 323, 325]
— crimes and crime rates, p. 1229 [2844]
— family and household income, pp. 709-710, 712, 721, 724-726 [1706-1708, 1712, 1728, 1733-1736]
— first ancestry, pp. 325, 327-328, 330 [823, 826, 829, 831]
— hours and earnings, p. 420 [1065]
— imports and exports, pp. 881, 903 [2031, 2135]
— marital status, women, p. 213 [524]
— population, pp. 75, 78, 81-82, 86, 101, 125, 128, 133, 136, 139, 143 [297-300, 302, 330, 369-370, 374-375, 383-386]
— poverty, pp. 746-749, 764, 788, 797, 799-800, 805-806, 808-811, 834, 837-838, 840-842 [1770-1771, 1773-1774, 1803, 1846, 1859-1860, 1863, 1865, 1872-1873, 1875, 1877-1878, 1880-1883, 1924, 1928, 1930, 1933-1937]
— revenues, p. 1219 [2814]

Huntsville, AL MSA
— establishments and employment, pp. 955, 960, 991 [2243,

Huntsville, AL MSA continued:
2252, 2317]
— occupancy, pp. 434-435, 445, 455, 512, 514, 516, 518, 527-528, 537, 547-548, 558, 570, 664, 685 [1095-1097, 1118, 1142, 1272, 1278, 1282, 1286, 1308-1309, 1330, 1354-1355, 1376, 1378, 1402, 1613-1614, 1660]
— population, pp. 113, 118 [350, 355]

Huron County, OH
— toxic chemicals, pp. 28, 48, 62, 69 [110, 197, 258, 289]

Huston-Tilotson College (Austin, TX)
— degrees conferred, pp. 286, 288, 290, 293, 295 [771, 773, 775, 777, 779]
— enrollment, pp. 297, 299 [781, 784]
— finances and expenditures, pp. 304, 307 [793, 796]

Hutchinson County, TX
— toxic chemicals, pp. 12, 24, 29, 35 [33, 92, 116, 143]

Iberia Parish, LA
— toxic chemicals, pp. 29, 35, 62 [114, 116, 142, 258]

Iberville Parish, LA
— toxic chemicals, pp. 8-11, 13, 15, 22, 25, 29, 34-35, 39-40, 42-44, 48, 59-60, 68 [19-20, 27, 29, 42, 49, 84, 96, 115, 139-140, 160, 163-164, 173-174, 176, 180, 196, 245, 248, 287]

Incline Village, NV
— travel, p. 1283 [3006]

Independence County, AR
— toxic chemicals, pp. 10, 45 [26, 183]

Indian River County, FL
— population, p. 91 [309-310]

Indiana University (Bloomington, IN)
— degrees conferred, pp. 288, 290-291, 295 [772, 774, 776, 778]
— enrollment, pp. 298, 300-304 [782-783, 786-788, 791-792]

Indiana University - Purdue University at Indianapolis (Indianapolis, IN)
— degrees conferred, p. 291 [776]
— finances and expenditures, p. 306 [794]

Indianapolis, IN
— airports, p. 1079 [2515]
— city government debt, pp. 1154-1166 [2665-2671, 2673-2680, 2683-2690]
— city government expenditures, pp. 1166-1189, 1213-1215 [2691-2716, 2719-2723, 2726-2737, 2739-2740, 2742-2743, 2797-2798, 2800, 2803-2804]
— city government revenues, pp. 1189-1213, 1216-1217 [2745-2751, 2753-2754, 2756-2767, 2769-2771, 2776-2780, 2782-2784, 2786-2796, 2806-2807, 2809]
— cost of living, p. 866 [1980]
— crimes and crime rates, pp. 1228, 1231-1232 [2840-2841, 2849, 2851-2852]
— distribution of employment, pp. 368-376, 383-385, 390-417 [935-954, 975-984, 995-1054]
— drug use, pp. 1233-1254, 1257-1267 [2856-2913, 2922-2955]
— employment, pp. 336-338, 364-366, 428-429 [835-838, 920, 924, 927, 930, 1080-1081, 1085]
— establishments and employment, pp. 962, 965 [2258, 2265]
— family and household income, pp. 706-707, 709, 712, 723, 727 [1701-1703, 1706, 1710, 1732, 1738]
— finances and expenditures, p. 309 [798-799]
— foods and food products, pp. 1071-1074 [2496-2501]

Numbers following p. or pp. are page references. Numbers in [ ] are table references.

1346

Numbers following p. or pp. are page references. Numbers in [ ] are table references.

Location Index

1347

Numbers following p. or pp. are page references. Numbers in [ ] are table references.

Numbers following p. or pp. are page references. Numbers in [ ] are table references.

Janesville – Beloit, WI MSA continued:
1906, 1912-1913, 1919, 1948]
Jarvis Christian College, TX (Hawkins, TX)
— degrees conferred, pp. 286, 288, 290, 293, 295 [771, 773, 775, 777, 779]
— enrollment, pp. 297, 299 [781, 784]
— finances and expenditures, pp. 304, 307 [793, 796]
Jasper, MO
— toxic chemicals, pp. 54, 56, 62 [222, 236, 260]
Jasper, TX
— toxic chemicals, p. 30 [121]
Jayuya County, PR
— toxic chemicals, p. 41 [166]
Jefferson, AL
— toxic chemicals, pp. 21-23, 33-34, 36, 45-47, 52, 60, 69 [79-80, 82, 85, 88, 132, 137, 147, 186, 191, 195, 216, 251, 290]
Jefferson, CO
— toxic chemicals, p. 52 [213]
Jefferson, KY
— county government expenditures, pp. 1116-1126 [2597-2598, 2600-2601, 2603-2605, 2607-2615]
— county government revenues, pp. 1127-1128, 1131-1140, 1142, 1144-1145, 1147-1148, 1151 [2616-2618, 2623-2626, 2628-2632, 2634-2638, 2644, 2648, 2650-2651, 2654-2655, 2663]
— county population, p. 116 [353]
— enrollment, p. 300 [785]
— teachers, pp. 309-310 [800-801]
— toxic chemicals, pp. 11, 14, 16, 19-20, 22, 26, 28, 32, 39, 41-43, 46, 49-51, 53, 55-56, 58-59, 61-62, 65-66, 68-69 [30, 47, 56, 69, 73, 81, 102, 110, 129-130, 160-161, 166, 171, 179, 189, 200, 204, 206, 211, 218, 230, 236, 240, 242, 244, 256-258, 274-276, 287-289]
Jefferson, MO
— cost of living, pp. 869, 871, 873, 875 [1988, 1995, 2001-2002, 2006]
— toxic chemicals, pp. 22, 28, 31, 45, 69 [83, 110, 124, 187, 291]
Jefferson, OH
— toxic chemicals, pp. 21, 36, 69 [79, 147, 291]
Jefferson, TX
— toxic chemicals, pp. 9-13, 17, 19-21, 23, 29, 32, 34-35, 40, 43-44, 46, 49-51, 53, 55-60, 62-63, 65-66, 70 [20, 22-23, 25, 29-30, 37, 41, 43, 65, 69, 75-76, 78, 85, 88, 115, 128, 139, 142-143, 163-165, 175, 180, 191, 200, 205, 207, 211, 218, 221, 230, 233-234, 238, 243, 245, 247-248, 260, 263, 273, 278, 293-294]
Jefferson, WI
— toxic chemicals, p. 9 [20]
Jefferson, WV
— toxic chemicals, pp. 10, 44 [27, 182]
Jefferson Parish, LA
— cost of living, p. 863 [1972]
— toxic chemicals, pp. 17-18, 20, 33, 44, 50-51, 54-55, 63, 66 [65-69, 75, 134, 180, 182, 206, 211, 221, 226, 265, 278]

Jersey City, NJ
— alcohol use, pp. 226-229 [553-564]
— cocaine and heroin use, pp. 229-232 [565-570, 572-574]
— crimes and crime rates, pp. 1223, 1227, 1229-1230, 1232-1233 [2822, 2835, 2843-2844, 2847-2848, 2854-2855]
— diseases, pp. 246-249 [633, 635, 638-639, 641]
— drug use, pp. 226, 233 [550-552, 578-580]
— drug use, marijuna, pp. 233-235 [581-589]
— eating habits, pp. 237-239 [597-602]
— employment, pp. 344-348, 354-359 [856-864, 866-869, 885-893, 895-900]
— exercise habits, pp. 239-242 [603-617]
— foods and food products, p. 1070 [2493]
— hours and earnings, p. 420 [1065]
— immigrants admitted, pp. 149, 151-167 [402, 407, 409, 411, 413-414, 416-436]
— imports and exports, pp. 877-878, 902 [2019-2020, 2129]
— land area, p. 6 [11]
— marital status, parents, p. 215 [528]
— naturalized citizens, pp. 174-186 [446-464]
— population, pp. 90, 113, 115, 118-119 [307, 350, 352, 355-356]
— refugees and asylees, pp. 190-200 [485-501]
— self-image, pp. 243-244 [618-623]
— steroid use, p. 232 [575-577]
— tobacco use, pp. 236-237 [591-596]
— youth risk behavior, pp. 244-246 [624-632]
Jersey Shore, NJ
— housing, p. 266 [703]
Jesup, GA
— prisons and prison population, pp. 1268-1270 [2959-2961, 2965-2966]
J.F. Drake Technical College (Huntsville, AL)
— degrees conferred, pp. 286, 288, 290, 293, 295 [771, 773, 775, 777, 779]
— enrollment, pp. 297, 299 [781, 784]
— finances and expenditures, pp. 304, 307 [793, 796]
Johnson C. Smith University (Charlotte, NC)
— degrees conferred, pp. 286, 288, 290, 293, 295 [771, 773, 775, 777, 779]
— enrollment, pp. 297, 299 [781, 784]
— finances and expenditures, pp. 305, 307 [793, 796]
Johnson City – Kingsport – Bristol, TN – VA MSA
— establishments and employment, pp. 1018, 1093 [2380, 2553]
— family and household income, pp. 713-716 [1713-1716, 1718-1719]
— first ancestry, pp. 315-316, 320, 325, 328 [808-809, 816, 823, 829]
— imports and exports, pp. 881, 903 [2031, 2135]
— marital status, men, p. 210 [519]
— marital status, women, pp. 213, 215 [524, 527]
— occupancy, pp. 457, 514, 547, 591-592, 617, 649, 657, 684 [1147, 1277, 1353, 1451-1452, 1510, 1581, 1600, 1657]
— population, pp. 74, 77, 80, 83, 85, 88, 113, 118, 127-130, 134, 138, 140-141 [297-300, 302-304, 350, 355, 373-378, 383-386]
— poverty, pp. 748-749, 755-757, 778-779, 824, 827, 829-831, 833, 847-849, 851-853 [1773-1774, 1785-1789, 1827-1829, 1904, 1910, 1914, 1916-1917, 1919, 1922, 1944-

Numbers following p. or pp. are page references. Numbers in [ ] are table references.

Johnson City–Kingsport–Bristol, TN–VA MSA continued:
   1949, 1951-1955]
Johnson County, IN
—toxic chemicals, p. 17 [64]
Johnson County, KS
—toxic chemicals, pp. 28, 66 [111, 280]
Johnson County, MO
—toxic chemicals, p. 20 [73]
Johnson County, TX
—toxic chemicals, p. 28 [110]
Johnstown, PA
—cost of living, p. 1081 [2524]
—family and household income, pp. 708, 714-718 [1705, 1715-1723]
—first ancestry, pp. 312, 318-319, 321-324, 326, 328-330 [803, 813, 815, 817-818, 820, 822, 825, 828, 830, 832]
—hours and earnings, p. 421 [1068, 1070]
—marital status, men, pp. 210, 212 [519, 522]
—marital status, women, p. 215 [527]
—population, pp. 75, 78, 80, 84, 86, 88, 128-132, 135, 138, 140-141 [297-300, 302, 304, 375-386]
—poverty, pp. 746, 749-751, 755-756, 779-780, 824, 829-831, 847-850, 852-854 [1769, 1774-1777, 1786-1788, 1828-1829, 1904, 1914, 1916-1917, 1919, 1944-1949, 1954-1957]
Johnstown, PA MSA
—occupancy, pp. 494, 514, 521, 559, 629, 649 [1231, 1277, 1294, 1378, 1536, 1581]
Jones County, TX
—toxic chemicals, p. 50 [207]
Joplin, MO
—family and household income, pp. 708, 713-718 [1705, 1713, 1715-1723]
—first ancestry, pp. 315-316 [808-809]
—imports and exports, p. 900 [2122]
—marital status, men, p. 210 [519]
—marital status, women, pp. 213, 215 [524, 527]
—population, pp. 75, 78, 80, 84, 87-88, 90, 109, 131-133, 137, 141 [297-300, 302-304, 306, 342, 379-381, 383-386]
—poverty, pp. 756-760, 779, 782-784, 787-789, 794-795, 823-824, 826-827, 829-835, 847, 849, 851-854 [1787, 1789, 1791, 1793-1796, 1827-1829, 1833-1835, 1838, 1843, 1845-1848, 1855, 1857, 1902, 1904, 1908, 1910, 1914, 1916-1917, 1919-1921, 1923, 1925, 1945, 1948-1949, 1952-1957]
Juneau, AK
—revenues, p. 1219 [2814]
Kalamazoo, MI
—asian population, pp. 94, 97-98 [317, 323, 325]
—family and household income, pp. 710-712, 721, 724, 727 [1707-1710, 1728, 1733, 1737]
—first ancestry, pp. 313, 315, 317, 320 [804, 808, 810, 815]
—marital status, men, p. 211 [520]
—marital status, women, p. 214 [525]
—population, pp. 75, 78, 80, 84, 86, 122-124, 134, 136, 139, 142 [297-300, 302, 364-368, 383-386]
—poverty, pp. 753, 784, 795, 799-801, 805, 834, 837, 839 [1782, 1838, 1856-1857, 1863-1864, 1866, 1873,

Kalamazoo, MI continued:
   1923, 1929, 1931]
—toxic chemicals, pp. 17-18, 37, 39, 41, 48, 57, 60, 63 [64-65, 67, 151, 160, 169, 198, 237, 250, 266]
Kalamazoo, MI MSA
—occupancy, pp. 449, 517, 549, 593, 653 [1128, 1285, 1358, 1454, 1590]
Kalamazoo–Battle Creek, MI MSA
—establishments and employment, p. 1093 [2553]
—imports and exports, pp. 879, 902 [2025-2026, 2132]
—population, pp. 113, 116, 118 [350, 354-355]
—tax-exempt establishments and employment, pp. 1004, 1009 [2345, 2355]
Kalaupapa, HI
—parks, p. 1279 [2986]
Kalawao County, HI
—population, pp. 91-92 [311-312]
Kalispell, MT
—cost of living, pp. 863-868 [1972, 1974, 1976, 1978, 1980, 1982, 1984, 1986]
—water and water use, p. 70 [295]
Kanawha County, WV
—toxic chemicals, pp. 17-19, 27-28, 31, 39-41, 44, 50-51, 57, 59-60, 62, 68 [64, 67-70, 104, 113, 123, 126, 158, 162, 165-166, 180, 205-206, 212, 239, 248, 250, 259-260, 285, 288]
Kane County, IL
—housing, p. 266 [701-702]
—toxic chemicals, p. 61 [256]
Kankakee, IL
—asian population, p. 96 [321]
—employment, pp. 359-360, 362-364 [902, 906, 912, 916, 918]
—family and household income, pp. 713, 719-721, 723 [1713, 1724, 1727-1728, 1731]
—first ancestry, pp. 313-315, 317-318, 321, 330 [804, 806-807, 811-812, 818, 832]
—occupancy, pp. 482, 634 [1204, 1547]
—population, pp. 76, 79-80, 83, 87-88, 113, 118, 122, 131, 135, 138-139, 143 [297-300, 302-303, 350, 355, 363, 379, 383-386]
—poverty, pp. 745-746, 760, 765-767, 802-803, 805, 809, 826, 828, 837, 840, 842 [1767, 1769, 1795, 1804-1807, 1867-1869, 1873, 1879, 1908, 1912, 1929, 1933, 1937]
—toxic chemicals, pp. 18, 26 [68, 101, 103]
Kansas City, MO–KS
—aliens, pp. 146-147 [387, 390, 393]
—asian population, p. 96 [321]
—city government debt, pp. 1154-1165 [2665-2671, 2673-2680, 2684-2689]
—city government expenditures, pp. 1166-1188, 1214 [2691-2715, 2721-2724, 2726, 2728-2737, 2739, 2741, 2800-2801]
—city government revenues, pp. 1190-1213 [2745-2751, 2753-2754, 2756-2762, 2764-2766, 2769-2771, 2776, 2778-2780, 2782-2793, 2796]
—consumer expenditures, pp. 218-222 [532-540]
—cost of living, pp. 873, 875 [2001, 2006]
—costs, p. 912 [2152-2155]
—crimes and crime rates, pp. 1225-1226, 1228-1229, 1231-1233

Numbers following p. or pp. are page references. Numbers in [ ] are table references.

Location Index

1351

Kansas City, MO – KS continued:
[2830-2833, 2840-2843, 2849-2853, 2855]
— diseases, p. 250 [646]
— distribution of employment, pp. 370-376, 385-390, 393-399, 402-408, 411-417 [945-954, 985-994, 1005-1014, 1025-1034, 1045-1054]
— drug use, pp. 1260-1262 [2930-2937]
— employment, pp. 336-338, 362, 365-367, 428-429 [835-838, 913, 925, 928, 931, 1082-1083, 1087]
— establishments and employment, pp. 916-927, 929-931, 933, 935-936, 942-969, 971-978, 980-988, 990-1003, 1015-1023, 1025-1044, 1049-1052, 1055, 1058-1066, 1068-1069, 1086-1087, 1089, 1092-1094, 1098 [2163-2164, 2166, 2168-2169, 2171, 2174, 2176-2177, 2179-2182, 2184-2186, 2188, 2191, 2195, 2197, 2201-2202, 2206-2209, 2214-2215, 2217, 2219-2234, 2236-2238, 2240-2245, 2247-2251, 2253, 2255-2257, 2259-2264, 2266-2267, 2269, 2271-2273, 2276-2291, 2294-2296, 2298, 2301-2302, 2305-2311, 2314-2315, 2318-2333, 2335-2337, 2339-2342, 2375-2379, 2381-2391, 2394-2407, 2409-2426, 2428-2433, 2443, 2445, 2447-2448, 2450, 2455, 2461, 2463-2465, 2467-2468, 2471, 2473-2476, 2478, 2482, 2484, 2536, 2538, 2543, 2551, 2553, 2555-2557, 2565]
— family and household income, pp. 706-707, 709, 723 [1701-1703, 1706, 1732]
— first ancestry, p. 313 [804]
— foods and food products, pp. 1071-1074 [2496-2501]
— general summary, pp. 1014-1015, 1046 [2371-2374, 2434-2435]
— home furnishings and equipment, p. 1074 [2502]
— hours and earnings, p. 423 [1076]
— housing, pp. 268-269 [709, 711-713, 716]
— imports and exports, pp. 879, 902 [2025, 2132]
— income, pp. 728-736 [1740-1752]
— land area, p. 6 [12]
— marital status, women, p. 213 [523]
— medicines, p. 1075 [2505-2506, 2509-2510]
— occupancy, pp. 432-433, 435-444, 447-448, 452-453, 456, 461-464, 466, 468, 470-476, 478-479, 481, 483, 486-487, 489-490, 492, 496-498, 501-503, 505-507, 509-510, 514, 518, 520-523, 526-527, 530-531, 533-534, 536, 538-541, 546, 548-550, 554-555, 557-561, 563-568, 570-573, 575-576, 578-580, 582-583, 586-587, 590, 593-600, 602, 604-607, 609-611, 613-615, 617-618, 621-622, 624, 627, 631-633, 636-637, 640-642, 644-645, 650, 654-656, 658-659, 662-663, 665, 667, 670-671, 674-679, 683, 686, 690-692, 694-701, 703 [1089-1091, 1095, 1099-1103, 1105, 1108, 1111, 1113-1114, 1116-1117, 1124-1125, 1134, 1136-1137, 1143, 1155-1161, 1163, 1166, 1170-1171, 1176-1177, 1179-1180, 1182-1185, 1187, 1189, 1195, 1197, 1200-1201, 1207, 1212-1214, 1220-1221, 1226-1227, 1236-1241, 1247, 1249, 1251, 1255, 1257-1258, 1260-1261, 1265, 1267, 1278, 1287, 1290-1293, 1296-1299, 1305, 1307, 1314-1315, 1322-1323, 1327, 1332-1336, 1338-1339, 1351, 1356-1357, 1359,

Kansas City, MO – KS continued:
1368-1369, 1371, 1375, 1377-1379, 1381, 1383-1384, 1387-1389, 1391, 1394-1397, 1399, 1404-1409, 1413, 1415-1417, 1421, 1424, 1426, 1429, 1434, 1439, 1441-1442, 1447, 1456-1457, 1460-1466, 1468, 1470-1471, 1475-1476, 1481-1482, 1485, 1487, 1490, 1492, 1494, 1499-1502, 1505, 1510-1513, 1517, 1521, 1525-1526, 1532, 1541-1545, 1551, 1554, 1561, 1563, 1565, 1569, 1571, 1582-1583, 1592, 1595-1597, 1601-1604, 1609-1612, 1616, 1619-1620, 1627-1629, 1637-1640, 1642-1644, 1646, 1654-1656, 1662-1663, 1672, 1674-1677, 1680, 1683, 1685-1686, 1688, 1691, 1693, 1695-1696, 1699-1700]
— population, pp. 74, 77, 80, 83, 85, 109, 111-113, 115, 118, 126, 133, 137, 139, 143 [297-300, 302, 343, 347, 349-351, 355, 370-371, 383-386]
— poverty, pp. 744-745, 748, 767-768, 803, 825, 831, 839 [1766, 1768, 1772, 1808-1809, 1870, 1907, 1918, 1932]
— poverty rates, pp. 742, 744 [1761, 1765]
— refugees and asylees, pp. 190-200 [485-501]
— restaurants, p. 1011 [2365]
— revenues, pp. 1112-1114, 1218, 1220 [2589-2596, 2810, 2813, 2816]
— tax-exempt establishments and employment, pp. 1003-1010 [2343, 2345-2353, 2355-2356]
— travel, p. 1282 [3004]
— unemployment, pp. 418-419 [1060, 1063]
— vacancies, p. 282 [767-768]
Kansas State University of Agriculture and Science (Manhattan, KS)
— degrees conferred, p. 292 [776]
Kay County, OK
— toxic chemicals, pp. 29, 50, 62, 67 [114, 116, 207, 261, 284]
Kenai Peninsula County, AK
— toxic chemicals, p. 20 [75]
Kenosha, WI
— employment, pp. 359-360, 362, 364 [902, 904, 906, 912, 918]
— hours and earnings, p. 422 [1071]
Kenosha, WI PMSA
— population, pp. 113, 118 [350, 355]
Kent County, DE
— toxic chemicals, p. 67 [281]
Kent County, MD
— toxic chemicals, p. 25 [98]
Kent County, MI
— toxic chemicals, pp. 49, 58, 65, 67-68 [204, 240, 242, 274, 281, 289]
Kent County, RI
— toxic chemicals, pp. 24, 54, 66 [90, 223, 277]
Kent County and Queen Anne's County, MD
— air quality, p. 4 [3]
Kenton County, KY
— toxic chemicals, p. 26 [102]
Kentucky State University (Frankfort, KY)
— degrees conferred, pp. 286, 288, 290, 293, 295 [771, 773, 775, 777, 779]
— enrollment, pp. 297, 299 [781, 784]
— finances and expenditures, pp. 305, 307 [793, 796]

Numbers following p. or pp. are page references. Numbers in [ ] are table references.

1352

Numbers following p. or pp. are page references. Numbers in [ ] are table references.

Location Index

Numbers following p. or pp. are page references. Numbers in [ ] are table references.

Lake County, IL continued:

— marital status, parents, p. 216 [529]

— toxic chemicals, pp. 34, 41, 52, 62, 68 [138, 166, 214, 258, 288]

Lake County, IN

— toxic chemicals, pp. 9-10, 21, 23, 33, 35, 38, 40-41, 44, 46-47, 51-53, 60, 66, 69 [23, 27, 79-80, 88, 132, 142, 154, 165-166, 179, 187, 195, 213, 216, 218, 248, 251, 278, 291]

Lake County, OH

— toxic chemicals, pp. 11, 28-29, 33, 37, 47, 65, 68 [30, 112, 115, 133-134, 149, 192, 274, 285]

Lake Geneva, WI

— housing, p. 266 [703]

Lakeland – Winter Haven, FL MSA

— construction, p. 913 [2158]

— crimes and crime rates, pp. 1222-1223, 1226 [2819, 2821, 2834]

— employment, p. 361 [909]

— establishments and employment, pp. 924, 952, 1025, 1059, 1061 [2180, 2235, 2395, 2464, 2469]

— family and household income, pp. 708, 715-719 [1705, 1717-1725]

— first ancestry, pp. 316, 330 [809, 831]

— geographic mobility, p. 207 [517]

— marital status, men, pp. 210, 212 [518-519, 522]

— marital status, women, p. 213 [524]

— occupancy, pp. 455, 484, 507, 514, 559, 590, 646 [1142, 1208, 1260, 1278, 1378, 1448, 1575]

— population, pp. 74, 77, 80, 83, 86, 90, 102, 114, 118, 128-132, 134, 137, 139, 143 [297-300, 302, 306, 332, 350, 355, 375-381, 383-386]

— poverty, pp. 749-751, 756-757, 779, 788, 796, 807-808, 826, 828, 834, 849-850, 853-854 [1775-1777, 1788-1789, 1828, 1845, 1858, 1875, 1877-1878, 1908, 1912, 1924, 1948-1949, 1955-1957]

Lamar County, TX

— toxic chemicals, p. 23 [86]

Lamesa, TX

— farms, p. 6 [9-10]

Lancaster, CA

— crimes and crime rates, p. 1229 [2844]

Lancaster, NE

— toxic chemicals, pp. 37, 65 [151, 274-275]

Lancaster, PA

— asian population, pp. 94, 96, 99 [318, 321, 326]

— family and household income, pp. 709, 713, 718-724 [1706, 1713, 1723-1733]

— first ancestry, pp. 318, 326, 329 [813, 825, 830]

— imports and exports, pp. 878, 902 [2019-2020, 2129]

— marital status, men, p. 210 [519]

— marital status, women, p. 213 [524]

— population, pp. 74, 77, 81, 83, 86-88, 90, 103, 105-106, 110, 135, 137, 140, 142 [297-300, 302-304, 306, 333, 337-338, 345, 383-386]

— poverty, pp. 744-746, 785, 790, 795, 827-829, 849, 854 [1766, 1768-1769, 1840, 1849, 1856-1857, 1911, 1913, 1915, 1948, 1958]

— toxic chemicals, pp. 22, 33, 36, 45, 52, 65 [84, 135, 145,

Lancaster, PA continued:

186, 214, 274]

Lancaster, PA MSA

— establishments and employment, pp. 984, 998, 1002, 1023, 1037, 1039, 1055-1056 [2302, 2332, 2341, 2390-2391, 2418, 2422, 2457-2458]

— occupancy, pp. 444, 484, 511, 536, 548, 559, 578-579, 611, 619, 628, 634, 647, 672, 685 [1117, 1209, 1271, 1327, 1355, 1378, 1421-1422, 1496, 1514, 1535, 1547, 1576, 1631-1632, 1660]

— population, pp. 114, 118 [350, 355]

Lancaster, SC

— toxic chemicals, pp. 9, 34, 39, 48 [23, 139, 157, 197]

Lander, WY

— weather and climate, p. 70 [296]

Lane College (Jackson, TN)

— degrees conferred, pp. 287-288, 290, 293, 295 [771, 773, 775, 777, 779]

— enrollment, pp. 297, 299 [781, 784]

— finances and expenditures, pp. 305, 307 [793, 796]

Langston University (Langston, OK)

— degrees conferred, pp. 287-288, 290, 293, 295 [771, 773, 775, 777, 779]

— enrollment, pp. 297, 299 [781, 784]

— finances and expenditures, pp. 305, 307 [793, 796]

Lansing, MI

— crimes and crime rates, p. 1224 [2825]

— housing, pp. 267, 269 [706, 714]

— parks, p. 7 [14]

Lansing Community College (Lansing, MI)

— degrees conferred, p. 286 [770]

Lansing – East Lansing, MI MSA

— asian population, pp. 94-98 [317, 319, 321, 323-324]

— establishments and employment, pp. 936, 990 [2209, 2315]

— family and household income, pp. 710, 723-725 [1707, 1731, 1733-1735]

— first ancestry, pp. 312-316, 318-320, 326-327 [802, 804-805, 808-810, 812, 814-815, 825-826]

— hours and earnings, pp. 420-422 [1065, 1067, 1069, 1072]

— marital status, men, p. 211 [520]

— marital status, women, p. 214 [525]

— occupancy, pp. 436, 468, 503, 537, 547, 559, 563, 570, 602, 628, 634-635, 637-638, 647, 669, 674 [1098, 1171, 1251, 1331, 1352, 1378, 1388, 1404, 1476, 1535, 1547, 1550, 1555-1556, 1577, 1624, 1635]

— population, pp. 74, 77, 80, 83, 86, 88, 114, 116, 118, 122-124, 133, 136, 140, 142 [297-300, 302-303, 350, 354-355, 364-368, 383-386]

— poverty, pp. 753, 759, 761-763, 783-785, 793, 797-798, 825, 836-838 [1782, 1793, 1797-1801, 1836, 1838-1840, 1854, 1860-1861, 1906, 1927, 1929, 1931]

Laramie County, WY

— toxic chemicals, pp. 20, 50 [76, 207]

Laredo, TX

— employment, pp. 361-362, 364 [908, 912, 918]

— family and household income, pp. 708, 713-715 [1704, 1714-1718]

— foods and food products, p. 1070 [2493]

— immigrants admitted, pp. 168-173 [437-445]

Numbers following p. or pp. are page references. Numbers in [ ] are table references.

Numbers following p. or pp. are page references. Numbers in [ ] are table references.

1356

Location Index

Numbers following p. or pp. are page references. Numbers in [ ] are table references.

Lexington, KY MSA
— city government expenditures, p. 1216 [2804]
— establishments and employment, pp. 962, 996, 1018, 1023, 1087 [2256, 2326, 2380, 2391, 2539]
— family and household income, pp. 711, 713, 727 [1709, 1713, 1737]
— first ancestry, pp. 316, 325-326, 329 [809, 823-824, 829]
— land area, p. 6 [12]
— marital status, women, p. 213 [523]
— occupancy, pp. 453, 484, 506, 514, 559, 619, 628, 649, 695 [1136, 1209, 1258, 1277, 1379, 1513, 1535, 1581, 1683]
— population, pp. 75, 77, 80, 84, 86, 88-90, 106, 114-115, 118, 124-127, 135, 137, 139, 142 [297-300, 302-303, 306-307, 338, 350-351, 355, 368-372, 383-386]
— poverty, pp. 798, 830 [1862, 1917]
— tax-exempt establishments and employment, p. 1004 [2344]

Lexington County, SC
— toxic chemicals, pp. 34, 62 [136, 260]

Liberty County, TX
— toxic chemicals, pp. 18, 28 [66, 113]

Licking County, OH
— toxic chemicals, p. 41 [169]

Lihue, HI
— cost of living, pp. 863-868 [1971, 1973, 1975, 1977, 1979, 1981, 1983, 1985]

Lima, OH
— cost of living, pp. 869-871, 873 [1988, 1991, 1995, 2001]
— family and household income, pp. 713, 717-718, 721-723 [1713, 1721-1723, 1728-1731]
— first ancestry, pp. 318, 329 [813, 830]
— hours and earnings, pp. 421-422 [1067, 1069, 1072]
— housing, pp. 267, 269 [706, 714]
— population, pp. 75, 78, 81-82, 86-87, 89, 135, 138-139, 142 [297-300, 302-303, 306, 383-386]
— poverty, pp. 745-746, 787, 805, 826, 829, 831 [1768-1769, 1843, 1872, 1908, 1915, 1919]

Lima, OH MSA
— occupancy, pp. 559, 628 [1378, 1535]

Limestone County, TX
— toxic chemicals, p. 36 [144]

Lincoln, NE
— asian population, p. 99 [326]
— family and household income, pp. 712-713, 719, 721-722 [1712-1713, 1725, 1729-1730]
— first ancestry, pp. 314-315, 318, 327 [806-807, 813, 826-827]
— housing, pp. 267, 269 [706, 714]
— marital status, men, p. 211 [520]
— marital status, women, p. 214 [525]
— naturalized citizens, pp. 174-186 [446-464]
— population, pp. 75, 78, 81, 83, 86, 89, 111, 119, 123-124, 133, 136, 140-141 [297-300, 302, 305, 346, 356, 365-368, 383-386]
— poverty, pp. 746, 753, 758, 761-762, 764, 780-781, 792, 795, 797-798, 825, 827, 839 [1770, 1782, 1792, 1797-1798, 1802, 1830, 1832, 1852, 1856-1857, 1860, 1862, 1906-1907, 1911, 1931]

Lincoln, NE continued:
— revenues, p. 1219 [2814]

Lincoln, NE MSA
— crimes and crime rates, p. 1223 [2821]
— occupancy, pp. 458, 511, 599, 611, 628, 647, 654 [1148, 1271, 1467, 1495, 1535, 1575, 1591]
— tax-exempt establishments and employment, p. 1004 [2344]

Lincoln County, KS
— population, p. 92 [312]

Lincoln County, WI
— toxic chemicals, p. 69 [291]

Lincoln Parish, LA
— toxic chemicals, p. 61 [257]

Lincoln University (Jefferson, MO)
— degrees conferred, pp. 287, 289-290, 293, 295 [771, 773, 775, 777, 779]
— enrollment, pp. 297, 299 [781, 784]
— finances and expenditures, pp. 305, 307 [793, 796]

Lincoln University (Lincoln University, PA)
— degrees conferred, pp. 287, 289-290, 293, 295 [771, 773, 775, 777, 779]
— enrollment, pp. 297, 299 [781, 784]
— finances and expenditures, pp. 305, 307 [793, 796]

Linn County, IA
— toxic chemicals, pp. 40, 62 [165, 259]

Linn County, OR
— toxic chemicals, p. 65 [273]

Little Rock, AR
— crimes and crime rates, pp. 1229-1230 [2844-2848]
— daycare, p. 223 [542]
— diseases, pp. 247-248, 250 [634, 637, 642]
— revenues, p. 1220 [2816]

Little Rock – North Little Rock, AR MSA
— crimes and crime rates, pp. 1222-1223, 1226, 1232 [2818-2821, 2823, 2834, 2854]
— establishments and employment, pp. 960, 1032, 1038 [2252, 2408, 2421]
— first ancestry, p. 327 [826]
— marital status, women, p. 213 [523]
— occupancy, pp. 436, 450, 453, 458, 481, 487, 499, 507, 511, 514, 519, 527, 538-539, 541, 547, 549, 557, 560, 590, 625, 628, 647, 654, 658, 675 [1099, 1132, 1138, 1148, 1202, 1216, 1244, 1260, 1271, 1278, 1288, 1308, 1332-1334, 1338, 1352, 1356, 1374, 1382, 1448, 1528, 1535, 1575, 1591, 1600, 1637]
— population, pp. 74, 77, 80, 84-85, 90, 114, 118, 134, 137, 139, 143 [297-300, 302, 306, 350, 355, 383-386]
— poverty, pp. 765-769, 785, 802-805, 808-811, 840 [1804-1807, 1809-1810, 1840, 1868-1873, 1877-1880, 1882-1883, 1932-1933]

Live Oak County, TX
— toxic chemicals, p. 10 [25]

Livingston County, MI
— toxic chemicals, p. 36 [144]

Livingston County, NY
— toxic chemicals, pp. 24, 35, 57, 63 [90-91, 140, 239, 266]

Livingstone College (Salisbury, NC)
— degrees conferred, pp. 287, 289-290, 293, 295 [771, 773, 775, 777, 779]

Numbers following p. or pp. are page references. Numbers in [ ] are table references.

1358

Location Index

Numbers following p. or pp. are page references. Numbers in [ ] are table references.

Numbers following p. or pp. are page references. Numbers in [ ] are table references.

Numbers following p. or pp. are page references. Numbers in [ ] are table references.

Numbers following p. or pp. are page references. Numbers in [ ] are table references.

Location Index

Numbers following p. or pp. are page references. Numbers in [ ] are table references.

Numbers following p. or pp. are page references. Numbers in [ ] are table references.

Location Index

Numbers following p. or pp. are page references. Numbers in [ ] are table references.

Numbers following p. or pp. are page references. Numbers in [ ] are table references.

Location Index

Numbers following p. or pp. are page references. Numbers in [ ] are table references.

1368

Numbers following p. or pp. are page references. Numbers in [ ] are table references.

Location Index

Minneapolis–St. Paul, MN–WI continued:
— tax-exempt establishments and employment,
  pp. 1003-1010 [2343-2354, 2356]
— unemployment, p. 419 [1061, 1063]
— vacancies, p. 282 [769]
— vital statistics, pp. 251-253 [651-656]

Mississippi, AR
— toxic chemicals, pp. 29, 32, 41, 49, 63, 67, 69 [114, 130,
  168, 201, 263, 282, 291]

Mississippi State University (Mississippi State, MS)
— degrees conferred, p. 292 [776]

Mississippi Valley State University (Itta Bena, MS)
— degrees conferred, pp. 287, 289, 291, 293, 295 [771, 773,
  775, 777, 779]
— enrollment, pp. 297, 299 [781, 784]
— finances and expenditures, pp. 305, 307 [793, 796]

Missoula, MT
— cost of living, pp. 870-871, 873 [1992, 1996, 2002]
— toxic chemicals, p. 29 [117]

Mobile, AL
— asian population, pp. 94, 99 [318, 326]
— crimes and crime rates, p. 1229 [2845]
— daycare, p. 223 [542, 544]
— diseases, pp. 247-248, 250 [634, 636-637, 642]
— family and household income, pp. 708, 713 [1704, 1714]
— first ancestry, pp. 325, 328 [823, 829]
— hours and earnings, p. 422 [1072]
— imports and exports, pp. 899, 901 [2121, 2125-2128]
— population, pp. 74, 77, 79, 84-85, 90, 115, 119, 133, 137-
  138, 143 [297-300, 302, 307, 351, 356, 383-386]
— poverty, pp. 751-758, 760, 765-769, 788, 790, 793, 801-806,
  808-811, 834, 837, 839-842, 850-852 [1778-1781,
  1783-1789, 1791, 1795-1796, 1804-1810, 1846,
  1849, 1854, 1866-1873, 1875, 1877-1883, 1924,
  1929, 1932-1937, 1950-1951, 1954]
— revenues, pp. 1219-1220 [2814, 2817]
— tax crime, p. 1272 [2974]
— toxic chemicals, pp. 12, 26, 29-31, 44-45, 48, 50-51, 57-59,
  64-66, 69-70 [34, 102, 114-115, 122-123, 125, 180,
  183, 196, 206, 212, 239, 241, 244, 268, 273, 278,
  293-294]

Mobile, AL MSA
— establishments and employment, pp. 943, 1024, 1042, 1098
  [2216, 2392, 2429, 2567]
— occupancy, pp. 451, 454, 456, 468, 480, 482, 487, 494, 507-
  508, 510-511, 517, 519, 527, 534, 541-543, 550,
  558, 560, 565, 588, 590-591, 616-617, 621-623,
  628, 643, 646, 648, 679-680, 687 [1132, 1139,
  1144-1145, 1172, 1199, 1204, 1215, 1232, 1262-
  1263, 1268-1269, 1284, 1288, 1307, 1324, 1340,
  1342-1343, 1360, 1376, 1382, 1392, 1443, 1449-
  1450, 1508, 1510, 1519-1520, 1523, 1534, 1567,
  1573-1574, 1579, 1647-1648, 1665]
— population, pp. 114, 118 [350, 355]

Modesto, CA
— asian population, pp. 93-96, 98-99 [317-321, 324, 326]
— family and household income, p. 713 [1713]
— first ancestry, pp. 323, 327 [821, 827]
— immigrants admitted, pp. 168-172 [437-444]

Modesto, CA continued:
— imports and exports, p. 880 [2027-2028]
— income, pp. 728, 730-731, 733 [1740, 1743, 1745, 1748]
— naturalized citizens, pp. 174-186 [446-464]
— population, pp. 75, 77, 81, 83, 86, 88-89, 99, 101-102, 104-105,
  108-111, 121, 133, 136, 140, 143 [297-300, 302-303,
  306, 327, 329, 331, 334-336, 340, 342, 344-347, 362-
  363, 383-386]
— poverty, pp. 744-745, 751-752, 758-765, 769-777, 780, 782,
  784-786, 788-792, 794, 796-800, 811-824, 826-828,
  833-835, 837-838, 843-846, 851-852 [1766-1768,
  1778-1780, 1791-1793, 1796-1803, 1811-1815, 1817-
  1824, 1830, 1834, 1838-1842, 1845-1846, 1848-1853,
  1855-1856, 1858-1865, 1884-1901, 1903, 1905, 1908,
  1911-1912, 1921, 1923-1926, 1928-1930, 1938, 1940,
  1942-1943, 1952, 1954]

Modesto, CA MSA
— crimes and crime rates, p. 1222 [2818-2819]
— establishments and employment, p. 1023 [2391]
— occupancy, pp. 436, 456, 458, 484, 508, 524, 544, 570, 589,
  606, 619, 660, 682 [1098, 1144, 1148, 1209, 1262,
  1300, 1347, 1404, 1446, 1485, 1513-1514, 1605, 1652]
— population, pp. 114, 118 [350, 355]

Monmouth, NJ
— county government expenditures, pp. 1116-1118, 1120-1126
  [2597-2601, 2605, 2608-2615]
— county government revenues, pp. 1127-1129, 1131, 1133-
  1141, 1143-1148, 1151 [2616-2618, 2623, 2626, 2628,
  2630-2633, 2635-2637, 2639-2640, 2642, 2646, 2648,
  2650, 2653-2655, 2663]
— county population, p. 116 [353]
— toxic chemicals, pp. 27, 38, 59, 63 [104, 155, 245, 264]

Monmouth–Ocean City, NJ PMSA
— diseases, pp. 247, 249 [635, 639]
— home ownership, p. 266 [699]
— hours and earnings, p. 420 [1065]
— imports and exports, pp. 878, 902 [2020, 2129]
— naturalized citizens, pp. 174-186 [446-464]
— population, pp. 114, 118 [350, 355]

Monongalia County, WV
— toxic chemicals, pp. 33, 57 [135, 238]

Monroe, AL
— toxic chemicals, pp. 30, 56 [121, 236]

Monroe, IN
— toxic chemicals, p. 65 [275]

Monroe, LA
— family and household income, pp. 708, 713-716 [1704, 1714-
  1715, 1717-1718]
— first ancestry, pp. 317-318, 320, 329 [811-812, 816, 829]
— imports and exports, p. 881 [2032]
— marital status, men, p. 212 [521]
— marital status, parents, p. 215 [528]
— marital status, women, p. 214 [526]
— population, pp. 75, 78-79, 84, 87, 101, 122, 135, 138, 143 [297-
  300, 302, 329, 363-364, 383-386]
— poverty, pp. 751-757, 765-768, 784-785, 793, 801-802, 804-
  811, 836, 840-842, 847, 850-852 [1778-1789, 1804-
  1807, 1810, 1838, 1840, 1854, 1866-1868, 1871-1880,
  1882-1883, 1927, 1933-1935, 1937, 1945, 1950-1953]

Numbers following p. or pp. are page references. Numbers in [ ] are table references.

Monroe, LA continued:
— revenues, p. 1219 [2814]
Monroe, LA MSA
— crimes and crime rates, p. 1222 [2818]
— occupancy, p. 458 [1148]
Monroe, MI
— cost of living, pp. 869, 871, 873 [1988, 1995, 2001-2002]
Monroe, MS
— toxic chemicals, pp. 29, 47, 52, 65, 68 [116, 195, 214, 273, 287]
Monroe, NY
— bridges, p. 1079 [2518]
— county government expenditures, pp. 1116-1122, 1124-1126 [2597-2605, 2608-2610, 2612-2615]
— county government revenues, pp. 1127-1151 [2616-2618, 2620, 2622-2623, 2625-2626, 2628-2633, 2635-2638, 2640, 2642, 2644, 2647-2650, 2653-2655, 2657, 2660-2663]
— county population, p. 116 [353]
— toxic chemicals, pp. 9, 11-14, 17, 35, 37, 42, 44, 46, 51, 60-63, 66, 68 [20, 29, 34, 41, 48, 64, 143, 148, 151, 170, 182, 189, 191, 212, 248, 250, 257, 260, 266, 277, 288]
Monroe, OH
— toxic chemicals, p. 44 [181]
Monroe, PA
— toxic chemicals, pp. 51, 53 [213, 220]
Monroe, TX
— poverty rates, p. 742 [1762]
Monterey Basin, CA
— travel, p. 1283 [3006]
Monterey County, CA
— livestock, p. 7 [13]
Montgomery, AL
— asian population, p. 98 [324]
— crimes and crime rates, p. 1229 [2845]
— family and household income, pp. 708, 714 [1704, 1714]
— first ancestry, pp. 325, 327-328 [823, 826, 829]
— imports and exports, p. 881 [2032]
— population, pp. 75, 77, 79, 84, 86, 109, 119, 134, 137-138, 144 [297-300, 302, 343, 356, 383-386]
— poverty, pp. 752-753, 755-757, 765-768, 784, 791, 801-811, 832, 840-842, 850 [1780-1781, 1785, 1788-1789, 1803-1810, 1838, 1851, 1866-1883, 1920, 1933-1937, 1950]
— revenues, pp. 1219-1220 [2814, 2817]
— toxic chemicals, pp. 35, 53, 67 [142, 221, 281]
Montgomery, AL MSA
— establishments and employment, p. 1024 [2393]
— occupancy, pp. 454-455, 467, 481, 489, 495, 511-512, 518, 560, 571, 602, 612, 674-675 [1140, 1142, 1170, 1202, 1220, 1234, 1270, 1272, 1286, 1382, 1405, 1476, 1498, 1636, 1638]
— population, pp. 114, 118 [350, 355]
Montgomery, IN
— toxic chemicals, p. 45 [184]
Montgomery, KS
— toxic chemicals, pp. 9, 40, 59 [23, 164, 247]

Montgomery, MD
— county government expenditures, pp. 1116-1118, 1122-1126 [2597-2599, 2601, 2609-2615]
— county government revenues, pp. 1127-1129, 1131-1141, 1143-1151 [2616-2618, 2623-2626, 2628-2637, 2640-2642, 2645-2648, 2650, 2653-2657, 2660, 2663]
— county population, p. 116 [353]
— enrollment, p. 300 [785]
— toxic chemicals, p. 18 [67]
Montgomery, NY
— imports and exports, p. 900 [2124]
Montgomery, OH
— county government expenditures, pp. 1116-1117, 1119-1126 [2597-2599, 2602-2603, 2606, 2608-2615]
— county government revenues, pp. 1127-1140, 1143-1149, 1151 [2616-2618, 2620, 2622-2623, 2625-2626, 2628, 2630-2637, 2647-2650, 2653-2654, 2656-2657, 2663]
— county population, p. 116 [353]
— toxic chemicals, pp. 22-23, 33, 40, 42, 61, 69 [84, 86, 132, 163, 171, 256, 289]
Montgomery, PA
— county government expenditures, pp. 1116-1118, 1120, 1122-1126 [2597-2601, 2604, 2606, 2609-2615]
— county government revenues, pp. 1127-1129, 1131, 1133-1140, 1143, 1146-1148, 1151 [2616-2618, 2623, 2626, 2628-2632, 2634-2637, 2645, 2647, 2652-2655, 2663]
— county population, p. 116 [353]
— population, p. 93 [315-316]
— toxic chemicals, pp. 8, 12, 22, 24, 27, 38, 42, 44, 48, 54, 67-68 [18, 34, 84, 91, 109, 155, 170, 181, 197, 226, 281, 285, 287]
Montgomery, TN
— toxic chemicals, pp. 27, 33, 37, 69 [109, 135, 148, 290]
Montgomery, TX
— toxic chemicals, p. 10 [24]
Montrose, CO
— cost of living, pp. 869-871, 873, 875 [1988, 1991, 1995, 2000, 2006]
— parks, p. 1279 [2986-2987]
Moore, TX
— toxic chemicals, pp. 10, 21, 46, 50, 56 [25, 77, 191, 207, 234]
Morehead City, NC
— parks, p. 1278 [2982]
Morehouse College (Atlanta, GA)
— degrees conferred, pp. 287, 289, 291, 293, 295 [771, 773, 775, 777, 779]
— enrollment, pp. 297, 299 [781, 784]
— finances and expenditures, pp. 305, 307 [793, 796]
Morehouse Parish, LA
— toxic chemicals, p. 31 [125]
Morehouse School of Medicine (Atlanta, GA)
— degrees conferred, pp. 287, 289, 291, 293, 295 [771, 773, 775, 777, 779]
— enrollment, pp. 297, 299 [781, 784]
— finances and expenditures, pp. 305, 307 [793, 796]
Morgan, AL
— toxic chemicals, pp. 17, 19, 26-28, 33, 38, 43, 46, 55-56, 65-66, 68 [62, 69, 101, 104, 109-110, 134, 156, 176-177, 191, 227, 232, 234, 275-276, 286, 288]

Morgan, IL
— toxic chemicals, pp. 18, 68 [68, 285]
Morgan, TN
— toxic chemicals, p. 62 [259]
Morgan State University (Baltimore, MD)
— degrees conferred, pp. 287, 289, 291, 293, 295 [771, 773, 775, 777, 779]
— enrollment, pp. 297, 299 [781, 784]
— finances and expenditures, pp. 305, 307 [793, 796]
Morgantown, WV
— prisons and prison population, pp. 1268-1269 [2959-2961]
Morris, NJ
— toxic chemicals, pp. 19, 22, 36, 54, 64 [70, 81, 144, 222, 271]
Morris Brown College (Atlanta, GA)
— degrees conferred, pp. 287, 289, 291, 293, 295 [771, 773, 775, 777, 779]
— enrollment, pp. 297, 299 [781, 784]
— finances and expenditures, pp. 305, 307 [793, 796]
Morris College (Sumter, SC)
— degrees conferred, pp. 287, 289, 291, 293, 295 [771, 773, 775, 777, 779]
— enrollment, pp. 297, 299 [781, 784]
— finances and expenditures, pp. 305, 307 [793, 796]
Morrison County, MN
— toxic chemicals, p. 27 [105]
Morton County, ND
— toxic chemicals, p. 9 [23]
Mosca, CO
— parks, p. 1279 [2986-2987]
Moultonboro, NH
— cost of living, pp. 864-868 [1973, 1975, 1977, 1979, 1983, 1985]
Mount Shasta, CA
— weather and climate, p. 70 [296]
Mountain View, CA
— ventures, p. 906 [2139]
Multnomah, OR
— county government expenditures, pp. 1116-1118, 1122, 1124-1125 [2597-2598, 2601, 2609-2610, 2612-2614]
— county government revenues, pp. 1127-1138, 1140, 1142, 1144, 1146-1148, 1151 [2616-2618, 2621-2626, 2628, 2630-2635, 2637, 2643, 2648-2649, 2653-2656, 2663]
— county population, p. 116 [353]
— population, p. 93 [316]
— toxic chemicals, pp. 12, 20, 32-35, 44, 56, 58 [37, 74, 128, 134, 137, 142, 181, 236, 242]
Muncie, IN
— cost of living, p. 869 [1989-1990]
— family and household income, p. 714 [1715]
— hours and earnings, p. 421 [1067]
— imports and exports, pp. 879, 899-900 [2026, 2119, 2124]
— marital status, men, p. 211 [520]
— marital status, women, p. 214 [525]
— population, pp. 76, 78-79, 84, 87, 110, 122-124, 129, 134, 137, 140, 142 [297-300, 302, 345, 364-368, 376, 383-386]

Muncie, IN continued:
— poverty, pp. 753, 778, 784, 794, 823-824, 832, 834, 847, 850 [1782, 1827, 1838, 1856, 1902, 1904, 1920, 1923-1924, 1945, 1950]
Muncie, IN MSA
— occupancy, pp. 444, 450, 464, 476-477, 493, 528-529, 570, 628, 642, 674 [1116, 1130, 1162, 1190, 1192, 1229, 1310, 1312, 1403, 1533, 1564, 1635]
Munising, MI
— parks, p. 1278 [2982]
Murfreesboro, TN
— parks, p. 1277 [2979]
Murray County, GA
— toxic chemicals, p. 27 [106]
Muscatine County, IA
— toxic chemicals, pp. 11, 18, 31, 63, 67 [30, 69, 123, 263, 282]
Muscogee County, GA
— toxic chemicals, pp. 18, 21-22, 24 [67, 80, 82, 91, 93]
Muskegon, MI
— family and household income, pp. 708, 714, 717, 719 [1705, 1715, 1721, 1724]
— first ancestry, pp. 313, 315-318, 320, 322-323, 326-328 [804, 807-808, 810-812, 815, 818, 820, 825, 827-828]
— marital status, men, p. 210 [518]
— population, pp. 75, 78, 81, 83, 86, 121-122, 133, 138-139, 143 [297-300, 302, 362-363, 383-386]
— poverty, pp. 745, 751-752, 758-759, 765-766, 780-783, 786-788, 801-802, 823, 826, 829, 851, 853-854 [1767, 1778-1780, 1791, 1793, 1804-1806, 1830, 1832-1833, 1835, 1841, 1844-1845, 1866-1868, 1902-1903, 1909, 1915, 1951, 1956-1957]
— toxic chemicals, pp. 10, 15, 21-22, 33, 46, 64 [27, 52, 78, 81, 133, 189, 267, 271]
— weather and climate, p. 70 [296]
Muskegon, MI MSA
— occupancy, pp. 450, 456, 469, 476-477, 480, 510-511, 513, 528, 544, 547, 551, 570 [1130, 1144, 1174, 1190, 1192, 1198, 1268, 1270, 1274, 1310, 1346, 1352, 1362, 1403]
Muskingum County, OH
— toxic chemicals, pp. 44, 53, 63 [181, 219, 265]
Muskogee County, OK
— toxic chemicals, p. 9 [23]
Myrtle Beach, SC MSA
— crimes and crime rates, pp. 1222-1223, 1226 [2819, 2821, 2834]
— establishments and employment, p. 979 [2293]
Nantucket, MA
— cost of living, pp. 866-868 [1979, 1981, 1983, 1985]
Naples, FL
— employment, pp. 339-344, 349-353 [841-855, 870-884]
— family and household income, pp. 710-711, 718, 720, 725-727 [1708-1710, 1722, 1727, 1735-1738]
— first ancestry, pp. 314, 316, 320-322, 324-326, 329-330 [805, 809, 815, 817-818, 821, 824-825, 831-832]
— geographic mobility, p. 207 [517]
— immigrants admitted, pp. 168-173 [437-445]
— imports and exports, p. 900 [2122]
— marital status, men, pp. 210, 212 [519, 522]

Numbers following p. or pp. are page references. Numbers in [ ] are table references.

Location Index

Numbers following p. or pp. are page references. Numbers in [ ] are table references.

1373

Nassau–Suffolk, NY PMSA continued:
— marital status, parents, p. 216 [529]
— naturalized citizens, pp. 174-186 [446-464]
— population, pp. 114, 118 [350, 355]
— unemployment, p. 419 [1064]
— vacancies, p. 282 [767]

National Park, CA
— parks, pp. 1276-1279 [2977-2978, 2980, 2983, 2986-2987]
— water and water use, p. 70 [295]

Navajo County, AZ
— toxic chemicals, p. 29 [117]

Nellis, NV
— prisons and prison population, pp. 1269-1270 [2962-2964]

Nelson County, ND
— population, p. 92 [312]

Nevada County, AR
— toxic chemicals, p. 36 [144]

New Bedford, MA
— cost of living, pp. 866-868 [1979, 1981, 1983, 1985]
— family and household income, p. 714 [1715]
— first ancestry, pp. 312, 314, 317-319, 323, 326 [802, 805, 811-812, 814, 820-821, 826]
— immigrants admitted, pp. 168-173 [438-445]
— imports and exports, pp. 879, 902 [2023-2024, 2131]
— marital status, men, p. 212 [522]
— marital status, women, p. 215 [527]
— naturalized citizens, pp. 174-186 [446-464]
— population, pp. 75, 78-79, 84, 86, 103, 105, 129-132, 134, 138, 140, 142 [297-300, 302, 333, 337, 376, 378-386]
— poverty, pp. 750-751, 770, 779-780, 811, 813, 816, 822-825, 844, 847, 851 [1775-1777, 1812, 1828-1829, 1884, 1886, 1892, 1902-1905, 1907, 1939, 1944, 1951]

New Bedford, MA MSA
— occupancy, pp. 456, 476-477, 487, 493, 511, 528, 531, 544, 548, 590, 621 [1145, 1190, 1192, 1215, 1228, 1270, 1310, 1316, 1346, 1354, 1449, 1519]

New Castle, DE
— toxic chemicals, pp. 10-12, 16, 21, 25, 29, 31, 38-39, 48, 54, 65, 68 [26, 29, 31-33, 56, 78, 95, 97, 115-116, 123, 154, 156, 160, 196, 224, 273, 287]

New Castle, PA
— cost of living, pp. 863-864, 866 [1971, 1975, 1981]

New Hanover County, NC
— toxic chemicals, pp. 33, 37, 39, 56 [132-133, 148, 157, 234]

New Haven, CT
— air quality, pp. 4-5 [1-2, 5-6]
— cost of living, p. 1080 [2522]
— crimes and crime rates, pp. 1229-1230 [2844, 2846-2848]
— diseases, pp. 247-249 [635, 638-639, 641]
— family and household income, p. 712 [1711]
— hours and earnings, p. 420 [1065]
— income, p. 736 [1753]
— offices, p. 906 [2140]
— population, p. 93 [315-316]
— tax crime, p. 1272 [2973]
— toxic chemicals, pp. 8, 16, 18, 21, 24, 34, 41-42, 44, 50-51, 53, 55, 59 [18, 58, 67, 78, 90-91, 139, 169-170, 182, 206, 212, 218-219, 227, 230, 248]

New Haven, CT MSA
— asian population, pp. 94-95 [317, 319]
— family and household income, pp. 707, 709-711, 723-727 [1702, 1706-1710, 1731-1738]
— first ancestry, pp. 312, 314, 318-321, 323-324, 327-328, 330 [803, 805, 812, 814-818, 820-822, 826, 828, 831]
— immigrants admitted, pp. 169, 173 [438-439, 445]
— imports and exports, pp. 879, 902 [2023-2024, 2131]
— marital status, men, pp. 211-212 [520, 522]
— marital status, women, p. 214 [525]
— occupancy, pp. 441, 444, 450, 464, 477-478, 480-481, 488, 495, 500, 511, 513, 526, 531, 549-551, 570, 575-576, 584, 592, 599, 614-615, 635, 648, 667, 687 [1111, 1116, 1130, 1162, 1192, 1194, 1199, 1202, 1216, 1234, 1245, 1270, 1275, 1304, 1316-1317, 1358, 1360-1361, 1403, 1414-1416, 1436, 1454, 1468, 1503-1504, 1550, 1579, 1621, 1665]
— population, pp. 74, 77, 80, 84-85, 89, 101, 103, 105-108, 135-136, 139, 143 [297-300, 302, 305, 329, 332-333, 337-340, 383-386]
— poverty, pp. 748, 751, 791, 796, 799, 805, 811-813, 815, 839, 847-848, 854 [1773, 1777, 1851, 1858, 1863, 1872, 1884-1886, 1889, 1931, 1944, 1946, 1958]

New London, CT
— toxic chemicals, pp. 11, 30-31, 53, 62 [30, 122, 124, 126, 219, 260]

New London–Norwich, CT–RI MSA
— asian population, p. 95 [320]
— establishments and employment, pp. 1056, 1099 [2458, 2567]
— family and household income, pp. 709-710, 720-726 [1706-1708, 1727-1736]
— first ancestry, pp. 312, 314, 316-324, 326, 328, 330 [802, 805, 810-812, 814, 816-818, 820-822, 824, 828, 831]
— hours and earnings, p. 420 [1065]
— immigrants admitted, p. 173 [445]
— imports and exports, pp. 879, 902 [2023-2024, 2131]
— occupancy, pp. 451, 476-477, 495-496, 510, 512-513, 516-517, 528-529, 531, 544, 551, 570, 585, 622, 630, 646, 652 [1133, 1190, 1192, 1234-1235, 1268-1269, 1274, 1282-1284, 1310, 1312, 1316, 1346, 1362, 1403, 1438, 1520, 1539, 1573-1574, 1587-1588]
— population, pp. 75, 78, 81-82, 86, 103, 105, 107, 111, 125, 133, 136, 140, 142 [297-300, 302, 333, 337, 339, 346, 369, 383-386]
— poverty, pp. 744-747, 760, 833, 854 [1766-1767, 1770-1771, 1796, 1921, 1958]

New Madrid County, MO
— toxic chemicals, pp. 44, 53 [181, 217]

New Orleans, LA
— alcohol use, pp. 226-229 [553-564]
— aliens, pp. 146-147 [388, 391, 394]
— asian population, p. 99 [326]
— chemicals, p. 5 [7]
— city government debt, pp. 1154-1165 [2665-2671, 2673-2680, 2684-2689]
— city government expenditures, pp. 1166-1187, 1189, 1213-1215 [2691-2706, 2708, 2710-2715, 2720-2726, 2728-2737, 2739, 2742, 2797-2798, 2802, 2804]
— city government revenues, pp. 1190-1213, 1217 [2745-2751,

Numbers following p. or pp. are page references. Numbers in [ ] are table references.

1374

Location Index

Numbers following p. or pp. are page references. Numbers in [ ] are table references.

New Philadelphia, OH
—travel, p. 1283 [3005]
New Port Richey, FL
— geographic mobility, p. 208 [517]
New York, NY
— air quality, pp. 4-5 [1-2, 5-6]
— airports, pp. 1078-1079 [2511, 2513-2515, 2517]
— alcohol use, pp. 226-229 [553-564]
— aliens, pp. 146-147 [388, 391, 394]
— apparel and apparel products, pp. 1046-1047 [2436-2439]
— bridges, p. 1079 [2518]
— cab drivers, p. 1080 [2519]
— cable television, p. 218 [530-531]
— city government debt, pp. 1154-1166 [2664-2680, 2683-2690]
— city government expenditures, pp. 1166-1189, 1213-1216 [2691-2706, 2708-2717, 2719, 2721-2743, 2797-2805]
— city government revenues, pp. 1189-1213, 1216-1217 [2744-2784, 2786-2796, 2806-2809]
— cocaine and heroin use, pp. 229-232 [565-570, 572-574]
— construction, p. 913 [2159]
— cost of living, pp. 863-874, 1080-1082 [1971, 1973, 1975, 1977, 1979, 1981, 1983, 1985, 1987, 1989-1990, 1993-1994, 1997-2000, 2003-2004, 2520-2523, 2525, 2530-2531, 2533-2534]
— costs, pp. 912-913 [2152-2157]
— crimes and crime rates, pp. 1223-1224, 1227-1229, 1231-1233 [2822-2825, 2835, 2842-2843, 2849-2850, 2852-2855]
— daycare, pp. 222-223 [541, 543]
— degrees conferred, p. 286 [770]
— diseases, pp. 246-250 [633, 635, 638-639, 641, 646]
— distribution of employment, pp. 368-417 [935-1054]
— drug use, pp. 226, 233 [550-552, 578-580]
— drug use, marijuna, pp. 233-235 [581-589]
— eating habits, pp. 237-239 [597-602]
— employment, pp. 336-338, 345-348, 354-367, 428-429 [833, 835-838, 857-864, 866-869, 885, 887-893, 895-901, 903, 905, 907, 911, 913, 915, 917, 919-924, 926-927, 929-930, 932-933, 1080-1081, 1084-1086, 1088]
— enrollment, p. 300 [785]
— establishments and employment, p. 938 [2210-2211]
— exercise habits, pp. 239-242 [603-617]
— finances and expenditures, pp. 309, 1276 [798-799, 2975]
— foods and food products, pp. 1069-1074 [2487-2493, 2496-2501]
— fortune 500 companies, p. 875 [2008]
— geographic mobility, p. 208 [517]
— home ownership, p. 266 [700]
— hotels and motels, pp. 1010-1011 [2357-2360, 2363]
— hours and earnings, pp. 420-422, 424 [1065-1066, 1070-1071, 1076-1078]
— housing, pp. 267-274, 276-277, 279 [707-708, 710, 715, 719-720, 723, 725, 729, 732, 734, 736, 746-747, 755]
— immigrants admitted, pp. 149-167 [401, 403, 405, 407, 409, 411, 413, 415-436]

New York, NY continued:
— imports and exports, pp. 875-877, 882-899, 901-902, 904 [2009-2018, 2033-2118, 2120-2121, 2125, 2129, 2136]
— income, pp. 728, 736 [1739, 1753]
— land area, p. 6 [12]
— libraries, pp. 1279-1280 [2988-2989]
— marital status, parents, p. 215 [528]
— naturalized citizens, pp. 174-186 [446-464]
— nonimmigrants admitted, pp. 186-189 [465-484]
— offices, pp. 906-907 [2141-2143, 2145-2146]
— parks, pp. 1276-1277 [2977-2978, 2980]
— political conventions, p. 1286 [3007-3009]
— population, pp. 85, 90, 92, 114-115, 118-119 [301, 308, 313-314, 350, 352, 355, 357]
— population, immigrants, p. 148 [397-399]
— poverty rates, pp. 742-743 [1760-1761, 1763, 1765]
— prisons and prison population, p. 1271 [2967-2969]
— refugees and asylees, pp. 190-200 [485-501]
— restaurants, pp. 1011-1012 [2365-2366, 2368-2370]
— revenues, pp. 1112-1114, 1217-1220 [2589-2596, 2810-2814, 2816-2817]
— self-image, pp. 243-244 [618-623]
— steroid use, p. 232 [575-577]
— tax crime, p. 1272 [2974]
— telephones, p. 1107 [2586-2587]
— television viewing, pp. 1281-1282 [2998-2999]
— tobacco use, pp. 236-237 [591-596]
— toxic chemicals, p. 7 [16]
— trade shows, p. 1286 [3010]
— travel, pp. 908, 1282 [2149-2151, 3001-3002]
— unemployment, pp. 417-419 [1055-1059, 1062, 1064]
— utilities, p. 1107 [2588]
— vacancies, p. 282 [766-767, 769]
— ventures, p. 906 [2138-2139]
— vital statistics, p. 254 [657-658]
— youth risk behavior, pp. 244-246 [624-632]
New York–Northern New Jersey–Long Island, NY–NJ–CT CMSA
— air quality, pp. 4-5 [3-4]
— asian population, pp. 93, 95, 97 [317, 319-320, 322-323]
— CMSA population, p. 121 [361]
— consumer expenditures, pp. 218-222 [532-540]
— cost of living, pp. 860-863 [1960-1969]
— employment, p. 339 [839-840]
— energy prices, pp. 1102-1107 [2570-2585]
— establishments and employment, pp. 916-932, 934-936, 942-947, 951-954, 956-961, 964-969, 971-985, 987-988, 990-994, 996-998, 1000-1002, 1016-1022, 1024-1027, 1030-1033, 1038-1043, 1047-1051, 1053-1060, 1063, 1065-1068, 1086-1099 [2162-2170, 2172-2187, 2189-2194, 2196-2200, 2203-2208, 2214-2217, 2219-2221, 2223, 2225-2226, 2233-2234, 2236, 2239-2241, 2244, 2246, 2248, 2251-2252, 2255, 2261-2263, 2266-2270, 2272-2274, 2276-2277, 2279-2283, 2285-2287, 2289-2291, 2293-2296, 2298-2302, 2304, 2308-2310, 2315, 2317-2319, 2322-2324, 2327-2329, 2332, 2337, 2339-2340, 2377-2378, 2381-2388, 2392-2396, 2398-2399, 2404, 2406, 2408-2410, 2422, 2424, 2427-2429, 2431-2433, 2440, 2442-2447, 2451-2453, 2455-2456, 2458-

Numbers following p. or pp. are page references. Numbers in [ ] are table references.

Numbers following p. or pp. are page references. Numbers in [ ] are table references.

Location Index

Numbers following p. or pp. are page references. Numbers in [ ] are table references.

Location Index

Oakland County Community College (Oakland... continued:
— enrollment, p. 302 [789]

Oakwood College (Huntsville, AL)
— degrees conferred, pp. 287, 289, 291, 294-295 [771, 773, 775, 777, 779]
— enrollment, pp. 297, 299 [781, 784]
— finances and expenditures, pp. 305, 307 [793, 796]

Ocala, FL
— family and household income, pp. 708, 714-718 [1705, 1716-1723]
— first ancestry, pp. 314, 316-318, 327, 330 [805, 809, 811-812, 826, 831]
— geographic mobility, p. 208 [517]
— immigrants admitted, p. 173 [445]
— marital status, men, pp. 210, 212 [518-519, 522]
— marital status, women, pp. 213, 215 [524, 527]
— population, pp. 75, 78, 80, 84, 86, 88, 100, 102-103, 106-107, 128-132, 134, 138-139, 142 [297-300, 302, 304, 328, 332-333, 337-339, 375-381, 383-386]
— poverty, pp. 749-750, 756-757, 769, 773, 777, 779-780, 784, 792, 801, 809, 826, 828, 830, 834, 849-850, 852-854 [1774-1777, 1787-1789, 1810, 1817, 1823, 1828-1830, 1837, 1852, 1866, 1880, 1909, 1912, 1916, 1924, 1948-1949, 1953-1955, 1957]

Ocala, FL MSA
— crimes and crime rates, pp. 1222, 1232 [2818, 2820, 2854]
— occupancy, pp. 444, 450, 476-477, 480, 484, 493, 495, 499-500, 511-512, 528, 531, 537, 544, 547, 570, 590, 689 [1116, 1130, 1190, 1192, 1198, 1208, 1228, 1230, 1234, 1242, 1244, 1270, 1274, 1310, 1316, 1330, 1346, 1352, 1403, 1448, 1668]

Ocean, MD
— housing, p. 266 [703]
— population, p. 93 [315]

Ocean County, NJ
— population, p. 93 [316]
— toxic chemicals, pp. 16, 39, 43, 54 [56, 58, 160, 177, 224]

Ocean Springs, MS
— parks, pp. 1278-1279 [2982, 2986-2987]

Odessa, TX
— employment, p. 361 [909]
— family and household income, pp. 708, 713-714, 717 [1704, 1714, 1716, 1721]
— immigrants admitted, pp. 169-171 [439-442]
— imports and exports, p. 881 [2032]
— marital status, men, p. 212 [521]
— occupancy, pp. 450, 456, 464, 476, 480, 492-493, 500, 511-512, 522, 529, 531, 537, 544, 547, 551, 657 [1130, 1144, 1162, 1190, 1198, 1228, 1230, 1244, 1270, 1274, 1295, 1312, 1316, 1330, 1346, 1352, 1362, 1599-1600]
— population, pp. 76, 79, 81, 83, 87, 89, 102, 105, 108-109, 121, 125, 133, 138, 140, 143 [297-300, 302, 305, 331, 336, 341, 343, 362-363, 370, 383-386]
— poverty, pp. 745, 751-756, 769-777, 781, 787, 808, 811-824, 826-830, 833, 835, 843-846, 850-854 [1767-1768, 1778-1781, 1783-1787, 1811-1824, 1831, 1843-1844, 1878, 1884-1901, 1903, 1905, 1909-1910, 1912, 1914, 1916-1917, 1922, 1925, 1938-1943,

Odessa, TX continued:
1949-1957]

Ogden, UT
— diseases, p. 250 [645]

Ogdensburg, NY
— imports and exports, pp. 899, 901 [2121, 2125]

Ogle County, IL
— toxic chemicals, p. 57 [238]

Ohio State University, Main Campus (Columbus, OH)
— degrees conferred, pp. 287, 289, 292, 294 [772, 774, 776, 778]
— enrollment, pp. 298, 300-304 [782-783, 786-788, 790-792]
— finances and expenditures, pp. 306, 308 [794-795, 797]

Ohio University, Main Campus (Athens, OH)
— degrees conferred, p. 292 [776]

Okeechobee County, FL
— toxic chemicals, p. 20 [76]

Oklahoma City, OK
— asian population, pp. 98-99 [325-326]
— city government debt, pp. 1154-1165 [2665-2671, 2673-2675, 2677-2680, 2684-2689]
— city government expenditures, pp. 1166-1188, 1214-1215 [2691-2706, 2708, 2710-2715, 2721-2723, 2726, 2728-2737, 2739, 2799, 2801]
— city government revenues, pp. 1190-1212 [2745-2751, 2753, 2755-2762, 2764-2766, 2769-2771, 2776, 2778-2780, 2782-2793]
— county government expenditures, pp. 1116-1120, 1122-1126 [2597-2598, 2601, 2603-2604, 2609-2615]
— county government revenues, pp. 1127-1129, 1131, 1133-1140, 1143, 1146-1149, 1151 [2616-2618, 2623, 2626, 2628, 2630-2632, 2634-2637, 2647, 2652-2655, 2657, 2663]
— county population, p. 116 [353]
— crimes and crime rates, pp. 1222, 1224-1226, 1228, 1231 [2820, 2827, 2829-2832, 2840-2841, 2849, 2851]
— diseases, pp. 248-249 [636-637, 640]
— distribution of employment, pp. 370-376, 385-390, 393-399, 402-408, 411-417 [945-954, 985-994, 1005-1014, 1025-1034, 1045-1054]
— employment, pp. 336-338, 361 [835-838, 909]
— establishments and employment, pp. 918, 935-936, 943, 949, 953, 956-957, 965, 969, 972, 984-986, 988, 990, 995, 1000, 1030, 1036, 1042, 1065 [2167, 2206, 2208, 2216, 2229, 2238, 2244, 2246, 2264, 2273, 2279, 2302, 2305, 2307, 2310-2311, 2315, 2325, 2335-2336, 2404, 2416, 2429, 2477]
— family and household income, pp. 706-707 [1701-1703]
— first ancestry, pp. 314-315, 330 [806, 808, 831]
— foods and food products, pp. 1071-1074 [2496-2501]
— hours and earnings, p. 424 [1076]
— housing, pp. 268-269 [709, 711, 716]
— imports and exports, p. 903 [2135]
— income, pp. 728-732, 734-736 [1740-1742, 1744-1746, 1749-1752]
— land area, p. 6 [12]
— marital status, men, p. 210 [518]
— marital status, women, p. 213 [523]
— occupancy, pp. 436-438, 443-444, 450, 476-477, 479-482, 491-493, 495, 499-500, 511-512, 520-521, 528-529, 531,

Numbers following p. or pp. are page references. Numbers in [ ] are table references.

1380

Numbers following p. or pp. are page references. Numbers in [ ] are table references.

Location Index

Numbers following p. or pp. are page references. Numbers in [ ] are table references.

Numbers following p. or pp. are page references. Numbers in [ ] are table references.

1384

Numbers following p. or pp. are page references. Numbers in [ ] are table references.

Location Index

1385

Philadelphia – Wilmington – Atlantic City,... continued:
    2255, 2257, 2259-2263, 2266-2269, 2271, 2274,
    2276-2278, 2280, 2282-2283, 2285-2290,
    2293, 2296, 2298-2301, 2303-2304, 2308, 2310-
    2311, 2318-2319, 2322-2326, 2328-2332, 2337,
    2341-2342, 2377, 2380, 2385-2386, 2389, 2391-
    2392, 2395-2396, 2399-2400, 2403-2404, 2407-
    2411, 2415, 2418, 2420-2421, 2423, 2431, 2440-
    2443, 2445-2447, 2450-2456, 2458-2462, 2464,
    2466-2468, 2470, 2472-2483, 2536-2538, 2540-
    2551, 2554-2555, 2557-2563]
— general summary, pp. 1014-1015, 1046 [2371-2374, 2434-
    2435]
— hours and earnings, pp. 422-423 [1073-1075]
— income, pp. 735-738 [1750-1752, 1754-1759]
— population, pp. 114, 116, 118, 120 [350, 354-355, 359-360]
— tax-exempt establishments and employment, pp. 1003,
    1005-1006, 1008-1010 [2343, 2346-2349, 2352,
    2354, 2356]
— vital statistics, pp. 251-253 [651-656]

Philadelphia – Wilmington – Trenton, PA – NJ – DE – MD CMSA
— asian population, pp. 93-95, 97 [317-319, 323]
— consumer expenditures, pp. 218-222 [532-540]
— cost of living, pp. 860-863 [1960-1969]
— energy prices, pp. 1102-1107 [2570-2585]
— family and household income, pp. 706-707, 709-711, 722-
    727 [1701-1703, 1706-1710, 1730-1738]
— first ancestry, pp. 312, 319-324, 326-328, 330 [803, 814-818,
    820, 822, 825-826, 828, 831]
— geographic mobility, pp. 204-207, 258-265 [502-516, 671-
    698]
— income, pp. 728-734 [1740-1749]
— marital status, men, pp. 211-212 [520-522]
— marital status, women, p. 214 [525-526]
— occupancy, pp. 432-435, 437-513, 515-537, 539-589, 591-
    620, 622-683, 685-703 [1089-1097, 1100-1129,
    1131-1132, 1134-1137, 1139-1143, 1145-1147,
    1149-1167, 1169-1189, 1191, 1193-1197, 1200-
    1203, 1205-1209, 1211-1214, 1216-1217, 1219-
    1223, 1225-1233, 1235-1242, 1244-1269, 1273-
    1275, 1279-1281, 1283-1284, 1286-1293, 1296-
    1299, 1301-1309, 1311-1316, 1318-1329, 1331,
    1334-1345, 1347-1349, 1351, 1353-1377, 1379-
    1402, 1405-1436, 1438-1445, 1447, 1450-1453,
    1455-1472, 1474-1497, 1499-1502, 1505-1517,
    1521-1547, 1549-1567, 1569-1574, 1577-1580,
    1582-1583, 1585-1587, 1590-1598, 1601-1620,
    1622-1623, 1625-1636, 1639-1647, 1649-1650,
    1653-1656, 1659-1700]
— population, pp. 74, 76, 80, 84-85, 89, 103, 105-106, 110,
    135-136, 139, 143 [297-300, 302, 305, 332-333,
    337-338, 345, 383-386]
— poverty, pp. 767-768, 794, 798-800, 803-808, 831, 837-839,
    841-842, 847, 854 [1808-1809, 1855, 1862-1865,
    1869-1871, 1873-1874, 1876-1877, 1918, 1928,
    1930, 1932, 1934, 1936, 1944, 1958]

Philander Smith College (Little Rock, AR)
— degrees conferred, pp. 287, 289, 291, 294-295 [771, 773,

Philander Smith College (Little Rock, AR) continued:
    775, 777, 779]
— enrollment, pp. 297, 299 [781, 784]
— finances and expenditures, pp. 305, 307 [793, 796]

Phillips County, AR
— toxic chemicals, pp. 13, 15, 19, 28, 61 [41, 50, 71, 112, 253]

Phoenix, AZ
— air quality, p. 4 [3]
— airports, pp. 1078-1079 [2513-2514, 2517]
— aliens, pp. 146-147 [389, 392, 395]
— asian population, pp. 94-95 [318-319]
— city government debt, p. 1166 [2690]
— city government expenditures, pp. 1188-1189, 1213-1216
    [2741-2743, 2797-2799, 2801-2803, 2805]
— city government revenues, pp. 1212-1213, 1216-1217 [2794-
    2796, 2806-2809]
— construction, p. 913 [2159]
— cost of living, p. 875 [2005]
— costs, pp. 912-913 [2152-2157]
— crimes and crime rates, p. 1224 [2824-2825]
— diseases, p. 250 [646]
— distribution of employment, pp. 368-382, 390-417 [935-974,
    995-1054]
— drug use, pp. 236, 1233-1267 [590, 2856-2887, 2889-2950,
    2952-2955]
— employment, pp. 336-338, 364-366, 428-429 [834-838, 920,
    924, 927, 930, 1080-1081, 1085]
— family and household income, pp. 706-707, 710, 712, 726-727
    [1701-1703, 1708, 1710, 1736, 1738]
— first ancestry, pp. 320, 322, 324, 330 [815, 819, 822, 832]
— foods and food products, pp. 1071-1074 [2496-2501]
— funeral prices, p. 224 [548-549]
— geographic mobility, p. 208 [517]
— home ownership, p. 266 [699]
— hours and earnings, p. 424 [1076-1077]
— housing, pp. 269, 271-275, 277-280 [718, 722, 724, 726, 728,
    730-731, 733, 735, 737-741, 748, 750-751, 753, 756,
    758-760]
— immigrants admitted, pp. 168, 170-173 [437, 440-444]
— income, pp. 728-734 [1740-1741, 1743-1746, 1748-1749]
— land area, p. 6 [12]
— libraries, p. 1280 [2988-2989]
— marital status, men, p. 210 [518]
— marital status, women, p. 213 [523]
— medicines, p. 1075 [2505-2506, 2509-2510]
— occupancy, pp. 432-435, 437-450, 452-455, 459, 461-468, 470-
    473, 475-480, 482-485, 491-492, 495-498, 500-504,
    506-507, 509-510, 512, 514, 516, 518-523, 525-530,
    532-537, 540-542, 544-546, 548-550, 553-564, 566-
    583, 586-589, 594-607, 609-610, 612-614, 616-621,
    625-627, 629, 631-633, 635-642, 644-645, 647-649,
    651-663, 666-673, 676-678, 680-686, 689-701, 703
    [1090, 1092, 1094, 1096-1097, 1100-1102, 1104-1105,
    1107-1109, 1111, 1113-1117, 1119-1121, 1123, 1125,
    1127, 1130, 1135, 1137, 1139, 1141, 1143, 1151,
    1155, 1157, 1159, 1161-1163, 1165, 1167, 1169, 1171,
    1175, 1177, 1179-1181, 1183, 1187, 1189, 1192-1193,
    1195, 1197, 1199, 1203, 1205, 1207, 1209, 1211,
    1225, 1227, 1233-1234, 1237, 1239, 1241, 1244, 1247,

Numbers following p. or pp. are page references. Numbers in [ ] are table references.

1386

Phoenix, AZ continued:

1249, 1251, 1255, 1259, 1261, 1265, 1267, 1272-
1273, 1277, 1281, 1283, 1287, 1289, 1291, 1293-
1294, 1297, 1299, 1303, 1305, 1307, 1309, 1313,
1315, 1319, 1321, 1323, 1325, 1327, 1329-1330,
1337-1339, 1341, 1345, 1349, 1351, 1354-1355,
1357, 1361, 1367, 1369, 1371, 1373, 1375, 1377,
1379, 1381, 1383, 1385, 1387, 1389, 1391, 1395-
1403, 1406-1411, 1413, 1416-1417, 1419, 1421,
1423-1425, 1427-1432, 1439, 1441-1443, 1445,
1447, 1457, 1459-1461, 1463-1471, 1473, 1475-
1477, 1480-1482, 1484-1487, 1491-1492, 1494,
1497, 1499-1503, 1508, 1510-1513, 1515, 1518,
1528, 1530-1532, 1537, 1541-1546, 1551-1556,
1558-1561, 1563-1564, 1569-1572, 1577-1578,
1581-1582, 1585-1589, 1591-1598, 1601-1608,
1610-1611, 1617-1620, 1622-1625, 1627-1630,
1632-1634, 1639-1645, 1649-1650, 1653-1656,
1659-1662, 1669-1674, 1676-1679, 1681-1688,
1690-1692, 1694-1696, 1699]
— population, pp. 74, 77, 81-82, 85, 89-90, 99, 102, 104-105,
109, 111-112, 115, 119, 125, 133, 136, 140, 143
[297-300, 302, 305, 308, 327, 331, 334, 336, 342,
346, 348, 351, 357, 369, 383-386]
— poverty, pp. 757-760, 769-777, 780-789, 794, 796, 811-822,
825, 827, 831-834, 843-846 [1790-1796, 1811-
1824, 1830-1847, 1855, 1858, 1884-1901, 1906-
1907, 1911, 1918, 1920-1924, 1938-1943]
— poverty rates, p. 742 [1761]
— prisons and prison population, pp. 1268-1271 [2959-2961,
2965-2966]
— revenues, pp. 1218-1219 [2810-2811, 2813, 2815-2816]
— sports activities, p. 1281 [2994]
— toxic chemicals, p. 8 [17]
— travel, pp. 908, 1282 [2149-2151, 3003]
— unemployment, pp. 417-418 [1055-1057]
— utilities, p. 1107 [2588]
— vacancies, pp. 280-281 [762-765]
— vital statistics, p. 254 [659-660]

Phoenix – Mesa, AZ MSA
— construction, p. 913 [2158]
— crimes and crime rates, p. 1223 [2822]
— employment, pp. 339-344, 349-353, 359-364, 367 [841-855,
870-884, 901, 905, 907, 909, 911, 915, 917, 933]
— establishments and employment, pp. 916-919, 921-928,
930-933, 935, 942-971, 973-985, 987-1003, 1015-
1043, 1047-1055, 1057-1069, 1086-1087, 1089,
1092, 1094, 1097-1098 [2163-2164, 2166-2169,
2174, 2176-2177, 2179-2182, 2184-2185, 2188,
2190, 2195-2197, 2199, 2201-2202, 2207, 2214-
2221, 2223-2242, 2244-2245, 2247, 2249-2251,
2253-2255, 2257, 2259-2263, 2266, 2268-2277,
2280, 2282-2283, 2285-2296, 2299-2302, 2304,
2308-2314, 2316-2319, 2321-2325, 2327-2329,
2331-2333, 2335-2339, 2341-2342, 2375-2379,
2381, 2383-2391, 2393-2397, 2399, 2401-2407,
2409-2415, 2417-2418, 2420-2426, 2429-2433,
2440-2443, 2445-2456, 2459-2466, 2468-2482,
2484, 2536, 2538-2539, 2543, 2552, 2555-2557,

Phoenix – Mesa, AZ MSA continued:
2564-2565]
— general summary, p. 1046 [2434]
— immigrants admitted, pp. 148-150, 154-167 [400, 403, 406,
415-436]
— imports and exports, pp. 878, 899-900, 902 [2021-2022, 2120,
2123, 2130]
— income, pp. 735-736 [1750-1752]
— naturalized citizens, pp. 174-186 [446-464]
— offices, p. 908 [2148]
— population, pp. 114, 118 [350, 355]
–- refugees and asylees, pp. 190-200 [485-501]
— tax-exempt establishments and employment, pp. 1003-1010
[2343, 2345-2348, 2350-2351, 2353-2354, 2356]
— vital statistics, pp. 251-253 [651-656]

Phoenix – Tucson, AZ
— foods and food products, pp. 1069-1070 [2487-2490]

Pickaway County, OH
— toxic chemicals, pp. 14-17, 40-41, 60 [47, 55-56, 63, 161, 165,
250]

Pierce, GA
— toxic chemicals, p. 22 [83]

Pierce, WA
— county government expenditures, pp. 1116-1118, 1122-1126
[2597-2598, 2601, 2609-2615]
— county government revenues, pp. 1127-1138, 1140, 1142,
1144-1148, 1151 [2616-2618, 2620, 2622-2626, 2628,
2630-2632, 2634-2635, 2637-2638, 2643, 2648-2650,
2653-2656, 2663]
— county population, p. 116 [353]
— toxic chemicals, p. 59 [244]

Pike, AL
— toxic chemicals, pp. 21-22, 45 [80, 82, 186]

Pike, IN
— toxic chemicals, p. 34 [137]

Pike, MO
— toxic chemicals, pp. 12, 20, 41 [33, 76, 169]

Pima, AZ
— toxic chemicals, pp. 25, 27 [94, 108]

Pima Community College (Pima, AZ)
— enrollment, pp. 302-303 [789, 791]

Pinal, AZ
— toxic chemicals, pp. 17, 20, 23, 33, 45, 61-62 [64, 74, 86, 135,
186, 257, 259]

Pine Bluff, AR
— chemical weapons, p. 6 [8]
— employment, pp. 344-348, 354-360, 362-364 [856-864, 866-
869, 885-893, 895-900, 906, 912, 916, 918]
— family and household income, pp. 708, 713-714 [1704, 1714-
1715]
— first ancestry, p. 329 [829]
— imports and exports, p. 881 [2032]
— marital status, men, p. 212 [522]
— marital status, women, p. 215 [526-527]
— population, pp. 76, 79-80, 83, 87, 108, 110, 122, 133, 138, 144
[297-300, 302, 341, 344, 364, 383-386]
— poverty, pp. 751-757, 760, 765-768, 779, 786-787, 795, 801-
811, 832, 840-842, 850-853 [1778-1781, 1783-1789,
1795, 1803-1807, 1810, 1828, 1841, 1844, 1857, 1866-

Numbers following p. or pp. are page references. Numbers in [ ] are table references.

Location Index

1387

Numbers following p. or pp. are page references. Numbers in [ ] are table references.

Numbers following p. or pp. are page references. Numbers in [ ] are table references.

Location Index

Numbers following p. or pp. are page references. Numbers in [ ] are table references.

Numbers following p. or pp. are page references. Numbers in [ ] are table references.

Location Index

Numbers following p. or pp. are page references. Numbers in [ ] are table references.

Raleigh, NC continued:
— population, pp. 90, 112, 115, 119 [307, 348, 351, 356]
Raleigh–Durham–Chapel Hill, NC MSA
— asian population, pp. 93, 95 [317, 319]
— cost of living, p. 871 [1994]
— establishments and employment, pp. 918, 935, 942, 953, 956-957, 965, 968, 978, 981, 985, 987, 989-991, 997-999, 1019, 1023, 1031, 1037, 1048, 1097 [2167, 2206, 2215, 2238, 2243, 2245-2247, 2264, 2271, 2290, 2297, 2305, 2308, 2312-2313, 2315-2317, 2328, 2331, 2333-2334, 2383, 2390-2391, 2406, 2418, 2441, 2564]
— family and household income, pp. 707, 709-712, 722-727 [1703, 1706-1710, 1712, 1730, 1732-1738]
— first ancestry, pp. 312, 316, 325, 327 [802, 809, 823-824, 826]
— hotels and motels, p. 1011 [2360]
— hours and earnings, pp. 420, 424 [1065, 1077]
— housing, p. 268 [712-713]
— imports and exports, pp. 880, 903 [2029, 2134]
— income, pp. 729, 732-733 [1741-1742, 1746-1747]
— marital status, men, pp. 211-212 [520-521]
— marital status, women, pp. 214-215 [525-526]
— occupancy, pp. 432-434, 436-437, 442-443, 445, 449-450, 452-453, 458-459, 462-471, 474-484, 488, 490-492, 495, 498, 500, 503-504, 510-511, 513, 515, 517, 520, 522, 526, 528, 530-531, 533, 537-538, 540-541, 543-544, 546-547, 549-550, 552-553, 555-561, 563-564, 570, 576-577, 579, 583-584, 592-593, 596, 598-600, 608, 611-612, 614, 616, 622-625, 628-629, 633, 635, 638-639, 648-650, 663-665, 667-668, 674, 679, 682-684, 686-689, 692, 695, 700 [1089, 1091, 1093, 1098, 1101, 1112-1113, 1116, 1119, 1128-1131, 1134, 1138, 1149-1151, 1158, 1160-1161, 1163-1166, 1170, 1172, 1174, 1176, 1178, 1184, 1186, 1188, 1190-1192, 1194, 1196, 1198, 1200, 1202-1203, 1206, 1208, 1217-1218, 1222, 1224, 1226, 1228, 1234, 1240, 1245, 1252, 1254, 1269-1270, 1274-1275, 1279-1280, 1284, 1292, 1296, 1306, 1309-1310, 1314, 1316-1317, 1322, 1330-1331, 1336, 1340, 1344, 1346, 1350-1353, 1358-1359, 1363-1364, 1366, 1370, 1372, 1374, 1376-1377, 1379-1380, 1384, 1388, 1390, 1403-1404, 1417-1418, 1423, 1433-1436, 1453-1456, 1462, 1465-1470, 1488, 1490, 1495-1497, 1503, 1506, 1508, 1521-1522, 1524, 1528, 1534, 1537, 1546, 1549-1550, 1557, 1559, 1578-1580, 1583, 1612-1615, 1621-1622, 1636, 1646, 1654-1658, 1663-1664, 1667-1668, 1675, 1682-1683, 1694]
— population, pp. 74, 77, 80, 83, 85, 112, 114, 118, 123-126, 134, 136, 138, 143 [297-300, 302, 347, 350, 355, 365-372, 383-386]
— poverty, pp. 747, 767-769, 794-795, 797-801, 803-806, 808, 810-811, 833, 839-842 [1771-1772, 1808-1810, 1855, 1857, 1860-1861, 1863, 1865-1866, 1869-1872, 1874, 1877, 1881-1883, 1922, 1932-1937]
— tax-exempt establishments and employment, pp. 1004, 1006-1009 [2344, 2349-2350, 2352, 2355]

Ralls County, MO
— toxic chemicals, pp. 8, 15, 54 [19, 50, 221]
Ramsey County, MN
— toxic chemicals, pp. 14, 23, 35, 40, 56-57 [47, 85, 143, 163, 236-237]
Rancho Santa Fe, CA
— travel, p. 1283 [3006]
Rancho Santiago College (Santa Ana, CA)
— enrollment, p. 302 [789]
Randolph County, NC
— toxic chemicals, p. 37 [151]
Rapid City, SD
— asian population, pp. 95, 98 [320, 325]
— crimes and crime rates, p. 1222 [2820]
— diseases, p. 250 [645]
— employment, pp. 359-361 [902, 906, 908]
— family and household income, pp. 708, 713, 715-719 [1705, 1713, 1717-1720, 1722-1724]
— first ancestry, pp. 314-316, 318, 322, 327 [806-807, 810, 813, 819, 827]
— hours and earnings, p. 421 [1068, 1070]
— occupancy, pp. 457, 495, 511, 513, 528, 531, 544, 546-547, 570, 669 [1146, 1234, 1270, 1274, 1310, 1316, 1346, 1350, 1352, 1403, 1626]
— population, pp. 76, 79, 81-82, 87, 101, 104, 108-109, 121, 124-126, 133, 137, 141-142 [297-300, 302, 330, 334, 341-343, 362-363, 368-369, 371, 383-386]
— poverty, pp. 744-745, 751-752, 757-760, 780-789, 823, 825-827, 829, 832, 834-836, 844, 852-854 [1766-1768, 1778-1779, 1790-1796, 1830-1835, 1837-1839, 1841-1848, 1902-1903, 1906, 1908, 1910, 1915, 1920-1921, 1923-1925, 1927, 1939, 1954, 1956-1957]
— revenues, p. 1219 [2814]
Rapides Parish, LA
— toxic chemicals, pp. 34, 56 [137, 236]
Ray Brook, NY
— prisons and prison population, pp. 1268-1269 [2959-2961]
Reading, PA
— family and household income, pp. 709, 720-723 [1706, 1726-1732]
— first ancestry, pp. 315, 318-319, 321-323, 326, 328-329 [808, 813-814, 817-818, 820, 825, 828, 830]
— marital status, men, pp. 210, 212 [519, 522]
— population, pp. 75, 77, 80, 83, 86, 88, 103-105, 128-132, 135, 137, 140, 142 [297-300, 302, 304, 333, 335, 337, 375-381, 383-386]
— poverty, pp. 749-751, 769-770, 789, 791, 796, 805, 811-813, 815, 824, 828, 845, 848-849, 854 [1774-1777, 1811-1812, 1848, 1850, 1858, 1872, 1884-1886, 1890, 1905, 1913, 1941, 1946, 1948, 1958]
Reading, PA MSA
— establishments and employment, pp. 1031, 1056 [2406, 2458]
— occupancy, pp. 495, 529, 544, 546, 558, 578, 653, 682 [1234, 1312, 1347, 1350, 1378, 1422, 1589, 1652]
— population, pp. 114, 118 [350, 355]
Red Willow County, NE
— toxic chemicals, p. 67 [282]
Redding, CA
— asian population, pp. 94, 96, 98 [318, 321, 324]

Numbers following p. or pp. are page references. Numbers in [ ] are table references.

Numbers following p. or pp. are page references. Numbers in [ ] are table references.

Numbers following p. or pp. are page references. Numbers in [ ] are table references.

Location Index

Rochester, MN continued:
1928, 1930, 1958]
— prisons and prison population, p. 1271 [2967-2969]

Rochester, NY
— asian population, p. 98 [324]
— city government expenditures, pp. 1188, 1215 [2741, 2802]
— city government revenues, pp. 1212, 1217 [2795, 2808-2809]
— cost of living, p. 874 [2003-2004]
— crimes and crime rates, pp. 1225-1226, 1228-1230 [2830-2832, 2842, 2845, 2848]
— diseases, p. 248 [636]
— distribution of employment, pp. 370-376, 385-390, 393-399, 402-408, 411-417 [945-954, 985-994, 1005-1014, 1025-1034, 1045-1054]
— establishments and employment, pp. 932, 935-936, 942, 946, 950, 955, 957, 975, 986, 989, 999, 1017, 1024, 1036-1037, 1050, 1052, 1060, 1068, 1087, 1099 [2200, 2206, 2208, 2215, 2222, 2232, 2241, 2246, 2284, 2307, 2313, 2333, 2378, 2392, 2417, 2419, 2444, 2449, 2465, 2483, 2539, 2569]
— family and household income, pp. 706-707, 709-711, 720-721, 723-727 [1701-1703, 1706-1709, 1727, 1729, 1731-1737]
— federal assistance, p. 258 [669]
— first ancestry, pp. 313-315, 319, 321-324, 328, 330 [804-805, 808, 814, 817-818, 820, 822, 828, 831]
— home ownership, p. 266 [699]
— hours and earnings, p. 420 [1065-1066]
— immigrants admitted, pp. 169, 173 [439, 445]
— imports and exports, pp. 878, 902 [2019, 2129]
— income, pp. 729-736 [1741-1742, 1744, 1746-1747, 1749-1752]
— land area, p. 6 [11]
— marital status, men, p. 212 [521]
— marital status, women, pp. 214-215 [525-526]
— medical insurance, p. 255 [665]
— occupancy, pp. 436, 447, 450, 452-453, 459, 469, 472, 481, 483, 491, 493, 499, 504, 512, 515, 521, 533, 546-548, 552, 556-558, 562, 566, 568, 570, 576, 578, 581, 584-586, 588, 592-593, 598, 603, 607, 611, 615-616, 640, 648, 650, 676-677, 683-686, 689, 693-695, 700, 703 [1098, 1123, 1125, 1131, 1135, 1138, 1151, 1173, 1181, 1200, 1206, 1224, 1228-1229, 1242, 1255, 1273, 1279, 1294, 1320, 1350-1351, 1353, 1355, 1365, 1373, 1375, 1377, 1386, 1395, 1399, 1404, 1417, 1420, 1428, 1435, 1438, 1440, 1443-1444, 1452, 1455-1456, 1467, 1477, 1486, 1496, 1505-1506, 1560, 1578, 1583-1584, 1640, 1643, 1656-1657, 1659-1660, 1663, 1669, 1677-1678, 1680-1681, 1694, 1699-1700]
— population, pp. 74, 77, 80, 83, 85, 90, 101, 103, 105, 110, 112, 114-115, 118-119, 121, 127, 134, 136, 139, 142 [297-300, 302, 307, 329, 332-333, 337, 345, 349-350, 352, 355-356, 362, 372, 383-386]
— poverty, pp. 793, 804, 811, 827, 831, 840, 848, 854 [1854, 1870, 1884, 1911, 1918, 1932, 1946, 1958]
— poverty rates, p. 743 [1764]
— refugees and asylees, pp. 190-200 [485-501]

Rochester, NY continued:
— revenues, p. 1220 [2817]
— tax-exempt establishments and employment, pp. 1004, 1006-1007, 1009 [2345, 2349-2350, 2355]
— unemployment, p. 419 [1061, 1063]
— vacancies, p. 282 [767]

Rock County, WI
— toxic chemicals, pp. 27, 32, 38-39, 41, 52 [109, 131, 156, 158, 166, 217]

Rock Island, IL
— cost of living, pp. 863-865, 869, 871, 873, 875 [1971, 1973, 1975, 1977, 1988, 1995, 2001, 2006]
— toxic chemicals, pp. 20, 33, 63 [73, 133, 266]

Rock Springs, WY
— cost of living, pp. 870, 872, 874 [1991-1992, 1996, 2002]

Rockbridge County, VA
— toxic chemicals, p. 22 [82]

Rockdale County, GA
— toxic chemicals, p. 52 [214]

Rockford, IL
— asian population, pp. 96, 98 [321, 324]
— cost of living, pp. 869-871, 873-875 [1988, 1991, 1995, 2001-2002, 2006]
— establishments and employment, pp. 963, 972, 1032, 1036 [2259, 2279, 2408, 2417]
— family and household income, pp. 709, 720-724 [1706, 1726-1727, 1729-1730, 1732-1733]
— first ancestry, pp. 313, 321-322, 327 [804, 818-819, 827]
— imports and exports, p. 879 [2025]
— population, pp. 75, 77, 80, 83, 86, 109, 114, 118, 127, 134, 137, 139, 142 [297-300, 302, 343, 350, 355, 373, 383-386]
— poverty, pp. 746, 748, 778, 782, 784, 800, 814, 824, 827-828, 854 [1769, 1773, 1825-1826, 1834, 1837, 1864, 1888, 1905, 1911-1912, 1958]

Rockingham County, NC
— toxic chemicals, p. 9 [22]

Rockingham County, VA
— toxic chemicals, pp. 31, 39, 43 [126, 158, 177]

Rockland County, NY
— toxic chemicals, pp. 14, 18 [48, 65]

Rogers County, OK
— toxic chemicals, p. 20 [76]

Roscommon County, MI
— population, p. 91 [309]

Roswell, NM
— cost of living, p. 868 [1984, 1986]

Rowan County, NC
— toxic chemicals, pp. 10, 12, 17, 19, 23, 38, 41 [27, 34, 62, 70-71, 86, 156, 165]

Russell County, AL
— toxic chemicals, p. 29 [116]

Rust College (Holly Springs, MS)
— degrees conferred, pp. 287, 289, 291, 294, 296 [771, 773, 775, 777, 779]
— enrollment, pp. 297, 299 [781, 784]
— finances and expenditures, pp. 305, 307 [793, 796]

Rutgers University (New Brunswick, NJ)
— degrees conferred, pp. 288, 290, 292 [772, 774, 776]

Numbers following p. or pp. are page references. Numbers in [ ] are table references.

Location Index

Numbers following p. or pp. are page references. Numbers in [ ] are table references.

Numbers following p. or pp. are page references. Numbers in [ ] are table references.

Location Index

Numbers following p. or pp. are page references. Numbers in [ ] are table references.

Numbers following p. or pp. are page references. Numbers in [ ] are table references.

Location Index

San Antonio, TX continued:

— immigrants admitted, pp. 148-150, 152-167, 169-172 [400, 402, 404, 406, 410, 414, 416-436, 438-443]

— imports and exports, pp. 881, 903 [2031, 2135]

— income, pp. 728-736 [1740-1741, 1743-1752]

— land area, p. 6 [12]

— libraries, p. 1280 [2988-2989]

— marital status, women, p. 215 [526]

— naturalized citizens, pp. 174-186 [446-464]

— occupancy, pp. 437-438, 440, 454-455, 460, 467, 476, 491, 494-495, 505, 509, 524-525, 529-531, 535, 538, 546, 557, 559, 572, 574, 577-578, 581, 588-591, 601-602, 606-607, 610, 615, 617, 625, 629-631, 634, 640-641, 649-650, 655, 660, 666-667, 669, 671, 676, 686, 690, 695-696, 698 [1102-1103, 1107-1108, 1139, 1143, 1152, 1154, 1168, 1189, 1223, 1231, 1233, 1256-1257, 1265, 1301-1302, 1312-1313, 1316, 1325, 1331, 1350, 1374, 1379, 1407-1408, 1412, 1418, 1422, 1427, 1443-1445, 1448, 1452, 1473, 1475, 1483, 1487, 1493-1494, 1504-1505, 1510, 1527, 1536, 1538, 1541, 1548, 1561-1562, 1580, 1584, 1594, 1605, 1617-1618, 1621, 1625, 1630, 1641, 1661, 1672, 1683-1684, 1689]

— population, pp. 74, 77, 81, 83, 85, 89-90, 99-102, 104-105, 110, 112, 114, 118-119, 122, 134, 136, 140, 143 [297-300, 302, 305, 308, 327-331, 334-336, 344, 348, 350, 355, 357, 363, 383-386]

— poverty, pp. 751-755, 768-777, 791, 793, 811-824, 826, 830-831, 843-847, 849-852 [1778-1781, 1783-1786, 1809, 1811-1824, 1851, 1853, 1884-1901, 1903, 1905, 1909, 1916-1918, 1938-1943, 1945, 1947, 1950-1954]

— poverty rates, pp. 742-743 [1760-1761, 1763, 1765]

— prisons and prison population, p. 1267 [2957-2958]

— revenues, pp. 1218-1220 [2811, 2813, 2817]

— tax crime, p. 1272 [2974]

— tax-exempt establishments and employment, pp. 1004, 1009 [2345, 2355]

— unemployment, pp. 417-418 [1055-1057]

— utilities, p. 1107 [2588]

— vacancies, p. 282 [767, 769]

San Benito County, CA

— toxic chemicals, p. 11 [32]

San Bernardino, CA

— county government expenditures, pp. 1116-1126 [2597-2598, 2600-2603, 2605, 2608-2615]

— county government revenues, pp. 1127-1129, 1131-1151 [2616-2618, 2620, 2623-2626, 2628, 2630-2638, 2640, 2643-2644, 2646, 2648-2650, 2652-2657, 2660-2663]

— county population, p. 116 [353]

— crimes and crime rates, pp. 1229-1230 [2844-2845, 2847-2848]

— geographic mobility, p. 208 [517]

— libraries, p. 1280 [2988-2989]

— livestock, p. 7 [13]

— toxic chemicals, pp. 15, 20, 30, 46, 69 [51, 74, 76, 120, 187, 291]

San Bernardino, CA continued:

— vacancies, p. 282 [766, 768]

San Diego, CA

— air quality, pp. 4-5 [1-6]

— airports, pp. 1078-1079 [2511, 2513-2514]

— alcohol use, pp. 226-229 [553-564]

— aliens, pp. 146-147 [389, 392, 395]

— asian population, pp. 94-96, 98-99 [318-322, 324-326]

— city government debt, pp. 1154-1166 [2665-2671, 2673-2675, 2677-2680, 2684-2690]

— city government expenditures, pp. 1166-1189, 1213-1216 [2691-2706, 2708, 2710-2715, 2721-2723, 2726, 2728-2737, 2739, 2742-2743, 2797-2799, 2801-2803, 2805]

— city government revenues, pp. 1189-1213, 1216-1217 [2744-2751, 2753, 2756-2762, 2764-2766, 2769-2772, 2776, 2778-2780, 2782-2796, 2806-2809]

— cocaine and heroin use, pp. 229-232 [565-570, 572-574]

— consumer expenditures, pp. 218-222 [532-540]

— cost of living, pp. 864, 866, 870, 875, 1080-1082 [1972, 1979, 1991-1992, 2005-2006, 2520, 2522, 2525, 2529]

— costs, pp. 912-913 [2152-2155]

— county government expenditures, pp. 1116-1126 [2597-2598, 2600-2602, 2605, 2608-2615]

— county government revenues, pp. 1127-1129, 1131-1151 [2616-2618, 2620, 2623-2626, 2628-2638, 2640, 2643, 2646, 2648-2650, 2652-2657, 2660-2663]

— county population, p. 116 [353]

— crimes and crime rates, pp. 1223-1224, 1226-1227 [2822, 2825, 2833, 2836, 2838]

— diseases, pp. 246, 248-250 [633, 638-639, 641, 646]

— distribution of employment, pp. 368-383, 385-417 [935-974, 985-1054]

— drug use, pp. 226, 233, 236, 1233-1267 [550-552, 578-580, 590, 2856-2945, 2947-2956]

— drug use, marijuana, pp. 233-235 [581-589]

— eating habits, pp. 237-239 [597-602]

— employment, pp. 336-338, 359, 364-367, 428-430 [835-838, 903, 921, 924, 927, 930, 933, 1080-1081, 1085, 1088]

— enrollment, p. 300 [785]

— establishments and employment, pp. 916-933, 935-936, 942-984, 986-1002, 1015-1019, 1021-1022, 1024-1026, 1028-1034, 1036, 1038-1043, 1047-1069, 1086-1089, 1092-1094, 1096-1098 [2163-2164, 2166-2169, 2171, 2174, 2176, 2179-2180, 2182, 2184-2185, 2188, 2190-2191, 2195-2197, 2199-2202, 2207-2209, 2214-2215, 2217-2237, 2239-2249, 2251-2257, 2259-2264, 2266, 2268-2271, 2273-2278, 2280-2283, 2285-2297, 2299-2301, 2303, 2306-2329, 2331-2341, 2375-2378, 2380-2382, 2387-2389, 2392-2395, 2397, 2401-2402, 2404-2406, 2408, 2410-2412, 2416-2417, 2420-2421, 2424-2426, 2428-2429, 2432-2433, 2440-2457, 2459-2462, 2464-2468, 2470-2480, 2482, 2484, 2536, 2538-2539, 2542-2543, 2551-2553, 2555-2557, 2560, 2562, 2564, 2567]

— exercise habits, pp. 239-242 [603-617]

— family and household income, pp. 706-707, 709-711, 723-727 [1701-1703, 1707-1710, 1732-1738]

— finances and expenditures, p. 309 [798-799]

— first ancestry, pp. 312, 314, 323-324, 327, 330 [802, 805, 821-

Numbers following p. or pp. are page references. Numbers in [ ] are table references.

1402

Numbers following p. or pp. are page references. Numbers in [ ] are table references.

Location Index

San Jose, CA continued:
— city government expenditures, pp. 1166-1189, 1213-1215 [2691-2706, 2708, 2710-2715, 2721-2723, 2726, 2728-2737, 2739, 2742-2743, 2797-2799, 2801-2803]
— city government revenues, pp. 1189-1213 [2744-2751, 2753, 2756-2766, 2769-2771, 2776, 2778-2780, 2782-2784, 2786-2793, 2796]
— cost of living, pp. 866-868, 870, 872, 875, 1080-1081 [1979, 1983, 1985, 1991-1992, 1996, 2005, 2520, 2525]
— crimes and crime rates, pp. 1224-1225, 1227 [2826, 2828, 2836, 2838]
— distribution of employment, pp. 370-376, 379-383, 393-399, 402-408, 411-417 [945-954, 965-974, 1005-1014, 1025-1034, 1045-1054]
— drug use, pp. 1233-1267 [2856-2887, 2889-2955]
— employment, pp. 336-338, 361, 364 [834-838, 907, 910, 921]
— family and household income, p. 712 [1711]
— geographic mobility, p. 208 [517]
— hotels and motels, p. 1011 [2360]
— hours and earnings, pp. 420, 424 [1065, 1076]
— housing, pp. 267-269 [707-708, 710, 715]
— immigrants admitted, pp. 149-150, 152-167 [401, 405-406, 410, 413, 415-436]
— imports and exports, pp. 876-877, 880, 882-900, 903-904 [2009-2016, 2027-2028, 2033-2092, 2094-2118, 2120, 2123, 2133, 2136]
— market shares, p. 940 [2212-2213]
— naturalized citizens, pp. 174-186 [446-464]
— occupancy, p. 280 [761]
— population, pp. 90, 112, 114, 118-119 [308, 348, 350, 355, 357]
— population, immigrants, p. 148 [397-398]
— postal service, p. 425 [1079]
— poverty rates, p. 742 [1761]
— refugees and asylees, pp. 190-200 [485-501]
— revenues, p. 1218 [2810, 2812-2813]
— unemployment, p. 419 [1062, 1064]
— utilities, p. 1108 [2588]
— vacancies, p. 282 [767]
— ventures, p. 906 [2139]
San Luis Obispo–Atascadero–Paso Robles, CA
— employment, pp. 339-344, 349-354 [841-855, 870-884]
San Mateo, CA
— county government expenditures, pp. 1116-1126 [2597-2598, 2600-2602, 2605, 2608-2615]
— county government revenues, pp. 1127-1129, 1131-1149, 1151 [2616-2618, 2620, 2623-2626, 2628, 2630-2638, 2640, 2643-2644, 2646, 2648-2650, 2652-2654, 2656-2657, 2663]
— county population, p. 116 [353]
— toxic chemicals, p. 48 [197]
San Patricio County, TX
— toxic chemicals, pp. 8-9, 25 [19-20, 97]
Sandstone, MN
— prisons and prison population, pp. 1268-1269 [2959-2961]
Sandusky, OH
— sports activities, p. 1280 [2990]

Sandusky, OH continued:
— toxic chemicals, pp. 15, 20, 33, 47, 57 [51, 74, 134, 194, 237]
Sangamon County, IL
— toxic chemicals, pp. 25, 37, 68 [98, 148, 285, 287]
Santa Ana, CA
— crimes and crime rates, pp. 1227-1228, 1231 [2836, 2838, 2842, 2850]
— employment, pp. 336-338 [835-838]
— hours and earnings, p. 424 [1076]
— land area, p. 6 [11]
— population, pp. 90, 112, 115 [307, 348, 352]
— population, immigrants, p. 148 [397-398]
— postal service, p. 425 [1079]
Santa Ana–Anaheim, CA
— geographic mobility, p. 208 [517]
Santa Barbara, CA
— toxic chemicals, p. 58 [244]
Santa Barbara–Santa Maria–Lompoc, CA MSA
— asian population, pp. 95-99 [319-324, 326]
— establishments and employment, pp. 936, 952, 955, 986, 989, 1025, 1044 [2209, 2235, 2243, 2306, 2312, 2394, 2433]
— family and household income, pp. 707, 709-711, 723-727 [1703, 1707-1710, 1732-1738]
— first ancestry, pp. 313-315, 323-324, 326 [803, 805, 807, 821-822, 824]
— immigrants admitted, pp. 168-173 [437-445]
— imports and exports, p. 903 [2133]
— income, pp. 728-733 [1740-1741, 1743, 1745-1746, 1748]
— marital status, men, p. 211 [520]
— marital status, women, p. 214 [525]
— occupancy, pp. 442, 467, 488, 512, 528, 531, 546, 584, 599, 602, 619, 653, 664-665, 667, 683 [1112, 1169, 1218, 1273, 1309, 1317, 1351, 1435, 1468, 1474, 1513-1514, 1589, 1613, 1616, 1621, 1655]
— population, pp. 75, 77, 81-82, 86, 89, 99, 101-105, 107-108, 110-111, 114, 118, 122-124, 133, 136, 140, 143 [297-300, 302, 305, 327, 329, 331-332, 334-336, 339-341, 344, 346-347, 350, 355, 364-368, 383-386]
— poverty, pp. 746, 753, 760-764, 769-777, 782-783, 786, 789, 791-792, 794-800, 811-822, 828, 833-835, 837-839, 843-846 [1770, 1782, 1796-1802, 1811-1824, 1834-1836, 1841, 1848, 1851, 1853, 1855-1861, 1863-1865, 1884-1901, 1912, 1921, 1923, 1926, 1928-1931, 1938-1943]
Santa Clara, CA
— county government expenditures, pp. 1116-1126 [2597-2598, 2600-2603, 2605, 2608-2615]
— county government revenues, pp. 1127-1129, 1131-1151 [2616-2618, 2620, 2623-2626, 2628, 2630-2638, 2640-2641, 2644, 2646, 2648-2650, 2652-2655, 2657, 2660-2663]
— county population, p. 116 [353]
— employment, p. 364 [921]
— toxic chemicals, pp. 14, 41-42, 46, 54, 64 [47, 165, 170, 189, 222, 271]
— ventures, p. 906 [2139]
— vital statistics, p. 254 [661]

Numbers following p. or pp. are page references. Numbers in [ ] are table references.

1405

Location Index

Numbers following p. or pp. are page references. Numbers in [ ] are table references.

Numbers following p. or pp. are page references. Numbers in [ ] are table references.

Location Index

1407

Seattle – Tacoma, WA continued:
2186, 2188, 2190-2191, 2195-2197, 2199-2202, 2206-2207, 2215-2220, 2222-2223, 2225-2228, 2232-2234, 2237-2242, 2247, 2249-2255, 2257, 2260-2263, 2266-2269, 2271-2272, 2275-2280, 2282-2283, 2285-2289, 2291, 2296, 2298-2301, 2303-2304, 2308-2312, 2314, 2318-2319, 2321-2324, 2328-2332, 2337, 2339, 2342, 2375-2376, 2382, 2384-2386, 2388-2390, 2392, 2395-2397, 2401, 2403, 2409-2410, 2412, 2414, 2420, 2427, 2430-2432, 2440-2446, 2451-2463, 2465-2466, 2468-2482, 2536, 2539-2542, 2544-2549, 2551-2552, 2554, 2558, 2562-2565, 2567]
— family and household income, pp. 706-707, 709-712, 720-727 [1701-1703, 1706-1710, 1726-1738]
— first ancestry, pp. 313-316, 322, 325, 327-330 [803, 805, 807, 810, 819, 824, 827-828, 830, 832]
— foods and food products, pp. 1069-1070 [2487-2490]
— general summary, pp. 1014-1015, 1046 [2371-2374, 2434-2435]
— hours and earnings, pp. 422-423 [1073-1075]
— housing, pp. 270, 272-273, 275-277, 280 [720, 726, 730, 741, 743, 750, 760]
— immigrants admitted, pp. 168-169, 171-173 [437-439, 441-444]
— income, pp. 728-739 [1740-1752, 1754-1759]
— job growth, p. 367 [934]
— marital status, men, p. 210 [518]
— marital status, women, p. 213 [523]
— occupancy, pp. 432-443, 445-455, 460-466, 468-480, 482-483, 485-486, 488-492, 495-530, 533-535, 537-550, 552-569, 571-577, 579-592, 594-616, 618-621, 623, 626-627, 629-667, 669-671, 673-674, 676-679, 681-703 [1090, 1092, 1094-1097, 1099-1105, 1107, 1109, 1111, 1113, 1115, 1118-1119, 1121, 1123-1127, 1129, 1131, 1133, 1135, 1137, 1139, 1141, 1143, 1153, 1155, 1157, 1159, 1161, 1163-1165, 1167, 1171, 1173, 1175, 1177, 1179, 1181, 1183, 1185, 1187, 1189, 1193-1195, 1197, 1199, 1203, 1207, 1211, 1213-1214, 1217, 1219, 1221, 1223-1225, 1227, 1233, 1235, 1237, 1239-1241, 1243, 1245-1249, 1251-1253, 1255, 1257, 1259, 1261-1263, 1265, 1267-1269, 1271, 1273, 1275, 1279, 1281, 1283-1285, 1287, 1289-1291, 1293, 1297-1301, 1303-1305, 1307, 1309, 1311, 1313, 1315, 1321, 1323, 1325, 1329, 1331, 1333, 1335, 1337, 1339, 1341-1343, 1347, 1349, 1351, 1353, 1355, 1357-1361, 1363, 1365, 1367, 1369, 1371, 1373, 1375, 1377, 1379, 1381, 1383, 1385-1387, 1389, 1391, 1393-1402, 1406-1411, 1413-1416, 1418-1420, 1423-1434, 1436-1437, 1439-1448, 1450, 1452, 1457-1466, 1468-1473, 1475-1495, 1497-1504, 1507-1508, 1511-1512, 1514-1515, 1517-1518, 1522-1524, 1529-1532, 1537, 1539-1546, 1548, 1550-1565, 1567-1573, 1576-1579, 1582-1587, 1589-1593, 1595-1598, 1600-1604, 1606-1615, 1617, 1619-1620, 1624-1630, 1633-1637, 1639, 1641-1645, 1647, 1650, 1652-1654, 1656, 1658-1659, 1661-1677, 1680-1683, 1685-

Seattle – Tacoma, WA continued:
1700]
— population, pp. 74, 76, 81-82, 85, 89, 104, 108-111, 114, 118, 120, 125-127, 133, 135, 140, 142 [297-300, 302, 305, 335, 340-347, 350, 355, 359-360, 369-373, 383-386]
— poverty, pp. 744, 747-748, 757-764, 780-786, 788-800, 804, 825, 828, 831, 833, 835-839, 854 [1766, 1771-1773, 1790-1791, 1793-1795, 1797-1803, 1830-1831, 1833-1835, 1838-1841, 1845, 1848-1865, 1870, 1906-1907, 1913, 1918, 1921, 1925-1931, 1958]
— tax-exempt establishments and employment, pp. 1004-1006, 1008-1010 [2343, 2346-2349, 2352-2356]
— television viewing, p. 1281 [2997-2998]
— vital statistics, pp. 251-253 [651-656]

Sebastian County, AR
— toxic chemicals, p. 26 [101]

Sebring, FL
— geographic mobility, p. 208 [517]

Sedgwick County, KS
— toxic chemicals, pp. 8, 11, 14, 16, 19, 29, 31-32, 39, 42-43, 49, 52, 54, 57-58, 63-64, 66-68 [19, 28-29, 47, 58, 71, 115, 125-126, 128, 160, 173-174, 176, 179, 201, 216, 226, 239, 241, 265, 267, 278, 281, 283, 288]

Selma University (Selma, AL)
— degrees conferred, pp. 287, 289, 291, 294, 296 [771, 773, 775, 777, 779]
— enrollment, pp. 297, 299 [781, 784]
— finances and expenditures, pp. 305, 307 [793, 796]

Seminole County, FL
— toxic chemicals, p. 66 [276]

Seneca County, OH
— toxic chemicals, pp. 12, 20-21 [33, 74, 79]

Sequoyah County, OK
— toxic chemicals, pp. 20, 23 [76, 85]

Sevier County, AR
— toxic chemicals, p. 56 [236]

Sexton Summit, OR
— weather and climate, p. 70 [296]

Seymour Johnson, NC
— prisons and prison population, pp. 1269-1270 [2962-2964]

Sharon, PA
— employment, pp. 359-360, 364 [902, 904, 906, 918]
— family and household income, pp. 708, 714-719 [1705, 1715, 1717-1719, 1721-1724]
— first ancestry, pp. 319, 321, 325-326, 328-330 [815, 817, 823, 825, 828, 830, 832]
— imports and exports, p. 900 [2122]
— marital status, men, pp. 210, 212 [519, 522]
— marital status, women, pp. 213, 215 [524, 527]
— occupancy, pp. 444, 480, 576, 578, 614 [1117, 1199, 1418, 1421-1422, 1503]
— population, pp. 76, 78, 80, 83, 87-88, 90, 112, 128-132, 135, 138, 140-141 [297-300, 302, 304, 306, 347, 374-386]
— poverty, pp. 749-751, 826, 829-830, 837, 847-849, 853-854 [1774-1777, 1909, 1914, 1916-1917, 1929, 1944, 1946, 1948, 1956-1957]

Sharp County, AR
— population, p. 91 [309-310]

Numbers following p. or pp. are page references. Numbers in [ ] are table references.

Location Index

Sioux City, IA – NE MSA
— asian population, pp. 94, 96, 98 [318, 321, 324]
— crimes and crime rates, pp. 1222, 1232 [2818, 2854]
— employment, p. 360 [904]
— family and household income, pp. 708, 713, 715-717, 719, 721 [1705, 1713, 1717, 1719-1720, 1725, 1729]
— first ancestry, pp. 314-315, 317-318, 322, 327 [806-808, 811, 813, 818-819, 827]
— hours and earnings, p. 421 [1068]
— occupancy, pp. 447, 499, 589, 614 [1123, 1242, 1445-1446, 1503]
— population, pp. 76, 79-80, 83, 87-88, 100, 104, 109, 122, 130, 132-133, 136, 140, 142 [297-300, 302-303, 328, 334, 342, 363, 377, 381-386]
— poverty, pp. 745, 751, 757-760, 763-764, 780-784, 786-787, 789-790, 793, 795-796, 798, 815, 823-827, 829, 832, 834, 836, 853 [1767-1768, 1777, 1790-1795, 1800, 1802-1803, 1830-1833, 1835, 1837, 1841-1843, 1847, 1850, 1854, 1857-1858, 1862, 1890, 1902-1904, 1906, 1908, 1910-1911, 1915, 1919-1920, 1924, 1927-1928, 1955-1956]
— toxic chemicals, p. 15 [50]

Sioux Falls, SD
— asian population, p. 98 [324]
— cost of living, pp. 870, 872, 1081 [1991-1992, 1996, 2527]
— crimes and crime rates, pp. 1222, 1230 [2820, 2846]
— family and household income, pp. 708, 713, 717-720, 722 [1705, 1713, 1720, 1722-1723, 1725, 1727, 1729]
— first ancestry, pp. 313-315, 318, 322, 327 [804, 806-808, 813, 819, 827]
— hours and earnings, p. 421 [1068, 1070]
— occupancy, pp. 631, 634 [1540, 1547]
— population, pp. 76, 78, 80, 84, 87-88, 109, 111, 121, 125-126, 132-133, 137, 141 [297-300, 302-303, 342, 346, 362, 369-371, 382-386]
— postal service, p. 425 [1079]
— poverty, pp. 744-747, 757-759, 780-781, 783-785, 787, 789, 791, 824-825, 829, 832-833, 854 [1766-1769, 1771, 1790-1794, 1830-1832, 1835, 1837-1839, 1843-1844, 1848, 1851, 1905-1907, 1915, 1919, 1922, 1957]
— revenues, pp. 1112-1114, 1219 [2589-2596, 2814-2815]

Skagit County, WA
— toxic chemicals, pp. 13, 59 [42, 247]

Slidell, LA
— cost of living, pp. 864-866 [1974, 1976, 1978]

Smith County, KS
— population, pp. 91-92 [311-312]

Smith County, TX
— toxic chemicals, p. 33 [134]

Snohomish County, WA
— toxic chemicals, pp. 28, 31, 42, 49 [110, 125, 170, 201]

Snowmass, CO
— sports activities, p. 1281 [2996]

Solano County, CA
— toxic chemicals, p. 64 [271]

Somerset County, NJ
— toxic chemicals, pp. 9, 14-15, 30, 32, 40, 43, 48, 57, 62 [22, 48, 51, 122, 128, 161, 178, 197, 239, 258]

Sonoma County, CA
— livestock, p. 7 [13]

South Bend, IN
— crimes and crime rates, p. 1230 [2846]
— hours and earnings, p. 422 [1071]
— population, pp. 114, 118 [350, 355]

South Bend – Mishawaka, IN
— asian population, p. 94 [318]
— family and household income, p. 721 [1728]
— first ancestry, pp. 312-313, 319, 323, 330 [803-804, 814-815, 820, 832]
— population, pp. 75, 78, 80, 84, 86, 89, 107, 124, 130, 134, 137, 139, 142 [297-300, 302, 305, 339, 367, 377, 383-386]
— poverty, pp. 751, 784, 797, 824, 828, 832, 854 [1777, 1838, 1859, 1905, 1913, 1920, 1957]

South Bend – Mishawaka, IN MSA
— occupancy, pp. 560, 588 [1382, 1443]

South Carolina State College (Orangeburg, SC)
— degrees conferred, pp. 287, 289, 291, 294, 296 [771, 773, 775, 777, 779]
— enrollment, pp. 297, 299 [781, 784]
— finances and expenditures, pp. 305, 307 [793, 796]

South Louisiana, LA
— chemicals, p. 5 [7]

South Padre Island, TX
— housing, p. 266 [703]

South Wellfleet, MA
— parks, pp. 1276-1278 [2977-2978, 2980, 2982-2983]

Southern Illinois University (Carbondale, IL)
— degrees conferred, pp. 288, 292 [772, 776]

Southern University and A& M College (Baton Rouge, LA)
— degrees conferred, pp. 287, 289, 291, 294, 296 [771, 773, 775, 777, 779]
— enrollment, pp. 297, 299 [781, 784]
— finances and expenditures, pp. 305, 307 [793, 796]

Southern University (New Orleans, LA)
— degrees conferred, pp. 287, 289, 291, 294, 296 [771, 773, 775, 777, 779]
— enrollment, pp. 297, 299 [781, 784]
— finances and expenditures, pp. 305, 307 [793, 796]

Southern University (Shreveport – Bossier City, LA)
— degrees conferred, pp. 287, 289, 291, 294, 296 [771, 773, 775, 777, 779]
— enrollment, pp. 297, 299 [781, 784]
— finances and expenditures, pp. 305, 307 [793, 796]

Southwestern Christian College (Terrell, TX)
— degrees conferred, pp. 287, 289, 291, 294, 296 [771, 773, 775, 777, 779]
— enrollment, pp. 297, 299 [781, 784]
— finances and expenditures, pp. 305, 308 [793, 796]

Southwestern College (Winfield, KS)
— degrees conferred, p. 295 [778]

Spartanburg County, SC
— toxic chemicals, pp. 10, 12, 16-17, 21, 24-25, 33, 37, 51 [24, 34, 56, 58, 62, 79, 92, 95, 133, 149, 212]

Spelman College (Atlanta, GA)
— degrees conferred, pp. 287, 289, 291, 294, 296 [771, 773, 775, 777, 779]
— enrollment, pp. 297, 299 [781, 784]

Numbers following p. or pp. are page references. Numbers in [ ] are table references.

Numbers following p. or pp. are page references. Numbers in [ ] are table references.

Location Index

Numbers following p. or pp. are page references. Numbers in [ ] are table references.

Numbers following p. or pp. are page references. Numbers in [ ] are table references.

Location Index

Numbers following p. or pp. are page references. Numbers in [ ] are table references.

Numbers following p. or pp. are page references. Numbers in [ ] are table references.

Location Index

1415

Toledo, OH continued:
— first ancestry, pp. 312-313, 317-319, 323, 326 [802, 804, 811, 813, 815, 820, 825]
— hours and earnings, pp. 421, 424 [1067, 1076]
— imports and exports, pp. 879, 903 [2025, 2132]
— occupancy, pp. 449, 454, 478, 488-489, 491, 507, 512, 519, 521, 539, 551, 576, 588, 591, 642, 674-675, 684 [1128, 1139, 1193, 1218, 1220, 1224, 1261, 1273, 1288, 1294, 1335, 1361, 1417, 1443, 1450, 1565, 1635, 1639, 1657]
— population, pp. 74, 77, 80, 84-85, 112, 119, 135, 137, 139, 142 [297-300, 302, 349, 355, 383-386]
— poverty, pp. 778, 839 [1825-1826, 1931]
— tax-exempt establishments and employment, p. 1007 [2350]

Tomahawk, WI
— travel, p. 1283 [3005]

Tooele, UT
— chemical weapons, p. 6 [8]
— toxic chemicals, pp. 30, 44, 66 [120, 179, 278]

Topeka, KS
— family and household income, pp. 719, 722 [1724-1725, 1730]
— first ancestry, pp. 319, 327, 329 [813, 827, 830]
— marital status, men, p. 210 [518]
— marital status, women, p. 213 [523]
— occupancy, pp. 521, 658, 680 [1294, 1600, 1648]
— population, pp. 75, 78, 80, 84, 86, 109, 126, 128, 132-133, 137, 139, 142 [297-300, 302, 342, 371, 375, 382-386]
— poverty, pp. 745, 749, 758-760, 764, 773, 781, 783-784, 788-790, 795, 807, 825, 828, 833, 835, 845 [1767, 1774, 1791-1793, 1795, 1802, 1817, 1831, 1835, 1838, 1846-1847, 1849, 1856, 1876, 1907, 1912, 1921, 1925-1926, 1941]
— tax crime, p. 1272 [2973]

Tougaloo College (Tougaloo, MS)
— degrees conferred, pp. 287, 289, 291, 294, 296 [771, 773, 775, 777, 779]
— enrollment, pp. 297, 300 [781, 784]
— finances and expenditures, pp. 305, 308 [793, 796]

Transylvania County, NC
— toxic chemicals, pp. 17, 37, 62 [62, 148, 260]

Traverse City, MI
— housing, p. 267 [703]

Travis, TX
— county government expenditures, pp. 1116-1117, 1119-1120, 1122-1126 [2597-2598, 2603-2604, 2609-2615]
— county government revenues, pp. 1127-1133, 1135-1136, 1138-1140, 1144-1148, 1151 [2616-2618, 2620, 2622-2626, 2630-2632, 2634-2637, 2648, 2650, 2653-2655, 2663]
— county population, p. 116 [353]
— prisons and prison population, p. 1267 [2958]
— toxic chemicals, pp. 10, 34, 44, 58 [24, 137, 181, 240]

Trenholm College (Montgomery, AL)
— degrees conferred, pp. 287, 289, 291, 294, 296 [771, 773, 775, 777, 779]

Trenholm College (Montgomery, AL) continued:
— enrollment, pp. 297, 300 [781, 784]
— finances and expenditures, pp. 305, 308 [793, 796]

Trenton, NJ
— cost of living, p. 1081 [2525]
— crimes and crime rates, p. 1223 [2822]
— hours and earnings, p. 420 [1065]
— income, p. 736 [1753]
— population, pp. 114, 119 [350, 355]

Troup County, GA
— toxic chemicals, pp. 21, 26 [80, 103]

Trumbull County, OH
— toxic chemicals, pp. 39, 46-47, 60, 69 [157, 187, 195, 251, 289]

Tucson, AZ
— asian population, pp. 95, 97-98 [319, 322, 325]
— city government expenditures, p. 1216 [2804]
— cost of living, p. 875 [2005]
— crimes and crime rates, pp. 1223, 1225-1226 [2821, 2830, 2832, 2834]
— daycare, p. 223 [542]
— diseases, pp. 248, 250 [636-637, 643]
— employment, pp. 336-338 [835-838]
— establishments and employment, pp. 952, 956, 960, 963, 969, 979, 989, 1041, 1062, 1087, 1092 [2235, 2243, 2252, 2259, 2273, 2292, 2312, 2428, 2471, 2539, 2552]
— first ancestry, pp. 312-313, 324 [802-803, 822]
— geographic mobility, p. 208 [517]
— hours and earnings, p. 424 [1076]
— housing, pp. 267-277, 279 [708, 710, 715, 719, 721, 723, 725, 727, 729, 732, 734, 736, 742, 746, 749, 755]
— immigrants admitted, pp. 168-173 [437-445]
— immigrants, illegal, p. 148 [396]
— imports and exports, pp. 878, 902 [2021-2022, 2130]
— income, pp. 728, 730-731, 733 [1740, 1743, 1745, 1748]
— marital status, men, p. 210 [518]
— marital status, women, p. 213 [523]
— occupancy, pp. 435, 491, 494, 514, 529, 546, 582, 584, 588, 613, 617, 622, 626, 629, 642-643, 649, 652, 665-666, 670, 683, 695, 703 [1097, 1224, 1231, 1277, 1311, 1351, 1431, 1435, 1444, 1500, 1509, 1521, 1530, 1536, 1566, 1581-1582, 1588, 1615-1616, 1618, 1626, 1655-1656, 1683, 1699]
— parks, p. 1279 [2986-2987]
— population, pp. 74, 77, 81, 83, 85, 89, 100-102, 104-105, 107, 109-110, 112, 114-115, 119, 133, 136, 140, 143 [297-300, 302, 305, 327, 329, 331, 334-336, 340, 342, 345, 347-348, 350-351, 355, 383-386]
— poverty, pp. 753-754, 757-760, 764, 769-777, 780-789, 794, 797, 811-822, 826-827, 832-835, 837, 843-846, 848, 850, 853 [1782-1784, 1790-1796, 1801, 1811-1824, 1830-1848, 1855, 1860, 1884-1901, 1908-1910, 1920-1926, 1929, 1938-1943, 1947, 1950, 1956]
— poverty rates, pp. 742-743 [1760-1761, 1763]
— prisons and prison population, pp. 1268-1269 [2959-2961]
— revenues, p. 1219 [2813-2814]
— tax-exempt establishments and employment, p. 1008 [2352]

Tulelake, CA
— parks, p. 1279 [2986-2987]

Numbers following p. or pp. are page references. Numbers in [ ] are table references.

1416

Numbers following p. or pp. are page references. Numbers in [ ] are table references.

Location Index

1417

Numbers following p. or pp. are page references. Numbers in [ ] are table references.

Numbers following p. or pp. are page references. Numbers in [ ] are table references.

1419

Numbers following p. or pp. are page references. Numbers in [ ] are table references.

Numbers following p. or pp. are page references. Numbers in [ ] are table references.

Location Index

Numbers following p. or pp. are page references. Numbers in [ ] are table references.

Location Index

Numbers following p. or pp. are page references. Numbers in [ ] are table references.

Numbers following p. or pp. are page references. Numbers in [ ] are table references.

1425

Location Index

Numbers following p. or pp. are page references. Numbers in [ ] are table references.

Numbers following p. or pp. are page references. Numbers in [ ] are table references.

Keyword Index

The Keyword Index lists every topic, company or business, agency, organization, brand, or personal name mentioned in *Gale City & Metro Rankings Reporter,* 2nd Edition tables. Each index citation is followed by page and table reference numbers. Page numbers are preceded by "p." or "pp." Page references do not necessarily identify the page on which a table begins. In cases where tables span two or more pages, references point to to the page on which the index term actually appears, which may be the second or subsequent page of a table. Table reference numbers appear in brackets ([]).

Numbers following p. or pp. are page references. Numbers in [ ] are table references.

Airports
— cargo volume, p. 1079 [2515]
— layovers, p. 1079 [2516]
— noise pollution, p. 1078 [2511-2512]
— on-time flights, p. 1078 [2513-2514]
— passengers, p. 1079 [2517]
— transportation, p. 1078 [2511-2512]

Albania
— asylees, p. 190 [486]
— refugees, p. 190 [486]

Alcohol use
— females, pp. 226-229 [553, 556, 559, 562]
— high schools, pp. 226-229 [553-564]
— males, pp. 227-229 [554, 557, 560, 563]
— youth, pp. 226-229 [553-564]

Aliens
— deportations, pp. 146-147 [387-395]

Allyl alcohol
— toxic releases, p. 19 [70]

Allyl chloride
— toxic releases, p. 19 [71]

Alpha-naphthylamine
— toxic releases, p. 19 [72]

Aluminum (fume or dust)
— toxic releases, p. 19 [73]

Aluminum oxide (fibrous forms)
— toxic releases, p. 20 [74]

American Indians
  See also: Native Americans
— population, p. 133 [383]

Ammonia
— toxic releases, p. 20 [75]

Ammonium nitrate (solution)
— toxic releases, p. 20 [76]

Ammonium sulfate (solution)
— toxic releases, p. 21 [77]

Amusement parks
— employment, p. 943 [2216]
— establishments, p. 943 [2216]

Anglers
  See also: Fishing; Salt-water anglers
— popular places, p. 1280 [2992]
— salt-water, p. 1281 [2995]

Aniline
— toxic releases, p. 21 [78]

Announcers
— blacks employed as, p. 439 [1106]
— men employed as, p. 573 [1411]
— whites employed as, p. 439 [1107]
— women employed as, p. 574 [1412]

Anthracene
— toxic releases, p. 21 [79]

Antimony
— toxic releases, p. 21 [80]

Antimony compounds
— toxic releases, p. 22 [81]

Apartment buildings
— construction prices, p. 912 [2155]

Apartments
— occupancy rates, p. 280 [761]
— rental rates, pp. 267, 269 [704, 717]

Apparel
— expenditures, p. 218 [533]
— export sales, pp. 875-876, 890 [2009-2010, 2075]

Apparel and accessory stores
— employment, p. 1047 [2440]
— establishments, p. 1047 [2440]

Apparel manufacturing
— earnings, p. 1047 [2438]
— employment, p. 1046 [2436]
— establishments, p. 1047 [2437]

Apprehensions
— illegal immigrants, p. 148 [396]

Arboreta and botanical or zoological gardens
— employment, p. 943 [2217]
— establishments, p. 943 [2217]

Architects
— blacks employed as, p. 440 [1108]
— men employed as, p. 574 [1413]
— whites employed as, p. 440 [1109]
— women employed as, p. 575 [1414]

Architectural services
— employment, p. 944 [2218]
— establishments, p. 944 [2218]

Archivists and curators
— blacks employed as, p. 441 [1110]
— men employed as, p. 575 [1415]
— whites employed as, p. 441 [1111]
— women employed as, p. 575 [1416]

Argentina
— nonimmigrants admitted to U.S., p. 188 [474]

Armored car services
— employment, p. 944 [2219]
— establishments, p. 944 [2219]

Arrestees
— cocaine use, pp. 1260-1261 [2931, 2935]
— drug use, pp. 1260-1262 [2930-2937]
— heroin use, pp. 1260, 1262 [2932, 2936]
— marijuana use, pp. 1261-1262 [2933, 2937]
— men, pp. 1261-1262 [2934-2937]
— women, p. 1260 [2930-2932]

Arsenic
— toxic releases, p. 22 [82]

Arsenic compounds
— toxic releases, p. 22 [83]

Art dealers
— employment, p. 1048 [2441]
— establishments, p. 1048 [2441]

Art, drama, and music teachers
— blacks employed as, p. 442 [1112]
— men employed as, p. 576 [1417]
— whites employed as, p. 442 [1113]
— women employed as, p. 576 [1418]

Artist printmakers
— blacks employed as, p. 519 [1290]
— men employed as, p. 655 [1595]
— whites employed as, p. 520 [1291]

Numbers following p. or pp. are page references. Numbers in [ ] are table references.

Numbers following p. or pp. are page references. Numbers in [ ] are table references.

Blacks continued:
— employed as physicians' assistants, p. 525 [1304]
— employed as physicists and astronomers, p. 527 [1308]
— employed as physics teachers, p. 528 [1310]
— employed as podiatrists, p. 529 [1312]
— employed as police and detectives, public service, p. 530 [1314]
— employed as political science teachers, p. 531 [1316]
— employed as power plant operators, p. 531 [1318]
— employed as precious stones and metals workers, p. 532 [1320]
— employed as printing press operators, p. 533 [1322]
— employed as private household cleaners and servants 534 [1324]
— employed as proofreaders, p. 535 [1326]
— employed as psychologists, p. 536 [1328]
— employed as psychology teachers, p. 537 [1330]
— employed as railroad brake, signal, and switch operators, p. 538 [1332]
— employed as railroad conductors and yardmasters, p. 539 [1334]
— employed as registered nurses, p. 539 [1336]
— employed as respiratory therapists, p. 540 [1338]
— employed as roofers, p. 541 [1340]
— employed as safe repairers, p. 506 [1258]
— employed as sailors and deckhands, p. 542 [1342]
— employed as sculptors, p. 519 [1290]
— employed as sheriffs, bailiffs, and other law enforcement officers, p. 543 [1344]
— employed as social work teachers, p. 544 [1346]
— employed as social workers, p. 545 [1348]
— employed as sociologists, p. 546 [1350]
— employed as sociology teachers, p. 546 [1352]
— employed as solderers and brazers, p. 547 [1354]
— employed as speech therapists, p. 548 [1356]
— employed as statisticians, p. 549 [1358]
— employed as stevedores, p. 550 [1360]
— employed as surveyors and mapping scientists, p. 551 [1362]
— employed as tailors, p. 552 [1364]
— employed as taxicab drivers and chauffeurs, p. 553 [1366]
— employed as teachers, elementary school, p. 554 [1368]
— employed as teachers, prekindergarten and kindergarten, p. 555 [1370]
— employed as teachers, secondary school, p. 556 [1372]
— employed as teachers, special education, p. 557 [1374]
— employed as technical writers, p. 558 [1376]
— employed as theology teachers, p. 558 [1378]
— employed as truck drivers, p. 559 [1380]
— employed as typesetters and compositors, p. 560 [1382]
— employed as typists, p. 561 [1384]
— employed as urban planners, p. 562 [1386]
— employed as veterinarians, p. 563 [1388]
— employed as water and sewage treatment plant operators, p. 564 [1390]
— employed as welders and cutters, p. 565 [1392]
— employed as welfare service aides, p. 566 [1394]
— executive, administrative, and managerial employment 383, 386 [976, 986]

Blacks continued:
— geographic mobility, pp. 261, 265 [681, 695]
— handlers, equipment cleaners, helpers, and laborers employment, pp. 383, 386 [977, 987]
— income, p. 728 [1739]
— inmigrants, p. 261 [681]
— machine operators, assemblers, and inspectors employment, pp. 383, 387 [978, 988]
— outmigrants, p. 265 [695]
— precision production, craft, and repair employment, p. 384, 387 [979, 989]
— professional specialty employment, pp. 384, 388 [980, 990]
— sales employment, pp. 384, 388 [981, 991]
— service occupations employment, pp. 384, 389 [982, 992]
— technicians and related support employment, p. 389 [993]
— technicians employment, p. 385 [983]
— transportation and material moving employment, p. 385, 390 [984, 994]
— university enrollment, p. 299 [784]

Boat dealers
— employment, p. 1049 [2444]
— establishments, p. 1049 [2444]

Boating
— marina service costs, p. 1280 [2993]
— marine diesel costs, p. 1280 [2991]
— towing rates, p. 1280 [2990]

Boats (ferry boats)
— fares, p. 1080 [2521]

Body weight
— females, p. 243 [618]
— high schools, p. 243 [618-620]
— males, p. 243 [619]
— youth, p. 243 [618-620]

Book stores
— employment, p. 1050 [2445]
— establishments, p. 1050 [2445]

Books, periodicals, and newspapers
— employment, p. 1016 [2377]
— establishments, p. 1016 [2377]

Bowling centers
— employment, p. 950 [2232]
— establishments, p. 950 [2232]

Brazers
— blacks employed as, p. 547 [1354]
— men employed as, p. 684 [1659]
— whites employed as, p. 548 [1355]
— women employed as, p. 685 [1660]

Breast surgeries
　See also: AIDS; Cancer; Diseases
— cancer, p. 250 [644-645]

Brick, stone, and related construction materials
— employment, p. 1017 [2378]
— establishments, p. 1017 [2378]

Bridge, lock, and lighthouse tenders
— blacks employed as, p. 450 [1132]
— men employed as, p. 585 [1437]
— whites employed as, p. 451 [1133]
— women employed as, p. 585 [1438]

Numbers following p. or pp. are page references. Numbers in [ ] are table references.

Keyword Index

1435

Numbers following p. or pp. are page references. Numbers in [ ] are table references.

Numbers following p. or pp. are page references. Numbers in [ ] are table references.

Keyword Index

Numbers following p. or pp. are page references. Numbers in [ ] are table references.

Numbers following p. or pp. are page references. Numbers in [ ] are table references.

Consumers
— expenditures, pp. 218-222 [532-540]
Container ports
— shipping, p. 1082 [2535]
Conventions
— Democratic Party, p. 1286 [3007]
— number booked, p. 1286 [3010]
— political parties, p. 1286 [3007-3009]
— Republican Party, p. 1286 [3008]
Cooks
— blacks employed as, p. 466 [1166]
— men employed as, pp. 600-601 [1471, 1473]
— whites employed as, p. 466 [1167]
— women employed as, p. 600 [1472]
Cooks (private household)
— blacks employed as, p. 466 [1168]
— men employed as, p. 601 [1473]
— whites employed as, p. 467 [1169]
— women employed as, p. 601 [1474]
Copper
— toxic releases, p. 33 [135]
Copper compounds
— toxic releases, p. 34 [136]
Coronary bypass surgery
— costs, p. 250 [646]
Correctional centers (federal)
— capacity, p. 1271 [2968]
— population, p. 1271 [2967]
— staff, p. 1271 [2969]
Correctional facilities (private)
— capacity, p. 1267 [2958]
— population, p. 1267 [2957]
Correctional institution officers
— blacks employed as, p. 467 [1170]
— men employed as, p. 602 [1475]
— whites employed as, p. 468 [1171]
— women employed as, p. 602 [1476]
Correctional institutions (federal)
— capacity, p. 1268 [2960]
— population, p. 1268 [2959]
— staff, p. 1269 [2961]
Costs
— burials, p. 224 [548]
— bus system operations, p. 1082 [2530]
— commuter rail system operations, p. 1082 [2531]
— coronary bypass surgery, p. 250 [646]
— cremations, p. 224 [549]
— daycare, pp. 222-223 [541-547]
— driving, p. 1081 [2527-2528]
— funerals, p. 224 [548-549]
— heat pumps, p. 913 [2156-2157]
— marina services, p. 1280 [2993]
— marine diesel, p. 1280 [2991]
— office space, p. 907 [2143-2144]
— subway system operations, p. 1082 [2534]
Counselors (educational and vocational)
— blacks employed as, p. 468 [1172]
— men employed as, p. 603 [1477]
— whites employed as, p. 469 [1173]

Counselors (educational and vocational) continued:
— women employed as, p. 603 [1478]
County governments
— revenues, pp. 1116-1151, 1196, 1201 [2597-2663, 2759, 2770]
Courier services (except by air)
— employment, p. 1087 [2539]
— establishments, p. 1087 [2539]
Craft
— employment, pp. 369, 373 [939, 949]
Craft-artists
— blacks employed as, p. 519 [1290]
— men employed as, p. 655 [1595]
— whites employed as, p. 520 [1291]
— women employed as, p. 656 [1596]
Credit unions
— employment, p. 918 [2167]
— establishments, p. 918 [2167]
Cremations
— costs, p. 224 [549]
Creosote
— toxic releases, p. 34 [137]
Cresol (mixed isomers)
— toxic releases, p. 34 [138]
Crimes
— murders, p. 1224 [2824-2825]
— property crimes, pp. 1225-1226 [2830-2833]
— rates, pp. 1229-1232 [2844-2853]
— serious, pp. 1224-1225, 1227 [2826-2829, 2836-2839]
— tax crimes, p. 1272 [2974]
— violent crimes, pp. 1228-1232, 1233 [2840-2853, 2855]
Cuba
— asylees, p. 192 [489]
— immigrants admitted to U.S., p. 151 [408-409]
— naturalized citizens of U.S., p. 176 [450]
— refugees, p. 192 [489]
Cumene
— toxic releases, p. 34 [139]
Cumene hydroperoxide
— toxic releases, p. 35 [140]
Cupferron
— toxic releases, p. 35 [141]
Customs districts
— exports, p. 899 [2121]
— imports, p. 901 [2125]
Cutters
— blacks employed as, p. 565 [1392]
— men employed as, p. 702 [1697]
— whites employed as, p. 565 [1393]
— women employed as, p. 702 [1698]
Cyanide compounds
— toxic releases, p. 35 [142]
Cyclohexane
— toxic releases, p. 35 [143]
Czech ancestry
— reported, p. 314 [806]
Dairy goats
— number, p. 7 [13]
Dairy products (except dried or canned)
— employment, p. 1020 [2384]

Numbers following p. or pp. are page references. Numbers in [ ] are table references.

Dairy products (except dried or canned) continued:
— establishments, p. 1020 [2384]
Dairy products stores
— employment, p. 1051 [2449]
— establishments, p. 1051 [2449]
Dance studios, schools, and halls
— employment, p. 959 [2250]
— establishments, p. 959 [2250]
Dancers
— blacks employed as, p. 469 [1174]
— men employed as, p. 604 [1479]
— whites employed as, p. 469 [1175]
— women employed as, p. 604 [1480]
Danish ancestry
— reported first ancestry, p. 315 [807]
Data processing schools
— employment, pp. 959, 1005 [2251, 2346]
— establishments, pp. 959, 1005 [2251, 2346]
Data processing services
— employment, p. 960 [2252]
-- establishments, p. 960 [2252]
Data-entry keyers
— blacks employed as, p. 470 [1176]
— men employed as, p. 604 [1481]
— whites employed as, p. 470 [1177]
— women employed as, p. 605 [1482]
Daycare
— costs, pp. 222-223 [541-547]
Death rates
— infants, p. 253 [656]
Deaths
— drug abuse, p. 254 [657-658]
— heroin use, p. 254 [657-658]
— methamphetamines, p. 254 [659-660]
— number, p. 252 [654]
— pollutants, p. 7 [16]
Debt
— governments, pp. 1166, 1191 [2690, 2747]
Decabromodiphenyl oxide
— toxic releases, p. 36 [144]
Deckhands
— blacks employed as, p. 542 [1342]
— men employed as, p. 679 [1647]
— whites employed as, p. 543 [1343]
— women employed as, p. 680 [1648]
Deep-sea foreign and domestic freight
— employment, p. 1087 [2540]
— establishments, p. 1087 [2540]
Degrees
— conferrals (associates), p. 286 [770-771]
— conferrals (bachelors), pp. 287-288 [772-773]
— conferrals (doctorates), pp. 289-290 [774-775]
— conferrals (masters), pp. 294-295 [778-779]
— conferrals (professional), pp. 291, 293 [776-777]
Deliveries
— Postal Service, p. 425 [1079]
Democratic Party
— conventions, p. 1286 [3007]

Demolitions
— costs, p. 258 [666-667]
— housing projects, p. 258 [666-668]
Dental assistants
— blacks employed as, p. 471 [1178]
— men employed as, p. 605 [1483]
— whites employed as, p. 471 [1179]
— women employed as, p. 606 [1484]
Dental hygienists
— blacks employed as, p. 472 [1180]
— men employed as, p. 606 [1485]
— whites employed as, p. 472 [1181]
— women employed as, p. 607 [1486]
Dental laboratories
— employment, p. 960 [2253]
— establishments, p. 960 [2253]
Dentists
— blacks employed as, p. 472 [1182]
— men employed as, p. 607 [1487]
— whites employed as, p. 473 [1183]
— women employed as, p. 607 [1488]
Department of Housing and Urban Development: See HUD
Department stores
— retail trade, p. 1069 [2485]
Department stores (excl. leased depts.)
— employment, p. 1052 [2450]
— establishments, p. 1052 [2450]
Deportations
— aliens, pp. 146-147 [387-395]
Depository institutions
— employment, p. 918 [2168]
— establishments, p. 918 [2168]
Destinations
— immigrants, p. 148 [399]
Detective agencies and protective services
— employment, p. 961 [2254]
— establishments, p. 961 [2254]
Detectives (public service)
— blacks employed as, p. 530 [1314]
— men employed as, p. 666 [1619]
— whites employed as, p. 530 [1315]
— women employed as, p. 667 [1620]
Detention centers (federal)
— capacity, p. 1271 [2968]
— population, p. 1271 [2967]
— staff, p. 1271 [2969]
Di(2-ethylhexyl) phthalate
— toxic releases, p. 36 [145]
Diaminotoluene (mixed isomers)
— toxic releases, p. 36 [146]
Dibenzofuran
— toxic releases, p. 36 [147]
Dibutyl phthalate
— toxic releases, p. 37 [148]
Dichlorobenzene (mixed isomers)
— toxic releases, p. 37 [149]
Dichlorobromomethane
— toxic releases, p. 37 [150]

Keyword Index

Numbers following p. or pp. are page references. Numbers in [ ] are table references.

Numbers following p. or pp. are page references. Numbers in [ ] are table references.

Numbers following p. or pp. are page references. Numbers in [ ] are table references.

Keyword Index

1443

Numbers following p. or pp. are page references. Numbers in [ ] are table references.

Numbers following p. or pp. are page references. Numbers in [ ] are table references.

Keyword Index

Numbers following p. or pp. are page references. Numbers in [ ] are table references.

Keyword Index

Numbers following p. or pp. are page references. Numbers in [ ] are table references.

1447

Numbers following p. or pp. are page references. Numbers in [ ] are table references.

Numbers following p. or pp. are page references. Numbers in [ ] are table references.

Numbers following p. or pp. are page references. Numbers in [ ] are table references.

Keyword Index

Numbers following p. or pp. are page references. Numbers in [ ] are table references.

1451

Numbers following p. or pp. are page references. Numbers in [ ] are table references.

Employment continued:
— women as air traffic controllers, p. 437 [1101]
— women as aircraft engine mechanics, p. 438 [1103]
— women as airplane pilots and navigators, p. 573 [1410]
— women as announcers, p. 574 [1412]
— women as architects, p. 575 [1414]
— women as archivists and curators, p. 575 [1416]
— women as artist printmakers, p. 656 [1596]
— women as art, drama, and music teachers, p. 576 [1418]
— women as astronomers, p. 664 [1614]
— women as athletes, p. 577 [1420]
— women as auctioneers, p. 578 [1422]
— women as auditors, p. 567 [1397]
— women as authors, p. 579 [1424]
— women as baggage porters and bellhops, p. 580 [1426]
— women as bailiffs, p. 681 [1650]
— women as bakers, p. 581 [1428]
— women as barbers, p. 582 [1430]
— women as bartenders, p. 583 [1432]
— women as bellhops, p. 580 [1426]
— women as biological and life scientists, p. 583 [1434]
— women as biological science teachers, p. 584 [1436]
— women as brazers, p. 685 [1660]
— women as bridge, lock, and lighthouse tenders, p. 585 [1438]
— women as bus drivers, p. 586 [1440]
— women as business and promotion agents, p. 587 [1442]
— women as business, commerce, and marketing teachers, p. 588 [1444]
— women as butchers and meat cutters, p. 589 [1446]
— women as cabinet makers and bench carpenters, p. 590 [1448]
— women as captains and other officers, fishing vessels 590 [1450]
— women as chauffeurs, p. 690 [1672]
— women as chemical engineers, p. 591 [1452]
— women as chemistry teachers, p. 592 [1454]
— women as chemists, except biochemists, p. 593 [1456]
— women as chief executives and general administrators, public administration, p. 594 [1458]
— women as child care workers, private household, p. 595 [1460]
— women as clergy, p. 596 [1462]
— women as compositors, p. 697 [1688]
— women as computer operators, p. 597 [1464]
— women as computer programmers, p. 598 [1466]
— women as computer science teachers, p. 599 [1468]
— women as computer systems analysts and scientists 600 [1470]
— women as cooks, p. 600 [1472]
— women as cooks, private household, p. 601 [1474]
— women as correctional institution officers, p. 602 [1476]
— women as counselors, educational and vocational, p. 603 [1478]
— women as craft-artists, p. 656 [1596]
— women as cutters, p. 702 [1698]
— women as dancers, p. 604 [1480]
— women as data-entry keyers, p. 605 [1482]
— women as deckhands, p. 680 [1648]

Employment continued:
— women as dental assistants, p. 606 [1484]
— women as dental hygienists, p. 607 [1486]
— women as dentists, p. 607 [1488]
— women as detectives | 667 | 1620
— women as dietitians, p. 608 [1490]
— women as directors, p. 568 [1399]
— women as dressmakers, p. 609 [1492]
— women as early childhood teacher's assistants, p. 610 [1494]
— women as earth, environmental, and marine science teachers, p. 611 [1496]
— women as economics teachers, p. 612 [1498]
— women as economists, p. 613 [1500]
— women as editors and reporters, p. 614 [1502]
— women as education teachers, p. 615 [1504]
— women as elevator operators, p. 615 [1506]
— women as English teachers, p. 616 [1508]
— women as explosives workers, p. 617 [1510]
— women as family child care providers, p. 618 [1512]
— women as farm workers, p. 619 [1514]
— women as fire inspection and fire prevention occupations 620 [1516]
— women as firefighting occupations, p. 621 [1518]
— women as fishers, p. 622 [1520]
— women as foreign language teachers, p. 623 [1522]
— women as forestry and conservation scientists, p. 623 [1524]
— women as funeral directors, p. 624 [1526]
— women as garbage collectors, p. 625 [1528]
— women as geologists and geodesists, p. 626 [1530]
— women as hairdressers and cosmetologists, p. 627 [1532]
— women as history teachers, p. 628 [1534]
— women as home economics teachers, p. 629 [1536]
— women as housemen, p. 644 [1570]
— women as housekeepers and butlers, p. 630 [1538]
— women as hunters and trappers, p. 630 [1540]
— women as insurance adjusters, examiners, and investigators, p. 631 [1542]
— women as interviewers, p. 632 [1544]
— women as judges, p. 633 [1546]
— women as labor relations managers, p. 656 [1598]
— women as launderers and ironers, p. 634 [1548]
— women as law teachers, p. 635 [1550]
— women as lawyers, p. 636 [1552]
— women as legal assistants, p. 637 [1554]
— women as legislators, p. 638 [1556]
— women as librarians, p. 639 [1558]
— women as library clerks, p. 640 [1560]
— women as licensed practical nurses, p. 641 [1562]
— women as locksmiths and safe repairers, p. 642 [1564]
— women as locomotive operating occupations, p. 642 [1566]
— women as longshore equipment operators, p. 643 [1568]
— women as maids and housemen, p. 644 [1570]
— women as mail carriers, postal service, p. 645 [1572]
— women as mapping scientists, p. 688 [1668]
— women as marine and naval architects, p. 646 [1574]
— women as marine life cultivation workers, p. 647 [1576]
— women as mathematical science teachers, p. 648 [1578]
— women as medical science teachers, p. 649 [1580]
— women as mining engineers, p. 649 [1582]

Numbers following p. or pp. are page references. Numbers in [ ] are table references.

Numbers following p. or pp. are page references. Numbers in [ ] are table references.

Numbers following p. or pp. are page references. Numbers in [ ] are table references.

Keyword Index

1455

Numbers following p. or pp. are page references. Numbers in [ ] are table references.

Numbers following p. or pp. are page references. Numbers in [ ] are table references.

Keyword Index

Numbers following p. or pp. are page references. Numbers in [ ] are table references.

Numbers following p. or pp. are page references. Numbers in [ ] are table references.

Keyword Index

Numbers following p. or pp. are page references. Numbers in [ ] are table references.

Numbers following p. or pp. are page references. Numbers in [ ] are table references.

Keyword Index

1461

Numbers following p. or pp. are page references. Numbers in [ ] are table references.

Handlers, equipment cleaners, helpers, and laborers
— blacks employed as, pp. 383, 386 [977, 987]
— Hispanics employed as, p. 377 [957]
— men employed as, p. 403 [1027]
— whites employed as, p. 394 [1007]
— women employed as, p. 412 [1047]

Hardware stores
— employment, p. 1058 [2463]
— establishments, p. 1058 [2463]

Hardware, plumbing, and heating equipment and supplies
— employment, p. 1026 [2397]
— establishments, p. 1026 [2397]

Hawaii
— visitors, p. 1282 [3003]

Health
— expenditures, p. 1214 [2800]

Health care
— Emergency Medical Services, p. 251 [650]
— Emergency Medical Services staff, p. 251 [649]
— Emergency Medical Services visits, p. 251 [647-648]
— expenditures, p. 220 [536]
— medical insurance, p. 255 [665]

Health maintenance organizations (HMOs)
— persons covered, p. 255 [665]

Health problems
— emergency room visits, p. 4 [1-2]
— hospital admissions, p. 5 [5-6]
— ozone exposure, pp. 4-5 [2, 6]

Health services
— employment, p. 967 [2269]
— establishments, p. 967 [2269]

Heat pumps
— construction, p. 913 [2156-2157]
— costs, p. 913 [2156-2157]

Heavy construction equipment rental and leasing
— employment, p. 968 [2270]
— establishments, p. 968 [2270]

Help supply services
— employment, p. 968 [2271]
— establishments, p. 968 [2271]

Helpers
— employment, pp. 368, 371 [937, 947]

Heptachlor
— toxic releases, p. 42 [172]

Heroin use
— arrestees, p. 1262 [2936]
— deaths, p. 254 [657-658]
— emergency room mentions, p. 231 [571]
— men, p. 1262 [2936]
— women, p. 1260 [2932]

Hexachloro-1,3-butadiene
— toxic releases, p. 42 [173]

Hexachlorobenzene
— toxic releases, p. 43 [174]

Hexachlorocyclopentadiene
— toxic releases, p. 43 [175]

Hexachloroethane
— toxic releases, p. 43 [176]

High schools
— alcohol, pp. 226-228 [553-561]
— alcohol use, p. 229 [562-564]
— body weight, p. 243 [618-620]
— cigarette use, p. 236 [591-593]
— cocaine, pp. 229-231 [565-570, 572-574]
— drug use (injected), p. 233 [578-580]
— food consumption, pp. 237-238 [597-599]
— fruit consumption, pp. 238-239 [600-602]
— guns, pp. 244-245 [624-626]
— illegal drugs, p. 226 [550-552]
— illegal steroid use, p. 232 [575-577]
— injected-drug use, p. 233 [578-580]
— marijuana, pp. 234-235 [584-589]
— marijuana use, pp. 233-234 [581-583]
— physical activity, pp. 240-242 [606-614]
— physical education, p. 242 [615-617]
— physical education classes, p. 239 [603-605]
— smokeless tobacco, p. 237 [594-596]
— steroid use (illegal), p. 232 [575-577]
— vegetable consumption, pp. 238-239 [600-602]
— weapons, pp. 245-246 [627-632]
— weight loss, pp. 243-244 [621-623]

Highways
— expenditures, p. 1214 [2801]

Hispanic Aleuts
— population, p. 104 [334]

Hispanic Eskimos
— population, p. 104 [334]

Hispanic female arrestees
— cocaine use, p. 1255 [2915]
— drug use, pp. 1254-1255 [2914-2917]
— marijuana use, p. 1255 [2916]
— opiates use, p. 1255 [2917]

Hispanic Indians
— population, p. 104 [334]

Hispanic male arrestees
— cocaine use, p. 1256 [2919]
— drug use, pp. 1256-1257 [2918-2921]
— marijuana use, p. 1256 [2920]
— opiates use, p. 1257 [2921]

Hispanic Pacific Islanders
— population, p. 104 [335]

Hispanics
— administrative support employment, pp. 376, 378 [955, 965]
— executive, administrative, and managerial employment, p. 377, 379-380 [956, 966, 969]
— geographic mobility, pp. 261, 264 [680, 694]
— handlers, equipment cleaners, and helpers employment 377 [957]
— inmigrants, p. 261 [680]
— machine operators, assemblers and inspectors, employment, p. 377 [958]
— machine operators, assemblers, and inspectors employment, p. 380 [968]
— outmigrants, p. 264 [694]
— precision production, craft, and repair employment, p. 377, 379-380 [959, 967, 969]
— professional specialties employment, pp. 377, 381 [960, 970]

Numbers following p. or pp. are page references. Numbers in [ ] are table references.

Numbers following p. or pp. are page references. Numbers in [ ] are table references.

Numbers following p. or pp. are page references. Numbers in [ ] are table references.

1465

Keyword Index

Numbers following p. or pp. are page references. Numbers in [ ] are table references.

Numbers following p. or pp. are page references. Numbers in [ ] are table references.

Keyword Index

Numbers following p. or pp. are page references. Numbers in [ ] are table references.

Keyword Index

Numbers following p. or pp. are page references. Numbers in [ ] are table references.

1469

Numbers following p. or pp. are page references. Numbers in [ ] are table references.

1470

Men continued:

— employed as dentists, p. 607 [1487]
— employed as detectives, p. 666 [1619]
— employed as dietitians, p. 608 [1489]
— employed as directors, p. 568 [1398]
— employed as dressmakers, p. 609 [1491]
— employed as early childhood teachers' assistants, p. 610 [1493]
— employed as earth, environmental, and marine science teachers, p. 611 [1495]
— employed as economics teachers, p. 611 [1497]
— employed as economists, p. 612 [1499]
— employed as editors and reporters, p. 613 [1501]
— employed as education teachers, p. 614 [1503]
— employed as elementary school teachers, p. 691 [1673]
— employed as elevator operators, p. 615 [1505]
— employed as English teachers, p. 616 [1507]
— employed as examiners, p. 631 [1541]
— employed as explosives workers, p. 617 [1509]
— employed as family child care providers, p. 618 [1511]
— employed as farm workers, p. 618 [1513]
— employed as fishers, p. 621 [1519]
— employed as foreign language teachers, p. 622 [1521]
— employed as forestry and conservation scientists, p. 623 [1523]
— employed as funeral directors, p. 624 [1525]
— employed as garbage collectors, p. 625 [1527]
— employed as general administrators, p. 594 [1457]
— employed as geologists and geodesists, p. 626 [1529]
— employed as hairdressers and cosmetologists, p. 626 [1531]
— employed as handlers, equipment cleaners, helpers, and laborers, p. 400 [1017]
— employed as history teachers, p. 627 [1533]
— employed as home economics teachers, p. 628 [1535]
— employed as housekeepers and butlers, p. 629 [1537]
— employed as housemen, p. 644 [1569]
— employed as hunters and trappers, p. 630 [1539]
— employed as insurance adjusters, examiners, and investigators, p. 631 [1541]
— employed as interviewers, p. 632 [1543]
— employed as ironers, p. 634 [1547]
— employed as judges, p. 633 [1545]
— employed as kindergarten teachers, p. 692 [1675]
— employed as labor relations managers, p. 656 [1597]
— employed as launderers and ironers, p. 634 [1547]
— employed as law teachers, p. 634 [1549]
— employed as lawyers, p. 635 [1551]
— employed as legal assistants, p. 636 [1553]
— employed as legislators, p. 637 [1555]
— employed as librarians, p. 638 [1557]
— employed as library clerks, p. 639 [1559]
— employed as licensed practical nurses, p. 640 [1561]
— employed as locksmiths and safe repairers, p. 641 [1563]
— employed as longshore equipment operators, p. 643 [1567]
— employed as machine operators, assemblers, and inspectors, pp. 400, 403 [1018, 1028]
— employed as maids and housemen, p. 644 [1569]

Men continued:

— employed as mail carriers, p. 645 [1571]
— employed as mail carriers (Postal Service), p. 645 [1571]
— employed as mapping scientists, p. 688 [1667]
— employed as marine and naval architects, p. 646 [1573]
— employed as marine life cultivation workers, p. 646 [1575]
— employed as marketing teachers, p. 587 [1443]
— employed as mathematical science teachers, p. 647 [1577]
— employed as meat cutters, p. 588 [1445]
— employed as medical science teachers, p. 648 [1579]
— employed as metal workers, p. 669 [1625]
— employed as mining engineers, p. 649 [1581]
— employed as motion picture projectionists, p. 650 [1583]
— employed as musicians and composers, p. 651 [1585]
— employed as nuclear engineers, p. 652 [1587]
— employed as nursery workers, p. 652 [1589]
— employed as occupational therapists, p. 653 [1591]
— employed as optometrists, p. 654 [1593]
— employed as painters, sculptors, craft artists, and artists printmakers, p. 655 [1595]
— employed as personnel and labor relations managers, p. 656 [1597]
— employed as petroleum engineers, p. 657 [1599]
— employed as pharmacists, p. 658 [1601]
— employed as photographers, p. 659 [1603]
— employed as physical education teachers, p. 660 [1605]
— employed as physical therapists, p. 661 [1607]
— employed as physicians, p. 663 [1611]
— employed as physicians' assistants, p. 662 [1609]
— employed as physicists and astronomers, p. 664 [1613]
— employed as physics teachers, p. 664 [1615]
— employed as podiatrists, p. 665 [1617]
— employed as police and detectives (public service), p. 666 [1619]
— employed as political science teachers, p. 667 [1621]
— employed as power plant operators, p. 668 [1623]
— employed as precious stones and metals workers, p. 669 [1625]
— employed as prekindergarten teachers, p. 692 [1675]
— employed as printing press operators, p. 670 [1627]
— employed as private household cleaners and servants, p. 671 [1629]
— employed as proofreaders, p. 672 [1631]
— employed as psychologists, p. 673 [1633]
— employed as psychology teachers, p. 674 [1635]
— employed as railroad brake, signal, and switch operators 674 [1637]
— employed as railroad conductors and yardmasters, p. 675 [1639]
— employed as registered nurses, p. 676 [1641]
— employed as reporters, p. 613 [1501]
— employed as respiratory therapists, p. 677 [1643]
— employed as roofers, p. 678 [1645]
— employed as safe repairers, p. 641 [1563]
— employed as sailors, p. 679 [1647]
— employed as scientists, p. 599 [1469]
— employed as sculptors, p. 655 [1595]
— employed as secondary school teachers, p. 692 [1677]
— employed as sheriffs, bailiffs, and other law enforcement

Numbers following p. or pp. are page references. Numbers in [ ] are table references.

Men continued:
officers, p. 680 [1649]
— employed as social work teachers, p. 681 [1651]
— employed as social workers, p. 682 [1653]
— employed as sociologists, p. 683 [1655]
— employed as sociology teachers, p. 684 [1657]
— employed as solderers, p. 684 [1659]
— employed as special education teachers, p. 693 [1679]
— employed as speech therapists, p. 685 [1661]
— employed as statisticians, p. 686 [1663]
— employed as stevedores, p. 687 [1665]
— employed as surveyors and mapping scientists, p. 688 [1667]
— employed as tailors, p. 689 [1669]
— employed as taxicab drivers and chauffeurs, p. 690 [1671]
— employed as teachers (elementary school), p. 691 [1673]
— employed as teachers (kindergarten and prekindergarten), p. 692 [1675]
— employed as teachers (secondary school), p. 692 [1677]
— employed as teachers (special education), p. 693 [1679]
— employed as technical writers, p. 694 [1681]
— employed as technicians, pp. 401, 407 [1023, 1033]
— employed as theology teachers, p. 695 [1683]
— employed as truck drivers, p. 696 [1685]
— employed as typesetters and compositors, p. 697 [1687]
— employed as typists, p. 698 [1689]
— employed as urban planners, p. 699 [1691]
— employed as veterinarians, p. 700 [1693]
— employed as water and sewage treatment plant operators, p. 701 [1695]
— employed as welders and cutters, p. 702 [1697]
— employed as welfare service aides, p. 703 [1699]
— employed as yardmasters, p. 675 [1639]
— employed in administrative support occupations, p. 399, 402, 408 [1015, 1025, 1035]
— employed in civilian labor force, p. 366 [927-929]
— employed in executive, administrative, and managerial employment, pp. 399, 402, 408 [1016, 1026, 1036]
— employed in fire inspection and fire prevention occupations, p. 619 [1515]
— employed in fire inspection occupations, p. 619 [1515]
— employed in firefighting occupations, p. 620 [1517]
— employed in locomotive operating occupations, p. 642 [1565]
— employed in precision production, craft, and repair occupations, pp. 400, 404 [1019, 1029]
— employed in professional specialties, pp. 400, 405 [1020, 1030]
— employed in protective services occupations, p. 569 [1400]
— employed in sales occupations, pp. 401, 405 [1021, 1031]
— employed in service occupations, pp. 401, 406 [1022, 1032]
— employed in transportation and material moving occupations, pp. 401, 407 [1024, 1034]
— employment-population ratio, pp. 428-429 [1080, 1082, 1086]
— heroin use, p. 1262 [2936]
— married, p. 210 [519]
— never married, p. 211 [520]
— separated from spouse, p. 211 [521]

Men continued:
— unemployment rate, pp. 417-418 [1055, 1058, 1060]
— university enrollment, p. 301 [788]
— widowed, p. 212 [522]
Men's and boys' clothing and accessory stores
— employment, p. 1062 [2470]
— establishments, p. 1062 [2470]
Men's and boys' clothing and furnishings
— employment, p. 1031 [2406]
— establishments, p. 1031 [2406]
Mercury
— toxic releases, p. 48 [196]
Mercury compounds
— toxic releases, p. 48 [197]
Metal products
— (fabricated), export sales, pp. 889-890 [2073-2074, 2078]
Metal workers
— men employed as, p. 669 [1625]
Metals (primary)
— export sales, pp. 887, 892 [2059-2060, 2086]
Metals and minerals (except petroleum)
— employment, p. 1031 [2407]
— establishments, p. 1031 [2407]
Metals service centers and offices
— employment, p. 1032 [2408]
— establishments, p. 1032 [2408]
Methamphetamines
— abuse, p. 236 [590]
— deaths, p. 254 [659-660]
Methanol
— toxic releases, p. 48 [198]
Methoxychlor
— toxic releases, p. 48 [199]
Methyl acrylate
— toxic releases, p. 48 [200]
Methyl ethyl ketone
— toxic releases, p. 49 [201]
Methyl hydrazine
— toxic releases, p. 49 [202]
Methyl iodide
— toxic releases, p. 49 [203]
Methyl isobutyl ketone
— toxic releases, p. 49 [204]
Methyl isocyanate
— toxic releases, p. 50 [205]
Methyl methacrylate
— toxic releases, p. 50 [206]
Methyl tert-butyl ether
— toxic releases, p. 50 [207]
Methylene bromide
— toxic releases, p. 50 [208]
Methylenebis(phenylisocyanate)
— toxic releases, p. 50 [209]
Metropolitan correctional centers (federal)
— capacity, p. 1271 [2968]
— population, p. 1271 [2967]
— staff, p. 1271 [2969]
Metropolitan detention centers (federal)
— capacity, p. 1271 [2968]

Numbers following p. or pp. are page references. Numbers in [ ] are table references.

Numbers following p. or pp. are page references. Numbers in [ ] are table references.

Numbers following p. or pp. are page references. Numbers in [ ] are table references.

Numbers following p. or pp. are page references. Numbers in [ ] are table references.

Numbers following p. or pp. are page references. Numbers in [ ] are table references.

Numbers following p. or pp. are page references. Numbers in [ ] are table references.

Numbers following p. or pp. are page references. Numbers in [ ] are table references.

Numbers following p. or pp. are page references. Numbers in [ ] are table references.

Keyword Index

Numbers following p. or pp. are page references. Numbers in [ ] are table references.

Numbers following p. or pp. are page references. Numbers in [ ] are table references.

Numbers following p. or pp. are page references. Numbers in [ ] are table references.

Keyword Index

1483

Numbers following p. or pp. are page references. Numbers in [ ] are table references.

Keyword Index

Numbers following p. or pp. are page references. Numbers in [ ] are table references.

Numbers following p. or pp. are page references. Numbers in [ ] are table references.

Numbers following p. or pp. are page references. Numbers in [ ] are table references.

Numbers following p. or pp. are page references. Numbers in [ ] are table references.

Numbers following p. or pp. are page references. Numbers in [ ] are table references.

Whites continued:
— employed as sailors and deckhands, p. 543 [1343]
— employed as sheriffs, bailiffs, and other law
  enforcement officers, p. 543 [1345]
— employed as social work teachers, p. 544 [1347]
— employed as social workers, p. 545 [1349]
— employed as sociologists, p. 546 [1351]
— employed as sociology teachers, p. 547 [1353]
— employed as solderers and brazers, p. 548 [1355]
— employed as speech therapists, p. 549 [1357]
— employed as statisticians, p. 550 [1359]
— employed as stevedores, p. 550 [1361]
— employed as surveyors and mapping scientists, p. 551
  [1363]
— employed as tailors, p. 552 [1365]
— employed as taxicab drivers and chauffeurs, p. 553 [1367]
— employed as teachers, elementary school, p. 554 [1369]
— employed as teachers, prekindergarten and
  kindergarten, p. 555 [1371]
— employed as teachers, secondary school, p. 556 [1373]
— employed as teachers, special education, p. 557 [1375]
— employed as technical writers, p. 558 [1377]
— employed as technicians, pp. 392, 398 [1003, 1013]
— employed as theology teachers, p. 559 [1379]
— employed as truck drivers, p. 560 [1381]
— employed as typesetters and compositors, p. 561 [1383]
— employed as typists, p. 562 [1385]
— employed as urban planners, p. 562 [1387]
— employed as veterinarians, p. 563 [1389]
— employed as water and sewage treatment plant
  operators, p. 564 [1391]
— employed as welders and cutters, p. 565 [1393]
— employed as welfare service aides, p. 566 [1395]
— employed in administrative support occupations, p. 390,
  393 [995, 1005]
— employed in executive, administrative, and managerial
  occupations, pp. 390, 393 [996, 1006]
— employed in precision production, craft, and repair
  occupations, pp. 391, 395 [999, 1009]
— employed in professional specialty occupations, p. 391,
  396 [1000, 1010]
— employed in sales occupations, pp. 392, 396 [1001, 1011]
— employed in service occupations, pp. 392, 397 [1002, 1012]
— employed in transportation and material moving
  occupations, pp. 392, 398 [1004, 1014]
— geographic mobility, pp. 261, 265 [682, 696]
— inmigrants, p. 261 [682]
— outmigrants, p. 265 [696]
— poverty, p. 778 [1825-1826]
Wholesale trade
— employment, p. 363 [915-916]
— employment growth, pp. 344, 348, 353, 359 [855, 869, 884,
  900]
— total, employment, p. 1042 [2431]
— total, establishments, p. 1042 [2431]
Widowed persons
— men, p. 212 [522]
— women, p. 215 [527]

Wine and distilled alcoholic beverages
— employment, p. 1043 [2432]
— establishments, p. 1043 [2432]
Women
  See also: Females
— administrative support employment, p. 411 [1045]
— arrestees, pp. 1260-1261 [2930-2933]
— business sales, p. 938 [2211]
— businesses owners, p. 938 [2210]
— cocaine use, p. 1260 [2931]
— college enrollment, p. 304 [792]
— divorced, p. 212 [523]
— drug use, pp. 1260-1261 [2930-2933]
— employed as accountants and auditors, p. 567 [1397]
— employed as actors and directors, p. 568 [1399]
— employed as administrators, protective services, p. 569 [1401]
— employed as aerospace engineers, p. 435 [1097]
— employed as agriculture and forestry teachers, p. 436 [1099]
— employed as air traffic controllers, p. 437 [1101]
— employed as aircraft engine mechanics, p. 438 [1103]
— employed as airplane pilots and navigators, p. 573 [1410]
— employed as announcers, p. 574 [1412]
— employed as architects, p. 575 [1414]
— employed as archivists and curators, p. 575 [1416]
— employed as art, drama, and music teachers, p. 576 [1418]
— employed as astronomers, p. 664 [1614]
— employed as athletes, p. 577 [1420]
— employed as auctioneers, p. 578 [1422]
— employed as auditors, p. 567 [1397]
— employed as authors, p. 579 [1424]
— employed as baggage porters and bellhops, p. 580 [1426]
— employed as bailiffs, p. 681 [1650]
— employed as bakers, p. 581 [1428]
— employed as barbers, p. 582 [1430]
— employed as bartenders, p. 583 [1432]
— employed as bellhops, p. 580 [1426]
— employed as biological and life scientists, p. 583 [1434]
— employed as biological science teachers, p. 584 [1436]
— employed as brazers, p. 685 [1660]
— employed as bridge, lock, and lighthouse tenders, p. 585
  [1438]
— employed as bus drivers, p. 586 [1440]
— employed as business and promotion agents, p. 587 [1442]
— employed as business, commerce, and marketing
  teachers, p. 588 [1444]
— employed as butchers and meat cutters, p. 589 [1446]
— employed as cabinet makers and bench carpenters, p. 590
  [1448]
— employed as captains and other officers, fishing vessels
  590 [1450]
— employed as chauffeurs, p. 690 [1672]
— employed as chemical engineers, p. 591 [1452]
— employed as chemistry teachers, p. 592 [1454]
— employed as chemists, except biochemists, p. 593 [1456]
— employed as chief executives and general administrators,
  public administration, p. 594 [1458]
— employed as child care workers, private household, p. 595
  [1460]
— employed as clergy, p. 596 [1462]

Numbers following p. or pp. are page references. Numbers in [ ] are table references.

Keyword Index

Numbers following p. or pp. are page references. Numbers in [ ] are table references.